MW00770021

DICTIONARY
of the
NEW TESTAMENT Use
of the OLD TESTAMENT

DICTIONARY *of the* NEW TESTAMENT Use *of the* OLD TESTAMENT

EDITED BY

G. K. Beale, D. A. Carson,
Benjamin L. Gladd,
and Andrew David Naselli

B
Baker Academic
a division of Baker Publishing Group
Grand Rapids, Michigan

Published by Baker Academic
a division of Baker Publishing Group
Grand Rapids, Michigan
www.bakeracademic.com

Printed in the United States of America

Library of Congress Cataloging in Publication Control Number: 2023014296
ISBN 9781540960047 (cloth)
ISBN 9781493442553 (ebook)
ISBN 9781493442560 (pdf)

Italics in Scripture quotations have been added for emphasis.

Baker Publishing Group publications use paper produced from sustainable forestry practices and post-consumer waste whenever possible.

23 24 25 26 27 28 29 7 6 5 4 3 2 1

Contents

Articles

Articles by Topic

Inner-Biblical Exegesis

Systematic Theology

Contributors

Andrew T. Abernethy *(Trinity Evangelical Divinity School)*
Wheaton College
Divine Warrior

T. Desmond Alexander *(Queen's University of Belfast)*
Union Theological College
Exodus, Book of; Holiness; Jerusalem

Christopher B. Ansberry *(Wheaton College)*
Grove City College
Proverbs, Book of

Richard E. Averbeck *(Annenberg Research Institute, Dropsie College)*
Trinity Evangelical Divinity School (emeritus)
Sacrifices and Offerings

S. M. Baugh *(University of California, Irvine)*
Westminster Seminary California (emeritus)
Ephesians, Letter to the

G. K. Beale *(University of Cambridge)*
Reformed Theological Seminary
Apostolic Hermeneutics: Description and Presuppositions; Colossians and Philemon, Letters to the; Method; Temple

Christopher A. Beetham *(Wheaton College)*
Zondervan
Quotation, Allusion, and Echo

Richard P. Belcher Jr. *(Westminster Theological Seminary)*
Reformed Theological Seminary
Ecclesiastes, Book of; Job, Book of

Craig Blaising *(ThD, Dallas Theological Seminary; PhD, University of Aberdeen)*
Southwestern Baptist Theological Seminary
History of Interpretation: 300 to 1800

Craig L. Blomberg *(University of Aberdeen)*
Denver Seminary (emeritus)
Jesus's Use of the Old Testament; Matthew, Gospel of

Chris Bruno *(Wheaton College)*
Training Leaders International
Ecclesiology

C. Hassell Bullock *(Hebrew Union College)*
Wheaton College (emeritus)
Psalms, Book of

Constantine R. Campbell *(Macquarie University)*
Sydney College of Divinity
Corporate Solidarity

Robert J. Cara *(Westminster Theological Seminary)*
Reformed Theological Seminary
Thessalonians, First and Second Letters to the

D. A. Carson *(University of Cambridge)*
Trinity Evangelical Divinity School (emeritus)
Apostolic Hermeneutics: Present-Day Imitation; John, Letters of

Mitchell Chase *(Southern Baptist Theological Seminary)*
Southern Baptist Theological Seminary
Daniel, Book of

Robert B. Chisholm Jr. *(Dallas Theological Seminary)*
Dallas Theological Seminary
Habakkuk, Book of

Sean Christensen *(Trinity Evangelical Divinity School)*
James, Letter of

E. Ray Clendenen *(University of Texas at Arlington)*
Lifeway Christian Resources
Malachi, Book of

Graham A. Cole *(Australian College of Theology)*
Trinity Evangelical Divinity School
Shalom; Wrath

C. John Collins *(University of Liverpool)*
Covenant Theological Seminary
Numbers, Book of

Jared Compton *(Trinity Evangelical Divinity School)*
Bethlehem College and Seminary
Corinthians, Second Letter to the

Brandon D. Crowe *(University of Edinburgh)*
Westminster Theological Seminary
Adam, First and Last; Mark, Gospel of; Prosopological Exegesis; Resurrection

John D. Currid *(University of Chicago)*
Reformed Theological Seminary
Enemies of the People of God; Feasts and Festivals; Leviticus, Book of

A. Andrew Das *(Union Theological Seminary in Virginia)*
Elmhurst University
Law

Karl Deenick *(Ridley College)*
Sydney Missionary and Bible College
Circumcision

Stephen G. Dempster *(University of Toronto)*
Crandall University (emeritus)
Genesis, Book of; Kingdom and King; Micah, Book of; Wilderness

Jason S. DeRouchie *(Southern Baptist Theological Seminary)*
Midwestern Baptist Theological Seminary
Covenant; Deuteronomy, Book of; Promises; Zephaniah, Book of

Daniel J. Ebert IV *(Trinity Evangelical Divinity School)*
Center for Biblical Studies, Philippines
Wisdom

Sam Emadi *(Southern Baptist Theological Seminary)*
Hunsinger Lane Baptist Church (Louisville, KY)
Typology

David Everson *(Hebrew Union College)*
Emmanuel Baptist Church (Mora, MN)
Targums: A Brief Introduction; Targums: Comparison with the NT Use of the OT; Targums: Thematic Parallels to the NT

John V. Fesko *(University of Aberdeen)*
Reformed Theological Seminary
Bibliology

Duane Garrett *(Baylor University)*
Southern Baptist Theological Seminary
Hosea, Book of; Joel, Book of; Lamentations, Book of

Simon Gathercole *(University of Durham)*
University of Cambridge
Abraham and Abrahamic Tradition; Son of Man

Radu Gheorghita *(University of Cambridge)*
Midwestern Baptist Theological Seminary
Septuagint: Background

Jonathan Gibson *(University of Cambridge)*
Westminster Theological Seminary
Obadiah, Book of

Andrew M. Gilhooley *(University of Pretoria)*
University of Pretoria
Sinai

Benjamin L. Gladd *(Wheaton College)*
Reformed Theological Seminary
Mystery

W. Edward Glenny *(PhD, University of Minnesota; ThD, Dallas Theological Seminary)*
University of Northwestern, St. Paul
Septuagint: Comparison with the NT Use of the OT

Graeme Goldsworthy *(Union Theological Seminary in Virginia)*
Moore Theological College (retired)
Israel and the Church, The Story of

Daniel M. Gurtner *(University of St. Andrews)*
Gateway Seminary
Dead Sea Scrolls, OT Use in; Dead Sea Scrolls, OT Use in: Comparison with NT Use of the OT; Dead Sea Scrolls: Thematic Parallels to the NT; Pseudepigrapha: A Brief Introduction; Pseudepigrapha: Comparison with the NT Use of the OT; Pseudepigrapha, NT Parallels in; Pseudepigrapha, NT Use of

George H. Guthrie *(Southwestern Baptist Theological Seminary)*
Regent College (Vancouver)
Hebrews, Letter to the

Matthew S. Harmon *(Wheaton College)*
Grace College and Theological Seminary
Galatians, Letter to the; Jude and the Second Letter of Peter; OT Use of the OT: Comparison with the NT Use of the OT; Philippians, Letter to the

Dana M. Harris *(Trinity Evangelical Divinity School)*
Trinity Evangelical Divinity School
Day of the Lord; Priest

J. Daniel Hays *(Southwestern Baptist Theological Seminary)*
Ouachita Baptist University and Southwestern Baptist Theological Seminary
Ezekiel, Book of; Samuel, Books of

Daniel R. Heimbach *(Drew University)*
Southeastern Baptist Theological Seminary
Ethics

Richard S. Hess *(Hebrew Union College)*
Denver Seminary
Joshua, Book of

Andrew E. Hill *(University of Michigan)*
Wheaton College (emeritus)
Chronicles, Books of; Zechariah, Book of

David Instone-Brewer *(University of Cambridge)*
Tyndale House, Cambridge
Mishnah, Talmud, and Midrashim, OT Use in; Mishnah, Talmud, and Midrashim, OT Use in: Comparison with NT Use of the OT; Mishnah, Talmud, and Midrashim: Thematic Parallels to the NT

Karen H. Jobes *(Westminster Theological Seminary)*
Wheaton College (emerita)
Greek Versions and the NT Quotations; Peter, First Letter of; Septuagint, NT Use of

Dennis E. Johnson *(Fuller Theological Seminary)*
Westminster Seminary California (emeritus)
Holy Spirit, Eschatological Role of

Jeremy Kimble *(Southeastern Baptist Theological Seminary)*
Cedarville University
Justice

Andreas J. Köstenberger *(Trinity Evangelical Divinity School)*
Biblical Foundations and Fellowship Raleigh (NC)
John, Gospel of; Mission

Jon C. Laansma *(University of Aberdeen)*
Wheaton College
Sabbath and Sunday

Peter H. W. Lau *(University of Sydney)*
University of Sydney
Ruth, Book of

Te-Li Lau *(Emory University)*
Trinity Evangelical Divinity School
Shame

Jonathan Leeman *(University of Wales)*
9Marks
Church

Richard Lints *(University of Notre Dame)*
Redeemer City-to-City (New York City)
Idolatry

Bryan Litfin *(University of Virginia)*
Liberty University
History of Interpretation: Early Church

Darian Lockett *(University of St. Andrews)*
Biola University
Canonical Interpretation

Phillip Marshall *(Southern Baptist Theological Seminary)*
Houston Christian University
Haggai, Book of

Oren Martin *(Southern Baptist Theological Seminary)*
Watermark Community Church (Dallas, TX)
Land; Literal Fulfillment

David L. Mathewson *(University of Aberdeen)*
Denver Seminary
Consummation

Sean McDonough *(University of St. Andrews)*
Gordon-Conwell Theological Seminary
Creation; Revelation, Book of; Satan

Catherine McDowell *(Harvard University)*
Gordon-Conwell Theological Seminary
Image of God

John D. Meade *(Southern Baptist Theological Seminary)*
Phoenix Seminary
Septuagint: Thematic Parallels to the NT

Christopher W. Morgan *(Mid-America Baptist Theological Seminary)*
California Baptist University
Glory of God; Love; Sin

Andrew David Naselli *(PhD, Trinity Evangelical Divinity School; PhD, Bob Jones University)*
Bethlehem College and Seminary
History of Interpretation: 1800 to Present; Serpent and Antichrist

Dane C. Ortlund *(Wheaton College)*
Naperville (IL) Presbyterian Church
Gospel

Ray Ortlund *(University of Aberdeen)*
Renewal Ministries
Marriage

John Oswalt *(Brandeis University)*
Asbury Theological Seminary
Isaiah, Book of

David W. Pao *(Harvard University)*
Trinity Evangelical Divinity School
Luke, Gospel of

David G. Peterson *(University of Manchester)*
Moore Theological College (emeritus)
Romans, Letter to the; Worship

Nicholas G. Piotrowski *(Wheaton College)*
Indianapolis Theological Seminary
Exodus, The

Stanley E. Porter *(University of Sheffield)*
McMaster Divinity College
Letter Couriers; Literacy in the Greco-Roman World; Orality; Rhetoric

Iain Provan *(University of Cambridge)*
Regent College (Vancouver)
Kings, Books of

O. Palmer Robertson *(Union Theological Seminary in Virginia)*
Consummation Ministries
New Areas for Exploration of the OT in the NT

Max F. Rogland *(Leiden University)*
Rose Hill Presbyterian Church (Columbia, SC)
Esther, Book of

Brian S. Rosner *(University of Cambridge)*
Ridley College
Biblical Theology; Corinthians, First Letter to the

David S. Schrock *(Southern Baptist Theological Seminary)*
Occoquan Bible Church (Woodbridge, VA)
Son of God; Typology

Mark A. Seifrid *(Princeton Theological Seminary)*
Concordia Seminary, St. Louis
Justification

Andrew G. Shead *(University of Cambridge)*
Moore Theological College
Jeremiah, Book of

Gary V. Smith *(Dropsie College for Hebrew and Cognate Languages)*
Union University
Amos, Book of; Ezra-Nehemiah, Books of

Mark L. Strauss *(University of Aberdeen)*
Bethel University
Exile and Restoration; Messiah

Brian J. Tabb *(London School of Theology)*
Bethlehem College and Seminary
Apocrypha: Comparison with the NT Use of the OT; Apocrypha, NT Use of; Apocrypha: Thematic Parallels to the NT; Apocrypha: Use of the OT

Alan J. Thompson *(Trinity Evangelical Divinity School)*
Sydney Missionary and Bible College
Acts, Book of

Daniel C. Timmer *(Trinity International University)*
Puritan Reformed Theological Seminary and Faculté de théologie évangélique (Montreal)
Jonah, Book of; Nahum Book of

Philip H. Towner *(University of Aberdeen)*
Pontificia Università Urbaniana (Rome)
Timothy and Titus, Letters to

Eric J. Tully *(University of Wisconsin–Madison)*
Trinity Evangelical Divinity School
Prophet

Miles V. Van Pelt *(Southern Baptist Theological Seminary)*
Reformed Theological Seminary
Judges, Book of; Song of Songs, Book of

Kevin J. Vanhoozer *(University of Cambridge)*
Trinity Evangelical Divinity School
Theological Interpretation of Scripture

Guy Prentiss Waters *(Duke University)*
Reformed Theological Seminary
Allegory

Stephen J. Wellum *(Trinity Evangelical Divinity School)*
Southern Baptist Theological Seminary
Christology

Joel White *(University of Dortmund, Germany)*
Freie Theologische Hochschule (Giessen, Germany)
Contextual and Noncontextual NT Use of the OT

Paul Williamson *(Queen's University of Belfast)*
Moore Theological College
Jews and Gentiles

Jonathan D. Worthington *(Durham University)*
Training Leaders International
Philo (1): Use of the OT; Philo (2): Influence on the NT; Philo (3): Comparison with NT Use of the OT; Philo (4): Thematic Parallels to the NT

Introduction

In the last few decades, the field known as "the use of the Old Testament in the New Testament" has blossomed. What was peripheral in the past has now taken center stage. At the annual Society of Biblical Literature conference, one need not wander far to stumble upon a paper devoted to the use of the OT in a particular NT passage. Indeed, entire SBL seminars are devoted exclusively to the cause, such as "Paul and Scripture" and "Scripture and 1 Corinthians." NT scholars are growing more aware of how NT authors, at key points in their arguments, often lean on specific OT passages, events, and concepts.

The fifth edition of the UBS *Greek New Testament* lists approximately 350 OT quotations in the NT (UBS^5, 857–63). The Gospel of Matthew, for example, contains about fifty-five OT quotations, whereas the other three Gospels together cite a total of sixty-five quotations (Blomberg, 1). In Paul's Letters there are about one hundred quotations. Regarding allusions, some scholars argue that the NT contains well over one thousand allusions. By way of comparison, the NT includes far fewer quotations of Jewish and pagan sources. Similarly, though the NT alludes to extrabiblical literature, it alludes to the OT far more frequently. The difference is staggering.

History of Interpretation

We start with a word about how we got here. A host of NT scholars in the late nineteenth and early twentieth centuries followed the lead of their OT colleagues and expended much energy examining what lies behind the NT documents in order to reconstruct the genesis of early Christianity. The next wave of scholarship became more concerned with the NT writings themselves and took interest in reading each NT book as a whole and appreciating its literary integrity. Around the mid-twentieth century, C. H. Dodd persuasively argued in *According to the Scriptures* that NT authors do not cite the OT detached from its original context but draw from the broad and immediate context of the OT. He concluded, "These [OT] sections were understood [by NT authors] as *wholes*, and particular verses or sentences were quoted from them rather as pointers to the whole context than as constituting testimonies in and for themselves" (Dodd, 126). Dodd's insight was a watershed moment for the field, setting the trajectory for years to come, though many scholars disagreed with his approach. The hermeneutical sapling that Dodd planted soon bore fruit in the ensuing decades as scholars, working with modern literary techniques, began to explore how NT authors employed the OT throughout their narratives and epistles.

The growing field of biblical theology, too, is part of this discussion. J. P. Gabler, often labeled the father of biblical theology, proposed in the late eighteenth century that the field of biblical studies should not be enslaved by dogmatics. This proposal gave way to countless historical-critical trends among NT scholars, but it also, in some sense, paved the way for various expressions of contemporary "biblical theology." Though the enterprise of "biblical theology" and its precise meaning have been the subject of tireless (and tired) debate in recent years, scholars have pursued a number of whole-Bible theologies. The last three decades have witnessed substantial interest in tracing various themes from Genesis to Revelation (e.g., covenant, creation, temple). Not coincidentally, much of this work is built upon the insights of those laboring in the trenches of the use of the OT in the NT. Furthermore, some NT biblical theologies, both in Germany and the United States, have more recently been keen to trace NT ideas back to the OT (e.g., Beale, Stuhlmacher).

Need for This Dictionary

With the torrent of publications on the use of the OT in the NT, the time is ripe for a dictionary dedicated to this rich and diverse field. What makes this field notoriously complex is its relationship to other scholarly disciplines and subdisciplines. Take, for example, the role of the LXX (or Old Greek) in the first century. Since most of the quotations in the NT are taken from the LXX, one cannot study how NT authors use the OT without also reflecting on the nature of the LXX itself and its various textual traditions. The relationship between the LXX and the MT must also be considered in the same breath. We should also be mindful of how sectors of Judaism made considerable use of the OT in their documents. What about the use of the OT in the OT? How do later OT prophets use the writings of earlier OT prophets? Do the NT authors cite the OT contextually? What role does systematic theology have in this discussion? Should we in the twenty-first century follow the hermeneutics of the apostles in the first century? As one can imagine, a host of scholars have thought deeply about such issues and offer wide-ranging answers, so at the heart of this project are essays dedicated to tackling such intricate hermeneutical matters.

This dictionary is written with its companion volume in mind, the *Commentary on the New Testament Use of the Old Testament* (*CNTUOT*). That book carefully investigates how each NT book quotes and alludes to the OT, highlighting the various hermeneutical permutations of the OT. This present volume continues that examination but on a synchronic level. More book-by-book reflection is needed. Where the *CNTUOT* examines each quotation and major allusion diachronically, a significant portion of this dictionary does so synchronically. The *CNTUOT* considers only how the NT uses the OT; it does not address how the OT uses the OT. This project attempts to redress this omission by furnishing separate essays on the use of the OT in each OT book.

Since biblical theology is indebted to careful study on how the OT is used in the NT, a third of this dictionary is dedicated to a wide range of biblical-theological topics. Those interested in how the two Testaments relate to each other on a hermeneutical level are often concerned with such prominent themes woven within them. Lastly, a handful of essays take up the important issue of the relationship between theology and inner-biblical exegesis. Exegesis does not take place within a vacuum, especially exegesis that is mindful of how the two Testaments are ultimately bound up with the person of Christ and the church. One's theological commitments profoundly shape such discussions.

Composition of This Dictionary

Though organized alphabetically, this dictionary is composed of five discrete types of entries (see the list of articles by topic).

1. Surveys of biblical books. These entries examine each book of the Bible at a synchronic level for its indebtedness to antecedent revelation. The NT essays summarize and update the *CNTUOT*. The OT surveys are responsible for tracing the influence of prior revelation in each OT book. When the author evaluates the use of the OT in Genesis, for example, the earlier parts of Genesis will be traced in the later parts. Likewise, the essay on Isaiah reflects upon the influence of the Pentateuch and how earlier OT traditions inform the book. Methodologically speaking, the OT surveys are inherently problematic as historical issues abound (dating, authorship, provenance, etc.). A way forward here is to rest upon a canonical approach. The authors of the OT essays in this dictionary depend upon the final shape of the canon as they discern the role of prior revelation. In addition, the contributors of the OT essays are encouraged to keep an eye on how the NT uses their respective OT books.

2. Biblical-theological topical essays. Approximately fifty essays trace prominent biblical-theological themes throughout both Testaments. Each essay studies a theme beginning in the OT and climaxing in the NT. Some themes are concretely embedded in the story line of the Bible (e.g., Adam, Abraham, the exodus, exile and restoration, Sinai). Other themes, while sensitive to the arc of the biblical narrative, tend to be more synthetic in nature (e.g., ethics, glory of God, holiness, justice, shame). In both cases, though, the contributors are responsible for rooting their discussions in the broad outline of the biblical story.

3. Jewish exegetical-traditions essays. One of the ways we appreciate how the NT uses the OT is to compare and contrast how Jewish literature did so in the Second Temple period and later. The task here is to uncover some of the more prominent interpretive techniques of the Jewish community. Such an endeavor is herculean in its own right, so we have assigned seven large essays to cover the use of the OT in some of the major sources of Jewish literature: Apocrypha, Dead Sea Scrolls, OT Pseudepigrapha, Philo, rabbinic literature (Mishnah, Talmud, Midrashim), Septuagint, and targums.

4. Inner-biblical exegesis. Nearly twenty essays take up a wide range of topics related to inner-biblical exegesis—method, definitions, presuppositions, literacy, letter couriers, apostolic hermeneutics, contextual use of the OT versus noncontextual use, history of research, typology, allegory, and so on. The strength of these essays lies in how the authors thoughtfully present the major views and furnish the reader with a curated and up-to-date bibliography.

5. Systematic theology. A considerable amount of theological and hermeneutical reflection has taken place in recent years, so five essays round out this dictionary by focusing on systematic categories that are related to the field of the use of the OT in the NT: theological interpretation of Scripture, bibliology, Christology, ecclesiology, and biblical theology. Theology and exegesis, especially exegesis that is aware of how NT authors incorporate the OT, is a deeply theological enterprise.

Bibliography. Beale, G. K., *A New Testament Biblical Theology* (Baker Academic, 2011); Blomberg, C., "Matthew," in *CNTUOT*, 1–109; Dodd, C. H., *According to the Scriptures* (Nisbet, 1952); Stuhlmacher, P., *Biblical Theology of the New Testament*, trans. and ed. D. P. Bailey (Eerdmans, 2018).

Abbreviations

General

Akk.	Akkadian
ANE	ancient Near East(ern)
Aram.	Aramaic
art(s).	article(s)
AT	author's translation
c.	century
ca.	circa
cf.	*confer,* compare
chap(s).	chapter(s)
col(s).	column(s)
d.	died
DSS	Dead Sea Scrolls
Eng.	English
esp.	especially
ET	English translation
fem.	feminine
fl.	flourished
frg(s).	fragment(s)
Gk.	Greek
HB	Hebrew Bible
Heb.	Hebrew
l(l).	line(s)
Lat.	Latin
lit.	literally
masc.	masculine
mg.	margin
MS(S)	manuscript(s)
n.	note
n.s.	new series
NT	New Testament
OT	Old Testament
par(s).	parallel(s)
pl.	plural
R.	Rabbi
sing.	singular
trans.	translated by
//	parallel(s)

Old Testament

Gen.	Genesis
Exod.	Exodus
Lev.	Leviticus
Num.	Numbers
Deut.	Deuteronomy
Josh.	Joshua
Judg.	Judges
Ruth	Ruth
1 Sam.	1 Samuel
2 Sam.	2 Samuel
1 Kings	1 Kings
2 Kings	2 Kings
1 Chron.	1 Chronicles
2 Chron.	2 Chronicles
Ezra	Ezra
Neh.	Nehemiah
Esther	Esther
Job	Job
Ps(s).	Psalm(s)
Prov.	Proverbs
Eccles.	Ecclesiastes
Song	Song of Songs
Isa.	Isaiah
Jer.	Jeremiah
Lam.	Lamentations
Ezek.	Ezekiel
Dan.	Daniel
Hosea	Hosea
Joel	Joel
Amos	Amos
Obad.	Obadiah
Jon.	Jonah
Mic.	Micah
Nah.	Nahum
Hab.	Habakkuk
Zeph.	Zephaniah
Hag.	Haggai
Zech.	Zechariah
Mal.	Malachi

New Testament

Matt.	Matthew
Mark	Mark
Luke	Luke
John	John
Acts	Acts
Rom.	Romans
1 Cor.	1 Corinthians
2 Cor.	2 Corinthians
Gal.	Galatians
Eph.	Ephesians
Phil.	Philippians
Col.	Colossians
1 Thess.	1 Thessalonians
2 Thess.	2 Thessalonians
1 Tim.	1 Timothy
2 Tim.	2 Timothy
Titus	Titus
Philem.	Philemon
Heb.	Hebrews
James	James
1 Pet.	1 Peter
2 Pet.	2 Peter
1 John	1 John
2 John	2 John
3 John	3 John
Jude	Jude
Rev.	Revelation

Ancient Texts, Types, and Versions

α′	Aquila
θ′	Theodotion
σ′	Symmachus
LXX	Septuagint
MT	Masoretic Text
OG	Old Greek
Vulg.	Vulgate

Modern Editions

NA[25]	*Novum Testamentum Graece.* Edited by [E. and E. Nestle], B. Aland et al., 25th rev. ed. Deutsche Bibelgesellschaft, 1963
NA[27]	*Novum Testamentum Graece.* Edited by [E. and E. Nestle], B. Aland et al., 27th rev. ed. Deutsche Bibelgesellschaft, 1993
NA[28]	*Novum Testamentum Graece.* Edited by [E. and E. Nestle], B. Aland et al., 28th rev. ed. Deutsche Bibelgesellschaft, 2012
UBS[4]	*The Greek New Testament.* Edited by B. Aland et al. 4th rev. ed. Deutsche Bibelgesellschaft, 1994
UBS[5]	*The Greek New Testament.* Edited by B. Aland et al. 5th rev. ed. Deutsche Bibelgesellschaft, 2014

Modern Versions

CEV	Contemporary English Version
CSB	Christian Standard Bible
ESV	English Standard Version
HCSB	Holman Christian Standard Bible
KJV	King James Version
NASB	New American Standard Bible
NEB	New English Bible
NET	The NET Bible (New English Translation)
NETS	New English Translation of the Septuagint
NIV	New International Version
NJPS	*Tanakh: The Holy Scriptures: The New JPS Translation according to the Traditional Hebrew Text*
NKJV	New King James Version
NLT	New Living Translation
NRSV	New Revised Standard Version
RSV	Revised Standard Version

Old Testament Apocrypha / Deuterocanonical Books

Add. Dan.	Additions to Daniel (= Pr. Azar., Sg. Three, Sus., and Bel)
Add. Esth.	Additions to Esther
Bar.	Baruch
Bel	Bel and the Dragon
1–2 Esd.	1–2 Esdras
Jdt.	Judith
1–2 Kgdms.	1–2 Kingdoms (= 1–2 Samuel)
3–4 Kgdms.	3–4 Kingdoms (= 1–2 Kings)
Let. Jer.	Letter of Jeremiah (= Baruch chap. 6)
1–4 Macc.	1–4 Maccabees
Pr. Azar.	Prayer of Azariah (often cited as part of the Song of the Three Jews)
Pr. Man.	Prayer of Manasseh
Ps. 151	Psalm 151
Sg. Three	Song of the Three Jews
Sir.	Sirach (Ecclesiasticus)
Sus.	Susanna
Tob.	Tobit
Wis.	Wisdom (of Solomon)

Old Testament Pseudepigrapha

Ahiqar	Ahiqar
Apoc. Ab.	Apocalypse of Abraham
Apoc. Adam	Apocalypse of Adam
Apoc. Dan.	Apocalypse of Daniel
Apoc. El. (C)	Coptic Apocalypse of Elijah
Apoc. El. (H)	Hebrew Apocalypse of Elijah
Apoc. Mos.	Apocalypse of Moses
Apoc. Sedr.	Apocalypse of Sedrach
Apoc. Zeph.	Apocalypse of Zephaniah
Apocr. Ezek.	Apocryphon of Ezekiel
Aris. Ex.	Aristeas the Exegete
Aristob.	Aristobulus
Artap.	Artapanus
As. Mos.	Assumption of Moses
2 Bar.	2 Baruch (Syriac Apocalypse)
3 Bar.	3 Baruch (Greek Apocalypse)
4 Bar.	4 Baruch (Paraleipomena Jeremiou)
Bk. Noah	Book of Noah
Cav. Tr.	Cave of Treasures
Cl. Mal.	Cleodemus Malchus
Dem.	Demetrius (the Chronographer)
El. Mod.	Eldad and Modad
1 En.	1 Enoch (Ethiopic Apocalypse)
2 En.	2 Enoch (Slavonic Apocalypse)
3 En.	3 Enoch (Hebrew Apocalypse)
Eup.	Eupolemus
Ezek. Trag.	Ezekiel the Tragedian
4 Ezra	4 Ezra
5 Apoc. Syr. Pss.	Five Apocryphal Syriac Psalms
Gk. Apoc. Ezra	Greek Apocalypse of Ezra
Hec. Ab.	Hecataeus of Abdera
Hel. Syn. Pr.	Hellenistic Synagogal Prayers
Hist. Jos.	History of Joseph
Hist. Rech.	History of the Rechabites
Jan. Jam.	Jannes and Jambres
Jos. Asen.	Joseph and Aseneth
Jub.	Jubilees
LAB	Liber antiquitatum biblicarum (Pseudo-Philo)
LAE	Life of Adam and Eve
Lad. Jac.	Ladder of Jacob
Let. Aris.	Letter of Aristeas
Liv. Pro.	Lives of the Prophets
Lost Tr.	The Lost Tribes
3 Macc.	3 Maccabees
4 Macc.	4 Maccabees
5 Macc.	5 Maccabees (Arabic)
Mart. Ascen. Isa.	Martyrdom and Ascension of Isaiah
Odes Sol.	Odes of Solomon
Ph. E. Poet	Philo the Epic Poet
Pr. Jac.	Prayer of Jacob
Pr. Jos.	Prayer of Joseph
Pr. Man.	Prayer of Manasseh
Pr. Mos.	Prayer of Moses
Ps.-Eup.	Pseudo-Eupolemus

Ps.-Hec. Pseudo-Hecataeus
Ps.-Orph. Pseudo-Orpheus
Ps.-Phoc. Pseudo-Phocylides
Pss. Sol. Psalms of Solomon
Ques. Ezra Questions of Ezra
Rev. Ezra Revelation of Ezra
Sib. Or. Sibylline Oracles
Syr. Men. Sentences of the Syriac Menander
T. Adam Testament of Adam
T. Job Testament of Job
T. Mos. Testament of Moses
T. Sol. Testament of Solomon
T. 3 Patr. Testaments of the Three Patriarchs
T. Ab. Testament of Abraham
T. Isaac Testament of Isaac
T. Jac. Testament of Jacob
T. 12 Patr. Testaments of the Twelve Patriarchs
T. Ash. Testament of Asher
T. Benj. Testament of Benjamin
T. Dan Testament of Dan
T. Gad Testament of Gad
T. Iss. Testament of Issachar
T. Jos. Testament of Joseph
T. Jud. Testament of Judah
T. Levi Testament of Levi
T. Naph. Testament of Naphtali
T. Reu. Testament of Reuben
T. Sim. Testament of Simeon
T. Zeb. Testament of Zebulun
Theod. Theodotus, *On the Jews*
Treat. Shem Treatise of Shem
Vis. Ezra Vision of Ezra

Dead Sea Scrolls

Qumran

Scrolls from Qumran are commonly identified by a cave number followed by a capital Q *and a document number. Scrolls that deviate from that pattern are listed below.*

ALD Aramaic Levi Document
CD Damascus Document
CD-A Damascus Document[a]
CD-B Damascus Document[b]
1QapGen ar Fragments of Genesis Apocryphon in Aramaic
1QH[a] Thanksgiving Hymns[a] (Hodayot[a])
1QH[b] Thanksgiving Hymns[b] (Hodayot[b])
1QIsa[a] Isaiah Scroll[a]
1QM War Scroll (Milḥamah)
1QpHab Pesher Habakkuk
1QS Rule of the Community (Serek Hayaḥad)
1QSa Rule of the Congregation (appendix a to 1QS)
1QSb Rule of the Blessings (appendix b to 1QS)
4QExod-Lev[f] 4QExodus-Leviticus[f]
4QJer[b,d] 4QJeremiah[b,d]
4QMMT Miqṣat Maʿaśê ha-Torah
4QpNah Nahum Pesher
4QS[a] Rule of the Community[a]
4QSam[a] 4QSamuel[a]
4QTest Testimonia
11QMelch Melchizedek

Wadi Murabbaʿat

Mur. 1 Exodus
Mur. 3 Isaiah
Mur. 4 Phylacteries
Mur. 88 XII (Minor Prophets)

Naḥal Ḥever

8Ḥev1 (8ḤevXII gr) Greek Scroll of the Minor Prophets

Masada

Mas1e Psalms[a]
Mas1k Songs of the Sabbath Sacrifice
Mas1l Apocryphon of Joshua

Mishnah, Talmud, and Related Literature

b. Babylonian Talmud
m. Mishnah
t. Tosefta
y. Jerusalem Talmud

Arakh. Arakhin
Avod. Zar. Avodah Zarah
Avot Avot
B. Bat. Bava Batra
B. Metz. Bava Metzi'a
B. Qam. Bava Qamma
Bekh. Bekhorot
Ber. Berakhot
Betzah Betzah (= Yom Tov)
Bik. Bikkurim
Demai Demai
Ed. Eduyyot
Eruv. Eruvin
Git. Gittin
Hag. Hagigah
Hal. Hallah
Hor. Horayot
Hul. Hullin
Kelim Kelim
Ker. Kerithot
Ketub. Ketubbot
Kil. Kil'ayim
Ma'as. Ma'aserot
Ma'as. Sh. Ma'aser Sheni
Mak. Makkot
Makhsh. Makhshirin
Me'il. Me'ilah
Meg. Megillah
Menah. Menahot
Mid. Middot

Mikw.	Mikwa'ot
Mo'ed	Mo'ed
Mo'ed Qat.	Mo'ed Qatan
Nash.	Nashim
Naz.	Nazir
Ned.	Nedarim
Neg.	Nega'im
Nez.	Neziqin
Nid.	Niddah
Ohal.	Ohalot
Or.	Orlah
Parah	Parah
Pe'ah	Pe'ah
Pesah.	Pesahim
Qidd.	Qiddushin
Qinnim	Qinnim
Qod.	Qodashim
Rosh Hash.	Rosh Hashanah
Sanh.	Sanhedrin
Seder	Seder
Shabb.	Shabbat
Sheqal.	Sheqalim
Shev.	Shevi'it
Shevu.	Shevu'ot
Sotah	Sotah
Sukkah	Sukkah
Ta'an.	Ta'anit
Tamid	Tamid
Tanh.	Tanhuma
Tehar.	Teharot
Tem.	Temurah
Ter.	Terumot
T. Yom.	Tevul Yom
Uq.	Uqtzin
Yad.	Yadayim
Yevam.	Yevamot
Yoma	Yoma (= Kippurim)
Zavim	Zavim
Zera.	Zera'im
Zevah.	Zevahim

Targums

Frg. Tg.	Fragmentary Targum(s)
Sam. Tg.	Samaritan Targum
Tg.	Targum + (biblical book) (e.g., Tg. Gen. = Targum Genesis)
Tg. Esth. I	First Targum of Esther
Tg. Esth. II	Second Targum of Esther
Tg. Jon.	Targum Jonathan
Tg. Ket.	Targum(s) of the Writings
Tg. Neb.	Targum of the Prophets
Tg. Neof.	Targum Neofiti
Tg. Onq.	Targum Onqelos
Tg. Ps.-J.	Targum Pseudo-Jonathan
Tg. Yer. I	Targum Yerushalmi I
Tg. Yer. II	Targum Yerushalmi II
Yem. Tg.	Yemenite Targum

Other Rabbinic Works

Ag. Ber.	Aggadat Bereshit
Avad.	Avadim
Avot R. Nat.	Avot of Rabbi Nathan
Der. Er. Rab.	Derekh Eretz Rabbah
Der. Er. Zut.	Derekh Eretz Zuta
Gem.	Gemara
Gerim	Gerim
Kallah	Kallah
Kallah Rab.	Kallah Rabbati
Kutim	Kutim
Mas. Qet.	Massekhtot Qetannot
Mas. Sop.	Masseketh Sopherim
Mek.	Mekilta
Mez.	Mezuzah
Midr.	Midrash (+ biblical book)
Pal.	Palestinian
Pesiq. Rab.	Pesiqta Rabbati
Pesiq. Rab Kah.	Pesiqta of Rab Kahana
Pirqe R. El.	Pirqe Rabbi Eliezer
Rab.	(biblical book) + Rabbah (e.g., Gen. Rab. = Genesis Rabbah)
S. Eli. Rab.	Seder Eliyahu Rabbah
S. Eli. Zut.	Seder Eliyahu Zuta
Sef. Torah	Sefer Torah
Sem.	Semahot
Shela	Shenei Luhot ha-Berit
Sifra	Sifra
Sifre	Sifre
Sof.	Soferim
S. Olam Rab.	Seder Olam Rabbah
Tan. d. El.	Tanna deve Eliyahu (= Seder Eliyahu Rabbah + Seder Eliyahu Zuta)
Tanh.	Tanhuma
Tef.	Tefillin
Tzitzit	Tzitzit
Yal.	Yalqut

Apostolic Fathers

Barn.	Barnabas
1–2 Clem.	1–2 Clement
Did.	Didache
Diogn.	Diognetus
Herm. Mand.	Shepherd of Hermas, Mandate(s)
Herm. Sim.	Shepherd of Hermas, Similitude(s)
Herm. Vis.	Shepherd of Hermas, Vision(s)
Ign. *Eph.*	Ignatius, *To the Ephesians*
Ign. *Magn.*	Ignatius, *To the Magnesians*
Ign. *Phld.*	Ignatius, *To the Philadelphians*
Ign. *Pol.*	Ignatius, *To Polycarp*
Ign. *Rom.*	Ignatius, *To the Romans*
Ign. *Smyrn.*	Ignatius, *To the Smyrnaeans*
Ign. *Trall.*	Ignatius, *To the Trallians*
Mart. Pol.	Martyrdom of Polycarp
Pol. *Phil.*	Polycarp, *To the Philippians*

Gnostic Texts / Nag Hammadi, Berlin, and Tchacos Codices

Gos. Truth — Gospel of Truth (I 3)
Trim. Prot. — Trimorphic Protennoia (XIII 1)

New Testament Apocrypha and Pseudepigrapha

Acts Pil. — Acts of Pilate
Gos. Pet. — Gospel of Peter
Gos. Thom. — Gospel of Thomas
Prot. Jas. — Protevangelium of James
Ps.-Mt. — Gospel of Pseudo-Matthew

Greek and Latin Works

Apuleius

Apol. — *Apologia (Pro se de magia)*

Aratus

Phaen. — *Phaenomena*

Aristophanes

Av. — *Aves*

Aristotle

Gen. an. — *Generation of Animals*
Hist. an. — *History of Animals*
Poet. — *Poetics*
Rhet. — *Rhetoric*

Augustine

Civ. — *The City of God*
Conf. — *Confessions*
Doctr. chr. — *Christian Instruction*
En. Ps. — *Enarrations on the Psalms*
Ep. — *Epistles*
Serm. Dom. — *Sermon on the Mount*

Aulus Gellius

Noct. att. — *Noctes atticae*

Cicero

Att. — *Epistulae ad Atticum*
De or. — *De oratore*
Inv. — *De inventione rhetorica*
Pis. — *In Pisonem*

Clement of Alexandria

Hyp. — *Hypotyposes*
Paed. — *Paedagogus*
Strom. — *Stromateis*

Cyril of Jerusalem

Cat. Lect. — *Catechetical Lectures*

Diodore of Tarsus

Comm. Ps. — *Commentary on the Psalms*

Ephrem the Syrian

Hymns Unl. Br. — *Hymns on Unleavened Bread*
Serm. Faith — *Sermons on Faith*

Epictetus

Diatr. — *Diatribai (Dissertationes)*

Epiphanius

Mens et pond. — *Of Measures and Weights*
Pan. — *Refutation of All Heresies*

Eusebius

Hist. eccl. — *Ecclesiastical History*
Praep. ev. — *Preparation for the Gospel*
Vit. Const. — *Life of Constantine*

Heraclitus

All. — *Allegoriae*

Herodotus

Hist. — *Histories*

Hesiod

Theog. — *Theogonia*

Hilary of Poitiers

Hom. Ps. — *Homilies on the Psalms*

Hippolytus

Comm. Dan. — *Commentarium in Danielem*
Haer. — *Refutatio omnium haeresium (Philosophoumena)*
Noet. — *Contra haeresin Noeti*

Homer

Od. — *Odyssey*

Irenaeus

Epid. — *Demonstration of the Apostolic Preaching*
Haer. — *Against Heresies*

Jerome

Comm. Ps. — *Commentarioli in Psalmos*
Comm. Tit. — *Commentariorum in Epistulam ad Titum liber*
Epist. — *Epistulae*
Pref. Gen. — *Preface to Genesis*
Vir. ill. — *De viris illustribus*

John Chrysostom

Hom. Gal. — *Homiliae in epistulam ad Galatas commentarius*

Josephus

Ag. Ap. — *Against Apion*
Ant. — *Jewish Antiquities*

J.W. — *Jewish War*
Life — *The Life*

Justin

1 Apol. — *First Apology*
Dial. — *Dialogue with Trypho*
Hort. — *Hortatory Address to the Greeks*

Lactantius

Inst. — *The Divine Institutes*

Longinus

Subl. — *On the Sublime*

Methodius of Olympus

Symp. — *Symposium*

Novatian

Trin. — *De trinitate*

Origen

Cels. — *Contra Celsum*
Comm. Jo. — *Commentarii in evangelium Joannis*
Comm. Matt. — *Commentarium in evangelium Matthaei*
Ep. Afr. — *Epistula ad Africanum*
Hom. Exod. — *Homiliae in Exodum*
Hom. Jer. — *Homiliae in Jeremiam*
Hom. Jes. Nav. — *In Jesu Nave homiliae xxvi*
Philoc. — *Philocalia*
Princ. — *De principiis (Peri archon)*

Philo

Abraham — *On the Life of Abraham*
Agriculture — *On Agriculture*
Alleg. Interp. — *Allegorical Interpretation*
Cherubim — *On the Cherubim*
Confusion — *On the Confusion of Tongues*
Creation — *On the Creation of the World*
Decalogue — *On the Decalogue*
Dreams — *On Dreams*
Drunkenness — *On Drunkenness*
Embassy — *On the Embassy to Gaius*
Eternity — *On the Eternity of the World*
Flaccus — *Against Flaccus*
Flight — *On Flight and Finding*
Giants — *On Giants*
Good Person — *That Every Good Person Is Free*
Heir — *Who Is the Heir?*
Hypothetica — *Hypothetica*
Joseph — *On the Life of Joseph*
Migration — *On the Migration of Abraham*
Moses — *On the Life of Moses*
Names — *On the Change of Names*
Planting — *On Planting*
Posterity — *On the Posterity of Cain*
Prelim. Studies — *On the Preliminary Studies*
Providence — *On Providence*
QE — *Questions and Answers on Exodus*
QG — *Questions and Answers on Genesis*
Rewards — *On Rewards and Punishments*
Sacrifices — *On the Sacrifices of Cain and Abel*
Sobriety — *On Sobriety*
Spec. Laws — *On the Special Laws*
Unchangeable — *That God Is Unchangeable*
Virtues — *On the Virtues*
Worse — *That the Worse Attacks the Better*

Plato

Ep. — *Epistulae*
Leg. — *Leges*
Resp. — *Respublica*
Tim. — *Timaeus*

Pliny the Elder

Nat. — *Naturalis historia*

Pliny the Younger

Ep. — *Epistulae*

Plutarch

Ages. — *Agesilaus*
Alex. — *Alexander*
Conj. praec. — *Conjugalia praecepta*
Demetr. — *Demetrius*
Luc. — *Lucullus*
Mor. — *Moralia*
Quaest. conv. — *Quaestionum convivialum libri IX*
Quaest. rom. — *Quaestiones romanae et graecae (Aetia romana et graeca)*

Porphyry

Antr. nymph. — *De antro nympharum*

Pseudo-Clementines

Recog. — *Recognitions*

Pseudo-Demetrius

De eloc. — *On Style*

Ptolemy

Flor. — *Letter to Flora*

Quintilian

Inst. — *Institutio oratoria*

Rufinus

Hist. — *Eusebii Historia ecclesiastica a Rufino translata et continuata*

Seneca

Ben. — *De beneficiis*
Clem. — *De clementia*
Ep. — *Epistulae morales*

Suetonius

Aug. *Divus Augustus*
Cal. *Gaius Caligula*
Dom. *Domitianus*

Tacitus

Hist. *Historiae*

Tertullian

Cult. fem. *The Apparel of Women*
Herm. *Against Hermogenes*
Jejun. *On Fasting, against the Psychics*
Marc. *Against Marcion*
Praescr. *Prescription against Heretics*
Prax. *Against Praxeas*
Res. *The Resurrection of the Flesh*

Theophilus

Autol. *To Autolycus*

Xenophon

Cyr. *Cyropaedia*
Mem. *Memorabilia*
Oec. *Oeconomicus*

Modern Works

AAWG Abhandlungen der Akademie der Wissenschaften in Göttingen
AB Anchor Bible
ABD *Anchor Bible Dictionary*. Edited by D. N. Freedman. 6 vols. Doubleday, 1992
AcBib Academia Biblica
AFECS Ad Fontes: Early Christian Sources
AGJU Arbeiten zur Geschichte des antiken Judentums und des Urchristentums
AIL Ancient Israel and Its Literature
AJA *American Journal of Archaeology*
ALGHJ Arbeiten zur Literatur und Geschichte des hellenistischen Judentums
ALNTS Ancient Literature for New Testament Studies
ALUOS *Annual of Leeds University Oriental Society*
AnBib Analecta biblica
ANF *Ante-Nicene Fathers*
ANRW *Aufstieg und Niedergang der römischen Welt*. Edited by H. Temporini and W. Haase. De Gruyter, 1972–
ANTC Abingdon New Testament Commentaries
AOAT Alter Orient und Altes Testament
AOTC Abingdon Old Testament Commentaries
APOT *The Apocrypha and Pseudepigrapha of the Old Testament*. Edited by R. H. Charles. 2 vols. Clarendon, 1913
ApOTC Apollos Old Testament Commentary
ArBib The Aramaic Bible
AS *Aramaic Studies*
ASBT Acadia Studies in Bible and Theology
ASNU Acta seminarii neotestamentici upsaliensis
AsTJ *Asbury Theological Journal*
ATD Das Alte Testament Deutsch
ATDan Acta theologica danica
ATR *Anglican Theological Review*
Aug *Augustinianum*
AUS American University Studies
AUSDDS Andrews University Seminary Doctoral Dissertation Series
AUSS *Andrews University Seminary Studies*
AYB Anchor Yale Bible
AYBD *Anchor Yale Bible Dictionary*. Ed. D. N. Freedman. 6 vols. Yale University Press, 1992
BA *Biblical Archaeologist*
BAFCS The Book of Acts in Its First Century Setting
BAGL *Biblical and Ancient Greek Linguistics*
BAR *Biblical Archaeology Review*
BASP *Bulletin of the American Society of Papyrologists*
BBET Beiträge zur biblischen Exegese und Theologie
BBR *Bulletin for Biblical Research*
BBRSup Bulletin for Biblical Research: Supplement Series
BCOTWP Baker Commentary on the Old Testament Wisdom and Psalms
BDAG W. Bauer, F. W. Danker, W. F. Arndt, and F. W. Gingrich. *Greek-English Lexicon of the New Testament and Other Early Christian Literature*. 3rd ed. University of Chicago Press, 2000
BDB F. Brown, S. R. Driver, and C. A. Briggs. *A Hebrew and English Lexicon of the Old Testament*. Clarendon, 1906
BDS BIBAL Dissertation Series
BEATAJ Beiträge zur Erforschung des Alten Testaments und des antiken Judentum
BECNT Baker Exegetical Commentary on the New Testament
BETL Bibliotheca ephemeridum theologicarum lovaniensium
BFCT Beiträge zur Förderung christlicher Theologie
BHHB Baylor Handbook on the Hebrew Bible
Bib *Biblica*
BibAC Bible in Ancient Christianity
BibInt *Biblical Interpretation*
BibInt Biblical Interpretation Series
BibOr Biblica et Orientalia
BIOSCS *Bulletin of the International Organization for Septuagint and Cognate Studies*
BIS Biblical Interpretation Series
BJRL *Bulletin of the John Rylands University Library of Manchester*
BJS Brown Judaic Studies

BJSUCSD Biblical and Judaic Studies from the University of California, San Diego
BLS Bible and Literature Series
BN *Biblische Notizen*
BNTC Black's New Testament Commentaries
BR *Biblical Research*
BRBS Brill's Readers in Biblical Studies
BRev *Bible Review*
BRS Biblical Resource Series
BSac *Bibliotheca sacra*
BSem Biblical Seminar
BSL Biblical Studies Library
BSR Biblioteca di scienze religiose
BST Bible Speaks Today
BTB *Biblical Theology Bulletin*
BTCP Biblical Theology for Christian Proclamation
BTFL Biblical Theology for Life
BTNT Biblical Theology of the New Testament
BTS Biblical Tools and Studies
BZABR Beihefte zur Zeitschrift für altorientalische und biblische Rechtsgeschichte
BZAW Beihefte zur Zeitschrift für die alttestamentliche Wissenschaft
BZNW Beihefte zur Zeitschrift für die neutestamentliche Wissenschaft
CAD *The Assyrian Dictionary of the Oriental Institute of the University of Chicago*. Oriental Institute of the University of Chicago, 1956–2006
CahRB Cahiers de la Revue biblique
CBC Cambridge Bible Commentary
CBET Contributions to Biblical Exegesis and Theology
CBQ *Catholic Biblical Quarterly*
CBQMS Catholic Biblical Quarterly Monograph Series
CBR *Currents in Biblical Research*
CC Continental Commentaries
CCP Cambridge Companions to Philosophy
CCT Contours of Christian Theology
CEJL Commentaries on Early Jewish Literature
CGTC Cambridge Greek Testament Commentary
Chm *Churchman*
CIJ *Corpus inscriptionum judaicarum*
CJT *Canadian Journal of Theology*
ClQ *Classical Quarterly*
CNNTE Context and Norms of New Testament Ethics
CNTUOT *Commentary on the New Testament Use of the Old Testament*. Edited by D. A. Carson and G. K. Beale. Baker Academic, 2007
Colloq *Colloquium*
CompNT Companions to the New Testament
ConBNT Coniectanea neotestamentica or Coniectanea biblica: New Testament Series
ConcC Concordia Commentary
COQG Christian Origins and the Question of God
CornBC Cornerstone Biblical Commentary
CQS Companion to the Qumran Scrolls
CRINT Compendia Rerum Iudaicarum ad Novum Testamentum
CSC Christian Standard Commentary
CSCO Corpus Scriptorum Christianorum Orientalium
CTC Christian Theology in Context
CTJ *Calvin Theological Journal*
CTL Cambridge Textbooks in Linguistics
CTM *Concordia Theological Monthly*
CTR *Criswell Theological Review*
CurBR *Currents in Biblical Research*
CurBS *Currents in Research: Biblical Studies*
CurTM *Currents in Theology and Mission*
CV *Communio Viatorum*
CWH Collected Works of Ruqaiya Hasan
CWS Classics of Western Spirituality
DBSJ *Detroit Baptist Seminary Journal*
DCH *Dictionary of Classical Hebrew*. Edited by D. J. A. Clines. 9 vols. Sheffield Phoenix Press, 1993–2014
DCLS Deuterocanonical and Cognate Literature Studies
Di *Dialog*
DJD Discoveries in the Judean Desert
DJG[1] *Dictionary of Jesus and the Gospels*. Edited by J. B. Green, S. McKnight, and I. H. Marshall. InterVarsity, 1992
DJG[2] *Dictionary of Jesus and the Gospels*. Edited by J. B. Green, J. K. Brown, and N. Perrin. 2nd ed. IVP Academic, 2013
DLNTD *Dictionary of the Later New Testament and Its Developments*. Edited by R. P. Martin and P. H. Davids. InterVarsity, 1997
DNTB *Dictionary of New Testament Background*. Edited by C. A. Evans and S. E. Porter. InterVarsity, 2000
DOTHB *Dictionary of the Old Testament: Historical Books*. Edited by B. T. Arnold and H. G. M. Williamson. InterVarsity, 2005
DOTP *Dictionary of the Old Testament: Pentateuch*. Edited by T. D. Alexander and D. W. Baker. InterVarsity, 2003
DOTPr *Dictionary of the Old Testament: Prophets*. Edited by M. J. Boda and J. G. McConville. IVP Academic, 2012
DOTWPW *Dictionary of the Old Testament: Wisdom, Poetry, and the Writings*. Edited by T. Longman III and P. Enns. InterVarsity, 2008
DPL *Dictionary of Paul and His Letters*. Edited by G. F. Hawthorne, R. P. Martin, and D. G. Reid. InterVarsity, 1993
DRev *Downside Review*
DSBOT Daily Study Bible: Old Testament
DSD *Dead Sea Discoveries*

DSI De Septuaginta Investigationes
DTIB *Dictionary for Theological Interpretation of the Bible*. Edited by K. J. Vanhoozer, C. G. Bartholomew, D. J. Treier, and N. T. Wright. Baker Academic, 2005
EBC *The Expositor's Bible Commentary with the New International Version*. 12 vols. Zondervan, 1976–92
EBCRE *The Expositor's Bible Commentary*. 13 vols. Rev. ed. Edited by T. Longman III and D. E. Garland. Zondervan, 2006–12
EBib Études bibliques
EBT Explorations in Biblical Theology
EBTC Evangelical Biblical Theology Commentary
ECC Eerdmans Critical Commentary
ECDSS Eerdmans Commentaries on the Dead Sea Scrolls
ECL Early Christianity and Its Literature
EDEJ *The Eerdmans Dictionary of Early Judaism*. Edited by J. J. Collins and D. C. Harlow. Eerdmans, 2010
EDSS *Encyclopedia of the Dead Sea Scrolls*. Edited by L. H. Schiffman and J. C. VanderKam. 2 vols. Oxford University Press, 2000
EEC Evangelical Exegetical Commentary
EJL Early Judaism and Its Literature
EKKNT Evangelisch-katholischer Kommentar zum Neuen Testament
EPSC Evangelical Press Study Commentaries
ESBT Essential Studies in Biblical Theology
EstBib *Estudios biblicos*
ESTJ *T&T Clark Encyclopedia of Second Temple Judaism*. Edited by D. M. Gurnter and L. T. Stuckenbruck. 2 vols. Bloomsbury T&T Clark, 2020
ESVEC ESV Expository Commentary
ETL *Ephemerides theologicae lovanienses*
EvQ *Evangelical Quarterly*
EvT *Evangelische Theologie*
ExAud *Ex Auditu*
ExpB Exploring the Bible
ExpTim *Expository Times*
FAT Forschungen zum Alten Testament
FBBS Facet Books, Biblical Series
FC The Fathers of the Church
FCT Formation of Christian Theology
FET Foundations of Evangelical Theology
FGM *The Dead Sea Scrolls: Study Edition*. Edited by F. García Martínez and E. J. C. Tigchelaar. 2 vols. Brill, 1997–98
FOTL Forms of the Old Testament Literature
FRLANT Forschungen zur Religion und Literatur des Alten und Neuen Testaments
FTS Frankfurter theologische Studien
GAP Guides to the Apocrypha and Pseudepigrapha
GKC *Gesenius' Hebrew Grammar*. Edited by E. Kautzsch. Translated by A. E. Cowley. 2nd ed. Clarendon, 1910
GorgBS Gorgias Biblical Studies
HALOT L. Koehler, W. Baumgartner, and J. J. Stamm. *The Hebrew and Aramaic Lexicon of the Old Testament*. Translated and edited under the supervision of M. E. J. Richardson. 4 vols. Brill, 1994–99
HBAI *Hebrew Bible and Ancient Israel*
HBI History of Biblical Interpretation Series
HBOT *Hebrew Bible / Old Testament: The History of Its Interpretation*. Edited by M. Saebø. 5 vols. Vandenhoeck & Ruprecht, 1996–2015
HBS History of Biblical Studies
HBT *Horizons in Biblical Theology*
HCOT Historical Commentary on the Old Testament
HDR Harvard Dissertations in Religion
Hen *Henoch*
Herm Hermeneia
HeyJ *Heythrop Journal*
HNT Handbuch zum Neuen Testament
HOTE Handbooks for Old Testament Exegesis
HRCS E. Hatch and H. A. Redpath. *Concordance to the Septuagint and Other Greek Versions of the Old Testament*. 2 vols. Clarendon, 1897. 2nd ed. Baker, 1998
HS *Hebrew Studies*
HSM Harvard Semitic Monographs
HSS Harvard Semitic Studies
HTKAT Herders theologischer Kommentar zum Alten Testament
HTR *Harvard Theological Review*
HTS Harvard Theological Studies
HUT Hermeneutische Untersuchungen zur Theologie
HvTSt *Hervormde teologiese studies*
IBC Interpretation: A Bible Commentary for Teaching and Preaching
ICC International Critical Commentary
IDB *The Interpreter's Dictionary of the Bible*. Edited by G. A. Buttrick. 4 vols. Abingdon, 1962
IDS *In die Skriflig*
IEJ *Israel Exploration Journal*
Imm *Immanuel*
Int *Interpretation*
ITC International Theological Commentary
IVPNTC IVP New Testament Commentaries
JAAR *Journal of the American Academy of Religion*
JAOS *Journal of the American Oriental Society*
JBL *Journal of Biblical Literature*
JBPR *Journal of Biblical and Pneumatological Research*
JCPS Jewish and Christian Perspective Series

JCT	T&T Clark Jewish and Christian Texts Series
JESOT	*Journal for the Evangelical Study of the Old Testament*
JETS	*Journal of the Evangelical Theological Society*
JGCJ	*Journal of Greco-Roman Christianity and Judaism*
JHebS	*Journal of Hebrew Scriptures*
JJS	*Journal of Jewish Studies*
JLE	*Journal of Lutheran Ethics*
JLSM	Janua Linguarum, Series Maior
JNES	*Journal of Near Eastern Studies*
JOTT	*Journal of Translation and Textlinguistics*
JPSBC	Jewish Publication Society Bible Commentary
JPSTC	Jewish Publication Society Torah Commentary
JR	*Journal of Religion*
JSHJ	*Journal for the Study of the Historical Jesus*
JSJ	*Journal for the Study of Judaism in the Persian, Hellenistic, and Roman Periods*
JSJSup	Journal for the Study of Judaism: Supplement Series
JSNT	*Journal for the Study of the New Testament*
JSNTSup	Journal for the Study of the New Testament: Supplement Series
JSOT	*Journal for the Study of the Old Testament*
JSOTSup	Journal for the Study of the Old Testament: Supplement Series
JSP	*Journal for the Study of the Pseudepigrapha*
JSPL	*Journal for the Study of Paul and His Letters*
JSPSup	Journal for the Study of the Pseudepigrapha: Supplement Series
JSS	*Journal of Semitic Studies*
JTI	*Journal of Theological Interpretation*
JTISup	Journal of Theological Interpretation Supplements
JTS	*Journal of Theological Studies*
JTSA	*Journal of Theology for Southern Africa*
KAT	Kommentar zum Alten Testament
KEL	Kregel Exegetical Library
LBS	Library of Biblical Studies
LCC	Library of Christian Classics
LCL	Loeb Classical Library
LEC	Library of Early Christianity
LHBOTS	Library of Hebrew Bible/Old Testament Studies
LNTS	Library of New Testament Studies
LPS	Library of Pauline Studies
LQ	*Lutheran Quarterly*
LSJ	H. G. Liddell, R. Scott, and H. S. Jones. *A Greek-English Lexicon*. 9th ed. with rev. supplement. Clarendon, 1996
LSTS	The Library of Second Temple Studies
MentC	Mentor Commentary
MJT	*Mid-America Journal of Theology*
MNTC	Moffatt New Testament Commentary
MNTS	McMaster New Testament Studies
MOP	*Między Oryginałem a Przekładem*
MSU	Mitteilungen des Septuaginta-Unternehmens
NABPRDS	National Association of Baptist Professors of Religion Dissertation Series
NAC	New American Commentary
NCBC	New Century Bible Commentary
NCHB	*The New Cambridge History of the Bible*. 4 vols. Edited by J. C. Paget, J. Schaper, R. Marsden, E. A. Matter, E. Cameron, and J. Riches. Cambridge University Press, 2012–16
NDBT	*New Dictionary of Biblical Theology*. Edited by T. D. Alexander and B. S. Rosner. InterVarsity, 2000
NDT	*New Dictionary of Theology*. Edited by S. B. Ferguson and D. F. Wright. Intervarsity, 1988
Neot	*Neotestamentica*
NIB	*The New Interpreter's Bible*. Edited by L. E. Keck. 12 vols. Abingdon, 1994–2004
NIBC	New International Biblical Commentary
NICNT	New International Commentary on the New Testament
NICOT	New International Commentary on the Old Testament
NIDB	*New Interpreter's Dictionary of the Bible*. Edited by K. D. Sakenfeld. 5 vols. Abingdon, 2006–9
NIDNTT	*New International Dictionary of New Testament Theology*. Edited by C. Brown. 4 vols. Zondervan, 1975–85
NIDOTTE	*New International Dictionary of Old Testament Theology and Exegesis*. Edited by W. A. VanGemeren. 5 vols. Zondervan, 1997
NIGTC	New International Greek Testament Commentary
NIVAC	NIV Application Commentary
NovT	*Novum Testamentum*
NovTSup	Supplements to Novum Testamentum
NPNF[1]	*Nicene and Post-Nicene Fathers*, Series 1
NPNF[2]	*Nicene and Post-Nicene Fathers*, Series 2
NSBT	New Studies in Biblical Theology
NTBT	G. K. Beale. *A New Testament Biblical Theology*. Baker Academic, 2011
NTC	The New Testament in Context
NTM	New Testament Monographs
NTOA	Novum Testamentum et Orbis Antiquus
NTR	New Testament Readings
NTS	*New Testament Studies*
NTSI	The New Testament and the Scriptures of Israel
NTTh	New Testament Theology
NTTS	New Testament Tools and Studies

NVBS New Voices in Biblical Studies
OBO Orbis biblicus et orientalis
OBT Overtures to Biblical Theology
OCA Orientalia Christiana Analecta
OCD *Oxford Classical Dictionary*. Edited by S. Hornblower, A. Spawforth, and E. Eidinow. 4th ed. Oxford University Press, 2012
OHDSS *Oxford Handbook of the Dead Sea Scrolls*. Edited by T. H. Lim and J. J. Collins. Oxford University Press, 2010
OTG Old Testament Guides
OTL Old Testament Library
OTP *Old Testament Pseudepigrapha*. Edited by J. H. Charlesworth. 2 vols. Doubleday, 1983–85
PACS Philo of Alexandria Commentary Series
PaSt Pauline Studies
PBM Paternoster Biblical Monographs
PBTM Paternoster Biblical and Theological Monographs
PhA Philosophia Antiqua
PIBA *Proceedings of the Irish Biblical Association*
PL Patrologia Latina [= Patrologiae Cursus Completus: Series Latina]. Edited by J.-P. Migne. 217 vols. Paris, 1844–64
PLCL *Philo in Ten Volumes (and Two Supplementary Volumes)*. English translation by F. H. Colson, G. H. Whitaker (and R. Marcus). 12 vols. LCL. William Heinemann; Harvard University Press, 1929–62
PNTC Pillar New Testament Commentary
PPS Popular Patristics Series
PresbRev *Presbyterian Review*
ProEccl *Pro Ecclesia*
PRSt *Perspectives in Religious Studies*
PrTMS Princeton Theological Monograph Series
PrW Preaching the Word
PS Pauline Studies
PTS Patristische Texte und Studien
PTSDSSP Princeton Theological Seminary Dead Sea Scrolls Project
RAD Reformed Academic Dissertations
RB *Revue biblique*
RBS Resources for Biblical Study
REC Reformed Expository Commentary
RevExp *Review and Expositor*
RevQ *Revue de Qumran*
RF&P *Reformed Faith & Practice*
RRJ *Review of Rabbinic Judaism*
RSMS Religious Studies Monograph Series
RTR *Reformed Theological Review*
RVV Religionsgeschichtliche Versuche und Vorarbeiten
SAIS Studies in the Aramaic Interpretation of Scripture
SAK *Studien zur Altägyptischen Kultur*
SANT Studien zum Alten und Neuen Testaments
SAOC Studies in Ancient Oriental Civilizations
SBB Stuttgarter biblische Beiträge
SBJT *Southern Baptist Journal of Theology*
SBLDS Society of Biblical Literature Dissertation Series
SBLEJL Society of Biblical Literature Early Judaism and Its Literature
SBLMS Society of Biblical Literature Monograph Series
SBLSCS Society of Biblical Literature Septuagint and Cognate Studies
SBLSP Society of Biblical Literature Seminar Papers
SBLSymS Society of Biblical Literature Symposium Series
SBS Sources for Biblical Study
SBSlov *Studia Biblica Slovaca*
SBT Studies in Biblical Theology
SCJR *Studies in Christian-Jewish Relations*
SCS Septuagint and Cognate Studies
SDSSRL Studies in the Dead Sea Scrolls and Related Literature
SE *Studia evangelica*
SECT Sources of Early Christian Thought
SemeiaSt Semeia Studies
SeptCS Septuagint Commentary Series
SFSHJ South Florida Studies in the History of Judaism
SHBC Smyth & Helwys Bible Commentary
SHCANE Studies in the History and Culture of the Ancient Near East
SJ Studia Judaica
SJCA Studies in Judaism and Christianity in Antiquity
SJOT *Scandinavian Journal of the Old Testament*
SJT *Scottish Journal of Theology*
SJud Studies in Judaism
SLTHS Siphrut: Literature and Theology of the Hebrew Scriptures
SNTSMS Society for New Testament Studies Monograph Series
SNTW Studies of the New Testament and Its World
SP Sacra Pagina
SPhA Studies in Philo of Alexandria
SPhilo *Studia Philonica*
SPhiloA *Studia Philonica Annual*
SSBT Short Studies in Biblical Theology
SSEJC Studies in Scripture in Early Judaism and Christianity
STDJ Studies on the Texts of the Desert of Judah
STR *Southeastern Theological Review*
Str-B H. L. Strack and P. Billerbeck. *Kommentar zum Neuen Testament aus Talmud und Midrasch*. 6 vols. Beck, 1922–61

StT — Studi e Testi, Biblioteca apostolica vaticana
SUNT — Studien zur Umwelt des Neuen Testaments
SVTP — Studia in Veteris Testamenti Pseudepigraphica
SwJT — *Southwestern Journal of Theology*
SymS — Symposium Series
TANZ — Texte und Arbeiten zum neutestamentlichen Zeitalter
TB — Theologische Bücherei: Neudrucke und Berichte aus dem 20. Jahrhundert
TBei — *Theologische Beiträge*
TBN — Themes in Biblical Narrative
TBT — *The Bible Today*
TC — Theology in Community Series
TDNT — *Theological Dictionary of the New Testament*. Edited by G. Kittel and G. Friedrich. Translated by G. W. Bromiley. 10 vols. Eerdmans, 1964–76
TDOT — *Theological Dictionary of the Old Testament*. Edited by G. J. Botterweck and H. Ringgren. Translated by J. T. Willis, G. W. Bromiley, and D. E. Green. 14 vols. Eerdmans, 1974–
TENTS — Texts and Editions for New Testament Study
TGST — Tesi Gregoriana: Serie Teologia
Them — *Themelios*
THNTC — Two Horizons New Testament Commentary
THOTC — Two Horizons Old Testament Commentary
ThTo — *Theology Today*
TJ — *Trinity Journal*
TLNT — C. Spicq. *Theological Lexicon of the New Testament*. Translated and edited by J. Ernest. 3 vols. Hendrickson, 1994
TLOT — *Theological Lexicon of the Old Testament*. Edited by E. Jenni, with assistance from C. Westermann. Translated by M. E. Biddle. 3 vols. Hendrickson, 1997
TLZ — *Theologische Literaturzeitung*
TMSJ — *The Master's Seminary Journal*
TNTC — Tyndale New Testament Commentaries
TOTC — Tyndale Old Testament Commentaries
TQ — *Theologische Quartalschrift*
TS — *Theological Studies*
TSAJ — Texte und Studien zum antiken Judentum
TTCS — Teach the Text Commentary Series
TWOT — *Theological Wordbook of the Old Testament*. Edited by R. L. Harris, G. L. Archer Jr., and B. K. Waltke. 2 vols. Moody, 1980
TynBul — *Tyndale Bulletin*
UBCS — Understanding the Bible Commentary Series
UCOP — University of Cambridge Oriental Publications
VC — *Vigiliae christianae*
VCSup — Supplements to Vigiliae christianae
VT — *Vetus Testamentum*
VTSup — Supplements to Vetus Testamentum
WAC — M. O. Wise, M. G. Abegg Jr., and E. M. Cook. *The Dead Sea Scrolls: A New Translation*. HarperCollins, 2005
WAW — Writings from the Ancient World
WBC — Word Biblical Commentary
WBT — Word Biblical Themes
WCF — Westminster Confession of Faith
WGRW — Writings from the Greco-Roman World
WMANT — Wissenschaftliche Monographien zum Alten und Neuen Testament
WTJ — *Westminster Theological Journal*
WTMS — Westminster Theological Monograph Series
WUNT — Wissenschaftliche Untersuchungen zum Neuen Testament
ZABR — *Zeitschrift für altorientalische und biblische Rechtgeschichte*
ZAW — *Zeitschrift für die alttestamentliche Wissenschaft*
ZCINT — Zondervan Critical Introductions to the New Testament
ZECNT — Zondervan Exegetical Commentary on the New Testament
ZECOT — Zondervan Exegetical Commentary on the Old Testament
ZNW — *Zeitschrift für die neutestamentliche Wissenschaft und die Kunde der älteren Kirche*
ZPE — *Zeitschrift für Papyrologie und Epigraphik*
ZTK — *Zeitschrift für Theologie und Kirche*

Abraham and Abrahamic Tradition

Abraham in the OT

In the beginning God created the heavens and the earth, and made man and woman in his own image. After the sin of Adam and Eve at the fall comes an accumulation of further evil, such that "the LORD saw how great the wickedness of the human race had become on the earth, and that every inclination of the thoughts of the human heart was only evil all the time" (Gen. 6:5). God therefore brings judgment upon the world, leaving only eight people remaining, Noah and his family. He then makes a covenant with Noah, promising not to curse the earth again or destroy all life (8:21), blessing Noah and his sons (9:1), and instructing Noah to repopulate the world (9:1–17). Immediately after these instructions from God, Noah gets drunk and curses his grandson, Ham's son Canaan. The covenant with Noah, therefore, is clearly not a solution to the problem of the world's sin. Indeed, immediately after the flood God declares it still to be true that "every inclination of the human heart is evil from childhood" (8:21). Through the line of his son Shem, Noah has a descendant Terah, who worships idols, not the true God (Gen. 11:10–26; Josh. 24:2). It is against this background that God calls Terah's son Abraham.

Abraham, who at this point is still named Abram, is first mentioned in Gen. 11. He is introduced as a son of Terah, married to Sarai (later Sarah), and uncle of Lot. In Gen. 17, as part of the terms of his covenant with Abraham, God says, "No longer will you be called Abram; your name will be Abraham, for I have made you a father of many nations" (Gen. 17:5). Thereafter in the Bible, except in two cases where both names are noted (1 Chron. 1:27; Neh. 9:7), he is called Abraham.

In Gen. 11 Abraham sets out with his father from Ur to journey to Canaan, but en route he settles in Haran. In Gen. 12, Abraham receives a promise: "I will make you into a great nation, and I will bless you; I will make your name great, and you will be a blessing. I will bless those who bless you, and whoever curses you I will curse; and all peoples on earth will be blessed through you" (12:2–3). God also promises Abraham the land of Canaan (12:7). In Gen. 15, the promise of the land is repeated (15:7), and God's commitment to multiply Abraham's descendants is intensified: "Look up at the sky and count the stars—if indeed you can count them. . . . So shall your offspring be" (15:5). In response, Abraham trusts the promise: "Abram believed the LORD, and he credited it to him as righteousness" (15:6). The promises to Abraham are therefore different from the covenant with Noah. Rather than commanding Noah to have children, God *promises* Abraham descendants; and God not only blesses Abraham, as he has blessed Noah's sons, but also decrees that Abraham himself will be a means of blessing for all nations.

In Gen. 17, the promise of numerous descendants for Abraham is reiterated and elaborated: Abraham will be the forefather of nations, and the ancestor of kings (17:6, 16). It is at this point that God commands Abraham to circumcise himself and requires that all his descendants also be circumcised (17:9–14). Circumcision is to be the "sign of the covenant" between Abraham and God (17:11). Abraham duly circumcises himself and all his household (17:23–27). In Gen. 22:16–17 the promise to Abraham is confirmed: "I swear by myself, declares the LORD, that because you have done this and have not withheld your son, your only son, I will surely bless you and make your descendants as numerous as the stars in the sky." Here God is not only promising but also taking an oath ("I swear by myself"), and the content of the oath is expressed in an emphatic Hebrew idiom (lit., "to bless I will bless you, and to multiply I will multiply").

This promise faces a difficulty: Sarah appears to be unable to have children. To obviate this problem Sarah and Abraham plan that he would have an heir through Sarah's slave Hagar, who then indeed gives birth to Abraham's first son, Ishmael (Gen. 16). But Ishmael, a result of a naturally schemed process, is not to be the heir. The heir is to be the miraculously conceived Isaac, born to Sarah in God's fulfillment of his promise (Gen. 21:1–2).

Genesis 25 records that Abraham had another wife (or concubine, in 1 Chron. 1:32), Keturah, who gave birth to six sons: Zimran, Jokshan, Medan, Midian, Ishbak, and Shuah (Gen. 25:2). After distributing property to all of his children in his lifetime, Abraham left everything he owned at his death to Isaac and died at the age of a hundred and seventy-five (25:5–7).

After Genesis, such is Abraham's significance that his name is frequently employed to identify God himself: "the God of Abraham, Isaac and Jacob/Israel" (Exod. 3:16; 1 Kings 18:36; 2 Chron. 30:6; cf. 1 Chron. 29:18), or "the God of Abraham, the God of Isaac and the God of Jacob" (Exod. 3:6, 15; 4:5), or even simply "the God of Abraham" (Ps. 47:9). In Isaiah, God goes so far as to call Abraham "my friend" (Isa. 41:8; cf. 2 Chron. 20:7).

The focus in the rest of the OT is on Abraham as the ancestor of the nation of Israel and the first recipient of God's covenant. When the Israelites suffer in Egypt, God remembers his covenant with Abraham (Exod. 2:24) and reaffirms his promise to Abraham that he would give them a land (6:7–8). When God threatens to destroy the nation, Moses appeals to God on the basis of his promise: "Remember your servants Abraham, Isaac and Israel, to whom you swore by your own self: 'I will make your descendants as numerous as the stars in the sky and I will give your descendants all this land I promised them, and it will be their inheritance forever'" (32:13). The rest of the OT contains numerous reaffirmations or recollections of the promises, especially to give Abraham's descendants the land (Lev. 26:40–45; Num. 32:11–12; Deut. 1:8; 26:10; 30:20; 34:4, etc.).

Early Jewish Interpretation

At least two motifs in early Jewish interpretation are especially relevant to the NT reception of Abraham, partly because Paul in particular appears to dispute some of the conventional ways in which Abraham is understood. These are encapsulated in a statement in Ben Sira (ca. 190 BC): "Abraham was a great father of many nations, and no-one was found like him in glory, who kept the Law of the most high and entered into covenant with him, and established the covenant in his flesh, and was found faithful in testing" (Sir. 44:19–20 AT). Abraham is both father of the nation and obedient to God.

First, then, Abraham is highlighted as father of the nation of Israel. Indeed, as seen in Ben Sira, he is the father of *nations*. One of his grandsons, Nebaioth son of Ishmael, was understood by Josephus to have been the ancestor of the Nabataeans (*Ant.* 1.12.4). According to 1 Macc. 12:21, Abraham is also the father of the Spartans. Primarily, however, Abraham was—through the line of Isaac and Jacob—the father of Israel, as the 1 Maccabees reference also makes clear when it says that the Spartans and the Jews have a common kinship. Or again, elsewhere, the phrases "the descendants of Abraham," "the children of the sainted Jacob," and "a people of your consecrated portion" are all ways of referring to Israel (3 Macc. 6:3).

Second, there is an emphasis on Abraham's piety. This is sometimes expressed in general terms as Abraham's sinlessness (Pr. Man. 8–9; T. Ab. 10:13). Sometimes it is connected with faithfulness in his trials, as in 1 Maccabees (ca. 100 BC): "Was not Abraham found faithful when tested, and it was reckoned to him as righteousness?" (1 Macc. 2:52). Similarly, Jubilees (ca. 150 BC) refers to the death of Sarah as "the tenth trial with which Abraham was tried, and he was found faithful, controlled of spirit. . . . He was found faithful and he was recorded as a friend of God in the heavenly tablets" (Jub. 19:8–9 AT). In the Mishnah (ca. AD 200), on the other hand, circumcision is the pinnacle of Abraham's piety: "Great is circumcision, for despite all the religious duties which our father Abraham performed, he was not called perfect until he was circumcised" (m. Ned. 3.11 AT). Among the Dead Sea Scrolls, Abraham's faithfulness and title of "friend of God" came "because he kept the commandments of God" (CD 3.2–4 AT).

Abraham in the NT

In the NT, Abraham is employed principally in four ways: as a type or comparandum of Christ, as father of God's universal people, as a type of Christian faith, and as the possessor of a reconfigured land.

Abraham and Christ. First, various NT authors employ the figure of Abraham and the promise made to him in a more or less directly christological manner. At a minimum, Abraham is an ancestor of Jesus (Matt. 1:2–16; Luke 3:23–38). Galatians takes the further step of identifying Jesus not as one of the promised descendants of Abraham but as *the* descendant: "Now the promises were made to Abraham and to his seed. It does not say, 'and to his seed*s*,' as if it were about plural seeds. Rather, it is about one: hence, '*to your seed*,' who is Christ" (Gal. 3:16 AT). Luke also goes further than merely seeing Abraham as part of Jesus's genealogy and says that Christ is the fulfillment of the promise. In the Magnificat, Mary sings that God "has helped his servant Israel, remembering to be merciful to Abraham and his descendants forever, just as he promised our ancestors" (Luke 1:54–55). This has taken place in the coming of Christ, understood here as the blessing promised to Abraham and his children. Shortly afterwards, in the Benedictus, Zechariah sings that in Christ, God has brought salvation to Israel "to show mercy to our ancestors and to remember his holy covenant, the oath he swore to our father Abraham" (1:72–73). Again, Christ is understood quite directly here as the fulfillment of what God promised to Abraham.

Elsewhere, comparisons are drawn between Abraham and Jesus. Romans implies that Abraham is a type of Christ. Abraham's body was already as good as dead, as was Sarah's womb (Rom. 4:19). Nevertheless, he became the father of many nations in accordance with the promise (4:16–17). While Abraham's faith foreshadows Christian faith, Abraham also foreshadows Jesus, because both were dead and yet are given life by the God who raises the dead.

John's Gospel draws a different comparison. Abraham is treated by Jews in the Gospel narrative as the defining, founding figure of the distant past. Yet Jesus as the incarnation of the preexistent Word is of greater antiquity than Abraham, who lived a millennium and a half earlier (John 8:58). Hence Jesus can say that, even in the patriarch's own time, Abraham saw Jesus's day and rejoiced (8:56). This perhaps alludes to a Jewish exegetical tradition—rooted in God's address to Abraham in the dark in Gen. 15:17–21—that Abraham not only received revelation *about* future glory but was actually shown it: "To him alone you revealed the end of times, secretly by night" (4 Ezra 3:14). It is not merely that Jesus is older than Abraham, however. The words "Before Abraham came into being, I am" imply that Christ belongs to the realm of eternally existent being, in contrast to Abraham and all the rest of creation, which "came into being" (John 8:58 AT; cf. 1:3).

Abraham and the people of God. Second, given Abraham's status as the founding father of the family of God, the question of who is a child of Abraham is central in the NT. In continuity with the OT, the NT defines the people of God in terms of Abrahamic descent, and this is expounded both negatively or exclusively, as well as positively or inclusively.

Negatively, already John the Baptist questions whether Abrahamic paternity understood in a biological or genealogical sense is significant on its own: "Do not think you can say to yourselves, 'We have Abraham as our father.' I tell you that out of these stones God can raise up children for Abraham" (Matt. 3:9; cf. Luke 3:8). The Baptist then warns that those who do not produce fruit will be cut down and thrown into the fire; just as in Jesus's parable of the rich man and Lazarus, in which the rich man is in hell even though he is a son of Abraham (Luke 16:24–27). Again, in John's Gospel, Jesus concedes that his Jewish opponents are the *seed* of Abraham, but their actions show that they are not really his *children* (John 8:37, 39).

Similarly, Paul explains in Romans how biological descent is not a sufficient condition of being an heir of Abraham. In this respect, Paul is continuing along the lines of Genesis, according to which only Isaac of Abraham's eight sons was his heir. This was true materially: "Abraham left everything he owned to Isaac" (Gen. 25:5). It was also true of the promised blessing: "It is through Isaac that your offspring will be reckoned" (Gen. 21:12). For Paul, as for John the Baptist and Jesus, Abrahamic descent must be evidenced in action: "And he is then also the father of the circumcised who not only are circumcised but who also follow in the footsteps of the faith that our father Abraham had before he was circumcised" (Rom. 4:12). Paul goes on to state that the relationship to Abraham is grounded in God's elective grace: "Nor because they are his descendants are they all Abraham's children. On the contrary, 'It is through Isaac that your offspring will be reckoned.' In other words, it is not the children by physical descent who are God's children, but it is the children of the promise who are regarded as Abraham's offspring" (Rom. 9:7–8). Paul grounds his argument here in the statement about Isaac in Gen. 21:12 noted earlier. The continuation of Isaac's line is also grounded in God's sovereign grace: "Not only that, but Rebekah's children were conceived at the same time by our father Isaac. Yet, before the twins were born or had done anything good or bad—in order that God's purpose in election might stand: not by works but by him who calls—she was told, 'The older will serve the younger'" (Rom. 9:10–12). Again, Paul's understanding of the set of Abraham's children excludes some, on the basis of the scriptural promises, who might have been assumed to belong in it. Alternatively, Gal. 4 classifies non-Christian Jews of the earthly Jerusalem not as Abraham's children but as Ishmaelite children of Hagar, because of (1) their persecution of Christians, in imitation of Ishmael's mockery of Isaac (Gal. 4:29; cf. Gen. 21:9); (2) their adherence to the law, which was given at Sinai in Arabia (Gal. 4:24–25); and (3) the resulting servitude, because this adherence to the law meant that they were still in the old age under slavery and the divine curse (3:10, 23–24; 4:1–3). There is emphasis throughout the NT, therefore, on how some who were assumed to be children of Abraham are in fact excluded from that family.

On the other hand, positively, the same scriptural promises also *include* those not expected to be a part of the family of Abraham. Zacchaeus, identified by his name (*Zakkai*) as a Jew, was a tax collector—a despised trade often referred to in rabbinic phrases such as "murderers, robbers and tax-collectors" (m. Ned. 3.4). In one rabbinic ruling, if a thief enters a house, only the part touched by the thief is defiled, but if a tax collector enters a house, the whole house automatically becomes unclean (m. Tehar. 7:6). In the parable of the Pharisee and the tax collector in Luke 18, the term comes at the end of a list: "robbers, evildoers, adulterers—or even like this tax collector" (v. 11). Yet in the following chapter, Zacchaeus shows the fruit that accords with repentance, giving half his wealth to the poor and repaying fourfold those he has cheated (Luke 19:8). As a result, Jesus declares, "Today salvation has come to this house, because this man, too, is a son of Abraham" (19:9). This salvation is rooted in Jesus's coming to rescue what was lost (19:10).

The focus in Paul, on the other hand, is on the inclusion of gentiles into Abraham's family. This is not because Jews are by default included: as we have seen, Abraham is "the father of the circumcised who not only are circumcised but who also follow in the footsteps of the faith that our father Abraham had" (Rom. 4:12). Rather, gentiles and Jews are included in the family of Abraham (1) on the same basis and (2) by the same means.

The basis is Christ himself. As was noted above in connection with Gal. 3:16, Christ is the singular seed of Abraham. This leads to the striking conclusion that there were in fact no independent descendants of Abraham in the time between the promise and the coming of Jesus. In fact, all believers are only secondarily descendants of Abraham, through being incorporated into Christ. This is stated clearly in Galatians: "So in Christ Jesus you are all children of God through faith, for all of you who were baptized into Christ have clothed yourselves with Christ. There is neither Jew nor Gentile, neither slave nor free, nor is there male and female, for you are all one in Christ Jesus. *If you belong to Christ, then you are Abraham's seed, and heirs according to the promise"* (3:26–29). The union with Christ brought about through baptism into Christ brings adoption into the family of God and the family of Abraham.

Just as inclusion in the family of Abraham comes on the same basis for all (namely, Christ), so it is through the same *means* (namely, faith). Abraham was the prototypical believer, as shown by Gen. 15:6, which Paul quotes in Gal. 3: "So also Abraham 'believed God, and it was credited to him as righteousness.' Understand, then, that those who have faith are children of Abraham. Scripture foresaw that God would justify the Gentiles by faith, and announced the gospel in advance to Abraham: 'All nations will be blessed through you.' So those who rely on faith are blessed along with Abraham, the man of faith" (3:6–9). On the principle that children imitate their fathers and are marked out by following in the footsteps of their fathers, all Christians are children of Abraham because they are marked by faith. The second quotation in this passage, from Gen. 12:3, applies this paternity principle to non-Jews, who have just as much access to faith as do Jews. As a result of being by faith, righteousness is not through observance of the law.

Paul arrives at a similar conclusion in Romans through a close reading of Gen. 12–17. We saw earlier the sequence of events in these chapters: promise (Gen. 12); reaffirmation of the promise, Abraham's justification, and the covenant (Gen. 15); circumcision (Gen. 17). In some early Jewish exegesis of these chapters, as we have seen, these events are read together as a single unit. By contrast, Paul emphasizes how in Gen. 15 Abraham is *already* justified by God: righteousness has already been reckoned or credited to him (Gen. 15:6). It is only afterward that the covenant of circumcision is instituted. Hence Paul argues, "Abraham's faith was credited to him as righteousness. Under what circumstances was it credited? Was it after he was circumcised, or before? It was not after, but before! And he received circumcision as a sign, a seal of the righteousness that he had by faith while he was still uncircumcised" (Rom. 4:9–11). Paul picks up on both the sequence (justification in Gen. 15 precedes circumcision in Gen. 17) and the language of circumcision being a "sign" of the covenant: in other words, circumcision is not the thing itself but a symbolic representation (Gen. 17:11). Paul glosses the word "sign," understanding it as a "seal." Again, then, circumcision is not righteousness or the covenant itself, but an attestation or confirmation of it. Hence justification does not come through works of observance of the law, for either Jews or gentiles (Rom. 4:1–8).

Abraham and Christian faith. The Abraham narrative is also explained in the NT to elucidate the character of faith. Paul draws together some of the strands of the Abraham narrative in his account of faith in Rom. 4: "Against all hope, Abraham in hope believed and so became the father of many nations, just as it had been said to him, 'So shall your offspring be.' Without weakening in his faith, he faced the fact that his body was as good as dead—since he was about a hundred years old—and that Sarah's womb was also dead. Yet he did not waver through unbelief regarding the promise of God, but was strengthened in his faith and gave glory to God, being fully persuaded that God had power to do what he had promised" (Rom. 4:18–21). Three elements from the Genesis narrative can be identified here. First, there is the "deadness" of Abraham and Sarah, which establishes that, left to their own devices, there would have been no possibility of a descendant for them: it was "against all hope." Second, Abraham's trust is not a generalized submission to a higher power but trust in a specific promise spoken by God. Third, it is a confidence in God's power to bring about what in the human sphere is the ultimate impossibility: bringing life from death. The reference to Abraham's trust in the God "who gives life to the dead and calls into being things that were not" (4:17) looks back to the trust in "God who justifies the ungodly" (4:5) and forward to trust "in him who raised Jesus our Lord from the dead" (4:24). Abraham "trusted in the God who enlivens the dead" (4:17), and so he foreshadows Christians who trust "in the one who raised Jesus our Lord from the dead" (4:24).

For some scholars, Abraham is understood as a type of Christ in Rom. 4, because just as Abraham has faith, so does Christ. Hence, on this view, Christ is a paradigm of faith, and therefore references to "faith *in* Christ" in Paul are really references to the "faith *of* Christ," the faith that Christ himself exercises. One of the chief difficulties with this approach is that Paul takes Gen. 15:6, "Abraham believed God, and it was credited to him as righteousness," as one of his key texts for justification or righteousness. It is important to note here that the words for "faith," "trust," and "believing" in Greek (the noun *pistis* and the verb *pisteuō*) are part of the same word-group. Similarly, the same is true for "righteousness" and "justification" (the noun *dikaiosynē* and the verb *dikaioō*). Hence, when Paul says "Abraham's believing → righteousness," that is the same as saying that "faith → justification"; the person believes and then is justified through that faith.

James is engaged in debate not with a traditional exegesis of Abraham in which his faith is conflated with circumcision and his other trials but with a caricature of Pauline teaching. We know of some who seem to have distorted Paul's teaching on the resurrection and concluded that for Christians "the resurrection has already taken place" (2 Tim. 2:18). Similarly, others amplified Paul's *distinction* between faith and works into an *opposition* between them, at least in practice. James contends with the person who "claims to have faith but has no deeds" and whose faith, since "it is not accompanied by action, is dead" (James 2:14, 17).

James's first argument is that such faith is essentially the same as the belief which the devil possesses—knowledge of truth about God without the right response. His second argument appeals to the Abraham narrative: "Was not our father Abraham considered righteous for what he did when he offered his son Isaac on the altar? You see that his faith and his actions were working together, and his faith was made complete by what he did" (2:21–22). He then goes on to quote the same passage used by Paul: Gen. 15:6. James, however, does not conflate faith and works: he accepts the two different terms, but says that faith and works function together and that faith is "made complete" or "fulfilled" by works. For James, works are a sine qua non of justification because without them faith would not be true justifying faith. In that sense, "a person is justified by deeds and not by faith alone" (2:24 AT). It is true faith, "made complete" or "fulfilled" by works, that justifies, not the naked kind of faith that even the devil possesses. It is faith "made complete" to which God's dealings with Abraham attest.

Abraham and the promise of land. As noted, outside of the Abraham narrative in Genesis, perhaps the principal application of the promise through much of the OT is to Israel's location in the land. There are two particular places in the NT where this element of the Abrahamic promise comes into focus, one more subtle and the other more explicit.

First, in Romans, Paul states as an assumption that "Abraham and his offspring received the promise that he would be heir of the world" (Rom. 4:13)—"heir of the world" in the sense not that the world leaves him an inheritance but that the world is his inheritance. There is no direct statement to this effect in the OT. Paul here probably combines the promises (1) that Abraham would receive land in Canaan in Gen. 12:7, (2) that he would be the ancestor of whole nations in Gen. 17:6, and (3) that he would be a blessing to all nations in Gen. 12:3. In Paul's day the gentile mission was already well underway (Rom. 15:19; Col. 1:23). The fact that Abraham's children are spread across the entire globe means that his inheritance is not confined to Canaan but is worldwide.

Second, Hebrews looks beyond the immediate entrance of Abraham into the promised land of Canaan and explains how he was in fact expecting more: "By faith Abraham, when called to go to a place he would later receive as his inheritance, obeyed and went, even though he did not know where he was going. By faith he made his home in the promised land like a stranger in a foreign country; he lived in tents, as did Isaac and Jacob, who were heirs with him of the same promise. For he was looking forward to the city with foundations, whose architect and builder is God" (11:8–10). Abraham did inherit the land of Canaan, but it was not his final destination—hence he was a stranger there, not just because in the past he originally came from somewhere else but also because his true future home was somewhere else. Abraham's camping in Canaan shows that he saw his time there as temporary because he was on his way to what Hebrews calls "the city of the living God, the heavenly Jerusalem" (12:22).

This creates a superficial conflict with Heb. 6, which seems to state that Abraham "received" (NIV) or "obtained" (ESV, HCSB) what he had been promised (Heb. 6:15). This can be understood as Abraham receiving a partial fulfillment of the promise, or an interim fulfillment in the sense that Canaan was a type of the heavenly Jerusalem. There is perhaps a clue in the word that Hebrews uses for this "receiving" or "obtaining," however, which does not always have the clear sense of "receive": it can also mean "happen upon" or "bump into," which would convey something less than taking full possession of what God has promised Abraham.

Conclusion

In sum, Abraham plays a very important role in biblical theology. As we have seen, God is even on occasion defined as being "the God of Abraham." Abraham's importance throughout Scripture is seen in how his trust in the promise, his faith leading to righteousness, and his reception of the covenant are frequently reaffirmed by God and recalled by his people. In the OT, he is the bearer of the covenant and the promise. In the NT, he plays a central role especially in the arguments in Paul's Epistles, as the apostle both explains the means of salvation and defines the people of God.

See also Circumcision; Covenant; Jews and Gentiles; Law

Bibliography. Adams, E., "Abraham's Faith and Gentile Disobedience," *JSNT* 65 (1997): 47–66; Bruce, F. F., "'Abraham Had Two Sons,'" *NTS* 22 (1975): 71–84; Gathercole, S., "Paul's Reevaluation of Torah, Abraham, and David in Romans 3:27–4:8," in *Where Is Boasting?* (Eerdmans, 2002), 216–51; Hansen, G. W., *Abraham in Galatians* (Sheffield Academic, 1989); Hess, R., P. E. Satterthwaite, and G. J. Wenham, eds., *He Swore an Oath*, 2nd ed. (Wipf & Stock, 2007); Jipp, J., "Rereading the Story of Abraham, Isaac, and 'Us' in Romans 4," *JSNT* 32, no. 2 (2009): 217–42; Moberly, R. W. L., "Abraham's Righteousness," in *Studies in the Pentateuch*, ed. J. A. Emerton (Brill, 1990), 103–30; Schliesser, B., *Abraham's Faith in Romans 4* (Mohr Siebeck, 2007); Shaw, D., "Romans 4 and the Justification of Abraham in Light of Perspectives New and Newer," *Them* 40 (2015): 50–62; Wenham, G. J., *Genesis 1–15*, WBC (Word, 1987); Wenham, *Genesis 16–50*, WBC (Word 1994).

Simon Gathercole

Acts, Book of

Broad summary statements in Acts (and also in Luke) concerning the Scriptures, numerous allusions to the wording and the themes of the OT, and approximately thirty explicit quotations in Acts of specific OT passages all indicate that the OT plays a significant role in Luke's account of the spread of the word following the ascension of Jesus. Luke's pervasive use of the OT in Acts makes it apparent that he expects his readers to be familiar with the patterns and promises of the OT so they can understand the significance of what he is saying about "these days" (3:24). Many have analyzed the details of Luke's usage with respect to matters such as text form, sources, introductory formulas, and hermeneutical issues (see Marshall, esp. the surveys on 513; see now also Meek, 1–23; Smith, 9–34; Pardigon, 40–97). We will briefly summarize some of these details before focusing on the broader theological significance of the OT for Luke's purposes in Acts.

Specific References to the OT

Table 1 identifies key data points, beginning with specific references to the OT (cf. Longenecker, 70–71; Steyn, 27–31; Meek, 137–44). These references include explicit quotations and statements that specifically relate the Scriptures as a whole to what is being said or done (cf. also Acts 13:15; 15:1, 5, 21; 18:13). Scholars disagree on the total number of explicit quotations, the differences depending on whether some quotations are combined (e.g., 1:20a–b; 7:31–34) and whether an introductory formula is identified (e.g., NA[28] lists thirty-six places in Acts where the OT is quoted). The Acts references below that aren't counted as explicit quotations are identified with square brackets (e.g., 3:18, 21, 24; 13:22). Although 13:22 is introduced with a reference to God's speech that is similar to statements in Acts 7 (cf. 7:3, 6, 7b, 33), it appears to be a summary conflation of Ps. 89:20; 1 Sam. 13:14; and Isa. 44:28 rather than a specific quotation of one particular text (Steyn, 166; Porter, "Composite," 89–92). Table 1 lists twenty-eight explicit quotations with introductory formulas (and 13:22) and ten references to the Scriptures as a whole (indicated in column 2 by italics) as a guide to the discussion that follows.

Table 1. References to the OT in Acts

Acts	OT	Speaker	Introduction
1:16, 20a	Ps. 69:25	Peter	the Scripture had to be fulfilled; the Holy Spirit spoke . . . through David concerning Judas; it is written in the Book of Psalms
1:20b	Ps. 109:8	Peter	it is written . . . and . . .
2:16–21	Joel 2:28–32	Peter	this is what was spoken by the prophet Joel; God says
2:25–28, 31	Ps. 16:8–11	Peter	David said about him; he was a prophet (v. 30)
2:34–35	Ps. 110:1	Peter	he [David] said
[3:18, 21, 24]	God . . . foretold through *all the prophets*; God . . . promised through *his holy prophets*; *all the prophets* who have spoken have foretold these days	Peter	
3:22–23	Deut. 18:15, 18, 19; Lev. 23:29	Peter	Moses said
3:25	Gen. 22:18; 26:4	Peter	[God] said to Abraham
4:11	Ps. 118:22	Peter	Jesus [Gk. this/he] is
4:25–26	Ps. 2:1–2	believers	[the Sovereign Lord] spoke by the Holy Spirit through the mouth of . . . David

Acts	OT	Speaker	Introduction
7:3	Gen. 12:1	Stephen	God said [to Abraham]
7:6–7a	Gen. 15:13–14; cf. Exod. 2:22	Stephen	God spoke to [Abraham]; God said
7:7b	Exod. 3:12	Stephen	God said
7:27–28	Exod. 2:14	Stephen	[the one fighting] said [to Moses]
7:31–32	Exod. 3:6	Stephen	[Moses] heard the Lord say
7:33–34	Exod. 3:5, 7–10	Stephen	the Lord said to [Moses]
7:37	Deut. 18:15	Stephen	Moses . . . told the Israelites
7:40	Exod. 32:1	Stephen	[the people] told Aaron
7:42–43	Amos 5:25–27	Stephen	this agrees with what is written in the book of the prophets
7:48–50	Isa. 66:1–2	Stephen	as the prophet says; says the Lord
8:30, 32–33, 35	Isa. 53:7–8	Luke, about the eunuch	reading Isaiah the prophet; the passage of Scripture; the prophet talking about; that very passage of Scripture
[10:43]	*all the prophets* testify about him	Peter	
[13:22]	[Ps. 89:20; 1 Sam. 13:14; Isa. 44:28]	Paul	God testified concerning [David]
[13:27, 29]	fulfilled the words [Gk. voices/sayings] of *the prophets* that are read; carried out [Gk. fulfilled] *all that was written* about him	Paul	
13:33	Ps. 2:7	Paul	as it is written in the second Psalm
13:34	Isa. 55:3	Paul	as God has said
13:35	Ps. 16:10	Paul	it is also stated elsewhere [or, in another (Psalm) he says]
13:40–41	Hab. 1:5	Paul	what the prophets have said
13:47	Isa. 49:6	Paul and Barnabas	the Lord has commanded us
15:15–18	Amos 9:11–12	James	the words of the prophets; as it is written; says the Lord
[17:2–3] [cf. also 17:17; 18:4, 19]	*the Scriptures*	Luke, about Paul	
[17:11]	*the Scriptures*	Luke, about Paul / the Bereans	
[18:24]	*the Scriptures*	Luke, about Apollos	
[18:28]	*the Scriptures*	Luke, about Apollos	
23:5	Exod. 22:28	Paul	it is written
[24:14]	everything that is in accordance with *the Law* and that is written in *the Prophets*	Paul	
[26:6–7, 22–23]	hope in *what God has promised*; what the *prophets and Moses* said	Paul	
[28:23]	from *the Law of Moses* and from *the Prophets*	Luke, about Paul	
28:25–27	Isa. 6:9–10	Paul	the Holy Spirit spoke; he said through Isaiah the prophet

Several observations about the use of OT quotations in Acts can be made just from the data of table 1:

1. All of the explicit quotations with introductory formulas appear in reports of direct speech or dialogue. That is, no explicit quotation with an introductory formula appears in narrative material.

2. Thus, the quotations are mostly from the lips of Peter (8), Stephen (10), and Paul (7, or 8 if 13:22 is included), with an additional quotation each from the believers in prayer (4:25–26) and James (15:15–18). A partial exception occurs when Luke informs readers of the passage the eunuch is reading from in the dialogue between the eunuch and Philip (8:30–35).

3. Most of the quotations, therefore, appear in the first half of Acts and, surprisingly, do not appear in Paul's defense speeches in Acts 22, 24, and 26. These, however, are primarily autobiographical defenses (and see the next point).

4. Although broad references to the prophets or to the Scriptures as a whole are found in the first half of Acts (3:18–24; 10:43; 13:27–29), they increase significantly in the second half of Acts (17:2–3, 11; 18:24, 28; 24:14; 26:6–7, 22–23; 28:23), being found in both narrative material and Paul's defenses in Acts 24, 26, and 28. These are similar to the global statements about the Scriptures found in the last chapter of Luke's Gospel (24:25–27, 45–48). These global statements are also an important window into Luke's use of the OT in Acts (Meek, 14–17).

5. The introductory formulas indicate that although the speakers can refer broadly to the authors as "the prophets" (13:40; 15:15; cf. 3:18, 21, 24; 10:43; 13:27), they also often refer to the author specifically by name, as they do of David (1:16; 2:25, 34; 4:25), Joel (2:16), Moses (3:22; 7:37), and Isaiah (8:30; 28:25; cf. 7:48). Sometimes the speakers refer to the location of the Scripture—for example, "the book of the prophets" (7:42; cf. 13:40; 15:15), "the Book of Psalms" (1:20), or, even more specifically, "the second Psalm" (13:33).

6. References to what "God said" often refer to actual statements made by God (e.g., 3:25; 7:3, 6, 31, 33; 13:34). Nevertheless, the view that Scripture is both divine and human speech frames Acts, as seen in the first and last quotations, both of which refer to the speech of the Holy Spirit and the human author (1:16; 28:25); in Peter's summaries stating that "God spoke by the mouth of his holy prophets" (3:21 [ESV]; cf. 3:18, 24); and the introduction to the quotation from Ps. 2 in Acts 4:25–26, which says that the Sovereign Lord "spoke by the Holy Spirit through . . . David."

7. Similarly, although the quotations are often introduced with reference to the speaker (e.g., David / Moses / the prophet says), this is not to be understood as downplaying the idea that these are written in Scripture. The combination of speech and writing is seen in 1:16–20 ("the Holy Spirit spoke . . . written in the Book of Psalms"); 8:30–35 ("the passage of Scripture . . . the prophet talking about"); 13:27–29 ("the words [Gk. voices/sayings] of the prophets . . . all that was written"); 13:33–35 ("written in the second Psalm . . . he [God] says" [ESV]); and 15:15–18 ("the words of the prophets . . . as it is written").

8. The majority of the citations come from the Pentateuch (11x) and the Psalms (8x, or 9x if 13:22 is included), followed by Isaiah (5x) and the Minor Prophets (4x). However, eight of the eleven Pentateuch citations are in Stephen's overview of the history of Israel. Although this is not reflected in table 1, the quotations largely follow the form of LXX Codex Alexandrinus (A), with some variations (Steyn, 250–57) that could be due to quotation from memory, different versions, or paraphrasing (Fitzmyer, 534). Some suggest that Luke's arguments depend on the LXX. Alternatively, the same argument could be made from both the LXX and the MT (Bock, 175–80; Marshall, 516; Meek, 131–32).

We will pause here briefly to touch on the most notable difference between the LXX and the MT: Acts 15:16–18 / Amos 9:11–12 refers to the restoration of the fallen "tent of David" (ESV; see Meek, 56–94). The term for "tent" by itself may be a reference to the eschatological temple that will be "rebuilt" (Bauckham). The same phrase in the LXX, however, is found elsewhere only in Isa. 16:5, where it appears to refer to the king in David's line who will rule in David's place or on his throne (cf. NLT, NET, NIV; Meek, 69; cf. also, e.g., LXX Ps. 77:67, where "tent of Joseph" parallels "tribe of Ephraim"). In Luke-Acts, this reference to David's tent picks up on the many other references to David and the fulfillment of promises to restore David's kingdom achieved through Jesus's resurrection and ascension to the throne of David (Luke 1:27, 32–33, 68–69; 2:4; Acts 2:30–36; 13:22–23, 32–35; Thompson, 123; Doble, 106; Miura, 187–94). The purpose of the restoration of the fallen tent of David is so that "the rest of mankind may seek the Lord, even all the Gentiles who bear my name, says the Lord" (Acts 15:17). The two main variations between the MT's "so that they might *possess* the remnant of *Edom*" and the NT's "so that the rest of *mankind* may *seek* the Lord" here are as follows: (1) the MT has the verb "possess," and the NT has the verb "seek"; and (2) the MT has "Edom" as the object of the verb possess, whereas the NT has "mankind" as the subject who will "seek the Lord." It is possible that the LXX is providing an interpretation of the MT. Thus, (1) "possession" in the context of Amos 9:12, in which the people are also "called by [God's] name," may indicate not conquest or submission by force but blessing and inclusion among God's people (cf. "called by God's name" in, e.g., Deut. 28:9–10; Isa. 43:7; Jer. 14:9; and, in the immediate context, the reference to Israel and the nations in Amos 9:7); (2) Edom, therefore, in the context of Amos 9:7, as the descendants of Esau, could be symbolic of the nations that will come under God's rule and blessing (cf. Isa. 19:23–25; Zech. 14:18–19; Ps. 87; Meek, 72–73). Thus, since God has "intervened to choose *a people for his name* from the Gentiles" (Acts 15:14, applying language used of Israel in Deut. 7:6; 14:2 to believing gentiles), James cites Amos 9:11–12 to confirm that gentiles who are called by God's name through believing in Jesus (Acts 10–11) are being joined together with believing Jews by God himself because the Davidic kingdom is established through Jesus (Acts 2:30). Thus, Amos 9 is "uniquely appropriate to James's argument" (Meek, 88) because it uniquely refers to the gentiles being called by the divine name (van de Sandt, 76–77).

9. Stephen's summary of Israel's history naturally includes references to that history. Thus, in Stephen's speech the distinction between explicit quotation, paraphrase, allusion, and biblical language can occasionally

be hard to determine (cf. Smith, 147–63). The same may be said to a lesser extent of Paul's synagogue sermon in Acts 13 (cf. 13:22).

10. In addition to providing information for summaries of Israel's history (Acts 7; 13:22), quotations also support the christological claims that Jesus is the suffering and risen Davidic Messiah, prophet like Moses, suffering servant, and ruling Lord (2:25–28, 34–35; 4:11; 8:32–33; 13:33–35). This christological function features in many of the broad summary statements about the OT as well (3:18; 10:43; 13:27, 29; 17:2–3, 11; 18:28; 26:22–23; 28:23). The quotations also warn of, or explain, the consequences for rejecting Christ (3:23; 13:40–41; 28:25–27; cf. also 7:42–43, 49–50), interpret Judas's betrayal and need for replacement (1:20), and identify the reason for opposition to followers of Jesus (4:25–26). Others explain the events of Pentecost (2:16–21), evidence divine support for the gentile mission (13:47; 15:16–18), and give a rationale for Paul's response to the high priest (23:5, though see below). Broader references to the current period as one of fulfillment are also seen in the global statements about Scripture (3:21, 24; 26:23; cf. 3:25).

Broader Uses of the OT

When we move beyond the explicit statements and quotations to allusions, biblical language, and themes, the pervasiveness of the Scriptures in Luke's account becomes even clearer. NA[28] lists approximately 230 allusions in Acts, many of which are significant for understanding the themes of Acts. For example, Acts 1:8 alludes to Isa. 32:15; 43:10–12; 44:8; and 49:6 (discussed further below); the phrase "in the last days" added in Acts 2:17 alludes to any number of OT texts but perhaps particularly Isa. 2:2, evoking Isaianic hopes for Israel and the nations and highlighting the eschatological significance of the events being narrated (Pao, 158); and Paul's Areopagus speech in Acts 17 may allude to Isa. 40:18–20; 45:18; and 66:1–2, as he provides a biblical framework for understanding God in contrast to idols (Pao, 193–97; Pardigon, 144–45). This sample, taken just from Isaiah, confirms the pervasiveness of the OT in Acts and should caution readers against assuming that the use of the OT is limited to speech material or even speech material for Jewish audiences, or that Luke only knew of the books explicitly quoted (Pentateuch, Psalms, the Minor Prophets, and Isaiah). Broader use of biblical phrases like "all the house of Israel" (2:36) and "the hand of the Lord" (11:21) adds to our sense of the pervasiveness of the Scriptures in Acts.

Psalms. More recent discussion has focused on broader structural influences of the OT on the narrative and theology of Acts (for a summary of the following, see Smith, 17–22). Peter Doble sees a broader framework in Acts derived from Psalms. Psalms is clearly significant in the programmatic speeches of Peter (Acts 2) and Paul (Acts 13), and both speeches cite Ps. 16. Furthermore, both Jesus and Peter cite Pss. 110 (Luke 20:41–44; Acts 2:32–35) and 118 (Luke 20:17; Acts 4:11). Psalms, therefore, is foundational to themes such as suffering, rejection, and Davidic kingship in Luke-Acts. Doble views the references to Psalms not as "proof texts" but "signals of [Luke's] narrative's theological *substructure*, the essential body of scripture revealing God's plan now fulfilled in Jesus" (90). This claim, while rightly recognizing the prominence of Psalms for the Christology of Luke-Acts, may unnecessarily raise to the level of primary influence what is more likely only of significant influence.

Isaiah. The number of lengthy quotations from and allusions to Isaiah in Luke-Acts—for example, the use of Isa. 53:7–8 in Acts 8:32–33 (cf. Luke 22:37), of Isa. 55:3 in Acts 13:34, and of the terms "servant" (Acts 3:13) and "Righteous One" (3:14; 7:52; 22:14; cf. Isa. 53:11)—point to the importance of Isaiah for understanding the Christology and soteriology of Acts. The use of Isa. 49:6 (Acts 13:47) and Isa. 6:9–10 (Acts 28:26–27) and the use of "servant" terminology to describe Paul's ministry (26:15–18) reveal the importance of Isaiah for understanding the ecclesiology of Acts and thus the definition of the people of God, the place of Israel, the gentile mission, and the roles of Paul and followers of Jesus (Koet; Beers). Furthermore, the large number of allusions and quotations from Isaiah may point to the broader influence of the Isaianic new-exodus program (esp. Isa. 40–55) in Acts (Pao; Mallen, *Isaiah*; Beers). The quotation from Isa. 40:3–5 early on in Luke (Luke 3:4–6) followed by references to Isaiah at key narrative locations in Acts (1:8; 13:46–47; 28:25–28) highlights not just the importance of Isaiah for Luke but, more significantly, the framework of the Isaianic new exodus as the context for understanding Acts (Pao).

Thus, this broader framework points to the presence in Acts of Isaianic themes such as the restoration of Israel, the word of God as the agent of the new exodus, the anti-idol polemic and the sovereignty of the Lord, and the inclusion of the gentiles (Pao, though the lattermost item in the list is transformed in Acts). The advantage of this thematic approach is that it moves beyond the separation of speech material (and the quotations mainly found there) from narrative material (and the allusions mainly found there) and the atomistic analysis of individual quotations (Mallen, *Isaiah*, 16; Pao, 8, 251). The "use" of the OT, here Isaiah in particular, in this approach incorporates these themes into a broader hermeneutical framework.

Whether or not one is convinced that the interpretive framework for Acts is primarily the Isaianic new exodus, the eschatological hopes of Isaiah are certainly prominent and important for understanding Luke's narrative account of the inauguration of the last days. To develop just one of the passages noted above, knowledge of the Isaianic allusions in Acts 1:8 helps readers to see that more than just the explicit quotations are important for recognizing Isaiah's importance for the interpretation of Acts.

Acts 1:6–8 has long been recognized as a key introduction to the rest of the book, in which the gospel spreads from Jerusalem. Recognizing the Isaianic allusions in Jesus's answer, however, alerts readers to the scriptural hope that is being fulfilled (Thompson, 103–8, building on Pao, 91–96). The apostles' question about the kingdom (1:6) arises in the context of the gatherings, in which Jesus's instructions about the promised coming of the Spirit in Jerusalem (1:4–5) are linked with his teaching about the kingdom (1:3). Not surprisingly, the apostles want to know how this scriptural promise of the Holy Spirit will play out with respect to the prophetic hopes for the people who received those promises. Thus, the apostles' question is not wrongheaded. Rather, it arises naturally in the context of Jesus's resurrection, his teaching about the kingdom, and the prophetic promise of the Spirit. For the sake of space, we will focus especially on Jesus's reference to Israel in 1:8.

In 1:8 Jesus actually answers the apostles' question about Israel (rather than rebuking them) and specifically refers to Israel in his answer. Apart from references to Jerusalem, and Judea and Samaria (i.e., Israel as the Southern and Northern Kingdoms; cf. Mic. 1:1, 5; Isa. 10:10–11; Ezek. 23:4; 37:15–28), the Isaianic phrases Jesus uses confirm that he is reassuring them concerning the prophetic hope for Israel. (1) His reference to the Holy Spirit coming "on you" (*eph' hymas*) reflects the wording of Israel's hope for the Spirit in the age to come in Isa. 32:15, which contains the phase "from on high," used by Jesus here in Acts 1 and also in Luke 24:49 (cf. also Isa. 32:15). (2) His promise that "you will be my witnesses" (*esesthe mou martyres*) reflects God's promise, in Isa. 43:10–12, that Israel will be transformed from a blind and disobedient servant into an obedient witness to God's salvation. (3) Jesus's promise that this witness will extend "to the end of the earth" (*heōs eschatou tēs gēs*) also reflects the promise that the servant of the Lord would not only restore Israel but also be "a light for the Gentiles, that my salvation may reach to the ends of the earth [*heōs eschatou tēs gēs*]" in Isa. 49:5–6 (cf. also 48:20; 62:11; Acts 13:47). Thus, by referring specifically to Israel in 1:8, and by using the language of the prophetic hope for Israel and the gentile nations, Jesus answers the apostles' question with a yes. Although they will not be able to work out the exact timing of God's plan, his promises for Israel are being fulfilled. Confirmation that the apostles' question about Israel is addressed by Jesus here is found in the following chapter. Peter addresses fellow Jews and residents of Jerusalem (2:14) as "Israelites" (2:22) and indeed as "all Israel" (2:36) when he declares to them the arrival of the prophetic hope of the last days in the pouring out of the promised Holy Spirit from the risen and ascended Lord Jesus (cf. the sequence of Israel then gentiles in 3:26; 15:16–17).

The Scriptures as "Prophecy"

Jesus's answer about the scriptural hope for God's people with reference to the language of Isaianic hopes is also a window into the broader understanding of the OT in Acts—namely, that the current era has been anticipated by the OT and is the outworking of the Father's plan there. In this sense the Scriptures as a whole are "prophetic." This is seen in part in the language of "fulfillment" in Acts (cf. the terms in 1:16 [regarding Judas and his replacement]; 3:18 [that the Messiah would suffer]; 13:27, 29 [regarding Christ's crucifixion]; 13:33 [regarding Christ's resurrection]). Luke particularly cites "the prophets" (13:40; 15:15), at times identifying an individual such as "the prophet Joel" (2:16) and "Isaiah the prophet" (8:30; 28:25; cf. 7:48). Moving beyond the prophetic books, we see that Moses, by implication, was also a prophet, as he spoke of "a prophet like me" to come (3:22; 7:37), and David, too, was a prophet (2:25; cf. Matt. 13:35). As noted above, however, it is not just specific prophets that Luke thinks point forward; he is fond of the word "all." God has "fulfilled what he had foretold through *all* the prophets" (Acts 3:18), "beginning with Samuel, *all* the prophets . . . have foretold these days" (3:24), and "*all* the prophets testify about him" (10:43). Sometimes it is simply "the prophets" whose words are fulfilled (13:27; 15:15). Furthermore, Paul states that he believes "*everything* that is in accordance with the Law and that is written in the Prophets" (24:14; cf. 28:23) and that the prophets and Moses anticipated the Messiah's suffering, resurrection, and proclamation to the gentiles (26:22–23). This understanding of Scripture as a whole as that which points forward picks up on the words of Jesus at the end of Luke's Gospel (24:27, 44). Thus, Paul's explanation of the events of Christ's death and resurrection comes from "the Scriptures" (Acts 17:2–3) and is examined on the basis of "the Scriptures" (17:11), such that Apollos's faithful proclamation that Jesus is the Christ is from "the Scriptures" (18:28).

As seen especially in the speeches and in the global statements about the Scriptures noted above, in Acts the focal point of this forward-looking aspect of the Scriptures is Jesus. His suffering and resurrection are highlighted in particular as the fulfillment of the Scriptures that makes possible the proclamation of forgiveness of sins in his name. Luke's multifaceted Christology is due in part to his conviction that Jesus fulfills *all* of the Scriptures (e.g., Luke 24:44). Jesus was the promised royal descendant of David (Acts 2:30–31; 13:23), the prophet of whom Moses spoke (3:22–23), the servant of the Lord (3:13, 26), and a man accredited by God (2:22) and anointed with the Holy Spirit (10:38). Yet, he also transcends those categories as David's risen and reigning Lord (2:34) who answers prayer (1:24; 7:59–60), knows and opens hearts (16:14), sends the Spirit (2:33), and saves those who call upon his name (2:21, 47). Much of this multifaceted Christology based on the comprehensive fulfillment of the Scriptures in Jesus is found in a condensed form in Peter's address in Acts 3:13–26. This brief summary contains (1) numerous titles used for Jesus (servant of the Lord, Holy and Righteous One, source of life, Messiah, Davidic king [implied by "beginning with Samuel"], prophet like Moses, seed of Abraham); (2) allusions to a wide variety of sections of the OT (Genesis, Deuteronomy, 2 Samuel, Isaiah, the prophets); and (3) global statements about the comprehensive nature of this fulfillment ("all" in 3:18, 24).

Yet, as indicated in the global statement in 3:24 and point 10 above regarding the quotations in Acts, the prophets "have foretold *these days*" (3:24). Therefore, the Scriptures also anticipate the pouring out of the Holy Spirit (2:16–21), the spread of the word beyond Jerusalem (Luke 24:47; Acts 1:8; 26:23), and blessing coming to the gentiles through Israel's Messiah (1:8; 3:25; 13:47; 15:17; 26:23; Porter, "Scripture"; Meek). Thus, these specific Scriptures, and the broader framework of the fulfillment of the Isaianic new exodus, also provide legitimation to the followers of Jesus, identifying them as "the Way," the true heirs of the Scriptures (24:14; cf. 9:2; 19:9, 23; 22:4; 24:22; on this ecclesiological argument, see Pao, 59–69).

Thus, Luke is not saying in Acts that followers of Jesus are finding something in the Scriptures that is not already there. The Scriptures themselves point forward and in this sense are "prophetic" (on the "proof from prophecy" discussion, see the summaries in Porter, "Scripture," 105–7; Meek, 5–7; Smith, 12–14). Just how they do so is something we will come to below.

The Scriptures Now Understood in Light of Jesus

Luke affirms that what is described in Acts is found in and anticipated by the Scriptures. However, in another sense Acts also portrays the Scriptures as being now better understood in light of the arrival of Jesus. To return to the list of uses of the quotations in point 10 above, we could say that there is a sense in which, although referring to a range of topics, all of those quotations are read in light of the arrival of Christ (cf. Meek, 132–33). In Peter's sermon, the arrival of the last days and the pouring out of the Holy Spirit promised in Joel 2 (Acts 2:16–21) have taken place because of the resurrection and ascension of Jesus (2:22–36). The promised mission to and inclusion of the gentiles take place because of his enthronement as the Davidic king and the restoration of the Davidic kingdom (15:16) and at his command (1:8; 13:47), by his provision, and according to his proclamation (1:8; 26:23). Even the scriptural explanation for the persecution of believers (4:25–26) refers to the opposition the anointed one would face and is understood to apply because the believers are identified with this suffering servant (4:13, 27–29). Stephen's outline of Israel's history in Acts 7 quotes and alludes to numerous Scriptures without explicit statements of "promise fulfillment." Yet even here, rejection of God's messengers culminates in the rejection of Jesus (7:9, 35, 37, 51–52). Paul's outline of Israel's history focuses on the pattern of God's gracious provisions of rescue, land, and leaders that culminates in Jesus (13:23).

This belief that all of Scripture is now to be understood in light of Jesus is perhaps also the case with what appears to be an exception to this usage in Acts 23:5. This quotation is often understood as Paul's acknowledgment of wrongdoing regarding his pronouncement of judgment upon the high priest and as an appeal to the continuing authority of the law. Several factors in the immediate context, however, suggest that Paul is being ironic in his use of Exod. 22:28 here and that this use, too, is informed by the arrival of Jesus. Is it likely that Paul did not know the high priest? In his immediately preceding account of his conversion, Paul mentions the high priest as one from whom he received permission to follow Christians to Damascus (22:5; cf. 9:1–2; 26:10). Is the high priest the ruler of God's people? The early chapters of Acts establish the replacement of the rulers of Israel by Jesus and his apostles as the leaders of God's true people (cf. "rulers" in 4:5–12, 18–20, 26, who are contrasted with the apostles, Jesus's authorized representatives over God's people). The immediately following context reaffirms the lordship of the risen Jesus over Paul's life (23:6–11). Thus, Paul's preceding accusation that the high priest is a "whitewashed wall" may mean that Paul's reply and citation of Exodus essentially state that the law-breaking behavior of the high priest means that while he is outwardly impressive, he is unrecognizable as the ruler of God's people. This resembles Jesus's denunciations of the Pharisees (cf. Matt. 23:27–28; Luke 11:37–44) and Ezekiel's judgments in Ezek. 13:10–16. Paul, therefore, is not "speaking evil"; he is speaking as a prophet, and this use of the OT is also informed by the arrival of Jesus, the true ruler of God's people.

According to Luke-Acts, Jesus himself taught the apostles how to interpret Scripture in light of him. Thus, although the two on the road to Emmaus were "slow to believe all that the prophets have spoken," they had Jesus explain to them what was said about himself "in all the Scriptures" (Luke 24:25–27). Likewise, in addition to reminding the disciples of his teaching about the fulfillment of everything written about him in the "Law of Moses, the Prophets and the Psalms," Jesus then "opened their minds so they could understand the Scriptures" (24:44–45). This is then further developed in Acts 1 when Jesus provides forty days of instruction about his resurrection, the kingdom of God, the promised Holy Spirit, and promises to Israel and the gentiles (Acts 1:3–8). The influence of Jesus upon the apostles and their interpretation of Scripture is indicated in Peter's use of Psalms in Acts 2 and 4 where he, like Jesus, cites Pss. 110 (Luke 20:41–44; Acts 2:32–35) and 118 (Luke 20:17; Acts 4:11).

While the Scriptures anticipate a Davidic king, a prophet like Moses, and a suffering servant, it is in Jesus, says Peter in Acts 3, that we see in one person what "all" the prophets were pointing to. Jesus sheds new light on the patterns and promises that were already there. This seems to be the way some OT texts are viewed as "fulfilled" in Acts. Thus, in 1:20, Pss. 69 and 109 are both psalms of David, and both concern betrayal. Building on Jesus's own teaching and the emphasis in Luke's Gospel on his identity as "great David's greater Son" (as James Montgomery describes Jesus in his hymn "Hail to the Lord's Anointed"), Peter's use of these psalms reflects a wider David typology (cf. Luke 1:32, 69; 2:4; 18:38–39; 20:41–44; Acts 2:25–34; 13:22–37; 15:16). That is, the patterns reflected in David's life culminate in his greater Son. Psalm 69 describes the pain the faithful Israelite experiences when being persecuted by his enemies, and v. 25 anticipates the ultimate removal of the enemies of David in an act of judgment. Likewise, the judgment and removal from a position of responsibility of one who repaid the friendship of the king with hatred and harm are, in Ps. 109:8, fulfilled in the ultimate betrayal of the one that David's rule anticipated.

This approach may also be behind Peter's use of Ps. 16 (LXX Ps. 15) in Acts 2. Because of the variations between the MT and LXX, particularly the translation of *šaḥat* ("pit") as *diaphthora* ("decay"), some see the argument for a bodily resurrection here as dependent on the LXX, such that the sense apparently shifts from being merely protection from death to being preservation after death and hence implying bodily resurrection (for the variations between the MT and LXX, see Steyn, 100–13; for links to other references to *hadēs* in the Psalms and the argument in Acts 2, see Doble, 90–95; for the similarity of conceptual argument, see Bock, 169–81).

Before citing Ps. 16, Peter specifies that the speaker is David but that David is speaking about Jesus ("David said about him . . . ," 2:25). In Peter's citation, David speaks in the first person about his confidence of the Lord's never-ending presence with him ("ever before me"). Because of this assurance of the Lord's presence, David is not shaken, he rejoices, and, as he says in the first indication that he is speaking about the Lord's presence after death, his "body" (*sarx*) can "rest in hope" (2:26; the shift from "security" [MT] to "hope" [LXX] still reflects trust; cf. Harriman, 249). In 2:27 David specifies that the basis for this assurance is his knowledge that the Lord "will not abandon me to the realm of the dead [*hadēs*]." This will be the key verse that Peter comes back to. Not only will he not be "abandoned" or "left behind" (LSJ, 470) in death; neither will the Lord "let your holy one see decay." The word for "decay" (*diaphthora*) refers to the rotting or destruction associated with the grave (Ezek. 21:31, "destruction"). In LXX Ps. 15:10 (MT 16:10) and often in the LXX, *diaphthora* translates the Hebrew *šaḥat* ("pit," "grave," "death"; cf. LXX Pss. 29:10 [30:10]; 54:24 [55:24, "pit of *decay*"]). Such extravagant language seems to press beyond mere preservation from death. Finally, the psalmist concludes with further statements of assurance of the Lord's never-ending presence ("paths of life . . . joy in your presence," Acts 2:28).

In 2:29–31 Peter argues that the references to the body in 2:26–27 indicate that although this psalm is spoken by David, it can't ultimately be about David because David "died and was buried" and his tomb is there for them to see (cf. 1 Kings 2:10; Neh. 3:16; Josephus, *Ant.* 7.392; cf. Harriman, 250). David did know, however, that God had "promised him on oath" that one of his descendants would rule (sit "on his throne"; cf. Ps. 132:11 [LXX 131:11], which looks back to 2 Sam. 7:13). Peter states, therefore, that the promise in the Davidic covenant of an everlasting rule is ultimately fulfilled in the rule of the one whom death cannot hold (Crowe, 25–27).

Peter's move from Ps. 16 to Jesus in Acts 2 could again reflect a David typology (as in 1:16–20) in which what is said by David or about him, his kingship, or his covenant anticipates a greater realization in the greater David to come. The supporting evidence that Peter gives in 2:31 suggests that he sees in this psalm extravagant language that could not have been fulfilled by David in the first instance but is fulfilled literally and ultimately in David's promised descendant (Kovalishyn). On the one hand, David points beyond his own experience. On the other hand, the bodily resurrection of Jesus, the greater David, shows what David and the promises to him were ultimately pointing to.

Thus, although in Acts the OT is viewed as forward looking and therefore, in a sense, "prophetic," it is understood to point forward in a range of ways, such that not only are specific prophecies such as the promised pouring out of the Holy Spirit fulfilled (Acts 2), but OT patterns also point forward to broader salvation-historical themes. After the arrival of the Davidic king, prophet, and deliverer par excellence, we now see more clearly the associated patterns of Scripture in light of his life, death, resurrection, and ascension. Readers such as Theophilus may be assured, therefore, that the outworking of God's saving rule in the spread of the word and the inclusion of Jews and gentiles together in the people of God is being accomplished by the risen Lord Jesus according to the patterns and promises of Scripture.

Bibliography. Bauckham, R., "James and the Gentiles (Acts 15:13–21)," in *History, Literature and Society in the Book of Acts*, ed. B. Witherington III (Cambridge University Press, 1996), 154–84; Beers, H., *The Followers of Jesus as the "Servant,"* LNTS 535 (T&T Clark, 2015); Bock, D. L., *Proclamation from Prophecy and Pattern* (JSOT Press, 1987); Crowe, B. D., *The Hope of Israel* (Baker Academic, 2020); Doble, P., "The Psalms in Luke-Acts," in *The Psalms in the New Testament*, ed. S. Moyise and M. J. J. Menken (T&T Clark, 2004), 83–117; Fitzmyer, J. A., "The Use of the Old Testament in Luke-Acts," in *Society of Biblical Literature 1992 Seminar Papers*, SBLSP

31 (Scholars Press, 1992), 524–38; Harriman, K. R., "'For David Said Concerning Him,'" *JTI* 11 (2017): 239–57; Koet, B. J., "Isaiah in Luke-Acts," in *Isaiah in the New Testament*, ed. S. Moyise and M. J. J. Menken (T&T Clark, 2005), 79–100; Kovalishyn, M. K., "David the Prophet?," *RF&P* 2, no. 3 (December 2017): 18–30; Longenecker, R. N., *Biblical Exegesis in the Apostolic Period*, 2nd ed. (Eerdmans, 1999); Mallen, P., "Genesis in Luke-Acts," in *Genesis in the New Testament*, ed. M. J. J. Menken and S. Moyise LNTS 466 (T&T Clark, 2012), 60–82; Mallen, *The Reading and Transformation of Isaiah in Luke-Acts*, LNTS 367 (T&T Clark, 2008); Marshall, I. H., "Acts," in *CNTUOT*, 513–606; Meek, J. A., *The Gentile Mission in Old Testament Citations in Acts*, LNTS 385 (T&T Clark, 2008); Miura, Y., *David in Luke-Acts*, WUNT 2/232 (Mohr Siebeck, 2007); Pao, D. W., *Acts and the Isaianic New Exodus*, WUNT 2/130 (Mohr Siebeck, 2000); Pardigon, F., *Paul against the Idols* (Pickwick, 2019); Porter, S. E., "Composite Citations in Luke-Acts," in *Composite Citations in Antiquity*, ed. S. A. Adams and S. M. Ehorn, LNTS 593 (T&T Clark, 2018), 62–93; Porter, "Scripture Justifies Mission," in *Hearing the Old Testament in the New Testament*, ed. S. E. Porter (Eerdmans, 2006), 104–26; Russam, D., "Deuteronomy in Luke-Acts," in *Deuteronomy in the New Testament*, ed. S. Moyise and M. J. J. Menken, LNTS 358 (T&T Clark, 2007), 63–81; Smith, S., *The Fate of the Jerusalem Temple in Luke-Acts*, LNTS 553 (T&T Clark, 2017); Steyn, G. J., *Septuagint Quotations in the Context of the Petrine and Pauline Speeches of the Acta Apostolorum*, CBET 12 (Kok Pharos, 1995); Thompson, A. J., *The Acts of the Risen Lord Jesus*, NSBT 27 (InterVarsity, 2011); van de Sandt, H., "The Minor Prophets in Luke-Acts," in *The Minor Prophets in the New Testament*, ed. M. J. J. Menken and S. Moyise, LNTS 377 (T&T Clark, 2009), 57–77.

Alan J. Thompson

Adam, First and Last

Adam is the first person in the Bible. This is not in doubt. Even so, Adam has been the subject of some of the most intense debate in recent years in the fields of theology and biblical studies. In a modern world suffused with science and driven by widespread belief in evolution, the biblical teaching on Adam has been reconsidered. Is it necessary for Adam to be the first human being? Does the Bible leave open other options? Some consider the *historicity* of Adam to be beside the point, since the OT is more interested in how Adam relates to Israel (Enns, 65–70). Yet others maintain that Adam must be the first actual human being (Versteeg, 1–67).

To understand Adam properly, we must consider how both the OT and NT use Adam. The consequences of a proper understanding of Adam are greater than some recognize. Though the question may seem abstract, inconclusive, or trivial, the NT does not leave open various possibilities for whether Adam existed or whether he was the first person. Instead, the NT *requires* us to understand Adam as a historical person who was indeed the first person in world history. The NT authors invoke the historical person of Adam, the first human being and the head of all humanity, to explain the historical realities of the work of Christ. The representative salvific work of Christ is tethered to the representative role of Adam as head of all humanity. According to Paul, Christ redeems those who descend from Adam; if there were people who did not descend from Adam, they would fall outside the parameters of the work of Christ. The NT authors do not leave room for a class of people who come from a source other than Adam.

In what follows I will consider the OT witness to Adam and his role as the head of humanity; the NT witness to Adam, especially in relation to Christ; and implications that Adam has for biblical theology.

Adam in the OT

Adam in Genesis. On the sixth day, God creates man and woman (Gen. 1:26–27). This summary account is given more detail in Gen. 2:7, where God makes Adam from the dust of the ground and breathes life into him. From Adam comes Eve (2:21–23)—and all other people. In Genesis, Adam is created by a special act of God, not as the result of an extended natural process of evolution—either theistic or Darwinian.

In Genesis the Lord enters into a relationship with Adam, the original head of humanity, giving him a probationary test in which he is not to eat from the tree of the knowledge of good and evil (2:16–17). If Adam transgresses this command, the penalty will be death (2:17). On the other hand, if Adam obeys, it is implied that he will experience eschatological life. Here Adam is not yet in possession of the highest life, but that goal is set before him (Bavinck, 564–67). Since the relationship between the Lord and Adam involves parties, stipulations, and sanctions, many historically have understood this relationship to be a covenant (WCF 7; Turretin, 8.3 [1:574–78]; Bavinck, 2:567–71). This covenant has been given various names, including the covenant of works, the covenant of creation, or the covenant of life. Though many have objected to the naming of this relationship as a covenant, especially since the term "covenant" is not used, such objections are not decisive. The term does not have to be used for the concept to be present. Further, Hosea 6:7 likely does refer to a covenant with Adam (see below). Furthermore, though Adam and Eve's marriage is not termed a covenant in Gen. 2, it is called that in Mal. 2:14. All this suggests that a covenant concept may be in mind with respect to the relationship between God and Adam, even though the word "covenant" is not used.

If the Lord's relationship with Adam takes the form of a covenant, then it is crucial to understand that covenant properly. First, this (and indeed any) covenant relationship between God and humanity must originate with God; he takes the initiative. Adam cannot put God in his debt; there is nothing Adam can do to *earn* eternal life on his own merits. Even if Adam were to obey God perfectly, he would not, strictly speaking, merit eternal life. This is where the term "covenant of works" has often been misunderstood. The covenant of works is not so named because it teaches that Adam could work his way to God. Instead, the covenant of works teaches that God offers to give Adam life if he obeys the stipulations of the divinely instituted covenant. The reward would not be proportional to his work.

Second, Adam is not only required to obey one arbitrary command. Adam is required to love and obey God entirely. He is called, with Eve, to be fruitful and multiply (Gen. 1:28). Adam is created upright (Eccles. 7:29); the law is written on his heart. He has no proclivity to sin, nor was he born a sinner. The probationary command given to Adam (Gen. 2:16–17) is a summary command that tests Adam's obedience to and trust in God in a special way (cf. Turretin 9.6.1 [1:604]; 9.8.7 [1:612]; Bavinck, 2:574; Vos, *Reformed Dogmatics*, 2:48–49).

Tragically, Adam fails, and through his actions sin enters the world. To be sure, Eve also plays a key role in the entrance of sin into the world, but in Scripture the covenantal responsibility resides primarily with Adam. Adam's representative actions explain the universality of sin and death, which affect everyone. Because of Adam's sin, the ground is cursed, work is hard, childbearing is painful, and death comes to all people (Gen. 3:16–19). Even so, despite their role in bringing sin into the world, Adam and Eve are not cast aside. God promises redemption through the seed of the woman (Gen. 3:15), who will eventually overcome the serpent. After his sin Adam does not serve as a representative whose actions count for others, but he does turn to the Lord and exhibit faith (cf. 3:20–21).

Following Adam's sin, Genesis recounts the proliferation of people and their sin and highlights the universality of death. Already in Gen. 4 sin is compared to a beast of prey preparing to pounce on Cain (4:7). From Adam's own family comes the first murder: Cain kills Abel (4:8). In Gen. 5 the effects of Adam's sin are evident in his genealogy, for in every generation those who are born die (excepting Enoch).

In brief, Adam's representative actions introduce into the world sin and death, which, the NT teaches, only the second and last Adam can overcome.

Pentateuch and Historical Books. Adam is not often mentioned by name in the OT after Gen. 1–5, but this does not lessen his importance. Throughout the OT, God's created order and the original estate occupied by Adam continue to be foundational. For example, the command for Adam and Eve to be fruitful and multiply (Gen. 1:28) is repeated in various ways throughout the Pentateuch (Gen. 9:1, 7; 35:11–12), and sometimes the commands become promises (Gen. 12:2–3; 17:2, 6, 8; 22:17–18; 26:3–4, 24; 28:13–14; see Beale, *New Testament Biblical Theology*, 46–54). Additionally, the promised land of Canaan is described in language that echoes the paradisiacal garden of Eden (Lev. 26:6–12). Both the tabernacle and the temple of Solomon in Jerusalem (1 Kings 6:14–36; 7:13–51; cf. 4:33 [MT/LXX 5:13]) also recall the garden of Eden (Beale, *Temple*; Morales). Likewise, the pattern of six days' work and one day's rest is codified in the Ten Commandments in a way that recalls God's work during the first, primordial week (Exod. 20:11).

Additionally, Adam's sin is recalled and echoed in various OT passages. It seems that Achan's sin is patterned after the actions of Eve in the garden (Gen. 3:6–8; Josh. 7:21; cf. 7:11, 15; Howard, 197), for which Adam was held responsible. Additionally, the nation of Israel in many ways recalls Adam. Though it would be going too far to say that Adam *is* Israel (Wright, 18–40), it is appropriate to note the extensive parallels between Adam and Israel. Like Adam, Israel is God's son (Gen. 5:1, 3; Exod. 4:22; Deut. 14:1; 32:5–6, 18–20), and both sons were or are called to covenantal obedience. The Lord offered or offers blessings and curses to both covenantal sons: If Adam disobeyed, he would die; if he obeyed fully, he would be granted eternal, eschatological life (Gen. 2:16–17). Similarly, if Israel obeys, they will experience long, blessed life in the promised land; if Israel disobeys, they will experience exile and curses (e.g., Lev. 26:3–39; Deut. 28).

Despite many similarities between Adam and Israel, significant differences are also apparent. Adam was created upright with the opportunity to receive eternal life by means of personal and perfect obedience. In contrast, all Israelites are, by nature and practice, sinners, and thus, no Israelite is in a position to inherit eternal life by means of his or her own perfect obedience. Likewise, Adam in his created state was not in need of redemption; the Israelites—all of whom are descended from Adam—are in need of redemption. The NT will explain that redemption is accomplished by one who is like Adam but better.

Adam's historicity is also apparent in biblical genealogies, such as in 1 Chron. 1:1. Given the importance of genealogies for legitimizing kings and priests, this passage confirms the interpretation of Genesis that says Adam really existed.

Psalms and Prophets. The problem of sin is assumed throughout the entire biblical corpus after Adam, and Adam's specific sin may also be recalled in the Prophets. Texts like Job 31:33 (Heb. *kəʾādām*) and Isa. 43:27 may refer to Adam, but a more prominent (if debated) text is Hosea 6:7. This is a difficult text to translate. The NIV reads, "As at Adam, they have broken the covenant; they were unfaithful to me there" (so also NRSV). In this translation, Adam is a place name rather than a personal name (cf. Josh. 3:16). However, this interpretation is problematic, and "Adam" is better taken as a reference to the first biblical man (so CSB, ESV). Several reasons support this. First, the Hebrew preposition (*kə*) seems less appropriate for referring to a place (where one might expect *bə*)—especially for referring to an obscure place like Adam, mentioned only in Joshua. Second, though Hosea 6 is more explicit, this passage is not exceptional in understanding the Bible to speak of a covenant with Adam. Key elements of a covenant are present in Gen. 1–3. Third, many ancient translations understand this passage to refer to the person of Adam (Crowe, *Last Adam*, 59–60). Fourth, a reference to Adam coheres well with the contents of Hosea, which frequently allude to covenantal texts from Genesis and the original created order (Curtis).

Psalm 8 also alludes to Adam. Echoing Gen. 1–2, David speaks of man being a little lower than the angels, crowned with glory and honor, with authority over other creatures. The language used for the authority entrusted to the son of man (*ben ʾādām*) in Ps. 8:4 (MT 8:5) is then echoed in Daniel's vision of the kingdom of the Son of Man, who rules over the beastly, ungodly kingdoms. Given the Adamic resonances of the royal rule of the Son of Man, Dan. 7 likely also alludes to Adam, a point that will be significant for the discussion of the Gospels below.

Adam in OT Apocrypha and Pseudepigrapha. The framework of the OT assumes that God is the creator of all humanity and has condescended to relate covenantally to his creatures, beginning with Adam. It is instructive that Adam is the focus of much elaboration in various noncanonical Jewish and Christian sources. Though space precludes interaction with these extracanonical elaborations, they do seem to reflect rather widespread interest in Adam near the time of the NT (e.g., Sir. 49:16; CD 3.20–21; 1QS 4.22–23; Apoc. Mos.; LAE; Jub. 2–4; T. Levi 18:10–14; 2 En. 30:11–14; Apoc. Adam). Such texts indicate that the interest in Adam as a foundational figure is much greater than one might conclude based on the sparse number of occurrences of Adam's name in the OT. This becomes even clearer in the NT.

Adam in the NT

Gospels and Acts. The Gospels present Jesus as a new Adam who overcomes the sin of the first Adam by his perfect obedience (Crowe, *Last Adam*). This is evident in the temptation account in Mark (1:12–13), in which Jesus obeys God and is with wild animals. This passing allusion probably echoes the original created order, in which Adam had dominion over the creatures and which was forfeited when he sinned. By his obedience Jesus overcomes the sin of the first Adam, and his presence in the wilderness suggests that Jesus is overcoming all that has been affected by the fall. Further, in Mark this passage is correlated to Jesus's obedience by which he binds the strong man (3:22–30; cf. Matt. 12:25–32), which has often been understood Adamically (Irenaeus, *Haer*. 3.18.6–7; 3.23.1; 5.21.1, 3; 5.22.1; Calvin, 2:72).

An emphasis similar to Mark's may be found in Luke. Immediately before Luke's temptation account comes Jesus's genealogy, tracing his ancestry all the way back to Adam, the son of God (3:38). When Jesus obeys in the following text (4:1–13), his obedience is therefore presented as that of a new Adam.

It is also likely that Jesus's preferred self-designation, "Son of Man" (or "the Son of Man" [*ho huios tou anthrōpou*]), alludes to Adam (Marcus). This is especially the case if the title derives largely from the "son of man" in Dan. 7:13–14, which seems to be the most persuasive option (cf. Matt. 26:64; Mark 14:62; Luke 22:69). As noted earlier, the son of man in Dan. 7 likely builds on the Adamic imagery of Gen. 1–2 and Ps. 8. When Jesus speaks of the work of the Son of Man, he speaks of himself as the new man who overcomes the sin of Adam. The authority of Jesus in his resurrected state probably also recalls Dan. 7 and therefore the first man as well (Matt. 28:18–20).

In the Gospel of John, Adamic resonances are particularly evident with respect to Jesus's crucifixion and resurrection. Adam was created with dominion, and Jesus is presented as a king in his crucifixion (though ironically). The words "behold Adam," spoken by God in Gen. 3:22, may be echoed in Pilate's words "behold the man" in John 19:5 (Litwa). After his resurrection Jesus is first seen in a garden, and Mary mistakes Jesus for the gardener (John 19:41; 20:15). This may recall Adam in the garden of Eden; many have seen this to be a biblical-theological theme that underscores that "what was lost in a garden is restored in a garden" (Moloney, 141n19).

In Acts the authority of the resurrected Christ over all people is related to Adam. In Athens, Paul tells the Areopagus, "From one man [God] made all the nations" (Acts 17:26). The phrase "from one" (*ex henos*) does not directly name Adam. However, the NIV is correct to interpret this as a reference to one man and thus to Adam himself. Paul then explains that God has appointed one man as judge over all peoples—Jesus of Nazareth, who has been raised from the dead. This means that all people everywhere should repent and turn to him (17:30–31). Paul relates the universality of humanity descended from Adam to the universality of the resurrected Lord over all peoples. Paul makes similar arguments in his letters (see below).

Before turning to the NT Epistles, we should also consider Adam's importance for Jesus's teaching. A key text is Jesus's discussion of marriage in Matt. 19. In response to the challenge about why Moses commanded divorce (19:7), Jesus appeals to God's original design for marriage in the days of Adam and Eve. Divorce was never the goal, for "at the beginning the Creator 'made them male and female' [*ho ktisas ap' archēs arsen kai thēly epoiēsen autous*]" (19:4). Jesus therefore grounds the eschatological ethics of the covenant community in the ethics of the original created order. He appeals to the marriage of Adam and Eve in the beginning to support the abiding validity of marriage in the present age.

NT Epistles. Paul alludes to Adam throughout his letters, especially in his crucial discussion on the relationship between Adam and Christ in Rom. 5:12–21. Here Paul organizes all of humanity under two covenant heads: Adam and Christ. The sin of one man, Adam, led to death and condemnation for all (5:12, 18). In contrast, the obedience of Jesus, the last Adam, leads to justification and life for all (5:18). As through Adam's disobedience the many are constituted (*katestathēsan*) sinners (5:19; Murray, 64–95), so through the obedience of one man the many are constituted righteous. Paul here explains the universality of sin and death, which entered the world through the representative actions of Adam. Paul also explains how the work of Christ pertains to humanity as a whole: Christ's actions lead to justification for all who trust in him. The solidarity of humanity—all natural people are represented by Adam—explains how Christ's actions can apply representatively as well. In Rom. 5 Paul does not merely give an illustration that stands regardless of whether Adam was historical. Paul's argument hinges on the unity of humanity in Adam. Just as Adam was a representative figure whose actions can be imputed to others (bringing death), so Christ is a representative figure whose actions can likewise be imputed to others (bringing life). Romans 5 provides the fundamental covenantal structure of Paul's soteriological thought: just as sin and death come by the representative actions of one man, so also justification and life come through the representative actions of one man (Crowe, "Obedience of Christ").

In 1 Cor. 15 Paul contrasts the first Adam with Jesus Christ, the last Adam (15:45). Fittingly, Paul also refers to Jesus as the second man (15:47). This points to Paul's conviction that Adam and Christ are the two most consequential figures of human history. And in this passage Paul again points to the resurrection authority of Jesus, whose dominion excels that of Adam. Through a man comes death; through a man comes the resurrection of the dead (15:21). Whereas the first Adam became a living being, the last Adam has become a life-giving Spirit. This does not mean that Paul equates Jesus with the Holy Spirit; rather, it refers to the close relationship between the resurrected Christ and the outpouring of the Spirit. The age of the resurrection is the age of the Spirit (Vos, "Eschatological Aspect"). For Paul, all people's identities are understood in relation either to Adam or to Christ; one's destiny hinges on one's relationship to one of these two men (15:48–49). Further, only those who are descended from Adam can be redeemed by Christ (Gaffin, 10–12). Paul's argument in 1 Cor. 15 requires Adam to be the progenitor of all humanity.

Adam also appears in 1 Tim. 2, where Paul discusses leadership in the church. In v. 13 Paul grounds the structure of church leadership in the order of creation. To be sure, this is a widely debated passage, but however one seeks to apply this passage, Adam is, for Paul, a real person with implications for the present. Paul further alludes to Adam in an array of passages (Rom. 1:21; 3:23; 7:14; Phil. 2:5–11; Col. 1:15, 18). In this light, the use of Ps. 8 may be another way for Paul, even if indirectly, to evoke the importance of the first man (cf. 1 Cor. 15:25–28; Eph. 1:20–23). Psalm 8 is also quoted in Heb. 2:5–9 to highlight the way Christ realizes the royal dignity of humanity. Less likely, though possible, is an allusion to Adam in Heb. 2:11, where "from one" (*ex henos*) most likely refers to God or possibly to a shared humanity (NIV: "from one family"). Here the point is most likely not that Jesus himself comes from Adam but rather that Christ, our Savior and forerunner, shares in the solidarity of all humanity.

One of the more explicit, if passing, references to Adam comes in Jude 14, where Enoch is identified as the seventh from Adam. Here Jude assumes the historicity of both Enoch and Adam in a way that recalls biblical genealogies. The NT authors agree with the evidence from the OT that Adam was a real human being. Further supporting this perspective is the strong emphasis on Adam in early Christian theology, such as we find in Irenaeus, Cyril of Alexandria, and *Cave of Treasures*, which extensively compares Adam and Christ (Crowe, *Last Adam*, 7–10).

Implications

It is difficult to overstate the significance of Adam for biblical theology—whether we speak of the first or last Adam. The two are closely correlated. Briefly, we should consider some historical, hermeneutical, and theological implications of Adam in Scripture.

In terms of historicity, the Bible requires us to affirm Adam as a historical person. Scripture leaves no ambiguity on this point. Adam was the first person in world history, created by a special act of God, and created sinless. Genesis 1–3 depicts the creation of the world, the good estate in which humanity was originally created, and the tragedy that ensued from the fall into sin. This is foundational for understanding the realities of sin and death in Scripture and common human experience.

Hermeneutically, one's approach to Adam is indicative of one's general approach to Scripture. Where the Bible speaks clearly, we must speak clearly. It is hermeneutically irresponsible to take clear texts—such as the many that deal with Adam—and treat them as though they are somehow unclear. To be sure, the biblical teaching on Adam challenges a number of modern-day perspectives and presuppositions, but we must submit to Scripture, even when it may seem difficult.

Theologically, the two-Adam structure is foundational for grasping the theology of the Bible. Were Adam not the first human being, then we would have to affirm either that (1) humans are created sinful or (2) there were other falls into sin that are not recounted in Scripture, which collectively affect all humanity. But the Bible affirms neither of these positions. The first position would make sin natural, make creation prone to evil, and implicate God in the sin of humanity. The second option severs the organic relationship of humanity and introduces different classes of people, some not derived from Adam, into the Bible. As noted above, this latter position is precluded by the teaching of 1 Corinthians.

In addition, the first and last Adam are crucial for understanding the representation of Christ and the way that we are saved. This is true not only because Adam was a representative in his pre-fall estate but also because of the means held out to him for eternal life: perfect obedience (Crowe, "Obedience of Christ"). When Adam fails, eternal life does not cease to be contingent upon perfect obedience. Yet, no person affected by Adam's sin can meet the standard of perfection. At the same time, since death came through a man, the resurrection must also come through a man. This highlights the need for the Son of God to become incarnate, fully human, yet not born by ordinary means. As one born of a virgin, Jesus is not implicated in Adam's sin. Further, our Savior must be divine in order to appease the wrath of God and raise us to eternal life. Thus, Jesus is one person with two natures: divine and human. As one who is fully human yet free from sin, Jesus realizes the standard of perfect obedience for eternal life. Jesus succeeds where Adam failed.

Biblical theology boils down to two men: Adam and Christ. Paul speaks of these two men as if they were the only two men in the world and from their belts hang all other people (Goodwin, 31).

See also Creation; Image of God; Messiah; Priest; Prophet; Sin

Bibliography. Bavinck, H., *Reformed Dogmatics*, ed. J. Bolt, trans. J. Vriend, 4 vols. (Baker Academic, 2003–8); Beale, G. K., *A New Testament Biblical Theology* (Baker Academic, 2011); Beale, *The Temple and the Church's Mission*, NSBT 17 (InterVarsity, 2004); Calvin, J., *Commentary on a Harmony of the Evangelists, Matthew, Mark, and Luke*, trans. and ed. W. Pringle, 3 vols. (repr., Baker Books, 2003); Crowe, B. D., *The Last Adam* (Baker Academic, 2017); Crowe, "The Passive *and* Active Obedience of Christ: Retrieving a Biblical Distinction," in *The Doctrine on Which the Church Stands or Falls*, ed. M. Barrett (Crossway, 2019), 437–64; Curtis, B. G., "Hosea 6:7 and the Covenant-Breaking like/at Adam," in *The Law Is Not of Faith*, ed. B. D. Estelle, J. V. Fesko, and D. Van-Drunen (P&R, 2009), 170–209; Enns, P., *The Evolution of Adam* (Brazos, 2012); Gaffin, R. B., Jr., *No Adam, No Gospel* (Westminster Seminary Press, 2015); Goodwin, T., *Christ Set Forth*, vol. 4 of *The Works of Thomas Goodwin* (James Nichol, 1862); Howard, D. M., Jr., *Joshua*, NAC 5 (Broadman & Holman, 1998); Litwa, M. D., "Behold Adam: A Reading of John 19:5," *HBT* 32 (2010): 129–43; Marcus, J., "Son of Man as Son of Adam," *RB* 110 (2003): 370–86; Moloney, F. J., *Love in the Gospel of John* (Baker Academic, 2013); Morales, L. M., *Who Shall Ascend the Mountain of the Lord?*, NSBT 37 (InterVarsity, 2015); Murray, J., *The Imputation of Adam's Sin* (Eerdmans, 1959); Philpot, J. M., "How Does Scripture Teach the Adam-Christ Typological Connection?," *SBJT* 21, no. 1 (2017): 145–52; Poythress, V. S., *Interpreting Eden* (Crossway, 2019); Turretin, F., *Institutes of Elenctic Theology*, trans. G. M. Giger, ed. J. T. Dennison Jr., vol. 1 (P&R, 1992); Versteeg, J. P., *Adam in the New Testament*, trans. R. B. Gaffin Jr., 2nd ed. (P&R, 2012); Vos, G., *Biblical Theology* (repr., Banner of Truth, 1975); Vos, "The Eschatological Aspect of the Pauline Conception of the Spirit," in *Redemptive History and Biblical Interpretation*, ed. R. B. Gaffin Jr. (P&R, 1980), 91–125; Vos, *Reformed Dogmatics*, ed. and trans. R. B. Gaffin Jr., 5 vols. (Lexham, 2012–16); Waters, G. P., "Theistic Evolution Is Incompatible with the Teachings of the New Testament," in *Theistic Evolution*, ed. J. P. Moreland et al. (Crossway, 2017), 879–926; Wright, N. T., *The Climax of the Covenant* (Fortress, 1992).

BRANDON D. CROWE

Adultery *See* Image of God; Marriage

Allegory

Few questions generate more confusion or controversy than the question of whether there is allegory in the NT. The verb *allēgoreō* appears in Jewish (Philo, Josephus, Athenagoras) and non-Jewish (Plutarch) Greek literature contemporary to the NT but occurs only once in the NT (Gal. 4:24). Within the early church, the term "allegory" came to denote the controversial method of interpretation championed by the Alexandrian father Origen. Origen, in fact, appealed to Gal. 4:24 to warrant his method of allegorizing the "Abrahamic history" (*Comm. Jo.* 20.67, 20.74; and yet see the contrasting claims of Chrysostom, *Hom. Gal.* 4:24, and Diodore of Tarsus and Theodore of Mopsuestia, cited in Froelich, 85–86, 95–98). Contemporary scholars, furthermore, have attempted to argue for allegory in the NT in places where the word does not appear. Paul's interpretation of Deut. 25:4 at 1 Cor. 9:8–9 and portions of the argument of Hebrews (particularly 7:1–10) have also been alleged to be specimens of NT allegory.

One's answer to the question of the presence of allegorical interpretation within the NT raises broader questions regarding the NT writers' use of the OT. If the NT writers approvingly engage in allegorical interpretation, what might the implications of that be for our understanding of their typological interpretation of the OT? If the NT writers' use of the OT is normative for Christian interpretation of the OT, is there warrant for allegorizing the OT today?

We will begin by reflecting upon the definition of allegory and exploring the history of allegory in the period leading up to the NT. We will then reflect upon the differences between typology and allegory. Finally, we will explore places in the NT where allegorical interpretation is alleged to surface—namely, select passages in Paul's Letters and in Hebrews. We will see that the allegorical methods of interpretation within antiquity find no parallel in the NT. The NT writers interpret the OT in ways fundamentally different from the way that certain Greek writers allegorize Homer and Hesiod and that Philo allegorizes the OT. What is alleged to be allegory within the NT is, upon closer and careful examination, typological interpretation of the OT.

Definition

Scholars have noted that how one defines allegory determines whether or not one will find allegory in the NT. For that reason, it is critical to be clear as to what allegory is and is not. The Greek verb *allēgoreō* is a compound formed from two Greek words, *agoreuō* ("speak") and *allos* ("other, another"). At root, allegory involves communicating something that is "other" than what one has said (see the definition of Heraclitus the Younger, *All.* 22). Allegory may be conceived in two distinct ways (Whitman, *Allegory*; Herren). At one level, allegory reflects a genre of literature. Within the NT, some of Jesus's parables arguably fall within this category (e.g., the parable of the sower). At another level, allegory denotes a mode of interpretation. Allegorical interpretation takes the details of a text and understands them in terms other than the apparent meaning of those details. Although such interpreters may believe that they are acting faithfully to the intention of the author, allegorical interpretation has no demonstrable foundation in the text itself.

In antiquity, the Greek noun *allēgoria* is a comparatively late term, and came to replace, by the time of the NT, an earlier term, *hyponoia* (Plutarch, *Mor.* 19). Both terms, however, denoted both the genre of allegory and allegorical methods of interpretation (for a fuller taxonomy of ancient allegory, see Young). Given this breadth of range, a brief survey of the history of allegory prior to the NT will help to provide the necessary context for taking up the question whether the NT writers employed allegory in their handling of the OT.

Allegory Prior to the NT

Allegory first surfaces in ancient Greek writers' interpretations of the myths of Homer and Hesiod. Beginning in the sixth century BC, interpreters responded to discomfort with Hesiod's primeval account of Kronos's castration of his father, Ouranos (*Theog.* 176–87), and Homer's account of the adulterous liaison of Ares and Aphrodite (*Od.* 8.266–369), to take but two examples. Theagenes of Rhegium (fl. late 6th c. BC) is among the first known writers who sought to defend the portrayals of the gods in Homer and Hesiod by allegorizing those portrayals. Allegorical interpreters sometimes represent the gods as material forces (Hera = air; Apollo = fire; Poseidon = water). They employed a "substitutionist" hermeneutic, in which the names of the gods and goddesses were thought to stand for natural realities (Herren). Along these lines, Stoic interpreters read ancient myths as scientific explanations of the physical world.

Plato, however, was dismissive of such readings of ancient myths. He did not attempt to retrieve scientific or moral meaning by means of substitution. Plato, rather, crafted new myths to express philosophical truth, the most famous of which is his "Allegory of the Cave" in the *Republic*. For Plato there are two realms: the realm of form and the realm of sense/shadow. That which is sense or shadow is a material and mutable reflection or approximation of eternal, spiritual form. One accesses the realm of form through the mind. The soul must recognize the realm of sense for its transience and impermanence. It must also employ the realm of sense to access the realm of idea.

Platonic philosophy spawned a new mode of allegory. The details of ancient myth, including the gods and their exploits, were seen as symbolic in character. They served to help readers to discern the relationship between the realm of sense and the realm of idea (Herren). This mode of allegory flourished well into the third century AD (Porphyry, *Antr. nymph.*). It differed from Stoic allegory in a couple of respects. It did not seek to generate meaning by substituting earthly realities for the gods and their actions. Rather, it saw the details of myths as symbolically pointing to realities pertaining to another realm. Stoic allegory reflected the materialism of its practitioners. Allegory in the Platonic tradition reflected Plato's two realms and the ultimacy of the realm of form or idea.

In the Hellenistic period, Jewish writers adopted allegorical methods in their interpretation of the OT. The Alexandrian Jew Philo (fl. AD 1–50) is best known for his allegorical interpretation of the Pentateuch. But Philo did not introduce allegory to Jewish interpretation. The Jewish writer Aristobulus of Alexandria and the Jewish text Letter of Aristeas, both ca. 100 BC, independently suggest that allegorical interpretation of the Pentateuch was an established practice before Philo.

But Philo, because his extant writings have been so fully preserved, is our best available window into the practice of Jewish allegory at the time of the NT. Philo wrote in part to commend Judaism to his learned non-Jewish contemporaries in Alexandria. He believed that Platonic truth could be demonstrated from the Torah. His allegorical readings of the Pentateuch—both its legislation and its narrative—were in service of that goal. Philo did not outrightly dismiss the concrete particulars of the Pentateuch, but he did see those details as pointers to philosophical truth. And so, for example, the account in Genesis of Abraham, Sarah, and Hagar, for

Philo, is read as an account of the passage of the soul (Abraham) from the learning of this world (Hagar) to the wisdom of God (Sarah) (*Alleg. Interp.* 3.244; *Cherubim* 3–10). Philo employed both substitutionist and symbolic modes of allegory in his writings. Philonic allegory, then, appears to have been characterized more by consistency of goal than by rigidity of method.

Allegory and Typology

Given that allegory was a hermeneutical commonplace among many ancient interpreters, the question arises whether allegory surfaces in the NT. In addressing this question, one must first reflect upon the typology of the NT writers. In doing so, one may more clearly discern how NT typology and ancient allegory are similar or different and, therefore, the degree to which they are or are not mutually compatible.

A type may be defined as "an event, a series of circumstances, or an aspect of the life of an individual or of the nation, which finds a parallel and a deeper realization in the incarnate life of our Lord, in his provision for the needs of men, or in his judgments and future reign." The "type" is "incomplete and preparatory," while the "antitype" is marked by "completeness and finality" (Foulkes, 366–67). Typology may be defined, then, as "the study of analogical correspondences between persons, events, institutions, and other things within the historical framework of God's special revelation, which, from a retrospective view, are of a prophetic nature. According to this definition, the essential characteristics of a type are: (1) analogical correspondence; (2) historicity; (3) forward-pointing; (4) escalation; (5) retrospection" (Beale, 29).

In light of these definitions, we may identify three basic elements of types and typology. First, a type, and its corresponding antitype, is historical in nature, whether it be a person, object, or event (Goppelt, 17–18). Second, the relationship between a type and its antitype is analogical in nature, not arbitrary. Furthermore, not only does the type point forward eschatologically to its antitype, but the antitype also represents an escalation or heightening within the analogical relationship of type and antitype. Third, the relationship between type and antitype is fully evident only from the perspective of revelatory fulfillment. It is the NT, in light of the finished work of Christ, that provides the vantage point by which OT types may be discerned with greatest clarity. The various type-antitype relationships of the Bible are not constructs of the NT writer but are discerned by the NT writer in light of the commencement, in Christ, of the last days (Beale).

Recognizing the diversity of allegorical methods employed by ancient writers, we may note three salient differences between typology and allegory. The first concerns the relationship of the original biblical text to that to which it corresponds. In a typological correspondence, the antitype "conveys" the "reality" of the type; in an allegorical relationship, the letter "disguise[s]" or "conceal[s]" the spiritual meaning to which it is related (Lampe and Woollcombe, 30). A typological correspondence is discernible from the letter of the text in a way that an allegorical correspondence simply is not. Furthermore, typology is concerned to interpret types within the broader literary and historical context of the texts in which those types fall. Allegory is not constrained by this context. Whether allegory is substitutionary or symbolic, it frequently isolates particular words from their immediate contexts in the interest of disclosing what are thought to be the deeper realities to which these words point.

The second difference between typology and allegory concerns the place and importance of history to each mode of interpretation. Typology is, at root, a historical enterprise. That is to say, the correspondences recognized by biblical typology are historical and eschatological in nature. Allegory is not necessarily indifferent to the narrative structure or progression of a text, but allegorical correspondences often stand independently of that structure or progression. More to the point, allegorical correspondences are fundamentally both vertical and conceptual/noetic. They are vertical in that they relate two realms that are spatially distanced (not historically distanced, as in typology). They are conceptual/noetic in that the lower realm points to ideas within the higher realm. As such, these ideas are static and need not be historical. While all typological relationships have a conceptual dimension to them, this conceptual dimension is a necessary but not a sufficient condition of such relationships. Typological relationships are fundamentally historical.

The third difference between typology and allegory concerns the nature of escalation or heightening in view in each. In typology, the antitype represents a heightening of the type in the sense that the type is historically provisional or incomplete, and the antitype is historically consummate or complete. There may be, furthermore, between the original type and the antitype any number of staged, intermediary types that carry the escalation to its intended goal. These intermediaries stand in an organic relationship to the type, to one another, and to the antitype. In allegory, escalation is ahistorical and conceptual in nature. The lower realm points, in concealed and obscure fashion, to the comparatively pure truth or idea contained in the higher realm. This interpretive framework is not historical but philosophical (Goppelt). Philonic allegory, for instance, is conducted within a broadly Platonic framework that effectively determines the referent of the biblical text and the character of the escalation between text and referent.

In light of these differences between typology and allegory, and in light of the inescapably historical character of biblical redemption and revelation, we do not expect to find instances of allegorical interpretation within the NT. The univocal message of the NT concerns Jesus Christ, who assumed true humanity, lived, died, and rose again in history, according to the Scriptures, for the salvation of sinners (1 Cor. 15:1–3). As the person and work of Christ are historical, OT foreshadowings of Christ must be understood along comparably historical lines. It would be unexpected, to say the least, to witness the NT writers attempting to draw philosophical claims about Christ in allegorical fashion from the text of the OT. Their convictions about Christ, rather, point us in one direction and one direction only—typology.

Allegory and the NT?

Some scholars, however, while acknowledging that the NT writers handle the OT typologically, also argue that the NT writers occasionally handle the OT allegorically (Longenecker; O'Keefe and Reno). Other scholars problematize the distinction between typology and allegory (Carter). There are three primary places in the NT where the question of allegory in relation to the interpretation of the OT surfaces: Paul's argument from Gen. 16 in Gal. 4:21–31; Paul's treatment of Deut. 25:4 in 1 Cor. 9:8–10; and the author of Hebrews' handling of the OT, particularly in Heb. 7–10. We will consider these passages and see that, in each case, the NT author is reading the OT typologically.

Galatians 4:21–31. Galatians 4:21–31 contains the only NT appearance of the verb *allēgoreō* (4:24; the cognate noun does not appear in the NT). Paul employs this verb approvingly, as a description of his explanation of Gen. 16 that follows in 4:24b–27. Paul's use of the verb *systoicheō* in 4:25 (also a NT *hapax legomenon*), which most translations render "corresponds to," serves to establish relationships between Sarah and Hagar (Gen. 16) and other later realities. In 4:25, Paul links Hagar to Mount Sinai, the present Jerusalem, slavery, and Hagar's children. In 4:26, Paul links Sarah to the Jerusalem above and to freedom and identifies her as the "mother" of believers. In 4:24b, Paul identifies each woman with a "covenant"—Hagar with Mount Sinai, who "bears children who are to be slaves," and Sarah with (implicitly and presumably) the Abrahamic covenant. Paul's handling of the text of Gen. 16, coupled with his use of the verb *allēgoreō* to describe that handling, then, raises the question whether Paul has undertaken an allegorical reading of the OT narrative.

To answer this question, one must first consider the place of Gal. 4:21–31 within the argument of the letter as a whole. Some commentators have seen it as a continuation of Paul's argument begun at 3:1. Others have seen it as the beginnings of Paul's exhortation, which continues in 5:1. It is likely that 4:21–31 does not sit comfortably in either category. The intervening plea of 4:8–20 sets 4:21–31 apart textually from the argumentation of 3:1–4:7. And, whereas the section concludes with an exhortation ("Get rid of the slave woman and her son," 4:30), itself a citation of Gen. 21:10, one is hard pressed to characterize the whole section as hortatory. Paul's chief concern here is the meaning of Scripture and its contemporary application. Even so, Paul recognizes that he is doing something different from his mode of argumentation earlier in Gal. 3:1–4:7, a difference expressed by the verb *allēgoreō*. A review of the progression of Paul's argument in 4:21–31 will clarify the manner in which he is handling the OT and point the way toward a definition of the verb *allēgoreō*.

In Gal. 4:21, Paul addresses those who seek to be "under the law" (*hypo nomon*). Paul has previously described being "under the law" as a state of captivity (3:23). Such persons stand in need of Christ's redemption (4:5). In view, then, are people who are relying upon the Mosaic law for justification (3:10). Paul's aim in the verses that follow is to persuade his readers of what the nature and consequences of being "under the law" truly are and to show that from Torah itself.

In the next two verses, Paul rehearses details found in Gen. 16–21. Abraham had a child, Ishmael, from a "slave woman," Hagar, and a child, Isaac, from a "free woman," Sarah (Gal. 4:22). Isaac was a child who was born "through promise" (4:22 AT; *di' epangelias*)—that is, according to God's promises extending back to Gen. 12:2. Ishmael, however, was born "according to the flesh" (*kata sarka*). Paul thus reminds his readers that Abraham's decision to conceive Ishmael was an act of unbelief.

In Gal. 4:24, Paul extends his argument beyond the text of Genesis. In 4:24–26, Paul identifies Hagar and Sarah with "two covenants," the Sinaitic and Abrahamic, respectively. He twice identifies Hagar with "slavery" (4:24–25), signaling a connection with readers who desire to be under the bondage of the law's regimen (4:21).

At first glance, it may appear that Paul is engaging in something like Philonic allegory (see Longenecker, 110–13). The verb "corresponds" (*systoichei*) serves to link Hagar with "the present city of Jerusalem" (4:25). By implication, Sarah, who is the "mother" of believers, corresponds to "the Jerusalem that is above" (4:26). The two Jerusalems are spatially distinguished. They are terrestrial and heavenly, respectively.

But, on closer inspection, Paul is not conjoining the details of biblical narrative to the spatial realms of sense and form. The descriptor "present" (Gk. *nyn*), after all, is temporal. Paul distinguishes the two Jerusalems eschatologically. The descriptor "above" serves to clarify in which Jerusalem the Galatian Christians participate. They do not participate in the present Jerusalem, characterized by law observance for justification. They participate presently in the eschatological Jerusalem. The eschatological character of this "Jerusalem" is evident in two ways. First, Paul's description of this latter Jerusalem as "above" finds a parallel in his description of Christ in 1 Corinthians. In contrast with Adam, the "earthly man," Christ is the "heavenly man." Believers in Christ (the "last Adam," 1 Cor. 15:45), correspondingly, are "those who are of heaven" (15:48). Second, believers, like Isaac, are "children of promise" (Gal. 4:28). We have been "born according to the Spirit" (AT), not "born according to the flesh," as Ishmael was (4:29). As Paul extends his contrast between the two "Jerusalems," he does so in terms of the fundamentally eschatological contrast between "flesh" and "Spirit." The contrast between the two Jerusalems in 4:25–26, then, is a thoroughly eschatological one.

The question then arises how Paul can conjoin Sarah with the Abrahamic covenant (and, in light of Paul's argument in Gal. 3:15–4:7: the new covenant as well) and Hagar with the Sinaitic covenant. Paul provides that answer in his citation of Isa. 54:1 in Gal. 4:27: "Rejoice, barren woman, who does not give birth; shout and cry out, she who does not have birth pangs; for the children of the desolate woman are more than of the woman who has a husband" (AT). A few chapters earlier, in Isa. 51:2, Isaiah has mentioned Sarah by name. Sarah is in view there as the one who has given birth to "Zion." Zion, in turn, is associated with fruitfulness, joy, gladness, and thanksgiving (51:3)—ideas that resurface in Isa. 54:1. The "Zion" of Isa. 51:3 is the eschatological Zion, which awaits YHWH's new-exodus deliverance (52:1–12). This deliverance will be accomplished through the work of YHWH's suffering servant (52:13–53:12).

It is in light of Isa. 51–54 that Paul associates the Sarah of Gen. 16–21 with the eschatological Zion. The eschatological Zion has been delivered by YHWH through the work of his servant, Christ. Paul's conjunction of Sarah, the Abrahamic covenant, eschatological Zion, and the new covenant represents the completion of a trajectory set forth by the prophet Isaiah and realized in Christ.

Given those associations, we may more readily grasp the rationale behind Paul's presentation of Hagar. If the "desolate/barren woman" of Isa. 54:1 is Sarah, then "the woman who has a husband" is surely Hagar (see Gen. 16:3). If Isaiah associates Sarah with eschatological Zion, then all that remains for Hagar is that which stands outside the realm of promise and redemption. And, for Paul, that is precisely "flesh" (Gal. 4:29) and "slavery" (4:24, 25). This pattern of association, in turn, accounts for Paul's conjunction of Hagar with the Sinaitic covenant. Paul, of course, does not bring the Mosaic covenant into view simpliciter in Galatians but rather as it is being (mis)used by his opponents in Galatia. Attempting to misuse the Mosaic covenant by seeking justification on the basis of obedience to its precepts is an expression of the flesh. This misuse characterizes not only Paul's opponents but also mainstream first-century Judaism—"the present city of Jerusalem" (4:25). Only the "children of promise"—Isaac and all believers in Christ—trace their birth to the Spirit and are true heirs, true sons (4:28–30). Thus, Hagar, her child, and Mount Sinai point forward to those of the present earthly Jerusalem who want to remain under the law for their justification, while Sarah and her child point typologically to the "Jerusalem that is above" of the new covenant. For Paul, these pairings do not lie outside the text of Scripture. They are found in the text of Scripture (see 4:21, 29).

In light of Paul's handling of the OT (Gen. 16–21; Isa. 51–54) in Gal. 4:21–31, what is the denotation of the verb *allēgoreō* in 4:25? Given Paul's pointedly eschatological reading of these texts, we may rule out allegory as practiced by the Stoics, Platonists, or Philo (contrast, in fact, Philo's reading of Gen. 21 at *Cherubim* 9). The verb indicates, rather, that Paul is reading the Torah in light of later revelation, Isaiah, and the fulfillment of the Law and the Prophets in the person and work of Jesus Christ.

Some interpreters have argued that neither typology nor allegory adequately describes Paul's interpretation in these verses (Hays, 116; cf. Jobes, 317–20), while others have argued that Paul blends typology and allegory (Harmon). But it seems more likely that Paul's argument is fundamentally typological. It meets the above-noted criteria of typology, while lacking any defining characteristic of allegory.

Why then does Paul employ the verb *allēgoreō* to introduce a typological argument? An initial answer lies in the fact that the verb does not necessarily denote the precise sense of allegory as practiced by the Stoics, the Platonists, or Philo. The verb's range of meaning was "broad[er]" in Paul's day (Silva, 636). LSJ, for instance, offers "speak figuratively *or* metaphorically" as one meaning for this verb. In light of Paul's treatment of Scripture in Gal. 4:21–31, the verb ("to speak of something other") should therefore here be rendered "interpreted figuratively" (see Moo, 295). The definition "interpreted allegorically" suggests a precision unsupported by the context of Gal. 4:21–31 and is therefore liable to mislead contemporary readers.

But why did Paul introduce this verb at all? Likely he does so to signal the distinction between his handling of Scripture in Gal. 3:15–4:7 and 4:21–31. What distinguishes these two sections of Galatians is not typology. Both arguments are fundamentally typological. What distinguishes the latter from the former is its sequencing, in concentrated fashion, of multiple texts of Scripture (Gen. 16; 21; Isa. 51–54) in a linear biblical-theological trajectory terminating in Christ. Paul's argument in Gal. 4:21–31, furthermore, rests upon the exegetical and biblical-theological foundation that he has laid in 3:15–4:7. The apostle assumes his readers' understanding of what he has already said about the Abrahamic, Mosaic, and new covenants ("promise," "law," and "faith," respectively). Galatians 4:21–31 also provides an ideal bridge to the hortatory portion of the letter beginning at 5:1: "It is for freedom that Christ has set us free. Stand firm, then, and do not let yourselves be burdened again by a yoke of slavery." This opening repeats the very concerns that Paul has highlighted in Gal. 4:21–31—slavery (in connection with the law) and freedom (in Christ). The verb *allēgoreō*, unique to Paul's Letters, highlights the unique function of 4:21–31 within the letter. What is not unique to 4:21–31, however, is the way in which Paul interprets the OT.

1 Corinthians 9:8–10. In 1 Cor. 9, Paul presents himself as an exemplar of the proper exercise of Christian liberty. For the sake of the gospel, Paul has voluntarily relinquished his right to remuneration for his labors (9:15–18). But although Paul suspends that right, he nevertheless insists to the Corinthians that he properly possesses that right. It is this latter point that is the burden of Paul's argument in 1 Cor. 9:1–18. In vv. 8–10, Paul quotes from "the Law of Moses": "Do not muzzle an ox while it is treading out the grain" (9:9a = Deut. 25:4). Paul then comments parenthetically, "Is it about oxen that God is concerned? Surely he says this for us, doesn't he? Yes, this was written for us, because whoever plows and threshes should be able to do so in the hope of sharing in the harvest" (9:9b–10). Paul therefore concludes from a Mosaic law governing the proper care of livestock that apostles should be remunerated for their labors.

Some scholars have pronounced Paul's argument allegorical and have advanced a number of arguments in support of that claim. First, the connection between animal husbandry (Deuteronomy) and ministerial provision (1 Corinthians) does not appear to be a typological one. Second, the adverb *pantōs* at 9:10, if translated "entirely" (as NRSV; "altogether," NASB, KJV), suggests that Paul is disavowing the meaning of the letter of Deut. 25:4 in favor of the interpretation proffered at 9:9–10.

Third, there are parallels with the way in which Philo handles such laws. Speaking of the Mosaic laws governing animal sacrifices, Philo argues, "For you will find that this exceeding accuracy of investigation into the animals, figuratively signifies the amelioration of your own disposition and conduct; for the law was not established for the sake of irrational animals, but for that of those who have intellect and reason" (*Spec. Laws* 1.259–60). Citing Deut. 25:4 at *Virtues* 145, Philo concludes, "For the man who has learnt the principles of humanity with respect to those natures which are devoid of sense, is never likely to err with respect to those which are endowed with life; and he who never attempts to act with severity towards creatures which have only life, is taught a long way off to take great care of those which are also blessed with reason" (*Virtues* 160). Philo argues that Mosaic laws addressing animals do not fundamentally concern the animals themselves. They are meant to instruct people, and particularly the way in which people are to treat other people. Philo's approach to these Mosaic laws in general is consistent with Paul's approach to Deut. 25:4 in particular.

On closer inspection, however, Paul is not engaging in an allegorical reading of Deut. 25:4. The adverb *pantōs*, in context, should be rendered "certainly" or "surely" (BDAG; cf. NIV, NET). Paul, then, does not set aside the sense of the letter of Deut. 25:4. Paul is simply saying that the meaning of Deut. 25:4 is not exhausted by its application to oxen. The law concerns "us" (*hēmas*).

The precise connection between oxen and apostles emerges from considering the genre of Paul's OT text—namely, law. Biblical law frequently legislates by providing an instance or circumstance that is representative of a broader class of related cases. Deuteronomy 25:4 provides for the welfare of working animals but not only animals. This law is concerned to ensure that anyone who works—whether animal or human—is not deprived of the rightful share of their labor. That Paul is thinking of Deut. 25:4 in these terms becomes clear when he describes the work of the apostles ("us," 10:10) in terms of plowing and threshing (10:10b) and sowing and reaping (10:11). For all the obvious differences, the apostles are in a position comparable to that of oxen, and the law of Deut. 25:4 applies to them.

As both Richard Hays and Anthony Thiselton have observed, this law of Deut. 25:4 sits within a larger legislative section of Deuteronomy (chaps. 24–25). For all their diversity, the laws of Deut. 24–25 are particularly concerned to promote the welfare of the vulnerable within Israel. Far from being an arbitrary or allegorical reading of Deut. 25:4, Paul's reading reflects the broader legislative concern of the portion of Deuteronomy from which this law is drawn.

It is this fact that likely accounts for any similarities of interpretation of Deut. 25:4 obtaining between Paul and Philo. Both interpreters recognize that Israel's legal obligations toward working animals exist within a wider framework of laws that address the just treatment of the needy and the vulnerable. As such, both Paul and Philo deny that this text's concern could be limited to oxen. To say this is not to concede that Paul has adopted Philonic allegorization of the laws of the Pentateuch. It is to say that, to the degree that Philo has read Deut. 25:4 within its immediate context, Paul agrees with that reading.

If Paul's reading of Deut. 25:4 is not allegorical, then how are we to characterize it? Certainly one would be hard pressed to argue for some kind of typological relationship between oxen and apostles. A more promising route would be to understand Paul's reading of this text along eschatologically informed analogical lines (Thiselton). Commentators observe that in the next chapter, Paul speaks of the new-covenant community as those "upon whom the ends of the ages have come" (10:11 AT). In that chapter, Paul pronounces old-covenant Israel to be "our ancestors" (10:1)—that is, the "ancestors" of new-covenant Christians. As such, the OT belongs to the new-covenant community no less than it did to the old-covenant community. The demand for justice reflected in Deut. 25:4 obliges God's people in all ages. Paul's reading and application of Deut. 25:4, however, reflect the changed eschatological circumstances of the people of God. As such, the moral principle that finds expression in Deut. 25:4 directs the new-covenant community to provide for the apostles from whose labors they spiritually profit.

Hebrews. Within twentieth-century scholarship, the study of Hebrews' use of the OT has explored what relationship there may be between Hebrews' and Philo's interpretations of the OT. The first half of the century's academic discussion emphasized similarities between the two writers, sometimes arguing for Hebrews' hermeneutical and conceptual dependence upon Philo. More recent scholarship, however, has accented their differences. For example, vocabulary within Hebrews that was formerly thought to have roots or background in the thought of Philo or Plato (e.g., *hypodeigma* and *skia*, 8:5; 9:23; 10:1; *eikōn*, 10:1) is now regarded as evidencing differences, not similarities or dependence, between Hebrews and Philo or Plato (Williamson; Hurst).

We may explore two dimensions of Hebrews that have suggested to some scholars an allegorical approach to the OT in Hebrews. The first is the way in which the author, throughout the letter but especially in Heb. 8–10, speaks of two vertical realities, the ephemeral creation inhabited by human beings and an abiding and superior heavenly reality. The second is the particular way in which the writer interprets Gen. 14 in Heb. 7:1–10.

Throughout the epistle, the author references "two distinct realms" (DeSilva, 27). The first realm is the creation, heaven and earth (1:10–12). Heaven and earth "will perish" and "wear out like a garment" (1:11). The "created things" are subject to being "shaken" (12:27). The second realm is the dwelling place of God and the exalted Christ (1:3; 10:12; 12:2), which the writer calls "heaven" (8:1) or "heaven itself" (9:24).

These two realms provide the framework within which the author addresses the priestly ministry of Christ in Heb. 8–10. In Heb. 8, the writer contrasts Christ's priestly ministry with that of the Levitical priests. Christ's ministry is carried out in the context of the "second" or "new" covenant (8:7–8), while the Levitical priests serve within the context of the "first" or "old" covenant (8:6–7). Corresponding to each covenant is a tent—Christ is "a minister in the holy places, in the true tent [*tēs skēnēs tēs alēthinēs*] that the Lord set up, not man" (8:2 ESV); the priests "serve a copy and shadow [*hypodeigmati kai skia*] of what is heavenly" (8:5 AT).

It is in the earthly tabernacle (note 9:1, *hagion kosmikon*), the writer continues, that priests continually offer "gifts and sacrifices . . . that cannot perfect the conscience of the worshiper" (9:9 ESV). But "through the greater and more perfect tent (not made with hands, that is, not of this creation)," Christ has offered himself as both priest and sacrifice (9:11 ESV). His sacrificial self-offering is "once for all," and so Christ's blood has "obtain[ed] an eternal redemption" and can "cleanse our consciences" (9:12, 14).

The author then reiterates this point that is so central to his argument. The "copies of the heavenly things [*hypodeigmata tōn en tois ouranois*]" had to be "purified" by the "sacrifices" prescribed by the Mosaic law (9:23). But "the heavenly things themselves [*auta de ta epourania*]" had to be purified "with better sacrifices [*kreittosin thysiais*] than these" (9:23). This has happened because "Christ has entered not into holy places made with hands, which are copies of the true things [*antitypa tōn alēthinōn*], but into heaven itself [*auton ton ouranon*]" (9:24 ESV). "The law has but a shadow [*skian*] of the good things to come" but not "the true form of these realities [*autēn tēn eikona tōn pragmatōn*]" (10:1 ESV).

There is, then, a correspondence between these two realms with respect to their tabernacles and the priestly activity within each. The tabernacle of the earthly realm is a shadow or copy of the tabernacle of the heavenly realm, which is the true tabernacle. The ministry conducted in the earthly tabernacle is ongoing, incomplete, and incapable of cleansing more than the body. The ministry conducted in the heavenly tabernacle is sufficient, perfect, and cleanses the conscience. It is in light of these realities that the author pronounces the sacrifice of Christ to be "better" than the Mosaic sacrifices (9:23), even as Christ mediates a "better" covenant with "better promises" (8:6 ESV).

Has the author of Hebrews allegorized the OT's presentation of the tabernacle, the Levitical priests, and their ministry at the priesthood by pointing to a higher, eternal, superior realm of which those OT realities are but dim reproductions? He has not. For one thing, the OT itself demonstrates that the earthly tabernacle was a copy of a heavenly reality. Furthermore, Hebrews' handling of the OT is typological. Complementing the author's vertical representation of the work of Christ in relation to the OT is a horizontal or eschatological representation of Christ and his work (Barrett, 363–65, 393). Christ's priestly ministry transpired in the space and time of this world. At the outset of the letter, the author insists that Christ's accomplished priestly work (1:3) has marked the dawn of the last days (*ep' eschatou tōn hēmerōn toutōn*, 1:2), the eschatological age of fulfillment. He did so having first become lower than the angels "for a little while [*brachy ti*]" (2:7 ESV). He was "crowned with glory and honor because of the suffering of death" (2:9 ESV) and was made "perfect through what he suffered" (2:10). Furthermore, his becoming a "merciful and faithful high priest in the service of God, to make propitiation for the sins of the people" required his becoming "like his brothers in every respect" (2:17 ESV). Christ could not be the kind of priest that he is now had not he lived and ministered in this earthly realm. Christ's accomplished priestly work of sacrifice took place in time, and its completion, in turn, has profound and defining temporal significance.

It is the eschatological dimension of Christ's priestly ministry that finds emphasis within Heb. 8–10 (Barrett). Christ is minister of a "second" or "new" covenant, which has displaced and rendered "obsolete" the "old" or "first" covenant (8:7, 13). This first covenant and its related Levitical priestly ministry pertained to this "present age [*ton kairon ton enestēkota*]" (9:9 ESV). The old covenant would obtain "until the time of reformation"—that is, the time appointed for Christ's priestly ministry to transpire in history (9:10 ESV).

In contrast with the priestly sacrifices of the old covenant, Christ offered himself "once for all" (9:12). In doing so, the author insists that, if Christ had not died once for all, "he would have had to suffer many times since the creation of the world." As it stands, he offered himself "once for all at the culmination of the ages" (9:26). It only remains for Christ to "appear a second time [*ek deuterou*], not to deal with sin but to save those who are eagerly waiting for him" (9:28 ESV). In the next chapter, that second appearance, significantly, is denominated by the temporal descriptor "the Day" (10:25). The sacrifice of Christ, then, is temporally situated between the beginning and the end of history and itself marks "the culmination of the ages."

How, then, may we represent the horizontal and vertical strands of the author's representation of Christ's priestly ministry? As Vos has noted, the OT presents an earthly "shadow" of heavenly reality (esp. the temple), and the NT presents the "substance" of "heavenly reality" (vertical). The OT shadow, moreover, "prefigures" the NT substance (horizontal). The horizontal and the vertical find integration insofar as the NT reality, temporally anticipated by the OT shadow, is none other than the *heavenly* reality. The author, then, depicts the ministry of Christ typologically even as he articulates a vertical dimension to his typology.

A second aspect of Hebrews' argument that some have alleged to be allegorical is the author's treatment of Gen. 14 in Heb. 7:1–10. In Heb. 7:3, the author claims an explicit correspondence between Melchizedek and the priestly "Son of God." This correspondence runs along two lines. In the first place, as Melchizedek, "king of righteousness" and "king of peace," is "without father or mother, without genealogy, without beginning of days or end of life" (7:2–3), he is like (*aphōmoiōmenos*) the eternal Son of God. Second, as Abraham presented a tithe to Melchizedek and was blessed by Melchizedek, so the Levites, descended from Abraham, acknowledged the superiority of Melchizedek (7:4–10). In this respect, Christ's priesthood is superior to the Levitical priesthood (see 7:11–19).

The correspondence that the author establishes between Melchizedek and Christ is sometimes said to be allegorical. Hebrews' etymologizing of Melchizedek's name finds parallel in ancient allegory (see Philo, *Alleg. Interp.* 3.79). The author isolates comparatively minor details from the Genesis narrative and capitalizes upon them to argue for the eternality and superiority of Christ, to whom Melchidezek points. Insofar as the correspondence is said to be verbal, vertical, and conceptual/noetic, the conclusion is drawn that Hebrews has engaged in allegorical exegesis of Gen. 14.

But the author is engaged in typological exegesis of Gen. 14. It must be remembered that the correspondence between Melchizedek and Christ is mediated by Ps. 110, twice cited in the text (Heb. 7:17, 21; cf. 5:6; 7:3). It is Ps. 110, according to the author, that testifies to the eternal priesthood of Christ, a priesthood that is after the order of Melchizedek and is "by the power of an indestructible life" (Heb. 7:16)—namely, his eternity as the Son of God. Accordingly, Ps. 110 views Gen. 14 to be typological of the eschatological reign of the priestly messiah. It is in light of the accomplished, sufficient, and final priestly work of the eternal Son of God (see Heb. 7:23–29; cf. 1:1–4) that the author interprets Gen. 14 by way of Ps. 110. The author does not thereby discard the literal meaning of Gen. 14. On the contrary, for Hebrews, the testimony of Ps. 110 in conjunction with the finished work of Christ illumines the meaning of Gen. 14, a text that all the while was eschatologically pointing forward to Jesus Christ (Williamson).

Conclusions and Implications

Having surveyed both allegory in antiquity and typology in the NT and having reviewed claims to allegory within certain texts of the NT, we have uncovered no indication that the NT writers undertake allegorical exegesis of the OT. The NT everywhere represents the work of the incarnate Christ as fundamentally and indispensably historical. That work, furthermore, marks the divinely ordained turning point or hinge of human history. The resurrection marked the dawn and inbreaking of the "last days" into history. The way in which the NT understands the OT to anticipate and prepare for the coming of Christ fully respects the historical character of his ministry. That is to say, the NT writers read the text of the OT typologically.

But it should not be thought that this study is a purely negative one. Our rehearsal of Paul and Hebrews has demonstrated the richness and nuance of NT typology. There is, for instance, a vertical component to the way in which each writer reads the text of the OT. Both Paul's exegesis of Gen. 16–21 and the author of Hebrews' exegesis of the Levitical priesthood and ministry run horizontally and vertically, and in ways that enrich our grasp of the correspondence between OT types and their antitype, Christ. We have also seen how NT typology frequently involves multiple texts from different sections of the OT canon. Paul interprets Gen. 16–21 by way of Isaiah, and the author of Hebrews interprets Gen. 14 by way of Ps. 110. NT typology is not a crudely drawn line between two points. Typology entails sophisticated and textured trajectories that often lead us artfully through substantial portions of the OT. Finally, we have seen that NT typology has clear ecclesiological and ethical dimensions. Paul's eschatological reading of Deut. 25:4 serves to illumine the nature and character of the new-covenant community, even as it models how the church is to read and apply Torah under the new covenant.

In this sense, the persistent question of the presence of allegory in the NT is an opportunity. It encourages readers of the NT to attend more closely to the ways in which the NT writers were reading the OT. And it helps us to see not only *that* but also *how* the entirety of Scripture is a book about Jesus Christ.

See also Literal Fulfillment; OT Use of the OT: Comparison with the NT Use of the OT; Typology; *Apostolic Hermeneutics articles*

Bibliography. Barrett, C. K., "The Eschatology of the Epistle to the Hebrews," in *The Background of the New Testament and Its Eschatology*, ed. W. D. Davies and D. Daube (Cambridge, 1956), 363–93; Beale, G. K., "Finding Christ in the Old Testament," *JETS* 63, no. 1 (2020): 25–50; Carter, C. A., *Interpreting Scripture with the Great Tradition* (Baker Academic, 2018); DeSilva, D. A., *Perseverance in Gratitude* (Eerdmans, 2000); Foulkes, F., "The Acts of God," in *The Right Doctrine from the Wrong Text?*, ed. G. K. Beale (Baker, 1994), 342–71; Froelich, K., trans. and ed., *Biblical Interpretation in the Early Church* (Fortress, 1984); Goppelt, L., *Typos*, trans. D. H. Madvig (Eerdmans, 1982); Harmon, M. S., "Allegory, Typology, or Something Else?," in *Studies in the Pauline Epistles*, ed. M. S. Harmon and J. E. Smith (Zondervan, 2014), 144–77; Hays, R. B., *Echoes of Scripture in the Letters of Paul* (Yale University Press, 1989); Herren, M., *The Anatomy of Myth* (Oxford, 2017); Hurst, L. D., *The Epistle to the Hebrews*, SNTSMS 65 (Cambridge, 1990); Jobes, K., "Jerusalem, Our Mother," *WTJ* 55, no. 2 (1993): 299–320; Lampe, G. W. H., and K. J. Woollcombe, *Essays on Typology*, SBT 22 (Allenson, 1957); Longenecker, R. N., *Biblical Exegesis in the Apostolic Period*, 2nd ed. (Eerdmans, 1999); Moo, D., *Galatians*, BECNT (Baker Academic, 2013); O'Keefe, J. J., and R. R. Reno, *Sanctified Vision* (Johns Hopkins University Press, 2005); Philo, *The Special Laws* and *On the Virtues*, in *The Works of Philo*, trans. C. D. Yonge (repr., Hendrickson, 1993); Silva, M., "Old Testament in Paul," in *DPL*, 630–42; Thiselton, A. T., *The First Epistle to the Corinthians*, NIGTC (Eerdmans, 2000); Vos, G., *The Teaching of the Epistle to the Hebrews* (Eerdmans, 1956); Whitman, J., *Allegory* (Clarendon, 1987); Whitman, ed., *Interpretation and Allegory* (Brill, 2003); Williamson, R., *Philo and the Epistle to the Hebrews*, ALGHJ 4 (Brill, 1970); Young, F. M., *Biblical Exegesis and the Formation of Christian Culture* (Cambridge University Press, 1997).

GUY PRENTISS WATERS

Allusion

See Quotation, Allusion, and Echo

Amos, Book of

Amos grew up in Judah in the small village of Tekoa, about twelve miles south of Jerusalem. His father was not a prophet, and Amos did not make his living by working at the Bethel temple (7:14–15). Rather, he earned a living by caring for sheep and a grove of sycamore trees that produced figs. The term *nōqēd* (1:1) defines his role as a manager in charge of a large flock of sheep and something like a chief foreman over the individual shepherds that led the sheep to pasture each day (Craigie, 29–33). He was probably born in Judah during the reign of the strong and prosperous King Uzziah, but his brief prophetic ministry was in the northern nation of Israel during the reign of Jeroboam II (ca. 793–753 BC). He prophesied about two years before a major earthquake struck (dated around 765–760 BC), an event he hints at in Amos 8:8 and 9:5 when he refers to the land rising and sinking. His ministry was unusual because he (like Jonah) left Judah and went to another nation (Israel) to deliver God's messages. Judah and Israel were enemies at this time (2 Chron. 25), so it is not surprising that a negative prophecy from a Judaean prophet was unwelcome. Amos apparently gave some of his messages in the capital city of Samaria (mentioned in 3:9, 12; 4:1; 6:1) and others at the Israelite temple in Bethel (7:10–17; 9:1–4). His ministry in Israel was cut short because he predicted the approaching death of Jeroboam II, the destruction of Israel (3:14–15), and the coming exile of the people of Israel (7:10–11). Although some conclude that Amos was immediately escorted out of the country by the Israelite authorities on charges of treachery, it is possible that this conflict only excluded Amos from speaking at the Bethel temple (Amos 7:13).

Essential Features of the Book of Amos

Composition. Amos was one of the first Hebrew scrolls to record information about a prophet's ministry and messages, although hundreds of years earlier prophets like Samuel, Nathan, and Gad (1 Chron. 29:29) wrote scrolls about the life of David that probably included some of their prophecies. There is no information about who recorded Amos's spoken words or when this was done, but it seems reasonable to assume that these messages were put in written form shortly after Amos returned to Judah. In contrast to this idea, Hans Walter Wolff (106–13) uses form and traditio-historical criticism to identify six stages in the compositional growth of this book over several centuries until it was completed in the postexilic era.

In contrast to the redactional approaches, others attribute all (or almost all) of these messages to Amos himself. Francis Andersen and David Freedman (194–99) reconstruct the chronological development of the book based on Amos's five visions in Amos 7–9 and connect these words to Amos or one of his disciples. Shalom Paul (6) rejects the "scissors-and-paste methods" of the redaction critics and joins a chorus of other authors who connect most of these messages to the prophet Amos (Paul; Smith; Hubbard; Stuart; Lessing).

Structure and message. The messages Amos spoke in Israel are divided into three major groupings. The structural components are fairly well defined by their form-critical features and content. The regular patterns found in Amos 1–2 are not employed in chaps. 3–6, and 7–9 contains a group of visions:

Part 1	The oracles against the nations	Chaps. 1–2
Part 2	Warning of judgment for Israel	Chaps. 3–6
Part 3	Visions and exhortations about the end	Chaps. 7–9

Following the superscription is a series of oracles against six foreign nations (1:3–2:3) and Judah (2:4–5), plus a longer climactic accusation against Israel (2:6–16). Each of these small oracles has common vocabulary ("For three acts of rebellion and for four, I will not vacillate . . . because you have . . . I will send fire" [AT]). The audience in Israel would naturally approve of the oracles against neighboring nations (including Judah in 2:4–5), but the people in Israel were no doubt shocked to hear Amos claim that God would destroy his own people in Israel.

The second part (Amos 3–6) explains in detail why God will judge Israel. God's roaring (like a lion) will bring a nation against Israel (3:11–12), and God will destroy the temple at Bethel and the homes of the wealthy (3:14–15) because of their sins. They must prepare to meet God (4:12) because their temple worship is unacceptable (4:1–5). They must seek God (5:3–4), not worship at the half-pagan temple at Bethel, and they must practice justice, because the day of the Lord (a day of darkness, not hope) will arrive soon and God will pour out his judgment on Israel (5:18–20).

The final unit (Amos 7–9) includes a controversy between Amos and a temple official at Bethel that takes place because Amos has predicted the fall of Israel and the death of their king (7:10–15). During the first two visions (a locust plague and a destructive fire), Amos prays, and God stops these disasters from happening (7:1–6), but soon God's patience ends (the vision of death in 8:1–3 and the destruction of the Bethel temple in 9:1–4), leaving little hope if the nation does not respond in repentance immediately. Amos's prophecies end not only with a reminder that the people's hope of divine protection is false (9:7–10) but also with the assurance that in the distant future God will restore the Davidic kingdom and bless their land with unlimited material blessings (9:11–15).

Literary Relationships Connected to Amos

The influence of earlier texts on Amos's preaching. There are several places where Amos seems to depend on earlier biblical texts. Many of these references to God's earlier activities function to legitimate Amos's claims about God's future actions. For example, in Amos 4:11 he warns that a destruction analogous to the complete destruction of Sodom and Gomorrah (Gen. 19, a common symbol of judgment that appears in Deut. 29:23; Isa. 13:19; Jer. 23:14) will come upon Israel if the people in the northern nation do not repent (Hasel, 71–76, connects the theme of repentance to a covenant tradition). Amos 2:4 accuses the Israelites of rejecting God's instructions and statutes, a reference to the law of Moses. This establishes the law as the standard by which the people will be evaluated, but no specific law is quoted in this instance. Instead, Amos accuses the people of being led astray by false alternatives that are inconsistent with the standards and requirements of the Torah. Amos 4:10 draws an analogy between God's coming judgment on Israel and God's past judgment on Egypt (Exod. 7–12), but no specific Egyptian plague is quoted. In addition to judging Israel's enemies, God will send disasters on his own people. Amos 2:10; 3:1; and 9:7 remind the listener of God's grace during the exodus, his caring for his people for forty years in the wilderness, and his conquest over the enemy nations living in the promised land, but now God warns that these gracious acts do not guarantee that he will never judge them if they continue in their sins. Amos 3:1–2 mentions God's gracious election of Israel (possibly drawing this idea from Deut. 7:6–7), and Amos 5:8 refers to the Noachian flood; together, these texts bring out the reality of God's past acts both of grace and of judgment. These warnings are intended to motivate the prophet's audience to follow God's instructions and enjoy his blessing. Based on these historical precedents and past literary predictions, those who fail to repent and turn to God will experience his wrath. Finally, Amos 4:13; 8:9; and 9:6 speak of God's great creative acts described in Gen. 1 and various psalms. In most of these examples the prophet Amos uses a past known event, what God did in a similar past situation, as an analogy or illustration to teach a lesson about the future that the Israelites will soon face. Will they repent and enjoy divine blessing, or refuse and face divine judgment?

Amos's influence on later prophetic teaching. The book of Amos had an impact on several later prophets in the OT. One example is found in the theme of the day of the Lord (Amos 5:18–20). Although there is no agreement on the origin of this concept (see Fensham; Černy), it is apparent that many of the people in the northern nation of Israel viewed it as a day of divine blessing, hope, and victory over their enemies. Amos astonishes his audience when he reverses this traditional understanding and proclaims that their day of the Lord will be a day of darkness and defeat. This idea (sometimes expressed simply as "on that day") is later picked up in Isa. 2:11–17 and used to refer to a time when God will humble the proud and defeat his enemies (cf. also 13:9), devastate the land, and remove people from the earth and the evil forces from the heavens (Isa. 24). Joel pictures the possibility of enduring the terrible devastation of the earth (Joel 1:15–20) on the gloomy day of the Lord (2:1–11) as a reason for his audience to "rend your heart and not your garments. Return to the LORD your God for he is gracious and compassionate" (2:13). Zephaniah refers to the approaching judgment of Jerusalem in 587 BC as an intermediate day of the Lord and encourages his readers to humble themselves and seek the Lord (Zeph. 1:7; 2:1–3; cf. Amos 5:4). Zechariah pictures the final battle for control of Jerusalem occurring on the future day of the Lord (Zech. 14), when God will defeat his enemies and establish his kingly rule.

Amos and the NT. In Acts, Stephen quotes from Amos 5:25–27 in his defense before the Sanhedrin (Acts 7:42–43), and James quotes from Amos 9:11–12 at the Jerusalem Council (Acts 15:16–18). These quotations do not fully agree with the MT of Amos and are heavily influenced by the LXX translation, the new context the speaker is addressing in Acts, and the hermeneutical principles the speakers apply in connecting two related situations.

Amos 5:25–27 addresses God's rejection of Hebrew worship happening at the temple at Bethel, where the people sacrifice to the golden calf and sing hymns of worship. This criticism is partially due to their unjust treatment of the weak and powerless (5:24), which ignores God's standards for justice. A second reason for God's displeasure is their focus on sacrifices instead of their heart relationship to God. A third factor is their worship of pagan gods in the wilderness (the golden calf at Sinai in Exod. 32–34) and in the time of Amos. So, Amos announces God's plan to send Israel into exile (5:27). This understanding of Amos 5:21–27 is complicated by a difficult Hebrew text. When interpreting the MT, one must come to a decision about the following questions: (1) Is Amos 5:25 a question or a statement? (2) Is 5:26a a question or a statement? (3) What is the vocalization and meaning of *skwt*, *mlkkm*, and *kywn*? Since the Greek translators did not know the names of all the ancient Assyrian gods mentioned in this verse, they had difficulty understanding what Amos was saying. The LXX makes 5:25 a statement and adds "not." Their misunderstanding of the unvocalized Hebrew text of 5:26 meant that *melek* (king) was misread as *mōlek* (the god Moloch), *sikkût* (the Assyrian god Sakkuth) was misread as *sukkôt* (tent, shrine), and *kîyûn* (the Assyrian god Kiyyun) was mistakenly read as *rhaiphan* by a Greek scribe. Thus, the LXX translation reads, "It was not to me that you offered victims and sacrifices for forty years in the wilderness, O house of Israel. You also took the tabernacle of Moloch and the star of the god Raiphan, the images you made for yourself to worship. So, I will carry you away beyond Damascus, says the Lord, the Almighty God is his name" (AT). When Stephen defends himself before the Sanhedrin in Acts 7, he probably quotes this LXX text from memory with only a few variations (Glenny, *Finding Meaning*, 181). Although the quotation is not perfectly exact, the key issue to consider is, Does Stephen twist or misconstrue the function or basic meaning of these OT verses? Aaron White suggests that these verses function "as a hermeneutical lens that draws together two eras of Israel by typology in order to reveal a pattern of Israelite behavior that extends into his day." Thus, Stephen sees an analogy between the hardened hearts in his day (Acts 7:51–53) and what the Israelites were doing both in the wilderness and in Amos's day (103). Darrell Bock suggests that Israel's "unfaithfulness had taken on a pattern or typology in the nation long before Stephen's time," and this sin extended itself through generations, "even beyond what Amos predicted" (299, 300). Stephen's point is that in each setting (the wilderness wandering, the time of Amos, and Stephen's day) the Israelites offered unacceptable sacrifices and singing to God, were unjust in their treatment of others, worshiped pagan gods, and resisted the leading of the Holy Spirit (Acts 7:51). Stephen is not just condemning the wilderness generation or the Israelites in the time of Amos; he is typologically applying the lessons from past failure to the audience he is addressing, since they are the culmination of the OT typological pattern.

In the wilderness, God was ready to destroy the whole nation for worshiping the golden calf (Exod. 32:10–11). Amos prophesied that unacceptable worship and unjust behavior would result in exile on the day of the Lord (Amos 5:27), and Stephen's audience is just as guilty as their fathers (Acts 7:51). Although the LXX is not a literal translation of every word in Amos 5:25–27, White concludes that the use of this text from Amos is harmonious with Luke's tradition of interpreting these prophecies as the authoritative words of God (103). Both Amos and Stephen see the people's injustice as being more determinative of their relationship to God than sacrifices. Both Amos and Stephen see Israel's repeated acceptance of idolatry as proof of the bankruptcy of their relationship to God, a bankruptcy that implies a similar fate (judgment on the day of the Lord) in each case. The textual differences (some significant) do not destroy these essential agreements. Injustice, idolatry, and empty ritual are unacceptable in Amos's day, and Stephen condemns the failure of the Israelite people of his day who seem to be following the same path as those in the wilderness and those of the time of Amos.

The second quotation from Amos appears in Acts 15:16–18 during the Jerusalem Council. This meeting deals with a disagreement within the early church over the necessity for the gentile converts to be circumcised and follow other Jewish regulations. This question arises, at least partly, because the uncircumcised gentiles in the household of Cornelius repented and received the Holy Spirit after Peter's preaching in Acts 10. Something similar happened when the gentiles responded positively to the preaching of Barnabas and Paul on their first missionary journey (Acts 13–14), so it seems that non-Jews can be converted and receive the Holy Spirit without first being circumcised. Other Jews believe that the gentiles must follow all the customs of Moses (including circumcision) to be saved and become part of the early church (Acts 15:1, 5). An important turning point in the discussion that leads to a decision is the LXX reading of Amos 9:11–12.

The Hebrew original, the LXX translation, and the words by James are similar but not identical. These differences are important but do not seriously impact the overall thrust of the message. For example, the suffix on "its ruins" is third-person masculine singular in Hebrew but third-person feminine singular in the LXX, while the MT "I will rebuild it" (third sing. suffix) is the same as the LXX "I will set up the parts of it" (third fem. sing. suffix). W. C. Kaiser (182–83) interprets the plural "their breaches" to refer to the restoration of the two kingdoms (Israel and Judah); the masculine singular "his ruins" to refer to David, not the feminine "tent"; and "rebuilding it" (fem. sing. suffix) to refer to the tent or the Davidic dynasty. However, the coming of Christ and the conversion of the gentiles provide new insights into this passage. The OT conception of the "tent of David" is no doubt more nationalistic and a rather utopian theological concept, while in Act 15 the meaning is being filled out and expanded in new ways with the establishment of the kingdom of God by the Davidic Jesus and the salvation of many gentiles. A comparison of these texts reveals their similarities and differences (see table 1).

The LXX of Amos harmonizes the suffixes in the Hebrew of Amos 9:11, making them all feminine singular and therefore referring to the tent of David, a metaphorical term describing the dynasty or kingdom of David, a kingdom the NT reader would connect to the kingdom that Jesus announced (Glenny, *Finding*, 6). The Hebrew "that they may possess the remnant of Edom" tends to carry military overtones, but the LXX more broadly has "that the rest of mankind may seek the Lord." The Hebrew of 9:12 refers to "dispossessing the remnant of Edom" (*yîrəšû ʾet-šəʾērît ʾĕdôm*) while the LXX refers to "the remnant of mankind seeking" (*ekzētēsōsin hoi kataloipoi tōn anthrōpōn*), a spiritual twist that may have arisen because of an alternative text. If the second *yod* (*y*, י) in *yyršw*, "they will possess," was carelessly written so that the line extended lower, the letter may have looked like a *dalet* (*d*, ד) which would give the word *ydršw*, "they will seek" (Gelston, 498). Alternative explanations have been proposed: (1) The translator may have understood "possess" as "a non-violent model for the incorporation of non-Israelite states in the eschatological Davidic empire" (Timmer, 468–79). This would involve establishing a positive control over people who gladly submit to Yahweh. (2) This variation may have arisen because of a theological influence from similarly worded passages (Isa. 19:16–25; Zech. 8:22; 14:2, 9) that refer to the nations seeking God. (3) This may just be the result of an inexact memory, providing the general sense of what Amos 9:11–12 says (Dines).

When James quotes this passage from the LXX, he takes some freedom (by deliberately making changes to it, by periphrastically giving the general sense of it from memory, or by purposely slanting its theological content). First, he omits a few words: "I will build up the fallen parts," which seem unnecessarily repetitive, and "as in the days of old." Further, he adds "known from of old" at the end and "after this I will return" at the beginning, plus he keeps the LXX reference to "mankind" instead of following the Hebrew "Edom." The most obvious change is "that men may seek the Lord" (in line with the LXX), in contrast to the Hebrew "that they may possess the remnant of Edom." Among the possible reasons for James following the LXX here are that he prefers the LXX as an interpretation of the Hebrew or that the LXX preserves the original Hebrew reading, which has become corrupted (Beale, 238–43). James's quotation of Amos settles the conflict so that the early church does not force the gentiles to be circumcised but rather requires them to avoid eating blood from a strangled animal, eating food offered to idols, and sexual immorality (Acts 15:29).

Table 1. Amos 9:11–12 in Hebrew, LXX, and Acts 15:16–18

Hebrew	LXX	James in Acts 15
in that day	in that day	after these things I will return
I will raise up the fallen tent of David	I will raise up the fallen tent of David	and I will rebuild the fallen tent of David
and I will repair their breaches	and I will rebuild its ruins	and I will rebuild its ruins
I will raise up its ruins	and I will set up the parts of it that are broken	and I will restore it
and I will rebuild it as in the days of old	and I will build it as in the ancient days	
that they may possess the remnant of Edom that the remnant of men and all the gentiles	that the rest of mankind may seek the Lord	
and all the nations that bear my name	and all the nations upon whom my name is called may seek me	and all the nations called by my name
declares the LORD who does this	says the Lord who does all these things	says the Lord who makes these things known from of old

Note: The translations are my own.

Bibliography. Andersen, F. I., and D. N. Freedman, *Amos*, AB (Doubleday, 1989); Beale, G. K., *The Temple and the Church's Mission*, NSBT 17 (InterVarsity, 2004); Bock, D. L., *Acts*, BECNT (Baker Academic, 2007); Carroll R., M. D., *A Prophet and His Oracles* (Westminster John Knox, 2002); Černy, L., *The Day of Yahweh and Some Relevant Problems* (University of Karlovy, 1948); Craigie, P. C., "Amos the NOQED in Light of Ugaritic," *Studies in Religion* 1 (1982): 29–33; Dines, M., "The Septuagint of Amos: A Study of Interpretation" (PhD diss., University of London, 1991); Eidevall, G., *Amos*, AYB (Yale University Press, 2017); Fensham, F. C., "A Possible Origin of the Concept of the Day of the Lord," *Biblical Essays* (Rege-Pers Beperk, 1966), 90–96; Gelston, A., "Some Hebrew Misreadings in the Septuagint of Amos," *VT* 52 (2002): 493–500; Glenny, W. E., *Finding Meaning in the Text* (Brill, 2009); Glenny, "Hebrew Misreadings or Free Translation in the Septuagint of Amos?," *VT* 57 (2007): 524–47; Glenny, "The Septuagint and Apostolic Hermeneutics," *BBR* 22 (2012): 1–25; Hasel, G. F., *Understanding the Book of Amos* (Baker, 1991); Hubbard, D., *Joel and Amos*, TOTC (InterVarsity, 1984); Kaiser, W. C., *The Uses of the Old Testament in the New* (Moody, 1985); Lessing, R. R., *Amos*, ConC (Concordia, 2009); Paul, S., *Joel and Amos*, Herm (Fortress, 1977); Smith, G. V., *Amos*, rev. ed. (Christian Focus, 1989); Stuart, D., *Hosea–Jonah*, WBC (Word, 1987); Timmer, D., "Possessing Edom and All the Nations over Whom YHWH's Name Is Called," *BBR* 29 (2019): 468–87; White, A. W., *The Prophets Agree* (Brill, 2020); Wolff, H. W., *Joel and Amos*, Herm (Fortress, 1977).

Gary V. Smith

Anthropology

See Adam, First and Last; Image of God

Antichrist

See Serpent and Antichrist

Apocrypha: Comparison with the NT Use of the OT

"Apocrypha" in Greek means "hidden things." This term refers to a collection of early Jewish writings from the Second Temple period that fall outside of the canonical Hebrew Scriptures. The designation "Apocrypha" for these noncanonical Jewish works may derive from the references to "hidden" or "sealed" books in OT and Jewish apocalyptic writings (e.g., Dan. 8:26; 12:4; 4 Ezra 12:37–38; cf. Stuckenbruck, 148). The Apocrypha include Wisdom literature, historical writings and stories, and supplements to biblical books in a collection roughly the same length as the NT. While it is challenging to identify one primary theme that unites these diverse works, deSilva explains that "the Apocrypha contain the testimony of faithful Jews who sought to live out their loyalty to God in a very troubled (and often hostile) world" (*Introducing*, 2).

While the order and contents of the Apocrypha are not fixed, the following Jewish works appear in one or more of the major codices of the Greek OT (Vaticanus, Sinaiticus, and Alexandrinus): 1 Esdras (also called Esdras A or 3 Ezra), Greek Esther (also called Additions to Esther), Judith, Tobit, 1–4 Maccabees, Ps. 151, the Prayer of Manasseh, Wisdom of Solomon, Sirach (also called Ecclesiasticus or the Wisdom of Ben Sira), Baruch (also called 1 Baruch), the Letter of Jeremiah, and Additions to Daniel (Prayer of Azariah; Song of the Three Jews; Susanna; Bel and the Dragon). For this article, these Jewish works constitute the OT Apocrypha. While Psalms of Solomon appears at the end of Codex Alexandrinus (following Sirach), it is typically excluded from modern editions of the Apocrypha and instead treated among the OT Pseudepigrapha. Some editions of the Apocrypha include 2 Esdras, which most scholars identify as a combination of three texts: a Jewish apocalypse known as 4 Ezra (2 Esd. 3–14) framed by two later Christian compositions (2 Esd. 1–2; 15–16). Third and Fourth Maccabees are sometimes excluded from the Apocrypha. Roman Catholics do not recognize these books as Scripture, while the Greek Orthodox Bible includes 3 Maccabees. However, they are Greek compositions that appear in at least one of the major Septuagint codices. Thus, this article includes 3–4 Maccabees within the Apocrypha while considering Psalms of Solomon and 4 Ezra to be among the OT Pseudepigrapha. Protestants do not consider the Apocrypha to be canonical, but the Orthodox and Roman Catholic traditions consider most of these writings to be authoritative Scripture.

This is the first of four entries on the OT Apocrypha and its use of Scripture. Here we compare seven representative examples in which the Apocrypha and the NT clearly cite or allude to the same biblical texts to discuss the following subjects: (1) the creation and fall of humanity, (2) the divine design of marriage, (3) Abraham's righteousness, (4) the command not to covet, (5) the promise of kingship, (6) the new exodus in the wilderness, and (7) the coming of Elijah.

Humanity's Creation and Fall: Gen. 2–3

Sirach and Wisdom of Solomon each reflect on the biblical account of humanity's creation and fall into sin. First, Ben Sira recounts that God created Adam "from the ground" and set him "above every living thing in the creation" (Sir. 33:10; 49:16 ESV; cf. Gen. 2:7). When the Lord made man "from the beginning," he "left him in the hand of his deliberation" (Sir. 15:14 NETS). This illustrates the principle that people face a choice between two ways—life and death (Sir. 15:17; cf. Deut. 30:19). Later, while contrasting the evil wife and the virtuous wife, he states, "From a woman sin had its beginning, and because of her we all die" (Sir. 25:24). Levison posits that this verse does not refer to Eve's sin but rather speaks proverbially about the evil wife, because of whom all husbands die. However, the traditional interpretation is more likely: Ben Sira here alludes to Eve's sin in Gen. 3:6. Though he does not elaborate on the theological significance of Eve's sin, he does affirm that it is the beginning of human sin and death (cf. Crenshaw, 764; Skehan and Di Lella, 348–49).

Wisdom of Solomon offers another perspective on humanity's creation and fall. The author writes, "For God created us for incorruption, and made us in the image of his own eternity, but through the devil's envy death entered the world, and those who belong to his company experience it" (Wis. 2:23–24). The reference to God's "image" (*eikōn*) alludes to Gen. 1:26, while "the devil's envy" likely refers to the crafty temptations of the serpent in Gen. 3 (Goff, 7–8; for similar Jewish interpretations, see Josephus, *Ant.* 1.40–43; 2 En. 31:3–6; LAE 12:1). In context, Wis. 2:23–24 supports the author's argument that the wicked who condemn the righteous are led astray because they do not know God's purposes (vv. 21–22). According to Wisdom, God neither made death nor delights in it (1:13). God created humans for immortality, but those who belong to the devil experience death (2:23–24). The author returns to the biblical creation story in 10:1–2, stating that "Wisdom protected the first-formed father of the world, when he alone had been created; she delivered him from his transgression, and gave him strength to rule all things." This clearly alludes to the biblical story of Adam's creation (Gen. 2:7), sin (3:6), and command to exercise dominion (1:28). The author moves beyond the Genesis account in referring to Adam's deliverance from sin, though without speculating about Adam's repentance as in LAE 4:3–5:2. Tobit 8:6 similarly affirms that God created Adam and Eve, from whom the human race originated.

Reflecting on Gen. 2–3, NT authors affirm that God created Adam as the first human being (Luke 3:38; Acts 17:26; 1 Cor. 15:45), the cunning serpent deceived Eve (2 Cor. 11:3; 1 Tim. 2:14), and death entered the world as a result of Adam's sin (Rom. 5:12). Moving beyond Sirach and Wisdom, Paul argues that sin, condemnation, and death spread to all people through the sin of the first man (Rom. 5:12, 15–19), such that "in Adam all die" (1 Cor. 15:22). The nearest Jewish parallel to Paul's thought comes in 4 Ezra 7:118, where the author laments that Adam's fall into sin was not his alone but "ours also" (cf. 4 Ezra 3:20–22; 7:11; 2 Bar. 48:42–43). However, Paul reflects a "more radical" understanding of sin's origin and effect on all people (Seifrid, 629). The apostle also explicates a more definitive solution to humanity's plight by presenting Adam as "a type" of Christ (Rom. 5:14 ESV), on account of whose obedience many receive the free gift of righteousness and "reign in life through the one man, Jesus Christ" (5:17–19).

The Divine Design of Marriage: Gen. 2:18–24

Jewish and NT authors frequently appeal to Gen. 2:18–24 to explain God's wise plan for human marriage and draw out theological and moral implications. Tobit 7–8 recounts the marriage of Tobit's pious son Tobias to his kinswoman Sarah, whose previous seven husbands were killed by a demon. On their wedding night, Tobias and Sarah pray for God's protection and recall that God made Eve for Adam to be his helper and support and that God said, "It is not good that the man should be alone; let us make a helper for him like himself" (Tob. 8:6). "You said" (*sy eipas*) introduces a precise quotation of Gen. 2:18 LXX. Tobias appeals to the biblical text as the basis of his own lawful marriage to Sarah, his suitable partner, and asks that God would show them mercy and bless them with long life together (Tob. 8:7). God providentially works to prepare and protect Tobias and Sarah for marriage, and this exemplary couple carefully follows the law and fulfills God's design for their lives (Ferrández Zaragoza, 149, 154). The couple's piety, purity, and prayerfulness suggest that their God-ordained union represents, in some sense, a return to the beginning before humanity's fall (cf. Ferrández Zaragoza, 156).

At the climax of the contest between Darius's bodyguards in 1 Esd. 3–4, young Zerubbabel proves his wisdom in expounding the strength of women. Alluding to Gen. 2:24, Zerubbabel tells the king, "A man leaves his own father, who brought him up, and his own country, and clings to his wife" and concludes that "women rule over you!" (1 Esd. 4:20, 22). This appeal to Gen. 2:24 highlights the power of the marriage bond, which endures for life, and demonstrates the priority of a man's love for his wife, which exceeds love for parents or country (1 Esd. 4:21, 25). In contrast, Tob. 8–9 presents Tobias urging his father-in-law Raguel to send him back to his own father immediately after his wedding (cf. Bird, 170).

The Gospels record that Jesus appeals to God's creative design for marriage "at the beginning" in response to the Pharisees' question about divorce (Matt. 19:3–4; cf. Mark 10:2, 6). Beginning with the rhetorical question "Haven't you read . . . ?" (Matt. 19:4), Christ offers a verbatim citation of Gen. 2:24 and concludes that since the husband and wife are "one flesh," no one should separate what God has joined together (Matt. 19:5–6).

Paul twice cites Gen. 2:24 in his letters. In 1 Cor. 6:12–20, he urges believers to flee from sexual immorality and glorify God with their body, which is a temple of the Spirit. Paul explains that the biblical text "The two will become one flesh" has clear ethical implications for the Corinthians: joining (*kollaō*) with a prostitute entails becoming "one with her in body" (v. 16). Such an immoral physical union is antithetical to believers' spiritual union with the Lord (v. 17). Thus, Paul appeals to Gen. 2:24 to explain "the intended permanence of sexual relationships" and thus underscores the seriousness of immoral sexual acts (Ciampa and Rosner, 713). In Eph. 5:31, he quotes Gen. 2:24 in the context of his extended teaching about the proper conduct of husbands and wives (Eph. 5:22–33). Surprisingly, Paul cites

Genesis here not to stress the one-flesh union in marriage but to explain the profound "mystery" of Christ's union with his church (v. 32; cf. Thielman, 826).

Thus, Jewish and NT authors affirm the foundational authority and enduring relevance of Gen. 2:18–24 to express God's design for human marriage, characterized by love and permanence. Jesus appeals to Gen. 2 to correct his contemporaries' permissive approach to divorce, which is also reflected in the Apocrypha (cf. Sir. 7:26; 25:26). Paul cites the same text to highlight the seriousness of sexual sin and to explain the spiritual bond of Christ with his people.

The Righteousness of Abraham: Gen. 15 and 22

Both Jewish and NT authors frequently appeal to Abraham, though with somewhat different emphases. In 1 Macc. 2:49–68, the great revolutionary leader Mattathias addresses his sons before he dies, urging them to be zealous for the law (v. 50). Mattathias charges, "Remember the deeds of the fathers, which they did in their generations; and receive great honor and an everlasting name" (v. 51 ESV). His survey of biblical heroes to emulate begins with the patriarch Abraham: "Was not Abraham found faithful when tested, and it was reckoned to him as righteousness?" (v. 52). Because some Jewish traditions recount ten trials of Abraham (e.g., Jub. 19:8), Francis Borchardt (34) reasons that this text "refers to his general quality of being rewarded when tested by God" rather than to a specific trial in Abraham's life. However, it is far more likely that 1 Macc. 2:52 alludes to the preeminent test in Abraham's life, the binding of Isaac, which is referenced frequently in Jewish literature and in the NT (e.g., 4 Macc. 13:12; 16:20; 18:11; Jub. 17:16; 18:1–16; Heb. 11:17–19; James 2:21). Moreover, the biblical account of Abraham's life refers to testing only in Gen. 22:1 (*peirazō*, LXX; *nissâ*, MT). Thus, Mattathias alludes to Abraham's faithfulness in offering Isaac when tested (Gen. 22) and combines this reference with an informal citation of Gen. 15:6b ("It was reckoned to him as righteousness," NETS). While Genesis does not explicitly refer to Abraham as faithful (*pistos*), 1 Macc. 2:52 conceptually recalls the commendations Abraham receives for fearing and obeying God in Gen. 22:12 and 18. Although Gen. 15:6 LXX highlights Abraham's faith (*pisteuō*), 1 Macc. 2:52 asserts that the patriarch's faithfulness (*pistos*) in testing is counted as righteousness. This is consistent with Mattathias's stress on the piety and zeal of other exemplars, such as Phinehas and Daniel (though he does mention the faith [*pisteuō*] of the three Jews saved from the fiery furnace [v. 59]). Thus, 1 Macc. 2:52 appeals to Abraham as a model covenant keeper whose example of faithfulness should inspire Mattathias's sons to zealous obedience to God's law. "The testing of Abraham parallels the situation the Maccabees now find themselves in" (Doran, 50).

Ben Sira similarly states that Abraham "proved faithful when he was tested [*en peirasmō heurethē pistos*]" (Sir. 44:20 AT). While the sage does not link Abraham's faithfulness with the declaration of his righteousness in Gen. 15:6 as does 1 Macc. 2:52, he emphasizes God's covenant with Abraham and the sure promises of blessing for the nations, numerous descendants, and the land for an inheritance (Sir. 44:19–22). Other Jewish authors similarly recall God's covenant with Abraham and the promise of land (Tob. 14:7; Bar. 2:34; 2 Macc. 1:2). Judith briefly recalls what God "did with Abraham, and how he tested Isaac," as an example of how God tests and admonishes his people (Jdt. 8:26).

Paul cites Gen. 15:6 in Rom. 4:3 to stress that God justifies the ungodly and reckons faith as righteousness apart from works. That Abraham is declared righteous before being circumcised signals that he is the father of all who share his faith (4:9–17). Similarly, in Gal. 3:6–8 the apostle quotes Gen. 15:6 together with the divine promise to bless all the nations in Abraham (Gen. 12:3; 18:18; 22:18). Paul clarifies that God's promise to Abraham antedates the giving of the law, which served to increase transgression until Christ—Abraham's "seed"—fulfilled that promise (Gal. 3:15–22). Through Christ, gentiles receive the promised blessing through faith and are counted as Abraham's offspring and heirs (3:14, 29). According to Heb. 11:17–19, Abraham, when tested, offered up Isaac "by faith" (*pistei*), being confident in God's promise (cf. Gen. 21:12) and in God's power to raise the dead. Thus, Rom. 4 and Gal. 3 cite Gen. 15:6 to teach the biblical principle that God justifies gentiles and Jews alike by faith apart from works.

The nearest NT parallel to 1 Macc. 2:52 is James 2:21–23, where James links Abraham's faith in God that was counted as righteousness (Gen. 15:6) with the patriarch's obedience in offering up Isaac on the altar (Gen. 22). James explains that Abraham was "justified by works" when he offered his son (James 2:21 ESV). Faith was active along with his works and was completed by those works (v. 22). The binding of Isaac revealed that Abraham feared God and obeyed his voice (Gen. 22:12, 18) and thus "fulfilled" the biblical declaration of his righteousness by faith in Gen. 15:6. Moo explains, "Abraham's faith, in its relationship to righteousness, found its ultimate significance and meaning in Abraham's life of obedience" (*James*, 138). James concludes by calling Abraham "God's friend" (James 2:23; cf. Isa. 41:8; Jub. 19:9), whose active faith offers an example for those tempted by friendship with the world (James 4:4). Thus, while 1 Macc. 2:52 refers to Abraham as a model of costly faithfulness to God, James 2:21–23 presents the patriarch as an example of true faith being accompanied by works (cf. v. 14). James affirms that Abraham's faith was counted as righteousness (Gen. 15:6) and explains that this faith was fulfilled and completed in the offering of Isaac (Gen. 22).

You Shall Not Covet: Exod. 20:17 and Deut. 5:21

Both 4 Maccabees and Romans cite the Decalogue's prohibition against coveting. The Ten Words conclude with the lengthy injunction against coveting your neighbor's wife, his house or field, his servants, his animals, or any other possessions of his (Exod. 20:17; Deut. 5:21 LXX). Interpreters have long debated whether the repeated prohibition "You shall not covet" (MT, *lōʾ taḥmōd*; LXX, *ouk epithymēseis*) in Exod. 20:17 and Deut. 5:21 should be read as two distinct commands or together as the tenth commandment (see DeRouchie, 93–126). Regardless, the Decalogue forbids sinfully desiring to have what belongs to another. "You shall not covet" addresses one's "inner feelings and thoughts," signaling that every area of one's life, not merely outward behavior, must conform to God's revealed standards (Alexander, 427). The prohibition against coveting functions as a "summary commandment" with a "uniquely comprehensive application" (Durham, 299–300), since craving what belongs to another is a first step toward committing murder, adultery, theft, or other violations of commandments.

Fourth Maccabees offers a sustained argument that "pious reason is absolute master of the passions" (1:1 NETS; cf. 6:31; 7:16; 13:1; 16:1; 18:2). After stating this thesis, the author demonstrates it with biblical precedents (1:30–3:18) followed by examples of the devout martyrs (3:19–18:24; cf. deSilva, *4 Maccabees*, xxvi–xxix). The author recounts how Joseph overcame sexual desire "by mental effort" (2:2), showing that reason rules over "every desire" (*pasēs epithymias*, 2:4). The author then cites what "the law says" in v. 5: "You shall not covet your neighbor's wife or anything that is your neighbor's." This quotation agrees precisely with the opening and concluding words of Exod. 20:17 and Deut. 5:21 LXX. The author concludes that since the law tells us not to covet, reason must be able to control desires.

Paul cites the tenth commandment twice, in Rom. 7:7 and 13:9. The apostle asserts, "I would not have known what coveting [*epithymian*] really was if the law had not said, 'You shall not covet [*ouk epithymēseis*]'" (7:7). Yet, sin "produced in me every kind of coveting [*epithymian*]" (7:8). Paul here cites "a truncated form of the Tenth Commandment," focusing on desire itself rather than particular manifestations (Timmins, 107–8). In Rom. 13:9, he cites the Decalogue's prohibitions against adultery, murder, theft, and coveting as "summed up" in the command "You shall love your neighbor as yourself," a verbatim citation of Lev. 19:18 LXX.

Paul and the author of 4 Maccabees each cite the prohibition of coveting as a representative summary of the Torah (Moo, *Romans*, 459); however, they reach precisely opposite conclusions about the command's implications (deSilva, *4 Maccabees*, 96). For the author of 4 Maccabees, the law not only expresses God's will but also empowers people to master sinful passions through reason. For Paul, though the commandment "promised life," it cannot curb sin at all and actually occasions more sin and leads to death (Rom. 7:10 ESV).

The Promise of Kingship: Gen. 49 and 2 Sam. 7

Both the Apocrypha and the NT recall the regal promises to Judah (Gen. 49:8–12) and the Lord's covenant with David (2 Sam. 7:12–16). Sirach 45:25 refers to "a covenant [*diathēkē*] with David, the son of Jesse, of the tribe of Judah: the king's heritage passes only from son to son" (AT). Here the sage likens the succession of kings in David's line to the heritage of Aaron the priest, which is for "his seed" (45:25 AT). Ben Sira's hymn celebrating the deeds of Israel's ancestors discusses David's selection as Israel's leader and his victories over his enemies (47:2–11). The section concludes by recalling that "the Lord took away David's sins and exalted his horn forever and gave him a covenant of kings and a glorious throne in Israel" (v. 11 AT). The sage alludes to 2 Sam. 7:12–16, where the Lord declares that he will establish the throne of David's son forever, as well as the promise to exalt David's horn (*keras*) in Ps. 89:24 (88:25 LXX) and Ps. 132:17 (131:17 LXX). When Ben Sira recounts the sin of Solomon and his successors, he expresses confidence that the Lord "will never give up his mercy" and "will never take away the seed of the one who loved him," recalling that "he gave a remnant to Jacob, and to David a root from him" (Sir. 47:22 AT). Ben Sira's reference to David's "root" (*rhiza*) likely alludes to the "root of Jesse" in Isa. 11:1 and 11:10 LXX. The sage expresses confidence in the enduring Davidic dynasty based on the Lord's promise that he will not remove his mercy from David's descendant but will establish his kingdom (2 Sam. 7:15–16).

Luke 1 similarly recalls the covenant promises to David, announcing that God will give to Jesus "the throne of his father David, and he will reign over Jacob's descendants forever" (vv. 32–33). The angel's words here include "significant conceptual parallels" with 2 Sam. 7:8–16 and Ps. 89 (Pao and Schnabel, 260). Likewise, Zechariah says that the God of Israel "has raised up a horn of salvation for us in the house of his servant David" (Luke 1:69). The Lord has thus "redeemed" his people (v. 68), accomplished what he declared by the prophets (v. 70), and remembered "his holy covenant" (v. 72). While Ben Sira asserts the general truth that God *will* remain faithful to his covenant promises to David, Luke 1 specifies that God *has* fulfilled those promises through the miraculous birth and unending reign of Jesus, David's long-awaited heir.

Both 1 Maccabees and Revelation allude to the description of Judah as "a lion's cub" (LXX, *skymnos leontos*) in Gen. 49:9, where the patriarch Jacob gathers his sons to declare what will happen in the last days (v. 1). He prophesies that Judah will be praised by his brothers and subdue his enemies (v. 8). Moreover, Israel's ruler will descend from Judah's line (v. 10). The MT describes the symbols of his regal authority ("scepter" and "staff"), while the LXX makes explicit that "a ruler [*archōn*] will not lack from Judah and a leader [*hēgoumenos*] from his thighs" and goes on to call Judah "the expectation of nations" (AT; on the interpretive difficulties in v. 10, see Wenham, 476–78).

Judas Maccabeus is compared to "a lion [*leonti*] in his deeds . . . a lion's cub [*skymnos*] roaring for prey" (1 Macc. 3:4), alluding to Gen. 49:9. In the previous chapter Mattathias declares that his son Judas shall be leader [*archōn*] of the army and charges his sons to pay back the nations (1 Macc. 2:66, 68). The author praises the great commander for extending Israel's glory (3:3), bringing salvation by his hand (3:6), and turning away wrath from Israel (3:8). Following their great military exploits, Judas and his brothers declare that "our enemies are crushed" (1 Macc. 4:36). Thus, the allusion to Gen. 49:9 in 1 Macc. 3:4 casts Judas Maccabeus as a royal leader of God's people. It recalls the patriarchal promise that his namesake, Judah, would produce a powerful, lion-like ruler who would conquer Israel's enemies and receive commendation from Israel. The author presents Judas not as a singular messianic ruler who fulfills ancient prophecy (as in the DSS, e.g., 1QSb 5.24–29; 4Q252 5.1–3) but as a great military hero like the judges who "save" Israel from their adversaries (1 Macc. 9:21; cf. Judg. 6:14–15; 10:1; 13:5).

In Rev. 5:5, one of the heavenly elders announces that "the Lion of the tribe of Judah, the Root of David, has triumphed." These messianic titles allude to Gen. 49:9 and Isa. 11:1, respectively. The image of the lion "suggests ferocity, destructiveness and irresistible strength" (Bauckham, 182). As a messianic symbol, the lion expresses the ancient hope of a powerful, formidable ruler of Israel. Taken together, the designations Lion of Judah and Root of David evoke biblical promises of the ideal king of God's people, who would execute true justice and slay the wicked. But Christ fulfills this promise ironically, as he triumphs initially as the slain Lamb (Rev. 5:5–7) who sits on heaven's throne (3:21) and will fulfill his messianic destiny as sovereign and judge of the nations at his regal return (19:11–16; cf. Isa. 11:4; Ps. 2:9; Tabb, 58).

The New Exodus in the Wilderness: Isa. 40

Baruch and the NT Gospels appeal to the new-exodus prophecy of Isa. 40. Baruch 5:7 quotes Isa. 40 as a promise of Israel's return from exile. The Baruch text prefaces an informal citation of Scripture with the introductory formula "God has ordered." This text exhibits the following verbal parallels to Isa. 40:4–5 LXX: "every mountain . . . be made low," "valleys filled," and divine "glory" (cf. Xeravits, 126). Baruch explains that God will make the ground level "so that Israel may walk safely in the glory of God" (5:7). In context, this appeal to Isa. 40 supports the writer's claim that God will remember his children who were led away by their enemies into exile and will "bring them back" to Jerusalem (Bar. 5:5–6). Drawing on other Isaianic imagery, Baruch describes Jerusalem taking off her garments of sorrow and being adorned by God and given an eternal name (5:1–4; cf. Isa. 52:1–2; 61:10; 62:2–4; Xeravits, 123–25). Thus, Baruch affirms the future fulfillment of Isaiah's prophecy that Israel will return from exile and be gloriously restored.

All four NT Gospels cite Isa. 40:3 to explain John's ministry of preparation for Christ (Matt. 3:3; Mark 1:3; Luke 3:4; John 1:23). The most extensive reference to Isa. 40 is Luke 3:4–6, which directly cites Isa. 40:3–5 LXX and introduces this scriptural appeal with the lengthy introductory formula "as it is written in the book of the words of Isaiah the prophet."

While Baruch, like other Jewish writers (e.g., Pss. Sol. 11:4–6), anticipates the future fulfillment of Isa. 40, Luke and the other evangelists stress that John's ministry in the wilderness signals the beginning of the promised new exodus of God's people. The Gospels make clear that Jesus is "the Lord" (*kyrios*) whose way John prepares. While Baruch reads Isa. 40 as a prophecy of Israel's future deliverance, Luke 3:6 emphasizes that Isaiah's prophecy of future salvation is good news for "all flesh," including the gentiles (cf. Acts 28:28). Further, Acts repeatedly refers to Jesus's followers as "the Way" (e.g., 9:2), which likely recalls the way of the Lord in Isa. 40:3 and links the Christian community to the fulfillment of God's promises to Israel (Pao, 67–68).

The Coming of Elijah: Mal. 4:5–6

In his encomium to Israel's heroes (Sir. 44–50), Ben Sira recounts the mighty ministry of Elijah, who "arose like fire," "brought down fire" by his prophetic words, and departed by "a whirlwind of fire" (48:1, 3, 9 ESV; cf. 2 Kings 1:10–12; 2:11). Ben Sira recounts how Elijah "shut up the heavens" and brought famine (48:2–3; cf. 1 Kings 17:1; 18:2), "raised a corpse from death" (Sir. 48:5; cf. 1 Kings 17:22), and brought kings to ruin (Sir. 48:6; cf. 1 Kings 21:19–24). The sage then declares that the great prophet is "ready at the appointed time, it is written, to calm the wrath of God before it breaks out in fury, to turn the heart of the father to the son, and to restore the tribes of Jacob" (v. 10 ESV). "It is written" (*katagrapheis*) introduces an informal citation of Mal. 4:5–6 (3:23–24 LXX), where God promises to send Elijah before the terrible day of the Lord to turn the people's hearts. The final line of Sir. 48:10 recalls not Malachi but Isa. 49:6, the prophecy of the Lord's servant who will "restore the tribes of Jacob." Patrick Skehan and Alexander Di Lella (534) suggest that this reference to Elijah's coming expresses "Ben Sira's messianic hope."

The NT on several occasions recalls the ministry of Elijah (Luke 4:25–26; Rom. 11:2–4; Heb. 11:35; James 5:17) and also reflects on Malachi's prophecy of Elijah's coming. In Luke 1:17, the angel informs Zechariah that his child, John, will go before the Lord "in the spirit and power of Elijah, to turn the hearts of the parents to their children . . . —to make ready a people prepared for the Lord." This announcement clearly alludes to Mal. 4:6 (3:23 LXX), though the verb *epistrepsai* ("turn") in Luke departs from Mal. 3:23 LXX (*apokatastēsei*). *Epistrepsai* closely parallels Sir. 48:10 and may be influenced by Ben Sira's treatment of Malachi's prophecy (Pao and Schnabel, 258), though *epistrepsai* could also reflect an alternate Greek text or independent translation of *hēšîb* ("return") in the Hebrew text of Mal. 4:6. Zechariah prophesies that John "will be called the prophet of the Most High" who "will go on before the Lord to prepare the way for him" (Luke 1:76). "The prophet" likely reiterates the expectation that John will minister "in the spirit and power of Elijah" (1:17), while John's ministry of preparation for the Lord alludes to Mal. 3:1 and Isa. 40:3 and anticipates the lengthy citation of Isa. 40:3–5 LXX in Luke 3:4–6.

Luke and Ben Sira similarly understand Mal. 4 to express the sure hope that God would send the prophet to restore Israel in advance of coming judgment. Ben Sira links Malachi's prophecy with the servant's work in Isa. 49:6, which may suggest that he views Elijah as a messianic figure. In contrast, Luke 1:17 announces the fulfillment of Mal. 4:5–6 in the prophetic ministry of John. Moreover, Luke 1:76 and John's own confession in 3:15–17 make clear that John is not the Messiah but prepares the way for the Lord's coming. Jesus reinforces the identification of John with "Elijah who is to come" in Matt. 11:14–15 (cf. 17:10–12).

Summary

The authors of the Apocrypha and the NT cite the Scriptures as the true and authoritative words of God. They quote and allude to biblical texts to understand God's wise plan for human beings in this world, to highlight biblical examples to follow, and to express confidence that God fulfills his promises. The seven representative examples above show that these Jewish and Christian writings apply the Scriptures in divergent ways that reflect their different presuppositions, particularly about the Messiah and the age to come. The apocryphal texts considered above affirm that God will remain faithful to his covenant promises to David, will send Elijah the prophet, and will save Israel. However, the NT stresses that God has already begun to fulfill these promises by sending Jesus, the long-awaited son of Abraham and son of David (Matt. 1:1), as well as his prophetic forerunner, John. Paul explains that Christ's righteousness offers the definitive solution to human sin and that Christ's relationship with his people is the profound mystery to which the institution of human marriage points. Moreover, while the Apocrypha stress the Jewish people's identity and calling as the people of God who must keep the holy law, the NT explains that Christ's coming brings salvation and blessing for all people, Jews and gentiles, who share the faith of Abraham.

See also OT Use of the OT: Comparison with the NT Use of the OT; *other Apocrypha articles; Dead Sea Scrolls articles; Mishnah, Talmud, and Midrashim articles; Philo articles; Pseudepigrapha articles; Septuagint articles; Targums articles*

Bibliography. Alexander, T. D., *Exodus*, ApOTC 2 (InterVarsity, 2017); Bauckham, R., *The Climax of Prophecy* (T&T Clark, 1993); Bird, M. F., *1 Esdras*, SeptCS (Brill, 2012); Borchardt, F., "Concepts of Scripture in 1 Maccabees," in *Early Christian Literature and Intertextuality*, ed. C. A. Evans and D. H. Zacharias, LNTS 391 (T&T Clark, 2009), 24–41; Ciampa, R. E., and B. S. Rosner, "1 Corinthians," in *CNTUOT*, 695–752; Crenshaw, J. L., "The Book of Sirach," in *NIB*, 5:601–867; DeRouchie, J. S., "Counting the Ten," in *For Our Good Always*, ed. J. S. DeRouchie, J. Gile, and K. Turner (Eisenbrauns, 2013), 93–126; deSilva, D. A., *4 Maccabees*, SeptCS (Brill, 2006); deSilva, *Introducing the Apocrypha*, 2nd ed. (Baker Academic, 2018); Doran, R., "1 Maccabees," in *NIB*, 4:1–178; Durham, J. I., *Exodus*, WBC 3 (Word, 1987); Ferrández Zaragoza, N., "La Oración de Tb 8, 5–9 en el Contexto del Libro y a la Luz de Gn 2,18," *EstBib* 74 (2016): 135–57; Goff, M., "Adam, the Angels and Eternal Life," in *Studies in the Book of Wisdom*, ed. G. G. Xeravits and J. Zsengellér, JSJSup 142 (Brill, 2010), 1–21; Levison, J. R., "Is Eve to Blame?," *CBQ* 47 (1985): 617–23; Moo, D. J., *The Letter of James*, PNTC (Eerdmans, 2000); Moo, *The Letter to the Romans*, 2nd ed., NICNT (Eerdmans, 2018); Pao, D. W., *Acts and the Isaianic New Exodus*, BSL (Baker Academic, 2002); Pao, D. W., and E. J. Schnabel, "Luke," in *CNTUOT*, 251–414; Seifrid, M. A., "Romans," in *CNTUOT*, 607–94; Skehan, P. W., and A. A. Di Lella, *The Wisdom of Ben Sira*, AB 39 (Doubleday, 1987); Stuckenbruck, L. T., "Apocrypha and Pseudepigrapha," in *The Eerdmans Dictionary of Early Judaism*, ed. J. J. Collins and D. C. Harlow (Eerdmans, 2010), 143–62; Tabb, B. J., *All Things New*, NSBT 48 (IVP Academic, 2019); Thielman, F. S., "Ephesians," in *CNTUOT*, 813–34; Timmins, W. N., *Romans 7 and Christian Identity*, SNTSMS 168 (Cambridge University Press, 2017); Wenham, G. J., *Genesis 1–15*, WBC 1 (Word, 1987); Xeravits, G. G., "The Biblical Background of the Psalms in Baruch 4:5–5:9," in *Studies on Baruch*, ed. S. A. Adams, DCLS 23 (de Gruyter, 2016), 97–134.

Brian J. Tabb

Apocrypha, NT Use of

The NT writers consistently cite the canonical Law, Prophets, and Writings as "the Scriptures" (*hai graphai*), yet they also show awareness of extrabiblical sources. Clear examples include Paul's citations of the Athenians' "poets" (Acts 17:28) and "a prophet" of Crete (Titus 1:12) and Jude's appeal to 1 Enoch 1:9 (Jude 14–15). The NT includes no formal citations of the early Jewish works collected in the Apocrypha, though scholars have suggested that these extracanonical writings were known to Jesus and NT authors and influenced them. This article sets forth criteria for establishing the NT writers' "use" of sources and then considers five representative examples of the Apocrypha's proposed influence on Matthew, Romans, and James.

Criteria for Discerning Use of Sources

Richard Hays's seven criteria for discerning intertextual echoes remain a standard reference point for biblical scholars (29–32; cf. Shaw, 234–45). (1) *Availability*: "Was the proposed source . . . available to the author and/or original readers?" (2) *Volume*: Does the text include "explicit repetition of words or syntactical patterns" from the source text, and is this source "distinctive or prominent"? (3) *Recurrence*: How often does the author "elsewhere cite or allude to the same scriptural passage"? (4) *Thematic Coherence*: "How well does the alleged echo fit into the line of argument" the author develops? (5) *Historical Plausibility*: Could the author "have intended the alleged meaning effect," and could readers grasp it? (6) *History of Interpretation*: Have other readers previously recognized this echo? (7) *Satisfaction*: "Does the proposed reading make sense" and "illuminate the surrounding discourse"? Some interpreters have criticized Hays for his imprecise terminology, for his emphasis on the readers' perceptions, and for combining criteria for identifying echoes with interpretive guidelines (see Porter, 36–40), and others have noted overlap between some of Hays's criteria (e.g., Litwak, 63; Beale, 32–35). Nevertheless, Hays's seven tests remain useful for assessing proposed allusions in Paul's writings and other texts.

The following discussion of the NT authors' proposed use of apocryphal texts employs Hays's criteria, with particular emphasis on the "availability" of these texts to NT authors and the "volume" of verbal and syntactical agreement between the NT text and the proposed source. While other articles in this dictionary compare the ways NT and apocryphal authors cite the OT and discuss thematic parallels between the two, this article focuses on the NT "use" of the OT Apocrypha.

You Have Heard It Said: Sirach and Matt. 5–6

Sirach is unique among the Apocrypha in that the author identifies himself using his own name—"Jesus son of Eleazar son of Sirach of Jerusalem" (Sir. 50:27)—and his grandson includes a preface that explains his own circumstances and reasons for translating the book from Hebrew into Greek. These details and internal evidence of the book allow scholars to firmly date the Hebrew composition to 196–175 BC and the Greek translation to sometime after 132 BC, when Ben Sira's grandson moved to Egypt (Sir. prologue 29; cf. deSilva, *Jewish Teachers,* 59). It is plausible that Ben Sira's work was available to Jesus in written or oral form, since Ben Sira was an esteemed scribe in Jerusalem who taught about two centuries before Jesus's birth (deSilva, *Jewish Teachers,* 84). The Sermon on the Mount includes a number of parallels to Ben Sira's teaching on anger, lust, oaths, almsgiving, prayer, and forgiveness. In fact, deSilva asserts, "The points of contact between Ben Sira's teachings and the recorded sayings of Jesus are so striking and numerous as to render it certain" that the latter knew and valued some of the former's sayings (*Jewish Teachers,* 68).

Ben Sira and Jesus address the sin of anger. Ben Sira observes that anger shortens one's life (Sir. 30:24) and stresses that "unjust anger cannot be justified" (1:22). People must not harbor wrath against another (28:3) or get angry for every wrong (10:6). Rather, the sage exhorts, "Remember the commandments and do not be angry [*mē mēnisēs*] with your neighbor" (28:7 ESV). In Matt. 5:21–48, Jesus repeatedly contrasts what disciples "have heard" about the law's interpretation with his own teaching as the one who fulfills the law (v. 17). In the first antithesis, Jesus declares that not only murderers but also whoever is angry with his brother "will be subject to judgment" (Matt. 5:21–22). He thus explains that anger is the root from which murder springs. DeSilva suggests that by linking the setting aside of anger with obedience to God's commands, Sirach offers a Jewish precedent for Jesus's teaching (*Jewish Teachers,* 68–69). There are thematic parallels between Sir. 28:7 and Matt. 5:21–22, but there is no explicit verbal repetition to demonstrate Jesus's dependence on Sirach. Moreover, Jesus moves well beyond Ben Sira's teaching by linking anger to the prohibition against murder and stressing the danger of eternal punishment.

Both teachers warn against the lust of the eye. Ben Sira urges, "Do not look intently at a virgin, lest you stumble [*skandalisthēs*] and incur penalties for her. . . . Do not look intently at beauty belonging to another" (Sir. 9:5, 8 ESV). Similarly, Jesus recalls the law's prohibition of adultery, then declares that "anyone who looks at a woman lustfully has already committed adultery with her in his heart" (Matt. 5:27–28). If one's eye or hand causes stumbling (*skandalizei*), Jesus reasons that it is better to lose a member than to go into hell (5:29–30). Thus, both teachers link lustful gazes with the commission of sinful sexual acts. Further, the texts each employ the verb *skandalizō*, a term used only by Sirach among the Greek OT and Apocrypha (Sir. 9:5; 23:8; 32:15; cf. Ps. Sol. 16:7). While these considerations suggest Ben Sira's possible influence on Jesus's teaching, the texts reflect quite different motivations for the instructions: Ben Sira cites the practical consequences of financial loss for fornication (e.g., Deut. 22:29), while Jesus warns of eternal punishment for those who indulge in sexual sin (noted by deSilva, *Jewish Teachers,* 69). Moreover, Ben Sira "blames a woman's beauty for the sinful lust . . . a man experiences" (Skehan and Di Lella, 219), an emphasis that is absent in Jesus's teaching. Additionally, Jesus identifies the lustful gaze as itself adulterous and not merely the first step toward sexual sin.

Sirach also cautions readers against invoking the divine name frequently in an oath (*horkos*), since "one who swears many oaths is full of iniquity" and whoever swears falsely "will not be justified" (Sir. 23:9, 11). This parallels Jesus's fourth antithesis, in which he recalls the ancient teaching, "You shall not swear falsely, but shall perform to the Lord what you have sworn [*horkous*]," then charges his disciples not to swear at all (Matt. 5:33–34 ESV). The source of Jesus's allusion to what "was said" is debated, though Lev. 19:12 is the most likely OT reference. Blomberg (25) acknowledges that Sir. 23:11 is "the closest intertestamental parallel" to Matt. 5:33. DeSilva suggests that "Jesus' instructions resemble a fence drawn around Ben Sira's position" (*Jewish Teachers*, 69). The texts employ common words for oaths (*horkos* and *omnyō*) but show no other verbal ties, though Ben Sira's statement that one swearing falsely "will not be justified" may parallel Jesus's declaration that "by your words you will be justified" (Matt. 12:37 ESV). While Ben Sira advises care and restraint with oaths, given the dangers of swearing falsely, Jesus categorically rejects oaths because all speech must be truthful.

Ben Sira and Jesus each employ a form of "like father, like son" reasoning when exhorting people to reflect God's own character (deSilva, *Jewish Teachers*, 71). Ben Sira counsels, "Be a father to orphans, and be like a husband to their mother; you will then be like a son of the Most High [*esē hōs huios hypsistou*]" (4:10), while one should not do good to evildoers, "for the Most High also hates sinners and will inflict punishment on the ungodly" (12:6). The sage makes a clear distinction: "Give to the one who is good, but do not help the sinner" (12:7). Ben Sira's counsel is consistent with the received saying that Jesus cites in Matt. 5:43: "Love your neighbor and hate your enemy." However, Jesus's "revolutionary" counter, "Love your enemies" (v. 44), has no parallel in Sirach or other Jewish writings (Hagner, 134). It is precisely by loving one's foes that disciples are shown to be sons of God, who shows kindness to the evil and the good (v. 45). DeSilva concedes that Jesus's call to love one's enemies represents "a radical extension of Ben Sira's teaching," since the sage sets clear limits for one's generosity while Jesus does not (*Jewish Teachers*, 71–72). However, Jesus's "radical extension" of Ben Sira's wisdom reverses and effectively refutes the sage's ethic that restricts love and good deeds to the devout neighbor. Piper (46) rightly concludes, "The argument of Sirach 12:6f is the precise opposite of Jesus' argument in Matt. 5:44f." This proposed allusion not only lacks clear verbal agreement but also fails to meet the tests of thematic coherence and satisfaction, since Jesus directly contradicts Ben Sira's ethics.

In Matt. 6:1–18, Jesus contrasts true righteousness and religious hypocrisy in almsgiving, prayer, and fasting—three hallmarks of Jewish piety. For example, Ben Sira explains that almsgiving atones for sin (Sir. 3:30) and likens it to "a signet ring with the Lord" (17:22). The sage counsels readers, "Lay up your treasure [*thes ton thēsauron sou*]" according to God's commands and "store up almsgiving in your treasury [*synkleison eleēmosynēn en tois tamieiois sou*]," confident that it "will rescue you from every disaster" (29:11–12; cf. Tob. 12:8–9).

DeSilva suggests that Sirach's instructions about storing up charity in one's treasury "are remarkably close" to Matt. 6:19–20, where Jesus teaches disciples to lay up treasures in heaven, not on earth (*Jewish Teachers*, 74). He acknowledges that for Ben Sira this treasury offers future help in this life to the generous person whereas Jesus's teaching concerns heavenly rewards (*Jewish Teachers*, 75). While there are thematic similarities between Sir. 29:11–12 and Matt. 6:19–21, the only verbal parallel is "your treasure" (*thēsauros sou*), which is insufficient grounds for establishing that Sirach directly influenced Jesus and/or Matthew.

There are several notable parallels between Ben Sira's and Jesus's instructions about prayer. First, the sage counsels, "Do not repeat yourself when you pray" (Sir. 7:14), while Jesus similarly teaches disciples that they need not pray like the gentiles, who suppose that God will hear them because of "their many words" (Matt. 6:7). Second, Jesus addresses God as "Father" in prayer (6:9), as does Ben Sira (Sir. 23:1, 4; 51:10). Third, Sirach urges people not to grow weary in prayer (7:10) and stresses that God hears the prayers of those who are humble, pious, poor, and oppressed (3:5; 4:6; 21:5; 35:16, 20–21; 51:11), highlighting the widow's complaint as a poignant example (35:17–18). Similarly, Jesus stresses God's readiness and willingness to answer his children's prayers (Matt. 7:11) and elsewhere presents a widow as a model of persistent prayer (Luke 18:1–8). Fourth, Ben Sira and Jesus each eschew hypocrisy in fasting and prayer (Sir. 34:31; Matt. 6:5–6, 16–18). These parallels may suggest that Sirach influenced Jesus's teaching on prayer in some way, given the recurrence of similar topics, though there is minimal verbal agreement between the texts.

Both Ben Sira and Jesus also connect extending forgiveness to other people with receiving forgiveness from God. The sage writes, "Forgive [*aphes*] your neighbor the wrong he has done, and then your sins will be pardoned when you pray. . . . Does he have no mercy toward someone like himself and yet pray concerning his own sins?" (Sir. 28:2, 4 ESV). Similarly, Jesus teaches disciples to pray, "Forgive [*aphes*] us our debts, as we also have forgiven [*aphēkamen*] our debtors" (Matt. 6:12). He then explains, "For if you forgive other people when they sin against you, your heavenly Father will also forgive you. But if you do not forgive others their sins, your Father will not forgive your sins" (6:14–15; cf. Mark 11:25). Jesus poignantly illustrates this point with his parable of the unforgiving servant (Matt. 18:23–35). Thus, deSilva concludes that the Lord's notable emphasis on forgiveness "did not originate with Jesus" but reflects Ben Sira's teaching two centuries prior (*Jewish*

Teachers, 73). Similarly, Keener (214) states that Matt. 6:14–15 “accords with one stream of Jewish wisdom tradition.”

Thus, of the various proposed parallels considered above, the influence of Sir. 28:2–4 on Matt. 6:14–15 is the most plausible. The firm dating of Sirach makes it likely that the text was available to Jesus and Matthew. These texts share not only thematic coherence but also some common wording, as both Jesus and Ben Sira clearly connect extending forgiveness to others with receiving forgiveness from God. For many of the other proposed parallels between Sirach and the Sermon on the Mount, Matthew's writings more closely align with the received teaching that Jesus recalls (“you have heard”) and then corrects or radically extends with his own teaching about true righteousness.

Come and Find Rest: Sir. 51 and Matt. 11:28–30

In addition to the proposed parallels between Sirach and the Sermon on the Mount, scholars have often linked Ben Sira's teaching with Jesus's famous invitation “Come to me . . . and I will give you rest” (Matt. 11:28; for the history of interpretation, see Betz, 11–20). Ben Sira concludes his book by recounting his own search for wisdom (Sir. 51:13–22) and then inviting readers to “draw near to me [*engisate pros me*] . . . and lodge in the house of instruction” (51:23). He adds, “Put your neck under the yoke [*hypo zygon*] and let your souls [*hē psychē hymōn*] receive instruction; it is to be found close by. See with your eyes that I have labored [*ekopiasa*] little and found for myself much rest [*anapausin*]” (51:26–27 ESV). The sage's invitation likely draws upon Wisdom's summons in Prov. 9:1–6 (cf. Skehan and Di Lella, 578), while references to the thirsty and the acquisition of wisdom “without money” (Sir. 51:24–25) may allude to Isa. 55:1.

The depiction of Wisdom in Sir. 51:23–27 (and 6:23–31) has exerted “a profound influence” on discussions of Matt. 11:28–30 (Charette, 290), as many scholars claim that Jesus models his teaching after Sirach (e.g., Keener, 349; France, 447; Hagner, 323; deSilva, *Jewish Teachers*, 78). Indeed, Matt. 11:28–30 and Sir. 51:23–27 share not only thematic affinities but also at least five verbal parallels in Greek: *pros me* (“to me”), *hai psychai hymōn* (“your souls”), *zygos* (“yoke”), *kopiaō* (“labor”), and *anapausis* (“rest”). Thus, Deutsch (130) concludes from these parallels to Sirach that Matt. 11:28–30 portrays Christ “not only as Wisdom incarnate, but as the Sage, the Teacher of wisdom.”

However, Jesus's promise that his disciples “will find rest for your souls” (Matt. 11:29) clearly alludes to Jer. 6:16 (Heb.), a point overlooked in some studies (e.g., Deutsch). Blaine Charette (297) argues that the proposed Sirach background to Matt. 11:28–30 “obscures the true intention of the evangelist,” who presents Jesus as the Messiah who fulfills Israel's hopes and offers “the eschatological blessing of rest.” Jesus does not present himself as a model sage who has labored in the study of the law “for all who seek wisdom” (Sir. 24:34); rather, he is “the Son” who knows the Father and reveals things hidden from “the wise” (Matt. 11:25–27).

Many scholars have concluded that Sir. 51:23–27 undoubtedly influenced Jesus's teaching in Matt. 11:28–30. The parallels between these texts fulfill many of the standard criteria for discerning allusions. It is historically plausible, though not certain, that Jesus would have been aware of Ben Sira's teaching. In addition to thematic coherence, the texts share a volume of common vocabulary. However, it is more difficult to discern whether this proposed allusion passes the final criterion, satisfaction—“the most important test” (Hays, 31). While Sir. 51:23–27 shares a number of verbal parallels to Matt. 11:28–30, in the end this proposed allusion more obscures than illuminates Jesus's teaching (Laansma, 196–200; Charette, 297). Indeed, “No Jewish teacher ever told another: Take up my yoke. This, however, is precisely what Jesus does” (Davies and Allison, 289). Jesus's “yoke” and the eschatological “rest” he offers have significantly different connotations than does Ben Sira's “yoke” of Torah that yields rewards in this life.

The Tongue Is Fire: Sir. 28:12–26 and James 3:1–12

According to deSilva (*Jewish Teachers*, 82), James, as Jewish Christian “wisdom literature,” resembles Sirach “very closely in terms of literary forms, argumentation, and topics.” DeSilva notes considerable parallels between how the two texts address the need to bridle one's tongue, given the dangers of careless speech, and suggests that James of Jerusalem draws upon Ben Sira's sagacious advice from two centuries earlier (*Jewish Teachers*, 82–85).

Sirach 28:12–26 reflects extensively on the dangers of sinful speech. Ben Sira notes that the same mouth can spread or snuff out a spark with either breath or spit (v. 12). He curses “the whisperer and double-tongued” in v. 13 and notes the injury caused by slander (“a third tongue” in Greek) in vv. 14–16. He explains that slander and angry words cause damage and death (vv. 17–21), perhaps drawing on Prov. 15:4 and 25:15 (Skehan and Di Lella, 365–66). The sage reasons that the tongue will neither prevail over the pious nor scorch them with its flame (v. 22), and then he warns readers to “make a door and a bolt for your mouth” and “balances and scales for your words . . . lest you err with your tongue” (vv. 25–26 ESV). Ben Sira also addresses the topic of speech in other passages. For example, he urges, “Be quick in your listening and in patience make a reply” (5:11 ESV). He notes, “Good repute and dishonor come from speaking, and a person's tongue is his downfall” (5:13 ESV). The sage also says, “A person may make a slip without intending it. Who has never sinned with his tongue?” (19:16 ESV).

James 3:1–12 reflects extensively on “the power and perils of the tongue” (Johnson, 254) and includes several parallels to Sirach. For example, James notes that "we all stumble in many ways" (James 3:2; cf. Sir. 19:16), asserts that "the tongue also is a fire" (James 3:6; cf. Sir. 28:22–23), and observes that "out of the same mouth come praise and cursing" (James 3:10; cf. Sir. 28:12).

However, the thematic overlap between James and Sirach does not demonstrate the former's dependence on the latter. Beyond the very common terms "tongue" (*glōssa*) and "mouth" (*stoma*) there are no clear verbal ties between James 3:1–12 and Sirach. Both authors reflect the traditional Jewish association of the tongue with fire (e.g., Prov. 16:27; 26:21; Pss. Sol. 12:1–2; cf. Allison, 535). Moreover, James is more radical than Ben Sira in claiming that the tongue is "set on fire by hell" and is untamable by human beings (James 3:6, 8), while the sage expresses confidence that the tongue "will not be master over the godly" (Sir. 28:22 ESV). Thus, while it is certainly possible that Ben Sira's teaching was available to James, the general thematic similarities between their teachings about the tongue do not prove that the brother of Jesus alludes to Sirach.

Idolatry and Immorality: Wis. 13–14 and Rom. 1:18–2:5

Wisdom of Solomon was probably the most well-known and influential book of the Apocrypha within the early church. It was cited in the second century AD by both Irenaeus and the Muratorian Canon (Kolarcik, 438). Writing sometime in the early Roman period, the author presents himself as Solomon, "the philosopher-king par excellence" (McGlynn, 68, 78). The book celebrates the eternal wisdom of God (e.g., Wis. 6:12–25), highlights the folly of idolatry (e.g., 13:1–15:19), and stresses God's unfailing help for Israel (e.g., 19:22).

Interpreters have often observed that Rom. 1:18–2:5 "has deep parallels in the early Jewish textual tradition"—particularly Wis. 13–15 (Linebaugh, "Wisdom," 37). Some argue that Paul consciously models his argument after Wisdom's template (e.g., Watson, 372; Dunn, 72). Scholars have documented numerous verbal parallels between Rom. 1:18–2:5 and Wisdom (e.g., Laato, 94–95; Sanday and Headlam, 51–52). The following are five clear examples: (1) According to Rom. 1:20 and Wis. 13:3–4, people "perceive" (*noeō*) God's "power" (*dynamis*) in his "creation" (*ktiseōs* / *ektisen auta*). (2) Rom. 1:21 states that people who did not act on their knowledge of God "became futile" (*emataiōthēsan*), and Wis. 13:1 says that all those ignorant of God were "futile" (*mataioi*) by nature. (3) Rom. 1:23 and Wis. 13:13 describe people idolatrously worshiping "an image of man" (*eikos . . . anthrōpou*). (4) Both authors refer to idolaters' "error" (*planē*, Rom. 1:27; *planaō*, Wis. 12:24; 13:6; 14:22). (5) Rom. 2:4 and Wis. 15:1 extol God's "kindness" (*chrēstos*) and "patience" (*makrothymos*), which should lead people to repentance (*eis metanoian*, Rom. 2:4; Wis. 11:23). Additionally, the "exchange" (*metallassō*) of natural for unnatural sexual relationships in Rom. 1:26 may parallel "sexual perversion" (*geneseōs enallagē*) in Wis. 14:26 (cf. Watson, 375).

Moreover, Wis. 13–14 and Rom. 1:18–32 present a parallel argument structure, as Linebaugh explains (*God*, 97–100; cf. Watson, 373–75). First, people do not worship the Creator, whose power they perceive (Wis. 13:1–9; Rom. 1:19–20). Second, they err by instead worshiping man-made idols (Wis. 13:10–14:11, 15–21; 15:7–13; Rom. 1:21–23). Third, their idolatry leads to increasing immorality (Wis. 14:12–14, 22–29; Rom. 1:24–31). Fourth, God's righteous judgment awaits those who practice such sins (Wis. 14:30–31; Rom. 1:32).

However, these parallel arguments serve different ends in Wisdom and Romans. Wisdom stresses that Israel is *different* than the nations that practice idolatry and immorality: "Knowing we are considered yours, we will not sin" (Wis. 15:2 AT; cf. v. 4). The author alludes to God's self-revelation in Exod. 34:6 (Wis. 15:1) yet "decontextualises divine mercy" by omitting any reference to Israel's disastrous idolatry in Exod. 32 (Linebaugh, *God*, 102–3). Paul's argument diverges sharply from Wisdom in Rom. 2 as he stresses that Israel is fundamentally *like* the nations who stand under God's judgment. The apostle presents the descent into pervasive idolatry and immorality not as a *gentile* problem but as a universal *human* predicament (Linebaugh, *God*, 120).

Do the parallels between Rom. 1:18–32 and Wis. 13–14 demonstrate that the apostle alludes to this apocryphal text? The book's dating and widespread influence suggest that Wisdom of Solomon was available to Paul (Bell, 75–76; deSilva, *Introducing*, 131, 157–60). The texts share multiple lexical and syntactical connections, parallel argumentation, and thematic coherence, and generations of scholars have proposed parallels to Wisdom in Rom. 1 and elsewhere in the letter (see Dodson, 2–13). These considerations all support the conclusion that Paul deliberately alludes to Wisdom in Rom. 1:18–32. However, "*textual dependence* serves the rhetorical function of establishing *theological difference*" (Linebaugh, *God*, 96). That is, the apostle does not simply rehearse Wisdom's analysis but engages this Jewish text and argues against its fundamental division between idolatrous gentiles and non-idolatrous Jews to demonstrate that "there is no distinction: for all have sinned" (Rom. 3:22–23 ESV).

Propitiation by Blood: Martyr Theology and Rom. 3:24–25

Scholars have proposed various influences and parallels for Paul's presentation of Jesus's death, including the vicarious deaths of the Jewish martyrs in 2 Maccabees and 4 Maccabees. Jarvis Williams (495) claims that this martyr theology "provided Paul with the fundamental (not the only) concepts that he needed to present Jesus' death as an atoning sacrifice and as a saving event in Rom. 3:21–26 to his Hellenistic Jewish and Gentile audience." He explains that martyr theology has roots in the OT and in other early Jewish texts, such as 2 Maccabees, which presents the Jewish martyrs "as atoning sacrifices and a saving event for the nation" (Williams, 500; contra Seeley, 87–89). These martyrs acknowledge that they suffer for their own sins (2 Macc. 7:32), yet they entreat God to be merciful (*hileōs*) to Israel and view their deaths as the means for ending the Almighty's just wrath against the nation (7:37–38).

Fourth Maccabees further develops this martyr theology and makes more explicit the sacrificial and salvific achievement of nine Jewish martyrs. In 6:28–29, the dying priest Eleazar asks God to be merciful (*hileōs genou*) to Israel, to satisfy the divine punishment (*arkestheis . . . dikē*), to effect purification (*katharsion*) by his blood, and to receive his life in exchange for theirs (*antipsychon autōn*). Eleazar's interpretation of his death employs OT sacrificial language (e.g., Lev. 16:19; 17:11) and recalls Moses's intercession on behalf of sinful Israel (Exod. 32:12; see Tabb, 84–85). In 4 Macc. 17:7–24, the author reflects on the martyrs' achievement, presenting them as not victims but victors in a noble contest. Some scholars interpret the martyrs' deaths as exemplary but not redemptive (e.g., Seeley, 87–89, 97–98), but such a reading obscures the author's claim that divine providence "saved" (*diesōsen*) Israel through their blood (17:22). Moreover, 4 Macc. 17:21–22 explains their deaths as vicarious sacrifices that purify the land (*tēn patrida katharisthēnai*), become a life-in-exchange (*antipsychon*) for the nation's sin, and serve as the metaphorical place of propitiation (*hilastērion*) for divine wrath (see Tabb, 91–92; Williams, 509–11).

Williams (510) observes that 4 Macc. 17:22 and Rom. 3:25 are the only instances where an author applies the term *hilastērion* for human beings' vicarious deaths. Bailey (156) explains that *hilastērion* is consistently used in two ways through the second century AD: to designate either Israel's mercy seat or votive offerings to pagan deities. He concludes that Paul uses *hilastērion* differently than 4 Macc. 17:22 does: Jesus's death is presented as the mercy seat, while the martyrs' deaths are "a propitiatory votive offering" (Bailey, 157–58). However, the sacrificial imagery in 4 Macc. 17:21–22, the familiarity of 4 Maccabees's author with the LXX, and the book's earlier reference to the cessation of temple sacrifices (4:20) suggest that the author refers to the martyrs' deaths as the metaphorical place where divine wrath is propitiated (Tabb, 94–96; Finlan, 200–203).

Scholars have suggested additional parallels between martyr theology and Rom. 3:21–26. For example, Williams (520) argues that Jesus and the martyrs die vicariously for others' sins, bring about cleansing, are the necessary price paid for atonement, and achieve salvation and reconciliation. He argues not for Paul's literary dependence on 4 Maccabees but for martyr theology's conceptual influence on the apostle (Williams, 495). This is an important caveat, since scholars have variously dated 4 Maccabees within the range AD 20–120 (see Tabb, 72–74; Klauck, 668; deSilva, *4 Maccabees*, xiv; van Henten, 73–82), though 2 Maccabees—the primary source for 4 Maccabees—dates to the 2nd century BC (Schwartz, 11–15).

The use of *hilastērion* for the deaths of Jesus and the martyrs is a unique verbal link between Rom. 3:25 and 4 Macc. 17:22, and these texts also both refer to blood (*haima*, 4 Macc. 6:29; 17:22; Rom. 3:25) and divine justice (*dikē*, 4 Macc. 6:28) or righteousness (*dikaiosynē*, Rom. 3:22). Other proposed parallels highlight conceptual similarities between the deaths of Jesus and the martyrs that receive further support elsewhere in Paul's writings. These parallels suggest that martyr theology influenced Paul's presentation of Jesus's death as a place of propitiation and means of salvation for sinners. However, the redemptive deaths of Jesus and the martyrs are also dissimilar in several crucial ways. First, Jesus did not in any sense suffer for his own sins, as the martyrs did (2 Macc. 7:32). Second, while the martyrs' noble deaths save *the nation* and move God to judge their enemies, Jesus saves "the ungodly" (Rom. 5:6), all who trust him, Jews and gentiles alike (3:26–31). Third, Paul stresses the unique redemptive-historical significance of Jesus's death, which fulfills the Law and the Prophets and deals with "former sins," not just Israel's predicament under tyranny.

Summary

This article has examined five representative examples of NT writers' proposed use of the Apocrypha by utilizing standard criteria for recognizing allusions. These examples include material from four major apocryphal texts (Sirach, Wisdom, 2 Maccabees, and 4 Maccabees) and three NT writings (Matthew, Romans, and James). This analysis has confirmed some of these proposed allusions, such as Paul's use of Wis. 13–14, martyr theology in Romans, and possibly the influence of Sirach on Jesus's teaching in Matt. 6:14–15. Other proposed allusions, such as those in Matt. 5:43–45 (Sir. 4:10; 7:6–7); 11:28–30 (Sir. 51:23–27); and James 3:1–12 (Sir. 28:12–26), illustrate thematic parallels but not demonstrable use of the Apocrypha by NT authors. Close comparison of select apocryphal and NT texts has revealed significant similarities in worldview, such as the close link between human forgiveness and divine forgiveness (Matt. 6:14–15; Sir. 28:2–4) and the belief that human blood is needed for the propitiation of divine wrath against sinners (4 Macc. 17:22; Rom. 3:25). This study has also highlighted significant differences in theological, ethical, and rhetorical emphases. For example, Jesus's charge to love one's own enemies directly contradicts Ben Sira's ethics (Matt. 5:44; Sir. 12:6–7), and his bold invitation to bear *his* yoke to find eschatological rest is far more radical than Ben Sira's call to submit to Torah's "yoke" to find rest in this life (Matt. 11:28–30; Sir. 51:23–27). Moreover, in perhaps the clearest example of the NT use of the Apocrypha, Paul's dependence on Wis. 13–14 sets up his theological argument over against Wisdom that Jews and gentiles alike are guilty before God (Rom. 1:18–2:5; 3:23).

See also OT Use of the OT: Comparison with the NT Use of the OT; *other Apocrypha articles; Dead Sea Scrolls articles; Mishnah, Talmud, and Midrashim articles; Targums articles; Philo articles; Pseudepigrapha articles; Septuagint articles*

Bibliography. Allison, D. C., *James*, ICC (Bloomsbury, 2013); Bailey, D. P., "Jesus as the Mercy Seat," *TynBul* 51 (2000): 155–58; Beale, G. K., *Handbook on the New Testament Use of the Old Testament* (Baker Academic, 2012); Bell, R. H., *No One Seeks for God*, WUNT 106 (Mohr Siebeck, 1998); Betz, H. D., "The Logion of the Easy Yoke and of Rest (Matt. 11:28–30)," *JBL* 86 (1967): 10–24; Blomberg, C. L., "Matthew," in *CNTUOT*, 1–110; Charette, B. B., "'To Proclaim Liberty to the Captives,'" *NTS* 38 (1992): 290–97; Davies, W. D., and D. C. Allison, *Matthew 8–18*, ICC (T&T Clark, 1991); deSilva, D. A., *4 Maccabees*, SeptCS (Brill, 2006); deSilva, *Introducing the Apocrypha*, 2nd ed. (Baker Academic, 2018); deSilva, *The Jewish Teachers of Jesus, James, and Jude* (Oxford University Press, 2012); Deutsch, C., *Hidden Wisdom and the Easy Yoke*, JSNTSup 18 (Sheffield Academic, 1987); Dodson, J. R., *The "Powers" of Personification*, BZNW 161 (de Gruyter, 2008); Dunn, J. D. G., *Romans 1–8*, WBC 38A (Word, 1988); Finlan, S., *The Background and Content of Paul's Cultic Atonement Metaphors*, AcBib 19 (Society of Biblical Literature, 2004); France, R. T., *The Gospel of Matthew*, NICNT (Eerdmans, 2007); Hagner, D. A., *Matthew 1–13*, WBC 33A (Word, 1993); Hays, R. B., *Echoes of Scripture in the Letters of Paul* (Yale University Press, 1989); Johnson, L. T., *The Letter of James*, AB 37A (Doubleday, 1995); Keener, C. S., *The Gospel of Matthew* (Eerdmans, 2009); Klauck, H.-J., *4. Makkabäerbuch*, Jüdische Schriften aus hellenistisch-römischer Zeit 3.6 (Gerd Mohn, 1989); Kolarcik, M., "The Book of Wisdom," in *NIB*, 5:437–600; Laansma, J., *"I Will Give You Rest,"* WUNT 2/98 (Mohr Siebeck, 1997); Laato, T., *Paul and Judaism*, SFSHJ 115 (Scholars Press, 1995); Linebaugh, J. A., *God, Grace, and Righteousness in Wisdom of Solomon and Paul's Letter to the Romans*, NovTSup 152 (Brill, 2013); Linebaugh, "Wisdom of Solomon and Romans 1:18–2:5," in *Reading Romans in Context*, ed. B. C. Blackwell (Zondervan, 2015), 36–44; Litwak, K. D., *Echoes of Scripture in Luke-Acts*, JSNTSup 282 (T&T Clark, 2005); McGlynn, M., "Solomon, Wisdom and the Philosopher-Kings," in *Studies in the Book of Wisdom*, ed. G. G. Xeravits and J. Zsengellér, JSJSup 142 (Brill, 2010), 61–82; Piper, J., *"Love your Enemies,"* SNTSMS 38 (Cambridge University Press, 1979); Porter, S. E., "Allusions and Echoes," in *As It Is Written*, ed. S. E. Porter and C. D. Stanley (Society of Biblical Literature, 2008), 29–40; Sanday, W., and A. C. Headlam, *Romans* (repr., T&T Clark, 1977); Schwartz, D. R., *2 Maccabees*, CEJL (de Gruyter, 2008); Seeley, D., *The Noble Death*, JSNTSup 28 (Sheffield Academic, 1990); Shaw, D. A., "Converted Imaginations?," *CBR* 11 (2013): 234–45; Skehan, P. W., and A. A. Di Lella, *The Wisdom of Ben Sira*, AB 39 (Doubleday, 1987); Tabb, B. J., *Suffering in Ancient Worldview*, LNTS 569 (Bloomsbury T&T Clark, 2017); van Henten, J. W., *The Maccabean Martyrs as Saviours of the Jewish People*, JSJSup 57 (Brill, 1997); Watson, F., *Paul and the Hermeneutics of Faith*, 2nd ed. (Bloomsbury T&T Clark, 2016); Williams, J. J., "Martyr Theology in Hellenistic Judaism and Paul's Conception of Jesus' Death in Romans 3:21–26," in *Christian Origins and Hellenistic Judaism*, ed. S. E. Porter and A. W. Pitts, TENTS 10 (Brill, 2013), 493–521.

Brian J. Tabb

Apocrypha: Thematic Parallels to the NT

The Jewish writings from the Second Temple period known as the Apocrypha include numerous verbal and thematic parallels with the NT. Many if not most of these parallels reflect the common formative influence of the OT Scriptures on these authors. The Apocrypha and the NT rehearse foundational elements of the biblical story, such as the creation of Adam and Eve (Tob. 8:6; Sir. 33:10; Acts 17:26), the flood (Wis. 10:4; Sir. 40:10; 44:17–18; 3 Macc. 2:4; 4 Macc. 15:31; Luke 17:27; 2 Pet. 2:5), God's promises to Abraham (Sir. 44:21; Acts 7:17; Rom. 4:13; Gal. 3:16–18; Heb. 6:13–15), and the exodus from Egypt (Jdt. 5:11–14; Bar. 1:19–20; 2:11; 1 Macc. 4:9; Acts 7:36; Jude 5). Each corpus appeals to the Mosaic law for authoritative ethical teaching (e.g., Tob. 7:12–13; 4 Macc. 2:5–6; Mark 7:10; 1 Cor. 9:9) and expresses the need to fear the Lord (Sir. 1:27; Acts 9:31; Col. 3:22). This article focuses on thematic parallels in five areas: (1) God's wisdom and character, (2) the identity of God's people, (3) the ethics of God's people, (4) the life of faith, and (5) salvation and judgment.

God's Wisdom and Character

The NT and Apocrypha together affirm that the Creator God has complete authority over his creation, that his plans and wisdom transcend the human ability to comprehend, and that his words are completely trustworthy and will come to pass.

The potter and clay. Ben Sira and Paul liken God to a potter who wisely molds the clay according to his own pleasure. In Sir. 33:7–15, the sage explains that the Most High has established opposites in creation according to his great wisdom (Skehan and Di Lella, 400). Though the sun shines equally each day, God sets apart some days and seasons as holy (vv. 7–9). Though all humanity is created from the ground, God blesses and exalts some people but curses and humbles others (vv. 9–12). Human beings are "like clay in the hand of the potter [*kerameus*], to be molded as he pleases" (v. 13). That is, the Creator God completely directs people's destinies according to his determination. The identification of God as the potter derives particularly from Jer. 18:1–6, where God directs the prophet to observe a potter fashioning clay as he pleases and then declares, "Like clay in the hand of the potter, so are you in my hand, Israel" (cf. Isa. 29:16; 45:9).

In Rom. 9:21, Paul similarly stresses the prerogative of the divine potter (*kerameus*) to fashion pottery for different uses "out of the same lump of clay." The apostle insists that God is completely free to show mercy to some who are prepared for glory while hardening others who are prepared for wrath (9:18, 22–23). To the objection that God unfairly blames those who cannot resist his will, Paul responds that the creature has no right to argue with the Creator and cites the rhetorical question in Isa. 29:16 LXX: "Shall what is formed say to the one who formed it, 'Why did you make me like this?'" (Rom. 9:20). Robert Jewett (594–95) argues that the apostle alludes to Wis. 15:7 in Rom. 9:20–21, given verbal and thematic links between the texts. However, in Wisdom the "potter" is a human worker who fashions "a futile god" from the same clay used for clean vessels (15:7–8). Paul's potter-clay analogy more closely parallels Sir. 33, sharing a common influence by the OT prophets. Sirach and Romans together insist that God has supreme authority over his creation, though Paul develops this further by stressing God's freedom to show mercy not only to Jews but also to gentiles whom he calls (Rom. 9:24).

God's unfailing word. Tobit 14 and Rom. 9 express confidence that God's word has not failed with respect to Israel's salvation (see Goodrich, 41–62). Tobit and Paul both speak about the fate of their fellow Israelites, their "brothers" (Tob. 14:4; Rom. 9:3–4 ESV). Tobit states that the prophets' words will surely come to pass and "none of all their words will fail" (14:4); Paul writes similarly, "It is not as though God's word had failed" (Rom. 9:6). Both also affirm that God will one day show mercy (*eleeō*) on Israel (Tob. 14:5; Rom. 11:31), and they express hope that gentiles will turn to the Lord (Tob. 14:6–7; Rom. 11:11, 25).

For Tobit, Israel's restoration entails the people's "return from their exile" to rebuild Jerusalem and its temple, which will lead all the nations to abandon their idols and "worship God in truth" (14:5–6). Richard Bauckham (433–59) observes that Tobit's vision of restoration includes the regathering of the scattered northern tribes, such as Tobit's tribe of Naphtali (1:1, 4; 7:3), and divine judgment upon their Assyrian captors (1:2; 14:15).

John Goodrich (62) reasons that Paul and Tobit "share similar eschatological perspectives on Israel's current salvation-historical location and future redemption." However, the apostle's salvation-historical perspective differs significantly from Tobit's. Paul declares that "Christ is the culmination of the law" and is "the Lord" who will save all who call on his name (Rom. 10:4, 9, 13; cf. Joel 2:32), while Tobit charges his son to "keep the law . . . and be merciful" as he waits for Israel's restoration (Tob. 14:9 ESV). Moreover, Paul stresses that salvation has come already to the gentiles "to make Israel envious" (Rom. 11:11), while Tobit envisions Israel's redemption prompting gentiles to abandon their idols (Tob. 14:5–6).

Who can search out God? Judith and Paul express in their own ways the OT conviction that no human being can search out God's thoughts (cf. Isa. 40:13; Job 11:7–8). When Judith hears that the people of Israel have convinced the city's magistrate to surrender to the Assyrians in five days, she rebukes the leaders for putting God to the test and setting themselves in his rightful place (Jdt. 8:9–13). She reasons, "You cannot plumb the depths of the human heart or understand the workings of the human mind; how do you expect to search out God, who made all these things, and find out his mind or comprehend his thought?" (8:14). Judith thus stresses their need for humility before God rather than their presumption (Wills, 264). The heroine warns them not to restrict the Lord's purposes with their plans, since "God is not like man, to be threatened" (8:16 ESV), alluding to Num. 23:19 LXX (cf. Gera, 279–80).

In 1 Cor. 2:6–16, Paul explains that he proclaims the wisdom of God revealed by the Spirit of God. He writes that "the Spirit searches all things, even the deep things of God" and that only the Spirit knows God's thoughts (vv. 10–11). Human beings cannot naturally grasp such things apart from divine revelation by the Spirit. Paul concludes with a citation of Isa. 40:13 LXX: "Who has known the mind of the Lord so as to instruct him?" While the expected answer to this rhetorical answer is "No one," the apostle surprisingly declares, "But we have the mind of Christ" (v. 16). He claims not superior individual insight but received spiritual wisdom that centers on Christ crucified (cf. Ciampa and Rosner, 702). Joseph Fitzmyer (180) suggests that Jdt. 8:14 expresses "a similar idea" to 1 Cor. 2:10 (cf. Rom. 11:33–34), yet while Judith emphasizes the inscrutability of God's thoughts, the apostle emphasizes the Spirit's revelation of God's mysterious wisdom for his people.

The Identity of God's People

The Apocrypha and the NT stress the identity and calling of Israel and the church, respectively, as God's holy people, who are Abraham's children and a royal priesthood.

The children of Abraham. Abraham is named twenty times in the Greek text of the Apocrypha and seventy-three times in the NT. Fourth Maccabees names Abraham nine times and also refers to noble Jewish martyrs as Abrahamites (9:21; 18:1, 20, 23). The author presents these martyrs as consummate examples of his thesis that "pious reason is absolute master of the passions" (1:1 NETS). In their willingness "to endure any suffering for the sake of God," these martyrs emulate Abraham's zeal for God and so prove themselves to be the patriarch's "true descendants" (16:19–20; 17:6; cf. Seim, 42). They die nobly for their devotion to the law as "children of Abraham," and they "live to God" like Abraham and receive the patriarch's welcome and praise (6:22; 7:19; 13:17; 16:25).

Luke's Gospel reflects a similar stress on Abraham, referring fifteen times to the patriarch. The speeches of Mary and Zechariah highlight God's faithfulness to his covenant promises to Abraham (Luke 1:54–55, 72–73; cf. Acts 3:25; 7:17). In Luke 3:8, John counters the Jews' confidence in their Abrahamic ancestry by announcing, "God can raise up children for Abraham" from stones. Jesus heals "a daughter of Abraham" from her afflictions (13:16) and surprisingly refers to the tax collector Zacchaeus as "a son of Abraham" (19:9). He also presents the patriarch welcoming a righteous beggar and excluding the wealthy Lazarus after their deaths (16:22–25). In Acts, Peter declares that "the God of our fathers" has glorified Jesus, and he recalls God's promise to bless all peoples through Abraham's seed (3:13, 25; cf. Gen. 22:18). Similarly, Paul announces the message of salvation to his "fellow children of Abraham" (Acts 13:26). Luke and Acts emphasize not Abraham's example of faithfulness but the fulfillment of God's promise given to the patriarch, which is good news even for the oppressed and the outcast.

While "no Gentile Christian is called a son or daughter of Abraham" in Luke-Acts (Seim, 40), Paul defines the "children of Abraham" as "those who have faith" (Gal. 3:7). The apostle identifies Christ as the singular seed of Abraham through whom God's blessings would flow to the nations (3:14, 16). He concludes that all who belong to Christ—Jews and gentiles alike—"are Abraham's seed, and heirs according to the promise" (3:29). Thus, Paul not only highlights God's sure promise to the patriarch but also explains how the nations experience these promised blessings through faith in Christ, Abraham's true son.

A kingdom of priests (Exod. 19:6). The books of 2 Maccabees, 1 Peter, and Revelation allude to the designation of Israel as "a royal priesthood and a holy nation [*basileion hierateuma kai ethnos hagion*]" (Exod. 19:6 LXX AT). Second Maccabees opens with two letters (1:1–2:18) that call readers to celebrate the temple's purification. The second letter recounts that God "has saved all his people" and has restored their inheritance as well as "the kingship and the priesthood and the consecration [*to basileion kai to hierateuma kai ton hagiasmon*], as he promised through the law" (2:17–18). The reference to God's promise signals a conscious appeal to the Scriptures, and multiple verbal parallels between 2 Macc. 2:17 and Exod. 19:6 confirm this allusion: *basileion* ("royal"/"kingship"), *hierateuma* ("priesthood"), and *hagiasmon/hagion* ("consecration"/"holy"; cf. Camponovo, 189–90). While Exod. 19:6 LXX refers to the nation itself as "a royal priesthood," 2 Maccabees refers to distinct institutions—"kingdom" and "priesthood"—that God has restored to Israel (cf. Schwartz, 168; Doran, 61). Odo Camponovo (190) reasons that since there were no Jewish kings at the time of the temple cleansing, "kingship" must refer to the people. Alternatively, Daniel Schwartz (168–69) suggests that *basileion* likely connotes simply the "independent rule" the nation enjoyed during the time of Judas Maccabeus. The purification of the temple and restoration of Israel's independent rule and priestly service suggest hope that God will "gather" his scattered people as he promised (Doran, 61–62; cf. Camponovo, 190).

Peter identifies his predominantly gentile readers as "a chosen people, a royal priesthood, a holy nation, God's special possession" (1 Pet. 2:9), alluding to Exod. 19:5–6 and Isa. 43:20–21 (Achtemeier, 163–66; Horrell, 128). The OT description of Israel as the special, holy people chosen by God to be a royal priesthood finds typological fulfillment in the church (Carson, 1030–31). Having received God's mercy and experienced a sort of new exodus out of darkness into light, believers in Christ have a new identity as "the people of God" and a new vocation to "declare the praises" of God as they offer acceptable spiritual sacrifices through Christ as priests (1 Pet. 2:5, 9–10).

The doxology in Rev. 1:5–6 praises Christ as the one who loved us, set us free from sins, and "made us to be a kingdom and priests to serve his God and Father." Here "kingdom" (*basileian*) and "priests" (*hiereis*) probably allude to Israel's designation as "a royal priesthood," indicating a typological fulfillment of Exod. 19:6 (Tabb, *All Things New*, 90–91). In Revelation as in Exodus, God saves his people by sacrifice for service as royal priests. Some scholars stress that the saints will "reign" and act as priests in the future resurrection but not in the present (Koester, 217; Schüssler Fiorenza, 123–24). However, Revelation more likely presents Christ's followers constituting a priestly kingdom already in an inaugurated and ironic way as they confess allegiance to the Lamb and conquer through faithful self-sacrifice (Tabb, *All Things New*, 91–92).

The Ethics of God's People

The ethical instructions given in the Apocrypha and the NT include a number of thematic parallels—for example, giving alms, fleeing immorality, joining those who weep, and avoiding idolatry.

Almsgiving and care for orphans and widows. The book of Tobit frequently highlights the importance of almsgiving and care for the poor. Tobit himself "performed many acts of charity [*eleēmosynas pollas*]" for his people and acted generously toward orphans and widows (1:3, 8). He instructs his son, Tobias, to "give alms [*poiei eleēmosynēn*] from your possessions to all who live uprightly, and do not let your eye begrudge the gift when you make it" (4:7 AT). Tobit counsels to feed the hungry, clothe the naked, and give surplus possessions away (4:16). He explains that God will see and reward generosity to the poor and reasons that "almsgiving delivers from death" (4:7, 10; cf. 12:9; Sir. 29:12; 40:24). Later, the angel Raphael says, "It is better to give alms than to lay up gold" (Tob. 12:8).

Jesus similarly instructs disciples to act generously toward the poor: "Sell your possessions, and give alms [*dote eleēmosynēn*]. Make purses for yourselves that do not wear out, an unfailing treasure in heaven" (Luke 12:33 NRSV). Jesus also reminds disciples that God sees and rewards almsgiving done in secret (Matt. 6:2–4). Jesus's instructions parallel Tobit and other Jewish writers, such as Ben Sira, but he also "radicalizes" the ethics of almsgiving (deSilva, *Jewish Teachers*, 94). Disciples of Jesus should not merely give to the godly (Tob. 4:7; Sir. 12:2, 4, 7); they should imitate God's lavish generosity by loving and doing good to "the ungrateful and the wicked" (Luke 6:35; cf. Matt. 5:44–45). Moreover, while Tobit's counsel to lay up "a good treasure for yourself against the day of necessity" (4:9) prepares for an uncertain future in which one might need charity from others, Jesus presents an eschatological motivation for generosity, as disciples store up heavenly treasure (Matt. 6:19–20; Luke 12:33; 18:22) and will be rewarded for their care for the poor and needy "when the Son of Man comes in his glory" (Matt. 25:31, 34–36).

Weep with those who weep. Ben Sira and Paul exhort readers to share in the sorrow of others. Ben Sira writes, "Do not lag behind those who weep, but mourn with those who mourn [*meta penthountōn penthēson*]" (Sir. 7:34 NETS). Since in v. 33 the sage urges generosity to the dead as well as the living, v. 34 most likely has in view one's duties toward the bereaved (Skehan and Di Lella, 208). Rather than keeping a comfortable distance from death and those who experience loss, it is better to join others in their weeping and thereby diminish their grief. Similarly, the apostle writes, "Rejoice with those who rejoice; mourn with those who mourn [*klaiein meta klaiontōn*]" (Rom. 12:15). In context, sharing with others—particularly fellow believers—in their joy and grief is an expression of the sincere love Paul calls for in v. 9. Such expressions of mutual sympathy require Christians to "share a common mind-set," as v. 16 explains (Moo, 800).

Jewett (767) calls Sir. 7:34 a "noteworthy" parallel with Rom. 12:15 and cites related maxims in Greek and rabbinic literature. While the sage counsels readers to join the bereaved in their mourning, the apostle appeals for readers to express sincere love for one another in both joy and sorrow.

Flee sexual immorality. The Apocrypha and the NT repeatedly warn against the dangers of sexual sin (*porneia*). For example, Tobit instructs his son, "Keep yourself . . . from all sexual immorality" (Tob. 4:12 AT). Tobias heeds this counsel and emphasizes his sexual purity on his wedding night (8:7). Similarly, Ben Sira writes, "Be ashamed of sexual immorality" (Sir. 41:17), and he explains that the adulterous woman disobeys God's law and commits offense against her husband (23:23). He also warns against lusting after a woman, whose beautiful appearance might seduce a man and cause him to stumble (9:5, 8–9). In 1 Cor. 6:18, Paul charges, "Flee from sexual immorality." Because "your body is a temple of the Holy Spirit" and "you were bought with a price," Paul urges the believer to "glorify God in your body" (6:19–20 ESV). While these texts all warn against immorality, they stress different motivations for sexual purity.

"Keep yourselves from idols." The Apocrypha and the NT include regular warnings against idolatry. The Letter of Jeremiah is "a sustained polemic against the worship of idols" (deSilva, *Introducing*, 230; cf. Moore, *Daniel, Esther, and Jeremiah*, 317). Drawing on the biblical critiques of idolatry (e.g., Deut. 4:27–28; Jer. 10:2–15), the author repeatedly stresses that idols of silver, gold, and wood "are not gods; so do not revere them" (Let. Jer. 16 ESV; cf. vv. 23, 29, 65, 69). Such idols are "false and cannot speak" (v. 8). They cannot see, feel, move, or help themselves; thus, they cannot help the weak or save people from death (vv. 19, 24–26, 36). Wisdom of Solomon similarly exposes the folly of trusting in "lifeless idols" and identifies the invention of idols as "the beginning of fornication" (14:12, 29). The tale with Daniel and Bel humorously illustrates the impotence of "man-made idols" and the need to worship "the living God, who created heaven and earth" (Bel 5 ESV). First Maccabees 1:43 recounts how a large number of Israelites sacrificed to idols in response to pressure from the gentile tyrant, and 2 Macc. 12:40–42 presents the deaths of Israelite soldiers with hidden idols as an act of divine judgment.

Similarly, Paul commands, "Flee from idolatry" (1 Cor. 10:14). The apostle reminds gentile readers that they were formally "led astray to mute idols" (12:2). He stresses the basic incompatibility of God and idols (2 Cor. 6:16). Idolatry is among "the acts of the flesh" that characterize people who will not inherit God's kingdom (Gal. 5:19–21; cf. 1 Cor. 6:9). Several NT texts urge gentile Christians not to eat food sacrificed to idols or practice sexual immorality (Acts 15:20, 29; 21:25; Rev. 2:14, 20). Moreover, in Rev. 9:20 plagues strike those who refuse to repent of idolatry, which parallels the account of God's judgment of the Canaanites in Wis. 12:9–11 (Beale, *Revelation*, 518). Revelation 9:20 also explains the true nature of idolatry by linking it with the worship of "demons" and echoing OT descriptions of idols' inability to see, hear, or walk (cf. Ps. 115:4–7; Dan. 5:23). NT writers do not conceive of idolatry simply as the worship of the pagan deities made of wood or stone that were ubiquitous in the Greco-Roman world. Paul characterizes greed as idolatry (Eph. 5:5; Col. 3:5), since "the greedy contravene God's exclusive rights to human love, trust, and obedience" (Rosner, 81). Similarly, John's appeal, "Keep yourselves from idols" (1 John 5:21), warns believers against embracing any alternative to Christ, "the true God and eternal life" (v. 20).

The Life of Faith

The Apocrypha and the NT call God's people to remain steadfast through testing and reflect on the OT motif of the righteous sufferer.

Faithfulness through testing. Ben Sira and James emphasize the need for steadfastness through testing. The sage writes, "Prepare your soul for testing [*peirasmos*]. Set straight your heart, and be steadfast, and do not be hasty in a time of distress" (Sir. 2:1–2 NETS). Readers must remain patient (*makrothymeō*) when humbled, because "gold is tested [*dokimazetai*] in the fire, and those found acceptable, in the furnace of humiliation" (2:4–5; cf. Wis. 3:5–6; 1 Pet. 1:6–7). Sirach 44:20 highlights the example of Abraham, who kept God's law and proved faithful when tested (*en peirasmō*). Thus, Ben Sira teaches that "by yielding to Torah, one may exemplify the faithfulness and obedience that characterises the path of wisdom" (Ellis, 94).

James calls readers to persevere in testing that they might be "mature and complete, not lacking anything" (1:4). He urges believers to rejoice in many trials (*peirasmois*), remembering that the testing (*dokimion*) of their faith produces perseverance (vv. 2–3). James 1:12 holds forth the promised "crown of life" as the reward for one who "perseveres under trial." James's discussion of human probation moves seamlessly from the noun *peirasmos* ("trial," vv. 2, 12) to the verb *peirazō* ("tempt," vv. 13–14; cf. Ellis, 26–27). James insists that God is *apeirastos* ("without temptation" [BDAG, 100], v. 13) and identifies people's sinful desires—not God—as the source of temptation. James illustrates his teaching by highlighting the "complete" faith of Abraham, the exemplary patience of the prophets, and the steadfastness of Job (2:22; 5:10–11). Ben Sira and James similarly emphasize the need to persevere through testing, though James diverges from the sage by offering an eschatological motivation for steadfast faith (1:12).

The suffering of the righteous. Wisdom and Luke's Gospel each develop the OT motif of the righteous sufferer. Wisdom 1–5 presents an extended contrast between the wicked, who summon death by their actions and words and will perish like chaff (1:16; 5:14), and the righteous, who are preserved by God and promised immortality (3:1; 5:15). The wicked persecute and condemn the righteous one, who calls God "his Father," claims to be the Lord's "servant" and "son," and awaits deliverance from his adversaries (2:13, 16, 18, 20 CEB). Yet, "the souls of the righteous are in the hand of God" (3:1), and they will experience "unexpected salvation" (5:2).

Scholars have often noted parallels between Wisdom and Luke's passion narrative (e.g., Beck, 43–47; Doble, 187–225). For example, Jesus's opponents question his sonship and taunt him with calls to save himself (Luke 22:70; 23:35, 37; cf. Wis. 2:18). In his death, Jesus is "righteous," calls on God as "Father," and commends his spirit into God's hands (Luke 23:46–47; cf. Wis. 2:16; 3:1). However, suffering serves a different purpose in Wisdom and Luke: the former presents God educating and testing the righteous through trials (Wis. 3:5), while Jesus's suffering is necessary, vicarious, and redemptive (Tabb, "Lucan Jesus," 296–97).

Wisdom and Luke allude to Isa. 52:13–53:12 and the lament psalms. In Wis. 2:13, the righteous man calls himself "the Lord's servant" (*pais kyriou*), recalling Isa. 52:13. Like Isaiah's servant, he is despised and misunderstood by opponents (Wis. 3:2; 5:4; Isa. 53:3–4), yet the vindication of God's *pais* in both texts prompts astonishment (Wis. 5:2; Isa. 52:15; cf. Nickelsburg, 83–87). However, Wisdom "makes no use of the idea of vicarious suffering" that is prominent in Isa. 53 (Suggs, 31). In Luke 22:37, Jesus emphatically cites Isa. 53:12 immediately before his arrest, which may suggest that Isa. 53 functions "as the hermeneutical key to the narrative of Jesus' suffering and death" (Pao and Schnabel, 385; cf. Tabb, "Lucan Jesus," 294–95). Wisdom 2:12–20 also includes a number of parallels to Psalms, such as the contrast between the "two ways" of the righteous, who will stand in God's presence, and the wicked, who will perish like chaff (Wis. 5:1, 14; Ps. 1:4–6; cf. Kolarcik, 462–64). In Luke 23:46–47 Jesus cites Ps. 31:5 (30:6 LXX) when entrusting himself to the Father's hands, and the centurion declares him *dikaios* (cf. Ps. 31:18), suggesting that Luke presents Jesus as "the royal righteous sufferer" (Jipp, 264). Moreover, Jesus's resurrection from the dead confirms his predictions and fulfills the Scriptures (Luke 24:6–8, 26–27).

Salvation and Judgment

The Apocrypha and the NT appeal to OT prophecies to explain the desecration of Israel's temple and to affirm that God will execute judgment according to human deeds and will bring salvation and restoration to his people just as he promised.

The abomination of desolation. The NT Gospels and 1 Maccabees refer to the desolating sacrifice prophesied by Daniel. First Maccabees recounts Israel's fateful "covenant" with the nations (1 Macc. 1:11; cf. Dan. 9:27) and the tyrant Antiochus IV's war against Egypt (1 Macc. 1:16–20; cf. Dan. 11:25–28). After the war, Antiochus built "a desolating sacrilege on the altar of burnt offering," erected altars in other Jewish towns, and destroyed copies of the Scriptures (1 Macc. 1:54–56). The phrase "desolating sacrilege" (*bdelygma erēmōseōs*) in v. 54 clearly recalls Dan. 9:27 (cf. 11:31; 12:11) and is the earliest interpretation of that text (Collins, 357). Later, when Antiochus learns that the Jews have routed his forces and torn down his abomination, he becomes sick from disappointment and recognizes his error (1 Macc. 6:5–13).

In Matt. 24, Jesus responds to his disciples' questions: "When will [the temple's destruction] happen, and what will be the sign of your coming and of the end of the age?" (v. 3). Jesus warns that Judean residents must flee when they "see standing in the holy place 'the abomination that causes desolation [*to bdelygma tēs erēmōseōs*],' spoken of through the prophet Daniel—let the reader understand" (Matt. 24:15–16; cf. Mark 13:14). The precise phrase "the abomination that causes desolation" occurs in Dan. 11:31 and 12:11 (cf. 9:27). Scholars typically identify Antiochus IV as the little "horn" (8:9) and the "contemptible person" (11:21) who would abolish temple sacrifice and set up the "abomination that causes desolation" (9:27), though this tyrant may be a type of a future antichrist figure (Longman, 43–44, 130). In Matt. 24, Jesus speaks not of Antiochus's past desecration of the temple but of some future event, which requires readers to exercise wisdom (cf. Dan. 12:10; France, 911–12). Some interpreters (e.g., Toussaint, 479–80) understand Matt. 24:15 to predict the actions of the man of lawlessness at history's end (2 Thess. 2:3–4). However, it is more likely that Jesus refers (at least primarily) to a horrifying event that will desecrate the temple before its destruction (cf. Matt. 24:2; for a survey of interpretive proposals, see Stein, 90–93). While "the abomination that causes desolation" in Daniel predicts the temple's desecration by Antiochus IV, Jesus applies Daniel's prophecy as a type of the defilement preceding the temple's destruction in AD 70, which may also prefigure the final rebellion of the man of lawlessness (2 Thess. 2:3–12).

Judgment according to works. Ben Sira and Paul both affirm the fittingness of God's judgment in accordance with human deeds. The sage writes, "As great as his mercy, so great is also his reproof; he will judge a man according to his works [*kata ta erga autou*]. . . . Each will receive according to his deeds [*kata ta erga autou*]" (Sir. 16:12, 14 AT). This reflects a consistent teaching throughout the OT that God pays back "each according to his works" (Prov. 24:12 AT; cf. Ps. 28:4; 62:12; Jer. 17:10; 50:29). Ben Sira explains that God knows every human deed (15:19) and will give everyone what they deserve; thus, sinners will not escape, and the godly will not be frustrated in the end (16:13). Later, the sage stresses that the Lord will not delay until he "repays vengeance on the nations" and "pays back each man according to his deeds [*kata tas praxeis autou*]" (Sir. 35:22–24 AT [vv. 20–22 LXX]).

The NT consistently affirms the OT principle that divine judgment corresponds to human deeds (cf. Matt. 16:27; Rom. 2:6; 2 Tim. 4:14; 1 Pet. 1:17; Rev. 2:23). In Rom. 2:6, the apostle states, "He will render to each one according to his works [*kata ta erga autou*]" (ESV). In Paul's argument, this principle of impartial judgment supports his warning in vv. 4–5 that Jews who presume on God's kindness and fail to repent will face eschatological wrath (Schreiner, 120). Thus, while Ben Sira expresses confidence that God will pay back the unrighteous nations and vindicate Israel, Paul stresses that God impartially administers punishment and reward to everyone by the same standard—to "the Jew first and also the Greek" (Rom. 2:9–10).

The new Jerusalem. Tobit, Baruch, and Revelation recall Isaiah's prophecies of Jerusalem's glorious future. Tobit confidently declares that the holy city will be restored in splendor: "Jerusalem will be built with sapphire and emerald," with walls, towers, battlements, and streets adorned with precious gems and gold (Tob. 13:16–17 ESV). Tobit's description of Jerusalem's renewed glory alludes to Isa. 54:11–12, and the rejoicing of the faithful in Tob. 13:14 recalls Isa. 66:10 (cf. Moore, *Tobit*, 281). Similarly, Baruch describes Israel's joyous salvation after the exile (4:22–24, 29, 36–37; 5:7) and the adornment of Jerusalem. Drawing on imagery from Isa. 52:1–2 and 61:10, the text says Jerusalem must arise, remove garments of affliction, and clothe herself with beauty, righteousness, and glory from God (5:1–2, 5; cf. Xeravits, 123).

Revelation 21 presents the new Jerusalem as the bejeweled bride of the Lamb and as the holy temple city; it represents the redeemed people of God and the place where God dwells with them forever (see Tabb, *All Things New*, 174–84). The "holy city" that comes down from heaven (21:2) contrasts sharply with the doomed harlot city, Babylon (14:8). John's depiction of the adorned bride (21:2, 10–11) alludes to Isa. 61:10 LXX (cf. 62:5). The jewels of Jerusalem's wall, foundations, and gate recall Isa. 54:11–12 LXX. Various details of Rev. 21:1–22:5, including the city's twelve gates, its perfect symmetry, and God's glorious presence, are patterned after Ezek. 40–48, signaling the fulfillment of Ezekiel's temple prophecy in the new creation (Beale, *Temple*, 350–52).

Summary

Thematic parallels between the Apocrypha and the NT reflect their common dependence on the OT. These authors present similar ethical instructions while reflecting different motivations. NT authors diverge significantly from the Apocrypha by defining God's people according to faith in Christ rather than Abrahamic ancestry, insisting that the eschaton has broken into history, and declaring that salvation has come to gentiles to make Israel jealous. Moreover, Jesus is the righteous servant par excellence, whose vicarious suffering and victorious resurrection fulfill the Scriptures and achieve salvation for God's people, both Jews and gentiles.

See also OT Use of the OT: Comparison with the NT Use of the OT; *other Apocrypha articles*; *Dead Sea Scrolls articles*; *Mishnah, Talmud, and Midrashim articles*; *Philo articles*; *Pseudepigrapha articles*; *Septuagint articles*; *Targums articles*

Bibliography. Achtemeier, P. J., *1 Peter*, Herm (Fortress, 1996); Bauckham, R., "Tobit as a Parable for the Exiles of Northern Israel," in *The Jewish World around the New Testament*, WUNT 233 (Mohr Siebeck, 2008), 433–59; Beale, G. K., *The Book of Revelation*, NIGTC (Eerdmans, 1999); Beale, *The Temple and the Church's*

Mission, NSBT 17 (InterVarsity, 2004); Beck, B. E., "Imitatio Christi and the Lucan Passion Narrative," in *Suffering and Martyrdom in the New Testament*, ed. W. Horbury and B. McNeil (Cambridge University Press, 1981), 28–47; Camponovo, O., *Königtum, Königsherrschaft und Reich Gottes in den frühjüdischen Schriften*, OBO 58 (Vandenhoeck & Ruprecht, 1984); Carson, D. A., "1 Peter," in *CNTUOT*, 1015–46; Ciampa, R. E., and B. S. Rosner, "1 Corinthians," in *CNTUOT*, 695–752; Collins, J. J., *Daniel*, Herm (Fortress, 1993); deSilva, D. A., *Introducing the Apocrypha*, 2nd ed. (Baker Academic, 2018); deSilva, *The Jewish Teachers of Jesus, James, and Jude* (Oxford University Press, 2012); Doble, P., *The Paradox of Salvation*, SNTSMS 87 (Cambridge University Press, 1996); Doran, R., *2 Maccabees*, Herm (Fortress, 2012); Ellis, N., *The Hermeneutics of Divine Testing*, WUNT 2/396 (Mohr Siebeck, 2015); Fitzmyer, J. A., *First Corinthians*, AB 32 (Yale University Press, 2008); France, R. T., *The Gospel of Matthew*, NICNT (Eerdmans, 2007); Gera, D. L., *Judith*, CEJL (de Gruyter, 2014); Goodrich, J. K., "The Word of God Has Not Failed," *TynBul* 67 (2016): 41–62; Horrell, D. G., "'Race,' 'Nation,' 'People,'" *NTS* 58 (2012): 123–43; Jewett, R., *Romans*, Herm (Fortress, 2007); Jipp, J. W., "Luke's Scriptural Suffering Messiah," *CBQ* 72 (2010): 255–74; Koester, C. R., *Revelation*, AB 38A (Yale University Press, 2014); Kolarcik, M., "The Book of Wisdom," in *NIB*, 5:437–600; Longman, T., III, *How to Read Daniel* (InterVarsity, 2020); Moo, D. J., *The Letter to the Romans*, 2nd ed., NICNT (Eerdmans, 2018); Moore, C. A., *Daniel, Esther, and Jeremiah: The Additions*, AB 44 (Doubleday, 1977); Moore, *Tobit*, AB 40A (Doubleday, 1996); Nickelsburg, G. W. E., *Resurrection, Immortality, and Eternal Life in Intertestamental Judaism and Early Christianity*, rev. ed. (Harvard University Press, 2006); Pao, D. W., and E. J. Schnabel, "Luke," in *CNTUOT*, 251–414; Rosner, B., "Soul Idolatry: Greed as Idolatry in the Bible," *ExAud* 15 (1999): 73–86; Schreiner, T. R., *Romans*, 2nd ed., BECNT (Baker Academic, 2018); Schüssler Fiorenza, E., *The Book of Revelation*, 2nd ed. (Fortress, 1998); Schwartz, D. R., *2 Maccabees*, CEJL (de Gruyter, 2008); Seim, T. K., "Abraham, Ancestor or Archetype?," in *Antiquity and Humanity*, ed. A. Y. Collins and M. M. Mitchell (Mohr Siebeck, 2001), 27–42; Skehan, P. W., and A. A. Di Lella, *The Wisdom of Ben Sira*, AB 39 (Doubleday, 1987); Stein, R. H., *Jesus, the Temple and the Coming Son of Man* (IVP Academic, 2014); Suggs, M. J., "Wisdom of Solomon 2:10–5," *JBL* 76 (1957): 26–33; Tabb, B. J., *All Things New*, NSBT 48 (IVP Academic, 2019); Tabb, "Is the Lucan Jesus a 'Martyr'?," *CBQ* 77 (2015): 280–301; Toussaint, S. D., "A Critique of the Preterist View of the Olivet Discourse," *BSac* 161 (2004): 469–90; Wills, L. M., *Judith*, Herm (Fortress, 2019); Xeravits, G. G., "The Biblical Background of the Psalms in Baruch 4:5–5:9," in *Studies on Baruch*, ed. S. A. Adams, DCLS 23 (de Gruyter, 2016), 97–134.

Brian J. Tabb

Apocrypha: Use of the OT

The Apocrypha are the collection of Jewish writings from the Second Temple period that are outside of the canonical Hebrew Scriptures but appear in one or more of the three major Septuagint codices (Vaticanus, Sinaiticus, and Alexandrinus). These works include wisdom and poetry (Wisdom of Solomon, Sirach, Prayer of Manasseh, Psalm 151), retellings of or supplements to biblical texts (additions to Esther and Daniel, Baruch, Letter of Jeremiah, 1 Esdras), and narratives (Tobit, Judith, 1–4 Maccabees). This article will consider representative examples of the numerous and varied references to the Scriptures in the Apocrypha.

Criteria for Discerning Use of Scripture

Gregory Beale (29, 31) defines a quotation as "a direct citation of an OT passage that is easily recognizable by its clear and unique verbal parallelism," while an allusion is "a brief expression consciously intended by an author to be dependent on an OT passage." If we follow these definitions, brief allusions to the Scriptures are very common in the Apocrypha, while direct citations are comparatively rare.

The apocryphal books only infrequently introduce biblical citations with introductory formulas. Tobit 2:6 refers to "the prophecy of Amos" to introduce a direct citation of Amos 8:10. Some variation of "Moses said" occurs four times in the corpus. Second Maccabees 1:29 alludes to Exod. 15:17; 2 Macc. 7:6 cites Deut. 32:36; and 4 Macc. 17:19 quotes Deut. 33:3. Second Maccabees 2:11 quotes Moses, but the source of the saying is unclear ("They were consumed because the sin offering had not been eaten"); this enigmatic citation may relate loosely to Lev. 10:16–20 (see Schwartz, 164). "The Lord said" introduces biblical references in Sus. 5, 53. The latter includes a verbatim citation of Exod. 23:7 LXX, while the source of the former appeal is unclear and appears to be crafted to suit the author's narrative (deSilva, *Introducing*, 253).

Fourth Maccabees 18:14–19 includes several explicit citation formulas: "the scripture of Isaiah" (*tēn Ēsaiou graphēn*; Isa. 43:2), "the songs of the psalmist David" (Ps. 34:19 [33:20 LXX]), "Solomon's proverb" (Prov. 3:18), "the query of Ezekiel" (Ezek. 37:3), and "the song that Moses taught" (Deut. 32:39). While the NT regularly introduces scriptural citations as *graphē*, 4 Macc. 18:14 offers the only such use in the Apocrypha. These writings frequently make general references to the law of Moses (e.g., Tob. 7:13) or "the words of the prophets" (e.g., Bar. 1:21). Biblical allusions in the Apocrypha are also commonly signaled by references to well-known biblical figures or stories (e.g., Sir. 44–49; 3 Macc. 2:4–7).

Presuppositions for Interpreting Scripture

Among Jews during the Second Temple period, "Scripture was on nearly everyone's mind" (Kugel, 122). Jews during this time, including the authors of the Apocrypha, shared four basic assumptions underlying their interpretation of Scripture (Kugel, 131–32; cf. Longenecker, 6–7).

First, Jewish interpreters assumed that "all of Scripture came from God and all of it was sacred" (Kugel, 132). For example, Sirach identifies the law as the perfect expression of God's eternal wisdom given to Israel as an inheritance (24:8–9, 23), Wisdom refers to "the imperishable light of the law" (18:4), and Tobit stresses the sure fulfillment of the prophets' words (14:4–8; cf. 1 Esd. 1:57).

Second, they assumed that biblical texts were "cryptic," with hidden meanings to uncover (Kugel, 132). For example, Ben Sira explains that the Most High "reveals the traces of hidden things" (Sir. 42:19) and that the scribe devoted to God's law will search out "the hidden meanings of proverbs" and "the obscurities of parables" (39:3).

Third, Jewish interpreters assumed that "Scripture was altogether harmonious in all its details and altogether true" and, moreover, that their own beliefs and practices were consistent with biblical teaching (Kugel, 132). The preface to Sirach explains that Ben Sira devoted himself to studying "the Law and the Prophets and the other books of our fathers" and wrote his book of wisdom to encourage others to "make even greater progress in living according to the law" (ESV). Likewise, in 2 Macc 15:9 and 4 Macc. 18:10 the faithful receive instruction and encouragement from "the law and the prophets."

Fourth, they believed that the Scriptures written long ago remained "altogether relevant to people in the interpreters' own day" (Kugel, 132). Thus, the Jews must seek guidance from the ancient text and carefully observe the laws about proper conduct. For example, 4 Maccabees commends adopting "a way of life in accordance with the law" (2:8; cf. 2:23; 5:16), and Tobit urges his son to "keep the law and the commandments . . . so that it may be well with you" (14:9 ESV).

The Abiding Authority of the Law

As devout Jews, the authors of the apocryphal books affirm the foundational contours of the biblical narrative: God created the world and human beings (Wis. 2:23; 11:17; 15:11; Sir. 15:14), delivered his people from Egypt (1 Macc. 4:9; 3 Macc. 6:4; Bar. 2:11; 2 Esd. 1:7), chose Jerusalem as the place for worship (Tob. 1:4), gave Israel the sacred law (Sir. 24:23), and must alone be worshiped and feared (Let. Jer. 5–6; Bel 5). These authors uniformly assume the law's divine truthfulness, supreme authority, and enduring relevance for God's people.

Throughout the Apocrypha, faithful Jews keep the law and appeal to its authoritative commands in all areas of life. In Tob. 6:13 and 7:12, levirate marriage is practiced according to the law of Moses (cf. Deut. 25:5–6). Tobit restates the law's directive to pay the worker his wages (4:14; cf. Lev. 19:13), affirms God's creational design for marriage (Tob. 8:6; cf. Gen. 2:18; 1 Esd. 4:20), and extends the command to honor one's father and mother to one's in-laws (Tob. 10:12; cf. Exod. 20:12). In 1 Maccabees, Judas dismisses soldiers, builds an altar, and offers sacrifice following the law's directives (*kata ton nomon*; 1 Macc. 3:56; 4:48, 53). Daniel invokes the authority of Exod. 23:7 to chastise the elders for unjustly condemning innocent Susanna (Sus. 53). First Esdras 5:48 recounts that the people offer sacrifices and celebrate the feast of booths "in accordance with the directions in the book of Moses the man of God." In 1 Esd. 8:82–85 (8:79–82 LXX), Ezra summarizes how the people have transgressed God's authoritative commands given by the prophets, citing "a medley" of several biblical texts, including Lev. 18:24–30 (Bird, 264).

First through Fourth Maccabees stress the law's authority over against competing claims to authority. The law given by the Creator God accords with nature and trains people in true virtue and proper worship (4 Macc. 5:23–25). Thus, when a gentile king or any human authority contradicts or sets aside the divine law (1 Macc. 1:41–50), the faithful must zealously obey God's commands (2:50). The devout martyrs stress their willingness to die rather than transgress the sacred law (2 Macc. 6:28; 7:30; 4 Macc. 6:27, 30; 13:9). The aged priest Eleazar in 3 Macc. 6:15 invokes the authority of God's word in Lev. 26:44 when he prays that God would not neglect his people in the land of their enemies "just as you have said."

Many of these books refer explicitly or implicitly to the covenantal framework of Deuteronomy. For example, Bar. 1:15–2:26 is a penitential prayer modeled after Dan. 9:4–19 in which the author recounts how "the Lord confirmed his word" (Bar. 2:1 ESV) by bringing upon sinful Israel the punishments threatened in Deuteronomy (see deSilva, *Introduction*, 222–23). In 2 Macc. 2:17–18, the author reflects on how God has saved his people and restored the inheritance, kingship, priesthood, and sanctification "as he promised through the law." He then expresses hope that soon God will show mercy and "will gather us from everywhere under heaven," alluding to Deut. 30:3–5. Similarly, the prayer in Tob. 13:2–6 alludes to Deuteronomy to affirm that no one can escape God's hand (Deut. 32:39), God will gather his scattered people (30:3), and God's people must turn to him with all their heart and soul (30:2). Thus, Tobit appeals to God's character and promise as the foundation for his hope of Israel's future restoration (Bauckham, 436).

The Fulfillment of Prophecy

Apocryphal books occasionally invoke the authority of biblical prophecy to indicate that the prophets' words either have come to pass or express Israel's future hope. Ben Sira entreats God to "raise up prophecies" and "let your prophets be found trustworthy" in his prayer for divine mercy for Israel (Sir. 36:20–21 AT [vv. 14–15 LXX]).

He asserts that the prophet Isaiah "was great and trustworthy in his visions" and that "he saw the future, and comforted the mourners in Zion," and "revealed what was to occur to the end of time" (Sir. 48:22, 24–25). Moreover, Ben Sira recounts that Jerusalem was destroyed "by the hand of Jeremiah" (49:6 AT).

Sirach 47:22 insists that "the Lord will never forsake his mercy" (AT; cf. 2 Sam. 7:15) and will never take away the seed of David but has given him "a root" (cf. Isa. 11:1). Patrick Skehan and Alexander Di Lella (528) assert that this text reflects "the Messianic hope of Ben Sira's day," though some scholars dismiss any messianic expectation in Sirach (cf. Collins, 108). Moreover, Sir. 48:10 notes that "it is written" that Elijah is ready "at the appointed time" to calm God's wrath, "to turn the heart of a father to a son and to restore the tribes of Jacob," a combined reference to Mal. 4:4–6 (3:22–24 LXX) and Isa. 49:6.

Tobit "remembered the prophecy of Amos" (Tob. 2:6), citing Amos 8:10. Amos indicts Israel for oppressing the poor (8:5–6) and prophesies that God will remember Israel's deeds and turn their feasts into mourning (8:7, 10). In Tob. 2:1–6, Tobit prepares to share the feast of Pentecost with the poor but learns of a poor man's murder. He buries the man's body and then eats in sorrow. Tobit quotes Amos 8:10 to highlight his own piety. The citation is ironic: Amos prophesies judgment on those who exploit the poor, but Tobit's feasting turns to mourning because he helps the poor (Nowell, 1002). Tobit's tears here also preview his anguished prayer in 3:1–6, where he grieves over his personal misfortunes and the reproaches he endures (Bauckham, 439).

Tobit 14 stresses the sure fulfillment of prophecy. On his deathbed, Tobit charges his son Tobias and his grandsons to leave Nineveh for Media because of prophesied judgment on the city (v. 4). The text of 14:4 is disputed: some manuscripts (e.g., Sinaiticus) refer to Nahum's prophecy against Assyria and Nineveh and the sure fulfillment of "everything that was spoken by the prophets of Israel" (NRSV; cf. NETS), while other manuscripts (e.g., Vaticanus) refer to "what Jonah the prophet said about Nineveh, that it will be overthrown" (ESV). A reference to Nahum's prophecy of coming destruction of Nineveh (Nah. 1:1; 2:8–10, 13; 3:18–19) fits the context of Tobit better than does Jonah, whose preaching led to Nineveh's repentance, not its demise (Fitzmyer, 326). In 14:5, Tobit confidently declares that Israel will receive mercy from God, return to the land, and rebuild Jerusalem and the temple "when the times of fulfillment shall come," summarizing various prophecies of Israel's postexilic restoration and reiterating Tobit's confidence in Jerusalem's glorious future (cf. 13:16–17). The use of *plēroō* ("fulfill") for prophetic fulfillment in 14:5 is unique within the Apocrypha. The book's final verse states that Tobit heard of the city's destruction before he died and "rejoiced over Nineveh" (14:15), illustrating Tobit's own piety and guaranteeing the fulfillment of the rest of the prophets' predictions (Bauckham, 448).

Baruch 5:7 alludes to Isa. 40:4–5 to express the hope of joyous salvation for Israel as "God has ordered." Baruch includes additional allusions to Isaiah's restoration prophecies, as in 4:29 ("everlasting joy," cf. Isa. 35:10), 4:30 ("comfort," cf. Isa. 40:1), and 5:1–2 ("put on . . . glory," cf. Isa. 52:1; "crown," cf. Isa. 61:10).

First Maccabees alludes to Daniel when describing Israel's disastrous "covenant with the Gentiles" (1 Macc. 1:11; Dan. 9:27) and Antiochus's invasion of Egypt (1 Macc. 1:16–20; cf. Dan. 11:25–28). The "desolating sacrilege" (*bdelygma erēmōseōs*) erected on the altar in 1 Macc. 1:54 also clearly recalls the book of Daniel (9:27; 11:31; 12:11). Jonathan Goldstein (45) contends that 1 Maccabees "seems to take delight in proving the oracles of Daniel false," but the evidence suggests that the author of 1 Maccabees interprets the tyrant's desecrating actions as a fulfillment of Daniel's prophecies. First Maccabees 3:4 likens Judas Maccabeus to "a lion" and "a lion's cub," which alludes to Jacob's famous deathbed prophecy of Judas's royal line (Gen. 49:9). The author then recalls the praise of Israel's king in Ps. 72:17 in 1 Macc. 3:9 ("his memory is blessed forever," AT), strengthening the picture of Judas as Israel's awaited king. At the same time, 1 Maccabees acknowledges the absence of prophets in Israel (9:27) and anticipates a future day when "a faithful prophet would arise" and instruct Israel (14:41 NETS; cf. 4:46; Deut. 18:15).

As they await martyrdom, the noble brothers and their mother express confidence that the Lord will have compassion on them "as Moses declared in his song" (2 Macc. 7:6; cf. Deut. 32:36). Fourth Maccabees claims that the martyrs' hopes of vindication have been fulfilled already (9:8; 17:18), citing for support Deut. 33:3 LXX: "All the sanctified are under your hands" (4 Macc. 17:19 AT). Deuteronomy recalls how God "spared" his holy people and gave them the law as an inheritance (33:3–4), and 4 Maccabees applies this text to the martyrs' immortal life in God's heavenly presence (see Tabb, 90–91).

Biblical Analogy or Illustration

The Apocrypha regularly appeal to OT people and events to illustrate a theological principle or draw an analogy between the Scriptures and the situations of the authors and their readers. Sometimes the analogical use of Scripture serves a hortatory aim: readers should "remember" biblical exemplars so they can imitate their piety amidst present adversity (e.g., 1 Macc. 2:51–60; 4 Macc. 18:10–19; Tob. 4:12).

The story of Judith evidently draws inspiration from the story of Jael and Sisera, where God delivers Israel by a woman's hand (Judg. 4:9; Jdt. 8:33; 16:5; see deSilva, *Introducing*, 95–96; White, 5). Judith appeals to Simeon's violent revenge against Shechem as an example of zeal for God (Jdt. 9:2–4; cf. Gen. 34:25–31; Jub. 30:2–6), reversing Jacob's curse on Simeon and Levi in Gen. 49:5–7 (deSilva, *Introducing*, 96). In contrast, 4 Macc.

2:19 chides Simeon and Levi for their anger and lack of temperance when they slaughtered the Shechemites. The author commends the example of Moses, who "controlled his anger by reason" when opposed by Dathan and Abiram in Num. 16:12–15 (4 Macc. 2:17).

Wisdom of Solomon appeals to various positive and negative examples from Genesis and Exodus (though avoiding proper names), illustrating the principle that "wisdom rescued from troubles those who served her" (Wis. 10:9). Enoch pleased God and was "taken up" (4:10; cf. Sir. 44:16). Wisdom protected Adam, "the first-formed father of the world," and steered "the righteous man" Noah in the ark (Wis. 10:1, 4). Wisdom recognized "the righteous man" Abraham and kept him strong (10:5), guided Jacob when he fled from Esau (10:10), and did not abandon Joseph when he was sold (10:13). Wisdom then rescued "a holy people and blameless race" from their oppressors (10:15), led them through the Red Sea (10:18), and prospered them by Moses, "a holy prophet" (11:1). In contrast, Cain killed his brother and perished (10:3), the "Five Cities" were burned for their wickedness (10:6), the Egyptians were drowned in the sea (10:19), and the Canaanites were destroyed for their detestable practices (12:3–6). Wisdom rehearses at length the biblical story of Israel's exodus from Egypt and preservation in the wilderness (11:1–14; 16:1–19:17). The author particularly highlights the greatness and fittingness of God's judgments on the Egyptians (11:16; 17:1; cf. 3 Macc. 2:6–7) and God's merciful discipline of and unfailing help for his people (Wis. 11:9; 19:22). Wisdom's treatment of the exodus events may move beyond analogy to typology, as the plagues against Egypt "become a prototype for God's present and future judgments of the world as well" (deSilva, *Introduction*, 145; Grabbe, 35, accepts typology in Wisdom "with caution").

Ben Sira demonstrates a "thorough familiarity" with the Scriptures as he extols the patriarchs, prophets, and other "famous men" (Sir. 44:1) to bolster his readers' resolve (Skehan and Di Lella, 500). Sirach's sweeping survey includes eight exemplars from the Pentateuch and stresses God's covenants. The list begins with Enoch, "an example of repentance" (44:16; cf. Philo, *Abraham* 17). Then Ben Sira names Noah (44:17–18), Abraham (44:19–21), Isaac and Jacob (44:22–23), Moses (44:23–45:5), Aaron (45:6–22), and Phinehas (45:23–24), highlighting the covenants God made with each of these heroes as well as with King David (45:25; cf. 47:11). The sage then praises Joshua and Caleb for leading Israel into its inheritance (46:1–10), the judges (46:11–12), Samuel the prophet (46:13–20), Nathan (47:1), David (47:2–11), his "wise son" Solomon (47:12–22; cf. 1 Kings 5:12), and the faithful kings Hezekiah and Josiah (48:17–22; 49:1–3). Ben Sira recalls the folly of Solomon (47:19–21) and the sins of Rehoboam, Jeroboam, and all the other kings who forsook the law (47:23–25; 49:4–5). Sirach also extols the deeds and ministries of the prophets Elijah and Elisha (48:1–16), Isaiah (48:20, 22–25), Jeremiah (49:6–7), Ezekiel (49:8), and the twelve prophets (49:10), as well as later leaders Zerubbabel, Jeshua, and Nehemiah (49:11–13). Sirach 49:14–16 concludes this expansive review with five individuals from Genesis: Enoch, Joseph, Shem, Seth, and Adam. Elsewhere Ben Sira likens the law's overflowing wisdom to the famous ancient rivers named in Gen. 2:10–14—the Pishon, Tigris, Euphrates, and Gihon—as well as to the Jordan at harvest time (Sir. 24:25–27).

In 1 Maccabees, the dying Mattathias summons his sons to "show zeal for the law" and "remember the deeds of the fathers" (2:50–51 ESV), naming Abraham, Joseph, Phinehas, Joshua, Caleb, David, Elijah, Hananiah, Azariah, Mishael, and Daniel (2:52–60; cf. 4 Macc. 18:10–19). In 3 Macc. 6:1–9, an aged priest summons God to show mercy to his people and invokes biblical examples of divine deliverance, including the exodus from Egypt and the rescue of the three friends from the fiery furnace, Daniel from the lions, and Jonah from the sea monster's belly. Similarly, 4 Maccabees appeals to Isaac's fearlessness when Abraham prepared to sacrifice him, to Daniel in the lion's den, and to Hananiah, Azariah, and Mishael in the fiery furnace as examples of faith in God and endurance of pain (16:20–23; cf. 18:11–13). Moreover, 18:14–19 includes a chain of biblical quotations that offer encouragement for those who willingly endure suffering out of loyalty to God (cf. deSilva, *4 Maccabees*, 260). The author here appeals to "the scripture of Isaiah" (Isa. 43:2), "the songs of the psalmist David" (Ps. 34:19 [33:20 LXX]), "Solomon's proverb" (Prov. 3:18), "the song that Moses taught" (Deut. 32:39), and "the query of Ezekiel" (Ezek. 37:3), the last of which may express not merely a biblical analogy but the prophetic hope of resurrection (Tabb, 117–18). Fourth Maccabees also illustrates its thesis that devout reason is master of the passions (1:1) by appealing to the example of Joseph overcoming sexual desire (2:2–6) and David pouring out his drink though he "was burning with thirst" (3:15). The Prayer of Manasseh contrasts the king's need for repentance with Abraham, Isaac, and Jacob, "who did not sin against you" (v. 8).

Multiple apocryphal books highlight Phinehas son of Eleazar as an exemplar of zeal for the Torah. Wisdom presents Phinehas as "a blameless man," the Lord's servant who acts as Israel's "champion" as he propitiates the divine wrath and puts an end to the disaster in the desert (18:20–21). Ben Sira similarly commends Phinehas as "zealous in the fear of the Lord" and recalls that God established with him "a covenant of peace" (Sir. 45:23–24 ESV). According to deSilva, 1 Maccabees presents Mattathias and Judas as "Phinehas redivivus" (*Introducing*, 279). Mattathias "burned with zeal for the law, just as Phinehas did against Zimri" (1 Macc. 2:26). He then summons his sons to "remember the deeds of the fathers" and highlights Phinehas's deep zeal (2:51, 54). Judas then "turned away wrath from Israel" by destroying the ungodly (3:8), again recalling the deeds of Phinehas (Num. 25:4, 11). Likewise, 4 Macc. 18:12 commends "the zeal of Phinehas," whose example the martyrs emulate.

Proverbial Use of Scripture

The authors of the Apocrypha often employ well-known biblical words and phrases to express a general proverbial truth consistent with Israel's Scriptures. Such usage may or may not draw attention to the original context of these words or phrases but reflects the author's deep familiarity with biblical language.

Sirach frequently uses biblical words and phrases proverbially and imitates the style of the biblical books he has devoted his life to studying (noted by his grandson in the prologue). Ben Sira regularly paraphrases sayings from Proverbs; for example, Sir. 1:14 ("To fear the Lord is the beginning of wisdom") restates Prov. 1:7, and Sir. 2:6 ("Trust in him . . . make your ways straight") adapts Prov. 3:5–6 (for additional illustrations, see Skehan and Di Lella, 43–44). Sirach 2:18 rephrases 2 Sam. 24:14—David's penitent response after the census—and generalizes it into a proverbial saying: "We will fall into the hands of the Lord and not into the hands of people" (ESV).

Judith reminds the elders that "God is not like man" (Jdt. 8:16 ESV), recalling Num. 23:19. She also draws on the Song of Moses when identifying God as "helper" and "defender" (Jdt. 9:11 AT; cf. Exod. 15:2) and declaring that "the Lord is a God who crushes wars" (Jdt. 16:2; cf. Exod. 15:3; for additional parallels with Exod. 15, see Wills, 287–88). In Tob. 5:1, Tobias answers his father Tobit, "I will do everything that you have commanded me," reflecting the formula of Josh. 1:16 to stress his pious obedience.

Wisdom frequently alludes to the Scriptures to stress the benefits of wisdom, God's providential care for the righteous, and the judgment that awaits the wicked. For example, the author affirms the proverbial truth that wisdom is "found by those who seek her" (Wis. 6:12; cf. Prov. 8:17). Alluding to Ps. 2:10, the author exhorts "rulers of the earth" and "kings" to love righteousness and learn wisdom or else face judgment (Wis. 1:1; 6:1). The wicked are like chaff driven by the wind (5:14; cf. Ps. 1:4), while the righteous are secure "in the hand of God" (Wis. 3:1; cf. Eccl. 9:1; Deut. 33:3; 4 Macc. 17:19). Wisdom 3:13–14 also states that the barren woman and the godly eunuch are "blessed," proverbial statements that reflect Isa. 54:1 and 56:4–5.

Expansion or Exposition of Biblical Accounts

Multiple books of the Apocrypha include expansions or expositions of biblical accounts. Sometimes the authors summarize or retell biblical material, while at other times they include stories, prayers, and other material to supplement the biblical text.

Wisdom retells various accounts of biblical history from creation through the wilderness wanderings (10:1–11:14), stressing the saving power of wisdom and the folly of neglecting it. The book also offers extended reflection on Solomon's prayer for wisdom (7:7–11; 9:1–18; 1 Kings 3:5–9).

First Esdras illustrates several literary features of other Jewish works (like Jubilees) that offer rewritten accounts of biblical history: (1) First Esdras retells and reinterprets the biblical narrative, (2) it combines biblical and nonbiblical material, (3) the author engages in implicit rather than overt interpretation, and (4) the book serves as a companion—not a substitute—for earlier biblical accounts (Bird, 8). First Esdras retells material from 2 Chron. 35–36, most of Ezra, and Neh. 7:73–8:13 (Bird, 2). It also inserts a long, entertaining story about a contest between three bodyguards of King Darius (1 Esd. 3–4). This account highlights the ascent of Zerubbabel, who is shown to be the wisest of the three guards and urges the king to fulfill his vow to build the temple (4:42–46).

Second Maccabees 1:18–2:15 recounts a narrative featuring the biblical figures Nehemiah and Jeremiah and "the Feast of the Fire" (1:18 AT), which does not appear in the OT. The author credits Nehemiah with building the temple (1:18), probably conflating the well-known governor who rebuilt Jerusalem's walls with an earlier Nehemiah who accompanied Zerubbabel, mentioned in Ezra 2:2; Neh. 7:7 (cf. Doran, 48).

The Prayer of Manasseh is a brief penitential prayer attributed to King Manasseh, presumably with reference to the time when he humbled himself before God during his imprisonment in Babylon (2 Chron. 33:12–13). This text may have been inspired by the reference to Manasseh's "prayer to his God" recorded in the Chronicles of the Kings of Israel (2 Chron. 33:18). Prayer of Manasseh parallels Ps. 51 in several places: v. 12 ("I have sinned, and my lawless acts I know," AT) alludes to Ps. 51:3 (50:5 LXX), while v. 14 ("according to your great mercy") recalls Ps. 51:1 (50:3 LXX). The author also depicts the Lord as "gracious and merciful . . . repenting concerning evils," alluding to Joel 2:13 LXX (Pr. Man. 7 AT; cf. Exod. 34:6).

The title of Psalm 151 ascribes this apocryphal psalm "to David as his own composition" (*idiographos eis Dauid*). Written in the first person from David's perspective, the psalm serves as "a liturgical retelling and abridgement of 1 Sam. 16–17" (deSilva, *Introducing*, 331). Psalm 151 rehearses how David tended Jesse's sheep (v. 1; cf. 1 Sam. 16:11), made an instrument (v. 2; cf. 1 Sam. 16:16), was anointed instead of his brothers (vv. 4–5; cf. 1 Sam. 16:6–13), and went out to meet the Philistine, beheaded him, and thus removed Israel's reproach (vv. 6–7; cf. 1 Sam. 17:36, 48, 51).

The Letter of Jeremiah presents itself as a communication of the prophet to the exiles, like the one in Jer. 29:1–28. It repeatedly charges readers not to fear idols, which are not gods (Let. Jer. 14, 22, 28, 64, 68), likely reflecting on Jer. 10:5. The author's extended polemic against the folly and impotence of idols also alludes to other biblical texts, such as Deut. 4:27–28; Ps. 115:3–8; and Isa. 46:6–7 (cf. deSilva, *Introducing*, 235).

The Greek version of Esther includes six major additions not found in the MT: (1) Mordecai's dream and the eunuchs' plot (11:2–12:6 [A 1–17]); (2) the king's letter authorizing the Jews' destruction (13:1–7 [B 1–7]); (3) two prayers by Mordecai and Esther (13:8–14:19 [C 1–30]); (4) Esther's dramatic reception by the king (15:1–16 [D 1–16]); (5) the king's letter reversing the earlier decree (16:1–24 [E 1–24]); and (6) the interpretation of Mordecai's dream and a brief postscript (10:4–11:1 [F 1–11]; cf. Reinhartz, 642; deSilva, *Introducing*, 112–14). While the Hebrew version of Esther lacks any explicit mention of God, Greek Esther repeatedly highlights God's role in the events of the story. For example, Mordecai sees "what God has determined to do" (11:12 NETS [A 11]), addresses the Lord as "King" and "God of Abraham" (13:9, 15 [C 2, 8]), and recalls how God made heaven and earth and redeemed Israel from Egypt (13:10, 16 [C 3, 9]).

The Greek editions of Daniel also contain significant additional material not found in the Hebrew-Aramaic book. After the faithful Jews are thrown into the fiery furnace in Dan. 3:23, the Greek text includes two long prayers joined by a brief narrative bridge. Prayer of Azariah is a prayer of confession that is similar to Dan. 9:4–19, while Song of the Three Jews is a hymn of praise that follows Ps. 136 in form and Ps. 148 in content (deSilva, *Introducing*, 244). These liturgical additions emphasize the wonder of God's saving power (Pr. Azar. 20; Sg. Three 66) in response to the pious prayers of his people. Greek Daniel also includes the legendary stories of Susanna (Dan. 13) and Bel and the Dragon (Dan. 14). In the former, Daniel saves Susanna after she is falsely accused of adultery, and the false witnesses are executed according to the law (Sus. 62; cf. Deut. 19:18–19; Apoc. Zeph. 6:10). In the latter, Daniel continues to worship "the living God" while refusing to revere "man-made idols" (Bel 5). He exposes the idol Bel as a fraud and destroys it (vv. 19–22). This tale may reflect the influence of Isa. 45:1–46:7 (deSilva, *Introducing*, 260), which recounts the fall of "Bel" (Isa. 46:1; cf. Bel 22) and stresses the uniqueness of the Creator God (Isa. 45:18, 21; cf. Bel 5) and the idols' impotence (Isa. 45:16, 20; 46:7; cf. Bel 6). Daniel also slays the Babylonians' revered dragon (Bel 23–27) and then survives for six days in the lions' den (31–42). During this time an angel transports the prophet Habakkuk to Babylon, where he brings dinner to Daniel (33–39; cf. Liv. Pro. 12:7).

Summary

The authors of the Apocrypha appeal extensively to the Scriptures for guidance and hope as they encourage readers to maintain their Jewish identity and remain faithful to God in the face of various challenges in a gentile-dominated world (cf. deSilva, *Introducing*, 2–3). They stress the abiding authority of the law of Moses, the sure fulfillment of the prophets' words, the dangers and folly of worshiping man-made idols, and various examples from the Scriptures of piety and zeal for the law that are worthy of emulation.

See also OT Use of the OT: Comparison with the NT Use of the OT; *other Apocrypha articles; Dead Sea Scrolls articles; Mishnah, Talmud, and Midrashim articles; Philo articles; Pseudepigrapha articles; Septuagint articles; Targums articles*

Bibliography. Bauckham, R., "Tobit as a Parable for the Exiles of Northern Israel," in *The Jewish World around the New Testament*, WUNT 233 (Mohr Siebeck, 2008), 433–59; Beale, G. K., *Handbook on the New Testament Use of the Old Testament* (Baker Academic, 2012); Bird, M. F., *1 Esdras*, SeptCS (Brill, 2012); Collins, J. J., *Jewish Wisdom in the Hellenistic Age*, OTL (Westminster John Knox, 1997); deSilva, D. A., *4 Maccabees*, SeptCS (Brill, 2006); deSilva, *Introducing the Apocrypha*, 2nd ed. (Baker Academic, 2018); Doran, R., *2 Maccabees*, Herm (Fortress, 2012); Fitzmyer, J. A., *Tobit*, CEJL (de Gruyter, 2003); Goldstein, J. A., *I Maccabees*, AB 41 (Doubleday, 1976); Grabbe, L. L., *Wisdom of Solomon*, GAP (Sheffield Academic, 1997); Kugel, J. L., "Early Jewish Biblical Interpretation," in *The Eerdmans Dictionary of Early Judaism*, ed. J. J. Collins and D. C. Harlow (Eerdmans, 2010), 121–41; Longenecker, R. N., *Biblical Exegesis in the Apostolic Period*, 2nd ed. (Eerdmans, 1999); Nowell, I., "The Book of Tobit," in *NIB*, 3:973–1072; Reinhartz, A., "Esther (Greek)," in *The Oxford Bible Commentary*, ed. John Muddiman and John Barton (Oxford University Press, 2007), 642–49; Schwartz, D. R., *2 Maccabees*, CEJL (de Gruyter, 2008); Skehan, P. W., and A. A. Di Lella, *The Wisdom of Ben Sira*, AB 39 (Doubleday, 1987); Tabb, B. J., *Suffering in Ancient Worldview*, LNTS 569 (Bloomsbury T&T Clark, 2017); White, S. A., "In the Steps of Jael and Deborah," in *"No One Spoke Ill of Her,"* ed. J. C. VanderKam (Scholars Press, 1992), 5–16; Wills, L. M., *Judith*, Herm (Fortress, 2019).

BRIAN J. TABB

Apostolic Hermeneutics: Description and Presuppositions

Analyzing the NT writers' interpretive and theological uses of the OT is a crucial step to understanding their reference to the OT. An aspect of this step is to reflect on what hermeneutical and theological presuppositions

This essay is a revision of G. K. Beale, *Handbook on the New Testament Use of the Old Testament* (Baker Academic, 2012), 13–25, 95–102, and of Beale, *A New Testament Biblical Theology* (Baker Academic, 2011), 651–749 (the latter work is abbreviated *NTBT* throughout the essay). These two works should be consulted to see the majority of the secondary sources appealed to in support.

underlie these uses. This essay explores these presuppositions. There are *at least* six presuppositions that can undergird a NT writer's use of the OT, though almost every one of them is debated to one degree or another. This essay briefly comments on the purported biblical origin of these presuppositions and the significance of the presuppositions for interpreting the OT in the NT. It is crucial to understand these presuppositions; without them it can be difficult to apprehend how a NT writer is interpreting the OT in line with its original meaning, which I believe is always the case to one extent or another.

Presuppositions of NT Writers in Interpreting the OT

Jesus and the apostles hold two grand assumptions that underlie these presuppositions. First, the OT Scriptures are "sacred" and are the Word of God. Therefore, all authoritative theological discussion must be based on and proceed from this sacred body of literature (on which, e.g., see Hays and Green, 130). For Jesus and his followers, what the OT said, God said; and what God said, the OT said (on which, see Warfield, 299–407). Second, and almost as ultimate, hearers and readers could not sufficiently understand Jesus and the apostles' theological presuppositions and interpretations of the OT without the aid of God's Spirit (on which, see, e.g., Ellis, *Old Testament*, 116–21; see 1 Cor. 2:6–16 for a classic formulation of this by Paul). These two more ultimate presuppositions are typically not discussed in connection with the following six presuppositions to be elaborated on, and so I include them here at the beginning.

At times, the following presuppositions also underlie the NT writers' interpretation of the OT. The purpose here is to elaborate on these assumptions, especially with respect to their biblical basis.

Corporate solidarity is a concept whereby one person represents many others. This concept has been well-discussed by H. W. Robinson (1964), though it was rightly qualified by later critics, some of whose sources are included in his bibliography (e.g., see Porter and esp. the introduction by Gene M. Tucker in Robinson's book [pp. 7–13], which surveys the various criticisms of Robinson's view; see also Ellis, *Prophecy*, 170–71, who discusses corporate solidarity or representation as an important presupposition in OT and NT studies).

In the OT, kings and prophets represented the nation Israel, and fathers represented families. The many people represented by one king, prophet, or father were looked upon as if they had done the righteous or sinful deed done by that representative, so that the many also received the same blessing or judgment for that deed as their representative. Among several examples of this concept in the NT is the sin and punishment of the first Adam, who represents all humanity, so that all humanity is seen to have committed Adam's sin and thus to be deserving of the punishment of that sin. In antithesis, Christ, the last Adam, performs an act of righteousness that results in resurrection life. He represents believing humanity, so that they are viewed as having done the righteous act and thus as deserving of resurrection life (see Rom. 5:12–19).

Christ as the Messiah represents true Israel of the OT and true Israel—the church—in the NT. This presupposition follows from the first. Christ represents Israel, and Christ does what Israel should have done but failed to do. Those who believe in Christ, whether Jew or gentile, become identified with him as the continuation of true Israel in her eschatological form. This presupposition is not new but is in the OT.

OT evidence for this presupposition. The ideas that the Messiah would represent latter-day Israel and the gentiles would become part of true end-time Israel are not merely NT presuppositions but have their roots in the OT itself.

Isaiah 49:3–6 is among the clearest statements in the OT that in the latter days the Messiah would sum up true Israel in himself. Here the servant is called "Israel": "He [the LORD] said to me, 'You are My Servant, Israel, in whom I will show My glory'" (v. 3 NASB). Part of his latter-day mission is "to raise up the tribes of Jacob and to restore the protected ones of Israel" (v. 6). Now, the servant cannot be the entire nation of Israel, since the sinful nation cannot restore itself. Neither can the servant be merely a faithful remnant of the nation, since the remnant is still sinful, and it would be redundant to say the remnant's mission was to restore the remnant (which "the protected ones" refers to in v. 6). Some have identified the servant with Isaiah, but there is no indication that he ever accomplishes such a mission, especially as further elaborated on in Isa. 53. Furthermore, he too is sinful and needs the healing mission explained there. Thus, the servant in Isa. 49:3 is best understood to be an individual messianic servant who will sum up Israel in himself and restore the remnant of Israel.

But how is the notion of the messianic servant summing up true Israel relevant to gentiles becoming true Israel in the eschaton? Since this servant is to be the summation of true Israel, all who want to identify with true Israel, whether Jew or gentile, will have to identify with him (which is the implication of Isa. 53). The OT implicitly connects the individual true Israel, the servant (or Israel's end-time king), and gentiles who identify with him. As we will see, the NT does so explicitly, and other OT passages prophesy that in the latter days converted gentiles will be identified as true Israelites. For example, Ps. 87 speaks of gentiles being "born" in Zion in the eschaton, so that they are considered as native-born Israelites:

> A Psalm of the sons of Korah. A Song.
> His foundation is in the holy mountains.
> The LORD loves the gates of Zion

More than all the other dwelling places of
Jacob.
Glorious things are spoken of you,
City of God. *Selah*
"I shall mention Rahab [Egypt] and Babylon
among those who know Me;
Behold, Philistia and Tyre with Cush: 'This one
was born there.'"
But of Zion it shall be said, "This one and that
one were born in her";
And the Most High Himself will establish her.
The LORD will count when He registers the
peoples,
"This one was born there." *Selah*
Then those who sing as well as those who play
the flutes will say,
"All my springs of joy are in you." (NASB)

The "glorious things" spoken of "Zion," the "city of God" (vv. 2–3), include the notion that the gentile nations will be considered to have been "born there" (v. 4). The reference to "there" in v. 4, where the nations are born, refers to "Zion" and the "city of God" in vv. 2–3. In v. 6, "the LORD will count when He registers the peoples" refers to a final, end-time accounting of the gentile peoples who "know Him" (v. 4) and who are considered true eschatological Israelites because they have been "born there" (v. 6b)—that is, in Zion, the city of God. Thus, people who have their national and ethnic origins among gentile nations will nevertheless be viewed as part of true end-time Israel.

Furthermore, Zech. 2:11 contains one of the rare OT uses of "My people" in reference to those outside of ethnic Israel: "Many nations will join themselves to the LORD in that day [i.e., the day of Israel's eschatological restoration] and will become *My people*. Then I will dwell in your midst, and you will know that the LORD of hosts has sent Me to you" (NASB). Elsewhere the name "My people" is almost always reserved for Israel (including its other three occurrences in Zechariah [8:7, 8; 13:9]). Again, the likelihood is that the nations in Zech. 2:11, who have made pilgrimage to Israel (see 2:11; 8:22–23), are considered to have become converts to Israel, so that they take on Israel's typical name of "My people."

Other OT passages could also be discussed that show gentiles will become true Israelites in the latter days (e.g., Isa. 19:18–25; 66:18–21; Ezek. 47:21–23).

NT evidence for this presupposition. The NT affirms that those who identify by faith with Christ, whether Jew or gentile, become identified with him as true eschatological Israel. This takes place when people identify by faith with Jesus as God's Son, and so they become adopted sons of God (Rom. 3:26–4:7; 8:12–25). Referring to Jesus as "the Son of God" is another way of referring to him as Israel, since this was one of the names by which Israel was called in the OT (note God's "son" in Exod. 4:22–23; Deut. 14:1; Ps. 2:7; Isa. 1:2, 4; 63:8; Hosea 1:10; 11:1; God's "firstborn" in Exod. 4:22; Jer. 31:9; cf. Ps. 89:27, which calls the coming Messiah God's "firstborn"). The title "Son of Man" is yet another way of alluding to him as Israel (Dan. 7:13 in its context; Ps. 80:17).

It is important to recall that Jesus's titles "Son of Man" and "Son of God" reflect the OT figures of both Adam and Israel (on which, see Beale, *NTBT*, 393–429).

The notion of Christians being part of God's Israelite family is expressed well in Galatians. This idea is based on the notion that there is one Messiah, who is identified with Israel and represents his people (which we have found above in Isa. 49). Paul views Christ to be the summation of true Israel and understands all whom Jesus represents, whether Jew or gentile, to be true Israel.

Galatians 3:16 indicates that Christ is the true Israelite seed promised to Abraham: "Now the promises were spoken to Abraham and to his seed. He does not say, 'And to seeds,' as referring to many, but rather to one, 'And to your seed,' that is, Christ" (NASB). Then Gal. 3:29 says that those who come into union with Christ also become the true Israelite seed promised to Abraham: "And if you belong to Christ, then you are Abraham's descendants [lit., "seed"], heirs according to promise" (cf. the similar concept in 3:26, "For you are all sons of God through faith in Christ Jesus," to 4:4–5, "God sent forth his Son . . . that we might receive the adoption as sons" [all NASB]). It is important to remember that the OT references to the "seed of Abraham" refer repeatedly and only to the people of Israel and not to gentiles, though the Israelite, Abrahamic seed was to bless gentiles (e.g., Gen. 12:7; 13:15–16; 15:5; 17:8; 22:17–18; 26:4; 32:12). The same is true in Judaism. The identification in Gal. 3:29 that both believing Jew and Greek (3:28) are Abraham's seed is, then, a reference to them as the continuation of true Israel. Again, in Gal. 4:28 Christians are said to be "like Isaac, . . . children of [the Abrahamic] promise" (NASB).

Following quite naturally on the heels of Paul's identification of Christians with Abraham's seed and the heavenly Jerusalem (Gal. 4:26–27) is the conclusion of Gal. 6:16. After Paul says "neither is circumcision anything nor uncircumcision, but a new creation" (v. 15 NASB), he says regarding "those who will walk by this rule" of no ethnic divisions in the new creation: "Peace and mercy be upon them—that is, upon the Israel of God" (AT). Thus, Jewish and gentile Christians together are called "the Israel of God," an identification virtually the same as in Gal. 3:29, where both are called "Abraham's seed." Some commentators, however, see that "peace and mercy" are pronounced here first on gentile Christians and then separately on Jewish Christians. This view is possible but improbable. Commentators are increasingly recognizing the identification of both Christian gentiles and Jews as "Israel" in 6:16, especially since one of the main points of the earlier part of the epistle is that there are no longer any ethnic distinctions between God's people. Consequently, Paul concludes the letter by saying that believing Jews and gentiles are the true "Israel of God."

Christ is also the embodiment of Israel and the fulfillment of Hosea's typological prophecy about Israel as a "son": "[Joseph] was there [in Egypt] until the death of Herod, that what was spoken by the Lord through the prophet might be fulfilled, saying, 'Out of Egypt did I call My Son'" (Matt. 2:15 AT). Matthew implicitly identifies Jesus's followers with him as the fulfillment of the "son" of Hosea 11:1 (cf. the implications of Jesus as "the Son of the living God" in Matt. 16:16 in Beale, *NTBT*, 406–12).

In Exod. 19:6 God says to Israel, "You shall be to Me a kingdom of priests," which likely means that as a whole nation they are to serve as kingly mediators of divine revelation between God and the unbelieving nations (see also Isa. 43:10–13). They are not faithful in this witnessing task. Therefore, God raises up a new priest-king, Jesus, and those identified with him are made a kingdom of priests, as expressed by Rev. 1:6; 5:10, which allude to Exod. 19:6 (so also 1 Pet. 2:9). Recall that Exod. 19:6 was a commission that Israel never fulfilled (cf. Isa. 40–55), but note the significance of "he made us" in Rev. 1:6 (AT; likewise 5:10), which means Christ has now empowered the church to be and do what Israel of old was not and could not do. The church is enabled by Christ to have unmediated access to God's presence and to be mediators of light to the nations.

Acts is important to discuss with respect to the gentiles participating in the promises of Israel. Some contend that when gentiles become believers in Acts, they become part of the beginning fulfillment of Israel's restoration prophecies. Despite this acknowledgment, these commentators argue that the gentile Christians do not come to be considered end-time Israel but instead exist alongside Israelite believers and continue in their primary identification as gentiles, albeit redeemed gentiles. However, Acts says that gentiles share equal footing with Jewish believers because they are to be viewed as true end-time Israel in identification with Jesus, the true Israel. Accordingly, the church, composed of believing Jews and gentiles, is the commencing fulfillment of the prophecies of Israel's restoration. In this respect, having discussed at the beginning of this section the servant of Isa. 49 as eschatological Israel, the citations of this prophecy in Luke-Acts will now be examined (see table 1).

Table 1. Isaiah 42 and 49 in Luke-Acts

Isa. 42 and 49	Isa. 42:6–7, 17 and 49:4, 6 in Luke-Acts
Isa. 49:3: "He said to me, 'You are My Servant, *Israel*, in Whom I will show My *glory*.'"	**With Application to Christ:** Luke 2:32: ". . . *a Light* of revelation *to the Gentiles*, and the *glory* of Your people *Israel*."
Isa. 49:5–6: "And now says the LORD, who formed Me from the womb to be His Servant, to bring Jacob back to Him, so that *Israel* might be gathered to him (for *I am glorified* in the sight of the LORD, and My God is My strength), He says, 'It is too small a thing that You should be My Servant to raise up the tribes of Jacob and to restore the preserved ones of Israel; *I will also make You a light of the nations so that My salvation may reach to the end of the earth*.'"	Acts 26:23: ". . . that the Christ was to suffer, and that by reason of His resurrection from the dead He would be the first to proclaim *light both to the Jewish people and to the Gentiles*."
Isa. 42:6b–7: "And I will appoint you as a covenant to the people, *as a light* to the nations, *to open blind eyes, to bring out prisoners from the dungeon* and those who dwell in *darkness* from the prison."	**With Application to Paul (and Others):** Acts 13:47: "For so the Lord has commanded us, '*I have placed You as a light for the Gentiles, that You may bring salvation to the end of the earth*.'"
See also Isa. 42:16: "*I will make darkness into light before them*."	Acts 26:17–18: "I am sending you, *to open their eyes* so that they may turn from *darkness* to *light* and from the *dominion of Satan* to God."

Note: Quotations are adapted from the NASB.

The quotations in Luke 2:32 and Acts 26:23 are applied to Christ's mission, which fulfills the servant Israel's mission in Isa. 49:1–6. Acts 13:47 views Paul and his colleagues to be fulfilling the same prophecy. It is likely the presupposition that the one Christ, Israel the servant, represents Paul and his special prophetic messengers, so that they also take on Christ's function—namely, the mission of Israel to be a light to the nations. In the very same manner, the servant prophecy of Isa. 42:6–7 is put on the shoulders of Paul in Acts 26:18, when he describes his mission as Christ's apostle.

Paul's identification with the servant Israel and his mission is pointed to further by reference to Paul being "a servant and . . . a witness" (Acts 26:16) in carrying out the servant's mission, a double designation also used in describing Israel's mission in Isa. 43:10: "You are my witnesses . . . and my servant." (See likewise 32:15; 43:12; 49:6, all of which refer to Israel [though 49:6 is the messianic servant] and are now applied to the apostles and, by implication, to their followers, though they do not uniquely fulfill the Isa. 42 and 49 prophecy in the way Paul does.) Thus, the salvation of the church is depicted as the end-time restoration of Israel.

There are many prophecies about Israel's restoration that are applied to and begin fulfillment in the church. The first relevant passage is Rom. 9:24–26: ". . . even us, whom He also called, not from among Jews only, but also from among Gentiles. As He says also in Hosea, 'I will call those who were not My people, "My people," and her who was not beloved, "Beloved." And it shall be that in the place where it was said to them, "you are not My people," there they shall be called sons of the living God'" (NASB). Here Paul quotes from Hosea 2:23 and 1:10. In each case the prophecy is about the restoration of Israel from captivity. At the end-time restoration, Israel will again be faithful and be called "My people" and "Beloved" and "Sons of the living God," whereas formerly in sin and rebellion in captivity Israel was called "Not God's people" and "Not beloved." What is striking in Rom. 9:25–26 is that not only Jews but also gentiles, "whom [God] also called" (v. 24), are seen to be the beginning fulfillment of these two restoration prophecies from Hosea (see Beale, *NTBT*, 707).

Several other OT prophecies about Israel's restoration are fulfilled in the church, but the scope of this essay does not allow for elaboration (Isa. 49:8 in 2 Cor. 6:2 [though apparently applied to Paul]; Lev. 26:11–12 and Ezek. 37:27 in 2 Cor. 6:16; Isa. 52:11 and Ezek. 11:17 and 20:34 in 2 Cor. 6:17; Isa. 54:1 in Gal. 4:27–29; Isa. 57:19 in Eph. 2:17; for discussion of these references, including Rom. 9:24–26, see Beale, *NTBT*, 705–28).

This discussion has significance for understanding what it means that the predominantly gentile church continues true Israel. Being identified with true Israel is neither a narrow parochial identification nor one that erases gentile identity. Rather, the church is also identified with what it means to be true Adam, especially in its identification with Jesus, the true Israel and last Adam. Consequently, for the church to be the beginning of true end-time Israel is to begin to be identified with the original purposes of Adam, of true humanity, which Christ has fulfilled.

Therefore, it is important to maintain that the church is not merely like Israel but actually *is* Israel. Converted gentiles were prophesied to come and to be identified with Israel and Israel's God in the latter days. Such eschatologically converted gentiles would become identified with Israel as had gentiles in the past, such as Rahab, Ruth, and Uriah. Their gentile identity was not eradicated, but they came to have a greater identity as true Israelites.

Consequently, it is not an "allegorical or spiritualizing hermeneutic" by which the predominantly gentile church is to be identified with Israel, but it is what we might call a "legal representative" or "corporate hermeneutic" that underlies this identification of the church. This second presupposition of Christ as true Israel and the church as true Israel is critical to understanding why OT promises of eschatological restoration are applied to Christ and the church in the NT, and why both are the inaugurated end-time fulfillment of the prophesied restoration of Israel.

There are numerous images, names, and prophecies of Israel that are applied to the church. Many others have seen that Christ and the church fulfill what is prophesied of Israel in the OT (France, 50–60, 75; Wright, 66–71, 87; LaRondelle; Beale, "Reconciliation"; Snodgrass, 27). The NT references cited above are merely the tip of the iceberg of a larger testimony to the church as being true Israel (see Beale, *NTBT*, 651–749, esp. 669–79).

History is unified by a wise and sovereign plan so that the earlier parts are designed to correspond and point to the later parts. This third presupposition is essential to the idea of "typology" (cf., e.g., Matt. 5:17; 11:13; 13:16–17; on typology, see Dodd, 128, 133; Foulkes; Hamilton). The temporal merisms applied to God's—and Christ's—relation to history show that reference to the beginning and end of history includes all events in between, and that these events are under their sovereign sphere (see Eccles. 3:1–11; Isa. 46:9–11; Rev. 1:4, 8, 17; 4:8; 21:6; 22:13; cf. Eph. 1:11). For example, Eccles. 3:1–11 (NASB) begins, "There is an appointed time for everything. And there is a time for every event under heaven." Then vv. 2–8 list several merisms to explain this ("a time to give birth and a time to die," v. 2; "a time to tear down and a time to build up," v. 3). The point is summarized in Eccles. 3:11: God "has made everything beautiful in his time" (AT) and he has done his work "from the beginning even to the end." God's sovereignty over history underlies the notion of typology, since what God has done in the past is designed by him to foreshadow future events; God shapes later events after earlier events.

The definition and nature of typology has been one of the thorniest issues to face in OT-in-the-NT studies in the twentieth and early twenty-first centuries. Part of this debate concerns the position of some who see the NT's typological interpretation of the OT to be close to allegory, an approach that reads foreign NT meanings into OT passages. Accordingly, some think typological interpretation has no continuity with the original meaning of OT texts and reads Christ or the church into OT passages that have nothing to do with either.

Therefore, this issue bears upon the question of the NT's continuity or discontinuity with the OT. One major question here is whether typology essentially indicates an analogy between the OT and NT or whether it also includes some kind of foreshadowing. Even among those who may include the notion of the forward-looking or prophetic element, most hold that typology is prophetic only from the NT writer's viewpoint and *not from the OT vantage point*. Many would qualify this further by saying that, although the OT author did not consciously intend to indicate any foreshadowing sense, the fuller divine intention did include it. Some who also hold to a *retrospective* prophetic view from the NT writer's viewpoint, however, may see this not as part of the fuller divine intention in the OT but as a completely new meaning given under inspiration. The last two positions, especially the last, view the NT's typological interpretation as not in line with the meaning of the OT passage. Some other scholars do not hold to any form of divine inspiration of Scripture and view the NT's typological interpretation of the OT to be a distortion of the OT intention.

The following definition of typology includes both analogy and a prophetic element: *the study of analogical correspondences among revealed truths about persons, events, institutions, and other things within the historical framework of God's special revelation, which, from a retrospective view, are of a prophetic nature and are escalated in their meaning.* According to this definition, the essential characteristics of a type are (1) analogical correspondence, (2) historicity, (3) a pointing forward (i.e., an aspect of foreshadowing or presignification), (4) escalation, and (5) retrospection.

But even when the immediate context of a passage does not indicate that something is being viewed typologically from the OT author's conscious vantage point, the wider canonical context of the OT usually provides hints or indicates that the passage is typological (for example, see Beale, *Handbook*, 133–47, on Isa. 22:22 in Rev. 3:7). This is affirmed by D. A. Carson (92–93):

> The NT writers insist that the OT can be rightly interpreted only if the entire revelation is kept in perspective as it is historically unfolded (e.g., Gal. 3:6–14). Hermeneutically this is not an innovation. OT writers drew lessons out of earlier salvation history, lessons difficult to perceive while that history was being lived, but lessons that retrospect would clarify (e.g., Asaph in Ps. 78; cf. on Matt. 13:35). Matthew does the same in the context of the fulfillment of OT hopes in Jesus Christ. We may therefore legitimately speak of a "fuller meaning" than any one text provides. But the appeal should be made, not to some hidden divine knowledge, but to the pattern of revelation up to that time—a pattern not yet adequately [or fully] discerned. The new revelation may therefore be truly new, yet at the same time capable of being checked against the old [and thus clarifying the older revelation].

Therefore, NT writers may interpret historical portions of the OT as having a forward-looking sense in the light of the whole OT canonical context. For example, various eschatological prophecies' portrayals of a coming king, priest, and prophet throughout OT revelation were so intrinsically similar to the historical descriptions of kings, priests, and prophets elsewhere in the OT that the latter were seen to contain the same pattern as the former (except for the historical failure) and thus to point forward to the ideal end-time figures who would perfectly carry out these roles.

There can be a variety of evidence within OT contexts themselves that a narration about a person, event, or institution contains a foreshadowing sense. One such indication is formulated by Gerhard von Rad. He observes that certain sections of the OT have repeated narrations of Yahweh commissioning people to fill certain offices (like those of the judges, prophets, priests, or kings). These narrations cluster repeated descriptions of a commission, the failure of the one commissioned, and judgment—and then the same cycle is repeated (accordingly, note the book of Judges and Isa. 22:15–25, as well as the rise and fall of the many kings as narrated in Kings and Chronicles). Von Rad sees a typological significance in these narratives. He contends that the literary clustering of repeated commissions and failures is evidence of a type within the OT itself. Furthermore, the forward-looking nature of these cyclic narratives of people and events can be discerned within the OT itself and often within each of the narratives themselves (see von Rad, 2:372–74; see also 2:384–85.). If von Rad is correct, and I believe he is, this would mean that we can recognize OT types as having a prophetic element even *before* the fuller revelation of their fulfillment in the NT.

There are various criteria for discerning types in the OT, but there is not space to elaborate on these here (see Beale, *Handbook*, 19–22). Likewise, we cannot address here whether or not modern readers can recognize types in the OT that are not recognized by the NT (see Beale, *Handbook*, 22–25, where I give an affirmative answer).

Typology can be called contextual exegesis within the framework of the canon since it primarily involves the interpretation and elucidation of the meaning of earlier parts of Scripture by later parts, which assumes an underlying presupposition of the unity of history.

The age of eschatological fulfillment has come in Christ. This fourth presupposition has its roots in the OT. The phrase "latter days" is prophetic and refers to a future time when (1) there will be a tribulation for Israel consisting of oppression (Ezek. 38:14–17), persecution (Dan. 10:14; 11:27–12:10), false teaching, deception, and apostasy (Dan. 10:14; 11:27–35); (2) after the tribulation Israel will seek the Lord (Hosea 3:4–5) and be delivered (Ezek. 38:14–16; Dan. 10:14; 12:1–13), and their enemies will be judged (Ezek. 38:14–16; Dan. 10:14; 11:40–45; 12:2; cf. also eschatological terms such as "time of the end" in Dan. 8:19; 11:40); (3) this deliverance and judgment will occur because a leader (messiah) from Israel will finally conquer all of its gentile enemies (Gen. 49:1, 8–12; Num. 24:14–19; Isa. 2:2–4; Mic. 4:1–3; Dan. 2:28–45; 10:14–12:10); (4) God will establish a kingdom on the earth and rule over it (Isa. 2:2–4; Mic. 4:1–3; Dan. 2:28–45) together with a Davidic king (Hosea 3:4–5); (5) after the time of tribulation and persecution, Dan. 11–12 says there will be a resurrection of the righteous and unrighteous (so Dan. 11:30–12:3 [see Beale, "Eschatological," 14]). The NT sees that fulfillment of the prophesied latter days has begun in the NT, though their consummation is still future (see, e.g., Mark 1:15; Acts 2:17; 1 Cor. 10:11; Gal. 4:4; 1 Tim. 4:1; 2 Tim. 3:1; Heb. 1:2; 9:26; 1 Pet. 1:20; 2 Pet. 3:3; 1 John 2:18; Jude 18).

Jesus is identified as divine. A fifth assumption is Jesus's identity as Yahweh incarnate. NT authors apply OT passages concerning Yahweh to Christ. Examples of this presupposition are found throughout the NT. The Synoptics, for example, narrate the stilling of the storm, wherein Jesus calms the chaotic waters (Mark 4:35–41 and par.). According to Ps. 89:8–10, only Yahweh possesses the power to still the sea. In his prologue, John reads the creation account of Gen. 1 and identifies Jesus as the eternal, creative "Word" (1:1–5). Later, after citing Isa. 53:1 and 6:10, John states, "Isaiah said this because he saw [Jesus's] glory and spoke about him" (12:38–41). Paul even places Jesus squarely within Israel's Shema (1 Cor. 8:4) and claims that Jesus was the "rock" that "accompanied" the first generation of Israelites in the wilderness (1 Cor. 10:4). Revelation, too, reuses symbols that are exclusively reserved for Yahweh in the OT and applies them to Jesus (e.g., Dan. 7:9 in Rev. 1:14). Many more examples could be given, but the point is clear enough: the apostles draw lines of correspondence between Yahweh in the OT and Jesus in the NT because they believe that Jesus is God.

This presupposition is rooted in the OT. For example, Isa. 9:6–7 refers to the coming Messiah as "Mighty God, Eternal Father" (NASB; see likewise Mic. 5:2; Ps. 110:1, among other texts expressing the deity of the coming Messiah).

Christ is the goal toward which the OT points and is the end-time center of redemptive history, which is the key to interpreting the earlier portions of the OT and its promises. This sixth presupposition is based partly on the above presuppositions about the unity of history and inaugurated eschatology. On these two grounds, it follows that the later parts of biblical history function as the broader context for interpreting earlier parts because they all have the same, ultimate, divine author who inspires the various human authors. One deduction from this premise is that, as the goal of the OT, Christ is the major lens through which to see the OT (on which see, e.g., Luke 24:25–27).

Conclusion

There is not space to argue more substantially for the biblical support of these six presuppositions. Other scholars working in this field have also recognized the viability of these assumptions. However, not all scholars agree that the NT writers had all these presuppositions. For example, some do not agree that Christ represents the true Israel of the OT *and* the true Israel—the church—in the NT. Some also would not accept the notion of inaugurated eschatology. For the most part, however, since the 1980s scholars have generally accepted that the NT writers possessed these presuppositions. I have dedicated most discussion to the second and third presuppositions because they are sometimes the hardest to comprehend for today's readers.

It is within the framework of these six presuppositions that the whole OT is perceived to point to the new covenant, eschatological age, via both direct prophecy and the indirect prophetic adumbration of Israel's history. This latter point is especially significant: OT history is understood as containing historical patterns that foreshadow the eschaton. Consequently, the nation of Israel, its kings, prophets, and priests, and its significant redemptive episodes compose the essential ingredients of this sacred history. This is what has been referred to above as "typology," defined as the study of correspondences between earlier and later escalated events, persons, institutions, and so forth within the historical framework of biblical revelation that have a prophetic function from a retrospective viewpoint. Typology is sometimes faulted for not being in line with original OT meanings because it sometimes refers to purely historical events as being prophetically "fulfilled" (cf. the introductory *plēroō* formula) when they appear not to be intended as prophecies from the OT author's perspective. But such an approach is understandable in view of its foundational assumptions that history is unified and that God has designed the earlier parts to correspond and point to the latter parts, especially to events that have happened in the age of eschatological fulfillment in Christ (see presuppositions 3–5). The concept of prophetic fulfillment should not be limited to fulfillment of direct verbal prophecies from the OT but should be broadened to include an indication of the "redemptive-historical relationship of the new, climactic revelation of God in Christ to the preparatory, incomplete revelation to and through Israel" (Moo, 191).

The broad, redemptive-historical perspective of these assumptions was the dominant framework within which Jesus and his followers thought, and it served as an ever-present heuristic guide to the OT. The matrix of these six perspectives is the lens through which the NT authors interpreted OT passages. Consideration of the immediate literary context of OT verses, which is what most interpreters affirm as an essential part of the historical-grammatical method, should therefore be supplemented by the canonical literary context, especially in the light of the last presupposition. In this respect, we need to consider that the NT may quote an earlier OT passage in a way that has been interpretively developed later in the OT canon. Sometimes an earlier OT text undergoes interpretive development by several subsequent OT texts, so that the canonical trajectory of that development is key to knowing how the NT understands the earlier OT text being cited.

When these six presuppositions are related closely to the NT's interpretative approach, they provide a satisfying explanation for C. H. Dodd's observations and conclusions, especially accounting for why the NT does not focus on verses independent of their OT contexts. The NT writers' selection of OT texts is not random or capricious or out of line with the original

OT meaning; rather, it is determined by this wider, overriding perspective, which views redemptive history as unified by an omnipotent and wise design. The unchanging principles of faith in God, God's faithfulness in fulfilling promises, the rebellion of the unbelieving, God's judgment of them, and his glory are expressed throughout this design. Therefore, the NT authors had an emphatic concern for overarching historical and canonical patterns and for significant persons (e.g., prophets, priests, and kings), institutions, and events that were essential constituents of such patterns. This emphasis was facilitated by the belief that Christ and the church now represent true Israel, so that it was attractive to see various segments and patterns of Israel's history from the OT as recapitulated in Christ and the church in the NT. This, then, was a holistic perspective guiding the writers away from concentrating on exegetically or theologically insignificant minutiae in passages and directing them to quote individual references as signposts to the broader redemptive-historical theme(s) that emerge from the immediate and larger OT context. Is this not the most likely explanation for the phenomenon in the NT of so few identical quotations from the same segments of the OT?

In addition, changed applications of the OT in general do not necessitate the conclusion that these passages have been misinterpreted, whether or not typology is involved. For example, Matthew applies to Jesus what the OT had intended for Israel (e.g., Matt. 2:4–22), and Paul applies to the church what had been intended for Israel (e.g., Rom. 9:24–26). Some believe the NT's affirmation that such prophecies about Israel are fulfilled in the Messiah or in the church is not in line with the original meaning of those prophecies. What should be challenged in these two kinds of apparently different applications (Matthew and Paul), however, is not their interpretation of the OT but the validity of the abovementioned presuppositional framework through which they interpret the OT, especially the assumption that Christ corporately represents true Israel and that all who identify with him by faith are considered part of true Israel. If these presuppositions are valid, then their interpretation of the OT in the two above categories of usage must also be plausible.

Nevertheless, it would be possible to hold these presuppositions and still interpret the OT noncontextually, as some scholars do. Along these lines, some scholars, especially those fueled by postmodern concerns, believe that the NT writers' presuppositions distort their interpretation of the OT, since these new presuppositions are foreign to the OT, having been created by the early Christian community in light of the coming of Christ. Accordingly, reading these foreign presuppositions into the OT skews the original meaning of the OT. What is often not acknowledged, however, is that every one of the above six presuppositions is rooted in the OT, as I have attempted to show briefly in this essay. Even the last presupposition about the Christ-oriented design of the OT is anticipated in the messianic strands of the OT beginning with Gen. 3:15 and developed, for example, in 49:9–10; Num. 24:17–19; Pss. 2; 89; Isa. 42; 49; 53; Zech. 9:9–10; 12:10.

In addition, it is true that what make the NT's use of the OT different from other early Jewish uses of the OT are its unique presuppositions, though there was a significant overlap of presuppositions with some early Jewish movements. For example, Qumran held in qualified ways to at least the first four presuppositions. They acknowledged corporate solidarity and considered themselves the true Israel. However, they did not believe Christ and the church were true Israel (first and second presuppositions above). They also held to inaugurated eschatology but not that the latter days had begun *in Christ and his coming* (fourth presupposition). The reason for the similarity of presuppositions among some of these Jewish groups is that they, too, modeled their interpretative approach on that of the OT itself. Thus, it is difficult to say that the NT community's presuppositions were radically new and the result of their own socially constructed mindset, unique to the first-century Christian context. Rather, these presuppositions go far back into the OT and span hundreds of years.

Consequently, the NT community's presuppositions are rooted in the OT, which I have noted especially in the first four presuppositions. For instance, the NT authors assumed they were living in the age of the eschaton, partly on the basis that the OT prophesies that the messianic age is to be an "eschatological" period (e.g., Gen. 49:1, 9–10; Num. 24:14–19; Hosea 3:5). There may be other presuppositions that could be discussed, but these are the most important.

The OT roots of the NT's presuppositions make it difficult to say that the NT's interpretive assumptions distort the meaning of OT texts. In this respect, the authors of both Testaments are part of a broadly related, interpretive community that shares the same general worldview and continues to develop earlier meanings with comparable hermeneutical perspectives as time goes on. These presuppositions aid in understanding that the NT's interpretations of the OT fall in line to varying degrees with the contextual meaning of the OT texts themselves and with legitimate extensions and applications of the meaning of OT texts. By interpreting the OT with these presuppositions, the NT writers were following the model of the grandest redemptive-historical interpreter: Jesus Christ (on which, see Luke 24:25–27).

See also Apostolic Hermeneutics: Present-Day Imitation; Contextual and Noncontextual NT Use of the OT; OT Use of the OT: Comparison with the NT Use of the OT; Typology

Bibliography. Beale, G. K., "The Eschatological Conception of New Testament Theology," in *"The Reader*

Must Understand," ed. K. E. Brower and M. W. Elliott (InterVarsity, 1997), 11–52; Beale, *Handbook on the New Testament Use of the Old Testament* (Baker Academic, 2012); Beale, *A New Testament Biblical Theology* (Baker Academic, 2011); Beale, "The Old Testament Background of Reconciliation in 2 Corinthians 5–7 and Its Bearing on the Literary Problem of 2 Corinthians 6:14–7:1," *NTS* 35 (1989): 550–81; Carson, D. A., "Matthew," in *EBC*, 8:1–599; Dodd, C. H., *According to the Scriptures* (Nisbet, 1952); Ellis, E. E., *Old Testament in Early Christianity* (Baker, 1991); Ellis, *Prophecy and Hermeneutic in Early Christianity* (Eerdmans, 1978); Foulkes, F., *The Acts of God* (Tyndale, 1958); France, R. T., *Jesus and the Old Testament* (Baker, 1971); Hamilton, J. M., Jr., *Typology* (Zondervan, 2022); Hays, R. B., and J. B. Green, "The Use of the Old Testament by New Testament Writers," in *Hearing the New Testament*, ed. J. B. Green, 2nd ed. (Eerdmans, 2010), 122–39; LaRondelle, H. K., *The Israel of God in Prophecy* (Andrews University Press, 1983); Moo, D. J., "The Problem of *Sensus Plenior*," in *Hermeneutics, Authority, and Canon*, ed. D. A. Carson and J. D. Woodbridge (Zondervan, 1986), 179–211; Porter, J. R., "Legal Aspects of Corporate Personality," *VT* 15 (1965): 361–80; Robinson, H. W., *Corporate Personality in Ancient Israel* (Fortress, 1964); Snodgrass, K., "Use of the Old Testament in the New," in *The Right Doctrine from the Wrong Texts?*, ed. G. K. Beale (Baker, 1994), 29–51; von Rad, G., *Old Testament Theology*, trans. D. M. G. Stalker, 2 vols. (Harper & Row, 1965); Warfield, B. B., *The Inspiration and Authority of the Bible* (Presbyterian & Reformed, 1948); Wright, N. T., "The Paul of History and the Apostle of Faith," *TynBul* 29 (1978): 61–88.

G. K. Beale

Apostolic Hermeneutics: Present-Day Imitation

"Apostolic Hermeneutics" is a convenient label to refer to the many ways in which the NT writers interpret the OT, even though not all NT writers are apostles and not all of the apostles contribute directly to the corpus of NT documents. This article explores the complex questions surrounding the extent to which contemporary interpreters may mirror the hermeneutics of the apostles—that is, the extent to which today's interpreters of Scripture may or even must follow the examples of the apostles as they interpret the Scriptures that have come down to them.

The Big Picture

Prior to about 1800, Christians tended not to speak of "Old Testament theology" and "New Testament theology" (Carson, "Theology"). From the earliest days of the church, of course, Christians recognized differences between the OT and the NT, and sometimes disputed what those differences meant. These were not merely theoretical debates, but existential: they were bound up with the very self-identity of believers. Not a few of the earliest Christian debates focused on such matters (as reported, e.g., in Galatians, Ephesians, Acts 15). Not until the nineteenth century, however, was there a large-scale and growing perception among many Christian scholars that the two corpora could not easily be woven into a single cloth. This led many to conclude that biblical theology should henceforth remain a purely descriptive and historical discipline, exploring what various believers held to be the truth while steadfastly refusing all attempts to construct a unified and normative canonical theology. By contrast, the same exegetical phenomena encouraged other scholars to focus attention on how the NT writers interpreted the OT texts—on the one hand, to preserve what was distinctive about OT theology (and indeed what was distinctive about the theology of each OT corpus) and, on the other hand, to go about constructing a whole-Bible biblical theology (*eine ganz biblische Theologie*).

Large Patterns

Many writers, springing from diverse theological backgrounds, have highlighted large theological themes that are carried over from the OT to the NT. Such studies also served to highlight numerous themes that did *not* get carried over from the OT to the NT. Otherwise put, energy was poured into establishing lines of both continuity and discontinuity between the Testaments. As the Bible was increasingly perceived to be a pastiche of diverse and fundamentally irreconcilable traditions, other voices inevitably articulated reasons for putting some of those traditions back together.

The influence of C. H. Dodd. One of the most seminal works in this connection is the brief but enormously influential book by C. H. Dodd, *According to the Scriptures: The Sub-structure of New Testament Theology*. Dodd argues that quotations from the OT must be interpreted in their fuller OT contexts, not evaluated as isolated prooftexts stripped of their contexts. As we will see, that thesis can be (and has been) challenged from time to time, but it holds in many places. Two caveats: (1) Dodd unnecessarily restricts the sweep of his study by considering only those OT quotations that are cited by at least two NT authors. In reality, his observations often hold true for those OT quotations that are cited or alluded to by only one NT author. (2) Dodd does not include in his study the many places (especially in the Apocalypse) where a NT writer deploys OT terminology and idiom but does not mean to invite the reader to call to mind the OT context—in the same way that someone may speak of the future stretching out "to the last syllable of recorded time," or may happily acknowledge that "this is the day that the Lord has made," without calling up, respectively, Macbeth or Psalm 18 (see esp. Beale, *Revelation*.) Nevertheless, Dodd's remarkable book has nurtured many contemporary impulses to uncover the ways in which NT writers pick up and develop OT themes. The questions then must be raised: Can contemporary students of Scripture duplicate the readings of the OT found in the NT, so as to tease out further canonical insight? Or are we shut in to discovering and repeating only what the NT writers themselves accomplished?

The Great Tradition. Recent years have witnessed many biblical interpreters distancing themselves from the dominant hermeneutical approaches of the last two centuries or so in favor of what is variously called premodern hermeneutics, or the hermeneutics of the Great Tradition. In particular, the Great Tradition, it is argued, flourished across the centuries before the rise of the historical-critical method. The Scriptures are grounded in God's supernatural self-disclosure, not least in such events as the giving of the law and the resurrection of Jesus. The recent return to an emphasis on the Great Tradition is intended to challenge biblical historical criticism, not least where methodological naturalism undergirds it. On this view, the Bible is in certain respects unlike other books. It is God's revelation and is grounded in the nature and activities of God who has sanctified human words and human processes for his own revelatory purposes. It follows, then, that the "act of reading a biblical text is not a secular act. It actually is a divine-human encounter" (Carter, 32), which in turn calls forth a special hermeneutic. How far we can duplicate such apostolic hermeneutics today will depend in no small measure on our ability to understand and adopt such hermeneutics when we read Scripture.

How the Great Tradition is to be understood is of course disputed. Four features of that tradition must be unpacked. First, if the label "Great Tradition" covers the dominant theological syntheses until the church withered under the naturalistic emphases of the Enlightenment, the sweep of its hermeneutical habits is shockingly broad. It is naive to imagine that one hermeneutical schema controlled the habits of all interpreters. One remembers the polarization between the Antiochene and Alexandrian schools; one cannot ignore the fourfold interpretive schemes that were already well developed by the end of the patristic period (literal, allegorical or typological, moral or prosopological, and anagogical interpretation). Some held that every scriptural passage demands that all four interpretive strategies be deployed, and pleaded apostolic warrant. Christian thinkers living in the heritage of the Reformation largely rejected this fourfold schema. With the passage of time exactly what was meant by some of the common labels skittered around from thinker to thinker. As we will see, terms such as "allegory" and "typology" reflected a wide range of meanings from scholar to scholar (and continue to do so today). In short, extraordinary diversity of both substance and hermeneutic flourished under the Great Tradition.

Second, the locus of the ultimate authoritative revelation was understood differently depending on one's tradition. For the Protestant, the locus of ultimate authority was Scripture itself; for the Catholic, it was a broader deposit given to the church (which in practice meant the magisterium). Both sides were of course committed to finding the supernatural voice of God's self-disclosure, but in practice its locus was disputed.

Third, this meant that not only the locus of the revealed authority was disputed but also the nature and locus of the hermeneutical axioms needed to interpret that revelation. Protestants found that revealed authority in Holy Writ, so therefore clear thinking about the hermeneutical axioms necessary for understanding that Holy Writ occupied much of their attention; on the Catholic side, appeal to apostolic hermeneutics meant, in practice, the hermeneutics of the church, whose interpretive grids were held to be apostolic. Dominant voices in the tradition of Roman Catholicism assigned interpretive authority to the magisterium. In other words, the interpretive key was not a literary matrix or a theological grid, but an ecclesiastical office, stretching from the pope down to the local priest. Others could read the Bible, of course (though they were not normally encouraged to do so), but as for what the Bible means, one was on the surest footing by consulting the magisterium: what the magisterium said the text meant, that was what the text meant. In other words, long before the onset of debates over the extent to which ordinary contemporary Christians are capable of pursuing *apostolic* hermeneutics, the Roman Catholic tradition had erected a barrier to limit the hermeneutical voice of ordinary Christians unless they followed the magisterial line (which Catholicism took to be the apostolic line).

Fourth, perhaps one can usefully speak of the hermeneutics of the Great Tradition (as opposed to the apostolic hermeneutics of the NT) if one envisages a potpourri of diverse interpretive grids that had certain things in common, followed by a substantial hermeneutical break in moving from the Great Tradition to the post-Enlightenment world. Strictly speaking, however, this was a break not so much in hermeneutics as in how one understands the very nature of Scripture. (On the nature of this divergence, see De Chirico.)

Summing up the impact of these features of the Great Tradition, we are driven to two unavoidable conclusions: (1) There was far more diversity in the hermeneutics of the Great Tradition than is commonly admitted. It is an error to claim that the Great Tradition maintained a monolithic hermeneutic that needs to be restored today. (2) While the Great Tradition was still dominant, a bifurcation of hermeneutical traditions developed between Catholicism and Protestantism. (Space prohibits the exploration of the hermeneutical impact of the earlier bifurcation between Catholicism and Orthodoxy.) On the Catholic side of the ledger, the growing reliance on the authority of the magisterium effected a certain hermeneutical order and coherence, but at the expense of sacrificing a reasoned and open hermeneutic, preferring hierarchical control. On the Protestant side of the ledger, the focus of attention was not on the degree to which contemporary scholars and preachers could duplicate the hermeneutics of the writers of the NT, but on what they perceived to be the urgent need for the restoration of Scripture's authority, over against what they held to be the usurpation of Roman Catholicism.

Select Trajectories in the Modern Period

Several phenomena developing during the last two and a half centuries or so have raised fresh questions about the hermeneutics presupposed by the writers of the NT documents, and, implicitly, by today's scholars as they ponder the extent to which they may duplicate the exegesis deployed by NT writers as they interpret OT texts. We may mention three.

Continuity and discontinuity. The first development concerns the lines of continuity and discontinuity between the OT and NT. These concerns captured attention and generated discussion from the earliest years of the church, long before the modern period. It is worth reminding ourselves of some of the roots of such division. No thinking gentile Christian during the first century could be unaware of the Jewish roots of their faith; no thinking Jewish Christian could ignore the tug of the Mosaic tradition. Jewish and gentile believers squabbled openly and sometimes heatedly. At the end of the day, the disputes turned on how to read and interpret the writings of what we today call the OT. Why observe the Jewish food laws if "Jesus declared all foods clean" (Mark 7:19)? Jesus was the Jewish Messiah: must not gentiles therefore be circumcised and become Jews before they could accept the Jewish Messiah as their own (cf. Gal. 2; 5:6; Rom. 4; Acts 15; 1 Cor. 7:18–20)? Paul writes, "One person considers one day more sacred than another; another considers every day alike. Each of them should be fully convinced in their own mind. Whoever regards one day as special does so to the Lord" (Rom. 14:5–6). The turning point, for him, is the Lord's death and impending return (14:9–10). Yet it is easy to see why some Jews regarded such theological advice as a kind of treason, a kind of blasphemy. How could they make common cause with alleged Christ-followers who discarded large swaths of the Torah with troubling ease? Paul can write, "Circumcision is nothing and uncircumcision is nothing. Keeping God's commands is what counts" (1 Cor. 7:19)—but understandably his opponent might respond, "Yes, but circumcision *is* one of God's commands!" It may be exhilarating and enchanting to be told that the old barriers that divided Jew and gentile are abolished, swept aside in the glorious vision of a new humanity (Eph. 2), but the prophets of the old covenant devoted much of their energy toward preserving the distinctions that separated the people of the covenant from the hordes of gentiles who surrounded them and threatened them with assimilation.

For the purposes of this essay, the point to note is that these fundamental differences that caused first-century Christians so much angst were addressed *by way of exegesis of biblical texts*. This is not to say that Christians did not recognize the revelatory claims at the heart of their faith: that is clear, for example, both in the accounts of Paul's conversion (Acts 8–9) and in his own self-understanding (Gal. 1–2). But what is striking is that when Paul wants to establish the rightness of his position, again and again he does so *by appealing to his exegesis of biblical texts*. Something similar could be said for Peter, John, and the author of Hebrews. In the second century, the tensions between these Jew/gentile polarities became so acute in the minds of Marcion and his followers that they ended up jettisoning the OT and substantial parts of the NT. What started out as differences in exegesis led the Marcionite side of the debate to go beyond exegesis to excision. Of course, the followers of Marcion were in the minority and were soon swept aside. But the point is that debates over questions of continuity and discontinuity between the Testaments regularly anchored their appeals in exegesis. In their own self-understanding, biblical interpreters were trying to preserve and imitate the exegesis of the earliest Christian writers.

In short, debates over the patterns of continuity and discontinuity between the Testaments stretch back into the earliest years of the church. There were debates over what those texts said, and thus over the hermeneutics deployed by the various interlocutors, but, with the exception of Marcion and some of his friends, not over the primacy of the text itself. There is no obvious case of a theologian arguing that it is improper to appeal to the same hermeneutical principles that the NT writers themselves used. But as we have seen, by about 1800 the rising emphasis on the discontinuities in our texts (e.g., between the OT and the NT, between different corpora within the OT and the NT, between alleged sources and final form of the text, worked out within an increasingly naturalist matrix) invited a new focus on the hermeneutics that was controlling the discussion. In the burgeoning exegetical freedoms that many scholars enjoyed, one of the things that was increasingly lost was any sense of obligation to work within the constraints of what were perceived to be apostolic hermeneutics.

Biblical theology. A second development was no less important—namely, the complicated rise of biblical theology. Apparently the expression "biblical theology" does not appear in the Western world until the beginning of the seventeenth century, when it was first used to refer to handbooks of biblical prooftexts summarizing Protestant systematic theology. By the time of the Pietists, "biblical theology" had taken on a new meaning: in his influential book *Pia Desideria* (1675), Philip Jacob Spener distinguishes his own "biblical theology" (which nurtured the Pietist movement) from the prevailing orthodoxy, which was "scholastic" or systematic theology. But the biggest jump in meaning surfaces influentially in the title of the inaugural address that J. P. Gabler delivered at the University of Altdorf in 1787. His title (in English translation) was *An Oration on the Proper Distinction between Biblical and Dogmatic Theology and the Specific Objectives of Each*. Gabler was trying to confront the endless theological disputations generated by (as he saw it) philosophical/theological debates grounded in finely tuned dogmatic positions that had little to do with the biblical texts. He proposed that what was needed was a commitment to *biblical* theology, what would today probably be called "exegetical theology." He dared to hope that after theologians had worked for a while on such biblical/exegetical theology, they would achieve greater unanimity as to what the Bible actually says. This would in turn facilitate agreement on how to put the pieces together—that is, on how to construct a dogmatic theology.

Time would show that many scholars were interested in pursuing the more rigorous biblical exegesis advocated by Gabler, but only a much smaller number yearned to make the synthetic leap back to systematics. For our purposes, the point to observe is that what Gabler was envisaging was not so much a new discipline as a renewed emphasis on the biblical texts themselves, in the hope that the concentration on the biblical texts would build up a wholesome unanimity that was trying to imitate the hermeneutics of the NT writers. In reality, it merely engendered as much diversity and disputation over the biblical texts themselves as over the large-scale systematic theologies that had held the primary focus of attention up to this point. What *did* develop, in due course, was the rise of what is now commonly called biblical theology. The terminology is disputed, but at the risk of reductionism we may make the following distinction. Systematic (or dogmatic) theology primarily deploys atemporal and logical forms of analysis to come to an understanding as to what the Bible is saying; biblical theology pays more attention to what is conveyed by the different literary genres, and especially by the temporal developments within the canon. Systematic theology asks questions such as, "What does the Bible say about God?"; biblical theology asks, "What is conveyed about God in the Wisdom literature? What does Isaiah contribute to our understanding of God, and how is that related to, say, the depiction of God in the Pentateuch? How does the theme of the atonement develop over time?"

The development of biblical theology did not take place in a straight line. Not a few scholars continue to insist that there is no such thing as biblical theology, which, in their view, sounds much too monolithic; there is, at best, a wide array of biblical theolo*gies*: the theology of Paul, the theology of Luke, and so forth, and, indeed, mutually incompatible theologies *within* Paul, *within* Luke, *within* Matthew. Others, more optimistic, argue that the cohesion and authority of Scripture can be traced out by carefully studying the biblical theology of the Bible. In any case, a great deal of this work, whether shaped to establish the wholeness and coherence of the Bible or to demonstrate its incoherence, is irrefragably tied to how later biblical writers use earlier writers, or, more specifically, to the question of apostolic hermeneutics.

Extracanonical sources. A third development was perhaps more important yet. Fired by new discoveries and by new ways of reading old texts, many scholars focused attention on how the Scriptures, especially the OT Scriptures, were cited and used by extracanonical sources. Not the least important of these sources have been the Qumran writings. If we can identify with some accuracy and verve how certain scribes, writing within a couple of centuries of the apostles, understood and applied the Scriptures, why should we think it strange if the NT writers understood and applied the same Scriptures in more or less the same ways? Analogous questions are raised by the discovery of the Nag Hammadi codices and the uncovering of new targums. These finds have led to an enormous amount of study focusing on, among other things, allegory, typology, and hook-word links.

Allegory. On the face of it, Paul seems to read parts of the OT historical narrative "allegorically" (Gal. 4:24 ESV; see further below). Many have argued that narrative parables convey only one point, so that when they seem to carry several points (e.g., cf. Mark 4:3–9 and 4:14–20) it is because they have been reshaped into allegories. So, in general, does this understanding of allegory justify referring to such passages as allegorical interpretation of Scripture? If the NT authors sometimes interpret the OT texts allegorically, is there any reason why we should not do so? Indeed, may not this be a mandate to do so? (Cf. Whitman; Young.) On the other hand, a slightly different definition of allegory may well skew our treatment of the subject significantly.

Typology. Typology sees correspondences between, on the one hand, people, institutions, and events in the past, and, on the other, people, institutions, and events in the present (or recent past). Often these parallels are ratcheted up in their most recent display. The many major treatments of the subject do not all agree (see Lampe and Woollcombe; Daniélou; Davidson; Goppelt; Hamilton), but there is a broad consensus that although typology can easily be abused, it nevertheless surfaces often when the NT cites the OT. There is also a growing recognition that typology is tightly tied to the notion of mystery, with its complex insistence that the gospel is simultaneously something that has been predicted in the past and is now being fulfilled, and something that has been hidden in the past and is now being revealed (see esp. Beale and Gladd; Carson, "Mystery"). To put it another way, readers of the NT soon learn to appreciate how the gospel is simultaneously the outgrowth of the old covenant, and something new—or, as J. H. Hutchinson puts it, we must wrestle with the newness of the new covenant. What is more disputed, as we will see, is the extent to which modern readers can appeal to typology to interpret earlier biblical texts, even when there is no unambiguous instance of the NT authors making the same leap.

Hook-word links. Not uncommonly, Jewish exegesis brings together apparently disparate passages by drawing attention to a common word that "hooks" the two passages together. An example often cited from the NT occurs in Rom. 4:1–12. There the apostle cites Gen. 15:6: "Abraham believed God, and it was *counted* to him as righteousness" (Rom. 4:3 ESV). As Paul works out his argument, he draws in Ps. 32:1–2: "Blessed is the man against whom the Lord *will not count* his sin" (Rom. 4:8 ESV). Thus, as Moyise (5–6) reads the passage in Romans, Paul equates "God *reckoning* [*counting*] righteousness to Abraham with God *not reckoning* [*counting*] sin to David," even though these two OT texts come from different periods of Israel's history and are written in different literary genres. The "catch-word link (reckoned, reckon) allows Paul to equate God *reckoning* righteousness to Abraham with God *not reckoning* sin to David" (5). Thus, Paul "deduces something that is not stated in Genesis 15, namely that God's reckoning righteousness to Abraham implies that his sins are forgiven" (5). Whatever one makes of this particular instance of hook-word links (on which, see below), there can be little doubt that such literary phenomena have enriched, but also rendered more complicated, our efforts to think clearly about the exegetical use of the OT by the NT writers, and therefore about the possibility of following their examples.

These three, of course—allegory, typology, and hook-word links—are but three examples of the many literary phenomena that surround the topic of this essay. (To survey highly varied literary phenomena in Jewish literature around the turn of the era, one might usefully consult Bowker, *Targums*; Instone-Brewer; see also the Dead Sea Scrolls articles and the Philo articles elsewhere in the dictionary.) But we may reflect briefly on these, as exemplary of many others, to demonstrate how many literary phenomena are afflicted with competing definitions that render large-scale agreement almost impossible.

Consider allegory. We have already observed how common it is for some scholars to detect allegory whenever a narrative parable makes many points as opposed to just one. If the story of the sower (or of the soils, as many prefer) is limited to making one point—perhaps that the fruitfulness of the Word of God in the life of people depends on their receptivity—we may assume we are dealing with a parable. But if there are numerous subsidiary points (e.g., the rocky soil and the other soils are all identified by their moral equivalents), then we must infer that the parable has been "allegorized." But not a few specialists in the parables argue that as long as the apparently subsidiary points all flow naturally out of the fundamental story, and indeed are virtually dictated by that story, then it is improper to detect allegory—that is, to label these subsidiary points in the narrative as allegorical interpretations or extrapolations. By contrast, when Philo insists that the three patriarchs, Abraham, Isaac, and Jacob, represent the three fundamentals of a Greek education, it is exceedingly difficult to warrant that conclusion by anything in the text of Genesis: the links found in a genuine allegory are established not by anything in the text, but by extratextual factors (see esp. Weder).

On such considerations, the parable of the sower in Mark 4 is not allegorized, while Philo frequently resorts to undisputed allegory. If we are going to make any advances in our attempts to decide whether today's interpreters are warranted in following the apostles in their appeal to "allegory," we had better find a way to decide what kind or kinds of "allegory" appear in the NT. Or again, a form of "allegory" is found in Gal. 4:24 (KJV: "which things are an allegory"; *allēgoreō*). But certainly in Paul's mind, the identity of the allegorical parallels is dictated not by extrabiblical realities but by Scripture itself: "Tell me," Paul writes, "you who want to be under the law, are you not aware of what the law says? . . . But what does Scripture say?" (Gal. 4:21, 30; see the article "Allegory" elsewhere in the dictionary). Small wonder, then, that most contemporary translations avoid the use of the English word "allegory" in Gal. 4:24: for example, the NIV reads, "These things are being taken figuratively." (Incidentally, one suspects that it is, in part, the effort to avoid technical terminology, with all of its propensity for over-specification, that has driven not a few contemporary writers to prefer rather hazy renderings such as "figural interpretation" and "echoes of Scripture" and the like [e.g., Hays, *Gospels*]. But reflecting on these developments would take us too far afield for the present discussion.)

Consider hook-word links. We have already observed how Paul's use of the hook word "reckon" or "count" in Rom. 4 allows him to draw together God's *counting* of righteousness to Abraham (Gen. 15:6) with his *not counting* sin to David. From this Moyise deduces that Paul is finding things in the OT text that are not really there. But it may be better to attempt a little more precision with respect to what is being linked, what is being counted. Thus, C. K. Barrett (85) argues that by introducing David, Paul is demonstrating that "'the counting of righteousness' [with Abraham] is equivalent to the 'not counting of sin' [with David] . . . [and so] justification . . . is neither the just evaluation of human merit (such as the Jew supposes Abraham to have had), nor the imparting of virtue, but [it is] forgiveness or acquittal" (cf. Bruner, 67). If that is the point of Paul's convening of two texts joined by a hook word, Moyise's hint about the inappropriateness of the apostolic exegesis is misplaced.

Conclusion. These reflections lead us to a subtle conclusion. Although it is true that the hermeneutical developments of the last two or three centuries that we have cursorily tracked and even more cursorily evaluated leave us with an astonishing array of options, it is also true that they leave us with some useful opportunities. For example, the developments within the field of biblical theology, although they have multiplied the options, have also opened up some interpretive choices regarding how to put together the Bible, choices that we had not previously seen. Again, although we may have become aware of the confounding subtleties lurking behind categories like "allegory" and "typology," we have also begun to see more clearly how these categories, far from laying new barriers against integrative thought, may open the doors to more credible engagement.

The Nub of the Challenge

So have we reached the place where we may confidently prescribe how closely contemporary biblical scholars are or are not warranted in adopting the exegetical practices of the NT authors? It is important to make it clear that we are not now trying to evaluate the worth or otherwise of any particular exegetical practice, as such practices have developed over the centuries. Rather, we are focusing on a much narrower question: To what extent may today's biblical scholars legitimately duplicate the exegetical practices of the apostles who lived and taught in the first generation of the church's life? We may usefully distinguish three positions:

First, the overwhelming majority of interpreters follow the patterns of their exegetical forebears: they plow similar exegetical furrows. This springs in part from the fact that biblical writers are themselves following the patterns of earlier biblical writers (cf. Graves; Witherington; Schnittjer). The resulting contemporary studies sometimes focus on how the Bible's entire story line unfolds (e.g., Hunter and Wellum), sometimes on the theology of one corpus (e.g., Gladd), sometimes on how one text or theme or narrative comes to be developed in highly diverse ways (e.g., Alexander; Adams and Domoney-Lyttle). Many argue that what is fresh or new in the ways in which the NT authors quote the OT is their set of christological presuppositions (e.g., Juel) or ecclesiological presuppositions (Hays, *Gospels*). Such approaches rarely set out to distill a set of hermeneutical keys that claim to unlock the sacred texts. Rather, such approaches seek to establish an organic and imaginative grid that "makes sense" of the ways in which NT writers handle Scripture, thereby authorizing contemporary interpreters to do the same (cf. Averbeck). The extent to which these grids find validation in the biblical texts varies enormously from scholar to scholar.

Second, some scholars sharply distance themselves from the hermeneutical stances adopted by the NT writers. One of the most notable of these is Barnabas Lindars, whose 1973 book *New Testament Apologetic* advances a novel thesis. Lindars argues that many of the quotations found in the NT share an identifiable characteristic: they are adduced by the NT writers in order to defend nascent Christianity, regardless of the fact that, if they are read soberly, the OT texts are being ripped out of their OT contexts. Such NT "apologetic" is shaped by Christian concerns to find support for their distinctive doctrines. At the level of words taken out of their contexts, they enjoy some superficial plausibility, but any serious reading of the texts demands that we acknowledge how utterly inappropriate they are when they remain nestled in the OT sources. The developing needs of the church to articulate and defend its growing body of doctrine determined both its choice and its use of OT texts.

For some scholars of more secular vision, this disjunction between the church's apologetic needs and its actual handling of Scripture fatally undermines the church's credibility when it comes to the exegesis of texts. For others (including Lindars), the church's doctrinal claims and apologetic needs can be safely disconnected from its exegesis of biblical texts. Christian doctrines emerged from the church's perception that the cross really did atone for sin, that Jesus really had risen from the dead, that the Spirit really had been poured out, and so forth—and if its handling of the biblical texts to support such faith claims is misguided and finally indefensible from an exegetical point of view, so be it: the truth claims themselves are not jeopardized, they are merely detached from any responsible reading of Scripture. Readers of the NT who insist on seeing a tighter connection between the church's faith and the church's handling of sacred Scripture will doubtless feel uncomfortable with this bifurcation.

Third, another approach has found favor among some modern interpreters. The form in which it is best known is articulated by Richard Longenecker (*Exegesis*). He argues that when the NT writers deploy exegesis that is grammatically above reproach and historically believable, we may happily follow their example, but when they resort to species of exegesis that are frankly "bizarre" (his word; Longenecker, "Who," 385), then we cannot follow them. Writing as he does out of a confessional framework, Longenecker, insists that divine inspiration protected the apostles from actual errors, not least when they appeal to variant texts, haggadah legends, and other textual maneuvers that we really cannot countenance today. We cannot claim for our interpretations the divine inspiration that the apostles enjoyed, so it is wiser, safer, and humbler not to appeal to divine interpretations for our own work but to restrict our efforts at interpretation to philological, grammatical, and historical analysis. We may repeat Paul's view that the rock that followed the Israelites really was Christ (1 Cor. 10:4), because that conclusion sprang from divine inspiration. But that does not warrant us to adopt similar exegetical procedures in our own exegesis (see also Thomas, and the discussion by Naselli in the article "History of Interpretation: 1800 to Present" elsewhere in the dictionary).

Longenecker has attracted a fair bit of negative criticism for his approach. At the risk of appealing to a caricature, we may say that liberals are suspicious of his stance because they do not buy into such a strong view of inspiration, while conservatives are suspicious of an approach to exegesis that rules out the possibility of making sense of the text. In any case, when he brought forth a new edition of his seminal book (*Exegesis*, 1999), Longenecker doubled down and devoted more pages to the defense of his thesis. In sum, he is advocating a position in which modern interpreters are authorized to follow their apostolic forebears when those forebears sound like contemporaries steeped in naturalism, and are directed away from them when the exegetical methods of those forebears seem to have been baptized in naivete and gullibility.

If one must retain a certain suspicion of what is going on in such passages, many argue, surely it is better simply to admit ignorance rather than to be quite so sure that responsible scholars must write off such exegetical practices. In short, we should adopt (such critics suggest) the stance of John Broadus in his 1886 commentary on Matthew. Whenever he came upon an OT quotation in the text of Matthew that he really did not understand, he simply acknowledged his ignorance and passed on to the next point.

One of Longenecker's most severe critics is Richard Hays (*Letters*). While Longenecker asserts that our Christian commitment "is to the reproduction of the apostolic faith and doctrine, and not necessarily to the specific apostolic exegetical practices" (*Exegesis*, 1999, xxxv), Hays retorts that such a view (1) "commits us to a peculiar intellectual schizophrenia in which we arbitrarily grant privileged status to past interpretations that we deem unjustifiable with regard to normal, sober hermeneutical canons," (2) "cuts the lifeline between Paul's time and ours," (3) fails to recognize that "'apostolic faith and doctrine' cannot be extricated so cleanly from apostolic exegesis," and (4) "is ironically unfaithful, in the most fundamental way, to the teaching of the apostle who insisted that 'the word is near you, in your mouth and in your hear heart'" (*Letters*, 180–82, 189). Longenecker (*Exegesis*, 1999, xxxvi) responds by asserting that where the two scholars disagree the fundamental issue is that Hays wants to tie together the resultant interpretations of Scripture with the "normativeness or exemplary status of the interpretive *methods*," whereas Longenecker insists that Scripture itself gives many examples of a distinction between, on the one hand, theology and exhortations and, on the other, the cultural means by which they are disclosed: dreams, the fleece of a sheep, the Urim and Thummim, the braying of a donkey, the casting of lots to determine the identity of the successor to Judas Iscariot, and so forth. In short, Longenecker wants to preserve the distinction between "(1) normative theological and ethical principles and (2) culturally conditioned methods and practices used in support and expression of those principles, which are described in the New Testament but are not set out as normative" (*Exegesis*, 1999, xxxvii).

Three responses are called for. (1) Although there is something to be said in favor of Longenecker's distinction between the (normative) content and the (nonnormative) method of disclosure, the examples he cites (e.g., the fleece of a sheep, the braying of a donkey, and the casting of lots) do not quite fit most of the disputed exegetical techniques. The fleece of a sheep, the braying of a donkey, and the casting of lots are clearly external to the content of the word of the Lord; by contrast, the type or the allegory or the hook word is *not* external, but is the substance of what is disclosed. A typology is not a distinguishable and separable means; it is inextricably part of the disclosure itself. (2) More traction could be gained from more evenhanded discussion of the most disputed passages. The citation of Ps. 40 in Heb. 10 does not necessarily drive us to the conclusion that the author is making a fundamental exegetical mistake about finding the incarnation in Ps. 40 (as the perusal of an array of the better commentaries on Hebrews makes clear). A little more exegetical nimbleness and flexibility might usefully be invoked before we are driven to impossible choices. (3) While initially Hays seems to be the one who is urging contemporary readers on to greater allegiance to the *methods* of disclosure (as Longenecker thinks of them), it soon becomes clear that in his view Paul's handling of Scripture authorizes in us a "bold hermeneutical privilege" that invites us to "create new figurations out of the texts that Paul read, . . . perhaps discerning correspondences that did not occur to Paul himself" and "to perform imaginative acts of interpretation" (Hays, *Letters*, 187–90). While calling us not to write off prematurely the modes of disclosure found in Scripture, Hays seems to be in danger of opening the door to indiscriminate imagination on the ground that we have the law written on our hearts.

The extent to which a contemporary reader of Scripture ought to duplicate the exegetical techniques of the NT writers as they interpret antecedent Scripture proves to be a remarkably intricate subject. When best treated, it may go a long way to enable us to handle the Bible as one book, however diverse its authors, genres, themes, and historical scope, and thus to enrich our grasp of the gospel of God.

See also Allegory; Apostolic Hermeneutics: Description and Presuppositions; Contextual and Noncontextual NT Use of the OT

Bibliography. Adams, S. A., and Z. Domoney-Lyttle, eds., *Abraham in Jewish and Early Christian Literature* (T&T Clark, 2019); Alexander, T. D., *Face to Face with*

God, ESBT (IVP Academic, 2022); Averbeck, R. E., *The Old Testament Law for the Life of the Church* (IVP Academic, 2022); Barrett, C. K., *The Epistle to the Romans*, 2nd ed., BNTC (Hendrickson, 1991); Beale, G. K., *John's Use of the Old Testament in Revelation*, JSNTSup 166 (Sheffield Academic, 1999); Beale, G. K., and B. L. Gladd, *Hidden but Now Revealed* (IVP Academic, 2014); Bowker, J., "Speeches in Acts," *NTS* 14 (1977): 96–111; Bowker, *The Targums and Rabbinic Literature* (Cambridge University Press, 1969); Broadus, J., *Commentary on the Gospel of Matthew* (American Baptist Publication Society, 1886); Bruner, F. D., *The Letter to the Romans* (Eerdmans, 2021); Carson, D. A., "Mystery and Fulfillment," in *Justification and Variegated Nomism*, vol. 2, *The Paradoxes of Paul*, ed. D. A. Carson, P. T. O'Brien, and M. A. Seifrid (Baker Academic, 2004), 393–436; Carson, "New Testament Theology," in *DLNTD*, 797–814; Carter, C. A., *Interpreting Scripture with the Great Tradition* (Baker Academic, 2018); Daniélou, J., *The Lord of History*, trans. N. Abercrombie (Longmans, 1958); Davidson, R., *Typology in Scripture* (Andrews University Press, 1981); De Chirico, L., *Same Words, Different Worlds* (Inter-Varsity, 2021); Dodd, C. H., *According to the Scriptures* (Nisbet, 1952); Gabler, J. P., *Oratio de justo discrimine Theologiae biblicae et dogmaticae regundisque recte utriusque finibus* (1787); Gladd, B. L., *From the Manger to the Throne* (Crossway, 2022); Goppelt, L., *Typos* (Eerdmans, 1982); Graves, M., *How Scripture Interprets Scripture* (Baker Academic, 2021); Hamilton, J. M., Jr., *Typology* (Zondervan, 2022); Hays, R. B., *Echoes of Scripture in the Gospels* (Baylor University Press, 2016); Hays, *Echoes of Scripture in the Letters of Paul* (Yale University Press, 1989); Hunter, T., and S. Wellum, *Christ from Beginning to End* (Zondervan, 2018); Hutchinson, J. H., *La nouveauté de la nouvelle alliance* (Excelsis, 2022); Instone-Brewer, D., *Techniques and Assumptions in Jewish Exegesis before 20 CE* (Mohr Siebeck, 1992); Jamieson, R. B., and T. R. Wittman, *Biblical Reasoning* (Baker Academic, 2022); Juel, D., *Messianic Exegesis* (Fortress, 1988); Lampe, G. W. H., and K. J. Woollcombe, *Essays in Typology* (SCM, 1957); Lindars, B., *New Testament Apologetic* (SCM, 1973); Longenecker, R. N., *Biblical Exegesis in the Apostolic Period* (Eerdmans, 1975; 2nd ed., 1999); Longenecker, "Can We Reproduce the Exegesis of the New Testament?" *TynBul* 21 (1970): 3–38; Longenecker, "'Who Is the Prophet Talking About?,'" in *The Right Doctrine from the Wrong Texts*, ed. G. K. Beale (Baker, 1994), 375–86; Morgan, R., *The Nature of New Testament Theology* (SCM, 1973); Moyise, S., "Can We Use the New Testament the Way the New Testament Authors Used the Old Testament?," *IDS* 36, no. 4 (2002): 1–18; Parker, B. E., and R. J. Lucas, eds., *Covenantal and Dispensational Theologies* (IVP Academic, 2022); Schnittjer, G. E., *The Old Testament Use of the Old Testament* (Zondervan, 2021); Spener, P. J., *Pia Desideria*, trans. T. G. Tappert (Fortress, 1964); Thomas, R., "The New Testament Use of the Old Testament," *TMSJ* 13 (2002): 79–98; Weder, H., *Die Gleichnisse Jesu als Metaphern* (Vandenhoeck & Ruprecht, 1980); Whitman, J., *Interpretation and Allegory* (Brill, 2000); Witherington, B., III, *Torah Old and New* (Fortress, 2018); Young, F., *Biblical Exegesis and the Formation of Christian Culture* (Cambridge University Press, 1997).

D. A. Carson

Atonement

See Sacrifices and Offerings

Authorial Intention

See Contextual and Noncontextual NT Use of the OT; Literal Fulfillment; OT Use of the OT: Comparison with the NT Use of the OT; *Apostolic Hermeneutics articles*

B

Baptism *See* Jews and Gentiles

Biblical Theology

What is biblical theology? And how does biblical theology relate to the subject of the NT use of the OT? To answer these questions, we need to consider (1) the different definitions of and approaches to biblical theology, (2) the challenges to and presuppositions of biblical theology, (3) examples of biblical theology within the Bible itself, (4) the many ways in which biblical theology connects the OT and NT, and (5) the themes that biblical theology uses to expound the theological message of the Bible. Biblical theology, properly undertaken, is essential for a rich understanding of the NT use of the OT. Indeed, biblical theology is integral to the process of discerning the meaning of the whole Bible and its application in today's world.

Definitions and Approaches

The discipline of biblical theology is variously defined and is pursued in a number of ways. E. W. Klink and D. R. Lockett distinguish five main types of biblical theology, citing a major proponent in each case: *historical description,* where the subject matter of biblical theology is the events "behind the text" and the focus of study is the historical and social contexts of the biblical documents (Barr); *history of redemption,* which concentrates on the progressive history of God's actions across the OT and NT, with Jesus Christ at the center (Carson); *worldview story,* which looks at the interconnected story line running through the biblical narrative and puts a premium on explicit narrative developments and the implied worldview of the authors/readers (Wright); *canonical criticism,* where the scope and sources of biblical theology are drawn from both the historical and ecclesial locations of the texts, the latter referring to an emphasis on the framework and guidance of the community of faith (Childs); and *theological construction,* with God, made known in Jesus Christ, as the primary subject matter, along with a focus on the goal of Scripture—namely, love of God and neighbor (Watson). Different understandings of biblical theology put more or less emphasis on "biblical" or "theology," and understand the terms differently.

Most published work claiming the name of biblical theology in the last thirty years, especially in series using the phrase in their titles (e.g., NSBT, BTFL, SSBT), is a version of the history-of-redemption approach. Still, even these definitions vary in terms of scope and emphasis:

- Biblical theology is "the study of the Bible on its own terms, . . . taking God's plan of redemption as the uniting theme of Scripture" (Kimble and Spellman, 2).
- "Biblical Theology, rightly defined, is nothing else than the exhibition of the organic progress of supernatural revelation in its historic continuity and multiformity" (Vos, 15).
- Biblical theology is "the interpretive perspective reflected in the way the biblical authors have presented their understanding of earlier Scripture, redemptive history, and the events they are describing" (Hamilton, 16).
- "Biblical theology studies how the whole Bible progresses, integrates, and climaxes in Christ" (DeRouchie, Martin, and Naselli, 20).
- Biblical theology "proceeds with historical and literary sensitivity and seeks to analyse and

> synthesize the Bible's teaching about God and his relations to the world on its own terms, maintaining sight of the Bible's overarching narrative and Christocentric focus" (Rosner, "Biblical Theology," 10).

In terms of method, some common elements of approach can be discerned. Biblical theology works inductively, using, as far as possible, the concepts and terms of the texts themselves, while still fully acknowledging their diversity of expression and point of view. It sees God as the main subject of Scripture and Jesus Christ as its climax. It seeks to understand the parts in relation to the whole, exploring the interactions of the literary, historical, and theological dimensions of the various biblical books and corpora. It takes the whole Bible into view and focuses on the Bible's unifying story line. It seeks to locate any biblical theme or passage in the larger narrative by asking questions about its backstory, the events of salvation history leading up to it, and its place in the Bible's story arc—that is, where it fits in the course of the big story. While systematic theology offers a contemporary articulation of Christian truth under topical headings primarily in propositional form, biblical theology expounds the grand narrative that unfolds across the whole canon. Making connections across the Bible is its signature move.

However, the contribution of biblical theology to understanding the Bible as a whole is not the whole story. As T. D. Alexander (1) explains, biblical theology "explores how the different biblical books contribute to its overall theological message and how in turn this overall message influences our appreciation of each book." Just as one can trace a biblical-theological theme through the Bible (see "Themes of Biblical Theology" below), so too can the theology of a single book of the Bible be expounded in the light of the theological message of the whole Bible, interpreting its distinctive meaning in the context of the whole. Studying the theology of Mark or Ephesians in the context of the rest of the Bible is no less an exercise in biblical theology than a study of the biblical-theological theme of covenant or kingdom across the entire canon of Scripture.

But biblical theology is not the final destination. It takes the raw materials unearthed by exegesis and assembles a foundation on which systematic theology, practical theology, and Christian ethics can safely build. Without biblical theology these other disciplines tend to produce incomplete and unstable structures.

Challenges and Presuppositions

The viability of undertaking biblical theology, understood as the investigation of the theological message of the whole Bible, assumes two things: that the Bible is a valid focus of study and that there is theological unity to the OT and NT that is predicated upon God's sovereign design of history.

Scholars such as William Wrede and Heikki Räisänen hold that biblical theology should be replaced by the study of the history of early Christian religion and beliefs and argue that a distinction between canonical and noncanonical early Christian literature is unwarranted. In this view the canon is a late and artificial decision of the church and orthodoxy an anachronistic construction read back into the first century. While the formation of the canon is a complicated matter, there is a strong case, as Peter Balla ("Challenges," 24; cf. *Challenges*) puts it, that "the church did not create the canon by some late decisions of synods and bishops, but recognized the authority of the NT writings in a process that began in the 1st century." Biblical theology's focus on the canonical writings can be justified historically.

There is also a theological case for privileging the books of the NT "from the fact that they were believed to be inspired by God" (Beckwith, 28). Others see no need to appeal to the divine authorship of Scripture and instead focus on the text of the biblical canon as a finished product on the grounds of ecclesial commitments (e.g., Childs). For most scholars engaged in doing biblical theology, the canon, for whatever reason, provides the boundaries and a basis for their work.

Biblical theology can also be challenged by objecting to the singularity of the second term in the phrase: some scholars argue that the Bible contains not one unified theology, but rather multiple theologies. Alongside an appeal to the inspiration of Scripture to defend its underlying unity, a historical case can also be made for a unified biblical message. The existence of early creeds in the NT referring to Jesus (e.g., 1 Cor. 12:3; Rom. 10:9; 1 John 4:15; Acts 8:37) or to God and Christ (e.g., 1 Cor. 8:6; 1 Tim. 6:13; 2 Tim. 4:1), summaries of the gospel (e.g., Rom. 1:3; 1 Cor. 15:3–5; 1 Pet. 3:18–22), and trinitarian formulations (e.g., Matt. 28:19; 2 Cor. 13:14), for example, point to a "basic theology" of the early Christians (see Balla, "Challenges," 25). Further, affirming the unity of Scripture does not negate paying attention to its diversity. Each book of the Bible displays unique purposes and distinctive themes. But the task of harmonizing the teaching of apparently discrepant texts, while ongoing, is not impossible and some development of thought across the canon can also be recognized. Biblical theology seeks to hold the unity and diversity of Scripture in delicate balance and to attend carefully to the distinctive contributions of each biblical book on its own terms. As Alexander (1) states, "The discipline of biblical theology affirms the theological unity of the Old and New Testaments, while recognizing the diversity of the biblical books in terms of content, genre and provenance."

Biblical Theology in the Bible

In one sense, biblical theology, as the study of the history of redemption, begins in the Bible itself. The developing narrative of God's saving activity is recalled and reflected upon at various points in both Testaments. For instance, "many psalms refer to incidents from Israel's history or in other ways reflect a biblical-theological perspective (Pss. 66–69, 76–78, 105–107, 147, 149)" (Satterthwaite, 46). There are also passages in the Synoptic Gospels, Acts, Paul's Letters, and Hebrews that recount the characters, events, and institutions of Israel's story in chronological order and at substantial length, providing a window into the way many early Christians effectively did biblical theology.

C. Bruno, J. Compton, and K. McFadden cite seven clear examples of explicit summaries of the OT story of Israel in the NT: (1) the genealogy in Matthew (1:1–17); (2) Jesus's parable of the tenants (Matt. 21:33–46 and pars.); (3) Stephen's speech (Acts 7); (4) Paul's sermon in Pisidian Antioch (Acts 13:16–31); (5) Paul's argument from salvation history in Gal. 3–4; (6) Paul's defense of God's faithfulness to Israel in Rom. 9–11; and (7) Hebrews' exhortation about persevering faith (chap. 11). Each of these passages tells Israel's story in a way that climaxes in Christ and continues in the life and mission of the church. God's judgment on sinners figures prominently in the retellings, especially in relation to exile as the covenant curse imposed on Israel for her unfaithfulness. The passages also highlight the lack of fulfillment of the promises to Abraham in Israel's story. The characters included in the summaries include exemplars to inspire faith, watershed figures (e.g., Abraham, Moses, David), and references to the law and its failure. The summaries also indicate that God himself is the main actor in the story: "The conclusion of Romans 9–11 reminds us that the goal of Israel's story is the glory of God" (Bruno, Compton, and McFadden, 196). Apostolic biblical theology represents a remarkable precedent in many respects for the discipline of redemption-historical biblical theology.

As it turns out, many NT books carry forward the narrative of God's saving activity from the OT in biblical-theological fashion. Even a cursory survey indicates that each of the four Gospels, for example, is firmly yet distinctively embedded in Israel's story through their respective selection and use of OT themes and texts (see Rosner, "Salvation History").

Matthew opens with words that allude to Israel's opening book (cf. 1:1 with Gen. 2:4) and a genealogy that ensures continuity of "Jesus Christ, the son of David, the son of Abraham" (1:1) with the story of Israel. Jesus, the Davidic Messiah, has come to announce that "the gospel of the kingdom" (4:23 ESV), the promised rule of God, is now to be realized in history. Matthew includes as many as fifty-five OT quotations to forge unmistakable links with God's saving activity in the past and to identify Jesus as the Christ who must suffer. Ten of these are introduced with the slightly varied formula, "This took place to fulfill . . ." More allusively, through intricate typology, a discerning of escalated patterns or analogies in history, Jesus is depicted as a new Moses who demands a "higher righteousness" and a new Israel who recapitulates the nation's history (rescued from Egypt, tempted in the wilderness, etc.) but without failure, and fulfills her destiny.

Mark describes the good news in terms of the fulfillment of Isaiah's prophecy of a new exodus (1:2–3; cf. Isa. 40:3; Mal. 3:1). Less overt than Matthew, Mark has explicit citations of the OT only at the opening of his account, in the passion narrative, and occasionally on the lips of Jesus. Yet his message that the climax of Israel's story has been reached is no less compelling. Jesus's messianic identity is made clear at his baptism (1:11: "You are my beloved son, in whom I am well pleased"), echoing the words of Ps. 2:7. The "tearing" open of the heavens in this scene (only in Mark; in Matthew and Luke the heavens are merely "opened") indicates that at last God has acted decisively to make good on his promises of salvation (cf. Isa. 64:1). OT passages and themes frequently underlie Mark's narrative.

Perhaps more than any other Gospel, Luke presents Jesus as the continuation of biblical history. His style of Greek, especially at the beginning of the Gospel (and also Acts) is reminiscent of the Greek translation of the OT. Whereas the OT for Matthew is largely a book of prophetic predictions, Luke emphasizes that God has bound himself to Israel with words of promise (e.g., to David, 1:30–32, 68–71 [2 Sam. 7:14]; to Abraham, 1:54–55, 72–73 [Gen. 12:1–3, etc.]), which are accomplished in Jesus. Jesus is also depicted as the interpreter of Scripture himself (24:25–49), for "all things which were written about [him] in the Law of Moses and the Prophets and the Psalms must be fulfilled" (v. 44 AT). In Acts, a salvation-historical approach to reading the OT is modeled in the speeches of Peter (2:16–36), Stephen (7:2–56), and Paul (13:16–41).

John's Gospel opens in 1:1–5 with a re-presentation of Gen. 1:1–3 connecting Jesus as the Word of God to the work of creation. OT antecedents then define the shape of the Messiah and his mission in John. The final revelation from God that Jesus brings and embodies is compared with that received and mediated by Moses. The signs he performs, recalling the "signs and wonders" of Moses, point to a new exodus. Jesus eclipses the great Jewish feasts and institutions that mark God's saving work in the past. As the "light of the world" and "living water" he fulfills the torch-lighting and water-pouring ceremonies of the Feast of Tabernacles. He replaces the Jerusalem temple and, by dying during Passover week, is the ultimate Jewish Passover sacrifice. He is also seen as the long-awaited "prophet like Moses" (6:14; 7:40; cf. Deut. 18:15).

Though rarely noticed, the practice of biblical theology goes back to the Bible itself.

Biblical-Theological Ways to Connect the OT and NT

Biblical theology and the NT use of the OT are inextricably related, especially if biblical theology is defined as the study of "the unfolding of the Old Testament in the New" (the subtitle of Beale's *A New Testament Biblical Theology*). Indeed, biblical theology uses every means possible to make connections between the Testaments in order to discern the theological message of the Bible. In one sense every article in this dictionary represents the building materials for biblical theology's task of theological construction. Beyond the careful study of OT quotations and allusions in the NT (see the article "Method," by G. K. Beale, elsewhere in this dictionary; and throughout *CNTUOT*), two ways of connecting the Testaments are commonly used in biblical theology: promise and fulfillment, and typology (see the articles "Promises," "Literal Fulfillment," and "Typology" elsewhere in this dictionary; cf. the article "Allegory"). And examples can be seen in the summaries of the Gospels' distinctive ways of rehearsing and extending salvation history in the previous section.

A third relationship—namely, OT influence in the NT without any specific literary connection (see Ciampa), or the influence of OT ideas—is just as important. The kingdom plays a significant role in many treatments of biblical theology. While the expression "kingdom of God/heaven" does not occur in the OT, the links of the NT concept to the OT are undeniable. They include the idea of the rule of God over creation, all creatures, the kingdoms of the world and, in a unique and special way, over his chosen and redeemed people, which is at the very heart of the message of the OT. The "kingdom" in the NT can be understood only against the backdrop of this rule and dominion, which is characteristically rejected by the human race and whose final stage is anticipated in the prophets in terms of radical renewal and completion.

The NT warning of the religious power of money offers a less obvious example of the NT use of OT themes. Jesus charged that people serve either God or mammon (i.e., possessions; Matt. 6:24; Luke 16:13). And Paul believed that some people's god is their belly (Rom. 16:18; Phil. 3:19) and condemned greed as a form of idol worship (Col. 3:5; Eph. 5:5). In none of these texts is there an allusion to or quotation of the OT. However, Jesus's and Paul's comparisons of greed with religion were more innovative in form or expression than in content (Rosner, *Greed*).

Two OT ideas, especially when read in the light of early Jewish interpretation, may be noted as preparing for the startling judgment that greed is idolatry. The solemn words "You shall have no other gods before me" (Exod. 20:3; Deut. 5:7) were early seen to have a comprehensive scope. The first commandment is not a warning against greed. However, as Martin Luther taught in his catechisms, it casts its bright light over all the others and is the source and fountain from which all the others spring. Ancient Jews took these words to be foundational to the rest of the Decalogue and in some sense all-embracing (Rosner, *Greed*, 71). In LAB 44:6–10, for example, the Ten Commandments are rephrased to make it clear that every one is broken by the making of idols. The prohibition of idolatry was understood as having a broad rather than narrow reach.

Further, the strong OT association of wealth with apostasy also anticipates the comparison of greed with religion. Several texts in Deuteronomy set the scene for this disturbing theme. The famous confession of Deut. 6:4 ("You shall love the LORD your God . . .") offers a positive restatement of the first commandment. Interestingly, the targumim of the Shema extend its relevance beyond the cultic and literal to a specific ethical application. Instead of enjoining the love of God with all one's heart, soul, and strength, it calls for full allegiance in terms of one's heart, soul, and possessions or money (Aram. *māmôn*). The identification of material things as a threat to fidelity to God is also underscored in Deut. 8, which warns those entering the promised land not to allow their prosperity to lead them to forget the Lord (Deut. 8:12–14). The lesson is reinforced in the Song of Moses in Deut. 32. Newly acquired wealth will lead the people into apostasy (see vv. 10–15): "Jeshurun ["the upright one," i.e., Israel] grew fat . . . and abandoned the God who made him" (v. 15 AT). Comparable warnings appear across the OT. For example, the sage prays that God will not give him riches, lest he "may have too much and disown [God] and say, 'Who is the LORD?'" (Prov. 30:7–9). Job explains, "If I have put my trust in gold or said to pure gold, 'You are my security,' . . . I would have been unfaithful to God on high" (Job 31:24–28).

Themes of Biblical Theology

J. M. Kimble and C. Spellman are representative of evangelical biblical theology in taking God's plan of redemption in Christ as the unifying theme of Scripture. Their survey of the grand story line of the Bible from Genesis to Revelation, showing how each division of the canon moves the overarching story forward, covers nine themes: God and his glory, kingdom, covenant, temple and priesthood, worship, messiah and atonement, salvation and judgment, Holy Spirit, and mission. J. S. DeRouchie, O. R. Martin, and A. D. Naselli similarly trace nine themes, also covering covenant, temple, and mission, and adding serpent, people of God, law, sabbath, land, and resurrection. It is noteworthy that all of these topics are explicitly theological, except serpent. The present volume includes many articles, including on most of the above, that fit the description of themes of biblical theology. In addition to theological topics, it includes figures such as Abraham, motifs like wilderness, abstract nouns like "love" and "shame," and concepts like holiness.

Such topics are ways of telling the Bible's big story (creation, fall, judgment, salvation, and consummation) and different lenses through which its essential message can be seen. One goal of biblical theology is to explore the Bible's theological message in fresh and unexpected ways. "Salvation," "covenant," "temple," and "mission" are not the only one-word answers to the question of what the Bible is about. Others include idolatry, violence, peace, victory, glory, and even clothes, cities, and serpents, to name but a few. These and many other themes use the full range of biblical-theological means of connecting the OT and NT, especially the development of OT themes and motifs. Most of them lead to the crucified, risen, ascended, and coming Lord Jesus Christ as the climax of the story.

The Bible is about idolatry, a prohibition that plays a central role in the Bible's overarching narrative (Rosner, *Greed*). The history of Israel is the story of the nation's struggle with idolatry. Despite dire warnings from Moses (Deut. 4:15–19; 7:1–5), the Israelites worshiped foreign gods, not only in Egypt (Josh. 24:14) but again in the promised land (Judg. 2:11–13; 17:1–18:31). Idolatry continued to be a snare in the days of David (1 Sam. 19:11–17) and especially Solomon (1 Kings 11:1–8), whose sin forced the division of the kingdom (1 Kings 11:9–13). With few exceptions idolatrous practices flourished in both Israel and Judah, and many of the prophets inveigh against the pollution of idols. The exile in Babylon renewed the confrontation, with Daniel and a few friends standing firm. And in the postexilic period, Malachi, Ezra, and Nehemiah opposed marriages with foreigners to remove the temptation. The new-covenant promises of Isaiah and Ezekiel envision God's people being cleansed and anointed with the Spirit and the removal of Israel's idols (e.g., Ezek. 36:26–36). Further, Isa. 45:5–6 reveals the Lord's determination to be known among the nations as the true and living God. In the NT those who continue to worship idols are excluded from the kingdom of God (1 Cor. 6:9; Rev. 9:20), and Jesus emerges as the incarnate icon (or image) of God (*eikōn tou theou*; 2 Cor. 4:4), the ultimate alternative to the worship of idols.

The Bible is about violence, brutal but sometimes ambiguous. It begins with the foundational premise that the fallen world, and humanity in particular, is violent. An entire episode of human history is sealed with the narrator's judgment that the earth was filled with violence (Gen. 6:11). We first encounter God's own violence in the flood, a divine judgment that destroys the greater part of human and animal life. But God's violence is different in that it is a function of his governance that is ultimately aimed toward the redemption of his creation. The Hebrew prophets foresaw in Jesus a new and powerful vision of this redemption in which violence is absorbed and transformed.

The Bible is about peace, the bringing together of warring parties. Peace is wished from one person to another, and people in general wish to live in peace, free from enemies and other dangers. However, peaceful relations between humans, as important as they might be, are not nearly so important as peace with God, which is achieved through sacrifice, in the end the sacrifice of Jesus Christ.

The Bible is about victory, which ultimately belongs to the Lord and is entirely his work. The Lord's military victories in the OT, which mark the high points of the national experience of pre- and early monarchical Israel, come about only when the people seek and obey him. Thus, it is no surprise when their disobedience leads to ignominious defeat and exile. Confidence that victory still belongs to the Lord is maintained in some of the psalms, where it is asserted that the Lord has conquered the cosmological forces of chaos, and in the prophets, who focus not on a decisive victory in the past but on the coming decisive demonstration of the victory of God in the future. In the NT, this victory of God is demonstrated supremely in the death and resurrection of the Lord Jesus Christ. Though the victory has been decisively achieved, its final celebration and realization await the day of the Lord that is yet to come.

The Bible is about glory radiant and ineffable, lost and regained. God's glorious presence, whether for salvation or destruction, is prominent in the key moments and central institutions of Israel's history and is decisively revealed in Jesus Christ. Through their sinful rebellion, human beings have forfeited the privilege, as image-bearers of God, of reflecting his glory. Paradoxically, we see the glory of God when Jesus is lifted up on the cross at his crucifixion. Through Christ, believers are restored to glory.

More mundanely, at first blush at least, the Bible is about clothes, used not only to denote community identity, signal social status, and enact legal agreements but also more significantly to illustrate God's redemptive activity. From the first act of mercy extended to fallen humanity, the covering of Adam and Eve with clothes, to the end of the age, when the community of the redeemed will be clothed with an imperishable, immortal, heavenly dwelling, the exchange and provision of garments portray God's gracious and redemptive activity. In the present age believers are to put on Christ, the conduct and lifestyle conducive to their status of being in union with him.

The Bible is about cities, in particular Jerusalem and Babylon and their fates and associations. Jerusalem as the religious center of the Holy Land, both originally and in its final restoration, represents the people of God. The word of God issues forth from Jerusalem, peoples gather in Jerusalem to honor God, and the messianic king will appear there victoriously. Conversely, Babylon serves as a symbol of wickedness. Babylon is the proud and wicked city that will be left uninhabited and in ruins, whose name will be cut off for all time. Christians are citizens of the Jerusalem above. The clash between the city of God and the city of Satan will come to a head in the age to come, with the fall of Babylon and the arrival of the new Jerusalem.

The Bible can even be said to be about serpents (Naselli), understood to include both snakes and dragons. Throughout the Bible, and most clearly in the first and last books, snakes deceive and dragons devour. The craftiness of the snake in Gen. 3 misleads Adam and Eve, which leads to their treachery and demise. God curses the snake and promises one who will crush it. In other parts of the Bible serpents, broadly understood, symbolize evil. This includes not only Satan but also Egypt and Pharaoh (Ezek. 32:2) and Babylon (Jer. 8:16–17; 51:34–35) as sea monsters, wicked leaders in Canaan and Moab as serpents needing to be crushed (Judg. 4:17–24; 5:24–27), King Herod as a murderous dragon (Matt. 2:13–18; cf. Exod. 1:8–22), the Pharisees as a hypocritical brood of vipers (Matt. 3:7–12; 12:33–37; 23:29–36), and false teachers in the NT as deceptive smooth talkers (Rom. 16:17–20; 2 Cor. 11:2–4, 13–15). In Rev. 12 and 20 the dragon is the ancient serpent who persecutes and murders God's people, and plans to annihilate his Messiah, but is ultimately conquered by the blood of the Lamb.

The Benefits of Biblical Theology

Graeme Goldsworthy notes four benefits of biblical theology that relate to its contribution to a deeper understanding of the NT use of the OT. Biblical theology promotes the following: a high view of the Bible by revealing its profound inner structures and big story, and the remarkable coherence of its imagery and themes; a high view of Jesus by showing that all the promises of God in the OT are yes in Christ (2 Cor. 1:20); a high view of the gospel by putting flesh on the bones of the NT's insistence that the key elements of the gospel are "according to the Scriptures" (1 Cor. 15:3–4); and a high view of the people of God by locating the church in the larger purposes of God.

In addition, by tracing the moral aspects of the unfolding biblical drama, biblical theology justifies "the development of a coherent overall theory of Christian ethics" (Hill, 100–101). And with respect to preaching, biblical theology helps the preacher to construct a worldview based on the shape of God's self-revelation in history and in the Bible, which gives impetus to a more effective apologetic (Adam).

In expounding the theology of the Bible, biblical theology is all about the relationship between the Testaments. But it is less an approach to the study of the OT in the NT than it is a synthesis of the results of such study. Without biblical theology the study of the NT use of the OT remains fragmented and incomplete. If the study of the use of the OT in the NT is the trees, biblical theology is the forest. It synthesizes the painstaking work of detailed analysis and enables a panoramic view of the glory of God in Christ.

See also Canonical Interpretation; Covenant; Theological Interpretation of Scripture

Bibliography. Adam, P., "Preaching and Biblical Theology," in *NDBT*, 104–12; Alexander T. D., "Biblical Theology," https://www.thegospelcoalition.org/essay/biblical-theology/; Balla, P., "Challenges to Biblical Theology," in *NDBT*, 20–27; Balla, *Challenges to New Testament Theology*, WUNT 2/95 (Mohr Siebeck, 1997); Barr, J., *The Concept of Biblical Theology* (Fortress, 1999); Beale, G. K., *Handbook on the New Testament Use of the Old Testament* (Baker Academic, 2012); Beale, *A New Testament Biblical Theology* (Baker Academic, 2011); Beckwith, R. T., "The Canon of Scripture," in *NDBT*, 27–34; Bruno, C., J. Compton, and K. McFadden, *Biblical Theology according to the Apostles* (IVP Academic, 2020); Carson, D. A., "New Testament Theology," in *DLNTD*, 796–814; Childs, B., *Biblical Theology of the Old and New Testaments* (Fortress, 1992); Ciampa, R. E., "Scriptural Language and Ideas," in *As It Is Written*, ed. S. N. Porter and C. D. Stanley, SBLSymS 50 (Society of Biblical Literature, 2008), 41–57; DeRouchie, J. S., O. R. Martin, and A. D. Naselli, *40 Questions about Biblical Theology* (Kregel, 2020); Goldsworthy, G., "Is Biblical Theology Viable?," in *Interpreting God's Plan*, ed. R. J. Gibson (Paternoster, 1998), 18–46; Hamilton, J., *What Is Biblical Theology?* (Crossway, 2013); Hill, M., "Biblical Theology and Ethics," in *Interpreting God's Plan*, ed. R. J. Gibson (Paternoster, 1998), 91–109; Kimble, J. M., and C. Spellman, *Invitation to Biblical Theology* (Kregel, 2020); Klink, E. W., III, and D. R. Lockett, *Understanding Biblical Theology* (Zondervan, 2012); Naselli, A. D., *The Serpent and the Serpent Slayer*, SSBT (Crossway, 2020); Räisänen, H., *Beyond New Testament Theology* (SCM, 1990); Rosner, B. S., "Biblical Theology," in *NDBT*, 3–11; Rosner, *Greed as Idolatry* (Eerdmans, 2007); Rosner, "Idolatry," in *Dictionary of Scripture and Ethics*, ed. J. Green et al. (Baker Academic, 2011), 392–94; Rosner, "Salvation History," in *DTIB*, 714–17; Satterthwaite, P. E., "Biblical History," in *NDBT*, 43–51; Stuhlmacher, P., *How to Do Biblical Theology* (Pickwick, 1995); Vos, G., *The Idea of Biblical Theology as a Science and as a Theological Discipline* (CrossReach, 2016); Watson, F., *Text and Truth* (T&T Clark, 1997); Wrede, W., "The Tasks and Methods of 'New Testament Theology,'" in *The Nature of New Testament Theology*, ed. and trans. R. Morgan (SCM, 1973), 68–116; Wright, N. T., *The New Testament and the People of God*, COQG 1 (SPCK, 1993).

Brian S. Rosner

Bibliology

Bibliology is the theological locus that covers the doctrine of Scripture and typically covers matters related to canon, inspiration and authority, inerrancy, clarity, and sufficiency. Canon concerns what books the church includes in the Scriptures; inspiration addresses the source of the books of Scripture; inerrancy speaks to the fact that the Scriptures do not contain errors; the clarity of Scripture indicates its perspicuity in matters of salvation and the sinner's duty; and sufficiency concerns Scripture's ability to inform and equip believers for salvation and the Christian life. This essay first explains each of these categories and then addresses how they rest on the necessary presupposition of the NT's use of the OT.

Canon

As early as the intertestamental period uninspired Jewish sources recognize that the OT Hebrew canon consists of what we know as the *Tanak*—the Torah, Nevi'im (Prophets), and Ketuvim (Writings). On the heels of the profaning of the altar, the people did not know how to proceed: "So they tore down the altar, and stored the stones in a convenient place on the temple hill until a prophet should come to tell what to do with them" (1 Macc. 4:45–46). This explanation indicates the absence of the prophets, which means the want of the revelation of God. The church historian Eusebius (ca. 260–339) records Philo of Alexandria's (ca. 25 BC–ca. AD 50) esteem for the law of Moses: "They [the Jews] have not altered even a single word of what had been written by him, but would rather endure to die ten thousand times, than yield to any persuasion contrary to his laws and customs" (Eusebius, *Praep. ev.* 8.6). Christ's own testimony on the road to Emmaus confirms these points when he explains the significance of his ministry: "Everything written about me in the Law of Moses, the Prophets, and the Psalms must be fulfilled" (Luke 24:44). Beyond this testimony, NT authors confirm a fixed OT canon where they refer to "Scripture" (John 10:35), "Holy Scriptures" (Rom. 1:2), or "sacred writings" (2 Tim. 3:15 ESV).

Internal evidence from the NT indicates that the authors understood their writings to be canonical and on the same authoritative footing as the OT canon. Peter warns the church that false teachers are twisting the writings of Paul "as they do the other Scriptures" (2 Pet. 3:16). In addition to this, NT authors refer to other books they have written, such as Luke referring to his Gospel (Acts 1:1), Paul referencing 1 Corinthians (2 Cor. 7:8), and Peter writing that 2 Peter is his "second letter" (2 Pet. 3:1). That Luke refers to his Gospel, Paul to his earlier letter to Corinth, and Peter acknowledges his first letter means that these NT authors confirm the legitimacy of their earlier letters; the letters were not pseudepigraphal, forgeries, or late post-apostolic additions. Paul charges the churches to read his letters publicly (1 Thess. 5:27; Col. 4:16) and usually signs his letters so the churches know they are authentic (2 Thess. 3:17). External evidence for the NT canon comes from church fathers and also appears in the Muratorian Fragment (AD 170). The Muratorian Fragment contains a list of the NT canon that includes all of the NT books except Hebrews, 1–2 Peter, and 3 John. Athanasius's *Paschal Letter* (AD 367) provides a list of the NT canon that matches its twenty-seven books. The OT and NT canons are significant especially in the light of Marcion of Sinope (AD 85–160), who rejected the OT and drastically reduced the NT canon to the Gospel of Luke and portions of Paul's Epistles.

The important doctrinal point to observe is that the church did not create the canon of Scripture but rather recognized what books had authority within the church. In the simplest of terms, the church did not give birth to the Bible; rather, the Bible gave birth to the church. The church recognized the sixty-six books of the Bible as canonical based on several criteria. First, they recognized the thirty-nine books of the OT as canonical. Second, they acknowledged the twenty-seven books of the NT as canonical based on the commission Jesus issued to the apostles, which entrusted them with his divine authority (John 16:12–15). The church recognized the various authors of the NT as eyewitnesses to the ministry of Christ or commissioned by Christ himself. The canons of the OT and NT set the stage for the NT's use of the OT, as the authors saw the NT canon as an organic part of the OT canon, for Jesus did not come "to abolish the Law or the Prophets" but to "fulfill them" (Matt. 5:17), and he built the church on the foundation of the NT apostles and prophets (Eph. 2:20).

Inspiration and Authority

Bibliology includes the doctrine of inspiration, which addresses matters related to the authorial source of the Scriptures. The Scriptures testify that they are God-breathed: "All Scripture is breathed out by God and profitable for teaching, for reproof, for correction, and for training in righteousness, that the man of God may be complete, equipped for every good work" (2 Tim. 3:16–17 ESV). Or as Peter explains, "Men spoke from God as they were carried along by the Holy Spirit" (2 Pet. 1:21 ESV). The Scriptures of the OT and NT possess authority because God is the author. There is even a sense in which God continues to speak through the Scriptures in the present, as the author of Hebrews quotes Ps. 95:7–11 and says, "Today, if you hear his voice . . ." (Heb. 3:7). The divine inspiration of the Scriptures does not diminish their human authorship. Statements such as "I, Paul, write . . ." (1 Cor. 16:21; Col. 4:18; 2 Thess. 3:17; cf. Philem. 19) or "I [Luke] . . . decided to write an orderly account" (Luke 1:3) indicate that these authors are writing using their knowledge, insights, and thoughts. The inspiration of Scripture does not turn the human authors into automatons. It does, however, mean that we must account for the dual authorship of Scripture, both God and human authors. Interpreters must account both for the immediate historical context, grammar, syntax, and location of any one passage of Scripture and its ultimate divine source (Swain, 35–60). In other words, the human author's original historical horizon is not ultimately determinative of the significance of a passage. Rather, its overall meaning rests within the whole of Scripture because even though the prophets "predicted the sufferings of Christ and the subsequent glories," they nevertheless "searched and inquired carefully, inquiring what person or time the Spirit of Christ in them was indicating" (1 Pet. 1:10–11 ESV). In other words, the prophets often prophesied more than they knew (see Beale, "Cognitive").

Historically, theologians have argued for the inspiration of the Scriptures on internal and external evidence. Historic Protestant confessions codify these points. In the Westminster Confession (1647), for example, internal evidence includes the "heavenliness of the matter, efficacy of the doctrine, the majesty of the style, the consent of all the parts, the scope of the whole (which is, to give all glory to God)." By all these things Scripture "abundantly evidence[s] itself to be the Word of God" (1.5). There are two chief external evidential considerations that demonstrate the inspiration of the Scriptures: (1) their power upon people, and (2) their providential preservation. First, the Scriptures evidence themselves to be of divine origin when a person repents of sin and believes in the promises of the gospel. Saul the Pharisee, for example, becomes Paul the apostle—a lion who was trying to devour the church becomes a lamb who now lays down his life for the church. Second, the providential preservation of the Scriptures from the fifteenth century BC (the likely time frame of the writing of the Pentateuch) to the first century (when the NT canon was completed) and the Scriptures' preservation over the last two thousand years serve as corroborating evidence of the divine origins of the Scriptures. At the same time, theologians do not rest the inspiration and authority of Scripture upon this internal and external evidence. As the Westminster Confession states, "The authority of the Holy Scripture, for which it ought to be believed, and obeyed, depends not upon the testimony of any man, or church; but wholly upon God (who is truth itself) the author thereof: and therefore it is to be received, because it is the Word of God" (1.4).

The inspiration of Scripture naturally invests the Bible with authority. In Roman Catholic theology the authority of the church stands on equal footing with Scripture because the church created the Bible. In Protestant theology tradition has an authoritative role but its authority is subservient to the authority of Scripture. In the words of the Westminster Confession, "The supreme judge by which all controversies of religion are to be determined, and all decrees of councils, opinions of ancient writers, doctrines of men, and private spirits, are to be examined, and in whose sentence we are to rest, can be no other but the Holy Spirit speaking in the Scripture" (1.10). The authority of Scripture rests on its divinity and its divinity is manifest in its trustworthiness. The NT authors, for example, all treat the OT for what they declare it to be, a God-breathed document, which is therefore trustworthy in all its assertions and authoritative in its declarations down to every jot and tittle (Barrett, 248).

Inerrancy

The inspiration of Scripture serves as the foundation for its inerrancy and infallibility. The infallibility of Scripture ensures that the Bible is reliable in all matters that it addresses and serves the purposes of God for the salvation of sinners. Correlatively, the Bible is also inerrant in that it is free from all falsehood and deceit. The inerrancy of the Scriptures is not limited to spiritual, redemptive, or religious themes. It extends also to matters of science and history ("Chicago Statement," arts. 11–12).

Inerrancy has sometimes been characterized as a recent, nineteenth-century, American invention created by the theologians of Old Princeton: Charles Hodge (1797–1878), A. A. Hodge (1823–86), and B. B. Warfield (1851–1921) (Rogers and McKim; Hodge and Warfield, "Inspiration"; Warfield, *Inspiration*). Yet, history tells a different story (Letham, 190–92). Theologians as early as Augustine (354–430) recognized the importance of an error-free Bible. In a letter to Jerome, Augustine writes, "For it seems to me that most disastrous consequences must follow upon our believing that anything false is found in the sacred books: that is to say, that the men by whom Scripture has been given to us, and committed to writing, did put down in these books anything false" (*Ep.* 28.3). Thomas Aquinas (1225–74) makes similar observations when he cites this same letter from Augustine to Jerome: "Only those books of Scripture which are called canonical have I learned to hold in such honor as to believe their authors have not erred in any way in writing them. But other authors I so read as not to deem everything in their works to be true, merely on account of their having so thought and written, whatever may have been their holiness and learning" (*Summa*, Ia, q. 1, art. 8).

Later Protestant theologians such as John Calvin (1509–64) tirelessly sought to harmonize seemingly contradictory passages of Scripture, especially in the Pentateuch and Gospels (Dowey, 90–105). Other Protestant theologians of the sixteenth century were blunt and explicit: "[The Bible] alone is without all error" (Bucanus, 42). Likewise, later post-Reformation theologians such as Francis Turretin (1623–87) affirmed that because the Bible is God-breathed and therefore divine, it is free from all error (*Institutes*, 2.3.3; 2.4.5–6). Turretin is especially relevant because his *Institutes* were used as a theological textbook at Old Princeton by the Hodges. In other words, the claims of biblical inerrancy are of great antiquity. But even the Roman Catholic Church at Vatican II (1962–65) affirms that "the books of Scripture must be acknowledged as teaching firmly, faithfully, and without error that truth which God wanted put into the sacred writings for the sake of our salvation" (*Dei Verbum*, 3.11). Inerrancy of Scripture, therefore, is not the claim of a small group of American nineteenth-century theologians but has wide historical and contemporary attestation among both Protestants and Catholics.

Clarity

Historically, the Protestant tradition has included the doctrine of the perspicuity (or clarity) of Scripture, which finds common expression in the Westminster Confession: "All things in Scripture are not alike plain in themselves, nor alike clear unto all: yet those things which are necessary to be known, believed, and observed for salvation, are so clearly propounded, and opened in some place of Scripture or other, that not only the learned, but the unlearned, in a due use of the ordinary means, may attain unto a sufficient understanding of them" (1.7). There are two important observations about the Confession's statement about the clarity of Scripture. First, it acknowledges that there are difficult passages of Scripture. Peter's comments about Paul's letters certainly come to mind: "There are some things in them that are hard to understand, which the ignorant and unstable twist to their own destruction, as they do the other Scriptures" (2 Pet. 3:16 ESV). The clarity of Scripture does not mean, therefore, that everything in the Scriptures is clear. Second, the clarity of Scripture specifically pertains to "those things which are necessary to be known, believed, and observed for salvation." For such things, the Scriptures are sufficiently clear that even a child can read and understand Scripture's overarching message. In the words of Gregory the Great (540–604), "As the divine word exercises the understanding of the wise by the mysteries it contains, so usually it comforts the simple by its surface meaning. It lays open what can nourish the little ones; it keeps in secret what lifts up the minds of loftier men in admiration. It is like a kind of river, so to speak, which is both shallow and deep, in which both the lamb may walk and the elephant may swim" (Gregory, 66).

At the same time, the Confession also identifies an important principle for seeking to understand the less than clear Scriptures. It states that Scripture addresses the same truths in other portions of Scripture. The clarity of Scripture rests on its inspiration. Because the triune God has inspired the Scriptures, the message from Genesis to Revelation is consistent. A correlative principle, therefore, of clarity is the *analogia Scripturae* ("the analogy of Scripture"). The Confession explains: "The infallible rule of interpretation of Scripture is the Scripture itself: and therefore, when there is a question about the true and full sense of any Scripture (which is not manifold, but one), it must be searched and known by other places that speak more clearly" (1.9). This principle simply stated is, Scripture interprets Scripture.

The analogy of Scripture rests upon the verbal and revelatory activity of the triune God. Whether in the individual passage or across the whole of the canon, God speaks, acts, and then speaks. In the opening lines of Genesis, God speaks, "Let there be light," which is then followed by the divine action of the creation of light (1:3). The Genesis account then follows this word ("Let there be light") and act ("and there was light") with a subsequent interpretive word, "And God saw that the light was good" (1:4). Word-act-word appears in this small pericope but also across the whole of the canon. The opening lines of Hebrews attest to this: "Long ago, at many times and in many ways, God spoke to our fathers by the prophets, but in these last days he has spoken to us by his Son" (Heb. 1:1–2 ESV). The OT is the anticipatory word-revelation of God. The act-revelation of the incarnation and ministry of Christ follows this anticipatory word. Then the subsequent NT interpretive word-revelation explains the significance of the earlier word-and-act revelations of God. In the simplest of terms, God is his own interpreter—Scripture interprets Scripture, the NT interprets the OT (Vos, 7).

Sufficiency

Scripture is also sufficient—that is, it addresses all things necessary for salvation and for living the Christian life (Barrett, 332–72). The French Confession (1559) summarizes this doctrine when it speaks of the word of God as "containing all that is necessary for the service of God and for our salvation." Because of its sufficiency, people are not allowed "to add to it, to take away from it, or to change it" (art. 5). Similar statements to this effect appear in other Protestant confessions such as the Westminster Confession of Faith (1.6). Protestant theologians aimed the sufficiency of Scripture at salvation and the Christian life and acknowledged that the Bible does not address many things. Scripture is not a rule, for example, for medical physicians, mathematicians, learning foreign languages, or teaching about astronomy; Scripture does not address every circumstance in life (Rutherford, 99). This does not mean Scripture is lacking but rather raises the question, For what did the triune God specifically design the Scriptures?

The Scriptures are the only means of discovering God's plan of redemption in Christ. They also explain fundamental truths that equip Christians to live the Christian life. As Paul writes to Timothy, "All Scripture is breathed out by God and profitable for teaching, for reproof, for correction, and for training in righteousness, that the man of God may be complete, equipped for every good work" (2 Tim. 3:16–17 ESV). Because the Scriptures originate from God, Christians must guard the sanctity of his Word and may not add to, delete, or modify anything in the Scriptures. Paul's warning to the Galatians regarding embracing another gospel speaks to the inviolability of God's word (Gal. 1:8–9). The sufficiency of Scripture does not negate but rather necessitates the illuminative and regenerative work of the Spirit because "the natural person does not accept the things of the Spirit of God, for they are folly to him, and he is not able to understand them because they are spiritually discerned" (1 Cor. 2:14). And sufficiency does not rule out the importance, utility, or necessity of general revelation, which addresses topics beyond the scope of the Scriptures (e.g., the natural order, science, medicine, or biology, among other subjects).

There are several examples of the sufficiency of Scripture throughout the Bible. Deuteronomy 1–3 recounts Israel's disobedience in the wilderness, after which God instructs the people through Moses, "You shall not add to the word that I command you, nor take from it, that you may keep the commandments of the LORD your God that I command you" (4:2 ESV). God's commands were sufficient for living in a manner that was pleasing to God. Notably, Jesus quotes Deut. 8:3, "Man does not live by bread alone, but man lives by every word that comes from the mouth of the LORD" (ESV), against Satan in his wilderness temptations (Matt. 4:4 // Luke 4:4). In the midst of his temptation, his Father's command was sufficient for him. A similar pattern unfolds with the Bereans in Acts 17. As Paul preached and taught, the Bereans "received the word with all eagerness, examining the Scriptures daily to see if these things were so" (Acts 17:11 ESV). These actions confirm that Scripture was both a final and sufficient authority for determining the veracity of Paul's teaching. Although the closing words of Revelation pertain immediately to the words of John's apocalypse, they nevertheless echo the earlier scriptural teaching about the sufficiency of Scripture from the OT: "I warn everyone who hears the words of the prophecy of this book: if anyone adds to them, God will add to him the plagues described in this book, and if anyone takes away from the words of the book of this prophecy, God will take away his share in the tree of life and in the holy city, which are described in this book" (Rev. 22:18–19 ESV). The sufficiency of Scripture stands in contrast to the Bible's characterization of human traditions. Jesus rebukes the religious leaders because they "leave the commandment of God and hold to the tradition of men" (Mark 7:8 ESV). Likewise, Paul warns against being taken "captive by philosophy and empty deceit, according to human tradition, according to the elemental spirits of the world, and not according to Christ" (Col. 2:8 ESV).

NT Use of the OT

The NT's use of the OT presupposes all of the aforementioned principles of bibliology: canon, inspiration and authority, inerrancy, clarity, and sufficiency. In the early church, challenges to the canon of Scripture came from Marcion, who rejected the OT and severely truncated the NT canon. Yet, the repeated quotations (approximately 350) and thousands of allusions and echoes to the OT show that the OT is vital to understanding the NT (Nicole, 137–38). In his efforts to refute Marcion's truncated canon, Irenaeus saw the unity of the canon in terms of Christ's recapitulation of Adam's person and work: "So *the Word was made flesh,* that, through that very flesh which sin had ruled and dominated, it should lose its force and be no longer in us. And therefore our Lord took that same original formation as [His] entry into flesh, so that He might draw near and contend on behalf of the fathers, and conquer by Adam that which by Adam had stricken us down" (*Epid.* 31 [trans. Robinson]). OT and NT are bound not merely by literary dependency of the latter upon the former but also by the inspiration and providential ordination of the word-act-word revelation in both Testaments.

First, regarding inspiration, when Paul says that "all Scripture is breathed out by God" (2 Tim. 3:16 ESV), he has the whole canon, both OT and NT, in view. Inspiration is a key building block in the understanding of canon, but it also plays a significant role in understanding the relationships between the Testaments. Some theologians locate the interpretive crux upon human authorship, intention, and original meaning. For example, Robert Thomas argues that "the OT must not receive multiple meanings by being read through the eyes of the NT" and that NT authors sometimes use OT passages in ways "entirely different from what was envisioned in corresponding OT contexts." In fact, NT authors often "disregarded the main thrust of the grammatical-historical meanings of the OT passages" (Thomas, 79–80, 83). For some, grammatical-historical interpretation is a sacrosanct rule that cannot be broken—that is, a text has one meaning determined by the original author's intent and understanding (Thomas, 86).

Several things work against such claims: (1) those who hold such views do not demonstrate how the unbreakable principle of the grammatical-historical interpretation originates from Scripture; (2) one cannot know what the original author envisioned; (3) while it is important to factor in authorship, historical context, and the grammar of a passage, all these factors only account for human authorship; (4) the Scriptures themselves say that human authors sometimes wrote more than they fully knew, as the prophets inquired "what person or time the Spirit of Christ in them was indicating when he predicted the sufferings of Christ and the subsequent glories" (1 Pet. 1:11 ESV); and (5) making grammatical-historical interpretation of the OT an inviolable principle requires that interpreters argue that NT authors misused OT texts.

Thomas (87) betrays this difficulty when he writes that NT authors "could assign such new meanings authoritatively because of the inspiration of what they wrote." Yet, this admission belies an important observation—by divine inspiration NT authors assign new meaning to OT texts. These are not radically new meanings, however, but organic, extended meanings that remain tethered to the original intent of the OT authors (Beale, "Doctrine"). Why does the inspiration of the Holy Spirit require that the Spirit assign an extended meaning to an OT text when the Holy Spirit inspired the original text to begin with? Applying Occam's razor to the question, is it not simpler to say that the Spirit of God inspired both OT and NT texts and that because of this divine inspiration, the NT is the divine, inerrant, infallible commentary on the OT? In other words, the human author does not take priority in the interpretive process but rather the divine author does. The Holy Spirit has inspired both Testaments, which binds the canon of Scripture together from Genesis to Revelation.

Second, if the triune God has breathed out all Scripture and God's revelation consists of both words and acts, then this means that not only are the *words* of OT revelation inspired but so are the providentially ordained *acts* that underly them. One of the clearest places where this emerges is in typology. Paul, for example, explains that Adam "was a type of the one who was to come" (Rom. 5:14 ESV). That Paul designates Adam as a *type* means that God specifically created and ordained Adam to prefigure Jesus. Paul was not adding new meaning to the creation narrative; rather, the Spirit used Paul to reveal God's authorial intent concerning Adam's significance. God reveals in terms of words and acts, which means that the whole OT contains prophetic persons, events, and institutions that in some way prefigure the person and work of the Messiah. As such, "God's promises shaped the way the biblical authors perceived, understood, and wrote" (Hamilton, 4). If God ordains persons, events, and institutions to prefigure his Son's revelation, then, given the word-act-word pattern and the divine inspiration of the whole canon, OT and NT are irrefragably joined. Whether Adam (Rom. 5:14), Moses (Heb. 3:1–3), Joshua (Heb. 4:8–10), Aaron (Heb. 7:11–23), David (Rev. 5:5; 22:16), Solomon (Luke 11:31), the tabernacle (John 1:14), the sacrifices (Heb. 8–9), Israel (Matt. 2:15), the promised land (Heb. 4:1–8), the flood (2 Pet. 2:4–5), or the judgment on Sodom and Gomorrah (Matt. 11:23–24; 2 Pet. 2:6–9)—these words and acts await their antitypical fulfillment in the act revelation of Christ and the subsequent interpretive word revelation of the NT. Consequently, "Scripture cannot be broken" (John 10:35 ESV). God inspired both Testaments, and thus the only way to understand the OT is to use the divinely inspired NT as God authoritatively explains his earlier word-act-word revelation.

The same relationship between the NT use of the OT undergirds the inerrancy, clarity, and sufficiency of Scripture. One of the aspects of inerrancy is the accuracy of the claims of Scripture, which is often showcased in terms of promises and prophecies fulfilled. In Paul's terms, "For all the promises of God find their Yes in him"—that is, in Christ (2 Cor. 1:20 ESV). Because the inerrant Scriptures find their source in the one and only true God, the only way to understand difficult or seemingly erroneous claims is to rest in the principle of the *analogy of Scripture*, the linchpin for the clarity of Scripture: "Inasmuch as all Scripture is the product of a single divine mind, interpretation must stay within the bounds of the analogy of Scripture and eschew hypotheses that would correct one Biblical passage by another, whether in the name of progressive revelation or of the imperfect enlightenment of the inspired writer's mind" ("Chicago Statement," 9). Scripture interpreting Scripture means using other portions of the Bible to interpret difficult portions or using the NT to interpret the OT. When God, for example, promised that the seed of the woman will crush the head of the serpent (Gen. 3:15) and that the seed of Abraham will be blessed (Gen. 12:1–2; 15:1–6; 22:15–18), we find the corresponding antiphonal NT response in the genealogies of Christ where Luke traces his descent back to Adam (Luke 3:38) and Matthew traces it back to Abraham (Matt. 1:2).

Likewise, the sufficiency of Scripture rests upon the principle of the NT's use of the OT. As God has spoken to his people in ages past, he continues to speak to his people in the present. Just as his word was sufficient to meet the needs of his people, his word is still sufficient to meet our needs. There is, however, an escalation from one Testament to the next, as we move from preparatory word-act-word revelation to consummatory word-act-word revelation. "God spoke to our fathers by the prophets, but in these last days he has spoken to us by his Son" (Heb. 1:1–2 ESV). For as the message that God declared through angels proved to be reliable and every transgression received its just retribution, how much more should we heed the definitive revelation of God in Christ (Heb. 2:2–3)? God fed Israel with manna from heaven, but in these last days he feeds us with the manna from heaven, Jesus Christ (John 6:31–33).

Conclusion

Bibliology includes the topics of canon, inspiration and authority, inerrancy, clarity, and sufficiency. All these topics are uniquely consistent with the NT's use of the OT because they all explicate in one way or another the fact that the triune God has inspired the whole canon of Scripture, and as covenant Lord his word possesses authority—it is trustworthy and thus inerrant, it is clear, and it is sufficient, whether for Israel or for the NT church.

See also Biblical Theology; Theological Interpretation of Scripture

Bibliography. Aquinas, T., *Summa Theologica* (Christian Classics, 1948); Athanasius, "Letter 39," in *NPNF*[2], 4:551–52; Augustine, "Letter 28: To Jerome," in *NPNF*[1], 1:251–53; Barrett, M., *God's Word Alone* (Zondervan Academic, 2016); Beale, G. K., "The Cognitive Peripheral Vision of Biblical Authors," *WTJ* 76, no. 2 (2014): 263–93; Beale, "Did Jesus and His Followers Preach the Right Doctrine from the Wrong Texts?," *Them* 14 (1989): 89–96; Bucanus, W., *Body of Divinity or Institutions of Christian Religion*, trans. R. Hill (Pakeman, Roper, and Tomlins, 1659); "The Chicago Statement on Biblical Inerrancy" (International Council on Biblical Inerrancy, 1978); *Dei Verbum*, in W. M. Abbot, *The Documents of Vatican II* (Guild, 1966); Dowey, E. A., Jr., *The Knowledge of God in Calvin's Theology*, 3rd ed. (Eerdmans, 1994); Eusebius, *Preparation for the Gospel*, part 1, trans. E. H. Gifford (Clarendon, 1903); *French Confession*, in *Reformed Confessions of the 16th and 17th Centuries in English Translation*, vol. 2, ed. J. T. Dennison Jr. (Reformation Heritage Books, 2010), 140–54; Gregory the Great, *Gregory the Great on the Song of Songs*, trans. M. DelCogliano (Liturgical Press, 2012); Hamilton, J. M., Jr., *Typology* (Zondervan Academic, 2022); Hodge, A. A., and B. B. Warfield, "Inspiration," *PresbRev* 6 (1881): 225–60; Irenaeus, *The Demonstration of the Apostolic Preaching*, trans. J. A. Robinson (SPCK, 1920); Letham, R., *Systematic Theology* (Crossway, 2019); Nicole, R., "New Testament Use of the Old Testament," in *Revelation and the Bible*, ed. C. F. H. Henry (Baker, 1958), 137–51; Rogers, J. B., and D. McKim, *The Authority and Interpretation of the Bible* (1979; repr., Wipf & Stock, 1999); Rutherford, S., *The Divine Right of Church Government and Excommunication* (John Field, 1646); Swain, S. R., *Trinity, Revelation, and Reading* (T&T Clark, 2011); Thomas, R., "The New Testament Use of the Old Testament," *TMSJ* 13, no. 1 (2002): 79–98; Turretin, F., *Institutes of Elenctic Theology*, 3 vols., trans. G. M. Giger, ed. J. T. Dennison Jr. (P&R, 1992–97); Vos, G., *Biblical Theology* (1948; repr., Banner of Truth, 1996); Warfield, B. B., *The Inspiration and Authority of the Bible* (repr., P&R, 2020); *Westminster Confession of Faith*, in *Reformed Confessions of the 16th and 17th Centuries*, vol. 4, ed. J. T. Dennison Jr. (Reformation Heritage Books, 2014), 231–72.

JOHN V. FESKO

Blessings, Covenant

See Covenant

C

Canonical Interpretation

Generally, canonical interpretation describes an approach that focuses not only on the content of Scripture but also the final canonized shape of the biblical text (or the final form) as the context for interpretation. A well-known proponent of canonical interpretation, Brevard Childs, argues, "The canonical form marks not only the place from which exegesis begins, but also the place at which it ends" (*New Testament as Canon*, 48). Both the content and form of Scripture are central for canonical interpretation, such that, in the words of John Sailhamer, "the final shape of [Scripture] is as important as the actual course of events that are recounted in it" ("Canonical Approach," 307).

Canonical interpretation privileges both the final form of an individual book of the Bible (e.g., the final Hebrew text of Genesis rather than a reconstruction of a previous set of traditions) and the final collection and arrangement of the entire Christian Bible. Therefore, although individual interpreters will have varying positions regarding critical issues (e.g., the multiple steps of composition for Isaiah or Philippians), canonical interpretation takes the final form of Isaiah and Philippians as the authoritative context for interpretation (though the text's tradition history retains hermeneutical significance). Furthermore, canonical interpretation views the collection and association (or ordering) of the texts in the OT and NT as significant to their meaning. For example, Genesis through Deuteronomy stands as a five-part sequence, such that each text deploys its meaning in the context of a collection called the Pentateuch. Similarly, Luke's Gospel, distanced from Acts by the placement of John, is situated as one of the four Gospels rather than the first volume of a two-part history of the early Christian movement, Acts being the second part. Thus, as Childs notes, the final form marks the beginning and ending of interpretation.

A Literary Approach or a New Method?

Because of the literary nature of the final form of the text, some understand canonical interpretation as merely a literary-critical approach. Lumped in with a host of literary-critical methods that began to challenge (and replace) historical-critical methods in the mid-twentieth century, the concern for canon is understood by some to be a literary approach to interpreting the text that is largely unconcerned with the text's history of origin. Focusing on the final form is, for some, a way of avoiding speculative historical reconstruction of composition or tedious tracing of sources underlying the final form of the text. Understood as a literary approach, canonical interpretation focuses on the literary shape of the texts as an end in itself, where interpretation can be completed without attending to the origins of the text.

For some (more postmodern) literary critics, the final form is a kind of jumping-off point where text and reader meet without concern for the text's compositional context at all. Here the whole question of the origins of the texts—author and audience—is a matter of secondary importance (perhaps even indifference), since what is of primary concern is the dynamic interchange between text and reader. Rather than being founded upon the historical qualities of the text (its context of origin or apostolic authorship), the authority of the Scriptures is bound up in their use in a particular believing community. The texts are used in an authoritative way because they have been found to be useful in shaping the religious sensibilities of a community.

But even critics of canonical interpretation argue that such (especially postmodern) views of the final form bear superficial resemblance to canonical interpretation.

Rather than merely a literary (or postmodern) approach, the final form, according to canonical interpretation, is the result of a historical process that begins with the circumstances of the text's composition and moves on to transmission and reception (collection and arrangement), the end of which bears the hermeneutical marks of earlier stages in that process. Thus, exegesis, for canonical interpretation, takes into account not only the history of the text's origin but also the history of its reception. The text's final form as it appears in the canon is the focus of exegesis and interpretation because it is the form of the text that not only was authored by prophets and apostles but also has been received as authoritative and functions as Scripture in the believing community. Canonical interpretation resists the historical-critical judgment that the issue of canon is a second-century phenomenon and therefore irrelevant to the study of the OT and NT.

In the end, canonical interpretation is not a new interpretive method or a new hermeneutic. One need not abandon other interpretive tools in order to appreciate the canonical context. In fact, canonical interpretation depends upon traditional historical-grammatical methods of interpretation in order to produce its observations. Though James Sanders adopts the label "canon criticism" (*Torah and Canon*) and thereby suggests a new method of interpretation, Childs insists that the label is unnecessary and misleading. He argues that canon criticism "implies that the concern with canon is viewed as another historical-critical technique which can take its place alongside of source criticism, form criticism, rhetorical criticism, and the like. I do not envision the approach to canon in this light" ("Canonical Shape," 54).

Depending upon the particular scholar, canonical interpretation is potentially compatible with all forms of historical-critical engagement. Childs argues, "The issue at stake in canon turns on establishing a stance from which the Bible is to be read as Sacred Scripture" ("Canonical Shape," 54). Therefore, canonical interpretation does not predetermine what kind of critical tools can be used in exegesis; rather, it is a stance or approach to the text of Scripture that shapes the entire process of interpretation. Mark Gignilliat (21) notes that canonical interpretation "identifies itself as a broad-ranging hermeneutic whose boundaries are marked by Christian commitments"—the particular Christian commitment being that of the basic unity of the canonical text.

Before I offer several examples of canonical interpretation, it will be necessary for me to define canon further. There has been extensive debate regarding the date and nature of the canon, and here it will be important to consider whether the definition of canon should be narrow or broad and whether canon and Scripture should be viewed as distinct or overlapping concepts.

Definition of Canon: Narrow or Broad?

In Gerald Sheppard's now somewhat well-known rubric, he describes two ways of defining canon—canon 1 ("norm") and canon 2 ("list")—demonstrating that both senses equally share historical warrant. In canon 1 the term refers to an authoritative set of teachings that shaped the early Christian community. Canon as "norm" or "rule of faith" functions as an authority within the Christian community—a rule or norm that defines faith and serves as a guiding principle for belief and practice (*norma normans*). Canon 2 refers to canon as a fixed collection (a "list") and stresses the delimitation of the collection. Coming only at the end of a lengthy process, canon as a fixed list is necessarily a later phenomenon. Thus, it denotes a closed collection of texts where outside texts could not be included and accepted texts could not be omitted (*norma normata*).

Those who adopt a narrow view of canon insist that it is appropriate to speak of canon only when there is direct evidence of a fixed list, usually at the end of the process of canonization. Discussing the significance of the partial canon list preserved in the Muratorian Fragment, Geoffrey Hahneman (406) argues, "To speak of a Christian 'canon' of scriptures is an anachronism before the second half of the fourth century because it is only after that time that Christian writers begin to employ the word [canon] . . . for a list of books counted as accepted scriptures." Hahneman's comment is typical of those arguing for a narrow understanding of canon. Closure, the moment in the formation process when the community finally fixes the number, order, and content of the collection, is *the* key characteristic of canon. According to the narrow or exclusive view, this official closure is necessary for there to be a canon at all. Eugene Ulrich (32) insists that this closure "represents a conscious, retrospective, official judgment." Of course, those taking this view are eventually forced to admit that the final and absolute listing of the biblical canon (whether in Jewish or Christian tradition) *never actually happened*. Michael Kruger (37) argues that the official and authoritative decision by the church regarding which texts are canonical or not "will not be found in the fourth century—nor even in the modern day, for that matter." Historically, there never was an official and definitive moment when the whole church decided upon a closed canon. Thus, there is no definitive fixing of the canon as Hahneman or Ulrich require. Stephen Chapman reasons that rather than a "minor point, this concession actually goes to the heart of the methodology employed, for why should one adopt as proper a definition of 'canon' that does not ever appear to have existed in reality?" ("Old Testament Canon," 136). Kruger (37) argues that the narrow or exclusive definition of canon appears to be anachronistic because such an officially closed list never existed. If canon never functioned historically as a final fixed list in this way, it seems better (following Sheppard) to consider a more nuanced understanding of canon—a broad notion of canon that incorporates both canon as list and canon as rule.

Another consequence of stressing canon as a fixed list is the emphasis placed upon the individuals or institutions supposedly responsible for the fixing. Harry Gamble argues, "Emphasis on the sharp distinctions furnished by *lists* tends to represent canonization more as *a process of exclusion* than of inclusion, *thus emphasizing polemical and apologetic moves*. This view also stresses the role of ecclesiastical authorities—bishops, synods, and councils—and downplays the importance of second-century controversies with heterodox movements" (271, emphasis added). The narrow view of canon understands the final list of canonical books as determined more by apologetic and institutional pressures than by a reception of these texts based upon an appreciation and understanding of their inner logic.

However, if the notion of canon is broadened to include its function as a rule or norm, one can, in turn, appreciate the internal qualities of the text. Childs argues, "The formation of the canon was not a late extrinsic validation of a corpus of writings, but involved a series of decisions deeply affecting the shape of the books. Although it is possible to distinguish different phases within the canonical process—the term canonization would then be reserved for the final fixing of the limits of scripture—the earlier decisions were not qualitatively different from the later" (*Introduction*, 59). That is, the pressures that led to the formation of the OT and NT were not exerted from the outside and were not manipulative of the texts themselves. The term "canon" cannot "be reserved for the final fixing of the limits of scripture" (*Introduction*, 59). What Childs is emphasizing here is that the texts themselves bore the characteristics of authority and canonical connection.

It was not an official listing of texts (by bishop or church) that gave the canon its authority; rather, the canonical process (composition, collection, and final association) left marks within the texts themselves such that those texts were received as Scripture. Therefore, the canonical (or final) form of the biblical texts constitutes not a secondary attribute or an anachronism but rather an intrinsic element of the literature itself. Canon is not merely "a late, ecclesiastical activity, external to the biblical literature itself, which was subsequently imposed on those writings"; rather, the church's "canonical consciousness" was from the beginning lying "deep within the New Testament literature itself" (Childs, *New Testament as Canon*, 21).

The broad notion of canon argues that the canon functioned as a rule or norm for the Christian community *before* becoming fixed in a final list. Therefore, as noted above, the development of the Christian canon was not due to an external force imposed upon the text by institutional pressures or motivated by political or apologetic concerns; rather, even before a more formal list of canonical texts developed, there was a growing recognition of the authority of these texts because of their intrinsic properties. In this way, in the words of Herman Ridderbos (25), "the canon is not a product of the church; rather the church is to be the product of the canon." Therefore, Chapman concludes that, understanding canon in a broad sense, the Christian church can be "said to have *inherited* a scriptural canon" ("Old Testament Canon," 140). Ridderbos (13) goes a step further, arguing that the "material authority of the canonical writings originates in the history of redemption because in that history the unique work of Jesus Christ himself comes to light." Naturally, the broad view of canon has implications for how one understands the relationship between Scripture and canon, an issue to be examined next.

Canon and Scripture

Understanding canon in narrow or broad terms directly affects one's view of how the terms "canon" and "Scripture" are related. Two positions predominate. The first position argues for a clear distinction between canon and Scripture. One of the original voices to oppose understanding canon and Scripture as overlapping terms is Albert Sundberg. Following Sundberg, John Barton (157–58) distinguishes "between the 'Scripture' which results from the growth of writings perceived as holy, and the 'canon' which represents official decisions to exclude from Scripture works deemed unsuitable." Barton's separation of Scripture and canon stresses the exclusive nature of canon, in which a definitive list of texts excludes and includes (canon 2).

James Barr argues for the sharp distinction between canon and Scripture because he sees a large gulf between the origins of the biblical material (composition) and the succeeding patristic period, in which these texts became canon (canonization). For Barr, before a fixed list of authoritative texts exists, a particular theological tradition might regard certain books as holy and having religious authority, but he insists these books would not be called "Scripture" because the boundary lines of the collection are not yet drawn. Furthermore, Barr (167) argues, "Canons are not particularly hermeneutical in their character. . . . This . . . is not their function."

A second view posits a necessarily close relationship between canon and Scripture. Both Sanders and Childs (along with Christopher Seitz, Sailhamer, and Chapman) argue that, historically, the term "canon" indicated both "norm" as well as "list" (see Sheppard above). Thus, a canon actually functions as a norm or rule within a community before being formalized as a fixed list. Furthermore, "this formalization is better understood as the recognition of an already-authoritative literary collection than as the conferral of authority" (Chapman, "Canon Debate," 278).

Softening the boundary line between Scripture and canon allows one to speak of canon as encompassing the entire process from composition to final canonization (rather than limiting canon to a final moment of fixing an exclusive list of books). Texts functioning as Scripture within a community of faith are already canonical in this regard. Childs argues, "The concept of canon was not a late, ecclesiastical ordering which was basically foreign to the material itself, but that canon-consciousness lay deep within the formation of the literature" (*Biblical Theology*, 70). Rather than something foreign to the text (something imposed on it from the outside), the texts were canonical by virtue of their intrinsic qualities. Thus, theologically, canon is best understood as an internal property of the text.

Canonical Interpretation

Because canonical interpretation is not a new criticism or hermeneutic, it is not possible to outline a canonical methodology consisting of a linear series of steps (Childs, "Toward Recovering," 126). In other words, there is no pristine canonical methodology or key hermeneutical concept that unlocks the Bible's message; rather, canonical interpretation insists that "the canon provides the arena in which the struggle for understanding takes place" (Childs, *Old Testament Theology*, 115). Good exegetical tools and skills will be necessary for right interpretation; however, the entire project must be guided by the overarching context of the canon. Rather than interpreting Scripture within the framework of promise and fulfillment, or redemptive history, or progressive covenantalism, canonical interpretation looks to the final form of the canon for such an overarching interpretive context (though, as the previous quotation of Ridderbos shows, some attempt to combine these frameworks with a notion of canon). For example, the canonical interpreter of, say, the Pentateuch, or the Book of the Twelve, or the Pauline corpus looks for clues embedded in the text as to the shape (and hermeneutical function) of that corpus, operating according to the text's own categories rather than categories of an overarching story line or historical schema.

As with all constructive biblical interpretation, the canonical approach values understanding the text in its historical and literary context. Exegetical tools that aid the reader in understanding the circumstances of the text's composition and the rhetorical and literary structure (and genre) of the text are a necessary exegetical point of entry. Another point of entry is the recognition that Scripture is a two-part canon and that the OT and NT are thus analyzed with regard to their structural similarities and dissimilarities. The historical or literal meaning of a particular text—identified by means of grammatical-historical exegesis—is, as it were, extended when viewed not only in the book-level context but also as part of a two-Testament Christian Scripture. Finally, canonical interpretation takes place within the specifically Christian claim that the Bible is a theological unity. Though the OT and NT have their own unique voices, they are equally the means by which God reveals himself. Without conflating the two Testaments, canonical interpretation sees a fundamental theological unity of Scripture such that both the OT and the NT ultimately refer to God's redemption in Jesus Christ. The interpreter must "encounter the biblical text from the full knowledge of the subject matter gained from hearing the voices of both Testaments." And particular to canonical interpretation is the fact that "the biblical text itself exerts theological pressure on the reader" to see the ultimate subject matter or theological reference (Childs, "Toward Recovering," 127).

By this point it should be clear that canonical interpretation is not a new or alternative method on the one hand and that it is an overarching theological approach to biblical interpretation on the other.

Canonical Interpretation: Examples

In order to illustrate canonical interpretation, the remainder of the article will present examples of biblical interpretation that focus on various aspects of canon.

Narrative seams in the Pentateuch and eschatology. Like Childs, Sailhamer dislikes the term "canon criticism," as he understands canon and criticism as opposing interests. Preferring the label "canonical theology," he argues that criticism inevitably leads to reading "behind" the text, focusing attention on the canon's developmental stages (not unlike Sanders). Like Childs, Sailhamer uses canon as a shorthand for the biblical text as it stood at the time of the formation of the canon. He speaks of a text-oriented approach to OT theology. In contrast to other canonical interpreters, Sailhamer generally understands insights from earlier layers of tradition history as not hermeneutically significant for interpretation. He insists that there is "an important distinction between the text of Scripture and the prehistory of that text. . . . Whatever prehistory we may be able to reconstruct for the text, it is not a source of revelation or inspired instruction" (*Introduction*, 84). Sailhamer's comment illustrates an internal tension within canonical interpretation—namely, the degree to which the results of tradition, form, or redaction criticism are helpful in exegesis. Most canonical interpreters agree that the final form of the text is the focus of interpretation, yet there is disagreement regarding the necessity of the text's prehistory for understanding textual meaning.

Sailhamer's work on the Pentateuch as a single book will provide an example of how canonical interpretation might guide one's understanding of OT theology. He identifies structures that not only reinforce the unity of the Pentateuch as a canonical subcollection but also argue for its fundamentally eschatological orientation. Sailhamer observes three "macro-structural junctures," made up of poetic discourses coming at the end of larger narrative units within the Pentateuch—Gen. 49, Num. 24, and Deut. 31. He calls attention to the repeated pattern and common terminology between the segments. "In each of the three segments, the central narrative figure (Jacob, Balaam, Moses) calls an audience together (imperative: Gen. 49:1; Num. 24:14; Deut. 31:28) and proclaims (cohortative: Gen. 49:1; Num. 24:14; Deut. 31:28) what will happen (Gen. 49:1; Num. 24:14; Deut. 31:29) in the 'end of days' (Gen. 49:1; Num. 24:14; Deut. 31:29)" ("Canonical Approach," 310).

The narrative in Gen. 49 acts like a prologue, indicating that the main character in the narrative, Jacob, has called his sons together in order to announce to them "that which will happen in the end of days" (Gen. 49:1b AT). Jacob's subsequent poetic discourse is set in the eschatological context of the "end of days." Similarly, the stories from Sinai and the wilderness function as a prologue to Balaam's poetic discourse in Num. 24. Once again, the discourse focuses on the "end of days" (Num. 24:14 AT). Finally, it functions as a kind of *inclusio* with the end of Deuteronomy. A narrative prologue fronts the poetic speeches by Moses. Just like Jacob, Moses has called together the elders of the tribes (Deut. 31:28) in order to announce the difficulties that "will happen in the end of days" (Deut. 31:29b AT).

Sailhamer argues that in the "seams connecting both poetic texts—Gen. 49 and Deut. 32—to the preceding narrative segments and using the same terminology the author has inserted an identical message to the reader as a clue that the poetic discourses are to be read 'eschatologically'" ("Canonical Approach," 310). He argues that the combination of macro-structure, narrative motifs, and specific terminology cannot be accidental, but rather indicates intentional canonical shaping. Such intentional elements in the text "reveal the work of the final composer or author of the Pentateuch" and, furthermore, reveal the "clear indication of the hermeneutic of this author" ("Canonical Approach," 311). Therefore, the shaping of the Pentateuch in this fashion suggests, theologically, that the historical narratives were refocused eschatologically. Sailhamer concludes that "one of the central concerns lying behind the final shape of the Pentateuch is an attempt to uncover an inherent relationship between the past and the future." Such a hermeneutic "leads to a form of 'narrative typology'" ("Canonical Approach," 311) that anticipates God's future work in the "end of days."

Formation of the OT canon: The Law and the Prophets. A canonical perspective understands that the overall shape of the OT has not come about by accident but bears intentional design. The shapers or editors who established the OT's major divisions (Pentateuch, Prophets, and Writings) also left indication of its overall structure. Several scholars have noted how Deut. 34:10–12 and Mal. 4:4–6 are not merely the final paragraphs of the Pentateuch and the prophetic corpus, respectively, but also "intentionally placed hermeneutical markers" that already respond "to the question of how the various subcollections of Old Testament scripture are to be read with respect to each other" (Chapman, "Canonical Approach," 122). Building on the work of Joseph Blenkinsopp and Rolf Rendtorff, Chapman, Sailhamer, and others note that the strong canonical links between the final paragraphs of the Pentateuch and of the Prophets, such that not only were the two collections drawn to a conclusion themselves but they also indicate a particular hermeneutical understanding of the whole into which the two subcollections fit.

First of all, according to Chapman, Deut. 34:10–12 and Mal. 4:4–6 are similar in that both passages are secondary, not written by the original author, and thus constitute a later shaping of the OT subcollections. Second, both passages focus on a particular individual characterized as a prophet: Moses and Elijah, respectively, both of whom performed signs and wonders. The first point is debatable. Many would argue that Mal. 4:4–6 is an original composition of the author, and some would insist the same for Deut. 34:10–12. Whether or not these passages involve redaction, the observation here is that the connections in the text suggest intentional canonical structuring. Moses is the key "prophet" in the Pentateuch, whereas Elijah is the central prophet in the Prophets (Sailhamer, "Canonical Approach," 314n28). Because of their remarkable similarity in form and content, these last verses of both the Pentateuch and the Prophets constitute the stitching that connects the two collections. Due to the variability of the tripartite structure of the OT (see Chapman, "Canonical Approach," 132–35), the seam connecting the Pentateuch and Prophets is likely stronger than that connecting the Prophets to the Writings. From this, Chapman argues that the relationship between the Pentateuch and the Prophets "is basic to the final shape of the canon as a whole" ("Canonical Approach," 135).

In addition to marking the threefold division of the OT, these canonical connections (or seams) suggest a particular way of understanding OT theology as well. Moses's promise of the future coming of a prophet (Deut. 18:15), in context, could be understood in either individual or corporate terms—in other words, it could be a promise of an individual eschatological prophet or the general office of the prophet. However, read in light of Deut. 34:10 ("No prophet has arisen again in Israel like Moses," CSB), it is clear that the promise refers to the future coming of an individual prophet. Sailhamer argues that Deut. 34:10–12 appears "to interpret the words of Moses in chap. 18 typologically and eschatologically, precisely the way these words are read in the NT (Acts 3:22; 7:37)" ("Canonical Approach," 315). If this reading is correct, then we see not only the intentional shaping but, further, the hermeneutical or theological framework of the OT canon.

However, this raises a key question: Were these passages (these seams) written and included in the text *in order* to give the OT canon a particular interpretive and theological framework? Or is it enough for a contemporary interpreter to read these passages in an intertextual way whether or not the interpretative or canonical framework was "intended by the literature's ancient tradents"? (Chapman, "Canonical Approach," 137). Sailhamer raises similar questions. He notes that, though inspired, Deut. 34 and Mal. 4 were likely not written by the original authors (Sailhamer, "Canonical Approach," 314). Sailhamer argues that reading Deut. 18 in light of Deut. 34 particularly discloses "firsthand the work and hermeneutic of those who collected and shaped the Hebrew canon"—those whom Chapman calls "tradents." He goes on to note that "we can also see that such a hermeneutic was not foreign or out of step with the final composition of the Pentateuch. On the contrary, in substance it is at one with that of the author of the Pentateuch" ("Canonical Approach," 314). Without the same language of authorship, Chapman also is careful to ground the inclusion of these canonical seams in the "actual historical process of the literature's development" ("Old Testament Canon," 137).

James and Jude as brackets for the Catholic Epistles. The opening of Jude includes this brief line about the author of the letter: "Jude, a servant of Jesus Christ and a brother of James" (Jude 1). At once this opening both draws attention to the family relationship between Jude and James as brothers of Jesus and effectively cues readers to think back to the Letter of James. Though it is unlikely that James and Jude exhibit literary dependence, the two letters share several key textual connections that indicate the presence of a framing device that defines the opening and closing boundaries of the canonical subcollection of the Catholic Epistles. There are several connections that draw together the openings of both letters. Negatively, James and Jude both intentionally omit any reference to their familial relation to Jesus, and neither refers to himself as an apostle. Furthermore, both letter openings include the self-description "a servant of Jesus Christ [*Iēsou Christou doulos*]" (James 1:1; Jude 1). The title itself is one of honor and authority most likely taken up from the OT. Additionally, Jude 1 draws a line of familial connection to James. That the name James needs no further identification is likely due to the fact that, after the death of James the son of Zebedee, the only James widely known in the early church merely by name would have been James the brother of Jesus and leader of the church in Jerusalem. The reference back to James in Jude 1 is taken as a reference to the Letter of James in some streams of reception (see Eusebius, *Hist. eccl.* 2.23.24–25). Later readers no doubt would have recognized the familial connection noted by Jude; however, the reference to James in Jude 1 would also have suggested, at a later time in the reception history of these texts, a connection between the letters themselves (Lockett, "James and Jude").

Furthermore, there is an intriguing connection between the ending of James and the ending of Jude. The final exhortation of James, situated just after a discussion of prayer, brings the letter to an abrupt end (almost a non-ending): "My brothers, if anyone among you wanders from the truth and someone brings him back, let him know that whoever brings back a sinner from his wandering will save his soul from death and will cover a multitude of sins" (James 5:19–20 ESV). Likewise, the final exhortation of Jude (and the Catholic Epistles as a whole) echoes James's call for redeeming an erring brother. "And have mercy on those who doubt [dispute]; save others [them] by snatching them out of the fire; to others [them] show mercy with fear, hating even the garment stained by the flesh" (Jude 22–23 ESV). Though the textual and exegetical issues are legion, this final passage just before Jude's benediction could likely be an exhortation to show mercy to the intruders who have been upsetting the faith of the community (Lockett, "Objects of Mercy"). Notice how mercy is to be offered with "fear" (reverential respect) for how the "garment" might be stained by the "flesh."

It is possible that these textual links led to reading James and Jude as the opening and closing texts of the Catholic Epistles collection. One hermeneutical insight stemming from this canonical shaping is that Jude's closing benediction could be read not only as the ending of Jude but also as the conclusion to the entire collection. The twofold benediction that God would "keep you from stumbling" and "make you stand in his presence without blemish with joy" in a general way summarizes themes running throughout the Catholic Epistles (v. 24 AT; Lockett, "James and Jude").

Diaspora and the people of God: James and 1 Peter. There are a significant number of lexical and thematic parallels between James and 1 Peter. Thirteen similarities in theme and vocabulary are of particular importance: (1) the address to the diaspora (James 1:1; 1 Pet. 1:1), (2) rejoicing in suffering (James 1:2; 1 Pet. 1:6–9), (3) proving of faith and perfection (James 1:3–4; 1 Pet. 1:7–9), (4) use of Isa. 40:6–8 (allusion in James 1:10–11; quotation in 1 Pet. 1:24–25), (5) birth through the divine word (James 1:18; 1 Pet. 1:23), (6) call to rid the self of evil (James 1:21; 1 Pet. 2:1), (7) quotation and interpretation of Lev. 19 (James 2:8, quoting Lev. 19:18b; James 2:1, 9, alluding to Lev. 19:15; 1 Pet. 1:16, quoting Lev. 19:2; 1 Pet. 1:22, alluding to Lev. 19:18b), (8) call to good conduct (James 3:13; 1 Pet. 2:12), (9) warning about desires at war within the self (James 4:1–2; 1 Pet. 2:11), (10) quotation of Prov. 3:34 LXX (James 4:6; 1 Pet. 5:5), (11) command to resist the devil (James 4:7; 1 Pet. 5:8–9), (12) promise that God will exalt those who humble themselves (James 4:10; 1 Pet. 5:6), and (13) quotation of Prov. 10:12 (James 5:20; 1 Pet. 4:8). In addition to these similarities in themes and terms, the sequence in which they are presented is strikingly uniform. The only deviations in their presentation occur between 4 and 5, between 6 and 7, then, finally, between 11 and 12.

The density of thematic and lexical similarity along with the uniformity in sequence could be evidence of some kind of compositional connection between the two letters (Lockett, "Use of Leviticus"). Whether or not there was literary dependence between the letters, these clear links draw the two texts together such that their first readers and subsequent compilers within the canonical process would have recognized their association. The textual connections between James and 1 Peter, read in the early Christian context, served as indicators or hermeneutical clues that encouraged reading the two texts together within the canonical subcollection of the Catholic Epistles. Though James and 1 Peter use the term "diaspora" differently, the shared term not only encourages a canonical reading of the two letters but also suggests a theological reality regarding the eschatological people of God—a people made up of both Jews and gentiles.

James addresses his readers as "the twelve tribes in the diaspora" (1:1 AT). Both "twelve tribes" and "diaspora" are most likely literal references to Jews living outside their homeland. Though at the time of writing the ten northern tribes had not been reconstituted from the time of the Assyrian invasion (notwithstanding Luke 2:36), the reference to "twelve tribes" is likely "not purely ideal, but indicates that the letter is intended for the whole diaspora, including not only the western but also the eastern diaspora, where descendants of the exiles of the northern tribes still . . . formed communities known and in communication with the rest of the Jewish world" (Bauckham, "James, 1 Peter," 154). That is, though "twelve tribes in the diaspora" refers to ethnic Jews outside the land of Israel, that does not limit the fact that it refers more broadly to the whole diaspora.

At the same time, James does not write to all Jews in the diaspora without distinction. This is both because James communicates as the leader of the early *Christian* movement and because his letter is not an attempt to convert his audience to faith in Christ (they already share the same faith; see 2:1). James, therefore, writes to Jewish followers of Jesus, yet he does not indicate a specifically Christian audience in the letter opening. This is likely indicative of how James understands the Christian movement. For him, Christians are not a specific sect, distinct from other Jews, but rather a "nucleus of the messianic renewal of the people of Israel which was [already] underway" (Bauckham, "James, 1 Peter," 154). Furthermore, the phrase "twelve tribes in the diaspora" evokes the general Jewish hope of the return of all the Jewish tribes from exile to the land of Israel—a program of renewal already initiated by Jesus in appointing the twelve apostles. This program of redemption is open to non-ethnic Israelites, as the example of Rahab demonstrates (2:25). Therefore, James's understanding of the people of God, even as a diaspora people, does not exclude gentiles, but "like Jesus' own mission, it is still focused on the messianic renewal of Israel as the necessary first stage in the messianic redemption *of the world*" (Bauckham, "James, 1 Peter," 155, emphasis added).

First Peter's use of "diaspora" marks his readers with a new identity as God's elect people. The bulk of the letter further unpacks this identity and its implications for his readers. Whereas the diaspora is indicative of Jewish identity in James, diaspora in 1 Peter is a way of describing gentile Christian identity theologically in the midst of a pagan world. Unlike James, 1 Peter addresses his readers as converts from a pagan life and society. Both letters, however, are similar in that neither is concerned to draw a distinction between Jewish and gentile followers of Jesus on the lines of purity or food laws. In fact, the entire question of relations between Jewish and gentile Christians is completely absent from both letters. The term "gentiles" is used throughout 1 Peter to refer not to non-Jews but to non-Christians (e.g., 2:12). This observation leads Richard Bauckham to argue that in 1 Peter the Jews "have simply dropped out of the picture altogether" ("James, 1 Peter," 160). Therefore, the language of diaspora, borrowed from the Jewish experience, is used in 1 Peter to draw a line of distinction between Christians and non-Christians.

Peter describes his diaspora readers as those who have experienced a new exodus where God has made those who were previously not a people to be his own elect people (Hosea 2:23; 1 Pet. 2:10). The image of "new birth" (1:3) likely also connects to the prophecy of Hosea, where those previously not God's people become "children of the living God" (Hosea 1:10). So, when 1 Peter describes his readers as those in the diaspora, it is in reference to a temporary diaspora. By means of the new exodus, Peter's readers are already the eschatological people of God; however, they still live presently as exiles among the gentiles. Rather than a *geographical* diaspora (as in James), 1 Peter's audience is in a *temporal* diaspora, living in the time between their present election and calling as God's people and their future inheritance at the revelation of Christ. It is within this in-between time (their diaspora) that Peter's audience must live out their new identity as God's holy people.

Though clearly distinct in many ways, the readers of James and those of 1 Peter are both experiencing diaspora as God's people; the theology of the two letters, when read together, helps clarify the identity of God's eschatological people. Bauckham notes, "If we read the catholic epistles in the order which at an early date came to be the accepted canonical order . . . then we read first a letter addressed only to Jewish Christians as the twelve tribes in the Diaspora and then a letter apparently addressed only to Gentile Christians as 'exiles of the diaspora,' to whom defining descriptions of Israel as God's people are applied" (*James*, 156). The theological result of reading James and 1 Peter in their canonical context is to announce the inclusion of gentiles into the eschatological people of God—a people in continuity with Israel via its Jewish Christian members while at the same time open to including those who previously had not been God's people (1 Pet. 2:10). Whereas James focuses on renewed Israel in his letter, he understands the messianic renewal of Israel as *the necessary first step* in the messianic redemption of the world. This theological perspective is evidenced all the more powerfully when James and 1 Peter are read in their canonical association. Therefore,

> the inclusion of Gentiles in the eschatological people of God is thus portrayed in the catholic letters in their own way just as clearly as in the Pauline corpus, reminding us that this was not confined to the Pauline mission but also happened, for example, in the church of Rome. . . . The sequence and relationship of James and 1 Peter portrays the priority of Israel (Rom. 1:16: "to the Jew first and also to the Greek"), Gentile Christians' indebtedness to Jewish believers (cf. Rom. 15:27), and also the full inclusion of Gentiles in the people of God. (Bauckham, *James*, 157)

The textual clues observed above suggest that as James and 1 Peter were received, collected, and arranged, they were understood as belonging to the Catholic Epistles collection and as witnessing, when read together, to God's purposes to renew the eschatological people of God—now including both Jews and gentiles.

See also Biblical Theology; Theological Interpretation of Scripture

Bibliography. Barr, J., *Holy Scripture* (Westminster, 1983); Barton, J., *Holy Writings, Sacred Text* (Westminster John Knox, 1998); Bauckham, R. J., *James: Wisdom of James* (Routledge, 1999); Bauckham, "James, 1 Peter, Jude and 2 Peter," in *A Vision for the Church*, ed. M. Bockmuehl and M. B. Thompson (T&T Clark, 1997), 153–66; Blenkinsopp, J., *Prophecy and Canon*, SJCA 3 (University of Notre Dame Press, 1977); Chapman, S. B., "The Canon Debate," *Journal of Theological Interpretation* 4, no. 2 (2010): 273–94; Chapman, "A Canonical Approach to Old Testament Theology?," *HBT* 25 (2003):121–45; Chapman, "The Old Testament Canon and Its Authority for the Christian Church," *ExAud* 19 (2003):125–48; Childs, B. S., *Biblical Theology of Old and New Testaments* (Fortress 1993); Childs, "The Canonical Shape of the Prophetic Literature," *Int* 32 (1978): 46–55; Childs, *Introduction to the Old Testament as Scripture* (Philadelphia: Fortress, 1979); Childs, *The New Testament as Canon* (SCM, 1984); Childs, *Old Testament Theology in a Canonical Context* (Fortress, 1985); Childs, "Toward Recovering Theological Exegesis," *ExAud* 16 (2000): 121–29; Gamble, H. Y., "New Testament Canon," in *The Canon Debate*, ed. L. M. McDonald and J. A. Sanders (Hendrickson, 2002), 267–94; Gignilliat, M. S., *Reading Scripture Canonically* (Baker Academic, 2019); Hahneman, G. M., "The Muratorian Fragment and the Origins of the New Testament Canon," in *The Canon Debate*, ed. L. M. McDonald and J. A. Sanders (Hendrickson, 2002), 405–15; Kruger, M. J., *Canon Revisited* (Crossway, 2012); Lockett, D. R., "James and Jude as Bookends to the Catholic Epistles," in *The Identity of Israel's God*, ed. M. Elliott, D. Collett, M. Gignilliat, and E. Radner (SBL Press, 2020); Lockett, "Objects of Mercy in Jude," *CBQ* 77 (2015): 322–36; Lockett, "The Use of Leviticus 19 in James and 1 Peter," *CBQ* 82 (2020): 456–72; McDonald, L. M., "The Integrity of the Biblical Canon in Light of Its Historical Development," *BBR* 6 (1996): 95–132; Painter, J., "The Johannine Epistles as Catholic Epistles," in *The Catholic Epistles and Apostolic Tradition*, ed. K.-W. Niebuhr and R. W. Wall (Baylor University Press, 2009), 239–305; Rendtorff, R., "The Place of Prophecy in the Theology of the Old Testament," in *Canon and Theology*, ed. R. Rendtorff, trans. M. Kohl, OBT (Fortress, 1993), 170–80; Ridderbos, H. N., *Redemptive History and the New Testament Scriptures* (Presbyterian and Reformed, 1963); Sailhamer, J. H., "The Canonical Approach to the OT," *JETS* 30 (1987): 307–15; Sailhamer, *Introduction to Old Testament Theology* (Zondervan, 1995); Sanders, J. A., *Torah and Canon* (Fortress, 1972); Sheppard, G. T., "Canon," in *Encyclopaedia of Religion*, ed. M. Eliade (Macmillan, 1987), 3:62–69; Ulrich, E., "Notion and Definition of Canon," in *The Canon Debate*, ed. L. M. McDonald and J. A. Sanders (Hendrickson, 2002).

DARIAN LOCKETT

Christology

The question Jesus asked his disciples is still alive today: "Who do people say I am?" (Mark 8:27). As in the first century, so today there is much confusion regarding Jesus's identity, even though most admit that Jesus is one of the most towering figures of history. The disciples respond to Jesus's question by listing some of the diverse answers of their day, yet every answer views Jesus only in the category of a mere human. Today, similar to Jesus's day, people continue to answer Jesus's question with varied and confused answers.

However, in complete contrast to these views of who Jesus is, Scripture *and* the confessional standards of Nicaea and Chalcedon answer correctly. Who is Jesus? Jesus is God the Son incarnate—the intra-trinitarian Son/Word who has always shared equally and fully the divine nature with the Father and Spirit (John 1:1–2; Col. 2:9), who in time became fully human by the addition of a human nature in order to redeem us from our sin by his life, death, and resurrection (Matt. 1:21; John 1:14; 1 Cor. 15:3–8). For this reason, Jesus is in a category all by himself as the exclusive and only Savior and Lord (John 14:6; Acts 4:12; Phil. 2:9–11).

Nevertheless, throughout church history, especially since the Enlightenment, some have questioned whether the theological formulations of Nicaea and Chalcedon are true to Scripture. Some have claimed that the church is guilty of distorting Scripture due to the influence of Hellenism (e.g., Bousset; Casey), or of modifying Jewish monotheism to think of Jesus as only functionally but not ontologically divine (e.g., Dunn;

Ehrman). Or, although better, others have argued that the NT presents a high Christology, yet later confessional standards "distort" Scripture by utilizing foreign theological vocabulary that leaves the biblical narratives and story behind (e.g., Wright, "Identity," 46–49; "Historical," 155–64).

Against these views, I contend that Nicaea and Chalcedon accurately read Scripture, albeit in *theological* language not found directly in Scripture (e.g., *homoousios, hypostasis*, etc.). Yet the language used, and theological "judgments" made (Yeago, 88), rightly understand and put together the biblical data in a way that faithfully renders who Jesus is from the entirety of Scripture. However, in order to draw this conclusion, one must approach and read Scripture on its own terms (i.e., according to its own claims, categories, metaphysical-theological framework, and unfolding story line). If Scripture is approached this way, then there is no discordance between the Jesus of the Bible and the Christ of the confessions.

Three steps will demonstrate this point: first, a brief discussion of method and how to read Scripture theologically; second, a sketch of five truths, rooted in the Bible's theological-metaphysical framework and covenantal plotline, that establishes how Jesus's identity as God the Son incarnate is progressively unveiled in the OT, which then comes to full light in the Son's incarnation and work in the NT; and third, a reflection on how Nicaea and Chalcedon are faithful renderings of Scripture and not distortions of it.

Reading Scripture Theologically

What we think Scripture is and how we read it are foundational for understanding Christ's identity in Scripture and later theological formulations. What is Scripture? Scripture is God's Word written through the agency of human authors unfolding God's eternal plan centered in Christ (2 Tim. 3:15–17; 2 Pet. 1:20–21; Matt. 5:17–20; Luke 24:25–27; Heb. 1:1–3), hence its authority and reliability. Minimally, this view entails that the Jesus presented in the text, though interpreted by the biblical authors, is the Jesus of history, and that their interpretation of him is God-given, accurate, and true. Although Scripture does not exhaustively describe Christ's identity (e.g., John 21:25), whatever it does say, it says infallibly and sufficiently.

In drawing theological/metaphysical conclusions about Christ's identity, we must read the Bible on its own terms. Scripture is our epistemological norm for comprehending who Jesus is apart from all historical-critical reconstructions of the text. In fact, attempts to understand Jesus's identity apart from the Bible's metanarrative and interpretive framework or to pick and choose parts of that framework while rejecting others only leads to speculative, subjective, and arbitrary interpretations of Jesus, which the various quests for the historical Jesus have done for centuries (Wellum, 39–77).

To read Scripture theologically, we must also remember that it is written over time. Revelation, alongside redemption, occurs progressively, largely demarcated by the biblical covenants. This entails that our reading of Scripture carefully traces out God's unfolding plan—the task of "biblical theology." Biblical theology is the exegetical and theological discipline that attempts to put together the entire canon in terms of its redemptive-historical progression (Rosner, 3–11). Scripture consists of many literary forms that require careful interpretation, but what unites biblical books is God's unfolding plan, starting in creation, accounting for the fall, unpacking God's redemptive promises through the covenants, and culminating in Jesus's coming and the ratification of a new covenant, which includes the inauguration of the new creation. To draw theological/metaphysical conclusions from Scripture, we must do so according to the Bible's own presentation and description of reality. This is necessary to identify Christ correctly. In fact, as God's plan unfolds, from creation to its fulfillment in Christ, Scripture gives the interpretive framework to grasp who Jesus is as God's eternal Son become flesh and the nature of his work.

Christ's Identity Revealed from Scripture's Plotline

How is Christ's identity unveiled in Scripture? It is revealed from the Bible's metanarrative beginning in Genesis. Jesus comes to us not *de novo* but rooted in the categories, content, and framework of the OT that reveal who he is, why he has come, and why he alone can redeem us. Individual texts in the NT make sense only when they are placed in the context of the OT. To establish the biblical identity of Christ, we must do so from the entirety of Scripture.

In fact, as we trace the Bible's plotline—starting in creation with its presentation of God as Creator and Lord, humans as image-sons created to know and serve God in covenant relationship, the entrance of sin into the world, and God's gracious promise and determination to redeem his people by a greater Adam, who is also identified with Yahweh—we discover that Scripture unveils the teaching that Jesus is *God the Son incarnate*. In other words, Christ's identity is disclosed to us across redemptive history as we discover how all of God's promises and various persons, events, and institutions are intended by God to anticipate, foreshadow, and typify the eternal Son to come. Yet it is not until the incarnation that he is fully revealed.

To demonstrate this point, we will sketch five truths that illustrate how Jesus's identity as God the Son incarnate is gradually unveiled across Scripture's covenantal story.

God the Creator-covenant Lord. To identify Christ in Scripture, especially as the divine Son, we must start with the strict monotheism of Scripture (e.g., Bauckham, *Jesus*; Capes; Hurtado; Loke; Tilling). In fact, this is where Paul begins at Athens (Acts 17:16–32). Given that the Athenians assumed a different god-world relationship than Scripture, Paul first establishes a biblical-theological/metaphysical framework so that his presentation of Christ will make sense on the Bible's own terms. Apart from doing so, the establishment of Christ's identity as the divine Son who shares the divine nature with the Father and Spirit will be less than biblical and misunderstood. In order to explain who Jesus is in relation to the one, true, and living God, Paul first establishes the Creator-creature distinction and identifies God as the Lord.

As Scripture opens, God is presented as the uncreated, independent, self-sufficient Creator of the universe who creates and rules all things by his word (Gen. 1–2; Ps. 50:12–14; Acts 17:24–25; cf. John 1:1). This truth establishes the Bible's central metaphysical distinction: the Creator-creature distinction and God's transcendent lordship over creation (Pss. 7:17; 9:2; 21:7; 97:9; 1 Kings 8:27; Isa. 6:1; Rev. 4:3). Yet, as Creator and Lord, God is also fully present and related to his creatures (immanent): he freely, powerfully, and purposefully sustains and governs all things to his desired end (Ps. 139:1–10; Acts 17:28; Eph. 1:11), but he is not identified with the world.

As the Creator, God rules over his creation with perfect power, knowledge, and justice (Pss. 9:8; 33:5; 139:1–4, 16; Isa. 46:9–11; Acts 4:27–28; Rom. 11:33–36). As Lord, God acts in, with, and through his creatures to accomplish his plan and purposes (Eph. 1:11). As a personal being, God commands, loves, and judges in a manner consistent with himself and according to the covenant relationships he has established with his creatures. Indeed, as we walk through redemptive history, God discloses himself not merely as uni-personal but as a unity of three persons: Father, Son, and Spirit (e.g., Matt. 28:18–20; John 1:1–18; 5:16–30; 17:1–5; 1 Cor. 8:5–6; 2 Cor. 13:14; Eph. 1:3–14). In fact, the trinitarian nature of God is disclosed with the unveiling of Christ as the divine Son, along with the Spirit of God.

God is also the Holy One (Gen. 2:1–3; Exod. 3:2–5; Lev. 11:44; Isa. 6:1–3). God's holiness means more than his being "set apart" since it is uniquely associated with his aseity ("life from himself"). God is categorically different in nature and existence from his creation; he shares his glory with no one (Isa. 42:8; 44:6–8). God's holiness entails his personal-moral perfection. He is "too pure to look on evil" and unable to tolerate wrong (Hab. 1:12–13; cf. Isa. 1:4–20; 35:8). When we sin against God, he must act with holy justice; however, he is the God who loves his people with a holy, covenant love (Hosea 11:9). God's holiness and love are never at odds (1 John 4:8; Rev. 4:8). Yet, as sin enters the world and God graciously promises to redeem us, a legitimate question arises as to how God will forgive our sins and remain true to himself—a question central to the Bible's unfolding plotline and Christ's identity.

This first truth of God's identity is vital in Scripture's identification of Christ. God's identity as the Creator-covenant Lord and the Creator-creature distinction establish a definite metaphysics to Scripture's interpretive framework. Specifically, Christ's identity is unveiled as it is tied to *this* God and *this* framework. Two points explain the significance of this point for identifying Christ.

First, as Scripture's story unfolds, beginning in Gen. 3:15—the seed of the woman—and then especially in the Prophets, the Messiah-Son to come will be human *but also identified with God*. For it is he who will fulfill all of God's promises, inaugurate God's saving reign, and share God's throne (Ps. 110)—something no mere human or angelic being can do (see Loke, 48–99).

In fact, one way that the NT teaches Christ's deity is by identifying Jesus with OT Yahweh texts (e.g., Rom. 10:9; 1 Cor. 12:3; Phil. 2:11; see Capes; Fee; Tilling) and applying *theos*, a word reserved for God, to Christ (John 1:1, 18; 20:28; Rom. 9:5; Titus 2:13; Heb. 1:8; 2 Pet. 1:1; see Harris). But in Scripture, no creature can share God's attributes (Col. 2:9), do God's works (Col. 1:15–20; Heb. 1:1–3), receive worship reserved for God alone (John 5:22–23; Heb. 1:6; Rev. 5:11–12), or bear God's name (John 8:58; Phil. 2:9–11) unless he is equal with God and thus, given monotheism, one who shares the one, identical divine nature (Levering, 47–74).

Second, given that God is the perfect standard of righteousness, sin before him is serious. As the Holy One, God is "the Judge of all the earth" who always does what is right (Gen. 18:25). But in promising to justify us before him (Gen. 15:6; Rom. 4:5), God must remain true to his own righteous demand against sin. But how can God remain just *and* justify the ungodly? In Scripture, this is *the* major question that drives the Bible's redemptive story. As God's plan is disclosed, this question is answered in a specific person—namely, the Messiah, who is the servant-son, who alone can redeem us *because he is more than a human son*. He is also the divine Son who becomes human to act as our representative and substitute (Rom. 3:21–26). As *God the Son*, he is able to satisfy his own righteous demand against us, and as *human*, he is able to satisfy the demands of covenant life for us as our new-covenant head.

Adam and the requirement of covenant obedience. Christ's identity can be grasped only if we also identify humans as image-sons and covenant creatures. Why? Because unless we go back to Adam and trace Scripture's link between the command to and curse of the first Adam, which is remedied only by the last Adam, we have little rationale for the incarnation of the divine Son, nor can we say why our Redeemer must be fully God and human (see Ps. 8; Heb. 2:5–18).

Scripture divides all people under two representative heads: the first Adam and the last Adam (Rom. 5:12–21;

1 Cor. 15:12–28). In God's plan, Adam is more than the first human; he is also humanity's representative and a *typos* of Christ, the last Adam (Rom. 5:14). Adam's headship defines what it means to be human, and sadly, by his representative-legal act of disobedience, he plunges all people into sin (Gen. 3; Rom. 3:23; 5:12–21).

God's demand for covenantal obedience is central to his relationship with us. Regardless of whether one speaks of a "creation covenant" (see Gentry and Wellum, 211–58, 666–85), God, as our Creator, demands complete loyalty and obedience from Adam as our head, and by extension from us (Gen. 2:15–17). The tree of the knowledge of good and evil tests whether Adam will be an obedient covenant-keeper. Adam disobeys, and the consequence of his action is not private. Post-fall, all people are born "in Adam"—guilty and corrupt. Adam's sin impacts the entire creation; we now live in an abnormal, cursed world that only God can remedy (Rom. 8:18–25), if he so chooses to act in grace. The tree of life holds out an implied promise of life. Yet, because of sin, God expels Adam from Eden, although there is a concealed hint of hope in God's promise of Gen. 3:15 and the unfolding covenants.

Why is this crucial for grasping Christ's identity in Scripture? Because what drives the Bible's story is the identification of *God's* promised provision as a *human* deliverer who will reverse the effects of Adam's disobedience, and one who is also greater than Adam. For redemption to occur, a human must render the required covenantal obedience for us. Yet the reversal of Adam's sin and all its disastrous effects will require more than a human. It will also require the divine Son, the true image of God (Col. 1:15; Heb. 1:3) to do what only God can do: to remove the curse, to pay for our sin, and to usher in a new creation. To underscore this point, we turn to the third truth.

The nature of the human problem. From Gen. 3 forward, Scripture teaches that Adam's disobedience brought sin into the world and humans under God's wrath (Rom. 5:12–21). God expels Adam and Eve from his presence due to sin, and the transmission of sin is universal. By Gen. 6, human sin has so multiplied that it results in a flood. Looking back on the course of human history, Paul confirms our universal problem: "There is no one righteous, not even one. . . . For all have sinned and fall short of the glory of God" (Rom. 3:10, 23). Adam's sin turned the created order upside down and brought on humanity the sentence of death (6:23). We, who were made to know and love God, are now under his righteous condemnation as his enemies and objects of his wrath (Eph. 2:1–3).

However, our sin *before* God creates a serious tension in the Bible's story and covenantal relationships—a tension that only God can resolve. God created humans to know him, to display his glory as his image-sons, and to rule over creation as his vice-regents (Gen. 1:26–28; Ps. 8). In the covenant, God promises to be our God, and that we will dwell in his presence (Exod. 6:7; Jer. 31:33). But given the nature of God and our sin before him, how can we dwell in his presence without experiencing his full judgment against our sin? God is holy and just, and we are not; he cannot overlook our sin. All of God's attributes are essential to him, including his holy justice. God is not like a human judge who adjudicates laws external to him; God *is* the law. Our sin is not against an abstract law; it is against *this* God, our Creator and Judge (Ps. 51:4). So, how can we have covenant peace without covenant obedience and the full payment of our sin? Even under the Mosaic covenant when God provided a means of atonement for Israel's sin (e.g., the sacrificial system, priesthood, tabernacle-temple; cf. Lev. 17:11), it was never sufficient in itself. Scripture teaches that the old covenant was a means to a larger end (Gal. 3:15–4:7). God intended to tutor Israel that a greater provision and covenant was necessary (Heb. 7–10), a point the prophets teach (see Jer. 31:31–34).

But the question arises: Given God's promise to redeem his people by his provision of a deliverer, what kind of person must he be? God created humans to rule over the world, but no one "in Adam" fully does so. Who, then, is able to establish God's saving rule (kingdom) on earth, to undo what Adam did by rendering full covenant obedience, and to satisfy God's holy demand against our sin? Ultimately, the *human* to come must be greater than Adam and, given that God cannot forgive our sins apart from satisfying his own moral demand against our sin, this human must be identified with *God*. The Messiah-Redeemer to come must identify with God in his nature and with us in ours, which is precisely what Scripture teaches as God's plan is unveiled through the covenants.

God himself redeems and re-creates through his obedient Son. After Adam's sin, God acts in grace by promising to reverse the effects of sin by *his* provision of the "seed of the woman" (Gen. 3:15 AT)—a promise that is given greater clarity over time. Although in embryonic form, we learn that the coming "seed" will destroy the works of Satan and restore goodness to the world. The promise creates the expectation that when it is finally realized, sin and death will be destroyed and God's saving rule will be established on earth. As God's plan unfolds, we discover who this Redeemer is and how he will save us. Three observations will develop this point.

First, *God's promise of a coming "seed" is unveiled through the covenants with Noah, Abraham, Israel, and David*. Each covenant adds to the development of the promise, which in due course anticipates the coming of an image-son who will be more than a mere human. How? God's promise of a coming human is foreshadowed by Adam, Noah, Moses, Israel, and David as types of the one to come. Yet, Scripture also identifies this "anointed one" (Messiah) with God since this Messiah-son does what only God can do—he inaugurates God's saving rule and shares God's throne (e.g., Pss. 2; 45; 110; Isa. 9:6–7; Ezek. 34).

Second, how does God's kingdom come in its redemptive, new-creation sense (Isa. 65:17)? As the OT unfolds, *God's saving reign is revealed and comes to this world in anticipatory form through the covenants and their heads—Adam, Noah, Abraham, and Israel, but uniquely through David and his sons.* Yet the OT repeatedly teaches that these covenant heads are insufficient; they are not the promised one—a truth especially evident in the Davidic covenant.

The Davidic covenant is the epitome of the OT covenants; it brings the previous covenants to a climax in the king (Gentry and Wellum, 443–85, 647–712). The covenant consists of God's promises about the establishment of David's house forever (2 Sam. 7:12–16), and, significantly, the Father-son relation established between God and the king (7:14; cf. Pss. 2; 89:26–27). This Father-son relation organically links the Davidic covenant back to the previous covenants and forward to Christ, David's greater Son (Carson, 13–42).

Regarding the former, "son" was first applied to *corporate* Israel (Exod. 4:22–23; cf. Hosea 11:1), but now it is the *individual* king, who, in himself, is "true Israel." He is the administrator of the covenant, thus representing both God's rule to the people and the people as a whole before God (2 Sam. 7:22–24). It also entails that the Davidic king fulfills the role of Adam; it is through *him* that God's rule is effected on earth (2 Sam. 7:19b; Gentry and Wellum, 456–59, 700–703; Crowe, 199–215). At the center of God's redemptive plan is the restoration of humanity's vice-regent role in creation via the seed. By the time we get to David, we now know it is through the Davidic king that creation will be restored. In the OT, this truth is borne out in many places, especially the Psalter, which envisions the Davidic son as executing a universal rule (e.g., Pss. 2; 8; 72; 110; cf. Isa. 11).

One further note: in the Davidic covenant, the Father-son relation is first in terms of Yahweh and the *human* king, but in the Prophets this king begins to break all human categories. How? David's greater Son is also identified with Yahweh so that he shares the divine name, rule, and throne. But, given the Creator-creature distinction, this places the king on the side of the Creator (Pss. 45:6; 110; Isa. 9:6; Dan. 7:14; cf. Heb. 1:5–14; Bauckham, "Christology"). Something similar occurs in the king/son-Spirit relation. God's Spirit is first poured out on various leaders in Israel, such as prophets, priests, and kings (e.g., Num. 11:16–18; 1 Sam. 16:13). But in the Prophets, David's greater Son has the Spirit unlike anyone else. One cannot think of *this* Son apart from the fullness of the Spirit (Isa. 11:1–3; 42:1; 61:1–3). Additionally, as a result of the Son's work, *he* will do what Yahweh does: pour out the Spirit on his people (Ezek. 36:25–27; Joel 2:28–32; cf. Acts 2). Already in the OT, in seed form, we have what blooms in the NT—namely, the distinct yet shared identity of the Father, Son, and Spirit (Matt. 28:18–20; John 1:1–2; 1 Cor. 8:5–6; 2 Cor. 3:18), which becomes the seedbed for later trinitarian reflection.

However, before we get to the Prophets, a problem arises in OT history. The Davidic kings disobey, yet the hope of salvation depends on them. God, as the covenant Lord, continues in his determination to keep his promise to bring forth the promised one, now specifically identified as the Davidic king, who will rule the world. But there is no faithful son-king who effects God's saving reign, which leads to the message of the Prophets and the anticipation of a new covenant.

To read the Prophets correctly, we must note their redemptive-historical location. All of the prophets write post-Davidic covenant, which reminds us that their message builds on what God has already revealed through the covenants in promises and typological patterns. The prophets are not only prosecutors of the covenant but also announce a future hope by recapitulating the past history of redemption and projecting it into the future (Goldsworthy, 123–32). They announce that God will keep his promises to redeem, and that *he* will do so through a faithful priest-king (Isa. 7:14; 9:6–7; 11:1–10; 42:1–9; 49:1–7; 52:13–53:12; 61:1–3; Jer. 23:5–6; 33:14–26; Ezek. 34:23–24; 37:24–28; cf. Ps. 110). In this priest-king, identified as the "servant of Yahweh," a new, everlasting covenant will come (Isa. 55:3), and with it the pouring of the Spirit (Ezek. 36–37; Joel 2:28–32), God's saving reign among the nations, the forgiveness of sin (Jer. 31:34), and a new creation (Isa. 65:17). The future hope of the Prophets is found in the new covenant.

All of the Prophets teach about the new covenant, but Jer. 31 is probably the most famous OT text. Jeremiah focuses on what is central to the new covenant—namely, the promise of the complete forgiveness of sin (Jer. 31:34). Under the Mosaic covenant, forgiveness of sin was normally granted via the sacrificial system, but it was never intended to be an end in itself. We know this because God announces that in the new covenant sin will be remembered "no more" (Jer. 31:34), which entails sin's full payment (Heb. 10:18). Jeremiah anticipates the perfect fellowship of God and his people and the dwelling of God with us in a new creation—ultimately the fulfillment of Gen. 3:15.

Third, we can now see how the OT plotline unveils Christ's identity as it moves to the NT. Who is able to fulfill all of *God's* promises, inaugurate *God's* saving rule, and forgive our sin? *God alone is the answer* (Isa. 43:11; 45:21) (Bauckham, *Jesus*, 182–85). After all, who can forgive sin and usher in a new creation, final judgment, and salvation other than God? No previous covenant mediator, or Israel as a nation, can do it; they have all failed. If salvation and judgment are to come, God himself must do it (Isa. 51:9; 52:10; 53:1; 59:16–17; cf. Ezek. 34) by a new and greater act of redemption/exodus, resulting in the ratification of a new and better covenant (Isa. 11:10–16; 40:3–5; 43:1–7; 55:3; Jer. 31:31–34).

However, alongside the fact that God must act to redeem, the OT also teaches that God will act through another David, a human "son," but a "son" who is identified with Yahweh. Isaiah pictures this well. This future king will sit on David's throne (Isa. 9:7) but he will also bear the titles/names of God (9:6). This king, though another David (11:1), is also David's Lord, who shares the divine rule (cf. Ps. 110:1; Ezek. 34). He will be the mediator of a new covenant; he will perfectly obey and act like Yahweh (Isa. 11:1–5), yet he will suffer for our sin to justify many (53:11). It is through him that forgiveness will come, for he is "the LORD our righteousness" (Jer. 23:5–6 AT). In him, OT hope and expectation are joined: Yahweh must save but through his King-Son—who is fully human yet also shares God's rule, throne, and name.

God's eternal Son becomes son. As the NT opens, it is Scripture's covenantal story that serves as the interpretive framework to identify who Jesus is, and which also unveils what was previously concealed (Heb. 1:1–3). Who is Jesus? He is the Son of the Father (John 5:16–30), the one who inaugurates *God's* kingdom and new-covenant age, thus identifying him with Yahweh in all of his actions. In Jesus, the forgiveness of sin is achieved (Mark 2:5; 1 Cor. 15:3), the eschatological Spirit is poured out (John 1:29–34; Acts 2), the new creation dawns (Luke 1:35; 1 Cor. 15:16–28; 2 Cor. 5:17; Eph. 2:10, 15), and all of God's promises are fulfilled (Matt. 5:17–20). But set within the OT context, this entails that Jesus is both the eternal Son of the Father (due to his identification with Yahweh) and the obedient human son-king (due to his incarnation). This is precisely how the NT presents Jesus.

In the NT, Jesus is clearly the *human* son (Matt. 1:1), who fulfills all the typological roles of the previous sons for our salvation (e.g., Adam [Luke 3:38], Israel [Exod. 4:22–23; Hosea 11:1], David [2 Sam. 7:14; Pss. 2; 16; 72; 110]). By his incarnation and work, Jesus becomes David's greater Son who inaugurates God's kingdom and is now seated on a throne, leading history to its consummation at his return (Matt. 28:18–20; Acts 2:32–36; Rom. 1:3–4; Phil. 2:9–11; Col. 1:15–20; Heb. 1). Jesus is the true Israel who by his obedience brings the nation's exile to its end in a new exodus (Matt. 2:15 [Hosea 11:1]; 3:15–17 [cf. Isa. 11:1–2; 42:1; 61:1]; 4:1–11; John 15:1–6 [Isa. 5:1–7]). Jesus is Abraham's true seed (Gal. 3:16) who constitutes his people as the true children of Abraham (Rom. 2:25–29; 4:9–22; Gal. 3:6–9). Jesus is the last Adam and the first man of the new creation (1 Cor. 15:21–22; Heb. 2:5–18). In his conception, the Spirit, parallel to the first creation (Gen. 1:2), overshadows Mary, which is the beginning of the new creation (Luke 1:35). In Jesus's baptism, he is identified as the promised Messiah, the Son of the Father, who receives the Spirit in full measure (Isa. 11:1–5; 61:1–2; Luke 4:14–21) and who pours out the Spirit on his people (Luke 3:16–17; John 20:21–23; Acts 2:1–36; 10:44–48; Gal. 3:26–4:7). Also, in his work, Jesus fulfills Adam's role of ruling over the creation as the obedient royal son-priest (Heb. 2:5–18 [Ps. 8]), evidenced by his healings and miracles tied to the inauguration of God's kingdom (Matt. 8–9).

But Jesus can do all this—that is, fulfill all of *God's* promises and inaugurate *God's* saving reign—only because he is the *divine* Son of the Father (Matt. 11:25–30; John 1:1–3; 5:16–30; 17:3) who assumed our humanity and lived, died, and was raised for our justification (Rom. 4:25). For it is only as the eternal "Word made flesh" (John 1:1, 14) that he can fulfill all the Law and the Prophets (Matt. 5:17–20; Luke 24:44–49), take on himself our sin and guilt, and make this world right by the ratification of a new covenant in his blood (Rom. 3:21–26; Eph. 1:7–10; Heb. 7–10).

For this reason, contra some biblical scholars (e.g., Dunn; Ehrman), the NT does not present a contradictory Christology that pits Jesus's ontology against his function. Instead, the NT follows a basic, unified pattern, grounded in the Bible's covenantal story that stresses a twofold truth regarding Jesus as Son and Lord. The first truth accents Christ's deity as the divine Son in relation to the Father and Spirit by identifying him with Yahweh as the Creator-covenant Lord, who alone rules, reigns, and redeems. The second truth accents the necessity of the incarnation and what Christ achieves as the incarnate Son, who, as our new covenant head, obeys for us in life and in death, thus securing our eternal salvation (e.g., Rom. 1:3–4; Phil. 2:6–11; Col. 1:15–20; Heb. 1:1–3; 5:8–10; see Bauckham, *Jesus*, 30–31; Wellum, 189–208).

In this way, from beginning to end, Scripture unveils Christ's identity. The OT anticipates Christ's coming and sows the seeds for what the NT announces. The NT brings to full light who Jesus is as God the Son incarnate, fully God and fully human, the eternal Word/Son of the Father made flesh (John 1:1, 14) for us and our salvation. This is the truth that Jesus teaches about himself (Matt. 11:25–30; 24:30; Mark 2:10; John 5:16–30; 8:58; cf. Loke, 134–93) and that the church confesses immediately (John 20:28; cf. Fee) and later systematizes with biblical fidelity in the confessional orthodoxy of Nicaea and Chalcedon, a final point to which we now turn.

Are Nicaea and Chalcedon Faithful to Scripture?

Determining whether Nicaea and Chalcedon are faithful to Scripture depends on what we think Scripture is and how we read it. As noted above, if we read Scripture on its own terms, we will conclude that the Jesus of the Bible *is* God the Son incarnate. Nicaea and Chalcedon, then, are not discordant voices but harmonious with Scripture. No doubt the theological language and categories of the confessions are not found directly in Scripture (e.g., *homoousios*, *hypostasis*, and in later theological reflection, *communicatio idiomatum*, the *extra*, *anhypostasia*, etc.). But the language used, and theological "judgments" made, accurately understand

and construct the biblical data in such a way that they faithfully render Christ's identity from all of Scripture (e.g., Yeago; Grillmeier, 3–9).

However, if we read Scripture not according to its own categories but instead in light of some "extratextual" framework that is foreign to the theology and presentation of Scripture (e.g., methodological naturalism tied to historical criticism, or some postmodern constructivism), then inevitably the Jesus discovered will not be the Jesus of the Bible or the Christ of the confessions. Instead, it will be a Jesus that reflects the extratextual system one starts with. For example, this lesson should have been learned by the various "quests for the historical Jesus"—a Jesus, it was assumed from the outset, who was not the Jesus of the Bible (see McGrath). Too often such a search took place within the confines of metaphysical and epistemological assumptions that were contrary to the metaphysics and worldview of Scripture. As such, the Jesus discovered was a reconstructed Jesus, removed from the Bible's theological framework and story line. A biblical, orthodox Christology—that which Nicaea and Chalcedon formulated—is rooted in a specific conception of God, Scripture, humans, etc., and apart from that theology/worldview it cannot stand.

But if we approach Scripture on its own terms, then, from Genesis to Revelation, it teaches us that Jesus is Lord (Phil. 2:6–11). And within Scripture's biblical-theological framework, to say that Jesus is Lord is to say that he is the eternal Son of the Father in relation to the Spirit, who shares the one, undivided divine nature (thus fully God), and due to his incarnation and work (thus fully human), Christ alone is Lord and Savior. Significantly, this is precisely what Nicaea and Chalcedon affirm: they have not left the biblical narratives behind (*pace* Wright, "Historical," 155–64); instead, they have faithfully identified and theologized about Christ Jesus.

No doubt, the confessions further reflect on Scripture, especially in regard to trinitarian relations and the nature of the incarnation. In fact, to take Scripture seriously demands that we do so, since systematic theology as an exercise in "faith seeking understanding" is "pressured" by the biblical texts to specify Christ's identity in terms of ontology (see Rowe, 306–8). For example, given Jesus's self-identity as the eternal Son of the Father, reflection must arise on how the Father and Son share the same divine nature along with the Spirit. Given the unity and aseity of the one Creator-covenant Lord, identifying Yahweh (*kyrios*) as both the Father and the Son "pressures" us to think in terms of the "nature-person" (*ousia-hypostasis*) distinction, eternal relations of origin, etc. (see Levering, 165–235; Ayres, 384–429). This kind of theological reflection is not the imposition of Hellenism on Scripture but precisely what Scripture demands. Or, given the truth of the Creator-creature distinction, reflection must arise on how we make sense of the divine Son becoming human and growing and learning (Luke 2:52). Or, given that the Son is fully God and omniscient, it is legitimate to ask why Jesus says he does not know certain things (Matt. 24:36). Scriptural teaching demands careful theological reflection and accounting for all the biblical data in the way that Scripture presents it.

In fact, this is what Nicaea and Chalcedon were doing. They were reflecting on Scripture in light of Scripture's own teaching, so that the church could faithfully confess, defend, and proclaim the God of the Bible as triune and Jesus as the eternal Son made flesh, our only Lord and Savior. They were not guilty of imposing the extratextual system of Hellenism on Scripture. The Christology of the confessions is rooted in the theological context of the OT, and in truth, christological heresy was more indebted to Greek philosophical categories than to Jewish or biblical ones. After all, it was Greek thought that had difficulty attributing full humanity and/or deity to Christ. Gnosticism and Arianism substituted alien views for the categories of Scripture (see Ayres; Grillmeier). In these false views, Jesus was no more than semi-divine—neither truly God nor truly human—something the church rejected as a denial of Scripture and thus heresy. Although Nicaea and Chalcedon employed extrabiblical language to theologize about Jesus, the language rightly identified the Christ of Scripture. This is why Nicaea and Chalcedon give us trinitarian theology and Christology that are in continuity with Scripture, not Greek thought.

It is also the reason why Nicaea and Chalcedon are rightly viewed as "rules of faith." Confessions are always secondary standards to Scripture, which is primary and foundational. However, because these confessions faithfully formulate biblical teaching, they rightly function as dogmatic "rules" for trinitarian and christological orthodoxy, which the church neglects to her peril. In our ongoing confession and proclamation of Christ as the only Lord and Savior, the church needs to stand on the shoulders of our confessional heritage, but even more significantly, the church needs to return repeatedly to Scripture to know, love, obey, and glory in our triune God in the face of God the Son incarnate, our Lord Jesus Christ.

See also Apostolic Hermeneutics articles; Septuagint articles

Bibliography. Ayres, L., *Nicaea and Its Legacy* (Oxford University Press, 2004); Bauckham, R., "Is 'High Human Christology' Sufficient?," *BBR* 27, no. 4 (2017): 503–25; Bauckham, *Jesus and the God of Israel* (Eerdmans, 2008); Bousset, W., *Kyrios Christos* (Abingdon, 1970); Capes, D., *The Divine Christ* (Baker Academic, 2018); Carson, D. A., *Jesus the Son of God* (Crossway, 2012); Casey, M., *From Jewish Prophet to Gentile God* (Westminster John Knox, 1991); Crowe, B., *The Last Adam* (Baker Academic, 2017); Dunn, J., *Christology in the Making*, 3rd ed. (SCM, 2003); Ehrman, B., *How Jesus Became God* (HarperOne, 2014);

Fee, G., *Pauline Christology* (Hendrickson, 2007); Gentry, P., and S. Wellum, *Kingdom through Covenant*, 2nd ed. (Crossway, 2018); Goldsworthy, G., *Christ-Centered Biblical Theology* (IVP Academic, 2012); Grillmeier, A., *From the Apostolic Age to Chalcedon (451)*, vol. 1 of *Christ in Christian Tradition*, trans. John Bowden, 2nd ed. (John Knox, 1975); Harris, M., *Jesus as God* (Baker, 1992); Hurtado, L., *Lord Jesus Christ* (Eerdmans, 2003); Levering, M., *Scripture and Metaphysics* (Blackwell, 2004); Loke, A., *The Origin of Divine Christology*, SNTSMS 169 (Cambridge University Press, 2017); McGrath, A., *The Making of Modern German Christology*, 2nd ed. (Wipf & Stock, 2005); Rosner, B., "Biblical Theology," in *NDBT*, 3–11; Rowe, C. K., "Biblical Pressure and Trinitarian Hermeneutics," *Pro Ecclesia* 11, no. 3 (2002): 295–312; Tilling, C., *Paul's Divine Christology* (Mohr Siebeck, 2012); Wellum, S., *God the Son Incarnate* (Crossway, 2016); Wright, N. T., "Historical Paul and 'Systematic Theology,'" in *Biblical Theology*, ed. C. Walsh and M. Elliott (Cascade Books, 2016), 147–64; Wright, "Jesus and the Identity of God," *Ex Auditu* 14 (1998): 42–56; Yeago, D. S., "The New Testament and the Nicene Dogma," in *The Theological Interpretation of Scripture*, ed. S. Fowl (Blackwell, 1997), 87–102.

STEPHEN J. WELLUM

Christus Victor *See* Divine Warrior

Chronicles, Books of

The books of Chronicles supplement the records of Samuel and Kings. The books of Samuel and Kings are considered part of what is often called the "Primary History" of the Old Testament (i.e., Genesis through Kings; see Freedman, 5–6). This connected narrative traces the rise and fall of the nation of Israel. Chronicles belongs to the "Secondary History" of the Old Testament, along with Ezra, Nehemiah, and Esther. Portions of these "Secondary" books retell the same story but from the perspective of the postexilic period of Hebrew history. They also update the story of Israel by reporting the fortunes of both the Hebrews who returned to Judah after the Babylonian exile and those who remained in Babylonia.

Literary Character

Chronicles may be classified broadly as history, since it is a continuous written narrative based on source materials and is devoted to particular subjects within a given time period (see Long, 250). Literary history is especially concerned with chronology and cause-effect relationships. The chronological span addressed in Chronicles is extensive, stretching from the patriarchs and matriarchs of Israel to the Babylonian exile—some fifteen-plus centuries. The Chronicler develops several cause-and-effect relationships in the narrative, including ones that explain the growth of Israel as a nation, the rise of Hebrew kingship, the subsequent loss of kingship, and foreign exile. In each case, these cause-and-effect relationships turn on the blessings and curses of the Mosaic covenant, contingent upon Israel's obedience to the covenant stipulations (cf. Lev. 26; Deut. 28).

The books of Chronicles are truly "chronicles" with regard to literary genre. As a literary form the chronicle is a prose composition consisting of a series of reports or selected events in third-person style, arranged and dated in chronological order (see Long, 246). The Chronicles also feature a rich collection of literary types, including genealogy (1 Chron. 3:1–9); list or catalog (1 Chron. 9:3–23; 2 Chron. 4:19–22); report (2 Chron. 9:1–12); letter (2 Chron. 30:6–9); prayer (1 Chron. 17:16–27); speech and sermon (1 Chron. 22:5–16; 2 Chron. 32:9–15); narrative (i.e., cast as a prophetic message, given the Chronicler's emphasis on the retribution principle and the need for repentance, 1 Chron. 17:4–14); song (1 Chron. 16:7–36); theological review (2 Chron. 21:20); and worship-festival summary. Steven McKenzie (43) identifies four basic genres in Chronicles: narrative, speech, list, and genealogy. This combination of literary forms and the well-developed plot structure of the two books confirm Chronicles as a literary work of considerable artistic merit (see Pratt, 199–202; also Japhet, 32: "The Chronicler wrote this history with full awareness of his task, its form, and meaning").

This artistry is seen in the various literary classifications assigned to Chronicles, including sermon, morality play, theology of hope, biography of God, and call to worship. Hugh Williamson (33) describes Chronicles as a "levitical sermon that both warns and encourages his audience." By sermon, we mean preaching, whether an oral or written public address. Rex Mason (223–25) has identified the essential characteristics of a sermon as follows: it appeals to some recognized source of authority, proclaims theological teaching about the nature and character of God, calls for some kind of response by the audience, and employs rhetorical devices designed to pique audience interest in the message. In each case, Chronicles fits the pattern of the sermonic literary form (see Hill, *Chronicles*, 32–33). Michael Wilcock (15–16) suggests Chronicles can be understood as a type of "morality play," a dramatization of a conflict between good and evil that yields an ethical lesson. In this case, the lesson is the turning of the heart or conscience toward God in view of the retribution principle rooted in covenant relationship with YHWH (see Wilcock, 15; Hill, *Chronicles*, 36; cf. Deut. 10:12–13).

The purpose of Chronicles is only secondarily to rekindle hope through the retelling of Israel's history, especially the story of Hebrew kingship. The Chronicler's primary purpose is to tell the story of the God of Hebrew history, a biography of the covenant-making and covenant-keeping God of Israel (see Hill, *Chronicles*, 38).

The "biography" as a literary form in the ancient world was a stylized account of the public and professional life of a significant individual in a given society. The primary purpose of the biography was to reshape or change the life of the reader through a literary encounter with a significant character portrayed as an ideal representative of the community. The Chronicler's litany of God's attributes and activities is impressive: his sovereign ruler as creator (2 Chron. 20:6), his election of Israel (1 Chron. 16:13, 17), his faithfulness to his word (1 Chron. 17:18–24), his responsiveness to prayer (2 Chron. 6:40; 7:12), and his justice (2 Chron. 19:7), goodness (2 Chron. 30:18–20), and mercy (2 Chron. 30:9). Ultimately, the Chronicler portrays God as one who is absolutely faithful to his covenant promises made to Israel, especially to David and his descendants (2 Chron. 6:14–15). He also reminds his audience that God is still looking for "those whose hearts are fully committed to him" (2 Chron. 16:9). The development of each of these themes naturally invites Chronicles's intertextual engagement with earlier scriptural resources.

Finally, Chronicles is a call to worship, the invitation that formally opens the liturgy by summoning the assembly of the faithful into God's presence (see Hill, *Chronicles*, 40–41). The call to worship is a hearty welcome to celebrate and praise God for who he is as the only true God and to thank him for what he has done to restore the pre-fall creation order and redeem fallen humanity. Certain portions of Chronicles emphasize temple worship (e.g., 1 Chron. 29:10–13; 2 Chron. 7:12–16), especially the pilgrimage festivals, which are presented as models for worship in postexilic Judah. There is a sense, however, in which the entirety of Chronicles is a call to worship because in the retelling of Israel's history we have the biography of God. This recitation of "salvation history" naturally elicits a response of praise and thanksgiving to the Lord (1 Chron. 16:8–10).

Historical Sources

One of the features of the chronicle as a literary genre is the overt appeal to supporting documents and validating external resources. Chronicles references a wide array of original source material:

Genealogical records: descendants of Simeon, 1 Chron. 4:33; descendants of Gad, 1 Chron. 5:17; descendants of Benjamin, 1 Chron. 7:9; descendants of Asher, 1 Chron. 7:40; all Israel, 1 Chron. 9:1; gatekeepers, 1 Chron. 9:22

Letters and official documents: David's temple plans, 1 Chron. 28:11–12; Sennacherib's letter, 2 Chron. 32:9–19; Hezekiah's Passover letter, 2 Chron. 30:6–9; proclamation of Cyrus, 2 Chron. 36:22–23

Other histories: "the book of the kings of Israel and Judah," 1 Chron. 9:1; "the book of the annals of King David," 1 Chron. 27:24; "the book of the kings of Judah and Israel," 2 Chron. 16:11; "the annotations on the book of the kings," 2 Chron. 24:27; "the book of the kings of Israel and Judah," 2 Chron. 27:7; "the annals of the kings of Israel," 2 Chron. 33:18; "the directions written by David king of Israel and by his son Solomon," 2 Chron. 35:4

Prophetic writings: "the records of Samuel the seer, the records of Nathan the prophet and the records of Gad the seer," 1 Chron. 29:29; "the prophecy of Ahijah the Shilonite and . . . the visions of Iddo the seer," 2 Chron. 9:29; "the records of Shemaiah the prophet and of Iddo the seer," 2 Chron. 12:15; "the annotations of the prophet Iddo," 2 Chron. 13:22; "the annals of Jehu son of Hanani, which are recorded in the book of the kings of Israel," 2 Chron. 20:34; the "events of Uzziah's reign . . . recorded by the prophet Isaiah son of Amoz," 2 Chron. 26:22; "the vision of the prophet Isaiah son of Amoz in the book of the kings of Judah and Israel," 2 Chron. 32:32; "the records of the seers," 2 Chron. 33:19

Many of the titles of the other histories and prophetic writings suggest overlapping rather than independent sources. Some are likely variant names for the two primary sources of the 1–2 Kings corpus: "the book of the annals of the kings of Judah" (e.g., 1 Kings 14:29) and "the book of the annals of the kings of Israel" (e.g., 1 Kings 15:31). The modification of the source citation formula to include the name "Israel" is in keeping with the Chronicler's purpose to unify the Hebrew tribes after the destruction of the divided monarchies (e.g., 2 Chron. 16:11 cites "the book of the kings of Judah and Israel," whereas the parallel in 1 Kings 15:23 cites only Judah).

The Chronicler highlights the role of the prophets as a positive force in Judah by interpolating references to them as advocates of repentance when the narrative in Kings preserves no such prophetic intervention. Clearly, the Chronicler makes reference to historical sources no longer extant (e.g., the genealogical records). More important is the recognition that the Chronicler relies principally on biblical books (presumably) previously established as Hebrew Scripture for his retelling of Israel's history—especially Samuel, Kings, and Psalms. This affirms the Chronicler's high regard for the received Scriptures of the Hebrew Bible; it also provides insight into the exegetical tradition of the later biblical writers as it relates to the selection, arrangement, and reshaping of excerpts from those anterior canonical documents (see Fishbane, 387).

Place in the Canon

The Hebrew title of the book is literally "the words of the days" or "the events," referring to the monarchies.

Table 1. Outline of Chronicles

(Select Samuel–Kings synoptic parallels are included.)

I. Genealogical prologue, 1 Chron. 1–9
  A. Patriarchs, 1 Chron. 1:1–2:2
  B. Israel's sons, 2:3–3:24
    [David's sons born at Hebron, 3:1–4a // 2 Sam. 3:2–5]
  C. Families of Judah, 4:1–23
  D. Simeon, 4:24–43
  E. Reuben, Gad, Manasseh, chap. 5
  F. Levi, chap. 6
  G. Issachar, Benjamin, Naphtali, Ephraim, Asher, chap. 7
  H. Saul, chap. 8
  I. Returning exiles, 9:1–34
  J. Saul's genealogy, 9:35–44
II. United monarchy, 1 Chron. 10–2 Chron. 9
  A. King Saul and King David contrasted, 1 Chron. 10–12
    1. Saul's death, chap. 10 // 1 Sam. 31:1–13
    2. David's ascension to kingship, chaps. 11–12
      [David becomes king over Israel, 11:1–3 // 2 Sam. 5:1–5]
      [David conquers Jerusalem, 11:4–9 // 2 Sam. 5:6–10]
      [David's mighty men, 11:10–47 // 2 Sam. 23:8–39]
  B. David and the ark of the covenant, chaps. 13–17
    1. Journey of the ark from Kiriath Jearim to Kidon, chap. 13 // 2 Sam. 6:1–11
    2. David's dynasty, 14:1–7
      [David's children born in Jerusalem, 14:3–7 // 2 Sam. 5:13–16]
    3. David defeats the Philistines, 14:8–17 // 2 Sam. 5:17–25
    4. The ark enters Jerusalem, chaps. 15–16
      [David brings the ark into Jerusalem, 15:1–16:6 // 2 Sam. 6:1–19a]
    5. The Davidic covenant, chap. 17 // 2 Sam. 7:1–17
  C. David's kingship, chaps. 18–20
    1. Territorial expansion, 18:1–13 // 2 Sam. 8:1–14
    2. David's royal officials, 18:14–17 // 2 Sam. 8:15–18
    3. David defeats the Ammonites, 19:1–20:3 // 2 Sam. 10:1–19
    4. Renewed war with the Philistines, 20:4–8
  D. David's preparations for the temple, 21:1–29:9
    1. David's census, 21:1–22:1 // 2 Sam. 24:1–25
    2. Securing building materials, 22:2–19
    3. Duties for Levites, chap. 23
    4. Priestly divisions, chap. 24
    5. Temple musicians, chap. 25
    6. Temple gatekeepers, chap. 26
    7. Military and political officials, chap. 27
    8. Temple architectural plans, chap. 28
    9. Gifts for temple construction, 29:1–9
  E. David's farewell and death, 29:10–30
    [Solomon named as successor, 29:20–22 // 1 Kings 1:28–53]
    [David's death, 29:26–30 // 1 Kings 2:10–12]

continued

F. Solomon's reign, 2 Chron. 1–9
    1. Solomon's ascension to kingship, chap. 1
        [Solomon's request for wisdom, 1:1–13 // 1 Kings 3:1–15]
    2. Construction of the temple, 2:1–5:1 // 1 Kings 5:1–6:38; 7:15–51
    3. Dedication of the temple, 5:2–7:22 // 1 Kings 8:1–9:9
    4. Solomon's activities, chaps. 8–9 // 1 Kings 9:10–10:39
        [Death of Solomon, 9:29–31 // 1 Kings 11:41–43]

III. Early history of Judah, 2 Chron. 10–32
- A. Four kings and the prophetic voice, 10:1–21:3
    1. Rehoboam, chaps. 10–12
        [Israel rebels against Rehoboam, 10:1–14 // 1 Kings 12:1–24]
    2. Abijah, 13:1–14:1a // 1 Kings 15:1–8
    3. Asa, 14:1b–16:14 // 1 Kings 15:9–24
    4. Jehoshaphat, 17:1–21:3
        [End of Jehoshaphat's reign, 20:31–21:3 // 1 Kings 22:41–50]
- B. Judah and the dynasty of Ahab, 21:4–23:21
    1. Jehoram, 21:4–20 // 1 Kings 8:16–24
    2. Ahaziah, 22:1–9 // 1 Kings 8:25–29
    3. Athaliah and Joash, 22:10–23:21 // 2 Kings 11:1–20
- C. Three kings and the decline of Judah, chaps. 24–26
    1. Joash, chap. 24 // 2 Kings 12
    2. Amaziah, chap. 25 // 2 Kings 14:1–22
    3. Uzziah, chap. 26 // 2 Kings 15:1–7
- D. Three kings and the Assyrian threat, chaps. 27–32
    1. Jotham, chap. 27 // 2 Kings 15:32–38
    2. Ahaz, chap. 28 // 2 Kings 16:1–20
    3. Hezekiah, chaps. 29–32 // 2 Kings 18:1–20:21

IV. Later history of Judah
- A. Three kings and repentance, 33:1–36:1
    1. Manasseh, 33:1–20 // 2 Kings 21:1–18
    2. Amon, 33:21–25 // 2 Kings 21:19–26
    3. Josiah, 34:1–36:1 // 2 Kings 22:1–23:30
        [Book of the Law found, 34:14–33 // 2 Kings 22:1–20]
- B. Four kings and the exile of Judah, 36:2–21
    1. Jehoahaz, 36:2–4 // 2 Kings 23:31–35
    2. Jehoiakim, 36:5–8 // 2 Kings 23:36–24:7
    3. Jehoiachin, 36:9–10 // 2 Kings 24:8–17
    4. Zedekiah, 36:11–14 // 2 Kings 24:18–20
    5. Fall of Jerusalem, 36:15–21 // 2 Kings 25:1–21

V. Epilogue: The edict of Cyrus, 36:22–23 // Ezra 1:1–3

The Hebrew book titles are characteristically taken from the first verse, but in this case the title phrase is found in 1 Chron. 27:24. Like Samuel and Kings, 1–2 Chronicles were originally one book. Chronicles follows Ezra-Nehemiah in the Hebrew Bible, suggesting it was either accepted into the OT canon at a later date or viewed as an appendix to the Writings collection. The Chronicler's interpretive and apologetic retelling of Israel's history was intended to awaken covenant faith and evoke hope in the beleaguered postexilic Jewish community. The larger structure of Chronicles accents this hopefulness in that the first book opens with the building of Solomon's temple (with gentile help) and the second book closes with the edict of a gentile king commanding the building of the second temple (2 Chron. 36:22–23). An expanded version of this tagline, the so-called Cyrus colophon in 2 Chronicles, appears in Ezra 1:1–4. The repetition of the decree of Cyrus binds the records of Ezra and Nehemiah with the history of the Chronicler. The connection of the Ezra-Nehemiah reforms with Israel's "temple history" reinforces the Chronicler's theocratic ideal and the expectation of a "new exodus." The emphasis on the Judahite monarchy instills hope for the restoration of Davidic kingship according to the promise of the Davidic covenant (2 Sam. 7; 1 Chron. 17).

Author

Jewish tradition ascribes the books of Chronicles to Ezra the scribe (b. B. Bat. 15a). Earlier biblical scholarship understood the books of Ezra, Nehemiah, and Chronicles to be the work of a single person, a "Chronicler" (cf. Tuell, 9–10, who reads them "together as a single, intentional narrative" but not necessarily the product of a single author). More recent study challenges the identification of the Chronicler with Ezra the scribe and raises numerous questions concerning the supposed literary and theological ties between Ezra-Nehemiah and Chronicles (see McKenzie, 21–27). It seems best to understand Chronicles and Ezra-Nehemiah as distinct compositions and to assign the books of Chronicles to an anonymous author/compiler, a "Chronicler" (e.g., Selman, *1 Chronicles*, 71; Klein, *1 Chronicles*, 17).

It is important to recognize the author and compiler of Chronicles as a pastor and theologian. As a pastor, the Chronicler's purpose is both instruction and exhortation. His narrative is a sermon, an exposition based on the pattern of failure and judgment, grace and restoration in Israel's history. As an exegete, the Chronicler employs two primary methods in his interpretation of Israel's history. The first is a form of biblical typology—that is, identifying formal correspondence between persons, institutions, and/or events of earlier biblical history with the same of later biblical history by way of foreshadowing (cf. Fishbane, 350–79; Ellis, 53–56). The second is now known as a form of inner-biblical exegesis—that is, the Bible's citation of itself as a historical and theological source (see Fishbane, 385–403; Menn, 55–79). The reinterpretation of earlier Scriptures by a later biblical writer is an OT example of what S. Lewis Johnson (39–51) has identified in the NT as the work of the Holy Spirit in "inspired exposition." In each case, the Chronicler's exegetical method assumes the supremacy of the earlier Hebrew Scriptures and models the principle of allowing Scripture to interpret Scripture (see Selman, *1 Chronicles*, 40–43). As a theologian, the Chronicler offers a recitation of Israel's history grounded in the theology of the covenants associated with Abraham, Moses, and David.

Date of Writing

The books of Chronicles, along with Ezra and Nehemiah, are probably among the latest books of the OT in terms of the date of composition. Biblical scholarship dates Chronicles anywhere from the ministries of Haggai and Zechariah (ca. 515 BC) to well into the Greek period (300 BC and later). If the genealogy of Zerubbabel is ordered in chronological sequence, then seven generations are counted from the exile of King Jehoiachin (ca. 597 BC to the Chronicler's own time; cf. 1 Chron. 3:17–21). Assuming a twenty-year generation, this internal evidence moves the date of (at least this portion of) Chronicles nearer 450 BC (cf. Selman, *1 Chronicles*, 71, who dates Chronicles around 400 BC, as does Klein, *1 Chronicles*, 16). The traditional dates cited for Ezra and Nehemiah and the widely acknowledged connections between Chronicles and Ezra-Nehemiah suggest a similar date (e.g., Boda, 8, posits an earlier date for Chronicles, around 425 BC). Given all the uncertainties, it seems reasonable to assign the compilation of Chronicles in its final form broadly to a date between the ministries of Ezra and Nehemiah (458–432 BC) and the eastern conquests of Alexander the Great (332–330 BC; McKenzie, 32, allows for a range between 400 and 300 BC for the date of Chronicles; cf. Knoppers, *1 Chronicles 1–9*, 116–17, who allows for a date ranging between the late fifth and mid-third century BC for the date of Chronicles).

Synoptic Parallels / Inner-Biblical Allusion

As noted previously, Chronicles retells the history of Israel from the perspective of the postexilic period. A restoration community of Hebrews is reestablished in Judah, and the second temple has been built in Jerusalem. The horrors of the fall of Jerusalem and the Babylonian exile are still a vivid and painful memory. The prospect that the event may be repeatable if the people violate YHWH's covenant and return to idol worship is a frightening specter. The Chronicler's retelling of Israel's history is based on the earlier scriptural source books of Samuel and Kings. His rehearsal of Hebrew history focuses on the faithfulness of God to his covenant word, with emphasis on the kingship in the Southern Kingdom of Judah.

According to Martin Selman, the Chronicler's message hinges on two words from God that emphasize divine promise and fulfillment: the dynastic covenant that God grants to David and his heirs, brokered by Nathan the prophet (1 Chron. 17:3–14), and God's response to Solomon's prayer at the dedication of the temple (2 Chron. 7:11–22; see Selman, *1 Chronicles*, 27). These special interests will inform the Chronicler's approach to the important intertextuality principle of selectivity in the utilization of particular passages from the precursor texts of Samuel and Kings: What is omitted? What is retained? What is added? And what is reshaped?

Regarding omissions, apart from the synoptic report of Israel's rebellion against Rehoboam (with some modification, 2 Chron. 10:1–11:4), the Chronicler gives less attention to the history of the Northern Kingdom of Israel. Notable exceptions include the report of the war between Asa and Baasha (1 Kings 15:16–24 // 2 Chron. 16:1–17:1) and the story of Micaiah the prophet and the death of Ahab (1 Kings 22:1–40 // 2 Chron. 18). Surprisingly, the Chronicler makes no mention of the prophets Elijah or Elisha despite his interest in the role of the prophets in relation to kingship.

Further, the moral failings of King David and the religious apostasy of King Solomon are overlooked. Likewise, the moral failures and religious apostasy of certain kings of Judah go unmentioned (e.g., the sins of Abijah are not referenced, 1 Kings 15:1–6 // 2 Chron. 13:1–2), while the reports of the goodness of kings like Asa (1 Kings 15:13–15 // 2 Chron. 15:16–19) and Jehoshaphat (1 Kings 22:41–50 // 2 Chron. 20:31–21:1) are naturally retained. In other cases, the full theological review of select Judahite kings, both the good and the evil, is reported by the Chronicler (e.g., King Jehoram, 2 Kings 8:16–22 // 2 Chron. 21:2–20). The author-compiler is not seeking to deceive or mislead in omitting certain of the negative reports and theological reviews related to kingship in Judah. Rather, he assumes the reader's working knowledge of the earlier Hebrew histories. The Chronicler is careful deliberately to select only those excerpts from Samuel and Kings that have a direct bearing on the worship life of the Israelite community or the theology of hope rooted in the restoration of Davidic kingship (see Hill, *Chronicles*, 29).

The books of Chronicles are considered a type of synoptic parallel due to the extensive overlap with the narratives of Samuel-Kings. The Chronicler's additions to Samuel-Kings reflect his pastoral concerns for religious reforms and spiritual renewal in postexilic Judah. Among the materials included in the expansions of Chronicles are David's preparations for the building of the Jerusalem temple, reorganization of the Levites, and prayer of blessing (1 Chron. 24–29); Asa's response to Azariah's prophecy (2 Chron. 15:1–15); Jehoshaphat's religious reforms and prayer for deliverance from enemies (2 Chron. 19:1–11; 20:1–30); the report of the military victories of Azariah/Uzziah (2 Chron. 26:6–15); Hezekiah's religious reforms and Passover celebration (2 Chron. 29–31); Manasseh's repentance (2 Chron. 31:11–17); and Josiah's religious reforms and Passover celebration (2 Chron. 35:1b–17).

The Chronicler's theological reshaping of the early Samuel-Kings narratives may be as subtle as a single word substitution in the synoptic parallel. For example, the insertion of the word "curses" (2 Chron. 34:24) for the term "words" (2 Kings 22:16) ties the prophecy of Huldah threatening exile for the sins of idolatry in Judah more concretely to the blessings-and-curses section of the Mosaic covenant (cf. Deut. 28:15–68). Roddy Braun offers an insightful discussion of the several variations between 2 Sam. 21–24 and 1 Chron. 21:1–22:1. Significant among his eight examples is the reference to "Satan" as the instigator of David's military census (1 Chron. 21:1), not YHWH (2 Sam. 24:1). Braun suggests that the reference to "Satan" ("Adversary," without the definite article) is probably the final stage in the OT development of "the Adversary" (with the definite article; cf. Job 1–2; Zech. 3:1). This figure is a member of YHWH's divine council who functions as an accuser of God's people and even incites them to do evil (see Braun, 216–17; cf. Walton, 53–57). Jewish piety may be an issue here as well, with the Chronicler seeking to avoid the direct association of God with the problem of evil. Mark Boda (174) suggests that the shift from YHWH to Satan as the instigator of the census came about because the Chronicler, "uncomfortable with the theological implications of the source, reworked the text guided by Num. 22:22–23." Gary Knoppers (*1 Chronicles 10–29*, 751) discounts the role of Persian dualism here, noting there is no inherently "dualistic view of reality" in Chronicles. The reference to Satan as the inciter of the census may reveal a subtle development in OT theology from the time of David to that of the Chronicler. As a result of God's progressive revelation, the Hebrews came to understand the agency of Satan in their approach to theodicy. That is, it is God's prerogative as sovereign Lord to use a Satan figure (whether a member of his divine council or Satan, the devil, himself) as his agent of testing and/or judgment to accomplish his redemptive purposes (Hill, *Chronicles*, 293; see Selman, *1 Chronicles*, 202–4; Firth, 542–43).

Chronicles and Psalms

Knoppers (*1 Chronicles 1–9*, 68) notes that in addition to the Chronicler's reuse of Joshua and Samuel-Kings, there are also citations and allusions to a variety of other earlier biblical texts, including Genesis, Exodus, Numbers, Deuteronomy, Isaiah, Jeremiah, Ezekiel, Zechariah, and Psalms. One example of the Chronicler's use of Psalms is the composite psalm found in 1 Chron. 16. The psalm appears to be a pastiche of selections from three different psalms presented as a "new" composition (Ps. 105:1–15 = 1 Chron. 16:8–22; Ps. 96:1–13 = 1 Chron 16:23–33; Ps. 106:1, 47–48 = 1 Chron. 16:34–36).

It is specifically tied to the celebration that accompanies the ark of the covenant's entry into Jerusalem and its installation in the special tent established for it by King David (1 Chron. 16:7). The passage provides a useful case study, illustrating the Chronicler's approach to intertextuality with respect to the selection, arrangement, and reshaping of precursor texts and the "authorial" point of view in the appropriation of these texts.

The Chronicler may have been influenced in the selection of psalmic material by the immediate context of the narrative in 1 Chron. 16:4. This account mentions that David appointed certain Levites to minister before the ark of the covenant by invoking (*zkr*), thanking (*ydh*), and praising (*hll*) the Lord God of Israel. These worship terms are scattered throughout the composite psalm in 1 Chron. 16 and provide a broad connective structure for the linking of the three source Psalms (*zkr*, vv. 12, 15; *ydh*, vv. 8, 34, 35; *hll*, vv. 10, 25, 36).

Interestingly, the three psalms pieced together by the Chronicler have no musical notations and no overt connections to David or Asaph. Yet, this composition is created to celebrate the return of the ark of God to Jerusalem and to interpret what this event means to Israel at this particular moment in her tumultuous history. A striking feature in the arrangement of the composite psalm is the chiastic structure or inverted parallelism of the imperative forms of *ydh* and *šîr* at the seams of the song of thanksgiving. This broad connective structure, which mirrors the worship response of "giving thanks" and "singing" to the Lord, evidences deliberate and skillful poetic arrangement on the part of the Chronicler (Hill, *Chronicles*, 239). The arrangement also provides thematic unity for the composition. Giving thanks and singing are appropriate declarations of praise offered to the God of Israel, creator, sustainer, and deliverer of his people—the Lord of the covenant.

One example of the Chronicler's reshaping of the earlier materials from Psalms in an attempt to retain poetic symmetry or to attain a new poetic synthesis is the substitution of "Israel" for "Abraham" in 16:13 (= Ps. 105:6). The change completes the perfect chiasmus of the A/B word pair "Israel/Jacob" (v. 13) and "Jacob/Israel" (v. 17).

The Chronicler's theological perspective or point of view very much informs his methodological approach to intertextuality. Each of the psalm selections utilized by the Chronicler in the composite psalm features covenantal themes, and for him these themes are embodied in the ark of the covenant. The first unit (16:8–22) accents God as a covenant maker and keeper and highlights Israel's unique place among the nations as the elect people of God (vv. 15–17). The reference to the land of Canaan as the "inheritance" of Israel is especially important in light of the recent Babylonian exile (v. 18). The second unit (16:23–33) extols God as creator and sovereign over all the nations and over all their gods (vv. 26, 30). The last unit (16:34–36) praises the goodness and mercy of the God of Israel's salvation. In addition, the composite psalm repeats the covenant name YHWH fifteen times.

Another way the Chronicler reshapes earlier historical source materials is by updating or explaining select texts for a later audience. Although not a synoptic parallel, the use of the Persian loan word *daric* as a measure for precious metal in 1 Chron. 29:7 demonstrates the Chronicler's willingness to update older language. The place name Baale-judah (2 Sam. 6:2) is updated with an explanatory phrase in the synoptic parallel ("that is, Kiriah-jearim," 1 Chron. 13:6). In another place, the Chronicler explains the reference to the earlier text with supplemental information (1 Kings 3:4, "Gibeon . . . the most important high place"; cf. 2 Chron. 1:3, "Gibeon, for God's tent of meeting was there"). There are also instances where variances in the synoptic parallels between Kings and Chronicles are not a matter of editorial reshaping; rather, the issue is one of Hebrew manuscript traditions upon which the synoptic parallels are based (see the discussion of the reading of Tadmor, a great caravan city northeast of Damascus [Palmyra in later Greek sources, 2 Chron. 8:4] for the place name Tamar [a small city near the south end of the Dead Sea, 1 Kings 9:18; cf. Ezek. 47:18–19; 48:28]; see Dillard, 64).

Chronicles in the NT

CNTUOT lists more than ninety references to the book of 1 Chronicles and more than 130 references to 2 Chronicles in the NT (1174–75). NA[28] cites twenty-six allusions to 1 Chronicles and fifty-four allusions to 2 Chronicles in the NT, compared to the mere two allusions cited in NA[25] (1 Chron. 16:35 in Acts 26:17; 2 Chron. 20:7 in James 2:23).

Approximately one-third of the NT allusions to 1 Chronicles are simply the citations of the names common to the genealogies of 1 Chron. 1–9 and the genealogical records of Jesus the Messiah found in Matt. 1 and Luke 3. Some of those names are included in other OT genealogical registers, making such specific connections tentative (e.g., Gen. 46:1–27; Ruth 4:18–22). A sampling of other suggested NT allusions to 1 Chronicles offers insight into the interpretive approaches and thematic emphases of the NT writers. In the possible allusion to 1 Chron. 16:35 in Acts 26:17, Israel's "deliverance" from the gentiles now takes the form of gospel mission to the nations by Paul and the early church (cf. Ps. 106:47; Isa. 42:6–7 [Israel as a "light to the nations"]; see Bock, 717–18). Interestingly, the allusion to the Davidic covenant (2 Sam. 7:5–16 // 1 Chron. 17:4–14) in Acts 7:45–46 focuses on the temple structure David desired to build for the God of Israel more than the Lord's establishment of the Davidic dynasty fulfilled, in part, in the Christ-event. The context of Stephen's speech indicates that the Solomonic and second temples were reminders that "God desired pure worship" (Keener, *Acts*, 1412–14). The declaration that Jesus is God's Son

(Heb. 1:5) illustrates the ambiguity and composite nature of the NT use of the OT at times, with three OT texts being typically cited as sources for the two quotations (Ps. 2:7; 2 Sam. 7:14 // 1 Chron. 17:13). The recognition of the status of Israel as "aliens and strangers" before God in David's benedictory prayer may be one of the few actual NT citations of 1 Chronicles (1 Chron. 29:15 in Heb. 11:13). Whether OT or NT, the metaphorical status of the Heb. *gēr* ("resident alien") underscores the transiency of life for the people of God (cf. Knoppers, *1 Chronicles 10–29*, 954).

Nearly one-fourth of NA[28]'s proposed allusions to 2 Chronicles concern the vision of the Lord sitting on his throne (2 Chron. 18:18), an image found across the OT (e.g., 1 Kings 22:19; Pss. 29:10; 99:1; Isa. 6:1; Ezek. 1:26; Dan. 7:9). The reference in Matt. 12:42 // Luke 11:31 to the queen of Sheba's visit to Jerusalem as attesting the glory of King Solomon alludes to 2 Chron. 9:1–12 (and its synoptic parallel, 1 Kings 10:1–13; cf. Matt. 6:29; Luke 12:27). Paul's acknowledgment of things that are "non-gods" (Gal. 4:8) may allude to Isa. 37:19; Jer. 2:11; 5:7; 16:20; or 2 Chron. 13:9. Or this may be an instance of a composite citation by which Paul categorizes the "non-gods as nonentities altogether" (Keener, *Galatians*, 354–55). The NT teaching that God shows no favoritism or partiality in his dealings with humanity is traced to 2 Chron. 19:7, which in turn is based on Deut. 10:17 (cf. Acts 10:34; Rom. 2:11; 1 Pet. 1:17). This serves as another example of the ambiguity and composite nature of NT allusions to the OT (and the misleading and/or incomplete nature of the OT references in NA[28]). The identification of Abraham as "God's friend" (James 2:23) may be a citation of 2 Chron. 20:7 or Isa. 41:8 or perhaps simply a summation of the Second Temple–era Jewish view of Abraham (cf. McKnight, 255). The report of the murder of Zechariah the priest in the courtyard of the temple (Matt. 23:35; Luke 11:51) is a reference to 2 Chron. 24:20–21, the only OT account of that episode. The review of Israel's long history of mockery and rejection of God's prophets prior to the Babylonian exile (2 Chron. 36:15–16) may provide the backdrop for the NT summation of the persecution of the OT prophets (Matt. 5:12; Luke 6:23; Acts 7:52); and according to NA[28], it may inform the parable of the tenants (Luke 20:9–16).

Conclusion

The Chronicler's message is largely "borrowed" from the written works of earlier prophets, poets, and kings who spoke "the word of the LORD." The Chronicler truly believes that the word of God stands forever (Isa. 40:8), assuming the words of God once delivered and preserved command equal authority when "preached" to a later generation of God's people. The epilogue of Chronicles (2 Chron. 36:22–23) concludes with the clause "and let him go up" (AT). The quotation of King Cyrus's proclamation permitting the return of Hebrew expatriates to Judah is broken off midsentence. The incomplete citation is both an invitation and a directive to his audience to participate in Second Temple worship (cf. Pss. 24:3; 122:4). Like the psalmist, the Chronicler understands that the worship of YHWH is the integrating factor for living a redeemed life in a fallen world (cf. Ps. 73:13–17). The Chronicler's message affirming the authority of God's word and the centrality of worship has currency for every generation of the people of God.

Bibliography. Bock, D. L., *Acts*, BECNT (Baker Academic, 2007); Boda, M. J. *1–2 Chronicles*, CBC (Tyndale House, 2010); Braun, R., *1 Chronicles*, WBC (Zondervan, 2015); Crockett, W. D., *A Harmony of the Books of Samuel, Kings, and Chronicles* (Baker, 1951); Dillard, R. B., *2 Chronicles*, WBC (Zondervan, 2015); Ellis, E. E., "The New Testament's Use of the Old Testament," in *Biblical Hermeneutics*, ed. B. Corely, S. Lemke, and G. Lovejoy (Broadman & Holman, 1996), 40–58; Endres, J. C., et al., *Chronicles and Its Synoptic Parallels in Samuel, Kings, and Related Biblical Texts* (Michael Glazier, 1998); Firth, D. G., *1 and 2 Samuel*, AOTC (Apollos, 2009); Fishbane, M., *Biblical Interpretation in Ancient Israel* (Clarendon, 1988); Freedman, D. N., *The Unity of the Hebrew Bible* (University of Michigan Press, 1991); Hill, A. E., *1 and 2 Chronicles*, NIVAC (Zondervan, 2004); Hill, "Patchwork Poetry or Reasoned Verse?," *VT* 33 (1983): 97–101; Japhet, S., *I and II Chronicles*, OTL (Westminster John Knox, 1993); Johnson, S. L., *The Old Testament in the New* (Zondervan, 1980); Keener, C. S., *Acts*, vol. 2 (Baker Academic, 2013); Keener, *Galatians* (Baker Academic, 2019); Klein, R. W., *1 Chronicles*, Herm (Fortress, 2006); Klein, *2 Chronicles*, Herm (Fortress, 2012); Knoppers, G. N., *1 Chronicles 1–9*, AB (Doubleday, 2003); Knoppers, *1 Chronicles 10–29*, AB (Doubleday, 2004); Kucová, L., et al., *Synoptic Perspectives*, LHBOTS (T&T Clark, 2020); Long, B. O., *1 Kings*, FOTL (Eerdmans, 1984); Mason, R., "Some Echoes of the Preaching in the Second Temple?" *ZAW* 96 (1984): 223–25; McConville, J. G., *I and II Chronicles*, DSBOT (Westminster, 1984); McKenzie, S. L., *I and II Chronicles*, AOTC (Abingdon, 2004); McKnight, S., *James*, NICNT (Eerdmans, 2011); Menn, E., "Inner-Biblical Exegesis in the Tanak," in *A History of Biblical Interpretation: The Ancient Period*, ed. A. J. Hauser and D. F. Watson (Eerdmans, 2003), 55–79; Newsome, J. D., ed., *A Synoptic Harmony of Samuel, Kings, and Chronicles* (Baker, 1986); Pratt, R. L. "First and Second Chronicles," in *A Complete Literary Guide to the Bible*, ed. L. Ryken and T. Longman (Zondervan, 1993), 193–205; Schnittjer, G. E., *Old Testament Use of Old Testament* (Zondervan, 2021); Selman, M. J., *1 Chronicles*, TOTC (InterVarsity, 1994); Selman, *2 Chronicles*, TOTC (InterVarsity, 1994); Tuell, S. S., *First and Second Chronicles*, IBC (John Knox, 2001); Walton, J. H., *Ancient Near Eastern Thought and the Old Testament*, 2nd ed. (Baker Academic, 2018); Wilcock, M., *The Message of Chronicles* (InterVarsity,

1987); Williamson, H. G. M., *1 and 2 Chronicles*, NCBC (Eerdmans, 1982).

Andrew E. Hill

Church

The Bible begins with two people assembled in a garden with God, followed by their exile from God's presence. It ends with the nations gathered from exile and assembled in a city with God once more (Rev. 21:24, 26; see also 7:9). The story in between chronicles how God gathers those nations to himself into a group collectively called the church. The story divides into multiple stages, which are distinguished from one another by successive and sometimes overlapping institutional structures.

Therefore, understanding what the church is, particularly with regard to its OT background, requires paying close attention to Scripture's movement from one stage to the next as well as the succession of institutional structures.

The Nature of Institutions and the Institutional Nature of the Church

More than most themes in biblical or systematic theology, the topic of the church has an institutional focus, which is to say, a moral focus. What is an "institution"? It is *an identity-defining and behavior-shaping rule structure*, such as the rules governing a handshake, auto insurance, home mortgages, or the US Congress. And every institution, from the handshake to Congress, depends upon moral evaluations. They also enable predictable social interactions, create social solidarity, and give meaning to human life.

Why emphasize the institutional nature of the church? First, the focus helps us to identify what or who the church is. The existence of any group, no matter how informal or formal, depends upon an institutional structure, some set of rules that define the group and mark off members from nonmembers. Such is the case of Adam and Eve in the garden, Israel in the land, the local church on earth, and the universal church in heaven. Each is constituted as a group by a set of rules.

Second, if the institutional focus is a moral focus, everything that the Bible affirms about the church bears significance for Christian discipleship—how Christians should follow Jesus together.

Third, turning to the focus of this essay, the OT provides us with countless institutions, which in turn provide the raw material—like bricks in a building—for understanding what the church is. The Bible includes many "images" for the church, like a holy nation, a royal priesthood, the temple, living sacrifices, adopted heirs, the bride, a flock, and dozens of others, most of which come from the OT. Recognizing that these images, in their OT instantiations, all possess an unseen skeleton, a rule structure and a set of moral evaluations, helps us grasp how they transfer to or even become the church, shaping its identity and ethic. The fact that the church is "a holy nation" (1 Pet. 2:9), for instance, means that the church is constituted from the standpoint of Christ's kingdom by the same rules that constitute a nation. Specifically, it's a community of people (1) united by an ultimate governing authority and (2) characterized by mutual recognition between ruler and ruled, which are the two criteria political scientists offer for defining a political community like a nation. In discipleship terms, therefore, members of the church (3) are accountable to teach one another everything their king commands (through preaching) and to give or rescind the markers of citizenship (through the ordinances) as if they were passports. In the same way, every NT image for the church possesses such a set of identity-defining and behavior-shaping requirements for the individual Christian and for the whole church, most of which have their background in the OT. What rules make a family a family, or a flock a flock, or an heir an heir? The church is constituted as the church by adopting the rules that make each one of these institutions what they are.

Here then is one way to describe what makes the church the church from the vantage point of the OT: through our covenantal union with Christ and his Spirit, the church both *represents* and has *internalized* many of the glorious institutions—rule structures—that the OT employs to anticipate the Messiah, his rule, and his people. We *become* the family to which all families on earth point. We *become* the nation to which Israel and all nations of the earth point. We *become* the temple to which Solomon's temple pointed. And so forth. That is, we represent and have internalized the "rules" that constitute each of these institutions.

Apart from understanding the OT's institutional landscape, then, it becomes difficult to speak about the church. A person reading the NT alone won't have the definitions of words it uses, like "people," "image," "bride," "family," "temple," "flock," "vine and branches," or "assembly." The OT provides the definitions to those words. Indeed, it is precisely that vast, diverse, and rich institutional landscape of the OT that makes the task of conceptualizing the church such a complex, beautiful, and glorious project.

Furthermore, recognizing that the church represents and internalizes *all* of these OT institutional structures offers one more lesson for our understanding of the church: we should not quickly prioritize one NT image over the others for defining the church, as theologians often do. Every image is necessary. How can we say the rules making the church a family mean more to God than the rules making it a body or a temple? In truth, no one image is enough because nothing like the church exists in all the world.

Macrostructure: Covenants

God's unfolding plan through the story of the Bible is held together by a series of covenants, which then set the context for how to interpret every other image or description for the church. They operate as a kind of macrostructure. Each micro institutional structure in Scripture—rules surrounding the tree of the knowledge of good and evil, civil governments, circumcision, sacrifice, holiness codes, the Great Commission, the Lord's Supper—regulates some aspect of life at those different covenantal stages.

The church shows up at the new-covenant point of the story line. Scholars sometimes define the church starting with the Trinity, a historical creed, or, again, a favorite image. Yet biblical-theological sensitivity recommends we define the church starting covenantally: the church is the people of the new covenant. Through his perfect life, substitutionary death, and resurrection, Jesus Christ purchased a people through this covenant (Matt. 26:28). Everything the church is and has comes from this covenant with him—who they are, how they gain access to God, what their purpose is. To translate biblical theology into the categories of systematic theology, ecclesiology is utterly subservient to Christology and a covenantal understanding of union with Christ.

Understanding the new covenant, in turn, requires understanding the previous covenants, which necessitates studying the OT. The earlier covenants set the terms for the new covenant. To use organic language, the DNA of God's covenant with Adam traces through to his covenant through Christ, like an infant growing into adulthood and presenting both continuity and discontinuity with the younger self.

The first two chapters of Genesis do not use the language of a covenant with Adam, perhaps because it was rooted in Adam's ontology: God created Adam in his image, and the covenantal purposes and moral boundaries of Adam's life followed inevitably from this creational fact. If function follows form, Adam the God-imager existed to image God, like a mirror that mirrors. Creational ontology, in other words, is covenantal. Specifically, Adam would image or represent God by creating and ruling, just like God creates and rules: "Be fruitful and increase in number; fill the earth and subdue it" (Gen. 1:28; cf. Ps. 8). The fact of being a God-imager also bears an implicit moral demand: he is to rule like God rules, be holy like God is holy, love what God loves, hate what God hates. He should not distort God's image like a wavy carnival mirror distorts. By virtue of creation, then, all humanity exists to represent God, his character, and his rule.

When humanity failed to keep God's covenant first through Adam and then through another Adam, Noah, God called out a special people through the chosen seed of Abraham to fulfill his original creation purposes: worship him by imaging or representing him. It is not the case that God had one set of purposes for all humanity (e.g., building cities) and another for his special people (e.g., worshiping him). Rather, God intends for all people to worship him by imaging or representing him as they do things like build cities. He gave this commission to Israel and its Davidic kings, and he provided them with a fuller exposition of his character as revealed in the Mosaic and Davidic covenants (Deut. 4:6–8; 17:14–20). When Israel and its kings failed to keep the Mosaic covenant, God promised a new covenant by which his people would again inhabit a kind of "Eden" (Ezek. 36:10–36). To this end, God himself came in the person of his Son to do what Adam, Israel, and David could not do: perfectly submit to the law of God and so image God. Jesus Christ, then, is the true Israel (Matt. 2:13–15) and the greater David (Matt. 22:43–45). He is Adam par excellence and "the image of the invisible God" (Col. 1:15).

Since ecclesiology is utterly subservient to Christology, this story line is crucial for understanding what the church is and how to frame its overall mission. By virtue of the church's covenantal inclusion in Christ, what Christ in his humanity is the church is. The church is a new-creation race—new Adams who are being "transformed into his image with ever increasing glory" (2 Cor. 3:18; cf. 5:17; Rom. 8:29; 1 Cor. 15:49; Col. 3:10), a holy nation and a new Israel (Gal. 6:16; 1 Pet. 2:9). Its overall mission, furthermore, matches what God intended for Adam and Israel but what the incarnate Son fulfilled: to glorify God by representing him accurately and comprehensively. "Be perfect, therefore, as your heavenly Father is perfect" (Matt. 5:48).

Sonship, Kingship, Priesthood, and Family

Yet the Bible explicates the covenantal ontology of imaging God through several other (institutional) themes—namely, sonship, kingship, priesthood, and family. These themes, therefore, also become central to Christ's identity and mission, and therefore to the church's as well.

God creates Adam in his image and likeness. Seth, Adam's son, then bears Adam's image and likeness (Gen. 5:3). The sonship theme, in other words, explicates or carries water for the imaging theme. Boys look like their fathers and—in the ancient world—follow their fathers vocationally, whether butchers, bakers, or candlestick makers. They image them. Adam in that regard was a son of God (Luke 3:38), a title eventually given to Israel (Exod. 4:22; Hosea 11:1), then to the Davidic king (2 Sam. 7:14; Ps. 2:7), then to the beloved, incarnate Son (Matt. 3:17), then to the church by virtue of its union with him. Who is the church? They are the sons of God and fellow heirs with Christ who possess all the rights and inheritance of sons (e.g., Gal. 4:5–6). What is the mission of the church as a whole? For starters, it's to live as sons (men and women alike), who work and love like the heavenly Father and Son (see John 17). (For the mission of local congregations, see the end of this article.)

If the imaging theme gives birth to the sonship theme, the sonship theme gives birth to the kingship theme.

Adam's father is not a butcher or baker but a king. Adam, therefore, was to rule as a king, as verified by God's commands to subdue and rule (see also Ps. 8).

Yet the kingship analogy is not straightforward. It comes with a twist. Adam was not an absolute monarch. Adam represented another king. His kingship was a mediating kingship—a priestly kingship. He was to fight off every God-defying intruder and to ensure the domain over which he ruled remain utterly consecrated to the glory of God. The kingly impulse to push the boundaries of Eden outward and subdue new territory was to be coupled with an inward and protective priestly impulse to "work" and "watch over" the garden like an Israelite priest, keeping the place where God dwelled holy (Gen. 2:15; Num. 3:7–8; 8:26; 18:5–6).

Once again, the Bible's covenantal structure allows one to trace these priest and king themes through the story line of Israel, to Christ, and finally to the church. God established separate lines of priests and kings through his covenants with Israel and David for the purpose of clarifying the duties of each, yet he also characterized the entire nation as a "kingdom of priests" (Exod. 19:6). These separate offices of priest and king were then "democratized" to every member of the new covenant in Jer. 31:34 (Beale, 733–37). Yet these two offices fix especially on one figure who would combine the roles of priest and king (Zech. 6:11–13). Christ then came as the perfect priest-king, offices that, once again, his people acquire by covenantal union (1 Pet. 2:9; Rev. 1:6). Who is the church? They are the priests and kings of God. What is its (universal) mission? Its members are to subdue all creation, whether as accountants, teachers, lawyers, mothers, artists, or any other thing, in a manner consecrated to God's holiness and mediating his rule, character, and fame.

One more theme emerges from Adam's sonship, which is family. Sonship, to state the obvious, is a familial image. Every family on earth points toward the fatherhood of God and, by implication, what it means to be constituted as the family of God (Eph. 3:14–15). Yet the familial theme also becomes crucial through God's promise to give Abraham many descendants. Genesis foregrounds the natural or physical nature of these descendants (e.g., Gen. 17:6–8), yet it also anticipates countless descendants by covenantal adoption: Abraham will be the "father of many nations," a household composed of Jews and gentiles alike (Gen. 17:3–5; cf. 15:5; Acts 2:21, 39; Rom. 4:16–18; Eph. 2:11–22). Paul then declares Christ to be "the seed" (Gal. 3:16; cf. Gen. 3:15; 22:17–18), yet his covenantal people are likewise adopted seed and full heirs of the promise (Gal. 3:29; Rom. 9:7–9; cf. Gal. 4:5; Eph. 1:5). Both credo- and paedobaptists affirm that descent or family membership by covenantal adoption moves to the foreground of what the church is. Paedobaptists preserve physical descent but move it to the background, which is why they define churches as consisting of "believers and their children." Credobaptists argue the *type* of the physical family gives way entirely to the *antitype* of an "unmixed" community consisting only of regenerate, new-creation believers, at least by design. Churches should therefore strive to admit only believers into their membership. Either way, who is the church? The family of God. What is its (universal) mission? To love and live together as family members, sharing an identity and caring for one another as families do.

Church as Bride, Temple, and More

As mentioned above, the OT landscape is filled with a variety of institutions that find their typological fulfillment in Christ and, by covenantal extension, the church. Sometimes the images of Christ's typological fulfillment and the church's covenantal identity emphasize Jesus's humanity and his likeness to his people. Both are identified as God's image-bearers, his children, his temple, and Israel. At other times, these images emphasize Christ's divinity and covenantal lordship. He is the bridegroom; the church is the bride. He is the covenantal head; the church is the covenantal body. He is the shepherd; the church is the flock. He is the vine; the church is the branches. And the order here never reverses. The covenantal head is never the body. Ecclesiology is subservient to Christology, and it must never be mystically fused with it. Creator and creature remain distinct, a point addressed further below.

Each image is worth unpacking because each is the shadow of a greater reality, and each teaches us about the church's identity, discipleship, and mission. The church as "bride" illustrates this point well. Paul recalls the creation imagery of a man leaving his parents and becoming one flesh with his wife (Eph. 5:31). He then explains that this creation institution points to something greater: "I am saying that it refers to Christ and the church" (v. 32 ESV). The lesson: God did not create marriage and then design churches to symbolize marriage. He designed the church, and then created marriage to symbolize the church and its relationship with Christ. For as powerful, civilization establishing, and central to human existence as marriage is, it is only a symbol or shadow of Christ and the church.

So too with Solomon's temple in the OT. The structure was magnificent (1 Kings 6; 2 Chron. 3–5). God's presence within was powerful (1 Kings 8:10–11; 2 Chron. 7:1–3). Yet more magnificent and powerful still was the presence of God in Christ, the true temple (John 2:19–21; Col. 2:9; Heb. 1:3). The church, too, has become God's temple, dwelling place, and house (1 Cor. 3:16–17; 2 Cor. 6:16; Eph. 2:21; Heb. 3:6; 1 Pet. 2:5), a reality more astounding than any physical structure.

Each image offers insight into the nature of Christian discipleship and how the church should live and work together. The temple image points to the call to holiness as we represent God's presence on earth (e.g., 2 Cor. 6:16). The body image points to the mutual dependence we bear toward one another (e.g., 1 Cor. 12:14–16). The branch image calls the church to abide continually in Christ and to bear fruit (John 15:5). The family image points to our shared identity and mutual responsibility (e.g., Mark 10:29–30; 1 Tim. 5:1–2). The pillar of truth image points to the church's work in declaring God's truth (1 Tim. 3:15). And so forth. What is the church? A bride, a temple, a body, a branch, the pillar of truth. What is its (universal) mission? To fulfill the realities and demands of each picture and institutional structure.

Church as Pneumatological

How does the church fulfill such a grandiose enterprise? God himself does it through his Spirit. If ecclesiology is subservient to Christology, it is dependent upon pneumatology. Christ's covenant unites the church to him not only *representationally* (Rom. 5:17) but also *spiritually* (see Acts 2:4, 17–18, 38). God's own Spirit has written his law upon their hearts (Jer. 31:33; Ezek. 36:27; 2 Cor. 3:3, 6).

Crucial here, then, is remembering what an institution is: a rule structure. When Christ fulfilled the law (Matt. 5:17), he fulfilled not just lists of laws like the Ten Commandments but all the institutional manifestations of the previous covenants. He fulfilled their rule structures. He acted the part of a God-imager as defined by the rules of imaging, a son as defined by the rules of sonship, a king as defined by the rules of kingship, a sacrificial lamb as defined by the rules of sacrificial lambs, a temple as defined by the rules of temple, a nation as defined by the rules of a nation, and so forth. Likewise, when the Spirit writes the law on the heart of a believer, he writes not just lists of laws but the rules that comprise each institutional structure. The heart of every born-again church member is "rewired" or "reprogrammed," like a switchboard being rewired or a computer being reprogrammed, so that it operates by a new set of rules. In this way, the church does not merely *represent* the family of God, a holy nation, and a royal priesthood; it *becomes* each of these things (cf. 1 Cor. 3:21b–23; 15:20–28).

The church has not yet experienced this reprogramming fully. Theologians refer to the time in between Christ's first and second comings as an already-not-yet season. Christ has already given the "firstfruits" of his Spirit to his people, but he's not yet given the Spirit in his fullness (Rom. 8:23–30). In the meantime, the old man and the new man, the flesh and the Spirit, abide together at war in each member.

Church as Body of Christ

The claim that the church *becomes* something through the Spirit raises a long-standing dispute concerning the NT's body-of-Christ image in particular. Theologians since Augustine have argued that the church is ontologically united to Christ as one person, head and body, and that the church is a prolongation of the incarnation. Together they are the "whole Christ," or *totus Christus*. The trouble with the various proposals of *totus Christus*, whether in robust Roman Catholic formulations or more tempered Protestant ones, is that the metaphysics remain unclear. At worst, they blur the lines between Creator and creature; at the least, they are susceptible to this misunderstanding. The same risk attends the Eastern Orthodox doctrine of theosis and what it means to "become partakers of the divine nature" (2 Pet. 1:4 ESV).

Yet an institutional and covenantal perspicuity, courtesy of the OT, guards against overly mystical and metaphysically vague presentations of biblical images and models of sanctification. To review the ground we've covered, the OT offers a concrete covenantal ontology: God created humanity in his image for the purpose of imaging his character and rule. And it offers a covenantal plan of salvation, a covenant Lord, and a covenantal people: a new Adam and perfect priest-king would fulfill the demands of the old covenant; then he would make a way for God's people to be forgiven and spiritually "rewired" or "reprogrammed" to keep God's law and enact the requirements of the OT's many institutions. All this means they would partake of the divine nature by imaging God's character and rule, representatively and (progressively) actually (see 2 Cor. 3:18). In short, the body-of-Christ image, like every image for the church, should be interpreted covenantally.

Church as *Ekklēsia*

Many other OT themes are crucial for understanding the church's identity, such as election or the entire host of soteriological themes like redemption, salvation, and more. Each theme requires attending to both continuities and discontinuities between the OT and NT, as attempted in the entire discussion above.

Yet one more area demands special attention—namely, the movement from ancient Israel as a geographically located kingdom to the church, which brings us to the word translated as "church" (*ekklēsia*) and to the church in its local expression. The discontinuity is easy for citizens of contemporary democracies to discern: While new covenant members anticipate a coming land at the eschaton, unlike Israel, they do not presently possess a land with borders and all the external trappings of a kingdom. Nor should the church as a church seek to assume the powers of civil governments, as the Davidic king possessed (Matt. 22:21). At the same time, there remains a subtle but crucial point of political and geographic continuity between old covenant and new: Like Israel, Jesus constituted his people according to the political rules of a kingdom. Also like Israel, he wants his people to be corporately visible, which requires geography. The church—not just individual Christians—needs to be seen, heard, and encountered as a communal witness to the kingdom of heaven. This seems to be at least one reason that Jesus names his people "my *ekklēsia*"—his assembly (Matt. 16:18). In so naming them he requires them to gather in his name, thereby occupying geographic space (Matt. 18:20). In that physical space, furthermore, the subjects of this king must declare everything he spoke, and they must mutually affirm their shared citizenship through covenantal signs—namely, baptism and the Supper, the latter of which is rooted in Israel's covenant meal, the Passover (Luke 22:8, 15). The gathered church, then, is the temporary, proleptic geography of Christ's kingdom. The remainder of this essay will unpack these points.

The primary word Jesus uses throughout the Gospels to describe his inaugurated rule is "kingdom." Then, seemingly out of nowhere, he promises to build his *ekklēsia* (Matt. 16:18; cf. 18:17). This word, which English Bible translators translate as "church," sounds religious to people today. Yet to readers of both the Greek version of the OT and classical Greek, *ekklēsia* was both political and spatial (see Acts 19:39). The ancient Greeks made political decisions in the *ekklēsia*, while the *ekklēsia* of the Lord served a crucial role in making God's kingdom visible among the people of Israel. God established his covenant with his people in the assembly (Deut. 9:10; 10:4; 18:16). His people read the words of the law every seven years in the assembly (Deut. 31:10–12, 30). And the people gathered to worship God in the assembly (Ps. 149:1). They knew politics and worship are one.

When God exiled Israel and Judah from the land, he effectively disbanded the assembly. Yet the prophet Joel, in the same breath in which he promised the outpouring of God's Spirit (Joel 2:28–32; Acts 2:17–21), also told Israel to "gather the people" and "consecrate the congregation"—the *ekklēsia* (Joel 2:16 ESV). Israel's entire political career and national history are pictured as a gathering, then a scattering through exile, and then a promise of another gathering. Against this OT backdrop, Jesus arrives and declares he will build his *ekklēsia* (Matt. 16:18). Here was the true end of exile for a new Israel, a new body politic, and the reconstituting of God's kingdom on earth.

Further, the word is spatial, requiring geography. An assembly gathers, with people standing or sitting shoulder to shoulder. Jesus then promises to consecrate such assemblies gathered "in his name" with keys of the kingdom in hand with his own presence. He is "there" and "among" them (Matt. 18:17–20; cf. 16:19), meaning he has deputized them to represent and speak for him when they render court-like judgments on the *what* and the *who* of the gospel—confessions and confessors.

Churches as Embassies of Heaven

To refer to the people of the new covenant is to refer to the universal church. The universal church is a heavenly and eschatological assembly of everyone—past, present, and future—who belongs to Christ's new covenant and kingdom (see Eph. 2:6; Col. 3:1, 3; Heb. 12:23). This membership in the heavenly assembly "shows up" on earth when Christians gather in the name of Christ and wield the keys through preaching the gospel and affirming one another in baptism and the Lord's Supper (see 1 Cor. 10:17). Those who gather in Christ's name possess authority to baptize in his name, and those with whom he dwells now he will dwell always (Matt. 18:20; 28:18–20). In short, the assembled local church is where the invisible universal church and the kingdom of God, originally promised to Abraham (Gen. 17:6; 35:11), become visible. It allows the nations to see, hear, even step inside the kingdom of God (see 1 Cor. 14:25).

Local churches, in other words, are embassies of Christ's kingdom. His kingdom authority sanctifies or consecrates space, much like the authority of the US government "consecrates" the space when a US embassy is built on foreign soil, making it American soil. Likewise, the gathered church or assembly is the temporary but visible geography of Christ's kingdom. It represents a power not from another place on the planet, but from heaven and the end of history.

In conclusion, the local church is a temporary institution suited to this moment of redemptive history in between Christ's first and second comings. It is an embassy in exile with a narrow mission: to *make* disciples and citizens and God's offspring. Specifically, it names or identifies these citizens of the kingdom through the ordinances and equips them to live as children of the heavenly Father through preaching. If the local church as an organized collective is an embassy, every member of the church is an ambassador. And each ambassador possesses a broad mission: to *be* disciples and citizens and sons. They are to image God the divine king in every domain of life, representing the culture and character and glory of heaven.

See also Covenant; Israel and the Church, The Story of

Bibliography. Beale, G. K., *A New Testament Biblical Theology* (Baker Academic, 2011); Clowney, E., "The Church as a Heavenly and Eschatological Community," in *The Church in the Bible and the World,* ed. D. A. Carson (1987; repr., Wipf & Stock, 2002); DeRouchie, J. S., "Counting Stars with Abraham and the Prophets," *JETS* 58, no. 3 (2015): 445–85; Gladd, B. L., *From Adam and Israel to the Church* (IVP Academic, 2019); Schreiner, T. R., "The People of the Promise," in *New Testament Theology* (Baker Academic, 2008), 675–754; Vanhoozer, K. J., "*Hocus Totus:* The Elusive Wholeness of Christ," *Pro Ecclesia* 29, no. 1 (2020), 31–42; Wellum, S. J., "Beyond Mere Ecclesiology," in *The Community of Jesus*, ed. K. H. Easley and C. Morgan (B&H, 2013), 183–212.

JONATHAN LEEMAN

Church Fathers

See History of Interpretation: Early Church

Circumcision

Circumcision is a central biblical idea. It is fundamental to the constitution of Israel (e.g., Gen. 17). It occurs at key turning points in redemptive history, such as Lev. 26 and Deut. 30, where God foreshadows the need for a "circumcision of the heart." It occurs in the Prophets as God looks ahead to greater acts of both judgment and redemption (e.g., Jer. 9:25; Isa. 52:1). In the NT it becomes the point of tension at the first-ever church council (Acts 15) and is almost the entire focus of Galatians and Rom. 2–4. Along the way, circumcision touches on crucial biblical themes, such as blamelessness and righteousness, faith, sacrifice, and the promised seed/Messiah. This article traces circumcision through the OT and NT in connection with those themes before finally considering the significance of physical circumcision and the meaning of circumcision of the heart.

Be Blameless

Circumcision first appears in the Bible in Gen. 17. God appears to Abraham and says, "I am God Almighty; walk before me, and be blameless, that I may make my covenant between me and you, and may multiply you greatly" (17:1–2 ESV).

God has previously promised to make Abraham a blessing to all nations (Gen. 12) and confirmed that in a covenant (Gen. 15). But now God suggests that the delivery of all that he has promised is somehow dependent on Abraham's blamelessness (Deenick, 19–21). Moreover, as a sign of this covenant Abraham shall circumcise himself and all the males in his house for the generations to come (17:10–11).

The expression "that I may make my covenant" is better rendered as "give [*ntn*] my covenant," in the sense of "that I may give what I have promised" (Deenick, 17–19). Numerous times through this passage and other passages in the Abrahamic narrative, God promises to "give" things. In each case, what is envisaged is the content of the promises (e.g., a father of many nations [17:5–6]; the land [17:8; also 12:7; 13:15, 17; 15:7]; a son through Sarah [17:16]; Ishmael to be a great nation [17:20]). So too here, God will deliver to Abraham all that he has promised him, but Abraham must walk before God blamelessly (17:1–2).

It is not uncommon for the requirement of blamelessness to be understood to mean little more than "faithful." But a careful examination of the term through the OT suggests otherwise (Deenick, 21–26). The term *tāmîm* generally means "complete" or "whole." It can refer, for instance, to a whole day or year (Lev. 23:15; Josh. 10:13) or the whole tail of a peace offering (Lev. 3:9). Yet the term is often used in a more theologically freighted manner to characterize the nature of a person's relationship with God. It is used to distinguish between the blameless and the wicked (Ps. 37:18–20; Prov. 2:21–22; 11:5, 20; 28:10, 18). And though, occasionally, *tāmîm* appears to mean merely "sincere" (Judg. 9:16, 19) or "truthful" (Amos 5:10), often it means far more.

For instance, God himself and his work, way, law, and knowledge are "perfect" (Deut. 32:4; 2 Sam. 22:26, 31; Ps. 18:25, 30 [vv. 26, 31 MT]; 19:7 [v. 8 MT]). Likewise, the king of Tyre is portrayed (somewhat exaggeratedly) using imagery reminiscent of the garden of Eden and is described as "blameless" before his fall into sin (Ezek. 28:15). So too, in an echo of God's command to Abraham, the one who can dwell on God's holy mountain is the one who "walks blamelessly" (Ps. 15:2). The connection of "blamelessness" with the character of God and the ideal of blamelessness as the condition of God's people both before the fall and eschatologically on God's holy mountain suggest that "blamelessness" represents utter perfection rather than merely sincerity or genuineness.

A similar understanding of "blameless" is also found in the Qumran material (Deenick, 106–11). Frequently, the term is used with a moral connotation—for example, "perfect holiness" (*tmym qdš*; e.g., CD 7.5; 20.2, 5, 7; 1QS 8.20), "perfect path" (*tmym drk*; e.g., 1QS 4.22; 8.10, 18, 21; 9.2, 5, 9; 1Q28a 1.28; 1QH[a] 9.36; 11Q5 27.3), or "walking perfectly" (*hwlkym tmym*; e.g., CD 2.15; 1QS 1.8; 2.2; 3.9; 8.18, 21; 9.6, 8, 9, 19; 1Q28b 1.2; 5.22). Such perfection requires not breaking a single word of the law of Moses (1QS 8.20–22), although restoration is possible in the case of negligence. Nevertheless, perfection does not belong to human beings but is a gift of God (1QH[a] 12.30–32).

Similarly, the terminology is used in an exacting way in the NT (Deenick, 97–105). The term used in the LXX most frequently to translate *tāmîm* is *amōmos*. In the NT, *amōmos* is used to describe Jesus himself as a lamb "without blemish" (Heb. 9:14; 1 Pet. 1:19). Likewise, Jesus will present his people on the last day as "blameless" or "without blemish" (Eph. 1:4; 5:27; Col. 1:22; Jude 24). The goal there is eschatological and represents the perfection and holiness necessary to live in the presence of God. The same is true of *amemptos*, the term used to translate *tāmîm* in the LXX of Gen. 17:1. For instance, Paul prays that God will establish the hearts of the Thessalonians as "blameless and holy in the presence of our God and Father when our Lord Jesus comes with all his holy ones" (1 Thess. 3:13). Another important term used in the LXX to translate *tāmîm* is *teleios*. While the meaning of *teleios* is much broader, it is still used in the NT in ways similar to the terms listed above. For instance, Paul works to present everyone "perfect in Christ" (Col. 1:28 AT). And Jesus states that the ultimate goal is to "be perfect, therefore, as your heavenly Father is perfect" (Matt. 5:48).

Blameless through Sacrifice

By instituting circumcision in the context of the command to be blameless, circumcision came to signify that requirement for absolute blamelessness (e.g., Isa.

52:1)—hence also its later attachment to obedience to the law (e.g., Acts 15:5; Gal. 5:3). The high demand of blamelessness, however, created a problem: How was Abraham to achieve it? Two things may be said in response.

First, the narrative of Genesis shows that whatever is required of Abraham, God means to fulfill it (Deenick, 29–32). As noted above, in Gen. 12 God calls Abraham and promises to make him a great nation and to bless the world through him. In Gen. 15 God confirms that commitment in a covenant. However, God's binding covenantal commitment is entered into unilaterally. In a covenant-making ceremony, both parties would normally walk down together between the animal pieces. But in Gen. 15 Abraham is asleep on the ground while God, in the form of a smoking fire pot and blazing torch, walks between the pieces alone (Gen. 15:17). The implication is profound: God means to do what he has promised, and its success does not depend on Abraham (Hamilton, 436–37).

Moreover, in Gen. 15, when Abraham believes God's promise, God reckons him to be righteous (Gen. 15:6). Righteousness and blamelessness have already been linked together in Genesis in the person of Noah: "Noah was a *righteous* man, *blameless* among the people of his time" (Gen. 6:9). But the terms are connected in other places too (e.g., Deut. 32:4; Job 12:4; Ps. 15:2; Prov. 11:5). Astonishingly, then, when God calls Abraham to blamelessness in Gen. 17, he has already reckoned him to possess it in Gen. 15. That is precisely Paul's point in Romans. Abraham was reckoned to be righteous by God long before God required him to be circumcised (Rom. 4:9–10). So, too, as Paul points out in Galatians, God's commitment to Abraham is promissory. And a promise, by definition, is independent of law (Gal. 3:18).

But second, while the fact that God would fulfill the requirements is clear, the mechanism by which God would do that is less clear. Nevertheless, an understanding of how "blamelessness" is used in the rest of the OT suggests that the sacrificial system is intended to answer precisely that question (Deenick, 26–29).

Of the ninety-one occurrences of *tāmîm* in the OT, fifty-one are within the context of the sacrificial system and refer to the animals that must be "spotless" or "without blemish." The purpose of the "spotless" animal sacrifice is to atone for the less-than-"spotless" life of the one bringing the offering (e.g., Lev. 1:4). Indeed, after Gen. 17:1 the next reference to blamelessness occurs in connection with the sacrificial system (Exod. 12:5), after which point it is used consistently in the Pentateuch to refer to "spotless" animals, with only five exceptions. The predominance of the sacrificial usage is telling. For an ancient Israelite, repeatedly bringing spotless animals for atonement and watching others bring such sacrifices would have functioned as a living commentary on how God intended for his people to be blameless when clearly they themselves were not—God would provide a spotless substitute to stand in their place.

That understanding of the "blamelessness" language is confirmed by the NT (Deenick, 97–104). We have already noted above that Jesus is described as a lamb "without blemish" (Heb. 9:14; 1 Pet. 1:19). In 1 Pet. 1:19 Jesus's blameless sacrifice becomes the means by which the people have been ransomed from a futile way of life in order to be holy as God is holy, while in Heb. 9:14 Jesus's blameless sacrifice purifies people from "dead works to serve the living God" (ESV). Similarly, in Col. 1:22, Jesus's death has made it possible for him to present his people as "holy and blameless" before God (ESV).

Testament of Benjamin 3.8 also contains a curious confirmation of the same ideas, stating that "a blameless one shall be delivered up for lawless men, and a sinless one shall die for ungodly men" (*APOT*). Irrespective of whether this is pre- or post-Christian (see Hengel, 137–38), it shows that others at the time of the NT saw the OT sacrificial language of blamelessness finding fulfillment in a blameless one dying on behalf of those who were not blameless.

In a similar way, the Qumran community also thought that the blameless sacrifices of the OT found fulfillment in the substitutionary perfect behavior of others (Deenick, 106–11). On a number of occasions, the perfect behavior of various members of the community is seen as atoning for the imperfect behavior of others (e.g., 1QS 8.1–4; 9.4–5). The Qumran material provides a useful foil to the NT since it highlights both a degree of commonality but also the unique contribution of the NT. Both see the OT sacrifices as finding fulfillment in genuine obedience and substitution. However, while Qumran sees that fulfillment in the community and its obedience, the NT sees the fulfillment in the perfect obedience of Jesus alone, typified in his substitutionary death.

Nevertheless, the key point is that the sacrificial system showed how it was possible for people who were not blameless to be reckoned blameless. And it also pointed forward to the prospect of a more substantial blamelessness in the obedient death of Jesus, the truly blameless substitute.

The Promised Seed

Circumcision indicates both God's requirement of blamelessness and, in the context of the sacrificial system, his commitment to making a blameless people for himself through a blameless sacrifice. Furthermore, circumcision signposts that the blameless sacrifice will come through a "seed" of Abraham.

In Gen. 17, God carefully distinguishes between those who will benefit from the blessings of the covenant, such as Sarah, Ishmael and the rest of Abraham's house, and Isaac, with whom God will "establish" (*hēqîm*) the covenant (Deenick, 39–44). Repeatedly, God tells Abraham that he will establish the covenant with Isaac (17:19, 21) and, more particularly, not with Ishmael (17:20–21). Indeed, although Ishmael and the other males in Abraham's house are circumcised, God specifically states that he will establish the covenant only with Isaac and "his seed after him," just as he established the covenant with Abraham and his seed after him—that is, Isaac (17:19 AT; cf. vv. 9–10; see Alexander, *Paradise*, 102).

Thus, although numerous people share in the covenant's blessings and sign, the covenant itself is made with a single line of descendants. That truth is reflected in the many references later in the OT to God's covenant with Abraham, Isaac, and Jacob (e.g., Exod. 2:24; Lev. 26:42; Num. 32:11; Deut. 1:8).

That pattern also fits the story line of Genesis and the book's interest in a "seed" (Deenick, 44–48). In Gen. 3:15, after the fall into sin, God promises Eve that from her will come a "seed" who will crush Satan's head. The search for that seed is carried on through the structure of Genesis (Alexander, "Genealogies"). Genesis is clearly structured around the term *tôlədôt* ("generations"; Gen. 2:4; 5:1; 6:9; 10:1; 11:10, 27; 25:12, 19; 36:1, 9; 37:2). Most of these sections focus on a particular individual, such as Adam (and Eve), Noah, Abraham, Isaac, Jacob, and so on (Hamilton, 9–10). So, too, these sections often contain genealogies that trace the line of descent from Eve through to Noah to Abraham and so on. It is in that framework that God promises to establish his covenant with Abraham and Isaac and his "seed" after him. The circumcision covenant, then, further specifies the line through which Eve's "seed" will come, while the following chapters trace out the continued interest in a single seed: it is Isaac, not Ishmael; Jacob, not Esau; and Joseph, not his eleven brothers (though the line ultimately passes to Judah [Gen. 49:8–12]). Moreover, the near sacrifice of Isaac in Gen. 22 hints at the way in which the sacrificial component of God's promise will be fulfilled through Abraham's seed.

Later, the Davidic covenant refines God's promise to Eve and Abraham even further. The resonances between Gen. 17 and the Davidic covenant are significant (Deenick, 32–39). For instance, David quotes to Solomon God's promise "If your descendants . . . walk faithfully before me with all their heart and soul, you will never fail to have a successor on the throne of Israel" (1 Kings 2:4). Like Abraham, David's descendants are to walk faithfully before God. The result of such obedience is that Solomon will not lack a descendant on the throne. Those ideas are repeated numerous times in connection with David and his sons (e.g., 1 Kings 3:6; 8:25; 9:4–7; 2 Kings 20:3; 2 Chron. 6:16; 7:17–20; Isa. 38:3). In other words, the obedience of David's sons becomes the condition for God's fulfillment of the covenant with David. Although the descriptions of David and his sons as "blameless" seem overly positive, like the descriptions of Noah (Gen. 6:9) and Zechariah and Elizabeth (Luke 1:6) they must be understood in the context of God's provision through sacrifice. God accepted David and his sons despite their imperfections in anticipation of a greater son who would walk before him blamelessly.

Again, these ideas find confirmation in the way the NT authors interpret the OT. The most obvious example is in Galatians. There Paul is engaged in an argument about the ongoing significance of circumcision. Remarkably, some of the Galatians are in danger of forfeiting Christ because of their insistence on circumcision (5:2). It is in that context that Paul makes the rather startling point that God's covenant with Abraham had only one descendant in mind—Christ (3:16). What makes the Galatians heirs of that promise, then, is not circumcision but their allegiance to and union with Christ, the true heir of Abraham (3:29)—an allegiance and union that are symbolized in baptism (3:26–27). In the light of the OT background, Paul's claim is not a fanciful invention but is deeply rooted in his understanding of the biblical-theological trajectories of the circumcision covenant.

Paul makes a similar move in Phil. 3. There, too, he is engaged in addressing a misunderstanding of circumcision. He warns against those who "mutilate the flesh" (3:2). In contrast, the real "circumcision" consists of those who "worship by the Spirit of God and glory in Christ Jesus and put no confidence in the flesh" (3:3 ESV). Paul then recounts his previous confidence before God on the basis of his circumcision, Jewish pedigree, zeal, and what he had considered his "blamelessness" and "righteousness" under the law. However, he now considers all that to be rubbish. The decisive tipping point is his realization that Jesus is the promised Messiah/Christ. Seven times he says that his chief goal now is to gain Christ, know Christ, be found in Christ, and so on, having a righteousness not from the law but from God through faith in Christ (3:7–11). The end result of identifying with Christ is becoming like him in his death, attaining to the resurrection from the dead, and thus being made perfect (3:10–12). Thus, for Paul, the privileges signified in circumcision and the promise of blamelessness and righteousness come not through circumcision itself but through the closest possible identification with Jesus as the Messiah and fulfillment of circumcision (Deenick, 128–30).

In Col. 2, Paul makes a similar point again. The Colossians have been "circumcised with a circumcision made without hands, by putting off the body of flesh, by the circumcision of Christ" (2:11 ESV). It appears that Paul means, as in Galatians and Philippians, that the Colossians are genuine heirs of Abraham together with Christ, having identified with Christ, especially in his death and resurrection (Deenick, 135–38).

It begins to become clear, then, why circumcision itself is the sign and not something else. Because the promise is about a male descendant, the sign of God's promise is attached to the part of the body responsible for procreation. This also makes sense of why circumcision ends with the arrival of Christ. It is because the promise has been fulfilled (Tuitiensis, *De Sancta Trinitate* 5.31). That, in turn, helps to explain why circumcision can be simultaneously a threat to the gospel (Gal. 5:2–3) and also a matter of complete indifference (1 Cor. 7:19). Insofar as people recognize that Jesus is the Christ and that trust in him is sufficient, circumcision does not matter. However, where circumcision comes to be viewed as essential to obtaining righteousness, it clouds the fact that the fulfillment of that promise lies in identification with Jesus through faith alone.

Physical Circumcision and the Individual

Thus, circumcision indicated God's requirement and provision of blamelessness through the blameless sacrifice of the seed of Abraham. But what did circumcision mean for the individual who received it?

Strikingly, right from the first moment that circumcision is instituted, there is a disconnect between those who receive the blessings of God's covenant with Abraham and those who are circumcised (Cohen, 13). For instance, Ishmael is circumcised even though God specifically excludes him from being a recipient of the covenant (Gen. 17:18–23). Sarah is included within the orbit of God's blessings to Abraham, yet she clearly does not receive the sign of circumcision (Gen. 17:15–16).

That disconnect between sign and recipient finds an important confirmation in the events of Josh. 5 (Deenick, 66–76). There God commands Israel to begin again the practice of circumcision (Josh. 5:2). For forty years in the wilderness the practice of circumcision has been in abeyance. The reason given for this pause is the disobedience of the people in the wilderness (Josh. 5:5–6). Because of their lack of faith in taking the land promised to Abraham, God swore that the wilderness generation would not enter the land (Num. 14:1–23). Indeed, there is a sense of reversal. What God had sworn (*šbʿ*) to Abraham, he later swore (*šbʿ*) the wilderness generation would not receive (Josh. 5:6). It seems that as a sign of the curse on the parents, the children were not circumcised for the forty-year period in the wilderness. Thus, those who have been circumcised (the parents) are excluded from the land, while those who are not circumcised (the children) will eventually inherit it.

But none of that compares with the stunning reversal of circumcision that Paul executes in Rom. 4 (see Deenick, 180–84). There Paul claims not simply that circumcision is neither essential nor a sign of special privilege for the Jews but, further, that it is a sign of God's purposes for the nations as well as the Jews (Morris, 203). Paul says in Rom. 4:11 that Abraham "received the sign of circumcision as a seal of the righteousness that he had by faith while he was still uncircumcised" (ESV). Paul's point is that only *after* Abraham is reckoned as righteous in Gen. 15 is he given circumcision, rather than being reckoned as righteous *on account* of his circumcision. The historical sequence of events is crucial. Abraham's circumcision seals and confirms the righteousness that he already possesses by faith. Paul also argues that Abraham's circumcision is in some way unique, such that it makes him the "father" of both the circumcised people who believe and the uncircumcised people who believe. Only for Abraham is circumcision properly a "seal." It is a further certification of the righteousness that God has reckoned him to possess by faith already in Gen. 15. Indeed, Paul argues that Abraham's circumcision is a sign not simply of righteousness by faith but of Abraham's righteousness by faith *while uncircumcised*, such that those who share his same faith while uncircumcised share in the same righteousness by faith that he received, whether they are Jews (Rom. 4:12) or gentiles (Rom. 4:11).

In that sense, further acts of circumcision do not "seal" those who received it. Rather, Abraham's circumcision seals *his* righteousness by faith. Further acts of circumcision point others back to what God has done for Abraham in order that recipients might see that righteousness is by faith, and it invites them, whether Jew or gentile, to share the same faith as Abraham and hence the same righteousness.

Circumcision of the Heart

That finally brings us to the OT metaphor of circumcision of the heart. The metaphorical use of circumcision occurs in a number of places in the OT (Lev. 26:41; Deut. 10:16; 30:6; Isa. 52:1; Jer. 4:4; 6:10; 9:25–26; Ezek. 44:7–9), but the key places are Lev. 26 and Deut. 10 and 30.

In Lev. 26 God calls the people to obedience. If they obey him, he will bless them in the land (Lev. 26:3–13). If they do not obey him, he will send curses upon them (Lev. 26:14–39). The expectation is that they will not obey him. But then God offers a startling reprieve in vv. 40–42. If the people "confess their sins" and "pay for their sin," God will remember his covenant with Abraham, Isaac, and Jacob. That confession and making of amends are also expressed in the language of "humbling" their "uncircumcised hearts." To speak of "humbling" rather than "circumcising" their "uncircumcised heart" gives us a key to the metaphor: circumcising one's heart is equivalent to humbling it (Bernat, 104–5). That corresponds with Jer. 4:4, too, where circumcising hearts means pursuing genuine repentance: returning to God and putting away their idols (Jer. 4:1; see Lemke, 303).

Likewise, in Deut. 10:16 Moses says, "Circumcise your hearts, therefore, and do not be stiff-necked any longer." The opposite of a stiff neck is a circumcised or supple heart that is humble before God. But it is more than that. In the previous chapter, Moses recounts the stubbornness of the people seen in the episode with the golden calf and at other times in the wilderness period. Yet Moses also recounts how he pleaded with God to forgive the people for their stubbornness. Significantly, however, the basis on which Moses pleaded for forgiveness was God's commitment to Abraham, Isaac, and Jacob. Likewise, the call to circumcise their hearts in 10:16 follows Moses's reminder that "the LORD set his heart in love on your fathers and chose their offspring after them" (ESV). Thus, the command to circumcise their hearts seems to involve more than mere humbling. It also includes an appropriation of God's grace grounded in his promise and commitment to Abraham and his seed (Deenick, 60–63).

Finally, in Deut. 30:6, God promises that what the people cannot do in circumcising their hearts, he will do for them: "The LORD your God will circumcise your hearts and the hearts of your descendants, so that you may love him with all your heart and with all your soul, and live." The end goal of that work is complete obedience and love for God. Nevertheless, that goal is not beyond them, but "the word is very near you; it is in your mouth and in your heart so you may obey it" (Deut. 30:14). As Paul notes, that word is the word of faith about Christ (Rom. 10:8). In Deuteronomy, the word is the word of promise to Abraham—Moses later tells the people to choose life, "that you may dwell in the land that the LORD swore to your fathers, to Abraham, to Isaac, and to Jacob" (Deut. 30:20 ESV; see Deenick, 64–66).

Similarly, in the NT, circumcision of the heart pertains to humble and repentant faith. In Rom. 2, Paul says that those who "keep the law's requirements" will be regarded as circumcised (2:26), not physically but in their hearts (2:29). What it means to "keep the law's requirements" is debated, but Paul's earlier reference to stubborn and unrepentant hearts (2:5) suggests that he has in view the same kind of issues as Moses does in Deut. 10:16: humble repentance and trust in God's promised Messiah. Moreover, there is good reason to believe that in the context, to "keep the law's requirements" means to keep that to which the law pointed—that is, Jesus (e.g., Rom. 3:21; 10:4; see Deenick, 143–70). In other words, the person with the circumcised heart is the one who humbly identifies with Christ, who is the fulfillment of God's promise to Abraham, as we have seen Paul argue in both Galatians and Phil. 3.

Circumcision signifies the need for blamelessness and for God's promise to provide it through a seed of Abraham. And circumcision invites people to receive that promise by humbling their hearts and trusting in God's promise to Abraham (i.e., circumcising their hearts). Ultimately, however, even that work is a work of God, as Deut. 30:6 suggests.

Such faith (or circumcision of the heart) was available to people in the OT as much as in the NT. However, what has changed now is the need to identify with Christ himself. In the OT period, believers humbly trusted in the seed who was promised, whereas now believers must put their trust in Jesus specifically.

With the coming of Christ, circumcision has become a matter largely of indifference, though if it is misunderstood, it can take a person away from the gospel. Beforehand, however, circumcision could not be so lightly discarded. Because God had commanded it to be done, obedience required it. Moreover, to abandon circumcision before the coming of Christ would have been to risk not communicating the gospel. Nevertheless, what always mattered was not circumcision itself but humble faith in the blameless seed of Abraham.

See also Covenant; Jews and Gentiles; Law

Bibliography. Alexander, T. D., *From Paradise to the Promised Land*, 3rd ed. (Baker Academic, 2012); Alexander, "Genealogies, Seed and the Compositional Unity of Genesis," *TynBul* 44 (1993): 255–70; Bernat, D. A., *Sign of the Covenant*, AIL 3 (Society of Biblical Literature, 2009); Blaschke, A., *Beschneidung*, TANZ 28 (Francke, 1998); Cohen, S. J. D., *Why Aren't Jewish Women Circumcised?* (University of California Press, 2005); Deenick, K., *Righteous by Promise*, NSBT 45 (Apollos, 2018); DeRouchie, J. S., "Circumcision in the Hebrew Bible and Targums," *BBR* 14 (2004): 175–203; Hamilton, V. P., *The Book of Genesis*, 2 vols., NICOT (Eerdmans, 1990–95); Hengel, M., "The Effective History of Isaiah 53 in the Pre-Christian Period," in *The Suffering Servant*, ed. B. Janowski and P. Stuhlmacher, trans. D. P. Bailey (Eerdmans, 2004), 75–146; Kline, M. G., *By Oath Consigned* (Eerdmans, 1968); Lemke, W. E., "Circumcision of the Heart," in *A God So Near*, ed. B. A. Strawn and N. R. Bowen (Eisenbrauns, 2003), 299–319; Livesey, N. E., *Circumcision as a Malleable Symbol*, WUNT 2/295 (Mohr Siebeck, 2010); Meade, J. D., "Circumcision of the Heart in Leviticus and Deuteronomy," *SBJT* 18, no. 3 (2014): 59–85; Morris, L. *The Epistle to the Romans*, PNTC (Eerdmans, 1988).

KARL DEENICK

Colossians and Philemon, Letters to the

Until recently there had been no book, monograph, or even article dedicated to a study of the OT in Colossians (on which, see below). One reason for such little scholarly attention to this subject is that there are no formal quotations or citations from the OT in Colossians. Numerous commentators find difficulty detecting even any allusions in the letter, although there are a number of them.

Neither of these tasks has been consistently carried out in past study of Colossians, except by G. K. Beale ("Colossians"; *Colossians* [passim]) and Chris Beetham, though significant essays on the subject have been written by Gordon Fee and Jerry Sumney. More recently, Paul Foster ("Echoes"; *Colossians*) has published two

This essay is a revision of G. K. Beale, *Colossians and Philemon*, BECNT (Grand Rapids: Baker Academic, 2019), 9–16.

essays that have been critical of the approach taken by Beetham, Fee, and myself. Foster argues that there is no conscious use of the OT within Colossians. I responded to Foster in a subsequent essay ("Old Testament"), contending that there are problems with his approach and, indeed, that there are significant allusions in the book.

Commentators offer various definitions of "allusion" and "echo" and posit various criteria for discernment of both. Some define an echo as unconscious and unintentional, others as conscious and intentional. Whether OT references are referred to as "allusions" or "echoes," the purpose in this entry is to argue the likelihood that Paul, to one degree or another, intends to make the reference. The goal is to point out, on a case-by-case basis, the clearest cumulative evidence for the presence of an intentional OT reference, regardless of how one wants to categorize it formally (i.e., as an echo or allusion).

Some Significant Allusions in Colossians

There cannot be full demonstration of the validity of allusions in this discussion (though for fuller analysis, see Beale, "Colossians"; *Colossians*; "Old Testament"). Being sensitive to the presence of OT allusions in Colossians has important significance for some greatly debated issues in Colossians, which also concern the important biblical-theological themes in the letter. For example, four specific OT allusions about the temple are applied to Christ and the church (1:9–10, 19; 2:9, 10).

One of these, Col. 1:19, explains why Christ should "come to have first place in everything" (v. 18b NASB). The combined wording of "well-pleased" (*eudokeō*) and "dwell" (*katoikeō*) in v. 19 also occurs in Ps. 67:17 LXX, the only such pairing in the LXX, and note that both texts also have *en autō* (see table 1).

Table 1. Shared Language in Ps. 67:17–18 LXX and Col. 1:19 (all AT)

Ps. 67:17–18 LXX	Col. 1:19
"God was well-pleased [*eudokēsen*] to dwell [*katoikein*] in it [i.e., Zion; Gk. *en autō*]. . . . The Lord will dwell [there] forever . . . in the holy place."	". . . because in him [*en autō*] all the fullness of deity was well-pleased [*eudokēsen*] to dwell [*katoikēsai*]."

The point is that God's tabernacling presence on earth is no longer in the earthly temple (the holy of holies) but is now expressed more greatly on earth in Christ, who eschatologically instantiates and typologically fulfills all that the temple represented. Thus, the reason that Christ should "come to have first place in everything" (v. 18b) is that he, being God, is the escalated form of God's holy of holies presence on earth. Colossians 2:9 and 10 refer back to this OT allusion in 1:19, respectively applying it again to Christ and then to believers, who are in union with Christ as the temple.

Why is Paul concerned to make so many temple allusions in such a short letter? The answer is that Paul wants to contrast the true temple in Christ, with which believers are identified, with the pseudo-claims of a heavenly temple experience by the false teachers. All the positive OT temple texts come before the most explicit piece of false teaching in the entire epistle (2:18). In fact, I think these preceding positive texts are key to recognizing that 2:18 concerns a false claim about a heavenly temple experience. The "fullness" (1:19; 2:9–10) that so many commentators discuss and debate (whether it is a polemic against a gnostic teaching or some other kind of false teaching) is best understood as the "fullness" of God in Christ as the new, end-time temple. Believers have all the "fullness" of Christ's presence in the temple that they need, in contrast to the empty "fullness" of temple experience offered by the false teachers. Accordingly, the OT background of the NT affects both the Christology of Colossians (Christ is the full divine expression of God's presence in the end-time temple) and the ecclesiology (the church is part of the latter-day temple, residing in the midst of the divine tabernacling presence).

Likewise, some of the OT allusions are crucial to substantiating the notion of Christ as the last Adam and end-time image of God (1:15) and of believers being identified in union with the last Adam and his image (3:9–10; cf. similarly the Gen. 1 allusions in Col. 1:6, 10 also with respect to implications for Christians being in God's image). An example is the use of Gen. 1:28 in Col. 1:6, 10, which is the first OT allusion in the epistle. The former is a part of the thanksgiving and the latter a part of a prayer based on the thanksgiving (see table 2). More discussion will be dedicated to this first allusion in Colossians because it is repeated, and it provides an example of how important the OT context is for understanding the interpretive use of OT allusions that occur later in Colossians (e.g., the temple allusions discussed earlier).

Table 2. Shared Language in Gen. 1:28 and Col. 1:6, 10

Gen. 1:28	Col. 1:6, 10
"*Increase* [*auxanesthe*] and *multiply* [*plēthynesthe*] and fill the earth . . . and rule over . . . *all the earth* [*pasēs tēs gēs*]." (LXX)	"In *all the world* [*en panti tō kosmō*] also it [i.e., the word of truth] is *bearing fruit* [*karpophoroumenon*] and *increasing* [*auxanomenon*]." (v. 6 NASB)
"Be *fruitful* [*pərû*] and multiply, and fill the earth . . . and rule . . . the earth." (NASB)	". . . *bearing fruit* [*karpophorountes*] in every good work and *increasing* [*auxanomenoi*] in the knowledge of God." (v. 10 NASB)

The Hebrew text may be the focus, since the LXX renders the Hebrew *pərû* ("bear fruit") by *auxanesthe* ("increase") and *rəbû* ("to multiply") by *plēthynesthe* ("to multiply"). The LXX is a viable rendering, since *auxanesthe* can have the connotation of the "increase" of fruit or of other organic growth (e.g., Isa. 61:11; 1 Cor. 3:6–7). The LXX may be combining both notions of "multiplying" and "bearing fruit" by its choice of *auxanesthe*, in order to anticipate the directly following reference to "multiplying." Paul appears to give perhaps a bit more of a literal rendering of the verbs by translating *pərû* by *karpophorountes* ("bear fruit") and *rəbû* ("to multiply") by *auxanesthe* as well as reproducing "all the earth" (cf. Gen. 1:26, 29 MT and 1:28 LXX).

One might understandably doubt that such an allusion exists in Col. 1 because, whereas Gen. 1 refers to the increase of humans on "all the earth" and their dominion over it, Col. 1:6 refers to the word of the gospel bearing fruit and increasing in all the world and 1:10 refers to good works as "bearing fruit" and to Christians' growth "in the knowledge of God [i.e., in God's word]." In this light, even if one were to persist in concluding that Paul is alluding to the Genesis text, it would seem still that one might have to conclude that the use is noncontextual, since Paul would be spiritualizing what Genesis applies to the physical growth of the human race.

There does appear, however, to be sufficient linguistic evidence to posit a probable and conscious allusion to Gen. 1:28. The repetition of the wording in Col. 1:10 highlights the earlier identical phrase and points further to Paul's conscious awareness of alluding to Gen. 1:28. Therefore, the question is whether or not Paul used the text to suit his own rhetorical purposes without being interested in the original meaning of Genesis. In order to answer this question, more analysis of Gen. 1:28 is needed.

It may be that Paul's use of the Gen. 1:28 language about the old creation, despite its apparently different application, is intended to indicate merely the general notion that a new creation has been inaugurated with believers because of their identification with Christ. But more may be in mind than this. Genesis 1:26–28 was a mandate to Adam (and his progeny) to reflect God's image (see Beale, *Temple*, 81–121). Part of ruling and subduing in the Gen. 1 mandate is to "be fruitful and multiply and fill" the earth with children who are to join Adam in reflecting God's image and in exercising kingly dominion over the earth.

Thus, Adam and Eve and their progeny were to be vice-regents and act as God's obedient children, reflecting God's ultimate glorious kingship over the earth. Already in Gen. 1–3, and relevant for Col. 1:6, 10, it is apparent that obedience to God's word is crucial to carrying out the task of Gen. 1:26, 28 (and disobedience led to failure: Gen. 3:2–4 includes at least three examples of misquotation or intentional twisting of the divine word in 2:16–17). Carrying out the mandate likely would have included ruling over the evil serpent by remembering and trusting in God's word in 2:16–17 (note the emphasis on what God "said" in 2:16; 3:1, 3).

Being fruitful and multiplying in Gen. 1:28 refers to the increase of Adam and Eve's progeny, who were also to reflect God's glorious image and be part of the vanguard movement, spreading out over the earth to fill it with divine glory. This assumes that spiritual instruction in God's word would be essential to Adam and Eve's raising of their children, since this would be crucial to their reflecting the divine image and fulfilling the mandate of bearing fruit and increasing.

Paul has tapped into one of the most important veins of the redemptive-historical story line of Scripture, albeit allusively. In fact, the mandate of Gen. 1:28 is repeated throughout the OT, as in Gen. 9:1, 6–7; 12:2; 17:2, 6, 8; 22:17–18; 26:3–4, 24; 28:3–4; 35:11–12; 47:27; Exod. 1:7; Lev. 26:9; Pss. 8:5–9; 107:38; Isa. 51:2; Jer. 3:16; 23:3; Ezek. 36:10–11, 29–30. Many of these contain the dual terminology of "increase and multiply," and several have the phrase "all the earth" (*pas* + *gē*) (cf. *kosmos* in Col. 1:6; cf. also 1 Chron. 29:10–12).

It is possible that we see in Col. 1:6, 10 the collective impact of these restatements upon Paul's thinking. If Paul is consciously alluding, at the least, to Gen. 1:28, how could he be appropriating this material? He appears to be focusing on the role of God's word in Gen. 2–3 in relation to carrying out the Adamic commission, so that part of carrying out the commission is faithfulness to God's word. This is highlighted in Col. 1:5–6, where "the word of truth" has finally begun expansion "in all the world . . . bearing fruit and increasing" in the way the first Adam should have spread it. This expansion, which should also have happened with each of the mandate's successive OT recipients, is now taking place "in" the Colossian believers, who have been "delivered from the domain of darkness and transferred . . . to the kingdom" (v. 13 AT). As believers continue to "bear fruit and increase," the commission of Gen. 1 is growing in them, with the inevitable result that it will expand to others. Verse 10 shows in what ways they are "bearing fruit and increasing": they are "bearing fruit *in every good work* and increasing *in the knowledge of God*." Reference to "the knowledge of God" is conceptually synonymous in a general way with the earlier mentioned "word of truth." The more one gains a knowledge of God's Word, the more one should "bear fruit" in good works.

In sum, Paul views believers as the progeny of the last Adam, fulfilling in him the mandate given to the first Adam, including growing in and obeying God's word. The Gen. 1:28 language applied to them in 1:6, 9–10 indicates that they are a part of the inaugurated new creation and are beginning to fulfill in Christ what has been left unfulfilled in the primordial mandate throughout the ages.

Another OT motif in Colossians is the "mystery" (Col. 1:26–27; 2:2–3), which is sometimes understood to be a polemic against proto-gnostic teaching. The "mystery" derives from the visionary prophecy of Daniel (Dan. 2:19–22, 28–30) and is best understood in the light of

Christ fulfilling the "mystery" of that text (especially being identified as the messianic "stone" of 2:35, 45 [parallel with the son of man in 7:13] that "filled the earth"). Daniel is a more viable influence on Paul's mystery concept than gnostic teachings.

An additional theme is that of the relationship of the OT law to the present Christian epoch. Especially Col. 2:16–17 shows that the OT food laws and holiday (holy day) laws are no longer binding, as they were in the OT period, because they were all foreshadows of Christ, who is the substance or fulfillment of these institutional laws. In particular, these laws revolve around worship of God at the temple, anticipating Christ as the focus of worship in the new temple. Likewise, physical circumcision in Israel foreshadows believers being spiritually "circumcised with a circumcision performed without hands . . . by the circumcision of Christ" (2:11 NASB; i.e., union with his death that separates him and believers from the old, sinful world).

Similarly, the notion of new creation (e.g., Col. 1:15–23; 2:20; 3:1–11) is to be viewed against an OT background. For example, the first creation in Gen. 1 is seen to be recapitulated in a new creation and on an escalated scale through Christ's resurrection (see 1:15–23).

The False Teaching in Colossae: The Use of the OT with Respect to OT Legalism and Apocalyptic Judaism

The first glimpse we get at some of the specifics of the erroneous teaching addressed in Colossians is in 2:16: "Therefore let no one act as your judge in regard to food or drink or in respect to a festival or a new moon or a Sabbath day" (AT). Recall that the false teaching is "not according to [based on] Christ . . . in [whom] all the fullness of deity dwells in bodily form" (2:8–9 AT). As I argued earlier, Paul emphasizes that Christ is the true end-time temple of God's presence and that believers "in him have been filled" with that tabernacling presence (2:10). Consequently, the error includes some false teaching about how to experience God's presence in the true heavenly temple. The false teachers did not deem being in Christ to be a sufficient experience of the temple. According to 2:16, this deviant teaching affirmed that obedience to OT dietary laws and ordinances about holy days was necessary in order to come into the presence of God in his heavenly temple. Colossians 2:21 repeats the food law requirement: "Do not handle! Do not taste! Do not touch!" Thus, "Let no one judge you" in 2:16 further develops "Be careful not to let anyone captivate you" in 2:8. Together, these emphasize the warning not to let the false philosophy dominate anyone (Moo, *Colossians*, 218).

Most commentators have mentioned only that these were dietary laws and decrees about holidays, the ongoing validity of which the false teachers were wrongly affirming. While this is true, most do not consider the primary purpose of these laws in the OT—namely, to enable the Israelite to enter into God's temple to worship him. These food laws in the present age were seen to have continuing validity for qualifying one for gaining an experience of heavenly temple worship (see Beale, *Colossians*, 214–19).

The Greek behind "a festival or a new moon or a Sabbath day" in 2:16 occurs as a triadic formula in the LXX, and early Judaism almost always linked them to temple sacrifices or temple worship; when the temple is not explicitly mentioned, it is likely assumed to be in mind to some degree since these feasts were held at the temple. While feasts, new moons, and Sabbaths were observed by some gentiles, the triadic formula is not found in pagan Greek contexts. That the food laws are to be understood primarily (though not exclusively) against an OT backdrop is also confirmed from Col. 2:17: these laws and the OT holidays were a "shadow of what is to come, but the substance is of Christ" (AT; cf. NKJV). Clearly, the OT rites and institutions were the shadow in mind here. This false teaching about dietary laws and holidays is rooted in a distortion of OT and Jewish ideas, especially related to the temple. This explains why Paul has already alluded to four OT temple texts, affirming either that Christ is the temple (1:19; 2:9) or that believers are part of this temple (1:9–10; 2:10). Thus, all the temple experience they need is in Christ; they do not need to pursue any other avenues to any other kind of temple involvement to have a fulfilling temple participation, such as that advocated by the false teaching. Therefore, the Colossian believers should not fear being judged for not following such a false teaching. The observation that these positive references to the temple are from the OT suggests a polemic against a false conception of the OT teaching about the temple.

Indeed, that the false teaching contains a clear strain of Jewish thought is explicitly in view in the further description of the false teaching in 2:18: "Let no one keep disqualifying you from your prize by delighting in self-abasement and the worship of the angels, taking his stand on visions he has seen, inflated without cause by his fleshly mind" (AT). The notion of "self-abasement," like the food laws, was likely designed to prepare for and enhance a visionary experience, such as heavenly visions of angels who are to be worshiped (or of angels worshiping).

The most contested verse of the whole epistle concerns the phrase in 2:18: *ha heoraken embateuōn*. The most straightforward rendering is "which things he has seen [the angels in heaven] when entering." The difficult Greek word *embateuōn* is best paraphrased as "entering into the innermost sanctuary." However, some commentators have doubted this translation because they see no reference elsewhere in the epistle to the temple. But this understanding of the difficult expression fits with Paul's repeated positive emphasis on Christ and believers as the true temple, which these commentators have failed to see. Paul's prior underscoring of the positive temple idea is designed as a polemic against the false teachers' claim that one can obtain experience of the heavenly temple apart from Christ (which may reflect some Hellenistic background). Thus, Col. 2:18 becomes the climax of Paul's presentation of the false teachers' position about having a heavenly temple experience that is not based on Christ (cf. 2:8 HCSB; 2:19). The Christians in Colossae should not fear being disqualified as first-class Christian citizens by the false teachers, and genuine believers' union with Christ as the temple is true and all they need. There is also a Hellenistic-pagan background to the false teaching, but this cannot be elaborated on here.

Other Uses of the OT in Colossians

Table 3 summarizes how Paul understands Christ's role in relation to various OT institutions and events.

Table 3. Christ in Relation to OT Themes

OT/Jewish Perspective	Paul in Colossians
Torah is Wisdom.	Christ is Wisdom (2:3; cf. 1:15–20).
Jerusalem temple is the locus of God's presence.	Christ is the new and greater temple and locus of the divine presence (1:19; 2:9), and saints are identified with Christ as the temple (2:10).
Physical circumcision is necessary for incorporation into the people of God.	Christ's death "cut him off" from the old world and does the same for believers who identify with him (2:11–13).
Festivals, new moons, and Sabbath days are to be kept.	Reality found in Christ of the new age (2:16–17).
Laws of clean and unclean food are to be maintained.	Reality found in Christ of the new age (2:16–17).
The exodus from Egypt results in Israel's redemption and inheritance in the land.	The end-time exodus in Christ of the church results in her redemption and inheritance of the kingdom (Col. 1:12–14).

Source: Adapted from Beetham, 251.

The use of the OT in Colossians plays a role in some of the most debated passages of the epistle. There is not space to refer to all the OT allusions in Colossians, but the reader can consult Beale ("Colossians"; *Colossians*) and Beetham for discussion of more of the allusions.

The OT in Philemon

I concluded in *CNTUOT* that there are no OT references in Philemon (see *CNTUOT*, 918).

Bibliography. Beale, G. K., "Colossians," in *CNTUOT*, 841–70; Beale, *Colossians, Philemon*, BECNT (Baker Academic, 2019); Beale, *Handbook on the New Testament Use of the Old Testament* (Baker Academic, 2012); Beale, "The Old Testament in Colossians," *JSNT* 41, no. 2 (2018): 261–74; Beale, *The Temple and the Church's Mission*, NSBT (Apollos, 2004); Beetham, C. A., *Echoes of Scripture in the Letter of Paul to the Colossians*, BibInt 96 (Brill, 2008); Fee, G. D., "Old Testament Intertextuality in Colossians," in *History and Exegesis*, ed. Aang-Won Son (T&T Clark, 2006), 201–21; Foster, P., *Colossians* (T&T Clark, 2016); Foster, "Echoes without Resonance," *JSNT* 38 (2015): 96–111; Hays, R. B., *The Conversion of the Imagination* (Eerdmans, 2005); Hays, *Echoes of Scripture in the Letters of Paul* (Yale University Press, 1989); Lucas, A. J., "Assessing Stanley E. Porter's Objections to Richard B. Hays's Notion of Metalepsis," *CBQ* 76 (2014): 93–111; Miller, G. D., "Intertextuality in Old Testament Research," *CurBR* 9 (2010): 283–309; Moo, D. J., *The Letters to the Colossians and to Philemon*, PNTC (Eerdmans, 2008); Shaw, D. A., "Converted Imaginations?," *CurBR* 11 (2013): 234–45; Sumney, J. L., "Writing 'in the Image' of Scripture," in *Paul and Scripture*, ed. C. D. Stanley, ECL 9 (Society of Biblical Literature, 2012), 185–229.

G. K. BEALE

Consummation

The biblical-theological story line moves consistently toward the goal of the consummate fulfillment of God's promises. The story begins with God creating the heavens and the earth, with human beings created in God's image as the pinnacle of his creative activity (Gen. 1–2). However, sin enters the world and ruins all aspects of God's good creation (Gen. 3). The rest of Scripture then moves inexorably toward the goal of the consummation of God's redemptive plan to restore humanity and all things affected by the fall. Though the NT is consistent in its testimony that the promises of eschatological salvation and the establishment of God's kingdom are fulfilled in an inaugural manner, the NT is likewise insistent that these promises have yet to reach their consummate fulfillment in God's redemptive plan at the second coming of Christ. This article considers the progress of the OT story line toward the consummation and the NT goal of the fulfillment of God's intention to consummate his redemptive purposes.

Consummation in the OT

OT indications of a future restoration of humanity and creation begin to take shape with the covenants made with Abraham and David. In the first redemptive covenant following the fall (Gen. 3), God promises that from Abraham will come a great nation who will possess a land, and the creation of this nation is to reach universal dimensions. Through Abraham all the nations of the earth will eventually be blessed (Gen. 12:1–2). This covenant is narrowed with the covenant that God makes with David (2 Sam. 7:14), which states that David's throne will be eternal, a promise that gets picked up elsewhere in anticipation of a climactic realization (cf. Pss. 2; 110; Isa. 9:6–7). One day the Davidic son's rule will encompass the entire earth (Ps. 2:8). The fullest expression of the consummate promises of God's intention to redeem all things comes in the prophetic texts, which demonstrate how the covenants with Abraham and David will be fulfilled.

Following their establishment in the land, the exile of Israel because of sin calls into question the fulfillment of God's promises made to his people through the covenants with Abraham and David. Therefore, the prophetic texts anticipate a day when God will restore Israel to the land promised to Abraham, gather them under a Davidic monarch, and judge their enemies. The prophets frequently use the term "day of the LORD" (cf. Isa. 13:6; Ezek. 30:2–3; Joel 1:15; 2:30–31; 3:14; Amos 5:18; Zeph. 1:7–18; Zech. 14:1) to refer to a seemingly imminent (but actually distant) future time when God will intervene to judge Israel and the nations (House, 187–201; Motyer, 615). That day will result in a time of restoration and prosperity for God's faithful people: Jerusalem itself will be rebuilt and adorned with precious jewels (Isa. 54:11–12), and the people will be united to God as his bride (Isa. 61–62). God will raise up his people and give them life (Ezek. 37:1–14). The dead will rise when God brings salvation (Isa. 26:19). Israel will be reunited in their land (Ezek. 36–37; cf. Isa. 40–55) under a Davidic king who will shepherd them and deliver them from their enemies (Ezek. 34:23–24; 37:24–25; Isa. 11:1–11). In the land, God will establish a new covenant relationship with his people, in which he will pour out his Spirit on them and give them a new heart, cleansing them from sin and enabling them to keep his commands (Ezek. 36:24–29; Joel 2:28–29). Jeremiah predicts a coming day when God will make a new covenant with his restored people, bringing cleansing from sin and writing his laws on the hearts of his people (Jer. 31:31–34). This new covenant will remedy the inefficiency of the old (Mosaic) covenant. At that time God's people will dwell in peace and security (33:1–9) under the rulership of a restored Davidic monarch (33:14–26). The restoration of the people and return to the land will bring about Edenic conditions (Isa. 41:18; Ezek. 36:35; 47:1–12) and will exhibit features of a new creation or abundant fruitfulness (Isa. 43:19; Ezek. 36:8–11; Jer. 31:12, 14), thus again restoring pre-fall conditions (Gen. 2). The establishment of a new covenant also means that God will dwell directly with his people (Ezek. 37:27; Joel. 3:16–17) in a rebuilt and renewed temple (Ezek. 40–48). The renewed land and temple will be a return to Edenic conditions, with the water and trees giving life to the land and to God's restored people (Ezek. 47:1–12; Gen. 2). Isaiah 65 (see below) depicts a day when the people will experience fruitfulness (v. 21) and harmony in the animal world (v. 25). The days of the people will be like a tree (v. 22). The LXX expands Isa. 65:22 to read "as the days of a tree *of life*" (*tou xylou tēs zōēs*), alluding to Gen. 2:9. According to Zechariah, a day will come when God's people will be restored to the land in Jerusalem and David's house will be restored (12:10; 13:1). The Lord will defeat the enemies of Jerusalem, and the city will experience unending light (14:7). Jerusalem will be the source of living water (14:8), and the Lord will rule over the entire earth from Jerusalem (14:9).

Beyond the restoration of God's people Israel, some prophetic texts anticipate the inclusion of gentiles in the blessings of renewal and restoration in fulfillment of the Abrahamic covenant, which says that Abraham will be a blessing to all the nations of the earth (Gen. 12:1–2). Perhaps more than any other prophetic text, Isaiah anticipates gentile inclusion in terms of the nations streaming to the restored Jerusalem. Nations will come to Zion to learn the ways of the Lord (Isa. 2:2–4). They will come to the light of the renewed Jerusalem (probably indicating their conversion) and will bring their wealth to it, contributing to its restoration (60; 66:19–21). Those from the nations will even function as priests (66:21). According to Zechariah, the nations who survive judgment will make a pilgrimage to Jerusalem to celebrate the feast of tabernacles (Zech. 14:16–19), and the entire city (not just the temple) will be sacred space (vv. 20–21).

While Israel does return to their land from exile, it is apparent that the prophetic promises in these texts are not fully realized in the temporal return to Palestine. The universal dimensions of the prophetic expectations of the full inclusion of the gentiles and the rule of God extending to the ends of the earth in fulfillment of God's promises to Abraham remain outstanding. The enemies of God and his people have yet to be judged. One day a "son of man" figure will come and judge the earthly kingdoms, replacing them with a kingdom that will never be destroyed (Dan. 7:13–14, 27). God will judge the entire earth (Isa. 24:1). Isaiah transcends expectations of the restoration of the people of God and the return to the land with promises of a new creative act (65:17–20). God will create new heavens and a new earth (Isa. 65:17; 66:22; cf. Gen. 1:1), with a new Jerusalem free of oppression and death (results of the fall; Isa. 65:20–23). Death will ultimately be defeated (25:8), and the dead will rise (26:19). In place of sorrow and death will be unending joy and life. The borders of the land will be expanded (26:15; Beale, *Biblical Theology*, 753). Thus, the OT prophetic expectations retain an unrealized dimension that awaits its consummate fulfillment. These expectations form the basis for the NT depictions of the consummation of God's redemptive plan.

Consummation in the NT

The consistent testimony of the NT is that the end-time promises anticipated in the OT prophetic texts have begun inaugurated fulfillment in the person of Jesus Christ. With the first coming of Christ the promised future kingdom of God had already drawn "near" (*engizō*); it was in the process of being fulfilled (Matt. 4:17; Mark 1:15; see Blomberg, 30–39). Yet Jesus's teaching and the rest of the NT are equally insistent that the end-time promises that find expression in the OT prophetic texts and inaugurated fulfillment in Jesus have yet to reach their consummate fulfillment.

Gospels. Alongside statements in Jesus's own teaching that the end-time kingdom is already being fulfilled in his person and ministry (e.g., Matt. 12:28) are statements that anticipate a consummate fulfillment of those promises. Jesus anticipates a future "renewal [*palingennesia*] of all things" (Matt. 19:28), perhaps a reference to a new creation (Blomberg, 380), that will take place when he comes to sit on his throne and judge with his disciples. The most detailed example is the so-called Olivet Discourse in Matt. 24 (see Mark 13; Luke 21). Jesus uses the word *parousia* several times to refer to his coming at the end of history to judge. Though some take the reference to the coming of the Son of Man as a reference to his coming in judgment upon Jerusalem in AD 70 (Wright, 339–68), it is more likely that *parousia* and the language of the dissolution of the constellations in Matt. 24:29 refer to the end-time return of Christ, when he will bring salvation and judgment. Though many signs will characterize the period of history leading up to the coming of Christ, including the destruction of Jerusalem in AD 70 ("the abomination that causes desolation," v. 15), the coming of the Son of Man will be evident in its "earth shaking" effects (v. 29)—a description that uses stereotypical apocalyptic language from Isa. 34:4. Yet Jesus is clear that even he does not know the time of his return, a fact that fosters vigilance and watchfulness on the part of his followers (24:36–25:46). Despite its realized eschatology (Blomberg, 674), John's Gospel likewise envisions the consummation of God's redemptive promises in the form of giving life to the people of God in the final resurrection (John 5:25; 6:39–40). Most likely, John is reflecting OT prophetic texts that envision the giving of life in the future new creation / restoration (Ezek. 37:5, 9, 10, 12–14; 47:7–12; Isa. 65:20–22; Zech. 14:8). Moreover, John, following Dan. 12:2, expects the future resurrection of both believers and unbelievers, in which the righteous will be raised to eternal life and the wicked to eternal judgment (John 5:28–29).

Pauline literature. The consummation of God's redemptive promises and plan is also developed in the Pauline corpus, which focuses particularly on the resurrection of God's people and the renewal of creation. God's plan is to one day reconcile everything in heaven and earth that was affected by the fall (Gen. 3) into its rightful place under the headship of Christ (Eph. 1:10; cf. Col. 1:16). Because of this, the church is to live by hope in the future coming of Christ, at which point he will consummate God's redemptive plan. According to Rom. 8, God's people await the future redemption when God will give life (*zōopoiēsei*, v. 11) to their mortal bodies (resurrection) through the Holy Spirit, who presently indwells them (vv. 11, 23). Alongside this redemption is the redemption of creation itself. The present creation groans, being subject to corruption because of the fall (vv. 19, 22), and awaits its final redemption and liberation from corruption (v. 21), a reference to the new creation (Moo, 517). The expectation of a future, eschatological resurrection receives even greater articulation in 1 Cor. 15. Christ's own physical resurrection, referred to with the imagery of "firstfruits" (*aparchē*), is a guarantee of the eschatological physical, bodily resurrection of the saints (15:20, 23), which will reverse the effects of Adam's sin, including physical (and spiritual) death (15:22, 45): Christ is the last Adam, who overturns the effects of the first Adam's fall. The physical resurrection of the saints is necessary for death to be ultimately swallowed up (v. 54; Isa. 25:8) and defeated, an event that will transpire when Christ returns (the parousia, 1 Cor. 15:23) and subdues all things under his feet and when all things find their place under the sovereign rule of God the Father (15:24–28). The subjection of all things under God's rule restores the original rule of God over creation (Gen. 1–2). Also, a physical transformation is necessary, since our present (fallen) bodies ("flesh and blood" [*sarx kai haima*], 1 Cor. 15:50) are not fit to inherit God's eternal kingdom, the new creation (vv. 50–54; cf. Rev. 21:1–22:5).

The hope in a future, bodily resurrection also plays a key role in Paul's instructions in 1 Thess. 4:13–18. The believers' hope is that, at the parousia of Christ, believers (both dead and alive) will be raised to live with Christ forever. The references to a parousia, "the voice of the archangel," "the trumpet," and the coming on the clouds (vv. 16–17) echo Jesus's teaching in Matt. 24:30–31. In 1 Thess. 5 Paul utilizes OT "day of the Lord" language (v. 2). The day of the Lord will bring both judgment and salvation. For unbelievers it will overtake them unexpectedly, and they will experience God's "wrath" (*orgēn*; v. 9), whereas believers will be prepared for it by being vigilant and watchful (5:6). For them the coming of Christ at the day of the Lord will bring about their final "salvation" (*sōtērian*; v. 9). In 2 Thessalonians Paul may be responding to an overreaction to or misunderstanding of what he has said in 1 Thessalonians. The Thessalonian believers thought that the day of the Lord promised in the OT had already arrived (2 Thess. 2:2). Paul writes to convince them that they are not yet in that day. On that day Christ "will be revealed" (*apokalypsei*, 1:7) from heaven with his holy angels. This day will mean judgment—exclusion from God's presence—for those who have oppressed God's people and refused the gospel (1:5–9). But this day will mean salvation for those who believe (v. 10). This dual emphasis on salvation and judgment is consistent with OT prophetic expectations of what will transpire at the coming day of the Lord. To prove that this day has not yet arrived, Paul appeals to three events that must still happen before the arrival of the day of the Lord: (1) the "rebellion" (*apostasia*), (2) the removal of the restrainer, and (3) the resulting revelation of the man of lawlessness (2:3–8). Though there is uncertainty as to exactly what Paul is referring to, Paul's point is that certain things have not yet happened that must happen before the day of the Lord arrives. When the man of lawlessness is finally revealed in the future (whoever he is or whatever it is), he will be overthrown at Christ's "coming" (*parousia*, v. 8).

2 Peter 3:10–13. In responding to the issue of the apparent delay of the eschatological "coming" (*parousia*) of Christ, Peter asserts that God's redemptive promises will certainly be consummated upon the arrival of the OT day of the Lord. Drawing on OT imagery, Peter envisions the dissolution of the present order as happening "with a roar" (2 Pet. 3:10; cf. Amos 1:2; Joel 4:16) and in fire and heat in an end-time judgment. Along with other NT authors, Peter asserts that the present earth "will pass away" (*pareleusontai*, 2 Pet. 3:10; cf. Matt. 5:18; 24:35; Mark 13:31; Luke 16:17; 21:33; 1 John 2:17; cf. Isa. 34:4; Rev. 6:14). Yet this passing away will take place to make way for a "new heavens and new earth" (*kainous . . . ouranous kai gēn kainēn*; 2 Pet. 3:13), a hope based on Isa. 65:17; 66:22; and other apocalyptic texts (Rev. 21:1; Jub. 1:29; 1 En. 45:4–5; 72:1; 91:16; 2 Bar. 32:6; 44:12; 57:2; 4 Ezra 7:75). It is unclear whether Peter envisions a literal destruction of the universe or the renewal of the present order. However, the overriding emphasis is not on cosmology but on the Lord's coming in eschatological judgment to lay bare all things (2 Pet. 3:10; Bauckham, *Jude, 2 Peter*, 315). The focus of this section, as with all eschatological texts in the NT, is hortatory: "What kind of people ought you to be? You ought to live holy and godly lives" (v. 11). The second coming of Christ is frequently a motivation for holy living throughout the NT (see the discussion on 1–2 Thessalonians above; cf. Heb. 10:25; James 5:7–8; 1 Pet. 4:7; 1 John 3:2–3).

Revelation. Though Revelation contains a number of "previews" of end-time judgment and salvation throughout its visions (e.g., 6:12–17; 7:9–17; 11:15–18), the lengthiest and most detailed articulation of the consummation of God's redemptive promises comes in the final chapters of the last book of the biblical canon. Chapters 19–22 are replete with allusions to the OT (see Fekkes; Mathewson; Tõniste) that form the basis for John's own conception of eschatological judgment and salvation, suggesting that all the OT prophetic hopes find their fulfillment in the consummate new creation in Rev. 21:1–22:5. The final chapters of Revelation provide a series of visions of consummate judgment and salvation precipitated by the second coming of Christ. In consistency with the OT prophetic texts, Rev. 19–22 envisions consummate *judgment* (19:11–20:15) and *salvation* (20:4–6; 21:1–22:5). Revelation 19:11–20:15 constitutes a series of removal scenes, where everything that opposes the full establishment of God's kingdom on earth is removed in a series of judgment scenes at the end of history. It is not clear whether these scenes in Rev. 19–20 indicate a series of chronological events or provide different perspectives on the same end-time event—namely, the coming of Christ to consummate the end-time judgment of God. End-time judgment begins with the emergence of God's agent of judgment, Christ the warrior on a white horse (19:11–21). The description of Christ as warrior resonates with OT texts (see, e.g., Pss. 2:9; 96:13; Isa. 11:4; Dan. 10:6). The battle scene itself reflects OT imagery (Ezek. 38–39). At this time the beast and false prophet, both introduced in Rev. 13, are thrown into the lake of fire. Moreover, all humanity that resists God and his kingdom is likewise removed. Most likely, the battle imagery metaphorically depicts a judgment scene rather than a literal battle. In Rev. 20 the dragon, Satan, receives the same fate as his beastly cohorts and, in a two-stage judgment (he is locked in the abyss, then let out to go into destruction), is also thrown into the lake of fire in judgment. Despite slightly different imagery, the battle of 20:7–10 is likely the same one as that of 19:11–21, since it also utilizes Ezek. 38–39. The first passage focuses on the defeat of the two beasts, while the second focuses on the defeat of Satan, thus reversing the order in which the figures were introduced in Rev. 12–13.

In the midst of Satan's judgment, the saints are vindicated in the millennium (20:4–6). Their coming to life alludes to Ezek. 37:4–6, 14. These verses in Revelation are much debated. Many have advocated an approach dubbed "premillennialism," in which the second coming of Christ precedes and inaugurates the period of the thousand-year reign. Though details differ (Chung and Mathewson), all premillennial interpretations have in common the idea that the millennium is a future period of time in which Christ and the saints will rule on earth. Another popular approach to interpreting this text is known as "amillennialism." It understands the thousand years as symbolic of Christ and the saints reigning from heaven during the entire church age. A third perspective known as "postmillennialism" is not currently as common (though during the Puritan period it was by far the most common view) and argues that the millennium is a future period of time, a golden age that the church, through its witness and through the work of the Holy Spirit, will establish on earth. At the end of this period, Christ will return to earth (hence the prefix "post-"). Nevertheless, the main function of the millennium is to vindicate and reward the people of God in the midst of Satan's judgment through their resurrection: since the fall, Satan has killed them and ruled over this world (Rev. 12–13); now, in a profound reversal, the saints come to life and reign. "The theological point of the millennium is solely to demonstrate the triumph of the martyrs: that those whom the beast put to death are those who will truly live—eschatologically, and that those who contested his right to rule and suffered for it will in the end rule as universally as he" (Bauckham, *Revelation*, 107). John envisions two resurrections: one for the righteous (20:4–5) and one for the unrighteous, which is a resurrection to judgment (20:12–15). Thus, following the resurrection and concomitant millennial reign of the saints, in a final sweeping-up act of judgment, all things are judged at the great white throne of Rev. 20:12–15. The unbelieving dead are raised for judgment—eternal separation from God in the lake of fire (20:12–13, 15). Included in this judgment is the earth itself, marred by sin and the fall and under the dominion of Satan.

At the end of Rev. 20 everything has been removed in order to make way for a new creative act in the form of "a new heaven and new earth" (Rev. 21:1; cf. Isa. 65:17). Furthermore, the saints have been raised (20:4–6) to new life in order to inhabit the new creation. The key term is *kainē* (21:1, 2, 5), an OT term (Isa. 43:19 LXX: *kaina*; 65:17 MT: *ḥădāšîm*) that indicates discontinuity with the old order and the qualitative newness of the new order of things. The new heavens and new earth, ultimately alluding to the first heavens and first earth (Gen. 1:1), recall Isaiah's prophesied new creation (Isa. 65:17). Though the metaphorical language of Revelation's visions makes it difficult to determine whether John envisions the destruction of the present order and a second creation *ex nihilo* or the renewal and transformation of the present order (Mathewson, 35–39), the vision probably depicts a renewal of the present creation (cf. Matt. 19:28; Rom. 8:20–21; 2 Pet. 3:9–10). In any case, at the center of the Christian hope for a consummate redemption is a physical creation, a natural corollary to the promise of physical resurrection bodies (1 Cor. 15; 1 Thess. 4:13–18; Rev. 20:4–6). Not only God's people but also all creation will be restored in a new creative act. At the center of the new creation stands the new-Jerusalem (21:2, 9–27), which fulfills OT expectations of a restored Jerusalem in Isa. 54:11–12; 60; 65:18, all texts to which John alludes (Mathewson). The new-Jerusalem imagery is combined with nuptial imagery, as the bride adorned in all her glory is now seen in her consummate state (21:2, 9–10, 19–20), fulfilling OT expectations of the restored people of God being his bride (Isa. 54:11–12; 61:10; 62:5; see Fekkes). This connection suggests that the city symbolizes the saints themselves rather than a physical structure. God establishes a new covenant relationship with his eschatological people: "They will be his people, and God himself will be with them and be their God" (Rev. 21:3; cf. Ezek. 37:27).

One of the most important subtexts for John's depiction of the consummation is Ezekiel's vision of a restored temple. John alludes to Ezek. 40–48 throughout his climactic vision, yet unlike Ezekiel, he does not envision a separate physical temple in the new creation (Rev. 21:22). Instead, John applies temple imagery to the entire city/people of God. The entire city is one large temple where God and the Lamb dwell. (Its layout, equal in width, height, and length [21:16], reflects the geometry of the holy of holies [1 Kings 6:20].) John reads Ezekiel's prophecy of a restored temple through his redemptive-historical lens of fulfillment in Christ. God and the Lamb's immediate dwelling with their people is what the temple, and the prophetic anticipations of a rebuilt temple, point to. God's luminous presence now suffuses the entire city (21:11, 23). Now that the reality has arrived, there is no need for a separate, physical temple to mediate God's presence with his people. The entire people of God are a temple in whose midst God and the Lamb's temple presence resides (21:22). The entire people of God are priests who wear the stones of the breastplate of the high priest and serve him in his presence (21:19–20; 22:3–4; cf. Exod. 28:17–20; Ezek. 28:13) so that they fulfill Adam's (Gen. 1–2) and Israel's (Exod. 19:6) vocation as kings and priests (on the stones in 21:19–20, see Beale, *Revelation*, 1080–88).

The new creation also reaches back to the garden of Eden (Rev. 22:1–2), echoing Gen. 2 and Ezek. 47:1–12. God's intention for humanity in the garden is consummately realized with unending life symbolized by the tree of life and water of life and with God's people serving as priests and ruling over creation (Rev. 22:3–5), the very things that Adam and Eve failed to do. Furthermore, echoing OT promises, the nations will also find their way into the new Jerusalem / new creation (21:24–26). This is problematic in that the nations have apparently been eliminated in judgment (Rev. 19–20). Their presence in the new creation after John's depiction of their complete destruction is probably for rhetorical effect, to indicate the complete nature of God's judgment and salvation and to demonstrate the options before the nations: repentance or judgment (Mathewson, 172–75). Their presence in the new creation should be understood as an end-time conversion of the nations at Christ's eschatological coming in fulfillment of OT texts (Isa. 2:2–4; 60:1–22). The most significant feature of the consummation of God's redemption promises in the new creation is God and the Lamb's presence in it with his people. God and the Lamb will dwell with their people, who will stand in their presence and see God's face. "And so the Bible ends, with a redeemed society dwelling on a new earth that has been purged of all evil, with God dwelling in the midst of his people. This is the goal of the long course of redemptive history" (Ladd, 632). Moreover, the goal of bringing final salvation to God's people results in bringing glory to God and the Lamb. "The sovereignty of God and Christ in redeeming and judging brings them glory, which is intended to motivate saints to worship God and reflect his glorious attributes through obedience to his word" (Beale, *Revelation*, 174).

See also Creation; Day of the Lord; Messiah; Resurrection

Bibliography. Bauckham, R. J., *Jude, 2 Peter*, WBC (Word, 1983); Bauckham, *Theology of Revelation* (Cambridge University Press, 1993); Beale, G. K., *The Book of Revelation*, NIGTC (Eerdmans, 1999); Beale, *A New Testament Biblical Theology* (Baker Academic, 2011);

Blomberg, C. L., *A New Testament Theology* (Baylor University Press, 2018); Chung, S. W., and D. L. Mathewson, *Models of Premillennialism* (Cascade, 2018); Fekkes, J., *Isaiah and Prophetic Traditions in the Book of Revelation*, JSNTSup 93 (JSOT Press, 1994); House, P. R., "The Day of the Lord," in *Central Themes in Biblical Theology*, ed. S. J. Hafemann and P. R. House (Baker Academic, 2007), 179–224; Ladd, G. E., *A Theology of the New Testament* (Eerdmans, 1974); Mathewson, D. L., *New Heavens and New Earth*, JSNTSup 238 (Sheffield Academic, 2003); Moo, D. J., *The Letter to the Romans*, 2nd ed., NICNT (Eerdmans, 2018); Motyer, J. A., "Judgment," in *NDBT*, 612–15; Tõniste, K., *The Ending of the Canon*, LNTS 526 (T&T Clark, 2016); Wright, N. T., *Jesus and the Victory of God*, COQG 2 (Fortress, 1996).

DAVID L. MATHEWSON

Contemporary Interpretation

See History of Interpretation: 1800 to Present

Contextual and Noncontextual NT Use of the OT

Many students of the Bible believe that when NT authors quote from the OT, they do so with little regard for the context of the quotation. They view the writers of the NT as gold miners who are interested only in the nugget, not the strata of rock from which it was extracted. For instance, S. V. McCasland famously argues in his eponymous article that "Matthew Twists the Scriptures," and he offers several examples in support of his view that Matthew tore OT texts out of their contexts and recontextualized them with alacrity. Many other scholars concur, and by no means only with regard to Matthew.

But is it true? To be sure, Matthew's use of the OT does strike modern readers as curious in places, at least at first glance. We cannot, however, hold Matthew or any other NT author to modern academic standards regarding the use of quotations; rather, they must be held to those standards of their own time and culture. Taken on their own terms and measured against the conventions of the day and the expectations of their audiences, the authors of the NT can be shown, demonstrably in most cases, to have been aware and respectful of the original contexts of the texts they quote or allude to.

What "Contextual Use" Implies

Respect for a contextual use of the OT was argued most clearly and convincingly seventy years ago by the Welsh scholar C. H. Dodd in a surprisingly thin book entitled *According to the Scriptures: The Substructure of New Testament Theology*. Dodd identifies fifteen OT texts that were quoted by at least two NT authors and comes to several conclusions on the basis of his study: (1) these texts played a decisive role in the formation of NT theological concepts, especially christological and soteriological ones; (2) when these texts are quoted, "the unit of reference was sometimes wider than the usually brief form of words actually quoted" (Dodd, 61); and (3) generally speaking, "the writers of the New Testament, in making use of passages from the Old Testament, remain true to the main intention of their writers" (Dodd, 130).

This is not to say—and Dodd does not say—that they make precisely the same hermeneutical use of the OT texts they quote as the original authors did. Arguably, no one who quotes a previous work ever does, except when he or she is summarizing or reviewing it. Indeed, the NT authors quite consciously and sometimes boldly interpret OT texts messianically that in their original context are not *explicitly* messianic. That comes as no surprise. They are not, after all, offering sterile and disinterested exegesis of OT texts, drawing out their meaning in a theological vacuum; rather, they are interpreting them based on their strong conviction that Jesus of Nazareth is, in fact, the promised Messiah who has inaugurated the end of the old age and the beginning of the new age. They do not, however, distort texts in such a way that their application would be incomprehensible to the original author. At least, that is the conclusion arrived at by Dodd.

Take Joel 2:28–32, one of the passages that Dodd draws on to demonstrate his thesis, as an example. Joel envisions a time when God will pour out his Spirit on "all flesh" (2:28 ESV). Prophetic speech and cosmic signs will be the result (2:30–31). In context Joel has the Israelites in view. Joel sees them scattered among the nations but also envisions a day when they will be gathered to Mount Zion in Jerusalem. All these events signal the beginning of a new epoch in salvation history, in which "everyone who calls on the name of the LORD will be saved" (Joel 2:32). In his Pentecost sermon in AD 30, a mere seven weeks after the resurrection of Jesus, Peter appropriates this text to interpret the phenomenon he and the other disciples are caught up in: speaking in other tongues (Acts 2:4). He states unequivocally that "this [the miracle of Pentecost] is what was spoken of by the prophet Joel" (Acts 2:16).

Did Joel precisely envision this scene in the context of the Jewish Feast of Pentecost in AD 30? Was he transported in the Spirit across time so that he might see this event and describe it? Probably not. It is even more doubtful that he foresaw that "calling on the name of the Lord" would entail confessing that "Jesus is Lord," as Paul proclaims with reference to this same prophecy (Rom. 10:9, 13). Still, Peter can hardly be accused of ripping Joel's prophecy out of its context. It is rather an example of contextual exegesis based on a particular conception of who Jesus is: the promised Messiah who according to Jewish expectations would be the one who transmits God's Spirit to God's people in the "latter days" (Acts 2:17, 33 AT).

Given Peter's presuppositions about Jesus's identity, his application of the prophecy of Joel to the events of Pentecost makes perfect sense, since Joel envisions an eschatological future that involves a familiar complex of OT themes: the day of the Lord (Joel 2:1–11), repentance by the people of Israel (2:12–17), and God turning back to Israel and renewing the land (2:18–27). The coming of the Messiah and his pouring out of God's Spirit on restored Israel were all part of this eschatological vision.

This was not a novel idea in early Judaism. In the Testament of Judah, a pseudepigraphical work from the mid-second century BC, "Judah," the progenitor of the Israelite tribe that bore his name, prophesies that "after this there shall arise for you a Star from Jacob in peace, and a man shall arise from my posterity like the Sun of righteousness, walking with the sons of men in gentleness and righteousness, and in him will be found no sin. *And the heavens will be opened upon him to pour out the spirit as a blessing of the Holy Father. And he will pour the spirit of grace on you*" (T. Jud. 24:1–3 *OTP*). Peter, then, is interpreting Joel's prophecy in a way that respects its original context and applies the text appropriately within the context of early Judaism/nascent Christianity. In this sense his use of the OT is doubly contextual.

"Doing Things" with OT Texts

There is, however, much more that needs to be said about the use NT authors make of OT texts. Our understanding of how texts work—all texts, not just biblical ones—was greatly enhanced as a result of the so-called "linguistic turn" in the twentieth century. The British philosopher of language J. L. Austin's *How to Do Things with Words*, first published in 1962, brought about a transformation in the way we think about speech acts. Austin was not the first to stress the function of language, but his cleverly titled and easily accessible book helped a broad audience understand that we can judge the success of a "locution"—a statement or utterance, whether spoken or written—only if we know what the speaker or author was hoping to accomplish by making it.

This has bearing on the issue we are concerned with because we cannot ultimately discern whether a NT author's use of an OT text may be considered contextual until we know what he intended to "do" with that quotation. As we noted above, NT authors do not always attempt to "do" the same thing with a quotation from the OT as its original author "did" with it. "Respecting the context" does not imply that, and much of the criticism aimed at NT authors regarding the use they make of OT quotations seems to ignore this fundamental insight.

Stated positively, we can affirm that a NT author has shown respect for the context of the OT quotation if it can be demonstrated that (1) he was aware of the context and (2) he did not attempt to "do" something with the quotation that is incompatible with its meaning within its original context.

When, for instance, Paul quotes the sixth commandment, along with several others, in Rom. 13:9, he does so with the intention of subsuming them under the commandment to "love your neighbor as yourself" (Lev. 19:18). In that narrow sense—one that ignores the pragmatic aspects of language ("doing things with words") and allows only for the most wooden and literal appropriation of a text—it could be said that the use Paul makes of the text is noncontextual. After all, he relativizes it by subordinating it to another law, one that was surely not in view when Moses propounded the Ten Commandments. In another sense, however, Paul can be shown to be drawing out the law's deeper intention. Taking his cue from Jesus (Matt. 22:39 pars.), he searches for and finds a principle in the law that captures the ethos behind the second tablet and brings this into the foreground.

Various Uses of OT Texts

In what follows, we will look at the various uses NT authors make of OT texts and offer examples of each species.

Fulfillment of prophecy. One of the most frequent uses made of OT texts by NT authors is the one that likely comes most immediately to the mind of modern readers of the Bible: an utterance that was intended to be prophetic within its original context is quoted or alluded to with a view toward establishing its fulfillment. Peter's quotation of Joel 2:28–32 in Acts 2:17–21, which we examined above, is an example of this, as is the first OT quotation in the NT: Isa. 7:14 in Matt. 1:23, to which we now turn our attention.

In Matt. 1:18–21, the evangelist recounts that Mary, who was engaged to Joseph, became pregnant with Jesus before they had sexual intercourse. How women become pregnant was no more a mystery then than now, and since Joseph knew that he was not the father of the child, he assumed that Mary had slept with another man. As he was contemplating ending the engagement (a step that in an early Jewish cultural context required initiating divorce proceedings), an angel appeared to him and told him that Mary had not been unfaithful to him; rather, the child she was carrying was created by a supernatural act of the Holy Spirit. The son she would bear should be named Jesus, for he would save his people from their sins. Matthew views this as the fulfillment of prophecy, as he explicitly states in Matt. 1:22, and he quotes the prophecy he has in view as follows: "The virgin will conceive and give birth to a son, and they will call him Immanuel" (1:23).

This quotation from Isa. 7:14 raises two questions regarding Matthew's use of Scripture. The first involves whether Isaiah really had a "virgin" in mind. There is no doubt that the English term accurately translates the word *parthenos*, the term used in the Septuagint (LXX), the Greek translation of the Hebrew Bible that was already widely used in the first century AD from which

Matthew is quoting. Many scholars argue, however, that *parthenos* is an unfortunate rendering of *ʿalmâ*, the term found in the Hebrew Bible in Isa. 7:14. They maintain that the Hebrew word does not denote "virginity" per se; rather, it means more generally "a young woman of marriageable age." That is why McCasland (144) argues that "Matthew twists the scripture" here: the evangelist's interpretation depends on the Greek translation, rather than the Hebrew original—that is, Matthew chose what he knew to be a skewed translation because it supported his interpretation.

Many highly respected scholars have argued, however, that the LXX translation is legitimate because it draws out the intention of the Isaianic text. None other than C. H. Gordon, a renowned Jewish scholar of Near Eastern languages and culture, argues that early use of *ʿalmâ* does, in fact, denote virginity, and E. J. Young (287), a highly accomplished student of Biblical Hebrew, could "confidently assert" that *ʿalmâ* was never used of a married woman. In other words, even if it could be shown against Gordon that, technically speaking, *parthenos* denotes a virgin while *ʿalmâ* does not, the latter term clearly *connotes* virginity in a culture where young women of marriageable age were simply assumed to be virgins.

The second problem has to do with the fact that in its original context the prophecy of a child born to a virgin/*parthenos*/*ʿalmâ* functions as a sign for King Ahaz—that is, it presumes fulfillment in his day (Isa. 7:16). The commentaries discuss whether the baby boy in question is a promised future son of the king or of Isaiah or perhaps of someone else altogether. There are, however, elements in the larger context of this prophetic word that point beyond mere initial fulfillment in the contemporary historical situation (Bauckham, 19–20). The promised son is described in terms that go well beyond what any king of Israel or Judah delivered, even allowing for an ample measure of hyperbole (Isa. 9:6–7). Further, as J. A. Motyer (123) pointed out fifty years ago, the Book of Immanuel (Isa. 7–11) anticipates the Assyrian invasion, Assyria's destruction, and the return from exile before the reign of the Davidic prince. In other words, even if Isaiah is expecting this prophecy to be initially fulfilled in his day, there is ample evidence that he looked forward to its ultimate fulfillment at a much later time.

Far from "twisting the scripture," then, Matthew shows a heightened awareness of the larger textual unit in which the prophecy he quotes is embedded. Clearly, he moves beyond the immediate historical situation presupposed by Isaiah and broadens the focus to include an eschatological horizon, but he does so because of his conviction that this is in view within the larger context of Isaiah's prophecy.

Typology. German theologian Leonhard Goppelt set out what has become a standard description of typology in his 1939 doctoral dissertation entitled "Typos" (Goppelt, 18–19): A "typology" accrues when a NT author identifies a correspondence between persons, events, or institutions in the OT (called "types") and the person and work of Christ or his church (the "antitypes"). At the outset, it should be noted that typology is a modern concept used to describe this phenomenon, not one that the Bible develops independently of prophecy (though the term *typos* is used by Paul in the way articulated above). That is to say that biblical authors do not distinguish between spoken prophecy and what we call typology. For them, it is one and the same whether God predicts future events in salvation history by using prophetic discourse to foretell, or cultural or historical developments to foreshadow them.

It is equally important to note that not just any happenstance correlation qualifies as a typology. A true typology presumes that God consciously and strategically places certain persons (e.g., Elijah; cf. Matt. 17:12–13), events (e.g., the conquest of the promised land; cf. Heb. 3:12–4:10), and institutions (e.g., the Feast of Passover; cf. 1 Cor. 5:6–8) in salvation history not only for purposes immediately relevant to their own context but also so that they might point ahead to larger realities that are subsequently fulfilled in Christ and his church. That is why biblical typology—as opposed to allegory—can claim to respect the context from which a type is taken. Thus, when a NT author's use of the OT is postulated to be typological, it should be demonstrable from the OT author's presuppositions, the underlying biblical narrative, or (at the very least) the OT canonical context that the presumed type does, in fact, point beyond itself, apart from the NT author's determination that this is so.

This presumes, of course, that God shapes history with a view toward facilitating typology, and that the NT authors' typological interpretations are inspired and authoritative. Scholars who deny one or both of these tenets therefore tend to view typology merely as a form of interpretation in which the perceived meaning of an OT text is generated solely by the imaginations of the NT authors. That, however, is not how the NT authors see it; for them, the perceived meaning inheres in the type itself. The *locus classicus* with regard to typology, 1 Cor. 10:1–11, is a case in point. In this passage, Paul warns the Corinthian believers not to trust in what they seem to have thought to be the apotropaic quality of baptism and the Lord's Supper—namely, that their mere participation in these rituals would protect them from God's judgment, regardless of whether they obeyed him or not. The apostle reminds them that at the outset of the exodus Israel experienced a baptism of sorts (crossing the Red Sea) and that during the wilderness wanderings the people ate "spiritual food" (manna) and drank "spiritual drink" (water drawn from barren boulders).

While these examples seem on the surface to have more the character of simple analogies, the first two are appropriated typologically elsewhere in the Bible. Paul is particularly interested in the last one. He states that the Israelites "drank from the spiritual rock that accompanied them, and that rock was Christ" (1 Cor. 10:4). The intended referent behind this enigmatic statement has been the cause of much speculation among NT scholars. Some point to a rabbinic tradition that envisions a sort of mobile well that followed Israel on its journeys through the wilderness. Others see a more general allusion to God, who is sometimes referred to as "the Rock" (cf. Gen. 49:24; Deut. 32:4). Neither of these theories, however, elucidates Paul's specific reference to Christ.

A more likely explanation takes its cue from the two pentateuchal texts that describe how water miraculously flowed from a rock in the desert. The first of these (Exod. 17:1–7) recounts how the people of Israel were on the verge of dying of thirst in the wilderness soon after their exodus from Egypt. They complain to Moses, who begs the Lord to intervene. The Lord proclaims that he will stand before Moses on a prominent rock at a place called Horeb. We should thus visualize the shekinah glory of God in the pillar of cloud hovering directly above the rock. God then instructs Moses to strike the rock with his staff. In order to do so, of course, Moses had to strike God, and this act of violence against God causes life-giving water to rush forth from the rock. The symbolic smiting of God, in other words, saves the people from death, and it is this aspect of the narrative that Paul seems to view as a type of Christ. The motif of the rock following Israel may simply be a creative way of combining this incident at the beginning of the wilderness sojourn with a second, similar one at the end of it (Num. 20:7–11). This accords with a well-attested early Jewish interpretive technique known as *gezerah shawah*, which interprets texts that exhibit verbal or thematic similarities in light of one another.

Paul's reading of these narratives, especially the first one, is certainly creative, but it would be wrong to construe it as noncontextual, as many commentators do, whether implicitly or explicitly. Rather, it is dependent upon very close attention to the details of the narrative and a respect for them that we do not see, for instance, in Philo's allegorical interpretation of the passage (*Alleg. Interp.* 2.86). Paul identifies a biblical motif here that accords with the servant's suffering to bring about the healing of his people (cf. Isa. 53:5) and ultimately with the death of Christ for the sins of many (1 Cor. 11:23–26). To his mind, this is not coincidental, but intended by God in its original context to point to the meaning it accrues in light of God's fuller revelation in Jesus Christ. Paul is clearly "doing" something new with the story of water flowing from the rock, but it flows from a careful reading of the text.

Analogy. Sometimes NT authors make use of OT texts to draw out the correspondences between persons or events in their contexts and similar ones in the OT without claiming that these are typologies in the sense outlined above. While analogical use of the OT clearly has a lot in common with typology, the main difference is that the latter claims that a predictive element inheres in the OT type, whereas the former does not. When drawing an analogy, NT authors are merely delineating a correspondence they see between their subject and a person, institution, or event in the OT without claiming that God had intentionally designed this correspondence to foreshadow that future person, institution, or event. They may do this to bolster their argument or simply to illustrate a point they want to drive home. It follows that, while authors who draw analogies from the OT are clearly aware of the historical and literary context of the texts they allude to, their readings are more concerned with the exigencies of their situations (though this is not incompatible with a close reading of the original context). In scholarly circles this is often referred to as "midrash," the technical term for this early Jewish and rabbinic method of interpretation. From the beginning, however, the term was used for any number of intertextual links to or among OT texts, and for our purposes, it is perhaps better to avoid it altogether.

Analogical use of OT texts ranges from brief allusions to more elaborate discourses that repeatedly invoke the correspondences between the NT author's subject and a text or tradition in the OT. An example of the former is Jesus's reference to Jonah in Matt. 12:40: "For as Jonah was three days and nights in the belly of a huge fish, so the Son of Man will be three days and three nights in the heart of the earth." Neither Jesus nor Matthew claims that Jonah's sojourn in the belly of the whale was a type of the death and resurrection of Jesus. In fact, the text's explicit use of simile makes it clear that this is simply an analogy drawn by Jesus. That being the case, it is astonishing how closely Jesus and Matthew pay attention to the original context. No attempt is made to suppress the temporal descriptor "three days and three nights," even though this does not correspond to the actual time that Jesus spent in the grave according to the Gospels.

An example of more elaborate analogical use of the OT can be found in John 6:25–59. There the evangelist recounts a dispute with Jews who were following Jesus after the feeding of the five thousand, hoping to see more miracles. They quote Scripture to Jesus (probably Neh. 9:15 or Ps. 78:24 [77:24 LXX]; both these texts are very similar to but not exactly the same as John 6:31), demanding another sign on the order of Moses's provision of manna for the people of Israel during the wilderness wanderings. They had just witnessed the multiplication of the bread and the fish (John 6:1–13), but that was not enough to satisfy their desire for sensational messianic signs. In response Jesus alludes to the miracle of the manna in the wilderness, repeatedly calling himself the true bread that has come down from heaven to give life to the world (6:33, 41, 48, 58). Some have seen a typology here, but it is interesting that neither Jesus nor John states this explicitly. This is perhaps because Jesus is not really comparing himself to the manna but contrasting himself with it (6:32). Manna was bread that spoiled (6:27); Jesus is the true bread of heaven. It is therefore perhaps best to view this as an example of an analogy rather than a typology, and it is important to note that the effectiveness of the analogy rests upon a very careful reading of the OT narrative that stressed the need to repeatedly gather the manna, which spoiled overnight and could not be kept, except on the day before the Sabbath (Exod. 16:19–30).

Allusion to underlying biblical narratives. Another very important but until recently less-analyzed use of the OT by NT authors is "metalepsis." Richard Hays, who introduced the concept to biblical studies, defines metalepsis as "a diachronic trope . . . [in which] a literary echo links the text in which it occurs to an earlier text, [and] the figurative effect of the echo can lie in the unstated or suppressed (transumed) points of resonance between the two texts" (20). In effect, Hays is simply extending Dodd's insight that NT authors often quote OT texts as a means of evoking their larger contexts (see above) to include more subtle allusions. Thus, according to Hays, biblical writers often refer to one part of a text or tradition in the OT, but the use they make of the text extends beyond the part they allude to so that they are implicitly interacting with the whole text or tradition. Metaleptic texts can stand alone and are comprehensible on a basic level without reference to an earlier text or tradition, but they also evoke much deeper levels of meaning that are accessible to those who are aware of the fuller narrative. A contemporary example of this literary phenomenon is the 2019 movie *The Joker*. Viewers who had never heard of Batman were enthralled by a story that is coherent and shockingly compelling in its own right, but those who had read the Batman comics or seen the Batman movies, from which the character of the Joker is taken, sensed that the Caped Crusader, who is never mentioned, was, so to speak, always just out of sight. They were aware, in other words, of many "suppressed points of resonance" (to use Hays's term) that add texture to the story and make it even more compelling.

In a similar way, NT authors sometimes make use of a seemingly simple word or phrase to evoke a complex biblical narrative. An intriguing example of this can be found in 1 Cor. 6 (see White, "Intertextual," 179–88). In this text Paul is admonishing the Corinthian believers not to sue each other in the civil law courts, which apparently was a problem in the church, but rather to solve their differences among themselves. In Greek, 1 Cor. 6:5 reads literally: "Is there not even one wise person among you who can *judge between his brother*?" Curiously, the noun "brother" is singular rather than plural, which seems nonsensical. Virtually all modern versions regard this as a grammatical error and correct it in translation, which is why English Bible readers are not aware of the anomaly. A little exegetical spadework, however, reveals that the oddly worded phrase "to judge . . . between a brother" is found in Deut. 1:16b LXX (where it woodenly translates idiomatic Hebrew). In that text Moses recounts how he appointed judges to hear disputes that arose among the people. Paul seems to be alluding to that text when he expresses his frustration that there are apparently no people present in the church in Corinth who can fill that role.

Paul's use of the OT here is illuminating in and of itself, but he also quotes Deut. 17:7 and then alludes to Dan. 7:22 immediately before he poses his solecistic rhetorical question (cf. 1 Cor. 5:13; 6:2–3). It is surely no coincidence that both of those OT texts are from passages that also address the topic of (very different) judicial competencies. When we put all of these together, something that as we noted above early Jewish interpreters were wont to do by means of *gezerah shawah*, it becomes clear that throughout 1 Cor. 5–6 Paul has an overarching biblical narrative in mind that runs something like this: Under the old covenant only a select group of individuals who had special access to the Spirit of God could judge disputes (Deut. 1:16; 17:7–13), but Daniel foresaw a day when all "the saints" would sit in judgment over the entire cosmos (Dan. 7:22). How can it be, then, that "the saints" in Corinth, all of whom have the Spirit of God (cf. 1 Cor. 1:2 with 2:12), are not capable of solving petty disputes on their own? Thus, what seemed to be a standalone allusion to Deut. 1:16 in 1 Cor. 6:5 becomes the key to unlocking a larger biblical narrative that adds theological depth to Paul's argument and exhorts the church to understand its high calling and live accordingly.

In some cases, large swaths of OT narrative serve as "prototypes" for the NT as they lay out their arguments (Beale, 81). Sometimes underlying narratives are metaleptically alluded to by a single verse. An example of this phenomenon is found in Rom. 10:19 (White, "Narrative," 199–201). There Paul quotes Deut. 32:21 as follows: "I will make you envious by those who are not a nation; I will make you angry by a nation that has no understanding." In this quotation from the so-called Song of Moses (Deut. 32:1–43) Paul discovers a divine purpose in Israel's rejection of the gospel and subsequent hardening, his subject in Rom. 9–11: the salvation of the gentiles is designed to provoke Israel to jealousy. A comparison of Deut. 32:1–43 with Rom. 9–11 reveals that Paul is not simply drawing on Deut. 32:21 to substantiate one point in his argument; rather, the Song of Moses serves as a template for the entire discourse. The song can be divided thematically into the following sections (McConville, 451):

1. Prologue: 32:1–3
2. Israel's election: 32:4–9
3. Israel's salvation: 32:10–14
4. Israel's rebellion against God: 32:15–18
5. Israel's rejection by God: 32:19–25
6. God's determination to have mercy on Israel: 32:26–43

Intriguingly, Rom. 9–11 is arranged along these same lines:

1. Israel's election (which has always involved a chosen remnant): 9:1–29
2. Israel's salvation (not yet accomplished): 9:30–10:4
3. Israel's rebellion against God (despite hearing the message): 10:5–21
4. Israel's rejection by God (except for the remnant): 11:1–10
5. God's determination to have mercy on Israel: 11:11–32

This brief comparison reveals that Paul is closely adhering to the structure of Deut. 32:1–43 in constructing his argument in Rom. 9–11. He is not, in other words, constructing his theology of Israel and the church out of whole cloth but recounting a fundamentally OT narrative that finds its fulfillment in Jesus Christ.

Another example of prototypical use of the OT is found in Rev. 4–5, for which Dan. 7 provides a blueprint. A side-by-side comparison of these two texts reveals a striking level of correspondence in their narrative flow. These are delineated by Greg Beale (81–82) as follows:

1. Introductory vision phraseology (Dan. 7:9 [cf. 7:2, 6–7]; Rev. 4:1)
2. The setting of a throne(s) in heaven (Dan. 7:9a; Rev. 4:2a [cf. 4:4a])
3. God is sitting on a throne (Dan. 7:9b; Rev. 4:2b)
4. The description of God's appearance on the throne (Dan. 7:9c; Rev. 4:3a)
5. Fire before the throne (Dan. 7:9d–10a; Rev. 4:5)
6. Heavenly servants surround the throne (Dan. 7:10b; Rev. 4:4b, 6b–10; 5:8, 11, 14)
7. Book(s) before the throne (Dan. 7:10c; Rev. 5:1–10)
8. The opening of the book(s) (Dan. 7:10d; Rev. 5:2–5, 9)
9. A divine (messianic) figure approaches God's throne in order to receive authority to reign forever over a kingdom (Dan. 7:13–14a; Rev. 5:5b–7, 9a, 12–13)
10. This kingdom includes all peoples, nations, and tongues (Dan. 7:14; Rev. 5:9b)
11. The seer's emotional distress on account of the vision (Dan. 7:15; Rev. 5:4)
12. The seer's reception of heavenly counsel concerning the vision from one among the heavenly throne servants (Dan. 7:16; Rev. 5:5a)
13. The saints are also given divine authority to reign over a kingdom (Dan. 7:18, 22, 27a; Rev. 5:10)
14. A concluding mention of God's eternal reign (Dan. 7:27b; Rev. 5:13–14)

Thus, the same fourteen elements from Dan. 7:9–27 are repeated in the same order (apart from small variations resulting from John's creative expansion of images).

These four functions—prophecy/fulfillment, typology, analogy, and metalepsis—account for the majority of instances in which NT authors make use of the OT. Though they sometimes employ the OT texts they interact with in unexpected ways, the use to which they put these texts is based on broadly contextual readings of them. Three other categories of use of the OT, all somewhat less tied to the context, but not nearly as common, are delineated below.

Symbolism. There are cases in which NT authors use OT texts and traditions as symbols. In everyday usage, a symbol is an image or object that points to or represents something beyond itself, like a flag or a siren and a flashing light. In literary terms, a symbol denotes a stock word or a phrase—quite often a proper noun—that has a specific referent in its original context and is used in another context to evoke some aspect of the original referent. Calling someone a "Benedict Arnold" (i.e., a traitor) or referring to someone's "Waterloo" (i.e., their demise) are modern examples of this literary phenomenon. It is not surprising that Revelation makes frequent use of symbols nor that many of these are drawn from the OT. One salient example can be found in Rev. 2:20, where the church in Thyatira is admonished because they tolerate "that woman Jezebel," who is promoting idol worship and sexual immorality in their midst. It is unlikely that the woman in question here actually bore that name (since it would have been unknown to gentile members of the congregation and odious to Jewish ones). Rather, John is evoking the OT figure of Jezebel, who drew away her husband Ahab, king of Israel, and with him the people to the worship of Baal (1 Kings 16:31; 21:25). John makes use of "Jezebel" as a convenient chiffer for a false prophetess. Another example from Revelation is the use of "Babylon" to refer to Rome (Rev. 17:5). Since Babylon was responsible for the destruction of the first temple in 586 BC, it is easy to see why the name was applied to the empire that destroyed the second temple in AD 70.

John makes more extensive use of symbols gleaned from the OT in Rev. 13:2a: "The beast I saw resembled a leopard, but had feet like those of a bear, and a mouth like that of a lion." These images are clearly drawn from Dan. 7:3–8, where four beasts—a lion, a bear, a leopard, and a "terrifying beast"—emerge from the sea. Daniel is told that the beasts represent four kingdoms (7:17), the final one more fearsome than all the others. John appropriates and reworks these symbols, combining the four beasts into one, probably in order to depict the transtemporal "kingdom" that has set itself up against God in various manifestations throughout history and in John's day was embodied by the unparalleled power and reach of the Roman Empire (see Beale, 71–72).

Allegory is a special case in which an author makes extended use of literary symbols to tell a story that refers to something beyond itself. Jesus made occasional use of allegory. An especially notable example is the parable of the vineyard, where the tenants of the vineyard represent the leaders of Israel and the servants represent the prophets (Mark 12:1–11 pars.). Though NT authors are not at all fond of allegory (in comparison to Philo, for example) and do not interpret the OT allegorically the way some of the church fathers do, Paul does on one occasion employ allegorical elements in the service of a larger typological reading of an OT tradition. In Gal. 4:21–31 he refers to Ishmael and Isaac, the two sons of Abraham, and notes that the former was born of Hagar, the slave woman, while the latter, the promised offspring, was the child of Sarah, the free woman. We are told that the former represents (lit. "is") Mount Sinai, where the Torah was handed down to Israel, whereas the latter represents Mount Zion and stands for the new covenant. Clearly, Hagar and Sarah are not mountains; they are real people. However, since one bore a son who was a slave and the other bore a son based on God's unconditional promise, they serve on the one hand as chiffers for the old and new covenants and on the other as types of two groups of descendants of Abraham: Jews under the old covenant and believers in Jesus.

In the case of symbolic and especially allegoric use, the NT author's main concern is not careful contextual use of the OT. However, it does presume that the author is aware of the original context since his application of the text depends on his drawing out a certain nuance within the text, and the success of the utterance (in speech-act theory, its "perlocutionary force") depends on his audience's ability to identify that nuance. Thus, for example, in order for John's reference to Jezebel in Rev. 2:20 to "work" (and we should not forget that he wanted to "do" something with it), his audience must know something about who Jezebel was. Thus, while symbolic use of the OT is not strictly contextual, it demonstrates awareness of the original context and cannot be entirely detached from it without becoming ineffective as a literary trope.

Illustration. Authors also employ what is sometimes called "gnomic usage." This occurs when NT authors draw on an OT text to illustrate a general principle or truth which is used to underline the abiding authority of the OT in new-covenant communities. One example of this can be found in 1 Cor. 9. In this chapter Paul is elaborating on the right of apostles to receive remuneration for their work. He begins by pointing to a couple of everyday examples to show what everyone affirms: that workers should be paid for the work they do. Then, in 1 Cor. 9:8–10 he turns to the Torah and quotes Deut. 25:4, which reads: "Do not muzzle an ox while it is treading out the grain." There is much discussion about this verse because Paul goes on to aver that it is not for oxen that God is concerned here, but "entirely" for us (9:10 NRSV). Some scholars argue that this is an example of noncontextual use because the OT text does, in fact, seem entirely concerned with oxen, not people, which would mean that Paul is misappropriating it for his purposes. In response, others have argued that the command may be proverbial in its original context, since it is surrounded by laws whose concern is clearly the welfare of human beings (cf. the discussion in Beale, 67–69). German OT scholar Heiko Wenzel has offered a novel solution (in a course lecture on the use of the OT in the NT, Freie Theologische Hochschule Giessen, Germany, April 2020). He pointed out that there would be no need to muzzle an ox to prevent it from eating the grain (i.e. the seeds) it is treading out. This is because oxen, like all bovines, eat forage (grain by-products like grass or hay); they cannot naturally digest grain, so they would not even try to eat it. Thus, the scenario the law envisions and sanctions, according to Wenzel, is that one farmer has borrowed another farmer's ox for a day to mill his grain (cf. Verbruggen, 705–6), but muzzles the animal after using it so that it won't eat the cattle feed he has harvested. The offense is akin to using a neighbor's car for a day or two and bringing it back with an empty tank. If Wenzel is right, then the text is, in fact, "entirely" concerned with preventing the exploitation of subsistence farmers rather than oxen, and Paul is using it quite properly to illustrate a general principle by referring to a relevant OT law.

It is possible, however, as noted above, that Deut. 25:4 is a proverb in its own right. In that case, Paul is using it, quite legitimately, in a broadly illustrative sense. There are other examples of this in the NT. Peter, for example, may be alluding to Prov. 26:11 in 2 Pet. 2:22, when he refers to a "true proverb" that states: "A dog returns to its own vomit." Peter is applying it to the false teachers of his day, who are clearly not in view in the OT passage, but it can hardly be argued that Peter is taking the proverb out of context. He captures the general sense of it—that people tend to fall back into their old and harmful ways—and adapts it to a new context. One could argue that this is exactly what proverbs are designed to "do." In this sense, the NT use of proverbial sayings from the OT must be deemed broadly contextual.

Dramatic effect. Sometimes authors make use of a text to bring about an emotional reaction on the part of the audience. This is sometimes referred to as "rhetorical use," but "rhetoric" is a broad term that can be used to refer to many different types of communication. We are interested in those cases where OT texts are employed to underline a particular point by means of dramatic tropes such as rhetorical questions, pleonasm, irony, etc. In such cases, the original context in which the text is embedded is not usually germane to the authors' purposes. For instance, when modern authors quote the first line of Hamlet's famous soliloquy—"To be or not to be, that is the question"—they are generally not trying to convey, as Hamlet was in context, that they are considering the pros and cons of taking their own life. Rather, quoting Shakespeare may be a way to add a touch of drama to a particularly difficult or momentous decision or even to evoke a sense of melodrama where no question is being considered at all.

One salient example of this is the florilegium (a catalog of quotations) that Paul composes in Rom. 3:10–18. In rapid succession he quotes from Pss. 14:1–3 (= 53:1–3); 5:9; 140:3; 10:7; Isa. 59:7 (cf. Prov. 1:16); and Ps. 36:1. All of these utterances stress the depravity of sinful human beings, and Paul groups them together for that reason alone, not because of any affinity they have for one another in their original context. He simply wants to impress upon his readers the consistent witness of Scripture to the desperate condition that human beings find themselves in apart from God's grace, and he effectively hammers this message home by means of the florilegium.

We should note that in two important ways Paul's use of Scripture for dramatic effect is unlike a modern speaker quoting Shakespeare's most famous utterance. First, Paul likely knew Psalms and Isaiah (not to mention the Torah and some of the other prophets) entirely by heart (cf. Sanders, 73–76). We can thus be sure that he was very aware of the original context of the quotations he gleaned from those works. Second, Paul has no love of dramatic effect for its own sake (1 Cor. 2:1–5). Rather, his rhetoric is always used in the service of persuading believers to adopt a new conviction (in Rom. 3:10–18, for instance, of the utter sinfulness of all human beings) or pursue some new course of action. Paul and the other NT writers are everywhere concerned, in other words, to use the Scriptures in line with their divine intent.

One important subcategory of the rhetorical use of Scripture is irony. This involves the application of a text in conscious opposition to its original intention. In that sense one could say that it is noncontextual, but in a more important sense, irony entails a sensitive reading of the original context. The NT author who makes ironic use of an OT text knows what the OT author intended to communicate—and intentionally turns it on its head. Further, irony "works" only if the reader is aware of what the NT author is doing; otherwise, it remains the author's private joke.

One particularly delicious example of the ironic use of the OT occurs toward the end of 1 Cor. 3. Over the course of the first three chapters of his letter to the Corinthians, Paul has been laying out his case that the death of Jesus on the cross appears to the world to be a total and ignominious defeat when it is actually God's greatest victory. What seems foolish in the eyes of human beings—a crucified Messiah—reveals the highest wisdom of God. Paul thus warns those who think they are wise to make sure they don't end up playing the fool. To substantiate his argument, he quotes Job 5:13 in 1 Cor. 3:19: "God catches the wise in their own cleverness" (AT). The irony is that it is Eliphaz, one of Job's three friends, who utters these words, and readers of Job know that Eliphaz becomes a prime example of someone who is tripped up by his own "wisdom." He thinks that it is Job whose foolishness has been laid open by God; in reality, he has only exposed his own "foolishness"—his utter lack of understanding of God and his ways.

Conclusion

In this article we surveyed a number of OT quotations and allusions. We saw how important it is to assess these in terms of the pragmatic aspect of communication, remembering that NT authors are trying to "do" things with the OT texts they interact with. We identified four main uses to which NT authors put their texts (fulfillment of prophecy, typology, analogy, and allusion to underlying biblical narratives) and three secondary uses (symbolism, illustration, and dramatic effect). In analyzing the main species of usage, we noted that, at least with regard to our limited sample, NT authors respect the context of the OT texts they quote or allude to. While the secondary categories involve usage that is in many cases somewhat detached from the original context, the NT authors demonstrate awareness of that context. In other words, they were consciously making unconventional use of the text and did so transparently. Still, a sensitivity to the original context could be documented and shown to have played an important role in the construction of the author's argument. Of course, it was not possible within this short space to prove that NT authors were aware of the original context of every OT text they quote or allude to, but that is not necessary. The examples proffered show a respect for the context that is not always apparent on a cursory reading of the text. At the very least, this should motivate modern readers of the NT to dig deeper before they decide, based on a cursory reading, that the authors are not interested in the original contexts of the OT texts they interact with. A closer reading will often prove that the opposite is the case, and based on patterns of usage analyzed here, the NT authors should certainly be given the benefit of the doubt.

See also Apostolic Hermeneutics: Description and Presuppositions; OT Use of the OT: Comparison with the NT Use of the OT; Typology

Bibliography. Austin, J. L., *How to Do Things with Words* (Clarendon, 1962); Bauckham, R., *Who Is God?* (Baker Academic, 2020); Beale, G. K., *Handbook on the New Testament Use of the Old Testament* (Baker Academic, 2012); Dodd, C. H., *According to the Scriptures* (Nisbet, 1953); Goppelt, L., *Typos* (Bertelsmann, 1939); Gordon, C. H., "'*Almah* in Isaiah 7:14," *JAAR* 21 (1953): 106; Hays, R. B., *Echoes of Scripture in the Letters of Paul* (Yale University Press, 1989); McCasland, S. V., "Matthew Twists the Scriptures," *JBL* 80 (1961): 143–48; McConville, J. G.,

Deuteronomy, AOTC (InterVarsity, 2002); Motyer, J. A., "Context and Content in the Interpretation of Isaiah 7:14," *TynBul* 21 (1970): 118–25; Sanders, E. P., *Paul: The Apostle's Life, Letters, and Thought* (Fortress, 2015); Verbruggen, J. L., "Of Muzzles and Oxen," *JETS* 49 (2006): 699–711; White, J. R., "Identifying Intertextual Exegesis in Paul," in *The Crucified Apostle*, ed. P. House and T. Wilson, WUNT 2/450 (Mohr Siebeck, 2017), 167–88; White, "N. T. Wright's Narrative Approach," in *God and the Faithfulness of Paul*, ed. C. Heilig, J. T. Hewitt, and M. F. Bird, WUNT 2/413 (Mohr Siebeck, 2016), 181–204; Young, E. J., *The Book of Isaiah: Chapters 1–18* (Eerdmans, 1965).

JOEL WHITE

Conversion *See* Jews and Gentiles

Corinthians, First Letter to the

Judged by the number of explicit citations, the OT seems to be of only marginal interest to 1 Corinthians. By any count, Romans has more than three times as many, with 1 Corinthians averaging as few as one per chapter, meaning several chapters have none. However, first impressions do not last, for on closer inspection the OT proves to be a major point of interest and a critical and formative source for the theology and ethics of the letter. Along with citations, there are innumerable allusions to the OT in 1 Corinthians, references to Jewish institutions and festivals such as the temple, priesthood, Passover, Unleavened Bread, and Firstfruits, phrases like "the things that are written" (4:6 AT) and "according to the Scriptures" (15:3, 4), references to biblical events using language that includes the readers (e.g., "our fathers" [10:1 ESV]), and teaching concerning the law of Moses (9:19–21; see Rosner, "Paul").

The backstory of Paul's work with the Corinthians also suggests that the Jewish Scriptures formed the basis of much of his original instruction to them. Paul poses the rhetorical question, "Do you not know?" (*ouk oidate*), ten times in the letter (3:16; 5:6; 6:2, 3, 9, 15, 16, 19; 9:13, 24) to chastise the church for not acting in accord with truths he had previously taught them (Barrett, 90). Most of these truths derive from Scripture, including topics such as the temple and its service, unleavened bread, judging the world and angels, and inheriting God's kingdom.

Rather than tracing the use of quotations and allusions sequentially through the letter (see Ciampa and Rosner), this essay considers the larger thematic and hermeneutical dimensions of the use of the OT in 1 Corinthians. Four books in particular are of critical importance for understanding 1 Corinthians—namely, Malachi, Isaiah, Deuteronomy, and Psalms.

Malachi and Temple Worship

There are three allusions to Malachi in 1 Corinthians, all of which relate to temple worship. First, in 3:12–15 Paul alludes to Mal. 3:2–3 in his discussion of the judgment of leaders who build God's temple, which is the church (3:16–17). The two texts use similar terminology (gold, silver, day, and fire) and both envisage a judgment in which fire consumes certain materials. The "temple" and its leaders are seen in relation to a judgment that will distinguish valid from ineffectual service. Malachi declares that "the Lord . . . will come to his temple" to judge the unrepentant (3:1–5), a belief that Paul echoes in 1 Cor. 3.

Second, in 10:21 Paul asserts the exclusivity of worship, over against idolatry, at the Lord's table. The expression "Lord's table" is used to refer to the altar in Mal. 1:7, 12. Paul's reference to the Lord's Supper as a participation at the Lord's table suggests the celebration of Christ's sacrifice now serves as the centerpiece for Christian worship as did the temple in the OT.

Third, an allusion to Malachi turns up in Paul's opening salutation and is the most important of the three. In 1 Cor. 1:2 Paul describes the Corinthians as united with "all those who call on the name of our Lord Jesus Christ in every place [*en panti topō*]" (AT). A key theme in Deuteronomy is the Lord's selection of one particular place where people would call on his name (understood to refer to Jerusalem). Repeated reference is made to "the place that the LORD your God will choose to have his name called upon" (Deut. 12:11 AT; cf. 12:21, 26; 14:23–24; 16:2, 6, 11; 17:8, 10; 26:2). However, rather than refer to that place, Paul says that the Corinthians join those who call on the name of the Lord "in every place." Paul is the only NT author to use the phrase (1 Cor. 1:2; 2 Cor. 2:14; 1 Thess. 1:8), and he uses it to refer to the worship of God that is spreading around the world through his ministry to the gentiles.

The expression echoes Mal. 1:11, which (in a context of frustration over the way the Lord is being worshiped in Jerusalem) prophesies a future time when gentiles would worship God "in every place": "For from the rising of the sun until its setting my name will be glorified among the gentiles and *in every place* [*en panti topō*] incense will be offered to my name and a pure offering, for my name is great among the gentiles, says the LORD Almighty" (AT; see Towner, 333). Significantly, in Rom. 15:16 Paul describes his gentile mission in cultic terms as "the priestly duty of proclaiming the gospel of God, so that the Gentiles might become an offering acceptable to God, sanctified by the Holy Spirit."

The allusion to Mal. 1:11 in 1 Cor. 1:2 suggests the Corinthians are part of the fulfillment of God's eschatological plan to be worshiped among all the gentiles. If Malachi's message was intended to help his audience come "to terms, mentally, spiritually and ethically, with the non-appearance of the new eschatological beginning" that had been expected with the return from exile (Koch, 179), Paul's goal in 1 Corinthians is to get the Corinthians to come to terms, mentally, spiritually, and ethically, with its appearance.

Paul's use of Malachi informs the purpose of the letter and introduces an image that carries on throughout (Rosner, "Church"). Paul identifies the church as the temple four times, on each occasion using *este*, the second-person plural of the verb "to be": 3:9 ("You are God's building"); 3:16 ("You are God's temple"); 3:17 ("You are that temple"); and 6:19 ("Your body is a temple of the Holy Spirit"). Many of the moral exhortations of the letter build on the image of the church as God's temple, including those associated with wisdom, purity, edification, and glory.

In 1 Cor. 1–4, Paul's work of laying the foundation of the garden-temple in Corinth was done as a "*wise* master builder" (1 Cor. 3:10 NASB; *sophos* is translated "skilled" in many modern English versions [e.g., RSV, NRSV, HCSB, ESV]). In the OT, those who built the tabernacle had to be wise (Exod. 31:6), and Solomon built his temple with wisdom (2 Chron. 2:12).

Paul's concern with the holiness of the Corinthians is signaled up front in 1:2 where he underscores the holy status of believers in three ways: they are the church belonging to God, sanctified in Christ Jesus, and saints by calling. The sheer redundancy tips off Paul's view that, as the rest of the letter indicates, they are not living up to their holy status. In the rest of 1 Corinthians purity issues are reflected in the identification of the readers as the temple of God (3:17) and the discussion of the moral implications of that understanding. The command to "clean out the old leaven" (5:7 NASB) and to "purge the evil person" from their midst (5:11–13 ESV) reflects the language of purity concerns, and Paul's command to avoid prostitutes is based on the radical impurity that would bring to their Spirit-indwelt temple (6:15–19). Purity concerns are also reflected in the issue of the children's uncleanness or holiness based on the status of the unbelieving husband (7:14) and in the concern not to provoke the Lord by drinking from both his cup and that of demons (10:21–22). As Michael Newton (52) points out, "Much of Paul's use of purity terminology centres upon his view that the believers constitute the Temple of God and as such enjoy the presence of God in their midst."

The term *oikodomeō* and its cognates are used in the LXX and NT of literally building the temple. Paul uses such terms to describe how he "built" the temple in Corinth (3:10, 12, 14). And Paul's call for the Corinthians to "build up / edify" (*oikodomeō*) fellow believers is the key ethical norm in chapters 8–14. Richard Bauckham (205) notes that "the frequently used metaphor of 'building' the Christian community is probably evidence of the widespread currency of the image of the church as the eschatological temple."

The theme of bringing glory to God pervades the whole letter, using a range of synonyms. Paul tells the church to "flee" sexual immorality (6:18) and idolatry (10:14) and instead to "glorify God" in sexual purity (6:20 ESV; *doxazō*) and proper worship (10:31; *doxa*). The Corinthians are to "boast" (or glory) in the Lord rather than human leaders (1:31; 3:21; both *kauchaomai*), worship in a fashion that brings glory and not dishonor to God in 11:2–16, and to await their own resurrection and glorification (chap. 15). As Greg Beale notes (252): "The purpose of the OT temple . . . was to house and show forth God's glory." As God's temple, the goal of Christians, both now and in the age to come, is the glory of God, "that God may be all in all" (15:28).

In 1 Corinthians, because the church is God's temple—a theme developed in connection with Malachi—church leaders must build wisely and the church must be pure, build one another up, and bring glory to God by shunning the pagan vices of sexual immorality and idolatry and by behaving respectfully in worship, all of which is a beginning fulfillment of OT temple prophecies.

Isaiah and Divine Wisdom

Paul's use of Isaiah in 1 Corinthians (esp. chaps. 1–4) is inextricably tied up with his understanding of the gospel, which he applies as the remedy to Corinthian factionalism. Paul's self-understanding as the prophetic herald of God's eschatological age in 1 Cor. 1:17, "Christ sent me . . . to *preach the gospel*" (*euangelizomai*), is indebted in his choice of words to Isa. 40:9; 52:7; and 61:1. Here, as Dickson (176) points out, "'secular' messenger language had been transposed to a higher, eschatological level, depicting the end-time herald(s) commissioned by Israel's God to announce his salvific reign." Paul's gospel heralding is an eschatological, divinely commissioned activity (Stuhlmacher, 156–65).

Richard Hays's summary of the use of the OT in 1 Cor. 1–4 is accurate ("Conversion," 402–3): "The backbone of the discussion in 1:18–3:23 is a series of six OT quotations (1:19; 1:31; 2:9; 2:16; 3:19; 3:20), [four of which are from Isaiah,] all taken from passages that depict God as one who acts to judge and save his people in ways that defy human imagination." Several scriptural allusions and motifs are also interspersed among the quotations and reinforce the same message.

In 1 Cor. 1:19 Paul quotes Isa. 29:14 to announce that God's eschatological judgment and salvation are taking place in the Corinthians' midst and to underscore that there is implacable opposition between human wisdom and the "word of the cross": "I will destroy the wisdom of the wise; the intelligence of the intelligent I will frustrate." The Corinthians who still value "the wisdom of the wise" have failed to notice God's apocalyptic judgment on such wisdom through the crucified Messiah. Isaiah's words are, for Paul, not just a judgment on ancient Judean leaders but also "an indictment of the rhetorical affectations of the Corinthians" (Hays, "Conversion," 404). The quotation helps establish that this observation is linked to the OT narrative of judgment and grace and shows that the paradox of the cross, foolishness to some but in reality power for salvation, is in accord with Scripture.

In 1 Cor. 1:20 Paul alludes to Isa. 33:18, which concerns the whereabouts of the chief officer, of the one who weighed the tribute, and of the one who counted the towers, a composite reference to the oppressors of God's people. It announces the end of their ascendancy and dominance. Both Isa. 33:18 and 1 Cor. 1:20 contain three questions beginning with the word "where" (*pou*), the only two places where this threefold repetition of *pou* appears in the LXX and NT. Both texts refer to the ineffectiveness of individuals who oppose God's people. Both contain rhetorical questions expecting the response, "Nowhere." In this light, the echo of Isa. 33:18 in 1 Cor. 1:20 recalls the overthrow by the Messiah of all those who oppose God and his people in the end time, reinforcing both the passage's Christology and eschatology.

Although we cannot be certain, Paul appears to include a loose quotation of Isa. 64:4 ("From of old no one has heard or perceived by the ear, no eye has seen a God besides you," ESV) in 1 Cor. 2:9. Both texts assert that no human being is able to understand the divine revelation without God's enabling. Isa. 64:4 concerns the uniqueness of God's plan of salvation, which remains hidden. Judgment against God's enemies also appears, as in the plea for divine intervention in 64:1 and the appearance of fire in 64:2 (cf. "to make your name known to your adversaries" in 64:2 also). In citing this Scripture Paul shows that the wisdom he preaches is nothing less than God's plan of salvation, which is being fulfilled in Paul's ministry.

In 2:16 Paul quotes the question from Isa. 40:13, "Who has known the mind of the Lord?" Paul's answer in the same verse is that "we have the mind of Christ." Isaiah 40:13, one of several rhetorical questions in 40:12–14, expects the answer, "No one." Isaiah 40:15–17 stresses further the gulf between humans and God: even "the nations are like a drop in the bucket." In context the "Spirit of the LORD" (40:13) that no one can know is God's plan of salvation (Isa. 11:2; 40:7; 59:19; 63:14). As H. H. D. Williams (214) observes, 40:13a could be paraphrased, "Who is able to comprehend the salvific plan of God?" Paul's audacious claim that we have the mind of Christ represents a biting ironic twist against the Corinthian elitists.

In 3:5–9 Paul deals with the Corinthians' preoccupation with specific leaders using an agricultural image. Hays (*Corinthians*) and Williams have detected an echo here of Isa. 5:1–7, a prominent text in early Jewish interpretation of Scripture. Overlapping features include the planting as the people of God, God's role as the chief worker and owner of the vineyard/field, the relative unimportance of human workers and their role as mediators. In particular, like 1 Cor. 3:5–9, Isa. 5:2 mixes both building and planting metaphors (cf. Jer. 18:9; 24:6; Ezek. 36:9–10).

Turning to architectural imagery to describe his role in Corinth, Paul echoes Isa. 3:3 in 1 Cor. 3:10 (Robertson and Plummer; Hübner). In 3:10 Paul refers to himself as "a wise master builder" (NASB). Both in Isa. 3:3 and here do we find the combination of *sophos* and *architektōn*. Both passages speak of wisdom and of judgment in relation to the leaders of God's people. The same terminology (*sophos* and *architektōn*) is applied to those who helped build Israel's tabernacle. For example, Exod. 35:31–32 LXX refers to a skilled workman of the tabernacle as "filled with a divine spirit of wisdom [*sophias*] . . . to be a master builder [*architektonein*] in all works of a master builder [*architektonias*] in order to form gold and silver . . . and works in stone" (AT). Similarly, Exod. 35:35 LXX describes a "master builder" of the "sanctuary."

Paul draws on texts from Isaiah to confirm that God is bringing to pass, through Paul, the eschatological fulfillment of salvation-history. Just as the new eschatological age has already dawned with the death and resurrection of Jesus Christ, so it is currently breaking into the old age through the preaching of Jesus Christ. Paul's message is not idle chatter or some good ideas but apocalyptic power (1 Cor. 4:20). As Paul proclaims and lives out "Christ crucified," all the structures of human existence are transformed, human pride is judged, and salvation comes to those who believe (1:17–25; cf. 1 Thess. 1:5). Paul's gospel brings the obedience of faith for the sake of Jesus Christ among the nations (Rom. 1:5; 16:26). So, Paul sees himself as not only proclaiming but also actively bringing about the new age of God's direct rule over the cosmos in both judgment and salvation. It is accomplished "by the power of signs and wonders, by the power of the Spirit of God" (Rom. 15:19 ESV). Similar themes emerge in 1 Cor. 2:6–11, which draws on apocalyptic motifs in Daniel (see especially Dan. 2:19–23 LXX).

In connection with apocalyptic motifs, Isaiah has a discernible "trajectory" that takes place across the book as a whole and within its individual sections (Webb, 30–31). This trajectory takes us from the existing world order (with its ruling powers: Israel, Assyria, and Babylon) to a new world order established by God. This happens via demolition and reconstruction, judgment and salvation, in that order. Its crucial transformative event is the justification that comes through the discipline of a suffering servant, and it climaxes in God's Spirit-empowered servants being sent out (e.g., Isa. 61:1) to preach the same two-edged message that divides the world into two groups: the judged and the saved (Webb, 30–33).

In Isaiah, as in 1 Cor. 1–4, there are therefore two types of wisdom: human and divine. Both types of wisdom are ultimately attempts at "salvation." There is the human idolatrous "wisdom" of the nations (cf. 1 Cor. 1:23), of their rulers and advisers (Isa. 10:12–14; 19:11–12; cf. 1 Cor. 2:6), which will be brought to nothing (cf. 1 Cor. 1:20). There is also the human "wisdom" of those within

Israel who recommend trust in foreign rulers, advisers ("the wise" and "the intelligent," Isa. 29:14; cf. 1 Cor. 1:19), and scribes (Isa. 33:18; Oropeza, 97–98); this, too, will be brought to nothing (1 Cor. 1:19–20), for they are, in fact, oppressive enemies of the Messiah and God's people (Williams, 88–100). The "wisdom" that trusts in foreign powers is wisdom that trusts in salvation by foreign gods—foolish idolatrous worship goes hand in hand with reliance upon Egypt, Assyria, and Babylon (Isa. 10:10–14; 44:17–20).

It is divine wisdom, however, that ultimately triumphs in Isaiah. There is a messianic figure introduced in 11:1, a "shoot . . . from the stump of Jesse," who is introduced with wisdom terminology: the Spirit of wisdom, understanding, counsel, and might will rest upon him (cf. 1 Cor. 2:10). Even though the "wise" in Israel are blind and deaf (Isa. 28:7, 12; 29:9–14; 30:9–11), when Israel is restored and her righteous king reappears, the blind and deaf will see and hear again (29:18; 30:20–22; 32:1–5; 33:17–22).

This king will put into effect God's plan of salvation, which is independent of human wisdom (Isa. 40:13–14, quoted in 1 Cor. 2:16). But, significantly, this salvific plan will come about in a strange and marvelous way. A suffering servant will come and suffer vicariously as a sacrifice for the sins of the people. The Servant Song of Isaiah 53 abounds in wisdom terminology, which is entirely consonant with the prominence of the wisdom motif throughout the whole of Isaiah. This servant will be wise (52:13), and by his knowledge he will justify many (53:11). In this way, he will silence and amaze the rulers of the nations (52:15, alluded to in 1 Cor. 2:9). So, the eschatological judgment, salvation, and vindication of those who wait patiently for God is an amazing, unheard of, unimaginable act of God's wisdom (Isa. 64:4; cf. 1 Cor. 2:9)—salvation through suffering. All are called, including gentiles, to come under the rule of King David, where they will find repentance and forgiveness of sins (Isa. 55:3–7) through God's remarkable, transcendent wisdom: "'For my thoughts are not your thoughts, neither are your ways my ways,' declares the LORD" (55:8). At this time, God's dwelling will be with the one who, like the suffering servant, is poor and broken in spirit and who trembles at God's word (66:1–2; cf. 53:4).

The ultimate outcome of God's salvation-historical plan in Isaiah is the glorification of God by the gentiles through worship in a new temple, with the corresponding judgment of those who refuse to submit to God (Isa. 56:6–7; 60:1–22; 62:2; 66:18–24). This could double as a summary of Paul's agenda in 1 Corinthians and lines up perfectly with Paul's gospel. Paul's astonishing message is that the suffering servant and the Davidic messiah king, who could be mistaken for two different figures in Isaiah, have both arrived in one and the same person: "We proclaim Christ crucified, a scandal for Jews and foolishness for gentiles, but to those who are called, both Jews and Greeks, Christ the power of God and the wisdom of God" (1:22–24 AT). All the eschatological expectations of the prophets, especially Isaiah, have come to fulfillment in this one man—in the suffering and exaltation of Christ, God's glory is fully revealed (cf. 2 Cor. 1:20).

Deuteronomy and the Grace of God

In 1 Cor. 5–10, quotations of Deuteronomy (13:5; 17:7; 19:19; 21:21; 22:21, 24; 24:7 in 5:13; 25:4 in 9:9) and numerous allusions accord the book a major role in the composition of the letter (Rosner, "Deuteronomy"; McDonough). The main material of Deuteronomy—namely, its laws—and the most famous texts, including the Shema and the Song of Moses, are strongly represented.

Many commentators mention Lev. 18:8 and 20:11 as the critical background to Paul's decision to expel the incestuous man in 1 Cor. 5, noting the shared terminology *gynaikos* and *patros*, "woman" and "father" (v. 2). However, two verses in Deuteronomy are just as likely to have influenced Paul. First, 27:20, "Cursed is anyone who sleeps with his father's wife," is perhaps the reason Paul "curses" the sinner in 1 Cor. 5. Second, 22:30, "A man is not to marry his father's wife," may have been the impetus for Paul to quote the Deuteronomic expulsion formula in 1 Cor. 5:13. A variation of that formula appears in Deut. 22:22 ("If a man is found sleeping with another man's wife . . . you must purge the evil from Israel"; cf. 22:24) and is presumably the penalty for the incest prohibited in 22:30.

First Corinthians 5:13b is a quotation of a frequent expression of the LXX of Deuteronomy, where it is used on six occasions to signal the execution of a variety of offenders (13:5 [13:6 LXX]; 17:7; 19:19; 21:21; 22:21, 24; 24:7; cf. Judg. 20:13 and the list of sins in 1 Cor. 5:9–10). The church must expel the wicked man in the hope of regaining him and above all to protect the community's standing before God and the world, teaching largely based on the Pentateuch, especially Deuteronomy, as v. 13b suggests.

The situations of Exod. 18 / Deut. 1:9–18 and 1 Cor. 6:1–6 are remarkably similar. Both Moses and Paul are overwhelmed by the judicial problems of the people of God. Both leaders decide to handle the more difficult cases themselves, with the Lord's help (cf. Exod. 18:19b; 1 Cor. 5:3–5), and appoint judges to adjudicate the lesser cases (see Exod. 18:21–22; Deut. 1:15; 1 Cor. 6:1b, 4, 5b) by deciding between their brothers (Rosner, "Moses").

The language of Deut. 6:4 ("The LORD our God, the LORD is one") governs Paul's wording and argument in 1 Cor. 8:4–6. Paul expands his opening statement that "there are many 'gods'" so as to allow the plurality of "lords" in the pagan world as well. Paul then "glosses 'God' with 'the Father,' and 'Lord' with 'Jesus Christ,' adding in each case an explanatory phrase: 'God' is the Father, 'from whom are all things and we to him,' and the 'Lord' is Jesus the Messiah, 'through whom are all things and we through him'" (Wright, 129). In this one text Paul simultaneously reaffirms strict Jewish monotheism and embeds Christ within the very definition of that one God/Lord of Israel.

Paul quotes Deut. 25:4 in 1 Cor. 9:9 to support his argument that he is entitled to compensation for the work of the ministry: "Do not muzzle the ox while it is treading out the grain." He argues that God's real concern is not for oxen (9:9b) but for "us" (9:10), the community of the last days (10:6, 11). Paul's use of the verse has been categorized in a variety of ways, most frequently as allegorizing (see Schrage, 2:298–300, and the views cited in Kaiser). It is probably more accurate to understand it as an argument from the lesser to the greater, as Jewish usage suggests (Instone-Brewer, 554).

In 1 Cor. 10:1–4 Paul uses the Israelites' experience of redemption, idolatry, and destruction as a prism through which the Corinthians are to understand their own eschatological situation. The reference to "baptism into Moses" is evidently formulated by Paul in order to make the metaphorical parallel as clear as possible. The divine provision of quail and manna is related in Exod. 16 and Num. 11 and celebrated in Deut. 8:3, 16; Neh. 9:20; Pss. 78:24; 105:40. The water from the rock is mentioned in Exod. 17:6 and Num. 20:8–11 and then celebrated in a series of texts including Deut. 8:15; Neh. 9:15; Pss. 78:20; 105:41; 114:8; Isa. 48:21. Paul calls the food and drink that were miraculously provided "spiritual" (*pneumatikos*) since he understands that they were provided by the Spirit and understands the elements of the Lord's Supper to also be food and drink of the Spirit who communicates the presence of Christ to his community.

In 1 Cor. 10:19–20 Paul recalls Deut. 32:17 to clarify the nature of his objection to participation in pagan religious meals. While Deut. 32:17 refers to the abhorrent unfaithfulness of Israel, most readers understand Paul to be speaking of the practices of the Corinthian Christians' pagan neighbors (as did many ancient scribes). Paul's other references to the scene of the golden calf in this context (and elsewhere) suggest that "Paul sees the Corinthian controversy about idol meat (v. 19) in double exposure with Israel's wilderness idolatry" (Hays, *Echoes*, 93). Thus, while the sacrifices referred to in both Deut. 32:17 and 1 Cor. 10:20 are pagan sacrifices, "Paul's real concern, like that of the Song of Moses, is that *God's own people* are becoming implicated in this 'abhorrent' practice" (Hays, *Corinthians*, 169). While the Corinthians may not have been tempted to offer sacrifices to pagan gods, by partaking in pagan religious meals they were still considered participants in the sacrifices themselves (thus the relevance of Paul's argument in 10:16–18 to his use of Deut. 32:17). Paul draws a broader theological conclusion (with clear ethical implications) from the statement about Israel's practice in Deut. 32:17. Since Israel's idolatrous sacrifices were offered to demons, idolatrous sacrifices in general should be similarly understood.

Paul's words in 1 Cor. 10:22, "Shall we provoke the Lord?" (ESV), echo the Lord's complaint against Israel in Deut. 32:21: "They have provoked me with what is no god, they have angered me by their idols" (AT). He essentially asks if he or the Corinthians would be foolish enough to follow in Israel's footsteps by participating in pagan worship as they did, provoking God by engaging in idolatrous associations or actions. Paul's follow-up question, "Are we stronger than he?" probably also reflects Deut. 32 and its emphasis on the strength of the Lord. According to Deut. 32, one of the purposes of the coming judgment will be to impress on the nation their lack of strength and the Lord's great power (cf. 32:30, 36–38). The motif of God's strength is also seen in the repeated use of the epithet "the Rock" in Deut. 32 (vv. 4, 15, 18, 30, 31), which the targumim understand as a figure for God's strength, most frequently translating it as "the Strong One" (see Rosner, *Paul*, 200). The motif relates to the Lord's strength as reflected in his power to protect or punish his people. Paul's question is designed not only to underscore the impotence of believers but also to stress the omnipotence of God: we are not stronger than the Strong One! It entails a frightening threat of judgment upon those Corinthian Christians who provoke God to jealousy.

Paul found in Deuteronomy and Moses a foreshadowing typological model and sympathetic ally. Both were concerned to explain to God's people an obedient response to God's grace in the light of the (new) exodus and (new) Passover. Both have the basic goal of securing the holiness and purity of that people in distinction from the nations and to promote the glory of God in "the land," in the case of Deuteronomy, or "in every place" (1 Cor. 1:2 ESV), as with 1 Corinthians. The apostle stops short of calling himself a second Moses, but he does compare and contrast his role as a "minister of a new covenant" with that of Moses in 2 Cor. 3.

Curiously, various elements in Deuteronomy strike a pessimistic note and point beyond the book to the need for the future decisive action of God. That little can be expected from God's people is signaled in Deut. 2 where they are unfavorably compared to the Moabites and Ammonites. It is also expressed throughout Deut. 5–11 where repeated calls to obey or remember (e.g., 5:1, 31–33; 6:1–14; 7:12–15) suggest a negative expectation. Israel's spiritual incapacity is repeatedly underscored (e.g., 29:4). Nothing less than a circumcision of the heart is required, which only God can perform (30:6; cf. 10:16). Moses predicts Israel's apostasy (31:16–18; 32:19–21, 26), and he himself dies outside the land (chap. 34), suggesting that there is little hope for the nation. Moses's song ends with the one reference to atonement in the entire book (32:43). The new-covenant teaching of Jeremiah and Ezekiel, in which the problem of the human heart is resolved, is thus anticipated in Deuteronomy (Millar).

In one sense, it is not only that 1 Corinthians looks back to Deuteronomy but also that Deuteronomy anticipates Paul's letter. The "later days," to which Deuteronomy 4:30 refers, "when you will return to the LORD your God and obey him," of which the Hebrew prophets also speak (cf. Jer. 23:20; 30:24; 48:47; 49:39; Ezek. 38:16; Dan. 2:28; 10:14; Hosea 3:5), is the time in which Paul locates the church of God in Corinth: the Corinthian believers are those "on whom the fulfillment of the ages has come" (1 Cor. 10:11 AT). Paul writes as a minister of the new covenant, a covenant that Deuteronomy does not name but ultimately anticipates.

Psalms and the Authority of Jesus Christ

Paul makes substantial use of various psalms throughout 1 Corinthians. In 1 Cor. 1:2, his description of Christians as "those who call on the name of the Lord" recalls similar language in Pss. 79:6; 80:18; 99:6; 116:4, 13. In 1 Cor. 3:20 Paul cites Ps. 94:11 ("The Lord knows that the thoughts of the wise are futile") to insist that God thwarts the plans of the wise. Paul's judgment in 1 Cor. 5:9–11 that the Corinthians should withdraw social contact from believers guilty of serious sins and not eat (*synesthiō*) with them echoes teaching in Ps. 101:5 (100:5 LXX): "He who slanders his neighbors secretly, he is banished; he who is of haughty looks and of a greedy heart, with him food is not shared [*synēsthion*]" (AT; Newton, 95). In 1 Cor. 10:1–13 Paul offers a typological interpretation of the exodus, wilderness wandering, and apostasy of Israel as a warning to the Corinthians not to fall into idolatry and sexual immorality, echoing similar appeals to Israel's history in Pss. 78 and 106 (cf. Neh. 9:5–37 and Deut. 32:1–43; Fee). In 1 Cor. 10:25–26 Paul infers from Ps. 24:1 ("The earth is the Lord's, and everything in it") that in certain contexts, since all food belongs to the Lord and comes from him, it can be received with thankfulness, regardless of how it has been used by others. In 1 Cor. 15:30 Paul's remark that the apostles are in constant danger from opponents of the gospel echoes the language of Pss. 44:22 and 119:109. And in 1 Cor. 15:36 the scornful rebuke, *aphrōn*, "Fool!" echoes Ps. 14:1 ("The fool [LXX *aphrōn*] says in his heart, 'There is no God'"; cf. Rom. 3:11–12).

However, Paul's most significant use of Psalms in the letter consists of an appeal to two psalms in 1 Cor. 15. In 15:25–27 Paul "alludes to Ps. 110:1 and Ps. 8:6 as prophecies of Christ's enthronement at the right hand of God and ultimate authority over all creation" (Hays, *Echoes*, 84). Together the two psalms support Paul's claim that all powers and authorities will be placed under Christ's feet and thus be subjected to God. Psalms 8 and 110 are also found together in Eph. 1:20–22 and Heb. 2:5–8. Paul's use of these psalms is significant not only for the topic of resurrection in 1 Cor. 15 but also as the basis for his insistence on the lordship and authority of Jesus Christ.

In 15:24–27 Paul deftly conjoins two psalms to make the points that Christ as the last Adam retrieved the situation the first Adam lost. It is an explicitly christological use of the OT with the OT notion of corporate representation as its presupposition; Christ represents his people (see 15:22–23). Hebrews 2:5–8 is comparable in its use of Pss. 8 and 110. There the glorious destiny of humankind to be crowned and receive dominion, which we failed to grasp, is fulfilled for us through Jesus.

First Corinthians 15:25 ("he has put all his enemies under his feet") alludes to Ps. 110:1 ("until I make your enemies a footstool for your feet"). The use of the psalm suggests that the referent of "he has put" (v. 25) is God (cf. v. 28). Paul interprets Ps. 8:6 in 1 Cor. 15:27 as applying to the Messiah, who brings to fulfillment God's intentions for humanity. The key word he finds in this psalm is *panta* (all things), which he inserts in the allusion to Ps. 110:1 in 1 Cor. 15:25, interpreting "all things" to include "death" (15:26).

Paul uses the two psalms to establish the authority and lordship of Christ, a key idea in the letter. If Corinthian problems can be attributed to their cultural background, Paul's various responses may be ascribed to his understanding of the crucified Christ's lordship over against all human and spiritual powers; in almost every case Paul pits Christ against the prevailing culture. He appeals for unity in the name of Christ (1:10), who is the power and wisdom of God (1:23–24) and the foundation of the church (3:11). The church must be cleansed of the incestuous man because of Christ's sacrifice (5:7). To have relations with a prostitute is to violate Christ (6:15). Eating food sacrificed to idols must be avoided for the sake of one for whom Christ died (8:11) and in imitation of Christ (11:1). With respect to head coverings, he notes that Christ is the head of every man (11:3). The Lord's Supper must be celebrated by discerning "the body" of Christ (11:29). Spiritual gifts are to be exercised in order to build up the body of Christ (12:27). The resurrection of believers is grounded in the resurrection of Christ (15:3–23). Finally, all of history is about the subjection of all things under Christ's feet and his presentation of the fully redeemed kingdom/creation to God the Father (15:24–28). Throughout the letter "Christ" and "Lord" appear over sixty times each and "Jesus" twenty-six times.

In connection with this, the nature of the eschatological temple and the glory that God is to receive through worldwide worship are understood in the light of the kingdom God has established through his Son, the universal Lord. The expectation that universal glory and worship would be given to God is at the heart of the significance of the lordship of Jesus Christ, whose postcrucifixion exaltation is understood by Paul and other NT authors to inaugurate the long-awaited time of the universal and eternal kingdom of God that would result in every knee bowing and every tongue confessing that "Jesus Christ is Lord, to the glory of God the Father" (Phil. 2:11; cf. Rev. 15:3–4). First Corinthians comes to a climax in chap. 15 with Paul's discussion of the resurrection as it relates to the ultimate triumph of Christ over all adversaries and the final transformation of our corruptible humanity into humanity that fully reflects God's glory. Significantly, Paul turns to two psalms to establish the relationship between Christ's resurrection, lordship, and reign, and God's ultimate glory (15:24–28).

Conclusion

It is possible to read 1 Corinthians without pondering Paul's use of Malachi, Isaiah, Deuteronomy, and Psalms. However, to do so is to read the text only superficially, as if Paul is simply responding ad hoc to problems in the church that he had heard about and that had been reported to him. The coherence of the letter, its big themes of wisdom, holiness, worship, edification, the glory of God, and the lordship of Christ, and its suffusion with the gospel of grace arising from Paul's mission and identity all stem from understanding the influence of these four books. Indeed, 1 Corinthians may be correctly described as "a hermeneutical event" (Hays, *Echoes*, 35), as a text best read in its inextricable and manifold relationship to the Scriptures of Israel.

Bibliography. Barrett, C. K., *A Commentary on the First Epistle to the Corinthians* (Black, 1971); Bauckham, R., *The Fate of the Dead*, NovTSup 93 (Brill, 1998); Beale, G. K., *The Temple and the Church's Mission* (InterVarsity, 2004); Ciampa, R., and B. Rosner, "1 Corinthians," in *CNTUOT*, 695–752; Dickson, J. P., *Mission-Commitment in Ancient Judaism and in the Pauline Communities*, WUNT 2/159 (Mohr Siebeck, 2003); Fee, G. D., *The First Epistle to the Corinthians*, 2nd ed, NICNT (Grand Rapids: Eerdmans, 2014); Hays, R. B., "The Conversion of the Imagination," *NTS* 45 (1999): 391–412; Hays, *Echoes of Scripture in the Letters of Paul* (Yale University Press, 1989); Hays, *First Corinthians*, IBC (John Knox, 1997); Hübner, H. *Biblische Theologie des Neuen Testaments*, 3 vols. (Vandenhoeck & Ruprecht, 1990–95); Instone-Brewer, D., "1 Corinthians 9:9–11," *NTS* 38 (1992): 554–65; Kaiser, W. C., Jr., "Current Crisis in Exegesis and the Apostolic Use of Deuteronomy 25:4 in 1 Corinthians 9:8–10," *JETS* 21 (1978): 3–18; Koch, K., *The Prophets*, trans. M. Kohl (Fortress, 1984); McDonough, S. M., "Competent to Judge," *JTS* 56 (2005): 99–102; Millar, J. G., *Now Choose Life* (Inter-Varsity, 1998); Newton, M., *The Concept of Purity at Qumran and in the Letters of Paul* (Cambridge University Press, 1985); Oropeza, B. J., "Echoes of Isaiah in the Rhetoric of Paul," in *The Intertexture of Apocalyptic Discourse in the New Testament*, ed. D. F. Watson (Society of Biblical Literature, 2002), 97–98; Robertson, A., and A. Plummer, *A Critical and Exegetical Commentary on the First Epistle of St. Paul to the Corinthians*, ICC (T&T Clark, 1911); Rosner, B. S., "The Church as Temple and Moral Exhortation in 1 Corinthians," in *Ecclesia and Ethics*, ed. E. A. Jones III et al. (Bloomsbury T&T Clark, 2016), 41–54; Rosner, "Deuteronomy in 1 and 2 Corinthians," in *Deuteronomy in the New Testament*, ed. M. J. J. Menken and S. Moyise, LNTS 358 (T&T Clark, 2007), 118–35; Rosner, "Moses Appointing Judges," *ZNW* 82 (1991): 275–78; Rosner, "Paul and the Law in 1 Corinthians," in *Scripture, Texts, and Tracings in 1 Corinthians*, ed. L. L. Belleville and B. J. Oropeza (Fortress Academic, 2019), 99–110; Rosner, *Paul, Scripture, and Ethics* (Baker, 1999); Schrage, W., *Der Erste Brief an die Korinther*, 4 vols., EKKNT (Benziger; Neukirchener Verlag, 1991–2001); Stuhlmacher, P., "The Pauline Gospel," in *The Gospel and the Gospels*, ed. P. Stuhlmacher (Eerdmans, 1991), 149–72; Towner, P. H., "The Pastoral Epistles," in *NDBT*, 330–36; Webb, B., *The Message of Isaiah*, BST (Inter-Varsity, 1996); Williams, H. H. D., *The Wisdom of the Wise* (Brill, 2001); Wright, N. T., "Monotheism, Christology, and Ethics," in *The Climax of the Covenant* (Fortress, 1992), 120–36.

Brian S. Rosner

Corinthians, Second Letter to the

For most of 2 Corinthians, Paul is in the dock. The letter begins and ends with him on trial. Even in the middle, when matters turn to the collection for the poor in Jerusalem, Paul's contested status makes an already delicate situation almost unbearably so: "I'm not commanding you, but I want to test the sincerity of your love" (8:8). While Paul explicitly cites the OT only fifteen times, it is his star witness. The OT proves that what the Corinthians have experienced as a result of his ministry are new-covenant experiences. In other words, the OT proves that Paul is who he claims to be—a minister of the new covenant—and that his local rivals, a group of so-called super-apostles, are not. Not every OT citation plays this role, but most do. And the others are not far afield. Two citations show that what Paul says about money is what God says about money. Two more show that how Paul acts aligns precisely with God's word. In short, if the Corinthians want proof that "Christ is speaking through [him]" (13:3), Paul gives it to them *in God's own words*.

Paul's use of the OT in 2 Corinthians, however, does more than this. Not only does it help us trace his argument, but it also reveals his hermeneutical assumptions. It tells us how Paul understands and interprets the OT and, therefore, how we should too. After all, if Paul's use of the OT was meant to be effective, if it was meant to persuade the Corinthians, then it must be based on a hermeneutic that can be tested by those without apostolic gifting, which is to say, by the Corinthians and others like them (see esp. 1:13).

Before looking at Paul's explicit citations, however, we should take a step back and say something about the fifteen explicit citations we've identified. After all, it's not always easy to tell when Paul is citing Scripture and when he's not (cf., e.g., what NA[28] and NA[27] do with Isa. 52:4 in 2 Cor. 6:17). For this reason, our discussion will take its cues from the citations identified in NA[28] (see table 1), with one exception. It will also include Paul's references to Gen. 1:3 and Isa. 9:2 (9:1 LXX) in 2 Cor. 4:6 (so also Balla). These references, though identified as allusions by NA[28], are prefaced by an introductory formula (*ho theos ho eipōn*) and followed by citations of Isaiah *in canonical order*: Isa. 49:8 (6:2), 52:11 (6:17), and 55:10 (9:10). Thus, both the introductory formula and the canonical ordering of Paul's explicit uses of Isaiah raise the "volume" of these allusions and justify including them along with Paul's other explicit citations. NA[28]'s list of citations, moreover, shows that Paul's attention is given to each part of the Hebrew canon. In fact, factoring in the allusions noted in NA[28], Paul's attention is almost equally divided between the Law (4 citations, 16 allusions), Prophets (8 citations, 18 allusions), and Writings (3 citations, 15 allusions) (see, similarly, Hafemann, "2 Corinthians," 246; *Servant*, 95–100; and for a survey of literature on the OT in 2 Corinthians, see Han, 3–15).

Table 1. OT Citations in 2 Corinthians

2 Cor.	OT
3:16	Exod. 34:34
4:13	Ps. 116:10
6:2	Isa. 49:8
6:16	Lev. 26:11–12
	Ezek. 37:27
6:17	Isa. 52:11
	Ezek. 20:34
6:18	2 Sam. 7:14
	2 Sam. 7:8
8:15	Exod. 16:18
9:7	Prov. 22:8
9:9	Ps. 112:9
9:10	Isa. 55:10
10:17	Jer. 9:23–24
13:1	Deut. 19:15

How Paul Uses the OT: Three Rhetorical Patterns

The body of Paul's letter divides into three parts: Paul defends himself (1:12–7:16), talks about the collection for the poor in Jerusalem (chaps. 8–9), and concludes once more defending himself (10:1–13:10). Within each part Paul uses the OT in a distinctive way to serve his larger rhetorical agenda. He uses the OT first as *witness*, then as *revelation*, and finally as *law*.

The OT as witness (1:12–7:16). In the first part of his letter Paul defends his ministry and uses the OT as a key witness in his defense (Gignilliat, "Follower," 99: "Paul's warrant of choice"; contra, e.g., Stanley, 97–98). He insists that if the Corinthians really wanted "proof" that Christ was speaking through him (13:3), then they needed to look no further than what God had already said in the OT. God's earlier word proved his legitimacy. Nine of Paul's fifteen citations in 2 Corinthians occur in this part of his letter and serve this purpose. If, as Paul will later say, a matter is settled by "two or three witnesses," what might the Corinthians say to nearly ten!

Anticipated glory (3:16). Paul cites Exod. 34:34 in 2 Cor. 3:16. The citation is part of a larger argument (3:1–18) in which Paul proves the legitimacy of his claim to be a minister of the new covenant. His proof consists of two appeals to the Corinthians' experience: the first to their experience of the Spirit (3:1–6) and the second to their experience of transforming glory (3:7–18).

First, Paul says that if the Spirit is present at Corinth, something he assumes none would deny (cf. 1 Cor. 12–14), then the new covenant has been ministered to them through Paul (for a similar argument, see Gal. 3:1–6). Along the way Paul alludes to two prophets—Jeremiah (31:31) and Ezekiel (36:27)—to establish the connection between their experience and OT expectation (2 Cor. 3:3, 6) and, therefore, to establish his claim.

Second, Paul says that if the Corinthians have experienced transforming glory, which, once more, he assumes none would deny, then they have experienced the effects of the new covenant as a result of his ministry. To support this connection between their experience of glory and the new covenant, Paul appeals to the Law, specifically to the story about God giving the old covenant to Moses in Exod. 34. Paul's argument progresses in four steps.

1. The old covenant's glory, which Paul establishes with an allusion to Exod. 34:29–30 (2 Cor. 3:7), anticipates the new covenant's greater glory (3:7–11). After all, if the prophets anticipate a new covenant, one that includes the promise of the Spirit, to say nothing of complete forgiveness of sins (Jer. 31:34), then that covenant must be even more glorious than the first.

2. The veiled glory characterizing Moses's ministry anticipates the unveiled, "very bold" (or, better, *open* qua *uninterrupted*) ministry of glory that characterizes the new covenant and indeed Paul's own ministry (3:12–13; see also 10:8; 13:10; cf. also 2:17; 4:2; 6:11). Once more Paul expects their experience will confirm what he says. Paul's argument, moreover, also implies that the new covenant's glory is superior, at least in this instance, simply in quantity rather than quality (on the antitheses in 3:7–11, cf. Hafemann, *Moses*, with Grindheim). Moses would don a veil whenever he finished speaking to Israel (3:13; cf. Exod. 34:33, 35) and, when he did, he kept Israel from an uninterrupted view of God's glory (on the specific nature of this glory—*eis to telos tou katargoumenou* [2 Cor. 3:13]—see Garrett, 752–55). Paul, however, never did this (4:3–6). (Why Moses donned a veil is an open question, turning in part on whether *pros to mē*

atenisai in v. 13 signals purpose or result; cf. Furnish, 207, with Guthrie, 221–22; see further the literature cited in Hafemann, *Servant,* 100–102).

3. Israel's failure to accept Paul's ministry did not undermine his legitimacy (3:14–15). Rather, it was simply one more instance of a tragic historical pattern. After all, this wasn't the first time Israel had resisted God's word (see, e.g., the commentary on the golden-calf incident in Exod. 32 in 33:3–4 and 34:9; see also Acts 22:18 and Rom. 9:30–33).

4. The Corinthians' transformed lives, moreover, prove that they have experienced the uninterrupted view of God's glory available in the new covenant (3:16–18). Moses's own experience in Exod. 34:34 of unveiled access to God's transforming glory anticipates the experience of every member of the new-covenant community (v. 16). Everyone who has the new-covenant Spirit has free (v. 17), unveiled access (v. 18) to glory, which leads inexorably to transformed lives.

Thus, the Corinthians' transformed lives prove the availability of uninterrupted glory and the presence of both the new covenant and its promised Spirit in Corinth. And this experience, Paul insists, began when he arrived in Corinth. All this to say, the Corinthians were themselves proof of Paul's authenticity; they were his letter of recommendation.

Anticipated light (4:6). Paul alludes to Isa. 9:2 (9:1 LXX) and Gen. 1:3 in 2 Cor. 4:6 (see also *eikona* in Gen. 1:26 LXX and *eikōn* in 2 Cor. 4:4). Once more he proves that his ministry fulfills and is, therefore, authenticated by OT expectation, this time by OT expectations about God's promised new creation. Paul says that his conversion/call (4:1, 6), a story likely well-known to the Corinthians (e.g., 1 Cor. 15:8–10), fulfilled God's promise to shine light and joy and peace on his people (cf. Isa. 9:6: "for . . . us"), beginning in Israel's darkest corners (Isa. 9:2; see Paul's self-deprecating autobiographical note in 1 Tim. 1:15; cf. 1 Cor. 15:9) and extending to the nations (cf. Isa. 49:6: "light for the Gentiles"; also 60:3; Acts 26:18; etc.).

Paul's experience of this anticipated mercy (4:1; cf. 1 Tim. 1:13, 16), therefore, explains what the Corinthians have experienced: Paul's tireless (4:1), straightforward (v. 2; cf. 3:12–13), and Jesus-centered ministry (4:5). What else could explain Paul's radical about-face if not an experience of "new creation"? In fact, it is the very nature of Paul's ministry that explains something else the Corinthians have witnessed: mixed responses to his ministry (vv. 3–4; cf. 2:15–16; 3:14–15). The "god of this age," Paul insists, opposes only ministry that reveals God's glory (cf. Acts 26:18). That god's activity, (in a way) like Moses's (2 Cor. 3:13), is designed to veil precisely what Paul displays. And this means that rejection is simply one more proof of Paul's authenticity.

Anticipated suffering (4:13). Paul cites Ps. 116:10 (115:1 LXX) in 2 Cor. 4:13. The Corinthians' objections notwithstanding, Paul's suffering does not contradict his claim to be God's minister. It places him, rather, in a long line of faithful, ministering sufferers, a line that happens to include Jesus himself (4:10–11) and many others from Israel's past (4:13). Each knew, as the Corinthians must, that suffering allows God to display his power in a special way (4:7), whether through sustaining a minister in the midst of suffering (4:8–9) or rescuing him (or *her;* see 6:18) out of it (4:10–11, 13; cf. Ps. 116:5–8).

What's more, if Paul's suffering contradicts his apostolic claims, then why have the Corinthians so obviously benefited from his ministry (4:12; see also 2:16; 3:1–6, 16–18)? What besides the presence of God's power could explain the powerful effects of his ministry? Moreover, it is this belief in the (paradoxical) association of God's power with human weakness that has sustained God's suffering ministers throughout history. Just like the righteous sufferers who have gone before him, Paul too is convinced that his weakness is only temporary, that it will benefit others, and, ultimately, that it will cause people to glorify God (4:14–15; cf. Ps. 116:17–19). So, were the Corinthians to write off Paul for having suffered, they would make nonsense of an OT pattern (4:13), a pattern that anticipates and climaxes in Jesus's own ministry (4:10–11), and they would make nonsense of their own experience of both Paul's suprahuman perseverance (4:8–9) and his effectiveness (4:12; also vv. 14b, 15a). And this is to say nothing of the effect such behavior (i.e., ingratitude) would have on God's glory (4:15b).

Anticipated ministry (6:2). Paul cites Isa. 49:8 in 2 Cor. 6:2. In the larger context (5:1–6:2) Paul says that Isaiah's promised new creation has arrived, at least initially, with Jesus's resurrection (5:15–17; cf. Isa. 43:18–19; 65:16b–23; 66:22–23; see Beale, *Biblical,* 527–38) and, therefore, that it has arrived in the lives of those connected to Jesus (5:17) and possessing his Spirit (5:5; cf. Isa. 42:1; 61:1; see also 44:3). "Now," Paul says, "is the time of God's favor" and the "day of salvation" (6:2, citing Isa. 49:8). Paul's ministry (5:18) is nothing less, therefore, than the continuation of Jesus's own ministry, of the servant's ministry, through whom God had long ago promised to bless Israel and the nations (Isa. 49:6; cf. Acts 13:47; also 26:16–18; see Cole, 195–213).

Paul says that he is "Christ's ambassador" and like Jesus continues to proclaim God's end-time "grace" and to display through his suffering and weakness God's new-creation power. This kind of display has been foreshadowed, as Paul has already said, every time God has preserved Israel's lamenting faithful (4:13). Or, as Paul says it here, in the prophetic words of Isaiah, "In the time of my favor I *heard* you, and in the day of salvation I *helped* you" (6:2; citing Isa. 49:8; cf. 49:5 with 2 Cor. 4:7–12). Both Paul's message and manner—ministry through *weakness*—map right on to Isaiah's servant, the Lord Jesus (cf. 4:10–12).

For the Corinthians, this means that to reject Paul, not least because he is suffering, would be to reject the very manner of the servant's ministry and the *anticipated* extension of the servant's ministry in all those who carry on his mission. Thus, for those able to read between the lines, Paul's appeal to be "reconciled to God" (5:20), given just before describing his ministry as an *extension* of Jesus's own, is simply another way of saying be "reconciled to *me*" (see, esp., 6:11–13; 7:2). Were they to continue holding him at arm's length they would risk having "receive[d] God's grace in vain" (6:1). Or, as he puts it later on, they would risk "fail[ing] the test" (13:5).

Anticipated responsibilities (6:16–18). Paul cites six OT texts in 2 Cor. 6:16–18, a section coming near the end of this first part of Paul's letter. He connects each to an exhortation given at the head (6:14) and tail (7:1) of this section (6:14–7:1), an exhortation, in fact, closely related to one he has just given in 6:11–13. There he urged the Corinthians to "open wide [their] hearts [to him]" (6:13; cf. 7:2). Here he turns the coin over: they must close their hearts to his unbelieving opponents (6:14; see also 11:12–15).

Once again Paul draws a tight line between his ministry and God's, implying that collusion with his opponents would be tantamount to collusion with *God's* enemy, Belial (6:15; see also 11:14). It would be like setting up an idol in *God's* temple, which is precisely what those with God's Spirit in Corinth had become (6:16a). Their status as God's temple is implied every time God says that he will one day "live with" and "walk among" his people (6:16b, citing Lev. 26:11–12; Ezek. 37:27; cf. Jer. 32:38). It is the status that God's end-time gift of the Spirit—the long-awaited return of the once-departed shekinah glory—always anticipated (cf. 3:1–6; 5:5; cf. Ezek. 10).

What this means, therefore, is that to reject God's grace, mediated through Paul, would be to reject God's long-awaited and finally given invitation to come home, to return from exile (see 6:17b, citing Ezek. 20:34 LXX, and alluding to v. 41; 6:18, citing 2 Sam. 7:8, 14, and alluding to Isa. 43:6). The choice, Paul insists, couldn't be starker: "Come out from them and be separate" or stay in Babylon (6:17a, citing Isa. 52:11).

Summary. The OT testifies against the Corinthians. It witnesses that they have failed to connect the dots between Paul's ministry and the Scripture's testimony. And, as a result, the OT warns the Corinthians that they risk repeating Israel's deadly mistake, stumbling over the servant by stumbling over his anticipated ambassador. The OT also witnessed that God's new creation was theirs for the having, if only they would open their hearts up to Paul and his gospel and put away his opponents and the unchristian behavior hiding in the shadow cast by their teaching (7:1; cf. also 12:19–21).

The OT as revelation (chaps. 8–9). In the second part of his letter, Paul turns to the delicate matter of the collection for the poor in Jerusalem and to the Corinthians' earlier promise to contribute to this collection. As in the first section of Paul's letter, here too the OT plays a key role. Paul uses it to show that what he says about the Corinthians' money is nothing less than what God has already said. In this case, it aligns not with anticipations latent in the OT, but rather with principles revealed in the OT.

The principle of equality (8:15). Paul cites Exod. 16:18 in 2 Cor. 8:15. The citation concludes an argument in which Paul urges the Corinthians to make good on their promise to give (8:1–15). After all, Paul notes, the Macedonians had given joyfully and generously, despite their severely restricted circumstances (v. 2). Their willingness to meet the needs of others, in fact, is exactly what one would expect from people claiming to follow the self-sacrificing Lord Jesus, who "became poor, so that [we] through his poverty might become rich" (v. 9). It is this willing love, not the extent of the Macedonians' or the Lord's generosity, that Paul wants the Corinthians to emulate (vv. 10–12). How much they gave, in other words, wasn't nearly as important as *why* they gave.

As for the amount given, Paul appeals to the principle of "equality" (vv. 13–15; see Balla, 775), where the "plenty" God gives to some is meant to be passed on to meet the "needs" of others (v. 14). And Paul finds this principle in the OT. When God told Israelite families to collect only enough manna to feed their households and no more, when all was said and done, no family had "too much" or "too little" (8:15, citing Exod. 16:18). Everybody had just enough; their needs were met (see Exod. 16:16, 18).

For the Corinthians, this means that any extra they have gathered is meant not for them but for those who do not have enough. Hoarding it, Paul surely implies, would be unbelief masquerading as wisdom (or, simply, stinginess). It would reveal that the Corinthians had forgotten where their "manna" comes from, both today's and tomorrow's (Hays, 87–91). Paul likely also wants to subtly warn the Corinthians about what happens to (or, better, what *eats*) plenty not given away (see Exod. 16:20).

The principle of reciprocity (9:9). Paul cites the OT three times in 9:6–15. Here at the end of his discussion about the collection, Paul once more talks about the Corinthians' "plenty" (8:14). Much of what he says is familiar: their plenty is from God and meant to be given away willingly—or, as Paul now puts it, "cheerfully" (9:7, citing Prov. 22:8 LXX). But Paul takes one further step. He makes explicit what was only implicit in his earlier discussion of Exod. 16:18 in 8:15. He insists that not only has God supplied their plenty, but he will also *re*supply it if it is given away.

Paul finds this principle of reciprocity revealed in Ps. 112:9 (111:9 LXX). When God's people in the past "freely scattered their gifts to the poor," God ensured that "their righteousness endures forever" (9:9). He ensures that his people never lack for gifts to freely scatter. It is another way of saying what Paul has already said at the beginning of this argument. "Whoever sows generously will also reap generously" (9:6). Seed scattered freely would lead to both a big harvest and, presumably, from this harvest more seed to scatter for the next season (Garland, 405). Paul reiterates this same principle using the language of Isa. 55:10 (2 Cor. 9:10). If God is the one who supplies "seed" to his people so that they'll have "bread" to share with those in need, then it goes without saying that he is also the one who can "increase" the amount of seed he gives and, thereby, "enlarge" his happily generous people's "harvest of righteousness" (see also "joy" in Isa. 55:12).

The Corinthians could, of course, hoard their plenty. But if they do, they will miss the compound interest that in God's economy accrues to the plenty that is given away. Plus, they would miss an opportunity to glorify God, benefit their kin, and contribute to the unity of God's family (9:11b–15).

Summary. Paul insists that everything he says about the Corinthians' money is based on principles revealed in God's word. By doing this, Paul subtly implies that should they fail to contribute, they would be out of alignment with God's word. There would be, in this case, reason for Paul to question the authenticity of *their* claim to be God's sons and daughters. But, should they give and thus keep in step with the principles Paul outlines from God's word, they would not only prove the integrity of their Christian confession but also provide one more witness to Paul's authenticity. After all, if not Paul, who was responsible for introducing the Corinthians to the grace that motivated such giving (see 8:7)? It wasn't, so far as we can tell, Paul's opponents (see 2:17; also 11:7–12).

The OT as law (10:1–13:10). In the third and final part of his letter, Paul once more defends his ministry, now explicitly mentioning his rivals in Corinth, a group of so-called super-apostles who had gained the ears and, indeed, hearts of some in Corinth (cf. 6:13; 7:2). Again, Paul calls the OT to his aid, insisting that its jurisdiction extends all the way to Corinth. What it says simply has to be obeyed. In fact, what one does with the OT's authority, Paul says, goes a long way toward identifying who is *and who is not* Christ's apostle.

The law of boasting (10:17). Paul cites Jer. 9:24 (9:23 LXX) in 2 Cor. 10:17. The citation comes near the end of an argument directly responding to the claims of Paul's rivals (10:12–18). Paul insists that his opponents evaluate their ministry and, therefore, his own by the wrong standard. Some in Corinth, in fact, have sadly followed suit (10:1–11). Not only is their standard terribly subjective ("they measure themselves by themselves," 10:12), but it also allows them to take credit for work they have not done in places they have not been assigned (10:13–15a, 16b). The practice is, at the very least, "not wise" (10:12). It is also clearly out of step with God's word.

The OT says that one must only boast in "the Lord" (10:17, citing Jer. 9:24)—that is, in work both *empowered* by the Lord and *assigned* by the Lord. And the implication for Paul's opponents and their sympathizers is devastating: How could these teachers be God's true coworkers when they so obviously fail to obey something God has said? This flagrant violation of God's law shows, as does Paul's obedience, who God's true apostle really is. Failing to see this, in fact, would have devastating consequences, this time not only for them (10:15b; cf. 6:16–18) or for other Christians (cf. 9:11–15) but also for their unbelieving neighbors. Continuing to stand against Paul would mean standing in the way of Paul's missionary activity in their city and beyond (10:15–16; see, once more, Ezek. 20:41). Sympathizing with Paul's disobedient rivals was bad enough; how much worse to get in the way of God's mission!

The law of witnesses (13:1). Paul's final citation of the OT is found in 13:1. Here he cites Deut. 19:15. The citation comes at the beginning of a final warning Paul issues, just before concluding his letter. It's a warning Paul intends to follow up on when he soon visits Corinth—this will be his third visit (13:1; see also, e.g., 9:4; 10:2; 12:14). Paul says that he will come ready to convict "those who sinned earlier or any of the others" (13:2)—that is, those standing against him, sympathizing with his rivals and refusing to repent of other behaviors that are out of step with their confession. Paul admits that he would rather they repent before his arrival (10:2, 11; 12:20–21; 13:10; cf. 2:1–3). But, barring that, he will come ready to establish their guilt just as God requires, "by the testimony of two or three witnesses" (13:1, citing Deut. 19:15). He has given them sufficient witnesses to establish his apostolicity; now he will provide sufficient witnesses to establish their inauthenticity (13:5), their guilt. Paul likely has in mind witnesses such as Timothy and Titus, along, perhaps, with the delegates assisting with the collection (8:18, 22; 12:18) and any others in Corinth who have been, either already (see, e.g., 7:9–16; cf. 2:5–11) or as a result of Paul's letter (13:10), reconciled to God and his apostle and have firsthand knowledge of the situation.

Summary. Paul appeals to the legal authority of the OT, letting the Corinthians—and his rivals—know that no one, not even Paul himself, stands outside of its authority. In fact, failure to obey what God has legislated is, Paul implies, one sure way to know who is and who is not in God's family.

How Paul Understands the OT: Three Hermeneutical Assumptions

Paul's use of the OT in 2 Corinthians sheds light not only on Paul's letter but also on Paul's hermeneutical assumptions (see, similarly, Bruno, Compton, and McFadden). When, for example, Paul proves the authenticity of his ministry by appealing to the presence of new-covenant realities at Corinth, this tells us not only how Paul uses the OT but also how he understands it. Paul assumes that the new covenant has been inaugurated.

Recognizing this then helps us to read Jeremiah's and Ezekiel's prophecies more like Paul does—that is, to read them better. Paul's use of the OT in 2 Corinthians, in fact, reveals at least three assumptions Paul has about the Bible and his place in the Bible's story.

Paul assumes that he lives in the age of fulfillment. If there's a hermeneutical first principle for Paul, it is this: the long-anticipated era of salvation, first announced to Adam and Eve (Gen. 3:15; cf. Gen. 1:3 and Isa. 9:2 in 2 Cor. 4:6), has arrived. And it has arrived by means of the death, burial, and resurrection of Israel's long-awaited Messiah, Jesus of Nazareth (5:14–21). The Corinthians' experience, Paul says, proves just this. They have experienced what Jeremiah and Ezekiel anticipated (3:3, 6; cf. Beale, *Handbook,* 56–57). God's law has at last been written on his people's hearts. And his Spirit has been given or, we might say, his shekinah glory has returned, this time to dwell not in the midst of God's people but, rather, inside them (6:16; cf. 1 Cor. 6:19). This signals for Paul that Israel's exile has finally ended (2 Cor. 6:17). "Now"—not later, not in a different era of God's story—"*now* is the day of salvation" (6:2). God's "new creation" has at last begun; the Corinthians who have been united to Christ have experienced its firstfruits (5:5, 17). To claim otherwise would make nonsense of their experience and would call into question Paul's integrity. Paul claims to be God's apostle, ministering Jeremiah's new covenant to any and all who would put their faith in God's crucified Messiah (3:6; 4:1, 7; etc.), just as Paul has done (4:4–6).

It should be noted, moreover, that Paul applies all these "promises" (see 1:20; 7:1) to gentiles, despite the fact that many of them in their original contexts refer to (ethnic) Israel (see, e.g., "people of Israel" and "people of Judah" in Jer. 31:31). It is, of course, true that the same prophets Paul cites anticipate gentile salvation (see, e.g., Jer. 12:14–17; Isa. 19:23–25; Ezek. 47:21–23), even in the surrounding contexts of some of the OT passages Paul cites (see, e.g., Isa. 49:6, 8; 58:3–8; Ezek. 20:41; 2 Sam. 7:19 mg.). And Paul hasn't lost sight of ethnic Israel, even though their situation looks rather bleak (see 2 Cor. 3:14–15). Paul will have more to say about all this in later letters, not least his next (see Rom. 9–11; see Scott, 91–93). Here, at least, Paul shows no hesitation to sweep gentiles into promises made to Israel. After all, once the Spirit had descended on the Corinthians (cf. Peter's experience in Acts 10:44–48), what else was Paul to do? He also shows no hesitation to suggest that every unbelieving gentile, as well as Jew, remains in exile (see Isa. 52:11 and Ezek. 20:34, 41 in 2 Cor. 6:17; Beale, "Reconciliation," 558–59). Thus, not only did Israel's exile not end in the Persian period, but it also continues to be the experience of *every* unbelieving human who remains "east of Eden."

Paul assumes that the OT points to Jesus, though not always in the same way. Paul begins 2 Corinthians maintaining that all God's promises are "yes" in Jesus (2 Cor. 1:20). But, curiously, *none* of the OT texts that Paul cites maintain that Jesus is their *only* referent. Some bypass Jesus altogether. For example, unlike Hebrews (3:1–6), Paul does not say Moses points to Jesus. Rather, he says Moses was a foil for his own ministry (2 Cor. 3:12–13). He also thinks Moses was a type of *every* believer (3:16; cf. Beale, *Handbook,* 57–66). This is also the way Paul reads Psalms in 2 Corinthians. For Paul, the suffering psalmist, elsewhere said to point to Jesus (Matt. 27:46, citing Ps. 22:1; see also Heb. 2:12, citing Ps. 22:22), points both to Jesus and to *every suffering new-covenant minister* (2 Cor. 4:10–14). More surprising is Paul's reading of Isaiah's Servant Songs, which, as we've already noted, Paul applies to himself (6:2; cf. Acts 13:47), likely because Jesus himself had done so at Paul's conversion (Acts 26:16–18; cf. 9:15). Paul knows the difference between his ministry and Jesus's (2 Cor. 5:14–15; cf. Gignilliat, "Now"), even while here and elsewhere the line between the two isn't quite as thick as we might expect (4:7–15; so, e.g., Campbell; see also Col. 1:24). Most surprising, however, is Paul's democratization of the Davidic covenant promise (2 Cor. 6:18, citing 2 Sam. 7:14 and alluding to Isa. 43:6; see Beale, "Reconciliation," 571–72; Webb, 54–55, including n. 4), applying to all God's "sons and daughters" what is elsewhere applied only to Jesus (see, e.g., Heb. 1:5; 5:5).

What this means, therefore, is that God's promises find their "yes" in Jesus in different ways. Or, we might say, the OT is "about" Jesus in different ways. Sometimes God's promises are "yes" in Jesus because he is the means that enables their fulfillment. He is the one who provides the atonement that activates Jeremiah's new-covenant promises (Jer. 31:34), who ascends on high and from his seat at God's right hand sends Ezekiel's promised Spirit (Acts 2:33; see also Eph. 4:8), thus enabling the righteous acts of God's people (see, e.g., those described in 2 Cor. 9:9, citing Ps. 112:9; so, e.g., Starling, 249–53). At other times, God's promises are "yes" in Jesus because he is the one they point to; he is their referent. He is the referent of God's promise to David's son in 2 Sam. 7:14; he is the one subtly latent in the Psalter's pattern of lamenting sufferers. But, even here, Paul tells us that these can just as easily apply to others, along with Jesus. The conviction expressed in 2 Cor. 1:20, therefore, need not lead to a flat-footed, "everything-points-to-Jesus-in-the-same-way" hermeneutic. Paul's christological hermeneutic in 2 Corinthians is simply more interesting than that.

Paul assumes that the OT is still authoritative. For Paul, the OT is not only *prospective,* whether of Christians or Jesus (or both), but also *prescriptive.* It reveals moral principles (cf. Beale, *Handbook,* 72–73). And it can teach these in unlikely places. Paul, after all, grounds his principle of equality in a *narrative* section of the Law (8:15, citing Exod. 16:18). This is, of course, precisely how Moses says the narrative should be read. Moses tells us that the story illustrates Israel's need for God's word (Deut. 8:3). Without it, without *ordering their lives by it*, Israel would be malnourished or worse (cf. Deut. 8:2: "keep his commands"). Thus, Paul's ethical hermeneutic simply takes its cues from Moses and finds in the narrative a word from the Lord meant to guide and, thus, nourish God's people (cf. 1 Cor. 10:1–13). What Paul does with the Psalter's poetry is similar (2 Cor. 9:9, citing Ps. 112:9). For Paul, the OT reveals principles that should order the lives of God's people. Yes, it says quite a lot about God's salvation-historical plan, not least about the One at the center of that plan. But the OT says more. The OT also teaches God's new-covenant people how to live in this liminal, wilderness period between the new exodus and full arrival of the new creation.

The OT, Paul insists, also still commands. Its authority can be expressed as law or imperative. Its jurisdiction extends to God's new-covenant people. Thus, what the Lord says through Jeremiah has to be obeyed. And when it is not, this is as good a signal as any that one might not be in God's family, much less in the role of God's spokesman as Paul's self-congratulating rivals claim to be. Similarly, Paul says that Deuteronomy's judicial prescriptions are as valid in this era of salvation history as they were in Moses's day, even though the covenant Moses ministered has been annulled (see *katargeō*, 3:7–11). This shouldn't surprise us, since God promised to write that very covenant's laws on his people's hearts (3:3, 6). Granted, this cannot mean that the law carries over completely, since Jesus (among others) says it does not (see, e.g., Mark 7:19). But it must mean that some laws do. Thus, just as the OT's promises are fulfilled in Jesus in different ways, so too are the OT's laws fulfilled in different ways (see, e.g., Matt. 5:17–20). Some are shadows (Heb. 10:1). Others are not. The same nuance required to understand 2 Cor. 1:20 is, therefore, required to flesh out the implications of 2 Cor. 13:1 (on this question, see, e.g., Hafemann, *Promise*, 192–96; Wellum).

Summary. Paul assumes that the Corinthians—and others with the Spirit—will agree with the way he reads the OT. We will agree that we are indeed living in the long-awaited era of salvation, that the OT prefigures not only Jesus but also us Christians, and that its ethical principles and moral injunctions continue to exercise their authority even in this new era in which we are living. Thus, keeping a close eye on Paul's use of the OT in 2 Corinthians puts to rest any doubts about Paul's authenticity and, at the same time, puts us in a place to read 2 Corinthians and the OT even better.

Bibliography. Balla, P., "2 Corinthians," in *CNTUOT*, 753–83; Barclay, J. M. G., "Manna and the Circulation of Grace," in *The Word Leaps the Gap*, ed. J. R. Wagner et al. (Eerdmans, 2008), 409–26; Beale, G. K., *Handbook on the New Testament Use of the Old Testament* (Baker Academic, 2012); Beale, *A New Testament Biblical Theology* (Baker Academic, 2011); Beale, "The Old Testament Background of Reconciliation in 2 Corinthians 5–7," *NTS* 35 (1989): 550–81; Belleville, L. L., *Reflections of Glory*, JSNTSup 52 (Sheffield Academic, 1991); Belleville, *2 Corinthians*, IVPNTC (InterVarsity, 1996); Bruno, C., J. Compton, and K. McFadden, *Biblical Theology according to the Apostles*, NSBT 52 (InterVarsity, 2020); Campbell, D. A., "2 Corinthians 4:13," *JBL* 128 (2009): 337–56; Cole, D. M. I., *Isaiah's Servant in Paul*, WUNT 553 (Mohr, 2021); Cover, M., *Lifting the Veil*, BZNW 210 (de Gruyter, 2015); Dumbrell, W. J., "The Newness of the New Covenant," *RTR* 61 (2002): 61–84; Furnish, V. P., *2 Corinthians*, AB (Doubleday, 1984); Garland, D. E., *2 Corinthians*, NAC 29 (Broadman & Holman, 1999); Garrett, D. A., "Veiled Hearts," *JETS* 53 (2010): 729–72; Gignilliat, M. S., *Paul and Isaiah's Servants* (T&T Clark, 2007); Gignilliat, "2 Corinthians 6:2," *WTJ* 67 (2005): 147–61; Gignilliat, "A Servant Follower of the Servant," *HBT* 26 (2004): 98–124; Greever, J. M., "'We Are the Temple of the Living God' (2 Corinthians 6:14–7:1)," *SBJT* 19, no. 3 (2015): 97–118; Grindheim, S., "The Law Kills but the Gospel Gives Life," *JSNT* 24 (2001): 97–115; Guthrie, G. H., *2 Corinthians*, BECNT (Baker Academic, 2015); Hafemann, S. J., *The God of Promise and the Life of Faith* (Crossway, 2001); Hafemann, *Paul: Servant of the New Covenant*, WUNT 435 (Mohr, 2020); Hafemann, *Paul, Moses, and the History of Israel*, WUNT 81 (Mohr, 1995); Hafemann, "Paul's Use of the Old Testament in 2 Corinthians," *Int* 52 (1998): 246–57; Han, P., *Swimming in the Sea of Scripture*, LNTS 519 (T&T Clark, 2016); Hays, R. B., *Echoes of Scripture in the Letters of Paul* (Yale University Press, 1989); Lalleman, H., "Paul's Self-Understanding in the Light of Jeremiah," in *A God of Faithfulness*, ed. J. A. Grant et al. (T&T Clark, 2011), 96–111; Rosner, B. S., "Deuteronomy in 1 and 2 Corinthians," in *Deuteronomy in the New Testament*, ed. M. J. J. Menken and S. Moyise, LNTS 358 (T&T Clark, 2007), 118–35; Scott, J. M., "The Use of Scripture in 2 Corinthians 6:16c–18 and Paul's Restoration Theology," *JSNT* 17 (1994): 73–99; Stanley, C. D., *Arguing with Scripture* (T&T Clark, 2004); Starling, D. I., "Meditations on a Slippery Citation," *JTI* 6 (2012): 241–55; Stegman, T., " Ἐπίστευσα, διὸ ἐλάλησα (2 Corinthians 4:13)," *CBQ* 69 (2007): 725–45; Stockhausen, C. K., "2 Corinthians 3 and the Principles of Pauline Exegesis," in *Paul and the Scriptures of Israel*, ed. C. A. Evans and J. A. Sanders (Sheffield Academic, 1993), 143–64; Watson, F., *Paul and the Hermeneutics of Faith* (T&T Clark, 2006); Webb, W., *Returning Home*, JSNTSup 85 (Sheffield Academic, 1993); Wellum, S. J., "Progressive Covenantalism and the Doing of Ethics," in *Progressive Covenantalism*, ed. B. E. Parker and S. J. Wellum (B&H Academic, 2016), 215–33; Wilson, J., "The Old Testament Sacrificial Context of 2 Corinthians 8–9," *BBR* 27 (2017): 361–78; Woodington, J. D., "A Precedented Approach," *JBL* 137 (2018): 1003–18; Wright, N. T., *The Climax of the Covenant* (Fortress, 1992).

Jared Compton

Corporate Solidarity

Corporate solidarity is a defining feature of NT teaching about the people of God. It refers simply to the notion that personal identity is shaped corporately rather than individualistically. While the Bible respects both "the one" and "the many," it is simply not possible to conceive of Christian identity without reference to the corporate entities to which every believer belongs.

The central theme that undergirds corporate solidarity in the NT is union with Christ. Paul is the primary teacher of union with Christ, though the theme resonates elsewhere in the NT, especially in John's Gospel, 1 John, and 1 Peter. Here we adopt the fourfold understanding of union with Christ developed in my *Paul and Union with Christ* (Campbell, 2012): *union*, *participation*, *identification*, and *incorporation*. These four concepts have varying degrees of resonance with the teaching of the OT, as especially Paul adopts OT images and metaphors for his articulation of union with Christ. Other NT authors also employ union with Christ to undergird corporate solidarity, as in John's vine imagery (John 15:1–8) and Peter's stone/temple imagery (1 Pet. 2:4–8), but the focus here will remain on Paul.

Corporate solidarity is grounded primarily in union with Christ, since each believer's personal union with him creates an indelible connection to all others "in Christ." Every person in Christ is connected to every other person in Christ through the Spirit. The corporate nature of union with Christ is emphasized in two of the four concepts I used to articulate union with Christ: identification and especially incorporation. We will briefly survey some key NT texts that illustrate union, participation, identification, and incorporation, while observing how they connect to the corporate solidarity of the OT.

Corporate Personality?

First it is necessary to address the question of so-called "corporate personality"—a concept that dominated much twentieth-century discussion of biblical corporate identity. Corporate personality is the concept that a group of people share together in the same "personality" or personal identity. It was a notion explored in early-twentieth-century sociology and applied to the OT, especially by H. Wheeler Robinson. Robinson identified a lack of a sense of individuality in primitive legislation and religion, as they dealt with people as members of a tribe, clan, or family rather than on the basis of a single life (S. Porter, 290). Key examples used to illustrate corporate personality include the death of Achan's family for his sin (Josh. 7), the use of "I" in Psalms, and the Servant Songs of Isaiah (S. Porter, 290). Robinson's theories, first published in 1926, went virtually unchallenged in biblical scholarship until the critiques of J. Porter (1965) and Rogerson (1970).

This has been a subject of much debate (see Timms, 40–47, for an overview of the discussion). Two issues are pertinent: First, does a concept of "corporate personality" exist in the OT, and if so, in what capacity? Second, does such a concept lie in the background of Paul's thought? In favor of the term's OT credibility and Pauline significance, Herman Ridderbos (62) claims that the single representative of a whole people stands in relationship with said people such that they are identified with their representative. Likewise, J. Christiaan Beker (310) regards Paul's "incorporation motif" as originating in the Jewish notion of corporate personality, with several of its components to be found in Paul. Sang-Won Son (27, 119) is also in favor of the concept and regards it as better than other explanations of "being in Christ" because "(1) it recognizes the locative use of the formula and (2) it conceives of Christ as a person."

Against the concept of corporate personality, Stanley Porter claims that this "sacred cow" is already dead "and is now more than ready to be buried" ("Two Myths," 298–99). He argues that the corporate life of Israel is better conveyed by the term "corporate representation." David Timms (47) regards the evidence for corporate personality in the OT as scant and debatable. John Rogerson suggests that adherence to the concept of corporate personality adds nothing but confusion and is based on anthropological theories that have long been abandoned ("Corporate Personality," 3, 14, 15). Alexander Wedderburn (352) holds a mediating position that acknowledges the difficulties of the term "corporate personality" while remaining "thoroughly appreciative of the idea expressed by it as long as exaggerated claims are not made for it."

If "corporate personality" is understood to refer to the solidarity of a tribe or nation in which one person serves as the representative of the whole, Robert Tannehill (29) suggests that "this has something to contribute to our understanding of Paul but is not a sufficient explanation of Paul's corporate or inclusive patterns of thought." The best evaluation of the evidence favors Stanley Porter's notion of "corporate representation," which retains the legitimacy of Israelite solidarity but not the problematic complexities of a shared personality. Nevertheless, as Tannehill and Jouette Bassler suggest, corporate representation does not account for Paul's thought in full and can only be a constituent factor therein.

Union with Christ

Union with Christ is defined as union, participation, identification, and incorporation—terms that together do justice to the widespread variety and nuance of Paul's language, theology, and ethical thought about our relatedness to Christ. Union conveys faith union with Christ, mutual indwelling, trinitarian, and nuptial notions. Participation refers to partaking in the events of Christ's narrative. Identification encapsulates believers' location in the realm of Christ and their allegiance to his lordship. Incorporation gathers up the corporate dimensions of membership in Christ's body. These terms provide sufficient breadth through which the various characteristics of union with Christ are to be understood—the notions of locality, identification, participation, incorporation, instrumentality, union, eschatology, and spiritual reality are all ably represented.

One of the most important questions that has engaged scholarship with respect to union with Christ has been whether antecedents to Paul's thought can be found in Greco-Roman or Jewish thought. Especially of interest in the first half of the twentieth century, this question has all but been abandoned in recent discussions.

First, moves by Rudolf Bultmann and others to anchor Paul's conception in Greco-Roman thought were never persuasive and have ultimately been rejected (Davies, 2). Greco-Roman parallels could only be used negatively, as it became increasingly clear that Paul did not follow such antecedents (Bousset, 164–66). The various species of pagan mysticism have little in common with Paul. Even the apparently parallel practice of baptism has been shown to convey a significantly different meaning for Paul when compared to Greco-Roman practice.

Second, Jewish theology of the Second Temple period informs Paul's categories of thought, forming the conceptual backdrop to his theological thinking (Macaskill, 103–27), but ultimately it does not account for the full-orbed nature of Pauline union with Christ (Wedderburn, 356). Albert Schweitzer (37) depended on late-Jewish apocalyptic eschatology for his reading of Paul, and while his insistence on the eschatological aspect of Pauline mysticism became influential, the rigidity with which he appropriated Paul in light of apocalyptic has largely been rejected (Davies, xi–xv, 10). Beyond apocalyptic eschatology, William Davies has pointed out various affinities between Paul and rabbinic Judaism, such as his distinction between the flesh and Spirit (17–20) and the Adamic representation of humanity (52–57). While such affinities are illuminating and no doubt resonate with Pauline theology, again they do not fully explicate Paul's conception of union with Christ, which remains startlingly original against his Jewish background.

Third, the OT has received comparatively little treatment on the question of antecedents to union with Christ. There are no parallels for Paul's entire conception of union with Christ to be found in the OT, nor is his union-with-Christ vocabulary to be found there. Some strands of Paul's thought, however, find antecedents in the OT, and these strands primarily relate to Pauline metaphors for union. The metaphors of marriage (Patterson, 692–99), temple, and clothing all find antecedents in the OT (Kim, 102). The contexts in which God refers to Israel as his bride are well known (e.g., Ezek. 16). The symbolic nature of the temple as the locality in which God dwells with his people is even better known (e.g., 1 Kings 8:27–30). Related to the temple cult, priestly garments were symbols of representation and mediation.

Each of these strands resonates well with Paul's metaphorical descriptions of union with Christ. Paul has reappropriated the divine marriage of the OT so that Christ is the husband and the church his bride. Temple imagery now refers to the people of God, among whom God dwells. Believers clothe themselves with Christ himself, the one true mediator. While Paul's christological configuration of marriage, temple, and clothing is boldly innovative, the OT antecedents to such themes are clear.

Nevertheless, the OT does not appear to anticipate such notions as mutual indwelling, the instrumentality of Christ, the otherworldly realm of Christ, and the body of Christ. Thus, while we may affirm that certain important strands of Paul's thought find antecedents in the OT, other major strands do not.

Union

Union conveys faith union with Christ, the mutual indwelling of Christ and believer, and trinitarian and nuptial notions. It is ultimately concerned with being spiritually united with Christ in a profound relationship of mutual indwelling. One of the key metaphors for such union is marriage, with Eph. 5:22–32 being the preeminent example.

In this extended discussion about husbands and wives, Paul offers the most explicit application of the metaphor of marriage to the relationship of Christ to his church. Lest it be argued that 5:22–30 merely depicts the relationship between Christ and the church as an illustration for husband-wife relations without explicitly denoting the church as the wife of Christ or Christ as her husband, 5:30–32 leaves no room for doubt. Quoting Gen. 2:24 in Eph. 5:30, Paul clarifies in 5:32 that he is talking about Christ and the church. It is to this relationship that Gen. 2:24 is applied, indicating that Christ is joined to his church as a husband to his wife and that the two are "one flesh." Son (155–56) summarizes the network of connections as follows: "A certain typological comparison exists between the two relationships and Gen. 2:24, that is, the marriage relationship between Adam and Eve. . . . The human marriage relationship between husband and wife is explained in the framework of the divine union between Christ and the church, and both are grounded in the 'one flesh' marriage union between Adam and Eve constituted in Gen. 2:24."

The metaphorical joining of husband and wife and their becoming one flesh indicate a profound union between Christ and the church. The metaphor is personal and implies a bond of intimacy that goes well beyond the other metaphors that Paul uses in portraying union with Christ. As for the immediate implications of this one-flesh union, Paul draws out several points in 5:22–30.

First, the intimate bond of the marriage union does not erase the distinctions between Christ and his bride. Rather than vague mysticism or "corporate personality," in which the identity of believers is dissipated through union with the divine, we see here that husband and wife are clearly distinguished—though united—and each has a particular role within the relationship.

Second, the church appropriately submits to Christ, her head (5:22–24). Thus, their one-flesh union neither undermines the lordship of Christ nor allows the church to indulge in disobedience. Submission is the church's only activity mentioned in the passage, which highlights both the significance of submission for the life of the church and her passivity in relation to the other aspects of the marriage relationship, as Christ takes responsibility for her.

Third, the marriage is prepared, instigated, and sustained by Christ, with the wife identified as the recipient of his care. Christ is the Savior of the body (5:23), having loved her and given himself for her (5:25). He makes her holy in order to present her to himself without blemish (5:26–27). He sustains her through provision and care (5:29). All of this underscores the reality that the one-flesh union with Christ is instigated by grace; it is not a union that believers "achieve" or approach through mystical disciplines or spiritual advancement. The church is entirely the beneficiary of Christ's advances toward her.

Finally, Paul's use of Gen. 2:24 demonstrates his willingness to view human marriage typologically. Marriage is a type that points forward to its antitype: Christ's marriage to his church.

Participation

Participation refers to partaking in the events of Christ's narrative. Since believers are united to Christ, they share in the defining moments of his story, such as his death, burial, resurrection, and ascension.

To be buried with Christ conveys participation with him in his death, so that believers share in this Christ-event in a conceptual or spiritual manner. The participatory nature of this concept is confirmed by the abundant presence of participation and identification motifs in the context of Rom. 6. In 6:3, Paul speaks of being baptized into Christ Jesus and in his death; believers have been joined with him in the likeness of his death (6:5), have been crucified with him (6:6), and have died and live with him (6:8).

In 6:6, we see the first of only two explicit references to crucifixion with Christ (cf. Gal. 2:19–20); it is clear that participation in the event of Christ's death is again in view. The use of crucifixion language is striking in a context in which death language is normative, and thus it underscores the historical particularity of the death of Christ; it is his actual crucifixion outside Jerusalem in about AD 33 that focuses our thoughts. Consequently, the language of co-crucifixion highlights the extraordinariness of participation in Christ's death—for Paul's first readers an event that occurred decades before their coming to faith in Christ. The notion of dying with Christ most likely conveys "participation in the salvation-historical effects of Christ's death as marking and effecting the end of the rule of sin and death" (Dunn, 322).

In 6:9, Christ's ongoing life proceeds from his resurrection from the dead. Since believers participate in Christ's resurrection (6:5), it follows that they also participate in the life of Christ that proceeds from it. In fact, 6:11 seems to confirm this conclusion: believers are alive to God in Christ Jesus.

Of the four images used to articulate union with Christ, participation seems to have the least OT precedent (though see R. Peterson, 30). While there appears to be little explicit evidence besides 2 Tim. 2:12, Joshua Jipp (165) argues that participation with Christ involves sharing in the royal rule of the promised Davidic king, which would offer a rich OT backdrop for the concept.

Identification

Identification refers to believers' location in the realm or dominion of Christ and their allegiance to his lordship. Tannehill develops the connection between dying and rising with Christ and the eschatology of the two realms through the concept of Christ as an inclusive figure. When Paul speaks of participating in Christ's death (see above), Tannehill (24) regards this "as entry into Christ, who is an inclusive or corporate person." Christ as an inclusive person is closely related to the concept of the new realm or dominion in Paul's thought: "Christ, as inclusive person, represents and embodies the new dominion in himself" (Tannehill, 24). For Tannehill, this concept of Christ as an inclusive figure is not dependent on the notion of "corporate personality," which has been falsely derived from the thought of the OT (see above). Rather, the inclusivity of Christ is dependent on the eschatological nature of his death and resurrection. Paul associates dying and rising with Christ with the end of the old dominion and the foundation of the new, and because of this they are eschatological events. And "because they are eschatological events, affecting the old dominion as a whole, they are also inclusive events" (Tannehill, 30). All people are included in one of these two dominions for good or for ill.

The notion of realm is seen in several passages. One realm is ruled by sin and death, while the other is ruled by grace and righteousness (Rom. 5:19–21). Membership in the latter realm requires fidelity to its values and principles (6:12–14), while membership in the former spells slavery (6:17–23). These two realms are also distinct as seen and unseen (2 Cor. 4:17–18). The ruler of the air has influence over those living according to the ways of the world (Eph. 2:1–3), while believers have been rescued from the domain of darkness and transferred into the kingdom of the Son (Col. 1:13–14). They have become children of the day and no longer belong to the night (1 Thess. 5:5–8).

In Col. 1:13–14 we observe a direct reference to the two opposing domains that constitute Paul's realm theology—"the domain of darkness" is that from which people need rescue. Paul's claim is that Christ has rescued believers from this domain "and transferred us into the kingdom of the Son he loves" (1:13 CSB). This "domain of darkness" also contrasts with the "light" mentioned in the previous verse—"The Father . . . has enabled you to share in the saints' inheritance in the light" (1:12 CSB). This "inheritance in the light" likely parallels "the kingdom of the Son"; the inheritance is found in "the light" rather than in the darkness. And it is found in the light because believers have been transferred to the realm of light, otherwise known as the kingdom of the Son.

There are obvious parallels here with the exodus, in which God rescues his people from the dominion of Egypt and, having redeemed them, establishes a covenant with them that constitutes them as a nation under God (McKnight, 124–25). The Israelites are transferred from the kingdom of Pharaoh to the direct rule of Yahweh. With such a clear parallel, it is reasonable to suppose that the whole of Paul's realm theology is grounded in the exodus event. It is, after all, the most significant salvation event in the OT, to which Paul often alludes. NT authors commonly find connections between the work of Christ and the blood sacrifice of the Passover lamb, salvation by that blood, and redemption out of slavery and into freedom. Paul's realm theology simply adds the notion of two dominions under which all of this occurs. Believers are redeemed by the blood of the Lamb, rescued out of slavery to sin, and transferred out of the dominion of evil to belong to the kingdom of Christ. The exodus is thus a type of which realm theology is the antitype (Campbell, *Hope of Glory*, 92).

Incorporation

Incorporation gathers up the corporate dimensions of membership in Christ's body. The key metaphors for incorporation are body, building, and temple.

1 Corinthians 12:12–27. Paul labors the point that each part does its work within the body of Christ and the diversity of its parts is essential to its proper functioning; it would do the body no good if each part were an eye (1 Cor. 12:17).

The key elements with respect to union with Christ pertain to vv. 12 and 27. Verse 12 makes the point that just as the body has many parts and is yet one body, so too is Christ. The body of Christ is one body with many parts and is analogous to a human body. Verse 27 underscores this reality with respect to believers themselves by stating that together they are the body of Christ and individually are members of it. They form one body and are parts of that body. Consequently, we see that the union that believers have with Christ has a totalizing effect on the one hand and a distinguishing effect on the other. Believers are the body of Christ; they are all made into one, forming a single corporate identity (Macaskill, 158). But believers are also individual parts of the body; their unity together does not quash their distinct and diverse otherness. The body has many different parts and is yet one body (1 Cor. 12:12–27). This oneness means that believers not only partake in Christ but also are joined to each other. The diversity of gifts and roles shared among its members serves to enhance the unity of the body as the body grows and is built up.

The body of Christ is one of Paul's most important metaphors for describing the nature of the church. If the church is Christ's body, of which he is head, the metaphor must convey connotations of union. "Generally speaking, the qualification of the church as the body of Christ is a denotation of the special, close relationship and communion that exist between Christ and his church" (Ridderbos, 362). The body is an organic being that is one in Christ and is also growing and maturing (Eph. 4:11–16). Christ is the head of the body, from whom and into whom the body grows. While the body grows by the work of God, it also builds itself through its supporting ligaments and tendons. It is striking, however, that such a central image for corporate solidarity is apparently without clear OT antecedent.

Ephesians 2:21–22. Speaking of the members of God's household (Eph. 2:19), which is built on the foundation of the apostles and prophets with Christ Jesus himself as the cornerstone (2:20; cf. Ps. 118:22; Isa. 28:16), Paul depicts God's people as a building growing into a holy temple. Unlike the previous references to God's people as temple, these two verses specify incorporation into Christ—and this explicitly, three times. Christ is the antecedent of the two relative pronouns in Eph. 2:21 and 2:22, such that the building is fitted together in him and is being built together in him for God's dwelling in the Spirit. Furthermore, the building is growing into a holy temple in the Lord: "If the presence of God is the feature that most essentially defines the temple, the indwelling of the Spirit so defines this congregation" (Campbell, "Earthly Symbol," 184). As David Peterson acknowledges, "Paul affirms in Ephesians that Christians in union with Christ fulfil the Temple ideal" (165).

Paul clearly applies the OT image of God's holy temple to the people of God, thus using that (once) concrete (so to speak) reality as a metaphor to convey something about the new-covenant congregation (Macaskill, 151–52). Rather than being built of stone, this temple consists of people; and rather than dwelling within a physical structure, which could be accessed by people to varying degrees, God's Spirit dwells within a people. The people of God constitute the "location" in which God dwells, and in that sense they have replaced the function of the temple of old. It is somewhat ironic that the temple is described as a building, since the metaphor has been used by Paul to make the point that the temple is no longer a building but a people. The temple is a people, not a building, and yet the people are described as a building—in a metaphorical sense, of course.

Conclusion

Corporate solidarity features in the NT through a web of interrelated images, all of which find their theological grounding in union with Christ. Believers collectively constitute the bride of Christ. They have died with him and have been raised with him for life within the realm of Christ's rule. Believers are individually members of the body of Christ, built together into him as the new temple in which God dwells by the Spirit. Christ is an eschatological inclusive person who draws his followers into a spiritual and corporate union with himself and all others in Christ. The corporate solidarity of the NT finds its source, means, and purpose in Christ himself.

Much NT teaching of corporate solidarity draws on OT imagery, which is transfigured into NT concepts. The original imagery is repurposed and given new significance in light of Christ. The nuptial dynamic between Yahweh and Israel is transfigured to Christ and the church. The transfer of God's people out of slavery in Egypt into the covenantal rule of Yahweh is transfigured to the spiritual transfer out of the kingdom of darkness into the kingdom of the Son. The temple as the designated physical dwelling place of God's presence within Israel is transfigured to the collective of Jews and gentiles built together in Christ as the house of the Spirit. These OT images are therefore types that find typological transfiguration and fulfillment in Christ. It is interesting, however, to note how few of these images are employed with explicit scriptural citation (cf. Eph. 5:31). Rather than being used with citation, these OT images are employed and understood within a shared conceptual universe.

While both OT and NT images convey corporate solidarity, there is no evidence to support the outdated concept of corporate personality. Though Christ is an inclusive figure and believers become "one" in him, individual personal identity is not displaced by the whole. Christ remains distinctly who he is (the head of the body and the husband of the church) and likewise individual believers retain their individuality within the whole (as distinct members of the body of Christ with individualized gifts and roles reflecting the body's diversity within its unity).

See also Abraham and Abrahamic Tradition; Adam, First and Last; Messiah

Bibliography. Bassler, J. M., *Navigating Paul* (Westminster John Knox, 2007); Beker, J. C., *Paul the Apostle* (T&T Clark, 1980); Bousset, W., *Kyrios Christos*, trans. J. E. Steely (Abingdon, 1970); Calvin, J., *Institutes of the Christian Religion*, ed. J. T. McNeill, trans. F. L. Battles (Westminster, 1960); Campbell, C. R., "From Earthly Symbol to Heavenly Reality," in *Exploring Exodus*, ed. B. S. Rosner and P. R. Williamson (Apollos, 2008), 177–95; Campbell, *Paul and the Hope of Glory* (Zondervan, 2020); Campbell, *Paul and Union with Christ* (Zondervan, 2012); Davies, W. D., *Paul and Rabbinic Judaism*, 3rd ed. (SPCK, 1970); Dunn, J. D. G., *Romans 1–8*, WBC (Word, 1988); Jipp, J. W., *Christ Is King* (Fortress, 2015); Kim, J. H., *The Significance of Clothing Imagery in the Pauline Corpus*, JSNTSup 268 (T&T Clark, 2004); Macaskill, G., *Union with Christ in the New Testament* (Oxford University Press, 2013); McKnight, S., *The Letter to the Colossians*, NICNT (Eerdmans, 2018); Patterson, R. D., "Metaphors of Marriage as Expressions of Divine-Human Relations," *JETS* 51 (2008): 689–702; Peterson, D., "The New Temple," in *Heaven and Earth*, ed. T. D. Alexander and S. Gathercole (Paternoster, 2004), 161–76; Peterson, R. A., *Salvation Applied by the Spirit* (Crossway, 2015); Porter, J. R., "The Legal Aspects of the Concept of 'Corporate Personality' in the Old Testament," *VT* 15 (1965): 361–80; Porter, S. E., "Two Myths: Corporate Personality and Language/Mentality Determinism," *SJT* 43 (1990): 289–307; Powers, D. G., *Salvation through Participation* (Leuven: Peeters, 2001); Ridderbos, H., *Paul: An Outline of His Theology*, trans. J. R. de Witt (Eerdmans, 1975); Robinson, H. W., *The Christian Doctrine of Man*, 3rd ed. (T&T Clark, 1926); Robinson, "The Hebrew Conception of Corporate Personality" (1935) and "The Group and the Individual in Israel" (1937), reprinted in *Corporate Personality in Ancient Israel* (Fortress, 1964); Rogerson, J. W., *Anthropology and the Old Testament* (Blackwell, 1978); Rogerson, "The Hebrew Conception of Corporate Personality: A Re-examination," *JTS* 21 (1970): 1–16; Schweitzer, A., *The Mysticism of Paul the Apostle*, trans. W. Montgomery (Johns Hopkins University Press, 1998); Son, S.-W., *Corporate Elements in Pauline Anthropology*, AnBib 148 (Pontifical Biblical Institute, 2001); Tannehill, R. C., *Dying and Rising with Christ* (de Gruyter, 1967; repr., Wipf & Stock, 2006); Timms, D., "The Pauline Use of *en Christo*" (PhD diss., Macquarie University, 2000); Wedderburn, A. J. M., *Baptism and Resurrection*, WUNT 44 (Mohr, 1987).

CONSTANTINE R. CAMPBELL

Cosmic Conflict

See Divine Warrior; Satan

Covenant

"Covenant" (Heb. *bərît*; Gk. *diathēkē*) is the Bible's term for "a chosen [as opposed to natural] relationship in which two parties make binding promises to each other," often with God as the witness (Schreiner, 13; cf. Hugenberger, 11). Thus, a covenant's core is a nonbiological, oath-bound relationship like those in clan alliances (Gen. 14:13), personal agreements (31:44), international treaties (Josh. 9:6; 1 Kings 15:19), national agreements (Jer. 34:8–10), and loyalty agreements (1 Sam. 20:14–17), including marriage (Mal. 2:14) (Gentry and Wellum, 162–63). Some scholars assert that "covenant" or "the covenantal kingdom" is *the* controlling center of the Christian canon (Eichrodt; Kline, *Kingdom*). Others have more modestly argued that the covenants' progression forms the backbone of Scripture's metanarrative (Gentry and Wellum, 31). Through covenants God relates to others, reverses sin's ruinous effects, and introduces his saving reign into the world. Each historical covenant includes both common and saving grace elements that Jesus's person and work culminate or realize. This study overviews the nature and interrelationships of the five main historical covenants between God and his creatures.

Adamic-Noahic Covenant

Adam's headship in the covenant with creation. Because the word "covenant" (*bərît*) first appears in Gen. 6:18 in relation to Noah, some question if God formally makes a covenant with creation through Adam (e.g., Williamson, *Sealed*, 52–58, 69–76). However, the substance of a covenant can exist without the term (2 Sam. 7; cf. Ps. 89:3). Furthermore, the Bible's earliest chapters depict the results of God's choosing to initiate a kinship-type bond with creation through Adam's representative headship (see Gen. 5:1–3; Jer. 33:20, 25), and this is the essence of a covenant (Niehaus, 1:46–50; Belcher, 64–66). While creation was "very good" (Gen. 1:31), it was incomplete. Thus, this elected relationship includes both God's pledge to providentially sustain (1:29–30) and humanity's conditional responsibility to bear his image as priest-kings who expand a God-dependent community and the garden sanctuary to the earth's ends (1:28; 2:15–17). When Adam transgressed this covenant, God cursed the earth and condemned humanity to spiritual and physical death (3:17; cf. Isa. 24:4–6; 43:27; Hosea 6:7).

Though Adam failed, his antitype—the last Adam, Jesus Christ—would succeed (Rom. 5:18) (Gentry and Wellum, 670–77; cf. Waters). Before announcing Adam's punishment, God curses the serpent and promises that the woman's male offspring would eventually destroy the evil one (Gen. 3:15–19). God then clothes his royal priests with animal-skin garments, likely because a substitutionary sacrifice was necessary to reestablish his relationship and partnership with them (3:20–21) (Kline, *Kingdom*, 145–53).

Covenant affirmation through Noah. After the flood, Yahweh fulfills his promise (Gen. 6:18) and establishes an "everlasting covenant" between himself and all living creatures on the earth, including Noah and his descendants. This singular covenant (*pace* Kline, *Kingdom*, 230–34; Van Pelt) included his promise to never again destroy all life with a flood (9:9–11, 16; cf. 8:22).

At least two features identify that God affirms with Noah his preexisting relationship with creation under Adam's headship (thus, the Adamic-Noahic *covenant* [singular]), though with some developments. First, parallels suggest that God recreates the world with Noah as covenant head: (1) (re-)creation begins in watery chaos (1:2 // 7:17–24); (2) the Spirit/wind moves (1:2 // 8:1); (3) God's image bearers steward creation (1:26–27 // 7:1–3; 9:2, 6); (4) animals are "according to their kinds" (1:21, 24–25 // 7:2–3, 14); (5) God blesses/commands human fruitfulness (1:28 // 9:1, 7), (6) designates food (1:29–30; 2:16 // 9:3), and (7) restricts food (2:17 // 9:4); (8) both families include father, mother, and three sons (4:1–2, 25 // 6:10; 7:13). Second, God's "establishing" (*hiphil qûm*) rather than "cutting/making" (*krt*) the Noahic covenant (*hēqîm bərît*; 6:18; 9:9) points to God's *affirming* or *sustaining* his earlier covenant with creation rather than his *initiating* (e.g., Gen. 15:18; Exod. 24:8) or *renewing* an old one either after it has been broken (e.g., Exod. 34:10) or with a new party (e.g., Josh. 24:25; 2 Chron. 34:31) (Dumbrell, 15–23; Niehaus, 1:192, 198–99; 2:139–74; Gentry and Wellum, 187–95; *pace* Williamson, *Abraham*, 195–203). Scripture applies affirmation language within the Noahic (Gen. 6:18; 9:11, 17), patriarchal (17:7, 21; Deut. 8:18), Mosaic (Lev. 26:9), and new (Ezek. 16:60, 62) covenants.

Additionally, God's affirmation with Noah develops the divine-creation relationship. Fear and a defense of human life now occur within humanity's dominion (Gen. 9:2, 6). God sanctions animal life as food (9:3; cf. 1:29), and he also guarantees the new context's perpetuity for redemption by specific promises and the covenant sign of the rainbow (9:12–17).

Abrahamic Covenant

After Shem, Ham, and Japheth's families multiply and rebel against God by exalting themselves, Yahweh confuses their languages and disperses some seventy nations across the globe (Gen. 11:8–9; cf. chap. 10). From one of them, he then distinguishes Abram and his offspring through whom he purposes to reverse the global curse and reconcile the world to himself.

God fulfills the covenant in two stages. Yahweh commissions Abram to "go" to Canaan and there "be a blessing." These two coordinated commands (12:1b, 2d) are each followed by one or more conditional promises (12:2abc, 3ab), and the second command-promise unit includes the ultimate promissory result, global blessing (12:3c) (on this structure, see table 1; cf. Gen. 17:1–2; Williamson, *Sealed*, 78–79; Dumbrell, 73–76; Gentry and Wellum, 266–70).

Table 1. Structure of Gen. 12:1–3

	And Yahweh said to Abram,	1
Stage 1: *Realized in the Mosaic Covenant*	"Go from your land . . .	b
	so that I may make you into a great nation,	2
	and may bless you,	b
	and may make your name great.	c
Stage 2: *Realized in the New Covenant*	Then be a blessing,	d
	so that I may bless those who bless you,	3
	but him who dishonors you I will curse,	b
	with the result that in you all the families of the ground may be blessed."	c

Both command-promise units identify how God would reverse the property and progeny punishments from Gen. 3:14–19 (Hamilton). They also foresee two major stages in salvation history (DeRouchie, *Understand*, 209–11). Stage one relates to Abraham fathering one nation in Canaan, which the Lord fulfills through the Mosaic covenant after Egypt afflicts Israel for four hundred years (15:13, 18; cf. Exod. 2:24; 6:4–5). Yahweh gives Israel Canaan for the twelve tribes during Joshua's days (Josh. 21:43–45; cf. Gen. 17:8), but it is not until David and Solomon reign that Israel's realm stretches from the border of Egypt to the Euphrates (2 Sam. 7:1; 1 Kings 4:20–21).

Stage two occurs when God's representative "blesses" the "clans/families/peoples" Yahweh had dispersed (Gen. 12:2d–3; cf. 10:32). Christ fulfills this stage by creating the new covenant community (Luke 1:54–55, 72–73). Genesis 17 contrasts Abraham fathering a single covenant nation in Canaan (17:7–8) with him fathering "many nations" (17:4–6; cf. 35:11), which fulfills the promise in 12:3 and 15:5 (cf. Rom. 4:16–17). Narrowing the promise of a singular "offspring" in Gen. 3:15, God will raise up the patriarch's biological "offspring" and multiply him like the stars (Gen. 15:3–5; cf. 22:17). He will be named through Isaac (21:12; cf. 17:19, 21), conquer his enemies' gate, and stand as the agent of blessing for all nations (22:17–18) (DeRouchie, "Counting"; "Lifting," 167–77). Although God anticipates that Abraham's descendants will inherit the singular "land" of "Canaan" and the larger suzerain state (15:18; 17:8), this singular offspring from Gen. 22:17–18 will inherit plural "lands" (26:3–4). Thus, God will overcome the world's curse, and Abraham will inherit "the world" (Rom. 4:13; cf. Ps. 2:8; Dan. 2:35; Matt. 5:5; Eph. 6:3).

The fulfillment of God's promises is both conditional and certain. The Abrahamic covenant testifies to the conditional nature *and* certain fulfillment of its promises. Conditionally, Abraham must "go" to the land and "be a blessing" there to overcome the curse and to bless the world (Gen. 12:1–3). For Yahweh to confirm the covenant, the patriarch must "walk before" God and "be blameless" (17:1–2). The covenant sign of circumcision reminds recipients of this priestly commission (cf. Exod. 19:5–6), portrays the curse of excision for violators, and distinguishes Abraham's offspring from all other peoples (see Kline, *Oath*; DeRouchie, "Circumcision," 182–89; Meade, "Meaning"). Alternatively, Yahweh stresses certain fulfillment through his self-imprecatory oath-sign and promise (Gen. 15:17–21; cf. Jer. 34:18; see Kline, *Oath*, 16–17, 41–42; Robertson, 7–15, 128–46; Hugenberger, 168–215; Gentry and Wellum, 286–94) and by swearing upon himself, following Abraham's faith-filled obedience wherein he nearly sacrificed Isaac (Gen. 22:16–18; cf. 26:3–5).

Hence, Yahweh's vow to fulfill both covenant stages ([1] great nation; [2] blessed world) responds to his covenant "son's" obedience (cf. Rom. 5:18–19; 8:4; Gentry and Wellum, 775–82). Using the infinitive absolute + *yiqtol* construction in Gen. 18:18 followed by the conditional reason + purpose statements in 18:19 highlights the certain yet contingent nature of God's promises (cf. Blaising and Bock, *Progressive*, 132–34). Abraham's covenant-mediating obedience secures initial fulfillment (Gen. 22:18; 26:5), but his faith rests in the promised obedience of his singular, male "offspring" (15:5–6).

The Abrahamic covenant parallels ancient royal grants, which obligated every generation to loyalty but made irrevocable or perpetual promises ensuring the pledged land or kingship would remain in the family, even if disloyal individuals forfeited their right to covenant blessings (Beckman, 109; cf. Weinfeld, 189–90; Knoppers, 683–92). Consequently, Paul contrasts the Abrahamic covenant's promissory quality with the Mosaic law-administration (Gal. 3:17–18; cf. Rom. 4:13–14).

The single Abrahamic covenant. Based on Gen. 12:1–3, Paul Williamson (*Abraham*, 212–14; *Sealed*, 89–91) argues that Yahweh initiates two distinct covenants with Abraham: (1) Gen. 15's temporary, national, and unilateral covenant, and (2) Gen. 17's eternal, international, and bilateral covenant. However, both chapters include national (Gen. 15:18; 17:7–8) and international (15:5; 17:4–6) elements. Later Scripture recognizes only a single "covenant" with the patriarchs (e.g., Exod. 2:24), and the switch from "cutting" (*krt*, Gen. 15:18) to affirming a covenant (Hiphil *qûm*, 17:7, 19, 21) strongly suggests a single covenant administration that develops over two redemptive-historical stages (Niehaus 2:103–74; Gentry and Wellum, 312–18). Both the Mosaic and new covenants fulfill different aspects of the single Abrahamic covenant.

Mosaic Covenant

The Mosaic covenant fulfills stage one of the Abrahamic covenant. After Yahweh brings Israel to Mount Sinai, he charges them to keep his "covenant" (Exod. 19:5), which will fulfill the first stage of his promises to Abraham (2:24; 6:4; cf. Dumbrell, 113–14). Such is clear when Moses pleads for the people's pardon after the golden-calf rebellion (32:13), which results in Yahweh's restoring the covenant (34:27–28) and in Moses's covenant renewal sermons at Moab (Deut. 1:8; 6:10).

After synthesizing (Exod. 20:1–17) and detailing (20:22–23:19) the covenant obligations, Yahweh formalizes the relationship (24:1–11). Leviticus and Deuteronomy's book of the law further develop the covenant through their holiness instructions and sanctions (cf. Lev. 10:10; Deut. 29:20; 30:10). This covenant guides Israel's historical evaluation, regulates prophetic declarations, supplies the Wisdom literature's framework, and governs God's people until the new covenant supersedes it at Christ's coming (Josh. 1:7–8; Mal. 4:4; Luke 16:16; cf. Gal. 3:23–26; Heb. 8:6–13).

The Mosaic covenant's sign was the Sabbath (Exod. 31:13–17). Yahweh institutes it to supply rest (Deut. 5:14) and to develop holiness by testing obedience and nurturing trust (Exod. 16:4–5, 23–26). Furthermore, the weekly and yearly Sabbath cycles remind Israel that through them and their Messiah Yahweh would reestablish right order in his world (cf. Matt. 11:27–12:8) by generating the sovereign peace he once enjoyed with creation (Gen. 2:1–3). The Sabbath represents a future reality for which both Israel and the world should hope (DeRouchie, *Understand*, 449–53).

The Mosaic covenant brings death. While the Mosaic covenant displays similarities to both second-millennium law codes and suzerain-vassal treaties (Kitchen, 283–89), its conditionality and revocability most approximate the latter. Yahweh's gift of lasting life and blessing depends upon Israel perfectly obeying all God's commands (Lev. 18:5; Deut. 8:1). Thus, in the old covenant, righteousness was the *goal* and not the *ground* (Deut. 6:25; cf. Rom. 9:30–32). Where disobedience prevailed, curse and death reigned (Deut. 27:26).

While a remnant of true believers existed in Israel (e.g., Moses, Rahab, Ruth, David, Isaiah; cf. Rom. 11:7), the majority needed heart surgery, for they were unrighteous, stubborn, unbelieving, and rebellious (Deut. 9:6–7, 23–24; 10:16; 31:27). Due to their spiritual inability (29:4), Israel should have recognized that their only hope was God reconciling them by grace through faith in his provision of a substitutionary sacrifice, which would atone for them if they realized their guilt and confessed their sins (Lev. 5:5–6; Num. 5:6–7). Any blessing they were to enjoy would be solely because of God's justifying grace apart from works (Rom. 9:30–32; cf. Gen. 15:6).

Nevertheless, Moses sees that Israel's stubbornness will lead them to rebel in the land and experience God's just exilic wrath (Deut. 4:25–28; 31:16–17). The lengthy covenant curse lists (Lev. 26:14–39; Deut. 28:15–68) forecast what is to come, and Israel's history unfolds just as Moses had predicted.

Because the Mosaic covenant era included a sustained hardness resulting in the people's destruction (Rom. 11:7–8), Paul rightly noted that "the law is not of faith" (Gal. 3:12 ESV) (see DeRouchie, "Leviticus"). The Mosaic covenant bore a ministry of condemnation (2 Cor. 3:9) and demonstrated both Israel's and the world's need for the promised deliverer (Rom. 3:19–22; 5:20; DeRouchie, "Condemnation").

The Mosaic covenant anticipates the new covenant. After exile, Yahweh would remember his covenant promises to the patriarchs (Lev. 26:42) and exodus generation (26:45), restore his people, transform the remnant's hearts, curse their enemies, and secure their life (Deut. 4:30–31; 30:1–14). Through Yahweh's promised Savior's new exodus, blessing, and global dominion (Num. 24:5–9, 17–19), other nations would gather to and rejoice in Yahweh (Deut. 32:43; 33:19), and this would ignite jealousy to draw Israelites back to God (32:21). In this age, the remnant would heed Moses's commandments (30:8) because a covenant-mediating prophet like Moses would supersede Moses's role (cf. 1 Tim. 2:5), clarify the divine word (Deut. 18:15, 18), and ensure its internalization within God's people (30:11–14; cf. Isa. 59:21). (On the eschatological nature of Deut. 30:11–14, see Coxhead; Smothers.)

Davidic Covenant

During the Mosaic covenant era after Israel settled the promised land, Yahweh advanced his promise of a coming royal Savior by pledging to David an eternal kingdom (2 Sam. 7:8–16; 1 Chron. 17:7–14). While the narrative accounts do not call the event a "covenant," other Scriptures do (2 Sam. 23:5; Ps. 89:3).

The nature of the Davidic covenant. God's covenant with David reveals that Scripture's promised Savior will come from David's royal line. In describing his prior (2 Sam. 7:8–9a) and subsequent (7:9b–11a) accomplishments for David, Yahweh echoes the Abrahamic covenant. Yahweh then vows that after David's death, he would build David a "house/dynasty" (7:11b–16). David's biological descendant ("offspring") would build a "house" for God's name, enjoy a lasting kingdom, and be Yahweh's royal son (7:12–15). David's house, kingdom, and throne would remain steadfast and established forever (7:16). In response, David recognizes that such promises bear hope and guidance for the world (7:19; Kaiser; Gentry and Wellum, 456–59). Thus, David's final words before death unpack his hope for this deliverer to work justice, overcome the curse, and establish a new creation (23:3–7).

Accounting for the royal son's potential for sin (7:14) and Solomon's belief that his temple fulfills God's promise that David's son would build Yahweh's "house" (1 Kings 8:18–20), Solomon initially and typologically fulfills God's promise of a royal son. Nevertheless, as with royal grants, Yahweh promised that the royal son's throne would last forever (2 Sam. 7:13, 16), insofar as the king obeyed (1 Kings 2:4). Thus, only a monarch with perfect obedience and an eternal reign would fulfill God's Davidic promises—facts manifest in the new covenant through Christ Jesus (Isa. 11:4–5; Acts 2:29–36; Gentry and Wellum, 459–80).

Other scriptural reflections on the Davidic covenant. The writing prophets identify the Savior of the Pentateuch and Former Prophets with David's seed and note that through him God will work a new exodus and new creation and reconcile many from Israel and other nations to himself (Isa. 9:7; Jer. 23:5–8; Amos 9:11–15; cf. Acts 15:16–18). The royal psalms also anticipate this Davidide, who will be Yahweh's "begotten son" (Ps. 2:7; cf. Acts 13:33), receive Yahweh's everlasting blessing (Ps. 21:6), fulfill the Davidic covenant promises (89:28–37), and inherit both the nations (2:8–9; cf. Rev. 5:9–10) and the Melchizedekian priesthood (Ps. 110:1–4; cf. Heb. 5:6).

New Covenant

The new covenant in Christ between God and his church realizes the hopes of Scripture's previous divine-human covenants. The new covenant solves the global problem of sin and death that the Adamic-Noahic covenant creates. It also fulfills the universal blessings promised to the patriarchs, overcomes the Mosaic administration's condemnation and realizes its restoration blessings, and embodies the Davidic kingdom hopes.

The OT terminology associated with the new covenant. Among the various labels the OT uses for the end-time relationship between Yahweh and those reconciled in Christ are "covenant" (Ezek. 16:62; Dan. 9:27; Zech. 9:11), "new covenant" (Jer. 31:31), "everlasting covenant" (Isa. 55:3; Jer. 32:40), and "covenant of peace" (Ezek. 34:25). Yahweh also tags the messianic servant himself a "covenant" (Isa. 42:6; 49:8; cf. 55:3; Dan. 9:27). The relationship is commonly associated with several other features:

- new exodus (Isa. 11:10–12, 15–16; Zech. 10:8–12; cf. Mark 1:1–3);
- new "David" (Jer. 23:5–6; 30:9; 33:15; Amos 9:11; cf. Luke 1:32–33; Rev. 5:5; 22:16);
- restoring past fortunes (Zeph. 3:20; *to a remnant of Israel/Judah:* Hosea 6:11; Joel 3:1; Amos 9:14; Zeph. 2:7; *to a remnant of other nations:* Jer. 48:47; Ezek. 16:53);
- new "heart" (Jer. 24:7; 32:39; cf. Deut. 30:6; Rom. 2:29);
- outpouring of God's Spirit (*on the messianic servant:* Isa. 42:1; 61:1; cf. Matt. 12:18–20; Luke 4:18–19; *on the people:* Isa. 32:15; Ezek. 36:27; Joel 2:28–29; cf. Acts 2:16–18);
- new "Jerusalem" (Isa. 2:2–4; 4:2–6; Jer. 3:16–17; cf. Gal. 4:25–26), which appears coterminous with a new creation (Isa. 43:19; 48:6; 65:17; 66:22; cf. Rev. 21:1–2).

From one perspective, the new covenant *affirms* Yahweh's original patriarchal covenant promises (*hēqîm bərît;* Ezek. 16:60, 62 with Lev. 26:42). But contrasting with the temporary Mosaic covenant, Christ mediates a *new, freshly initiated* covenant (*kārat bərît;* Jer. 31:31; 32:40). (For alternative approaches to Ezek. 16:59–63, see Niehaus 2:165–69; Gentry and Wellum, 585–88.) This covenant's newness brings righteousness and contrasts with the old Mosaic covenant that "brought death" and "condemnation" (Jer. 31:32; 2 Cor. 3:6–7, 9, 14). Hebrews' author notes that because of Christ the new covenant supersedes the Mosaic covenant, which is now becoming "obsolete and outdated" and "will soon disappear" (Heb. 8:6–8, 13).

The OT's depiction of the new covenant community. The prophets portray the new covenant in national terms (Jer. 31:36; Mic. 4:7; cf. 1 Pet. 2:9). Nevertheless, they also testify that the restored community includes a remnant from Israel/Judah (Isa. 10:20–22; Zeph. 2:7, 9) and—fulfilling the Abrahamic promises—many from other nations (Amos 9:12). Because of the righteous servant-person's substitutionary sacrifice and victorious resurrection (Isa. 53:10–11; Zech. 12:10; 13:1), Yahweh incorporates the latter peoples into his single people (Isa. 19:24–25; Jer. 12:16) so they enjoy new birth certificates identified with the new Jerusalem (Ps. 87) (DeRouchie, "Counting"). Thus, God counts as Abraham's offspring the single "Israel of God" (Gal. 3:29; 6:16) whom Yahweh's servant-person "Israel" justifies (Isa. 45:25; 49:3; 53:11). These peoples are Christ's church and God's new "holy nation" (1 Pet. 2:9) identified with the heavenly "Jerusalem" (Gal. 4:25–26; Heb. 12:22).

The NT sets forth how the new covenant is realized. Jesus's ministry inaugurates the new covenant and God's end-time reign that the OT anticipates (Matt. 26:28–29). Christ is Abraham's singular, male "offspring" (Gal. 3:16). Through him believers from every nation become God's children and inherit every promise (3:8, 14, 28–29) (Collins; DeRouchie and Meyer; DeRouchie, "Counting").

Many faithful evangelicals, especially in paedobaptist circles, claim that Christ has only partially inaugurated the new covenant, thus allowing both regenerate and nonregenerate covenant membership (e.g., Pratt, 172; Dumbrell, 269–72; Swain, 566–69). The use of perfect verbs in Heb. 8:6, 13, however, suggests that Christ has fully initiated (though not brought to completion) the new covenant, which means not just some but all of its members are already experiencing the internal transformation that God promised (Heb. 8:8–12; Jer. 31:31–34). Furthermore, we know that "[Christ] *has made perfect* [*teteleiōken*] forever those who are being made holy" (Heb. 10:14)—that is, those who are part of the new covenant, in whose hearts Yahweh has already put his law and whose sins he remembers "no more" (10:16–17; cf. Jer. 31:33–34). Such teaching reaffirms that only those who actually "share in Christ," the new covenant priestly mediator, "hold [their] original conviction firmly to the very end" (Heb. 3:14), for sustained sinning results in punishment (10:26–27). One does not over-realize the new covenant by stressing that membership comes only by faith in Christ's priestly-salvific work (Wellum).

Within the Abrahamic covenant, physical circumcision depicts an excising curse, marks one for God's service, and typologically foreshadows a heart circumcision that would enact the required devotion (Kline, *Oath*; DeRouchie, "Circumcision"; Meade, "Meaning," "Flesh"). Until Christ's coming, for most Israelites the sign announced only their coming punishment rather than actual loyalty. However, in his death, Jesus underwent the excising curse to which the physical circumcision pointed (Col. 2:11; cf. 1:22; Gal. 3:13; Kline, *Oath*) and secured the new covenant's sign of promised heart circumcision for those believing in him, thus identifying the new people of God as true "Jews" (Rom. 2:28–29; Phil. 3:3; Meade, "Flesh"). Baptizing believers in the triune God's name externally testifies to this inward reality (Matt. 28:19). Rather than replacing circumcision in the flesh, water baptism symbolizes primarily the believer's union with Christ in his death and resulting resurrection (Rom. 6:3–4; Col. 2:11–12) and secondarily the believer's cleansing from sin (Heb. 10:22; 1 Pet. 3:21). Because heart circumcision as the antitype is now realized among all new covenant members, physical circumcision as a type is no longer necessary (1 Cor. 7:19; Gal. 5:6).

Along with the onetime rite of water baptism, gathered members of Christ's church regularly partake of the Lord's Supper (1 Cor. 11:17–20, 22) in order to remember Christ (11:25) and receive spiritual nourishment (10:16–17; cf. John 6:53–57, 63). We eat bread signifying his body given for his people, and we drink the Lord's cup signifying the new covenant in his blood (1 Cor. 11:23–26; cf. Luke 22:20).

Summary

The Bible's story line progresses through the historical covenants between God and his people. Jesus fulfills each covenant in different ways. The Adamic-Noahic covenant with creation establishes the crisis and context of global curse and common grace out of which the other covenants clarify God's solution and saving grace. The Abrahamic covenant forecasts the hope of Christ and new creation through its conditional-yet-certain kingdom promises of land(s), seed, blessing, and divine presence. The remaining covenants clarify how God fulfilled these promises in two progressive stages. In the Mosaic covenant (stage 1) Abraham's offspring as a single nation experience blessing but then curse, which results in their exile from the promised land. The Davidic covenant recalls the promises of a royal deliverer and declares the specific line through whom he will rise. Then the new covenant (stage 2) realizes these hopes in an already/not-yet way through the person and perfect obedience of Christ Jesus, whose kingdom work overcomes the curse with universal blessing, makes Abraham the father of many nations to the ends of the earth, and reconciles all things to God through the new creation.

For fair overviews of various theological systems' understandings of how the historical covenants progress, integrate, and climax in Christ, see Merkle. For dispensationalism, see Blaising and Bock, *Israel*; *Progressive*; Saucy; Vlach. For new-covenant theology and progressive covenantalism, see Wells and Zaspel; Wellum and Parker; Gentry and Wellum. For covenant theology, see Kline, *Kingdom*; Horton; and Waters, Reid, and Muether.

See also Abraham and Abrahamic Tradition; Adam, First and Last; Ethics; Jews and Gentiles; Kingdom and King; Law

Bibliography. Beckman, G. M., *Hittite Diplomatic Texts*, ed. H. A. Hoffner Jr., 2nd ed., WAW 7 (Scholars Press, 1999); Belcher, R. P., Jr., "The Covenant of Works in the Old Testament," in Waters, Reid, and Muether, *Covenant Theology*, 63–78; Blaising, C. A., and D. L. Bock, eds., *Dispensationalism, Israel and the Church* (Zondervan, 1992); Blaising and Bock, *Progressive Dispensationalism* (Baker, 1993); Collins, C. J., "Galatians 3:16," *TynBul* 54 (2003): 75–86; Coxhead, S. R., "Deuteronomy 30:11–14 as a Prophecy of the New Covenant in Christ," *WTJ* 68 (2006): 305–20; DeRouchie, J. S., "Circumcision in the Hebrew Bible and Targums," *BBR* 14, no. 2 (2004): 175–203; DeRouchie, "Counting Stars with Abraham and the Prophets," *JETS* 58, no. 3 (2015): 445–85; DeRouchie, "From Condemnation to Righteousness," *SBJT* 18, no. 3 (2014): 87–118; DeRouchie, *How to Understand and Apply the Old Testament* (P&R, 2017); DeRouchie, "Lifting the Veil," *SBJT* 22, no. 3 (2018): 157–79; DeRouchie, "The Use of Leviticus 18:5 in Galatians 3:12," *Them* 45, no. 2 (2020): 240–59; DeRouchie, J. S., and J. C. Meyer, "Christ or Family as the 'Seed' of Promise?," *SBJT* 14, no. 3 (2010): 36–48; Dumbrell, W. J., *Covenant and Creation*, 2nd ed. (Paternoster, 2013); Eichrodt, W., *Theology of the Old Testament*, trans. J. A. Baker, 2 vols., OTL (Westminster, 1961, 1967); Gentry, P. J., and S. J. Wellum, *Kingdom through Covenant*, 2nd ed. (Crossway, 2018); Hamilton, J. M., Jr., "The Seed of the Woman and the Blessing of Abraham," *TynBul* 58 (2007): 253–73; Horton, M., *Introducing Covenant Theology* (Baker Academic, 2006); Hugenberger, G. P., *Marriage as a Covenant* (Baker, 1994); Kaiser, W. C., Jr., "The Blessing of David," in *The Law and The Prophets*, ed. J. H. Skilton (P&R, 1974), 298–318; Kitchen, K. A., *On the Reliability of the Old Testament* (Eerdmans, 2003); Kline, M. G., *By Oath Consigned* (Eerdmans, 1968); Kline, *Kingdom Prologue* (Wipf & Stock, 2006); Knoppers, G. N., "Ancient Near Eastern Royal Grants and the Davidic Covenant," *JAOS* 116 (1996): 670–97; Meade, J. D., "Circumcision of Flesh to Circumcision of Heart," in Wellum and Parker, *Progressive Covenantalism*, 127–58; Meade, "The Meaning of Circumcision in Israel," *SBJT* 20, no. 1 (2016): 35–54; Merkle, B. L., *Discontinuity to Continuity* (Lexham, 2020); Niehaus, J. J., *Biblical Theology*, 2 vols. (Lexham, 2014, 2017); Pratt, R. L., "Infant Baptism in the New Covenant," in *The Case for Covenantal Infant Baptism*, ed. G. Strawbridge (P&R, 2003), 156–74; Robertson, O. P., *The Christ of the Covenants* (P&R, 1980); Saucy, R., *The Case for Progressive Dispensationalism* (Zondervan, 1993); Schreiner, T. R., *Covenant and God's Purpose for the World*, SSBT (Crossway, 2017); Smothers, C. J., "In Your Mouth and in Your Heart" (PhD diss., Southern Baptist Theological Seminary, 2018); Swain, S. R., "New Covenant Theologies," in Waters, Reid, and Muether, *Covenant Theology*, 551–69; Van Pelt, M. V., "The Noahic Covenant of the Covenant of Grace," in Waters, Reid, and Muether, *Covenant Theology*, 111–32; Vlach, M. J., *Dispensationalism*, 2nd ed. (Theological Studies, 2017); Waters, G. P., "The Covenant of Works in the New Testament," in Waters, Reid, and Muether, *Covenant Theology*, 79–97; Waters, G. P., J. N. Reid, and J. R. Muether, eds., *Covenant Theology* (Crossway, 2020); Weinfeld, M., "The Covenant of Grant in the Old Testament and the Ancient Near East," *JAOS* 90 (1970): 184–203; Wells, T., and F. G. Zaspel, *New Covenant Theology* (New Covenant Media, 2002); Wellum, S. J., "The New Covenant Work of Christ," in *From Heaven He Came and Sought Her*, ed. D. Gibson and J. Gibson (Crossway, 2013), 517–40; Wellum, S. J., and B. E. Parker, eds., *Progressive Covenantalism* (B&H Academic, 2016); Williamson, P. R., *Abraham, Israel, and the Nations*, JSOTSup 315 (Sheffield Academic, 2001); Williamson, *Sealed with an Oath*, NSBT 23 (InterVarsity, 2007).

JASON S. DEROUCHIE

Creation

The NT, along with early Judaism at large, presupposes that God is "the Maker of heaven and earth" (Ps. 146:6; see, e.g., Mark 10:6; Acts 17:24–31; 1 Cor. 8:6; Heb. 11:3; Rev. 4:11). Thus, even when an explicit OT citation is not in view, the creation theology of the OT profoundly shapes NT theology. The OT, of course, has creation at its very foundation: "In the beginning God made the heavens and the earth" (Gen. 1:1). While the narration of primal events did not always employ the seven-day schema of Genesis (see, e.g., Ps. 104), God's act of calling things into being is presupposed throughout the remainder of the OT. Thus, in the flood narrative, for instance, the rain from above coupled with inundation from below represents a reversal of the separation of the waters in Gen. 1. The flood is a kind of de-creation, followed by a new creation in which dry land appears (8:14), and Noah and his family are commanded like Adam and Eve to "be fruitful and multiply" (8:17). In the same way, the seminal event of the exodus involves the wind/Spirit of God blowing over the waters so that dry land appears as the gateway to new life for Israel.

Synoptic Gospels

Jesus's ministry as depicted in the Synoptics reflects an OT/Jewish affirmation of God's ongoing concern for the world he has created. God's providential care for the world is particularly evident in texts like Matt. 6:25–34.

The creation accounts in Genesis play an important role in Jesus's marriage ethic. When some Pharisees ask Jesus if a man may divorce his wife for any reason, he replies, "Haven't you read . . . that at the beginning the Creator 'made them male and female,' and said, 'For this reason a man will leave his father and mother and be united to his wife, and the two will become one flesh?' So they are no longer two, but one flesh. Therefore what God has joined together, let no one separate" (Matt. 19:4–6). The advent of the kingdom of God does not mean the renunciation of the created order but rather a return to God's initial plan for marriage as articulated in Genesis.

The follow-up discussion has important implications for Jesus's view of the Law in relation to creation. When the Pharisees protest that Moses permitted divorce, Jesus says, "Moses permitted you to divorce your wives because your hearts were hard. But it was not this way from the beginning" (Matt. 19:8). This anticipates Paul's more detailed analysis of the Law as an interim measure subject to revision upon the advent of the Messiah. God's intent revealed in the creation, rather than the Sinai covenant, sets the standard for human conduct with respect to marriage (cf. France, 713–14).

As R. S. Barbour has aptly summarized, Jesus "not only brings the marvelous newness and freshness of God's coming Kingdom (already mysteriously present); he also brings the original, primal, rightness of things, which any man who is really human can recognize, into focus once more. In Him the old and the new become one without confusion and without separation; and that is the secret of the Kingdom" (31–32).

Jesus's control over the created order is an important theme in the Synoptics, and the so-called nature miracles are saturated with OT imagery. The feeding of the five thousand (Matt. 14:13–21; Mark 6:30–44; Luke 9:10–17; John 6:1–15) has overtones of the exodus account (a point made explicit in John's account [John 6:1–15]). The curious miracle of walking on the water (Matt. 14:22–33; Mark 6:45–52; John 6:16–21; curious in that it does not directly meet a human need, as is the case in almost all the other mighty works) finds its significance by way of allusion to Job 9, a passage centered on the power and inscrutability of God as revealed in his creative acts. When we read that Jesus came to the disciples "walking upon the sea" (Matt. 14:25 ESV), this is an almost verbatim note from Job 9:8 LXX; even more interesting is the detail in Mark 6:48 that Jesus "meant to pass by them" (ESV); the verb here, *parelthein*, is the same one used in Job 9:11 LXX: "If [God] should *pass me by* I would not know it" (AT; cf. also YHWH "passing by" Moses in Exod. 33:18–19). Thus, characteristics ascribed to God in Job are here predicated of Jesus—a powerful example of the often subtle high Christology to be found in the Synoptics (cf. Edwards, 197–99). A similar point, equally dependent on a recognition of the OT, is made in the other sea miracle: the stilling of the storm. When the disciples cry out, "Who then is this, that even the wind and the sea obey him?" (Matt. 8:27 AT; Mark 4:41; Luke 8:25), the thoughtful reader is meant to answer this by recourse to texts like Ps. 107:28–29: "Then they cried out to the LORD in their trouble, and he brought them out of their distress. He stilled the storm to a whisper; the waves of the sea were hushed." Again, Jesus is said to do what only YHWH can do.

The creation ordinance of the *Sabbath* also plays a critical role in the Synoptics (and John will in typical fashion tease out in greater detail some of that toward which the Synoptics gesture). Jesus keeps the Sabbath to the extent that he can serve as a popular teacher in the milieu of first-century Judaism, yet he offers some pointed challenges to contemporary attitudes to its observance. His own attitude is aptly summed up in the conclusion to the incident of the disciples plucking grain on the Sabbath: "The Sabbath was made for man, not man for the Sabbath. So the Son of Man is Lord even of the Sabbath" (Mark 2:27–28). On the one hand, Jesus privileges the love command and human need over a hyperscrupulous assessment of Sabbath practice; at the same time, he declares that as the Son of Man (a reference to Dan. 7:13; he also makes a transparent allusion to his status as Davidic Messiah by referring to 1 Sam. 21:1–5) he is the ultimate arbiter of appropriate Sabbath practice (cf. Edwards, 96–97).

Jesus's Sabbath *healings* make a profound theological point, most clearly seen in the healing of the bent-over woman in Luke 13:10–17. Jesus first shows an awareness of inner-Jewish debate when he refers to people watering oxen and donkeys on the Sabbath (Luke 13:15; cf. Deut. 5:14; m. Eruv. 2:1–6; Marshall, 558–59). More critically, he insists that it is perfectly fitting for the woman to be healed on the Sabbath (note the "ought" in ESV of v. 16; the verb *dei* could equally be rendered "must" or "is necessary"), since she has been deprived by Satan of truly celebrating the goodness of God's creation, one of the pillars of OT Sabbath observance (Exod. 20:11; the other rationale, the *deliverance* from bondage in Egypt [Deut. 5:15], could of course equally apply in her case). Jesus is bringing creation to its appointed goal.

Of course, this mission ultimately involves Jesus's death, and it is significant that this death implicates the created order as well. This is seen most dramatically in Matthew. Prior to his crucifixion, Jesus details the cosmic disturbances that will attend his return: "Immediately after the distress of those days 'the sun will be darkened, and the moon will not give its light; the stars will fall from the sky, and the heavenly bodies will be shaken'" (Matt. 24:29). This celestial dissolution draws upon several OT texts, including Isa. 34:4, Ezek. 32:7, and Joel 2:1–10, all of which make the point that judgmental de-creation precedes redemptive re-creation (cf. France, 921–23). What Matthew brings out with particular force is how the death of Jesus itself initiates a prelude of this cosmic catastrophe: the sun fails to shine (Matt. 27:45), and the earth quakes and tombs split open, followed by a proto-resurrection (27:50–54). The entire sequence is modeled after Ezek. 37 (cf. Senior, "Death") and suggests that the death of Jesus mysteriously inaugurates the end-time de-creation and restoration. As Isaac Watts brilliantly captures in his hymn "Alas and Did My Savior Bleed," "Well might the sun in darkness hide and shut his glories in / When Christ the mighty maker died for man the creature's sin."

Gospel of John

John is arguably the greatest single resource for creation theology in the NT. He begins with a transparent allusion to Gen. 1: "In the beginning was the Word, and the Word was with God, and the Word was God. . . . Through him all things were made" (John 1:1, 3). John thus sees Jesus as the creation-bringing divine utterance of Gen. 1, with an assist from Ps. 33:6, "By the *word* of the LORD the heavens were made." John then makes note of the *light* Jesus brings, which is neither *understood* nor *overcome* by sinful humanity (John 1:5, 10). This is a creative reading of Gen. 1 that moves imperceptibly from Jesus's involvement in primal creation to the fresh creative word he utters throughout his public ministry (cf. McDonough), and from material realities (the separation of literal light and darkness in the beginning) to spiritual or relational realities (the separation of believers and unbelievers that is such a prominent feature of the subsequent narrative).

Since Jesus is the eternal Word of God, his mighty works in John can be seen as both the restoration of primal creation (as Barbour suggests) and as the inauguration of new creation. Thus, the "first of [Jesus's] signs," turning water into wine at the wedding feast in Cana (John 2:1–12), serves as a present blessing to the nuptials of the young couple and as a transparent allusion to the "new wine" of the kingdom, which will culminate in the messianic banquet in the new heavens and earth (cf. Mark 2:22; here, as often, John is best read against a presumed background of the Synoptic tradition; see Bauckham, *Testimony*).

This is seen even more dramatically in the healing of the man born blind. Jesus's words first recall the light motif from John's prologue and Gen. 1: "While I am in the world, I am the light of the world" (John 9:5). Jesus's unusual healing technique—making mud and smearing it on the man's eyes—evokes the creation of mankind; while the word for "mud," *pēlos*, does not appear in the LXX of Gen. 1 or 2, it does show up as a cipher for the stuff of humanity in numerous other LXX texts (e.g., 2 Kgdms. 22:43; Ps. 17:43 [ET 18:42]; Job 10:9; 30:19; 33:6); it also represents humanity in Qumran (1QS 11.22; 1QH[a] 9.23; 11.25; 18.5–6) and secular Greek texts (Aristophanes, *Av.* 686; Epictetus, *Diatr.* 4.11.27).

Finally, we may note the central thread of *Sabbath* in John's Gospel. As in the Synoptics, Sabbath healings (including the healing of the blind man above) are a flashpoint of controversy between Jesus and his opponents. When the Jerusalem authorities confront him over the Sabbath healing of the paralytic, Jesus responds, "My Father is always at his work to this day, and I too am working" (John 5:17). The idea that God can work on the Sabbath seems to have been accepted by at least some rabbis: "'Wretch! Is not a man permitted to carry on the Sabbath in his own courtyard?' He replied, 'Yes.' Whereupon they said to him, 'Both the higher and lower regions are the courtyard of God, as it says, *The whole earth is full of His glory* (Isa. VI, 3), and even if a man carries a distance of his own height, does he transgress?' The others agreed. 'Then,' said they, 'it is written, *Do I not fill heaven and earth?*'" (Exod. Rab. 30.9, cited in Barrett, 256).

Equally important is the fact that Jesus repeatedly discusses the *work* he is doing on earth (e.g., John 4:34; 17:4). This climaxes in his declaration on the cross, "It is finished" (19:30). We might suspect that a Gospel that begins with a reference to Gen. 1 and repeatedly speaks of Jesus working would culminate in some sort of Sabbath. This is confirmed in the very next verse: John 19:31 twice mentions the Sabbath (necessitating the need for speeding up the death of Jesus). Jesus's re-creative work culminates in his death on the cross.

Romans

Concerns with creation bookend the first major section of Romans, chaps. 1–8. Although Paul does not overtly cite Genesis in his opening salvo against gentile sin, God's creation of the world is the foundation for his critique: gentiles are without excuse for their sin, "for since the creation of the world God's invisible qualities—his eternal power and divine nature—have been clearly seen, being understood from what has been made" (1:20). The root sin of the gentiles is idolatry, which is again directly linked to the creation: "They exchanged the truth about God for a lie, and worshiped and served created things rather than the Creator—who is forever praised. Amen" (1:25). It is likely that Paul singles out homosexual acts for extended treatment because his Jewish readers would have perceived them to be contrary to the created sexual order (1:26–27; cf. Moo, 113–17). While there is continued debate about precisely what sort of knowledge people can glean about God from looking at the world, it is clear that Paul brings gentile sinners to account on the basis of God's creation of all things.

Creation is certainly relevant to the intervening chapters—note especially how Paul characterizes Abraham's God as one "who gives life to the dead and calls into being things that were not" (4:17), an early affirmation of the doctrine of creation *ex nihilo*. But Paul brings the theme to the fore once more in chap. 8: "The creation waits in eager expectation for the children of God to be revealed" since it "was subjected to frustration, not by its own choice, but by the will of the one who subjected it" (Rom. 8:19–20) and cannot be freed from its futility until humanity is put in the right with God. Although the precise language of futility does not appear in Gen. 3 (Paul's use of *mataiotēs* here may result from its prominence in the LXX of Qoheleth), the reality of it does, and it is likely Paul had that curse passage in mind as he wrote Rom. 8 (cf. Moo, 515–16).

First Corinthians

While 1 Corinthians can appear as a hodgepodge of passages directed to the congregation's myriad problems, it is in fact a cohesive message centered on the need to emulate Christ in our loving service to one another. One of the subtle threads that ties the letter together is creation. In the course of questioning the Corinthians' commitment to social status and recommending the cross as the antidote to such thinking, Paul alludes to creation *ex nihilo*: "God chose the lowly things of this world and the despised things—and the things that are not—to nullify the things that are, so that no one may boast before him" (1:28–29). God's exaltation of social "nobodies" (like most of the Corinthians!) is predicated on his power to create things out of nothing.

Creation is also in view in one of Paul's most audacious christological formulas: 1 Cor. 8:6 reads (literally), "But for us one God, the Father, from whom are all things and we to him; and one Lord, Jesus Christ, through whom are all things and we through him." While the diction is terse, the second half refers to the common early Christian confession that Christ was the agent of creation (see McDonough, esp. 150–71). The audacity lies in Paul's reworking of the foundational Jewish confession, the Shema of Deut. 6:4: "Hear, O Israel: The LORD our God, the LORD is one." Jesus as "Lord" is thus incorporated into the divine identity (Bauckham, *Crucified*, 28). Paul's point in context is that Jesus has been the vehicle of God's blessings since the beginning; thus, Paul states in 10:4 that the water-giving rock in the wilderness wanderings *was* Christ (and the high Christology theme is reinforced, as the "rock" also alludes to the designation of God in Deut. 32:4).

In 1 Cor. 11, Paul applies the binitarian creation formula of 8:6 to worship practices in Corinth. The passage has been the source of much debate concerning its implications for relationships between the sexes, and we cannot solve that problem here (if anywhere). But we should at least note that, for Paul, the creation coming "from" the Father and "through" the Son is mirrored in the woman coming "from" the man and the man "through" the woman (drawing especially on the narrative in Gen. 2:21–23).

The letter climaxes with Paul's extensive discussion of the resurrection in 1 Cor. 15, a passage filled with creation motifs. He summarizes God's program for history in vv. 20–28, and he begins naturally enough with Adam, and particularly his role in the introduction of universal death. The solution to this dilemma in Christ involves one of Paul's most subtle but powerful OT allusions: "For he must reign until he has put all his enemies under his feet. The last enemy to be destroyed is death. For he 'has put everything under his feet'" (15:25–27). Note the double appearance of the phrase "under his feet"—this is a classic example of *gezerah shawah*, a Jewish exegetical technique by which two (or more) passages are brought together on the basis of common vocabulary. The first reference to "under his feet" comes from Ps. 110, the second from Ps. 8, and the juxtaposition is of the utmost theological importance. Psalm 110 is the quintessential messianic psalm quoted numerous times in the NT, including by Jesus himself (Matt. 22:44; Mark 12:36): "The LORD says to my Lord, 'Sit at my right hand until I make your enemies your footstool'" (ESV). Psalm 8, meanwhile, evokes Gen. 1 and extols God for his glory as it is revealed in his creation of the cosmos. The psalm highlights the central role of humanity in the creation narrative and marvels that God has "put all things under his feet" (v. 6 ESV). By putting these two texts together, Paul makes the point that the Messiah's mission consists in bringing the creation project (to use Colin Gunton's term) to its goal.

Creation theology rooted in the OT also informs Paul's discussion of the nature of our resurrected bodies. A resurrected body may seem unthinkable to a sophisticated "spiritual" Greek person, but such a one should consider that God gives bodies to each thing as he desires (15:38). Since that includes the universally revered heavenly bodies (1 Cor. 15:40–41; cf. Gen. 1:14), skeptics should realize that giving believers a glorified resurrection body is well within God's demonstrated capabilities. The introduction of the heavenly bodies is likely occasioned by Dan. 12:3 in his passage on the resurrection: "Those who are wise will shine like the brightness of the heavens; and those who lead many to righteousness, like the stars forever and ever." Adam's merely earthly nature (1 Cor. 15:45; cf. Gen. 2:7) cannot attain to the glory of God; we need a body able to withstand the outpouring of God's spirit, and this can only be given to us by the man "from heaven," Jesus (15:47–49 ESV; note also the "image" language drawn from Gen. 1:26; 5:1–3).

The upshot of all this for the present day is that the work of the Corinthians in the Lord is not *in vain*—the threat of vanity pervades 1 Cor. 15 (see vv. 2, 10, 14, 17, 29–32), and its reversal here is (as in Rom. 8) in deliberate contrast to the curse on human labor in Gen. 3.

Colossians

Creation is a crucial leitmotif in Colossians. Even before the creation-centered "hymn to Christ," Paul twice makes use of Gen. 1:28: The gospel is "bearing fruit and growing" in the whole world (Col. 1:6), a Greek translation of the Hebrew verbs for "being fruitful and multiplying" in Genesis. The progress of the gospel in Paul's day represents a new-covenant fulfillment of the command to Adam and Eve. Paul then prays that the Colossians will be "bearing fruit in every good work and increasing in the knowledge of God" (1:10 ESV), using the same verbs as in v. 6.

The "hymn" in 1:15–20 begins with God creating the world through Christ, and then expresses his redemptive work in strict parallelism with this creative work (McDonough, 172–91). The "image" language in v. 15 recalls the creation account, though here Christ is likely seen as the proto-image in whose likeness Adam is created (see below on 3:10, and Stettler); the vision of the enthroned God in Ezek. 1 may have also contributed to Paul's thought here, as Ezekiel reports that "high above on the throne was a figure like that of a man" (Ezek. 1:26). The repeated use of "everything" in the hymn shows the cosmic scope of God's creative and redemptive work through Christ.

Finally, the creation narrative grounds Paul's ethical instructions in Col. 3. The Colossians are to "take off" the "old [man]" with its deceptive and malicious practices and "put on the new [man], which is being renewed in knowledge in the image of its Creator" (3:9–10). The allusion to Gen. 1:26 is evident. But Paul now has in view the *new creation*, the restoration of the full image and likeness which was tarnished by the fall. The fact that this "new [man]" currently exists side by side, so to speak, with the "old [man]" shows an already/not-yet dynamic that pervades the NT's teaching on the new creation of the person. Thus, in this passage, the Colossians are said to be already "raised with Christ" (3:1). In a similar way, Jesus can say, "A day is coming *and now is* when the dead will hear the voice of the Son of God and the ones who hear will live" (John 5:25 AT); and Paul can write to the Corinthians that "if anyone is in Christ, there is a new creation" (2 Cor. 5:17 NRSV).

Pastoral Epistles

The Pastoral Epistles are often dismissed by modern critics as the work of late first-century ecclesiastical busybodies looking to clamp down on a chaotic, charismatic church. A recognition of the creation theology that lies behind the Pastorals can give us a renewed appreciation for their function in the canon. In essence, the Pastorals remind us that even in the dawning of the new age, the rhythms of the initial creation remain relevant for the life of the church. This is evident in the well-known passage concerning a woman's need to learn "in all submissiveness" in 1 Tim. 2:9–15. The precise nature of such "submission" and its place in the contemporary church continue to be debated, and we need not solve that question here—but the critical thing is that Paul believes the primal events of the creation still have a bearing on the church. His rationale for a woman not "having authority over a man" is that "Adam was formed first, then Eve. And Adam was not deceived; it was the woman who was deceived and became a transgressor" (2:13–14 AT). The question of how "childbearing" is meant to "save" the woman is equally vexing (2:15), but Paul may be alluding to the protevangelium in Gen. 3:15, where the seed of the woman will crush the serpent's head, a promise that the NT seems to couple with the messianic birth of Isa. 7:14; 66:7 (cf. Rev. 12; Mounce, 143–49).

An equally critical allusion to Genesis undergirds Paul's affirmation of marriage and food in 1 Tim. 4:4:

"For everything God created is good, and nothing is to be rejected if it is received with thanksgiving." The notion of creation's *goodness* is clearly rooted in Gen. 1 and serves as a counter to the world-renouncing practice of some in Timothy's congregation. But the significance of the citation goes beyond marriage and food. Coupled with 1 Tim. 2, the positive note on created order provides the theological basis for Paul's instruction throughout the Pastorals: because God's creation was *and remains* fundamentally good, the church is not to slough off created realities as irrelevant to their faith and practice. To take but one example, while differences between male and female may be *relativized to some degree* in the present (Gal. 3:28), and while those differences may in some sense obsolesce at the end of time (Matt. 22:30), we still live at present in the good creation of Gen. 1, and this created order is to be respected.

Hebrews

With respect to creation, Hebrews lives within the tension between the present "shakable" world order and the "unshakable" order to come. The author handles this tension with great subtlety. He begins by affirming that God made "the ages" through Christ (Heb. 1:2 AT). (He also includes the detail from Ps. 2:8 that Christ is the "heir of all things," and gives us the only direct statement of the creation of angels in 1:7.) Thus, the present age is not dismissed as worthless (God is the one "through whom and on account of whom all things exist" [2:10 AT], and Jesus is worthy of honor as the builder of God's "house" [3:3; cf. Num. 12:7]), but it is seen as the stepping stone to the greater age to come.

The crucial verses are 12:26–27: "His voice shook the earth then, and now he has promised, saying, 'Yet once more I will shake not only the earth but also the heaven.' By 'yet once more' he signifies the removal of what can be shaken, as of created things in order that what cannot be shaken may remain" (AT). The OT background is key to understanding this text. "Yet once more I will shake" is drawn from Hag. 2:6, but the notion of an unshakable world comes from the LXX of Pss. 92:1 and 95:10: both contain "the world which will not be shaken" (*tēn oikoumenēn hētis ou saleuthēsetai*). The author of Hebrews appears to have concluded from a comparison of Haggai and the Psalms that there must be two worlds: the present shakable one, and a future unshakable one, the age to come.

James

James roots his well-known imperatives in a rich theology of God's *unity*, which is meant to be mirrored in the cohesion of the community and the integrity of believers' lives. Central to this theology is God's power and goodness as revealed in creation. James wants his listeners' faith to be rooted in the perfect goodness and generosity of the giving God: "Every good gift and every perfect gift is from above, coming down from the Father of lights, who does not change like shifting shadows. He chose to give us birth through the word of truth, that we might be a kind of firstfruits of his creatures" (1:17–18 AT). The expression "Father of lights" likely refers to God's creation of the heavenly bodies in Gen. 1:14 (cf. Martin, 40–41). The meanings of "word of truth" and "firstfruits of his creatures" are debated, with some seeing a reference to the primal creation of humans and others to the life-giving power of the gospel. The latter seems more likely in context (especially given the prominence of the "word" of the gospel throughout the NT), but in either case the emphasis lies on God's creative speech as first articulated in Gen. 1 (cf. Martin, 40–41).

The creation narratives deeply inform James's account of speech ethics in chap. 3. He notes ironically that although humans have tamed every animal, they have not yet found a way to tame their own tongues (3:7–8; cf. Gen. 1:28). When he condemns a split tongue that blesses God while cursing fellow humans, he unmasks this hypocrisy by reference to the creation of Adam in the beginning: "With the tongue we praise our Lord and Father, and with it we curse human beings, who have been made in God's likeness" (James 3:9). Notably, he does not distinguish here between believers and unbelievers: for James, people at large remain those created in the image of God, and therefore they must be treated with respect.

Revelation

It is appropriate that the canon's final book should bring the promise of its first book to fruition. God is praised as Creator at key points in Revelation (4:11; 14:7), and the book reaches its climax with a vision of Eden restored and enhanced: "Then the angel showed me the river of the water of life, as clear as crystal, flowing from the throne of God and of the Lamb down the middle of the great street of the city. On each side of the river stood the tree of life, bearing twelve crops of fruit, yielding its fruit every month. And the leaves of the tree are for the healing of the nations" (22:1–2).

See also Adam, First and Last; Consummation

Bibliography. Barbour, R. S., "Creation, Wisdom, and Christ," in *Creation, Christ, and Culture,* ed. R. W. A. McKinney (T&T Clark, 1976), 22–42; Barrett, C. K., *The Gospel according to St. John* (Westminster, 1978); Bauckham, R., *God Crucified* (Eerdmans, 1998); Bauckham, *The Testimony of the Beloved Disciple* (Baker Academic, 2007); Beale, G. K., *A New Testament Biblical Theology* (Baker Academic, 2011); Edwards, J. R., *The Gospel according to Mark,* PNTC (Eerdmans, 2002); "Exodus Rabbah," in *Midrash Rabbah,* trans. S. M. Lehrman (Soncino, 1939), 3:1–581; France, R. T., *The Gospel of Matthew,* NICNT (Eerdmans, 2007); Gunton, C. E., *The Triune Creator* (T&T Clark, 2001); Marshall, I. H., *The Gospel of Luke,* NIGTC (Eerdmans, 1978); Martin, R. P., *James,* WBC

(Zondervan, 1988); McDonough, S. M., *Christ as Creator* (Oxford University Press, 2009); Moo, D., *The Epistle to the Romans,* NICNT (Eerdmans, 1996); Mounce, W., *Pastoral Epistles,* WBC (Thomas Nelson, 2000); Senior, D., "The Death of Jesus and the Resurrection of the Holy Ones (Mt 27:51–53)," *CBQ* 38 (1976): 312–29; Senior, *The Passion of Jesus in the Gospel of Matthew* (Liturgical Press, 1990); Stettler, C., *Der Kolosserhymnus* (Mohr Siebeck, 2000).

SEAN MCDONOUGH

Curses, Covenant

See Covenant

D

Daniel, Book of

In the sixth century BC, a young Israelite named Daniel emerges in biblical history, and his story unfolds over a decades-long exile to Babylon. The Babylonian army takes him captive in 605 BC, when he is a teenager, and he gives his final prophecy in 536 BC (Dan. 10:1), when he is in his eighties. The book does not refer to his parents or any siblings, but it showcases his faith and providential positions in pagan administrations. When the book opens, Babylon is in power, but Daniel's life extends through Babylon's fall to the Medo-Persians in 539 BC. Although exiled from the promised land, Daniel does not return once the Medo-Persians permit the Israelites to rebuild and restore their former lives. In this book, Daniel becomes an exile and probably dies outside the land of promise (1:6; 12:13).

Essential Features of the Book of Daniel

Composition. The book of Daniel is from the hand of the man whose name it bears. There is no compelling evidence that another author is more likely than he. First-person references in the visionary sections (e.g., 7:2; 8:1; 9:2; 10:2) provide an internal claim to Danielic authorship. He completed the composition of the book sometime after his final vision, in 536 BC (10:1), though he wrote parts of the book earlier (7:1).

Some scholars have been skeptical of a sixth-century composition because of the detailed prophecies, and according to these scholars, such historical predictions indicate composition after the events themselves (see Greidanus, 5–8). Prophecies in Dan. 8 and 11 speak of future Greek activities and victories centuries after the prophet lived, so higher-critical scholars assert a second-century BC date of composition (Goldingay, 206–7). But this assertion presumes an anti-supernatural posture toward the book. Jesus treated the prophet Daniel as a historical figure who prophesied (Matt. 24:15). With a presupposition that treats the book of Daniel as historical and canonical, readers will be engaging a work composed in the sixth century BC that both reports events contemporary with the prophet and foretells events far beyond his day.

Structure. Scholars consistently observe the Hebrew-Aramaic-Hebrew design in the book of Daniel. Chapters 1 and 8–12 frame an Aramaic section (chaps. 2–7). This Aramaic section is a chiasmus (Gentry, 26–28). Chapter 1 provides the background to Daniel's presence in Babylon, and it illustrates his faithfulness to Yahweh, a key theme in the book. The Aramaic chiasm then unfolds like this:

- A Four earthly kingdoms and God's everlasting kingdom (Dan. 2)
  - B The deliverance of the faithful from judgment (Dan. 3)
    - C Judgment on Babylonian arrogance (Dan. 4)
    - C′ Judgment on Babylonian arrogance (Dan. 5)
  - B′ The deliverance of the faithful from judgment (Dan. 6)
- A′ Four earthly kingdoms and God's everlasting kingdom (Dan. 7)

After the Aramaic chiasmus, the language returns to Hebrew (Dan. 8–12). These final chapters are also a chiasmus (Chase, "Daniel," 25, 106–7):

- A A vision about Persia and Greece (Dan. 8)
  - B The promise of ultimate Jubilee (Dan. 9)
- A′ A vision about Persia and Greece (Dan. 10–12)

The genre shifts from primarily narrative (chaps. 1–6) to primarily prophecy (chaps. 7–12). In Dan. 1–6, there are six stories—one per chapter—that move forward chronologically. In chap. 1, Daniel is faithful during his recent exile to a foreign land. In chap. 2, Daniel interprets the Babylonian king Nebuchadnezzar's dream about present and future empires that lead to the establishment of a heavenly kingdom. In chap. 3, Shadrach, Meshach, and Abednego show steadfastness, like their friend Daniel, and miraculously emerge from a fiery furnace. In chap. 4, the Lord humbles the self-exalting Nebuchadnezzar, who finally extols the power and justice of God. In chap. 5, the Babylonian king Belshazzar presides over a banquet where God's judgment is revealed through ominous writing on a wall. In chap. 6, during the new administration of the Medo-Persians, God delivers Daniel from a den of lions that conspirators have manipulated the king into using as a royal punishment.

Then the chronology resets as Dan. 7–12 begins (7:1; 8:1; 9:1; 10:1). This second set of six chapters contains four visions (chaps. 7; 8; 9; 10–12), with the fourth being the longest vision as well as the conclusion to the book. In chap. 7, Daniel sees a vision of four earthly empires that are inferior to the everlasting reign of one like a son of man. In chap. 8, Daniel sees a vision about the Greeks conquering the Persians as well as about a future Greek king who will severely persecute the people of God. In chap. 9, while Daniel is interceding for the Israelites and confessing their sins, Gabriel reveals that the greatest act of atonement and Jubilee will be accomplished by the Messiah in the distant future. In chaps. 10–12, Daniel receives a vision connecting again to the future Greek victory over the Persians, and it expands on the malicious Greek king who will oppose and terrorize the people of God.

Message. The book of Daniel reports faithfulness in the face of exile with hope for deliverance on both the near and far horizons. On the near horizon, Daniel himself will live through the exile and the Israelites' release from captivity. His contemporaries can trust that God has not forgotten the captive Israelites and will bring them back to the land of promise. On the far horizon, the people need a deliverance deeper than any mere political ruler can bring. One day God will establish an everlasting kingdom, accomplish atonement for sinners, and bring about the ultimate vindication for God's people through resurrection and judgment. The message of the book, therefore, is primarily for those beyond the days of Daniel. He is told to seal his book (12:4, 9), for its various prophecies pertain to later times. The miraculous deliverances and the promise of future resurrection should shape the obedience of the readers so that they live for the praise of God amid the snares and sufferings intrinsic to life in earthly kingdoms.

Daniel and the OT

The book of Daniel has thematic and lexical links to earlier parts of the OT, particularly the Pentateuch. Due to young Daniel's faithfulness to God, he evidently is well steeped in prior divine revelation. The narratives and prophecies of his book confirm his biblical convictions and biblical worldview. The following six examples illustrate how the book of Daniel connects to earlier parts of the OT.

Covenant curses. In the opening chapter of the book, Nebuchadnezzar's army comes against the city of Jerusalem to besiege it (1:1–2). God has warned about the rise of a foreign adversary in the covenant curses of the Pentateuch (Lev. 26:31–33; Deut. 28:49–50). The Lord gives Judah's king into Nebuchadnezzar's hand, along with vessels from the Jerusalem temple (Dan. 1:2). The first two verses of the book narrate God's faithfulness to judge his law-rejecting, idol-worshiping people. According to the book of Daniel, then, God is faithful to bring about what he promised in the days of Moses. If the covenant curses of the Pentateuch are not understood as part of the background to 1:1–2, the reader will not sense the impact of how the story of Daniel begins.

Later in the book, after the Medo-Persians defeat the Babylonians, the prophet Daniel is praying (Dan. 9:1–3). His prayer reflects the awareness of promised judgments—covenant curses—that God would bring upon the rebellious Israelites. Daniel's prayer highlights the rejection of God's prophets (9:6, 10) and the consequent curse of exile that Moses speaks about in the Pentateuch (9:11–12). The covenant curses (Lev. 26; Deut. 28) foretell the state of calamity that Daniel is living through (Dan. 9:13–14).

The sovereignty of God. The book of Daniel exalts the living God as sovereign over all people, all things, all events. The Lord gives Judah into Babylonian captivity (1:2). He grants wisdom and discernment to Daniel and Daniel's friends (1:17). He raises up empires and brings down kings (2:21; 4:33; 5:30–31). He makes known the future because he has decreed what will happen (2:22, 28). He thwarts the murderous plots against his people (3:25–27; 6:22–23). He reveals to Daniel that a future figure will have comprehensive and everlasting dominion (7:13–14). Not even death will prove beyond God's power (12:2–3). Everyone who lives—including their very breath—is in the hands of the living God (5:23).

The divine sovereignty in the book of Daniel is consistent with earlier biblical depictions of God. He made the heavens and earth from nothing (Gen. 1:1–31), he flooded the earth (6:9–8:19), he gave life to Sarah's barren womb (21:1–2), and he sent Joseph to Egypt with intentions that differed from those of Joseph's malicious brothers (45:4–8; 50:20). The God of Daniel is the God of Genesis. He is also the mighty God of the exodus, who brought out his firstborn son Israel and crushed the Egyptian army with walls of water (Exod. 12–14).

His power is greater than all human obstacles, and he reigns supreme over all the gods of the nations. When readers see the revelation and wonders in the book of Daniel, they see the work of a sovereign God who has been exercising his authority on cosmic and microscopic levels since Gen. 1.

False worship. Unsurprisingly, pagan empires practice pagan worship. Nebuchadnezzar commands the worship of an image (Dan. 3:1–7), and Belshazzar praises false gods at a banquet (5:1–4). Yet in the first and second commandments that God pronounced at Mount Sinai, the Israelites are prohibited from worshiping other gods or representing the true God with images (Exod. 20:1–6). The exclusivity of true worship is a factor in the lives of Daniel and his three friends, for they face pressure to compromise and to engage in idolatry. The refusal of false worship could cost them their lives.

In Dan. 3, Daniel's friends—Shadrach, Meshach, and Abednego—face death in a fiery furnace if they refuse to bow and worship the golden image that Nebuchadnezzar has set up (Dan. 3:4–6). But they know that idolatry is wicked before the Lord. They resolve to die rather than worship what is not God (3:16–18). Later in the book, conspirators in the Persian administration seek to trap Daniel by using his Godward devotion against him. They convince the king to sign an ordinance that calls for prayer to be made only to the king for thirty days, lest the lawbreaker perish in a den of lions (6:7–9). But Daniel refuses to pray to anyone except the Lord (6:10–13). Calling upon the name of any idol, or any human king, would be idolatrous, and Daniel resolves to be faithful to God.

Shadows of Joseph. The prophet Daniel is a dream interpreter and experiences promotion and vindication in a territory outside the promised land. These features parallel the character of Joseph in Gen. 37–50 (Hamilton, 229–32). Joseph is a dream interpreter (Gen. 40–41) who experiences promotion and vindication in a territory outside the promised land (41:37–57). Although Joseph is in Egypt and Daniel is in Babylon, the similarities between these two characters are intentional. The narratives in Daniel portray the exiled prophet as a new Joseph in a foreign land.

The shadows of Joseph in the story of Daniel are confirmed by a unique expression. In Dan. 5, Belshazzar summons Daniel to interpret some spontaneous writing on a wall, and he describes Daniel as someone with "the spirit of the gods" (Dan. 5:14). Throughout the OT, the phrase "the spirit of the gods" appears elsewhere only in the Joseph narratives. After hearing the interpretation of a dream, the pharaoh says Joseph has "the spirit of the gods" (Gen. 41:38 mg.). Both Joseph and Daniel go into a form of exile when they are teenagers, and their lives of faithfulness and gift of dream interpretation invite the reader to ponder these—and other—parallels. Both men overcome the temptation to compromise their integrity, interpret the dreams of a monarch, and serve a pagan administration in a high-ranking capacity.

The end of exile. Although Daniel enters captivity under the Babylonian regime, he explains that another empire will succeed Babylon (Dan. 2:37–39). This subsequent empire is that of the Medo-Persians, who conquer Babylon in 539 BC (5:30–31; 9:1–2). With a new empire in power over the Israelites, the end of the exile arrives. During the first year that the Israelites are under the Medo-Persians, Daniel is praying that God will fulfill his promises to restore his people to their promised land (Dan. 9).

Daniel anticipates the end of exile because earlier OT statements anticipate it. In fact, before his prayer in 9:4–19, he meditates on Jeremiah's prophecies about the seventy years of judgment that God would bring to an end (9:2; Jer. 25:12). At the temple dedication, King Solomon anticipated a day when God's people would be alienated from the holy land and holy sanctuary (1 Kings 8:46). But if the exiled people would pray toward Jerusalem with confession and contrition, God would hear their prayer and restore them (8:46–51; cf. vv. 30, 33–34, 38–39). Solomon's words shape Daniel's prayer practice, for Daniel prays toward Jerusalem (Dan. 6:10).

Seventy sevens. While Daniel's intercessory prayer will be answered, the angel Gabriel appears with a revelation about a greater deliverance in the future (Dan. 9:1–23). The "seventy years" of Jeremiah are multiplied. Gabriel speaks about "seventy sevens" decreed by God that will lead to a covenant being made and atonement being accomplished (Dan. 9:24, 26–27). Daniel has been praying for the seventy-year judgment to end so that restoration and exodus from Babylon can begin. A period of "seventy sevens" prepares readers for an even greater restoration and exodus than that which Daniel's contemporaries experience in his day.

The OT background to Gabriel's revelation is Lev. 25 (Gentry, 33–34). According to the Lord, the Israelites must count seven sevens of years, with forty-nine years setting up the Year of Jubilee (Lev. 25:8). When Gabriel speaks about seventy sevens (Dan. 9:24), the Levitical background allows a multiplication of the numbers to 490 (70 × 7). If 49 years in Lev. 25 set up the Year of Jubilee, then 490 years set up a tenfold Jubilee.

Daniel and the NT

The book of Daniel is a source of teaching, quotation, and allusion for the Gospels, Acts, the Epistles, and Revelation. The following six examples illustrate such usage.

Daniel 2 and the expanding stone. During the passion week, Jesus tells a parable about wicked tenants who will face judgment for killing a vineyard owner's son (Luke 20:14–16). Jesus says the tenants' rejection of the son is what the OT said would happen: "The stone the builders rejected has become the cornerstone" (Luke 20:17, quoting Ps. 118:22). But the stone language on the lips of Jesus does not stop there. Jesus says in the next verse, "Everyone who falls on that stone will be broken to pieces; anyone on whom it falls will be crushed" (Luke 20:18).

The combination of images alludes to the interpretation of Nebuchadnezzar's dream in Dan. 2 (Steinmann, 140). According to Jesus, a stone will break people into pieces, and according to the dream of Nebuchadnezzar, a stone will break into pieces a statue of metals (Dan. 2:34–35, 45). This stone will then become a great mountain and fill the earth (2:35). The prophet Daniel interprets the stone as God's everlasting kingdom, which will subdue all other kingdoms (2:44–45).

In the parable of the tenants in Luke 20, Jesus is the son who will be killed. He is the cornerstone who will be rejected. He is also the stone who will break those who fall on him and who will crush those he falls upon. Jesus is identifying himself as the stone from Dan. 2:34–35. He is bringing the everlasting kingdom that Nebuchadnezzar dreamed about. In the ministry of Christ, the kingdom of God is at hand (Mark 1:14–15). The resurrected and ascended Christ will subject all enemies under his feet, including the last enemy—death (1 Cor. 15:25–26). The dominion of Christ—the stone—will extend over all things, like the stone (in Nebuchadnezzar's dream) that becomes a mountain and fills the earth.

The allusion by Jesus to Dan. 2:34–35 helps identify the historical empires that fulfilled Nebuchadnezzar's dream. According to 2:31–35, the Babylonian king foresees four metals (which represent four empires) and then a crushing stone (which represents God's everlasting kingdom). The identity of these metals has been a subject of dispute among interpreters (see Steinmann, 144–57). Are these four empires the Babylonians, the Medes, the Persians, and the Greeks? Or are the four empires the Babylonians, the Medo-Persians, the Greeks, and the Romans? Since Jesus is the stone that came during the reign of the Romans, the fourth kingdom in Dan. 2:31–35 must be the Roman Empire, meaning that the previous three are the Babylonian, Medo-Persian, and Greek Empires (see Josephus, *Ant.* 10.11.7).

Daniel 7 and the Son of Man. One of the NT's most used passages from the book of Daniel is 7:13–14 (see Steinmann, 355–60; Kim, 1–14). In a vision, one like a son of man comes with the clouds to the Ancient of Days and receives all dominion and authority over all peoples, nations, and languages. The picture is of heavenly exaltation and vindication. The mysterious "son of man" figure shares the authority of God and is served by the nations as God is. A royal son who exercises dominion recalls Gen. 1–2, where Adam is God's image bearer and viceregent. The son of man in Dan. 7 is an Adamic figure who fulfills the Edenic responsibility to subdue and rule.

"Son of Man" is the title Jesus most frequently attributes to himself (e.g., Mark 9:31; 10:33). At his Jewish trial, Jesus invokes Dan. 7 in front of the high priest (Hamilton, 189–90). Jesus tells him, "You will see the Son of Man sitting at the right hand of the Mighty One and coming on the clouds of heaven" (Mark 14:62). The response of the high priest confirms that Jesus's claim—if untrue—is blasphemy (14:63–64). When Jesus is crucified, the narrative teaches that the vindication of the Son of Man comes through the humiliation of the Son of Man.

Acts and Revelation also include allusions to Dan. 7:13–14. Several weeks after the resurrection of Jesus, he ascends before the eyes of his disciples, and a cloud takes him out of sight (Acts 1:9). In the book of Revelation, a vision identifies the Son of Man figure with the ascended and victorious Jesus. John sees an occupied throne, and the conquering Son of David approaches the throne (Rev. 5:1–7). Then Jesus is worshiped (5:8–12). The subsequent breaking of the seals (6:1–8:5) demonstrates the authority and dominion of Christ.

Daniel 9 and the anointed one. In the first verse of the NT, Matthew announces Jesus as "the son of David" (Matt. 1:1). As the promised king, Jesus is the anointed one, the Messiah. The hope for a son from David's line is rooted in 2 Sam. 7:12–13, where God (through Nathan the prophet) tells David that a future son will reign. The words of Gabriel to Daniel build on this prophecy of a future king (Dan. 9:24–27), and the NT announces that Jesus fulfills this role. Jesus is the anointed one who dies and establishes a new covenant (Matt. 21:9; Luke 22:20).

According to the angelic revelation in Dan. 9, a future anointed one is crucial to God's promise of a tenfold Jubilee (9:24–25). The anointed one is a covenant maker, and his work will bring an end to sacrifices (9:27; see Gentry and Wellum, 636–43). The OT era will end with this promise unfulfilled. Even though the Persians conquer the Babylonians and release the Israelites from captivity, no son of David ascends to the throne in Jerusalem during these days. Nevertheless, Dan. 9:24–27 perpetuates the hope for an anointed one.

In the Gospels, Jesus is the covenant-making anointed one. He dies with a royal title inscribed about his head (Mark 15:26). As the prophecies in Dan. 9:24 and 9:27 indicate, Jesus makes atonement for sin and ends the purpose of sacrificial offerings (Mark 15:38; John 19:30).

Daniel 10 and the apocalyptic Jesus. The opening vision of Revelation depicts a glorious and fearsome Christ. He is clothed with a long robe and has a golden sash around his chest (Rev. 1:13), his eyes are like fire (v. 14), his feet are like bronze, and his voice is mighty like the roar of many waters (v. 15). In response to this sight, John falls at his feet like a dead man, but Christ puts his hand upon John for reassurance (v. 17). This encounter alludes to Dan. 10 (Beale, 154–77).

The fourth vision in the book of Daniel (10:1–12:13) begins with a figure appearing to the prophet. Daniel beholds a man clothed in linen with a belt around his waist (10:5). This imposing figure has eyes of fire and legs of bronze; his voice is powerful (v. 6). The prophet beholds this heavenly figure and falls to the ground (v. 9). In response to Daniel's posture, the figure puts his hand upon him for reassurance (vv. 10–11).

The allusion in Rev. 1 to Dan. 10 may identify the heavenly figure (whom the OT prophet encounters) as the preincarnate Son of God (Steinmann, 497–501). But perhaps the correspondences between the figures and their actions in Dan. 10 and Rev. 1 are meant to portray the apocalyptic Christ with imposing and fearsome imagery, Dan. 10 being an appropriate source for such imagery (Hamilton, 146).

Daniel 11 and the prediction of judgment. During the days leading to his death on the cross, Jesus issues a prediction of judgment from the Mount of Olives. He tells his disciples, "So when you see standing in the holy place 'the abomination that causes desolation,' spoken of through the prophet Daniel—let the reader understand—then let those who are in Judea flee to the mountains" (Matt. 24:15–16). Interpreters dispute the meaning of Jesus's words. But if "this generation" that will witness these things (Matt. 24:34) is the generation of Jesus's contemporaries, then he is probably warning about the near-horizon destruction of Jerusalem that the Roman army will inflict in AD 70. If people do not flee from the region, they could be caught in warfare and thus killed.

The warning from Jesus explicitly mentions a prophecy of Daniel, and the language about an abomination of desolation connects the reader to Daniel's fourth vision (Dan. 10–12). In Dan. 11, the prophet hears about an insidious person who will arise to inflict terror upon God's people. "His armed forces will rise up to desecrate the temple fortress and will abolish the daily sacrifice. Then they will set up the abomination that causes desolation" (11:31). This is the source of allusion in Jesus's words (Matt. 24:15; Hamilton, 187).

After the Greeks conquer the Medo-Persians, a Greek ruler will one day arise and persecute the Israelites, profaning their sanctuary. Historically, this was fulfilled in approximately 167 BC when Antiochus IV Epiphanes profaned the Jerusalem temple and disrupted the sacrificial system. When Jesus alludes to what the prophet Daniel has prophesied, the fulfillment of Daniel's prophecy has already happened, so Jesus is invoking Daniel's prophetic words and their fulfillment in Antiochus as a pattern or type of what Jesus's own contemporaries will experience.

Just as the speaker to Daniel prophesies about a foreign army coming against the Jerusalem temple (Dan. 11:31), Jesus prophesies about an army coming against the temple (Luke 21:20–22). Just as the prophecy in the book of Daniel foretells the disruption of the sacrificial system (Dan. 11:31), Jesus prophesies that an abomination causing desolation will stand in the holy place, thus profaning the temple and disrupting the system of offerings (Matt. 24:15; Mark 13:14). As Jesus expresses his warning in this way (using the language of Dan. 11:31), the hearers and readers must know he is warning about terror coming upon the temple, just as the prophecies in the book of Daniel foretold what happened during the second century BC.

Daniel 12 and the general resurrection. The book of Daniel narrates judgments and vindications, but the ultimate hope of judgment and vindication appears at the end of the final prophecy. Near the end of Daniel's fourth vision (Dan. 10–12), the prophet hears about a day of reckoning and resurrection: "Multitudes who sleep in the dust of the earth will awake: some to everlasting life, others to shame and everlasting contempt" (12:2; see Mihalios, 31–51). The general resurrection will establish eternal states: the saints will enjoy everlasting life, but the wicked will face everlasting shame.

Jesus uses the language of Dan. 12:2 when he speaks of the future judgment that the Son of Man will execute: "Do not be amazed at this, for a time is coming when all who are in their graves will hear his voice and come out—those who have done what is good will rise to live, and those who have done what is evil will rise to be condemned" (John 5:28–29; see Mihalios, 101–23). Daniel 12:2 is the only OT text that explicitly promises a bodily resurrection for both the righteous and the wicked, making it the background to Jesus's words (see Greidanus, 388–89; Chase, "Daniel," 159). And when Jesus says, "The men of Nineveh will stand up at the judgment with this generation and condemn it" (Matt. 12:41), he is alluding again to Dan. 12:2, for "standing up" refers to rising in resurrection.

Paul alludes to Dan. 12:2 when he references "a resurrection of both the righteous and the wicked" (Acts 24:15; Steinmann, 47). The two categories—the righteous and the wicked—parallel the promise in Dan. 12:2 that some people will rise to everlasting life and others to everlasting contempt. Paul preaches a general resurrection because he believes (and uses) the words in Dan. 12:2. This Pauline conviction is confirmed by his teaching elsewhere: "For we must all appear before the judgment seat of Christ, so that each of us may receive what is due us for the things done while in the body, whether good or bad" (2 Cor. 5:10; Chase, "Influence," 129–30). Paul has clarified the meaning of Dan. 12:2. All people will rise from death in order to appear before Christ the righteous judge, and this will be the time when eternal states are established for the righteous and the wicked. The wicked will receive the wages of sin, while the righteous will enjoy the unending gift of life in Christ Jesus.

Bibliography. Beale, G. K., *The Use of Daniel in Jewish Apocalyptic Literature and in the Revelation of St. John* (Wipf & Stock, 1984); Chase, M. L., "Daniel," *Daniel–Malachi*, ESVEC 7 (Crossway, 2018), 17–169; Chase, "The Influence of Dan. 12:2 on the Pauline Epistles," *CTR* 16, no. 1 (2018): 123–32; Gentry, P. J., "Daniel's Seventy Weeks and the New Exodus," *SBJT* 14, no. 1 (2010): 26–44;

Gentry, P. J., and S. J. Wellum, *Kingdom through Covenant*, 2nd ed. (Crossway, 2018); Goldingay, J. E., *Daniel*, WBC (Nelson, 1989); Greidanus, S., *Preaching Christ from Daniel* (Eerdmans, 2012); Hamilton, J. M., *With the Clouds of Heaven* (IVP Academic, 2014); Kim, S., *The "Son of Man" as the Son of God*, WUNT 30 (J. C. B. Mohr, 1983); Mihalios, S., *The Danielic Eschatological Hour in the Johannine Literature*, LNTS (T&T Clark, 2011); Steinmann, A. E., *Daniel*, ConcC (Concordia, 2008).

MITCHELL CHASE

David *See* Messiah; Son of God

Day of the Lord

The word for "day" in both Hebrew (*yôm*) and Greek (*hēmera*) can denote either a division of time (e.g., a twenty-four-hour period), a specific historical period (e.g., the days of Noah), or a future eschatological event, such as the final judgment. The exact expression "day of the LORD" (*yôm YHWH*; *[hē] hēmera [tou] kyriou*) and related references, such as "the day," "that day," or "the last days," frequently occur in conjunction with either God's intervention in historical events (such as the locust plague in Joel) or eschatology, referring to the final judgment and the restoration of all things at the end of the age. This expression and related concepts are especially frequent in the OT prophetic corpus. NT occurrences draw upon OT eschatology as well as OT apocalyptic concepts that were developed in later Jewish apocalyptic writings. (A distinction can be made between eschatological, referring to the last things or last days, and apocalyptic, referring to a literary genre or a worldview—although the two overlap.) Although numerous older studies treat the day of the Lord, scholarly attention has dwindled of late. This may be due, in part, to questions of methodology. Some older studies limit their scope to the exact Hebrew or Greek expression (or an even smaller subset), whereas others include a matrix of related expressions, concepts, and themes.

This article first considers the expression's origin and OT usage, focusing on both explicit and implicit references within the prophetic corpus. It then briefly identifies a few developments from apocalyptic Jewish writings in the centuries leading up to the composition of the NT before surveying the NT appropriation of this concept. Finally, several implications for biblical theology and hermeneutics are presented. The focus here is on the canonical form of books discussed; hence questions of sources and redactional layers are not considered.

The Day of the Lord in the OT

The day of the Lord figures prominently in the prophetic corpus, particularly the Minor Prophets, where it is usually associated with a time of future (often imminent) judgment or restoration. The exact expression "day of the LORD" (*yôm YHWH*) occurs sixteen times: Isa. 13:6, 9; Ezek. 13:5; Joel 1:15; 2:1, 11, 31 (MT 3:4); 3:14 (MT 4:14); Amos 5:18 (2x), 20; Obad. 15; Zeph. 1:7, 14 (2x); Mal. 4:5 (MT 3:23). A few scholars limit their discussion to these occurrences (e.g., Hoffman). However, variant expressions such as "day of the LORD's anger" (e.g., Lam. 2:22) seem to indicate the same complex of events associated with a future time of divine intervention. Indeed, the expression "that day" often evokes the entire cluster of themes (both positive and negative) associated with the day of the Lord (e.g., Isa. 5:30; 10:20). Related expressions include "the last days" (Isa. 2:2; Mic. 4:1) or "days to come" (Ezek. 38:16; Dan. 2:28). Thus, the concept of the day of the Lord extends beyond the expression *yôm YHWH*. An interesting example of the "day" outside of the prophetic corpus occurs in Job 20:28, where Zophar refers to the judgment that comes upon the godless individual in terms of "the day of God's wrath."

Origin of the expression "day of the LORD." There is general agreement that the expression "day of the LORD" was in use prior to the prophets' writings. There is no consensus, however, concerning the term's origin. Sigmund Mowinckel proposes that the expression indicated an enthronement festival of Yahweh, although this proposal has not gained wide acceptance. Others draw upon the work of Gerhard von Rad, who grounds the expression in the presentation of the Lord as the divine warrior who engages in holy warfare and defeats his enemies, often understood as other nations. The prophets appropriate this imagery to indicate a future time in which the Lord's enemies, including his own people when they reject their covenantal commitments and follow foreign gods, will be judged. In this way the expression offers both warning and hope (Barker, 132). The complex of images associated with the day of the Lord, however, is not identical to the divine-warrior motif, even if that motif contributed to the expression's origin and development. Thus, determining the precise origin of the concept or the expression may not be possible. The approach here traces both the expression and the concept somewhat chronologically, beginning with preexilic prophets and concluding with postexilic ones.

Early Minor Prophets and Isaiah. The earliest example of this expression appears to be Amos 5:18–20, where it seems to represent a well-known concept. This passage suggests that the concept originally had positive associations as indicated by the reference to light, which could have metaphorically indicated prosperity (Barton, 69) or the expectation that the Lord would intervene and defeat Israel's (foreign) enemies. Amos refutes this false hope by explicitly linking the day of the Lord with darkness, not light (5:18–20), and calling it the "day of disaster" (6:3). He introduces this theme early on. Amos 1:14 describes the "day of battle," when the Lord will judge the nations surrounding Israel.

Amos 2 shifts the focus onto Israel and proclaims that even brave warriors will flee the battle naked "on that day" (2:16; cf. 3:14). Significant in Amos is the reversal of expectation concerning the day of the Lord: God's wrath would be directed against the nation itself, not just its foreign enemies, although there is also hope for the future restoration of the shelter of David (9:11).

Joel 2:1–2 describes a day of "darkness and gloom," of "clouds and thick darkness" (ESV; cf. 2:31; 3:14–15). The invasion of locusts (Joel 1) anticipates the invading army of the Lord (Joel 2). The sheer horror and the cosmic dimensions of this event are heightened by the rhetorical question that dramatically closes the extended description of the day of the Lord (Joel 2:1–11): Who can endure such a day? Rather than answer this question directly, Joel 2:12–17 shows that the only hope for the future is a wholehearted return to the Lord. In response to the prayers of the people, the Lord has pity and promises future restoration. The expression "after this / afterward" in Joel 2:28 indicates the eschatological nature of the "great and dreadful day of the LORD" (v. 31), when the outpouring of the Spirit and salvation for those who call upon the name of the Lord occur (2:28–32). Joel 3:14–16 stresses the nearness of the day and further describes it as a time of refuge for God's people. Indeed, Joel 2:32 promises a remnant who will be delivered in Zion (cf. Obad. 17). In Joel 3:1–3, "in those days" refers to the day of the Lord, when the nations are gathered for judgment in the Valley of Jehoshaphat ("Yahweh judges"; v. 2) because of the great evil they have committed against the Lord's inheritance, both his people and his land. This passage reveals the reversal that accompanies the coming day of the Lord, where the restoration of Jerusalem is described in both Edenic and eschatological terms—indeed, a spring of water will flow forth from the house of the Lord (3:18).

A prominent feature of Zephaniah's depiction of the "day of the Lord" is its cosmic scope where the whole earth and all of humanity are destroyed (1:1–7; 18). This great day is the "day of the LORD's sacrifice" (v. 8) and "wrath" (v. 15) that are directed against idolators (1:7–18; cf. 2:1–2). Indeed, the torrent of descriptors (e.g., "anguish," "trouble," "ruin," "darkness," "gloom") of this day in 1:15 intensifies the day's horror. It will cause people to grope around as if blind (v. 17). On this day, silver and gold are of no use (v. 18); only humility and repentance may possibly offer shelter (2:3). Yet "that day" is also associated with a future time of purification and restoration for Zion (3:9–20).

Rolf Rentdorff argues that the complex of themes associated with the day of the Lord is clarified and amplified when the Minor Prophets are studied as a unit in their canonical arrangement. He argues that early readers of Amos may have been shaped by Joel's presentation of the day of the Lord, which precedes Amos canonically. Similarly, Joel, Amos, and Zephaniah all link the day with a call to repentance. This canonical reading helps both to show development of the "day of the Lord" theme and to highlight the distinctive contributions of each prophet.

In Isaiah, the day of the Lord is often associated with destruction (e.g., 13:6, 9; cf. 24:21). In Isa. 13, the depiction of the Lord as a divine warrior is particularly pronounced, with God summoning his army to judge Babylon. It is a day that the Lord has prepared for those who exalt themselves and worship foreign idols (2:12, 17). On that day, people will throw away their idols and flee from the Lord's presence and majesty (2:19–21). For those who oppress the poor, it is a "day of punishment" (10:3 ESV). In Isa. 34:8, the day is linked with "vengeance" against Edom and is accompanied by the destruction of human activity and "a return to nature" (Barker, 138). Yet, the theme is also associated with the remnant and its restoration (4:2–6).

Later Minor Prophets, Jeremiah, and Ezekiel. In later prophets, the day of the Lord continues themes found in earlier writings. For example, although not using the expression "day of the LORD," Jer. 46:10 describes a "day of vengeance" against Egypt for its self-exaltation. Similarly, Ezek. 30:3 foretells doom for Egypt and the nations (cf. Obad. 15) using the imagery of gloom and darkness. Yet, the day is also a time of judgment against false teachers among God's people (Ezek. 13:5). Judah's possessions will be plundered on the day of the Lord (Zech. 14:1), although there will also be purification and restoration, and the Lord himself will fight for Jerusalem (12:1–9; 13:1–6; 14:1–11).

The final book of the OT (also the conclusion to the Book of the Twelve), Malachi, further develops the "day of the Lord" concept. Like Joel, Malachi wonders who can endure the day of the Lord's coming (3:2). The twofold association of the day of the Lord with judgment and restoration is also evident in Malachi, where the day when God acts (3:17) is a time of compassion for the righteous and burning judgment for evildoers (4:1). The prophecy in Mal. 4:5 that Elijah will return in the "great and dreadful day of the LORD" was later understood to refer to John the Baptist (e.g., Matt. 11:13–14; Mark 9:13), thereby providing a link between the OT expectation of the day of the Lord and the NT.

The Day of the Lord in the NT

As with the OT, the "day of the Lord" (*[hē] hēmera [tou] kyriou*) in the NT is fused with a complex of related themes and events, such as the Lord's "coming" (*parousia*), "appearing" (*epiphaneia*), and "revelation" (*apokalypsis*). The expression "day of the Lord" occurs in Acts 2:20 (in the citation of Joel 2:28–32); 1 Cor. 5:5; 1 Thess. 5:2; 2 Thess. 2:2; and 2 Pet. 3:10. As with the OT, the expression is further referenced by related terms, including simply "that day" or "those days."

As noted, the concept's eschatological and apocalyptic implications were further developed in other Second Temple writings, such as 1 Enoch, 4 Ezra, and 2 Baruch, although the expression "the day of the Lord" is rare. Part of this apocalyptic worldview included the concept of two ages/worlds: the present age/world and the age/world to come (e.g., 4 Ezra 7:50). With the coming of the kingdom in Jesus, however, these ages were understood to overlap such that the kingdom arrived with Jesus's incarnation (Mark 1:15; Luke 11:20) but would be fully present on a future "day" (Matt. 26:29). This already/not-yet paradox is a key aspect of inaugurated eschatology. Another development from Jewish apocalyptic writings is a shift from judgment on the nations to judgment upon individuals (Hiers, "Judgment," 80).

The Gospels and Acts. The expression the "day of the Lord" does not occur in any of the Gospels, yet Jesus uses expressions such as "on that day," or simply "the day" or "that day," to refer to future judgment or the kingdom's consummation. For example, in Matt. 7:22, Jesus warns that not everyone who says to him, "Lord, Lord," "on that day" will be able to enter the kingdom of heaven. Similarly, in Luke 17, Jesus replies to the Pharisees' query concerning when the kingdom of God will come (v. 20) by linking this event back to the judgment in the "days" of Noah (vv. 26–27) and Lot (vv. 28–29) and warning that "the day" that the Son of Man is revealed will similarly catch those who are unprepared off guard (v. 30). This passage includes the notable expression "the days of the Son of Man" (vv. 22, 26; cf. v. 24; cf. Matt. 24:36–37). The judgment associated with the coming of the Son of Man can also be referred to as "those days" (e.g., Mark 13:17, 20, 24). Similar to Joel 2 (cf. Hag. 2:6, 21), the "day" is associated with signs in the heavens and cosmic shaking (Luke 21:25–27) that indicate that the kingdom is near (v. 31). In Luke 21:34, Jesus warns that "that day" will be like a trap for those weighed down by sin and anxiety. Matthew is unique among the Synoptics with the expression the "day of judgment" (Matt. 10:15; 11:22, 24; 12:36). A reference to the day of the Lord is probably implied in the parable of the ten virgins, where Jesus teaches about the future coming of the kingdom (25:1) and refers to the event as "the day" (25:13). During his final meal with his disciples, Jesus informs them that he will not drink the fruit of the vine again until he partakes of it with the disciples on "that day" in the future kingdom (Matt. 26:29 // Mark 14:25). The exact timing of "that day," however, is known only by the Father (Matt. 24:36 // Mark 13:32).

John's Gospel uses the phrases "on the last day" or simply "that day." Jesus assures his listeners that he will lose none of those whom the Father has given him and will raise them up on "the last day" (6:39, 40, 44, 54), but he warns that those who reject him will be condemned on "the last day" (12:48). Martha affirms that Lazarus will be raised at the resurrection on "the last day" (11:24). In his final instructions to his disciples, Jesus assures them that on "that day" they will know that Jesus is one with the Father and they are one with Jesus (14:20; cf. 16:23, 26).

In summary, Jesus's teaching associates the day of the Lord with his return, which will be a time of terror and judgment for unbelievers and a time of great joy for believers. The connection between the "day of the Lord" and messianic expectations is not present in the OT, whereas it is assumed in the NT (see Vander Hart).

The only occurrence of the expression the "day of the Lord" in Acts is found in 2:20, which is part of an extended citation of Joel 2:28–32. This citation also includes the expression "in those days" (Acts 2:18). The citation is part of Peter's speech (vv. 14–36) in which he links the outpouring of the Spirit taking place before him to Joel's prophecy. In Paul's speech before the Areopagus, he refers to "a day" set by God for judgment through the "man he has appointed" (17:31).

Pauline Epistles. Both the concept and the expression "day of the Lord" are prevalent in Pauline theology, where it is understood in conjunction with Paul's understanding of inaugurated eschatology, the so-called already/not-yet. It is also closely associated with the apocalyptic understanding of two ages (e.g., the present age and the age to come in Eph. 1:21). For Paul, the new age has begun with the death and resurrection of Jesus Christ. Although the two ages overlap, they are distinct. As Con Campbell (65) notes, "This present age is one of sin and death, while the age to come is one of judgment and salvation." In Paul, the "day of the Lord Yahweh" becomes the "day of the Lord Jesus Christ" (Kreitzer, 259). Yet, whereas the day of the Lord in the OT is associated with God's future defeat of his enemies, the day of the Lord for Paul is associated with the complete defeat of these enemies already begun in Christ (Campbell, 132). There are several closely related variants of this expression, such as "the day of our Lord Jesus Christ" (1 Cor. 1:8), "the day of [our] Lord Jesus" (2 Cor. 1:14), "the day of Christ Jesus" (Phil. 1:6), and "the day of Christ" (1:10; 2:16). Paul's substitution of "Christ" and/or "Jesus" for "Lord" reveals his understanding that Jesus Christ now fulfills the role previously ascribed to Yahweh. As with Jesus's own teaching, the expression is linked with a future time of judgment, often in conjunction with Paul's desire that his audience be found blameless at that time and his urging present obedience and faithfulness. In the Pauline Epistles, the day of the Lord is closely associated with the parousia. Additionally, the concept of the day of the Lord is connected with the "revelation" (*apokalypsis*) of Jesus Christ (e.g., 1 Cor. 1:7–8) and his "appearing" (*epiphaneia*, e.g., 2 Tim. 1:10; Kreitzer, 259). These related lexemes and concepts "signal" the day of the Lord (Campbell, 122). Thus, the concept of the day of the Lord spans the breadth of Paul's Epistles, where the "day" may also be indicated by the "hour" (*hōra*) and the "end" (*telos*). (A similar understanding of "hour" occurs in John's Gospel and Epistles; e.g., John 2:4; 7:30; 8:20; 12:23, 27; 17:1; 1 John 2:18.) Moreover, the "day" in the Pauline Epistles is often associated with the believers' resurrection, their inheritance, and eternal life.

Paul offers an extended discussion on the day of the Lord in 1 Thess. 5:1–11. Perhaps as an allusion to Jesus's teaching (e.g., Matt. 24:42–44 // Luke 12:39–40), the day is compared to "a thief in the night" that will catch the unprepared off guard (v. 2). But Paul is confident that the Thessalonians will not be surprised by "this day" (v. 4). In this passage, Paul also associates "day" with righteous behavior and "night" with sinful activities. Context suggests that the concept of the day of the Lord is also intended in 1 Thess. 4:13–18. The expression also occurs in 2 Thess. 2:2 as part of an extended discussion of the Lord's coming and final defeat of the "lawless one" (2:1–12). The reference to "that day" (v. 3) clearly indicates the day of the Lord. This letter includes the expression "on the day he comes" (1:10), which is associated with the revelation of the Lord Jesus (v. 7) and glorification of his people (v. 10). Matthew Aernie (xvii, 146–47) argues that the use of legal language in 2 Thess. 1 indicates that Paul understands the day of the Lord as "a court day." He encourages the persecuted Thessalonians to persevere, knowing that they will be vindicated by the Lord on that day.

The day of the Lord factors prominently in the Corinthian correspondence. In his opening thanksgiving, Paul assures the Corinthians that the Lord will keep them firm until the end so that they will be blameless on the "day of the Lord Jesus Christ" (1 Cor. 1:8). In 1 Cor. 3:13, the true nature (precious or worthless) of those who build upon the foundation that Paul has laid will be brought to light on "the day" (note the allusions to Mal. 3:1–3; 4:1 in 1 Cor. 3:10–15). The theme of judgment is particularly pronounced in 1 Cor. 5:5, where the individual who has committed unspeakable sexual immorality is to be handed over "to Satan for the destruction of his flesh, so that his spirit might be saved on the day of the Lord." The focus in 1 Cor. 15 on judgment and resurrection suggests that the concept is also in view there. In his explanation of why he was unable to visit Corinth, Paul hopes that the Corinthians will gain understanding of these circumstances such that they will be able to boast of Paul and his companions in the "day of the Lord Jesus" (2 Cor. 1:14). The expression "day of salvation" occurs in 2 Cor. 6:2 (citing Isa. 49:8) as part of Paul's extended discussion of the ministry of reconciliation in 5:11–6:2. In this verse Paul declares that this promised day of salvation is indeed this present time.

Similar themes occur elsewhere in Paul's writings. In Rom. 2, Paul warns of the "day of God's wrath" (v. 5, likely alluding to Zeph. 1:14) when God's righteous judgment will occur (cf. Rom. 2:16). The association of "day" (and implicitly the dawning age to come) with righteousness, and "night" (and implicitly the present age) with evil is clear in Rom. 13:11–14, where the day is near (v. 12).

Paul assures the Philippians that the one who has begun a good work in them will complete it on the "day of Christ Jesus" (1:6). He prays that they will mature so as to be found blameless on the "day of Christ" (1:10). They will become so as they practice humility and avoid complaining, so that Paul can boast about them on the "day of Christ" (2:16). In Eph. 4:30, Paul warns of grieving the Holy Spirit in whom believers are "sealed for the day of redemption." Finally, in 2 Tim. 1:12, Paul expresses his confidence that Christ Jesus can guard what Paul has "entrusted to him until that day." He prays that God will show mercy on Onesiphorus, who helped Paul, "on that day" (1:18). He notes the terrible evil that will occur "in the last days" (3:1) but is confident of "the crown of righteousness" that awaits him "on that day" (4:8).

General Epistles and Revelation. The theme of the day of the Lord occurs in the General Epistles, particularly 2 Peter. In his discussion of false teachers, Peter speaks of the punishment in store for the unrighteous "on the day of judgment" (2:9). The "last days" (3:3) will be a time in which people will mock the delay of the Lord's return. Just as the flood waters previously judged mockers (3:6), so too the ungodly in the present day will experience destruction on "the day of judgment" (3:7). "The day of the Lord will come like a thief" (3:10; cf. Matt. 24:42–44 // Luke 12:39–40) and is imminent (3:12). Similarly, Jude 6 describes the severe judgment that will come upon the ungodly in the "great day." By contrast, John uses the "day of judgment" to indicate the confidence and lack of fear that believers will have because of God's perfect love (1 John 4:17). The expression "last days" occurs in Heb. 1:2 in connection with God's final and complete revelation in the Son. The recipients of Hebrews are exhorted to persevere and not forsake meeting together as they see the "day" approaching (Heb. 10:25).

The concept of the day of the Lord flows through Revelation, with its focus on judgment, the coming of the Lord, the eradication of evil, and the restoration of the heavens and earth. Specific references to the day of the Lord are, however, more limited. The terrors that unfold after the sixth seal is broken are described in terms of the "great day" of the wrath of the one on the throne and of the Lamb (6:17; cf. Joel 2:11; Zeph. 1:14). A reference to the "day" occurs in conjunction with the sixth bowl, where demonic spirits gather for battle on the "great day of God Almighty" (16:14)—about which the Lamb declares that he comes like a thief (16:15).

Biblical-Theological and Hermeneutical Implications

The expression "day of the Lord" has numerous implications for biblical theology and hermeneutics. Perhaps the first is the certainty of a future time of judgment, when the ultimate reckoning of sin, injustice, and evil occurs and when the righteous are vindicated and rewarded. In the NT, this future judgment is fused with the parousia of Jesus Christ and the resurrection of the dead. On that day, the present age will end and the age to come will finally be ushered in. As Campbell (129) notes, "Indeed, it is the coming of Christ—his revelation from heaven—that establishes the *day* for what it is. It is the eschatological era ushered in by the Lord's coming and appearance." It is thus a time of both fear and terror for the ungodly and of hope and joy for believers. It will be a time of separating those who may enter or inherit the kingdom from those who will be excluded from it.

Second, the day of the Lord is associated with imminence, although its precise timing is unknown. Thus, the prophets could exhort the covenant community to repent in view of the nearness of this day. Similarly, Jesus urges his followers to be watchful and prepared, since the day will come like a thief in the night. Paul refers to the day to urge his audiences to live blameless lives, to persevere, and to remain diligent in their present tribulations. The biblical presentation of the day of the Lord is accompanied by a clear sense of expectation and exhortation to be prepared and to persevere considering its unknowable and likely surprising timing.

Finally, the day of the Lord involves a reversal of fallen creation and the restoration and reconciliation of all things. All that was ruptured in the first humans' rebellious refusal to trust God's goodness and perfect provision is now reconciled back to the Father through the perfect work of the Son. The hopes of the prophets for the restoration of Zion and its remnant will be fully realized on the day of the Lord when all the ungodly are judged, evil is finally eradicated, the redeemed are vindicated, and the new Jerusalem descends from heaven thereby ushering in the new creation.

Throughout the biblical witness, the terror and hope associated with the day of the Lord are fused, indicating that God's righteous judgment of evil cannot be separated from his reconciliation of all things. For those whose hope is in the risen Lord, the day of the Lord anticipates joyful worship, but for those who have rejected the Son of God, it is a day of terror, dread, and judgment.

See also Consummation; Divine Warrior; Messiah; Resurrection

Bibliography. Aernie, M. D., *Forensic Language and the Day of the Lord Motif in Second Thessalonians 1 and the Effects on the Meaning of the Text*, WTMS (Wipf & Stock, 2011); Barker, J. D., "Day of the Lord," in *DOTP*, 132–43; Barton, J., "The Day of Yahweh in the Minor Prophets," in *Biblical and Near Eastern Essays*, ed. C. McCarthy and J. F. Healy, JSOTSup 375 (T&T Clark International, 2004), 68–79; Campbell, C. R., *Paul and the Hope of Glory* (Zondervan, 2020); Cathcart, K. J., "The Day of Yahweh," in *ABD*, 2:84–85; Delling, G., "*hēmera*," in *TDNT*, 2:943–53; Hiers, R. H., "Day of Christ," in *ABD*, 2:76–79; Hiers, "Day of Judgment," in *ABD*, 2:79–82; Hiers, "Day of the Lord," in *ABD*, 2:82–83; Hoffmann, Y., "The Day of the Lord as a Concept and a Term in Prophetic Literature," *ZAW* 93 (1981): 37–50; Kreitzer, L. J., "Eschatology," in *DOTP*, 253–69; Mowinckel, S., *He That Cometh*, trans. G. W. Anderson (Abingdon, 1954); Paul, S. M., *Amos*, Herm (Fortress, 1991); Rendtorff, R., "Alas for the Day!," in *God in the Fray*, ed. T. Linafelt and T. K. Beal (Fortress, 1998), 186–97; Rendtorff, "How to Read the Book of the Twelve as a Theological Unity," in *Reading and Hearing the Book of the Twelve*, ed. J. D. Nogalski and M. A. Sweeney, SBLSymS 36 (Scholars Press, 2000), 75–87; Schreiner, T. R., *Paul, Apostle of God's Glory in Christ* (InterVarsity, 2001); Vander Hart, M. D., "The Transition of the Old Testament Day of the Lord into the New Testament Day of the Lord Jesus Christ," *MJT* 9 (1993): 3–25; Verhoef, P. A., "*yôm*," in *NIDOTTE*, 2:419–24; von Rad, G., "The Origin of the Concept of the Day of Yahweh," *JSS* 4 (1959): 97–108.

DANA M. HARRIS

Dead Sea Scrolls, OT Use in

Discovered in the deserts of the Judean wilderness between 1947 and 1956, the Dead Sea Scrolls furnish a treasure of literary material from a Jewish group roughly contemporary to the writings of the NT. This Jewish "community" (*yaḥad*), like the early Christians, was deeply shaped by the writings of the OT. These Scrolls were found in the environs of Khirbet Qumran (de Vaux; Magness), along the northwest coast of the Dead Sea, where the dry environment preserved an enormous cache of about nine hundred ancient documents dating from around 250 BCE to 68 CE, written in Hebrew, Aramaic, and Greek (García Martínez). About one-fourth of this material is comprised of biblical texts, the vast majority of which are quite fragmentary and small. The exceptions are Isaiah (1QIsa[a]), which is preserved nearly in its entirety (see the article "Dead Sea Scrolls, OT Use in: Comparison with NT Use of the OT" elsewhere in the dictionary), and the book of Esther, which alone among the texts of the OT is not found at Qumran.

In addition to the biblical material at Qumran, a large assortment of writings expand upon or "rewrite" biblical narratives, such as Jubilees, or develop ideas based on obscure biblical figures, such as 1 Enoch. All bear unmistakable traces of influence from the OT. Many of these reflect the distinctly "sectarian" nature of the *yaḥad* that preserved them and often relate to rules and legal matters and "illustrate the community's intentional separation from other Jews" (Elledge, 190). Foremost is the Rule of the Community (1QS; 4Q255–264; 5Q11), which is often regarded as a charter document of the practices and beliefs of the Qumran sect. Other works of a similar nature are the Rule of the Congregation (1QSa), the Rule of Blessings (1QSb), and the Damascus Document (4Q266–273; 5Q12; 6Q15; CD). The War Scroll (1QM; 4Q490–497; translations from DSS taken from García Martínez and Tigchelaar unless otherwise noted) depicts an eschatological battle between the "sons of light" and the "sons of darkness." Legal materials are also found in the Halakic Letter (4QMMT [4Q394–399]) and the Temple Scroll (11Q19–20; 4Q524). The pesharim (e.g., 1QpHab; 1Q14–15; 4Q161–164; 4Q167–171; 4Q173), or commentaries, explain much about the community's self-understanding and interpretation of Scripture.

The Scrolls contain an extensive collection of liturgical writings (Falk, *Prayers*; Penner), such as the Thanksgiving Hymns (Hodayot; 1QH[a]; 4Q427–433) and the Angelic Liturgy (Songs of the Sabbath Sacrifice; 4Q400–407; 11Q17). The latter is a collection of hymns depicting angelic priests offering heavenly sacrifices that coincide with earthly worship. Wisdom writings, such as the Book of Mysteries (1Q27; 4Q299–301) and 4QInstruction (4Q415–418; 4Q423), are also found among the Dead Sea Scrolls (Goff), as are apocalyptic texts, such as the book of Daniel (1Q71–72; 4Q112–116; 6Q7) and segments of 1 Enoch (1Q19a–b [?]; 4Q201–212). Other apocalypses were otherwise unknown until the discovery of the Scrolls, including the Messianic Apocalypse (4Q521), the Aramaic Apocalypse (4Q246), and an assortment of texts associated with the new Jerusalem (1Q32; 2Q24; 4Q232; 4Q554–555; 5Q15; 11Q18). All these Jewish writings bear some marks of the influence of the OT and illustrate to varying degrees the hermeneutical lenses of the community that preserved them.

Pesharim

The most important documents of the Dead Sea Scrolls for exhibiting biblical interpretation are found in a genre of literature known as the pesharim (see Goldman). These ancient writings, found only among the Dead Sea Scrolls, contain a quotation from a biblical text that the author considers to be prophetic (e.g., Hosea, Zephaniah, Micah, Nahum, Habakkuk, Isaiah, Psalms), followed by an explicit statement regarding its "interpretation" (*pšr*), then an explanation relating that biblical text to the Qumran group's own setting (Vermes, 90–91). As such it is often regarded as a new, divine revelation (Elliger, 155–57) made known to a particular priest, typically identified as the "Teacher of Righteousness" (1QpHab 7.5; Goldman, 600). These are regarded as "continuous pesher" (Carmignac, "Qumrân," 361), of which examples are found on Isaiah (4Q161–165), Hosea (4Q166–167), Micah (4Q14), Nahum (4Q169), Zephaniah (1Q15; 4Q170), and Psalms (1Q16; 4Q171; 4Q173). However, there is some debate about the nature and extent of these classifications (Dimant, "Pesharim," 244–48; Horgan, "Habakkuk"; Lim; Campbell).

Pesher on Habakkuk. A commentary on Habakkuk was found in Qumran Cave 1 in 1947 (Brownlee, "Habakkuk"; Horgan, "Habakkuk", 157–85). This manuscript, 1QpHab, dates to the second half of the first century BC. Habakkuk himself prophesies that the Lord will raise up the Chaldeans to punish the wickedness of Judah (Hab. 1:2–6) and describes the violent destruction they will bring (1:7–11). When Habakkuk issues a complaint (1:12–2:1), the Lord responds with a pronouncement of future judgment upon the Chaldeans (2:3–20). Moreover, the prophecy that "the vision awaits its appointed time; it hastens to the end—it will not lie. . . . It will surely come; it will not delay" (2:3 ESV) is taken by the Qumran sect to indicate that Habakkuk's prophecies pertain to the future, not Habakkuk's own time, and so create an opportunity for the later interpreter to read the prophecy in light of his own setting.

Clear examples of this are found throughout the Habakkuk pesher. For instance, early in Habakkuk, the prophet exhorts the nations to observe what the Lord is doing in Judah: "I am going to do something in your days that you would not believe, even if you were told" (Hab. 1:5). The Qumran interpreter regards this as a prediction of what occurred in their own group's history (1QpHab 1.17–2.10). Specifically, it claims this refers to a "Man of the Lie" and his followers, who have "not [obeyed the words of] the Teacher of Righteousness from the mouth of God" (1QpHab 2.1–3 WAC). Appearing in the Last Days (1QpHab 2.5–6), these people are "trai[tors to the] New [Covenant], because they did not believe in God's covenant [and desecrated] His holy name" (1QpHab 2.3–4). This Man of the Lie appears to be a member of the Qumran group who would not accept the teachings of the leader, and perhaps founder, known as the Teacher of Righteousness (cf. Hab. 1:13 and 1QpHab 5.8–12; Hab. 2:15 and 1QpHab 11.2–8). While the Habakkuk text says nothing of a man of the lie or a community teacher, 1QpHab exploits the "you could not believe" of Habakkuk 1:5 to identify it as a rhetorical statement not about the astonishing things God would do but about the actual unbelief in the *yaḥad*'s own experience.

Since the Qumran interpreters apply the prophecies of Habakkuk to their own time, they regard future prophecies against the Chaldeans as a cipher for the Romans (called "Kittim"; cf. Gen. 10:4) and view the prophecy of vindication for God's people in the light of Roman oppression in the first century BC. So, the utterance that the oppressive Chaldeans "sweep by like the wind and go on, guilty men, whose own might is their god" (Hab. 1:11 ESV) is applied to the Roman Kittim: "This refe[rs t]o the rulers of the Kittim, who cross the land by the advice of a family of sinn[ers]: each before his fellow, [their] rulers come, one after the other, to devastate the la[nd]" (1QpHab 4.10–13 WAC). With the Kittim being the Romans, the advice of "a family of sinners" is the counsel of the Roman senate, who issued instructions for changes of leadership (consults) in the Roman occupiers annually (cf. also Hab. 1:16 and 1QpHab 6.2–5). Again the biblical prophecy is removed from its original setting, and the opponents of Israel in Habakkuk become a cipher for the opponents of the Jews at Qumran.

Pesher on Nahum. Another important commentary on the OT is found in the pesher on Nahum. In its original setting, Nahum is a prophecy anticipating the Lord's imminent judgment on Assyria and its capital city of Nineveh (Nah. 1:1; 3:19). The prophet compares that city to the den of a lion where its young will be killed and do no more harm (2:11–12) and likens it to a prostitute whose shame will be exposed (3:5–7). The pesher on Nahum (4Q169) is more fragmentary than the Habakkuk pesher, covering portions of the first two chapters and much of the third, but enough is preserved to exhibit some of its hermeneutic. It is like the Habakkuk pesher in its mention of the Kittim but unique in its mention of individual names.

Nahum's prophecy regarding the lion and its cub (Nah. 2:11b) is interpreted in frgs. 3–4. Here the older lion is "[Deme]trius, king of Greece, who sought to come to Jerusalem through the counsel of the Flattery-Seekers; [but the city never fell into the] power of the kings of Greece from Antiochus until the appearance of the rulers of the Kittim; but afterwards it will be trampled" (4Q169 3–4.1.1–4 WAC). The person here is Demetrius III Philopator Akairos (95–88 BC; Josephus, *Ant.* 13.370), king of Seleucid Syria, who attacked Jerusalem at the request of its inhabitants, so brutal was the rule of Alexander Jannaeus, who reigned as king and high priest from 103 to 76 BC in Judea (Josephus, *Ant.* 13.372–76; *J.W.* 1.90–92). "Flattery-Seekers" or "seekers after smooth things" is a pejorative reference to the Pharisees, whereas the Antiochus mentioned is Antiochus IV Epiphanes (175–164 BC), whose prohibition of the practice of Judaism triggered the Maccabean revolt (166–160 BC; 1 Macc. 1–4). For the eschatological community at Qumran, the prophecy of Nahum furnishes suitable material in which to see their own experiences, though as with the Habakkuk pesher, suitable points of correspondence and contextual ciphers are utilized.

In another notable example, Nahum says, "The lion killed enough for his cubs and strangled the prey for his mate" (Nah. 2:12). This is interpreted at Qumran in reference "to the Lion of Wrath who would kill some of his nobles and the men of his party" (4Q169 3–4.1.5 WAC). This "Lion of Wrath" is Alexander Jannaeus, king of Judah. Nahum further describes this lion as "filling his lairs with the kill and his dens with the prey" (Nah. 2:12), and in interpreting this statement the pesher again looks to Alexander Jannaeus: "This refers to the Lion of Wrath [. . . ven]geance against the Flattery-Seekers, because he used to hang men alive" (4Q169 3–4.1.6b–7 WAC). Alexander was known to have publicly crucified eight hundred opponents (Pharisees) while he murdered their wives and children in front of them in Jerusalem (88 BC; Josephus, *J.W.* 1.96–97; *Ant.* 13.179–80). In this regard the Nahum pesher not only continues to affirm the familiar hermeneutic we have seen above but also provides some historical points of connection that aid in dating the document and the community that composed and preserved it.

Pesher on the Psalms. The pesher on Psalms (4Q171; 4Q173; 1Q16) is the largest from Qumran. Its five columns quote and interpret primarily portions of Pss. 37, 45, 60, 68, 108, and 129 (Jokiranta, 457). The Qumran interpreter regards the psalms as predictive in nature and, as with the other pesharim, associated with the sect's own setting. For instance, where the psalmist says, "The LORD makes firm the steps of the one who delights in him; though he may stumble, he will not fall, for the LORD upholds him with his hand" (Ps. 37:23–24), the commentator regards the "righteous" as the Teacher of Righteousness and the "wicked" as his opponents (4Q171 1–2.3.15–17). Similarly, the psalmist says, "The wicked lie in wait for the righteous, intent on putting them to death; but the LORD will not leave them in the power of the wicked or let them be condemned when brought to trial" (Ps. 37:32–33). The commentary asserts that "[t]his refers to the Wicked [Pri]est who ob[serv]es the Righ[teous Man and seeks] to kill him" (4Q171 1–2.4.8 WAC). However, the commentary continues, "God will not le[ave him] and will not [condemn him when] he comes to trial" (line 9 WAC). Instead, "to the [wicked God will give] his just [des]serts, by putting him into the power of the tyrant[s of] the Gentiles to do with him [what they want]" (lines 9–10 WAC). This is taken as righteous vindication of God's oppressed righteous people among the Qumran sect, particularly the Teacher of Righteousness.

Pesharim on Isaiah. Six texts from Qumran, dating as early as 100 BC, are identified as commentaries on Isaiah (3Q4; 4Q161–165; Lundberg, 256). Of these, only a few merit explanation here. 4Q161 cites segments from Isa. 10:20–11:5 concerning God's promise to deliver his people from the threats of Assyria. The reference to the hewing down of Israel's opponents (10:33–34) is understood as a reference to the Kittim (i.e., the Romans; 4Q161 8–10.3.3–8). The rod from Jesse's stock (Isa. 11:1) is regarded as the "[Branch of] David, who will appear in the Las[t Days]" (4Q161 8–10.3.17 WAC). God "[will give him] a glorious [th]rone, [a sacred] crown, and elegan[t] garments" (line 19 WAC), and "he will rule over all the G[enti]les" (line 20 WAC). The single fragment 4Q162 cites and comments upon verses from Isa. 5. The calamities of Isa. 5:5–6 are taken to refer to "the Last Days, when the land itself is condemned by sword and famine; so it shall be at the time when the land is punished" (4Q162 2.1–2). The wicked of Isa. 5:11–14 are interpreted as "the Men of Mockery [Pharisees] who are in Jerusalem. They are the ones 'who have rejected the Law of the LORD, and the word of Israel's Holy One they have cast off. For this reason He became very angry with His people'" (4Q162 2.6–8 WAC, citing Isa. 5:24–25). 4Q164, consisting of three fragments, cites Isa. 54:11–12 concerning the restoration of Jerusalem with walls of precious stones (cf. Rev. 21:12–21; Horgan, *Pesharim*).

Pesher on Hosea. The pesher on Hosea (4Q166–167) purports to be interpretations of the biblical text that were revealed to the Teacher of Righteousness (cf. 1QpHab 7.1–5). Hosea's prophecies are directed toward the Northern Kingdom of Israel before its conquest in 722 BC by Assyria, and the Qumran interpreter applies them to his own community before the onset of the Roman conquest in 63 BC (Horgan, "Hosea," 246). The prophet regards the exile and calamities upon Israel as recompense for turning to Baal and forsaking the Lord (Hosea 2:8–14). In the commentary those who lead them astray (4Q166 2.5) are people who teach incorrect interpretations of the torah, likely judged against those of the Teacher of Righteousness (cf. 1QpHab 5.7–12). The judgment of famine (4Q166 2.12) is likely that which preceded the arrival of Pompey (63 BC). The reference to "her feasts, her new moons, her Sabbaths, and all her appointed feasts" (Hosea 2:11 ESV) is likely a reference to the 364-day calendar followed by the *yaḥad* (4Q166 2.15–16) as opposed to the lunisolar calendar followed by the Jews in Jerusalem (cf. Jub. 6:34–35; 1QpHab 11.3–8; 4Q171 1–10.4.7–8; Horgan, "Hosea," 247). Finally, the prophecy regarding a "lion to Ephraim" and "a young lion to the house of Judah" (Hosea 5:14 ESV) is interpreted as the "Lion of Wrath" (4Q167 2.2), most likely Alexander Jannaeus (cf. 4Q169 3–4.1.5–6; Josephus, *J.W.* 1.113). Contentious issues such as calendar come into play, and again historical references to the community's experience are evident.

Additional pesharim. The pesher on Micah (1Q14) is attested in a single fragmentary manuscript from Qumran. Despite its disconnected nature, references to Mic. 1:2–9; 6:14–16; 7:6–9 (?); and 7:17 are evident, as are terms such as "the Teacher of Righteousness." This Teacher "[shall teach the law to his par]ty and to all those who are willing to be added to the chosen of [God, the ones who observe the law] in the party of the *Yaḥad* who will be saved on the Day of [Judgment]" (1Q14 8–10.6–9 WAC). It also mentions his enemy, Samaria (Mic. 1:5–6), called "the Spouter of Lies" who will lead astray the simple-hearted (1Q14 8–9.4–5; see M. Collins, "Micah," 375). Other pesharim include a few lines of a single fragment commenting on Mal. 3:16–18 (4Q253a) and seven fragments of a work known as the Pesher of the Periods (*pšr ʿl hqṣym*; 4Q180–181). The latter is an interpretation not of texts, as are the other pesharim, but of history (Dimant, "Periods").

Conclusion. The pesharim of Qumran provide a rich tapestry of the use of the OT in the Dead Sea Scrolls. They are composed by the community itself and in each instance make it clear what text they are citing and how it is interpreted, much like modern commentaries. This aids in identifying a consistent hermeneutical pattern by which the Qumran interpreter regards statements, including prophecies, from the OT as immediately relevant for their own setting. Where opponents are named in the OT, they become "code" for a corresponding opponent in the Qumran setting. Implicitly, the oppression of Israel in the prophetic writings of the OT is readily seen as the oppression of the Qumran sect. Even where no authoritative figure is mentioned in the OT, the sectarians see in them implicit references to the Teacher of Righteousness, an authoritative and honored figure in the group's own history, whose teachings are prophetic in nature.

Thematic Commentaries

In addition to the pesharim, there are other commentaries that do not use the word "pesher" (interpretation). These are regarded as "thematic pesher" or "thematic commentaries" (Carmignac, "Qumrân," 361). Such a text "adduces verses from diverse prophecies linked together by a common topic" (Goldman, 601), though which works belong to this category is the subject of some debate (Lim, 46–53). Nevertheless, they are commentaries that prove illuminating for understanding the interpretation of the OT at Qumran.

Florilegium. A prominent example of this kind of material is found in 4Q174, known as the Eschatological Midrash (Steudel) or, more commonly, Florilegium, which means "anthology" and reflects the diversity of cited biblical sources upon which the author comments. In this instance the author's attention is upon the Davidic dynasty espoused in 2 Sam. 7 and Pss. 1–2, which the author reads eschatologically in light of his own setting (Campbell, 33–44). Where the biblical author asserts that the Lord will establish a secure place for Israel (2 Sam. 7:10), the Qumran interpreter understands an eschatological "house" (*hbyt*) that "[he will establish] for [him] in the last days" (4Q174 1.1.2–3 FGM). Furthermore, the Qumran interpreter invokes Exod. 15:17–18 for support, which says nothing of shelter for a people but rather the abode and sanctuary of the Lord (*miqdāš ʾădōnāy*). Where the biblical author asserts that God will "give you rest from all your enemies" (2 Sam. 7:11), the Qumran interpreter regards this as a prophecy against the "sons of Belial" for their oppression of the "s[ons of] lig[ht]" (4Q174 1.1.7–9). Samuel's account of God's promise to build a "house" (*byt*) for David, raising up his seed and establishing the throne of his kingdom forever (2 Sam. 7:12–14), is regarded as referring to the "branch of David" (*ṣmḥ dwyd*), a messianic figure who "will arise with the Interpreter of the law who [will rise up] in Zi[on in] the [l]ast days" (4Q174 1.1.10–12; cf. Amos 9:11; Tzoref, "Florilegium," 212). The collation of biblical verses allows the Qumran interpreter to speculate on concepts in line with his eschatological perspectives.

Testimonia. Another anthology of biblical texts is Testimonia (4Q175). It is divided into four sections, stringing together texts from the OT without explicit commentary but in a manner that indicates the Qumran sectarians' contemporizing interpretation of Scripture (Rietz, 532). For instance, the first three sections are related to the subject of future leaders: the prophet like Moses (Deut. 5:28–29; 18:18–19; 4Q175 1–8), followed by the "star from Jacob" and "scepter from Israel" (Num. 24:15–17 AT; 4Q175 9–13), which likely refer to a priestly and a royal messianic figure, respectively. Then it presents Moses's blessing on Levi (Deut. 33:8–11; 4Q175 14–20), which likely emphasizes a future priestly figure or at least a priestly (Levitical) role in interpreting Scripture (Rietz, 531). The fourth paragraph relates to Joshua's curses on those who fortify Jerusalem (or Jericho?; cf. Josh. 6:26) but is dependent on not biblical tradition but the Apocryphon of Joshua (4Q378–379; 4Q522; 5Q9; Mas1l). This is likely in reference to Simon Maccabeus and his sons, Judas and Mattathias (Cross, 111–15). As in the pesharim, we see here historical references relevant for the Qumran sect. But we also see, as in the Florilegium, a compiling of texts according to the interpreters' eschatological outlooks.

Melchizedek Scroll. A similar phenomenon occurs in the fascinating thematic pesher called the Melchizedek Scroll (11Q13), which is a composite document of a number of fragments dating from the second century BC (Puech). This text draws from the biblical account where Melchizedek, the priest/king of Salem, receives a tenth of Abram's spoils from kings he defeated and blesses Abram (Gen. 14:18–20). Other than the mention of an eternal priesthood in the order of Melchizedek (Ps. 110:4), the OT says nothing about him. The central portion of the manuscript (col. 2) begins with discussion of the Year of Jubilee and the year of remission and release (Lev. 25:13; Deut. 15:2). These verses seem to be treated as a unit, with a singular interpretation: "[The interpretation (*pšrw*)] is that it applies [to the L]ast Days [*l'ḥryt hymym*] and concerns the captives" (11Q13 2.4 WAC). This in turn is cited as being in accord with the prophecy of Isaiah, "to proclaim the Jubilee to the captives" (Isa. 61:1 AT). These Isaianic "captives" will be assigned to the "inheritance of Melchizedek," who restores them and proclaims their liberty and forgiveness (11Q13 2.5–6 WAC). Atonement shall be made "for all the Sons of [Light] and the peopl[e who are pre]destined to Mel[chi]zedek" (11Q13 2.8 WAC) at a time appointed as the "year of grace of Melchizedek" (*lšnt hrṣwn lmlky ṣdk*, 2.9 WAC) or "the year of Melchiz[edek]'s favor" (WAC; cf. Isa. 61:2). This is also the time of Melchizedek's armies, along with a nation of the holy ones of God, to establish a rule of judgment (11Q13 2.9), for which the interpreter cites Ps. 82:1: "God presides in the great assembly; he renders judgment among the 'gods.'" Then, where that same psalmist asks how long God will judge unjustly and show partiality to the wicked (Ps. 82:2; 11Q13 2.10), the Qumran author adds his interpretation. This, he urges, applies to Belial and all the forces of evil and wickedness: "Melchizedek will thoroughly prosecute the vengeance required by Go[d's] statutes. [In that day he will de]liv[er them from the power] of Belial, and from the power of all the sp[irits predestined to him]" (11Q13 2.13 WAC). It is noteworthy that Melchizedek receives an eschatological role with respect to the Qumran sectarians that is entirely absent from the accounts of the OT.

Conclusion. Unlike the pesharim on individual books, the point of focus in the thematic pesharim is not a single text for expansion but the collation of texts. The Qumran interpreter then is able to undertake what may be regarded as a biblical theology of sorts, in that he seeks to trace out a topic with verses he deems relevant to the task. However, as with the pesharim, what texts he deems relevant is largely determined by his own hermeneutic, in which he regards his own community, its interests and outlooks, as determinative. Also like the authors of pesharim, the interpreters in thematic pesharim are comfortable with decoding a figure from the biblical text to their own setting and interests.

Rewritten Scripture

In addition to commentaries, there are other ways in which biblical interpretation at Qumran is exhibited. One of these is the way in which a Qumran interpreter largely reproduces biblical texts without quoting or alluding to the narrative but rather by paraphrasing, expanding, or rewriting it. Some of these reproduce the biblical text nearly verbatim while inserting nonbiblical narratives into the account. But there is some debate as to how to classify these. Some regard these works as parabiblical or parascriptural. The latter gets to the heart of the matter, as it serves "as an umbrella term for a broad class of texts that in various ways extend the authority of Scripture by imitation and interpretation" (Falk, *Parabiblical Texts*, 7). The term "rewritten Scripture," however, is favorable because it recognizes the literary phenomena with which the original text is handled and the authoritative nature of the resulting text, especially in relation to the original. These include portions of 1 Enoch and Jubilees (Nickelsburg), which are found among the Dead Sea Scrolls but are treated elsewhere as being among the OT Pseudepigrapha. Molly Zahn explains that the writings unique to the Dead Sea reproduce "substantial portions of one or more biblical books, but modify the scriptural text by means of addition, omission, paraphrase, rearrangement, or other types of changes" (*OHDSS*, 323). Among the Scrolls, pride of place for the rewritten-Scripture texts belongs to the Genesis Apocryphon and the Temple Scroll. Since these do not quote biblical texts but rather paraphrase and rewrite, summaries of the contents will illustrate the manner in which they interpret the OT.

The Genesis Apocryphon. The Genesis Apocryphon was entirely unknown until its discovery on the floor, rather than in jars, in Cave 1 at Qumran in 1947 (1Q20 or 1QapGen). It is written in Aramaic and dates from early in the first century AD (Fitzmyer, 25–26; Falk, *Parabiblical Texts*, 28; Machiela, 136–37). Of the twenty-two columns that survive, only five (cols. 2, 19–22) are substantially legible. Fragments comprise an additional column, labelled "col. 0" and placed at the beginning, though its proper location is uncertain.

It narrates stories of Enoch, Lamech, Noah, and Abram related to accounts in Gen. 6–15. As a pseudepigraphon, it presents many of these accounts in the first person (Lamech, Enoch, and Noah). Yet as a rewritten Scripture it contains considerable additions, omissions, and various amendments to the biblical account. Abraham's account, also given in the first person, is expanded from the biblical account of his sojourn in Egypt (cf. Gen. 12:10–20), though later (1Q20 21.23–22.34), curiously, the narrative adheres closely to Gen. 14 and gives its account of Abraham in the third person. The extant text can be divided simply into three main sections, containing the account of the miraculous birth of Noah (cols. 0–5), the life of Noah and an account of the flood (cols. 5–18), and a narrative about Abram, which is incomplete (cols. 19–22?).

While the apocryphon's treatment of Genesis overlaps with Enochic writings (e.g., 1 En. 106–107 and the Book of Giants) and Jubilees (e.g., the chronology of Abram and Sarai in Egypt and the division of the earth), the work is largely unique. The author's interpretation of Genesis is best regarded as "interpretive reworkings, intended to alleviate difficulties in Genesis" (Machiela, 131). It is "mostly a relatively free paraphrase that is often expansive but sometimes abbreviated" (Falk, *Parabiblical Texts,* 94). But there are exceptions, such as instances of a literal rendering of the Hebrew resembling the tradition of the Samaritan Pentateuch and the Septuagint over the MT (Gurtner, 285).

In its treatment of Genesis the author also exhibits some unevenness in the handling of material, most notably in the accounts of Noah and Abram (Machiela, 131). Though there is a similar amount of material between the two, Noah receives considerably more attention than Abram in the Genesis Apocryphon. Furthermore, Noah's presentation draws from Genesis but is supplemented by a great deal of external material, much of which is known from other ancient sources. And there are very few translations from the Genesis account in the Noah narratives (e.g., 1Q20 6.23; 10.12; 11.11, 18; 12.1, 9, 10, 13; Fitzmyer, 39; Falk, *Parabiblical Texts,* 95). In contrast, the accounts of Abram are much less developed, though their extrabiblical material is unique to the Genesis Apocryphon (Machiela, 131) and there are many instances of translation (Falk, *Parabiblical Texts,* 95).

The work is by no means intended to replace Genesis. It is an exegetical work based upon that book and "was meant to be read *alongside* the authoritative text" (Machiela, 142, emphasis original). The work intends to fill in material not explicit in the text, address particular interpretative uncertainties, and draw connections between people and events in the narrative and so becomes the "proper lens through which to read Genesis" (Machiela, 142). Falk explains that the work serves to make the Scripture more clear, systematic, and lively, but he underscores the uncertainty of the context in which it did so—a school, synagogue, or home, whether it was educational or liturgical, for educational or apologetic purposes (*Parabiblical Texts,* 41–42).

The Temple Scroll. Also of a legal nature but of a very different character, the Temple Scroll (11Q19) is an extensive document, dating from around 120 BC (Schiffman, 19–32, 487–504), that recasts large portions of Exodus through Deuteronomy, two-thirds of its content pertaining to God's instruction for building the temple. It describes Moses's second ascent up Sinai (Exod. 34), intertwined with prohibitions of idolatry (Deut. 7), and is presented as God's special revelation to Moses. In cols. 3–13, it provides intricate detail for the construction of the sanctuary, drawing from 2 Chron. 3 and 1 Kings 6 as well as Ezekiel, with particular attention to its furnishings, drawing from those of the tabernacle (Exod. 25–27; 36–38). Despite drawing from biblical texts here and later, the description does not correspond to any of Israel's sanctuaries. Instead, it utilizes the biblical blueprint for some sort of new temple to be constructed in the future. This is followed by instructions for observing festivals and sacrifices (cols. 13–29), seemingly advocating a solar, 364-day calendar configuration like other Qumran and Second Temple texts (Jubilees and 1 Enoch; cf. Lev. 23; Num. 28–29). The next segment (cols. 30–65) describes the structures surrounding the sanctuary, along with the temple courts, in a concentric square configuration in which there is an inner court (priests), middle court (healthy males), and outer court (for celebrants of the festivals). The latter two courts each bear twelve gates named for the tribes of Israel but depicted on a scale so massive as to be incompatible with the topography of Jerusalem and the Kidron Valley. Concern for purity (cols. 44–52) is taken from Lev. 11–15 and relates to the sanctuary and the temple's environs. The last section contains an assortment of laws from Deut. 13–17 (cols. 51–55), and the document ends with the author's reworking of Deut. 18–23 (cols. 60–66), with particular concerns regarding sexual-purity laws (Lev. 18; 20).

Conclusion. The literature of rewritten Scripture at Qumran illustrates at least two things about the sect's understanding of the OT. First, it illustrates the importance of the biblical text that they both preserve and supplement by their numerous expansions. Second, it shows an abiding authority of the texts from the OT that, in their rewriting, they seek to contextualize to their own setting.

Additional Qumran Texts

The OT is utilized in many other ways in the Dead Sea Scrolls. Biblical laws, drawn primarily from the Pentateuch (esp. Exod. 20:22–23:33; Lev. 17–26; Deut. 12–26), form the base of *legal texts* particular to Qumran. The Damascus Document (CD) was previously known from two medieval manuscripts (CD-A and B) found in the storeroom of a synagogue in Old Cairo, the Cairo Genizah. It was supplemented significantly by the discovery of ten ancient copies of the same work at Qumran (4Q266–273; 5Q12; 6Q15), which include regulations for priests, ritual purity, relations with gentiles, and Sabbath observance. The Temple Scroll (11Q19), which is also regarded as rewritten Scripture, uses materials from Exod. 34–Deut. 23 to explain legal topics pertaining to the temple complex, purity, and a festival calendar. Interpretation of biblical texts is at the heart of 4QMMT (Miqṣat Maʿaśê ha-Torah, "Some of the Works of the Torah"), which appears in six manuscripts that treat legal matters via a letter framed as a legal debate, with the common refrain "our opinion" or "we say" (*ʾnḥnw ʾwmrym*) indicating its points of disagreement with the (unknown) correspondent. The points of disagreement are strictly legal in nature, based on biblical instructions from the law and often finding affinities in later rabbinic literature. They concern a wide variety of biblical matters, such as the correct time to eat the peace offering (Lev. 7:11–17; 4Q394 3–7.2.9–12), the preparation of the red heifer (Num. 19:2–10; m. Parah 3:7; 4Q394 3–7.2.13–17), or contact with the skins of a dead animal (Lev. 11:25, 29; 4Q397 2.22–23). But it also addresses legal matters not found in the Torah, such as bringing animal hides into the temple (4Q394 3–7.2.17–20; m. Hul. 9:2) and handling the skins and bones of unclean animals (4Q397 1–2.21–22; m. Yad. 4:6). Additional subjects pertain to tithes, unsuitable marriages, and liquid streams. These legal documents give indications of how the Qumran sect regarded the continuing authority of biblical law in their own day as well as illustrate their particular interpretation and application in their own legal concerns.

A diverse assortment of religious *poetic and liturgical works,* all deeply influenced by the OT, also reveal Qumran's interpretation of biblical texts. The most prominent of these are the Thanksgiving Hymns (1QH[a]; 1QH[b]; 4Q427–432) and the Songs of the Sabbath Sacrifice (4Q400–407; 11Q17; Mas1k). The Thanksgiving Hymns ("Hodayot") are a collection of hymns directed to God, many of which begin, "I give thanks to you" (*ʾwdkh;* AT). They are preserved in seven manuscripts in all and date to the middle of the Hasmonean period. The texts contain approximately twenty-five psalms that are individual rather than communal in nature. Like the biblical psalms, they are used to evoke the feelings and beliefs of the worshiper. But they will also speak to the person and claims of opponents, whom they describe as "teachers of lies and seers of falsehood" (1QH[a] 12.9–10; translations in this paragraph are from García Martínez and Tigchelaar). They have sought to "change your law" (*lhmyr twrtkh;* 1QH[a] 12.10). The author also speaks of God's law that "you [God] engraved in my heart" (*ʾšr šnnth blbby;* 1QH[a] 12.10) in language resonating with adherence to wisdom (Prov. 3:3; 7:3). This illustrates how foundational the law is to the author, who elsewhere repeats familiar themes found in the biblical psalms—for example, God as creator, the lowliness of humanity, the violence done to the righteous by the wicked and subsequent vindication from God, the wisdom given by God to the righteous, and the place of the righteous singing praises to God—in portions particularly resonating with the biblical texts (VanderKam, *Today,* 63–64).

The Qumran sect's high regard for the OT and strict interpretation of it creates a fundamental problem: How does one adhere to a strict hermeneutic, including for cultic worship, without access to the Jerusalem temple? In some respects, Qumran liturgies and corporate worship likely address these concerns. Among these is the Angelic Liturgy, a work comprised of thirteen poems allotted to Sabbaths for one-fourth of a calendar year, based on a 364-day calendar. It is to be performed as a corporate liturgy, and it uses a repetitive style that may serve to enhance meditation. In this work, which is strongly influenced by the language of Ezek. 1, the worshiper accompanies an angelic priest into the heavenly temple. In addition to depictions of the roles of the heavenly priests (songs 1 and 2), the worshiper experiences praises and blessings pronounced by the angelic priests within the heavenly sanctuary (songs 6–8). Other songs take the worshiper on a virtual tour through the heavenly sanctuary, first through the entrance (song 9) and then through the sanctuary's veils (song 10) to the inner sanctuary, where shapes on the walls are animated (song 11). In the sanctuary one also encounters God's throne and the angelic priests wearing their priestly garments (song 13). The work concludes with an abbreviated tour in the reverse direction. All the cultic furnishings and practices are based, to varying degrees and in various ways, on biblical instruction.

Conclusion

Evidence for how the OT was interpreted by the Jewish sect at Qumran by no means suffers from a want of materials. The pesharim are replete with explicit citations of biblical texts and contextual applications from the interpreter. They illustrate how the sectarians viewed the prophetic utterances of biblical texts as applicable to their own setting and circumstances, through viewing the OT prophecies as directly or typologically fulfilled in their community, though other uses are also found. Inevitably, the promises of God to Israel in the OT are applied to the *yaḥad* at Qumran. The judgments of God upon Israel's enemies, even where explicitly identified with particular people and nations in the Bible, are applied (plausibly typologically) by the *yaḥad* to their own opponents—Jew or gentile. Scriptures are both preserved and "rewritten" in a manner that demonstrates the concern for the narrative of the Bible on the one hand and keen interest in the development of their own eschatological views on the other. Distinctive sectarian laws are deeply informed by the OT, as are the poetic and liturgical writings. Together this material does not provide an entirely uniform model for how Qumran interpreted the Bible. But it does furnish today's readers with a sense of the importance of the biblical texts preserved among these curious Jews in the Judean Desert as well as the lengths to which they would go to underscore the relevance of the Scriptures for their own unique context.

See also OT Use of the OT: Comparison with the NT Use of the OT; *other Dead Sea Scrolls articles; Mishnah, Talmud, and Midrashim articles; Philo articles; Pseudepigrapha articles; Septuagint articles; Targums articles*

Bibliography. Bernstein, M. J., "What Has Happened to the Laws? The Treatment of Legal Material in 4QReworked Pentateuch," *DSD* 15 (2008): 24–49; Bockmuehl, M., "The Dead Sea Scrolls and the Origins of Biblical Commentary," in *Text, Thought, and Practice in Qumran and Early Christianity,* ed. R. Clements and D. R. Schwartz, STDJ 84 (Brill, 2009), 3–30; Brooke, G. J., "Qumran Pesher," *RevQ* 10 (1979): 483–503; Brooke, "Thematic Commentaries on Prophetic Scriptures," in *Biblical Interpretation at Qumran,* ed. M. Henze, SDSSRL (Eerdmans, 2005), 134–57; Brooke, G. J., D. K. Falk, E. J. C. Tigchelaar, and M. M. Zahn, eds., *The Scrolls and Biblical Traditions,* STDJ 103 (Brill, 2012); Brownlee, W. H., "Biblical Interpretation among the Sectaries of the Dead Sea Scrolls," *BA* 19 (1951): 54–76; Brownlee, "The Habakkuk Commentary," in *The Isaiah Manuscript and the Habakkuk Commentary,* ed. M. Burrows with the assistance of J. C. Trever and W. H. Brownlee (American School of Oriental Research, 1950), xix–xxi, lv–lxi; Campbell, J. G., *The Exegetical Texts,* CQS 4 (T&T Clark, 2007); Carmignac, J., "Le document de Qumrân sur Melkisédeq," *RevQ* 7 (1969–71): 343–78; Carmignac, "Notes sur les Peshârîm," *RevQ* 3 (1962): 505–38; Charlesworth, J. H., ed., *The Bible and the Dead Sea Scrolls* (Baylor University Press, 2006); Collins, J. J., *The "Dead Sea Scrolls,"* Lives of Great Religious Books (Princeton University Press, 2013); Collins, J. J., "The Transformation of the Torah in Second Temple Judaism," *JSJ* 43 (2012): 455–74; Collins, M. A., "Micah, Pesher of," *ESTJ* 1:374–75; Collins, M. A., *The Use of Sobriquets in the Qumran Dead Sea Scrolls,* LSTS 67 (T&T Clark, 2009); Crawford, S. W., *The Temple Scroll and Related Texts,* CQS 2 (Sheffield Academic, 2000); Cross, F. M., *The Ancient Library at Qumran,* 3rd ed. (Augsburg Fortress, 2000); Davila, J. R., *Liturgical Works,* ECDSS 6 (Eerdmans, 2000); Davila, "The Macrocosmic Temple, Scriptural Exegesis, and the Songs of the Sabbath Sacrifice," *DSD* 9, no. 1 (2002): 1–19; de Troyer, K., and A. Lange, eds., *Reading the Present in the Qumran Library* (Society of Biblical Literature, 2005); de Vaux, R., *Archaeology and the Dead Sea Scrolls* (Oxford University Press, 1973); Dimant, D., "Pesharim, Qumran," *ABD* 5:244–51; Dimant, "The Pesher of the Periods (4Q180–181)," *ESTJ* 1:422–24; Elledge, C. D., "Dead Sea Scrolls," *ESTJ* 2:190–93; Elliger, K., *Studien zum Habakuk Kommentar vom Toten Meer* (Mohr-Siebeck, 1953); Falk, D. K., *Daily, Sabbath, and Festival Prayers in the Dead Sea Scrolls,* STDJ 27 (Brill, 1998); Falk, *The Parabiblical Texts,* LSTS 63 (T&T Clark, 2007); Fishbane, M., *Biblical Interpretation in Ancient Israel* (Clarendon, 1985); Fitzmyer, J. A., *The Genesis Apocryphon of Qumran Cave 1 (1Q20),* BibOr 18B, 2nd ed. (Pontifical Biblical Institute, 2004); Flint, P. W., ed., *The Bible at Qumran* (Eerdmans, 2001); García Martínez, F., "The Contents of the Manuscripts from the Caves of Qumran," in *The Caves of Qumran,* ed. M. Fidanzio, STDJ 118 (Brill, 2016), 67–79; García Martínez, F., and E. J. C. Tigchelaar, *The Dead Sea Scrolls Study Edition,* 2 vols. (Brill, 1997–1998); Goff, M. J., *Discerning Wisdom,* VTSup 116 (Brill, 2007); Goldman, L., "Pesharim," *ESTJ* 2:600–602; Gurtner, D. M., *Introducing the Pseudepigrapha of Second Temple Judaism* (Baker, 2020); Harrington, H. K., *The Purity Texts,* CQS 5 (T&T Clark, 2004); Hempel, C., *The Damascus Texts* (Sheffield Academic, 2000); Horgan, M. P., "Habakkuk Pesher," in *Pesharim, Other Commentary, and Related Texts,* ed. J. H. Charlesworth et al., PTSDSSP 6B (Westminster John Knox, 2002), 157–85; Horgan, "Hosea, Pesher of," *ESTJ* 1:246–47; Horgan, *Pesharim,* CBQMS 8 (Catholic Biblical Association, 1979); Jassen, A. P., "Pesharim and the Rise of Commentary in Early Jewish Interpretation," *DSD* 19 (2012): 363–98; Jokiranta, J., "Psalms, Pesher on," *ESTJ* 1:457–59; Katzin, D., "The Use of Scripture in 4Q175," *DSD* 20 (2013): 200–36; Levinson, B. M., *A More Perfect Torah* (Eisenbrauns, 2013); Lim, T. H., *Pesharim,* CQS 3 (Sheffield Academic, 2002); Lundberg, M. J., "Isaiah, Pesher of," *ESTJ* 1:256–58; Machiela, D. A., *The Dead Sea Genesis Apocryphon,* STDJ 79 (Brill, 2009); Magness, J., *The Archaeology of Qumran and the Dead Sea Scrolls* (Eerdmans, 2002); Mason, E. F., *"You Are a Priest Forever,"* STDJ 74 (Brill, 2008); Nickelsburg, G. W. E., "The Bible Rewritten and Expanded," in *Jewish Writings of the Second Temple Period,* ed. M. E. Stone, CRINT 2/2 (Fortress, 1984), 89–156; Penner, J., *Patterns of Daily Prayer in Second Temple Judaism,* STDJ 104 (Brill, 2012); Puech, É., "Notes sur le manuscrit de XIQMelkîsèdeq," *RevQ* 12 (1987): 483–513; Rietz, H. W. M., "Testimonia (4Q175)," *ESTJ* 1:530–33; Schiffman, L., *The Courtyards of the House of the Lord,* STDJ 75 (Brill, 2008); Schuller, E. M., "Recent Scholarship on the Hodayot 1993–2010," *CBR* 19 (2011): 119–62; Segal, M., "Between Bible and Rewritten Bible," in *Biblical Interpretation at Qumran,* ed. M. Henze, SDSSRL (Eerdmans, 2005), 10–28; Steudel, A., *Der Midrasch zur Eschatologie,* STDJ 13 (Brill, 1994); Strugnell, J., "The Angelic Liturgy at Qumran," in *Congress Volume: Oxford 1959,* VTSup 7 (Brill, 1960), 318–45; Swanson, D. D., *The Temple Scroll and the Bible* (Brill, 1995); Tzoref, S., "Florilegium (4Q174)," *ESTJ* 1:212; Tzoref, "Genesis Commentaries (4Q252–254, 254a)," *ESTJ* 1:220–22; VanderKam, J. C., *The Dead Sea Scrolls and the Bible* (Eerdmans, 2012); VanderKam, *The Dead Sea Scrolls Today,* 2nd ed. (Eerdmans, 2010); Vermes, G., "The Qumran Interpretation of Scripture in Its Historical Setting," *ALUOS* 6 (1969): 85–97; Wise, M. O., *A Critical Study of the Temple Scroll from Qumran Cave 11* (University of Chicago Press, 1990); Yadin, Y., *The Temple Scroll* (Weidenfeld & Nicolson, 1985); Zahn,

M. M., *Rethinking Rewritten Scripture*, STDJ 95 (Brill, 2011); Zahn, "Rewritten Scripture," in *OHDSS*, 323–36.

DANIEL M. GURTNER

Dead Sea Scrolls, OT Use in: Comparison with NT Use of the OT

As noted elsewhere ("Dead Sea Scrolls, Use of the OT in"), the Dead Sea Scrolls furnish an unprecedented cache of about nine hundred ancient documents. About one-fourth of this material is comprised of biblical texts. Of these, most attested are Psalms (thirty-six "copies"), Deuteronomy (twenty-nine), and Isaiah (twenty-one). Notably, this proportion and priority are known to reflect usages by the NT authors as well. These three books are followed by Exodus (seventeen); Genesis (fifteen); Leviticus (thirteen); then Daniel, Numbers, and the twelve Minor Prophets (each with eight); followed by Jeremiah and Ezekiel (six each). The books of Samuel, Job, Song of Solomon, Ruth, and Lamentations are each attested by four copies. Three copies each were found of Judges, Kings, and Ecclesiastes; two each of Joshua and Proverbs; and one each of Ezra-Nehemiah and Chronicles. Most of these (137 of 202 copies of biblical MSS) were found in Cave 4 (VanderKam, 29–31).

James VanderKam remarks that these proportions give an accurate reflection of the emphases of the Qumran group. The abundance of Psalms could be used for the worship, meditation, and prooftexting known to occur among the Qumran *yaḥad* (community). Narratives such as the Pentateuch provide them with historical examples, while legal books (Exodus through Deuteronomy) undergird the communal living formed by the group. The prophecies from Isaiah furnish them with an assortment of predictions in which to identify their eschatological leader. Perhaps modest importance for the Qumran group accounts for the sparse attention to some historical books (Joshua, Judges, Samuel, Kings, Ezra, Nehemiah, and Chronicles) and the absence of Esther (VanderKam, 31–32).

Though nearly all biblical texts from Qumran are fragmentary, one prominent exception is worth mentioning: the book of Isaiah (1QIsa[a]). This is a complete manuscript of Isaiah found in 1947 and is the only completely preserved copy of any biblical book. It was copied not later than 75 BC, consists of fifty-four columns an average of 26 centimeters in height, and has a total length of 7.34 meters (Ulrich, 258–61). Being a thousand years older than the MT makes it an important witness to the text of Isaiah around the time of the NT. Textually, it contributes to scores of minor variants between it, the MT, other Qumran manuscripts, and the Septuagint. There are seven more substantial instances (one to four and one-half verses) in which the MT contains readings not found in the Isaiah Scroll (2:9b–10; 34:17b–35:2; 37:4–7; 38:20b–22; 40:7aβ–8a, 14b–16; 63:3).

Scripture was also preserved among the Dead Sea Scrolls in the form of phylacteries (Heb. *tepîllîm*; Aram. *təpîllîn*) and mezuzot. These are excerpts of texts from the Torah that were typically written on animal skin and placed in leather containers. Phylacteries were attached by leather thongs to the forehead and the hand, a practice based on a literal understanding of Exod. 13:9 (cf. 13:16; Deut. 6:8; 11:18) in which a biblical text is to be "a sign on your hand and a reminder [or emblem] on your forehead." Mezuzot were attached to the gates and doorposts of homes in fulfillment of the instruction to "write them on the doorframes of your houses and on your gates" (Deut. 6:9; 11:20). Fragments of twenty-six texts from phylacteries were found at Qumran, containing Exod. 12:43–13:16; Deut. 5:1–6:9; 10:12–11:21; and sometimes Deut. 32. Mezuzot from Qumran contain portions of Exodus (Exod. 20:7–12 [4Q149]; 14:1–4 [4Q154]; 13:11–16 [4Q155]) and Deuteronomy (Deut. 10:12–11:1 [8Q4]).

Qumran material is valuable for the interpreter of the NT for at least two reasons. First, it provides an abundance of manuscripts that predate the MT by a millennium. These readings are preserved primarily in Hebrew but also in Greek and furnish the interpreter with textual options potentially available for the authors of the NT. When examining the NT authors' use of the OT, the interpreter is thereby furnished with highly accessible ancient witnesses to an authentic text that existed, in most instances, decades or even a century or more prior to the writing of the NT. For this reason, I have carefully collated the primary citations of the OT in the NT, noted where the OT text quoted in the NT is extant among the Scrolls, and catalogued them in table 1.

Table 1. Qumran Manuscripts of OT Texts Cited in the NT

OT Text	NT Citation	DSS Manuscript of OT Text
Genesis		
Gen. 1:27	Matt. 19:4; Mark 10:6	4Q4; 4Q10
Gen. 2:2	Heb. 4:4	4Q10
Gen. 2:7	1 Cor. 15:45	4Q7
Gen. 21:10	Gal. 4:30	4Q365; 4Q252
Gen. 48:4	Acts 7:5	4Q1

OT Text	NT Citation	DSS Manuscript of OT Text
Exodus		
Exod. 1:8	Acts 7:18	4Q1
Exod. 2:14 LXX	Acts 7:27–28	4Q13
Exod. 2:22	Acts 7:6	4Q11
Exod. 3:7–10	Acts 7:34	4Q1; 4Q377 1.1.9
Exod. 9:16	Rom. 9:17	4Q14

OT Text	NT Citation	DSS Manuscript of OT Text
Exod. 12:46	John 19:36	4Q11; 4Q14; 4Q128; 4Q136; 4Q140; 4Q37
Exod. 13:2	Luke 2:23	4Q37; 4Q154; 4Q132; 4Q145; Mur. 4; 1Q13
Exod. 13:12	Luke 2:23	4Q129; 4Q133; 4Q155; 4Q22
Exod. 13:15	Luke 2:23	4Q129; 4Q133; 4Q155; 4Q135; 4Q15
Exod. 20:11	Acts 4:24; 14:15	4Q149
Exod. 20:12 // Deut. 5:16	Matt. 15:4; Mark 7:10; Eph. 6:2–3	4Q149; 4Q158
Exod. 22:27 (ET 22:28)	Acts 23:5	4Q22
Exod. 32:6	1 Cor. 10:7	4Q22
Exod. 33:19	Rom. 9:15	4Q22
Leviticus		
Lev. 11:44	1 Pet. 1:16	4Q365
Lev. 19:2	1 Pet. 1:16	11Q1; 4Q367
Lev. 19:12	Matt. 5:33	4Q367
Lev. 23:29	Acts 3:23	11Q1
Lev. 26:12	2 Cor. 6:16	4Q119
Numbers		
Num. 12:7	Heb. 3:2, 5	4Q23; 4Q27
Num. 16:5	2 Tim. 2:19	4Q27
Num. 30:2	Matt. 5:33	4Q27
Deuteronomy		
Deut. 5:16	Matt. 15:4; Mark 7:10; Eph. 6:2–3	4Q142; 4Q134; 1Q13; 4Q137; 4Q41; 4Q129; 4Q139
Deut. 5:21	Rom. 7:7	4Q37
Deut. 6:4	Mark 12:29, 32	4Q135; 4Q140; 4Q130; 4Q43; Mur. 4
Deut. 6:5	Matt. 22:37; Mark 12:30, 33; Luke 10:27	4Q140; 4Q43; 4Q130; 4Q150; 4Q152; Mur. 4
Deut. 8:3	Matt. 4:4; Luke 4:4	4Q30; 4Q33
Deut. 9:19	Heb. 12:21	4Q30
Deut. 10:20	Matt. 4:10; Luke 4:8	4Q128; 4Q138; 4Q151
Deut. 17:7	1 Cor. 5:13	4Q30
Deut. 18:15–20	Acts 3:22	4Q33
Deut. 19:15	Matt. 18:16; 2 Cor. 13:11; 1 Tim. 5:19	4Q38a
Deut. 21:23	Gal. 3:13	4Q36
Deut. 25:4	1 Cor. 9:9; 1 Tim. 5:8	4Q33
Deut. 25:5	Matt. 22:24; Mark 12:19; Luke 20:28	4Q33
Deut. 27:26	Gal. 3:10, 13	4Q30
Deut. 29:3 (ET 29:4)	Rom. 11:8	4Q39
Deut. 29:17 (ET 29:18)	Heb. 12:15	4Q30 1.2
Deut. 30:12	Rom. 10:6	4Q29
Deut. 30:14	Rom. 10:8	4Q29
Deut. 31:6	Heb. 13:5	1Q5
Deut. 32:21	Rom. 10:19	1Q5
Deut. 32:35	Rom. 12:19; Heb. 10:30	4Q45
Deut. 32:43	Rom. 15:10; Heb. 1:6 (citing LXX)	4Q44
2 Samuel		
2 Sam. 7:8	2 Cor. 6:18	Ps151A 7 (11Q5 28.10–11)
Psalms		
Ps. 2:1	Acts 4:25	11Q7
Ps. 2:7	Acts 13:33; Heb. 1:5; 5:5	3Q2; 11Q7
Ps. 5:10 (ET 5:9)	Rom. 3:13	4Q83
Ps. 6:4 (ET 6:3)	John 12:27	11Q8
Ps. 14:1–3	Rom. 3:10–12	11Q7
Ps. 16:8–11	Acts 2:25–28	4Q85
Ps. 16:10	Acts 13:35	4Q85
Ps. 19:5 (ET 19:4)	Rom. 10:18	11Q7
Ps. 22:14 (ET 22:13)	1 Pet. 5:8	4Q88
Ps. 35:19	John 15:25	4Q98
Ps. 43:5	Mark 14:34	1Q12
Ps. 45:7 (ET 45:6)	Heb. 1:9	11Q8
Ps. 51:6 (ET 51:4)	Rom. 3:4	4Q91; 4Q85
Ps. 53:2–4 (ET 53:1–3)	Rom. 3:10–12	4Q83; 4Q85
Ps. 69:10 (ET 69:9)	John 2:17; Rom. 15:3	4Q83
Ps. 82:6	John 10:34	MasP[a] (Mas1e)
Ps. 94:11	1 Cor. 3:20	4Q84
Ps. 94:14	Rom. 11:2	4Q84
Ps. 95:7–8	Heb. 3:15; 4:7	4Q94
Ps. 95:7–11	Heb. 3:7–11	1Q10; 4Q94
Ps. 95:11	Heb. 4:3, 5	1Q10
Ps. 102:26–28 (ET 102:25–27)	Heb. 1:10–12	4Q84
Ps. 104:4	Heb. 1:7	4Q31; 11Q5; 4Q86; 4Q93
Ps. 104:12	Matt. 13:32; Mark 4:32; Luke 13:19	4Q93
Ps. 107:26	Rom. 10:7	4Q88
Ps. 112:9	2 Cor. 9:9	4Q98f
Ps. 116:10	2 Cor. 4:13	4Q96
Ps. 118:6	Heb. 13:6	4Q84
Ps. 118:26	Matt. 21:9; 23:39; Mark 11:9; John 12:13; Luke 13:35; 19:38	4Q84; 11Q5
Ps. 119:32	2 Cor. 6:11	1Q10
Ps. 135:14	Heb. 10:30	4Q92
Ps. 139:14	Rev. 15:3	11Q5
Ps. 140:4 (ET 140:3)	Rom. 3:13	11Q5
Ps. 145:17	Rev. 15:3	4Q408 3+3a.6; 11Q5
Ps. 148:1	Matt. 21:9; Mark 11:10	11Q5
Ecclesiastes		
Eccles. 7:20	Rom. 3:10	4Q109
Isaiah		
Isa. 1:9	Rom. 9:29	1QIsa[a]; Mur. 3
Isa. 6:3	Rev. 4:8	1QIsa[a]; 4Q60
Isa. 6:9 LXX	Matt. 13:14; Mark 4:12; Acts 28:26	1QIsa[a]; 4Q162
Isa. 6:10	John 12:40	1QIsa[a]; 4Q60
Isa. 7:14	Matt. 1:23	1QIsa[a]
Isa. 8:10	Matt. 1:23	1QIsa[a]; 4Q59; 4Q60
Isa. 8:12	1 Pet. 3:14	1QIsa[a]; 4Q59; 4Q60; 4Q65
Isa. 8:13	1 Pet. 3:15	1QIsa[a]; 4Q59; 4Q60; 4Q65
Isa. 8:14	Rom. 9:33; 1 Pet. 2:8	1QIsa[a]; 4Q59; 4Q65
Isa. 10:3	1 Pet. 2:12	1QIsa[a]; 4Q59
Isa. 10:22	Rom. 9:27	1QIsa[a]
Isa. 11:2	1 Pet. 4:14	1QIsa[a]
Isa. 11:10	Rom. 15:12	1QIsa[a]; 4Q57
Isa. 12:2	Heb. 2:13	1QIsa[a]; 4Q59; 4Q56
Isa. 13:10	Matt. 24:29; Mark 13:24	1QIsa[a]; 4Q56

OT Text	NT Citation	DSS Manuscript of OT Text
Isa. 22:13	1 Cor. 15:32	1QIsa^{a}; 4Q57; 1Q8; 4Q55
Isa. 25:8	1 Cor. 15:54; Rev. 7:17; 21:4	1QIsa^{a}; 4Q57
Isa. 26:20 LXX	Heb. 10:37	1QIsa^{a}
Isa. 28:11	1 Cor. 14:21	1QIsa^{a}; 4Q57
Isa. 28:16	Rom. 9:33; 10:11; 1 Pet. 2:6	1QIsa^{a}; 1Q8; 4Q60
Isa. 29:14	1 Cor. 1:19	1QIsa^{a}
Isa. 35:4	John 12:15	1QIsa^{a}; 1Q8
Isa. 35:5	Matt. 11:5; Luke 7:22	1QIsa^{a}; 1Q8
Isa. 40:3	Matt. 3:3; Mark 1:3; John 1:23	1QIsa^{a}; 4Q56; 1Q8
Isa. 40:13	Rom. 11:34; 1 Cor. 2:16	1QIsa^{a}
Isa. 42:1–4	Matt. 12:18–21	1QIsa^{a}; 4Q56
Isa. 42:12	1 Pet. 2:9 (?)	1QIsa^{a}; 4Q56
Isa. 42:18	Matt. 11:5; Luke 7:22	1QIsa^{a}; 4Q61
Isa. 45:21	Mark 12:32; Acts 15:18	1QIsa^{a}; 4Q56
Isa. 45:23	Rom. 14:11	1QIsa^{a}; 4Q56
Isa. 49:8	2 Cor. 6:2	1QIsa^{a}; 1Q8; 4Q58
Isa. 49:10	Rev. 7:16	1QIsa^{a}; 4Q58
Isa. 52:4	2 Cor. 6:17	1QIsa^{a}; 4Q58
Isa. 52:7	Rom. 10:15	1QIsa^{a}; 1Q8; 4Q56
Isa. 52:11	2 Cor. 6:17	1QIsa^{a}; 1Q8; 4Q57
Isa. 52:15	Rom. 15:21	1QIsa^{a}; 4Q57; 1Q8
Isa. 53:1	John 12:38; Rom. 10:16	1QIsa^{a}; 1Q8; 4Q57
Isa. 53:4	Matt. 8:17; 1 Pet. 2:24	1QIsa^{a}; 1Q8
Isa. 53:5	1 Pet. 2:24	1QIsa^{a}; 1Q8
Isa. 53:6	1 Pet. 2:25	1QIsa^{a}; 1Q8; 4Q57
Isa. 53:7–8	Acts 8:32–33	1QIsa^{a}; 1Q8; 4Q57; 4Q58
Isa. 53:12	Luke 22:37; 1 Pet. 2:24	1QIsa^{a}; 1Q8; 4Q56; 4Q57; 4Q58
Isa. 54:1	Gal. 4:27	1QIsa^{a}; 1Q8; 4Q58
Isa. 54:13	John 6:45	1QIsa^{a}; 4Q57; 4Q69a
Isa. 55:3	Acts 13:34	1QIsa^{a}; 1Q8
Isa. 55:10	2 Cor. 9:10	1QIsa^{a}; 1Q8
Isa. 56:7	Matt. 21:13; Mark 11:17; Luke 19:46	1QIsa^{a}; 4Q62a
Isa. 59:7	Rom. 3:15–17	1QIsa^{a}; 1Q8
Isa. 59:20	Rom. 11:26	1QIsa^{a}; 1Q8
Isa. 61:1–2	Luke 4:18–19	1QIsa^{a}; 1Q8; 4Q56
Isa. 62:11	Matt. 21:5	1QIsa^{a}; 1Q8
Isa. 65:2	Rom. 10:21	1QIsa^{a}
Isa. 66:2	Acts 7:50	1QIsa^{a}; 1Q8
Isa. 66:14	John 16:22	1QIsa^{a}; 1Q8
Isa. 66:24	Mark 9:48	1QIsa^{a}; 1Q8; 4Q56; 4Q57
Jeremiah		
Jer. 9:22–23 (ET 9:23–24)	1 Cor. 1:31; 2 Cor. 10:17	4Q71
Jer. 12:3	James 5:5	4Q70
Jer. 12:15	Acts 15:16	4Q70
Jer. 22:24	Rom. 14:11	4Q72
Ezekiel		
Ezek. 5:11	Rom. 14:11	11Q4
Hosea		
Hosea 1:6	1 Pet. 2:10	4Q79
Hosea 1:9	1 Pet. 2:10	4Q79
Hosea 2:1	Rom. 9:26–27	4Q79; 4Q82
Hosea 2:25 (ET 2:23)	Rom. 9:25; 1 Pet. 2:10	4Q82
Amos		
Amos 3:13	Rev. 4:8; 15:3	4Q78
Jonah		
Jon. 2:1 (ET 1:17)	Matt. 12:40	4Q76; 8Ḥev1
Micah		
Mic. 5:1, 3 (ET 5:2, 4)	Matt. 2:6	8Ḥev1
Habakkuk		
Hab. 1:5	Acts 13:41	8Ḥev1; Mur. 88
Hab. 2:3	Heb. 10:37	Mur. 88; 8Ḥev1
Hab. 2:4	Rom. 1:17; Gal. 3:11; Heb. 10:38	Mur. 88; 4Q82 (?)
Haggai		
Hag. 2:6	Heb. 12:26	Mur. 88
Hag. 2:21	Heb. 12:26	Mur. 88; 4Q80
Zechariah		
Zech. 3:2	Jude 9	8Ḥev1; 4Q80
Zech. 12:10	John 19:37; Rev. 1:7	4Q80
Malachi		
Mal. 3:1	Matt. 11:10; Mark 1:2; Luke 7:27	4Q76
Mal. 3:17	1 Pet. 2:9	4Q76
Mal. 3:23 (ET 4:5)	Matt. 17:10; Mark 9:11	4Q76

A second reason the Qumran material is valuable for the interpreter of the NT is that it yields scores of examples of how the Qumran interpreters used and interpreted the same OT texts cited by NT authors. For this reason, I have also carefully collated the primary citations of OT texts that are cited in both the NT and the Dead Sea Scrolls and catalogued them in table 2.

Table 2. OT Texts Cited in Both the NT and DSS

OT Text Cited	NT Citation	DSS Citation
Gen. 1:27	Matt. 19:4; Mark 10:6	4Q504 8(recto).4; 6Q15 1.3; CD-A 4.21
Gen. 2:7	1 Cor. 15:45	1QH^{a} 11.21–22; 4Q504 8(verso).4–5
Gen. 2:24	Matt. 19:5; Mark 10:7–8; 1 Cor. 6:16; Eph. 5:31	4Q418 10.4–6
Gen. 12:3	Gal. 3:8; Rev. 1:7	ALD 10.12 (59)
Gen. 14:17–20	Heb. 7:1	ALD 8–10, 13; 1QApGen ar (1Q20) 22.12–26
Gen. 15:6	Rom. 4:3, 9, 22; Gal. 3:6; James 2:23	4Q398 14–17.2.7 (C 31 = 4QpapMMT^{c})
Gen. 15:13–14	Acts 7:6	ALD 11.2 (63)
Exod. 19:5–6	1 Pet. 2:9	ALD 4.7 (3c)
Exod. 20:12 // Deut. 5:16	Matt. 15:4; Mark 7:10; Eph. 6:2	4Q416 2.3.15–19 (4QInstruction^{b} = 4Q418 9–10)
Lev. 12:8	Luke 2:24	4Q266 6.2.12–13 (= 4QDamascusDocument^{a})
Lev. 18:5	Rom. 10:5; Gal. 3:12	CD-A 3.15–16
Lev. 19:12	Matt. 5:33	CD-A 15.3

OT Text Cited	NT Citation	DSS Citation
Lev. 19:18	Matt. 5:43; 19:19; 22:39; Mark 12:31, 33; Luke 10:27; Rom. 12:19; 13:9; Gal. 5:14; James 2:8	CD-A 6.20–21; 9.2
Deut. 18:15–20	Acts 3:22	4Q375 1.1.1; 4Q158 6.6–8; 4Q175 5–8
Deut. 29:17 (ET 29:18)	Heb. 12:15	1QH[a] 12.15
Deut. 31:6	Heb. 13:5	1Q33 15.7–9
2 Sam. 7:14	2 Cor. 6:18; Heb. 1:5; Rev. 21:7	4Q174 1.1.10–12
Ps. 2:1	Acts 4:25	4Q174 3.18–19
Ps. 22:14 (ET 22:13)	1 Pet. 5:8	1QH[a] 13.12–13
Ps. 41:10 (ET 41:9)	John 13:18	1QH[a] 13.25–26
Isa. 6:3	Rev. 4:8	1QH[a] 8.12
Isa. 10:22	Rom. 9:27	4Q161 2–6.2.1–7
Isa. 11:2	1 Pet. 4:14	1QH[a] 6.36; ALD 3.6 (1av.8); 1QS 4.3; 4Q444 1.3; 4Q161 8–10.3.11–16
Isa. 22:13	1 Cor. 15:32	4Q177 1.12–13
Isa. 28:11	1 Cor. 14:21	1QH[a] 10.20–21; 12.17; 4Q430 1.4
Isa. 28:16	Rom. 9:33; 10:11; 1 Pet. 2:6	1QS 8.7–8; 4Q259 2.16
Isa. 29:14	1 Cor. 1:19	1Q33 18.10
Isa. 40:3	Matt. 3:3; Mark 1:3; John 1:23	4Q176 1–2.1.4; 1QS 8.11–16; 9.19–20; ALD 2.5 (1av.7); 4Q256 18.3; 4Q258 8.4; 4Q259 3.19
Isa. 40:13	Rom. 11:34; 1 Cor. 2:16	4Q511 30.6
Isa. 49:10	Rev. 7:16	1QH[a] 16.5, 17
Isa. 52:7	Rom. 10:15	11Q13 2.15–16, 23
Isa. 61:1–2	Luke 4:18–19	1QH[a] 23.15–16; 4Q521 2.2 + 4.12; 11Q13 2.9, 19–20
Jer. 31:31–34	Heb. 8:8–12; 10:16–17	CD-A 6.19; 8.21; CD-B 19.33–34; 20.12; 1Q28b 5.21
Amos 9:11	Acts 15:16	4Q174 1.1.12–13; CD-A 7.16
Hab. 1:5	Acts 13:41	1QpHab 1.15–17; 2.1–10
Hab. 2:4	Rom. 1:17; Gal. 3:11; Heb. 10:38	1QpHab 7.11–17; 8.1–3
Zech. 9:9	Matt. 21:5; John 12:15	1Q33 19.5; 4Q492 1.5
Zech. 13:7	Matt. 26:31; Mark 14:27	CD-B 19.7–9

This material in table 2, which is the primary interest for the present purposes, furnishes interpreters with the hermeneutical uses of the OT and so provides points of comparison with their use in the NT. The exercise of comparing and contrasting usages can illustrate similarities and/or differences in the hermeneutics and beliefs of the Qumran sectarians on the one hand and the authors of the NT on the other. At the outset, however, it is important to be aware that the NT authors are often using the texts in a distinct way. Specifically, the NT, especially in the Gospels, frequently uses language of "fulfillment" of an OT text in the setting of the life and ministry of Jesus (see Stuckenbruck, 143). Qumran texts never use such language, and though they commonly expect biblical texts to be interpreted and applied in light of the interpreters' own setting, their usage lacks the explicitly telic nature of the NT use. Also, the Qumran citations of Scripture appear in wide varieties of Qumran documents: not only parabiblical texts and rewritten Scripture but also the pesharim, with their distinct formulaic usages (Stuckenbruck, 143–44). Add to this an assortment of legal material and liturgies, and one quickly recognizes that not only the differing contexts but also the differing genres are factors in comparing the use of the OT in the Dead Sea Scrolls and in the NT. Nevertheless, comparative analysis is fruitful, as some of the more prominent examples may illustrate.

Genesis 15:6: Counted as Righteousness

Context of Gen. 15:6. In Gen. 12:1 the Lord calls Abram to leave his home and kindred for a land God himself will show him. The Lord promises to make Abram "a great nation" (*gôy gādôl*), so Abram and his wife, Sarai, set out for Canaan (12:2–5). When they arrive at Shechem, then inhabited by the Canaanites, the Lord promises to Abram that the land will be given to Abram's offspring, so Abram builds an altar to the Lord there (12:6–7). After a sojourn in Egypt (12:10–13:2), Abram and Sarai return to the altar he built, call upon the name of the Lord (13:4), and then settle in the land of Canaan (13:12). There the Lord again speaks to Abram, promising to give all the land he sees to him and his offspring forever (13:14–15). Then he promises to make his offspring "like the dust of the earth, so that if anyone could count the dust, then your offspring could be counted" (13:16). He settles by the oaks of Mamre and builds another altar to the Lord (13:18). Later, in Gen. 15, the word of the Lord comes to Abram in a vision (*bammaḥăzeh*), telling him that he will have his own heir, his very own son (15:4), and that his descendants will be as numerous as the stars of the heavens (Gen. 15:5). Then, the author of Genesis says, Abram "believed the LORD" (*wəheʾĕmin bayhwāh*), and it was "credited to him as righteousness" (*wayyaḥšəbehā lô ṣədāqâ*; LXX *kai elogisthē autō eis dikaiosynēn*). The statement is important in the Pentateuch, for the verb *hʾmn* is more often used in negative contexts for unbelief (e.g., Gen. 45:26; Exod. 4:8; Num. 14:11; 20:12; Deut. 1:32; 9:23; Wenham, 329). Perhaps it is fitting then that here it is counted as righteousness, a notion found elsewhere of Phinehas (Ps. 106:31). Whereas "righteousness" (*ṣədāqâ*) is a positive act of human activity in the OT (e.g., Gen.

6:9; 7:1; 18:23, 25, 26; 20:4), here it is uniquely tied not to an action but to faith, a point that is developed by later authors.

Genesis 15:6 in the NT. The exemplary faith of Abraham receives considerable attention in the NT. Specifically, the text of Gen. 15:6 is utilized four times by Paul (Rom. 4:3, 9, 22; Gal. 3:6) and once by James (James 2:23).

Romans. Beginning in Rom. 3:20, Paul explains that no one will be justified (*dikaiōthēsetai*) by works of the law (*ex ergōn nomou*) but that now the righteousness of God (*dikaiosynē theou*) is manifest apart from the law (*chōris nomou*, 3:21; cf. 3:28). Instead, this righteousness is through faith in Jesus Christ (*dia pisteōs Iēsou Christou*, 3:22) to all who believe—Jew or gentile—since all people are in equal standing, sinners who have fallen short of the glory of God (3:22–23, 29–30). As an example of justification by faith being equally for Jews and gentiles, Paul evokes the example of Abraham, "our forefather according to the flesh" (4:1). Here Paul cites our verse from Gen. 15:6: "Abraham believed God, and it was credited to him as righteousness" (*episteusen de Abraam tō theō kai elogisthē autō eis dikaiosynēn*, Rom. 4:3). Paul's rendering, save the change from *Abram* to *Abraam* (which does not occur until Gen. 17:5) and the inclusion of a postpositive *de*, follows the LXX verbatim, which is itself nearly a precise rendering from the MT aside from the addition of Abram's name.

> Abraham believed God, and it was credited to him as righteousness. (Rom. 4:3)
>
> Abram believed the LORD, and he credited it to him as righteousness. (Gen. 15:6)
>
> And Abram believed God, and it was reckoned to him as righteousness. (Gen. 15:6 NETS)

Paul goes on in Rom. 4 to explain his point: The language of "counting" (*logizomai*) is not suitable for the one who works (*ergazomai*) to earn wages (*misthos*), so what was counted to Abram as righteousness was a gift (*kata charin*) acquired by believing in God (*pisteuō*). Moreover, when Abram's faith "was counted to" him "as righteousness" (*elogisthē tō Abraam hē pistis eis dikaiosynēn*, again a citation of Gen. 15:6), Abraham had not yet been circumcised (Rom. 4:9–10). This means that whatever "work" circumcision may be, even for Abraham it was received only *after* he was credited righteousness. Or simply put, Abraham, the ancestral father of Judaism, was credited righteousness *by faith* while he was still a gentile. So, now he is the father of all those "who also follow in the footsteps of the faith" that he had (Rom. 4:12). Above, we saw the circumstances under which Abram believed: having been given a promise several times regarding his offspring when as yet he had none. Then, when he was an old man ("about a hundred years old," Rom. 4:19), he still believed. "No unbelief made him waver" (4:20 ESV), and he was "fully convinced" that God could do what he promised (4:21 ESV). So, his faith is "counted to him as righteousness" (*elogisthē autō eis dikaiosynēn*, 4:22—the final reference to Gen. 15:6). Paul's illustration culminates in its application: just like with Abraham, righteousness is also "for us who believe in him who raised Jesus our Lord from the dead" (Rom. 4:24 AT). The importance here for Paul is that the righteousness credited to Abraham is not a declaration of a quality of Abraham's own but rather something external from him—meaning, from God—that is in response to Abraham's expression of faith (Longenecker, 496).

Galatians. Similarly, in Galatians, Paul confronts readers who have deserted Christ and turned to a "different gospel" (*heteron euangelion*, 1:6). There is debate as to what this "other gospel" is, but readers of Galatians know that, at the very least, it is brought by some "who trouble" the Galatians and "distort the gospel of Christ" (1:7 ESV). It is in some sense "contrary to" the one preached by Paul, and its advocates are accursed (1:8–9). But somehow the Galatians have been "bewitched" (3:1) and seem to be relying on "works of the law" (*ex ergōn nomou*, Gal. 3:2; cf. 3:5) rather than "hearing with faith" (*ex akoēs pisteōs*, 3:2 ESV; cf. 3:5). The kind of "faith" Paul has in mind is modeled by Abraham (*kathōs Abraam*, 3:6). And here Paul explains precisely the kind of faith that was modeled, quoting Gen. 15:6:

> Abraham "believed God, and it was credited to him as righteousness." (Gal. 3:6)
>
> Abraham believed God, and it was credited to him as righteousness. (Rom. 4:3)
>
> Abram believed the LORD, and he credited it to him as righteousness. (Gen. 15:6)
>
> Abram believed God, and it was reckoned to him as righteousness. (Gen. 15:6 NETS)

The wording here juxtaposes the verb (*episteusen*) and its subject (Abraham) but is otherwise identical to the Rom. 4 citation. His point is that the nature of Abraham's justification—by faith—is indicative of those who are the true "sons of Abraham" (Gal. 3:7 ESV). By contrast, those who depend on justification from works of the law (*ergōn nomou*) are in fact under a curse (3:10; cf. Deut. 27:26).

James. The Letter of James addresses the same issue of justification and the faith of Abraham from Gen. 15:6, but in a rather different context. Rather than addressing a justification by works of the law (Gal. 3:6) or by a faith accessible to Jew and gentile alike (Rom. 4:3, 9, 22), James is addressing one who claims to have faith (*pistis*) that has no works (*erga*) of any kind, even the most basic of communal charity among Christians. The question is whether such a "faith" can save him (James

2:14). He offers a clear illustration of someone seeing a person in need and wishing them well but doing nothing to aid them, and James asks, rhetorically, what good that is (2:15–16). Then he asserts that this kind of faith, which is a "faith by itself" that "does not have works," is not a saving faith but rather "is dead" (2:17 ESV). Those who merely have faith without accompanying works have nothing to show for it (2:18). Then James indicates the kind of "faith" he has in mind: "You believe that there is one God. Good! Even the demons believe that—and shudder" (2:19). The indication is that James's notion of a "faith" that does not save is one that can be shared with a demon, which is often regarded as "intellectual assent"—belief in factual matters without corresponding and illustrative behavior. Here it is worth noting that Paul does not use the *pistis* word group in this manner. James explains that "faith apart from works is useless" (*hē pistis chōris tōn ergōn argē estin*) and offers the example of Abraham, who was "justified by works" (*ex ergōn edikaiōthē*) when he offered up Isaac on the altar (2:20–21 ESV). This is in reference to the near sacrifice of Isaac (Gen. 22:1–18), which takes place in a context removed from Gen. 15:6 but seemingly puts in jeopardy the very offspring promised to Abram in Gen. 15:4. The point, James asserts, is that it is the kind of faith Abraham had, which "was active along with his works" (*hē pistis synērgei tois ergois autou*) and "completed by his works" (*ek tōn ergōn hē pistis eteleiōthē*), that is in view (2:22 ESV). And this fulfills the Scripture of Gen. 15:6: "Abraham believed God, and it was credited to him as righteousness" (*episteusen de Abraam tō theō, kai elogisthē autō eis dikaiosynēn*, James 2:23). The text here is identical to that cited in Rom. 4:3:

> Abraham believed God, and it was credited to him as righteousness. (James 2:23)
>
> Abraham believed God, and it was credited to him as righteousness. (Rom. 4:3)
>
> Abram believed the LORD, and he credited it to him as righteousness. (Gen. 15:6)
>
> Abram believed God, and it was reckoned to him as righteousness. (Gen. 15:6 NETS)

So, he concludes, a person is justified by works and not by faith alone (James 2:24). James's use of Gen. 15:6, then, is to explain to readers that the kind of faith spoken of in Gen. 15:6 is the kind that Abraham himself possessed and that is accompanied by the work of Gen. 22. It is in this sense that the "Scripture" (Gen. 15:6) was fulfilled. For James, the faith exhibited in Gen. 22 is the only truly legitimate and saving faith, the faith that raises the believer above the merely intellectual assent of demonic faith. And it is precisely this kind of faith—which is exhibited by the appropriately accompanying work—by which one is justified. A faith *without* such action is likely what James means when he says that one is considered righteous "not by faith alone" (James 2:24). It is a "faith" devoid of an accompanying work—a conception that Paul does not seem to consider—that cannot justify.

The NT, then, utilizes the citation of Gen. 15:6 to indicate the exemplary faith of Abraham, but in different ways. Paul reminds his readers that Abraham was, in effect, a gentile when he was justified and had no law by which to be justified. Moreover, it was his belief, contrary to all appearances, that justified him. James complements that view by citing Abraham as having exhibited an exemplary faith that had direct bearing on his actions, a quality of the very faith about which Paul too writes. We will see, however, that the sectarians at Qumran, in a very important document, understand that same verse and its implications in a considerably different way that serves their own sectarian interests.

Genesis 15:6 in the Dead Sea Scrolls. Abraham is a towering figure in Second Temple Judaism, and the scene in Gen. 15:6 is the subject of some reflection (e.g., Philo, *Abraham* 262; *Unchangeable* 4; Jub. 18:6; 1 Macc. 2:52). Among the Dead Sea Scrolls, Gen. 15:6 is quoted in 4QMMT (Miqṣat Maʿaśê ha-Torah), frequently referred to as the Halakic Letter. Written in the form of a letter, the document is a sectarian polemic written to an influential leader in Jerusalem and is generally agreed to reflect the early history of the Qumran sectarian group and the development of Jewish halakah in the second century BC. It is attested in six (4Q394–399), possibly seven (4Q313), manuscripts that can be reconstructed into a composite document (Qimron and Strugnell). It begins with an opening formulation, now lost, followed by an exposition on the calendar (Section A, 4Q394 3–7.1.1–3). Then, in Section B (4Q394 3–7.1–2; 4Q397 1–2; 4Q394 3–7.2; 4Q396 1–2.1; 4Q394 8.3–4; 4Q396 1–2.3–4) is the body of the letter, primarily addressing the mixture of what is holy with what is profane. These comprise a list of twenty-four examples of how the impure is being allowed to mix with the pure and so profane what is holy. The reader is exhorted to follow the example of the author and separate from those who practice such things.

In Section C (4Q397 14–21; 4Q398 11–13; 14–17.2) the author issues a warning of destruction to those who violate these rules (cf. Deut. 7:26), thus explaining why the author (and his community) have separated themselves from such uncleanness (C, lines 4–9). He exhorts them to do the same (lines 10–16). This is followed by two sets of illustrations of blessings and curses from Israel's past (lines 17–21, 23–26) and another warning (lines 21–23). At the very end comes a final exhortation (lines 23–32, from 4Q398 14–17.2.1–8 = 4Q399 1–2): The author claims that he has written to the recipient "some of the works of the law" (*mqṣt mʿśy htwrh*, C, line 27 WAC) for the readers that they may "possess insight and knowledge of the law" (line 28 AT). They will keep from the counsel of Belial (line 29) and find "it will be reckoned to you as righteousness" (*wnḥšbh lk lṣdqh*; AT). This means that they have "done what is right and good" before God (31 AT). The phrase is found in two places in the OT: The first, in reference to Abraham, is Gen. 15:6. But the author of MMT makes no reference to Abraham, so another possibility from the OT is worth considering—namely, the actions of Phinehas as referenced in Ps. 106:30–31. Phinehas is known from an episode in Num. 25, when Israel lived in Shittim and "the people began to whore with the daughters of Moab" (25:1 ESV). They bowed down to other gods and angered the Lord (25:2–3), who instructed Moses to strike down the chiefs of the people that the Lord's anger might be turned away from Israel (25:4–5). When an Israelite brought a Midianite woman to his family, Phinehas interceded by driving a spear through both the Israelite and the woman, and thus "the plague against the Israelites was stopped" (25:8). And though twenty-four thousand died (25:9), the Lord explicitly said that Phinehas by his action "has turned my anger away from the Israelites" (25:11). Recalling this, the psalmist celebrates the zeal of Phinehas, when he "stood up and intervened, and the plague was checked" (Ps. 106:30). This act, the psalmist continues, "was credited to him as righteousness [*wattēḥāšeb lô liṣdāqâ*] for endless generations to come" (106:31). The language here is nearly verbatim from Gen. 15:6. Comparison with the 4QMMT C 31 text reads as follows:

> And he credited it to him as righteousness. (Gen. 15:6)
>
> This was credited to him as righteousness. (Ps. 106:31)
>
> It will be reckoned to you as righteousness (4QMMT C 31 WAC)

A few distinctions can be instructive. First, note that the usage of the phrase in MMT is devoid of any reference either to Abra(ha)m or belief or to an act of Phinehas. The cause of the reckoning of righteousness is, contextually, bound to the author's understanding of halakah and the reader's adoption of it. Second, the Genesis *qal* imperfect *yaḥšəbehā* and the psalmist's *tēḥāšeb* (*niphal* imperfect) parallel the MMT *niphal* perfect, but all draw from the same root, *ḥšb*. Third and finally, the biblical indication that the righteousness was counted "to him" (*lw*; Abraham and Phinehas, respectively) naturally becomes in MMT the second person, "to you" (*lk*, the obedient readers). So, where the biblical texts attribute "righteousness" to the one who by faith believed the promises of God despite all external appearances (Abraham) or who acts in such a way on behalf of Israel to avert the righteous judgment of God (Phinehas), the Qumran text attributes it to the reader who (rightly) separates himself from the Jerusalem cult, where the sanctity of its worship is compromised by mixture with the profane.

The notion of "righteousness" (*ṣdq, ṣdqh*) is regarded as "a hallmark of Qumran theology" (Charlesworth, 781). It is foremost an attribute of God. For example, in the Hodayot, God alone, not people, is the worker of righteousness (1QH[a] 12.31–32; cf. 1QH[a] 8.28; 1QS 11.12–16). It is by God's righteousness that humans are cleansed from guilt (1QH[a] 12.36–37). The members of the Qumran *yaḥad* separated themselves from what they perceived as the improprieties of the Jerusalem temple cult to form their own sect (Mathews). In the present world, righteousness is lacking, even among the elect (cf. 1QH[a] 17.14–15; 1Q27 1.5–6). So, they are seldom described as righteous themselves but rather are called the "the sons of righteousness" (*bny ṣdq*; AT; 1QS 3.20, 22; 9.14; 1QM 13.10; 4Q259 3.10; 4Q424 3.10; 4Q502 1.10; 4Q503 48–50.8). In their outlook, personal righteousness is reserved for the Sons of Light at the end of time (1QS 3.15–16; 4.23–26; 11.12–16; cf. 1QH[a] 5.34–36; 14.4–35; 19.4–14; 1Q27 1.6). Perhaps the purpose of the Community Rule (1QS) is to prepare initiates for this in their commitment "to perform truth and righteousness and justice upon the earth" (1QS 1.5–6 AT; cf. 1QS 3.20). The "Teacher of Righteousness," to whom God has revealed the mysteries of his will (1QpHab 7.1–4), is himself righteous, in contrast to the "Wicked Priest" in Jerusalem (1QpHab 1.12–13 WAC). And the "righteous" who live by faith (Hab. 2:4) are defined in terms of loyalty to the Teacher (1QpHab 7.17), specifically "observing the Law" (FGM) among those "whom God will free from the house of judgment" (1QpHab 8.1–20 WAC). The reason for such freedom, the interpreter says, is "on account of their toil and of their loyalty to the Teacher of Righteousness" (1QpHab 7.2–3 FGM; cf. 1QS 8.15; 1QpHab 8.1–2). And their place in the wilderness is to prepare the way of the Lord by expounding the Law (1QS 8.1–17). The result, then, at Qumran is clearly the attribution of righteousness to the one who adheres to the proper teachings of Torah, especially as expounded by the Teacher.

Comparison. Literary affinities between Paul and MMT, including reference to "works of the law" and the citation of Gen. 15:6, have elicited much discussion among interpreters of the NT (e.g., Doering; Dunn, 1–97). Paul's appeal especially in Galatians may be in direct opposition to the kind of notion present in MMT. Paul's citation of Gen. 15:6 shows that it was the faith of Abraham that was regarded as righteousness (Gal. 3:6), and he insists that "works of the law" will by no means bring about justification (2:16). It may be the kind of "works of the law" advocated in 4QMMT that Paul regards as the teaching of "false brothers" (2:4 ESV). Though there is no evidence of Paul directly opposing the Qumran sectarians, the common language of "works of the Law" does give evidence from antiquity that there were in fact some Jews, those responsible for 4QMMT, that regarded some aspect of obedience to Torah as taught by the Teacher as the means of acquiring righteousness. For James the notion of being credited righteousness on the basis of legal or cultic regulations is absent. Rather, the righteousness that is credited in James's usage of Gen. 15:6 is one that is demonstrated by faith. Conversely, the component of faith in James, even at its bare level of intellectual assent, is entirely absent from all Qumran material.

Isaiah 40:3: Prepare the Way of the Lord

Isaiah 40:3 in its Isaianic context. Isaiah 40:3 occurs in a context in which the prophet announces the eschatological coming of the Lord to shepherd his sheep (40:1–11). This is good news, since in the face of threats to Jerusalem, God's might prevails over enemy nations and pagan gods. He rules over history and will one day establish justice on earth (40:12–42:13). The role of the prophet, then, is to prepare God's people for the coming of God himself. Isaiah 40 begins with an exhortation to comfort the people (40:1), a notion that in Isaiah is frequently associated with some blessing to the people, whether simply joy, restoration of land, or some kind of redemption (12:1; 30:18; 49:13; 51:3, 12; 52:9; 61:2; 66:13). The ones who are to do this are unidentified, though readers know there is more than one (Isaiah's *naḥămû*, "comfort," is plural). Readers simply know that God has instructed certain individuals to comfort his people and speak tenderly to Jerusalem (40:2) three things: first, "that her hard service has been completed," which may refer to military service, meaning that God here announces the end of Jerusalem's warfare (Smith, 94); second, "that her sin has been paid for," which is surely done by God (cf. 43:25; 44:22; 53:6–12; 55:7); third, "that she has received from the LORD's hand double for all her sins." This last statement is unclear, though in the context it must refer to something positive, as it is to be regarded as good news. Isaiah 40:3 announces "a voice of one calling" and then provides the content of what he calls. The content of what he announces has to do with making appropriate preparations for a time when all flesh will see God (40:5; cf. 62:10–11). It is regarded as analogous to a royal edict to repair roads on which a king will soon come (Smith, 95–96). So, the exhortations to "prepare the way" and "make straight" paths (40:3) pertain to the leveling out of uneven spots on this metaphorical highway for God. Fullness of divine justice will be established (40:4), and God's majestic deliverance will be evident to all (40:5; cf. Exod. 24:9–18). Though people are but temporary, the word of God stands forever (Isa. 40:6–8). Good tidings will be brought to Zion, Jerusalem, and the towns of Judah: "Here is your God" (40:9). He comes in power and tends his flock like a shepherd (40:10–11).

Isaiah 40:3 in the NT. Isaiah 40:3 is cited three times in the NT, all in the Gospels and all in reference to John the Baptist (Mark 1:3; Matt. 3:3; John 1:23). The first citation (Mark 1:3) occurs at the beginning of the evangelist's narrative of "the gospel of Jesus Christ" (1:1 ESV). Initially that good news is said to be in accordance with the prophet Isaiah: "Behold, I send my messenger before your face, who will prepare your way" (Mark 1:2 ESV). The difficulty is that the first citation comes not from Isaiah but Mal. 3:1, which is in turn an allusion to Exod. 23:20.

> I will send my messenger ahead of you, who will prepare your way. (Mark 1:2)

> And look, *I am sending my angel in front of you* in order to guard you on the way in order to bring you into the land that I prepared for you. (Exod. 23:20 NETS)

> *Behold, I am sending my messenger,* and he will oversee the way *before me.* (Mal. 3:1 NETS)

The context of Exod. 23:20 describes this as the role of the "angel of the Lord" (LXX *angelos kyriou;* MT *malak yhwh*), who goes before the camp of the sons of Israel (see also Exod. 23:20, 23; 32:34; 33:2). In Malachi there is an announcement that a messenger will be sent by the Lord to prepare the Lord's way in coming to his temple (3:1; cf. Ezek. 43:2–4; Hag. 1:8). Importantly, Malachi later (4:5) identifies the messenger as Elijah, whom God will send before the "day of the LORD." In light of Malachi's context, Mark's readers are to anticipate a direct, personal intervention on the part of God, with a forerunner making this announcement, who contextually is equated with John the Baptist. The notion of "preparing the way" (*hos kataskeuasei tēn hodon sou*) probably looks proleptically to the Isa. 40:3 citation to follow. Mark's attribution of these Exodus/Malachi citations to Isaiah likely results from the influence of an Isaianic notion of the coming of God for salvation. In juxtaposing the Exod. 23 / Mal. 3 citation with that of Isa. 40:3 (in Mark 1:3), Mark has indicated that the former is to be interpreted through the lens of the latter. Specifically, "preparing the way" in Mark 1:2 is equivalent to Mark 1:3's "Prepare the way of the Lord." These texts are melded here because of the messenger that begins God's inbreaking into eschatological deliverance, here through John the Baptist.

Mark's citation of Isa. 40:3 is found in Mark 1:3 and follows the LXX nearly verbatim:

> *A voice of one crying out in the wilderness: "Prepare the way of the Lord; make straight the paths* of our God." (Isa. 40:3 NETS)

> *A voice of one calling in the wilderness, "Prepare the way for the Lord, make straight paths* for him." (Mark 1:3)

The only difference is how it ends. Whereas the LXX ends with "the way of our God" (*tas tribous tou theou hēmōn*), Mark ends with "his ways" (*tas tribous autou;* AT). Perhaps Mark is familiar with a Greek text that differs from the LXX. This is possible, and the reading *autou* is attested and is likewise reflected in Matt. 3:3

and Luke 3:4. To whom Mark refers with his addition of *autou* is found from Isaiah, where the presumption seems to be that God's people are in need and only God himself is able to intervene effectively. Where the voice of Isa. 40:3 announces that Yahweh himself is coming, Mark identifies the announcer as John the Baptist, and the one coming is Jesus (Mark 1:4–9), all in direct prophetic fulfillment of Mal. 3:1 and Isa. 40:3.

Matthew's context is similar to that of Mark but less complicated. After an extended birth narrative of Jesus (Matt. 1–2), John the Baptist appears in the wilderness of Judea (3:1). Following John's exhortation to repent (3:2), the evangelist explains that John is the one spoken of "by the prophet Isaiah" (*dia Ēsaiou tou prophētou*) and then quotes Isaiah: "The voice of one crying in the wilderness: 'Prepare the way of the Lord; make his paths straight'" (3:3 ESV; Matthew's account is identical to that of Mark 1:3). Making the association with Elijah all the clearer, the First Evangelist describes John's attire in terms of "camel's hair" and a "leather belt around his waist" (Matt. 3:4; cf. 2 Kings 1:8; Zech. 13:4). Matthew ties this prophetic fulfillment only to Isa. 40:3 and not to Mal. 3:1, which Mark includes.

Finally, Isa. 40:3 is cited in the Gospel of John (1:23) in a context identical to those of Mark and Matthew, but in characteristically explanatory form. John the Baptist, though not known by that designation in the Fourth Gospel, is said to bear witness about Christ (the Word) while acknowledging that he himself is not the Christ (John 1:15–20). When asked about his identity, he claims to be the one (*egō*) spoken about in Isaiah the prophet (*kathōs eipen Ēsaias ho prophētēs*), citing Isa. 40:3:

> A voice of one crying out in the wilderness: "Prepare the way of the Lord; make straight the paths of our God." (Isa. 40:3 NETS)

> I am the voice of one calling in the wilderness, "Make straight the way for the Lord." (John 1:23)

John omits the reference to making straight his paths (*eutheias poieite tas tribous tou theou hēmōn*), and rather than the familiar *hetoimasate* used in LXX Isaiah and Mark/Matthew, John uses *euthynate* (from *euthynō*). The evangelist goes on to explain the nature and role of John in answer to questions from those sent by the Pharisees regarding his baptism (1:24–25). He announces the coming of one among them, whom they presently do not know and the strap of whose sandal he is unworthy to untie (1:26–27). When he, Jesus, arrives at John's baptism, John testifies that this is indeed he, "the Lamb of God, who takes away the sin of the world" (1:29). So, in the Fourth Gospel the citation not only serves to identify John's role in fulfillment of the Isaianic prophecy but also is quickly and explicitly tied with his testimony about the identity of Jesus as the "Lamb of God."

Isaiah 40:3 in the Dead Sea Scrolls. The identical text from Isa. 40:3 is famously cited in the Rule of the Community, since the work describes itself as "the book of the order of the *yaḥad*" (4QS[a] 1.1 AT; *sēper serek hayyaḥad*). It was found in multiple copies at Qumran and dates between the late second century BC and mid-first century AD. It contains the regulations, the teachings, and some liturgies for the Qumran community, as well as rites of initiation. The first text describes the conscription of initiates to the *yaḥad* who are to "separate from the session of perverse men to go into the wilderness, there to prepare the way of truth" (1QS 8.13 WAC). They find justification for this wilderness separation in Isa. 40:3: "In the wilderness prepare the way of the LORD; make straight in the desert a highway for our God" (ESV; cf. 1QS 8.14). These initiates are beginning to fulfill the Isa. 40:3 prophecy. The telling aspect of this is how the Qumran sectarians explain what it means to prepare the way of the Lord and precisely how that is done. For them, the interpretation follows: "This means the expounding of the Law, decreed by God through Moses for obedience, that being defined by what has been revealed for each age, and by what the prophets have revealed by His holy spirit" (1QS 8.15–16 WAC). It is important to observe that at Qumran the expounding of the law is explicitly tied with the interpretation of it by the Teacher of Righteousness, whose interpretation is regarded as divinely inspired. This is clarified later in the Community Rule, where each person is exhorted to "walk blamelessly with his fellow, guided by what has been revealed to them," which is regarded as "preparing the way in the desert" (1QS 9.19 WAC) and again pertains to legal instructions and keeping oneself "from perversity" in beginning prophetic fulfillment of Isa. 40:3 (1QS 9.21 WAC; cf. 4Q176 1–2.1.4).

Comparison. Isaiah 40:3 furnishes both the Dead Sea Scrolls and early Christianity with a fulcrum in the respective groups' self-identities. For the Jews at Qumran, they themselves are the ones preparing for the Isaianic coming of God and do so by study of Torah in accord with their Teacher. For the NT, the one preparing for the Isaianic coming of God is John the Baptist, and the coming of God himself is seen in the incarnate Christ. While scholars often debate the connotations for the respective communities in historical-critical rubrics, at a textual and theological level it is clear that the Christotelic reading of the Isaianic prophecy itself is of decisive importance, as with other OT citations shared between Qumran and the NT.

Conclusion

The comparison of the NT with the Dead Sea Scrolls could go on much further, examining many other OT prophetic texts that both corpuses understand to have been fulfilled. Notably, the mention of a prophet like Moses (Deut. 18:15–20) is applied to Christ in Acts 3:22 but also applied distinctly, though ambiguously, in the

Reworked Pentateuch (4Q158 6.6–8) and the Testimonia (4Q175 5–8). The designation of a son of David to rule on his father's throne forever (2 Sam. 7:14) is also applied to Christ numerous times in Matthew alone (Matt. 1:1, 20; 9:27; 12:23; 15:22; 20:30, 31; etc.), whereas at Qumran it is taken to refer to the "branch of David" who will rise up with the Interpreter of the Law (4Q174 1.1.11–12; cf. Amos 9:11). The Isaianic declaration of the Spirit of the Lord being upon an eschatological figure to proclaim the year of the Lord's favor (Isa. 61:1–2) is conflated with Isaiah 58:6 in Luke 4:18–19, presenting Jesus as an Isaianic bringer of eschatological Jubilee (Gurtner). Isaiah 61 is likewise conflated with other eschatological texts (e.g., 1QH[a] 23.15–16; 4Q521 2.2 + 4.12), also in a Jubilee context in the Melchizedek Scroll (11Q13 2.9, 19–20). The "new covenant" text from Jeremiah (Jer. 31:31–33) is seen as accomplished in the person and work of Christ (Heb. 8:8–12; 10:16–17), yet for the Qumran sectarians it is regarded as integral to their own community (CD-A 6.19; 8.21; CD-B 19.33–34; 20.12; 1Q28b 5.21). The exhortation to the daughters of Zion to rejoice at the coming of her King (Zech. 9:9) is cited with reference to the humility of Jesus's entry into Jerusalem (Matt. 21:5). At Qumran it becomes a war cry of sorts in an eschatological battle (1Q33 19.5; 4Q492 1.5). These and others could be explored further, but in many cases interpreters find that what distinguishes the NT reading from those of Qumran, and indeed of other Jewish writings in antiquity, is the Christ-event. The person and work of Jesus of Nazareth furnish early Christians with a Christotelic lens by which, in various ways, the NT authors read how the OT prophecies have been fulfilled.

See also OT Use of the OT: Comparison with the NT Use of the OT; *other Dead Sea Scrolls articles; Mishnah, Talmud, and Midrashim articles; Philo articles; Pseudepigrapha articles; Septuagint articles; Targums articles*

Bibliography. Bauckham, R., *James* (Routledge, 1999); Brooke, G. J., "Isaiah 40.3 and the Wilderness Community," in *New Qumran Texts and Studies*, ed. G. J. Brooke and F. G. Martínez, STDJ 15 (Brill, 1994), 117–32; Charlesworth, J. H., "Righteousness," *EDSS* 2:781–82; Doering, L., "4QMMT and the Letters of Paul," in *The Dead Sea Scrolls and Pauline Literature*, ed. J.-S. Rey, STDJ 102 (Brill, 2014), 69–87; Dunn, J. D. G., *The New Perspective on Paul*, rev. ed. (Eerdmans, 2005); Gurtner, D. M., "Luke's Isaianic Jubilee," in *From Creation to New Creation*, ed. D. Gurtner and B. Gladd (Hendrickson, 2013), 123–46; Hempel, C., *The Qumran Rule Texts in Context*, TSAJ 154 (Mohr Siebeck, 2013); Longenecker, R. N., *The Epistle to the Romans*, NIGTC (Eerdmans, 2016); Mathews, M., "Righteousness and Justice," *ESTJ* 2:671–73; Metso, S., *The Serekh Texts*, LSTS 62 (T&T Clark, 2007); Przybylski, B., "*Tsedeq, Tsedaqah, and Tsaddiq* in the Dead Sea Scrolls," in *Righteousness in Matthew and His World of Thought*, SNTSMS 41 (Cambridge University Press, 1980), 13–38; Qimron, E., and J. Strugnell, *Qumran Cave 4*, DJD 10 (Clarendon, 1994); Reed, S., "Physical Features of Excerpted Torah Texts," in *Jewish and Christian Scripture as Artifact and Canon*, ed. C. Evans and D. Zacharias (T&T Clark, 2009), 82–104; Smith, G. V., *Isaiah 40–66*, NAC (B&H, 2009); Snodgrass, K., "Streams of Tradition Emerging from Isaiah 40:1–5 and Their Adaptation in the NT," *JSNT* 8 (1980): 24–45; Stuckenbruck, L., "The Dead Sea Scrolls and the New Testament," in *Qumran and the Bible*, ed. N. Dávid and A. Lange (Peeters, 2010), 131–70; Tov, E., "Appendix: Phylacteries (Tefillin) and Mezuzot," in *Revised Lists of the Texts from the Judaean Desert* (Clarendon, 2010), 131–32; Ulrich, E., "Isaiah Scroll (1QIsa[a])," *ESTJ* 1:258–61; VanderKam, J. C., *The Dead Sea Scrolls Today*, 2nd ed. (Eerdmans, 2010); Wenham, G. J., *Genesis 1–15*, WBC (Nelson, 1987).

Daniel M. Gurtner

Dead Sea Scrolls: Thematic Parallels to the NT

Creation

Creation and new creation in the OT and NT. Creation is an important theme for both the OT and NT, and various aspects of it come into play in the Dead Sea Scrolls as well. The account of Gen. 1 begins with darkness, and the earth itself is without form and is void (v. 2). God speaks into existence light (v. 3); sky (v. 6); earth (v. 10); its vegetation (v. 11); the sun, moon, and stars (vv. 14–19); living creatures of the sea and air (vv. 20–23); and living creatures of the earth (vv. 24–25). God creates all these in the formulaic "let there be . . . and there was" manner. God also names, observes, and declares all of this to be "good." Finally, God makes man in his image and likeness, male and female; blesses them; and gives them dominion over the earth (vv. 26–30). At the end of six days, God is finished and declares all that he has made "very good" (v. 31). Then God "rested" on the seventh day (2:1–3). The subsequent account (2:4–3:24) brings into focus one particular day in the making of heaven and earth, when the Lord God makes "man" (*hāʾādām*) from the dust of the ground (*min-hāʾădāmâ*) and he becomes a living creature (*wayəhî hāʾādām lənepeš ḥayyâ*, 2:4–7). This day also includes the creation of the garden in Eden, instructions for the forbidden tree, the creation of "woman" and the serpent's temptation of Adam and Eve, and their subsequent fall and expulsion from the garden (Gen. 3). The flood, too, may be regarded as a re-creation, when God repeats his instruction to Noah and his sons, "Be fruitful and increase in number and fill the earth" (9:1; cf. 1:28). Later Isaiah speaks of creating "new heavens and a new earth. The former things will not be remembered, nor will they come to mind" (65:17). Presumably this is because the earth is "utterly broken" and "split apart" (24:19 ESV) and "the heavens will vanish like smoke" (51:6; cf. 34:4). In Isaiah this re-creative act of God is his kingdom, where he dwells among a transformed people, devoid of sin, death, and destruction (48:13; cf. 66:15–24; Smith, 718).

In the NT, creation appears in John 1:1, which recalls the "in the beginning" of Gen. 1:1 to recount the activity of "the Word" (*ho logos*, John 1:1–9). Thus, the recounting of creation bears a decidedly Christocentric focus, ascribing to Christ the means by which creation came about (cf. also 1 Cor. 8:6; Col. 1:15; Heb. 1:2). Elsewhere Paul affirms that creation itself bears witness to God's attributes sufficiently for him to be known by humanity (Rom. 1:20). Later Paul explains that creation itself is in bondage to corruption and longs to be set free (8:19–23).

The concept of the "new creation" (*kainē ktisis*) in the NT refers to God's renewal or restoration of creation in the eschatological age. This present creation is depicted in its transitionary longing as it awaits something future (Rom. 8:19–22; cf. Heb. 2:5). The most explicit depiction of the new creation is in Rev. 21–22, where it is described as "a new heaven and a new earth" (*ouranon kainon kai gēn kainēn*) but its details are given in terms of a new Jerusalem and a heavenly temple. In this dazzling account the visionary explains that the first earth has passed away (21:1) and sees the new Jerusalem descend (21:2), and all of the ensuing vision pertains to the holy city, the one seated on a throne, and the message to the church (21:3–22:21).

Creation in the Dead Sea Scrolls. The Dead Sea Scrolls do not clearly furnish readers with a systematic view of creation, but several texts provide glimpses of their perspectives in a few categories directly related to the creation accounts of the OT. The Scrolls give some account of *Adam and the fall* in Words of the Luminaries (4Q504 8; translations from DSS taken from García Martínez and Tigchelaar unless otherwise noted), which presents a prayer for each day of the week (line 1). It is a fragmentary text that paraphrases Gen. 1–3, with extant portions highlighting 1:26 and 2:7–8. It describes Adam as "our [fat]her, you fashioned in the image of [your] glory" (line 4). The breath of life was blown into his nostrils, along with intelligence and knowledge (line 5). He was placed in the garden and was to govern it (line 5). The remainder is fragmentary, but what can be made out—God "imposed on him not to tu[rn away . . .]" (line 8), "everlasting generations" (line 11), and filling the earth "with [vi]olence and she[d innocent blood . . .]" (line 14)—suggests that the account of the fall as well as Adam's rule over creation was used in a weekly liturgical cycle (cf. CD 3.20; 10.8; 4Q422 1.1.6–12; 4Q423 2.1–7).

God's role in creation is often presented as the *basis for worship*, such as in hymnic literature, notably the Hymn to the Creator (11Q5 26.9–15). This text, like those of the Hebrew Bible (e.g., Pss. 89:5–7; 135:7; Jer. 10:12–13; 51:13–16), credits the wisdom of God with creating all things and is replete with praise to God for it. It begins with a litany of praises to God for his attributes (11Q5 26.9–11a) before recounting God's creative work. It recounts how God separated light from darkness, inspiring awe among the angels (lines 11b–12). Then it describes in majestic terms the creation of mountains with produce for sustaining life and how God established the world with his wisdom and spread out the heavens with his knowledge (lines 13–15). Other hymnic writings from Qumran likewise point to creation as a basis for offering praise to God, particularly the Hodayot, or Thanksgiving Hymns. Here, too, one finds praise to God for the wisdom by which he established creation (1QH^{a} 9.7–8). Its orderliness is reflective of the character of God (1QH^{a} 9.11–13; 1QM 10.11–16; 4Q422 2–6.2.12). The Hodayot also acclaim him for stretching out the heavens and establishing by his wisdom and power all they contain (1QH^{a} 9.9–11, 13–15). All of this is created for God's own pleasure and glory (1QH^{a} 9.9–10, 14–15, 19–20).

The Dead Sea Scrolls also look to facets of creation to articulate their views of the origins and nature of *good and evil*. This is seen most clearly in the Treatise on the Two Spirits (1QS 3.13–4.25), an exposition for the *miskal* (spiritual director) in teaching the "Sons of Light" (members of the Qumran group; 1QS 3.13). God foreknows the deeds of people he created (4Q180 1.2–3), including those who would turn aside (CD 2.7–8). It teaches that God designed all things before they were made and also created the laws that govern them (1QS 3.15–17a). Then it explains that God made humans to rule the world and placed within them the spirit of truth and of deceit, from which come generations of truth and deceit (1QS 3.17b–19). The Prince of Light leads the children of light in the truth, while the Angel of Darkness leads the sons of deceit in the paths of wickedness (1QS 3.20–4.24) until the "appointed end and the new creation" (1QS 4.25 FGM). So, God's created order is equipped with two controlling spirits, which both affirm the ultimate sovereignty of God over his creation while accommodating human sin. Moreover, whereas creation observes laws established by God, humankind does not (1Q34 3.2.1–3; cf. 4Q418 126.2.5). Indeed, the orderliness of God's creation is utilized as an exhortation to people to live in wisdom and understanding (1Q26; 4Q415–418; 4Q423; 4Q146 1, 7, 10).

Creation is a decisive factor in maintaining what became a contentious issue in Second Temple Judaism in general and within the Dead Sea Scrolls in particular—namely, the matter of the proper *calendar*. Feasts and festivals observed by Jews and prescribed in the OT fell on different days, so determining which calendar should be used was important, and this was largely determined by the created order. For instance, the Astronomical Book (1 En. 72–82), which dates to the third century BC, knows of a solar calendar of 364 days (1 En. 72:32; 74:10) and a lunar or lunisolar calendar of 354 days (1 En. 73; 78:6–17). Moreover, Sirach (ca. 175 BC) insists that the moon, rather than the sun, marks the changing of seasons (43:6–8; 50:6; VanderKam, 27). Jubilees (ca. 160–150 BC), however, insists that Israel "shall guard the years in this number, three hundred and sixty-four days, and it will be a complete year" (6:32a *OTP*). Furthermore, it continues, "no one shall corrupt its (appointed) time from its days or from its feasts because all (of the appointed times) will arrive in them according to their testimony, and they will not pass over a day, and they will not corrupt a feast" (6:32b *OTP*). The lunar calendar is correspondingly condemned (6:34). In this context the Dead Sea Scrolls, too, have a deep concern for calendar matters (see Talmon; Glessmer). The presence of the Astronomical Book at Qumran (4Q208–211) shows that the sect was familiar with the two calendrical options. Furthermore, the discovery of Jubilees at Qumran (1Q17–18; 2Q19–20; 3Q5; 4Q176; 4Q216; 4Q218–224; 11Q12) confirms that sect's preference for the solar calendar, as does the evidence from the Community Rule (1QS 1.8–15; 9.26–10.8; cf. CD 16.2–4). This comes to bear in the Temple Scroll (11QTemple 12–29), which utilizes the solar calendar for prescribing the dates of a number of festival holidays. And the Psalms Scroll (11Q5) explains that David wrote 364 songs, one for each day of the year, and fifty-two songs, one for each Sabbath of the year (11Q5 27.2–11). The solar calendar was also important for the Mishmarot (*mišmārôt*)—that is, accounts of the service of groups of priests who are on duty to offer sacrifices in the temple (1 Chron. 9:23; 26:2; Neh. 7:3; 12:9)—of which many are found at Qumran (1QM 2.1–2; 4Q321–330; Jacobus, "Mishmarot," 510–11).

Comparison. The Dead Sea Scrolls and the NT share a common outlook on creation as a display of God's majesty and grounds for worship. Whereas the NT commonly refers to creation itself and the new creation inaugurated in Christ, such notions are almost entirely absent from the Scrolls. The Scrolls show little interest in the creative process articulated in Gen. 1–3 but instead focus on particular aspects that suit their own interests—especially the calendar, a notion almost entirely absent from the NT.

Resurrection

Resurrection in the OT and NT. There is little explicit material about resurrection in the OT. To be sure, one finds narratives of people who have died coming back to life, such as the son of the widow of Zarephath (1 Kings 17:17–24) or the son of the Shunammite woman (2 Kings 4:31–37; cf. 13:20–21). These miraculous events likely serve to authenticate the prophetic ministries of Elijah and Elisha by showing how people are reanimated to their prior form of existence. Other passages may hint at resurrection, such as the notion that God will not "let [his] holy one see corruption" (Ps. 16:10 ESV; cf. 49:14–15). Still others seem clearer (Job 19:26; Isa. 26:19), but it is the prophecy of Ezekiel (37:1–14) that explicitly references physical resurrection, here in terms of the hope of national rebirth. The prophet is led by the Lord to a valley full of very dry bones (37:1–2) and told to prophesy the word of the Lord over these bones (37:3–4). The prophecy is that the Lord will cause breath to enter the bones and they shall live, and the language of the prophecy includes graphically physical terms: the laying of sinews and covering of flesh, the opening of graves and raising of bodies, and the bringing of the people into the land of Israel (37:5–14). Daniel also foresees a time of deliverance (12:1) in which the "multitudes who sleep in the dust of the earth will awake" (12:2), some to everlasting life (cf. Isa. 65:20–22) and others to shame and contempt (Dan. 12:2; cf. Isa. 66:24). Here it seems evident that there is some kind of individual, bodily resurrection particularly for vindication of unjustly persecuted righteous people, which becomes more developed in the NT, beginning with the bodily resurrection of Jesus (1 Cor. 15). Here Paul, writing around AD 55, draws attention to the earlier apostolic teaching under which they were converted (1 Cor. 15:1, 3; cf. Acts 18:1–18)—namely, that Christ died for our sins (15:3), was buried (15:4a), was raised on the third day "in accordance to the Scriptures" (*kata tas graphas*, 15:4b ESV), and appeared to many, including Paul (15:5–8). Christ's resurrection, which is unquestionably physical (15:35–53), exhibits the defeat of death (Rom. 6:9; 1 Cor. 15:55; Heb. 2:14; Acts 2:24) and is the basis on which Christians also may hope to be raised from the dead (1 Cor. 15:52).

Resurrection in the Dead Sea Scrolls. There is some debate as to whether the Scrolls attest to resurrection at all. The argument of Émile Puech claiming extensive evidence has been widely critiqued (see especially Collins, 111–28). In the Treatise on the Two Spirits (1QS 3.13–4.25), the author asserts that adherence to the teachings of the sons of truth will be rewarded with "plentiful peace in long life, fruitful offspring with all everlasting blessings, eternal enjoyment with endless life [*ʿwlmym bḥyy*, or "life everlasting" WAC], and a crown of glory with majestic raiment in eternal light" (1QS 4.6–8 FGM). But the meaning here is not entirely clear and could correspond with Qumran teachings elsewhere ("he who gives life to the dead of his people," *[yqy]m hmḥyh ʾt mty ʿmw*, 4Q521 7 + 5.2.6; or Pseudo-Ezekiel[a], 4Q385). The Messianic Apocalypse (4Q521), building on Isa. 61:1 (cf. also 51:14; Ps. 146:5–9), declares that among the "marvelous acts" that God will do for the downtrodden righteous, he "will heal the badly wounded and will make the dead live, he will proclaim good news to the poor" (4Q521 2.2.12 AT). The phrase "make the dead live" or "cause the dead to live" (*yḥyh wmtym*) suggests bodily resurrection. Moreover, those who have done good before the Lord are destined to die, but "the Reviver [rai]ses the dead of His people" (4Q521 5.2.4–6), again suggesting bodily resurrection. Elsewhere, in Pseudo-Ezekiel[a] (4Q385), the author comments on Ezek. 37:4–10 when he says, "And a great many people [revi]ved" (*wyḥyw w]yʿ[m]d ʿm rb ʾnšym*, 4Q385 2.8; cf. 4Q386 1–2). Though there remains uncertainty as to whether this text originates at Qumran or not (Nickelsburg), its preservation among the Scrolls requires serious consideration. Hints of resurrection are found among the Hodayot, which mention God saving the author's life "from the pit, and from the Sheol of Abaddon" (1QH[a] 11.19 FGM) and lifting him "up to an everlasting height, so that I can walk on a boundless plain" (1QH[a] 11.20 FGM; cf. 1QH[a] 19.10–17). But it is unclear whether these texts speak to a future, eschatological resurrection (Puech, 2:366–81) or a metaphorical depiction of entry into the community (Kuhn, 44–88). Similarly, an Aramaic pseudo-Daniel text (4Q245) makes ambiguous reference to "[. . . th]ey then shall rise" (*[. . . ʾ]ln ʾdyn yqwmwn*) in the context of the wicked (4Q245 2.2–6), but it is too fragmentary for scholars to discern its meaning. In the final analysis most scholars remain skeptical, or at least uncertain, as to whether the Qumran sectarians believed in any sort of resurrection. Perhaps the evidence is simply too scant to be clear one way or the other. Regardless, it is evident that resurrection does not find any degree of prominence within Qumran writings.

Temple

Temple in the OT and NT. King David seeks to construct a permanent and more suitable dwelling for Israel's God (2 Sam. 7:2) that is patterned after the tabernacle, but it is ultimately built by his son, Solomon. The structure is largely stone (limestone?), while the interior is lined with cedar and overlaid with gold that features engravings of cherubim, palms, and flowers (1 Kings 6:15–29). It is divided into two main sections, the holy place (*hêkāl*) and the "most holy place," or "holy of holies" (*dĕbîr*) (1 Kings 6:16–18). Within the most holy place stands the ark of the covenant, with its two golden cherubim stationed atop its lid, wings outstretched so as to reach the walls of the room (1 Kings 6:23–28; 2 Chron. 3:10–13). Within the holy place there are various additional cultic furnishings (1 Kings 6:20–22).

The temple is dedicated by Solomon (1 Kings 8:22–61; 2 Chron. 6:12–42), and the glory of the Lord dwells within it (1 Kings 8:10–11; 2 Chron. 5:13–14). Eventually, Nebuchadnezzar of Babylon loots the temple and palace (cf. 2 Chron. 36:7) and carries the king and a significant part of the population into captivity (2 Kings 24:1–17), and by 586 BC the temple is destroyed (25:11–12). Putting an end to this captivity, Cyrus, king of Persia, permits Jews to return to Jerusalem and rebuild their temple (2 Chron. 36:23; Ezra 1:1–4). The return begins in 538 BC, and the ensuing temple is similar to that of Solomon, though apparently lacking its adornment (Ezra 3:12–13; Hag. 2:3). The temple is known as that of Zerubbabel, governor during that period, who restores the sacred vessels and provides for further building (Ezra 1:6–11; 6:3–8:36), though it is not completed until 516 BC (Ezra 5–6). Daniel's vision (Dan. 7–12) anticipates a renewal of the temple as part of God's eschatological triumph (12:11–12; cf. Ezek. 40–47; Zech. 1:16–17).

In the time of the NT the temple was rebuilt yet again, this time under Herod the Great (37–4 BC), who began his work on the temple in 20–19 BC (cf. Josephus, *Ant.* 15.380–87; *J.W.* 1.401–2). Much of it was designed according to OT regulations, though it was nearly double the size of the Solomonic temple (Josephus, *J.W.* 1.401–2). The temple proper (*naos*) was finished in about eighteen months, although eight years were required for the courts and considerably longer for the entire complex (John 2:20 records forty-six years).

The temple naturally figures prominently in the ministry of Jesus, and sometimes participation in cultic worship seems to be presumed (Matt. 5:23–24; 8:4 and pars.). But even this is in proper perspective where Jesus states that God desires "mercy, not sacrifice" (9:13; 12:7) and insists that "something greater than the temple is here" (12:6; cf. 17:24–27). It is also the scene of his "triumphal entry" into Jerusalem (21:1–11 and pars.), the "cleansing" of the temple (Mark 11:12–17 and pars.), and healings and teachings (Mark 11:27–13:2; 14:49 and pars.). Jesus is accused of threatening to destroy the temple (Mark 14:59; 15:29 and pars.), but John clarifies that the temple about which he speaks is his body (John 2:19–21).

In Acts the Jerusalem temple is a frequent place for the meeting of early Christians (2:46–47) and the teaching of the apostles (3:1–10; 5:19–26; 21:26–31; cf. 25:8; 26:21). Elsewhere in the NT the church becomes God's temple (1 Cor. 3:16–17; Eph. 2:21). Revelation sees a temple in heaven where God dwells (11:1–2, 19), from which angels issue forth (14:15–17) and from which God speaks (16:1, 17). Finally, in the new Jerusalem the Lord God Almighty and the Lamb become the temple (21:22).

Temple in the Dead Sea Scrolls. The members of the Qumran sect seem to have separated themselves from the Jerusalem temple, but whether they rejected it entirely or instead hoped for restorations of its conservative practices of ritual purity is debated. Qumran documents are, of course, replete with condemnations of the cultic practices in Jerusalem, with their frequent references to the high priest as the "Wicked Priest" (1QpHab 1.13; 8.8–9; 9.9; 11.4–5) who has defiled God's sanctuary (12.8–9), robbed the poor (8.12; 9.5; 10.1; 12.10), and accumulated personal wealth (cf. 12.9; 4Q169 1.11). Some documents (CD-A 1.3) speak of God's anger toward the temple, where improper services are conducted (CD-A 4.1, 18–19; 4Q394 8.3.5; 4Q396 1.1; 2.1, 6, 8, 10; cf. CD-A 3.18–19), cultic orders are changed (CD 3.6; 1Q22 1.8–10; 4Q390 1), and forbidden marriages take place (CD-A 5.6; cf. Jub. 30:15–17), causing the temple to become contaminated and rendering the cult ineffective (CD-A 6.12–13; cf. CD-A 6.16; CD-B 20.23; 4Q390 2.1; 1 En. 89:73). To compensate, the *yaḥad* (community) seems to have considered its practices a necessary, sufficient, and temporary substitute for the cultic practices of the Jerusalem temple (1QS 4; 5.6; 8.11; cf. 4Q258 1.1.4; 2.2.6–7; 1Q34 + 1Q34bis 3.2.1–8; 4Q511 35.3). Similarly, Josephus says, "God himself . . . turned away from our city . . . because he deemed the temple to be no longer a clean dwelling place for Him" (*Ant.* 20.166 [LCL]; cf. Josephus, *J.W.* 5.19). With such negative views of the temple, the question arises as to how such a sect of conservative Jews, keenly concerned to observe torah, could observe its cultic regulations without access to an operating temple cult. This is a complicated matter that is addressed partly through communal activity of the sectarians and partly through their own developed notions of temple.

Building on the vision of Ezek. 40–48, the Qumran New Jerusalem document (5Q15; 4Q554–555; 11Q18; 1Q32; 2Q24) provides an angelic tour of the heavenly city and its eschatological temple. The city itself is likely an idealized one, generally thought to be too large to be realistic (measuring about eighteen by thirteen miles). No description of the temple itself survives, only mention of it and narratives of priests and their activities (11Q18 15.1–5; 14.2.1–5; 13.1–7; 2Q24 4.1–18). The Temple Scroll (11Q19) reads as revelation to Moses that is like the one he received for the fashioning of the tabernacle (Exod. 34), but it is also integrated with laws against idolatry (Deut. 7). Though the first column is lost, the second seems to indicate it is a direct revelation from God to Moses at Sinai. It gives instructions for the sanctuary (cols. 3–13) and its surrounding courts (cols. 30–47; cf. 2 Chron. 3; 1 Kings 6), all depicted three concentric square courts with the sanctuary in the center, as well as regulations for purity (cols. 44–51; cf. Lev. 11–15). The temple is an idealized rather than actual temple, and scholars debate its role at Qumran. The notion of a heavenly sanctuary finds robust expression in Songs of the Sabbath Sacrifice (4Q400–407; 11Q17; Mas1k). This unique liturgical composition is difficult to construct, since about one-third of it is lost and another third is preserved in small fragments. Each of these thirteen "songs" is designed to be recited, likely corporately, for each Sabbath and repeated four times each year, based on the 364-day calendar. As a whole, the work recounts the activities of an angelic priesthood conducting sacrifices in a heavenly sanctuary, accompanying the priest as he passes through the veils into the sanctuary, where angelic priests, garbed in high-priestly attire, conduct their ministry.

Finally, in a play on words, the Jews at Qumran regard their fellowship as a temple of sorts (*byt,* "house," but used also of the temple as God's house). They refer to their members as "the house of truth in Israel" (*byt h'mt byśr'l,* 1QS 5.6 FGM; cf. 1QS 8.5, 9), a "holy house for Aaron" (*byt qwdš l'hrwn,* 1QS 8.8–9), and "a house of the Community for Israel" (*byt yḥd lyśr'l,* 1QS 9.6; cf. 4Q258 1.1.5; 4Q511 35.3: "God makes (some) hol[y] for himself like an everlasting sanctuary [*lmqdš ʿwlmym*]").

Exodus

Exodus in the OT and NT. The departure (Gk. *exodos*) of Israel occurs after 430 years of bondage in Egypt (Exod. 12:31–51). The Lord, in a pillar of cloud by day and a pillar of fire by night, leads Israel out of Egypt (13:17–22), only to be pursued by Pharaoh and trapped against the Red Sea (14:1–20). Moses stretches out his hand over the sea, and the Lord drives back the waters, enabling Israel to pass through on dry ground (14:21–22). When the Egyptians follow, the Lord causes the waters to return and cover them, saving Israel and causing great rejoicing (14:23–15:21). God's mighty deliverance is often evoked as a means of exhortation to Israel (esp. Pss. 77; 78; 80; 105; 106; 136; Ezek. 20; cf. Dan. 9:15–16) and anticipates a new, eschatological deliverance for God's dispersed people (Isa. 51:9–11; 56:7–8; 57:14; 63:7–19; 66:7–9, 18–23).

Though there is little explicit mention of the exodus event itself in the NT, there are recognizable traces of it, such as the opening of Mark (1:1–3), utilizing the notion of God sending an angel before Israel (Exod. 23:20) eschatologically in the framework of the good news for which John the Baptist prepares the way (cf. Mal. 3:1; 4:5; Isa. 52:7; 61:1–2). Some regard Jesus's baptism as an exodus-like passing through the waters (Mark 1:10 and pars.) and the declaration of the "beloved Son" (Mark 1:11 ESV and pars.) as an identification of Jesus as Israel's servant-deliverer (cf. Ps. 2:7; Isa. 42:1). Others include the depiction of Jesus as a new Moses bringing about a greater exodus-like deliverance (Matt. 4–7; Heb. 3:1–11) and departure from slavery (Rom. 6–8). In Revelation, John evokes images of the Exodus plagues to depict his scenes of judgment (8:2–9:21; 15:1–16:21).

Exodus in the Dead Sea Scrolls. References to the exodus event itself are relatively sparse in the Dead Sea Scrolls. Yet the book of Exodus is widely attested, with manuscripts dating as early as the third century BC (4QExod-Lev^{f}). And the several manuscripts in which it is preserved suggest the importance of it within the Qumran community (1Q2; 2Q2–4; 4Q1; 4Q11; 4Q13–22; cf. Mur. 1.4–5). There are no clear citations of the key text (Exod. 14:21–22) evident among the Scrolls. The Damascus Document mentions the exodus as "the first deliverance of Israel" (*bmzmtw bhwšʿ yśr'l,* CD-A 5.19), implying, without explanation, another. Elsewhere the Scrolls speak of the Babylonian exile as Israel being "delivered up to Egypt a second time" (4Q462 1.13; Wold, 279–98). In these instances it becomes a metaphor for deliverance of God's people, but it is not a major theme at Qumran.

Conclusion

Resurrection is a subject where the Dead Sea Scrolls and the NT part company in significant ways. Though the OT contains but hints at the idea, it becomes a foundational teaching for the NT, beginning with the bodily resurrection of Christ as a doctrinal necessity and historical reality. For both Jews at Qumran and early Christianity, participation in the cultic sacrifices of the Jerusalem temple is not part of their respective religious commitments. Whereas Christians participated to some degree in temple activities, the atoning sacrifice of Christ entirely supplants the sacrifices of the temple and, indeed, is the object to which those sacrifices were intended to point. For the Qumran sectarians the temple is essential for their understanding of obedience to torah, yet the present cult is impure and unclean, rendering it, in their view, preferable to isolate themselves in the wilderness and devise compensations for corporate worship and fanciful notions of a heavenly sanctuary. Both the NT and the Scrolls foresee a new Jerusalem, but as is typical, early Christian regard for the centrality of Christ as himself the temple creates a sharp distinction from the conception found in the Scrolls. Despite the importance of the exodus event in Israelite history and the attention it receives elsewhere in the OT, there is little explicit mention of it in the NT or the Dead Sea Scrolls. Cumulatively, comparison of OT concepts found in both the Scrolls and the NT illustrates the diversity with which the respective communities can read and utilize the same material.

See also OT Use of the OT: Comparison with the NT Use of the OT; *other Dead Sea Scrolls articles; Mishnah, Talmud, and Midrashim articles; Philo articles; Pseudepigrapha articles; Septuagint articles; Targums articles*

Bibliography. Abegg, M. G., "The Calendar at Qumran," in *The Judaism of Qumran*, ed. A. J. Avery-Peck, J. Neusner, and B. D. Chilton (Brill, 2001), 1:145–71; Busink, T. A., *Der Tempel von Jerusalem, von Salomo bis Herodes*, Studia Francisci Scholten memoriae dicata 3 (Brill, 1990); Chazon, E., "The Creation and Fall of Adam in the Dead Sea Scrolls," in *The Book of Genesis in Jewish and Oriental Christian Interpretation*, ed. J. Frishman and L. van Rompay (Peeters, 1997), 13–24; Chazon, "Human and Angelic Prayer in Light of the Dead Sea Scrolls," in *Liturgical Perspectives*, ed. E. Chazon, R. Clements, and Avital Pinnick, STDJ 48 (Brill, 2003), 35–47; Collins, J. J., *Apocalypticism in the Dead Sea Scrolls* (Routledge, 1997); Crawford, S. W., "Exodus in the Dead Sea Scrolls," in *The Book of Exodus*, ed. T. B. Dozeman, C. A. Evans, and J. N. Lohr, VTSup 164 (Brill, 2014), 305–21; Crawford, *The Temple Scroll and Related Texts*, CQS 2 (Sheffield Academic, 2000); Davies, P. R., "The Ideology of the Temple in the Damascus Document," *JJS* 33 (1982): 287–301; Davila, J. R., *Liturgical Works*, ECDSS (Eerdmans, 2001); Davila, "The Macrocosmic Temple, Scriptural Exegesis, and the Songs of the Sabbath Sacrifice," *DSD* 9, no. 1 (2002): 1–19; Dimant, D., "4QFlorilegium and the Idea of the Community as Temple," in *Hellenica et Judaica*, ed. A. Caquot, M. Hadas-Lebel, and J. Riaud (Peeters, 1986), 165–89; Dimant, "Men as Angels," in *Religion and Politics in the Ancient Near East*, ed. A. Berlin (University Press of Maryland, 1996), 93–103; Elledge, C. D., "Resurrection," *ESTJ* 2:656–58; Elledge, *Resurrection of the Dead in Early Judaism, 200 BCE–CE 200* (Oxford University Press, 2017); García Martínez, F., and E. J. C. Tigchelaar, *The Dead Sea Scrolls Study Edition*, 2 vols. (Brill, 1997–98); Glessmer, U., "Calendars in the Qumran Scrolls," in *The Dead Sea Scrolls after Fifty Years*, ed. P. Flint and J. C. VanderKam (Brill, 1998–99), 2:213–78; Gurtner, D. M., "Danielic Influence at the Intersection of Matthew and the Dead Sea Scrolls," in *Matthew within Judaism*, ed. D. M. Gurtner and A. Runesson, ECL 27 (SBL Press, 2020), 307–27; Gurtner, *Invitation to the Pseudepigrapha of Second Temple Judaism* (Baker Academic, 2020); Hobbins, J. F., "Resurrection in the Daniel Tradition and Other Writings at Qumran," in *The Book of Daniel*, ed. J. J. Collins and P. W. Flint (Brill, 2002), 2:395–420; Jacobus, H. R., "Calendars in the Qumran Collection," in *The Dead Sea Scrolls at Qumran and the Concept of a Library*, ed. S. W. Crawford and C. Wassen, STDJ 116 (Brill, 2016), 217–43; Jacobus, "Mishmarot," *ESTJ* 2:510–11; Kuhn, H.-W., *Enderwartung und gegenwärtiges Heil*, SUNT 4 (Vandenhoeck & Ruprecht, 1966); Levenson, J. D., *Resurrection and the Restoration of Israel* (Yale University Press, 2006); Longacre, D., "A Contextualized Approach to the Hebrew Dead Sea Scrolls Containing Exodus" (PhD diss., University of Birmingham, 2015); Maier, J., *Die Tempelrolle vom Toten Meer und das "Neue Jerusalem"* (Ernst Reinhardt, 1997); Newsom, C., *Songs of the Sabbath Sacrifice*, HSS 27 (Scholars Press, 1985); Nickelsburg, G. W. E., *Resurrection, Immortality, and Eternal Life in Intertestamental Judaism*, rev. ed., HTS 56 (Harvard University Press, 2007); Puech, É., *La croyance des Esséniens en la vie future*, 2 vols., Ebib 21–22 (Cerf, 1993); Riska, M., *The House of the Lord* (Vandenhoeck & Ruprecht, 2007); Riska, *The Temple Scroll and the Biblical Text Traditions* (Finnish Exegetical Society, 2001); Sanderson, J. E., *An Exodus Scroll from Qumran*, HSS 30 (Scholars Press, 1986); Schiffman, L., *The Courtyards of the House of the Lord*, STDJ 75 (Brill, 2008); Smith, G. V., *Isaiah 40–66*, NAC (B&H, 2009); Swanson, D. D., *The Temple Scroll and the Bible* (Brill, 1995); Tabor, J. D., and M. O. Wise, "4Q521 'On Resurrection' and the Synoptic Gospel Tradition," *JSP* 10 (1992): 149–62; Talmon, S., "The Calendar of the Covenanters of the Judean Desert," in *The World of Qumran from Within* (Magnes, 1989), 147–85; VanderKam, J. C., *Calendars in the Dead Sea Scrolls* (Routledge, 1998); Wentling, J. L., "Unraveling the Relationship between 11QT, the Eschatological Temple, and the Qumran Community," *RevQ* 14 (1989): 61–73; Wise, M. O., *A Critical Study of the Temple Scroll from Qumran Cave 11*, SAOC 49 (University of Chicago Press, 1990); Wold, B. G., "Revelation's Plague Septets," *Echoes from the Caves*, ed. F. G. Martínez, STDJ 85 (Brill, 2009), 279–98; Yadin, Y., *The Temple Scroll I–III* (Israel Exploration Society, 1983).

DANIEL M. GURTNER

Death *See* Creation

Demons *See* Satan

Deuteronomy, Book of

Perhaps no other book has influenced biblical thought like Deuteronomy. From Scripture's perspective, Moses's Deuteronomic messages formalize the post-exodus generations' old-covenant relationship with God by providing them a constitution for life in the promised land. It also helps later seers, sages, sovereigns, and songwriters to unravel the movement of Israel's history from entrance into the land to exile. Finally, it enables readers to grasp the nature of covenant responsibility and the possibility of lasting covenant relationship and to hope for the age of restoration beyond curse associated with a covenant-mediating prophet like but greater than Moses, under whose ministry Yahweh would transform hearts and empower love and obedience.

Deuteronomy's Hermeneutics

Deuteronomy stands climactically as the last installment in the Pentateuch and narrates the last days of Moses's life by highlighting his "words" to Israel in the region of the Jordan in the wilderness (Deut. 1:1) and "the terms of the covenant the LORD commanded Moses to make with the Israelites in Moab, in addition to the covenant he made with them at Horeb" (29:1). Deuteronomy not only stands as the last book in the Pentateuch's literary sequence but also explicitly builds on the preceding story and distinguishes the Horeb (i.e., Sinai) covenant materials of Exodus, Leviticus, and Numbers from those bound up in Deuteronomy, which presents itself as covenant renewal. This may be why the Greek translator rendered the book *deutero-nomos* ("second law"; cf. 17:18).

Moses himself calls Deuteronomy's "words" and "terms" "this Book of the Law" (29:21; 30:10; 31:26), and this embedded book or scroll shapes the bulk of Deuteronomy and addresses the nature and possibility of Israel's lasting covenant relationship. The narrator stresses that by proclaiming and writing the messages in his lawbook, Moses "legally enforced" (*piel* of *bʾr*, rendered "expound" in the NIV) the law as covenantally binding instruction for future Israelite generations (1:5; cf. 27:8; so Braulik and Lohfink).

Examples of allusions to earlier pentateuchal narratives. Deuteronomy includes numerous general recollections from Genesis of Yahweh's choice of the patriarchs and his promise of land to them (e.g., Deut. 1:8; 6:10; 7:12–13; 10:22; 29:12). It also incorporates many historical flashbacks to Exodus and Numbers, including the exodus (e.g., Deut. 4:34, 37–38; 29:2–3; cf. Exod. 4–15), revelation at Horeb (e.g., Deut. 4:9–14; 5:2–33; cf. Exod. 19–20), rebellion at Horeb (Deut. 9:8–10:11; cf. Exod. 32–34), and numerous wilderness events like the rebellion at Kadesh (e.g., Deut. 1:19–45; cf. Num. 13–14), the movement past Edom, Moab, and Ammon (Deut. 2:1–23; cf. Num. 20:14–21:20), the Transjordan's conquest (Deut. 2:24–3:20; cf. Num. 21:21–35), and the episode with Balaam and the Moabites (Deut. 23:4–5; cf. Num. 22–24). Through such narrative rehashing, Moses warns of the seriousness of sin, grounds the covenant at Moab in a context of Yahweh's past grace, and motivates present and future Israelite generations to love the Lord and pursue righteousness.

Recalling Yahweh's covenant with and promises to the fathers. Deuteronomy is clear that what Yahweh has done for Israel through the exodus, covenant at Horeb, preservation through the wilderness, and renewed covenant at Moab is a direct outworking of what God promised to the patriarchs. Moses speaks of the Israelite "fathers" (*ʾābôt*) around fifty times in Deuteronomy, referring regularly to "the land I/Yahweh swore to the fathers" (Deut. 1:8, 35; 6:10, 18, 23; 7:13; 8:1; 9:5; 10:11; 11:9, 21; 19:8; 26:3, 15; 28:11; 30:20; 31:7, 20; cf. 1:21), "the God of your/our fathers" (1:11, 21; 4:1; 6:3; 12:1; 26:7; 27:3; cf. 29:25), and "the covenant/oath that I/Yahweh made with your fathers" (4:31; 7:12; 8:18; 29:12–13; cf. 5:3; 29:25). In addition, seven times Deuteronomy uses the patriarchal name formula ("Abraham, Isaac, and Jacob"), five of which stand appositionally to "the fathers" (1:8; 6:10; 9:5; 29:13; 30:20; cf. 9:27; 34:4). Deuteronomy also associates "your fathers" with the seventy who "went down into Egypt" (10:22; cf. 26:5). Because the book gives no further information regarding these elements, it assumes prior knowledge of Genesis's historical traditions.

Against the deconstructive, redactional approaches of higher critics and against the transgenerational rhetorical views of Jerry Hwang (*Remembrance*) and Bill Arnold, Israel's "fathers" in Deuteronomy are always the patriarchs (i.e., Abraham, Isaac, and Jacob) and the generations associated with them (Tigay, 61). Along with those texts explicitly naming the patriarchs, others necessarily refer to the patriarchs by way of temporal signals (e.g., 1:11, 21, 35; 4:37; 6:23; 7:8; 8:3, 16; 10:11, 15, 22) and/or their inclusion of key phrases from the original name formula text in 1:8 (e.g., 4:1, 31; 6:18; 7:12–13; 8:1; 11:9, 21) (see esp. Arnold, 12–17, 19–27). The remaining texts (e.g., 6:3; 8:18) lack any clues suggesting a referent besides the patriarchs.

Moses's narrative reuse of the revelation and rebellion at Horeb. Deuteronomy 5–11 shapes the first movement within Deuteronomy's second main address (chaps. 5–26). While its primary genre is prophetic exhortation, Moses often recasts past narratives to substantiate his sermonic appeals. Consider two examples.

5:2–31. Deuteronomy 5:1 opens with three conjoined charges. The first is an imperative ("*Hear* . . . the decrees and laws") and the second and third charges build upon it ("*Learn* them and *be sure* to follow them"). Before adding further exhortation in 5:32–33, 5:2–31 recalls Yahweh's covenant-making acts at Horeb to clarify why Israel must listen to Moses's commands. Israel must listen since at Horeb God made a covenant with Israel (not the patriarchs, 5:2–3), who not only experienced the Horeb theophany and the giving of the Ten Words (5:4–22) but also saw Moses installed as the covenant mediator. Deuteronomy 5:23–27 details how the people requested Moses's mediatorship, and then 5:28–31 identifies that Yahweh appointed him to the role.

Both Exod. 20 and Deut. 5 include similar but not identical versions of the Ten Words (see below). Exodus 20 simply notes that *the people* requested that Moses mediate between them and Yahweh (Exod. 20:18–19), whereas Deuteronomy highlights specifically that it was the congregation's *representatives* who entreated the prophet (Deut. 5:23–27). Deuteronomy 5:28–31 notes specifically that Yahweh heard the leaders' request and directed Moses—elements not present in Exod. 20.

The account in Exod. 20 is short and functions to conclude the initial narrative record of the Sinai revelation. In contrast, in Deut. 5 Moses recalls this history as motivation for heeding his present instruction. He narrates in more specific and personal ways and by this validates his role as Yahweh's mouthpiece. The Moab generation and all those receiving his written instruction in future generations need to heed the decrees and laws he is about to declare (5:1, 32) *because* they requested and Yahweh appointed him as covenant mediator (5:2–31).

9:7–10:11. As in Deut. 5, the main genre of 9:1–10:11 is prophetic exhortation, as highlighted by the directive charge in 9:3: "But be assured today that the LORD your God—he is the one who goes across ahead of you—is a devouring fire" (NIV adapted). Israel must take their sin seriously, or God's punishment on the Anakites will also befall them! To support this warning, Moses again uses narrative retelling, this time of Israel's Horeb and wilderness rebellions. After emphasizing Israel's stubbornness (9:4–6), Moses calls the people to remember how they rebelled in the wilderness, thus arousing God's just anger (9:7). He supplies three examples (Horeb, 9:8–21; Taberah, Massah, and Kibroth Hattaavah, 9:22; Kadesh Barnea, 9:23), but he develops only the first, likely because it was at Horeb that Israel experienced most vividly the devouring fire of God. Throughout Moses's retelling, he assumes that his hearers are familiar with the various accounts, but his fresh narration emphasizes in greater ways the danger in which unrighteous Israel now finds themselves before God.

Moses's narrative retelling opens by declaring how "at Horeb you aroused the LORD's wrath so that he was angry enough to destroy you" (Deut. 9:8; cf. Exod. 32:7–10). Moses then recalls the Horeb rebellion and emphasizes Israel's doom more than he does in Exod. 32. After noting that Yahweh announced Israel's sin (Deut. 9:12), Moses places God's statement of intent to destroy in its own speech act (9:13–14). The prophet then fails to recount his initial prayer and God's response (cf. Exod. 32:11–14). He instead immediately details that he descended from the mountain and smashed the covenant documents (Deut. 9:15–17) to build a sense of foreboding about the people's future. Indeed, it is only after Moses recalls his second season of intercession (9:18), highlights Israel's evil and God's wrath (9:18–19), gives further narrative delay (9:20–24), returns to overview his prayer (9:25–29), and digresses on a brief excursus (10:1–9) that we finally learn that the Lord listened to the prophet's prayer and that "it was not his will to destroy you" (10:10). Rather, he purposed for Moses to lead the people into the land that he swore to give to the patriarchs (10:11). (For more, see Hayes; Hwang, "Theophany.")

Moses's account of the rebellion at Horeb in no way contradicts the narrative in Exod. 32. Nevertheless, the changes in Deut. 9–10 elevate the seriousness of Moses's original charge in 9:3 that Israel must know Yahweh as "a devouring fire." The changes also prepare the listener for the inference in 10:12, "And now, Israel, what does the LORD your God ask of you but to fear the LORD your God?" Moses draws on a well-known past event to heighten Israel's sense of need to pursue the Lord.

Examples of allusions to earlier pentateuchal laws. Moses's instruction also often recalls earlier laws in Exodus, Leviticus, and Numbers (e.g., Deut. 5:6–21 [Exod. 20:1–17]; 14:3–21 [Lev. 11:1–28]; 14:21 [Exod. 23:19; 34:26]; 16:16–17 [Exod. 23:14–17]; 19:15 [Num. 35:30]; 22:9–11 [Lev. 19:19]; 24:8 [Lev. 13–14]). This material and his additional commands build upon and finalize Israel's constitutional documents that together are to guide and govern the people's faith and practice in the promised land.

The Decalogue in Deut. 5:6–21. In Deut. 5:6–21 Moses recasts the Decalogue from Exod. 20:1–17 when he includes it in validating his prophetic role as mediator. The most substantial changes come in relation to the call to keep the Sabbath and the prohibition on coveting a neighbor's wife. (For more, see DeRouchie, "Counting"; "Making".)

Keep the Sabbath. Exodus 20:8–11 calls household heads to "remember the Sabbath day" (v. 8) and grounds the call to not work on the Sabbath in Yahweh's making the world in six days but having rested on the Sabbath (v. 11). It ends by noting how Yahweh "blessed the Sabbath and made it holy" (v. 11). In contrast, Deut. 5:12–15 charges people to "observe the Sabbath day . . . as the LORD your God has commanded you" (v. 12). This addition emphasizes the lasting relevance of Yahweh's words for this new generation. Moses adds humanitarian love as a purpose for prohibiting work among all household members and living property: "so that your male and female servants may rest, as you do" (v. 14; cf. Exod. 23:12; Deut. 12:12, 18; 16:11, 14). Finally, Moses further grounds the call to keep the Sabbath by recalling Israel's slavery in Egypt (5:15), which not only treats the present generation as if they were the ones God redeemed but also places the first creation in parallel with the exodus, thus treating the latter as a new creation. The Lord rescued Israel from slavery, and so they must now value his image in others by letting all rest on the seventh day.

Never covet your neighbor's wife. Exodus's command to never "covet" one's neighbor's wife, male or female servant, ox or donkey, or anything that is his follows the initial charge to never "covet" a "neighbor's house" (Exod. 20:17). In Deuteronomy, Moses swaps "house" and "wife," thus placing the prohibition against coveting a neighbor's wife on its own line (Deut. 5:21). In light of Deuteronomy's stress on the rights of the vulnerable, especially women (e.g., Deut. 10:17–18; 12:12; 15:12; 20:7; 21:10–17; 22:13–21, 23–29), Daniel Block ("Covet," 462) is likely correct to see "a deliberate effort to ensure the elevated status of the wife in a family unit and to foreclose any temptation to use the Exodus version of the command to justify men's treatment of their wives as if they were mere property, along with the rest of the household possessions" (cf. Schnittjer, 103–4). Thus, Moses highlights that household heads must seek to preserve others' rights and not only their own.

The Decalogue version in Deut. 5:6–21 stands distinct in several ways from the one in Exod. 20:1–17. Nevertheless, Moses treats this new record as the very Ten Words God spoke out of the fire at the mountain (Deut. 5:4–5, 22 with 4:12–13 and 10:4). This is the thrust of the twice stated subordinate clause, "as the LORD your God has commanded you" (5:12, 16). Yahweh clearly allowed his unchanging revelation to find fresh motivation and new application within this new context, while not commanding anything new.

The three pilgrimage feasts in Deut. 16:16–17. Both Exod. 23:14–17 and Deut. 16:16–17 mandate that "three times a year all your men must appear before the [Sovereign] LORD" (Exod. 23:17; Deut. 16:16) to celebrate "the Festival of Unleavened Bread," "the Festival of Harvest/Weeks," and "the Festival of Ingathering/Tabernacles" (Exod. 23:15–16; Deut. 16:16). "No one shall appear before the LORD empty-handed" (Deut. 16:16; cf. Exod. 23:15). The semantic parallels between the Book of the Covenant and Deuteronomy are clear, but Deuteronomy makes advances in two ways: (1) It stresses that the celebration must occur "at the place [Yahweh] will choose" (Deut. 16:16; cf. vv. 2, 6, 7, 11, 15). (2) Whereas Exod. 23:14–17 highlights the need for crop gifts (cf. Num. 15:18–21), Deuteronomy's silence on the nature of the gift and its stress on giving in "proportion to the way the LORD your God has blessed you" (16:17) opens the door for the greater economic diversification that would naturally come with urbanization (so Schnittjer, 129). These elements directly relate to how Deuteronomy emphasizes that the decentralized people, settled independently throughout the promised land, must continue to prioritize the centralized sanctuary at the site God designates (12:5, 11). To that place they must bring their offerings "because the LORD your God has blessed you" (12:7). Moses's Deuteronomic legislation supplements the earlier law by identifying how Israel should heed it in the time of settlement.

Handling skin disease in Deut. 24:8–9. In Deut. 24:8–9, Moses writes, "In cases of defiling skin diseases, be very careful to do exactly as the Levitical priests instruct you. You must follow carefully what I have commanded them. Remember what the LORD your God did to Miriam along the way after you came out of Egypt." Moses directs these words to the congregation, and their need to "follow carefully what I have commanded" the Levitical priests likely refers "to the instructions relating to the various forms of leprosy as they appear in Lev. 13–14" (Weinfeld, *Deuteronomy 1–11*, 30). This is significant since many liberal scholars assert that Deuteronomy shows no dependence on the priestly/holiness materials in Leviticus. Importantly, Leviticus explicitly identifies that Yahweh has given Moses (and Aaron) instructions for how the priests are to respond when met by a member of the assembly with leprous disease (Lev. 13:2–3; 14:2–3). Detailed guidelines follow. In contrast, in Deuteronomy Moses is speaking to the whole congregation, and there is no need to inform them of the specific instructions for the priests. The religious leaders will know what to do; the congregants need only go to them and heed their instructions. (For more, see Kilchör, "Reception.") To add further motivation, Moses recalls Miriam's skin disease with which God punished her while Israel journeyed through the wilderness en route to the promised land (Num. 12:10–15). Moses has a host of earlier written materials (and memories) available when he is preaching his Deuteronomic messages.

Deuteronomy's hermeneutical and theological strategy. In Deuteronomy Moses assumes, repurposes, and supplements earlier materials. At least three factors appear to have guided Deuteronomy's hermeneutical principles: (1) the desire to stress the lasting significance and certain fulfillment of past promises; (2) the need to motivate present and future loyalty by recalling past experience; and (3) the demand to indicate the abiding authority, implications, and fresh applications of past instruction.

Stressing the lasting significance and certain fulfillment of past promises. Moses regularly recalls the patriarchs, most commonly in relation to Yahweh's promises to them. He evokes the promise of the land (1) to urge Israel to enter and possess it (Deut. 1:8), (2) to emphasize how sin prevented many from enjoying the land (1:35), (3) to stress that Israel must remain covenantally faithful to flourish and endure in the land (6:18; 7:12–13; 8:1), (4) to note how the land promise motivated Yahweh's saving activity and blessing (9:5, 27; 26:15), (5) to reaffirm how the land promise will be fulfilled (31:7), and (6) to mark the certainty of this fulfillment as the context for future ethics (26:3) and disobedience (31:20). Moses points to Yahweh as the patriarchs' God to identify him as the one who made a covenant with them (29:25), who promised them that he would multiply Israel (1:11; 6:3) and give them the land (1:21; 4:1), and who by these promises is motivated to save his people (26:7). Moses also stresses the certainty that Yahweh will fulfill the covenant that he swore to them (4:31; 8:18).

Motivating loyalty by recalling past experience. In Deuteronomy, three different times Moses draws on Israel's encounter with God at Horeb to motivate the people's present loyalty. The prophet urges them not to engage in idolatry since Yahweh's theophany at the mountain included no form (4:9–24). Moses then charges Israel to heed his voice because Yahweh approved their request that Moses mediate the covenant (chap. 5). Finally, Moses recalls Israel's rebellion with the golden calf to ground his charge that they know Yahweh as a consuming fire and to emphasize the grave danger of disloyalty (9:3–21, 25–29; 10:10–11). In each instance, the prophet substantiates his present appeals by recalling past narratives that identify the nature of God, the seriousness of sin, and/or the sweet, undeserving nature of divine mercy. Past experience should influence present ethics.

Indicating the abiding authority, implications, and fresh applications of past instruction. Moses's messages in Deuteronomy identify awareness of the Decalogue from Exod. 20:1–17, the Book of the Covenant in 20:22–23:33, and the priestly instructions in Leviticus. What Moses does not explicitly recall, he still appears to assume, and there is no reason to think the earlier covenant materials bear anything but abiding authority for Deuteronomy's audience. Moses's changes in Deut. 5:6–21 identify how he could curb potential misinterpretations or misapplications while retaining the same central thrust of the Ten Words. His minor additions in Deut. 16:16–17 to the instruction regarding the pilgrimage feasts apply the earlier law to the prospect of a decentralized people who will be dispersed throughout the promised land, with some separated from the central sanctuary and some living in urban rather than agrarian contexts. The law in Deut. 24:8–9 regarding how to treat skin disease stresses the abiding authority of Leviticus's instructions to the priests but now identifies their lasting implications for the congregation at large. In all, Deuteronomy supplements rather than replaces or amends what comes before (see Kilchör, *Mosetora*; "Reception"; Schnittjer, 73–153).

Deuteronomy as Foundation to the Rest of the OT

Moses stressed the canonical nature of his words (Deut. 4:2; 12:32) and instructed the priests and elders to read the book of the *tôrâ* publicly every seven years (31:10–11). It was this *tôrâ* that was to guide Israel's kings (17:18–19) and stand as a perpetual witness against the people (31:26). Deuteronomy supplied Israel with a theological framework for understanding their relationship with God (e.g., 6:4–9, 20–25) and the covenant history that was to come (4:25–31; 30:1–14; 31:16–18, 26–29). Furthermore, its structural echoes of ancient Near Eastern treaties and law codes highlight how its covenant guidelines and motivating sanctions (29:1) were politically binding on all future generations until the prophet mediating the new covenant (18:15–19) would arise (see Kitchen, 283–89; Huddleston, 30–66). Hence, Deuteronomy's influence on subsequent OT literature is not surprising.

The book stands as the foundation of what some term the "Deuteronomistic History," as is clear from the way its vocabulary and perspective pervade Joshua through Kings (for lists, see Weinfeld, *School*, 320–65). However, against the historical-critical consensus, the Deuteronomic flavor of the covenant history is likely due not to a Deuteronomistic redaction of the whole but to Deuteronomy's influence on the later writings (see Richter).

The OT's historical-narrative books regularly characterize Moses's law as the benchmark for proper conduct (e.g., Josh. 1:7, 13; 1 Kings 2:3) and often quote or allude to Deuteronomy (e.g., Judg. 3:6 [Deut. 7:3]; 2 Kings 14:6 and 2 Chron. 25:4 [Deut. 24:16]; 2 Kings 23:25 [Deut. 6:5]; Neh. 1:5 and Dan. 9:4 [Deut. 7:9]). They also pervasively assume that the reader should judge the history of the covenant people by the foundational covenant materials of the Pentateuch (e.g., Judg. 2:15 and Dan. 9:11–13 [Deut. 28:15–68]).

Deuteronomy also highly influenced Israel's writing prophets (e.g., Jer. 23:21–22; Zech. 7:11–12; cf. Dan. 9:10). They use Moses's law to guide their teaching and indictments (e.g., Isa. 8:16, 20; Jer. 2:8; 6:19; Ezek. 7:26; 22:26; Hosea 4:6; Hab. 1:4; Zeph. 3:4), cite Deuteronomy (e.g., Isa. 6:10 [Deut. 29:4]; Jer. 3:1 [Deut. 24:1–4]; Ezek. 36:24 [Deut. 30:4–5]; Hosea 13:5–6 [Deut. 8:12, 14]), and understand Israel's failure to keep the law as God's reason for punishing them (e.g., Jer. 44:23; Ezek. 20:21; Hosea 8:1; Amos 2:4). Additionally, the prophetic warnings of punishment and promises of salvation often recast Moses's old-covenant curses (e.g., Isa. 1:9–10 [Deut. 29:23]; Hab. 1:8 [Deut. 28:49]; Zeph. 1:13 [Deut. 28:30]) and restoration blessings (e.g., Jer. 29:13–14; Ezek. 36:24–27; Zeph. 3:20 [Deut. 4:29–30; 30:2–5]). Until the end of the OT age, Yahweh urges the postexilic community, "Remember the law of my servant Moses, the decrees and laws I gave him at Horeb for all Israel" (Mal. 4:4; cf. 3:7).

Finally, Deuteronomy shows close ties with Israel's wisdom tradition. The motif of fearing Yahweh that gives rise to faithful ethics theologically grounds both Deuteronomy's covenant piety and the wisdom books of Job, Proverbs, and Ecclesiastes (Deut. 5:29; Job 1:9; Prov. 1:7; Eccles. 12:13; see Block, "Fear"). Other links are evident, including their didactic style (Deut. 6:4; 9:1; Prov. 4:7; 5:7), stress on teaching and learning (Deut. 4:1; 5:1; Prov. 1:2–6), choice between two ways (Deut. 30:19; Prov. 12:28), focus on God as a father disciplining his son (Deut. 8:5–6; Prov. 3:11–12), promise of extended life for keeping commands (Deut. 4:40; Prov. 3:1–2), and many others. The covenant relationship that Deuteronomy formalizes most likely provides the context out of which Israel's wisdom teaching grew (so, too, Grant; Block, "Fear"). Wisdom seeks to live out the life framed by the law, as the various principles of godliness are applied in all of life's circumstances.

In sum, later OT authors cite Deuteronomy for various reasons. These include (1) to indicate the direct fulfillment of Deuteronomic curses (e.g., Deut. 28:22 in Amos 4:9; Deut. 28:28–29 in Isa. 59:10); (2) to reassert predictions about Israel and the broader world's future that still await both typological (e.g., Deut. 30:2–4 in Neh. 1:9) and direct (e.g., Deut. 30:2–4 in Ezek. 36:24–28 and Zeph. 3:20) fulfillment; (3) to illustrate the application of Deuteronomy (e.g., Deut. 27:5 in Josh. 8:31; Deut. 24:16 in 2 Kings 14:6); and (4) to signal the abiding authority of Moses's law-covenant in the OT age (Mal. 4:4), often by noting its violation (e.g., Deut. 7:3–4 in Judg. 3:6; Deut. 8:11–16 in Hosea 13:5–6).

Deuteronomy and the NT

An overview of NT uses of Deuteronomy. According to the index in UBS[4], the NT quotes or alludes to Deuteronomy at least 194x, which ranks it fifth in frequency after Isaiah (414x), Psalms (410x), Exodus (244x), and Genesis (236x). Among the frequent verbal parallels are numerous references to the Ten Words (e.g., Matt. 5:21; Rom. 13:9; James 2:11), the Shema (e.g., Mark 12:29–33), and various other legal declarations (e.g., Gal. 3:13 [Deut. 21:23]; 3:10 [Deut. 27:26]), predictions (e.g., Acts 3:22; 7:37 [Deut. 18:15]), and promises (e.g., Rom. 12:19; Heb. 10:30 [Deut. 32:35]). Within Rom. 9–11, Paul notes that Israel's spiritual disability continues "to this very day" (Rom. 11:8 [Deut. 29:4]; cf. 2 Cor. 3:14), how God is fulfilling Moses's predictions of the nearness of the new-covenant word (Rom. 10:6–8 [Deut. 30:12–14]), and Israel's jealousy over gentile salvation (Rom. 10:19; 11:13–14; 15:10 [Deut. 32:21, 43]). We thus see the NT authors using Deuteronomy in numerous ways, including (1) direct prophetic fulfillment (e.g., Deut. 30:6 in Rom. 2:29; Deut. 30:12–14 in Rom. 10:6–8); (2) typological fulfillment (e.g., Deut. 18:15–19 in Acts 3:22–26 and 7:37, 52); (3) analogical use (e.g., Deut. 25:4 in 1 Cor. 9:9–10; 1 Tim. 5:17–18); and (4) continued abiding authority (e.g., Deut. 5:16 in Eph. 6:2–3; see below). (For an initial overview of how various NT books use Deuteronomy, see Moyise and Menken; cf. *CNTUOT*; Lincicum.).

One example: The testing of God's Son in Luke 4:1–13. All three Synoptic Gospels include Jesus's "temptation narrative" (Matt. 4:1–11; Mark 1:12–13; Luke 4:1–13), wherein the devil operates as the agent of God's testing his Son. In Luke, in each of his three encounters with the devil Jesus cites Deuteronomy as Scripture to which Satan himself is accountable.

At the first test, the devil wants Jesus to prove his divine sonship by turning stones to bread to alleviate his hunger from his extended fast (Luke 4:3). Jesus responds by citing from Deut. 8 ("Man shall not live on bread alone," v. 3), wherein Moses urges the wilderness generation to "remember" how Yahweh has tested them to demonstrate how his word rather than manna sustains life (vv. 2–4; cf. 29:6), to "know" that Yahweh disciplines them as a father does a son (v. 5), and to "observe" God's commands (v. 6). As God's greater Son and Israel's representative, Jesus learns from God, submits to his Father's discipline, and heeds his word.

The devil then promises to grant Jesus authority over all the earth's kingdoms if he would worship the devil as the world's ruler (Luke 4:5–7). Jesus would eventually have "all authority in heaven and on earth" (Matt. 28:18; cf. Dan. 7:13–14; Phil. 2:9), but the devil proposes a messianic triumph without tribulation. Jesus responds by quoting Deut. 6:13: "Worship the Lord your God and serve him only" (Luke 4:8). Jesus slightly alters his citation of Deut. 6:13 while remaining true to the verse's original sense to counter the devil's desire for worship.

For Luke, the climax of Jesus's tests comes when the devil cites Scripture. Bringing Jesus to the pinnacle of the temple, the devil again urges him to prove his divine sonship, this time by casting himself down. The devil supports his charge by quoting Ps. 91:11–12, which promises that God will protect his own by intervening with angels (Luke 4:10–11). Jesus opposes the devil by citing Moses's words in Deut. 6:16: "It is said, 'Do not put the Lord your God to the test'" (Luke 4:12; cf. Exod. 17:1–7). Moses notes that Israel tested Yahweh in the wilderness, but Jesus refuses to repeat Israel's sin.

For Jesus, the OT bears abiding canonical authority, and the devil himself is subject to it. By narrating Jesus's victory over temptation, Luke vindicates God's claim that Jesus is his "Son" (Luke 3:22; cf. 1:32, 35; 3:38). As God's Son, Jesus stands as the antitypical Adam/humanity (Gen. 5:1–3; Luke 3:38), obeying where Adam had failed (cf. Osborne, 367–68). Jesus is also the new Israel (Exod. 4:22–23; Jer. 31:9; Hosea 11:1), who remains faithful in his wilderness temptation where Israel did not (see Pao and Schnabel, 286–87; Osborne, 369–70).

Bibliography. Arnold, B. T., "Reexamining the 'Fathers' in Deuteronomy's Framework," in *Torah and Tradition*, ed. K. Spronk and H. Barstad (Brill, 2017), 10–41; Block, D. I., "The Fear of YHWH," in *The Triumph of Grace* (Cascade, 2017), 283–311; Block, "'You Shall Not Covet Your Neighbor's Wife,'" *JETS* 53, no. 3 (2010): 449–74; Braulik, G., and N. Lohfink, "Deuteronomium 1,5," in *Textarbeit*, ed. K. Kiesow and T. Meurer, AOAT 294 (Ugarit-Verlag, 2003), 34–51; DeRouchie, J. S., "Counting the Ten," in DeRouchie, Gile, and Turner, *For Our Good Always*, 93–125; DeRouchie, "Making the Ten Count," in DeRouchie, Gile, and Turner, *For Our Good Always*, 415–40; DeRouchie, J. S., J. Gile, and K. J. Turner, eds., *For Our Good Always* (Eisenbrauns, 2013); Grant, J. A., "Wisdom and Covenant," in *DOTWPW*, 858–63; Hayes, C. E., "Golden Calf Stories," in *The Idea of Biblical Interpretation*, ed. H. Najman and J. H. Newman, JSJSup 83 (Brill, 2004), 45–94; Huddleston, N. A., "Ancient Near Eastern Treaty Traditions and Their Implications for Interpreting Deuteronomy," in *Sepher Torath Mosheh*, ed. D. I. Block and R. L. Schultz (Hendrickson, 2017), 30–77; Hwang, J., *The Rhetoric of Remembrance*, SLTHS 8 (Eisenbrauns, 2012); Hwang, "The Rhetoric of Theophany," in DeRouchie, Gile, and Turner, *For Our Good Always*, 145–64; Kilchör, B., *Mosetora und Jahwetora*, BZABR 21 (Harrassowitz, 2015); Kilchör, "The Reception of Priestly Laws in Deuteronomy and Deuteronomy's Target Audience," in *Exploring the Composition of the Pentateuch*, ed. L. S. Baker Jr., K. Bergland, F. A. Masotti, and A. R. Wells, BBRSup 27 (Eisenbrauns, 2020), 213–25; Kitchen, K. A., *On the Reliability of the Old Testament* (Eerdmans, 2003); Lincicum, D., *Paul and the Early Jewish Encounter with Deuteronomy* (Baker Academic, 2013); Moyise, S., and M. J. J. Menken, eds., *Deuteronomy in the New Testament*, LNTS 358 (T&T Clark, 2007); Osborne, G. R. "Testing God's Son," in DeRouchie, Gile, and Turner, *For Our Good Always*, 365–87; Pao, D. W., and E. J. Schnabel, "Luke," in *CNTUOT*, 251–414; Richter, S. L., "Deuteronomistic History," in *DOTHB*, 219–30; Schnittjer, G. E., *Old Testament Use of Old Testament* (Zondervan, 2021); Tigay, J. H., *Deuteronomy*, JPSTC (Jewish Publication Society, 1996); Weinfeld, M., *Deuteronomy 1–11*, AB (Doubleday, 1991); Weinfeld, *Deuteronomy and the Deuteronomic School* (Clarendon, 1972).

Jason S. DeRouchie

Divine Commission

See Adam, First and Last; Image of God

Divine Warrior

Among the many threads woven across the two-Testament canon, the concept of God as Divine Warrior might pose the greatest challenge to the faith of the faithful. There is no getting away from the conviction across both Testaments that God acts in both the earthly and heavenly spheres as Divine Warrior. The aim of this article is to survey the Divine Warrior thread from the Pentateuch to Revelation.

Divine Warrior in the OT

The tripartite division of the Hebrew Bible offers a coordinated witness to God as Divine Warrior and the people of God's responses to their warrior God.

Torah. Where does the depiction of God as Divine Warrior first appear within the OT story line? For some (Levenson; Cross; contra Tsumura), it is when God defeats forces of chaos, particularly the sea, to establish an ordered world in creation (Gen. 1:1–2:3; Ps. 74:12–17). All ambiguity subsides when we move forward to God's deliverance of Israel from Egypt. After God parts the sea, Israel crosses safely and the Egyptian hordes drown. Israel and Moses then sing, "The Lord is a warrior; the Lord is his name; Pharaoh's chariots and his army he has hurled into the sea" (Exod. 15:3–4). Some scholars interpret this event in light of ancient myths where Marduk and Baal conquer the dangerous gods of the sea—Tiamat and Yam—but Sa-Moon Kang (123–25) is correct that the sea is YHWH's weapon, not his foe, in Exodus. As Moses's song continues, an ancient Near Eastern pattern unfolds where victorious sea battles (Day, 97–101) result in temple building ("You will bring them in and plant them on the mountain of your inheritance—the place, Lord, you made for your dwelling, the sanctuary," Exod. 15:17) and enthronement as king ("The Lord reigns for ever and ever," 15:18). What the Israelites express in song about the Lord as a saving warrior is on display across the narratives in Exod. 1–14 (Trimm). Israel's God harnesses creation, causes panic, and sends an angelic destroyer all with the purpose of making himself known as the Lord, the saving warrior who fights for his people. This foundational moment in Israel's history offers a pattern that recurs throughout the OT: "The Lord will fight for you; you need only to be still" (14:14).

The emphasis upon the Lord fighting for Israel continues amid their journey to Sinai. When the Amalekites attack Israel, this is an attack against the Lord's throne (Exod. 17:16). Moses makes it clear that the Divine Warrior is the one granting victory and that success against the Amalekites therefore waxes and wanes depending upon whether Moses's arms are raised while holding the staff of God (17:9–13). The pattern of divine intervention continues in Israel's journey to the edge of the promised land, where it is the Lord who gives Arad (Num. 21:1–3) and Bashan (21:34) into the hands of Israel. Deuteronomy 33, the final song in the Pentateuch (Miller), opens with a vision of the Lord coming from Sinai with his army (v. 2) as their king (v. 5) and concludes by extolling him: "He is your shield and helper and your glorious sword. Your enemies will cower before you, and you will tread on their heights" (33:29). In God's saving interventions in Egypt and in the journey to Sinai and Canaan, the Divine Warrior motif in the Pentateuch shows that Israel should be ready to trust that the Lord will go before them as they take the land of promise

(Deut. 7:17–24). Yet, Israel is warned that the Divine Warrior will wage war against Israel if they are not faithful to the stipulations given at Sinai (Deut. 7:26).

Former Prophets. The conquest of Canaan results in Israel obtaining only a small portion of the promised land: the east-central area (Jericho and the Ai region), the southeast-central area (the Gibeon region), and the northeast area (the Hazor region). The meagerness of this procurement, however, has nothing to do with YHWH's inability, as all of Israel's victories depend upon the Divine Warrior's intervention (von Rad, 41–52). After God parts the Jordan River (Josh. 3) and Israel consecrates itself to be the Lord's holy army at Gilgal (5:2–12), a heavenly being, identified as the commander of the Lord's army, is a proxy for God (5:13–15). He assures Joshua, "I have delivered Jericho into your hands" (6:2), and the military strategy for taking Jericho points to warfare by the Holy One. Seven priests with trumpets march before the ark of the covenant—a symbol of God's royal presence—in the midst of Israel's army as they circle Jericho once a day for the first six days and seven times on the seventh day. As the trumpets blast and the army shouts, the walls collapse, and Israel destroys the entire city in fiery devotion, as *ḥērem*, to God. Nearby, at Ai, after an initial failure, Israel again is victorious when Joshua holds a javelin toward Ai (8:18, 26). When Israel fights against the anti-Gibeon coalition, the Lord casts hailstones at Israel's enemies (10:11) and causes the sun to stand still in order to lengthen the day to ensure Israel's success (10:13). The account ends, "Surely the LORD was fighting for Israel" (10:14). Israel's northern campaign is also a success because "the LORD gave [the northern coalition] into the hand of Israel" (11:8). Thus, just as Israel's deliverance from Egypt depends entirely upon the Divine Warrior, so too does Israel's possession of Canaan.

Conflict plagues Israel's existence in the land, yet the Divine Warrior continually intervenes to deliver his people, even amid Israel's perpetual disobedience. As the cycle of judges reveals, time after time God raises up a deliverer for his people. Through Ehud, the Lord gives Moab into Israel's hands (Judg. 3:28). Just as Deborah prophesies, honor goes to a woman (Jael) when the Lord delivers Sisera into her hands (4:9, 23). When the Midianites oppress Israel, God has Gideon select only three hundred soldiers, causes panic within the enemy's camp (7:22), and vanquishes the Midianites. God's Spirit even empowers suspect judges like Jephthah (11:29) and Samson (14:19; 15:14–15) to afflict the Ammonites and Philistines. The theme continues during the monarchy. The Spirit empowers King Saul to rescue an Israelite city from the Ammonites (1 Sam. 11:6). God's presence enables David to defeat Israel's enemies too (e.g., 2 Sam. 5:6–10). During the divided monarchy, one of the most dramatic interventions by the Divine Warrior in the entire Bible occurs when the angel of the Lord "put to death a hundred and eighty-five thousand in the Assyrian camp" (2 Kings 19:35).

In view of this backdrop of the Divine Warrior's successes on behalf of and through Israel, the failures of Israel in battle stand out. When Israel cannot take Ai, it is due to Achan's sin (Josh. 7). When God sells Israel into the hands of other nations in Judges, it is because they have done evil. When the ark—a priestly good-luck charm—is confiscated by the Philistines and Israel falls to them, this is an indictment against Eli's family (1 Sam. 4). Eventually, the tide turns against Israel and Judah as they plummet further and further into sin and apostasy. Assyria and then Babylon take them captive, and the temple is destroyed. By the end of the Former Prophets, the Divine Warrior seems to have ceased fighting on Israel's behalf; they no longer possess the land that the Divine Warrior fought to give them in Joshua. Even worse, the Divine Warrior now seems to be fighting against Israel—a point developed more explicitly in the Latter Prophets.

Latter Prophets. The writing prophets, Isaiah through Malachi, offer two distinct insights on the Divine Warrior motif. The book of Isaiah will be illustrative for this corpus. First, as stated above, the Latter Prophets envisage the Divine Warrior as now fighting against Israel (Longman and Reid, 48–60). In Isaiah's opening chapter, God declares, "Ah! I will vent my wrath on my foes and avenge myself on my enemies" (1:24). When this line is viewed in isolation, who the Lord's foes and enemies are is not clear. The next line disambiguates: "I will turn my hand against you" (1:25). The "you" is Zion; God's chosen nation is now his enemy. God is fighting against them, using Assyria (e.g., 7:17; 10:5) and, later, Babylon (39:5–7; cf. Hab. 1:6) to punish his people for rebellion against him. As ghastly as it seems for God to use wicked nations as instruments to punish Israel, the prophets also make it clear that the Divine Warrior will bring judgment upon Babylon as well (Isa. 13–14; Jer. 50–51). Thus, the Latter Prophets offer a vantage point on Israel and Judah's devastation at the hands of world powers: the Divine Warrior himself is wielding these empires as weapons against his very own people, who are now his enemies due to their sin.

Second, the Latter Prophets are unique in their eschatological depiction of the Divine Warrior. Two of the most striking passages—both of which influence the NT—are Isa. 59:15–20 and 63:1–6 (Abernethy, 83–102). In YHWH's astonishment over seeing neither justice nor one to intervene regarding justice (59:15–16a), he takes matters into his own "arm": "His own arm achieved salvation for him" (59:16b). God's "arm" is often a metaphor for his powerful intervention within history, particularly the exodus event (Exod. 6:6; 15:16; Deut. 4:34; 5:15; 7:19; 9:29; 11:2; 26:8; Ps. 77:15). He arrays himself in battle armor, with righteousness as his breastplate, salvation as his helmet, vengeance as his garments, and a cloak of zeal (Isa. 59:17). Strikingly, there is no mention of offensive weapons; instead, as was common in the ancient world, the focus is upon how the garments reflect the nature of the person who is wearing them (e.g., Job 29:14; Ps. 109:29). These garments reveal the Divine Warrior's essence and motivation. The Lord is a warrior who detests injustice, so he enters the fray out of zeal to set right all that is wrong ("righteousness") and to save. The "enemies" and "foes" against whom the Lord will wage battle extend to the entire world ("he will repay the islands") yet also include those among Israel who do not repent (Isa. 59:18–19). Those "who repent of their sins" will experience the Divine Warrior's intervention as redemption (59:20).

Isaiah 63:1–6 depicts the Divine Warrior returning from battle wearing bloodied garments. As in 59:15–20, the Lord, finding no one to help, takes matters into his own "arm": "My own arm achieved salvation for me" (63:5). He achieves this salvation by trampling the nations as one tramples grapes in a winepress (63:3, 6). Although gruesome, the Divine Warrior invites us to interpret his actions salvifically: "It is I, proclaiming victory [*ṣədāqâ*], mighty to save" (63:1). Thus, Isa. 59 and 63 prophesy that the Divine Warrior who has acted through his arm in the exodus to save Israel will act again in a climactic, eschatological fashion to judge evil across the entire world (including in Israel) and to save his faithful servants (including those from the nations).

Writings. The Writings relate to the core of the Torah and Prophets, so it is not surprising that they express the Divine Warrior motif. Within the Psalter, there are numerous psalms pertinent to our topic: Pss. 18, 21, 24, 29, 46, 47, 66, 68, 76, 93, 96, 97, 98, 114, 124, 125, and 136 (Longman, 274). There are numerous overlaps among these psalms: (1) natural phenomena (including fire and lightning) as weapons (18:9–15; 21:9; 29:7; 68:4, 8, 33; 97:2–4); (2) human enemies of Israel as targets (18:14; 21:8–9; 66:3; 68:1–2, 21); (3) allusions to the exodus and parting of the sea (66:6; 114:1–3; 136:12–13); (4) an end of warfare (46:9–10; 76:3); (5) victory underscoring divine kingship (24:7–10; 29:10–11; 47:2; 68:24; 97:1); (6) an international scope (46:9–10; 66:7; 96:3; 98:3); and (7) warfare culminating at the sanctuary (68:17; 114:2). The Divine Warrior whose actions are recounted in Israel's historical narratives and whose saving judgments are prophesied about is the subject of Israel's praises as they celebrate their victorious king.

Thus, throughout all the sections of the OT, the biblical authors portray God as a Divine Warrior. Within the Torah, the Lord is a Divine Warrior who defeats Israel's oppressor—Egypt—and, when Israel is en route to the promised land, menacing nations. Within the Former Prophets, the Divine Warrior continues to fight on Israel's behalf as they begin to settle Canaan, yet Israel's unrelenting rebellion against the Lord culminates in the Divine Warrior waging war against Israel and Judah through Assyria and Babylon. The Latter Prophets depict the Divine Warrior's battle against his own people and look to the eschatological future, when God will come in climactic military might to save his faithful servants and judge the rebellious. In the Writings, the Divine Warrior motif is most apparent in the Psalter, where one finds Israel praising God for the very actions on display in the Torah and Prophets.

Divine Warrior in the NT

The Divine Warrior motif in the NT corresponds to the OT's witness, but the NT distinctly emphasizes the spiritual and heavenly realities that God overcomes. It would be a mistake, however, to make a simple dichotomy by claiming that the Divine Warrior conquers physical realities like human nations in the OT while he conquers spiritual realities in the NT. In the OT, the Lord's victories over the nations lead to spiritual freedom for Israel and demonstrate his power over the "gods" of the time; in the NT (especially Revelation) the victories of God include his punishing the wicked human nations, not merely evil forces. So, the Testaments exhibit a difference in emphasis on the Divine Warrior motif, not a dichotomy.

The Gospels and Acts. The Gospels and Acts present Jesus as the Divine Warrior who has come to conquer death, Satan, and demons.

Driving out demons. Just as God "drove out" Israel's enemies from Canaan (*ekballō* LXX; e.g., Deut. 11:23; Josh. 24:18), so Jesus "drives out" demons. On one occasion, Pharisees claim that Jesus drives out demons only by Beelzebul. Jesus argues that Satan would not drive out Satan. Instead, "If it is by the Spirit of God that I drive out demons, then the kingdom of God has come upon you" (Matt. 12:28; cf. 8:12, 16, 31). On another occasion, Jesus drives out a legion of demons from the tormented man in the region of the Gadarenes (Mark 5:1–20). When they enter pigs and drown in the sea, this may allude to the exodus event, where the Egyptian hordes drown in the sea. In line with this exodus theme, just before this account in Mark, Jesus shows his exodus-like power over the sea when he calms the storm (4:35–41).

Satan falls like lightning. Jesus's statement "I saw Satan fall like lightning from heaven" (Luke 10:18) coordinates divine warfare on earth with heavenly warfare. Jesus says this after the seventy-two return and report, "Even the demons submit to us in your name" (10:17). Some interpret Luke 10:18 as a statement concerning Satan's prehistoric fall, as a reference to Christ's victory over Satan in his incarnation or death and resurrection, or even as a prophecy about Satan's fall at the end of time. Ming Gao (100–135), however, convincingly argues that Jesus understands the exorcisms by his disciples on earth to be in coordination with God's victory over Satan in that moment in the heavenly place. In addition, Jesus overcomes Satan when he resists temptation in the wilderness. Thus, the Divine Warrior—Jesus—grants authority to his followers to contribute to God's battle against Satan, where the battle on earth corresponds with the battle in heaven.

The victorious Son of Man. Jesus chooses not to call upon myriads of angelic warriors as he is apprehended (Matt. 26:53), but this does not mean he relinquishes his role as Divine Warrior. Instead, the concluding chapters of the Gospels put Jesus's role as Divine Warrior into finer view. Jesus cryptically informs the Sanhedrin, "From now on you will see the Son of Man sitting at the right hand of the Mighty One and coming on the clouds of heaven" (26:64). Although the man before them seems unimpressive and is destined to die a shameful death, they will soon view him quite differently. He will be known as the one of whom Dan. 7:13 prophesied, the one who receives from the Ancient of Days power and dominion over all. The reversal of Jesus's status comes into view when Matthew reports signs of the eschatological day of the Lord in conjunction with Jesus's death: darkness and earthquakes (Matt. 27:45, 51; see Johnson). Eschatological judgment in Jesus's death does not receive the final word; Jesus "emerges as triumphant Son of God" (Longman and Reid, 132) as tombs burst open, the dead rise, and Jesus is resurrected. The Divine Warrior has conquered death.

Pauline Epistles. Paul's Epistles interpret the significance of the life, death, resurrection, ascension, and second coming of Jesus and apply it to the church. Retrospectively, Paul declares that at the cross God "disarmed the powers and authorities, . . . triumphing over them by the cross" (Col. 2:15). These powers and authorities are spiritual forces holding people captive in sinful behavior and the resulting sentence of death—such spirits may promote idolatry and false conceptions about life and religion (2:8, 11). At the cross, however, Christ displays that he is "head over every power and authority" (2:10) when his death conquers the power of sin over the flesh and sin (2:11, 13–14), and his resurrection offers hope for a new life (2:12). Thus, the cross is where the Divine Warrior triumphs over the forces and condemnation of sin and death.

Prospectively, Paul still awaits the complete destruction of death and of "all dominion, authority and power" (1 Cor. 15:24). Some of the Corinthians are questioning the resurrection of the dead, so Paul clarifies that Christ is the firstfruits of victory (15:20, 23) and will come again to actualize the victory for his people—"The last enemy to be destroyed is death" (1 Cor. 15:26). Thus, although the cross signals a decisive blow to the powers and authorities of this world in Christ's victory, Paul expects the ultimate destruction of death, dominion, authorities, and powers when Christ comes again.

In between the past and future victories of Christ, Paul expects God's people to participate in the Divine Warrior's mission (Neufeld). In Isa. 59:15–20, God is the Divine Warrior arraying himself in battle attire. In Eph. 6, Paul exhorts believers to put on the very armor God himself puts on in Isaiah: the breastplate of righteousness and helmet of salvation (Eph. 6:14, 17). What is more, the Ephesians also have an offensive weapon, the "sword of the Spirit, which is the word of God" (6:17). This armor is to protect believers from and enable believers to fight "against the rulers, against the authorities, against the powers of this dark world and against the spiritual forces of evil in the heavenly realms" (6:12).

Revelation. The book of Revelation opens by announcing that Christ "is coming with the clouds" (1:7), a statement reminiscent of Dan. 7:13 (quoted by Jesus in Matt. 26:64) when the Son of Man comes to establish his dominion. This Christ is the one with eyes "like blazing fire" (Rev. 1:14) and a "sharp, double-edged sword" coming from his mouth (1:16). Revelation's most developed subsequent depiction of Christ as Divine Warrior echoes back to this opening chapter. In Revelation 19, a rider named "Faithful and True" is waging war (19:11). He has eyes like "blazing fire" and a "sharp sword" coming out of his mouth (19:12, 15), unmistakably identifying him as the Christ encountered in Rev. 1. Armies follow him, but they are not clothed in battle armor. Instead, the Divine Warrior himself "treads the winepress of the fury of the wrath of God Almighty" (19:15; cf. 14:9–11, 19–20), which refers to Isa. 63. Although the beast and the kings of the earth with their armies prepare to fight against the Divine Warrior, there is no challenge in the battle. We are simply told of the outcome—the beast and false prophet are cast into the lake of fire and the kings and their armies are slain by the sword of Christ's mouth (Rev. 19:19–21). What is more, the Divine Warrior sends Satan and death itself into the lake of fire (20:10, 14) along with those whose names are not written in the book of life (20:15). Although there are ranges of opinion on how to interpret this symbolism throughout Revelation (Collins), Revelation depicts Christ as the Divine Warrior, the conquering Lamb, whose victory over evil and judgment of the wicked in his first and second comings assure the faithful that their king is far greater than all others.

Conclusion

By tracing the Divine Warrior motif across the Testaments, the unity and diversity of the Bible's witness to this aspect of God are on full display. Throughout the Bible, God as the Divine Warrior is responsible for victory, but the strategies he uses are diverse: plagues and sea; a raised staff or javelin; marching, the ark, and trumpets; ambush; hailstones and the sun standing still; a woman and her tent peg; judges and kings in Israel; the angel of death; foreign empires; a spoken word; an unlikely cross; and a church armed with the sword of the Spirit. Throughout the Bible, the recipients of God's wrath vary as well: threats to Israel such as Egypt, Amalek, Moab, Canaanite nations, the Philistines, Assyria, and Babylon; rebels against God, including Israel and Judah; spiritual forces set against God, including sin, death, demons, and Satan; and those not in the book of life. The overwhelming impression of Scripture's witness is that the church can rest assured that the Divine Warrior has fought and will continue to fight victoriously against all powers that threaten his good purposes for his delivered people.

See also Consummation; Day of the Lord; Exodus, The; Messiah

Bibliography. Abernethy, A. T., *The Book of Isaiah and God's Kingdom*, NSBT 40 (IVP Academic, 2016); Collins, A. Y., *The Combat Myth in the Book of Revelation*, HDR 9 (Edwards Brothers, 1976); Cross, F. M., *Canaanite Myth and Hebrew Epic* (Harvard University Press, 1973); Day, J., *God's Conflict with the Dragon and the Sea*, UCOP 35 (Cambridge University Press, 1985); Gao, M., *Heaven and Earth in Luke-Acts* (Langham Partnership, 2017); Johnson, R. M., *I See Dead People* (P&R, 2019); Kang, S.-M., *Divine War in the Old Testament and in the Ancient Near East*, BZAW 177 (de Gruyter, 1989); Levenson, J. D., *Creation and the Persistence of Evil* (Princeton University Press, 1988); Longman, T., III, "Psalm 98: A Divine Warrior Victory Song," *JETS* 27 (1984): 267–74; Longman, T., III, and D. G. Reid, *God Is a Warrior* (Zondervan, 1995); Miller, P. D., *The Divine Warrior in Early Israel*, HSM 5 (Harvard University Press, 1973); Neufeld, T. R. Y., *Put on the Armour of God*, JSOTSup 140 (Sheffield Academic, 1997); Trimm, C., *"YHWH Fights for Them!,"* GorgBS 58 (Gorgias, 2014); Tsumura, D., *Creation and Destruction* (Eisenbrauns, 2005); von Rad, G., *Holy War in Ancient Israel*, trans. M. J. Dawn (Eerdmans, 1991).

Andrew T. Abernethy

Dodd, C. H.

See History of Interpretation: 1800 to Present

E

Ecclesiastes, Book of

Ecclesiastes is a difficult book to understand because of a variety of views concerning authorship, date of composition, and the relationship between the positive and negative statements in the book. The lack of consensus among commentators on these issues also makes it a challenge to comprehend the message of the book. Is the author Solomon, the only king after David to rule over all of Israel in Jerusalem, as stated in 1:12, or is Qoheleth presenting himself as Solomon to make a point about the pursuit of meaning in life (see below)? Some date the book as late as the third century BC to address the allure of Greek thought to the Jewish people (Krüger, 21–22). How one relates the positive statements of the book to the negative statements can lead to opposite conclusions. For example, Ecclesiastes is seen by some as the quintessence of skepticism and by others as the quintessence of piety (Ogden, 9–10). Decisions made on these questions affect the understanding of what other OT passages would have been available for the author to interact with. Because of limited space this article will primarily focus on relationships between Ecclesiastes and the Pentateuch, with some discussion of Proverbs (for broader associations, see Dell and Kynes). I approach Ecclesiastes with the belief that it is a first-person autobiography (1:12–12:7) written from an "under the sun" view; the added third-person frame (1:1–11; 12:8–14) points to the true foundation of wisdom so that the book acts as a warning against speculative wisdom (Belcher, *Finding Favour*, 63–67). I use "Qoheleth" to refer to the first-person autobiography and "Ecclesiastes" to refer to the whole book (all translations of Ecclesiastes are mine).

Ecclesiastes and Genesis

Many authors have commented on possible allusions between Ecclesiastes and Genesis. The more obvious examples will be discussed.

***The name Abel and the key word* hebel.** The word *hebel* is the motto of Ecclesiastes. It occurs in a superlative refrain at the beginning of the book (1:1) and at the beginning of the epilogue (12:8). It also occurs about thirty-eight times to characterize the various aspects of life that Qoheleth examines. This is his main conclusion about life. Whether one understands the word to mean brevity, futility, or meaninglessness, it is a negative conclusion about what one experiences in life.

The name Abel in Gen. 4 is the same word as *hebel* in Ecclesiastes. Abel's life reflects the negative connotations of the term in Ecclesiastes. God accepted Abel's offering, but he did not accept Cain's offering. Cain became angry and murdered his brother, a clear example of a righteous person experiencing injustice. Qoheleth examines many things in life that are just as frustrating, including the fact that the righteous do not experience the blessings they should experience while the wicked prosper (3:16; 7:15; 9:1–3), and he concludes that such scenarios are *hebel*. Abel's name fits his experience in life and lines up with Qoheleth's conclusions about life (Clemens, 7). It is hard to say, however, whether Qoheleth is alluding to the person called Abel, because there is no specific reference to his experience of injustice.

The cycles of nature and the created order. Following the motto (1:2) and the key question of the book (1:3) is a description of the natural world (1:4–7) and human activity within the world (1:8–11). Some see allusions between Eccles. 1:4–7 and the created order of Gen. 1 or the permanence of seasons in Gen. 8:22 (Forman, 257).

The order established at creation and affirmed after the flood is the foundational background from which life on the earth continues, but whether this passage in Ecclesiastes is deliberately referring to Gen. 1 or 8 is harder to establish. Apart from common vocabulary related to the sun (*šemeš*), the wind (*rûaḥ*), and the streams (*naḥal*), there is no significant linguistic overlap between these texts. General theological and thematic links between the two texts are possible, although Ecclesiastes seems to be presenting a negative view of the futility of the created order (for a positive interpretation, see Whybray) in line with the *hebel* motto and the "weariness" of all things in 1:8 (Longman, *Ecclesiastes*, 69). Qoheleth highlights the incongruity between creation functioning according to its beneficial design (Gen. 1:31) and the futility of his description, an ironic contrast between what is and what ought to be (Good, 30).

Qoheleth and Solomon. The relationship between Qoheleth and Solomon has been a subject of debate, particularly since the Enlightenment. A few continue to argue that Qoheleth is Solomon (Garrett, 257–64; Belcher, *Ecclesiastes*, 14–24), leaving no need for him to allude to anyone more powerful than himself. On the other hand, most argue that Qoheleth is not Solomon and that Ecclesiastes alludes to the description of Solomon in 1 Kings. Qoheleth assumes the literary persona of King Solomon in 1:13–2:26 (Longman, *Ecclesiastes*, 22; Fox, 159, 373) in order to show that even someone such as a powerful king who has access to all the benefits of life is not able to find meaning in those activities. If Solomon cannot discover the meaning of life in these areas, no one else can (Longman, "Qoheleth," 52). Although Solomon is alluded to in Eccles. 1:1 and 12, there are few linguistic connections between Ecclesiastes and 1 Kings, unless one sees a subtle allusion between Qoheleth and the verb *qāhal* in 1 Kings 8. "Qoheleth" is a feminine singular participle that functions as a professional designation. It is derived from the root *qāhal*, which means "to gather together, assemble." The root is used several times in various forms in relationship to Solomon when he dedicates the newly built temple (1 Kings 8:1, 2, 14, 22, 55, 65). Tremper Longman ("Qoheleth," 48) concludes that "Assembler" (Qoheleth) may be an intertextual reference to 1 Kings 8 and a subtle hint that Solomon is the referent.

Whoever one understands Qoheleth to be, he has the means to carry out his search for meaning in all the activities mentioned in 2:1–11. This passage has been compared with royal inscriptions from ancient Near Eastern kings (Seow, 151), but others see possible connections between Eccles. 2:4–6 and Gen. 1–2 (Krüger, 65; Verheij). Qoheleth built houses, planted vineyards, and made for himself gardens and parks in which he also planted fruit trees and made pools of water to water the growing trees. This description is supposed to be reminiscent of God planting the garden of Eden as well as providing fruit trees and a river to water the garden (Verheij). There are a few linguistic connections between these two texts, such as the verb "to plant" (*nāṭaʿ*), the noun "garden" (*gān*), and a reference to "fruit trees" (*ʿēṣ pərî*), but these are common words (Dell, 7–8). In Eccles. 2:4–6, the verb "to plant" is used not with "garden" but with "vineyard," and there are many gardens, not merely one. Reflecting on Gen. 1–3, one could argue that a king should exercise his dominion so as to understand the world God has made and to bring order to it. Qoheleth would respond that the activities described in 2:1–11 do not further the quest for meaning in life. He presents another ironic incongruity because there should be profit to labor (Gen. 1:26–28), even after the fall (Prov. 14:23). He concludes that although there is some pleasure in the work, there is no profit, because everything is *hebel* (2:11).

The fall and its results. The tenor of Ecclesiastes is that human life is lived in a broken world. This conclusion comes from his search for meaning in life and his conclusion that the human heart is wicked (Eccles. 7:20). Qoheleth actively searches for "the sum of things" (7:25), using the word *ḥešbôn*, which means "an accounting" and in context refers to the search for an explanation of how the world works. Qoheleth has already found that wisdom is inaccessible (7:23–24), and in 7:25 he begins the conclusion of his search to know the sum of things, which includes both "wisdom" and "the wickedness of folly and foolishness that is madness" (see also 1:17). Qoheleth reflects on several things he has found, but his foundational conclusion is "that God has made mankind upright but they have sought out many schemes" (7:29). Qoheleth refers to the original creation of *ʾādām* (the generic use referring to humanity) as upright (*yāšār*), a term that has ethical connotations when used of humans. This term is not used in Gen. 1–2, but it brings to mind the statement of the goodness of God's creation in Gen. 1:31 (Bartholomew, *Ecclesiastes*, 268). Thus, humans have messed up the world because they are messed up. Confirmation of this conclusion comes in Qoheleth's comment concerning what he has found among men and women. He has only found one man among a thousand who is upright, but he has not found one such woman among them (7:28). Rather, he has found more bitter than death the woman who is a snare (7:26). Perhaps this conclusion is a reference to Eve's role in the garden and the results of sin on the marriage relationship (Gen. 3:16), but it seems more likely that it is an allusion to the adulterous woman in Prov. 5:4 and 7:23. Qoheleth has not found a Prov. 31 woman in his search, nor hardly any upright men, because humanity is corrupt. The depth of corruption is analogous to the description in Gen. 6:5 that every intention of the thoughts of human hearts is only evil continually.

The effect of wickedness on the earth and the trouble of living in a world suffering under the curse of sin permeate Ecclesiastes. Not only is the human heart "full of evil" (8:11; 9:3), as in Gen. 6:5, but in Qoheleth's view everything in the world under the sun is characterized by futility (1:2; 12:8). The one result of disobedience of God's command clearly stated in Gen. 2:17 was death, which affected everything in Adam's world. In Qoheleth's view, death is a fog that hangs over everything and ultimately makes life *hebel*. It clouds the future of life on earth by bringing uncertainty into people's lives, because no one knows when death will strike (3:22; 6:12). It ends earthly existence, and there is little hope for any life or activity after death (9:10). More specifically, things that felt the sting of the curse in Gen. 3 are things that Qoheleth highlights in his "under the sun" perspective. For example, Qoheleth's view of God is analogous to Adam and Eve's response to God after they sinned. They fled from God in fear when he came into the garden. God is seen as part of the problem because he gave Eve to Adam (Gen. 3:12) and has made it difficult for people to understand his work in the world (Eccles. 3:11). Qoheleth even says in a proverb that humans are not able to straighten what God has made crooked (7:13). God is recognized as the Creator (12:1), but he is a distant God (5:2) who does not solve the issues with which Qoheleth is wrestling even when he could have been brought in to solve the problem (3:16–21; 9:1–6). God acts in an arbitrary way toward the righteous and the wicked (3:16; 7:15–18; 8:10–15). Qoheleth uses only "Elohim" to refer to God, not "Yahweh," the covenant name of God that is common in Proverbs. Thus, Qoheleth exhibits little passion for God or desire for God above everything else in life, as in Ps. 73:23–28 (Belcher, *Finding Favour*, 178–80).

The toil of work. Work is given to human beings by God before the fall and is significantly affected by the curse of sin. Work becomes difficult because now the cursed ground does not cooperate but instead produces thorns and thistles (Gen. 3:15–16). The frustration of work is hinted at in Gen. 3: work will produce pain (3:17), and Adam (*'ādām*) will have to sweat (3:19) in order to eat bread until he returns to the ground (*'ădāmâ*). Although there is little linguistic overlap with Gen. 3:17–19, Qoheleth highlights and expands on the frustrating nature of work (Anderson, 106, 113). Ecclesiastes begins with the question of whether there is any profit to human labor (1:3). The term "profit" (*yitrôn*) is a commercial term that refers to some kind of gain or surplus. The word for "labor" (*'āmāl*) has strong negative connotations (Num. 23:21; Job 4:8; Prov. 24:2). Qoheleth answers the question of 1:3 in 2:10–11, after the description of his extensive activities in 2:1–8. The answer is that there was no profit to his labor because it was all characterized by futility (*hebel*) and a striving after the wind. However, he did find enjoyment in his labor, which he characterizes as his "portion" (*ḥēleq*). This portion will be associated with calls to enjoyment (3:22; 5:19; 9:9) where eating, drinking, and life's pleasures are to be embraced, an ironic use that presents the incongruity between what Qoheleth experiences and the profit one would expect from labor.

Anthropology: The nature of human beings. Not only does the fall affect work, but it also has a tremendous impact on the nature and place of human beings in God's world. Both Genesis and Ecclesiastes talk about the physical constitution of human beings in similar ways. Humans are made of dust and will return to dust at death (Gen. 2:7; 3:19; Eccles. 3:20; 12:7). Gen. 2:7 states that God formed Adam of the dust of the ground and breathed into his nostrils the breath of life (*nəšāmâ*) so that Adam became a living being (*nepeš ḥayyâ*). The breath of life is the life-sustaining principle embodied in human beings that comes from God (Mathews, 197). Animals also have it (Gen. 7:22) and so are also called "living creatures" (NASB) in Gen. 1:20–21, 24; 9:10. Qoheleth uses "spirit" (*rûaḥ*) rather than "breath of life" to refer to this life-sustaining principle so that the loss of spirit brings death. Both Genesis and Qoheleth affirm that humans and animals have the same breath, are made of dust, return to dust, and go to the same place, which could be a reference to the grave, where the physical body returns to dust. Qoheleth is dependent on Genesis in his view of the constitution of humans and animals, but based on his experience he does not clearly affirm that the destiny of the two is different, because they have the same fate. Thus, he concludes, "So, human beings have no advantage over the animals, for everything is senseless [*hebel*]" (3:19). He presents another ironic incongruity because he is not sure whether the spirits of human beings ascend upward or whether the spirits of animals descend to the earth (3:21). Although the question "Who knows?" may be open-ended in Jon. 3:9 and Joel 2:14, for Qoheleth it is a closed question because no one really knows (Crenshaw, 274–88). There is no emphasis on the special place given to human beings within God's creation, even though they are made in the image of God. When Qoheleth later affirms that at death "the dust returns to the earth as it was and the spirit returns to God who gave it" (12:7), he could be affirming that God is the source of life (Fox, 331) or describing a return to a pre-life situation (Longman, *Ecclesiastes*, 273). But if there is a glimmer of hope, here it is diminished by the superlative refrain that everything is *hebel* (12:8).

Ecclesiastes and Numbers

After the spies search out (*tûr*) the land and all but Joshua and Caleb bring back a bad report, a section of laws follows, including the need for tassels on the garments of the Israelites to help them remember to do the commandments of Yahweh "and not follow [*tûr*] after your own heart and your own eyes" (Num. 15:39 NASB). The linguistic connections are not particularly strong between Num. 15:39 and Eccles. 11:9. They both use common words for "heart" and "eyes," but Ecclesiastes uses the verb *hālak* while Numbers uses the verb *tûr*. However, it is striking that the exhortations of each passage seem to contradict each other. The Numbers passage encourages the Israelites not to follow their heart and eyes, because that will lead them astray, whereas Eccles. 11:9 encourages young people, "Walk in the ways of your heart and in the sight of your eyes, but know that concerning all these things God may bring you into judgment." Such different advice is bound to raise questions about the relationship between these two texts. Sirach 5:2 seems to reject Qoheleth's advice, and the rabbis have questions about it (Kynes, 16). Some argue that Qoheleth is exhorting young people to enjoy life to its full capacity because God will judge them for things they did not enjoy (Seow, 371). Will Kynes (21) sees support for this view from the broader spy narrative of Numbers, where Moses's command to spy out the land (13:17–18) leads to a good report where it would be appropriate to follow their eyes and heart in desiring and taking the land God had promised to give them. As with Eccles. 11:9, the Israelites must give an account for the good they saw and did not enjoy.

Kynes's arguments notwithstanding, Qoheleth's advice in 11:9 is best understood as another ironic incongruity that goes against the grain of Num. 15:39. Although the verb *tûr* is not used in Eccles. 11:9, Qoheleth uses it elsewhere, with negative conclusions drawn about the search itself. Qoheleth has not been able to discover the sum of things (7:25–27), everything done under the sun is *hebel* (1:13), and even cheering the body with wine proves unprofitable (2:3, 10–11). This fits with the view that the calls to enjoyment involve only limited benefits from labor, not benefits on the level of profit. The context of 11:7–12:7 also supports this view because it encourages young people to make use of every opportunity during the time of youth before the darkness of the future comes. It starts with light (11:7–8), but darkness begins to dominate and puts a damper on everything until death comes. Qoheleth's pattern is to encourage the enjoyment of life and then give warnings concerning the future, with the future mainly focused on life under the sun, as seen in 11:8–12:1 (Belcher, *Ecclesiastes*, 378).

Ecclesiastes and Deuteronomy

Ecclesiastes 5:1–7 (MT 4:17–5:6), which alludes to Deut. 23:21–22 (MT 23:22–23) and 4:39, has been called the most explicit example of intertextuality in Ecclesiastes (Schoors, 48). It is a unit set apart by imperatives that offers instruction concerning proper behavior in worship. The main issue is how one should understand the intent of Qoheleth's admonitions (for positive assessments, see Eaton, 97–100). How one understands Qoheleth's view of God in 1:12–12:7 makes a big difference in one's understanding of this passage. The larger context of 4:1–6:9 has the theme of unfulfilled expectations toward political power (4:1–3, 13–16; 5:8–9) and wealth (5:10–6:9), which leads to a cautious approach to God (Belcher, *Ecclesiastes*, 193). A case can be made that the same approach is expressed in 5:1–7.

Caution before God is expressed in the several admonitions in 5:1–2 where one's attitude toward approaching the temple and prayer is in view: "Watch your step," "do not be quick to speak," and "let your words be few" because "God is in heaven and you are on the earth" (Longman, *Ecclesiastes*, 150). The statement about God seems to allude to Deut. 4:39, which states that "the LORD is God in heaven above and on the earth below." Both use the phrase *hāʾĕlōhîm baššāmayim*, but the differences include the fact that Qoheleth never uses the name "Yahweh" for God and that it is not God who is on the earth, but "you." Qoheleth adapts the passage in Deuteronomy to draw a sharp distinction between God and human beings (Schoors, 52), another ironic use to make his point. There is a lot of debate about the proverb in 5:3, but the point is that since many words come from the mouth of a fool, words should be few. Thus, to avoid acting like a fool, one should be cautious in prayer before a God who is distant.

The second half of this text deals with making vows (5:4–7). Qoheleth's advice in 5:4 is remarkably similar to the law on vows in Deut. 23:21 (for comparisons of the texts, see Levinson, 29). Both passages point out the negative consequences of not fulfilling a vow. The major differences are that Qoheleth uses "Elohim" instead of "Yahweh," replaces the stronger prohibition *lōʾ* with the weaker *ʿal*, and replaces the theological motivating clause in Deuteronomy, which says that "the LORD your God will certainly demand it of you and you will be guilty of sin," with advice about the danger of making empty promises, "for there is no delight in fools." Instead of calling the failure to fulfill a vow a sin (*ḥēṭʾ*), Qoheleth calls it a "mistake" (*šəgāgâ*). This mistake is serious because it could lead to punishment: "Why should God be angry with your words and destroy the work of your hands?" Although some understand punishment by God as being in tension with his noninvolvement in the world or as an "orthodox gloss," it fits with Qoheleth's idea of a hidden, unfathomable God whose actions in the world are not certain or understandable by human beings (Schoors, 54). Instead of using senseless words, one should fear God, which means being cautious before him (Longman, "Fear of God," 16).

Ecclesiastes and Proverbs

Proverbs sets forth the blessings that come from the way of wisdom but also recognizes the difficulties of life, thus providing a nuanced view of the deed-consequence relationship (Belcher, *Finding Favour*, 39–51). Qoheleth addresses many of the same issues as Proverbs but from an under-the-sun view that is based on observations lacking a solid foundation (Longman, *Ecclesiastes*, 32–39; for more positive approaches to the message of Qoheleth, see Eaton; Ogden). Proverbs clearly teaches the two ways (2:9–22; 9:1–6, 13–18), but Qoheleth wants to search both the way of wisdom and the way of madness and folly (1:17; 7:15–18). Thus, he highlights situations where the wicked prosper and the righteous suffer (3:16; 8:10–11, 14; 9:2). Proverbs praises the benefits of wisdom

(3:1–26). Qoheleth recognizes that wisdom has benefits over folly but questions his own pursuit of wisdom because what happens to the fool also happens to the wise (2:12–16). Qoheleth struggles with the reality that it does not make any difference in life whether one follows wisdom or foolishness (9:1–6). Concerning labor, both Proverbs and Qoheleth use the word *ʿāmāl*, which stresses the difficult nature of labor, but Proverbs asserts that there is profit to labor (14:23), and Qoheleth denies it (2:11). Proverbs uses the covenant name of God, "Yahweh," because he is very involved in life situations (16:9; 19:21; 21:30–31). Qoheleth uses only the name "Elohim" because God is a distant God who is not brought in to solve the problems with which he is wrestling, even when there is opportunity to do so (3:19–22; 9:1–6). The right view comes in the epilogue, where the dangers of speculative wisdom are confronted with the proper view of the fear of God related to the commandments of God (12:13–14).

Ecclesiastes and the NT

The most obvious allusion to Ecclesiastes in the NT is the use of the noun *mataiotēs* in Rom. 8:20, where Paul speaks of the creation being subject to futility with the hope that it will be set free from its bondage to corruption. This noun is the Greek translation of *hebel* in the LXX of Ecclesiastes. Paul's assessment resonates with Qoheleth's description of the world struggling under the effects of the curse. Paul's analogical use of the universal principle of corruption is also used in other places in Romans. The verb *mataioō* in Rom. 1:21 describes the futility of the thinking of those who suppress the truth and move further into corruption, an apt description of the perspective of Qoheleth (Bartholomew, "Intertextuality of Ecclesiastes," 231). Paul's indictment of all humanity under the power of sin in Rom. 3:10 may draw on Eccles. 7:20 (Seifrid, 616). Qoheleth understands the power of sin that Paul describes, but Paul is clearer on the possibility of redemption because of the person and work of Christ, who has taken upon himself the curse of sin and the futility of life. We have seen in the resurrection of Christ the power of the new creation, which will free creation from the bondage of corruption and obtain the freedom of the glory of the children of God.

Bibliography. Anderson, W. H. U., "The Curse of Work in Qoheleth," *EvQ* 70 (1998): 99–113; Bartholomew, C. G., *Ecclesiastes* (Baker Academic, 2009); Bartholomew, "The Intertextuality of Ecclesiastes and the New Testament," in *Reading Ecclesiastes Intertextually*, ed. K. Dell and W. Kynes (T&T Clark, 2014), 226–39; Belcher, R. P., Jr., *Ecclesiastes*, Mentor Commentary (Christian Focus, 2017); Belcher, *Finding Favour in the Sight of God* (IVP Academic, 2018); Clemens, D. M., "The Law of Sin and Death," *Them* 19 (1994): 5–8; Crenshaw, J. L., "The Expression *MÎ YÔDĒA'* in the Hebrew Bible," *VT* 36 (1986): 274–88; Dell, K., "Exploring Intertextual Links between Ecclesiastes and Gen. 1–11," in *Reading Ecclesiastes Intertextually*, ed. K. Dell and W. Kynes, 3–14; Dell, K., and W. Kynes, eds., *Reading Ecclesiastes Intertextually* (Bloomsbury T&T Clark, 2014); Eaton, M. A., *Ecclesiastes*, TOTC (InterVarsity, 1983); Forman, C. C., "Koheleth's Use of Genesis," *JSS* 5 (1960): 256–63; Fox, M. V., *A Time to Tear Down and a Time to Build Up* (Eerdmans, 1999); Garrett, D. A., *Proverbs, Ecclesiastes, Song of Songs*, NAC (Broadman & Holman, 1993); Good, E. M., *Irony in the Old Testament* (Almond, 1981); Krüger, T., *Qoheleth*, Herm (Fortress, 2004); Kynes, W., "Follow Your Heart and Do Not Say It Was a Mistake," in *Reading Ecclesiastes Intertextually*, ed. K. Dell and W. Kynes, 15–27; Levinson, B. M., "'Better That You Should Not Vow Than That You Vow and Not Fulfill,'" in *Reading Ecclesiastes Intertextually*, ed. K. Dell and W. Kynes, 28–41; Longman, T., III, *The Book of Ecclesiastes* (Eerdmans, 1998); Longman, "'The Fear of God' in the Book of Ecclesiastes," *BBR* 25, no. 1 (2015): 13–21; Longman, "Qoheleth as Solomon," in *Reading Ecclesiastes Intertextually*, ed. K. Dell and W. Kynes, 42–57; Mathews, K. A., *Genesis 1–11:26*, NAC (Broadman & Holman, 1996); Ogden, G., *Qoheleth* (Sheffield Academic, 1987); Schoors, A., "(Mis)use of Intertextuality in Qoheleth Exegesis," in *Congress Volume: Oslo 1998*, ed. A. Lemaire and M. Sæbø (Brill, 2000), 45–59; Seifrid, M. A., "Romans," in *CNTUOT*, 607–94; Seow, C. L., *Ecclesiastes*, AB (Doubleday, 1997); Verheij, A., "Paradise Retried," *JSOT* 50 (1991): 113–15; Whybray, R. N., "Ecclesiastes 1.5–7 and the Wonders of Nature," *JSOT* 41 (1988): 105–12.

Richard P. Belcher Jr.

Ecclesiology

In what follows, we will consider areas of continuity and discontinuity between the old- and new-covenant people of God. At the outset, some might object to the term "ecclesiology" being applied in both OT and NT, for the term is sometimes narrowly defined as the study of the NT church. However, it is better to frame ecclesiology as the nature and structure of how God's covenant people are governed and how they relate to one another and the Lord throughout history. This understanding of the word would then encompass the whole scope of redemptive history. Moreover, the word *ekklēsia* refers to the "called out" ones; this applies to both the OT and NT people of God, so it is fitting to consider both eras under the heading of "ecclesiology."

It is clear that God has gathered a people to himself throughout redemptive history, and he always has given this people clear instructions for their ongoing life together. In this essay, we will consider how the structure, shepherds, and symbols given to God's covenant people both remain and change within the main biblical covenants, with a particular emphasis on the shift from old to new covenants with the coming of Christ and his fulfillment of the old covenant.

Pre-Mosaic Ecclesiology

Garden of Eden. Some continue to doubt that Adam and Eve entered into a covenant in the garden; however, in light of the rest of the biblical evidence, a covenant is the best way to understand the relationship between God and his people in the garden (see, e.g., Dumbrell, 1–58). Regardless of whether one considers God's relationship with Adam and Eve a covenant, the structure of how his people relate to him and one another is clear and can be distinguished from what one finds in later covenant administrations. God's people, Adam and Eve, are to live under God's direct rule, sustained by him and eventually sharing in the tree of life. Whether they ever ate from the tree of life, the fruit of the tree was necessary for their long-term life and sustenance (Gen. 3:22). Moreover, as we see throughout redemptive history, God's people in Gen. 1–2 are defined by their relationship with him in bearing his "image." That is, both Adam and Eve are constituted as God's people by nature of their creation by him and their commission to fulfill the task to which he commissions them (1:27–30). The commission given to Adam and Eve, and later repeated in a modified form to Noah (9:1), functions as the governance given to the people of God. They are to live under his direct rule, seeking to fulfill the commission he has given them. Thus, from creation onward God's people gather under his rule and are sustained by his grace.

Abraham. After the fall, God bars his people from the life-giving tree and reconfigures this covenantal arrangement. God requires sacrifices as a means of approaching him (both Cain and Abel apparently understand that they are to offer some form of sacrifice, Gen. 4:3–5). Though the reasons for its acceptance are unclear, only Abel's sacrifice is acceptable to God, most likely because of Abel's true faith in the Lord (Heb. 11:4). Regardless, although the nature of the relationship between God and his people has changed after the fall, the essential structure of God's direct revelation to his people under his leadership remains the same. They are to relate to God through his revealed will. However, to commune with him, an additional step—sacrifice—is now required.

Much the same could be said about the nature of the relationship between God and his covenant people during the Abrahamic period, for here we also find the patriarchs offering sacrifices to the Lord (e.g., Gen. 31:54; 46:1). However, when the rite of circumcision is introduced, it marks out the people of God in a new way. It becomes the entrance rite for God's covenant people and serves as a "sign of the covenant" between God and his people (Gen. 17:11). As Bobby Jamieson (75) describes it, circumcision is a "covenant initiating oath-sign."

The Lord commands Abraham and his descendants to circumcise all their male children on the eighth day after their birth. This command applies to both Abraham and everyone in his household (17:12–14). In this rite, we see God's people clearly marked out in distinction from the rest of the world. Whereas the covenant sign of the rainbow given to Noah was between God and "all life on the earth" (9:17), the institution of circumcision marks out the covenant people of God, Abraham's household and descendants, in distinction from the rest of the world. The institution of circumcision could be, in a sense, the formal beginning of ecclesiology in the OT, for if the topic treats the nature and structure of the people of God, here for the first time an institution is commanded that marks out who the people of God are and are not.

In the Abrahamic covenant (and the Mosaic covenant, as we will observe below), the covenant members include the entire household. Many will debate how this principle develops in the new covenant, yet this "genealogical principle" is clear throughout the OT. The people of God consisted of households—adult covenant members, children, and even servants (Gen. 17:27).

Under the covenant with Abraham, the people of God are marked out by circumcision and continue to be governed by the direct commission of God. Abraham is called by God for a specific action: to go out from his family to the place to which God was commanding him to go (Gen. 12:1). However, all his offspring are included in the covenant and in the commission to be a blessing to the nations (12:3). This arrangement continues without modification until the Mosaic covenant, at which point the structure, shepherds, and symbols of the people of God are clarified in more detail. Following this, in the new-covenant era, these institutions are continued but also modified as they are fulfilled in Christ and his people. In the rest of this essay, we will give these two covenant administrations primary attention.

Old-Covenant Ecclesiology

Old-covenant structure and signs. Although God reveals his law directly to Moses on Mount Sinai, the law addresses the whole nation of Israel, the descendants of Abraham, thus establishing continuity between the covenant with Abraham and the covenant with Israel at Sinai. Yet the exodus from Egypt also constitutes the beginning of a new era in which the Lord has delivered his people from slavery and distinguishes them from the rest of the world in a new way. The Lord delivers his people from slavery through the plagues, which culminate in the Passover events, and the sacrificed lamb serves as a substitute for the death of the firstborn sons in Israel. The anniversary of this decisive plague and sacrifice is to be the beginning of the new year for the nation of Israel (Exod. 12:2). Thus, the nation is both new and not new in that it is a continuation of the covenant people descended from Abraham but has now received instructions on how to order their lives and worship.

Under the terms of the Mosaic covenant, Israel continues to be marked out by the rite of circumcision as the covenant-initiating oath-sign, just as was the case under the covenant with Abraham (see DeRouchie). The instructions given earlier in Genesis are repeated in Lev. 12:3: all male children born in Israel are to be circumcised on the eighth day, and this circumcision marks them out as part of the covenant people of God. Though women do not receive the same sign, those born or married into these families are also counted as covenant members. For example, Naomi and her daughter-in-law Ruth are considered members of God's people (Ruth 1:16–17). In the Mosaic covenant, the genealogical principle continues. The covenant people of God include adults, children, and all other members of the household: slaves, sojourners, and others. To be a part of Israel was, if one was a male, to be circumcised, and to be circumcised was to be a member of the covenant people. Additionally, those marked out by circumcision take on the obligations of the covenant, including both blessing for faithfulness and cursing for those who break the covenant (on this theme, see Kline, "Signs"; "Signs: Second"; *Consigned*).

While membership of the covenant people remains essentially the same as it did in the Abrahamic covenant, their overall structure and organization, along with proper worship of the Lord, are all given much more detailed attention in the law. The intricacies of the cultic instructions in the Torah are beyond the scope of this essay; however, to properly understand the ecclesiology of OT Israel we will review the main structure and symbols God requires under the law.

Added to the entrance rite of circumcision given to all male children in Israel, the law introduces a structure that includes annual feasts, festivals, and sacrifices, all of which revolve around the tabernacle (and later the temple). Exodus 23 lists three major festivals in Israel. If circumcision functions as the covenant-initiating oath-sign, then the annual observance of the Passover and the subsequent festivals that follow function as "renewing oath-signs." As we will discuss below, Jamieson rightly considers the Lord's Table as the renewing oath-sign of the new covenant, but he does not give attention to the Passover and the related festivals in Israel as renewal signs (Jamieson, 116). Since the covenant initiation sign is required for entrance to Passover, the Passover feast in particular functions in concert with the sign of circumcision as the "oath-signs" of the law (Exod. 12:43–48). That is, they are the signs that the people of God receive for both entrance into (through circumcision) and the renewal of the covenant (through the Passover feast).

As noted above, the annual Passover festival marks the beginning of the year in Israel; God also commands that a series of annual feasts follow this. Immediately after the Passover, which commemorates the exodus through the substitution of the Passover lamb, the Festival of Unleavened Bread continues this celebration of freedom from slavery in Egypt (Exod. 23:15). Shortly after this was the "Festival of Harvest" to celebrate the Lord's provision for his people (Exod. 23:16a). The third major festival in Israel's calendar was to be the Festival of Ingathering (Sukkoth), also known as the Festival of Tabernacles. This feast was celebrated at the end of the year (Exod. 23:16b). We could add the Day of Atonement (Yom Kippur) to these three major festivals as perhaps the most sacred day in Israel's calendar (Lev. 16). These festivals all focus Israel's attention on the Lord's deliverance through sacrifice and his ongoing provision for the life of his people. Added to the entrance rite of circumcision, these serve as renewal rites for God's covenant people under the Mosaic law.

Along with the major events in the calendar, the more frequent rhythm of Israel's calendar was the weekly observance of the Sabbath day. Though the Sabbath command is rooted in the creation week of Gen. 1–2, the formal institution of this commandment does not come until Exod. 20:8–11 as part of the Decalogue (see Shead). Israel is to keep the Sabbath holy by refraining from labor on the seventh day of the week as an exercise of trust in the Lord. It is not clear in the law that this was to be a day when they were to gather for corporate worship; rather, this day was intended for rest from daily labor as an expression of trust in God.

Later synagogue practice on the Sabbath more closely approximated the liturgy of early Christian worship, but in its original setting the Sabbath day did not require Israelites to participate in what we might call a worship service. Rather, it was to be a day of rest that reflects the patterns of the Lord's work in the creation week. This rest takes a particular focus in the NT and Christ's fulfillment of this institution. Closely related to the Sabbath, the Lord also commands Israel to observe a Sabbath Year in which they would give the land rest from normal cultivation and planting, living on the natural growth of the land, as well as a Jubilee Year every seventh Sabbath year (every forty-nine years). During this year, the debts of the people and obligations of servanthood are absolved (see Bruno).

Israel was to observe a regular calendar of both weekly Sabbaths and annual festivals as reminders of the Lord's creating and saving work. The sacrificial system functions alongside these regular events as an ongoing means of approaching God. Whereas Genesis describes the patriarchs offering sacrifices, the people are given more precise instructions for offering sacrifices in the instructions of the law. Again, we need not detail the intricacies of the law's instructions. The law gives us instructions on five kinds of offerings (see table 1).

Table 1. Types of Offerings in Israel

Offering	Instructions	Purpose
Burnt	Lev. 1:3–17	Atonement for sin
Grain	Lev. 2:1–16	Pleasing aroma and devotion to the Lord
Peace	Lev. 3:1–17; 7:11–21	Thanksgiving, paying a vow, or freewill devotion to the Lord
Sin	Lev. 4:1–5:13	Atonement for sin and impurity
Guilt	Lev. 5:14–6:7	Payment for sin

The purposes of these sacrifices overlap at several points, but in all of them, the people of God approach him through the sacrifices that the priests offered. Generally, the sacrifices are the means by which God's people deal with their sin and express their devotion and thanksgiving to him.

In all of these institutions, the covenant people of God were marked out by observing these "oath-rite symbols." The entrance rite of both the Abrahamic and Mosaic covenant people of God is circumcision. The renewal rites are found in the ongoing observance of the calendar events (Sabbath, feasts) and the regular practice of sacrifices. These structures and symbols mark out the people of God from the world and serve as his instructions for the regular worship of his people. The primary leaders and guides who administer these structures and symbols were to be the Levitical priests and later the Davidic kings.

Despite all their intricacy, these sacrifices remain incomplete and insufficient for lasting fellowship between God and his people. As Hebrews notes, the priests had to offer sacrifices first for themselves and then for the sin of the people (Heb. 7:27). Moreover, these sacrifices were offered year after year without respite. In many cases, Israel failed to uphold the yearly observance of the Passover and other required observances. However, even if they had kept them faithfully, they would have discovered that the feasts and calendar days also pointed beyond themselves to greater fulfillments yet to come, for as Hebrews also instructs us, the old-covenant people of God never fully entered the rest that the Lord designed for his people (Heb. 4:1–13). These days were a shadow, but the substance and fulfillment of these days are found in Christ (Col. 2:17). We will return to the christological fulfillment of the structure and symbols of the old covenant below, but first we will consider the leaders or shepherds of Israel.

Shepherds. During the exodus and the conquest, Moses and then Joshua serve as unique leaders in Israel; their office is never quite duplicated. The judges take up this mantle to some degree, and the Lord also appoints priests to serve as shepherds and leaders in Israel overseeing gathered worship and sacrifices. Later, kings and prophets serve as shepherds and leaders of the people of God.

In Exod. 18, we see Moses functioning as the judge of Israel. All of the people with questions or disputes would come to him for decisions (Exod. 18:13). Seeing this, his father-in-law, Jethro the Midianite, suggests that Moses institute a system of judges to rule over the people (18:21–26). It is unclear how long the particulars of this system are intended to last, yet they provide at least a short-term structure for Moses to function as the de facto chief executive of the people of God through the wilderness wanderings. However, Moses not only functions as judge and leader in Israel but also has a prophetic role in conveying the words of the Lord to the people (see the frequent use of the phrase "you shall say to the people of Israel" [Exod. 20:22; 30:31 ESV; cf. 33:5; Lev. 9:3; 20:2]; cf. also Deut. 18:15). Beyond this, Moses also has a priestly role in ordaining the Levitical priests though not an official priest himself (Lev. 8:1–30). This role is later passed to Joshua, whom the Lord commissions to lead the people into the promised land (Deut. 31:14–15). Joshua functions as judge and leader and conveys the word of the Lord to the people (Josh. 20:2), but he does not have a priestly role. Apart from their roles as leaders in battles against Israel's oppressors, the later judges are more limited to administrative and executive functions only. In sum, Moses functions in a sense as king, prophet, and priest, Joshua as king and prophet, and the later judges until Samuel as kingly figures. With the prophet Samuel, these three functions are brought back together before being divided again in the monarchy as kings, priests, and prophets take on more formal functions. All in some sense serve as shepherds of the people of God, but the ministry of the priests is particularly focused on the gathered worship of the people of God. Regardless of how the functions and formal office of prophet, priest, and king are exercised in Israel, none are able to lead God's people into lasting obedience. Israel's leaders continually lead the people into sin and failure until the culminating judgment of the exile.

Priests. In their years in Egypt, the nation had naturally organized itself according to its descent from the sons of Jacob, the twelve patriarchs. This organization is codified during the exodus and wilderness wanderings and then in their settlement in the promised land after the conquest. Of particular note for our purposes are the instructions given to the priests with respect to their organization, their service in the temple, and their ongoing ministry among the people.

The law is well known for its intricate instructions about the priests' role in the sacrificial system and their service in the temple. We need not explore these instructions in detail other than to observe that in their role as ministers in the temple, the priests function as vital spiritual leaders in Israel. The priests themselves are responsible for maintaining the ongoing work surrounding the tabernacle and later temple, and the Levites' duties are spread more widely both inside and outside of the temple (see Num. 18). As the sacrifices and festivals were the primary way that the people of God sought forgiveness of sins and expressed thanksgiving and devotion to God, the priests were the primary mediators between the people and God in formal worship.

Prophets. While they were certainly called by the Lord, Israel's prophets did not hold a formal office with ordination or anointing in the manner of the kingship or priesthood. Nonetheless, the prophets, especially in the later parts of the monarchy, come to serve an important role in calling the people of God back to fidelity to his covenant. The ministries of Isaiah, Jeremiah, and Ezekiel warn of the impending exiles and call the people, particularly their leaders, back to the Lord.

Kings. In Deuteronomy, the Lord instructs the future kings to write out the law and know it well so that they may model law-keeping to the people (Deut. 17:18–20; on this them, see Anizor). Later, under David and Solomon, the king has a close association with the temple. David prepares for the construction of the temple and his son Solomon supervises its actual production and leads in its dedication.

As with the structure and symbols of the old covenant itself, the ministry of Israel's shepherds is incomplete and insufficient. The ministry of the priests is incomplete, for they are never able to finally and fully deal with the sin of the people. The prophets are ultimately insufficient, for despite their faithful proclamation of the word of the Lord, Israel and its leaders fail to return to covenant fidelity. God had always intended for many in Israel to fail to listen to the prophets, yet there is a sense in which the ministry of the prophets is incomplete, for God's covenant people have not returned to him (Isa. 6:8–13). Finally, the kings fail to rule as God intended. From David's failure with Bathsheba in 2 Sam. 11 to Zedekiah's pride in 2 Chron. 36, the kings of Israel and Judah fail to model obedience to the law. Rather than self-giving rulers, they are often self-seeking shepherds; consequently, the Lord himself would see to it that his people would be governed by a faithful shepherd-king (Ezek. 34:1–24).

Despite these insufficiencies and failures throughout the old-covenant era, the Lord preserves a faithful remnant within his larger covenant people. When the prophet Elijah laments that he alone is left, the Lord informs him that a faithful remnant of seven thousand have not bowed the knee to Baal (1 Kings 19:18). The outward structures and signs of the covenant are insufficient, yet the Lord has preserved a remnant for himself within the old-covenant community. Thus, even in the old covenant, there is a distinction between external signs and structures and the internal realities of a circumcised heart (so Deut. 10:16; 30:6). In the new covenant, the need for internal transformation is clarified as we see that the structure, signs, and shepherds of the people of God from the OT are fulfilled in Christ and subsequently transformed for the new-covenant church.

New-Covenant Ecclesiology

In general, there is a move toward simplicity and fulfillment in the new-covenant structures. However, this does not mean that the nature and structure of the people of God is a "merely spiritual" community; rather, in the new covenant, we see the structure, signs, and shepherding care of God's people fulfilled in Christ and subsequently transformed in the church.

New-covenant structure and signs. Whereas the old-covenant people of God were marked out by the circumcision of every male son, the new-covenant people of God are marked out by baptism. To use Jamieson's language again, baptism is then the initiating oath-sign of the new covenant (Jamieson, 116). The OT looks forward to the day when circumcision of the body would be fulfilled by the circumcision of the heart. In Col. 2, Paul refers to this as "a circumcision not performed by human hands" but "by Christ" (v. 11). This kind of circumcision is an image of conversion and regeneration. This spiritual circumcision is then signified by physical baptism (v. 12). This sign seals our union with Christ in his death and resurrection (Rom. 6:1–3), for Christ fulfills the new-covenant promises.

We might, therefore, say that just as physical circumcision points forward to the new-covenant reality of the circumcision of the heart, baptism points backward to this same reality. Christians are divided on whether the genealogical principle of the Abrahamic covenant continues with baptism, but the connection between circumcision of the heart and baptism favors reserving this sign for those who have been regenerated (Schreiner, 75–80). This is also consistent with the expectation of Jer. 31:34. Whereas the Lord had preserved a faithful remnant within the old-covenant community, all members of the new-covenant community are expected to know the Lord. In any case, baptism has replaced circumcision as the entrance rite of the new covenant. The NT indicates that all who receive baptism are members of the new-covenant people of God and are proper recipients of its ongoing discipline and instruction (Matt. 28:18–20).

We also see the Passover and its related feasts and sacrifices fulfilled in the Lord's Supper. The Passover lamb pointed forward to the greater sacrifice of the Lamb of God, who takes away the sin of the world (John 1:29). During the Last Supper, Christ explains that the bread and wine that they are consuming at that Passover table will continue as the symbol of his body and blood that are to be offered on the cross (Luke 22:14–20). Consequently, as Jamieson (120) summarizes, "The Lord's Supper is a transformation of the Passover, a communal participation in the benefits of Jesus' death, the renewing oath-sign of the new covenant."

Thus, the only symbols mandated for the NT people of God are baptism and the Lord's Supper. As always, however, the people of God are sustained by his Word and its accompanying signs. In the new-covenant era, these signs are the sacraments of baptism and the Lord's Table.

If the signs of the old covenant find their fulfillment in baptism and the Lord's Table, then we can then ask whether and how the old-covenant structures for worship and life find their fulfillment in the new-covenant church. The NT sometimes speaks of sacrifices, but these are now spiritual in nature because the sacrificial system has reached its fulfillment in Christ (see, e.g., 1 Pet. 2:5). As we will see below, this is now possible because the entire people of God have become a holy priesthood and even a new temple, a spiritual house.

The structure of the people of God in the old covenant was primarily shaped by the sacrifices and the calendar laid out in the law of Moses, but the new-covenant people of God are structured around the simpler pattern of the Lord's Day gathering for worship, instruction in the Word, gathering at the Lord's Table, and fellowship together (Acts 2:42). The sacrificial system finds fulfillment in the person and work of Christ (as does the Levitical priesthood, as we will see below). The sacrifices offered year after year to deal with the sin of the people are no longer necessary, for Christ "sacrificed for their sins once for all when he offered himself" (Heb. 7:27). The shadows of the OT calendar and festivals find their fulfillment in and through Christ. This fulfillment is true of the Sabbath as well. Regardless of whether they affirm the Lord's Day as a Christian Sabbath or see the Sabbath principle fulfilled in some other way, all Christians agree that the Sabbath day is transformed and fulfilled in Christ (see the essays in Carson).

While Christian theologians continue to debate some of the particulars of how the gathered people of God are to structure their churches and order their time, all new-covenant believers agree that the old-covenant law finds fulfillment in Christ. Moreover, all agree that the Lord Jesus also fulfills the tasks of the leaders and shepherds in Israel.

New-covenant shepherd(s) and flock. Not only does the sacrificial system find its fulfillment in and through Christ, but the priesthood itself does as well. As noted above, he is the greater priest who brings the Levitical priesthood to its end (Heb. 7:11–28). God instructs the priests under the law to lead the people of God in seeking forgiveness and offering thanksgiving. In the new covenant, God's people come to him only through Christ (1 Tim. 2:5). Jesus is also the prophet promised in Deut. 18:15, for he is the one who now speaks for God to his people in the fullest possible way (Heb. 1:2). Finally, he is the true king, the faithful Davidic shepherd who rules over the people of God (Ezek. 34:23–24). Because of their union with Christ, the true prophet, priest, and king, God's new-covenant people also share in the fulfillment of these roles to some degree.

Paul indicates that saints will share the reign of Christ in some manner: "If we endure, we will also reign with him" (2 Tim. 2:12). This reign echoes the exaltation of the "son of man" figure in Dan. 7. Regardless of how one interprets the "son of man" sayings in the NT, it is difficult to avoid seeing the interplay between the people of God and their single representative in Dan. 7. As many have noted, the "son of man" figure in Dan. 7:13–14 is the single ruler who is "given dominion and glory and a kingdom" (ESV). However, Dan. 7:18 clearly indicates that the "saints of the Most High" are those who "receive the kingdom" (ESV). In contrast to the four kings whose reigns will be temporary and end in disaster, the saints will receive and possess an eternal kingdom and participate in the reign of the son of man (Meadowcroft). Therefore, the king represents the people and the people of God in some sense share in the reign of the king. Following the exaltation of Jesus in his ascension to the Father, the people of God are both united to the Messiah and called to imitate his mission and call—in this case, in the reign of the saints in the kingdom of God.

The new-covenant people of God also share in the new priesthood of Jesus. Like Israel, those who are connected to Jesus the Messiah are to be "a royal priesthood" (1 Pet. 2:9). In other words, because the church is attached to Jesus, the true and final priest, it shares his task and commission. The move to have non-Israelites included in the priesthood should not have surprised the first generation of Christians, for Isa. 66:21 looks forward to the day when God "will select some of them [the gentiles] also to be priests and Levites."

Christ is the true prophet, and the church, therefore, plays a prophetic role in the world today. The proclamation of the Word of God indeed takes on a special prominence for teachers and preachers in the church, yet all members of the church are called to a prophetic role in some sense. The two witnesses of Rev. 11:3–12 likely symbolize the church. As G. K. Beale (573) notes, the witnesses "represent the whole community of faith, whose primary function is to be a prophetic witness." All members of the new-covenant people of God have been given the shared commission to speak on behalf of Christ and thus fulfill a prophetic role (Matt. 28:18–20).

Finally, although Christ is the true shepherd and king of God's new-covenant people, he has appointed elders who care for the people of God the way that Christ intends (1 Pet. 5:1–4). Again, while there is a measure of disagreement among Christians about how this office is to function, who is qualified to hold the office, whether it is to be divided into bishops and priests or one pastor/shepherd/elder office, and how these shepherds are to relate, all orthodox Christian groups recognize that under the ultimate authority of Christ, he has appointed "undershepherds" to care for his people (1 Tim. 3:1–7). Alongside this group, most also recognize a second office, deacons, who help serve in the church in various ways (1 Tim. 3:8–13).

Conclusion

I have defined ecclesiology as the nature and structure of how God's covenant people are governed and relate to one another and the Lord. Often these structures look quite different among the old- and new-covenant people of God. Nonetheless, they share continuity in that the old-covenant structure, symbols, and shepherds all find fulfillment in the person and work of Christ and the ongoing new-covenant realities are rooted in Christ's ongoing work. From this, we can see that the new covenant people of God share in these fulfilled realities while living out their calling as prophets, priests, and kings in the world now and in the age to come.

See also Church; Covenant; Israel and the Church, The Story of

Bibliography. Anizor, U., *Kings and Priests* (Pickwick, 2014); Beale, G. K., *The Book of Revelation*, NIGTC (Eerdmans, 1999); Bruno, C. R., "'Jesus Is Our Jubilee' . . . but How?," *JETS* 53 (2010): 81–101; Calvin, J., *Institutes of the Christian Religion*, ed. J. T. McNeill, trans. F. L. Battles (Westminster, 1960); Carson, D. A., ed., *From Sabbath to Lord's Day* (Wipf & Stock, 1999); Dempster, S. G., *Dominion and Dynasty*, NSBT (InterVarsity, 2003); DeRouchie, J. S., "Circumcision in the Hebrew Bible and Targums," *BBR* 14 (2004): 175–203; Dumbrell, W. J., *Covenant and Creation* (Paternoster, 2013); Jamieson, B., *Going Public* (B&H Academic, 2015); Kline, M., *By Oath Consigned* (Eerdmans, 1968); Kline, "Oath and Ordeal Signs," *WTJ* 27 (1965): 115–139; Kline, "Oath and Ordeal Signs: Second Article," *WTJ* 28 (1965): 1–37; Meadowcroft, T., "'One like a Son of Man' in the Court of the Foreign King," *JTI* 10 (2016): 245–63; Schreiner, T. R., "Baptism in the Epistles," in *Believers Baptism*, ed. T. R. Schreiner and S. D. Wright (B&H, 2006), 67–96; Shead, A. G., "Sabbath," in *NDBT*, 745–50.

Chris Bruno

Echoes

See Quotation, Allusion, and Echo

Enemies of the People of God

This side of the fall, God's people have always had enemies. That reality is part of the warp and woof of the life of the covenant people. This hostility has taken on various forms throughout history, but the truth is, as Jesus warns his people in the NT, "if the world hates you, keep in mind that it hated me first. . . . If they persecuted me, they will persecute you also" (John 15:18–20). The world's animosity may ebb and flow against God's people, but it has always been there, from the beginning of human existence, and it will last until the end of humankind's earthly days. We begin our study by considering the first enemy to appear in the Scriptures. That being winds up to be the greatest and most formidable adversary that God's people will ever face.

The Serpent in the Garden

At the close of the creation account in Gen. 1, "God saw all that he had made, and it was very good" (1:31). However, in Gen. 3:1, a new character appears in the story; the verse begins with a disjunctive *vav* ("now") that indicates an interruption to the story in order to introduce this additional creature. This new character is "the serpent," and one should take note of the use of the definite article that denotes the presence of *one* particular being. The word for "serpent" is the common one in Hebrew for snakes in general (cf. Exod. 4:2–3). People of the ancient Near East had a multifaceted view of snakes: some embraced snakes as a means of protection, and others feared snakes. "Thus they regarded the snake as both friend and fiend, protector and enemy, and the personification of the sacred and the profane. Some snakes were to be worshipped; others were to be considered incarnations of evil" (Currid, *Ancient Egypt*, 88). In Gen. 3, the serpent is obviously a manifestation of evil and an enemy to humanity.

Although some scholars dismiss the belief that the serpent in the garden is some type of manifestation of Satan (Tate, 466–67), the NT firmly and explicitly testifies to that identification (see John 8:44; Rev. 12:9; 20:2). The Hebrew term for "Satan" *(śāṭān)* commonly means "adversary," and it derives from a verb that signifies "to bear a grudge/cherish animosity" (*HALOT*, 2:918). The word can refer to human enemies (e.g., 1 Sam. 29:4) but also is used specifically of Satan as the personification of evil. For the latter, the Hebrew text normally employs a definite article ("the adversary"; see Zech. 3:1–2; Job 1–2 [14x]). The NT writers also employ the name "Satan" (Gk. *Satanas*) to refer to a personal being and sometimes attach the definite article to it (e.g., Matt. 12:26).

Satan's first recorded act is the part he plays in the temptation and fall of humans into sin (Gen. 3:1–6). His actions against humankind are malevolent and monstrous. Jesus comments on Satan's nature and activity in the garden when he says, "He was a murderer from the beginning, not holding to the truth, for there is no truth in him. When he lies, he speaks his native language, for he is a liar and the father of lies" (John 8:44). When God condemns the serpent for his role in the fall of humankind, he sets up a new order in which he announces, "I will put enmity between you and the woman, and between your offspring and hers; he will crush your head, and you will strike his heel" (Gen. 3:15). The term "enmity" (Heb. *ʾêbâ*) is fronted in the original text for emphasis (i.e., "enmity I will put"). That term signifies that one party is an enemy to another (*HALOT*, 1:35–36). This noun appears five times in the OT, and in each case it reflects hostile intent that can lead to outright murder (e.g., Num. 35:21–22; Ezek. 25:15).

The bitter antagonism extends beyond the conflict between the serpent and the woman. It reaches to all succeeding generations—that is, to the "offspring" of the serpent and the "offspring" of the woman. This Hebrew term (*zeraʿ*) commonly means "seed," and its usage often reflects human lineage or posterity. The idea of seed signifying future generations is verified in ancient Near Eastern documents: for example, the Merenptah Stela from Egypt (late thirteenth century BC) describes Israel as in a destroyed state by saying, "Their seed is not." It is important to define these two offsprings/seeds. The generational descent is referring not to physical lineage but to spiritual posterity. The serpent, a fallen angel, does not have the power of physical reproduction (cf. Mark 12:25). Yet a person can be a child of Satan by will, heart, and intent. Jesus, in fact, assails the Pharisees by saying, "You belong to your father, the devil" (John 8:44).

The offspring of the woman is clearly defined by the apostle John when he describes the conflict between the two seeds near the close of human history. He says, "When the dragon saw that he had been hurled to the earth, he pursued the woman who had given birth to the male child. . . . Then the dragon was enraged at the woman and went off to wage war against the rest of her offspring—those who keep God's commands and hold fast their testimony about Jesus" (Rev. 12:13–17). All of human history, according to the Scriptures, attests to the unfolding nature of this conflict. And the church needs to be continually reminded of the reality of this enmity that needs to be viewed with spiritual and eternal eyes. As Paul says, "Put on the full armor of God, so that you take your stand against the devil's schemes. For our struggle is not against flesh and blood, but against the rulers, against the authorities, against the powers of this dark world and against the spiritual forces of evil in the heavenly realms" (Eph. 6:11–12).

Immediate Consequences of Enmity (Genesis)

The promise of enmity between the seed of the serpent and the seed of the woman takes on various forms in the history of humankind. Adam and Eve witness an immediate, initial fulfillment in the tragic history of their first two sons, Cain and Abel. Although both children are physically descended from Adam and Eve, they are spiritual descendants of two different lines. John tells us that Cain "belonged to the evil one and murdered his brother" (1 John 3:12a), making him the first human in the line of the serpent's seed. Abel, in contrast, is a man of faith (Matt. 23:35; Heb. 11:4). Cain's carnal bent is demonstrated by his callous, rebellious worship recorded in Gen. 4:3–7. After being admonished by God, Cain kills Abel in the field. "And why did he murder him? Because his own actions were evil and his brother's were righteous" (1 John 3:12b). Thus, the seed of the serpent strikes quickly at the seed of the woman, and perhaps ultimately it is an attempt to prevent the coming of the promised one of Gen. 3:15 (see below).

The Scriptures then record the struggle between the two lines by tracing the genealogical descent of the lines of Cain and his brother Seth, who replaces Abel (Gen. 4:25). Cain's lineage, registered in Gen. 4:17–18, concludes with Lamech, who is the seventh generation from Adam. He is a most profane man, the first polygamist, who arrogantly boasts of having killed someone for having slightly wounded him (Gen. 4:23). Umberto Cassuto (244) comments on this genealogy, "Not only does violence prevail in the world, but it is precisely in deeds of violence that those generations gloried . . . the very qualities that are ethically reprehensible, and are hateful in the sight of the Lord, are esteemed in the eyes of men." Seth's lineage is recorded in Gen. 5, and it also culminates in a person named Lamech (vv. 25–31). This second Lamech feels the pain of God's curse on creation and then displays hope that his son Noah (Heb. name = "rest") would bring relief and rest from the existing misery and corruption. The author is contrasting the two Lamechs: one hopes for deliverance, and the other glories in his shame and violence.

The unfolding of this theme of enmity between the two lines is evident in Scripture from this point on, although we cannot take the time to consider all its complexities. One further example from Genesis may help to clarify this theme. In Gen. 25:19–34, the twins Esau and Jacob are born to Isaac and Rebekah. The twins' relationship from the beginning is defined by enmity and contention. The first indicator of conflict is in v. 22: "The babies jostled each other within her." The verb used there is one that commonly means "to crush" (*HALOT*, 2:908). Rebekah then asks the Lord why this is happening, and he responds with a prophecy that the enmity between the two children symbolizes enmity between two peoples. The fulfillment of this prophecy comes in the ongoing conflicts between the sons of Jacob (the Israelites) and the sons of Esau (the Edomites), who stand outside the line of God's covenant promises.

The second indicator of conflict occurs at the twins' birth (vv. 24–26). When Esau is born, Jacob follows, grasping the heel of his brother. The symbolism is obvious: the younger brother is holding on to the older, as if he is not going to let him out first. Jacob's name reflects that action; it is a cognate of the word "heel" in Hebrew. Jacob is "one who takes by the heel," which carries with it the idea of being one who supplants through scheming (Mathews and Mims, 185–95).

Jacob lives up to his name in the succeeding story of Esau's selling of his birthright to him (vv. 27–34). In that episode, not only are we to consider Jacob's plotting, but also our attention is drawn "to the deliberateness of Esau's action. . . . He did not fall under some sudden temptation, but . . . he deliberately and wilfully 'despised his birthright'" (Bullinger, 211). The author of Hebrews comments on the contrast between the two men: to Esau, the things of the earth mean more than the promises of God, and therefore, Heb. 12:16 calls him a "godless" or "profane" (KJV) man. A chapter earlier, the writer calls Jacob an heir (with Abraham) "of the same promise" (11:9). Jacob certainly is not sinless, but he belongs to the seed of the woman through whom the promise will be fulfilled.

Expansion of Enmity

The following book, Exodus, is crucial in the development of the seed conflict. No longer is enmity limited to two individuals (e.g., Cain and Abel, Esau and Jacob); now it expands to include two peoples or nations. The conflict now extends to the covenant people of God in opposition to the people of Egypt, who are outside the covenant. The enmity between the two is evident immediately in Exod. 1, in which Pharaoh attempts to destroy the people of God through a series of increasingly malevolent acts. First, he oppresses the people of God by setting slave masters over them and forcing them to build the store cities of Pithom and Rameses; this forced labor is compulsory, burdensome toil (Exod. 1:11). The Hebrew word for "forced labor" is used later of the much-hated unpaid slave labor during the reigns of Solomon and Rehoboam (1 Kings 11:28). This plan of population control does not work, but, ironically, causes the people of Israel to increase in number (Exod. 1:12–13).

Pharaoh then responds by ordering male infanticide to be performed on the Hebrew children by their midwives (Exod. 1:15–16). This destruction of only males by royal decree is perhaps for a variety of reasons: first, it lessens the number of future soldiers to fight against Egypt (cf. v. 10); second, females could easily be assimilated into Egyptian society through intermarriage; third, "blood-lines and status were continued through male lineage" (Currid, *Exodus*, 1:52), and the discontinuation of male lineage would help stamp out the people of Israel; finally, the male infanticide was an attempt to destroy the promised coming male deliverer (Gen. 3:15; see below). The theme of the destruction of male infants in order to prevent the appearance of a redeemer echoes into the NT. In that time, Jesus is born into a situation of severe persecution of the people of God, in which the ruler Herod orders the destruction of the male infants of Bethlehem (Matt. 2:16). He is attempting to prevent the coming of the "king of the Jews" foretold in the Scriptures as told to him by the teachers of the law (Matt. 2:2–6). Ironically, Jesus escapes the massacre when his family flees to Egypt (Matt. 2:13).

Pharaoh is not dissuaded by the fact that, despite the ordered slaughter, the Hebrews continue to multiply (Exod. 1:20). Finally, he orders a direct holocaust to be perpetrated by his own people: whenever a son is born to the Hebrews, the Egyptians are to throw him in the Nile River. The seed of the serpent is to massacre the male descendants of the seed of the woman. In an ironic twist, God "hurled" the Egyptian army into the Red Sea and so destroys the elite males of Egypt (Exod. 15:1). The word "hurled" in that verse is a synonym of the word "throw" used in Exod. 1:22. The plots and schemes of the Egyptians turn back upon themselves.

The ancient Egyptians believed Pharaoh to be the incarnation of the god Ra in human form. The biblical writers are quite aware of the cult of Ra in Egypt, so they use obvious wordplays on the name of the Egyptian god Ra and the Hebrew concept of *raʿ* ("evil"). Salient allusions are found in Exod. 5:19; 10:10; 32:12, 22; Num. 11:1; 20:5; and Deut. 9:18. These double entendres are for the purpose of ridiculing Pharaoh as the embodiment of Egypt's chief deity (Rendsburg).

Yahweh, who violently judges Egypt and delivers the Hebrews, further advances the enmity between the two peoples. The extended plague account demonstrates that God fights on behalf of the seed of the woman and judges the seed of the serpent. In fact, the plague account foreshadows the plagues that God will use to strike the followers of Satan at the end of time. In Rev. 16, John has a vision of God's wrath against those who conspire with the dragon/serpent. God uses five of the ten plagues of Egypt against the seed of the serpent in that chapter: turning water to blood (vv. 3–4), multiplication of frogs (vv. 13–14), sores (v. 2), hail (v. 21), and darkness (v. 10). The plague account in Exod. 7–12 serves as a model or paradigm of judgment that will come upon all unbelievers; it is a mere foretaste of the final days.

The enmity between Egypt and Israel in the exodus event functions as an archetype for many of the conflicts that Israel has with her enemies. The conflict in Egypt echoes and reverberates into the battle of the five kings of the Canaanite confederation against the Israelite army in Josh. 10 (Currid, "Echoes"). The exodus pattern continues in the conflict between Israel and Philistia in the ark episode of 1 Sam. 4–7 (Daube, 73–78; see esp. Estelle).

These literary echoes are perhaps most prominent when Israel's later prophets use the exodus incident as a paradigm for God's rescue of his people out of the oppression of Babylon. For example, God promises in Ezek. 20:33–38 that he will return the exiled Hebrews to their land, using imagery and language of the exodus. He will gather them with "a mighty hand and an outstretched arm"; this is the exact language for God's work in Egypt (Exod. 6:6; Deut. 26:8; etc.). Then he will take them into the wilderness and judge them "as I judged your ancestors in the wilderness of the land of Egypt" (v. 36; cf. Zech. 10:9–11).

Like Egypt, Babylon is a paradigm for the seed of the serpent in the Scriptures. Babylon in the OT is the archenemy of God's people: they destroy Solomon's temple in Jerusalem and send away the people into exile (ca. 586 BC). Babylon is the site where rebellious humanity builds the tower of Babel (Gen. 11:1–9) under the leadership of Nimrod, a descendant of Noah's recalcitrant son, Ham (Gen. 10:8–10). In the NT, John uses the name "Babylon the Great" to represent the Roman Empire (Rev.

14:8; 16:19; 17:5; etc.), which, like Babylon, destroyed the temple in Jerusalem and severely oppressed the people of God in the first century AD. In John's writings, however, "Babylon the Great" may also generally represent the entire ungodly world, its manners, and the way it treats the people of God. Babylon, therefore, symbolizes the world's opposition to God and his people.

These two great persecutions, one in Egypt and one in Babylon, bookend Israel's occupancy of the land of promise (serving as an *inclusio*). The centuries between them are filled with continual conflict between Israel and her enemies, both internally and externally. In Gen. 15:18–21, God promises Abraham that his descendants ("seed"; cf. Gen. 3:15) will inherit the land of Canaan. Implicit to the promise, however, is a warning that ten people groups already inhabit the land. This formula of groups is repeated ten times in the Torah, although never again with the full number of groups (Exod. 3:8, 17; 13:5; 23:23, 28; 33:2; 34:11; Num. 13:29; Deut. 7:1; 20:17). Enmity between these peoples and Israel becomes clear when God commands his people to annihilate them, bringing to bear the *ḥērem* (the "ban") upon them (Exod. 23:23; Deut. 7:1). This internal conflict continues even after Israel conquers the land of Canaan (e.g., Judg. 1:27–36).

Throughout her history, Israel is also often at war with the immediately surrounding pagan nations. During the wilderness wanderings after the escape from Egypt, the Hebrews clash with the Edomites (Num. 20:20), the Moabites (21:21–35), and the Amalekites (Exod. 17:8–16). Hostile engagement continues between Israel and these three peoples well into the period of Israel's settlement in the land of Canaan. After the initial clash with the Amalekites on the way to Canaan, Moses comments, "Because hands were lifted up against the throne of the LORD, the LORD will be at war against the Amalekites from generation to generation" (Exod. 17:16). During the united monarchy (ca. 1050–930 BC), Israel repeatedly exchanges blows with the "uncircumcised" Philistines, who have settled on the southern coastal plain of the Mediterranean Sea. The bottom line is that the people of God have never lacked enemies to struggle with from the seed of the serpent.

Victory and Defeat

Wars inevitably come to a conclusion. In Gen. 3:15, God not only establishes enmity between the two seeds but also promises a resolution to the hostilities. In the final two lines of the verse, God announces there will come a climactic clash between two persons in the two lines. "He" (masc. sing. pronoun) will crush "your" (masc. sing. pronoun) head, and "you" (masc. sing. pronoun) will strike "his" (masc. sing. pronoun) heel. The pronouns "you" and "your" obviously refer to the serpent, because he is the one to whom God is speaking. The other combatant is unidentified. Some commentators believe that "he" and "his" do not designate an individual but merely refer to the "offspring" of the earlier line in the verse. In other words, it restates that the two seeds will clash throughout history (e.g., Westermann, 355). Collins convincingly argues against that position and demonstrates that one is right in seeing an individual as the referent here ("Syntactical Note"). Consequently, Gen. 3:15 is to be understood as the beginning of the messianic promise that unfolds throughout the remainder of Scripture (Alexander, 19–39). The messianic interpretation has a long history, dating to the Septuagint (LXX) of the third to second centuries BC, and the NT confirms it (Martin).

The two belligerents will strike one another. The verbs the NIV translates "crush" and "strike" are the same in the original Hebrew: they underscore the violence of the blows that will be given (BDB, 983). The body parts that will be struck highlight the primacy of the "he" over the serpent: The blow to the serpent is to the head, which probably reflects a mortal, deadly wound. The serpent will strike the "he" on the heel, a wound that would not be fatal. In addition, the preeminence of the one coming to do battle with the serpent is emphasized by the order of the combatants in the text. In the first two conflicts of Gen. 3:15, the serpent ("you"/"your") is mentioned first; now, in the final tier of conflict, the "he" is placed in the opening position. This alternation (chiasm) affirms the supremacy of the messianic figure in the battle.

Who is this "he" of Gen. 3:15 who will crush the head of the serpent? "One major clue is found in the New Testament where Jesus is portrayed as in the direct lineage of Adam and Eve in Luke 3; Christ is thus being portrayed as a direct male descendant of the woman. It is further significant that immediately after the genealogy, Jesus is led by the Spirit in the wilderness in order to battle Satan. The champion sallies forth to engage the enemy, as it were, head-on. Thus begins a raging war that reaches its climax at the cross where the Messiah lands a mortal blow to the head of the serpent" (Currid, "Echoes"). In Gen. 3:15, God promises that one will come to defeat the first and greatest enemy of his people. Collins rightly concludes, "Genesis fosters a messianic expectation, of which this verse is the headwaters" (*Genesis*, 157). In the coming of Christ, this expectation is fulfilled. The author of Hebrews expresses it well when he states that Jesus came that "he might break the power of him who has the power of death—that is, the devil" (Heb. 2:14).

Not only did Christ vanquish Satan at the cross, but he also defeated the followers of the evil one, as Paul says: "Having disarmed the powers and authorities, he made a public spectacle of them, triumphing over them by the cross" (Col. 2:15). Ironically, Christ does to the enemies of God what they had done to him by marching him through Jerusalem disdainfully to the cross. Jesus, to the contrary, makes a spectacle of them by defeating them through the cross.

The Last Enemy

In Gen. 2:16–17, God gives man a law that requires obedience: he is forbidden to eat from the tree of the knowledge of good and evil. If he disobeys, he will bear the consequences. God's warning to the man is direct when he says, "You will certainly die." The syntax of this threat in the original Hebrew consists of an infinitive absolute verb preceding an imperfective of the same verb. In other words, a direct translation would be, "Dying, you will die." This construction is a common Hebrew method of intensification, and it implies certainty in the result. When humankind disobeys God's commandment, God plunges all humanity into sin and its resultant death sentence. As Paul comments, "The wages of sin is death" (Rom. 6:23), and, "Death reigned through that one man" (Rom. 5:17).

Paul further declares, "The last enemy to be destroyed is death" (1 Cor. 15:26). And indeed, it has been conquered. The one who vanquished Satan and his followers is also the one who triumphed over death. Paul identifies him as "our Savior, Christ Jesus, who has destroyed death" (2 Tim. 1:10). Christ has been victorious over this last enemy and has given victory to God's people over it as well. Paul's great doxology in 1 Cor. 15:54–57 is a fitting reminder: "'Death has been swallowed up in victory.' 'Where, O death, is your victory? Where, O death, is your sting?' The sting of death is sin, and the power of sin is the law. But thanks be to God! He gives us the victory through our Lord Jesus Christ."

Conclusion

Although God's people throughout history have been beset with various types of formidable foes—Satan, demons, pagan nations, ungodly rulers, and others—those enemies have not prevailed, and will not. Consider, for example, the many powerful nation-states that beleaguered and persecuted God's people, such as Assyria, Babylon, Egypt, Philistia, and Rome. Where are those enemy nations today? They are all in the dustbin of history. But where are God's people? They are yet here and thriving upon the earth. And the true church will last forever, despite its many enemies, because believers "are more than conquerors through him who loved us" (Rom. 8:37).

See also Consummation; Day of the Lord; Divine Warrior; Messiah

Bibliography. Alexander, T. D., "Messianic Ideology in the Book of Genesis," in *The Lord's Anointed*, ed. P. Satterthwaite, R. Hess, and G. Wenham (Paternoster, 1995), 19–39; Bullinger, E. W., *Figures of Speech Used in the Bible* (Eyre & Spottiswoode, 1898); Cassuto, U., *A Commentary on the Book of Genesis* (Magnes, 1961); Collins, C. J., *Genesis 1–4* (P&R, 2006); Collins, "A Syntactical Note (Gen. 3:15)," *TB* 48 (1997): 139–48; Currid, J. D., "Adam and the Beginning of the Covenant of Grace," in *Covenant Theology*, ed. G. P. Waters, J. R. Muether, and J. N. Reid (Crossway, 2020); Currid, *Ancient Egypt and the Old Testament* (Baker, 1997); Currid, "Echoes of Egypt and the Exodus in the Battle of the Five Kings (Josh. 10:10–15)," in *The Law, the Prophets, and the Writings*, ed. A. King, R. Osborne, and J. Philpot (B&H Academic, 2021); Currid, *Exodus*, 2 vols., EPSC (Evangelical Press, 2000–2001); Daube, D., *The Exodus Pattern in the Bible* (Faber & Faber, 1963); Estelle, B. D., *Echoes of Exodus* (IVP Academic, 2018); Martin, R. A., "The Earliest Messianic Interpretation of Gen. 3:15," *JBL* 84 (1965): 425–27; Mathews, V. H., and F. Mims, "Jacob the Trickster and Heir of the Covenant," *PRSt* 12 (1985): 185–95; Rendsburg, G. A., "The Egyptian Sun-God Ra in the Pentateuch," *Hen* 10 (1988): 3–15; Tate, M., "Satan in the Old Testament," *RevExp* 89 (1992): 461–74; Westermann, C., *Genesis 1–11* (Augsburg, 1984).

JOHN D. CURRID

Ephesians, Letter to the

In Ephesians Paul shows how fully he is steeped in the OT. It comes out not only in the few direct quotations of OT passages but also in allusions marked by both linguistic and conceptual connections. To appreciate how ancient authors could be shaped in their thinking by authoritative literature, one has only to read the kind of Greco-Roman authors with which the pre-Christian Ephesians would have been familiar. Such authors integrated quotations and various kinds of allusions into their works from their own classic poets, playwrights, and historians in similar fashion to how NT authors use the OT (cf. Stanley). Likewise, Paul's thinking in Ephesians has been fully shaped by the OT, which he sees as fundamentally fulfilled in the Lord Jesus Christ (1:10), a fulfillment in which Paul was himself a foundational participant (2:20; cf. 3:5; 4:11) as the apostle to the gentiles (3:1–13).

In his *CNTUOT* entry on Ephesians, Frank S. Thielman surveys eight passages where Paul either cites the OT directly or integrates it in various ways into his epistle: 1:20–23; 2:13–17; 3:1–13; 4:7–11; 4:17–5:20; 5:31–32; 6:1–3; and 6:10–17. Thielman's longest discussion naturally falls on 4:7–11, where Paul's use of Ps. 68 has led to quite a bit of discussion in scholarly literature (Thielman, 819–24).

Two preliminary details need to be highlighted for our brief update of Thielman's treatment of Ephesians. First, Paul is confined (3:1, 13; 4:1; 6:20) and may not have had access to written books of the OT at the time of writing this epistle. It would be perfectly understandable if Paul quoted OT texts from memory with minor variations from the written sources. On the other hand, it is possible that Paul had books, and especially "parchments," brought to him while in custody (2 Tim.

4:13). The latter probably denotes a codex-like notebook made from parchment (Lat. *membrana*), which could possibly have been used by Paul for his notes or even for a collection of quotations (cf. Hezser, 95–98). Regardless, Paul probably relies on his excellent memory if not on written sources for his OT citations.

Second, since Thielman wrote his essay, much work on what are sometimes simply called OT allusions has been going on in biblical scholarship and has a bearing on Paul's employment of the OT in Ephesians (Beale). This dictionary reports on this work in many places, but the survey work found in David Allen, Christopher Bruno, and Bryan Estelle will be summarized next. Then we will update consideration of some of the places in Ephesians discussed by Thielman and conclude with an example of an OT "echo" in Ephesians.

Citations and Allusions

Allen surveys the field of the NT use of the OT in a recent article where he identifies this as a maturing subdiscipline of NT studies (4–5). Allen's main orientation is to divide the use of the OT into "micro" and "macro" readings of NT passages against their OT backgrounds: "'Micro' readings are more concerned with fine textual detail and are cautious about more expanded interpretation; 'macro' ones are driven by them and utilize what may otherwise seem to be a fairly minor echo to generate a wider narrative or story" (11).

The essay by Bruno also surveys the field generally (311–19). He proposes a standard treatment of the NT author's verbal and conceptual links to the OT and considers the effects of the citations on the original and modern readers, yet his contribution is to endorse the view advanced by Poythress in a series of essays relating the divine authorship of Scripture to our analysis of the use of the OT by the NT. This means that in addition to evaluating the human author's context and historical circumstances, one must also read a passage in light of the development of Scripture to that point in redemptive revelation and then read the passage in light of the whole Bible because of its ultimate divine origin (Bruno, 319; cf. Beale, 24–25).

While not commenting on Ephesians itself, nevertheless, Estelle provides a helpful introductory survey of the "inner-biblical" OT use of the OT as well as the NT use of the OT textual relationships as a preview for his own development of the idea of "echoes" of the exodus theme in Scripture. What makes his survey particularly helpful is his reading not only in biblical scholarship but also in literary theory and linguistics more broadly. The result is a nicely nuanced taxonomy of five ways that texts and authors use other authors and their texts: (1) evocation and influence; (2) quotation; (3) subtle citation; (4) allusion; and (5) echoes and reminiscence (Estelle, 30–34). He divides a passage into these categories through looking at shared language (linguistic links), shared content, and shared form (28–30).

The idea of "shared form" in particular, Estelle notes, has received little attention (29–30). In Ephesians, for instance, the opening benediction (1:3; *berekah*) form is clearly derived and adapted from a well-known OT and Jewish form of prayer (cf. 2 Cor. 1:3; 1 Pet. 1:3; Baugh, 76). Although "echo" has been discussed in NT studies at least since Richard Hays's influential work on Paul, Estelle's use of this category differs from Hays's by maintaining "a divine-author centered approach" on the issue: "The divine authorial intent may mean that human authors say more than they recognize at the time" (Estelle, 36). Estelle's work as a whole illustrates echo as a biblical motif manifest throughout biblical literature even where linguistic links may not be present.

Ephesians 1–2

While the OT references in the first two chapters of Ephesians are slight and passing, they lay down a foundation for the book as a whole as building on the theme of Christ bringing peoples together from throughout this creation into an inaugurated new creation. This messianic work is presented in 1:15–23 as Paul reports on his prayer that the Ephesians may know the overwhelming power of God unleashed toward them when he raised Christ from the dead and seated him in supreme dominion over all things.

Paul picks up language used in the OT in Isa. 40:26 ("his great power and mighty strength") and Ps. 147:5 ("mighty in power") when he expresses God's "incomparably great power for us who believe" and "mighty strength" (Eph. 1:19). The OT references are to God's strength exercised in creation, which Paul appropriates to describe God's creative might in inaugurating the new creation in Christ. This new-creation reference is fleshed out a little more in the passing quotation of Ps. 8:6 ("You put everything under [his] feet") and Ps. 110:1 ("Sit at my right hand until I make your enemies a footstool for your feet") in Eph. 1:22. Psalm 8 in particular references the exaltation of the human race in the person of Adam over this creation in the beginning, while Paul in Ephesians references Christ as a second Adam exalted over the new creation (cf. 1 Cor. 15:20–28; Heb. 2:5–9; Thielman, 814–17; Owens, *Beginning*, 131–42).

The new-creation references continue in 2:11–22, where Christ has created one new human race under his headship in the church (esp. 2:15; see 2:10), which takes the form, at present, of a temple as an earthly dwelling place for God through the Spirit (2:20–22). This new-creation temple imagery consisting of unified Jewish and gentile believers has been seen as built on the "framework" of Ezek. 37 (Suh; see also Foster on Eph. 3:19 and Baugh, 453–54, on 5:18). The proclamation of peace bringing together into one body those "far away" and those "near" (2:13, 17) is a reference developed particularly from Isaiah's prophecy of future restoration from exile for repentant people: "'I have seen their ways, but I will heal them; I will guide them and restore comfort to Israel's mourners, creating praise on their lips. Peace, peace, to those far and near,' says the LORD. 'And I will heal them'" (Isa. 57:18–19; cf. 52:7). Mark Owens (*Beginning*, 149–52) holds this in continuity with Paul's new-creation theme in Ephesians and other books regarding the "one new human" (2:15 AT; cf. Thielman, 817–18).

Ephesians 4:7–11

Paul's use of Ps. 68 (LXX 67) in 4:7–11 is one of the more debated NT passages that use the OT (cf. Thielman, 819–25; Ehorn). Paul introduces the psalm with the unusual phrase *dio legei* (see below), leading the audience to expect a fairly precise wording of the OT, even given the presumption mentioned above that Paul would likely have to rely on memory rather than a written text while in custody. The wording is quite close between Ps. 68:18 (LXX 67:19; MT 68:19) ("When you ascended on high, you took many captives; you received gifts from people, even from the rebellious—that you, LORD God, might dwell there") and Eph. 4:8 ("When he ascended on high, he took many captives and gave gifts to his people"), with the change of person from "you" to "he" and the resulting change of relevant verb forms being a minor accommodation of the passage to a new setting. The nexus of contention centers on Paul's change of the Lord's reception of gifts in the psalm to Christ's giving of gifts in Ephesians, which gifts turn out to be people called to serve his church (4:11).

To explain Paul's shift from "receive" to "give," scholars have a range of opinions, extending from seeing Paul as simply misquoting the psalm, to saying he is using a translation that has this wording, to suggesting he is engaging in a loose kind of paraphrasing comment (*midrash pesher*) (see the survey in Ehorn, 97–109). One of the more compelling views is that Paul is not mechanically quoting one portion of Ps. 68 but interpreting the whole of it in light of its fulfillment in Christ, the triumphant Divine Warrior who is portrayed in the psalm (cf. Gombis, "Cosmic Lordship"; Gombis, *Drama*; Lunde and Dunne; Baugh, 320–26). This explanation seems especially attractive when one considers a possible intertextual allusion to Isaiah here as well (Wilder).

Examination of Ps. 68 shows it to be a song of Yahweh's deliverance of his people from his and their enemies by saving them from death (v. 20), after which he ascends on high to dwell among his people in peace. The women divide the spoils of battle (v. 12), and the conquered kings of the earth bear gifts of tribute to the divine victor (v. 29) as the whole world is called on to worship the Lord (vv. 31–32). Then Yahweh, enthroned in his holy place (v. 24) with his loyal subjects attending him, distributes "power and strength to his people" (v. 35). These themes of triumph and the gentiles streaming in to worship the Lord, as well as the Lord's largesse from the riches of his grace, are also prominent concerns throughout Ephesians (e.g., 1:15–23; 2:11–22; 3:5–13; cf. Baugh, 325–26).

However, the key to Paul's use of Ps. 68 in 4:7–11 is actually in the unusual way he introduces the reference with the phrase *dio legei* ("for this reason it says"). Unfortunately, scholars usually refer to this phrase as a citation "formula," sometimes referencing a few places where the phrase appears elsewhere in the NT and in Philo, and give it no further analysis (e.g., Thielman, 820–22). In consequence, they miss Paul's important view of the relation of the OT to Christ's fulfillment indicated by this introductory phrase.

First off, the conjunction *dio* is not very common in the NT, with Paul using it twenty-six times out of its fifty-two total appearances. Contrast this with the nearly seventy times the true quotation formula *gegraptai* ("it stands written") appears in the NT. Next, the phrase *dio legei* does introduce Scripture quotations in Eph. 5:14; Heb. 10:5; and James 4:6 (cf. Heb. 3:7), but in the first and last of these passages it has the same significance as in the four passages normally referenced in Philo (see, e.g., Thielman, 821; cf. *dio legetai* in Philo, *Drunkenness* 166)—that is, it gives the moral standard or foundation for some idea being true or for an exhortation (see Baugh, 435–38, for discussion of Eph. 5:14).

The critical idea comes from the conjunction *dio*, which is derived from the preposition *dia* and the neuter relative pronoun *ho* referencing a previous statement or passage. *Dio* marks what follows as an inference or result from the previous thing, that previous things being presented as its cause, reason, or rationale. For example, after Paul says that Abraham exercised a strong faith in God and his promise without wavering (Rom. 4:20–21), he writes, "That is why [*dio*] his faith was 'counted to him as righteousness'" (v. 22). It was *because* of Abraham's faith that, in consequence, God justified him by that faith.

We expect OT prophecy to form the reason or rationale for later NT fulfillment. But in Eph. 4:7–8, Paul reverses the causation: the ascended Christ graciously distributes gifts to his church, and it is for this reason (*dio*) that Scripture says, "When he ascended on high." Paul's statement and logic are clear: what gave rise to Ps. 68 speaking of ascent and gift giving was Christ's ascent and gift giving. It is an announcement ahead of time of the good news of Christ, much like the "preproclamation of the gospel" (*proeuangelizomai*) Abraham heard, which Paul mentions in Gal. 3:8 (cf. Heb. 10:5; see further discussion in Baugh, 321–22, 329–31).

Ephesians 6:10–17

One could say that Eph. 6:10–17 is a favorite passage in the church and a source for much vivid preaching, with its catalog of ancient weapons and armor. It is also a prominent place for discussion of Christian warfare against evil spiritual powers (Adewuya). The passage's OT background in Isaiah is clear and pretty fully discussed in the literature (e.g., Thielman, 830–33), but Paul blends this OT background with contemporary literature and culture familiar to the Ephesians (see below).

Isaiah's reference to God himself as the Divine Warrior who acts on behalf of his people is prominent in Eph. 6:13–17, particularly his battle gear (see Isa. 59:15b–17; 61:10). Reference to taking up armor and battle is also found in Rom. 13:12–14; 2 Cor. 10:3–5; 1 Thess. 5:8. See also Wis. 5:15–23, which some believe shapes Ephesians, though more likely both are independently influenced by Isaiah (cf. Pss. Sol. 17:32–35). Standing behind this battle imagery is Israel's God as Divine Warrior fighting on their behalf.

This Divine Warrior is the Messiah equipped with the Spirit of the Lord (Isa. 11:1–4), with Isa. 11:5 in the LXX reading, "And his waist has been belted with righteousness and his loins bound up with truth" (AT; cf. Eph. 6:14). The Lord Jesus has definitively won the battle over all enemies and risen from the dead in triumph and absolute, new-creation sovereignty (1:19–22; 2:4–6; 4:8–10). So, now his followers put on "the armor of light" because they have clothed themselves "with the Lord Jesus Christ" (Rom. 13:12, 14) and conduct their warfare in this life equipped with the Lord's own (defensive) armament. As such, the Lord's people carry on their own advance of the new-creation victory won by the Lord as they proclaim "the gospel of peace" (Eph. 6:15) to the whole world (so Owens, "Spiritual Warfare").

While OT imagery and passages clearly inform Eph. 6:10–17, Paul has also woven into this passage two elements drawn from his audience's world. First, the schemes and deceit of the devil and of his human allies in 6:11 demonstrate their shameful qualities in contrast with the honor and virtues of Jesus and of his followers. This portrait of the contestants stands against a classical background, especially in the warfare in Homer (so Asher; cf. Baugh, 540). Second, the word *palē*, used only in 6:12 in the NT and often rendered "struggle" (NASB, NIV), refers to "wrestling" (so KJV, ESV), which often occurred in ancient battles that had devolved into hand-to-hand combat in armor, where being thrown to the ground rather than remaining "standing" (6:11, 13–14) could spell a soldier's doom (see Gudorf). The background of 6:10–17, then, is not only the OT references to the divine armor and battle equipment from Isaiah but also ideas from epic literature and from common wrestling contests familiar to Paul's contemporaries from their world (see Baugh, 543–45).

New Exodus in Ephesians

The theme of new creation is a common thread throughout Ephesians. One further motif in the book is an "echo" of the new exodus accomplished by Christ in the compact theme of "redemption from slavery to inheritance," which Estelle (284–85) discusses in a very brief survey of the exodus motif in Col. 1:12–14. We can also find this motif in Ephesians where this redemption (1:7; 4:30) brings both Jews and gentiles together as God's own prized possession (1:14) into a "glorious inheritance" (1:18; cf. 1:11, 14) in Christ—even gentiles who were formerly separated from "the covenants of the promise" (2:12) and alienated from all hope and from God under the tyranny of "the ruler of the kingdom of the air" (2:2) but are now "fellow citizens with God's people" (2:19; cf. 2:11–12) in "the kingdom of Christ and of God" (5:5). The "breaking down" of the dividing wall was accomplished in Christ's great victory through the cross, resulting in peace (2:14–16; cf. 1:19–22). Hence, Christ Jesus even took captivity captive in his triumphal ascent on high to fill all things (4:8–10).

Conclusion

Work on Ephesians since Thielman's entry has focused on Paul's development of the new-creation theme, especially against a background in Isaiah. Going forward, more reflection upon different kinds of allusion and echoes may prove fruitful for seeing how OT themes such as temple-building play a role in shaping Ephesians. The Jewish literary background is not the only source of Paul's inspiration, such that further reflection would also prove fruitful for seeing how Paul blends into his teaching in Ephesians themes from the audience's own Greco-Roman background related to topics such as adoption, citizenship, or warfare.

Bibliography. Adewuya, J. A., "The Spiritual Powers of Ephesians 6:10–18 in the Light of African Pentecostal Spirituality," *BBR* 22 (2012): 251–58; Allen, D. M., "Introduction: The Study of the Use of the Old Testament in the New," *JSNT* 38 (2015): 3–16; Asher, J. R., "An Unworthy Foe," *JBL* 130 (2011): 729–48; Baugh, S. M., *Ephesians*, EEC (Lexham, 2016); Beale, G. K., *Handbook on the New Testament Use of the Old Testament* (Baker Academic, 2012); Bruno, C. R., "Readers, Authors, and the Divine Author," *WTJ* 71 (2009): 311–21; Ehorn, S. M., "The Use of Psalm 68(67).19 in Ephesians 4.8," *CBR* 12 (2012): 96–120; Estelle, B. D., *Echoes of Exodus* (IVP Academic, 2018); Foster, R. L., "'A Temple in the Lord Filled to the Fullness of God,'" *NovT* 49 (2007): 85–96; Gombis, T. G., "Cosmic Lordship and Divine Gift-Giving," *NovT* 47 (2005): 367–80; Gombis, *The Drama of Ephesians* (InterVarsity, 2010); Gudorf, M. E., "The Use of πάλη in Ephesians 6:12," *JBL* 117 (1998): 331–35; Hays, R. B., *Echoes of Scripture in the Letters of Paul* (Yale University Press, 1989); Hezser, C., *Jewish Literacy in Roman Palestine*, TSAJ 81 (Mohr Siebeck, 2001); Lim, T. H., "Qumran Scholarship and the Study of the Old Testament in the New Testament," *JSNT* 38 (2015): 68–80; Lunde, J. M., and J. A. Dunne, "Paul's Creative and Contextual Use of Psalm 68 in Ephesians 4:8," *WTJ* 74 (2012): 99–117; Owens, M. D., *As It Was in the Beginning* (Pickwick, 2015); Owens, "Spiritual Warfare and the Church's Mission according to Ephesians 6:10–17," *TynBul* 67 (2016): 87–103;

Stanley, C. D., "Paul and Homer," *NovT* 32 (1990): 48–78; Suh, R. H., "The Use of Ezek. 37 in Ephesians 2," *JETS* 50 (2007): 715–33; Thielman, F. S., "Ephesians," in *CNTUOT*, 813–33; Wilder, W. N., "The Use (or Abuse) of Power in High Places," *BBR* 20 (2010): 185–200.

S. M. BAUGH

Esther, Book of

The book of Esther presents the story of the exiled Jewish community living in ancient Persia during the reign of Ahasuerus. Hadassah, better known as Esther, is a beautiful Jewish exile selected by Ahasuerus to replace Queen Vashti after she is deposed. Esther's cousin / adoptive father Mordecai obtains a place of prominence in the king's court, where he proves his loyalty by preventing a plot against the king's life. A conflict arises between Mordecai and the king's top advisor, Haman, who seeks a royal decree to have Mordecai and all his people annihilated. To obtain "relief and deliverance" (Esther 4:14), Mordecai urges Esther to intercede with the king on behalf of her people, ultimately leading to several ironic reversals: Haman, who is the "enemy of the Jews" (8:1), and his sons are hung on a tree instead of Mordecai (7:10; 9:14); a counterdecree is issued, allowing the Jews to take preemptive action against their aggressors (8:11); and many Persian citizens declare themselves to be Jews (8:17; cf. 9:27). The festival of Purim is instituted in commemoration, and Mordecai is elevated as second in rank to the king (10:2).

Critical Issues in the Study of Esther

Questions of dating and canonicity affect considerations of the book's potential use of prior Scripture and its availability or desirability as a potential source text for other writers. Scholars propose a variety of dates for Esther's composition, typically ranging from the late Persian to early Hellenistic periods, and the process of its acceptance into both the Jewish and Christian canons was more complicated than with most biblical books (see Beckwith, 288–97, 311–18, 322–23). Two additional issues particularly relevant to the subject of intertextuality may be singled out.

Compositional matters: Three distinct textual traditions. Esther exhibits a complex history of textual development, witnessed to by the traditional Hebrew text and by two distinct Greek versions, the LXX and the so-called Alpha Text. The Alpha Text and LXX include numerous references to God and to religious practices that are lacking in the MT, a phenomenon also observable in the two targumim to Esther (Ego). Moreover, both the Alpha Text and the LXX (the latter followed by the Vulgate) feature various "additions"—that is, full pericopae not found in the Hebrew text that consist of visions, prayers, letters, and other expansions. The question of *which* version of the book is received as canonical thus has a significant impact on its literary and theological analysis.

Theological issues: The absence of God. It is well known that the MT of Esther lacks any reference to God, giving the book a "secular" appearance. Moreover, it fails to mention any rituals or institutions that might point to a deity, such as prayer, temples, sacrifices, and the like, even when such a reference might be expected (e.g., Esther 4:16 speaks of fasting without mentioning prayer). This peculiarity has been a major factor in discussions of the book's canonicity. Additionally, some have questioned the morality of the protagonists as presented in the MT: the actions of Esther and Mordecai can appear either morally ambiguous or sinfully vengeful (Anderson, 38). Such features are mitigated significantly in the Greek versions, which depict Esther in a more explicitly positive light (Harvey, 225–29).

Despite God's noticeable "absence" from the Hebrew version, the book's theological message is usually explained in terms of divine providence, revealed in the impossibly complex chain of events that ultimately results in deliverance for the Jews. However, Esther is unlike some narratives that explicitly identify God's sovereignty as the cause of a happy outcome from dire circumstances (e.g., Gen. 45:5, 7; 50:20). The MT's silence concerning God is best attributed to the author's understated literary strategy, which seeks to convey the tenuous sociopolitical situation of the exilic Jewish community, in which God "seemed" to have gone into hiding (Rogland, "Cult," 101).

Esther's Use of OT Scripture

Increasingly, scholars are recognizing Esther's subtle but pervasive use of Scripture (Firth, 34). Clearly, the book feels very much at home within the canonical literature of the OT. Of the various intertextual proposals in the scholarly literature, some are almost universally accepted.

The Joseph narrative (Gen. 37–50). It is now virtually axiomatic in Esther scholarship to note the influences of the Joseph story (e.g., Grossman, 210–13, 222): Mordecai's trajectory in the narrative bears obvious resemblances to Joseph's career as a displaced Jew in a foreign land who rises to "second" (*mišneh*) in power (Esther 10:3; cf. Gen. 41:40). This general thematic parallel is confirmed by many verbal connections between the two narratives, some of which serve to compare Mordecai to Joseph or to contrast Haman with him (Link and Emerson, 132–37). Such links include a "signet ring" being "removed" from the king's "hand" and given to a top advisor and Joseph and Mordecai being "clothed" luxuriously and "made to ride" with a crier "calling out" before them (Gen. 41:42–43; Esther 6:9, 11; 8:2). Along with other passages, the influence of the Joseph narrative on the presentation of Mordecai develops the trajectory of a second-Adam typology within the OT canon (Link and Emerson, 138–41).

The exodus and Passover narratives. Numerous parallels between Moses, on the one hand, and Esther and Mordecai, on the other, often with a distinctly ironic twist, have led J. William Whedbee (129–90) to describe both narratives as "comedies of deliverance." As with Esther, scholars have noted the absence of God in the opening chapters of Exodus (Cowan, 1–24). The theme of deliverance from a royal directive to exterminate the Jews, with the establishment of a commemorative festival as a result, naturally leads one to draw comparisons between the two narratives. Early evidence of a Passover-Purim association is found in the Peshitta of Esther 9:26 ("Therefore they called these days Purim, in accord with the name Passover") and in the Jerusalem Talmud (y. Meg. 1:5), in which R. Helbo links the redemption of Purim with that of Passover (Wechsler). It is especially noteworthy that the decree for the Jews' destruction is issued on 13 Nisan (Esther 3:12)—that is, on the day before the Passover celebration (Exod. 12:6, 18). It is inconceivable that the ironic significance of this date would be lost on a Jewish audience in the Second Temple period.

Saul and Agag, Israel and Amalek, Mordecai and Haman. In 1 Sam. 15, King Saul, the son of Kish from the tribe of Benjamin, is commanded to devote the Amalekites to destruction, including Agag their king. He refuses to do so, necessitating Samuel's intervention (1 Sam. 15:33). Amalek is Israel's prototypical archenemy from their earliest days in the wilderness following the deliverance from Egypt. In Exod. 17 the Lord declared that he would "have war with Amalek from generation to generation" (v. 16 AT)—realized numerous times in the Pentateuch and the book of Judges—and that eventually he would "blot out the memory of Amalek from under heaven" (v. 14 AT). This expectation can be viewed as a fulfillment of the Lord's promise to Abraham to "curse" those who dishonor him and his descendants (Gen. 12:3). Saul's summons to engage in *ḥērem* warfare thus reveals the Amalekites' "cursed" status and represents the continuation of Israel's earlier conflicts with them.

With this background in mind, Haman's designation as an "Agagite" (Esther 3:1) and Mordecai's lineage as a Benjaminite and a descendant of Kish (2:5) invite the reader to view their conflict as a recapitulation of this ongoing warfare "from generation to generation." The eventual triumph of Esther and Mordecai over Haman undoes Saul's earlier failure with respect to King Agag and fulfills the divine oracle of Exod. 17 concerning Amalek's destruction (Bowman, 102). In this way, what ostensibly begins as a bitter interpersonal rivalry between two members of the royal court is ultimately revealed to have a deeper theological significance as an act of Yahweh's "holy war": just as the biblical *ḥērem* represents the expression of God's curse, so also the judicial execution of Haman by "hanging him on a tree" indicates that he has been cursed by God (Deut. 21:22–23).

This reading is confirmed by the application of holy-war principles to the remaining "enemies of the Jews" in Esther (Jobes, *Esther*, 167–69, 196–99; Wetter, 157–62). For example, the Jews' refusal to "lay a hand on the plunder" (Esther 9:10, 15 AT) even though it is permitted by the king's decree (8:11) indicates that they understand their actions to be those of the *ḥērem*. Similarly, the "dread" (*paḥad*) that falls upon the enemies of the Jews in 9:2–3—otherwise inexplicable for opponents of a "scattered and dispersed" minority group (3:8 AT)—is best explained as the fulfillment of the Lord's promise to send *paḥad* upon his foes when the Israelites engage in holy war (Exod. 15:16; Deut. 2:25; 11:25; see Wetter, 159–60). Just as holy war resulted in "rest" for God's people (Deut. 12:10; 25:19; Josh. 23:1; etc.), so also the Jews' *ḥērem* against their enemies in Persia achieves "rest" in Esther 9:22 (Wetter, 162).

The evocation of holy-war concepts in Esther helps fill in what initially appear to be "gaps" in the narrative. First, it indicates that the actions of Mordecai and Esther regarding Haman individually or the Jews' enemies collectively are to be viewed not as a character flaw but as faithfulness to an implicit divine directive (Jobes, *Esther*, 168; Wetter, 158). The royal decrees that they help craft are thus to be appreciated by the reader ultimately as expressions of divine judgment. Second, the successful outcome of the *ḥērem* is yet another subtle pointer to the Lord's presence in Esther, since holy war is carried out in the conviction that victory will be attained not by human might but by Yahweh, the Divine Warrior (Stuart, 395–96; Jobes, *Esther*, 190).

The various instances of holy war stemming from this ancient conflict between Israel and Amalek should be understood as the outworking of an even more fundamental biblical motif—namely, the warfare prophesied between the "seed" (Heb. *zeraʿ*) of Eve and of the serpent in Gen. 3:15 (see Dowden, 6, 181; Van 't Veer, 9–10). Pharaoh's slaughter of the Hebrew male children in Exod. 1 and Herod's attempt to destroy the newly born Messiah in Matt. 2 are likewise examples of this conflict that are taken up and woven into the stunning intertextual tapestry of Rev. 12, which makes their satanic origin explicit. The similarities between these events and Haman's plotted annihilation of all Jews throughout the Persian Empire are a clear invitation to interpret the events of Esther as another satanic attempt upon the people of God. The use of *zeraʿ* in the narrative to designate the people or descendants of Mordecai and the Jews (6:13; 9:27, 28, 31; 10:3) confirms the linkage with Gen. 3:15, indicating that the book represents a fulfillment of the ancient typological pattern. At the same time, however, Esther does not present the events of the narrative as the final and climactic fulfillment of this pattern, and in this way it encourages the reader to look beyond the success of Mordecai for an even greater one yet to come (cf. Link and Emerson, 136–37).

Evocations of temple and cultic imagery. Various writers have observed that Ahasuerus's palace is described in terms reminiscent of the temple structure (e.g., Grossman, 22–24), such as its featuring of an "inner" and an "outer" court (Esther 5:1; 6:4). Several other similarities between the Persian court and the temple are also observable (Rogland, "Cult"). For example, the designation of Bigthana and Teresh as "guardians of the threshold" (*šōmərê hassap*; Esther 2:21) is noteworthy, since the phrase is used exclusively for temple guardians elsewhere in the OT (e.g., 2 Kings 12:10; 1 Chron. 9:19), while *raṣim* is used consistently of royal guards (e.g., 1 Kings 14:27). The casting of the lot, or *pûr*, so central to the book's plot by providing the name of the festival it establishes, was viewed as a sacred, sometimes priestly, duty in the OT as well as in other ancient literature (Rogland, "Cult," 103–4). The "blue and purple" cloth used for palace hangings (Esther 1:6) and for Mordecai's garb (8:15) evoke the colors of the sanctuary (e.g., Exod. 25:4).

Frei (15) contends that typological significance emerges from the combination of characters and eventful circumstances. As a corollary to this it may be added that the narrative setting of those characters and circumstances also serves this end. The "cultic" descriptions of the Persian palace complex thus point toward Ahasuerus's role as a God figure: like Yahweh, Ahasuerus "displays" the riches of his "royal glory" and "the splendor of his great majesty" (Esther 1:4 AT; cf. Exod. 33:18; Deut. 5:24). This realization in turn allows the roles of the other main characters to find their place around this dynamic and points toward other theologically substantive themes in addition to that of divine providence. According to Lewis, for example, the conflicted relationship between the Jews and Ahasuerus points toward their conflicted relationship with Yahweh, their divine sovereign. In addition, the theme of exclusion from or reception into the king's presence points toward the Jews' role as an intercessory people, embodied particularly by Esther and Mordecai (Rogland, "And So").

Summary. Not surprisingly, the book of Esther draws significantly from the Pentateuch and Former Prophets, although references to the Latter Prophets and Writings have also been suggested and are deserving of further study. Esther's avoidance of quotation formulas in favor of more subtle intertextual cues coheres with the author's literary strategy of depicting a world in which God appears to be absent. In general, the author's method of exegesis may be best characterized as largely "typological" in approach (Talmon, 437). Thus, Mordecai is presented as a second Joseph (and thereby a second Adam), Purim appears as a new exodus and Passover, and so on. This typology is often recapitulative in nature, though at times it takes on a prophetic or mantological cast (cf. Fishbane) insofar as the author treats the continuing warfare of Israel and Amalek as culminating in the conflict between Mordecai and Haman. In view of many of the critical questions pertaining to the scholarly study of the book mentioned above, it should be noted that Esther's rich use of Scripture has profound implications for discussions of the book's canonical status and for adding nuance to the common impression of the book's "secularity."

The Use of Esther in Second Temple Judaism

One inevitable result of Esther's postexilic provenance is that it is rarely or never used by other OT books. On the other hand, there is no doubt that the work was known in its Hebrew and Greek forms in the Second Temple period. Post-NT interaction with Esther is amply attested in the mishnaic and talmudic literature, most obviously in the tractate Megillah, dedicated to the reading of the scroll, along with rabbinic exegesis in two separate targumic traditions and in the midrash. Many, though not necessarily all, of these exegetical traditions postdate the NT era, but in Qumran and Josephus we find testimony to the existence and use of Esther either predating or roughly contemporaneous with the NT.

Qumran. No biblical manuscripts of Esther have been discovered at Qumran, a fact typically attributed to the community's avoidance of Purim in their liturgical calendar, though the book's absence could simply be a result of its relative brevity combined with the "accidental" nature of archaeological discovery (White Crawford, 269). Nevertheless, the evidence is mounting that the book was known to the scribes of the Qumran community. Esther's influence has been discerned in the Genesis Apocryphon and the Temple Scroll (De Troyer), among other suggestions (e.g., Koller, 129–30).

Josephus. Josephus clearly views Esther as canonical (Beckwith, 315), and he provides a thorough retelling of the book's narrative in *Ant.* 11.184–296. Among other things, he presents Esther and Mordecai in an exalted light, omitting features that might have been viewed as unflattering to a Hellenistic readership (Feldman, *Studies*, 513). Thus, for example, Josephus states that Esther was "of the royal family" (*Ant.* 11.185) and that Mordecai was "one of the chief men of the Jews" (*Ant.* 11.198). He also explains that Mordecai did not bow before Haman out of "wisdom" and because it was forbidden by his native law (*Ant.* 11.210), even though the MT leaves it unexplained. Josephus's reading generally accords with the approach of the ancient versions, which fill in many of the "gaps" presented by the MT.

The Use of Esther in the NT

Neither the characters of the book of Esther nor the chief events of the narrative are explicitly mentioned in the NT. Likewise, the observance of Purim emphasized in Esther is never clearly indicated in the NT, though some suggest it is the unnamed festival in John 5:1

(Bowman, 99–132) or that it has influenced Rev. 11:13 (Bauckham, 281–82). These lacunae have led to the assertion that the NT never quotes Esther (e.g., Anderson, 42), but this is misleading at best: when one considers broader forms of intertextuality in addition to direct quotation, it becomes evident that the book exercises some degree of influence on the NT writers (for the fullest survey to date, see Lees, 129–66).

The clearest instance of a likely NT quotation of the book of Esther occurs in the Markan account of Herod's vow to give Herodias's daughter "up to half [his] kingdom" (Mark 6:22–23). Unlike the other synoptic material, Mark's version uniquely shares the distinctive phrasing of Ahasuerus's offer to Esther (Esther 5:3, 6; 7:2), which is widely taken as intentional (Nolan; for other possible echoes in the Markan pericope, see Aus, *Water*). The fact that Herodias's daughter asks for John the Baptist's head, just as Haman intended to ask the king to execute Mordecai (Esther 6:4), creates a stark contrast with Esther's humble request for the life of her people (Esther 7:3–4).

Goulder suggests that the Matthean passion narrative was crafted to correspond to the festival of Purim. In contrast to Luke, Matthew locates the parable of the wedding banquet during the passion week, and Goulder (214) argues that it has been crafted as a kind of "Christian parable on the book of Esther," with its themes of an invitation to the banquet of a "king" (not simply "a certain man" as in Luke 14:16), messengers announcing the banquet's readiness, the refusal of invitees (cf. Vashti), and the punishment of a wicked guest. David Lees (172–80) has provided some necessary corrections of Goulder's work but nevertheless supports the basic notion of Esther's influence on the parable, and he has drawn attention to other material from the Matthean passion narrative that suggests Esther was an intended intertext (for the possible influence of Esther on the Markan and Johannine passion narratives, see Aus, 1–27, and Bowman, respectively). This includes some uniquely Matthean material characterizing Judas that invites comparisons with Haman, such as the clearer focus on his financial incentive for betrayal and the inclusion of his death (Lees, 208–28). A particularly significant datum is Matthew's distinctive phrasing in the cry "Let him be crucified! [*Staurōthētō*]" (Matt. 27:22–23), in contrast to *staurōson* (Mark 15:13–14; John 19:6) or *staurou* (Luke 23:21–23). The only LXX attestations of the verb occur in LXX Esther 7:9 and 8:12 (= Addition E 18; the Alpha Text utilizes the verb *kremannymi*), with the king declaring, "Let him be crucified! [*Staurōthētō*]" in LXX Esther 7:9. The verb's exclusive use in LXX Esther and the shared distinctive wording make an intended echo highly probable. This resonance was noted early in the Christian exegetical tradition (Thornton), which found the potential analogy between Christ's crucifixion and Haman's execution awkward. Lees (254) argues, however, that the Matthean use of Esther is subtly crafted in such a way as "to clarify that Jesus is not to be viewed as Haman, and yet, through their respective crucifixions salvation comes to the Jewish people."

Another passage displaying significant intertextual connections to Esther is Gal. 2:14, where Paul utilizes the verb *ioudaizō* to refer to "living like a Jew." The only other occurrence of this verb in biblical Greek is LXX Esther 8:17, which states that "many of the nations were circumcised and were 'Judaizing'" (*polloi tōn ethnōn perietemonto kai ioudaizon*, AT; the MT lacks the reference to circumcision). Paul strongly opposes the pressure being exerted on the Galatian believers to "Judaize" by submitting to circumcision (Gal. 2:3; 5:2–3, 6, 11; 6:12–13, 15) and observing other elements of the Mosaic law such as the religious calendar (cf. Gal. 4:10). Based on Paul's emphatic condemnation of gentile "Judaizing" in Galatians, Lees (376) argues that Esther's use of *ioudaizō* is likewise condemnatory, pointing to the following clause in Esther 8:17 ("for fear of the Jews had fallen on them," ESV) as hinting at a lack of heartfelt conversion. However, the element of fear is presented positively in 9:2 (see the discussion of holy war above), and there is no negative connotation to the gentile proselytes mentioned in 9:27. The condemnation of "Judaizing" in Galatians, in contrast to the positive view of it in Esther, should be attributed to Paul's redemptive-historical focus on Christ as the fulfillment of the law: Paul's argument in Gal. 2 does not hinge on the supposed genuineness of the gentiles' conversion. Paul addresses the gentiles not as "false converts" but as those who are in danger of "falling away from grace" (Gal. 5:4). Thus, his argument is based on the redemptive-historical reality that "the fullness of time had come" in the sending of the Christ (4:4–5 ESV), with the result that "there is neither Jew nor Gentile" for those baptized into him (3:28). Nevertheless, Galatians and LXX Esther uniquely share the same verb *ioudaizō* and explicitly deal with gentilic conversion and circumcision, making the probability of intended intertextual usage extremely high.

Relatedly, it can be argued that the book of Esther informs those NT passages that speak positively of the church as a "diaspora" (James 1:1; 1 Pet. 1:1; cf. John 11:52) and that thereby affirm the new redemptive-historical economy in which there is no longer a central geographical hub for the people of God (cf. Gal. 4:26; Heb. 12:22). Examples of gentilic conversion in the OT involve either a relocation to Israel (e.g., Ruth 1:16–17) or, in the case of Naaman, taking "two mule loads of earth" from Israel back to Aram (2 Kings 5:17 ESV). In contrast, Esther's generally positive stance toward gentiles and their conversion includes "no emphasis on the Land whatsoever" (Fuller, 131). The loosened nexus between the land and religious belief, identity, and practice suggests that "the book of Esther can be read as the story of the transformation of the *exile* into the *Diaspora*" (Levenson, 15). While the theological understanding of the Babylonian exile, the diaspora, and the restoration in Second Temple Judaism is a complex and hotly contested subject (Piotrowski), not all perspectives on these events were negative, and one can observe positive approaches that embraced a diasporic lifestyle (Scott, 181–82). Though the Jews are described as "exiled" in MT Esther 2:6 (*glh*) or even more negatively in the LXX as "captive" (*aichmalōtos/aichmalōteuō*), it is noteworthy that Haman describes them in Esther 3:8 as "scattered"/"dispersed" (LXX *diaspeirō*; cf. LXX Deut. 4:27; 28:64). Feldman ("Concept," 160) argues that Josephus, like the biblical account, puts this latter designation in the mouth of Haman precisely because this "scattering" is not to be viewed negatively, which is further confirmed by Josephus's own original embellishments not drawn from the MT or LXX. In terms of the canon of OT Scripture, it appears to be the book of Esther above all that prepares for more positive views on the diaspora in Second Temple Judaism, views that are seen in full flower in the NT's embrace of the church's "scattered" state and the opportunities that it presents for the gentile mission.

Summary

The use of Esther in the NT is clearly an underdeveloped field of study. This is not surprising, given the lack of manuscript attestation from Qumran, the scholarly debates concerning the book's canonical status in Second Temple Judaism, and the subtlety of its own usage of Scripture and of the proposed NT references to it. Nevertheless, when one is attuned to a broader range of intertextual usage beyond simple quotation, the influence of Esther on the NT consists of more than just "a few slight allusions" (so Firth, 34–35). The common assertion that the book has been ignored by the NT is therefore in need of serious revision. Future research will need to take the multiple textual witnesses of the book into account, including possible references to the Additions to Esther (see, *inter alia*, Jobes, *Alpha-Text*, 190; Levenson, 40) as well as the exegetical traditions of Second Temple Judaism that have shaped the book's reception (Lees, 165).

Bibliography. Anderson, B. W., "The Place of the Book of Esther in the Christian Bible," *JR* 30 (1950): 32–43; Aus, R. D., *Barabbas and Esther and Other Studies in the Judaic Illumination of Earliest Christianity* (Scholars Press, 1992); Aus, *Water into Wine and the Beheading of John the Baptist* (Scholars Press, 1988); Bauckham, R., *The Climax of Prophecy* (T&T Clark, 1992); Beckwith, R., *The Old Testament Canon of the New Testament Church and Its Background in Early Judaism* (Eerdmans, 1985); Bowman, J., *The Fourth Gospel and the Jews* (Pickwick, 1975); Cowen, D., *Theology in Exodus* (Westminster John Knox, 1994); De Troyer, K., "Once More, the So-Called Esther Fragments of Cave 4," *RevQ* 19 (2000): 401–22; Dowden, L., *Exalting Jesus in Esther* (Holman Reference, 2019); Ego, B., "Retelling the Story of Esther in Targum Sheni in Light of Septuagint Traditions," in *The Targums in the Light of Traditions of the Second Temple Period*, ed. T. Legrand and J. Joosten (Brill, 2014), 72–83; Feldman, L. H., "The Concept of Exile in Josephus," in *Exile: Old Testament, Jewish, and Christian Conceptions*, ed. J. M. Scott (Brill, 1997), 145–72; Feldman, *Studies in Josephus' Rewritten Bible* (Brill, 1998); Firth, D. G., *The Message of Esther* (InterVarsity, 2010); Fishbane, M., *Biblical Interpretation in Ancient Israel* (Clarendon, 1988); Frei, H., *The Eclipse of Biblical Narrative* (Yale University Press, 1974); Fuller, M. E., *The Restoration of Israel* (de Gruyter, 2006); Goulder, M., *The Evangelists' Calendar* (SPCK, 1978); Harvey, C. D., *Finding Morality in the Diaspora?* (de Gruyter, 2003); Grossman, J., *Esther*, Siphrut 6 (Eisenbrauns, 2011); Jobes, K. H., *The Alpha-Text of Esther* (Scholars Press, 1996); Jobes, *Esther*, NIVAC (Zondervan, 1999); Koller, A., *Esther in Ancient Jewish Thought* (Cambridge University Press, 2014); Lees, D. M., "Intertextual Ripples of the Book of Esther" (PhD diss., Free University of Amsterdam, 2018); Levenson, J. D., *Esther*, OTL (Westminster John Knox, 1997); Lewis, S., "Narrative Analogy and the Theological Message of Esther" (PhD diss., Westminster Theological Seminary, 2018); Link, P. J., Jr., and M. Y. Emerson, "Searching for the Second Adam," *SBJT* 21, no. 1 (2017): 123–44; Nolan, M., "Esther in the New Testament," *PIBA* 15 (1992): 60–65; Piotrowski, N. G., "The Concept of Exile in Late Second Temple Judaism," *CBR* 15 (2017): 214–47; Rogland, M., "'And So I Will Go unto the King,'" in *Faithful Ministry*, ed. M. Rogland (Wipf & Stock, 2019), 153–67; Rogland, "The Cult of Esther," *JSOT* 44 (2019): 99–114; Scott, J. M., "Exile and the Self-Understanding of Diaspora Jews in the Second Temple Period," in *Exile: Old Testament, Jewish, and Christian Conceptions*, ed. J. M. Scott (Brill, 1997), 173–218; Stuart, D. K., *Exodus*, NAC (B&H, 2006); Talmon, S., "Wisdom in the Book of Esther," *VT* 13 (1963): 419–55; Thornton, T. C. G., "The Crucifixion of Haman and the Scandal of the Cross," *JTS* 37 (1986): 419–26; Van 't Veer, M. B., *De Jodenhaat gedateerd naar Christus* (Knoop en Niemeijer, 1938); Wechsler, M. G., "The Purim-Passover Connection," *JBL* 117 (1998): 321–35; Wetter, A.-M., "Speaking from the Gaps," in *Reflections on the Silence of God*, ed. E. J. H. Becking (Brill, 2013), 153–67; Whedbee, J. W., *The Bible and the Comic Vision* (Fortress, 2002); White Crawford, S., "Esther, Book of," in *EDSS*, 1:269–70.

MAX F. ROGLAND

Ethics

For those considering how the NT uses the OT, one far-reaching question concerns whether the Bible incorporates a single, unified ethics or two. Does the Bible reveal and employ a single ethics that is good for everyone for all time, or does it reveal and employ two different ethics involving different standards for different people at different times—one in the OT and another in the NT, one for ancient Israel and another for the church, one relevant before the cross and another relevant after the cross? Or is there perhaps an old ethics that starts in the OT, continues for unbelievers today, and is passing away and a new inbreaking ethics inaugurated by Christ that supplants the old ethics as the kingdom of God takes over the world?

One interpretation sees the Bible presenting a single ethics, while the other sees it presenting a form of dualism according to which the NT introduces an ethics that is different than the one that applies in the OT. This difference has divided Christians throughout history. For example, although Martin Luther launched the Protestant Reformation, he did not break with monastic notions assuming a dualistic view of biblical ethics, and this dualistic interpretation continues in the ethical teaching of John Howard Yoder and Stanley Hauerwas. In contrast, John Calvin follows Augustine in holding to a single ethics throughout the Bible, and this unitary interpretation continues in the teaching of Carl F. H. Henry, Oliver O'Donovan, and most evangelicals today. This article affirms the unitary interpretation of biblical ethics and argues that ethics in the NT does not replace ethics in the OT but rather clarifies and extends the ongoing relevance of a single ethics expressing the unchanging character of God.

Continuity and Discontinuity

Whether there is one ethics or two in the Bible is complicated by how Scripture transitions from an old covenant to a new covenant, since this raises questions about the way moral law in the OT relates to gospel and grace in the NT. A shift between the two covenants generating some sort of discontinuity does occur. But does this shift necessitate replacing one ethics with another? And especially, does discontinuity between the covenants in any way affect how moral law in the OT relates to the ethical teaching of Jesus and the apostles? Dealing with these questions has led to seven views: hard continuity, moderately hard continuity, mild continuity, hard discontinuity, moderately hard discontinuity, mild discontinuity, and complete moral continuity mixed with complete ceremonial and civil discontinuity. Three favor forms of continuity, three favor forms of discontinuity, and one balances these approaches in a way that affirms a unitary view of biblical ethics.

Hard continuity holds that any law issued by God must endure no matter what it concerns. Proponents argue that Christ, in the NT, keeps every OT stipulation and never discontinues any, meaning that we must as well. No one holds this view anymore, but it was applied rigidly in the first century by some members of the church in Jerusalem (Acts 11:2–3; 15:1; Gal. 2:12). These early Christians disrupted church unity by denying full membership to gentile converts who did not follow all Jewish practices (Acts 15:1–2; Gal. 2:15–16). This view divided the faithful until it was rejected by the first church council (Acts 15).

Moderately hard continuity affirms moral and civil continuity between the OT and NT and holds that although ceremonial laws apply differently now, they also remain relevant. Proponents realize the NT institutes a new worship system and agree that rules governing the old worship system do not have the same role as before. But OT ceremonial rules have not ceased; rather, they either are less relevant now than before or apply differently now than before. Thus, dietary rules might be qualified by food science, rules on priestly garments modified by culture, and Sabbath requirements adapted to express the spirit rather than letter of the law.

Mild continuity goes beyond moderately hard continuity by asserting that any sort of OT law can cease. But this is a continuity view because any particular OT law must pertain unless the NT somewhere says that it no longer applies. So, if the NT says nothing about discontinuing a particular OT law, that law still applies.

Hard discontinuity holds that nothing stipulated in the OT remains relevant for NT believers. Proponents believe the OT has no ongoing ethical authority and only offers historic background because the work and teaching of Christ supersede everything God did before then. They conclude that moral laws in the OT, whether expressed in creation or promulgated at Sinai, are all discontinued and replaced by the grace of God, love of Christ, and inner guidance of the Holy Spirit. The grace of God in the NT introduces a new and different ethics for a new and different dispensation, or Christ in the NT does away with lower ethical standards temporarily permitted in the OT and replaces them with higher ethical standards that will last forever. Consequently, some things that used to be ethical in the OT have become unethical, while some things that used to be unethical have become ethical. For example, some Christian pacifists consider war ethical in the OT but not in the NT.

Moderately hard discontinuity assumes discontinuity affects all OT laws but also recognizes that many OT norms are repeated in the ethical teaching of Jesus and the apostles. Proponents see no principle governing which OT laws continue, and they think Jesus in the NT indeed introduced a new ethics referred to as the law of Christ or law of love. So, even though they admit repetition occurs, they still say the Bible has two different ethical systems. Repetition is explained as divine prerogative apart from any governing principle.

Mild discontinuity goes beyond moderately hard discontinuity by thinking a governing principle determines which OT norms continue in the NT. It is, in a way, similar to mild continuity but differs by reversing that view. Mild continuity says *everything* the OT requires must be relevant unless the NT says otherwise, and mild discontinuity says *nothing* the OT requires can be relevant unless the NT says otherwise. So, unless the NT repeats an OT requirement, mild discontinuity says it no longer applies. But if the NT reaffirms something the OT requires, then not only does that requirement continue, but anything else in the OT relating to it continues as well.

For mild continuity all that matters is whether an OT norm is or is not explicitly abrogated in the NT, and for mild discontinuity all that matters is whether an OT norm is or is not explicitly reaffirmed in the NT. But neither accounts for categorical differences in OT law or for the significance of divine immutability. Dealing with these concerns leads to the next and last view on how ethics in the OT relates to ethics in the NT.

Early on, the church declared Marcion (AD 85–160) heretical for teaching Christ had proclaimed a love ethic that makes OT ethics terribly bad and wrong. Since then most Christians have related the Testaments according to a principle of *complete moral continuity mixed with complete ceremonial and civil discontinuity*. This last view discerns different categories of law in the OT, and although labels for these categories have not always been used, most Christians throughout history have accepted them by treating moral laws in the OT, especially the Ten Commandments, as ongoing while thinking other OT laws no longer apply.

The problem with treating all OT laws from a discontinuity stance is that doing so makes biblical ethics clash with divine immutability. God acts and reacts, is pleased and grieved, and rewards and punishes. But God's character never changes (Num. 23:19; Ps. 102:27; Mal. 3:6; Heb. 1:12; James 1:17). He is "the same yesterday, today, and forever" (Heb. 13:8). OT moral laws reveal what conforming to God's unchangeable character requires, so when Peter quotes the OT and commands his audience to be holy as God is holy (1 Pet. 1:15–16; Lev. 11:44–45; 19:2; 20:7), he must be demonstrating that OT moral laws remain relevant.

Problems also arise from treating all OT laws from a continuity stance, first, because the NT clearly discontinues some OT requirements and, second, because continuity positions do not deal with the differing functions and purposes of biblical laws. Continuity views all assume *any* OT law in *any* category must still apply unless it is explicitly discontinued. But since the NT never mentions discontinuing the OT death penalty for rebellious children (Deut. 21:18–21), this would mean we should still be executing such children. No one holding any continuity view defends doing so, but the position follows from what is assumed.

The main problem with the first six views comes from thinking that one thing settles the relevance of every OT law, moral or otherwise, the same way and that every OT law must therefore be either continuous or discontinuous unless an exception modifies how that one thing applies. The solution is to recognize different categories of law in the OT and to interpret these different categories separately. Doing so treats laws in the same category the same and laws in other categories differently. Complete moral continuity mixed with complete ceremonial and civil discontinuity treats God's moral law in the OT as universal, timeless, and unchanging and thus continued in the NT, and it treats other categories of law in the OT as localized, time-bound, and subject to change and thus discontinued in the NT.

But this last view must still deal with how the NT makes contrasting claims about the way Christians relate to OT laws. On the one hand, Paul says, "Don't let anyone judge you in regard to food and drink or in the matter of a festival or a new moon or a Sabbath day" (Col. 2:16), and in Hebrews we are told OT laws applied only for a time (Heb. 9:9–10). On the other hand, Jesus declares, "Until heaven and earth pass away, not the smallest letter or one stroke of a letter will pass from the law" (Matt. 5:18), and Paul says OT laws still are "holy and just and good" (Rom. 7:12), were issued "for us" (1 Cor. 9:10), remain profitable for "training in righteousness" (2 Tim. 3:16), and are not rendered irrelevant by faith in Christ (Rom. 3:31).

How should we interpret these claims? Either we dismiss ethics in the NT as contradictory, or we accept it as noncontradictory based on distinguishing different categories of OT law. If ethics in the NT really is noncontradictory, then these claims must concern different things and not the same thing. Moral laws in the OT must still apply in the NT, while other OT stipulations do not. One principle must govern laws classified as moral and another govern laws classified otherwise. Having explained and affirmed complete moral continuity mixed with complete ceremonial and civil discontinuity, we turn now to examine three areas where the NT relates to OT ethics in ways often contested by those denying a unified view of biblical ethics.

The OT Ethic of War Continues in the New

The area most debated when considering whether OT ethics continues in the NT concerns going to war. God in the OT sanctions war on justified grounds, but does Jesus change that when rebuking Peter's use of the sword in Gethsemane (Matt. 26:52; John 18:11)? The NT authorizes rulers to exercise deadly force in the course of their duties (Rom. 13:4), but is that just for unbelievers, because Christians are prevented now from holding positions that require making life-or-death decisions? Amish, Mennonite, and Swiss Brethren Christians believe so and have held to their convictions, sometimes at great cost. Jesus did not resist going to the cross, but neither was he a pacifist. Jesus in the NT never discontinued any OT moral norm, including the authorization of going to war.

There are two ethics of war in the OT—a crusade ethic for wars led by God for spiritual reasons, which involves sparing no one (Deut. 20:16–17), and a just-war ethic for wars led by rulers responsible for ensuring justice and national security (Deut. 20:1–15). Both ethics are affirmed again in the NT. The just-war ethic is reaffirmed in the NT for rulers needing to fight justified battles (Luke 14:31), punish wrong behavior (Rom. 13:4; 1 Pet. 2:14), and preserve civil tranquility (1 Tim. 2:2), and the crusade ethic will apply again at the end of human history in the last battles led by Jesus against armies led by the devil (Rev. 19:17–21; 20:7–9).

But this complication aside, most debate dealing with this area focuses on whether Jesus replaces the OT just-war ethic with a new pacifist ethic. The NT shows that Jesus was no warmonger but also that he never started a new war ethic. Jesus is the Prince of Peace (Isa. 9:6; cf. Luke 1:79). But the peace Jesus offers is the reconciling of sinners to God, not the causing of wars to cease in a world filled with sinners at odds with God prior to the millennial kingdom or at the very end of history (Isa. 2:4; Mic. 4:3). Pacifists read civil nonviolence into nearly every place "peace" is mentioned in the NT. But the peace of reconciling sinners to God and the peace of civil nonviolence are not the same thing, and Jesus even warns not to expect one to cause the other under present circumstances (Matt. 24:9; John 16:33).

In the only place Jesus addresses "peace" in the sense of civil nonviolence, he denies teaching pacifism. Rather, Jesus says, "Don't assume that I came to bring peace [nonviolence] on the earth. I did not come to bring peace [nonviolence], but a sword" (Matt. 10:34). Since he acknowledges the reality that kings calculate their odds of winning before launching into battle (Luke 14:31–32), it is apparent that Jesus does not condemn the notion that good kings must sometimes go to war. And of course, Jesus does not practice nonviolence when driving money changers from the temple with a whip (John 2:15).

When pacifists appeal to how Jesus rebukes Peter's use of the sword and goes to the cross without resisting, they misread these events in ways contrary to instructions Jesus gives earlier that same evening. During the Last Supper Jesus tells his disciples to acquire and carry swords because they will need them after he leaves (Luke 22:36). So, when Jesus rebukes Peter a few hours later, he is not doing away with OT ethics relating to war but rather is preventing Peter from hindering his mission. Jesus goes to the cross not to launch a pacifist ethic but to be "the Lamb of God who takes away the sin of the world" (John 1:29).

We must remember too that Jesus is one with the Father (John 10:30; 14:9) and thus identified with God in the OT (Col. 1:15–20). Jesus is eternal and predates the incarnation. He was before Abraham (John 8:58) and as "commander of the LORD's army" (Josh. 5:14) was the one who led Israel in defeating Jericho. Making this connection is important because ethics in the Bible reveals and expresses the unchanging character of God (Ps. 102:27; Mal. 3:6; James 1:17). The character of God is constant throughout Scripture, so biblical ethics must be as well. Thus, because God in the OT held war is sometimes ethically justified, this means Jesus does as well—not only because he leads armies and goes to war in the OT prior to the incarnation but also, and mainly, because Jesus is the eternal and always-present God who never changes. The OT war ethic continues in the NT because "Jesus Christ is the same yesterday and today and forever" (Heb. 13:8).

Moral Aspects of OT Sabbath Keeping Continue in the NT

Another area debated when considering the NT use of OT ethics concerns Sabbath keeping. OT Sabbath requirements have ceremonial, civil, and moral aspects, and Jesus disputes these with religious teachers of his day more than any other area of OT law. Some think Jesus does away with the fourth commandment, and others think he changes the ethical portion of the fourth commandment along with other aspects. But the NT shows that Jesus affirms the ongoing ethical relevance of the fourth commandment even while discontinuing its ceremonial and civil aspects. The Sabbath ethic portrayed in the NT remains the same as in the OT even though its expression differs.

The ethical element in the fourth commandment obligates us to honor God's sovereignty over work, rest, and the way we use time. It holds us accountable to God for how spiritual life intersects with and affects material life, and this intersection is as important now as ever. In the NT, Jesus, Paul, and the author of Hebrews (Matt. 12:11–12; Rom. 14:5–12; Heb. 10:25) all stress how the Sabbath ethic is now, and always has been, more about respecting God's sovereignty over work, rest, and how we use time than about how this respect is expressed. Of course, the NT extensively modifies how respect for God's sovereignty in this area gets expressed. The day for corporate worship shifts from Saturday to Sunday (Acts 20:7; 1 Cor. 16:2), Sabbath keeping on other days is permitted, and honoring the Sabbath all the time is allowed as well (Rom. 14:5). But Christians also are cautioned not to let this increased freedom of expression hinder gathering for corporate worship (Heb. 10:25). So, although ways of expressing the Sabbath ethic are loosened in the NT, the ethic itself retains its full force.

Jesus does not alter the Sabbath ethic, but he does address several misinterpretations. Jesus teaches that interpreting the Sabbath ethic properly depends on understanding four things: (1) that God desires a heart of mercy over ritual practices (Matt. 12:7); (2) that God's authority must not be confused with human authorities (Matt. 12:8); (3) that the Sabbath does not interfere with religious duties, serving people in need, or handling emergencies (Matt. 12:11–12; Luke 13:15–16); and (4) that God gave it to enhance and not to diminish human welfare (Mark 2:27). That Jesus gives so much attention to proper interpretation clearly shows he does not set aside the Sabbath ethic but rather affirms its ongoing relevance.

The NT reveals that Jesus never sins (2 Cor. 5:21; Heb. 4:15; 1 Pet. 2:22; 1 John 3:5), is spotless (1 Pet. 1:19), and is blameless (Heb. 9:14), and this means he lives up to everything God's moral law requires. So, although Jesus discontinues OT ceremonial stipulations (cf. Mark 7:19), he still perfectly obeys what the Sabbath ethic requires (Matt. 5:17). Thus, Jesus distinguishes the ethical component of the fourth commandment from its other aspects. The Holy Spirit, too, makes a similar distinction when discontinuing OT dietary laws in a vision to Peter (Acts 10:15; 11:9). Paul does the same in relation to ceremonial and civil aspects of the Sabbath law (Rom. 14:5–6). And the first church council announces that church membership does not require keeping OT ceremonial requirements (Acts 15:28–29). Ceremonial and civil aspects of the OT Sabbath law do fall away in the NT. But the ethic sustaining the fourth commandment remains in force (Rom. 14:6–7; Heb. 10:25), and this is most evident where Hebrews says "a Sabbath rest remains for God's people" (Heb. 4:9) and after that says that practicing this Sabbath rest still keeps Christians from "disobedience" (Heb. 4:11).

The OT Moral Law Continues in the NT

A third area debated when discussing NT use of OT ethics concerns the way OT moral law is affected by NT references to the passing of Mosaic stipulations. What does Paul mean by saying something "chiseled in letters on stones" was "set aside" (2 Cor. 3:7, 11)? Is he saying OT moral laws cease in the NT? If not, what else could he mean? Interpreting this correctly requires realizing Paul in 2 Cor. 3 is contrasting two ministries, one of condemnation and one of justification. He is addressing how two ministries have different tasks, not contrasting two ways of attempting the same task.

Paul does address OT moral law when referring to "letters on stones." But he is not saying that moral law ceases in the NT or that the NT introduces a different ethics replacing OT moral law. Rather, Paul is saying OT moral law drives people to the gospel and that function ceases after people accept the gospel. God's moral law does not save and never did (Gal. 2:16; 3:11). It merely reveals the ethical standards God requires (Rom. 7:7). Saving sinners requires something else, not a new ethic but something able to save sinners from what the same ongoing ethic says we deserve. In other words, it requires the gospel. The moral law says we deserve death; the gospel says Christ died in our place. The gospel does not do away with moral law or replace one ethics with another. Rather, it says Christ solved the problem of condemnation for failing standards we cannot meet on our own (Rom. 8:1). That is why Paul says, "Do we then nullify the law through faith? Absolutely not! On the contrary, we uphold the law" (Rom. 3:31).

What Paul says has been "set aside" by Christ (2 Cor. 3:11) is not the ongoing relevance of God's moral law but something God's moral law stops doing after a person comes to faith—namely, driving that person toward accepting the gospel. He is distinguishing not between ethics in the NT and ethics in the OT but rather between the differing effects of the same ongoing ethics on unbelievers and believers.

When Paul elsewhere contrasts "a righteousness of my own from the law" with "the righteousness from God based on faith" (Phil. 3:9), he is contrasting not different ethical systems but different ways people try to satisfy what an ongoing ethics requires: some attempt it on their own without Christ, and others trust Christ as doing it for them. The righteous perfection God demands is measured the same way throughout Scripture. Moral law shows us that "all have sinned and fall short of the glory of God" (Rom. 3:23) and that escaping deserved punishment requires a "gift of God" (Rom. 6:23). God's moral law must be satisfied one way or another. If we rely on ourselves, we will die, but if we trust Christ instead, we will live (Rom. 6:23). And no matter what course we take, God's moral law is unchanged throughout Scripture.

The enduring nature of God's moral law also is affirmed where Paul mentions "the glory of God" in Rom. 3:23. This expression indicates a fixed ethical standard also known as the "holiness of God" or "righteousness of God." It is an enduringly normative measure by which all is judged and to which all must conform the same way in both the OT and NT (Lev. 11:44–45; 19:2; 20:7; 1 Pet. 1:15–16). Throughout the Bible, moral law is nothing other than God revealing what conforming to his character requires. There is no difference between God's moral law, God's holiness, and God's righteousness, and therefore, God's moral law must be as constant, consistent, enduring, and relevant as God himself (Num. 23:19; Ps. 102:27; Mal. 3:6; Heb. 1:12; James 1:17).

Finally, when Jesus says nothing in the law will pass away "until heaven and earth pass away" (Matt. 5:18), he means everything God's moral law requires must and will continue as long as creation continues. So, when Paul says Christ "made of no effect the law consisting of commands and expressed in regulations" (Eph. 2:15), he must be saying Christ has done away with ceremonial laws excluding non-Jews from Jewish worship practices and cannot be saying God's moral law no longer applies. Jesus affirms continuity of a single, unitary ethics so fixed and unchanging it endures as long as heaven and earth endure, and Paul says only that what Christ did on the cross does away with OT ceremonial regulations.

Summary

There are three major problems with thinking ethics in the OT is different from ethics in the NT: doing so misconceives the nature of moral law, conflicts with the affirming of divine immutability, and vitiates the gospel. Denying the Bible teaches a single, unitary ethics overlooks how moral law comes from God, reveals the character of God, and holds us accountable to God.

Because the character of God never changes and ethics in the Bible expresses what conforming to his character requires, supposing biblical ethics changes between the OT and NT is not compatible with the doctrine of divine immutability. Finally, denying that the Bible teaches a single, unitary ethics also vitiates the gospel because, if OT moral law does not apply in the NT, there is no sin problem to solve (Rom. 4:15). A single, unitary ethics throughout Scripture is what necessitates the death of Christ and makes the gospel good news.

Those thinking ethics in the NT differs from ethics in the OT must either deny that biblical ethics expresses the character of God or say that the character of God changes between the OT and NT. If biblical ethics expresses the character of God and the character of God never changes, then ethics in the NT must be the same as in the OT. There must be a single unitary ethic throughout.

Some things change between the OT and NT, and some do not. A new covenant replaces an old covenant (Jer. 31:31; Matt. 26:28; Mark 14:24; Luke 22:20; 1 Cor. 11:25). Ceremonial practices change from one worship system to another (Mark 7:19; Acts 10:15). Believers are freed from the curse of the law because the punishment we deserve for falling short is paid by Christ (Gal. 3:13; Rom. 6:23). Christians no longer fear the coming wrath of God (John 3:36; 1 Thess. 1:10). There is no final death for those who have "passed from death to life" (John 5:24 ESV; cf. 1 John 3:14; 1 Cor. 15:56). And the Holy Spirit now enables believers to live increasingly worthy lives (John 14:26; Gal. 5:16–18, 25; Col. 1:10–12). But what holiness means and requires is the same yesterday, today, and forever. Sin is measured the same way yesterday, today, and forever. And the unearned righteousness of Christ credited to us by the gospel is measured the same way yesterday, today, and forever. The righteousness of God has not changed, because the character of God has not changed. Obligation to conform to the character of God has not changed and still governs all we say, do, and desire. We must still obey God, and we love him and should want nothing else. Conditions change and covenants change. But biblical ethics transcends time and place because it is and always has been concerned with nothing other than conforming humanity to God, who never changes.

See also Covenant; Holy Spirit, Eschatological Role of; Law

Bibliography. Carson, D. A., "The Tripartite Division of the Law," in *From Creation to New Creation*, ed. D. M. Gurtner and B. L. Gladd (Hendrickson, 2013), 223–36; Feinberg, J. S., ed., *Continuity and Discontinuity* (Crossway, 1988); Fuller, D. P., *Gospel and Law* (Eerdmans, 1980); Kaiser, W. C., Jr., "New Approaches to Old Testament Ethics," *JETS* 35 (1992): 289–97; O'Donovan, O., "Towards an Interpretation of Biblical Ethics," *TynBul* 27 (1976): 54–78; Poythress, V. S., *The Shadow of Christ in the Law of Moses* (P&R, 1991); Ross, P. S., *From the Finger of God* (Christian Focus, 2010); Sprinkle, J. M., *Biblical Law and Its Relevance* (University Press of America, 2005); Westerholm, S., *Israel's Law and the Ways of the Lord* (InterVarsity, 1995); Wright, C. J. H., *An Eye for an Eye* (InterVarsity, 1983).

DANIEL R. HEIMBACH

Evil Spirits

See Satan

Exegesis, Contemporary

See History of Interpretation: 1800 to Present

Exegesis, Early Church

See History of Interpretation: Early Church

Exile and Restoration

The theme of exile refers to the expulsion from or loss of one's home and an accompanying sense of alienation, weakness, insecurity, and vulnerability. While the term most commonly refers to the Babylonian exile of the sixth century BC, the theme of exile and restoration is central to the whole of the biblical narrative.

Precursors to Israel's Exile and Restoration

Adam and Eve: Expulsion from paradise. The expulsion of Adam and Eve from the garden sets the stage for all subsequent exiles. In the beginning of the biblical story, God creates an ideal world and places the first humans in a place of safety and security, with all the resources necessary for them to flourish. Their role is to provide guardianship over God's creation. The only condition for blessing is obedience. Yet Adam and Eve succumb to temptation and disobey God. The result is expulsion (exile) from Eden (Gen. 3:24) and the entrance of sin and death into the world (Rom. 5:12). The rest of the biblical narrative may be viewed as God's purpose and plan to bring humanity out of exile to a restored relationship with their God.

The Abrahamic covenant: The promise of a homeland. The restoration plan is initiated through God's covenant with Abraham. God calls Abraham to leave the security and comfort of his homeland and venture to an unknown place. In turn God promises to give Abraham a great name, a new homeland and a great nation, and blessings for himself and for all nations (Gen. 12; 15; 17). Though Abraham resides in Canaan only "as a foreigner" (i.e., in exile; cf. Heb. 11:9), God promises him "the whole land of Canaan . . . as an everlasting possession to you and your descendants after you; and I will be their God" (Gen. 17:8). Here the relationship with God ("I will be their God") is linked to a place of security in the land.

The exodus: Paradigm for restoration after exile. Israel's sojourn in Egypt begins as an act of deliverance from famine, when God takes the evil intended by Joseph's brothers and turns it into good—"the saving of many lives" (Gen. 50:20). Yet redemption turns to exile when a new king arises in Egypt who does not know Joseph and enslaves the Israelites (Exod. 1:8). The exodus from Egypt thus represents not only the greatest act of redemption in the OT (see the "Exodus, Book of" article elsewhere in this volume) but also the means of restoration from exile to the land God promised to Abraham. In the account of the burning bush, God tells Moses, "I have indeed seen the misery of my people in Egypt. . . . So I have come down to rescue them from the hand of the Egyptians and to *bring them up out of that land into a good and spacious land, a land flowing with milk and honey*" (Exod. 3:7–8). The exodus marks a return from exile to the homeland God has promised Abraham and the patriarchs.

The OT repeatedly recalls the exodus to remind Israel of their national identity as the people of God. The common refrain is "I am the LORD, who brought you up out of Egypt to be your God" (Lev. 11:45; cf. Exod. 13:3, 9, 14, 16; 32:11; Deut. 6:21; 9:26; 26:8; Jer. 32:21; Dan. 9:15; Hosea 11:1; etc.). In response, God calls Israel to "be holy, because I am holy" (Lev. 11:45)—a people set apart to God.

Israel's years of exile as slaves in Egypt should result in compassion for those who are exiles and outsiders. A consistent refrain throughout the Hebrew Scriptures is to love and treat with justice the weak and vulnerable within Israel. Deuteronomy 24:17 cautions, "Do not deprive the foreigner or the fatherless of justice, or take the cloak of the widow as a pledge." The reason follows: "Remember that you were slaves in Egypt and the LORD your God redeemed you from there" (Deut. 24:18).

The Mosaic covenant: With disobedience comes exile. Israel's reestablishment in the land is contingent upon obedience, and from this point on in the biblical narrative, covenant faithfulness, exile, and restoration are inextricably linked together. In the covenant God establishes with Israel at Mount Sinai, there are promises of blessings, peace, and prosperity if Israel will keep God's commands:

> If you follow my decrees and are careful to obey my commands, I will send you rain in its season, and the ground will yield its crops. . . . I will grant peace in the land. . . . I will look on you with favor and make you fruitful and increase your numbers, and I will keep my covenant with you. . . . I will walk among you and be your God, and you will be my people. I am the LORD your God, who brought you out of Egypt. (Lev. 26:3–13; cf. Deut. 28:1–14)

But if Israel breaks God's commands and worships idols, the land will be devastated, and the people will be scattered among the nations:

> But if you will not listen to me and carry out all these commands . . . and so violate my covenant, then I will do this to you: I will bring on you sudden terror, wasting diseases and fever that will destroy your sight and sap your strength. You will plant seed in vain, because your enemies will eat it. I will set my face against you so that you will be defeated by your enemies. . . . I will scatter you among the nations. . . . Your land will be laid waste, and your cities will lie in ruins. (Lev. 26:14–33; cf. Deut. 28:15–68)

This threat of destruction and exile is consistently followed by promises of restoration:

> But if they will confess their sins . . . I will remember my covenant with Jacob and my covenant with Isaac and my covenant with Abraham, and I will remember the land. For the land will be deserted by them and will enjoy its sabbaths while it lies desolate without them. . . . But for their sake I will remember the covenant with their ancestors whom I brought out of Egypt in the sight of the nations to be their God. I am the LORD. (Lev. 26:40–45; cf. Deut. 30)

Incomplete conquest and the period of Judges: Spiritual exile within the land. The conquest of Canaan, though a partial fulfillment of the Abrahamic covenant, lies incomplete at the beginning of Judges. We see here that the promise of restoration after exile is more than merely occupying the land. There is a spiritual exile when Israel's disobedience results in alienation from God. When Joshua gives his farewell address, he warns that disobedience will mean that "the LORD's anger will burn against you, and you will quickly perish from the good land he has given you" (Josh. 23:16). Spiritual exile can also mean foreign oppression. Throughout the period of the judges, Israel remains in the land but is repeatedly oppressed by the nations around them. The pattern of sin and oppression followed by repentance and redemption in Judges is analogous to exile and restoration.

The Assyrian and Babylonian Exiles

The failure of God's people and their kings to honor God's covenant eventually results in exile, as the pentateuchal commands have warned. The Assyrian Empire conquers the Northern Kingdom of Israel in 722 BC, taking many of the people into exile and repopulating the land with foreigners (whose intermarriage with the Israelites, according to 2 Kings 17:24–41, results in the Samaritan race). The Southern Kingdom of Judah remains a nation for 136 years but eventually succumbs to Nebuchadnezzar, king of the Neo-Babylonian Empire. In 605 BC, Nebuchadnezzar defeats Egypt and brings Judah into his sphere of influence. A series of deportations follows (597, 586, 581). In 587–586, Nebuchadnezzar besieges Jerusalem, eventually destroying the city and its temple. The Babylonians have a policy of assimilating conquered people into the Babylonian way of life by bringing the best and the brightest to be indoctrinated in Babylon, for which reason Daniel and his friends are taken at this time (Dan. 1:3–7).

Restoration from Exile Predicted and Fulfilled

Jeremiah predicted that the exile would last seventy years (Jer. 25:12; 29:10; cf. 2 Chron. 36:21), a period that may be calculated approximately from the destruction of the temple in 586 BC to its reconstruction and rededication in 516 BC. God raises up the Persian king Cyrus, who conquers the Babylonian Empire in 539 BC and issues decrees allowing the Jews to return to their homeland and rebuild Jerusalem and the temple (Ezra 1:1–4; 6:3–5). A first group returns under the leadership of Zerubbabel, who becomes governor of Judea and lays the foundations for a new temple. A second group comes back under the leadership of Ezra in 457 BC. A third group returns with Nehemiah in 444 BC to rebuild the walls of Jerusalem. The prophets Haggai and Zechariah urge God's people to finish building the temple.

The return from exile as a new exodus. Because of the significance of the exodus in Israel's history, it is not surprising that the prophets draw on exodus imagery to describe the regathering of Israel after exile. In Hosea 2:14–15, Israel's restoration (symbolized by the restoration of Hosea's wife, Gomer) is described as Yahweh bringing her into the wilderness where he will speak tenderly to her: "There she will respond as in the days of her youth, as in the day she came up out of Egypt."

A new and greater exodus is also described in Jer. 23: "'So then, the days are coming,' declares the LORD, 'when people will no longer say, "As surely as the LORD lives, who brought the Israelites up out of Egypt," but they will say, "As surely as the LORD lives, who brought the descendants of Israel up out of the land of the north and out of all the countries where he had banished them." Then they will live in their own land'" (Jer. 23:7–8; cf. 16:14–15).

Ezekiel 36–37 also provides the promise of restoration after exile. Yahweh will once again gather his people to their promised land (36:24, 28, 33–36; 37:12, 14). He will give them a new heart and a new spirit (36:26; 37:1–14). Israel and Judah will be reunited as one nation (37:15–23), and David will be their king forever (37:24–25). The Lord will once again dwell in their presence and will make an everlasting covenant of peace with them (37:26–27).

The greatest prophet of restoration is Isaiah. In Isa. 11, written under the threat of Assyrian exile, the Lord promises one day to gather "a second time" the surviving remnant of his people. He will "raise a banner for the nations" and bring back "the exiles of Israel." He will gather "the scattered people of Judah" from the far reaches of the world (vv. 11–12). "There will be a highway for the remnant of his people . . . from Assyria, as there was when Israel came up from Egypt" (v. 16). The reference to a *second* return in v. 11 (the first being the first exodus), together with the exodus imagery in vv. 15–16, clearly presents the eschatological regathering of exiled Israel as a new exodus. Yet the restoration goes beyond the first exodus in scope and substance. "The wolf will live with the lamb, the leopard will lie down with the goat, the calf and the lion and the yearling together; and a little child will lead them. . . . They will neither harm nor destroy on all my holy mountain, for the earth will be filled with the knowledge of the LORD as the waters cover the sea" (11:6–9). Here we have images not just of a regathered and restored nation but of an eschatological renewal of creation and a return to Eden-like conditions.

The Book of Consolation (Isa. 40–55). The most pervasive restoration / new-exodus imagery in the Prophets appears in Isa. 40–55, appropriately called the Book of Consolation, since from its opening words the prophet announces a message of comfort and salvation for the exiles in Babylon (40:1). The new-exodus announcement forms an *inclusio*, beginning and ending the Book of Consolation (40:3–5; 55:12–13). The nation has received just punishment for their sins (40:2). Yahweh is about to come to their aid, triumphantly revealing himself so that all people will see his glory (40:3–5). At various points the first exodus provides the model. As Yahweh brought Israel out of Egypt, so he will lead them forth again (Isa. 42:16; 48:20; 49:9–10; 52:12; 55:12). In the first exodus Yahweh delivered his people as a mighty warrior (51:9; cf. Exod. 15:3), defeating horse and chariot at the Red Sea (Isa. 43:16–17; cf. Exod. 14:25, 28; 15:10, 21). So again with his mighty arm (40:10; 51:9–10; 52:10) he will "march out like a champion" (42:13) to defeat Israel's oppressors (cf. 49:24–26; 51:22–23). As he dried up the sea and led his people through (51:10), so again he will lead them through waters and fire (43:1–2, 16). The pillar of cloud and fire that went before the people (Exod. 13:21–22) and moved behind to protect them from the Egyptians (Exod. 14:19–20) is recalled as Yahweh becomes both front and rear guard (Isa. 52:12). He not only brings them out but also sustains them in the wilderness. As he caused water to flow from the rock (48:21; cf. Exod. 17:2–7; Num. 20:8) and provided food for his people, so he will now provide streams in the desert (41:17–20; 43:19–21; 49:10), feeding and shepherding his people on the way (40:11; 49:9).

The Isaianic new exodus is not just a repetition of the first. It surpasses it in many respects. Whereas the Israelites had to celebrate the Passover in haste in the first exodus (Deut. 16:3; cf. Exod. 12:11), the exiles "will not leave in haste" (Isa. 52:12). They "will go out in joy and be led forth in peace" (Isa. 55:12), without the dangers and terrors that accompanied the wilderness generation (Anderson, "Exodus Typology," 191). Repeatedly the prophet points out that this is something new and creative that Yahweh is doing: "Forget the former things; do not dwell on the past. See, I am doing a new thing!" (Isa. 43:18–19; cf. 42:9; 48:3, 6–7).

Israel's salvation will be a glorious renewal. There will be a rebuilding of the country and its cities and a new apportionment of the land (49:8, 17–21; 54:11–14). Israel's enemies will be defeated (41:11–12; 49:26; 54:15–17). The mighty nations of the world will come and offer homage (45:14; 49:7, 22–23). Jerusalem and the temple will be restored and made more glorious than ever (44:28; 49:16–17; 54:11–12).

There are again clear eschatological implications in the promises of Eden-like restoration (51:3); transformation of the wilderness into rivers, pastures, and gardens (41:18–19; 43:19; 49:9); and the eternal duration of Yahweh's salvation (45:17; 54:10, 15–17).

Though the new exodus is described as the triumphant return of Yahweh himself and a revelation of his glory (40:3–5, 10–11), his human instrument is the pagan king Cyrus, astonishingly called Yahweh's "anointed" and "shepherd" (44:28; 45:1; cf. 41:1–5, 21–29; 45:9–13; 46:9–11; 48:12–16).

Exile and Restoration in Second Temple Judaism

While the return of the Jews from exile confirms God's promises and provides assurance that Israel remains God's people, the relatively small number of Jews who return and the difficulties they encounter seem hardly to live up to the descriptions of a glorious return of Yahweh to bring his people back and of the Eden-like restoration of creation that would follow (Isa. 11:6–9; 41:18–19; 43:19; 49:9; 51:3).

Various scholars have proposed that many Jews of the first century AD considered Israel to be in exile still. Iain Duguid (477) points out that the return of the Jews fell far short of the great expectations raised by the visions of Jeremiah and Ezekiel: "Israel's land was still governed by foreigners, not by a descendant of the line of David; many (the diaspora) were still scattered through other lands; and those who returned persisted in all kinds of sin. . . . Because of the people's hardness of heart, the exile was in some respects still a reality." The shekinah glory, which filled the temple at Solomon's dedication of the temple and which departed from the temple in Ezekiel's vision, is nowhere said to return to Jerusalem in Second Temple literature. N. T. Wright (*New Testament*, 268–69) similarly asserts, "Most Jews of this period, it seems, would have answered the question 'where are we?' in language which, reduced to its simplest form, meant: we are still in exile. . . . Although she had come back from Babylon, the glorious message of the prophets remained unfulfilled. Israel still remained in thrall to foreigners; worse, Israel's god had not returned to Zion" (cf. Wright, *Paul*, 139–63).

This theme of Israel still being in exile appears in a wide range of literature. Tobit (third century BC) asserts that "they all will return from their exile and will rebuild Jerusalem in splendor; and in it the temple of God will be rebuilt, just as the prophets of Israel have said concerning it. Then the nations in the whole world will all be converted and worship God in truth. They will all abandon their idols, which deceitfully have led them into their error; and in righteousness they will praise the eternal God" (Tob. 14:5–7). From Tobit's perspective the promised restoration is still future and will result in global transformation for both Israel and the nations. The implication, of course, is that the exile has not yet ended for Israel, despite the meager return of some Jews from Babylon.

The Qumran sectarians similarly viewed Israel as a nation in exile. In their view, however, their own community represented the righteous remnant of Israel who were finding God's "way" in the wilderness. The Damascus Document reads, "For when they were unfaithful in forsaking him, he hid his face from Israel and from his sanctuary and delivered them up to the sword. However, when he remembered the covenant of the very first, he saved a remnant for Israel and did not deliver them up to be destruction" (CD 1.3–11, trans. García Martínez).

Even during Maccabean times, when the Hasmonean dynasty established a kingdom that rivaled in scope and influence the united kingdom of David and Solomon, there was a sense that the exile would not end until all of Israel returned to the land. Jonathan Maccabeus prays in 2 Maccabees, "Gather together our scattered people, set free those who are slaves among the Gentiles, . . . and let the Gentiles know that you are our God. Punish those who oppress and are insolent with pride. Plant your people in your holy place, as Moses promised" (1:27–29 NRSV).

This Israel-still-in-exile motif has important implications as we turn to the NT's perspective on exile and restoration.

Exile and Restoration in the NT

The Gospels and Acts. Matthew's genealogy, which contains three (Matt. 1:11, 12, 17) of the four explicit references to the exile in the NT (cf. Acts 7:43), confirms the significance of this event in Israel's religious life. The genealogy is structured around three sections of fourteen generations, from Abraham to David, from David to the Babylonian exile, and from the exile to Christ. Considering the profound importance of the Abrahamic and Davidic covenants for NT theology, it is remarkable that the exile is placed beside them as seminal events in Israel's history.

Though the exile is only occasionally explicitly referred to in the NT, the theme of restoration after exile plays a significant role in NT theology, especially when new-exodus imagery is factored in.

1. John the Baptist is described in all four Gospels with language from Isa. 40:3 as the "voice" of one crying out in the wilderness to prepare the way

for the Lord (Matt. 3:3; Mark 1:3; Luke 3:4; John 1:23). As noted above, in Isaiah this passage is the joyful announcement that God will triumphantly lead his people out of their Babylonian exile to the promised land. The evangelists clearly view the coming of Jesus the Messiah as God's restoration of his people from exile.

2. Rikk Watts sees Mark's attribution of the mixed quote from Mal. 3:1 and Isa. 40:3 in Mark 1:2–3 to "Isaiah the prophet" as intentionally placing the whole of the Markan narrative under the banner of the Isaianic new exodus. David Pao (5) similarly sees "the scriptural story that provides the hermeneutical framework of Acts" as "none other than the foundation story of Exodus as developed and transformed through the Isaianic corpus."
3. The portrayal in the Synoptics of Jesus as the new Israel and as a new Moses has implications for this theme of exile. Jesus's family seeks refuge as exiles in Egypt until God calls his "son" out of Egypt (Matt. 2:15) just as he did for Israel in the exodus (Hosea 11:1). The mourning for the innocents slaughtered in Bethlehem parallels the weeping that accompanied the Babylonian exile (Matt. 2:17–18, citing Jer. 31:15). Jesus's temptation in the wilderness is analogous to Israel's wilderness wanderings, as Jesus resists the same temptations to which Israel succumbed (Matt. 4:1–11; Luke 4:1–13). Like Moses, Jesus goes up to a mountain to deliver his inaugural kingdom address, the Sermon on the Mount (Matt. 5–7), and then again to reveal his glory to his disciples in the transfiguration (Mark 9:2–13 and pars.). In Luke, the topic of conversation between Jesus, Moses, and Elijah is the "departure" (9:31, Gk. *exodos*) that Jesus is about to accomplish in Jerusalem. It appears that Luke is presenting Jesus's death, resurrection, and ascension as the accomplishment of a new exodus that will bring God's people out of spiritual exile into their true home.

Paul: Exile as slavery to sin and death. Though Paul nowhere explicitly refers to the Babylonian exile, his description of humanity as alienated from God and as slaves to sin and death is an exilic image (Rom. 6:15–23). In various contexts Paul presents the gentile mission as restoration from exile. He cites Isa. 11:10 from the LXX to show that when the "Root of Jesse" (= the Messiah) will arise to rule over the nations, "in him the Gentiles will hope" (Rom. 15:12). Similarly, in Rom. 9:25–26 he applies Hosea 1:10; 2:23—originally referring to the renewal of Israel—to the inclusion of the gentiles into the people of God.

The proclamation of the gospel is also identified by Paul with passages related to renewal after exile: "How beautiful are the feet of those who bring good news!" (Rom. 10:15, citing Isa. 52:7; cf. Isa. 53:1 in Rom. 10:16; Isa. 57:19 in Eph. 2:17). So, too, Israel's ultimate restoration is related to restoration from exile. In Rom. 9:27–28, the present remnant of Israel that is saved is likened to the remnant after the Assyrian conquest (Isa. 10:22–23), and in Rom. 11 Paul's description of unbelieving Israel as branches cut off from the vine suggests an image of exiles in need of restoration. Though Israel is presently alienated from God and cut off from the covenant, the day will come when the faith of the gentiles will provoke them to jealousy and "all Israel will be saved" (Rom. 11:26). In language reminiscent of the new-exodus return from Babylon, Paul affirms that "the deliverer will come from Zion; he will turn godlessness away from Jacob. And this is my covenant with them when I take away their sins" (Rom. 11:26–27; cf. Isa. 59:20, 21; 27:9).

Hebrews: In search of a city whose builder and architect is God. The writer to the Hebrews develops the theme of exile with reference to Israel's wilderness wanderings (Heb. 3:7–4:11). According to Ps. 95:11, because of their hardness of heart, Israel failed to enter God's "rest" and so wandered in the wilderness for forty years. Nor did Joshua provide them with rest (Heb. 4:8). A promise of "Sabbath-rest" (v. 9)—an analogy for salvation—therefore remains for the people of God. The readers are encouraged to "make every effort to enter that rest, so that no one will perish by following [the Israelites'] example of disobedience" (4:11).

The theme of exile is also prominent in Heb. 11, the celebration of persevering faith. Abraham left his homeland to go to a place he did not know, so that even in the promised land, he lived in tents "like a stranger in a foreign country" (11:8–9). Exile thus symbolizes those who persevered in faith even though they had not yet received what was promised: "All these people were still living by faith when they died. They did not receive the things promised; they only saw them and welcomed them from a distance, admitting that they were foreigners and strangers on earth. People who say such things show that they are looking for a country of their own . . . a heavenly one. Therefore God is not ashamed to be called their God, for he has prepared a city for them" (11:13–16).

First Peter and James: Aliens and strangers in a foreign land. The theme of believers as exiles living in a foreign land is most prominent in 1 Peter. The readers are addressed as "God's elect, exiles scattered throughout the provinces of Pontus, Galatia, Cappadocia, Asia and Bithynia" (1 Pet. 1:1). As "foreigners and exiles" they are not part of this evil world system and so are to "abstain from sinful desires, which wage war against your soul" (2:11). Though they are politically and militarily powerless by virtue of their status as outsiders and foreigners, the Spirit's transforming power allows them to "live such good lives among the pagans that, though they accuse you of doing wrong, they may see your good deeds and glorify God on the day he visits us" (2:12). James, too, addresses his readers as exiles: "the twelve tribes scattered among the nations" (James 1:1). Though this status leaves them vulnerable to exploitation and abuse (1:2, 12; 2:6–7), if they ask, God will provide them with the wisdom to live lives of faith and godliness (1:5).

Revelation: The final restoration. The theme of restoration after exile finds its ultimate resolution in the closing chapters of Revelation. The creation of a new heaven and a new earth represents the believer's true and final home, a place of complete safety and security and the antithesis of exile (21:1–2; cf. Isa. 65:17). In fulfillment of the Deuteronomistic promises, the new Jerusalem represents a place where God will dwell with his people and will be their God (Rev. 21:3; cf. John 14:2–3). There will be no need for a temple, because God's presence will be unmediated: "The Lord God Almighty and the Lamb are its temple" (21:22). There will be no sun or moon, "for the glory of God gives it light, and the Lamb is its lamp" (21:23). The gates will never be shut, because there will be no night there (21:25; 22:5) and thus no threats from thieves or enemies. All the dangers associated with exile—hunger, thirst, exposure, exploitation, and abuse—will be removed. Most significantly, citizenship in this city of God is available to all who come humbly by faith: "The Spirit and the bride say, 'Come!' And let the one who hears say, 'Come!' Let the one who is thirsty come; and let the one who wishes take the free gift of the water of life" (22:17).

See also Adam, First and Last; Exodus, The; Jews and Gentiles

Bibliography. Ackroyd, P. R., *Exile and Restoration*, OTL (Westminster John Knox, 1968); Anderson, B. W., "Exodus and Covenant in Second Isaiah and Prophetic Tradition," in *Magnalia Dei*, ed. F. M. Cross, W. E. Lemke, and P. D. Miller Jr. (Doubleday, 1976), 339–60; Anderson, "Exodus Typology in Second Isaiah," in *Israel's Prophetic Heritage*, ed. B. W. Anderson and W. Harrelson (Harper, 1962), 177–95; Brueggeman, W., *Cadences of Home* (Westminster John Knox, 1997); Duguid, I. M., "Exile," in *NDBT*, 475–78; Elliott, J. H., *A Home for the Homeless* (Fortress, 1981); Evans, C. A., "Jesus and the Continuing Exile of Israel," in *Jesus and the Restoration of Israel*, ed. C. C. Newman (InterVarsity, 1999), 77–100; Klein, R. W., *Israel in Exile*, OBT (Fortress, 1979); Knibb, M. A., "The Exile in the Literature of the Intertestamental Period," *HeyJ* 17 (1976): 253–72; Mánek, J., "The New Exodus in the Books of Luke," *NovT* 2 (1958): 8–23; Martínez, F. G., *The Dead Sea Scrolls Translated* (Eerdmans, 1996); Mbuvi, A. M., *Temple, Exile and Identity in 1 Peter*, LNTS 345 (T&T Clark, 2007); Nixon, R. E., *The Exodus in the New Testament* (Tyndale, 1963); Pao, D., *Acts and the Isaianic New Exodus*, BSL (Baker Academic, 2002); Radner, E., *Time and the Word* (Eerdmans, 2016); Scott, J. M., ed., *Exile*, JSJSup 56 (Brill, 1997); Watts, R. E., *Isaiah's New Exodus in Mark* (Baker Academic, 2001); Wright, N. T., *Jesus and the Victory of God* (Fortress, 1999); Wright, *The New Testament and the People of God* (Fortress, 1992); Wright, *Paul and the Faithfulness of God* (Fortress, 2013).

MARK L. STRAUSS

Exodus, Book of

Exodus gets its English title from the Greek word *exodos*, meaning "going out," a reference in Exod. 19:1 to the departure of the Israelites from Egypt. While the title "going out" encapsulates well the first half of the book, chaps. 19–40 center on God's "coming down" to live among the Israelites. God's rendezvous with the Israelites at Mount Sinai is highly significant theologically, for it reflects a partial restoration of the divine-human relationship that was broken due to Adam and Eve's disobedience in the garden of Eden (Gen. 3).

Key Themes in Exodus

Although Exodus may give the impression of being composed of disparate materials, these are closely integrated under the theme of "knowing God." The plot of Exodus revolves around how the Israelites come to experience God in a more personal way. This is reflected in the climax toward which the book moves, when God comes to dwell among the Israelites (Exod. 40:34–38). This more intimate relationship, however, requires making a covenant or treaty, through which the Israelites commit themselves voluntarily to be God's "treasured possession" (19:5). If they are obedient to God and keep the covenant, they will be a "kingdom of priests and a holy nation" (19:6).

By entering into a solemn agreement at Mount Sinai, the Israelites take God to be their divine king and promise him their exclusive allegiance (24:3, 7; cf. 19:8). This master-servant relationship contrasts sharply with a comparable relationship that is introduced at the start of Exodus, when the Israelites are enslaved by the king of Egypt. While Pharaoh, who is viewed by his people as a deity, forcibly subjects the Israelites to the harshest of conditions, the Lord invites them to submit voluntarily to his rule over them and offers them rest, the Sabbath being the sign of the covenant (31:12–17). Pharaoh conscripts the Israelites to construct store cities from straw and clay, but Yahweh commissions them to manufacture from the finest of materials a royal tent for his glory. The Israelites' master-slave experiences with Pharaoh and Yahweh are diametrically opposite; the two masters are very different.

This contrast between Pharaoh and Yahweh is introduced at the start of Exodus. Pharaoh's attitude toward the Israelites is presented as running counter to God's creation mandate for humanity. The brief report of the Israelites being fruitful and multiplying and filling the land (1:7) recalls God's instructions in Gen. 1:28. Pharaoh, however, prevents the Israelites from flourishing. Against this background, God sends Moses to lead the Israelites out of Egypt. Importantly, through this process of redemption from slavery (reflected in the use of the verb *gā'al*, "to redeem," in Exod. 6:6; 15:13), God makes himself known to both the Israelites and the Egyptians.

The theme of knowing God is highlighted in Pharaoh's response to Moses: "Who is Yahweh that I should heed him by releasing Israel? I do not know Yahweh, and moreover, I will not release Israel" (Exod. 5:2 AT). In the light of Pharaoh's ignorance of Yahweh, subsequent episodes abound with references to making Yahweh known (6:3–7; 7:5, 17; 8:10, 22; 9:4, 16, 29; 10:1–2; 11:7; 14:4, 18). The divinely initiated supernatural events in Egypt are designed to reveal God's power. When these events are later followed by the destruction of Pharaoh's chariot force at the Lake of Reeds, the Israelites testify through song to the awesome majesty and power of God as he redeems them from the cruel servitude imposed upon them by the king of Egypt (15:1–13).

God, however, is not simply interested in demonstrating that he is more powerful than Pharaoh. Exodus draws out other important aspects of God's nature. The most prominent of these is his holiness. Moses encounters God's holy nature when God calls to him from the burning bush (3:4–5). God's presence sanctifies the ground around the bush. Later, at the same mountain, the Israelites are required to be sanctified before they can ascend the mountain in safety (19:10–15, 21–25). A similar pattern is evident when Aaron is appointed to serve as high priest in the tabernacle, which spatially resembles Mount Sinai (Rodriguez, 127–45). Before Aaron and his sons can approach God, they need to partake in a complex consecration ritual.

In Exodus only those who are holy may approach God to know him relationally. Exodus records three consecration rituals that shed light on the process by which alienated people may come closer to God. The first of these is Passover. To deliver the Israelite firstborn males from death, the Passover ritual sanctifies them so that they belong to God (Num. 3:13; 8:17; cf. Exod. 13:2). While no explicit explanation is given in Exod. 12, the narrative implies that the firstborn males are ransomed from death through the sacrifice of the Passover animals (reflected in the use of the verb *pādâ* in 13:13, 15), purified through the sprinkling of blood, and sanctified through eating the sacrificial meat with unleavened bread (Alexander, "Passover Sacrifice," 1–24; supplemented in Alexander, *Exodus*, 211–34). Subsequently, the firstborn males are ransomed by the Levites (Num. 3:12–13, 45–51; 8:16–18). As a result, the Levites, being holier than other Israelites, are enabled to come closer to God as they serve in the tabernacle.

A second consecration ritual takes place when the Israelites commit themselves to the covenant at Mount Sinai. Initially, the mountain is out of bounds to everyone apart from Moses. After offering whole-burnt and fellowship sacrifices and sprinkling blood on the people, some of the prominent leaders of the Israelites ascend the lower slopes of Mount Sinai. Whereas previously they were divinely prohibited from touching the mountain (Exod. 19:12–13, 21–24), those who are consecrated have the remarkable privilege of seeing God, if only from a distance and not fully (24:9–11).

The final consecration ritual described in Exodus involves the appointment of Aaron as high priest and his sons as priests. The instructions for this ritual are very detailed (Exod. 29), but clear parallels exist with the previous two consecration rituals, involving the making of whole-burnt and fellowship offerings, the sprinkling of blood, and the eating of the sacrificial meat with unleavened bread.

As these different rituals reveal, the process of knowing God relationally requires the Israelites to be made holy by God (cf. Exod. 31:13; Lev. 20:8; 21:15, 23; 22:9, 16, 32). Beyond the necessity of being sanctified through a special sacrificial ritual, the covenant obligations given at Mount Sinai underline that being God's holy people has important ethical implications for the Israelites (cf. Exod. 22:31; Lev. 19:2; 20:7). God's own holiness is to be reflected in his people's moral perfection.

The special covenant relationship established between God and the Israelites at Mount Sinai facilitates God's plans for the people. The events at Mount Sinai prepare for the creation of Jerusalem as the holy-mountain city of God. This outcome is anticipated when the Israelites celebrate in song their divine rescue in Exod. 15. After highlighting how God has rescued them from the violent aspirations of the Egyptian charioteers, the song concludes by looking to a future when the Israelites will dwell with God on his holy mountain (Exod. 15:17). However, before they come to this mountain, God brings them to another mountain to prepare the people for life in his presence. Like Passover, which was to be celebrated annually to recall God's redemption of the Israelites from slavery, the events of Mount Sinai are recalled through the daily cultic activities associated with the tabernacle, which resemble Mount Sinai (Alexander, *Exodus*, 562–65).

In the micro-story of Exodus we see modeled the macro-story of the entire Bible, for Exodus informs our understanding of God's redemptive plan for the whole earth. As savior and king, God redeems people from satanic control, ransoms them from death, purifies them from defilement, and sanctifies them so that they may become a royal priesthood and a holy nation. Exodus reveals how one nation is rescued by God and enabled to live in his presence, but this paradigm will be escalated to include every nation, for the Exodus story prefigures future developments that will end with God's holy presence filling the whole world.

Exodus as a Sequel to Genesis

As the second book of the Bible, Exodus continues the story that unfolds in Genesis and is meant to be read as a direct sequel. While some allusions to Genesis in Exodus are very obvious, others are brief and subtle. All, however, influence to varying degrees how the text of Exodus should be interpreted. A knowledge of Genesis shapes our reading of Exodus.

Israel in Egypt. The opening verses of Exodus make it immediately apparent that what follows is intended to be read as a sequel to Genesis. Chronologically, Exodus continues where Genesis finishes, with the narrative flowing directly from one book to the other. Exodus opens with the words, "These are the names of the sons of Israel who went to Egypt." This same wording comes in Gen. 46:8, which introduces a list of all those who went down into Egypt from Canaan. The Genesis passage concludes by noting that those who went to Egypt "were seventy" (Gen. 46:27), a total that is echoed in Exod. 1:5. However, the order of the names in Exod. 1:2–4 does not reflect Gen. 46:8–25; it resembles more closely Gen. 35:23–26, which in turn follows the birth order recorded in Gen. 29:31–30:24; 35:16–18. The reference to Joseph's death in Exod. 1:6 creates a bridge back to the final verses of Genesis (Gen. 50:22–26).

Various elements in the opening verses of Exodus are unintelligible without a prior knowledge of Genesis. The wording of Exod. 1:1 presupposes that the reader understands that the names "Israel" and "Jacob" refer to the same person (cf. Gen. 32:28). No explanation is given in Exod. 1:1–5 to explain why Jacob's family migrates to Egypt, and nothing is said to account for Joseph being there already. Remarkably, without an awareness of Genesis the reader of Exodus would not even know that Joseph is Jacob's son. Nor would the reader appreciate the significance of the observation in 1:8 that there arose a new pharaoh who did not know Joseph. Why would any Egyptian king be expected to know a foreign immigrant? Genesis provides the answer, telling of Joseph's significant contribution to the welfare of the Egyptians as a nation and the positive attitude of an earlier pharaoh to Joseph and his family (Gen. 41:41–45; 47:1–12). The new pharaoh, possibly belonging to a new dynasty (Sarna, 5), has no knowledge of what Joseph did in the past and therefore feels no obligation to treat the Israelites well. A background knowledge of Genesis is essential to understanding the new developments narrated at the start of Exodus.

The creation mandate. Although only seventy Israelites migrate to Egypt, their remarkable increase in number becomes a cause of concern for the new pharaoh. This massive explosion in the population is conveyed in Exod. 1:7 through four verbs that signify growth and through the statement that "the land was filled with them." The four verbs conveying numerical growth occur together only here. Usually only two of these verbs are used in combination (e.g., Gen. 8:17; 9:1; 17:20; 28:3; 35:11; 47:27; 48:4), three occurring together only in exceptional cases (9:7). Strikingly, all four verbs of growth in Exod. 1:7 "mirror the language of creation (Gen. 1:28 and 9:1–2)" (Fox, 241; cf. Ackerman, 76–77). The extraordinary growth of the Israelites gives every appearance of fulfilling God's command to humanity in Gen. 1:28, which is later repeated to Noah and his family after the "re-creation" of the earth following the flood (Gen. 9:7; cf. 9:1). In addition, given that the Hebrew noun *ʾereṣ* can be rendered either "earth" or "land/country," the comment that "the land [*ʾereṣ*] was filled with them" in Exod. 1:7 echoes the divine command in Gen. 1:28 to "fill the earth [*ʾereṣ*]." With good reason, Terence Fretheim (25) views the parallels between Exod. 1:7 and Gen. 1:28 as indicating that the Israelites are fulfilling God's creation mandate under his blessing. The verbs signaling numerical growth in Exod. 1:7 also recall the divine promises made to the patriarchs Abraham, Isaac, and Jacob concerning numerous descendants (Gen. 12:2; 13:16; 15:5; 17:2, 6; 22:17; 26:4, 24; 28:14; 35:11; 46:3; 48:4; cf. 28:3). Pharaoh's attempt to stop the numerical growth of the Israelites presents him as directly opposing God's plan for humanity. By reading Exodus in the light of Genesis, it becomes apparent that from the outset Pharaoh's actions are antithetical to God's will.

God's covenant with the patriarchs. The opening verses of Exodus presuppose that the reader is familiar with the story of Joseph's rise to prominence in Egypt and the subsequent relocation of Jacob's family from Canaan to Egypt. A further recurring allusion to Genesis is introduced at the end of Exod. 2 when the narrator records, "God heard their groaning and he remembered his covenant with Abraham, with Isaac and with Jacob" (2:24). To remember a covenant means to fulfill the obligations that were promised when the covenant was made. To anyone without a prior knowledge of Genesis, the reference to a covenant in Exod. 2:24 would be puzzling.

The significance of God's covenant with the patriarchs is fleshed out in Exod. 3 when God calls Moses to bring the Israelites out of Egypt. Making Moses aware of his concern for the oppressed Israelites, God states that, having observed the affliction of the people, he will rescue them from Egypt and bring them into the land of Canaan (Exod. 3:7–10). God's words recall not only the references to seeing, hearing, and knowing in Exod. 2:24–25 but also, more importantly, the covenant that God made with Abraham in Gen. 15. God informed the patriarch, "Know for certain that for four hundred years your descendants will be strangers in a country not their own and that they will be enslaved and mistreated there. But I will punish the nation they serve as slaves, and afterward they will come out with great possessions" (Gen. 15:13–14). Gen. 15 goes on to record that God made a covenant with Abraham, promising his descendants "the land of the Kenites, Kenizzites, Kadmonites, Hittites, Perizzites, Rephaites, Amorites, Canaanites, Girgashites and Jebusites" (15:19–21). The repetition of six of these names in Exod. 3:8 reinforces the link between the two passages. The importance of

God's covenant with Abraham for the rescue of the Israelites is underlined by what God instructs Moses to tell the elders of Israel in Exod. 3:16–17. God's rescue of the Israelites from slavery in Egypt will lead to their taking possession of the land of Canaan. The promise of land to the descendants of Abraham, Isaac, and Jacob is a significant motif in Genesis (see Gen. 12:7; 15:13–21; 17:8; 24:7; 26:2–5; 28:13–15; 35:12; 48:4). Knowledge of this promise underlies Joseph's request that his bones be returned to Canaan (Gen. 50:25) and the fulfillment of this request (Exod. 13:19).

God's speech to Moses in Exod. 3:7–10 indicates that the rescue of the Israelites from slavery occurs because of God's covenant with Abraham. Confirmation of this comes later in Exodus when the narrator records that the Israelites were in Egypt for 430 years (12:40–41), an observation that resonates with the four hundred years mentioned in Gen. 15:13.

References to God's covenant with the patriarchs occur elsewhere in Exodus. When Moses becomes disillusioned after Pharaoh's refusal to release the Israelites, God reminds Moses of his pledge to give the land of Canaan to Abraham, Isaac, and Jacob (6:2–5). God then instructs Moses to tell the Israelites of this divine commitment (6:6–8). Exodus 6:6–7 recalls Gen. 15:13–14 and 15:18; meanwhile, Exod. 6:2 and 6:4 probably allude to Gen. 17:1 and 17:8, respectively. The expression "established my covenant" (Exod. 6:4) alludes to Gen. 17:7–8, which also mentions that Abraham's descendants will possess the "land of Canaan."

The introduction of specific allusions to Gen. 17 is significant because the covenant of circumcision does not simply expand upon the divine promise of land in Gen. 15. In Gen. 17 God promises to make Abraham the father of many nations; Gen. 15 focuses simply on Abraham being the father of one nation. Genesis 17 adds an entirely new dimension, moving beyond the guarantee of land to Abraham's descendants in Gen. 15.

The covenant introduced in Gen. 17 differs from the covenant of Gen. 15 in substantial ways while incorporating the guarantee of land. Whereas the covenant of Gen. 15 focuses exclusively on Abraham's biological descendants taking possession of the land of Canaan, the covenant of circumcision is closely tied to the idea that through one of Abraham's descendants all the nations of the earth will be blessed (cf. Gen. 22:18). In the light of this, it is worth observing how circumcision, the sign of the Gen. 17 covenant, is tied into the account of God's deliverance of the Israelites from Egypt. Only those males who are circumcised may participate in the Passover (Exod. 12:44, 48). This requirement underscores that the covenant of circumcision is a prerequisite for being included among those who identify with the Israelites' experience of being redeemed by God. Even Moses is not excluded from this requirement, as the short, enigmatic passage of Exod. 4:24–26 reveals.

Since God's intervention in Egypt on behalf of the Israelites is motivated by his covenant with Abraham, Isaac, and Jacob (2:24; 6:5), it is not surprising that Moses draws attention to this covenant when God threatens to destroy the Israelites after they make the golden idol at Mount Sinai (32:7–14). Here is a further allusion to Genesis.

It is often suggested that the covenant at Mount Sinai is closely tied to the Abrahamic covenant (e.g., Dumbrell, 80–81, 89–90; Gentry and Wellum, 323–24, 326). However, the two covenants have very different functions. The Abrahamic covenant is about Abraham being the father of many nations (Gen. 17:4–5). The Sinai covenant is about the Israelites being God's special possession through obeying him and keeping the covenant. The difference between the two covenants is highlighted by Paul in Gal. 3, where he draws an important distinction between the promises associated with Abraham and the law associated with Mount Sinai.

While the Sinai covenant differs in function from the Abrahamic covenant, there are aspects of the covenant obligations that allude back to Genesis. The prohibitions against killing and adultery (Exod. 20:13–14) are best understood in the light of what Genesis has to say about marriage and the value of human life (Gen. 2:24; 9:5–6; cf. Alexander, *Exodus*, 414–20). The commandment concerning the Sabbath refers to God resting on the seventh day (Exod. 20:11; cf. Gen. 2:2–3). However, subtle variations in wording indicate that the Sabbath of the Decalogue is not to be equated in every way with the "seventh day." They merely share common features. God sanctifies both days, and both involve rest from all work (cf. Shead, 746). For the Israelites at Mount Sinai, keeping the Sabbath is a reminder that God has delivered them from harsh labor in order (1) to give them rest and (2) to transform them into a holy nation.

The tabernacle and the garden of Eden. The Sinai covenant is designed to bring the Israelites into a closer relationship with God. If the Israelites keep the covenant, they will become a royal priesthood (Exod. 19:6), enjoying the status that Adam and Eve had before they were expelled from Eden. A return to Edenic conditions is partially reflected in the account of the construction of the tabernacle, which shares features in common with the garden of Eden. However, links between the final chapters of Exodus and the opening chapters of Genesis are insufficient to justify the long-standing Jewish tradition that the construction of the tabernacle marks the climax of creation (cf. Propp, 675–76). The tabernacle, as a model of the cosmos, foreshadows a future time when God's glory will fill the whole world (Alexander, *From Eden*, 31–42).

The gifting of Bezalel "with the Spirit of God" recalls the opening chapter of Genesis, where the "Spirit of God" hovers over the surface of the waters in preparation for God's ordering and filling an earth that is formless and empty (Gen. 1:2). A connection between

God's making the world and Bezalel's constructing the tabernacle is further suggested by the mention of *kol-məlā'kâ*, "all kinds of skills" (Exod. 31:3), which comes also in Gen. 2:3, where it is translated "all the work." As Richard Middleton (87) remarks, "These verbal resonances suggest that Bezalel's discerning artistry in tabernacle building images God's own construction of the cosmos."

Exodus in the NT

The exodus story vividly illustrates how alienated human beings are reconciled to a holy God, but the outcome did not result in the complete removal of all the barriers that separate the people from God. Despite everything that happens, even Moses is still not permitted to see the face of God (Exod. 33:18–23). In the light of this, it is no surprise that the Israelites' deliverance from Egypt and their subsequent relationship with God become the basis in other OT books, especially Isaiah, for believing in another and greater exodus.

Against the background of an OT expectation of a further exodus, the Exodus paradigm of salvation is embraced by NT writers to explain the life, death, resurrection, and ascension of Jesus Christ. Central to this is Jesus's death at Passover. Paul underscores the Passover nature of Jesus's death by commenting briefly, "For Christ, our Passover lamb, has been sacrificed" (1 Cor. 5:7). Peter describes Jesus Christ as "a lamb without blemish or defect" (1 Pet. 1:19). While this phrase by itself could refer to other sacrifices, the context implies a Passover connection. Peter states that those who are ransomed by Christ's blood (1:18) become "a royal priesthood, a holy nation, God's special possession" (2:9), echoing the exodus story (Exod. 19:6).

John's Gospel offers the most developed use of the exodus story in presenting its account of Jesus. At the heart of this presentation lies the belief that Jesus Christ, as a Passover sacrifice, brings eternal life to those threatened with death. Unlike the Synoptic Gospel writers, John records three occasions when Jesus is present at Passover celebrations in Jerusalem (John 2:13; 6:4; 11:55). Interestingly, John places the death of Jesus after a series of signs that resemble, but in a contrasting way, the signs and wonders that occurred in Egypt. Whereas the signs and wonders in Exodus have a negative impact on people (e.g., water into blood), climaxing in the death of the Egyptian firstborn males, the signs recorded in John's Gospel have a positive impact (e.g., water into wine), climaxing in resurrection life. While some NT scholars have reservations about linking John the Baptist's remark about Jesus being the "Lamb of God" (1:29, 36) with the Passover lamb, this association is by far the most obvious in the light of the entire Gospel, a link confirmed by John's observation that Jesus's bones, like those of the Passover sacrifice, were not broken (19:31–37; cf. Exod. 12:46; Num. 9:12). When the Egyptian Passover is viewed as a consecration ritual, it is not difficult to understand why John the Baptist states that the "Lamb of God . . . takes away the sin of the world" (John 1:29). Elsewhere in John's Gospel the Passover provides a helpful paradigm for understanding Jesus's remarks about eating his flesh and drinking his blood (John 6:53–58; see Hoskins, "Deliverance") and about being freed from slavery to sin (John 8:34–36; see Hoskins, "Freedom").

A new covenant. An important component in the process by which the Israelites are brought into a more intimate relationship with Yahweh is the initiation of a covenant relationship. After redeeming the Israelites from slavery in Egypt, God invites them to serve him exclusively through establishing a friendship treaty. Despite promising Yahweh total obedience, the Israelites quickly display their lack of faithfulness, breaking the obligations placed upon them by the covenant sealed at Mount Sinai. The biblical account of their later history testifies to their persistent disobedience. Consequently, their unique relationship with God is constantly strained. Centuries after their deliverance from Egypt, the prophet Jeremiah intimates that God will establish a new covenant with his people that will result in greater obedience (Jer. 31:31–34; cf. Isa. 54:10; 55:3; 61:8; Jer. 32:40; Ezek. 34:25; 37:26–27). This promise of a new covenant is later associated with Jesus Christ (Luke 22:20; 1 Cor. 11:25; 2 Cor. 3:6), with the author of Hebrews boldly asserting its superiority over the older Sinai covenant (8:8; 9:15; 12:24). Whereas the theophany accompanying the Sinai covenant filled the Israelites with fear, the new covenant is linked to a less intimidating experience as people come to "Mount Zion, to the city of the living God, the heavenly Jerusalem" (Heb. 12:18–24; cf. Rev. 21:1–4).

As the Sinai covenant resulted in God coming to dwell among his people, the new covenant is associated with God coming to dwell in his people through the Holy Spirit. Consequently, the NT witnesses to the Jerusalem temple being replaced by a new temple composed of the followers of Jesus (Eph. 2:19–21). In line with this, the Aaronic high priesthood and cultic practices linked to the Sinai covenant become redundant, as high-priestly activity is relocated from the model of the heavenly temple to the true temple itself (Heb. 7:12). As the Holy Spirit under the old covenant endowed individual Israelites with special gifts to manufacture the tabernacle, so too with the new covenant the Holy Spirit imparts grace gifts for the building of the organic temple. Drawing on this analogy, Paul sees himself as a master builder, like Bezalel, whose service is to lay a foundation on which others can build (1 Cor. 3:10; cf. Exod. 31:2–5; 35:30–35).

The consecration rituals of Exodus draw attention to the importance of being holy in order to approach God. Reflecting the sacrificial nature of these rituals, the author of Hebrews writes, "We have been made holy through the sacrifice of the body of Jesus Christ once for all" (10:10). He later adds, "And so Jesus also suffered outside the city gate to make the people holy through his own blood" (13:12). Since Jesus is "the one who makes people holy" (Heb. 2:11), his followers are regularly addressed as "holy ones" or "saints" by Paul (e.g., Rom. 1:7; 1 Cor. 1:2; 2 Cor. 1:1; Eph. 1:1; Phil. 1:1; Col. 1:2). The sanctification of believers, which is linked to the indwelling of the Holy Spirit, coincides with conversion (Peterson).

These examples of NT allusions to the Exodus account of how God and the Israelites come into a covenant relationship do not exhaust all possible connections. They merely illustrate how the OT story is used typologically to provide a framework for understanding how God redeems people from the powers of evil, ransoms them from death, purifies them from defilement, and sanctifies them in order to establish a special covenant relationship with them. At the heart of this process stands Jesus Christ, the Lamb of God, the ultimate Passover sacrifice.

Bibliography. Ackerman, J. S., "The Literary Context of the Moses Birth Story (Exod. 1–2)," in *Literary Interpretations of Biblical Narratives*, ed. K. R. R. Gros Louis, J. S. Ackerman, and T. S. Warshaw (Abingdon, 1974), 74–119; Alexander, T. D., *Exodus*, ApOTC (Apollos, 2017); Alexander, *From Eden to the New Jerusalem* (Kregel, 2009); Alexander, "The Passover Sacrifice," in *Sacrifice in the Bible*, ed. R. T. Beckwith and M. Selman (Baker, 1995), 1–24; Dumbrell, W. J., *Covenant and Creation* (Paternoster, 1984); Fox, E., *Genesis and Exodus* (Schocken, 1991); Fretheim, T. E., *Exodus*, IBC (John Knox, 1991); Gentry, P. J., and S. J. Wellum, *Kingdom through Covenant* (Crossway, 2012); Hoskins, P. M., "Deliverance from Death by the True Passover Lamb," *JETS* 52 (2009): 285–99; Hoskins, "Freedom from Slavery to Sin and the Devil," *TJ* 31 (2010): 47–63; Middleton, J. R., *The Liberating Image* (Brazos, 2005); Morales, L. M., *The Tabernacle Pre-Figured* (Peeters, 2012); Peterson, D., *Possessed by God* (Apollos, 1995); Propp, W. H. C., *Exodus 19–40*, AB (Doubleday, 2006); Rodriguez, A. M., "Sanctuary Theology in the Book of Exodus," *AUSS* 24 (1986): 127–45; Sarna, N. M., *Exodus*, JPSTC (Jewish Publication Society of America, 1991); Shead, A. G., "Sabbath," in *NDBT*, 745–50.

T. Desmond Alexander

Exodus, The

"Israel is my firstborn son, and I told you, 'Let my son go that he may worship me.'" As Yahweh's simple command to Pharaoh, these words of Exod. 4:22–23 are pregnant with meaning for understanding the premise and goals of everything that occurs in Israel's historic exodus from Egypt. In turn, the events of the exodus form typological patterns that do not merely repeat in describing new situations but develop and carry the rest of the Bible to its eschatological telos.

The Exodus

It is insufficient to define the exodus simply as Israel's departure from Egypt, and it is an unfruitful reduction to cast it merely in political or sociological terms. Rather, the exodus is *cosmic* from beginning to end. *The exodus is Yahweh's quintessential act of international self-revelation and redemption that brings Israel through the wilderness to his sacred presence and forms them into a covenantal worshiping people through the blood of the Passover lamb, all in measured fulfillment of his purposes in creation and in eschatological expectation of a new world.* This is all captured in the following eight exodus subthemes.

Redemption unto life and "rest." At its most basic level, the exodus is Yahweh's paradigmatic act of salvation. As the book of Exodus opens, Israel faces two problems: they are ruthlessly made to work under a slavish yoke (1:11–14; cf. 2:11, 23; 5:4–19; 6:6–7; cf. Deut. 26:6–7), and they are threatened with extinction (1:15–16, 22; cf. 5:21; 14:5–12). In the exodus, therefore, Israel's three-day journey (3:18; 5:3; 8:27; cf. Num. 33:8) delivers them from death to life (foreshadowed in 2:10) in a typological resurrection (Morales, *Exodus*) as they are "brought up/out" from Egypt (3:12, 17; 6:6, 11; 7:2; 13:18; cf. Deut. 26:8). This new life, in turn, is marked by "rest" (5:5; 16:23; 23:12), which is Yahweh's explicit goal in 33:14.

By the blood of the Passover lamb. The night of the Passover is another threat to life, but the firstborn sons of Israel—representing their entire families—survive the angel of death because the blood of an unblemished lamb is applied to the doorposts of their homes (12:7, 12–13, 23). The lamb serves as a substitutionary atonement for those in the home: the lambs were killed (12:6, 21) in place of the sons (12:13, 23). Additionally, the qualities of the lamb (12:5, 8), those who eat it (12:4, 16), and the way the blood is applied (12:22) resemble the process for setting apart individual priests within Israel (Exod. 29; Lev. 8). Thus, Israel becomes Yahweh's "kingdom of priests" (Exod. 19:6) as the Passover atones for Israel's sins, saves them from death, and qualifies them to worship in the divine presence (Alexander, 104–7). The emphasis on commemorating this night forever (12:2–3, 14–20, 24–27) underscores the Passover's significance for Israel's self-understanding and its role in shaping future hopes.

Through the wilderness. Yahweh's leading Israel through the wilderness is critical to understanding the exodus (3:18; 5:1–3; 7:16; 8:27; cf. Deut. 8:2, 14–16; 29:5; 32:10; Pss. 78:19, 52; 105:39–41; Ezek. 20:10). The "road/way" through the desert (Exod. 13:18, 21; 23:20) is the path of forming, trial, and refining (see Talmon), as Yahweh leads them by the glory cloud and fire (13:21–22; cf. Num. 9:15–23; Deut. 8:2). Thus, the theme of suffering and testing before glory and inheritance pervades the biblical metanarrative, as does the emphasis that

Yahweh is with his people in all afflictions as he carries them "on eagles' wings" to himself (Exod. 19:4; cf. Deut. 32:11–12).

To the sacred place of worship. The ultimate purpose of the exodus is to bring Israel into the place where they can worship and dwell with Yahweh (Exod. 3:12, 18; 4:22–23; 5:1, 3; 7:16; 8:1, 20; 9:1, 13; 10:3, 7–9, 26; 12:31; 15:13; 19:1–2; 32:34). At the outset, Yahweh commissions Moses not only to bring Israel out but also to bring them *to* a particular place: the "good" land (3:8). The exodus will not be complete, therefore, until Israel enters Canaan. First, however, they must stop at the very mountain where Moses stood (3:12), a three-day journey from Egypt (3:18; 5:3; 8:27; 15:22). The area is called "holy ground" because Yahweh's presence resides there (3:5). This is Mount Sinai where, after another three days (19:11, 16), Yahweh descends with thunder, lightning, cloud, trumpets, smoke, fire, and earthquake (19:16–20). Thus, in the exodus Yahweh goes from Mount Sinai to "visit" his people (3:16; 4:31; 13:19; cf. Gen. 50:24) and bring them to himself so they can worship him there.

Once there, Moses ascends and enters into the cloud on the seventh day (24:15–16). Israel is then to remain at Mount Sinai until they have crafted the tabernacle, made with the treasures of Egypt (3:21–22; 11:2; 12:35–36; 25:3; 38:24–31; cf. Gen. 15:14; Pss. 68:18; 105:37). The climax to the entire narrative comes after the tabernacle is completed when the glory cloud of Yahweh's presence takes up permanent residence therein (40:34–38). Thus, Yahweh "dwells in their midst" (25:8–9; 29:42–46). Insofar as the tabernacle is made to look like Eden (25:31–40; 26:1, 31; cf. Gen. 1:6–12; 2:9, 12; 3:24), filling it with God's glory is both reminiscent of the prefall creation and a typological realization of Yahweh's intention of filling the whole creation with his glory in the latter days (Estelle, 105, 318–22). Subsequently, the tabernacle becomes the center of religions life, and the sacrificial system—especially that of the Day of Atonement—becomes the means by which Yahweh can continue to dwell among sinful people (Lev. 16:1–34; 20:7–8, 26; 21:8).

Yahweh is the God of gods. The exodus is also Yahweh's historic, public, international self-announcement, for he alone is God (Deut. 4:32–39). Moses asks, "What is his name?" (Exod. 3:13) and Pharaoh snarls, "Who is Yahweh, that I should obey him?" (5:2 AT). Throughout the book Yahweh explains time and again his rationale for all his mighty deeds: "so that [Moses, Israel, Pharaoh, Egypt, and all the nations] may know I am Yahweh" (6:6–7; 7:5, 17; 8:10, 22; 9:29; 10:2; 14:4, 18; 16:12; 29:46; 31:13; etc.; cf. also Deut. 4:35; 7:9; Ezek. 20:12, 26). Thus, the exodus is performed "in the sight of the nations" (Lev. 26:45; cf. Exod. 15:13–16; Ps. 98:1–3: Ezek. 20:9, 14, 22), so that Yahweh may receive global renown (Exod. 9:14–16; 18:1, 11; cf. Josh. 2:8–11; 9:8–9).

Miracles and prophecy through Moses. The exodus is accomplished through Yahweh's "mighty hand" and "outstretched arm" performing "signs and wonders" (Exod. 3:20; 6:6; 7:3; 13:3, 14; Deut. 4:34; 5:15; 6:22; 7:19; 26:8; Neh. 9:10; Pss. 135:9; 136:11–12; Jer. 32:20–21). The apex is the parting of the Red Sea (Exod. 14:21–15:21; Pss. 77:16–19; 78:12–14; 106:7–9), but the plagues (Exod. 7:14–12:32), "filling" and "satisfying" Israel with bread (Exod. 16; Pss. 78:25; 105:40), and the provision of water (Exod. 15:22–25; 17:1–7; Num. 20:8; Ps. 78:15–16) are also part and parcel of the exodus. In addition to revealing Yahweh's glory, these miracles also become the matrix inside of which "his servant Moses" is believed as a prophet (Exod. 4:8–16; 14:31) and in turn become paradigmatic of the great eschatological prophet par excellence "like Moses" (Deut. 18:15, 18; 34:10–12).

Judgment on Israel's enemies. The ten plagues constitute Yahweh's judgment upon both Pharaoh and Egypt's gods (Exod. 6:6; 12:12; cf. Num. 33:4) because of their false claims to deity and sovereignty (Currid, 108–13, 118–20). Because Pharaoh refuses to let Israel go, his own firstborn is killed, whereas the Passover lamb protects Israel's sons (12:29; cf. 4:23). In the end, Pharaoh and his army die in the Red Sea as Israel comes out alive (14:13–14, 23–30; 15:1–10; foreshadowed in 1:15–2:10).

Israel is Yahweh's "Son." Conversely, *Israel* is Yahweh's "firstborn son" (4:22). As the Sovereign's collective "son," Israel is his corporate viceroy over all creation (19:5–6). The subsequent crowning of Israel's king (Deut. 17:14–20) is downstream from this and anticipates Yahweh's intention to rule the world through his appointed "son" (cf. 2 Sam. 7:12–14; Ps. 2).

Genesis Prelude

The exodus is not exclusively Israel's story, however, but a *cosmic* story. All of the subthemes mentioned above are first vocalized in the creation account and the call of Abraham. Eden is the abode of the one true Creator God on a mountaintop (cf. Gen. 2:10–14; Ezek. 28:11–15). The glory cloud begins to redress this lost presence as it resides in the Eden-esque tabernacle (Morales, *Tabernacle*, 245–77). Life pervaded creation, but death is the mark of the human condition outside of Eden (Gen 2:7, 17; 3:19)—Israel is saved from death many times in the exodus, thus experiencing a typological resurrection. The Creator originally achieves "rest" on the final day of creation (2:1–3), and in the exodus Israel "rests" from Pharaoh's burdens. Adam is a king and priest (1:28; 2:15), and Israel again takes up that mantle. Adam begins in a good land, while the wilderness, the place of thorns and thistles, is the opposite of Eden (3:17–18). Israel's wilderness wanderings are thus a microcosm of humanity's expulsion from Eden, and so the exodus results in a return to the presence of God. In short, Pharaoh's death leading to the building of the tabernacle is a modicum of fulfilling Gen. 3:15.

Abraham's story also prefigures the exodus in several ways (Morales, *Exodus*, 19–36). Principally, the covenant-cutting ceremony of Gen. 15 foretells the exodus: Abraham's children will be in bondage (15:13; cf. Exod. 1:11), but God himself will lead them with fire and smoke/cloud (Gen. 15:17; cf. Exod. 13:21–22; 14:19–25) "between the pieces" (*gəzārîm*; Gen. 15:17; cf. esp. Ps. 136:13 MT) in order to enter into covenant with them (Gen. 15:18; cf. Exod. 24:3–8) and give them the land (Gen. 15:7, 16, 18–20; cf. Exod. 3:8; Deut. 26:8–9). Equally, the substitution of the ram (Gen. 22:13) for Abraham's "son" (22:2, 3, 6, 9–10, 12–13, 16) on the third day (22:4) prefigures the Passover, serving also as a typological resurrection (cf. Heb. 11:19).

Observing these links to Genesis situates the exodus within a larger cosmic metadrama, seen in creation and Abraham's call. It casts the exodus as a temporal-spatial fulfillment of the Creator's purposes in Eden and as a foretaste of his completion of those purposes in the eschaton when his glorious presence will fill the whole earth. The exodus is, therefore, a down payment and promise to the earth and all who dwell therein.

Land, Rest, Son, and Temple in the Good Land

The final goals of the exodus are not accomplished until Israel worships Yahweh in the good land (Exod. 3:8, 17; 23:20; Deut. 26:8–9) promised to Abraham (Gen. 12:6–7; 15:18–21; 17:8), the designated place of rest with a permanent temple built by Yahweh's son (Exod. 15:17; cf. Neh. 9:15; Pss. 78:52–55; 105:43–44).

The book of Joshua, therefore, continues with pervasive exodus tropes. The conquest begins with another water crossing (3:13; cf. Exod. 15:8) on dry ground (3:17; cf. Exod. 14:16). Just like Moses, Joshua is told he is entering sacred space (5:15; cf. Exod. 3:5). Rahab has a Passover-like experience (2:18–19; 6:17), intimating that broader goal of incorporating gentiles into this exodus-salvation (cf. Gen. 12:3; Exod. 12:38). And Yahweh's great name is known, for the nations have heard of his mighty hand (2:9–11; 4:23–24; 9:9). All this leads to giving Israel "a place of rest" (1:13 ESV; cf. 21:43–44) so that Israel will serve/worship Yahweh (24:14–28). Joshua is therefore to be understood as the penultimate stage of the exodus: attaining rest in the special place where Yahweh is exclusively worshiped.

The ultimate stage, then, is for Yahweh's son to establish the Creator's permanent sacred abode on earth by building the temple (cf. Exod. 15:17). Therefore, Solomon is called Yahweh's "son" (2 Sam. 7:14), who obtains "rest" (2 Sam. 7:1, 11; 1 Kings 4:25; 8:56) and builds the temple (2 Sam. 7:13; 1 Kings 5–8), which is then filled with Yahweh's glory (1 Kings 8:10–11; cf. Exod. 40:34–38) "so that all the peoples of the earth may know [Yahweh's] name and fear [him]" (1 Kings 8:43; cf. 10:6–9, 23–25). Several other details in 1 Kings 6–8, especially the calendar (6:1; 8:16, 21, 53), further connect the exodus to Solomon's temple, the latter marking the completion of the former (Frisch, 5–11; cf. esp. Pss. 68:15–18; 78:54). With 1 Kings 8 the cycle is complete: Yahweh leaves Sinai to get his people and bring them there where they build a tabernacle so he can travel with them until permanently residing in his temple on Mount Zion—the holy abode that emulates Eden (1 Kings 6:18, 23–36; 7:18–26, 36, 42) and anticipates a new creation.

The retelling of the exodus is not just for the sake of historical review but also serves as comparative prelude to other great acts of redemption (Deut. 7:17–19; Judg. 6:7–10, 13; 2 Sam. 7:6; Pss. 80:8–14; 106:4–47; 114:1–8; Isa. 63:10–14; Ezek. 20:1–26; Hosea 11:1, 11; Acts 7:17–44). It grounds ethics (Lev. 25:42, 55) and instructs the next generation (Ps. 78:1–4). And Yahweh's very nature/uniqueness is understood against the backdrop of the exodus (2 Sam. 7:23; Jon. 4:2). The exodus, therefore, provides a kind of logic of history and the lingua franca of redemptive history (Ruth 2:12; 3:9; 1 Sam. 4–6; 1 Kings 11–14; 17–18; Ps. 23:2–5).

The Exile as Exodus Reversal

Tragically, the great accomplishment of the exodus's goals in 1 Kings 8–10 is not permanent. David's sons are unfaithful and so the nation goes into exile. Naturally, this can only be described as the exodus run in reverse. They "go out" *from the land* (Ezek. 36:20; Jer. 15:1). The temple is destroyed (2 Kings 24–25) and Yahweh's glory departs (Ezek. 11:22–23). The "son" is dethroned (2 Kings 25:6–7; Mic. 5:1; cf. 2 Sam. 7:14b). Relational monikers given to Israel in the exodus are stripped away (Hosea 1:6, 9; cf. Exod. 3:7, 10; 33:19). They are afflicted with diseases akin to the plagues in Egypt (Deut. 28:27, 58–61; Amos 4:10). Yahweh's mighty "outstretched arm" is *against* them (Jer. 21:5; Ezek. 6:14) "in the sight of the nations" (Ezek. 5:8). And most tellingly, Israel is driven back into the wilderness (Hosea 12:9) through which they "return to Egypt" (Deut. 28:68; Isa. 10:24; Jer. 2:17–18; Hosea 8:13; 9:3, 17). Creation is therefore undone (Isa. 13; 24; Ezek. 6:14), and the bitter irony is that *in judgment* Israel will know that [he is] Yahweh (Ezek. 6:14; 7:4, 27; 12:15–16; etc.). Thus, by the end of the historical narrative the nations no longer seek the wisdom of Yahweh's son but have again placed their yoke on Israel (Isa. 47:6).

The Eschatological Vision

As Israel finds themselves again under foreign, idol-worshiping domination outside the good land, they need nothing less than another miraculous, nation-forming deliverance that reveals Yahweh's glory and brings them back to his sacred abode. Not surprisingly, therefore, Israel's return from exile is described as a *new exodus* (cf. esp. Isa. 11:11, 16; 43:18–19; Jer. 16:14–15; 23:7–8; Mic. 7:15). While the prophets each employ exodus themes with their own nuances, in toto they create a mosaic of Israel's future in terms of an eschatological exodus. Yahweh will again bring Israel out (Isa. 48:20; 49:9; 52:11; 55:12; Ezek. 20:38, 41; Zech. 2:6) from under their foreign yoke/burden (Isa. 9:4; 10:26–27; 14:25; Jer. 30:8; Ezek. 34:27). Yahweh will again be with Israel

(Isa. 43:5; 52:12; Ezek. 11:16; Zech. 2:10–11) as he leads them out of captivity along the road/way (Isa. 9:1; 35:8; 40:3; 42:16; 43:16, 19; 49:9–11), into the desert (Isa. 40:3; 43:19; Ezek. 20:35–36; Hosea 2:14–15) and passing again through mighty waters (Isa. 10:26; 11:15; 42:15; 43:2, 16; 51:9–11). This new exodus will be attended with miracles like the first exodus, such as giving water (Isa. 41:17–18; 43:20; 48:21; 49:10) and feeding multitudes (Isa. 49:9; Ezek. 34:11–16) by Yahweh's "mighty hand and outstretched arm" (Ezek. 20:33–34; cf. also Isa. 11:11; 40:10; 51:9; Joel 2:30). It will necessitate a new Passover-like sacrifice (Isa. 53:4–10) and is described with resurrection imagery just as the first exodus (Ezek. 37:1–14; Hosea 13:14) "on the third day" (Hosea 6:1–2). Ezekiel 37:13 says, "And you shall know that I am Yahweh *when* I open your graves and raise you from your graves, O my people" (AT). Yahweh's end goal is once again to lead his people back to worship in his sacred abode (Isa. 35:10; 43:21; 51:11; 52:8; Ezek. 20:40; Mic. 4:6–7; Zech. 2:7, 12). All this is done as Yahweh judges the nations like he did Pharaoh's army (Isa. 10:25–26; 43:17; Jer. 25:12; Ezek. 25:1–26:6; 38:17–23; Mic. 7:15–17). And, as with the first exodus, Yahweh performs this great deliverance in the sight of the nations (Ezek. 20:41; 28:25; Isa. 52:10) so that all will know that he is Yahweh (Isa. 11:9; 41:20; 48:9–11; Ezek. 20:38–44; 34:27, 30; 36:23, 36; 37:6, 12–14; 39:28; etc.; cf. also the Isa. 40:5/55:13 *inclusio*; Jer. 16:21; 31:34; Zech. 2:9, 11).

Isaiah in particular emphasizes that all this can only be accomplished through an eschatological Moses-like figure called "Yahweh's servant" (who also has *divine* qualities; compare 52:13 with 6:1; 57:15). He takes the name, identity, and mission of Israel upon himself (41:8–9; 42:1–6, 19; 45:4–6) in order to bear their suffering and affliction in this exile-as-Egypt experience (53:4, 7, 11–13; cf. esp. Exod. 1:11–14; see Ceresko). He gives his life as an atoning self-sacrifice (52:15; 53:5, 8, 12; cf. Lev. 16:22), and thereby opens the door to pardon sins (40:1–2) and gather both Israel and gentiles to himself (49:1–6). His death and resurrection (53:10) are the funnel through which the new exodus must pass, and the effect is to create a faithful community of international "servants of Yahweh" (54:16–17; 56:6–8; cf. Lev. 25:55).

There are also significant ways that the new exodus will surpass the original. (1) The eschatological exodus will result in the desert being turned into a new creation (Isa. 35:1, 6; 41:18–20; 43:19–20; 44:3–4; 51:3; 55:12–13; Ezek. 36:35; Hosea 2:14–23), which the filling of the tabernacle with the glory cloud adumbrated. (2) While the first exodus climaxed with the construction of the tabernacle and then the temple (Exod. 25–31; 35–40), filled with Yahweh's glory (Exod. 40:34–38; 1 Kings 8:10–11), this new exodus ends in a *cosmic* temple (Isa. 2:2–4; Ezek. 40–48; Mic. 4:1) filled with Yahweh's glory (Ezek. 43:1–5). (3) It will include gentiles as redeemed Israel / "the servant" becomes "a light for the nations that [Yahweh's] salvation may reach to the end of the earth" (Isa. 49:6 ESV; cf. 11:10–11, 16; 19:23; 42:6; 52:10, 15; 56:6–8; Mic. 4:1–2; Zech. 2:11; Mal. 1:11). (4) Yahweh will create a new humanity with "circumcised hearts," made to walk in his ways (Deut. 30:1–6; Jer. 31:33; Ezek. 11:18–20; 37:26–28). (5) And all this means that when the new exodus fully commences, it will be irreversible; never again will the people of God "return to Egypt!"

In sum, the new exodus is not a repeat of the original exodus, or some copied pattern, but a *completion* of the original exodus, a permanent, eschatological realization of its goals: Yahweh's special people, including gentiles, planted in a new creation that serves as Yahweh's cosmic temple.

With the historic return from exile there is a near-horizon fulfillment of these visions (Ezra 1:2–3). The temple is even rebuilt with the silver and gold of Babylon (Ezra 1:6–7; 7:11–20). But it is not a thorough fulfillment (cf. Neh. 9:36), and so Malachi hopes for a truly eschatological "road/way" to a new temple (Mal. 3:1–4). Second Temple Jewish authors showed the same reflection and hope (1 Macc. 8:18; 14:26; Tob. 13:4–5, 15; Bar. 5:6; Sir. 36:10–11; Jub. 17:3; 22:14; 32:19; 1 En. 5:7; 28:1; 29:1; Pss. Sol. 17:27; 1QS 9.16–21; Josephus, *Ant.* 11.75; 20.97–99; *J.W.* 2.258–63). All this sets the stage for extraordinarily thick exodus imagery in the NT.

The First Eschatological Horizons

Throughout the NT the language, themes, and emphases of the original exodus and the prophetic new exodus are employed to describe Jesus's life, death, and resurrection, the origins of the church, the Christian experience, and the eternal state.

Matthew and Mark. In Matt. 2, Jesus's birth parallels the circumstances surrounding Moses's birth (Exod. 1–2). On the OT eschatological timetable, such a parallel forecasts the great end-time new exodus led by this new Moses. This is prophetically validated when Matt. 2:15 announces the "fulfillment" of Hosea 11:1, "Out of Egypt I have called my son," when Jesus escapes Herod "by night." Subsequently, John the Baptist preaches "in the wilderness" to prepare the Isaianic "way of the Lord" (Matt. 3:3; cf. Isa. 40:3; cf. also Matt. 11:10) that will reform Israel in a new exodus at the end of the exile (Piotrowski). This becomes further evident when, in his first recorded actions, Jesus recapitulates the exodus in Matt. 3–7 (Kennedy). Just as Israel was called Yahweh's son, passed through the waters into the desert, and went up onto the mountain to receive the Decalogue, so too Jesus passes through the waters of baptism, where God declares him to be his Son (3:16–17), immediately enters into the wilderness to be tempted for forty days (4:1–11), and proceeds up a mountain to teach on the law (5:1, 17–48). In short, Matthew demonstrates how Jesus is the true Son of God, commencing his eschatological exodus—fulfilling the expectations and responsibilities laid out by the prophets.

Jesus's teaching and miracles then demonstrate that his followers comprise the eschatological Israel with him in the new exodus. He teaches them to call God their "Father" (Matt. 5:16, 48; 6:1, 4, 6, 8, 14, 18, 26, 32; 7:11; 10:20, 29; 13:43; 18:14; 23:9; 28:19) and that they too are "sons" (Matt. 5:9, 45; 13:38). Equally, the Lord's Prayer includes a plea for ongoing sustenance within, and advancement of, the new exodus: the cry that the Father's name would be hallowed (6:9) comes from the new-exodus language of Ezek. 36:23, and the prayer for "our daily bread" (6:11) recalls the original exodus (Exod. 16:4; Ps. 78:25). The feeding of the five thousand in Matt. 14:13–21 clearly echoes the feeding with manna in Exod. 16, refracted through Ezek. 34:11–16, 23–24. Jesus's description of his death as a "ransom for many" (20:28) is resonant of Exod. 6:6 and Isa. 53:12. Matthew also emphasizes that Jesus's Last Supper (26:17–30) is a Passover meal (v. 19), thereby filling in the theological implications of his impending death: he is the eschatological lamb who will die to forgive the "sins" of "many" (26:28; cf. Exod. 12:1–3; Isa. 53:12). By eating this covenant meal (cf. Exod. 24:8–11), the new "twelve" become the eschatological priesthood to the nations (cf. Matt. 28:18–20).

Mark has some similar dynamics. But unique to the Second Gospel is the opening combined quotation of Exod. 23:20, Isa. 40:3, and Mal. 3:1, each of which uses exodus/new-exodus language of Yahweh bringing his people to his sacred dwelling. The composite quotation, therefore, creates new-exodus expectations and prepares the reader to hear even faint echoes of the exodus throughout (Watts). Jesus is called God's Son (Mark 1:11; cf. Exod. 4:22) and enters the wilderness (1:12–13; cf. Exod. 13:18). The setting is constantly "along the sea" in the first half of the Gospel (1:16; 2:13; 3:7; 4:1; cf. Exod. 14:9) and then "on the way" in the second half (8:27; 9:33–34; 10:32, 46, 52; 11:8; cf. Exod. 13:17–22; 23:20). Jesus stretches out his hand (1:41; cf. Exod. 8:6, 17; 10:22; 14:21, 27), calls a paralytic a "son" and forgives his sins (2:5; cf. Exod. 4:22; 34:6–7), and finally heals him "so that you may know" the glory of God (2:10, 12; cf. Exod. 6:7; 8:10, 22; 9:14, 29; 14:4, 18; etc.). Jesus goes up onto a mountain and calls the twelve (3:13–14; cf. Exod. 24:4), and after saving them from the waters (4:35–41) he sends demons into a herd of pigs that rush into the sea and drown (5:13; cf. Exod. 14:23, 28; 15:4–5, 19). Jesus "sees" his disciples "about the fourth watch" and means to "pass by them" (6:48; cf. Exod. 14:24; 33:22; 34:6) before declaring "I am" (6:50 AT; cf. Exod. 3:14). Jesus predicts his resurrection "after three days" (8:31; 9:31; 10:34; cf. Exod. 3:18; 5:3) before giving his life as a "ransom/redemption" (10:45; 14:24; cf. Exod. 6:6). Any of these terms by themselves would not create a legitimate intertext with the exodus tradition, but collectively within the exodus/new-exodus frame selected by the Exodus-Isaiah-Malachi quotation in 1:2–3 they are powerful reverberations.

Equally, much of the language of the Isaianic new exodus (Isa. 40–55) also pervades Mark: at "a desolate place . . . they all ate" (6:32, 44 ESV; cf. Isa. 49:8–10); "he came to them walking on the sea" (6:48–49 ESV; cf. Isa. 43:16); "I am" (6:50 AT; cf. Isa. 41:4; 43:10–11, 25); "to serve, and to give his life as a ransom for many" (10:43, 45; cf. Isa. 52:13, 15; 53:11–12); "my blood of the covenant, which is poured out for many" (14:24; cf. Isa. 52:15; 53:12); "Pilate was amazed" (*thaumazein*; 15:5; cf. LXX Isa. 52:15). With the thorough exodus expectation and accompanying echoes, Mark reads as the fulfillment of Isaiah's long-awaited new exodus hopes.

Luke-Acts. Luke also explains Jesus's birth in new exodus tones: God has "remembered" his promises to Abraham (1:54–55, 72–73; cf. Exod. 2:24), and "visited" (1:68, 78; 7:16; 19:44; cf. Exod. 4:31) and "redeemed" his people (1:68; 2:38; 24:21; cf. Exod. 6:6; 13:15; 15:13). Uniquely though, Luke calls Jesus's death and resurrection his *exodon* (9:31; cf. LXX Exod. 19:1; Num. 33:38; 3 Kgdms. 6:1; Ps. 104:38; cf. also Luke 24:50) in which Jesus releases his people from the reign of sin and Satan (Garrett). As with the first exodus, and foreseen in the prophets, this new exodus climaxes in the creation of the eschatological dwelling place of God as Jesus's followers are filled with the Spirit throughout Acts (Beale; cf. also 1 Cor. 3:17; 2 Cor. 6:16; Eph. 2:19–22; 1 Pet. 2:4–5). Stephen's speech confirms this in Acts 7:7—Israel was brought out to worship "in this place," and now Acts 7 is the hinge for the Spirit of God to cover the earth.

Structurally speaking, new-exodus Isaianic quotations are used at determinative moments in Luke-Acts (Pao, 70–110).

- Isa. 40:3–5 in Luke 3:4–6
- Isa. 42:7; 52:7; 58:6d; 61:1–2 in Luke 4:17–19
- Isa. 42:1; 43:9–12; 49:6 in Luke 24:47 and Acts 1:8
- Isa. 53:7–8 in Acts 8:28–33
- Isa. 55:3 and 49:6 in Acts 13:34, 46–47
- Isa. 6:9–10 in Acts 28:26–27

This has the effect of presenting the entire narrative of Luke-Acts as a fulfillment of Isaiah's new-exodus expectations. Believers are now those on "the Way" with the Lord (Pao, 51–69; Acts 9:2; 19:9, 23; 22:4; 24:14, 22). In all, "Acts cannot be properly understood apart from the wider context of the Isaianic New Exodus" (Pao, 19).

John. John's Gospel brings together creation themes (1:1–5) with those of the exodus (1:14–18) and new exodus (1:23; cf. Isa. 40:3). Whereas Moses was forbidden from seeing God's glory (Exod. 33:18–20), John says he and the apostles "have seen his glory" as God has "made his dwelling among us" (1:14). Moreover, John the Baptist calls Jesus "the Lamb of God, who takes away the sin of the world" (1:29; cf. v. 36), placing his death on the same theological trajectory as the original Passover, only now reaching to provide atonement for the nations as well (10:15–16; 11:51–52; cf. Isa. 53:7–12). To reinforce this John continually emphasizes how Jesus's death corresponds to the celebration of Passover (12:1; 13:1; 19:14), with his body being treated as the original Passover lamb was (19:29–38; cf. Exod. 12:10, 22, 46; Num. 9:12).

In the Fourth Gospel Jesus's miracles are inversely parallel to the plagues of Egypt. In the exodus the signs spelled death for the Egyptians; now Jesus's signs are sources of life. Jesus's "first sign" (2:11 AT) turns water into wine, and his "second sign" (4:54) raises a "son" from the brink of death. In John 6, the feeding of the five thousand occurs on a mountain (v. 3) at the time of Passover (v. 4), a clear parallel to the feeding in the wilderness (vv. 30–33; cf. also esp. Ezek. 34:11–14). Jesus gathers up the eschatological Israel (cf. John 6:12–13), and the people conclude he is "the Prophet" like Moses (v. 14). John also stands out for how Jesus draws upon the divine name in Exod. 3:14; 6:2 in his many "I am" statements (6:20, 35; 8:12, 58; 10:7, 11; 11:25; 14:6; 15:1; cf. also Isa. 41:4; 43:15), showing he is not merely like Moses, but he is Yahweh himself among his sojourning people.

Thus, the Gospels and Acts present Jesus as leading the eschatological new exodus, as the new Moses and Passover lamb, and even as Yahweh himself with his people "on the way."

The Epistles. In the Epistles the language of the exodus is taken up to describe the Christian life. In Rom. 8:14–30 (AT) the exodus becomes the story for the all the people of God, all of creation, and even God himself (Keesmaat). Specifically, sin is akin to Israel's captivity under Pharaoh, but Christians are no longer in such "bondage" (v. 15; cf. Exod. 6:6; 13:13–14; 20:2) because they are "led by the Spirit" as "sons of God" (v. 14; cf. Exod. 6:6; 15:13; Deut. 32:5–6, 12, 18–20; Isa. 63:11–14; Jer. 31:9) who are being conformed to the image of Christ the "firstborn" son (v. 29), and therefore "heirs" with Christ (v. 17). Through this sonship the creation will also be "set free from its bondage" (vv. 19–21) and "groaning" (v. 22; cf. Exod. 2:23–24; 6:5), which God himself also endures (8:23, 26)! This collection of exodus terms demonstrates that to Paul the prophets' new exodus is fulfilled in liberation from the bondage to sin and coming into an inheritance in the new creation (cf. also Rom. 6:6–7, 12–14; Gal. 3:23–4:11; 5:1; Col. 1:11–14).

Paul also sees the experiences of the exodus/wilderness generation as "types" (*typoi*) of the Christian life that help believers understand "temptations" they face (1 Cor. 10:1, 6, 11, 13). As participants of the new covenant, however, believers have hearts written on by the Spirit (2 Cor. 3:1–6). And the Lord's Supper amounts to the eschatological expression of the Passover. "For Christ, our Passover Lamb, has been sacrificed" (1 Cor. 5:7) and Christians now eat "in remembrance" of Jesus (1 Cor. 11:24–25; cf. Exod. 12:14; 13:3).

First Peter also teaches Christians to understand themselves as being in the midst of the eschatological exodus. They have been "redeemed" by "the precious blood of Christ, a lamb without blemish or defect" (1 Pet. 1:18–19; cf. 2:22–24; Exod. 6:6; 12:5; Isa. 53; Rev. 5:6, 9) "in these last times" (1 Pet. 1:20). Indeed, it is the efficacious voice / word / good news of the Isaianic new exodus that has created the community of believers (1 Pet. 1:23–25; cf. Isa. 40:6–9). Now they comprise God's "chosen people, a royal priesthood, a holy nation, God's special possession" (1 Pet. 2:9; cf. Exod. 19:5–6; Isa. 43:18–21), and are given the exodus names once stripped in the exile (1 Pet. 2:10; cf. Hosea 1:6, 9; 2:23).

In sum, the Christian life is one of "faith," contrary to the wilderness generation, who could not enter God's "rest" (Heb. 3:7–4:3; cf. also Jude 5). But the land is a typological figure of heaven itself (Heb. 4:4–8). Christians are therefore exhorted—and called to exhort one another—to see through the deceits of sin and endure with believing hearts to the end (3:12–14). Only so will they receive the ultimate and eternal "rest" of God (4:9–11) that the land had intimated (4:8). All the same, this Christian sojourn is not like the original coming to Sinai (12:18–21) but rather a participation in "the church of the firstborn" at the foot of "Mount Zion, . . . the city of the living God, the heavenly Jerusalem" (12:22–23).

The Final Eschatological Horizon

Revelation also reverberates with several exodus themes to explain the Christian life, especially amid persecutions. God provides believers with "two wings of a great eagle" to escape into the wilderness (Rev. 12:14; cf. Exod. 19:4), as they serve as God's "kingdom and priests" (Rev. 1:5–6; 5:9–10).

And Revelation tells of the dawning of the eternal state, the new creation, as the final and complete eschatological exodus. Lightning, thunder, trumpets, earthquakes, and fire of the Mount Sinai theophany (Exod. 19:16–20) are used to describe visions of God (Rev. 4:5–6; cf. also Exod. 24:10, 17), especially the return of Jesus Christ, who now "reigns for ever and ever" (11:15–19; 16:15–21; cf. also esp. Exod. 15:18). Each of these involve theophanic judgment on those oppressing God's people and in turn create the eternal worshiping community. Revelation 15:3 even says they "sang the song of God's servant Moses and of the Lamb" (cf. Exod. 15:1; Isa. 42:10–13; 54:1; 55:12) in view of the judgment of exodus-like plagues (Rev. 15:1; 16:1–14).

Finally, the last barrier between Egypt and coming to the mountain of Yahweh was the Red Sea. In full eschatological realization John sees "a new heaven and a new earth" where "there was no longer any sea" (Rev. 21:1). This is likely not a statement on the absence of vast bodies of water in "God's dwelling place . . . now among people" (21:3), but the final divide between this world where Satan had been "deceiving the nations" (20:3, 8) and the eternal land of promise (Mathewson; cf. esp. Isa. 43:16–21; 51:9–11). The Creator's victory over the sea is the prelude to his divine presence and the indestructible covenant reality wherein "they will be his people, and God himself will be with them and be their God" (Rev. 21:3).

Conclusion

The use of exodus imagery across the Bible does not simply serve an aesthetic function, nor capitalize on mnemonic devices, but reveals the historic exodus as a local typological event adumbrating the final cosmic-wide dwelling of the presence of God. Fulfillment to that end is like a rolling horizon. As the Bible progresses, the horizon expands before the reader: the place of worship to which the exodus leads is first Mount Sinai, then the tabernacle, then the land, then the temple on Mount Zion, then forecasted into the future by Israel's prophets. Finally, Jesus's ministry comprises the new exodus that is then experienced by his church, the eschatological temple, in anticipation of "the new heavens and the new earth."

Moreover, the exodus sketches an outline of the gospel: Israel is brought out of bondage from death to life through a sacrifice and made into a worshiping community that is called to trust Yahweh in the desert, all in expectation of a new world. So too, Christians are delivered from their slavery to sin and made alive by Jesus's self-sacrifice and resurrection, now to worship and trust/believe him as they live in the already/not-yet new creation. Thus, the eschatological new exodus has happened in Jesus's ministry, is happening in the experience of Christians, and will happen at the end of the age.

See also Covenant; Exile and Restoration; Law

Bibliography. Alexander, T. D., *From Paradise to the Promised Land*, 4th ed. (Baker Academic, 2022); Beale, G. K., "The Descent of the Eschatological Temple in the Form of the Spirit at Pentecost: Part 1," *TynBul* 56 (2005): 73–102; Ceresko, A. R., "The Rhetorical Strategy of the Fourth Servant Song (Isaiah 52:13–53:12)," *CBQ* 56 (1994): 42–55; Currid, J. D., *Ancient Egypt and the Old Testament* (Baker, 1997); Ehorn, S., ed., *Exodus in the New Testament*, LNTS 663 (Bloomsbury T&T Clark, 2022); Estelle, B. D., *Echoes of Exodus* (IVP Academic, 2018); Fishbane, M., "The 'Exodus' Motif/The Paradigm of Historical Renewal," in *Biblical Text and Texture* (OneWorld, 1998), 121–40; Fox, M. R., ed., *Reverberations of the Exodus in Scripture* (Pickwick, 2014); Frisch, A., "The Exodus Motif in 1 Kings 1–14," *JSOT* 87 (2000): 3–21; Garrett, S. R., "Exodus from Bondage," *CBQ* 52 (1990): 656–80; Holland, T., *Contours of Pauline Theology* (Mentor, 2004); Idestrom, R. G. S., "Echoes of the Book of Exodus in Ezekiel," *JSOT* 33 (2009): 489–510; Keesmaat, S. C., "Exodus and the Intertextual Transformation of Tradition in Romans 8.14–30," *JSNT* 54 (1994): 29–56; Kennedy, J., *The Recapitulation of Israel*, WUNT 2/257 (Mohr Siebeck, 2008); Mathewson D., "New Exodus as a Background for 'The Sea Was No More' in Revelation 21:1c," *TJ* 24 (2003): 243–58; Morales, L. M., *The Tabernacle Pre-figured*, BTS 15 (Peeters, 2012); Morales, *Exodus Old and New*, ESBT (InterVarsity, 2020); Ninow, F., *Indicators of Typology within the Old Testament* (Peter Lang, 2001); Pao, D. W., *Acts and the Isaianic New Exodus*, WUNT 2/130 (Mohr Siebeck, 2000); Piotrowski, N. G., *Matthew's New David at the End of Exile*, NovTSup 170 (Brill, 2016); Smith, D. L., "The Use of 'New Exodus' in New Testament Scholarship," *CBR* 14 (2016): 207–43; Talmon, S., "The Desert Motif in the Bible and Qumran Literature," in *Literary Studies in the Hebrew Bible* (Magnes, 1993), 216–54; Watts, R. E., *Isaiah's New Exodus in Mark*, WUNT 2/88 (Mohr Siebeck, 1997).

NICHOLAS G. PIOTROWSKI

Ezekiel, Book of

Ezekiel and Jeremiah were contemporaries, with Ezekiel's prophetic ministry coming slightly later in history, overlapping the second half of Jeremiah's. The theological context and the message of both prophets are

Table 1. Outline of Ezekiel

I. Loss of Yahweh's presence, and judgment on Jerusalem (1:1–24:27)
  A. The glory of Yahweh and the call of Ezekiel (1:1–3:27)
  B. Object lessons of judgment (4:1–7:27)
  C. The glory of Yahweh leaves the temple of Jerusalem (8:1–11:25)
  D. The exile dramatized (12:1–28)
  E. Ezekiel condemns the false prophets (13:1–23)
  F. Judgment on Jerusalem announced (14:1–16:63)
  G. Judgment on Jerusalem arrives (17:1–24:27)
II. Judgment on the nations (25:1–32:32)
III. God's restored presence and the new temple (33:1–48:35)
  A. From judgment to hope: Yahweh the shepherd will cleanse them and give them a new heart (33:1–36:38)
  B. Yahweh gives new life to those who are profoundly dead (37:1–28)
  C. A future invasion, but the enemy is defeated (38:1–39:29)
  D. The glorious new temple and the restored presence of Yahweh (40:1–48:35)

similar in many regards, even if they were in two very different locations. The young priest Ezekiel was one of the ten thousand Judahites taken into exile by the Babylonians in 597 BC, after King Jehoiachin surrendered. Thus, he was in Babylonian exile when God called him to be a prophet. Part of Ezekiel's message was delivered in the years leading up to the fall and destruction of Jerusalem in 587 or 586 BC (in between the two exiles), but part of his message was delivered after the fall and destruction of Jerusalem (including the temple) and in light of that devastating event.

The Structure and Message of Ezekiel

The overall message of Ezekiel parallels that proclaimed by several other prophets and epitomized by Jeremiah: (1) You (Judah) have broken the covenant Yahweh made with you at Sinai (defined by Exodus–Deuteronomy); you need to repent and turn back to Yahweh. (2) Since there is no repentance, judgment is coming, both on Judah and on the surrounding nations. (3) Yet there is hope beyond the judgment for a glorious, future restoration brought by Yahweh and his Davidic king. Intertwined throughout this message in Ezekiel are the interrelated central themes of Yahweh's presence, Yahweh's power, and Yahweh's glory. The book can be outlined as seen in table 1 (from Hays and Duvall, 358–60; Hays, 200–201).

The Use of the Torah, the Former and Latter Prophets, and Psalms in Ezekiel: An Overview

Since the book of Ezekiel was written toward the end of the canonical OT, it is no surprise that the book makes use of a wide range of earlier materials (as well as contemporary material such as Jeremiah). Ezekiel makes reference to people, events, places, practices, structures, conversations, theological statements, phrases, themes, imagery, and various other aspects from all five books of the Torah (especially Exodus, Leviticus, and Deuteronomy), the former prophets 1–2 Samuel and especially 1–2 Kings, and the Latter Prophets Isaiah, Amos, Hosea, Zephaniah, and especially Jeremiah (Kutsko, 10–14; Kohn, 94–95, 103–4; Carley, 13–81; Gile, 1–16, 214–20; Zimmerli, 1:41–52). On the other hand, Ezekiel never mentions by name any of these sources (Zimmerli, 1:45–46). His use of Psalms is limited but still evident.

Although Ezekiel does contain at least one lengthy direct quotation (Zeph. 1:18, quoted in Ezek. 7:19) and dozens of very close phrase citations, most of his intertextual usage falls into the category of allusion or thematic reuse, often with an emphatic expansion, usually reflective of the current theological situation in which Ezekiel lives. For example, probably building on the Deuteronomic concept of covenant, Hosea presents Israel as the unfaithful, harlot-like wife of Yahweh (Hosea 1:2; 2:4–15). Jeremiah employs this theme as well (Jer. 2:1–3:5) but then also expands it into an Israel/Judah "two-sisters" concept of unfaithfulness (3:6–25). Ezekiel takes this imagery and expands it even further through two very long chapters (Ezek. 16, 23), even adding a third sister, Sodom (16:46–58; Carley, 55).

The point of an allusion or reference often lies in the similarity between the two texts or sometimes just in the reality of the referent text. Yet sometimes the point seems to lie in the differences or in the expansions. For example, in Jeremiah, as part of the promised new covenant relationship, Yahweh promises to put his *torah* within them (31:33), while in Ezekiel he promises to put his *Spirit* within them (36:27), stressing the empowerment of his very presence.

Likewise, the call of Ezekiel in chap. 1 has allusions to the call of Isaiah in Isa. 6, but the point may lie in Ezek. 1's stark differences: the change in location (exile in Babylonia, stressing the mobility of Yahweh), the fiery windstorm (connecting to the exodus story), and the frequency of the term *rûaḥ* (spirit) (Duvall and Hays, 135; Zimmerli, 1:108–10).

In addition, the issue of literary intertextuality in Ezekiel is complicated by the fact that just about every text in Ezekiel is either part of a vision that Yahweh gives to him (1:1–3:15; 8:1–11:25; 40:1–49) or direct speech from Yahweh himself. Indeed, the majority of the chapters in Ezekiel begin with "The word of Yahweh came to me," followed by direct discourse from Yahweh. So, the prophet Ezekiel is not simply using earlier literary works to create a new document; rather, Yahweh is speaking to him and through him to Judah on the basis of Yahweh's earlier history with them (as recorded in the earlier documents). As Ezekiel seeks to understand and record what Yahweh has revealed to him, no doubt he is reliant on this earlier (and contemporary, like Jeremiah) material for his understanding, his phraseology, even much of his basic theological terminology (see the discussion of the similar situation for John, the author of Revelation, in Beale and McDonough, 1084–85). No doubt Ezekiel assumes that his audience is likewise familiar with the earlier sources as well, will hear his message in that context, and will recognize his intended allusion-based connections to those texts.

The Use of the Torah, the Former and Latter Prophets, and Psalms in Ezekiel: Examples

Many of the numerous allusions and references in Ezekiel can be grouped into several central, often interrelated topics: the exodus, the presence of Yahweh and the temple/tabernacle, and shepherds and the new covenant. This section will discuss each of these topics before giving a brief list of other miscellaneous intertextual usages.

The exodus. The exodus event, the central paradigm for deliverance in the OT, lies at the heart of Yahweh's relationship with Israel/Judah, and it is thus no surprise that references and allusions to the exodus are frequent in Ezekiel. One of the central aspects of the exodus is that it included both well-deserved judgment (on the Egyptians) and gracious deliverance (for the Israelites). Ezekiel picks up on both aspects, paralleling the upcoming actions of Yahweh with his past actions in the exodus, actions by which he judged his enemies and saved his people. One of the most noticeable connections is the phrase "Then you/they will know that I am Yahweh." This phrase occurs frequently throughout Exodus (e.g., 6:7; 7:5, 17; 8:22; 10:2 AT). The message in Exodus conveyed by this phrase is that everyone will eventually know who Yahweh is by the actions he carries out, either in terrible judgment (Pharaoh and the Egyptians) or in spectacular deliverance (Israel and those who go out with Israel). John F. Evans (1, 8) notes that this phrase and similar variations occur over seventy times in Ezekiel. The citation of this phrase in Ezekiel is analogous to its usage in Exodus. As in the time of the exodus, Yahweh is now bringing about a second great central event of deliverance, and everyone will know/experience Yahweh through these actions, either as the great deliverer or the great judge/destroyer of his enemies.

In the book of Ezekiel the exodus event not only is viewed as one of the most critical aspects of Israel's past history and her relationship with Yahweh, reflecting the very character of Yahweh, but also provides the paradigm for her future. Ezekiel 20, in particular, uses the exodus event in this manner. Ezekiel 20:1–29 recounts the various phases of the historical exodus while stressing the disobedience of Israel in the wilderness (in contrast to Yahweh's continual gracious provision). Then, in 20:30–44—still using the exodus motif as a paradigm—Ezekiel moves to the future, describing another time in the wilderness (the exile) followed by a new exodus in which Yahweh brings the people into the new promised land (Block, 1:52–55; Zimmerli, 1:41, 63). The new-exodus theme, in which Yahweh will regather the scattered exiles and bring them back to the land, echoes throughout Ezek. 11–37 (Block, 1:55–56). Ezekiel alludes to the exodus event not just as a pattern or paradigm for deliverance but also as an indication of the scale or significance of the upcoming deliverance. The exodus was not just one deliverance event among many; it is *the* deliverance event in their history. Ezekiel's allusions to the exodus and his new-exodus theme imply that the coming deliverance is parallel not just in character but also in scale and significance.

The presence of Yahweh and the temple/tabernacle. The presence of Yahweh living in the midst of Israel is one of the central themes in Ezekiel. In Ezek. 1 the prophet encounters the mobile presence of Yahweh while in exile. In Ezek. 8–11, in response to Judah's obstinate and continued idolatry, Yahweh, who has been residing in the temple since 1 Kings 8:10–11 (as he had previously been residing in the tabernacle since Exod. 40:34), departs from the temple to abandon Judah and Jerusalem to their enemies in judgment. Then, in Ezek. 43:1–5, in the culmination of the restoration, the glory of Yahweh (i.e., his presence) returns to the new temple (described in Ezek. 40–48). The final words of the book of Ezekiel are "And the name of the city from that time on will be: THE LORD IS THERE" (48:35). This presentation in Ezekiel of Yahweh and his relationship to the temple pulls from dozens of texts and images in earlier material, including the fiery descent of Yahweh to Mount Sinai (Exod. 19), the instructions for building the tabernacle and the descent of Yahweh into the tabernacle (Exod. 25–31; 33–40), the presence of Yahweh in Israel's midst as the central blessing of the exodus and the covenant (e.g., Exod. 29:45–46), and the construction of the temple and the occupation of the temple by Yahweh (1 Kings 6–8). The allusion to the theme of Yahweh's presence, especially in the exodus and in covenant-making contexts, again is used analogously and paradigmatically. The exodus is the central deliverance event in Israel's history, accompanied by the establishment of the covenant at Sinai. At the heart of that deliverance and the covenant was the presence of Yahweh. Ezekiel is stressing that a new deliverance and covenant establishment by Yahweh is coming and that it will match—even surpass—the exodus event and covenant.

Likewise, the description of the new temple in Ezek. 40–48 is replete with imagery from the Torah, especially Leviticus. The terminology "before Yahweh," used over sixty times in Leviticus in regard to worshiping in the presence of Yahweh, is likewise frequent throughout Ezekiel (in various related forms), especially Ezek. 43–48. Once again, Ezekiel depicts the coming reestablished presence of Yahweh and the coming new relationship he will have with his people as analogous to that previously seen in the Torah.

Numerous other texts are alluded to as well. Ezekiel 47 describes a life-giving river flowing out of the temple (where the presence of Yahweh resides) down to the Dead Sea. This carries strong allusions to the river that waters the garden of Eden in Gen. 2:10–14 (cf. also Ps. 46:4), suggesting a final return to the Edenic situation of life in the garden blessed by the presence of Yahweh (Duvall and Hays, 147; Clements, 71–72, 107; Zimmerli, 2:510–11). Finally, the division of the land into the old tribal allotments in Ezek. 48 certainly parallels the allotment of the land back in Josh. 13–19. As above, here we see that the coming deliverance and reestablishment of Yahweh's presence in the book of Ezekiel are portrayed as analogous to earlier positive and central events in Israel's history. Yet Ezekiel often pushes beyond the parallels, indicating that the coming deliverance will be even more spectacular than the old one.

Shepherd imagery and the coming (new) covenant. In a climactic culmination of OT eschatological hope, Ezek. 34, along with 37:24–28, uses extensive shepherd imagery to depict how Yahweh will restore/regather his people and reestablish his covenant with them. These two passages pull together themes, motifs, images, and promises from across the OT, especially from Genesis, Leviticus, Numbers, 2 Samuel, 1 Kings, Isaiah, Jeremiah, Hosea, Micah, and Psalms (Block, 2:285–306; Zimmerli, 2:213–21).

In an extended analogy in which Israel / the people of God are compared to sheep, Yahweh pronounces judgment on the current "bad shepherds" (current leaders) of Israel (Ezek. 34:1–10) and then declares that he himself will now shepherd the flock, regathering them and establishing justice (34:11–22). He then shifts from referring to himself as the shepherd to referring to David his servant as the shepherd (34:23–31), concluding with a description of the coming covenant of peace, which is characterized with the traditional tripartite formula of relationship (I will be your God; you will be my people; I will dwell in your midst / be among you / be with you).

While the shepherd imagery in Ezek. 34 echoes a number of texts (Gen. 48:15; Num. 27:17; 1 Kings 22:17; Ps. 23; Mic. 2:12; 4:6–8), the primary background for much of it is Jer. 23:1–8 (Zimmerli, 2:45). In Jer. 23 the destructive current leaders are compared to bad shepherds. Yahweh then declares that he himself will regather the scattered flock and that a Davidic king will rule justly and righteously. Ezekiel 34 utilizes this same imagery but expands it by incorporating other covenant-related concepts drawn from other texts as well (Lev. 26; Isa. 54; Jer. 31).

The shepherd imagery of Yahweh's Davidic king regathering his people culminates in a discussion of a new reestablished covenant relationship, the "covenant of peace" (34:25–31; 36:24–38), in which Yahweh will pour out his Spirit on his people, underscoring the tripartite relationship (I will be your God; you will be my people; I will dwell in your midst). In these passages Ezekiel appears to be expanding on the new covenant of Jer. 31:31–33 as well as other associated texts in Jeremiah, such as 32:37–41. Indeed, Gerhard von Rad (235) comments, "There are striking parallels with Jer. XXXI.31ff.; one feels that Ezekiel must somehow have had Jeremiah's prophecies in front of him." Yet note Ezekiel's primary expansion. While in Jer. 31:33 the tripartite formula is "I will put my *law* [*torah*] in their minds [midst] and write it on their hearts. I will be their God, and they will be my people," Ezek. 36:27–28 reads, "I will put my *Spirit* in you. . . . You will be my people, and I will be your God" (Duvall and Hays, 141–44; Block, 2:356–57).

The "covenant of peace" (Ezek. 34:25) also probably alludes to Isa. 54:10 ("Yet my unfailing love for you will not be shaken nor my covenant of peace be removed"). There are also numerous linguistic and theological connections between Ezek. 34:25–30 and Lev. 26:4–13. One highly significant difference, however, is that in contrast to the conditional nature of Lev. 26:4–13, Ezek. 34:25–30 drops all aspects of conditionality. There are no human preconditions or calls to repentance prior to Yahweh's spectacular fulfillment of the prophecy (Block, 2:303–5).

Ezekiel uses the phrase "covenant of peace" to refer to the messianic age, a time that includes peace from the wild animals (34:25). This suggests an allusion to Isa. 11:6–9. The inclusion of a restoration of crops, trees, and other vegetation (34:27, 29), however, suggests a more likely connection to Hosea 2:21–23. Daniel Block (2:307) notes that these two aspects, famine and wild animals, apparently serve to represent the entire range of possible disasters and judgments.

Ezekiel 36:24 describes a new exodus. In that context, the material that follows in 36:25–28 (and note that 36:26 is almost an exact quotation of 11:19) is probably alluding to Deut. 30:6–8: "The LORD your God will circumcise your hearts and the hearts of your descendants, so that you may love him with all your heart and with all your soul, and live" (Block, 2:354).

Other intertextual uses: A brief selected list. There are numerous other intertextual usages throughout Ezekiel. For example, in Ezek. 1 the prophet sees the mobile throne of Yahweh accompanied by four rather bizarre creatures. Here Ezekiel seems to struggle to describe them, referring to them vaguely as "living creatures." However, when Ezekiel sees these same creatures at the temple in Jerusalem, he clearly identifies them as cherubim (Ezek. 10:15), probably because of his familiarity with cherubim associated with the tabernacle (Exod. 25:18–26:31; 36:8–37:9) and the temple (1 Kings 6:23–8:7).

Note also the similarity between Ezek. 3:3 ("'Son of man, eat this scroll I am giving you and fill your stomach with it.' So I ate it, and it tasted as sweet as honey in my mouth") and Jer. 15:16 ("When your words came, I ate them; they were my joy and my heart's delight") (Zimmerli, 1:44–45). Ellen F. Davis (50–51) suggests that in both cases the point is to connect the spoken word with the written word. When Ezekiel eats the word of Yahweh, it is already in written form, underscoring the importance of the written word for Ezekiel, as was also evident in the prophecies of Jeremiah.

Ezekiel 3 also has several connections to 1–2 Kings. The command from Yahweh in Ezek. 3:4, "Speak my words," uses the root *dbr* twice: as a verb, meaning "to speak," and as a noun, meaning "word." This twofold use of *dbr* shows up similarly three times in 1 Kings 13 (13:17, 18, 32; Zimmerli, 1:43). Likewise, the action of the Spirit on Ezekiel in 3:12–14 (see also 11:24; 43:5) is similar to the reference to the Spirit and Elijah in 2 Kings 2:16. Furthermore, Ezekiel's use of the phrase "The hand of the LORD was on me" in 3:22 (see also 1:3; 3:14) recalls the same usage in the preclassical prophets (2 Kings 3:15).

Ezekiel 7:2 and 7:6 declare, "The end has come." This is probably alluding to Amos 8:2, where the identical phrase occurs ("The time is ripe," NIV) (Raitt, 71). Similarly, Ezek. 7:26 states, "They will go searching [in vain] for a vision from the prophet, priestly instruction in the law will cease, the counsel of the elders will come to an end." This text appears to cite Jer. 18:18, indicating through contrast that what Jeremiah's opponents say has no merit: "The teaching of the law by the priest will not cease, nor will counsel from the wise, nor the word from the prophets."

An interesting feature of Ezek. 8:1, repeated also in 14:1 and 20:1, is that God's vision or revelation came on the prophet "while I was sitting in my house and the elders of Judah were sitting before me." This description does not occur in any of the other literary prophets, but it does occur in almost identical form in 2 Kings 6:32 regarding Elisha (Zimmerli, 1:43).

In Jer. 7 Yahweh instructs Jeremiah to stand at the gate of the temple (7:2) and to pronounce judgment on those coming in through the gates. The people in Jerusalem feel safe to do "these detestable things" (7:10) and then to come into the temple, implying that they think Yahweh cannot see them. Yahweh, however, points out in 7:11 that he does see them (NIV renders the phrase as "I have been watching," but a more literal rendering would read, "I see!"). Yahweh then declares, "I will thrust you from my presence" (7:15). Ezekiel 8 contains numerous parallels, but with graphic expansion. Yahweh takes Ezekiel on a tour of the entire temple, starting with the north gate (8:3). Yahweh refers repeatedly to the terrible idolatrous sins being committed as "detestable things" (8:6, 9, 13, 15, 17). The people are quoted as saying, "The LORD does not see us" (8:12, repeated in 9:9), while the text repeatedly records Yahweh either telling Ezekiel to *see* or asking him, "Do you *see*?" (8:6, 9, 12, 13, 15, 17). The consequences are that these things "will drive me far from my sanctuary" (8:6). Because of this terrible widespread sin right in the temple, Yahweh concludes by saying, "Although they shout in my ears, I will not listen to them" (8:18). This echoes Yahweh's sentiment back in Jer. 11:11, "Although they cry out to me, I will not listen to them."

Ezekiel 12:2 declares, "They have eyes to see but do not see and ears to hear but do not hear, for they are a rebellious people." This description occurs in similar fashion both in Isa. 6:9: "Be ever hearing, but never understanding; be ever seeing, but never perceiving"; and more directly in Jer. 5:21: "you foolish and senseless people, who have eyes but do not see, who have ears but do not hear" (Zimmerli, 1:45).

Ezekiel 13's condemnation of the false prophets is quite similar to Jeremiah's frequent condemnation of this same group (Jer. 6:13–15; 8:10–12; 23:13–24; Rochester, 207). In reference to these false prophets (and other leaders), the verse "They lead my people astray, saying, 'Peace,' when there is no peace" (Ezek. 13:10) bears strong resemblance to Jer. 6:13–14: "Prophets and priests alike, all practice deceit. . . . 'Peace, peace,' they say, when there is no peace" (see also Jer. 8:11). Likewise, Ezek. 14:1–11, dealing with false prophecy and idolatry, is similar in vocabulary and style to Lev. 17 (Block, 1:423–24; Zimmerli, 1:35, 48).

Ezekiel 22:17–22 provides another example of Ezekiel's tendency to expand material. Isaiah 1:22 and 25 briefly mention the imagery of dross removed during the refining of silver as a picture of judgment. Ezekiel develops this image into an entire paragraph (22:17–22) with similar meaning (Zimmerli, 1:32).

Drinking the "cup" as a metaphor for judgment in Ezek. 23:31–34 probably derives from a similar usage in Jer. 25:15–26, but Jeremiah uses it for judgment on the nations, while Ezekiel uses it to represent the past devastation on Samaria, which is now coming on Jerusalem (Zimmerli, 1:45). Also, Ezek. 29–32 makes several references to Jer. 46 in regard to judgment on Egypt (Nevader, 168–72).

Although interpreting allusions in Ezekiel to his contemporary Jeremiah is complicated by issues of compositional chronology, it may be helpful to note that Jeremiah's proclamation of judgment on the Egyptians in Jer. 46 is in the context of their defeat at Carchemish in 605 BC (Jer. 46:2). Ezekiel dates his prophecy to around eighteen years later (587 BC; Ezek. 29:1). Perhaps his allusion to Jer. 46 is drawing an analogous comparison. That is, Ezekiel proclaims that in the near future the Egyptians will be defeated just as certainly as they were at Carchemish back in 605 BC, in the well-known event Jeremiah prophesied about.

Another connection back to 1–2 Kings is in the terminology of Ezek. 33:33, "Then they will know that a prophet has been among them." In 2 Kings 5:8, Elisha sends orders to bring the Syrian Naaman to him, declaring, "And he will know that there is a prophet in Israel" (Zimmerli, 1:43).

Finally, in the description of the new temple in Ezek. 40–48, there is no mention of the ark of the covenant. This is probably in keeping with Ezekiel's emphasis, similar to a theme in Jer. 3:16–17, on the coming reestablishment of Yahweh's presence, which will be in parallel with the presence of God experienced in Israel's past, only with some distinctive differences that portray this new presence and new covenant as superior and even more spectacular.

Use of Ezekiel in the NT

As the book of Ezekiel prophesies the future restoration and return of Yahweh, it interweaves and expands a number of the most significant messianic themes from the OT: the coming righteous, messianic Davidic king; the return of the presence of Yahweh as shepherd and king; a new covenant relationship in which the presence of Yahweh is established by his Spirit, placed within his people; ultimate victory over Yahweh's enemies; and the establishment of a new "temple" where Yahweh's holy presence will dwell forever. The NT presents Jesus Christ as the fulfillment and culmination of these promises. Thus, it is no surprise to see allusions, echoes, and direct references to Ezekiel throughout the NT wherever these themes appear. Among the many references, three clusters stand out: Jesus as the Good Shepherd in John's Gospel (using Ezek. 34), the coming of the Spirit at Pentecost in Acts 2 (using Ezek. 36–37), and the future temple and other imagery (harlot, future battle, etc.) throughout Revelation (using primarily Ezek. 16; 37–48).

When Jesus identifies himself as the Good Shepherd in John 10, he is clearly drawing a connection to Ezekiel's prophecy in Ezek. 34. Note the important messianic implications flowing out of this identification, for in Ezek. 34 the coming Shepherd is depicted both as Yahweh himself and as his servant David. Furthermore, it is this same coming Shepherd who will both restore Yahweh's people and judge his enemies. It is through this coming Shepherd that Yahweh's new covenant of peace will be established, along with a new presence of Yahweh in the midst of his people. Besides John 10, the image of Israel as sheep and of Jesus as the Great Shepherd occurs in numerous other NT passages as well (Matt. 2:6; 9:36; 25:32; 26:31; Luke 15:4; Heb. 13:20; 1 Pet. 2:25). While these passages also sometimes refer directly or indirectly to other OT texts (e.g., Jer. 23:1–4; Mic. 5:4; Zech. 13:7), all of them imply an allusion to Ezek. 34, which contains the most extensive discussion and development of the messianic shepherd in the OT.

The prophecies of the covenant of peace brought by the Great Shepherd (Ezek. 34), the placing of Yahweh's Spirit within his people (Ezek. 36:24–28), and the establishment of the "new covenant" (Jer. 31:31) all relate to the tripartite statement of covenant relationship: I will be your God; you will be my people; I will dwell in your midst (or among you). These three prophecies find fulfillment in Christ and the church in the NT. The new way of experiencing the presence of God in the new covenant relationship ("I will put my Spirit in you") is prophesied in Ezek. 36:24–28 (and in Joel 2) and finds fulfillment in the NT in Acts 2 when the Holy Spirit comes and fills the new people of God. Furthermore, the Spirit, wind, and fire imagery of Acts 2 draws not only from Ezek. 36:24–28 but also from 1:4; 13:13; and 37:1–28.

Finally, Revelation makes extensive use of Ezekiel throughout the book, especially Rev. 20–22. Indeed, Ezekiel is one of the most influential OT books in Revelation. John seems to understand his own identity as similar to Ezekiel's. Many of John's central images draw on images in Ezekiel (e.g., the harlot of Rev. 17; cf. Ezek. 16). Toward the end of Revelation the use of Ezekiel is even more extensive. In fact, "John models his narrative of the final battle, judgment, and new Jerusalem precisely on Ezek. 37–48" (Beale and McDonough, 1082), which has not yet come to fulfillment but surely will. Revelation 20:8, for example, explicitly connects the upcoming battle to the Gog and Magog battle in Ezek. 38–39. With reference to the coming new heavens and new earth, Rev. 21:3 declares, "Look! God's dwelling place is now among the people, and he will dwell with them. They will be his people, and God himself will be with them and be their God." This is a clear connection to and fulfillment of Ezek. 36:24–28; 37:27–28; and 43:7, similarly restating the tripartite covenant formula. Also, as with Ezek. 47, Rev. 22 describes a river flowing from the presence of God, creating a fertile land with trees that bring healing.

Bibliography. Beale, G. K., and S. M. McDonough, "Revelation," in *CNTUOT*, 1081–1161; Block, D. I., *The Book of Ezekiel*, 2 vols., NICOT (Eerdmans, 1997–98); Carley, K. W., *Ezekiel among the Prophets*, SBT 31 (Allenson, 1975); Clements, R. E., *God and Temple* (Fortress, 1965); Davis, E. F., *Swallowing the Scroll*, JSOTSup 78 (Almond, 1989); Duvall, J. S., and J. D. Hays, *God's Relational Presence* (Baker Academic, 2019); Evans, J. F., *You Shall Know That I Am Yahweh*, BBRSup 25 (Eisenbrauns, 2019); Gile, J., *Ezekiel and the World of Deuteronomy*, LHBOTS 703 (T&T Clark, 2021); Hays, J. D., *The Message of the Prophets* (Zondervan, 2010); Hays, J. D., and J. S. Duvall, *The Baker Illustrated Bible Handbook* (Baker Books, 2011); Kohn, R. L., *New Heart and a New Soul*, JSOTSup 358 (Sheffield Academic, 2002); Kutsko, J. F., *Between Heaven and Earth*, BJSUCSD 7 (Eisenbrauns, 2000); Nevader, M., "YHWH and the Kings of Middle Earth," in *Concerning the Nations*, ed. E. K. Holt, H. C. P. Kim, and A. Mein, JSOTSup 612 (Bloomsbury, 2015); Raitt, T. M., *A Theology of Exile* (Fortress, 1977); Rochester, K. M., *Prophetic Ministry in Jeremiah and Ezekiel*, CBET 65 (Peeters, 2012); von Rad, G., *Old Testament Theology*, vol. 2, trans. D. M. G. Stalker, OTL (1962–65; repr., Westminster John Knox, 2001); Zimmerli, W., *Ezekiel*, trans. R. E. Clements, 2 vols., Herm (Fortress, 1979, 1983).

J. DANIEL HAYS

Ezra-Nehemiah, Books of

Ezra was the son of Seraiah, the high priest, and his genealogy goes all the way back to the first high priest, Aaron (Ezra 7:1–5), but Ezra was a scribe, not a high priest. Ezra's father experienced the military conquest of Jerusalem and the burning of the temple and was forcibly exiled to Babylon by Nebuzaradan, the captain of the Babylonian king's guard (2 Kings 26:18), in 587 BC. Ezra was born in Babylon, spent several years training to be a scribe, taught the Torah of Moses (Ezra 7:10), and led a caravan of Israelites back to Jerusalem (Ezra 7:6). He regularly read from the scrolls to the people (Neh. 8; cf. 13:1–5) and was actively involved with the dedication of the wall around Jerusalem. There is no information about his death.

Nehemiah was the son of Hacaliah and the brother of Hanani (Neh. 1:1–2). Nehemiah initially lived in the Persian capital of Susa (Neh. 1:1), where he served as the cupbearer for the Persian king Artaxerxes I (1:11). One part of his ministry involved encouraging people to end the reproach on God's name by rebuilding the wall and gates of Jerusalem (2:17–18). He served as the political governor of Judah for over twelve years (10:1), encouraged people to persevere in spite of opposition (4:14), and enforced the statutes of the covenant agreement (10:28–39; 13:1–31).

Essential Features of Ezra-Nehemiah

Composition. The final form of Ezra-Nehemiah appears to be one unified book produced by a narrator who based it on numerous Jewish historical (Ezra 8:1–14) and temple documents (Ezra 2) plus Aramaic letters from local (Ezra 5:8–16), provincial (Ezra 6:6–12), and national (Ezra 6:1–12) Persian authorities. Some treat these sources as authentic documents that were faithfully preserved and represent what actually happened (Breneman). Others find several different sources that were placed in sequence and edited together by the Chronicler (Cross). Still others view these editorial insertions as expressions of an ideological slant (a utopian perspective, according to Cataldo). Finally, some picture the composition process as involving a continually growing corpus with multiple layers of additions and numerous redactional comments over an extensive period of reflection and growth (Wright; Böhler; Pakkala). Each of these approaches has some supporting evidence, but the more complicated and extended the process is thought to be, the more speculative the theory becomes. The analysis below argues for a unified literary interpretation centered on the theme of the restoration of God's worshiping community based on ancient documents that legitimate the narrator's claims. The first-person "I/we" terminology suggests that the narrator of the story bases his composition on the written memoirs of Ezra and Nehemiah, but there is no way of knowing how faithfully the narrator quotes these sources. Hugh Williamson (xxxiii–xxxv) proposes that Ezra 1–6 was composed last in order to justify and make routine the reforms happening at the Jerusalem temple. Since the Samaritans were establishing separate traditions and building their own temple on Mount Gerizim, and since there were splits among the Jerusalem priesthood, there was a need to overcome the disarray and normalize new values. The remnant's beliefs and culture were built on the traditions of the past, and the Jerusalem community was the legitimate continuation of God's people of the time of the first temple (Clines, 24). The method, purpose, or plan of composition is not explicitly explained anywhere, but structural analysis identifies the smaller subunits of text that fit together to form the completed composition (Ezra 1–6; 7–10; Neh. 1–7; 8–10; 11–13). At some point (as early as 400 BC) these shorter narratives and lists were collected together and published (Williamson, xxxv).

Structure and message. Almost all interpreters recognize that the book of Ezra naturally divides into two parts: (1) God restores the people to Jerusalem and restores worship before the time of Ezra and Nehemiah (Ezra 1–6); (2) Ezra comes with another caravan of people, and he restores the holy seed of Israel by resolving the problem of inappropriate marriages to foreigners who worship other gods (Ezra 7–10). The third literary unit (Neh. 1–7) primarily describes the need for the people to persevere through the troubles associated with restoring Jerusalem's wall, but many interpreters place Neh. 5 after Neh. 13 because it is not about the restoration of the wall (Throntveit, 122). There is widespread confusion and disagreement over the structure of Neh. 8–13, because chaps. 8–10 appear to come from the Ezra Memoirs. To alleviate some of these problems, it seems best to make Neh. 8–10 a separate, almost parenthetical, segment concerning the confession of sins and covenant renewal. The final section (Neh. 11–13) picks up the theme of increasing the number of people living in Jerusalem from Neh. 7 and the dedication of the wall from Neh. 6, but this segment ends with a very anticlimactic condemnation of the Israelites in Neh. 13 because they are unfaithful to the earlier covenant commitments made in Neh. 10:28–39. The consistent theological theme throughout these paragraphs is that God has been providentially guiding the Israelite leaders Zerubbabel, Ezra, Nehemiah, Haggai, and Zechariah (Ezra 5:1; 7:6, 9; Neh. 2:8, 20; 7:5; cf. 13:14, 22, 29); the Israelite people (Ezra 1:5; 3:11; 5:5; 8:18, 22, 31; Neh. 1:8–9; 4:15; 9:9–37); and the Persian kings (Cyrus in Ezra 1:1; Darius in Ezra 6:8, 22; 7:28; Artaxerxes in Neh. 2:8, 18) to accomplish his will.

The Hermeneutics of Ezra-Nehemiah

Ezra-Nehemiah reports that the leaders of the Israelites used a variety of literary resources to support their arguments in favor of maintaining a godly worshiping community in Jerusalem that lived by the covenant promises and stipulations. These supporting written sources included (1) Persian and Israelite historical documents, used to justify an action or change; (2) covenant instructions and warnings in penitential prayers, used to remind people of earlier promises about the future; and (3) records concerning feasts, offerings, temple regulations, singing instructions by David, and Mosaic commandments, used to regulate behavior and purify the community.

The use of Israelite and Persian documents. The Persian proclamation by Cyrus in Ezra 1:2–4 originally functioned as permission to immigrate to Jerusalem, but in the context of Ezra's ministry it serves as a justification for living in Judah and for the restoration of worship at the temple (5:13, 15). David Clines (36) suggests that the Hebrew slant of the document may be due to the influence of a Jewish scribe who recorded this proclamation, but without the original it is impossible to know whether this scribe changed anything or, if so, what the changes were. Tattenai's letter (Ezra 5:7–16) and Darius's decrees (Ezra 6:3–12) reproduce two interesting interpretations of the past. The Israelite scribe's summary includes an honest admission of failures and a defense of Israel's action based on Cyrus's decree (5:13–15). Meanwhile, the Persian document in 6:3–5 says nothing about past rebellion but supports the Hebrew claims about the temple vessels being returned (5:15; 6:5), so the negative report by the Israelites in 5:11–15 is ignored and permission is granted to finish the temple. The narrator uses the Hebrew document recording the names of the true Israelites moving to Jerusalem in Ezra 2 / Neh. 7 to identify the authentic holy Israelite seed that should move into Jerusalem after the wall is rebuilt (Neh. 11–12). These documents justify and legitimate the action taken as appropriate and in tune with historical Persian records.

The use of earlier instruction by Moses and David. The Ezra and Nehemiah Memoirs repeatedly justify an activity to reassure the reader that these two leaders are following the instructions given to Moses or David. Music is performed at the dedication of the altar as David instructed them (Ezra 3:10) and at the dedication of the wall (Neh. 12:24, 45). In addition, genuine worship and the correction of behavior are based on what is written in "the Law of Moses," which Ezra reads and teaches to the Israelites (Ezra 3:2; 6:18) and to provincial judges (7:25). Ezra bases his reforms on the law of God (Neh. 8:2, 8, 14, 18; 9:3; 10:29, 34; cf. Ezra 9:1; 10:2; Neh. 9:13, 16, 26), and Nehemiah does the same (Neh. 13:1–3), but neither quotes any specific verses.

The quotation of earlier verses, especially in penitential prayers. When the Israelites praise God in Ezra 3:11, they quote Ps. 136:1, and when they renew their covenant with God in Neh. 10:28–39, they base their new commitments on instructions in the law about not marrying foreign wives (Neh. 10:30; cf. Deut. 7:3), the yearly tithe (Neh. 10:32; cf. Exod. 30:11–16), the bringing of firstfruits (Neh. 10:35–36; cf. Exod. 13:2; 23:19), and a tithe of the tithe for the priests serving at the central sanctuary (Neh. 10:38; cf. Num. 18:26).

The three penitential prayers in Ezra 9:6–15; Neh. 1:5–11; and Neh. 9:5b–37 heavily depend on earlier texts. All three prayers confess sins and admit that the Israelites did not follow all the instructions in the covenant (Ezra 9:7, 10–11; Neh. 1:6–7; 9:16, 26, 29, 34). They recognize that in the past God was gracious, compassionate, and just (Ezra 9:8, 13, 15; Neh. 1:5, 10; 9:17, 27–28, 31, 33), and there is a ray of hope near the end of each prayer (Ezra 9:8–9; Neh. 1:9–11; 9:32).

Since each penitential prayer arises out of a unique setting, the topics, requests, and quotations are different. The news that some Israelites did not separate themselves from the neighboring peoples of the lands (Ezra 9:1) sharply contrasts their inappropriate acts with God's instructions in the covenant in Deut. 7:3 and with their earlier decision to separate themselves from the peoples of the lands in Ezra 4:1–5 (around 536 BC).

An examination of two verses (11–12) of the prayer in Ezra 9:6–15 reveals the thought basis (or the phrase basis) for his prayer (see table 1).

Table 1. Ezra 9:11–12 and Possible Sources

Ezra	Phrase	Possible Source
9:11c	The land you are going to possess	Deut. 7:1
9:11d	is a polluted land, polluted by the peoples of the lands	Lev. 18:24, 30
9:11d	with their abominations	Lev. 18:24, 30; Deut. 7:25–26; 12:31; 18:9, 12; 20:18; 22:5; 23:19 [MT 23:18]; 24:4; 25:16; 27:15
9:11e	which fill it end to end with their impurities.	2 Kings 10:21; 21:16
9:12ab	So now, do not give your daughters to their sons and do not take their daughters for your sons.	Deut. 7:3
9:12c	And do not seek for their peace or goodness forever	Deut. 23:7 [MT 23:6]
9:12d	in order that you will be strong	Deut. 11:8
9:12e	and eat the good things in the land	Deut. 6:11
9:12f	and you will inherit it for your sons forever.	Deut. 1:38–39

Note: The translations in the table are my own.

Frequently, one must conclude that several of these clauses

> appear to be an extended allusion that rises to the level of being a modified quotation. Most of the terms are the same, though the subject of the verbs and the pronominal suffixes are singular in Deuteronomy (referring to the nation as a whole), but plural in Ezra because he wanted to apply these words to the individuals who had committed these sins. These grammatical changes indicate that making an exact copy (a modern definition of a quotation) was not Ezra's main desire; instead, he was motivated to communicate these thoughts in terms that people would easily recognize as deuteronomic. (Smith, "Influence," 354)

In Deuteronomy this meant that the Israelites should kill all the Canaanites when they entered the land, because intermarriage might encourage Israelites to worship pagan gods (7:1–7). But in Ezra's day there are no instructions to annihilate the Samaritans; instead, this command implies they should not intermarry with any of the non-Israelite people (9:1–4). The means of accomplishing God's will has changed, but the principle of neither marrying nor seeking the prosperity of non-Israelites is still valid.

The second penitential prayer (Neh. 1:5–11) shows strong dependence on earlier texts. Its structure powerfully communicates biblical principles in a unique pattern. When the prayer is arranged in grammatical and syntactical terms, 1:5–11 exhibits balance and repetition (see Smith, *Ezra-Nehemiah*, 253).

1:5a Vocative address to YHWH
 1:6 Jussive request, "let, may"
  1:8 Conditional, "if unfaithful" clause, plus apodosis "I will scatter"
   1:9a Conditional, "if you return" clause
  1:9b Conditional, "if scattered" clause, plus apodosis "I will gather"
1:11 Vocative address to God
 1:11 Jussive request, "may, let"

The outer pattern of the prayer at the beginning (1:5–6) and the end (v. 11a) has a vocative address that calls on God to listen actively and respond to their request. The jussives (1:6, 11) express a strong desire (GKC §109) for YHWH to pay attention both to the distress and reproach of Jerusalem (described in 1:3) and to this prayer. Nehemiah 1:8d–9 addresses the theology of restoration by quoting the guiding principles God explained years ago. The "if" clause in 1:9 justifies understanding the two preceding clauses as conditional to express the covenant theology of this prayer. The logic is as follows: (1) sin will lead to scattering, (2) but if people repent, turn to YHWH, and confess their sins, (3) then God will gather the people he scattered. With Israelites still scattered in Assyria, Babylon, and Egypt and only a small remnant now living around Jerusalem, a fuller restoration will require more people to return to God and to their land. The implication of this prayer is that God will bring complete restoration if the people restore their relationship with YHWH.

The following examination of phrases in Nehemiah's prayer in 1:5–9 explores the nature of these connections, including the canonical recontextualization in the reuse of phrases from Deuteronomy. (Translations in the comparison are my own.)

1. Nehemiah 1:5 states, "O YHWH, the God of heaven, the great and awesome God, who keeps the covenant and loving-kindness to those who love him and to those who keep his commandments." It is quite similar to Deut. 7:9 ("YHWH your God, he is God, the faithful God, who keeps covenant and his steadfast loving-kindness to those who love him and keep his commandments"), 7:21 ("YHWH your God is in your midst, a great and awesome God"), and 10:17. Although Nehemiah's prayer is not an exact quotation of Deuteronomy, Nehemiah's word choice and phraseology reveal a strong dependence on Deuteronomy. The new contextualized variation in Nehemiah uses the popular postexilic title "God of heaven" (1:5).

2. The first half of Lev. 26:40 reads, "If they confess their iniquity and the iniquity of their fathers, in their unfaithfulness against me . . ." Nehemiah 1:6 includes similar terminology (e.g., "confess"; "I and my father's house"; cf. "If you are unfaithful . . ." [1:8]). The thoughts of Lev. 26:40 may be somewhere in the general background of the memory of Nehemiah, but this is not a quotation so much as a general allusion that draws an analogy between the past and the present situation. The terms "we sinned" in Neh. 1:6 and "iniquity" in Lev. 26:40 do not match. The common use of "unfaithful" (*mā'al*) in postexilic writings is likely a cultural preference rather than an aspect of literary dependence.

3. "I will scatter you among the people" in Neh. 1:8 is quite similar to "YHWH will scatter you among the peoples" in Deut. 4:27 or "YHWH will scatter you among all the peoples" in Deut. 28:64. Nehemiah 1:9 ("If you were scattered to the ends of the heavens, from there I will gather them") is written in terminology very similar to that found in Deut. 30:4 ("If you are scattered to the ends of the heavens, from there YHWH your God will gather you"). The Lord's scattering of people is a common theme (Lev. 26:33; Deut. 28:64; Ps. 44:11; Jer. 9:16; Ezek. 6:8; 11:16; 12:15; 20:23; 22:15; 36:19; Joel 3:2; Zech. 10:9), so it is impossible to identify the literary source the narrator used. This allusion demonstrates that the theology of Deuteronomy is a legitimate authority in this new situation.

4. Nehemiah 1:9a ("[if] you return to me and [if] you keep my commandments . . . and [if] you do them") is similar to but not exactly the same as Deut. 30:2 ("you return to YHWH your God and listen to his voice according to all that I have commanded you today"). The third phrase ("and [if] you do them") is not in Deuteronomy. This quotation affirms that the conditions for restoration have not changed.

5. Nehemiah 1:9b has the phrase "if you were scattered to the ends of the heavens" and the positive promise "from there I will gather you unto this place." These reflect Deut. 30:4 ("and if you are scattered to the ends of heaven, from there YHWH your God will gather you"). The Deuteronomy quotation assures the audience that God's prophetic intentions have not changed.

6. Nehemiah 1:9f ("unto the place where I chose for my name to dwell") is almost an exact quotation of Deut. 12:11 and 12:5 ("the place YHWH your God will choose for his name to dwell"), showing the analogy between the past and the present ways God deals with his people.

The third prayer (Neh. 9:5b–31) has many quotations of earlier texts about creation (v. 6), Abram (vv. 7–9), the exodus (vv. 9–11), the wilderness journey (vv. 12–16), God's gracious compassion after repeated failures (vv. 16–31), and the Judahites' present situation under Persia (vv. 32–38a). An examination of the phrases in one section of this prayer illustrates the high degree of dependence on other passages in the Pentateuch.

Table 2. Possible Sources of the Words in Neh. 9:5b–8

Neh. 9:5b Ps. 106:48	Praise YHWH your God Praise YHWH the God of Israel
Neh. 9:5c Ps. 106:48	From everlasting to everlasting From everlasting to everlasting
Neh. 9:6a, 7a Isa. 37:16 2 Kings 19:19	You are YHWH alone You [YHWH] alone are God You are YHWH God alone
Neh. 9:6b Deut. 10:14	You made the heavens To YHWH your God belong the heavens
Neh. 9:6c Deut. 10:14	The highest heavens, the earth, and all that is in it The highest heaven and all their hosts
Neh. 9:7c Gen. 15:7	And brought him out of Ur of the Chaldees I brought you out of Ur of Chaldees
Neh. 9:7d Gen. 17:5	You established his name Abraham And your name will be Abraham
Neh. 9:8a Gen. 15:6	He was faithful before you He believed in YHWH
Neh. 9:8b Gen. 15:18	You cut a covenant with him Yahweh cut a covenant with Abraham
Neh. 9:8c Gen. 15:19–21	To give him the land of the Canaanites, Hittites, Amorites, Perizzites, Jebusites, Girgashites Hittites, Perizzites, Rephaim, Amorites, Canaanites, Girgashites, and the Jebusites
Neh. 9:8d Gen. 15:18 Neh. 9:8e Deut. 9:5	To give it to his seed To your seed I will give And you established your words To establish the word

Note: See Smith, *Ezra-Nehemiah*, 388. All translations in the table are my own.

All three prayers recognize that the people did not keep the laws, make observations about the history of the nation, and briefly look to the future, but Ezra 9 seems to be much more pessimistic and fearful that another judgment looms in the near future. In contrast, Neh. 1 seems to be more optimistic, emphasizing God's greatness, steadfast loving-kindness, preservation of the covenant (Neh. 1:5), and great compassion. In Neh. 9, Nehemiah believes God will gather more of his people from the far corners of the world (cf. Neh. 1:9) and has the power to redeem them from their present slavery to Persia (Neh. 9:32–38). He expects a positive answer because God gives success to those who fear him (Neh. 1:10) and because they are renewing their covenant with God (Neh. 10).

The difference in these prayers is partially due to the different historical settings and the theological relationship between God and his people in three different periods. Ezra is present in Jerusalem with the sinful people who have intermarried with the pagan people of the land, so he is troubled and worried. In Neh. 1 Nehemiah is in Susa and realizes that with God's help he might be able to change the future situation in Jerusalem through his relationship with the king (Neh. 1:11), and following Neh. 9 the people are listening to the law, repenting of sins, and preparing to renew their covenant with God (Neh. 10).

Nehemiah knows that God keeps his covenant, for God acts in steadfast love and power (1:5) and redeems Israel (1:10), but Ezra's emphasis in Ezra 9 is on their embarrassment, their shame and guilt, and God's anger. Ezra is so pessimistic (Ezra 9:13) that he expects that there will not even be a remnant of Israel left in the future (9:14). However, the prayer in Neh. 9 fully recognizes the nation's sins but balances that with God's compassion. There is hope if the people renew their covenant relationship with God.

Nehemiah's two prayers are based on Judah's positive covenant relationship because of the greatness of God's grace, power, and promises in Deuteronomy. Ezra's prayer is focused on covenant breaking and expects destruction for those who do not repent. Deuteronomy's explanation of the covenant puts these two ideas side by side. So, Ezra knows repentance is necessary if there will ever be any hope (Deut. 4:25–31; 30:1–4). The situation of Ezra's audience determines how he should pray and the level of hope he should project. The positive response of the audience in Ezra 10 suggests that Ezra made a wise choice of words.

The negative and the positive sides of the covenant relationship in Deuteronomy are equally important; but the key is to know the needs of the audience so that one can emphasize what is needed at the proper time. Nehemiah is not in front of a sinful Israelite audience in Judah (Neh. 1–2), so he neither sees the sinful acts that Ezra mentions nor experiences the hopelessness that Ezra feels. Nehemiah admits that past sin was the core problem that resulted in the scattering of the nation of Israel (Neh. 1:6–7), but he is much more interested in God's ability to gather his people, rebuild the walls, and do awesome things through his strong outstretched arm (Neh. 1:10). Deuteronomy's covenant theology provides a sound theological foundation for him to understand both the scattering and the gathering (Neh. 1:8–9). His desire is for God to take away the reproach of the remnant in Jerusalem, for that is the need he is aware of (Neh. 1:2–3). Thus, one learns that at times God's people need to be convicted of sin so that they will repent, but at other times they need to be uplifted and reminded of God's greatness and power so that they will have hope. Although every verse in Deuteronomy is true, most verses apply only to contextually relevant parallel situations.

NT Use of Ezra-Nehemiah

There are no direct quotations of Ezra-Nehemiah in the NT or even significant allusions. UBS[5] does give a few references in its "Index of Quotations and Allusions" to some possible allusions: Ezra 3:2 in Matt. 1:12 and Luke 3:27; Ezra 4:3 and 9:1–10:44 in John 4:9; Ezra 9:3 in Matt. 26:65; Ezra 9:7 in Luke 21:24; Neh. 9:6 in Rev. 10:6; Neh. 9:15 in John 6:31; Neh. 9:36 in John 8:33; Neh. 10:37 in Rom. 11:16; and Neh. 11:1 in Matt. 4:5. However, none are strongly connected to a phrase (at least two words) in the text of Ezra-Nehemiah.

Bibliography. Bautch, R. J., *Developments in Genre between Post-Exilic Penitential Prayers and the Psalms of Communal Lament*, AcBib 7 (Society of Biblical Literature, 2003); Becking, B., *Ezra-Nehemiah*, HCOT (Peeters, 2016); Blenkinsopp, J., *Ezra-Nehemiah*, OTL (Westminster, 1988); Boda, M. J., "Praying the Traditions," *TynBul* 48 (1997): 55–70; Böhler, D., *Die Heilige Stadt in Esras und Esra-Nehemia*, OBO 158 (Vandenhoeck & Ruprecht, 1997); Breneman, M., *Ezra, Nehemiah, Esther*, NAC (Broadman & Holman, 1993); Cataldo, J., "Utopia in Agony," in *Worlds That Could Not Be*, ed. S. J. Schweitzer and F. Uhlenbruch, LBS (T&T Clark, 2016), 144–70; Clines, D. J., *Ezra, Nehemiah, Esther*, NCBC (Eerdmans, 1984); Cross, F., "A Reconstruction of the Judean Restoration," *JBL* 21 (1975): 4–18; Fensham, F. C., *The Books of Ezra and Nehemiah*, NICOT (Eerdmans, 1982); Laird, D., *Negotiating Power in Ezra-Nehemiah* (SBL Press, 2016); Pakkala, J., *Ezra the Scribe*, BZAW 347 (de Gruyter, 2004); Pakkala, "The Original Independence of the Ezra Story in Ezra 7–10 and Nehemiah 8," *BN* 129 (2006): 17–24; Smith, G. V., *Ezra-Nehemiah*, ZECOT (Zondervan, 2022); Smith, "The Influence of Deuteronomy on Intercessory Prayers in Ezra and Nehemiah," in *For Our Good Always*, ed. J. S. DeRouchie, J. Giles, and K. Turner (Eisenbrauns, 2013), 345–64; Steinmann, A. E., *Ezra and Nehemiah*, ConC (Concordia, 2010); Throntveit, M., *Ezra-Nehemiah*, IBC (John Knox,1992); Williamson, H. G. M. "The Aramaic Documents in Ezra Revisited," *JTS* 59 (2009): 41–62; Williamson, *Ezra, Nehemiah*, WBC (Word, 1985); Wright, J., *Rebuilding Identity*, BZAW 348 (de Gruyter, 2004).

Gary V. Smith

F

Feasts and Festivals

It is likely that the ancient Israelites followed various calendars during their occupancy of the land of promise. They obviously held to a solar/lunar calendar that is in evidence as early as Gen. 1. On the fourth day of creation, "God said, 'Let there be lights in the vault of the sky to separate the day from the night, and let them serve as signs to mark sacred times, and days and years'" (1:14). The OT, however, does not present a full solar/lunar calendar, and thus, a detailed knowledge of its specific usage in Israel is uncertain. The reality is that "information about these matters must be gleaned from occasional often incidental references to dates, days, months, seasons, and years" (Vanderkam, 814).

Although an agricultural calendar is not directly communicated in the OT, the Israelites also maintained one based on the types of crops that they produced. Ancient Israel was primarily a farming economy, so they likely followed an annual calendar based on agricultural practice. At the Israelite site of Gezer, archaeologists discovered a limestone tablet from the tenth century BC that contains a school text of an agricultural calendar written in ancient Hebrew (AT):

> His two months are olive harvesting,
> His two months are planting grain,
> His two months are late planting,
> His month is hoeing flax,
> His month is barley harvest,
> His month is harvest and festivals,
> His two months are vine tending,
> His month is summer fruit.

Perhaps the most detailed calendar in ancient Israel is the festal or cultic calendar that is first elucidated in the Pentateuch. Five cultic calendars, in various degrees of detail, appear there: Exod. 23:10–19; 34:18–26; Lev. 23; Num. 28–29; and Deut. 16:1–17 (see Queen-Sutherland, 76–87).

Leviticus 23 is probably the most systematic and standardized presentation of the cultic calendar in Israel. Because of its highly organized and structured design, some scholars date Lev. 23 to a very late compositional time in the history of Israel (see Porter, 177–79). "In reality, it appears that the Leviticus calendar is earlier than those in either Deuteronomy or Numbers, and the latter in particular is clearly dependent on Leviticus" (Currid, *Leviticus*, 299).

The cultic calendar of Israel is structured upon three foundational national pilgrim festivals that the people are required to celebrate annually. These are the Passover / Feast of Unleavened Bread (Lev. 23:4–8), the Feast of Weeks (Lev. 23:15–22), and the Feast of Booths (Lev. 23:33–43). At the very core and heart of these festivals is weekly Sabbath observance: the Sabbath is the first appointed time set by God in Lev. 23.

Sabbath (Lev. 23:3)

The Sabbath is the "Sabbath of sabbatical observance" (v. 3 AT; *šabbat šabbātôn*; see BDB, 992). This construction is a superlative in Hebrew that underscores that the seventh day has been distinctly set apart from the other days of the week (cf. its usage in Exod. 31:15). Being the first festival established by God (Gen. 2:1–3), it is foundational to the Hebrew festal calendar. Its structural importance to the calendar is evident in Lev. 23, in which *seven* festivals are presented, and most of them appear in the *seventh* month of the calendar (Wenham, 301).

The text underscores the all-pervasive and ubiquitous nature of the command for Israel to keep the Sabbath: the phrase "wherever you live" (*bəkōl môšəbōtêkem*) is commonly translated as "in all your dwelling places." This means that the Sabbath is not something merely to be observed in the temple or by the priests but that this weekly festival, no matter where one lives, binds all Israel. For further study, see the "Sabbath and Sunday" article elsewhere in the dictionary.

Passover and the Feast of Unleavened Bread (Lev. 23:4–8)

The first annual feast of the cultic calendar is Passover. It is celebrated on the fourteenth day of the first month, the month of Abib, in the spring (see Exod. 13:4; 23:15; 34:18). In postexilic times, it is referred to as the month of Nisan (Neh. 2:1; Esther 3:7). In Lev. 23, the Passover festival receives only cursory examination and description: it is likely that the author assumes the audience's knowledge of the grand Passover narration of Exod. 12:1–28.

The Hebrew term for Passover is *pesaḥ*, and it is first used of the festival in Exod. 12:11. It is the principal word employed in the Bible referring to the celebration of God's having redeemed Israel out of the land of Egypt. The feast does commemorate that deliverance, but its essential purpose is to bring glory to the Lord for his work of deliverance: "It is the LORD's Passover" (Exod. 12:11).

Passover is to be celebrated in the first month of the Hebrew cultic calendar. The new year thus coincides with a new beginning that is born of Israel's redemption from Egypt. God commands at least four times in Exod. 12 that the people of God are to keep the Passover in perpetuity—that is, "for the generations to come . . . a lasting ordinance" (v. 14). The second Passover celebration occurs at Mount Sinai "in the first month of the second year after they came out of Egypt" (Num. 9:1).

There is no evidence to suggest that Israel celebrated Passover during the thirty-nine years of wandering between Sinai and the Jordan River. After Israel crossed the river into the land of promise, they encamped at Gilgal and celebrated the Passover "on the fourteenth day of the month" (Josh. 5:10). With the recording of the Passover in Josh. 5, a thematic, inverted structure may be observed that covers Israel's escape from Egypt, the wanderings, and the entrance into Canaan:

Exod. 12:43–50	Circumcision/Passover
Exod. 14	Parting of the Red Sea
Exod. 15–Josh. 2	Wilderness wanderings
Josh. 3	Parting of the Jordan River
Josh. 5:1–12	Circumcision/Passover

Passover serves as the bookends of the account. As such, the symmetrical structure underscores that the slavery in Egypt is over, redemption has taken place, and there is a new beginning in the land of promise.

Passover does not appear in the OT again until the reign of the Judean king Hezekiah (716–687 BC). Well over five hundred years have passed from the celebration at the Jordan River to the time of Hezekiah. Does this mean that Passover was never celebrated during those many centuries? We are uncertain, although its appearances in the historical literature are tied only to particular orthodox reforms in the nation's history (2 Kings 23; 2 Chron. 30). At best, we can say that the celebration of Passover during Israel's existence in the land was sporadic.

Seventy years after the destruction of Jerusalem at the hands of the Babylonians, the returned exiles rebuild the temple. They finish in 516 BC, seventy years after its ruination. One of the first acts of the people is the celebration of the Passover: "On the fourteenth day of the first month, the exiles celebrated the Passover" (Ezra 6:19). Again, the Passover signals deliverance and new beginnings.

During the Second Temple period, Passover was commonly celebrated. Josephus mentions it frequently in his works *Jewish Antiquities* and *Jewish War*. In one text, he records the number of people who came to Jerusalem for Passover: "So these high priests, upon the coming of the feast which is called Passover . . . found the number of sacrifices was two hundred and fifty-six thousand five hundred; which, upon the allowance of no more than ten that feast together, amounts to two million seven hundred thousand and two hundred persons" (*J.W.* 6.9.3). Those numbers are obviously inflated, as E. P. Sanders (126) appropriately remarks: "No one believes the largest of these figures, though other ancient writers also refer to enormous crowds." Still, the number of pilgrims at Passover was immense, and Sanders (128) concludes that there were "300,000 to 500,000 people attending the festivals, especially Passover."

The roots of the early church were found in the OT, and Passover took on a deep, profound meaning as typological of the deliverance to be brought by a coming messianic redeemer. As Kenneth Mathews (202) says, "It pointed to the ultimate deliverance provided by Jesus who was the Passover lamb for the forgiveness of sins and liberation of those who were destined for death in sinful servitude." The final week of Jesus's life coincides with preparation for and celebration of the Passover. The Last Supper, in which Jesus celebrates the Passover meal with his disciples, occurs on the night of his arrest (John 11:55; 13:1). In that meal, Jesus interprets the Passover as a foreshadowing of his coming and ministry. Two of the elements of the meal are wine and bread: the wine symbolizes the blood of the lamb that was shed for the Israelites in Egypt, and the bread signifies the bread that the Hebrews carried on their backs when they left Egypt quickly. In Matt. 26:26–28, Jesus proclaims that the wine is a figure of his blood, which removes the sins of his people, and the bread is a figure of his body, which is hung on the cross for sinners. Jesus is claiming that he is the Passover lamb; as Paul says, "For Christ, our Passover lamb, has been sacrificed" (1 Cor. 5:7).

God commanded that his people would celebrate Passover in perpetuity (Exod. 12:14, 17, 24), and when Christians partake of the Lord's Supper they are, in fact, doing that. The Scots Confession of 1560 highlights that theological truth:

> As the fathers under the Law, besides the reality of the sacrifices, had two chief sacraments, that is, circumcision and the Passover, and those who rejected these were not reckoned among God's people; so do we acknowledge and confess that now in the time of the gospel we have two chief sacraments, which alone were instituted by the Lord Jesus and commanded to be used by all who will be counted members of his body, that is, Baptism and the Supper or Table of the Lord Jesus, also called the Communion of His Body and Blood.

A main reason that Christians celebrate Passover in this way is to remind them that Christ delivered his people from death and darkness and brought them to newness of life.

The Feast of Unleavened Bread begins the day after the Passover "on the fifteenth day of that month" (Lev. 23:6). Although they are two separate feasts, they are quite naturally tied together: the NT authors often combine the two, calling Passover "the first day of the Festival of Unleavened Bread" (Matt. 26:17; Mark 14:12), as does Josephus (*Ant.* 2.14.6). The Feast of Unleavened Bread particularly commemorates the rapidity of the escape of the Hebrews from Egypt after the sacrifice of the Passover (Exod. 12:17–20).

The celebration is called a "festival/feast" (*ḥag*; Lev. 23:6). This noun derives from a root meaning "to make a pilgrimage" (BDB, 290; cf. the Arabic *haj* to Mecca). This term perhaps anticipates the time when Israel will be in the land of promise and the people will be required to travel to Jerusalem to celebrate this festival. It is to last for seven days, and the Hebrews are allowed to eat only bread without yeast during the length of the feast. They are also to "remove leaven out of your houses" (Exod. 12:15 ESV), a command designed to keep the people from inadvertently using leaven in their food.

Like Passover, the Feast of Unleavened Bread appears to have been kept by the Israelites mainly in times of revival and reform. The OT mentions it being celebrated in the days of Solomon (2 Chron. 8:13), during the reforms of Hezekiah (2 Chron. 30:13, 21) and Josiah (2 Chron. 35:17), and during the return immediately after the rebuilding of the temple (Ezra 6:22).

The Feast of Firstfruits (Lev. 23:9–14)

During the Feast of Unleavened Bread the Israelites are also to celebrate the Festival of Firstfruits: it "began after the Sabbath in the week of Unleavened Bread" (Rooker, 286). The celebration is a one-day affair that commemorates the beginning of the harvest season in Israel. The ritual begins with the offerer bringing a bundle of sheaves of the first grain to the priest; the grain is probably barley, since it is the first grain crop to ripen. The priest then waves the bundle before Yahweh in order to dedicate the beginning of the harvest period as a blessing of God to his people. The wave offering is accompanied by various other offerings in order to acknowledge God's blessing of produce to Israel.

With regard to the NT period, it is critical to observe that the resurrection of Jesus Christ occurs on the first day after the Sabbath during the Feast of Unleavened Bread (Matt. 27:62; 28:1). Jesus rises from the dead on the day of the Feast of Firstfruits. This is not accidental: Christ's resurrection from the dead fulfills the Feast of Firstfruits. Paul comments poignantly that "Christ has indeed been raised from the dead, the firstfruits of those who have fallen asleep" (1 Cor. 15:20). Because of the resurrection of Christ, the eternal harvest has now begun.

The Feast of Weeks (Lev. 23:15–22)

The second pilgrimage feast is called either the Feast of Weeks (Exod. 34:22; *šābuʿōt*) or the Feast of Harvest (Exod. 23:16). It marks the end of the grain harvest, and worshipers are to present "an offering of new grain to the LORD" (Lev. 23:16). "The purpose of the celebration is to recognize Yahweh as the provider of crops, and that he is deserving of the first fruits of produce" (Currid, *Exodus*, 121).

The feast is a one-day affair that is to be celebrated seven weeks after the sheaf ritual of the Feast of Firstfruits. The exact day it is to be held is a matter of debate (Hartley, 385–86). It is a great day of celebration and a fitting climax to the harvest season (Deut. 16:11). In addition to the grain offering, three prominent sacrifices are offered on the day: the whole burnt offering (Lev. 1), the sin offering (Lev. 4–5), and the peace offering (Lev. 3). These are generous offerings that reflect gratitude of the people for God's abundant blessings upon them.

The Feast of Weeks is mentioned only one other time in the OT outside the Pentateuch, during the time of Solomon (2 Chron. 8:13). We do know that it was held during the intertestamental period because it is mentioned in Jub. 22:1, 2 Macc. 12:31, and Tobit 2:1. Josephus, in the first century AD, provides several accounts of the festival, which he calls by the Greek name "Pentecost" (*Ant.* 3.10.6; 13.8.4; 17.10.2; *J.W.* 1.13.3). The entire rabbinic tractate Bikkurim in the Mishnah describes the offerings of the firstfruits during the time of Shavuot. Sometime after the destruction of the second temple in Jerusalem, rabbinic Judaism associated the Feast of Weeks with God's giving of the torah on Mount Sinai. Some Jewish traditions maintain that King David was born and died on Shavuot.

The Feast of Weeks serves as an important time setting for a major event in the early church. Jesus is crucified at Passover (1 Cor. 5:7), and then, seven weeks later, comes the celebration of the Feast of Weeks / Pentecost (= "fiftieth day" in Gk.). On that day, the Holy Spirit fills the gathered members of the church, and they begin to speak in various languages, declaring the wonders and glory of God (Acts 2:1–11). Because the day is a pilgrim festival, many are there to hear the gospel preached, both Jews and gentiles. Many are converted to the Christian faith (Acts 2:41). The tie between this event and the Feast of Weeks is implicit: those who come to faith in Christ at Pentecost are the "harvest" and "firstfruits" of the early church.

Although Pentecost's commemoration of the giving of the law on Mount Sinai has a late attestation, some scholars believe it reflects an earlier tradition. If this is true, it "is significant for Christian Pentecost, because at Pentecost the coming of the Holy Spirit, who wrote the law on the human heart, replaced the old administration by the law that was written on the rock" (Waltke, 295n16).

The Feast of Booths (Lev. 23:33–43)

On the fifteenth day of the seventh month, five days after the Day of Atonement (see below), the Israelites are to celebrate a third pilgrimage, called the Feast of Booths. This feast commemorates God's leading the people through the wilderness from Egypt to the land of promise and his provision for them in great measure on their travels (v. 43). It also anticipates that God will continue to "bless you in all your harvest and in all the work of your hands" (Deut. 16:15). The Feast of Booths is to be a joyful affair.

The festival lasts for seven days, and during that time the Hebrews are to live in temporary shelters they have constructed (v. 42). The word "booths" (*sukkôt*) derives from a verbal root that means "to cover over," and it specifically refers to putting a roof on a temporary shelter (cf. Gen. 33:17; Isa. 1:8; see Levine, 161). Some commentators argue that the word "booth"/"cover" refers not to Israelite temporary shelters but rather to "God's protective cloud [that] shielded them in the wilderness as a booth protects one from the elements" (Tigay, 469). Although support for the latter interpretation is not as strong as for the former, both underscore the purpose of the festival: to praise God for his protection and care in the wilderness.

Solomon's reign is the only preexilic era in which the Israelites are explicitly said to celebrate this feast. However, after the death of Solomon, Jeroboam I sets up an imitation Feast of Booths in the Northern Kingdom so that his people will not be lured to travel to Jerusalem to celebrate it (1 Kings 12:25–33; note in v. 32 that Jeroboam's feast is on the fifteenth day of the eighth month, not the seventh month). The prophet Zechariah foresees a time when all nations will gather yearly in Jerusalem to celebrate the Feast of Booths/ Tabernacles. After the exile, the leaders of Jerusalem in Nehemiah's time study the Torah with Ezra, and they discover that the word commands them to keep the Feast of Booths. The people of God obey: "The whole company that had returned from exile built temporary shelters and lived in them. From the days of Joshua son of Nun until that day, the Israelites had not celebrated it like this. And their joy was very great" (Neh. 8:17). The point is not that Israel had not celebrated the feast since the time of Joshua; rather, the people in Nehemiah's day are joyful over their return to the land in the same way as the Israelites rejoiced in entering the land in Joshua's day.

This festival is called the Feast of Tabernacles in the NT. By the first century AD, it had become a spectacular affair. Apparently, during the Second Temple period, one of the central rituals of the feast was the daily procession of the priests to the pool of Siloam. There they would fill up jars with water and carry them back to the temple. Then the priests would pour water down the temple steps as they chanted Isa. 12:3, "With joy you will draw water from the wells of salvation" (see b. Sukkah 48b; 51a; 51b). One purpose of the ritual was to remind people of God's deliverance of Israel from Egypt and his guiding them to the land of promise. It also pointed to the fruitfulness that God gave to his people by providing water for them by rain (b. Sukkah 48b).

It is likely that this water ritual is the setting for Jesus's teaching in John 7:37–38. The Feast of Booths has reached its climax "on the last and greatest day of the festival." At this point, Jesus stands before the crowds and proclaims, "Let anyone who is thirsty come to me and drink." He obviously is speaking metaphorically: if anyone is in need of salvation, in need of spiritual drink, then that person needs to come to Jesus. Jesus is the fulfillment of what the Feast of Booths anticipates; he is, in a sense, the "rain" that God promised to pour out in the messianic dispensation.

In addition to these three pilgrim festivals, Lev. 23 includes three other feasts, which are not pilgrimages to the sanctuary but are important for the Hebrew cultic calendar: the Feast of Trumpets, the Day of Atonement, and the Feast of Firstfruits.

The Feast of Trumpets (Lev. 23:23–25)

As the Sabbath is the holy day of the calendar week, the seventh month "is the most sacred and festive month in the Hebrew calendar" (Currid, *Leviticus*, 306). This month begins with "a day for you to sound the trumpets" (Num. 29:1). The day is celebratory, as it marks the end of one agricultural year and the beginning of the next one (Wenham, 305). In postexilic Judaism, the Feast of

Trumpets came to be known as Rosh Hashanah (Heb. "the head of the year")—that is, New Year's Day.

The day is announced with a series of trumpet blasts. Often this activity is carried out for the purpose of calling people to a public event, such as worship or war (e.g., Ps. 81:3; BDB, 930). It is a day of a solemn congregational assembly and one on which no labor is to be done. According to Num. 29:1–6, the day is a lively time of sacrifice: it includes a whole-burnt offering and a sin offering in addition to the daily sacrifices.

The purpose of the Feast of Trumpets is to call and make ready the people of Israel for the momentous events that will soon follow in the seventh month. It is a day of spiritual preparation, particularly for the tenth day of the seventh month, which is the Day of Atonement (see below). In v. 24, the feast is named a "memorial" (Heb. *zikkārôn*). That term indicates that the trumpets are also calling Israel to a time of recollection of what God has done for them.

Day of Atonement (Lev. 23:26–32)

Although this one-day festival is briefly related in the text before us, it receives detailed description in Lev. 16. This day, Yom Kippur, is the culmination of the worship of Israel for the calendar year: this is the great day of deliverance in which the sins of Israel are dealt with. The word "atonement" (Heb. *kippurîm*) is a plural noun in Hebrew, and this likely signifies the superlative sense: this day denotes complete atonement. The Israelites are to humble themselves on this day by acting with contrition and self-denial.

The central figure in the critical events of the day is the high priest. In preparation for the day's activities at the sanctuary, he first collects a young bull and a ram that he will later offer up for atonement for himself and his family (Lev. 16:6, 11). Before that ritual, he bathes and clothes himself with high-priestly garments. These are unadorned vestments that reflect the humility and submission of the high priest as he enters the most holy place. Targum Yerushalmi says that there is no gold on the garments so that no one is reminded of the golden calf (Snaith, 78).

After the high priest offers the bull as a sin offering for himself and his family, he oversees the ceremony of lots involving two goats. One lot falls on a goat that is sacrificed to Yahweh, and the other lot falls on the "scapegoat." This term is *ʿăzāʾzēl*, a noun that means the "entire removal" of something (BDB, 736). The name describes its function. The high priest lays his hands on the animal, symbolically transferring the sin of Israel to the creature. He then hands the animal over to a man who takes it into the wilderness and releases it (Lev. 16:20–22).

After the ceremony of lots, the high priest enters the holy of holies to perform atoning work through blood sacrifice (Lev. 16:11–19). His first act there is to burn incense to create a vapor or mist in the room; this is to prevent the high priest from clearly seeing the presence of God. It is for his protection; the mist is "to shroud the Seat of Grace, the sight of which, as explicitly stated in the text, may kill even Aaron" (Haran, 113–29). The high priest then splashes the blood of the sacrifice on the mercy seat, which serves as a purification offering for Israel. Once he finishes that atoning work, he comes out to the altar to perform further expiatory and propitiatory work (Lev. 16:18–19).

The sacrifices of the Day of Atonement are not in themselves efficacious to cover sin (expiation) or to stay God's wrath (propitiation). Hebrews 10:4 is clear when it says, "It is impossible for the blood of bulls and goats to take away sins" (cf. v. 11). But that does not mean that those sacrifices are meaningless in the OT. They are shadows or types of the atoning work of Christ, the ultimate high priest. OT believers obtained forgiveness and acceptance with God only as they offered sacrifices in true penitence and in faith in the coming redeemer. Believers throughout time are redeemed only by the sacrificial work of Christ (see 1 Pet. 1:18–19).

The Day of Atonement is not specifically mentioned in the OT after the Pentateuch. "It is curious that no specific reference to the day of atonement occurs elsewhere in the Old Testament, despite the periodic occurrence of certain significant events in the seventh month" (Harrison, 175). Texts from the Second Temple period, including the literature from Qumran, frequently cite the Day of Atonement as the most important festival in Judaism (Kalimi).

A strong case can be made that the Day of Atonement functions as the setting for Paul's classic declaration of Christ's atonement in Rom. 3:21–26 (Moo, 231–37; Schreiner, 191–95). At the heart of his argument, Paul uses the Greek word *hilastērion*, which refers to the "mercy seat" on top of the ark of the covenant in the inner sanctuary. The end of v. 24 could appropriately be rendered as "the redemption which is in Christ Jesus, whom God displayed publicly as a mercy seat in his blood through faith." Therefore, Jesus functions as the high priest (Heb. 9:11), the place of the sprinkled blood, and the sacrificial victim all at the same time. His sacrifice is the final Day of Atonement for the people of God.

The fulfillment of the Day of Atonement in the coming of Christ bears all the marks of typology. Typology has four essential characteristics: both events must be historical, there must be real correspondences between the two events, heightening must occur from the earlier event to the later, and some evidence of God's ordination of the type must be seen (Currid, "Typology"). All these elements are obviously and clearly found in this relationship.

Summary

The festal calendar of Lev. 23 is an important part of the setting for the NT. "Nowhere is the continuity between the testaments so clear as in the calendar" (Wenham, 306). The early church understood that three of the major Hebrew festivals were fulfilled in the coming of Christ: Passover became Good Friday, the Feast of Firstfruits became Easter, and the Feast of Weeks became Pentecost. "This correspondence indicates that these feasts had a preparatory role anticipating what would be accomplished in the coming of Christ, since they all, like the Old Testament sacrifices, pointed to him" (Rooker, 291).

See also Covenant; Exile and Restoration; Exodus, The

Bibliography. Currid, J. D., *Exodus*, vol. 2, EPSC (Evangelical Press, 2001); Currid, *Leviticus*, EPSC (Evangelical Press, 2004); Currid, "Recognition and Use of Typology in Preaching," *RTR* 53 (1994): 115–29; Haran, M., "The Uses of Incense in the Ancient Israelite Ritual," *VT* 10 (1960): 113–29; Harrison, R. K., *Leviticus*, TOTC (Inter-Varsity, 1980); Hartley, J. E., *Leviticus*, WBC (Word, 1992); Josephus, *Jewish Wars*, in *The Works of Josephus*, trans. W. Whiston (Hendrickson, 1987), 543–772; Kalimi, I., "The Day of Atonement in the Late Second Temple Period," *RRJ* 14 (2011): 71–91; Levine, B. A., *Leviticus*, JPSTC (Jewish Publication Society, 1989); Mathews, K. A., *Leviticus*, PrW (Crossway, 2009); Moo, D., *The Epistle to the Romans*, NICNT (Eerdmans, 1996); Porter, J. R., *Leviticus*, CBC (Cambridge University Press, 1976); Queen-Sutherland, K., "Cultic Calendars in the Old Testament," *Faith and Mission* 8 (1991): 76–87; Rooker, M., *Leviticus*, NAC (Broadman & Holman, 2000); Sanders, E. P., *Judaism: Practice and Belief, 63 BCE–66 CE* (SCM, 1992); Schreiner, T., *Romans*, BECNT (Baker, 1998); Snaith, N., *Leviticus and Numbers*, NCBC (Attic, 1969); Tigay, J. H., *Deuteronomy*, JPSTC (Jewish Publication Society, 1996); Vanderkam, J. C., "Calendars," in *ABD*, 1:814–20; Waltke, B. K., *An Old Testament Theology* (Zondervan, 2007); Wenham, G., *The Book of Leviticus*, NICOT (Eerdmans, 1979).

John D. Currid

Fornication

See Marriage

Fulfillment

See Literal Fulfillment; Mystery

[G]

Galatians, Letter to the

The influence of the OT Scriptures on Paul's argument and theology in Galatians, and even on the structure of the letter, is pervasive. This influence happens at both the conscious/explicit level (e.g., Paul specifically cites and alludes to key OT passages that further his argument) and the subconscious/implicit level (e.g., various OT texts, themes, and motifs shape his thinking in ways that he may not always be consciously aware of while writing the letter; see esp. Ciampa). Scripture runs like a current throughout Galatians—sometimes on the surface, other times slightly below—that forms the very substructure of how Paul thinks, argues, and communicates his message. Stated another way, the OT Scriptures are one of the lenses (the other being the gospel of Jesus Christ) through which Paul views all of life. In one sense, Paul's fundamental disagreement with the opponents in Galatia is hermeneutical, rooted in a different understanding of the relationship between the OT Scriptures and what Christ has accomplished through his life, death, and resurrection. Therefore, the significant amount of scholarship on various aspects of the use of the OT in Galatians should come as no surprise. This brief article will first survey which OT passages Paul engages and then summarize how he engages those texts.

The OT Passages Paul Engages in Galatians

Paul draws from a number of different OT books in Galatians (see chart in Harmon, *Galatians*, 474–78), but four stand out in particular: Genesis, Leviticus, Deuteronomy, and Isaiah. This pattern aligns with the Pauline corpus as a whole, where these books are also among the most frequently cited and alluded to.

Genesis. The thesis statement (3:6–9) of Paul's extended argument in 3:1–5:1 is shaped by a combination of God declaring Abraham righteous by faith (Gen. 15:6) and the promise to bless all the nations in him (Gen. 12:3; 18:18; 22:18). This Abraham-shaped faith is the paradigm for believers' faith in Christ. In explaining the relationship between the Abrahamic promise and the Mosaic law (Gal. 3:15–18), Paul draws on the covenant-ratification ceremony of Gen. 15:7–21 and the promise of Isaac as the singular seed who will inherit the promises in Gen. 17:1–10, 19–21; 22:18. Paul concludes the argument of 3:1–5:1 with a reading of Gen. 16–21 (mediated through Isa. 54:1 and its larger context) to demonstrate that the Abrahamic promises have been fulfilled in Christ and in those born according to the Spirit (Gal. 4:21–5:1).

Exodus. On the thematic level, there are multiple links to Exodus: the nexus of God as Father, sonship, adoption, and inheritance (Gal. 4:4–7; cf. Exod. 4:22–23); the connection between God's glory and forgiveness of sins (Gal. 1:4–5; cf. Exod. 34:6–7); and the reference to leaven (Gal. 5:9; cf. Exod. 12:15–20; 13:3–10). The language of "so quickly deserting" the true gospel (Gal. 1:6) may echo Israel's apostasy with the golden calf in Exod. 32–34.

Leviticus. Paul cites Lev. 18:5 ("The one who does them will live by them," AT) as the fundamental principle of the Mosaic law covenant (Gal. 3:12), then likely echoes the same text in Gal. 5:3 (see further Sprinkle). In Gal. 5:14, he summarizes the entire law with a citation of Lev. 19:18 ("You shall love your neighbor as yourself," AT). In saying that the law came "by the hand of a mediator" (Gal. 3:19 AT), Paul likely echoes Lev. 26:46, where the various commandments are said to be given "by the hand of Moses" (AT). The call to live in the freedom

Christ purchased rather than the yoke of slavery (Gal. 5:1) parallels God bringing his people out of Egypt and breaking the yoke of their slavery (Lev. 26:13).

Numbers. The wish for grace and peace (Gal. 1:3) may echo the well-known Aaronic blessing of Num. 6:24–26. By stressing his pre-Christian zeal for the traditions of his fathers (Gal. 1:14), Paul may have seen himself in the mold of Phinehas, who atoned for Israel's idolatry by zealously guarding the purity of Israel (Num. 25:1–13). The reference to Christ being cursed because he was hung on a tree (Gal. 3:13) may echo the execution of the chiefs of the Israelites for their idolatry (Num. 25:1–4).

Deuteronomy. To explain why a curse rests on those who rely on works of the law (Gal. 3:10), Paul cites a combination of Deut. 27:26; 28:58. He likely echoes those same texts later in Gal. 5:3 when stressing the need to keep the whole law. Citing Deut. 21:23 ("Cursed is everyone who is hanged on a tree") enables Paul to explain how Christ became a curse for his people (Gal. 3:13). More subtly, the pronouncement of a curse on those who preach a different gospel may echo the judgment for false prophets in Deut. 13. The reminder that "God is one" (Gal. 3:20) certainly alludes to the Shema (Deut. 6:4) or its reappropriation in Zech. 14:9.

Isaiah. While the quotation from Isa. 54:1 in Gal. 4:27 is the only explicit citation from Isaiah, there are numerous allusions and echoes throughout Galatians (Harmon, *Free*). Isaiah 40–66 provides a broad structural framework for Paul's argument, theology, and structure in Galatians (Beale, *Handbook*, 86–87). More specifically, Isa. 49–54 appears to form a broad conceptual substructure to Gal. 1–4. Paul describes his apostolic call in language that is borrowed from the servant of Yahweh in Isa. 49 (Gal. 1:15–16) and that produces residual echoes later in the letter (1:24; 2:2, 20; 4:11). Jesus's death is portrayed in light of the suffering servant from Isa. 53 (Gal. 2:20; 3:13; 4:4–6). The argument in Gal. 3:1–5:1 begins with a call to look to Abraham and trust in God's promises to him (Isa. 51:1–8) as the foundation for being a son of Abraham (Gal. 3:6–9). It climaxes with the announcement that all who believe in Christ are sons of the Jerusalem above (Gal. 4:27), grounded in a citation of Isa. 54:1. As the suffering servant from Isa. 53 (Gal. 3:13), Christ enables the gift of the Spirit to come to Jew and gentile alike in fulfillment of the Abrahamic promise (Gal. 3:14) as anticipated in Isa. 44:3–5. As the servant, Jesus also leads his people in the Isaianic new exodus (Gal. 4:1–7). Although this Isaianic substructure does not seem to continue through Gal. 5–6, those chapters do contain a number of echoes of, allusions to, and thematic parallels to Isa. 40–66. Just as God has promised (Isa. 32:15–20; 57:15–21; 63:11–14), his Spirit empowers his people to walk in obedience and produce fruit (Gal. 5:18, 22–23). The new creation that results from Christ's work (Gal. 6:15) is rooted in the repeated new-creation motifs and references in Isaiah (Isa. 43:18–20; 65:17–25). Even the final blessing of peace and mercy on the Israel of God (Gal. 6:16) likely has its roots in Isa. 54:10 (Beale, "Peace"). Additionally, there are a number of similarities between Galatians and Isa. 40–66 on the thematic level, including (1) the restoration of Jerusalem, (2) forgiveness of sins, (3) return from exile through a new exodus that transforms creation itself, (4) salvation extending to the nations, and (5) the enigmatic servant figure. This Isaianic narrative substructure supports Paul's larger argument in Galatians that God has fulfilled the promises to Abraham in and through Jesus Christ, who as the Isaianic suffering servant has inaugurated the return from exile through a new exodus that culminates in a new creation in which all who believe in Christ participate, regardless of their ethnicity, gender, or socioeconomic status.

The rest of the Prophets. Paul cites Hab. 2:4 ("The righteous shall live by faith," AT) to demonstrate that no one can be justified by the law (Gal. 3:11) and anticipates this citation in Gal. 2:20 when he stresses that he lives by faith in Christ. Jeremiah's repeated use of the language of building up and tearing down (1:10; 24:6–7; 31:27–28) may supply the background for similar language regarding the Mosaic law (Gal. 2:18). The assertion that "God is one" in connection with the giving of the law (Gal. 3:20) may allude to Zech. 14:9, where similar language expresses the universal reign of God over all the nations (Bruno, 162–98). Paul may be drawing on Hosea 8:1–7; 10:12–13 when he warns about the dangers of sowing to the flesh and reaping destruction (Gal. 6:8). The Spirit battling the desires of the flesh and the necessity of walking in/by the Spirit (Gal. 5:16–26) likely are rooted in the promised gift of God's Spirit in Ezek. 11:19–20; 36:26–27.

The Historical Books. Although the connection would, admittedly, be subtle, Paul may echo the Achan story (Josh. 7; 1 Chron. 2:7) when he refers to the opponents as those troubling the Galatians (Gal. 1:7–9). Some have seen the story of Elijah (1 Kings 19:14–15) behind Paul's trip to Arabia in Gal. 1:17 (Wright, "Elijah"). God's promise to David in 2 Sam. 7:12–16 (along with Ps. 2:7) likely forms at least part of the backdrop for the summary of the gospel in terms of God sending both his Son to redeem his people and the Spirit of his Son into their hearts (Gal. 4:4–7; see Scott, 121–86).

Wisdom literature. Paul's assertion that no one is justified by works of the law (Gal. 2:16; 3:11) is a partial citation of Ps. 143:2. That increases the likelihood that being led by the Spirit (Gal. 5:18) echoes Ps. 143:10. Proverbs 30:14 may find an echo in Paul's warning about biting and devouring one another (Gal. 5:15). The principle of reaping what one sows (Gal. 6:7) occurs several places in Wisdom literature (Job 4:8; Prov. 22:8; Eccles. 11:4).

Paul's Level of Engagement with the OT Scriptures in Galatians

In general terms the different forms of OT influence range from direct citations to thematic parallels, with allusions and echoes falling on the spectrum between them (see Harmon, *Free*, 26–39). Paul does more than engage isolated scriptural texts throughout the letter as if he is merely interested in citing an authoritative text to enhance the rhetorical force of his argument. While his citations and allusions are understandable on their own terms within the immediate context of Galatians, they regularly take on a far greater depth of meaning when their original OT contexts are considered. Paul's engagement with Scripture in Galatians falls into four broad categories (drawn from Beale, *Handbook*, 55–93), with his use of the term "allegory" in Gal. 4:21–5:1 warranting special consideration.

Narrative framework. A number of different narrative frameworks for Galatians have been proposed (see the survey in Das). In addition to the Isaianic narrative discussed above, proposals include the faith(fulness) of Jesus (Hays); gentile influx into Zion (Donaldson); sin, exile, and restoration (Wright, *Climax*); Abraham's faithfulness/obedience (Longenecker); exodus (Wilder); and new exodus (Scott). The number of proposals with valid supporting evidence suggests a number of overlapping and interlocking narratives that shape Paul's argument and theology at various points in Galatians.

Fulfillment. Throughout Galatians, Paul asserts or implies fulfillment of OT promises and types/patterns. Although he uses explicit fulfillment language only in 5:14 (where the whole law is said to be fulfilled in living out Lev. 19:18) and 6:2 (where it is not linked to an OT text), Paul clearly presents Scripture as being fulfilled at various points in the letter. He sees his own life and ministry in some sense as the fulfillment of the mission of the servant in Isa. 49 (Gal. 1:10, 15–16, 24; 2:2). The death of Jesus fulfills the description of the suffering servant of Isa. 53 (Gal. 1:4; 2:20; 3:13; 4:4–6). Believers experience the Spirit in fulfillment of God's OT promises (Gal. 3:2, 5, 14; 5:16–24 // Isa. 32:15–20; 44:1–5; Ezek. 36:26–27). The nations are being blessed through the gospel in fulfillment of God's promise to Abraham (Gal. 3:8–9 // Gen. 12:3; 18:18; 22:18). As the singular seed of Abraham, Jesus receives the inheritance promised to Abraham (Gal. 3:16–18 // Gen. 17:7–10, 19–21; 22:18; Isa. 41:8; 53:10; 54:3) and shares it with all who are united to him by faith (Gal. 3:26–4:7). Through him the hope of Jew and gentile together acknowledging the universal reign of the one true God has come to pass (Gal. 3:19–20 // Zech. 14:9). The promised new exodus that was to come about through a suffering servant and result in a new creation has been fulfilled in Christ (Gal. 4:1–7; 6:15 // Isa. 41:17–20; 51:9–10; 52:13–53:12), as has the promise of a new Jerusalem that produces children free from their slavery to sin (Gal. 4:27 // Isa. 54:1). Paul concludes the letter by praying for God's people to experience the peace and mercy that were promised through the new covenant (Gal. 6:16 // Isa. 54:10).

Authoritative support. Paul uses Scripture to provide authoritative support for various claims. Thus, he can assert that no flesh will be justified by works of the law (Gal. 2:16) on the basis of Ps. 143:2. Since Abraham was justified by faith (Gen. 15:6), it naturally follows that believers are also (Gal. 3:6). Those who rely on the law fall under a curse (Gal. 3:10), as Deut. 27:26; 28:58 make clear. Since Hab. 2:4 clearly establishes that the righteous shall live by faith, it is evident that no one can be justified by the law (Gal. 3:11). Indeed, Lev. 18:5 makes it clear that the law is not of faith (Gal. 3:12). That Jesus took our curse upon himself (Gal. 3:13) is supported by citing the curse that rests on those hanged on a tree (Deut. 21:23). Paul knows that those who sow to the flesh will reap destruction because Hosea 8:1–7; 10:12–13 make a similar assertion.

Example. Paul also illustrates various points through the use of an OT example. Referring to the opponents as those troubling the Galatians (Gal. 1:7–9) echoes the story of Achan troubling Israel. Paul's own preconversion zeal for the law (Gal. 1:13–14) echoes Phinehas's zeal to preserve the purity of Israel (Num. 25:1–13). The story of Abraham's two sons from different women (Gen. 16–21) illustrates the relationship between flesh and spirit (Gal. 4:21–5:1), while Sarah's command to Abraham to cast out Hagar and her son Ishmael (Gen. 21:10) is a picture of what God commands the Galatians to do to the opponents (Gal. 4:29).

Allegory. Paul's use of the Greek verb *allēgoreō* (Gal. 4:24)—translated as "allegory" in many English versions—has challenged interpreters for centuries (see the helpful and concise summary in Keener, 402–10). Debate swirls around whether Paul's use of Scripture in 4:21–5:1 is best described as allegory, typology, or something else. At minimum it is an example of figural interpretation, in which the meaning extends beyond the literal sense. Further complicating matters is the tendency to import distinctions between allegory and typology forged in the early Christian debates between the Alexandrian and Antiochene schools of interpretation (third and fourth centuries) back into Paul's first-century Jewish context. In those later discussions, typology is distinguished from allegory on the basis of the former being rooted in the historical and textual correspondences in the text and the latter imposing a theological, philosophical, or textual framework that reveals hidden meanings that are otherwise unseen. Yet it is open to debate whether such distinctions were relevant for first-century Jewish hermeneutics (Gignilliat, "Allegory," 137–41). Based on parallels with Philo's use of *allēgoreō*, however, it is possible to understand this verb as having the sense of "reading a text through the lens of another textual, philosophical, or theological framework to reveal a fuller meaning" (Harmon, "Allegory," 150).

Perhaps instead of an either-or approach, a both-and conclusion is appropriate. What Paul actually does in Gal. 4:21–5:1 is a combination of typology and allegory. It is typology in that it depends on real historical and textual correspondences intended by the authors of Genesis and Isaiah. Yet it is also allegory (in the sense of the term used by Philo, not in the later Alexandrian sense) because those correspondences are more fully revealed through the use of the textual and theological framework provided by Isa. 54:1 and its surrounding context (Harmon, "Allegory"). It should be stressed that Paul is not imposing a theological meaning that was formerly completely hidden. Rather, Paul understands more fully what was revealed earlier in the OT, with Isa. 54:1 and its surrounding context further illuminating meaning that is embedded within the Genesis narrative itself.

Conclusion

Paul's use of Scripture in Galatians will continue to prompt further study, despite the large amount of scholarship it has already generated. The rich mixture of citations, allusions, echoes, and thematic parallels combined with the theological complexities of Paul's argument are a siren song that will likely prove irresistible for the foreseeable future.

Bibliography. Beale, G. K., *Handbook on the New Testament Use of the Old Testament* (Baker Academic, 2012); Beale, "The Old Testament Background of Paul's Reference to 'the Fruit of the Spirit' in Galatians 5:22," *BBR* 15 (2005): 1–38; Beale, "Peace and Mercy upon the Israel of God," *Bib* 80 (1999): 204–23; Bruno, C. R., *"God Is One,"* LNTS 497 (Bloomsbury, 2013); Caneday, A. B., "Covenant Lineage Allegorically Prefigured," *SBTJ* 14 (2010): 50–77; Ciampa, R. E., *The Presence and Function of Scripture in Galatians 1 and 2*, WUNT 2/102 (Mohr Siebeck, 1998); Das, A. A., *Paul and the Stories of Israel* (Fortress, 2016); Di Mattei, S., "Paul's Allegory of the Two Covenants (Gal. 4.21–31) in Light of First-Century Hellenistic Rhetoric and Jewish Hermeneutics," *NTS* 52 (2006): 102–22; Donaldson, T. L., "The 'Curse of the Law' and the Inclusion of the Gentiles," *NTS* 32 (1986): 94–112; Dunne, J. A., *Persecution and Participation in Galatians*, WUNT 2/454 (Mohr Siebeck, 2017); Gignilliat, M., "Isaiah's Offspring," *BBR* 25 (2016): 205–23; Gignilliat, "Paul, Allegory, and the Plain Sense of Scripture," *JTI* 2 (2008): 135–46; Harmon, M. S., "Allegory, Typology, or Something Else?," in *Studies in the Pauline Epistles*, ed. M. S. Harmon and J. E. Smith (Zondervan, 2014), 144–58; Harmon, *Galatians*, EBTC (Lexham, 2021); Harmon, *She Must and Shall Go Free*, BZNW 168 (de Gruyter, 2010); Hays, R. B., *The Faith of Jesus Christ*, 2nd ed., BRS (Eerdmans, 2002); Jobes, K. H., "Jerusalem, Our Mother," *WTJ* 55 (1993): 299–320; Keener, C. S., *Galatians* (Baker Academic, 2019); Lincicum, D., *Paul and the Early Jewish Encounter with Deuteronomy*, WUNT 2/284 (Mohr Siebeck, 2010); Longenecker, B. W., *The Triumph of Abraham's God* (Abingdon, 1998); Scott, J. M., *Adoption as Sons of God*, WUNT 2/48 (Mohr Siebeck, 1992); Silva, M., "Galatians," in *CNTUOT*, 785–812; Sprinkle, P. M., *Law and Life*, WUNT 2/241 (Mohr Siebeck, 2008); Wakefield, A. H., *Where to Live*, AcBib 14 (Brill, 2003); Wilder, W. N., *Echoes of the Exodus Narrative in the Context and Background of Galatians 5:18*, SBL 23 (Lang, 2001); Willitts, J., "Isa. 54,1 in Gal. 4,24b–27," *ZNW* 96 (2005): 188–210; Wright, N. T., *The Climax of the Covenant* (Fortress, 1992); Wright, "Paul, Arabia, and Elijah (Galatians 1:17)," *JBL* 115 (1996): 683–92.

MATTHEW S. HARMON

Genesis, Book of

Genesis has pride of place at the beginning of the Bible. As such it plays a critical role in providing the essential frame of reference for the rest of Scripture. Like the introductory scenes in a great drama, it describes the setting, the main characters, and the plotline of the Bible. Without Genesis, the rest of the Bible is left hanging in the air. For instance, if the Bible started with Exodus, one would have to ask, Who are these Israelites? How did they end up in Egypt? What is the real significance of their persecution? Why did their God liberate them? But with Genesis as the backstory, all these questions are explained. And the universal significance of Israel's liberation is clearly highlighted. In Israel's salvation lies the secret to the world's salvation.

Structure of the Book

Genesis is divided into a prologue and ten "chapters," each with a similar genealogical heading: "These are the generations of X" (2:4 ESV; 5:1; 6:9; 10:1; 11:10, 27; 25:12, 19; 36:1 [cf. v. 9]; 37:2). In each of these titles, X has been introduced in the previous story line and is further developed in the ensuing narrative. Thus, the prologue (1:1–2:3) deals with the creation of heaven and earth, and this creation is further developed in 2:4–4:26 with the creation of humanity in its garden paradise and their expulsion because of disobedience. Consequently, Adam and his family (introduced in the previous section) are followed down to Noah in the next chapter (5:1–6:8), and in the subsequent narrative the Noah story is elaborated (6:9–9:29). Thus, a line is traced from creation and the first humans, made to rule the world, to the person of Judah, who will someday rule the world again (49:8–12). This link between the world and Israel can also be discerned if the chapters are grouped into two divisions of five each. The first deals with universal history (2:4–11:26), and the second with a family history (11:27–50:26).

Major Themes

Creation. Genesis provides the foundation for the superstructure of the rest of the Bible. It describes the transcendent Creator and his creation of the cosmos, including the earth and all its varied life along with the climax of creation, humanity, made in God's image. This is not so much an exhaustive scientific description as a theologically rich depiction of God's transcendence and his loving care for his creation, and especially humanity. He speaks and reality jumps into being. Humans are far from an afterthought; they are creatures elevated to be covenant partners with God. The prologue of Genesis (1:1–2:3) describes this in general terms with a panoramic description of the creative acts of God, while 2:4–2:25 focuses on the creation of humanity, its vocation as God's representative in his creation, and the consequent importance of human obedience to the divine word. All of this is fundamental to understanding the rest of the biblical story, the task and purpose of humanity, and its ultimate responsibility to God.

Problem and solution. After an introductory prologue (1:1–2:3), the first five "chapters" of the book (2:4–11:26) consist of a number of catastrophes (the fall, Gen. 3; fratricide, 4:1–16; bloodlust, 4:17–24; the flood, 6:8–9:17; the tower of Babel, 11:1–9) and largely present a universal perspective, while the last five "chapters" (11:27–50:26) consist of a number of blessings and focus on one family through four generations. Read together, the first section describes the problem with the world and the second sketches the beginning of a solution. The problem is the pandemic of sin, death, and divine judgment caused by human disobedience to the divine word (Gen. 3), which affects everyone and everything. The world is cursed, and the word "curse" occurs five times (3:14, 17; 4:11; 5:29; 9:25), highlighting this problem. The solution, however, for this world under curse is found in the family of Abraham. In fact, the key text at the beginning of the second section functions as a preview of the rest of Genesis, if not the Bible. Five times the word "bless" occurs as if to reinforce the reversal of the curse (12:1–3). The point is not lost to the perceptive audience: in Abraham and his seed, the curses will be reversed and the blessed world of Gen. 1–2 will be restored.

Later passages in Genesis highlight this theme of blessing as Abraham and his descendants partially fulfill the divine mandate to humanity at the beginning to be fruitful, multiply, and have dominion over the earth. In the midst of death and barrenness, they are promised that they will have numerous descendants and that kings will emerge from their progeny (Gen. 1:28; 12:2; 13:14–18; 15:5; 17:4–16; 18:18; 22:17–18; 24:60; 26:3–5; 28:13–15; 35:11–12).

In addition, there are many allusions in the rest of the OT to a coming restoration of creation as a result of God's salvation for the world. Psalm 72 speaks of the Israelite king who will bless the nations and bring about an Eden-like paradise; similar imagery is found in Ezek. 36:24–36. Isaiah and Hosea describe a new creation where animals will live in harmony with humanity, the serpent will be destroyed, and death will be no more (Isa. 25–27; 65:17–25; Hosea 2:16–23; cf. Amos 9:13–15; Joel 3:18). All these texts assume that something has gone wrong with creation and Israel; nonetheless, creation will be restored in a coming redemption (cf. Isa. 24–25; Hosea 6:7).

Themes of the family history. In the family history of the second section, three of the four generations of a family are followed and in each there is a programmatic statement at the beginning that provides the lens through which the narrative is viewed. These are God's word to Abraham in 12:1–3, God's word to Rebekah in 25:23, and Joseph's two dreams in 37:6–7, 9. The word to Abraham is a word of blessing to him personally, that he will become a great nation and provide a descendant (or descendants) through whom the world will be blessed. The entire subsequent narrative is about the miraculous birth of Isaac—the beginning of a nation (Gen. 21)—and the procurement of a small plot of ground for this nation (Gen. 23). The ensuing Jacob cycle is determined by the oracle to Rebekah that the younger of her twins, Jacob, would inherit the blessing. Finally, the Joseph story is governed by the dreams of Joseph as he rises to power above his brothers, becomes second-in-command over Egypt, and from his position of power blesses the world.

Throughout the family history there are intertextual links. Thus, Rebekah's decision to follow in Abraham's footsteps by leaving Mesopotamia echoes his decision to leave Ur. Her decision expressed in one word ("I will go" [*'ēlēk*], 24:58) captures the laconic verb used to describe her future father-in-law's past decision ("he went" [*wayyēlek*], 12:4). Likewise, Abraham's duplicity emerges in that of his son (12:10–20; 20:1–18; 26:6–11). Jacob deceives his firstborn brother to obtain a blessing, but Laban deceives Jacob by marrying him to his undesired firstborn daughter. Jacob deceives his father by wearing goatskin on his arms (27:16), while Jacob's sons trick him when they bring him Joseph's torn coat smeared with a goat's blood (37:31–35). Tamar engages in seduction in order to further the promise of children for Judah's line (38:14–19), while in the very next chapter Potiphar's wife seeks to seduce Joseph for sexual gratification (39:7–14). Moreover, it is difficult not to see Joseph in his rule over Egypt and with his wisdom to bless the nations (Gen. 41–49) as a partial fulfillment of the promise to Abraham of worldwide blessing (12:3).

Covenant family themes are developed in the rest of the OT as well. The covenant with Abraham, Isaac, and Jacob functions as a leitmotif of God's salvation for his people throughout Scripture (Exod. 2:24; 3:16; Lev. 26:42; Mic. 7:20; Neh. 9:7). Hosea remembers Jacob's wrestling in the womb and with God to encourage Israel (12:3–4). Jeremiah recalls Jacob's deception to indicate depravity (9:4). Joseph functions as a type of God's protection and providence (Ps. 105:16–22).

Genesis 3:15: The Protevangelium

While it has become very common to deny the significance of the promise to the woman in the curse on the serpent—that enmity would be placed between the serpent's seed and her seed, and would lead eventually to a crushing defeat for the serpent—this text occupies a pivotal, strategic position in Genesis. After its announcement, there is an extraordinary concern for genealogical precision and a focus on human descendants, which suggests the hope for a descendant or descendants who will defeat the power of the serpent and restore the original conditions of life in the garden—namely, harmonious relationships between God and humanity, humans among themselves, and humanity and nature. The conflict between the two lines is drawn out in the birth of the first two children, Cain and Abel (4:1–16), and then in two lines of descendants. The first line (Cain's) culminates in Lamech steeped in sin, who boasts in bloodlust (4:17–24), and the second (Seth's) climaxes in another Lamech (Gen. 5), who hopes that his newly born child will bring relief from God's curse on the earth. It is thus no coincidence that the genealogical trajectory of Genesis is narrowed down to Abraham and his descendants (12:1–3), one of whom is promised dominion over the world (49:8–12).

The rest of the OT makes clear that a Davidic ruler from the tribe of Judah will someday come and trample on the serpent (Isa. 9:5–6; 11:1–10; Ps. 72). In this greater son of David lies the world's hope. This hope is based not only on the genealogical trajectory of Genesis that narrows this down to a ruler from the tribe of Judah but also on the developing narrative in which a covenant is made with David, that he would always have a ruler on the throne (2 Sam. 7). Such a ruler would eventually rule the world and bring about God's salvation (Pss. 2; 72).

NT Development

It is not accidental that Genesis, the first and foundational book of the OT, is referenced many times in the NT both explicitly and implicitly. Its many foundational themes provide the conceptual substructure to the theology of the NT. The NT's description of the new creation assumes the old creation of Genesis. Christ as the second Adam is based on the first Adam of Genesis. Thus, the universal curse in Genesis is reversed by the universal blessing provided in Jesus, which results in nothing less than a new creation. In fact, the conclusion to the NT compares the new creation to the old creation to show the superiority of the former. A number of scholars have pointed out these similarities (e.g., Dumbrell; Waltke). They sum up the profound importance of Genesis for comprehending the significance of what has happened in the NT. Some of the parallels are listed in table 1. The beginning of the OT and the ending of the NT thus provide bookends for the biblical story.

Table 1. Parallels between Revelation and Genesis

Revelation	Genesis
New heaven and new earth (21:1)	Old heaven and old earth (chaps. 1–2)
No sea (21:1)	Creation of the sea (1:2, 9–10)
No death (21:4)	Death (chaps. 2–5)
No pain or tears (21:4)	Pain and sweat (3:16–19)
First things passed away (21:4)	First things (chaps. 1–3)
No sun and moon (21:23)	Sun and moon (1:14–19)
No night (21:25)	Night (1:3–5)
River of life with trees of life (22:1–4)	River with one tree of life (2:9–14)
No curse (22:3)	Curse (3:14–15, 17–19)

Many other examples could be added. This article simply touches on the most important ones. Many of these could be categorized as allusions, analogies, or types of Genesis texts, as well as fulfillments of ancient prophecies. Some texts are used simply to provide a rationale for institutions (e.g., marriage) and doctrines (e.g., justification). Many supply examples to be emulated (e.g., Abraham) or avoided (e.g., Esau).

The Synoptic Gospels. The first example is at the beginning of the NT in Matthew. Matthew opens his Gospel with the following words: "The book of the genealogy of Jesus the Messiah, the Son of David, the Son of Abraham." This explicitly connects Matthew with Genesis, in particular Gen. 5:1: "The book of the genealogy of Adam" (AT). In fact, "genealogy" in Matt. 1:1 renders the Greek word *genesis*. This Gospel is thus a new Genesis.

The genealogy that follows traces Jesus's genealogy from Abraham to David, and from David to Jesus. The first seven members mentioned in the genealogy all come from Genesis: Abraham, Isaac, Jacob, Judah, Perez, Zerah, and Tamar. Matthew begins with Abraham because of the covenant made with him and the promise that in his seed all the nations of the earth would be blessed (Gen. 12:3). It is not a coincidence that Matthew ends with Jesus's great commission to his followers to go into the whole world and make disciples of all nations (28:19–20). This text is showing that Jesus is the fulfillment of the Abrahamic promise of blessing.

Jesus uses Genesis to provide the original overarching basis for the institution of marriage and for the prohibition of divorce. He cites the creation of male and female in Gen. 1:27 and their being joined in marriage in 2:24 for his interpretation that an indissoluble human bond has resulted (Matt. 19:4–5; cf. Mark 10:6–8). Jesus later sketches a long trajectory of persecution of the righteous (Matt. 23:35) stretching from Cain's murder of Abel (Gen. 4:1–16) to Zechariah's martyrdom (2 Chron. 24:21–22). Analogy is key here not only in the murder of one righteous person at both ends of the Hebrew Bible but also in the cries for justice (Gen. 4:10; 2 Chron. 24:22). Jesus also uses typology to describe the relationship between the first major judgment in the flood at the beginning of the world and his prediction of the final judgment at the end of the world (Gen. 6:9–7:24; Matt. 24:37–39).

Jesus uses language of God's supernatural power in Sarah's birth of Isaac to educate his disciples about his power to make disciples in the kingdom. The disbelieving Sarah is rebuked by an angel's question, "Is anything too hard for Yahweh?" (Gen. 18:14 AT). With similar language, Jesus rebukes his disciples who believe that it is impossible to enter the kingdom: "With human beings it is impossible but with God all things are possible" (Matt. 19:26 AT; cf. Mark 10:27). The angel Gabriel uses the same language to answer Mary's question about how she can be a mother without having sexual relations with a man (Luke 1:37; cf. Rom. 9:9).

A typological parallel is drawn between Sodom and the cities that reject the preaching of the disciples. Any of the cities that reject the kingdom message will merit far worse judgment than Sodom. They are more culpable because the announcement that comes to them is far clearer and more salvific (Matt. 10:15; 11:23; Gen. 18:20–19:28).

The divine voice at Jesus's baptism alludes to the sacrifice of Isaac: "This is *my son, my beloved one,* in whom I am well pleased" (Matt. 3:17 AT). Jesus is not only equipped by the Spirit descending on him like a dove but also identified with Abraham's child of promise and the ordeal of the Akedah, an ordeal from which he, unlike Isaac, will not be rescued (Matt. 3:17; Mark 1:11; Luke 3:22; cf. Gen. 22:2).

When the Sadducees wish to take up their heretical view of the denial of a resurrection, they invoke the levirate law, regarding the necessity for the next of kin to marry a widow without any male heirs. The Gospels use virtually the exact wording of Gen. 38:8 (cf. Deut. 25:5). Judah says to Onan, "Go into the widow of your brother, and do the levirate act, and raise seed up for your brother" (AT; cf. Matt. 22:24; Mark 12:19; Luke 20:28). The Sadducees use such a law to suggest the absurdity of resurrection by hypothesizing a sequence of seven brothers who marry the same widow, and who each die without having a child. They then ask Jesus for the identity of the real husband in the resurrection. Jesus questions the underlying premise of the question with two points: they know neither the Scriptures nor the power of God. Citing Exod. 3:6, he proves that the resurrection is taught from the OT since God would never be identified as the God of the dead. Further, the power of God indicates that marriage will be obsolete in the new world, so the conundrum of the right marriage partner is solved (Matt. 22:29–33).

Finally, after his resurrection in Luke, Jesus joins two distraught disciples on the road to Emmaus. Their hopes have been dashed because of the recent death of Jesus, whom they believed was the Messiah, the hope of Israel. Jesus reeducates them and is finally recognized by them when they break bread with him (Luke 24:13–34). This new transforming vision that comes with eating is the direct foil to Adam and Eve's new but very different vision of the world when they eat the forbidden fruit (Gen. 3:5–7).

John's Gospel. John begins his Gospel with a direct echo of Gen. 1 by stating that the Word was in the beginning with God and everything was created by the Word (John 1:1–3). This is a reflection on the power of God's word as the agent of creation in the beginning of Genesis. As John continues, he states that this Word became incarnate in Jesus Christ (1:14). Later in the Gospel there is a reference to the serpent in Gen. 3, when Jesus is confronting the duplicitous religious leaders. He says, "You belong to your father, the devil, and you want to carry out your father's desires. He was a murderer from the beginning, not holding to the truth, for there is no truth in him. When he lies, he speaks his native language, for he is a liar and the father of lies" (John 8:44). This is probably a reference to the serpent's speech in Gen. 3:4 when he told the first woman in the garden that she would not die if she ate from the forbidden fruit.

John includes several references to Abraham. At one point, Jesus states, "Your father Abraham rejoiced to see my day; he saw it and was glad" (John 8:56 CSB). This may refer to the general coming of the descendant/s who would bless the world (Gen. 12:3) or to the specific descendant who would be like the sacrificial lamb offered in the place of Isaac (22:13).

Jacob also appears in John's Gospel as Jesus meets a Samaritan woman at a well outside Samaria, a well that went back to the patriarchal period. Jacob had given this land to his son Joseph (John 4:5–6, 12; Gen. 33:19; Josh. 24:32; cf. Gen. 48:22). Jesus's meeting this future disciple may further echo Jacob's encounter with Rachel, his future wife (Gen. 29:1–11). The point is that Jesus gives living water that satisfies the soul rather than physical water that satisfies the body temporarily. Jacob also features in the account of Nathaniel's conversion (John 1:45–51). When Jesus meets Nathaniel, he speaks of him as an Israelite in whom there is no deceit, probably in contrast to the deceitful Jacob (John 1:47; Gen. 27:36; cf. Jer. 9:4). When Nathaniel is amazed at Jesus's prescience, Jesus further develops the Jacob typology by telling Nathaniel that he will be even more amazed when he sees heaven opened and the angels of God ascending and descending on the Son of Man (John 1:50–51). This evokes the story of Jacob's dream when he sees angels descending and ascending on a ladder to heaven that comes down near his head (Gen. 28:12). Jesus is the promised one who will finally unite heaven and earth!

When Pilate presents Jesus to the Jews, he declares, "Behold the Man!" (John 19:5 AT). Alan Richardson observes that John here presents God's original intention, the new Adam, the messianic king. And when Jesus is taken out to be crucified, his cross is erected at Golgotha, the place of the skull (Matt. 27:33; Mark 15:22; Luke 23:33; John 19:17). There may be an allusion here to the seed of the woman who would crush the head of the seed of the serpent but be wounded in the process. The resurrection that follows takes place in a garden, where

Mary mistakes the gardener for Jesus (John 20:11–18). Here, the new Adam takes up his role as the first gardener and meets his new bride, Mary, in a new Eden. The fall has been reversed.

Finally, after the resurrected Jesus meets his disciples and breathes into them the Holy Spirit, he commissions them with a message of forgiveness (John 20:19–23). This recalls the creation of Adam in Gen. 2:7 when God breathed into him the breath of life and indicates that Jesus is making a new humanity through the gift of the Holy Spirit and the message of forgiveness.

Acts and Paul. In Acts, Paul refers to creation in Genesis when he declares to the Athenians that God made the world and everything in it, giving to every creature life and breath, making from one person every nation of humanity, even appointing the times and the boundaries of their countries (Acts 17:24–26; Gen. 1–2; 10). He further describes human beings as the offspring of God (Acts 17:29), which is an echo of the image of God and sonship (Gen. 1:27–28; 5:1–3; cf. Luke 3:38).

But most of the references to Genesis in Acts derive from Stephen's speech to the Sanhedrin when he presents a history of Israel to persuade his hearers that Christ is the goal of the OT and that they are directly implicated in his death (Acts 7). He begins with God's call of Abraham in Gen. 12 (Acts 7:2–3) and traces the history of the patriarchs from Abraham to Joseph, including their burials in Canaan (Acts 7:16, combining Gen. 23; 25:9–10; 33:19; 35:29; cf. Josh. 24:32). He specifically mentions the delay in the promise regarding the possession of the land because of the Egyptian sojourn (Acts 7:5–7; Gen. 15:3–18); the covenant of circumcision (Acts 7:8a; Gen. 17); the birth and circumcision of Isaac (Acts 7:8b; Gen. 21); the birth of Jacob (Gen. 25:21–26) and the twelve patriarchs (Acts 7:8c; Gen. 29:31–35:18); and the story of Joseph (Acts 7:9–16; Gen. 37–50).

One other passage in Acts reinforces the importance of the promise to Abraham, which is reiterated throughout Genesis (Acts 3:25; Gen. 12:3; 18:18; 22:18; 26:4; 28:14). In Peter's speech to a Jewish audience (Acts 3:11–26), he speaks of the promise to Abraham that through his seed all peoples of the earth would be blessed (Gen. 12:3). He explains that when God raised up his servant Jesus, he sent him to the Jews first, so that they might first experience this blessing through repentance and faith (3:25–26). Thus, Jesus is regarded as the fulfillment of this prophecy.

Genesis also plays a large part in the substructure of Pauline thought. In Rom. 1, Paul grounds his thesis of universal condemnation in the gentiles' distortion of the created works all around them (Gen. 1), worshiping and serving the creature instead of the Creator (Rom. 1:18–26). This probably alludes to Adam's creation and fall. When Paul wishes to show that justification by faith has its precedent before the law was given, he uses the example of Abraham being justified by faith before his circumcision (Rom. 4; Gen. 15–17). Paul cites a form of the key text, that Abraham's faith was credited to him for righteousness, three times (Rom. 4:3, 9, 22; Gen. 15:6). He goes to great lengths to emphasize Abraham's faith: when he considered his one-hundred-year-old body as good as dead, as also that of his ninety-year-old wife, he still kept believing, growing stronger in faith (Rom. 4:19–20). While a close reading of Genesis does show Abraham doubting (Gen. 15:1–5; 16:1–16; 17:17), Paul is probably summarizing the entire trajectory of his life.

Paul also uses the Adam-Christ typology to show the nature and extent of Christ's salvation. Adam's sin has plunged the whole world into sin and death, but the second Adam, Jesus Christ, has provided salvation. His obedience has made the gift of righteousness, and hence eternal life, available to all (Rom. 5:12–19; Gen. 1–3).

In dealing with the doctrine of election, Paul shows how Abraham's seed is found in the chosen seed of Isaac, the child of the promise, and not the child of the flesh, Ishmael (Rom. 9:6–9). Whereas Ishmael was born of human initiative and human potency, Isaac, the miracle child, was born of supernatural power (Rom. 9:7–9; Gen. 16; 18:10–14). Paul then proceeds to illustrate the doctrine of election by showing that God chose Jacob over Esau while they were still in the womb, before they could perform any action whatsoever, whether good or evil (Rom. 9:10–13; Gen. 25:19–26). Finally, Paul refers to a promise that is true not only of the Messiah but also of his followers. Utilizing the promise that the woman's seed would defeat the seed of the serpent, he writes to his Roman audience that the "God of peace will soon crush Satan under your feet" (Rom. 16:20; cf. Gen. 3:15).

Paul also deals with a problem in worship in the church at Corinth by recalling the creation of the first man and woman in Gen. 2. Evidently in the Corinthian church, the cultural custom was for women, and not men, to wear head coverings. Paul argues that the custom is based on a creational order. The man does not need a head covering because he is the image and glory of God whereas the woman requires one because she is the image and glory of man. This assumes the temporal sequence of the man being created first, followed by the woman. The man is thus not from the woman, but vice versa, as part of the man was taken from his body and formed into a woman. At the same time, Paul notes that in birth the man also comes from the woman (1 Cor. 11:7–12), so that man and woman have a coequal and codependent status.

Similarly, Paul uses the typology of the first and second Adams to defend a key doctrine in the Christian faith—namely, the resurrection of the dead at the last day, a doctrine that was being denied in the Corinthian church because of an incipient Gnosticism (1 Cor. 15:45–49; Gen. 1–2). Thus, the first Adam died, but the second Adam lives and will resurrect believers at his return in the future. He is the firstfruits of their future resurrection. Thus, the two resurrections—Christ's in the middle of history and his people's at the end of history—are inextricable. To deny the one is to deny the other (1 Cor. 15:1–34). The resurrection of Christ is not just an addendum to their faith but its heart (1 Cor. 15:1–3, 12–18).

Paul draws another analogy when combating false apostles in the church who are derogating him and elevating themselves. He compares them to the serpent who deceived Eve with its lies (Gen. 3:1–7). Correspondingly, the Corinthians are like an innocent woman in danger of being deceived by these later manifestations of the serpent (2 Cor. 11:1–4).

Another reference to Genesis in the Corinthian correspondence occurs when Paul is instructing about sexual immorality (1 Cor. 6:12–20). In a culture of rampant sexual immorality, he shows the sacred significance of the sexual act: it is not just a temporary union of bodies for pleasure; it is a holy, permanent union. Consequently, Paul argues that prostitution, a common practice in Corinth, is unthinkable, because an invisible union will persist long after the physical separation. Paul grounds this truth in Gen. 2 where the basis of marriage is found in the two genders being joined in the sexual act: the two are now one flesh (2:24).

In Galatians, Paul uses texts employed in Romans to stress the importance of justification by faith. False teachers have infiltrated the Galatian churches, asserting that faith in Christ is insufficient for salvation and must be accompanied by performance of the Jewish law. Thus, he challenges the Galatians to determine whether their salvation was by the works of the law or by the hearing of faith. And lest they be confused by these alternatives, he cites Gen. 15:6, "Abraham 'believed God, and it was credited to him as righteousness'" (Gal. 3:6). To reinforce his point, Paul states that the promise of Gen. 12:3 that in Abraham's seed all nations of the earth would be blessed proves that God has justified the ungodly through faith as those who believe are blessed with the man of faith, Abraham (Gal. 3:8–9). To show that the Galatians should rely on faith in Christ rather than human ability, Paul draws an analogy between the way of the law, which depends on human ability, and the way of the Spirit, which requires faith. Indeed, the two children of Abraham illustrate these two ways (Gal. 4:21–25; Gen. 16; 21). Ishmael is born of the slave woman, Hagar, and represents the way of the flesh—the way of human power—whereas Isaac is born of the free woman, Sarah, and stands for the way of faith. As a result, Abraham sends Hagar and Ishmael away from his family so that they do not receive the true inheritance, which comes only to the faithful (Gal. 4:29–30; Gen. 21:9–10).

The letters to Ephesus and Colossae can be grouped together since they cover similar content. Creation texts are mentioned at the beginning of Colossians with the stunning point that Christ is the true image of the invisible God, the firstborn of all creation, and that he was before all things and by him all things consist (Col. 1:15–17). Paul is showing the superiority of Christ to every created thing, and the backdrop for his assertion is the creation narrative in Genesis. Likewise, Paul uses the idea of the first and second Adam to show believers that they have been created in the image of the new man, created in righteousness, holiness, and truth, and that they have put off the old man, which was corrupted according to deceitful desires (Eph. 4:21–24; Col. 3:9–11). And when Paul wishes to instruct husbands and wives in their proper relationship to each other, he urges that husbands love their wives as Christ loves the church, and that wives submit to their husbands as to Christ (Eph. 5:22–33). Paul grounds this truth in Christ's relationship to the church, which is shown to be a great mystery reflected in the creation of the male and female at the beginning, in which the woman is built from the man as a separate creation, which explains their attraction to each other and their reunion again in marriage (Gen. 2:18–25). This results in the institution of marriage whereby a man leaves his parents and cleaves to his wife, and they become one flesh (Eph. 5:31; Gen. 2:24).

Hebrews and the Catholic Letters. Hebrews is probably addressed to Jewish Christians and as a result has many references to the OT. Its main purpose is to place the superiority of Christ before its audience. He is the great Creator (1:1–4; Gen. 1:1–3) who has brought about a superlative redemption. Thus, the Sabbath points to an eschatological rest for the people of God as people rest from their dead works to trust in Christ (4:4; Gen. 2:2). Abel's blood, which cries out for justice, is contrasted with Christ's blood, which pleads for mercy (12:24; Gen. 4:10). Melchizedek, the priest-king in Genesis, functions as a type of Christ (Heb. 7; Gen. 14:18–20). The great chapter on faith (Heb. 11) is a virtual roll call of OT figures, many of whom are found in Genesis (Abel, Enoch, Abraham, Sarah, Isaac, Jacob) and are great examples of faith in God's promise. Even Abraham's hospitality (13:1–2; Gen. 18:1–14) and Esau's greed (12:16–17; Gen. 25:29–33) serve respectively as an exhortation and a warning.

In the Catholic Letters, James uses texts from Genesis to show the importance of a faith that works. Christian speech that praises God is incongruous with curses on humans made in his image (3:9–10; Gen. 1:27). Similarly, the example of Abraham's sacrifice of Isaac shows that a living faith must issue in action (James 2:20–24; Gen. 22:1–18; cf. 15:6).

In 1 and 2 Peter, Genesis notably features in several texts. The salvation of Noah during the flood points forward to the baptism of Christians (1 Pet. 3:20–21; Gen. 6–9). The flood itself serves as a sign of future judgment (2 Pet. 3:4–6). Peter also alludes to the time before the flood when fallen angels caused such havoc that they were imprisoned. By virtue of his death Christ was able to preach to them (1 Pet. 3:19–21; 2 Pet. 2:4; Gen. 6:1–7:24). The salvation of Lot from Sodom functions as a model for future salvation of the godly (2 Pet. 2:6–9;

Gen. 19:1–16). Finally, Sarah is presented as a model for Christian women (1 Pet. 3:6; Gen. 18:12).

Jude, like 2 Peter, has similar OT references. He uses the examples of Cain (v. 11), the fallen angels (v. 6), and the destruction of Sodom and Gomorrah (v. 7) to warn his audience of false teachers, immorality, and the consequent judgment of God. Jude uses the example of Enoch, the seventh from Adam according to Gen. 5 (Jude 14–15), to announce coming judgment on all the ungodly. While Jude cites a prophecy from the Book of Enoch (1 En. 1:9), the example of Enoch, who walked with God in a generation of wickedness, contributes to the importance of keeping the faith despite hostile circumstances.

First John uses an explicit reference to Cain and Abel to show the difference between the children of God and those of the devil. After commanding his audience to love one another and thereby prove that they are God's children, John cites the example of Cain, who hated his brother because of his righteous behavior (1 John 3:11–18; Gen. 4:3–8). The description of God as pure light echoes God's first creative act in Genesis (1 John 1:5; Gen. 1:3). And John's description of the love of the world as comprising the lust of the flesh, the lust of the eyes, and the pride of life alludes to the first temptation when Eve saw the forbidden fruit as good for food, desirable to the eyes, and coveted for wisdom (1 John 2:15–17; Gen. 3:6).

Revelation. Revelation has many allusions to the OT and is thus a fitting bookend to the Scriptures. Some of the echoes and allusions have been noted at the beginning of this essay. But there are others scattered throughout the book, such as the tree of life in the garden of Eden (Rev. 2:7; 22:14; 19; Gen. 2:8–9; 3:22, 24), the judgment of Sodom (Rev. 9:2; 20:10; Gen. 19), and Jesus as the Lion from the tribe of Judah (Rev. 5:5; Gen. 49:9–10).

Bibliography. Alexander, T. D., "Royal Expectations in Genesis to Kings," *TynBul* 49 (1998): 191–212; Clines, D. J. A., *The Theme of the Pentateuch* (JSOT Press, 1978); Dempster, S. G., "'He Believed the LORD,'" in *The Doctrine on Which the Church Stands or Falls*, ed. M. Barrett (Crossway, 2019), 41–66; Dumbrell, W. J., *The End of the Beginning* (Wipf & Stock, 2001); Hooker, M., "Adam in Romans 1," *NTS* 6 (1960): 297–306; Johnson, M. D., *The Purpose of the Biblical Genealogies* (Cambridge University Press, 1969); Kim, J.-W., "Explicit Quotations from Genesis in the Context of Stephen's Speech in Acts," *Neot* 41 (2007): 341–60; Lohr, J. N., "Righteous Abel, Wicked Cain," *CBQ* 71 (2009): 485–96; Menken, M. J. J., and S. Moyise, eds., *Genesis in the New Testament* (T&T Clark, 2012); Minear, P. S., *Christians and the New Creation* (John Knox, 1994); Pate, C. M., "Genesis 1–3," *CTR* 10, no. 2 (2013): 3–25; Richardson, A., *The Gospel according to St. John* (SCM, 1959); Sailhamer, J. H., *The Pentateuch as Narrative* (Zondervan, 1992); Schnittjer, G., "The Blessing of Judah as Generative Expectation," *BibSac* 177 (2020): 15–39; Schnittjer, *Old Testament Use of the Old Testament* (Zondervan, 2021); Spurgeon, A. B., "1 Timothy 2:13–15," *JETS* 56 (2013): 543–56; von Rad, G., *Genesis* (Westminster, 1973); Waltke, B. K., *Old Testament Theology* (Zondervan, 2007).

STEPHEN G. DEMPSTER

Gentiles *See* Jews and Gentiles

Glory of God

God's glory appears in every major part of the Bible and affects every major doctrine. It is also notoriously hard to define.

The Meaning(s) of Glory

Terminology. "Glory" normally translates the Hebrew term *kābōd* and the Greek term *doxa*. *Kābōd* stems from a root that means "weight" or "heaviness" (Longman, 48). Depending on its form, it could have the sense of honorable, dignified, exalted, or revered. C. John Collins (581) explains that it became "a technical term for God's manifest presence." It is similar in many respects to the concept of God's name in the OT.

According to Sverre Aalen, *doxa* in secular Greek refers to an opinion, conjecture, repute, praise, or fame. He maintains that the concepts were transformed by the Septuagint and that *doxa* translated *kābōd* and took on the same meaning, referring to God's manifestation of his person, presence, and/or works, especially his power, judgment, and salvation.

Biblical usage. At a basic level, it is helpful to notice that the glory of God is referenced in the Bible as an adjective, sometimes a noun, and sometimes a verb. God is glorious (adjective), reveals his glory (noun), and is to be glorified (verb).

More particularly, the Bible speaks of the glory of God in several senses (Morgan, "Toward").

First, glory is used as *a designation for God himself*. God is the "Majestic Glory" (2 Pet. 1:17). This rare phrase is apparently a Hebrew way of referring to God without stating his name.

Second, glory sometimes refers to *an internal characteristic, attribute, or a summary of attributes of God*. God is intrinsically glorious in the sense of fullness, sufficiency, majesty, beauty, and splendor (Ps. 24:7–10; Acts 7:2; Eph. 1:17).

Third, the Bible frequently speaks of glory as *God's presence*. Exodus recounts the glory cloud (Exod. 13–14; 16:7; 20; 24), manifestations to Moses (chaps. 3–4; 32–34), and God's presence in the tabernacle (29:43; 40:34–38). God's glorious presence is also highlighted in the ark of the covenant (1 Sam. 4:21–22), temple (1 Kings 8:10–11), eschatological temple (Ezek. 43:1–5), Christ (John 1:1–18), the Holy Spirit (John 14–16), and heaven (Rev. 21–22).

Fourth, the Bible depicts glory as *the display of God's attributes, perfections, or person*. John's Gospel speaks of glory in this way, as Jesus performs "signs" that manifest his glory (2:11). The Bible uses various terms for this concept, but the idea is clear: God glorifies himself in displaying himself. His mercy, grace, justice, and wrath are all displayed in salvation and judgment (cf. Rom. 9:20–23; Eph. 2:4–10).

A fifth connotation of glory is as *the ultimate goal of the display of God's attributes, perfections, or person*. Exodus and Ezekiel are replete with passages that unfold God's actions for the sake of his name or in order that people will know he is the Lord (e.g., Exod. 6:7; Ezek. 5:13; 6:7–14). Paul points out that God chooses, adopts, redeems, and seals us "to the praise of the glory of his grace" (Eph. 1:6 AT; cf. vv. 12, 14).

Sixth, glory sometimes connotes *heaven or eschatological consummation of the experience of God's presence.* Hebrews 2:10 speaks of "bringing many sons to glory" (ESV). Philippians 4:19 offers the covenant promise, "my God will supply every need of yours according to his riches in glory in Christ Jesus" (ESV). Believers are prepared for glory (Rom. 9:23) and will be raised "in glory" (1 Cor. 15:43).

Seventh, glory may be used in connection with *the worship or exaltation of God.* Psalm 29:2 urges, "Ascribe to the LORD the glory due his name." At Jesus's birth, the heavenly host resounds with "glory to God in the highest" and the shepherds are "glorifying and praising God" (Luke 2:14, 20; see Newman, "Glory"). Further, the Bible is filled with doxologies linking worship to glory: "To the only wise God be glory forever through Christ Jesus" (Rom. 16:27). Glorifying God is a way of life for God's people (cf. Matt. 5:13–16), who glorify God in their bodies (1 Cor. 6:20), relationships (1 Cor. 10:31), and spiritual gifts (1 Pet. 4:11).

These multiple usages of glory are distinct but related. The triune God who is glorious displays his glory, largely through his creation, image-bearers, providence, and redemptive acts. God's people respond by glorifying him. God receives glory and, through uniting his people to Christ, shares his glory with them—all to his glory. Put differently, glory is *possessed*: God's presence and intrinsic glory (Exod. 40:34–38; Isa. 42:8). Second, glory is *displayed*: God shows his glory in creation (Ps. 19:1), providence (Ps. 104:31), humanity (Ps. 8:4–5), and salvation (Exod. 14:13–18; Acts 3:13–15; see Packer). Third, glory is *ascribed*: believers glorify God (Ps. 115:1; Rev. 19:1). Fourth, glory is *received*: God accepts their glorifying of him (Ps. 29:1–2; Rev. 4:9–11). Fifth, glory is *shared*: God graciously communicates his glory with his people in redemption, making them increasingly glorious in Christ (2 Cor. 3:18; 2 Thess. 2:14). Sixth, glory is *purposed*: all this redounds to God's glory (Rom. 11:36; Eph. 1:3–14).

Usage in theology. Theologians often speak of the glory of God in intrinsic and extrinsic terms. God is intrinsically glorious, in the sense of fullness, sufficiency, majesty, honor, worth, beauty, weight, and splendor. God's glory is also extrinsic, a "dazzling theater," as John Calvin put it (*Institutes* 1.5.8; 2.6.1).

Jonathan Edwards (230–31) views God's glory as intrinsic and a communication of himself that may be seen, marveled at, and rejoiced in. John Gerstner (2:34) explains, "In the sermon on Psalm 89:6 Edwards had the glory of God consisting in God's greatness (natural attribute) and goodness (moral attribute). So glory is another word used for the sum total of all divine excellencies. It refers to the internal as well as manifestative glory. The latter amounts to a setting forth of the attributes in their reality and fullness."

More recently, J. I. Packer designates it as "fundamental to God" and refers to God's glory as the "excellence and praiseworthiness set forth in display" (271–72). John Piper teaches, "The glory of God is the outward radiance of the intrinsic beauty and greatness of his manifold perfections" (*Dangerous*, 81).

OT scholars tend to come at this differently. Some, like C. John Collins, underscore God's glory as his manifest presence. Ray Ortlund Jr. speaks similarly, but also ties glory to God's nature and beauty: "His glory is the fiery radiance of his very nature. It is his blazing beauty. . . . The glory of the Lord . . . is God himself becoming visible, God bringing his presence down to us, God displaying his beauty before us" (237). Others, like John Hartley, view God's glory as the manifestation of his essence. Hartley follows C. Vriezen (150) here, who defines glory as "the radiant power of [God's] Being, as it were the external manifestation of [God's] mysterious holiness."

Despite the apparent differences, there is a shared understanding of God's glory as the extrinsic manifestation of something intrinsic. This is because Scripture plainly links the extrinsic display of God's glory to a variety of his attributes, works, and terms that stress his person and nature. God's glory relates to his holiness (Isa. 6:1–8; Rev. 4–5), uniqueness (Isa. 42:8), power (Exod. 13:21–22), beauty, majesty, and goodness. God's glory is also tied to his work in creation (Ps. 19), salvation (Eph. 1–2), providence (Exod. 16:10–12; 40:36–38), judgment (2 Thess. 1:8–9), and victory (Exod. 14:15–18). God's glory is linked to his very nature: God's presence, name, holiness, face, Spirit, fullness, and honor (McConville, 156–57; Newman, 396; Waltke, 474).

So God's glory is the extrinsic display of his attributes, works, and the totality of his nature. These are interrelated. God's activities of creation, providence, salvation, and judgment are all for his glory. In these works, God sets forth various attributes on display. For example, in Exodus, God acts so that others will recognize his utter uniqueness and power. In Romans, God's saving action displays his righteousness, justice, wrath, power, mercy, and glory (3:21–26; 9:20–23). In Ephesians, God acts for the ultimate display of at least three attributes: grace (1:6), kindness (2:4–10), and wisdom (3:10–11).

In doing so, God acts unto his ultimate end—his glory. Edwards (243) is helpful: "The thing signified by that name, the glory of God, when spoken of as the supreme and ultimate end of all God's works, is the emanation and true external expression of God's internal glory and fullness . . . or, in other words, God's internal glory, in a true and just exhibition, or external existence of it."

The Biblical Story and God's Glory

God's glory has been called "the foundational theme of New Testament theology" (Schreiner, 135), biblical theology in general (Hamilton, 37–65), and God's ultimate end (Edwards, 231). It is a key theme in the biblical story.

Creation and God's glory. God reveals his glory in creation: "The heavens declare the glory of God" (Ps. 19:1). "Since the creation of the world," humans have seen God's "eternal power and divine nature" in the things he has made (Rom. 1:20). The transcendent Creator shows his sovereignty in creation, for as divine King he effects his will by his mere word (Gen. 1:3). God also reveals his goodness in creation, as the steady refrain testifies: "And God saw that it was good" (1:10, 12, 18, 21, 25).

God especially reveals his glory in his creation of humans as persons made in his image (1:26–28). In doing so, God invests his image-bearers with glory, honor, and dominion. David marvels, "You have . . . crowned him with glory and honor. You have given him dominion over the works of your hands" (Ps. 8:5–6 ESV). Sinclair Ferguson (139–40) explains, "In Scripture, image and glory are interrelated ideas. As the image of God, man was created to reflect, express and participate in the glory of God, in miniature, creaturely form." All creation testifies to God's glory, and humans uniquely bear God's image, serving as his representatives and stewards.

The fall and God's glory. In Gen. 1–2, God blesses Adam and Eve with an unhindered relationship with him, intimate enjoyment of each other, and delegated authority over creation. God gives only one prohibition: not to eat of the tree of the knowledge of good and evil. Sadly, in Gen. 3, Adam and Eve disobey God's command. Their rebellion brings God's justice. The couple feels shame, estrangement from and fear toward God, and they try to hide from him (3:7–10). They are alienated from each other, and pain and sorrow follow (3:10–21). Even worse, God banishes the couple from his glorious presence in Eden, a temple-garden (3:22–24; Beale, *Theology*, 29–46).

Sin devastates God's image-bearers, whom he made to reflect his glory. The Bible describes sin as a failure to keep God's law (1 John 3:4), an absence of his righteousness (Rom. 1:18), a lack of reverence for God (Jude 15), and a falling "short of the glory of God" (Rom. 3:23). Proud humans soon attempt to advance their name rather than God's name and glory (Gen. 11:1–9), a clear manifestation of idolatry (see Beale, *Worship*, 15–20). Paul's words pertain to all humans since the fall, although not all worship physical images: they "exchanged the glory of the immortal God" for an image (Rom. 1:23; cf. 1 John 5:21). Sin is a failure to image the Creator to the world, a failure to honor God as he is due, a worshiping of the creature rather than the Creator (Rom. 1:21–23). Sin is trading the glory of God for something less (Ps. 106:20; Jer. 2:11–12). Richard Gaffin captures the sad condition of image-bearers since the fall:

> For Paul the essence of human sin is the rebellion of the creature against the Creator in whose image he has been made, a renouncing of the truth of the creaturely dependence that divine image-bearing entails, for the lie of human self-sufficiency and independence from God. This deeply rooted revolt is such that human beings refuse to acknowledge God's glory evident in the entire creation and evident particularly in and to themselves because they, uniquely as creatures, are God's image. The creaturely capacities given with being that image, capacities to be for God, for doing his will and obeying his law, are instead directed against him in devoting to self or some other creature the worship and service due to him alone. The result of sin is not the loss of the divine image but its defacement or distortion, the loss of image-bearing integrity. In this sense all human beings are sinners who "fall short of the glory of God." ("Epistles," 147)

Redemption and God's glory. Thankfully, God does not destroy humanity for cosmic treason but graciously works to redeem it and the cosmos. In redemption, God begins to restore his glory in his image-bearers. He intends to restore humans as full image-bearers who will reflect his glory.

God calls Abraham from idolatry and enters into covenant with him and his descendants (Gen. 12:1–3; 17:7). God promises to give Abraham a land, to make him into a great nation, and through him to bless all peoples (12:3). From Abraham come Isaac and then Jacob, whose name God changes to Israel and from whom God brings twelve tribes and a nation. God identifies his glory with his people Israel (Isa. 40:5; 43:6–7; 60:1). He promises to bless them so that they will bless the nations, who will glorify him. When Egypt enslaves the covenant people, God redeems them through Moses, showing his glory in plagues and exodus so all will know he is incomparable (Exod. 9:16). He also displays his glory through theophanies, the giving of the law, and the tabernacle and temple. God's presence guides his people as they occupy the promised land under Joshua. God gives Israel kings. Under David the kingdom grows, and God renews his covenant with his people. He promises to make David's descendants into a dynasty and to establish the throne of one of them forever (2 Sam. 7:16). Solomon builds a temple to manifest God's presence. Solomon does much right, but his disobedience leads to the kingdom splitting into Northern (Israel) and Southern (Judah) Kingdoms.

God sends prophets to turn his sinful people away from worthless idols and back to himself, the uniquely glorious God. These prophets call the people to covenant faithfulness and warn of the judgment that will come if they fail to repent. Nevertheless, the people repeatedly rebel. In response, God sends the Northern Kingdom into captivity to Assyria (722 BC) and the Southern Kingdom into captivity to Babylon (586 BC). Through the prophets, God also promises to send a deliverer (Isa. 9:6–7; 52:13–53:12). The prophets yearn for Israel to become what God intended—glorious (Isa. 60–66)—when the Messiah arrives. God promises to restore his people to their land (Jer. 25:11–12), and he does so under Ezra and Nehemiah. The people rebuild the walls of Jerusalem and build a second temple. Yet the OT ends with God's people continuing to turn away from him (Malachi).

Four hundred years later, God sends his Son as the promised Messiah, suffering servant, King of Israel, and Savior of the world. As the Messiah, Jesus is glorious, but not as expected. The Jews hope for a political leader to restore Israel to its former glory. But Jesus's redemption and his glory are deeper than anticipated, for he is the Lord of glory, the radiance of God's glory, even Yahweh himself (James 2:1; Heb. 1:3; Dan. 7:13–14). Jesus the Messiah is the eternal Son, intrinsically glorious, who humbles himself to become a man (John 1:1–18; Phil. 2:5–11). Both lowly shepherds and glorious angelic hosts mark his birth (Luke 2:1–20). His signs witness to his glorious identity and the presence of God's kingdom (John 2:11; 11:4, 38–44). In the transfiguration, Jesus's glory shines (Mark 9:2–13; 2 Pet. 1:16–21).

Jesus chooses twelve disciples to lead his messianic community. He brings God's kingdom by casting out demons, doing miracles, and preaching good news. Jewish leaders oppose him. The Sanhedrin condemns Jesus in an illegal trial, and Pontius Pilate crucifies him. Humanly speaking, Jesus dies as a victim in a dreadfully evil act. Yet his death fulfills God's eternal plan, and Jesus succeeds in his mission to seek and save the lost. His glory is linked with his suffering and death (John 17:1–5). The cross is also Jesus's path to glory (1 Pet. 1:10–11). The cross displays God's glory by showing his righteousness, patience, and grace (Rom. 3:24–26). Jesus not only bears the world's sin in death but also is raised from the dead. His resurrection confirms his identity, defeats sin and death, gives new life to believers, and promises their future resurrection. He is raised by the glory of the Father unto glory, exalted to the highest status (Rom. 6:4; Phil. 2:9–11; Heb. 2:9). He ascends gloriously and reigns gloriously (1 Tim. 3:16; Acts 7:55–56).

Jesus tells his disciples to take the gospel to all nations, fulfilling God's promise to bless all peoples through Abraham. They are to disciple others, who will do the same. On Pentecost, Jesus sends his Spirit, who forms the church as the NT people of God. The early church is committed to evangelism (Acts 2:38–41), fellowship (vv. 42–47), ministry (vv. 42–46), and worship (v. 46). The church faces persecution, but some Jews and many gentiles trust Christ, and churches are planted. They teach sound doctrine, correct error, and call believers to live for God. The apostles teach that the Father plans salvation, the Son accomplishes it, and the Spirit applies it. God calls, regenerates, declares righteous, and adopts into his family all who trust Christ. God is making his people increasingly holy and glorious in Christ (2 Cor. 3:17–18).

The glorious triune God manifests his glory and, through union with Christ, shares it with his people. Paul praises God's mighty power that produces "glory in the church and in Christ Jesus" (Eph. 3:20–21). Paul depicts the church in glorious language: it is "the fullness of him who fills all in all" and "a dwelling place for God" (1:23; 2:22 ESV). Even more than creation, the church is the theater of and witness to God's glory (3:10–11). As God's people love and seek him, he gives them joy, which in turn brings him glory (as Mary exemplifies [Luke 1:46–47]). God is glorified in us as the church as we love and delight in him (Piper, *Desiring*, 31–50). The church is now being sanctified, and one day Christ will present it "to himself in splendor, without spot or wrinkle or any such thing, that she might be holy and without blemish" (Eph. 5:27 ESV). Indeed, the church is a new humanity, a people displaying God's glory and testifying that God's mission of cosmic reconciliation is well underway and heading toward the grand finale of history (1:10–11; 2:14–16; 3:10–11). In the meantime, the church glorifies God through its worship and its character, which has been transformed by the Spirit to communicate God's communicable attributes. As the church is marked by love, holiness, goodness, justice, and faithfulness, God is reflected and thus glorified (Morgan, "Church").

The consummation and God's glory. The biblical drama of God's glory culminates in the consummation, which is also characterized by glory. Jesus will finish what he has started, and his return will be glorious (Matt. 16:27; Luke 21:27; Titus 2:13), as will his victory, judgment, and punishment of the wicked (2 Thess. 1:6–11; Rev. 20:11–15). Most of all, Jesus's revelation of himself in the new creation will be glorious in the church and cosmos (Rom. 8:21; Eph. 5:27; Rev. 21–22).

Having been justified by faith, then, we "rejoice in the hope of the glory of God" (Rom. 5:2 ESV). Because we have been united to Christ, whom the Father raised from the dead by his glory (6:4), we too have new life. Though we may suffer now, God guides history to his intended goals, including glorifying us with Christ (8:17). This entails "the glory that will be revealed in us" (v. 18), "the freedom of the glory" of God's children (v. 21 ESV), our ultimate conformity to Christ's image (v. 29), and our glorification (v. 30).

Moreover, God will bring "many sons to glory" (Heb. 2:10 ESV). God prepared such glory for us "beforehand"

(Rom. 9:23 ESV), and, because of our union with Christ and his resurrection, our bodies will likewise be raised in glory (1 Cor. 15:42–58).

Paul shows that our union with Christ is "to the praise of his glorious grace" and "glory" (Eph. 1:6, 12, 14) and results in personal and cosmic redemption (vv. 3–14), even our "glorious inheritance" from "the Father of glory" (vv. 17–18 ESV). The landmark consummation passage is Rev. 21–22. Just as Gen. 1–2 shows that the biblical story begins with God's creation of the heavens and the earth, Rev. 21–22 shows that it ends with God's creation of a new heaven and a new earth. The story begins with the goodness of creation and ends with the goodness of the new creation. The story begins with God dwelling with his people in a garden-temple and ends with God dwelling with his people in heaven, a new earth-city-garden-temple.

The glory of God is manifested in the new creation (Isa. 66:22–23; Rom. 8:18–27; Rev. 21–22). And since God's extrinsic glory is communicated to his people in salvation history, it relates to the already/not-yet tension. God's glory is now being displayed, and yet its ultimate display is still future (1 John 3:2). As G. K. Beale observes, "The sovereignty of God and Christ in redeeming and judging brings them glory, which is intended to motivate saints to worship God and reflect his glorious attributes through obedience to his word" (*Revelation*, 174). Further, "nothing from the old world will be able to hinder God's glorious presence from completely filling the new cosmos" or "hinder the saints from unceasing access to that divine presence" (*Revelation*, 1115).

Once and for all, God's victory is consummated. God's judgment is final, sin is vanquished, justice prevails, holiness predominates, and God's glory is unobstructed. God's eternal plan of cosmic reconciliation in Christ is actualized, and God is "all in all" (1 Cor. 15:28). As a part of his victory, God casts the devil and his demons into the lake of fire, where they are "tormented day and night forever and ever" (Rev. 20:10). Then God judges everyone: powerbrokers, those deemed nobodies, and everyone in between. "Anyone whose name was not found written in the book of life was thrown into the lake of fire" (v. 15). God consigns to hell all who are not of the people of Jesus (cf. Dan. 12:1; Rev. 13:8; 21:8, 27).

Magnificently, the new heaven and new earth arrive, and God dwells with his covenant people (21:3, 7), comforts them (v. 4), and renews all things (v. 5). John depicts heaven as a glorious temple, multinational and holy (vv. 9–27). God's people rightly bear his image, serving and worshiping him, reigning with him, and knowing him directly (22:1–5). God receives the worship he is due and blesses humans beyond measure, as they finally live to the fullest the realities of being created in his image and showing his glory. And throughout it all, God is glorified.

Summary: The drama of God's glory. As humans, we refused to acknowledge God's glory and instead sought our own, forfeiting the glory he intended for us as his image-bearers. By his grace, however, through union with Christ, God restores us as image-bearers to participate in and reflect his glory. We are recipients of glory, are being transformed in glory, and will be sharers of glory. Our salvation is from sin to glory. We have received great grace: we who exchanged the glory of God for idols and rebelled against his glory have been, are being, and will be transformed by the very glory we despised and rejected! Even more, through union with Christ, together we are the church, the new humanity, the firstfruits of the new creation, bearing God's image, displaying how life ought to be, and making known the wisdom of God.

All of this redounds to his glory, as God in his manifold perfections is exhibited, known, rejoiced in, and prized. In this sense, the entire biblical plot—creation, fall, redemption, and consummation—is the drama of God's glory. Edwards (247) captures it well: "The whole is *of* God, and *in* God, and *to* God; and he is the beginning, middle, and end."

See also Adam, First and Last; Consummation; Image of God; Temple

Bibliography. Aalen, S., "*doxa*," in *NIDNTT*, 2:44–48; Beale, G. K., *The Book of Revelation*, NIGTC (Eerdmans, 1999); Beale, *A New Testament Biblical Theology* (Baker Academic, 2011); Beale, *We Become What We Worship* (IVP Academic, 2008); Calvin, J., *Institutes of the Christian Religion*, ed. J. T. McNeill, trans. F. L. Battles, 2 vols. (Westminster, 1960); Collins, C. J., "*kabod*," in *NIDOTTE*, 2:577–87; Edwards, J. "The End for Which God Created the World," in *God's Passion for His Glory*, ed. J. Piper (Crossway, 1998), 125–252; Emerson, M. Y., and C. W. Morgan, "The Glory of God in 2 Corinthians," *SBJT* 19, no. 3 (2015): 21–39; Ferguson, S. B., *The Holy Spirit*, CCT (InterVarsity, 1996); Gaffin, R. B., Jr., "Glory, Glorification," in *DPL*, 348–50; Gaffin, "The Glory of God in Paul's Epistles," in Morgan and Peterson, *The Glory of God*, 127–52; Gerstner, J. H., *The Rational, Biblical Theology of Jonathan Edwards*, 3 vols. (Berean, 1993); Grudem, W., *Systematic Theology* (Zondervan, 1994); Hamilton, J. M., Jr., *The Glory of God in Salvation through Judgment* (Crossway, 2010); Hartley, J. E., "Holy and Holiness, Clean and Unclean," in *DOTP*, 420–31; Kaiser, W. C., *The Majesty of God in the Old Testament* (Baker Academic, 2007); Kline, M. G., *Images of the Spirit* (Baker, 1980); Longman, T., III, "The Glory of God in the Old Testament," in Morgan and Peterson, *The Glory of God*, 47–78; McConville, J. G., "God's Name and God's Glory," *TynBul* 30 (1979): 149–64; Morgan, C. W., *Christian Theology*, with R. A. Peterson (B&H Academic, 2020); Morgan, "The Church and God's Glory," in *The Community of Jesus*, ed. K. H. Easley and C. W. Morgan (B&H Academic, 2013), 213–35; Morgan, "Toward a Theology of the Glory of God," in Morgan and Peterson, *The Glory of God*, 153–87; Morgan, C. W., and R. A. Peterson, eds., *The Glory of God*, TC 2 (Crossway, 2010); Newman, C. C., "Glory," in *DLNTD*, 394–400; Newman, *Paul's Glory-Christology*, NovTSup 69 (Brill, 1991); Ortlund, R. C., Jr., *Isaiah*, PrW (Crossway, 2005); Packer, J. I., "The Glory of God," in *NDT*, 271–72; Piper, J., *The Dangerous Duty of Delight* (Multnomah, 2011); Piper, *Desiring God* (Multnomah, 2003); Ross, A. P., *Creation and Blessing* (Baker, 1997); Schreiner, T. R., *Paul, Apostle of God's Glory in Christ* (InterVarsity, 2001); Sivonen, M., "The *Doxa* Motif in Paul" (PhD. diss., University of Helsinki, 2018); Vriezen, C., *An Outline of Old Testament Theology* (Branford, 1966); Waltke, B. K., with C. Yu, *An Old Testament Theology* (Zondervan, 2007).

CHRISTOPHER W. MORGAN

Gospel

It is difficult to think of a more comprehensive single term to capture the message of the Bible than "gospel" (*euangelion*). And unlike some popular teaching that may give the impression that it is the NT that gives us the gospel while the OT provides something else, the NT writers themselves see the gospel as the fulfillment of the Hebrew Scriptures. Put the other way round, the OT provides both the categories and the historical run-up without which the fullness of the NT "gospel" is greatly impoverished or even meaningless. Mark opens with Jesus summoning belief "in the gospel" as a matter of appropriate responding to "the time" being "fulfilled" (Mark 1:15 ESV). Paul opens his letter to the Romans by speaking of "the gospel of God, promised beforehand through the prophets in the holy Scriptures" (Rom. 1:1–2 AT). Peter understands the ever-abiding "word of the Lord" of Isa. 40:8 as "the good news that was preached [*to euangelisthen*] to you" (1 Pet. 1:25 ESV).

Clearly the apostles understood their own ministry to be the heralding and handing down of an ancient message that had come to fulfillment, if in surprising ways, in Jesus Christ. But in what ways is the NT gospel informed and illuminated by the OT? This question deserves careful consideration, for if the apostles understood the gospel to be not only the key umbrella moniker for the content of the early church's preaching but also the fulfillment of an incomplete OT narrative history, then understanding what "the gospel" is and how it is informed by the OT is basic to understanding the message of the Bible.

The noun *euangelion* occurs seventy-five times in the NT (seventy-six if the occurrence in Mark 16:15 is included), with the associated verbal form *euangelizō* (variously translated) occurring another fifty-four times (plus one occurrence of *proeuangelizomai*, Gal. 3:8). Both the noun and the verb are spread fairly indiscriminately across the NT corpus, though with a notable absence in the Johannine literature (no instances of the *euang-* word root in John or 1–3 John; three in Revelation) and a preponderance in the thirteen letters traditionally ascribed to Paul (sixty of the seventy-five occurrences of *euangelion* and twenty-one of the fifty-four occurrences of *euangelizō*).

Defining "Gospel"

What do the NT authors mean by "gospel," and how does the OT inform their use and meaning? We will focus in this essay on explicit uses of the *euang-* word root since they are so abundant, though we should not lose sight of James Barr's insight that a concept may be present even when the word is not. With regard to the gospel, one thinks, for instance, of Paul's reference to "the sound words of our Lord Jesus Christ and the teaching that accords with godliness" (1 Tim. 6:3 AT)—probably a general reference to what Paul elsewhere calls "the gospel" or "my gospel," though here in 1 Tim. 6 without that exact word.

We should be crystal clear on our terms before engaging the biblical data, not least when considering a word that has been the victim of such wide-ranging definition, especially in recent decades. In some quarters the "gospel" refers to what God has done in Christ for the salvation of sinners in distinction from anything believers do in response. Biblically speaking, however, this is reductionistic, since at times the NT speaks of "obeying" the gospel (Rom. 10:16; 2 Thess. 1:8; 1 Pet. 4:17 ESV). In other quarters the gospel is set opposite divine judgment, but Paul has no trouble speaking of "that day when, according to my gospel, God judges the secrets of men" (Rom. 2:16 ESV). In the years surrounding the dawn of the twenty-first century, much NT scholarship defined the Pauline gospel as a centrally horizontal matter having to do with gentile inclusion rather than a vertical matter having to do with an individual's salvation before a righteous God, but this has been shown to be an exaggeration (see, e.g., Carson, O'Brien, and Seifrid). This "new perspective" is now not so new, and attention has shifted to other readings of the NT gospel such as that of Douglas Campbell and others, whose critique of so-called "justification theory" sees God's wrath and justice as erroneously elevated to a central place and as thus constructing an overly "contractual" gospel, arguing instead that the gospel has to do with a warmly benevolent deity. But this too has been held at arm's length by most scholars, as it creates an either/or where a both/and is more representative of apostolic teaching. And the tides of NT scholarship roll on.

Sticking close to the text, we can establish that the biblical gospel is, as its etymology suggests (*eu* + *angelia*), an announcement of good news or glad tidings. But news of what, in particular? And why is it good? This essay's survey of the NT's use of gospel language against its OT background leads us to see the gospel as *christological*, for the good news is centrally an announcement brought by and embodied in a person and his work, especially in his death and resurrection; *eschatological*, announcing the arrival of the climactic time in world history; *soteriological*, because this news is good in that it delivers humans from their deepest, most entrenched, and otherwise intractable plight; *ethical*, in the sense that this good news not only provides entrance into but also nurturing of the new life in Christ; and *global*, as the good news of divine deliverance is for all the nations. We will see these elements as we work through OT gospel language in the NT.

OT Antecedents

Going back at least to Adolf Deissmann, a strain of NT (especially Pauline) scholarship has persisted in viewing the NT notion of "gospel" against its Roman background and the announcement of "good news" from the battlefield or upon a new emperor's accession to the throne (Wright). Yet as has been shown (e.g., Barclay; Kim, *Christ*; Kim, "Paul"), this claim has been overblown. One finds occasional use of *euang-* language in noncanonical sources in and around the time of the NT, such as Cicero (*Att.* 2.3.1; 13.40.1), Plutarch (*Ages.* 33.4; *Demetr.* 17.5), and Josephus (*J.W.* 2.420; 4.618, 656), who use the word generally to speak of circumstantial fortune in military or everyday affairs. But secular use of *euang-* language is disproportionately light compared to the biblical usage. It is the OT that the apostles quote extensively in the NT, not least in their explications of the gospel, and there is almost a complete absence of explicit quotations from secular Greek society (with a few notable exceptions, such as Acts 17:28), even if we concede that Judaism was itself affected in various ways by the Greco-Roman world (Hengel; Stuhlmacher). So, we turn our attention to the OT and the Greek translations of it that the apostles quote.

The LXX uses the noun *euangelia* (which does not appear in the NT) five times, the noun *euangelion* one time, and the verb *euangelizō* twenty-three times (all translating various forms of *bāśar*, "to preach, bear tidings, gladden with good tidings"), with stability of usage across the OG, Theodotion, Symmachus, and Aquila. These twenty-six total occurrences break down into two rough categories, generally aligning with the genre in which they appear. In the historical narratives of the OT we find the *euang-* root denoting the bearing of news, often but not always clearly good news, from one location to another. Thus, several of the twenty-six instances cluster in 2 Sam. 18, the account of Ahimaaz and the Cushite bringing the news of Absalom's death to David (2 Sam. 18:20, 22, 25, 27, 31). Similar uses are seen in 1 Sam. 31:9 (echoed in 1 Chron. 10:9) and 2 Sam. 4:10, which speak of Saul's death as a matter of ostensible "good news," though David laments the news and demands that it not be published (2 Sam. 1:17–27); 1 Kings 1:42, where Jonathan the son of Abiathar allegedly carries "good news"; and 2 Kings 7:9, where the four lepers come across the deserted camp of the Syrians and account it a matter of "good news."

In poetry sections and especially the Prophets, however, *euang-* language shifts notably from communicating news on the horizontal plane to a use more vertical in orientation. No longer is it human events and victories that form a message of good news; now it is Yahweh's own deliverance of his people that comprises the message of good news. This is not to say that the "good news" reported in the Historical Books would not have been interpreted by the readers of these books in a theocentric way as a matter of divine deliverance. But in poetry and the Prophets, divine deliverance is in the foreground. Indeed, the very nature of the deliverance shifts. From military and political "good news" in the Historical Books comes a shift to a deeper message of good news, the announcement of deliverance not only from one's enemies without but also one's sins within. This is not to say the prophetic good news is individual and "spiritual" only; it is corporate, holistic, and even cosmic. But the prophetic hope is of deliverance not merely from hostile nations but also from Israel's more basic problem—one not beyond but within Israel's own borders.

The root occurs three times in the Psalms, each time referring to an announcement of divine salvation flowing from Yahweh's steadfast love and faithfulness to his covenant commitments (Pss. 40:9; 68:11; 96:2). Possibly of relevance to NT references to the gospel (given the close association between the gospel and the spread of divine blessing to the gentiles), the latter two texts come in contexts that speak of God's kingship over all the nations of the earth.

The remaining instances of *euang-* in the OT are the most significant for informing our understanding of the NT gospel. Leaving aside Jer. 20:15, where the prophet laments "the man who brought the news [*ho euangelisamenos*] to my father, 'A son is born to you,' making him very glad" (ESV), we are left with six occurrences (Joel 2:32; Nah. 1:15; Isa. 40:9; 52:7; 60:6; 61:1), of which three are explicitly quoted in the NT (Isa. 40:9; 52:7; 61:1). A fourth, Nah. 1:15, echoes Isa. 52:7 and will not receive separate attention. In these prophetic texts we arrive at the heart of OT precedence for NT use of gospel language.

Joel 2:32 uses the verb *euangelizomai* immediately after the block quoted by Peter at Pentecost (Acts 2:17–21). The verb itself is not quoted by Peter (Luke records Peter leaving off the second half of Joel 2:32), but we remember that the apostles cite the OT with broader reference to the surrounding OT context (Dodd; those in his wake). The LXX renders *ûbaśśərîdîm* ("and among the survivors," a word commonly referring to the remnant) with *kai euangelizomenoi*, with both the Hebrew and Greek then speaking of this group of people as those escaping and being called or summoned by the Lord. Those who "escape," "whom the Lord calls," are those to whom, according to the LXX translators, "the gospel is preached." All this comes in the context of Joel's famous prophetic declaration of the coming day of the Lord, when the Spirit will be poured out and the latter days will dawn. This use of *euang-* is thus tightly associated with the cluster of phenomena in Joel 2 ushering in the new age, which Peter claims at Pentecost to have been launched in the resurrection of Jesus (Acts 2:17–21, 29–32; cf. Rom. 10:13).

Isaiah is the key OT book for understanding the meaning of the gospel from a whole-Bible perspective. All four instances of *euang-* occur in the second half of the book, as the tone shifts from confrontation (Isa. 1–39) to assurance (Isa. 40–66). The first instance (40:9), embedded in one of the most consoling passages in all the Bible, announces the good news that Yahweh is determined to come to his people clothed in the utter might of a regal judge (40:10) and yet in the tender gentleness of a caring shepherd (40:11). While Isa. 40:9 is not quoted in the NT, Peter quotes the immediately preceding passage (40:6–8) and explicitly interprets its reference to "the word of God" as "the good news that was preached [*to euangelisthen*] to you" (1 Pet. 1:24–25 ESV). Peter thus takes the gospel to be the abiding promise of God—in the context of Isa. 40, the promise to draw near in comforting restoration of his people—and in Peter's usage it is a word through which believers today are born again (1 Pet. 1:23).

As with Isa. 40:9 (and Nah. 1:15), Isa. 52:7 speaks of news so good that it requires proclamation from a mountaintop, even Zion itself, the pinnacle on which all God's promises find culminating expression. Arguably the most significant OT text for understanding the NT gospel, Isa. 52:7 is quoted in Rom. 10:15 as a prophetic anticipation of the preaching of the death and resurrection of Christ to receptive gentiles amid largely unreceptive Israelites. In Isaiah's context the "good news"—which most immediately is set parallel to "peace," "news of happiness," and "salvation"—more broadly reflects the assurances of God that his people's self-wrought miseries under Babylonian captivity and felt estrangement from God will soon be reversed, their shame turned into glory, and their fortunes returned in an escalated and invincible way. These themes continue in the two later occurrences of *euang-* language in Isaiah, which speak of the abundance and glories of the nations rolling by sheer grace into the lap of God's people (Isa. 60:6) and the announcement of good news that pulls God's people out of a plight so grave that the worst of human adversities—poverty, brokenheartedness, imprisonment, and mourning—are used to express it (Isa. 61:1). The latter text is quoted by Jesus as having found its fulfillment in him (Luke 4:16–21).

In summary, the OT *euangelion* is good news of deliverance—in the Historical Books, good news of battlefield deliverance; in the later OT, good news of exilic deliverance that not only restores circumstantially but also announces the return of God himself to launch the latter days and gather up all the OT promises of restoration and shalom despite his people's large-scale settled recalcitrance and sin-riddled undeservedness.

Gospel in the NT

The announcing of a gospel launches the fourfold witness to Jesus in what came to be identified as the Gospel accounts of Matthew, Mark, Luke, and John (Mark 1:1, 14–15; Matt. 4:23; Luke 4:18). Yet the bulk of NT occurrences (for both the noun and the verb) come in Paul's Letters, which will therefore be our focus when we consider the rest of the NT beyond the Gospels.

Gospels. The verb *euangelizō* occurs mainly in Luke (10x, with one occurrence in Matthew) while the noun *euangelion* is found exclusively in Matthew (4x) and Mark (8x). Neither occurs in John. While Matthew does not use *euang-* language conspicuously in the opening chapters of his Gospel, Mark and Luke both do, and each in ways clearly informed by the OT, though more subtly in Luke's case.

Mark's Gospel is particularly significant for understanding the gospel in the sweep of the biblical story line. The account opens, "The beginning of the gospel of Jesus Christ" (Mark 1:1 ESV). The language of "beginning" may seem to suggest that the gospel is something entirely new, an irruption unanticipated by the OT. Yet Mark then immediately quotes Isaiah and Malachi to introduce John, who will then introduce Jesus, the bringer of the longed-for new exodus (Watts), an exodus not out of economic slavery but out of spiritual slavery into the real promised land of forgiveness and a restored relationship with God. The cumulative effect of various curious narrative details throughout Mark 1—the language of "beginning" echoing Gen. 1:1; the identification of Jesus as "the Son of God" and thus the promised Davidic heir; the way in which Jesus is "cast out," tempted by Satan, and dwells with the wild animals (1:12–13 AT)—lead to the conclusion that Mark is presenting Jesus as a second Adam, one who succeeds where Adam failed. And the announcement of this intervention, in which the Son of David will give his life on behalf of others (10:45) and, rising, will launch the new age, is captured in the single word *euangelion*, placed conspicuously at the heading of the account (1:1) and then used twice in the summation of Jesus's ministry (1:14–15). Throughout the rest of Mark the *euangelion* serves as shorthand for the message by and about Jesus (8:35; 10:29), a message to be "proclaimed" to all the world (13:10; 14:9). Matthew has parallel uses to these latter texts (Matt. 24:14; 26:13), though his account tends to refer to the gospel as "the gospel *of the kingdom*" (4:23; 9:35; 24:14 ESV), a phrase that ties in to Matthew's pervasive theme of the kingdom of heaven.

We find Luke's ten uses of the verb *euangelizō* mainly clustered toward the beginning of the Gospel (all but two in the first nine chapters), with the use in 4:18, quoting Isa. 61:1, of defining, even paradigmatic, significance. Jesus has just launched his public ministry (4:14–15). And he begins by entering a synagogue and claiming himself to be the fulfillment of the anointed Messiah of Isa. 61 (Luke 4:21), a passage that promises both in its immediate and broader contexts divine deliverance from all Israel's troubles and sins before the watching nations—deliverance in which God will align himself with his people's sorrows (Isa. 63:9) as their Father (63:16; 64:8), tearing asunder the heavens in an act of re-creation (64:1; 65:17–25) in merciful defiance of his people's continued hard-heartedness (65:2–3). The "good news" that is proclaimed throughout Luke's Gospel (2:10; 4:43; 8:1; 9:6) is neither purely circumstantial, nor merely individual, nor primarily future. It is nothing less than the quiet explosion onto human history of the longed-for new age in which God would bring to fulfillment his promise of heaven on earth, the presence here and now—despite the ongoing presence of the old order and the misery and death that mark it—of what was expected to happen at the end of history. This Isaianic and eschatological significance of the gospel is reflected in Jesus's words to John the Baptist's messengers about Jesus's multifaceted ministry undoing the fall and restoring men and women to who they were created to be, words that conclude with the climactic hearing of "good news preached" (7:22 // Matt. 11:5 ESV). And as in Mark's opening, we find in Luke that the *euangelion* is a matter both of continuity with the OT (4:17–21), fulfilling ancient promises, and of discontinuity (16:16), bringing unprecedented clarity and knowledge.

The rest of the NT. The *euangelion* as articulated throughout the rest of the NT fits cleanly with what we have found in the Gospels. Sometimes scholars have portrayed the Gospels as proclaiming the kingdom and Paul the gospel. But the very categories of "gospel" and "kingdom" heavily overlap. Moreover, given that the content of the apostolic gospel centers on Christ's death and resurrection, it makes sense that Jesus, preaching as he is *before* his death, would focus on the kingdom, whereas Paul, ministering a generation later, would focus on Christ's death and resurrection. The key point for our purposes as we transition to the rest of the NT is that here, as in the Gospels, we find the *euangelion* to be an announcement of something God has done in fulfillment of previously incomplete OT trajectories. While it is acceptable for "the gospel" to be reduced to "four spiritual laws" or other nutshell presentations for the sake of contextualized evangelistic efforts, the gospel must be understood by believers to be not abstract but deeply historically embedded.

We cannot treat every one of the seventeen uses of *euang-* language in Acts and the eighty-one uses in the thirteen Pauline Epistles. So, we will take Romans as a way into Paul's understanding of the gospel, as Romans is the most systematic and perhaps the least specifically contextualized writing of his. And right at the start of this letter Paul speaks of "the gospel of God, which he promised beforehand through his prophets in the holy Scriptures, concerning his Son, who was descended from David according to the flesh and was declared to be the Son of God in power according to the Spirit of holiness by his resurrection from the dead, Jesus Christ our Lord, through whom we have received grace and apostleship to bring about the obedience of faith for the sake of his name among all the nations" (Rom. 1:1–5 ESV). Amid much that could be said about this pregnant opening to Romans, what immediately stands out is the explicit redemptive-historical wedding of the gospel to prophetic anticipations in the OT. Indeed, this introduction to Romans is an effective summary of Paul's teaching on the gospel. Two elements are worth highlighting, elements that reflect Paul's broader use of *euang-* language, both of which flow from OT history. First, what comes through most clearly as Paul piles up explanatory phrases to unpack the gospel is that the gospel is not a bare formula but finds its locus and meaning in a person—Jesus, the Son of God, descended from David (1:3–4, 9; cf. 2 Tim. 2:8). Second, this gospel is for the whole world, not just Israel (1:5). These two aspects of the gospel recur throughout Paul's Letters.

Viewing Paul's Letters panoramically, we see that the gospel is the heart of Paul's calling (Acts 20:24; 1 Cor. 1:17); is of divine origin (Gal. 1:11–12) and "of first importance" (1 Cor. 15:3); is a message not centrally embodied or enacted or intuited but proclaimed (1 Cor. 9:14; 2 Cor. 2:12; 1 Thess. 2:9) and then personally appropriated (2 Cor. 9:13); makes specific truth claims (Eph. 1:13; Col. 1:5; 1 Tim. 1:10–11); has inherent power (Rom. 1:16; Col. 1:6; 1 Thess. 1:5) for the strengthening of God's people (Rom. 16:25); is easily diluted and thus requires careful defense (Gal. 1:6; 2 Cor. 11:4; Phil. 1:7, 16); is veiled to fallen humans (2 Cor. 4:3–4); offers salvation (Eph. 1:13) and peace (6:15) and glory (2 Thess. 2:14) and resurrection life (2 Tim. 1:10); is accessed by self-divesting faith (Col. 1:23), is the means by which one begins a life in Christ and by which one is nurtured in that life (1 Cor. 15:1–2; Gal. 2:14); summons believers to nobility of life (Phil. 1:27); and is available to gentiles no less than to Jews (2 Cor. 10:16).

In short, the gospel is the climactic revelation in Christ's life, death, and resurrection of the salvation begun in the OT. Thus, Paul can speak of "the mystery of the gospel" (Eph. 6:19), "mystery" referring to the revealing here, at the pinnacle of redemptive history, of what was present but hidden in times past (Ridderbos, 44–53). And so we are reminded once more that the NT gospel is a matter of both continuity and discontinuity—continuity in that Paul's gospel fulfills OT trajectories and also is in accord with traditions he himself has received (1 Cor. 11:23; 15:3), discontinuity in that his gospel was received by divine revelation (Gal. 1:11–12), a communication so deeply personal and transforming that he sometimes refers to it as "my gospel" (Rom. 2:16; 16:25; 2 Tim. 2:8), signifying his unique apostolic role in preserving the *euangelion* and especially his distinct calling to bring it to the gentiles (Gal. 2:2, 7–9). This inter-ethnic dimension of Paul's gospel, evident in many of Paul's uses of *euang-* language (e.g., Rom. 11:28; 15:16, 19; Eph. 3:6), flows from the vision of Isa. 40–66 that God's restoring work would sweep up the nations in its blessings and not be restricted to Israel.

Yet the ethnic and international (horizontal) elements of the gospel ought not to be played off against its more basic moral and spiritual (vertical) dimensions, as has sometimes been done in more recent NT scholarship. Indeed, it is precisely by tracking closely with OT antecedents to the *euangelion* that we see both the fundamental saving nature of the good news and its ethnically embracing implications, for the deliverance of God in Isaiah and throughout the OT focuses first on Israel and the forgiveness of her sins and then on the worldwide inclusion of the nations in that salvation. Thus, in perhaps the key text in all of Paul's Letters for understanding how he views the gospel as against its OT background (Rom. 10:15), he quotes Isa. 52:7 (= Nah. 1:15; understood as of eschatological significance in various quarters of the Judaism of the time, e.g., 11QMelch 2.15–16; Pss. Sol. 11:1–2) in commending the global import of the good news about Jesus. And the extrapolation of God's favor out from ethnic Israel to the whole world is itself reflective of the realization of eschatological promises (e.g., Eph. 3:8–11).

Conclusion

What Geerhardus Vos argued a century ago with regard to Paul's theology can be applied to the whole of the NT: to understand the eschatology of the apostles is to understand their theology as a whole, for the entire apostolic tradition is colored by the conviction that the latter days have dawned in Christ, as they interpret the Christ-event in light of the OT. And the single most effective summary of this apostolic kerygma is captured by the term *euangelion*.

In closing, we return to the five pillar marks of the gospel identified above—the good news as taught in the NT and as informed by the OT is *christological, eschatological, soteriological, ethical*, and *global*. On this side of our biblical survey we can further clarify that these five elements can be roughly understood to be concentric circles radiating outward, with Christ himself at the center. The gospel is fundamentally a message about Christ, who gathers up all the OT promises in himself. Christ is *the* message of Christianity, a point that NT scholars as divergent as Dunn (722–30) and Warfield (265–319) can argue with equal verve (*christological*). But Christ is not a Savior divorced from history; rather, he is rooted in it, indeed culminating it—more than this, he actually launches, in his death and resurrection, the eschaton, the new age promised by the prophets (*eschatological*). This gospel saves from divine wrath and human ruin (*soteriological*), transforms morally (*ethical*), and is offered to all nations (*global*).

But these necessary concomitants to the biblical gospel begin to move toward the implications as distinct from the essence of the gospel. The good news itself is the announcement that in Jesus the last days have dawned and in him penitent sinners are forgiven of their sins and reconciled to God in accord with OT anticipations. The snowballing hopes and promises rumbling and building through the Hebrew Scriptures come to their climax and fulfillment in the gospel of Jesus Christ, with the promise that one day the old age, in the present time overlapping with the new age, will fall away as the promises of the gospel come to final consummation in the new heavens and the new earth.

See also Covenant; Justice; Law; Messiah

Bibliography. Barclay, J. M. G., *Pauline Churches and Diaspora Jews*, WUNT 275 (Mohr Siebeck, 2011); Barr, J., *The Semantics of Biblical Language* (Oxford University Press, 1961); Campbell, D., *The Deliverance of God* (Eerdmans, 2013); Carson, D. A., P. T. O'Brien, and M. A. Seifrid, eds., *Justification and Variegated Nomism*, 2 vols. (Baker Academic, 2001, 2004); Deissmann, A., *Bible Studies*, trans. A. Grieve (T&T Clark, 1901); Dodd, C. H., *According to the Scriptures* (Nisbet, 1953); Dunn, J. D. G., *The Theology of Paul the Apostle* (Eerdmans, 1998); Hengel, M., *Judaism and Hellenism* (SCM, 1974); Kim, S., *Christ and Caesar* (Eerdmans, 2008); Kim, "Paul and the Roman Empire," in *God and the Faithfulness of Paul*, ed. C. Heilig, J. T. Hewitt, and M. F. Bird (Fortress, 2017), 277–308; Ridderbos, H., *Paul*, trans. J. R. de Witt (Eerdmans, 1975); Stuhlmacher, P., *Biblische Theologie des Neuen Testaments*, 2 vols., 3rd ed. (Vandenhoeck & Ruprecht, 2005); Vos, G., *The Pauline Eschatology* (repr., P&R, 1994); Warfield, B. B., *The Person and Work of Christ* (Benediction Classics, 2015); Watts, R. E. *Isaiah's New Exodus in Mark* (Baker Academic, 2001); Wright, N. T., *Paul and the Faithfulness of God* (Fortress, 2013).

DANE C. ORTLUND

Grace *See* Gospel; Justice

Greek Versions and the NT Quotations

The availability of several versions of the Bible—for instance, the many English versions we enjoy today—is not a uniquely modern circumstance. Although it is common to refer to the ancient Greek version of the Hebrew Bible as "the Septuagint," there was actually more than one Greek version in circulation during the NT period. The first Greek translation of the Jewish Scriptures is believed to have been made of the Pentateuch in the third century BC, with translations of other books of the Hebrew corpus subsequently made by other translators at other times and places (Jobes and Silva, 13–33). The initial translation of most canonical Hebrew books may have been completed by the middle of the second century BC when Ben Sira's grandson wrote the prologue to a Greek translation he made of his grandfather's work (the apocryphal text now known as Sirach or Ecclesiasticus). He mentions a Greek translation of "the Law itself, the Prophecies, and the rest of the books," which "differ not a little when read in the original" (NRSV), suggesting some perceived inadequacy in translated texts (Jobes and Silva, 20n18, 32).

Probably due to influence of the Hasmonean dynasty in Palestine, the first Greek translation of the Hebrew Bible began to be revised possibly even before all the books of the extant Hebrew canon had been translated (Jobes and Silva, 28, 106, 337). Also, during the early Christian era, Jewish translators made new translations or significant revisions to previously existing translations. Although some of these texts have survived in manuscript fragments or in quotations by ancient authors, it is possible that some Greek versions available to the NT writers are not now extant. Furthermore, during the pre- and early Christian era the text of the Septuagint was being revised to make it more literally follow a contemporaneous Hebrew text that was probably not identical to the extant MT. Given multiple forms of both Hebrew *Vorlagen* and Greek versions, it is difficult to know precisely which Greek text of the Hebrew Bible was available to readers around the Jewish Mediterranean diaspora (Alexandria, Palestine, Asia Minor, Greece, Rome) or specifically what form of the Greek OT text the NT writers cite.

The First Greek Translation

The scholarly consensus is that the first Greek translation of the Hebrew Pentateuch was made in the third century BC, probably in Alexandria, Egypt, in response to the religious and linguistic needs of the large Greek-speaking Jewish community living there (Jobes and Silva, 13–24). The term "Septuagint" (*hoi hebdomēkonta*), which originally referred to only the Pentateuch, was extended to refer to the first Greek translation of other books of the Hebrew Scriptures that followed at other times and probably other places, perhaps in Palestine and Asia Minor. However, in modern scholarship the original translations of the respective books outside the Pentateuch are preferably referred to as the "Old Greek" (OG) version. The complete corpus of the Pentateuch and the rest of the Hebrew canon as a unity is designated LXX/OG.

The original LXX translators would have used Hebrew manuscripts of the Scriptures contemporary to their time—that is, two or three centuries before the NT was produced and before the Hebrew text became stable during the first century of this era. By AD 100 the Hebrew text had become more standardized, but it was not until several centuries later that the form known as the MT took shape (Silva, 632). There was ample time for the Hebrew text to develop and change from the text used by the LXX/OG translators, and this may account for some differences between the LXX/OG and the MT.

Furthermore, even before the entire Hebrew canon existed in Greek translation, the previously translated books likely underwent revision (Jobes and Silva, 25, 28). One significant manuscript witness to this revisional activity that predates the Christian era is the Minor Prophets Scroll (8ḤevXII gr) from Naḥal Ḥever, which displays correction toward a Hebrew text (Marcos, 109; Steyn, 698). We must realize that "the origin and the development of 'the LXX' was a long textual transmission process which involved different translators at different places and different times, that it differs quite markedly from book to book, consists of different revisions, versions, strands and layers, and of 'shorter and longer texts' [when compared to the MT]" (Steyn, 698).

The historical prominence of the Septuagint was sealed when it was later adopted by the Christian church as its official Bible, the Greek language being the lingua franca of the Roman Empire. Its text was most likely not identical to the pristine version of the original translation due to the usual vicissitudes of manuscript transmission as well as deliberate revisions, especially during the Hasmonean period (Kreuzer, "'Old Greek,'" 225–37).

The Later Translations or Revisions of the Three

Ancient writers also referred to translations attributed specifically to Aquila, Theodotion, and Symmachus, sometimes referred to together as "the Three" (translators), although they did not collaborate and they worked separately at different times and locations (Jobes and Silva, 24–30). Little is known about these men, and none of these three versions have survived as a whole; they exist only in a few manuscript fragments, in patristic quotations, and in notes in the margins of manuscripts of biblical books. It has generally been believed that the adoption of the Septuagint by the Christian church and its eventual rejection by the synagogue provided the motivation for new versions that would more faithfully, by some measure, reflect the Hebrew texts. But some of the revisions displayed in the Three are also found in pre-Christian manuscripts, so other incentives may have prompted such versions. These incentives might include the influence of exegetical methods and rabbinic interpretation on translation technique, or a pedagogic need for an "interlinear" style translation, or the increased prominence of the proto-MT Hebrew text form requiring revision of the Greek translation away from its original Hebrew *Vorlage* and toward a proto-MT text (Marcos, 109–110).

In some places the NT writers quote a Greek form of the Hebrew Scripture that is also found in one or more of the versions attributed to the Three but that differs from the LXX/OG. Such occurrences suggest the

NT writer used a Greek version other than the LXX/OG that was evidently in circulation and that later became the source text for the later work of the Three. Collated extant readings from the Three can be found in the secondary apparatus of the Göttingen critical edition *Septuaginta*, using the abbreviations α′ (Aquila), σ′ (Symmachus), and θ′ (Theodotion) or, where the Three agree, (οἱ) γ′ (see Jobes and Silva, 152–55, 381–84).

Aquila of Pontus (ca. AD 140). Ancient testimony claims that Aquila was a resident of Sinope in Pontus, Asia Minor (Jobes and Silva, 26–28). It is said he was related to Emperor Hadrian, who commissioned Aquila to oversee the building of Aelia Capitolina in AD 135 on the ruins of Jerusalem, which had been destroyed in AD 70. After converting to Judaism, he also undertook a new translation of the Hebrew text that was accepted in his day, seeking to correct perceived deficiencies in the then-available Greek versions. His translation method followed the principle of one-to-one lexical correspondences, even "translating" Hebrew particles and some word endings at the expense of Greek syntax and grammar. He translated a given Hebrew word with the same Greek word throughout, even if context would indicate a better lexical choice. Aquila put the Greek words in the same order as the Hebrew, resulting in poorly formed Greek sentences. He may have produced this work as an aid to accessing the Hebrew text for people who had minimal knowledge of Hebrew, in which case the translation would have been similar to the English glosses in modern interlinear Bibles. Aquila's translation became the Greek text form used in the synagogue for several centuries. The rabbinic works of that era quote Aquila but not the LXX/OG.

The NT contains some indications that Aquila revised a Greek OT text that was known to some NT writers. For instance, 1 Pet. 2:8 uses a paraphrase of a Greek version of Isa. 8:14 to describe the stone laid in Zion in relation to those who reject it as a stone of stumbling (*lithos proskommatos*) and a rock of temptation to sin (*petra skandalou*). In the latter phrase, Peter follows not Isa. 8:14 OG, which reads *petras ptōmati*, but a reading found in the later Greek version attributed to Aquila, as does Paul in Rom. 9:33.

On February 8, 533, Emperor Justinian decreed, "Those who read Greek shall use the Septuagint tradition, which is more accurate than all the others. . . . We give permission to use also Akilas's [Aquila's] translation" (Jobes and Silva, 31). Aquila remained the standard Jewish Greek Scripture until the Arabic invasion in the seventh century, when the Greek language ceased to be the lingua franca.

Theodotion (late second century AD). Theodotion is believed to have lived in Ephesus in the late first or second century (Jobes and Silva, 28–29). He apparently took an existing Greek translation of the Hebrew Scriptures and revised it toward a preferred Hebrew text form. Some of his renderings that were once thought to be distinctive of his work are now known to have existed a century or two before he lived. For example, Heb. 11:33 quotes Dan. 6:22 (OG/MT 6:23) in a form that matches the rendering attributed to Theodotion, "God shut the mouth of the lions" rather than the OG reading, "God saved me from the lions." There are two complete extant versions of the Greek Daniel: the OG and Theodotion's (θ′), though the role of the historical Theodotion in producing it is debated. "Theodotion's" translation of Daniel apparently supplanted the OG version, which was widely regarded as defective (cf. the prologue to Sirach mentioned above). See also Paul's quotation of Isa. 25:8 in 1 Cor. 15:54, which disagrees with the OG but agrees with the rendering later attributed to Theodotion (Silva, 633a; Beale). Recognition of these readings led to the proposal of a "proto-Theodotion version" that circulated in the first century and that later became the basis of Theodotion's revision work.

An extant pre-Christian scroll of the Greek Minor Prophets (8ḤevXII gr) confirms that a version containing elements once ascribed to Theodotion was in fact already in use prior to the NT. The rendering of the Hebrew phrase *wgm* with the Greek *kaige* was considered a distinctive trait of Theodotion's "*kaige* recension," but it is now believed that those texts do represent not a unified recension but rather a translation style used within a Greek version that later became the basis for Theodotion's work. The largest number of Theodotionic texts, now referred to as the "*kaige* group," are preserved in Septuagintal manuscripts of Job, Proverbs, Isaiah, Jeremiah, and Ezekiel. Song of Songs, Lamentations, and Ruth may have been first translated into Greek by the same Jewish scholars responsible for the revision that produced the *kaige* group (van der Kooij, 203). Theodotion was known to Irenaeus, Epiphanius, and Jerome (Marcos, 142).

Symmachus (ca. AD 200). Symmachus is believed to have produced a Greek version of the Hebrew Scriptures around AD 200 for the Jewish community at Caesarea in Palestine (Jobes and Silva, 29–30). Despite the existence of both Aquila's and Theodotion's translations, there was apparently a need for a reliable translation of the then-preferred Hebrew Scriptures in a Greek style suitable for native Greek readers. Symmachus's work on the Pentateuch and the Major Prophets displays the best biblical Greek style and a high degree of clarity and accuracy. On the basis of syntactic and lexical characteristics, scholars can reasonably conclude that Symmachus knew Aquila's translation, and probably Theodotion's, as well as the LXX/OG. The Christian writers Epiphanius, Eusebius, Jerome, and Palladius knew of Symmachus (Marcos, 124).

The Versions Known to Origen (ca. AD 185–254)

Origen, a Christian theologian of Alexandria, Egypt, who eventually settled in Caesarea in Palestine, undertook an apologetic project known as the Hexapla. He was not interested in the text-critical task of determining original readings; rather, his work was intended to ascertain the fidelity of the Christian Greek OT by a thorough comparison of various Greek translations of the Hebrew Scriptures. Inscribed in adjacent columns, Origen included a Hebrew text, a transliteration of the Hebrew text into Greek letters, the translations of the Three, and the LXX/OG version. Origen apparently produced a revised Greek version that probably commingled his source texts, making the task of pre-Hexaplaric textual criticism extremely difficult. For some OT books Origen also possessed three anonymous Greek translations of the Hebrew Scriptures known as the Quinta, Sexta, and Septima, about which little is otherwise known (Jobes and Silva, 30–31; Marcos, 155–73).

The Lucianic recension. Lucian of Antioch was a Syrian who lived in the middle of the third century and died a Christian martyr in AD 312 (Jobes and Silva, 46–48). He apparently updated an existing Greek text of some books of both the OT and NT by inserting additions from the Three in the OT text, replacing pronouns with proper names, making implicit subjects or objects explicit, substituting synonyms, and replacing Hellenistic forms with Attic (Marcos, 230–31). It is believed Lucian used the Greek OT text produced by Origen for at least some books, producing what is now known as the Lucianic or Antiochene recension.

The presence of so-called Lucianic readings attested long before Lucian lived has led scholars to propose a "proto-Lucianic text"—at least for the Historical Books—that had already been revised toward a Hebrew text. For instance, Rom. 10:15 quotes Isa. 52:7 but deviates from the OG, instead agreeing with some witnesses to the much later Lucianic recension that stands closer to the Hebrew text (Wilk, 257; Spottorno 1991). A large number of "Septuagint" manuscripts contain the Lucianic revisions, especially in Psalms, the Prophets, Joshua, Samuel-Kings, Chronicles, and Job. Scholars have not been able to identify any Lucianic revisions within the Pentateuch.

The mutual influence of the Greek versions. The existence of other Greek versions of the Hebrew Scriptures alongside the LXX/OG is indisputable. These versions may have also been based on, or corrected toward, a Hebrew text that was different than the *Vorlage* translated by the LXX/OG translators, as there were at least three Hebrew texts in circulation: the proto-MT, the proto-Samaritan, and the Hebrew parent text of the Septuagint. Both by scribal transmission and by deliberate revision, the texts of these several Greek versions influenced one another in ways that can be gleaned only by detailed comparison of the manuscripts themselves. Other than Origen's methodical work, nothing is known of the textual history of the origin and circulation of the various texts. Virtually every extant manuscript of the Greek Bible is an admixture of readings from various sources and stages in the transmission of the biblical texts, making the task of textual criticism extremely difficult. Moreover, the Judean Desert materials confirm the existence of more than one Hebrew version of the Jewish Scriptures at the time of the NT. Modern scholars cannot assume that the MT was the Hebrew *Vorlage* of any or all of the Greek versions throughout their full extent, even though it is now the only complete Hebrew text available to scholars. The relationships between the texts of the Hebrew and Greek versions of the OT and between the NT quotations and their source texts are complex, to say the least.

The Relationship of NT Quotations to Their Source Texts

The study of the OT quotations in the NT involves some methodological issues: (1) identifying what counts as a quotation; (2) deciding if the quotation "agrees with" the LXX/OG, the MT, both, or neither; (3) determining whether any perceived differences are due to a source text that is no longer extant (of text-critical value) or have been introduced by the NT writer (of exegetical value). Typically, only probable or possible conclusions can be reached, but that is the nature of historical research. This type of textual analysis may then figure into further discussions about the quality of the Hebrew of the MT and about whether the LXX/OG or other Greek versions preserve, in a given place, an older reading of a Hebrew proto-MT text that had become corrupted.

Although the MT as presented in the medieval (AD 1008) manuscript Leningradensis (Leningrad Codex B 19a) is the only extant full text of the Hebrew Bible, it has textual problems in places, which has become more evident with the examination of the Hebrew scrolls from Qumran, which are about a millennium older. While confirming the antiquity and overall quality of the transmission of the consonantal text of the extant MT, the Judean Desert materials also confirm the existence of other Hebrew texts that agree with the LXX/OG against the MT. This indicates that the LXX/OG and other Greek versions may bear witness, in principle, to the oldest Hebrew text retrievable by scholars, because the Hebrew *Vorlagen* from which the LXX/OG translations were made were older than the Qumran Hebrew scrolls by two centuries or more. However, before concluding that the LXX/OG preserves an older and better reading than the MT, one must be confident of having the pristine Greek translation from which transmission errors and subsequent revisions have been removed, and then one must consider if the translator introduced what appear to be deviations from the presumed Hebrew *Vorlage*, either by error or by intention due to translation style or interpretation. A retroversion of this hypothetical pristine Greek text back into its presumed Hebrew *Vorlage* therefore provides an additional, albeit hypothetical, Hebrew witness that can be used in textual criticism of the Hebrew text (see Swete, 441–57; Tov, *Septuagint*). For instance, Tov argues that Jeremiah existed in two distinct literary forms that differ in length and sequence.

The shorter, older Hebrew edition from which the extant OG Jeremiah was translated was later expanded to become the extant MT text. Notably, distinctive features of OG Jeremiah as retroverted into Hebrew by Tov are indeed found in 4QJer[b,d] in chaps. 9–10 and 43 (Tov, *Textual*, 286–88).

In terms of agreement between NT quotations and their source texts, there are five general categories of possible relationships:

1. NT = LXX/OG = MT
2. NT = MT ≠ LXX/OG
3. NT = LXX/OG ≠ MT
4. NT ≠ LXX/OG ≠ MT
5. Cases that are too debatable or complex to be classified into one of the previous four categories

The work of deciding the relationships among the three texts (MT, LXX/OG, NT quotation) must involve determining the original reading of the NT text and then comparing its text form to the MT and to a standard reconstructed text of the LXX/OG, either the Rahlfs-Hanhart edition or the Göttingen *Septuaginta* for those volumes in existence (but note that sometimes these two critical editions have different reconstructions of the Greek—e.g., Hosea 2:1). However, as explained above, the LXX/OG was not the only Greek version of the Hebrew Bible in circulation at the time the NT books were written, and there were already revisions of the Jewish Scriptures that moved the Greek text closer to a Hebrew text, which may or may not have been the proto-MT or the Hebrew *Vorlage* from which the LXX/OG translators had originally worked. When a NT quotation stands closer to the MT than does the LXX/OG reading, it was once thought that the NT writer had provided his own Greek translation of the Hebrew. While this is plausible in some cases, it may also be that the NT writer is simply using a Greek version that had already been revised toward a contemporaneous Hebrew proto-MT text.

In spite of the debate about what constitutes a quotation, how many there are in the NT, and the somewhat subjective nature of what "agreement" means when a quotation in the NT is compared to its source text in the OT, Moisés Silva's analysis of the explicit OT quotations in Paul's writings, discussed in the following paragraphs, is instructive (Silva, 631).

Category 1: Paul = LXX/OG = MT. This equivalence is what Bible readers might expect based on modern assumptions that the LXX/OG accurately translates the MT and that the NT writer accurately quotes his source text. Of the 107 quotations in Paul identified by Silva, forty-two, or about 39 percent, show agreement across all three texts in all matters of substance (e.g., Joel 2:32 [MT 3:5] in Rom. 10:13, see below). Although such agreement among all three texts (English, Greek, and Hebrew) is probably what most uninitiated English readers expect, it is not the case with the majority of quotations. This may produce confusion when an English-Bible reader flips to the OT to check a quotation and finds that the two do not agree (see categories 3 and 4 below).

But even where the quotation in the NT appears to agree with both LXX/OG and MT, the exegete will do well to consider further which text was more likely in the mind of the NT writer, the Hebrew or the Greek, for the immediate context of the quoted verse in the Hebrew text and the Greek version may differ in relevant ways, particularly when allusions to and metaleptic echoes of the OT in the NT text are in view. As one author says, "The context around nearly every citation includes phrases and statements that are reminiscent of the contexts to which the passages originally belong" (Wilk, 261).

The NT context of the quotation must also be carefully considered. For instance, Rom. 10:13 quotes Joel 2:32 OG (MT 3:5) in agreement with both the MT and the OG, "Everyone who calls on the name of the Lord will be saved." But the immediate context of Rom. 10:11–12 indicates something of further interest. In 10:11 Paul quotes Isa. 28:16 but agrees with neither the OG nor the MT by adding *pas* ("everyone") and changing the OG verb from aorist subjunctive to the future indicative. In so doing, Paul adapts his quotation of Isa. 28:16 in anticipation of the prophecy from Joel 2:32 OG that he then quotes in 10:13, "For '*everyone* who calls upon the name of the Lord will be saved,'" a quotation that includes *pas*. "He also underlined the universal scope of salvation in Christ asserted in Rom. 10:12: 'For there is no distinction between Jew and Greek; the same Lord is Lord of all and bestows his riches upon *all* who call upon him'" (Wilk, 259, italics added). In other words, the textual form of one quotation can influence the textual form of another in the immediate context in support of the NT author's purposes.

Category 2: Paul = MT ≠ LXX/OG. In many cases, however, the MT and the LXX/OG present two different readings. Paul's quotations agree with the MT against the LXX/OG in only seven of 107 cases, or about 6 percent. And where Paul's quotation does agree with the extant MT, the question remains whether he provided a Greek translation of the Hebrew proto-MT himself or was simply quoting a Greek OT text that had already been corrected toward the proto-MT.

The cases where the MT and the LXX/OG present different readings are explained, in general terms, by either a free translation technique used by the translator of the Greek OT version, or a mistranslation of the Hebrew, or a Hebrew *Vorlage* used by the Greek OT translator that differed from what would much later become the MT extant today (or possibly a mix of more than one of these). Each and every case must be considered on its own merits. The discernment of the reason for disagreement in any given case is important for the *text-critical task*. But there is also the possibility that the NT writer deliberately paraphrases or revises the OT quotation, which is of exegetical significance. Discerning changes intentionally made by the NT writer is of great importance to the *exegetical task*, for it may suggest highlighted themes or motifs. (In the case of OT quotations in the Synoptic Gospels, another level of consideration is how the literary relationships among them, and subsequent textual transmission, may have affected the text of the quotations.)

For instance, Hab. 2:4 in Gal. 3:11 agrees more closely with the MT than with the OG, which includes the conjunction *de* and the genitive pronoun *mou*, neither of which are present in Gal. 3:11. It is possible that Paul corrects the Greek to agree with the MT reading, but would that kind of meticulous textual conformity have been Paul's intent? More likely, this appears to be a revision by Paul himself because of the way the quotation sits in his argument, in which he does not wish to include even a mild adversative (Kreuzer, *Bible*, 246).

Habakkuk 2:4 is also quoted in Rom. 1:17, *ho de dikaios ek pisteōs*, agreeing exactly with the first five words of the OG text form. In comparison, the reconstruction of Hab. 2:4 in the Greek Minor Prophets Scroll from Naḥal Ḥever, which tends to isomorphize the Hebrew, probably read, [*en autō kai di*] *kaios en pistei autou*. This reconstructed reading of missing letters (*en autō kai di*), based on the spacing in the scroll, appears to agree with the translation ascribed to Aquila and with the MT's third-person pronoun *autou* (Kreuzer, *Bible*, 244). Therefore, Paul's quotation in Rom. 1:17 suggests that he was still using the OG version and not the *kaige* text form when he wrote Romans. Furthermore, "it is remarkable that the Greek text presupposes a personal suffix of the first-person singular instead of the third person," which Paul omits altogether from his quotation to generalize the statement (Kreuzer, *Bible*, 245).

Category 3: Paul = LXX/OG ≠ MT. More often than not, where the LXX/OG and MT disagree, Paul's quotation agrees with the reconstructed LXX/OG (Rahlfs or the Göttingen *Septuaginta*) against the MT—seventeen of 107 quotations, or about 16 percent. For instance, 2 Cor. 13:1 quotes Deut. 19:15, agreeing with the LXX ("every matter") against the MT ("a matter") with the inclusion of *pan* ("every"). But at the same time, the quotation disagrees with both the MT and the LXX by not repeating *epi stomatos* ("by mouth"), and therefore, this quotation could also be classified in category 4. This is a good example of how difficult it can be to judge "agreement" when some element(s) of the quotation agree and others disagree with the presumed source text.

The complexity of the textual study of the NT quotations of the OT is exemplified by the well-known example of Luke's quotation of Amos 9:11–12 in Acts 15:13–18 (NT = LXX/OG ≠ MT), "so that the rest of mankind and all the nations may seek [me]" (AT), where the MT reads, "so that they may possess the remnant of Edom and all the nations" (see Jobes and Silva, 214–15). The OG translator may have misread a *dalet* for a *yod*, reading the Hebrew verb as "to seek" instead of "to inherit"; ignored the Hebrew direct-object marker; and then read the name "Edom" as *ʾādām* ("mankind"). A second way to read these differences is as evidence of intentional redactional activity that took place when Obadiah, with its oracle against Edom, was placed directly after Amos in the proto-MT sequence of the Twelve. (The sequence of the Twelve in the MT is different from the sequence in the OG.) In this case, it has been argued that the OG preserves the older reading of the Hebrew, though there is no manuscript evidence that attests the retroverted OG reading. A third explanation of the difference is that the OG translator was contextualizing the prophecy for a larger, more general audience by reading a part, the gentile nation of Edom, for the whole of all nations. The "possession of Edom" was then interpreted to be a human response of seeking for God, that God might claim (possess) his own. The plot thickens when we consider whether James was quoting a Hebrew text of Amos or a Greek text at the Jerusalem Council. Furthermore, regardless of which language James spoke at the council, Luke, the gentile, Greek-speaking author of Acts, may have had access only to the OG Amos. Or even if he was aware the Hebrew text was different, he may have used the OG quotation because it better supported his theme of the universality of the gospel.

Category 4: Paul ≠ LXX/OG ≠ MT. In the second-largest category, thirty-one of 107 quotations, or about 29 percent, Paul agrees with neither the LXX/OG nor the MT. It is among these quotations that Paul may provide his own translation of a Hebrew text or may quote a Greek version that is no longer extant. For instance, Paul may translate Job 5:13 himself when he quotes it in 1 Cor. 3:19, because the rendering agrees with neither the MT nor the OG and the Greek stands a little closer to the MT. A distinctive word choice, *panourgia* ("craftiness"), has suggested to some that Paul uses a Greek text that has been corrected toward the MT and that will later be revised by Symmachus, where the same word is found in Prov. 8:12 (Silva, 633a). Note that examples in this category present evidence that the Greek OT manuscripts were *not* in these places corrected to agree with the NT.

If a quotation in the NT agrees with neither the MT nor the LXX/OG but does agree with the quotation as found in another writer, then it is more likely that the NT writer was simply using one of the other Greek versions in circulation. For instance, the quotation of Gen. 2:2 in Heb. 4:4 agrees exactly with Philo's quotation of Gen. 2:2 (*Posterity* 64) while differing from both the critically reconstructed LXX reading ("on the *sixth* day") and, in more minor ways, the MT (Steyn, 705). Since a direct literary influence between Philo and the author of Hebrews is unlikely, it is more likely that both use a Greek version of Gen. 2:2, perhaps circulating in Alexandria, that differs from both the (proto-)MT and the LXX. Or did a Christian editor at some later time revise Philo's quotation to agree with the NT's Heb. 4:4? In either case, it would be an error to attribute the differences to a deliberate revision of the quotation by the writer of Hebrews. This example highlights how inaccurate it would be to say simply that the writer of Heb. 4:4 uses "the Septuagint," for the quotation does not agree with the LXX/OG but probably comes from a Greek text, otherwise unknown to us, that Hebrews and Philo both use.

Because of the revered place of the MT both historically and theologically, it can be startling to realize that so many NT quotations of the OT do not agree with the MT. This can be unsettling for those who revere the MT as an inspired text and who perhaps further assume that an inspired NT writer would use only an inspired OT text. Such a line of thinking led Augustine to argue that the Septuagint translation—and *only* the Septuagint among all the Greek versions of the OT—*was* inspired (*Civ.* 18.42–44). This idea is rejected by the Protestant doctrine of Scripture, which recognizes only the biblical autographs and *no* translation as divinely inspired. Although the Greek versions of the OT are not inspired texts, the quotations of the OT in the NT are, nevertheless, God's divine word by virtue of *the inspiration of the NT text itself*.

Gert Steyn (699) observes, "One can hardly speak today anymore in general of 'the LXX' with the assumption that we have a reconstructed and standardized text available in order to use in comparative studies with the explicit quotations in the NT." For both the text-critical and the exegetical task, the analysis of NT quotations of the OT must go beyond comparison to the MT and the critical editions of the LXX/OG to consider the possibility that another Greek OT version is the source text. Nevertheless, despite the inherent difficulties, the NT quotations of the OT are in principle the oldest witness to the Greek version(s) of the Jewish Scriptures. The NT predates the great uncial codices by a few centuries and provides a witness to the OT text as it stood long before the work of Origen, which, while serving his purposes, almost hopelessly confused the Greek OT textual traditions.

The Transmission History of NT Quotations of the OT

The textual history of quotations of the OT in the NT also aids in textual criticism of the Greek versions of the OT, for the NT quotations, as they were written, are themselves a pre-Hexaplaric witness, earlier by three or four centuries than the four major uncials (Jobes and Silva, 208–11). This is especially true if the NT quotations present an independent witness of the quoted OT text unaffected by mutual interference during the period of scribal transmission. The current scholarly consensus is that

> the Septuagint and New Testament scriptures were transmitted independently of each other for a surprisingly long period. Typically, the New Testament quotations did not influence the Septuagint text and vice versa. These general observations are not without exceptions. But these exceptions can be identified and thus separated from the main strands of the transmission. As a consequence, the early Christian quotations bear a greater authority, not only for interpreting them in the Christian context, but also for locating them in the textual history of the Septuagint. They contribute to our understanding of the Septuagint, beginning with Old Greek and continuing to Roman times. (de Vries and Karrer, 16)

An exception to this generality is found in Papyrus 46, where the most probable explanation for its readings at Rom. 9:27; Heb. 5:6; 7:17, 21 is LXX/OG influence on the respective quotations of the OT (de Vries, 89–91).

Because the NT quotations are important text-critical evidence for the Greek OT, if a NT reading is stable (i.e., there are no variant readings in NT MSS) and it presents a textual difference within the Greek OT quotation, it is imperative to decide if the difference is introduced by the NT author or is simply the Greek OT text known to the NT author. If introduced by the NT writer, it is valuable for exegesis of the NT passage but of no value for textual criticism of the Greek OT text, for it could not have been present in the Greek OT text (Jobes and Silva, 210). But if the variant indicates that the reading was already in existence, then it is strong and important text-critical evidence for the text of the Greek OT as it existed at the time the NT was written.

To complete an example of the textual history of a quotation in the NT in relation to its source text, consider again the example of Isa. 28:16 quoted in Rom. 9:33 ("the one who believes") and again in Rom. 10:11 ("everyone who believes"). The critical OG text of Isa. 28:16 agrees with the MT, which does not have *pas* ("everyone") except in one ninth-century minuscule (407). The quotation of Isa. 28:16 in Rom. 9:33 agrees with the OG, which also agrees with the MT; however, the same quotation in Rom. 10:11 includes the word *pas* and so agrees with neither the OG nor the MT. It is likely that Paul modified the quotation of Isa. 28:16 in Rom. 10:11, adding *pas* to highlight his point about the universality of salvation, which is explicitly stated in the next verse, Rom. 10:11. During the subsequent transmission of the text of Romans, a later scribe altered the quotation of Isa. 28:16 in Rom. 9:33 to agree with Rom. 10:11. Finally, the scribe of the one ninth-century OG manuscript of Isaiah revised the text of OG Isaiah by adding the word *pas* to a manuscript of Isa. 28:16 to agree with Rom. 10:11 (Jobes and Silva, 211).

Earlier scholars tended to assume that the NT manuscripts and Greek OT manuscripts often influenced one another during scribal transmission, as when Christian scribes may have "corrected" either the NT quotation or its Greek OT source text to agree with the corresponding text. Based on this assumption, text-critical decisions for original readings in the LXX/OG manuscripts were sometimes made for the reading that did *not* agree with the NT quotations. More recent scholarship that has examined the manuscripts of NT quotations challenges that assumption with evidence that, "typically, the New Testament quotations did not influence the Septuagint and vice versa" (de Vries and Karrer, 16). The evidence where the NT writer disagrees with the LXX/OG without either the NT manuscripts or LXX/OG manuscripts being harmonized to agree suggests that scribes did *not* routinely make such revisions. (See Jobes, "Septuagint," for discussion of similar conclusions based on the OT quotations in 1 Peter.) "The transmission of the books of the Septuagint and the New Testament occurred, in large measure, independently to at least the 5th and 6th centuries" (de Vries and Karrer, 8). One apparent exception is that parallel revisions of *style* in both the Greek OT and NT parts of a given codex display stylistic preferences of the scriptorium (de Vries and Karrer, 9). Nevertheless, even this cannot be assumed as a general principle, and each case must be individually considered.

Bibliography. Beale, G. K., "A Reconsideration of the Text of Daniel in the Apocalypse," *Bib* 67 (1986): 539–43; de Vries, J., "The Textual History of the Scriptural Quotations in the New Testament," in de Vries and Karrer, *Textual History*, 79–92; de Vries, J., and M. Karrer, eds., *Textual History and the Reception of Scripture in Early Christianity*, SCS 60 (Society of Biblical Literature, 2013); Jobes, K., "The Septuagint Textual Tradition in 1 Peter," in Kraus and Wooden, *Septuagint Research*, 312–33; Jobes, K. H., and M. Silva, *Invitation to the Septuagint* (Baker Academic, 2015); Kraus, W., and R. G. Wooden, eds., *Septuagint Research Issues and Challenges in the Study of the Greek Jewish Scriptures*, SCS 53 (Society of Biblical Literature, 2006); Kreuzer, S., *The Bible in Greek*, SCS 63 (SBL Press, 2015); Kreuzer, "From 'Old Greek' to the Recensions," in Kraus and Wooden, *Septuagint Research*, 225–37; Marcos, N. F., *The Septuagint in Context* (Brill, 2001); Silva, M., "Old Testament in Paul," in *DPL*, 630–42; Spottorno, M. V., "The Lucianic Text of Kings in the New Testament," in *VII Congress of the International Organization for Septuagint and Cognate Studies*, ed. C. E. Cox, SCS 31 (Scholars Press, 1991), 279–84; Steyn, G. J., "Which 'LXX' are We Talking about in NT Scholarship?," in *Die Septuaginta*, ed. M. Karrer and W. Kraus, WUNT 219 (Mohr Siebeck, 2008), 697–707; Swete, H. B., *An Introduction to the Old Testament in Greek*, rev. R. R. Ottley (Hendrickson, 1989); Tov, E., "Lucian and Proto-Lucian," in *The Greek and Hebrew Bible* (Leiden, 1999), 477–88; Tov, *The Text-Critical Use of the Septuagint in Biblical Research*, 3rd ed. (Eisenbrauns, 2015); Tov, *Textual Criticism of the Hebrew Bible*, 3rd ed. (Fortress, 2012); Wilk, F., "The Letters of Paul as Witnesses to and for the Septuagint Text," in Kraus and Wooden, *Septuagint Research*, 253–71.

KAREN H. JOBES

H

Habakkuk, Book of

Setting

Habakkuk prophesied in the late seventh and early sixth centuries BC, during the final days of the kingdom of Judah. The book contains material from different points in the prophet's career (Roberts, 82–84). In 1:5–6 the Lord says the rise of the Babylonian Empire will surprise the nations. This would have been so prior to their victory over the Egyptians at Carchemish in 605 BC. Other texts (1:6–11, 15–17; 2:5–17) depict the Babylonians as a mighty empire with an established reputation for being cruel and proud. This would have been the case after their victory at Carchemish and in conjunction with the subsequent expansion of their dominance. The prophet anticipates a devastating invasion of Judah. This must refer to the Babylonian invasion of 597 BC (2 Kings 24:10–17) and/or the culminating invasion of 588–586 BC, when they destroyed the Jerusalem temple (2 Kings 25).

Structure and Message

The heading in 1:1 designates the book (or perhaps the first two chapters) as a "prophecy" (or "oracle"). The Hebrew term *maśśāʾ*, which is derived from a verb meaning "lift up," often refers to a burden or load. When used of prophetic judgment speeches, it may depict them as "heavy" messages the prophet must carry and unload. Another option is that the noun reflects the idiom "lift up the voice," in which case it refers merely to the message the prophet proclaims (see Cook, 27–29.)

A second heading in 3:1 designates what follows as a "prayer," reflecting the petition of 3:2 and the affirmation of confidence in 3:16–19. Verses 3–15 expand upon the petition by rehearsing the famous "deeds" the prophet asks the Lord to repeat. Some consider this final chapter of the book to be secondary, a position supported by the chapter's omission from the Habakkuk commentary found at Qumran. But the chapter rounds out the book's message and structure (see below) and appears both in the Greek Minor Prophets scroll found at Naḥal Ḥever, dating to the first century AD, and in a text found at Murabbaʿat, dating to the second century AD (Haak, 3, 5; Thompson, 41–42).

The book takes the form of a dialogue (Chisholm, 433–34):

1. Habakkuk's lament (1:2–4): The prophet laments that violent oppressors are perpetrating injustice throughout society.
2. The Lord's response (1:5–11): The Lord announces he is raising up the violent Babylonians, who will conquer nations.
3. Habakkuk's objection (1:12–2:1): The prophet objects that the Lord's plan does not solve but escalates the problem of injustice in the world.
4. The Lord's response (2:2–20): The Lord assures Habakkuk he will in due time punish the Babylonians. In the meantime, the righteous will be sustained by their faithfulness.
5. Habakkuk's prayer (3:1–19): Habakkuk asks the Lord to renew his mighty deeds from Israel's past and declares his confidence in the Lord's ability to sustain him.

Use of Antecedent Scripture

Habakkuk 1:8. The book of Habakkuk contains several allusions to antecedent Scripture. For example, in 1:8 the Lord speaks of an enemy that comes "from afar" and is like an eagle. This combination occurs only here and in Deut. 28:49, suggesting the Lord is alluding to that passage. If so, this indicates that the Babylonian invasion implements the threatened judgments (i.e., "curses") against those who have broken their covenant with the Lord (cf. Hab. 1:4).

Habakkuk 1:12. In 1:12 the prophet addresses the Lord as "my Holy One" and "Rock." This pair of titles occurs only here and in Hannah's Song, where she declares "there is no one holy" like the Lord and "there is no Rock" like Israel's God (1 Sam. 2:2). The basis for Hannah's affirmation of the Lord's incomparability is his sovereignty over death and life (2:6), as evidenced by his capacity to give a barren woman like her a child (2:5). The titles point to his transcendence and ability to protect his people, much as rocky terrain can provide for one who is in danger a relatively inaccessible refuge (cf. 1 Sam. 24:2).

Habakkuk's use of the titles is ironic when compared to Hannah's Song. God's holiness refers first and foremost to his transcendence as cosmic King. Hannah has this in mind when she affirms that no one is "holy" (v. 2) like the Lord. Habakkuk shares this view, for he acknowledges the Lord's sovereign control over the Babylonians as his instrument of judgment (1:12b). The Lord's holiness encompasses his moral authority, which he possesses by reason of his sovereign position. A corollary of the Lord's holiness is his commitment to justice, which Habakkuk has in mind when he states, "Your eyes are too pure to look on evil; you cannot tolerate wrongdoing. Why then do you tolerate the treacherous? Why are you silent while the wicked swallow up those more righteous than themselves?" (1:13). By addressing the Lord as his Holy One, Habakkuk highlights the tension he sees in the Lord's use of the arrogant, wicked Babylonians to judge Judah. How can the holy God use such evil people to accomplish his purposes and thereby seemingly violate his holy character (see Whitehead, 270–71; Patterson, 158; Barker and Bailey, 312; Floyd, 109)? His use of "Rock" is also ironic, since Hannah uses this title to refer to God as a protector, a theme she highlights when she says the Lord guards his followers and shatters their enemies (1 Sam. 2:9–10). By calling God "Rock," Habakkuk highlights the incongruity he sees in Israel's protector allowing the Babylonians to crush the nation he protects (Roberts, 103).

In addition to alluding to the Song of Hannah, Habakkuk likely has the Song of Moses (Deut. 32) in mind, where the epithet "Rock" is first used of the Lord. In this song Moses previews Israel's history, speaking from a vantage point in the future. The Lord, Israel's Rock (v. 4), is faithful and just. He formed, cared for, and protected his people (vv. 5–14). But Israel rebelled against its Creator, Protector or "Rock," and Deliverer (vv. 15–18). Consequently, the Lord removed his protection from his people and allowed foreigners to conquer them. Yet the Lord remains the true Rock (vv. 30–31) who is superior to the foreigners' gods, referred to as "their rock" (v. 31). A day will come when the Lord will show mercy to his people (v. 36) and avenge them (vv. 40–43). The foreigners' gods ("the rock they took refuge in") will be unable to protect them (vv. 37–39).

The Song of Moses provides a framework within which to understand Habakkuk's dilemma and protest. Moses makes it clear the Lord, Israel's Rock, is perfectly just, a truth Habakkuk also affirms (1:13). However, if his people disobey him, as Habakkuk's generation has done, the Lord will punish them. This is the answer to Habakkuk's question, as expressed in 1:13. Yet the Song of Moses also affirms that the Lord will eventually punish the foreign conquerors of his people. This may explain why Habakkuk describes Babylonian wickedness in such detail (1:13–17). Understood against the backdrop of the Song of Moses, Habakkuk's words, which are a mixture of accusation (against sinful Babylon) and lament, function as an appeal to the Lord to implement judgment against his people's enemies.

Habakkuk 2:12–14. The allusions to both Hannah's Song and Moses's Song provide just one example of how a cluster of antecedent texts is used in Habakkuk. Another example appears in the woe oracle in 2:12–14. In 2:12 the Lord pronounces a "woe" against the one "who builds a city with bloodshed and establishes a town by injustice." This echoes Mic. 3:10, which denounces one who builds "Zion with bloodshed and Jerusalem with wickedness." Only in these two texts does the expression "builds with bloodshed" occur. The referent differs in the two texts. Micah is describing corrupt leaders in Zion, while Habakkuk has the Babylonians in view. Yet there is a unifying theme: the perpetration of injustice, which results in devastating judgment upon the perpetrator.

Habakkuk 2:14 anticipates a time when knowledge of the Lord's glory will cover the earth as the waters cover the sea. This echoes Isa. 11:9, which envisions knowledge of the Lord filling the earth as the waters cover the sea. The primary difference between the two texts is the inclusion of "glory" in Hab. 2:14. Isaiah speaks of the time when a new David, pictured as a root from Jesse, will establish a kingdom of justice and peace through the energizing power of the Lord's Spirit. The people of the earth will know the Lord in that they will recognize his moral authority and submit to his will (cf. Jer. 22:15–16). In Habakkuk the Lord's glory, his royal splendor, fills the earth in the context of his judgment upon the Babylonians. The greedy Babylonians rob other nations and destroy lands and cities (2:4–13), attributing their success to their idol gods (2:18–19; cf. 1:16). But the Lord's judgment will turn Babylon's "glory" to shame (2:16) and reveal his royal splendor to the earth.

Habakkuk gives a "different application" of Isa. 11:9, but not a "radically" different one (Schultz, 328). The texts share a common theme: future recognition of the Lord's royal position. Habakkuk fuses Isa. 11:9 (note esp. the metaphor of the waters covering the sea) with Isa. 6:3, which describes the whole earth being full of the Lord's glory.

Habakkuk 3:2–15. In his prayer Habakkuk draws on theophany imagery from a cluster of antecedent texts. He asks the Lord to "repeat" (literally "revive") his mighty acts (3:2). He expands upon his request (3:3–15) by rehearsing these famous deeds in "a poetic montage of various events in which the Lord intervened in Israel's early history" (Chisholm, 434; cf. Whitehead, 275; Wendland, 603). The prophet's expectation is that history will repeat itself as the Lord unleashes his judgment on the Babylonians (cf. 2:4–20).

The montage begins with the Lord's march from the southeast, specifically from Teman and Mount Paran (3:3). There is an echo of Deut. 33:2, where the Lord comes from Sinai and reveals himself from Seir and Mount Paran as he assembles his people, leads them into the promised land, and defeats their enemies (cf. 33:26–29). Habakkuk's desire to have this event repeated is consistent with Judg. 5:4–5, where Deborah speaks of the Lord, the God of Sinai, marching from Seir/Edom to do battle for his people (cf. Ps. 68:7–8). The Lord, the mighty warrior of Moses's day, was alive and well and fully capable of delivering his people in Deborah's time. Habakkuk is confident he can do the same in his day (cf. Hab. 1:12a; 3:6b).

There is another echo of Judg. 5:4 in Habakkuk's prayer. In 3:12–13 he depicts the Lord striding (or marching) through the earth in anger and coming out to deliver his people. The verbs *ṣʿd*, "stride, march," and *yṣʾ*, "come out," appear in parallel in Judg. 5:4a, where the Lord marches out to do battle.

As in Deut. 33:2, the Lord's arrival is accompanied by brightness (3:4). He appears in splendor (*nōgah*), as in 2 Sam. 22:13 // Ps. 18:12, where David uses this term of the Lord's brightness as he descends from the sky to deliver him from the surging water of death.

Habakkuk's montage contains other echoes of 2 Sam. 22 // Ps. 18:

1. The warrior motif of shooting arrows appears in Hab. 3:11, where the sun and moon are paralyzed "at the glint" of the Lord's "flying arrows." In 2 Sam. 22:15 // Ps. 18:14 the Lord shoots his arrows and scatters his enemies.
2. The Lord does battle on behalf of his people and his "anointed one" (3:13). The language is reminiscent of 2 Sam. 22:51 // Ps. 18:50, where the Lord gives his "anointed one" victories. Hannah's Song may be in the background here, for she anticipated a time when the Lord would strengthen his king and enable his "anointed one" to raise his horn in victory (1 Sam. 2:10). In both 2 Sam. 22:51 // Ps. 18:50 and 1 Sam. 2:10 the "anointed one" is clearly Israel's ruler, since the term stands in parallel with "king." In Hab. 3:13 the referent may be different, since "anointed one" stands in parallel with "people," suggesting the nation is in view. (A few Hebrew manuscripts, as well as two major LXX witnesses [Vaticanus and Sinaiticus] read the plural here, "anointed ones.") Even if the referent is different, the texts are linked conceptually in that the Lord intervenes for his anointed servant, whether it is the corporate entity Israel or the nation's king.
3. The Lord tramples on the sea (*yām*) and the abundant waters (*mayim rabbîm*) (3:15), which symbolize nations that oppose him (cf. 3:12). Likewise, in 2 Sam. 22:16–17 // Ps. 18:15–16 the Lord attacks the sea (*yām*) and delivers David from the overwhelming abundant waters (*mayim rabbîm*) that symbolize his deadly (cf. v. 5) enemies (v. 17).

Some of the imagery common to Hab. 3 and 2 Sam. 22 // Ps. 18 also appears in Ps. 77. (There is no consensus on the date of Ps. 77, but a case can be made for it antedating Habakkuk. See Terrien, 557.) In this poetic account of the Red Sea crossing, the psalmist says the Lord's "arrows flashed back and forth" (v. 17), and he depicts the Lord leading his people through the sea (*yām*) and the abundant waters (*mayim rabbîm*) (v. 19), which he casts in an adversarial role (cf. v. 16). Beyond this use of imagery, Ps. 77, if it was written earlier than Habakkuk, may have influenced the book at a more fundamental level. During his crisis (Ps. 77:1–4), the psalmist recalled "the former days" and "the years of long ago" (77:5) and the Lord's mighty deeds (77:10–12), specifically the powerful acts associated with the exodus (77:14–20). In other words, like Habakkuk, he looked to the past to gain confidence regarding the future as he longed for a renewal of divine favor and mercy (cf. 77:7–9).

A particularly significant allusion appears in Habakkuk's prayer when he states that "sun and moon stood still in the heavens" (3:11). This recalls the account in Josh. 10:12–14, which tells how the Lord caused the sun and moon to stand still in the sky, allowing Israel to annihilate their Canaanite enemies. The verb *dmm*, "be motionless, quiet," appears twice in Josh. 10:12–14, but the verb *ʿmd*, "stand, stand still" (cf. Hab. 3:11) is also used with both the moon (Josh. 10:13a) and sun (10:13b) as subject. The antecedent texts surveyed above are from poetic theophanies, which describe the Lord's historical acts of intervention in figurative language. However, the description of the sun and moon standing still derives from a narrative account of the Lord's victory over the Canaanites. The prophet is eager to see the Lord intervene in history again in the same remarkable way he did in the days of Joshua.

To summarize, the theme that unites this cluster of antecedent theophany texts and Hab. 3:2–15 is the Lord's intervention on behalf of his people. In each passage he comes in power to deliver his people from their enemies. The cluster encompasses several historical events, including the exodus (Ps. 77, if indeed it is antecedent), the conquest of Canaan (Deut. 33), Deborah and Barak's victory over the Canaanites (Judg. 5), and David's battles with Israel's enemies (2 Sam. 22 // Ps. 18) as anticipated in Hannah's Song (1 Sam. 2:10). Habakkuk longs to see the Lord intervene in such power once more, this time against the Babylonians.

Habakkuk 3:19. The preceding survey reveals several intertextual links between Habakkuk's prayer and 1 Sam. 22 // Ps. 18. Yet another appears in Habakkuk's declaration of confidence at the end of his prayer. The prophet knows difficult times are coming yet is confident in the Lord's ability to sustain the righteous (cf. 2:4), even when food is scarce (3:17). He declares, "The Sovereign LORD is my strength; he makes my feet like the feet of a deer, he enables me to tread on the heights" (3:19). One hears an echo of 2 Sam. 22:34 // Ps. 18:33: "He makes my feet like the feet of a deer; he causes me to stand on the heights." Habakkuk uses different verbs (*śym* and *drk*) than David (*šwh* and *ʿmd*), but both texts express the theme of the Lord providing stability for those who face a challenge—whether it is enemies on the battlefield (in David's case) or the reality of starvation in the aftermath of military defeat (in Habakkuk's case).

Summary of Habakkuk's use of antecedent texts. While verbatim quotation in Habakkuk, if present, is limited to words and phrases, we see evidence of paraphrase and detect verbal links that establish allusion and signal thematic correlation between passages. While allusion is sometimes made to a single text (see 1:8; 2:12; 3:19), one also detects the use of combinations (1:12) or clusters (2:12–14; 3:2–15), as table 1 shows.

Thematic correlation through allusion has a variety of functions in Habakkuk:

1. On at least three occasions the text to which allusion is made provides a theological framework or pattern that enables one to put into proper perspective statements by the Lord or the prophet. In 1:8 the Lord's allusion to one of the covenant curses of Deut. 28 indicates the coming judgment is punishment for covenant violations. Habakkuk's use of the divine title "Rock" in 1:12 invites comparison with Deut. 32, where this title is prominent. Viewing Deut. 32 as the backdrop for the prophet's appeal enables one to see the full import of his statement, which is more than a mere protest. The link to Ps. 77 in Hab. 3:2 prompts one to view that psalm as a framework for Habakkuk's prayer, in which the prophet, like the psalmist, looks back to the Lord's mighty deeds to gain confidence for the future.

Table 1. Habakkuk's Use of Antecedent Texts

Habakkuk	Verbal Link(s)	Text(s) to Which Allusion Is Made
1:8	from afar, like an eagle	Deut. 28:49
1:12	Holy One Rock	1 Sam. 2:2 1 Sam. 2:2; Deut. 32:4, 15, 18, 30–31
2:12	builds . . . with bloodshed	Mic. 3:10
2:14	earth . . . filled with the knowledge of the glory of the LORD as the waters cover the sea	Isa. 11:9 (combined with Isa. 6:3)
3:2	your deeds	Ps. 77:12
3:3	from Mount Paran	Deut. 33:2 (cf. Judg. 5:4–5)
3:4	splendor	2 Sam. 22:13 // Ps. 18:12 (cf. Deut. 33:2)
3:11	sun and moon stood still	Josh. 10:12–14
3:11	arrows	2 Sam. 22:15 // Ps. 18:14; Ps. 77:17
3:12–13	strides, comes out	Judg. 5:4
3:13	anointed one	1 Sam. 2:10; 2 Sam. 22:51 // Ps. 18:50
3:15	sea, abundant waters	2 Sam. 22:16–17 // Ps. 18:15–16; Ps. 77:19
3:19	my feet like the feet of a deer, on the heights	2 Sam. 22:34 // Ps. 18:33

2. In 1:12 the prophet uses a pair of divine titles found in 1 Sam. 2:2 to set up an ironic contrast with Hannah's Song. Hannah used the titles to celebrate the Lord's intervention on her behalf. But Habakkuk, by addressing Israel's protector in this way, highlights the incongruity he sees in the Lord's decision to use the Babylonians as his instrument of judgment.
3. Allusion sometimes links passages that share general themes, though the historical circumstances surrounding the passages differ. In Hab. 2:12–14 the Lord uses allusion to highlight two themes. The first theme, that perpetration of injustice brings devastating judgment upon the perpetrator, is found in both 2:12, which depicts Babylon as building a city through violence, and Mic. 3:10, which speaks of Zion's corrupt leaders doing the same. The second theme, the future widespread recognition of the Lord's royal authority, appears in both Hab. 2:14, where the Lord reveals his royal splendor to the earth by judging Babylon, and Isa. 11:9, which anticipates a kingdom of justice and peace existing in a time when the earth will know the Lord. In Hab. 3:19 one also detects a linking

of passages sharing a general theme. Habakkuk, anticipating the harsh realities of impending judgment, alludes to 2 Sam. 22:34 // Ps. 18:33, where David celebrates the Lord's enablement in battle. In both passages the Lord provides stability for those who trust him in the face of difficulties.

4. In his prayer (3:2–15) Habakkuk alludes to a cluster of passages as he asks the Lord to reactualize his mighty deeds of old. Habakkuk longs to see the Lord intervene in the same powerful way he has delivered his people throughout their history. By clustering allusions to various events, he highlights the Lord's ability to save.

The NT's Use of Habakkuk

Four NT passages quote from Habakkuk, once from Hab. 1:5 (Acts 13:41) and three times from Hab. 2:4 (Rom. 1:17; Gal. 3:11; Heb. 10:38).

Habakkuk 1:5. In his message in Pisidian Antioch, Paul urges his audience to find forgiveness from sin through the resurrected Jesus. He concludes his appeal by warning them to take heed (Acts 13:41). Attributing the citation to the "prophets," he quotes Hab. 1:5 in a form close to the LXX version, which addresses the listeners as "scoffers." In the original context the Lord announces he is raising up the Babylonians to judge his sinful people. In Paul's context the remarkable, unbelievable act of God pertains to the resurrection of Jesus and justification by faith in him. The connection is rather loose, but there is a common theme that links the texts: people must pay careful attention when the Lord acts in a remarkable new way. One ignores the Lord's intervention at one's peril (see Wall, 249–52; Thomas, 166).

Habakkuk 2:4. The meaning of Hab. 2:4 has been debated. The passage is best translated "See, the one whose desires are not upright faints, but the godly one lives by his integrity" (Chisholm, 437). The pronoun "his" in 2:4b could refer to the prophecy as reliable (see 2:2–3; in this case the translation would be "its reliability") or to God's faithfulness. (The LXX reads [literally] "faith/faithfulness of me," with the first-person pronoun referring to the speaker, God, and functioning either as a subjective genitive ["my faithfulness"] or an objective genitive ["faith in me"].) But the most likely referent is the "godly (one)" mentioned just before this. In this case the text affirms that the godly, in contrast to those who are not upright, will be sustained through the coming trial by their upright character and commitment to God.

In 2:4 "godly (one)" (*ṣaddîq*) is used collectively to refer to the innocent, godly people who are being oppressed. This same word describes the innocent victims of oppression in Judah (1:4) and the innocent among the nations who will be swallowed up by the Babylonians (1:13; cf. Hunn, 89). The verb "lives" refers here to physical preservation (cf. 3:16–19). The term translated "integrity" (*ʾĕmûnâ*) refers to "faithfulness" or "allegiance." The word's primary meaning is "firmness, steadiness" (cf. Exod. 17:12). When used of human character and conduct, it pertains to reliability (see Prov. 12:17, 22; Isa. 59:4; Jer. 5:3; 9:3) and integrity (see 2 Kings 12:15; 22:7; Jer. 5:1).

In Rom. 1:17 Paul quotes Hab. 2:4 as proof that "the righteousness of God" is "by faith." In Gal. 3:11 he cites Hab. 2:4 to prove one "is justified before God" by "faith," not by the law. In both cases Paul omits the pronoun "his" with "faith." As noted above, in the OT the term *ʾĕmûnâ* refers to one's character, not necessarily faith. Yet a righteous lifestyle, even in OT times, is based upon an unwavering commitment to God coupled with trust in God's promise to reward and protect his loyal followers. One sees this in the conclusion to Habakkuk's prayer, where trust in God's character and in his ability to save (cf. 3:18–19) sustains Habakkuk. Faith and faithfulness are two sides of the same coin, and their close connection explains Paul's use of Hab. 2:4 (see Patterson, 221; Wendland, 621). (For a more in-depth discussion of Paul's use of Hab. 2:4, see the articles on Romans and Galatians.)

Hebrews 10:37–38 cites Hab. 2:3b–4 in a textual form similar to the LXX. Yet there are differences: the author of Hebrews puts the pronoun "my" with "righteous one," omits the pronoun "my" with "faith," and reverses the order of clauses in v. 4. He urges his readers to remain faithful despite their trials, for God will eventually reward their perseverance. This is consistent with the original meaning of Hab. 2:4, where the Lord reminds the prophet that persistent faithfulness will sustain the godly.

Bibliography. Barker, K. L., and W. Bailey, *Micah, Nahum, Habakkuk, Zephaniah*, NAC (Broadman & Holman, 1998); Chisholm, R. B., Jr., *Handbook on the Prophets* (Baker Academic, 2002); Cook, P. M., *A Sign and a Wonder*, VTSup 147 (Brill, 2011); Floyd, M. H., *Minor Prophets: Part 2*, FOTL 22 (Eerdmans, 2000); Haak, R. D., *Habakkuk*, VTSup 44 (Brill, 1992); Hunn, D., "*Pistis Christou* in Galatians," *TynBul* 63 (2012): 75–91; Patterson, R. D., *Nahum, Habakkuk, Zephaniah*, WEC (Moody, 1991); Roberts, J. J. M., *Nahum, Habakkuk, and Zephaniah*, OTL (Westminster John Knox, 1991); Schultz, R. L., *The Search for Quotation*, JSOTSup 180 (Sheffield Academic, 1999); Terrien, S., *The Psalms*, ECC (Eerdmans, 2003); Thomas, H. A., *Habakkuk*, THOTC (Eerdmans, 2018); Thompson, M. E., "Prayer, Oracle and Theophany," *TynBul* 44 (1993): 33–53; Wall, R. W., "The Function of LXX Hab. 1:5 in the Book of Acts," *BBR* 10 (2000): 247–58; Wendland, E., "'The Righteous Live by Their Faith' in a Holy God," *JETS* 42 (1999): 591–628; Whitehead, P., "Habakkuk and the Problem of Suffering," *JTI* 10 (2016): 265–81.

Robert B. Chisholm Jr.

Haggai, Book of

The Book of Haggai presents the oracles of the postexilic prophet Haggai. The name "Haggai" occurs 11x in the OT (Hag. 1:1, 3, 12, 13; 2:1, 10, 13, 14, 20; Ezra 5:1; 6:14). After some seventy years of exile in Babylon, now under Persian rule, the Israelites are permitted to return to their homeland through the decree of Cyrus in 538 BC (2 Chron. 36:22–23; Ezra 1:1–4). Zerubbabel the son of Shealtiel and Jeshua the son of Jozadak return to Jerusalem among the exiles and take on leadership roles in the community (Ezra 2:2; 3:8; 4:2–3; 5:2). At the site of the former Solomonic temple they rebuild the altar and begin to offer sacrifices again (Ezra 3). However, the attempts to rebuild the temple structure come to a halt for sixteen years due to opposition from local leaders; during this time, they take care of their own situations, building their homes and providing for themselves. The impetus to pick up the building project again arrives in the form of two prophetic figures, Haggai and Zechariah: "Then Zerubbabel . . . and Joshua . . . arose and began to rebuild the house of God that is in Jerusalem, and the prophets of God were with them, supporting them" (Ezra 5:1–2 ESV).

The completion of the "house" occurs "on the third day of the month of Adar, in the sixth year of the reign of Darius" (Ezra 6:15 ESV), approximately four years after the prophetic word first came to Haggai (August 29, 520 BC; see Hag. 1:1). His ministry stretches through some fifteen weeks during the second year of the reign of Darius, after which time Haggai recedes into the background while Zechariah continues (until Darius's fourth year). We know very little of Haggai otherwise. In Hag. 1:1 he is simply designated as "Haggai the prophet," and in 1:13 as "the messenger of YHWH" who speaks "with the message of YHWH" (AT). All in all, questions related to his name and its significance or to his birth location, age, or priestly connections can only yield speculation. Alec Motyer (964) describes Haggai as "thoroughly orthodox" in that, despite only a single reference to the covenant (2:5), "he taught in the direct line of the Mosaic exodus-Sinaitic tradition and its Davidic development." His Yahwistic faith is evident from his frequent designation for God as YHWH throughout the book (35x); those occurrences include the collocations "YHWH of hosts" (14x), "YHWH their God" (2x), and "YHWH of hosts their God" (1x).

Structure and Message of the Book

The book of Haggai is structured around six prophetic oracles: (1) 1:1–2; (2) 1:3–11; (3) 1:13; (4) 1:15b–2:9; (5) 2:10–19; (6) 2:20–23. These oracles form two major sections of three oracles each. In section one (1:1–15a), YHWH uses the prophet to stir the Judeans out of spiritual lethargy to rebuild the temple destroyed by the Babylonians. In section two (1:15b–2:23), YHWH assures them that he is present to bless their efforts and ensure the meaningfulness of their work.

Haggai's first address (1:1–2) situates the prophetic message in the "second year of Darius the king, in the sixth month, on the first day of the month" (ESV; August 29, 520 BC). On this new moon festival day, only the leaders Zerubbabel and Joshua are addressed. Prefacing his oracle with the messenger formula ("thus says YHWH"), Haggai assures the postexilic community that this first prophetic utterance since returning to the land indeed comes directly from God. His indictment concerns the people's apathy toward rebuilding the house of YHWH, as they proclaim with certainty it is not time for (re)building.

Haggai's second prophetic utterance confronts the people as a whole (1:3–11) later that day. It is a sad tale of two timetables and two houses: they have said that it is *not the time* to (re)build YHWH's house (1:2), but YHWH now asks, "*Is it a time* for you yourselves to dwell in your paneled houses, while this house lies in ruins?" (1:4 ESV). Leaving YHWH's house desolate, they are chastised for "each running to" his own house (1:9 AT), a metaphor for busying oneself with his house and its necessities. Doubly exhorting them to self-reflection (1:5, 7), YHWH insists that the people realize that the absence of dew and produce is not the result of impersonal meteorological and agricultural forces; it is the result of divine agency as YHWH, in an artful play on words, has called for a drought (*ḥōreb*) because the people have left the temple a ruin (or "desolate," *ḥārēb*, 1:10–11). The oracle forcefully issues a call to action with the promise that God's pleasure and glory are bound up in completing the work (1:8–9).

Structurally, the first two oracles of Hag. 1:1–11 together form a unit, presenting YHWH's indictment and summons for the people to rebuild. Then the last segment of the book's first half chronicles a corresponding answer to the summons. Here we find a historical narrative of the people's obedient response to the prophet's preaching (1:12–15), with Haggai's third oracle (1:13) skillfully embedded within that narrative. This oracle supplies an all-important promise in direct divine speech ("I am with you"), which itself is framed by no less than three indications of the divine name YHWH as the source of this promise: Haggai as "the messenger of YHWH" speaking "by the message of YHWH" punctuates the end of the speech as "the oracle of YHWH" (*nəʾum-YHWH*, frequently rendered in English translation as "declares the LORD").

The second half of Haggai (1:15b–2:23) contains the last three oracles and extends hope about the glorious nature of the rebuilding and the blessing the people will have with God. The fourth oracle (1:15b–2:9) comes seven weeks later (October 17, 520 BC). YHWH addresses their discouragement about the apparently insignificant nature of their endeavor (compared to Solomon's temple, 2:3), summoning them to "be strong," "work," and "fear not" (2:4–5 ESV), assuring them of his exodus-like presence (2:4–5) and his shaking of nature and nations to ensure resources for a house of unrivaled glory (2:6–9).

The fifth oracle (2:10–19) comes sixty days later on December 18, 520 BC. Appealing to priestly teaching that uncleanness (unlike holiness) can pass to other things by contact (2:11–13), Haggai explains that the people's uncleanness (resulting from offerings at a disregarded temple site) has resulted in their present experience of want and distress (2:14). Nevertheless, engaging in the temple construction will meet with YHWH's blessing going forward (2:18–19).

Later that day, Haggai addresses his sixth and final oracle to Zerubbabel alone (2:20–23). Returning to the theme of shaking nature and nations, Haggai contemplates not the adornment of the temple-house but a cataclysmic and eschatological shaking where the establishment (or renewal) of another house—a Davidic house—comes into focus. Using the language of election, service, and signets, God promises to exercise his kingly authority through David's descendant Zerubbabel.

Inner-Biblical Links with the OT

As a prophet standing on the far end of OT biblical history, Haggai prophesies and writes with a significant corpus of canonical material at his disposal. It is therefore not surprising to discover a plethora of specific texts or textual themes appropriated by Haggai from prior revelation. An author's use of an existing text or textual tradition has been described as "intertextuality" and can range along a spectrum from overt uses (direct and sometimes extensive quotation with citation formulas, or unsourced but clear quotations of one or more clauses) to allusions (the clear evoking of prior texts via use of several words or mention of characters from the source) to echoes (the most subtle form, consisting of perhaps a single word or phrase, nodding backward toward something a literate reader would recognize) (for these distinctions see Hays, *Paul*, 2–33; Hays, *Gospels*, 10–11; Rogland, 8–9). Since "intertextuality" has many definitions and much philosophical baggage in relation to postmodernism, it is probably better to use the phrase "inner-biblical exegesis." Max Rogland (8) points out that such "textual 'reuse' can serve a variety of purposes such as providing a 'prooftext' to an argument or evoking textual coloring of some kind."

Table 1 lists inner-biblical connections in the order they appear in Haggai, rather than thematically. Where prior texts apply to a particular part of the verse, language has been added to clarify which part of the verse is in view. Due to the constraints on space, we will treat only a handful of passages (primarily related to the theme of temple-building) to give a sense of how Haggai appropriates prior revelation. For NT uses of Haggai, see *CNTUOT*.

Table 1. Inner-Biblical Citations in Haggai

Passages	Possible Inner-Biblical Connections
1:1	by the hand of Moses: Exod. 9:35; 35:29; Lev. 8:36; Num. 4:37, etc. prophets: Isa. 20:2; Jer. 37:2; 50:1; Ezek. 38:17; Zech. 7:7, 12
1:2	"this people" as negative expression: Jer. 6:19, 21; 7:16, 33; 8:5; 9:15; 11:14; 13:10; 14:11; 15:1; 16:5; 19:11; 21:8; 23:33; 32:42; 33:24; 36:7 house of YHWH to be built: Zech. 8:9
1:5, 7	see discussion
1:6	Hosea 4:10; Mic. 6:14–15
1:8	see discussion
1:9	Jer. 8:15; 14:19
1:10	Lev. 26:4, 19–20; Deut. 11:17; 28:23; 32:22; 1 Kings 17:1; Zech. 8:12
1:11	Deut. 7:13; 11:14; 12:17; 14:23; 18:4; 28:33, 51; Hosea 2:8–9; Joel 1:10
1:12	Deut. 4:10; 13:5, 12; 17:13; 19:20; 21:21; 31:12–13; 1 Sam. 12:14
1:13	Gen. 26:24; 28:15; Deut. 31:23; Isa. 43:2, 5; Jer. 1:8, 19; 15:20; 30:11; 42:11; 46:28
1:14	see discussion
2:4–5	see discussion
2:6	"in a little while": Isa. 10:25; Jer. 51:33; Hosea 1:4 (cf. Isa. 29:17, with restoration) shaking/earthquake motif: Isa. 24:17–20; Ezek. 38:19b–20; Joel 2:10, 30–31; 3:15–16; Zech. 14:4–5
2:6–9, 21	see discussion
2:10–14	Lev. 6:25, 27; 7:19; 11:24–28; 22:4–7; Num. 19:22
2:13	Lev. 22:4; Num. 5:2; 9:6, 7, 10; 19:13
2:14	Israel as a nation (Heb. *gôy*) (neutral): Exod. 19:6; 33:13; Zeph. 2:9; Ps. 33:12 Israel as a nation (Heb. *gôy*) (negative): Deut. 32:28; Judg. 2:20; Isa. 1:4; 10:6; Jer. 5:9, 29; 7:28; 9:9 (MT v. 8); Ezek. 2:3; Mal. 3:9
2:15, 18	"set your heart": see discussion at Hag. 1:5, 7 founding of the temple: Zech. 8:9
2:16	Isa. 5:2; Hosea 9:2
2:17	Deut. 28:22; Amos 4:9
2:19	Deut. 8:8; 28:1–14; 1 Kings 4:25; Isa. 36:16; Mic. 4:4
2:21–22	see discussion
2:23	see discussion

Haggai 1:5, 7. These two verses might echo passages in the Torah. Although the expression in Hag. 1:5, 7 (*śîmû ləbabkem ʿal-darkêkem*, literally "set your heart upon your ways" but frequently glossed "consider your ways") is not used in Exod. 7:23, Pharaoh is there described as one who "did not take even this to heart" (*wəlōʾ-šāt libbô gam-lāzōʾt*). More intriguing is Exod. 9:20–21, which describes two contrasting responses by the Egyptians to the threatened plague of hail (*bārād*, Exod. 9:22; cf. Hag. 2:17): some "feared the word of YHWH" (cf. Hag. 1:12)

and protected the slaves and livestock, but others "did not set [their] heart upon the word of YHWH" (*lōʾ-śām libbô ʾel-dəbar YHWH*) and eventually suffered for it (AT). Haggai may be suggesting that some of the Egyptians had more sense than God's people. A final allusion might be Deut. 32:46, where Moses uses identical wording except for the prepositional phrase: "Set your heart on all these words" (*śîmû ləbabkem ləkol-haddəbārîm*). The way that Haggai leans upon the covenantal passages of Leviticus and Deuteronomy, and the covenant lawsuit context of the Song of Moses in Deut. 32, suggests that Hag. 1:5, 7 echoes this text.

Haggai 1:8. The command "Go up into the mountains and bring down timber" echoes 2 Chron. 2:8–9 (cf. 1 Kings 5:6), where Solomon asks for wood to be sent from Tyre for the building of the great and wonderful house of YHWH. Here, however, it is the Judeans themselves who must willingly go and bring it. A consequence of their building is that YHWH "will take pleasure" in it and "be glorified." A text like Lev. 1:3–4 may form the background for the first of these statements. Verse 3 uses a cognate noun (*rāṣôn*), while v. 4 employs a form of the same verb used in Hag. 1:8 (*rāṣâ*). The semantic connection is clear: to complete the temple "will achieve the status of an acceptable offering in which the Lord will take pleasure" (Verhoef, 67). Although in prior OT revelation the *niphal* forms of *kbd* with first-person inflections ("I am / will be glorified") occur in conjunction with divine judgment (see Exod. 14:4, 17–18; Lev. 10:3; Ezek. 28:22; 39:13), here it occurs as a result of their obedient rebuilding. In addition, the verbal root *kbd* very likely triggers associations with the noun *kābôd* ("glory") and the revelation of YHWH's theophanous glory at Sinai (Exod. 24:16, 17; 29:43; 40:34, 35; Lev. 9:6, 23).

Haggai 1:14. A number of antecedent texts and concepts are at play in this verse. First, Haggai describes YHWH's work in Zerubbabel, Joshua, and the remnant of the people by using a collocation of the *hiphil* verb *ʿûr* with the noun *rûaḥ*; this results in their building the house of YHWH. Interestingly, the ear attuned to this collocation likely recognizes that throughout OT revelation, when God is the subject, the spirits of the ones he stirs up are usually pagans for the purpose of executing judgment: Pul king of Assyria (= Tiglath-pileser [1 Chron. 5:26]), the Philistines and the Arabians (2 Chron. 21:16–17), a destroyer against Babylon (Jer. 51:1), the kings of the Medes (Jer. 51:11). God as the subject of this verb (but without *rûaḥ* as object) also occurs in similar judgment contexts: a gathering of great nations against Babylon (Jer. 50:9), the Medes (Isa. 13:17–19), and Cyrus (Isa. 41:25; 45:13). But in restoring Israel to the land, God reverses the pattern (2 Chron. 36:22–23 and Ezra 1:1): he stirs up the spirit of Cyrus for blessing to Israel! Whereas frequently the spirit of a pagan king is stirred to tear down the people of Israel and others, here it effects the building of a house for YHWH, the result of divine sovereignty (fulfilling YHWH's word by Jeremiah). Ezra 1:5 and Hag. 1:14 apply this work of YHWH to the Israelites themselves: Ezra speaks of the leaders, the priests and Levites, and everyone "whose spirit God had stirred to . . . rebuild the house of YHWH," and Haggai likewise speaks of YHWH stirring up the spirit of the Israelites (not the pagan kings) to rebuild.

Second, Haggai's description of the physical response to YHWH's stirring bears remarkable similarities to the description of tabernacle construction in Exod. 35–40. Haggai says that they performed *məlāʾkâ* ("work") on the house; of the thirty-three occurrences of this noun in Exodus, twenty-one apply to preparations for and construction of the tabernacle (35:21, 24, 29, 31, 33, 35 [2x]; 36:1–8 [10x]; 38:24 [2x]; 39:43; 40:33). Among these Exodus texts two seem especially likely to have influenced Haggai. First, in addition to mention of the "work" on the divine dwelling place ("tent of meeting" in Exodus, "house of YHWH" in Haggai), Exod. 35:21 shares with Hag. 1:14 the expressions "they came" and "they brought," and description of "the spirit" moving them to the work (but with a twist here: in Haggai, YHWH is the active agent, stirring their spirit). The other text is Exod. 35:29. It uses *bəyad-mōšeh* (cf. *bəyad-ḥaggay* in Hag. 1:1, 3; 2:1), mentions "all the men and women, the people of Israel" (cf. "all the remnant of the people" in Hag. 1:14), and employs the noun *məlāʾkâ* ("work") with the verb *ʿāśâ* ("to do")—all in the context of their heart moving them to bring material as a freewill offering for working on the tabernacle. Haggai and the people, then, appear as a kind of postexilic Moses/Israel, where God's prophet is again calling for the people to invest in the construction of a dwelling place for God in their midst.

Haggai 2:4–5. Anyone in an Israelite context hearing Haggai's summons to "be strong" (*ḥăzaq*) and "not fear" (*ʾal-tîrāʾû*) in light of the presence of YHWH (2:4–5) would likely sense a familiar ring from earlier exhortations to others: Israel (Deut. 31:6; Isa. 35:4; 2 Chron. 32:7–8), Joshua (Deut. 31:7–8, 23; Josh. 1:5–9 [but with synonyms for "fear"]), and Solomon (1 Chron. 22:13; 28:20). Haggai 2:4–5 may simply echo the full range of these texts, or one particular passage may be in view. Several elements match 1 Chron. 28:20: the verbs "be strong," "do/work," and "do not fear," and the promise of divine presence. Both passages further share the context of encouragement to build a house for God. Like a prior son of David (Solomon), in this new day Zerubbabel, Joshua, and the remnant people also receive exhortations and promises to likewise engage in temple-building until the task is complete.

Haggai's mention in 2:5 of "the word that I [YHWH] covenanted with you" (AT) when Israel left Egypt and "my Spirit" abiding among them appear to draw upon Exod. 25:1–8; 35:4–29; 36:2–7. The present generation is reminded of a previous one's generous, obedient giving of gold, silver, and other supplies to build the first divine dwelling place as part of their covenant obligation to the Lord. It is as if YHWH were saying, "Commit your energy and resources, for just as I provided the exodus community with an abundance so that I might dwell among them (Exod. 25:8), so I will provide an abundance for you, if you will contribute and work for a temple that can be even more glorious than the first."

Finally, Zech. 8:9–13 later seems to take up Hag. 2:4–5, along with the other verses in Haggai that reference YHWH's removal of blessing from the work of their hands. The Zechariah section is framed by the expression "let your hands be strong" in 8:9 and 8:13 (the same verbal root, *ḥzq*, as in Hag. 2:4) and uses the same command "do not fear" in 8:13 (*ʾal-tîrāʾû*). He explicitly mentions former prophets (8:9) in the days prior to rebuilding (probably Haggai and Zechariah himself) and the poor conditions the people faced (8:10). However, Zechariah now promises a reversal of what YHWH had done before their commitment to rebuild, where judgment will give way to blessing and peace (8:11–13).

Haggai 2:6–9 and 2:21. The two shakings in Hag. 2:6–9 and 2:21 appear to have some direct connection to Joel 3 (translations ESV). In Joel 3:2 (MT 4:2), the *gôyim* are mentioned twice: "I will gather all *the nations*" (for judgment) because they "have scattered [my people] *among the nations* and have divided up my land." In 3:4–6, God moves from the general term "(all) the nations" to address specifically "Tyre and Sidon, and all the regions of Philistia" (v. 4), which appear to be stand-ins for the nations. God explains why he will judge: "For you have taken *my silver and my gold*, and have carried *my rich treasures into your temples*" (v. 5). It seems that the language of Hag. 2:6–9 is reversing what these nations have been rebuked for having done to the Israelites in Joel. The lexico-semantic links between Joel 3:5 and Hag. 2:7–8 are clear: "silver and gold"; "my rich treasures" (*maḥămadday*; cf. *ḥemdat kol-haggôyim* in Hag. 2:7); "you have carried" (*hiphil* of *bôʾ*; Hag. 2:7 has a *qal* form with *ḥemdat kol-haggôyim* as the subject); "into your temples" (Haggai uses "house" but still refers to the temple). So the silver and gold that belonged to YHWH, treasures the nations took from Israel to use on their pagan temples, God will now shake out of the nations for the building and glorifying of the new temple so that its glory excels the prior one.

Scholars disagree on whether "I will fill this house with glory" (2:7) refers to God's theophanous glory-presence or to the riches of the nations. If the former, then the language of the glory of YHWH filling the tabernacle/temple would be in view (Exod. 40:34, 35; 1 Kings 8:11; 2 Chron. 5:14). If the latter, then Haggai could possibly be appropriating texts like Ps. 72:10 and especially Isa. 60 with its reference throughout to glory, silver and gold, the abundance and wealth of kings and nations coming into Israel, and the glorifying of God's sanctuary. Revelation 21, then, would be taking this language from Haggai and Isaiah and applying it to the new Jerusalem with the mention of God's presence (v. 3), glory and radiance (vv. 10–11), the precious things making up the city (vv. 15–21), the presence of God without a physical temple (v. 22), the glory of God giving light (v. 23), and the nations and kings bringing their "glory" into it (vv. 24–27).

Haggai 2:21–22. For comments on the shaking of the cosmos and countries, see discussion on Hag. 2:6–9. The text of Hag. 2:22 has a significant number of potential inner-biblical links. First, God's activity of "overthrowing" is first mentioned canonically in the overthrow of Sodom and Gomorrah (Gen. 19:25, 29). Interestingly, this early account forms a paradigm or point of comparison for subsequent mentions of God's overthrowing other people and nations (see Deut. 29:23; Isa. 13:19; Jer. 20:16; Amos 4:11; Lam. 4:6). A few other OT texts relay God's threats to overthrow, but without comparisons to Sodom and Gomorrah (see 2 Kings 21:13; Jon. 3:4). In Hag. 2:22 the object of "overthrow" (*hpk*) is a construct chain, "the throne of kingdoms" (*kissēʾ mamlākôt*). This chain occurs elsewhere in the OT most frequently to describe the Israelite king or the Davidic throne (Deut. 17:18; 2 Sam. 7:13; 1 Kings 9:5; 2 Chron. 23:20); the words also co-occur outside of a construct chain with reference to the Davidic monarchy (2 Sam. 3:10; 7:16; Isa. 9:6). In Hag. 2:22, however, the thrones to be overthrown are clearly those of the world, perhaps in anticipation of the Davidic promise to come in v. 23.

Second, the picture in Hag. 2:22 of God overthrowing chariots and their riders (*merkābâ wərōkəbêhā*) and of horses and their riders (*sûsîm wərōkəbêhem*) going down clearly alludes to the exodus, especially as it is portrayed in the Song of the Sea in Exod. 15:1 ("horse and its rider," *sûs wərōkəbô*), 15:4 ("the chariots of Pharaoh," *markəbōt parʿōh*), and 15:5 ("they went down to the depths," *yārədû bimṣôlōt*). The victory over Egypt in the original exodus forms a powerful paradigm for the decisive, future work of God to crush his enemies as he establishes his presence and power on behalf of his people.

Third, Hag. 2:22 presents the image of men falling, "everyone by the sword of his brother/fellow" (AT). This theme of internecine fighting and mutually assured self-destruction at the Lord's hands can be found in Judg. 7:22; 1 Sam. 14:20; 2 Chron. 20:23; Ezek. 38:21; Zech. 14:13.

Haggai 2:23. This verse draws upon a number of OT passages. First, when YHWH says to Zerubbabel, "I will take you," he is employing a verb that can have the sense of special selection, as in the case of Israel (Exod. 6:7), Abraham (Josh. 24:3), and David (2 Sam. 7:8). The Davidic overtones of the final passage are likely in view, as it continues with the description of Zerubbabel as "my servant" (*ʿabdî*). This title is applied to David 31x in the OT (e.g., 2 Sam. 3:18; 7:5, 8, 26; Ezek. 34:23; 37:24), as well as to figures in David's line: Hezekiah (2 Chron. 32:16) and the one called "my servant, the Branch" (Zech. 3:8; cf. 6:12).

Second, YHWH tells Zerubbabel that he will make him "like a signet ring" (*kaḥôtām*). Seals and signets are mentioned 14x in the OT; however, the idea of a *person* functioning as a signet ring suggests dependence on Jeremiah here. According to Jer. 22:24, Jehoiachin (one of the final Davidic kings) is told on oath by YHWH that "even if you . . . were a signet ring on my right hand, I would still pull you off." Removal of Jehoiachin as a signet ring means denying to him the authority to function as the Davidic king. Haggai 2:23 is a dramatic reversal: YHWH intends to use Zerubbabel as a signet ring to reestablish David's throne.

The final Davidic allusion occurs in the explanatory clause given for this special treatment of Zerubbabel: "For I have chosen you" (*kî-bəkā bāḥartî*). The same verb is used of God's choosing David (instead of others) in 1 Sam. 16:8–10; 2 Sam. 6:21; 1 Kings 8:16; 11:34.

Above all, it seems that 2 Sam. 7 is probably the most prominent passage influencing Hag. 2:23. Recall that in 2 Sam. 7, David has proposed to build YHWH a house. YHWH says instead that he will build a house for David. YHWH begins by reminding David of his selection in v. 8 ("I took you"). By evoking 2 Sam. 7:8, Haggai likely intends the hearer to remember the entire context of this passage: God has been "with you" (v. 9); YHWH promises a "place" for his people (v. 10; cf. the promise in Hag. 2:9 of God providing peace "in this place [the temple]"); David's house will involve rulers in his dynastic line, for whom God will establish "his kingdom" (vv. 12, 13, 16—the same Hebrew word used in Hag. 2:22 for the "kingdoms" that he will overthrow); God will provide to David a son who will build YHWH a house for his name (v. 13). Of course, in David's immediate purview this refers to Solomon. But Haggai, by appropriating this text for his current timeframe, appears to portray Zerubbabel as a second son of David, one who will build a new house for YHWH and in whom the future of the Davidic house's fortunes will be reversed from the destruction Jehoiachin had experienced.

Bibliography. Baldwin, J., *Haggai, Zechariah, Malachi*, TOTC (InterVarsity, 1972); Cody, A., "When Is the Chosen People Called a Gôy?," *VT* 14 (1964): 1–6; Hays, R. B., *Echoes of Scripture in the Gospels* (Baylor University Press, 2016); Hays, *Echoes of Scripture in the Letters of Paul* (Yale University Press, 1989); Herbert G. M., "'This People' and 'This Nation' in Haggai," *VT* 18 (1968): 190–97; Jacobs, M., *The Books of Haggai and Malachi*, NICOT (Eerdmans, 2017); Motyer, J. A., "Haggai," in *The Minor Prophets*, ed. T. E. McComiskey, 3 vols. (Baker, 1998), 3:963–1002; Rogland, M., *Haggai and Zechariah 1–8*, BHHB (Baylor University Press, 2016); Verhoef, P. A., *The Books of Haggai and Malachi*, NICOT (Eerdmans, 1987).

PHILLIP MARSHALL

Harris, J. Rendel

See History of Interpretation: 1800 to Present

Hays, Richard B.

See Quotation, Allusion, and Echo

Hebrews, Letter to the

The growth of scholarly attention to the NT book of Hebrews has been explosive in recent decades, and particular interest in the author's use of the OT continues to expand accordingly with substantive studies offered in the form of monographs, journal articles, and conference presentations. In my *CNTUOT* entry on Hebrews, I note that the power of Hebrews' appropriation of the Jewish Scriptures stems from an integration of rhetorical and rabbinic skills, wielded forcefully and pastorally in the elucidation of a profoundly Christocentric vision of theology. Thus, through the very blood and bone of this message that we call Hebrews flows the OT, at every hand the author taking up texts, topics, events, persons, or institutions drawn from the older-covenant writings and bringing them to bear in powerful arguments for the hearers to endure in following Jesus, the Son of God and high priest of the new covenant.

OT Ties to Hebrews

Quotations and allusions. In the *CNTUOT* I survey forty-eight passages where the author either quotes the OT directly or makes overt allusion to a scriptural text or texts: 1:2, 3, 4, 5a, 5b, 6, 7, 8–9, 10–12, 13; 2:6–8a, 12, 13, 16–18; 3:2–5, 7–11, 15–19; 4:3–7; 4:4; 5:5, 6, 7–9; 6:4–6, 7–8, 14, 18, 20; 7:1–4, 17, 21; 8:1, 5, 8–12; 9:20, 23, 28; 10:5–9, 12–13, 16–17, 27, 28, 30, 37–38; 11:1–40; 12:2, 5b–6, 12–13, 15, 18–21, 26b; 13:5, 11. In these passages I note thirty-seven quotations, forty overt allusions, and a number of places where very faint allusions to the OT text may be detected. Following Richard Hays, I use the term "echoes" to refer to more faint allusions.

The quotations normally follow introductory formulae that present the words as falling from the lips of God, most often using forms of *legō*. Moreover, there is an implicit trinitarianism to Hebrews (Pierce), with twenty-three quotations presented as spoken by God, four placed on the lips of Christ, and four others attributed to the Holy Spirit. Those passages constituting the words of human beings, while ultimately considered to be divine in origin, have introductions that are presented as issuing from a human context or perspective (e.g., 2:6; 9:20; 12:21). The odd introductory formula at Heb. 2:6, "But there is a place where someone has testified . . . ," may utilize ambiguity to retain the general emphasis on God as the speaker of Scripture.

As for allusions and echoes, Hebrews' language is permeated with such, as we see right from the book's introduction. For example, at the very heart of the introduction's description of the Son, Heb. 1:3 alludes to a passage that will come up repeatedly throughout the discourse: "He *sat down at the right hand* of the Majesty in heaven" (*ekathisen en dexia tēs megalōsynēs en hypsēlois*); this allusion to Ps. 110:1 (109:1 LXX) proclaims the exaltation of Christ by evoking the psalm passage.

This use of Ps. 110:1 to evoke the Son's status brings us to an echo in the introduction, one that is often missed. At Heb. 1:4 we find "So he became as much superior to the angels as *the name* he has inherited is superior to theirs." When the author writes of "the name he has inherited" (*keklēronomēken onoma*), he alludes to the broader context of 2 Sam. 7:14, a verse he proceeds to quote (Heb. 1:5). In that context the Lord gives King David an oracle through the prophet Nathan (2 Sam. 7:4–17). In 2 Sam. 7:10–17 the oracle shifts to the Lord's promises for the future, including the work and status of David's son. The term "name" (Heb. *šēm*; Gk. *onoma*) plays an important role in the chapter. God promises David that he will make his name great like the names of the greatest people of the earth (2 Sam. 7:9). Furthermore, David's son will build a house for God's name even as God establishes the son's throne forever (2 Sam. 7:13), and the result will be that both the name of God's people and the name of the Lord himself will be magnified (7:23, 26).

Text form. Sorting out the textual tradition behind Hebrews has coursed a winding path in scholarly discussions but in the past half century has tended to focus on the author's eclectic use of a variety of traditions (e.g., McCullough); nevertheless, all agree that Hebrews is oriented to a Greek text form. Moreover, Radu Gheorghita, for example, makes the case for the profound theological and exegetical orientation of Hebrews' author to the LXX, that textual tradition shaping his theological messages in the book. Furthermore, Gert Steyn proposes that the author's particular *Vorlage* hails from an Egyptian context. Another main vein of discussion concerns the author's own adjustment of his text form at hand for stylistic purposes or to communicate a point of theology and/or exhortation (Bateman, 240; Leschert, 245–47; Hughes, 59; Jobes, 181–91).

Which books influence Hebrews the most? By far the most influential portions of the OT on Hebrews are Psalms and the Pentateuch. Of the quotations and overt allusions in the book, 44 percent come from the former, and 31 percent from the latter. The remaining evocations of the OT stem primarily from the prophets, accounting for 18 percent (primarily Isaiah and Jeremiah, with one quotation each from Habakkuk and Haggai), with the remaining quotations and allusions coming from only two historical books, 2 Samuel and Joshua, and Proverbs (which provides only one). Generally speaking, the framework of Hebrews' discourse may be read as interweaving christological exposition and reflection, grounded especially in Psalms, and exhortation to community action, drawn from various parts of Scripture but most especially from redemptive history found in the Pentateuch. For example, one can consider the profound impact of Deuteronomy on the book's exhortation material (D. Allen). However, forming perhaps the most significant passage for the backbone of the book's Christology, the author focuses especially on Ps. 110 (Compton), a text used in orienting the discussion to the heavenly realm and the exaltation of Christ (Ps. 110:1) and the appointment of Christ as high priest (Ps. 110:4). Psalm 110 plays a central role in a broader network of key passages that knit together the author's sermon.

Methods of appropriation and argument and their role in the book. The author utilizes numerous rabbinic techniques of appropriation in his handling of the OT, including the catena (a string of OT texts), verbal analogy, argument from lesser to greater, the art of dispelling confusion, midrashic commentary on a text, argument from the literal meaning of a word, the example list, and, throughout, reinforcement of an idea or exhortation with a quotation (Guthrie, "Hebrews"). These methods shape Hebrews into a powerful act of communication.

A "string of pearls" and verbal analogy. Hebrews 1:5–2:4 offers good examples of each of the first three of these methods. The grouping of texts in 1:5–14 constitutes a catena, or "string of pearls" (*ḥāraz*), a method of appropriation used by teachers in broader Judaism of the day, by which related scriptural texts were "chained" together via catchwords or verbal analogy (*gəzērâ šāwâ*). In mounting an impressive string of quotations offered one after another, the effect was to build overwhelming evidence for a particular point under discussion. Here the author of Hebrews uses the method to drive home the unquestionable superiority of the Son to the angels.

The catena of 1:5–14 is made up of three pairs of texts followed by the quotation of Ps. 110:1. Each of the pairs is joined by verbal analogy, the author bringing together passages on the basis of a shared word or words. For example, the first two passages, Ps. 2:7 and 2 Sam. 7:14, are brought together by the common use of the words *huios* ("son") and *egō* ("I") as well as the verb of being, *ei/esomai/estai* ("you are," "I will be," "he will be"). Notice also that both of these OT texts proclaim a unique status for the Son in relation to God the Father. In essence, the first pair thus asserts the superiority of the Son to the angels by virtue of the Son's unique relationship to the Father.

The author brings together the second pair of passages, Deut. 32:43 LXX (cf. Ps. 97:7 [96:7 LXX]) and Ps. 104:4 (103:4 LXX), quoted at Heb. 1:6–7, on the basis of the catchword "angels" (*angeloi*). On the one hand, clearly the angelic beings are inferior to the Son in that they worship him (Deut. 32:43 LXX). On the other hand, the second quotation in this pair, Ps. 104:4, is found in a psalm of praise to God as Lord of creation. The translators of the Greek rendering have interpreted the "messengers" of the Hebrew text as "angels" (*angeloi*; cf. Gen. Rab. 21:9; Exod. Rab. 15:6, 22; 25:2; Deut. Rab. 9:3), tapping into a significant stratum of OT thought that associates the angelic beings with the winds and lightning of the storms on which God rides, a motif expressed in Jewish works of the broader Second Temple period (e.g., Jub. 2:2; T. Adam 1:12; 1QH[a] 9.9b–12). Thus, the psalm proclaims that the angels are inferior in status to the Son; whereas he is exalted to a place of highest honor and majesty, they are his servants. Together, the second pair of texts in the catena argues for the Son's superiority on the basis of the inferior action and status of the angels.

The third and final pair of texts in this string of pearls (Heb. 1:8–12) is made up of Ps. 45:6–7 (45:7–8 MT; 44:7–8 LXX; L. Allen) and Ps. 102:25–27 (102:26–28 MT; 101:26–28 LXX), brought together by their common and extensive use of the Greek pronoun *sy* ("you"; five times in each passage). For the author of Hebrews these proclamations concerning the Son tell us of his exalted nature and position, which set him far above the angels. According to the first of these psalms, the Son has an eternal throne and thus has been set above his companions. Psalm 102:25–27, on the other hand, proclaims the Son as the eternal creator of the heavens and earth and as the one who will terminate them in the end. Hebrews' use of this powerful psalm echoes an emphasis in the NT on the Son as creator and terminator of the world (John 1:3; 1 Cor. 8:6; Col. 1:16; Heb. 2:5, 8; cf. 1 Cor. 15:28). Furthermore, in harmony with Ps. 45:6–7, Ps. 102:25–27 drives home the eternal nature of the Son as not bound to the transitory nature of the world.

The final, culminating quote of the catena of texts in Heb. 1:5–14, Ps. 110:1 (Ps. 109:1 LXX) stands alone rather than in tandem with another passage, marking its heightened significance in the broader discourse (1:3; 8:1; 10:12; 12:2). It recalls the allusion to the same verse in the book's introduction (1:3), forming a bracket, or *inclusio*, around Heb. 1. It also offers a fitting culmination for the catena, embodying a resounding proclamation of the Son's enthronement at the right hand of God. So, the string of texts in 1:5–14 uses the angels as a reference point to drive home the unquestionable majesty and status of the Son, thus prompting a deep reverence for Christ and the word of salvation.

Argument from lesser to greater. This clear picture of the superiority of the Son and the deep reverence for him above his angelic servants in turn lays the foundation for the *argument from lesser to greater* (*qal wahomer*) found at Heb. 2:2–4. An argument from lesser to greater (sometimes called an *a fortiori* argument) suggests that if something is true in a lesser situation, it certainly is true in a greater situation and has greater implications. Following this logic, the argument at Heb. 2:2–4 asserts that if rejecting the law of God, which was delivered through angels—beings clearly inferior to the Son—resulted in devastating punishment (the "lesser" situation in this argument), it is certainly true that the rejection of the word of salvation delivered through the superior Son of God deserves even greater punishment! The author of Hebrews uses this type of argument at several other places throughout the book (9:13–14; 10:26–29; 12:9, 25–27).

Dispelling confusion and midrashic commentary. Psalm 8:4–6, quoted and expounded with midrashic commentary at Heb. 2:5–9, has verbal analogy with the quotation of Ps. 110:1 at Heb. 1:13. The author reads the passages, one in light of the other, as messianic (as with 1 Cor. 15:25–27; Eph. 1:20–22), referring to the submission of either "enemies" (Ps. 110:1) or "all things" (Ps. 8:6) under "the feet" (*tōn podōn*) of Christ. The reference to the subjugation of "the world to come" at Heb. 2:5 points back to the quotation of Ps. 110:1 at Heb. 1:13 ("*until* I make your enemies a footstool for your feet").

Psalm 8, in its original OT context, celebrates the glory of God and the dignity of human beings in their role vis-à-vis the rest of the created order, and there has been some debate concerning whether the appropriation of the psalm by Hebrews is anthropological or christological (Guthrie and Quinn). Quinn and I suggest that from the "if" (which anticipates the submission of all things to Christ at the end of the age) onward it should be read profoundly as *both*, the anthropology of the psalm taken up and fulfilled in the Christology. In essence, the Son, the last Adam, has succeeded where the first Adam failed in the divine commission to rule over God's creation. Moreover, Ps. 8:4–6 contains elements of both exaltation ("crowned him with glory and honor") and incarnation ("made him a little lower than the angels") and thus serves as a fitting trigger of transition from a focus on the exaltation of Christ in Heb. 1 to a focus on incarnation in 2:10–18.

I use the label "midrashic" not to denote a genre of rabbinic literature but to signify that the author offers a running (albeit brief here) explanation, or commentary, on a text. The author's midrashic commentary on Ps. 8:4–6 (Heb. 2:8b–9) employs a rabbinic technique called "dispelling confusion." With the technique a rabbi takes an apparent contradiction between two passages and explains why there is no contradiction between the two. The "contradiction" seemingly addressed by Hebrews concerns the *timing* of the subjugation of things to the Son. Has this already occurred ("You . . . put everything under his feet"; Ps. 8:6 // Heb. 2:8), or will the subjugation occur at the end of the age ("until I make your enemies a footstool for your feet"; Ps. 110:1 // Heb. 1:13)? The author of Hebrews dissipates the potential confusion by explaining that indeed all things have been subjected to Christ's rule already: "For in subjecting everything to him, he left nothing that is not subject to him," Heb. 2:8b CSB). Yet, the author reads Ps. 110:1 as meaning that from the standpoint of human experience, we do not yet *perceive* all things as in subjection to

Christ ("As it is, we do not yet see everything subjected to him," Heb. 2:8c CSB).

Literal meaning of a word or phrase and its implications. Hebrews clearly holds that every word of Scripture has significance or implications, and rabbis of the day could evince this axiom by building an argument on a single word or phrase from a text under consideration. For example, having presented the longest quotation in the NT (Jer. 31:31–34 [38:31–34 LXX]; Heb. 8:8–12), the author of Hebrews seizes on a single word from the quotation, the word rendered "new" (*kainēn*), for comment! He writes ever so briefly, "By calling this covenant 'new,' he has made the first one obsolete; and what is obsolete and outdated will soon disappear" (Heb. 8:13). Thus, the implication is drawn from the meaning of the word *kainēn*.

Example list. The crafting of "example lists" (*exempla*) to drive home with power an exhortation finds expression in various parts of ancient literature (e.g., 4 Ezra; Cicero, *De oratore*; Philo; Damascus Document; 1 Maccabees). Although they are presented in the form of exposition, *exempla* function to present so many examples related to a desired response that the hearers will be challenged to act (Cosby, *Function*). Consequently, they are hortatory in nature. Our great "Hall of Faith" in Heb. 11 takes up this technique, presenting great, marginalized heroes of faith in chronological order (Eisenbaum, *Jewish*). Exhibiting *pistis* ("faith"), the term employed anaphorically to drive home the author's point, the heroes provide an unrelenting and extensive witness to this mode of life as foundational for the people of God, especially in times of great difficulty.

Theological Axioms behind the Author's Uses of the OT

One of the most significant conversations in recent discussions concerns the axioms behind Hebrews' use of the OT (e.g., Docherty, 179–81). This emphasis calls to mind, for instance, Daniel Patte's 1975 work *Early Jewish Hermeneutics in Palestine*, in which he points to axioms behind the targums (Patte, 65–74). Here we seek to address the theological convictions evident in Hebrews's appropriation of the OT text.

Scripture is God's authoritative words. Hebrews presents the words of Scripture as the words of God and therefore as words of inherent authority, both proclaiming what is true and calling people to adhere to or respond to its truth with obedience (Docherty, 180–81, 197). We see this, for example, in the introductory formulae throughout, by which Scripture is presented as the very words of God (e.g., "he says" or "God says"). The author also demonstrates this conviction in his use of reinforcement, an exhortation or proposition bolstered simply by quoting an authoritative text, as if the text's inherent authority is self-evident. For instance, at Heb. 13:5 we find the exhortation "Keep your lives free from the love of money and be content with what you have," which is immediately reinforced with "because God has said, 'Never will I leave you; never will I forsake you,'" the quotation taken from Deut. 31:6.

Scripture is inspired in the particulars. The author of Hebrews quotes his source texts faithfully and demonstrates a conviction that the particulars of the scriptural texts are significant. As demonstrated by the author's seizing on the literal meaning of a word in his commentary on a text (described above), the very words of Scripture are seen as significant. This conviction also manifests in midrashic commentary, as the author capitalizes on words from a quoted passage, weaving them into an exhortation, as at 3:12–13, where, having quoted Ps. 95:7–11, he emphasizes words from the quotation: "See to it, brothers and sisters, that none of you has a sinful, unbelieving heart that turns away from the living God. But encourage one another daily, as long as it is called 'Today,' so that none of you may be hardened by sin's deceitfulness" (Heb. 3:12–13). Here the author picks up on the terms from the psalm rendered in English as "today," "day," "heart," "hear," "enter," "test," "rest," "unbelief," and "swear." He culminates the exhortation with a repetition of the first part of the psalm, "Today, if you hear his voice, do not harden your hearts as in the rebellion." Thus, the particular words of Scripture are seen as relevant to a contemporary context, holding authority over the hearers. We also see the axiom at work as the author even attends to particular word order within a passage (Docherty, 180), as with his treatment of Ps. 40:6–8 at Heb. 10:5–10. Having quoted the passage in 10:5–7, the author then emphasizes what the psalmist said "first" and what followed after, commenting, "He sets aside the first [part of the passage] to establish the second [part of the passage]." The argument hinges on the specific ordering of propositions within the text of Scripture.

Scripture is inherently a coherent, interconnected whole. Themes in the broader original context of a citation may make that portion of Scripture especially fit to be considered in unison with other passages containing similar themes in their broader contexts, a point made in my work on the "string of pearls" found at Heb. 1:5–14 (Guthrie, "Hebrews," 928; see Docherty, 194–95). Consequently, the Scriptures are conceived as being coherent and inherently interconnected in terms of both meaning and significance, for they all originate with God himself. Therefore, a passage of Scripture can be read in light of other passages of Scripture, or various passages may be considered together on the basis of themes they have in common. Accordingly, the Scriptures, as spoken by God, are understood by the author of Hebrews as a unified whole (Docherty, 197). This axiom also constitutes the foundation of verbal analogy, by which a rabbi would pull two passages together to consider one in light of the other. For example, at Heb. 4:3–5 the author begins to explain the nature of the "rest" denied to the wilderness generation in Ps. 95:11, a passage quoted just a few verses earlier (Heb. 3:11). The author sets alongside this passage Gen. 2:2, another text that mentions God's rest: "On the seventh day God rested from all his work" (Heb. 4:4). The interpreter then reads the "rest" of Ps. 95:11 in light of God's act of "rest" in Gen. 2:2, concluding that Ps. 95 speaks of a Sabbath rest that remains for the people of God, a rest in which people cease from their own works as God did from his on the seventh day (Heb. 4:9–10). Association by verbal analogy thus flows from a general conviction in strands of Second Temple Judaism that Scripture is to be explained by Scripture, since all Scripture, as voiced by God, is thus synthetic, a coherent whole and completely true.

Scripture and a synthetic view of history. A final axiom speaks of the historical orientation of Scripture in Second Temple Judaism. Since God, as the Lord of all of history, is the one speaking, a synthetic view of Scripture, as coherent and interconnected, works in conjunction with a synthetic view of history. In other words, the Scriptures are historically situated and also express truths about history past, present, and future. As God's revelation unfolds through the ages of biblical history, latter points of revelation gather to themselves earlier revelation like interpretive magnets, for the one true God is working out his will in human history, speaking about his work through the ages of biblical revelation (Patte, 66–68). For Hebrews, Scripture is read through the lens of an apocalyptic layout of history that divides it into three great ages: the time before the coming of the Messiah, the "last days" initiated with the coming of the Messiah, and the age to come (Heb. 1:1–2; 12:26–27; Mackie). Thus, revelation especially finds a telescopic focus in the Christ-event, which gathers to itself, in Hebrews, layers of texts from the Jewish Scriptures that are used to express the significance of the person and work of God's Son.

For example, Hebrews clearly holds to a typological relationship between institutions of the old-covenant era and the fulfillment in Christ, the practices of the old covenant having been taken up into the new covenant (see Ounsworth; Ribbens; Cockerill, 56; Heb. 4:1–10; 5:1–10; 7:1–10:18). Furthermore, Christ, in his high-priestly work of redemption, inaugurated dynamics that will culminate at the end of the age. In his exaltation he has been enthroned as Lord, but his vanquishing of all of his enemies will not take place until the end of the age (Heb. 1:13; 2:5–9). Thus, Hebrews reads both Scripture and all of history as profoundly Christocentric (Cockerill, 56–57). For Hebrews this is why the Scriptures are always a fresh word, relevant for hearers through the ages, able to be placed in new contexts in the world (Docherty, 177). The God of Hebrews, his exalted Christ, and the Holy Spirit live and continue to speak to people through the living voice of Scripture.

The OT and the Message of Hebrews

In 1959 G. B. Caird suggested that Hebrews' discourse was built around four key OT texts: Ps. 8 (Heb. 2); Ps. 95 (Heb. 3); Ps. 110 (Heb. 5–7); and Jer. 31 (Heb. 8–10). In 1975 Richard Longenecker (175–85) played off Caird's work, adding that 1:3–2:4, with its catena of OT texts, must be figured into the equation as well, and two decades later, in 1996, R. T. France extended the discussion further by adding the expositions of Hab. 2:3c–4 and Prov. 3:11–12 found in Heb. 10–12. Thus, France (259) noted a total of seven expositions, highlighting "digressions" or exhortations that followed on the heels of the expositional sections. Also in 1996 and influenced by the seminal work of Caird, John Walters (59–70) offered an analysis similar to France's, following France in observing that Hebrews builds on six key citations (Pss. 8; 95; 110; Jer. 31; Hab. 2; Prov. 3) plus the catena of Heb. 1. Walters's contribution consisted of noting the integration of the scriptural expositions with paraenesis in Hebrews. These studies suggest that Hebrews consists of a backbone of key passages that drive the discourse, while integrating a host of other quotations, allusions, echoes, and general references into the overall message.

My assessment of the unfolding message of Hebrews, as built around key OT texts and theology, has numerous points in common with these proposals but also some variance with them. As noted above, Hebrews conceives of God as speaking his message into the world, and that message has culminated in a supreme word of salvation delivered in the person, work, and words of his Son (Heb. 1:1–4; 2:1–4). Those who respond positively to God's word, through faith, will inherit the blessings of new-covenant salvation (6:9, 11–12; 9:15; 10:36, 39; 12:22–24, 28), while those who reject that word face devastating punishment (2:3; 4:12–13; 6:4–8; 10:26–31; 12:29). "It is a dreadful thing to fall into the hands of the living God!" (10:31).

The first two chapters of Hebrews are launched and anchored by Ps. 110:1 (Heb. 1:3, 13), with its orientation to the Son of God as the enthroned Lord of the universe (1:5–14) whose word of salvation must be embraced (2:1–4). The early church held forth this psalm as a fulfilled prophecy of the Messiah's exaltation to the right hand of God following his resurrection (e.g., Acts 2:34) and as a herald of the manifestation of his authority at the end of the age, when all his enemies will be dealt the final blow (1 Cor. 15:25). At Heb. 2:5–8 the author quotes Ps. 8:4–6, reading that psalm in tandem with Ps. 110:1, the two psalms considered together on the basis of verbal analogy (Ps. 110:1 and Ps. 8 have in common a reference to *tōn podōn*, "the feet"). Originally written as a reflection on the status of human beings in creation, Ps. 8 also functions as a prophetic word anticipating the end-time Adam, the ultimate human who will fulfill the commission given to our first ancestors (Gen. 1:28). Thus, the appropriation of Ps. 8 by Hebrews should be read as both profoundly anthropological and christological, with the former taken up into and fulfilled in the latter. The quotation of Ps. 8 also moves the discourse thematically from the exaltation of Christ to a focus on the incarnation (Heb. 2:10–18), which had to take place for the Son to die for the sons and daughters of God (2:10–18) and for the Son to be appointed "from among the people" as a high priest (5:1; cf. 2:17–18; 4:14–16).

Having begun with an exposition of the person and status of the Son of God in chaps. 1–2, the author now turns to the topic of faithfulness, anchored by the quotation of Ps. 95 at Heb. 3:7–11. Yet, to launch this topic, he begins with the faithfulness of the Son of God himself, highlighted by a favorable comparison with faithful Moses (3:1–6). Moses was faithful as a servant, whereas the Son was faithful as a son over the house of God (3:5–6). The author's ultimate aim, of course, is to encourage faithfulness on the part of the hearers (3:6b).

In 3:7–19 the writer of Hebrews then considers the negative example of the wilderness wanderers, recounted in Ps. 95. Most significantly for our author, the quoted portion of the psalm culminates with God's oath, "They shall never enter my rest" (Heb. 3:11). Commenting on the passage in midrashic fashion (see above), 3:12–19 offers a strong exhortation not to follow the example of those who fell in the wilderness, capitalizing on a restatement of the psalm's first exhortation: "Today, if you hear his voice, do not harden your hearts as you did in the rebellion" (Heb. 3:7–8; Ps. 95:7c–8 [94:7c–8 LXX]).

Inherent in this psalm of warning, however, our author finds a promise for the people of God, especially as the psalm is read in light of Gen. 2:2 (Heb. 4:1–11), with which Ps. 95:11 has verbal analogy (both passages refer to forms of the word "rest," *katapausin/katepausen*). God's "rest," spoken of in Gen. 2:2, still remains for the people of God, who respond to God in faith rather than with disobedience and unbelief (3:19–4:3). Like the wilderness wanderers of the OT era who anticipated a promised land, the hearers of Hebrews have a word of good news preached to them, but they must add faith to their hearing of God's word to enter God's true Sabbath rest (4:9), the inheritance he has for them.

With 5:1–10, Ps. 110:4 moves to the forefront of the discourse, transitioning the primary christological focus to the appointment or ordination of the Son as a great high priest (5:1–7:28). In Heb. 4:16–5:10 the author has numerous echoes of ordination material from Lev. 7:28–9:24 (Guthrie, "Layering"), but the foundation for the whole of 5:1–10 and 7:1–28 is Ps. 110:4, with its declaration of the Son as the appointed high priest according to the order of Melchizedek. Once that ordination is established as superior to the old-covenant system of priesthood (7:11–28), the author turns to the superiority of Jesus's new-covenant offering (8:3–10:18), argued from the decisive forgiveness found in Jer. 31:31–34, a passage that forms the backbone of Heb. 8:3–10:18.

Around that backbone, and with reflection on the old-covenant system of worship (9:1–10), Hebrews argues for the superiority of Christ's sacrifice on the basis of its heavenly location (8:1–2; 9:11, 24), its blood (that of Christ, not of animals; 9:12–14), and its decisive nature. Unlike the sacrifices of the old-covenant system, Christ's Day of Atonement sacrifice only had to be made once for all time (7:27; 9:12, 25–28; 10:10, 12). One of the primary theological discussions of recent years concerns the sacrificial work of Christ as oriented to the heavenly tabernacle (see esp. Moffitt; Gäbel; Jamieson). The atoning work of Christ, which was initiated on the cross in Christ's death, reached its culmination in the heavenly holy of holies as the resurrected Lord presented himself as high priest before God the Father (9:11–12, 24; 10:12). Accordingly, Christ is the typological fulfillment to whom the priests and sacrifices of the OT pointed.

The high-priestly Christology of the book lays the groundwork for the hortatory material in Hebrews. For instance, the conflation of Isa. 26:20 and Hab. 2:3 at 10:37–38 launches the author's focus on "faith" that carries through the example list in Heb. 11, even as it offers a prophetic warning concerning the coming of the Messiah at the end of the age. At that coming, which will take place "in just a very little while" (9:37; cf. Isa. 26:20), those who are righteous, who live by faith (Hab. 2:4), will be distinguished from those who shrink back in faithlessness and experience destruction (Heb. 10:39). Additionally, the quotation of Habakkuk's word on faith becomes paradigmatic, a template of godly living exemplified in lives of the OT faithful (Heb. 11). Consequently, the faith motif also is associated with the strong emphasis on endurance in the rolling exhortations of Heb. 10:32–12:17, a theme amplified in the quotation of Prov. 3:11–12 at Heb. 12:5–6 (Croy). Hebrews labels that proverbial word as a "word of encouragement" to those who are God's "sons." The author, of course, draws an analogy between the heavenly Father's discipline and that of earthly fathers, again making an argument from lesser to greater (Heb. 12:9). Yet, the author appropriates the proverb itself as a direct word of declaration to God's children.

The perspective held by the author of Hebrews is that the exalted, high-priestly person and work of God's Son provide a firm foundation for persevering, running the race in obedience to God's word of salvation (12:1–2). In the new covenant, God's people worship him with thankful reverence and awe (12:28) and live well for him in the world (Heb. 13:1–6). Unlike the fallen wanderers of the OT (3:7–19) who trembled before Mount Sinai at the establishment of the old covenant (12:18–21), the true people of the new covenant have arrived at the place of God's presence, the city of the living God, with its holy of holies that now stands open for his priestly people to draw near, since they have been cleansed from sin decisively (10:19–25; 12:22–24). Moreover, when at the end of the age God fulfills the prophetic word of

Hag. 2:6, "Once more I will shake not only the earth but also the heavens" (Heb. 12:26b), God's people will be manifest as belonging to a kingdom that cannot be shaken (Heb. 12:27–28).

Bibliography. Allen, D. M., *Deuteronomy and Exhortation in Hebrews*, WUNT 2/238 (Mohr Siebeck, 2008); Allen, L. C., "Psalm 45:7–8 (6–7) in Old and New Testament Settings," in *Christ the Lord*, ed. H. H. Rowdon (Inter-Varsity, 1982), 220–42; Barrett, C. K., "The Eschatology of the Epistle to the Hebrews," in *The Background of the New Testament and Its Eschatology*, ed. W. D. Davies and D. Daube (Cambridge University Press, 1956), 363–93; Barth, M., "The Old Testament in Hebrews," in *Issues in New Testament Interpretation*, ed. W. Klassen and G. F. Snyder (Harper & Row, 1962), 65–78; Bateman, H., *Early Jewish Hermeneutics and Hebrews 1:5–13*, AUS 193 (Lang, 1997); Caird, G. B., "The Exegetical Method of the Epistle to the Hebrews," *CJT* 5 (1959): 44–51; Clements, R. E., "The Use of the Old Testament in Hebrews," *SwJT* 28 (1985): 36–45; Cobrink, H., "Some Thoughts on the OT Citations in the Epistle to the Hebrews," *Neot* 5 (1971): 22–36; Cockerill, G. L., *The Epistle to the Hebrews*, NICNT (Eerdmans, 2012); Cohn-Sherbok, D., "Paul and Rabbinic Exegesis," *SJT* 35 (1982): 117–32; Compton, J., *Psalm 110 and the Logic of Hebrews*, LNTS 537 (Bloomsbury T&T Clark, 2015); Cosby, M. R., *The Rhetorical Composition and Function of Hebrews 11 in the Light of Example Lists in Antiquity* (Mercer University Press, 1988); Cosby, "The Rhetorical Composition of Hebrews 11," *JBL* 107 (1988): 257–73; Croy, N. C., *Endurance in Suffering*, SNTSMS 98 (Cambridge University Press, 1998); D'Angelo, M. R., *Moses in the Letter to the Hebrews*, SBLDS 42 (Scholars Press, 1979); Docherty, S. E., *The Use of the Old Testament in Hebrews*, WUNT 2/260 (Mohr Siebeck, 2009); Dodd, C. H., *According to the Scriptures* (Nisbet, 1961); Eisenbaum, P., "Heroes and History in Hebrews 11," in *Early Christian Interpretation of the Scriptures of Israel*, ed. C. Evans and J. A. Sanders, JSNTSup 148 (Sheffield Academic, 1997): 380–96; Eisenbaum, *The Jewish Heroes of Christian History*, SBLDS 156 (Scholars Press, 1997); Ellingworth, P., "The Old Testament in Hebrews" (PhD diss., University of Aberdeen, 1977); Ellis, E. E., *Paul's Use of the Old Testament* (Baker, 1981); Ellis, *Prophecy and Hermeneutic in Early Christianity* (Eerdmans, 1978); Enns, P., "The Interpretation of Psalm 95 in Hebrews 3.1–4:13," in *Early Christian Interpretation of the Scriptures of Israel*, ed. C. Evans and J. A. Sanders, JSNTSup 148 (Sheffield Academic, 1997), 352–63; Filson, F., *"Yesterday,"* SBT (Alec R. Allenson, 1967); Fitzmyer, J. A., "'Now This Melchizedek' (Heb. 7:1)," *CBQ* 25 (1963): 305–21; France, R. T., "The Writer of Hebrews as a Biblical Expositor," *TynBul* 47 (1996): 245–76; Gäbel, G., *Die Kulttheologie des Hebräerbriefes*, WUNT 2/212 (Mohr Siebeck, 2006); Gheorghita, R., *The Role of the Septuagint in Hebrews*, WUNT 2/160 (Mohr Siebeck, 2003); Guthrie, G. H. "Hebrews," in *CNTUOT*, 919–95; Guthrie, "Hebrews' Use of the Old Testament: Recent Trends in Research," *CBR* 1 (2003): 271–94; Guthrie, "High Priestly Sacrifice and 'Intertextual Layering' in Hebrews" (presented at the Hebrews Section of the Society of Biblical Literature, national meeting, San Diego, 2019); Guthrie, "Old Testament in Hebrews," in *Dictionary of the Latter New Testament and Its Developments*, ed. R. P. Martin and P. H. Davids (InterVarsity, 1997), 841–50; Guthrie, *The Structure of Hebrews*, NovTSup 73 (Brill, 1994); Guthrie, G. H., and R. D. Quinn, "A Discourse Analysis of the Use of Psalm 8:4–6 in Hebrews 2:5–9," *JETS* 49 (2006): 235–46; Harris, M. J. "The Translation and Significance of *ho theos* in Hebrews 1:8–9," *TynBul* 36 (1985): 129–62; Harris, "The Translation of Elohim in Psalm 45:7–8," *TynBul* 35 (1984): 65–89; Hays, R. B., *Echoes of Scripture in the Letters of Paul* (Yale University Press, 1989); Hughes, G., *Hebrews and Hermeneutics* (Cambridge University Press, 1979); Jamieson, R. B., *Jesus' Death and Heavenly Offering in Hebrews*, SNTSMS 172 (Cambridge University Press, 2019); Jobes, K., "The Function of Paronomasia in Hebrews 10.5–7," *TJ* 13 (1992): 181–91; Katz, P., "The Quotations from Deuteronomy in Hebrews," *ZNW* 49 (1958): 213–23; Kibbe, M. H., *Godly Fear or Ungodly Failure?*, BZNW 216 (de Gruyter, 2016); Kistemaker, S., *The Psalm Citations in the Epistle to the Hebrews* (Soest, 1961); Laansma, J., *"I Will Give You Rest,"* WUNT 2/98 (Mohr Siebeck, 1997); Leschert, D., *Hermeneutical Foundations of Hebrews*, NABPRDS 10 (Mellen, 1994); Loader, W. R. G., "Christ at the Right Hand," *NTS* 24 (1977–78): 199–217; Longenecker, R. N., *Biblical Exegesis in the Apostolic Period* (Eerdmans, 1975); Mackie, S. D., *Eschatology and Exhortation in the Epistle to the Hebrews*, WUNT 2/223 (Mohr Siebeck, 2007); Mathewson, D., "Reading Heb. 6:4–6 in Light of the Old Testament," *WTJ* 61 (1999): 209–25; McCullough, J. C., "The Old Testament Quotations in Hebrews," *NTS* 26 (1979–1980): 363–79; McNamara, M., "Melchizedek: Gen. 14, 17–20 in the Targums, in Rabbinic and Early Christian Literature," *Bib* 81 (2000): 1–31; Moffitt, D. M., *Atonement and the Logic of Resurrection in the Epistle to the Hebrews*, NovTSup 141 (Brill, 2011); Motyer, S. "The Psalm Quotations of Hebrews 1," *TynBul* 50 (1999): 3–22; Ounsworth, R., *Joshua Typology in the New Testament*, WUNT 2/328 (Mohr Siebeck, 2012); Overland, P., "Did the Sage Draw from the Shema?," *CBQ* 62 (2000): 424–40; Patte, D., *Early Jewish Hermeneutic in Palestine*, SBLDS (Scholars Press, 1975); Pierce, M., *Divine Discourse in the Epistle to the Hebrews*, SNTSMS 178 (Cambridge University Press, 2020); Ribbens, B. J., *Levitical Sacrifice and Heavenly Cult in Hebrews*, BZNW 222 (de Gruyter, 2016); Silva, M., "The New Testament Use of the Old Testament," in *Scripture and Truth*, ed. D. A. Carson and J. W. Woodbridge (Zondervan, 1983), 147–65; Steyn, G. J., *A Quest for the Assumed LXX Vorlage of the Explicit Quotations in Hebrews*, FRLANT 235 (Vandenhoeck & Ruprecht, 2011); Strobel, A., "Die Psalmengrundlage der Gethsemane-Parallele Hbr. 5,7ff," *ZNW* 45 (1954):

252–66; Thomas, K. J., "The Old Testament Citations in Hebrews," *NTS* 11 (1965): 303–25; Thompson, J. W., "Structure and Purpose of the Catena in Heb. 1:5–13," *CBQ* 38 (1976): 352–63; Walters, J. R., "The Rhetorical Arrangement of Hebrews," *AsTJ* 51 (1996): 59–70.

GEORGE H. GUTHRIE

History of Interpretation: Early Church

The early church's encounter with the OT was variegated and multiform, like the Christian movement itself. No single approach or exegetical method was used by all the ancient Christians as a monolithic bloc. Subgroups within the church created hermeneutical trajectories that distinguished them from other communities. Therefore, substantial diversity of interpretation can be discerned across a wide geographic area.

The one unifying aspect of early Christian hermeneutics was the pervasive insistence that the OT must be filtered through the lens of Jesus Christ and the NT in order for one to discern its true meaning. Yet even here, the precise method for appropriating the Jewish Scriptures via the Christian corpus was hotly debated. Perceptions about the relationship between the two Testaments evolved dramatically over the first five centuries of church history.

The term "early church" needs definition for the purposes of this article. Many persons, movements, and sects in antiquity identified themselves with the name of Jesus or considered themselves to be his followers. Within the limited parameters of this article, the focus will be on the body of writers who are associated with what came to prevail as "orthodoxy" and who formed the so-called Great Church as opposed to various Gnostics, Marcionites, Montanists, Encratites, and other "heretical" Jesus-worshiping communities.

Yet even among the orthodox church fathers, interpretive variety can be—indeed, must be—taken into account. In particular, regional differences can often be seen, especially as regards the language used for textual commentary or in the Scripture version itself. Interpreters who wrote in Latin, Greek, or Syriac or who were reading the Vetus Latina / Vulgate, the LXX, or the Peshitta encountered a substantially different text and therefore had different comments about it.

Another factor that created interpretive diversity was the emergence of distinct camps within the church, or what are sometimes called "schools," which possessed their own stances on key biblical texts. The leaders of these schools perceived their differences to hinge upon distinct hermeneutical presuppositions. However, they did not perceive their interlocutors to be entirely outside the Christian movement like heretics would be. The most obvious example of this phenomenon was the emergence in the third century of the Alexandrian and Antiochene schools of interpretation (see below).

In short, early Christian interpretation of the OT was marked by both widespread *unity* around the premise that this corpus must be interpreted in light of the NT and substantial *diversity* about what exegetical methods ought to be used to do so.

The Early Christian Concept of an "Old Testament"

The church fathers did not manufacture the concept of an OT; they received it directly from the apostolic witness. But what was meant by "testament"? Over time, Christians began to think of this term as a body of writings instead of the divine arrangement that those writings described. However, before the OT was Scripture, it was a God-given covenant.

In the LXX, the Greek word *diathēkē* translates the Hebrew *bərît*, a covenant made by God in which the terms are set forth by divine mandate. It is for this reason that the word "testament" is a common translation of *diathēkē*, since a testament is a declaration of purpose or intent (which is often, though not always, expressed at death, as in the case of a last will and testament). God's testament is his divine declaration of what he intends to do and what his covenant people's obligations shall be.

The juxtaposition of the word "new" (*kainos*) with *diathēkē* appears in the LXX at Jer. 38:31 (MT 31:31), where a new covenant is predicted by the prophet. This obviously implies the existence of an older covenant—namely, the previous arrangement under which God's people have related to him. So, when the NT picks up this pairing of words—whether in the mouth of Jesus at the Last Supper (Luke 22:20), in the writings of Paul (1 Cor. 11:25; 2 Cor. 3:6), or elsewhere (Heb. 8:6–13; 9:15)—the expectation is for a new relational arrangement due to a new declaration of divine intent, not the bequest of a new written corpus.

The existence of an "old" covenant is not merely implied but is explicitly mentioned in the Bible. The key chapter is 2 Cor. 3, especially v. 14, which sets the word *palaios* in conjunction with *diathēkē*. Paul writes, "But their [i.e., the Israelites'] minds were made dull, for to this day the same veil remains when the old covenant is read. It has not been removed, because only in Christ is it taken away." Clearly, Paul's expression *palaias diathēkēs* includes documents that could be "read." A written text is the instrument of revelation for the divine arrangement. However, the written text is not primary. Paul is more concerned with two "ministries" (*diakonia*, vv. 7–8): one of death, the other of the Spirit.

In addition to *kainos* and *palaios*, Heb. 8:7–8, 13 (cf. 9:15) similarly juxtaposes the words "first" (*prōtos*) and "second" (*deuteros*) with *diathēkē*. Here the meaning is oriented exclusively toward a cult system, not Scriptures that could be read. In both Paul and Hebrews, the foremost understanding of a *diathēkē* is a divine disposition for proper worship. Though a written text necessarily serves as the vehicle for the covenant's communication, this meaning is secondary.

Due to this received biblical witness, the church fathers believed that the coming of Jesus Christ had ushered in the new arrangement, prophesied long ago by Jeremiah, under which God would now interact with his people. The new covenant was revealed in a body of apostolic writings that explained its differences from the old covenant. Over time, this textual nuance of "covenant/testament" came to the fore, superseding the more basic idea of a divine arrangement. But it did not start out that way.

What the church fathers of the second century meant by the "old covenant" was the outdated arrangement that God had pursued with the Jews through the Mosaic law but that was no longer in force (Barn. 4:8; Justin, *Dial.* 10–11; Clement of Alexandria, *Strom.* 1.29.182.2). In Irenaeus of Lyons, the covenants are construed as two salvation arrangements, the "law" and the "gospel" (*Haer.* 4.9.1). Yet Irenaeus also gave the term "testament" a noteworthy textual nuance when he offered direct quotations from both sets of literature and envisioned them as a conjoined pair (*Haer.* 4.15.2; 4.28.1–2). Irenaeus was followed more obviously by Tertullian, the first Christian writer to be preserved in Latin and the man who owns the distinction of giving us the terms *vetus testamentum* and *novum testamentum* (*Marc.* 4.6.1; 4.9.3; 4.22.3; *Prax.* 15.1; *Praescr.* 30.9; *Jejun.* 14.1). Clearly, Tertullian had books in mind when he spoke of the biblical testaments , for he also called them "documents" or "records" (*instrumenta*; see esp. *Marc.* 4.1.1; and *Res.* 33.1; *Herm.* 19.1; 20.4; *Praescr.* 38.2–3, 8). Around this same time, Melito of Sardis reported that his journey to the Holy Land had helped him determine "the books of the Old Testament" (Eusebius, *Hist. eccl.* 4.26.14). Clement of Alexandria likewise described the two testaments as sources of God's words, together forming "the Scriptures" (*Strom.* 5.13.84.3–85.2), whose "sequence" or "succession" (*akolouthia*) is so conjoined that they essentially form a single testament in distinct times (*Strom.* 7.16.100.5–6; 7.17.107.5).

From the third century on, the textual meaning of *diathēkē* became at least as common as, and eventually eclipsed, the covenant or divine-arrangement meaning (e.g., Origen, *Princ.* 4.1.1; *Comm. Jo.* 5.8; Novatian, *Trin.* 9.2; 10.1; 17.3–6; 26.20; 30.1; Methodius, *Symp.* 10.2; Lactantius, *Inst.* 4.20.4; Cyril of Jerusalem, *Cat. Lect.* 4.33). This change reflected the ancient church's pronounced exegetical turn toward interior dogmatic debates (Trinity, Christology) instead of polemical exchanges with Jewish interlocutors about who truly possessed the covenant. The need in the new Constantinian empire for an authoritative biblical text (Eusebius, *Vit. Const.* 4.36) also played a role in solidifying the concept of the OT as a book. By the age of the canon lists and uncial manuscripts of the late fourth and early fifth centuries, the term "Old Testament" in the ancient church normally referred to a collection of sacred writings instead of an arrangement for divine relationship (Kinzig, 534), though the original meaning was never entirely forgotten.

Hermeneutical Trajectories in the Early Church

Beginnings. The so-called apostolic fathers and Greek apologists of the early second century did not possess a sophisticated textual hermeneutic (although the latter group was more adept at navigating the pagan intellectual currents than the former). Their interests were primarily pastoral, which in their context of cultural hostility required a robust concern for apologetics. To the extent that these writers focused on the OT, their efforts were geared mostly toward displaying ancient predictions of Christ to skeptical opponents.

The primary opponents to whom fulfilled prophecies might be expected to appeal were the Jews, since they too accepted the OT as authoritative. Yet prophetic proofs of Christ were thought to appeal to a pagan audience as well. The conservative culture of Greco-Roman antiquity respected the Jewish Scriptures for, if nothing else, their sheer antiquity. Oracles from long ago that could be construed as predicting Christ were viewed by the earliest Christian writers as a useful tool to persuade both pagans and Jews. (Whether those interlocutors actually were convinced is a different question.)

Generally speaking, the interpretive method of the Christian writers in the first half of the second century can be called typological. The term refers to a one-to-one correspondence between a thing, person, or event in the OT (the *typos*) and the Christian counterpart to which it pointed ahead (the *antitypos*). Initially, patristic typology took a simplistic "just as then, so also now" approach. The earlier item was not integrally or systematically related to the later but only served as an indistinct pointer toward the future fulfillment. The language of "shadow" and "reality" was often used, harkening back to Plato's cave analogy (*Resp.* 514a–517a) and the NT (Col. 2:17; Heb. 8:5; 10:1). Another common pair of descriptors was "temporal" and "eternal." This way of connecting the type and the antitype highlighted the tenuous, feeble, or transient relationship between them.

Examples of patristic typological interpretations include some that had explicit biblical warrant, such as Adam or Melchizedek being compared to Christ (Rom. 5:12–19; 1 Cor. 15:22, 45–49; Heb. 6:20–7:28), the bronze serpent of the wilderness being compared to the cross (John 3:14–15), and the temple sacrifices being compared to the once-and-for-all atonement (Heb. 10:1–18). But the church fathers also made extrabiblical extrapolations, such as the crossing of the Red Sea being compared to baptism (Origen, *Hom. Exod.* 5.1; Cyril of Jerusalem, *Cat. Lect.* 19; possibly alluded to in 1 Cor. 10:2), the scarlet cord of Rahab to the rivulet of Christ's blood (Justin, *Dial.* 111; Origen, *Hom. Jes. Nav.* 3.5), and Eve to the Virgin Mary (Justin, *Dial.* 100; Irenaeus, *Haer.* 3.22.4). Not all of the earliest Christian interpreters indulged in typologies to the same degree. Ignatius of Antioch rarely referred to the OT in his seven epistles, while the Epistle of Barnabas is full of such references, as is Justin Martyr's *Dialogue with Trypho*.

Many early Christian apologists derived source material for their typologies from collections of excerpted OT texts known as *testimonia*. Enthusiastic scholarly research on this topic can be traced to J. R. Harris's *Testimonies Part 1* (1916) and *Part II* (1920), which together have had a significant impact on early-Christian studies. The subsequent scholarly research trajectory focused on the study of extant lists, such as those found in Cyprian's *To Quirinius*, and/or the discernment of such lists behind the OT quotations of patristic apologists or even the NT itself. The Christians of the first through third centuries encountered both circulating testimony documents containing OT references (used for apologetic and/or liturgical purposes) and whole OT books. Only the ancient writers with access to a significant library would have encountered the entire OT as a collection. Furthermore, it is likely that the NT writers had much of the OT memorized and could draw from that source. This would not, however, have been the case for patristic writers of a gentile background, who instead were often dependent on the *testimonia* collections.

A new synthesis. The somewhat primitive typological approach of the first Christians began to give way to a more systematic and integrative approach under Irenaeus in the late second century. The bishop of Lyons attempted to propound a *hypothesis* of the faith—that is, a story arc in which the two Testaments formed a single plotline that recounted a unified saga of divine redemption and recapitulation (*Haer.* 1.9.3–4; Hefner; Norris). An important aspect of this innovation was the borrowing of the church's creedal material, known as the rule of faith (*regula fidei*), from its original context of baptismal catechesis to serve as a hermeneutical key. The rule of faith helpfully summarized, in a succinct and memorable fashion, the Christian metanarrative that the entire Bible proclaimed in greater detail. With this development, there was no longer just a shadowy correspondence between old and new but a plotline that joined the two Testaments into a coherent story, a kind of divine drama.

Tertullian adopted Irenaeus's integrative hermeneutical approach with gusto. For both of these writers, Marcionism provided a strong impetus not only to affirm that the twin revelations of the Creator and his Christ are linked but also to discern an inextricable and intimate relationship between them. Tertullian writes that the emergence of the NT from the Old "is achieved through reshaping, through amplification, through progress, just like fruit is separated from seed, though fruit comes out of seed. So also, the gospel is separated from the law because it advances from out of the law—something other than the law, but not alien to it, different, though not opposed" (*Marc.* 4.11.11 AT; cf. 4.6). By the turn of the third century, the ancient church was operating with a much more systematic—indeed, organic—understanding of the relationship between the two Testaments.

The Latin West. In the ancient church, the use of Latin as a medium for written communication lagged behind Greek until the third century. Even after the Latin tongue was widely adopted in the church, OT exegesis continued to retain the polemical tone that had been initiated by Tertullian's *Against the Jews*. This can be seen in Novatian's *On Jewish Foods*, a refutation of the OT dietary laws, as well as his earlier treatments of circumcision and the Sabbath (which are not extant), or in Cyprian's *To Quirinius*, which is a stream of biblical prooftexts for anti-Judaic and christological points. The Latin writers of Africa, Italy, and Gaul did not begin to publish commentaries—that is, sustained biblical exegesis for the sake of Christian edification, not polemics—until the late fourth century. A little earlier, Victorinus of Pettau did write a commentary on the Genesis creation narrative, and Reticius of Autun published a commentary on the Song of Songs, but these works have not survived.

The absence of true commentary in the West was due in part to the lack of a respectable version of the Bible in Latin. The so-called *Vetus Latina* was a notoriously wooden translation of the LXX and the Greek NT, not just to the point of being hard on the Ciceronian ear but being so slavish to the original as to be ungrammatical. It was a Bible for the common people, and they loved it as such, even if the erudite Christians couldn't quite bring themselves to engage with it. So beloved was this time-tested Latin version that, as Augustine tells it, when Jerome dared in his Vulgate to change the name of the plant that grew over Jonah's head (4:6) from a "gourd" to "ivy," a riot broke out in church (*Letter* 71.3.5; cf. *Letter* 82.5.35). Nevertheless, Jerome's much more respectable Vulgate eventually won the day, not only because of his reputation as a learned scholar but also because of his willingness to translate from the "Hebraic truth" (a common phrase in Jerome's parlance; see, e.g., *Letter* 78.9; 112.20) of the Jewish Scriptures instead of the LXX ("The truth must be squeezed out of the Hebrew books," Jerome, *Letter* 20.2; cf. 48.19).

With the rise of textual scholars and/or theologians like Jerome, Augustine, Ambrose, and Hilary of Poitiers, the late fourth century finally began to produce Latin commentaries on the OT for their own sake. Jerome stands out because he went to Syria and Bethlehem where, virtually alone among the Western church fathers, he learned Hebrew in order to appreciate the original text of the OT as well as rabbinic exegesis of it. Although Augustine likewise recognized the importance of linguistic research, including examination of the original Hebrew, he preferred the authority of the

LXX to both the Hebrew and the Old Latin (*Doctr. chr.* 2.15.22).

In terms of exegetical principles, the Latin writers of this era, though not as oriented toward Jewish polemics as their forebears, still employed a robust christological hermeneutic. In this they were guided by the four main NT passages that validated messianic interpretation of the OT through signs and figures: Luke 24:27, "And beginning with Moses and all the Prophets, he explained to them what was said in all the Scriptures concerning himself"; John 5:39, 46, "These are the very Scriptures that testify about me. . . . If you believed Moses, you would believe me, for he wrote about me"; 2 Cor. 3:6, "The letter kills, but the Spirit gives life" (cf. v. 16, "But whenever anyone turns to the Lord, the [interpretive] veil is taken away"); and Gal. 4:24, "These things are being taken figuratively." Together, these four texts gave the church fathers explicit warrant to find Christ or Christian truth throughout the OT, for it was put there intentionally by the Holy Spirit.

It was precisely such christological exegesis that had converted Augustine once he finally listened to a Christian Platonist like Ambrose expound the spiritual meaning of the OT. Augustine writes, "I rejoiced that the old Scriptures of the law and the prophets were laid before me to be perused, not anymore with the eye to which they seemed most absurd before . . . but now with delight I heard Ambrose, in his sermons to the people, often recommend earnestly this text as a rule: 'The letter kills, but the Spirit gives life'; and by drawing aside the mystic veil, Ambrose spiritually laid open that which, when accepted according to the 'letter,' had seemed to teach perverse doctrines" (*Conf.* 6.4.6; *NPNF*[1], 1:92, adapted). Augustine's discovery that the OT wasn't limited to crude Jewish myths and outdated laws but could be interpreted spiritually to speak about Christ was a revelation that set this dissolute and heterodox rhetor on a new ecclesial trajectory. However, it wasn't the late fourth-century churchmen of the Latin West who first recognized the OT's manifold interpretive richness. It was the school of Alexandria and especially its greatest teacher, Origen.

The school of Alexandria. The precise origins of Christianity in Alexandria are difficult to determine. Gnostics functioned there from an early time—for example, Basilides during Emperor Hadrian's reign (AD 117–38) (Clement of Alexandria, *Strom.* 7.17.106.4). A foundational apostolic presence is not out of the question, though the traditions that name John Mark as the first bishop are mentioned no earlier than Eusebius (*Hist. eccl.* 2.16.1). The proto-orthodox church emerges with distinct lines only in the late second and early third centuries under Clement of Alexandria (fl. 180–215) and Origen (fl. 204–30). Both men are associated with Alexandria's catechetical school (Eusebius, *Hist. eccl.* 5.10–11; 6.3.3; 6.6.1), whose ostensible purpose was prebaptismal instruction but which also served as a kind of intellectual hub for Christian scholars in the erudite Alexandrian milieu.

The church's exegetes at Alexandria could draw from a hallowed tradition of allegorical interpretation. The pre-Christian Greek philosophers had allegorized the crude aspects of the Homeric myths to find lasting philosophical truth (Heraclitus Homericus, *All.* 1.1–2; 5.1–16; cf. Origen, *Cels.* 6.42). Likewise, Hellenistic Judaism—preeminently Philo—had applied this method to the OT to find alternatives to traditional rabbinic exegesis (Philo, *Rewards* 11.61–65; *Creation* 54.154; 56.157). The Christian Gnostics had availed themselves of the allegorical method as well: some of the law was "figurative and symbolic" (*typikon kai symbolikon*), said Ptolemy (*Flor.* 5.1–8, in Epiphanius, *Pan.* 33). Ultimately, the difference was not in the methodology but in the final outcome. In each case, an authoritative text was interpreted to "say something other" (the etymology of *allēgoria*) than its plain meaning. Whether that alternate output was Greek philosophical truths, Jewish wisdom, esoteric speculations about cosmology and angels, or prophecies about Jesus of Nazareth depended on which kind of exegete was availing himself of allegory.

Christian allegory at Alexandria is especially associated with Origen, who not only used the method frequently but also codified its use for later generations (a tradition that would be long-lasting and highly influential; de Lubac). Although Origen claimed there was hidden meaning to be uncovered throughout the biblical text, in practice he usually applied the method only to the OT, since the New was overtly christological already. Sometimes these meanings were put into a twofold, threefold, or fourfold approach. But whatever the number used in the scheme, the central distinction was always between the plain, literal, grammatical meaning and various kinds of alternate, higher, or spiritual meanings.

Origen appeals (rather obscurely, it must be admitted) to Prov. 22:20–21 as the basis for his three-tiered exegetical approach. His Greek Bible says, "Do thou portray them threefold [*trissōs*] in counsel and knowledge, that thou mayest answer words of truth to those who question thee" (Butterworth, 275). From this word of Solomonic advice, Origen discerned three progressively higher levels of interpretation that corresponded to the tripartite human constitution. They were (1) the "flesh of the scripture, this name being given to the obvious interpretation"; (2) a middle level for persons of moderate Christian progress, identified as "the soul" of the text; and (3) a highest level for "the man who is perfect"—that is, who can be "edified by the spiritual law" (*Princ.* 4.2.4, Butterworth).

This threefold interpretive scheme fulfilled Origen's programmatic statement a little earlier: "Now the reason why [the heretics] hold false opinions and make impious or ignorant assertions about God appears to be nothing else but this, that scripture is not understood in its spiritual sense, but is interpreted according to the bare letter. . . . That there are certain mystical revelations made known through the divine scriptures is believed by all, even by the simplest of those who are adherents of the word; but what these revelations are, fair-minded and humble men confess that they do not know" (*Princ.* 4.2.2, Butterworth). Though Origen humbly confessed that the mystical revelations were hard to discern, he nevertheless made a lifetime career of expounding them through expansive allegorical interpretation of the OT.

Origen explained the multitiered nature of the Bible in *Princ.* 4.2.8–9. He focused on the OT, which he called "a record dealing with the visible creation, the formation of man and the successive descendants of the first human beings until the time when they became many." Origen also mentioned the accounts of "wars" and "conquerors" as well as the "written system of law" through which "the laws of truth are prophetically indicated." Origen argued that "the bodily part of the scriptures"—that is, the plain meaning of these OT accounts—could improve the multitude as much as they were capable of receiving it (Butterworth).

However, Origen went on to say that "the Word of God [i.e., Christ the Logos] has arranged for certain stumbling-blocks, as it were, and hindrances and impossibilities to be inserted in the midst of the law and the history," things that "did not happen, occasionally something which could not happen, and occasionally something which might have happened but in fact did not." These "impossibilities are recorded in the law for the sake of the more skillful and inquiring readers" who, by devoting themselves "to the toil of examining what is written," are able to uncover "a meaning worthy of God" in "the writings which were previous to the coming of Christ" (*Princ.* 4.2.9, Butterworth).

Thus, for Origen, the OT text had variable value depending on the skill and spiritual maturity of the interpreter. Ordinary Christians could benefit from the literal sense. But for the more advanced reader, a higher, spiritual meaning about Christ could be teased out from the difficulties—or even impossibilities—that had been lodged in the sacred text for Christian adepts to recognize at a later time. Allegory was the God-ordained means for overcoming these stumbling blocks in the "body" of the OT, prompting a deeper search for a completely different meaning. This exegetical willingness to leave the literal sense behind through allegory was the main dividing line between the exegetes of Alexandria and Antioch.

The school of Antioch. Biblical hermeneutics at Antioch can be viewed as a response to Alexandria or an antecedent to it. On the one hand, the Antiochenes were well aware of what their counterparts down at Alexandria were doing, and they actively sought to refute it. On the other hand, the Antiochene exegetical method had a long pedigree of its own. The pagan rhetorical tradition at Antioch, which emphasized the scholarly study of texts with attention to history and philology, contributed greatly to the literalism of the Antiochene school. The Christians in Antioch were also in relationship with the Jewish community from the very beginning (Acts 11:19–26; Ign. *Magn.* 8:1–2; 10:3; Ign. *Phld.* 6:1), and this conservative interpretive community was by no means enamored with Philonian allegory. Thus, textual literalism ruled the day at Antioch.

In this context, "literalism" (i.e., an emphasis on the "letter") refers to one or more of the following: (1) focusing solely on the text's wording, (2) understanding individual words according to their normal meaning, (3) attending to the "plain sense" of words within their surrounding sentence, (4) discerning the overall logic of an argument or narrative, and (5) accepting the text's intended reference to the material or earthly world, whether present, historical, or prophetic (Young, 188–89). These literalistic principles were fundamental at Antioch. The Alexandrian school often employed them as well before launching into the more speculative allegorical forays that the Antiochenes decried.

The primary writers of the school of Antioch were Diodore of Tarsus (d. 390), John Chrysostom (349–407), Theodore of Mopsuestia (350–428), and Theodoret of Cyrus (393–ca. 460). All of these writers argued for literal-historical modes of interpretation and/or were critical of Alexandrian allegory. Forerunners of the Antiochene theological outlook, though not organized into a formal "school," included Paul of Samosata and Dorotheus in the late third century and Lucian of Antioch and Eustathius in the early fourth. Eustathius left us the tract *On the Witch* (or *"Belly-Myther") of Endor against Origen*, which criticizes allegory for dehistoricizing the biblical text.

The distinction between typology, allegory, and the Antiochene method known as *theōria* has often been overstated. All three methods were ways of finding Christian meaning in OT texts that did not obviously refer to Christianity. Hard lines between these methodological approaches should not be drawn, for the definitions are somewhat fluid. Various patristic writers could intermingle their methods freely or could use different methods but arrive at the same exegetical conclusions.

That being said, the Antiochene school did believe its hermeneutical method diverged from the practice of Alexandria. Diodore of Tarsus made this critique in the prologue to his *Commentary on the Psalms*: "We will not shrink from the truth but will expound it according to the historical substance [*historia*] and the plain literal sense [*lexis*]. . . . One thing is to be watched, however: *theōria* must never be understood as doing away with the underlying sense; it would then be no longer *theōria* but allegory." The Alexandrians are in Diodore's mind when he continues, "But those who pretend to 'improve' Scripture and who are wise in their own conceit have introduced allegory because they are careless about the historical substance, or they simply abuse it" (Froehlich, 85–86).

The debate between Alexandria's and Antioch's ways of reading the OT centered on whether the NT ever gave warrant for an allegorical approach. Key Alexandrian proofs for the legitimacy of this method were the rock that gave water to the Israelites, which signified Christ (Exod. 17:1–7; Num. 20:1–13; 1 Cor. 10:4–6), and the unmuzzled ox treading grain, which proved the apostolic workers were worthy of their wages (Deut. 25:4; 1 Cor. 9:9–10; 1 Tim. 5:18). However, the most important text of all, because it used the verb *allēgoreō*, was Gal. 4:24, "These things are being taken figuratively: The women [i.e., Sarah and Hagar] represent two covenants."

Diodore comments about this important passage, "[Paul's] use of the word [allegory] and his application is different from that of the Greeks. The Greeks speak of allegory when something is understood in one way but said in another. . . . Holy Scripture does not speak of allegory in this way" (*Comm. Ps.* 118.preface; Froehlich, 87–88). In other words, Gal. 4:24 cannot be used to justify the application of Hellenistic allegorical principles to the OT, despite Paul's use of the word. Diodore goes on to explain that Antioch's approach "does not repudiate in any way the underlying prior history, but 'theorizes,' that is, it develops a higher vision [*theōria*] of other but similar events in addition, without abrogating history." Unfortunately, says Diodore, the Alexandrians "follow not the apostle's intention but their own vain imagination, forcing the reader to take one thing for another" (Froehlich, 86).

Generally speaking, the school of Antioch, more so than Alexandria, validated Israel's history as important in its own right. For example, the Minor Prophets were addressing political issues of their own day, not hiding christological prophecies everywhere in their words. The distinctive approach of the Antiochenes was to emphasize—much like the local rhetorical schools—the *pragmata* and *historia* of a text (Hill, 9–10, 139–40). Their method of *theōria* allowed them to find some future ecclesial meanings but not nearly as often as Alexandrian allegory. And the Antiochenes were adamantly unwilling to treat the literal sense like Origen sometimes did: as an error or absurdity inserted into the OT text by God to prompt a search for an alternate interpretation. Rather, the literal sense was always the basis for whatever higher meaning would be constructed. All the ancient Christians read the OT "spiritually" and thus christologically, just not equally as often nor by exactly the same methods.

As a long-standing Hellenistic city that had been founded in the wake of Alexander the Great's conquests, Antioch's primary language of commerce, scholarship, and public discourse—and thus of its scriptural exegesis—was Greek. But Antioch was the western terminus of the Silk Road, a trade network that stretched across much of Asia. As such, Antioch was in contact with cities to its east that sat in the uneasy borderland between the Roman Empire and the Parthian and Sasanian Empires. There, the primary language of Christian Scripture, liturgy, and artistic expression was Syriac. This reality created a third linguistic and geographical node of early Christianity, distinct from the Latin West and the Greek East: the Syriac church of Persia and Mesopotamia.

The schools of Edessa and Nisibis. As with Alexandria, the origins of Syriac Christianity are shrouded in mystery. Yet by all accounts, Jewish Christianity was an important foundation for the church that arose in Syria and Mesopotamia. Belief in Jesus of Nazareth traveled early to Damascus (Acts 9:1–2, 19). The flight of the Jerusalem church around the time of the temple's destruction pushed many refugees into the Transjordan region (Eusebius, *Hist. eccl.* 3.5.3; Epiphanius, *Pan.* 29.7.7–8; 30.2.7–9). From these early centers, a form of Christianity with a pronounced Hebraic flavor soon spread into Edessa, Osrhoene, Nisibis, and even the Persian Empire. The movement was surprisingly rural, involving many small villages. The famous house church at Dura-Europos, which is securely dated to the mid-third century, gives physical attestation to the presence of Christians in the Parthian borderlands by this time.

In addition to Jewish Christianity of various overlapping types (Ebionites, Nazoreans, Elkesaites, Mandaeans), the early Syriac church also was influenced by heterodox or quasi-Gnostic teachers such as Tatian (late second century), Bardaisan (d. 222), and Mani (d. 276).

The OT of the Syriac church was the Peshitta, which was translated from the Hebrew in the second century by scholars from a Jewish Christian milieu. The source text was normally the proto-MT, though midrashim and targumim influenced the translation. Theologically and liturgically, Syriac Christianity tended to stay closer to its Jewish roots than in Greek- or Latin-speaking areas. For example, robust connections were maintained between the Passover meal and the Christian Eucharist, Torah was read aloud from a bema, and Sabbath blessings were offered by the community (Rouwhorst). The Pseudo-Clementines, extant from the fourth century but based upon earlier texts, valorize Peter and James as advocates of Jewish Christianity. This literature also makes Moses the forerunner of Christ (*Recog.* 4.5) and traces the continuous history of God's people from creation, through Abraham, to the early church (*Recog.* 1.27–74).

The earliest "orthodox" Syriac writers were Aphrahat (fl. 337–45) and Ephrem the Syrian (306–73). Both writers identified with the catholic church of the Roman Empire and therefore vigorously critiqued Judaism, though with a greater degree of understanding (or even respect) than most of their Greek and Latin contemporaries. Several of Aphrahat's twenty-three *Demonstrations* offered polemical ammunition to a Christian friend about Jewish topics such as circumcision (11), the Passover feast (12), the Sabbath (13), avoidance of certain foods (15), the election of the gentiles in Israel's place (16), the Messiah as the Son of God (17), and the Jews' false hope of reunification from their diaspora (19). The twenty-third *Demonstration* traced the messianic line of blessing from Adam to Christ (23.13–46), at which point it was transferred to the gentiles based on the principle that the grape of God's blessing was contained in the grape cluster of Israel until the anointed king was killed, Jerusalem was destroyed, and grace was removed from the Jews (23.1, 46–47; Isa. 65:8–9). Aphrahat's citations of the Peshitta were frequent, and his interpretation tended toward reasonable literalism and copious historical proofs. While symbols abounded, true allegory was not present in his work.

Ephrem the Syrian composed sermons, commentaries, apologetic treatises, and, most famously, liturgical songs. Though his engagement with Judaism was more forceful than that of Aphrahat, at times even hostile enough to be called anti-Semitic (*Serm. Faith* 3; *Hymns Unl. Br.* 19), Ephrem nonetheless viewed the OT as replete with goodness and blessing. In his *Hymns on Virginity* 28–30, Ephrem used artistic metaphors to portray the unity and harmony of God's revelation. Jesus Christ gathered the "scattered symbols" of the Torah along with the "prototypes" of the gospel and the "powers and signs" of nature to paint a rich portrait of himself and his Father (28.2, McVey). Christ the Word took into his hands the two harps of the OT and NT—"the temporal harp and the true harp"—and played from them a single, harmonious song, complemented by the "third harp" of nature (29.1–5, McVey). Although new royal sculptures were rightly fashioned as a king matured, the old statues were not discarded, since they, too, portrayed truth (28.10, McVey). Like Aphrahat, Ephrem's interpretation of the OT discovered rich symbolism and abundant imagery that foreshadowed the coming of Christ, but he did not employ allegory in the Alexandrian sense of the term.

Ephrem was born at Nisibis, where he helped to build a thriving center of Christian intellectual productivity that could be called a "school." But when Rome ceded Nisibis to Persia in 363, Ephrem moved to the safer confines of Edessa and reestablished his school there. Decades later, the Syriac church came to be influenced by the Antiochene cleric Nestorius (ca. 381–451) and his dyophysite Christology. After the Council of Chalcedon in 451, the school at Edessa was shut down in 489 for its Nestorian leanings and so moved back to Nisibis. In the subsequent centuries, Nisibis went on to become a major center of Christian learning in Persia. Interpretation there tended to be literal and grammatical. Due to the influence of Theodore of Mopsuestia, the later Nisibene scholars viewed far fewer OT texts as messianic than in Aphrahat and Ephrem's day.

The Interpretation of the OT in Early Christian Art

Early Christian writers were not the only interpreters of the OT; so too were the ancient church's artists. Selection of imagery was not always dictated by the clerical elite. Sometimes the scenes were chosen by common fossors or workshop artisans or by the patrons who commissioned the works, while in other instances (such as the extravagant floor mosaics of the Patriarchal Basilica at Aquileia) the local-church leadership and/or wealthy donors were more heavily involved.

The physical locus for early Christian artistic expression included the frescoes of the Roman catacombs (late second century on); sarcophagi (late third century on); movables such as small statues, liturgical implements, religious icons, and luxury arts (primarily fourth century on); and mosaic art on the floors, walls, and ceilings of basilicas (post-Constantinian). The unique house church at Dura-Europos (240s) preserves images, in its baptistery, of Adam and Eve covering their pudenda and David slaying Goliath, reminding worshipers of original sin and their triumph over the enemy.

Christian artists used OT imagery often because much of this corpus was narrative and thus susceptible to visual representation. However, artistic license was bound by strict communal expectations. The execution of scenes normally bore a close relationship to the church's textual tradition of interpretation. As in the written sources, so with art, the narratives of the OT were filtered through the NT to give them the proper theological meaning or spiritual significance. For the early Christians more so than the pagans, the written word and the artistic image existed in a mutually reinforcing relationship because of Scripture's authority and standardizing influence.

Some of the most common OT figures and scenes in pre-Constantinian art were Adam and Eve, who symbolized temptation or sin (Rom. 5:12–21; 1 Cor. 15:22, 45–49; 2 Cor. 11:3; 1 Tim. 2:13–14); Noah, whose ark represented the church's safe refuge from the world and judgment and whose waters, conversely, offered cleansing and salvation through baptism, as signaled by a dove (Matt. 3:16; 24:37–39; 1 Tim. 1:19–20; 1 Pet. 3:20–21; 2 Pet. 2:5); the binding of Isaac, who, with his father, Abraham, was a sign of great faith and who also served as a type of Christ, since he was a sacrificial son who bore wood upon his shoulders (Gal. 4:21–31; Heb. 11:17–19; James 2:21–24); Moses striking the rock, which had baptismal connotations and depicted the offer of living water from the Savior, flowing from his side for healing and cleansing (John 4:10–15; 7:37–39; 19:34; 1 Cor. 10:1–4; Eph. 5:25–27; 1 John 5:6–8; Rev. 21:6; 22:1–2); Daniel and the three Hebrew youths, who gave vivid OT expression to the ancient Christians' experience of persecution, being vulnerable yet faithful as they faced danger until, like their Lord, they were resurrected from confinement and triumphed over Satan's power (2 Tim. 4:17; Heb. 11:32–34; 1 Pet. 5:8); and Jonah, the most common image in early Christian art, seen especially in funerary contexts such as sarcophagi or the catacombs because of the tripartite cycle of Jonah being swallowed by the sea monster (= death), Jonah being vomited forth (= resurrection), and Jonah being at rest under a garden vine (= paradise; Matt. 12:38–41; 16:4; Luke 11:29–32).

After the rise of Constantine, the church's artistic expression grew significantly more complex. The quality of execution improved with the greater financial investment available, since art was now patronized by the ecclesiastical and imperial elites. Greater attention was given to Jesus as an enthroned cosmic ruler as well as to the saints and martyrs. Depictions of Noah and Jonah became less common, while at the same time new biblical images began to appear, such as scenes from the life of Christ or representations of Peter and Paul (Jensen, 20). Of course, the prior OT imagery by no means disappeared; only now it could be represented on a grand scale (e.g., Abel, Abraham, Melchizedek, Moses, Isaiah, and Jeremiah as precursors of Christ in the mosaics of the sixth-century Basilica of San Vitale in Ravenna). From the ancient period on, Christian art, like Christian exegesis, embraced the saying of Jesus in John 5:39, "These are the very Scriptures that testify about me."

Although patristic interpretive methodologies often varied according to time or place, the one constant among the early Christians was their deep love for Holy Scripture. In no age of church history was the Bible more studied, contemplated, and cherished than during the patristic era. Concerning such high regard for divine revelation, the ancients have much to teach us.

See also Allegory; Apostolic Hermeneutics: Description and Presuppositions; Messiah; Typology; *other History of Interpretation articles*

Bibliography. Brock, S. P., *The Bible in the Syriac Tradition* (Gorgias, 2006); Butterworth, G. W., *Origen: On First Principles* (Peter Smith, 1973); de Lubac, H., *Medieval Exegesis*, trans. M. Sebanc, 2 vols. (Eerdmans, 1998); de Margerie, B., *The Latin Fathers*, vol. 2 of *An Introduction to the History of Exegesis*, trans. P. de Fontnouvelle (St. Bede's, 1995); Ferguson, E., "The Covenant Idea in the Second Century," in *Texts and Testaments*, ed. W. E. March (Trinity University Press, 1980), 135–62; Ferguson, ed., *The Bible in the Early Church*, vol. 2 of *Studies in Early Christianity* (Garland, 1993); Froehlich, K., *Biblical Interpretation in the Early Church*, ed. W. G. Rusch, SECT (Fortress, 1984); Graves, M., ed., *Biblical Interpretation in the Early Church*, series ed. G. Kalantzis, AFECS (Fortress, 2017); Harris, J. R., *Testimonies: Part I* and *Part II* (Cambridge University Press, 1916, 1920); Hauser, A. J., and D. F. Watson, eds., *The Ancient Period*, vol. 1 of *A History of Biblical Interpretation* (Eerdmans, 1990); Hefner, P. J., "Saint Irenaeus and the Hypothesis of Faith," *Di* 2 (1963): 300–306; Hill, R. C., *Reading the Old Testament in Antioch*, ed. J. Bingham, BibAC 5 (Society of Biblical Literature, 2005); Hovhanessian, V. S., ed., *The Old Testament as Authoritative Scripture in the Early Churches of the East* (Lang, 2010); Jensen, R. M., *Understanding Early Christian Art* (Routledge, 2000); Kannengiesser, C., *Handbook of Patristic Exegesis*, ed. J. Bingham, 2 vols., BibAC (Brill, 2004); Kinzig, W., "Καινὴ διαθήκη," *JTS* 45 (October 1994): 519–44; Kugel, J. L., and R. A. Greer, *Early Biblical Interpretation*, ed. W. A. Meeks, LEC (Westminster, 1986); McDonald, L. M., and J. A. Sanders, eds., *The Canon Debate* (Hendrickson, 2002); McVey, K. E., *Ephrem the Syrian: Hymns*, ed. B. McGinn, CWS (Paulist Press, 1989); Norris, R. A., "Theology and Language in Irenaeus of Lyons," *ATR* 76 (1994): 285–95; Rouwhorst, G., "Jewish Liturgical Traditions in Early Syriac Christianity," *VC* 51 (1997): 72–93; Sæbø, M., *Antiquity*, vol. 1.1 of *Hebrew Bible, Old Testament: The History of Its Interpretation* (Vandenhoeck & Ruprecht, 1996); Simonetti, M., *Biblical Interpretation in the Early Church*, ed. A. Bergquist, M. Bockmuehl, and W. Horbury, trans. J. A. Hughes (T&T Clark, 1994); Young, F., *Biblical Exegesis and the Formation of Christian Culture* (Cambridge University Press, 1997).

BRYAN LITFIN

History of Interpretation: 300 to 1800

The fourth century has been called "the Golden Age of Greek Patristic Literature" (Quasten, 1). Although it opened with the most severe empire-wide persecution of the Christian church in Roman history (the Great Persecution of 303–13), the subsequent peace saw a dramatic change in the relationship of church and state and the rise and flourishing of gifted church leaders whose literary output formed the classical expression of Christian theology. Practically all this writing in one way or another had to do with the interpretation of Scripture. With Paul, the church believed that "all Scripture is inspired by God and profitable" (2 Tim. 3:16 RSV) for the education and mission of the church. That mission became more critical with the great influx of people into the churches once Christianity was officially recognized.

Classical Christian Interpretive Methods

Interpretation was needed, of course, to help people from a pagan background understand writings of a different culture, speaking of religious matters that were new to them. Two primary problems confronted the interpreter. First, the Bible used in the churches, the Septuagint, was a Greek translation of the OT that sounded rough and unsophisticated to cultured Roman ears. This Greek OT was used together with NT writings, which were written in Koine (common) Greek, not the elevated style Hellenists and Romans might expect of writings inspired by God. Hardly any of the Christian bishops and teachers of the fourth century knew Hebrew (Jerome was an exception), and it would not be until the modern era that the literary features of Hebrew narrative and poetry would be understood and appreciated. A second, more substantial problem, however, was the fact that the OT, and even portions of the NT, had to do with the history of the Jewish people and the structure and practice of the Jewish religion. The problem was clearly identified and addressed by the third-century biblical scholar Origen of Alexandria in his handbook on hermeneutics, *On First Principles*: How is a book about Jewish people and the practice of Jewish religion to be interpreted for the education of Christian people in the Christian religion?

The question was acute at a time when Christianity and Judaism were officially distinguished and yet were in competition for the evangelization/proselytization of pagans attracted to the God of the Bible. To answer it, Origen turned to Paul's discussion of a problem in the Jewish reading of Moses in 2 Cor. 3, where Paul draws a distinction between the letter and the spirit (3:6). Origen took this to refer to two levels of meaning in the biblical text—one literal and one spiritual. Both Jews and Christians could understand the text literally, but only Christians could perceive the spiritual sense. This answer set the trajectory for the Christian interpretation of Scripture to the Middle Ages and beyond.

Literal interpretation. Interpretation according to the letter, or literal interpretation, sought the obvious, natural meaning of the words of the text, which would not normally be problematic except for unrecognized words, especially names of people and places, unfamiliar customs, and unusual grammatical, syntactical forms, which are sometimes due to translation. By virtue of their grammatical and rhetorical training, Christian interpreters were skilled in lexical analysis and compositional techniques. Patristic commentaries often provide the meanings of unfamiliar words and offer paraphrastic renderings of unclear constructions. Of special interest, however, was etymology for the meanings of names, which were thought to be clues to the sense of the text in which they appear. Interpreters typically consulted or created lists of etymologies for that purpose.

Confidence in the original form of the text formed a necessary element of literal interpretation. Patristic commentators used the LXX but were aware of other Greek translations. In the third century, Origen created the Hexapla as a tool for textual analysis containing the Hebrew text, a transliterated version of the Hebrew text in Greek letters, the LXX, and other Greek translations set side by side in parallel columns. This tool was still in use in the fourth century and some such comparative study can be seen in the commentaries of that era. Jerome would advance textual study in reference to the Hebrew text of the OT and by the production of a more accurate and stylistic Latin text. Concern for textual accuracy to the extent of the interpreter's competency characterizes the tradition of Christian commentary.

By a literal interpretation of the NT, Christian interpreters exposited the doctrinal content of the Christian faith. As the centuries progressed, the propriety of the literal sense as Christianity's doctrinal foundation was repeatedly reaffirmed. The problem, however, was what to do with a literal interpretation of the OT.

Spiritual interpretation. Christian interpretation of Scripture was formed in a cultural context in which allegorical and mystical hermeneutical practices were well known. Hellenistic philosophers had applied allegorical interpretative techniques to Homer to convert unseemly narratives into philosophical cosmological description or ethical prescriptions. Philo of Alexandria, a Jewish philosopher of the first century AD, pioneered the application of these techniques to the interpretation of the Hebrew Scriptures, and his work was exemplary for the Christian Alexandrians Clement and Origen. But Christian spiritual interpretation did not merely transfer pagan hermeneutics to Scripture. Christian interpreters turned to a set of NT texts from the Gospels and Epistles, especially the Pauline Epistles and Hebrews (which was thought to be Pauline), that relate Jesus Christ, his ministry and salvific work, and the church formed by and in him to OT events, institutions, and even to its overall message, using language such as "type," "mystery," "allegory," "testimony," "fulfillment," and "spirit" (versus "letter"). Whereas patristic commentators sometimes claimed to see Hellenistic or Philonic philosophical and cosmological teachings in biblical texts, for the most part they sought to show Christ, his accomplishments, and his superior teaching as the hidden meaning of the OT. Their consensus on the abrogation and supersession of Israel in the progression from the OT to the NT informed their reading of Christ in the OT. It was here, in this hidden sense, that the identity of the OT as Christian Scripture was to be found.

The language used by Christian interpreters for this spiritual sense included several terms used mostly interchangeably but sometimes with nuanced differences. As already noted, "spiritual" reflects Paul's distinction between letter and spirit in 2 Cor. 3:6. "Allegorical" refers to a meaning other (*allos*) than the literal sense, as in the above-mentioned philosophical interpretation of poetic texts. Justification for its Christian use was traced to Paul in Gal. 4. By the end of the patristic era, when used in distinction from other spiritual senses, it came to indicate the theological or doctrinal sense of a passage. "Mystical" derives from Paul's references to things hidden in the Law or Prophets now revealed through Christ (see, e.g., Rom. 16:25). Over time, it came to be used in accordance with Hellenistic spatial metaphysics—a meaning metaphysically *higher* or *deeper* than the material world of appearances. In that sense, it overlaps with "anagogical," which also refers to a higher meaning and could be used interchangeably with "allegorical." When distinguished from allegory, it typically refers to the heavenly realities of Christian hope. "Tropological" means figurative, but when used distinctively alongside the other terms, it indicates the moral significance to be drawn from a passage. "Theoria" refers to contemplation. It was the Antiochene term of choice for spiritual meaning. "Typological" interpretation has come to be distinguished from allegory in recent times, but a terminological distinction is not clearly evident for much of Christian history. Recognition of types is frequent in Christian interpretation and based on NT practice. While allegory was criticized at times for excess, the commended practice of spiritual interpretation tends to be more typological, stressing a relationship between persons, events, and institutions across the Testaments.

A basic twofold distinction prevails through much of traditional Christian interpretation, based on the letter/spirit distinction drawn from 2 Cor. 3:6, with the various terms above being used to indicate the spiritual sense. In one passage, Origen speaks of three sense levels corresponding to a trichotomous anthropology, in which a moral sense intervenes between a literal, bodily sense and a spiritual sense (*Princ.* 4.2.4). Rarely, however, does Origen expound three senses in any given passage. Medieval interpreters implement his trifold analysis much more frequently. Also, John Cassian, as discussed below in "Latin Patristic Interpretation," recommends distinguishing four sense levels, but again, those who adopt that analysis are not consistent, reverting often to a basic twofold distinction.

For the practice of spiritual interpretation, the establishment of the precise text and its literal interpretation were foundational. One was not supposed to invent and simply impose a spiritual meaning. (Allegory sometimes did just that.) It was to be suggested by something in the text. This could be peculiarities in grammar or syntax, or in the narrative. Origen speaks of factual impossibilities or errors in the narrative designed to move the reader to seek Scripture's inspired truth on a higher level. (Some followed him on this point, but by the late fourth century opposition grew on this and other matters leading to a condemnation of Origen in the sixth century.) Objects in the text might also suggest spiritual meaning. Pagan learning might be called upon here to reveal some insight about the nature, attributes, history, or circumstances of things that could be windows to a higher meaning. The definitions of words are suggestive, especially etymologies revealing the secrets of people and place names. On the latter, topography adds needed information. Numerology might be applied to reveal secrets of numbers. The data gathered by these various means would then be used to suggest something in the NT or generally in the rule of faith by virtue of the link of a similar word or concept. The principle here is that Scripture interprets Scripture.

The establishment of the rule of faith from the literal sense was crucial as a guide to spiritual interpretation. Augustine clarifies that doctrine is to be based on the literal sense alone. Spiritual interpretation is used to reveal the harmony of doctrinal truth from the OT to the NT. In line with this is the limiting principle that an interpretation of Scripture needs to be worthy of God. This again connects to the rule of faith but also to the overall presentation of the attributes and works of God in Scripture.

Greek Patristic Interpretation

Perhaps the most well-known Christian writer at the beginning of the fourth century was the church historian *Eusebius of Caesarea* (ca. 265–ca. 340), who as bishop oversaw the work of the famous Christian library in that city where Origen, after leaving Alexandria, had written much of his exegetical work. Eusebius produced commentaries on the Psalms, Isaiah, and a synopsis on the Gospels. Fragments of other commentaries have been preserved in the catenae (florilegia from the fifth century onwards containing excerpts from Greek patristic commentators usually identified together with the biblical text, oftentimes in parallel columns). By way of reference tools, Eusebius published his *Onomasticon*, which identified biblical place names, often reflective of his personal acquaintance with that land. His exegesis typically identifies, in Origenist fashion, a literal sense for the text followed by a spiritual interpretation directing the reader to Christ and NT realities on the basis of suggestive words or ideas in the text, especially etymologies. Eusebius's hermeneutic distinctively emphasizes the fulfillment of messianic prophecy in the life and work of Jesus. In this, he carries forward the older Christian apologetic tradition and publishes its quintessential expression in his *Demonstration of the Gospel*. Eusebius is also important for his construal of the theological coherence of the OT and the NT in which he postulates that Jewish law was the development and particularization of a pre-Mosaic ethical monotheism. With the incarnation of the Logos, the particular Jewish expression has been superseded and the original revelation has been clarified by Jesus Christ. Spiritual interpretation must be applied to the OT to de-particularize that text and show the harmony between the Testaments.

Whereas Eusebius wavered in the face of the Arian controversy of the early fourth century and onward, the Alexandrian bishops Alexander and his famous successor *Athanasius of Alexandria* (ca. 296–373) were resolute defenders of the theology of the Nicene Creed (325). Athanasius published several highly influential treatises laying out the hermeneutical and exegetical justification of the conciliar definition. The syntactical structure of the creedal statement and much of its vocabulary were taken directly from Scripture, and the nonbiblical language (e.g., *homoousios*) was intended as a summative interpretation of both didactic and figurative biblical expressions. The Arian controversy was a dispute about biblical hermeneutics (Kannengiesser, *Holy*, 1). Common to both sides was the conviction that Scripture, both OT and NT, proclaimed Christ. The question had to do with what it supposedly said about the essential being of Christ. Apparently beginning as a dispute over the interpretation of the Wisdom text of Prov. 8, which in typical patristic fashion was seen as speaking of Christ, the argument proceeded by an examination of the verbs of the text and the contexts of their usage elsewhere in Scripture. Athanasius lays out several hermeneutical terms for readers to keep in mind: the *ethos* and *idioma*, or custom and style of biblical expression; the *skopos*, or the scope or aim of biblical revelation (namely, Christ in his double reality of God and man); and the *dianoia*, or true sense inherent in Scripture, in contrast to the *epinoia*, or meanings that are actually products of the reader's imagination. Much of the polemical argument involved extensive lexical, grammatical, and syntactical analysis of NT texts on the person and incarnation of the Son of God. This shows that in this controversy, the theological sense was necessarily tied to the linguistic, semantic, and syntactical structure of Scripture. Looking back over this and other similar controversies, Augustine later advises that the theological sense, while it can be illustrated by spiritual interpretation, must first be established on the basis of the literal sense of Scripture.

We have no clearly authentic commentaries from Athanasius, but his *Letter to Marcellinus on the Interpretation of the Psalms* has been esteemed through the ages as a devotional classic, even being incorporated into the Codex Alexandrinus for an introduction to the Psalter. It presents Christ as the scope of the Psalter while distinguishing individual psalms as designed for the healing and reordering of the soul. His *Festal Letters* are a study in the typological reading of the Passover in relation to the atonement of Christ, connecting that reading to the NT teaching on faith.

Probably the best fourth-century representative of Origenist exegesis was *Didymus the Blind* (ca. 313–ca. 397), an ascetic and teacher in Alexandria. Didymus produced commentaries on many biblical books, especially on Wisdom literature and prophetic books, many of which were destroyed after the sixth-century condemnation of Origen (although fragments were preserved in the catena). In typical Origenist fashion, Didymus first identifies the literal sense of a text and then presents a spiritual or moral meaning, suggested by words present in the text, their usage elsewhere in Scripture, and any etymological meanings thought to be associated with them.

Respect for Origen's contribution to biblical hermeneutics can be seen in the work of the late-fourth-century Cappadocian Fathers. Sometime before 378, *Gregory Nazianzus* (ca. 329–ca. 390), who included studies under Didymus in his portfolio of educational experiences, and *Basil of Caesarea* (330–379) published the *Philocalia*, a compilation of excerpts from the works of Origen, as a tribute to the Alexandrian and in promotion of his hermeneutical method. Basil himself displays the art of spiritual exegesis in his *Homilies on the Psalms* together with moral instruction tied at times to the literal sense. However, in Basil's *Hexaemeron*, an exegetical examination of Gen. 1, he criticizes allegory and even on occasion Origen's interpretation of that text.

A more consistent example of spiritual interpretation can be found in the later works of Basil's younger brother, *Gregory of Nyssa* (ca. 335–ca. 395). Gregory defends allegory explicitly in his treatise *On the Inscriptions of the Psalms* and in his commentary on the Song of Songs. Gregory's *Life of Moses* is an allegory on the ascent of the soul in the knowledge of God.

Cappadocian theology affirmed the incomprehensibility of God against Neo-Arianism. For Gregory of Nyssa, knowing God takes place as a mystical advance of the soul through divinization in Christ. It is tied to the progressive understanding of Scripture in its spiritual sense.

Traditionally, surveys of the Christian use of the Bible distinguish an Alexandrian "school" from an Antiochene one. These are thought to constitute two trajectories defining early Christian biblical interpretation, the former emphasizing spiritual interpretation and the latter literal interpretation. The classification is simplistic yet not without some merit. As Francis Young (734–35) has noted, it is better to see Antiochene interpreters as debate participants within a common tradition. One would be warranted in seeing "Antiochene hermeneutics" as part of the broader critique of Origenism beginning in the latter part of the fourth century, which went beyond the Cappadocian doctrinal differences to include hermeneutical practice as well—not a rejection of spiritual interpretation per se but a correction, reformulation, and restriction of its proper use.

The label "Antiochene school" primarily refers to the work of *Diodore of Tarsus* (d. ca. 390, a contemporary of Didymus) and his two students, *John Chrysostom* (ca. 349–407) and *Theodore of Mopsuestia* (ca. 350–428). Theodore is remembered as "the blessed interpreter" in Syriac Christianity, and his influence can be traced through the centuries of Syriac biblical commentators. *Theodoret of Cyrus* (ca. 393–ca. 466) is usually included as an Antiochene, but he is often an exception to the Antiochene literalism.

Diodore wrote commentaries on all the books of the OT and some of the NT writings, of which only fragments in the catena and his commentary on Pss. 1–50 have survived. Many writings of Theodore have survived in Syriac translation as well as in Greek or Latin translation. They are well represented in the catena.

The basic complaint of Diodore and Theodore against Origenistic allegorization is that it appears to take the slightest excuse for transitioning away from the literal sense to a supposed meaning that has nothing to do with it. These Antiochenes do recognize a higher sense to Scripture, which they label as *theoria*. However, unlike allegory, *theoria* maintains a relationship to *historia*, the narrative flow of the text. Sometimes *theoria* appears to be what today is called typology, but not always. The Antiochenes are keen to distinguish various levels of figuration in Scripture including parable and riddles and even allegory conceived as a trope rather than as a technique of the interpreter. Theodore's commentaries are highly paraphrastic, tracing the literal meaning of words in their given textual sequence and dealing with historical matters of people and places as they arise. His commentaries appear to be composed for his own scholarly purposes and are mostly devoid of homiletical content. Typically, he sets forth an introductory hypothesis for his comments on a portion of text.

Distinctive to these Antiochenes is their view on the fulfillment of OT prophecy, which they take in many cases to occur either within the narrative history of OT Scripture or in intertestamental history. They assign historical fulfillment to the Psalter in the same way. Only some psalms and some prophecies were regarded as truly messianic. However, they did acknowledge hyperbolic language, which could be applied to more than one time, place, or person.

John Chrysostom avoided not only allegory but also any discussion of hermeneutical methodology. Chrysostom's work is almost entirely homiletical and paraenetical. He is a quintessential example of drawing moral instruction from Scripture and presenting it sermonically to the church with polished skill. His practice fits well with the moral use of Scripture that all Christian expositors, including the Alexandrians, affirmed. This accounts for his great popularity and the extensive preservation of his works.

Latin Patristic Interpretation

Origen's legacy was transferred to the Latin West through the influential ministries and writings of bishops Ambrose and Augustine and the scholarly works of Jerome. From them we can trace contributions to the late shaping of the Western biblical tradition by Cassian, Cassiodorus, Gregory, and Bede.

Ambrose of Milan (ca. 339–397) was only a catechumen at the time he was chosen for the episcopal see in Milan. He thoroughly immersed himself in the study of Scripture and theology and was profoundly impressed with the works of Philo and Origen, interacting with them by name in his own exegetical work. Most of Ambrose's biblical work was on the OT in the form of commentaries, exegetical treatises, and sermons. His only work on the NT was on the Gospel of Luke in which he was dependent on Eusebius of Caesarea. Ambrose distinguishes the meaning of Scripture on three levels: literal, moral, and spiritual/doctrinal (corresponding to Origen's three levels). He makes frequent use of etymologies and the principle of Scripture interpreting Scripture through suggestive words, names, and places. Even animals could signify virtues or spiritual practices. Inspired by Origen, Ambrose sermonically interprets Song of Songs spiritually as the soul's love for Christ with great literary and rhetorical skill, profoundly influencing Augustine and helping to change his opinion of Scripture. Ambrose addresses both textual difficulties in the alternate translations and historical questions in the textual narrative, but his goal is to derive the spiritual meaning for the full edification of his people doctrinally and morally.

Jerome (ca. 347–419), the highly educated philologist, pursued the life of an ascetic scholar. He was excellent in Latin, mastered Greek, and acquired a working knowledge of Hebrew, which was rare in his day. He studied theology and exegesis under Apollinaris of Laodicea, Gregory Nazianzus, and Didymus the Blind, and was profoundly influenced by the scholarly exegetical works of Origen. Jerome wrote commentaries on both OT and NT books, many of which repeat Origen's interpretations or follow his multilevel approach. In the late-fourth-century Origenist controversy, Jerome distinguished Origen the exegete from Origen the speculative theologian. While condemning the latter, he sought to preserve the former, translating several of Origen's works into Latin.

However, more important than his commentaries was Jerome's textual and translation work offering revisions of the Latin biblical text based on a critical study of Greek versions by means of Origen's Hexapla. Not satisfied with this, Jerome proceeded to create a new Latin translation of the OT based on the Hebrew text. The project took about fifteen years, being completed in 405/406. While not widely accepted at first, it would eventually be recognized with the title Vulgate and became the definitive Latin translation of the OT until the modern era.

Ambrose's approach to Scripture profoundly influenced *Augustine* (354–430), who found in the former bishop's spiritual interpretation a pathway to overcome his objections to the crude style of his Latin Bible and the unseemliness of its narratives. In the course of his life of biblical scholarship, consisting of sermons, commentaries, and topical treatments of both OT and NT passages, he would grow in his appreciation for Scripture in its literal sense also.

From Augustine we have the significant work *On Christian Doctrine*, which sets forth his theoretical understanding of hermeneutics based on the distinction between signs (*signa*) and things (*res*). Words are signs that refer to things, although they can never do so with complete adequacy. Furthermore, things may also function as signs of other things, especially material things functioning as signs of transcendent things. The sign function of things creates a hermeneutical challenge for understanding the words that refer to them. A full understanding of the truth of biblical communication requires careful study of each stage in the referential sequence: (1) identification of the correct words for the text; (2) lexical, grammatical, and rhetorical study of those words; (3) a knowledge of the world of things to which those words refer (which may rely on pagan science and history); and (4) a knowledge of God and transcendent things, which requires initial instruction in the church's rule of faith (which itself is to be demonstrated from the literal sense of clear passages of Scripture, especially in the NT). Added to this was Augustine's identification of the goal of Christian instruction—namely, love (1 Tim. 1:5). Following the legacy of Origenist hermeneutics by noting etymologies and tracing lexical usage and conceptual echoes elsewhere in Scripture, the interpreter with a basic understanding of Scripture's message and intended effect could proceed to interpret a specific text of Scripture, identifying what was to be interpreted literally and what should be understood spiritually. Most of the OT was interpreted spiritually. More important to Augustine than the correct interpretation of a particular passage was an overall knowledge of truth and an alignment of one's life with the aim of Scripture, which was love. An inaccurate interpretation could be tolerated so long as the rule of faith was maintained and Christian love promoted.

Also important for the history of biblical interpretation was Augustine's adaptation of Tyconius's *Book of Rules* (see Augustine, *Doctr. chr.* 3). This *Tyconius* (d. ca. 400), a Donatist theologian, published in his *Book of Rules* a hermeneutic "utterly independent of and indifferent to earlier (and especially Greek) modes of interpretation" (Fredrikson, 855). Composed primarily, but not solely, for the interpretation of Revelation, its influence can be seen in Augustine's own interpretation of Rev. 20 in *City of God*, and it continued to shape Western commentaries on Revelation for centuries afterwards. The seven rules (seven in relation to the seven-sealed scroll of Rev. 5) were not rules to be applied by the interpreter but rules supposedly employed by the Holy Spirit in forming the composition of Scripture, rules that the interpreter needs to recognize as inherent in the text in order to perceive its meaning correctly. There are seven rules: (1) The Lord and His Body—some references to the Lord may speak of his body, the church, and vice versa; (2) The Lord's Bipartate Body—the church has a mixed nature, containing both the good and the wicked; (3) The Promises and the Law—law, or works, and faith have a complex, complementary relationship; (4) The Particular and the General—particular persons and events in narrative may conceal general truths; (5) Times—precise numbers may be figures for spiritual truths; (6) Recapitulation—narrative sequence may actually be reiteration or repetition; and (7) The Devil and His Body—references to the devil may be to his followers or vice versa (see Fredriksen, 854).

The application of these rules allowed for a profound historicizing of biblical prophecy and apocalyptic, shifting meaning away from future conditions associated with the coming of the Lord to the present conditions of the church. This was different from the mystical/spiritual approach of Hellenistic hermeneutics. However, the two approaches are found together in the heritage of Christian hermeneutics.

The impact of Augustine on the Western tradition theologically and hermeneutically is incalculable, shaping the Christian mind through the Middle Ages to the Reformation and even down to the modern era.

While many Latin expositors may be mentioned, four in particular contributed to the terminology and shape of Western practice.

John Cassian (ca. 360–ca. 433) was a contemporary of Augustine who sided against him in the Pelagian controversy, developing a position that would come to be known as semi-Pelagianism. Most important for hermeneutics was his threefold classification of spiritual knowledge, which when added to the literal sense yielded the famous four levels of sense known through the Middle Ages: literal, tropological, allegorical, and anagogical (*Conferences* 14.8.1). In this distinctive usage, tropology refers to the moral sense, allegory to the doctrinal or theological sense, and anagogy to the heavenly, eschatological sense of the text.

Cassidorus (ca. 490–ca. 580), a theological follower of Augustine, is most important for his extensive application of rhetorical analysis to exegesis, with the technical identification of tropes and figures of speech.

Gregory the Great (ca. 540–604), bishop of Rome, famous for his homilies and commentaries, is traditionally considered one of the four great fathers of the Western church, alongside Ambrose, Augustine, and Jerome. Gregory compares his hermeneutical practice to building a house: laying a foundation with the literal sense, raising the walls of doctrinal truth through allegorical interpretation, and then completing the finishing work with the moral sense. This follows the trifold division in Origen and Ambrose, except that Gregory inverts the order of the allegorical and moral senses. His threefold scheme competes with Cassian's delineation of four senses in the works of medieval commentators. Moral transformation is the goal, and Scripture is seen as a mirror revealing the conditions of the soul in sin and grace. Gregory recommends meditative rumination upon Scripture for maximum benefit. His masterpiece, the multivolume *Moral Reflections on Job*, is an extended reflective piece ranging through the different sense levels. He traditionally interprets Job as a type of Christ, but noticeable is the application of Tyconius's rules of alternating head/body references, of the reality of the bipartite body applied to the struggle of the Christian life, and of the spiritual significance of numbers.

Bede (ca. 673–735), from whom we have the earliest history of the English church, quotes extensively from earlier patristic commentaries but often provides original insights on the various levels of meaning. He does not follow a rigid classification of senses, sometimes noting only a literal/spiritual distinction. But he is aware of Cassian's categories and uses them when he believes it is appropriate. Bede's great contribution is the wealth of information he brings to his task, reflecting the well-supplied monastic library of Northumbria where he spent practically his entire life. He set an example of erudition on details of the literal sense as a necessary foundation for spiritual interpretation.

The Middle Ages

The Carolingian Renaissance brought a renewed emphasis on Latin proficiency and literacy, which in the study of Scripture meant careful grammatical and lexical study of the Latin text. But it also meant literacy in the Latin patristic commentary tradition. Ninth-century church councils required ecclesiastics to study Scripture according to the wisdom of the fathers. Marginal notations began to appear in works identifying their patristic sources by initials (Levy, 57). In *Paschasius Radbertus* (ca. 790–ca. 860), *Haimo of Auxerre* (ca. 800–ca. 865), and *John Scotus Eriugena* (ca. 810–ca 877), grammatical exegesis moves back and forth between the biblical text and patristic commentary.

In the eleventh century, biblical scholarship was promoted in monastic schools. Following Augustine's encouragement of learning from classical sources and the example of Cassiodorus, special attention was given to the study of logic and rhetoric with a view to their use as hermeneutical tools for understanding Scripture. *Bruno of Rheims*, known for his commentaries on Psalms and the Pauline Epistles, exposited Paul in the structure of Ciceronian rhetoric. *Lanfranc of Bec*, archbishop of Canterbury (d. 1089), however, sought to show the distinctiveness of Pauline argument with respect to these classical forms.

The twelfth century saw the rise of urban monasteries, such as the Augustinian Abby of St. Victor, founded in Paris by William of Champeaux. *Hugh of St. Victor* (d. 1142) became well known for his attention to the literal sense as the necessary grounding for all spiritual senses. Hugh stressed the need for, and personally modeled, a detailed knowledge of the range of biblical facts. These constituted the "honeycomb" that must be duly grasped and properly squeezed in order to obtain the honey of the spiritual sense. Some move from the text to the spiritual sense too quickly. Careful attention to and meditation on the details of the literal text is crucial to avoid mistakes at the spiritual level. Hugh's dependence on Augustine's explanation of the move from words to earthly things to spiritual truths is clear. Origen and Gregory the Great are also cited in his work, and he follows Gregory's adaptation of Origen's three levels as history, allegory, and tropology, although he notes that not every text contains all three. Moral meaning is the goal of exposition. Prayer and spiritual discipline are its proper context. In his work *On the Sacraments*, he states his intent to present the allegorical meaning of Scripture. The sacramental path to spiritual blessedness is the goal of every Christian and simultaneously the goal of exposition. Accordingly, one can trace the development and influence of sacramental theology in the Middle Ages by its presence in explanations of the allegorical sense of Scripture.

Andrew of St. Victor (d. 1175) followed Hugh's lead on the importance of the literal sense to the extent of engaging with Jewish rabbinical sources for a more accurate knowledge of the OT text. At this time rabbinical scholars such as Rabbi Solomon ben Isaac of Troyes, known as Rashi (1040–1105), and his grandson, Rabbi Samuel ben Meir, known as Rashbam, were developing the hermeneutical method of peshat. This method stressed a "plain sense" reading of texts in their broader biblical contexts with attention to narrative flow. Other rabbinical scholars, such as Rabbi Eliezer of Beaugency, developed features of literary analysis such as flashback and foreshadowing. While it is unclear how much Hebrew Andrew actually knew, his extensive reference to the Hebrew text and use of rabbinical exposition was unprecedented in the Middle Ages.

The cathedral school at Laon in the twelfth century appears to have been the origin of the *Glossa ordinaria*, which contributed significantly to medieval biblical study. The *Glossa* was a verse-by-verse commentary on the entire Bible containing the biblical text with interlinear grammatical notes and marginal comments from patristic and early medieval interpreters as well comments by the glossator. The *Glossa* became the standard commentary for biblical study down to the time of the Reformation. Martin Luther consulted it in the sixteenth century in his preparations of lectures on Psalms and Romans.

The *Glossa* became so commonly used that *Robert of Melun* (d. 1167) complained that study of the *Glossa* was replacing exegesis of the biblical text. In his own hermeneutical practice, Robert reaffirmed many of the common features of medieval interpretation, stressing the necessity of moving from OT figure to NT reality. The subject matter of Scripture was Christ and the sacraments. Pagan liberal arts of the trivium and the quadrivium were foundational for understanding the literal sense.

As a contribution to the literal study of the text, *Peter Comestor* (d. 1178/79) produced the *Historia scholastica*, which purported to be a factual history of the world from creation to the ascension, following the biblical narrative and adding information and detail from pagan sources. This was meant to provide material for the literal sense but was also filled with allegorical comments. It became a standard work and was itself glossed by later contributors.

Hugh of St. Cher (ca. 1190–1263) drew upon the *Glossa ordinaria* and the *Historia scholastica* to produce a commentary for preachers on the entire Bible in 1236 under the title *Postillae in totam Bibliam*. "Postil" thereby enters the lexicon as a general term for commentary, usually with a special orientation to preaching. Also in the thirteenth century, *Thomas Aquinas* (ca. 1225–1274) reaffirmed many of the principles already mentioned but is noted for applying to the Bible the fourfold causal system of Aristotle.

In the fourteenth century, *Nicholas of Lyra* (ca. 1270–1349) produced the highly influential *Postillae litteralis* (1322–33), a commentary on the entire Bible focused on the literal sense. Nicholas noted that problems in interpreting the literal sense could arise from copyist mistakes in textual transmission, from translation mistakes, and from poor expressions coming down in the form of traditional commentary. Significantly, Nicholas stressed the need to go back to the Hebrew text of the OT, citing Jerome as an example of this principle. Somehow, he acquired a knowledge of Hebrew and drew frequently on rabbinic sources such as Rashi for lexical analysis.

Also consequential for later developments in hermeneutics, Nicholas formulated the notion of a double literal sense. This, he felt, was necessary to counter Jewish criticism of Christian exegesis. According to Nicholas, one needed to recognize that the letter of Scripture may contain both a historical and a spiritual sense *within the letter*. The first could be recognized by Jews but only Christians could grasp the second, without which one did not have a true understanding of the literal sense. Nicholas developed his notion of the double literal sense from Tyconius's third rule of the duality of promise and law, which Augustine reformulated as letter and spirit (*Doctr. chr.* 3). Essentially this move allowed typology to be reconceptualized as an aspect of the literal sense. Accordingly, a prophecy about Solomon could be seen as *literally* fulfilled in both Solomon and Jesus with a typological link between the fulfillments.

Expanding the hermeneutical task, Nicholas also affirmed the traditional three levels of spiritual meaning going back to Cassian, now with spiritual meaning extending throughout all four levels, although he acknowledged that not every sense was present in every text. As a special work on the tropological sense, he published *Postilla moralis* in 1339.

Finally, it should be noted that Nicholas advocated for the following fourfold structural symmetry between the Testaments: Law-Gospel, History-Acts, Wisdom-Epistles, and Prophecy-Apocalypse (Levy, 240–42). The structure emphasized the legal character of the gospel, a common medieval view that would be challenged by the Reformers. However, Nicholas's structure also has the OT ending with the Prophets, which naturally raised the question about Maccabees. Nicholas dismissed it as noncanonical, appealing to Jerome for support. On that matter, as well as for his emphasis on and concept of a double literal sense, he would be appreciated by the Reformation.

The Renaissance

The Renaissance beginning in the fifteenth century brought a renewed interest in classical literature, both pagan and patristic, as well as in the Bible. The invention of printing made classical material widely available to scholarly demand. Philological skills in classical languages of Latin, Greek, and Hebrew were nurtured and editions of texts and new translations produced. With respect to the Bible, Renaissance philology brought a renewed concern for accuracy on the literal level, which, as traditionally noted, was foundational for the spiritual use of Scripture.

The concern for an accurate translation of the Bible from Greek and Hebrew into Latin was exemplified by *Giannozzo Manetti* (1396–1459), who translated most of the NT and some of the OT before his death. *Lorenzo Valla* (ca. 1406–57), who famously proved the *Donation of Constantine* to be a forgery, produced extensive grammatical, lexical, and literary notes on the Greek text of the NT with suggestions for a revised Latin translation. His work was published by Erasmus in 1505. The first Latin grammar on the Hebrew language was published by *Johannes Reuchlin* (1454/55–1522) in 1506, based on the medieval rabbinic Hebrew grammar (published in Hebrew) by David Kimchi (Radak) (1160–1235). This was of inestimable importance for OT exegesis in the Reformation era.

Just two years later (1508), *Jean Lefèvre* (ca. 1455–1536) published his *Fivefold Psalter* (*Quincuplex Psalterium*) containing three versions attributed to Jerome, the Old Latin Version, and Lefèvre's own edition with notes, paraphrase, and a brief commentary. Luther would later use Lefèvre's *Psalter* to prepare his lectures on Psalms in 1513. However, Lefèvre is especially to be noted for developing Nicholas of Lyre's double literal sense. On the one hand, a historical literal sense understood Psalms with respect to David and Israel, but a proper and true literal sense interpreted them with respect to Christ and the church. The distinction between the two literal senses was that of the letter and the spirit (2 Cor. 3:6). This allowed a pursuit of historical and contextual study while affirming a typological approach to the whole of Scripture that seemed to accord with the NT use of the OT.

Lefèvre also published a commentary on the Pauline Epistles offering corrections to the Vulgate based on the Greek text. His own reading of Paul was consistent with late medieval Catholicism in merging law and gospel, but it is especially focused on the mystical union of the believer with Christ similar to the mysticism of Nicholas of Cusa (1401–64), whose works Lefèvre also edited and published.

Most importantly, *Erasmus of Rotterdam* (ca. 1466–1536) produced a reliable edition of the Greek text of the NT in 1515 and offered an improved Latin translation on that basis. The scholarly work of Erasmus was extensive, but his text of the NT was of chief importance for subsequent biblical and theological study. He himself held to a devotional, moralistic Christianity that avoided the path of the Reformers. He acknowledged his indebtedness to Origen and Augustine for understanding the spiritual meaning of Scripture, perceived in the relationship of words to material things to spiritual truths. Like Gregory, he typically interpreted Scripture with respect to its literal, allegorical, and tropological senses with the moral sense being his primary concern and the goal of his work.

The Reformation

Martin Luther (1483–1546), whose posting of the Ninety-Five Theses in 1517 is typically regarded as the beginning of the Reformation, lectured on Scripture throughout his faculty service at Wittenburg. He published commentaries, particularly on Psalms and the Letters of Paul, and his sermons were transcribed and published as well. His various pastoral and theological writings and even his hymns engage with the interpretation of Scripture. He wrote introductions to the Testaments and famously translated the Bible into German, a work that he rightly recognized was itself an act of interpretation. Luther could engage with multiple levels of meaning, drawing allegorical or tropological meanings particularly in sermons to make a doctrinal point or press an application. However, he came to reject that approach in favor of a double literal sense that contained a prophetic bearing toward Christ. Most importantly, however, Luther developed from his study of Paul an understanding of the righteousness of God as a forensic gift, of faith as personal trust, of the human condition in sin and grace, and of a soteriological Christology structured by the dialectic of the cross and the resurrection. Most important was his development of Paul's distinction between law and grace into a hermeneutical principle, the dialectic of law and gospel. The law, in this sense, is the condemnatory message of Scripture confronting our works, whereas the gospel is that which offers forgiveness and promises blessing and life to faith. The dialectical contrast between the two translates to a dialectical contrast between the Testaments. This had the effect of nullifying the entire medieval interpretation of the NT gospel as a higher, more perfect form of the OT law, with its concomitant view of the Christian life as sacramentally assisted moral progress toward perfection. On the other hand, law and gospel, as Luther understood it, pervaded both Testaments, constituting an ever-present dialectic confronting the reader of Scripture and pointing to Christ. Whereas the law/gospel contrast and its associated Pauline topics, especially faith, pervade Luther's works, perhaps the clearest expression of it can be found in the *Loci communes* (first edition 1521) of his associate, *Philipp Melanchthon* (1497–1560). The *Loci* was a theology manual consisting of Pauline themes more or less as they appear in Romans. Law and gospel receive a separate listing in that work in which theological instruction occurs as an exposition of Scripture.

Huldrych Zwingli (1484–1531) became pastor of the Grossmunster in Zurich in 1519. He was fully trained in the textual study of Greek and Latin classics and patristic literature, but the publication of Erasmus's text of the NT profoundly affected him. He embraced the concept of reform based on Scripture and Luther's key insight of justification by faith. But Zwingli remained pastorally focused on moral instruction. He preached through the whole of Scripture, and his sermons became the basis for published commentaries.

To educate the clergy, Zwingli created a school in Zurich that included an ongoing seminar focused on the exegesis of the text of Scripture. Philological study of the text in Hebrew, Greek, and Latin was the primary purpose of this exegesis along with rhetorical analysis identifying tropes and figures of speech.

Zwingli could refer at times to different senses, distinguishing a mystical or moral sense from the literal meaning of the text. But he was critical of allegory and could speak of a spiritual sense contained within the literal, in a manner similar to Lefèvre. Perception of this literal-spiritual sense, he believed, was made possible by the illumination of the Holy Spirit, an emphasis noticeably different from Luther. To discover it, Zwingli stressed the importance of prayer and a conviction regarding meaning following one's own study of the text apart from consulting commentaries. Unlike later spiritualists, however, Zwingli kept illumination tethered to the text of Scripture; it did not constitute an independent revelation.

Controversy arose in 1525, when some students in Zwingli's exegetical seminar denounced the practice of infant baptism as contrary to NT teaching. Their break from Zwingli was the genesis of the Swiss Anabaptist movement. Zwingli in response argued for a covenant unity between the Testaments that allowed for a typological relationship between OT circumcision and NT baptism. His view was elaborated by his successor in Zurich, *Heinrich Bullinger* (1504–75), in his publication *The One and Eternal Testament or Covenant of God* (1534). Bullinger attributed to Zwingli the hermeneutical insight of one eternal covenant embracing both Testaments as the framework for the Bible's unified theological message.

John Calvin (1509–64) lectured and preached extensively through Scripture in Geneva. His commentaries on the OT and NT (except Revelation) are still used today. His *Institutes of the Christian Religion* was composed as a guide to understanding Scripture, and his various tracts and treatises address theological topics on the basis of Scripture, which he viewed as inspired and of supreme authority.

Calvin's typical approach combines grammatical and lexical study of the words of the text with rhetorical analysis, identifying and clarifying tropes and figures of speech, for the goal of succinctly explaining or paraphrasing the author's intended meaning. To this end he was able to use a growing set of recently published lexical and grammatical tools for the study of Greek, Hebrew, and Latin. The goal of this exegesis was similar to that expressed by earlier interpreters: to make the text useful for Christian living. However, Calvin criticizes his predecessors (e.g., Augustine) for their recourse to allegory instead of laboring for what he calls "the original and simple sense of the text" (*Commentary on Galatians* 4:22). The accuracy of an interpretation is for him more important than its perceived usefulness (contrary to Augustine in *On Christian Doctrine*). Scripture, being inspired by God, is inherently useful and will accomplish its purpose if the interpreter will stand back and let the text speak (Opitz, 433–34). Scripture needs to be presented simply, directly. Calvin criticizes even some Reformers (such as Martin Bucer) whose verbosity hinders the reader from directly grasping the sense of the text. Although he criticizes allegory, Calvin does affirm a double literal sense in which a typological reference to Christ was seen in conjunction with the grammatical, historical meaning of the words. Similar to Zwingli, he stresses the illumination of the Holy Spirit for understanding the full sense of Scripture but maintains the connection of Word and Spirit. Also, in agreement with the Zurich Reformers, he speaks of one covenant uniting OT and NT, with the church appearing in different ages. However, he also affirms with Luther and Melanchthon the dialectic of law and gospel. Both emphases are crucial for understanding Scripture. Their relationship is not fully explained by Calvin. That would be taken up, debated, and refined in the developing tradition of covenant or federal theology from the late sixteenth century to the present day.

By eschewing allegory and relying instead upon a typology within the literal sense for the Bible's unified presentation of Christ, the Reformers of Zurich and Geneva set the direction for a tradition that would have to address and explain historical differences as part of the Bible's unified theological message. As a partial answer, Calvin employs the concept of accommodation, suggesting differences in human capacity for revelation. But he also speaks of institutional and structural changes that mark a positive advance in divine revelation leading up to Christ, a view that is important for the development of redemption-history biblical theology in the Reformed tradition.

It is difficult to assess Anabaptism's hermeneutical theory and practice because of the intense persecution that severely limited scholarly reflection in that movement. One exception that offers a window into the Anabaptist use of Scripture is *Pilgram Marpeck* (ca. 1495–1556).

Marpeck affirms a Reformation emphasis on faith as personal trust with a soteriology centered on union with Christ. Salvific union with Christ is a theme that can be found in Luther and is especially highlighted in Calvin. However, Marpeck is not as clear on forensic justification. Faith's knowledge comes from Scripture through the illumination of the Holy Spirit, an emphasis that can be traced to Zwingli. Contrary to some accusations against Anabaptists, Marpeck does not separate Word and Spirit.

The key difference from the Magisterial Reformers, however, is Marpeck's rejection of the analogy between OT circumcision and NT baptism. Marpeck insists that the NT covenant does not equal the OT covenant. OT ethics are not NT ethics. The OT "church" is not the same reality as the NT church, and the salvific experience of OT saints is not the same as that of NT saints. There is progress in revelation moving from OT promise to NT fulfillment. Promise points to and leads to fulfillment, but the experience of promise and the experience of fulfillment are essentially different.

This is an interpretation that emphasizes the newness of the NT in relationship to the OT, the transition from old to new taking place in and through the historical work of Christ. Typology is affirmed in the relationship of OT and NT, but type and antitype are distinct in experience. This way of reading salvation history also carries a futurist eschatology since the blessings of salvation are progressively fulfilled in time, being realized in and through Christ historically. The final fulfillment is yet to be realized in and through a realistic future coming. Regrettably, this Anabaptist reading of Scripture was suppressed by widespread and extremely cruel persecution. Not until the modern era would another approach this radical seriously be considered.

In spite of a developing unified covenant approach to the testamental relationship, some within the Reformed movement were willing to explore the implications of a future literal fulfillment of the ethnic, national, and even territorial promises of God to Israel. In Strassbourg, in the late 1520s, *Martin Cellarius* and *Wolfgang Capito*, part of Martin Bucer's scholarly network, published works arguing for an ethnic and territorial future for Israel (in Palestine!) as the natural and literal sense of OT prophecies (Hobbs, 474–76). The view was rejected and suppressed by Bucer, whose traditional views on typology prevailed. However, the expectation of the future conversion of Jews in relation to the literal sense of OT prophecies was nurtured in sixteenth-century English Puritanism and would remain influential in English theological thought to the modern era (see Murray). English Puritanism would come to include a chiliast orientation through the work of *Joseph Mede* (1586–1638), professor at Christ's College, Cambridge, whose *Clavis Apocalyptica* (1627) offered an organic, chronological interpretation of the visions of Revelation (in contrast to a Tyconian-Augustinian reading), climaxing in a future millennial kingdom on earth prior to the eternal state.

Traditions of Protestant orthodoxy in the late sixteenth and early seventeenth centuries preserved and promoted the hermeneutical practices of the Reformers. These post-Reformation orthodox scholars strongly maintained the doctrine of the inspiration of Scripture and the primacy of the literal sense as the bearer of theological truth. Accordingly, they promoted philological and grammatical study of Scripture. However, in the late sixteenth century, both Lutheran and Reformed theologians added a scholastic, Aristotelian framework to their theological, exegetical work, which the Reformers had rejected. This outlook appears to account for the tendency of post-Reformation orthodox scholars to construe biblical syntax, of whatever genre, in the manner of formal propositions subject to syllogistic reasoning for apologetic and polemical goals. This approach of proof-texting appears to have contributed to the brittleness of an already fractured theological discourse. Even so, however, there are many examples of the continuance of Reformation-style homiletical and pastoral exposition of Scripture.

Handbooks on hermeneutics by seventeenth-century Protestant orthodox authors focus on philological and grammatical exegesis as well as providing guidelines for proper recognition of Scripture's allegorical or spiritual sense according to the rule of faith set forth in the Protestant confessions. In some of these works, such as the handbook on hermeneutics by *Salomon Glassius* (1593–1656), a clear distinction is made between typology and allegory, although, within proper limits, both are affirmed. While biblical hermeneutics shared aspects of general hermeneutics, especially in the advancing field of philology, the special character of Scripture as the inspired Word of God had to be acknowledged, and this was directly tied to recognition of its spiritual, primarily typological meaning.

The work of *Johannes Cocceius* (1603–69) is important for both its contribution to philological study, emphasizing the contextual nature of verbal meaning, and the positing of a chronological, progressive salvation history, structuring and unifying the canon of Scripture. Through his teaching career at Bremen, Franeker, and Leiden, Cocceius published widely on philology, biblical exegesis (with commentaries on every biblical book), and theology. Most importantly, his *Doctrine of the Covenant and Testament of God* (first edition 1648) set forth his view of salvation history as a series of "abrogations" of the effects of the covenant of works toward the full manifestation of the covenant of grace in the eschatological kingdom of God. Significantly, he projected a yet future progression of history toward the kingdom by his prophetic interpretation of the letters to the seven churches in Rev. 2–3. This view of Scripture and history was quite influential in English Puritanism and German Pietism, even extending to the modern era.

The movement of Pietism can be seen as developing and intensifying Reformation emphases such as the importance of prayer, piety, and the illumination of the Spirit for understanding Scripture in contrast to the Scholastic trajectory that had developed in post-Reformation orthodoxy. *Philipp Jakob Spener* (1635–1705) sought to remedy the persistent lack of biblical literacy among the laity by organizing structures promoting Bible reading and study. While the goal was familiarity with all of Scripture, special focus was given to NT Epistles as the core of instruction for the Christian life. Spener's program of reform is set forth in his influential work *Pia desideria* (1675), which also includes a futurist expectation of the fulfillment of prophecies in both the OT and the NT Apocalypse. *August Hermann Francke* (1663–1727), professor of oriental languages and then of theology at the University of Halle, continued the work of Spener. He offers a detailed analysis of the hermeneutical task involving the "husk" and the "kernel" of Scripture—the former having to do with the letter while the latter concerned the true or proper literal sense. This was an analytical development of Luther's double literal sense. Analyzing the "husk" meant addressing the historical, grammatical, and structural/thematic sense of the text. But the "kernel" could be grasped only by a regenerate mind under the illumination of the Holy Spirit. This true or proper literal sense joins the words' meaning with their theological coherence in relation to Christ, and joins practical implication and application to the life of the believer. *Johann Jakob Rambach* (1693–1735) gave further clarity to this method and is recognized for clearly distinguishing the place of application in the process of hermeneutical understanding.

Pietism took a different turn in the work of *Johann Jakob Schütz* (1640–90) and *Gottfried Arnold* (1666–1714), separating from the state-recognized church to form independent congregations. These radical Pietists were chiliasts, who, while stressing the literal sense as the husk of Scripture, emphasized a mystical affective union with Christ as the kernel.

Pietism made a major contribution in the area of textual criticism. Franke's successor at Halle, *Johann Heinrich Michaelis* (1668–1738), prepared the first critical text of the Hebrew Bible, the *Biblia Hebraica*, along with a three-volume philological commentary, entitled *Adnotations*, in 1720. *Johann Albrecht Bengel* (1687–1752), inspired by Michaelis, produced a critical text of the NT, the *Novum Testamentum Graecum*, with a critical apparatus, in 1734. Bengel was the first to group manuscripts into families and is regarded by many as the father of modern textual criticism. He also published an accompanying commentary, the *Gnomon Novi Testamenti*, in 1742, together with a new Latin translation. Bengel's work was used with appreciation for generations. For his own hermeneutical approach, Bengel was an idiosyncratic chiliast, whose major concern was tracing the chronological structure of the biblical narrative, affixing dates to the creation of the world and the future coming of Christ.

A different direction in post-Reformation hermeneutics was pursued by *Hugo Grotius* (1583–1645). Essentially, Grotius sought to interpret the literal sense of Scripture with special interest in its historical context (understood as the narrative historical context) but without concern for the typological-christological or mystical aspect of the literal sense. Grotius was a highly recognized legal scholar of humanist training who also excelled in philological and textual work. He was the first to bring the Codex Alexandrinus into text-critical study and was well read in classical, patristic, and rabbinic sources. He wrote commentaries on Scripture which were widely used and appreciated for the wealth of information and depth of insight elucidating the meaning and significance of the biblical text, with lengthy discussions of exegetical problems and development of biblical themes. Grotius's historical-contextual exegesis is markedly different from the acontextual, ahistorical rationalist deductive proof-texting approach to Scripture in much of post-Reformation orthodoxy. It also differs from the devotional and even mystical interpretation of Pietists. Grotius was a forerunner of the later field of biblical criticism, although he himself still upheld the authority of Scripture and accepted biblical narrative in a manner that would later be dismissed as naively precritical.

Enlightenment and Early Modern

The fracturing of Western Christianity through attempts to reform it became a convenient excuse for political realignment that plunged Europe into the Thirty Years War (1618–48). The aftermath saw a religious, philosophical, scientific, and political reaction against the classical claims of Christianity, including its view of the Bible.

In England, one aspect of this reaction can be traced to *Herbert of Cherbury* (1582–1648), whose call for a philosophical religion embracing a simple monotheism and morality was answered by a succession of influential writings shaping the religious-philosophical movement known as Deism. This movement criticized the idea of miracles in general and especially religious claims of miracles, including those reported in the Bible. Such reports had to be critically rejected or reinterpreted in a nonsupernatural manner.

The most significant critique of establishment Christianity, however, came from the Dutch-Jewish philosopher *Baruch Spinoza* (1632–77), who published his *Tractatus Theologico-Politicus* in 1670. Spinoza not only rejected miracle reports but also drew attention to compositional, redactional, and transcriptional features that revealed human authorial activity in a manner that had mostly been ignored or had been used as occasions to seek a spiritual meaning. Spinoza questioned many traditional attributions of authorship for the biblical books, including the Mosaic authorship of the Pentateuch. The ideas of divine inspiration and spiritual illumination were rejected, and Spinoza pressed for interpreting Scripture in a natural manner as one would any other book. Under this perspective, the historical-contextual interpretation of Scripture developed by Grotius was now critical of Scripture's narrative framework.

In Germany, *Herman Samuel Reimarus* (1694–1768) was convinced by the writings of the English Deists of a religion of reason and universal morality, and he was persuaded that such was the true teaching of Jesus Christ. Reimarus criticized reports of miracles in both the OT and the NT. Even the report of the resurrection of Jesus had to be rejected as historically impossible. Reimarus tried to separate a "true," rationalist Jesus from the NT accounts, which came from his disciples and were false interpretations of him. The NT interpretations of OT prophecies as messianic prophecies fulfilled in Jesus had to be rejected as allegories. Literal interpretation needed to refer them to the historical context of the OT prophet, not the future context of the NT. Likewise, Jesus also should be interpreted in his first-century Roman political context.

Reimarus did not publish his views during his lifetime. They were discovered by *Gotthold Ephraim Lessing* (1729–81) in the Wolffenbüttel library and published by him in installments beginning in 1771. Lessing offered a theoretical defense not only of Reimarus but of the Enlightenment itself as the progressive dawn of reason in the mind of primitive and superstitious humanity. As reason became clear, primitive ideas would be overcome. When reading primitive literature, like the Bible, one needed to discern the light of the eternal truths of reason through the particular historical expressions that attempted to convey but necessarily clouded them. One needed, in the language of Paul, to distinguish the spirit from the letter (2 Cor. 3:6) with reason being the true referent of "spirit." In 1793/94, *Immanuel Kant* (1724–1804) would defend such a move as an enlightened form of allegorical interpretation.

The rationalist criticism of the contents of Scripture conditioned many late-eighteenth-century contributions important for the direction of biblical studies. For example, *Johann Philipp Gabler* (1753–1826) famously distinguished biblical theology as a distinct discipline from dogmatic theology. Biblical theology would be developed in different ways in subsequent decades, but Gabler's view of it involved de-particularizing biblical ideas so as to distill their supposed pure, general (rational), conceptual form. *Johann Salomo Semler* (1725–91) helped launch the modern study of the canon with his *Treatise on the Free Investigation of the Canon* (1771–75). Semler demonstrated historically a fluidity in the canonical boundaries for Jews and early Christians. His purpose was to encourage Christians of his day to be open to sources of enlightenment beyond the traditional canonical boundaries of their own church confessions.

As the eighteenth century closed, *Johann David Michaelis* (1717–91) and *Johann Gottfried Eichhorn* (1752–1827) published respectively an *Introduction to the New Testament* (1750) and an *Introduction to the Old Testament* (1780–83), addressing authorship, date, historical background, and other issues that were judged to be preliminary to the grammatical study of the text. They are both important for emphasizing the historical condition of the contents of the biblical books, including their themes, ideas, and concepts. The titles of their works have come to define subfields of biblical scholarship.

Around the same time, *Johann August Ernesti* (1707–81) first published his influential hermeneutical textbook *Institutio interpretis Novi Testamenti* (1761), which was translated into English in 1827 (US) and 1832/33 (UK) under the titles *Elements of Interpretation* and *Principles of Biblical Interpretation*, respectively. This can be seen as a modest, conservative adaptation of the rationalist disposition against mysticism and the proof-texting methods of scholasticism. Ernesti was a classical scholar and eminent philologist who clearly and cogently defended the propriety of literal interpretation, focusing on the meaning of the words of the text in their historical contexts and in accordance with authorial usage and style. Ernesti was concerned not with making ancient texts relevant (in contrast to the patristic concern expressed at the beginning of this survey) but with establishing the true meaning of their words. Spiritual interpretation, in Ernesti's view, was a lazy neglect of the hard work of historical-grammatical interpretation. Neither did he have any patience for the historical-prophetic reading of biblical narrative and chronology.

Conclusion

This survey has traced Christian interpretation of the Bible from the fourth century to the eighteenth, from Eusebius, who valued Origen's legacy of spiritual interpretation, to Ernesti, who rejected it. Both men contributed to the philological and textual study of Scripture as understood in their day as they sought to expound Scripture's literal sense. The eighteenth century ended with the political revolution in France and the philosophical revolution of Immanuel Kant. Both would have an impact on biblical interpretation as a new century began.

See also other History of Interpretation articles

Bibliography. Augustine, *On Christian Doctrine*, trans. D. W. Robertson Jr. (Prentice Hall, 1958); Chau, W.-S., *The Letter and the Spirit* (Lang, 1995); Coggins, R. J., and J. L. Houlden, eds., *A Dictionary of Biblical Interpretation* (SCM, 1990); Ernest, J. D., *The Bible in Athanasius of Alexandria* (Brill, 2004); Evans, G. R., *The Language and Logic of the Bible* (Cambridge University Press, 1984); Fredriksen, P., "Tyconius," in *Augustine through the Ages*, ed. A. D. Fitzgerald (Eerdmans, 1999); Hobbs, R. G., "Pluriformity of Early Reformation Scriptural Interpretation," in *HBOT*, 2:452–511; Kannengiesser, C., ed., *Handbook of Patristic Exegesis*, 2 vols. (Brill, 2004); Kannengiesser, *Holy Scripture and Hellenistic Hermeneutics in Alexandrian Christology* (Center for Hermeneutical Studies, 1982); Krey, P. D. W., and Lesley Smith, eds., *Nicholas of Lyra* (Brill, 2000); Levy, I. C., *Introducing Medieval Biblical Interpretation* (Baker Academic, 2018); McKim, D. K., ed., *Dictionary of Major Biblical Interpreters* (InterVarsity, 2007); Murray, I. H., *The Puritan Hope* (Banner of Truth Trust, 1971); Opitz, P., "The Exegetical and Hermeneutical Work of John Oecolampadius, Huldrych Zwingli and John Calvin," in *HBOT*, 2:407–51; Origen, *On First Principles*, trans. G. W. Butterworth (Peter Smith, 1973); Quasten, J., *The Golden Age of Greek Patristic Literature from the Council of Nicea to the Council of Chalcedon*, vol. 3 of *Patrology* (Spectrum Publishers, 1960); Reventlow, H. G., *History of Biblical Interpretation*, trans. L. G. Perdue and J. O. Duke, 4 vols. (Society of Biblical Literature, 2009–10); Runia, D. T., *Philo in Early Christian Literature* (Fortress, 1993); Smalley, B., *The Study of the Bible in the Middle Ages* (University of Notre Dame Press, 1964); Tyconius, *The Book of Rules*, trans. W. S. Babcock (Scholars Press, 1989); Young, F., "Traditions of Exegesis," in *NCHB*, 1:734–51.

CRAIG BLAISING

History of Interpretation: 1800 to Present

"In the past God spoke to our ancestors through the prophets at many times and in various ways, but in these last days he has spoken to us by his Son" (Heb. 1:1–2). *How do the OT and NT relate to each other?* Over the past two hundred years, exegetes and theologians have answered this question at many times and in various ways. The different approaches are dizzying, and it is impossible to comprehensively describe and evaluate them in a short essay. This essay surveys the various approaches by concisely highlighting twelve of them that have been influential. The format is to explain a view and then reply to it.

1. The OT and NT Collect Religious Writings That Are Contradictory and Not Coherent

Position. The OT contradicts itself; the NT contradicts itself; and the OT and NT contradict each other. Thus, the OT and NT are not a consistent, unified whole but collections of religious writings that are contradictory and not coherent.

This position flows out of Enlightenment rationalism, according to which the basis of what we think and do is autonomous reason—not our sense experience or religious beliefs based on authoritative revelation. This approach interprets the Bible as an evolved collection of fallible human documents—a method that Baruch Spinoza (1632–77) helped mainstream (cf. Gignilliat, 15–36).

This was the context in 1787 when J. P. Gabler argued that dogmatic theology was insufficiently sensitive to the text of Scripture and that scholars should study the whole Bible free from the constraints of dogmatic theology. The trend in academic biblical studies in the 1800s was to view the Bible as diverse and disunified. G. L. Bauer helped lead this shift to atomize biblical studies when he published his OT theology (1796) and NT theology (1800–1802) *separately*. Once it became common for scholars to be experts in only the OT or only the NT, an increased narrowing followed, from experts in the NT to experts in Luke's writings to experts in Luke's Gospel to experts in Q studies. "From around 1870, for approximately a century, 'biblical theology,' in the sense of the writing of works on the theology of OT and NT together, to all intents and purposes ceased to exist" (Scobie, 18).

Enlightenment rationalism influenced biblical studies to use a naturalistic version of historical criticism. Historical criticism studies the human aspects of a text—the sort of topics an introduction to a biblical commentary addresses (who wrote the book; where, when, to whom, and why he wrote it; its genre and textual history). The Tübingen school—influential NT scholars in Germany led by F. C. Baur (1792–1860)—led the charge to approach the Bible as a fallible historical document. Baur sharply distinguished Peter and Paul, and he viewed NT Christianity as part of a massive first- and second-century whole in which the NT was a later reaction to actual Christianity and its supposed "heresies" like Gnosticism.

This approach developed into the history-of-religions school—historical criticism that presupposed that religious movements and documents influence one another apart from any supernatural causes. This framework once again changed how scholars studied the OT (e.g., W. M. L. de Wette, 1780–1849) and the NT (e.g., W. Wrede, 1859–1906): a so-called OT theology or NT theology is impossible; instead one should study the *history* of religious movements rather than study select literature from documents that we call the OT and NT. Scholars who pushed back against this rationalistic approach include J. C. K. von Hofmann, Adolf Schlatter, Leonhard Goppelt, and Oscar Cullman (cf. Carson, "Theology," 796–99; Scobie, 9–28; Yarbrough). (For a summary of biblical interpretation from 1800 to 1975, see Bray, 221–460.)

Response. This rationalist approach rejects historic Christian orthodoxy, particularly regarding the doctrines of Scripture and providence. (1) Regarding Scripture, is the Bible God-breathed (inspired), entirely true and thus without error (inerrant), incapable of error (infallible), and our final authority (*sola Scriptura*)? If so, then the entire Bible coheres and does not contradict itself (see Feinberg, 31–425). (2) Regarding providence, does God sovereignly work out his plan in human history? If so, then God has brilliantly planned and superintended the persons, events, and institutions in the OT and NT (see Carson, "Providence"). "We sometimes need reminding that the NT authors would not have understood the OT in terms of any of the dominant historical-critical orthodoxies of the last century and a half" (Beale and Carson, xxviii; in reply to Baur, see Hartog).

2. The OT Is Inferior to the NT

Position. The OT is lower in status and quality than the NT. This conclusion was common among those who thought the OT and NT contradict each other (see approach 1 above). Gerald Bray explains, "The older view that the two Testaments were one was gradually abandoned, as ideas of progress in religion became common. By 1900 only the most conservative theologians still held it, and they had mostly opted out of the critical enterprise. The Old Testament was seen by almost everyone as an earlier stage of religious development, superseded by the teachings of Christ" (Bray, 300).

Friedrich Schleiermacher (1768–1834), a leading proponent of theological liberalism, demoted the OT as inferior to the NT but still part of Scripture. In his doctrine of Scripture, he mentions the OT only briefly in this postscript: "The Old Testament Scriptures owe their place in our Bible partly to the appeals the New Testament Scriptures make to them, partly to the historical connexion of Christian worship with the Jewish Synagogue; but the Old Testament Scriptures do not on that account share the normative dignity or the inspiration of the New" (Schleiermacher, 608).

Adolf von Harnack (1851–1930), also a leading proponent of theological liberalism, rejected the OT as part of the Christian canon for today (cf. Goppelt, 3–4). This approach is basically a rationalist version of Marcion, the most influential heretic in the second century. One section of Harnack's book on Marcion has this thesis: "The rejection of the Old Testament in the second century was a mistake which the great church rightly avoided; to maintain it in the sixteenth century was a fate from which the Reformation was not yet able to escape; but still to preserve it in Protestantism as a canonical document since the nineteenth century is the consequence of a religious and ecclesiastical crippling" (Harnack, 134).

Response. The early church and Reformers rightly recognized both the OT and NT as canonical—as equally Christian Scripture (see Feinberg, 429–564; Meade and Gurry, 107–66).

3. The OT Has Meaning according to Historical-Critical Methods and according to Scripture's Final Canonical Form

Position. Bible interpreters should embrace both a historical-critical method and a canonical approach. Brevard Childs (1923–2007) epitomizes this unusual combination, which simultaneously embraces aspects of Enlightenment rationalism and presupposes the church-recognized canon. Childs bucked the trend of atomizing OT and NT studies by interpreting Scripture as a canonical whole with a unified, coherent message (Childs, 70–79). Although he employed the tools of historical criticism, he ultimately jettisoned historical questions and asked broader theological questions about *the literary narrative as a whole* irrespective of whether the events actually happened in history as the text records.

Response. Childs's canonical reading does not depend on whether the text reports accurately about people and events in real history. He treats the canon as a narrative whole—a final form we must not tamper with—and reduces historical criticism to busywork that does not affect the theological canonical reading (cf. Carson, "Theology," 804, 807). Thus, Al Wolters concludes, "Childs has essentially accepted the claims of mainline historical criticism to be wearing the mantle of value-free scientific objectivity and autonomous rationality and has accommodated this to a dualistic Christian construal of the relationship of nature and grace. By failing to challenge, either philosophically or religiously, the ideological nature of aggressively secular biblical criticism, he has set himself the difficult—I would argue: ultimately impossible—task of defending orthodox Christian theology while in principle conceding its historical basis to biblical criticism" (Wolters, 191–92; cf. Noble).

4. It Is Impossible to Objectively Interpret the OT and NT

Position. We cannot objectively interpret Scripture because meaning and interpretation are subjective. A text does not have a "correct" meaning for us to discover; what determines the meaning is what we presuppose (e.g., Hanson, 13). Forms of postmodernism question whether interpreters can transcend their own context and determine a text's meaning (cf. Beale, *Handbook*, 11–12).

Response. What we presuppose does indeed play a critical role in how we read and apply Scripture, and our faith (not pure unaided reason) at least partly accounts for what we presuppose. But it is ultimately nonsensical and disastrous to the Christian faith to deny that interpreters can know the true meaning of the biblical text; we can never know fully like God knows, but we can know truly even if that knowledge is partial (see Carson, *Gagging*; Vanhoozer). Whether an interpreter thinks the NT validly uses the OT depends significantly on whether one accepts what the NT authors presuppose. (This section condenses and updates Moo and Naselli, 713.)

5. NT Authors Interpret the OT out of Context as a Power Move to Persuade Readers to Submit

Position. The primary concern of NT authors like Paul when they use the OT is not to interpret it in its literary context but to use it rhetorically in a way that persuades readers to obey them. In other words, they are not concerned mainly with what OT authors originally meant but instead with using the OT as a power move to induce their audience to submit (e.g., Stanley, *Arguing*).

At least two arguments support this view of Paul's letters: (1) Most of Paul's audience could not read Greek or Hebrew. (2) Most of Paul's audience were recently converted gentiles who could not appreciate the literary and theological significance of OT quotations and allusions.

Response. In reply to the first argument, one did not need to be able to read Greek or Hebrew to understand Scripture since when the church gathered, someone would read Scripture aloud (cf. Col. 4:16; Rev. 1:3). (See the article "Literacy in the Greco-Roman World" elsewhere in the dictionary.)

In reply to the second argument, that is true, but at least four factors mitigate it: (1) Some of the audience were Jewish Christians who understood and appreciated the OT references. (2) Some of the gentiles in the audience were familiar with the Jewish synagogue and the OT. (3) Local churches read and reread Scripture aloud as well as taught and preached Scripture, so new believers would increasingly understand OT connections. A text means what the text's author meant to communicate through his written words; what a reader can understand does not determine what a text means. (4) Many ancient common people who were illiterate were orally and culturally literate. That is, they listened to great works of the ancient world and even memorized some passages. They could do the same with Scripture. (This section condenses and updates Beale, *Handbook*, 9–11, with permission.)

6. NT Authors Take Their OT Quotations from Proof Texts Compiled to Argue That Jesus Is the Messiah

Position. NT authors presupposed that the crucified and resurrected Jesus is the Messiah and then chose OT quotations from a list that Christians had compiled for apologetic purposes. They used those OT quotations outside of their literary contexts.

This view has two variations: (1) The source of the OT passages that the NT cites is a testimony book, which collects proof texts (*testimonia*) to strengthen Christian apologetics (see Harris). (2) The source of the OT passages that the NT cites is not a single testimony book but various excerpts of OT passages that early Christians circulated: "The investigator should approach the Pauline materials with the working assumption that Paul drew his quotations directly from written sources (i.e., a collection of passages excerpted from biblical scrolls) and not from memory, unless the evidence indicates a different practice in a particular situation" (Stanley, *Paul*, 79).

Response. (1) Lists of OT quotations likely existed, but it does not follow that the NT authors quoted the OT out of context. The NT authors—especially Paul, a former Pharisee—had marinated in the OT by memorizing it, hearing it read, and reading it in scrolls they could access (see Lincicum). (2) This view considers only explicit quotations, but the NT alludes to the OT thousands of times (see the article "Quotation, Allusion, and Echo" elsewhere in the dictionary). (This section condenses and updates Beale, *Handbook*, 6–7, with permission.)

7. NT Authors Ransack and Distort the OT to Argue That Jesus Is the Messiah

Position. After the NT authors believed that the crucified and resurrected Jesus is the Messiah, they hurriedly searched the OT for proof and then used OT proof texts in an eisegetical manner. They twisted OT passages out of their literary contexts—sometimes by deliberately altering the text itself—to answer Jewish objections to Jesus being the Messiah (Lindars, 17–31, 283–86). For example, "the work of Jesus, as remembered and interpreted by the Church, itself became the definition of Messiah's function" (Lindars, 153), so the NT authors read passages like Isa. 53 in light of their conviction that Jesus is the Messiah (Lindars, 75–88, 135, 153–54, 234–37, 248, 252–53, 257–58). Similarly, the early church needed to come up with an explanation for Judas Iscariot's apostasy to vindicate Jesus for choosing him, so they searched the OT for an explanation and altered the meaning of Pss. 41 and 109 and Zech. 11 (Lindars, 98–99, 109–10, 116–22, 263).

Response. In reply, what falsifies this view is demonstrating that NT authors consistently interpreted the OT in its literary context. (See the third reply to approach 8; approaches 9, 11, and 12; and the article "Contextual and Noncontextual NT Use of the OT" elsewhere in the dictionary.)

8. NT Authors Interpret the OT with Exegetical Methods Common in Second Temple Judaism to Argue That Jesus Is the Messiah

Position. NT authors interpreted the OT with Jewish methods of interpretation that were popular at the time with the goal of proving that Jesus is the Messiah. Some describe these methods as "midrash" (particularly for mainstream rabbinic Judaism) or "pesher" (particularly for the Dead Sea Scrolls). (See the articles elsewhere in the dictionary on the Dead Sea Scrolls; on the Mishnah, Talmud, and Midrashim; and on the targums; cf. the articles on the Apocrypha, on Philo, and on the Pseudepigrapha.) Such interpretive methods are generally unconvincing to modern interpreters, but they were convincing to people in the first century (Longenecker). Peter Enns (103–55) argues that evaluating whether the NT validly uses the OT depends solely on ancient standards—even if from our perspective NT authors distort OT passages by wrongly reading Christ into them.

Response. (1) Lists of interpretational rules (middot) such as the seven attributed to Rabbi Hillel or the thirteen to Rabbi Ishmael did not *govern* how NT authors interpret the OT. To the contrary, NT authors and other post-OT Jewish authors share the interpretive tendencies of OT authors. Gary Schnittjer (860–61) explains,

> All of the so-called Judaic interpretive techniques are nothing more than observations of commonplace exegetical tendencies within Israel's Scriptures. Since these interpretive tendencies are not unusual but widely disseminated in the Hebrew Scriptures it is not clear why the authors of the New Testament would need to consult proto-rabbinic exegetical scholarship or vice versa. It seems entirely natural that those who studied the Hebrew Bible, like the authors of the New Testament and the Judaic scholars of late antiquity, could independently and coincidentally emulate the sorts of interpretive interventions found within Israel's Scriptures. Claims of dependence on something other than Israel's Scriptures for exegetical phenomena pervasive within Israel's Scriptures need to provide evidence of this dependence—as well as explaining why extravagant explanations of dependence are necessary for ordinary interpretive maneuvers.

(2) It is helpful to distinguish an interpretational method from what an author presupposes while employing that method. The method of applying an OT text to a new situation (e.g., identifying a person or event in the OT with a later one, connecting several OT passages, or modifying an OT text) is a surface-level issue; the crucial under-the-surface issue is what an author presupposes about Scripture and salvation history. NT authors presuppose that the OT is God-breathed, that God has sovereignly worked out his saving plan in human history, and that Jesus the Messiah fulfills the OT (see Moo and Naselli, 716–17; cf. Beale, *Handbook*, 95–102).

(3) NT authors interpret the OT contextually (see Beale, *Handbook*, 1–5; cf. 103–32). A significant hermeneutical difference between non-Christian Jewish exegetes and NT authors is that non-Christian Jews elevated the law as the interpretational grid when they read the OT while NT authors read the OT in its historical sequence (e.g., Rom. 4; Gal. 3; Heb. 3:7–4:13; 7:1–28; see Carson, "Fulfillment," 410–12; Carson, "Three More," 40–42).

Carson explains why Enns's view is implausible:

> Enns is more respectful [than Lindars], but it is difficult to see how his position differs substantively from that of Lindars, except that he wants to validate these various approaches to the Old Testament partly on the ground that the hermeneutics involved were already in use (we might call this the "Hey, everybody's doing it" defense), and partly on the ground that he himself accepts, as a "gift of faith," that Jesus really is the Messiah. This really will not do. The New Testament writers, for all that they understand that acceptance of who Jesus is comes as a gift of the Spirit (1 Cor. 2:14), never stint at giving *reasons* for the hope that lies within them, *including reasons for reading the Bible as they do.* The "fulfillment" terminology they deploy is too rich and varied to allow us to imagine that they are merely reading in what is in fact not there. [1] They would be the first to admit that *in their own psychological history* the recognition of Jesus came before their understanding of the Old Testament; but they would see this as evidence of moral blindness. [2] As a result, they would be the first to insist, with their transformed hermeneutic (not least the reading of the sacred texts in salvation-historical sequence), that *the Scriptures themselves can be shown to anticipate a suffering Servant-King, a Priest-King, a new High Priest,* and so forth. In other words, Enns develops the first point but disavows the second. The result is that he fails to see how Christian belief is *genuinely* warranted by Scripture. (Carson, "Three More," 44–45; cf. Beale, *Erosion,* 85–122)

9. NT Authors Often Implicitly Include the Larger OT Literary Context When They Quote the OT

Position. NT quotations of the OT are not isolated proof texts from so-called testimony books but the result of responsible exegesis. C. H. Dodd argued for this hermeneutical warrant in 1952:

> The method included, first, the *selection* of certain large sections of the Old Testament scriptures, especially from Isaiah, Jeremiah and certain minor prophets, and from the Psalms. These sections were understood as *wholes,* and particular verses or sentences were quoted from them rather as pointers to the whole context than as constituting testimonies in and for themselves. At the same time, detached sentences from other parts of the Old Testament could be adduced to illustrate or elucidate the meaning of the main section under consideration. But in the fundamental passages it is *total context* that is in view, and is the basis of the argument. (Dodd, 126; cf. Baird, 3:44)

Richard Hays argues for a more complex approach that he labels "intertextuality—the imbedding of fragments of an earlier text within a later one" (Hays, 14). When NT authors explicitly quote an OT passage, the quotation is the tip of an iceberg with far-ranging intertextual relationships. Hays agrees with but goes beyond Dodd by perceiving "echoes" that NT quotations and allusions awaken (e.g., Isa. 52:5 in Rom. 2:24; Hays, 45–46). Over the past few decades, scholars have shifted from focusing on the roughly 350 OT quotations in the NT to mapping the interplay between OT quotations, allusions, and conceptual parallels. (See the article "Quotation, Allusion, and Echo" elsewhere in the dictionary.)

Response. Dodd's argument is persuasive, but a challenge for Hays's approach is convincingly identifying and proving specific echoes (see Moo and Naselli, 723–25; cf. Beale, *Handbook,* 29–40; Emadi, "Intertextuality").

10. NT Authors Usually Interpret the OT in Its Literary Context but Occasionally with Inspired (and Unrepeatable) Subjectivity; OT Passages Have a Single Meaning Identical to What OT Authors Consciously Intended

Position. NT authors used the OT in two ways: either in accord with the OT passage's single, grammatical-historical meaning or not. Most uses reflect the single meaning that the OT author consciously intended. In the relatively few cases in which NT authors do not interpret OT passages in their literary contexts, NT authors subjectively apply OT passages "to situations *entirely different* from what was envisioned in corresponding OT contexts. They *disregarded* the main thrust of the grammatical-historical meanings of the OT passages and applied those passages in different ways to suit the different points they were putting across" (Thomas, 83 [italics added]). NT authors do this with a hermeneutic that we cannot reproduce (e.g., Matt. 2:15 and Hosea 11:1; Rom. 10:20 and Isa. 65:1). Why is it permissible for NT authors to interpret the OT noncontextually but not permissible for us to interpret the OT that way? "The NT writers could assign such new meanings authoritatively because of the inspiration of what they wrote" (Thomas, 87).

Response. (1) This view does not adequately explain why NT authors would appeal to the OT for support if such an appeal was not based on a demonstrable connection. If Christianity is right that Jesus the Messiah fulfills the OT (contra modern Judaism), then it is difficult to validate Christianity's claim apart from demonstrating that the NT consistently respects the OT literary context (cf. Moo and Naselli, 712–13). (2) NT authors do not get a free pass for bizarre interpretations (even if they used Jewish methods of interpretation that were popular at the time) simply because what they wrote is God-breathed. They model how to interpret any part of the Bible in light of the whole (contra Longenecker, xxxiv–xxxix; see approach 12 below).

11. NT Authors Consistently Interpret OT Passages in Their Literary Contexts, and OT Passages Have a Single Meaning Identical to What OT Authors Consciously Intended

Position. NT authors do not find additional or expanded meanings in OT passages but instead interpret OT passages in accord with their single meaning. This is the case when NT authors apply OT passages or draw out what OT passages imply. *Meaning* is what an OT author consciously intended to communicate through his written words, and *significance* includes implications or unintended consequences that are consistent with the meaning. An axiom of this approach is that NT authors may not find more or different *meaning* in OT passages than what OT human authors consciously intended, but NT authors may identify *significance* in OT passages that OT authors did not consciously intend (see Kaiser; Chou; Vlach).

Response. This view commendably argues that NT authors consistently interpret the OT in its literary and theological context, so there is considerable overlap between this approach and the next one below. But must the meaning of an OT passage be identical with what its human author consciously intended? Sometimes NT authors seem to attribute to OT passages more meaning than OT authors consciously intended. For example, King David writes in Ps. 2:7 that the Lord says to the king of Israel at his coronation, "You are my son; today I have become your father." The NT cites Ps. 2:7 as the warrant for three conclusions that do not seem identical with what David consciously intended: (1) Jesus is that "son," and "today" is the day Jesus rose from the dead (Acts 13:32–33); (2) Jesus is better than angels (Heb. 1:5); and (3) the Father appointed Christ to serve as the great high priest (Heb. 5:4–5). (Cf. Moo and Naselli, 719–22.)

12. NT Authors Consistently Interpret OT Passages in Their Literary Contexts, and OT Passages May Have an Expanded Meaning That the Divine Author Intended but That the Human Author Did Not Consciously Intend

This approach builds on the view that NT authors often implicitly include the larger OT literary context when they quote the OT (approach 9), and it has a lot in common with the previous view (approach 11). Three related components distinguish this approach from the previous one: (1) the "what" is an expanded meaning; (2) the "why" is a canonical approach; and (3) the "how" is typology. Scholars who basically align with this approach include Patrick Fairbairn, Geerhardus Vos, Leonhard Goppelt, Graeme Goldsworthy, Douglas Moo, Stephen Wellum, James Hamilton, Jason DeRouchie, and the four editors of this volume.

An expanded meaning. An OT passage may have an expanded meaning that its human author did not consciously intend but that the passage's divine author did intend. It is that divine intention that NT authors occasionally refer to when they discern an expanded meaning in an OT passage. "Expanded meaning" means not that an OT passage's meaning *changes* but that in retrospect one may recognize an expanded meaning that the OT human author did not consciously intend but that the divine author intended from the beginning.

An aspect of this concept is *sensus plenior* (i.e., fuller sense). The classic definition of *sensus plenior* is "that additional deeper meaning, intended by God but not clearly intended by the human author, which is seen to exist in the words of a biblical text (or group of texts, or even a whole book) when they are studied in the light of further revelation or development in the understanding of revelation" (Brown, 92). For Raymond Brown and other Roman Catholics, the basis for validating *sensus plenior* is "development in the understanding of revelation," which includes the magisterium; thus, *sensus plenior* is a way to justify concepts with poor scriptural support such as Mariology. Protestants confine the basis for validating *sensus plenior* to further revelation in the NT.

There are three common objections to *sensus plenior:* (1) It is easily abused. (2) It undermines the NT's apologetic arguments. (3) It contradicts inspiration.

In reply, (1) The misuse of a concept does not automatically invalidate it. (2) What an interpreter presupposes about Scripture, providence, and Jesus is more decisive than one's interpretational method. Also, the NT uses the OT not solely to evangelize but also to inform and assure Christians. (3) The doctrine of inspiration allows that God may intend more than (but never less than) what the OT human author intended. "The Chicago Statement on Biblical Hermeneutics" puts it this way: "The single meaning of a prophet's words includes, but is not restricted to, the understanding of those words by the prophet and necessarily involves the intention of God evidenced in the fulfillment of those words" (art. 18; cf. Compton). The progress from an OT passage to a NT passage (like "Out of Egypt I called my son" in Hosea 11:1 and Matt. 2:15) is like an acorn developing into an oak tree (i.e., an organic connection of continuity and progression), not like an acorn developing into a grapevine (i.e., no organic connection). (Cf. Beale, "Hosea"; Plummer.)

Expanded meaning is a viable concept, but it does not specify on what historical and theological basis NT authors discern expanded meanings in some OT passages. What gives it explanatory power is a canonical approach and typology.

A canonical approach. The basis of recognizing an expanded meaning that the divine author intended but that the OT human author did not consciously intend is a canonical approach. A canonical approach views the whole Bible as the ultimate literary context for interpreting an OT passage. The whole canon has unity because it has a single divine author. OT authors may have suspected what they wrote to be pregnant with meanings they did not comprehend, but even if they did not have such an inkling, OT authors would not object to how NT authors use the OT. That is, Hosea would not have objected, "What in the world is Matthew doing with 'Out of Egypt I called my son'? I was referring to the Israelites, not Jesus. Matthew twisted my words out of context" (e.g., McCasland, 144). The divine author does not intend a meaning *contrary to* what the OT human authors intended to communicate through their words; God may intend more but not less than what the human authors intended. A canonical approach builds on the salvation-historical story of the Bible that unfolds through the covenants and climaxes in Jesus fulfilling the OT (Matt. 5:17; 11:13; Rom. 10:4). This approach follows the pattern of how the OT uses the OT (see the article "OT Use of the OT, Comparison to the NT" elsewhere in the dictionary; Schnittjer).

Typology. The means of recognizing an expanded meaning that the divine author intended but that the OT human author did not consciously intend is typology. Typology analyzes how NT persons, events, and institutions (i.e., antitypes) fulfill OT persons, events, and institutions (i.e., types) by repeating the OT situations at a deeper, climactic level in salvation history (cf. Baker, 180). Typology is picture prophecy in which a type *prophesies* an antitype (DeRouchie, 60–62, 185–86, 189; contra Baker, 181; Goldingay, 31, 214). In other words, an antitype *fulfills* a type.

Typology includes at least four elements: analogy, historicity, foreshadowing, and escalation.

Analogy: The type and antitype are analogous. A type (such as King David, the exodus, or the sacrificial system) and its antitype (Jesus) compare to each other in a significant way.

Historicity: The type and antitype occur in real history. Allegory creates a symbolic world that is not necessarily based on actual history, but typology is always based on actual history. The meaning of an allegory depends on an extratextual grid, but the meaning of typology depends on historical events that the text narrates and explains (Carson, "Fulfillment," 404; Beale and Carson, xxvi; see the article "Allegory" elsewhere in the dictionary). For example, Adam is the covenantal head of the original creation, and Christ is the covenantal head of the new creation (Rom. 5:12–21; 1 Cor. 15:21–22, 45–49); Paul's argument that Adam is a type of Christ necessarily implies that Adam really existed as the first human being (see Philpot).

Foreshadowing: God sovereignly designed the type to foreshadow the antitype. The antitype is consistent with what the OT human author of a type intended to communicate. The OT human author may be aware that what he writes is prophetically forward-looking in a predictive sense; that is, he is conscious that what he writes is part of a typological trajectory that will climax in the Messiah. Typology "is always divinely predictive and usually intentionally so on the part of the human author" (DeRouchie, 287; cf. Beale, "Cognitive"; Hamilton).

But sometimes the OT human author may not be conscious of that connection, and one may discern that God-intended typological connection retrospectively with a canonical approach (cf. Beale, *Handbook*, 14–15; Gentry and Wellum, 132; Bock, 261–73; Chase, 59–62). An example of retrospective typology is Paul's use of Isaiah and Job in Rom. 11:34–35 (Naselli, *From Typology*, 117–45). Carson ("Fulfillment," 406) explains,

> When Paul (or, for that matter, some other New Testament writer) claims that something or other connected with the gospel is the (typological) fulfillment of some old covenant pattern, he may not necessarily be claiming that everyone connected with the old covenant type understood the pattern to be pointing forward, but he is certainly claiming that God himself designed it to be pointing forward. In other words *when* the type was *discovered* to be a type (at some point along the trajectory of its repeated pattern? only after its culmination?)—i.e., when it was discovered to be a pattern that pointed to the future—is not determinative for its classification as a type.

So if an OT human author of a type were able to look forward in time and see how a NT author would interpret Jesus in light of what the OT author wrote, the OT author might respond something like this: "That's beautiful! I did not fully understand what everything I wrote implies. I was not fully conscious of how what I wrote was part of a typological trajectory that climaxes in Jesus the Messiah. But now I see that what I wrote is wonderfully consistent with what this NT author wrote. Praise God for masterfully designing it that way!" (cf. Plummer, 57). NT authors presuppose that (1) God ordered OT history to prefigure and anticipate his climactic redemptive acts; (2) the NT records those redemptive acts; and (3) the whole canonical context illuminates what OT passages mean.

Escalation: The antitype escalates the type from shadow to reality by climaxing in Jesus. The antitype surpasses the type (Col. 2:17). Typology shows how the OT points to Jesus (cf. Luke 24:27, 44; John 5:39; 2 Cor. 1:20; Heb. 1:1–3).

Some argue that we can identify a person, event, or institution as a type only if the NT specifically labels it as a type (e.g., Zuck, 175–81, who identifies only seventeen types in Scripture). That approach may seem safe, neat, and tidy, but it is too restrictive. When the author of Hebrews mentions various types related to the tabernacle, he says as an aside, "But we cannot discuss these things in detail now" (Heb. 9:5). That implies that there are typological connections that Scripture does not fully explain.

NT authors "never claimed to have mentioned all Old Testament types. So if Jesus is the most accurate interpreter of the Old Testament who ever lived, and if those who wrote in his name also interpreted and preached the Old Testament the way in which he instructed them, then our interpretation of the Old Testament will be more faithful when it is closest to theirs. If we imitate the biblical authors, we will inevitably identify types that are not in the New Testament" (Chase, 52). One of the joys of interpreting the Bible is to responsibly trace typological connections by following the example of NT authors—types such as the temple, the Noahic flood, the land, and Joseph (see the articles "Temple" and "Land" elsewhere in the dictionary; Yoshikawa; Emadi, *From Prisoner to Prince*; cf. the article "Typology" elsewhere in the dictionary; Beale, *Handbook*, 13–25; Hamilton, 17–28). (Parts of this section condense and update Moo and Naselli, 725–37; Naselli, "How.")

Conclusion

Over the past two hundred years, academics have taken many different approaches to how the OT and NT relate to each other. This essay surveys a dozen of those ways. Some of the approaches are incompatible with an evangelical view of Scripture and providence (especially approaches 1, 2, 4, 5, and 7), and evangelical academics continue to investigate how the NT uses the OT (especially approaches 11 and 12). The editors of this volume hope that its 140-plus essays profitably contribute to the ongoing study of this complex and weighty topic as we constantly remember what the Lord says in Isa. 66:2: "These are the ones I look on with favor: those who are humble and contrite in spirit, and who tremble at my word."

See also other History of Interpretation articles

Bibliography. Baird, W., *History of New Testament Research*, 3 vols. (Fortress, 1992–2013); Baker, D. L., *Two Testaments, One Bible*, 3rd ed. (InterVarsity, 2010); Beale, G. K., "The Cognitive Peripheral Vision of Biblical Authors," *WTJ* 76 (2014): 263–93; Beale, *The Erosion of Inerrancy in Evangelicalism* (Crossway, 2008); Beale, *Handbook on the New Testament Use of the Old Testament* (Baker Academic, 2012); Beale, "The Use of Hosea 11:1 in Matthew 2:15: One More Time," *JETS* 55 (2012): 697–715; Beale, G. K., and D. A. Carson, "Introduction," in *CNTUOT*, xxiii–xxviii; Bock, D. L., "Scripture Citing Scripture," in *Interpreting the New Testament Text*, ed. D. L. Bock and B. M. Fanning (Crossway, 2006), 255–76; Bray, G., *Biblical Interpretation* (InterVarsity, 1996); Brown, R. E., *The* Sensus Plenior *of Sacred Scripture* (St. Mary's University, 1955); Carson, D. A., *The Gagging of God* (Zondervan, 1996); Carson, "Mystery and Fulfillment," in *The Paradoxes of Paul*, vol. 2 of *Justification and Variegated Nomism*, ed. D. A. Carson, P. T. O'Brien, and M. A. Seifrid, WUNT 2/181 (Baker Academic, 2004), 393–436; Carson, "The Mystery of Providence," in *How Long, O Lord?*, 2nd ed. (Baker Academic, 2006), 177–203; Carson, "New Testament Theology," in *DLNTD*, 796–814; Carson, "Three More Books on the Bible," *TJ* 27 (2006): 1–62; Chase, M. L., *40 Questions about Typology and Allegory* (Kregel, 2020); "The Chicago Statement on Biblical Hermeneutics" (International Council on Biblical Inerrancy, 1982); Childs, B. S., *Biblical Theology of the Old and New Testaments* (Fortress, 1993); Chou, A., *The Hermeneutics of the Biblical Writers* (Kregel, 2018); Compton, J. M., "Shared Intentions?," *Them* 33, no. 3 (2008): 23–33; DeRouchie, J. S., "Redemptive-Historical, Christocentric Approach," with responses and rejoinder, in *Five Views of Christ in the Old Testament*, ed. B. J. Tabb and A. M. King, Counterpoints (Zondervan, 2022), 181–211 (also 56–62, 112–17, 163–69, 234–37, 284–89); Dodd, C. H., *According to the Scriptures* (Nisbet, 1952); Emadi, S., *From Prisoner to Prince*, NSBT 59 (InterVarsity, 2022); Emadi, "Intertextuality in New Testament Scholarship," *CurBR* 14 (2015): 8–23; Enns, P., *Inspiration and Incarnation*, 2nd ed. (Baker Academic, 2015); Feinberg, J. S., *Light in a Dark Place*, FET (Crossway, 2018); Gentry, P. J., and S. J. Wellum, *Kingdom through Covenant*, 2nd ed. (Crossway, 2018); Gignilliat, M. S., *A Brief History of Old Testament Criticism* (Zondervan, 2012); Goldingay, J., "First Testament Approach," in *Five Views of Christ in the Old Testament*, ed. B. J. Tabb and A. M. King, Counterpoints (Zondervan, 2022), 21–45 (also 69–71, 101–6, 152–57, 212–16, 266–71); Goppelt, L., *Typos*, trans. D. H. Madvig (Eerdmans, 1982); Hamilton, J. M., Jr., *Typology* (Zondervan, 2022); Hanson, A. T., *The New Testament Interpretation of Scripture* (SPCK, 1980); Harnack, A. von, *Marcion*, trans. J. E. Steely and L. D. Bierma (Labyrinth, 1990); Harris, J. R., *Testimonies*, 2 vols. (Cambridge University Press, 1916–20); Hartog, P. A., ed., *Orthodoxy and Heresy in Early Christian Contexts* (Pickwick, 2015); Hays, R. B., *Echoes of Scripture in the Letters of Paul* (Yale University Press, 1989); Kaiser, W. C., Jr., *The Uses of the Old Testament in the New* (Moody, 1985); Lincicum, D., "Paul and the *Testimonia*," *JETS* 51 (2008): 297–308; Lindars, B., *New Testament Apologetic* (Westminster, 1961); Longenecker, R. N., *Biblical Exegesis in the Apostolic Period*, 2nd ed. (Eerdmans, 1999); McCasland, S. V., "Matthew Twists the Scripture," *JBL* 80 (1961): 143–48; Meade, J. D., and P. J. Gurry, *Scribes and Scripture* (Crossway, 2022); Moo, D. J., and A. D. Naselli, "The Problem of the New Testament's Use of the Old Testament," in *The Enduring Authority of the Christian Scriptures*, ed. D. A. Carson (Eerdmans, 2016), 702–46; Naselli, A. D., *From Typology to Doxology* (Pickwick, 2012); Naselli, "How Should Biblical Theology Approach Typology?," in *40 Questions about Biblical Theology*, by J. S. DeRouchie, O. R. Martin, and A. D. Naselli (Kregel, 2020), 81–88; Noble, P. R., *The Canonical Approach*, BibInt 16 (Brill, 1995); Philpot, J. M., "How Does Scripture Teach the Adam-Christ Typological Connection?," *SBJT* 21, no. 1 (2017): 145–52; Plummer, R. L., "Righteousness and Peace Kiss," *SBJT* 14, no. 2 (2010): 54–61; Schleiermacher, F., *The Christian Faith*, 3rd ed. (Bloomsbury T&T Clark, 2016); Schnittjer, G. E., *Old Testament Use of Old Testament* (Zondervan, 2021); Scobie, C. H. H., *The Ways of Our God* (Eerdmans, 2002); Stanley, C. D., *Arguing with Scripture* (T&T Clark, 2004); Stanley, *Paul and the Language of Scripture*, SNTSMS 69 (Cambridge University Press, 1992); Thomas, R. L., "The New Testament Use of the Old Testament," *TMSJ* 13 (2002): 79–98; Vanhoozer, K. J., *Is There a Meaning in This Text?* (Zondervan, 1998); Vlach, M. J., *The Old in the New* (Kress, 2021); Wolters, A., "Reading the Gospels

Canonically," in *Reading the Gospels Today*, ed. S. E. Porter (Eerdmans, 2004), 172–92; Yarbrough, R. W., *The Salvation Historical Fallacy?*, HBI 2 (Deo, 2004); Yoshikawa, S. T., "The Prototypical Use of the Noahic Flood in the New Testament" (PhD diss., Trinity Evangelical Divinity School, 2004); Zuck, R. B., *Basic Bible Interpretation* (Victor, 1991).

ANDREW DAVID NASELLI

Holiness

Of all the divine attributes mentioned in the Bible, holiness is perhaps the most significant but possibly also the most difficult to comprehend. As the prophet Isaiah records, the seraphim proclaim in God's presence, "Holy, holy, holy is the LORD Almighty" (6:3). Experiencing a similar vision of God, the apostle John observes that the "four living creatures" never stop saying day and night, "Holy, holy, holy is the Lord God Almighty" (Rev. 4:8). Holiness is intimately linked to God, for he alone is innately holy and the ultimate manifestation of holiness (1 Sam. 2:2; cf. Isa. 40:25; Rev. 15:4).

Holy, Clean, and Unclean

To understand the concept of holiness in the Bible, Exodus and Leviticus provide a vital foundation. Holiness gains prominence in these books as they narrate the story of how God, the Holy One, comes to dwell among the Israelites. God's holy presence has profound implications for the Israelites as they live in proximity to him. Whereas Exodus reveals how people, who are not innately holy, are sanctified in order to approach God in safety, Leviticus addresses the issue of how people, who are by nature prone to being unholy, may continue to exist near a holy deity. Together, Exodus and Leviticus establish holiness as a significant theological concept in the Bible.

Four important categories shape the world of the ancient Israelites in Leviticus. God instructs the Levitical priests to "distinguish between the holy and the common, between the unclean and the clean" (10:10). This instruction highlights two boundaries that are to be carefully maintained. The first concerns the distinction between what is holy and what is common. This distinction separates everything that is associated with the tabernacle, where God lives, from everything outside the tabernacle's curtain-enclosed courtyard. God's presence makes the portable sanctuary and everything linked to it holy.

The second boundary, involving clean and unclean, separates the Israelite camp and everything inside it, including the tabernacle, from everything outside the camp. Consequently, the Israelites view themselves in general terms as clean, while all other nations are unclean. This distinction is reinforced on a daily basis by the restriction of the Israelites' diet to "clean" food (Lev. 11; Wenham, "Theology," 6–15).

God's instruction in Lev. 10:10 mentions four categories, creating two boundaries. In reality everything can be classified as holy, clean, or unclean (on the understanding that everything holy was also clean but not everything clean was holy). For this reason, only the concepts of holy, clean, and unclean are mentioned frequently in Leviticus; the Hebrew term *ḥōl* ("common") occurs only in Lev. 10:10. Hebrew words based on the root *qādaš* (e.g., "holy," "holiness," "sanctify") come 152 times in Leviticus, representing about one-fifth of all OT occurrences. The adjectives *ṭāhôr* ("clean") and *ṭāmēʾ* ("unclean") and their associated terms occur 74 and 132 times in Leviticus, respectively, accounting for more than one-third of all occurrences of *ṭāhôr* terminology and more than half of all occurrences of *ṭāmēʾ* terminology in the OT. The frequency with which these terms are mentioned in Leviticus underlines the importance of the categories holy, clean, and unclean.

Differing Degrees of Holiness and Uncleanness

Exodus and Leviticus reveal that within the broad categories of holy, clean, and unclean, further distinctions exist. The portable sanctuary consists of three distinct sections. The tent is divided into two rooms: the most holy place (or holy of holies) and the holy place. God dwells in the most holy place, giving it the highest degree of holiness. Within the most holy place is the ark of the covenant, which functions as the footstool of the divine throne (1 Chron. 28:2; cf. Pss. 99:5; 132:7). A cherubim-decorated curtain separates the most holy place from the holy place. Three golden items—the incense altar, the lampstand, and the table for the bread of the Presence—all stand in the holy place, which has a lower level of holiness than the most holy place. The curtain-enclosed courtyard surrounding the tent is also holy but to a lesser degree. Within the courtyard are located the altar and laver, both made of bronze.

Even the curtains that cover the tent reflect differing degrees of holiness, with the innermost curtain being made of linen, another layer of cloth outside this being made of goat hair, and finally two outer layers being made of animal skins. These materials go from the most holy to the least holy. Maintaining such distinctions may explain the unusual regulation against mixing linen and wool (Deut. 22:11).

The graduated degrees of holiness in the different sections of the portable sanctuary are apparent in other ways. Only the high priest may enter the most holy place; other priests have access to the holy place, and non-priestly Israelites may enter only the courtyard. The most holy place is constructed from the most valuable and most highly crafted materials. Less valuable and less ornate materials are used for the holy place and the courtyard, with clear distinctions being introduced between these two areas (e.g., gold for the holy place, bronze for the courtyard). From a different perspective, Jacob Milgrom (*Studies*, 78–79) observes that differing levels of sin are atoned for in different sections of the sanctuary: "the individual's inadvertent misdemeanors" are purged upon the outer altar; "the inadvertent misdemeanor of the high priest or the entire community" is expiated in the holy place; "wanton, unrepented sin" is atoned for in the holy of holies by the high priest. The greater the sin, the more it encroaches upon the holiness of the tabernacle.

The graduated levels of holiness evidenced in the portable sanctuary are paralleled by different intensities of uncleanness. This is reflected, for example, in the steps necessary to remove uncleanness. The regulations of Leviticus reveal that anyone touching the carcass of an animal remains unclean until the evening, but anyone carrying the carcass must also wash his or her clothes to become ritually clean (11:24–28, 39–40). Differing levels of uncleanness are also evident in the degree to which uncleanness is passed on to other people or objects. Only more serious forms of uncleanness can affect other people or objects. If a man has intercourse with a woman during her monthly period, he becomes unclean for seven days, and he makes unclean any bed on which he lies (15:24). Whoever touches this bed becomes unclean, but only for one day, and their uncleanness does not affect other people or objects (15:27).

Within the Israelite camp that surrounds the tabernacle, a subtle distinction in cleanness exists between the tribe of Levi and all other tribes. As reflected in Num. 3–4, the Levites camp immediately around all four sides of the portable sanctuary and are assigned duties associated with the daily maintenance and transportation of the tabernacle. These duties require them to have a level of cleanness greater than that of other Israelites.

Within this world structured around the categories of holy, clean, and unclean, the Israelites imbibe an understanding of the concept of holiness. The people are reminded about these concepts constantly. They are not merely religious ideas associated with cultic activities; they touch upon the most common activities (e.g., diet; Lev. 11) and the most intimate aspects of life (e.g., sexual relations; Lev. 15:24). No area of human existence is excluded.

For the Israelites, God is the supreme manifestation and sole source of holiness. The more one moves away from God, who dwells in the most holy place, the less holy everything becomes. Whereas holiness is associated with God, uncleanness represents the antithesis of everything holy. Holiness and uncleanness are incompatible. Nothing unclean can come near to God. For this reason, the priests who serve in the tabernacle must be vigilant to remain holy; this applies especially to the high priest. For the Israelites, people, places, objects, and even periods of time could be located on a spectrum based on the tripartite classification of holy, clean, and unclean. This spectrum runs from ultimate holiness to ultimate uncleanness, with the category of clean being in the middle (Jenson).

Since God alone is intrinsically holy, he is the sole source of holiness. His presence sanctifies anything that he touches. This is true for the most holy place within the tabernacle. It is equally true when he descends upon Mount Sinai. Holiness emanates from God, making the mountain holy. Only God can sanctify others. As he reminds the Israelites, "I am the LORD, who makes you holy" (Lev. 20:8; cf. 21:8, 15, 23; 22:9, 16, 32). Holiness is unattainable for humans but for the grace of God.

By observing what distinguishes one level of holiness or uncleanness from another, the Israelites are enabled to form a better understanding of holiness. As people or objects move from uncleanness toward greater holiness, there is an increasing intensity in terms of perfection and purity (Wenham, *Leviticus*, 18–25). The priests who offer sacrifices at the bronze altar must not have any physical deformities (Lev. 21:16–23). Similarly, the animals that are sacrificed at the altar are normally expected to be without defect (Lev. 1:3, 10; 3:1, 6; 4:3, 23, 28, 32; 5:15, 18; 6:6; 9:2–3; 14:10; 22:19–25; 23:12, 18; cf. Exod. 12:5). In line with this emphasis upon perfection, the high priest, as the holiest of priests, must adhere to stricter rules regarding marriage, purity, and contact with corpses. In marked contrast, uncleanness is associated with imperfection. Leviticus 13–15 highlights various reasons for people becoming unclean. One facet of this concerns skin diseases that blemish a person's appearance (Lev. 13:1–46).

In a world where perfection and imperfection are associated with holiness and uncleanness, respectively, it is no surprise that these categories are mapped onto the moral behavior of people. The call to live holy lives requires perfect behavior. Being a holy nation has ethical implications. With good reason, the principal obligations of the Sinai covenant, as revealed by God in the Decalogue (Exod. 20:2–17), are not restricted to the Israelites' relationship with God but include their behavior toward others. When the Ten Commandments are later recorded on stone tablets, they are placed within the ark of the covenant, a further indicator that holiness and morality are closely linked. This relationship is reflected in Lev. 17–19, which sets out the high moral demands that God places upon the Israelites.

The bond between holiness and perfect behavior is conveyed in Ps. 24: "Who may ascend the mountain of the LORD? Who may stand in his holy place? The one who has clean hands and a pure heart, who does not trust in an idol or swear by a false god" (vv. 3–4). Psalm 15 expresses the similar sentiment that only the morally blameless may live on God's holy mountain. The prophet Habakkuk assumes that God's holiness is incompatible with immoral behavior. Adressing God as "my Holy One" (1:12), he remarks, "Your eyes are too pure to look on evil; you cannot tolerate wrongdoing" (1:13).

Life and Death

Another important general pattern emerges within the regulations of Leviticus: holiness is linked to life, but uncleanness is associated with death. This distinction is reflected in the animals that are classified as clean and therefore suitable for eating and those that are designated unclean and unsuitable for consumption (Lev. 11:2–47; cf. Deut. 14:3–20). Whereas all clean animals are herbivores, all mammals classified as unclean have claws and are by nature carnivores (Lev. 11:2–8; cf. Deut. 14:4–8). As predators they bring death to other creatures. The same principle appears to be true as regards the birds that are classified unclean (Lev. 11:13–19; cf. Deut. 20:11–18). Insofar as the Hebrew names of the birds can be identified with particular species, they all appear to be birds of prey.

Uncleanness is also associated with death in other ways. Those who are declared unclean by a priest must wear torn clothes and have unkempt hair, signs that they are in mourning (Lev. 13:45). Touching a human corpse makes a person unclean (Num. 19:11–16). The high priest is not permitted to come close to any corpse, including those of his parents (Lev. 21:11). He is also prohibited from tearing his clothes or having unkempt hair (Lev. 21:10). Other priests are permitted to have contact with those who have died, but only for their closest relatives (Lev. 21:1–4).

In the light of the three categories—holy, clean, and unclean—the Israelites see themselves as living in a world that is predominantly unclean, from which God has rescued them so that they might become a holy nation (Exod. 19:6). However, apart from the priests and select others who have a holy status (e.g., Nazarites; Num. 6:1–21), most of the nation belongs to the category of clean. Yet, the people struggle to maintain even this lower level of perfection and purity. They live in a world where sin and death constantly threaten to defile. People are by nature unclean, especially due to their immoral activity.

In all likelihood these differing aspects of uncleanness recall humanity's alienation from God (cf. Harper). When Adam and Eve are expelled from the garden of Eden for disobeying God, they are punished by death and barred from the "tree of life" (Gen. 3:22–24). Expulsion from God's presence pushes humanity into the realm of death.

The regulations of Leviticus reveal that uncleanness, like holiness, is dynamic in nature, having the power to defile anything that comes into contact with it. The book of Haggai highlights this: "A person defiled by contact with a dead body" defiles "bread or stew, . . . wine, olive oil or other food" (2:11–13).

The dynamic aspect of uncleanness explains why the immoral actions of people are a source of defilement that may even extend to the point of polluting the holiness of the tabernacle. To address this consequence the Israelites are required to offer purification (or sin) offerings (Lev. 4:1–5:13; 6:24–30). The Day of Atonement ritual performs a similar service for the whole nation (Lev. 16). Without the removal of the defilement that is due to human sin, the tabernacle could not function as a divine dwelling. The book of Ezekiel highlights this reality by describing how God abandons the Jerusalem temple due to the Israelites' idolatry, which is practiced even within the sanctuary itself (Ezek. 8–11).

The link between uncleanness and death may explain why Leviticus gives so much attention to the use of blood to reverse the impact of uncleanness. Leviticus 17:11 highlights the atoning nature of blood: "For the life of a creature is in the blood, and I have given it to you to make atonement for yourselves on the altar; it is the blood that makes atonement for one's life." Whereas uncleanness is associated with death, holiness is associated with life, symbolized by blood.

The Process of Consecration

As one who is compassionate and gracious (Exod. 34:6–7), God provides processes for people to be delivered from the domain of death and uncleanness so that they may become holy as he is holy. The details of these God-given rituals vary depending upon the extent of uncleanness that needs to be removed or the level of holiness that needs to be acquired. While the circumstances prompting rituals to be undertaken may vary, a common pattern is evident that usually involves the cleansing of the relevant party, the payment of a ransom, the purification of objects within the tabernacle, and contact with something holy to sanctify the person.

Of the various consecration rituals recorded in the OT, the most detailed concerns the high priest. Due to his role in approaching God, the high priest needs to be holier than all other Israelites. Exodus 29:1–37 records the instructions for the consecration of the high priest and his sons, but the implementation is narrated in Lev. 8. The ritual involves a series of actions that are repeated daily for seven days.

Aaron and his sons are washed with water (Lev. 8:6) and anointed with oil (8:12). Then a bull is sacrificed as a purification (or sin) offering to cleanse the bronze altar (8:14–17). This altar needs to be purified from human defilement because it has been manufactured by people. Blood from the bull is put on the corners of the altar. Blood taken from purification offerings is applied only to objects linked to the tabernacle, never to people (Milgrom, *Leviticus*, 529). Next, a ram is sacrificed as a burnt offering (8:18–21). Aaron and his sons lay their hands on the ram to indicate that it represents them. The life of the ram is given to ransom the lives of Aaron and his sons. A second ram is sacrificed, probably as a peace (or fellowship) offering (cf. 3:1–17; 7:11–21). On this occasion selected parts of the ram are placed upon the altar. Some blood from this sacrifice is daubed on the lobe of Aaron's right ear, on the thumb of his right hand, and on the big toe of his right foot to cleanse him from defilement (8:23). This process is repeated for Aaron's sons (8:24). The remaining blood of the sacrifice is thrown against the sides of the bronze altar. Subsequently, some of this blood is taken from the altar and sprinkled, along with oil, on Aaron and his garments and on his sons and their garments. This blood, which has been made holy through contact with the altar, makes Aaron and his sons holy (8:30; Averbeck, 1004). Finally, Aaron and his sons eat meat from the second ram along with unleavened bread (8:31–32; cf. 8:2). By eating the meat, which is holy, they are sanctified.

This complex ritual, involving the sacrifice of three animals, is repeated for seven days, underlining that it is not easy to attain the highest degree of holiness granted to the Israelites by God. Even after all that Aaron does to be sanctified to a high level, he is still prohibited from encountering God directly. When he enters daily the holy place, an ornate curtain separates him from the footstool of the divine throne in the most holy place. Only on the Day of Atonement, and under special conditions, is he permitted to go beyond the curtain (Lev. 16:2–34).

The process for consecrating Aaron and his sons provides the fullest insight into how people are sanctified. Interestingly, this elaborate consecration ritual has features in common with both Passover (Exod. 12:1–30) and the ritual undertaken by the Israelites when the covenant is sealed at Mount Sinai (Exod. 24:3–11).

At Passover the firstborn male Israelites are delivered from death by making a sacrifice, sprinkling blood on the doorframes of the Israelite homes, and eating the sacrificial meat with unleavened bread. Exodus 13:2 implies that this ritual consecrates all the firstborn males to God, an idea that is confirmed in Numbers when the Levites become substitutes for the firstborn males in a process based on the principle of a ransom being paid (3:12–13, 45–51; 8:16–18; cf. Exod. 13:13). Due to this substitution, the Levites enjoy a holier status than other Israelites. This holier status may be traced back to the Passover ritual, which consists of elements that resemble the consecration ritual for the priests (Exod. 29; Lev. 8). A ransom is paid through the sacrifice of the Passover animal, the Israelite homes are purified through the application of blood, and the people are made holy through eating sacrificial meat and unleavened bread (Alexander, 211–34).

With regard to the covenant at Mount Sinai, the Israelites are initially prohibited from ascending the mountain due to its holy nature. To prepare for God's descent upon the mountain, the people are to consecrate themselves (Exod. 19:10, 14–15). This, however, does not make them sufficiently holy to ascend the mountain. Consequently, the sealing of the covenant is marked by a consecration ritual involving the sacrifice of burnt and fellowship offerings and the sprinkling of blood on the people. After this ritual takes place, some of the more prominent Israelites ascend the slope of the mountain, where they eat and drink and are permitted to see God from a distance (Exod. 24:9–11). While the narrative does not elaborate upon the details of the ritual that takes place, it clearly imparts to those involved a degree of holiness that permits them to move toward God in safety. Prior to this, God has solemnly warned that anyone ascending the mountain should be put to death (Exod. 19:12–13, 21–24).

In considering the similarities between these three consecration rituals, it is highly significant that the tabernacle is viewed by the Israelites as resembling Mount Sinai. Both have a tripartite structure, with an altar at the lowest/outermost location and the divine presence at the highest/innermost location (Sarna, 203). Entering the tabernacle parallels ascending the mountain. The historical experience of the Israelites at Mount Sinai shapes the liturgy of the tabernacle and, later, the temple.

The consecration rituals recorded in Exodus and Leviticus emphasize that sinful people may approach God only after they have been sanctified. However, despite all that happens at Mount Sinai, the people never attain a degree of holiness that permits them to enter the most holy place. Moreover, the regulations of Leviticus assume a world where death, uncleanness, and evil are daily realities. Against this background, the construction of the tabernacle, itself a model of the world, heralds a time when God's glory will fill the whole earth, bringing an end to uncleanness and everything associated with it.

Holiness in the NT

The NT frequently alludes to the concepts of holiness and uncleanness in ways that correspond with the outlook of the OT. The Gospels highlight, however, that Jesus is not defiled by what is unclean, as might have been expected. On the contrary, through physical contact, he makes clean those with skin diseases (Matt. 8:1–4; Mark 1:40–44; Luke 5:12–14) and bodily discharges (Matt. 9:20–22; Mark 5:24–34; Luke 8:42–48). He even restores life to the dead (Matt. 9:18–26; Mark 5:35–43; Luke 7:11–17; 8:49–56; John 11:38–44). Jesus's holy nature is acknowledged by his disciples (John 6:69; cf. Acts 3:14; 4:27, 30; Heb. 7:26) and even by unclean spirits (Mark 1:24; Luke 4:34). Luke observes that the angel Gabriel tells Mary, "The holy one to be born will be called the Son of God" (Luke 1:35). These features point toward the divinity of Jesus.

In his teaching, Jesus criticizes the Pharisees and the teachers of the law for focusing on minor aspects of ritual purity while neglecting the major causes of uncleanness (cf. Matt. 23:23–28; Luke 11:37–41). Responding to the Pharisees' criticism of his disciples for not washing their hands, Jesus says, "What comes out of a person is what defiles them. For it is from within, out of a person's heart, that evil thoughts come—sexual immorality, theft, murder, adultery, greed, malice, deceit, lewdness, envy, slander, arrogance and folly. All these evils come from inside and defile a person" (Mark 7:20–23; cf. Matt. 15:17–20). Reflecting the OT association of holiness with perfection, Jesus challenges his followers to be perfect as their heavenly Father is perfect (Matt. 5:48).

Excluding Revelation, there are over thirty references in the NT to Jesus's followers being called "saints" or "holy people" (e.g., Acts 9:13; Rom. 1:7; cf. 15:25). Behind this designation lies the belief that the death of Jesus sanctifies those who believe in him. The author of Hebrews speaks of Jesus as "the one who makes people holy" (Heb. 2:11; cf. Acts 26:18; 1 Cor. 1:2). Later, he writes, "We have been made holy through the sacrifice of the body of Jesus Christ once for all" (Heb. 10:10; cf. 10:14; Col. 1:22). He subsequently states, "Jesus also suffered outside the city gate to make the people holy through his own blood" (Heb. 13:12). Succinctly, Paul refers to Jesus as the Paschal lamb (1 Cor. 5:7), reflecting how the Gospels develop in complementary ways the significance of Jesus's death at the time of Passover. Peter also associates the death of Jesus with consecration, drawing on imagery from Exodus (1 Pet. 1:18–19; 2:9). Similarly, purification is associated with the sacrificial death of Jesus Christ: "The blood of Jesus, his Son, purifies us from all sin" (1 John 1:7; cf. 1:9; John 15:3; Titus 2:14; Heb. 1:3). As David Peterson (547) notes, "Sanctification in the NT is an integral part of the redemptive work of Jesus Christ. It is regularly portrayed as a once-for-all, definitive act and is primarily to do with the holy status or position of those who are 'in Christ.'"

The sanctifying activity of Jesus is linked to the role of the Holy Spirit. Over ninety times in the Bible the Spirit of God is called the Holy Spirit, underlining the Spirit's holy nature. On three occasions Jesus and the Holy Spirit are mentioned together as actively involved in the consecration of believers (1 Cor. 6:11; Heb. 10:29; 1 Pet. 1:2). As God's presence made holy the tabernacle, the presence of the Holy Spirit within believers sanctifies them so that they become "a dwelling in which God lives by his Spirit" (Eph. 2:22; cf. 1 Cor. 3:16–17; 6:19; 2 Cor. 6:16).

In the light of their sanctification by Christ and the Holy Spirit, which is linked to conversion, believers are to live holy lives. Peter exhorts this most clearly, quoting Leviticus: "But just as he who called you is holy, so be holy in all you do; for it is written: 'Be holy, because I am holy'" (1 Pet. 1:15–16; cf. Rom. 6:19, 22; 2 Cor. 1:12; Eph. 4:24; Col. 3:12; 1 Thess. 2:10; 3:13; 1 Tim. 2:15; Titus 1:8; 2 Pet. 3:11). The author of Hebrews likewise underlines the importance of holiness: "Make every effort to live in peace with everyone and to be holy; without holiness no one will see the Lord" (12:14). Paul warns believers to shun wickedness and immorality, "for God did not call us to be impure, but to live a holy life" (1 Thess. 4:7; cf. 1 Cor. 1:2; 2 Cor. 12:21; Eph. 4:19; 5:3; 1 Thess. 4:3–4).

Holiness is clearly linked to behavior that is morally exemplary. Believers must purify themselves: "Since we have these promises, dear friends, let us purify ourselves from everything that contaminates body and spirit, perfecting holiness out of reverence for God" (2 Cor. 7:1; cf. James 4:8). The author of Hebrews describes God as a father who disciplines his children to produce holiness of character: "God disciplines us for our good, in order that we may share in his holiness" (Heb. 12:10; cf. 1 Thess. 5:23).

While the clean-unclean barrier between Jew and gentile is abolished through the replacement of the first/old covenant by a second/new covenant, the followers of Jesus continue to live in a world where sin and death remain to be defeated fully. Against this background, the NT, like the OT, anticipates a time when the earth will be renewed and holy people will live in God's holy presence in a holy place (Thomas, 53–69). In his vision of "the Holy City, the new Jerusalem," the apostle John sees a golden city that resembles an enormous holy of holies. Due to its holy nature, John observes, "Nothing impure will ever enter it, nor will anyone who does what is shameful or deceitful, but only those whose names are written in the Lamb's book of life" (Rev. 21:27; cf. v. 8). Remarkably, those who reside in the Holy City will see God's face, and "his name will be on their foreheads" (22:4), a comment that recalls how the Aaronic high priest wore on his forehead a pure-gold plate engraved with the words "HOLY TO THE LORD" (Exod. 28:36).

See also Glory of God; Priest; Temple

Bibliography. Alexander, T. D., *Exodus*, ApOTC (Apollos, 2017); Averbeck, R. E., "Offerings and Sacrifices," in *NIDOTTE*, 4:996–1022; Harper, G. G., *"I Will Walk among You"* (Eisenbrauns, 2018); Jenson, P. P., *Graded Holiness* (JSOT Press, 1992); Milgrom, J., *Leviticus 1–16*, CC (Doubleday, 1991); Milgrom, *Studies in Cultic Theology and Terminology* (Brill, 1983); Peterson, D. G., "Holiness," in *NDBT*, 544–50; Sarna, N. M., *Exploring Exodus* (Schocken, 1996); Thomas, G. J., "A Holy God among a Holy People in a Holy Place," in *"The Reader Must Understand,"* ed. K. E. Brower and M. W. Elliott (Apollos, 1997), 53–69; Wenham, G. J., *The Book of Leviticus*, NICOT (Eerdmans, 1979); Wenham, "The Theology of Unclean Food," *EvQ* 53 (1981): 6–15.

T. DESMOND ALEXANDER

Holy Spirit, Eschatological Role of

Israel's prophets, Jesus himself, and the NT authors associated the Holy Spirit's fullest revelation and operation in redemptive history with the long-awaited arrival of "the last days," which would be inaugurated through the incarnation, saving mission, and exaltation of the Messiah. The prophets foresaw a future outpouring of the Spirit on God's people, transforming their hearts to obey God's law (Ezek. 36:25–27; 37:1–14; cf. Isa. 44:1–5) and empowering them all to speak God's word (Joel 2:28–29). Following predictions by John the forerunner (Luke 3:16–17) and Jesus himself (Acts 1:6–8), the apostles identified this "last days" outpouring of the Spirit with the events of Pentecost, when their ascended Lord bestowed the Spirit's power to declare in the dialects of the nations the mighty deeds that God had done in Jesus (Acts 2:1–36). In his seminal essay on Paul's connection of the Spirit with the last days, Geerhardus Vos rightly observed that "the connection of the Spirit with eschatology reached back into the Old Testament" ("Eschatological Aspect," 95).

Although Pentecost marked the redemptive-historical, eschatological watershed in the Holy Spirit's engagement with the people of God, both OT and NT affirm that the Spirit was present and active in the created order (Gen. 1:2) and the covenant community (Isa. 63:10–14) from the beginning. Fulfilling their preliminary role in the history of revelation, Israel's ancient Scriptures are more restrained than the NT in describing the Spirit's operations, especially with respect to his sanctifying work in believers (Warfield, 146–51). Nevertheless, the Spirit's activity in Israel's communal experience and his prominence in prophetic promises of "last days" blessedness are the interpretive context for the NT's announcement that Christ's life-giving Spirit now empowers new-covenant ministry (2 Cor. 3:1–17).

The biblical witness to the Holy Spirit's role at the "last days" climax of God's redemptive plan can be summed up in four broad themes: the Spirit of life, the Spirit of revelation, the Spirit of wisdom, and the Spirit of glory.

The Spirit of Life

The Niceno-Constantinopolitan Creed (AD 381) describes the Holy Spirit as "the Lord and Giver of life." Three OT motifs related to the Spirit's life-imparting power are carried into and developed in the NT: creation, resurrection, and agricultural fertility.

Creation. In the Genesis creation account, the Spirit (*rûaḥ*, LXX *pneuma*) of God is portrayed in the imagery of a bird "hovering" (*məraḥepet*) over the waters of a "formless" (*tōhû*) earth (Gen. 1:2). Later, Moses uses the same imagery to portray Israel's exodus from Egypt under the Lord's protective wings: "in a barren and howling waste [*tōhû*]" he protected Israel like an eagle that "hovers [*yəraḥēp*] over its young" (Deut. 32:10–12). This avian imagery thus links the Spirit's role at creation with the pillar of cloud and fire that led and protected Israel as they emerged from slavery and trekked through the wilderness (Isa. 63:11–14; Neh. 9:19–20) (Kline, 13–16). Although Jesus's reception of the Spirit in his baptism was primarily a messianic anointing for his royal mission (Luke 4:1, 16–21; Acts 10:38), the descent of the Spirit in the form of a dove (Luke 3:22) also evokes the imagery of Gen. 1:2 to signal that a new creation is dawning with the appearance of this last, faithful Adam (Luke 3:23–38).

The Spirit's *life-imparting* role at creation is shown in the vivification of Adam, as God "breathed into [*nāpaḥ*, LXX *emphysaō*] his nostrils the breath of life [*nišmat ḥayyim*, LXX *pnoē zōēs*], and the man became a living being" (Gen. 2:7). Echoes of this terminology in the account of the resurrection of the widow's son through Elijah (LXX *emphysaō*, 1 Kings 17:21) and Ezekiel's vision of Israel's slain corpses revivified by the Lord's Spirit (*nāpaḥ*, LXX *emphysaō*; *rûaḥ*, LXX *pneuma zōēs*, Ezek. 37:5–6, 9–10; see 36:23–27) direct hopes forward toward a future, eschatological "inbreathing" of the Spirit to restore life to God's people (Beale, 560–62). After his resurrection, Jesus "breathed into" (*emphysaō*) his disciples with the words "Receive the Holy Spirit," sending them out on mission (John 20:21–23). Although scholars debate whether this is an alternative perspective to Luke's Pentecost narrative (Acts 2) or an enacted prophecy of the Spirit's post-ascension outpouring, the allusion to the creation of Adam is clear.

Paul shows a further implication, both eschatological and christological, from the account of Adam's creation: "So it is written: 'The first man Adam became a living being'; the last Adam, a life-giving Spirit" (1 Cor. 15:45). Christ's resurrection is the moment when he, the last Adam, became a "life-giving Spirit" (*pneuma zōopoioun*; Gaffin, 18–19). The contrast between first Adam and last lies in the power of the risen Christ to convey his resurrection life, through God's Spirit (Rom. 8:10–11), to those who are united to him. Even apart from the disastrous consequences of Adam's fall (Rom. 5:12–21; 1 Cor. 15:21–28), the initial creation of Adam as a living being, vivified by the breath of God, foreshadowed a "last days" new creation in which a last Adam would bring others to life by the dynamic of God's Spirit (Vos, "Eschatological Aspect," 105–7).

Resurrection and heart renewal. Ezekiel's vision of resurrection in the valley of dry bones (Ezek. 37:1–10) looks not only back to Adam's creation but also forward to Israel's return from exile and heart transformation by the power and grace of God. The vision is interpreted both before and after the prophet receives it (36:24–30; 37:11–14; see also 39:25–29). Israel's "death" is exile from the promised land, the covenant curse for their treason against their God (Deut. 28:49–68). Israel's "resurrection" will come when the Lord regathers his dispersed people and replaces their heart of stone with a heart of flesh, with a new spirit—"*my* Spirit"—cleansing their defilement ("sprinkle clean water") and enabling them to obey his commands (Ezek. 36:24–27).

This historical trajectory—covenant violation, covenant curse, and subsequent restoration through God's faithful mercy—was forecast by Moses in Deuteronomy (4:25–31; 28:15–30:10). Moses predicted that after dispersion in exile, in "later days" (*bəʾaḥărit hayyāmîm*, LXX *ep' eschatō tōn hēmerōn*) Israel would return to the Lord and obey him (4:30). God's sovereign grace would cause this change of heart: "The LORD your God will circumcise your hearts and the hearts of your descendants, so that you may love him with all your heart and with all your soul, and live" (30:6). Ezekiel's vision makes explicit that the Spirit of God will effect this heart transformation. The same promise appears also in the new-covenant promise spoken through Jeremiah: "I will put my law in their minds and write it on their hearts" (31:31–34).

NT authors announce the fulfillment of the prophetic promises concerning God's eschatological bestowal of his Spirit to generate life and heart-transforming holiness. Sometimes NT texts blend imagery and terminology from various OT sources. Jesus speaks with Nicodemus, Israel's teacher, about birth from above "of water and the Spirit," which is necessary for anyone to see and enter God's kingdom, now inaugurated by the arrival of the messianic king (John 3:3–5). He probably alludes to Ezek. 36:25–26, though water appears as a metaphor for the Spirit in other prophecies as well (see below). Paul contrasts his new-covenant ministry to the ministry of Moses, since the former entails the inscription of God's will not on stone tablets but "on tablets of human hearts" through "the Spirit of the living God"—the Spirit who "gives life" (2 Cor. 3:3–6). This passage and its context (3:1–4:6) contain echoes of Sinai (Exod. 31:18; 34:1, 27–35), the new-covenant promise of Jer. 31, and the stone/heart contrast of Ezek. 36. In Rom. 2:28–29 Paul evokes Moses' heart-circumcision metaphor (Deut. 30:6; see 10:16; Jer. 4:4; 9:25–26) to describe the Spirit's vivifying and sanctifying work, contrasting "outward and physical" circumcision with "circumcision of the heart, by the Spirit." The exalted Messiah has brought the Spirit in eschatological power to transform hearts.

Paul traces the gracious exchange of deserved death under covenant curse for blessed life under divine favor back to God's covenant commitment to Abraham, the promise of the Spirit's life-imparting presence: "Christ redeemed us from the curse of the law by becoming a curse for us . . . in order that the blessing given to Abraham might come to the Gentiles through Christ Jesus, so that by faith we might receive the promise of the Spirit" (Gal. 3:13–14). Like Isaac, believers of every nationality are Abraham's children of promise, "born by the power of the Spirit" (4:28–29). In Christ, who is Abraham's singular "seed," all who belong to Christ have become Abraham's seed (3:16, 29), walking, led, and living by the Spirit (5:16, 18, 25).

Fruitfulness. A related prophetic metaphor of the Spirit's eschatological arrival is the outpouring of rain on parched earth, generating fruitfulness. Israel's spiritual barrenness is like dry, thirsty soil in an uncultivated wilderness, so the promised last-days salvation is pictured as fertility-restoring rainfall. Israel's farmlands will be deserted "till the Spirit is poured on us from on high, and the desert becomes a fertile field" (Isa. 32:14–17). "I will pour water on the thirsty land, and streams on the dry ground; I will pour my Spirit on your offspring, and my blessing on your descendants," and as a result they will flourish, gladly acclaiming the Lord as their owner (Isa. 44:3–5). Prophets portray Israel's return from exile in the imagery of abundant waters flowing through wastelands, quenching human thirst and making plant life flourish (Isa. 35:6–7; 49:8–10; 51:3; Jer. 31:8–9).

NT authors allude to the prophets' rainfall and rivers imagery to announce that the longed-for last-days outpouring of God's Spirit has arrived. Although the "pouring out" of the Spirit may also allude to royal and prophetic anointing with oil (see below), the prophets' use of this meteorological imagery to express the life-imparting, fruit-producing power of the Spirit's arrival also influences NT usage. Like parched earth, Christian believers have been "given the one Spirit to drink [*potizō*, an irrigation metaphor also in 1 Cor. 3:6–9; see LXX Gen. 13:10]" (1 Cor. 12:13; Dunn, 130–31). As a result, believers bear the fruit (*karpos*) of the Spirit (Gal. 5:22–23), just as OT prophets foresaw that the downpour of the Spirit from heaven would produce the fruit of righteousness (Isa. 37:30–32; 45:8; see Zech. 8:11–13; Beale, 583–88). In fact, NT authors expect to see Spirit-produced "fruit of righteousness" flourishing in believers' relationships (Phil. 1:11; cf. Heb. 12:11). The author of Hebrews draws on the prophetic imagery of rainfall irrigating farmland to reinforce his solemn call to persevering faith, in view of the blessing of the Spirit's presence in the Christian community, bringing "the powers of the coming age" (Heb. 6:4–8; cf. 2:4).

Related to the prophetic image of the Spirit descending as rainfall on parched soil is the metaphor of the Spirit as refreshing water that quenches human thirst. Jesus promises to give to a Samaritan woman "living water" that dispels thirst forever because it springs up from within the individual. The eschatological moment has arrived when Jewish-Samaritan disputes over earthly worship sites become moot, transcended by God-pleasing worship "in Spirit and in truth" (John 4:10–14, 19–23). Later, at the Feast of Tabernacles, the annual commemoration of God's provision of light, manna, and water during Israel's trek in the wilderness, Jesus announces, "Let anyone who is thirsty come to me and drink. Whoever believes in me, as Scripture has said, rivers of living water will flow from within them" (John 7:37–38). This NT use of the OT receives much comment, since the wording that Jesus attributes to "Scripture" appears in no specific OT passage (Carson, 321–29; Köstenberger, 451–55). Various OT sources for water imagery in general have been proposed (Isa. 12:1–3; 58:11; Zech. 14:6–9; etc.). The context of the "last and greatest day of the feast" suggests that the water-pouring rites associated with Tabernacles (m. Sukkah 4) are in view and that Jesus alludes to the Lord's miraculous provision of water from the rock (Exod. 17:1–7; cf. Num. 20:1–13). From Neh. 8–9 we learn that, after returning from exile, when repentant Israelites observed the Feast of Tabernacles, they praised their Lord for his provision in the wilderness long ago, which included the pillar of cloud and fire, God's good laws, bread from heaven and water from the rock, and "your good Spirit to instruct them" (9:12–20). John interprets the imagery of Jesus's promise and places it in eschatological perspective: "By this he meant the Spirit, whom those who believed in him *were later to receive*. Up to that time the Spirit *had not been given*, since Jesus had not yet been glorified" (John 7:39). If an allusion to the flow of water from the rock at Massah is intended, Jesus anticipates Paul's typological interpretation in 1 Cor. 10:3–4: when Israel drank "the same spiritual [*pneumatikos*] drink" from "the spiritual [*pneumatikos*] rock"—namely, Christ—their nourishment was a foretaste of blessings experienced by Christian believers, "on whom the culmination of the ages has come" (10:11).

The Spirit of Revelation

On the day of Pentecost, Peter's quotation and application of Joel 2:28–32 (MT and LXX 3:1–5) emphasize that the outpouring of the Spirit upon *all* of God's servants, male and female, old and young, would bring about a vast expansion of gifts to convey divine revelation (dreaming dreams, seeing visions, prophesying; Acts 2:1–21, 33, 38–39). "Filled with the Holy Spirit" to speak Spirit-given words (2:4; cf. Luke 1:15, 41, 67), Peter sharpens the eschatological focus of Joel's prophecy, replacing the prophet's generic "afterward" [*ʾaḥărê-kēn*, LXX *meta tauta*] with "in the last days" [*en tais eschatais hēmerais*], an eschatologically charged expression found elsewhere in the prophets (*bəʾaḥărît hayyāmîm*, Isa. 2:2; Ezek. 38:16; Hosea 3:5; *ep' eschatō/eschatou/eschatōn tōn hēmerōn*, Num. 24:14; Deut. 4:30; Jer. 23:20; 30:24 [LXX 37:24]; Dan. 2:28; 10:14).

The background of Joel's prophecy is Moses's desire, centuries earlier, "I wish that all the LORD's people were prophets and that the LORD would put his Spirit on them!" (Num. 11:29). In due time, Moses's longing became "the promise of the Father," and it is fulfilled as the risen and ascended Christ pours out the Spirit upon his expectant followers (Acts 1:4; 2:33). The Spirit signaled his descent upon the ancient elders of Moses's day by moving them to "prophesy," showing everyone that their utterance did not originate from themselves. But, Moses notes, they "did not do so again" (Num. 11:25). Henceforth the Spirit continued to give those elders wisdom, enabling them to judge their fellow Israelites. For the church under the new covenant, as for those ancient elders, the Spirit signals his initial descent by enabling "all" to speak "the wonders of God" in diverse dialects, fulfilling Joel's prophecy of a universally distributed prophetic gift (Acts 1:14–15; 2:2–4, 11, 16–18).

After Pentecost, although the Spirit is poured out on all who are in Christ, since all have been baptized into one body by the Spirit (1 Cor. 12:13), not all believers prophesy (vv. 29–30). No single gift of the Spirit is distributed to all believers, but the Spirit equips each and every member to minister grace to others in the body (12:7)—a marked expansion of ministerial gifting in contrast to the OT era, in which the Spirit's ministry-qualifying operations focused on specific leaders, particularly prophets, judges, and kings (Warfield, 138–45).

Luke sets Pentecost in a wider biblical-theological framework through allusions to the motifs of Spirit and servant in Isaiah. Parallels between the launch of Jesus's ministry in Luke's Gospel and that of his church in Acts invite comparison. At Jesus's baptism and anointing by the Spirit for his mission, the Father's voice (Luke 3:22) evokes OT terminology to identify him as both Messiah ("my Son," Ps. 2:7) and servant ("in whom I am well pleased," Isa. 42:1). Jesus begins his ministry in the Spirit's power by declaring that the servant's words, "The Spirit of the Lord is on me, because he has anointed me to proclaim good news to the poor" (Isa. 61:1–2; cf. 42:6–7), have been fulfilled in his reading of that Scripture (Luke 4:14–21). Following the pattern set by their Master, God's people receive his promise (Luke 24:48–49; Acts 1:8) that God's Spirit will come upon them (Isa. 32:15; 44:3–5), that in his power they will fulfill the role of the Lord's servant and witnesses (43:10–12; 44:6–8). As he was anointed by the Spirit for his mission, so at Pentecost Jesus—no longer suffering servant but now exalted Lord—bestows the Spirit on his assembled followers, and all speak God's wonders in the languages of the nations (Acts 2:1–4). Apostles have a distinctive calling to bear witness to his resurrection (Acts 1:8, 22; 2:32; 3:15; 10:39–41; 13:31). Yet God's Spirit, the divine witness (Acts 5:32), is given to *all who obey God*. So, the word spreads through the witness of all Christ's followers, as persecution scatters them toward the earth's ends (Acts 8:1–4; 11:19–21). Thus, Israel's calling as the Lord's Spirit-enabled servant and witness is fulfilled first in Jesus the faithful Israel and then in those who follow him, who testify "to the ends of the earth" that he alone is the living God and Savior (Acts 4:13; 13:47; see Isa. 43:10–12; 44:6–8; 45:21–23; Johnson, *Message*, 32–52; Johnson, "Jesus against Idols").

The Spirit of Royal Wisdom

The OT shows the Spirit of God coming upon designated leaders to impart strength so they can defend the people of God and administer justice with wisdom. Before the monarchy, the Lord repeatedly responds to his wayward people's desperate pleas for relief from foreign invaders by raising up judges. The Lord's Spirit comes upon, "clothe[s]" (Gideon), or "rushe[s] upon" (Samson) these individuals, overcoming their weaknesses and impelling them to courageous combat against their enemies (Judg. 3:10; 6:34; 11:29; 13:25; 14:19; 15:14; cf. 14:6). The royal anointing of Israel's first two kings, Saul and David, is likewise accompanied by the Spirit's "rushing upon" them (1 Sam. 10:6, 10; 11:6; 16:13). These outpourings of the Spirit fortify the newly anointed kings to lead Israel into battle against their oppressors (1 Sam. 11, 17).

These bestowals of the Lord's Spirit upon judges and kings are the background for the messianic prophecy in Isa. 11. The "stump of Jesse" portrays the impending humiliation of the dynasty of David, Jesse's son (v. 1). That a branch will emerge from this stump shows that the Lord has not abandoned his covenant commitment to maintain David's dynasty in perpetuity (vv. 10–16; cf. 2 Sam. 7:12–17; 23:5; Ps. 89). Rather, that royal house will be restored to ascendancy through a Davidic descendant: "The Spirit of the LORD shall rest upon him [LXX *ep' auton*]—the Spirit of wisdom and of understanding, the Spirit of counsel and of might, the Spirit of the knowledge and fear of the LORD" (Isa. 11:2 ESV). The result of the Spirit's resting on the Davidic "branch" is his administration of discerning and impartial justice that aids the needy and brings destruction on the wicked—the king's proper role (Isa. 11:3–5).

These OT motifs of royal anointing and the Spirit's empowerment at the outset of a king's reign appear in the Gospel accounts of Jesus's baptism by John. The Spirit descends on him (*ep' auton*) while a voice from heaven addresses Jesus, "You are my Son" (Luke 3:22; cf. Matt. 3:16–17), alluding to the Lord's address to his anointed in Ps. 2:6–7. Allusions to Isa. 10–11 in the Lukan context (1:78: "rising sun" [*anatolē*, which glosses *ṣemaḥ*, "branch," in Ezek. 16:7; Zech. 6:12]; 2:40: "wisdom"; 3:9: "ax . . . at the root of the trees" [Isa. 10:33–34]; 3:16: "more powerful" [*ischyroteros*]) and the reference to anointing by the Spirit in Isa. 61:1–2, the text read by Jesus in the synagogue (Luke 4:17–21), reinforce the conclusion that the Isaianic promise of the branch from Jesse's stock is among the major OT tributaries that converge at Jesus's baptism (Pao and Schnabel, 280). Peter's words to Cornelius in Acts 10:38 further confirm this: "God *anointed* Jesus of Nazareth with *the Holy Spirit* and power, and . . . he went around . . . healing all who were under the power of the devil, because God was with him." Consequently, the Spirit leads the newly anointed Messiah into the wilderness to join battle with the enemy (Luke 4:1–13); and following his initial victory, "Jesus returned to Galilee in the power of the Spirit" (4:14) to liberate those oppressed (4:18) by Satan and his evil forces (4:33–36). Matthew identifies Jesus's healing ministry—in obscurity, not for publicity—as fulfillment of Isaiah's prophecy of a chosen servant upon whom God has put his Spirit, equipping him to bring justice and hope to the gentiles (Matt. 12:15–21; Isa. 42:1–4).

The church's last-days anointing with the Spirit, like her Lord's, has royal as well as prophetic overtones. Just as the Davidic and divine Son's anointing with God's Spirit at his baptism arms him for his messianic warfare against the forces of darkness, so also at Pentecost Jesus, now the exalted Christ, pours out the Spirit on his people to empower them to advance his kingdom conquest to earth's ends. So, the church boldly testifies in word and deed, and the domain of darkness cannot withstand the redemptive light that spreads to the gentile nations (Acts 6:10; 8:7; 13:6–12, 44–49; 16:16–18; 19:12–16). Ages earlier, Moses's successor, Joshua, "filled with the spirit of wisdom" (Deut. 34:9; cf. Num. 27:18–23), led God's people in conquest of the promised land—God's light had pierced pagan darkness. So also in the last days, Stephen, Philip, and Barnabas are distinguished as "full of the Spirit and wisdom" (Acts 6:3; cf. 11:24), and through their witness the light of God's word moves out from Jerusalem, into Judea and Samaria, and on to the ends of the earth, into regions previously benighted in religious compromise (Samaria) and pagan darkness (Acts 8:4–40; 14:8–20; 17:16–34).

The Spirit of Glory

The apex of last-days blessing foreseen by the OT prophets is the restoration of communion between God and his human creatures, the renewal of "God with us" reality in a temple that will be immune to defilement and destruction. Eden was a sanctuary that Adam was charged to serve and to guard (Gen. 2:15), just as Israel's priests would later serve sanctuaries and guard them from trespass by anyone unclean (Num. 1:53; 3:5–10, 38; 18:3–5). Adam and Eve's banishment from the garden foreshadowed Israel's exile from God's holy land and the despoiling of God's holy house on Mount Zion. But the prophets foresee a future sanctuary that will exceed in glory the splendors of Eden and of Solomon's temple (Isa. 2:1–4; 25:6–9; Ezek. 40–48; etc.).

Sensory phenomena signaled the Lord's descent on Mount Sinai, making it a sanctuary on earth, terrifying with the display of God's presence (Exod. 19:16–20; 20:18; 24:15–17). There Moses saw a heavenly sanctuary, the pattern for an earthly tabernacle in which God would dwell in the center of Israel's camp (25:9). Upon this tent's completion, it was overshadowed (*episkiazō*; 40:35 LXX; cf. Matt. 17:5) and filled with divine glory of such radiance that not even Moses could enter (Exod. 40:34–35). This light of God's presence had been visible in the pillar of cloud and fire that protected Israel and led them through the sea to freedom (13:21–22; 14:19). Later OT texts identify that visible splendor with the angel of God's presence and the Spirit of the Lord (Isa. 63:10–14; Neh. 9:12–13, 19–20). The same stunning glory later irradiated the temple constructed under Solomon (1 Kings 8:10–11). Nevertheless, even as Israel's sanctuaries (tabernacle, temple) functioned as meeting places of the Lord with his people, OT voices signaled the inadequacy of these physical dwellings of God (1 Kings 8:27; Isa. 66:1–2). NT voices develop these OT hints that those material, mutable sanctuaries could only foreshadow God's *personal*, *permanent* indwelling in his people, now present in these last days (see Acts 7:44–50; Heb. 9:1–8, 11–12, 24).

Jesus himself is the preeminent fulfillment of the ancient "God with us" institutions, for he is the Word who "became flesh and dwelt [*skēnoō*, cognate of *skēnē*, "tent"] among us" (John 1:14 ESV). His conception is miraculous and mysterious, as the Holy Spirit comes upon his virgin mother and the power of the Most High overshadows (*episkiazō*) her, just as the glory cloud overshadowed the tabernacle (Luke 1:35). Christ's appearance as Messiah begins a new era in the history of worship, in which issues of geographical locale become moot and "true worshipers will worship the Father in the Spirit and in truth" (John 4:19–26). His body becomes the "temple" destroyed by God's enemies but raised on the third day (John 2:18–22) by the power of God's Spirit (Rom. 1:4; 1 Cor. 15:45).

Derived from Jesus's centrality as the eschatological temple is the identity of his church as the new, Spirit- and glory-filled dwelling place of God. At Pentecost, the audible and visible phenomena that demonstrate the descent of the Spirit echo the wind and fire of Sinai (Philo, *Decalogue*, 33–35, 46–49). Specifically, the tongues of fire that "rest" (*kathizō*) on each believer, as Christ baptizes "with the Holy Spirit and fire" (Luke 3:16), signify that the Spirit's "filling" (*pimplēmi*, Acts 2:4) of them constitutes them as his eschatological temple, filled with his glory as surely as the tabernacle was "filled" with the glory of the Lord (*pimplēmi*, LXX Exod. 40:34–35) and his fiery cloud "rested" (*skiazō*) on it (LXX Num. 9:18–22; Beale, 592–613; Johnson, *Message*, 57–60).

The allusions to Sinai, tabernacle, and temple at Pentecost are developed in the NT Epistles' use of the OT to characterize the church as the fulfillment of God's determined purpose to dwell with his people. Gentile believers, formerly distant from the living God, his community, and his sanctuary, are now being incorporated and rising "to become a holy temple in the Lord . . . , built together to become a dwelling in which God lives by his Spirit" (Eph. 2:11–22). Because the church is "God's temple" in which "God's Spirit dwells," he jealously protects its purity (1 Cor. 3:16–17; cf. 6:19; 2 Cor. 6:16–18).

Peter interweaves imagery from the tabernacle and OT prophetic visions to encourage suffering churches that their distress signifies not God's absence but his intimate presence (1 Pet. 4:12–17). When fiery trials befall Christ's people, it shows that "the Spirit of glory and of God rests [*anapauō*] on you" (4:14), just as the cloud and fire overshadowed the tabernacle (Exod. 40:34–38) and the temple eventually became the "resting place" of the Lord's ark (1 Chron. 6:31 [LXX 6:16, *katapausis*]; 28:2 [*anapausis*]; see Ps. 132:7–8, 14). Ezekiel saw that the judgment of those complicit in Judah's sin would "begin" (*archomai*) from God's holy place (*qādōš*, LXX *hagios*) with the elders who were "in front of the house [*bāyit*, LXX *oikos*]" (Ezek. 9:6 AT). So also the suffering of the church as God's house (*oikos*) in the "last times" (1 Pet. 1:20; cf. 1:5) signals the beginning (*archomai*) of judgment from the house of God, a purging that will spread out to destroy those who disobey God's gospel (4:17–18). The fire (*pyrōsis*, *pyr*) of this inaugurated eschatological judgment, however, refines faith and proves it genuine (1:7). Malachi announced that the Lord would come suddenly to his temple as a refiner's fire (*pyr*) to purify Levites like gold and silver, fit to present offerings acceptable to the Lord (Mal. 3:1–4). Likewise, the church's present sufferings show the Lord's presence in his new spiritual (Spirit-ual) house (*oikos pneumatikos*), the sanctuary in which a new "holy priesthood" offers spiritual sacrifices acceptable to God through Jesus Christ (1 Pet. 2:4–5).

See also Covenant; Ethics; Temple

Bibliography. Beale, G. K., *A New Testament Biblical Theology* (Baker Academic, 2011); Carson, D. A., *The Gospel according to John*, PNTC (Eerdmans, 1991); Dunn, J. D. G., *Baptism in the Holy Spirit*, SBT 2/15 (Allenson, 1970); Ferguson, S. B., *The Holy Spirit* (InterVarsity, 1996); Gaffin, R. B., Jr., *Perspectives on Pentecost* (Presbyterian & Reformed, 1979); Johnson, D. E., "Jesus against Idols," *WTJ* 52, no. 2 (1990): 343–53; Johnson, *The Message of Acts in the History of Redemption* (P&R, 1997); Kline, M. G., *Images of the Spirit* (Baker, 1986); Köstenberger, A. J., "John," in *CNTUOT*, 415–512; Pao, D. W., and E. Schnabel, "Luke" in *CNTUOT*, 251–414; Vos, G., "The Eschatological Aspect of the Pauline Conception of the Spirit," in *Redemptive History and Biblical Interpretation*, ed. R. B. Gaffin Jr. (Presbyterian & Reformed, 1980), 91–125; Vos, *The Pauline Eschatology* (1930; repr. P&R, 1994); Warfield, B. B., "The Spirit of God in the Old Testament" (1895), in *Biblical and Theological Studies*, ed. S. G. Craig (Presbyterian & Reformed, 1952), 127–56.

Dennis E. Johnson

Hope *See* Consummation

Hosea, Book of

Hosea son of Beeri prophesied in Israel (the Northern Kingdom) in the eighth century BC, beginning in the reign of Jeroboam II (793–753) and continuing through the fall of Samaria at the end of Hoshea's reign in 722. He died probably around 715 (Moon, 4–5). His ministry thus began with Israel as a prosperous and expanding empire and ended with the nation obliterated, its capital city a ruin, and its people scattered.

Essential Features of the Book of Hosea

Composition. The book ostensibly comes from Hosea himself; it never suggests that anyone else had a hand in its composition. Even so, scholars routinely ascribe parts of the book—especially texts that relate to Judah—to secondary sources (Childs, 377–78; Wolff, xxxi–xxxii), and some more radical theories propose highly complex redaction histories for the book, with little of the text coming from the man Hosea (Yee; Harper). However, we have no compelling evidence that the material of the book is not from Hosea or that the prophet himself was not involved in the final editorial process (Garrett, 24–25). The superscription implies that, using messages and oracles that Hosea delivered throughout his career, the final form of the book was put together in Judah during the reign of Hezekiah (Dearman, 5–8; Moon, 12–13). This presumably took place after the fall of Samaria.

Structure and message. The one structural element of Hosea that almost all interpreters agree upon is that there is a break between Hosea 1–3 and 4–14 (Ward; Buss, 6–37; Wolff; Andersen and Freedman; Hubbard; Dearman; Moon). Beyond that, there is little consensus. The distinctive nature of chaps. 1–3 is obvious. They concern Hosea's marriage to the promiscuous Gomer. The account is a vivid representation of the apostasy and punishment of Israel. Gomer never appears again after chap. 3, and the metaphor of Israel as the wayward wife is scarcely present in chaps. 4–14.

One may suggest that chaps. 4–14 are structured as follows: First, there is a series of complaints and warnings in which the number three is prominent (chaps. 4–7). This begins with a general indictment (chaps. 4–5), giving three oracles that allude to the names of Hosea's three children. The first oracle (4:1–3) speaks of the crime of "bloodshed," an allusion to the "bloodshed" associated with Jezreel (1:4). The second (4:4–14) speaks of three guilty segments of the population: the priests, the common people, and the women. This part of the text is associated with the child Lo-Ammi ("not my people"), as it three times refers to "my people" (4:6, 8, 12). The third (4:15–5:15) gives a series of three warnings (4:15–19; 5:1–7; 5:8–15), concluding in 5:12–15 with severe judgments (YHWH will be like gangrene to Israel's wound, and like a lion, he will savagely tear into the nation). This corresponds to the name of Lo-Ruhamah ("not pitied"). After this, Hosea gives three exhortations to repent (6:1–3), followed by three metaphors describing YHWH's vexation: the morning cloud that quickly disappears and gives no rain (6:4–7:2), the madhouse bakery (7:3–10), and the silly dove that flits back and forth in a vain search for help (7:11–16).

Second is a chiastic series of condemnation oracles (8:1–10:10):

- A Warfare and exile (8:1–3)
  - B Unworthy kings and the bull idol of Samaria (8:4–6)
    - C Prostitution, barrenness, and exile (8:7–10)
      - D Israel's altars and palaces (8:11–14)
        - E Prostitution, barrenness, and exile (9:1–6)
          - F Hostility toward the prophets (9:7–9)
        - E′ Barrenness and exile (9:10–14)
      - D′ The shrine at Gilgal and the unworthy rulers (9:15)
    - C′ Barrenness and exile (9:16–17)
  - B′ Many altars, disdain for kings, and the bull idol of Samaria (10:1–8)
- A′ Warfare and exile (10:9–10)

The third major section concerns YHWH's vexation over Israel, with a focus on the story of Jacob (10:11–13:14b). It is another chiasmus:

- A Divine vexation (10:11–11:11)
  - B Jacob and his heirs (11:12–12:8)
    - C Prophetic parables of condemnation (12:9–11)
  - B′ Jacob and his heirs (12:12–13:3)
- A′ Divine complaint and decision (13:4–14b)

In the last major division of the book (13:14c–14:8), Hosea laments over Israel and issues a final appeal for repentance (13:14c–14:3), and YHWH responds with a promise of mercy (14:4–8). The book ends with a wisdom postscript (14:9).

The Hermeneutics of Hosea

Two features of Hosea stand out. First, it can be highly obscure, with the meaning of the Hebrew difficult to translate or, if translatable, difficult to interpret. The problems with the Hebrew are sometimes due to textual corruption and may also reflect the idiosyncrasies of a northern dialect of Hebrew, but there is more to it than that. The text is intentionally opaque, requiring the reader to ponder it thoroughly. Hosea himself says as much in the final verse of the book, asserting that the "wise" and "discerning" understand these things but the "rebellious" stumble in them (14:9). Second, Hosea is replete with allusions to prior OT texts. Recognition of these allusions is a key to interpreting the book. In many passages, the meaning of Hosea is altogether lost if one does not comprehend the existence and significance of these allusions.

Examples of OT allusion. At the very beginning of his book, Hosea alludes to an episode from Israel's history: "Call his name Jezreel, for very soon I will bring a Jezreel-like massacre upon the house of Jehu" (1:4 AT). Jehu slaughtered the household of Ahab and the priests of Baal, an event associated with Jezreel, the place of Naboth's vineyard (2 Kings 9–10). What Jehu did to an earlier apostate dynasty shall be done to Jehu's dynasty.

Hosea several times condemns his contemporaries by alluding to prior persons and events. Hosea 6:7–9 states, "Like Adam, they violate covenant; they are unfaithful to me there. Gilead is a city of wicked men, stained with footprints of blood. As marauders lie in ambush for a man, so do bands of priests. [Along the] way they murdered at Shechem, committing shameful crimes" (AT). As the man Adam was the first to violate God's command (Gen. 3), so also the Israelites of the town of Adam (located by the Jordan River) are faithless to the covenant. As Gilead slaughtered many Ephraimites who were in flight after a defeat inflicted by Jephthah (Judg. 12:4–6), thereby leaving the town marked with "footprints of blood," so also the Gilead contemporary with Hosea is still a treacherous city. And as Levi deceived and murdered the men of Shechem (Gen. 34:25–26), so also the priests contemporary with Hosea are little better than a band of thugs. In addition, Hosea retells the story of Jacob (Hosea 12:3–4) to make the point that his heirs, the Israelites, were much like Jacob the schemer but, unlike him, were not redeemed and transformed by an encounter with God.

Hosea also alludes to the Law, particularly Deuteronomy (Cassuto). Hosea 4:2 indicts Israel with the words "There is only cursing, lying and murder, stealing and adultery." This points to the Decalogue (Exod. 20:7, 13–16; Deut. 5:11, 17–20). YHWH in Hosea 13:6 laments, "When I fed them, they became satisfied. When they were satisfied, they became proud. Thus, they forgot me" (AT). Deut. 8:11 states, "Take care that you do not forget YHWH your God" (AT).

Hosea's hermeneutical strategy. Hosea employs three principal strategies in alluding to prior biblical texts. He first employs recurrence, whereby a later generation in some manner repeats the behavior of a prior generation. This happens in the aforementioned case of Hosea 6:7–9, in which the people in the town of Adam repeat the disobedience of the man Adam, the people of Gilead continue the treachery of their ancestors, and the priests at Shechem repeat the brutality of Levi. In these cases, the later generation continues the behavior of a prior generation. But sometimes the later generation reverses a prior text. Thus, Hosea 9:14 calls on YHWH to give the women of Israel dry breasts and miscarrying wombs; this reverses the blessing of Gen. 49:25. So also the curse of Hosea 9:6, that the Israelite refugees will be buried in Egypt, reverses Jacob's dying wish in Gen. 47:29, that he not be buried in Egypt.

A second strategy of Hosea is to create a link between the one and the many. Usually the "one" will be some ancestral figure, and the "many" will be his descendants. This, too, occurs in the above cases of Adam, Jacob, and Levi.

Hosea's third strategy is to link an eschatological work of God to some corresponding event in Israel's history. Once again, the later work may either repeat or reverse the prior work. Hosea 1:10 promises to make Israel as numerous as the sand on the shore, a repetition of Gen. 22:17 (cf. also Hosea 2:18 to Gen. 1:22). Hosea 2:14, however, where YHWH promises to allure Israel into the wilderness to save her, reverses Num. 14:32–34, where Israel is condemned to wander in the wilderness as punishment for the rebellion at Kadesh-barnea.

Hosea never explicitly exegetes a passage to which he alludes. He does not claim that his use of a text is its contextual interpretation. Thus, he does not claim that Genesis, in its account of Levi at Shechem, predicts that the priests would be violent men. On the other hand, he is not arbitrary, imposing an alien meaning on a passage. He never allegorizes. Instead, he sees a generic, typological connection between the historical context of the source passage (Levi at Shechem) and a contemporary manifestation (violent priests at Shechem). One could thus say that, for Hosea, the contemporary event "fulfills" the prior text even though the prior text does not explicitly predict anything.

Hosea and the NT

Hosea is a critical test for the legitimacy of the NT's use of the OT. In particular, the use of Hosea 11:1 in Matt. 2:15 is often cited as a textbook example of a NT author taking an OT text out of context and inappropriately presenting it as messianic prophecy. Confronting this problem, Christian interpreters sometimes adopt peculiar strategies to find a way to affirm the legitimacy of Matthew's handling of Hosea. They may assert that Matthew is employing a Jewish midrashic manner of interpretation, they may defend a quasi-allegorical interpretation (as in the "theological interpretation of Scripture" movement), or they may simply assert that the "Jesus event" has so changed how the apostles read the OT that they are, in effect, free to impose new meanings upon it. But would Hosea have recognized the legitimacy of any of this? Probably not. Hosea frequently alludes to or employs prior Scripture, but he does not employ any of the above methods. It is better to take Hosea's hermeneutics as a starting point and consider whether the apostles followed the method pioneered by Hosea himself. If so, then we can affirm the legitimacy, from Hosea's perspective, of the NT's handling of his book.

Hosea 11:1 and Matt. 2:15. Hosea 11:1 reads, "When Israel was a boy, I loved him; and I called my son out of Egypt" (AT). This concerns the exodus from Egypt. It does not speak of a future event (it says, "I called my son," and not, "I will call my son"). Although some have tried to turn this verse into a univocal prediction of the Messiah's future departure from Egypt (Sailhamer), this is not persuasive (McCartney and Enns). Besides the tense of the verbs, one may raise other objections to a messianic interpretation. First, Hosea explicitly identifies the "boy" as "Israel" and not as the Messiah. Second, 11:2 says that YHWH's "son" sacrificed to Baal, something Christians would be loath to attribute to Jesus. Third, Israel is portrayed as a rebellious "heifer" in Hosea 10:11–15 and as a faithless "son" in Hosea 11:1–4. Both are metaphors, and neither is to be taken literally. Fourth, Hosea repeatedly refers to the exodus (2:15;

11:5; 12:9, 13; 13:4). The event is a major theme in the book, and there is no reason to suppose that 11:1 concerns something else. Nevertheless, Matt. 2:15 does cite Hosea 11:1b and assert that it was "fulfilled" when Jesus returned with Mary and Joseph from Egypt. We must, therefore, try to understand what Matthew is saying and whether it can be justified.

To begin with, Matthew does not say that Hosea predicted Jesus's return from Egypt; he says that Jesus's return "fulfilled" Hosea's words. The former would imply that Hosea specifically and knowingly told his readers that the Messiah would spend time in Egypt and then come back; the latter requires only that Hosea's words spoke to a typological theme or pattern and that what Jesus did constituted a recurrence of the pattern. The word "fulfill" can be used of a prediction if it is clear that the text in question makes a prediction. For example, Mal. 4:5 states, "Look, I will send you the prophet Elijah before the great and terrible day of YHWH comes" (AT). This is explicitly predictive. Jesus alludes to this verse in asserting that John the Baptist is the coming "Elijah" (Matt. 11:14; 17:10–12), implying that John "fulfilled" Malachi's prediction. But Hosea 11:1 is historical retrospection; as such, the "fulfillment" must be typological rather than predictive.

Typological fulfillment is a recurring motif in Matthew. Just as Israel went down into both the Red Sea and the Jordan River, so also Jesus was baptized in the Jordan. He spent forty days in the wilderness, just as Israel spent forty years in the wilderness. He gave his law on a mountain (Matt. 5–7), just as YHWH gave the law to Israel from Mount Sinai. He fed the crowds in the wilderness (14:15–21; 15:32–38), just as YHWH gave manna to Israel in the wilderness. In no case did the relevant OT passage explicitly predict anything about the Messiah, but in every case the Messiah fulfilled a pattern established in the OT.

Matthew thus follows the hermeneutic of recurrence, as does Hosea. In the above examples, Matthew leaves the OT allusions unstated, requiring the reader to reflect and analyze in order to recognize the implicit typological pattern. Even in his citation of Hosea 11:1, where he makes his source text explicit, Matthew does no exegesis and gives no explanation. Hosea, as we have seen, alludes to events in Israel's history, sometimes explicitly (as when he recites incidents from the life of Jacob) and sometimes not (as when he does no more than mention Shechem to allude to Gen. 34). But neither Matthew nor Hosea fully unpacks prior texts, and neither claims that their use of a text constitutes its "true" or hidden meaning. In both Hosea and Matthew, Israel's narrative history establishes patterns or types of behavior, and that behavior is "fulfilled" in a later generation (Hosea) or in the life of the Messiah (Matthew). Both books demand that the readers engage the text perceptively.

Furthermore, both Hosea and Matthew employ representational typology, in which the actions of the one and the actions of the many mirror each other. In Hosea, the prior behavior of the one (Jacob or Levi) is reflected in the subsequent behavior of the many (the whole of Israel or the priests). In Matthew, the prior activity of the many (Israel coming out of Egypt or spending forty years in the wilderness) is mirrored in the subsequent activity of the one, Jesus. We have also seen that in his allusions to OT texts, Hosea may see either repetition or reversal. In Matthew, Jesus repeats incidents from the history of Israel (he comes out of Egypt), but he also reverses the prior analogues (unlike the rebellious "son" of Hosea 11:2, Jesus is obedient). In short, the validity of Matthew's interpretation is not established by proving that Hosea 11:1 is actually a prediction, nor should we resort to allegorizing, to rabbinical or sectarian Jewish models, or to some other arbitrary manner of handling either text. Instead, Matthew is vindicated because he employs precisely the same methods that Hosea himself employed (see also Beale).

We should also say a word about an ancient Christian mode of handling such problems, *sensus plenior* (the "more complete meaning"). The method asserts that the prophet, led by the Spirit, included in his message a prediction that the prophet himself did not recognize but that the Spirit intended. Thus, Hosea was referring only to the exodus when he wrote, "I called my son out of Egypt," but the Spirit intended it as a hidden prediction of Jesus's Egyptian sojourn. By itself, *sensus plenior* is arbitrary and of little value. We have no way of knowing what God secretly intended, and in context, Hosea 11:1 clearly speaks of the exodus. If, however, we first establish the typological linkage between Hosea and Matthew and do so independently of any special appeals to the secret intentions of God, we can then come back and take a fresh look at *sensus plenior*. It is remarkable, after all, that Hosea uses the metaphor of the "son" in his allusion to the exodus. He could have spoken nonmetaphorically ("my people") or used another common metaphor (Israel as God's flock, or vine, or fig tree). But the clause "I called my son out of Egypt" has a strikingly literal fulfillment when applied to Jesus, and it is probably for this reason that Matthew explicitly cites the Hosea text. We may thus assert the validity of *sensus plenior*, or at least the concept, without depending upon the device to save the NT's use of the OT.

Hosea 6:2 and 1 Cor. 15:4. Paul says that he preached "that Christ died for our sins according to the Scriptures, that he was buried, that he was raised on the third day according to the Scriptures" (1 Cor. 15:3–4). Notwithstanding Jesus's assertion that Jonah's three days in the sea were analogous to Jesus's three days in the earth (Matt. 12:40), the only OT text that explicitly speaks of resurrection on the third day is Hosea 6:2 (see also Conzelmann, 256). Alluding to Jonah, Jesus focuses on time spent in the domain of death and its function as a sign. But Paul focuses more on sin, punishment, death, and resurrection. For this, Hosea 6:1–2 is more apposite: "Come, let us return to YHWH! He has torn us up, but he will heal us; he has struck us, but he will bind our wounds. He will restore life after two days, on the third day he will raise us, that we may live in his presence" (AT).

Once again, the Hosea text is not a prediction. It is an exhortation; Hosea wants his people to repent so that YHWH may forgive and restore them. In context, Hosea's "three days" are not to be taken literally. They stand for an undefined short space of time: If Israel will come back to YHWH, they will be amazed at how quickly God will respond and heal them. Attempts to turn Hosea 6:2 into a more direct prediction of Jesus's death and resurrection are not persuasive (e.g., Dempster argues that in the OT a three-day period leads to a salvific event and thus Hosea 6:2 must point to Jesus's resurrection, but counterexamples are common, such as Gen. 30:36; 40:16–19).

Paul's claim, that Jesus's death "for our sins" and resurrection "on the third day" fulfilled "the Scriptures" (1 Cor 15:3–4), applies the hermeneutic of recurrence to Hosea 6:2. The one (Jesus) recapitulated the story of the many (Israel). As Israel was wounded and died for its sins, so also Christ was wounded and died for ours. As Israel was promised renewal "on the third day," so Christ, the firstfruits of the great eschatological renewal, was raised on the third day. Furthermore, there is a reversal pattern: Israel, because of its disobedience, did not experience resurrection on the third day, but Jesus, through his obedience, did experience it. In Paul's theology, the pattern of recurrence is extended forward into the experience of the church: as Christ died and rose on the third day, so also we died and rose with him. Paul states, "I was crucified with Christ. I no longer live, but Christ lives in me. The life I now live in the flesh, I live by faith in the Son of God, who loved me and gave himself for me" (Gal. 2:19b–20 AT). Paul thus sees the theology of the one and the many operating in two directions: the one, Jesus, was the ideal servant and fulfilled the task of the many, Israel; the many, the church, find resurrection and release from sin in the experience of the one, Jesus.

We can apply the general concept of *sensus plenior* to Hosea 6:2 after the fact, so to speak, not to validate Paul's use of the text but to recognize the uncanny verbal correspondence between the OT text and the NT doctrine: resurrection occurs "on the third day." With this we can affirm Peter's claim that the "Spirit of Christ" spoke in advance through the prophets about Jesus's suffering and glory (1 Pet. 1:11).

Hosea 13:14b and 1 Cor. 15:55. Paul, loosely citing Isa. 25:8a ("[YHWH] will swallow up death forever") and Hosea 13:14b, celebrates Christ's triumph over death: "When this corruptible [body] is clothed in incorruptibility, and this mortal [body] is clothed in immortality, then the written word will come to pass: 'Death has been swallowed in victory! Where is your victory, Death? Where is your sting, Death?'" (1 Cor. 15:54–55 AT). In this case, the principal problem for the Christian expositor is not that Paul seems to wrench the Hosea passage from its context but that the Hosea passage itself appears to be incoherent. Hosea 13:14 (ESV) reads, "I shall ransom them from the power of Sheol; I shall redeem them from Death. / O Death, where are your plagues? O Sheol, where is your sting? Compassion is hidden from my eyes." YHWH appears to assert in one breath that he will ransom his people from death and that he will have no compassion on them.

The solution is to recognize that the final line of 13:14, "Compassion is hidden from my eyes," belongs with the next verse. As mentioned in the structural analysis above, 10:11–13:14b is a chiasmus that begins with YHWH's expression of vexation over what to do with wayward Israel (10:11–11:11) and ends with his decision to judge them and yet redeem them from death (13:4–14b). The end of v. 14 does not belong with this passage; it introduces Hosea's complaint. Recognized as the words of Hosea (and not of YHWH), "Compassion is hidden from my eyes" does not mean "I will show no compassion." It means, "In light of the ruin I see coming for Israel, I see no evidence of compassion." Hosea 13:14c–15 should be therefore translated, "I don't see any compassion! Although [Ephraim] prospers among his brothers, YHWH's east wind will come, rising up from the wilderness! His fountain will fail; his spring will dry up! [An enemy] will plunder [his] treasury of all its precious booty!" This is Hosea's dismayed response to YHWH's promise to redeem Israel from death. The prophet is asserting that he sees nothing but disaster on the horizon for Israel. After Hosea completes his complaint, YHWH responds with reassurance that he will, in fact, heal Israel and make it thrive again (14:4–8). For our purposes, the main point is this: the final line of 13:14 does not belong with the other lines of the verse, and we can disregard it when analyzing 13:14b and its relationship to 1 Cor. 15:54–55.

In context, Hosea 13:14ab promises eschatological restoration after God has judged Israel. The promise to redeem them from death is not hyperbole. It implies that the promised restoration will be more than a national regathering; it addresses the most urgent of all human concerns and our ultimate enemy, death. It gives no specifics regarding how or in what manner death will be defanged, but it does imply an eternal and eschatological Israel. Paul, therefore, is not appropriating this text illegitimately when he asserts that the resurrection of Jesus fulfills the hope of eschatological victory over death. For Paul, the mystery that surrounds Hosea's promise of victory over death has been answered in Christ.

Bibliography. Andersen, F. I., and D. N. Freedman, *Hosea*, AB (Doubleday, 1980); Beale, G. K., "The Use of Hosea 11:1 in Matthew 2:15," *JETS* 55 (2012): 697–715;

Buss, M. J., *The Prophetic Word of Hosea* (Töpelmann, 1969); Cassuto, U., "The Prophet Hosea and the Books of the Pentateuch," in *Biblical and Oriental Studies* (Magnes, 1973), 79–100; Childs, B. S., *Introduction to the Old Testament as Scripture* (Fortress, 1979); Conzelmann, H., *1 Corinthians*, Herm (Fortress, 1975); Dearman, J. A., *The Book of Hosea*, NICOT (Eerdmans, 2010); Dempster, S., "From Slight Peg to Cornerstone to Capstone," *WTJ* 76 (2014): 371–409; Garrett, D. A., *Hosea, Joel*, NAC (Broadman & Holman, 1997); Harper, W. R., *Amos and Hosea*, ICC (Scribner's Sons, 1905); Hubbard, D. A., *Hosea*, TOTC (InterVarsity, 1989); McCartney, D. G., and P. Enns, "Matthew and Hosea," *WTJ* 63 (2001): 97–105; Moon, J. N., *Hosea*, ApOTC (InterVarsity, 2018); Sailhamer, J. H., "Hosea 11:1 and Matthew 2:15," *WTJ* 63 (2001): 87–96; Ward, J. M., *Hosea* (Harper & Row, 1966); Wolff, H. W., *Hosea*, Herm (Fortress, 1974); Yee, G., *Composition and Tradition in the Book of Hosea* (Scholars Press, 1985).

DUANE GARRETT

Human Being

See Adam, First and Last; Image of God

I

Idolatry

The biblical account of idolatry is rooted in the image-making dynamic that runs across the breadth of the canon. At the heart of this pattern is an intrinsic reflective relationship rooted in worship. The *imago Dei* (image of God / *ṣelem ʾĕlōhîm*) in the opening chapters of Genesis refers to the humans God creates, whom God intended to reflect him by means of worshiping him. Idolatry is the practice that turns this reflective relationship upside down. Instead of worshiping God, humans craft an idol and worship it. In both instances, human identity is rooted in what they worship (cf. Beale, 15–36). The surprising end to this story in the NT is that the perfect image of God (Jesus) enters into human history in visible form and both restores the image in God's people and breaks the powers of the idols (cf. Blocher).

It is important to note that at the point where *imago Dei* language drops out in the OT (Gen. 11), the language of idolatry becomes prominent. Outside of Israel's primeval history (Gen. 1–11), *ṣelem* (image) does not occur again with *ʾĕlōhîm* (God), nor with any other positive designation as a reflection or representation of God. Where *ṣelem* does occur (e.g., Num. 33:52; 2 Kings 11:18; 2 Chron. 23:17; Ezek. 7:20; Amos 5:26) there are always negative overtones associated with the reflection/image.

In the ancient Near East, idols reflected the deities to which they pointed. The Hebrew term for "image" (*ṣelem*) has the semantic range to include idols as well, having the substantive denotation of making visible what was not readily seen. Across the OT, when *ṣelem* is used negatively, it becomes allied with a host of other Hebrew terms casting a pejorative tone onto Israel's dalliances with these foreign gods. Other terms for idols included *pesel* (carved or graven image—e.g., Exod. 20:4; Deut. 5:8; 27:15; Isa. 44:10–20), *tərāpîm* (family idols—e.g., Judg. 17:5; 18:14–20; 1 Sam. 19:13; Hosea 3:4), *ʾāwen* (plain idol—Isa. 41:29; 66:3), and *semel* (carved likeness—e.g., Deut. 4:16).

In the ancient Near East, kings functioned as vice-regents of distant deities, imaging those deities in the discharge of their duties. Surrounded by nations where idol making and idol worship were common, Israel was called to be utterly unique. There were to be no material images of an invisible deity among the Israelites. In neighboring cultures carved statues abounded as the visible representations of invisible deities in whom the hopes of the nations resided. By contrast, in Israel there were to be no carved images because God had already made a concrete image both visible and tangible to all who would look—namely, humankind.

The dialectic of YHWH's faithfulness and Israel's unfaithfulness animates large portions of the OT narrative from Gen. 12 onward. The narrative of the exodus from Egypt is followed quickly by the precarious journey into the Sinai wilderness. Israel is in dire need of sustenance and a navigator. They are met with a surprising series of displays of YHWH's faithfulness to them. Geographical guidance is provided by a pillar of fire at night and a moving cloud during the day. Water comes from a rock. Bread descends from heaven. Quail are mysteriously provided out of the skies. Yet Israel cannot quite accept that God would continue to provide for them.

The first commandment given at Sinai (Exod. 20) is the central principle of the covenant relationship established at Sinai and with the second commandment forms an important context to understand the future history of idolatry. Israel was to have no other gods before YHWH. Theirs was a relationship whose bonds were not to be violated by the entry of any third party into the unique intimacy of the relationship. YHWH understood well Israel's natural disposition to stray from the intimacy of this relationship. There were no other gods in the metaphysical universe. There was not a pantheon of deities to rival YHWH. Why then does YHWH enact laws about other gods if in fact, ontologically speaking, there are no other divine beings? It is because the fragility of the human heart disposed it to yearn for safety and security on its own terms (cf. Halbertal).

In the second commandment, the language of "image" is turned upside down theologically and represents the profaning of the human person in their divine-like activity (Exod. 20:4–6; Deut. 5:8–10). The warning against making carved images is a warning against mistaking the created order for the Creator. The created order often appears to pose the most imminent threats to Israel's safety and significance. Storms, famines, and military enemies all pose great dangers to a small nomadic group of Semitic tribes in the ancient world. How could they combat the forces arrayed against them if not by their own cunning and craftsmanship? The second commandment is centrally articulating that Israel's safety and security have already been warranted by YHWH.

Turning the Story Upside Down

The landmark OT text regarding idolatry is Exod. 32, which records the golden-calf incident. It is a paradigmatic text that echoes across the rest of the OT. Running from Exod. 32:1 to 33:6, the account of the golden calf is carefully crafted in Exodus. It is framed by an initial ascent up the mountain, followed by descent, and concluding with an ascent and final descent. At the outset, Israel cannot grasp how God would care for them in the wilderness, most especially without their anointed leader present, who has ascended up the mountain into the cloud. As a result, they craft a molten image of a cow that will give them food in the desert, likely modeled upon the agrarian idols of Egypt, whence Israel had recently departed. Israel appears to attribute their deliverance from Egypt to the golden calf they have just made (Exod. 32:5). In the cloud on top of the mountain, YHWH tells Moses that the Israelites are "your people, whom you brought up out of Egypt" (Exod. 32:7). Moses responds in turn by reminding God that they are "your people, whom you brought out of Egypt" (Exod. 32:11). The question of "belonging" is the critical question in the narrative and continues throughout the rest of the canon. To whom do the people belong? And to whom do they confess ownership? These are the questions of identity at the heart of the story of idol making in Exod. 32. YHWH's covenantal ownership of Israel was threatened by their attempt to grant ownership rights to the idols. And significantly, Israel's security was threatened in this change of ownership. Their purpose and significance became as fragile as the calf that could be made one day and smelted out of existence the next. From this point forward in Israel's history, acts of rebellion are characterized by appeal to the calf's attributes—a stiff neck, a hard heart, ears that cannot hear, and eyes that cannot see. The sensory malfunction language often used in the OT with reference to rebellion resonates from here in the golden-calf episode (cf. Beale, chap. 6).

The canonical echoes of the Sinai episode reinforce its enduring significance for Israel's future relationship to YHWH. In Moses's song recorded in Deut. 32, there is a strong interplay between the idols made by the people and the people themselves. The idols are "no gods," and the people become as a result of their idols "no people."

In Num. 33, YHWH issues a warning regarding the gods/idols Israel will confront on the other side of the Jordan when they go in to possess the promised land. The "rebellion in the desert" serves as the reminder of Israel's fragile status. YHWH instructs Israel to "destroy all their figured stones and destroy all their metal images and demolish all their high places" when they enter the promised land (33:52 AT).

In 2 Kings 11:18 and the parallel account in 2 Chron. 23:17, the images/idols of Baal are destroyed with the recognition that they are powerless competitors to YHWH but powerful competitors for Israel's loyalties. Israel had ceased to be YHWH's possession and had become instead the possession of the idols.

Nehemiah's recounting of redemptive history at the rebuilding of the temple calls to mind both God's great act of deliverance from Egypt and Israel's "great blasphemy" of the molten calf (Neh. 9). Stephen's speech in Acts 7 that reviews Israel's history similarly connects Moses's rule as the redeemer of Israel in bringing them out of Egypt by the power of God and the people's rebellion in requiring Aaron to make a golden calf to lead them. Israel's hymnody likewise connects God's great act of redemption in the exodus and Israel's contrasting act of infidelity: "At Horeb they made a calf and worshiped an idol cast from metal. They exchanged their Glory for an image of a bull, which eats grass. They forgot the God who saved them, who had done great things in Egypt" (Ps. 106:19–21 NIV, modified).

Israel's prophets often refer to Israel's hard-heartedness, their stiff necks, and their having ears but not hearing and eyes but not seeing (e.g., Isa. 6:9; 44:18; Jer. 5:21; 7:26; 17:23; Ezek. 3:7; 12:2; Zech. 7:11; cf. 2 Chron. 30:8; 36:13; Neh. 9:16–17; Job 41:24; Pss. 95:8; 115:5–6). Thus, the people were becoming as spiritually inanimate as the idols that they worshiped. Jeremiah refers to the idols as scarecrows. They look like living persons but are not able to talk or walk (Jer. 10:5). There was no life in the idols, and therefore they could not be life-giving.

The prophet Isaiah offers the clearest and richest denunciation of idolatry in the period of the monarchy. The second half of Isaiah opens with four spiraling poems, each in turn having to do with the confrontation between YHWH and the gods of the nations. In Isa. 40, the idol maker is portrayed as God-like in his creative abilities. But unlike God, the idol maker becomes faint and his strength wears out. He becomes hungry and thirsty as all humans do. But God does not grow weary or faint, and further, in that familiar refrain of Isa. 40:31, "those who hope in the LORD will renew their strength. They will soar on wings like eagles; they will run and not grow weary, they will walk and not be faint."

At a certain point Isaiah's argument becomes satirical. The idol maker cuts down trees to make his idols. He uses some of the wood for cooking, some of it for heating, and the rest of it to make his idols/gods, as if the scraps of wood were worthy objects of worship. The satire unveils the genuine irrationality of idolatry. The idol maker has ventured to make his own idol as the means to control his own significance and safety.

In Isa. 44 the idols are said to be "empty/nothing" (*tōhû*, 44:9), hearkening back to the formless and void (*tōhû* and *bōhû*) earth in Gen. 1:2. The emptiness of the idol, however, belies the arrogance of the project. The idol maker had supposed that he was creating a deity. The rhetorical question Isaiah implies is, "Who indeed could possibly make his or her own god?" In other words, what sense does it make to say that the god who made us is made by us?

A final comment on the OT use of idolatry: the language of marital infidelity was a root metaphor in the OT to make explicit the character of idolatry (cf. Exod. 34:14–15; Lev. 20:5; Judg. 2:17; 1 Chron. 5:25; Isa. 1:21; 23:17; Jer. 3:8–9; Ezek. 16:17; Hosea 4:12–13; Mic. 1:7). "To go whoring after other gods" was a common way to speak of idolatry. Picturing God as the bridegroom and Israel as his bride construes the history of Israel as a sacred romance. The bridegroom searches out the bride and redeems her from troubles. The bride is not always careful to keep interlopers out of the marriage bed. She often plays the harlot. In the later prophets especially (Isa. 61–62; Jer. 25; 33; Ezek. 16; Hosea 3), YHWH's faithful love of Israel stands in stark contrast to Israel's faithlessness.

Turning the Upside-Down Story Right Side Up

In the NT the *imago dei* is most directly connected to Christ (2 Cor. 4:4; Col. 1:15). Christ is the "exact representation" and that by which the invisible God has become visible (Heb. 1:3; John 1:18). Christ is the perfect image who suffers in our place and for our redemption (Eph. 5:25–26). As a consequence, human identity is most clearly seen in Christ, the one in whom, through whom, and for whom humankind was made (1 Cor. 8:6; Col. 1:16). Surprisingly, it turns out that God does have a concrete and visible image, and though this may appear as grounds for accusing Christianity of idolatry, the apostles claim that the visibility of Christ as the image of God (*eikōn tou theou*) precisely inverts the corrupted order of idolatry. In Christ, the Creator has entered into creation and thereby recreated the cosmic order after his image.

The idols represent the inversion of the original theological order of representation and reflection. They depict an exchange of the glory of God for the foolishness of this world (Rom. 1:23). The practices of idolatry assume that the gods are beings adequately represented by objects of gold or silver and able to be shaped and molded by their worshipers (Acts 17:29). These practices pervaded the Greco-Roman world and were difficult for newly converted Christians to repudiate in their entirety. The religious customs associated with the temple cults were often considered normative for all citizens of the empire. Rejecting those customs entailed dissonance with imperial rule and inevitably put Christians at risk. The opposite danger was just as real as well. Showing any kind of loyalty to the idols would constitute unfaithfulness to Christ and thereby put one's place in the covenant at risk (1 Cor. 10:14; 1 John 5:21).

Gentile nations thought of idolatry in positive and beneficial terms. Idols were physical representations of the locally worshiped gods. As the cult of the emperor grew in the first century, temples were constructed to the pantheon of the Greco-Roman gods with the emperor now included (cf. Price). These "national" gods and their idols were to be respected and revered across the breadth of the empire (cf. Biguzzi). Christianity was clearly not in step with the religious impulses of the empire.

In Jesus's interaction with the Pharisees, there is only one prominent place where idolatry is even implicitly mentioned. In Mark 12:13–17 (pars. Matt. 22:15–22; Luke 20:19–26), the Pharisees ask Jesus whether Jews should pay taxes to Caesar. The question implicitly asks whether the image of Caesar on the coins used to pay taxes constitutes idolatry. The coin requested by Jesus did in fact portray the emperor as the *pontifex maximus* (high priest) of the Roman religion. In his response to the query of the Pharisees, Jesus understands the challenge but resists the assumptions behind the question. Treating another human as God is wrong. But does paying taxes to Caesar entail treating him as God? Jesus reasons that the emperor can be recognized as important to the well-being of the empire without also attributing to him divine powers. In this sense Jesus is demythologizing the emerging emperor cult—Caesar is not God—while also granting the emperor his right to collect taxes for the well-being of the people. This becomes the pattern for Paul in dealing with food offered to idols. If the idols are treated as divine, then Christians should abstain from the food offered to them. But if the idols are treated as simply blocks of gold or silver, then eating food offered to them is permissible.

The emperor cult became more aggressive after Jesus's death, extremely so under Domitian (emperor from AD 81 to 96), demanding a test of loyalty from all

Roman citizens because of the imperial claim to deity. This would have been quite different under Augustus and Tiberius, the emperors in Jesus's time, during which time no such test existed (cf. Marcus). Relinquishing the coin to the tax collectors in Jesus's day amounted to no more than an affirmation that Caesar possessed some form of civil authority. Undoubtedly, had Jesus been confronted with a claim about the alleged deity of the emperor, he would have steadfastly denied it. Toward the end of the first century, Christians faced this precise situation. As Revelation manifests, martyrdom was the cost of refusing the emperor's test of loyalty and denying his claim to deity.

It is somewhat surprising to find that greed is included as an idolatry-related vice in the NT. No concrete relation of greed to the temple cults of the Greco-Roman world is apparent, and yet Paul denounces greed as idolatrous in Col. 3:5 and Eph. 5:5. No other vices in the NT are listed in such straightforward connection to the larger theological umbrella of idolatry. Why greed? The initial clue might come from the reminder that idolatry is fundamentally defective worship. It is rooted in the desire to replace God as the proper object of worship with an alternative. The Scriptures confront any number of alternatives, including money. Jesus's warnings against trying to serve two masters, God and mammon, is a pungent reminder that money is all too often treated as an alternative deity to the living God (Matt. 6:24; Luke 16:14). Treating greed as a form of idolatry simply affirms that money, though not intrinsically evil, can nonetheless be worshiped as an idol (cf. Rosner, *Greed*).

At the Jerusalem Council in Acts 15 the apostles effectively head off a schism in the early church by affirming together that gentile converts to Christianity need not be circumcised. This boundary marker between Jews and gentiles would no longer be a marker between Jewish Christians and gentile Christians according to the council. However, the apostles are clear that the gentile converts ought to avoid idolatry—most likely a reference to the temple cults of gentiles where idol worship took place in honor of local as well as imperial deities. These temple cults were often accompanied by temple prostitutes, whose presence underscored for the apostles the connections between idolatry and adultery.

At the Jerusalem Council, the apostles drew a strong line around the temple cults themselves, and thereby drew a strong linkage between idolatry, sexual immorality, and certain dietary habits (cf. Rom. 2:22; 1 Cor. 5; 8; Gal. 5). The apostolic decree at the conclusion of the Jerusalem Council is representative of these concerns. That decree insists that gentile Christians, as would have been the case for Jewish Christians, should "abstain from the things polluted by idols, and from sexual immorality, and from what has been strangled" (Acts 15:20 ESV). These same concerns are repeated in Rom. 2:22; 1 Cor. 5; 8; and Gal. 5. In each of these passages comes the encouragement to resist the dominant religious practices of the Greco-Roman world in which they lived while fully cognizant of the need to survive in that idolatrous world.

In Rom. 1, Paul describes a great and terrible theological exchange concerning the practice of idolatry. The glory of God is exchanged for images of every sort of creature: men and birds and land animals and even reptiles (1:23). This description of the tragic exchange at the center of idolatry is a Pauline way of providing a big picture of human corruption. The apostle issues the familiar canonical claim that there is no comparison between the Creator and the creature, and yet humans have persuaded themselves into thinking that other created things will satisfy their deepest longings.

Important contrasts throughout Paul's argument in Rom. 1 illuminate the emotional power of idolatry. Hoping to hold down the truth, humans are held down by unrighteousness (1:18). That which can plainly be seen is exchanged for darkness (1:20–21). Though they know God, they do not know God (1:21). Claiming to be wise, they become fools (1:22). The glory of God is exchanged for a dim image. The shadow is embraced rather than the reality (1:23). Refusing to honor God, they dishonor themselves (1:24). Truth is exchanged for a lie. (1:25). In each of these the created order is turned upside down or inside out.

This great exchange follows the pattern of Israel's idolatries. Israel had been baptized into Moses in the cloud and the sea (1 Cor. 10:2). They were given a new identity in these nation-defining episodes. The sea quite clearly points to the surprising crossing of the Red Sea at the command of Moses. The cloud recalls the divine presence that hovered over Israel as they wandered in the Sinai wilderness after the Red Sea crossing. Paul also references the episode of the manna in Exod. 16 and the water from the rock in Exod. 17. Israel's rebellion evidenced in the golden-calf episode is all the more striking when set in the context of Yahweh's provisions for them. Israel had witnessed the shrines to the Egyptian gods while in captivity in that land. Though they sustained a separate identity from the Egyptians, they inevitably accommodated their religious practices to their surrounding context. Paul references this pattern of Israel's idolatry as a paradigm of the temptations of idolatries in Corinth (1 Cor. 10:11). Temptations arise whenever the Creator is confused with the creation.

In 1 Cor. 10, Paul follows out another familiar line of argument against idolatry. There he turns his attention to Isa. 44, where nonliving idols represent nonexistent gods. Paul admonishes the Corinthians to flee from idolatry because the gods represented do not actually exist. In this light they surely cannot provide any grounds for hope in the face of adversity. Paul's initial response is to treat the idols with the respect they deserve—namely, none. Therefore, he encourages the Corinthians not to have any qualm of conscience about eating meat that may have been offered to the idols (v. 25). However, Paul prohibits practices associated with idol worship. There is to be no dalliance with any object, real or imagined, that challenges God's sole unique status as the singular Creator and Redeemer. There are to be no other gods in the hearts of God's people. From this angle, one should abstain from eating meat offered to idols if it encourages the practices of idolatry in even the slightest way.

Two significant episodes should be mentioned from Acts that narrate the precariousness of refusing to bow before the idols. In Acts 7, Stephen reminds the Jewish ruling court that Israel's long history of idolatry is embedded in Israel's habits. The paradigm act of idolatry of Exod. 32 was followed by the continual habit of borrowing the patterns of worship from the surrounding nations. Stephen cites Amos 5 as evidence from Israel's own history of the pattern of idolatry. He infers from the golde-calf episode that all future idolatry that the prophets later condemned had its origins in the wilderness. Even the worship of Moloch and Rephan by the Northern Kingdom, which Amos cites, is linked to the pattern that began in the Sinai wilderness.

In Acts 17, Paul confronts the common religious idolatry of the Greco-Roman world at Athens, a city filled with idols in a way likely more pervasive than in other Greco-Roman cities of comparable size. Its long and distinguished history had in part been tied to the heritage of temples and statues dedicated to a variety of emperors and gods. There were also several altars to unknown gods to ensure that no gods were omitted from their rightful place within the pantheon of gods represented at Athens. The Athenian idols were considered a sign of its cultural significance. Paul's critique of idolatry in Athens would likely have struck the Athenian elites as quite odd.

The critical hinge that Paul's argument turns on concerns whether it makes sense to suppose that the Creator of the world could be fashioned out of gold or silver. It is God who created humankind, not the reverse. God is not an image that could be formed from the imagination or creativity of human artists. Paul claims that it would be illogical to suppose that humans could find their safety and significance by creating the god who gave them meaning in the first place.

What surely marks out the NT as the fulfillment of the OT is the claim that the *imago Dei* attains a unique status in the person of Jesus Christ, not merely as a human but as the perfect image of God. It is not an abstract metaphysical claim but primarily a confession about salvation. The claim that Jesus is the "image of the invisible God" (Col. 1:15) is the means to establish that God is renewing/restoring/redeeming his people into his image. As the image of God, Jesus is "reconciling to himself all things, whether on earth or in heaven, making peace by the blood of his cross" (Col. 1:20 AT). In Christ, God became visible. In John 14, when Jesus responded to Philip's request to show them the Father, he said, "The one who has seen Me has seen the Father" (14:9 NASB).

In 2 Cor. 4, the gospel is the glory of Christ, whose light illuminates those with eyes that had formerly been blinded by idolatry. The "god of this world" (*ho theos tou aiōnos*), like the golden calf, had blinded all those who sought security and purpose at its feet. The idol had refashioned its worshipers after its own image—blind and dumb. Christ, in an act of re-creation, restored the "inner nature" (*ho esō hēmōn*) in an ironic reversal, the second creation being enacted by one who was also the very image/likeness of God.

If idolatry is the theological act of honoring the creature above the Creator, Jesus is the one who reverses that theological move by reconstituting the *imago Dei* with the full reflection of the divine glory in his own person. Jesus is the true human image in contrast to the false idol. The image of God in humans was marred by Adam's fall but restored in Christ. Idols represent the attempt to find significance and security by the works of one's own hands. By contrast, Jesus is the one whose significance and security from beginning to end are found not in the labors of his own hands but in sacrificing his life for others in covenantal obedience to his Father. Though he is equal with God, he does not consider that status as grounds to assert control on his own terms (Phil. 2:6–8). Rather, he willingly obeys his Father even at the cost of his own life. He is the inverted idol of God, the one who humbles himself to the point of death on a cross.

See also Adam, First and Last; Image of God

Bibliography. Achtemeier, P., "Gods Made with Hands," *ExAud* 15 (1999): 43–61; Barr, J., "The Image of God in the Book of Genesis," *BJRL* 51 (1968): 11–26; Beale, G. K., *We Become What We Worship* (IVP Academic, 2008); Berkouwer, G. C., *Man: The Image of God* (Eerdmans, 1962); Biguzzi, G., "Ephesus, Its Artemision, Its Temple to the Flavian Emperors, and Idolatry in Revelation," *NovT* 40 (1998): 276–90; Blocher, H., *In the Beginning* (InterVarsity, 1987); Bonnington, M., "Fleeing Idolatry," in *Idolatry*, ed. S. Barton (T&T Clark 2007), 107–19; Bray, G., "The Significance of God's Image in Man," *TynBul* 42 (1991): 195–225; Cassuto, U., *A Commentary on the Book of Genesis: Part One* (Magnes, 1989); Clines, D. J. A., "Humanity as the Image of God," in *On the Way to the Postmodern*, 2 vols., JSOTSup 292–93 (Sheffield Academic, 1998), 2:447–97; Halbertal, M., *Idolatry* (Harvard University Press, 1992); Keller, T., *Counterfeit Gods* (Dutton, 2009); Keyes, D., "The Idol Factory," in *No God but God*, ed. O. Guiness and J. Seel (Moody, 1992); Kline, M., *Images of the Spirit* (Eerdmans, 1980); Kutsko, J. F., "Will the Real *Selem Elohim* Please Stand Up?," *SBLSP* 37 (1998): 55–85; Levenson, J., "The Temple and the World," *JR* 64 (1984): 139–58; Lints, R., *Identity and Idolatry* (IVP Academic, 2015); Lints, "Imaging and Idolatry," in *Personal Identity in Theological Perspective*, ed. R. Lints, M. Horton, and M. Talbot (Eerdmans, 2006), 204–25; Lints, "Introduction to a Theological Concept of Personhood," in *Personal Identity in Theological Perspective*, ed. R. Lints, M. Horton, and M. Talbot (Eerdmans, 2006), 1–10; Marcus, J., "Idolatry in the New Testament," *Int* 60, no. 2 (2006): 152–64; McDowell, C., *The Image of God in Eden* (Eisenbrauns, 2009); Ortlund, R. C., Jr., *Whoredom* (Eerdmans, 1996); Price, S. R. F., *Rituals and Power* (Cambridge University Press, 1984); Rosner, B., "The Concept of Idolatry," *Them* 24 (1991): 21–30; Rosner, *Greed as Idolatry* (Eerdmans, 2009); Rowe, C. K., "New Testament Iconography?," in *Picturing the New Testament*, WUNT 2/193 (Mohr Siebeck, 2005), 289–312.

RICHARD LINTS

Image of God

In the past several years alone numerous substantial studies on the *imago Dei* have been published (Herring, Lints, McConville, McDowell, Peterson), yet basic questions about the meaning of this phrase remain. When applied to humans, does it refer primarily to their mental likeness to God? Is it a relational term? Does it suggest physical similarity to God, or does it, rather, indicate human qualities, gifts, and abilities that reflect God? Further, what is the relationship between humans, as created *in* God's image, and Jesus, whom Paul identifies as "*the* image of the invisible God" (Col. 1:15)? Are there other individuals or groups that Scripture describes as created in God's image? If so, what is the relationship among them?

The key to understanding the *imago Dei*, whether in the context of human creation, as a proclamation of Jesus's identity, or as applied to ancient Israel, to the church, or to individual Christians, lies in the biblical usage of the phrase in the early chapters of Genesis. We also need to give thoughtful consideration to the meaning of the relevant terms within their broader historical context and to the genre and the specific literary contexts in which they appear. After determining the meaning of "image" and "likeness" in Gen. 1:26–27; 5:1–3; and 9:5–7, we will consider how this concept is manifest in a unique way with corporate Israel. We will then turn to the NT where Paul and other NT writers identify Jesus as *the* image of God (Col. 1:15) before concluding with a study of the church, corporately and individually, as bearers of God's image.

The "Image of God" in Genesis

Image and likeness in Gen. 1:26–28. The first three references to the image of God appear in the opening chapter of the Bible:

> God said, "Let us make humanity in our image [*bəṣalmēnû*] and according to our likeness [*kidmûtēnû*] and let them rule over the fish of the sea and over the birds of the sky and over the beasts and over all the earth, and over every creeping creature on the earth." So God created humanity in his image. In the image of God he created it [*'ōtô*]. Male and female he created them. Then God blessed them and God said to them, "Be fruitful and multiply. Fill the earth and subdue it. Rule over the fish of the sea and the birds of the sky, and over every living thing that moves on the earth." (AT)

According to Gen. 1:26–28 *ṣelem* and *dəmût* possess a reflective quality. Humanity is made *in* God's image and *according to* his likeness, meaning that there is some level of correspondence between the original and those patterned after it. The immediate context suggests that the means by which humanity reflects God is twofold: dominion (1:26, 28) and fruitfulness (1:28). At God's appointment, male and female are to rule over (*ûrədû*) creation and subdue (*wəkibšuhā*) the earth in imitation of God's rule and authority. Similarly, as God created the first human pair, male and female are to multiply and fill the earth through procreative acts of their own (2:24–25). Thus, being made in God's image and according to his likeness includes *both ruling and procreative functions.*

Image and likeness in Gen. 5:1–3. Genesis 5:1–3 preserves the only other instance where "image" and "likeness" are paired within the OT:

> This is the book of the generations of humanity. On the day when God created humanity in the likeness of God he made it [*'ōtô*]. Male and female he created them, and he blessed them and called their name (named them) "humanity" on the day they were created. When Adam had lived 130 years he fathered a son in his likeness and according to his image, and he called his name (named him) Seth. The days of Adam after he fathered Seth were 800 years, and he fathered other sons and daughters. (AT)

In Gen. 5:3 "image" and "likeness" are physical and relational terms associated with procreation. Adam *fathered* Seth. Consequently, Seth is Adam's *kin* and *kind*. Specifically, he is Adam's *son*. As a member of the human race, Seth's function, like his parents', is to rule, to subdue, and to be fruitful and multiply. What Gen. 5:1–3 makes explicit is that image and likeness is *the language of sonship*.

Image in Gen. 9:6. The third and final use of "image" (this time without "likeness") in Genesis occurs in Gen. 9:5–7:

> And indeed/surely for your lifeblood I will require a reckoning (demand an accounting): from every beast I will require it. And from each human being I will require a reckoning for the life of another human being. Whoever sheds human blood, by humans shall his blood be shed, because in the image of God he [God] made humanity. Now be fruitful and multiply. Swarm/teem on the earth and multiply on/in it. (AT)

As with 5:1–3, Gen. 9:6–7 looks back to creation. Homicide requires the death of the offender because, as the Hebrew word order emphasizes, *in the image of God* he (God) made humanity. This explanation indicates the high value God places on human life, but it does not explain what it means to be created in the image and likeness of God. Why is the death penalty required for homicide?

In 2 Chron. 24:22 a group of rebellious Israelites murders the priest Zechariah. As he dies he cries out, "May the LORD see and *avenge* [*wəyîdrōš*]!" (ESV). Psalm 9 also recognizes God as Israel's divine avenger. Israel is commanded to praise the Lord, "for he who avenges shed blood [*dōreš dāmîm*] is mindful of them" (Ps. 9:11–12 [MT 9:12–13]). In ancient Israel avenging the blood of a murdered family member was the responsibility of the *gō'ēl*, or "kinsman redeemer." We are familiar with the role of the *gō'ēl* from the book of Ruth, where Boaz, kinsman of the deceased Mahlon, fulfills the duty of the redeemer by marrying the widowed Ruth and assuming responsibility for her mother-in-law, Naomi. Although not mentioned in Ruth, a *gō'ēl*'s responsibility also included avenging the death of a murdered family member (Num. 35:19, 21, 24, 27; Deut. 19:6, 12; Josh. 20:3, 5, 9; 2 Sam. 14:11). This particular role was known as the *gō'ēl haddām*, or "the blood avenger." Given Zechariah's dying plea for the Lord to avenge his death, and the psalmist's praise of God as one who avenges the shed blood of his people, Israel apparently understood the Lord to be their blood avenger. As the father of his people, and, hence, their closest male "relative," Yahweh was Israel's *gō'ēl*. He rescued and redeemed them, he cared and provided for them, and when one of his kin was murdered, he avenged their wrongful death (cf. Zech. 2:8 [MT 2:12]). The reason for the death penalty in the case of homicide, as Gen. 9:6 states, is because humanity is made in God's image—that is, *humans ultimately belong to the family of God*. To kill someone is to murder one of God's family members. As the paterfamilias of humanity and thus its *gō'ēl* / blood avenger, the Lord demands life for life.

To be created in the image and likeness of another has both functional and ontological implications. In Gen. 1 it refers to humanity's function *to rule as God's representative*, and *to (pro)create (i.e., multiply, fill the earth) in imitation of God's creative acts*. Genesis 5:1–3 emphasizes the ontological aspect: to be made in Adam's image and likeness defines Seth as a member of Adam's kind—that is, as a human being. They are kin, specifically father and son. This same emphasis on image as kin underlies the reason for the death penalty in the case of homicide (9:6). As those made in God's image, humans are members of God's family. As humanity's paterfamilias, God, the *gō'ēl* / blood avenger, demands life for life.

Given that both Gen. 5:3 and 9:6 connect image and likeness with kinship/sonship, and that both of these texts appeal to Gen. 1:26–28, is there any indication in Gen. 1 itself that to be created in God's image and likeness defines humans ontologically as "sons" or "children" of God? In Gen. 1 there *is* an emphasis on the relationship of one generation to the next. *Ten times in seven verses alone* (Gen. 1:11–12, 21–25) the author notes the creation of the plants and animals "according to its/their kind." While humanity will also procreate "according to their own kind" (cf. Gen. 5:3), Gen. 1 declares instead that male and female were created in the image and according to the likeness *of God*. Humanity is distinct from the rest of creation because, on some level, it is made "according to God's kind." Without divinizing humanity, the early chapters of Genesis seem to agree that to be made in God's image and likeness is to be his royal son/child.

The genre of Gen. 1. Genre plays a crucial role in understanding these terms as well, but the question to which genre Gen. 1 belongs has proven difficult to answer. Is it history? Is it poetry? Should it be classified as a liturgical text, or a hymn? Several scholars have noted its affinities with ancient Near Eastern temple building texts, including its seven-day structure (Fisher, 319; Beale). They conclude that Gen. 1 is not simply the story of creation *but an account of God constructing his macro-temple, the heavens and the earth*. Later biblical texts concur. Psalm 104:2–3, 5 depicts the Lord as the earth's master builder, "stretching out the heavens like a tent. . . . He lays the beams of his chambers on the waters . . . He set the earth on its foundations, so that it should never be moved" (ESV). In Job 38:4–11 God is the divine carpenter who laid the foundation of the earth, determined its measurements, stretched the line, sunk its bases, laid its cornerstone, and added bars and doors. Isaiah 66 identifies heaven and the earth as the very throne room of God's cosmic palace-temple. God then asks, "What is the house that you would build for me, and what is the place of my rest? *All these things my hand has made, and so all these things came to be*" (66:1–2a). These reflections on Gen. 1 further support the idea that when God created the heavens and the earth he was constructing his cosmic temple.

What significance does this bear on our interpretation of image and likeness? By defining humanity as created in the image and likeness of God in the context of a temple, the author of Isaiah makes a bold and daring pronouncement: *God is represented not by man-made statues of silver and gold but by living, breathing human beings that he himself creates*. Rather than manifesting God, as the statue of a god was thought to do, human beings represent God in the world by ruling, subduing, creating, and cultivating as his vice-regents over creation.

Image and likeness in the ancient Near East. The use of royal images as representatives of a king's presence, sovereignty, and power was a common practice in the ancient Near East. One example is a statue of Hadad-yis'i, the governor of Guzan in the ninth century BC, found at Tell Fekheriye in Syria. A bilingual

Aramaic-Akkadian inscription on the statue refers to it as both "the image" and "the likeness" of the governor, with terms cognate to those in Gen. 1:26–27 (Millard and Bordreuil). Textual evidence indicates that in the ancient Near Eastern world, "image" meant more than merely "representative." The cognate Akkadian term *ṣalmu* occurs in the Assyrian Tukulti-Ninurta hymn (mid- to late 13th c. BC), where it refers to the king as both a statue and the god's son. Similarly, an Egyptian wisdom text from the Tenth Dynasty identifies humans born of the god as *snnw*, "image," referring to a statue (Lorton, 131–32). In context, however, it clearly refers to offspring, who are the "images" (children) of the god. Further, synonyms for "image" and "likeness" appear in the beginning of the Babylonian creation story, the Enuma Elish, to denote the children of the gods. For these reasons, it seems all the more likely that "image" and "likeness" in Gen. 1 are *double entendres*. God's people represent him in the world as his living "statuettes," but they do so because they are, first, his royal children.

Image and likeness in Gen. 2? Although Gen. 2:5–3:24 presents a view of human creation different from the previous chapter, it does seem to develop the functional aspect of *ṣelem* and *dəmût* embedded in these terms as they are used in Gen. 1:26–27. Specifically, it portrays Adam as a royal figure whose responsibility it is to care for and cultivate God's garden. He is to make it fruitful and to cause its vegetation to reproduce in imitation of God, *the gardener par excellence* (2:8), in whose image Adam was made.

To understand Adam's role in the garden of Eden we must first ask who, in the cultural world of the OT, tended royal and sacred gardens and parks. Although servants would have done the actual labor, Mesopotamian royal ideology ascribes this role *to the king*. He bore the title "gardener" (NU-KIRI$_6$/*nukaribbu*) and "farmer, cultivator" (ENGAR/*ikkaru*), and was credited with harvesting rare trees and plants from conquered lands and cultivating them (making them fruitful and causing them to multiply) within his own royal and sacred gardens, as a display of his, and his god's, sovereignty over those lands (see NU-KIRI$_6$/*nukaribbu* in CAD N/2, 323–27; ENGAR/*ikkaru* in CAD I/J, 49–55; Widengren, 1–19; Callendar, 61–62). Solomon was also known for his vast botanical knowledge: "He spoke of trees, from the cedar that is in Lebanon to the hyssop that grows out of the wall" (1 Kings 4:33 ESV). Similarly, in Eccl. 2:4b–6 the king of Jerusalem claims, "I built houses and planted vineyards for myself. I made myself gardens and parks, and I planted in them all kinds of fruit trees. I made for myself pools from which to water the forest of growing trees." Commentators have thus concluded that Adam's role as cultivator and caretaker of the garden was a *royal* task, in the tradition of ancient Near Eastern monarchs. What the Genesis author suggests, however, is that what is later manifested as a royal task among kings of the ancient Near East was originally a *human* function. To care for creation and to cultivate it was one way that humanity was intended to function as God's image.

Finally, as many have noted, the verbs used for Adam's role "to work and to guard" the garden (*šmr* and *ʿbd*, Gen. 2:15 AT), are the same verbs used to describe the duties of the Levites who are to guard and serve (minister) at the tabernacle (Num. 3:7–8; 8:26; 18:5–6). Thus, scholars have determined that the use of *šmr* and *ʿbd* to describe Adam's work in the garden indicates that he served not only as a royal administrator of the kingdom but also as a priest of Yahweh's "sanctuary" in Eden. This idea is not without precedent in the ancient Near East. One of the titles borne by Assyrian kings was *šangû*, a term that denotes the king's role as the divinely appointed chief priest who participates in rituals and is responsible for the provision and maintenance of all the sanctuaries in his jurisdiction. This dual office is also well attested in earlier Sumerian royal hymns and inscriptions in which the king was appointed as the high priest of his domain (Seux, 228–29; van Driel, 173). What some identify as a priestly role for Adam was simply part of what it meant to be human—to cultivate God's sacred garden and to serve and worship him. Perhaps we should understand instead that Israel's priests were assigned this particular aspect of God's original creational intent for humanity. After the fall, it was reserved for and embodied by the Levites, for a time, until this priestly role would be distributed once again to all of God's people (1 Pet. 2:9).

In sum, the terms *ṣelem* and *dəmût* in Gen. 1 are multivalent. They define humanity both ontologically, as sons or children of God, and functionally, as those who rule and subdue, multiply and fill, represent God, and serve and worship him, in part, by tending and cultivating his good creation.

Corporate Israel as the "Image and Son" of God

The opening chapter of Exodus notes, "The people of Israel were fruitful and increased greatly; they multiplied and grew exceedingly strong, so that the land was filled with them" (Exod. 1:7). As many have recognized, this language echoes Gen. 1:28. It intentionally links God's people, Israel, with humanity in Gen. 1, to show that God's original creational intent was moving forward. Despite sin and rebellion, all nations would indeed be blessed, as God had promised, through Abraham's descendants. Even more, God's original creational intent—for his people to multiply and fill the land—was coming to pass through Israel.

Given this connection in Exod. 1:7 between Israel and humanity in Gen. 1, we should not be surprised to read, "Then you [Moses] shall say to Pharaoh, 'Thus says the LORD, "My son, my firstborn, is Israel, and I say to you, release my son that he may serve/worship [*ʿbd*, cf. Gen. 2:15] me." But if you refuse to release him, I will indeed kill your firstborn son'" (Exod. 4:22–23 AT). Not only does the text identify Israel explicitly as God's "son," and notably his *firstborn* son, but also Yahweh demonstrates himself to be Israel's divine kinsman (*gō'ēl*) who will carry out his role as the avenger of blood. This is similar to God's response in Gen. 9:5–6, which implies that Yahweh is the kinsman of his people, humanity (cf. *pdh*, "to ransom," and *g'l*, "to redeem," in Jer. 31:11 ESV).

In addition to the intentional link between Israel and humanity in Exod. 1:7 (cf. Gen. 1:26–28), and the explicit identification of Israel as Yahweh's son in Exod. 4, we also see the royal and priestly aspects given to humanity at creation resurface in Israel—for example, in Exod. 19:5–6, "If you will indeed obey my voice and keep my covenant, you shall be my treasured possession among all peoples, for all the earth is mine; and you shall be to me a kingdom of priests and a holy nation." These human roles were assigned to Israel so that they might demonstrate what it meant to be human. As Michael Goheen puts it, Israel was to be "an attractive sign before all nations of what God had intended in the beginning, and of the goal toward which he was moving: the restoration of all creation and human life from the corruption of sin" (25). This was to be accomplished not only through sacrifice, prayer, studying the Torah, abstaining from idolatry, and observing religious feasts and festivals, but by the way Israel used their resources, how they treated their employees, how they conducted business, and how they cared for the poor—all before the watching eyes of the nations (Lev. 19:9–10, 13, 35–36). Israel was commanded not to glean the edges of the field, not to strip the vineyards bare or to gather the fallen grapes, not to steal, lie, oppress, rob, commit injustice, slander, hate, or seek vengeance. They were to use honest weights and measurements so as not to increase their own wealth by cheating the buyer (Lev. 19). As Israel conformed to the law, the law would conform them to the image and likeness of the Father. Although the OT does not describe Israel explicitly as created in God's image and likeness (*ṣelem* and *dəmût*), this is implied by their position as firstborn son and royal priest. Through obedience Israel would manifest its true identity as a people created in the image of God, and thus show the nations God's original creational intent for all of humanity.

Christ as the Image

The *imago Dei* comes to its fullest expression in Jesus, whom Paul identifies explicitly as "the image of the invisible God" (*eikōn tou theou tou aoratou*, Col. 1:15). By contrasting "image" (*eikōn*) with "invisible" (*aoratos*), Paul emphasizes that God the Father, largely unseen until Jesus's arrival, *has been made visible in Christ*. However, Jesus is not merely a *representation* of God. By using the language of Gen. 1:26–27 (*eikōn*), Paul creates a series of significant contrasts that reveal Jesus's identity. First, whereas humanity was created *in* the image of God (*kat' eikona theou*, Gen. 1:27), Jesus *is* the image of God (*hos estin eikōn tou theou*, Col. 1:15). Whereas humanity was created *as* God's royal representative, to rule and subdue creation on God's behalf (Gen. 1:26, 28), Jesus *is himself* the king (Col. 1:13). Whereas humanity *represents* God visibly on the earth, Jesus *manifests* God visibly on the earth. By declaring, "For by him all things were created, in heaven and on earth [*en tois ouranois kai epi tēs gēs*; cf. LXX of Gen. 1:1: *en archē epoiēsen ho theos ton ouranon kai tēn gēn*], visible and invisible, whether thrones or dominions or rulers or authorities—all things were created through him and for him. And he is before all things, and in him all things hold together" (Col. 1:15–16), Paul identifies Jesus with none other than Elohim of Gen. 1.

Further, Paul's use of *eikōn* to designate Jesus as *the* image of God (Col. 1:15) may be an intentional contrast with false images, which the LXX refers to with the same term over fifteen times (Deut. 4:16; 2 Kings 11:18; 2 Chron. 33:7; Isa. 40:19; Hosea 13:2; Ezek. 7:20; 16:17; Dan. 2:31, 34, 35; 3:1, 2, 3, 5, 7, 10, 12, 15). In his rant against idolatry (*eikōn*/idol in LXX Isa. 40:19), Isaiah proclaims Yahweh as the *sole creator* and the *exclusive sovereign over all authorities* (Isa. 40:21–26). Given this background, it is not surprising that Paul would describe Jesus as the *eikōn* of God who created all things, in heaven and on earth, including all thrones, dominions, rulers, and authorities (Col. 1:16). He identifies Jesus not only with Elohim of Gen. 1, but also as the *true, living* image of God, over and against lifeless man-made idols that were worshiped in ancient Israel and in Jesus's day, including at Colossae (Magie).

It is also worth considering that Paul's use of *eikōn* in Col. 1:15 without the prepositions that appear in Gen. 1:26–27 (*kata* in the LXX, *bə*/*kə* in the MT) suggests that Jesus is the *archetype after which humanity is patterned*. That is, to be created in the image of God is to be made according to the likeness *of Christ*, who is "before all things" (Col. 1:17). Just as Jesus is the template for the *new* humanity, created by the Spirit (2 Cor. 3:18), he was the template for *original* humanity, also created by the Spirit (Gen. 1:2; 2:7). Thus, to bear Christ's image (1 Cor. 15:49; Rom. 8:29) and to be transformed into his likeness (2 Cor. 3:18) imply the restoration of humanity's original identity, function, and purpose—to rule, subdue, cultivate, be fruitful and multiply, and extend the blessing and presence of God in the world.

Christians as Children and "Images" of God

Many of the NT authors mention this transformation. Having borne the image of Adam, those who belong to Christ will also bear his image, as humanity did prior to the fall (1 Cor. 15:49; see also Gladd, 302–3). As "sons of God" we will be fully restored through *the* Son, who is "the firstborn *among many brothers*" (Rom. 8:29; cf. Heb. 2:11–15). Our transformation into Christ's likeness results not only in the restoration of our sonship to God; we also gain the added blessing of becoming *the younger siblings of Christ*! We will share a family resemblance with our Father and our elder Brother that will be recognizable (1 John 3:1–2). Our resurrected bodies will resemble the radiant face of Moses as he descended Mount Sinai, the glorified bodies of Moses and Elijah on the Mount of Transfiguration (Luke 9:30–31), and the body of Jesus himself, whose face "shone like the sun" (Matt. 17:2) and whose clothing was "dazzling white" (Luke 9:29; cf. Rev. 1:16b, 3:4–5; 4:4; 10:1). What's more, our family resemblance will be manifest in our character: our thoughts, motives, desires, and actions will be aligned with the character of God our Father and Christ our Brother. After referring to believers as a new creation "in the likeness of God [which] has been created in righteousness and holiness and truth" (Eph. 4:23–24 AT), Paul says we will speak the truth, turn from sin, and abandon corrupt talk for that which is good and builds up (4:25–29). We will put away bitterness, wrath, anger, clamor, slander, and malice and be kind to one another, tenderhearted, and forgiving—walking in love (4:31–5:2). Like our Father and elder Brother, we will eschew sexual immorality, impurity, covetousness, filthiness, foolish talk, and crude joking (5:3–4). This is what it means to be made in God's image and to belong to the family of God. We will be like him when we see him as he is (1 John 3:2).

Conclusion

It is critically important for our understanding of God and the divine-human relationship, and for realizing our identity and purpose in this world, to have a proper sense of the *imago Dei*. Genesis 1 associates it with ruling and procreation but also, based on 5:1–3, with sonship. To be created in God's image and likeness is, first and foremost, to be his child. Genesis 9 further emphasizes the kinship aspect of the *imago Dei* by showing that the "life for life" principle is based on the idea that humans belong to the family of God. God avenges their life because he is their divine paterfamilias.

Given that Gen. 1 commemorates God's construction of his macro-temple, to be created in God's image and likeness implies that humans are in some way comparable to "statuettes." Indeed, they are living images, who represent God in the world. Further, they are to be cultivators of God's good creation, as they work and serve the Lord in his cosmic temple.

As humanity multiplied, they were to fill the earth, bearing God's presence and blessing as their numbers expanded. After the fall Israel took on the role of son and royal priest, serving as the vehicle through whom God's light would come to the nations (Isa. 49:6). Where Israel failed, however, Jesus succeeded. He is *the* image of God—the true, living manifestation of the Father, God's faithful firstborn son, our elder brother, and the template after which humanity was originally created. God's people will be re-created, again formed after the pattern of Christ. Like Moses and Elijah atop the Mount of Transfiguration, we will bear God's glory—a physical, outward sign that marks our (re)creation in God's image and membership in his family. To be changed into the likeness of Christ means nothing less than the restoration of our status as God's children (Rev. 21:3, 7) and a new era of ruling, cultivating, and worshiping God, for eternity.

See also Adam, First and Last; Image of God; Son of God

Bibliography. Beale, G. K., "Eden, the Temple, and the Church's Mission in the New Creation," *JETS* 48 (2005): 5–31; Callendar, D., *Adam in Myth and History* (Eisenbrauns, 2000); Fisher, L. R., "Creation at Ugarit and in the Old Testament," *VT* 15 (1965): 313–24; Garr, R. W., "'Image' and 'Likeness' in the Inscription from Tell Fakhariyeh," *IEJ* 50 (2000): 227–34; Gladd, B. L., "The Last Adam as the 'Life Giving Spirit' Revisited," *WTJ* 71 (2009): 297–309; Goheen, M., *A Light to the Nations* (Baker Academic, 2011); Herring, S. L., *Divine Substitution* (Vandenhoeck & Ruprecht, 2013); Klein, J., "The Coronation and Consecration of Šulgi in the Ekur (Šulgi G)," in *Ah, Assyira*, ed. M. Cogan and I. Eph'al (Magnes, 1991), 292–313; Lints, R., *Identity and Idolatry* (IVP Academic, 2015); Lorton, D., "God's Beneficient Creation," *SAK* 20 (1993): 125–55; Magie, D., "Egyptian Deities in Asia Minor in Inscriptions and on Coins," *AJA* 57 (1953): 163–87; McConville, J. G., *Being Human in God's World* (Baker Academic, 2016); McDowell, C., *The Image of God in the Garden of Eden* (Eisenbrauns, 2015); McDowell, "In the Image of God He Created Them," in *The Image of God in an Image Driven Age*, ed. B. F. Jones and J. W. Barbeau (IVP Academic, 2016), 29–46; Millard, A. R., and P. Bordreuil, "A Statue from Syria with Assyrian and Aramaic Inscriptions," *BA* 45 (1982): 135–41; Peterson, R. S., *The* Imago Dei *as Human Identity* (Eisenbrauns, 2015); Seux, M. J., *Epithetes* (Letouzey et Ane, 1967); van Driel, G., *Cult of Aššur* (van Gorcum, 1969); Widengren, G., *The King and the Tree of Life in Ancient Near Eastern Religion* (Almqvist & Wiksell, 1951).

CATHERINE McDOWELL

Intertextuality

See Quotation, Allusion, and Echo; Theological Interpretation of Scripture

Introductory Formulas of Quotations

See Quotation, Allusion, and Echo

Isaiah, Book of

Isaiah son of Amoz prophesied in Judah (the Southern Kingdom) in the eighth century BC, from at least the death of Uzziah (6:1) until the departure of Sennacherib upon the destruction of his army (37:37). The probable dates of these events are 739 and 701 BC. Thus, Isaiah's ministry occurred during the last days of Israel (the Northern Kingdom) and the threat that Assyria would also destroy Judah. Ahaz and Hezekiah were the kings with whom Isaiah had dealings. In both cases he called upon the kings to trust Yahweh to deliver them. Ahaz refused, but Hezekiah, in extremity, did exercise such trust, and Yahweh vindicated it, demonstrating his unique nature and power. However, as the book has it, Isaiah foresees a day when Judah would not be delivered but would be taken into captivity in Babylon. Realizing that such an event would seem to contradict his proclamation of Yahweh's uniqueness, Isaiah predicts that Yahweh will defeat the Babylonian gods and restore his people to their land.

Essential Features of the Book of Isaiah

Composition. The book ostensibly comes from Isaiah himself; it never suggests that anyone else had a hand in its composition. The initial superscription (1:1) naming Isaiah is repeated in 2:1, and Isaiah is depicted speaking to both Ahaz (7:1–17) and Hezekiah (37:5–7, 21–35). No other person is named or identified as speaking. Nevertheless, it has become increasingly common since the late eighteenth century to deny that Isaiah wrote the entire book. This is primarily because Isaiah is not named after chap. 39 and because chaps. 40–66 seem to be addressed to the exiles in Babylon (40–55) and possibly to the returnees from the exile (56–66). Additionally, it is noted that the content of chaps. 40–66 is different from that of chaps. 1–39. It is also claimed that differing style and vocabulary indicate a different author.

Solutions to these problems have proliferated. Initially, it was suggested that there were two authors: Isaiah and an unnamed prophet who wrote chaps. 40–66 during and after the exile. Then a third author was proposed for chaps. 56–66. At the present time, it is suggested that Isaiah son of Amoz only wrote a small portion of the book and that successions of his followers across the next several centuries carried out a process of continual revision until the book reached its present form in the fourth century BC. However, it must be pointed out that there is no objective evidence for any of this. That being so, the book ought to be interpreted as a whole, as its form obviously intends us to do.

Structure and message. There is general agreement that there are two main divisions in the book: chaps. 1–39 and 40–66. There is also wide agreement, although by no means universal, that 40–66 should be further subdivided between 40–55 and 56–66. Within these major units, there is some consensus concerning sections: chaps. 1–12; 13–23; 24–27; 28–35; 36–39; 40–48; 49–55; 56–59; 60–62; 63–66. But there is no agreement on how these sections relate to one another. A glance at major commentaries will make this point very clearly. Two primary factors have influenced my own proposal: (1) the emphasis on servanthood in chaps. 40–66, and (2) the *inclusio* of the mission to the nations in 2:1–5 and 66:18–24 (which has its own *inclusio* with 56:1–8). In the first place, then, just as the NT tells the reader how to read the OT, Isa. 40–66 tells the reader how to read chaps. 1–39—that is, with a focus on Israel's role as servant. But what is the purpose of that servanthood? It is that the nations might come to know Yahweh, the only God. In that light, see table 1 for an outline of the book.

Table 1. Outline of Isaiah

- I. 1–6 The call to servanthood: problem and solution
- II. 7–39 Trust: the basis of servanthood
  - A. 7–12 Trust refused, but the nations trust instead
  - B. 13–35 Lessons in trust
    - 1. 13–23 The folly of trusting the nations
    - 2. 24–27 Yahweh, sovereign of the nations
    - 3. 28–33 Woe to those who will not wait for Yahweh
    - 4. 34–35 Conclusion: a desert or a garden?
  - C. 36–39 Trust proven but then abandoned
- III. 40–55 Grace: the motive and means of servanthood
  - A. 40 Grace: Yahweh's desire, ability, and determination to redeem
  - B. 41–48 Grace: the motive of servanthood; Yahweh's servants
    - 1. 41–46 Yahweh versus the gods of Babylon
    - 2. 47–48 Implications of Yahweh's uniqueness
  - C. 49–55 Grace: the means of servanthood; Yahweh's servant
    - 1. 49:1–52:12 Anticipation
    - 2. 52:13–53:12 Revelation
    - 3. 54–55 Invitation
- IV. 56–66 Righteousness: character of servanthood
  - A. 56:1–8 Righteous foreigners and eunuchs
  - B. 56:9–59:15a Unrighteous Israel
  - C. 59:15b–21 The Divine Warrior
  - D. 60:1–22 The glory of Zion
  - E. 61:1–3 The anointed one: oaks of righteousness
  - D′. 61:4–62:12 The righteousness of Zion
  - C′. 63:1–6 The Divine Warrior
  - B′. 63:7–66:17 Unrighteous Israel
  - A′. 66:18–24 Righteous foreigners

In brief, the message of the book is that Yahweh alone is God of all the earth, that he is love, truth, and goodness (in short, holy), and that he desires a relationship with humans in which they recognize these things and mirror them in their own lives. However, the only way into such a relationship is through trusting surrender of their lives into Yahweh's hands, something that fallen humans are never willing to do. They trust humanity, as exemplified in the great nations, much more than they trust him. The result is inevitably destruction at the hands of those nations. What Yahweh wants is for a people who, instead of denying him and trusting the nations to their own destruction, will rather trust him and, being delivered from the nations, will draw them into trusting and worshiping him as well.

Hezekiah proves that Yahweh is trustworthy, but when he has an opportunity to reveal Yahweh's glory to the nations he fails. Clearly, he is not the promised anointed one who will lead the world into the wholeness, the shalom, that Yahweh has promised. Furthermore, Isaiah knows that Judah will not trust Yahweh in the coming years and that Yahweh will remove his protecting hand from them. So, what will motivate them to abandon themselves to trusting him? The answer is grace, Yahweh's refusal to let his people go, to let the nations swallow them up. Far from abandoning them, he will use them as the evidence in his court case against the Babylonian gods, in which he will prove that they are not gods at all. He alone can do a new thing, something that has never happened before, the return of a people from captivity.

But how can Yahweh do that? Yes, he can in his own sovereignty take his people out of the hand of mighty Babylon and restore them to their land. But how can he restore them to himself? How can a holy God use an unholy people as his servants? Sin and its effects cannot simply be ignored. The complex sacrificial system announced that point with unmistakable clarity. The answer is the servant. The servant will take the people's, and the world's, sin upon himself and present them to Yahweh as clean and whole. How such a thing should be possible is beyond human rationality, but God's thoughts and ways are not ours.

So, why does the book not end at that point? First, Yahweh wants to share his character with his people; that is why he delivered them from the grasp of sin. If they continue to live in ways that defy his holy character, then the deliverance was for nothing. But second, there is the mission. Israel is Yahweh's servant to accomplish what? By their transformed lives they are to draw the nations to the mountain of the house of Yahweh, there to learn his ways. As the suffering servant he has come to bear the sins of the servants and carry away their guilt. But as the Divine Warrior he comes to destroy the power of darkness in their lives and to arise as the dawn in their lives. As "oaks of righteousness," as the bride, "the holy people," they will presage a new heaven and a new earth and will call all nations into a fellowship with Yahweh that is eternal.

The Hermeneutics of Isaiah

It is no accident that Isaiah has been called "the Prince of the Prophets." This book, in beautiful poetry and prose, contains the most complete compendium of biblical theology that is to be found in any single book of the Bible. It takes the reader from creation to the new heaven and new earth. It contains the clearest statements of monotheism and transcendence. It has the most developed exploration of the complexities of sin, as well as the most powerful statement of substitutionary atonement. The depth of theology is accompanied by gripping images beginning with the abandoned hut in a cucumber patch of chap. 1 and extending all the way to the burned, decaying bodies of rebels in chap. 66.

This literary and theological richness has meant that interpreting the book has been a daunting task through all the centuries since its writing. Nevertheless, that being said, there are some features that may provide a key to interpretation. One of the most striking features that unifies the book is the phrase "the Holy One of Israel." This phrase occurs 25x in the book (26x if one includes "the Holy One of Jacob" in 29:23). It seems likely that the frequency of the phrase and its distribution throughout the book (13x in chaps. 1–39 and 13x in chaps. 40–66) is the result of the impact of the vision of chap. 6. The two elements in the phrase, "Holy One" and "of Israel," serve to highlight the two primary facets of Yahweh's nature that the book emphasizes: his transcendence and his immanence.

While it is not possible to separate transcendence and immanence in the various parts of the book, there is some value in looking at their relative treatments. In chaps. 1–39 transcendence particularly is expressed in the contrast between Yahweh and the nations. Why would one trust the nations of humanity when the one who made the nations and who will judge the nations has invited you into a relationship with himself (cf. 31:1–3)? His immanence appears in his promise to care for his people if they will only trust him; he "waits to be gracious to [them]" (30:18 ESV). In chaps. 40–66 his transcendence is particularly seen in his absolute distinction from the so-called gods. There is none like him (45:18), and Babylon's sin is that she has arrogated that distinction for herself (47:8, 10). But even more explicitly than in the earlier division, the two elements are closely intertwined in chaps. 40–66. Here, very frequently "the Holy One of Israel" is identified as "your Redeemer" (e.g., 43:14). It is precisely because he is the transcendent Creator that he can break into the cosmos and redeem his people from the power of the nations and the effects of their sin.

Another important interpretive key is the universalism of the book. Beginning in chap. 2 and continuing through the final division of the book, chaps. 56–66, it is unmistakable that the salvation of Judah and Jerusalem is not for them alone but for the world. Yahweh is to be trusted so that Judah and Jerusalem, God's servants, may demonstrate to the world, by means of the servant, that Yahweh alone is God and, as such, is the sole Savior of the world. This theme unites the book and projects the book into the NT era.

Isaiah and the NT

Along with Genesis, Deuteronomy, and Psalms, Isaiah is frequently referred to in the NT. Ben Witherington (13) has argued that when "echoes" are considered, only Psalms is more often referred to. Part of the reason for the heavy usage of Isaiah (411x according to Witherington, 13–18) is the previously mentioned fact that of all the OT books, Isaiah has the most references to the Messiah. Thus, as the NT writers sought to show that Jesus was indeed the one promised in the OT, they would obviously turn to Isaiah. But Witherington (4) argues that there is another factor: Psalms and Isaiah are poetic (Psalms entirely so, and Isaiah heavily so). Given that poetry appeals more to the affective and less to the cognitive, this means that statements can be multivalent, carrying a surplus of meaning. Thus, in Witherington's words (348), the NT writers found in Psalms and Isaiah a deep well of meaning upon which to draw as they sought to understand and explicate the Christ event.

It is impossible in this short compass to examine even a small portion of the more than four hundred usages of Isaiah that are found in the NT. But it is possible to discuss several representative examples of the various types of usage. We may identify four of these: they are "echoes," "allusions," "analogies," and "predictions." Echoes may result from the writer's familiarity with the text of Isaiah so that Isaianic language may be used even when the writer is not aware of doing so. Allusions typically involve an intentional use but simply as a literary device in which the original context is of no particular interest to the NT author. Analogies involve a fuller treatment of the original context in which the writer is saying that his or her situation is similar to that of the original author: "This is like that." Finally, there are predictions in which the NT writer is saying that the OT author was consciously and intentionally pointing to something in NT times when he or she spoke the original words: "This is that." (There is considerable disagreement about these categories and precisely how they should be defined, particularly as to intentionality. See the article "Quotation Allusion, and Echo" by Chris Beetham, elsewhere in the dictionary.)

Echoes. It is probably in Revelation that the largest number of "echoes" of Isaiah appear. It has been argued that Isaiah is in the background of the entire book although there are very few direct quotations to be found. How many of these are conscious and how many are unconscious is very difficult to say. But it is evident that John believes himself to be part of the whole prophetic tradition, and that there is a direct continuity between what is happening to him and what the Scriptures have portrayed. In addition, he is saturated with Scripture, especially with Isaiah. These things being so, we should not be surprised if Isaianic language bubbles up everywhere (Fekkes, 102).

An example of a multiple echo is found in Rev. 19:13–15, where the Divine Warrior wears a robe dipped in blood and has a sword coming out of his mouth. The robe dipped in blood is reminiscent of Isa. 63:3, where the Warrior coming up from Edom has a garment spattered with blood like the garment of one who has been treading grapes in the wine vat. The reference to the sword reminds one of Isa. 11:4, where it is said that the promised one "will strike the earth with the rod of his mouth and slay the wicked with the breath of his lips" (AT).

In Rev. 5:9 and 14:3 the "new song" is an echo of Isaiah's "new song" in 42:10 (as well as 6x in Psalms). Other echoes appear in 2:17, "a new name" (Isa. 65:15); 4:8, "Holy, holy, holy is the Lord God Almighty" (Isa. 6:3); and 15:4, "all nations will come and worship before you" (Isa. 66:23). It seems likely that the description of God as the one who "sits on the throne" (4:2; 5:1; 6:16; 7:10, etc.) is also an echo of Isa. 6.

Echoes found in other NT books include Luke 3:8, "We have Abraham as our father" (Isa. 51:2); 1 Cor. 1:17, "to preach the gospel" (Isa. 52:7; 61:1); 2 Cor. 9:10, "seed to the sower and bread for food" (Isa. 55:10); Phil. 2:10–11, "every knee should bow . . . and every tongue confess" (Isa. 45:23); and Heb. 9:28, "sacrificed once to take away the sins of many" (Isa. 53:12).

Allusions. With an allusion, an author or speaker is making an appeal to an audience through the use of some material that they have in common. As stated above, I am distinguishing an allusion from an analogy by the degree of theological continuity between the original and the citation. An analogy presupposes such continuity, while an allusion does not. Witherington (463) suggests that many of the hearers/readers might not have had the knowledge that these references call for but that the writers wanted to push those hearers/readers to seek out that knowledge, perhaps from the couriers who brought the letter.

When John calls the city built on seven hills (Rev. 17:9, manifestly Rome) Babylon (17:5), he is alluding to Isa. 13–14 and 47, where Babylon represents that human pride that exalts itself against God and brings destruction upon itself. Interestingly, some of the language in Revelation that is used to describe Babylon, especially her prostitution, is very similar to that used of Tyre in Isa. 23, at the end of the oracles against the nations headed up by Babylon in chap. 13.

Another probable allusion is found in Jesus's parable of the vineyard in Matt. 21:33–41. The allusion would be to the vineyard of bitter grapes in Isa. 5. In Isaiah the vineyard itself produces the bad grapes. In Matthew it is the tenants of the vineyard who refuse to give the owner the rent that is due him. But the overall point is similar: the owner of the vineyard is not receiving what he has a right to expect from the vineyard.

Many of these allusive uses are what Witherington calls "homiletical" (346). That is, they are used to illustrate or reinforce a point being made. There is less concern for how the material is used in its original setting (but see Matthew's apparent awareness of the context of Isa. 5 [Matt. 21:33–40]). Paul is a prime example of such usage. In Rom. 2:24, speaking of Jews who are proud of their law while at the same time breaking it, he alludes to Isa. 52:5, which speaks of God's name being blasphemed because of the people's defeat by their enemies. In Rom. 3:17 he alludes to Isa. 59:7–8, "The way of peace they do not know," in his catena of quotations establishing that none is righteous. In Rom. 9:20–21, when he asks whether God could not harden the Jews' hearts if he so chose, he makes use of Isaiah's two illustrations where the pot dares to challenge the potter about what he is making (29:16; 45:9). Other examples may be found in Rom. 9:27–29 and 10:20–21.

Other homiletical allusions appear in Stephen's sermon recorded in Acts 7 and in Jesus's words in Mark 9:48. Stephen uses Isa. 66:1–2 to reinforce his statement that the "temple" is not finally intended to be a building, and Jesus, speaking of hell, makes use of Isa. 66:24 with its depiction of a place of death and decay.

Analogies. When a NT writer draws an analogy with an Isaianic passage, he is paying attention to the prophet's argument and while not necessarily saying that the prophet had the future in mind. He is arguing that there is a genuine parallel between the two situations. The most prominent example of this is the use of Isa. 6:9–10. The NT quotes this two-verse passage more than any other (Matt. 13:14–15; Mark 4:12; Luke 8:10; John 12:40; Acts 7:51; 28:26–27; Rom. 11:8). Jesus uses it to explain his use of parables, and the apostles use it to make sense of the Jewish rejection of the gospel. Just as Isaiah's message seemed to have hardened the hearts of his hearers, so did the gospel.

Jesus uses Isaiah in this way frequently. In Matt. 24:29, when he speaks of the end of the world, he draws upon Isaiah's poetic description of the ends of Babylon (13:10) and Edom (34:4). In Matt. 15:8–9 (Mark 7:6–7) he argues that when Isaiah excoriated his people for their superficial religion, he was describing the people of Jesus's day as well. In all three of the Synoptics (Matt. 21:13; Mark 11:17; Luke 19:46) Jesus is reported as quoting Isa. 56:7 when he drives the money changers from the temple. As in Isaiah, the temple was to be "a house of prayer for all nations."

While Paul uses Isaiah allusively in Rom. 9 and 10, it can also be argued that he uses the prophet analogically as well. In 9:27–29 he argues that just as Isaiah saw that only a remnant would return from exile (Isa. 10:22–23), so also only a remnant would respond to the gospel. Another analogical use is to be found in Gal. 4:27, where the apostle applies the promise Isaiah has made to the earthly Jerusalem (54:1) to the spiritual Zion.

Predictions. Many interpreters who would be more or less in agreement with the previous three categories will differ at this point. One issue is whether a specific prediction of the future is possible. But a second issue has to do with the intention of the OT writers and whether in certain instances they understood themselves to be making a prediction or not. When the NT writers claim that something has been predicted by an OT prophet, there is a tendency on the part of persons in both of these camps to see the NT writers as, in some sense, misusing the OT materials.

A good example of this latter position is found in regard to the well-known Isa. 7:14: "A virgin shall conceive and bear a son and shall call his name Immanuel" (AT). It will be claimed, justly on the basis of the surrounding context, that Isaiah was talking not about some figure in the distant future but about a child to be born within a year of the pronouncement. That being so, according to these scholars, Matthew has misused an ancient statement that really had nothing to do with Jesus simply because the Greek translation happened to use the Greek word meaning "virgin," something that was not in Isaiah's intention. Or, somewhat more generously, Matthew has filled the ancient statement with further meaning.

While there is no question of the immediate application of the sign (Isa. 7:15–17), Isaiah's use of the unusual word *ʿalmâ* is important. It is an ambiguous word, unlike either "young woman" (*naʿărâ*) or "virgin" (*bətûlâ*). If the only significance of the sign was for the immediate future, "young woman" or even "woman" would have been adequate. In its other usages *ʿalmâ* refers to a young woman of marriageable age. In the cases where her marital status can be determined, she is yet unmarried. By implication, then, she is a virgin. Why did Isaiah use the ambiguous term? Precisely because the significance of this sign that God was with his people would not be exhausted in the deliverance from Syria and Israel that Isaiah was predicting. In the future Immanuel would be truly present with his people in their human flesh as a result of a virgin birth. The LXX decision, five hundred years after the initial application of the sign had occurred, to translate the Hebrew with *parthenos*, "virgin," rather than a Greek term for "young woman" is strong evidence as to the understanding by Jewish interpreters of Isaiah's ultimate intention. Thus, Matthew has used the term as Isaiah intended, neither misusing it nor filling it with additional (unintended) meaning.

This then has a bearing on how Isa. 9:1–7 (MT 8:23–9:6) should be understood (Matt. 4:14–16; Luke 1:32–33, 79; John 7:42). Who is the "child" intended here? Was it Hezekiah, who was to bring light to the northern regions of Israel, where the Assyrian depredations first occurred? Or was it Immanuel, the Mighty God, who would bring light to those who had plunged themselves into darkness by refusing "the law and the testimony" (8:19–20 AT)? If we correctly understand Isa. 7:14 and what it says about Immanuel, it becomes clear that Isaiah's intent far exceeds a successor for Ahaz, and that the NT writers were correct in thinking so.

This understanding is further supported by Isa. 11. This is not a poetic description of the expected reign of Hezekiah. The person predicted here, while certainly described poetically, is not the typical ancient Near Eastern king, establishing and maintaining a dominion through the use of military force. In fact, what he brings about is exactly the opposite of this. It is virtually a new heaven and new earth (note that 11:9 is directly quoted in 65:25). Thus, when the NT writers draw upon this passage to speak of Christ, they are using it within the full intent of Isaiah (Rom. 15:10; 2 Thess. 2:6).

It is not clear whether Isaiah saw himself as predicting the forerunner of Jesus when he spoke the words now recorded as 40:3 or not. Matthew certainly takes them that way (3:3). John the evangelist has John the Baptist appropriating the position for himself (John 1:23), while Mark (1:1–3) and Luke (3:4–6) use more nuanced language ("as it is written in Isaiah the prophet"). This may be an example of the prophet's not having a full revelation of the implications of what the Spirit was leading him to say. The appearance of the reference in all four Gospels supports such an understanding.

Be that as it may, there is no doubt that the NT writers were correct when they understood Isaiah to be referring to Christ in his description of the individual servant in 42:1–9; 49:1–12; 50:4–9; and 52:13–53:12. So Matthew cites 42:1–4 (12:18–21), and Paul cites 49:6 (Acts 13:47). Jesus himself alludes to 50:6 and 53:12 (Mark 10:34 and Luke 22:37). It is generally accepted that Jesus himself explained to his disciples the connections between himself and Isaiah's servant, if not before the resurrection, then after (cf. John 12:38; Luke 24:27). Thus, when the Ethiopian eunuch inquires of Philip whom the prophet was speaking of in the material now found in Isa. 53, Philip is immediately ready to preach Christ from that passage. Isaiah 61:1–2 is intended to be the capstone of all the servant passages. This is made evident by the direct parallel with 42:7. Thus, when Jesus uses 61:1–2 to introduce his messianic mission, stating that the prediction has been fulfilled in him, he is signaling his understanding of the entire complex, beginning in Isa. 40. It may be that when the evangelists begin the exposition of Jesus's ministry with their indication that 40:3 is referring to John the Baptist, they are making the same point.

Bibliography. Evans, C. A., *To See and Not Perceive*, JSOTSup 64 (Sheffield Academic, 1989); Fekkes, J., *Isaiah and Prophetic Traditions in the Book of Revelation*, JSNTSup 93 (JSOT Press, 1994); Hays, R. B., *Echoes of Scripture in the Gospels* (Baylor University Press, 2017); Mallen, P., *The Reading and Transformation of Isaiah in Luke-Acts*, LNTS 367 (T&T Clark, 2008); Moyise, S., and M. J. J. Menken, eds., *Isaiah in the New Testament* (T&T Clark, 2005); Schneck, R., *Isaiah in the Gospel of Mark, I-VIII*, BDS 1 (BIBAL Press, 1994); Wagner, J. R., *Heralds of the Good News* (Brill, 2003); Watts, R., *Isaiah's New Exodus and Mark* (Baker Academic, 2001); Wilk, F., "Paul as User, Interpreter, and Reader of the Book of Isaiah," in *Reading the Bible Intertextually*, ed. R. B. Hayes, S. Alkier, and L. A. Huizinga (Baylor University Press, 2009), 83–99; Witherington, B., III, *Isaiah Old and New* (Fortress, 2017).

JOHN OSWALT

Israel *See* Church; Israel and the Church, The Story of

Israel and the Church, The Story of

To tell the story of Israel and the church we must take account of two streams in the biblical narrative that are distinct throughout while being closely linked. The first concerns the whole of creation with humanity at its pinnacle, created in God's image and likeness, and exercising dominion over creation. The second is about one nation that is chosen from within fallen humanity and has a God-given purpose involving all nations. The convergence of these two streams constitutes the NT understanding of the church as the people of God.

The Wider Narrative

The nation of Israel is only part of the wider humanity that began with the creation of Adam and Eve and their placement in the garden of Eden. In a similar way the NT tells how the church began with one who is called the last Adam (1 Cor. 15:45). The first congregation consisted of Jews in Jerusalem. But the church soon began to include gentiles, who are also part of the wider humanity. How Israel and the gentiles relate in the OT's view of the people of God, and in the NT's view of the church, is our concern here.

The narrative begins with Yahweh, the Creator of all the earth and of the heavens above. Although the biblical story largely focuses on Yahweh and his dealings with Israel, he always remains Sovereign Lord over all creation. Within this universal sovereignty is Yahweh's distinctive role as the covenant God of Israel. The stories of Israel and the gentiles are closely connected but should not be confused.

Israel begins with the descendants of Abram through Isaac's son Jacob (Israel). The election of Abram continues a historical process that goes back to the beginning of the fallen world and to Abel, the son of Adam and Eve, who was chosen over his brother Cain. The chosen line, traced through Gen. 3–11, recommences with

Seth and continues with Noah, Shem, Tehra (Abram's father), and then Israel (1 Chron. 1:1–27; Luke 3:23–38). However, the election of Israel as God's special people descended from Abram has ramifications for all nations (Gen. 12:3).

Abram's name is changed to Abraham (father of a multitude). The initial promises made to him include four main things: his descendants will be very numerous; they will inherit the land of Canaan; they will be a special people to God; and through them all the nations of the earth will be blessed (Gen. 12:1–3; 15:1–6; 17:1–8). This covenant is restated to Abraham's son Isaac, and then to Isaac's son Jacob (Israel), and thus is made with all Israel as a people. The role of Israel as mediator of God's blessing to the wider humanity continues into the NT and plays a vital role in our understanding of the NT and its use of the OT.

Israel's enslavement in Egypt is resolved by the miraculous redemption event of the exodus and the bringing of the people to Sinai. Here they are constituted as a nation under the Sinai covenant or law. God tells them that their obedience to his covenant will establish them as "my treasured possession among all peoples, for all the earth is mine." They will be "a kingdom of priests and a holy nation" (Exod. 19:4–6 ESV). Thus, Israel is designated as having a priestly ministry beyond itself while remaining a unique, holy nation among all peoples. The Sinai covenant is prefaced by reference to Israel's privileged role of being the mediator of God's blessings to all humanity.

The Attributes of Israel

A number of attributes make Israel identifiable as the unique people of God. The process of election that began with Abel and Seth leads to the calling of one man to be the father of many nations but particularly of Israel. First, to Israel exclusively belong the oracles of God, including the covenants (Exod. 2:23–25; 6:1–8; 19:1–8; Rom. 3:1–2; 9:4–5). God spoke uniquely to Israel as the people at the center of his purpose to establish his kingdom.

Second, only Israel experienced the redemptive event of the exodus from captivity, the giving of the law, and the assurance of belonging to God: "I am the LORD your God, who brought you out of Egypt, out of the land of slavery" (Exod. 20:2). The exodus becomes the historical paradigm for defining Israel's exclusive relationship to Yahweh (e.g., Exod. 29:45–46; Lev. 25:38; 26:13; Deut. 16:6; Judg. 2:1; 1 Sam. 10:18; 1 Chron. 17:21; Pss. 106:7–8; 114:1–8; Hosea 12:13; 13:4).

Third, the promises of the covenant concerning the land of Canaan are initially fulfilled by Israel's possession of the land, even though disobedience causes the process of possessing it to be protracted and painful. This land, described as a land "flowing with milk and honey" (Exod. 3:8), is the place where God blesses them abundantly (Deut. 28:1–14). Echoes here of the garden of Eden later become direct prophetic predictions (Isa. 51:3; Ezek. 36:35). Numbers, Joshua, and Judges tell of the unbelief and idolatry that plague Israel's entry into and possession of the land. First Samuel relates the unsettled times as Israel strives to consolidate its national integrity and possession of Canaan in the face of many foes.

Fourth, the city of Jerusalem becomes the focal point of God's promises during the rule of David. God had promised to make his name dwell in a place to be revealed (Deut. 12:5–7; 16:1–2, 6; 26:1–2; 1 Kings 14:21). King David captures the Jebusite fortress of Zion (Jerusalem), which he names "the City of David" (2 Sam. 5:9; cf. 6:10, 12, 16). When the temple is built and the ark brought there, Jerusalem also comes to be known as the city of God (Pss. 46:4; 48:1–2, 8; 87:1–3). It is the place where God makes his name to dwell.

Fifth, the temple of Solomon is established as the permanent dwelling place of God—that is, where he caused his name to dwell. Solomon understood that this dignity did not mean that God was somehow confined to the ark in the temple (1 Kings 8:27–30; cf. Isa. 66:1), a fact not lost later to Stephen when he challenged the Jews over their adherence to the Jerusalem temple (Acts 7:44–50). Nevertheless, as the tabernacle had been, the temple becomes for Israel the tangible symbol of God's presence among his people. The ministry of both tabernacle and temple provides for the reconciliation of sinful subjects and the maintenance of Israel's fellowship with Yahweh.

Sixth, the royal dynasty or house of David becomes the focus of Yahweh's rule in Israel. Provision for kingship had been made in the Deuteronomic law (Deut. 17:14–20), but Israel's desire for a king was corrupted by the desire to be like other nations (1 Sam. 8:1–9). The first king, Saul, begins well but is ultimately rejected for his unbelief (1 Sam. 15:10–11, 26–28). Samuel the prophet is sent to anoint a new king approved by God, and so David becomes the anointed one. David endures much tribulation until the death of Saul. First, he is recognized as king over Judah (2 Sam. 2:4), and then over all Israel (2 Sam. 5:1–5). David's desire to build a temple in Jerusalem is rejected in favor of his son. Instead, God covenants with David that his dynasty will rule forever; David's son will be God's son (2 Sam. 7:1–16). God's covenant with Israel is summarized as "I will . . . be your God, and you will be my people" (Lev. 26:12; Jer. 7:23; 11:4; Ezek. 11:20; cf. 36:28). It is here personalized in Yahweh's promise concerning David's son: "I will be his father, and he will be my son" (2 Sam. 7:14). Israel has already been named as the son of God (Exod. 4:22; cf. Hosea 11:1), and the son of David is now named as the son of God and the representative of all Israel.

The tangible evidence of Israel being the chosen people of God, then, is that God redeemed them from captivity to dwell in the promised land, the place he prepared for them; the focus of the land is the city of God, Jerusalem; the focus of the city is the temple, which speaks of God's being in their midst; and over all is God's king, who mediates the rule of God himself. The heart of all this is "Immanuel": God is with us.

Empirical and Spiritual Israel

The unconditional nature of the covenant promises lies in the emphasis of so many of the promises made: God is going to bring about his purposes. There is a fundamental connection between the sovereignty of God and human responsibility that will characterize the whole biblical narrative. God's sovereignty means that his purposes will not fail, despite the constant expressions of the people's idolatry, unbelief, and disobedience.

The conditional nature of the covenant lies in the blessings of God being contingent on the obedience of the people (Gen. 18:17–19; Exod. 19:5; Lev. 26:3–4, 14–39; Deut. 28:15–68). The development of the nation is fraught with difficulties due to disobedience and unbelief. Nevertheless, there is a clear development from the promises made to Abraham, through the history surveyed above, to the glory of Solomon's kingdom centered on Jerusalem and the temple (1 Kings 8–10). This is the zenith of Israel's history, but it is soon tarnished by Solomon's disobedience (1 Kings 11:1–13). From there on, despite a few valiant attempts at reform by kings such as Asa, Jehoshaphat, Hezekiah, and Josiah, Israel's glory fades as Assyria destroys the Northern Kingdom of Israel in 722 BC, and then Babylon wreaks destruction on Judah in 586 BC.

During this period of decline leading to the eventual destruction of both parts of the kingdom, a new and significant movement arises. Yahweh sends a new order of prophets that we know as the writing prophets (or Latter Prophets). They bring a new eschatological dimension to the revelation of the salvation-history process. Speaking within specific aspects of the nation's history, these prophets present a three-point message to both Israel and Judah. First, there is the accusation of covenant breaking. Second, their dire threats of God's judgment on covenant breaking seem to indicate the possibility that all God's promises will be obliterated. Third, and most significantly for the way the NT takes up the story of Israel, is the element of the assurance of Israel's final salvation and how it will benefit the nations. God's promises and purposes will not fail.

The tension between the unconditional and the conditional elements of the covenant raises the question of how, in the face of Israel's constant disobedience, the kingdom of God that is centered on this nation will ever be established. The Latter Prophets provide the answer in at least two ways: first, there will be a faithful remnant out of the whole people who will inherit the promises; and second, Yahweh will do a work of renewal in the whole of creation including the faithful of both Israel and the nations (Isa. 65:17–18; 66:22; Jer. 23:3–4; Joel 2:28–32; Mic. 2:12; 4:6–7; 5:7–9; Zeph. 2:7; 3:12–13; Zech. 8:1–8, 11–13). The internalized covenant foreshadowed by Moses will become a new covenant written on their hearts (Deut. 30:6; Jer. 31:31–34; Ezek. 36:25–28). The resurrection of the nation will mark the fulfillment of God's promises, and a Davidic king will rule over them (Jer. 23:1–8; 33:14–22; Ezek. 37:11–14; Dan. 12:1–2). The prophets foreshadow the renewal and perfection of creation, the covenant, the land, Zion, the temple, and the Davidic rule—everything that was subject to frustration and judgment on account of the sin of humankind (Rom. 8:19–23).

The Nations in the OT

The nations in the OT are characterized by their relationship to God's people Israel. They are at enmity with Israel whenever, and wherever, they threaten the integrity of God's promises to Israel. On the upside is the promise of the covenant that Israel will mediate blessings to all the nations of the earth. Nevertheless, the promise of Gen. 12:3 does not translate into a program of mission to the nations by Israel. Rather, Israel as the people of God will have an effect on the surrounding nations when they live consistently with their identity as the people of God (Deut. 4:5–8; Isa. 2:2–4; 66:18–20; Zech. 8:20–23).

While a few notable gentiles come into Israel (e.g., Ruth and Rahab), the fulfillment of the promise of blessing to the nations is not given detailed treatment until we come to the eschatology of the Latter Prophets. The ingathering of the gentiles is contingent upon the final salvation of Israel on the day of the Lord. Although there will be an inflow of gentiles centered on the renewed temple in Jerusalem, those so blessed are still distinguished from ethnic Israelites until the consummation (Isa. 2:1–4; 19:18–25; 25:6–8). This accords with the original promise to Abraham (Gen. 12:3).

Israel's Fulfillment in the NT

Israel's fulfillment in the NT is twofold: the person of Jesus as the ideal Israelite and the Jewish disciples of Jesus who then form the first church in Jerusalem. According to Matthew, Jesus is the son of David, the son of Abraham (1:1). He fulfills the role of Israel in his "exodus" from Egypt (2:15). He accomplishes Israel's righteousness in his baptism and again as God's well-pleasing son (3:13–17). He comes not to destroy the Law and the Prophets but to fulfill them (5:17), and he claims that the Scriptures about Israel testify to him (Luke 24:27, 44–49; John 5:39–47). Every reference to Jesus as the Son of David points to this identity as the representative and true Israel. The "I am" sayings of Jesus in John's Gospel all relate to OT themes. Thus, for example, "I am the bread of life" (John 6:35) recalls the feeding of Israel with manna (Exod. 16:1–12); "I am the good shepherd" (John 10:11) is a link with Israel's ideal king foretold in Jer. 23:3–4 and Ezek. 34:11–24; and "I am the true vine" (John 15:1–5) identifies Jesus as Israel, God's vine in Isa. 5:1–7; 27:2–6; and Ps. 80:8–16.

Paul theologizes on Jesus as fulfilling the promises to Israel in his resurrection (Acts 13:32–33) and asserts that all God's promises find their "yes" in him (2 Cor. 1:20). Looking to 2 Sam. 7:12–14, Paul identifies the gospel as revealed in the OT, as concerning the Son of David, who is shown to be the Son of God through his resurrection (Rom. 1:1–4). In both passages there is a conflation of Son of David and Son of God. Jesus then fulfills the vital attributes of Israel: he is the new temple (John 2:19–22) and the new Davidic king, which together are the central focus of Israel. He is the minister of the new covenant (Luke 22:20; Heb. 8:6–13).

When it comes to the disciples, the apostles, and the followers of Jesus, everything points to their being seen as the faithful remnant of Israel. The Twelve reflect the twelve tribes of Israel; they are sent to the lost sheep of Israel (Matt. 10:5–15) and will one day judge the twelve tribes of Israel (Matt. 19:28).

The Nations in the NT

Luke's account of the postresurrection address of Jesus concludes with Jesus outlining his hermeneutic principle: "He opened their minds so they could understand the Scriptures" (Luke 24:45–47). It centers on the death and resurrection of Christ and the preaching of repentance and forgiveness to all nations, beginning with Jerusalem. This evangel will emanate from Jerusalem to the whole world. Luke's further account in Acts 1:6–8 also indicates Jerusalem as the starting point for mission into the whole world. There is little evidence of this outreach until Paul is designated as apostle to the gentiles and begins his missionary travels (9:15; 13:1–3, 44–48). The dynamic of Paul's mission is significant: after declaring that he is turning to the gentiles, he goes first to a Jewish synagogue as the way to reach gentile God-fearers (14:1). It seems Paul understands the OT covenant dynamic as continuing in that Israel remains the mediator of salvation to the gentiles.

Israel and the Church in the NT

There is considerable controversy among biblical scholars over the relationship of Israel to the church in the NT. Three main perspectives will suffice to show the broad spectrum of opinion.

Dispensationalism. First, one form of premillennialism (Christ returns before a thousand-year rule on earth) is classic dispensationalism. First promoted in the 1830s, it asserts a separation of the fulfillment of the earthly promises to Israel and the heavenly promises relating to the church, promises that are not predicted in OT prophecy. This means that God has a twofold plan of salvation: the earthly Jewish kingdom and the heavenly church. Dispensationalists criticize the more common view of the one kingdom of God's church combining believing Jews and believing gentiles as "replacement theology." The church is seen as replacing Israel and, indeed, there are those who designate the church as the new Israel. Dispensationalism is itself vulnerable to a critique of its apparently arbitrary division of Scripture into seven separate dispensations. It raises further questions concerning the way it interprets the NT by its literalistic reading of the OT. The NT itself is silent about the kind of literalistic fulfillment of prophecy anticipated by dispensationalism.

Covenant theology. The second position we may loosely characterize as Reformed or covenant theology, which asserts a complete identity of the new, or true, Israel and the church. This supersessionist view (the church supersedes Israel) commonly expresses the position of those known as postmillennialists (the world is largely Christianized before Christ's return) and amillennialists (the present age is the millennial rule of Christ). The strength of this position is its hermeneutic based on the Christology of the NT. Prophecy is interpreted not in a literalistic way but christologically. Broadly speaking, its hermeneutic is one that interprets the OT in the light of God's final revelation in Christ and the NT. It is, however, open to criticism for apparently overlooking the NT's distinctions between Jew and gentile in the church.

Postsupersessionism. The third position should not be interpreted as simply trying to find a balance between dispensationalism and covenantal supersessionism. It may be characterized as postsupersessionism. It aims to maintain the NT perspective on the relationship of Jew and gentile in the church, and to evaluate the extent to which the OT dynamic of Israel and the nations shapes the NT teaching on the church. This is crucial for understanding the NT use of the OT.

There are two important treatments of an Adam-Christ typology in Paul (Rom. 5:12–19 and 1 Cor. 15:20–23, 42–49). Christ is the last Adam, in whom the unity of humankind in relation to the Creator is restored. Thus, since the incarnation of the God-man remains and the humanity of Christ is not discarded in heaven, the last Adam points to the one new man in Christ in the consummation. This suggests that the distinctions between redeemed Israel and the redeemed gentiles will have no real significance in the consummation of the kingdom of God.

The NT presents three aspects of the fulfillment of the OT promises. First, all prophecy is fulfilled in Jesus; second, all prophecy goes on being fulfilled in the church and in the world through the preaching of the gospel; and third, all prophecy will be fulfilled universally in the consummation at the return of Christ. Jesus is the fulfiller of Israel and its promises. But he is also the Word who created all things, and he is the new creation in whom the believer participates (John 1:1–3; 3:1–8; 2 Cor. 5:17; Eph. 1:9–10; Col. 1:15–20; Heb. 1:1–3; 1 Pet. 1:3, 23). Christ transforms both OT strands: creation, including all humanity, and Israel as God's elect nation.

While the NT has much to tell us about the return of Christ in glory and the consummation, its main message is to the age of the church as it awaits this consummation. We note the Israel-gentile perspective in the Gospels as they treat the time of Jesus here on earth. The ascension and Pentecost bring us to the present age of the church and the propagation of the gospel to the world.

Postsupersessionism emphasizes the maintenance of the dynamic of the OT in that Israel, not gentile believers, was given the status of a nation of priests through whom the nations would find blessing. Only Israel was under the tutelage of the law of Sinai (Gal. 3:23–29). Although there is salvation only in Christ, gentiles come to faith in Christ by a different way (Rom. 2:12–16). The church is not, as dispensationalism says, a virtual afterthought because of Israel's refusal to accept the kingdom offered by Jesus. On the contrary, the gospel of Christ is the ultimate focus of the dynamic of Israel's faith and the promises of God in the OT. A Jew coming to Jesus in faith is not converting to a different religion but is fulfilling his or her OT faith. Gentiles come to Jesus as those blessed because of Israel's election.

Because of the division of the apostolate with Peter as apostle to the circumcision and Paul as apostle to the uncircumcision (Acts 13:46–47; Gal. 1:15–16; 2:7–8), some commentators suggest that we should assess the Epistles of Peter as written specifically to Jewish Christians. The Epistle to the Hebrews also makes sense as addressed to Jewish Christians. If this is so, these documents could support the idea that all the attributes of Israel are not yet applied to gentile Christians. Rather, they maintain the Israel/gentile perspective of the OT.

The tension in the present age of the church between the "now" and the "'not yet" is expressed in the unity-distinction of the present empirical life of Christians and the life to come already possessed by faith in Christ (Eph. 2:5–6; Col. 3:1–4; Heb. 12:22–24; 1 John 3:1–3). Passages like Gal. 3:28 express a particularized unity, in this case in the sinner's justification, but do not eliminate other essential distinctions, such as between men and women. Paul may appear to eliminate all distinctions between Jew and gentile in referring to "one new man" in Christ (Eph. 2:13–16 ESV), but his treatment of the plan of God for Israel in Rom. 9–11 would suggest otherwise. The distinction is actually between the "now" and the "not yet."

Postsupersessionism thus rejects the notion that the church is the new Israel. Instead, it sees the church as containing both the "new" or "spiritual" Israel along with the saved ("blessed") gentiles. The distinction may be finally and fully removed in the consummation, but the NT does not unambiguously suggest this. The last book of the canon is arguably the most OT-oriented book of the NT. Israel and all humanity appear to be without distinction in the final scene of the new and heavenly Jerusalem, the focus of Israel, merged with the new Eden, the focus of Adam (Rev. 21–22). Nevertheless, John still preserves the distinction in the great vision in Rev. 7. He appears to maintain the dynamic of salvation expressed in the covenant with Abraham. Thus, the perfect number of the redeemed of Israel, the 144,000, is juxtaposed with the great multitude out of every nation, tribe, and language group, as they are all gathered before the throne of God. The distinctions are ultimately resolved in the fact that, in Christ, there is one new humanity (Eph. 2:15).

Conclusion

In the NT, the true Israel is first Christ, and then those Jews who are "in Christ" through faith in Jesus the Messiah. The story of Israel does not evaporate in the NT. Throughout the present age of the church, it continues to be the story of the chosen nation with a ministry of priesthood to the wider world. The saving acts of God, leading to the recovery of God's "good creation" from before the entrance of sin, do not eliminate all reference to the dynamic of Israel under the covenant when we come to the emergence of the church. Classic dispensationalism is correct in rejecting the idea that the (mainly gentile) church replaces Israel and is heir to all its promises. But it is in error in mainly interpreting the NT by the OT and in finally separating Israel from the church. A key theological principle is at stake here—namely, the unity-distinction principle (also critical for both Christology and trinitarian theology). This keeps us aware of the way unity (without fusion) and distinction (without separation) are present in so many relationships which are often erroneously treated as "either/or." In its concern to maintain the distinction between Jew and gentile in God's purposes, dispensationalism actually completely separates them and destroys any unity.

Covenant theology is correct in seeking to interpret the OT by the Christology of the NT but is in error when it fails to note the continuation of important distinctions in the NT between Jew and gentile. This supersessionist concern to maintain unity under the gospel actually is in danger of fusing the place of Israel and the church, which may be regarded as a tendency to reinterpret the NT as a purely gentile document.

The postsupersessionist reaction to both dispensationalism and covenant theology seeks to redress certain popular and academic tendencies in the interpretation of both the OT and the NT. We modern Christians are often inclined to interpret every biblical text as written directly to us and about us. While all Scripture is rightly regarded as God's Word to us and for us (2 Tim. 3:16–17), a word written originally to Jews must be understood as speaking to the distinctive situation of Israel before God. The difficulty we all face when we come to appropriating the NT Scriptures and applying them to our (mostly gentile) Christian lives is how to discern the originally intended recipients of any text, and how that awareness affects our understanding of the text. Any text that clearly addresses Jewish Christians needs to be carefully evaluated for its application to gentiles.

Dispensationalism's separation of God's salvation plan for Jews from his plan for the church leads to the designation of some sections of the NT as belonging to Israel and not the church. Such separation is unsustainable. Nevertheless, it is a warning for covenantalists not to merge Israel and the gentiles to the point where the church is perceived not only historically as a gentile thing but also as theologically gentile. For example, we should regard Paul's treatment of Jew and gentile in Rom. 9–11 as integral to the whole argument of that epistle. Paul has already set the tone in Rom. 1:16: "I am not ashamed of the gospel, because it is the power of God for the salvation of everyone who believes, first for the Jew, then for the gentile" (AT).

See also Church; Covenant

Bibliography. Athas, G., "Reflections on Scripture," in Robinson, *Selected Works,* 125–39; Beale, G. K., "The Church as the Transformed and Restored Eschatological Israel" and "The Church as the Transformed and Restored Eschatological Israel (Continued)," in *A New Testament Biblical Theology* (Baker Academic, 2011), 651–749; Dumbrell, W. J., "Johannine Eschatology," in *The Search for Order* (Grand Rapids: Baker, 1994), 235–58; Gutbrod, W., "*Israēl,*" in *TDNT,* 3:375–91; König, A., *The Eclipse of Christ in Eschatology* (Eerdmans, 1989); Köstenberger, A. J., and P. T. O'Brien, *Salvation to the Ends of the Earth,* NSBT 11 (Apollos, 2001); Ladd, G. E., *A Theology of the New Testament* (Eerdmans, 1974), 537–39; Martin-Achard, R., *A Light to the Nations,* trans. J. P. Smith (Oliver & Boyd, 1962); McComiskey, T., *The Covenants of Promise* (Baker, 1987); Meyer, R., "Israel," in *NIDNTT,* 2:304–16; Pakula, M., "A Biblical Theology of Israel in the New Testament," in Robinson, *Selected Works,* 1:105–12; Pate, C. M., et al., *The Story of Israel* (InterVarsity; Apollos, 2004); Richardson, A., *An Introduction to the Theology of the New Testament* (SCM, 1958), 266–90; Robinson, D. W. B., *Faith's Framework* (Paternoster, 1985); Robinson, *Selected Works,* 2 vols., ed. P. G. Bolt and M. D. Thompson (Australian Church Record, 2008); Schreiner, T. R., *New Testament Theology* (Baker Academic, 2008).

GRAEME GOLDSWORTHY

J

James, Letter of

Few readers of Scripture, when probed about the use of the OT in the NT, think foremost of the Epistle of James. The letter contains few clear citations of Scripture and has received comparatively little attention from scholars relative to the Gospels and the Pauline corpus. Yet from the letter's outset, with its address to "the twelve tribes in the diaspora" (1:1 AT), through the closing verse (5:20), an apparent allusion to Prov. 10:12, one finds an author whose teaching and thought are centered on the OT. The form and function of James's teaching have been rightly compared to the Jewish wisdom tradition (cf. esp. Bauckham), but the influence of the OT itself manifests in various forms. James writes at multiple points with the wisdom of a sage but elsewhere adopts the balance of fiery rebuke and pastoral compassion reminiscent of the OT prophets (e.g., 4:4, 9; 5:1–6) and reflects deeply on the implications of the law for those under the lordship of Christ (cf. 1:15; 2:1–13, 19; 4:11–12).

In an encouraging development, the brief time since D. A. Carson's entry on the book of James in *CNTUOT* has seen some of the first monograph-length treatments of James's use of the OT (Christensen; Foster; Morales). To appreciate the function of the OT in James's epistle, the reader stands to benefit from an awareness of the traditional forces that influence his thinking. In his trenchant handling of the book, Carson calls attention to three key features that characterize the use of the OT in James (Carson, 997). First, as with many of the NT texts, the great majority of citations and allusions in the book are sourced from the LXX. Second, James's instruction bears many similarities to OT Wisdom literature and Second Temple Jewish interpretation, including contrasts typical of the two-ways motif. Third, the specific wisdom instruction that James includes also demonstrates multiple affinities with the teaching of Jesus. The second of these three observations, in particular, is worthy of additional discussion for its relation to the use of the OT. This entry, therefore, expands upon the groundwork established by Carson. We attempt to detail the attributes that make James's use of the OT unique, examining material ranging from prominent source texts to key examples that demonstrate his hermeneutic.

Wisdom and Tradition

James's use of the OT is notable for both what it includes and what it excludes. Unlike other NT texts, the book stands apart for its lack of reference to messianic and eschatological prophetic OT texts. The minimal christological content derived from the OT is less a theological statement than a reflection of the purpose and genre of the letter itself. With the pastoral intent we might imagine James having, as the leader of the Jerusalem church, he writes primarily to demarcate and clarify the path forward for his readers in their faith. Notably, for James this is the path characterized by unwavering devotion (1:5–8; 4:8), purity from the world (1:27; 3:17; 4:4, 8; cf. Lockett), and wholeness/perfection (esp. 1:4).

Though some scholars resist paraenesis as a genre classification, the highly prescriptive nature of the book of James has led many scholars to compare the text to other forms of contemporary exhortative instruction. The works of Richard Bauckham (29–111) and Luke Cheung, in particular, have helped clarify the genre of the letter by demonstrating multiple ways in which the text is an extension of Jewish wisdom instruction. While direct citations and allusions to OT wisdom texts are rare apart from Prov. 3:34 (James 4:6) and Prov. 10:12

(James 5:20), the frequent use of short, aphoristic sayings is a hallmark of James and characteristic of wisdom instruction. Bauckham (76–78) demonstrates that even the infrequent direct reference to wisdom texts is in fact a distinguishing mark of the Jewish sage, who sought to adapt and develop the insights of his mentor(s). For James, this helps account for the numerous thematic and linguistic overlaps between his instruction and that of his primary influences—the OT itself and especially Jesus as its authoritative interpreter. Clear citations of the OT are relatively uncommon, given this aspect of wisdom instruction, but where they do occur they function in an authoritative manner (Lev. 19:18 in James 2:8; Gen. 15:6 in James 2:23; cf. Lockett, 169).

In his articulation of what constitutes a life of perfection and wisdom from above (cf. 3:15), James demonstrates a clear knowledge of interpretive traditions that precede him. At multiple points, his use of the OT and supplemental examples aligns closely with Second Temple Jewish and rabbinic texts (e.g., cf. James 2:1–4 with t. Sanh. 6:2A–J; b. Shevu. 30a; Avot R. Nat. A22a; Sifre Devarim pisqa 144). Knowledge of traditional precedents can aid the reader at multiple points in the epistle. This includes conclusions to some of the vexing exegetical questions in the letter. Yet at the same time, James is by no means beholden to tradition. For example, his use of OT exemplars demonstrates a willingness to align with traditional interpretation (Abraham and Rahab in 2:21–25) and also to vary from such tradition with his own reflection on the OT narrative (Elijah in 5:17–18). In the examples that follow, we provide a brief glimpse into arguably the key OT text for James's instruction as well as specific examples that demonstrate the confluence of wisdom and tradition in the epistle.

Leviticus 19

The love command from Lev. 19:18 in James 2:8 stands as one of the clearest OT references in the book, with the text directly matching that of the LXX. The command itself plays a prominent role in the entire reflection on the law in James 2:1–13, with the broader context of Lev. 19 also included with James's admonition against partiality. The use of the OT text in this section is noteworthy for two parallels shared with Jewish tradition and, in the first case, with James's NT contemporaries.

First, commensurate with Second Temple, rabbinic, and other NT writers, James references the love command of Lev. 19:18 in discussion of the Decalogue and as a summary statement for the Law as a whole (cf., e.g., Sifra Qedoshim 4:7B; Jub. 7:20–21; Philo, *Hypothetica* 7.1–9; Matt. 19:16–24; 22:37–40; Mark 12:29–33; Luke 10:25–37; Rom. 13:9; Gal. 5:14). The additional identification of the love command as the "royal law" (*nomon basilikon*) in a unit that speaks of Jesus as "the Lord of glory" (2:1) and the inheritance of the kingdom for his disciples (2:5) is telling. For James, Lev. 19:18 is the overarching principle of kingdom ethics that reflects the instruction of the king himself (see the discussion in Allison, *James*, 401–5).

Second, James once again stands close to Second Temple and rabbinic texts by treating Lev. 19:18 in conjunction with aspects of its contextual unit. This application of the text is unsurprising in light of the summary function of the love command noted above. In particular, ethical instruction from a variety of Second Temple and rabbinic texts betrays a clear tendency to treat Lev. 19:18 alongside the preceding exhortations of Lev. 19:15–18. James Kugel and Christopher Chandler have provided helpful insight on this exegetical tradition by noting several examples in the literature of Qumran (e.g., CD-A 6.20–7.5; 8.1b–7a), additional Second Temple wisdom and ethical instruction (e.g., T. Gad 4:1–3; T. Zeb. 7:2; 8:1–6; Sir. 19:5–20:3), and the rabbis (e.g., Sifra Qedoshim 4:4B–C). Chandler's work is especially relevant, as it demonstrates James's proximity to contemporaneous Jewish exegetes in applying the love command (Lev. 19:18; James 2:8) as the basis for impartiality (Lev. 19:15; James 2:1–9). These two traditional trajectories give the reader insight into the power of James's argument. He seamlessly weaves together traditional concentration on the ethics of the law with Jesus's holistic view of neighborly love as its paradigmatic summary.

Given the widespread use of Lev. 19 in Jewish wisdom and ethical instruction, its inclusion in the Letter of James is unsurprising. However, the breadth of its influence on the letter was underappreciated until Luke Timothy Johnson's seminal article in 1982. Noting the significant reflection on Lev. 19:15–18 in James 2:1–9, Johnson (125) argues that where an author demonstrates a clear penchant for a source document, the likelihood of further references to the same source is heightened (Johnson, 392). Based on this "clustering effect," Johnson identifies five other potential allusions to Lev. 19 within the letter (Lev. 19:16 in James 4:11–12; Lev. 19:13 in James 5:4; Lev. 19:18a in James 5:9; Lev. 19:12 in James 5:12; and Lev. 19:17b in James 5:20; see Johnson 393-94).

Supporting evidence for Johnson's five additional allusions varies, and one's conclusion likely depends on the strength attributed to the "clustering effect." A decent claim can be made for the allusion to Lev. 19:16 in James 4:11–12. There, despite possessing only thematic rather than verbal agreement with the OT text, the use of the noun *plēsion* ("neighbor") in James 4:12 with reference to the *adelphon* ("brother") in the prior verse suggests a relationship to Lev. 19:16. Similarly, a strong case can be made for an allusion to Lev. 19:17–18 in James 5:20. Like the Leviticus text, James welds together the unlikely partnership of rebuke and love, closing with a statement from Prov. 10:12 rather than the love command previously referenced in James 2:8. Other suggestions are more difficult to substantiate. For example, as Johnson (394–96) concedes, James 5:4, which is said to reflect

Lev. 19:13, also shares close verbal correspondence with Mal. 3:5, and the alleged reference to Lev. 19:18a in James 5:9 can be linked only as a thematic allusion. Nevertheless, the evidence is enough to support the conclusion that James's wisdom instruction relies heavily on Lev. 19 and that this OT chapter bears the broadest influence on his epistle. As Bauckham (143) notes, this is especially noteworthy given the fact that the main exposition of the letter appears to begin (2:1) and end (5:19–20) with reflection on Lev. 19 (this structure suggests a prototypical use of Lev. 19 in James, according to Beale's classification, 80–89).

James 1:9–11

The first direct reference to an OT text in the letter also presents one of its most frequently debated exegetical questions. The syntax of James 1:9–10 raises the key question before the introduction of the OT text itself. Although the statement of v. 9 includes both an explicit verb and subject with attributive adjective ("And let the humble brother boast in his high position"), the contrast presented in v. 10 lacks both the verb and explicit subject of the adjective ("and the rich [person] in his humble position"). The logic of the parallelism certainly suggests the implied *kauchasthō* verb in v. 10, but the question is whether the same logic necessarily applies to the substantive (*ho adelphos*), which would suggest a reference to the rich within the Christian community. If one resists the implied "brother" in v. 10, the result suggests that the implied "boasting" is ironic and that the target of James's caustic remark is likely external to the community (Christensen, 120–21).

The OT allusion that immediately follows (1:10b–11) offers important insight into this exegetical stalemate. The natural imagery referenced—namely, the "grass" and "fading flower" appearing in vv. 10–11—uses common OT metaphors (e.g., Job 14:2; Pss. 37:2; 90:5–6; 103:15–16; Isa. 40:6–8). Nevertheless, a careful comparison demonstrates the high likelihood of Isa. 40:6–8 being the source text. Only it and James contain the exact phrase "like the flower of grass" (*hōs anthos chortou*, LXX Isa. 40:6) and forms of the verbs *xērainō* and *ekpiptō* (Christensen, 116–18; Morales, 86). This raises another important question related to the similes of Isa. 40:6–8 that James employs. Douglas Moo frames it well: "The question is properly what the image of the fading flower refers to: eschatological judgment or simple transitoriness?" (Moo, 67). Although many commentators simply conclude the latter, applying the allusion in a broad, gnomic sense, the question is worthy of further scrutiny.

Both the OT and the book of Isaiah itself demonstrate three ways in which natural imagery similar to Isa. 40:6–8 are applied: (1) with reference to general transience, (2) in a polemic against wicked people external to God's community, and (3) in a polemic against unfaithful Israel (Davidson). The introductory poem of Isa. 40—namely, 40:1–11—forms one of the key passages of the entire book. With its significant implications for redemptive history, it is also one of the most oft-referenced passages in subsequent Jewish traditional texts and the NT. Despite this prevalence, explicit references to 40:6–8 are relatively uncommon. What the traditional texts lack in frequency of references to 40:6–8 they make up for in consistency. In fact, every reference to this particular section of the Isaianic new-exodus passage occurs in the context of the judgment of God's enemies (2 Bar. 82:3–8; 4Q185 1.8–12; Tg. Isa. 40:6–8; Gen. Rab. 53:3; Midr. Ps. 1:20; see Penner, 204–5). The targum is especially striking for its correspondence to James 1:9–11, as both clarify the focus of the judgment relative to LXX Isa. 40:6–8 (the wicked in Targum Isaiah, the rich in James 1:10) and include an expanded causal clause explaining the agency of judgment.

These parallels support the strong likelihood that James applies Isa. 40:6–8 not as a general reminder of the transience of all humanity but as a poignant indictment of a specific group that he identifies as "the rich." To return to the exegetical stalemate noted at the outset of this section, the judgment emphasis supports the purposeful omission of "brother" in James 1:10a and a reading of "the rich" as external to the Christian community. Thus, writing to a community facing forms of oppression from those of greater socioeconomic means, James draws upon the judgment imagery of Isa. 40:6–8 in order to remind the community of the value of unwavering faith in Christ and his eternal kingdom (cf. 2:5).

James 5:19–20

The closing material in the Letter of James has often been viewed as a set of scattered exhortations. However, the parallels between James and Jewish wisdom instruction explain the relatively short, aphoristic content, including the closing phrase, drawn from Prov. 10:12 (see Bauckham, 65–66, for James's preference for closing units with aphorisms; note also Allison, "Liturgical"). Even if the forms of the closing section and final verse are explainable, the use of the OT raises two questions of interest. First, unlike the use of Prov. 10:12 in 1 Pet. 4:8 and the LXX text of Proverbs, James says that it is the person who brings back a wayward sinner, rather than "love," that covers sins. This unique adaptation begs the question, What accounts for the change? The answer to this question impacts the second question—namely, the difficult exegetical matter of whose sins are "covered" (*kalyptō*), the wandering sinner or the one who returns them to the right path?

At first glance, a connection between love and rebuke appears tangential at best. But here again the connection between James and Jewish wisdom literature brings clarity, as these two virtues are frequently connected (Prov. 3:12; 9:8; 13:24; 27:5–6; cf. Sir 18:13; see Christensen, 157–62; Corley, 161). In light of Lev. 19:17–18's outsized significance elsewhere in the epistle, it is noteworthy that these themes also coalesce there. These two factors form the basis for Johnson's view of a thematic allusion to Lev. 19:17b (398). Such an allusion explains the replacement of the "love" subject from Prov. 10:12 with the lengthier subject of the rebuke/correction of the wayward, uniting them in line with the example of Lev. 19:17–18. Additional evidence provides further support to Johnson's claim of the fusion of Lev. 19 and Prov. 10:12 in the text of James 5:20. Multiple scholars have noted the thematic resonance between the concept of rebuke from Lev. 19:17 and the speech-ethics emphasis inherent in Prov. 10 (Milgrom, 1647; Kugel, 50). Second Temple Jewish literature also provides multiple examples of merging the rebuke command of Lev. 19:17 with Proverbs and other wisdom texts (Sir. 19:5–20:3; Testament of Gad; 1QS 5.24–6.1; CD 9.2–8; see Corley, 171–72). Given these precedents, it is likely that James is reexpressing the insight of Lev. 19:17–18 in combination with the second clause of Prov. 10:12.

Once again, interpretive tradition lends insight into the exegetical question at hand. In the instances where Jewish writers reflect on the combination of love and rebuke in Lev. 19:17–18, they consistently highlight the act of rebuke or correction as a means of preventing further sin for the one doing the correcting (CD 9.2–8; CD-A 6.20–21; 1QS 5.24–6.1; T. Gad 4:1–3; 6:1–5; b. Arakh. 16b). These function as repeated warnings that vengeance, grudge bearing, and slander are real threats to the community and are antithetical to the kingdom virtue of love. If James draws upon the background of Lev. 19:17–18 in order to emphasize the importance of correction within the community, then the inclusion of the aphorism from Prov. 10:12 likely conveys a similar sentiment to these traditions (Christensen, 159–61). Thus, although the change of subject in the second clause of James 5:20 is syntactically awkward, the use of the OT supports the covering of further sin for the one acting to restore the wayward sinner.

OT Exemplars

James draws upon OT characters to a far greater extent than most NT writers, with Abraham (2:21–23), Rahab (2:25), the prophets collectively (5:10), Job (5:11), and Elijah (5:17) serving as paradigmatic examples of action driven by unwavering faith. Two key observations are worth noting. First, the characters are seamlessly introduced in the context of James's argument. The audience is assumed to have broad familiarity with the details of their respective stories and their relevance to his point in the context of the letter. Second, often aligning with the themes that we have noted above, the character portrayals stand very close to their representation in Jewish tradition.

For example, while James's emphasis on Job's "perseverance" (*tēn hypomonēn*) can be regarded as implicit to the OT text, it is developed prominently in subsequent tradition, most notably in Sirach and the Testament of Job. However, the reference to Elijah stands as the key contrast to this harmony with tradition and serves as a reminder of James's willingness to veer from traditional emphasis at times. Whereas Elijah's story, as detailed in 1 Kings 17:1–18:46, was embellished in traditional accounts (e.g., Sir. 48:1–10), James stresses his common frailty (see Foster, 165–90; Kamell Kovalishyn). By emphasizing Elijah's "sameness" (*homoiopathēs hēmin*), James brings his audience into proximity with Elijah's own experience and provides a powerful example that unites his immediate exhortation toward prayer with his overarching emphasis on enduring faith.

On account of its implications for the theology of James 2:14–26, as well as efforts to assess the harmony of the account relative to Paul's writings, the example of Abraham and use of Gen. 15:6 stand as the most scrutinized aspects of the OT in the epistle. Little discussion can be added to Carson's excellent analysis of the passage in *CNTUOT* (Carson, 1003–5). By uniting Abraham's obedience in the event of the Akedah (Gen. 22) with the qualitative statement about his faith from Gen. 15:6, James stands closer to traditional Jewish accounts than the careful chronological treatment in the works of Paul (Rom. 4; Gal. 3). Given James's portrayal of Abraham in this manner as one whose faith was evidenced and completed by obedient action, the pairing with Rahab should not be glossed over. Both characters exemplify James's charge toward unwavering faith that manifests in action, even when that action comes at great risk or discomfort (see Foster, 104–27).

Conclusion

While numerous other suggestions for OT influence upon the epistle have been raised, this article has attempted to draw attention to the material OT texts and influences in James's letter. The various studies published since Carson's *CNTUOT* article represent a promising start, but significant opportunity remains for assessing and clarifying James's use of the OT in relation to Jewish tradition and the teaching of Jesus himself. The overarching role of the OT throughout the letter—especially in key sections that underscore his thesis—demonstrates the central significance of the OT and its traditional interpreters in James's particular form of wisdom instruction.

Bibliography. Allison, D. C., *James*, ICC (Bloomsbury T&T Clark, 2013); Allison, "A Liturgical Tradition behind the Ending of James," *JSNT* 34 (2011): 3–18; Bauckham, R., *James*, NTR (Routledge, 1999); Beale, G. K., *Handbook on the New Testament Use of the Old Testament* (Baker Academic, 2012); Carson, D. A., "James," in *CNTUOT*, 997–1013; Chandler, C. N., "'Love Your Neighbour as Yourself' (Lev. 19:18b) in Early Jewish-Christian Exegetical Practice and Missional Formation," in *"What Does the Scripture Say?,"* ed. C. A. Evans and H. D. Zacharias, LNTS 469 (T&T Clark, 2012), 12–56;

Cheung, L. L., *The Genre, Composition and Hermeneutics of the Epistle of James* (Paternoster, 2003); Christensen, S. M., *The Relationship between the Epistles of James and 1 Peter* (PhD diss., Trinity Evangelical Divinity School, 2018); Corley, J., *Ben Sira's Teaching on Friendship*, BJS 316 (Brown Judaic Studies, 2002); Davidson, R., "The Imagery of Isa. 40:6–8 in Tradition and Interpretation," in *Quest for Context and Meaning*, ed. C. A. Evans and S. Talmon, BibInt 28 (Brill, 1997), 37–55; Foster, R. J., *The Significance of Exemplars for the Interpretation of the Letter of James*, WUNT 2/376 (Mohr Siebeck, 2014); Johnson, L. T., "The Use of Lev. 19 in the Letter of James," *JBL* 101 (1982): 391–401; Kamell Kovalishyn, M. "The Prayer of Elijah in James 5," *JBL* 137 (2018): 1027–45; Kugel, J. L., "On Hidden Hatred and Open Reproach," *HTR* 80 (1987): 43–61; Lockett, D. R., *Purity and Worldview in the Epistle of James*, LNTS 366 (T&T Clark, 2008); Milgrom, J., *Leviticus 17–22*, AB (Doubleday, 2000); Moo, D. L., *The Letter of James*, PNTC (Eerdmans, 2000); Morales, N. R., *Poor and Rich in James*, BBRSup 20 (Pennsylvania State University Press, 2018); Penner, T. C., *The Epistle of James and Eschatology*, JSNTSup 121 (Sheffield Academic, 1996).

SEAN CHRISTENSEN

Jeremiah, Book of

Jeremiah prophesied from Josiah's thirteenth year (627 BC), or perhaps from the discovery of the Book of the Law in 622, through to some years after Jerusalem's fall in 586. His preaching was shaped by Josiah's reforms, bitterly opposed by Jehoiakim (609–597), and dubiously received by Zedekiah (597–586), whose political situation was parlous. His few supporters included the scribe Baruch, who wrote down Jeremiah's words and composed biographical material. From these records a series of "books" was produced (25:13; 30:2; 36:2, 32; 45:1; 51:60), culminating in the book of Jeremiah, written for Judeans in exile. Thus, there are two "original audiences": the first listeners and the first readers.

Essential Features of the Book of Jeremiah

Composition. The diversity of materials (poetry, sermons, biography) and the nature of inter-Judean rivalries during and after exile have resulted in a wide range of views about the book's origin. Some locate its composition largely during the lifetime of the prophet and shortly thereafter, with an addendum (52:31–34) dating to ca. 560; others discern layers of redaction into Hellenistic times. We find no firm grounds within the text to exclude the former view. Jeremiah concluded his ministry in Egypt, where it seems he produced the first complete edition of his book, a version reflected in the Septuagint. Some time later, perhaps with Seraiah (Jer. 51:59), Jeremiah reorganized and expanded the book, shaping its message for a Babylonian readership (Lundbom, *Closer*, 23–32). Individual units, especially the prose, were tightened up structurally and their message sharpened, with greater prominence given to Babylon and its king; the oracles against the nations, which followed 25:13, were moved to the end of the book, with Babylon given the climactic final position; and the book as a whole was framed as an enactment of the divine word in all the nations (Shead, "Text").

Structure and message. It follows that the structure of the book is highly intentional. It is organized around the major disjunctive heading usually translated "The word which came to Jeremiah from the LORD" (7:1; 11:1; 18:1; 21:1; 25:1; 30:1; 32:1; 34:1, 8; 35:1; 40:1; 44:1). The word of the Lord is in effect the book's main character. Its speaker, Jeremiah, embodies the word and receives the people's hostility toward it. In the book's *first movement* we see the word tearing down the nation's institutions, rendered void by covenant abandonment. The *second movement* begins in 605 BC—the year Nebuchadnezzar rose to power—with the theological crisis of a people unresponsive to a supposedly irresistible word (25:1–3); it ends with Jeremiah's announcement of restored fortunes, made once his message of a seventy-year exile prevails over Hananiah's message of swift restoration. The book then cycles back twice to the year 605 to observe the word of God at work from different perspectives (35:1; 45:1). The *third movement* shows the word finally doing what it said, as Jerusalem falls and the people, including Jeremiah, are scattered among the nations. The horizon of the *fourth movement* is global, as the word lays waste to the world, from Egypt to Babylon. While there can be no peace for Jeremiah's listeners, a day will come when the nation is raised from death as a new covenant transforms the people inwardly. This day will be realized when Babylon falls and Judah lives again (50:4–20). For the moment, however, exiled readers live between judgment and hope (chap. 52) (Shead, *Mouth*, 87–105). (See table 1, "The Four Movements of Jeremiah.")

Jeremiah's Use of Scripture

Jeremiah is the longest book in the Bible by word count, and almost every other OT book either uses or is used by it. Its most significant sources are Deuteronomy, Isaiah, Hosea, and Psalms, followed by Genesis, Exodus, 2 Kings, Ezekiel, Joel, Amos, and Micah. William Holladay and Walter Brueggemann have the best surveys in English.

Jeremiah and Deuteronomy. Deuteronomy colors every part of Jeremiah, from the Decalogue (cited in 7:9), to derived laws (3:1–5 // Deut. 24:1–4), to ethics (5:28; 7:6; 22:3; 22:16 // Deut. 10:18; 15:11), to Moses's final appeal in Deut. 30:15, cited ironically in 21:8 ("See, I am setting before you the way of life and the way of death"). The book's prose is shot through with the diction of Deuteronomy, often with a distinctive Jeremianic twist. However, one foundational text underlies Jeremiah's entire ministry: Deut. 29:16–21. It provides

Table 1. The Four Movements of Jeremiah

First Movement	
The word of the Lord announces Judah's destruction and its speaker is crushed	
1	Call and commissioning
2–6	Yahweh: scorned husband, angry warrior
7–10	The temple corrupted
11–17	The covenant dismantled
18–20	The elect rejected
21–24	The throne vacated
Second Movement	
The word of the Lord vindicates its speaker and offers true hope to deaf listeners	
25–29	Seventy years, not two
30–34	Peace, but not now
Third Movement	
The word of the Lord destroys the nation it created and plants seeds of new life	
35–39	The word destroys Jerusalem
40–43	The word scatters the remnant
44	God's word will stand
Fourth Movement	
The word of the Lord destroys the nations and draws a new nation from the wreckage	
45	Baruch, whose scroll preserved the word
46:1–51:58	The word will destroy nations and raise Israel
51:59–64	Seraiah, whose scroll marks Babylon's fall
52	Appendix: back to the present

the rationale for his message of judgment, the source of endless exegetical and theological rumination, and the bedrock of his confidence over decades of fruitless preaching and violent opposition. Within this text a single verse stands out as Jeremiah's favorite: "When someone hears the words of this oath and they bless themselves in their heart, thinking, 'I will have peace, *even though I follow the stubbornness of my heart*,' this will result in the sweeping away of the watered land together with the dry" (Deut. 29:19 AT).

The italicized phrase occurs again eight times in Jeremiah, and just once elsewhere (3:17; 7:24; 9:14; 11:8; 13:10; 16:12; 18:12; 23:17; Ps. 81:12). Its use in 16:12 is definitive. Jeremiah has announced the end of life in Judah to bemused listeners who ask, "What wrong have we done?" (16:10). His two-part answer begins (16:11) by accusing their ancestors with a Deuteronomic trio of verbs: they have followed, served, and worshiped other gods—a trio that always ends in exile (Deut. 8:19; 29:26; Josh. 23:16; 1 Kings 9:6). Secondly, although exile was always a possibility, Jeremiah's generation is uniquely culpable: "You are following the stubbornness of your evil hearts" (16:12). The context of this phrase in Deuteronomy is the oath sworn to Abraham to give his descendants the land (Deut. 29:12–15), an oath that might tempt someone to persist in idolatry on the basis that God would have no choice but to honor his oath (29:16–19). This is the sin of which Jeremiah's listeners were newly guilty. Josiah's reading of the Law Book (2 Kings 23:2) had made them the most theologically educated generation in memory; but having understood God's covenantal love, their decision cynically to exploit it corrupted their hearts beyond repair—a theme explored in Jer. 17. Deuteronomy 29:20 continues, "The LORD will never be willing to forgive them. . . . All the curses written in this book will fall on them." This is the origin of Jeremiah's confidence, unshaken by twenty-three years of fruitless preaching (25:3).

Jeremiah returns repeatedly to the surrounding context of Deut. 29:19. (1) Moses's exhortation begins in Egypt, where "you saw among them their detestable images" (Deut. 29:17). Jeremiah's first three major units likewise begin in Egypt (2:5–6, 17–19; 7:22–26; 11:7–8). Judah has returned to Egypt, and not simply to gain an ally against Babylon. (2) Moses continues, "Make sure there is no man or woman . . . whose heart turns away from the LORD our God to go and worship the gods of those nations; make sure there is no root among you that produces such bitter poison" (Deut. 29:18). The "bitter poison" of idolatry is reworked in Jer. 9:15 and 23:15, but the two-step of "turning away from Yahweh" followed by "going after other gods" (worked out more fully in Deut. 29:25–26) perfuses Jeremiah's message from start to finish. (3) Moses's key sentence, "I will have peace, even though I follow the stubbornness of my heart" (Deut. 29:19 AT), shapes Jeremiah's *preaching*. "Peace" is his one-word summary of the message of the false prophets (4:10; 6:14; 8:15; 14:13, 19; 23:17; 28:9), a message that feeds the people's deepest desires and enables them to exercise their hypocrisy with complete confidence. (4) It also shapes Jeremiah's *book*, as successive uses of the key phrase chart Judah's downfall. In 7:24 the exodus generation serves as a warning, who "followed the stubbornness of their evil hearts" (AT); by 11:8 this stubbornness has become perennial. In 13:10 Jeremiah's listeners, addressed as "they," are characterized with the key sentence for the first time; in 16:2 "they" becomes "you"; and in 18:12 the sentence is put directly onto their lips: "We will all follow the stubbornness of our evil hearts." (5) This tipping point is followed by a poem (18:13–17) with numerous links to Deut. 29:19–24: "disaster on the watered land" (29:19 // Jer. 18:14); "the whole land will be a burning waste" (29:23 // Jer. 18:16a); "all the nations will ask" (29:24 // Jer. 18:16b). (6) Moses's closing summary (Deut. 29:25–28) ends with the verb "uproot" (*ntš*), occurring only here in the Pentateuch. Jeremiah 1:10 expands this verb with five others to form the prophet's mission statement, a refrain that recurs throughout the book.

It is against this background that we should understand Jeremiah's presentation as a prophet like Moses (1:6–9 // Deut. 18:18), albeit one denied the Mosaic ministry of intercession, for Yahweh will no longer forgive (14:10–12; 15:1). Jeremiah's immersion in Deuteronomy results in a rich variety of usage, along with a number of interpretive techniques explaining in various ways how the covenant curses of Deuteronomy are coming on his generation.

Rhetorical and theological inversions. Jeremiah 11 opens with two expository sermons on a topic sentence taken from Deut. 29:9, "Listen to the terms of this covenant" (11:2; cf. vv. 3, 6, 8), which vv. 3a, 6a turn into fresh words of prophecy. In the first sermon (11:2–5) Jeremiah effectively reenacts Deut. 27, which concludes, "'Cursed is anyone who does not uphold the words of this law by carrying them out.' Then all the people shall say, 'Amen!'" (27:26). This summarizing self-curse is split and used to bracket Jeremiah's sermon. Inside the bracket are two elements. First, Jeremiah strengthens the opening malediction by reminding his listeners that before he gave the law, God acted in mercy and power to rescue them (drawing on Deut. 4:20). Second, Deut. 27:1–10 is summarized in reverse order. God, not Moses, becomes its speaker ("I said"), and his words are presented as a command given to Israel at the point of their rescue. Jeremiah 7:23 uses similar techniques, but 11:3–5 reveals the sheer virtuosity of his preaching:

> "'Cursed is the one who does not obey the terms of this covenant [Deut. 27:26a]—the terms I commanded your ancestors when I brought them out of Egypt, out of the iron-smelting furnace' [4:20]. I said, 'Obey me and do everything I command you [27:10], and you will be my people, and I will be your God [27:9]. Then I will fulfill the oath I swore to your ancestors [27:3b], to give them a land flowing with milk and honey'—the land you possess today" [27:3a]. I answered, "Amen, LORD" [27:26b].

Jeremiah's basic analysis of Deut. 27:1–10 is, "Here in the land of blessing, given by oath, you have become God's people, so obey him." But by reversing the order of his source text and sandwiching it between the halves of Deut. 27:26 Jeremiah reminds his listeners that failure to obey puts a curse over the whole enterprise. Making obedience the initial condition has the effect of inserting a silent negative into Moses's argument: "If you [do not] obey me, you will [not] be my people, I will [not] keep my oath, and you will [not] keep the land." Finally, by pinning the whole thing to the moment of rescue from Egypt he raises the stakes: How could one think of spurning a God like this? And if one did, how could one hope to escape his justice? Surely there could only ever be one result: the loss of the land. The sophisticated inversion by which Jeremiah draws out the meaning of the text for his listeners is a sermonic equivalent of the rhetorical inversions and subversions that punctuate his poetry. His words are prophetic speech-acts that place the listeners under the covenant curses of Deuteronomy, and do so according to Scripture.

Modified citation. At a number of points Jeremiah modifies his sermon text to reinforce his topic sentence, beginning with 11:3b (see above), where he replaces "law" (Deut. 27:26a) with "covenant." His second sermon (11:6b–8), a summary of Deut. 29:16–21, goes further. It begins with the rebellious generation of the exodus (11:7 // Deut. 29:16) and traces a direct line to Jeremiah's audience by inserting "until today," seeing the first generation as typological of Jeremiah's, and punctuating the entire path with strong warnings. Jeremiah then pluralizes the words of the individual who decides to follow the stubbornness of his or her own heart (Deut. 29:19), applying them to the entire nation, and concludes with a phrase from his topic sentence, "all the terms of the covenant," in place of Deuteronomy's "every curse written in this book": "But they did not listen or pay attention; instead, they followed the stubbornness of their evil hearts. So I brought on them all the terms [NIV: curses] of the covenant I had commanded them to follow but that they did not keep" (Jer. 11:8). The sermon closes the hermeneutical gap between the generations by the technique of modified citation.

Analogy by allusion. The unique triad "Show no mercy [*ḥml*], pity [*ḥws*], or compassion [*rḥm*]" features twice, once with Yahweh as subject (13:14), and once with Nebuchadnezzar as Yahweh's instrument of holy war against Jerusalem (21:7). The triad adapts Deut. 13:8, which required any idolatry within Israel to be exterminated without mercy, pity, or concealment (outside Ezekiel this is the only other verse where "mercy" and "pity" come together). But Jeremiah alters "concealment" to "compassion," a word used just twice in Deuteronomy. The first occurrence comes later on in the same passage (Deut. 13:17): when an idolatrous town has been devoted to destruction, Yahweh will turn from his anger and have compassion on them. Ultimately (Deut. 30:3), Yahweh will turn and have compassion after the nation's idolatry has led to national destruction. The choice of this word allows Jeremiah to plant the seeds of future restoration in his language of destruction. An exposition of the covenant implications of idolatry would be incomplete without including the end goal of promise-keeping through compassion—a word Jeremiah uses positively only of postexilic restoration (12:15; 30:18; 31:20; 33:26; 42:12). The twist is that God's compassion is extended to all nations (12:14–17).

Poetry elaborated and applied. Deuteronomy 32 was a significant source for Jeremiah's poetry (Lundbom lists forty borrowings [*Jeremiah 1–20*, 110–14]). The opening poem in Jeremiah (2:2–3) has been inspired by Deut. 32:10–14, but Jeremiah takes it in a new direction by subsuming every blessing of the covenant into one relationship. The barren wilderness gives way not to the fruitful land but to the fruitful bride. The question, "What fault [ʿāwel] did your ancestors find in me?" (Jer. 2:5) alludes to Deut. 32:4, "a faithful God and without fault [ʿāwel], upright and just" (AT). The mocking question and wish in 2:28—"Where then are the gods . . . ? Let them come if they can save you!"—draw on Deut. 32:37–38.

Poems of response follow Jeremiah's sermons, just as Deut. 32 follows Moses's sermons. In the first of these poetic collections (Jer. 8–10), Yahweh gives idolatrous Judah "poisoned water" (8:14) and sends "venomous snakes" (8:17), embellishments of Deut. 32:32–33. These references bracket the onrushing army coming to devour the nation (8:15–16) and clarify that this is God's doing. God's power, not his weakness, is the cause of Judah's downfall—which is the message of Deut. 32:30–35. Yahweh is not just a stronger god; he is God beyond compare, and his incomparability is elaborated in 10:6–10 (// Deut. 32:31, 39). It is this God who is "the Portion of Jacob" (10:16 // Deut. 32:9).

In the logic of Moses's song, God saw and determined the future of idolatrous Israel (Deut. 32:20, "see . . . their end"), a future that would have been averted only if Israel wisely discerned "their end" (32:29). In Jer. 12:4 the people have become convinced that God does not "see [their] end" (ESV)—citing Deut. 32:20. It is this stupidity, as much as their wickedness, that blights the land, and in 12:7–9 Yahweh thrice names and rejects "my inheritance," a probable reference back to Deut. 32:9. Jeremiah applies the message of the poem, not just its images.

Jeremiah's other sources. Jeremiah touches on most phases of Israel's history, a history his message often inverts and nullifies. His call (1:5–9; cf. 15:1) points back to that of *Moses* (Exod. 4:10); like *Pharaoh,* Babylon is "refusing to let them go" (Jer. 50:33 // Exod. 4:23); the *exodus* is reversed in Jer. 22:11 and chaps. 42–44; *Balaam's* words (Num. 24:17; also 21:27–30) are reprised in the Moab oracle (Jer. 48:45–46); the judgment anticipated by *Joshua* (Josh. 23:15) will be reversed in Jer. 32:42; *Jephthah's* speech to the Ammonite king (Judg. 11:24) opens the oracle against Ammon (Jer. 49:1–2); Jer. 15:9 reverses *Hannah's* song (1 Sam. 2:5); but the *Davidic* covenant (2 Sam. 7:16) is reaffirmed in Jer. 33:17. A number of Jeremiah's sources merit specific attention.

Dalit Rom-Shiloni identifies nine functions of pentateuchal traditions in Jeremiah: they authorize Jeremiah's status as a prophet; characterize the people's sinfulness; describe their status before God; demonstrate covenant breaches; describe Israel's interactions with the nations; demonstrate God's nature; intensify the description of destruction; designate redemption; and structure Jeremiah's concept of exile ("Actualization," 258–61). These functions are enabled by a range of hermeneutical methods, as illustrated by Jeremiah's use of Genesis.

The theology of Genesis is universal and may simply be reemployed (e.g., "Is anything too hard for the LORD?" [Jer. 32:17, 27 // Gen. 18:14]). The same goes for cosmology. Images of uncreation, for example, are part of Jeremiah's world-picture (4:23, 25 // Gen. 1:2; 2:5). The *concept* of uncreation, however, applies to Judah's future by cosmological-historical typology (on this and the following typologies, see Fishbane, 354–79). In contrast, the more analogical likening of Babylon's fall to the tower of Babel (51:53, "Even if Babylon ascends to the heavens . . .") rests on a spatial typology. Historical typology is the natural means of connection to the patriarchs. God's promise to fulfill his creation mandate (Gen 1:28; 9:1) by making Abraham "fruitful and increase" (Gen. 17:20; 35:11) is echoed in Jer. 29:6, though Abraham is named just once (33:26). Finally, Jeremiah wields the Jacob story against his listeners by means of biographical typology: Jacob the deceiver was the father of the nation, and these are his children (9:4–5 // Gen. 35:10–12). Often the prophet exploits shared knowledge of the Genesis narratives to unsettle and disturb his audience. Jeremiah 15:8 subverts the promise of offspring to Abraham in Gen. 22:17; in Jer. 20:16 the prophet calls the curse of Sodom and Gomorrah upon himself (Gen. 19:25). The God of Genesis determines the fate of every nation and of creation itself, but he deprives Jeremiah's listeners of the security found in his promise to Abraham.

Jeremiah's use of texts from Leviticus (Rom-Shiloni, "Forest") is less well recognized. There are isolated uses of cultic terminology (e.g., "accept [a sacrifice]," 14:12; "the horns of their altars," 17:1; or the reworking of Lev. 22:14–16 in 2:3); but there is also contextual exegesis, notably, of Lev. 26:14–45, as indicated by the use of "abhor" (*gʿl*), a verb found with this sense only in Lev. 26:11, 15, 30, 43, 44; Ezek. 16:45; and Jer. 14:19–21. Jeremiah's confession is virtually a summary of the Leviticus passage, bracketed by Lev. 26:44 (common words are italicized): "Have you *rejected* [// Lev. 26:44] Judah completely? Do you *abhor* [NIV: despise] Zion [// 26:30]? Why have you *afflicted* us [// 26:24] so that we cannot be healed? . . . We acknowledge our wickedness, LORD, and *the guilt of our ancestors* [// 26:40] . . . *Remember* [// 26:45] your *covenant* with us and do not *break* it [// 26:44]." In Lev. 26 Yahweh's "abhoring" of Israel culminates in exile, and he will "remember the covenant" by preserving the exiled remnant. Jeremiah recognizes that Judah is guilty of all the crimes of Lev. 26, but he begs the Lord to limit his judgment by preserving them from exile. This is a type of "covert legal exegesis" (Fishbane, 144), but its genre—prayer, not narrative—allows Jeremiah to plead for the prediction to be revised (cf. Fishbane, 467–71). Yahweh's rejection of this Moses-like intercession (15:1) only reinforces the message of Lev. 26.

Kings is the companion volume to Jeremiah. As Acts does for Paul's Epistles, Kings supplies Jeremiah's immediate historical and theological context, especially the events and characters of 2 Kings 21–25. The perspective of Kings on the fall of Jerusalem is expressed in Jer. 21:3–7; 27:5–22; 37:17–21; 38:14–28. Solomon's palace (1 Kings 7:2) is alluded to in 21:14; 22:7, 15, 23, and Yahweh's speech to Solomon (1 Kings 9:9) in 22:9. The narrator's condemnation of Manasseh in 2 Kings 21:12, 16 is partially cited in 7:6; 19:3–4; 22:3, 17; and Huldah's oracle in 2 Kings 22:16–20 (itself an exposition of Deut. 32:15–22) is alluded to in 1:16; 7:20; 8:19, and elsewhere. Jehoiakim's response to the reading of the scroll (36:24) is compared unfavorably to that of Josiah (2 Kings 22:11). The close relationship of the two books is cemented by the common text in 2 Kings 25 and Jer. 52, an appendix to "the words of Jeremiah" (51:64). An abbreviated version of the same narrative is found in Jer. 39. The relationship of these chapters is complex, as they seem to have taken shape concurrently, in the early exilic period, and each is adapted to its own context (e.g., the unique comment about Zedekiah in 52:11b). Jeremiah 52 functions both to frame the book and to step back from the dramatic visions of Babylon's fall (chaps. 50–51) into the prosaic present, deferring but not extinguishing the hope of restoration. Tying the two works together in this way mutually reinforces their authority.

Only Deuteronomy is more significant than Isaiah, whose words Jeremiah closely studied (e.g., the Moab oracle, 48:5, 31, 34, 37–38 // Isa. 15:2–6; Jer. 48:29, 31–33, 35–36 // Isa. 16:6–12). The prophet Jeremiah was part of a vigorous debate on the interpretation of Scripture, to which the book of Isaiah was central. Jerusalem's deliverance from Sennacherib in 701 and Isaiah's words concerning Zion gave Hananiah confidence that the exile of 597 would be short-lived (28:2 // Isa. 14:25; cf. Jer. 26:19). For Jeremiah, too, Isaiah had direct relevance. A nation would invade from afar (5:15–17 // Isa. 5:26–29); Judah would experience pain like a woman in labor (4:31 // Isa. 13:8); her punishment would be like the smelting of silver (6:27–30 // Isa. 1:21–25); "the anger of Yahweh will not turn back" (23:20 AT // Isa. 5:25, etc.); but the enemy will eventually be judged (25:12–13 // Isa. 14:25–27) and a Davidic branch arise (23:1–8 // Isa. 11) (Sweeney). Both Jeremiah and Hananiah agreed on this basic schema, but Jeremiah insisted that because of Judah's hypocrisy Isaiah's future hope was not applicable. Jeremiah's reading of Isaiah was shaped, as Hananiah's was not, by setting Judah's behavior against the covenantal standards of Deuteronomy.

Jeremiah stood self-consciously in the prophetic tradition of the eighth century (Lalleman, *Tradition*), and the legal citation of Mic. 3:12 in Jer. 26:18—among the earliest recorded citations of canonical Scripture—suggests the availability of written prophecy. Hosea, whose life and message intersected before Jeremiah's did, is referenced over fifty times. Jeremiah takes over Hosea's marriage metaphor (Jer. 2–3; cf. Hosea 1–3), his keyword "return" (*šûb*), and his imagery of wounding and healing (Hosea 5:13; 6:1; 7:1; 11:3; 14:4). Amos inspired Jeremiah's preaching: his subversive rhetoric; his role as an intercessor; his theology of Israel's history (2:30; cf. Amos 4:6–11) and of creation (4:28; 13:16; cf. Amos 5:8; 8:9); his visions (1:11; cf. Amos 7:8). These and many other "homiletical elaborations" of earlier prophets (Fishbane, 461) serve to place Jeremiah and his listeners firmly within a long history: "Though the LORD has sent all his servants the prophets to you again and again, you have not listened or paid any attention" (25:4). At the same time, Jeremiah's hope for a future David (23:5–6) continues the prophetic tradition arising from 2 Sam. 7:12–16 by taking elements from Amos 9:11 and Isa. 11:1–2 and refocusing them on his own context. Closer to home, Zephaniah, supporter of Josiah's reforms, is referenced just sixteen times. Nahum and Jeremiah's contemporary Habakkuk are rarely used.

The catena in 10:23–25 (// Prov. 16:9; 20:24; Pss. 6:1; 79:6–7) draws on psalms that fit the situation of prophet and nation and bespeak a deep familiarity with liturgical and wisdom traditions. Language from the psalms permeates Jer. 2–20, with individual lament characterizing the prophet's confessions; however, direction of dependence is not always clear (e.g., Jer. 20:8–10 // Ps. 31:12–13 [MT 31:11–12]; 20:11, 13 // Ps. 35:4, 10). Psalms function as both prophecy (Jer. 7:12, 14 // Ps. 78:60) and Scripture (Jer. 12:1–2; 17:5–8 // Ps. 1). Wisdom is especially prominent in Jer. 7–10 (Allen). Keeping the law is wise (4:22–23; 8:7–8; cf. Deut. 4:6) because it is the blueprint for a flourishing society, land, and creation (4:22; 5:22; 10:12 // Prov. 10:8; 8:29; 3:19, respectively; cf. Dell).

In short, while Jeremiah's use of sources often seems spontaneous, the natural mode of expression of a mind steeped in Scripture, he is never lazy. He carefully analyzes history through the lens of the covenant at Horeb and strives to show, with biblical-theological rigor, how Judah's future will flow from her past. Jeremiah's contested claim to be sent from God withstood scrutiny precisely because his preaching was according to the Scriptures (26:17–19).

Jeremiah's Influence on Later Texts

The language Ezekiel shares with Jeremiah points both to a common stock of phrases and ideas, and to dependence—assuming not only that Ezekiel heard Jeremiah preach (Holladay, 84) but also that an edition of Jeremiah reached Babylon relatively early in the exile. Like Jeremiah, Ezekiel must suffer opposition but stand firm, eat God's words and speak them to deaf listeners (Ezek. 2–3 // Jer. 1), and perform symbolic actions that draw his life into his message (Ezek. 4–5 // Jer. 13; 27; 32). Ezekiel condemns false prophets (Ezek. 13 // Jer. 23), depicts Jerusalem as an unfaithful woman (Ezek. 16 // Jer. 2–4), and attacks Israel's shepherds (Ezek. 34 // Jer. 23:1–4). The books share distinctive phrases, such as (among many others), "The word of Yahweh came to me" (21x in Jeremiah, 41x in Ezekiel, 14x elsewhere); "sword, famine, plague" (15x in Jeremiah, 7x in Ezekiel,

2x elsewhere); "See, I am against [you]" (6x in Jeremiah, 14x in Ezekiel, 2x elsewhere); and, of course, the new covenant promise (Ezek. 11:19; 36:26 // Jer. 31:33).

Later books draw upon Jeremiah both as prophecy fulfilled and as a model for covenant faithfulness. Jeremiah 25:8–14 is the model for Dan. 9, and Jer. 30–33 for Zech. 8:2–19 (Assis). Much of Nehemiah's program was inspired by Jeremiah, from his closing the gates on the Sabbath to his prayers (Shepherd). The figure of Jeremiah—especially his faithfulness in a context of idolatry, and his prayers for Jerusalem—became more prominent in later Judaism, as reflected in Baruch; Epistle of Jeremiah; 2 Macc. 2:4–12; 15:12–16; Josephus (e.g., *J.W.*, 5.391–93); and many other still later works.

Jeremiah and the NT

Jeremiah is named just three times in the NT (Matt. 2:17; 16:14; 27:9). The largest numbers of citations and allusions per NA[27] are in Matthew (26), Luke-Acts (40), Romans (11), the Corinthian letters (11), Hebrews (13), and Revelation (76).

The OT citations in Matthew's infancy narrative tell the story of "Immanuel" who "will save his people from their sins" (Matt. 1:21–22). He will be the shepherd of his people in a new exodus (1:23–3:3). "Rachel weeping for her children" (2:18 // Jer. 31:15) sits in the middle of this story. In Jer. 31, Rachel's tears are for the death of the nation, but she is told to dry them because God will bring his people back and make a new covenant with them. In Matthew likewise, seeing the Jeremiah passage as a typological foreshadowing, the slaughter of children anticipates both the death of God's Son and the new covenant his blood will achieve. The presence of weeping Rachel strengthens the connection between Matt. 1:21 and Jer. 31:34, as Matthew anticipates the "blood of the covenant, which is poured out for many *for the forgiveness of sins*" (Matt. 26:28; see Niederhofer).

In Matt. 16:14 Jeremiah is popularly considered a messianic figure. At the same time, when Jesus offers "rest for your souls" (11:29 // Jer. 6:16) and calls the temple a "den of robbers" (21:13 // Jer. 7:11), he puts himself in Yahweh's place, not Jeremiah's. A "cluster of images" in Matt. 27:4–8—Judas's confession to having shed "innocent blood," the renaming of a potter's field, and the linking of burial and bloodshed to it—links the citation that follows to Jer. 19, whose theme fits "Matthew's emphasis . . . that the Jewish leaders who resist and condemn [Jesus] are actually bringing God's judgment down on themselves and on their land" (Blomberg, 95–96). This is the first time in Jeremiah that we have seen the prophet suffering bodily (Jer. 20:2), and Matthew's implied exegetical insight is that the "innocent blood" with which the valley is filled (Jer. 19:4) includes Jeremiah's, who therefore functions as a Christ-figure.

Jeremiah was a major influence on Paul's self-understanding. On balance, Jer. 1:5 makes the best antecedent for Gal. 1:15–16, "God, who *set me apart* from *my mother's womb* and called me by his grace, was pleased to reveal his Son in me so that I might *preach him among the Gentiles*" (Lalleman, "Self-Understanding"). Called like Jeremiah, Paul brought a message of "tearing down" and "building up" (2 Cor. 10:8; 13:10 // Jer. 1:10) as he fought those who claimed falsely to be apostles and boasted in themselves, not God (1 Cor. 1:31; 2 Cor. 10:17 // Jer. 9:23–24). Paul's sufferings bore a Jeremiah-like testimony to his gospel (2 Cor. 10:1–12:10). The rejection of this gospel by the people of Israel is accounted for in a Jeremianic fashion as well, both negatively with language of uncircumcised hearts (Rom. 2:25–27 // Jer. 9:26) and positively by God's plan to make a new pot from the old lump of clay (Rom. 9:21 // Jer. 18:4–10)—namely, a new Israel into which the gentiles are grafted (Rom. 11:19 // Jer. 11:16; see Reasoner). Finally, the way in which Paul's letters preserve his authoritative word and presence at a distance finds its precedent and model in Jeremiah (Doering, 560–62).

According to Jer. 31:34b, the reason Yahweh can write his law on Israel's heart is because "[he] will forgive their wickedness" (Shead, *Mouth*, 196–204). What kind of forgiveness can transform the forgiven person inwardly? For the author of Hebrews, who quotes and exegetes Jer. 31:31–34 at length (Heb. 8:8–12; 10:16–17), only Christ can fulfill such a prophecy. The blood of Christ not only obtains eternal redemption, but also "cleanse[s] our consciences from acts that lead to death" (Heb. 9:12, 14). Herein lies the newness of the "new covenant" (Luke 22:20; 1 Cor. 11:25; cf. Matt. 26:28).

John, in Revelation, is a great blender of the prophets; what may be said of Jeremiah applies to Isaiah and Ezekiel as well. Sometimes John applies Jeremiah with careful discipline. The sufferings of the Judeans (Jer. 15:2) are applied to the followers of Christ (Rev. 13:10); the elect of Israel are protected from a harm (Rev. 7:1–2) that echoes the judgment of non-Israelite Elam (Jer. 49:34–39). At other times, John uses images from Jeremiah more freely, such as the wormwood fed to people (Jer. 9:15) and prophets (23:15), which in Rev. 8:10–11 blights the earth; or the images of God as searcher of hearts and minds (Rev. 2:23 // Jer. 17:10) and spring of living water (Rev. 7:17; 21:6 // Jer. 2:13; see Collins). The Babylon oracle in Jer. 50–51, together with oracles from Isaiah and Ezekiel, lives again in the prophecies concerning "Babylon" (Rev. 17–18). The use of a code name for Rome echoes "Sheshak" in Jer. 25:26; 51:41. Rome's status as world power and its (Nero's) persecution of Christians legitimize this hermeneutical equivalence. The cosmic, suprahistorical imagery of verses like Jer. 51:41, 48–49, 52 justifies a hermeneutic whereby the command "Come out!" (Rev. 18:4) and the promise that Babylon's evil will be returned upon her function as typological foreshadowings not just of Christ's historical victory over death and calling into being of his church, but of the eschatological consummation of his work.

Bibliography. Allen, L. C., "The Structural Role of Wisdom in Jeremiah," in *Riddles and Revelations,* ed. M. J. Boda, R. L. Meek, and W. R. Osborne (Bloomsbury Academic, 2018), 95–108; Assis, E., "Zechariah 8 and Its Allusions to Jeremiah 30–33 and Deutero-Isaiah," *JHebS* 11 (2011): 2–21; Blomberg, C. L., "Matthew," in *CNTUOT,* 1–109; Brueggemann, W., *The Theology of the Book of Jeremiah* (Cambridge University Press, 2007); Collins, A. Y., "Jeremiah in the Book of Revelation," in Najman and Schmid, *Jeremiah's Scriptures,* 523–31; Dell, K. J., "Jeremiah, Creation and Wisdom," in *Perspectives on Wisdom,* ed. J. Jarick (Bloomsbury T&T Clark, 2016), 375–90; Doering, L., "The Commissioning of Paul," in Najman and Schmid, *Jeremiah's Scriptures,* 570–90; Fishbane, M., *Biblical Interpretation in Ancient Israel* (Clarendon, 1985); Holladay, W. L., *Jeremiah 2,* Herm (Fortress, 1989); Lalleman, H., *Jeremiah in Prophetic Tradition* (Peeters, 2000); Lalleman, "Paul's Self-Understanding in the Light of Jeremiah," in *A God of Faithfulness,* ed. J. A. Grant, A. Lo, and G. J. Wenham (T&T Clark, 2011), 96–111; Lundbom, J. R., *Jeremiah 1–20,* AB (Doubleday, 1999); Lundbom, *Jeremiah Closer Up* (Sheffield Phoenix, 2010); Najman, H., and K. Schmid, eds., *Jeremiah's Scriptures* (Brill, 2017); Niederhofer, V., "The Jeremianic Covenant Theology and Its Impact in the Gospel of Matthew," in Najman and Schmid, *Jeremiah's Scriptures,* 532–43; Reasoner, M., "The Redemptive Inversions of Jeremiah in Romans 9–11," *Bib* 95, no. 3 (2014): 388–404; Rom-Shiloni, D., "Actualization of Pentateuchal Legal Traditions in Jeremiah," *ZABR* 15 (2009): 254–81; Rom-Shiloni, "The Forest and the Trees," in *Congress Volume Stellenbosch 2016,* ed. L. C. Jonker, G. R. Kotzé, and C. M. Maier (Brill, 2017), 56–92; Shead, A. G., *A Mouth Full of Fire* (Apollos, 2012); Shead, "The Text of Jeremiah (MT and LXX)," in *The Book of Jeremiah,* ed. J. R. Lundbom, C. A. Evans, and B. A. Anderson (Brill, 2018), 255–79; Shepherd, D., "Is the Governor Also among the Prophets?," in *Prophets, Prophecy, and Ancient Israelite Historiography,* ed. M. J. Boda and L. M. Wray Beal (Eisenbrauns, 2013), 209–27; Sweeney, M. A., "Jeremiah's Reflection on the Isaian Royal Promise," in *Uprooting and Planting,* ed. John Goldingay (T&T Clark, 2007), 308–21.

Andrew G. Shead

Jerusalem

In a collection of woodcut maps first published in 1581, a German pastor, Heinrich Bünting, produced a fascinating figurative map of the world using a cloverleaf-inspired design. In the map the three leaves represent the continents of Europe, Asia, and Africa. America, described as "the new world," features in a lower corner of the map, and "Engeland" is portrayed as an island above Europe. At the center of the map Bünting prominently places Jerusalem, a vivid acknowledgment of the city's importance for the whole world. This graphic portrayal of the city at the center of the world reflects well the significance of Jerusalem within the Bible. However, the biblical picture is more complicated than Bünting's map suggests.

In the Bible the name "Jerusalem" refers to an elevated location in the Judean mountains between the Mediterranean Sea and the Dead Sea, but it is also associated with two other locations, neither of which is on the present earth. In Galatians, Paul contrasts the earthly Jerusalem with a "Jerusalem that is above" (4:26). Elsewhere, Hebrews refers to a "heavenly Jerusalem" (12:22). Sharing this understanding of a Jerusalem located in heaven, Revelation concludes by recording how the apostle John "saw the Holy City, the new Jerusalem, coming down out of heaven from God" (21:2; cf. 3:12; 21:10) to be located on a "new earth" (21:1). John's vision of the "new Jerusalem" represents the climax to which God's redemptive activity has been progressing throughout history. This concluding vision underlines the centrality of Jerusalem in God's purposes for the whole world.

While narrative books of the OT vastly prefer the designation "Jerusalem" for the city, poetic books (esp. Psalms, Isaiah, Jeremiah, and Lamentations) often refer to it as "Zion," sometimes in parallel with Jerusalem (e.g., Lam. 1:17; 2:10, 13). The name "Zion" occurs infrequently in the NT, with all but two occurrences (Heb. 12:22; Rev. 14:1) coming in quotations derived from the OT (Matt. 21:5; John 12:15; Rom. 9:33; 11:26; 1 Pet. 2:6).

Jerusalem's Rise to Prominence

Jerusalem is undoubtedly a highly significant location in the Bible. It first comes to prominence when the city is captured by King David. Prior to this, Jerusalem, known as Jebus, was controlled by the Jebusites, who are always mentioned last in lists of inhabitants of the land (e.g., Gen. 15:19–21; Exod. 3:17; 13:5; 23:23; 33:2; 34:11; Deut. 20:17). This feature possibly suggests they were the last to be conquered by the Israelites (Sarna, 14). David's capture of Jerusalem marks the final stage in the Israelite conquest of Canaan. Previous attempts to possess the city failed (Josh. 15:63; Judg. 1:21). After establishing Jerusalem as the capital of his kingdom, David reigns over all Israel and Judah for thirty-three years (2 Sam. 5:5). Prior to this, David reigned over Judah for seven years and six months in Hebron.

There are grounds for possibly associating Jerusalem with Melchizedek, king of Salem (Gen. 14:18), given the similarity in the names Salem and Jerusalem (cf. Ps. 76:2). Abraham's near sacrifice of Isaac may have taken place close to Jerusalem. In Gen. 22 the location is simply described as being in the "region of Moriah"; 2 Chron. 3:1, which records the only other occurrence of the name in the OT, refers to "Mount Moriah" as the location of the temple at Jerusalem. While these tentative links are interesting, they are not given any essential theological significance in the rest of Scripture.

The Temple City

After capturing Jerusalem, David brings to the city the ark of the covenant (2 Sam. 6:1–19). As the footstool of the heavenly throne (1 Chron. 28:2; cf. Pss. 99:5; 132:7), the ark is intimately linked to God's presence and sovereignty. Consequently, Jerusalem becomes the location where God places his name and the location to which the Israelites are expected to travel in order to appear before their God. God's majestic presence in Jerusalem is confirmed through the building of an ornate palace/temple during the reign of Solomon (1 Kings 6–8). The Hebrew term *hêkāl* denotes a royal residence, whether a palace for a human king or a temple for a divine king. The author of Kings records how God's glory fills the newly constructed building as it had previously filled the tabernacle (1 Kings 8:10–11; cf. Exod. 40:34–35). Jerusalem, "the city of our God" (Ps. 48:8), provides a natural opportunity for people to live near God. By replacing the portable sanctuary (the tabernacle) with a palace/temple, Solomon establishes Jerusalem as the location of God's permanent abode. This sets Jerusalem apart from all other cities; it becomes the city of God (e.g., Pss. 46:4; 135:21).

For its residents Jerusalem is a source of blessing because of God's presence (e.g., Pss. 128:5–6; 133:1–3; 134:3; 147:12–14; cf. Creach, 124–34). Captives returning to the city are filled with laughter and joy (Ps. 126:1–2; cf. 137:6). Zion is "perfect in beauty" (Ps. 50:2), "the joy of the whole earth" (Ps. 48:2). With good reason the psalmist proclaims, "The LORD loves the gates of Zion more than all the other dwellings of Jacob. Glorious things are said of you, city of God" (Ps. 87:2–3).

The opportunity to dwell in the city of God takes on added significance when viewed against the story of Adam and Eve's expulsion from God's presence in the garden of Eden. In the light of humanity's alienation from God, Jerusalem offers hope. Appropriately, the architecture of the Jerusalem temple recalls the garden paradise from which Adam and Eve were expelled (Stager, 38–47).

For those who cannot live in Jerusalem, the city becomes a pilgrim destination for worshiping Yahweh at the annual festivals. Those who make the journey are profoundly blessed (Ps. 84:5–7). As Mark Smith (109) remarks:

> In sum, the pilgrimage was like visiting paradise and temporarily recapturing the primordial peaceful and abundant relationship with God. It involved both holiness and pleasure, sacred and aesthetic space. It was an experience imbued with holiness, the beauty of the divine dwelling, and the very presence of God. The pilgrims' experience in the Temple was global in its effects. It saturated the psalmists' senses with all kinds of wonders: abundant food and incense, music and singing, gold and silver, palm trees, water and cherubs. This joyful experience led further to an experience of awe and holiness in the presence of God.

The Royal City

Although God's presence by itself is sufficient to explain the significance of Jerusalem, another aspect must not be overlooked. God's choice of Jerusalem is intimately connected to his choice of David, who will establish a royal dynasty. The author of Ps. 78 highlights how, in the time of Samuel, God rejected "the tent of Joseph and did not choose the tribe of Ephraim," choosing rather "the tribe of Judah" and "David his servant" (Ps. 78:67–70 CSB; cf. 132:13–18; Jer. 7:12–15; 26:6, 9). In affirming his choice of the tribe of Judah, and of David as king, God also chooses "Mount Zion, which he loved" (Ps. 78:68). Behind these choices stands an expectation that is first introduced in Genesis regarding a future king who will bring God's blessing to the nations of the earth (Alexander, "Expectations"; "Regal").

This expectation builds upon the idea that at creation God endows Adam and Eve with the status of viceregents, commissioning them to rule over all other earthly creatures on his behalf. Unfortunately, because the human couple succumb to the serpent's misrepresentation of God and eat from the tree of the knowledge of good and evil, God expels them from the garden of Eden. No longer are they or their descendants able to govern on God's behalf.

In appointing David as king in Jerusalem, God reestablishes the role of viceregent, linking it specifically to the Davidic dynasty. This outcome is reflected in Ps. 2, which records God as saying, "I have installed my king on Zion, my holy mountain" (2:6). In response, the king replies, "I will proclaim the LORD's decree: He said to me, 'You are my son; today I have become your father'" (2:7).

Behind the wording of Ps. 2 lie the events recorded in 2 Sam. 7. This significant chapter records how David proposes to build a house (palace/temple) for God (see Goswell). Although God rejects David's proposal as inappropriate, he nevertheless responds by committing to build an everlasting house (dynasty) for David. The events of this chapter forge a strong bond between the Davidic dynasty and God's palace/temple in Jerusalem, as the divine and the human thrones are set up in the same city. This confirms the viceregent status of the Davidic king, who is subject to God. The significance of this bond is underlined by God's creating a father-son relationship between himself and the Davidic king (2 Sam. 7:14).

Holy Mountain City

In addition to being a royal city, Jerusalem is viewed in the OT as a holy mountain city. As the psalmist observes, "He has founded his city on the holy mountain" (Ps. 87:1). This mountain aspect of Jerusalem is developed more fully in Ps. 48, which begins with these words: "Great is the LORD, and most worthy of praise, in the city of our God, his holy mountain. Beautiful in its loftiness, the joy of the whole earth, like the heights of Zaphon is Mount Zion, the city of the Great King" (48:1–2; cf. 125:1).

While some scholars suggest that this mountain tradition finds its roots in Canaanite mythology (Clifford), the Israelite concept of the holy mountain includes important features that set it apart as distinctive (Roberts). Particularly significant is that God's mountain abode is holy. This has important implications for the city, for it brings into consideration the moral behavior of those who dwell there. As the author of Ps. 24 states, "Who may ascend the mountain of the LORD? Who may stand in his holy place? The one who has clean hands and a pure heart, who does not trust in an idol or swear by a false god" (Ps. 24:3–4). The same sentiment is expounded in more detail in Ps. 15, emphasizing the moral dimension of being holy. In the light of these expectations the prophets critique Jerusalem on account of its immorality, pronouncing God's condemnation upon its inhabitants (e.g., Isa. 1; Jer. 2; Ezek. 5:8–12).

The concept of the holy city may be traced back to the exodus from Egypt. When the Israelites extol God for delivering them from the imminent violence of the Egyptian charioteers at the Lake of Reeds, their song concludes by announcing God's future plan for them: "You will bring them in and plant them on the mountain of your inheritance—the place, LORD, you made for your dwelling, the sanctuary, Lord, your hands established. The LORD reigns for ever and ever" (Exod. 15:17–18). These words express their hope of living with God on the mountain where he will establish his sanctuary or holy place. This hope eventually results in Jerusalem becoming the holy mountain city where God dwells with his people.

However, before the Israelites arrive in the promised land, God deliberately leads them to another holy mountain, Mount Sinai, where he enters into a unique covenant relationship with the Israelites. In different ways, the events at Mount Sinai prepare the people to live with God in his holy mountain city. At Mount Sinai the Israelites gain an understanding of God's holy nature and the moral demands that need to be met in order to be a holy nation. While initially Mount Sinai is off limits to the people due to God's holy presence (Exod. 19:10–15, 21–24), through the sacrificial ritual that seals the covenant relationship, the Israelites are consecrated, enabling their representatives to ascend the slopes of the holy mountain (24:2–13). This development paves the way for the people to live on God's holy mountain in the promised land.

By way of anticipating this future development, God comes to dwell with the Israelites at Mount Sinai in preparation for their dwelling with him on his holy mountain. This is confirmed through the construction of the tabernacle, which is designated a *miškān* or dwelling place. Additionally, through the giving of the Decalogue and the book of the covenant, God provides the people with moral instruction so that they may be holy as he is holy.

To underline the importance of all that takes place at Mount Sinai in preparation for the Israelites' residence with God on his holy mountain, the cultic rituals associated with the tabernacle recall the process by which the covenant was sealed at Mount Sinai. Intentionally, the spatial layout of the tabernacle resembles Mount Sinai, with both having a tripartite arrangement. Symbolically, the Israelites transport Mount Sinai to Mount Zion.

The Decimated City

Although Jerusalem takes on the mantle of the city of God, its residents live immoral lives and abandon their covenant commitment to God. As Deuteronomy warns, failure to obey God will ultimately lead to punishment involving exile (Deut. 28:64–68). Kings narrates how the kingdoms of Israel and Judah turn from God, resulting in subjugation to the nations of Assyria and Babylon, respectively. As regards Judah, considerable blame is laid at the feet of certain Davidic kings, an ironic development given the special role that the Davidic dynasty had in establishing Jerusalem as the city of God. Of all the prophetic condemnations of Jerusalem, Isaiah's short parable conveys well God's sense of disappointment concerning the inhabitants of Jerusalem; their behavior resembles bitter grapes (Isa. 5:1–5). The consequences for Jerusalem are devastating. God summons the Babylonians to capture the city, raze its walls, destroy the temple, and end the rule of the Davidic dynasty over the nation.

The fall of Jerusalem to the Babylonians in 586 BC is calamitous in the light of how God preserved Jerusalem and the Davidic dynasty in the face of similar threats in the past. The Assyrian army of Sennacherib failed to take Jerusalem, due to divine intervention, but no such aid is forthcoming when the Babylonians besiege the city. At the price of being labeled a traitor, the prophet Jeremiah warns that those already exiled to Babylon will be more secure than those remaining in Jerusalem. His words sound heretical to those who have developed a mistaken belief in the inviolability of Jerusalem due to God's presence (Ollenburger). As the book of Ezekiel reveals, Jerusalem is so defiled by the idolatry of its residents that God can no longer remain within the city.

The destruction of Jerusalem by the Babylonians is highly ironic, for Babylon has become within Israelite tradition the archetypal opposite of Jerusalem. It represents, more than any other city, human disdain toward God. The early chapters of Genesis come to a climax by describing the construction of Babylon (Gen. 11:1–9; *bābel* is the Hebrew name for Babylon). The builders of Babel/Babylon set their sights on overthrowing God by ascending to heaven itself. Isaiah's portrayal of the king of Babylon reflects this aspiration to be equal to God.

Isaiah records the king's ambition: "I will ascend to the heavens; I will raise my throne above the stars of God; I will sit enthroned on the mount of assembly, on the utmost heights of Mount Zaphon. I will ascend above the tops of the clouds; I will make myself like the Most High" (14:13–14). Although Babylon appears to win in the conflict with Jerusalem, the OT prophets predict the restoration of Jerusalem, anticipating that the future city will far exceed in splendor preexilic Jerusalem.

A New Jerusalem

Lamentations graphically reveals God's severe judgment against Jerusalem. Yet God does not abandon the concept of a holy mountain city where he will dwell with his people, who are under the authority of a Davidic king. As Donald Gowan observes, the eschatological hope of the OT is focused on Jerusalem. In keeping with God's redemptive plan, the concept of Jerusalem as the city of God becomes the goal of a greater vision, as God's past dealings with Israel provide a model or type for his future actions (see Goldsworthy). This envisaged Jerusalem, however, will be a cosmopolitan city in which the nations of the earth live in God's holy presence under a righteous Davidic king. As Israel received divine instruction at Mount Sinai, so the nations will come to the mountain of God to be instructed, resulting in universal peace (Mic. 4:1–4; Isa. 2:2–4). "Jerusalem becomes, in the prophetic vision, a symbol of God's final work of salvation for all the nations, who unite in their knowledge and worship of him. In all this Jerusalem—the historical city—recedes into the background" (McConville, 47; cf. Thomas, 913: "Zion becomes a symbol of new creation and redeemed humanity that lives before God without sin, death or pain because God rules in its midst").

The collected oracles of the prophet Isaiah convey well this hope, centered on a new Jerusalem, of a transformed world (see Webb, 65–84; G. Smith, 42–51). The book of Isaiah begins by focusing on God's rejection of a corrupt Jerusalem at the end of the eighth century BC. In marked contrast, it ends by describing a radically different Jerusalem that is precious to God (Isa. 62:1–5, 12). Importantly, Isaiah associates the divine creation of a resplendent Jerusalem with the creation of a new heavens and new earth (65:17–18), using language that recalls the opening verse of Genesis. This new Jerusalem will not simply evolve out of the earthly Jerusalem of Isaiah's day but will come into existence through a second creation. To underline this sense of new creation, Isaiah highlights how the natural environment will be characterized by harmony in place of violence (Isa. 65:25; cf. 11:6–9).

Isaiah's vision of a new Jerusalem goes far beyond anything that is achieved when the Persian king Cyrus sends Judean exiles back to the decimated Jerusalem at the end of the sixth century BC. Isaiah predicts this restoration under Cyrus, envisaging the rebuilding of the temple and the city (Isa. 44:28). Strikingly, Cyrus is designated the Lord's anointed (Isa. 45:1), recalling the anointing of David (1 Sam. 16:1–13). However, Isaiah's portrait of a gentile king coming to the rescue of Jerusalem is overshadowed by references to another individual who will play a vital role in establishing the new Jerusalem. As a light to the nations (Isa. 49:6), this "servant of the LORD" will bear the iniquity of others so that they may experience peace with God (Isa. 53:4–12). In keeping with God's commitment to establish David's dynasty forever, the "servant" displays characteristics of a Davidic king (Zehnder, 231–82).

The Jerusalem that Isaiah envisages is not simply a city to be inhabited by a future generation. Various indications in Isaiah suggest that this city will be inhabited by those who are raised to life after death. Drawing on the imagery of exiles returning from captivity, Isaiah speaks of "those the LORD has rescued" entering "Zion with singing" and experiencing "everlasting joy" (Isa. 35:10). Those living in Isaiah's new Jerusalem will not experience death (cf. Isa. 25:7–8). Belief in an eternal, heavenly Jerusalem is reflected in Jewish writing from the intertestamental period (see Fuller Dow, 127–31) as well as in the NT.

The prophet Ezekiel also envisages a future Jerusalem that will be a holy-mountain temple-city. His knowledge of this city comes from a series of visions that he receives, appropriately, on a very high mountain (40:2). The visions are recorded in Ezek. 40–48. As various scholars observe, these visions are largely symbolic in nature: "All in all Ezekiel's scheme appears highly contrived, casting doubt on any interpretation that expects a literal fulfillment of his plan" (Block, 502). Among everything that he witnesses, Ezekiel envisages a time when the holy mountain sanctuary of Jerusalem will be undefiled by human sin: "All . . . will be most holy" (43:12; cf. 43:6–11). The symbolic nature of the vision is reinforced by the description of the ever-expanding river that flows out of the temple, bringing life to the Dead Sea (47:1–12).

The restoration of Jerusalem after the Babylonian exile serves as a reminder that God has not abandoned his plan to establish on the earth a holy city where he will dwell with his people. The gradual reconstruction of the city, beginning with the temple, offers hope that God will reinstate the Davidic dynasty. Whereas in the past he rejected the tent of Joseph and Shiloh, the prophets of the exilic period anticipate the enthronement of a Davidic monarchy (Jer. 23:5–6; 33:14–26; Ezek. 34:23–31; 37:24–28; cf. Zech. 9:9–10). Once more Jerusalem will welcome a Davidic king. However, he will be no ordinary king.

The Heavenly Jerusalem

Against the background of how the concept of Jerusalem is developed in the OT, the NT maintains the importance of the city in God's redemptive plan. But like the OT, the NT envisages a corrupt Jerusalem being replaced by a new, eternal Jerusalem. At the heart of this transition stands Jesus of Nazareth, whom the NT writers unanimously affirm is the promised Davidic king, the Anointed One (or "Christ" or "Messiah").

Drawing on the significance of the relationship between Jerusalem and the Davidic king, Luke observes how the prophetess Anna associates the birth of the infant Jesus with the "redemption of Jerusalem" (Luke 2:38). Yet Luke's Gospel, like the other Synoptic Gospels, gives prominence to Jesus's public ministry in Galilee, a sign perhaps that, contrary to the expectations of many of Jesus's contemporaries, earthly Jerusalem will not be at the center of the kingdom that he has come to establish. Matthew's repeated references to the "kingdom of heaven" may well serve a similar purpose.

When Luke focuses on Jesus's journey to Jerusalem, a distinctive feature of his Gospel, he does not describe Jerusalem as the ultimate destination: "As the time approached for him to be taken up to heaven, Jesus resolutely set out for Jerusalem" (Luke 9:51). For Luke, Jesus's ascension to heaven is of primary importance; this is where he will be enthroned as king at the right hand of God the Father.

Luke's emphasis on the ascension of Jesus, underlined by its prominence at the end of his Gospel and at the start of Acts (Luke 24:50–53; Acts 1:6–11), harmonizes with his observation that the coming of the Holy Spirit upon believers marks a transition from God residing in the Jerusalem temple to the church becoming God's dwelling place through the Holy Spirit (Beale, 201–16). God moves from living among his people to living within them. This relocation diminishes the importance of Jerusalem as the temple city, a development that is in keeping with Jesus's prediction that the temple will be destroyed (Matt. 24:2; Mark 13:2; Luke 21:6).

Recognizing the significance of Jerusalem in God's redemptive plan, Jesus expresses his deep concern for the well-being of the city's inhabitants. However, he also acknowledges its rejection of God (e.g., Matt. 23:37–39; Luke 13:33–34; 19:41–44) and speaks of it as the location where he will be executed (Matt. 16:21; 20:17–18). Although he is welcomed into Jerusalem as the "son of David," his subsequent death, instigated by the religious elite, underlines the city's antipathy toward God. God's plans under the new covenant inaugurated by Jesus center on a heavenly Jerusalem.

This shift of location is noted by Paul in Galatians. Using the story of Abraham's relationship with Sarah and Hagar as an illustration, Paul contrasts the "present Jerusalem" with the "Jerusalem above" (4:21–31). In line with this, he informs the believers in Philippi, "Our citizenship is in heaven" (Phil. 3:20).

Paul is not alone in contemplating a heavenly Jerusalem. The author of Hebrews also writes of "the heavenly Jerusalem," which is "the city of the living God" (12:22). He subsequently remarks, "For here we have no lasting city, but we seek the city that is to come" (13:14 ESV). This belief in a "city that is to come" has previously been mentioned in connection with the patriarch Abraham, who looked forward in faith to "a better country, that is, a heavenly one" (11:16 ESV). "For he was looking forward to the city that has foundations, whose designer and builder is God" (11:10 ESV). During his lifetime on earth Abraham never inhabited this city, but the author of Hebrews anticipates a future time when his readers will reside in this city with Abraham and the other patriarchs (cf. 11:39–40). This outcome resonates with the expectations of the future that are encapsulated by Jesus in the Beatitudes, which say that, alongside other positive developments, the meek shall inherit the earth and see God (Matt. 5:3–12).

The crowning vision of Revelation depicts the descent of a heavenly city, a new Jerusalem, to a new earth. This marks the climax of God's redemptive activity, fulfilling his original intention when the first earth was created (Alexander, *City*). Echoes of the entire biblical story permeate John's vision of the new Jerusalem. The splendor and enormity of the city reflect the majesty of the one whose throne is established there. John's vision highlights the holiness of the city, alongside its elevated location. The city is home to all those who have been redeemed by the Lamb, who enjoy the ultimate experience of seeing the face of God (Rev. 22:4).

See also Jews and Gentiles; Temple

Bibliography. Alexander, T. D., *The City of God and the Goal of Creation* (Crossway, 2018); Alexander, "The Regal Dimension of the תלדות־יעקב," in *Reading the Law*, ed. J. G. McConville and K. Möller (T&T Clark, 2007), 196–212; Alexander, "Royal Expectations in Genesis to Kings," *TynBul* 49 (1998): 191–212; Beale, G. K., *The Temple and the Church's Mission* (Apollos, 2004); Block, D. I., *The Book of Ezekiel: Chapters 25–48*, NICOT (Eerdmans, 1998); Clifford, R. J., *The Cosmic Mountain in Canaan and the Old Testament* (Harvard University Press, 1972); Creach, J. F. D., *The Destiny of the Righteous in the Psalms* (Chalice, 2008); Fuller Dow, L. K., *Images of Zion* (Sheffield Phoenix, 2010); Goldsworthy, G., *Christ-Centered Biblical Theology* (Apollos, 2012); Goswell, G., "Why Did God Say No to David?," *JSOT* 43 (2019): 556–70; Gowan, D. E., *Eschatology in the Old Testament* (Fortress, 1986); McConville, J. G., "Jerusalem in the Old Testament," in *Jerusalem Past and Present in the Purposes of God*, ed. P. W. L. Walker (Deo Gloria Trust, 1992), 21–51; Morales, L. M., *The Tabernacle Pre-Figured* (Peeters, 2012); Ollenburger, B. C., *Zion, City of the Great King* (JSOT Press, 1987); Roberts, J. J. M., "Davidic Origin of the Zion Tradition," *JBL* 92 (1973): 329–44; Sarna, N. M., *Exodus* (Jewish Publication Society, 1991); Smith, G. V., "Isaiah 65–66," *BSac* 171 (2014): 42–51; Smith, M. S., *The Pilgrimage Pattern in Exodus* (Sheffield Academic, 1997); Stager, L. E., "Jerusalem as Eden," *BAR* 26 (2000): 38–47, 66; Thomas, H. A.,

"Zion," in *Dictionary of the Old Testament: Prophets*, ed. M. J. Boda and J. G. McConville (IVP Academic, 2012), 907–14; Webb, B. G., "Zion in Transformation," in *The Bible in Three Dimensions*, ed. D. J. A. Clines, S. E. Fowl, and S. E. Porter (JSOT Press, 1990), 65–84; Zehnder, M., "The Enigmatic Figure of the 'Servant of the Lord,'" in *New Studies in the Book of Isaiah*, ed. M. Zehnder (Gorgias, 2014), 231–82.

T. Desmond Alexander

Jesus's Use of the OT

The life and ministry of Jesus were permeated by use of the OT, regardless of which Gospel one reads. Questions of the trustworthiness of the accounts lie largely outside the scope of this article, but a good case can be made for the reliability of Jesus's explicit quotations of the OT (Blomberg; for Luke, cf. Kimball). Apart from criteria of authenticity used on specific passages, scholars are more likely to accept what appears in the oldest Gospel sources (almost certainly Mark and probably Q). But distinctively, Matthean, Lukan, and even Johannine material can be deemed credible by standard historical methods too. Throughout, Jesus employs explicit fulfillment formulae as well as other introductions that show he is intentionally referencing Scripture. In addition to quotations, one may find numerous allusions and echoes as well as actions that Jesus undertakes based on OT backgrounds. Isaiah, Psalms, and Deuteronomy are Jesus's most cited books, but texts appear from many parts of the Law, Prophets, and Writings.

The Gospel of Mark

Fulfillment of prophecy. Mark 7:5–8 critiques a group of scribes and Pharisees for following "the tradition of the elders" (the oral law), which are merely human rules, concerning ritual handwashing without genuine worship of God. Jesus introduces Isa. 29:13 by declaring, "Isaiah was right when he prophesied about you." Yet the OT text is not a future-referring one but an indictment of the Israelites in Isaiah's day. Jesus is interpreting the text typologically, seeing a new recurrence of the same behavior and attitudes in his day. He then turns to two laws mandating respect for parents (Exod. 20:12; 21:17), clearly believing the moral principles to be enduring, and he berates those who use the corban practice to avoid responsibility to care for their parents (Mark 7:9–13). This leads him to contrast internal and external purity, concluding that only that which comes out of a person, from their heart, including evil thoughts, can defile them (vv. 14–23). From this Mark infers that "Jesus declared all foods clean" (v. 19b). Almost certainly, this represents the Christian understanding of Jesus's teaching when Mark wrote, most likely in the sixties, rather than something the disciples understood on the spot, since it took Peter's vision of unclean animals accompanied by God's command to kill and eat them (Acts 10), a decade or more after Jesus's death, to convince them of the full significance of Jesus's teaching.

The one place in Mark where Jesus refers to actual fulfillment of Scripture is 14:49, where the timing and manner of Jesus's arrest and the events that follow are in view. Nothing indicates which passage(s) Jesus has in mind, but given his predilection elsewhere for the suffering-servant texts in Isaiah (esp. 52:13–53:12), one or more of them seems likely. In Mark 12:10–11, Jesus quotes Ps. 118:22–23 on the stone the builders rejected becoming the cornerstone, introducing it with "Have you not read this passage of Scripture?" In context, the quoted passage is about an event in the psalmist's day (Ps. 118:24), most likely the coronation of a king. But Jesus sees the pattern repeating in his "triumphal entry." Were there the language of fulfillment here, it would be a case of multiple fulfillment. Jesus could well have a more direct single fulfillment in view in Mark 14:27, when he predicts the disciples "will all fall away" and then quotes Zech. 13:7. There is no other obvious biblical example of a shepherd being struck and the "sheep" scattered after Zechariah's time.

Legal applications and principles derived from narrative and poetry. Even as Jesus looks forward to a new era in salvation history when the law will no longer always apply in the same way it did before his death and resurrection, there is no indication that he ever breaks one of the written laws of Scripture. So, he encourages the leper he heals to follow the Mosaic command to receive a priestly confirmation of his cleansing and to offer the appropriate temple sacrifices (Mark 1:44). He argues from the lesser to the greater in appealing to OT precedent for violating the Sabbath (2:26). In the debate with some Pharisees about divorce (10:6–8), he returns to "first principles" by quoting Gen. 1:27 and 2:24. And he cites key moral commandments in his interaction with the rich young ruler (Mark 10:19).

In reminding the temple throng that it is written, "My house will be called a house of prayer for all nations" (Mark 11:17), Jesus quotes Isa. 56:7. In one sense this is a timeless statement of the purpose of the gentile court, but in an eschatological context, Isaiah was also looking forward to the messianic age, when gentiles would much more widely come to worship Israel's God. The statement that too many have made it a "den of robbers" (in the sense of a nationalist stronghold; Barrett) quotes Jer. 7:11 in a context where too many are trusting (wrongly) in the temple as a refuge that they believe God would never destroy (7:4, 14–15).

Jesus cleverly derives support from the narrative of the burning bush for the reality of resurrection life (Mark 12:26; Exod. 3:6). In repartee with the Sadducees, who believe that doctrine can be established only from the five books of Torah, he cannot appeal to clearer OT passages on resurrection. Various suggestions have been offered as to the moves involved in deriving the idea that God is the God of the living rather than the dead from the present tense in "I am the God of Abraham," but what matters is that it is a hermeneutic that leaves his interrogators without a response.

The most positive interaction Jesus has with a questioner takes place during his last day of teaching in the temple when he refers to the double love command (Deut. 6:4–5; Lev. 19:18) as the greatest in the law (Mark 12:29–31), but even then he gives only a weak compliment to the lawyer, telling him that he is "not far from the kingdom of God" (v. 34). The climax of his teaching, however, comes when he turns the tables on his questioners and asks them about Ps. 110:1 ("The Lord said to my Lord: 'Sit at my right hand until I put your enemies under your feet'"). His question, though not phrased exactly this way, amounts to asking who the second "Lord" is above David, the author of the psalm. For the logic to be persuasive he must assume that most would recognize that it is the Messiah. But if the Messiah is above the king of Israel, he must be more than merely a human political and military ruler (Mark 12:35–37).

Scriptural language used without introduction. In numerous instances Jesus quotes the OT without any tip-off that he is doing so. Answering the question of why he speaks in parables, he replies, "So that, 'they may be ever seeing but never perceiving, and ever hearing but never understanding; otherwise they might turn again and be forgiven!'" (Mark 4:12; cf. Isa. 6:9–10). Originally, the quotation was part of Isaiah's prophetic commission to pronounce judgment on an already rebellious Israel; now Jesus is reapplying it to those who have already rejected him in the first century. But just as Isa. 6:13 promised a righteous remnant, so some will respond positively. Parables do not merely conceal but also reveal, at least for those who have ears to hear.

In Mark 13:24–25, Jesus combines Isa. 13:10 and 34:4 to refer to the cosmic signs that will accompany his return. In their contexts in Isaiah, they probably refer metaphorically to upheavals within Israel's world as God punishes the nations that oppress her. Still, 34:4 can be more easily seen as perhaps only eschatological, and the addition of one verse to another from a different context often meant that the second was interpreting the first (Adams and Ehorn). So, Jesus may see a direct fulfillment in his second coming. But he uses no introductory formula that requires us to speak of fulfillment at all. The same is true of his uses of Dan. 7:13 in Mark 13:26 and 14:62 and of Dan. 9:27; 11:31; 12:11 in Mark 13:14. The "abomination that causes desolation" in the latter cluster of passages was believed by some Jews to have been fulfilled by Antiochus Epiphanes's desecration of the temple in 167 BC (1 Macc. 1:57; 4:8). But Jesus applies it to the coming destruction of the rebuilt temple in AD 70, while he sees the Son of Man coming on the clouds of heaven as climaxing in his second coming.

Perhaps Jesus's most enigmatic repetition of scriptural language appears in Mark 15:34, when he cries out from the cross, "My God, my God, why have you forsaken me?" This reuses the language of Ps. 22:1. Ancient Jews knew their Scriptures extraordinarily well and often referred to only one small part of a larger passage, recognizing that their listeners would know the entire context. Has Jesus chosen this passage to recite because he knows the psalm ends with the triumph and vindication of the speaker (vv. 22–31)? It is hard to know, but a good case can be made that he has (Porter, 153–77).

Allusions and other references. Relevant OT backgrounds can be found for almost every passage in Mark. A few obvious and/or important examples are worth mentioning. The sickle used in the harvest in the parable of the seed growing secretly (Mark 4:29 alludes to Joel 3:13) reinforces the suggestion that Jesus is using the imagery eschatologically. Calming the storms and walking on water (Mark 4:35–41; 6:45–52) could very well be Jesus's intentional illustration of Job 9:8, where Yahweh (and he alone) "treads on the waves of the sea," and Ps. 107:29–30, where he calms storms and brings those in boats to safe haven. Feeding the multitudes in the wilderness almost certainly is intended to call to mind God's provision of manna during the Israelites' wandering for forty years (Exod. 16:13–35).

When the disciples ask Jesus why the scribes say Elijah must come before the Messiah (if he is the Messiah, they haven't seen Elijah), they most likely have Mal. 4:5 in mind. Jesus replies that Elijah has come and people have done to him what they pleased, a probable reference to John the Baptist and his execution (cf. Mark 6:14–29). While Mark does not quote Zech. 9:9 the way Matthew and Luke do, Jesus's entrance into Jerusalem on a donkey to the acclaim of the crowds seems to be an intentional fulfillment of what may well be a very direct messianic prophecy.

The detailed description of the vineyard in the parable of the wicked tenants (Mark 12:1–12) makes one think of the same list of elements in Isaiah's song of the vineyard (Isa. 5:1–7). Both passages are parables of judgment on the disobedient in Israel.

Conclusion. Most of the introductory formulae more common to Matthew or other later Gospel writers find at least one exemplar in Mark, suggesting Jesus was the origin for these various OT uses. The most explicit citations, especially from the prophetic literature, also consistently appear in polemical contexts with Jesus's antagonists, for whom Scripture is a central authority. But at least with the issue of ritual purity, Jesus anticipates a time when a major break from past practice will take place. Jesus himself turns to the OT for justification for his favorite title for himself, "Son of Man," while other concepts like Messiah and Lord, even if less common, are similarly buttressed. In a number of instances Jesus is linking himself, however indirectly, with Yahweh himself.

The Sayings in Q

"Q" in this article is merely shorthand for material common to Matthew and Luke but not found in Mark and does not presuppose that it was one definable written source, though it may have been. The common convention of using Luke's chapter and verse references preceded by Q will be used to save space.

Quotations with introductions. Three times in Q 4:1–13 Jesus refutes the devil's temptations by citing what "is written" in Scripture, each time from Deuteronomy (8:3; 6:13, 16): humanity should not live on bread alone, they should worship only the Lord, and they should not put him to the test, respectively. All of these are fundamental moral or spiritual principles that remain timeless. Jesus in Q 7:27 quotes Mal. 3:1—about God sending his messenger to prepare the way before God suddenly comes to his temple—and identifies John the Baptist as the messenger. The text in Malachi is not a messianic prophecy but a prediction of what Yahweh himself will do. Jesus is then filling the role of Yahweh!

Quotations without introductions. Q 12:51 and 12:53 do not use an introductory formula but are so close in wording to Mic. 7:6 that Jesus surely has it in mind. The religious divisions within households in ancient Israel are being repeated in the first century. Jesus does not ask his followers to provoke such strife, but he recognizes its inevitability when not all in one family have the same spiritual allegiance. Q 13:35 anticipates a future day when many in Israel will see him returning and will again declare, as people did in the times of the psalmist, "Blessed is he who comes in the name of the Lord" (Ps. 118:26). Jesus rehearses the miracles that will characterize the messianic age as itemized in Isa. 35:5–6 as part of his reply to John the Baptist's followers who have come asking on behalf of their imprisoned master if Jesus is indeed the coming one (Q 7:22).

References to OT individuals and events. Q also contains a number of Jesus's references to well-known characters and events in the Hebrew Scriptures. Q 13:28 refers to the patriarchs Abraham, Isaac, and Jacob as representatives of faithful Israel who will be part of the kingdom even when not all of their Jewish descendants will. Jesus predicts more dire judgment on the Galilean villages who saw his miracles (but nevertheless rejected him) than on Sodom and Gomorrah, proverbial for their wickedness in early OT times (Q 10:12), and on Tyre and Sidon, archenemies of Israel in later OT times (vv. 13–14). Jesus promises his opponents no sign other than the sign of Jonah (his death and resurrection) in Q 11:29. He goes on to note that the repentant Ninevites, from the capital of hostile Assyria, like another powerful foreigner, the queen of Sheba, will condemn those in Jesus's day who fail to repent (vv. 30–32). Q 11:51 threatens punishment on "this generation" for all the blood shed by the murders of the prophets from Abel to Zechariah, while 17:26–27 refers back to the days of Noah. Q 16:16, finally, separates the era of the Law and the Prophets from John, recognizing the progress of salvation history.

Material Unique to Matthew

A major emphasis of Jesus in teaching found only in Matthew is his fulfillment of the Hebrew Scriptures. He declares he has not come to abolish them, but instead of contrasting that with its natural opposite (preserving them), he says he has come to fulfill them—to bring them to their intended goal and full meaning (Matt. 5:17; cf. 7:12 and McKnight). Contrary to many who argue that Matthew's church still follows all of the Law unchanged and who point to Jesus's insistence that not the smallest part of the Law will disappear until heaven and earth do (5:18a), his declaration continues, "until everything is accomplished" (5:18b). With respect to the validity of animal sacrifices, everything is accomplished with his work on the cross, and believers must not continue them, not even Jewish believers. Every other category of law must be assessed similarly (Banks; France).

The antitheses in Jesus's Sermon on the Mount (Matt. 5:21–48) start to flesh out this principle. It is often said that they question only Pharisaic halakah, but in overturning the law of retaliation ("an eye for an eye," vv. 38–42), they seem to go further to envision a new age when even the written law does not function in the same way it once did. In controversies over associating with the wicked and with "working" on the Sabbath, Matthew twice records additional words of Jesus (9:13; 12:7) quoting Hosea 6:6 ("I desire mercy, not sacrifice"). This defends his behavior via the OT, but since actual sacrifices are not the issue, he must be generalizing to something like the contrast between moral and ritual laws. Because he has no parallel to Mark 7:19b, Matthew has been said to be more conservative about the dietary law, but since he preserves Jesus's teaching about only what comes out of a person as defiling them (Matt. 15:17–20), this is hard to maintain. In 24:20, Matthew reports Jesus telling the disciples to pray not just that their flight as persecution increases not occur in the winter (cf. Mark 13:18) but also that it not take place on a Sabbath. But this scarcely means Matthew or his churches still kept the Sabbath any more than they kept "winter." Both are hindrances to travel in a country that overall is still law-abiding, one due to the weather and the other due to the unavailability of services.

In Matt. 21:16, Jesus justifies the children's praises of him by quoting Ps. 8:3 LXX on the identical topic, introduced with the rhetorical question "Have you never read . . . ?" This is merely the reapplication of a general principle to a new context. The same is true of the legal requirement for two or three witnesses (Deut. 19:15). Jesus quotes this principle in his teaching on church discipline as a reason for an aggrieved person who receives no satisfaction from approaching the offender privately to then take one or two people with them (Matt. 18:16).

The original person plus one or two others adds up to two or three.

Material Unique to Luke

Probably the most important uniquely Lukan passage in which Jesus quotes the OT is Luke 4:16–21. Here he takes the Isaiah scroll in the Nazareth synagogue, unrolls it to Isa. 61:1–2, and quotes the author's pronouncement that the Lord's Spirit is on him to announce good news to the poor and healing to all kinds of broken people. It is the favorable year of the Lord, a reference to Jubilee (Lev. 25:8–54). Then he astonishes his audience by declaring that this Scripture is fulfilled that day in his people's hearing, obviously referring to his own person and ministry. Interspersed is a phrase from Isa. 58:6 on freeing the oppressed, which Jesus may add as an interpretive gloss based on his prior knowledge of the passage, a common ancient Jewish practice for readers or interpreters of Scripture (cf. the whole targumic tradition). That Jesus's ministry includes healing the physically sick people who are itemized in Isa. 61:1 is a reminder that the physical and spiritual blessings of the gospel must be kept together, even though physical healing is never guaranteed in this life.

Like Mark and Matthew, Luke has a reference to the double love command as the heart of the Law. But here it comes from a lawyer who is discussing eternal life with Jesus, and it forms the prelude to the parable of the good Samaritan (Luke 10:25–37). Jesus nevertheless affirms the lawyer's assessment; what they disagree is on the definition of a neighbor in the command to love one's neighbor. In Luke 22:37, Jesus cites Isa. 53:12a as what was "written" and therefore must be fulfilled—namely, his being numbered among the lawless (in his crucifixion). Here we have reasonably direct fulfillment, especially since the excerpt of Isaiah is sandwiched between explicit statements of the servant's ministry of substitutionary atonement (vv. 11, 12b).

In additional comments of Jesus in Luke, we also read of how, in the end times, things will become so bad that people will want the mountains to fall on them to end everything (23:30, reapplying the language of Hosea 10:8). Jesus also repeats language from Ps. 31:5 in his dying words to his Father, "Into your hands I commit my spirit" (Luke 23:46), which was also a common bedtime prayer for children. Finally, Luke shows that Jesus sees fulfillment of all of Scripture as central, just as Matthew does, when in Luke 24:25–27 and 44–47 he rebukes Cleopas and his companion for failing to believe everything written about him and then explains to the Eleven how everything about him in "the Law of Moses, the Prophets and the Psalms" had to be fulfilled in him.

The Gospel of John

The most explicit quotations of the OT by Jesus in John begin in John 6:31 and 6:45 with citations of Ps. 78:24 and Isa. 54:13, respectively. The overall form of Jesus's Capernaum synagogue sermon, in which he embeds these quotes, is a characteristically Jewish proem midrash, which starts with a key text, moves on to a related one, and circles back to the original topic at the end. The source of the "Scripture" in John 7:37–38 that refers to rivers of living water flowing from the believer (or possibly Christ) is less clear. Some combination of Isa. 58:11 with Prov. 4:23; 5:15; or Zech. 14:8 seems likely.

Jesus's great "I am" statement of John 8:58 probably cites Exod. 3:14 but may also allude to one or more of the "I am he" statements of Isaiah (41:4; 43:10, 13; etc.). In John 10:34, Jesus cites Ps. 82:6 to justify his acceptance of the title "Son of God." After all, the psalmist referred to powerful people in Israel as "gods," which seems to be an even loftier claim. Embedded in this dialogue is an important affirmation that Jesus and his opponents share: Scripture cannot be broken (10:35), which suggests both its authority and its unity. What differs is their interpretation and their understanding of how it applies in the age of Jeremiah's new covenant (Jer. 31:31–33).

Classic typology appears in John 13:18, as a statement about an enemy of David (Ps. 41:9) is said to be fulfilled in Judas's betrayal of Jesus. The pattern that first involved the king of Israel and his opponent is reenacted in the life of the greater king of Israel. Similar typology reappears in the use in John 15:25 of Pss. 35:19 and 69:4 (see further Clark-Soles, 314–15).

Just as Matthew and Luke depict Jesus making sweeping, programmatic statements about him fulfilling Scripture more generally, so too does John. In 5:39 and 5:46, he reminds the Jewish leaders that they study the Scriptures daily. If only they rightly understood them, if they truly believed Moses, who pointed ahead to a greater person to come who would be like him and who was to be followed (Deut. 18:15), they would accept that their Bible points to Jesus, and they would believe him. Other primary uses of Scripture by Jesus appear in John 3:3–15 with the story of the serpent on the pole on the wilderness (Num. 21:9), in 4:34 with the sowing and reaping in the fields "white for harvest" (cf. Amos 9:13), and in 8:14–17 with the appeal to the principle of two or three witnesses (Deut. 19:15) (Anderson).

Most of Jesus's explicit quotations of Scripture in John's Gospel again appear in polemical contexts, usually in reply to religious leaders (Sheridan). Jesus employs the Bible's authority to refute their charges. But charges of Johannine anti-Semitism are refuted by the fact that Jesus and all his first followers also were Jewish.

Observations and Conclusions

Despite numerous studies of a given evangelist's or Gospel source's singly attested use of the OT, there is little to set off any given use of Scripture as dramatically different from any other or from Jesus's own use. Even Matthew, who doubles the number of quotations in general and the number of fulfillment quotations in particular, reuses the same introductions, the same kinds of fulfillments, and the same applications of the Law, Prophets, and Writings as can already be found in passages attributed to Jesus in Mark and Q. To the extent that differing themes characterize the various Gospels and their sources, and given the widespread use of the OT to support those themes, one will find certain nuances and changes of emphasis. But these derive from the varying themes more than any varying approaches to the Hebrew Bible. One original, creative mind lies behind the diversity of approaches to Scripture; therefore, it is not the case that the diverse Gospel sources all independently produced them (Evans). The amount of typology utilized makes it unlikely that the Gospel writers invented history to match the prophecies; only after events that reminded people of something in the OT was anyone likely to draw the connection.

Matthew, Luke, and John, all in their own ways, stress that Jesus claimed to fulfill the Scriptures as a whole, not just numerous individual texts, while for Mark fulfillment of God's purposes more generally functions as a headline over his Gospel (1:15). This is to say not that every verse or minor subdivision in the OT somehow testifies to Jesus but that everything that does point to him in the Scriptures is now being fulfilled. Of course, Jesus's eschatological teaching separates what the OT nowhere unambiguously separates, which is why Christians speak of his first and second comings. Topics Jesus supports with prophecy include especially the end of exile (McComiskey), the new exodus (Patterson and Travers), and his role as suffering servant (Moo), with its effects of both judgment and vindication (Bryan).

Nor is it just prophecy, whether direct, multiple, or typological, that is brought to its intended completion in Jesus, but all of the Law, Prophets, and Writings as a whole. Interpretations of Jesus's view of the OT that see it as dividing the old-covenant Scriptures into an abiding moral law versus a temporally limited civil and ceremonial law are not unfaithful to his general pattern and spirit. But an added nuance is needed: every part of Scripture applies in some way to the believer, but none can be applied correctly until one understands how it is fulfilled in Christ. And that fulfillment may vary from a major commandment being transferred over intact to the new age, as with nine of the ten commandments (all but the Sabbath command) to a practice altogether done away with, except in a spiritual or symbolic sense, as with the sacrificial laws now giving way to Christ's once-for-all atonement (Klein, Blomberg, and Hubbard, 443–49). It is difficult to improve on Loader's summary (523–24): "A reconstruction of Jesus' attitude toward the Law needs then to take into account diverse strands of tradition: the radically humane Jesus; the culturally conservative Jesus; the theologically strict Jesus in issues of morality; the Jesus who is like popular Hellenistic preachers, Jewish and non-Jewish; the Jesus who gives priority to ethical behaviours and attitudes above ritual and cultic Law; the Jesus who shares [John the Baptist's] eschatology, but claims its partial fulfilment."

See also John, Gospel of; Luke, Gospel of; Mark, Gospel of; Matthew, Gospel of

Bibliography. Adams, S. A., and S. M. Ehorn, eds., *New Testament Uses*, vol. 2 of *Composite Citations in Antiquity* (T&T Clark, 2018); Ahearne-Kroll, S., *The Psalms of Lament in Mark's Passion* (Cambridge University Press, 2007); Anderson, P. N., "The Fulfilled Word in the Gospel of John," *The Gospel of John*, vol. 4 of *Biblical Interpretation in Early Christian Gospels*, ed. T. R. Hatina (Bloomsbury T&T Clark, 2020), 57–82; Banks, R., *Jesus and the Law in the Synoptic Tradition* (Cambridge University Press, 1975); Barrett, C. K., "The House of Prayer and the Den of Thieves," in *Jesus und Paulus*, ed. E. E. Ellis and E. Grässer (Vandenhoeck & Ruprecht, 1978), 13–20; Blomberg, C. L., "Reflections on Jesus' View of the Old Testament," in *The Enduring Authority of the Christian Scriptures*, ed. D. A. Carson (Eerdmans, 2016), 669–701; Bryan, S. M., *Jesus and Israel's Traditions of Judgement and Restoration* (Cambridge University Press, 2002); Clark-Soles, J., *Scripture Cannot Be Broken* (Brill, 2003); Cope, O. L., *Matthew* (Catholic Biblical Association of America, 1976); Ellis, E. E., "How Jesus Interpreted His Bible," *CTR* 3 (1989): 341–51; Ellis, "Jesus' Use of the Old Testament and the Genesis of New Testament Christology," *BBR* 3 (1993): 59–75; Evans, C. A., "Why Did the New Testament Writers Appeal to the Old Testament?," *JSNT* 38 (2015): 36–48; Evans, C. A., and W. R. Stegner, eds., *The Gospels and the Scriptures of Israel* (JSOT Press, 1994); France, R. T., *Jesus and the Old Testament* (Tyndale, 1971); Hägerland, T., *Jesus and the Scriptures* (Bloomsbury T&T Clark, 2016); Hanson, A. T., *The Living Utterances of God* (Darton, Longman and Todd, 1983); Hays, R. B., *Echoes of Scripture in the Gospels* (Baylor University Press, 2016); Hays, *Reading Backwards* (Baylor University Press, 2014); Holmén, T., *Jesus and Jewish Covenant Thinking* (Brill, 2001); Juel, D., *Messianic Exegesis* (Fortress, 1987); Kimball, C. A., *Jesus' Use of the Old Testament in Luke* (Sheffield Academic, 1994); Klein, W. W., C. L. Blomberg, and R. L. Hubbard Jr., *Introduction to Biblical Interpretation*, 3rd ed. (Zondervan, 2017); Loader, W. R. G., *Jesus' Attitude towards the Law*, WUNT 2/97 (Mohr Siebeck, 1997); Marcus, J., *The Way of the Lord* (T&T Clark, 1992); McComiskey, D. S., "Exile and Restoration from Exile in the Scriptural Quotations and Allusions of Jesus," *JETS* 53 (2010): 673–96; McKnight, S., *The Jesus Creed* (Paraclete, 2004); Meyer, B. F., "Appointed Deed, Appointed Doer," in *Authenticating the Activities of Jesus*, ed. B. D. Chilton and C. A. Evans (Brill, 1998), 155–76; Montanaro, A., "The Use of the Old Testament Quotations in John's Gospel," *NovT* 59 (2017): 147–70; Moo, D. J., *The Old Testament in the Gospel Passion Narratives* (Almond, 1988); Moyise, S., "Jesus and Isaiah," *Neot* 40 (2009): 49–70; Moyise, *Jesus and Scripture* (Baker Academic, 2010); Myers, A. D., and

B. G. Schuchard, eds., *Abiding Words* (SBL Press, 2015); O'Brien, K., *The Use of Scripture in the Markan Passion Narrative* (T&T Clark, 2010); Patterson, R. D., and M. E. Travers, "Contours in the Exodus Motif in Jesus' Earthly Ministry," *WTJ* 66 (2004): 25–47; Porter, S. E., ed., *Hearing the Old Testament in the New Testament* (Eerdmans, 2006); Powery, E. B. *Jesus Reads Scripture* (Brill, 2003); Sheridan, R., *Retelling Scripture* (Brill, 2012); Tan, K. H., *The Zion Traditions and the Aims of Jesus* (Cambridge University Press, 1997); Tasker, R. V. G., *Our Lord's Use of the Old Testament* (Pickering & Inglis, 1956); Wenham, J., *Christ and the Bible* (Wipf & Stock, 2009).

CRAIG L. BLOMBERG

Jews and Gentiles

From a biblical-theological perspective, Jews and gentiles both share a significant part in God's plan and purpose for creation. According to the OT, God's choice of Abraham and his biological descendants served a much broader objective: blessing not just for the nation of Israel but for all peoples on earth (Gen. 12:2–3; 22:18). According to the NT, this divine objective is finally achieved through faith in Jesus—the seed of Abraham who makes the prospect of international blessing a reality (Gal. 3:8–29), reconciling both Jew and gentile to God and creating "one new humanity" through the cross (Eph. 2:11–22). Thus, the eschatological goal in Christian Scripture is for a single people of God, "persons from every tribe and language and people and nation," in whom God's plans for a priestly kingdom are ultimately realized (Rev. 5:9–10; cf. Exod. 19:6; 1 Pet. 2:9).

God's Goal for Creation

Whatever their differences, both Gen. 1 and 2 portray humans as "the pinnacle of God's creative activity" (Williamson, 45). Their special status is underlined by the unique responsibility they are given: to work and care for the garden (Gen. 2:15) and to fill the earth and subdue it (Gen. 1:28). It may thus be inferred that God's creative purpose is to extend the borders of Eden—including the blessing experienced there—throughout the entire earth (see, e.g., Gladd, 9–21). While rebellion against God (Gen. 3) disrupts this global objective, it does not end it. Rather, in the immediate aftermath of human rebellion, God announces that the seed of the woman will crush the serpent's head (3:14–15). It is with the latter, the skull-crushing seed of the woman, that the rest of Genesis—and indeed the OT—is primarily concerned. While Eve may mistakenly have assumed his arrival with the birth of her firstborn (4:1), it quickly becomes evident that the promised line of descent will actually be traced through Seth (5:3).

God's Covenant with Creation

Before the flood, the promised line of seed is traced to Noah, highlighting the significance of his deliverance: through God's grace the promised seed is preserved, and creation's future is divinely guaranteed by covenant. This solemn commitment is made not only with Noah and his descendants but also with every living creature (Gen. 9:10). This suggests that God's purposes encompass not just humanity but all creation. Yet the special role of humanity in attaining this universal goal is again underlined: Noah and his sons are to fulfill God's mandate to "be fruitful and increase in number; multiply on the earth and increase upon it" (9:7; cf. 1:28). While the related idea of subduing the earth and ruling over the rest of creation is now conspicuously absent (9:1, 7; although cf. 9:1 LXX), God's global purpose is once more reflected in this divine mandate for humanity to populate the whole earth. And this is given further expression even after Genesis narrows its focus to one particular family and the promises God makes concerning Abraham and his descendants.

God's Blessing of Abraham and His Descendants

Genesis 12:2–3 is a seminal text for biblical theology as a whole and for the relationship between Jews and gentiles in particular. Here we discover not only God's plans for Abraham and his descendants but also their significance in God's broader plan—namely, to bless "all the families of the earth" (ESV). While some have understood v. 3 to suggest that other nations might simply *wish* for such blessing (cf. Gen. 48:20; Zech. 8:13) rather than actually experience it, this would be "decidedly anti-climactic" (Dumbrell, 77), especially in a context that appears to anticipate such blessing as being the norm by using the plural ("*those* who bless you," v. 3a) to depict it. Moreover, elsewhere in the Abraham narrative (e.g., Gen. 18:18) a mere wish by other nations hardly explains Abraham's international significance or God's compulsion to share with him his intention to destroy Sodom. This, and the fact that the prospect of blessing is related to the person of Abraham rather than simply his name, suggest that Abraham and his seed will be instrumental in securing such anticipated blessing for the nations (Gen. 17:4–5; 22:18; 26:4; cf. 35:11; 49:10). Thus understood, Abraham will be the "father of multitudinous nations" (Gen. 17:4 AT) by mediating divine blessing to them rather than merely being their biological progenitor. Indeed, the latter idea is excluded by the simple fact that only two biblical nations—the Israelites and the Edomites—could actually trace their physical ancestry back to Abraham and Sarah (cf. Gen. 17:16). There is thus a decidedly international dimension in the ancestral narratives (cf. Gen. 49:10b) despite their immediate focus on Abraham and his biological descendants. This is also the case for the rest of the Pentateuch, where the relationship between Israel and the nations is further developed.

Israel's Mission: A Light to the Nations

In Exodus and beyond, the role of Israel as a light to the nations begins to take shape. The initial obstacle to the fulfillment of God's plan—Egypt's attempt to obstruct, first, Israel's population explosion and, subsequently, their exodus from Egypt—becomes an opportunity to teach Israel (Exod. 6:2–8; 10:2; 14:31), Egypt (Exod. 7:5; 11:7; 14:4, 18), and the surrounding nations (Exod. 15:14–16; 18:1, 8–11) about the power and sovereignty of Yahweh, Israel's covenant God. Israel's unique relationship with God, the primary focus from Exod. 19 to the end of the Pentateuch, serves to underline further the nation's raison d'être as a "kingdom of priests and a holy nation" (Exod. 19:6; cf. Deut. 7:6)—that is, to model God's kingdom and make such appealing to surrounding nations (Deut. 4:5–8; 26:16–19; cf. Num. 23:8–10, 21–24; 24:5–9).

However, as the Torah anticipates—and as the rest of the OT confirms—Israel does not maintain its distinctiveness as God's special people; rather, by becoming just like its surrounding neighbors, Israel provokes divine judgment, something that could potentially jeopardize God's plans to make his name known in all the earth (Exod. 9:16; cf. Ezek. 36:16–23). Consequently, rather than serving as a witness to the nations in a positive sense (see, e.g., 2 Kings 19:19 // Isa. 37:20), Israel functions in a more negative role—attesting to covenantal curse rather than to covenantal blessing (Lev. 26:32; Deut. 28:25; cf. Jer. 15:4; 24:9; 29:18; 34:17; Joel 2:17–18). Nevertheless, as the prophetic corpus underlines, such divine judgment will not be God's final word. Out of the ashes of exile God will reestablish his kingdom through a new exodus and a new covenant that will create a new Israel in which the promises to Abraham—for both Israel and the nations—will find complete fulfillment.

The OT's Eschatological Vision: Incorporation of Gentiles into the People of God

While hope for a postexilic restoration of Israel is frequently attested in Israel's prophetic texts, its global or international ramifications also attract significant attention—particularly in the case of Isaiah.

From its opening chapters Isaiah anticipates a positive international response ("all nations," "many peoples") to Yahweh and his instruction "in the last days" (Isa. 2:2–4; cf. Mic. 4:1–3) reflecting "relational, attitudinal, and moral-behavioral transformation" (Schultz, 131). Such expansion is also foreshadowed in the honor conferred on "Galilee of the nations" (Isa. 9:1–2; cf. Matt. 4:15–16) and possibly further envisaged under the rule of the future Davidic king (Isa. 11:9–11; cf. Ps. 72:17b). While this second exodus may focus more especially on the dispersed *Israelite* remnant (cf. Isa. 11:12–16), the two concepts—the gathering of Israel and the rallying of the nations—are integrally related (cf. 12:4–5). While certainly not the major focus, Isaiah's oracles against foreign nations also suggest hope and reconciliation for some, though not all, of Israel's former enemies (cf. 14:1; 18:7; 19:18–25). In a similar vein, the following section (Isa. 24–27) depicts a global response of praise to Yahweh (24:14–15), whose blessings incorporate "*all* peoples" (25:6–8; cf. 26:18–19).

Gentile inclusion is likewise attested in the second part of the book (Isa. 40–66), where the servant is said to be "a light for the Gentiles" (42:6–7; cf. 49:6–7; 51:4–5; 52:14–15) and to "bring justice to the nations" (42:1, 4) and where God's salvation extends "to the ends of the earth" (49:6) and calls for an international response (42:10–12; 45:22–24; cf. 49:26; 52:10). The servant's role in relation to such is arguably highlighted in Isa. 55:5, where the singular subject ("you"; cf. the pl. form in 55:1–3) successfully summons "nations" to himself (Oswalt, 439–40). In accord with such a universal call, the following chapter highlights the future inclusiveness of God's people (56:3–8; cf. Deut. 23:1–8)—namely, those who keep his covenant (Isa. 56:1–4, 6; cf. 56:9–57:21). Such international inclusion reaches a fitting climax in the book's final chapters, where, despite a more subservient role, nations, their kings, and their wealth come to Zion's everlasting light—that is, to Yahweh (60:3–11). God's rebellious people are sharply distinguished here from his "servants"/"chosen ones" (65:1–16; cf. 66:2–17); only the latter will inherit God's permanent blessings (65:9–10, 19–23) and proclaim his glory among the nations (66:19). Consequently (66:20–21; cf. Isa. 56), "erstwhile Gentiles are gathered as brothers" (Motyer, 542), and "all flesh will come and bow down before the LORD" (66:23 AT). Indeed, gentiles in the eschaton will be considered part of true Israel (Ps. 87) and faithful servants of Yahweh (Isa. 56:6–7)—even in the most consecrated role imaginable: priests and Levites (see 66:20–21).

Although he is appointed as "a prophet to the nations" (Jer. 1:5), Jeremiah's role is primarily a negative one (1:10), announcing their coming destruction (cf. 25:15–38; 46:1–51:64). In contrast with Israel, eschatological reversal for the nations receives only minimal attention. Even so, some of the same prospects reflected in Isaiah are articulated: the gathering of all nations to Jerusalem to honor Yahweh (3:17a); an attitudinal, relational, or ethical transformation (3:17b; 4:2b; 16:19b–20), or at least the possibility of such; and their incorporation among God's people (12:14–17).

Ezekiel's hope for the nations seems even more muted (see Ezek. 29:13–16; 47:21–23; cf. also 47:12 with Rev. 22:3); like Isaiah's and Jeremiah's, his oracles against foreign nations (Ezek. 25–32) anticipate Israel's restoration at their expense (28:25–26; 29:21). Moreover, the oft-repeated recognition formula ("They will know that I am Yahweh") speaks mostly of intellectual acknowledgment rather than attitudinal transformation (although cf. Ezek. 38:16, 20, 23; 39:7, 21–24, 27).

By contrast, the Minor Prophets occasionally articulate the hope of gentile inclusion in the latter-day people of God. For example, Amos anticipates a restored Davidic kingdom that will "possess the remnant of Edom and all the nations that bear my [Yahweh's] name" (Amos 9:12, a text cited [from the LXX] by James to validate the inclusion of gentile believers within the NT church; cf. Acts 15:13–17). As noted above, Micah anticipates the same prospect as Isaiah (Mic. 4:1–3). Moreover, he likewise looks forward to a Davidic ruler whose "greatness will reach to the ends of the earth" (Mic. 5:4) and an influx of people—arguably including gentile converts as well as Jewish exiles—from all over the earth (Mic. 7:12). Zechariah similarly envisages such an ingathering (Zech. 8:7–8, 20–23) but more clearly highlights the incorporation of gentiles (cf. Zech. 2:11 [MT 2:15]; 8:22; 14:16).

Given this eschatological vision in the OT, it is hardly surprising to see the nations being invited (e.g., Pss. 33:8; 47:1; 96:7–9; 117:1; 148:7; see also Pss. 67; 98) to join with Israel in praising God, a realistic expectation (e.g., 22:27; 86:9) that will ultimately find fulfillment in Zion (87:4–5; 102:15, 22).

Jesus, the Promised Messiah and "Light of the World"

Significantly, the NT proclaims that the anticipated Messiah (i.e., God's anointed king) has come in the person of Jesus (e.g., Matt. 1:17–18; 2:1–6; 11:2; 16:16; 23:10; Mark 1:1–3; 9:41; Luke 2:11, 26; John 1:41; 4:25–26; 20:31; Acts 2:31; 5:42; Rev. 12:10)—"the son of David" and "the son of Abraham" (Matt. 1:1; cf. 1:17; Luke 1:27, 68–75; 2 Tim. 2:8; Rev. 5:5; 22:16). As such, Jesus is the promised royal "seed" and heir to God's covenant promises (Luke 1:31–33; Acts 13:32–38; Gal. 3:16), the one who saves his people (Matt. 1:21; Luke 1:68–75; Acts 13:38–39) and the one through whom "all peoples on earth will be blessed" (Acts 3:25; Gal. 3:7–9, 13–14). Moreover, as the Isaianic "servant," Jesus is "the light of the world" (John 8:12; 9:5; cf. 1:4; 3:19; Luke 2:30–32; 4:18–19; Acts 26:23)—a role inherited by his disciples and apostles (Matt. 5:14; Acts 13:47; 26:16–18; Eph. 5:8), who will evangelize and make disciples of "all nations" (Matt. 24:14; 28:19), beginning at Jerusalem (Luke 24:47) but expanding "to the ends of the earth" (Acts 1:8; cf. John 10:16). Accordingly, God's plans and promises for both Jews and gentiles converge and are fulfilled in Jesus and his church (Rom. 15:8–12), who together constitute the true "seed of Abraham" (Gal. 3:26–29) and "Israel of God" (Gal. 6:16)—the church through its union with Christ.

The Church as the New Covenant People of God

The idea that non-Jews or foreigners could become part of the covenant community / people of God is therefore not a NT novelty; it is already evinced or foreshadowed in the OT (see, e.g., Exod. 12:19; Ruth 1:16; cf. Deut. 23:8) and plainly expected to occur on a much greater scale in the future (see the earlier section "The OT's Eschatological Vision"). The beginning of such ingathering of gentiles is alluded to within the Gospels (e.g., Matt. 8:5–13; 15:21–28; cf. 25:31–46; Luke 13:29) despite Jesus's earthly ministry focusing chiefly on "the lost sheep of Israel" (Matt. 10:5–6; 15:24). The evangelism of Jews remains a priority in Acts, where the apostles preach first to Jews and only subsequently to gentiles (Acts 13:46–47; 18:5–6; cf. 3:26; Rom. 1:16).

However, the door of faith that God opens to these gentiles (Acts 14:27) soon brings Barnabas and Paul—God's "apostle to the Gentiles" (Rom. 1:5; 11:13; Gal. 2:8; cf. Acts 9:15)—into sharp conflict with those (viz., the Judaizers) who insist that circumcision and law-keeping are necessary for gentile salvation (Acts 15:1–2, 5; cf. Gal. 1–2). Paul firmly resists any such notion, maintaining that gentiles are incorporated within the new covenant community solely on the basis of their Christian faith (Rom. 1:17; 9:30; Gal. 3:7–14, 26; Eph. 2:8–9; Col. 1:21–23; 2 Thess. 1:10). In this respect gentile Christians are really no different from their Jewish siblings, who are likewise saved through faith rather than works of the law (Acts 20:21; Rom. 1:16–17; 3:21–30; 4:16–5:2; Gal. 2:15–16; cf. Acts 11:21; 15:11) and are thus brought into a *new* covenant relationship with God through union with Christ (Eph. 1:3–14). Accordingly, being "in Christ" transcends all ethnic, gender, and social divisions (1 Cor. 12:13; Gal. 3:28–29; Col. 3:11), not least the "dividing wall of hostility" (Eph. 2:14) between Jews and gentiles (Rom. 10:12; Eph. 2:11–22). Thus, those who "once were far away"—"excluded from citizenship in Israel and foreigners to the covenants of promise, without hope and without God in the world"—have "now in Christ Jesus . . . been brought near by the blood of Christ" (Eph. 2:12–13) and are "no longer foreigners and strangers, but fellow citizens with God's people and also members of his household" (Eph. 2:19). As such, gentiles have become "heirs together with Israel, members together of one body, and sharers together in the promise in Christ Jesus" (Eph. 3:6). While Paul speaks of this—both here and elsewhere—as a "mystery" not previously made known (Eph. 3:3–5, 8–11; cf. Rom. 16:25–26; Eph. 1:9–10; Col. 1:26–27), he is referring to *how* this union has been achieved (cf. Eph. 5:32) rather than to the incorporation of gentiles per se (cf. Rom. 15:8–12; Gal. 3:8).

More controversial, however, is the question of ethnic Israel's status in light of the new covenant and its more inclusive focus. As attested in Acts, the evangelism of gentiles comes partly at Israel's expense, mainly due to the latter's unbelief (cf. Acts 13:46–48; 18:6; 22:18–21; 28:26–28). Israel's rejection of God's Messiah and the apostolic message raises the specter that Paul addresses in Rom. 9–11—namely, that God's promises and purposes for Israel have somehow failed. Paul insists otherwise, emphasizing that (1) God's promises apply only to the spiritual descendants of Abraham (Rom. 9:6–8); (2) the objects of God's mercy include not only Jews but also gentiles (Rom. 9:23–26); (3) everyone—whether Jew or gentile—"who calls on the name of the

Lord will be saved" (Rom. 10:13); (4) there remains an Israelite "remnant chosen by grace" (Rom. 11:5); (5) the people of Israel have not stumbled "so as to fall beyond recovery" (Rom. 11:11) but can be "grafted into their own olive tree" (Rom. 11:24); and (6) "all Israel will be saved" (Rom. 11:26). Rather than suggesting "a future salvation for ethnic Israel"—whether understood simply in terms of a future mass conversion or including both eschatological conversion and national restoration (Lucas, 235–36)—Paul is more likely alluding (cf. Rom. 11:25b) to an ongoing phenomenon that is taking place throughout the present era (see Beale and Gladd, 82–88). In any case, he certainly is insisting that "salvation can be found in one place only: within the one community made up of those who believe in Jesus Christ. . . . Jews, like Gentiles, can be saved only by responding to the gospel and being grafted into the one people of God" (Moo, 725–26).

The NT's Eschatological Vision: The New Jerusalem and New Creation

We might therefore expect that as coheirs to the covenant promises, both Jewish and gentile believers enjoy and anticipate all the riches of God's inheritance. Such is precisely what we find in the future hope held out in the NT—where this includes even the territorial dimension of God's promise, albeit in a global or cosmic sense (Matt. 5:5; cf. Rom. 4:13). Thus understood, gentiles participate not just in the promise of "blessing" but also in the promise of "land"—both of which find their culmination in the ultimate *seed* of Abraham (Gal. 3:16–18, 29). Therefore, "in Christ, God's blessings of 'seed' and land are [both] becoming universalized, just as the OT itself anticipated would happen in the age of fulfilment" (DeRouchie, 33–34).

In keeping with this, the OT's restoration hope for a new creation (Isa. 65:17–18; 66:22)—an Eden-like paradise (Ezek. 36:35; 47:12; cf. Amos 9:13–15; Isa. 30:23–25; Jer. 31:12) in which the "sound of weeping and of crying will be heard no more" (Isa. 65:19)—finds its ultimate fulfillment in the NT's eschatological vision of a "new heaven and a new earth" (2 Pet. 3:13; Rev. 21:1), with its "new Jerusalem" (Rev. 21:2–22:5), in which "'there will be no more death' [cf. Isa. 25:8] or mourning or crying or pain, for the old order of things has passed away" (Rev. 21:4). Most significantly, this eschatological inheritance is for all God's people (cf. Col. 1:12; Heb. 9:15; 1 Pet. 1:4)—those who through Christ are victorious (Rev. 21:7) and whose names are recorded in the Lamb's book of life (Rev. 21:27). This inheritance is not simply reserved in heaven for one nation but is for "persons from every tribe and language and people and nation"—that is, all those whom the Lamb has made "to be a kingdom and priests to serve our God" and who thus "will reign on the earth" (Rev. 5:9–10). While the promised eternal inheritance is evidently not all-inclusive in a universalist sense (cf. Rev. 21:8, 27; 22:14–15), plainly this new Jerusalem does not have any ethnic or national barriers; rather, "the nations will walk by its light, and the kings of the earth will bring their splendor into it. . . . The glory and honor of the nations will be brought into it" (Rev. 21:24–26). Thus, the influx of nations and their wealth anticipated in Isa. 60:3–5 is ultimately fulfilled in terms not of the old Jerusalem and its temple but rather of the new Jerusalem—the eschatological city and eternal dwelling of God.

See also Circumcision; Covenant; Feasts and Festivals

Bibliography. Beale, G. K., and B. L. Gladd, *Hidden but Now Revealed* (InterVarsity, 2014); DeRouchie, J. S., "Father of a Multitude of Nations," in *Progressive Covenantalism*, ed. S. J. Wellum and B. E. Parker (B&H Academic, 2016), 7–38; Dumbrell, W. J., *Covenant and Creation* (Paternoster, 2013); Gladd, B. L., *From Adam and Israel to the Church* (InterVarsity, 2019); Lucas, R. J., "The Dispensational Appeal to Romans 11 and the Nature of Israel's Future Salvation," in *Progressive Covenantalism*, ed. S. J. Wellum and B. E. Parker (B&H Academic, 2016), 235–53; Moo, D. J., *The Epistle to the Romans*, NICNT (Eerdmans, 1996); Motyer, J. A., *The Prophecy of Isaiah* (InterVarsity, 1993); Oswalt, J. *The Book of Isaiah: Chapters 40–66*, NICOT (Eerdmans, 1998); Schultz, R. L., "Nationalism and Universalism in Isaiah," in *Interpreting Isaiah*, ed. D. G. Firth and H. G. M. Williamson (InterVarsity, 2009), 122–44; Williamson, P. R., *Sealed with an Oath*, NSBT 23 (InterVarsity, 2007).

PAUL WILLIAMSON

Job, Book of

There are many challenges in understanding the book of Job. It is composed of many different parts representing different participants in the debate, which revolves around the suffering of Job. This article will examine the final form of the book to investigate the possible use it makes of other passages in the OT. Differing opinions concerning the date of composition of Job and other OT books impact which sources scholars think are available to Job. Whether someone takes a diachronic or a synchronic approach also impacts how one views relationships between texts. Several resources list possible connections of Job to other OT literature (Driver and Gray, lxvii–lxviii; Hartley, 11–13). Other sources discuss connections between Job and the OT (Fishbane, "Discourse," 86–98; Dell and Kynes). This article examines representative examples of connections between Job and other OT Scriptures. It also briefly reflects on NT connections.

Job and Genesis

The availability of Genesis as a source to which Job could allude is not a problem for those who date Genesis early—either as connected to Moses (Steinmann, 3–8) or as a preexilic document (Wenham, xliv)—or late if Job is also dated late (Driver and Gray, 46–47).

***Job's use of* ʾādām.** The word *ʾādām* in Job mainly refers to humanity, but three times it may refer to the first man, Adam (15:7; 20:4; 31:33). The first two instances occur in the second cycle of speeches, where Eliphaz and Zophar are discussing with Job the reasons for his suffering. Eliphaz asks a rhetorical question in 15:7 that expects a "no" answer: "Are you the first man [*ʾādām*] ever born? Were you brought forth before the hills?" These questions refer back to the creation of the world and are a specific response to Job's claim that his wisdom is not inferior to the friends' wisdom (Job 13:1). Thus, Eliphaz raises doubts about Job's source of wisdom. If Job were the first man ever born, a clear allusion to Adam, then he could claim a special source of wisdom. But since that is not the case, then Job has no advantage over the friends and cannot claim that his wisdom is greater than theirs. Zophar argues that even though the wicked may experience joy, it lasts for only a moment. Job should understand this ancient teaching that goes back to when *ʾādām* was placed on the earth (20:4). Zophar either uses *ʾādām* in a generic sense, referring to human beings, or he alludes to Adam.

The third use of *ʾādām* that might be an allusion to Adam occurs in the final speech of Job (31:33). He declares his innocence with an oath that calls down curses on himself if he has committed any of the forms of wicked behavior he lists. Using the phrase *kəʾādām*, he rejects the notion that he has concealed his transgressions by hiding iniquity in his heart. This phrase could be translated either "as Adam" or "as people." If the reference is to Adam, the idea is that Adam tried to cover up his sin by making coverings for himself and by hiding from God. If the reference is to people in general, the idea is that it is a common reaction for people to cover up their sin. This would fit well with the way *ʾādām* is used in most of its occurrences in Job. Of course, such a response did originate with Adam. Job 15:7 is the clearest reference to Adam, and the other two texts make sense if Adam is in view (Oeming, 27).

Job 3 and Gen. 1. A negative allusion exists between Job's desire that his day be darkness in 3:4 and the creation of light on the first day in Gen. 1:3. Michael Fishbane expands the connections between Job 3 and the days of Gen. 1:1–2:4a by seeing allusions between Job 3 and every day in Genesis except day three. He calls Job's speech a counter-cosmic incantation that systematically reverses the acts of creation and articulates Job's absolute and unrestrained death wish for himself and the entire creation ("Jeremiah," 153–55). Although the parallels between Job 3 and the days of Gen. 1:1–2:4a are very general and not that convincing, the call on darkness to curse the day of Job's birth (3:1–10) has the same impact for which Fishbane argues. On the first day of creation God creates light with the command, "Let there be light" (*yəhî ʾôr*). The separation of light from darkness is the foundational beginning of the rest of the acts of creation. Concerning the day of his birth, Job pleads in 3:4, "That day, let there be darkness" (*yəhî ḥōšek*, AT). Job associates darkness with the event of his birth (3:4–9). Darkness dominates this section as Job expresses his desire that the day of his birth be obliterated. By this allusion he is calling for a reversal of the acts of creation, because if there had been no light on the first day, the rest of creation would not have occurred. Job curses the day of his birth because if he had not been born, he would not be suffering (v. 10).

Job 42:2 and Gen. 11:6. In Gen. 11:6b, Yahweh declares concerning the gathering of people at the tower of Babel, "Then nothing they plan to do will be impossible for them." Job in his second response to Yahweh asserts, "I know that you can do all things; no purpose of yours can be thwarted" (42:2). Although the two contexts are different, the same thought is expressed. Both texts use the verbal phrase *lōʾ yibbāṣēr* (the verb is translated as "impossible" and "thwart," respectively). Genesis 11:6 uses the verb *zāmam* ("plan"), and Job 42:2 uses the noun *məzimmâ* ("purpose"). Are these linguistic connections enough to establish an allusion? Fishbane ("Discourse," 90–91) asks why Job uses the noun *məzimmâ* for God's purposes when the word has a negative connotation in Wisdom literature (Job 21:27; Jer. 11:15; Prov. 12:2). The negative use of this noun leads Norman Habel to argue that Job is making a "friendly barb" to God because he does not use the word "plan" (*ʿēṣâ*), which God used when he confronted Job (38:2). Job may be referring to the original "scheme" devised by Yahweh and Satan to test Job's integrity (Habel, 581). Although *məzimmâ* frequently refers to a wicked plan, negative connotations derive from the context, not the term itself. It is used with the morally neutral sense of "purpose, intention, thinking" (*DCH*, 5:209). Thus, there is no problem with Job using *məzimmâ* to refer to Yahweh's purposes (Clines, *Job 38–42*, 1205). Job's use of the form of the verb *yibbāṣēr* is a bit unusual. The noun *məzimmâ* is feminine, so one would expect a feminine verb, but the verb Job uses is masculine, and it is the same form that occurs in Gen. 11:6b. Fishbane argues that the verb is carried over into Job as a frozen form and concludes that the ungrammatical usage suggests that Gen. 11:6 is both the ironic target and the source of Job's rhetoric (Fishbane, "Discourse," 91). Although it appears that the people at the tower of Babel would be able to do whatever they purpose, God hinders their plans and scatters them over the earth. Job has learned that God is the only one who is able sovereignly to carry out all of his purposes, including allowing Job, an innocent person, to suffer (Longman, 449).

Job 42:17 and Gen. 25:8; 35:29. Job's death is described in ways that parallel the deaths of two patriarchs, Abraham and Isaac.

> And so Job died [*wayyāmot*], an old man [*zāqēn*] and full of days [*ûśəbaʿ*]. (Job 42:17)

> Then Abraham breathed his last and died [*wayyāmot*] at a good old age, an old man [*zāqēn*] and full of years [*wəśābēaʿ*]; and he was gathered to his people. (Gen. 25:8)

> Then he [Isaac] breathed his last and died [*wayyāmot*] and was gathered to his people, old [*zāqēn*] and full of years [*ûśəbaʿ yāmîm*]. (Gen. 35:29)

The description of Abraham's death is the longest, Isaac's is shorter, and Job's is the shortest. All three descriptions use three terms in the same order: the word for "death," the word for "old," and the descriptive phrase "full of years," with a shortened phrase used for Abraham. All three also live long lives. Job lives 140 years after his suffering, Abraham lives 175 years, and Isaac lives 180 years. The similarity in the ways their deaths are described places Job on the same level as Abraham and Isaac. The same order of the three terms and the fact that the description of Job's death is a shortened form could point to an allusion to the deaths of the patriarchs. Job's death is an appropriate ending to a life devoted to God even through the struggles of his suffering. Job was as great in his death as he was in his life (Habel, 586).

Job, Psalms, and Proverbs

When discussing Job's relationships to Psalms and Proverbs, the subject of the date of Job becomes more important. If Job is dated in the exilic or postexilic periods, there is no problem with Job alluding to Psalms and Proverbs; plus, many other books come into play with which Job might be interacting, such as Jeremiah (Dell) and Isa. 40–55 (Kynes). Some argue that a precise date for the final form of the book is neither possible to determine nor important for interpretation (Longman, 27). If such is the case, then a synchronic approach becomes the best way to understand Job's allusions. Dell (107) states, "Texts may speak to each other, and to us, regardless of whether any author intended a connection or any situation gave rise to the connection." For diachronic approaches, the date of the book is more important. If the final form of the book is dated before the exile, such as a date during the proliferation of Wisdom literature during Solomon's reign in 1 Kings 4:20–34 (Belcher 2018, 11–14), Job could be interacting with Ps. 8, written by David. If Job is dated earlier than David, then it is unlikely it is interacting with Ps. 8. There is a general consensus that Job 7:17 is a parody of Ps. 8:4–6 to make a point about the status of human beings. But is it possible that Job and his friends, who are non-Israelites, are interacting with each other out of their own wisdom tradition and using general concepts that are integral to wisdom discussions later reflected in Israel's Wisdom literature? The following discussion tries to set the parameters of such an approach.

Job's friends appeal to their own traditions of wisdom. At the beginning of the book, Job is called "the greatest man among all the people of the East" (1:3). "People of the East" (*bənē-qedem*) refers to a distinct group of people outside of Israel. The "East" could refer to the area east of Palestine in the vicinity of Edom, which could be the location of the land of Uz (1:1), or the area northeast of Palestine associated with Aram/Syria (Hartley, 65–66, 69). Because Job is a non-Israelite from the area east of Palestine, it is natural to conclude that Job is part of the people of the East (Clines, *Job 1–20*, 15). Solomon's wisdom is said to be greater than that of the people of the East (*bənē-qedem*) and that of Egypt (1 Kings 4:30 [5:10 MT]). A connection is made between the wisdom tradition of Job and his friends and that of Solomon.

The wisdom tradition to which the friends of Job appeal is associated with the God of the patriarchs. The book of Job uses names for God that the patriarchs and other OT Scriptures use, such as El, El Shaddai, Eloah, Elohim, and especially Yahweh. In 4:12–16 Eliphaz describes a vision where he receives a word that gives him supernatural insight (Clines, *Job 1–20*, 128–29). This wisdom is verified by observation through careful investigation of human experience (5:27) and nature (8:11–19). It has also been handed down from their fathers so that the friends can appeal to the tradition of the fathers (8:8–10), an ancient and time-tested tradition of previous generations (Longman, 158). It would not be surprising if this wisdom tradition covered topics that Israel's Wisdom literature also covers, because of its association with God and because it is common for Israel's Wisdom literature to be similar to the wisdom literature of the ancient Near East (Kitchen, 552–66).

When Job in 7:17 uses the phrase "What is mankind that . . ." (*mâ-ʾěnôš kî*), it is commonly assumed that he is alluding to Ps. 8:4 with the purpose of giving a parody of its message. There is evidence, however, that this question is commonly asked in a variety of contexts where the purpose of the question is to assert that the person in view is unworthy of or unable to do the action described in the following clause. So, the question in Ps. 8:4a, "What is mankind that you make so much of them?" means that humans are unworthy of divine consideration. Job's use of the question in 7:17 has the same meaning. The difference between Job 7 and Ps. 8 is what each does with the question. Job confirms the lowliness of humanity with regard to God, whereas Ps. 8 contrasts this view by proclaiming the majestic place of human beings in God's creation (Van Leeuwen, 210).

It is easy to focus on the use of this question in Ps. 8 and Job 7 and not recognize the flexibility of the form of this question, its widespread use in Scripture, and its occurrence in the Amarna letters. G. W. Coats discusses the simplest form of this question as having two elements. The first element is composed of a nominal sentence introduced by an interrogative particle (*mâ* or *mî*) and followed by a personal pronoun, a proper name, or a noun. The second element is a verbal sentence connected to the introductory question with *kî*, or *'ăšer*, or a *waw* consecutive with an imperfect verb. He lists numerous passages as following this simple form: Exod. 5:2; 16:7; Num. 16:11; Judg. 9:38; 1 Sam. 17:26; 2 Sam. 9:8; 2 Kings 8:13. In each case the purpose of the question is to assert that the person in view is unworthy of or unable to do the action described in the following clause. He also discusses the evidence from twenty-five Amarna letters that exhibit the same twofold structure and parallel the form and use of the question in Hebrew. He concludes, "Consistent structure and characteristic diction mark a basic genre, a stereo-typed formula" (Coats, 14–16). The stylistic form, the broad use, and the common meaning of this question raise the possibility that this is a quasi-proverbial formula that had become a common saying (Van Leeuwen, 210).

It is not surprising that this question is also used several times in Job and Psalms. In Ps. 144:3 the question parallels the question in Ps. 8:4, "What is man . . . the son of man . . . ?" (ESV), except the words *'ĕnôš* and *'ādām* are switched. The question is followed by a statement in 144:4 that human beings (*'ādām*) are like a breath (*hebel*). The king in his present need (144:7–8, 11) identifies himself with the common lot of humans (*'ādām*). He appeals to Yahweh, his superior, for deliverance out of his own sense of weakness, vulnerability, and trust (Van Leeuwen, 211). Job 15:14 asks the question "What are mortals, that [*mâ-'ĕnôš kî*] they could be pure?" This question expects a negative answer and is used by Eliphaz as an indirect rebuke of Job (Habel, 255). Job 21:15 uses the formula in an ironic way by placing the question in the mouth of the wicked, "Who is the Almighty, that [*mah-šadday kî*] we should serve him?" The wicked insult God by declaring that he is a nobody and they will therefore not serve him. The variety of the use of this formula, even in this small sample, suggests the free literary use of a common oral formula (Van Leeuwen, 213).

Will Kynes (29) has the most complete analysis of Job's allusions to Psalms. He develops a comprehensive eight-step process that seeks to interpret them both historically and hermeneutically with the use of both diachronic and synchronic approaches. The purpose of the diachronic step is to see which direction of dependence is possible, or probable, but conclusions based on this evidence are tenuous because inner-biblical parallels can often be interpreted in either direction. There is disagreement among scholars concerning the direction of dependence between Job and Psalms, but if Job is dated between the fifth and third centuries, as Kynes affirms, there is no definitive evidence to preclude the possibility of Job's diachronic dependence on Psalms. He also acknowledges, however, that the same thing could be said about Psalms' dependence on Job. Even though he believes he presents a strong case of Job's use of Psalms, it is only a probable explanation of the lexical and thematic connections between the texts (Kynes, 49–51).

Kynes (65) rejects Van Leeuwen's conclusion—that is, that the formulaic question in Job 7 is independent of Ps. 8—as resting on a false disjunction. Even if the question is formulaic, Job 7 could also be alluding to Ps. 8 based on thematic connections between the two passages. Also, Job 19:9 uses the word "crown," as does Ps. 8:5, and Job 25:5–6 uses a phrase that includes the moon and the stars, as does Ps. 8:3 (Kynes, 73–75). The issue is not whether a comparison of the two texts is profitable on a synchronic level but whether the author of Job had Ps. 8 in mind when he wrote Job 7. Kynes (89–92) emphasizes the intention of the human author, particularly in his discussion of the use of the two clauses in Ps. 107:40, which are almost exactly reproduced in two different verses of Job 12 (Ps. 107:40a in Job 12:21a; Ps. 107:40b in Job 12:24b). Job 12:22 repeats the parallel terms "darkness" and "deep darkness" from Ps. 107:10 and 14. Job 12:23 omits the hope of restoration after exile that occurs in Ps. 107:38–41. Two phrases used in Job 12:25 appear in 107:14 and 27, where they describe prisoners as being in darkness and sailors on the sea as staggering like drunken men. These two phrases, however, are general descriptions. If Job is using Ps. 107 as a subtext, one would expect the parallels to be more numerous. Also, the fact that Ps. 107 emphasizes that some of the people are suffering because of their sin does not make it a good comparison with Job, who is not suffering because of his sin.

Synchronic connections become important when Job, Psalms, and Proverbs become part of the canon of Scripture. It is natural to compare texts that deal with similar ideas and express them in similar ways. Thus, one would expect Job 7 and Ps. 8's views of humankind to be compared and contrasted in light of the common phrase "What is mankind?" (*mâ-'ĕnôš*). Kynes (5) refers to John Calvin as following the traditional view that Job was written before Psalms while anticipating readings between the two that are common today. In Calvin's sermon (133) on Job 7, he states that Job's words are contrary to Ps. 8. Calvin, however, focuses not on the human author but on the divine author. In his sermon on Job 7:7–15, he says we ought to seek the intent of the Holy Spirit and that Job at times speaks after the manner of what we are taught by the Spirit even though such things were not written down in the time of Job (127–28). In light of Kynes's admission, based on diachronic considerations, that the direction of dependence is not definitive (see above), it is possible that Ps. 8 is a response to Job's negative views in Job 7.

The book of Job explores the common wisdom theme of the relationship between suffering and sin in reference to the justice of God, a theme that is also prevalent in Proverbs. Therefore, it makes sense to compare the two books. Proverbs is nuanced in its view of the relationship between deeds and the consequences that follow (Belcher, *Favour*, 39–52). It is a misunderstanding to draw a mechanical relationship between deed and consequence for three reasons: (1) many proverbs are not meant to be universal statements; (2) wealth is recognized as a relative good instead of an absolute good (Prov. 16:8, 19); and (3) there are always extenuating circumstances in life, such as injustice (Prov. 13:23) and the sovereignty of God (Prov. 16:9; 21:30–31). Early in the first round of speeches, Eliphaz expresses a more nuanced view of the deed-consequence relationship (Job 5:17–18) that reflects the teaching of Prov. 3:11–12. The discipline of God is a blessing because God not only wounds but also heals (Crenshaw, 180, argues that a common wisdom tradition also explains the similarities between Job 5:17–18; Prov. 3:11–12; and Deut. 32:39). The friends also accuse Job of sin, citing it as the cause of his suffering. They describe the wicked in ways that are similar to descriptions of the wicked in Proverbs. The phrase "the lamp of the wicked will be put out" (AT) is used in Prov. 13:9b in contrast to the light of the righteous and in 24:20b as showing the end of the wicked. Bildad uses a similar phrase in Job 18:5a and 6b to describe the end of the wicked as a warning to Job, implying that Job will experience this fate. Bildad also uses the phrase "his strong steps are hampered" (18:7 AT), which is similar to Prov. 4:12a, "When you walk your steps will not be hampered." Proverbs uses the phrase with the negative to describe the one who walks the way of wisdom, and Bildad uses it without the negative to describe the wicked. Both Job 26:6 and Prov. 15:11a describe Sheol and Abaddon as being exposed before God. Proverbs uses it to show the omniscience of God, who knows the hearts of human beings, and Job uses it as part of his argument for the omnipotence of God, whose ways are not always comprehended by human beings. Part of God's omnipotence is that "he marks out the horizon on the face of the waters" (Job 26:10a), which is similar to a phrase that Lady Wisdom uses in Prov. 8:27b to describe her existence at creation. Several times, Proverbs asserts that wisdom is more valuable than wealth, including gold, silver, and jewels (3:14–15; 8:11, 19). Job comes to the same conclusion in Job 28:15–19. Thus, it is not unusual for two wisdom books to discuss similar ideas and themes.

Job and the NT

There is a probable allusion in Phil. 1:19 to the LXX of Job 13:16 (see Hays; cf. Silva, 836). Both passages have in common the phrase *touto moi apobēsetai eis sōtērian* ("This will turn out for my deliverance"). Job is suffering, Paul is in prison, and both are confident they will be delivered. The basis for Job's confidence is expressed in the next clause: "for no godless person would dare come before him [God]." Paul's confidence rests in the prayers of God's people and the help of the Spirit of Christ. In both contexts there is the prospect of death (Job 13:15; Phil. 1:20). Job's righteous character is appealed to in Ezek. 14:14 to show that even Job could not stop the destruction of Jerusalem. Job is also appealed to in James 5:11 as an example of someone who persevered in suffering. Job is a type of an innocent sufferer, much like Abel and the prophets, but is fulfilled ultimately in the suffering of Jesus Christ (Belcher, *Job*, 53–55). Many in the first century found it hard to believe that the one who claimed to be the Son of God could die a criminal's death (Matt. 27:42–43). Clearly, the wisdom of God, which appears to be foolishness to many people, is wiser and more powerful than human wisdom (1 Cor. 1:18–25), because Christ's suffering accomplishes God's plan for our salvation (2 Cor. 5:21). In Rom. 11:34–35, Paul's doxological conclusion to Rom. 9–11, he uses Job 41:11a (41:3a MT) in 11:35 to show that God does not owe humans anything, which in Job's situation means not even an explanation for suffering (Naselli). The proper response to God's sovereign, inscrutable wisdom is praise.

Bibliography. Belcher, R. P., Jr., *Finding Favour in the Sight of God* (IVP Academic, 2018); Belcher, *Job* (Christian Focus, 2017); Calvin, J., *Sermons on Job*, trans. R. R. McGregor (Banner of Truth Trust, 1993); Clines, D. J. A., *Job 1–20*, WBC (Thomas Nelson, 1989); Clines, *Job 38–42*, WBC (Thomas Nelson, 2011); Coats, G. W., "Self-abasement and Insult Formulas," *JBL* 89 (1970): 14–26; Crenshaw, J. L., "Divine Discipline in Job 5:17–18, Proverbs 3:11–12, Deuteronomy 32:39, and Beyond," in Dell and Kynes, *Reading Job Intertextually*, 178–89; Dell, K., "'Cursed Be the Day I Was Born!,'" in Dell and Kynes, *Reading Job Intertextually*, 106–17; Dell, K., and W. Kynes, eds., *Reading Job Intertextually* (T&T Clark, 2013); Driver, S. R., and G. B. Gray, *Job*, ICC (T&T Clark, 1921); Fishbane, M. "The Book of Job and Inner-Biblical Discourse," in *The Voice from the Whirlwind*, ed. L. G. Perdue and W. C. Gilpin (Abingdon, 1992), 86–98; Fishbane, "Jeremiah IV 23–26 and Job III 3–13," *VT* 21 (1971): 151–67; Habel, N. C., *The Book of Job*, OTL (Westminster, 1985); Hartley, J. E., *The Book of Job*, NICOT (Eerdmans, 1988); Hays, R. B., *Echoes of Scripture in the Letters of Paul* (Yale University Press, 1989); Kitchen, K., "Proverbs 2," in *Dictionary of the Old Testament: Wisdom, Poetry and Writings*, ed. T. Longman III and P. Enns (IVP Academic, 2008), 552–66; Kynes, W., *My Psalm Has Turned into Weeping* (de Gruyter, 2012); Longman, T., III, *Job*, BCOTWP (Baker Academic, 2012); Naselli, A. D., *From Typology to Doxology* (Pickwick, 2012); Oeming, M., "To Be Adam or Not To Be Adam," in Dell and Kynes, *Reading Job Intertextually*, 19–29; Silva, M., "Philippians," in *CNTUOT*, 835–39; Steinmann, A., *Genesis*, TOTC (IVP Academic, 2019); Van Leeuwen, R. C., "Psalm 8.5 and Job 7.17–18," in *The World of the Aramaeans*, ed. M. Daviau, J. W. Weavers, and M. Weigl (Sheffield Academic, 2001), 1:205–15; Wenham, G. J., *Genesis 1–15*, WBC (Word, 1987).

Richard P. Belcher Jr.

Joel, Book of

Joel famously speaks of a terrible locust plague, and it contains the text cited by Peter in his Pentecost sermon (Joel 2:28–32, cited in Acts 2:17–21). But Joel is also a paradigmatic text. It establishes rules for how biblical prophecy is to be read. Its brevity and thematic consistency allow us to recognize a rhetorical pattern that is difficult to spot in larger books.

Date of Composition

Nothing is known of Joel son of Pethuel. The date of the book's composition is disputed, with some arguing it is from the ninth century and thus the oldest of the prophetic books (Archer, 305), and others asserting it is a postexilic text (Barton, 15; Dillard and Longman, 365). In all probability, the book was written after the fall of Samaria in 722 and before the fall of Jerusalem in 586, perhaps in the late seventh or early sixth century (Garrett, *Joel*, 286–94). Notably, there was a severe drought in the time of Jeremiah (Jer. 14), and the locust plague of Joel was accompanied by drought (1:12, 17, 20).

Against some interpreters (Barton, 5–14; Hiebert; Pfeiffer, 574–75; Smith, Ward, and Bewer, 49–67), no compelling evidence suggests that multiple hands or a complex redaction history lie behind Joel. The book is unified and is reasonably taken to be the product of a single mind (Barker, 6–12; Marcus, 65–66; Prinsloo).

Structure and Message

Many who argue that Joel is a composite work do so on the basis of the disparate range of topics it addresses. But the book does have a unifying theme, as well as a structure that coherently reflects that theme. In order to demonstrate this, however, one must first examine the enemy described in 2:1–11, 20.

The northern army of 2:1–11, 20. Joel 1 describes a devastating locust plague and drought. Joel 2:1–11, however, is an account of YHWH's "army" attacking Jerusalem, with 2:20 describing the destruction of that army. The question is whether this army is made up of locusts, thus continuing the account in chap. 1, or of humans, describing a new, different threat.

Two pieces of evidence might support the locust interpretation. First, elements in the portrayal of the army are reminiscent of a locust plague. For example, they are horse-like (2:4), and a locust somewhat resembles a horse's head. Second, the army is said to be "like" soldiers (2:7), which implies that they are in fact not soldiers. However, neither claim is compelling. Since the account of the army comes on the heels of the recital of the locust plague, one would expect that the army would be described in terms that recall the locusts. The locusts and the human army are of the same type (YHWH's army), and the literary account draws out visual parallels between the two. And of course, the human army would possess actual horses. There is also precedent in ancient Near Eastern texts for describing human armies as locusts (Andiñach).

Also, the use of "like" is misleading. The Hebrew "like" (*kə*) does not necessarily refer to two different but analogous things; it can imply that something fulfills an ideal. English does the same. If a commander tells his soldiers to behave "like men" in the face of the enemy, he implies not that they are something other than literal men but that they should fulfill the ideal of manhood. So also, when Joel says that the locust plague "comes like destruction from the Almighty" (1:15), he does not mean that it is not really from God. When Jer. 6:23 says the Babylonian army will advance "lined up like men in battle formation," it means that they will perform a textbook example of a battle maneuver, not that they are not literally an army (see also Ezek. 26:10; Zech. 14:3). When the enemy in Joel 2:7 advances "like warriors," they behave just as one would expect of a battle-hardened, hostile army.

Other pieces of evidence preclude the "locust" interpretation of 2:1–11, 20. The Hebrew of 2:8 states that the army remains in formation and does not become disorganized or swerve aside in the face of "weapons" (*šelaḥ*, perhaps pikes, but especially projectiles such as javelins and arrows). But locusts do not advance in ranks, and no sane person would try to stop a locust swarm by shooting arrows at it. At the climactic moment in the army's assault, it scales the walls and breaks into houses within the city (2:9). While the presence of locusts inside people's homes was a nuisance, they did all of their destruction out in the fields, orchards, and vineyards. For a human army, the objective was to plunder inside the city walls and houses. Finally, the army in 2:20 is called the "northerner." But locust plagues in Israel did not and do not come from the north. They breed in the Sudan and enter Israel from the south (Garrett, *Exodus*, 324–26). The great Mesopotamian powers of Assyria and Babylon, however, are routinely described as out of the north (e.g., Jer. 1:14–15; 4:6; 6:1, 22; 10:22; Ezek. 26:7). If, as suggested above, Joel is a late preexilic text, it was written in the memory of the Assyrian crisis and in anticipation of the Babylonian onslaught. But the army of 2:1–11, 20 is assuredly human, not locust.

The arrangement of the oracles. The various oracles of Joel are discrete and easily distinguished from one another. The book begins with two parallel onslaughts, the locusts (1:1–20) and the northern army (2:1–11). This is followed by a call for repentance and mourning (2:12–17). After this comes a series of oracles promising salvation for Israel, including an introduction (2:18–19), the destruction of the northern army (2:20), the restoration of the land after the drought and locust plague (2:21–27), the gift of the Spirit (2:28–32), and the judgment on the gentile armies at the valley of Jehoshaphat (3:1–21).

These oracles begin with a carefully laid out chiasmus. It concerns the assault by the locusts and the northern army and the restoration of Israel after those calamities.

- A Punishment: The locust plague (1:2–20)
  - B Punishment: The northern army (2:1–11)
    - C Transition: Repentance and response (2:12–19)
  - B′ Forgiveness: The northern army destroyed (2:20)
- A′ Forgiveness: The locust-ravaged land restored (2:21–27)

The chiasmus concerns historical Israel: Jerusalem has suffered from a locust plague and will suffer from a Babylonian invasion, but it will recover from both. The extravagant language of 2:20 is not to be taken literally; it is a poetic and hyperbolic portrayal of the fall of the northern enemy. By implication, Jerusalem will be restored after the northern enemy that conquers it falls. The historical fulfillment of this is the collapse of the Neo-Babylonian Empire and the subsequent return of the Jews from exile. Second, a call to repentance sits at the pivotal, central position in the chiasmus, implying that YHWH will save his people when they return to him. This reflects the theology of repentance and restoration found in Deut. 30:1–10.

Two subsequent prophecies move from the historical to the eschatological, echoing the two salvation prophecies in 2:20–27:

- A″ The Spirit poured on all people (2:28–32), echoing the healing of the land in 2:21–27
  - B″ All nations destroyed (3:1–21), echoing the destruction of the northern army in 2:20.

God's salvation of Israel from locusts and from Babylonians is presented as an analogue for eschatological salvation. As God destroyed the northern army, so he will destroy all the armies of the nations in the great day of judgment. And as God sends the rain that heals the land after the drought and locust plague, so the Spirit will heal the people's failure to bear fruit for God. The Spirit will be "poured out" as though it were a liquid (2:28), an apt counterpart to the healing rains. Put another way, the locusts anticipate the Babylonians, who in turn anticipate the nations' battle against God in the eschatological valley of Jehoshaphat. The rain that renews the scorched land anticipates the Spirit that renews the people.

The day of YHWH as the unifying theme. The unity of Joel consists in how it links its oracles: The locust plague foreshadows the northern invasion, and God's redemption of historical Israel from these calamities foreshadows his eschatological salvation. More fundamentally, a single idea, the "day of YHWH," characterizes all these events. The locust plague initiates the dreadful day of YHWH (1:15). The northern army comes against Jerusalem on the day of YHWH, which is a "day of darkness and gloom, a day of clouds and blackness" (2:1–2). The healing of the land after the locust plague also will happen when YHWH does "great things" and "wonders" in Judah (2:21, 26), and even the pouring out of the Spirit is accompanied by the dreadful signs of the day of YHWH (2:30–31). In the final battle, at the valley called "Jehoshaphat" (3:2), the sun, moon, and stars go dark because it is the day of YHWH (3:14–15). In short, every major event of Joel is described as the day of YHWH. The locust plague, the invasion by the northern army, and the other climactic events are all manifestations of a single ideal or pattern, the day of YHWH. This is the core message of the book: the day of YHWH manifests itself in both historical and eschatological events, and these events may be either acts of judgment or acts of salvation. The day of YHWH is the unifying theme and central topic of the book.

The Hermeneutics of Joel

The day of YHWH as a type. Scholars interpreting the day of YHWH typically follow the lead of either Gerhard von Rad, who associates the concept with holy war, or G. W. Ahlström, who associates it with Israel's cultic calendar. Neither interpretation works well in Joel. Against von Rad, the sending of rain and then the coming of the Spirit are not in any sense martial events, and yet both are presented as dramatic works of God, the latter being most explicitly connected with the day of YHWH. Against Ahlström, the cultic portion of Joel, the call to repentance (2:12–17), is the only section that *lacks* any trappings of the day of YHWH.

Many Christians, upon hearing the phrase "the day of the Lord," would assume that it means the last judgment. To be sure, the ferocious account of YHWH's wrath poured out on the nations in the "valley of decision" (3:14) poetically portrays God's final, eschatological judgment on the world. But the locust plague that struck historical Israel is no less a fulfillment of the day of YHWH, even if much less severe in degree. The same is true of the Babylonian invasion or, as a saving event, the coming of the Spirit. Each experience is an authentic fulfillment of the day. This means that the day of YHWH is not a single event but a type, a theological ideal that unfolds in history and in the eschaton, and that singular acts of God may at various times interrupt the normal flow of human experience. Each act may legitimately be regarded as the day of YHWH. Even so, the concept cannot be pluralized; one may not speak of the "days of YHWH." It is a single ideal with many manifestations.

Joel's hermeneutic and OT prophecy. Outside of narrative texts, one rarely finds the prophets making single, specific predictions (the narrative in Isa. 38:5 is such a prediction: God would grant an additional fifteen years to Hezekiah's life). Instead, the great prophetic texts employ types or thematic ideals similar to Joel's day of YHWH. Joel asserts that the day of YHWH will be fulfilled in various ways at various times. Generally, the later fulfillments are more severe or magnificent than the earlier ones, with the greatest fulfillments being eschatological. Often, the text employs language that is in part metaphorical and sometimes hyperbolic, making interpretation difficult (the northern army in 2:20 is like a great beast whose slain body will span the width of Israel and create a stench; the last judgment is a battle in which the armies of the world fight YHWH in the valley of Jehoshaphat). But the heart of the issue is this: the prophets will often speak of a "type" or "prophetic ideal" that will manifest itself in various ways. Accordingly, the day of YHWH is a prophesied event that finds several fulfillments in the OT and its climactic fulfillment in the NT.

This hermeneutic is often the key to unraveling problems in prophetic texts. To give a single example from outside Joel, who is Isaiah's servant of YHWH? Isaiah 49:3 directly asserts that Israel is the servant, but 49:5–6 seems to contradict this, saying that the servant has a mission to Israel and then to the nations. Isaiah 50:4–9 presents the faithful prophet as the suffering servant of YHWH. Isaiah 53 then presents the servant as a singular, messianic figure who uniquely suffers and dies vicariously. How can these disparate portraits be reconciled? The solution is not to regard one answer as correct to the exclusion of the others but to recognize that all fulfill, in varying degrees, the type of the servant of YHWH.

Joel and the OT

Joel, like most biblical books, frequently draws upon the language of the OT. It has many verbal parallels to the account of the locust plague in Exod. 10, implying that what God once did to Egypt he now has done to Judah. Joel's promise that the Spirit will come upon all people fulfills the desire of Moses in Num. 11:16–29. It is doubtful, however, that Joel should be regarded as a "midrashic treatment" of Exod. 10 or that resignification is the key to understanding Joel (against Strazicich, 159–62). Joel gives little attention to the exodus event. Employment of common language does not mean that the latter text is hermeneutically dependent on the earlier text. Similarly, it is doubtful that Joel 2:28–32 "is directly reflecting upon Num. 11:1–12:8," if by that one means Joel is principally concerned with fulfilling that passage (against Dillard, 90). The focus in Numbers is on Moses's desire for a universal prophetic gift. The focus in Joel is on the Spirit's ability to heal and save the people (Joel 2:32), a fulfillment of Deut. 30:6. In this, prophetic charisma is evidence of the Spirit's presence but is not the main point. By analogy, Peter's citation of Joel and (by extension) allusion to Num. 11 does not mean that for Peter a universal gift of prophecy is the main point. The glossolalia of Pentecost is proof that the Spirit has come and the new covenant has begun, but it does not imply that everyone in the church will be a prophet, notwithstanding Moses's wish. Even a genuine allusion is not always the key to a text's meaning.

Joel and the NT

Joel and Pentecost. Within Joel, the pouring out of the Spirit on all flesh is an eschatological fulfillment of the day of YHWH, the counterpart to the rains that heal the land after drought and locusts. In Acts, the gift of the Spirit is the beginning of the new covenant, a manifestation of God's saving power in the aftermath of the resurrection of Christ. The meaning of the Spirit's arrival in both Joel and Acts is thus coherent.

In his sermon, Peter quotes the entire Joel prophecy about the Spirit's outpouring (Joel 2:28–32; Acts 2:16–21). He claims that the glossolalia experienced at the temple fulfills Joel's prophecy (Acts 2:16), but Joel also mentions dreams, visions, blood, fire, smoke, and the darkening of the sun and moon. These things do not happen on the day of Pentecost. Some suggest that the signs in the heavens that occurred at Jesus's crucifixion (Matt. 27:45) fulfilled the prediction that the heavenly bodies would go dark (Bruce, 69), but it is not clear that an event that took place prior to Pentecost can be retrospectively applied to the events of that day. Another explanation is that the darkening of the sky in Joel is a metaphor for Jesus's conflict with Satan (Kerrigan). Bede took the blood to mean the blood from Jesus's side, the fire to be the Holy Spirit, and the smoke to symbolize penitential mourning (Barrett, 137). But these allegorizing interpretations are not persuasive. Classic dispensationalists argue that the Pentecost event did not in fact fulfill Joel's prophecy but was only analogous to it; the actual fulfillment will come in either the tribulation or the millennium (English, 930; Walvoord, 228–34). This contradicts the text; Peter plainly asserts that the Pentecost event fulfills Joel.

One may make two observations relevant to this problem. First, Peter subtly modifies the Joel text. Where Joel has "and afterward, it will be" (Joel 2:28 [3:1 MT] AT), Peter says, "And in the last days, it will be" (Acts 2:17). Peter understands the Joel text to be speaking of the eschatological era, the "last days" (see Isa. 2:2; Mic. 4:1). Second, Joel does not necessarily imply that people will receive the Spirit, have visionary dreams, and see blood and fire and the sun and moon go dark all in the same day. The apocalyptic signs are a cue to the reader that this, like the judgment on all nations in the valley of Jehoshaphat, is an eschatological event.

Peter implies, and the rest of the NT more fully develops, that the Pentecost experience marked the beginning of the era of the new covenant. This includes the gift of the Spirit, the acceptance of the gospel among the gentiles, and the anticipation of the cataclysmic events that will accompany the judgment on all the earth. Although the darkening of the sky at Jesus's crucifixion may well be anticipatory of this, that is not the reason for Peter's citing the whole of Joel's prophecy. Rather, it is that the gift of the Spirit marks the beginning of the eschaton, an era that begins with the gift of the Spirit and ends in cataclysmic judgment on the world.

We may well wonder why the Spirit came on Pentecost (the "Feast of Weeks," described in Exod. 34:22; Lev. 23:15–16; Deut. 16:9–10). This festival celebrates the completion of the grain harvest, Israel's principal bulwark against famine and starvation. Second Temple literature suggests that this festival was accompanied by sumptuous feasting (Tob. 2:1–2). This celebration of abundance has an obvious counterpart in Joel, with its lamentation over locusts, drought, and famine (1:1–20) and its anticipation of the rains that will restore the land (2:21–27). As noted above, a typological link joins the rains that restore Israel's harvests and the Spirit, who heals the people of their sin. Thus, Pentecost is the appropriate moment for the coming of the Spirit.

Joel and the locusts of Revelation. The "locusts" of Rev. 9:1–11 allude to the locust event of Joel 1 (and also to the locusts of Exod. 10:12–20). Revelation's locust creatures come up from the shaft of the abyss, which may be analogous to how, in a severe locust plague, the first generation lays eggs in the ground and the second generation thus emerges from the ground to devour whatever vegetation remains (Aune, 529). Joel's locust plague seems to be such an event, with the first generation coming from the south and the second arising from their eggs (Thompson). Also, the five-month extent of the plague of Rev. 9:5 may reflect the normal chronology of such a severe locust event.

But the passages are radically different. The locusts of Joel are insects that devour vegetation. The "locusts" of Revelation are composite beasts similar to what we see elsewhere in Revelation, and they cannot be identified with any natural creature. In addition to their astonishing appearance, they have as king over them the angel called Abaddon and Apollyon (contrast Prov. 30:27). Finally, and constituting a decisive difference from the locusts of Joel 1, the locust-like creatures of Revelation do not harm vegetation but torment unrepentant humans (9:4).

Beyond the fact that Joel's locust plague is identified as the day of YHWH and the Revelation plague is an apocalyptic event, there is little connection between the two texts, and it would be a mistake to treat one as the interpretive key to the other. Revelation can draw on the imagery of OT passages without implying either that it determines the meaning of the earlier texts or that the earlier texts provide the meaning of Revelation (but see Beale, 493–504). Joel's locusts are ordinary and literal; one may doubt whether Revelation intends a literal meaning for its locusts. They are metaphorical representations of the agony and despair that beset those who worship the beast. However, just as the locust plague anticipated greater, more terrible events in Joel, so the "locusts" of Revelation anticipate more terrible judgments on those who worship the beast.

Bibliography. Ahlström, G. W., *Joel and the Temple Cult of Jerusalem* (Brill, 1971); Andiñach, P. R., "The Locusts in the Message of Joel," *VT* 42 (1992): 433–41; Archer, G. L., *A Survey of Old Testament Introduction* (Moody, 1974); Aune, D. E., *Revelation 6–16*, WBC (Thomas Nelson, 1998); Barker, J., *From the Depths of Despair to the Promise of Presence* (Eisenbrauns, 2014); Barrett, C. K., *Acts*, vol. 1, ICC (T&T Clark, 2004); Barton, J., *Joel and Obadiah*, OTL (Westminster John Knox, 2001); Beale, G. K., *The Book of Revelation*, NIGTC (Eerdmans, 1999); Bruce, F. F., *The Book of Acts*, NICNT (Eerdmans, 1954); Dillard, R. B., "Intrabiblical Exegesis and Effusion of the Spirit in Joel," in *Creator, Redeemer, Consummator*, ed. H. Griffith and J. R. Muether (Wipf & Stock, 2007), 87–93; Dillard, R. B., and T. Longman III, *An Introduction to the Old Testament* (Zondervan, 1994); English, E. S., *The New Scofield Reference Bible* (Oxford University Press, 1967); Garrett, D. A., *A Commentary on Exodus*, KEL (Kregel, 2014); Garrett, *Hosea, Joel*, NAC (Broadman & Holman, 1997); Hiebert, T., "Joel, Book of," in *ABD*, 873–80; Kerrigan, A., "The 'Sensus Plenior' of Joel III, 1–5 in Act., II, 14–36," in *Sacra Pagina*, ed. J. Coppens (Duculot, 1959), 295–313; Marcus, D., "Nonrecurring Doublets in Joel," *CBQ* 56 (1994): 56–67; Pfeiffer, R. H., *Introduction to the Old Testament* (Harper & Brothers, 1941); Prinsloo, W. S., "The Unity of the Book of Joel," *ZAW* 104 (1992): 66–81; Smith, J. M. P., W. H. Ward, and J. A. Bewer, *Micah, Zephaniah, Nahum, Habakkuk, Obadiah and Joel*, ICC (Scribner's Sons, 1911); Strazicich, J., *Joel's Use of Scripture and Scripture's Use of Joel* (Brill, 2007); Thompson, J. A., "Joel's Locusts in the Light of Near Eastern Parallels," *JNES* 14 (1955): 52–55; von Rad, G., "Origin of the Concept of the Day of Yahweh," *JSS* 4 (1959): 97–108; Walvoord, J., *The Holy Spirit* (Dunham, 1954).

DUANE GARRETT

John, Gospel of

John's use of the OT is so thoroughgoing and comprehensive that it cannot be properly appreciated merely in terms of explicit quotations or even implicit echoes or allusions. Rather, John's overall worldview is thoroughly grounded in the Hebrew Scriptures, and this leads him to refer to OT texts and concepts numerous times, whether explicitly or implicitly (Köstenberger, *Theology*, 277–310; Klink; cf. Schlatter). On a foundational level, this pertains particularly to the Genesis creation and fall narratives, which provide John with the polarities of light and darkness and of life and death. In addition, John anchors his account of the mission of Jesus in key OT figures, institutions, and events such as Abraham, Moses, the exodus, Passover, and the temple.

Most striking is John's dependence on Isaiah both in terms of theological concepts and specific phrases (Hamilton; Young). This includes John's "sending Christology" of Jesus as the Word who came from God, accomplished his mission, and subsequently returned to the One who sent him. It also pertains to the figure of the Son of Man, who has been "lifted up" in fulfillment of Isaiah's portrait of the messianic servant of the Lord. The entire first half of John's Gospel, "The Book of Signs," may be patterned after Isaiah's theology of signs (Köstenberger, "Appropriation," 376–86) and appropriately ends with a dual quotation from both major portions of Isaiah. John here engages in theodicy, demonstrating that Israel's rejection of the Messiah is divinely willed and fulfills OT prophecy (Evans).

Other notable OT connections include those with the prophetic books of Ezekiel and Zechariah (Manning). The former supplies John with the notion that with Jesus, there will be one flock and one shepherd, uniting believing Jews and gentiles in one body (Köstenberger, "Shepherd"). John also echoes Ezekiel's vision of a spiritual restoration of God's people. Zechariah provides the picture of the humble Messiah entering Jerusalem on a lowly donkey and the figure of the God-Messiah who is pierced for the transgressions of God's people. The book of Psalms, especially the psalms of David, contributes to John's portrait of the Messiah as the righteous sufferer who is hated for no legitimate reason (Brunson; Daly-Denton).

In addition, numerous other motifs and symbols can be traced back to OT influence on how John views the world and the mission of Jesus, who is the incarnate Word, the Messiah, and the Son of God (Carson, "John"; Freed; Köstenberger, "John"; Menken; Schuchard). What is more, John reflects Jesus's own use of Scripture with reference to himself (France). In what follows, we will survey John's use of the OT following the contours of the Johannine narrative, moving from the prologue (1:1–18) to the Book of Signs (1:19–12:50), the Book of Exaltation (chaps. 13–20), and the epilogue (chap. 21). We will conclude with some final observations on John's use of the OT.

Prologue (1:1–18)

The Johannine gospel drama depicts Jesus's mission within the purview of the cosmic conflict between God and the Messiah on one side and Satan and the world on the other. The Gospel opens with an unmistakable allusion to the opening of Genesis: "In the beginning." This signals to the reader that John consciously links God's acts in creation with the mission of Jesus. In the first instance, God, "in the beginning," created the universe. In the second instance, John writes, "In the beginning was the Word, and the Word was with God, and the Word was God" (1:1). That same Word that had existed eternally prior to creation and through whom everything had been spoken into being, had now, in Jesus, become flesh and pitched his tent among his people. John and his fellow apostles have seen God's glory in Jesus, the unique, one-of-a-kind Son from the Father, and are bearing witness to what they had seen (1:14; cf. 1 John 1:1–4).

In addition, John connects Jesus's coming to the previous history of God's dealings with his people. In particular, he links the revelation mediated by Jesus with the antecedent revelation mediated by Moses (the law): "For the law was given through Moses; grace and truth came through Jesus Christ" (1:17). The Exodus account of the giving of the law, with its reference to Moses's inability to see God and live (33:20), forms the backdrop for John's introduction of Jesus. While "no one has ever seen God," including Moses, through whom the law was given, Jesus, "the one-of-a-kind Son, himself God, who is at the Father's side, he has made him known" (1:18 AT). By juxtaposing the respective types of revelation mediated by Moses and Jesus, John shines a spotlight on the massive escalation of divine self-disclosure brought by Jesus. As John testifies, "We have seen his glory" (1:14). The glory Moses could not see, John and his fellow apostles have seen, and they have inherited eternal life.

The Book of Signs (1:19–12:50)

Jesus as superior to his messianic forerunner. The account of Jesus's mission appropriately takes its point of departure with John the Baptist, who identifies himself as "the voice of one crying out in the wilderness, 'Make straight the way of the Lord'" (1:23 ESV; cf. Isa. 40:3). This first explicit OT quotation in John's Gospel presents John the Baptist as the herald of the new exodus that would be effected by Jesus the Messiah. In keeping with the OT context, the Baptist understands that he, the voice himself, is relatively insignificant when compared to the one to whom his message points: "He must increase; I must decrease" (3:30 AT; Köstenberger, "John," 424–28). The Baptist's relative insignificance is consistently emphasized throughout the early chapters of John's Gospel in order to highlight the gulf separating him and Jesus.

The Baptist is the best man; Jesus is the bridegroom (3:29). The Baptist is from earth; Jesus is from heaven (3:31). The Baptist is a lamp that shone for a little while; Jesus is the light of the world (5:35; 8:12; 9:5). The Baptist came to bear witness to the light; Jesus is the true light that has come into the world (1:6–8). The Baptist came before Jesus, yet Jesus ranks above him because he preexisted eternally with God the Father (1:15). In fact, the Baptist is not even worthy to untie the straps of Jesus's sandals (1:27). John performs no sign; Jesus works numerous signs identifying him as the Messiah (10:40–42; 12:36–37; 20:30–31). Thus, by literary *inclusio* (1:19–34 and 10:40–42), the entire Book of Signs is framed as a comparison between the humble role of the Baptist as a witness to Jesus and Jesus as the light and signs-working Messiah.

Jesus as the agent of new creation. The first week of Jesus's ministry is cast in terms of a week of the new creation Jesus inaugurated. On day one, John identifies himself in keeping with Isaiah's prophecy (1:19–28). On day two, "the next day," he identifies Jesus as the "Lamb of God" and "Son of God" (1:29, 34). On day three, "the next day," he reiterates his testimony regarding Jesus as the "Lamb of God" and points several of his followers to Jesus (1:35–42). On day four, "the next day," Jesus calls additional followers, including Philip (who believed Jesus was the one "of whom Moses in the Law and also the prophets wrote" [1:45 ESV]) and Nathanael, whose confession that Jesus is "Son of God" and "King of Israel" (1:49 ESV) elicits Jesus's comparison of the revelation brought by him with the revelation God provided to Israel on Jacob's ladder at Bethel (1:51; cf. Gen. 28:12).

Jesus as the fulfillment of patriarchal history. The allusion to Jacob, in turn, is one of several references to patriarchal history in the early chapters of John's Gospel. At the Cana wedding, Jesus's mother tells the servants, "Do whatever he tells you," likely an allusion to Pharaoh's words regarding Joseph (2:5; cf. Gen. 41:55). The subsequent reference to God giving his only Son harks back to Abraham's almost-sacrifice of his "only son" Isaac (3:16; cf. Gen. 22); and Jesus's encounter with the Samaritan woman takes place "near the field that Jacob had given to his son Joseph," in close proximity to Jacob's well (4:5–6 ESV). This cluster of patriarchal references in the so-called Cana Cycle (chaps. 2–4) sets Jesus's early mission within the context of the "holy history" of the past (Davies). Just as God was at work in a redemptive and revelatory manner in antecedent salvation history, so now Jesus is on the scene building on, and yet transcending, hints and manifestations of God's earlier work in and for Israel.

Jesus as the messianic bridegroom. In keeping with the presentation of Jesus's first week of ministry in terms of a new creation, the beginning of the Cana Cycle opens with the time marker "on the third day" (2:1). In addition to possibly alluding to Jesus's resurrection on the third day (cf. 2:18), this completes the first week of Jesus's mission. The Cana Cycle (chaps. 2–4) has begun. Fittingly, it opens with Jesus's first messianic sign at a wedding, which may hint that Jesus himself is the messianic bridegroom (cf. 3:29). The barrenness of contemporary Judaism stands in marked contrast to Jesus, the Messiah, who produces an abundance of wine, which in turn serves as an emblem of the joy and celebration he has come to bring (see, e.g., Isa. 25:6; Jer. 31:12–14). In this way, Jesus is cast as the one who has come to restore Judaism and to fulfill her hopes of the end-time messianic banquet.

Jesus as the fulfillment of Jewish festivals. Each major section of the Book of Signs features one Passover. The first is found toward the beginning of the Cana Cycle, which shows Jesus in Jerusalem (2:13). The second is found toward the beginning of the Festival Cycle (chaps. 5–10), at 6:4, which Jesus spends in Galilee. The third and final Passover featured in John is found toward the end of the Book of Signs, in the bridge section of chaps. 11–12, when Jesus is shown to attend his final Passover in Jerusalem at the dawn of his crucifixion (11:55; cf. 13:1). Festival references are particularly pronounced in the Festival Cycle, which features an unnamed feast (5:1), the Passover (6:3), the Feast of Tabernacles (7:2), and the Feast of Dedication (10:22). In this way, John shows Jesus as the fulfillment of the Jewish festival calendar (Köstenberger, *Theology*, chap. 10). As to Passover, Jesus is the "Lamb of God" (1:29, 36) whose legs are not broken (19:36; cf. Exod. 12:46); as to Tabernacles, Jesus is the giver of "living water" (4:10–11) and the "light of the world" (8:12; 9:5); as to Dedication, which celebrated the Jewish liberation from Seleucid sacrilege, Jesus is the truth that sets people free (8:32; 14:6). In addition, Jesus is also cast as the replacement for and fulfillment of the temple, the new temple (2:18–21; cf. 4:23–24).

Jesus as the new temple. Jesus's appearance at the temple at the occasion of his first recorded Passover elicits John's second explicit OT quotation. When Jesus authoritatively cleanses the temple, a possible second (Jerusalem) sign (cf. 2:23; 3:2; Köstenberger, "Seventh"), Jesus's followers remember Ps. 69—"Zeal for your house will consume me" (v. 9)—which Jesus fulfills by way of typology as the righteous (Davidic) sufferer whose zeal for God results in affliction by his own people (cf. 15:25; 19:24, 28–30) (Bryan; Köstenberger, "John," 431–34). Later, after Jesus has been crucified and risen on the third day, they "believed the Scripture and the word that Jesus had spoken" regarding the destruction and rebuilding of the "temple," which in reality was Jesus's body (2:21–22 ESV). If, as is likely, John composed his Gospel sometime after the destruction of the physical temple in Jerusalem (Köstenberger, "Destruction"), the message to his readers would have been unmistakable: God had judged Israel and the temple because of people's corrupt worship there, yet he had raised Jesus as its replacement and fulfillment (Hoskins).

Jesus as the lifted-up Son of Man. The account of Jesus's encounter with Nicodemus, the "teacher of Israel," is replete with OT antecedents. Jesus's words regarding a new, spiritual birth most likely echo new-creation motifs in Ezekiel, whereby water symbolizes spiritual cleansing and the new birth invokes God's promise of "a new heart" and "a new spirit" (3:3, 5; cf. esp. Ezek. 36:25–27). Jesus's words regarding Moses lifting up a snake in the wilderness recount Israel's wilderness wanderings during the exodus, with additional resonances from Isaiah's language of YHWH's servant being "lifted up" and from Daniel's mysterious figure of a "son of man" (3:14; cf. 8:28; 12:32; Num. 21:8; Isa. 52:13; Dan. 7:13). By way of typology, looking in faith at the lifted-up Jesus corresponds to looking in faith at the lifted-up bronze serpent in the wilderness, yet by way of escalation, believers in Jesus receive eternal life, while the Israelites in the wilderness only had their physical lives preserved. In this way, Jesus's conversation with Nicodemus is situated within the context of the scriptural account of Israel's exodus and the prophetic hope and expectation of a restored people of God and a lifted-up servant who would die for people's transgressions and thus be paradoxically honored and exalted by God.

Jesus as the fulfillment of sacred space. Jesus's encounter with the Samaritan woman, as noted above, takes place within the matrix of previous "holy history," involving Jacob and Joseph. In addition, the conversation takes place within view of Mount Gerizim, which invokes reminiscences of Moses's instruction of the people of Israel on the verge of entering the promised land. There, Moses sets before them both a blessing and a curse. The Israelites must not succumb to idolatry when entering Canaan but love and serve only the God who has made a covenant with them: "And when the LORD your God brings you into the land that you are entering to take possession of it, you shall set the blessing on Mount Gerizim" (Deut. 11:29 ESV; cf. chap. 28). The Samaritan version of the Pentateuch holds that Moses's instruction included the building of a sanctuary on Mount Gerizim that, Samaritans claimed, was superior even to the temple in Jerusalem. In the present context, John's message is clear: Jesus is superior to both Mount Gerizim and the Jerusalem temple; he is the fulfillment of all of patriarchal history and supersedes even Moses's instructions to Israel prior to entering the promised land (Davies).

Jesus as Lord of the Sabbath. Just as the Cana Cycle features parallel yet contrasting portraits of two individuals—Nicodemus and the Samaritan woman—in order to contrast their respective faith or lack thereof, so the Festival Cycle features parallel yet contrasting portraits of two more individuals, a lame man and a blind man, both of whom are healed by Jesus on a Sabbath. In both cases, the evangelist withholds the information that the healing took place on a Sabbath until later in the narrative (5:9; 9:14; cf. 7:21–24). In both cases, Jesus's opponents cast aspersions on him for breaking the Sabbath. In the context of both healings, Jesus is charged with blasphemy on account of his implicit claim to deity and authority over the Sabbath (5:18; 10:33). The two healed men, for their part, offer starkly differing responses: the lame man reports Jesus to the authorities while the blind man, blind no more, first confesses Jesus as a prophet, then identifies himself as his disciple, and in the end professes faith in Jesus as Lord and worships him (9:17, 27, 38). In the context of this account of contrasting faiths, Jesus is identified as aligned with God the Creator who is Lord of the Sabbath: "The Father and I are one" (10:30).

Jesus as the life-giving bread. While the feeding of the five thousand is featured in all four Gospels, only in John do we find the Bread of Life Discourse (chap. 6), where a Johannine sign is connected with an "I am" statement. In addition to Jesus showing himself to be the Messiah by performing a sign, the Fourth Evangelist shows how the sign underlies Jesus's identity as the "bread of life." Thus, what the Synoptics present as a miraculous multiplication of loaves and fish resulting in the feeding of the multitude, John's Gospel transposes into a messianic sign whose significance is elaborated upon in the discourse that follows (Köstenberger, "Transposition"). The division among Jesus's disciples that ensues marks a major watershed in John, leaving only the Twelve as a believing remnant whom Jesus will equip for mission in the second half of the Gospel. The exodus motif is front and center, as the crowds invoke the scriptural record of their ancestors' partaking of the manna in the wilderness (6:31; cf. Exod. 16:4, 15; Ps. 78:24). Thus, Jesus is also cast as the new Moses who will lead God's people on a new exodus and feed them with the new manna. This "bread from heaven," Jesus explains, is his very own flesh and blood, which those who believe in him must ingest in order to receive eternal life. In this way, the Fourth Evangelist significantly aids and advances his readers' understanding of the significance of the feeding of the multitude as he shows it to be grounded in Jesus's own identity. What is more, Jesus invokes the words of Isaiah, who envisioned that in the last days "they will all be taught by God" (6:45; cf. Isa. 54:13). In Jesus's teaching, this day has now arrived (Köstenberger, "John," 448–50).

Jesus as the light of the world. At the heart of the Festival Cycle is Jesus's appearance and discourse at the Feast of Tabernacles (chaps. 7–8), which continues the exodus theme struck in the previous chapter. This festival, celebrated in September or October, commemorated Israel's wilderness wanderings for an entire week during which booths were erected and various water-pouring and torch-lighting ceremonies took place. On the final day of the festival, Jesus invokes an unidentified Scripture, saying regarding the one who believed in him, "Out of his heart will flow rivers of living water" (7:38 ESV). The evangelist explains that this refers to the Spirit whom those who believed in Jesus would receive following Jesus's glorification (7:39). Not only would Jesus satisfy people's spiritual thirst, but his followers, too, would be sources of life-giving nourishment. Later, Jesus identifies himself as the "light of the world" (8:12; cf. 9:5), again pointing to his fulfillment of festal symbolism with regard to the water-pouring and torch-lighting ceremonies performed during Tabernacles.

Jesus is greater than Abraham. In keeping with John's emphasis on Jesus's fulfillment of patriarchal history and his superiority over previous figures in holy history, he shows Jesus engaged in dispute with some "Jews who had believed him" (8:31). As it turns out, this belief operates only on the most superficial of levels, as Jesus challenges them to remain in his word. While acknowledging that these Jews are ethnically Abraham's descendants, he goes on to assert that spiritually they are children of the devil because they are trying to kill him (8:37). Being a descendent of Abraham *physically* is not enough; faith in Jesus the Messiah is required. The discussion escalates yet further and culminates in Jesus's assertion that he existed before Abraham, at which his Jewish opponents again pick up stones to throw at him on account of perceived blasphemy (8:58–59). Yet, rightly understood, Jesus is greater than Abraham, just as he is greater than Jacob (4:12) and Moses (5:45–47).

Jesus is the good shepherd. Near the conclusion of the Festival Cycle, Jesus identifies himself as the "good shepherd," an image rife with OT connections (10:11). The people of Israel are frequently likened to sheep, and God to a loving, caring shepherd (e.g., Pss. 23:1; 100:3). Yet at the same time, prophets such as Ezekiel denounce Israel's leaders as irresponsible shepherds who care nothing for the sheep entrusted to them but instead exploit the sheep and enrich themselves at the sheep's expense (Ezek. 34). While Jesus's followers listen to his voice and are safe in his care, his opponents are not even among his sheep (John 10:26). What is more, as the supreme proof of his love, Jesus will give his life for his sheep, as he has authority to lay down his life and to take it up again (10:15, 17–18). Also, Jesus will be a shepherd not only for believing Jews but also for believing gentiles, so that both will be united in one flock under one shepherd, fulfilling Ezekiel's vision of God sending a shepherd who would unite God's people as one community under his leadership (10:16; cf. 11:51–52; Ezek. 34:23; 37:24; Köstenberger, "Shepherd").

Jesus is the resurrection and the life. The account of the raising of Lazarus, the seventh, climactic sign of Jesus in John's Gospel, reveals that Jesus has life in himself and thus is able to restore life to the dead (11:25; cf. 1:4; 5:26). While the hope of resurrection was only nascent in OT times and typically conceived in corporate terms (e.g., Ezek. 37), the expectation of individual resurrection can be found in a few places (Job 19:25; Dan. 12:2). Nevertheless, even in the first century, Jewish eschatology continued to hold to a view of two ages, the present age and the age to come, and resurrection was expected only in the age to come. Earlier in John's Gospel, Jesus affirmed that he is the end-time judge and agent of resurrection (5:25–29). In the account of the raising of Lazarus, however, Jesus is shown to transcend any dichotomous thinking. When Jesus tells Martha that he will raise her brother, she responds that, yes, she knows that he will raise him on the last day; yet Jesus retorts that, no, he will raise her brother *right now* (11:23–25)! In this way, Martha serves as a representative of Jewish eschatology while Jesus serves as a representative, if one can put it that way, of Johannine eschatology, according to which Jesus is intrinsically the life-giver and thus the future has invaded the present. Jesus has come to give abundant resurrection life, not only in the future but also in the here and now (10:10). In the Johannine narrative, where the presence of Lazarus at Jesus's anointing and beyond serves as indisputable, irrefutable evidence in support of Jesus's claims, Lazarus turns out to be the final trigger setting in motion Jesus's demise (cf. 12:1–2, 9–11, 17–19).

Jesus is the humble servant-king. Like the other Gospels, John includes the account of Jesus's triumphal entry into Jerusalem. He recounts how the crowds waved palm branches at Jesus's arrival and hailed him as the king of Israel (12:13; cf. Ps. 118:25). John adds that Jesus was seated on a donkey in fulfillment of Zechariah's prophecy (Zech. 9:9; cf. Zeph. 3:14–16; Köstenberger, "John," 470–74). Not only does Jesus evoke reminiscences of King Solomon's entrance into the city, but he also, by the manner in which he rides into Jerusalem, accentuates the meek and humble nature of his kingship. His entry may have been triumphal (albeit met with at least partial misunderstanding), but it was not triumphalist. As Jesus later testifies to Pontius Pilate, the Roman governor, his kingdom is not of this world (18:36). What is more, his kingdom is not built on power; it is built on truth (18:37). Ironically, therefore, while Pilate perceives Jesus as "the king of the Jews" and the Jews exclaim that they have no king but Caesar, betraying their messianic hope, Jesus is both king of Israel and king of the world, yet not in worldly, nationalistic terms but in spiritual terms that transcend ethnic descent, political affiliation, or any other external conception of identity. However, Jesus will be king not only over the spiritual realm but also over the complete physical realm at the consummation.

Jesus's rejection fulfills biblical prophecy. The Book of Signs closes on an ominous note of rejection. Already at the halfway point, on the heels of Jesus's Bread of Life Discourse, John notes that many of Jesus's disciples stop following him and signals that one of the Twelve, Judas, is a traitor (6:60–71). Now act 1 of the Johannine drama closes with a dual prophecy from Isaiah, averring that Jewish unbelief in Jesus is divinely willed and part of God's sovereign purpose. First, the evangelist notes that Jesus's signs have been met with persistent unbelief, just as Isaiah had prophesied (12:38; cf. Isa. 53:1; Brendsel). Second, he asserts that the Jewish authorities representing the nation neither *would* nor *could* believe, so that Isaiah's prophecy might be fulfilled that God blinded people's eyes and hardened their hearts so they could not see or understand (12:40; cf. Isa. 6:10; Köstenberger, "John," 476–83). One might legitimately ask how God can still hold people responsible for rejecting Christ when he has sovereignly hardened their hearts so they cannot believe. However, John and other biblical writers such as Paul hold divine sovereignty in tension with human responsibility and affirm both (see also 8:47; 10:25–26; 14:17; cf. Rom. 9–11; Köstenberger, *Theology*, 457–508; Carson, *Sovereignty*). With this, the Book of Signs closes on a note of Jewish rejection of the Messiah. The next book will open with Jesus gathering and equipping a believing remnant, his new messianic community, in order to commission this group subsequent to his crucifixion, burial, and resurrection.

The Book of Exaltation (Chaps. 13–20)

Act 2 of the Johannine drama is often called "The Book of Glory," but "The Book of Exaltation" may be a better description, as Jesus displays God's glory *throughout* John's Gospel (see, e.g., 1:14; 2:11; 9:3). This may be one important reason why John does not feature the account of the transfiguration: Jesus's glory is not confined to one striking manifestation; it is consistently displayed in everything Jesus says and does (cf. 1:14–18). One structural feature that demarcates chaps. 13–20 as a major new unit is that chap. 13 begins with a new introduction or preamble. While it is not as lengthy or extensive as the prologue that introduces the Gospel in its entirety, this preamble does set the tone for the passion narrative that it introduces. Rightly understood, therefore, 13:1–3 serves as an introduction not merely of the footwashing, or even the Farewell Discourse (chaps. 13–17), but of the entire passion narrative which, more narrowly, comprises chaps. 18–20.

In this preamble, readers are told that it is now the time before the Passover (reiterating 11:55). John stresses Jesus's foreknowledge of the events that are about to transpire. He notes Jesus's imminent departure and return to the Father (a shorthand and euphemism for the cross, burial, resurrection, and ascension) and states that Jesus loved his own to the end—that is, not merely at the footwashing (which serves as an anticipatory glimpse of Jesus's cruciform love) but ultimately at the cross (13:1; cf. 3:16). While Judas's betrayal had yet to happen historically, the evangelist, taking up the mantle of omniscient narrator, presents the betrayal as already a fait accompli: the devil had already put it into Judas's heart to betray Jesus (13:2). Judas's treachery, too, took place in fulfillment of Scripture (13:18; cf. Ps. 41:9; see also John 17:12). Again, Jesus is typologically depicted as the righteous sufferer who trusts in God's sovereign providence in the face of adversity. Yet Jesus is secure in his relationship with God the Father and cognizant of his supernatural origins and destiny (13:3). In this way, the stage is set, not merely for the footwashing or the Farewell Discourse, but for the entire second act of the Johannine drama—"The Book of Exaltation." It is here that Jesus gathers and equips his new messianic community for their mission.

Jesus's preparation of his messianic community. The literary form in which John conveys this historical event for his readers is that of a farewell discourse. This is a biblical genre first found in the Pentateuch in the farewell speeches of the patriarchs (cf. Gen. 49). It is even more pronounced in Moses's farewell speech to the people of Israel prior to their entrance into the promised land, which constitutes all of Deuteronomy. In the Second Temple period, the testamentary genre flourished and gave rise to works such as Testaments of the Twelve Patriarchs. Thus, by presenting Jesus's teaching in chaps. 13–17 in the form of a farewell discourse, John builds on a rich tradition of farewell discourses in both biblical and extrabiblical literature (see also Josh. 23–24; 1 Sam. 12; 1 Kings 2:1–12; 1 Chron. 28–29; Lacomara; Kellum). Such discourses typically include elements such as predictions of a person's death and departure, predictions of future challenges for one's sons or followers, arrangements regarding succession, exhortations to moral conduct, a concluding commission, an affirmation of God's covenant promises, and a final doxology (Moloney, 377–78). In Jesus's case, however, he will be gone only "for a little while," after which his followers would see him again (13:33; 14:19; 16:16–19). Also, Jesus's instruction focuses on the future rather than, as was common, on the past.

The mission of the exalted Jesus. In his final instruction, Jesus urges his followers to love one another (13:34; 15:17); comforts them in their hour of need (13:36; 14:1–3, 18, 27–28); and announces the arrival of "another helping presence," the Holy Spirit, who, unlike Jesus, would not merely be *with* them but take up residence *within* them (14:16–18 AT; cf. 14:26; 15:26; 16:7). Thus, rather than focus on his imminent *absence*, Jesus dwells on his continued *presence* with his disciples as mediated through the Holy Spirit. This is what Harold Attridge calls a "bending" of the conventional testamentary genre (3–21, esp. 9–10, 17–18). Perhaps most importantly, the underlying assumption of the entire Farewell Discourse (and of the entire second act) is that while from a historical vantage point the crucifixion is still future, spiritually speaking Jesus has *already* been exalted. And it is from this vantage point of anticipated exaltation that Jesus speaks to his original disciples and acts at the arrest and the crucifixion, and that John writes his passion narrative. For all practical purposes, Jesus's mission has already been completed (cf. 17:4; 19:30); thus the focus in the second half of John's Gospel is on the mission of Jesus's followers: prayers directed to the exalted Jesus will be answered (14:13); Jesus will commission his followers (17:18; 20:21) and send his Spirit to empower their mission (proleptically enacted at 20:22); and the disciples will be taken into the orbit of the loving and unified relationship of Father, Son, and Spirit (chap. 17; Köstenberger, *Missions*; Köstenberger and Swain, 149–64). Against the backdrop of the OT depiction of Israel as God's vineyard, Jesus is portrayed as the vine and his followers as the branches; this makes Jesus the typological fulfillment of Israel and symbolizes the organic nature of his relationship with believers (15:1–8; cf. Isa. 5:1–7; Ps. 80:8–16; Ezek. 15). At the same time, as they go about their mission, they will be hated by the world, again in fulfillment of scriptural expectation; in this way, they will follow in the footsteps of Jesus, who is typologically depicted as the righteous Davidic sufferer (John 15:18, 25; cf. Pss. 35:19; 69:4; Köstenberger, "John," 493–95).

The passion narrative. The passion narrative proper reiterates Jesus's foreknowledge at the occasion of his arrest (18:4, 9; cf. 13:1–3). John all but assumes Jesus's Jewish trial before Caiaphas (cf. 18:24, 28) and instead focuses primarily on his Roman trial before Pilate (18:28–19:16). In keeping with repeated explicit and implicit references to Jesus's deity throughout the Gospel (1:1, 18; 5:18; 8:58–59; 10:30), the ultimate charge the Jewish leaders bring against Jesus is that of blasphemy (19:7). In the end, Pilate (who alone has judicial authority to pronounce a death-by-crucifixion verdict) reluctantly hands Jesus over to be crucified. Pilate calls Jesus "your King" (19:14 ESV) and has an inscription written, "Jesus of Nazareth, the King of the Jews" (19:19); the Jewish authorities, for their part, in an astonishing and brazen rejection of their messianic hope, deny having any king other than Caesar (19:15). In this way, John makes clear that Jesus's kingdom is not of this world (18:36) and that the kingdom of God—a central part of the Synoptic presentation of Jesus—is not ethnically but spiritually defined. Instead, John habitually speaks of eternal life, which those who believe in Jesus will inherit (e.g., 3:16; 20:30–31; Köstenberger, *Theology*, 284–87).

The crucifixion. The account of Jesus's crucifixion features several explicit OT quotations, which contrasts with the relatively sparing use of direct citations up to this point in the second act and accentuates the fulfillment of Scripture by various details associated with the death of Jesus. Three aspects of Jesus's crucifixion in particular are highlighted as fulfilled by the evangelist: (1) the soldiers present at the crucifixion cast lots for Jesus's garment rather than tearing it into pieces (19:24; cf. Ps. 22:18); (2) the soldiers do not break Jesus's legs because he is already dead (19:36; cf. Exod. 12:46; Num. 9:12; Ps. 34:20); (3) the soldiers pierce Jesus's side, and blood and water emanate from it (19:37; cf. Zech. 12:10; see also 1 John 5:6; Rev. 1:7). Jesus's untorn robe may represent the unity of God's kingdom; his unbroken legs may point to Jesus as God's Passover lamb and symbolize God's preservation of the righteous sufferer; and the piercing of Jesus in place of the piercing of YHWH portrays Jesus as included in the identity of YHWH. In addition, the evangelist asserts that this information reflects eyewitness testimony and is therefore accurate and recorded for the purpose that his readers might believe (19:35; cf. 20:30–31; 21:24–25). What is at stake here is primarily to certify that Jesus died a real death. He really died and was really buried; thus, the resurrection was a real, bodily resurrection. Later, a form of Gnosticism would assert that Jesus only *appeared* to be human (docetism). Perhaps John argues against a precursor of this heresy here. Also, the demonstration that every detail surrounding Jesus's crucifixion fulfills biblical prophecy (whether found in the Law, the Prophets, or the Psalms) shows that the crucifixion was divinely willed and sovereignly superintended, which strikes a similar note as the one sounded at the end of the Book of Signs (cf. 12:36–41; note that starting with 12:38, John uses the introductory formula "so that Scripture might be fulfilled"). Divine sovereignty and human responsibility work hand in hand, and God uses even the actions of unbelieving Roman soldiers to accomplish his divinely foreknown and foreordained purposes.

Epilogue (Chap. 21)

The epilogue features Jesus's final resurrection appearance recorded in this Gospel. Peter is transformed from fisherman to shepherd. In this way, his three denials of Jesus are offset by three affirmations of his love for Jesus. Jesus also predicts that Peter will eventually die a martyr's death, just as Jesus himself died to give his life for his sheep (21:19; cf. 12:33). By contrast, the author of the Gospel, called "the disciple whom Jesus loved," would fulfill his ministry by bearing written witness to Jesus (21:24–25; cf. 1:18). Peter's role as shepherd, as mentioned, stands in a rich trajectory of God being the shepherd of his people and of Jesus being the "good shepherd" in contrast to Israel's faithless shepherds.

Final Observations

John's Gospel is steeped in the Hebrew Scriptures. Explicit quotations are clustered especially around Jesus's crucifixion. The second half of John's Gospel contains multiple "fulfillment quotations." Yet a mere focus on direct citations only captures a small portion of John's grounding in antecedent revelation. In fact, John sets Jesus's coming within a matrix of biblical theology that ranges from creation to new creation, from God's covenant with Israel through Moses and the exodus to a new exodus heralded by John the Baptist. In addition, the book features a rich tapestry of allusions, such as God's people as his flock (chap. 10) and branches of the vine (chap. 15).

What is more, John derives major planks in his entire theology and Christology from OT concepts. One of the most distinguished examples is John's sending Christology, which he most likely derives from Isaiah's depiction of the word of God that is sent on an earthly mission and returns to him once its mission has been accomplished. Isaiah's portrayal of the suffering servant as being lifted up and highly exalted is taken up by John in his depiction of Jesus as the lifted-up Son of Man who dies on the cross and is subsequently exalted by resurrection and ascension. Also noteworthy is John's theology of signs, which harks back to Moses's mighty deeds at the exodus as well as prophetic signs by individuals such as Isaiah (Köstenberger, "Appropriation"). Isaiah also supplies John with the rationale for his theodicy in view of Israel's obduracy (Evans).

All in all, John combines a large variety of antecedent biblical strands and motifs and shows how they all culminate in Jesus. Thus, his OT use is Christotelic in nature, showing how biblical revelation ultimately points to Jesus, who fulfills the OT messianic vision in both word and deed.

Bibliography. Attridge, H. W., "Genre-Bending in the Fourth Gospel," *JBL* 121 (2002): 3–21; Brendsel, D. J., *"Isaiah Saw His Glory,"* BZNW 208 (de Gruyter, 2014); Brunson, A. C., *Psalm 118 in the Gospel of John,* WUNT

158 (Mohr Siebeck, 2003); Bryan, S. M., "Consumed by Zeal," *BBR* 21 (2011): 479–94; Carson, D. A., *Divine Sovereignty and Human Responsibility* (John Knox, 1981); Carson, "John and the Johannine Epistles," in *It Is Written*, ed. D. A. Carson and H. G. M. Williamson (Cambridge University Press, 1988), 245–64; Daly-Denton, M., *David in the Fourth Gospel*, AGJU 47 (Brill, 2004); Davies, W. D., *The Gospel and the Land* (University of California Press, 1974); Evans, C. A., "Obduracy and the Lord's Servant," in *Early Jewish and Christian Exegesis*, ed. C. A. Evans and W. F. Stinespring, Homage 10 (Scholars Press, 1987), 221–36; France, R. T., *Jesus and the Old Testament* (Tyndale, 1971); Freed, E. D., *Old Testament Quotations in the Gospel of John*, NovTSup 11 (Brill, 1965); Hamilton, J., "The Influencer of Isaiah on the Gospel of John," *Perichoresis* 5, no. 2 (2007): 139–62; Hoskins, P. M., *Jesus as the Fulfillment of the Temple in the Gospel of John*, PBM (Paternoster, 2008); Kellum, L. S., "Farewell Discourse," in *DJG*[1], 266–69; Klink, E. W., III, "Light of the World," in *Cosmology and New Testament Theology*, ed. J. T. Pennington and S. M. McDonough, LNTS 355 (T&T Clark, 2008), 74–89; Köstenberger, A. J., "The Destruction of the Second Temple and the Composition of the Fourth Gospel," in *Challenging Perspectives on the Gospel of John*, ed. J. Lierman, WUNT 2/219 (Mohr Siebeck, 2006), 69–108; Köstenberger, "Jesus the Good Shepherd Who Will Also Bring Other Sheep," *BBR* 12 (2002): 67–96; Köstenberger, "John," in *CNTUOT*, 415–512; Köstenberger, "John's Appropriation of Isaiah's Signs Theology," *Them* 43, no. 3 (2018): 376–86; Köstenberger, "John's Transposition Theology," in *Earliest Christian History*, ed. M. F. Bird and J. Maston, WUNT 2/320 (Mohr Siebeck, 2012), 191–226; Köstenberger, *The Missions of Jesus and the Disciples according to the Fourth Gospel* (Eerdmans, 1998); Köstenberger, "The Seventh Johannine Sign," *BBR* 5 (1995): 87–103; Köstenberger, *A Theology of John's Gospel and Letters* (Zondervan, 2009); Köstenberger, A. J., and S. Swain, *Father, Son and Spirit*, NSBT 24 (IVP Academic, 2008); Lacomara, A., "Deuteronomy and the Farewell Discourse (John 13:31–16:33)," *CBQ* 36 (1974): 65–84; Manning, G. T., *Echoes of a Prophet*, JSNTSup 270 (T&T Clark, 2004); Menken, M. J. J., *Old Testament Quotations in the Fourth Gospel*, CBET 15 (Kok, 1996); Moloney, F. J., *The Gospel of John*, SP 4 (Liturgical Press, 1998); Schlatter, A., *Der Evangelist Johannes*, 2nd ed. (Calwer, 1948); Schuchard, B. G., *Scripture within Scripture*, SBLDS 133 (Scholars Press, 1992); Smith, R. H., "Exodus Typology in the Fourth Gospel," *JBL* 81 (1962): 329–42; Young, F. W., "A Study of the Relation of Isaiah to the Fourth Gospel," *ZNW* 46 (1955): 215–33.

ANDREAS J. KÖSTENBERGER

John, Letters of

Few documents in the NT sustain as wide a range of interpretations as do the Johannine Epistles (cf. von Wahlde)—on matters dealing with their provenance, literary genres, primary themes, social context, place in early church history, and more. These disputed matters inevitably have a bearing on how we think antecedent Scriptures are used in the Johannine Epistles.

Disputed Introductory Matters

Until about two hundred years ago, the overwhelming majority of Johannine scholars held that the apostle John wrote the Fourth Gospel, the Johannine Epistles, and (probably) the Apocalypse (assuming the "John" of Rev. 1:4 is a reference to the apostle). That is now a minority position. Today it is more common to argue that the author of the Fourth Gospel and the author of the Johannine Epistles emerged from the same Johannine "school" or "community," and that the original John was not in any case the apostle but some ill-defined elder.

Similarly, it was once commonly agreed that the Fourth Gospel was likely written first, followed by the Johannine Epistles and the Apocalypse. This was predicated in part on the belief that the Gospel is primarily evangelistic, while the Epistles were understood to address established churches—and many would expect evangelism to predate the discipling of believers. When popular scholarly opinion increasingly argued that neither were written to win people to Christ but were calculated to deepen the readers' theological maturation, there was less reason to think that the composition of the Gospel preceded that of the Epistles. In any case, another wave of scholarly opinion has washed over this scene and changed the landscape. A substantial minority of Johannine scholars hold that the Gospel was produced in two or more editions. That opens up the possibility that one or more of the Epistles were written and published between editions of the Gospel (cf. Culpepper and Anderson). The speculations become increasingly complex (and decreasingly verifiable!) the more layers one postulates for both the Gospel and the Epistles (e.g., von Wahlde, vol. 3). Inevitably, the creative proposals have become so numerous that there are almost as many proposals as there are Johannine scholars, which has led some to speak of the balkanization of Johannine scholarship (Carson, "Balkanization"). Of course, it is important to recognize that there have always been some scholars who defend the older view, the view supported by the church fathers: the apostle John wrote the Gospel and the Epistles, the former with the primary purpose of evangelism and the latter primarily to edify the saints.

Further, the order of composition of the Epistles has long been debated. After all, their canonical order is determined by their relative length (longest to shortest), but this has no necessary bearing on their chronological order. (Similarly for the Pauline Epistles, whose canonical order is established by two principles: letters to churches come before letters to individuals, and longer letters precede shorter letters, with the exception of Ephesians, which succeeds Galatians despite being slightly longer.) Occasionally those commenting on the Johannine Epistles have felt free to change the order (e.g., Marshall; Strecker). The vocabulary, themes, and style of 1 and 2 John are so similar that there is good reason for thinking they came from the same hand. Moreover, 2 and 3 John boast their own similarities. Both come from the "elder," and both deal with the question of hospitality, though from opposite angles: 3 John urges hospitality, while 2 John specifies when hospitality is to be withheld. By their opening and closing lines, both 2 and 3 John show themselves to be letters, while 1 John appears to be sermonic. Karen Jobes (28–29) plausibly suggests that 1 John was first preached in the elder's church shortly after the schism to which he alludes (cf. 1 John 2:18–19) and then circulated to nearby churches facing the same problem. Quite possibly 2 John served as a cover letter to 1 John. For whatever reason, Diotrephes, a leader in another church to which 1 John was sent, did not accept the bearer of 1 and 2 John, prompting the elder to write to his friend Gaius so as to circumnavigate the blockade set up by Diotrephes (3 John). The truth of the matter is that the Johannine Epistles are so brief that it is difficult to be certain about the details of the schism. In 2 John, one can identify the doctrinal issue that lies at the heart of the division and observe that it has some parallels in 1 John (see 2 John 7–9; cf. 1 John 2:22; 4:2, 3). By contrast, although it is clear that a schism lurks behind the text of 3 John, there is no unambiguous identification in 3 John of a doctrinal aberration. Yet at the same time many commentators rightly acknowledge that it is almost impossible to read the Epistles without postulating some such relationship as that suggested here.

Disputed Subject Matter

As mentioned a little earlier, 1 John is remarkable for the number and variety of interpretations it has generated. These interpretations easily become controlling grids that shape the work and theology of those who adopt them. In the paragraphs that immediately follow, some of these interpretive grids are briefly identified, along with some brief comments when they shed light on how John handles antecedent biblical material.

First, virtually every commentator draws attention to the way John deploys a limited number of themes and then cycles through them several times (e.g., on the importance of love, see 1 John 2:9–11; 3:10b–18; 4:7–12, 16–21; 5:1–3). This kind of repetition makes it possible to "find" structures in 1 John predicated on parallelism. Indeed, the number of books and articles written during the last century, and given over to the literary structures in 1 John, is rather high (e.g., Feuillet; Thomas, "Literary"). The bearing of this structural emphasis on the way in which John refers to antecedent Scriptures will become clearer after the next example.

Second, the massive commentary on the Johannine Epistles by Raymond Brown in the Anchor Bible series has one characteristic that makes it unique. Although the work is both detailed and comprehensive, what stands out about this commentary is its controlling thesis: every section of 1 John, Brown argues, takes up one or more sections of the Fourth Gospel, and develops them, modifies them, applies them, comments on them, or refracts them in some way. In part, this is no more than the common recognition that the Gospel and the Epistles, especially 1 John, work with the same themes. Yet Brown is saying much more than this. He adds specificity to the connections he draws between the works, the more so since before writing his commentary on the Epistles, he wrote a two-volume work on the Gospel. He is not claiming merely that in the Epistles the apostle draws thematic connections with themes in the Gospel but that every pericope in the Epistles includes specific allusions to concrete passages in the Gospel. Although Brown's commentary is enormously informed and evocative, we must acknowledge that his central thesis has not proved convincing to most other Johannine scholars. Nevertheless, Brown's thesis exposes an important reality: to the extent that the Epistles *do* allude to earlier material, they do so without using unambiguous direct quotations. The alleged references to earlier material are so disputable that few scholars line up to concur on the list. In other words, both the structural parallels (see the previous section) and the alleged allusions to earlier material are so little constrained by exact quotations that we are forced to recognize that substantive word-for-word quotation does not appear to be an element in the apostle's style. That should warn us to exercise suitable caution when we try to identify specific OT quotations or allusions in the Johannine Epistles.

Third, one of the most influential commentaries on 1 John to appear in the last hundred years or so carries the evocative title *The Tests of Life*. The author, Robert Law, finds three "tests of life" in 1 John: the truth test, the obedience test (or the moral test), and the love test (or the social test). One is truly a child of God and a follower of Jesus if one "passes" all three—and it is not "best two out of three," with a lot of grading on the curve. To not believe the truth, not obey the Christ, or not love fellow Christians is to deny the Father and the Son. But despite this black-and-white scenario (see esp. 1 John 3:7–10), there is hope that is grounded in the cross (2:2; 4:10). This analysis by Law is not wrong, but it has contributed to an unending discussion about whether or not 1 John is a polemical document. Those who are happy to identify with the "polemical" label point out how decisively John speaks against the antichrists, those who "went out from us" and who "did not really belong to us" (2:19), and how they can be identified. On the other hand, those who prefer to think of 1 John as a sermon of edification rather than a sermon of polemics point out that the book is written for believers to read, to help them be a little more discerning and a lot more shaped by a sharp handling of the three "tests." Many commentaries use some variant of this analysis to outline the dominant message of the book. Others think, probably rightly, that 1 John is simultaneously polemical and edifying. By building its readers up, it is also warning them to avoid various poisonous alternatives; by identifying the failed alternatives, it is helping its readers to become more mature. One cannot help but remember the words of the old song "Love and Marriage": "You can't have one without the other."

Fourth, until the last three decades or so, many commentators cast the Epistles (especially 1 John and 2 John) against a gnostic or docetic background. This is not to deny that other backgrounds have been suggested, including wisdom literature, the Dead Sea Scrolls, and even apocalyptic sources. But probably no contextual background has been more enduring than docetic Gnosticism, perhaps in particular Valentinian Gnosticism. This is not to say that all who appealed to such backgrounds came to the same conclusions. We can find a range all the way from Rudolf Bultmann, whose reconstructions turn in part on the way he aligns his recovered "sources" with some form or other of Gnosticism, to John Stott, who understands the christological error that constitutes the "lie" in 1 and 2 John to be bound up with docetism, and whose analysis generates a much more traditional commentary. But once again, the diversity of putative sources to which John allegedly makes allusion is so varied that it is very difficult to imagine direct dependence. The evidence is simply too flimsy. Today this reality is increasingly recognized, not least because the gnostic and docetic documents on which such theories are based are simply too late to justify Johannine dependence on them (King). The result is that such things as the doctrinal error on which the schism apparently rests cannot with confidence be mapped onto nascent docetism, and this reality drives not a few commentators to be more cautious about claims to finding specific allusions to ostensibly antecedent material. The evidence is sufficiently slender that it compels us to be reticent about how John uses his sources (cf. Jobes; Yarbrough; Köstenberger; Kruse).

Fifth, a number of commentators and writers of monographs have fastened onto one word or controlling theme in such a way that the Epistles, or at least 1 John, are spun in a well-defined direction. In theory, this should provide an opportunity to align suitable quotations from the OT to support this tilt in the interpretation of the text, but in no case is this what we find. For example, Terry Griffith fastens onto the closing words of 1 John 5—namely, "keep yourselves from idols"—and makes a good case for a polemic forged in a Jewish, not gnostic, context, but his argument does not turn on unambiguous quotations from the LXX. Several works fasten onto the atonement passages, 1 John 2:1–2 and 4:7–10 (e.g., Do; Armitage; Morgan-Wynne), but the same thing must be said. The analysis of the schism that Stephen Smalley finds in 1 John sounds more like a twentieth-century dispute than a first-century one, but in any case provides no locus for extensive allusions to the OT. The commentary by John Thomas (*1 John*) tilts the emphasis in 1 John toward the work of the Spirit, but with no gain in allusions to the OT. The innovative work by Matthew Jensen, who leans on the literary/rhetorical method of Wolfgang Iser to open up "gaps" in the flow of 1 John 1:1–5 and 1:6–2:11 that demand to be filled in by NT references that focus on Jesus's resurrection, deserves high praise for its innovation and rigor but does not open up new connections between the Epistles and the OT. The creative source- and redaction-critical theory of Jörg Frey pictures the evangelist "remembering" the history of Jesus (which expression in Frey's hands includes creating ostensibly "historical" narrative out of whole cloth) in such a way that the Christology (i.e., the theology) shapes and controls the "history": his title is *Theology and History in the Fourth Gospel*, and the sequence of the first two nouns discloses the agenda. (For more detailed interaction, see Carson, review of *Theology and History*.) But once again we are carried no further in our quest.

Two Strong Allusions to the OT

Two prefatory notes will clarify this section. (1) On a strong definition of "quotation," a definition that includes the specification that it must be made up of at least three or four words, there is no OT quotation in the Johannine Epistles. (2) On a very loose definition of "allusion," doubtless there are many OT allusions in 1 John, since 1 John deals with such themes as sin, atonement, love, obedience, faith, and much more—and of course such themes are generously sprinkled through the OT canon. But their occurrence is so frequent that it is very difficult to map specific references to, say, "sin" or "atonement" in 1 John onto the OT. But there are two tight allusions in 1 John to the OT—that is, allusions to specific OT passages—one that is universally acknowledged and one that is sometimes disputed or overlooked.

First, in 1 John 3:12, we find mention of Cain: "Do not be like Cain, who belonged to the evil one and murdered his brother." "Cain" is an unusual name; there can be no doubt that John is referring to the Cain of Gen. 4, even though John does not *quote* Gen. 4. In late Jewish literature, Cain, the first murderer, became the archetypical sinner. That is the way he is presented here. In Jude 11, "the way of Cain" is identified as false teaching. In both passages, the reference is specific, and Cain himself carries negative exemplary force.

The second allusion, in 1 John 2:27, is initially rather puzzling: "As for you, the anointing you received from him remains in you, and you do not need anyone to teach you. But as his anointing teaches you about all things and as that anointing is real, not counterfeit—just as it has taught you, remain in him." John tells his readers they do not need anyone to teach them, because they already have the anointing. Probably this is a way of referring to the activity of the Spirit, who (Jesus had taught them) would lead them into all truth (John 16:13). But what does John think *he* is doing, but teaching them? He tells his readers that they do not need anyone to teach them, meaning, of course, that they do not need the secessionists to teach them. Doubtless when he himself is teaching them, he views his teaching activity as an extension of the Spirit's ministry. Perhaps the secessionists claimed they had some kind of anointing that the rest of the Christians did not have—and John tells them they do not need what the secessionists are offering because John's readers *do* have the anointing (of the Spirit). And suddenly it is difficult to avoid seeing the allusion to Jer. 31:31–34. Jeremiah foresees the coming of the new covenant. When that arrives, various things will happen, not the least important of which is this: "No longer will they teach their neighbor, or say to one another, 'Know the LORD,' because they will all know me, from the least of them to the greatest" (Jer. 31:34). Under the terms of the old covenant, there were designated people whose task it was to teach the rest of the covenant people to know the Lord; indeed, they had special endowment and commission to do just that, for the old covenant was a tribal-mediating covenant (see further Carson, "'No Need'"). But under the terms of the new covenant, no longer will certain designated people say "Know the LORD" because they will *all* have the anointing. If 1 John 2:27 alludes to Jer. 31:34, the apostle is advancing his argument by saying that under the transformed circumstances of the new covenant there can be no place for people to promote themselves to a privileged inside track with God, for all of God's true people share the same anointing. In short, 1 John 2:27 alludes to Jer. 31 in order to claim that the promised blessings of the new covenant are fulfilling the promises of the OT prophet.

Bibliography. Armitage, C., *Atonement and Ethics in 1 John* (T&T Clark, 2021); Bennett, T. A., *1–3 John*, THNTC (Eerdmans, 2021); Brown, R. E., *The Epistles of John*, AB 30 (Doubleday, 1982); Bultmann, R., *The Johannine Epistles*, Herm (Fortress, 1973); Carson, D. A., "The Challenge of the Balkanization of Johannine Studies," in *John, Jesus, and History*, vol. 1, *Critical Appraisals of Critical Views*, ed. P. N. Anderson, F. Just, and T. Thatcher (Society of Biblical Literature, 2007), 133–64; Carson, "1–3 John," in *CNTUOT*, 1063–67; Carson, "John and the Johannine Epistles," in *It Is Written*, ed. D. A. Carson and H. G. M. Williamson (Cambridge University Press, 1988), 246–64; Carson, review of *Theology and History in the Fourth Gospel*, by Jörg Frey, *JETS* 62, no. 4 (2019): 832–36; Carson, "'You Have No Need That Anyone Should Teach You,'" in *The New Testament in Its First-Century Setting*, ed. P. J. Williams, A. D. Clarke, P. Head, and D. Instone-Brewer (Eerdmans, 2004), 269–80; Culpepper, R. A., and P. N. Anderson, *Communities in Dispute* (SBL Press, 2014); Culy, M. M., *1, 2, 3 John* (Baylor University Press, 2004); Denault, P., *Le côté obscure de la vie chrétienne* (Publications Chrétiennes, 2018); Do, Toan, *Re-thinking the Death of Jesus* (Peeters, 2014); Feuillet, A., "Étude structurale de la première Épître de Saint Jean," in *Neues Testament und Geschichte*, ed. H. Baltensweiler and B. Reicke (Theologischer Verlag, 1972), 307–27; Frey, J., *Theology and History in the Fourth Gospel* (Baylor University Press, 2018); Griffith, T., *Keep Yourselves from Idols*, JSNTSup 233 (Sheffield Academic, 2002); Heil, J. P., *1–3 John* (Cascade, 2015); Jensen, M. D., *Affirming the Resurrection of the Incarnate Christ*, SNTSMS 153 (Cambridge University Press, 2012); Jobes, K. H., *1, 2, 3 John*, ZECNT (Zondervan, 2014); King, K. L., "'The Gnostic Myth,'" in *Christianity in the Second Century*, ed. J. C. Paget and J. Lieu (Cambridge University Press, 2017), 122–50; Klauck, H.-J., *Studien zum Korpus der johanneischen Schriften*, WUNT 439 (Mohr Siebeck, 2020); Köstenberger, A. J., *A Theology of John's Gospel and Letters*, BTNT (Zondervan, 2009); Kruse, C. G., *The Letters of John*, 2nd ed., PNTC (Eerdmans, 2020); Lamb, D. A., *Text, Context and the Johannine Community*, LNTS 477 (Bloomsbury, 2014); Law, R., *The Tests of Life*, 3rd ed. (T&T Clark, 1914); Marshall, I. H., *The Epistles of John*, NICNT (Eerdmans, 1978); Morgan-Wynne, J., *The Cross in the Johannine Writings* (Pickwick, 2011); Paget, J. C., and J. Lieu, *Christianity in the Second Century* (Cambridge University Press, 2017); Schuchard, B. G., *1–3 John*, ConcC (Concordia, 2012); Smalley, S. S., *1, 2, 3 John*, WBC (Word, 1984); Stott, J. R. W., *The Letters of John*, TNTC (Tyndale, 1964); Strecker, G., *The Johannine Letters*, Herm (Fortress, 1995); Thomas, J. C., *1 John, 2 John, 3 John*, The Pentecostal Commentary (T&T Clark, 2004); Thomas, "The Literary Structure of 1 John," *NovT* 40 (1998): 369–81; Van der Watt, J. G., *Rethinking the Ethics of John*, WUNT 291 (Mohr Siebeck, 2012); von Wahlde, U. C., *The Gospel and Letters of John*, 3 vols., ECC (Eerdmans, 2010); Yarbrough, R. W., *1–3 John*, BECNT (Baker Academic, 2008).

D. A. CARSON

Jonah, Book of

The book of Jonah is anonymous, but the prophet who is one of its central characters and came from Gath-hepher in the territory of Zebulun is known from 2 Kings 14:25. That passage refers to his earlier prophecy of uncertain date regarding the restoration of the Northern Kingdom under Jeroboam II (ca. 789–748 BC). The book of Jonah does not state when it was composed, so the time of its composition must be inferred from relevant information in the text. The book's few Aramaisms are often adduced as proof for its exilic or postexilic origin, but their paucity and randomness do not suggest Aramaic influence. Their significance for dating is further limited by the proximity of Israelite (northern) Hebrew to

Aramaic-speaking populations from the eighth century onward (Shitrit, 165). These factors, along with syntax that is a "superb" example of eighth-century classical Hebrew (Niccacci) and the book's presumption that Assyria's strength and violence are well known, make likely an eighth-century date of composition, probably near the time of Assyria's resurgence under Tiglath-Pileser III (ca. 745–727 BC).

Essential Features of the Book of Jonah

Composition. The unity of the book as a whole is rarely questioned apart from chap. 2 (see Wöhrle, and contrast Spronk). Arguments against the authenticity of the psalm in Jon. 2 are usually based on the shift from prose in the surrounding narrative to poetry in the psalm itself, the psalm's different vocabulary, and the ostensibly contradictory images of the rebellious prophet in chap. 1 over against the repentant prophet in chap. 2 (cf. Wolff, 78–79, 128–31). With respect to the first two points, shifts in genre and vocabulary are common in ancient Near Eastern literature and so do not threaten the book's unity (Holm, 271–72). The degree of tension between the presentations of Jonah in chap. 2 and elsewhere in the book will be discussed below.

Structure and message. The following structure emphasizes several contrasts that are key to the author's message, especially between Jonah and the sailors (chaps. 1–2) and between Jonah and YHWH (chaps. 3–4):

Chap. 1	Jonah's flight from YHWH, the sailors' turn to YHWH, and Jonah's deliverance
Chap. 2	Jonah's psalm
Chap. 3	Jonah's message to Nineveh, Nineveh's repentance, and God's response
Chap. 4	Jonah's response to God's mercy to Nineveh, God's response to Jonah

The book uses the unprecedented sending of Jonah to Nineveh to expose the danger of smug presumption among those who know a good deal about God (epitomized by the prophet himself), to demonstrate God's commitment to bring good to the nations through his people (Gen. 12:1–3; Exod. 19:5–6), and to glorify God's grace and compassion in saving sinners regardless of their ethnicity or initial level of knowledge about him (cf. Stek; Timmer).

The disobedient prophet who believes he can flee from God's presence also symbolizes the Northern Kingdom of Israel: quite familiar with who YHWH is, but largely unwilling to live in submission to him (Kim, 504–7, also compares Jeroboam II and Nineveh's ruler). The non-Israelite sailors are a perfect foil for the prophet and his homeland. They are initially without any knowledge of YHWH, but after hearing only a few words of God's power, sovereignty, and justice they come to revere him and prove their profound and exclusive commitment to him by their actions (1:16). The prophet, after attempting to avoid his mission by drowning, crafts a hymn that recognizes YHWH's deliverance (Youngblood, 105) while portraying God as responsible for his recent near-death experience (2:3, contrast 1:12), makes no mention of his astounding rejection of and flight from the divine commission (1:3; Yates, 231), and strangely emphasizes his persistent belief that YHWH would save him (2:4, 7) more than God's gracious intervention (2:6, 9d) (Youngblood, 114–15; Timmer, 83–84). While Jonah's "looking toward" YHWH in prayer shows that he depended on God for deliverance (Youngblood, 111–12), it is less clear that he repented or fully embraced his mission (Benckhuysen, 12–13), a point that chap. 4 develops further (Vaillancourt, 183; Wendland, 389).

In the second half of the book the Ninevites respond much like the sailors to Jonah's message of impending judgment, although there is no claim that they turned away from their gods. Still, their repentance is significant, and they even realize that it cannot oblige God to deliver them (3:9–10). In the face of Nineveh's repentance, Jonah finally reveals that he initially rejected the divine commission because he feared that YHWH would show grace and compassion to Nineveh, which in his eyes could not be a legitimate recipient of it. YHWH rebuts Jonah's misuse of the divine character and misunderstanding of grace, and puts before Jonah—and the reader—the fact that those who experience God's gracious deliverance should celebrate that deliverance and glorify God for it (cf. 2:9) when he graciously shares it with others.

Jonah's Use of the OT

Jonah's extensive use of the OT includes quotations, allusions, and "echoes." Jonathan Magonet (44–50, 65–84), Hyun Kim, and Scott Noegel extensively analyze Jonah's inner-biblical interpretation (Craig, 102–4, lists others). The following examples include texts with strong lexical ties as well as texts whose surface-level ties to Jonah are less obvious but whose semantic overlap is significant. Some allusions demonstrate the relevance of the earlier text's context for its reuse (cf. Turner's "broad reference" [578]). In many cases dependence or influence is assumed but cannot be proved due to the difficulty of dating the source text (esp. various psalms). In such cases, the biblical authors' understanding of revelation and the canon as establishing a unique universe of discourse (Dempster, 95–96) may adequately explain the consistent and widespread transmission of theological "ideas and phraseology" (Sasson, 23) in ancient Israel apart from literary dependence.

Jonah and Jer. 26; 36. Gary Yates identifies numerous conceptual and lexical similarities or differences between Jonah and Jeremiah (esp. Jer. 26 and 36) that function ironically or inversely. The sailors respond to Jonah's unintentional and indirect testimony about

YHWH whereas Jeremiah's audience rejects him and his intentionally delivered message (Yates, 227); both prophets find themselves in life-threatening situations, albeit for very different reasons (Yates, 231); both their intended audiences are guilty of "evil" (*rāʿâ*; Yates, 225); and Jonah the unfaithful prophet apparently refuses to intercede for his fellow travelers while Jeremiah the faithful prophet intercedes despite a divine prohibition against doing so (Jer. 14; Yates, 234).

Jonah 1 and Ps. 107:23–32. Jonah 1 and Ps. 107:23–31 share lexical and thematic elements that suggest a close relationship between them, even if it seems likely that Ps. 107 reuses Jonah (the psalm's references to the return from exile require that it be later; contrast Magonet, 81–82). In both texts, the main characters (all but Jonah are non-Israelites) board a ship (*ʾonîyâ*, Ps. 107:23; Jon. 1:3) that once on the sea (*yām*, Ps. 107:23; Jon. 1:4) encounters wind (*rûaḥ*, Ps. 107:25; Jon. 1:4) and storm (*saʿar*/*səʿārâ*, Ps. 107:25; Jon. 1:4). The overwhelmed sailors cannot remedy the situation (Ps. 107:27; Jon. 1:5, 13) and so cry out for divine help (Ps. 107:28, to YHWH; Jon. 1:5, to their gods). YHWH quiets the storm (*šātaq*, Ps. 107:30; Jon. 1:11, 12), and the sailors are encouraged to (Ps. 107:31) or do (Jon. 1:16) recognize YHWH's sovereignty and faithful character (*ḥesed*, Ps. 107:31; cf. Jon. 2:8 [MT 2:9]). If the author of Ps. 107 had the book of Jonah before him, he does not mention the prophet, presumes the non-Israelite origins of the mariners, and juxtaposes YHWH's grace and his covenant faithfulness to Israelites in an analogical interpretation of Jon. 1.

Jonah 1:9 and Ps. 95:5. Carl Bosma (77–79) argues that Ps. 95:5 ("sea . . . made . . . formed . . . dry land") is the closest of several parallels to Jon. 1:9 ("made the sea and the dry land"), and that the "subversive polemic against the gods" in the immediate context of the psalm "polemically unmasks the Canaanite deities," including Yam. Jonah's reuse of Scripture thus accepts its enduring authority as the basis for a critique of the sailors' gods, which explains the sudden appearance of their great fear in the following verse (Jon. 1:10), once they realize that they are threatened by YHWH's anger.

Jonah 1:14 and Pss. 115:3 // 135:6. The verbal pair "do . . . please" with YHWH as the subject is rare and ties this verse to Pss. 115:3; 135:6. More significant resonances arise from these psalms' critique of idolatry (115:4–8; 135:15–18), affirmations of YHWH's unique sovereignty (115:16; 135:5), and encouragements to trust in him (115:9–11; 135:14, 19–21) (Timmer, 72–74; Bosma, 85; Sasson, 135–36). The echo of these psalms in the description of the sailors' newfound belief in YHWH's unique deity and trustworthiness affirms the abiding authority of these psalms and makes the sailors the spiritual peers of faithful Israelites while casting Jonah in an unfavorable light.

Jonah 1:16 and Ps. 50:15–16. Apart from legislative contexts, the occurrence of the pair "offer sacrifices and pay/make vows" in close proximity is quite rare (e.g., 1 Sam. 1:21; Pss. 50:14; 66:13; 116:14, 17, 18; Isa. 19:21). All these cases except the last make this behavior typical for faithful Israelites, while the Isaiah passage foresees that non-Israelites will exhibit the same attachment to YHWH. The use of the phrase here is quite possibly drawn from Ps. 50:14, whose sharp separation between faithful (50:5, 14–15) and unfaithful Israelites (50:16) perfectly suits the message of the book of Jonah. Attributing these actions to the non-Israelite sailors shows that they can have authentic relationships with YHWH *outside* eschatological settings like Isa. 19:21, and so Jon. 1 presents a very limited but notable fulfillment of such prophecies.

Jonah 2:2 and various psalms. The opening line of Jonah's prayer ("I called out of my distress to YHWH and he heard me" [AT]) is quite close to Ps. 120:1 ("To YHWH in my distress I called and he answered me" [AT]; Benckhuysen, 17; Magonet, 46; Sasson adds Ps. 130:1–2; Lam. 3:55–56). Magonet notes the change in word order, which, if Jonah is dependent on the psalm, adds a note of egocentricity by putting the first-person verb at the head of the hymn's first clause. Be that as it may, the ironic reuse of individual laments at various places in Jonah's prayer glosses over the sin that caused Jonah's distress, in contrast to the oppression of the "righteous sufferer" in many such laments, including Ps. 120. Kevin Youngblood (105) and Jack Sasson (168) also note several lexical and semantic parallels between Jon. 2:2a and Ps. 18:6, which includes a reference to YHWH's temple (cf. Jon. 2:4).

The presence of several consecutive shared lexemes suggests that the second half of Jon. 2:2 probably echoes Ps. 31:23 ("you heard . . . my voice . . . [when] I cried for help" [*šwʿ*]; Potgieter, 160; other uses of portions of Ps. 31 later in Jon. 2 corroborate this claim). Psalm 31 presents the lament of one who trusts in YHWH (Ps. 31:14; see vv. 3, 4, etc.) despite opposition from his enemies (31:4, 8), and like other such psalms, it affirms YHWH's faithfulness (*ḥesed*, 31:16) and goodness (31:19) for "those who fear" YHWH. These contextual elements add irony to the psalm's reuse here, since Jonah's disobedience and willingness to die rather than go to Nineveh prove that he does not fear YHWH while the non-Israelite sailors learn to fear YHWH in mere moments.

Jonah 2:3 and Ps. 42:8. Although several passages are close to Jonah's "all your billows and waves pass over me" (AT; cf. Pss. 18:5–6; 88:7; Mic. 7:9; Sasson, 173–76), Ps. 42:7 offers the only exact parallel (Sasson, 176; Magonet, 44). This quotation is heavy with irony: the psalmist laments the oppression of his God-denying enemies and consequent distance from the Jerusalem temple, while Jonah laments literal waves and billows that pass over him because he has removed himself as far as possible from the temple by attempting to flee a divine commission that might bring YHWH's grace to the nations (cf. 1 Kings 8:41–43; Isa. 56:7).

Jonah 2:4 and various psalms. Shared lexemes and semantics in the first half of Jon. 2:4 ("I said, 'I have been expelled from your sight'" [AT]) lead many to hear an echo of Ps. 31:22 here ("I said, 'I have been cut off from your sight'" [AT]; Magonet, 45; Potgieter, 160; Brenner, 185; Dell, 94). Magonet (45) also points out that the "nevertheless . . ." (*ʾākēn*) in the same verse (MT 31:23) highlights the psalmist's "gratitude to God," while in Jonah a similar word (*ʾak*; MT 2:5) makes Jonah "very firmly the subject of what follows." In another irony, Jonah aligns himself with faithful worshipers who persist in prayer despite being at a great distance from the temple by echoing (if only faintly) other passages in Psalms (cf. Pss. 18:6; 28:2; 134:2; 138:2; Youngblood, 108).

Jonah 2:5 and Ps. 69:2. Of the various texts upon which Jonah might draw here (Sasson, 183, notes Pss. 18:5; 30:3; 69:2; 103:4; Lam. 3:54), Magonet (47) cautiously identifies Ps. 69:2 as most likely in light of the shared phrase "waters . . . my life," while Noegel (247) translates the same phrase as "like a hunger" and connects it to the appetite of Sheol (cf. "belly" in 2:2). The presence of themes like the psalmist's innocence of certain offenses (Ps. 69:4) and guiltiness of others (69:5), his zeal for YHWH's house (69:9), his figurative death by drowning (69:14–15), and the faithful and merciful divine character (69:13, 16) as the only hope of salvation (69:29) arise from the psalm as a whole. These themes contrast its author with Jonah, who never clearly recognizes his sin but celebrates his deliverance from death.

Jonah 2:7 and Ps. 107. The most proximate comparable use of the rare verb "faint" here (*ʿâṭap*; cf. Pss. 61:2 [MT 61:3]; 77:3 [77:4]; 102:1; 107:5; 142:3 [MT 142:4]; 143:4; Lam. 2:11, 12) appears with the same verbal conjugation and verbal object "life" (*nepeš*) in Ps. 107:5 (cf. Brenner, 185; Magonet, 48, argues for Ps. 142:3 or 143:4, noting that the author of Jonah might have replaced "spirit" in those texts, or Ps. 77:3 with "life" given that term's prominence in Jon. 2). If the author has indeed drawn on Ps. 107 here (or vice versa), the psalm's emphasis on YHWH's *ḥesed* (107:1 and passim) in delivering from exile, imprisonment, affliction, and dangers at sea that are broadly attributed to their sin (107:11, 17) is salient and contrasts with Jonah's silence regarding his sin in another example of irony or inversion.

Youngblood (117) sees Jonah's descent toward the land of the dead in Jon. 2:6–7 as "the antithesis of Israel's exodus" (cf. Noegel, 244–48, who argues that the sea is described in primordial terms here). He notes the shared use of "sea" and "reeds" (cf. Exod. 15:4, through which Israel passes safely), "mountain(s)" (Israel will be planted on the "mountain of [YHWH's] inheritance," 15:17), and the "land" promised to Israel (versus the "earth" that swallowed the Egyptians, 15:12). The different referents and semantics of many of these lexemes in their respective contexts make this comparison rather uncertain. In particular, the "Sea of Reeds" is a title, while the connection between "seas" and "reeds" is generic and semantically flexible (Sasson, 185), and YHWH's mountain is Zion, not Sinai.

Jonah 2:8 and Ps. 31:6–7. The rarity of the phrase "regard empty vapor" (i.e., worship idols) makes clear that a lexical link exists between Ps. 31:6 and Jon. 2:8 (Magonet, 45; Youngblood, 112; Potgieter, 159). Sasson (195–96) notes varying levels of correspondence between this verse as a whole and Deut. 32:21; Pss. 16:4; 71:9; Jer. 8:19; Hosea 4:10; and Zech. 10:2. Both Ps. 31 and Jon. 2:8 denounce idolaters, although against Magonet (46), it is unlikely that Jonah is "more tolerant" of such persons than the psalmist. Despite presumably having heard the sailors' remarkable prayer to YHWH, Jonah's reference to them as "those who abandon their mercy" (AT; cf. Deut. 32:21) is both mistaken and an invitation to critique Jonah, who enjoys some measure of mercy but shows no concern for the mariners' physical or spiritual well-being (cf. Ps. 31:7; for a somewhat different interpretation, see Vaillancourt, 183–84).

Jonah 2:9 and Ps. 3:8. Youngblood (114) notes that the rare form used here for "salvation" is used elsewhere only in Pss. 3:2 (MT 3:3); 80:2 (80:3); Isa. 62:1. The general recognition that "salvation belongs to YHWH" echoes Ps. 3:8 and may be a simultaneous reference to Ps. 3:2, 8, or a broad reference to 3:2–8 and its context (Magonet, 49; Wendland, 391). This link to Ps. 3 invites the reader to compare David, who was forced to flee from Absalom during a coup d'état, with Jonah, who chose to flee YHWH's call to prophesy against Nineveh.

Jonah 3:9–10 and Exod. 32:12–14; Jer. 26; 36. The words of Nineveh's ruler in 3:9 that express the hope that God would "turn from his fierce anger" are drawn from Exod. 32:12 and anticipate the fuller quotation of Exod. 34:6–7 in Jon. 4 (Kelly, 826; Wendland, 391; Magonet, 71; Benckhuysen, 22). In Jon. 3:10 the phrase "and God relented . . . to do to them" (AT) is a quotation of Exod. 32:14, modified only slightly by the addition of "He did not do it." These quotations from the Sinai pericope establish an analogy between Israel and Nineveh and identify YHWH's free grace as the basis for the deliverance of both Israel at Sinai and Nineveh in Jonah's day. The divine relenting should be understood in relation to the implicit condition of repentance, which nonetheless does not bind God to respond mercifully (Jon. 3:9; cf. Joel 2:14; Jer. 18:7–8). The episode of Nineveh's repentance and deliverance as a whole reflects the implicit qualification of many prophetic oracles of judgment, although Jonah shows no clear literary dependence on the later formulation of this principle in Jer. 18:7–8 (contra Dell, 91; cf. also Jer. 26:3, 15; Ezek. 18:21–23; Wendland, 391, adds 2 Sam. 12:22).

Jonah 4:2 and Exod. 34:6–7. The quotation of parts of Exod. 34:6–7 by the prophet in Jon. 4:2 is the book's literary and dramatic peak. Jonah prefers death to living in a world where YHWH indiscriminately shares his grace, classically (but not exclusively) shown to Israel at Mount Sinai, with groups that Jonah considers unqualified. This use of Exod. 34:6–7 is notable for being the only text that applies it directly to non-Israelites (Timmer, 122), and so is a striking case of analogy in which YHWH's mercy puts Israel and Nineveh on equal footing. The addition of "relents concerning calamity" (AT) is found elsewhere only in Joel 2 (Kelly, 807; Benckhuysen, 24), but that text's apparently late date makes Jonah's dependence upon it unlikely.

Jonah and the NT

Matthew and Luke see a clear typological relationship between Jonah and Jesus. John Stek (44–45) sees Jesus's death and deliverance as facets of the "sign of Jonah," as do Youngblood (115–17) and Michael Andrews, who broadens the death element to include Jesus's suffering from Gethsemane onward. In Matt. 12:38–42, the sign entails time in Sheol, deliverance from the grave (12:40; Gladd, 45), and Jesus's preaching, which must be met with repentance. Luke 11:29–32 is shorter, but includes Jonah's role as a sign and (perhaps) as a preacher of repentance (Bock, 1095–97). In both Matthew and Luke, the typological relationship between Jesus and Jonah simultaneously contrasts repentant Nineveh with Jesus's unrepentant detractors (Matt. 12:41; Luke 11:32). Mark 4:35–41 establishes a contrastive typological relationship between the disobedient Jonah, who is sleeping when he should not be (Jon. 1:5), and Jesus, whose sleep demonstrates his faith (Gladd, 138).

Jonah's role in the OT as the only prophet sent to the nations makes his unique ministry the first point on a trajectory that runs through the eschatology of the OT and becomes a central theme in the NT, beginning with the arrival of the magi (Matt. 2:1–12) and Simeon's song (Luke 2:32, Luke's first reference to gentiles) and being partially inaugurated in Jesus's occasional ministry in gentile areas (Matt. 8:28–34; 15:21–28 // Mark 7:24–30; cf. Matt. 4:15; Luke 4:24–30). The sign function of Jesus's death and resurrection underlies the apostolic preaching of the gospel (e.g., Acts 3:15; 4:2, 10; 10:38–43; Rom. 1:1–4; 1 Pet. 1:1–4), while the sustained rejection of the apostles' message by many Jews prompts them to turn to the gentiles, blending Jonah typology with the fulfillment of the Isaianic servant's mission to the nations (Acts 13:46–48).

Bibliography. Andrews, M. W., "The Sign of Jonah," *JETS* 61, no. 1 (2018): 105–19; Benckhuysen, A. W., "Revisiting the Psalm of Jonah," *CTJ* 47 (2012): 5–31; Bock, D. L., *Luke 9:51–24:53*, BECNT (Baker Academic, 1996); Bosma, C. J., "Jonah 1:9—An Example of Elenctic Testimony," *CTJ* 48 (2013): 65–90; Brenner, A., "Jonah's Poem out of and within Its Context," in *Among the Prophets*, ed. P. R. Davies and D. J. A. Clines (Sheffield Academic, 1993), 183–92; Craig, K. M., Jr., "Jonah in Recent Research," *CurBS* 7 (1999): 97–118; Dell, K., "Reinventing the Wheel," in *After the Exile*, ed. J. Barton and D. J. Reimer (Mercer University Press, 1996), 85–102; Dempster, S. G., "Torah, Torah, Torah," in *Exploring the Origins of the Bible*, ed. C. A. Evans and E. Tov (Baker Academic, 2008), 87–128; Gladd, B. L., *Handbook on the Gospels* (Baker Academic, 2021); Holm, T. L., "Ancient Near Eastern Literature," in *A Companion to the Ancient Near East*, 2nd ed., ed. D. Snell (Blackwell, 2007), 269–88; Kelly, J. R., "Joel, Jonah, and the YHWH Creed," *JBL* 132 (2013): 805–26; Kim H. C. P., "Jonah Read Intertextually," *JBL* 126 (2007): 497–528; Magonet, J., *Form and Meaning*, BBET (Lang, 1976); Niccacci, A., "Syntactic Analysis of Jonah," *Liber Annus* 46 (1996): 9–32; Noegel, S., "Jonah and Leviathan," *Hen* 37 (2015): 236–60; Potgieter, J. H., "David in Consultation with the Prophets," in *"My Spirit at Rest in the North Country" (Zechariah 6:8)*, ed. H. M. Niemann and M. Augustin, BEATAJ 57 (Lang, 2011), 153–63; Sasson, J. M., *Jonah*, AB (Doubleday, 1990); Shitrit, T., "Aramaic Loanwords and Borrowing," in *Encyclopedia of Hebrew Language and Linguistics*, ed. G. Khan, 4 vols. (Brill, 2013), 1:164–69; Spronk, K., "Jonah, Nahum, and the Book of the Twelve," *JHebS* 9 (2009), https://doi.org/10.5508/jhs.2009.v9.a8; Stead, M. R., *The Intertextuality of Zechariah 1–8*, LHBOTS 506 (T&T Clark, 2009); Stek, J., "The Message of the Book of Jonah," *CTJ* 4 (1969): 23–50; Timmer, D. C., *A Gracious and Compassionate God*, NSBT 26 (Apollos, 2011); Turner, I., "Going Beyond What Is Written or Learning to Read?," *JETS* 61, no. 3 (2018): 577–94; Vaillancourt, I. J., "The Pious Prayer of an Imperfect Prophet," *JESOT* 4, no. 2 (2015): 171–89; Wendland, E., "Text Analysis and the Genre of Jonah (Part 2)," *JETS* 39, no. 3 (1996): 373–95; Wöhrle, J., "A Prophetic Reflection on Divine Forgiveness," *JHebS* 9 (2009), https://doi.org/10.5508/jhs.2009.v9.a7; Wolff, H. W., *Obadiah and Jonah*, CC (Augsburg, 1986); Yates, G., "The 'Weeping Prophet' and 'Pouting Prophet' in Dialogue," *JETS* 59, no. 2 (2016): 223–39; Youngblood, K., *Jonah*, ZECOT (Zondervan, 2013).

DANIEL C. TIMMER

Joshua, Book of

The book of Joshua is named after the leader of Israel and successor of Moses. In Greek his name is identical to the NT name of Jesus. It carries the sense of "the Lord saves" or "the Lord is salvation."

The assurances and promises of the Pentateuch form the context for Joshua. The book describes the realization of the promise of land God gave to Abraham and his successors in Genesis (Gen. 12:1–3, 7; 13:14–17; 15:17–28; 17:8; 22:17; 28:4; 35:12) and onward through the exodus and the subsequent period (Exod. 3:8, 17; 34:24; Lev. 20:24; Num. 14:8; Deut. 6:10; 9:5; 11:9; 26:1–3; 28:52; Josh. 1:2). Joshua is a direct fulfillment of these promises.

The book of Joshua resembles royal land grants of the ancient Near East, especially the West Semitic world of the second millennium BC. As is the case in various grants, a sequence of contents parallels the overall structure of Joshua: encounter with the land (chaps. 1–5); defeat of enemies, especially those in the land (chaps. 6–12); allotment of the land to those loyal to the victor (chaps. 13–21); and a concern about holding the land and passing it on to successors in the future (chaps. 22–24). In this perspective God is the great king and victor, while Joshua and Israel form the vassal recipient(s) of the land grant. God decides to give the land as part of the covenant agreement that Israel enters into before the events of Joshua (Deut. 28). As an indication that this earlier passage remains an abiding authority, Joshua and Israel reaffirm this covenant agreement at the end of the book as Joshua's life draws to a close (Josh. 23–24).

The Crossing (Josh. 1–5)

The key to the success of the granting of the land does not lie in the might or power of Joshua or of his Israelite army. Instead, it lies with the presence of God as part of his covenant response and blessing for his people. This is clear in the opening speech, with which God charges Joshua and all who will follow him (Josh. 1:1–9). Verses 1–2 connect directly with the preceding chapter, Deut. 34, and serve as its fulfillment. Moses's death is recounted. The death creates a power vacuum. However, God's presence continues to protect and guide the people through the appointment of Joshua as leader and full successor to Moses. Verses 2–5 lay out the program that will occupy the book and life of Joshua, so that each verse summarizes and provides a blueprint for the rest of the book: crossing the Jordan and entering the land (v. 2 = chaps. 1–5), acquiring every place toward which Israel moves (v. 3 = chaps. 6–12), detailing the map of the allotted land (v. 4 = chaps. 13–21), and completing the work with covenant renewals and rededications (v. 5 = chaps. 22–24).

Joshua 1:5 doubles as an introduction to the second half of the speech, which exhorts the listeners to faithful obedience and identifies the source of the success they can achieve. Verse 8 is a favorite memory verse that emphasizes keeping the book of the law, meditating on it, and obeying it. However, many overlook the promised presence of God that envelopes this command with two explicit statements in v. 5 ("I will be with you. I will never abandon you") and one explicit statement in v. 9 ("Wherever you go the LORD your God will be with you" [both AT]). Joshua will not succeed because he obeys the book of the law; he will succeed because God is present with him to enable him to obey the book of the law. This is a direct fulfillment of God's promised presence (Exod. 33:14).

God reaches out to Joshua and promises his presence for the success of the mission (Josh. 1:5–9). God exalts Joshua (3:7) just as he did Abram (Gen. 12:2). In a similar manner, the text compares that honoring of Joshua's leadership with the honoring of Moses's leadership (Josh. 4:14). God works through dramatic miracles, especially in his special presence in the ark of the covenant (Exod. 25; 37), typifying God's presence among his people in the OT. The onward movement of the ark, begun when Israel left Sinai (Num. 10:33–36), continues in the opening chapters. As represented by the ark, God leads his people. Neither natural barriers, such as the Jordan River (Josh. 3–4), nor human constructions, such as Jericho (chap. 6), can obstruct the onward movement of God and his people. This continues until the ark reaches its goal and final resting place in Jerusalem (2 Sam. 6; 1 Chron. 15) and in the temple (1 Kings 8; 2 Chron. 5). The presence of God, with redeeming love and holiness, extends beyond Israel to include others. Most of all, Rahab represents a faithful Canaanite who believes in God. In one of the most profound confessions of faith in the OT (Josh. 2:9–11), Rahab asserts her belief in Israel's God. She begins with "I know." This contrasts ironically with the repeated "I don't know" in vv. 4, 5. What she denies to the agents of Jericho's king contrasts with what she openly proclaims to the representatives of Israel and Israel's God. Rahab separates from the Canaanites and identifies with the Israelites. The confession forms a concentric structure:

A The LORD has given you this land
  B and . . . a great fear of you has fallen on us . . .
    C All who live in this country are melting in fear because of you.
      D We have heard . . .
        E the LORD dried up the water of the Red Sea . . .
        E′ what you did to Sihon and Og . . .
      D′ When we heard of it,
    C′ our hearts melted in fear
  B′ and everyone's courage failed because of you,
A′ for the LORD your God is God in heaven above and on the earth below. (Josh 2:9–11)

The first and last lines confess God's power over creation and his ability to give the land to Israel (cf. Gen. 1; Pss. 24:1; 50:10–12; Isa. 40:10, 12–15, 21–28; Job 38–41). As lines B and C (and B′ and C′) describe the fear God's acts have instilled in the Canaanites, the reader finds that Rahab's words establish a direct fulfillment of the prophecy of Exod. 15:15–16, a prophecy given in the Song of the Sea at the time of Israel's crossing of the Red Sea in the exodus. In the center is the confession of God's historic acts of redemption on behalf of his people. The exodus (Exod. 14–15) at the birth of Israel and the defeat of Sihon and Og (Num. 21; Deut. 3) as the latest event of God's salvation of his people form the paradigmatic events of salvation and preservation. They are types of the manner in which God works.

As a type of the new believer, Rahab participates in the Passover celebration that Israel celebrates (Josh. 5). Along with the Feast of Unleavened Bread (celebrated with the seven-day event of a daily journey around Jericho), Rahab fulfills the salvation event commanded in Exod. 12:1–11, 43. Rahab, unable to join Israel at that point, nevertheless opens her window and faces away from Canaanite Jericho and toward incoming Israel (Josh. 2:18–19). The scarlet cord alludes to the blood spread over the door, and the gathering of the family recalls another part of this family-oriented feast.

The sovereign presence of God continues with the crossing of the Jordan River, where the ark guarantees that the waters will be held back and that Israel will cross on dry ground (Josh. 3–4). God does "amazing things" (3:5), the same term that describes the plagues that he sent against Egypt (Exod. 3:20). The "living God" is one who elsewhere (Ps. 84:2; Hosea 1:10) is close to his people and performs great acts for them. God causes the waters to pile up in a "heap," an antitype to the Red Sea crossing (Exod. 15:8; Ps. 78:13). The statement that "all Israel passed by" (Josh. 3:17) fulfills the divine word of 1:2, where the key verb "pass by" (used twenty-one times in Josh. 3:1–5:1) occurs. The pile of stones forms the "memorial" of the crossing (Josh. 4:6–7) as a symbol for future generations. It recalls the "memorials" of the exodus and Passover (Exod. 12:14; 13:9), of the first military victory against Amalek (Exod. 17:14), and of special feasts and offerings (Lev. 23:24; Num. 5:15, 18; 10:10; 31:54). It is the first of seven stone memorials erected in the promised land (Josh. 7:26; 8:28–29, 32; 10:27; 22:34; 24:26; 1 Sam. 7:12). God exalts Joshua for following his word (Josh. 4:13–14). God's purpose for this miracle reaches beyond Israel as a fulfillment to grant revelation of himself to all the nations of the earth (Josh. 4:24), fulfilling Abraham's call to bless all peoples (Gen. 12:1–3) and realizing the role of Israel as a royal priesthood for everyone in the world (Exod. 19:6). The crossing of the Jordan moves the ark closer to where it will reside in the later temple of Solomon to which all nations might look to find answers by prayer (1 Kings 8:41–43; Isa. 56:7; Matt. 21:13; Luke 19:46) and to which all peoples might come to learn of God (Isa. 2:1–4; Mic. 4:1–5).

Circumcision (Josh. 5:2–12), the great symbol of God's covenant with his people (Gen. 17:8–13), must precede the central celebration of the covenant, Passover (Exod. 12:48). In an example of irony, if the earlier generation "died" (Heb. root *tmm*) in disobedience, this generation "completes" (Heb. root *tmm*) circumcision in obedience (Josh. 5:5–8). God stops giving the manna (Exod. 16:31–34), which was to teach Israel to rely on him (Deut. 8:3, 16; Matt. 4:1–4), when Israel enters the land, where the food of the barley harvest becomes available (Josh. 5:11–12; 24:13), fulfilling the assurance of the richness of the promised land (Deut. 6:10–11). This will become the food for the Feast of Unleavened Bread, celebrated during the seven days that Israel marches around Jericho (5:10).

The Battles (Josh. 6–12)

God's sovereignty ensures that the Israelites defeat Jericho and Ai (Josh. 6; 8), destroy the southern coalition and its towns and villages (chap. 10), and defeat the northern coalition, with its forces led by the general of Hazor (chap. 11). In the midst of these events God renews his covenant with Israel (8:30–35), analogous to the renewal at the end of the book (chaps. 23–24). Whoever violates the covenant is punished in the harshest manner (7:11–15; 23:16). However, divine covenant mercy and love deliver Rahab from doomed Jericho. So important is the concern for the salvation of Rahab and her family that Josh. 6:16–25 devotes nearly as many Hebrew words (86) as are used to describe the defeat and destruction of Jericho (102). The seven-day march not only corresponds to the seven days of Unleavened Bread but also, like other "seventh" occurrences, describes a special event that God brings to a conclusion (Gen. 7:4, 10; Exod. 7:25; 29:37; 1 Sam. 13:8; 1 Kings 8:65; 2 Chron. 30:22–23; Neh. 8:18). Compare the seven priests and seven trumpets (Josh. 6:4, 13, 15, 16).

The battles, like what has preceded (Josh. 1:2; 2:8–11; 5:1), are the work of God (6:2; cf. the assurances of Pss. 18:43; 54:7; 56:13; 71:23; 86:13; 116:8). The loud noise of the horns (Josh. 6:4–5) accompanies processions of the ark and of Israel (Num. 10:2–6; 2 Sam. 6:15–16). The devotion to God of all Jericho (Josh. 6:17), as Israel did to the armies of Sihon and Og (Num. 21:2–4; Deut. 2:34; 3:6; Josh. 2:10), directly fulfills the commands of what Israel was to do to the sinful Canaanites in order to prevent them from seducing God's people to worship their deities (Gen. 15:16; Deut. 20:17–18). The curse on any who later inhabit the destroyed site (Josh. 6:26) applies an earlier command concerning any place where other gods are worshiped (Deut. 13:16; cf. 1 Kings 16:34). The plunder that is not destroyed goes to God, according to Joshua's command (Josh. 6:18), foreshadowing the revelation of Achan's sin in the next chapter.

Achan's sin as a departure from the covenant (Josh. 7) ironically contrasts with Rahab's entering into the covenant with God's people (Josh. 2; 6). The long genealogy of Achan (7:1), the longest in the book of Joshua, connects him and his sin with all of Israel. In another irony, the loss of thirty-six of the force sent to Ai (7:5) indicates God is not with Israel and leads to a reaction of melting in fear—a reversal of the effect Israel had on the Canaanites (2:11; 5:1).

God is gracious and compassionate (Exod. 34:6–7) not only in saving Rahab (Josh. 2; 6) but also in protecting Israel against Canaanite armies (chaps. 6–11), in providing allotments for Caleb and Joshua (14:6–15; 19:49–51) and for all Israel, in granting extra land for Israel to clear (17:14–18), in providing safety for the unintentional killer (chap. 20), and in providing cities and towns for the Levites (chap. 21). Joshua's challenge that foreigners would wipe out Israel's name and challenge God's own great name echoes Moses (Exod. 32:9–14; Num. 14:13–16; Deut. 9:28–29). The same verb with which God describes Israel's sin here (Josh. 7:11) ironically alludes to in the crossing of the Jordan (1:2) and in the crossing against Jericho (6:7). Israel would not witness the further miracle of crossing against Ai, because it had crossed against God. The sin of one affects all in many different areas. The "devoted things" from Jericho belonged to God (6:18–19, 24). Because Israel stole these things, God would treat Israel as "devoted things." In another irony, as Israel devoted Jericho to fire, so the one who did these sinful acts would be destroyed by fire (6:24–26; 7:15). Although the name Achan has no etymology in Hebrew, "Achor" in the Valley of Achor refers to "trouble" and is used as a nickname. So, Achan is called Achor in 1 Chron. 2:8 and in the LXX account of Josh. 7, in fulfillment of who Achan became.

The destruction of Ai (Josh. 8) begins with divine direction (unlike chap. 7) and the concern not to be afraid or discouraged. The first part of God's charge in Josh. 8:1 is a repeated charge to Joshua in Josh. 1:5–9, here used again in an analogous situation. The expression also occurs in 1 Chron. 22:13; 28:20, where David charges his son Solomon to undertake the task of building the temple. Here as well God's chosen leader faces a great test. The ruse tactic that Joshua uses against Ai is analogous to the deception that the tribes of Israel use against Gibeon in Judg. 20, where, as with Ai, they succeed after initial failures. Following the account of the victory, the Hebrew text records a covenant renewal (Josh. 8:30–35). Israel erects an altar on Mount Ebal where offerings are given (8:30–32 directly fulfills Deut. 27:4–8). Half of Israel stands at Mount Gerizim, and half at Mount Ebal to the south (Josh. 8:33, again fulfilling Deut. 27:12–13).

Due to Achan's sin and its consequences, the kings of Canaan no longer fear Israel, because they know Israel can be defeated (contrast Josh. 5:1 with 9:1–2). They gather together to attack the Israelites (9:1–2). The Gibeonites, however, fear Israel and try to make a treaty with them. Despite their deception (9:4), the Gibeonites follow Rahab in making a confession regarding Israel's God and his acts of salvation against Egypt and Sihon and Og (9:9–10; cf. 2:9–11). The oath sworn before God has abiding authority (9:15, 19; cf. Gen. 26:26–31; Exod. 20:7; Lev. 19:12; Deut. 5:11; 1 Sam. 14:24; 20:8; Ezek. 16:59–60). The designation of the Gibeonites as woodcutters and water carriers (Josh. 9:21–23) fulfills the command of how non-Israelites will live in the promised land (Deut. 29:11).

As the southern coalition gathers against Gibeon and the latter calls Israel for aid, God alludes to and repeats his promises that he has given Israel the victory and therefore they need not fear to go to war (Josh. 10:8; cf. 1:2, 5–9; 6:2; 8:1). In 10:16–27 the central part of the conflict and victory is recalled. Joshua and Israel defeat and kill those who led their armies to fight against Gibeon and Israel. The Israelites place their feet on the necks of the Canaanite kings as a symbol of the latter's defeat (Ps. 110:1). The repeated attack and destruction of fortified centers throughout the south directly fulfill the commands of Deut. 20:16–18, which specify that the population centers must be destroyed.

Joshua 11 turns to the northern coalition, led by Jabin of Hazor, who perhaps reflects a dynastic name related to the Jabin of Hazor of Judg. 4–5, where Deborah and Barak will again bring Israel victory. Horses and chariots occupy the center of the northern army (Josh. 11:4). These are the most sophisticated weapons of the age, symbolizing military power and guaranteeing success (Exod. 14:9, 23; Deut. 11:4; 20:1; 1 Kings 20:1, 21). Accompanied by an army like the sand on the seashore (Josh. 11:4; cf. Gen. 22:17; 1 Sam. 13:5), this assured victory ironically becomes a defeat (again, cf. Exod. 14–15). The section on battles concludes with a list of the peoples and towns that God gives to his people, typifying all the land they will occupy (Josh. 13–21).

The Allotment (Josh. 13–21)

A large part of the book concerns the allotment of the promised land through its mapping and distribution (Josh. 13–21). This unique, material expression of the covenant provides a physical connection between each Israelite and God, in every place they might live in that land. It directly fulfills the general promise of Gen. 12:7; 13:14–17.

The text begins with a notice that Joshua has grown old ("old and advancing in years," Josh. 13:1 AT), an expression repeated in 23:1. It occurs elsewhere only of Abraham and Sarah in Gen. 18:11, of Abraham in 24:1, and of Solomon in 1 Kings 1:1. In every case the individual faces a great task. Sarah will give birth to an heir. Abraham will find a wife for his son, Isaac. David will appoint his son Solomon as his successor. In Josh. 13, Joshua begins to allocate the lands to the various tribes. In Josh. 23, he renews the covenant with God and calls all Israel to follow God.

Chapter 13 fulfills the description of the land of Canaan to be given (as in Josh. 1:4) before it outlines the direct fulfillment of the allotment of the land east of the Jordan River (13:8–33) that was given by Moses to the tribes of Reuben and Gad and half of Manasseh (Num. 32:33–42; Deut. 3:8–17). The land west of the Jordan has not yet been allotted.

Joshua 14 reviews the allotment and then describes Caleb's allotment. Like Joshua, Caleb had believed God had given Israel the land (Num. 13:30; 14:24, 30, 38; 26:65; 32:12). His allotment in the tribe of Judah at Hebron and the allotment of Joshua (Josh. 19:49–50) frame the tribal lands on the west side of the Jordan River. Only Joshua and Caleb are types of those who follow the Lord with a whole heart (Num. 32:12; Deut. 1:36; Josh. 14:8, 9, 14).

As with the tribes east of the Jordan River, the general sequence of allotments for those west of the Jordan River moves from south to north. The allotment in the south thus begins with Judah, whose preeminence analogically occurs in Numbers (2:9; 10:14) and Judges (1:1–2; 20:18). The story of Aksah, daughter of Caleb, who approaches her father, requests something from him, and receives it, analogically recalls the experience of Rebekah (Gen. 21:61–67), and has further allusion to the inheritance rights obtained from Moses by the daughters of Zelophehad (Num. 27:1–11; 36:1–13; Josh. 17:3–6). Aksah is the wife of Othniel, who becomes the first judge (Judg. 3:7–11). This couple thus provides a faithful link between the generation of Joshua and those of the judges.

Chapters 16–17 outline the allotments of Ephraim and Manasseh, the two tribes who are sons of Joseph (Gen. 48:14, 19) and thus typify the special role of Rachel. These settlements in the central hill country will form the center of the Northern Kingdom of Israel. The blessing of these two tribes is illustrated by their larger size, where Manasseh alone covers both sides of the Jordan River, and by the needed expansion of Manasseh in the virgin highlands of the central hill country (Josh. 17:14–18). The story of Zelophehad's daughters (17:3–6) and their inheritance directly fulfills Moses's works and demonstrates the exceptional grace of Moses allowing the daughters to inherit the land (Num. 27:1–11; 36:1–13).

The remaining tribes are allotted in Josh. 19. This chapter follows a lengthy description of Benjamin (18:11–28), the other Rachel tribe blessed to become part of Judah and the Southern Kingdom. The mention of the resettlement of the Danite territory in the town of Dan (north of the Sea of Galilee, Josh. 19:47) anticipates Judg. 18 and the story of the brutal conquest of that town as well as the installation of an illicit priest and religious cult there. Both the resettlement and the fact that Dan is the last tribe to receive an allotment serve both as an analogy of the negative evaluation of that tribe's false religious practices later and as a fulfillment of Gen. 49:17 and Deut. 33:22.

Joshua 20 precisely fulfills the promised cities of refuge, towns east and west of the Jordan River to which a citizen who accidentally kills another Israelite can find refuge from the vendetta of the dead person's family (cf. Exod. 21:12–14; Num. 35:6–34; Deut. 4:41–43). In contrast to other cultures, where the killer was forced to flee the country, these cities of refuge enable the faithful Israelite caught up in such a tragedy to remain in the land that God has given as part of the covenant and to continue as a member of God's people.

The Levitical towns of Josh. 21 provide homes for the Levites, the tribe that typifies the firstborn of all Israel given back to God (Num. 3:41, 45; 8:18). They have no land allotted to them but are an analogy to the firstfruits of the land (Exod. 23:19; Num. 28:26; Deut. 26:2, 10), a token of which is returned to God to acknowledge the whole of the harvest as his gift. Scattered across the promised land and often located near Canaanite strongholds, these towns will fulfill their purpose as centers from which the Levites can teach concerning God's word and faith (Lev. 10:11). The allotments thus conclude with a gift back to God of these towns as a token of all the land he has given to Israel.

The Covenant Renewal (Josh. 22–24)

Quoting a great deal from Deuteronomy as now fulfilled, Joshua renews the covenant with Israel in chap. 23 and again in 24:1–28. These "last words" express what the "servant of the LORD" (24:29) considers most important for the people to hear. They provide an analogy to the final testimonies of Jacob (Gen. 48–49), Joseph (Gen. 50:22–26), Moses (Deut. 1–33), and later David (1 Kings 2:1–9).

The final notes of Josh. 24:29–33 record the burial of Joshua as a direct fulfillment of the promise that the generation of God's people who went down to Egypt would anticipate this generation, which has now returned and inherited the promised land (Gen. 50:24; Exod. 13:19). While Joshua's death and burial (Josh. 24:29–30) bring this generation of Israel to an end, the notices of the high priest Eleazar's death and the succession by his heroic son Phinehas (Exod. 6:23, 25; 29:9; Num. 25:1–11) provide hope that something of the godly influence of Joshua and Eleazar will continue into the following generations.

Allusions in the New Testament

Matthew 28:18–20 analogically applies the importance of the presence of God to Joshua's mission in Josh. 1:5-9. There Jesus sends forth his disciples, commanding them to baptize and to teach others to obey God's law, with the promise of Jesus's presence as the means to achieve success in the mission.

Rahab's confession of God's works in Josh. 2:9–11, and of the exodus specifically, provides a type of the one who confesses the great act of salvation in the NT, that of Jesus's death and resurrection. Like Rom. 10:9, confession and belief in what God has done form the basis for salvation. God does not change in his purpose. Rahab finds salvation, and her confession serves analogically as a model for future generations. She becomes a member of Hebrews' hall of fame (Heb. 11:31), and the demonstration of her righteousness in hiding the spies is recalled in James 2:25.

The battles of Israel in Joshua form a type of the Christian's life where the believer is called to believe and to enter into the victory (Rom. 8:37; Eph. 2:8–9).

In terms of allotments, Judah's first place has been noted. Further, Judah's presentation of the most complete and detailed boundary description of any tribe, followed by the longest list of towns (subdivided by region, Josh. 15:20–63), points to a special recognition of Judah that anticipates how from it would come the line of David and of Jesus Christ (Mic. 5:2; Matt. 1–2). If the Levitical cities provided the special servants of God as a place from which to teach the covenant, the role of the Levites to live out and to instruct in God's law also shows a type of the disciples and pastors who would teach the new covenant (Acts 2:44–47; Rom. 15:26–27; Phil. 4:10–18).

The tribes east of the Jordan are the first group singled out for a special assertion of loyalty in Josh. 1:12–18 and become the first to receive their allotment (chap. 13). In chap. 22 they are the last group singled out to distinguish (1) what was essential to God, the unity of the people and their worship at an altar in the promised land; and (2) what was unessential, living west of the Jordan River. They provide an analogy to the call for Christians to distinguish what is central to discipleship and what is peripheral (e.g., 1 Cor. 3; 8; 2 Cor. 6:14-18; 2 John 7-11).

The record of the last words of Joshua (24:2–27), as a summary of what is closest to the heart of this "Jesus" of the OT, provides a model and anticipates both Simeon's words over the infant Jesus (Luke 2:25-35) and the words of Jesus before his death (especially John 14–17).

Bibliography. Brueggemann, W. A., *The Land*, OBT (Fortress, 2002); Earl, D. S., *Reading Joshua as Christian Scripture*, JTISup 2 (Eisenbrauns, 2010); Hess, R. S., "Introduction to Joshua and Notes," in *NIV Biblical Theology Study Bible*, ed. D. A. Carson et al. (Zondervan, 2018), 345–83; Hess, *Joshua*, TOTC 6 (IVP Academic, 2008); Wright, C. J. H., *Walking in the Ways of the Lord* (Apollos, 1995).

RICHARD S. HESS

Jude and the Second Letter of Peter

Second Peter and Jude present a fascinating case study in the way that NT authors draw upon the OT, for at least three reasons (cf. Carson, 1047). First, the obvious overlap between these two letters indicates that either (1) 2 Peter borrows from Jude, (2) Jude borrows from 2 Peter, or (3) both borrow from a common source. Although the prevailing view among scholars is the first option, none of the conclusions in this essay depend on a particular conclusion. But the overlap does raise the question of the extent to which both authors share the same approach to engaging OT texts. Second, both Jude and (to a lesser degree) 2 Peter display an awareness of Second Temple Jewish literature that shows up not only in direct references to such literature but also potentially in the way that these authors interpret OT texts. Indeed, some contend that 2 Peter and Jude's interpretations of OT texts are so mediated through those Second Temple Jewish texts and traditions that how those texts interpret the OT is simply adopted by 2 Peter and Jude. But, as D. A. Carson observes, clear dependence is often difficult to demonstrate conclusively (1047). Third, both 2 Peter and Jude regularly refer to OT people and events in ways that make it difficult to pinpoint a particular passage or in a manner that assumes the reader's preexisting knowledge of that person or event. As a result, it can be difficult to determine the OT text form these NT authors use.

Broadly speaking, 2 Peter and Jude use the OT in connection with three theological themes: the Word of God, God's judgment on his enemies and salvation of his people, and the return of Christ to consummate a new creation.

The Word of God

In 2 Peter, the apostle uses several OT echoes to illustrate the nature of Scripture (i.e., "prophetic message," 1:19). By calling it "a light shining in a dark place" (1:19), Peter echoes texts in Psalms that portray God's Word as "giving light to the eyes" (19:8) and a "lamp for my feet, a light to my path" (119:105). Psalm 119:130 is especially pertinent: "The unfolding of your words gives light; it gives understanding to the simple." The light of God's prophetic word will continue to shine in this dark world "until the day dawns and the morning star rises in your hearts" (2 Pet. 1:19). Peter uses the OT symbol of the dawning of the day as a metaphor for the arrival of God's eschatological acts (Isa. 9:2; Mal. 4:2; Luke 1:78–79) and the comfort it will bring to God's people (Pss. 37:6; 46:5; 130:6). Thus, when Christ the "morning star" (in fulfillment of Num. 24:17–19; see below) returns, it will signal the arrival of God's climactic eschatological act and bring true comfort to his people.

God's word is also the means by which he created and judged the world. The assertion that "by God's word . . . the earth was formed out of water and by water" (2 Pet. 3:5) is a clear allusion to Gen. 1:9–10 (cf. Pss. 24:2; 102:25), where God commands the waters under the sky to be gathered in one place so that the dry ground (which he calls earth) can appear. This same combination of God's word and water was also the means of judgment when "the world of that time was deluged and destroyed" (2 Pet. 3:6), an obvious allusion to the flood account of Gen. 6–8. Peter sees in the flood a pattern of final judgment when he asserts that "by the same word the present heavens and earth are reserved for fire, being kept for the day of judgment and destruction of the ungodly" (2 Pet. 3:7). Since God had promised never to destroy the earth again through a flood (Gen 9:11), the final judgment on this present creation will come through fire. Yet even with this difference, Peter clearly sees the flood as a historical event designed by God (i.e., a type) to anticipate the far greater reality of final judgment (i.e., antitype), and a key point of continuity between the type and antitype is the power and authority of God's word.

Judgment and Salvation

Although they use different OT examples, both 2 Peter and Jude make significant claims about Jesus's identity as a starting point for their warnings about the certainty of God's severe judgment on his enemies. Peter authenticates his eyewitness status by briefly recounting the transfiguration, specifically noting the Father's affirmation, "This is my Son, whom I love; with him I am well pleased" (2 Pet. 1:17). In these words Peter identifies Jesus as the fulfillment of three OT figures. As the Son of God he is the promised Davidic king foretold in Ps. 2:7. Referring to him as the Son whom the Father loves identifies him with Isaac (Gen. 22:2, 12, 16), portraying Jesus as the sacrifice provided by the Father. Lastly, Jesus is the Isaianic servant (Isa. 42:1), the one with whom God is well pleased because he embodies what Israel was called to be but never was. By referring to Jesus as the "morning star" just a few verses later (2 Pet. 1:19), Peter has in view Balaam's prophecy that a star that will come out of Jacob to rule the nations (Num. 24:17–19), which Peter envisions happening when Christ returns. Peter uses this mixture of direct promise fulfillment and indirect typological fulfillment to present Jesus as the fulfillment of the OT hope.

By contrast, Jude uses the exodus as his starting point but does so in a provocative manner. Regardless of whether the text originally read "Jesus" (NA[28]) or "Lord" (NA[27], which in the context is still a reference to Jesus), Jude's larger point stands unaffected: it was the Lord Jesus who "delivered his people out of Egypt, but later destroyed those who did not believe" (Jude 5). Like many other biblical authors before him, Jude sees the exodus as a type of the redemption accomplished by Jesus. But in line with 1 Cor. 10:1–13 and Heb. 3:7–13, Jude warns that just as the Lord judged the Israelites who did not persevere in faith, so too the Lord Jesus will destroy those who fall away from "the faith that was once for all entrusted to God's holy people" (Jude 3). Likely drawing upon the events of Num. 13–14 (Schreiner, 446), Jude sees a typological connection between the Israelites and believers with an escalation of the severity of judgment in light of the greater redemption that believers have experienced.

Shared Allusions. From these respective starting points, 2 Peter and Jude enumerate a series of shared OT allusions as a warning of the judgment that will come upon false teachers and those who follow them in their rejection of the gospel and its moral entailments. They draw upon Gen. 6:1–4 (as well as Jewish interpretations of this passage; see, e.g., Jub. 4:15–5:9; T. Reu. 5:6–7; T. Naph. 3:5) to depict the angels who transgressed their appointed boundaries and were consigned to the gloomy darkness until judgment day as a picture of what awaits the licentious false teachers (2 Pet. 2:4; Jude 6). While Jude is more specific about the nature of their sin than 2 Peter, both authors arrive at the same conclusion regarding God's judgment for their sin. God's judgment on Sodom and Gomorrah (Gen. 18–19) is the second shared allusion (2 Pet. 2:6-8; Jude 7); both 2 Peter and Jude see in their fiery judgment a picture of the eternal judgment that will come on all the ungodly. As in the first allusion, Jude is more specific about the sin in view ("sexual immorality and perversion") than 2 Peter ("depraved conduct," 2:7). But more significantly, 2 Peter interweaves an additional allusion of righteous Lot being rescued from that judgment (see below). The third shared allusion is the prophet Balaam, whom the Moabite king Balak solicited to curse Israel (Num. 22–24). Following the lead of several OT texts that present Balaam as an example of those who put stumbling blocks before God's people (Deut. 23:5–6; Josh. 13:22; 24:9; Neh. 13:2; Mic. 6:5; cf. Rev. 2:14), both Jude and 2 Peter see the greed that motivated Balaam's actions as analogous to the pursuit of financial gain that drives the false teachers (2 Pet. 2:15–16; Jude 11). Here again, 2 Peter provides more detail, noting not only Balaam's greed but also God's rebuke of the false prophet through a speechless donkey. Determining whether these allusions are simply analogies used to emphasize a universal point (i.e., God's certain judgment on those who rebel against him) or installments in a typological pattern that will culminate in God's eschatological judgment on the last day is difficult.

Unique to 2 Peter. Following the sequence of Genesis, 2 Peter moves from rebellious angels to a general allusion to the flood (Gen. 6–9). Second Peter sees in the flood a picture of both judgment on the ancient world and deliverance for Noah ("a preacher of righteousness") and his family (2 Pet. 2:5). Given that Peter later uses the flood as a type of the final judgment coming on the present world (3:6), it seems likely that it is also an installation in a typological pattern. As noted above, in addition to sharing the use of God's judgment on Sodom and Gomorrah with Jude, 2 Pet. 2:7–8 also incorporates the rescue of righteous Lot (Gen. 19:1–22), "who was distressed by the depraved conduct of the lawless" and "was tormented in his righteous soul by the lawless deeds he saw and heard." Peter interweaves these types of judgment and salvation to prove his claim that "the Lord knows how to rescue the godly from trials and to hold the unrighteous for punishment on the day of judgment" (2:9). For Peter, this typological pattern of God rescuing the righteous from trials while keeping the unrighteous under punishment for judgment anticipates the last day, when God brings final judgment on his enemies and consummates the salvation of his people in a new creation (3:10–13). That final judgment is further described in fiery terms, which likely echoes the similar destruction of Sodom and Gomorrah (2:6) as well as later OT texts that also echo or allude to Gen. 19:24 (e.g., Ezek. 38:22; cf. Rev. 20:9–15). As with the flood, God's fiery judgment on Sodom and Gomorrah is a type of final judgment. Peter describes those who depart from the true gospel as an illustration of Prov. 26:11 when he compares them to dogs who return to their vomit (2 Pet. 2:20). As a result, their final state is worse than before they claimed to know Jesus (2 Pet. 2:21).

Unique to Jude. Jude uses three distinct OT allusions to describe the false teachers. The first is related to Jewish traditions surrounding Moses's death (Deut. 34) reflected in Testament of Moses (Bauckham, 65–76), which recounts a dispute between the archangel Michael and Satan over the body of Moses. Rather than rebuke Satan based on his own authority, Michael simply says, "The Lord rebuke you!" (Jude 9). Zechariah 3:2 uses an almost identical phrase when Yahweh rebukes Satan for his accusations against Joshua the high priest. Jude's logic appears to be that "unlike Michael, the false teachers assumed for themselves the authority to make blasphemous judgments about angelic beings. If someone as powerful and holy as the archangel Michael declined to make a charge that was clearly correct, how much more restraint should mere humans exercise in rendering judgments against angelic beings they barely understand?" (Harmon, "Jude," 513–14). The accusation that the false teachers "have taken the way of Cain" (Jude 11) is the second unique allusion. This may be a general allusion to Cain's hatred for and murder of his brother Abel (Gen. 4:1–16), but Jewish literature also attributed to him greed, violence, lust, and, perhaps most relevant for Jude, the leading of people into wickedness (Jub. 4:31; T. Benj. 7:1–5; Apoc. Ab. 24:3–5; Apoc. Mos. 2:1–4; 3:1–3; 40:4–5; 1 En. 22:7; see Bauckham, 79–80). Elsewhere in the NT Cain is remembered as a murderer and serves as an example of the hatred that leads to murder (1 John 3:12). Jude's familiarity with Jewish tradition may suggest he sees Cain as an analogy of the false teachers, whose immorality extends beyond general wickedness to leading others astray. In his final distinctive allusion, Jude links the false teachers with those who "have been destroyed in Korah's rebellion" (Jude 11). This broad allusion assumes the reader is familiar with the story found in Num. 16, where Korah leads a rebellion against Moses's leadership. Yahweh judges not only Korah and his followers by causing the ground to open and swallow them alive but also those who grumbled that the judgment was too severe by sending a plague upon them. Later Jewish literature portrayed Korah as "the classic example of the antinomian heretic" (Bauckham, 83). Jude sees the false teachers as modern-day Korahs, undermining the leadership of God's people and thus destined for destruction. These OT allusions serve as analogies to depict Jude's opponents in light of notorious OT figures.

In his poetic description of the false teachers Jude uses language that may echo OT texts. Referring to them as "shepherds who feed only themselves" (Jude 12) may recall Ezek. 34:1–8, where Yahweh condemns Israel's leaders for their exploitation of the people. Jude 12 refers to the false teachers as "clouds without rain," a potential echo of Prov. 25:14, which asserts, "Like clouds and wind without rain is one who boasts of gifts never given." The false teachers may give the appearance of offering the life-giving sustenance of the living water of the gospel, but in reality their promises are empty. Jude then switches metaphors: the false teachers are also "wild waves of the sea, foaming up their shame" (Jude 13). Isaiah 57:20 similarly describes the wicked as "like the tossing sea, which cannot rest, whose waves cast up mire and mud." Just as waves dredge filth from the bottom of the sea and toss it to the surface, so the ungodliness of the false teachers overflows for others to see. Describing the false teachers as "wandering stars" (Jude 13) may be an ironic echo of Dan. 12:3, which refers to resurrected saints as shining "like the stars forever and ever." Jude 16 also refers to the opponents as "grumblers," which in light of the reference to the exodus (Jude 5) and use of similar language elsewhere in the NT may allude to Israel's grumbling in the wilderness (e.g., Exod. 16). The faintness of such potential echoes (with perhaps the exception of Ezek. 34:1–8) makes it difficult to know whether Jude has specific OT texts in view or is merely drawing upon stock-in-trade biblical imagery.

A brief word must also be said regarding Jude's citation of 1 En. 1:9. By introducing Enoch as "the seventh from Adam" (Jude 14) he alludes to Gen. 5:21–24, which describes Enoch (in the seventh generation from Adam) being taken up into heaven by God because he walked with God. As a result, Jewish literature portrayed Enoch as a recipient of heavenly visions and revelations, recorded in a series of books named after him. The specific language of 1 En. 1:9 quoted in Jude 14–15 likely borrows language from Deut. 33:2 ("The LORD came from Sinai . . . with ten thousand holy ones" [CSB]) and perhaps Dan. 7:9–10 ("The Ancient of Days took his seat. . . . Thousands upon thousands attended him; ten thousand times ten thousand stood before him"). The fact that Jude sees in 1 En. 1:9 a genuine prophecy does not entail that he regarded the entirety of 1 Enoch as inspired, authoritative, canonical Scripture (Moo, 271–74; Schreiner, 566–69). Jude uses this text to reinforce the certainty of God's coming judgment on those who, like the false teachers, lead God's people astray through their heterodoxy and heteropraxy.

The Return of Christ and the New Creation

Although Christ's return is mentioned in Jude (vv. 14–15, 21, 24–25), it is far more prominent in 2 Peter. In response to false teachers scoffing at the promise of Christ's return (2 Pet. 3:3–4), Peter draws on several OT texts to reassure believers that God will in fact keep his promises. Peter draws language from Ps. 90:4 as an abiding authority to establish the validity of his claim that "with the Lord a day is like a thousand years, and a thousand years are like a day" (2 Pet. 3:8). Just as Yahweh commanded Habakkuk to wait for the eschatological fulfillment of his promises even "if it seems slow" (Hab. 2:3 ESV), so too Peter reminds believers that "the Lord is not slow in keeping his promise, as some understand slowness. Instead he is patient with you, not wanting anyone to perish, but everyone to come to repentance" (2 Pet. 3:9). Likely drawing on Jewish tradition, Peter ties the timing of the last day with the repentance of God's people (Bauckham, 312–13). But believers can hasten the coming day of God (3:12), language that may be drawn from Isa. 60:22, where in reference to the consummation of his promises Yahweh says "in its time I will hasten it" (ESV). In light of Isa. 60:22, some Jewish texts (Sir. 36:8; 2 Bar. 20:1–2; 54:1; 83:1) speak of God hastening the end, sometimes in connection with Israel's repentance (Carson, 1059–60).

Peter's description of the consummation depends largely on several texts from Isaiah. Based on God's promise that believers "are looking forward to a new heaven and a new earth, where righteousness dwells" (2 Pet. 3:13). Peter reaffirms the certain fulfillment of Yahweh's promise in Isa. 65:17 that he "will create new heavens and a new earth," though the promise of new creation in Isaiah goes well beyond this specific text (cf. 43:16–21; 51:3; 66:22). Describing this new creation as a place "where righteousness dwells" may further draw language from Isa. 32:16 ("The LORD's justice will dwell in the desert, his righteousness live in the fertile field") and 60:21 ("Then all your people will be righteous and they will possess the land forever"). Peter draws on these OT texts to reassure believers that God will keep his promises and motivate them to pursue lives of righteousness as they await the consummation (2 Pet. 3:11–13).

Conclusion

The frequently allusive manner in which 2 Peter and Jude use the OT assumes the reader is so familiar with those OT persons and events that even a name or a brief phrase is enough to evoke the entire OT context of that reference. Indeed, perhaps the most striking feature of their use of the OT is that, despite the large number of allusions and potential echoes, there are very few, if any, direct and obvious citations (depending, of course, on how one defines citation). The primary way both authors use the OT is a blend of analogies and typology, with the line between those categories not always clear. Their poetic descriptions of false teachers draw stock-in-trade language from the OT. And the extent to which their use of the OT is mediated through Jewish interpretive traditions remains a pressing question that scholars will continue to debate.

Bibliography. Bauckham, R. J., *Jude, 2 Peter,* WBC (Word, 1988); Brown, D. E., "The Use of the Old Testament in 2 Peter 2:4–10A" (PhD diss., Trinity Evangelical Divinity School, 2002); Callan, T., "Use of the Letter of Jude by the Second Letter of Peter," *Bib* 85 (2004): 42–64; Carson, D. A., "2 Peter," in *CNTUOT,* 1047–61; Cassuto, U., "The Episode of the Sons of God and the Daughters of Man," in *Biblical and Oriental Studies,* trans. I. Abrahams (Magnes, 1973), 1:29–40; Charles, J. D., "The Angels under Reserve in 2 Peter and Jude," *BBR* 15 (2005): 39–48; Clines, D. J. A., "The Significance of the 'Sons of God' Episode (Genesis 6:1–4) in the Context of the 'Primeval History' (Genesis 1–11)," *JSOT* 13 (1979): 33–46; Davids, P. H., *The Letters of 2 Peter and Jude,* PNTC (Eerdmans, 2006); Dexinger, F., *Sturz der Göttersöhne; oder, Engel vor der Sintflut?,* WBT 13 (Herder, 1966); García Martínez, F. "Interpretations of the Flood in the Dead Sea Scrolls," in *Interpretations of the Flood,* ed. F. García Martínez and G. P. Luttikhuizen, TBN 1 (Brill, 1999), 86–108; Green, G. L., *Jude and 2 Peter,* BECNT (Baker Academic, 2008); Harmon, M. S., *The God Who Judges and Saves* (Crossway, 2023); Harmon, "Jude," in *Hebrews–Revelation,* ed. I. M. Duguid, J. M. Hamilton Jr., and J. Sklar, ESVEC (Crossway, 2018), 501–24; Harmon, "2 Peter," in *Hebrews–Revelation,* ed. I. M. Duguid, J. M. Hamilton Jr., and J. Sklar, ESVEC (Crossway, 2018), 363–410; Jackson, D. R., *Enochic Judaism,* LSTS 49 (T&T Clark, 2004); Kelly, J. N. D., *The Epistles of Peter and of Jude,* BNTC (Black, 1969); Kline, M. G., "Divine Kingship and Genesis 6:1–4," *WTJ* 24 (1961–1962): 184–204; Kline, *Kingdom Prologue* (1993; repr., Wipf & Stock, 2006); Kraftchick, S. J., *Jude, 2 Peter,* ANTC (Abingdon, 2002); Loader, J. A., *A Tale of Two Cities,* CBET 1 (Kok, 1990); Moo, D. J., *2 Peter, Jude,* NIVAC (Zondervan, 1996); Morschauser, S., "'Hospitality,' Hostiles, and Hostages," *JSOT* 27 (2003): 461–85; Muddiman, J., "The Assumption of Moses and the Epistle of Jude," in *Moses in Biblical and Extra-Biblical Traditions,* ed. A. Graupner and M. Wolter, BZAW 372 (de Gruyter, 2007); Neyrey, J. H., *2 Peter, Jude,* AB (Doubleday, 1993); Savelle, C. H., "Canonical and Extracanonical Portraits of Balaam," *BSac* 166 (2009): 387–404; Schreiner, T. R., *1, 2 Peter, Jude,* CSC (Broadman & Holman, 2020); VanGemeren, W. A., "The Sons of God in Genesis 6:1–4," *WTJ* 43 (1981): 320–48; Yoshikawa, S. T., "The Prototypical Use of the Noahic Flood in the New Testament" (PhD diss., Trinity Evangelical Divinity School, 2004).

MATTHEW S. HARMON

Judges, Book of

Judges is the second book in the second section of the Hebrew Bible known collectively as the Prophets (cf. Luke 24:44). This collection consists of two subsections known as the Former and Latter Prophets. Each subsection consists of four books. The Former Prophets are Joshua, Judges, Samuel, and Kings. The Latter Prophets are Isaiah, Jeremiah, Ezekiel, and the Twelve. The Former Prophets record the history of Israel's tenure in the land of Canaan, from the crossing of the Jordan River in Joshua to the destruction of Jerusalem and the Babylonian exile as recorded in 2 Kings 25. One of the primary concerns of this section of Scripture is to document and record the faithfulness of YHWH to keep all his promises that were made to the house of Israel through Moses (Josh. 21:45; 23:14; 1 Kings 8:56) in the midst of Israel's persistent idolatry and unfaithfulness to the Mosaic covenant (e.g., Judg. 2:1–3). YHWH's faithfulness in the Former Prophets also consists of fulfilling the promise to expel Israel from the land when their breach of that covenant reaches its fullness. This is clearly expressed in Josh. 23:15–16 (AT): "And just as every good thing has come upon you which YHWH your God has promised you, so will YHWH bring upon you every evil thing until he has destroyed you from this good land which YHWH your God has given to you. *When* you violate the covenant of YHWH your God that he commanded you, and you go and serve other gods, and you bow down to them, *then* the anger of YHWH will burn against you, and you will quickly perish from the good land that he had given to you."

As covenantal books, the Latter Prophets indict Israel for their unfaithfulness to the Mosaic covenant, while the Former Prophets officially document Israel's persistent infidelity toward YHWH. It is this persistent infidelity as expressed in Josh. 23 that serves as the backdrop to Judges.

Judges records the history of the nation of Israel from the death of Joshua (Judg. 1:1; 2:8) up to a period of time prior to the establishment of the monarchy through Samuel, the last of the so-called judges (ca. 1360–1084 BC). The refrain that gives this book its internal structure (see below) aptly characterizes the life of Israel during that time: "And the children of Israel did that which was evil in the eyes of YHWH" (Judg. 3:7; 6:1; with variations in 3:12; 4:1; 10:6; 13:1).

The Hebrew title of this book is the masculine plural form of the word for "judge" (*šōpəṭîm*), the designation for the office of the leaders presented in this book. These judges were raised up by YHWH to deliver his people from the oppression caused by their own idolatry, to secure the rest of the land, and to promote fidelity to YHWH by keeping the covenant (Judg. 2:16–19; 1 Sam. 12:19–25). They did not render judicial decrees. Rather, they brought *judgment* on those foreign nations who oppressed God's people.

Date and Authorship

Judges, like all of the books of the Former Prophets, is an anonymous composition of unknown date. Some traditions suggest that Samuel may have been the author (b. B. Bat. 14b–15a), but this is impossible to verify even though we know that Samuel wrote and kept records (1 Sam. 10:25; 1 Chron. 29:29). The four references to kingship in Judges (17:6; 18:1; 19:1; 21:25), and the strong pro-Judah and anti-Benjamin polemic in the introductions and conclusions that frame the book, suggest a period of composition after the establishment of the monarchy. Additionally, the author's reference to "the day of the captivity of the land" in 18:30 may suggest an exilic or postexilic date. Perhaps someone like Samuel recorded the internal narratives of the judges while the introductions and conclusions to the book were added later in a final stage of composition (cf. Van Pelt, 512–13).

Structure

The structure of the book is one of its most striking features. It contains two introductions (1:1–2:5; 2:6–3:6) and two corresponding conclusions (17:1–18:31; 19:1–21:25). The introductions and conclusions focus on Israel's idolatry and inability to possess the land promised to them by YHWH. Between these are six major judge episodes, six minor judge references, and one anti-judge figure (Abimelech). The so-called minor judges consist of only one to three verses and do not contain any of the formulaic elements of the major judge episodes but rather serve to mark or introduce major judge episodes. For example, the three minor judges Ibzan, Elon, and Abdon (12:8–15) precede the Samson narratives and mark it as the final and climactic judge episode in the book.

The following seven formulaic elements are often found in the major judge narratives: (1) Israel does evil in the eyes of YHWH; (2) YHWH gives or sells his people into the hand of the enemy; (3) Israel cries out; (4) YHWH raises up a judge to deliver; (5) the enemy is defeated; (6) the land has rest; (7) the judge dies. The first major judge, Othniel, serves as a succinct and complete paradigm for these seven elements (3:7–11; cf. Block, 146–47).

The six major judges are presented in two triads: Othniel, Ehud, and Deborah/Barak and then Gideon, Jephthah, and Samson (cf. Chisholm, 251–53). These triads are explicitly marked by their introductory formulas. In the accounts of Othniel and Gideon, the people of Israel do that which is evil in the eyes of YHWH (3:7; 6:1). In the two accounts that follow each of these two initial judges, the people of God *continue* to do evil in the eyes of YHWH (3:12; 4:1; 10:6; 13:1). The differences in the opening formulas are more striking in Hebrew.

The arrangement of Judges is not chronological but rather theological. The structure of the book as a whole appears to be modeled after the days of creation presented in Gen. 1:1–2:3 (Van Pelt, 513–15). Genesis 1 opens with a brief introduction (1:1–2) followed by six creation days (1:3–31) presented in two triads that climax on the seventh day with YHWH enthroned as Sabbath King (2:1–3). That is, Genesis takes us from chaos to cosmos in two triads of days that climax in YHWH's kingship over that cosmos. In Judges, however, we move from relative cosmos in the days of Joshua to the chaos of the final chapters of Judges through the presentation of two triads of judge narratives. In this case, there is no king in Israel, a tacit rejection of YHWH's kingship over his people during that period of Israel's history. In other words, the structure of Judges portrays the "uncreation" of Israel as they persist in their idolatry. Table 1 illustrates the literary structure of Judges modeled after the presentation of the days of creation (Van Pelt, 515).

Table 1. Parallel Structures in Judges and Gen. 1:1-2:3

The Structure of Judges		The Structure of Genesis	
Two Introductions 1:1–2:5 2:6–3:6		**Introduction** 1:1–2	
1. Othniel 3:7–11	**4. Gideon** 6:1–8:35	**Day 1** 1:3–5	**Day 4** 1:14–19
2. Ehud 3:12–30	**5. Jephthah** 10:6–12:7	**Day 2** 1:6–8	**Day 5** 1:20–23
3. Deborah/Barak 4:1–5:31	**6. Samson/Samson** 13:1–16:31	**Day 3** 1:9–13	**Day 6** 1:24–31
Two Conclusions 17:1–18:31 19:1–21:25		**Day 7** 2:1–3	

Source: Miles V. Van Pelt, "Judges," in *Deuteronomy–Ruth*, ed. Ian M. Duguid, James M. Hamilton Jr., and Jay Sklar, ESVEC 2 (Crossway, 2021), 515. Copyright © 2021. Used by permission of Crossway, a publishing ministry of Good News Publishers, Wheaton, IL 60187, www.crossway.org.

Another striking parallel in structure between the six days of creation and the six major judge narratives is the design of episodes three and six. In Gen. 1, days three and six are *double creation days*. On day three, God creates the dry land (vv. 9–10) and then vegetation (vv. 11–12), both of which are independently characterized as "good." On day six, God creates animals (vv. 24–25) and then mankind (vv. 26–31), both of which are again independently characterized as "[very] good." In Judges, the third and sixth major judge narratives are *double judge narratives*. The third major judge narrative includes two main figures, Deborah and Barak, and two accounts, the narrative account in chap. 4 and the poetic account in chap. 5. In the sixth major judge narrative, the account of Samson is clearly divided into two main sections marked by the repetition of a concluding formula indicating that Samson judged Israel for twenty years during the time of Philistine oppression (15:20; 16:31). The repetition of a concluding formula is the same technique employed in Gen. 1 to mark the two parts of the double creation days. Once again, literary parallels of these types suggest that the author of Judges has intentionally modeled the structure of the book after the pattern of the days of creation in Genesis (paragraph adapted from Van Pelt, 315n3).

Inner-Biblical Connections

In terms of the economy of redemptive history, the judges serve as types of Christ. They are raised up by the Lord, are empowered by the Spirit, deliver God's people from oppression, and secure Israel's inheritance (rest) in the land (2:16, 18; 3:9–11). The lives and work of the judges and their associates connect back with God's words and deeds in earlier parts of Scripture and anticipate the life and work of Christ as presented in the NT.

The Pentateuch in Judges. As indicated above, the macrostructure of Judges is patterned after the days of creation as presented in Gen. 1:1–2:3. In addition to this structural connection, several more specific features in the Pentateuch connect with Judges.

In Gen. 3:15, the Lord promised that the seed of the woman would crush the head of the serpent. A typological echo of this promise is hinted at twice in Judges. In the first instance, Jael drives a tent peg through the head of Sisera, the commander of the army of Jabin king of Canaan (4:21; 5:24–27). In the poetic retelling of this event, Deborah and Barak sang, "She struck Sisera; she crushed his head; she shattered and pierced his temple" (5:26 ESV). In a second instance, an unknown woman taking refuge in a tower throws down a large millstone, striking the anti-judge Abimelech and crushing his skull (9:53). In this instance, the Hebrew word for "skull" is the same one used for the location of the crucifixion of Jesus. "And they brought him to the place called Golgotha (which means Place of the Skull)" (Mark 15:22 ESV; cf. Matt. 27:33; John 19:17).

In Judg. 11, under the influence of the Spirit, Jephthah makes a vow that would require him to sacrifice his daughter if the Lord would give him victory over Israel's oppressors. The author is careful to highlight her status as Jephthah's only child: "She was his only child; besides her he had neither son nor daughter" (11:34 ESV). The word for "only child" here is the same word applied to Isaac in Gen. 22:2 when Abraham is commanded to sacrifice his only son. In both instances, the type of sacrifice required is also the same: a whole burnt offering (Gen. 22:2; Judg. 11:31). As such, both sacrifices serve as types of the sacrifice that the Father would make of his only Son to save and deliver his people (cf. John 1:18; 3:16, 18; Heb. 11:17).

In Judg. 19:14–30, the men of Benjamin of Gibeah surround a house where a Levite and his concubine are lodging as visitors for the night. The men of the city demand that the Levite be brought out so that they might engage in illicit sexual activity with him. The events recorded in Judg. 19 closely resemble the events recorded in Gen. 19:1–11, when the two angels spent the night with Lot in Sodom. There are at least ten points of similarity between these events (cf. Van Pelt, 664–65; Block, 520):

1. Travelers arrive at a town in the evening.
2. A host urges the guests not to spend the night in the town square/gate.
3. The host is a sojourner, not a native of the city.
4. All the men in the city surround the house.
5. The men of the city make the same demand of the host (cf. the striking verbal parallels in Gen. 19:5; Judg. 19:22).
6. The host goes out to the men of the city and leaves the visitors in the house.
7. The host pleads with the men of the city not to do this wicked thing (cf. Gen. 19:7; Judg. 19:23).
8. The host offers two women as a substitute for the men (cf. Gen. 19:8; Judg. 19:24).
9. The men of the city do not want the women as a substitute.
10. All the inhabitants of the city are eventually destroyed, and the city is burned with fire.

The close connection between the events recorded in Gen. 19 and Judg. 19 serves to characterize the Benjaminites of Gibeah as Sodomites. In other words, God's people have become Canaanite, a people to be purged from the land at that time (cf. Josh. 23:15–16). Later, when Israel rejects YHWH as their king and asks for a king like all the other nations (1 Sam. 8:4–9), it is harrowing to discover that the Lord gives them exactly what they demand, a king from Benjamin of Gibeah, a Canaanite king in kind (1 Sam. 9:1; 10:26). The sinful behavior of the Sodomites serves as a type of sinful behavior that is repeated throughout the OT and NT, along with the complete judgment that follows (cf. Deut. 29:23; 32:32; Isa. 1:9, 10; 3:9; 13:19; Jer. 23:14; 49:18; 50:40; Lam. 4:6; Amos 4:11; Zeph. 2:9; Matt. 10:15; 11:24; Rom. 9:29; 2 Pet. 2:6; Jude 7; Rev. 11:8).

The call of Moses in Exod. 3 serves as the literary model for the call of Gideon in Judg. 6. Gideon is the fourth major judge and is raised up by YHWH and empowered by the Spirit to deliver God's people from the oppression of the Midianites. Those features common to each call narrative are identified below (cf. Van Pelt, 574; Shalom-Guy, 15–16):

1. Reference to Midian (Exod. 3:1; Judg. 6:11)
2. Angel of the Lord appears (Exod. 3:2; Judg. 6:11–12)
3. Promise of divine presence (Exod. 3:12; Judg. 6:12, 16)
4. Deliverance from Egypt (Exod. 3:7–8; Judg. 6:13)
5. Objection of the person called (Exod. 3:11; Judg. 6:15)
6. Commission to deliver (Exod. 3:10; Judg. 6:16)
7. Confirming sign (Exod. 3:12; Judg. 6:17)

With the patterning of Gideon's call after the call of Moses, the author is clearly portraying Gideon as a second Moses figure (see Wong; Shalom-Guy). In a similar way, Israel's deliverance from Egypt is also rehearsed in Judges. God's deliverance of his people in Judg. 4–5 is patterned after the events of Exod. 14–15. Both accounts begin with God delivering his people followed by a poetic retelling of the events. In Exodus, Moses and Miriam lead in song. In Judges, Deborah and Barak lead. In Judg. 5:4–5, YHWH leads the battle in a great storm theophany in the tradition of Sinai (Niehaus, 281–82; Poythress, 286–87). He swiftly defeats the enemy with their horses by washing them away in the "ancient torrent" (5:21–22), recalling how God defeated the Egyptians at the Red Sea. Just as YHWH threw into confusion (*wayyāhām*) the camp of Egypt (Exod. 14:24), so he also threw into confusion (*wayyāhām*) Sisera with all of his chariots (Judg. 4:15). These intentional connections establish patterns of redemption that continue to appear and unfold across the canon (Josh. 10:10; 1 Sam. 7:10; 2 Sam. 22:15; 2 Chron. 15:6).

In Exod. 23:23–33, YHWH warns his people against worshiping the gods of the Canaanites since their expulsion from the land will be gradual until Israel increases in number to fully occupy the land: "Little by little I will drive them out before you until you are fruitful and inherit the land" (v. 30 AT). This section ends with what becomes a programmatic verse for the events recorded in Judges: "They shall not dwell in your land lest they cause you to sin against me. For if you worship their gods, then it will become a *snare* to you" (Exod. 23:33 AT). Judges records Israel's failure to expel the Canaanites from the land. They also worship their gods and become trapped in that "snare" just as YHWH had warned (Judg. 2:1–3).

Israel's inclination and proclivity toward idolatry are one of the reasons that YHWH forbids them from making covenants, showing mercy, or intermarrying with the people of the land (Deut. 7:1–4). This is one reason why YHWH commands that the Canaanites be removed from the land by putting them to the ban (*ḥrm*)—that is, devoting them to complete destruction (Deut. 7:5–7). In the end, however, Israel will be expelled from the land due to their incessant and ever-worsening idolatry, as Judges clearly sets forth. YHWH knows this and makes it known to Moses at the end of his life: "And the Lord said to Moses, 'Behold, you are about to lie down with your fathers. Then this people will rise and whore after the foreign gods among them in the land that they are entering, and they will forsake me and break my covenant that I have made with them'" (Deut. 31:16 ESV; cf. 29:24–28; 30:18; 31:17–21). Deuteronomy constitutes an important theological lens through which to examine the message of Judges, which serves as the beginning of the fulfillment of Moses's prophetic word.

Judges in the Prophets. Joshua 15:16–19 records the account of Othniel's victory over Kiriath-sepher and his marriage to Achsah, the daughter of Caleb. This account is repeated almost verbatim in Judg. 1:12–15 amid the report of Judah's mostly successful occupation of the land allotted to them by Joshua and Moses. The account is repeated in order to highlight the prominent role of the tribe of Judah in Judges, a prominence that will continue to develop through David and then ultimately through Jesus.

The account of the death of Joshua is first recorded in Josh. 24:29–30 and then twice more in the book of Judges, first in 1:1 and then again in 2:7–8. The accounts in Judges mark the beginnings of the two introductions to the central judge narratives (1:1–2:5; 2:6–3:6). Additionally, the reference to the death of Joshua in Judg. 1:1 serves as a literary link between Joshua and Judges in the same way that the reference to the death of Moses in Josh. 1:1 (cf. Deut. 34:5–8) serves as a literary link between Deuteronomy and Joshua. The opening line of each book is formulaic: "And it was after the death of Moses" (Josh. 1:1 AT); "And it was after the death of Joshua" (Judg. 1:1 AT). The significance of the death of a covenant mediator is a major theme in the Gospels.

In the book of Samuel, Eli serves as a judge. After his death, it is recorded that "he judged Israel forty years" (1 Sam. 4:18 AT). Forty years are also associated with Othniel (Judg. 3:11), Deborah and Barak (Judg. 5:31), and Gideon (Judg. 8:28). It is also the number of years of Philistine oppression before the Lord raised up Samson as the last judge in Judges (Judg. 13:1).

Samson and Samuel share a number of significant features in common. They are both born to a barren woman (Judg. 13:2; 1 Sam. 1:2). They are both declared Nazirites from birth (Judg. 13:5; 1 Sam. 1:11). They both serve as judges (Judg. 15:20; 16:31; 1 Sam. 7:15). They both serve as forerunners to a king and the monarchy in Israel. In the case of Samson, the angel of YHWH tells his mother that Samson "will *begin* to save Israel from the hand of the Philistines" (13:5 AT). It was King David who finished the work that Samson was commissioned to begin, first by defeating their champion Goliath (1 Sam. 17), and then by subduing all the enemies of the land (2 Sam. 7:1). As forerunners to the coming king, both Samson and Samuel serve as types of John the Baptist (see below).

In 1 Sam. 12, Samuel rehearses the history of YHWH's faithfulness to Israel. In the midst of this rehearsal, Samuel identifies a selection of judges through whom YHWH delivered. "YHWH sent Jerub Baal [Gideon] and Barak and Jephthah and Samuel, and he delivered you from the hand of your enemy all around, and you lived in security" (v. 11 AT). A similar list appears in Heb. 11:32, once again highlighting faith and faithfulness.

Judges anticipates the establishment of the monarchy in Samuel. The two conclusions to the book are structured by a programmatic statement repeated four times: "In those days there was not a king in Israel" (Judg. 17:6; 18:1; 19:1; 21:25 AT). This expression serves as a tacit rejection of YHWH's kingship and explains the progressive corruption of Israel as those who did "what was right in their own eyes" (Judg. 17:6; 21:25 AT). The rejection of YHWH's kingship in Israel is made explicit when Israel requests a king like all the surrounding nations. "And YHWH said to Samuel, 'Listen to the voice of the people, to all that they are saying to you. For they have not rejected you, but they have rejected me from being king over them'" (1 Sam. 8:7).

In terms of Israel's early monarchy, Judges also anticipates the conflict between Saul and David and their royal dynasties. Saul is a Benjaminite from Gibeah. David is a Judahite from Bethlehem who will later make Jerusalem his royal city. Saul is a king rejected by YHWH (1 Sam. 13:13–14), but David is a king with whom YHWH makes an eternal covenant (2 Sam. 7:5–17; Ps. 89:3–4). In Judg. 1, the prominence of Judah is exemplified by the nineteen-verse account of the tribe's success in occupation (vv. 2–20) immediately followed by the one-verse account of Benjamin's failure to drive out the Jebusites from Jerusalem and their subsequent and long-standing cohabitation with them (v. 21). Then, in the second conclusion to the book, the tribe of Benjamin, and specifically the men of Gibeah, are characterized as Sodomites. When Israel is called into battle against the tribe of Benjamin to purge the evil from their midst, YHWH commands that the tribe of Judah go up first and lead in battle (20:18). In these subtle ways, Judges anticipates Israel's monarchy and its early struggles.

The Latter Prophets contain no explicit references to Judges. However, there is a formulaic, stock phrase that appears both in the book of Judges and in the Latter Prophets. Each of the six major judge narratives in Judges begins with a statement that Israel had done evil in the eyes of YHWH (3:7, 12; 4:1; 6:1; 10:6; 13:1). This evil is always idolatry. Moses hints at this reality at the end of his life when he states, "For I know that after my death you will surely act corruptly and turn aside from the way that I have commanded you. And in the days to come evil will befall you, *because you will do what is evil in the sight of the Lord*, provoking him to anger through the work of your hands" (Deut. 31:29 ESV; cf. 4:25). In the Latter Prophets, this becomes an idiom for Israel's persistent idolatry. For example, in Jer. 7:30, YHWH says through the prophet, "For the sons of Judah have done evil in my sight, declares the LORD. They have set their detestable things in the house that is called by my name, to defile it" (ESV). Other examples include Isa. 66:4; Jer. 32:30; 52:2. This same expression is also used for those kings in Samuel and Kings who both commit and promote idolatry through the monarchy (1 Kings. 11:6; 14:22; 15:26, 34; 16:19, 25; 21:20, 25, etc.).

Judges in the Writings. Psalm 106 is a historical psalm that rehearses the faithfulness of YHWH to Israel from their deliverance out of Egypt up through the period of the judges. Verses 34–46 (27 percent of the psalm) are dedicated to the events recorded in Judges. It begins with Israel's failure to expel the inhabitants of the land followed by their subsequent cohabitation with those they fail to expel (vv. 34–35). These verses coordinate with the two introductions in Judg. 1:1–3:6. The remaining verses rehearse the judge cycles that constitute the core of Judges. Israel engages in idolatry (vv. 36–39). YHWH gives them into the hands of their oppressors (vv. 40–42). YHWH delivers them numerous times (v. 43) when they cry out in their distress (v. 44). We are told that YHWH does this because he remembers his covenant and so relents from his wrath and acts in accordance with his abundant steadfast love (v. 45) in order that we might give thanks to his holy name and boast in his praise (v. 47). Psalm 106 is using the events recorded in Judges as evidence of YHWH's faithfulness to the covenant in the context of Israel's sinfulness. This contrast highlights YHWH's steadfast love according to a pattern established in Deut. 32. Verses 1–25 of this song constitute a covenant lawsuit in which YHWH indicts Israel for their violation of the covenant. Then, in vv. 26–43, he turns in compassion to promise the restoration of his people and their inheritance.

Ruth, the fourth book in the Writings, opens with a reference to the period of the judges. It begins, "In the days of the judging of the judges, there was a famine in the land" (AT). In this way, the events recorded in Ruth find a chronological context that establishes a point of comparison with Judges. During the time of the judges, God's people do evil in his eyes. The foreigner Ruth, by way of contrast, does that which is right in his eyes. This is why Ruth is characterized as a "woman of strength" in 3:11. She represents the real-life example of the woman described in Prov. 31:10–31. She is the only woman in the whole of the Hebrew Bible to receive this impressive approbation. The close connection between Prov. 31:10 and Ruth 3:11 is likely the reason that Ruth follows Proverbs in the Hebrew Bible.

Judges in the NT. There are a number of interesting connections between Judges and the NT. First, as stated above, the judges serve as types of Christ, prefiguring the life and ministry of Jesus. Like the judges, Jesus is a savior (Judg. 2:16; 3:9, 15; Matt. 1:21; Luke 2:11) raised up (sent) by the Father (Judg. 2:16, 18; 3:9, 15; 6:14; Matt. 10:40; John 4:34; Acts 3:22; 7:37) and empowered by the Spirit (Judg. 3:10; 6:34; 11:29; 14:6; Matt. 3:16; 4:1; 12:28; John 1:32; Heb. 9:14) to deliver God's people and secure rest in the context of their inheritance (Judg. 3:11, 30; 5:31; 8:28; Matt. 11:28–29; Heb. 4:3–11).

Additionally, the presentation of the life of John the Baptist in the Gospels appears to have been modeled on the life of Samson, the final and climactic judge in Judges. The following list illustrates some of the major points of comparison (from Van Pelt, 623):

1. Both accounts begin with significant birth narratives (Judg. 13; Luke 1:5–25).
2. Both mothers are barren (Judg. 13:2; Luke 1:7).
3. Both are declared to be Nazirites for life prior to birth (Judg. 13:3–5; Luke 1:15).
4. Both births are announced by the angel of the Lord (Judg. 13:3; Luke 1:11).
5. Both fathers struggle with believing the news of the angel of the Lord (Judg. 13:16–17; Luke 1:18–20).
6. Both birth narratives record the commission or task of each figure (Judg. 13:5; Luke 1:16–17).
7. Both Samson and John the Baptist are betrayed by women (Delilah and the daughter of Herodias), resulting in their eventual deaths (Judg. 16:1–22; Matt. 14:1–12).
8. Both men serve as forerunners to a coming king who achieves rest for his people (2 Sam. 7:1; Matt. 11:28).

These points of comparison demonstrate that Samson is a type of John the Baptist, a climactic covenant official who prepares the way for the coming of the king. However, Samson may also serve as a type of Christ in the way that he serves as a judge. Barry Webb (418–19) identifies Samson as a type of Christ in this way:

> Christian readers can hardly fail to notice a number of points of correspondence between the broad structure of Samson's career and that of Christ: his annunciation by a divine messenger, his marvelous conception, his holiness as a Nazirite, his endowment with the Spirit, his rejection by his own people, his being handed over by their leaders, the mocking and scorn he suffered at their hands, and the way his calling was consummated in his death, by which he defeated the god Dagon and laid the foundation for a deliverance to be fully realized in a day to come. The correspondences are too numerous, and too germane to who Samson was, for what he achieved to be simply brushed aside as fanciful. The fact is that when the story is read in the context of the Bible as a whole, we discover even here, in the most unlikely of places, intimations of things to come.

Many of the events in the life and ministry of Samson serve as a type of the life and ministry of Jesus. Samson is a savior raised up by the Lord to deliver his people, but is ultimately rejected by those people, handed over to the enemy, and achieves his greatest victory in his death. Perhaps Samson is not the incredulous character that so many consider him to be.

In 1 Cor. 7:15, Paul appears to permit divorce when an unbelieving spouse leaves a believing spouse. Judges 19:2 may provide the background for this allowance. Here it is stated that the Levite's concubine was unfaithful to him by leaving him and returning to the house of her father—that is, she abandoned him. The verb used to describe the unfaithfulness of the concubine (*znh*), is the same verb used to describe the unfaithfulness of Israel to YHWH at this time (rendered "whored" in Judg. 2:17; 8:27; 8:33 ESV).

Finally, the most explicit connection between Judges and the NT is found in Heb. 11. In v. 32, four of the major judges (Gideon, Barak, Samson, and Jephthah) appear together with David and Samuel as men of faith who "conquered kingdoms, enforced justice, obtained promises, stopped the mouths of lions, quenched the power of fire, escaped the edge of the sword, were made strong out of weakness, became mighty in war, put foreign armies to flight" (Heb. 11:33–34 ESV). These judges are further described as men "of whom the world was not worthy" (v. 38 ESV) and so "commended for their faith" (v. 39). The reception of the judges in the NT as types of Christ and men commended for their faith and service in the kingdom of God should significantly shape our interpretation of the judges. As types of Christ, these judges remain faithful to their callings by continuing to help us fix our own eyes on Christ even today (12:12).

Bibliography. Block, D. I., *Judges, Ruth*, NAC (Broadman & Holman, 1999); Chisholm, R. B., Jr., "The Chronology of the Book of Judges," *JETS* 52 (2009): 247–55; Hugenberger, G. P., *Judges*, ApOTC (IVP Academic, forthcoming); Niehaus, J. J., *God at Sinai* (Zondervan, 1995); Poythress, V. S., *Theophany* (Crossway, 2018); Ryan, R., *Judges* (Sheffield Phoenix, 2007); Shalom-Guy, H., "The Call Narratives of Gideon and Moses," *JHebS* 11 (2011): 2–19; Van Pelt, M. V., "Judges," in *Deuteronomy–Ruth*, ESVEC 2 (Crossway, 2021), 509–675; Webb, B. G., *The Book of Judges*, NICOT (Eerdmans, 2012); Wong, G. T. K., "Gideon: A New Moses?," in *Reflection and Refraction*, ed. R. Rezetko, T. H. Lim, and W. B. Aucker, VTSup 113 (Brill, 2007), 529–45.

MILES V. VAN PELT

Judgment

See Consummation; Day of the Lord

Justice

"Justice" is a term heard frequently in various places, such as discussions held by political commentators, courtrooms where attorneys are deliberating, and academic discussions surrounding the humanities. Increasingly, in the West the term is used in a rather subjective way, as challenges to long-standing moral and cultural constructs continue to proliferate. Indeed, there seems to be a continual push toward understanding justice as merely respecting the rights of another. However, when such rights come into complete conflict with other viewpoints, identity politics ensues, and seemingly, the one with the loudest voice within that particular sphere wins the day, calling into question what was truly accomplished.

Justice as seen in the Scriptures, however, reveals objective truth that endures in all generations and transcends all cultures concerning God's holy and upright character, our natural inability to act in just ways, and the call for us to live out righteousness and justice as God's people. Biblically defined and understood, justice is rendering to each person what is their due, whether reward or punishment, based on an objective moral standard of rightness, which is in accordance with God's character and revealed in God's word. Put more simply, biblical justice is the rendering of righteous judgment (see Leeman). Feinberg notes that if one is to be just, they must do what is right according to God's standards, for he is the standard of what is ethically and morally right and wrong (*No One*, 345). Thus, one must understand what is right in God's eyes before vying for one's rights.

Several terms in Scripture may be rendered "justice"; here we will focus on those used most frequently. The Hebrew term *mišpāṭ* occurs 415 times in the OT, with the majority of occurrences in Psalms (65), Ezekiel (43), Isaiah (42), Jeremiah (32), Proverbs (20). This term has a range of meaning, including justice, judgment, rules, ruling, and decision. Another Hebrew word, *ṣedeq*, denotes the doing of justice. In many contexts where these terms are used, the issue at hand is injustice in the midst of God's people and a call from God's law or his prophets to punish the lawbreaker and assist the oppressed and weak.

In the NT the term *dikaiōsynē*, along with its various cognates, depicts the ideas of justice, righteousness, and judgment. These terms are seen in a variety of places within the NT, with a definite concentration in Romans, which depicts a righteous/just God who justly condemns both Jews and gentiles in sin. However, by means of the work of Christ, God the Father is both just and justifier in making sinners a part of his people and declaring them to be righteous by virtue of their faith in and union with Christ.

In thinking through the concept of justice it is imperative that one understands how it relates to God and then, by virtue of this reality, how it relates to God's covenant people as well as to those outside the covenant community. This will allow readers to discern how God brings about justice both by means of saving and by means of judging. Thus, our primary concern is to sketch, albeit briefly, a biblical rendering of justice and finally to consider how the concept of justice relates to biblical theology and hermeneutics.

Justice and the OT

The first occurrence of the Hebrew terms in the OT are found in a conversation between God and Abraham. In the first instance, God proclaims that he chose Abraham and his descendants to bless the nations "by doing righteousness and justice" (Gen. 18:19 ESV). Subsequently, when God pronounces that he will destroy Sodom and Gomorrah in their wickedness, Abraham appeals to God's justice, asking him not to punish the righteous along with the wicked (Gen. 18:25). Thus, even in this first instance, one sees a call to humanity to act justly based on the just standards and character of God. We will first observe God's just character and then see how this understanding of God's justice impacts the call for humanity to be just and be treated justly.

The justice of God. The justice of God is seen right from the start. Man and woman are created in God's image to reflect his glory and exercise dominion over the face of the earth (Gen. 1:26–28). In other words, they are to exercise just rule under God and his righteous standards. God blesses Adam and Eve, who are to function as his vice-regents, and places them in a garden where they will experience blessing and God's presence, provided they obey God's command not to eat from the tree of the knowledge of good and evil (2:15–17). They, however, succumb to temptation, rebel, and partake of the forbidden fruit (3:1–7). Consequences (3:8–19) including exile from Eden (3:23–24) come as a result.

God proclaims, due to the choice to rebel against his command, that humans are now in a sinful state, and seemingly, if they partake of the tree of life, they will live forever in this state (3:22). Therefore, he drives Adam and Eve from the garden of Eden and places an angel at the entrance of the garden to keep people from partaking of the tree of life (3:23–24). Thus, God removes humanity from his blessing, immediate presence, and protection. In other words, he renders judgment because his just standard has been violated.

Beyond Eden we see the same God, who possesses a righteous and just character and has established a moral order for the universe under which all creatures must abide and by which they are judged. Even an unbelieving person, such as Pharaoh, recognizes that God is "right" or "just" (Exod. 9:27) due to his intrinsic character. He is the great, mighty, and awesome God who is not partial but executes justice for the downtrodden, the poor, and the marginalized (Deut. 10:17; cf. 2 Chron. 19:7; Pss. 10:14–18; 146:5–8). All of his ways are just and upright (Deut. 32:4). In the context of prayers of confession, the nation of Israel recognizes their sin and how God has acted justly in disciplining them (2 Chron. 12:6; Ezra 9:15; Neh. 9:33).

The psalmist also speaks much of the justice of God. These varying prayers cry out for justice to be done and judgment to be rendered in light of the work of enemies that surround God's people (Ps. 5:8). There are cries for deliverance based on God's righteousness, which endures forever (31:1; 71:2; 111:3; 143:1). Many of the psalmists reaffirm the just nature of God's character, how he loves the righteous deeds of his people, and how the upright will be with him in his presence (e.g., 11:7). He is to be praised because he loves righteousness and justice and will establish equity on earth (33:5; 99:4; 145:6–7). His justice and righteousness are expansive, reaching to the heavens (71:19), and serve as the foundation of his throne, characterizing his rule and reign (97:1–2; cf. 119:137). There is no contradiction: our God is full of grace and mercy and yet completely righteous in his dealings with humanity (116:5; 145:17). He justly exalts those who exult in his name (Ps. 89:15–16).

The prophets also speak to God's justice, declaring that he exercises right judgment in all of his ways. In the discipline of wicked Israel, in which God sends them into exile, he shows himself to be "exalted in justice" and "holy in righteousness" (Isa. 5:16 ESV; cf. Lam. 1:18; Dan. 9:7, 16). No one has taught God the path of justice; his intrinsic character is just, demonstrated in the declaration and execution of right judgments (Isa. 40:14; 45:19, 23–24). He is incomparable to any idol, the one and only true God who will bring about righteousness and salvation amid an unrighteous people (Isa. 46:12–13; 51:1–6). In the midst of a crooked and sinful nation, where justice and righteousness are denied, the Lord is displeased that there is no justice and instead only oppression and transgression (Isa. 59:1–14). The Lord sees and considers such activity and attitudes to be evil, and thus he puts on righteousness as a garment and deals with such injustice (Isa. 59:15–18). He shows himself to be just in all of his ways while Israel and the nations parade themselves in unrighteous ways (Zeph. 3:1–5).

The justice of humanity. The OT depicts a perfectly just God who renders right judgments upon humanity, and he calls his people to be set apart among the other nations to a pattern of just living (Gen. 18:19). In the law, which is perfectly righteous/just (Deut. 4:8), God calls his people to justice, which includes returning a wandering animal, even if it is an enemy's (Exod. 23:4–5); allowing the poor and the sojourner access to gleanings from the harvest (Lev. 19:10); and giving a hired person his wages in a timely manner (Lev. 19:13; Harbin, 699). Israel is to refrain from spreading false reports, bearing false witness, or receiving bribes, all of which would be examples of perverting justice (Exod. 23:1–9). Within a courtroom there is to be no injustice, but impartial rendering of judgment whether those involved are rich or poor (Lev. 19:15; Deut. 16:18–20). This is especially needful in a culture where judges, not juries, render a verdict and false accusations and bribery are the favored devices of injustice (cf. 1 Sam. 8:3; Jer. 5:26–28; Prov. 17:23; 19:28). Judges must render justice in the fear of God, knowing they act on behalf of the Lord (2 Chron. 19:5–7).

God is calling for a just people, who serve as eyes to the blind, feet to the lame, and a father to the needy (Job 29:14–16). Israel is often blind to their lack of justice, thinking themselves to be a nation that does righteousness and thus expecting God to render them righteous judgments (Isa. 58:1–2). And yet, God sees through their external hypocrisy stemming from corrupt hearts and calls them to hate oppression and care for the needy (Isa. 58:3–12). Justice must be rendered even in mundane business transactions (Lev. 19:35–36; cf. Hosea 12:6–7). In all, God's people are to be generous, not spending all their means on themselves but loving their neighbors and caring for their needs.

Among the people, the king serves a crucial role as it relates to justice. Under the monarchy, the king is called to write out and know the law so that he will fear the Lord and serve as an example and representative for the nation of Israel (Deut. 17:14–20; cf. Prov. 2:1–9). He is the final arbiter of justice in the land (2 Sam. 8:15; 15:3–4; 1 Kings 3:28; 10:9; Ps. 72:1–2; Prov. 20:8; 29:4), though always in a secondary sense, as God is the one who ultimately grants justice (Prov. 29:26). As such, kings are warned about rendering unjust judgments, and they are called to acknowledge God's knowledge of all such affairs and the consequences for all their unrighteous ways (Jer. 21:11–12; 22:1–5; Mic. 3:1–3, 9–11). As one observes the kingship in Israel and the rendering of justice, particularly through the eyes of the prophets, one discerns abysmal failure.

The way of wickedness is an abomination to the Lord, but he loves those who pursue righteousness (Prov. 15:9). When justice is done, the righteous are overjoyed, and the wicked terrified (21:15). Those who observe justice and do righteousness are promised blessing from the Lord (Ps. 106:3). The problem is that humanity fails in this sense, since no one living is righteous/just before God of their own accord (143:2). The prophets rebuke Israel for their extortion, robbery, oppression, and succumbing to bribery, calling them instead to do good, seek justice, not exploit the vulnerable, and care for the needs of the widow and the poor (Isa. 1:16–17; 5:23; Ezek. 22:29; Birch, 436).

Daniel rightly recognizes the sin of the nation before a just God, confessing that they in their unrighteousness have fallen short of his will and acknowledging their need of his grace (Dan. 9:4–19). The call of a just God is for his people to do justly and love mercy and walk humbly with him (Mic. 6:8; cf. Hosea 14:9; Amos 5:12–24). God's people should "render true judgments," showing kindness and mercy especially to those who have no social standing, but the people made their hearts "diamond-hard" (Zech. 7:9–12 ESV). This is why the prophets have an eschatological focus, pointing forward to how a just God will redeem a people and give them new hearts that are enabled to walk in justice before him (Jer. 31:31–34; Ezek. 36:25–27).

Despite the full display of their unjust deeds, God will save a people for himself at the end of history or in the "latter days." He will make a covenant with them and betroth them to himself in righteousness and justice (Hosea 2:19; cf. Jer. 9:23–24), and he will be faithful and righteous in dealing with them (Zech. 8:8). The prophets declare that this salvation of an unjust people by a holy God will occur by means of his servant, the Messiah. This coming Messiah will love righteousness/justice and hate wickedness (Ps. 45:6–7; cf. Heb. 1:8–9). He will judge with equity, justice, and faithfulness on behalf of the poor and the meek (Isa. 11:1–5; Jer. 23:5). He is declared to be a king who is righteous/just and possessing salvation (Zech. 9:9; cf. Matt. 21:5). This salvation of a people will come about through a coming servant suffering on behalf of humanity and bearing their sins (Isa. 53:1–10); this righteous/just one will "make many to be accounted righteous" (Isa. 53:11 ESV). People are declared just/righteous by God by means of faith in him and, specifically, this coming suffering servant (Hab. 2:4; cf. Rom. 1:17; Gal. 3:11; Heb. 10:38).

Justice in the NT

The justice of God. The NT reiterates precisely what is seen in the OT—namely, that God is perfectly just and calls his people to walk in justice. Jesus the Messiah—who will one day serve as the righteous judge of all of humanity, particularly concerning their care for others (Matt. 25:31–46)—even on the cross is declared by the Roman centurion to be innocent/righteous (*dikaios*; Luke 23:47). The apostles declare Jesus to be "the Holy and Righteous One" (Acts 3:14; cf. 7:52; 22:14) who is to be recognized as such by repentance and faith for salvation. The holy and just God makes a way of salvation for unrighteous people through Christ. Paul labors to demonstrate in Rom. 9–11 that, in saving a people consisting of both Jews and gentiles, God is in no way unjust (Rom. 9:14). He has mercy on whomever he wills and hardens according to his sovereignty (Rom. 9:18). As John Piper asserts, "God cannot be faulted with a disposition or conduct that contradicts the truth of who he is. This truth is that he is infinitely glorious and worthy of all honor and thanks (Rom. 1:21). God is totally devoted to uphold and display this truth in all his actions [including divine election]" (Piper, 95–96; cf. Moo, 591–92). God judges justly and impartially all of humanity according to each one's deeds (1 Pet. 1:17; cf. Ps. 62:12), rendering salvation or condemnation.

Our deeds alone do not earn us a right relationship with the just God, because we have all sinned (Rom. 3:23), are by nature children of wrath (Eph. 2:3), and stand condemned under God's wrath (John 3:36). We operate in unjust ways, like the Pharisees (Luke 11:42; cf. John 7:24). We seek to justify ourselves, pointing to deeds that can never truly save us from condemnation under God's righteous decrees (Luke 18:9–14). However, if we confess our sins and have faith in Jesus Christ, God is faithful and just to forgive us of all our sins (1 John 1:9; cf. Luke 18:13–14). Thus, the justice of God is revealed in its fullest at the cross, where Jesus is put forward as a propitiation. Jesus's identity as the Son of God and his work of penal substitution uphold God's justice in the atonement (Treat, 225–26). This same salvation is what the OT prophets anticipate: an unjust people who are justified and then live out righteousness.

The justice of God in salvation and judgment. Paul speaks of this salvation in his magnificent Letter to the Romans. The first part of this epistle is concerned with showing how sinful and condemned all of humanity, Jew and gentile, is before the righteous God (Rom. 1:18–3:20). No one can be made right with God by works of the law, but the righteousness of God is made manifest to those who have faith in Jesus (Rom. 3:21–22). All are sinners but can be justified by God's grace through faith in Jesus, who is the wrath-absorbing sacrifice for us on behalf of our sins (Rom. 3:23–25). He took our sins that we might become his righteousness (2 Cor. 5:21). This, Paul says, is the key to how a just God can render a judgment of righteousness for guilty sinners—namely, because Jesus paid the price for our sins (Isa. 53:1–11; cf. 1 Pet. 3:18). The gospel, therefore, promises pardon from God's just wrath against sin. Before human judges, the Savior was unjustly tried and executed (Isa. 53:8). From the divine perspective, however, Jesus's death satisfied God's justice (Rom. 3:26). Thus, God remains a righteous judge, executing justice even as he justifies those sinners who believe in Christ (Luke 18:14; Gal. 3:11–13; 1 Pet. 2:23; Shogren, 440–41). As such, the just God justly justifies the unjust.

Having been justified, the people of God are called to act in just ways, similar to the call of the OT prophets. We do not act as the ultimate judge, since God is Judge of all (James 4:11–12; cf. Rom. 12:19–21; 1 Thess. 4:6). Instead, Christians act justly by thinking on things that are just (Phil. 4:8); caring for those in need, such as widows and orphans; and by treating employees and fellow humans with dignity (James 1:27; 5:1–9; cf. Luke 18:1–19:10; see Hays). We are called as God's people to love and good works on behalf of others (Gal. 6:10). We are to do justice and, most importantly, proclaim the word of justice as seen in Scripture, of a righteous God, a sinful people, and a redeeming Messiah (see DeYoung and Gilbert, 223–39; Keller, 216). For those who are elect, redeemed by faith in Christ, God will someday render perfect justice through salvation at the final judgment (Luke 18:7–8). However, those outside of this confession and belief in the Messiah will suffer just judgment for their sins (Rev. 16:5–7). Christ will one day righteously judge and make war against those who are opposed to him, and they will meet God's judgment in the lake of fire (19:11; 20:11–15). Thus, acting in total and perfect justice, God will manifest that justice in salvation and judgment forever.

Biblical-Theological and Hermeneutical Implications

One must consider, when thinking through the topic of justice and how it is rendered, that as Feinberg (*Continuity*) highlights, there is both continuity and discontinuity across the Testaments. One cannot simply render judgments regarding the understanding or application of the concept of justice without considering developments across redemptive history. This is true when thinking of both the justice of God as well as that of God's people.

Concerning God's justice, God renders righteous judgment from the very beginning of Scripture, dealing justly with humanity in that time. One can also observe, however, that God "passed over former sins" (Rom. 3:25 ESV), not executing absolute and total justice upon creation in an immediate sense, which would have meant eternal condemnation. This does not demean God's justice but looks ahead to the way in which God would justly justify a people. Thus, the OT also points forward to the time when he will implement absolute and final justice over all creation (Ps. 98:9; Eccles. 3:16; Isa. 28:5–6; 29:19–21), which includes the salvation of a people in righteousness. Likewise, the NT emphasizes the approaching final judgment, when all people will be evaluated according to their works (Rom. 2:5; 3:5–6; Rev. 20:13; Shogren, 441). The God who is the same yesterday, today, and forever (Heb. 13:8) is a just God, as seen in the entirety of Scripture, and this justice is rendered in salvation and judgment across the Testaments ultimately because of the work of Christ.

Thus, what was anticipated in the OT came to fulfillment in the NT regarding the Messiah and his work. He would save a people and, in the end, set up a kingdom of justice. Gary Shogren notes that Ps. 72 is a prayer for a king who would protect the poor, "a psalm that looks beyond Solomon to an ideal just king." The OT predicts that the Messiah will execute justice on God's behalf (Isa. 9:7; 11:3–4; 16:4–5; 28:17), and in the NT Jesus begins to carry out the Father's justice while on earth (Matt. 12:18–21; John 5:28–30). Still, it is in the future that he will execute God's will over all (Acts 17:31; Rev. 19:11; Shogren, 441). God's justice, therefore, is displayed in Christ's first coming, when he inaugurates his kingdom, and will be consummated when he judges all at his second coming, bringing about the full establishment of his eternal kingdom. The full display of God's righteous judgment comes into display with the coming of Christ, and thus, the full concept of justice is progressively revealed in Scripture.

Regarding the people of God, one can observe certain distinctives between Israel and the church when reading OT passages about justice and applying them to today's circumstances. For example, theocratic Israel in the OT was predominantly an agrarian culture, and much of the application regarding justice centered on the handling of resources and treatment of employees.

Israel is told, for instance, that they should not glean the corners of their fields but rather leave this excess for the poor and sojourner (Lev. 19:9–10; 23:22). The ground for this command is simply "I am the LORD your God," thus linking God's righteous character to that of his people. Or one could consider the Year of Jubilee, wherein Israel is to allow the land to rest, restore land to the rightful owner, and release individuals from perpetual servitude (Lev. 25:8–55). Again, the motivation given for these commands stems from God's own character and from the fact that he has redeemed them to be his covenant people (Lev. 25:17, 38, 55).

Since we are a people under the new covenant, these kinds of OT commands regarding justice cannot simply be applied to us today. First, on a basic level, we do not operate under the Mosaic covenant, and many of us do not operate within an agrarian context. Second, we must understand how these kinds of commands concerning justice come to us through the person and work of Christ. Christ came to inaugurate his kingdom, and we await its full consummation (Matt. 6:9–10; 12:28). In his first coming he came not to abolish the law but to fulfill it (Matt. 5:17), and in his fulfilling of the law there are nuances of transformation of which one must be aware. For example, regarding justice to be rendered in the Year of Jubilee, when we view Lev. 25 in light of Isa. 61, it would seem that this event was meant, at least in some sense, to be eschatological in nature (Bruno, 94). This is further seen when we consider Luke 4:17–19, where Jesus proclaims in a synagogue in Nazareth that he is the fulfillment of Isa. 61:1–2. Christopher Bruno notes, "While other aspects of Jubilee, particularly physical and economic relief, are present in the ministry of Jesus, they are pointers to a greater reality, namely, the forgiveness of sin and the restoration of the relationship between God and his people" (99). Thus, as the Year of Jubilee is an institution in Israel's covenant relationship with God, one must understand it both in its near context and in the way it is now to operate among a new-covenant people. Jesus models and teaches about justice being rendered under the new covenant, but primarily the liberty to be enjoyed is that of the forgiveness of sins. This is due to his work on the cross and the nature of his kingdom as one that grows by means of making and multiplying disciples of Jesus (Matt. 28:18–20). We must not grow weary in rendering right judgments and caring for others, especially for those of the household of faith (Gal. 6:10; cf. James 1:27), but the issue of justice must be rightly placed within the context of how God renders ultimate justice to his people—namely, through belief in the gospel of Jesus Christ. The most just thing we can do for all of humanity is to proclaim the good news by which they can be justly justified and transformed so as to render justice increasingly in creation.

This brief biblical-theological and hermeneutical sketch demonstrates that justice is tightly tethered to one's understanding of God's character, the progression of the covenants, the work of Christ, the nature of the kingdom of God, and the relationship between Israel and the church. God demonstrates his righteousness throughout redemptive history, but it is essential to consider Jesus's person and work to integrate fully his justification of an unrighteous people. Through his life, death, and resurrection, Jesus inaugurated a kingdom, which is made up of his followers, who are transformed by grace and faith to render justice in all they do as God's people. The further we move away from the emphasis on forgiven sin and the restoration of the relationship between God and his people by means of the gospel, the further we move away from a NT understanding of justice. Yes, we are to care for the poor, the widow, and the orphan and to render right judgments that will lead to fair practices and nonexploitation, and we are to do so in a variety of ways. And the best way to lead others toward that end is to proclaim how the just God justly justifies the unjust, to declare that this good news is to be received by faith, and to see the Spirit continue to transform a people to live in increasing righteousness.

See also Consummation; Covenant; Day of the Lord; Gospel

Bibliography. Birch, B. C., "Justice," in *Dictionary of Scripture and Ethics*, ed. J. B. Green (Baker Academic, 2011), 433–37; Bruno, C. R., "Jesus Is Our Jubilee . . . But How?," *JETS* 53 (2010): 81–101; DeYoung, K., and G. Gilbert, *What Is the Mission of the Church?* (Crossway, 2011); Feinberg, J. S., *Continuity and Discontinuity* (Crossway, 1988); Feinberg, *No One Like Him* (Crossway, 2001); Harbin, M. A., "Jubilee and Social Justice," *JETS* 54 (2011): 685–99; Hays, J. D., "'Sell Everything You Have and Give to the Poor,'" *JETS* 55 (2012): 43–63; Keller, T., *Generous Justice* (Dutton, 2010); Leeman, J., *What Is Justice?* (Crossway, forthcoming); Moo, D. J., *The Epistle to the Romans*, NICNT (Eerdmans, 1996); Piper, J., *The Justification of God*, 2nd ed. (Baker, 1993); Shogren, G. S., "Justice," in *Evangelical Dictionary of Biblical Theology*, ed. W. A. Elwell (Baker, 1996), 440–43; Treat, J. R., *The Crucified King* (Zondervan, 2014).

JEREMY KIMBLE

Justification

Christian understandings of justification long have been associated with Paul, with his arguments in Galatians and Romans, and especially with the cluster of texts in these letters and others that speak of God's saving work in Jesus Christ as the justification of the fallen and sinful human being (Rom. 1:16–17; 3:1–26; 4:1–5:21; Gal. 2:11–21; 3:6–14, 23–29). These texts are supplemented by the response to the message of Paul found in the Letter of James, which likewise has played a significant role in Christian conceptions of God's justifying work (James 2:14–26). Alongside them stand various passages in the Pauline corpus (inter alia, Phil. 3:6–9; 1 Cor. 1:30; 6:11; 2 Cor. 3:9; 5:17, 21) and Luke-Acts (Luke 18:9–14; Acts 13:38). The contention between God and the world that runs through John's Gospel and into the Apocalypse is also relevant to the theme of justification, although seldom explored (John 16:8–10; Rev. 16:5–7).

It is apparent from Paul's appeals to the Scriptures that his language concerning justification is shaped by Jewish tradition and the Scriptures. This conceptual framework differs from Hellenistic thought in significant ways. Paul's arguments concerning justification deal with first-century Jewish issues that are vital to the life of the gentile congregations in Galatia, Rome, and elsewhere that have emerged from the proclamation of Jesus as Messiah. Christian living and Christian identity are at stake, along with the question of Christian hope.

The Background and Context of Justification in Scripture and Early Judaism

The English term "justification" normally is associated with the idea of divine recognition and approval of a person standing before the final divine judgment. "Righteousness" often signifies personal rectitude or moral virtue. In its individualistic connotations, English usage differs from that of both Hebrew and Greek, which bear social and creational dimensions. In many instances the biblical terms that appear in English as "justification" and "righteousness" might be rendered as "justice" and are associated with a rightly ordered creation (LXX Isa. 45:7–9; 48:18–19; 51:1; 53:11).

The scope of the references to "justification" in Paul's Letters as well as in other NT writings becomes apparent within the broader field of conceptions of "righteousness" and "justice" derived from Scripture and present in early Judaism. It quickly becomes clear from a survey of the usage of *dikaioō* in the LXX (48x) that the verb "justify" consistently bears a distinct "forensic" connotation. The same applies to the usage of cognate nouns and adjectives in contexts that speak of a justifying act. This forensic connotation goes beyond the human relation with God to include social relations—that is, recognition and approval by others (Sir. 10:29; 13:3; 18:22; Luke 16:15) and thus also a self-relation based on this approval (Sir. 7:5; Luke 10:29). The theme of recognition and the self-understanding that emerges from it resonate with Paul's statements about "justification" in the human-divine relation and the final divine judgment. Paul appeals to LXX Ps. 31:1–2 (MT 32:1–2) in Rom. 4:7–8 and thereby links the forgiveness of sins and the Lord's "not counting" sin to "the *blessing*" of God's "reckoning righteousness apart from works." Forgiveness thus expresses an essential element of Paul's understanding of God's justifying work in Christ. The question of human identity and the *source* of recognition and approval—namely, whether it comes directly from God or is granted by human beings—is likewise included within the debate over faith and the "works of the law" (Rom. 4:9–12).

The most frequent context of the verb *dikaioō* within Scripture and Jewish tradition is that of a contention, in which two parties dispute opposing claims to justice. These contentions generally involve the calling of witnesses and often entail the introduction of a third party bearing authority, such as a priest, judge, or king, who is to adjudicate the contested matter (cf. Exod. 23:6–7; Deut. 25:1–2; 2 Sam. 15:2–4; Isa. 50:8). The contention itself, however, remains a dispute over justice between the two parties. The "judges" of Israel are known as such because as "charismatic leaders" raised up by the Lord, their essential task is judging—whether in favor of Israel over against its adversaries or within Israel over internal disputes (Ruth 1:1). The later role of the king likewise is essentially that of "ruling and judging" in righteousness, a hope that appears prominently in the promise of the coming "root of Jesse" (Isa. 11:1–10).

In biblical understanding, the administration of justice is to be an act of mediating the judgments of God. Both priests and, later, kings are the Lord's anointed, and his ruling and judging are entrusted to them. At the opening of Deuteronomy, Moses thus reminds the appointed judges that "judgment belongs to God" (Deut. 1:17). Correspondingly, Ps. 72, which is attributed to Solomon, begins with the petition "God, give your judgments to the king and the just outcome that is yours to the king's son" (Ps. 72:1 AT). At the same time, within Israel there is direct access to God in the temple, where those with complaints might present their appeals for vindication—that is, for "justification" (1 Kings 8:31–32; 2 Chron. 6:22–23). Appeals to God for justice likewise appear frequently within Psalms (cf. Pss. 9; 10; 35; 82), as do the celebrations of God's judgments (Ps. 98).

God's acts of judgment arise from his authority as king not merely of Israel but of the entire creation (Gen. 18:25; Pss. 24; 47; 98). In his saving act of judgment, he makes Israel his people and himself Israel's king (Exod. 15:1–18; Pss. 44:1–8; 47). References to God's ruling, judging, and effecting justice and righteousness consequently are associated with the Lord acting as king, as is especially prominent in the royal psalms (Pss. 93–99) and in Isaiah (41:21–24; 43:8–21). "Justification" and the "righteousness of God" presuppose the conceptual framework of the ruling and judging God. The Lord intervenes both on behalf of the oppressed and, as the one true God and Creator, for his own cause both in contention with his people (Hosea 4:1–17; Mic. 6:1–8) and with the world and its idols (Isa. 41:1–7, 21–29; 43:8–28; 45:9–13).

The psalmists are aware that the Lord acts not merely with respect to the injustice of nations and peoples but also in response to individual wrongs (Pss. 5; 7:1–8; 9; 10). The psalmist who appeals to the Lord to judge and destroy his enemy is nevertheless aware of his own guilt as well as that of all who live and petitions the Lord not to contend with him (143:2). Correspondingly, other psalms speak of the blessing of forgiveness before God (Pss. 32; 51). As noted above, Paul takes up these themes of individual guilt and forgiveness directly from these psalms (Rom. 3:20; 4:6–8; Gal. 2:16).

The role of God as ruler and judge—whether of Israel or the nations—makes clear that justification is not to be understood in terms of God's covenant faithfulness toward Israel (contrary to the view of N. T. Wright). The universal dimension of the divine judgments speaks against this interpretation, as does the awareness that God's judgments fall on individuals, not merely on nations. That is not to say that God's faithfulness to his people Israel is irrelevant to the biblical understanding of God's justifying acts. These acts are described in Scripture as an expression of the Lord's faithfulness to his word of promise (Isa. 40:8; 45:23–24; 55:9–11). The fulfillment of that promise in the judgment on behalf of Israel takes place, however, as an unanticipated event. It follows Israel's violation of its covenantal relationship with the Lord (Isa. 42:18–25; 43:22–28). The sheer wonder of the Lord's saving righteousness is apparent in Isaiah, where the Lord announces that he will prevail in his contention with the idols, the nations, and his own people in fulfillment of his own word by saving his people and the nations in spite of themselves (44:1–5, 21–23; 45:8–13). The Lord himself creates righteousness. His justifying act has no basis in Israel's faithfulness. Just the opposite is true: it comes in the face of Israel's rebellion. The covenant has been broken. Israel's history is reduced to null in the wake of the judgment that has fallen upon it (42:10–25; 43:22–28; 46:3–12; 48:1–22; 50:1–3). Saving righteousness arises from the Lord, the Creator, who in an act of judgment establishes his right and his righteousness in the world, manifesting that he is the one true God (45:18–25). In the wake of judgment, the Lord promises a new covenant with his people (Jer. 31:31–34; Isa. 59:15–21; Ezek. 37:20–28). To construe "God's righteousness" and his justifying work as "covenant faithfulness" is to forget that salvation is constituted in judgment. It is to forget that God's righteousness must be revealed (Ps. 98:1–3; Rom. 1:16–17).

The judgments of Israel's kings also are regarded as establishing justice in ever new ways within the world. Righteousness is not a stable and fixed reality. It has to be sought again and again: "Justice, justice you shall pursue" (Deut. 16:20 AT). The appeal to the Lord to "give [his] judgments to the king and the just outcome that is [his] to the king's son" presupposes this need to find justice (Ps. 72:1). The story of Solomon's celebrated judgment concerning the contested infant is a dramatic example of the discovery of justice in new and unexpected circumstances (1 Kings 3:23–28). In a certain respect, the concentration on Torah and the development of halakah in early Judaism resulted from the absence of rulers who could establish justice in the changing circumstances of Israel's life. Within Israel's earlier life, the judgment of a king established law. Thus, for example, David's pronouncement that those who stay with the baggage and those who go into battle share equally in the spoils becomes law: "He made it a statute and judgment in Israel until this day" (1 Sam. 30:25 AT). The decisions of priests in an earlier period are characterized in the same way (Deut. 17:8–13).

The world, as the Scriptures present it, is not a peaceful Eden, even if the memory of that well-ordered world, full of righteousness and peace, remains. It is instead a battleground where oppression, violence, and bloodshed rage, a place in which the just and righteous order of the Creator is constantly under siege. Righteousness and order are not a given and unchanging reality for Israel but a gift of God in a world that has been invaded by evil. Consequently, in contrast with Hellenistic thought, the world is seen as bearing a "broken goodness" that can be repaired only by divine intervention. The Hellenistic understanding of "distributive justice" is certainly present within Scripture (Pss. 18:20–30; 62:9–12), but it is not the final and decisive element of the biblical understanding. The Lord makes himself known in acts of triumph over evil and in the forgiveness of sins. For this reason, in the context of God's justifying acts, "righteousness" is understood as a saving righteousness that brings justice to a rebellious and broken world (Isa. 51:1–6; 53:11). This usage stands in contrast to normal Hellenistic usage in which "to justify" meant to condemn and punish. While the punishment of evil is presupposed in the establishing of righteousness, it is the salvific righteousness itself that stands at the center of attention and transcends anything that its recipients have earned or deserved. The Lord creates righteousness anew within the broken creation.

This establishing of justice makes clear that the judgments rendered are regarded as effective. Verdicts are viewed synthetically, joined to the enactments of the judgment they require. Verdict and vindication can be distinguished, but they are not separated. This perspective finds linguistic expression. In Hebrew, as well as in the Greek of the LXX and the NT, "justification" and "righteousness" signify vindication and justice effected. Thus, David *performs* just judgment and righteousness for (or "upon," LXX) all Israel (2 Sam. 8:15). The same synthetic conception of justification may be seen in Paul's word that Jesus has been raised "for our justification" (Rom. 4:25) and in his reminder to the Corinthians that they "have been washed, made holy, justified" in the name of Jesus and by the Spirit (1 Cor. 6:11 AT). Justification and sanctification thus are not distinct elements within an order of salvation. They are differing dimensions of one salvation in the crucified and risen Lord. Justification takes place in a divine performative speech act. Indeed, it is the *ultimate* performative speech act, which transcends all others: it creates righteousness and justice and re-creates the human being.

The Background and Context of Paul's Message of Justification

The NT witness to God's justifying work in Jesus is a theological elaboration of the common early Christian confession "that Christ died for our sins according to the Scriptures, and that he was entombed, and that he was raised on the third day, according to the Scriptures" (1 Cor. 15:3–4 AT). This early confession twice refers to the Scriptures as its basis, once in reference to the death of Jesus and once in reference to his resurrection. In both instances an interpretive word is attached to the narration: Christ died *for our sins*. He was raised *on the third day*.

Paul's message of justification is nothing other than the further interpretive restatement of this gospel in response to the question of the relationship between the gospel of Christ and the law of God given to Israel. It is no accident that this articulation of the gospel is found in Paul's Letters: his mission to the gentiles demands it. It consequently bears a hermeneutical element: God's justifying work in Christ transcends the law and thereby brings it to fulfillment (Rom. 13:8–14; Gal. 5:13–14; 6:2, 14–16).

As is the case for the earliest confession of the gospel itself, Paul's message of justification is the interpretation of Jesus's cross and resurrection. Both elements of the saving event are included within his announcement of God's justifying work. Justification takes place through "the redemption that is in Christ Jesus" (Rom. 3:24 ESV; cf. Isa. 43:1; 44:22–24; 63:4), whom God purposed to be his "mercy seat" (Rom. 3:25 AT; cf. Exod. 25:17–22; Lev. 16:12–15). Paul thereby points not merely to the death of Christ but to the crucified and risen Lord as the mercy seat of God. The same thought appears in Rom. 5:9–10. In Rom. 4:25, Paul announces that "our justification" has taken place through the resurrection of the crucified Jesus. Likewise, in Gal. 2:19–21, he describes righteousness as coming to him through his being crucified with Christ and given a new life. Paul thus understands justification as the justification of the ungodly through God's fulfillment of his saving promise to Abraham in the resurrection of the crucified Jesus (Rom. 4), in whom we are incorporated and who is given to us in faith. The "peace with God" that is ours in justification (5:1) is given to us "through our Lord, Jesus Christ." Our faith is the divinely worked response to the gift of peace and life already given in the crucified and risen Christ. With Paul, justification is a confession of the crucified *and risen* Lord.

The justifying event of Christ's cross and resurrection is forensic in nature, as is especially clear in Gal. 3:13, where Paul speaks of Christ redeeming "us"—both Jews and gentiles—"from the curse of the law" so that the divine blessing of Abraham might come to reality in Christ (Gal. 3:13–14). Justification takes place in a dynamic exchange in which Christ takes on the reality of our sin, becoming what we are, in order that we might become what he is in his righteousness (2 Cor. 5:21).

The law, with its demands, exposes every human being in their subjection to the power of sin, according to Paul. It lays bare the attempt of all human beings to justify themselves despite their godlessness, lies, oppression, and violence (Rom. 3:9–20). Even the law-observant Jew is manifest as a "sinner" (Gal. 2:15–17). This apostolic assertion is not limited to the first century. It speaks to all the pious, up to the present. The setting of Paul's message of justification is that of the contention between God and every fallen human being, who all tragically live under sin's power (Rom. 3:9; 5:12; 7:7–13; Gal. 3:22). Echoing Ps. 51:5, Paul presents this contention in dramatic terms. Every human being shall be exposed as a liar. God shall be justified in his words and shall triumph when he enters into judgment (Rom. 3:4). This description of the state of the world recalls the Lord's contention with the idols, the nations, and his people as it appears in Isaiah (41:1–7, 21–29; 42:10–25; 43:8–28; 44:6–20; 45:9–46:13; 48:1–22). It likewise anticipates the final judgment (Rom. 14:10–12; Gal. 6:5; 2 Cor. 5:10). As Paul's following announcement of the manifestation of God's righteousness makes clear, it also speaks of Jesus's cross and resurrection (Rom. 3:21). In this justifying event the contention between God and the rebellious and idolatrous human being is resolved. Justification is therefore simultaneously the justification of God and the justification of the fallen human being, through the wonder of God's redeeming love in Christ. God has "demonstrated" his righteousness so that he might be recognized as "just and the justifier" of the one who "is of the faith that comes from Jesus" (Rom. 3:26 AT). Our justification is our judgment, and vice versa.

As Paul's language in Rom. 3:26 makes clear, this justification is to be understood in individual terms. As noted above, he goes on to describe justification as the "blessing" of forgiveness of sins that was granted to David and to Abraham and that is granted to each one who, with Abraham, believes (Rom. 4:6–8; Ps. 32:1–2). Similarly, he speaks in Galatians both of God's recognition and acceptance of believers as his "sons" and as heirs of the world and of their Spirit-mediated recognition of God as Father (Gal. 4:6–9). The personal, existential, and experiential dimension of Paul's message of justification is not to be ignored.

His message, however, remains social and creational. God's work in Jesus rectifies the long period of his patience, in which he ignored the sins that were committed, the deceit, oppression, and violence that terrorize this world (Rom. 3:9–20, 26). The justified have been thrust into the service of God's righteousness on the battleground of this world (Rom. 6). Their service is that of witness and suffering with Christ. As those who belong to God through Christ, they come under attack by the forces of the enslaved creation. They thus share in the contention between God and the world. They are, as the psalmist complains, "sheep given to slaughter" (Rom. 8:36 AT; Ps. 44:22). They nevertheless shall not be condemned but shall be justified over against the world by Christ, the one who died and has been raised and who intercedes for them (Rom. 8:34).

Paul presents justification as a redeeming event located in the crucified and risen Christ (Rom. 3:24–26). In him are we made to be the righteousness of God (2 Cor. 5:21). In Christ the blessing of Abraham has come about. Prefigured in Isaac, he is the one seed of Abraham (Gal. 3:14, 16). In Christ, and only in Christ, we are "sons of God" and "Abraham's seed" (3:26, 29 ESV). By God's doing, we have been placed "in Christ," who is our righteousness—and our holiness and wisdom (1 Cor. 1:30). Our righteousness remains outside of us in him.

Correspondingly, the event of justification cannot be reduced to a mere transaction, forensic though it is. Nor does it represent a simple turn in redemptive history. It is the incursion of the eschaton into the present world in Jesus Christ. Paul thus announces that "the righteousness of God" has been revealed in the gospel, just as the psalmist before him celebrated the revelation of God's righteousness in his saving judgment before the eyes of the world (Ps. 98). Both the psalmist and Paul still await the final revelation of God's righteousness. But the gospel of the crucified and risen Jesus that Paul announces, in which the righteousness of God is revealed, is no mere event in the course of history. Jesus, the seed of David, is set apart as the Son of God by his "resurrection from among the dead" (Rom. 1:3–4 AT). The newness of life given to believers is their present participation in Jesus's resurrection. The night has passed; the day has come (13:8–14). Paul's "*but now* the righteousness of God has been manifested" is the announcement of the eschatological moment of the fulfillment of Scripture in the crucified and risen Christ and the gospel that proclaims him (3:21 ESV). Salvation has arrived. In Christ we have been justified. The kingdom of God has intersected human history in Jesus (14:17). That we must still give account of ourselves before God's "judgment seat" (*bēma)* emerges from this intersection of the eschaton with the world in Christ as the paradox of the life of faith (14:10–12). Justified by faith, we seek our justification in Christ (Gal. 2:16–17) and "wait for the hope of righteousness" (5:5 ESV).

The justifying event is mediated to human beings by the faith that is given in Christ and distributed through the apostolic witness. The prior faith of Israel and its patriarchs notwithstanding, this faith is a unique, eschatological reality. It has come only as Christ has come (Gal. 3:23–26). It comes from the apostolic message that echoes and fulfills the prophetic voice of Isaiah (Rom. 10:16–17; Isa. 53:1). The apostolic message furthermore has its origin in the "word of Christ"—namely, the word that God has spoken to the world in the incarnate, crucified, and risen Jesus (Rom. 10:17; cf. 10:6–8). Consequently, for Paul, "faith" is no mere human disposition, nor can it be transposed to its linguistic and conceptual counterpart, the idea of "faithfulness." Faith is determined by its content. Paul speaks of "the faith of Christ," not as Jesus's faith(fulness) but as the faith that has Christ as its content and that comes from him (Rom. 3:22, 26; Gal. 2:20; 3:22; Phil. 3:9).

The proclamation of the gospel and the call to faith correspondingly bear a universal scope. The righteousness of God revealed in it is "for the Jew first and also for the Greek" (Rom. 1:16–17 AT). It is this universal, apostolic proclamation of justifying faith that Paul defends in Rom. 1–4 and Gal. 3–4. The question at stake in both instances is the relationship of the law to God's saving work in Jesus. As one called as an apostle and set apart for the gospel, Paul recognizes that "a person is justified by faith apart from the works of the law" (Rom. 3:28).

Two inseparable but distinct issues are at stake in this judgment. First, works of the law are excluded from justification and therewith from the determination of our standing at the final judgment. Paul addresses this question in his subsequent appeal to the figure of Abraham: the childless Abraham, in believing the word of promise, believed the God who justifies the ungodly (Rom. 4:1–5). Righteousness was accounted to him apart from his works: this promise to Abraham appears at the single point in the narrative in which Abraham does nothing. God alone acts (Gen. 15:6). Paul presents the figure of Abraham in a related way in Gal. 3:6–29. In both instances, he reinterprets the figure of Abraham on the basis of Scripture in dissent with early Jewish tradition. There Abraham was understood as the paradigm of keeping the law and a law-based covenant of circumcision (Sir. 44:19–21). Paul presents Abraham as the father of the justifying faith of the ungodly. His circumcision is the sign of this justifying faith.

Second, in Romans and Galatians, as well as in Philippians, "justification by faith alone" clearly has to do with the constitution of human identity and the identity of the people of God. Is it necessary to become circumcised, to commit oneself to the law, and to become Jewish in order to be justified before God at the final moment of judgment? Is it necessary to be recognized as such by others? Or does justification rest in a divine act in Jesus that brought the eschaton into the world, transcended the law, and brought its fulfillment (Gal. 3:28)?

Jewish identity was constituted not merely by descent from Abraham or the mark of circumcision but by commitment to the law and the practice of it. The earliest Christians, whether Jew or gentile, had to come to terms with what it meant to believe in Jesus and to affirm the Scriptures that announced the demands of the law. We need not suppose that many of them were troubled by guilt or that they imagined that they had to earn their salvation. Paul's contrast between grace and indebted reward (Rom. 4:4–5) is not a characterization of the early

Jewish understanding of attaining salvation. It represents the apostle's judgment concerning the meaning of "works" and any sort of value attached to them. The problem in earliest Christianity, as well as in the early Judaism out of which it grew, was the unreflective mixing of grace with a requirement of works for salvation.

James on Justification

The brief discussion of justification in the Letter of James almost certainly represents a Jewish Christian response to Paul's message (James 2:14–26). It is unlikely, however, that James attacks Paul in this response. He does not name the apostle, nor does he directly engage Paul's argument, even if he takes up the same themes and appeals to Gen. 15:6, one of the fundamental Pauline texts on justification. James instead provides a warning and corrective to anyone who would turn Paul's argument into a slogan. Perhaps he senses this danger with Paul himself. Even if he does, he does not reject the Pauline message. James takes up the word of the divine reckoning of righteousness to Abraham, interprets it in light of Abraham's sacrifice of Isaac—Jewish tradition regarded the act as effectively completed—and presents it as the fulfillment of the promise of "friendship with God" that is implicit within the divine reckoning of righteousness. Abraham's faith in the promise of descendants had its completion in the sacrifice of Isaac (James 2:21–22; cf. Heb. 11:17–19). The Scripture that announced Abraham's justification came to fulfillment in the same act (James 2:23). A faith without works is a mere spoken faith and not a saving faith (2:18–21, 26). Paul, in his own way, takes the same position, even threatening his hearers with failing to share in the kingdom as it arrives in this world (Gal. 5). Correspondingly, the Jacobian appeal to the justification of Rahab, the harlot, shows that James, too, understands the divine work of justification as the justification of the ungodly (James 2:25; Heb. 11:31).

See also Justice; Law

Bibliography. Bovati, P., *Re-establishing Justice*, ed. M. J. Smith, JSOTSup 105 (JSOT Press, 1994); Carson, D. A., P. T. O'Brien, and M. A. Seifrid, eds., *Justification and Variegated Nomism*, 2 vols. (Baker Academic, 2001, 2004); Kim, S., *Justification and God's Kingdom* (Mohr Siebeck, 2018); Klaiber, W., *Justified before God* (Abingdon, 2006); Laato, T., "Justification according to James," *TJ* 18 (1997): 43–84; Levin, C., "Altes Testament und Rechtfertigung," *ZTK* 96 (1999): 161–76; Prothro, J. B., *Both Judge and Justifier*, WUNT 2/461 (Mohr Siebeck, 2018); Seifrid, M., *Christ, Our Righteousness*, NSBT 9 (InterVarsity, 2000); Stuhlmacher, P., *Biblical Theology of the New Testament*, trans. and ed. D. P. Bailey (Eerdmans, 2018); Wright, N. T., *Paul and the Faithfulness of God*, COQG 4 (Fortress, 2013).

Mark A. Seifrid

K

Kingdom and King

The concepts of kingdom and king in the NT are best understood in terms of their OT background. Both terms are important since a kingdom represents the territory, domain, and people over which the king extends his rule and law. When Jesus begins his ministry, it can be summed up in the sentence "Repent, for the kingdom of heaven is near!" (Matt. 4:17 NET). The concept of God's kingdom is central to his teaching. John the Baptist has the same message and is regarded as the forerunner of Jesus (Matt. 3:2). This message is electric with relevance. Why? To understand it, the OT backstory is fundamental.

The OT Background

The terminology for the kingdom of God is rare in Israel's Scriptures and predominates in late books (e.g., Dan. 4:3 [3:33 MT]; 7:14; 1 Chron. 28:5; 2 Chron. 13:8). The concept, however, is foundational. Key moments throughout the OT include the expectation of a king from the line of David who will usher in a kingdom of universal peace. This is found in the prophets as well as in other writings. For example, in Ps. 2 the anointing of a Davidic king means that the nations must accept his authority or be destroyed because the entire earth will be given to him as an inheritance. Psalm 72 strikes the same note of Davidic kingship resulting in a universal kingdom of shalom. At many places in the prophets, such an ideal state of affairs is due to the advent of a Davidic king who will destroy the wicked, save the oppressed, and transform nature (Isa. 9:5–7; 11:1–10; Ezek. 34:20–31; Hosea 2:16–23; Joel 3:18; Amos 9:11–15; Mic. 5:2–4 [5:1–3 MT]; Zech. 9:9–11; 14:8–21).

Where did this eschatological hope come from? It is clearly in the covenant that God made with David that he would always have a ruler who would eventually reign over the world (2 Sam. 7; cf. Pss. 89; 132). But the germ of this idea is there from the earliest times in Israel. Hannah looks forward to a king who will bring a new world order to the ends of the earth (1 Sam. 2:1–10). So does Balaam before her in his prophecies of a star emerging from Jacob to crush Israel's enemies and of a lion-like, triumphant warrior (Num. 23:24; 24:9, 17–19). Prior to Balaam, Jacob on his deathbed sees a lion from the tribe of Judah receiving obeisance from the nations and bringing about such a renewal of nature that grapevines can be used as hitching posts for donkeys (Gen. 49:8–12). This is an elaboration of an earlier oracle given to him that he would beget a line of kings (Gen. 35:11). And prior to Jacob, God prophesied to Abram that all the nations would be blessed through his seed and that kings would spring from this line (Gen. 12:3; 17:6). This trajectory should put to rest the idea that kingship was a foreign element in Israel, a reversion to paganism and antithetical to Israel's covenantal roots. What was rejected in Israel was a kingship like the other nations, in which the king had autonomous power (cf. 1 Sam. 8:6–18). Rather, the only acceptable kingship was a monarch who would represent God and embody the Torah's teachings (Deut. 17:14–20).

But can this hope be traced back even further than the patriarchs? If one reads the OT as a story beginning with creation, one can clearly see the origin of this trajectory in the creation of the first pair of human beings. God created humanity in his image and likeness to rule the creation, to exercise sovereignty and dominion over his world. The language in Gen. 1:26–28 is replete with royal imagery, and this regal language is the theme of a later psalm: human beings have been made a little less than God and all things have been placed under their feet (Ps. 8:5–8). This last image was common in the ancient world as kings were often portrayed in a regal pose of domination with animals and enemies under their feet. As a result, the first king and queen are Adam and Eve, and they are to extend the divine rule over the world in such a way as to image God in the temple of his creation. They miserably fail in their task by listening to the serpent and not to God. What is the consequence? Certainly curse and death, but God is not finished with them. He promises that the seed of the woman will engage in a war with the seed of the serpent but that someday victory will come for the woman because a descendant will administer a lethal blow to the seed of the serpent (Gen. 3:15).

This is no less than a battle for the world, which is now regarded as under the hegemony of the serpent; God, however, is going to restore the kingdom to its rightful heirs. Eventually a human conqueror will emerge from the descendants of the woman and bring about this restoration. Thus, human beings will bring again God's kingdom to earth. The will of God will be done on earth as it is in heaven. This idea of divinely acknowledged rule by human beings on the earth is essential for the kingdom of God. The OT makes clear that while God is the ruler over the kings of the earth, and over all reality, his rule is not yet acknowledged on the earth. The earth is cursed as a result, and human beings are largely under the control of the serpent.

The rest of the OT is an unfolding of this plot, hence the concern for both genealogy and geography. A human descendant will establish God's rule and God's presence throughout created space: the king will have a kingdom. From Abraham, the Israelite nation is established as a place where the worship of the true God takes place and from which the human descendant will emerge. God's law is given to protect the nation from the contamination of pagan ways. Under it, the nation is to be a light to the rest of the world. God shows himself faithful to Israel in many and various ways, even though his people fail repeatedly. Someday all wrongs will be righted as a king from the line of David emerges to bring about this shalom. As David Howard (34) remarks, "Israel's kingdom was a symbol of God's reign on earth" and "its king God's vice-regent." This ideal was projected into the future in a universal way. Kingship was eschatologized and universalized. Thus, the kingdom of the serpent would be destroyed forever, and all would acknowledge the universal reign of God (Zech. 14:9). In fact, in Micah this person is called a ruler (*môšēl*) and the anagram of this title beautifully captures the peace (*šālôm*) that his universal reign will bring (Mic. 5:2–4 [MT 5:1–3]).

The Gospels

This irruption of the kingdom into the world is the OT hope, so John the Baptist's announcement of the kingdom and the coming king expects God's arrival in the person of the Messiah, the new Adam, to rule the world. Thus, Matthew opens his Gospel with the genealogy of Jesus, the son of David, the son of Abraham (Matt. 1:1–17). Here is the coming one who will bless the entire world. There is an entire network of Scriptures that understand the Davidic king to be God's son who will someday rule the world, through whom all nations of the earth will be blessed. As if to underline this point, Matthew organizes the genealogy of Jesus into three groups of fourteen: Abraham to David, David to the exile, the exile to Jesus. The Hebrew letters for David have the numerical value of fourteen!

Jesus's descent from David is emphasized in Luke's Gospel when Gabriel announces to Mary that she will be the mother of the Messiah with language invoking OT kingdom passages. She is told that her son will inherit the throne of David and a kingdom that will never end (Luke 1:31–33; Isa. 9:5–6). Then Mary sings a song foretelling the logic of this new world order that the birth of her son will launch. Using language from the Song of Hannah, she sings in her Magnificat of the mighty being pulled down from their thrones and the humble being exalted, and she sees this all as a direct fulfillment of the covenant with Abraham (Luke 1:46–55; cf. 1 Sam. 2:1–10).

Zechariah echoes and expands on Mary's words when his son, John the Baptist, is born. A mighty savior from the line of David will be given who has been predicted by the prophets and will save Israel from its enemies, shining light in darkness and ushering in the way of peace (Luke 1:68–79).

Soon wise men from the east come to worship a new king whose birth has been announced in the heavens (Matt. 2:1–2). This echoes the prophecy of Balaam, who had envisioned a star rising out of Jacob who would bring about the defeat of evil powers (Num. 24:17). When Herod demands to know the location of the birth of this new king, Jewish priests and teachers tell him that the king will be born in Bethlehem according to the prophecy of Micah (Mic. 5:2–4). The actual birth of this child is announced not by a few angels or important personages as in miraculous OT births (Gen. 18:1–10; Judg. 13) but by a heavenly host of angels, to show it is the birth par excellence (Luke 2:8–14). The passage in Micah indicates that this king will have a universal rule marked by peace.

The traveling sages present Jesus with gifts worthy of royalty, fulfilling another OT prophecy (Isa. 60:6). Accordingly, when Jesus is baptized with the Spirit at the Jordan River, he hears the words, "You are my beloved Son, in whom I find delight" (Matt. 3:17 AT). Two references here relate to kingship: in Ps. 2 the Davidic king is anointed to be God's son and to have universal dominion, and in Isa. 42:1–6 God's servant is the one whom God commissions to bring justice to the world. In Isaiah the mission will be achieved gradually, not instantly, demanding considerable endurance from the king. Though exhausting, the mission will not finally exhaust him (Isa. 42:3–4). In this mission the king will be different from those of the nations; he will comfort the exhausted and revive the fainthearted, and he will not draw attention to himself and his achievements in the process. Moreover, by using the term "beloved Son," the voice from heaven may well draw on the story of the sacrifice of Isaac in Gen. 22, where a father offers up his beloved son as a sacrifice to God. In line with the Isaiah passage, the idea of kingship is associated with suffering (cf. Isa. 53).

After his baptism, Jesus immediately proceeds to the desert, where he fasts, prays, and meditates on the divine word and his mission as the Son of God (Matt. 4:1–11). Here he encounters the tempter and does battle with the one who holds the world under his power, the prince of darkness. Jesus is constantly tested to prove his sonship, but nowhere more powerfully than in the last temptation in Matthew when he is offered all the kingdoms of the world held under Satan's sway and bondage, if he but bows down and worships Satan. The allusion in Matt. 4:8–9 is to Dan. 7, where the son of man will eventually receive all the kingdoms of the world, but Jesus knows it will happen only if he fulfills the divine will. There is no shortcut. Satan offers an alternative to kingship that bypasses the path of suffering on the cross, but Jesus firmly rejects it. Adam, the first human king, fails in the garden against the serpent's temptation and loses his kingship, but Jesus, the second Adam, succeeds in the desert and maintains his royal status.

When Jesus leaves the desert after defeating and dethroning Satan, he moves into the devil's domain in the northern part of Judea, Galilee of the nations, and he begins to announce the coming of the kingdom; his message can be summed up in the sentence "Repent, for the kingdom of heaven is near!" (Matt. 4:17 NET). This is no less than an invasion of the kingdom of God into human history, brilliant light coming into the midst of a dark world. Matthew regards this as a fulfillment of Isaiah's ancient prophecy of a Davidic king who will become a universal ruler: "Land of Zebulun . . . Galilee of the Gentiles—the people living in darkness have seen a great light" (Matt. 4:13–16). With this quote the larger context of Isaiah is invoked: "For to us a child is born. . . . And he will be called Wonderful Counselor, Mighty God, Everlasting Father, Prince of Peace. Of the greatness of his government and peace there will be no end. He will reign on David's throne and over his kingdom" (Isa. 9:6–7).

Hence, Jesus begins his healing ministry amid his preaching of the good news of the kingdom. Satan's kingdom is clearly being despoiled, as Jesus later points out when he is accused of being in league with Satan after healing a demon-possessed man (Matt. 12:22–32). The accusation comes immediately after the crowd's response to this miracle that Jesus must be the messianic king, the son of David (12:23). Jesus answers his accusers by stating that Satan would never cast out Satan since a house divided against itself cannot stand. Then he states, "If it is by the Spirit of God that I drive out demons, then the kingdom of God has come upon you." He elaborates, "Or again, how can anyone enter a strong man's house and carry off his possessions unless he first ties up the strong man? Then he can plunder his house" (12:28–29; cf. Isa. 49:24–25). Clearly the kingdom of God is being enlarged because the strong man in charge of the kingdom of darkness has been bound.

That the kingdom is making gradual inroads into Satan's domain is shown by Jesus's Sermon on the Mount (Matt. 5–7), which functions as the constitution of the kingdom. The beatitudes indicate both a present and a future orientation. The first and last ones indicate that Jesus's disciples enjoy a present status in the kingdom while the beatitudes in between indicate the kingdom in its fullness has not yet arrived. Thus, while the poor of spirit are enjoying the kingdom of heaven (5:3), the meek have not yet inherited the earth (5:5). Moreover, when Jesus teaches his disciples how to pray, he utilizes this concept of the OT kingdom as God's reign. They are urged to pray for both the name of God and the kingdom of God: "Let your name be sanctified, let your kingdom come, let your will be done on earth as it is in heaven" (6:9–10 AT). Joining God's name and kingship evokes Zech. 14:9. Jesus is therefore teaching his disciples to pray for the arrival of that day when God's sovereignty will be established over and recognized throughout the world.

Some of Jesus's miracles have a rich OT background dealing with sovereignty and kingship. One of the key demonstrations of sovereignty in ancient Israel is God's mastery over the hostile storms. God is able to still a hostile storm with a word, where sailors were desperately crying to him for help, proving his sovereignty (Ps. 107:23–32; cf. Gen. 1:2–3; Exod. 15). Jesus does the same when his disciples cry out to him for help in the storm on the Sea of Galilee. Similarly, when describing God's sovereignty in creation, Job remarks, "He alone stretches out the heavens and treads on the waves of the sea" (Job 9:8). Jesus is no different when he walks on the water coming to his disciples to relieve their distress (Matt. 14:22–34).

Jesus's kingly rule is demonstrated by the healing of a crippled man on the Sabbath (Matt. 9:1–8). When he forgives the sin of the man first, some are offended. Then, to show that he has divine authority to do so, he heals the man. This proves that he is the Son of Man coming on the clouds of heaven to rule the world (Dan. 7:13–14). Jesus later removes any ambiguity about his fulfillment of this text at his trial when he solemnly declares under oath, "From now on you will see the Son of Man sitting at the right hand of the Mighty One and coming on the clouds of heaven" (Matt. 26:64). The high priest's immediate charge of blasphemy reveals that he understands Jesus's words only too well.

In other miracles Jesus functions as the royal servant of Yahweh who is on a mission to bring his rule to the ends of the earth but in a different way than that of most rulers, who are concerned for power and status. After healing many people, he admonishes them not to broadcast their healing to fulfill the prophecy of Isaiah: "Here is my servant whom I have chosen. . . . He will not quarrel or cry out; no one will hear his voice in the streets" (Matt. 12:18–21). This is the longest OT citation in Matthew and it testifies to quiet, faithful service and eventual universal kingship. This king and his kingdom are unique. Jesus teaches his disciples that they must imitate this principle of regal service in their own lives. His ultimate argument for the pathway of royal service is his own example of coming not to be served but to serve and give his life as a ransom for many (cf. Mark 10:35–45). Jesus has in mind the entire context of Isa. 40–55, where God's faithful servant who reigns on high with him stoops to the depths and gives his life in place of his people (Isa. 52:13–53:12).

Jesus reaffirms the reality of the kingdom to correct any misunderstanding of the nature of his mission. First will come salvation, later judgment. At the announcement of his mission at his hometown of Nazareth, recorded in Luke, Jesus reads a portion of Isaiah at the synagogue, identifying his mission with the predicted anointed servant of Yahweh: "The Spirit of the Lord is on me, because he has anointed me to proclaim good news to the poor . . . to set the oppressed free, to proclaim the year of the Lord's favor" (Luke 4:18–19; Isa. 61:1–2a). In this reading Jesus omits "to proclaim . . . the day of vengeance of our God, to comfort all those who mourn" (Isa. 61:2b). Thus, first will come salvation and then judgment. They will not be simultaneous.

The same is implied later when the now imprisoned John the Baptist expresses doubt about Jesus's messianic role. After all, the wicked are not burning up like chaff and Herod is continuing his despotic rule. Jesus instructs John to revise his kingdom timetable, telling him that the miracles of God's future kingdom predicted in Isaiah are now being fulfilled: "The blind receive sight, the lame walk, lepers are cleansed, the deaf hear, the dead are raised, and good news is proclaimed to the poor" (Matt. 11:4–5; cf. Isa. 35:5–6; 61:1). The day of judgment is being delayed so that the kingdom can advance.

When Jesus enters Jerusalem riding on a donkey, he fulfills the OT promises regarding the return to Zion of its king and the exaltation of Jerusalem to be the city of light in the world of darkness, both of which are described throughout Isa. 40–66. But the Gospel writers explicitly cite this act of Jesus as fulfilling Zech. 9:9–11 (cf. Matt. 21:5; Mark 11:5; John 12:15). He rides not on a warhorse but on a lowly donkey to show the peaceful nature of his kingdom. However, when the Gospel writers cite this text, they omit the elimination of war and the global dimensions of peace. The point is that these aspects of the reign and kingdom of the Messiah will come at a later time. The kingdom is going to come in installments.

That is precisely the point of some of Jesus's teachings about the kingdom. The preaching of the kingdom is like seed sown in different types of soil. It has different effects in different soils, but eventually it will bring forth a great harvest in the good soil (Matt. 13:1–9, 18–23). Again, the kingdom is like leaven that is kneaded into flour, gradually leavening the whole loaf of bread (Matt. 13:33).

The kingdom, however, is not an ordinary political kingdom. In fact, Jesus says that his kingdom is not of this world (John 18:36). Otherwise, he would send legions of angels to overpower his enemies (Matt. 26:53). But allegiance to the king must be accepted into people's hearts, not coerced, to bring a change from the inside out. Thus, his disciples are like the new Jerusalem of Isa. 60, who shine their light of good works into a world of darkness (Matt. 5:14–16).

After the resurrection, Jesus is installed as the new king at the right hand of God. With all the authority of heaven and earth, the prophecy about the son of man in Dan. 7 is now realized as Jesus sends his disciples to all the nations (Matt. 28:18–20; cf. Dan. 7:14). In a very real sense, then, his saints are also given the rule of the nations (Dan. 7:27). Their question about whether Christ is going to restore the kingdom after the resurrection in Acts betrays a distorted understanding. It is not going to happen as they think with shock and awe as one might gather from a cursory reading of OT texts, but rather as they wait for empowerment from on high with the gift of the Holy Spirit. Then they will be the king's witnesses in all of Judea, Samaria, even unto the ends of the earth (Acts 1:6–8).

Acts and Paul

It is this announcement in Acts 1:6–8 that motivates the disciples in Acts as they spread out in the task of world evangelism. They boldly speak of a new king, Jesus, who will not tolerate any rivals. James proves from the OT that through Jesus and the message to the gentiles, God is rebuilding the fallen kingdom of David "so that the rest of humanity may seek the Lord" (Acts 15:17 NET; Amos 9:12 LXX).

Opposition to this kingdom leads to persecution and imprisonment of early Christians. This results in members of the early church reading Israel's Scriptures and seeing their situation in the light of Ps. 2, where the newly appointed Davidic king experiences resistance from ancient monarchs: "Indeed Herod and Pontius Pilate met together with the Gentiles and the people of Israel in this city to conspire against your holy servant Jesus, whom you anointed" (Acts 4:28). Jesus is the climactic fulfillment of the king of Ps. 2, to whom all the nations of the earth will be given as his inheritance.

As one considers the Pauline corpus of letters, many of the same points are underscored. Jesus Christ is the Lord of Glory but also the one from the seed of David (Rom. 1:3–4). His reign has been inaugurated with his resurrection, and he will reign until all enemies are placed under his feet, with the last enemy being death (1 Cor. 15). Citing a catena of OT texts in Rom. 15, Paul sees his mission to the gentiles as fulfilling this great commission (15:9 [= Ps. 18:49], 10 [= Deut. 32:43], 11 [= Ps. 117:1]). The catena climaxes with the prophecy of a Davidic descendant ruling the nations: "The Root of Jesse will spring up, one who will arise to rule over the nations; in him the Gentiles will hope" (15:12 [= Isa. 11:10 LXX]). In Paul's concluding prayer in Romans, he discerns the ultimate goal of his ministry: all the nations will come to experience the obedience that comes from faith in the Messiah (Rom. 16:26).

This goal compels Paul to announce the good news. He conceives of the kingdom of God in terms of inaugurated eschatology. The kingdom has come in Jesus Christ and this new king is right now through his disciples calling people to submit to his lordship and be filled with the Holy Spirit, thus creating a new society of love and forgiveness. Outside this society is the kingdom of darkness where the flesh rules rather than the Spirit, and where Satan, the prince of the power of the air, still holds sway (Eph. 2:1–3; Gal. 1:4; Col. 1:13). But the final goal of history is not in doubt. In Philippians, Paul uses the language of Isa. 45 and applies it to Christ. He states that someday every knee will bow and every tongue confess that Jesus Christ is Lord (Phil. 2:10–11 [= Isa. 45:23]).

Hebrews and the Catholic Letters

In Hebrews, the kingdom of God is emphasized in a number of ways with citations from the OT. The writer cites Ps. 8, which describes the royal dignity of the human race, crowned with glory and honor (Heb. 2:5–15). They were created to have dominion over the world: all things were to be placed under their feet. But the writer points out that human beings have forfeited this grand destiny. All things are not presently under the dominion of human beings, "for we do not see all things under their power" (Heb. 2:8 AT). However, we do see Jesus, who was for a short while made lower than the angels, crowned with glory and honor because he submitted to death "to deliver human beings from the power of the devil that they might be delivered from the slavery of the fear of death" (2:14–15 AT). Christ has restored the original glory, majesty, and destiny of humanity.

Human royalty is emphasized as well by Peter, who writes to his audience reminding them of their identity in a collage of texts from the OT. They are an elect race, a priestly kingdom, a holy nation, an extraordinary people. Their purpose is that they might declare the praises "of the one who called you from darkness into his marvelous light" (1 Pet. 2:9 AT). Regal servant language defining Israel's status at Sinai (Exod. 19:5–6) is joined with terminology describing God's equipping of his servant after an exodus-like experience (Isa. 43:20).

Revelation

Since Revelation describes the consummation of God's kingdom in the world, it is replete with images from the OT that enhance its message. From the very beginning it celebrates the new status of Christians, who have been not only forgiven and washed with the blood of Christ but also made "into a line of kings and priests to serve God" (Rev. 1:6 AT). This is language that is again borrowed from God's covenant with Israel at Sinai (Exod. 19:5–6). In John's first vision he collapses as a dead man when he sees the exalted Christ, whom he depicts as the Son of Man and the Ancient of Days in Dan. 7 and the divine angel in Dan. 10 (Rev. 1:9–20). John is granted this vision during a time of crisis for the young church to show that despite what circumstances might suggest in a hostile world, Jesus Christ is the ruler of all the kings of the earth (Rev. 1:5) and his word must be obeyed at all costs (Rev. 2–3). And to those in the church at Thyatira who are faithful, Christ promises authority over the nations and an iron scepter with which to reign (Rev. 2:26–27; cf. Ps. 2:8–9).

When John is transported to heaven to see what will transpire on the earth in the future, his first vision is a visit to the throne room of heaven and earth, where he sees Jesus Christ as the lion from the tribe of Judah and as a slain lamb on a throne (Rev. 4–5). Both images are central to the Christian faith. They depict the suffering and royalty of the Messiah. He who suffered to make salvation possible is now seated on the throne to bring all of history to its conclusion. Both images are indebted to the OT, the conquering lion from Genesis (49:8–12) and the lamb from the many sacrificial passages where domestic animals are offered up as sacrifices on behalf of the people (Gen. 22; Exod. 12; Lev. 1–7; 16).

The vision also shows Christ making his disciples kings and priests unto God so that they reign over the earth, much like the commissioning of Israel at Sinai (Rev. 5:10; Exod. 19:5–6). The vision concludes with the twenty-four elders along with the four living creatures bowing before the throne on which Christ and God are seated. It is a powerful statement of the OT and NT people of God united in praise, as the twelve tribes are joined by the twelve apostles, who join with all creation in ascribing glory, laud, and honor to their king.

Later, Christ is depicted being born. He is slated to rule the nations with an iron rod (Rev. 12:5; Ps. 2:8–9). He engages in battle with the dragon, representing Satan, who seeks to maintain his rule on the earth. Finally, Revelation pictures believers in the new heaven and new earth, in the city of God, portrayed as a garden city of Eden, reigning with Christ forever and ever. The long-awaited kingdom begun in ancient Israel, reaching out with a global mission in Christ and the early church, has finally arrived. "The kingdom of the world has become the kingdom of our Lord and of his Messiah, and he will reign forever and ever" (Rev. 11:15). This is the fulfillment of the destiny for which humanity was made in the beginning (Rev. 22:1–4; Gen. 1:26–28), as they will reign with him forever and ever (Rev. 22:4).

See also Covenant; Holy Spirit, Eschatological Role of; Messiah

Bibliography. Block, D. I., "The Spiritual and Ethical Foundations of Messianic Kingship," in *The Triumph of Grace* (Wipf & Stock, 2017), 335–48; Boling, R. G., *Judges*, AB (Doubleday, 1975); Dempster, S. G., "Hannah's Song, a New World Order and the Right Side of History," in *Ecclesia Semper Reformanda Est*, ed. D. B. Barker, M. A. G. Haykin, and B. Howson (Joshua Press, 2016), 3–32; Du Plessis, I. J., "The Relation between the Old and the New Testaments from the Perspective of Kingship/Kingdom including the Messianic Motif," *Neot* 14 (1981): 42–61; Dumbrell, W. J., "Spirit and Kingdom of God in the Old Testament," *RTR* 33 (1974): 1–10; Goswell, G. R., "The Shape of Kingship in Deut. 17," *TJ* 38 (2017): 169–81; Howard, D. M., Jr., "The Case for Kingship in the Old Testament Narrative Books and the Psalms," *TJ* 9 (1988): 19–35; Patrick, D., "The Kingdom of God in the Old Testament," in *The Kingdom of God in Twentieth Century Interpretation*, ed. W. Willis (Wipf & Stock, 2020), 67–80; Roberts, J. J. M., "In Defense of the Monarchy," in *The Bible and the Ancient Near East* (Eisenbrauns, 2002), 358–75; Selman, M. J., "The Kingdom of God in the Old Testament," *TynBul* 40 (1989): 161–83; Waltke, B. K., with C. Yu, *An Old Testament Theology* (Zondervan, 2007); Wifall, W., "Genesis 3:15: A Protoevangelium," *CBQ* 36 (1974): 361–65.

STEPHEN G. DEMPSTER

Kings, Books of

As the last book of the Former Prophets, 1–2 Kings looks back on a significant amount of earlier scriptural material in all manner of explicit and more subtle ways. It draws above all on Exodus and Deuteronomy in articulating its message, but also on the other books in various measures. This brief reflection will focus on the importance of the Pentateuch for our reading of 1–2 Kings, before describing some aspects of the use of these books in the NT.

Genesis

We begin in the beginning, with the biblical creation story in Gen. 1–2. Precisely because ancient Near Eastern temples were designed to reflect in their architecture and furniture people's fundamental beliefs about the cosmos, the Genesis creation story inevitably informs the descriptions in Kings about true and false worship in the Jerusalem temple. Positively, the bronze "sea" mentioned in 1 Kings 7:23–47 represents the forces of watery chaos subdued and brought to order by the Lord in Gen. 1:2–10, although Exod. 30:18–21 and 40:30–32 also suggest a practical function for such a water receptacle within the courts of (in that case) the tabernacle. Negatively, the story of King Manasseh's idolatrous rule in 2 Kings 21 includes an important reference to his worship of "the starry hosts" (sun, moon, and stars, vv. 3, 5). It is a powerful way of clarifying that Manasseh has ceased to believe in the one true God, the Creator of heaven and earth, and therefore the Lord *of* hosts (e.g., 1 Kings 18:15)—not merely one god *among* the hosts. The well-versed reader remembers in this respect the explicit injunction in Deut. 4:19 (cf. 2 Kings 17:16) not to bow down to precisely this heavenly array. The early chapters of Genesis also provide us with an early parallel in Enoch to God's later "taking up" of Elijah into the heavens (Gen. 5:24; 2 Kings 2:1–12). Moreover, they give us a geographical context within which to make sense both of Solomon's great wealth in 1 Kings 9–10 (gold pours into his royal court from Ophir, Gen. 10:29; 1 Kings 9:28) and the visit of the queen of Sheba (Gen. 10:28; 1 Kings 10:1). The economic reach of Solomon is vast, we learn, and his fame is global (cf. 1 Kings 4:29–34).

More important to the story of Solomon and of 1–2 Kings as a whole, however, is the promise to Abraham in Gen. 12:1–3, along with the associated covenant first mentioned in Gen. 15. This promise—the obstacles to and progress toward its fulfillment—dominates the preceding narrative in Genesis through Samuel, and as we read the description of wise Solomon's kingdom in 1 Kings 4, it is easy to imagine that we have finally arrived at the promise's intended outcome.

Internally to God's chosen people, we learn that under Solomon's rule "Judah and Israel . . . ate . . . drank and . . . were happy" and the people were "as numerous as the sand on the seashore" (1 Kings 4:20). This reminds us very much of Gen. 22:17, which promises, "I will surely bless you and make your descendants as numerous as the stars in the sky and as the sand on the seashore." Indeed, the area of Solomonic rule in the region corresponds to the ideal extent of Israel's dominion as promised to Abraham in Gen. 15:18; he "ruled over all the kingdoms from the Euphrates River to the land of the Philistines, as far as the border of Egypt" (1 Kings 4:21)—that is, from Tiphsah, on the Euphrates, to Gaza, in the far south of Philistia (4:24). Externally, people from all nations "came to listen to Solomon's wisdom, sent by all the kings of the world, who had heard of his wisdom" (1 Kings 4:34). This reminds us of the part of the Abrahamic promise pertaining to blessing on the gentile nations (Gen. 12:3).

Both aspects of the promise are picked up again in Solomon's prayer in 1 Kings 8. His land is the one given to the fathers (i.e., the patriarchs, vv. 34, 40) as an inheritance (v. 36; cf. Deut. 4:37–38)—a land, though, that now has a temple built in it toward which "the foreigner who does not belong to your people Israel but has come from a distant land because of your name" may pray in expectation of an answer from God (1 Kings 8:41–43; cf. Gen. 17:1–8). This is a blessing on the gentiles indeed. The promise to Abraham is also referenced in 2 Kings 13:22–24, in the context of the oppression of northern Israel by Hazael king of Aram. In these circumstances, we read, "the LORD was gracious to them and had compassion and showed concern for them because of his covenant with Abraham, Isaac and Jacob" (v. 23). This covenant is the fundamental reason for God's help in the midst of foreign oppression.

As we come to the end of Genesis, we encounter in the Joseph story some interesting details that become important in 1 Kings as the narrative about Solomon's flourishing empire gives way to the story of how it collapsed (1 Kings 11–12). The apostate king is challenged by enemies, the first of whom is Hadad (11:14), who like Joseph finds favor with the Egyptians (11:18; cf. Gen. 39:4) and marries an Egyptian wife (1 Kings 11:19; cf. Gen. 41:45). Later Hadad pleads with Pharaoh to let him go (1 Kings 11:21–22), recalling the Israelite plea in Exodus (e.g., Exod. 5:1; 7:16; 8:1). The Kings authors draw on both Genesis and Exodus here to prepare the way for what will shortly become an extended comparison between Rehoboam and Pharaoh, as well as between Moses and another Solomonic enemy, Jeroboam, who also finds himself at one point in his life in Egypt (1 Kings 11:40).

Exodus

The stark contrast between Israel, on the one hand, and Egypt, on the other, is fundamentally important to the Pentateuch, and it is not surprising that the authors of Kings should develop this same contrast in characterizing the conflict between faithful and unfaithful Israel in the monarchic period. So it is that King Solomon's ultimate apostasy, involving marriages to many foreign princesses (1 Kings 11:1–13), is already foreshadowed early in his reign by his marriage to his *Egyptian* wife (1 Kings 3:1). His son Rehoboam is later characterized in numerous different ways as "Egyptian" in his treatment of his own people. Summoned to Shechem by "all Israel" (12:1)—to the very city where Joseph's bones are buried (Josh. 24:32)—Rehoboam is faced by their complaint that they are no longer the people delivered from slavery in Egypt. They have become instead once more a people suffering "harsh labor" (1 Kings 12:4; cf. Exod. 1:14; 2:23). Rehoboam now announces his intention that the Davidic line will continue to rule in a Pharaoh-like manner. Just like Pharaoh in Exodus, he increases the oppression (1 Kings 12:14; cf. Exod. 5)—an outcome described in a way that recalls God's hardening of Pharaoh's heart (1 Kings 12:15; cf. Exod. 4:21; 7:3–4, 13).

Jeroboam, in this story, plays Moses to Rehoboam's Pharaoh. Apparently reluctant, like Moses (Exod. 4:1–17), to take on the role of liberator—the MT of 1 Kings 12:2 tells us that he initially remained in Egypt when he heard about the events in Shechem—he eventually steps up to lead northern Israel out from under Rehoboam's yoke (1 Kings 12:20). No sooner has he done so, however, than he begins to be painted in the colors not of Moses but of Aaron. Fearing that the presence of the temple in Jerusalem (1 Kings 12:27) will subvert his rule, he builds centers of worship within his own territory at Dan and Bethel, constructing golden calves as focal points for worship at these sanctuaries (cf. Aaron in Exod. 32). His words to his subjects in 1 Kings 12:28—"Here are your gods, Israel, who brought you up out of Egypt"—are almost exactly those with which the people greet the construction of the first calf in Exod. 32:4. Like Aaron, Jeroboam then proceeds to announce a festival on a date "of his own choosing" (cf. Exod. 32:5)—the new king's version of the Feast of Tabernacles, celebrated in Jerusalem in the seventh rather than the eighth month (1 Kings 12:33; cf. 8:2; Lev. 23:33–43). Like Aaron in all these respects, 2 Kings 17:21 will later confirm that Jeroboam thereby committed "a great sin" (Exod. 32:21, 30–31).

This exploration of who are the true Israelites, standing in line with Moses, and who are "the Egyptians" among them, then extends throughout the remainder of 1–2 Kings in all kinds of ways and at all kinds of levels. Elijah is clearly identified, for example, as standing on the correct side of the line, whatever his weaknesses may have been. Miraculously preserved in the wilderness by God's provision of "bread and meat," just like the Israelites after the exodus (1 Kings 17:6; cf. Exod. 16:8, 12–13), he is later also supplied with water along with food in the midst of a drought (1 Kings 17:7–16; cf. Exod. 17:1–7). On Mount Carmel, in 1 Kings 18, he rebuilds an "altar of the LORD" using twelve stones, reminding the Israelites of their true identity as the Lord's people and calling them back to Mosaic faith (1 Kings 18:30–31; cf. Gen. 35:10). In this context his suggestion to King Ahab, in the aftermath of his encounter with the living God, that he should "eat and drink," takes on the tones of an invitation to covenant renewal (1 Kings 18:41; cf. Exod. 24:4, 11).

In 1 Kings 19 Elijah then unexpectedly retreats in the face of Queen Jezebel's threats, finding himself, like Moses and his people, on a journey to "Horeb, the mountain of God" (v. 8; cf. Exod. 3:1). The "forty days and forty nights" of his travels and the provision of food for the journey recall Israel's wandering in the wilderness (Num. 14:33–34) almost as much as Moses's first sojourn on the mountain (Exod. 24:18). Casting Elijah's story against this background account already raises important questions: Will Elijah be like the servant Moses or like stubborn Israel when he gets to his destination? Will he, like Moses, see God (Exod. 33:12–23), and will it make any difference to his life? Privileged like Moses indeed to encounter God on the mountain, Elijah is in fact slow to understand what it means, and perhaps unwilling to do so. Nevertheless, he remains generally faithful to the Lord—the kind of prophet who, like Moses, is able to call down fire from heaven (1 Kings 18:38; 2 Kings 1:10; cf. Exod. 9:22–26) as well as to cross bodies of water on dry land (2 Kings 2:7–8; cf. Exod. 14:15–31, esp. vv. 21–22). His successor, Elisha, is painted in similar colors. He too, Moses-like and carrying a powerful staff (2 Kings 4:29; cf. Exod. 14:16; 17:9), parts the waters and crosses on dry land (2 Kings 2:13–14).

Elijah's opponent King Ahab, on the other hand, is resolutely "Egyptian." We see this in 1 Kings 21, for example, where he covets Naboth's vineyard in Jezreel. Naboth's refusal to sell this property marks him out as a faithful Yahwist who is obedient to Torah: all of the promised land belonged not to the families who technically "owned" it but to God, who had, through Joshua, allocated its various parts to the tribes as their inheritance (e.g., Josh. 13:7). It was not open to individual Israelites to sell land in perpetuity. The fact that Ahab wanted to turn Naboth's property into a "vegetable garden" (1 Kings 21:2) is especially significant; the phrase occurs elsewhere in the OT only in Deut. 11:10, where a contrast is offered between Egypt (a vegetable garden requiring human care) and the promised land (which "the LORD your God cares for" [11:12]). This is a king who wants to turn Israel (God's vine, Isa. 3:13–15) into Egypt. In pursuing this dream, having already broken the Ten Commandments pertaining to idolatry and coveting, he and his wife go on to break various others concerning false testimony, murder, and theft (1 Kings 21:1–6, 13–19; cf. Exod. 20:13–17).

So it is throughout 1–2 Kings: its authors constantly signal to their readers, by referring and alluding to Exodus, how we are to interpret what is happening in the period of the later monarchy. For the most part the Israelites are understood to have "sinned against the LORD their God, who had brought them out of Egypt" (2 Kings 17:7), reminding us of the prologue to the Ten Commandments in Exod. 20:2. The foundational requirement in those commandments is of course that God's people must have "no other gods before [him]" (Exod. 20:3), and it is this most central commandment that the Israelites of the later monarchy forgot, as they "worshiped other gods" and "idols" (2 Kings 17:7, 12; cf. Exod. 20:4–5). All of this was done with the stubbornness and pride of those who had come out of Egypt in the first place—a famously "stiff-necked" people (2 Kings 17:14; cf., e.g., Exod. 32:9).

Leviticus and Numbers

To a great extent the reference to and use of Leviticus and Numbers in 1–2 Kings relates to topics already covered above. To grasp the righteousness of Joash with respect to his fundraising campaign in 2 Kings 12 requires that the reader is aware of the content of Lev. 4–7. Leviticus 23:33–43 describes the correct way of celebrating the Feast of Tabernacles, against which Jeroboam's innovations in 1 Kings 12 must be measured. Likewise, if we are to understand the problems with Jeroboam's new priesthood described in that chapter, we must recognize the important distinction developed in Num. 3–4 between those set apart by God for priestly service and the people to whom they minister. Naboth's refusal to sell his land to Ahab must be read against the background of the rules pertaining to land in Lev. 25:8–24, and the manner of his death in the light of Lev. 24:15–16.

An important new connection must be noted between the rules pertaining to skin disfigurements (often referred to as "leprosy" in our translations) in Lev. 13–14 and the Naaman story in 2 Kings 5. Naaman the Syrian has contracted such a skin disease (just like the people described in 2 Kings 7:3–20), which signifies to the reader ritual uncleanness or defilement—the judgment of God, in fact (cf. Num. 12:1–15). Naaman is therefore someone who is in every sense "outside the camp," in Levitical terms—both a foreigner and a "leper." Yet in this story he becomes an insider by way of washing seven times in the Jordan (2 Kings 5:10). The instruction to do so is heard first of all as involving merely *ritual* cleansing: "Couldn't I wash in [other rivers] and be cleansed?" This is precisely the language of Lev. 13:7, 35; 14:2, 23, 32 ("cleansed") and 14:8–9 ("wash"). Naaman's complaint is that he came to Israel to have the leprosy *removed*, and he has been offered *ritual cleansing* instead. His servants put him right, however, and he is healed.

Another new connection pertains to the bronze snake fashioned by Moses in the wilderness (Num. 21:4–9) and apparently later deposited in the temple in Jerusalem along with other religious items from the Mosaic age (1 Kings 8:1–9). To our surprise we read in 2 Kings 18:4 that King Hezekiah of Judah broke this snake into pieces in the course of his religious reform. Here we have a respectable ancient relic, then, drawn unfortunately into the worship of the Canaanite fertility cult because of its association with life-giving power (in both the Numbers story and ancient Near Eastern thinking more generally), and thus eventually requiring the drastic treatment meted out to it by Hezekiah in this narrative.

Deuteronomy

The language and ideas of Deuteronomy abound in 1–2 Kings, as first King Solomon, and then almost all the succeeding kings of Israel and Judah, are weighed in relation to the Mosaic law code and found wanting. It is not that Solomon does nothing well. In his temple-building, for example, he does admirably, standing right in line with Deuteronomy in many larger and smaller ways (e.g., 1 Kings 6:7 [cf. Deut. 27:5–6]; 8:9 [cf. Deut. 10:1–5]). Again, his prayer in 1 Kings 8 explicitly picks up phraseology from Deuteronomy (e.g., 8:41–43 [cf. Deut. 4:34; 5:15]; 8:51 [cf. Deut. 4:20]). It speaks of the promised land as an "inheritance" (1 Kings 8:36; cf. Deut. 4:37–38), and its various "woes" have been selected for consideration precisely because they appear in the list of covenant curses related to disobedience in Deut. 28:15–68 (esp. vv. 21–25, 36–37). Solomon's desire in this prayer is that God should cause his people to walk in his ways, so that "all the peoples of the earth may know that the LORD is God and that there is no other" (1 Kings 8:60; cf. Deut. 4:35). Yet he recognizes the alternative possibility: that the people will serve other gods, in which case the temple will become a ruin to be scoffed at by passersby (1 Kings 9:8; cf. Deut. 29:22–28).

This later disobedience is already foreshadowed, unfortunately, in Solomon's own life. He marries an Egyptian wife, even though intermarriage with foreigners is explicitly banned in Deut. 7:3. In due course he proceeds to break other aspects of the Deuteronomic law as well. He accumulates horses, even returning to Egypt to acquire them (1 Kings 4:26, 28; 10:26–29; cf. Deut. 17:16). He takes "many wives," so that his heart is "led astray," and he also accumulates large amounts of gold (1 Kings 9:10–10:29; 11:1–8; cf. Deut. 17:17). Point by point, he departs from "the law of the king" as laid down in Deut. 17. Specifically, he is said to have "loved" and "held fast" to his various wives rather than to God (1 Kings 11:1–2; cf. Deut. 6:5; 10:12, 20; 11:1, 22; 13:4; 30:20).

The kings who follow Solomon are likewise explicitly assessed in terms of their adherence to Deuteronomic law. There is Jeroboam, for example, who builds a temple outside Jerusalem that infringes on the prohibition in Deut. 12 and fashions idols for worship in defiance of a passage like Deut. 4:15–24. Under Rehoboam's leadership, Judah sets up "sacred stones" like those of the Canaanites in Deut. 12:3 and makes use of the "shrine prostitutes" forbidden in 23:17–18 (1 Kings 14:23–24). A full understanding of the portrayal of Ahab's treatment of Naboth in 1 Kings 21 depends on our knowledge not only of the already noted contrast in Deut. 11:10–12 between Egypt as "a vegetable garden" requiring human care and the promised land, which "the LORD your God cares for," but also of the legal roles of both elders and witnesses in Deut. 19:11–21; 21:1–9, 18–21. Later, the piety of Amaziah is emphasized in 2 Kings 14:6 as he adheres to the "Law of Moses" (rather than to custom) in dealing with the families of those who had murdered his father (cf. Deut. 24:16).

It is not surprising that the overall summary of the history of the monarchy that is later provided in 2 Kings 17:1–17 should likewise draw heavily on Deuteronomy. The Israelites throughout this period, we are told, copied "the nations around them" whom the Lord had ordered them not to imitate (2 Kings 17:15; cf. Deut. 7; 18:9–12)—and whom "the LORD had driven out before them" (2 Kings 17:8). Because they have copied the Canaanites, the Israelites now meet the same fate; they are driven out of the promised land. Not even the righteous kings Hezekiah and Josiah could save them. The former completes a religious reform described in language that clearly recalls Deut. 12:1–7 (2 Kings 18:4–6) and faces down an Assyrian emperor who promises the citizens of Jerusalem a new "promised land" just like their own (2 Kings 18:32; cf. Deut. 8:7–9). Hezekiah is a true worshiper of the living God—one who understands that Yahweh is God alone, Creator of "heaven and earth" and "God over all the kingdoms of the earth" (2 Kings 19:15; cf. Deut. 4:32–40), and that the gods of the other nations are but wood and stone (2 Kings 19:18; cf. Deut. 4:28). Josiah, for his part, is the ideal king who does not turn from God's law "to the right or to the left" (2 Kings 22:2; cf. Deut. 17:20). Presented with the newly recovered "Book of the Law" (2 Kings 22:8; cf. Deut. 28:61; 29:21; 30:10; 31:26), he responds to its message piously, setting in motion his own reform. At its heart lies a renewal of the covenant between the Lord and his people to which Deuteronomy is the supreme witness (2 Kings 23:2–3; cf. Deut. 5:2–3; 29:1–28). It is founded on the royal promise to "follow the LORD" and wholeheartedly "keep his commands, statutes and decrees" (2 Kings 23:3; cf. Deut. 6:17). Josiah's reform is more all-encompassing than Hezekiah's, not least in the celebration of the Passover "as it is written in this Book of the Covenant" (2 Kings 23:21; cf. Deut. 16:1–8). There is simply no king like Josiah when it comes to turning to the Lord (2 Kings 23:24–25); he does so, in fact, "with all his heart and with all his soul and with all his strength, in accordance with all the Law of Moses" (23:25; cf. Deut. 6:5). Yet Judah's fate is already sealed (2 Kings 23:26–30).

By the end of 2 Kings, then, the threats of Deuteronomy appear to have overwhelmed the promises (Deut. 4:25–27). The covenant has failed—or so it seems.

1–2 Kings in the NT

The huge impact of 1–2 Kings on the NT is well illustrated by attending briefly to just three of Kings' main characters. The first is Solomon, the wise king who turned in the end to apostasy (1 Kings 11:1–8). Although Solomon was initially blessed by God, divine wrath eventually fell on his royal house, although not as severely as the reader might have initially expected (11:12–13, 32, 34, 36), and not eternally (11:39). This ending to the Solomon story implies that the hope expressed in Solomon's prayer of 1 Kings 8:22–53 is not futile—the hope that after the covenant has seemingly failed, God will forgive. The promise to David of an eternal throne will be discovered still to stand. In the NT, of course—the new covenant—Jesus is identified as *the* Son of David toward whom this Davidic promise ultimately points (Matt. 1:1–16; 21:1–11; 22:41–46), *the* king who sits upon David's throne (Luke 1:32–33; John 18:28–40; Acts 2:29–36). Jesus is the one greater than Solomon, to whose wisdom people should listen, as the queen of Sheba had listened to her contemporary (Matt. 12:42; Luke 11:31; cf. also Matt. 13:54; Luke 2:40, 52).

Some of this wisdom pertains to dealing well with wealth, and King Solomon's famous "splendor" features in Jesus's teaching on this theme (Matt. 6:25–34; Luke 12:22–31) in contexts where believers are instructed not to allow concern about material needs to interfere with the seeking of God's kingdom. Here Solomon is a warning and example to the NT believer. More generally the NT is, like the Solomon story, very much aware of the inadequacies of and dangers inherent in a wisdom that is simply "from below" but to which the Christian might be attracted (e.g., Rom. 1:21–25; Col. 2:8; James 3:13–18), over against the wisdom "from above" that is characteristically revealed to "children" (Luke 10:21)—to those who are not wise by worldly standards at all (e.g., 1 Cor. 1:26–31; cf. 1 Kings 3:7).

Our second exemplary character is the flawed prophet Elijah—in so many ways similar to Moses, even to the extent of "dying" on the other side of the Jordan (2 Kings 2:7–12; Deut. 34:1–8), but also to Jonah, the grudging, disobedient servant of God (1 Kings 19). Unlike Solomon, Elijah makes an appearance "in person" in the NT, standing on the Mount of Transfiguration alongside Moses and Jesus (Matt. 17:1–13; Mark 9:2–13; Luke 9:28–36). The main point in all three Gospels is that Jesus is greater than both those other prophets privileged to meet with God on a mountain. Elsewhere Elijah functions typologically in respect to Jesus. He does so explicitly in Luke 4:24–26, where Jesus's mission embraces the gentiles just as Elijah's did. The greatest of the prophets is to exercise his ministry in ways analogous to his predecessor. There are implicit connections as well. Angels minister to Jesus in the wilderness (1 Kings 19:5–8; Matt. 4:1–11); he opposes Baal(-Zebub), dealing firmly with the "possessed" (1 Kings 18:20–40; 2 Kings 1:2–17; Matt. 12:22–28; Luke 11:14–20); he performs miracles of provision and healing (1 Kings 17:7–24; Matt. 14:13–21; 15:29–39; Luke 7:11–17); and in the end he ascends into heaven (2 Kings 2:11; Acts 1:2).

In all these ways and more, the NT portrait of Jesus builds on the portrait of Elijah in Kings. Yet it is not Jesus who is most often connected with Elijah in the Gospels; it is John the Baptist. Here "Elijah" prepares the way for God's final victory over the powers of darkness, appearing before the ministry of Jesus begins, dressed like Elijah (2 Kings 1:8; cf. Matt. 3:4; Mark 1:6) and warning of the coming kingdom of God. He is identified as the Elijah to come by an angel in Luke 1:11–17 and by Jesus in Matt. 11:1–19; 17:11–13; Mark 9:11–13.

Like Solomon, Elijah not only functions in the NT as a type of Jesus (and in this case, of John the Baptist as well) but also appears as "someone just like us," one of the people of God. Christians can learn valuable lessons from Elijah's life, the NT writers affirm—whether about the way in which God works with "remnants" of his people (Rom. 11:1–10; the remnant theme remains important throughout Kings), or faith (Heb. 11:32–39), or prayer (James 5:13–18).

Finally, we turn to Elisha, who is explicitly mentioned only once in the NT, in Luke 4:27, where he also functions typologically in respect to Jesus. Jesus's mission embraces the gentiles, as the mission of Elisha did; what Jesus will do is analogous to what Elisha did when healing the Aramean soldier Naaman. However, there is in the Gospels certainly no shortage of implicit connections between the two men as well. For example, Jesus heals lepers, just like Elisha (2 Kings 5; Matt. 8:1–4; 10:8; 11:5; Mark 1:40–45; Luke 5:12–16; 7:22; 17:11–19; cf. also John 9:1–12 for a different kind of healing story that has analogies to the Naaman narrative). Jesus transforms water (2 Kings 2:19–22; John 2:1–11) and suspends the laws of gravity in relation to it (2 Kings 6:1–7; Matt. 14:22–33; Mark 6:45–51; John 6:16–21). He raises the dead (2 Kings 4:8–37; Mark 5:21–24, 35–43; Luke 7:11–17; John 11:17–44) and multiplies food (2 Kings 4:1–7, 42–44; Matt. 14:13–21; 15:29–39; Mark 6:30–44; 8:1–10; Luke 9:10–17; John 6:1–15). He does all this especially for the benefit of the humble, who are generally more open to God's salvation than the great. He mediates salvation, but he also brings judgment. He utters prophetic curses (2 Kings 2:23–24; Matt. 21:18–22; Mark 11:12–14, 20–21; cf. also Matt. 25:41). He comes so that those who see will become blind, even as those who are blind gain their sight (2 Kings 6:8–23; John 9:35–41; 12:37–41). He is the initiator of the coming of God's kingdom, when all will know divine justice (Matt. 13:36–43, etc.).

Bibliography. Aberbach, M., and L. Smolar, "Aaron, Jeroboam, and the Golden Calves," *JBL* 86, no. 2 (1967): 129–40; Berman, J. A., "Law Code as Plot Template in Biblical Narrative," *JSOT* 40, no. 3 (2016): 337–49; Bottini, G. C., "Continuity and Innovation in Biblical Tradition," *SBSlov* 11, no. 2 (2019): 120–29; Brueggemann, W., *1 & 2 Kings*, SHBC 8 (Smyth & Helwys, 2000); Chun, S. M., "To Reform or Not to Reform," in *Characters and Characterization in the Book of Kings*, ed. K. Bodner and B. J. M. Johnson, LHBOTS 670 (T&T Clark, 2020), 250–68; Dharamraj, H., *A Prophet like Moses?*, PBM (Paternoster, 2011); Hays, J. D., "Has the Narrator Come to Praise Solomon or to Bury Him?," *JSOT* 28, no. 2 (2003): 149–74; Hobbs, T. R., *1, 2 Kings*, WBT (Word, 1989); Hobbs, *2 Kings*, WBC (Word, 1985); House, P. R., *1, 2 Kings*, NAC (Broadman & Holman, 1995); Huddleston, J. "What Would Elijah and Elisha Do?," *JTI* 5, no. 2 (2011): 265–81; Markl, D., "No Future without Moses," *JBL* 133,no. 4 (2014): 711–28; Morales, L. M., ed., *Cult and Cosmos*, BTS 18 (Peeters, 2014); Nelson, R. D., *First and Second Kings*, IBC (John Knox, 1987); Provan, I. W., "An Ambivalent Hero," in *Characters and Characterization in the Book of Kings*, ed. K. Bodner and B. J. M. Johnson, LHBOTS 670 (T&T Clark, 2020), 135–51; Provan, *1 and 2 Kings*, NIBC (Hendrickson, 1995); Provan, *1 & 2 Kings*, OTG (Sheffield Academic, 1997); Provan, *1 and 2 Kings*, UBCS (Baker Books, 2012); Provan, I. W., V. P. Long, and T. Longman, III, *A Biblical History of Israel*, 2nd ed. (Westminster John Knox, 2015); Viviano, P. A., "Glory Lost," in *The Age of Solomon*, ed. L. K. Handy, SHCANE 11 (Brill, 1997), 336–47.

Iain Provan

L

Lamentations, Book of

Lamentations is a liturgy of five poems mourning the destruction of Jerusalem at the hands of the Babylonians in 586 BC. Similar poems grieving the destruction of great cities appear very early in the ancient Near East. Sumerian lamentation poems over the cities of Ur, Nippur, Uruk, and Eridu (late third millennium) have been found. Furthermore, there is evidence for the persistence of this genre through the second and first millennia (Gwaltney). Scholars debate whether this body of texts influenced the biblical poets (Salters, 13–15), but it seems likely that they were at least aware of the genre (Hillers, 32–39).

Essential Features of Lamentations

Composition. Jewish tradition ascribes Lamentations to Jeremiah. There are certain verbal parallels between Jeremiah and Lamentations. For example, both speak of the poet's eyes overflowing with tears (Jer. 9:1, 18 [8:23; 9:17 MT]; 13:17; 14:17; Lam. 1:16; 2:11; 3:48–49). On the other hand, Jewish tradition apparently ascribes the book to Jeremiah because of 2 Chron. 35:25, which states that Jeremiah composed a lament over King Josiah after his death. But Lamentations says nothing about Josiah and cannot be the text to which Chronicles refers. Moreover, the Hebrew text of Lamentations has no prologue and does not ascribe the work to Jeremiah. Also, Lam. 4:19–20 alludes to Zedekiah's failed attempt to escape Jerusalem at the end of the siege (2 Kings 25:4–5), and it implies that the poet was with Zedekiah at this time (Lam. 4:19: "They chased us"). But Jeremiah was confined to the "court of the guard" when the city fell (Jer. 38:28 ESV; 39:13–14). Also, if Jeremiah did compose the laments, it is difficult to understand why they were not included in his book. All things considered, the case that Jeremiah composed Lamentations is not fully compelling.

Even so, Lamentations may have been written in the exilic period and soon after Jerusalem's fall; it need not be postexilic. The book presents the agonies of Jerusalem's populace as a recent and ongoing event; it does not look on the calamity as something from the distant past. Both Jer. 41:5 and Zech. 7:3–5 imply that ritual lamentation over Jerusalem began almost immediately after the city fell. Thus, even if Jeremiah did not compose the book, it is not necessarily a late, postexilic work (see also Salters, 9–10; Harrison, 200–201).

The acrostic pattern. The essential structure of Lamentations is obvious: it contains five poems, with one poem per chapter. Each of the first four poems is an acrostic following the twenty-two letters of the original Hebrew alphabet, from *aleph* to *tav*, and the last poem is not acrostic but is twenty-two verses long and, in that sense, mimics the acrostic pattern.

Why does Lamentations employ the acrostic pattern? A simple and fairly obvious explanation is that acrostic poems are easier to memorize for public recitation. Or the acrostic pattern may be used for aesthetic or structural purposes and in some way to help convey the message of the book (House, 306–7). Another possibility is that an acrostic conveys the idea that the subject has been fully covered, like saying that one has looked at every issue from *a* to *z* (Huey, 445). Certainly, the acrostics do have one structural function: they make it obvious where each poem begins and ends.

Elsewhere in the Bible, however, acrostic poems typically have a didactic function. Acrostic poems include Pss. 34; 37; 111; 112; 119; 145; Prov. 31:10–31. Psalm 34:11 reads, "Come, children, listen to me, and I will teach you the fear of YHWH," while Ps. 145:4 asserts, "One generation commends your works to another; they describe your heroic acts" (both AT). Psalm 37 exhorts the reader, via an acrostic list of arguments and appeals, not to envy the prosperity of the wicked. Psalm 111 lists the praiseworthy qualities of YHWH; its counterpart, Ps. 112, lists the virtues of those who fear YHWH. Psalm 119 gives a recitation on the value of Torah, while Prov. 31:10–31 instructs the reader on the virtues of the good wife. This suggests that Lamentations is more than a liturgical text for an annual ceremony of mourning. The reader is expected to ponder the words and take lessons from them. Perhaps Lam. 5, which is entirely a prayer, is non-acrostic because it is thought inappropriate to offer a prayer that employs an instructional motif, as though God needed teaching.

One curious feature is that chap. 1 follows the normal order of the Hebrew alphabet but chaps. 2–4 slightly deviate from this. In the currently accepted order, the letter *ayin* is followed by the letter *pe*, but the acrostics in Lam. 2–4 reverse this order, so that *pe* is followed by *ayin*. This suggests that a different poet, with a different understanding of the order of the alphabet, composed chaps. 2–4. But we do not know. One thing, however, is clear: each of the five poems is distinct from the others, with each coming from a specific perspective and each giving a specific message. The poems are not redundant.

The five lament poems. Lamentations 1 focuses on the metaphor of Jerusalem as a woman, Lady Zion. The poem alternates between two perspectives: In 1:1–9b, 10–11b, 17, the poet grieves over her suffering (Lady Zion is represented in the third person). But in 1:9c, 11c–16, 18–22, Lady Zion herself cries out over her pain (she speaks in the first person). She once had been a queen but is now a widow and slave (1:1); her lovers have betrayed her, and she wanders among the nations (1:2–3); her children wander in destitution (1:4–6); and she is impoverished and receives no pity (1:7–11). She calls out to both God and the nations, but no one heeds her (1:12–22).

Lamentations 2 describes Jerusalem's suffering from a prophetic perspective. Like a prophet, the poet knows the emotional state, purposes, and actions of God (2:1–8). As is common among the prophetic texts, he alternates between declaring that Lady Zion brought this suffering on herself and expressing deep sorrow over her suffering. Formulaic constructions common among the prophets also appear here. Fire represents the wrath of God both in Lam. 2:1–9 and in the prophets (e.g., Isa. 5:24; 9:19; 29:6; 30:27, 30; 33:14; 47:14; 66:15; Jer. 4:4; 15:14; 21:12; Ezek. 15:7; 21:31; Nah. 1:6). God in his anger has thrown down Jerusalem from heaven to earth (Lam. 2:1; Isa. 14:12–15). The Jerusalem sanctuary, now laid low, was God's "footstool" (Lam. 2:1; Isa. 60:13). God has brought Jerusalem's fortifications down (Lam. 2:2; Isa. 25:12). God has come upon the "garden" that was Jerusalem and broken down its "booth" (Lam. 2:6; Isa. 1:8; 5:5). God despises Israel's rituals of worship and has brought them to an end (Lam. 2:6–7; Isa. 1:13–14). Jerusalem's gates are smashed and lie in the dirt (Lam. 2:9; Isa. 45:2). The prophet's eyes are exhausted from weeping (Lam. 2:11; Jer. 9:1). The prophet appeals for ritual mourning (Lam. 2:18–19; Joel 2:12–17). Young and old, both men and women, lie dead in the streets of Jerusalem (Lam. 2:21; Ezek. 9:6). At the end of the poem, Lady Zion herself speaks, complaining that YHWH's punishment was too harsh (Lam. 2:20–22).

Lamentations 3 reads more like a standard psalm of lament, written by a man who himself was witness to the calamity and who suffered personal loss. He ascribes his sufferings to God, who has beaten him (3:1), trapped him like the dead in Sheol (3:6), and mangled him as a bear or lion would (3:10). Even so, he places his hope in God (3:21–32) and calls the people to repentance (3:33–41). Until God acts to save, however, he can only weep and look toward heaven (3:48–55). But he is so confident of God's salvation that he can preemptively thank God for it (3:56–66).

Lamentations 4 is perhaps the most severe poem of all, being an unvarnished account of the agonies of Jerusalem. There is little personification of the city, and the poet is neither a prophet nor a representative citizen. The lament simply recounts how bad things are. The wealth the city once held is all gone, and people have nothing to give to their starving children (4:1–5). The survivors look like corpses (4:6–9). They resort to cannibalism (4:10). The priests formerly had to remain separate from common people because of the holiness of their work, but now even they must behave as though they were lepers (4:13–16). Enemies have chased down the Jews and their king like predators seeking prey (4:17–20). The only comfort they can take is that their enemy, Edom, will soon be as they are (4:21–22).

Lamentations 5 is entirely a prayer to God, and it is voiced by the people of Jerusalem (it uses the first-person plural throughout). Most of the prayer is taken up with a recital of the suffering the people have endured, and it closes with a plaintive question, asking whether God has abandoned them forever (5:20, 22).

Lamentations and the NT

To all appearances, the NT never directly cites Lamentations. There is an echo of Lam. 3:45 ("You have made us scum and refuse in the midst of the peoples," AT) in 1 Cor. 4:13b ("We have become like the scum of the world, the filth of all people, to this very day"). Even so, and despite the paucity of apostolic citations of the book, Lamentations develops several themes that are central to NT theology.

The suffering servant and Lam. 3. In Lam. 3, a single man speaks of his intense suffering in the context of the fall of Jerusalem. This individual, regardless of the experiences of the poet behind the text, is an idealized and representative figure. This is not autobiography; the specific events spoken of (e.g., "The enemy slew my children") did not actually befall the poet. But he does say that YHWH broke his bones (3:4), blocked his path (3:9), shot him with arrows (3:12), and broke his teeth (3:16), among other afflictions. But the man is not simply a personification of Jerusalem's suffering. To the contrary, he is mocked and despised by his own people (3:14). His sufferings include those of the Jerusalem populace but are also of a higher order, as he is afflicted by both the nations and the Jews.

The OT has the theological ideal of the suffering servant, a figure most eloquently portrayed in Isa. 53. But this is not the only place where the ideal appears. It can be seen in the intercession by a long-suffering Moses in Exod. 32–34, in the prayers of David, and in the agonies of Jeremiah. The servant's sufferings come from God even though they are administered by evil people, and the suffering always has a redemptive purpose. The passion of Jesus is the ultimate but not the only realization of this ideal, as illustrated by the ordeals of the OT heroes. Paul, too, says that his sufferings fill up "what is lacking in the afflictions of Christ" (Col. 1:24 AT), and his awareness of his role as a suffering servant may be behind his apparent use of Lam. 3:45 in 1 Cor. 4:13. Remarkably, Lam. 3:1 begins, "I am the man," a phrase uncannily echoed in the words of Pilate, "Behold, the man!" (John 19:5 AT), suggesting that all the agonies that befell Jerusalem were concentrated upon Jesus. That is, the cross was the most profound fulfillment of Lam. 3. Jesus himself was acutely conscious of the connection between his ordeal and those of the city (Luke 23:28–31).

Jesus may have been consciously drawing upon Lam. 3:30 ("Let him offer a cheek to one who would strike him and let him have his fill of reproach," AT) in his admonition to "turn the other cheek" in response to a slap (Matt. 5:39). Also, the evangelists may have regarded the beatings Jesus endured as a fulfillment of Lam. 3:30 (see Matt. 26:67–68; 27:30–31; Mark 15:19; Luke 22:63–64; John 19:1–5). One may add to this Lam. 3:15 ("He has filled me with bitter herbs and given me gall to drink") and compare it to Matt. 27:34, which says that Jesus was given wine mixed with gall to drink. In context, Lam. 3:15, 30 describe the sufferings of the sinner. He has repented of his sin and placed his hope in God, but he must endure cruelty inflicted upon him as part of the process of his redemption.

Similarly, Lam. 3:25–27 is a series of three sayings that begin with the word *ṭôb*, "good." The Hebrew is somewhat obscure (Salters, 230–33; Hillers, 115), but it can be rendered without emendation as "YHWH is good to one who places hope in him, to the person who seeks him. [YHWH is] good, so one should be patient and silently [await] YHWH's salvation. [This is] good for a man: that he should bear the yoke of his youth." The word "youth" (*nəʿûrîm*) reflects the familiar idea of the "sins of one's youth" (Job 13:26; Ps. 25:7; Jer. 3:25), and the three verses assert that if Israel will patiently and in faith bear the pain that their sins have brought upon them, God will forgive and heal. If this ideal is applied to Jesus's exhortation in Matt. 5:39, the implication is that turning the other cheek is more than just showing patience toward hateful people. Enduring hostility is an essential quality of those who are truly repentant and is part of working out one's salvation. Although sinless, Jesus in his passion took on the role of the older, wiser penitent who quietly bears the consequences of his earlier misdeeds. In this, too, Jesus fulfilled the most profound meaning of Lam. 3.

The fallen city. As noted above, Lamentations follows an ancient literary genre, the lament over a fallen city. This is especially true in chap. 1, where Jerusalem is a lady who has grievously suffered. Throughout the OT, cities are personified as women. This metaphor implies that the city is a thing of beauty, and it draws upon the feminine ideals of mother, wife, and daughter. She nurtures her children, is the home to her husband, and is the object of tender affection from her parents, who strive to protect her. Every city has a dark side—poverty, crime, oppression, and filth—but the metaphor is fundamentally positive, implying that she is attractive, nurturing, and an object of devotion. The image of the city as a weeping woman is especially redolent, provoking sympathy in the reader by drawing upon the experience of seeing women weep over their deceased children.

The OT has other poems that focus on fallen cities, but these are often taunts and not laments (Isa. 14; Nah. 3). Revelation 18, however, gives a series of laments over the apocalyptic "Babylon." Although it makes use of several texts from the prophets (cf. Nah. 3:4 to Rev. 17:16; Jer. 51:7 to Rev. 18:3), the laments over Babylon especially echo motifs from Lamentations, albeit at times in an inverted form. Jerusalem is Lady Zion, and Babylon is the great prostitute. As Jerusalem was once a princess (Lam. 1:1), so Babylon calls herself a queen (Rev. 18:7). As Jerusalem once had great wealth but lost it all (Lam. 4:1–2), so also shall Babylon (Rev. 18:11–13). Both Jerusalem and Babylon are punished by God. Jerusalem is the apostate city of God, and Babylon is the mother city of paganism and imperial power. That is, both cities stand at the head of their respective typological ideals. The parallels are telling: the lamentation over Babylon is not a taunt or ironic; it is, like the lament over Jerusalem, real. Babylon, for all its sins, is a great city, and its fall entails great human suffering. Revelation expresses deep sorrow over the corruption that undoes all the good that human society may achieve.

The lament over Jerusalem also reappears in the words of Jesus, most obviously in his weeping over the city. She is the city who kills the prophets and stones those who are sent to her, and she is destined to be "desolate" (Matt. 23:37–38). But there may be in Jesus's sayings yet another echo of Lam. 1.

In Lam. 1:14, Lady Jerusalem says that her sin has become a yoke around her neck. The metaphor of the yoke, representing servitude, is common in the Bible (Lev. 26:13; Deut. 28:48; 1 Kings 12:10; Isa. 9:4; Jer. 27:8), but it is peculiar to portray sin as a yoke. This leads us to Matt. 11, where Jesus appears to make a severe non sequitur. After lamenting the sin, unbelief, and coming destruction of the Jewish cities of Chorazin, Bethsaida, and Capernaum, he abruptly declares that all who are burdened should come to him because his yoke is easy (Matt. 11:20–30). This abrupt shift is generally attributed to a redactional process. "The text stands in sharp contrast to the woes pronounced on the Galilean cities. . . . It is an assured result of research that Matt. 11:25–30 is not a unitary text but that we have here three logia" (Luz, 156). But this may not be correct. Jesus's lament over the cities' destruction at the hands of enemy armies and the metaphor of the yoke recall Lam. 1, and this may be behind the sudden shift in Jesus's speech. Sin, as Lady Zion discovered, is a terrible burden. Cities that bear this yoke are destined for destruction. But Jesus calls upon people in Chorazin, Bethsaida, and Capernaum to take up his yoke. Understood in this manner, the yoke they should cast off is not simply their hardships and worries; it is their sin. Perhaps Jesus is saying that everyone must bear some yoke. One will either bear a yoke of sin, as do the cities Jesus denounces, or bear a yoke of discipleship.

Jesus's prayer (Matt. 11:25–27) may also echo Lamentations. In Lam. 1:14–16, Lady Zion declares first that her sin is a yoke and then that God has "rejected" her warriors (v. 15) and her children are desolate (v. 16). Jesus asserts that the Father has hidden the truth from the wise and revealed it to small children (Matt. 11:25). To be sure, the idea that God reveals his message to children and not to the wise owes more to Ps. 8:2 than it does to Lamentations (see Matt. 21:16). Even so, mutatis mutandis, there is a parallel between Lam. 1 and Matthew. In Lamentations, confidence in warriors turns the people from God and leads to their children being left desolate. In Matthew, confidence in the scribes and teachers leads people to reject Jesus. Only the children whom the Father has chosen will see the light of the gospel.

Israel rejected. As described above, Lam. 3 describes the travails of Jerusalem from the standpoint of a single man, the poet. Besides recounting the sorrows he has endured, he declares that all this has happened because of the sin he and his fellow citizens committed. He asserts that God is compassionate, however, and he calls upon his people to endure the suffering laid upon them with patience, knowing that God will ultimately redeem. After the poet models how the people should pray (v. 42), the people respond with vv. 43–47 (as marked by the first-person plural forms).

The prayer, however, is not what we might expect—namely, a lengthy recitation of their guilt and a plea for restoration after the pattern of Dan. 9:4–19. Instead, they mention only once and in passing that they have sinned (3:42a), and even here they complain that God has not forgiven them (3:42b). What follows is a recital of how badly God has treated them. God has dealt with them only in anger and has been pitiless in his slaughter of the Jews (v. 43). He has cut himself off from their prayers (v. 44). He has made the nations treat the Jews like scum (v. 45). Their enemies swallow them down (v. 46), and on every side they see only terrors and snares (v. 47). The contrast between this litany of complaint and the pious, contrite appeal of the poet (3:22–41) is striking.

True, OT prayer is typically characterized by surprising bluntness in complaining to God (see Pss. 44:23; 74:1; 77:7). Even so, it is impossible to deny that their prayer is very long on blaming God and very short on contrition. One may respond to this text apologetically (e.g., House, 421–22, treats all of vv. 42–66 as the prayer of the poet, erasing the distinctive use of first-person plural forms in vv. 42–47, and so claims that the poet ends up on the side of the angels). Yet another approach, one that also treats all of vv. 42–66 as the poet's prayer, argues that he is simply unable to maintain his pious stance and yields to his skepticism (Bier). Against both of these, it is better to see the poet's words as distinct from those of the people. The complaining tone reappears in Lam. 5, in which the people continue to speak primarily of their suffering and even declare, "Our fathers sinned and are no more, and we bear their punishment" (5:7 AT; contrast Jer. 31:29). There is a real tension between what the poet recommends and what the people actually pray.

The sorrow and confusion of the people's prayer is real, and it anticipates the tragic history of the Jewish suffering under the nations. At the same time, it suggests that they have not yet been given the grace to make a true return to God. The promise of Deut. 30:1–10, that God would circumcise their hearts and they would return to him with sincere repentance, is not yet fulfilled. In this, the appeal of the poet and the response of the people are echoed in Paul's anguish in Rom. 9–11 over the mystery of Israel's unbelief. The bleak tone of Lamentations continues to the very end of the book, where Israel wonders if God has forever rejected them and if his anger knows no limits (5:22). This despairing tone is not a "problem" in Lamentations; it is an essential feature. It tells us what the exile really means for Israel, implying that an end to their suffering will not come about until there is a great work of God, when he changes their hearts.

Bibliography. Bier, M., "'We Have Sinned and Rebelled; You Have Not Forgiven,'" *BibInt* 22 (2014): 146–67; Gwaltney, W. C., "The Biblical Book of Lamentations in the Context of Near Eastern Lament Literature," in *Scripture in Context II*, ed. W. Hallo, J. Moyer, and L. Perdue (Eisenbrauns, 1983), 191–211; Harrison, R. K., *Jeremiah and Lamentations*, TOTC (InterVarsity, 1973); Hillers, D. R., *Lamentations*, AB (Yale University Press, 2008); House, P. R., "Lamentations," in *Song of Songs and Lamentations*, by D. Garrett and P. R. House, WBC (Thomas Nelson, 2004), 267–473; Huey, F. B., *Jeremiah, Lamentations*, NAC (Broadman & Holman, 1993); Luz, U., *Matthew 8–20*, Herm (Fortress, 2001); Salters, R. B., *Lamentations*, ICC (T&T Clark, 2010).

Duane Garrett

Land

The promise of land to Abram recaptures and advances what was lost in Eden, and will be fulfilled through Abraham's offspring who will remake a new and better Eden (Dempster, 48). The promised land, then, anticipates an even greater land to come. Although the territorial promise initially relates to Israel's settlement in the land of Canaan, by divine design it also points to something far more expansive, which the NT reveals. Our primary concern is to track the progression of the land promise through the biblical covenants until it reaches its final fulfillment in the new creation in Christ.

The Land and the OT

The promises made to Abraham in Genesis occupy a special place in the promise of land. The events of Gen. 1–11, however, are more than simply a prologue. In many ways they are paradigmatic, for they reflect the movement from sin to exile to restoration, all of which cycle through the rest of the OT. In other words, God's promises to Abram address the curse of the ground and Adam's expulsion from Eden brought about by sin (Gen. 3:17–19, 23). Though the gracious act of salvation is illustrated with Noah, it is with Abram that a new beginning and blueprint are revealed.

God graciously interrupts the escalation of sin and death emanating from and through Adam by promising blessing to and through Abram. The word "bless" occurs five times in the call of the patriarch (12:1–3), the gracious counterbalance to the five "curses" against fallen creation and humanity (3:14, 17b; 4:11; 8:21; 9:25) (Gentry and Wellum, 260–61). The call of Abram resurrects God's blessing. For example, whereas Adam and Eve experience exile from their homeland (3:24), God calls Abram out of Ur and promises him land that will restore the blessings of Eden. Just as Adam and Eve receive the promise of restoration in the programmatic prophecy of Gen. 3:15, so the promise to Abram clarifies the means through which God will bring his people back from exile into a new place of blessing.

God's covenant with Abraham recovers the universal purpose of Adam in terms of the blessing of both offspring and land. The universal scope of Eden narrows to the land of Canaan, thus allowing Canaan to serve as a microcosm of what God intended for all humanity. In time Canaan would expand with the proliferation of Abraham's offspring. When Gen. 22:17–18 and 26:3–4 are taken together, the immediate context of the Abrahamic covenant points to a universal expansion of the territorial promise (more on this point below) and begins to establish the type or pattern that points both back to Eden and forward to the ultimate fulfillment of the promise that would eventually encompass the entire world.

Furthermore, in the Abrahamic covenant there are both national (Gen. 12:2, "nation") and international (17:4–6, "nations") components (Williamson, 19). Genesis 15 is a covenant God made with Abraham and his "seed," and Gen. 17, which (re)affirms this covenant after it is doubted in chap. 16, broadens the category of "seed" (Alexander, "Seed," 770). Also, God changes Abram's name to Abraham, for God made him "the father of a multitude of nations" (17:5 ESV). An intended ambiguity exists, then, for Abraham's "seed" *both* encompasses a multitude of nations (chap. 17) *and* relates to an individual descendant (22:17b) who will mediate blessing to all the nations of the earth.

When these texts are put together, the ultimate inheritors of the patriarchal promises are not restricted to a national entity but extend to an international community. God's programmatic agenda for humanity after Eden begins with the formation of a nation through Abraham and points forward to an international people, a theme picked up later in the Prophets. It's difficult to see how any national borders could exhaust the territorial promise, for the multiplication of descendants naturally expands the territorial borders until the earth is filled.

Though there is significant progression and fulfillment of the land promises under leaders such as Moses, Joshua, David, and Solomon, the prophets bring back into focus the Abrahamic promises and advance the pattern of fulfillment in various ways and stages, including both a physical and a spiritual return with national and international results (Martin, 95–114). For example, Isaiah describes Israel's return from exile in both imminent and distant ways, as well as in language resembling the exodus (e.g., Isa. 11; 35; 51:9–11; 52:11–12). The first return from exile is a physical release and return to the land that God's servant Cyrus will accomplish (42:18–43:21; 44:24–45:1; cf. Ezra 1:1–3). But though this return is another fulfillment of God's promised restoration, it in no way compares to the prophets' final vision. Indeed, a deeper captivity kept Israel from being fully restored. That is, though the people are taken out of idolatrous nations, Yahweh still needs to take idolatry out of the people. God's servant-king would accomplish this restoration by bringing back Israel so that God's salvation may reach the nations (Isa. 49–53). Forgiveness will come through God's (individual) servant, who will deliver his (corporate) servant Israel (42:1–9; 49:1–6), redeem his people (9:2–7), rule over his people (11:1–5), and atone for sin by suffering, dying, and taking the punishment upon himself that they deserve (42:1–9; 49:5–6; 50:4–9; 52:13–53:12).

Furthermore, the servant's substitutionary atonement will initiate a new covenant that will enable both Israel *and* the nations to enjoy the blessings of both the Abrahamic and Davidic covenants (Isa. 54–55; cf. 19:19–25). Such an international redemption had been God's plan since Abraham had received the word of promise. Moreover, a Davidic king will bless and rule the nations because God has made him leader and commander of the peoples (55:4–5). This connects to the servant-king in Isa. 53, whose self-offering and resurrection enable him to fulfill God's Davidic covenant promises and to serve as the basis for the new or everlasting covenant. Astonishingly, not only does Isaiah tag the remnant of ethnic Israelites as the Lord's servants (Isa. 65:13–25), but he also employs the same designation for redeemed foreigners from the nations (56:6). Furthermore, in fulfillment of the Abrahamic covenant, the Lord will give his *name* and *blessing* to his servants in the land (65:13–16; cf. Gen. 12:3; 17:5; 22:18; 26:4). The servant-person's saving work, therefore, creates *servants,* and all—transformed Israelites and foreigners—will go to Jerusalem as God's holy mountain in a pilgrimage of worship (Isa. 2:2–4; 27:13; cf. Mic. 4:1–5).

But Isaiah proceeds to describe more splendidly the result of this new order. Isaiah 65:17–66:24 succinctly summarizes the end-time themes that occur throughout the entire book and elaborates on the hope of restoration to the city of Jerusalem and the land in otherworldly language that describes astounding realities (cf. Isa. 2:1–4; 4:2–6; 9:1–7; 11:1–10). When the various strands are drawn together, Isaiah's vision of final restoration involves a new heavens and new earth (65:17; 66:22), a new Jerusalem (65:18–19; cf. 4:2–6), and a holy mountain, Zion (65:25; cf. 2:1–4; 4:2–6). Moreover, in fulfillment of the promises to and covenant with Abraham, God will give them a new *name* and they will receive *blessing* in the *land* by the God of truth (65:15–16). By the end of Isaiah, then, this temple-mountain-city is coextensive with the new heavens and new earth, which resounds with astonishing Eden-like realities cast in terms of God's kingdom coming to and filling the earth.

In similar order, in Jeremiah, God promises to take back his people if they return, and "then nations shall bless themselves in him, and in him shall they glory" (Jer. 4:1–2 ESV). This reference identifies how God would fulfill his promises to Abraham (e.g., Gen. 12:3; 22:18) if Israel would repent and glorify God. As in Isaiah, the prophet sees the nations being a part of the restoration of Israel and Judah, and realizing this cosmological and teleological goal will fulfill the Abrahamic promises (Jer. 12:14–17). Jeremiah 12 intriguingly speaks of an exile, not just for Judah but also for Yahweh's evil neighbors "who touch the heritage that I have given my people Israel to inherit" (12:14 ESV). Astonishingly, in v. 15, after Yahweh plucks up each people from their land, he will again have compassion on them, and he will "bring them in again each to his heritage and each to his land" (ESV). And in the end, when Yahweh brings all the exiles home, if the nations learn to swear by Yahweh's name, "then they shall be built up in the midst of my people" (v. 16 ESV). Furthermore, Jeremiah proclaims that Israel will return from exile in terms of a new exodus (16:14–15).

Then, in chaps. 30–33 Jeremiah unfolds the great promises of salvation and offers hope beyond the exile that will come in the form of a new covenant and return to the land. Of particular importance is 31:38–40, which concerns the rebuilding and expansion of Jerusalem. In addition to the restoration of Davidic leadership (30:8–11), priesthood (31:14), and people (31:31–34), the restoration of the city completes the glorious reversal of Jeremiah's pronouncements of judgment. Though the city had been destroyed, the future age of redemption will see its restoration *and more*. Therefore, the new Jerusalem will be both different and expanded from the old, and the rebuilt city will become the center of God's presence among his people (3:14–18; cf. Isa. 65:17; 66:22; Rev. 21:3).

Jeremiah describes the restoration of both people and place in the future and pins these hopes on a Davidic leader, a righteous branch who, interestingly, combines both king and priest. This king-priest will secure a new covenant for his people as certain as God's covenant with day and night, make them dwell securely in the land, and multiply the offspring of David to be as numerous as the sands of the sea in fulfillment of his covenant with Abraham (33:14–26). Moreover, Jer. 31:35–40 hints that this new covenant would operate within the contours of a new creation.

In similar fashion, Ezekiel prophesies that the renewed people will be purified in heart and spirit, and they will be one flock under a new David (Ezek. 34–37). As a result, "the nations will know that I the LORD make Israel holy, when my sanctuary is among them forever" (37:28). Whereas God had been a sanctuary to the exiles "for a little while" (11:16), his presence will be with them forever. He will make a new covenant (36:16–38), which will deal with their sin and finally reconcile them to Yahweh, so that he can say, "They will be my people, and I will be their God" (37:23; cf. v. 27). In order for this restoration to come, however, God must create a holy people from nothing. And to be sure, he will accomplish his new creation. Indeed, Ezekiel uses the language of resurrection to illustrate the promise of Israel's return to a new life in their own land from the deathlike existence of exile. In other words, the restoration to the land is linked with the resurrection motif. The dead will be brought to life so that they too may participate in the restoration. But Ezekiel's vision of restoration does not stop with Israel. Like similar passages throughout the writing prophets, Ezekiel indicates that the restoration will have international significance (16:59–63).

Ezekiel continues with his program by envisioning in chaps. 40–48 a rebuilt temple with revitalized worship. That is, a new humanity is first (re-)created (Ezek. 37) and then placed in a new temple-Eden (Ezek. 40–48). The climactic vision in chaps. 40–48 describes the fulfillment of the promises of chaps. 1–39. In a significant passage, Ezek. 37:25–28 pulls together various strands of the new place for God's people and prepares the way for even more glorious promises in chaps. 40–48 (cf. 43:7–9). It is significant, then, that Ezekiel ends with a vision of a purified land with boundaries situated around a new temple complex. More specifically, Ezek. 47:1–12 contains an abundance of Edenic imagery and describes a paradisiacal temple that extends to encompass the entire land. Significantly, Ezekiel uses language similar to Jeremiah's regarding a measuring line extending the boundaries outward (Ezek. 47:3; Jer. 31:39; cf. Zech. 2). Thus, the promise concerning the renewed Israel living in the land under a new David is fulfilled in the vision of a temple, recreating an Edenic context, the boundaries of which are coterminous with the land. Ezekiel, then, in line with the other prophets, describes astounding hope for the future that includes transformed land and human nature—a new and better Eden enlarged with one immense river of life and many trees of life. From a canonical perspective, Rev. 21–22 presents this worldwide temple as the new heaven and new earth in light of the fulfillment of Christ (Beale, 348–53).

The Land and the NT

The NT presents an already/not-yet fulfillment of the land promises in the OT. More specifically, the NT presents the land promised to Abraham and his offspring to be finally fulfilled in the (physical) new creation as a result of the person and work of Christ. At this time in salvation history, however, the fulfillment is focused primarily on Christ, who himself has inaugurated a new creation through his resurrection. That is, God's covenant presence and blessing are found in Christ, and those united to him by faith in his death, resurrection, and ascension receive their inheritance, rest, and every spiritual blessing in the heavenly places in him (Eph. 1:3). In the present, believers live as exiles (1 Pet. 1:1; 2:11) between the inauguration and consummation of the kingdom and anticipate the final fulfillment and enjoyment of these covenant blessings in his presence in the new heaven and new earth (Rev. 21–22). A look at selected passages demonstrates this work.

In Matthew, a connection with land is introduced in 2:15 (cf. Hosea 11:1). In the context of Hosea, God recalls the history of Israel, God's son (Exod. 4:22–23), when he delivered them out of Egypt in fulfillment of his promises to give them their own land. But Hosea 11:2–7 goes on to lament how Israel has wandered away from the Lord and to predict their future return to exile (11:5). Another exodus was needed. This exodus event became central in the life of Israel, to which later revelation would attest. As God's revelation progresses through Israel's successes and failures, an even greater exodus begins to be anticipated (Isa. 43:16–21; 51:9–11; Jer. 16:14–15; 31:31–34; Hosea 2:14–15; 11:10–11). Within this typological milieu, Hosea is looking for a saving visitation from the Lord. This point is important, for what Matthew sees is something Hosea himself has already seen. Matthew is rightly putting together God's organic and progressive revelation in chronological order to demonstrate that God's true Son has arrived to accomplish a greater exodus in fulfillment of his promises (Carson, "Matthew," 92). As a result, Matthew now sees Jesus as the locus of true Israel, which he goes on to show in Jesus's testing in the wilderness, the giving of a "new law" in the Sermon on the Mount, and revelation of Jesus as the true Son.

Second, "land" also appears in Matt. 5:5. The verb "inherit" in the OT is often linked to Israel's entering into and possessing the land (e.g., Deut. 4:1; 16:20; Isa. 57:13). A few observations are important for interpreting Matt. 5:5 and the use of Ps. 37. To begin, Ps. 37 looks over the eschatological horizon (vv. 18, 29), in which the familiar theme of inheriting the land is promised as a future hope to those who faithfully wait for the Lord (vv. 3, 9, 11, 18, 22, 29, 34). This eschatological orientation is further confirmed by the fact that Ps. 37 was recognized as messianic in Jesus's day (Carson, "Matthew," 133). Likewise, the Beatitudes are framed within the inaugurated eschatological context of the kingdom, which is evidenced by the repetition of present blessing (Matt. 5:3, 10) and future blessings (vv. 4–9). Hence Matthew, like the rest of the NT, is picking up and advancing the eschatological trajectory of Ps. 37. However, the ultimate fulfillment should not be spiritualized into some kind of non-territorial space. In fact, for Matthew, the culmination of God's promises will result in the renewal of all things (19:27–28), when God's kingdom on earth reflects his kingdom in heaven (6:10).

Finally, in a passage laden with OT imagery, Jesus lays claim to what was (temporarily) experienced in Israel's life in the land: rest (Matt. 11:28–30). Rest, once promised and given by God to obedient Israel in the land, is no longer centered in a geographical territory. Rather, it is now bound up in and given by Christ, which testifies to his divine identity. Significantly, "you will find rest for your souls" echoes Jer. 6:16, where it is the reward Yahweh offers to those who search for the good way and walk in it. Furthermore, the rest promised to David (2 Sam. 7:11) and experienced under Solomon (1 Chron. 22:9)—only to be forfeited as a result of sin—is now given under the yoke of the true Davidic son. Thus, Jesus now shares in the divine activity of giving and fulfilling the promises of rest, which likely brings to mind God's rest after creation and Israel's Sabbath rest.

Now, at last, after the burden and toil experienced in the garden after the fall (Gen. 3:17–19), under Israel's slavery in Egypt (Exod. 6:6), and presently under the demands of Rome, rest is given to and experienced by those who are related to Jesus.

In John 15, Jesus says, "I am the true vine" (v. 1). Vineyard imagery was common in the ancient world, and one familiar with the OT would understand the connection Jesus was making (e.g., Isa. 5:1–7; 27:2–6; Ps. 80:8–16; Ezek. 15:1–8; 17:1–21; Hosea 10:1–2). This imagery was a symbol for Israel, God's covenant people, and consistently stressed Israel's disobedience and failure to bear fruit no matter how much God tended to and cultivated her. Thus, God would judge Israel by the hands of other nations (see Isa. 5). Surprisingly, though, it is not a nation or people that is the vine; it is Jesus. That the vine is Jesus, not the church, is intentional. The Lord is viewed in his representative capacity, the Son of God and Son of Man who dies and rises so that a new people might come into being and bring forth fruit for God. Indeed, Jesus is the true vine—the true Israel—and his disciples are now the branches.

Perhaps the most important OT passage for John 15 is Ps. 80, for it brings together the themes of vine and son of man (Carson, *John*, 513). This psalm is a prayer for the restoration of Israel, a vine that God brought out of Egypt, planted in the land, and blessed (vv. 8–9). Just as God has delivered and planted his people in the past, so the psalmist is praying for salvation in the future, which presumably includes restoration to the land. However, John 15 indicates that a redemptive-historical shift has taken place. The true vine *now* is not apostate Israel but Jesus himself, and the place of blessing is in him. Now, if exiled Israel wants to be restored, then they must be rightly related to Jesus and planted in him.

In Paul, the fulfillment of the land promise in relation to Christ is further confirmed in Rom. 4:13, which builds on his previous argument, defines the content of the promise to Abraham, and explains what it is—namely, that Abraham would "inherit" the world. While the land initially promised to Abraham and his descendants extended to the borders of Canaan, both the pattern and trajectory of the OT show that as his offspring multiplied and filled the earth, so also would the boundaries of the land encompass the earth. Of particular importance is Gen. 26:3–4, where the unique plural "lands," when read in conjunction with the oath to which it alludes in Gen. 22:17–18, makes clear that Abraham's seed will possess/inherit the gate of his enemies. This, together with Gen. 22:17, provides exegetical footing for Paul's assertion that Abraham would inherit the world. Paul, then, is demonstrating sound biblical exegesis, informed by Scripture's redemptive-historical story line, by putting all three elements of the covenant together (Schreiner, 435). Therefore, in light of Christ—Abraham's (singular) offspring (Gal. 3)—Abraham and his (corporate) offspring will inherit the world as people, both Jew and gentile, come to faith in Jesus Christ.

For Paul and Peter, the concepts of inheritance and sonship, which relate to Israel in the OT, expand. For example, in Col. 1:12–13 the combination of terms such as "inheritance," "deliverance," and "transfer" bring to mind the exodus. Thus, there is an eschatological reward for believers who experience a better exodus in Christ that escalates from the OT inheritance of the promised land to the NT inheritance of final salvation. Furthermore, inheritance in Paul is connected with sonship, for the OT demonstrates that God's son is Israel (Exod. 4:22) and the inheritance is the land. In the NT, however, Paul understands all God's people—both Jew and gentile—to be sons of God through faith in Jesus Christ, and if they are Christ's then they are Abraham's offspring, inheritors according to the promise (Gal. 3:26, 29; cf. 4:7; Rom. 8:17). Since Christ is God's Son par excellence, then those who are in Christ receive their inheritance in him as they await the final fulfillment of God's promises. Moreover, they are sealed with the promised Holy Spirit, who is the guarantee of their inheritance until they acquire possession of it (Eph. 1:13–14; cf. Ezek. 36:26–27; 37:14; Joel 2:28–30). Thus, the Christian's inheritance looks to the not yet.

Likewise, Peter praises God for the church's certain salvation, for through the resurrection of Jesus and because of God's great mercy they have been "begotten anew" to a living hope (1 Pet. 1:3 AT; cf. 1:23), to an imperishable inheritance (1:4), and by God's power are kept through faith for the salvation to be revealed (1:5). Peter likely selects the language of inheritance to describe what awaits Christians and understands the inheritance no longer in terms of a land promised to Israel but rather in terms of the end-time hope that lies before them. For Peter, like Paul, the background of the idea of inheritance is the OT. In other words, Peter's use of the term is understood in light of Christ and his fulfillment. The future fulfillment of God's promise, however, should not be understood as merely spiritual. This hope is still physical, for we learn from 2 Peter that it will be realized in a new heaven and a new earth (2 Pet. 3:13; cf. Rev. 21:1–22:5). But it transcends and leaves behind the shadow of the land of Canaan.

In Heb. 3:7–4:13, rest in Canaan functions as a type of God's heavenly rest in Gen. 2 and Ps. 95. The rest that came with entering the land under Joshua points back to creation; however, the land was not completely conquered (cf., e.g., Josh. 13). This rest anticipated the eschatological rest for the people of God, which David announced in Ps. 95. As the OT demonstrates, rest in the land was no longer possible. But God's rest is available for all who believe and obey. As long as it is called "today," then, God's people are not exhorted to return to the type of rest in the land of Canaan. Rather, they are exhorted to enter God's eschatological rest that comes through a newfound relationship with Christ (Heb. 3:6).

In Heb. 11:8–22, the author emphasizes Abraham's obedient response to God's command to go to a place that he would receive as an inheritance (vv. 8–10). According to v. 9, "by faith [Abraham] went to live in the land of promise, as in a foreign land, living in tents with Isaac and Jacob, heirs with him of the same promise" (ESV). The image of the patriarchs living in tents stresses the fact that mere entry into the land did not result in the attainment of the promised inheritance. Then immediately it says that "he was looking forward to the city that has foundations, whose designer and builder is God" (v. 10 ESV). The logical relationship between vv. 9 and 10 is important to note. Abraham looked for the land of promise "because" he was looking to the city with foundations. The pointed contrast between "the land of promise" and "a foreign land" serves to show the unsettled life of Abraham. That is, entrance into the promised land had brought no settlement. Hence, Abraham looked beyond his present scene to the unseen blessing, for the land pointed beyond itself. According to the author, then, the patriarchs knew that the land of promise was not the ultimate fulfillment since they were dwelling as strangers and exiles (11:13). This point is underscored in v. 16, "But as it is, they desire a better country, that is, a heavenly one. Therefore God is not ashamed to be called their God, for he has prepared for them a city" (ESV).

That the land of Canaan was not ultimately the fulfillment of the promise is confirmed in that the patriarchs died there without receiving the things promised (11:13). However, the land of Canaan was not merely a rest stop. Rather, it was the *promised land*—the land Abraham and his offspring received as their inheritance. From there they continuously waited for the appearance of the city of God, of which they were already members by virtue of God's call and promise. This city is later referred to as the heavenly homeland (11:16), the city of the living God, heavenly Jerusalem (12:22), the unshakable kingdom (12:28), and the abiding city that is to come (13:14). Indeed, they looked beyond Canaan to a *new* heaven and *new* earth—a *new* Jerusalem. Again, the promised land pointed to something greater.

Given its beginning, Scripture's ending should not surprise us. The final place of the kingdom in Revelation—the new creation—appears as the consummation of a complex biblical continuum reaching back to creation. This consummation depicts the new heaven and new earth as a paradisiacal new Eden (cf. Gen. 2:10–14 and Rev. 22:1–2; Gen. 3:22–24 and Rev. 22:2; Gen. 2:11–12 and Rev. 22:18–21; Gen. 3:8 and Rev. 21:3–5), new Jerusalem (21:2), and cosmological temple (21:22) that is, in climax of the covenants, filled with God's presence (21:3). Moreover, the end also relates to Israel's universalized land promises that reach back through the prophets to Abraham all the way to Eden. In fulfillment of the promise to Abraham that "in you all the families of the earth shall be blessed" (Gen. 12:3 ESV), ransomed people from every tribe, tongue, people, and nation (Rev. 5:9) are given a new creation. In this new creation, the geographical boundaries of this place expand to the entire new creation in ways that remarkably reflect the visions of the prophets. That is, Rev. 21–22 dazzlingly displays the future fulfillment of the prophets, and the entire OT, by collapsing temple, city, and land into one paradisiacal end-time picture portraying God's covenant presence with his people.

This final picture at the end depicts a glorious return of God's people living in his place under his rule, thereby tying together the creation and placement of man in Eden, the redemption of Israel, and, finally, God's eschatological purposes to bring blessing to the world. In other words, the pattern Eden anticipated has not merely been regained and the promised land possessed, but it has been radically transformed through the life, death, resurrection, ascension, and rule of the triumphant Lamb, who won a new creation for his people. Indeed, the kingdom of the world will become "the kingdom of our Lord and of his Christ, and he shall reign forever and ever" (11:15 ESV; cf. Pss. 2; 8). God's people in Christ will once again dwell in the land—forever.

See also Covenant; Law; Literal Fulfillment; Promises

Bibliography. Alexander, T. D., "Beyond Borders," in *The Land of Promise*, ed. P. Johnston and P. Walker (InterVarsity, 2000), 35–50; Alexander, *From Eden to the New Jerusalem* (InterVarsity, 2008); Alexander, "Seed," in *NDBT*, 769–73; Beale, G. K., *The Temple in the Church's Mission*, NSBT (InterVarsity, 2004); Carson, D. A., *The Gospel according to John*, PNTC (Eerdmans, 1991); Carson, "Matthew," in *EBC*, 8:3–599; Dempster, S. G., *Dominion and Dynasty*, NSBT (InterVarsity, 2003); Gentry, P. J., and S. J. Wellum, *Kingdom through Covenant*, 2nd ed. (Crossway, 2018); Martin, O. R., *Bound for the Promised Land*, NSBT (InterVarsity, 2015); Schreiner, T. R., *Romans*, 2nd ed., BECNT (Baker Academic, 2018); Williamson, P. R., "Promise and Fulfillment," in *The Land of Promise*, ed. P. Johnston and P. Walker (InterVarsity, 2000), 15–34.

Oren Martin

Law

The Mosaic Law (Heb. *tôrâ*; Gk. *nomos*) includes God's instruction and promises (e.g., Job 22:22; Ps. 94:12; Prov. 1:8; 4:2; 13:14; Isa. 2:3; 42:4; 51:4; Mal. 2:6–8). The root meaning of *tôrâ* is to "teach" (Deut. 6:1). Wisdom literature therefore draws on Torah to promote righteous living (e.g., Prov. 3:1). Most instances, however, refer to doing what the Torah (Law) commands. *Tôrâ* frequently serves as the direct object of verbs, indicating the commands that are to be done. One is to "keep," "walk in," "do," or "obey" *tôrâ*; one "breaks," "transgresses," "rejects," or "does violence to" it. *Tôrâ* is used synonymously with "commandment(s)," "statute(s)," "rule(s)," and "testimony(ies)." Likewise, in the NT *nomos* may refer to the Scriptures (e.g., Matt. 22:36; Luke 10:26; John 7:49; Rom. 3:21; Gal. 4:21) but most frequently refers to what is commanded (e.g., Matt. 5:18; cf. 5:19; 22:36; 23:23; Luke 2:22–24, 27, 39; Acts 23:3; John 7:19, 23, 51; 8:17; 19:7; Rom. 2:12, 23, 25; 3:20; 4:15; 5:20; 7:2, 3, 5, 7; Gal. 2:16; 3:10, 12). Each of the NT authors grapples afresh with the role of the law and the performance or fulfillment of its commands—whether moral or cultic—in the lives of those in Christ.

Law in the OT

The Mosaic legislation is embedded within a narration of origins. From the beginning God promises blessings for obedience and curses for disobedience. The first commandment comes with God's blessing: "Be fruitful, multiply, and fill the earth" (Gen. 1:28 AT). Genesis 2:16–17 threatens a curse: the man is not to eat of the tree of the knowledge of good and evil, or in that day he will die. In lieu of a legal code, an unwritten law of conscience should have condemned Cain, because of his surrender to envy (4:7), and the wickedness of the generations that followed (6:5, 11). Humanity's story narrows to a single man, Abraham, who places his trust in the God who calls him to leave his ancestral home (15:6). He and his household later receive circumcision as a sign of their faith (Gen. 17). While enslaved in a foreign land, the promised offspring forget the God of Abraham; however, God does not forget them but brings them forth from the land of their captivity into the wilderness and to freedom (cf. Heb. 3:7–4:13).

God gives the Law in the context of this relationship (Exod. 19–24), a relationship soon tragically broken but mercifully restored (Exod. 32–34). The covenant at Sinai/Horeb constitutes a priestly kingdom and holy nation devoted to the Lord (Exod. 19:5–6; cf. Rom. 9–11). Introducing the law are the Ten Commandments, themselves introduced by a reminder of how God has already acted on Israel's behalf (Exod. 20:2). This relationship with God (the first tablet) precedes and grounds relationships with others (the second tablet). The law governs even secret thoughts and deliberations (Exod. 20:17; Lev. 19:17–18, 33–34; Deut. 5:21; cf. Rom. 7:7–12).

The book of the covenant follows, being delivered to Moses, the people's representative. It interprets and elaborates on the Decalogue (Exod. 20:14, 18–22; 21:1; cf. Matt. 5:21–32). No priests or kings are mentioned, since God acts to right the scales of justice for the priestly people through lay judges and elders (Exod. 21:23–34; cf. Lev. 24:19–20; Deut. 19:21; 32:25; Matt. 5:39–41). Instructions on the tabernacle sandwich Exod. 32–34's golden-calf incident, which culminates in the veiled Moses acting as the representative-turned-mediator of God's holy presence (cf. 2 Cor. 3:11, 13–14). The tabernacle is but a physical and spatial version of Moses's mediation (cf. Heb. 8:1–10:18). Leviticus 1–7 continues the tabernacle laws, followed by the instructions for the high priest in Lev. 8–9 (cf. Heb. 4:14–10:18); cultic purity in Lev. 11–15, including even the food the people eat (Lev. 11; cf. Mark 7:15–23; Matt. 15:11, 17) and the diseases that afflict them (Lev. 14:2–32; cf. Matt. 8:1–4); and atoning sacrifice for sin in Lev. 16 (cf. Rom. 3:25–26). The Holiness Code of Lev. 17–26 is epitomized in Lev. 19:2: "You shall be holy, for I the LORD your God am holy" (ESV). That chapter expands on the Ten Commandments as an expression of love (Lev. 19:18, 34; cf. Matt. 7:12; 22:34–40; 23:5–7, 23; Luke 10:25–37; Rom. 13:8–10; Gal. 5:14). Killing, for instance, includes even anger and desires for revenge (Lev. 19:17; cf. Matt. 5:21–22).

In Deuteronomy, the second law, Moses teaches a new generation before they cross the Jordan without him (cf. Deut. 1:1; Luke 6:12–7:49). Israel remains God's chosen people (Deut. 7:6; 10:14–15). Laws are repeated, such as the commands for sacred days and festivals, whether Sabbath, Passover, Unleavened Bread, Weeks, or Booths (e.g., Deut. 5:12; 16:1–17; cf. Lev. 23; Matt. 12:1–14; John 5:1–18; 6:1–71; 7:37–39; Acts 2). Deuteronomy "democratizes" the people's holiness before an impartial God, with implications even for the strangers in their midst (Deut. 10:17). Even the runaway slave enjoys rights among God's people (Deut. 23:15–16; cf. Philemon). Citizens establish courts, militia, and even the kingship from among the brothers. Deuteronomy 27–28 concludes the code with a listing of blessings and curses, including, ultimately, exile. The much lengthier sections on the impending curses testify to what will prove impossible for the people (Deut. 27:26; cf. Gal. 3:10). God will have to intervene to create obedient hearts (Deut. 29:3–4; 30:1–10; cf. Jer. 31:31–34).

Deuteronomy 6:4–9, like Lev. 19, serves as a partial summary of the laws encapsulated in the Ten Commandments (cf. Mark 12:28–31). Leviticus 19 groups together several commandments that govern relations among people and concludes, "You shall love your neighbor as yourself" (Lev. 19:18; cf. v. 34). Jesus's comment that Deut. 6:4–5 and Lev. 19:18 are the greatest commands would not have surprised his peers (Mark 12:28–31; cf. John 13:34), or Rabbi Hillel (b. Shabb. 31a) or the author of Tobit (Tob. 4:15) in the years before: "What you hate, do not do to anyone." "The rest is commentary."

Paul

Paul's discussions of Moses's Law have long been a matter of controversy and have not been easily extricated from larger issues pertaining to his ancestral faith. E. P. Sanders's 1977 *Paul and Palestinian Judaism* championed a "new perspective" on Judaism: The long-standing consensus of Jewish legalism in Paul's day and among the Tannaim (the rabbis from AD 70–200) was without foundation. The Jews obeyed God's commands to *remain* in a relationship God had graciously and freely entered into with them as an elect people. Dale Allison demonstrates the value of Sanders's work even for the study of the

Gospels. If Paul, however, was not responding to Jewish legalism, what, then, was his concern with Law observance? Heikki Räisänen thinks Paul is simply inconsistent. James D. G. Dunn, on the other hand, recognizes consistency: the apostle rejects a nationalistic misuse of the Law requiring the gentiles for their salvation to be circumcised and observe Sabbath and food laws (the "works of the Law," Gk. *erga nomou*).

Despite the popularity of Dunn's new perspective on Paul, some Second Temple and Tannaitic texts may still be fairly described as attributing salvation to the performance of the Law. Further, Paul regularly critiques the Law itself, without any particular emphasis on the boundary-marking elements of circumcision, Sabbath, and food laws (e.g., Rom. 3:20–22; 4:13–14; 5:13, 20; 7:4, 7–8; Gal. 2:19, 21; 3:11–13, 17–18; 4:21; 5:4). Paul faults failure to obey the Law (Rom. 7:14–25; Gal. 3:10). Also difficult for the new perspective is Paul's contrast of salvation by faith in/of Christ with works or the works of the law (Gal. 2:16; 3:2, 5, 10; Rom. 3:20, 28). The Law is based on doing (Gal. 3:12), not on faith and promise (Rom. 4:15–16). According to Rom. 4:2–5, Abraham was saved not by works, as if he had merited payment, but by God's gracious gift, whereas Israel thought it could obtain righteousness by pursuing the Law on the basis of its works (Rom. 9:31–32). Paul therefore contrasts believing and doing (Rom. 10:4–8). He considers his achievements under the Law worthless compared to what he enjoys in Christ (Phil. 3:3–9). This reading of the undisputed letters dovetails with the contrast of human works/performance with salvation by God's grace through faith in Eph. 2:8–9 and Titus 3:5.

Paul interprets the gracious elements in Judaism in terms of Christ, who alone atones for sin (Gal. 3:13; Rom. 3:25–26). The temple cult and sacrifices are understood in term of Christ (1 Cor. 3:9–17; 6:19; Phil. 2:17; 4:18; 2 Cor. 6:14–7:1; Rom. 12:1). Apart from a gracious framework, non-Christ-believing Jews inevitably fail to obey God's Law (Rom. 2:17–29; 3:11–19). The Law, intended for life (7:10), is co-opted by and increases with sin (5:13; 7:7–25). Knowing God's Law, though a privilege, only reveals disobedience (2:1–3:20; esp. 3:10–12, 20). The Law imprisons (Gal. 3:22–23), brings a curse (3:10), and holds people "under" its power (3:22; 4:5, 9), leading to slavery (4:21–26) and death (2 Cor. 3:7). Paul takes as obvious that no one does all that the Law commands and thus all fall under its condemnation (Gal. 3:10; cf. 1 Kings 8:46; Prov. 20:9; Eccles. 7:20). The Mosaic Law was for a limited time (Gal. 3:19), but now the fullness of time has come (4:4–5). Believers are no longer under the Law and are released from it, since Christ is the end (goal) of the Law (Rom. 6:14; 7:2, 6; 10:4). To be "under the Law" is to go back in time to an era that Paul says has come to an end (Gal. 3:24–25). Christ believers, instead, are led by the Spirit (Gal. 5:18; Rom. 6:14–15). Since God saves on the basis of Christ and not of the Mosaic Law, as a *consequence* of Paul's Christ-centered reasoning, gentiles may be included in that salvation as well.

Scholars debate whether Paul's *nomos* may mean "principle" or consistently refers to the Mosaic torah (1 Cor. 9:20–21; Rom. 3:27; 7:21, 23, 25; 8:2; Gal. 6:2). Prior to Gal. 6:2 every previous instance of *nomos* in Galatians refers to Moses's Law. Even Gal. 6:2 may be taken as the Law understood through the lens of Christ's love, a love described in terms of the moral precepts of the Law (Gal. 2:20; 5:14; cf. Rom. 13:8–10, citing the Decalogue; Eph. 6:2–3). Paul therefore continues to appeal to the Law as *a* warrant for Christian behavior (e.g., 1 Cor. 9:8–9; cf. Deut. 25:4). On the other hand, cultic elements in the Law such as circumcision, Sabbath, and food laws are not applicable for gentile Christ believers (Lev. 11:1–44; Deut. 14:3–21; 1 Cor. 7:19; Gal. 5:6; 6:15; Rom. 14:5–6, 14, 20). The theocratic, civil elements of the Law no longer apply to Christ-believing assemblies, who are expected to obey the Roman authorities (Rom. 13:1–7).

Mark

Moses and Elijah, representing the Law and the Prophets, appear with Jesus on the Mount of Transfiguration, and yet the voice from heaven subordinates them to Jesus's ministry as the "beloved Son" (Mark 9:2–8). The disciples are to listen to him, the one who fulfills the promise of a prophet whom the people are to heed (Deut. 18:15). Jesus directs the rich young ruler to the necessity of keeping the Decalogue's commands (Mark 10:19), which should ultimately lead him to follow Jesus (10:20–22). The Law must be interpreted in light of the greater authority of Christ. When a scribe asks Jesus which commandment is the most important (Mark 12:18–34), Jesus points to the love of God and neighbor but then describes that love as relativizing burnt offerings (Mark 12:33; cf. 15:38; Deut. 6:4–5; Lev. 19:18). This scribe is "not far" from a kingdom realized in Christ himself, who is then described as enthroned at God's right hand (Mark 12:35–37).

As for the Law's cultic concerns, lepers were not to be touched and were to remain outside the camp, and yet Jesus heals by touching a leper, apparently undefiled by the contact (Mark 1:40–45; cf. Lev. 13:46). In Mark 5:24–34 a hemorrhaging woman touches Jesus (5:27, 28, 30, 31). This should render him unclean (Lev. 15:25–27), and yet Mark remains unconcerned. Jesus ignores the prohibition against touching dead bodies as he touches and raises a dead girl (Mark 5:41; cf. Lev. 21:1, 11; 22:4; Num. 5:2). The prophesied messianic feast of the new age has arrived (Isa. 25:6). Jesus's disciples are not to fast; the new wine is being placed in *new* wineskins (Mark 2:18–22). Even the Sabbath is to be observed as interpreted by the Lord of the Sabbath, who allows for a higher level of activity on the holy day than expected (Mark 2:24–28; 3:3–5). Jesus declares all foods clean, since the food laws represent merely external matters unable to effect true purity (Mark 7:15, 18–23). Although Mark does not present a fuller theology of the Mosaic Law, some laws are clearly no longer normative since Christ's coming, and certainly the extrabiblical traditions of the elders are not (7:8–9). Mark's Jesus even appeals, against Moses, to God's original purpose in creation (10:2–9). Nevertheless, other elements of the Law remain in effect. For instance, one must still honor parents in accordance with the Decalogue (Mark 7:9–13).

Matthew

In Matt. 5:17–20 Jesus emphasizes the continuing validity of the Law: Each "dot" and "iota" is to be accomplished with a righteousness exceeding the professionals. He commends temple sacrifice (Matt. 5:23–24) and tithing (23:23). The disciples even seem expected to observe the Sabbath (12:1–14; 24:20). Matthew stresses the Law's fulfillment in Christ, who is greater than both David and the temple as the Sabbath's Lord (12:3–6, 8). As in Mark, Jesus claims that food does not render a person unclean (Matt. 15:11; cf. Lev. 11:1–44; Deut. 14:3–21), although Matthew removes Mark 7:19's explicit elimination of the kosher/nonkosher distinction. Jesus sends the leper to the priests not to be cleansed—Jesus has already done that—but as a testimony to them (Matt. 8:1–4; cf. Lev. 14). He declares "sons" to be "free" from the temple tax in Matt. 17:26. As he is greater than the temple, the laws must be understood in terms of him (12:5–6), and one day the temple will be no more (chap. 24). In other words, while under the old covenant one may sacrifice (5:24; 9:13; 12:7), tithe (23:23), and observe Sabbath (24:20), Matthew anticipates changes with the arrival of the new era in Christ—and yet, one is still to love God and neighbor with the new wineskins (9:14–17; 22:34–40). The Law and the Prophets were in effect "until" John and the time of their rightful fulfillment (11:13).

As Jesus offers a fuller and stricter interpretation of the Law's true meaning, he contrasts what was said by Moses with what he himself has said (Matt. 5:21–22, 27–28, 31–32, 33–34, 38–39, 43–44). To overlook anger in the prohibition against murder is to miss the sin within human hearts (Matt. 5:21–22; Exod. 20:13; cf. Prov. 14:29; 22:24; 29:22). Adultery includes even lust (Matt. 5:27–28; Job 31:1; Prov. 6:23–25). Jesus permits divorce for sexual sin but underlines that divorce and remarriage are not God's intention (Matt. 5:31–32; 19:8). Such obedience is due a perfect God (5:48). This radical demand requires Jesus's saving work in the face of human evil and transgression (15:18–19; 19:3–9; 19:21–22; 20:28).

In his torah teaching, Jesus criticizes human traditions/additions, including those pertaining to eating with "sinners" (9:11), fasting (9:14), observing the Sabbath (12:2, 10), handwashing (15:1–2, 12, 20), and divorce (19:3). Even Jesus's prohibition of oaths (allowed by the Law in Num. 30; Josh. 9:20) appears to be targeting a Pharisaic system designed to avoid telling the truth (Matt. 23:16, 18–22). Thus, Jesus himself swears an oath (Matt. 26:63–64; cf. Rom. 1:9; 2 Cor. 1:23; Gal. 1:20; Phil. 1:8; Heb. 6:13–18). In Matt. 5:38–39 Jesus corrects a misuse of the justice system in which a person uses civic penalties to exact personal revenge against someone (civil penalties in Exod. 21:22–25; Lev. 24:17–22; Deut. 19:21; personal revenge prohibited in Lev. 19:18; Deut. 32:35; cf. Prov. 20:22; 24:29; Rom. 12:19–13:7). Jesus is the final authority on the interpretation of the torah and is to be obeyed (28:20).

Luke-Acts

Luke's Gospel opens with Zechariah and Elizabeth walking blamelessly in the Lord's commandments and statutes (Luke 1:6, 9; cf. Deut. 4:40), John and Jesus being circumcised on the eighth day (Luke 1:58; 2:21; cf. Lev. 12:3), and Joseph and Mary observing purification laws and consecrating Jesus as the firstborn (Luke 2:22–24, 27; Exod. 13:2; Lev. 12:8). The twelve-year-old Jesus and his parents travel to Jerusalem to observe Passover (Luke 2:41–52; cf. Exod. 34:22–23; Deut. 16:1–8). Luke, early on, appears to encourage Law observance.

Jesus in his ministry defends healing on the Sabbath as lawful activity and justifies his disciples' behavior on that day (Luke 6:1–5, 9; 14:1–6). When charged with Sabbath violation for healing a crippled woman, Jesus notes his opponents' hypocrisy (13:10–17). He declares a lawyer "correct" in his interpretation of the mandates to love God and neighbor (10:25–26; Deut. 6:5; Lev. 19:18): "Do this and you will live" (Luke 10:28). He affirms the rich ruler's belief that the commandments are a means of inheriting eternal life (18:18, 20). Although the Law and the Prophets were only until John, the next verse affirms the eternal validity of the Law (16:16–17).

After the resurrection in Luke's Gospel and then in Acts, Jesus's followers continue to observe the Sabbath (Luke 23:56), worship God at the appropriate hours at the temple (Luke 24:53; Acts 2:46; 3:1; 5:12–13, 20–21, 42), and observe the Feast of Weeks (Acts 2:1). Even Jewish priests join the movement (6:7). At one point, Peter and John go to the temple at the ninth hour, the time of the evening burnt offering (3:1). "False witnesses" charge Stephen with speaking against the Law and the customs of Moses, but Stephen shows how *they* had disobeyed the law (6:13–14; 7:53). Even gentiles are to observe certain Mosaic laws (15:20–21, repeated in 15:29; 21:25). Paul circumcises Timothy (16:3), takes a Nazirite vow (18:18; cf. Num. 6:2, 18), purifies himself at Jerusalem, and pays for his men's sacrifices (Acts 21:21–24, 26). Luke thereby proves false the charge that Paul supported Jews abandoning the Law and circumcision (21:21, 24; cf. 22:12; 23:3; 25:8; 28:17).

Jesus's ministry represents the fulfillment of the Law and the Prophets, which were in effect until John (Luke 16:16; 24:27, 44; cf. 4:16–21). Jesus's interpretation of Mosaic Law is normative and often more radical. For instance, although remarriage appears permissible in Deut. 24:1–4, Jesus rules it out altogether (Luke 16:18). As in Matthew and Mark, Jesus touches lepers and the dead daughter whom he raises (Luke 5:12–15; 8:40–56), and he requires his hearers to heed his *own* teachings and commands. Jesus is the new David and Lord of the Sabbath, so his disciples are authorized to pick grain on the Sabbath, and he even heals on that day (6:1–11; 13:10–17 [uniquely Lukan]). The rebellious son of Deut. 21:18–21 is no longer stoned (Luke 15:11–32). Jesus transforms how the commandments are to be observed.

Stephen offers a case in point: he affirms circumcision (Acts 7:8), Moses (7:20–22, 36, 38), the Law (7:38, 53), and the tabernacle (7:44–45), and yet there is a grain of truth behind the false witness against him (6:11, 13–14), as he criticizes excessive temple veneration (7:48–50). He appears to lump his critics in with those who stood against Moses and the prophets (7:9, 23–29, 35–40).

A new era, nevertheless, is dawning. Peter receives a vision declaring unclean foods as clean (Acts 10:9–16; 10:44–11:18; cf. Lev. 11:1–44; Deut. 14:3–21)—albeit to justify gentiles as clean and rightful recipients of the gospel message. The burdensome yoke of the Law—even for Jews—is not to be placed on the gentiles, who need not be circumcised (Acts 15:7–11, 19, 24; cf. Gen. 17:9–14; Lev. 12:3). Even Paul's own Law observance appears to be for pragmatic reasons rather than a soteriological necessity (Acts 18:18; 21:21–26; cf. 1 Cor. 9:20–21). *Both* Jews and gentiles are saved by the grace of the Lord Jesus and not by Moses's Law (Acts 13:38–39; 15:11). While Jews continue to observe the Law, gentiles are not to obey the Law fully or be circumcised.

Gentiles are to abstain from things polluted by idols, from what has been strangled, and from sexual immorality (Acts 15:20; cf. 15:29; 21:25). These prohibitions may not be limited to pagan temple activities, as some suppose, since avoiding eating meat with blood is a broader prohibition. The prohibitions may stem from Lev. 17–18 as commands for gentiles living in the midst of Israel. On the other hand, Lev. 17–18 does not mention meat offered to idols or idolatry, and other laws for resident aliens are not mentioned. Although circumcision and the Law are not necessary for salvation, the focus in Acts 15 is on sexual sins and sensitive matters that might otherwise prevent Jews and gentiles from coming together for meals. These prohibitions do not constitute a new Law but allow gentiles to "do well," or do what is wise and proper (15:29). The decree is for every city where synagogues are present (Acts 15:21).

Some have contended that Timothy's circumcision in Acts 16:3 demonstrates *Luke's* emphasis on Paul's Law observance whereas Paul, in his own account, does not circumcise Titus (Gal. 2:3). Timothy is a different case than Titus, however. Timothy has a Jewish mother and thus is considered an ethnic Jew. To take an uncircumcised Jew into the synagogues would be an offense. Paul defers to Jewish sensibilities. In 1 Cor. 9:19–23 Paul adapts to the customs of those to whom he is ministering. Titus, on the other hand, is a gentile, and for him to be circumcised would signal its necessity for gentiles.

Paul's pragmatism is again on display with his visit to Jerusalem, his arrest, and his subsequent hearings in Acts 21:17–26:32. Jews charge Paul with teaching diaspora Jews to abandon circumcision and Moses (21:20–21). Paul nevertheless agrees with James as a Jew to submit to a Nazirite vow (21:23–24, 26; cf. 18:18). When charged with speaking against the Jews, their temple, and the Mosaic Law, he stresses his respect for Jewish customs (21:28, 22:12; 24:6, 18). He urges the high priest to observe the Law and apologizes to him (23:3, 5). He affirms the Law and the Prophets (24:14; cf. 26:2, 6–7). While not required for salvation, it remains customary for Jews to observe the Law.

John

John stresses Jesus's divine identity (1:1, 18; 20:28). Yahweh is his people's past and future Shepherd, so Jesus as the Good Shepherd gives his life for the sheep (John 10:11–18; Ps. 23:1; Ezek. 34:11–16, 23–24). The vineyard of the Lord is Israel, even as Jesus is the true vine who bears fruit (Isa. 5:1–7; John 15:1–8). Jesus is the true Passover Lamb (John 18:14, 28, 39). He works on the Sabbath because his Father is working (5:1–9, 17). The Jews immediately recognize this as a claim of being equal with God (5:18).

Jesus's words and the Father's testimony supply the Law's two witnesses to the truth of his ministry (John 8:16–18). The Law itself bears witness to Christ; consequently, those who do not believe in Jesus are not able to interpret the Law rightly (1:45; 5:38–39, 46). The temple points to Jesus as the true temple (2:19–22; cf. 4:21, 42). The manna in the wilderness points to Jesus, the true bread from heaven for the life of the world (6:25–29, 51–54). The lighting ritual points to Jesus as the light of the world (8:12). John's many types—like Moses's lifting up the snake (3:14–15)—all point to Christ. To reject Jesus is to violate the Law, since Moses wrote about him (5:39–47; 7:19; cf. Deut. 6:4–5). The Sabbath law must be interpreted, then, in light of the Son's coming and his Sabbath healing (John 5:1–9; 7:22–23). Followers of Jesus will be Law observant in a more profound sense (7:23; 9:28).

At the same time, the grace of Christ is superior to that of the Law (John 1:16: "instead of"). Jesus provides the disciples *his own* commandments (1:17; 13:34; 14:15, 21, 23–24; 15:10) as opposed to "their Law" (15:25) or "your Law" (10:34; cf. 7:19; 8:17). Included in these is the commandment to love one another as Christ has loved them (13:34; 15:12, 17). The focus is not on keeping laws but on loving as Jesus loved. Since Jesus does the Father's will, to love as Christ loved fulfills the purpose of the Law (5:19; 8:29).

1 John

As in John's Gospel, those who know God keep his commandments (1 John 2:3–4). First John's command is not a new one but "from the beginning" (2:7–11 ESV). What is "new" is the age that has arrived with Jesus Christ (2:8). The commands are linked to the "truth," understood in terms of Christ (1:6, 8). Keeping commandments is to do God's "word" (2:6, 7–8, 14), and the "word of life" (1:1–3) is Jesus Christ (2:22–23; 4:2–3; 5:6). God's command is to believe in Jesus and to love one another (2:7, 9, 11; 3:23). Love for others stems from loving God and obeying the commandments (4:7–21; 5:2–3). Such love of God is possible only for those born of God, who have been rescued from sin by Christ's atoning sacrifice (4:9–10).

James

James includes Jews outside the land of Israel among his addressees (1:1). A partial observance of the Law is insufficient. James criticizes especially favoritism at the expense of the poor (2:1–13; cf. Lev. 19:15, 18). One must keep and practice the entire Law, or else one is a Law-breaker (James 2:10). To defame others is to defame the law (4:11). James does not mention circumcision, Sabbath, food laws, or the law's cultic components (cf. Hebrews) even though he is writing to Jews. He highlights, rather, the Decalogue (2:8–11).

James's "Law of liberty" and "royal Law" frees people so that they can observe God's will (1:25; 2:8, 12 [citing Lev. 19:18]). These verses parallel similar claims in Paul (Rom. 8:3–4: the Law in the hands of the Spirit of life has set believers free from the Law in the hands of sin and death; Gal. 6:2: the Law in the hands of Christ is fulfilled by Christian love; also Rom. 7:10, 12). James 1:25 and 2:12 are in contexts of doing God's will and are never severed from the context of the "word of truth," which powerfully creates believers and new life (1:18–25; 2:8–13). The "implanted" word (1:21 ESV) recalls the promises of the new covenant in Jer. 31:33–34. Thus, when James refers to doing the word (1:22–23), fulfilling the "royal law" (2:8), or the "law of liberty" (1:25; 2:12), in context this is the obedience created by the word of the gospel. With the divinely created obedience of the Lawgiver's royal Law of liberty (4:12), the cultic elements, circumcision, the food laws, and the Sabbath are no longer in effect and thus go unmentioned.

Hebrews

The Mosaic covenant, established in the wilderness, is now surpassed by a heavenly covenant (Heb. 12:18–29). The old covenant was a partial and preliminary revelation (1:1–3), and Moses is contrasted with Christ (3:1–6). The new covenant fulfills the old but also renders Sinai obsolete (8:7–13). To return to the old is to abandon Christ's sacrificial work on the cross (cf. 6:4–8; 10:26–31; 12:25–29). The author of Hebrews does not want the readers to revert to Levitical sacrifice or to the Aaronic priesthood, which pointed forward as shadows to the substance in Christ. The old institutions do not forgive sins. That takes place only through the once-for-all sacrifice of Christ and in the new covenant (8:7, 13; 9:1, 11–14, 18, 23–28; 10:1–18).

The Mosaic Law pointed forward, and its tabernacle anticipated a true tabernacle in heaven (10:1; cf. 8:1–6; 9:1–10). The Law was mediated by angels, but the message of salvation came through Jesus Christ. Angels validated Moses's Law, but Jesus's message was confirmed by his first hearers and by signs and wonders from God. The Mosaic Law included penalties for disobedience, and so does the new covenant (2:2–4). Apostasy incurred God's wrath in the old covenant, and the same is true in the new covenant, with God's redemptive work in Christ (10:26–31). Moses and Jesus both served or serve priestly roles, but Jesus is greater than Moses as the builder is greater than the house itself and as the son is over a servant (2:17; 3:1–6). Both were or are faithful, but Moses testified to Jesus. The new covenant's priesthood and sacrifices surpass the old covenant's, with Jesus as the high priest at a better sanctuary (4:14–5:10; 7:1–10:18). The change in priesthood also reflects the change of law (7:11–12). The "weak" Law did not bring any sort of perfection or atonement for sin (7:18–19; cf. 10:1, 4), had its faults (8:7), and has been changed (7:12; cf. 8:13; 10:8–9). The entire old covenant has been superseded by the new covenant and a superior cult with an entirely different law (7:12; 13:9–16).

Similarly, the promises of land and rest point to the heavenly city and Sabbath rest (3:7–4:13; 11:9–10, 13–16; 12:22; 13:14). Whereas the wilderness generation failed to enter God's rest, the present generation is urged to be faithful and to enjoy God's Sabbath rest. Both generations were preached the gospel message to enter the heavenly rest, and both faced the danger of failing to heed this offer (3:12–13; 4:1, 2, 6, 11).

Hebrews regularly contrasts the requirements and punishments of the Sinai covenant with what is required for those belonging to Christ (2:1–4; 9:6–10, 15–24; 10:26–31; 12:25–29; 13:9–12). The law is now written on hearts (8:7–13; Jer. 31:31–34). What these commands are is not always clear, but the author exhorts his readers while acknowledging the cleansing of sins through Christ's death (Heb. 13). The author reduces the Mosaic Law largely to its cultic elements and does not cite it as an ethical norm. The readers are, rather, to show compassion on fellow believers, including those in prison (10:34; 13:3); they should show hospitality to strangers, as did Abraham and Lot (13:2); they are not to love money but should trust God for their needs (13:5–6); they are to avoid sexual sin (13:4)—all consistent with OT morality. Financial sacrifices for those in need replace animal sacrifices (13:15–16). Hebrews therefore admonishes a new covenant ethic.

Conclusion

Each NT author offers a distinctive approach to the law, and yet there is significant overlap. The NT authors are unanimous in seeing the OT law as pointing forward as a witness to what has taken place in Jesus's saving work. As for the law's regulations and requirements, the Christ believer "fulfills" that law and obeys it as directed through the lens of Christ and his Spirit.

See also Circumcision; Covenant; Feasts and Festivals; Jesus's Use of the OT; Jews and Gentiles; Justice; Love; Sacrifices and Offerings; Sinai; Temple; Wilderness

Bibliography. Allison, D. C., Jr., "Jesus and the Covenant," *JSNT* 29 (1987): 57–78; Bahnsen, G. L., et al., *Five Views on Law and Gospel* (Zondervan, 1993); Das, A. A., *Paul and the Jews*, LPS (Hendrickson, 2003); Das, "Paul and the Law," in *Paul Unbound*, ed. M. D. Given (Hendrickson, 2009), 99–116; Dunn, J. D. G., *The New Perspective on Paul*, WUNT 185 (Mohr Siebeck, 2005); Loader, W. R. G., *Jesus' Attitude towards the Law*, WUNT 2/97 (Mohr Siebeck, 1997); McKnight, S., *The Letter of James*, NICNT (Eerdmans, 2011); Patrick, D., "Law in the OT," in *NIDB*, 3:602–14; Patrick, *Old Testament Law* (John Knox, 1985); Räisänen, H., "The Law as a Theme of 'New Testament Theology,'" in *Jesus, Paul, and Torah*, JSNTSup 43 (Sheffield Academic, 1992), 252–77; Räisänen, *Paul and the Law* (Fortress, 1983); Sanders, E. P., *Paul and Palestinian Judaism* (Fortress, 1977); Schreiner, T. R., *40 Questions about Christians and Biblical Law* (Kregel, 2010); Thielman, F., *The Law and the New Testament*, CompNT (Crossroad, 1999).

A. ANDREW DAS

Letter Couriers

This essay addresses the question of the nature of letter couriers in the ancient world, and in particular in the Greco-Roman world in which the NT was written. It is easy to overlook the mechanics of letter conveyance and the role of the letter courier since little to nothing is made of these elements within the NT and the letters that were sent were ostensibly delivered to their intended destinations. However, the delivery of a letter was a more complex situation than one might at first imagine, and the role of the letter courier is itself far more complex than might at first appear. In this essay, I will address two major issues regarding letter couriers. First, I address the history of letter delivery in the ancient world in order to establish what the possibilities were for letter conveyance. Second, I address the role of the letter courier and what may have been expected of such a person within the letter conveyance system. Letter couriers play an important role not just in the physical dissemination of letters but also in their reception and interpretation.

A Brief History of Letter Delivery in the Ancient World

The postal system of the ancient world of the Mediterranean can be divided into two types: the official postal service and the private postal service. Since possibly the Assyrians and certainly the Persians, we have known of sophisticated official postal services in the ancient world. There was, however, no developed private postal service, certainly not during the Roman era. I will discuss the official postal service within the ancient world first, followed by the means of sending mail for those in the private sector. (In what follows, I summarize the descriptions regarding the ancient postal services given by Epp, 393–407; Harmon; Klauck, 60–65; Llewelyn, "Conveyance," 2–22; "Sending," 339–49; White, 214–15.)

The earliest postal system for which we have significant documentation was apparently developed by the Persians in the sixth century BC. This system, established by Cyrus, is referred to in several ancient sources. The structure of the system is recounted in a passage from the ancient Greek historian Herodotus (*Hist.* 8.98.1–2; cf. 3.126), who recounts the relay system that the Persians developed, with one rider per day of the journey transporting the mail by horse. Xenophon, the later Greek historian, mentions how quick the system is in delivering the post, based upon the relay system (*Cyr.* 8.6.17–18). This postal system, probably headed by a government official (see Plutarch, *Alex.* 18), was used for official purposes, including government and military communication, but was also apparently used by the king and other officials within the government for personal matters. A road system was also developed alongside the postal system to facilitate empire-wide communication and transportation. The cost of maintaining the 1,700 miles of the system was paid by those within whose territory the roads ran. We get an idea of how effective the system was from the book of Esther. On two occasions—once when Haman executes his order to kill the Jews (3:12–13) and once when Mordecai, through King Ahasuerus, countermands that order (8:10)—the Persian system of letter delivery is mentioned in the Bible and noted for its speed and effectiveness. Josephus also refers to those who sent out the announcement of Ahasuerus's wedding (*Ant.* 11.203).

Since the Greek empire consisted of individual city-states, even if in leagues, no similar postal system developed in Greece. It was Alexander the Great's capture of Persia that inspired the Greeks to develop their own postal system for the Hellenistic Empire. Alexander's successors, the Diadochi, reorganized the Persian postal system for their own areas of influence, and thus Antigonus I developed such a system in Asia Minor and Greece, and the Seleucids and Ptolemies did similarly in Syria and Egypt, respectively. The Egyptian system, as one might expect, focused upon the course of the Nile for north-south delivery of letters (by horse) and packages (by boat) but also developed a series of east-west delivery systems for letters (by foot) and packages (by camel).

Rome improved upon these early postal systems. Its postal system, called the *cursus publicus*, was inaugurated by Julius Caesar but fully instigated by Augustus as one means of uniting his growing empire. Augustus's system apparently began with carriers transporting mail by foot around Italy and other western areas, but he then expanded the system and adapted it to the eastern Greek/Persian system. Suetonius, the Roman historian, mentions the postal system in his account of Augustus's life (*Aug.* 49.3). Rome initially used the relay system but then introduced the use of carts of various sorts to carry the mail. It eventually abandoned the relay system for one in which the same rider proceeded along the entire distance, changing animals at designated places. The system was not as fast as the Persian system with its relayed riders but probably improved reliability (since one rider went from start to finish), and riders could, some think, cover up to fifty miles in a day. The carriers were issued special papers (a diploma) that designated their privileges.

This Roman postal system was designed to serve the Roman Empire, and so it was designed for governmental correspondence, including both administrative and military matters. Sometimes the military used the road system for its own purposes and movements. This does not mean that private citizens did not sometimes use the official postal system, by perhaps having a carrier transport a letter or package for them, or that officials did not use the system for some of their personal business. Almost assuredly they did. However, it would have been more usual for those who could afford it to hire special governmental couriers, called *tabellarii*, or have their own servants make the journey (on *tabellarii*, see Llewelyn, "Sending," 342–48, although it is not entirely certain who the *tabellarii* were or how they functioned in relation to the official Roman postal system). But this was reserved for those with financial means. There were also select soldiers who sometimes delivered the mail, especially for the emperor. Other functions also developed along with the system. These included the *frumentarii*, who were postal carriers responsible for the delivery of especially important mail, and they took on the characteristics of a kind of secret police.

For most people, however, there was effectively no official postal service, and hence no simple and relatively reliable means of delivering letters or other documents or goods. There are three major ways that the post was delivered for those who did not hold official positions. As mentioned above, the wealthy could afford to send one of their own servants or to use a special courier to send their mail. Second, a group of people could hire one of the special governmental couriers to carry mail for the entire group. There apparently were some local tax officers who banded together to hire private couriers who could also be used by others. This was still costly. The third option—and one that was used by the vast majority of people—was to entrust one's letter or letters to someone who happened to be traveling in the direction that one wished the letter to go. In an ideal situation, this person might have been a friend, so as to help guarantee the reliability of the delivery. In other instances, this person might have been a businessman traveling with a camel caravan and other businessmen, or even a complete stranger who was passing through on the way toward the desired destination of the letter.

As a result, postal delivery for nongovernmental letters and packages was unreliable. Many circumstances could thwart the successful delivery of a letter or a package. The addressee might not be found, or the address might be insufficient. Or the letter carrier might not arrive. Or the person might lose the letter, delay its delivery, access confidential information, or even steal a package. We have papyri that record what is being sent in packages so that the recipient can check the package against the list to ensure that everything has arrived, going so far as to ask the recipient to write back in confirmation.

The Roles and Responsibilities of Letter Couriers

In light of the discussion above, we will concentrate upon the possible roles and responsibilities of letter couriers for nongovernmental letters. Some have, on occasion, raised the question of whether Paul utilized the official postal service as a means of his correspondence with some of his churches, and in particular to deliver some of the letters that he sent to them. This question is sometimes raised in relation to the Letter to the Philippians. Near the end of the letter, Paul sends greetings and says that among those who send greetings are "those who belong to Caesar's household" (Phil. 4:22). This has prompted the question, first, of the origin of Paul's letter and, second, whether those members of Caesar's household had anything to do with the postal system and carrying this letter to the Philippians. There has been much discussion of the origin of Paul's imprisonment letters, and Philippians in particular, with most scholars believing that Rome is the most likely option (Porter, 62–68). However, several of the other options, such as Caesarea, Ephesus, and even Corinth, were imperial cities in the sense that they had a strong Roman influence and even presence, and so it is difficult to know from origin—as uncertain as it may or may not be—what that means in relationship to the Roman government. The second issue concerns Caesar's household and whether any of those in the household would have been among the special couriers of the postal system, *tabellarii*. The first difficulty in making this assessment is that it is difficult to establish exactly who the *tabellarii* were and how they functioned. Stephen Llewelyn raises several questions regarding whether those referred to in Philippians as being in Caesar's household could be *tabellarii*. The first difficulty is that *tabellarii* may not have been able to use the Roman governmental postal system. We simply do not know enough about the *tabellarii*, the diplomas they were given, and what these diplomas may or may not have allowed for them in relation to the Roman postal system. Second, there is no indication by Paul in Philippians that the members of Caesar's household were *tabellarii*, since the members of the household comprised a wide range of positions from lower-level to relatively high administrative positions. A third difficulty is that there is no indication in the letter that its couriers may have been Christians since the number of Christians and their likelihood as letter couriers would have been small. A fourth and final difficulty is that there is no need for the hypothesis. The hypothesis seems to have been formulated because of a need for a clear means of communication between Paul and the Philippians. However, the route to be traveled—probably to and from Rome (although this location is not required)—was well and frequently traversed (Llewelyn, "Sending," 342–48).

So, without the public postal system available, we must examine the role of the letter courier in relation to the possible private means available. Before we are able to do that, we should probably establish the major reasons for sending a letter in the ancient world. Letters had three primary purposes: to establish and maintain relationships (as a substitute for the author's personal presence), to form a dialogical interchange in which one side conveys something or responds to the other (probably information, but not necessarily only information), and to provide a permanent record of the interaction between the two parties (Porter, 140–41). Each one of these is important. Much has been made of Robert Funk's statement about the importance of the letter as conveying Paul's apostolic presence, and thereby apostolic authority. It is questionable whether the letter itself conveys the apostolic authority, as Paul seems to continue to have numerous problems with some of his churches, but there is definitely a sense in which the letter conveys the apostle's presence—though probably no more so than other letters in the ancient world. We have records of many personal letters from the ancient world where a personal presence is created by means of the written letter, whether a husband to a wife, or a child to a parent, or the like. Further, it is often thought that language is primarily used simply to convey information. The conveyance of information can often be important in a letter, but one must be careful how one defines information. The "information" of a letter may relate to things (donkeys, citrus plants, olives, etc.) as well as to thoughts and feelings (friendship, recommendation, etc.). Finally, many letters of the ancient world provided a permanent record of the interaction between parties. The reasons for this vary, from ensuring faithful delivery of the letter and/or goods to much more personal reasons regarding the status of the relationships involved.

As a result, we can outline a number of different functions of the letter courier.

Deliver the letter. The first, and most obvious, responsibility of the letter courier was to ensure that the letter was delivered to its proper destination. This was not necessarily an easy task, as travel could involve not only the road system but also travel by sea, along with all the potential dangers of such travel (Richards, 189–200). As we saw above, ensuring the delivery of a letter was perhaps a more difficult task than one might first realize. It is worth asking how it was that the NT letters were constructed so that they would arrive at their proper destination. If they were sent by personal friends who knew the recipients (either a church or individual), then it may have been very straightforward: a simple address on the back of the letter. However, as Llewelyn points out, letters were addressed many ways due to varying needs for clarity. A letter to a small village might be relatively easy to address, but a letter to a major city, such as Rome (or a place that had several church groups), may have required much more, especially if the letter courier did not know the recipients very well or at all. Some of the ways of addressing letters include an attached label specifying the directions, a separate sheet of papyrus with directions, the verso of the letter containing the directions along with the address, and indications of ways to find the destination other than directions. Sometimes directions were also given for the sending of a return letter (Llewelyn, "Conveyance," 29–43). We can imagine that any number of these may have been used by NT authors, even if they were entrusting their letters to friends, since some of the addressees found in the letters themselves are not altogether clear as to their specific point of destination.

Before we discuss specific letter couriers and then their further responsibilities, we should discuss the question of the difference between letter carriers and emissaries or envoys. We know that Paul used a number of emissaries or envoys—that is, people who represented him and worked on his behalf in relationship with the churches for which he felt responsibility. There are a number of emissaries mentioned in the Pauline Letters (Llewelyn, "Conveyance," 55): Artemas (Titus 3:12), Crescens (2 Tim. 4:10), Epaphras (Col. 1:7–8), Erastus (2 Tim. 4:20; cf. Acts 19:22), Silas (2 Cor. 1:19; cf. Acts 17:14), Timothy (1 Cor. 4:17; 2 Cor. 1:19; Phil. 2:19–23; 1 Thess. 3:2–6; 1 Tim. 1:3–4; cf. Acts 17:14; 19:22), Titus (2 Cor. 7:6–7; 8:6–7, 16–24; 9:5; 12:17–18; 2 Tim. 4:10; Titus 1:5), and Tychicus (Eph. 6:21–22; Col. 4:7–9; 2 Tim. 4:12; Titus 3:12). These emissaries or envoys appear to be people within the scope of the Pauline mission who act on behalf of Paul, conveying information, receiving information, helping to spread the gospel, and doing other kinds of ministry functions on behalf of the apostle (on the importance of envoys, see Mitchell,

"Envoys"). Such emissaries were an important part of the Pauline missionary venture. However, these emissaries or envoys were not necessarily letter couriers. They may have simply gone with oral instructions from Paul or even just with the commission of performing a necessary task and then reporting back to him about the progress of the gospel.

Still, these two functions may have overlapped. We do not have complete information for the letters of the NT, but we believe that the following were letter couriers (not all letters give an indication of the courier) (see Llewelyn, "Conveyance," 51–54; expanded by Harmon, 136–45, on whom the following discussion is dependent; cf. Head, "Named," 279–82; Porter, passim on the various letters).

Phoebe. In Rom. 16:1–2, Paul states, "I commend to you our sister Phoebe, a deacon of the church in Cenchreae. I ask you to receive her in the Lord in a way worthy of his people and to give her any help she may need from you, for she has been the benefactor of many people, including me." This passage does not identify Phoebe as the letter carrier, but it does commend her to the recipients, a feature that many scholars consider indicative of being the letter carrier.

Timothy. First Corinthians 4:17 may indicate that Timothy carried 1 Corinthians to the Corinthians, although most scholars do not accept this in light of 1 Cor. 16:10, which seems more tenuous on Timothy's arrival (contra Harmon, 140–41, who follows Mitchell, *Paul*, 222–23, on interpreting 1 Cor. 16:10). Timothy would still be an emissary, instructed to remind the Corinthians of Paul's life in Christ and what he teaches elsewhere. In Phil. 2:19–24, Paul states that he is hoping to send Timothy to the Philippians soon. The passage does not say that he is intending to send a letter by Timothy, but the commendation of him is followed by the commendation of Epaphroditus, who is also being sent.

Titus. Titus is thought to have possibly been the one who delivered either 1 Corinthians (2 Cor. 12:18) or Paul's "tearful letter" (2 Cor. 7:12–14) or even 2 Corinthians (2 Cor. 8:16–24). Titus was clearly relieved at the response of the Corinthians if he delivered the tearful letter. If he is the one carrying 2 Corinthians, he is said to be coming with enthusiasm as a partner and coworker of Paul.

Epaphroditus. In Phil. 2:25–30, Paul states that he finds it necessary to send Epaphroditus to the Philippians. The interesting fact is that Epaphroditus appears to have been sent first from the Philippians to Paul and acted as their messenger, but now he is acting as Paul's.

Tychicus. Colossians 4:7–9 speaks of Tychicus bringing information to inform the Colossians about Paul and encourage them. He is said to be accompanied by Onesimus. Many think that Tychicus was the carrier of the letter.

Onesimus. It has recently been (re)argued that Onesimus is the carrier of the Letter to Philemon, rather than Tychicus, Timothy, or an otherwise unspecified carrier (Head, "Onesimus," notes that the traditional view is Onesimus, held by many from Jerome and Chrysostom to the present).

These examples do not constitute a large body of strong evidence regarding Pauline letter carriers, and offer even less as to the role of the letter carrier, besides that of physically transmitting the letter to the intended recipients.

The task of the letter courier was not finished upon delivery of the letter. A range of functions has been suggested for the letter courier, even if we do not get clear indications from the NT letters what those functions may have been specifically in relation to the NT itself. Comments made in a number of documentary papyri indicate that the letter courier served an important role not just in ensuring the arrival of the letter but also in its presentation and even understanding. I will discuss five additional tasks and functions of the letter courier (see Richards, 182–85, 201–4; Harmon, 134–36; cf. Head, "Named").

Deliver goods. As we have already observed, the Roman postal system was designed for more than simply letters. It was designed for letters and packages. Similarly, those who were not able to avail themselves of the official Roman system needed to send both documents and goods (one might argue that a letter was just a small form of goods or package). Many of the documentary papyri that have survived from the ancient world are financial documents that record various financial transactions, such as the buying, selling, sending, and receiving of goods. Just as governments needed to communicate and move equipment, so did individuals. However, the risks of moving goods for individuals were much greater because they had to be entrusted to individuals. This accounts for the fact that those sending goods often looked for those they knew to send their goods—to help ensure their safe arrival. This also accounts for the accompanying letters in which those sending goods would specify what the courier was carrying, such as money or various items, sometimes even listed. This would serve to ensure that the goods—all of the goods—were delivered as they were supposed to be.

Read the letter. Scholars often comment that the reading of the letter by the courier was an expectation in the ancient world, and many discussions of the letter courier include the reading of letters as one of the courier's duties (e.g., Botha, 417–19, who treats the discussion as a matter of rhetoric; Richards, 202; Harmon, 135–36). This seems to make logical sense in the light of the relatively widespread illiteracy in the Greco-Roman world (Stanley, *Arguing*, 63). An opposition is often drawn within the Greco-Roman world between orality and literacy, to the point that some scholars emphasize one over the other. The debate over how to think about these two factors has been ongoing over the last century or more. In many ways, this is a false disjunction. There are varying types of literacy of which one may speak, including differences in being able to actively and passively use language, as well as being able to read and/or write. There is no denying that orality was important in the ancient world, and we cannot minimize the fact that probably the great majority of people in the ancient world were illiterate if by that we mean that they were unable to read and write. However, this fails to note that the Greco-Roman world was a literate culture. By that, I mean that even those who were functionally illiterate within the world of the first century lived within a world in which written documents played a major role, to the point that they could not survive without the use of and dependence upon such documents. We can see evidence of this in many different ways. Even if, as William Harris (266–67) has estimated, only about 15 percent of people in the ancient world were literate (although this figure has been challenged by, e.g., Humphrey; Bagnall), virtually all of them were dependent upon written documents for their existence and livelihood, especially in the Roman bureaucratic world. Even those who were illiterate were expected to communicate with others in permanent ways, issue or sign receipts, perhaps sign contracts, and file Roman census reports at appropriate times in which they acknowledged their possessions. Even if they could not write these documents themselves, or even read them without the help of someone else, they were required to hire someone to write these documents for them, and they had to live by the terms of their legal obligations.

In such a world, someone who could read a letter was valuable, and a letter courier who could read would arguably often have to do so especially in a context such as Paul writing to a congregation where many, if not most, of those present would not have been able to read for themselves. Harmon points out that Xenophon in his *Hellenica* (7.1.39) speaks about a gathering of Thebans to hear a letter from the king read by a Persian to them (135n25). But Peter Head claims that he "did not find any evidence that any particular letter-carrier was also expected to read the letter aloud to the recipient" ("Named," 297, cited by Harmon, 135n25). Head even thinks there is some evidence against it. Head does admit that perhaps the evidence is limited and perhaps is not something to be remarked upon in such letters, and he even suggests that other letters might reveal such a practice. Nevertheless, there is minimal to no evidence from documentary letters of the letter courier reading the letter to the recipients.

There are several considerations to note here. The first is suggested by Head himself—namely, that "perhaps . . . we should not think of the letter-carrier as the most obvious candidate to recite the letter" ("Named," 297). In other words, it may still be the case due to the nature of the literate culture of the time that the letter was read to the recipient(s) but not by the letter courier. A second consideration is that Paul seems to provide evidence that he expected his letters, or at least some of them, to be read aloud by someone to the audience. Paul states at the end of 1 Thessalonians, "I charge you before the Lord to have this letter read to all the brothers and sisters" (5:27). Again, in Col. 4:16, Paul states, "After this letter has been read to you, see that it is also read in the church of the Laodiceans and that you in turn read the letter from Laodicea."

I will make several observations about these comments in the Pauline Letters. The first is that the admonition for reading aloud is placed at the end of the letter in both instances. This would appear to require that the letter courier either already know the contents of the letter—a possibility we will discuss further below—or that the reading is a subsequent act and not an initial one. In fact, the language seems to indicate that in both instances there is an admonition for subsequent readings to be made before the entire congregation. However, it would also appear that the initial reading is being made before the congregation, which would imply reading aloud, as Acts 15:30–32 seems to indicate (although not a Pauline letter). A third consideration is the passage from Xenophon cited above regarding an authority figure's letter being read before a group. A fourth consideration is, as Luther Stirewalt (19) has suggested, that Paul's Letters may not be forms of expanded personal letters but rather be based upon models of official letters and treated in that way. This may be in harmony with the pattern of the third consideration.

In sum, a letter courier may have been, in some circumstances, responsible for reading a letter aloud to the recipient. However, this is not a given since someone else may have read the letter if the recipient were illiterate. It appears that it would have been more likely that the letter courier read the letter, or at least gave the letter over to someone to read aloud if there were a group gathered to hear the letter. This certainly seems to have been the procedure, and it was followed in subsequent readings as well.

Provide additional information. A letter courier might also have provided additional information not included within the letter. A number of scholars have determined that the letter courier provided additional information to the readers (see Doty, 37; Richards, 183–84, 201–2; Head, "Ancient"; "Named," 296; Harmon, 134–35). Head calls it "extending the communication initiated by the letter" ("Named," 296). By that, he seems to mean that the letter courier, because of an association with the letter writer, was able to provide further information and extend the knowledge of the readers. The nature of this extended information apparently varied considerably. Documentary papyri and other ancient documents indicate that sometimes the additional information extended what was found in the letter, while at other times the information provided was not related to the material in the letter but was perhaps information that was more appropriate to be conveyed orally than in written form.

Randolph Richards provides two examples of such extended information in the NT (201–2). The first illustrates how others may have conveyed information by means of the letter courier in addition to the letter. In 1 Cor. 1:11, Paul says, "Some from Chloe's household have informed me that there are quarrels among you," which may well indicate that additional information was given to Paul about the Corinthian situation by the member of Chloe's household that brought the letter from Corinth. Paul then deals with those matters in 1 Cor. 1–6, before he states in 7:1, "Now for the matters you wrote about," thus indicating that he has concluded responding to the additional information and is now addressing the content of the letter. In Eph. 6:21–22, Paul says to the Ephesians, "Tychicus, the dear brother and faithful servant in the Lord [and probably the letter courier], will tell you everything, so that you also may know how I am and what I am doing." Richards wonders whether the matter concerns Paul's imprisonment (see 6:20). In any case, Paul continues: "I am sending him to you for this very purpose, that you may know how we are, and that you may encourage him" (6:22). That is, Paul states that one of the purposes of Tychicus being sent to the Ephesians with the letter is to convey additional information about Paul's situation, information that Tychicus as an associate of Paul knows and is authorized to convey. We might add a third example from outside of the Pauline Letters. In Acts 15:30–32, Judas and Silas, two of the letter couriers of the letter from Jerusalem to Antioch (along with Paul and Barnabas), are said to encourage and strengthen the church after they read the letter.

Serve as an envoy or emissary. We have already distinguished between an envoy and a letter courier. There were apparently many Pauline emissaries or envoys who were not letter couriers. Some of them have been noted above. There may have been some letter couriers who were not envoys or emissaries, but that appears to be much less likely. Named letter couriers in particular seem to have this function (Head, "Ancient," 219). The nature of the letter carriers' task, at least for those who carried Paul's letters, appears to have been, as noted above, to establish and/or maintain a relationship between Paul and his audience (a basic epistolary function), to serve as Paul's representative in his absence (one of the related basic letter functions), to represent Paul's teachings and directives to the recipients, including both the letter and any additional information (as noted above), to gather the information that Paul should know and convey this information back to Paul, to continue to build up various churches when Paul had to move on to other locations (Llewelyn, "Conveyance," 55), and any number of other functions of such a representative. The role of the Pauline envoy has been more widely recognized in more recent research (Mitchell, "Envoys"; cf. Harmon, 141–45), especially as scholars have come to appreciate more fully that the Pauline mission involved more than just the individual Paul but a group of traveling companions who ministered throughout the eastern Mediterranean. Paul may have been at the center of this group, but he relied upon a host of others to be engaged in important communication with his churches and even individuals.

Interpret Paul's letters, including the use of the OT. A number of scholars have recently emphasized that one of the possible functions of the Pauline letter courier was to interpret Paul's letters, including and perhaps especially his uses of the OT. This possible function of the letter courier goes further than the idea simply of adding information, as it requires a level of understanding of Paul that is perhaps more in line with the role of the envoy or emissary who speaks not just the words of Paul but with the voice and authority of Paul. In discussing the reception of Paul's Letter to the Romans and the audience's familiarity with the OT, Ross Wagner (38) states that "it is quite likely that the bearers of Paul's letters were charged by the apostle with the further responsibility of helping to interpret them." Greg Beale (10) goes further by focusing in particular upon apprehending the meaning of OT references for an early Christian audience that, for the most part, were recently converted gentiles who were not conversant with the Scriptures of Israel. There has been a challenge to this position that argues that, while Paul's audience may have been relatively ignorant of the Scriptures of Israel, Paul provided all that was necessary within the literary context and used his authority to establish the meaning in that particular context (e.g., Stanley, *Arguing*, 36–61; "Pearls"; see Abasciano for a response to Stanley). Such a position would tend to minimize the function of the letter courier—or any other interpreter—for understanding Paul's letters and the use of the OT. There is admittedly something to be said for the integrity of an epistolary argument; however, texts in general are not nearly so clear as some seem to think that they are, and Paul's are no different, so that, even if Paul may not have directly advocated it, it is entirely likely that questions of interpretation of his letters arose—in fact, we know that they did (see 2 Pet. 3:16)—that led to his letter couriers or other emissaries engaging in early Pauline interpretation.

Final Thoughts regarding Letter Couriers

Despite the abundance of documentary papyri, as well as the NT letters, we know surprisingly little about the roles that the letter courier played in the process, besides the obvious one of delivering the letter to the intended audience—and they didn't always successfully do that. The most that we can do is to use analogies from other literature, from history, and from the documentary papyri, as well as the NT, to provide a rough grid of the kinds of roles and functions that letter couriers may have played. We may acknowledge that their primary task was to ensure that the letter was delivered, a task that was not necessarily that easy, even with communication in the Greco-Roman world as advanced as it was. As far as other possible functions of the letter courier—such as delivering goods, reading letters aloud, providing additional information, serving as envoys, and interpreting Paul and his use of the OT—we have some good basis for thinking that at least some of these tasks were performed at least some of the time. We cannot eliminate any of them from consideration, but we may rightly question whether they were always expected to play a role in the delivery of a letter. Letter couriers for documentary letters certainly held additional responsibilities, whether ensuring that goods arrived or providing some additional information, but the case is more complex for the NT letters. We have tantalizing information about the role that Paul's letter couriers and envoys may have played in the letter delivery system, but we must be careful not to overextend and overgeneralize. The evidence that we have examined above seems to indicate that the function of the letter courier may have varied according to each individual letter and situation.

Conclusion

The Roman postal system, based upon Persian and Hellenistic precedents, was one of the several marvels of the Roman bureaucracy and provided a means for reliable communication throughout the Roman Empire. However, this system would not have been available to most people, as they were not part of the Roman governmental hierarchy. The vast majority of people were required to find other means to communicate by written correspondence, including relying upon a variety of much more casual and ad hoc means. This does not mean that these informal systems were not used—they were in fact widely relied upon and proved reasonably reliable, all things considered—but that the role of the letter courier took on a special character. I have attempted to discuss and outline some of the major functions of the letter courier in the Greco-Roman world, especially as that courier functioned in relation to the NT letters. The evidence that we have is suggestive that the letter courier played, at least on occasion and in part, a vital role beyond that of simply delivering the letter to its intended recipient. However, we must remain skeptical about the full extent of that role.

See also Literacy in the Greco-Roman World; *Septuagint articles*

Bibliography. Abasciano, B. J., "Diamonds in the Rough," *NovT* 49 (2007): 153–83; Bagnall, R. S., *Everyday Writing in the Graeco-Roman East* (University of California Press, 2011); Beale, G. K., *Handbook on the New Testament Use of the Old Testament* (Baker Academic, 2012); Botha, P. J. J., "The Verbal Art of the Pauline Letters," in *Rhetoric and the New Testament*, ed. S. E. Porter and T. H. Olbricht (Sheffield Academic, 1993), 409–28; Doty, W. G., *Letters in Primitive Christianity* (Fortress, 1973); Epp, E. J., "New Testament Papyrus Manuscripts and Letter Carrying in Greco-Roman Times" (1991), repr. in *Perspectives on New Testament Textual Criticism*, NovTSup 116 (Brill, 2005), 383–409; Funk, R. W., "The Apostolic Parousia," in *Christian History and Interpretation*, ed. W. R. Farmer, C. F. D. Moule, and R. R. Niebuhr (Cambridge University Press, 1967), 249–68; Harmon, M. S., "Letter Carriers and Paul's Use of Scripture," *JSPL* 4 (2014): 129–48; Harris, W. V., *Ancient Literacy* (Harvard University Press, 1989); Head, Peter M., "Letter Carriers in the Ancient Jewish Epistolary Material," in *Jewish and Christian Scripture as Artifact and Canon*, ed. C. A. Evans and H. D. Zacharias (T&T Clark, 2009), 203–19; Head, "Named Letter-Carriers among the Oxyrhynchus Papyri," *JSNT* 31 (2009): 279–99; Head, "Onesimus the Letter Carrier and the Initial Reception of Paul's Letter to Philemon," *JTS* 71 (2020): 628–56; Humphrey, J. H., ed., *Literacy in the Roman World* (Journal of Roman Archaeology, 1991); Klauck, Hans-Josef, *Ancient Letters and the New Testament* (Baylor University Press, 2006); Llewelyn, S. R., "The Conveyance of Letters," in *New Documents Illustrating Early Christianity*, vol. 7, ed. S. R. Llewelyn (Eerdmans, 1994), 1–57; Llewelyn, "Sending Letters in the Ancient World," *TynBul* 46 (1995): 337–56; Mitchell, M. M., "New Testament Envoys in the Context of Greco-Roman Diplomatic and Epistolary Conventions," *JBL* 111 (1992): 641–62; Mitchell, *Paul and the Rhetoric of Reconciliation* (1992; repr., Westminster John Knox, 1993); Porter, S. E., *The Apostle Paul* (Eerdmans, 2016); Richards, E. R., *Paul and First-Century Letter Writing* (InterVarsity, 2004); Stanley, C. D., *Arguing with Scripture* (T&T Clark, 2004); Stanley, "'Pearls before Swine,'" *NovT* 41 (1999): 124–44; Stirewalt, M. L., *Paul the Letter Writer* (Eerdmans, 2003); Wagner, J. R., *Heralds of the Good News* (Brill, 2002); White, J. L., *Light from Ancient Letters* (Fortress, 1986).

STANLEY E. PORTER

Leviticus, Book of

The title "Leviticus" comes from the Latin Vulgate, which has adapted it from the LXX. The Greek word is *leuitikon*, an adjective meaning "Levitical" or "that which pertains to the Levites." This is perhaps not the best heading for the book, first of all because the name "Levite" appears in the document only four times, and these in the span of two verses (25:32–33). The book actually has more to do with directions for the entire congregation of Israel and for the priests rather than the entire tribe of Levi. An old adage is appropriate here: "All priests are Levites, but not all Levites are priests." Later Jewish scribes (Tannaitic period, ca. 200

BC–AD 200) were more accurate when they called the book the *torat kohanim*—that is, "the book of the priests" or "the manual of the priests."

The title of the book in the Hebrew Bible is *wayyiqrāʾ*, which is the opening word of the text, meaning "and he called." This is a common Hebrew practice; so, for instance, the book of Exodus is titled *wəʾēlleh šəmôt*, which are the opening two words of the Hebrew text, meaning "and these are the names of."

Structure and Genre

In the Hebrew canon, Leviticus is the middle book of the Pentateuch, and thus some consider it "the heart of the Pentateuch's narrative" (Morales, 27). This is perhaps an overstatement, since Leviticus builds on the central theme of the Pentateuch presented at the end of Exodus. Exodus has closed with a description of the construction of the tabernacle and God descending in theophanic form into the holy of holies (40:34–38). There, God will meet with his people through a sacrificial system under the oversight and mediation of a priesthood. The tabernacle is at the heart of Hebrew worship and ritual. What are now needed are rules to regulate the practices of worship in Israel at the tabernacle (and later at the temple). That is a major purpose of Leviticus and one of the main reasons it was placed in the canon immediately after Exodus.

Leviticus is similar to a modern book of church order: it contains a series of manuals or directories that specify how the OT church is to operate and worship. There are six self-contained manuals in the book (Currid, *Leviticus*, 18–19):

- Directory 1: Manual of sacrifice for the entire congregation (1:1–6:7)
- Directory 2: Manual of sacrifice for the priesthood (6:8–7:38)
- Directory 3: Cleanliness Code (11:1–15:33)
- Directory 4: Manual of the Day of Atonement for the high priest (16:1–34)
- Directory 5: Holiness Code (17:1–26:46)
- Directory 6: Manual for the funding of the sanctuary (27:1–34)

These six directories are legislative. In fact, only two passages in the entire book are not regulatory, and those are the incidents of chaps. 8–10 and 24:10–23. The first narrative deals with the ordination of the priesthood, the beginning of formal worship in the tabernacle, and the profanation of worship led by Nadab and Abihu. The second narrative recounts the stoning of the blasphemer. Both of these accounts, however, are related to the surrounding legislative prescriptions. Both serve as examples or illustrations of the legal points being made in their contexts by the biblical writer.

Composition

No book in the OT claims divine origination as frequently as Leviticus. Thirty-eight times in twenty-seven chapters the text says, "The LORD said to Moses . . ." (Rooker, 39). The opening words of the book state, "The LORD called to Moses and spoke to him from the tent of meeting" (1:1). And the document ends with the statement, "These are the commands the LORD gave Moses" (27:34). These two verses serve as an *inclusio*, thus underscoring one of the author's principal teachings: the means and methods of Israel's worship and set-apartness are revealed from God to his people. That truth is further emphasized by the fact that each of the six directories of formal worship begins with "The LORD said to Moses . . ." (6:8; 11:1; 16:2; 17:1; 27:1; cf. 1:1).

The rest of the OT confirms the view that the book came from the Lord and was delivered by the hand of Moses (e.g., 2 Chron. 23:18; 30:16; 35:12). The NT additionally bears witness to the revelation of Leviticus from God to Moses (see Matt. 8:2–4; Luke 2:22; Rom. 10:5). The fact of the matter for the biblical authors was that "Leviticus is a narrative about God speaking to Moses repeatedly" (Vasholz, 11).

Traditional Judaism held to the belief that God revealed the torah, including Leviticus, to Moses at Mount Sinai and then Moses recorded the words of God (e.g., Rabbi Akiva [AD 50–135] in Zevah. 115b; Levine, xxvi). The early church agreed. For example, in the first century AD, Clement of Rome wrote, "The blessed Moses . . . noted down in the sacred books all the instructions which were given him" (1 Clem. 43:1, quoted in Wells, 191). And the second-century AD church father Justin Martyr comments, "The History of Moses is by far more ancient than all profane histories . . . which he wrote in the Hebrew character by the Divine inspiration" (*Hort.* 12; Wells, 186–91). This has been the dominant position of the church through the centuries.

Modern source criticism disagrees with the traditional views of the formation and composition of Leviticus. It argues forcefully that the book was compiled from a variety of different sources over a long period of time. The book, therefore, had a complex development. Early source critics believed that Leviticus belonged to the priestly stratum called P and that priests produced it during the postexilic period (ca. fifth century BC). Later critics determined that P itself was comprised of multiple sources, such as a self-contained document called H (= Holiness Code) found in Lev. 17–26. Many argue that P edited H. Another position says that, in fact, H edited P (Milgrom, 27). Such are the diverse speculations that dominate the study of source criticism.

Leviticus in the Rest of the OT

The teachings of Leviticus are commonly found and cited in the remainder of the OT. Regarding previous historical material in Genesis and Exodus, Leviticus codifies laws already in practice. Michael Fishbane (95) is right when he says, "The received legal codes are thus a literary expression of ancient Israelite legal wisdom." In other words, many of the regulations of Leviticus have a long history prior to their codification and standardization at Sinai. For example, the first three offerings enumerated in the Levitical manual of sacrifice (1:1–3:17) were already practiced by God's people: the burnt offering (Gen. 8:20; 22:3), the grain offering (Gen. 4:3), and the peace offering (Exod. 20:24; 24:5). A priesthood also existed prior to its codification in Leviticus. Adam, the first human, served as a priest in the temple of the garden of Eden (Beale, 9–24). Melchizedek was a "priest of God Most High" (Gen. 14:18). According to Exod. 19:6, God proclaimed that his people would be "a kingdom of priests."

In addition to codification, Leviticus contains echoes of earlier material from Genesis and Exodus. For instance, the tabernacle, in which the priests serve as regulated by the laws of Leviticus, is an echo of the original garden temple of Eden, where Adam served as priest. The tabernacle reflects the very presence of God with his people, as did the first temple in Eden (Lev. 9:6, 23).

Many of the laws of Leviticus are also a direct fulfillment of earlier commands, particularly from Exodus. For instance, in Exod. 29:44, God says that he will consecrate the tabernacle and the priesthood in the future. That promise is fulfilled in Lev. 8, in which Moses anoints both the tabernacle (v. 10) and the priesthood (v. 30) and thus consecrates them.

The later books of the OT allude to Leviticus in a myriad of ways. As an example, I will briefly consider Ezekiel's use of the Holiness Code (Lev. 17–26). Scholars have long understood that Ezekiel responds to the crisis of the exile by preaching to the people of his day, using that passage extensively (see, in particular, Lyons, 12–26). First, Ezekiel sees that the Holiness Code is authoritative for the people of his day, and he appeals to it often (e.g., Ezek. 18:6–9). Second, he uses the Holiness Code to bring accusations of disobedience against the people (e.g., 22:7–12), including numerous sexual laws (e.g., 18:6; 22:10). Third, the prophet uses the conditional covenantal judgments of Lev. 26:14–39 and applies them as soon coming to pass against the people of his day (see esp. Ezek. 14:13–21). And finally, Ezekiel draws on the very images of the conditional covenantal blessings of Lev. 26:1–13 to point to a future eschaton. He pronounces that one day God's people will be free from harmful beasts (Ezek. 34:25) and that they will not be exploited by other nations (34:28). It will be a time of great abundance in rain and crop yield (34:26–27). In that day, God will cause his people to be fruitful and multiply (36:29–30). The Immanuel principle will be central to their existence (36:28).

Leviticus in the NT

Leviticus was at one time the first book of the Hebrew Bible read and studied in the synagogue (Wenham, vii). In the church, however, little attention is paid to it, for it seems to be full of rules and regulations that have nothing to do with or say to the church. Really, what application could there be to the modern church regarding food laws, rules for skin diseases, and precepts of house fungi? How could such archaic rules have any significance to the church? This is a complicated and hard issue, and we can only do some initial digging here. However, we can certainly provide a broad picture and a window into the issue by considering some of the major motifs of Leviticus and how they relate to the NT. We will consider three major themes of Leviticus and their relationship to the NT: the sacrificial system, the priesthood, and the concept of holiness.

The Hebrew sacrificial system. The sacrificial system laid down in Leviticus and followed throughout the OT has ceased for the people of God. The system is now fulfilled in the coming of Jesus Christ. Christ offered himself as the final sacrifice, once and for all, for the people of God (Heb. 10:8–14). They no longer need a physical, temporal sanctuary in which the animal sacrifices take place, because "the Lord God Almighty and the Lamb are its temple" (Rev. 21:22). The sacrifices themselves are unnecessary because of Christ's atoning sacrifice on the cross, his resurrection, and his ascension to the heavenly temple.

It would be a mistake, however, to assume that because the work of Christ abrogated the sacrificial system of Leviticus, it is not important for the church to study it. The reality is that the sacrificial laws of Leviticus serve as pointers and shadows of the work of Christ; they are forerunners of his final atoning work. By studying Leviticus, the church realizes the depth and pervasiveness of human sin and sees that there is a wide chasm between a holy God and an unholy people. The sacrificial laws underscore the absolute necessity of atonement in humanity's being made right with God. And while the sacrificial system demonstrates these things, it also reflects its own insufficiency to meet these needs. The author of Hebrews tells us that "it is impossible for the blood of bulls and goats to take away sins" (10:4). The Hebrew sacrificial system was not efficacious in and of itself, but it pointed to something greater to come, and that is the fulfillment of the sacrificial system in the person and work of Jesus Christ.

One may rightly ask, How, then, were OT believers made right with God if not by the sacrificial system delineated in Leviticus and elsewhere? In other words, how was peace attained between a righteous God and sinful humanity prior to the cross of Christ? How were sins forgiven and reconciliation procured? Throughout church history, many commentators have argued that people in the OT were saved by keeping torah. This is a great error. Paul argues vehemently against it, because "no one will be declared righteous in God's sight by the works of the law" (Rom. 3:20; cf. 3:23; Gal. 2:16). The reality is that no individual can keep torah (James 2:10).

Consequently, no human is saved and made right with God by keeping the law. Torah, in other words, is not the solution to humanity's sin and alienation from God. Its purposes are to show clearly humanity's sin (Rom. 3:20) and to be a "guardian" or tutor (Gal. 3:24) to lead humanity to the true solution to their condition.

The sacrifices in Leviticus served as types or pointers to the atoning work of Christ. Persons in the OT obtained forgiveness and acceptance from God only as they offered these sacrifices in true penitence and faith in the coming Redeemer. The sacrificial system was merely a shadow of what was to come—that is, the final, ultimate sacrifice of God's only Son, Jesus Christ. It is only through the sacrifice of Christ that anyone is saved and made right with God. In addition, one needs to be careful not to say that OT believers were saved by the promise of the coming Redeemer. No one is saved by a promise. People are saved only through the reality of the fulfillment of the promise in the coming and work of Jesus Christ.

Perhaps the most striking shadow of the Levitical sacrificial system that points to Christ is the Day of Atonement (Lev. 16). A strong case can be made that Paul refers to the Day of Atonement in his classic statement on atonement in Rom. 3:21–26 (Schreiner, 191–95; Moo, 231–37). At the heart of this passage is Paul's use of the word *hilastērion*, which can be translated as "mercy seat" and ought to be understood in reference to the lid of the ark of the covenant in the holy of holies in the tabernacle/temple (Exod. 25:17–22). An alternate reading of Rom. 3:24b–25a would be "the redemption that is in Christ Jesus, whom God displayed publicly as a mercy seat in his blood through faith." In other words, Christ was the final, ultimate sacrifice offered on the Day of Atonement.

The priesthood. The overseer and administrator of the sacrificial system in Israel is the Aaronic priesthood. Leviticus 8 describes the consecration and ordination of that priesthood at the command of Yahweh. Throughout the chapter, the formulaic phrase "as Yahweh commanded" appears seven times, and it provides structure and symmetry to the passage (Klingbeil, 509–19). Leviticus 9 then records the first sacrifices offered by Aaron in the tabernacle on his own behalf as high priest, on behalf of the priesthood, and on behalf of the people of Israel. It needs to be underscored that the Israelite priesthood presents offerings not only for the people but also for themselves, because they are also sinful and weak. The author of Hebrews understands this well when he says, "For the law appoints as high priests men in all their weakness" (7:28). In addition, the sacrifices offered by and through the priesthood are continuous—that is, day after day, week after week, month after month, and year after year, the priests monotonously and repeatedly offer the same sacrifices for all Israel. There appears to be no finality to it.

There is, however, impermanence to the Aaronic priesthood itself. As the writer to the Hebrews says, "Now there have been many of those priests, since death prevented them from continuing in office" (7:23). And as well, the Aaronic priesthood has ended; it ceased to exist after the destruction of the Second Temple in AD 70. There is finality in that reality.

Christ, however, has come as the final high priest, but not according to the priesthood of Aaron, which has ended. Psalm 110 is the most frequently cited messianic psalm in the NT. Yahweh says to the Messiah that he will be a great king with utmost authority and a royal priest "in the order of Melchizedek" (v. 4). Melchizedek is introduced in Gen. 14 as both a priest and a king. The combination of these two offices, while not unusual in the ancient Near East, was rare, if not nonexistent, in Israel. Its uniqueness in Israel becomes a sign for the coming Messiah, who will combine the two offices in his person (Ps. 110; Zech. 6:12–13).

The author of Hebrews deals in detail with the relationship between Melchizedek and the Messiah, and he argues that Jesus Christ is the fulfillment of Ps. 110; he even quotes Ps. 110:4 twice to underscore that relationship (5:6; 7:17). In Heb. 7, the author establishes that the priestly order of Melchizedek finds its climax and fulfillment in Jesus. The topic is complex and lengthy, so we will consider only the first three verses of chap. 7, which lay the groundwork for the teaching by drawing parallels between Jesus and Melchizedek (Currid, *Genesis*, 289).

1. Melchizedek is described as a priestly king, and Jesus is the same (v. 1).
2. Melchizedek's name means "king of righteousness," and his office is "king of peace/Salem"; righteousness and peace are two characteristics of the Messiah's reign (v. 2).
3. Melchizedek is not of the Aaronic line. Jesus, as well, descends not from that priestly line but from the tribe of Judah (vv. 3, 14).
4. Genesis does not record the birth or death of Melchizedek, and this is symbolic of the eternal priesthood of Jesus: "Resembling the Son of God, he remains a priest forever" (v. 3). Jesus, like Melchizedek, "has a permanent priesthood" because he continues forever (v. 24).

Melchizedek, the priestly king at the time of Abraham, is a type or foreshadowing of Jesus Christ. He is a historical figure who points ahead to the priestly kingship of Jesus. He is the shadow, while Christ is the reality.

According to the author of Hebrews, Jesus is not merely the fulfillment and climax of the OT priesthood but, further, the final, ultimate high priest. He is the eternal, sinless high priest who offers himself as the sacrificial victim. The writer of Hebrews proclaims this point poignantly when he says, "Such a high priest truly meets our need—one who is holy, blameless, pure, set apart from sinners, exalted above the heavens. Unlike the other high priests, he does not need to offer sacrifices day after day, first for his own sins, and then for the sins of the people. He sacrificed for their sins once for all when he offered himself" (7:26–27). Andrew Jukes (43) puts it well: "Christ is the offering, Christ is the priest, Christ is the offerer."

Holiness. Another dominant motif of Leviticus is holiness. In fact, an entire manual or directory is dedicated to it, often referred to as the Holiness Code (Lev. 17–26). The Hebrew term for "holiness" is the root *qdš*, and it is used frequently in this manual (e.g., 20:7–8; 21:8, 15, 23; 22:9, 16, 32). It commonly means "to be set apart, wholly other, unique, uncommon." Thomas McComiskey (786–89) rightly defines it like this: "A basic element of Israelite religion was the maintenance of an inviolable distinction between the spheres of the sacred and the common or profane." Israel was to be different than the world, especially as they related to the nations surrounding them.

The foundation of and paradigm for Israel's holiness is the holiness of God. In Lev. 19:2, God declares to the people through Moses, "Be holy because I, the LORD your God, am holy." God's essential nature is one of holiness (Isa. 6:3). His people are called to emulate him—that is, to think and act like him. Holiness is therefore *imitatio Dei* (imitation of God).

The Holiness Code makes clear that every area of life is subject to the concept of holiness. So, for example, Lev. 19 alone addresses family life (v. 3), the sacrificial system (vv. 5–8), economics (vv. 9–10), societal relationships (vv. 11–14, 17–18), judicial issues (vv. 15–16), and worship (v. 4). No area of life is isolated from the concept of holiness. All things are to be brought under the lordship of God and subject to his teachings and statutes. As one author remarks, "No area of life is exempt from the demand to be holy, for Israel is separated as a holy people to Yahweh" (Dumbrell, 44).

Holiness is not merely found in the Holiness Code; it pervades the entire book of Leviticus. For example, Lev. 11:1–23 describes the dietary restrictions, or kashrut laws, that God places upon Israel. The purpose of these laws has been a matter of debate for ages. Some believe they are primarily hygienic; others see them as polemical against foreign, pagan worship; and still others understand them to be merely arbitrary distinctions (see discussion in Currid, *Leviticus*, 140–43). The key to understanding the dietary laws is found later in the chapter, where God tells his people not to defile themselves with unclean animals: "I am the LORD your God; consecrate yourselves and be holy, because I am holy. Do not make yourselves unclean by any creature that moves along the ground" (11:44). The food distinctions are primarily symbolic of holiness—that is, "the division into clean foods and unclean foods corresponded to the division between holy Israel and the Gentile world" (Wenham, 170). Clean animals represent set-apart Israel, and unclean animals the common, pagan nations. Consequently, whenever the people of Israel eat, they are reminded of their position as the set-apart people of God. The purpose of the food laws is to "imbue the mind of Israel with moral distinctions" (Bonar, 210).

The issue of the application of the food laws to the early church was a major source of conflict (see Acts 15). They were no longer binding (see 10:10–16), because the covenant relationship was no longer centered in the physical nation of Israel but extended to all peoples, regardless of nationality. In other words, the kashrut was not to be kept by the church because these laws did not symbolize the holiness or set-apart nature of the people of God.

Even with the abrogation of laws such as the food restrictions, it would be a mistake to dismiss the concept of holiness as applying to the church. When speaking to the church throughout the world, Peter says, "As obedient children, do not conform to the evil desires you had when you lived in ignorance. But just as he who called you is holy, so be holy in all you do; for it is written: 'Be holy, because I am holy'" (1 Pet. 1:14–16). Peter here quotes Lev. 11:44 as yet applicable to the church. Holiness is *imitatio Dei*—that is, emulation of God. The people of God today are yet called to do that and bring every area of life under the lordship of Christ. As Paul says, "So whether you eat or drink or whatever you do, do it all for the glory of God" (1 Cor. 10:31), and, "Whatever you do, whether in word or deed, do it all in the name of the Lord Jesus" (Col. 3:17).

Sacrifices, priesthood, and holiness are only three examples of the rich connections between Leviticus and the NT. Other areas of study are equally fertile, such as the Hebrew calendar in Leviticus and its fulfillment in the NT (see my article "Feasts and Festivals" elsewhere in the dictionary).

Conclusion

For the Christian, the heart of Leviticus is the teaching of the great depth and seriousness of human sin. Humankind's unholiness separates them from a holy God; there is a deep chasm between God and humanity. Leviticus, however, teaches that the chasm may be bridged and that people can be made right with God. Reconciliation requires atonement. But the cultic system of Leviticus is insufficient; it cannot make atonement for humankind's sin or bring peace between God and humanity. It points to the need for something greater. It demands a final, sufficient sacrifice offered by a final, sufficient high priest for a final, sufficient atonement. More than any other book in the OT, Leviticus foreshadows and prefigures the coming of the Messiah and his final work of atonement.

Bibliography. Beale, G. K., "Adam as the First Priest in Eden as the Garden Temple," *SBJT* 22, no. 2 (2018): 9–24; Bonar, A., *Leviticus* (Banner of Truth, 1966); Brown, C. A., "The Peace Offerings and Pauline Soteriology," *Imm* 24–25 (1990): 59–76; Currid, J. D., *Genesis*, vol. 1, EPSC (Evangelical Press, 2003); Currid, *Leviticus*, EPSC (Evangelical Press, 2004); de Moor, J. C., "The Peace Offering in Israel and Ugarit," in *Schrift en utileg* (Kok, 1970), 112–17; Dumbrell, W., *The Faith of Israel* (Baker, 1988); Fishbane, M., *Biblical Interpretation in Ancient Israel* (Clarendon, 1988); Jukes, A., *The Law of the Offerings in Leviticus I–VII Considered* (James Nisbit, 1847); Klingbeil, G. A., "The Syntactic Structure of the Ritual of Ordination (Lev. 8)," *Bib* 77 (1996): 509–19; Levine, B. A., *Leviticus*, JPSTC (Jewish Publication Society, 1989); Lyons, M. A., "Transformation of Law," in *Transforming Visions*, ed. W. A. Tooman and M. A. Lyons (Pickwick, 2010), 1–32; McComiskey, T. E., "Holiness," in *TWOT*, 2:786–89; Milgrom, J., *Leviticus 1–16*, AB (Doubleday, 1991); Moo, D., *The Epistle to the Romans*, NICNT (Eerdmans, 1996); Morales, L. M., *Who Shall Ascend the Mountain of the Lord?* (IVP Academic, 2015); Rooker, M., *Leviticus*, NAC (Broadman & Holman, 2000); Schreiner, T., *Romans*, BECNT (Baker, 1998); Vasholz, R. I., *Leviticus*, MentC (Christian Focus, 2007); Wells, N. W., "The Ante-Nicene Fathers and the Mosaic Origin of the Pentateuch," *The Old Testament Student* 3 (1884): 186–91; Wenham, G., *The Book of Leviticus*, NICOT (Eerdmans, 1979).

JOHN D. CURRID

Lindars, Barnabas

See History of Interpretation: 1800 to Present

Literacy in the Greco-Roman World

The problem of literacy and orality in the Greco-Roman world is much larger than the question of literacy in regard to the NT. The field of classical studies has faced a similar set of questions. The discussion of orality and literacy arguably goes back to Josephus, who made observations on Homer's not having written his poems (Josephus, *Ag. Ap.* 1.11–12). The subject was taken up with earnestness in the eighteenth century with the rise of historical criticism. François Hédelin doubted Homer's existence because he left no writings; Richard Bentley endorsed the oral growth of the Homeric poems; Robert Wood argued that Homer was an oral poet and could not write; and Friedrich Wolf argued for later redaction of Homer's written texts originating from an oral poet. In the nineteenth century, Karl Lachmann and later Ulrich von Wilamowitz-Moellendorff argued for a composite Homeric text, a mix of written and oral features. Then in the twentieth century, Milman Parry, followed by his student Albert Lord, argued for the oral-formulaic theory of composition based upon Yugoslavian folk singers, a theory that continues to be important in classical studies with implications for NT studies (Foley, 2–10). In NT studies a similar progression occurred regarding orality and literacy, even if not reaching so far back. In the eighteenth century, J. G. von Herder was the first to recognize that Christianity originated with preaching rather than with written texts. A concern for oral transmission was taken up in full force by the form critics of the 1920s and the redaction critics of the 1950s. The oral dimension of the NT came into its own with the work of scholars such as Birger Gerhardsson, Kenneth Bailey, and Werner Kelber, and has continued to be developed in light of the burgeoning field of media studies (Loubser, *Oral*, 87).

Growing recognition of the role of ancient orality has raised the question of the rate of literacy in the ancient world. There have been various opinions on this. Before the recognition of the importance of orality, there was a belief that the ancient world was generally literate. As H. H. Tanzer (83) stated, "Everybody could read and almost everybody could, and apparently did, write" (cited in Harris, *Ancient*, 9), at least in Pompeii, and the papyrologist C. H. Roberts (48) as late as 1970 believed that the world of the NT was "a literate world . . . at almost all levels" (cited in Harris, *Ancient*, 9). Since that time, with wider consideration of orality and its influence, the literacy rates have been greatly revised downward and some precision in estimates has been attempted, to the point that J. A. Loubser contends that "an estimated 3%–10% of the total population of the [Roman] Empire were conversant with a high manuscript culture" (*Oral*, 88–89). There is quite a bit of difference between these two positions. What Rosalind Thomas (4) says of the Greeks is probably true of those who are investigating the Greco-Roman world and hence the world of the NT: "Scholars have indeed tended to see Greece as a literate or an oral society according to their predominant interests or tastes." Nevertheless, a consensus of sorts has emerged around the findings of the classicist William Harris, even if his views have not been without reproach and have left room for further question. Harris estimates that 10 to 20 percent of Roman males and less than 10 percent of Roman women were literate, so the "overall level of literacy is likely to have been below 15%" (*Ancient*, 267; see also Gamble, *Books*, 2–10; for responses to Harris, see Humphrey). It is difficult to know if Harris is correct in his estimate because there are so many unknown variables, including a recent attempt to be sure that what has been called "everyday writing," including graffiti, ostraca, and the like, is taken into account as evidence of wider literacy (Bagnall). Nevertheless, Harris's figure (or one much like it) is often used in NT studies. Even if it is on the lower side, Keith Hopkins (135) estimates that this would mean over two million adult men in the Roman Empire could read, and this large number would have exerted a significant influence on society and culture as a whole.

Complicating Factors in Estimating Literacy in Antiquity

There are many complicating factors in estimating literacy in antiquity. I will identify three of them that are the most obvious. Nevertheless, despite their being obvious, they make any conclusions difficult to firmly sustain. These three factors are ambiguity in defining literacy, the lack of evidence, and the multilingual nature of the Mediterranean world of the first century.

Ambiguity of the concept of literacy. The concept of literacy is difficult to define. Sociolinguists define literacy in a number of different ways, based upon several different variables. Some of these variables include active versus passive literacy, primary versus secondary languages, reading versus writing, registerial variation, and lingua franca. These merit brief explanations, because each one of them influences what we mean when we speak of literacy (cf. Baetens Beardsmore, 1–42, for helpful discussion).

Active literacy involves the ability to instigate and direct linguistic events, as opposed to passively being able to respond to such events. An active language user is able to initiate and direct a conversation or possibly read a document or even write (or dictate) a document, while a passive user may be able to understand a conversation but may be unable to respond to it and may well be unable to read or write. There are obviously varying degrees of active and passive literacy, depending upon some of the other factors mentioned below. It would appear safe to say that there are usually more people with passive literacy within a population than there are those with active literacy, no matter how such an estimation is made. The result of such complexity is for some to speak of "semi-literates" (Botha, "Greco-Roman," 199). This is probably not the best term to use, as it implies a singular cline or continuum. The point of the discussion here is that there are complex sets of variables, so that one may be literate in one area but not literate in another.

Primary and secondary language use revolves around diachronic issues, such as first language acquisition versus second or subsequent language acquisition. Multilingualism is not a static concept, but its functionality varies depending upon the linguistic environment. Depending upon one's circumstances, one may have primary language facility with limited secondary language ability, or one may have primary language attrition and secondary language competence. The age of acquisition also may influence one's linguistic competence. The ancient world, including the Greco-Roman world, was a functional multilingual environment in which virtually everyone would have a primary language but many, if not most, would also have a secondary language or languages. Their competence in these may have varied from language to language over time and environment.

Reading and writing are often joined together as if they are the same linguistic activity, when they are two very different linguistic activities. The ability to read a language does not guarantee the ability to write in the language, although the ability to write a language probably means that the person is able to read it. The two, reading and writing, are different linguistic processes. It is almost assuredly the case that, in the ancient Greco-Roman world, more people could read than write. As Harris states, "Among the inhabitants of the [Roman] empire in general, though a few used writings heavily and though some knew how to use written texts without being literate, for most, the written word remained inaccessible" (*Ancient*, 232).

Literacy must also take into account registerial variation. Language is used in varying registers—that is, language according to its use, rather than according to its user. Thus, authors may vary their language depending upon the circumstances in which they use it. Various so-called dialects reflect user-based features, such as accent, but register reflects the situational context in which language is used. Literacy may vary according to one's engagement with and facility in these various registers. The ability to produce and even read a receipt or simple letter engages a particular type of register, whereas the ability to read and understand a literary text or a complex treatise requires engagement with other types of registers. A language user may not be capable of using all register varieties within a language.

The last element to mention is lingua franca. A lingua franca is defined by Bernard Comrie (982) as "where a mixed speech community uses a natural language as a convenient general medium." This common natural language unites linguistically diverse groups on the basis of social, economic, or educational factors. The lingua franca of the Roman Empire, at least in the east, was Greek on the basis of Alexander's conquests that united the eastern Mediterranean. The result was that Greek was in widespread use by a variety of people for whom their first language was other than Greek (e.g., Aramaic for many Jews in Palestine) but who wished or found it necessary to communicate with the occupying powers and their local rulers, whether they were Roman officials or client kings.

Lack of linguistic evidence. The second major complicating factor is simply the lack of direct evidence. This is, of course, a problem with much study of the ancient world, especially with reference to contemporary categories of discussion. We cannot examine the population of the Greco-Roman world to determine their type or level of literacy. The only evidence that we have, because of this, is indirect evidence, even though this evidence is substantial. This substantial evidence includes at least five areas for consideration: government institutions, education, religion, literary texts, and documentary texts. The Roman government was notoriously bureaucratic and kept an abundance of written records, as did their subordinate governments, which implies that these were written and read, at least by a portion of the population. These documents include census reports on people and property, official edicts of various sorts, records of various meetings, and similar documents. These documents required literacy for production and consumption. The Greco-Roman educational system had two major levels to it, the lower of which exposed students to both speaking and writing. Their writing was based upon imitation of the models of others (e.g., classical authors, rhetorical handbooks, epistolary types, etc.). However, it is also well known that even the grammar school education was elitist and not available to the wider population. Some religions, although not all, within the Greco-Roman world were literary religions, in that they had sacred texts that were important to them. Judaism is perhaps the best known of these, with its written Scriptures first in Hebrew and Aramaic and then translated into Greek in Egypt beginning in the second century BC. There was already a widely developed literary tradition within the Greco-Roman world, focused primarily on Alexandrian scholarship. Alexandrian scholarship was responsible for the preservation and transmission of what we would call the classical tradition, with authors such as Homer and the Greek tragedians, as well as others, copied and preserved, such as in the great library at Alexandria. This led to the development of a scholarly tradition for the transmission and editing of classical texts. Finally, there is an abundance of documentary texts, mostly on papyri. These papyri included letters, receipts, lists, and a variety of other ephemera, produced and received by those transacting business within the Greco-Roman world. The letter tradition itself is significant, although we also realize that many letter "writers" made use of scribes and may well also have required readers for the letters they received.

This evidence is abundant and significant, but even though we are aware of it, it is difficult to quantify the types and levels of literacy of the population as a whole. We know that there must have been literate people who were able not only to speak various languages as required but also to read and write them. The evidence above makes this clear. However, we do not know how significant a percentage of the population would have maintained various levels of literacy in relationship to this body of evidence.

Multilingualism of the Mediterranean world. The Mediterranean world was multilingual, on the basis of its complex history. This is especially true of the eastern Mediterranean, which served as a throughway to connect Egypt and Africa with Asia and Europe. Many major armies marched through Palestine on their way out of or into one of these other areas. Some of these incursions included the exodus of the Jewish people from Egypt into Palestine, the invasions of the Assyrians and then the Babylonians, the Greek invasion of Alexander the Great, various battles back and forth between the Ptolemies and Seleucids, and then the coming of the Romans. Each of these movements would have constituted not only a military effort but also a cultural and even a linguistic event. Each left its imprint in various ways upon the area. One result was the multilingualism that characterizes Greco-Roman Palestine. "Superdiversity" is a term that has recently been devised to describe linguistic environments in which there is complex and intensified multilingualism (Blommaert). The Roman world of the first century reflects ancient superdiversity and its accompanying linguistic complexity. Superdiversity in the ancient world recognizes that there were diverse indigenous linguistic varieties that were then intermingled by users of a variety of other languages. These languages were introduced through widespread trade and travel, but also through major military conquests, especially the Hellenistic conquest of Alexander the Great in the third century BC and the Roman conquest of the first century BC, that imposed extra-indigenous varieties upon the existent population. The result had an important effect upon literacy as individual users balance the demands of the superdiversity.

Within the Greco-Roman world, some languages had greater prestige than others on the basis of a complex mix of cultural, military, socioeconomic, educational, historical, and other factors—many of them having nothing to do with the languages themselves (on prestige language, see Hudson, 30–34; Downes, 185–96). The Greco-Roman world was complex regarding prestige languages, with Latin in the west and Greek in the east as the prestige languages of the empire. However, within more localized linguistic environments, there may have been local prestige languages. For example, for the Jewish population of Palestine, their religious prestige language may have been Hebrew, their cultural prestige language may have been Aramaic, but their intercultural prestige language was Greek. The place of prestige languages would have had an impact on literacy, so that some within a culture had a greater chance of literacy in one language over another due to its prestige.

Major Issues in Greco-Roman Literacy

There are various issues that emerge in any discussion of Greco-Roman literacy. These are related to the complicating factors mentioned above and constitute some of the important issues that are raised when the topic of literacy is discussed in an ancient context. These include orality versus literacy, the role of writing, reading out loud and silently, the place of scribes, the role of education, the place of libraries, the elite, literacy and power, and the book trade.

Orality versus literacy. As mentioned above, there have been various positions regarding the degrees of literacy within the Greco-Roman world. Since it is so difficult to quantify what is meant by literacy (see above), the views have tended to be polarized—that is, arguing for a primarily literate or a largely illiterate Greco-Roman culture. For many of those arguing these positions, literacy is equated with the role, importance, and use of written texts. Thus, on the one hand, Charles Talbert (101–2) argues that "Christianity emerged in a Mediterranean culture that was not illiterate. Education was widespread. Books were produced on a scale heretofore unknown. A large reading public consumed prose written with a rhetorical cast" (cf. Hurtado). On the other hand, Harris has called this kind of position "a philologist's idealized view of the ancient world" ("Epigraphy," 88–89). We have already observed Harris's view on literacy in the Greco-Roman world. Catherine Hezser (*Jewish*, 503) goes further and states that "Jewish society in Palestine, in both the early and late imperial period, was characterized by lower literacy and more restricted use of texts than the Greco-Roman society in which it was a part." She thus concludes that this finding "must lead to a new assessment of our understanding of ancient Judaism as a 'book religion' and a greater emphasis on other, nontextual forms of religious expression." She later, however, argues that literacy rates in Jerusalem were higher than elsewhere in Palestine and that Greek literacy surpassed Hebrew and Aramaic literacy in Palestine ("Jewish," 60), but without devoting sufficient attention to Greek as the evidence clearly warrants (cf. Harris, "Epigraphy"; Bar-Ilan).

A third position, however, that has grown in significance in more recent times is to recognize the Greco-Roman world as primarily an oral culture (see Harris, *Ancient*; Botha, "Literacy"; for Jewish society in Palestine, see Gamble, "Literacy"; Heszer, *Jewish*; "Jewish"), but also recognize that one does not need to choose between literacy as a facility with written texts or illiteracy as no facility with written texts. In other words, one can argue that the Greco-Roman world as an oral culture was also a literate culture, in that it depends upon the use, transmission, and preservation of oral tradition. Scholars who find such oral culture in the Greco-Roman period often look back to earlier times, especially the classical period, in which there was a highly developed oral culture found in both ancient Greece and then Rome (Havelock, 29). This means that various kinds of technical knowledge that might later be thought of as being dependent upon written documentation were preserved and transmitted by oral means as a form of oral technology (Couch, 593). In that sense, dependence upon oral transmission, even if formally illiterate, does not mean that those involved have restricted cognitive ability (Camp). Walter Ong (112) has argued that this kind of oral consciousness remained in place much longer than the Greco-Roman period, even up to and including the Middle Ages.

This position addresses a very important issue within the ancient world: the fact that there was a valuation of and reliance upon orality. However, for an oral culture, there was a significant amount of written documentation, arguably far more in the Greco-Roman world than in any previous culture (and probably many since). The only way to explain the relationship is to argue that, even if literacy rates were low, there existed what one might well call a literate culture. Even those who were formally illiterate—that is, unable to read or write—came into regular and inevitable contact with the literate world by means of written documents that they were required to use in day-to-day life (Bowman; cf. Hezser, *Jewish*, 24; Bagnall, 27–53). This means that even an illiterate person had to engage with literate culture in regular ways in order to make one's way through life—such as the writing of a document, the reading of a letter, the attestation to land ownership, the acknowledgment of receipt of a shipment of grain, or the filing of a census report.

The role of writing. The immediately preceding section makes clear that writing, which is one of several factors in establishing and demonstrating literacy, was a very important element within the Greco-Roman literate culture. It is a truism to state this, but every culture that has produced written documents has placed a value upon writing, some clearly more than others. Many of the documents that were found in the remains of the Mycenaean Empire were nonliterary documents devoted primarily to the recording of financial transactions. Nevertheless, even if the Myceneans did not develop a robust written literary culture (their oral culture was the basis of the Homeric epics), they valued writing sufficiently to record financial matters. There are many imaginable reasons for use of writing, including simply the complexity of the records involved or the desire not to have to worry about such things while one was more interested in other matters. Such a perspective has led many to believe, as does Loubser, that "writing was seen as secondary to the spoken word and regarded as supportive of it" ("Orality," 63). Similar sentiments are often made about Jewish culture, with its regard for the "living voice" (attributed to Papias in Eusebius, *Hist. eccl.* 3.39.4, but it is a relatively common phrase and sentiment; see Botha, "Living," 751–52). Writing may be secondary and supportive (I will not enter into the dispute over that at this point), but it is necessary nevertheless if one desires preservation of any document, regardless of its literary or documentary or fiduciary value, beyond the memory of the individuals who know the information. The Romans seemed to realize this, even if writing developed relatively late for them.

Thomas Habinek has looked not just at writing in Rome but how writing developed in Rome. He asks the questions, "How does the social impact and significance of literacy at Rome change over time? How do the uses of literacy at Rome differ from those found in other ancient societies? What do Roman practices of reading and writing tell us about the Roman understanding of what writing is and is not?" (115). He answers his questions by surveying the rise in written artifacts in Roman times. He concludes that there are two major reasons: one he calls "proprietorial, as in the marking of territory or indications of ownership and financial responsibility," while the other "speaks to a particular form of sociability" (119). The latter take the form of dedications to people (not gods), commemorations, and written attestations of social responsibilities. Harris offers a helpful list of forty-one uses of writing (*Ancient*, 26–27). Although his list is for the Greeks, the amount of overlap with Habinek's two broad categories is significant. An examination of the categories, and of the individual instances, indicates that there are some functions of writing whose purposes could not be achieved without writing.

Reading aloud and silently. There has been much confusion, especially within NT studies, regarding the place of reading aloud or silently. As noted above, the ability to read is a manifestation of one type of literacy, and no doubt an important one. The further issue, however, is whether the ancients were able to read silently or whether they only read aloud. In a linguistic culture where only a few people (even if an indeterminate number) are able to read and where there is a limit to the number of books (see below), reading aloud would be a normal activity. This would allow those without their own reading materials or unable to read to hear the text. We see instances of this occurring in the Bible, such as Luke 4:16–30, when Jesus reads the text from Isaiah in the Nazareth synagogue.

The conditions mentioned above, along with biblical instances, have indicated to some that reading aloud was the norm, with some arguing that it was almost an inviolable norm. Paul Achtemeier makes a well-known case that there was no writing done that was not meant for auditory pronouncement. He bases this argument on a variety of factors, including the nature of ancient oral culture, Greek continuous writing (without spaces), and the use of rhetorical and mnemonic features in writing, among some possible others. Many have followed Achtemeier in this position. This is intriguing, since three years later the historian Frank Gilliard marshaled numerous examples from as early as the fifth century BC (Euripides, Aristophanes, and apparently Alexander the Great, Julius Caesar, Cicero, and Augustus) to well into the Christian era (Augustine) of people reading silently (with further examples in Gavrilov, esp. 70–71). One of the instances often used to illustrate reading aloud is the fourth-century Christian writer Ambrose, who is said to have been able to read to himself, something upon which Augustine remarks (*Conf.* 6.3.3). Clearly, what Augustine finds remarkable is not simply that Ambrose could read to himself but that he only read to himself.

These more complete findings do not minimize the importance of reading aloud, as that would have been part of the literate culture that relied upon those who could read aloud reading to those who were unable to read. However, these findings do mitigate at least some of the emphasis upon orality at the expense of writing. They recognize that reading was a more diverse activity than some have thought and could well have been used in a wider range of circumstances than those who posit simply audible reading alone.

Productive literacy in literate culture. To have a literate culture, one must have literary artifacts, by which I mean examples of written documents that form both the basis of this literate culture and hence the object of written literacy. There is much that can be said about the development of written documents of various types, but as discussed above, for a variety of reasons even in oral cultures, written documents have long occupied an important place, even if seen to be of secondary importance (a claim that is worth challenging). The huge remains of documentary papyri, only a small portion of which have been published, well illustrate how, even within a primarily illiterate population, literate culture is operative. This wealth of documents—including not only letters but also the remains of lived life, such as receipts, accounts, contracts, wills, deeds, titles to land, reports, notes, census documents, governmental documents, and many others—illustrates the dependence of Greco-Roman culture upon written texts and hence upon literacy. We have already noted how even those who were functionally illiterate were dependent upon these documents and hence required means of access to such documents. There are two areas to mention further.

The first area is the role and function of scribes. In an environment where literacy is limited, such that even if someone could read they perhaps could not write, there is a need for scribes. In fact, scribes occupied a major functional role within ancient literate culture and were certainly used by those who were functionally illiterate but were also used by those who could read and write. History has recorded for us some of these scribes, such as Cicero's Tiro and Paul's Tertius, among others. Scribes were a mainstay within community life and occupied positions of authority within civic life. Scribes had varying levels of formal training and ability and hence charged varying amounts for their work. Their importance is illustrated in documentary papyri that record a scribe writing a papyrus for someone who was illiterate. Such people required a scribe to participate more fully in literate culture and record documents important to their lives, businesses, and other activities.

Book culture is another area to mention. Book culture involves many variables, including several mentioned above. I mention here publication and the book trade.

Publication of a manuscript included many of the factors mentioned above, including the use of scribes. However, the publication process itself was surprisingly much like that of modern publication. Raymond Starr has defined the two major spheres in which the production of a publishable manuscript occurred. The first sphere is what we might call prepublication, when the author writes and then revises the manuscript on the basis of a close circle of friends and even servants and scribes who helped in the editorial process. Papyrus was relatively cheap in the ancient world, despite what some have contended, and so there were plenty of materials available if there were people who were able (i.e., literate) to produce the manuscripts involved. The second sphere involves publication. Once authors believed that their work was worthy of publication, they distributed copies to their friends. Once the manuscript was in the hands of their friends, it could be considered published, because then there was access to it for others. Those interested in the manuscript could borrow a copy of it to have their own copy made, and dissemination would transpire in this way. The role of the book trade is one that increased over time. At first, the book trade was relatively limited—although we know that even classical Greece had an abundance of books—because the publication and distribution of manuscripts occurred on the basis of circles of friendship. However, booksellers came into business mostly focusing upon a location, and they would accumulate copies of various books that would then be available for others to copy. By the time of the first century, it appears that there was a recognizable book trade in the Greco-Roman world, with books available to those of the artisan class and higher at often reasonable prices (Phillips). There was not a lot of money to be made in publication by authors, but there must have been some rewards—if not monetary, then in terms of prestige or power or other intangible benefits—to make it tempting to engage in pseudepigraphy. Several ancient authors, Galen being perhaps the best known, were outraged to find works falsely attributed to them being sold in bookshops. As a result, a number of major authors from the ancient world have had pseudepigraphs attributed to them (Porter and Pitts, 21–26).

Publication and the growing book trade provide incentives for literacy. However, the process of book production and the book trade itself show various types of literacy among individuals. Members of an author's household (the householder in most instances would have been a person of some means) would have had to be literate in order to aid in the publication process, such as functioning as readers, editors, or copyists. The greater distribution of books indicates the growth of literacy among an expanding segment of the general public.

Literacy support. Literacy was supported within the Greco-Roman world in numerous ways. Some sought it of necessity, such as those who needed to access written documents. However, the opportunity to become literate would have been limited by a variety of other societal factors, such as access to education. It has been noted that some people were attracted to particular types of literature and often were involved in its publication and its authors. This could include a range of authors, from Homer, who was widely supported, edited, copied, and recopied in the Greco-Roman world, to sacred texts such as the Septuagint, especially by those who had religious motivations (Gamble, *Books*, 85).

There were also what might be termed public institutions that supported literacy. These include schools and libraries. I have already noted the Greco-Roman educational system. Whereas traditionally scholars have depicted a tripartite system with elementary, grammar, and then rhetorical school, more recent research seems to indicate a bipartite system of grammar school and rhetorical school (Porter and Pitts, 15–20). The grammar school was more inclusive, was probably geared to the needs of a given location or region, and may have often assumed some prior preparation for study, such as knowledge of the alphabet. Grammar school was followed by rhetorical education. There is no doubt that oral culture played a significant role in the educational system, but it is also true that written texts were an integral part of every level of education, from learning the alphabet, to learning to write syllables and words, to beginning to transcribe texts, to beginning to compose letters, to engaging in rudimentary rhetorical exercises (the *progymnasmata*), not to mention the rhetorical handbooks that may or may not have played a part in advanced education. "The Poet" (i.e., Homer), other poets, the tragedians such as Euripides, and other similar writers were the focus of the curriculum. Students learned to read, write, and explain these texts, engaging both oral and written abilities. Libraries were also important for the promotion of literacy, as they stood as monuments to the products of literacy in a way that the sheer mass accumulation of documentary texts never could. Libraries were an embodiment of the notion mentioned above that written texts were necessary as a means of preserving and even memorializing important people or events that may otherwise have been forgotten. Major libraries grew up especially in Alexandria and Ephesus, but there were many private libraries as well, some of which may have been more important than the larger ones in the preservation of literate culture (Kenyon, 65; cf. Dix). The Alexandrian library was reputed (by Aristeas) to desire to contain a copy of every book in existence (Let. Aris. 9). These libraries, both large and small, were probably in large part responsible for the preservation of many of the authors of the ancient world whose works would otherwise have perished once the few copies of their works had worn out and then been discarded when readers were no longer interested in them, much like a paperback at a garage sale. The libraries became not just an elitist symbol of wealth and power but also important preservers and protectors of literate culture and with it literacy itself as they retained copies of what were considered the materials most worth preserving and protecting.

Literacy and power. We cannot end this discussion without mentioning the relationship between literacy and power. It is easy to believe that literacy in its fullest sense would have been elitist, reserved for only the small upper echelons in Greco-Roman society, and power along with it as one was able to create and interpret written artifacts that were not accessible to others (see Bowman and Woolf, 1, quoting Pattison, viii: "Literacy is always connected with power"). There is a sense in which this is true, because the elite upper classes had wealth and hence access to education, whether in schools or from tutors. In fact, it appears to be a trope within Greco-Roman culture to depict oneself as being able to write as a means of demonstrating membership in the elite or upper classes. We do have evidence that those in the upper classes were often able to read and write, and often the elite engaged in writing their own documents by hand as a sign of power and as a demonstration of social prestige (McDonnell). However, we also know that reading and writing were not reserved for the elite. Whereas the elite may have engaged in writing their own documents, such as a letter to a friend, they did not apparently engage in the copying of documents. For such things they relied upon others. We know that scribes and similar functionaries (e.g., *grammateus*) occupied a particular stratum within society as an important functionary within the civil system that conveyed status and even power (Bowman and Woolf, 10). We also know that some freedmen and also slaves were taught to read and write, if for nothing else than being able to copy manuscripts for others, including the elite. However, we also must recognize that literacy was a force in democratization of culture, even if only to a small extent. The elite were not interested in copying manuscripts. For that task, others had to be recruited, those who were not members of the elite. This of necessity opened up literacy to a variety of others, including slaves and servants, some of whom would become freedmen. This would eventually, even if slowly, open up access for education and then literacy to a greater number of people who would be required to assume the tasks of practitioners of literacy within the ancient world. This increase in literacy was the product of the Roman Empire, or at least the product of its administrative needs. Much of this increase occurred from the second century AD on, and it involved a range of different forms of written artifacts, some of them not as important as others. Nevertheless, the groundwork for it was already laid in early imperial Rome with the expansion of the empire. An expanded empire required greater documentation and written communication, as is seen in grain shipment reports and receipts, contracts, and storage agreements, and as individuals who lived in various parts of the empire filed their census reports and laid claim to land and other property (Woolf). These bureaucratic requirements fostered the increase of literate culture across the socioeconomic strata as all participated in it.

Final Considerations in Understanding Greco-Roman Literacy

In this final section, I outline some of the ways forward in the discussion. While many more things could be said about Greco-Roman literacy, I identify two.

First, discussion of literacy probably requires a much more nuanced approach, what William Johnson (625) calls a "sociology of reading"—that is, a sociological contextualization of what is involved in reading that calls into question whether one can legitimately "speak of 'literacy' and 'reading' in antiquity as though these were one thing for all groups of people and all types of texts over the course of a millennium" or more. Johnson identifies three factors here: the people involved, the types of texts, and the span of time. As I mentioned above, a factor not often considered is register theory. In other words, one might well wish to consider not just how language functions—that is, whether it is oral or written, and whether those engaged are illiterate or literate and to what degree—but how literacy functions differently in various typical contextual situations. In other words, one might consider how literacy functions in the dictating, writing, and reading of letters as opposed to other texts, by the author and by the reader(s), and in what kinds of situations. Esther Eidinow and Claire Taylor have certainly pushed matters forward in this respect by their study of letters written on pieces of lead. Their goal is not to deal with the larger topic of literacy but the more focused questions of "(i) the social status of and relationships between the correspondences, (ii) the character of their communication, and (iii) the different kinds of literacy that existed in ancient Greece during this period" (32). This and probably more can be garnered from representative texts with a more fully developed linguistic approach that asks these kinds of questions.

Second, one should be cautious about creating false dilemmas between possibilities in the discussion of literacy. Such bifurcations fall victim to all the problems of the fallacy of the law of the excluded middle. We have seen some of these problems above. It is easy to talk about orality versus literacy, literacy versus illiteracy, speaking versus writing, and any number of other false oppositions (Robbins, 77, where he expands the notions of types of culture), when there are usually various intermediate positions that are worth considering. I have posited above that one way of addressing some of these is through the discussion of literate culture, even if we are speaking of a culture in which only a percentage of people had some level of literacy (to varying degrees and of varying types) and an arguably larger percentage of people did not have this kind of literacy but were, nevertheless, themselves dependent upon and even contributors to a literate environment—that is, an environment where, even with oral culture, there was a place for written artifacts.

Conclusion

Oral culture has been a focus of discussion in recent biblical studies. This essay has attempted to introduce some of the considerations regarding literacy, especially in a Greco-Roman context. This is not an easy discussion to have, because there are many problems involved in such a topic, depending upon both conceptual and evidential factors. Nevertheless, the topic of literacy, not as opposed to oral culture but as a companion to it, helps us to understand the context in which the NT documents were produced as part of a literate culture within the Greco-Roman world. There are also some obvious implications for how literacy would influence the use of texts within the ancient world depending upon one's access to them. This has direct bearing upon how the OT would have been understood and transmitted and then finally reconceptualized in the NT.

See also Letter Couriers; Rhetoric; *Septuagint articles*

Bibliography. Achtemeier, P. J., "*Omne Verbum Sonat*," *JBL* 109 (1990): 3–27; Baetans Beardsmore, H., *Bilingualism*, 2nd ed. (Multilingual Matters, 1986); Bagnall, R. S., *Everyday Writing in the Graeco-Roman East* (University of California Press, 2011); Bar-Ilan, M., "Illiteracy in the Land of Israel in the First Centuries CE," in *Essays in the Social Scientific Study of Judaism and Jewish Society*, ed. S. Fishbane and S. Schoenfeld (Ktav, 1992), 46–61; Blommaert, J., *Ethnography, Superdiversity and Linguistic Landscapes* (Multilingual Matters, 2013); Botha, P. J. J., "Greco-Roman Literacy as Setting for New Testament Writings," *Neot* 26 (1992): 195–215; Botha, "Living Voice and Lifeless Letters," *HvTSt* 49 (1993): 742–59; Bowman, A. K., "Literacy in the Roman Empire," in *Literacy in the Roman World*, ed. J. H. Humphrey (Journal of Roman Archaeology, 1991), 119–31; Bowman, A. K., and G. Woolf, "Literacy and Power in the Ancient World," in *Literacy and Power in the Ancient World*, ed. A. K. Bowman and G. Woolf (Cambridge University Press, 1994), 1–16; Camp, C. V., "Oralities, Literacies, and Colonialism in Antiquity and Contemporary Scholarship," in *Orality, Literacy, and Colonialism in Antiquity*, ed. J. A. Draper, SemeiaSt 47 (Society of Biblical Literature, 2004), 193–217; Comrie, B., "Languages of the World," in *An Encyclopaedia of Language*, ed. N. E. Collinge (Routledge, 1992), 956–83; Couch, C. J., "Oral Technologies," *The Sociological Quarterly* 30 (1989): 587–602; Dix, K., "'Public Libraries' in Ancient Rome," *Library & Culture* 29 (1994): 282–96; Downes, W., *Language and Society*, 2nd ed. (Cambridge University Press, 1998); Eidinow, E., and C. Taylor, "Lead-Letter Days," *The Classical Quarterly* 60 (2010): 30–62; Foley, J. M., *The Theory of Oral Composition* (Indiana University Press, 1988); Gamble, H. Y., *Books and Readers in the Early Church* (Yale University Press, 1995); Gamble, "Literacy and Book Culture," in *DNTB*, 644–48; Gavrilov, A. K., "Techniques of Reading in Classical Antiquity," *The Classical Quarterly* 47 (1997): 56–73; Gilliard, F. D., "More Silent Reading in Antiquity," *JBL* 112 (1993): 68–94; Habinek, T., "Situating Literacy at Rome," in *Ancient Literacies*, ed. W. A. Johnson and H. N. Parker (Oxford University Press, 2009), 114–40; Harris, W. V., *Ancient Literacy* (Harvard University Press, 1989); Harris, "Literacy and Epigraphy, I," *ZPE* 52 (1983): 87–111; Havelock, E. A., *The Literate Revolution in Greece and Its Cultural Consequences* (Princeton University Press, 1982); Hezser, C., "Jewish Literacy and Languages in First-Century Roman Palestine," in *The Languages of Palestine at the Time of Jesus*, ed. C. Morrison, BibOr 89 (Pontifical Biblical Institute, 2020), 58–77; Hezser, *Jewish Literacy in Roman Palestine*, TSAJ 81 (Mohr Siebeck, 2001); Hopkins, K., "Conquest by Book," in *Literacy in the Roman World*, ed. J. H. Humphrey (Journal of Roman Archaeology, 1991), 133–58; Hudson, R., *Sociolinguistics*, 2nd ed., CTL (Cambridge University Press, 1996); Humphrey, J. H., ed., *Literacy in the Roman World* (Journal of Roman Archaeology, 1991); Hurtado, L. W., "Greco-Roman Textuality and the Gospel of Mark," *BBR* 7 (1997): 91–106; Johnson, W. A., "Toward a Sociology of Reading in Classical Antiquity," *American Journal of Philology* 121 (2000): 593–627; Kenyon, F. G., *Books and Readers in Ancient Greece and Rome* (Clarendon, 1932); Loubser, J. A., *Oral and Manuscript Culture in the Bible* (Sun Press, 2007); Loubser, "Orality and Literacy in the Pauline Corpus," *Neot* 29 (1995): 61–74; McDonnell, M., "Writing, Copying, and Autograph Manuscripts in Ancient Rome," *ClQ* 46 (1996): 469–91; Ong, W. J., *Orality and Literacy* (Routledge, 1982); Pattison, R., *On Literacy* (Oxford University Press, 1982); Phillips, J. J., "Book Prices and Roman Literacy," *The Classical World* 79 (1985): 36–38; Porter, S. E., and A. W. Pitts, "Paul's Bible, His Education and His Access to the Scriptures of Israel," *JGCJ* 5 (2008): 9–40; Robbins, V. K., "Oral, Rhetorical, and Literary Culture," *Semeia* 65 (1995): 75–91; Roberts, C. H., "Books in the Graeco-Roman World and the New Testament," in *The Cambridge History of the Bible*, vol. 1, ed. P. R. Ackroyd and C. F. Evans (Cambridge University Press, 1970), 48–66; Starr, R. J., "The Circulation of Literary Texts in the Roman World," *ClQ* 37 (1987): 213–23; Talbert, C. H., "Oral and Independent or Literary and Interdependent," in *The Relationships among the Gospels*, ed. W. O. Walker, Jr. (Trinity University Press, 1978), 93–102; Tanzer, H. H., *The Common People of Pompeii* (Johns Hopkins University Press, 1939); Thomas, R., *Literacy and Orality in Ancient Greece* (Cambridge University Press, 1992); Woolf, G., "Literacy or Literacies in Rome?," in *Ancient Literacies*, ed. W. A. Johnson and H. N. Parker (Oxford University Press, 2009), 46–68.

STANLEY E. PORTER

Literal Fulfillment

Difficulty has arisen in biblical interpretation when considering the issue of the fulfillment of God's promises. For many, this difficulty is perhaps most clearly seen in the promises to Israel in the OT. More specifically, OT prophecies regarding God's promise to restore the nation of Israel include returning from exile, restoring Jerusalem, rebuilding the temple, and reinstituting the sacrificial system. Some of these promises are initially fulfilled within the OT itself, such as returning to the land and rebuilding the temple, yet these fulfillments fall far short of how the prophetic language describes them. The question becomes, then, How precisely are these promises fulfilled? Should they be taken literally, or literalistically? Must the nation Israel remain distinct from gentiles, having its own land with its own temple and sacrificial system? Since these promises are not fulfilled in this exact way in the NT, must an eschatological view demand a future (millennial) age in which these prophecies are fulfilled? Or do these promises reach their ultimate fulfillment in Christ and all that he achieved through his atoning life, death, burial, resurrection, and ascension, which will culminate in a new heavens and new earth in which both Jew and gentile will dwell with God forever?

This article proceeds in four steps to understand the fulfillment of God's promises. First, it discusses the issue of authorial intent in biblical interpretation. Second, it provides an interpretive framework for understanding the fulfillment of God's promises. Third, it discusses the interpretive issue of literal fulfillment. And fourth, it applies this interpretive framework to God's OT promises and offers examples of how they are fulfilled in the NT, both initially in Christ's first coming and finally in his return to make all things new.

Divine and Human Authorial Intent

Scripture is God's word through human authors. This entails that the final meaning of any text is made most clearly known in the light of *all* Scripture. The process of understanding the meaning of a text, then, begins with interpreting the grammatical-historical context, proceeds through the redemptive-historical character of Scripture as it looks back to prior revelation, and reaches its fullness in the context of the whole canon. This way of interpretation honors the nature of Scripture as a both fully divine and fully human word. Meaning, then, is not limited exclusively to what the human author knew or intended, but ultimately extends to what God intended, which becomes clearer as revelation progresses until it reaches its fullness in Christ. That is, given the nature of Scripture, biblical interpretation must allow for a fuller meaning that does not disagree with or go against what the human author wrote. In fact, the meaning deepens, extends, and develops until reaching its culmination in Christ (see Moo and Naselli; Beale and Gladd). We can substantiate this extension and development that the NT makes known by reading OT texts as the NT authors did—namely, as part of a completed, canonical, christological whole. Therefore, in reading and citing the OT, the NT authors through the Holy Spirit are given insight into the divinely intended meaning of earlier Scripture. God's end-time work in Christ and the gift of the Spirit, then, enable the NT authors to read the OT with new—indeed, with Spirit-filled christological—eyes. Furthermore, the Holy Spirit regenerates and illumines readers of the canonical Scriptures to understand what God has spoken in his Son, who fulfills his saving promises that have been written down for the eye of faith to see (1 Cor. 2:10–16).

The Interpretive Framework of Scripture

The nature of Scripture and divine-human authorial intent provide an important interpretive framework for understanding how God fulfills his promises. First, the dual authorship of Scripture shapes how the interpreter understands the fulfillment of God's promises. On the one hand, because God is the primary author, Scripture displays a remarkable unity that makes known the mystery of God's will to unite all things in Christ (Eph. 1:9–10). On the other hand, because of the various secondary human authors, Scripture displays remarkable diversity through the history of redemption. Sound biblical interpretation, therefore, must consider the intention of the author as conveyed through various literary forms. Taken together, then, when genres such as prophecy include symbols and shadows, or types, of things to come as part of divine revelation, then interpretation must allow for a fulfillment that extends beyond, yet does not contravene, the human author, especially when revealed in the NT. Second, because of this unity and diversity, or unity through diversity, biblical interpretation should consider the progressive stages of revelation along Scripture's covenantal structure that escalate from OT promise to NT fulfillment in the person and new-covenant work of Christ. Finally, biblical interpretation should keep the whole canon in view even when studying the various parts. That is, we must read every passage in the context of the completed canon since God intended from the beginning that his later words and works should build upon and bring to fulfillment his earlier words and works, so that in some sense all Scripture reveals one long, diverse but unified process of God speaking and acting.

Interpreters must give attention to the OT and NT as the Testaments progressively reach their fulfillment in Christ. Scripture is a unity because God has declared the end from the beginning in order to accomplish his redemptive purposes (Isa. 46:10). So, to interpret his Word rightly is not merely to survey the individual parts but to see how each part fits into the whole of God's plan that culminates in Christ. Because the OT and NT constitute the whole of God's authoritative Word, they integrate and cohere with one another. This coherence is evident when studying the parts in light of the whole, in which the whole makes sense of the individual parts. To analyze and synthesize Scripture well, then, one must study it in context, and Scripture itself contains the context necessary for determining how God's promises are fulfilled. More specifically, when analyzing and synthesizing the OT and NT, it is important to consider the immediate, covenantal/epochal, and canonical/christological horizons (Lints). A brief comment on these horizons will aid in understanding the fulfillment of God's promises in Christ disclosed to us in Scripture.

Literal Fulfillment

The word "literal" is difficult to define because of its abuse in our modern context and its use in dispensational and nondispensational debates. Used correctly, the term captures a text's genre(s) and literary conventions. One can interpret a text "literally" without meaning "physically," because interpretation must account for figures of speech, wordplays, and so on contained within the passage (see Poythress, 82–86). The chasm between dispensational and nondispensational theologies, particularly on the issue of fulfillment, has often been cast in terms of "literal versus nonliteral" fulfillment. Both sides cite so-called literal interpretation, yet they settle on opposite ends of the spectrum when it comes to issues such as the relationship between Israel and the church, the fulfillment of the land promises, the rebuilding of the temple, the reinstitution of the sacrificial system, and the second coming of Christ in relation to the millennium. This reality suggests that the issue is not literal versus nonliteral but rather what constitutes the very nature of Scripture as a dually authored text and, flowing from it, its interpretation. Therefore, more precision is needed when it comes to the issue of literal versus nonliteral fulfillment. In other words, the so-called literal fulfillment of God's promises demands not a literalistic or "physical" fulfillment but rather fulfillment that accords with the type of speech it is.

For example, those who interpret the Bible literalistically may insist that a passage such as Isa. 65:19–20 refers to a future millennial state and cannot be a fulfillment of the new creation because, although it describes something better than life in the present, it is not as good as life in the new earth. But such an interpretation does not adequately take into account the nature of prophetic language, as well as how this passage is picked up in Rev. 21. From Isaiah's perspective, how could he adequately describe the glory and splendor of the presence and power of God finally breaking into history to create a new heaven and a new earth? Yet, enough continuity exists between the original prophecy and its unexpected fulfillment for NT hearers and readers to recognize their connection. Indeed, the fulfillment far exceeds its original vision precisely because God's Messiah, the Word who became flesh, far exceeds human imagination!

Typological Fulfillment

One way Scripture displays God's promise and fulfillment is through typology. The NT consistently demonstrates that God's saving promises have been fulfilled in and through the person and work of Jesus Christ. That is, the NT authors interpret the eschatological promises through the lens of all that Christ accomplished through his life, obedience, suffering, death, burial, resurrection, and ascension. For example, Jesus's own person and work provide his disciples the interpretive key for understanding the OT in relation to him (Luke 24:27, 44), and had his opponents rightly understood the words of Moses, they would have believed in Jesus, for Moses wrote of him (John 5:46; cf. Deut. 18:15–22; Acts 3:17–26). In other words, had they truly known and believed God, then they would have seen *in Christ* that God fulfills his promises. Indeed, all the promises of God find their "Yes" *in him* (2 Cor. 1:20). Christ Jesus is the final revelation of God (John 1:14; Heb. 1:1–2), the second and last Adam (Rom. 5:12–21; 1 Cor. 15:45), and Abraham's offspring (Matt. 1:1; Gal. 3:16). He is the true, obedient Son (Matt. 2:15; 3:17; cf. Exod. 4:22; Ps. 89:27) who accomplishes a better exodus from the greater enemy of sin (Col. 1:12–13), the true temple through whom is given better access to God (John 1:14; 2:18–22), the life-giving vine(yard) who, unlike unfaithful Israel, bears fruit (John 15:1–11; cf. Isa. 5; Hosea 9:10), and the great high priest and sacrifice of a better covenant (Heb. 7–8). He is David's greater Son and King (Matt. 1:1; 22:41–46; Rom. 1:2–3), the true Shepherd (John 10; Ezek. 34; Ps. 23), the better Solomon in whom are hidden all the treasures of wisdom and knowledge (Matt. 12:42; Col. 2:3), and the great "I am" who preexists Abraham (John 8:58; cf. Exod. 3:14). And in the end, he is the Lord and Christ who wins a better kingdom, the new heaven and new earth, which is brilliantly described in a complex of OT imagery such as a paradisiacal new Eden, new Jerusalem, and cosmological temple that is, in the climax of the covenants, filled with God's presence (Rev. 21–22; Isa. 65:17; 66:22; Ezek. 40–48).

At the same time, however, the fulfillment of these promises comes in two stages. Although through Christ the decisive victory has *already* been won, it is *not yet* fully realized. So, the initial stage of fulfillment builds off the literal sense in the OT but also extends it (Beale, *Theology*, 511). For example, the promise of resurrection in the OT begins with believers being raised spiritually from the dead in Christ but will end in their bodily resurrection and glorification. Likewise, promises to rebuild the temple and reinstitute sacrifices have been fulfilled in Christ, the Word who became flesh and "templed" among us (John 1:14) and the sacrificial Lamb of God who takes away the sin of the world (1:29). Moreover, the church—composed of both Jew and gentile believers in Christ—is the temple of God (1 Cor. 3:16). Nevertheless, these promises will not be consummated until Christ returns and God finally dwells with his people in the new creation, in which there is no temple, "because the Lord God the Almighty and the Lamb are its temple" (Rev. 21:22). The person and work of Christ, then, in an already/not-yet framework, provide the interpretive key for rightly understanding the fulfillment of God's promises. The first advent of Jesus not only fulfills prophetic and messianic expectations revealed in the OT but also extends them. This extension and transformation is demonstrated in NT themes such as fulfillment, typology, kingdom, covenant, and land.

Typology in Matthew. The opening verses of Matthew provide a helpful link regarding the relationship with the OT expectation of restoration and fulfillment. Matthew writes, "The book of the genealogy of Jesus Christ, the son of David, the son of Abraham" (1:1 ESV). Matthew's language is significant because the phrase "book of the genealogy" (*biblos geneseōs*) is found in only two places in the LXX (Gen. 2:4; 5:1). Thus, Matthew opens by deliberately connecting his account of the gospel to Genesis, which recounts the story of the people of Abraham, Isaac, and Jacob. These two occurrences in the biblical story line are important to consider in order to understand Matthew's conception of fulfillment.

Genesis 2:4 gives the account of God's creation of the heavens and the earth, and 5:1 begins a new genealogical tree after the fall that emphasizes the continuation of humanity and a re-creation through the Noahic covenant. Thus, it is momentous that Matt. 1:1 is only the third place in the canon that this phrase is used. In other words, Matthew connects Jesus to the first creation (Gen. 1:1), the post-fall re-creation (Gen. 5:1) where the image of God is proliferated, and now to the dawning of a new creation. Like John's opening words, "In the beginning" (1:1), Matthew commences his Gospel with a new book of beginnings that links prior history with God's saving purposes. Through his genealogy, then, Matthew weaves together key threads from Israel's story and continues the story begun in the OT. Thus, Matthew advances new-creation themes through the genealogy of the Messiah and indicates that the fulfillment of the OT has been inaugurated through the historic event of Jesus Christ (see France, *Matthew*, chap. 5). And although Matthew does not include an exhaustive list of Jesus's genealogical history, the fact that he is strategically fitting the Messiah's history into a pattern indicates that he is making not so much a physiological observation as a theological reflection on the working out of God's purposes. The genealogy shows that the era of preparation is now complete, and the stage is set for the dawning of the fulfillment of God's saving, messianic promises.

Matthew paints a complete picture, from the beginning of Israel's history to its end, or goal, by the way he frames his genealogy of the Messiah in three balanced periods of fourteen generations each. Matthew points his readers to the arrival of the Messiah who has come in fulfillment of the Davidic promises of a kingdom and the Abrahamic promises of international blessing (cf. also Matt. 3:9; 8:11). Moreover, Matthew includes the unexpected: the exile. Hence, it appears that the long-awaited return from exile has dawned.

Going further into Matthew's conception of fulfillment is Matt. 2:15, a quotation from Hosea 11:1. Hosea is recalling the history of Israel, God's son (Exod. 4:22–23), when God delivered them out of Egypt. This fulfilled God's promise to call out a people from bondage and give them their own land. But Hosea 11:2–7 goes on to lament how Israel has wandered away from the Lord and to predict a future return to exile (11:5). Like her ancestors, Israel was unfaithful to her covenant God. As a result, another exodus was needed. This new exodus event became central in the life of Israel, to which later revelation would attest. As God's revelation progresses through Israel's successes and failures, an even greater exodus is anticipated (Hosea 2:14–15; 11:10–11; cf. Isa. 43:16–21; 51:9–11; Jer. 16:14–15; 31:31–34). In other words, Hosea moves from retrospect to prospect, both recalling the first exodus and predicting a new one. Thus, the exodus from Egypt forms a type or pattern of a greater salvation to come. This point is important, for what Matthew views in his own context is something seen by Hosea himself, albeit unclearly. In other words, Matthew is not reading into Hosea what is not there; rather, what has been promised and predicted through Hosea is now being revealed to Matthew. Indeed, God's true and better Son has arrived to accomplish a greater exodus in fulfillment of his promises. As a result, Matthew now sees Jesus, God's true and obedient Son, as the fulfillment of Israel, which he goes on to demonstrate (e.g., Matt. 4:1–11).

It is at this point that one comes into contact with typology in Matthew, which is instructive for understanding typology throughout the NT. Jesus is the typological fulfillment of Israel, for he is the true Israel who fulfills the promises made to Abraham and David. Hence the Messiah, God's obedient Son in the flesh, has come to perform a new and greater exodus for the people of God and restore them from exile. In this greater exodus, God brings his people out of bondage to sin *and* he will also bring them into the abundant blessings of his Son, something which rebellious Israel did not permanently enjoy (Col. 1:13–14). Although Israel made it out of Egypt, they did not permanently enter God's blessing because of their failure to keep his covenant. Unlike the exodus under the leadership of Moses, then, through the liberating work of Jesus, God definitively brings his people out of captivity and into the place of redemptive blessing.

Matthew's typology presents an important issue for understanding the fulfillment of God's promises. Typology involves correspondence(s) between initial persons, events, and institutions and later ones. That is, God's past dealings with his people serve as patterns, or types, for his future dealings with his people. For example, OT prophets anticipate and look for a new prophet, new David, new exodus, new covenant, and a new city of God; the old had thus become a type or shadow of the new, for it pointed forward to it. Subsequently, the NT authors saw in Christ and his work the fulfillment, or antitype, of these prophetic hopes.

Components of typology. There are several important components in typology. First, typology gives attention to textual and historical/theological correspondences that develop across the canon. These correspondences provide the hermeneutical controls for linking types with their antitype(s). Second, typology is prospective and prophetic. That is, God intentionally planned certain persons, events, and institutions in redemptive history *in order that* they would serve later redemptive—and christological—realities. Third, typology stresses escalation as the OT story line moves forward to its NT fulfillment. As a result, the OT is incomplete as to the working out of God's purposes and thus cannot be *fully* understood apart from its fulfillment in the NT. Promises in the OT point forward to their fulfillment(s), and the type is fulfilled and surpassed by its antitype. Finally, these typological connections find their ultimate fulfillment in the person and work of Christ. In making typological connections—types with their antitypes—promises and fulfillments are linked. Such typological connections are made clear by textual and historical connections that are developed both within the OT itself and then from the OT to the NT.

The kingdom of God. For example, when Jesus arrives on the historical scene, the eschatological promises of God to David and Israel concerning his kingdom rule have not yet been fulfilled. In fact, Israel had long been under their enemies' rule. What the NT writers repeatedly demonstrate, however, is that the various streams of God's eschatological promises reach their fulfillment in the living waters of the true King, Jesus Christ. For example, Luke records Jesus quoting Isa. 61:1–2, a passage that predicts a time when God will break into history to establish his kingdom. He says, "The Spirit of the Lord is upon me, because he has anointed me to proclaim good news to the poor. He has sent me to proclaim liberty to the captives and recovering of sight to the blind, to set at liberty those who are oppressed, to proclaim the year of the Lord's favor" (4:18–19 ESV). Jesus then declares that the time of fulfillment is now: "Today this Scripture has been fulfilled in your hearing" (4:21). Whereas Mark describes Jesus's message in terms of the nearness of the kingdom (1:14–15), Luke stresses the nearness of the person. In other words, with the king comes the kingdom. Jesus is saying to his hometown audience that the time they have been longing for is now here, and it is found in him.

Furthermore, the signs that the kingdom of God has arrived in the person and mission of Jesus are numerous. For example, Jesus casts out demons (Matt. 12:28; Luke 11:20), demonstrates victory over Satan (Luke 10:18), performs miracles (Matt. 11:2–5), bestows forgiveness (Mark 2:10; cf. Isa. 33:24; Mic. 7:18–20; Zech. 13:1), and proclaims that the eschatological promises of the kingdom have come (Matt. 11:5; Mark 1:15). In fact, the position of Mark 1:15 within the structure of Mark's Gospel indicates that the proclamation of the kingdom of God is at the heart of Jesus's preaching. Luke teaches the presence of the kingdom when he recounts how the Pharisees ask Jesus when the kingdom of God will come. Jesus responds by saying, "The kingdom of God is not coming in ways that can be observed, nor will they say, 'Look, here it is!' or 'There!' for behold, the kingdom of God is in the midst of you" (Luke 17:20–21). Instead of looking for outward signs of the presence of a primarily political kingdom, Jesus is saying that the Pharisees ought to realize that the kingdom of God is presently in their midst, in the person of Jesus himself, and that faith in him is necessary for entrance into it.

Outside of the Gospels, the NT also confirms the arrival of the kingdom. In Acts, the references to the kingdom at the beginning and end (1:3, 6; 28:23, 31), the emphasis on the comprehensive teaching of the kingdom attached to these references, the explanation of the kingdom by Jesus to his disciples, and the fact that Luke ends on the subject of the kingdom of God collectively show that these verses frame the entirety of Acts and serve as a hermeneutical lens through which to interpret it. Likewise, Paul demonstrates the inbreaking of the kingdom as a result of the rule and reign of the risen and redeeming Christ (e.g., Rom. 14:17; 1 Cor. 4:19–20; 15:20–28; Col. 1:13–14), and that those who inherit the kingdom will evidence it in the present (e.g., 1 Cor. 4:20–21; Gal. 5:21; Eph. 5:5). Indeed, God has fulfilled his promises to the fathers and to David, from whom "God has brought to Israel a Savior, Jesus, as he promised" (Acts 13:23 ESV). And this Savior brings his saving blessings not only to Israel but also to the nations (Acts 13:46–47). Believers in Christ are a new creation (2 Cor. 5:17), which has broken into the present as a result of the cross of Christ (Gal. 6:14–15), yet they live in the present evil age (Gal. 1:4; Rom. 8:18–25) and await the resurrection of their bodies in the future (2 Cor. 5:1–10). In Hebrews, believers have presently received the kingdom that cannot be shaken, but a day is coming when things on earth and heaven will be shaken and removed, and the consummation of God's purposes will be complete (Heb. 12:26–28).

It appears throughout the NT, then, that God's kingdom has finally arrived in the person and finished work of Jesus, through whom blessings are received. Yet, the fulfillment takes place in a surprising way, for God's saving promises are inaugurated but not yet consummated. That is, the kingdom of God is already but not yet here. For example, in Matt. 6:10 Jesus instructs his disciples to pray, "Your kingdom come, your will be done, on earth as it is in heaven." Also, those who do the will of God will enter into the kingdom (Matt. 7:21), but the ones who do not will enter into judgment (Matt. 7:22–23). The parables of the sower, mustard seed, and leaven (Matt. 13; cf. Mark 4; Luke 8) are explicitly presented as revealing a mystery—namely, how Jesus's kingdom teaching encompasses more than a single catastrophic event. The spiritual kingdom is present because the King-Messiah is present, but his reign will not be fully and physically established until his second coming.

Likewise, Paul depicts the kingdom as both present and future. He is confident that the Lord will ultimately rescue him and bring him safely into his kingdom (2 Tim. 4:18). He also believes that the unrighteous will not enter the kingdom of God (1 Cor. 6:9). The future tense of the verbs indicates that Paul is referring to the future kingdom. In 2 Pet. 1:11 the readers are exhorted to cultivate godly qualities so that "there will be richly provided for you an entrance into the eternal kingdom of our Lord and Savior Jesus Christ" (ESV). And finally, Revelation looks forward to the end of history when Christ will return, reward the faithful, and punish the disobedient. Therefore, Christians should be challenged and encouraged to live faithfully in the present (2:1–3:22) and run with endurance, even in the face of persecution (1:9; 13:10; 14:12).

The NT message of the inaugurated yet not finally consummated kingdom as a result of the life, death, resurrection, and ascension of Christ is crucial in understanding the fulfillment of OT promises. Jesus's inauguration of the kingdom is an important stage in the advancement of God's rule, set in motion from the time of Adam and Eve's exile from the garden. Through the covenants, promises, and mighty acts of the Lord to and through Israel, God displays his authority and reestablishes his kingdom at various points. Through the prophets he promises a future time in which he will decisively break into history and perform a new saving work for his people. The calling of Abraham, the exodus, the conquest, the allotment of land, the Davidic dynasty, the temple, and the restoration from exile display progressive fulfillments of his kingdom promises. However, with the coming of Jesus, the Son of God, the Word-become-flesh, God climactically and decisively breaks into history and inaugurates his kingdom program until the day when the kingdom of the world will become the kingdom of the Lord and of his Christ, "and he will reign for ever and ever" (Rev. 11:15).

A new covenant. The OT also promises a new covenant (Jer. 31:31–34; cf. Deut. 30:6; Isa. 24:5; 42:6; 54:13; 55:1–5; Ezek. 11:19–20; 34:20–31; 37:15–28; 39:29; Joel 2:28–29). The new covenant would have a purpose similar to the Mosaic covenant—that is, to bring the covenant blessings back into the present experience of Israel. The previous covenants, then, culminate in the new covenant, for this covenant gathers up the promises made throughout the OT (e.g., an inheritance; a divine-human relationship; offspring; blessing on a national and international scale). Hence, there are certain elements of continuity between the prior covenants and the new covenant. For example, the latter includes the presently divided "house of Israel" and "house of Judah" (i.e., it projects a unified people; Jer. 31:31), emphasizes obedience (Jer. 31:33; Ezek. 36:25–27; Isa. 42:1–4; 51:4–8), focuses on offspring (Jer. 31:36; 33:22; Ezek. 36:37)—particularly a royal seed (Jer. 33:15–26; Ezek. 37:24–25; Isa. 55:3)—and, in the end, will fulfill the repeated covenant refrain: "I will be their God, and they will be my people" (Jer. 31:33; cf. 7:23; 11:4; 24:7; 30:22; 31:1; 32:38; Exod. 29:45; Lev. 26:12; Ezek. 11:20; 37:23, 27). Therefore, though it introduces something new in God's purposes for his people, it must not be viewed in opposition to the previous covenants.

Despite its continuity, however, it is not *entirely* like the previous (Mosaic) covenant (Jer. 31:32). For example, the new covenant will secure the radical transformation of the heart (Jer. 31:33a; Ezek. 36:26), a more intimate relationship with God in which they will all know Yahweh (Jer. 31:33b–34; Ezek. 36:27), and an inviolability unlike the Mosaic covenant (Jer. 31:32). All of these new-covenant blessings will come because God will provide full and final forgiveness of sin (Jer. 31:34; Ezek. 36:29, 33). Through the new covenant, then, God will fulfill his promises and secure his eschatological purposes for his people and the world.

The new covenant makes clear that God is determined to finish what he began in the previous covenants—namely, to make a people for himself and reverse the curses of Eden. Although the new covenant is often cast in national terms (e.g., Jer. 31:36–40; 33:6–16; Ezek. 36:24–38; 37:11–28), it will also have international significance (e.g., Jer. 4:2; 12:16–17; Ezek. 16:53–63; 36:36; 37:28). Its universal scope is depicted most clearly in Isaiah (42:6–7; 49:6; 55:3–5; 56:4–8; 66:18–24). Furthermore, the new covenant projects the ultimate fulfillment of the divine promises to make a worldwide people for God onto a suffering servant—an obedient Israelite who will serve a corporate Israel—in a new heavens and new earth (Isa. 65:17; 66:22). For example, Isa. 42:6–7 says that the Lord will give his servant "as a covenant for the people, a light for the nations, to open the eyes that are blind, to bring out the prisoners from the dungeon, from the prison those who sit in darkness" (ESV). Furthermore, Ezek. 37:26–27 reveals that Yahweh will *multiply* the nation, which alludes to the promises to Abraham to multiply his offspring. Thus, the new covenant is presented as the climactic and ultimate fulfillment of the covenants that God established with the patriarchs, the nation of Israel, and David / David's son (Isa. 9:6–7; 11:1–10; Jer. 23:5–6; 33:14–26; Ezek. 34:23–24; 37:24–28) to multiply and fill the earth with his people, both Jew and gentile. This fulfillment would come through a covenant enacted on better promises because of the One—the obedient Son—who will fulfill it (Heb. 8–10).

The new covenant also promises a place for God's people. In other words, this new, transformed people will return to a better land. For example, Isaiah brings into focus God's cosmological intentions for his creation just as he had designed in the garden of Eden. Isaiah 65:17, for instance, reveals that God will "create new heavens and a new earth, and the former things shall not be remembered or come into mind" (ESV). This prophetic declaration is nothing short of a profound hope of a return to an Edenic paradise. Furthermore, the ensuing picture of the new heavens and new earth reads like a reversal of the devastating effects brought into creation by Adam's sin: there will be no more weeping (v. 19) and no more death (v. 20), they will subdue the land and enjoy the fruit of its bountiful provision (v. 21), exercise dominion (vv. 22, 25), and fill the earth with their descendants (v. 23). Likewise, Hosea 2:16–23 says that God will forge a new relationship with his people who were formerly "Not my people" (v. 23), and creation will be renewed such that his people will know him and experience eternal peace. This new world reflects both the former splendor of Eden as well as the restored and expanded future reality of the new creation that will "remain" forever. Thus, the new covenant in the end will "Edenize" the entire earth and will serve as the means through which God will bring his people back into his kingdom forever.

When it comes to the issue of land, however, dispensationalists arrive at a different conclusion by appealing to a so-called literal hermeneutic. How, then, should one make sense of their argument? To begin, one must know what constitutes dispensational theology in order to understand how it reaches its conclusions. While dispensationalism is not monolithic, all varieties of dispensationalism derive a biblical theology from an interconnected set of convictions (see Feinberg). First, the sine qua non of dispensationalism is the way it distinguishes between the nation of Israel and the church. Second, dispensationalists affirm that if "an OT prophecy or promise is made unconditionally to a given people and is still unfulfilled to them even in the NT era, then the prophecy must still be fulfilled to them" (Feinberg, 76). Third, dispensationalism believes that proper hermeneutics require "literal" interpretation by employing a limited grammatical-historical approach that focuses on what the human author intended. That is, the NT does not reinterpret or spiritualize the promises to Israel such that they apply to the church. John Feinberg (76) writes, "Lack of repetition in the NT does not render an OT teaching inoperative during the NT era so long as nothing explicitly or implicitly cancels it." Feinberg's contention applies to typology as well. In other words, both type and antitype must have their own meaning even if they have a typological relation to the other. As a result, the NT antitype, or fulfillment, does not cancel the meaning of the OT type (79). Thus, dispensationalists prioritize the OT above the NT (Vlach, *Dispensationalism*, 17). Furthermore, dispensationalists distinguish themselves from nondispensationalists by insisting that the OT be taken on its own terms rather than reinterpreted in the light of the NT. So, for example, if God promised to Israel a return to the land, or a rebuilding of the temple with the reinstitution of sacrifices, and it is still unfulfilled to them in the NT, then God *must* fulfill that promise in the future. For dispensationalists, then, God demonstrates his faithfulness by keeping his promises to the nation of Israel.

Dispensationalists contend that if God's promises to Israel are unconditional, then national Israel alone must ultimately fulfill them in the future, regardless of how the NT fulfills the OT promises (Feinberg, 77–83). However, some progressive dispensationalists, who go beyond earlier dispensationalists in their understanding of typology, allow the church to typologically fulfill some of the OT promises for Israel. Nevertheless, they assert that, even though the antitype in a real sense fulfills the type, this fulfillment is only partial. That is, though the church initially fulfills OT promises spiritually, it does not receive the physical promises to Israel. For example, on the issue of land, the progressive dispensationalist view maintains that, although some spiritual aspects are applied to the church, God will still fulfill the territorial aspects of his promise to national Israel in the future. Therefore, the original promises to the nation of Israel must still be kept, even if they apply in partial ways to the church.

Does this view correctly understand how Christ fulfills the OT promises? Although progressive dispensationalism should be commended for attempting to apply the inaugurated eschatology of the NT, for various reasons this view does not correctly account for the already/not-yet character of the kingdom or the nature of typological fulfillment in Scripture. First, the way they apply inaugurated eschatology is not accurate *at this point*. While there is an already/not-yet nature to the kingdom in the NT, this eschatological perspective does not *merely* mean that part of the kingdom is present now with the church and part of it (i.e., the physical land) will be present later for national Israel. Instead, the NT shows that Christ has *already* fulfilled *all* of God's saving promises and that these promises are expanding where Christ is present—in the church now, which is one new "man" composed of both Jews and gentiles in Christ (Eph. 2:11–22), and finally in the consummated new creation.

Second, the NT presents Christ's person and work as both fulfilling and completing OT types. It is not that the church simply replaces Israel. Rather, Christ represents and fulfills the identity, purpose, and mission of Israel as the true obedient Son, temple, vine, prophet, priest, and king—and then bestows blessings to his people, believing Jews and gentiles alike. Hence, all who are included *in Christ* receive every spiritual blessing in Christ as they await their future inheritance, the new creation. In other words, believing Israel receives not less but more: the whole earth! (This point leaves open the possibility of a future salvation for ethnic Jews [see Rom. 9–11].)

This interpretation aligns with the way the Bible consistently treats types as eschatologically escalating or intensifying in the progression from type to antitype and from promise to fulfillment. OT types do not merely correspond analogically to the NT antitype, but they serve as "a shadow of the good things to come" (Heb. 10:1; cf. Col. 2:17). At this point, then, though dispensationalists agree that the promises to Israel are fulfilled in the new heaven and new earth, they still want to maintain that God will fulfill his nationalistic promises to Israel by supplying a geopolitical state to his redeemed Jewish people separate from gentile Christians in the millennial age. But this is incorrect for two reasons.

First, God fulfills all his promises in relation to Christ and gives them to believing Jews and gentiles *equally* as the church (Eph. 2:11–22). Second, other types such as prophets, Levitical priests, Davidic kings, circumcision, temple, and sacrifices are not waiting for God to fulfill them in the consummation but instead are already fulfilled, having reached their terminus and telos in Christ. They have already arrived at their divinely appointed end, regardless of the already/not-yet aspect of Christ's work. In other words, when Christ comes, *he* as the antitype is the true Son, prophet, priest, king, vine, temple, covenant, and sacrifice. And such realities should inform our understanding of the promises of land as well.

Conclusion

In the end, the final place of the kingdom—the new heaven and new earth—described in Rev. 21–22 appears as the consummation of complex imagery that reaches all the way back to Genesis. This consummation depicts the new heaven and new earth as a paradisiacal new Eden, new Jerusalem, and cosmological temple that is, in the climax of the covenants, filled with God's presence. Moreover, the end also relates to Israel's universalized promises that reach back past Abraham all the way to Eden. In fulfillment of the promise to Abraham that "in you all the families of the earth shall be blessed" (Gen. 12:3 ESV), ransomed people from every tribe, tongue, people, and nation (Rev. 5:9) are restored to a new creation with its new Jerusalem reminiscent of Eden. In this new creation, the geographical boundaries of the land expand to the entire new creation in ways that remarkably reflect the visions of the prophets such as Isaiah, Jeremiah, and Ezekiel. Revelation 21–22 interprets the future fulfillment of the prophets by collapsing temple, city, and land into one paradisiacal end-time picture portraying the final reality of God's covenant presence with his people. The final chapters of Revelation, then, describe in glorious detail the culmination of all God's covenant promises brought about by a better King who wins a better creation for his people.

See also OT Use of the OT: Comparison with the NT Use of the OT; Typology; *Apostolic Hermeneutics articles*

Bibliography. Beale, G. K., *Handbook on the New Testament Use of the Old Testament* (Baker Academic, 2012); Beale, *A New Testament Biblical Theology* (Baker Academic, 2011); Beale, ed., *The Right Doctrine from the Wrong Texts?* (Baker, 1994); Beale, G. K., and B. Gladd, *Hidden but Now Revealed* (IVP Academic, 2014); Blaising, C. A., "Dispensationalism," in *Dispensationalism, Israel and the Church*, ed. C. A. Blaising and D. L. Bock (Zondervan, 1992), 13–34; Carson, D. A., "Recent Developments in the Doctrine of Scripture," in *Hermeneutics, Authority, and Canon*, ed. D. A. Carson and J. D. Woodbridge (1986; repr., Wipf & Stock, 2005); Feinberg, J. S., "Systems of Discontinuity," in *Continuity and Discontinuity*, ed. J. S. Feinberg (Crossway, 1988), 63–86; France, R. T., *Matthew: Evangelist and Teacher* (1989; repr., Wipf & Stock, 2004); Gentry, P. J., and S. J. Wellum, *Kingdom through Covenant*, 2nd ed. (Crossway, 2018); Karlberg, M. W., "The Significance of Israel in Biblical Typology," *JETS* 31 (1988): 257–69; Lints, R., *The Fabric of Theology* (Eerdmans, 1993); Moo, D. J., and A. D. Naselli, "The Problem of the New Testament's Use of the Old Testament," in *The Enduring Authority of the Christian Scriptures*, ed. D. A. Carson (Eerdmans, 2016); Poythress, V. S., *Understanding Dispensationalism*, 2nd ed. (P&R, 1994); Vanhoozer, K. J., *Is There a Meaning in This Text?* (Zondervan, 1998); Vlach, M. J., *Dispensationalism* (Theological Studies Press, 2008); Vlach, "What Is Dispensationalism?," in *Christ's Prophetic Plans*, ed. J. MacArthur and R. Mayhue (Moody, 2012), 19–38; Woodbridge, J. D., *Biblical Authority* (Zondervan, 1982).

OREN MARTIN

Life *See* Creation

Lord's Supper *See* Feasts and Festivals

Love

Love in the OT

Genesis. Although the word "love" is absent in Gen. 1–2, God's love shines in creation. We see it in his making Adam and Eve in his image, giving them dominion, and pronouncing "all that he had made . . . very good" (1:27–28, 31). The psalmist declares, "The earth is filled with your love, LORD" (Ps. 119:64). Although it too lacks the word, Gen. 3:15 displays God's redemptive love. No sooner had Adam and Eve sinned than God promised to crush the head of "that ancient serpent called the devil, or Satan" (Rev. 12:9). God's love appears when Noah finds "favor in the eyes of the LORD" (Gen. 6:8) and after the flood, when God appoints the rainbow to highlight his promise of forbearance with humanity (9:8–17). God chooses Abraham, an idolater, and ultimately makes him the father of believing Jews and gentiles (Rom. 4:11–12). God's covenant with Israel is similar to other ancient Near Eastern treaties in form (Exod. 20:2–17), but it is also "startling because no other nation in the ancient world is known to have claimed a covenant with its deity" (House, 117). In love God pledges to be God to Abraham and his descendants (Gen. 17).

Exodus. This book is replete with God's love. "Probably no event in Israel's history rivals the exodus for its theological importance" (House, 89). The exodus reveals God's uniqueness, greatness, sovereignty, justice, power, and also his deep love for the patriarchs and their descendants (Exod. 12–15). Moreover, the exodus "acts as a chief paradigm for salvation, as evidence of God's love for Israel and as a spur toward loving obedience on the part of God's people in the rest of Scripture" (House, 89). The Ten Commandments reveal God's holiness and justice, *and* his love. He loved the Israelites enough to be their God, to redeem them from Egyptian bondage (Exod. 20:2), and to jealously guard their love for him alone (vv. 3–6). All the Ten Commandments summon the people to love their Redeemer and Lord wholeheartedly: the first four do so directly, and the last six demand love for God by loving neighbors (Matt. 22:37–40). In Exod. 34:6–7 God reveals his name and character. This revelation profoundly affects the rest of the OT (e.g., Neh. 9:17; Ps. 86:15; Joel 2:13; Jon. 4:2). He is "the LORD, the LORD, the compassionate and gracious God, slow to anger, abounding in love and faithfulness, maintaining love to thousands, and forgiving wickedness, rebellion and sin. Yet he does not leave the guilty unpunished." Note how God's love is consistent with his wrath and judgment, as he is slow to wrath and does punish the guilty. God's love is not equal in proportion with his wrath, however, as he abounds in love but is slow to wrath. Further, his judgment extends to a few generations, whereas his love extends to a thousand generations.

Leviticus. Moses teaches Israel to be holy as God is holy (Lev. 19:2). Living according to God's holiness requires them to "love your neighbor as yourself" (v. 18). Indeed, central to being God's holy people is living in love. Such love includes very ordinary tasks: leaving gleanings for the poor and sojourners when harvesting, dealing honestly with one another, paying workers on time, showing kindness to those who have disabilities, defending the lives and reputations of neighbors, and refusing to bear grudges (vv. 9–18).

Numbers. God's love abounds in the priestly blessing of his people, identifying them as belonging to the Lord: "The LORD bless you and keep you; the LORD make his face shine on you and be gracious to you; the LORD turn his face toward you and give you peace" (Num. 6:24–26).

Deuteronomy. Moses makes clear in Deuteronomy that God's choice of Israel is based solely on his love. "Israel was to love Yahweh because he first loved her" (Waltke, 509). "The LORD did not set his affection on you and choose you because you were more numerous than other peoples, for you were the fewest of all peoples. But it was because the LORD loved you and kept the oath he swore to your ancestors that he brought you out with a mighty hand and redeemed you from the land of slavery" (Deut. 7:7–8). God chooses Israel alone "out of all the peoples on the face of the earth" (7:6; 14:2) because of his great love for them (4:37; 10:15). Moreover, God's love is ongoing. Bruce Waltke (508) observes, "Like a father, he cares for Israel. He fights for his firstborn son (Deut. 3:22), going before Israel (1:30), driving out the nations (4:38). . . . He provides for and protects Israel (11:10–12). . . . He bears them (1:31) and disciplines them (8:5)."

William Dyrness cites the classic passage teaching that because of God's faithfulness to Israel, he expects undivided love in return. Deuteronomy 6:5 commands "a love arising from the whole person . . . which attaches itself to God in a personal way and which naturally issues in a life of loyalty and commitment" (Dyrness, 163). Further, "the law has significance only within the framework of relationships already established by covenant" (Dumbrell, 123). Thus, love is "an active commitment arising out of God's prior choice" expressed "in outward conformity to what God requires of Israel . . . from a rightly aligned heart" (124–25). Of course, this applies to individuals. But Paul House (171) rightly says that Deuteronomy "stresses love for a God who creates a holy community. Yahweh creates the community through election, deliverance, guidance and revelation, all of which show that the Lord loves Israel."

Historical books. Nehemiah entreats God on the basis of his love for Israel: "Because of your great compassion you did not abandon them in the wilderness" (Neh. 9:19) but guided, taught, and gave them manna and water. In disobedience Israel had failed to drive out the Canaanites from the promised land. This fulfilled God's prediction that his people would forsake him and embrace Canaanite gods. Respectively, Judges and Ruth illumine the absence and presence of love for God and others. Judges, filled with Israel's spiritual adultery, tells how Israel's misplaced love leads to its "Canaanization." By contrast, Boaz and Ruth display love for God and others (Ruth 2:10–12). In grace God includes their son in the line of David and Christ (4:21–22; Matt. 1:1–16).

Key historical narratives tell how "out of love for David the Lord places his son on the throne, and out of love for God Solomon fulfills his father's dream of a temple for Yahweh" (House, 524). God makes a covenant with David, promising to care for Judah and foretelling the eternal reign of David's descendent (2 Sam. 7:13–16; cf. 1 Kings 15:3–5). Spurning Yahweh's love and covenant, Jeroboam establishes his own religion opposed to that in Jerusalem (1 Kings 12:25–33). The sins of the Northern Kingdom's later kings are gauged by how much they emulate Jeroboam (e.g., 15:34). His idolatry eventually brings exile (2 Kings 17:21–23). Contrasting Joshua's opening chapters and 2 Kings' closing ones is tragic: In the former Israel seizes Jericho by God's power as they start to possess the promised land. In the latter the Babylonians seize the land.

Psalms. Israel's inspired songs sing of God's love for all his creatures (Ps. 145:9–16), all humans (8:3–4), and especially his covenant people (103:8–13). Indeed, "You, Lord, are forgiving and good, abounding in *love* to all who call to you" (86:5). The word "love" here is *ḥesed*, a key word used over one hundred times in the Psalms. "Israel experienced God not only as high and lifted up, as awful in holiness, but also as turning toward them in loving-kindness." *Ḥesed* "lies at the heart of the biblical revelation of God" (Dyrness, 58). *Ḥesed* is included in God's self-revelation in Exod. 34:6 and occurs in every line of Ps. 136: "His *love* endures forever." It communicates God's loyal love to his covenant people. God requires *ḥesed* of them as well (Duguid): "And what does the LORD require of you? To act justly and to love *mercy* [*ḥesed*] and to walk humbly with your God" (Mic. 6:8).

Song of Solomon. "No Old Testament text approximates the Genesis situation [Gen. 2:25] as closely as do the lovers' statements in Song of Solomon . . . to the extent that one can draw analogies between God's love for Israel and the love reflected" here (House, 465). The purity of love in the Song contrasts vividly with Israel's adulterous love for God in Hosea 1–3.

Isaiah. In spite of Israel's unfaithfulness to Yahweh and rejection of his prophets, his love remains steadfast: "Though the mountains be shaken and the hills be removed, yet my unfailing love for you will not be shaken" (Isa. 54:10; cf. 63:7). Though Israel feels forsaken by the Lord, it is not so. "Can a mother forget the baby at her breast and have no compassion on the child she has borne? Though she may forget, I will not forget you!" (49:15). Indeed, "the return [to the land in 539 BC] will prove God's love for Israel" (House, 207).

Jeremiah. God sends Jeremiah to give Judah another chance to repent and be spared captivity (Jer. 18:7–8) but the people refuse. In the midst of Jeremiah's severe messages, he recalls God's comforting words, "I have loved you with an everlasting love; I have drawn you with unfailing kindness" (31:3). God opposes his rebellious people but still loves them. "Is not Ephraim my dear son, the child in whom I delight? Though I often speak against him, I still remember him. Therefore my heart yearns for him; I have great compassion for him" (31:20). Despite Judah's covenant breaking and coming Babylonian captivity, God promises to make a new covenant with them. Unlike the Mosaic covenant that Israel broke, God will fulfill the new covenant by giving his people new obedient hearts, forgiving their sins, and bringing them to know him (31:31–34). Indeed, the new covenant "will occur because of the love Yahweh has had for Israel from their first days" (House, 318).

Ezekiel. The prophet Ezekiel, in exile in Babylon because of Israel's sins, reveals God's love: "As surely as I live, declares the Sovereign LORD, I take no pleasure in the death of the wicked, but rather that they turn from their ways and live. Turn! Turn from your evil ways! Why will you die, people of Israel?" (Ezek. 33:11). "As the prophets have shown decisively, exile cannot separate the faithful from Yahweh's covenant love" (House, 417).

Hosea. "In the prophets—especially Hosea—the expression of love reaches its highest expression" (Dyrness, 60). "The canon saves the most heartrending evidence for Yahweh's covenant love and remnant faithfulness until now" (House, 350). No prophet ever heard harder words than Hosea, "Go, show your love to your wife again, though she is . . . an adulteress. Love her as the LORD loves the Israelites, though they turn to other gods" (3:1). House (348) explains, "By loving this woman despite her failure to remain faithful to him, Hosea's marriage to Gomer demonstrates for Israel the persevering love of God for a constantly straying Israel." Hosea conveys God's strong emotion, "My heart is changed within me; all my compassion is aroused. I will not carry out my fierce anger, nor will I turn and devastate Ephraim. For I am God, and not man—the Holy One among you. I will not come in wrath" (11:8–9 AT).

Jonah. The book of Jonah communicates the Lord's love and mercy toward all nations. Jonah's refusal to obey the Lord and preach to Israel's political enemies is the foil for this message. When the Lord spares Jonah and he preaches to the Assyrians, things turn out as he had feared (Jon. 4:2). "God saw . . . how they turned from their evil ways," and "he had compassion and did not bring upon them the destruction he had threatened" (3:10 AT).

Micah and Zephaniah. Micah and Zephaniah celebrate God's love and forgiveness for wayward Israel, "Who is a God like you, who pardons sin and forgives the transgression of the remnant of his inheritance? You do not stay angry forever but delight to show mercy. You will again have compassion on us; you will tread our sins underfoot and hurl all our iniquities into the depths of the sea" (Mic. 7:18–19). "The LORD your God is with you, the Mighty Warrior who saves. He will take great delight in you; in his love he will no longer rebuke you, but will rejoice over you with singing" (Zeph. 3:17).

Love in the NT

When the NT proclaims God's love, it is not changing the subject of the biblical story. "The careful reader of the Old Testament is fully prepared for the New Testament's absorption with the love of God at the cross of Jesus" (Ortlund, 49).

Synoptic Gospels. Jesus reveals the love of God as never before. God shows kindness to all humans, for he gives sunshine and rain to all (Matt. 5:45). Ladd (82) points out "a new element in [Jesus's] teaching about God, namely God is the seeking God." We see this in Jesus's parables of the lost sheep, lost coin, and lost son in Luke 15, which reveal God's persistent love. Jesus shows God's love for the unlovely, including Zacchaeus, a wealthy chief tax collector, who welcomes Jesus into his house. After pronouncing Zacchaeus saved, Jesus proclaims his gracious motive for ministry: "The Son of Man came to seek and to save the lost" (Luke 19:10). With OT imagery, Matthew describes leaderless people whom Jesus loves: "When he saw the crowds, he had compassion on them, because they were harassed and helpless, like sheep without a shepherd" (Matt. 9:36; cf. Num. 27:17; 1 Kings 22:17). The Father intensely loves his "little ones" (Matt. 18:10; Schreiner, 132). In love, Jesus introduces a way to address God—as "Abba" or Father (Mark 14:36). In a parable, Jesus teaches that God has mercy on the humble. God rejects the Pharisee who exalts himself but accepts the tax collector who cries, "God, have mercy on me, a sinner" (Luke 18:13). Love for God is also a command, as Jesus summarizes OT ethics, "Love the Lord your God with all your heart and with all your soul and with all your mind. . . . Love your neighbor as yourself" (Matt. 22:37, 39). Further, Jesus clarifies a "neighbor" to mean anyone in need (Luke 10:25–37), even enemies (Matt. 5:44). God's love includes the Father's love for the Son, proclaimed at Jesus's baptism and transfiguration (Matt. 3:17; 17:5). And Jesus teaches that "the love of God cannot be understood apart from the holiness and the judgment of God" (Schreiner, 126), which prepares us for the doctrine of Christ's atonement.

John. The love of God shines brightly in the Fourth Gospel. As in the Synoptics, the Father loves the Son, but here this truth is on Jesus's lips: "My Father loves me" (10:17; cf. 15:9). Jesus prays, "Father, . . . you loved me before the creation of the world" (17:24). A reciprocal truth is that Jesus loves the Father and obeys him (10:18), even to the cross (14:30–31). Left to themselves people do not love God (5:42); rather, they "loved darkness instead of light because their deeds were evil" (3:19). Nevertheless, God loves the world, which hates him, and gives his Son to save all who believe (3:16). Jesus loves his own to the end, laying down his life for them (13:1; 15:13). Jesus shares the Father's love with them (15:9), and the Father himself loves them (16:27; 17:23). Although before salvation people are loved by the world, once they come to know Christ the world hates them (15:19). Jesus insists, "If you love me, keep my commands" (14:15). Love for Jesus issues in obedience (14:21, 23; 15:10), and those who disobey him show that they do not love him (14:24). Disciples who love and obey Jesus will know special fellowship with the Father and the Son (14:21, 23). "Jesus' whole ethic in John is summed up in love" (Ladd, 279). "Jesus models sacrificial and humble love in washing the disciples' feet" and chiefly in dying for them (13:12–17, 34–35; Schreiner, 706). Akin to the Synoptics' teaching, "Love your neighbor as yourself," Jesus teaches in John's Gospel, "A new command I give you: Love one another" (13:34; 15:17). Jesus's love for his people is the measure of this love (13:34; 15:12). Loving obedience to Jesus makes God's love known to others (13:35). "The disciples, says Jesus, should love one another because doing so will enhance their mission to the world" (13:35; Thielman, 208).

Paul. God's love is trinitarian. The Father loves his Son (Col. 1:13). And the persons of the Trinity love us: the Father (2 Thess. 2:16), the Son (Eph. 5:25), and the Holy Spirit (2 Cor. 13:14). God's love is boundless; it cannot be measured, though the apostle tries (Eph. 3:17–19).

God's love is undeserved: "But God demonstrates his own love for us in this: While we were still sinners, Christ died for us" (Rom. 5:8). Moreover, God's love for the spiritually dead is the epitome of grace (Eph. 2:4–5). "God's choosing or electing people to salvation is often attributed to his love [as we saw in Deut. 7:7–8]. Paul draws on the OT here" (Schreiner, 341). Paul writes, "In love he predestined us for adoption" (Eph. 1:4–5). Again, "For we know, brothers and sisters loved by God, that he has chosen you" (1 Thess. 1:4).

God's love leads to our salvation. Love is the motive of the Father in sending his Son to the cross for us (Rom. 5:8). It is also the Son's motive in dying in our place (Gal. 2:20). God's motive in applying salvation is the same—"But because of his great love for us, God, who is rich in mercy, made us alive with Christ even when we were dead in transgressions" (Eph. 2:4–5; cf. Titus 3:4–7). God's love keeps us saved to the end: "For I am convinced that neither death nor life, neither angels nor demons, neither the present nor the future, nor any powers, neither height nor depth, nor anything else in all creation, will be able to separate us from the love of God that is in Christ Jesus our Lord" (Rom. 8:35–39).

Love characterizes the church. The apostle rejoices to hear of the churches' love: "We always thank God, the Father of our Lord Jesus Christ, when we pray for you, because we have heard of your faith in Christ Jesus and of the love you have for all God's people" (Col. 1:3–4). It is God who teaches his people to love, and Paul prays for love to increase: "Now about your love for one another we do not need to write to you, for you yourselves have been taught by God to love each other. And in fact, you do love all of God's family throughout Macedonia. Yet we urge you, brothers and sisters, to do so more and more" (1 Thess. 4:9–10).

Love is the focus in the Christian life, for Paul enjoins believers to bear "with one another in love" (Eph. 4:2), to speak "the truth in love" (4:15), and to "walk in the way of love" (5:2). Christ is our example of love (Eph. 5:2, 25), and love is the first fruit that the Spirit produces in us (Gal. 5:22). The command to love one another is central to Pauline ethics (Lev. 19:18; Rom. 13:8–10; Gal. 5:13–15).

Love is only as good as its object. Paul warns of misplaced loves, including love of self (2 Tim. 3:2), Demas's love of "this world" (4:10), and "the love of money," which "is a root of all kinds of evil" (1 Tim. 6:10).

Love propels evangelism (2 Cor. 5:14). Paul thanks Christ for appointing him "to his service" even though he persecuted the church. Christ poured out grace, faith, and love "abundantly" on Paul, who consequently proclaimed "Christ Jesus came into the world to save sinners—of whom I am the worst" (1 Tim. 1:12–15).

The most celebrated passage on love in Paul is 1 Cor. 13. "The chapter is primarily about living in Christian community in a way that glorifies God, and that is by learning to treat other members of Christ's body the way God has treated us—with self-sacrificing, other-oriented love" (Ciampa and Rosner, 619). Without love the spiritual gifts are useless (vv. 1–3), and only love, not the gifts, endures (vv. 8–12). In between Paul personifies love to describe its key attributes (vv. 4–7). Love is patient, enduring difficult people. Love is kind and not jealous, since it wants the best for others. Love is not self-promoting or proud, but humble and servant-oriented. Love is pure, clean, and holy. Love does not insist on its own way but focuses on how to generously bless others. Love is neither irritable nor resentful but is long-suffering and forgiving. Love advocates for justice and endorses truth. Love bears, believes, and hopes, refusing to be suspicious, cynical, or pessimistic about others. And love keeps on loving, persevering in relationships because people matter. In the context of frustrating circumstances and people, love appears as patience. In the context of the successes of others, love does not allow envy but rejoices with those who rejoice. In the context of one's own successes, love refrains from self-promotion and practices humility. In the context of the sin of another, love appears as forgiveness and not keeping track of wrongs. In each case, God's people love, genuinely desiring the good of others and serving them for their good.

Hebrews. The writer urges professing Hebrew Christians not to leave the faith because of persecution. God remembers his people's labor and love for him shown in ministry to other believers (Heb. 6:10). The writer urges his readers to persevere, remembering that "the Lord disciplines the one he loves" (12:6). The readers must "spur one another on toward love and good deeds," especially in difficult circumstances (10:24).

James. James twice describes believers as "those who love" God (1:12; 2:5). The loving God cares for the widows and orphans, and so must his people (1:26–27). "Kindness to the needy is God-like. We sustain aliens, widows, and orphans because he sustains aliens, widows, and orphans" (Doriani, 59). Further, God loves the poor and opposes partiality, and so must his people, who are to be characterized by mercy and love (2:1–13; see his use of Lev. 19:18). Indeed, true faith works. Or even better, true faith loves (2:14–26). True wisdom blesses others, showing itself in peace, mercy, considerateness, and impartiality (chap. 3). God himself is merciful and compassionate (5:11; cf. Exod. 34:6–7).

1 Peter. Peter tells of believers loving and trusting Christ, whom they have not seen (1 Pet. 1:8). They must "love one another deeply, from the heart" (1:22; cf. 4:8). Peter's "specific directives . . . summarize the pathway and beauty of love in human relationships" (Schreiner, 670).

2 Peter. Peter extols love in 2 Pet. 1:7 by putting it at the end of a list of virtues, a position showing "its status as the sum of the other virtues" (Thielman, 529). Peter recalls hearing the Father assert his love for his Son on the Mount of Transfiguration (1:17).

1 John. John teaches that "God's love, which originates in himself (4:7–8) and was manifested in his Son (9–10), is made complete in his people (12)" (Stott, 167). John stresses that "God is light" (holiness, 1:5) and "God is love" (4:8; cf. v. 16). John highlights God's initiative in loving us "by sending his Son to die in our place as an atoning sacrifice for our sin (4:10, 19)" (Thielman, 553). John exults in the magnitude of God's love: "See what great love the Father has lavished on us, that we should be called children of God!" (3:1). All who know God love their brothers and sisters in the faith; all lacking this love do not know God (2:9–11; 3:10; 4:20–21). "Love . . . is not an empty claim but an active, practical assistance of those in need" (Thielman, 553; see 3:18). Jesus is our great example of love (3:16). God assures us of salvation because God's perfect love "drives out fear" (4:17–18).

2–3 John. The false teachers fail the test of truth because they deny the incarnation. "The gospel and the other two letters provide moving expressions of the importance of the love command. Third John provides an example of this command at work" (Thielman, 568), for though Diotrephes refuses hospitality to itinerant missionaries, Gaius provides it.

Jude. "The grace of God frames Jude's letter, for he commences by reminding readers that . . . God has specially set his love upon them, and they are protected and kept from the designs of the intruders by Jesus Christ himself (Jude 1). The letter concludes with a doxology (Jude 24–25) that returns to the theme of God's sustaining love" (Schreiner, 157–58). Jude thus highlights God's grace in his letter condemning false teachers.

Revelation. Believers rejoice that Jesus loves and redeems them through his sacrifice (1:5). God loves and defends his people (20:9). Jesus loves his own enough to correct those halfhearted in their faith and invites them to repent and to fellowship with him (3:19–20). God acknowledges when people love him more than their own lives and persevere in Christ (12:11).

Synthesis

"God is love. Everything we know about him teaches us that, and every encounter we have with him expresses it. God's love for us is deep and all-embracing, but it is not the warmhearted sentimentality that often goes by the name of love today" (Bray, 17). We have seen that both Testaments highlight God's love. Along the way, three massive truths about love stand out: God's love for us, our love for God, and our love for one another. According to 1 John 4:7–12, these truths interrelate (see Morgan, "Trinity's Love").

First, God is loving (4:8). He seeks the good of others and eternally gives of himself for their good. His love is intrinsic, eternal, permanent, objective, and inseparably interrelated to all his divine attributes. It is expressed within the Trinity, as the Father loves the Son, the Son loves the Father, each loves the Spirit, and so forth (see also John 6; 10; 17).

Second, God's own trinitarian love is shared with us and leads to our love for God. God's love is especially displayed through the Father's sending his one and only Son into the world via the incarnation to be a propitiation for our sins (1 John 4:9–10). God's love enables our new life and love for God. In particular, God's love initiates our salvation (v. 10), gives rise to our new life/birth (vv. 7, 9), and leads to our love for God (vv. 7–12)—all through uniting us to Christ and his saving work.

Third, God's love for us and our love for God lead to our love for others. The Spirit gives us new life and communicates God's love through us back to God. We love God because he first loved us. That we love God shows we are born of God, as does our love for others (4:7–8). The Spirit communicates God's love *to us*; the Spirit communicates God's love *through us back to God*; and the Spirit communicates God's love *through us toward others*. The love we give ultimately flows from, reflects, and is defined by God's own love. Just as God genuinely seeks the good of others and gives himself for their good, as his people we, too, genuinely seek the good of others and give ourselves for their good. As we love, God's love is shining through us, extending his love to others, and reaching his intended goals (4:11–12). It is no wonder that John urges, "Beloved, let us love one another," and, "Beloved, if God so loved us, we also ought to love one another" (vv. 7, 11 ESV).

See also Covenant

Bibliography. Bray, G. B., *God Is Love* (Crossway, 2012); Carson, D. A., *The Difficult Doctrine of the Love of God* (Crossway, 2000); Ciampa, R. E., and B. S. Rosner, *The First Letter to the Corinthians*, PNTC (Eerdmans, 2010); Doriani, D. M., *James*, REC (P&R, 2007); Duguid, I., "Loyal-Love (Hesed)," https://www.ligonier.org/learn/articles/loyal-love-hesed/; Dumbrell, W. J., *Covenant and Creation* (Thomas Nelson, 1985); Dunn, J. D. G., *The Theology of the Apostle Paul* (Eerdmans, 1998); Dyrness, W., *Themes in Old Testament Theology* (InterVarsity, 1979); Edwards, J., *Charity and Its Fruits* (repr., Soli Deo Gloria, 2005); House, P. R., *Old Testament Theology* (InterVarsity, 1998); Ladd, G. E., *A Theology of the New Testament* (Eerdmans, 1974); Mahony, J. W., "Love in the Triune Community?," in Morgan, *The Love of God*, 95–127; Morgan, C. W., *Christian Theology*, with R. A. Peterson (B&H Academic, 2020); Morgan, "How Does the Trinity's Love Shape Our Love for One Another?," in Morgan, *The Love of God*, 129–42; Morgan, ed., *The Love of God* (Crossway, 2016); Morris, L., *Testaments of Love* (Eerdmans, 1981); Ortlund, R., Jr., "Is the God of the Old Testament a God of Love?," in Morgan, *The Love of God*, 33–49; Schreiner, T. R., *New Testament Theology* (Baker Academic, 2008); Stott, J. R. W., *The Letters of John*, TNTC (repr., Eerdmans, 1990); Thielman, F., *Theology of the New Testament* (Zondervan, 2005); Vanhoozer, K., ed., *Nothing Greater, Nothing Better* (Eerdmans, 2001):Waltke, B. K., *Old Testament Theology* (Zondervan, 2007).

CHRISTOPHER W. MORGAN

Luke, Gospel of

The importance of the OT in Luke is best illustrated by its concluding chapter, where Jesus speaks with the two disciples on their way to Emmaus and explains "beginning with Moses and all the Prophets . . . what was said in all the Scriptures concerning himself" (Luke 24:27). This statement does not merely point to the particular messianic prophecies contained in the OT but also suggests that "all the Scriptures" point toward Jesus, whose mission and significance cannot be understood apart from these writings.

The importance of the OT is also reflected in the more than thirty explicit quotations as well as hundreds of allusions contained in this Gospel (see Kimball, 206–12, who identifies 439 allusions to the OT in Luke). From the explicit quotations, Luke is clearly dependent on the LXX, though the presence of Hebrew source texts behind the traditions available to Luke in his citation of particular OT passages cannot be denied (Bock, 271). That Luke is dependent on the LXX may suggest that he is a gentile who is not able to read Hebrew. That a gentile can constantly use and interact with OT traditions may suggest that he and his audience are God-fearers (*phoboumenos ton theon; sebomenos ton theon*), a label that recurs throughout the second volume of Luke's writings (Acts 10:2, 22, 35; 13:16, 26, 50; 16:14; 17:4, 17; 18:7) and pertains to gentiles who worship God but are not full proselytes. If so, they would be familiar with the LXX either from their participation in synagogue worship or from their training in the OT (cf. Acts 17:10–15; 18:24–28). As a companion of Paul (16:10–17; 20:5–15; 21:1–18; 27:1–28:16; cf. Col. 4:14; 2 Tim. 4:11; Philem. 24), Luke may also be influenced by the apostle's handling of the

OT texts and may have access to *testimonia*—collections of OT passages on selected themes relevant for early Christian teaching and apologetics (Albl).

This survey will examine the distinct uses of the OT in the four sections of Luke before highlighting the several themes that emerge from these uses.

Luke 1–2

The Lukan birth narrative contains only one set of quotations on the faithfulness of Jesus's parents to the stipulations of the OT laws (2:23–24; cf. Exod. 13:2, 12, 15; Lev. 12:8), but the influence of the OT goes beyond these explicit quotations. First, the distinct shift from the polished Greek sentence of Luke 1:1–4 to the notable presence of Semitism in the birth narrative proper has suggested to some the presence of Semitic sources behind this narrative, though the Lukan hand can be felt throughout the section. A better explanation is to consider these as Septuagintalisms that point to an intentional imitation of the language of the Greek OT. If so, Luke is signaling to the readers to consider his work as "biblical history" that testifies to the continuation of God's redemptive work.

This continuity of the act of God is also underlined by the use of the barren-woman motif, one that appears at critical junctures in the history of Israel: Sarah (Gen. 18), Rebekah (Gen. 25), Rachel (Gen. 30), the mother of Samson (Judg. 13), and Hannah (1 Sam. 1–2). Within the OT, this motif has already been applied to Israel (cf. 1 Sam. 2:5, 9) and is further extended to the future deliverance of God's people (cf. Isa. 54:1) and to the eschatological reversal brought about by the gracious act of God. In light of the sustained interest in this motif that extends to the rabbinic period (cf. Pesiq. Rab Kah. 20.2; Callaway, 122), Luke's evocation of it at the beginning of his narrative (1:7) signals not only the continuity of God's work among his people but also the fulfillment of God's eschatological promise to Israel.

The dawn of this eschatological age is most clearly marked by the heavy saturation of prophetic activities in Luke 1–2, especially when the absence of such activities is noted in some segments of Second Temple Jewish traditions (cf. 1 Macc. 9:27; 14:41). Various individual characters, including John the Baptist (1:15), Elizabeth (1:41), Zechariah (1:67), Simeon (2:25–27), and Anna (2:36) testify to the work of this prophetic Spirit, which finds its climax in Mary's conception of the "Son of God" (1:35). The significance of the presence of these various characters is explained only in Luke's second volume, when Peter testifies to the arrival of the eschatological age: "In the last days, God says, I will pour out my Spirit on all people. Your sons and daughters will prophesy, your young men will see visions, your old men will dream dreams. Even on my servants, both men and women, I will pour out my Spirit in those days, and they will prophesy" (Acts 2:17–18 [Joel 2:28–29]).

Luke 3:1–9:50

Two lengthy quotations from Isaiah provide an interpretative framework for the reading of this section as well as the entire Lukan writings. The main body of this Gospel is introduced by an extended quotation from Isa. 40:3–5 in Luke 3:4–6. The narrow application of this quotation to the life and ministry of John the Baptist cannot be denied, especially since "to make ready a people prepared for the Lord" in Luke 1:17 and "you will go on before the Lord to prepare the way for him" in 1:76, both applied to John the Baptist, allude to Isa. 40:3, which is quoted here in Luke 3:4: "Prepare the way for the Lord." Nevertheless, the significance of this lengthy quotation for Luke's writings extends beyond this immediate context. First, the inclusion of the clause "and all people will see God's salvation" (3:6 [Isa. 40:5]) anticipates the second volume of Luke's writings, which provides an account of the conversion of gentiles, an account that culminates in the statement that "God's salvation has been sent to the Gentiles" (Acts 28:28). Second, the identification of the church as "the Way" (*hē hodos*) in Acts (9:2; 19:9, 23; 22:4; 24:14, 22) can also be traced back to the call to "prepare the way [*tēn hodon*] for the Lord." Some Jews claimed to be heirs of God's promises to his people by identifying themselves as "the Way" (*derek*, 1QS 9.16–21; CD 1.11–13; 2.5–7); here Luke claims that the fulfillment of such promises can be found only in the community of the gospel.

The significance of this quotation lies also in the content and nature of the passage quoted. First, in the OT (Mal. 3:1) and in Second Temple Jewish traditions (Bar. 5:6–9; Ps. Sol. 8:17; T. Mos. 10:4; 1 En. 1:6–7; 1QS 8.13–16; 9.16–21; Davis, 61–102), Isa. 40:3 has repeatedly been used in an eschatological sense. Luke's use here echoes this long tradition as he points to the arrival of this new era. Second, Isa. 40:3–5 is situated within Isa. 40:1–11, the prologue to Isa. 40–55. As such, it lays out the basic framework for the program of God's redemptive work: the restoration of the people of God (Isa. 40:1–2, 9–11), the universal revelation of the glory/salvation of God (40:3–5), and the power of the Word of God and the fragility of human beings (40:6–8). This framework provides a lens through which the mission of Jesus and the church can be understood within the wider redemptive work of God (cf. Pao).

The second extended quotation appears in the Nazareth sermon of Jesus in Luke 4:18–19, where Isa. 61:1–2a and 58:6 are used to define Jesus's mission and ministry. Luke places this episode before Jesus's Capernaum ministry (cf. Mark 6:1–6) to underline the programmatic nature of this sermon. The inclusion of Isa. 58:6 ("to set the oppressed free [*aphesei*]") in the quotation from Isa. 61:1–2a is possibly prompted by the key word *aphesis* in Isa. 61:1c ("to proclaim freedom [*aphesin*] for the captives"). More important, the omission of Isa. 61:2b ("and the day of vengeance of our God") allows the quotation to end with the word "favor" (*dektos*), a word that is picked up in Jesus's comments that follow: "No prophet is accepted [*dektos*] in his hometown" (4:24). The tragic message is clear: while God has forgiven his people and finds them acceptable despite their disobedience, they refuse to accept this gospel.

In its original context in Isaiah, the various descriptors in this quotation ("the poor," "the prisoners," "the blind," and "the oppressed") are all directed to one group of people—the people of God who are in exile. The proclamation of "the year of the Lord's favor" is therefore a declaration of the arrival of the promised salvation. The programmatic nature of this declaration is made clear in 7:22 when Jesus uses the literal/physical sense of these descriptors in pointing to his ministry as the embodiment of the fulfillment of God's promises.

The programmatic nature of this Nazareth sermon is also illustrated by the responses to Jesus's proclamation of the arrival of the eschatological salvation. First, in response to those who question his identity (4:22), Jesus introduces his fate as a prophet rejected by his own people (4:24). The original meaning of the saying ("No prophet is accepted in his hometown") points to the different responses Jesus has received from those in Nazareth and Capernaum; but in its wider narrative context, this saying points to Jesus as a prophet rejected by God's own people. Corresponding to the Jewish rejection of Jesus is the note on the extension of the gospel to the gentiles, illustrated by the stories of Elijah and Elisha (4:25–27). These twin emphases on the Jewish rejection of the gospel and the inclusion of the gentiles will dominate the remaining narrative throughout the Lukan writings.

The proclamation of the arrival of God's eschatological salvation and the Jewish rejection of this salvation become the foci of this section, and both are reinforced by uses of Isaiah. In the beatitudes and woes that introduce the Lukan Sermon on the Plain, for example, Isa. 61:1–2 is again evoked with references to "the poor" (6:20), "comfort" (6:24), and mourning (6:25), and the reversal of the fortunes of the people of God presupposes that which was introduced in the Nazareth sermon (for a parallel use of Isa. 61:1–2 in the Qumran documents, see 1QH[a] 23[top].12–15; Allison, 104–6). The recognition of the use of Isaianic language here is important; the focus of the beatitudes is not the virtues and good deeds performed by those who are to enter the kingdom of God but the state of oppression in which God's people find themselves, a state that will be reversed by God with the arrival of God's kingdom through his Son, Jesus Christ.

As in the Nazareth scene, the proclamation of the arrival of God's kingdom is again followed by a note on the rejection of that kingdom. The allusion to Isa. 6:9 within the parable of the sower (8:10) provides a statement on the Jewish rejection of the gospel: "Though seeing, they may not see; though hearing, they may not understand." In its original context, this obduracy theme serves as an indictment against Israel for their refusal to be faithful to God. Thus, in Luke it underscores the rebellious act of the Jews as they follow their ancestors in rejecting the work of God. Unlike Matthew (13:14–15), however, the full quotation of Isa. 6:9–10 is reserved for the end of Luke's work (Acts 28:26–27), when a final warning to God's people is issued (see below). Luke's note on Jewish rejection provides an appropriate conclusion to this section as Jesus points to his death as the culmination of the opposition by the leaders of the Jews (9:22; cf. 9:44).

Luke 9:51–19:44

Unlike Mark (10:1–52) and Matthew (19:1–20:34), Luke includes a lengthy central section that depicts Jesus's journey from Galilee to Jerusalem. Despite its form being a "travel narrative," its content does not focus on traveling, as reflected in the lack of a detailed itinerary. Numerous proposals have been made in an attempt to explain this discrepancy between form and content, the most fruitful of which focuses on the use of the OT in this section. Significant linguistic parallels to Deuteronomy have long been recognized, and C. F. Evans has further suggested that the passages within this central section are organized following the order of Deut. 1–26. Subsequent studies have affirmed the significant presence of Deuteronomy within this section, but most remain unconvinced of Evans's suggestion of a strict parallel structure between this section and a portion of Deuteronomy.

A more fruitful approach is represented by David Moessner, who argues for a thematic parallel and suggests that the passages within this central section correspond to four recurring themes in Deuteronomy: (1) the Jewish contemporaries of Jesus can be compared to the faithless wilderness generation of old (11:29–32; 12:54–13:9; 17:20–37); (2) like Moses, Jesus is sent by God to call his people to repent (10:1–16; 11:14–54; 12:54–13:9; 13:22–30; 14:15–24; 15:1–32; 17:22–37; 19:1–27); (3) but God's prophet is again rejected by his people (9:52–58; 10:25–37; 11:37–54; 12:35–53; 13:22–35; 14:1–27; 16:19–31; 19:1–10, 38–44); and (4) as a result, destruction will come upon this rebellious people (11:31–32, 50–51; 12:57–59; 13:24–30, 35; 14:24; 17:26–30; 19:27, 41–44).

While Deuteronomic influence may not be equally evident in these individual passages, this reading is consistent with the way this central section is introduced. In the final paragraph of the previous section, one finds Jesus on the mountain with Moses and Elijah (9:30), with the former likely referring to the paradigmatic prophet and the latter the eschatological prophet (cf. Deut. Rab. 3:17 [on 10:1]; C. A. Evans, 81; Mareček). This is reinforced by the conclusion of this transfiguration narrative when the voice from heaven takes up the words of Moses, who is understood as pointing forward to his eschatological successor: "Listen to him" (9:35 [Deut. 18:15]). Not only is the Mosaic-prophetic paradigm evoked, but the uniquely Lukan note on the conversation among Jesus, Moses, and Elijah on Jesus's "exodus" (*tēn exodon*, 9:31) may also allude to the historical exodus event (cf. Exod. 19:1; Num. 33:38). If so, Luke is already marking his central section as an "exodus" journey where Jesus, the eschatological Mosaic prophet, calls God's people to repent.

Beyond the influence of Deuteronomy, other OT passages also play a role in this central section. Two passages concerning the inheritance of eternal life contain explicit quotations of the OT. First, in Luke 10:27 one finds the use of Deut. 6:5 and Lev. 19:18. As part of the Shema, Deut. 6:5 belongs to the central confession of the Jews (m. Ber. 1:1–4). In this Lukan context, however, the focus is on the definition of "neighbor" in Lev. 19:18, as further explicated in the parable of the good Samaritan that follows. For many Jews, "neighbor" would refer to a fellow Israelite (Mek. Exod. 21:35; *TDNT* 6:315). Departing from the expected trilogy of "priests, Levite, and people" (1 Chron. 28:21; Ezra 7:7, 13; 10:5; Neh. 7:73; 8:13; cf. 1QS 2.11, 19–21; Gourges), the inclusion of the Samaritan therefore questions the narrower Jewish identification of the boundary of God's people. Moreover, as "priest" and "Levite" are cultic markers, and as the conflict between Jews and Samaritans often centered on cultic matters (cf. John 4:20), the Samaritan's reception of the one lying on the ground can be considered as a way to approach God. This is consistent with the portrayal of the Samaritan who, after being healed, "threw himself at Jesus' feet" (Luke 17:16), an act considered "to give praise to God" (17:18).

The OT is also explicitly quoted in the second passage on inheriting eternal life, though the focus now returns to the central confession of Israel in the affirmation of the one God. The seventh, sixth, eighth, ninth, and fifth commandments are evoked in 18:20 (cf. Exod. 20:12–16; Deut. 5:16–20), but it is the allusion to the tenth, on coveting (Exod. 20:17; Deut. 5:21), that forms the climax of this passage: "Sell everything you have and give to the poor, and you will have treasure in heaven. Then come, follow me" (Luke 18:22). In its original context, the tenth commandment forms the basis of the "ethical" commandments that precede, since acts of coveting reflect the failure to worship the one and only God. In this Lukan context, Jesus's call for the ruler to sell all that he has to follow him becomes a commentary on Jesus's own identity. Jesus takes on the role of God the Father in demanding absolute allegiance and faithfulness. As such, Jesus's question "Why do you call me good?" (18:19) is not a denial of his own goodness but a challenge to the ruler to recognize Jesus's own status and identity as one to be identified with God who alone is good (cf. 1 Chron. 16:34; 2 Chron. 5:13; Pss. 34:8; 118:1, 29).

Finally, Luke's allusion to Ps. 118:26 in 13:35 deserves a brief note. This is the first use of Ps. 118 in this Gospel, and it anticipates the use of the same clause in 19:38 with the additional explicit identification of Jesus as "the king" (*ho basileus*). Psalm 118 provides a framework for the depiction of both the rejection and subsequent exaltation of Jesus the king (see discussion below). In this context, "he who comes" (*ho erchomenos*) echoes the earlier question of John the Baptist (7:19), one that may already have alluded to this psalm. Unlike in Matt. 23:39, the use of Ps. 118:26 here refers less to Jesus's second coming than to his entry into Jerusalem. This verse therefore becomes both a critique and a call to repentance. It is a critique of the Jews, as this quote follows a note on the desolation of their house (cf. Jer. 12:7), which anticipates their rejection of the king who is to enter Jerusalem; it is a call to repentance in that only those who recognize Jesus as the messianic king can "see" him again.

In Luke 19:38, the insertion of "the king" and the description of Jesus's entry into Jerusalem (19:32–37) may also evoke Zech. 9:9: "See, your king comes to you, righteous and victorious, lowly and riding on a donkey, on a colt, the foal of a donkey." The use of both Ps. 118:26 and Zech. 9:9 paves the way for the description of the tragic end of the earthly mission of Jesus the king, one who is rejected by his own people. Ironically, when Jesus is hung on the cross, he is publicly identified as "the king of the Jews" (23:38). With these references, Jesus is no longer simply portrayed as a Deuteronomic prophet; he is also the messianic king whose rejection merely anticipates his subsequent exaltation when he is to be recognized as "both Lord and Messiah" (Acts 2:36).

Luke 19:45–24:53

Luke's final section witnesses a marked increase in the explicit use of the OT. Isaiah continues to play a notable role in this section in marking the dawn of an eschatological era with Jesus's death and exaltation. This section begins with the temple-cleansing narrative, which contains a quotation from Isa. 56:7 followed by an allusion to Jer. 7:11 (Luke 19:46; for the use of Jeremiah as a symbol of judgment on Israel, see Luke 9:51 [Jer. 21:10]; 11:47–50 [Jer. 7:25–26]; 13:35a [Jer. 12:7; 22:5]; 19:41 [Jer. 9:1; 13:17; 22:10]; 21:5–38 [Jer. 4:23–28]; Hays). The focus on the inclusion of the gentiles in God's eschatological salvation, noted in Isa. 56:7, is consistent with the Lukan use of Isa. 40:5 in Luke 3:6. In this context, however, the quotation from Jeremiah makes it clear that the failure to include the gentiles stems from the desecration of the temple cult by God's own people. That the focus here is on the criticism of the Jews may explain why the phrase "for all nations" (*pasin tois ethnesin*, Isa. 56:7c) is omitted. Nevertheless, the two are related in that the extension of the salvation to the gentiles (cf. Isa. 40:5) only follows the cleansing of God's own city (cf. Isa. 40:1–2, 9–11).

A similar hint of a gentile mission can also be found in Jesus's application of Isa. 53:12 to himself: "And he was numbered with the transgressors" (Luke 22:37a). The emphatic note that this verse from Isaiah's fourth

Servant Song applies to Jesus himself ("I tell you that this must be fulfilled in me. Yes, what is written about me is reaching its fulfillment," 22:37b) points to its christological use in this context of Jesus's suffering. The immediate fulfillment of this verse may be found in the description of Jesus being placed among the "criminals" in 23:33. Nevertheless, a wider application is also possible, since in its Isaianic context "transgressors" (*anomoi*) can refer to those outside of God's covenant (e.g., Isa. 10:6; 66:3; cf. Pss. Sol. 17:11, 18; *TDNT* 4:1087); if so, to be "numbered with the transgressors" is to be identified with the outcasts and those outside the covenantal community. In its Lukan context, this quotation immediately follows Jesus's call to his disciples to take up their purses, bags, swords, and cloak (22:36), equipment necessary for missionary traveling (cf. 9:1–6; 10:1–12). An anticipation of a gentile mission is therefore possible even in the passion account.

The final use of Isaiah in Luke can be found in the call of Jesus to his disciples to remain in Jerusalem until they have been clothed "with power from on high" (*ex hypsous dynamin,* 24:49). When this verse is read together with "You will receive power when the Holy Spirit comes on you" (*epelthontos tou hagiou pneumatos eph' hymas*) of Acts 1:8 in reference to the same event, it is clear that Isa. 32:15 lies behind both: "till the Spirit is poured on us from on high" (*heōs an epelthē eph' hymas pneuma aph' hypsēlou,* LXX). The coming of the Spirit signals the beginning of a new age when God restores his people and reveals his glory for all to witness. This note echoes Isa. 61:1 as it appears in Luke 4:18 while anticipating the dramatic manifestation of the Spirit in Acts that lays the foundation for the mission of the church.

While the figure of the Isaianic suffering servant is often understood to play a significant role in the Gospel passion narratives, it is Psalms that appears to play the central role in Luke's final section (cf. Doble; Miura; Jipp). Quotations and allusions to these psalms alone provide a sustained narrative of Jesus's suffering in these chapters. The use of Ps. 118:22 in Luke 20:17 ("The stone the builders rejected has become the cornerstone") provides the framework in which Jesus's death is to be understood: his death belongs to God's salvific plan, but he will be vindicated. This vindication is underlined by the use of Ps. 110:1 in Luke 20:42–43 ("The Lord said to my Lord: 'Sit at my right hand until I make your enemies a footstool for your feet'"), a part of which is reiterated in 22:69 ("The Son of Man will be seated at the right hand of the mighty God"). The royal messianic identity of Jesus is implied in the uses of these psalms, and his final exaltation is affirmed as God declares victory over the forces of evil.

The narrower account of Jesus's crucifixion (23:32–46) is also saturated with allusions to Psalms, as in this quotation of the final words of Jesus: "Father, into your hands I commit my spirit" (23:46 [Ps. 31:5]). This final and climactic saying of the earthly Jesus, which portrays him as the righteous sufferer that is familiar in Psalms, provides a critical interpretive lens through which the entire account is to be understood. This portrayal is reinforced by the numerous allusions that precede: "They divided up his clothes by casting lots" (23:34b [cf. Ps. 22:18]); "He saved others; let him save himself" (23:35b [cf. Pss. 22:8; 89:19–20]); "They offered him wine vinegar" (23:36 [cf. Ps. 69:21]); "All those who knew him . . . stood at a distance, watching these things" (23:49a [cf. Ps. 38:11]). In light of these references, it should also be understood that Jesus is portrayed as the "servant" (*pais*) figure in Psalms (69:17; 86:16; see also the superscription of Ps. 18, which identifies David as "the servant of the LORD"), especially since in Luke's second volume a psalm (2:1) is used in reference to Jesus, God's "servant" (*pais,* Acts 4:25; cf. 3:13, 26; 4:27, 30).

That Deuteronomy, Isaiah, and Psalms play a particularly important role in this Gospel may explain the unique three-part descriptors found only here in the NT: "Everything must be fulfilled that is written about me in the Law of Moses, the Prophets and the Psalms" (24:44b).

Significant Lukan Themes Constructed through the Use of the OT

Moving beyond a survey of some of the OT quotations and allusions in the various sections of this Gospel, the following will highlight three of the foci or functions of these interactions.

Identity of Jesus. Luke's Christology is constructed through the use of OT language and traditions. Three major christological constructions will be considered here. First, at critical junctures of Luke's narrative, Jesus is presented as a prophet. At the beginning of Jesus's ministry, the use of Isa. 61:1–2 and 58:6 identifies Jesus as the one who fulfills the mission of the eschatological prophet. This is made explicit in 4:24 when Jesus considers himself one of the prophets rejected by their own people. The use of the Elijah-Elisha stories in 4:25–27 further suggests that the mission to the gentiles is to be considered part of the mission of God's eschatological prophet.

Marking the beginning of Luke's central section, language from the prophetic traditions further identifies Jesus as a prophet destined to suffer in Jerusalem (Croatto). The use of the NT *hapax legomenon analēmpsis* ("taken up," 9:51) recalls the prophet Elijah, who was likewise "taken up" (*anelēmphthē,* 2 Kings 2:11) to heaven. That Jesus "set his face" (*autos to prosōpon estērisen,* 9:51) to Jerusalem likewise belongs to the language of the prophets who proclaim judgment on Jerusalem and on God's own people (cf. Jer. 21:10; Ezek. 6:2; 13:17; 14:8; 15:7; 20:46; 21:2). That Jesus "sent messengers on ahead" (Luke 9:52) also recalls those who share the burden of Moses in Num. 11:16–17. These allusions, combined with the previous note on Jesus's exodus journey (Luke 9:31), point to Jesus's prophetic mission and identity. As Luke begins his final section with the prophetic act of cleansing the temple, accompanied by the use of Isa. 56:7 and Jer. 7:11, he further reinforces this portrayal of Jesus as God's prophet.

Beyond the saturation of language from the prophetic traditions at critical junctures of Luke's narrative, one finds Jesus being recognized as "a great prophet" (7:16; cf. 7:39) by the crowd. At the end of Luke's narrative, two disciples also identify Jesus as "a prophet, powerful in word and deed before God and all the people" (24:19). While these may not be considered statements by reliable witnesses, the explicit application of Deut. 18:15–19 to Jesus by Peter in Acts 3:22–23 clearly reflects Luke's own opinion: "For Moses said, 'The Lord your God will raise up for you a prophet like me from among your own people; you must listen to everything he tells you. Anyone who does not listen to him will be completely cut off from their people'" (cf. Acts 7:37).

The emphasis on Jesus as prophet not only provides continuity between the OT and the eschatological mission of Jesus but also allows Jesus's followers to follow in his footsteps as they seek to continue the prophetic mission of Jesus among God's people and beyond. Even the Jews are considered "heirs of the prophets" (Acts 3:25). Jesus's followers who are persecuted as he was are now considered in the line of rejected prophets (7:52).

Though the prophetic mission of Jesus is emphasized in Luke's writings, he is never considered merely "one of the prophets of long ago [who] has come back to life" (Luke 9:19), as some among the Jewish crowd say. In response to those who claim that Jesus is a (mere) prophet, Peter provides a clear confession that Jesus is "God's Messiah" (9:20). The first use of the title "Messiah" (*christos*) appears in 2:11, where it is used with "Lord" (*kyrios*) within a context where the Davidic royal messianic tradition is evoked: "Today in the town of David a Savior has been born to you; he is the Messiah, the Lord." The exact formulation of the two titles, *christos kyrios*, appears nowhere else in the LXX and NT, but its appearance in a notable extracanonical psalm that depicts the royal messianic figure that is to come (Pss. Sol. 17:32) paves the way for this Lukan descriptor.

The second construction relates to the sonship language. In the account of Jesus's baptism, the heavenly voice proclaims, "You are my Son" (3:22). This likely evokes Ps. 2:7 ("You are my son; today I have become your father"), where Jesus is identified as the royal Davidic figure, an identification anticipated already in Luke 1–2 (cf. 1:32–33, 68–79). The heavenly voice from the transfiguration narrative begins in a similar fashion, "This is my Son" (9:35), a formulation that is also drawn from the same tradition.

The use of the title "Messiah" with "son of David" appears in Luke 20:41. The link between "Messiah" and "David" can already be found in the account of the establishment of the eternal covenant with David's house in 2 Sam. 7:14–17, which is reiterated in the royal psalms (e.g., Ps. 89:29–37). Significantly, in this Lukan context, the identification between these two is immediately followed by the use of another royal psalm where the two titles are explicated by the third, "Lord" (*kyrios*; 20:42–43 [Ps. 110:1]). In the second volume of Luke's writings, the use of Ps. 110:1 in Acts 2:34–35 is likewise immediately followed by the titles "Lord" and "Messiah" in reference to Jesus's exaltation: "God has made this Jesus, whom you crucified, both Lord and Messiah" (Acts 2:36). Within the wider Lukan narrative, this Davidic messianic figure fits well within the prophetic traditions of Israel that anticipate the establishment of a Davidic dynasty and the restoration of Israel (cf. Acts 13:34 [Isa. 55:3]; Strauss).

The third construction to be considered is the suffering-servant figure. Jesus is identified as "servant" (*pais*) only in Acts (3:13, 26; 4:27, 30), but the reference to the fourth Servant Song in Luke 22:37 (Isa. 53:12) suggests to some that the suffering Jesus of Luke's passion narrative should be read in light of the Isaianic suffering-servant figure (Green). Nevertheless, the repeated use of Psalms in the account of Jesus's crucifixion (23:32–46, see above), as well as the explicit identification of David as God's "servant," followed by a quote from Ps. 2:1 in Acts 4:25, argues for the dominance of the righteous-sufferer paradigm of Psalms in situating the "servant" references (Jipp). The influence of the Isaianic servant figure, however, cannot be denied in light of its importance in early Christian writings.

Identity of the church. Beyond the identity of Jesus, the significance of his mission for both Israel and the gentiles is another concern reflected in Luke's use of the OT. Already in Luke 2:30–32 the fates of these two communities are intertwined. The "salvation" that is "prepared" for "all nations" (2:30–31) anticipates the quotation from Isa. 40:3–5 in Luke 3:4–6 ("Prepare the way for the Lord. . . . All people will see God's salvation"), and "a light for revelation to the Gentiles" (2:32a) alludes to Isa. 42:6 and 49:6. This concern for the gentiles is, at this point in the narrative, for "the glory of your people Israel" (2:32b), and the use of "light" with "glory" recalls Isa. 60:1: "Arise, shine, for your light has come, and the glory of the LORD rises upon you." The relationship between the two is maintained through the end of the Gospel, where the gospel that is to be preached "to all nations" is one that finds its "beginning at Jerusalem" (24:47), a framework already laid out in Isa. 40:1–11, which is evoked by the extended quotation from Isa. 40:3–5 in Luke 3:4–6.

As the narrative develops, however, it becomes clear that this salvation is rejected by the Jews, though the mission to the gentiles continues. The Jewish rejection of the gospel dominates the narrative of Luke, while the mission to the gentiles becomes the focus of a major part of Acts. In Luke, immediately following the proclamation of "the year of the Lord's favor" in the Nazareth sermon (4:19 [Isa. 61:2]), Jesus's own statement that "no prophet is accepted in his hometown" (4:24) becomes part of this programmatic passage for the entire Gospel. As noted above, the use of Deuteronomy in Luke's central section and of Psalms in the passion narrative draws attention to Jesus as the prophet rejected by his own people to the point of death. These scriptural references point to a long history of Israel refusing to acknowledge God's redemptive work since the wilderness generation. Stephen's recounting of OT history in Acts 7 provides an apt commentary on the behavior of the Jews, who are again compared to their ancestors: "Was there ever a prophet your ancestors did not persecute? They even killed those who predicted the coming of the Righteous One. And now you have betrayed and murdered him" (7:52).

This account of the mission to the Jews would not be complete without a note on the striking use of Isa. 6:9–10 at the end of Luke's two-volume work. In the context of Isaiah, the first part of the book (Isa. 1–39) is best captured by the call narrative in Isa. 6:1–12, where the focus of the message to be proclaimed is one of judgment on God's people. The reversal in the second part of Isaiah points to God's gracious deliverance of this rebellious people with the dawn of the eschatological salvation (Isa. 40–55), a focus best captured in the call narrative in Isa. 40:1–11. In the Lukan writings, this Isaianic reversal is, ironically, once again reversed. Luke uses Isa. 40 at the beginning of the account of Jesus's ministry (3:4–6) and Isa. 6 at the end of his narrative of the early Christian mission (Acts 28:26–27); the judgment-to-salvation message of Isaiah becomes a salvation-to-judgment message. Though Luke does not claim to provide the final word on the Jewish response to the gospel, this entire narrative does provide an explanation of why a community that claims to be the heirs of the OT promises consists of an increasing number of gentiles.

Continuity between Jesus and the church. The use of Isa. 6 and 40 at the beginning and end of the Lukan writings is unique. While the extensive use of the OT in Luke clearly points to the continuity between the OT and the age of fulfillment, the use of the OT in Luke-Acts also provides continuity between the mission of Jesus and that of the early church. This departs from the use of the OT in the one-volume Gospels precisely because they omit an account of the history of the early Christian movement. Two examples will suffice.

First, at the end of Luke's Gospel one finds a quotation formula without the presence of an exact quotation from the OT: "This is what is written: The Messiah will suffer and rise from the dead on the third day, and repentance for the forgiveness of sins will be preached in his name to all nations, beginning at Jerusalem" (24:46–47). While there is discussion surrounding what OT sources constitute the various parts of this statement, the point remains clear: the OT promises are to unite both volumes of Luke's writings, and the fate of the Messiah (in Luke) is not to be separated from the mission "to all nations" (in Acts). The mission of the church is therefore an integral part of the mission of Jesus, and both are fulfillments of God's promises of old.

Finally, the use of Ps. 118 should again be noted. The repeated uses of this psalm form a framework within which both Luke and Acts are to be understood (Wagner). Evoked in both Luke (13:35; 19:38 [Ps. 118:26]) and Acts (4:11 [Ps. 118:22]), Ps. 118 points to both the human rejection and divine vindication of Jesus the Messiah, whose suffering and exaltation aim at calling even those who reject him to repentance (Acts 5:31; cf. Ps. 118:16). This is the pattern of God's redemptive work in the OT, and one that reemerges in a dramatic way in the account of the mission of Jesus the Messiah.

Bibliography. Achtemeier, P. J., "*Omne verbum sonat,*" *JBL* 109 (1990): 3–27; Albl, M. C., *"And Scripture Cannot Be Broken,"* NovTSup 96 (Brill, 1999); Allison, D. C., *The Intertextual Jesus* (Trinity Press International, 2000); Bock, D. L., *Proclamation from Prophecy and Pattern,* JSNTSup 12 (Sheffield Academic, 1987); Callaway, M., *Sing, O Barren One,* SBLDS 91 (Scholars Press, 1986); Croatto, J. S., "Jesus, Prophet like Elijah, and Prophet-Teacher like Moses in Luke-Acts," *JBL* 124 (2005): 451–65; Davis, C. J., *The Name and Way of the Lord,* JSNTSup 129 (Sheffield Academic, 1996); Doble, P., "Luke 24.26, 44—Songs of God's Servant," *JSNT* 28 (2006): 267–83; Evans, C. A., "The Function of the Elijah/Elisha Narratives in Luke's Ethic of Election," in *Luke and Scripture,* ed. C. A. Evans and J. A. Sanders (Fortress, 1993), 70–83; Evans, C. F., "The Central Section of St. Luke's Gospels," in *Studies in the Gospels,* ed. D. E. Nineham (Blackwell, 1955), 37–53; Gourges, M., "The Priest, the Levite, and the Samaritan Revisited," *JBL* 117 (1998): 709–13; Green, J. N., "The Death of Jesus, God's Servant," in *Reimaging the Death of the Lukan Jesus,* ed. D. D. Sylva (Hain, 1990), 1–28; Ham, C. A., *The Coming King and the Rejected Shepherd,* NTM 4 (Sheffield Phoenix, 2005); Hays, J. D., "The Persecuted Prophet and Judgment on Jerusalem," *BBR* 25 (2015): 453–73; Jipp, J. W., "Luke's Scriptural Suffering Messiah," *CBQ* 72 (2010): 255–74; Kimball, C. A., *Jesus's Exposition of the Old Testament in Luke's Gospel,* JSNTSup 94 (Sheffield Academic, 1994); Lanier, G. R., *Old Testament Conceptual Metaphors and the Christology of Luke's Gospel,* LNTS 591 (T&T Clark, 2018); Mareček, P., "Elijah: His Role and Importance in the Gospel of Luke," *Studia Biblica Slovaca* 12 (2020): 51–70; Miura, Y., *David in Luke-Acts,* WUNT 2/232 (Mohr Siebeck, 2007); Moessner, D. P., *Lord of the Banquet* (Fortress, 1989); Moo, D. J., *The Old Testament in the Gospel Passion Narratives* (Almond, 1983); Moyise, S., *The Old Testament in the New* (Continuum, 2001); Pao, D. W., *Acts and the Isaianic New Exodus,* WUNT 2/130 (Mohr Siebeck, 2000); Pao, D. W., and E. Schnabel, "Luke," in *CNTUOT,* 251–414; Porter, S. E., ed., *Hearing the Old Testament in the New Testament* (Eerdmans, 2006); Strauss, M. L., *The Davidic Messiah in Luke-Acts,* JSNTSup 110 (Sheffield Academic, 1995); Stronstad, R.,

The Charismatic Theology of St. Luke, 2nd ed. (Baker Academic, 2012); Swartley, W. M., *Israel's Scripture Traditions and the Synoptic Gospels* (Hendrickson, 1994); Wagner, J. R., "Psalm 118 in Luke-Acts," in *Early Christian Interpretation of the Scriptures of Israel*, ed. C. A. Evans and J. A. Sanders, JSNTSup 148 (Sheffield Academic, 1997), 154–78; Wright, N. T., *The New Testament and the People of God*, COQG (Fortress, 1992).

DAVID W. PAO

LXX

See Septuagint articles

M

Malachi, Book of

As the prophet Malachi addresses God's people, he faces a failure of leadership as well as hypocrisy, spiritual apathy, cynicism, and greed.

Setting

Author. The uniqueness of the name "Malachi" (Heb. *mal'ākî*), meaning "my messenger" (from *mal'āk*, "messenger/angel"), and its use with that meaning in 3:1 ("I am sending my messenger," AT) have convinced many scholars of the book's anonymity (e.g., Rudolph, 247–48). The reference in Mal. 3:1, however, may be a play on the name of the prophet, as Mic. 7:18 alludes to the meaning of the prophet's name ("Who is like Yah?"). The name "Malachi" on a late-monarchy jar handle from Arad shows the name to be authentic (Hess, 702).

Date. Malachi contains sufficient chronological clues for scholars to date its composition in the reign of Darius I (521–486 BC) or Xerxes (486–465 BC), sometime between about 500 and 460 BC. Andrew Hill (53–55) believes Darius's reign is more likely, but Michael Fox (21) argues cogently for Xerxes.

Structure and Message

Structure. Many scholars regard as axiomatic the argument, first made in 1959 by Egon Pfeiffer, that Malachi comprises six disputations and perhaps one or two final appendices (4:4, 5–6 [Heb. 3:22, 23–24]). A few, however, join me in considering this approach inconsistent, problematic, and inadequate (e.g., Floyd, 564–67). The book covers three major topics: "(1) the priests' responsibility to honor Yahweh's name in 1:2–2:9, (2) Yahweh's demand that his people treat each other with kindness and faithfulness in 2:10–3:6, and (3) Yahweh's demand that his people treat their possessions with faith in God's provisions, mercy toward those in need, and obedience to his instructions in 3:7–4:6" (Clendenen, "Passionate Prophet," 209). The use of assertion-objection-response in Malachi is a rhetorical device to make vivid the sinful attitudes and behavior that the prophet discerns in his audience (Clendenen, "Malachi," 222–23).

Message. Malachi's call to return to the Lord's ways as set forth in the Torah (3:7; 4:4) is motivated by what God has done in the past—"I have loved you" (1:2)—and by a future day of judgment on the arrogant and the wicked (4:1) and of compassion and reward for the faithful who fear Yahweh (3:16–18).

Inner-biblical Connections

Our purpose is both to analyze how Malachi uses previous texts and also to consider its use in the NT.

Yahweh's love (1:2–5). The people's disputation of Yahweh's love in 1:2 is met initially by a history lesson based on their knowledge of Gen. 25–36. The verb for love, *'āhab*, is used several times in Deuteronomy (and elsewhere) either of choosing for relationship (4:37; 7:6–8; 10:14–15) or of loyalty in that relationship (5:10; 6:5; 7:13; etc.), and both senses are in view in Mal. 1:2–5. The former is foregrounded in Mal. 1:2, where the allusion is to Gen. 25:26. God's choice of Jacob over Esau was unmerited and resulted in God's permanent relationship with Israel. This is the element picked up by Paul, who applies it typologically to the true Israel in Rom. 9:10–13.

Although the pairing of "love" and "hate" is not used of God in Genesis, it is used of Jacob choosing Rachel and rejecting Leah in Gen. 29 and appears similarly in Deut. 21:15–17. With no indication of a connection to those passages, Malachi applies the expression to God's choice of Jacob over Esau in Rebekah's womb (Gen. 25:22–23), which Paul quotes along with Mal. 1:2b–3a. This allows God's hating of Esau in Mal. 1:3a to do double duty. In the context of v. 2 it expresses God's *not choosing* Esau as the seed of promise. But in the context of vv. 3b–4 it expresses God's becoming an *enemy* to Esau's descendants the Edomites for their wickedness (cf. Hosea 9:15; Pss. 5:5; 11:5). God's love in terms of election becomes his love in terms of faithfulness and grace. If God did not love Israel, he would have wiped them out for their wickedness as he did Edom (cf. Mal. 3:6).

In Mal. 1:3–4 the prophet depends on his audience knowing Edom's recent history and probably at least some of the prophecies of Edom's fall (Kessler, "Unity," 229), which elucidate Edom's wickedness. About a dozen texts have been suggested as Malachi's sources, but the language they share is mostly "conventional curse or judgement language" from the OT and the ancient Near East (Gibson, 53–55).

Jonathan Gibson's careful analysis of lexical parallels leads him to conclude that six passages have the highest level of probability of being Malachi's source texts, especially Isa. 34:5–15; Ezek. 35:2–15; and Joel 3:19–20. Ezekiel 35 is the most likely, partly because of the recurring use of the root *šmm*, "desolate" (Gibson, 59–60, 62). Table 1 shows the degree of lexical overlap (the order following Malachi's text).

Table 1. Lexical Overlap between Mal. 1:2–4 and Possible Source Texts

Hebrew word	Mal. 1:2–4	Isa. 34:5–15	Jer. 49:7–22	Ezek. 25:12–14	Ezek. 35:2–15	Joel 3:19–20 [LXX 4:19–20]	Obadiah
ʿēśāw	Esau		Esau				Esau
śym	turned				turned		
har	mountains		mountain		mount		
šmm	wasteland		desolation		desolate	wasteland	
naḥălâ	inheritance				inheritance		
midbār	desert					desert	
tan	jackals	jackals					
ʾĕdôm	Edom	Edom	Edom	Edom	Edom	Edom	
ḥrb	ruins	desolate	ruin	wasteland	ruin		
gĕbûl	country						border
ʿôlām	forever	forever	forever		perpetual	forever	forever

In the light of these pre-texts, Mal. 1:3 could have concluded with "as I prophesied," and this is likely what Malachi's audience is expected to understand. Then v. 4 extends the desolation of the past into a prophesied unending future, echoing Isa. 34:10; Jer. 49:13; and Ezek. 35:9.

Indictment of the priests (1:6–2:9). This extended section, which uses texts from Leviticus, Deuteronomy, and Ezekiel, is unified by its addressing "you priests" in 1:6 and 2:1 (cf. 2:7) and by its repetition of many terms, such as "name," "fear," "honor," "despise," and "face."

The pericope is divided by the repeated vocative "you priests" and the consequential adverb *wəʿattâ*, "so now" (2:1 AT). The focus in 1:6–14 is on the priests' failure to oversee properly the offerings. Malachi uses the terms *leḥem*, "food," and *šulḥan*, "table," to invoke the concept of a host feeding his guests at his table, such as "the king's table" (1 Sam. 20:29; 1 Kings 4:27 [MT 5:7]), "David's table" (2 Sam. 9:7–13), and "Jezebel's table" (1 Kings 18:19; cf. "the Lord's table" in 1 Cor. 10:21).

Only Malachi speaks of "despising" (*bzh*) Yahweh's name (1:6), though "profaning" (*ḥll*) the name, used in 1:12, occurs often elsewhere, especially in Leviticus and Ezekiel. Of the nineteen references to "profaning" Yahweh's "name" in the OT, nine are in Ezekiel, involving the "nations" (20:9, 14, 22; 36:20–23; 39:7). Malachi 1:12 may allude to Ezek. 36:23, which speaks of the greatness of God's name, which Israel has profaned among the nations. The postexilic priests' negligence echoes preexilic Israel's idolatry (Weyde, 148). But rather than just vindicating his name in the nations' eyes, as in Ezekiel, Malachi declares, to the shame of Israel's priesthood, that true worship of Yahweh will pass to the nations themselves!

Several scholars propose that Mal. 1:7–14 draws especially on Lev. 22:17–25 (Weyde, 118–22; Gibson, 85–90; Kessler, *Maleachi*, 63). But although the conceptual parallel is clear and some lexical items determined by the topic are shared ("vow," "altar," "food," "blind," "accept," "deformed/defective," "male"), the case for dependence is debatable. Although the concurrence of *mošḥāt*, describing a "defective" sacrifice only in Lev. 22:25 and Mal. 1:14, may be significant (cf. Weyde, 119–20), several key terms are different (e.g., *qrb* in Leviticus versus *ngš* in Malachi, specific offerings, and specific defects). The prophet is surely familiar with Mosaic sacrificial law, and Karl William Weyde may be correct that he uses Lev. 22:17–25 and even Deut. 15:21 "in a rather free manner" (133).

Malachi 2:1–9 confronts the priests' unfaithfulness as teachers of Torah (cf. Lev. 10:11; Deut. 33:10; Jer. 18:18; Ezek. 7:26; Mic. 3:11; 2 Chron. 15:3; 17:7–9) and warns of an impending curse on the priests and their descendants for their ritual negligence (2:1–3; Clendenen, "Malachi," 287). The term for "the curse" in 2:2, *hammǝʾērâ*, is definite and occurs in this form only three times: 2:2; 3:9 (*bammǝʾērâ*); and Deut. 28:20. Malachi is alluding to the covenant curses of Deut. 28:15–68, although he narrows their focus from the nation to the priesthood (cf., however, 1:14). The threat in Deut. 28:20—"Yahweh will send [*šlḥ*] against you [sg.] the curse, the confusion, and the rebuke" (AT; cf. Mal. 2:3; 3:11)—is made first-person in Mal. 2:2: "I will send [*šlḥ*] against you [pl.] the curse" (AT).

The nature of 2:2–3 is identified in 2:1 and 2:4 as *hammiṣwâ hazzōʾt*. Elsewhere meaning "this command," it is here "this decree" concerning (*ʾel*) the priests (cf. Nah. 1:14, using the related verb *ṣwh*: "Yahweh has decreed concerning [*ʿal*] you" [AT]). This decree serves as a final warning of the certain consequences of failure to obey. According to Gibson (93), "Malachi surely intended a wordplay: what is against the priests is an 'admonition,' a 'judgement' for not keeping the 'command' associated with their office, which, ironically, primarily involved teaching [the commands of Yahweh]" (cf. Weyde, 171; Stuart, "Malachi," 1310–11).

According to Michael Fishbane, 1:6–2:9 is essentially the prophet's exegesis of the priestly blessing in Num. 6:23–27, showing how they have "despised the divine name and service" and are threatened with "suspension of the divine blessing" (332–33). Several lexical parallels may be noted (see table 2).

Table 2. Lexical Parallels between Num. 6:23–27 and Mal. 1:6–2:9

Num. 6:23–27 (AT)	Mal. 1:6–2:9 (AT)
23 Tell Aaron and his sons, "Thus you are to **bless** the Israelites. Say to them, 24 'May YHWH **bless** you and protect you; 25 may YHWH make his **face** shine on you and **be gracious** to you; 26 may YHWH **lift up his face** to you and **give** [*śym*] you **peace**.'" 27 So they will **place** [*śym*] **my name on** the Israelites, and I will **bless** them.	2:2 "I will curse your **blessings.**" 1:9 "Appease the **face** of God that he may **be gracious** to us. . . . Will he **lift up** the **faces** of any of you?" 2:5 "My covenant was with him life and **peace**, and I gave [these] to him." 2:2 "And if you don't **place** [*śym*] **upon** the heart to give glory to **my name** . . ."

The verb *ḥnn*, "be gracious," occurs in the jussive third-person ("may he be gracious") only five times in the OT, and only in Num. 6:25 and Mal. 1:9 does it begin with the conjunction *waw* ("*and/that* may he be gracious"). Malachi even curses them with their own blessings (cf. Stuart, "Malachi," 1296–97).

Malachi speaks of these priests in 2:4–9 as governed by a divinely instituted "covenant with/of Levi" (a phrase used only here), which they have violated (like Deuteronomy [cf. 18:1], Malachi avoids distinguishing priests and Levites). Using similar terms, Neh. 13:29 describes priestly intermarriage as defiling "the covenant of the priesthood and of the Levites." Malachi portrays a past, ideal era of Israel's priesthood during which God entered into a covenant with "[the tribe of] Levi," bestowing "life and peace" on him and expecting, in return, reverence and awe (2:5) as well as "true instruction," a life of "peace and integrity," and the practice of "turn[ing] many from iniquity" (2:6 AT).

Although the term "covenant" is not found in Exod. 32:26–29, Scott Hahn (155–56; cf. Hugenberger, 157) argues cogently that "the initial point of origin for the 'covenant with Levi' is at Sinai, following the golden calf incident" (contra Garrett, 519–22; Stuart, *Exodus*, 682). Although the idiom "fill the hand," meaning "ordain," was used earlier of Aaron and his sons (Exod. 28:41; 29:9), in 32:29 it is used more broadly of the sons of Levi (cf. Mal. 3:3), who receive "a blessing" they will pronounce on others (Num. 6:23–24; Deut. 10:8–9; 33:8–11). Their support is later assured by "a permanent [*ʿôlām*] covenant of salt before YHWH" (Num. 18:19 AT; cf. Hahn, 157).

A later demonstration of zeal by Aaron's grandson Phinehas in Num. 25:6–15 leads to a divine grant of "my covenant of peace" (perhaps alluded to in Mal. 2:5–6) and a "permanent [*ʿôlām*] priesthood" (25:12–13 AT; cf. Exod. 29:9; 40:15), which narrows the recipients to Phinehas's descendants (Hahn, 157–60). The Levitical responsibility to teach the Torah (Mal. 2:6–7) reflects Deut. 33:10, although it is probably not an allusion (cf. Gibson, 101–5). Though Malachi's priests are suffering for their covenant violation (2:8–9), the covenant remains valid (2:4, "so that my covenant with Levi may continue"). Resolution, described in 3:1–4, will require drastic measures.

Judah's unfaithfulness (2:10–16). Malachi's second issue is Judah's violation of their (Mosaic) covenant with their one divine "Father" and "Creator" (cf. Deut. 32:5–6; Isa. 64:8; Jesus's Jewish opponents may allude to Mal. 2:10 in John 8:41; cf. Menken, 93–94) by committing treacherous acts against covenant siblings (2:10, "each against his brother" [AT]). Malachi, however, focuses on the treachery of men violating marriage covenants witnessed by

God (2:14) and even marrying foreign, idol-worshiping women (2:11; cf. Clendenen, "Malachi," 321–36).

Many have judged 2:15a to be unintelligible, and countless interpretations have been suggested. Gordon Hugenberger offers a reasonable interpretation in which the first "one" (indefinite *'eḥad*) alludes to Gen. 2:24 and refers to the marital oneness of the original paradigmatic couple (132–67; cf. Clendenen, "Malachi," 349–57).

Malachi 2:16 is also challenging (cf. Clendenen, "Malachi," 357–70). The verbs *śn'*, "to hate," and *šlḥ*, "to send away/divorce," occur together only three times in a marital context (cf. Deut. 22:13–19; 24:1–4), and the husband is the subject of both verbs, which involve rejecting his wife. Malachi probably speaks to men who were using Deut. 24:3 to justify divorce for any reason except "something shameful" (Deut. 24:1; Clendenen, "Malachi," 359–70; cf. Kessler, *Maleachi*, 214). God's condemning response is, "If he hates [his wife], divorcing [her], he covers his garment with violence/oppression" (AT).

Yahweh's response to Judah's grumbling (2:17–3:6). In 3:1–6 God condescends to answer Judah's impertinent question in 2:17, "Where is the God of justice?" His ironic answer is essentially, "I'll give you the justice you deserve" (Clendenen, "Messenger," 84–85). He begins in 3:1 by announcing that prior to "the Lord" (*hā'ādôn*) coming to "his temple," he will send "my messenger" (*mal'ākî*). This prophecy, echoed in 4:5 (MT 3:23) with the added identification "Elijah," points to a human prophetic agent associated with the well-known "day of Yahweh" (cf. "the day" in 3:2). The messenger's task to "clear the way" uses the verb *pnh* and the noun *derek*, a phrase occurring only three other times in the OT (Isa. 40:3; 57:14; 62:10). It refers to *God's* "way" only in Isa. 40:3, which, as Mark 1:2–3 recognizes, suggests identifying Malachi's "messenger" with Isaiah's "voice" (Clendenen, "Messenger," 86). The NT recognizes this messenger prophecy as being fulfilled by John the Baptist, Jesus's forerunner (Matt. 11:10–14; Mark 9:11–13; Luke 7:27; Acts 13:23–25), as is also the case with Isaiah's "voice" (Matt. 3:3; Luke 3:4; John 1:23).

The NT quotations of Mal. 3:1 in Matt. 11:10; Mark 1:2–3; Luke 7:27 all identify Jesus with "the Lord" and therefore with Yahweh. They also add the phrase "ahead of you," which may allude to Exod. 23:20. Similarities exist, but so do differences.

> Exod. 23:20 (AT): **Behold**, I am **sending** a **messenger** before you to guard you on the way.
>
> Mal. 3:1 (AT): **Behold**, I am **sending** my **messenger**, and he will prepare a way before me.

The two messengers differ in nature (angel versus prophet) and function (to guard and lead versus to induce repentance). Perhaps Malachi's use of Exodus language "foresees another exodus" in which judgment will be prominent (Beale, 695), but Malachi's intention is not transparent (cf. Gibson, 173; Snyman, 131).

Gibson also makes a cogent argument that the question in Mal. 3:2, "But who can endure the day of his coming?" alludes to Joel 2:11 ("Indeed, great is the day of Yahweh and very dreadful, and who can endure it?" [AT]), which adds to Malachi's use of irony and surprise: "suddenly" (3:5 AT) to them will come judgment rather than vindication (2:17) or comfort (Isa. 40:3) or protection and guidance (Exod. 23:20; Gibson, 177–80; cf. Clendenen, "Messenger," 93).

Malachi 3:5 gives an exemplary list of those against whom the Lord will bring judgment. The concern for adultery, withholding wages, and oppressing widows and orphans is echoed in the NT with terminology from the LXX of this verse in James 1:27; 4:4; and 5:4 (cf. Jobes, 139–41; Johnson, 302).

A divine intervention by a "messenger of the covenant" (3:1) will bring fiery judgment to refine and purify "the sons of Levi" (3:2–4 AT; cf. 2:4). This fits the context of the Lord's coming to his temple (cf. Matt. 21:12) and the importance of the Levites in 1:6–2:9, which suggests that their covenant will endure (2:4).

This endurance is explicit in Jer. 33:14–26, where the Levitical covenant is intertwined with the Davidic covenant. Its permanence is also expressed in Num. 18:19 and 25:13 (cf. Exod. 40:15). The intersection of the two covenants also occurs in Zech. 3 and 6:9–15 and is hinted at in Mal. 3:1–4 (with no clear allusion to these passages), all of which probably point to a messiah who will be priest as well as king (cf. Clendenen, "Messenger," 100–101; Wolters, 186–96; Hahn, 136–75).

A literal Levitical priesthood under the new covenant in the messianic kingdom appears to be ruled out in Heb. 7–8 by the "better" eternal priesthood of the Judahite Jesus (though his mother was a "relative" of the Levitical Elizabeth, Luke 1:36) as the typological fulfillment of Melchizedek, king of Salem and "priest of God Most High" (Gen. 14:18), as predicted in Ps. 110:4 (cf. Heb. 7:15–18; Schreiner, 221–30). God's intention that Israel would be a "kingdom of priests" to the nations (Exod. 19:6) was not thwarted, but fulfillment required a temporary splitting of king and priest because of Israel's sin. The split would continue conceptually after hints were given of (1) the provisional nature of the Levitical covenant (e.g., Isa. 56:6–7; 61:5–6; 66:1–4, 18–21; cf. Hahn, 168–69) and (2) a future reuniting of king and priest in the deus ex machina of a Melchizedekian messiah (e.g., Ps. 110:4), who would unite in himself Jews and gentiles in a royal priesthood (1 Pet. 2:5–9), including many sons of Levi (Acts 4:36; 6:7).

Tithes and blessings (3:7–12). Whereas negative commands to "stop" doing those things are dominant in Mal. 1:2–3:6, positive commands conclude the book: "Return!" in 3:7 and "Remember!" in 4:4. Malachi 3:7 echoes Zech. 1:2–6a (esp. v. 3) with the reference to Judah's disobedient ancestors and the identical call to "return to me, and I will return to you." This shows by analogy that repentance is still called for and possible. Whereas Zechariah points to past results of stubborn rebellion, Malachi's focus is only on how ingrained is their disobedience, exemplified by their ingratitude and consequent rejection of God's right to redistribute a tenth of their produce according to Mosaic legislation (cf. Lev. 27:30–32; Num. 18:21–32; Deut. 12:5–19; 14:22–27).

As a result, God points out in Mal. 3:9, "By the curse you are being cursed" (AT), using the term (*hammǝʾērâ*) that in 2:2 represents the covenant curses of Deut. 28, which are still operative. The phrase "the fruit of your land," found six times in Deut. 28, twice with the verb for "devour" (vv. 33, 51), is found with the same verb in Mal. 3:11. Malachi's use of the verb "rebuke" (*gʿr*) in 3:11 (and 2:3) may also allude to the curse in Deut. 28:20 (cf. Gibson, 192–93). If they will repent, God will "open the floodgates of heaven" (3:10) and flood them with blessings, a reverse allusion to the judgment in Gen. 7:11 and 8:2 (cf. 2 Kings 7:2, 19).

Coming day of reward and judgment (3:13–4:3). Judah's withholding of their tithes shows their bitterness toward God for his perceived unfaithfulness in not rewarding their superficial and dishonest worship (3:13–15). Besides these self-righteous ones and the prospering wicked they envy (3:15) is a third group of genuine believers whose speech to "one another" (3:16) is evidently the opposite of the self-righteous. On the coming day of judgment, these will be spared as members of God's "treasured possession" (*sǝgullâ*, 3:17), the "kingdom of priests and . . . holy nation" that many in Israel have forfeited (Exod. 19:5; cf. Deut. 7:6; 14:2; 26:18; Ps. 135:4).

Final command (4:4–6). Many scholars see 4:4–6 as an editorial addition to the book intended to conclude the Prophets with a repetition of Josh. 1:7, to link it to the Pentateuch with the reference to Moses, and even to link it to Ps. 1 and the Writings with the reference to the Torah (cf. Snyman, 182–87). Gibson effectively points out the weaknesses in this view (215–35). Although "Moses my servant" occurs elsewhere only in Josh. 1:2 and 1:7 (ESV; cf. "my servant Moses" in Num. 12:7, 8; 2 Kings 21:8), which may point to an allusion, early variations in canonical book order must be acknowledged. Malachi may be using God's warning for Joshua to "observe" the Torah, "which Moses my servant commanded you" (Josh. 1:7 AT), as an instructive analogy. God is now calling for Israel to "remember" the Torah, "which I commanded [Moses] at Horeb for all Israel" but which they have forgotten (Mal. 4:4 AT). Also, as "life and peace" (2:5; cf. Prov. 3:2) have always depended on Israel's response to God's instruction through Moses, so it will be on the day of Yahweh. As "all Israel" entered "the great and fearsome" wilderness with God's instruction after breaking God's covenant at Horeb (Deut. 1:19 AT; cf. 9:7–8), so Israel will enter "the great and fearsome day of Yahweh" with Moses's instruction (Mal. 4:5). The typological connection to Horeb in Malachi may be intended to add weight to Yahweh's warning.

The exact phrase "before the coming great and fearsome day of Yahweh" (AT) occurs elsewhere only in Joel 2:31. There the stress is on vindication, deliverance, and blessing for all God's people who will turn (*šûb*) to him with all their heart and gather for prayers of contrition (2:12–17). As in Mal. 3:2 citing Joel 3:11, Malachi uses Joel ironically again to warn that the experience of individuals on that day will depend on whether they fulfill Joel's conditions and thus join those who fear Yahweh (Mal. 3:16–17) and remember his Torah.

Many parallels exist between Moses and Elijah that may explain the latter's role in Malachi and their consequent appearance together on the Mount of Transfiguration (Matt. 17:1–13; Mark 9:2–13; Luke 9:28–36)—most notably their theophanic encounters with God at "Horeb, the mountain of God" (Exod. 3:1; 1 Kings 19:8). The role to be played by the eschatological prophet calls for someone "in the spirit and power of Elijah" (Luke 1:17), suggesting a typological relationship between Elijah and John. However, a direct fulfillment of Mal. 4:6 is indicated by John's mission to "turn the hearts of the fathers to the children" (AT). Gabriel's description of John's role, which exceeds the wording of Mal. 4:6, probably involves a contextual interpretation suggested by Mal. 2:6 (the ideal priest "turned many from iniquity" [ESV]) and 3:7 ("Return to me, and I will return to you"), both of which use the verb *šûb*, "turn, return." Jesus may echo this interpretation of 4:6 when he says, "Elijah is coming and will restore all things" (Matt. 17:11 AT; cf. Mark 9:12). On differences between the MT and LXX of Mal. 4:6 (and also Sir. 48:10) and Luke's Greek text, see Pao and Schnabel (258). Despite NT fulfillments of much of Malachi, however, there remains the time when "the sun of righteousness will rise with healing in its wings" (4:2 AT) and the Messiah will be celebrated and served by all the nations "in every place" (1:11).

Bibliography. Beale, G. K., *A New Testament Biblical Theology* (Baker Academic, 2011); Clendenen, E. R., "Malachi," in *Haggai, Malachi*, by R. A. Taylor and E. R. Clendenen, NAC (Broadman & Holman, 2004); Clendenen, "'Messenger of the Covenant' in Malachi 3:1 Once Again," *JETS* 62 (2019): 81–102; Clendenen, "A Passionate Prophet," *BBR* 23 (2013): 207–21; Fishbane, M., *Biblical Interpretation in Ancient Israel* (Oxford University Press, 1985); Floyd, M. H., *Minor Prophets: Part Two*, FOTL 22 (Eerdmans, 2000); Fox, R. M., *A Message from the Great King* (Eisenbrauns, 2015); Garrett, D. A., "Levi, Levites," in *DOTP*, 519–22; Gibson, J., *Covenant Continuity and Fidelity*, LHBOTS 625 (Bloomsbury T&T Clark, 2016); Hahn, S. W., *Kinship by Covenant* (Yale University Press, 2009); Hess, R. S., *The Old Testament* (Baker Academic, 2016); Hill, A. E., *Malachi*, AB (Doubleday, 1998); Hugenberger, G. P., *Marriage as a Covenant* (Baker, 1994);

Jobes, K. H., "The Minor Prophets in James, 1 & 2 Peter and Jude," in *The Minor Prophets in the New Testament*, ed. M. J. J. Menken and S. Moyise (T&T Clark, 2009), 135–53; Johnson, L. T., *The Letter of James*, AB (Doubleday, 1995); Kessler, R., *Maleachi*, HTKAT (Herder, 2011); Kessler, "The Unity of Malachi and Its Relation to the Book of the Twelve," in *Perspectives on the Formation of the Book of the Twelve*, ed. R. Albertz et al. (de Gruyter, 2012), 223–36; Menken, M. J. J., "The Minor Prophets in John's Gospel," in *The Minor Prophets in the New Testament*, ed. M. J. J. Menken and S. Moyise (T&T Clark, 2009), 79–96; Pao, D. W., and E. J. Schnabel, "Luke," in *CNTUOT*, 251–414; Pfeiffer, E., "Die Disputationsworte im Buche Maleachi," *EvT* 19 (1959): 546–68; Rudolph, W., *Haggai-Sacharja-Maleachi*, KAT (Gerd Mohn, 1976); Schreiner, T. R., *Commentary on Hebrews*, BTCP (Holman Reference, 2015); Snyman, S. D., *Malachi*, HCOT (Peeters, 2015); Stuart, D. K., *Exodus*, NAC (B&H, 2006); Stuart, "Malachi," in *The Minor Prophets*, ed. T. E. McComiskey (Baker, 1998), 3:1245–396; Weyde, K. W., *Prophecy and Teaching* (de Gruyter, 2000); Wolters, A., *Zechariah*, HCOT (Peeters, 2014).

E. Ray Clendenen

Manuscripts, NT

See Septuagint articles

Manuscripts, OT

See Septuagint articles

Mark, Gospel of

To understand the Gospel of Mark and its Christology requires paying careful attention to its interaction with the OT (see Hays, *Gospels*, 15–103). In some passages Mark quotes the OT explicitly—perhaps around thirty times. Yet frequently Mark's OT references are more allusive. For this latter reason, it could be misleading to focus exclusively on Mark's more explicit uses of the OT. Instead, we must adopt a more holistic understanding of the way that the OT informs Mark's narrative. Mark's more explicit quotations are like the tip of the iceberg that reveal a larger structural role of the OT beneath the surface (see Hays, "Who?," 206–8).

It is also important to note that the criteria (and terminology) one uses to determine "quotations" and "allusions" are debated (see the article "Quotation, Allusion, and Echo" elsewhere in the dictionary). I do not intend to address these terms or the method one uses to identify OT references. For simplicity, I will simply speak of more explicit *citations*, and less explicit *allusions*. Table 1 (drawn especially from NA[28], which I utilize throughout) provides a possible list of the more explicit OT quotations in Mark—whether or not they include an introductory formula (e.g., "it is written").

In what follows I consider various ways Mark engages the OT, with a particular eye to christological and redemptive-historical issues. First, I consider Mark's use of the OT up to Peter's confession at Caesarea Philippi (Mark 1:1–8:30). Second, I consider the use of Scripture after the Caesarea Philippi episode (8:31–16:8; for this structure, cf. Edwards, 20–21).

The OT in Mark 1:1–8:30

Mark 1:1–15. The beginning of Mark's Gospel points to a new "beginning" (*archē*) of the gospel through Christ. This language may evoke the beginning of Scripture (Gen. 1:1: *en archē*; cf. John 1:1).

Immediately after this, supporting this new beginning, comes one of the most important OT references in Mark (Mark 1:2–3). Here Mark introduces a quotation as originating from Isaiah, but it is actually a composite citation from Exod. 23:20; Mal. 3:1; and Isa. 40:3 (see esp. Watts, *Exodus*, 53–90). Mark looks back to the first exodus and the way of Israel through the wilderness (Exod. 23:20) and combines this with the eschatological expectations of Mal. 3:1, which speaks of the messenger who would come to prepare the way for the Lord in judgment. These texts are combined with the main thrust of Mark's quotation, which comes from Isa. 40:3 in Mark 1:3. Isaiah 40 looks forward to Israel's great day of deliverance and consolation, which would be a new, greater exodus. If the first exodus was the paradigm of redemption in the days of Moses, Isaiah speaks of a greater, more lasting exodus when God comes to bring final redemption for his people. This is the message of "good news" in Isa. 40:9 (LXX: *euangelizō*), which correlates to the good news in Mark 1:1 and throughout the Gospel. That Mark identifies this composite quotation as coming from Isaiah highlights the Isaianic contours of the eschatological new exodus that correlates to the new work of redemption that comes through Christ (Watts, *Exodus*, 88–90; Marcus, *Way*, 18–20; Hays, *Echoes*, 21; see also Watts, "Mark," 119–20).

Further, this composite quotation communicates divine Christology. In Isa. 40:3 the one whose way needs to be prepared is the Lord, who has no rivals (see Isa. 40:12–31). Yet in Mark it is Jesus the Lord (*kyrios*) whose way is prepared in the wilderness. Thus, Jesus is identified with the Lord of Isa. 40:3. As Craig Keener (1:305) has argued, "Mark [like the Gospel of John] also believes Jesus is deity: his reapplication of the 'Lord' of Isa 40:3 to Jesus (Mark 1:3) can be understood in no other way."

John the Baptist's appearance and ministry (1:4–8) also build on OT eschatological expectations. John is dressed like Elijah, with camel hair and a belt of leather (2 Kings 1:8; Mark 1:6). This coheres with the anticipation in Mal. 4:5–6 of the return of Elijah: though Elijah did appear with Jesus on the Mount of Transfiguration, Jesus makes clear that it was actually John the Baptist who fulfilled Mal. 4 (see Mark 9:13; cf. Matt. 17:13). Further, John's baptism most likely builds on OT

Table 1. Explicit OT Quotations in Mark

Markan Text	OT Text(s)	Introductory Formula?	Comments / Usage
1:2–3	Exod. 23:20; Isa. 40:3; Mal. 3:1	Yes	Composite citation; Isaianic new exodus
2:25–26	1 Sam. 21:1–6	Yes	A summary, not a precise quotation; David and holy bread at Nob
4:12	Isa. 6:9–10	No	Purpose of parables
6:34	Num. 27:17; 2 Chron. 18:16 (see also Jdt. 11:19)	No	Sheep without a shepherd
7:6–7	Isa. 29:13	Yes	Critique of hypocrisy
7:10a	Exod. 20:12; Deut. 5:16	Yes	Fifth commandment
7:10b	Exod. 21:17	Yes	Death penalty for breaking fifth commandment
8:18	Jer. 5:21	No	Lack of spiritual understanding
9:48	Isa. 66:24	No	Punishment of God's enemies
10:6	Gen. 1:27 (see also Gen. 5:2)	No	Creation of man and woman
10:7–8	Gen. 2:24	No	Marriage of man and woman
10:19	Exod. 20:12–16; Deut. 5:16–20 (Exod. 21:10? Prov. 17:5? Sir. 4:1?)	Yes	Fifth through ninth commandments ("Do not defraud" source uncertain)
11:9–10	Ps. 118:25–26	No	Royal expectations of Davidic Son
11:17a	Isa. 56:7	Yes	Temple's design: house of prayer for all nations
11:17b	Jer. 7:11	No	Temple's reality: den of violent bandits
12:10–11	Ps. 118:22–23	Yes	Jesus as rejected cornerstone
12:26	Exod. 3:6	Yes	God's promises and the resurrection
12:29–30	Deut. 6:4–5	Yes	Shema and first great commandment
12:31	Lev. 19:18	Yes	Second great commandment
12:32	Deut. 6:4	No	Scribe's response: God is one
12:32	Isa. 45:21; possibly Deut. 4:35	No	Scribe's response: none other but God
12:33	Deut. 6:5	No	Scribe's response: love for God
12:33	Lev. 19:18	No	Scribe's response: love for neighbor
12:36	Ps. 110:1	Yes	David's Son and David's Lord
13:14	Dan. 11:31; 12:11	No	"Abomination of Desolation"
13:24–25	Isa. 13:10; 34:4; Joel 2:10	No	Cosmic judgment
13:26	Dan. 7:13–14	No	Son of Man coming with clouds
14:27	Zech. 13:7	Yes	"Strike the shepherd"
14:34	Ps. 42:5, 11; 43:5	No	Anguish of soul
14:62	Ps. 110:1; Dan. 7:13	No	Composite quotation; future coming and vindication of Son of Man
15:24	Ps. 22:19	No	Divided garments
15:34	Ps. 22:2	No	Cry of dereliction

expectations of eschatological, final cleansing from sin (e.g., Jer. 31:31–34; Ezek. 36:25–26, 33; 37:23; Zech. 13:1; see Vos, 315–16).

Jesus's baptism (1:9–11) should also be understood in light of the OT. When Jesus comes up out of the water, Mark's Gospel is unique in saying the heavens were "ripped open" (*schizomenous*, 1:10). Scholars often point out the likely background here from Isa. 64:1 [63:19 MT/LXX]: "Oh that you would rend the heavens and come down!" (ESV). Whereas the term for "rend" in the LXX is "open" (*anoigō*), in the MT the Hebrew verb *qāraʿ* seems to provide the background for Mark's use of *schizō* (so, e.g., Hays, *Echoes*, 18; Watts, "Mark," 120–22; Marcus, *Mark 1–8*, 159). This context in Isaiah looks back to the glorious work of the Lord in the exodus (63:7–14), bemoans the suffering of God's people, and looks forward to a new day of redemption like the first exodus (63:15–64:12). The cry to "rend the heavens and come down" is thus a cry of God's people for a new work of redemption. For Mark, this work begins in earnest once Jesus is baptized and begins his public ministry. The voice from heaven affirming Jesus's sonship recalls Ps. 2:7 ("You are my son") and Isa. 42:1 ("I am well pleased," *rāṣtâ napšî*), along with the language of "beloved" (*agapētos*) from Gen. 22:2 (e.g., Lane, 57) or perhaps reflecting *bəḥîrî* from Isa. 42:1 MT (so Cranfield, 55). If so, then the heavenly voice identifies Jesus as the true Davidic king, the servant of Isaiah, and the true son of Abraham (cf. also Matt. 1:1).

In the temptation account (1:12–13), Jesus is likely portrayed as a new Adam whose peaceful presence with the wild animals (recalling the paradise of Eden) signifies that he ushers in the era of peace envisioned by the prophets (Isa. 11:1–9; 65:25; see Crowe, 25–27, 74–80). For, indeed, the covenantal blessings included protection from wild animals (Lev. 26:6), while the covenantal curses included the threat of wild animals (Lev. 26:21–22). At the same time, Jesus's forty-day temptation in the wilderness may recall David's wilderness trials after his anointing as king (see esp. 1 Sam. 20–31), prior to his consolidation of and open rule over the kingdom. Additionally, the wilderness context again suggests that a new exodus is at hand (see also Exod. 23:29–31).

Immediately after this, Jesus announces the good news of the kingdom (Mark 1:14–15). The good news likely finds a background in texts such as Isa. 40:9 (noted above) and 52:7 (see Pennington, 14–16). The servant of Isaiah looms large in Mark, for Jesus is the servant of whom Isaiah spoke (see esp. Marcus, *Way*, 186–96), who will give his life as a ransom for many (Mark 10:45). The kingdom of which Jesus speaks in this context evokes the Lord's promise to David of a kingdom that would never end (e.g., 2 Sam. 7:14–16; Ps. 132:11–12).

Mark 1:16–8:30. Fishers of people. Jesus's next action in Mark is to call disciples whom he will make fishers of people (1:16–20). It has been argued that this image is one of judgment, coming from Amos 4 (see Hays, *Echoes*, 24–25). Yet one could also argue that this is a more positive theme, since by catching people the disciples are presumably gathering them into the kingdom of God that they might escape judgment, perhaps also participating in a new exodus (see, e.g., Jer. 16:14–16, noted in Marcus, *Mark 1–8*, 184; see also John 21:11, perhaps drawing from Ezek. 47:9–10; cf. Bauckham, *Testimony*, 271–84).

Son of Man. Jesus's most common self-designation in Mark is Son of Man, which occurs for the first time in 2:1–12. Jesus's use of the designation is cryptic, and scholars disagree on its background, and whether it is even a title. It seems best to appreciate that this phrase is less clear at the beginning of the Gospel but becomes clearer as the Gospel progresses. By the end of Mark we know much more about not only the suffering of the Son of Man (8:31; 9:31; 10:33–34) but also his future vindication and glory. In Mark 13:26; 14:62 Jesus seems rather clearly to speak of the Son of Man coming with the clouds in language from Dan. 7:13–14, which brings clarity to earlier uses of "Son of Man" as well.

Further, in Dan. 7 the human dimensions of the Son of Man's kingdom stand in contrast to the beastly, ungodly kingdoms. The designation Son of Man therefore speaks to the true humanity of Jesus in language that quite likely evokes Adam's original estate. Daniel 7 builds on the "son of man" reference in Ps. 8:4 (8:5 MT/LXX), which itself reflects Adam's original created state in Gen. 1–2, and likely points to Jesus's role as a new Adam who has come to rectify the problems deriving from the first Adam (see Crowe, 38–40; see also Marcus, "Son").

Highlighting the divine authority of the Son of Man in Mark 2:1–12 is Jesus's authority to forgive sins (2:5, 10). In the OT God forgives sins (e.g., Exod. 34:6–7; Num. 14:19; 1 Kings 8:30; Ps. 32:1–2, 5; 51:2, 7–9; 103:3; 130:4; Isa. 1:18; 6:7; 43:25). Indeed, the opponents' question in Mark 2:7 probably invokes the language of the Shema. "Who is able to forgive sins except one—namely, God [*ei mē heis ho theos*]?" (AT) likely recalls *kyrios ho theos hēmōn kyrios heis estin* ("The LORD our God, the LORD is one") from Deut. 6:4 (see Lee, 153–74). If so, then the passage revolves to a significant degree on the authority of Jesus as Son of Man in relation to the identity of God. Jesus's authority to heal the paralyzed man illustrates his divine authority to forgive sins (2:10–12). Additionally, Jesus's knowledge of the men's thoughts (2:6) likely also points to his deity—in this case, to know the heart in the way only God knows (e.g., Gen. 6:5; 1 Sam. 16:7; Pss. 94:11; 139:2, 4, 23; Isa. 66:18).

Another important passage for understanding the christological dimensions of the OT is Mark 2:23–28. Three issues are pertinent from this text. First, we must ask what OT passage Jesus envisions when he mentions the passage about Abiathar, when he seems to refer rather to the passage about Ahimelech (1 Sam. 21:1–6). Mark did not simply get this wrong (cf. Marcus, *Mark 1–8*, 241). More likely possibilities are that Abiathar is the more familiar priest (so possibly Cranfield, 116), and/or Mark's preposition *epi* in 2:26 may refer only to the "passage about" rather than "time when" (see Lane, 115–16). Abiathar is also the priest who brought the priestly ephod to David (1 Sam. 30:7), which may highlight royal-priestly themes also in Mark 2 (see below).

Second, why were David and his men not wrong to eat the bread set apart for the priests? The most likely answers are (1) that the moral law to care for human life is superior to ceremonial laws (see Bavinck, 77, 80–82, 86–87), and/or (2) that David's role as a royal-priestly figure typologically anticipates the work of Christ as an even greater royal-priestly figure, as illustrated by the statement in 2:28 (cf. Edwards, 95–96).

Third, Jesus speaks of his lordship over the Sabbath as Son of Man (Mark 2:27–28). In 2:27 Jesus assumes the creation of humanity as the apex of creation and speaks of the Sabbath in a way that reflects that created order. Indeed, humanity was created prior to the Sabbath (Hendriksen, 108). But since Jesus is the authoritative man as (divine) Son of Man (see 2:10–12), he has authority not only over all of humanity but also over the day that was created for the benefit of humanity. In other words, if Jesus has authority over the greater (humanity), then he has authority also over the lesser (the Sabbath day). Jesus does not violate the Sabbath but shows us its true intention (see also Mark 3:4). Here again "Son of Man" is an authoritative title, especially when coupled with the term "Lord" (*kyrios*), which is an important christological predication in Mark (see Johansson; see also Garland, 258).

Binding the strong man. In Mark 3:22–30 Jesus is accused of being possessed by Beelzebul. In Mark this means the devil (see 3:22), but it could derive from Beelzebub (= "lord of the flies") in 2 Kings 1:2–3 (see also Davies and Allison, 2:195), or is perhaps better translated as "lord of the house," in light of *zəbūl* (= "habitation"; see *HALOT*, 1:263) in texts like 1 Kings 8:13; Ps. 49:14 (v. 15 MT); Isa. 63:15; Hab. 3:11 (following Marcus, *Mark 1–8*, 272). Here Jesus speaks of himself as the stronger man (cf. Mark 1:7) who binds the strong man—that is, the devil. At least two OT allusions here are worth considering. First, this may be again Adamic imagery, for 3:22–30 evokes the temptation account of 1:12–13 (on the literary structure, see Shively, 1–2, 154–63; Best, 12). Second, the language may also evoke Babylon as a strong man who held God's people in captivity (Isa. 49:24–25, noted in, e.g., Watts, "Mark," 145–48). Similar themes arise in the healing of the Gadarene demoniac (Mark 5:1–20).

Purpose of parables. In Jesus's explanation of the parables (4:10–12), he quotes Isa. 6:9–10 to indicate typological use of the OT. As was true of Isaiah's ministry, Jesus's prophetic ministry will elicit unbelief (see, e.g., Mark 3:6, 22, 30), and those who do not believe are held responsible for that unbelief (cf. 14:21). At the same time, divine revelation is given to those with eyes to see and ears to hear (see 4:11). This is a theme we see throughout Mark. Later Jesus will quote Jer. 5:21 and apply it typologically even to the disciples: "Having eyes do you not see, and having ears do you not hear?" (Mark 8:18 ESV). This will be illustrated by the two-stage healing of the blind man (8:22–25) and will be further highlighted by Peter's inadequate understanding at Caesarea Philippi (see 8:27–33).

The law, Christology, and redemptive history. The OT law plays a significant role throughout Mark. Because of the law Herod has John the Baptist arrested (Mark 6:16–18). At least two aspects of the OT seem to be in view here. First, according to Lev. 18:16, it is not lawful to marry the wife of one's brother. Second, to take another man's wife is adulterous and violates God's original intention (cf. Mal. 2:16; Matt. 5:32). Later (Mark 10:2–12) Jesus explains that although Deut. 24:1 allowed divorce in the Mosaic law, it was not God's design from the beginning. Instead, drawing on the abiding authority of Gen. 1:27 (see also 5:2) and 2:24, Jesus affirms that marriage is to be a lifelong commitment of a man and a woman, and this should characterize the ethics of his disciples.

Debates about the law play a key role in Mark 7. In response to the critique that he and his disciples do not ritually wash their hands before they eat, Jesus quotes Isa. 29:13 typologically to point out the hypocrisy of those who wash outwardly while inwardly their hearts are far from God, and who reject the law of God in favor of human traditions. This recalls the judgments pronounced against God's own people in Isaiah's day. Jesus illustrates their hypocrisy by showing how his opponents violate the fifth commandment, to honor one's father and mother (Exod. 20:12; Deut. 5:16; see also Exod. 21:17), by substituting a human command whereby money is offered to God instead of used to support one's parents, which violates the clear teaching of God's law, which has an abiding authority. Jesus also clarifies that external impurity does not lead us to sin; rather, sin comes from sinful hearts (7:15–23). Here Jesus teaches that the law is spiritual and permanent. Yet he also teaches that there is a shift with respect to the law in the context of redemptive history, for in 7:19 Jesus declares all foods clean. The coming of Christ thus marks a new stage in the application of the law, with the moral aspects more clearly delineated from the ceremonial aspects. Thus, later NT teaching on the freedom of believers to avoid food regulations finds its foundation in Christ's own teaching (e.g., Acts 10:10–16, 28, 34–35; 1 Cor. 10:24–27).

Miracles and the OT. The OT is also important to understand the ways Jesus reveals his messianic identity to his disciples. When Jesus raises a girl who died (Mark 5:35–43), he demonstrates divine authority to grant life (e.g., Deut. 32:39; cf. Bauckham, *Testimony*, 246–48). In Mark 6:34 Jesus identifies the crowds as sheep without a shepherd, likely invoking Num. 27:17; 2 Chron. 18:16 typologically. Mark 6:34 thus employs royal, messianic imagery from the OT: the Messiah will guide his people in peace (see Jer. 23:1–8; Ezek. 34:23–31; see Block, 275–76, 296). Interestingly, "shepherd" language is also used of the Lord himself (see Ps. 23; Ezek. 34:1–16), suggesting a close relationship between the messianic shepherd and the Lord. In Mark, Jesus is the new David who shepherds the sheep, and as Son of God is himself divine. Indeed, when Jesus feeds the five thousand, he not only is embodying messianic anticipations of a coming prophet like Moses (cf. John 6:14–15) but also parallels the Lord, who provided the Israelites bread from heaven and was expected to provide a future feast in the wilderness (see Neh. 9:15; Ps. 78:24; Isa. 25:6; see also John 6:31–32; see further Davies and Allison, 2:481–85; Lane, 232). The abundance of Jesus's baskets left over after feeding five thousand men also recalls, even as it is greater than, when Elisha fed one hundred men from twenty loaves and some grain and had some left over (2 Kings 4:42–44; e.g., Lane, 229–31).

Twice Jesus calms a storm. In Mark 4:35–41 Jesus is asleep in the stern of the ship when the disciples rouse him and cry out that they are perishing. In his sleeping during a troublesome time, Jesus models the trust in God's care we see in Ps. 3:5 (cf. Jon. 1:4–6). Further, it has been argued that the rousing of Jesus recalls Ps. 44:23 ("Awake! Why are you sleeping, O Lord? Rouse yourself! Do not reject us forever!" ESV)—the sovereign one who is roused to save his people, which thus highlights Jesus's divinity (Marcus, *Mark 1–8*, 338). Jesus's stilling of the sea with a word recalls the authority of the Lord from the OT (Ps. 65:6–7; 107:28–29), including the exodus imagery of triumphing over the waters (so Marcus, *Mark 1–8*, 338).

Similarly, in Mark 6:45–52 Jesus again calms a storm, but this time without a word. In this instance, Jesus walks on the sea, recalling the path of the Lord in the exodus (see Ps. 77:16–20). Further, that Jesus wanted to "pass by" his disciples (6:48) likely echoes Job 9:8 and other theophanic texts in which the Lord's glory passes by his people (e.g., Exod. 33:19–22; 1 Kings 19:11; cf. Hays, *Echoes*, 70–73).

Two unique Markan healings (7:32–37; 8:22–26) invoke the OT to point to the dawning of the messianic age through Jesus. In Mark 7:32 the rare term *mogilalos* ("difficult of speech") fulfills Isa. 35:5–6, which speaks of the deaf speaking and the blind seeing as part of the description of the coming messianic age (see also 7:37; cf. France, *Mark*, 302; see also France, *Matthew*, 424–25). Similarly, the two-stage healing of the blind man in Mark 8:22–26 may also speak of the direct fulfillment of Isa. 35:5–7. Both these healings propel the narrative forward to Peter's confession of Jesus as the Christ.

The OT in Mark 8:31–16:8

Mark 8:31–10:52. Transfiguration and the suffering servant. After Peter confesses Jesus as the Christ—that is, the Messiah who would take the reins of the Davidic kingdom (see 8:29)—Jesus predicts his death and resurrection three times (see 8:31–33; 9:30–32; 10:32–34; see Lane, 292–94; Marcus, *Mark 8–16*, 604). Jesus speaks about his role as Son of Man, but also invokes the language of Isaiah's Servant Songs (Isa. 42; 49; 50; 52–53; so Marcus, *Way*, 187–90). This can be found in Mark 10:45, where the Son of Man who gives his life (*psychē*) as a ransom for many (*pollōn*) likely evokes Isa. 53:12 (so Marcus, *Way*, 187). Other OT texts that serve as background to this text include Dan. 7:13–14 (used ironically, for the Son of Man should be served) and Ps. 49:7–8 (only the Son of Man can give his life as a ransom). Similarly, Mark 10:34 may allude to the spitting on the Isaianic servant (Isa. 50:6; also noted by Marcus, *Way*, 189–90). In the preceding context Jesus teaches the need to deal decisively with sin, which is dangerous and can lead to hell (9:47). Jesus invokes the last verse of Isaiah (66:24) to speak of the future of God's enemies whose "worm does not die and the fire is not quenched" (Mark 9:48 ESV). Jesus may also allude in 9:49 to Lev. 2:13 ("salted with fire"). This is a difficult verse, but salt and fire in Mark 9:49 "appear to be symbols of the trials and cost of discipleship" (Edwards, 296), though it may refer to the fire of the Holy Spirit (see Watts, "Mark," 194–96; Marcus, *Mark 8–16*, 698).

After Jesus's first prediction of his death and resurrection comes the transfiguration (9:1–8). Appearing with Jesus on the mount are Moses and Elijah. As is commonly noted, both figures were associated with eschatological expectations (see also Mark 6:15; 8:28). But it is also noteworthy that both Moses and Elijah were witnesses of theophany (Exod. 33:17–23; 1 Kings 19:11–18). To see Jesus on the Mount of Transfiguration is to see the glorious, divine Son of God. Further, the heavenly voice tells the disciples to listen to Jesus, citing Deut. 18:15. Jesus is the prophet whom Moses predicted, and attention focuses here on Jesus more than Moses or Elijah. The glory that is unveiled in the transfiguration anticipates the glory of the returning Son of Man from Dan. 7:13–14, noted elsewhere in Mark (13:26; 14:61–62).

Challenge to the rich man. In 10:17–22 Jesus challenges the man who wants to know what he can do to inherit eternal life. Jesus quotes at least four of the Ten Commandments from the so-called second table of the law (a fifth commandment is of uncertain source; cf. Exod. 21:10; Sir. 4:1; see also Prov. 17:5, suggested by Skehan and Di Lella, 165). The man's obedience was insufficient to inherit eternal life (10:21–22), and Jesus may well be assuming the principle "do this and live" from Lev. 18:5 to highlight the man's inadequate obedience (see further Crowe, 181–82). Further, in the opening exchange Jesus may allude to Deut. 6:4 when he speaks of only God as good in 10:18 (*ei mē heis ho theos*; so Lee, 175–93), and it has even been suggested that Jesus's challenge for the man to follow him recalls the first commandment (Cranfield, 330).

Mark 11:1–16:8. Triumphal entry, the temple, and controversies. Explicit appeal to the OT increases after the triumphal entry, where Jesus enters as Son of David (see also 10:46–52). Though it is not cited in Mark, the colt on which Jesus rode must be taken as a fulfillment of Zech. 9:9 (see Matt. 21:4–5; John 12:15). When Jesus enters Jerusalem the crowds greet him with the messianic acclamation derived from Ps. 118:25–26, which may reflect *hôšîʿâ nāʾ* from the MT, since "Hosanna" is not present in the LXX. In Mark 12:10–11 Jesus speaks of himself as the rejected cornerstone, which also derives from Ps. 118 (vv. 22–23). This is temple language, as Ps.

118 points typologically to Jesus, who is the reality to which the physical temple pointed. In his resurrection Jesus will be seen as the precious cornerstone: rejected by men, but accepted and precious to God (see 1 Pet. 2:6). Soon after the triumphal entry Jesus approaches the temple (Mark 11:11), fulfilling Mal. 3:1 (see Mark 1:2).

Jesus's cursing of the fig tree (11:12–14, 20) must be understood in relation to Jesus's actions in the temple, when Jesus overturned the tables of the money changers and would not allow anyone to carry vessels through the temple (11:15–16). Here at least two aspects are worth considering. First, Jesus appears to be critiquing the temple authorities for making it a profit center (cf. John 2:16; see also Bauckham, "Demonstration"). Second, Jesus may be focusing especially on the temple's sacrificial system and pointing to the true atonement that he provides (see Garland, 490–93). Jesus then quotes two OT passages. The first is Isa. 56:7 and the expectation that in the future the temple will be a house of prayer for all nations. Instead, Jesus states that it had become a den of armed bandits (*lēstai*), quoting Jer. 7:11. This context in Jeremiah is one of misplaced trust in the temple in spite of the people's continued resistance to the voice of God. Jesus's critique of the temple, employing Jer. 7:11 typologically, is clarified by the cursing of the fig tree, which is a prophetic-parabolic action that suggests the faithlessness of Israel, which in the OT could be illustrated by a barren fig tree (see esp. Jer. 8:13; so Snodgrass, 259).

Several controversies in Mark 12 center on the OT. In the question about paying taxes to Caesar (12:13–17), the rejoinder of "Whose image is on the coin?" has often been taken as an echo of humanity made in God's image (Gen. 1:26–27; see already Ign. *Magn.* 5:2). Following this comes a question from the Sadducees about the resurrection (Mark 12:18–27), whom Jesus critiques because they know neither the Scriptures nor the power of God (12:24). Jesus then explains from Exod. 3:6 that God's covenant promises are unbreakable, and points to fulfillment in the resurrection age, for God is the God not of the dead but of the living.

Next comes a question about the greatest commandment in the OT (Mark 12:28–34). Jesus quotes Deut. 6:4–5 to speak of love for God as the first great commandment and adds Lev. 19:18 as the second great commandment. Jesus focuses on the moral dimensions of the OT, specifically love for God and neighbor. To this the scribe responds positively, affirming that God is one (Deut. 6:4) and has no rivals (Isa. 45:21; possibly Deut. 4:35). This scribe further echoes a theme consistent with what we find in Mark 7 and elsewhere, that God desires mercy more than burnt offerings (e.g., Ps. 40:6; 51:17; 1 Sam. 15:22; Hosea 6:6). If the great commandment focuses on the oneness of God, then the quotation of Ps. 110:1 that follows in Mark 12:35–37 encourages readers to understand that the identity of the one God includes both Father and Son (Johansson, 116–19; Lee, 112–30). Psalm 110:1 is used typologically to show that Jesus is both David's son (descended from David according to the flesh) and David's Lord (the preexistent Son who will reign at God's right hand in his state of exaltation).

Mark 13 is one of the most difficult portions of the Gospel to interpret, and much hinges on one's understanding of the OT. The divisions of the tribulation that pits family members against one another (13:12) recalls the language of Mic. 7:6. The abomination of desolation in 13:14 echoes the phrasing of Dan. 11:31; 12:11. This abomination came to pass in the first instance under Antiochus IV, who profaned the temple around 167 BC (see 1 Macc. 1:54). This historical event is used eschatologically in Mark 13 to speak about another abomination, perhaps under Caligula or Titus in the first century. If so, this first-century, eschatological abomination may well also prefigure typologically a final, consummate abomination (see 2 Thess. 2:3–4 and discussion in Edwards, 396–400).

A second copse of murky texts comes in Mark 13:24–25, which seems to allude to Isa. 13:10; 34:4; Joel 2:10, but without verbatim agreement with any one text (see further Watts, "Mark," 225–27). Mark 13:24–25 clearly speaks of judgment, but the specifics are difficult to tease out. Mark 13:24 may have a preliminary fulfillment at the death of Christ (15:33), and it may point to the coming judgment on the generation of Jesus's day when the temple is destroyed (see 13:5–23), but it seems to have a future, cosmic judgment in view concerning "that day" (13:24–27). The language from Isa. 13:10 (along with Joel 2:10), though it comes in the context about the judgment of Babylon (see Isa. 13:1), speaks more broadly about the judgment of the whole world on the "day of the LORD" (13:6–13; cf. Motyer, 136–40; Oswalt, 303–8), and that is the way that Mark seems to use it as well. Further supporting this more cosmic dimension is the allusion in Mark 13:26 to the coming of the Son of Man with power and glory from Dan. 7:13–14. This event most likely refers to the second coming of Christ, which is anticipated in the glory of the transfiguration (see also 14:61–62).

Last Supper, trial, and death. William Lane (487) argues that Isa. 53:4–12 and Pss. 22 and 69 are key to understanding the suffering of Christ in light of the will of God. Jesus's Last Supper, a Passover meal (Mark 14:12), recalls the first Passover (Exod. 12:1–6) and the yearly celebration of Passover commanded in the OT. Indeed, throughout Mark's passion account we find echoes of the exodus, confirming that the redemption Jesus is accomplishing is the long-awaited new exodus. The betrayal of Jesus predicted in 14:18 fulfills Ps. 41:9 (Lane, 503). A summary statement in Mark 14:21 affirms that (1) the Son of Man will be handed over just as it has been written in the Scriptures (see also 14:49), but also (2) the sinner is responsible for his actions. In 14:24 Jesus refers to his blood as the blood of the covenant, in language that recalls the blood sprinkled at Sinai (Exod. 24:6–8; Lane, 507). Jesus institutes a new covenant, one that is greater than the Mosaic covenant, for he pours out his own blood "for many" (*hyper pollōn*), which couches Jesus's actions as the suffering servant (Isa. 53:12).

Later, Jesus predicts all his disciples will scatter when he (the shepherd) is struck, which seems to be a direct fulfillment of Zech. 13:7. In his prayer in Gethsemane Jesus employs the language of anguish from Pss. 42:5, 11; 43:5 (Mark 14:34), which may be categorized as a rhetorical or perhaps typological use of the OT. It is highly probable that the psalmists' hope in God for salvation is also assumed in Jesus's prayer.

The OT also plays a key role in Jesus's trial. Those assembled against Jesus do not have sufficient witnesses for a capital offense, which requires two witnesses to agree (Deut. 17:6; 19:15; cf. Mark 14:55–59). One of the most important christological scenes in Mark comes in 14:62, where Jesus confirms he is the Christ, the Son of the Blessed One (see 14:61). Jesus responds, "I am [*egō eimi*], and you will see the Son of Man seated at the right hand of Power, and coming with the clouds of heaven" (14:62 ESV). While *egō eimi* may reflect language of Isa. 40–55 (see Bauckham, *Testimony*, 245–50) and/or Exod. 3, the Son of Man coming with the clouds alludes to Dan. 7:13, and his sitting "at the right hand of Power" refers to Ps. 110:1. Thus, Jesus speaks of his future exaltation, when he will come with the clouds after being installed at God's right hand (see, e.g., Cranfield, 444; Marcus, *Mark 8–16*, 1008). Here the return of Christ is most likely in view, which may be implied by the logic of Ps. 110 itself (Smith and Vaillancourt). Jesus thus invokes the OT to speak of his unique authority as David's son and David's Lord, the divine Son of Man who will in the future come with the clouds.

Further allusions to Isaiah and Psalms come in Mark 15. When Jesus is silent before his accusers (15:5), this likely fulfills Isa. 53:7 (see also Acts 8:32; Marcus, *Way*, 189). Looming large in Mark 15 is the role of Ps. 22, an important prophetic psalm about the suffering and vindication of the Davidic king, which is quoted at least two times. In Mark 15:24 those who are crucifying Jesus cast lots and divide his garments (Ps. 22:18). In Mark 15:34 Jesus quotes Ps. 22:1 ("My God, my God, why have you forsaken me?"), referring to Jesus's bearing the penalty for sin as the Son of David. A third reference likely comes when the people wag their heads in Mark 15:29 (Ps. 22:7; see Gladd, 192–94). It is likely, as is commonly noted, that the wider context of Ps. 22 is assumed throughout Mark 15. Psalm 22 does not end in despair but transitions in 22:22 to speak of God's deliverance (e.g., Gladd, 194; Waltke and Houston, 377). David's suffering and vindication foreshadow typologically the greater suffering of the Son of David. The darkness that covers the land at the death of Jesus (Mark 15:33) may evoke the plagues of the exodus (Exod. 10:21–23), as well as the darkness of gloom prophesied by Amos 8:9–10 (see Ortlund and Beale). When the temple curtain is torn in two (Mark 15:38), the verb used is again *schizō* which may (like 1:11) recall the apocalyptic hope of Isa. 64:1 (63:19 MT).

Resurrection and ending of Mark. Not only does Jesus's death fulfill Scripture, but so also does his resurrection. At least three times in Mark, Jesus has shown the necessity of the resurrection. Although in Mark this is not explicitly related to the fulfillment of Scripture, in some Markan texts the resurrection finds precedent in the OT (e.g., Ps. 118:22–23 in Mark 12:10–11). Further, Jesus has shown that the Sadducees did not understand the Scriptures indicating that there is indeed a resurrection (12:24–27). Likewise, elsewhere in the NT the resurrection is seen to be a scriptural necessity (e.g., Luke 24:25–27, 44–47; Acts 15:16–18; 26:6–8, 22–23), and there is enough evidence in the text to conclude that Mark shares that perspective.

The fear of the women at the empty tomb (16:5–8) is likely taken to be in the manner of "fear and trembling" that we find throughout the Scriptures as the appropriate response to theophany or the reality of the presence of God (e.g., Job 4:12–16; Ps. 2:11–12; see also Mark 5:33, 42; 6:51–52; 9:6; 1 Cor. 2:3; 2 Cor. 7:15; Phil. 2:12; Eph. 6:5, noted in Catchpole, 7–10; see also Hurtado, 439–40). Here Mark's Gospel most likely ends: with an affirmation of the resurrected Christ, remembering the scriptural promise that he sits at God's right hand and will come again with the clouds (Ps. 110:1; Dan. 7:13; Mark 14:62).

Conclusion

The OT is clearly important in Mark. Though it is difficult to make sweeping summaries about Mark's quotations, here I venture some concluding observations.

1. In Mark 1–10, prior to the passion narrative, one observes a focus on texts from the Pentateuch (esp. Exodus) and Isaiah.
2. In the passion narrative (Mark 11–16) one finds an even greater concentration of OT quotations, with more examples coming from Psalms, in addition to the Pentateuch and Prophets (including Daniel).
3. Mark typically follows LXX text forms in these quotations, but some of Mark's allusions to the OT may also reveal knowledge of the Hebrew text.
4. The historical and literary contexts of OT texts are important in Mark, and the typological use of the OT is particularly noteworthy.
5. The OT does not pass away, but it finds its realization in Christ and his work. We thus do well to consider the christological implications of Mark's use of the OT, along with the redemptive-historical development of the OT that is evident with the advent of the new era in Christ. Passages that apply to the "Lord" (YHWH) in the OT can be applied

to Jesus in Mark (e.g., Isa. 40:3). As divine Son, Jesus forgives sins and raises the dead. Yet he is also presented as the true Adam and true Son of David, emphasizing his humanity. Jesus is both David's Son and David's Lord.

Bibliography. Bauckham, R., "Jesus' Demonstration in the Temple," in *Law and Religion*, ed. B. Lindars (James Clarke, 1988), 72–89; Bauckham, *The Testimony of the Beloved Disciple* (Baker Academic, 2007); Bavinck, H., *The Duties of the Christian Life*, vol. 2 of *Reformed Ethics*, ed. J. Bolt (Baker Academic, 2021); Beale, G. K., *Handbook on the New Testament Use of the Old Testament* (Baker Academic, 2012); Best, E., *The Temptation and the Passion*, 2nd ed., SNTSMS 2 (Cambridge University Press, 1990); Block, D. I., *The Book of Ezekiel: Chapters 25–48*, NICOT (Eerdmans, 1998); Calvin, J., *Commentary on a Harmony of the Evangelists*, trans. and ed. W. Pringle, 3 vols. (repr., Baker Books, 2003); Catchpole, D., "The Fearful Silence of the Women at the Tomb," *JTSA* 18 (1977): 3–10; Cranfield, C. E. B., *The Gospel according to St. Mark*, CGTC (Cambridge University Press, 1963); Crowe, B. D., *The Last Adam* (Baker Academic, 2017); Davies, W. D., and D. C. Allison Jr., *The Gospel according to St. Matthew*, 3 vols., ICC (T&T Clark, 1988–97); Edwards, J. R., *The Gospel according to Mark*, PNTC (Eerdmans, 2002); France, R. T., *The Gospel of Mark*, NIGTC (Eerdmans, 2002); France, *The Gospel of Matthew*, NICNT (Eerdmans, 2007); Garland, D. E., *A Theology of Mark's Gospel*, BTNT (Zondervan, 2015); Gladd, B. L., *Handbook on the Gospels* (Baker Academic, 2021); Hays, R. B., *Echoes of Scripture in the Gospels* (Baylor University Press, 2016); Hays, "'Who Has Believed Our Message?,'" *SBL 1998 Seminar Papers*, SBLSP 37, 2 vols. (Scholars Press, 1998), 1:205–25; Hendriksen, W., *Exposition of the Gospel according to Mark*, NTC (Baker, 1975); Hurtado, L. W., "The Women, the Tomb, and the Climax of Mark," in *A Wandering Galilean*, ed. Z. Rodgers et al., JSJSup 132 (Brill, 2009), 427–50; Johansson, D., "*Kyrios* in the Gospel of Mark," *JSNT* 33 (2010): 101–24; Keener, C. S., *The Gospel of John*, 2 vols. (Hendrickson, 2004); Lane, W. L., *The Gospel according to Mark*, NICNT (Eerdmans, 1974); Lee, J. J. R., *The Christological Rereading of the Shema (Deut 6:4) in Mark's Gospel*, WUNT 2/533 (Mohr Siebeck, 2020); Marcus, J., *Mark 1–8*, AB (Doubleday, 2000); Marcus, *Mark 8–16*, AB (Yale University Press, 2009); Marcus, "The Son of Man as Son of Adam, Part II: Exegesis," *RB* 110 (2003): 370–86; Marcus, *The Way of the Lord*, SNTW (T&T Clark, 1993); Motyer, J. A., *The Prophecy of Isaiah* (InterVarsity, 1993); Ortlund, D. C., and G. K. Beale, "Darkness over the Whole Land," *WTJ* 75 (2013): 221–38; Oswalt, J. N., *The Book of Isaiah: Chapters 1–39*, NICOT (Eerdmans, 1986); Pennington, J. T., *Reading the Gospels Wisely* (Baker Academic, 2012); Shively, E. E., *Apocalyptic Imagination in the Gospel of Mark*, BZNW 189 (de Gruyter, 2012); Skehan, P. W., and A. A. Di Lella, *The Wisdom of Ben Sira*, AB (Doubleday, 1987); Smith, M. J., and I. J. Vaillancourt, "Enthroned and Coming to Reign," *JBL* 141 (2022): 513–31; Snodgrass, K. R., *Stories with Intent* (Eerdmans, 2008); Vos, G., *Biblical Theology* (Banner of Truth, 1975); Waltke, B. K., and J. M. Houston, with E. Moore, *The Psalms as Christian Worship* (Eerdmans, 2010); Watts, R. E., *Isaiah's New Exodus and Mark*, WUNT 2/88 (Mohr Siebeck, 1997); Watts, "Mark," in *CNTUOT*, 111–249.

BRANDON D. CROWE

Marriage

Opening the Bible for its teachings on marriage, one would profitably turn to Gen. 2, Eph. 5, 1 Pet. 3, or some other familiar text. Such passages stand out, obviously, and they reveal much. But the Bible has more to say about marriage than can be discerned from various passages along the way. The Bible itself, taken as a whole, is united by a marital theme. The original creation was the home of the first marriage, with Adam and Eve (Gen. 2:18–25). The final creation will be the home of the ultimate marriage, with Christ and his bride (Rev. 19:6–9; 21:1–2, 9). Marriage is not, therefore, just another biblical teaching among others; marriage is one of the overall concepts defining the Bible as a coherent whole. This is so because the great message of the Bible is the love of Christ for his people, and his love is of a marital nature. Marriage reveals the mystery of the gospel itself (Eph. 5:31–32).

Our approach here will be, first, to establish what the OT teaches about marriage. Our interest is not in the marital practices among the covenanted people. At times their behavior was unbiblical to the point of becoming bizarre (Gen. 29:31–30:24). So, we purpose to consider only those OT passages that define and describe marriage with normative authority. Second, we will enrich these foundational understandings with the NT's development of the relevant OT texts. We will find that the NT's development of the OT on marriage elevates the biblical vision from present concerns for personal happiness to the heights of eschatological ultimacy and cosmic renewal.

Marriage in the OT

The equal dignity of the two human sexes is clearly declared in the creation account: "So God created man in his own image, in the image of God he created him; male and female he created them" (Gen. 1:27 ESV). As image-bearers of God, man and woman exercise royal dominion over the lower creation (1:26, 28). This biblical account of human identity leaves no room for anyone held down in subservience. Indeed, Gen. 1:27 is the first verse in the Bible structured with the parallel lines of OT poetry. The text *celebrates* the unique and glorious stature of man and woman under God. By striking contrast, the Babylonian account of creation does not even mention the distinct creation of male and of female.

The two sexes come together in marriage in Gen. 2, where the Bible defines marriage as God means it to be: "For this reason a man will leave his father and mother and be united to his wife, and they will become one flesh" (Gen. 2:24 AT). The point of this verse is to show the ongoing relevance of what God accomplished in the garden of Eden. With the phrase "for this reason," the author turns from looking back to the primal events in Eden, looks around at the broken world of today, and speaks to all post-Eden people, pointing back to God's gift of the first marriage between Adam and Eve as definitional for all marriages in all places and at all times.

As in Gen. 1, the vision of Gen. 2 is uplifting but also somewhat baffling. It is uplifting because, when the Lord God introduces the first woman to the first man, Adam greets her with rhapsodic joy and relief: "This is now bone of my bones and flesh of my flesh; she shall be called 'woman,' for she was taken out of man" (2:23). In the first recorded human words, the man, far from feeling threatened by the woman's obvious equality with himself, rejoices over her as his perfect match. In that spirit of gentle, happy confidence in God's wise gift, the author then endorses this Edenic pattern as normative. That is the whole point of v. 24. But Gen. 2 is also somewhat baffling, because the sensitive reader will wonder why marriage deserves to be featured so prominently in the precedent-setting opening chapters of the entire Bible. Only the NT can finally resolve that mystery.

The distinctive meaning of marriage sets it apart from all other human relationships. Genesis 2:24 sums it up as "one flesh." The word "flesh" suggests mortality (Ps. 78:39), while the word "one" requires comprehensive unity in mutual giving and receiving. The divine pattern for marriage, from the beginning, has always been *one mortal life fully shared*. Neither the husband nor the wife may mark off any part of their individual existence with a "no trespassing" sign, blocking out the open sharing that marriage simply *is*. True marriage entails the courageous risk of total commitment and the tender vulnerability of total openness—but with no shame: "The man and his wife were both naked, and they felt no shame" (Gen. 2:25 AT). What we see, then, in the audacity of "one flesh" is one man and one woman for one lifetime coming together in an all-encompassing union with no boundaries.

As the biblical story moves to the fall narrative of Gen. 3, marriage remains prominent. But now it is the disruptive confusion of marriage that brings the divine order of creation to ruin beyond all human remedies. The wife is misled by satanic temptation (Gen. 3:13; 1 Tim. 2:14), while the husband allows the evil to progress without a word (Gen. 3:6), each one violating their one-flesh union premised in a shared loyalty to God. As a result, the divine decree gives them up to sorrow and suffering in marriage: "To the woman he said, '. . . Your desire will be for your husband, and he will rule over you'" (3:16). The point of this "oracle of destiny" (Kidner, 71) is discernible from the similar language in Gen. 4:7: "It [sin] desires to have you, but you must rule over it." If we apply the logic of that expression to Gen. 3:16, the sense becomes clear. Fallen married couples will be buffeted by two perennial temptations. The woman will be inclined to control ("desire") her husband, and the husband will be inclined to dominate ("rule") his wife, the two of them spiraling down into mutual incomprehension, frustration, isolation, and misery. Under the judgment of God, the lovely harmony of Eden dissolves into the historic "battle of the sexes." We see, then, the enduring marital tragedy of Gen. 3. When, in Adam, we broke from God, we lost more than God. In losing God, we lost everything we ourselves cherish as happy and humane, especially in marriage. And part of our enduring legacy of lostness is our lack of awareness of what marriage is meant to be and our lack of capacity to live up to its true glory.

The rest of the Bible includes accounts of sometimes beautiful and sometimes ugly marriages, depending on whether men and women are putting their hope in God or in themselves. But more prominently, the Bible also tells the gospel story of God's love creating and purifying a bride for his Son. The primary burden of Scripture is not to address the human betrayals of marriage but to announce the good news of God's covenantal faithfulness to his people.

The brokenness of fallen married people is assumed in and judged by the seventh commandment: "You shall not commit adultery" (Exod. 20:14). Apparently, we need to be told how bizarre sexual sin really is—comparable to groveling in idolatry "with stone and wood" (Jer. 3:9). Questions 137–39 of the Westminster Larger Catechism open up the breadth and depth of this holy and wise commandment. For example, "What are the sins forbidden in the seventh commandment?" Answer: "The sins forbidden in the seventh commandment, besides the neglect of the duties required, are adultery, fornication, rape, incest, sodomy and all unnatural lusts"—for starters.

The prophets boldly and lengthily extend the seventh commandment, with shocking degrees of imaginative application, to God's sacred covenant with the nation of Israel (Isa. 1:21; Jer. 2:2, 20, 32; 3:1–10; 13:25–27; Ezek. 16; 23; Hosea 1:1–9; 2:2–13; 3:1–5). What is noteworthy at this point is the increasingly clear connection between the relational model of human marriage and the covenantal bond between the Lord and his people Israel.

But the Wisdom literature, though warning all readers that sexual sin is costly and painful folly (Prov. 2:16–19), also rejoices in the glories of exuberant human sexuality within the covenant of biblical marriage (Prov. 5:15–19; Song of Songs, passim). The purpose of the sages is to help men flourish as men, and women flourish as women, especially within the delicate beauty of married sexuality.

The OT's witness to marriage, then, develops along two parallel lines: the man-with-woman relationship of one flesh (in its ideal state, its fallen brokenness, and its continuing beauty) and the Yahweh-with-Israel relationship of one loyalty (in its pristine originality, its violated tragedies, and its ultimate restoration). These various threads are woven together with finality in the NT.

Marriage in the NT

Three NT passages quote or allude to the key OT text on marriage—its definition in Gen. 2:24. But before we survey those illuminating passages, our attention is first drawn to Jesus in Matt. 5:27–28, where he says, "You have heard that it was said, 'You shall not commit adultery.' But I tell you that anyone who looks at a woman lustfully has already committed adultery with her in his heart." Responding not to the seventh commandment but to the oral tradition ("you have heard") that had grown up around the commandment and had limited and even trivialized the scope of its relevance, Jesus recovers the full authority of the OT commandment, and he is blunt about it. A woman's sexuality is so sacred, so worthy of protection, that even *a thought* invading her privacy offends the God who sees all. The fact that a thought in the mind of a watching man might never enter her experience or even her awareness makes no difference. Her sexuality per se remains inviolate in the sight of God.

Now the three NT uses of Gen. 2:24 lead us into the fullness of NT revelation of the gospel. The first is found in Matt. 19:3–6, where Jesus responds to the hairsplitting legalistic hermeneutics of the Pharisees on divorce:

> Some Pharisees came to him to test him. They asked, "Is it lawful for a man to divorce his wife for any and every reason?"
>
> "Haven't you read," he replied, "that at the beginning the Creator 'made them male and female,' and said, 'For this reason a man will leave his father and mother and be united to his wife, and the two will become one flesh'? So they are no longer two, but one flesh. Therefore what God has joined together, let no one separate."

The Pharisees wish to debate divorce, but Jesus wants them to rediscover marriage. Only then can they rightly consider divorce. So, our Lord thinks his way past the divorce text of Deut. 24:1–4, all the way back to Gen. 1:27 and God's original creation of male and female. The Pharisees' whole approach to marriage and divorce is with furrowed brows, as if the dynamics of manhood and womanhood are fundamentally problematic. But Jesus looks back to their original creation as a glory to rejoice over.

Then Jesus quotes Gen. 2:24—and that as spoken not by Moses but by the Creator, since the true intent of the OT cannot be rightly perceived until we have considered the text not only at the historical level but also at the ultimate theological level. In doing so, Jesus strengthens our understanding of marriage in two ways.

First, in agreement with the Greek textual tradition, he reads that "*the two* will become one flesh." At one level, this is obvious from the facts of the matter. But even the OT kings found a way around the obvious (1 Kings 11:3). And it is as if Jesus anticipates the distortions of marriage in our own day, so that he reaffirms explicitly that the two, male and female, and they only, shall become one in marriage.

Second, Jesus unveils for the first time a deeper reality hidden within the human commonplaces of a man and woman getting married: "What God has joined together . . ." The word "become" in "the two shall become one flesh" is nondescript. Jesus reveals the deeper reality and glory of it: God is there, joining the man and the woman together as they marry. Thus, Jesus asserts directly what Malachi had suggested indirectly (Mal. 2:14–15). When a man and woman get married today, God himself creates a new reality in this world that had not existed before. Every lawful marriage is a wonder of God and worthy to be preserved: "Let no one separate." This is just as true of every imperfect marriage in the world today as it was of the perfect marriage of Adam and Eve in the garden of Eden so long ago.

The second NT use of Gen. 2:24 is found in 1 Cor. 6:15–18a, where Paul instructs the early church in his theology of the human body:

> Do you not know that your bodies are members of Christ himself? Shall I then take the members of Christ and unite them with a prostitute? Never! Do you not know that he who unites himself with a prostitute is one with her in body? For it is said, "The two will become one flesh." But whoever is united with the Lord is one with him in spirit.
>
> Flee from sexual immorality.

Without this astonishing NT revelation, it might never occur to us that our bodies are limbs and organs and members of Christ himself. It might otherwise have seemed an impertinence to think such a thing. But Paul is clear and even insistent about it. To strengthen his assertion and to connect it explicitly with our sexuality, Paul quotes the final phrase of Gen. 2:24: "The two will become one flesh." The one-flesh union of marriage he juxtaposes with the mere physical coupling of sex with a prostitute: "one with her in body." Then Paul adds another bold assertion to complete the picture: "But whoever is united with the Lord is one with him in spirit."

Paul proposes, then, three categories of relationships. First, unmarried sex is a one-body union. Second, married sex is a one-flesh union—one mortal life fully shared, as we saw in Gen. 2. Third, devotion to Christ is a one-spirit union. Thus, Paul makes explicit that human sexuality, male and female in marriage, is analogous to our ultimate relationship with Christ himself. Marriage, therefore, legitimately serves as a picture of our ultimate and eternal union with Christ. And Christian sexual ethics cannot be dismissed as a petty taboo but must be revered as an entailment of the gospel itself and worthy of our most reverent loyalty.

The third NT use of Gen. 2:24 is found in Eph. 5:28–32, where Paul's thinking rises to the ultimate significance of human marriage:

> In this same way, husbands ought to love their wives as their own bodies. He who loves his wife loves himself. After all, no one ever hated their own body, but they feed and care for their body, just as Christ does the church—for we are members of his body. "For this reason a man will leave his father and mother and be united to his wife, and the two will become one flesh." This is a profound mystery—but I am talking about Christ and the church.

The striking thing about this use of Gen. 2:24 is Paul's premise in v. 30: "For we are members of his body." We could not be more near and dear to our Lord. To quote John Calvin, "We are so joined to [Christ] that he does not have anything of his own which he does not share with us." Our risen Lord identifies with us that intimately and fully. Amazingly, we are *members of his body*. Now, where does Paul go next in his thinking? To Gen. 2:24, which he quotes in v. 31. The flow of thought back in the Genesis account was this: Eve was made from Adam's very body. Therefore, marriage is the (re)union of man and woman as one flesh. But now, in the new context of the gospel fully revealed, the flow of thought is this: We are united with Christ as his body. Therefore, marriage displays the ultimate union of Christ and his people in the form of a healthy, one-flesh marriage, such as Eph. 5:22–33 describes. In other words, the deepest reason why a man and a woman fall in love and get married goes beyond their own romance and hormones and other merely human factors; the deepest reason for this very human and common experience is found in the whole drama of human history—namely, the Son of God, with a loving heart and a self-sacrificial purpose, pursuing and winning his bride forever. Eschatological salvation is the final—and the breathtaking—explanation for God's gift of our sexuality and marriage. No wonder, then, that Paul comments in v. 32, "This is a profound mystery." It is why the Book of Common Prayer has long taught us that marriage is "an honorable estate, instituted of God, signifying unto us the mystical union that is betwixt Christ and his Church." The NT shines the full light of the gospel on this OT gift, showing us its true glory, so long hidden from our eyes but now revealed in Christ.

Before the NT ties all the threads together in Revelation, 1 Pet. 3:3–6 instructs Christian wives in the holiness of marriage by appealing to OT precedent:

> Your beauty should not come from outward adornment, such as elaborate hairstyles and the wearing of gold jewelry or fine clothes. Rather, it should be that of your inner self, the unfading beauty of a gentle and quiet spirit, which is of great worth in God's sight. For this is the way the holy women of the past who put their hope in God used to adorn themselves. They submitted themselves to their own husbands, like Sarah, who obeyed Abraham and called him her lord. You are her daughters if you do what is right and do not give way to fear.

Unlike the brilliant unveiling of a heretofore hidden insight in Eph. 5, here Peter appeals to the OT for an inspiring moral example. Sarah can and should be admired not only for her lifelong journey with Abraham, living by faith in God's promises, but also for the particular moment when, though laughing in disbelief, she nevertheless put her hope in God and yielded to Abraham as "my master" (Gen. 18:12 AT). Peter's larger point in the passage is how Christian wives should conduct themselves in relation to husbands who "do not believe the word" (3:1). What does that imply about Abraham, in the logic of Peter's argument? He was not always an inspiring example himself (Gen. 12:11–13). But there still is a way for a Christian woman to respond to a husband when he is less than Christian, and the OT offers a guiding example.

The NT pulls many themes together in Revelation. Not surprisingly, the marriage theme stands out clearly. Standing in stark contrast with "the great prostitute" of this world (17:1–6), "the bride" has made herself ready for the wedding supper of the Lamb (19:6–9). The true church will no longer be a persecuted minority, struggling through this present evil age, but she will be a whole new world, with no rivals, but with only her Lover (21:1–2, 9–10).

The astonishing vision thus imparted through the biblical gospel is the finality of divine love. The laws of physics do not lift our minds to the highest level of reality; it is the love of God that claims ultimacy. And from the beginning, the beautiful but simple drama of man and woman in marriage provides the typological profile of this unfolding gospel grandeur, making the truth of redemption more easily recognizable and alluring along the way. The profound meaning of male and female united in marriage positions the gospel to be received not only as a theological argument but also as a love story—indeed, a work of art.

See also Adam, First and Last; Creation; Image of God

Bibliography. Andreades, S. A., *Engendered* (Weaver, 2015); Girgis, S., R. T. Anderson, and R. P. George, *What Is Marriage?* (Encounter, 2012); Kidner, D., *Genesis*, TOTC (InterVarsity, 1971); Ortlund, R. C., Jr., *God's Unfaithful Wife* (InterVarsity, 1996); Ortlund, *Marriage and the Mystery of the Gospel* (Crossway, 2016); Piper, J., and W. Grudem, eds., *Recovering Biblical Manhood and Womanhood* (Crossway, 1991); Stienstra, N., *YHWH Is the Husband of His People* (Kok Pharos, 1993).

Ray Ortlund

Matthew, Gospel of

The Gospel of Matthew brims with all kinds of uses of the OT. In approximately fifty-five places, Matthew's wording is similar enough to be called a quotation (compared with about sixty-five in the other three Gospels put together). About twenty of these texts are unique to Matthew. Twelve times Matthew explicitly refers to Scriptures being "fulfilled." Countless allusions to and possible echoes of the Hebrew Bible further demonstrate how steeped in the OT Matthew is. Key themes and titles for Jesus draw on still more OT background.

The fulfillment or completion of the sacred narrative of Israel in Jesus can in fact be viewed as the central message of this Gospel (Spadaro; France, 166–205). The densest cluster of quotations appears in the first four chapters, which introduce Jesus first as a baby and then as he prepares for ministry. The Sermon on the Mount (chaps. 5–7) presents the heart of his message of the kingdom, with its thesis statement appearing in 5:17: "Do not think that I have come to abolish the Law or the Prophets; I have not come to abolish them but to fulfill them." The rest of the sermon, especially 5:21–48, illustrates the many novel ways Jesus relates to Scripture, summed up in the famous Golden Rule ("So in everything, do to others what you would have them do to you"), precisely because "this sums up the Law and the Prophets" (7:12)—a two-part reference to the entire OT.

The plot of Matthew then unfolds, revealing Jesus's authority in word and deed, the increasing polarization his ministry causes in Israel, and the impending judgment on the majority of Israel's leaders and many others in the nation, even as they think they are condemning him. The new covenant of Jeremiah (Jer. 31:31–34) is being inaugurated, and what began as a uniquely Jewish mission (Matt. 10:5–6) must now incorporate all peoples of the world (28:18–20). Herman Waetjen (17) aptly summarizes, "Matthew . . . tells the story of Jesus' fulfillment of Israel's Scriptures as the consummation of Israel's history in which God's New Israel is established as God's New Humanity."

Fulfillment Quotations

Three broad categories of fulfillment appear. Occasionally, an OT passage may directly predict what Matthew recognizes has now occurred. Commonly, there is a provisional fulfillment within the OT itself, but the context of the prophecy suggests still more to come. Frequently, too, Matthew employs typology—the recognition of significant, recurring patterns of events in redemptive history that can be attributed only to God (Goppelt; Hays).

Direct fulfillment. Matthew 8:17 ("He took up our infirmities and bore our diseases") quotes Isaiah's fourth Servant Song (Isa. 53:4). The first Servant Song (42:1–9) comes in a context that identifies the servant as Israel (41:8–9), though even then Matthew observes a second referent (see below). By the final Servant Song (52:13–53:12), only an individual can be in view, because he bears Israel's suffering in its place. The Isaianic passage focuses more on spiritual healing; Matthew applies it to a series of physical healings (Matt. 8:1–17). There *is* healing in the atonement, but when and how that healing comes is up to God.

Matthew 21:5 forms an even clearer example, as Jesus rides into Jerusalem on a donkey to fulfill Zech. 9:9. This is how Israel's messianic king will enter the holy city, in glory and triumph, as Jesus's contemporaries recognize. But they fail to recall that this is also a "lowly" entrance on a humble beast of burden by one who comes in peace (v. 10).

Multiple fulfillment. The most famous example of multiple fulfillment is no doubt the first in Matthew. Isaiah 7:14 predicts that a young woman of marriageable age (Heb. *ʿalmâ*) will conceive and bear a son who will be called "God with us" ("Immanuel"). The verses immediately following show that some fulfillment must have occurred within the prophet's lifetime, because the two nations threatening Judah will be laid waste before this child knows right from wrong (vv. 15–16; cf. 8:8). By 9:6, however, the son who is born can be called "Wonderful Counselor, Mighty God, Everlasting Father, Prince of Peace," and his reign in the line of David will never end (v. 7). Clearly, no one before Jesus fulfills that role. Matthew, moreover, follows the LXX in translating *ʿalmâ* as "virgin" (*parthenos*), seeing that woman ultimately as Mary, Jesus's mother. Hints of other pre-Christian messianic interpretations of this passage suggest Matthew was not the first to understand Isaiah in this fashion (Hengel and Bailey).

Still in the context of Isa. 9 (vv. 1–2), Matt. 4:16 fulfills the promise that those living in darkness in Galilee would see a great light. Originally, this referred at least to the return of Israelites from exile. Yet the birth of the son who is also "Mighty God" in this context shows that there had to be more fulfillment to come—the spiritual illumination that the Messiah would provide.

As noted above, Isa. 42:1–4, quoted in Matt. 12:18–21, must have originally referred to Israel modeling godliness before the nations of the world. Nevertheless, by the time the Servant Songs climax in a single individual who suffers for his people's sins, a second stage of fulfillment for the servant appears throughout. Beaton (192) phrases it well: "Jesus [is] royal messiah, . . . the Spirit-endowed, compassionate servant of the Lord whose words and deeds evinced the justice anticipated with the advent of the messiah and the inauguration of the Kingdom of God."

The only fulfillment quotation that Matthew takes over from a canonical source is in 13:13–15, citing Isa. 6:9–10 (cf. Mark 4:12, but without the word "fulfill"). It is also the only fulfillment quotation that cites a specific passage, which is attributed to Jesus. Originally, the prophet was to pronounce judgment on the rebellious Israelites in his day, but the chapter ended with the prediction of a remnant that would also be judged, followed by a stump of "holy seed" (Isa. 6:13). So, Jesus is justified in seeing repeated cycles of fulfillment of Israel's obduracy.

Typological fulfillment. We now turn to what may be called "a reasoned practice that assumes a divinely intended correspondence between God's saving activity at different times in the history of redemption" (Hagner, lvi). Hosea 11:1 is explicitly about the exodus, with Israel as God's son. But remarkably, the same circumstances attend the beginning of the new covenant—God's liberator coming out of Egypt, heading for Israel. The believer in Yahweh's providence could not see this as a chance coincidence; it must be God's hand, bringing a new exodus. The meaning of the OT is "filled full" (another meaning of the Gk. *plēroō*).

Although the OT does not contain fulfillment quotations per se, the concept of typology is certainly present. Already in Jer. 31:15, the prophet refers to the mothers in Israel lamenting the departure of their sons in captivity to Babylon as "Rachel weeping for her children . . . because they are no more." Rachel was Jacob's wife and had died centuries earlier. Yet she could be personified as mourning all of her children going down to Egypt, perhaps even anticipating the slavery they would later experience there, including the killing of the newborn boys. All Matthew is doing in 2:17–18 is applying the language once again to refer to the mothers in and around Bethlehem (which included Ramah), who are distraught over the loss of their children to the swords of Herod's soldiers.

The use of Ps. 78:2 in Matt. 13:35 might be Matthew's most unexpected fulfillment quotation, given all the possible meanings of the Hebrew *māšāl* ("proverb," "riddle," "taunt," "wise saying," "mystery," etc.), but "parable" is one such meaning. The psalm, moreover, does refer to God's revealing things previously hidden, which is what Jesus's parables do. So, a typological reprise of a similar pattern of revelation does fit ancient Jewish uses of that form of fulfillment (Cope).

Matthew 27:9–10 seems to combine language from Zech. 11:12–13 and from Jer. 19:1–13 and/or 32:6–9. The language of Zechariah is clearer, but Jewish practice sometimes identifies only one of two sources for a composite quotation when the other is more obscure, precisely since it would not be as easily recognized. In any event, the recurrence of the paltry sum of thirty pieces of silver and the purchase of a potter's field are obviously striking enough for Matthew to credit the event to typological fulfillment (Moo).

The fulfillment of Scripture in Matt. 2:23 has proved particularly puzzling because no OT text ever refers to anyone being called a Nazarene. But this is also the one place where Matthew refers to "prophets" in the plural, so he may have in mind a more general theme. The most common suggestion is that the consonants in the Hebrew for "Nazarene" (*nṣr*; vowel points had not yet been invented) suggested the messianic "Branch," or *nēṣer*, of Isa. 11:1.

Finally, Matt. 26:54 and 56 speak of the Scriptures and the prophets in the plural being fulfilled with reference to the manner of Jesus's arrest and execution, but without any quotation or combination of OT phrases. They may well be referring back to v. 31, which quotes Zech. 13:7, though not with a fulfillment formula, along with Isaiah's suffering-servant texts, especially 52:13–53:12.

Quotations from What Was Spoken or Written

Other clear quotations of the OT in Matthew are introduced with wording like "it is written," "prophesied," or "spoken through the prophet." Of these, the first is the most common in Second Temple Jewish literature, though a majority of OT quotations in that literature do not employ any introductory formula (Chester). Interestingly, we again find both direct and multiple fulfillment, even without the word "fulfillment" in the text. We also find a handful of more declarative principles or outright commands. But there are no unambiguous examples of typology, suggesting that Matthew recognizes that a reference to "fulfillment" is necessary for his readers to consider typology as an option.

Direct fulfillment. Micah 5:2 is about as straightforward a prediction as one finds in the prophetic literature. Candidates for the messiah who are not born in Bethlehem need not apply! Of course, Matt. 2:6 manages to complicate matters slightly by adding the words "by no means" before "least." But Matthew is not contradicting Micah's analysis of Bethlehem's size but is rather saying that now that the Messiah has come, Bethlehem is no longer insignificant.

Malachi 3:1, on the other hand, has an ambiguity in its original context. Since the Lord is first of all Yahweh, might the "messenger" be the Messiah? But once Jesus has applied the divine title to himself, the one preparing for his coming must be someone else. Malachi 4:5 supplies the OT prophet's identification: the messenger is Elijah. Because Elijah never died but was taken up in a chariot to heaven, many Second Temple Jewish ideas about his return sprang up. Jesus himself builds on this concept when he identifies John the Baptist as the fulfillment of that prophecy (Matt. 11:10; cf. Luke 7:27), as Matt. 11:14 clarifies. Most likely Jesus means what Luke 1:17 makes explicit, that John came "in the spirit and power of Elijah," not that he was the literal OT prophet descended back to earth.

Matthew 24:15 refers to "the abomination that causes desolation" about whom Daniel spoke (cf. Dan. 9:27; 11:31; 12:11). While we cannot exclude altogether the possibility that Jesus, like 1 Macc. 1:57 and 4:38, finds a provisional fulfillment in Antiochus's desecration of the temple in 167 BC, he gives no hint of any fulfillment other than that of a future sacrilege. In the flow of thought of Matt. 24, he most likely has the Roman destruction of the temple in AD 70 in view.

Zechariah 13:7, as used in Matt. 26:31, at first glance would seem to be a case of pure typology. The actions surrounding a Davidic king in the prophet's day are being repeated in the treatment of Jesus, the messianic shepherd-king. The larger context of Zech. 12–14, however, has enough messianic overtones, especially with its repeated "on that day" (12:3, 4, 6, 8, 9, 11; 13:1, 2, 4; 14:4, 6, 8, 9, 13, 20, 21), that probably this is direct fulfillment.

Multiple fulfillment. Isaiah 40:3 has been taken as directly fulfilled by John the Baptist (Matt. 3:3 and pars.). Yet it is likely that its first referent is preparation for the return of the Israelites from exile in the time of the Persian Empire. But the larger context of complete transformation of the landscape, even if taken metaphorically, suggests something more decisive; hence, John the Baptist senses that it still needs to be fulfilled as the messianic era dawns.

Isaiah 29:13, in the present tense, is even more clearly about the disobedient Israelites of Isaiah's day. But the scenario of superficial allegiance with fundamentally disloyal hearts repeats itself even more dramatically with the Jewish leaders' scrupulous obedience to purity laws, written and unwritten, despite unclean heart attitudes (Matt. 15:8–9 and par.).

Isaiah 56:7 is harder to categorize. The prophet is looking ahead, potentially to the messianic age, when the temple "will be called a house of prayer for all nations." So perhaps we should think of direct fulfillment in Jesus's day, explaining his outrage that the temple is not fulfilling its purpose. On the other hand, his specific objection—that commerce related to the purchase of sacrificial animals is keeping the gentiles from worshiping in their court—addresses a recent problem caused by Caiaphas's moving the "market" from the Kidron Ravine to the temple precincts. The temple may have been functioning properly before that shift, and Jesus wants it to do so again (Matt. 21:13). The OT passage he cites next (Jer. 7:11) was originally a rhetorical question about the temple in Jeremiah's day ("Has this house, which bears my Name, become a den of robbers to you?"). Clearly, Matthew sees that corruption repeated, so multiple fulfillment may be the best label for both citations.

Principles and commands based in Scripture. Jesus can appeal to OT passages to underscore that they have an abiding authority. Without specific language about fulfillment, Jesus can employ introductions about what "is written," what "you have heard," or what "God said." Jesus cites Deuteronomy three times in this way to refute Satan in the wilderness, explaining that humans do not live by bread alone, that one should not test God but should worship him only (Matt. 4:4, 7, 10 // Deut. 8:3; 6:16, 13; cf. Luke 4:1–13). Even the devil cites Scripture (Ps. 91:11–12) but misapplies it out of context (Matt. 4:6 and par.).

Six times in the antitheses of the Sermon on the Mount, Jesus quotes OT commands (Exod. 20:13, 14; Deut. 24:1; Lev. 19:12; Exod. 21:24 // Lev. 24:20; Lev. 19:18) only to reinterpret them (Matt. 5:21, 27, 31, 33, 38, 43). Because the final quotation adds "hate your enemy" to the command to "love your neighbor," and because Jesus says in each case, "you have heard" (rather than "it is written"), many think Jesus is overturning merely the oral law of the Pharisees. But it would be odd to give five examples unambiguously from the written law of Moses and then expect listeners to retroject, based solely on a partial addition in the last quotation, the idea that this is only oral law. Besides, commands like those to obliterate the Canaanite armies in Joshua's conquest certainly sound like hating one's enemy!

Finally, in Matt. 15:4 Jesus reaffirms the command to honor one's parents (Exod. 20:12) and notes the command to put to death the person who curses their parents (21:17) as a foil to the Jewish leaders' corrupt corban practice, which prevents them from honoring their parents and may even metaphorically curse them (Matt. 15:5–6). In each of the above instances, a distinctive authority is being attributed to the Hebrew Scriptures.

Other Kinds of Scripture Quotations

In many instances, Matthew clearly quotes the OT but without any of the standard introductory formulae, and occasionally without any introduction at all. These passages typically do not claim any kind of prophetic fulfillment, though in one or two cases some kind may be implied.

What Jesus's opponents should know. On four occasions, Jesus defends himself against criticism by certain Jewish leaders with a question like "Have you never read . . . ?" followed by an OT quotation. In Matt. 19:4–5, he expects the Pharisees who are trying to embroil him in their debates about divorce to know Gen. 1:27 and 2:24 on the original purposes and permanence of marriage. In Matt. 21:16, he appeals to Ps. 8:2 to justify to some chief priests and scribes how even little children praised God, just as they were crying "Hosanna!" to Jesus as he entered the temple precincts. In Matt. 21:42, he appends the cornerstone saying of Ps. 118:22–23 to his parable of the wicked tenants with a similar question to certain chief priests and Pharisees. In Matt. 22:32, finally, he asks if the Sadducees haven't read specifically what God said to *them* in the account of Moses at the burning bush when he declared, "I am the God of Abraham, the God of Isaac, and the God of Jacob" (Exod. 3:6).

On two other occasions Matthew does not include an actual quotation from Scripture but still describes Jesus asking if certain leaders haven't read about specific biblical events. In 12:3 and 5, he asks in turn, "Haven't you read what David did . . . ?" and, "Haven't you read in the Law . . . ?" In the first case he refers to David eating the sacred showbread when he and his men were in great need (1 Sam. 21:1–6); in the second he cites the legal principle that the priests work on the Sabbath in the temple without being guilty of breaking the law (Num. 28:9–10). That Jesus's critics in each case are individuals from the leadership sects in Israel makes it appropriate for him to assume that they can read and should have read the sacred Scriptures, even when a majority of Israelites are at least partly illiterate.

In two cases, Jesus introduces a Scripture with a statement that functions similarly to his rhetorical questions. In Matt. 9:13, he tells a group of Pharisees, "Go and learn what this means, 'I desire mercy, not sacrifice'" (Hosea 6:6), prioritizing the moral above the ritual law when he associates with tax collectors and sinners. He could just as easily ask, "Have you not read . . . ?" This way, however, the focus is even more strongly on the fact that they have not understood the text as they should have. In Matt. 12:7, Jesus again cites Hosea 6:6, again with a group of Pharisees, this time to support his disciples "harvesting" grain on a Sabbath to satisfy their hunger.

Other questions. When Jesus uses questions to address his critics, he is simply replicating what they often do with him. In one instance, the question addressed to Jesus actually cites Scripture. Deuteronomy 24:1 permitted divorce in certain instances, or so the Pharisees understood it, though they debated what those circumstances were. So, in Matt. 19:7, they ask Jesus about this text when he has just appeared to exclude divorce altogether.

In Matt. 22:37–39, Jesus cites the double love command (Deut. 6:5; Lev. 19:18) to answer a lawyer's question about the greatest commandment. He echoes his language in the Sermon on the Mount (7:12) when he adds, "All the Law and the Prophets hang on these two commandments." Once again, we are reminded how central fulfillment is for Matthew.

A very influential use of the OT by Jesus will reappear several more times in the NT—citing Ps. 110:1 in Matt. 22:44. He has avoided the traps embedded in several questions addressed to him during his teaching in the temple. Now he turns the tables on his questioners and asks, in essence, how a psalm he accepts as authored by David could refer to two people as "Lord" above the king of Israel unless one were the Messiah and unless that Messiah were more than a merely human descendant of David. No one is able to answer him, nor does anyone ask him further questions (v. 46). Here direct prophetic fulfillment is implicit in Jesus's indirect self-reference.

Specifying key laws or principles. Other contexts that lead to someone quoting a command from the law include the rich young ruler's query about which commandments Jesus has in mind when he tells him to obey them (Matt. 19:17–18a). Jesus replies with selections from the Decalogue and the command to neighbor love (vv. 18b–19). In 18:16, without any question or even an introductory formula, Jesus explains the need for one or two witnesses to accompany a believer who has been sinned against by a fellow church member. He simply states the policy and then transitions to Scripture: "so that 'every matter may be established by the testimony of two or three witnesses'" (Deut. 19:15). A frequently misinterpreted use of the OT appears in Matt. 26:11 ("The poor you will always have with you"), a paraphrase of Deut. 15:11a ("There will always be poor people in the land"). Ironically, this is not an excuse for doing nothing to help the poor; exactly the opposite is true. The Deuteronomic verse continues: "Therefore I command you to be openhanded toward your fellow Israelites who are poor and needy in your land" (v. 11b).

Miscellaneous. In a number of Gospel contexts, Jesus prefaces a declaration with the words "I have (not) come to . . . ," explaining a purpose of his mission (Matt. 5:17; Mark 2:17 and par.; John 6:38; 10:10). In Matt. 10:34–35 (cf. Luke 12:49), Jesus says that he has "not come to bring peace, but a sword" and to set the members of a household against one another (where their religious allegiances do not mesh). He breaks into the language of Mic. 7:6 without any introduction, no doubt seeing the behavior of the Israelites' divided loyalty in Micah's day playing itself out again in the people's polarized response to his ministry. With respect to his return, Jesus uses the imagery of Isa. 13:10 and 34:4, which speaks of cosmic upheavals concerning the day of the Lord and of judgment against the nations. If there were a fulfillment formula, we would have multiple fulfillments, against Israel's enemies in OT times and at the end of the age, but Jesus is just reapplying biblical language to his return. He does the same when he alludes to the Son of Man coming on the clouds (Dan. 7:13) in Matt. 24:30 and 26:64; even though this is not couched in terms of fulfillment, it is likely referring to a future fulfillment.

As he hangs on the cross, Jesus utters his horrible cry of dereliction (Matt. 27:46, "My God, my God, why have you forsaken me?"), quoting Ps. 22:1. Even though he does not use explicit fulfillment language, Jesus echoes the feelings David had when his enemies were attacking him. If it is not typological, it is at least analogical. More so than with any other quotations in Matthew, one wonders if the common Jewish principle of implying a much larger context of a passage than just what is cited comes into play. After all, the psalm ends on a note of triumph as David is vindicated and all the earth hears the praise of the Lord, with many turning to him (vv. 22–31), just as Jesus's resurrection leads to the Great Commission and many becoming believers. Finally, the crowds who shout "Hosanna!" to the Lord at the so-called triumphal entry (Matt. 21:9; cf. Ps. 118:25) trigger Jesus's response about Israel similarly crying when he returns, "Blessed is he who comes in the name of the Lord" (118:26).

Allusions

Matthew is so full of allusions to the OT that it is difficult to choose the most important. But a study of Matthew's use of the OT would certainly be incomplete if we didn't mention the genealogy of Jesus (1:2–17), with all the names and details furnished from the Hebrew Scriptures. The voice at the baptism (3:17) and transfiguration (17:5) alludes to a combination of Ps. 2:7 with Isa. 42:1 and Deut. 18:15, respectively, showing Jesus as both the messianic king and suffering servant. The beatitudes about those who mourn, are meek, and are pure in heart (Matt. 5:4, 5, 8) allude to Isa. 61:1, Pss. 37:11, and 24:3–4, respectively. Jonah 1:17 appears so clearly in Matt. 12:40 that some would call it a quotation. Isaiah's Song of the Vineyard (Isa. 5:1–7) furnishes the imagery for the beginning of Jesus's parable of wicked tenants (Matt. 21:33). The Sadducees virtually quote the provisions for levirate marriage (Matt. 22:24) in Deut. 25:5. And the details at the crucifixion of offering Jesus wine mixed with gall (Matt. 27:34) and casting lots for his garments (v. 35) typologically allude to Pss. 69:21 and 22:18, respectively. Many other allusions could be added.

Uses of Various Portions of the OT

Matthew clearly sees elements of what have been called the moral, ritual (or ceremonial), and civil law all as relevant and authoritative for his day, even if the ritual and civil law are often creatively reapplied in ways appropriate for the new covenant. These categories, of course, do not appear in the Bible itself, despite their widespread use throughout church history. All three major sections of the Hebrew Scriptures—the Law, the Prophets, and the Writings—are well represented. As with the NT in general, the three books most often quoted are Isaiah, Psalms, and Deuteronomy, which gives us one major book each of the Prophets, the Writings, and the Law, in that order. Matthew clearly cites Isaiah the most, no matter what is counted as a quotation or an allusion. Deuteronomy comes in second, but only if its parallels to the laws in Exodus are included. Otherwise, Psalms edges it out. But the exact numbers are not important compared to how each book is used. We will look briefly at the six OT books Matthew most frequently cites.

Isaiah. One of the unexpected results of a book-by-book examination of the OT sources Matthew utilizes is that almost every quotation from Isaiah involves multiple fulfillment (Blomberg, "Interpreting"). A lot of this most likely stems from the amount of Isaiah that looks ahead to either the Assyrian or Babylonian exiles and yet consistently envisions restoration for Israel beyond those punishments for the nation's disobedience. That several of the quotations Matthew cites come from Isaiah's first thirty-nine chapters reminds us that Isaiah is not as neatly divided into short-term prophecy (chaps. 1–39) and long-term, more eschatological restoration (chaps. 40–66) as many have alleged. Isaiah has the most extensive treatment of the glories of Israel's return from exile, blending at times into millennial conditions and even the new heavens and new earth (Isa. 65:17). Isaiah itself couches the return from exile as a new exodus, fairly inviting later writers to see additional fulfillment when events warrant it.

The Servant Songs also contribute significantly to Matthew's use of Isaiah. Even if the servant is explicitly identified as Israel prior to the first Servant Song, as one progresses through the remaining Servant Songs more details suggest a specific person until the one who dies an atoning death for the people of Israel must be an individual.

Psalms. The many occasions when David suffered lead Matthew naturally to draw frequent typological comparisons with Jesus, especially since he is David's royal descendant. The literary genre of a psalm does not lend itself to genuine, future-referring prophecy nearly as often, but patterns in the experiences of David and his greater Son prove rife for comparison, especially with the themes of the humiliation and subsequent exaltation of the righteous sufferer.

Deuteronomy and Exodus. Moses's historical reprise of Israel's obedience and disobedience as God's children sets Matthew up nicely for showing how Jesus recapitulates the mandate for Israel with consistent obedience as Yahweh's Son (Crowe). The legal material can likewise be mined for principles that Jesus still finds valuable for his followers. It is hard always to know whether Matthew thinks of Deuteronomy or Exodus as his primary source, especially for the Ten Commandments, but both books are involved at multiple points.

Jeremiah. Jeremiah is best known for his largely unrelenting message of judgment against Israel for its rebellion against God. But his prophesied new covenant plays a role in Matthew, as in the rest of the NT, quite out of proportion to the small amount of material directly about it. In Jesus's day, Second Temple Judaism had already mined Jeremiah for both of these themes repeatedly (Knowles; Whitters).

Zechariah. In Zechariah the themes are more christological. Matthew's two main reasons for citing Zechariah are to highlight the messianic shepherd as royal and rejected (Ham). He also remains humble as he is rejected (Moss).

Correlation with Matthew's Theological Emphases

Not surprisingly, when a NT author uses the OT to highlight fulfillment of prophecy, by whatever mode, most of that prophecy will focus on the person and ministry of Jesus. Just about every significant christological title in Matthew is deeply embedded in Scripture, as are numerous other themes. Space forbids discussion of all but the more distinctive christological titles.

Son of David. Of the more distinctive titles of Matthew, none is more frequently shown to be rooted in the OT than "Son of David" (Zacharias; Piotrowski). Jesus is the royal messianic shepherd descended from David from the opening verse, where the title "Son of David" first appears. David is a key focus of the genealogy (Matt. 1:1–17), while his healing role (highlighted in Matthew) is stressed in Ezek. 34–36 and 2 Sam. 5:6–8. Jesus's behavior is compared with David's in 1 Sam. 21:1–6, and Judas's with Ahitophel's, both of whom hang themselves when their rebellions against their masters fail (Matt. 27:5; 2 Sam. 17:23). But even if Matthew adds a number of these connections with David, they are all clearly based in Jesus's own claims about the Messiah being David's Lord, which draw on Ps. 110:1. Jesus's Davidic role as shepherd, a compassionate shepherd (Matt. 9:36; 14:14; 15:32; 20:34), unlike the false shepherds in Ezekiel's day, shows that the main contrast Matthew develops is between Jesus and the Israelite rulers and leaders of his day, not with every last person within the nation (Turner).

New/greater Moses. Just as Moses is miraculously preserved while the baby boys around him are being killed (Exod. 2), so also is Jesus after the massacre instigated by Herod the Great. Like Moses, Jesus has to be brought out of Egypt to the land of Israel. In Matthew, he is particularly a teacher, inculcating the ethics of the new covenant, especially in a great sermon delivered on a mountain, just as Moses gave the ethical mandates of the law he received at Mount Sinai. The five extended discourses of Jesus in Matthew (chaps. 5–7, 10, 13, 18, 23–25) have been likened to the five books of the Law from Moses (Allison). If one adds material already present in Matthew's sources, we may note that Moses is present at the transfiguration, where God commands that people listen to Jesus, just as Moses predicted a prophet would arise who would be like him and to whom the people must listen (Deut. 18:15–18).

Son of Abraham, Immanuel, and Wisdom. Three other titles are often seen as more significant for Matthew than for the other Gospel writers, even though none occupies as much of his attention as Son of David or new Moses. "Son of Abraham" also appears in 1:1 and determines where Matthew begins his genealogy (1:2; unlike Luke, who goes all the way back to Adam and God [3:38]). This gives Jesus even more ancient Israelite pedigree than just his Davidic lineage, but it also prepares him to be a messiah for gentiles, since the children of Abraham were progenitors of both Jews and gentiles. "Immanuel" ("God with us," Isa. 7:14) forms an *inclusio* with the last verse of the Gospel (Kupp), where Jesus promises to be with his disciples always (1:23; 28:20). Wisdom appears classically in 11:16–19 and 11:25–30, where she is personified as in Prov. 8–9 and speaks in language very similar to Sir. 51:23–27. While the NT never technically quotes the OT Apocrypha, sometimes its allusions come very close to sounding like partial quotations, as here. Matthew's emphasis on Wisdom may also reflect his understanding of Solomon as a unique son of David, given his great reputation for wisdom and his transmission of so many proverbs (Witherington).

Matthew's Structure

Some have attempted to discern an outline for Matthew where every section is dictated by the OT quotations that appear within it (e.g., Patrick). The inconsistent frequency of their appearance makes this somewhat implausible, but a large portion of the Gospel can be so structured (Schreiner, 42–43). A good portion of the genealogy of Matt. 1:1–17 comes from the Hebrew Scriptures. Many have seen the five fulfillment quotations of chaps. 1–2 as governing the choice of details in 1:18–2:23 surrounding Jesus's infancy. Scriptural quotations and composite allusions highlight the ministry of John the Baptist, Jesus's baptism, the temptation of Jesus, and the beginning of his ministry in 3:1–4:17.

The Sermon on the Mount quotes Scripture only in the antitheses of 5:21–48, but the message is framed by references to the Law and the Prophets (5:17; 7:12). Isaiah's prophecy about the servant healing people's diseases (Isa. 53:4; Matt. 8:17) strictly applies as a summary only of Matt. 8:1–16, but given the prominence of healings among the ten miracles of chaps. 8–9, it could be viewed as to some extent guiding the choice of material in this larger section. The use of Mic. 7:6 in Matt. 10:35 specifically governs only 10:34–38, but given that Jesus's missionary speech is dominated by the hostility the disciples can eventually accept, the Micah passage could be viewed as the central thrust of the chapter.

The OT quotations in 11:10 and 12:18–21 hardly account for everything in chaps. 11–12. Still, the first quotation is about the ministry of John the Baptist, who is a focal point for much of chap. 11, and the second is about the servant accepting abuse without quarrelling, which similarly pervades much of chap. 12. Matthew 13:14–15 and 13:35 more clearly quote the OT to explain the purpose and model for Jesus teaching in parables, which encompasses all of 13:1–52. The longest stretch of Matthew with little explicit quotation of the OT is 13:53–18:35, but this section includes Jesus's withdrawal from Galilee for gentile territory (esp. chaps. 14–15), where the OT would be less understood, and the first stage of the road to the cross, which is unified by Jesus's own triple passion prediction (16:21; 17:22–23; 20:18–19). What OT quotations do appear in these chapters are much more tied to specific incidents and tend to be about correct behavior (ritual handwashing, divorce and remarriage, the demands of the rich young ruler) rather than any kind of prophecy.

With the last week of Jesus's life (chaps. 21–28), OT quotations reappear again in clusters, though never to such an extent that they appear to govern Matthew's choice of a whole series of episodes to narrate. The view that the passion narrative is merely prophecy historicized fails at this point. The clusters of frequent quotations surrounding both Jesus's infancy and his death include many instances of typology that would not naturally have suggested themselves to anyone until after events actually happened that reminded people of the OT texts. So, it is unlikely that Matthew merely creates "history" out of a collage of OT quotations.

Conclusion

Matthew is the Gospel most steeped in the OT. The theme of the fulfillment of Scripture unites his narrative. But the kinds of fulfillment, like other uses of Scripture, are too diverse to be interpreted all in the same way (Nolland, 36, gives additional categories). Each finds some precedent in both Mark and Second Temple Judaism. Above all, each functions in service of demonstrating that Jesus is the Davidic Messiah to whom all the peoples of the world owe allegiance.

Bibliography. Allison, D. C., Jr., *The New Moses* (Fortress, 1993); Barrett, M., *Canon, Covenant, and Christology* (InterVarsity, 2020); Beale, G. K., *Handbook on the New Testament Use of the Old Testament* (Baker Academic, 2012); Beaton, R., *Isaiah's Christ in Matthew's Gospel* (Cambridge University Press, 2002); Blomberg, C. L., "Interpreting Old Testament Prophetic Literature in Matthew," *TJ* 23 (2002): 17–33; Blomberg, "Matthew," in *CNTUOT*, 1–109; Chester, A., "Citing the Old Testament," in *It Is Written*, ed. D. A. Carson and H. G. M. Williamson (Cambridge University Press, 1988), 141–69; Cope, O. L., *Matthew* (Catholic Biblical Association of America, 1976); Crowe, B. D., *The Obedient Son* (de Gruyter, 2012); France, R. T., *Matthew* (Paternoster, 1989; repr., Wipf & Stock, 2004); Goppelt, L., *Typos* (Eerdmans, 1982); Gundry, R. H., *The Use of the Old Testament in St. Matthew's Gospel with Special Reference to the Messianic Hope* (Brill, 1967); Hagner, D. A., *Matthew 1–13*, WBC (Word, 1993); Ham, C. A., *The Coming King and the Rejected Shepherd* (Sheffield Phoenix, 2005); Hatina, T. R., ed., *The Gospel of Matthew*, vol. 2 of *Biblical Interpretation in Early Christian Gospels* (T&T Clark, 2008); Hays, R. B., *Reading Backwards* (Baylor University Press, 2014); Hengel, M., and D. P. Bailey, "The Effective History of Isaiah 53 in the Pre-Christian Period," in *The Suffering Servant*, ed. B. Janowski and P. Stuhlmacher (Eerdmans, 2004), 75–146; Knowles, M., *Jeremiah in Matthew's Gospel* (Sheffield Academic, 1993); Kupp, D. D., *Matthew's Emmanuel* (Cambridge University Press, 1996); Menken, M. J. J., *Matthew's Bible* (Leuven University Press, 2004); Moo, D. J., *The Old Testament in the Gospel Passion Narratives* (Almond, 1983); Moss, C. M., *The Zechariah Tradition and the Gospel of Matthew* (de Gruyter, 2008); Nolland, J., *The Gospel of Matthew*, NIGTC (Eerdmans, 2005); Patrick, J. E., "Matthew's Pesher Gospel Structured around Ten Messianic Citations of Isaiah," *JTS* 61 (2010): 43–81; Piotrowski, N. G., *Matthew's New David at the End of Exile* (Brill, 2017); Schreiner, P., *Matthew, Disciple and Scribe* (Baker Academic, 2019); Spadaro, M. C., *Reading as the Climactic Fulfillment of the Hebrew Story* (Wipf & Stock, 2015); Stendahl, K., *The School of St. Matthew* (Gleerup, 1954); Turner, D. L., *Israel's Last Prophet* (Fortress, 2015); Waetjen, H. C., *Matthew's Theology of Fulfillment, Its Universality and Its Ethnicity* (Bloomsbury T&T Clark, 2017); Whitters, M. F., "Jesus in the Footsteps of Jeremiah," *CBQ* 68 (2006): 229–47; Witherington, Ben, III, *Matthew* (Smyth & Helwys, 2006); Zacharias, H. D., *Matthew's Presentation of the Son of David* (Bloomsbury T&T Clark, 2017).

CRAIG L. BLOMBERG

Memory *See* Orality

Messiah

The Hebrew term "messiah" (*māšîaḥ*) means "anointed" or "anointed one." The term appears twice in the NT in Greek transliteration as *messias* (John 1:41; 4:25), but the great majority of NT references utilize the Greek translation, *christos*, usually rendered in English as "Christ." In the OT, "anointed one" can refer to anyone set apart to God for a particular task and is used in the OT with reference to prophets (1 Kings 19:16; Ps. 105:15), priests (Lev. 4:3, 5, 16; 6:22), and kings. The term is even used of Cyrus the Great (Isa. 45:1), who is chosen by God as the agent to return God's people from exile and allow the rebuilding of the temple in Jerusalem. The term's most common OT use is with reference to the king of Israel, God's chosen instrument for ruling his people (1 Sam. 2:10). It is first used of Saul, Israel's first king, whom David refuses to kill since he is "the LORD's anointed" (1 Sam. 24:6, 10; 26:9, 11, 16, 23; 2 Sam. 1:14). Yet it is David himself, the man after God's own heart, who becomes the model and prototype for the one called "Messiah"—the eschatological ruler from David's line.

If we were to limit our study to the use of the term "messiah" in the OT, this would be a very short article, since the Hebrew term *māšîaḥ* is used, at most, once in the OT with reference to the eschatological king (Dan. 9:25–26)—and this reference is greatly debated. If, however, we expand our study to the *messianic idea* in Israel and in the NT, the topic becomes encyclopedic. We will therefore limit our study to the origin of the messianic idea in the Davidic-promise tradition, a brief survey of its development in the OT and in Second Temple Judaism, and the use of these "messianic" passages in NT writers.

Messiah in the OT

The Davidic-promise tradition. The original justification for Israel's monarchy may be found in God's mandate for humanity to reign over creation as his vice-regent (Gen. 1:28). Yet its historical foundation is to be found in God's choice of David to be king following the rejection of Saul (1 Sam. 13:14; 16:1). The Davidic covenant (2 Sam. 7:5–16; cf. 1 Chron. 17:4–14) serves as the legitimizing document for the Davidic dynasty. The episode begins with a statement of the Lord's consolidation of David's throne and David's desire to build a house (= temple) for Yahweh. Yahweh answers by deferring the task of temple-building to David's son Solomon and says that instead the Lord will build a "house" (= dynasty) for David. The promise that follows has its initial focus on Solomon: God will raise up David's offspring to succeed him; he is the one who will build a house for Yahweh; God will establish a father-son relationship with him; when he sins, the Lord will discipline him. Yet despite Solomon's failure, God's loving-kindness will remain forever with David: "Your house and your kingdom will endure forever before me" (2 Sam. 7:16).

Although this passage is the first explicit affirmation of the eternal legitimacy of the Davidic throne, it has intertextual connections with passages that appear earlier in the biblical narrative. Here the Deuteronomistic promise of a secure homeland for Israel following the exodus (Deut. 3:20; 12:9–10; Josh. 1:15) is linked to the Davidic dynasty (2 Sam. 7:10). The covenant with David thus becomes an extension of the Sinaitic covenant.

Intertextual connections can also be seen in two other pentateuchal texts that affirm the Davidic dynasty. In the patriarchal blessings of Gen. 49, Jacob prophesies,

> You are a lion's cub, Judah;
> you return from the prey. . . .
> The scepter will not depart from Judah,
> nor the ruler's staff from between his feet,
> until he to whom it belongs [or Shiloh] shall
> come. (Gen. 49:9–10)

Judah, David's tribe, is here identified as the ruling tribe from which Israel's king will come. While the original significance of Shiloh is greatly debated, it likely means "to whom it belongs" (NIV), a reference to the establishment of the Davidic dynasty and ultimately (assuming a messianic perspective) to the eschatological king who will establish that throne forever.

Balaam's third and fourth oracles (Num. 24:3–9, 15–24) are closely related to Gen. 49, since they contain almost identical language related to a lion (Gen. 49:9; Num. 24:9) as well as scepter and ruling imagery (Num. 24:7, 17). Although Num. 24 speaks more generally of the king from "Jacob," there is little doubt that the Davidic dynasty is in view.

Ideal kingship and the royal psalms. The affirmation and idealization of the Davidic dynasty find poetic expression in the royal psalms (Pss. 2, 18, 21, 45, 72, 89, 110, 132, etc.). These psalms, likely composed for a variety of court occasions during the Davidic dynasty, celebrate God's choice of David and his descendants. Intertextual echoes of the Davidic covenant appear throughout: the promise of an eternal throne for David's descendants (21:4; 45:17; 89:5, 30, 37; 132:11–12), a father-son relationship with God (2:7; 89:27–28; 110:3), and victory over enemies and security in the land (2:8–9; 18:31–42; 21:8–12; 45:5; 72:8–11; 89:22–26; 110:1–2; 132:17–18).

The expanding Davidic-promise tradition in the Prophets. The glorious and idealized reigns of David and Solomon are followed by the division of the kingdom and repeated foreign intervention, first by the Assyrians and then by the Babylonians. The many spiritual failures of the kings of Israel and Judah, together with political setbacks, prompt hopes among the prophets of Israel and Judah for a return to the glory days of the Davidic dynasty and the fulfillment of God's promise to David. These hopes come to their most exalted literary and theological expression in the prophecies of Isaiah. In the midst of the threats posed to Judah—first by the Syro-Ephraimite alliance and then by the Assyrian invasion—Isaiah prophesies the restoration of the Davidic dynasty in glorious splendor. A Davidic heir will be born (Isa. 9:6), a shoot sprouting from the root of Jesse (11:1). Like David, he will be endowed with the Spirit of the Lord, providing wisdom and insight (11:2–3; cf. 1 Sam. 16:13). His words will carry judging power: with the breath of his lips and the rod of his mouth he will destroy the wicked (Isa. 11:4). He will establish an eternal kingdom of peace, justice, and righteousness, reigning on David's throne forever (9:1–7; 11:1–16). His throne names are extraordinary: "Wonderful Counselor, Mighty God, Everlasting Father, Prince of Peace" (9:6). Isaiah's contemporary Micah also predicts the fulfillment of God's promise to David with the coming of a new Davidic ruler. He will be born in Bethlehem (Mic. 5:2, the birthplace of David) and, like David, "will stand and shepherd his flock in the strength of the LORD" (5:4).

When the Davidic dynasty collapses with the destruction of Jerusalem and the Babylonian exile under King Nebuchadnezzar, prophetic hopes turn to a time of future restoration when the Davidic throne will be restored. Jeremiah predicts that one day a righteous "shoot" (echoes of Isa. 11:1) of David will sprout anew, reigning wisely and establishing God's justice (Jer. 23:5–6 AT). Ezekiel similarly prophesies that God will one day regather his people and restore them to their land. He will raise up a new David, a shepherd-king, who will guide and protect God's people against false shepherds—that is, the present leaders of Israel (Ezek. 36:24–38). Ezekiel draws together elements of both the Davidic and Sinai covenants. The Sinaitic formula "I will dwell among the Israelites and be their God" (Exod. 29:45; cf. Lev. 26:12) becomes "I, the LORD, will be their God, and my servant David will be prince among them" (Ezek. 34:24).

The Second Temple Period: The Emergence of "the Messiah"

The postexilic and Second Temple periods saw the waxing and waning of messianic hopes in Israel. In the postexilic period, messianic expectations were no doubt aroused following the decree of Cyrus the Great, which allowed the return to the land, the rebuilding of the temple, and the establishment of Zerubbabel (a Davidic descendant) as governor. Yet when Zerubbabel passed from the scene and the priestly leadership assumed a more prominent political as well as religious role, hopes for a Davidic messiah tended to be set aside or pushed into the distant future. This was especially true during the Maccabean period, when the Hasmonean priest-kings ruled in place of a Davidic king. First Maccabees acknowledges that "David, because he was merciful, inherited the throne of the kingdom forever" (1 Macc. 2:57), yet it also says that God had ordained that the Hasmonean priest-king (Simon in this case) "should be their leader and high priest forever, until a trustworthy prophet should arise" (14:41). As long as they were in power, the ruling Hasmoneans were clearly content to postpone the Davidic reign until the eschatological future.

Yet the corruption of the Hasmonean dynasty and divisions within Israel resulted in renewed Davidic hopes among other groups in Judaism. The classic expression of Second Temple messianism appears in Psalms of Solomon, a collection of hymns that arose in Pharisaic circles in the first century BC. Writing against both the corruption of the Hasmoneans and the rising hegemony of Rome, the author calls on God to "raise up for them their king, the son of David, to rule over your servant Israel. . . . Undergird him with strength to destroy the unrighteous rulers, to purge Jerusalem from gentiles who trample her to destruction" (Pss. Sol. 17:21–23 *OTP*). The description of the Messiah draws heavily from the OT Davidic-promise tradition (esp. Isa. 11:1–5, but also Pss. 2:9; 89:24; Jer. 23:5–6; Ezek. 34:23–24; 37:24–25; Num. 24:17; etc.). The eschatological king is a powerful warrior and judge who has supernatural power and wisdom from the Lord to judge the wicked and establish God's righteous reign (Pss. Sol. 17:25). Two titles are particularly noteworthy in the Psalms of Solomon because of their originality. The first is "Son of David," which appears here for the first time in Jewish literature as a title for the Messiah (Pss. Sol. 17:21 AT). It will become a favorite messianic title in Matthew's Gospel and in later rabbinic Judaism. The other new title is *christos kyrios*, "Messiah, the Lord" or "the Anointed Lord" (Pss. Sol. 17:30 AT). While the expression "the LORD's Anointed" (*məšîaḥ YHWH; christos kyriou*) is a common designation in Judaism for Israel's king, ascribing the title "Lord" to the Messiah is unprecedented (cf. Luke 2:11). Here and elsewhere in Second Temple Judaism, "messiah" is on its way to becoming a technical term for the end-time king from David's line.

Similar expectations for a conquering messiah appear in the (probably) Essene community that produced the Dead Sea Scrolls. In the priest-led community at Qumran, however, we find two messiahs (or "anointed ones"), a royal messiah from the line of David and a priestly messiah from Aaron's line (1QS 9.11; 1Q28a 2.11–21; 1Q28b 4.24–29; 4Q175 11–12), with the priestly messiah functioning as guide and counselor for the royal one. The royal messiah is a warrior king after the model of Isa. 11:1–5, who destroys the unrighteous and rules the nations with a rod of iron (4Q174 1.1.10–13; 4Q161; 4Q252 1–5). These Qumran texts draw from a variety of the Davidic texts discussed above (Gen. 49:10; Num. 24:17; 2 Sam. 7:11–14; Pss. 2; 89; Isa. 11:1–5; Jer. 23:5–6; 33:15–17; Ezek. 34:23–24; 37:24–25; Amos 9:11).

It is important to conclude this section by noting that first-century Judaism displays significant diversity with reference to messianic figures and eschatological hopes (Neusner et al.). In some texts God himself is described as savior. In others a mediator or messianic figure acts on God's behalf. These mediators are sometimes described in primarily human terms; at other times, they are portrayed in language suggesting an exalted heavenly figure. Often they are identified as a Davidic heir. In other cases, traditional messianic texts are applied to an agent of salvation, but no Davidic connection is made (cf. the "son of man" in 1 Enoch).

While we must acknowledge this diversity, the most widespread and pervasive messianic expectations in Second Temple Judaism center on an eschatological king from David's line who will establish God's righteous rule.

The Messiah in the NT Use of the OT

When we open the pages of the NT, "Messiah" has clearly become a well-established title and category. This is evident in Luke 3, for example, where the people wonder whether John the Baptist might be "the Messiah" (cf. Matt. 1:17; 2:4; Mark 8:29; 12:35; 14:61; Luke 2:11, 26; etc.).

Matthew. Matthew's Gospel has rightly been called the "Gospel of the Messiah," since it is the most Jewish of the Gospels and draws deeply from the Jewish Scriptures. There is an assumption throughout Matthew that "Messiah" is a well-established category within Judaism and that the coming of Jesus the Messiah represents the dawn of eschatological salvation. Matthew begins with "the genealogy of Jesus the Messiah the son of David, the son of Abraham" (1:1). The genealogy is structured around two covenants (Abrahamic, Davidic) and three epochs of fourteen generations each, climaxing in the coming of the Messiah: Abraham to David, David to the Babylonian exile, and the exile "to the Messiah" (1:17). David's prominence is clear from a gematria on his name, which in Hebrew adds up to fourteen.

This emphasis on Jesus the Messiah as the fulfillment of Scripture and the climax of salvation history continues throughout Matthew. When Herod asks his religious advisors where the Messiah is to be born, they cite Mic. 5:2 to confirm the Bethlehem birthplace (2:4–6). Clear echoes of the Davidic-promise tradition can be seen in the divine sonship of the Messiah expressed in Peter's confession that Jesus is "the Messiah, the Son of the living God" (16:16), and the high priest's question at Jesus's trial, "Tell us if you are the Messiah, the Son of God" (26:63; cf. 2 Sam. 7:14; Pss. 2:7; 89:27).

Yet there is also a measure of surprise and discontinuity with Matthew's OT Christology. At one point John the Baptist—hearing of the "deeds of the Messiah"—sends his disciples to ask Jesus whether he is indeed the "Coming One" (= the Messiah). The narrative implies that his doubts were sparked by Jesus's ministry of teaching, healings, and exorcisms, which did not seem to be the actions of the Davidic warrior-king. Jesus responds by pointing to Isaianic promises related to the restoration of creation: the lame will walk, the blind will see, and the deaf will hear (Matt. 11:2–6, citing Isa. 35:5–6; 61:1). Jesus's conclusion, "Blessed is anyone who does not stumble on account of me," is not just Jesus's words to John but also Matthew's message to those who would reject Jesus because he did not restore Israel's kingdom in the way many had hoped.

Discontinuity is also seen when Jesus cites Ps. 110:1–2 to challenge the Pharisees as to how the Messiah can be both David's "son" (and so subordinate to him) and David's "Lord" (and so superior). Though no explicit answer is given, the implication is that Jesus's messiahship surpasses traditional expectations.

Mark. Though Mark cites far fewer OT prophecies than Matthew, he clearly sees Jesus's messiahship as the fulfillment of OT hopes and expectations. His first line identifies his story as "the good news about Jesus the Messiah" and immediately connects this to the fulfillment of Scripture, "as it is written in Isaiah the prophet . . ." In this way, Mark places the whole Jesus-event under the banner of Isaianic eschatological salvation (Watts).

The rest of Mark's Gospel can be seen as the gradual revelation of Jesus's messiahship. At his baptism the Father affirms it with an allusion to Ps. 2:7 ("This is my Son"). Throughout Jesus's Galilean ministry the demons know it (1:24, 34; 5:7). Yet it is not until the midpoint of Mark's story that the first human character acknowledges it. Peter, when asked by Jesus, "Who do you say that I am?" responds as representative of the Twelve: "You are the Messiah" (8:29). Yet like the blind man who at first sees only partially (8:24), Peter's vision is only partial. Jesus now reveals that his messiahship will entail suffering and sacrifice (8:31). Peter rebukes him for such defeatist talk, but Jesus rebukes him back, accusing him of satanic ambition and a merely human perspective (8:32–33).

From this point in the narrative, Mark's emphasis shifts from confirming Jesus's messiahship on the basis of his authoritative words and actions to demonstrating that Jesus will accomplish the messianic task through sacrifice and suffering. Three times Jesus predicts his death and resurrection (8:31; 9:31–32; 10:33–34); each time the disciples misunderstand and reveal their own pride and desire for self-aggrandizement (8:32; 9:33–34; 10:35–41). Jesus then teaches about cross-bearing discipleship and self-sacrificial leadership (8:34–38; 9:35–37; 10:42–45). These episodes climax at the end of the third cycle, as Jesus announces that "even the Son of Man did not come to be served, but to serve, and to give his life as a ransom for many" (10:45). The statement alludes to Isa. 53:11 and the role of Isaiah's suffering servant of the Lord. The Messiah's role at his first coming is not to crush the Roman legions but to defeat humanity's greatest foes—Satan, sin, and death.

The last great revelation of Jesus's messiahship comes at the climax of the passion narrative. The centurion at the foot of the cross sees how Jesus dies and acknowledges, "Surely this man was the Son of God!" (15:39). Ironically, a gentile centurion is the first to recognize that *in his suffering and death* Jesus fulfills the mission of the Messiah. In this way Mark alludes to where the gospel is going (to the gentiles) and how it will get there (through the suffering and sacrifice of God's people).

Luke-Acts. Luke's overall purpose in writing is the *confirmation of the gospel* (Luke 1:1–4). He is seeking to demonstrate that Jesus is indeed the Messiah and that the church represents the people of God in the new age of salvation. Four themes in particular relate Luke's messianic Christology to this apologetic purpose.

1. The first is a strong promise-and-fulfillment theme. Although Luke quotes the OT directly much less than Matthew, his narrative is permeated with OT allusions and motifs, demonstrating the *continuity* between Judaism and Christianity. Jesus's messiahship, for example, is introduced in thoroughly traditional terms. Gabriel announces to Mary that Jesus "will be great and will be called the Son of the Most High. The Lord God will give him the throne of his father David. . . . His kingdom will never end" (Luke 1:32–33). This is a traditional Jewish messianism right out of 2 Sam. 7; Ps. 89; Isa. 9, 11; and so on. Similar descriptions appear repeatedly in Luke's birth narrative. Jesus will be "a horn of salvation . . . in the house of his servant David" (Luke 1:69; cf. Pss. 89:24; 132:17). He is "the Messiah, the Lord," a Savior born in Bethlehem, the town of David (Luke 2:11; cf. Mic. 5:2). He is the "Lord's Anointed" (Luke 2:26 AT) who will bring about the "consolation of Israel" (2:25) and the "redemption of Jerusalem" (2:38).

2. A second fulfillment theme in Luke-Acts related to Jesus's messiahship is the salvation of the gentiles. In response to those attacking the gentile mission (and Paul, the apostle to the gentiles), Luke's narrative confirms that according to Scripture the Messiah's role was meant

to be "a light for revelation to the Gentiles" (Luke 2:32; also Acts 13:47; both cite Isa. 49:6; cf. Acts 26:23) and that the restoration of the Davidic reign would herald the time "that the rest of mankind may seek the Lord, even all the Gentiles who bear my name" (Acts 15:16–17, citing Amos 9:11 LXX).

3. A third messianic theme with apologetic significance is the suffering role of the Messiah. Against those who would say that the crucifixion negates Jesus's claim to be the Messiah, Luke counters that all along it was God's purpose that the Messiah would accomplish salvation through his death and resurrection. This theme comes to its clearest expression in Luke's account of the Emmaus disciples (Luke 24:13–35). When the two express to their fellow traveler (the incognito Jesus) their disappointment that the prophet Jesus did not turn out to be the one to redeem Israel (i.e., the Messiah), Jesus rebukes them for their spiritual dullness and responds, "Did not the Messiah have to suffer these things and then enter his glory?" (24:26), a point he subsequently proves from "all the Scriptures" (24:27). This is the first explicit reference in Luke-Acts to the suffering of *the Messiah* (always "the Son of Man" before this). The theme that the Messiah must suffer then continues throughout the rest of Luke-Acts (Luke 24:46; Acts 3:18; 17:3; 26:23).

4. Luke's fourth important messianic theme is the exaltation-enthronement of the Messiah at God's right hand, which serves as an apologetic response to those who would claim that Jesus could not be the Messiah because his kingdom did not come. Luke counters that Jesus's ascension represents his enthronement as Davidic Messiah. In Peter's speech on the day of Pentecost, he cites Ps. 16:8–11 ("You will not abandon me to the realm of the dead") to show that David predicted the resurrection of the Messiah (Acts 2:25–29) and that Peter identified it as the fulfillment of God's promise to place one of David's descendants on his throne (2:30–32, citing Ps. 132:11). Jesus's ascension/exaltation therefore represents his vindication and glorious enthronement as Messiah and Lord (Acts 2:33–36, citing Ps. 110:1).

John. The Fourth Gospel shows little interest in traditional messianic expectations. There is no genealogy nor any explicit connection to Jesus's Davidic ancestry. It is Jesus's heavenly origin and divine sonship that are stressed. Yet John does not deny Jesus's messiahship. Indeed, his whole purpose in writing is "that you may believe that Jesus is the Messiah, the Son of God, and that by believing you may have life in his name" (John 20:31). Throughout the Gospel, debate among the Jews centers on whether Jesus is indeed the Messiah (1:41; 4:25, 29; 7:26–27, 31; 9:22; 10:24; 11:27; 12:34).

John's only reference to David and to traditional messianic expectations appears in 7:41–42, where the Jews are divided concerning Jesus and some ask, "How can the Messiah come from Galilee? Does not Scripture say that the Messiah will come from David's descendants and from Bethlehem, the town where David lived?" Some scholars claim that John is here rejecting traditional Davidic messianism in favor of a divine and heavenly Messiah. More likely, this is typical Johannine irony—an insider's wink at his readers. The Jews think that Jesus's Galilean origin disqualifies him from being the Messiah. Yet they are ignorant of what Jesus's followers know: Jesus was actually born in Bethlehem and has legitimate Davidic ancestry. Though his true origin is from heaven and his identity as the Word made flesh goes well beyond Jewish expectations, Jesus is indeed the fulfillment of OT expectations for the Messiah.

Paul. While Paul, like John, strongly affirms Jesus's deity and divine sonship, nevertheless traditional Davidic messianism is an essential theological *foundation* for his high Christology. Paul's magnum opus, the letter to the Roman church, begins by affirming Jesus's status as the Davidic Messiah. In what is likely an early Christian hymn, Paul affirms that the gospel God promised beforehand through the prophets concerned his Son, "who as to his earthly life was a descendant of David" (Rom. 1:3). The combination of Davidic ancestry and divine sonship echoes 2 Sam. 7:14; Pss. 2:7; 89:27–29. Later in Romans, when Paul affirms the privileges attributed to Israel, he writes that "from them is traced the human ancestry of the Messiah" (Rom. 9:5; cf. 2 Tim. 2:8). Davidic messianism is the presupposition and foundation of Paul's divine Christology.

Paul's fundamental (and paradoxical) assertion that "Christ died for our sins" (1 Cor. 15:3) no doubt brings together OT images related to both the Davidic Messiah and the Isaianic servant. Yet echoes of traditional Davidic messianism are to be found at various points in Paul's Letters, especially in his statements on the exaltation of Christ and the consummation of the kingdom. Alluding to the messianic Ps. 110, Paul asserts that Christ "must reign until he has put all his enemies under his feet" (1 Cor. 15:25) and that by virtue of his resurrection and exaltation, Christ is "at the right hand of God . . . interceding for us" (Rom. 8:34; cf. Eph. 1:20; Col. 3:1). In Rom. 15:12 Paul quotes Isa. 11:10 to justify the gentile mission: "The Root of Jesse . . . will arise to rule over the nations; in him the Gentiles will hope."

Hebrews. One would not expect the Letter to the Hebrews to have much traditional messianism, since the author's Christology dwells so strongly on Jesus's role as the great high priest whose once-for-all sacrifice for sins provides eternal redemption. Nevertheless, OT texts related to the Davidic-promise tradition play two significant roles. First, the author cites several messianic texts to confirm that Jesus is the Son of God and is therefore greater than the angels (Heb. 1:5, citing 2 Sam. 7:14; Ps. 2:7). Second, while Jesus's non-Levitical lineage through Judah might appear to disqualify him from the priesthood in Israel, in fact it confirms its legitimacy. The Levitical sacrifices, offered year after year by a flawed high priest, were ultimately unable to provide true or final forgiveness of sins. Through his Melchizedekian priesthood (a right likely claimed by the Davidic kings; Ps. 110:4), Jesus establishes a new priesthood and a new covenant, which provides authentic knowledge of God, the law written on hearts, and eternal forgiveness of sins (Heb. 7–10).

Revelation. Revelation contains perhaps the most traditional messianic descriptions in the NT. At his return, Jesus the Messiah will come as conquering king to establish an eternal reign of peace, justice, and righteousness. The rider on the white horse who has a sharp sword coming out of his mouth and who rules the nations with an iron scepter (Rev. 19:11–16) recalls the "shoot . . . from the stump of Jesse" who will "strike the earth with the rod of his mouth" (Isa. 11:1, 4) and the enthroned Davidic Son of God, who will "break them with a rod of iron" (Ps. 2:9). Jesus is "the Lion of the tribe of Judah, the Root of David" (Rev. 5:5; cf. Gen. 49:8–10; Isa. 11:1; Jer. 23:5–6), who, because of his role as the Lamb who was slain (Rev. 5:6, 9), is worthy to bring human history to its consummation.

While much of the rest of the NT wrestles with the question of how Jesus can be the Messiah since he apparently did not fulfill the expected role of subjugating every power and authority and establishing God's eternal kingdom, in Revelation the kingdom arrives in all its glory; heaven comes to earth, and "the Root and the Offspring of David," the "bright Morning Star," invites all who are thirsty to come and receive the free gift of the water of life (Rev. 22:16–17). With the return of the Messiah, God's kingdom arrives on earth as it is in heaven.

See also Adam, First and Last; Image of God; Kingdom and King; Son of God

Bibliography. Charlesworth, J. H., ed., *The Messiah* (Fortress, 1992); Charlesworth, ed., *Qumran-Messianism* (Mohr Siebeck, 1998); Collins, J. J., *The Scepter and the Star*, 2nd ed. (Eerdmans, 2010); Evans, C. A., "Messianism," in *DNTB*, 698–707; Hess, R. S., and M. D. Carroll R., eds., *Israel's Messiah in the Bible and the Dead Sea Scrolls* (Baker Academic, 2003); Horbury, W., *Jewish Messianism and the Cult of Christ* (SCM, 1998); Neusner, J., et al., eds., *Judaisms and Their Messiahs at the Turn of the Christian Era* (Cambridge University Press, 1987); Oegema, G. S., *The Anointed and His People* (Sheffield Academic, 1998); Porter, S. E., ed., *The Messiah in the Old and New Testaments* (Eerdmans, 2007); Satterthwaite, P. E., R. S. Hess, and G. J. Wenham, *The Lord's Anointed* (Paternoster, 1995); Strauss, M. L., *The Davidic Messiah in Luke-Acts* (Sheffield Academic, 1995); Watts, R., *Isaiah's New Exodus in Mark* (Baker Academic, 2000).

Mark L. Strauss

Metalepsis

See Quotation, Allusion, and Echo

Method

This essay represents one approach to interpreting the OT in the NT. It is not the only method nor will following it guarantee the interpreter a true or exhaustive meaning.

The reasons for this are manifold. First, interpreters are fallible creatures: despite whatever procedure they are following, their fallibility extends to their ability to interpret. Second, the task of interpretation is not merely a science but also a literary art, which defies strict rules. Third, no one person can exhaustively understand what another has said, whether that be understanding what someone has said or written in the modern setting or in the ancient world. An authorial speech act is "thick," and it is impossible for any one interpreter to unravel all the layers of meaning within it.

Nevertheless, we can retrieve some meaning from what has been said or written. Good interpretations can uncover layers of meaning that result in sufficient understanding of a biblical passage. In this respect, the guidelines offered below are not prescriptions or formulas that will ultimately lead to correct interpretations. Rather, the procedures discussed here suggest different angles from which we can look at a passage. When all these approaches are put together, they will provide the potential for gaining a cumulatively better understanding of the way the NT interprets the OT. Additional angles of viewing a text could certainly be added to the ones covered here, angles that will result in further understanding. To analyze an OT reference by following the ninefold approach described here will take some work, but I believe it will enable the researcher to better understand the passage at hand.

The aim of this essay is to obtain a better understanding of the way the NT is related to the OT at those points where the NT refers to the OT. The ultimate purpose in this exercise is to help interpreters more clearly to hear and apprehend the living word of the living God (cf. Acts 7:38), so that we may encounter God increasingly and know him more deeply, and, as a result, think and do those things that honor God.

Overview

I begin with an overview of the approach before elaborating on each of the nine steps. (I first encountered the essence of this approach in a class on the OT in the NT taught by S. L. Johnson in the mid-1970s at Dallas Theological Seminary; likewise, see Snodgrass, 48–49, whose approach is very similar but only briefly set forth.)

This essay is a revision of G. K. Beale, *Handbook on the New Testament Use of the Old Testament* (Baker Academic, 2012), 41–55. This section of the *Handbook* should be consulted to see the majority of the secondary sources appealed to in support and the broader discussion of this topic.

1. Identify the OT reference. Is it a quotation or allusion? If it is an allusion, then there must be validation that it is an allusion, judging by certain criteria.
2. Perform an initial analysis of the broad and immediate NT context where the OT reference occurs.
3. Analyze the OT context both broadly and immediately, especially the paragraph in which the quotation or allusion occurs.
4. Survey any use of the OT text in early and late Judaism that might be of relevance to the NT appropriation of the OT text.
5. Compare the texts (including their textual variants): NT, LXX, MT, targums, and early Jewish citations (DSS, the Pseudepigrapha, Josephus, Philo). Underline or color-code the various differences.
6. Analyze the author's textual use of the OT: Which text does the author rely on, or is the author making his own rendering, and how does this bear on the interpretation of the OT text?
7. Analyze the author's interpretive (hermeneutical) use of the OT.
8. Analyze the author's theological use of the OT.
9. Analyze the author's rhetorical use of the OT.

Elaboration

Here each of the nine steps listed above will be elaborated.

1. Identify the OT reference. Is it a quotation or allusion? If it is an allusion, then there must be validation that it is an allusion, judging by certain criteria. This step has been addressed elsewhere in the dictionary (see the article "Quotations, Allusion, and Echo"). Therefore, I will proceed to the next step.

2. Perform an initial analysis of the broad and immediate NT context where the OT reference occurs. Overview of the broad NT context. Try to discover the occasion for the particular NT book in which the OT quotation occurs. Why was the book written? To whom? These questions are easier to answer in epistolary literature but harder in the Gospels and Acts. Next, gather an overview of the outline of the entire NT book in which the OT reference occurs. Try as best as possible to discern the way the argument develops logically throughout the book, paying special attention to the main themes of the paragraphs and how they appear to relate. Since this is a massive task in itself, it is advisable that after a reading of the entire biblical book and reflection on how the argument develops, the introductions of two or three substantive commentaries on the biblical book should be consulted. Pay special attention to how these commentaries outline the book (and break down the major literary units) and how they trace the progress of thought throughout the book. Combine your own views with what you consider to be the best views of the commentaries and construct a tentative working outline of the book, showing how its argument develops.

Overview of the immediate NT context. Then pay special attention to how the chapter in which your quotation occurs appears to fit into the overall argument of the biblical book. More specifically, how does the paragraph in which the quotation occurs fit into the argument of the chapter itself? Is it a basis or purpose for what has preceded or for what follows? Is it a detailed explanation or interpretation of what has gone before or perhaps a summary of what is to follow? Is it an inference or result of what has preceded? Is it a response to a preceding narration of an event or conversation between two parties? Does it indicate the means by which something in the surrounding context is accomplished? Is it a contrast or comparison to something in the context? Does the paragraph answer a preceding question? Is it perhaps part of a series of statements in the chapter that have no logical relationship to one another? At a later point in the procedure, more in-depth interpretation of the paragraph itself will take place.

3. Analyze the OT context both broadly and immediately, especially the paragraph in which the quotation or allusion occurs. This is crucial! It may provide previously unnoticed insights into the OT citation or allusion. One should go into the exegetical depths of the Hebrew text (or the English text, if the researcher does not know Hebrew). Here one should interpret the OT on its own grounds and within its own redemptive-historical context, without allowing the NT text to influence the interpretation, since it represents a later stage of redemptive history.

Overview of the broad OT context. First, the researcher should go through the same process as discussed in the preceding step concerning the NT context, though now applying this to the broad OT context from which the NT draws its reference.

Overview of the immediate OT context. One now focuses on the very OT paragraph from which the NT has taken its reference. Here one tries to employ all the angles of OT exegetical practice when studying the literary unit that contains the OT quotation. Accordingly, the interpreter should be aware of how the focus paragraph logically fits into the flow of thought in the chapter, and the same questions asked just above for the NT context apply here also. Then the flow of thought within the paragraph should be traced, especially to ascertain how the part that is quoted fits into that flow. Here again, the various questions just asked above for the NT should be asked about how each of the verses (or propositions) relate to one another in the paragraph under focus. How does the quotation fit into the logical development of thought in the paragraph?

Other interpretative questions should be asked about the paragraph, especially since they may have potential bearing on the material providing the NT quotation: Is there a major textual, grammatical, syntactical, lexical, theological, genre, historical-background (in the ancient Near East), or figure-of-speech problem in the paragraph? In this regard, the student should consult Douglas Stuart's *Old Testament Exegesis* for an elaboration of these interpretative problems and how to go about addressing them.

Relate the OT quotation to what comes earlier and later in the canonical Scriptures. First, how does the historical and redemptive epoch of this OT passage relate to the earlier or later stages of redemptive history within the OT itself?

Second, try to determine if the quotation in its original literary context is itself a quotation of or allusion to an earlier written OT text (or even to an earlier passage in the book in which it occurs). Or is the quotation repeated or alluded to later in the OT (or even by a later passage in the book in which it occurs)? If either is the case, the interpreter will need to go to the earlier or later text and analyze it in the same way as described above for the focus text in order to try to determine how the focus text is using the earlier text or being used by the later OT text. There are some aids in trying to discover whether the focus quotation is a development of or being developed by another OT passage. First, check the outer and bottom margins of the Hebrew text. Second, check the margins of the major English translations. Third, use concordances to search for unique word combinations that perhaps can be found only in the focus text and one or two other OT texts. Finally, Gary Schnittjer's *Old Testament Use of Old Testament* is a very helpful source that identifies many of the earlier references of the OT that are alluded to and used in later parts of the OT.

If such unique word combinations are found elsewhere in the OT, they are good candidates to consider as either allusions to the OT focus text or as being alluded to by the focus passage. If we find that two or three other later OT texts allude to the focus text, for example, then there is the possibility of tracing the interpretive or theological trajectory of its use. This is an important exercise to conduct since there is always the possibility that a NT writer may refer to an earlier OT text but understand it through the interpretative lens of a later OT passage that alludes to the earlier one. Or it is possible that a NT writer could refer to a later OT text but understand it through the interpretative lens of an earlier OT text to which the later text alludes. In such cases, if the interpreter is unaware of such connections, the NT writer's interpretation of the OT quotation or allusion may be hard to understand. In this respect, we are entering into the realm of biblical theology and face some key questions: How are several OT passages literarily and interpretatively linked? How do such linkages relate to the NT author's use of a particular OT passage? It is also possible that a NT writer might be influenced by some OT theme (found in multiple passages) through which he understands the OT text to which he is making reference (e.g., see Rom. 3:10–18 with respect to the theme of sinful depravity).

Tentatively apply the findings from this step to the NT quotation: Are there similarities in theme or argument? Do the OT and NT quotation and allusion address similar problems? And so on.

4. Survey any use of the OT text in early and late Judaism that might be of relevance to the NT appropriation of the OT text. One must become acquainted with the various primary sources in early and late Judaism in English translation. (An annotated bibliography of the relevant Jewish sources is found in Beale, chap. 6. Some of the Hebrew and Greek editions of these sources are cited for those who know the biblical languages.)

The purpose of this step is to discover how Judaism independently understood the same OT passages that the NT has cited. Therefore, one should consult Scripture indices in these various Jewish works. The indices will direct the reader to the particular page in the Jewish source where the specific OT passage is discussed. In addition, there are commentaries on historical backgrounds that the researcher may consult to see if a NT passage contains a Jewish or Greco-Roman background. These commentaries will often be helpful in showing where there is an independent Jewish interpretation of the same OT references that appear in the NT. (These background commentaries are also in the annotated bibliography in Beale, chap. 6.)

Explain the relevance of Jewish background for the use of the OT passage in the NT. This is a threefold task. First, collect all the citations and discussions in Judaism of the specific OT text under focus. Second, summarize any patterns, trends, similar uses, or similar ideas observable in these Jewish uses of the OT text. Third, compare these Jewish uses in their own Jewish contexts to the way the OT text is used in the NT and its context. Here it is important to evaluate whether the non-Christian Jewish uses are similar to the NT use. If so, does the Jewish use give a better understanding of the NT use? Sometimes looking at a NT employment of the OT through the lens of a non-Christian Jewish use brings new vistas of perspective.

In this respect, one would not necessarily conclude that the NT text is literarily dependent on the earlier or contemporary Jewish use, though this is possible. (Here I invoke the warning of Sandmel, "Parallelomania," who warns of the temptation too often to see dependence by one writer on an earlier writer; see also Donaldson; cf. Bauckham, 207–20.) Both Judaism and the NT could be drawing on a common stock of understandings of OT texts that was in general circulation at the time. In such cases, primarily Jewish writings contemporaneous with or earlier than the NT are crucial for consideration, since the perspectives they express would have had opportunity to circulate in first-century Palestinian culture and reflect a common stock of tradition potentially known to a NT writer. Later Jewish interpretations (sources from the second century and later) may still be relevant to one degree or another, especially when corroborating but not directly dependent on earlier Jewish interpretations, since they may reflect earlier traditions existing at the time of the first century. Nevertheless, when there is only later evidence, it must be treated cautiously and not viewed as having significant bearing on the way the NT has understood an OT reference.

More typical, in my view, is that both Judaism and the NT writers are going back to some of the same OT texts and interpreting them for their own communities. The different segments of early Judaism (e.g., Qumran, Palestinian Judaism, Alexandrian Judaism, apocalyptic Judaism) did not primarily learn their interpretative approach to the OT from one another, nor was early Christianity primarily dependent on any of these segments of Judaism for their understanding of how to approach the OT. Rather, it is more likely that both the NT writers and early Jewish interpreters patterned their interpretation of the OT after the way later OT writers interpreted earlier OT passages (see the article "OT Use of the OT: Comparison with the NT Use of the OT" elsewhere in the dictionary).

Accordingly, it is beneficial to look at Jewish interpretations of the same OT texts as those cited in the NT in the same way that we look at modern commentaries. There are very good commentaries, some that are so-so, and others that are not very insightful. I am sure that many readers have consulted a commentary on an OT passage and had an "Aha!" moment. The commentary discussion provided an interpretation that we had never thought of before, and the new perspective caused us to look at the biblical passage in a new way and to see what was really there in the first place. Obviously it is absurd to think that the OT passage is dependent on a contemporary commentary. Nevertheless, the commentary may provide insight into the original meaning of the passage. Once given the new perspective, the interpretation may be demonstrated really to lie in the ancient biblical text.

The same is true with Jewish interpretations of OT texts, whether they come from early or late Judaism. They can serve as commentaries, fostering a better understanding of the way Christian writers interpret the same OT passages. Indeed, if we find value in consulting modern commentaries, why would we not avail ourselves of ancient commentaries, which are closer to the time when the NT writings were composed and may have been privy to patterns of thinking in common with the NT writers themselves? References in early Judaism (second century BC to second century AD) are more relevant than those in later Judaism (third to sixth century AD and onward). The obvious reason (to reiterate) for this is that a first-century NT writer could have been familiar with or influenced by ideas from early Jewish references but not those that developed after the first century AD. Nevertheless, it is possible that notions found in post-first-century Jewish references existed in earlier oral sources or traditions with which a NT author could have been familiar.

There surely will be Jewish interpretations of the OT that are the opposite of the NT's use of the same passage. In such cases the Jewish use shows how unique the early NT writers and Judaism itself were, especially where several early Jewish sources have interpretations antithetical to those of the NT. In such cases we can grow to appreciate the uniqueness of the NT witness in the context of its Jewish environment. At other times, the relationship of Jewish interpretations to the NT may be unclear. There may be cases where Jewish interpretations offer neither reinforcing nor contrasting interpretations that contribute to any useful understanding of the NT reference. Therefore, at the conclusion of this analysis, there should be a *tentative* comparison of the way the OT text is used by Jewish writers with the way it is used in the NT text.

Illustration of the relevance of Jewish background for the use of the OT in the NT. Here we could adduce many examples of how Jewish interpretations of OT texts have shed interesting light on the same texts cited in the NT. A number of examples may be found in *CNTUOT*, which often includes a section dealing with how Judaism understood a quotation and what bearing this may or may not have on the NT use (reference may be made to other works on the NT's use of the OT, as well as more technical commentaries on the NT).

5. Compare the texts (including their textual variants): NT, LXX, MT, targums, and early Jewish citations (DSS, the Pseudepigrapha, Josephus, Philo). Underline or color-code the various differences. For example, see Beale, 49, where there are textual comparisons of Isa. 6:9–10 in John 12:40 (in the MT, LXX, and NT). The following kinds of comparisons are to be made: (1) triple agreement is portrayed as regular text; (2) double agreement is portrayed in italics; (3) unique elements (grammar, terminology) are underlined; (4) change in word order is portrayed with double underlining. Not every minute change can be shown according to this fourfold scheme, but the significant ones are exhibited. Making these comparisons in Hebrew and Greek provides better precision and more clarity.

6. Analyze the author's textual use of the OT: Which text does the author rely on, or is the author making his own rendering, and how does this bear on the interpretation of the OT text? In this section major changes among the Hebrew, LXX, and NT texts should be noted. In light of those changes, one should try to ascertain on what OT text the author is dependent or if the author is making his own interpretive paraphrase. How this bears on the interpretation of the OT text will be discussed in the next section.

7. Analyze the author's interpretive (hermeneutical) use of the OT. Study the immediate NT context, especially the paragraph in which the quotation or allusion occurs. At the conclusion of this part of the study, it is important to survey the possible categorical uses of the OT in the NT (see the article "Contextual and Noncontextual NT Use of the OT" elsewhere in the dictionary) to decide which may be in mind. For example, the NT author may be indicating direct prophetic fulfillment, indirect typological fulfillment, an analogy, an abiding truth, an irony, and so on.

Overview of the immediate context. The broad context of the quotation in the NT has already been explored in step 2 above. Now, as in the OT analysis section (step 3 above), one focuses on the very paragraph in which the NT quotation is found. Here one tries to employ all the angles of NT exegetical practice when studying the literary unit that contains the OT quotation. Accordingly, after the interpreter has determined how the focus paragraph logically fits into the flow of thought in the chapter, the flow of thought within the paragraph should be traced, especially with a view to how the quoted part fits into that flow. Here again, the various questions asked in step 2 should be asked about how each of the verses (or propositions) relates to the others in the paragraph under focus. How does the quotation fit into the development of thought in the paragraph?

Other interpretive questions should be asked about the paragraph, especially since they may have potential bearing on the material providing the NT quotation: Is there a major problem in the paragraph concerning issues of textual criticism, grammar, syntax, word meanings, theology, genre, historical background (any helpful Jewish interpretation of the OT passage), or figures of speech? In this regard, the student should consult Gordon D. Fee's *New Testament Exegesis* for elaboration of many of these interpretive problems and how to go about addressing them.

Relate the quotation to other quotations from or allusions to the same OT passage elsewhere in the NT. There are several aids to help one become aware of other NT quotations or allusions to the same OT text outside the passage of focus. These are mentioned and discussed in Beale, chap. 2. If other uses within the NT are found, the interpreter would need to go to those other texts and analyze them in the same way as described above for the focus text; the goal is to determine how the use in the focus text is to be compared with the other interpretive uses elsewhere in the NT. The time spent in analyzing these other uses will likely be less than the time already spent researching the use of the OT in the focus text, since a number of the steps will have already been accomplished. The practical demands of time (whether on account of pastoral ministry or the limits of a scholarly project) will impose certain limitations on how much further exploration of these other texts can be done.

If there are differences of interpretation or of interpretive emphasis between the focus text and the other parallel OT uses, then these need to be spelled out clearly. Do the other uses shed any light on the use in the focus text? Do they pose difficult questions or problems for how the focus text is related to them? These questions enter into the realm of biblical theology: How are several NT uses of the same OT texts interpretively and theologically linked? How do such linkages relate to the NT author's use of a particular OT passage in the focus text?

Relate the quotation to other quotations from or allusions to the same OT passage elsewhere in post-NT literature. This primarily involves looking to the NT Apocrypha (see Hennecke and Schneemelcher) and the church fathers (esp. of the second century AD). There are two main sources for finding where the church fathers quote or allude to the OT. First, the most thorough source is *Biblia Patristica* (Allenbach et al., eds.), which gives references to both the OT and the NT. A second source, though less exhaustive, is the massive set of *Ante-Nicene Fathers* (Coxe, Robertson, and Donaldson, eds.; helpful for studying the meaning of words in the Apostolic Fathers are the following: the lexicon of Kraft, *Clavis Patrum Apostolicorum*, and Goodspeed, *Index Patristicus*); in addition, note *Nicene and Post-Nicene Fathers* (Schaff, ed. [Series 1]; Schaff and Wace, eds. [Series 2]). At the end of each volume is a Scripture index, which allows one easily to find references to the OT in the particular fathers found translated in each volume (though vols. 2 and 14 of *NPNF*[2] do not contain a Scripture index; see also Jurgens, *The Faith of the Early Fathers*, which has both topical and Scripture indexes).

Survey the possible categorical uses of the OT in the NT. At the conclusion of this part of the study, survey the possible categorical uses of the OT in the NT (again, see the article "Contextual and Noncontextual NT Use of the OT" elsewhere in the dictionary) to decide which may be in mind. How do the conclusions reached so far in this part of the study point to or indicate which categorical use is intended? All of the conclusions reached so far in the steps of this chapter (up through the present step) should be brought to bear in attempting to answer this question.

8. Analyze the author's theological use of the OT. After determining the interpretive use of the OT passage, a theological question should be asked: To what part of theology does this use of the OT passage contribute? Here the categories of systematic theology, biblical theology, and so-called constructive theology are surveyed in order to reflect on the theological use. One can consult the table of contents of some of the standard systematic theologies to recognize the categories of systematic theology that may be relevant to the passage in question (see, e.g., Bavinck, *Reformed Dogmatics*; Berkhof, *Systematic Theology*; Hodge, *Systematic Theology*; Turretin, *Institutes of Elenctic Theology*; Grudem, *Systematic Theology*). For example, all systematic theologies include the categories of Christology, ecclesiology, and pneumatology. Some uses of the OT in the NT pertain to each of these particular categories. Accordingly, with respect to Christology, there are some cases where an OT passage describing God is applied to Christ (e.g., see Matt. 3:3; John 1:23); with regard to ecclesiology, many NT passages take OT prophecies about Israel and apply them to the church (e.g., Rom. 9:26; 10:13); concerning pneumatology, several NT passages cite the OT (e.g., Luke 4:18–19; Acts 2:17–21).

One should also be aware of the categories of biblical theology. A source that will make one more aware of the relevant categories of biblical theology is *The New Dictionary of Biblical Theology* (Alexander and Rosner, eds.; see also Elwell, ed., *Evangelical Dictionary of Biblical Theology*; Léon-Dufour, ed., *Dictionary of Biblical Theology*; and the volumes in the New Studies in Biblical Theology series, edited by D. A. Carson). For example, among important biblical-theological categories to which OT-in-the-NT uses may contribute are the "restoration of Israel," "inaugurated eschatology," "the second exodus," recapitulations of Eden, the temple, the image of God, and so on.

Another important aspect of considering the theological use is to try to discern what theological presuppositions might underlie the interpretive use. Certain uses may appear strange or hard to understand in relation to the original meaning of the OT passage. In some of these cases, a NT writer may be understanding the OT text through the lens of a NT presupposition. In the light of the writers' presuppositions, their use of the OT may become more understandable and explainable. The main presuppositions that are relevant for consideration are the following, though the validity of some of these is debated (for elaboration of these presuppositions, see the article "Apostolic Hermeneutics: Description and Presuppositions" elsewhere in the dictionary):

1. Corporate solidarity or representation is assumed.
2. On the basis of point 1, Christ is viewed as representing the *true Israel* of the OT *and* the true Israel—the church—in the NT.
3. *History is unified* by a wise and sovereign plan so that the earlier parts are designed to correspond and point to the later parts.
4. The age of *eschatological fulfillment* has come in Christ but has not been fully consummated.
5. As a consequence of point 4, it may be deduced that the later parts of biblical history function as the broader context to interpret earlier parts because they all have the same ultimate divine author, who inspires the various human authors. One deduction from this premise is that the divine Christ and his glory as the end-time center and goal of redemptive history are the *key to interpreting the earlier portions of the OT and its promises.*
6. *Jesus is identified as divine.*

These presuppositions have their roots in the OT itself. Again, keep in mind that all of the conclusions reached so far in the various steps of this chapter will contribute to a better understanding of the theological use of the OT.

9. Analyze the author's rhetorical use of the OT. What was the author's purpose in referring to the OT? What is the final intended force of the statement, especially with respect to moving the readers in a particular direction theologically or ethically? This may be harder to discern in the Gospels and Acts but a bit easier in epistolary literature, where the occasion for writing and the problems being addressed by the NT writers are more explicitly stated. As before, remember that the conclusions reached in all of the various steps of this chapter will help toward a better understanding of the rhetorical use of the OT.

Conclusion

This essay has laid out a ninefold approach to interpreting the OT in the NT. There are certainly other possible approaches and angles from which to study OT references in the NT. However, the nine elements discussed here are the bare necessities of studying this topic.

See also Apostolic Hermeneutics articles

Bibliography. Alexander, T. D., and B. S. Rosner, eds., *The New Dictionary of Biblical Theology* (InterVarsity, 2001); Allenbach, J., et al., eds., *Biblia Patristica*, 7 vols. + supplement (Centre national de la recherche scientifique, 1975–) [this source also includes an index of apocryphal references, available online at http://www.biblindex.mom.fr/]; Bauckham, R., *The Jewish World around the New Testament* (Baker Academic, 2010); Bavinck, H., *Reformed Dogmatics*, 4 vols. (Baker Academic, 2003–8); Beale, G. K., *Handbook on the New Testament Use of the Old Testament* (Baker Academic, 2012); Berkhof, L., *Systematic Theology*, 11th ed. (Eerdmans, 1969); Coxe, A. C., A. Robertson, and J. Donaldson, eds., *Ante-Nicene Fathers*, 10 vols. (1885–96; repr., Hendrickson, 1999) [vol. 10 contains a Scripture index; all volumes online at http://www.ccel.org/fathers.html]; Donaldson, T. L., "Parallels," *EvQ* 55 (1983): 193–210; Elwell, W. A., ed., *Evangelical Dictionary of Biblical Theology* (Baker, 1996); Fee, G. D., *New Testament Exegesis*, 3rd ed. (Westminster, 2002); Goodspeed, E. J., *Index Patristicus* (Allenson, 1907); Grudem, W., *Systematic Theology*, 2nd ed. (Zondervan, 2020); Hennecke, E., and W. Schneemelcher, eds., *New Testament Apocrypha*, 2 vols. (Westminster, 1963–65); Hodge, C., *Systematic Theology*, 3 vols. (1871–73; repr., Eerdmans, 1973); Holmes, M. W., *The Apostolic Fathers* (Baker, 1999) [this is a very helpful aid that has the Greek text on the left and the corresponding English translation on the facing page]; Jurgens, W., *The Faith of the Early Fathers*, 3 vols. (Liturgical Press, 1970–79) [this source has both topical and Scripture indexes];

Kraft, H., *Clavis Patrum Apostolicorum* (Kösel, 1963); Léon-Dufour, X., ed., *Dictionary of Biblical Theology* (Desclée, 1967); Sandmel, S., "Parallelomania," *JBL* 81 (1962): 1–13; Schaff, P., ed., *The Nicene and Post-Nicene Fathers*, Series 1, 15 vols. (1886–99; repr., Hendrickson, 1994) [online at http://www.ccel.org/fathers.html]; Schaff, P., and H. Wace, eds., *The Nicene and Post-Nicene Fathers*, Series 2, 14 vols. (1890–1900; repr., Hendrickson, 1994) [online at http://www.ccel.org/fathers.html]; Schnittjer, G. E., *Old Testament Use of Old Testament* (Zondervan, 2021); Snodgrass, K., "The Use of the Old Testament in the New," in *The Right Doctrine from the Wrong Texts?*, ed. G. K. Beale (Baker, 1994), 29–51; Stuart, D. K., *Old Testament Exegesis* (Westminster, 1980); Turretin, F., *Institutes of Elenctic Theology*, 3 vols. (P&R, 1992–97).

G. K. Beale

Micah, Book of

The prophecy of Micah is the sixth of the Minor Prophets in the Hebrew Bible, the third in the Septuagint. Micah, a contemporary of Isaiah, prophesied concerning Jerusalem at the end of the eighth century BC (Mic. 1:1). His hometown, Moresheth, was a farming community near the fertile coastal plain bordering on the Philistine town of Gath (1:1, 14). He predicts the destruction of the Northern Kingdom under the Assyrians (1:2–7) and a similar destruction to his own nation of Judah because of rampant covenant violation (1:8–16; 3:1–12). The corruption is so pervasive that hardly one loyal follower of Yahweh remains, and the people seem blind to the coming Assyrian juggernaut of God's judgment (7:1–6). Beyond the judgment, the prophet looks to the future, envisioning a pure Jerusalem and holy temple that will be elevated to the supreme place in the world. True justice will flow from these, and they will be the center of world peace (4:1–5). Parallel to this elevation of the sanctuary, an exalted messianic figure will come, born in Bethlehem, a new David, who will establish this peace (5:2–4). Micah's preaching produces repentance in King Hezekiah, and Judah is spared imminent disaster (Jer. 26:18–19). The Assyrians retreat without capturing Jerusalem (2 Kings 18–19).

Structure of the Book

There are multiple ways to look at Micah's structure, but probably the most accurate is to view it as either a two-part (1:1–5:15; 6:1–7:20) or three-part structure (1:1–2:13; 3:1–5:15; 6:1–7:20). The tripartite structure is more symmetrical and balanced, suggesting editorial intention. The command to hear begins each major section (1:2; 3:1; 6:1), and each section contains judgment speeches balanced with salvation oracles (1:1–2:11 and 2:12–13; 3:1–12 and 4:1–5:15; 6:1–7:7 and 7:8–20). The book makes clear that the Southern Kingdom of Judah, like the Northern Kingdom of Israel, is headed for judgment because of covenant violation. Despite the coming judgment, however, God's promise to Abraham remains intact, and the entire world will be blessed with peace at the end of history as God's sovereign reign over the world is finally established.

Major Themes

Justice. One of the strongest condemnations of the people of God by Micah was the juxtaposition of intense concern for religious ritual and performance with a failure to live out their faith in the daily routines of life, whether in the workplace, the home, the village, the city gate, or the temple. This explains Micah's ridicule of the one-off performances of religious devotion in which people competed with each other for celebrity status, whether giving year-old calves for burnt offerings, thousands of rams, or ten thousand rivers of oil. The hyperbole is clearly satirical, and Micah contrasts this with the requirements of Yahweh, which focus on a daily life of service: to seek justice, to love mercy, and to walk humbly with God (6:6–8). The people are more concerned with following the statutes of Omri, the unjust northern king, than those of Yahweh (6:16). The contamination of injustice has left the land devoid of faithful Yahweh followers (7:2). Worst of all, the religious leaders have led the way in the corruption in their preference for economic profits over God and people (3:11).

Although Micah's denunciations of Israel's injustice are prophetic revelations granted to him, they should not be surprising. The Torah's covenantal demands and its abiding authority are clear, and the people have failed to observe its requirements. The Torah is a revelation that in its broad sweep of commands is aimed at inculcating a wholehearted love for God and a love for neighbor equal to love of self. To reflect the values of the Torah is to reflect the character of God himself, and thus Israel is to be a holy nation, distinct from the rest of the world in its reflection of the divine character. Injustice is the clear violation of the command to love one's neighbor, which is formulated legally in the second half of Israel's Decalogue. This results from covetousness (prohibited in the tenth commandment), which results from idolatry (forbidden in the first two commands). Micah's constant references to injustice throughout his prophecies target Israel's avarice (coveting wealth), which he denounces unequivocally (2:1–2). It amounts to an idol that can never satisfy the human heart (cf. 1:5–7). No amount of sacrifices or tithes could compensate for this. Indeed, it is sacrilege. This explains why Micah's succinct history of salvation—divine mercy has delivered Israel from Egyptian bondage and led them through the wilderness into the promised land (6:1–5)—should have led to a concern for justice, mercy, and following in the way of the Torah (6:8).

Zion and scion. At the center of the book stands the temple on Mount Zion. It had become a place of venality and corruption in Micah's time, and he predicts a day when it will be destroyed—in fact, he is the first prophet to announce the destruction of Jerusalem and its temple—and be replaced by a temple that will rise above all other places of worship and from which the word of the Lord would go forth to beckon the nations to come and end the blight of war (3:9–4:5). At this newly resurrected temple the nations will meet with Yahweh and be instructed in the right way to live, and their transformed hearts will reshape their instruments of war and destruction into ones suited for peace and production. Alongside this exaltation of Zion will come the exaltation of a scion from David's line, from Bethlehem, whose greatness will eventually reach the ends of the earth (5:2–4). This scion will shepherd the people, and his rise coincides with the emergence of a remnant of followers, who will effectively bless the nations who accept them (the dew in 5:7) or curse the ones opposing them (the lion in 5:8–9).

These two ideas of the temple, which stands for the earthly throne of the heavenly Yahweh, and the human monarch who is a representative of the heavenly king are rooted in earlier revelation. David had wanted to build a house (a temple) for Yahweh, but Yahweh would not allow him this privilege. Instead, Yahweh would build a house for David (a dynasty) that would never lack a ruler (2 Sam. 7). This Davidic covenant (cf. Ps. 89:3) itself springs from earlier statements in Scripture in which Jacob had prophesied of a great conqueror from the tribe of Judah who would transform nature and to whom the nations would pay homage (Gen. 49:8–12). This would in effect reestablish human beings as the image of God in his universe, seeking justice and loving mercy as a result of their communion with God.

Patriarchal promises. Micah uses a number of key texts from Genesis that contribute to a more fully orbed view of the salvation he envisages in Mic. 4–5. Thus, he describes the return from exile as "the gathering of the lame . . . who have suffered at my hand" (4:6–7 AT). Here is an allusion to Jacob's struggle with Yahweh at the Jabbok, from which he emerges maimed but transformed (Gen. 32). Similarly, he describes the gathered exiles as the tower of the flock (literally, "the tower of Eder"), which alludes to a location near Bethlehem where Rachel died giving birth (Gen. 35:21) and thus may suggest the renewal of the Davidic empire after a time of suffering. Moreover, the references to the renewed remnant as being both "dew" to friends and "a lion" to enemies refer not only to later patriarchal promises (Gen. 27:28; 49:8–10) but also to God's original promise to bless those who bless Abraham and curse those who curse him (Gen. 12:3). Micah concludes with the attribute formula (Exod. 34:6–7) and a focus of God's forgiveness of the people, which is grounded in the Abrahamic covenant: "You will be faithful to Jacob and show love to Abraham, as you pledged on oath to our ancestors in days long ago." This means that Israel's sins will be trodden underfoot and hurled into the bottom of the sea like Pharaoh's horsemen (Mic. 7:19–20; cf. Exod. 15). Israel's ancient salvation from Egypt has been magnified to an ultimate degree.

NT Development

These themes resonate in the NT, either explicitly or implicitly. The theme of a messianic deliverer coming to establish world peace and to be born in Bethlehem is found at the beginning of the NT, in Matthew (2:1–18). When sages from the east journey to Jerusalem following a sign in the heavens indicating the birth of a new king, they end up enquiring where the new king has been born. King Herod discovers from Jewish scholars that Bethlehem is the birthplace, since this was prophesied by Micah (Matt. 2:6; cf. Mic. 5:2–4). Herod provides the travelers with the information and then asks them to return on their way home so he too can have the opportunity to worship. The sages then travel to Bethlehem, where they worship the infant Jesus, the newly born king, but return another way because of a divine warning. When Herod discovers their deception, he sends soldiers to murder infants in the vicinity of Bethlehem to ensure the death of the Messiah.

Matthew's citation of Micah is part of a series of citations used to show that Jesus is the predicted Messiah from the OT and the fulfillment of OT prophecy (Matt. 1:22–23 [= Isa. 7:14]; 2:15 [= Hosea 11:1]; 2:18 [= Jer. 31:15]). Matthew combines this text from Micah with God's announcement in 2 Samuel that David would be a shepherd and ruler of Israel (2 Sam. 5:2; cf. Matt. 2:6b).

Interestingly, the wording of the citation from Micah does not precisely follow the extant Masoretic Text or the Septuagint but seems to be a concise abridgment of both. However, there does seem to be a major difference between Micah and Matthew: Micah says that Bethlehem is insignificant among the thousands/chiefs of Judah, while Matthew declares in his citation that Bethlehem is by no means least among the rulers of Judah. Matthew's loose translation appears like a blatant contradiction. Nonetheless, although this translation is not formally equivalent, it brings out the essential meaning of the Micah passage in which insignificant Bethlehem becomes important because it is the birthplace of the Messiah.

John's Gospel picks up on the same theme of the birth of Jesus in Bethlehem. Here the Jewish audience of Jesus discusses how their knowledge about the Messiah's credentials contradicts Jesus's claims. "On hearing his words, some of the people said, 'Surely this man is the Prophet.' Others said, 'He is the Messiah.' Still others asked, 'How can the Messiah come from Galilee? Does not Scripture say that the Messiah will come from David's descendants and from Bethlehem, the town where David lived?' Thus the people were divided because of Jesus. Some wanted to seize him, but no one laid a hand on him" (John 7:40–44). John reveals the people's ignorance as a way of affirming Jesus's claim to be the Messiah.

But there are other explicit references to Micah. When discussing coming persecution to his disciples, Jesus warns them to have no illusions about his demands and the possible consequences, and thus he cites Mic. 7:6:

> Do not suppose that I have come to bring peace to the earth. I did not come to bring peace, but a sword. For I have come to turn "*a man against his father, a daughter against her mother, a daughter-in-law against her mother-in-law—a man's enemies will be the members of his own household.*" Anyone who loves their father or mother more than me is not worthy of me; anyone who loves their son or daughter more than me is not worthy of me. Whoever does not take up their cross and follow me is not worthy of me. Whoever finds their life will lose it, and whoever loses their life for my sake will find it. (Matt. 10:34–39)

In his context, Micah is stressing the rampant corruption throughout his nation because of covenant violation. The result is a total breakdown of trust, in which one's own family will become one's enemies. In an analogous way Jesus uses the same text to describe the importance of maintaining loyalty to him on the part of his disciples as they deal with the division that will be caused by following him. This family division will put one's loyalty to the test as Christ's lordship even transcends familial bonds.

The parallel passage in Luke does not emphasize loyalty as much but uses the passage in the context of the coming of the Son of Man. One must be prepared for incredible persecution, even within one's own family, as the day approaches (Luke 12:49–53). Mark makes this eschatological context more explicit and widens the circle of persecution beyond the family, concluding that "everyone will hate you because of me," but the one who endures to the end will be saved (Mark 13:12–13).

One more explicit reference to Micah is found when Jesus curses a fig tree for appearing to have leaves and no fruit. This occurs in two different temporal contexts in the Gospels, but with the same general setting. In Matthew, after cleansing the temple and spending the night in Bethany, he returns to the city and observes a fig tree (21:18–22). Because it has bloomed leaves, he approaches it to get some fruit, but he finds it barren. Consequently, he curses it. The disciples are astonished that it withers so quickly, and Jesus uses the miracle as an object lesson on faith. Faith can not only wither fig trees on demand but also move mountains. Jesus is pointing out the emptiness of religion that seems to be alive (the leaves) but is barren of real faith (no figs). That is what had happened to the temple. It had become an emporium instead of a house of prayer. In Mark, the same story is spread over two days (Mark 11:12–14, 20–25).

It is no accident that Jesus uses this image of the fig tree and its barrenness to describe the lack of true faith. Micah laments the lack of true religion in his nation using the same image: "What misery is mine! I am like one who gathers summer fruit at the gleaning of the vineyard; there is no cluster of grapes to eat, none of the early figs that I crave. The faithful have been swept from the land; not one upright person remains. Everyone lies in wait to shed blood; they hunt each other with nets" (Mic. 7:1–2). For both Jesus and Micah, this sign of total corruption indicates the country is ripe for judgment. The temple, the place of prayer, has become a den of robbers, and both city and temple must be destroyed.

Jesus probably also refers to Micah when he excoriates the religious leaders of his day for their insincere practice of their faith (Matt. 23:23). He uses a text from Micah that criticizes outlandish one-off sacrifices and instead commends a heart that continually seeks justice, loves mercy, and walks humbly with God (6:8). While Jesus seems to criticize the opposite types of sacrifices—punctilious, regular religious behavior that ensures even the smallest herbs are tithed (the mint, the dill, and the cumin)—he in fact makes the same point as Micah. External religious performance has become more important than the weightier matters of the Torah: a life seeking justice, mercy, and faith. Clearly these three terms match the same triad in Micah.

There are a few other allusions to Micah in the NT. When Jesus is struck on the face with a rod before being crucified (Matt. 27:30), there may be an allusion to the ruler of Judah being struck on the head as a sign of humiliation by the Assyrians at the turn of the seventh century BC (Mic. 5:1).

At the end of Zechariah's hymn at the birth of his son John, he sings, "He has helped Israel, his servant, and remembered mercy, just as he has spoken to our fathers, to Abraham and his descendants forever" (Luke 1:54–55 AT). This is probably an allusion to the end of Micah's hymn that closes his book: "You will be faithful to Jacob, and show love [LXX "mercy"] to Abraham, as you pledged on oath to our ancestors in days long ago" (Mic. 7:20).

There also may be two more allusions to Micah. At the center of the book Micah prophesies the destruction of the temple because of the total corruption of the people: judges, prophets, and priests. The temple mount will become nothing but a plowed field in a forest (3:12). And this is really the prediction of the end of the age since the very next passage indicates a resurrection of the temple in the last days, when the Torah will go out to the nations and they will beat their swords into plowshares and their spears into pruning hooks (4:1–5). This death-resurrection motif in Micah is similar to the death-resurrection complex at the heart of the NT. On the one hand, Jesus describes the end of an old age with the destruction of the temple (Matt. 24:2), which is seen as part of the complex of events signifying the end of the age. But with his resurrection, the Holy Spirit empowers his disciples who go out from Jerusalem to Samaria and the ends of the earth with their message of forgiveness and good news (Acts 1:8), and the essential message is peace (cf. Mic. 4:3).

Similarly, Jesus himself regards his body as the temple of God and says, "Destroy this temple, and I will raise it again in three days" (John 2:19). The destruction of this temple (divine judgment for human sin) and its resurrection (salvation for the world) stand at the heart of the NT as they stand at the heart of Micah.

Bibliography. Alfaro, J. I., *Justice and Loyalty*, ITC (Eerdmans, 1989); Beale, G. K., *Handbook of the New Testament Use of the Old Testament* (Baker Academic, 2012); Blomberg, C. L., "Matthew," in *CNTUOT*, 1–109; Dempster, S. G., *Micah*, THOTC (Eerdmans, 2017); Dennison, J. T., Jr., "Micah's Bethlehem and Matthew's," *Kerux* 22 (2007): 4–11; Rudolph, W., *Micha, Nahum, Habakuk, Zephanja*, KAT (Gütersloher Verlagshaus, 1975); Schnittjer, G. E., *Old Testament Use of the Old Testament* (Eerdmans, 2021); Stendahl, K., *The School of St. Matthew and Its Use of the Old Testament* (Fortress, 1968); Waltke, B. K., *A Commentary on Micah* (Eerdmans, 2007).

STEPHEN G. DEMPSTER

Midrash

See Apostolic Hermeneutics articles

Midrashim

See Mishnah, Talmud, and Midrashim articles

Mishnah, Talmud, and Midrashim, OT Use in

Rabbinic traditions are avoided by many NT scholars because they are difficult to date. Their written records do not start until about AD 200 and even the Talmuds contain fifth-century material. So it is correct to be skeptical when looking for material that dates back to NT times in these writings.

During the last century a great deal of critical work has now established that these written collections do preserve significant portions of material that existed in the early first century. These older traditions had been preserved by a systematic and believable process of memorization. Birger Gerhardsson's presentation of this evidence in 1961 was initially dismissed due to a damaging review by Jacob Neusner, as he himself admitted (foreword to the 1998 reprint of Gerhardsson's *Memory and Manuscript*). Neusner had asserted that rabbinic materials could not be regarded as earlier than their first written version. His energetic work in this area, which included authoring hundreds of books, convinced most NT scholars. However, Neusner's continuing research gradually brought him to reassess his conclusions, and he came to recognize that ancient material had indeed been preserved among the later traditions. He helped rehabilitate Gerhardsson's work by writing a foreword for the 1998 edition, in which he regretted his initial assessment. He similarly wrote a foreword for the first volume of my *Traditions of the Rabbis from the Era of the New Testament*, agreeing with the project of identifying rabbinic material that can be used as background to the NT.

It is difficult to date specific ancient material, especially as it is clear that later editors both added to older traditions and inserted them into later discussions, usually without any signal concerning their age other than the names of rabbis. The names and dates of rabbis are fairly well established but traditions are sometimes ascribed to different rabbis, so the use of names to date material is questionable. Neusner found a way of confirming that such dating was indeed possible. He notes that much of rabbinic literature is made up of case law, in that a judgment made in one case is used as the basis of later discussions and decisions, just as in modern case law. This means that one can place most legal traditions in a relative chronology, because a law that relies on another law must be later than it. Having done this with large bodies of traditions, Neusner then compares this chronology with the relative dates of the rabbis that these traditions are ascribed to—and they match. His conclusion, which is generally accepted, is that we can use named rabbis to date a halakic (i.e., legal) tradition, because even though it may occasionally be assigned to the wrong rabbi, this is normally a contemporary of the correct one.

An important and significant gap remains: we cannot (yet) safely use this method to date haggadic traditions—that is, the nonlegal material found in midrashim (commentaries) and biographical accounts or stories within the Talmud. Nor can we date traditions in targums, because they are not attributed to named rabbis; for these, we have to rely on interpretations found or implied in the Septuagint. Nevertheless, a significant body of material can be used, with care, as background for the NT. This is not often useful for theology, because the material that can be dated is concerned with how to actually obey the law, and exactly what is commanded or prohibited, rather than what we can learn about God.

The rabbis revealed a great deal about how they interpret the sacred text, while deducing what the law says. Because they are keen to ensure accurate interpretations, they discuss which interpretive techniques can be used safely. They decide that some are useful for discovering meaning, while others are useful only to illustrate or confirm an interpretation that is already established. Those useful for discovery are used mainly before AD 70, while those useful for confirmation are more popular after that.

The dividing line of AD 70 runs through Jewish history as clearly as the BC/AD division runs through Christian history. When Jerusalem fell, the Romans not only destroyed the temple but also nearly destroyed Judaism itself, including all its scholarly history. The story is recorded that Yohanan ben Zakkai had the foresight to escape Jerusalem by pretending to be dead. He was carried out in a coffin by his disciples, supposedly for burial. Instead, they carried him to the Roman commander Vespasian. Yohanan quoted to him Isa. 10:34: "Lebanon will fall by the Majestic One" (ESV) and thereby predicted that Vespasian would become emperor. Vespasian was flattered, or at least he realized that Yohanan would be no trouble, and gave him and his disciples a home at Yavneh (Jamnia), where they established the only academy that survived the destruction (b. Git. 56ab).

We do not learn why Yohanan identifies "Lebanon" with Jerusalem, though we have a record of discussions about this by later rabbis (b. Yoma 39b). The only explanation that involves Yohanan himself is the story that forty years earlier (i.e., about AD 30) the temple doors had portentously opened themselves during the night. Yohanan had said to them, "O Temple, why do you frighten us? We know that you will end up destroyed. For it has been said: *Open your doors, O Lebanon, that the fire may devour your cedars!* [Zech. 11:1]" (y. Yoma 6:3 [Neusner]; cf. b. Yoma 39b). This is similar in time and significance to the account of Matt. 27:51.

The Judaism of Yavneh was very different from that of any Jewish group that had preceded it. Although it was based on the same sacred text, which was initially interpreted in the same way, it had lost its variety and divisiveness. Only one group of scholars had survived, and they knew that all their learning had almost been lost. All the traditions of the Sadducees, Qumran separatists, and the numerous other groups (we know only some of their names) had been lost. Those who survived decided on a new path.

Previously each rabbi had taught his own halakah (i.e., "way" or rules based on Torah), so that a dispute resulted in dissension and the creation of yet another small group. The smallness of these groups is seen in the fact that all "the house" or "school of Hillel" and "school of Shammai" were able to meet in one upper room (m. Shabb. 1:4), so they likely numbered fewer than one hundred altogether. Rulings from that period include six from the "school of Gamaliel"—the rabbi connected with Paul—which implies that each influential rabbi founded a group that followed his distinct halakah.

At Yavneh they decided that everyone would remain united by following the same halakah. Any disputes were discussed and then decided by a vote that all agreed to follow, on pain of excommunication.

Their discussions were recorded first in the Mishnah (ca. AD 200) and Tosefta (ca. AD 300), and then in two commentaries on the Mishnah: the Jerusalem Talmud (ca. AD 400) recording debates in Palestine, and the Babylonian Talmud (ca. AD 500) recording different though often related debates that occurred hundreds of miles away. These collections of debates all follow the same structure of six orders each with about ten respective tractates, each covering a specific topic, though only the Mishnah includes all of them.

The starting points for most topics are traditions from authorities revered among the survivors at Yavneh, the most important authority being Hillel. His traditions are mostly preserved in a collection of about 360 disputes between Hillelites and Shammaites recorded in a standard form, an example of which is found in the opening of the first tractate Berakhot, on prayer:

> **The school of Shammai say: At evening every man should recline to recite and at morning they should stand.** For it is said: *And when you lie down and when you rise* [Deut. 6:7c].
>
> **And the school of Hillel say: Every man should recite according to his way.** For it is said: *When you walk in the way [you are]* [Deut. 6:7b]. (m. Ber. 1:3 AT)

The sections in bold were probably the original memorized form. The disciples who had to learn this already knew that the question concerned reciting the Shema. They also knew that "way" (*derek*) was ambiguous in Hebrew, as in English, so it could refer to walking down a "way" or the "way" you were already doing something. This standard format with minimal wording helped to make the debate easy to memorize. The Scripture proofs are usually obvious and often missing, which suggests that they were added later. However, it is likely that they accurately reflect the original reasoning, because the Shammaites (who did not survive AD 70) often have a stronger scriptural basis for their rulings.

This new emphasis on unity at Yavneh created a new way of reasoning. Before a vote was taken at Yavneh, Scripture could be used to support contrary points of view, as in the example just given. But once a vote was taken, Scripture was mainly used to support or illustrate the conclusion. This means that prior to AD 70, the most important exegetical techniques were those that could determine the meaning of a text. But after AD 70 a new type of exegesis was needed—one that supported conclusions that had already been established, which often required new creative exegetical techniques.

Lists of Exegetical Techniques

Techniques of exegesis were later codified into lists of middot: seven techniques attributed to Hillel, thirteen to R. Ishmael (which effectively include all of Hillel's), and thirty-two to Eliezer b. Jose HaGelili (which includes about half of Ishmael's). Hillel was almost certainly not the author of the first list, and the other two authors are equally uncertain. However, the existence of three lists, which progressively encompass and replace the smaller, implies a chronological development in the techniques that were used.

The first two are lists of techniques that seek the *peshat* meaning—that is, the "plain" or primary sense of a passage. The third list contains many techniques for finding the *derash*—that is, the "hidden" or secondary meanings. *Derash* meanings do not supplant the *peshat* meaning but are regarded as a complementary exploration of the full meaning of the text. Techniques that uncover the *derash* include allegory and wordplay (e.g., puns).

Before AD 70, the main purpose of exegesis was to discover the meaning of the text and convince rivals about the "correct" interpretation, so the *peshat* techniques were used almost exclusively. Some *derash* techniques can possibly be identified in Qumran and Philonic exegeses. They both could experiment with *derash* because their writings address their own followers, so they did not have to convince anyone. Palestinian Pharisees, however, were surrounded by rival groups each with a different halakah. To show that their halakah was based on Scripture, they required *peshat* techniques. But after AD 70, when they had reached agreement by debate and a vote, *derash* techniques could illustrate and teach their conclusions. These techniques could be used to discover scriptural foundations for matters not plainly taught in the text.

Two very productive *derash* techniques were limitation (*miut*) and extension (*ribui*). If a law contains one of the common particles *min* ("from"), *raq* ("except"), or *ʾak* ("only"), then this implies an unwritten limitation to that law supposedly passed down verbally from Moses. Similarly, if a law contains *kōl* ("all"), *ʾet* ("with"), *gam* ("also"), or *ʾap* ("also"), this implies an unwritten extension. This was especially persuasive if the particle appeared to be superfluous—that is, its absence would not change the meaning of the text. For example, it was already decided that the execution of a pregnant adulteress should not be postponed till after she gave birth (m. Arakh. 1:4), and later they looked for scriptural support for this. Rabbi Joseph (early fourth century) managed to derive it from "also" (*gam*), which can be regarded as otherwise superfluous in Deut. 22:22 (b. Arakh. 7a).

These and similar techniques allowed scholars to find scriptural support for any tradition, old or new. However, there were guidelines that prevented their misuse. It was understood that using such techniques of exegesis, "no man can propound on his own [authority]" (b. Pesah. 66a; y. Pesah. 6:1, 39a AT). In other words, if something is already taught with authority, you can use this type of exegesis to confirm it or illustrate it, but you cannot use it to establish a new meaning on your own authority. Only a few exegetical techniques could be used to establish the meaning of a text, though frustratingly, a specific list has not survived.

This distinction between interpretive techniques that can establish what the text means and techniques that can only confirm established teaching is found in a key passage that became the foundation for teaching exegesis: Hillel's debate about Passover on a Sabbath.

Hillel's Interpretive Techniques

The interpretive techniques of Hillel were made famous when he was a relatively obscure scholar freshly arrived in Jerusalem from Babylon. Disaster had struck: the recently adopted Roman calendar had placed Passover on a Sabbath. The older, supplanted calendar has been preserved for us at Qumran by those who decided to leave the temple rather than celebrate festivals on the "wrong" days. By having exactly fifty-two weeks per year (i.e., 364 days) they were able to make Passover always fall on a Tuesday. It also ensured that every major feast fell on a weekday so that "no-one should offer anything upon the altar on the Sabbath except the sacrifice of the Sabbath" (CD 11.17–18 [García Martínez]).

Passover required a lot of preparatory work by the common people, some of which was expressly forbidden on a Sabbath. This included carrying a knife to the temple, with which to slaughter their lamb and extract the offerings of fat for the altar. Hillel started his career as he would continue it—by defending the ordinary person who was trying to keep the law. He argued at length that Passover was permitted on the Sabbath. Immediately after this, they asked what to do about the ordinary people. Hillel answered, "Let them be; the holy spirit is on them" (which is perhaps the earliest rabbinic reference to the holy spirit). He said this because he had spotted them doing something clever: they put the knife into the wool of their lamb that walked with them, so they did not break the Sabbath law because the knife was carried by the lamb, and not by them. After making their offering, they could wait till sunset ended the Sabbath, and then carry home the knife and the carcass.

The oldest version of this tradition is in Tosefta, though it was clearly recorded long after the event, because Hillel is afforded respect that he would not have had at the time. Hillel made four arguments:

> One time the fourteenth happened to be on a Sabbath. They asked Hillel the Elder: Does Passover override the Sabbath?
>
> He said to them: Do we have [only] one Passover in a year which overrides the Sabbath? We have more than three hundred Passovers in a year and they [all] override the Sabbath.
>
> [Everyone in] the whole temple court joined [to listen to] him.
>
> [1] He said to them [by *heqesh*]: The tamid [daily burnt offering] is a collective offering and the Passover is a collective offering.

Just as the tamid is a collective offering and overrides the Sabbath, so also Passover is a collective offering [so it] overrides the Sabbath.

[2] Another thing [by *gezerah shawah*]: It is said concerning tamid: *Its appointed time* [Num. 28:2]. And it is said concerning Passover: *Its appointed time* [Num. 9:2].

Just as tamid, concerning which is said: *Its appointed time,* overrides the Sabbath, so also the paschal sacrifice concerning which is said: *Its appointed time,* overrides the Sabbath.

[3] And further [by] *qal wahomer*: And just as tamid, concerning which one is not liable to be cut off, overrides the Sabbath, [so also] Passover, concerning which one *is* liable to be cut off—is it not logical that it overrides the Sabbath?

[4] And further, I have received from my masters: that Passover overrides the Sabbath. (t. Pesah. 4:13–14 AT; cf. y. Pesah. 6:1; y. Shabb. 19:1; b. Pesah. 66ab)

This tradition resulted in the early list of seven exegetical techniques being attributed to Hillel. However, we have no examples of Hillel using most of them, and the list does not include *heqesh,* which he did use on this occasion, so it is unlikely the list was authored by him.

We will now look at the most important exegetical techniques, starting with those used by Hillel in this tradition, and instances of the same techniques in the NT.

Heqesh and *Gezerah Shawah*

The techniques of *heqesh* and *gezerah shawah* can be used to unite disparate texts or topics. *Heqesh* unites them by finding a shared description, and *gezerah shawah* finds a shared phrase. When they are united in this way, a detail from one can be applied to the other. Hillel uses *heqesh* by pointing out that both Passover and the daily burnt offering could be described as community offerings—that is, a single animal for several people. Each daily burnt offering was for the whole nation, and each paschal offering was for a whole household. He also uses *gezerah shawah* to unite them by the phrase "its appointed time," which is used concerning each of them in different texts.

Clearly, both techniques are open to abuse, because the description or phrase found to be shared may have nothing to do with the issue. In this case, the shared feature (the fact that the offering will be made for several people) has nothing to do with the Sabbath. However, the shared phrase ("its appointed time") refers to the day on which the offering is permitted, so it could be regarded as related to the Sabbath issue.

The rabbis recognized the potential weakness of these techniques. They did not allow the use of either to establish the interpretation of a verse, though they could be used to support an interpretation that was already established in a more secure way. The Talmud points this out in words that are placed into the mouths of Hillel's detractors on the day: "No man can propound a *gezerah shawah* on his own [authority]" (b. Pesah. 66a; y. Pesah. 6:1, 39a AT). They do not bother to point out that if a *gezerah shawah* is unsafe, then the weaker *heqesh* is certainly not sufficient to establish an interpretation.

It is therefore somewhat surprising to find Jesus citing an exegesis that uses this technique to establish his teaching about monogamy. When asked about divorce, he starts by teaching about marriage: "Have you not read that he who created them from the beginning made them male and female [Gen. 1:27], and said: 'Therefore a man shall leave his father and his mother and hold fast to his wife, and the two shall become one flesh' [Gen. 2:24]?" (Matt. 19:4–5 AT; cf. Mark 10:6–8). This is very similar to the start of a scriptural proof at Qumran in support of monogamy: "The foundation of creation is '*male and female he created them*' [Gen. 1:27]. And those who entered [Noah's] ark *went in two by two into the ark* [7:9]" (CD 4.21–5.1, based on García Martínez). Both Matthew and Mark precede their quotations with something similar to the opening phrase "the foundation of creation" (CD 4.21): "the beginning of creation" (Mark 10:6), and "created them from the beginning" (Matt. 19:4 AT). The differences may be due to translation from Aramaic or oral transmission. This phrase suggests that Jesus was citing a common teaching that was transmitted with this standard introduction. The exegesis has been abbreviated in the Gospels by omitting the second quotation, perhaps to save space in the Gospel, and perhaps because there was no need to spell it out.

The Qumran version is similarly abbreviated because it omits the final crucial words "male and female" in Gen. 7:9. These words link the verses, so the technique used is *gezerah shawah.* When the verses are linked, the detail "two" from Gen. 7:9 can be applied to Gen. 1:27 to show that man had only one wife at creation. Therefore, all marriages that follow that pattern should consist of only two people.

This exegesis was not invented by Jesus, because the Qumran version predates him, so his inclusion of the traditional opening was presumably to help his listeners recognize something they had heard before.

This is followed by another well-established exegesis, using the targumic method of adding to the text in order to explain its meaning. When quoting Gen. 2:24, the Gospels add the word "two": "*The two* shall become one flesh." This exegesis, too, would not have been regarded as an invention of Jesus, because the same insertion is found in the Septuagint, Peshitta, Samaritan Pentateuch, Vulgate, Targum Pseudo-Jonathan, and Targum Neofiti.

Neither of these exegetical techniques can be used to determine the meaning of the text, but they can establish or illustrate a meaning already accepted. This is probably why the Gospels present the teaching in a way that emphasizes that it is already traditional, so Jesus is merely agreeing with it.

Qal wahomer

The *qal wahomer* technique could be used to establish the meaning of a passage even without relying on tradition: "A man may infer a ruling using *qal wahomer* on his own [authority]" (b. Nid. 19b AT; cf. b. Pesah. 66a). *Qal wahomer* is reasoning from *qal* (small or minor) and *homer* (large or major), which is an aspect of reasoning found in most systems of logic and law. If a minor thing is a crime, then something greater must also be so. If an unimportant or unlikely person has a right, then a more important or more obvious candidate must have at least an equal right.

Hillel points out that failing to keep Passover was penalized by being cut off from Israel, but this penalty is not recorded for a priest who fails to present the daily offering. He reasons that this makes the Passover more important than the daily offering. He can thereby reason that if the less important offering can override Sabbath restrictions, then certainly the more important offering should override them.

Paul uses the same reasoning to overrule the law of levirate marriages. The law ruled that if a woman is widowed without a son to inherit the name and property of his father, a brother-in-law must offer to marry her. Paul reasons that a widow has the right "to marry anyone she wishes" (1 Cor. 7:39). He does not state his reasoning, but it is fairly obvious. Paul's phrase is identical to the essential wording of a standard divorce certificate, without which the certificate would be invalid. Jews allowed the addition of one restriction—you could demand that the new husband be Jewish—and Paul added an equivalent restriction: "But he must belong to the Lord."

Paul appears to be reasoning by *qal wahomer*: if a divorced woman has this right when her marriage is ended by man, then surely a widowed woman has this right when her marriage is ended by death—that is, by God. We can be fairly confident that Paul was reasoning in this way because Josephus uses similar language (*Ant.* 4.255–56) and R. Ashi uses identical reasoning to officially end the law of levirate marriage four hundred years later (b. Qidd. 13b).

Tradition

Although many rulings are based on exegesis, the most important ground for any rabbinic teaching is ultimately tradition. When Hillel's exegetical reasoning fails to convince his skeptical audience, he ends with, "I have received from my masters." This appears to be an argument that they do not attempt to refute—or, at least, not in the recorded versions.

In the world of post–AD 70 Judaism, Hillel's teachers were regarded as the most important men of their generation, so quoting them as authorities would be an unassailable argument. However, this would have made the preceding series of exegetical arguments redundant, so it is likely that this final clinching conclusion was added later. This is not to say that tradition was less important in the Jewish world before AD 70, but each group had their own sources of tradition, so it was difficult to quote someone who would convince your rivals.

Whether or not Hillel himself added the argument from tradition, this conclusion became increasingly important. This is because his debate became a source for discussing the various strengths and weaknesses of these forms of exegesis. As a result, in the talmudic versions of the debate, counterarguments for each of his proofs were put into the lips of the temple authorities. This transformed the story into a useful way to teach exegetical reasoning, but the result was that all of Hillel's arguments appear to be undermined. The addition of a tradition from the highest authorities was therefore needed to establish Hillel's important conclusion unassailably for following generations.

In the Gospels, Jesus is portrayed as opposed to reliance on tradition (Matt. 15:2–6; Mark 7:3–13), and the people marvel that he does not rely on tradition when he teaches (Matt. 7:28–29 // Mark 1:22). This might suggest that Christians would subsequently reject tradition as a source of authority, but this did not occur. When Paul gives a series of arguments to support his contention that women should cover their heads during worship, his final argument is, "We have no other practice—nor do the churches of God." (1 Cor. 11:16). This closes the debate in the same way that the argument from tradition does for Hillel.

Contradiction

When one text contradicts another, there must be a solution. Because the rabbis regarded Scripture as inspired, the solution could not be a simple error. And because they used the whole of Scripture as the source of law, the solution could not be that a phrase was vague or approximate. This made contradictions particularly problematic from an apologetic point of view. However, these same contradictions could become a source of new teaching.

For example, the Sadducees (sometimes called Boethusians) believed the omer (the first sheaf of harvest) should be offered fifty days after the Passover, counting from the Sabbath of that week (Lev. 23:9–10, 15–16). However, the Pharisees said one should start counting from the first day of Passover, whatever day of the week this was. Yohanan b. Zakkai was credited with proving the Sadducees wrong when he said to one, "Fool! Is not our perfect Torah [better] than your insignificant mumbling? One text says: *You shall count fifty days* [Lev. 23:16] and one text says: *They shall be seven complete weeks* [i.e., forty-nine days] [Lev. 23:15]. How [can this be]? Now [one speaks] concerning a Festival Day that falls on a Sabbath, and [one speaks] concerning a Festival

Day that falls on a non-Sabbath day" (b. Menaḥ. 65b AT). He points out that the two descriptions can both be correct: if Passover week starts on a Sabbath the gap is forty-nine days, and if it starts on a Friday the gap till the seventh Sabbath is fifty days. This means the Pharisees are correct to start counting on the first day, and not on the Sabbath. This debate would have occurred between the time the Roman calendar was adopted in the second century BC and the demise of the Sadducees in AD 70. However, the unrealistically disrespectful description of the Sadducees (who are represented by "one old man who was babbling" immediately before this excerpt) suggests this was probably recorded after AD 70.

This technique is used in Heb. 3–4, which points out that Scripture says Israel "rested" in the land (1 Kings 8:56) but also that this "rest" was still to come (Ps. 95:11). Hebrews solves this by pointing to a third text that says God "rested from all his work" (Gen. 2:2). From this the author argues there is another, different type of rest waiting for God's people when they rest from all their work. This reasoning works properly only in Greek because 1 Kings 8:56 and Ps. 95:11 both use *katapausis* in Greek and *mənûḥâ* in Hebrew, while Gen. 2:2 uses *katapauō* but in Hebrew has *šābat* instead of *mənûḥâ*. This makes it likely (though not certain) that the exegesis is a Christian invention, or possibly that it originated in Alexandria, where exegesis often depends on the LXX (as seen in Philo).

Redundancy

Rabbinic lawyers interpreted Scripture as though God was the perfect legislator. This means that no word or phrase should be redundant, so a word that appears to be superfluous must be conveying some other meaning that a careful exegete can discover.

For example, the Hillelites noticed the word "matter" or "cause" (*dābār*) was redundant in the proof text for divorce due to adultery (Deut. 24:1).

> **The school of Shammai say: A man may not divorce his wife, except if he finds in her a cause: [i.e.] indecency [*dbr ʿrwh*].** For it is said: *Because he found in her a cause of indecency* [*ʿrwt dbr*, Deut. 24:1].
>
> **And the school of Hillel say: Even if she spoiled the broth,** for it is said: [any] *cause* [*dbr*].
>
> The school of Hillel said to the school of Shammai: Since it said *cause*, why did it [also] say *indecency*? And since it said *indecency*, why did it [also] say *cause*?
>
> [It needed both] because if it said *cause* and it did not [also] say *indecency* I could say: She who is divorced for a *cause* may be permitted to remarry, but she who is divorced for *indecency* may not be permitted to remarry. . . .
>
> And if it said *indecency* and did not [also] say *cause*, I could say: She may go [into divorce] for *indecency*, [but] she may not go [into divorce] for a *cause*. (m. Git. 9:10 with the continuation in Sifre Deut. 269, AT; cf. b. Git. 90a; y. Git. 9:11, 54b)

The likely original summary is in bold, though there is no reason to doubt the genuineness of the exegesis that was attached later. The Hillelites reasoned that even if the word *dābār* were omitted from Deut. 24:1, the verse would still teach about a divorce due to adultery, so this word would be redundant.

No reply by Shammai follows the Hillelites' longer explanation, which assumes rather than explains Hillel's conclusion, so it was almost certainly added after the demise of the Shammaites in AD 70. Nevertheless, it likely represents the way they reasoned, though the Shammaites probably had a longer defense.

Josephus (*Ant.* 4.253), Philo (*Spec. Laws* 3.5 [LCL 5.30]), and Matt. 19:3 contain the phrase "any cause," thus preserving Hillel's conclusion—namely, that *dābār* must refer to reasons for divorce other than adultery, and because no restrictions are named, this must mean "any cause," even something as minor as a single burnt meal. They could then explain the apparent redundancy: if the cause was "indecency," one could reason this was so serious that the guilty party could not remarry.

The Shammaites counter that Deut. 24:1 refers to nothing "except . . . a [single] cause: indecency." They express this by reversing the order of the words in Deut. 24:1, from *ʿrwt dbr* to *dbr ʿrwh*. This is recorded almost word by word in the Greek of Matt. 5:32: "except for a cause [*logou* = *dbr*] of indecency [*porneias* = *ʿrwh*]."

This debate illustrates how abbreviation of debates can cause misunderstandings. Even the long accounts in Mark 10 and Matt. 19 abbreviate as much as the rabbinic records, and this is abbreviated even further in the summary statements (Matt. 5:31–32; Luke 16:18). A similar summary of the Shammaites' conclusion was recorded long after their demise, in an early fourth-century debate: "A man should not divorce his wife except he found indecency in her" (y. Sotah 1:1, 1a AT). The context implies these rabbis thought that the Shammaites had taught divorce was allowed for nothing except adultery. Actually, the Shammaites taught that Deut. 24:1 allowed divorce for nothing but adultery. Like the Hillelites, they taught other grounds for divorce were found in Exod. 21:10–11—though they disagreed on the details (m. Git. 5:6–7). So, we should bear in mind that rabbis themselves could be confused by their own abbreviation of debates.

Allegory

Allegory is very rarely found in rabbinic exegesis before AD 70, and perhaps never, because the following example may originate later. However, it is included because this is very similar to Qumran pesher ("interpretation"), which identifies words or concepts in a text by simply stating "this means: . . ." with little effort to explain the connection. Allegory makes connections fit with one another by using analogy, as practiced by Philo and the church fathers. It occurs only once in rabbinic traditions that can possibly be dated before AD 70.

> He [Hananiah, chief of the priests, mid-first century] used to say: *Do not look on me for I am black, tanned by the sun* [Song 1:6].
>
> These are the leaders of Judah who removed the yoke of the Holy One (Blessed be He) from over them and enthroned over them a king of flesh and blood. (Avot R. Nat. A 20 AT)

Hananiah was a temple official, and this probably refers to the time Agrippa I, a half-Jew, was allowed to read the Torah in the temple—an act that some welcomed (m. Sotah 7:8). This is allegory because he gives little reason to make this identification, other than referring to the context in Canticles: "My own vineyard I had to neglect"—which would have been regarded as a reference to Jerusalem (Isa. 5).

Paul's "allegorizing" in Gal. 4:22–31 is a complex attempt to line up Hagar and Sarah with Sinai and Jerusalem representing the old and the new covenant of slavery and freedom. This is quite different from anything found in rabbinic exegeses or even at Qumran. It is closer to the elaborate allegories found in Philo. It is tempting to regard this as Paul's attempt to show that he can allegorize as well as Apollos, who came from North Africa and may thus have learned from Philo. Apollos was so celebrated for his preaching skills that some preferred him to Paul (Acts 18:24; 1 Cor. 1:12; 3:4–6). Though some see Paul using allegory in Gal. 4, others see him using a typological reasoning (on which, see the article "Allegory" by G. Waters elsewhere in the dictionary).

Pragmatism

Occasionally decisions were made without any basis in Scripture for pragmatic reasons. These might be justified or illustrated by Scripture, but those recording the reasons are sometimes honest enough to say it is "for the sake of peace" or "for the sake of the world." We know that this was an officially recognized reason for decisions because a number of them are collected together in the Mishnah (m. Git. 4:2–5:5). For example, there was a difficult case of a man who was half a slave—perhaps because he was jointly owned and one master released him (as was normal at age thirty):

> **He who is half-slave and half-free serves his master one day, and [serves] himself one day—the words of the school of Hillel.**
>
> **Said to them the school of Shammai, "You have benefited his master, but you have not benefited him.** To marry a slave girl is not possible, for half of him is free. [And to marry] a free woman is not possible, for half of him is a slave. Shall he refrain [from marriage]? But was not the world made only for procreation, as it is said, *He created it not a waste, he formed it to be inhabited* [Isa. 45:18].
>
> But: For the benefit of the world, they force his master to free him. And [the slave] writes him a bond covering half his value.
>
> And the school of Hillel reverted to teach in accord with the opinion of the school of Shammai. (m. Git. 4:5; m. Ed. 1:13 AT)

Both schools agreed that it was the duty of a man to have children, but a slave can marry only a slave, and a free person can marry only a free person, so half a slave cannot marry anyone. The Shammaites ruled that the master must give up his half-ownership and the slave will repay him his value when he can. This conclusion was so convincing that even the Hillelites changed their minds to support it. This is almost certainly a genuine decision by Shammaites because the Hillelites reverted to follow their opinion—which is an account they would not have invented after AD 70, when Judaism was essentially led by Hillelites.

The reason given is not exegetical but pragmatic: "for the benefit of the world." The verb *tqn* translated "benefit" means "to straighten, set in order." This pragmatic reason is often translated "for the order of the world," but is translated here "for the benefit of the world" in order to make a verbal link with the same vocabulary used for "You have benefited his master, but you have not benefited him." This is expressed elsewhere in other ways: "for the benefit of the altar" (e.g., m. Git. 5:5) and "for the sake [*drk*] of peace" (e.g., t. Git. 3:14[18]).

Fee argues that Paul uses this form of argument when he says that those who have been abandoned by nonbelieving partners are released because "God has called you to peace" (1 Cor. 7:15 ESV).

Jesus may also refer to this when he justifies his own decision to not marry, which contradicts the Jewish principle (accepted by Hillelites and Shammaites in this debate) that all men should procreate. He says that some become "eunuchs for the sake of the kingdom of heaven" (Matt. 19:12), which may be a deliberate contrast to "for the sake of this world."

Conclusion

The types of rabbinic exegetical techniques found in the NT tend to reflect those that were being used in rabbinic Judaism before AD 70. The *peshat* meaning was important when disputes abounded within Judaism, because each group needed to prove to others that their beliefs and practices reflected Scripture. The early Christians shared these same concerns in their interactions with Judaism. After AD 70, when Jews agreed to a common halakah, so they all had the same practices and largely had the same beliefs, the *derash* meanings were sought to support and illustrate what everyone agreed on. This involved a set of exegetical techniques that are largely absent from the NT, though some (such as allegory) perhaps make a cursory appearance.

See also OT Use of the OT: Comparison with the NT Use of the OT; *other Mishnah, Talmud, and Midrashim articles*; *Dead Sea Scrolls articles*; *Philo articles*; *Septuagint articles*; *Targums articles*

Bibliography. Epstein, I., et al., *The Babylonian Talmud*, 18 vols. (Soncino, 1952); Fee, G. D., *The First Epistle to the Corinthians*, rev. ed., NICNT (Eerdmans, 2014); García Martínez, F., and E. J. C. Tigchelaar, *The Dead Sea Scrolls*, 2 vols. (Eerdmans, 1997–98); Gerhardsson, B., *Memory and Manuscript*, ASNU 22 (Gleerup, 1961; repr., Eerdmans, 1998); Heineman, J., *Prayer in the Talmud*, SJ 9 (de Gruyter, 1977); Instone-Brewer, D., "The Eighteen Benedictions and the Minim Before 70 CE," *JTS*, n.s., 54 (2003): 25–44; Instone-Brewer, *Techniques and Assumptions in Jewish Exegesis Before 70 CE*, TSAJ 30 (Mohr Siebeck, 1992); Instone-Brewer, *Traditions of the Rabbis from the Era of the New Testament*, vols. 1, 2A (Eerdmans, 2004–11); Kasher, D., trans., Avot D'Rabbi Natan, Sefaria, accessed November 8, 2022, https://www.sefaria.org/Avot_D'Rabbi_Natan; McNamara, M., et al., *The Aramaic Bible*, 22 vols. (Liturgical Press, 1990–2007); Neusner, J., foreword to *Memory and Manuscript: Oral Tradition and Written Transmission in Rabbinic Judaism and Early Christianity; with Tradition and Transmission in Early Christianity*, by B. Gerhardsson, trans. E. J. Sharpe (Eerdmans, 1998), xxv–xlvi; Neusner, *Mishnah* (Yale University Press, 1988); Neusner, *The Tosefta Translated from the Hebrew*, 6 vols. (Ktav, 1977–86); Neusner, J., et al., *The Talmud of the Land of Israel*, 34 vols. (University of Chicago Press, 1982–95); Vermes, G., "Pre-Mishnaic Jewish Worship and the Phylacteries from the Dead Sea," *VT* 9 (1959): 65–72; Vermes, "The Story of Balaam," in *Scripture and Tradition in Judaism* (Brill, 1961), 127–77.

David Instone-Brewer

Mishnah, Talmud, and Midrashim, OT Use in: Comparison with NT Use of the OT

The early traditions of rabbinic Judaism are rarely concerned with the same passages as those exegeted in the NT. The NT is, understandably, largely interested in texts concerning the Messiah and those needed to establish theology that is distinct from mainstream Judaism, and most of these are from outside the Torah. By contrast, datable rabbinic traditions come from legal texts, so they are mainly citing the Torah.

We should not conclude that Jews in NT times were uninterested in the Scriptures outside the Torah. This may, of course, have been the case for the Sadducees, though we only know this from what non-Sadducees have said. The Qumran fragments cover the whole OT, and judging from what has survived, the most popular books were Psalms, Deuteronomy, and Isaiah. Commentaries on non-Torah books have survived, but these were codified relatively late, and dating methods used for halakic traditions do not work well in these collections.

Synagogue worship included a Torah reading followed by haftarah from the Prophets. This practice may have started when Antiochus IV forbade the reading of Torah in the second century BC, so they read a section from the Prophets that reminded them of the reading they would have had. They continued reading these passages alongside the Torah when this was possible again. Jesus's reading from Isaiah in Luke 4:16–19 may be a haftarah, because it follows the rule that the reading should end on something reflecting "the consolation of Israel" (which Heineman, 228, traces back to 2 Macc. 8:23). We cannot be sure what the Torah reading would have been because the pre–AD 70 lectionary was different and did not survive.

There are, nevertheless, a few texts that are exegeted both in the NT and rabbinic traditions.

Rock That Followed

Paul refers to a "rock that followed them" from which all of Israel drank "the same spiritual drink," because "that Rock was Christ" (1 Cor. 10:4 AT). This refers to the two occasions when Moses struck a rock to produce water during their wilderness wanderings—at the start of their journey and at the end. The first (Exod. 17:1–7) was just before their early victory over Amalek at Rephidim (v. 8), though it says they called the place "Massah and Meribah" (v. 7—i.e., "testing" and "quarreling"). The second (Num. 20:10–13) was at Kadesh (v. 1), where Moses was reprimanded for striking the rock twice, which resulted in him dying before they reached the promised land. Just after this they found the well, as narrated in Num. 21:16–18.

God tells Moses that these waters at Kadesh are "the waters of Meribah" (Num. 20:13). This led early commentators to conclude that although the two locations are far apart, the waters and the rock are the same, so the rock must have followed them. E. Earle Ellis and others point out this likely relates to ideas that are recorded in targums and midrashim (e.g., Mek. Exod. 17:6; Num. Rab. 1:2). These traditions cannot be dated, but similar ideas are also in Pseudo-Philo, which probably originated in the first century: "The water of Mara followed them in the desert forty years," and again, "A well of water followed them" (LAB 1:15; 10:7 AT).

The earliest rabbinic tradition that refers to this very literal interpretation is the following:

> And so the well which was with the Israelites in the wilderness was a rock, the size of a large round vessel,

> surging and gurgling upward, as from the mouth of this little flask, rising with them up onto the mountains, and going down with them into the valleys.
>
> Wherever the Israelites would encamp, it made camp with them, on a high place, opposite the entry of the Tent of Meeting.
>
> The princes of Israel come and surround it with their staffs, and they sing a song concerning it: *Spring up, O Well! Sing to it! [The well which the princes dug, which the nobles of the people delved with the scepter and with their staves]* [Num 21:17–18].
>
> And they well upward like a pillar on high, and each one [of the princes] draws water with his staff, each one for his tribe and each one for his family, as it is said: *The well which the princes dug*. (t. Sukkah 3:11, based on Neusner)

There is no attribution to help date this tradition, but the similarities to LAB are significant. The Qumran community also expressed great interest in the account of the well, though they had an allegorical interpretation that did not attempt to express a literal meaning:

> God remembered the Covenant with the forefathers, and he raised from Aaron men of discernment and from Israel men of wisdom, and He caused them to hear. And they dug the Well: *the well which the princes dug, which the nobles of the people delved with the stave* [Num. 21:18]. The *Well* is the Law, and those who dug it were the converts of Israel who went out of the land of Judah to sojourn in the land of Damascus. God called them all *princes* because they sought Him, and their renown was disputed by no man. The *Stave* is the Interpreter of the Law of whom Isaiah said . . . [Isa. 54:16] . . . And the *nobles of the people* are those who come to dig the *Well* with the staves with which the *Stave* ordained that they should walk in all the age of wickedness—and without them they shall find nothing—until he comes who shall teach righteousness at the end of days. (CD 6.2–11, based on García Martínez)

Compared to this, Paul's interpretation goes beyond allegory or typology. He was not saying that this rock was *like* Christ, but it *was* Christ. The fact that the rock moved around the wilderness showed it had volition. This suggests it was a Christophany, similar to the fourth man in the fiery furnace (Dan. 3:25) or the third angel who went to see Abraham (Gen. 18:22). This enables Paul to say that the Israelites had spiritual drink, as if it came directly from Christ.

The Ox Eats the Grain

Practical support for Christian workers is called for in 1 Cor. 9:9–11 and 1 Tim. 5:17–18, both arguing from the law, "Do not muzzle an ox while it is treading out the grain" (Deut. 25:4).

Paul asks rhetorically if the purpose of this law is to demonstrate God's compassion to his creatures. His formulation expects a negative answer, though this is sometimes cited as an example of the humane character of the Law (Philo, *Virtues* 145–46; Josephus, *Ant.* 4.233). However, Jews rejected appealing to God's compassion in this way. One of the guidelines for public prayer was, "If a man said [in his prayer]: 'To a bird's nest do Thy mercies extend' [cf. Deut. 22:7] . . . they put him to silence" (m. Ber. 5:3; m. Meg. 4:9 AT). This is because it was forbidden to praise God for his compassion to animals, as if the laws are "springing from compassion," because this might detract from the strict observance of a decree (b. Ber. 33b; cf. y. Ber. 5:3 AT).

Paul expects his readers to know that the law of the unmuzzled ox is not solely or even primarily concerned with animal welfare. It is the basis for most of the laws concerning workers' rights in rabbinic discussions. They interpret the law in a similar way to other legislative systems, including modern ones: whatever right belonged to an individual must apply also to anyone more important. Therefore, if an ox has the right to enjoy some of the product of his work, then so does a farm slave and any other farm worker through his wages; and workers in other occupations therefore had similar rights.

Paul summarizes a laborer's rights: "The plowman should plow in hope and the thresher thresh in hope of sharing in the crop" (1 Cor. 9:10 ESV). This is equivalent to the legal summary in the Mishnah that a worker may partake of crops they worked on before the harvest and crops they worked on after harvest: "And these [have the right to] eat [the produce on which they labor] by [right accorded to them in] the Torah: he who labours on what is as yet unplucked [may eat from the produce] at the end of the time of processing; [and he who labours] on plucked produce [may eat from the produce] before processing is done" (m. B. Metz. 7:2, based on Neusner). This ruling is the start and basis for all decisions on workers' rights and payment of wages in the tractate Bava Metzi'a. As usual, the scriptural grounds for this are not stated in the Mishnah, but we find them in the Talmud.

> It follows *a minori*, from an ox: if an ox, which does not eat of what is attached, may nevertheless eat of what is detached; then a man, who may eat of what is attached, may surely eat of what is detached! As for an ox, [it may be argued] that [this privilege] is because you are forbidden to muzzle him; can you assume the same of man, whom you are not forbidden to muzzle?
>
> But then let the muzzling of man be interdicted, *a fortiori*, from an ox: if you must not muzzle an ox, whose life you are not bidden to preserve, then man, whose life you are bidden to preserve, you must surely not muzzle him! (b. B. Metz. 87a, based on Epstein)

There are no competing exegeses so there is no reason to doubt this was the accepted origin of this branch of law.

Paul and the rabbis of his time were interpreting the law of the ox literally and extending that law using *qal wahomer*. The rabbis applied this not just to farm workers but to all workers, which would include Christian pastors.

Son Called from Egypt

Matthew 2 uses the OT in a way that appears to depend on *derash*-style exegetical techniques. It refers to Mic. 5:2–4; Hosea 11:1; and Jer. 31:15 at vv. 6, 15, and 18, respectively. The author regards these as convincing examples of fulfilled prophecy (vv. 5, 15, 17). Geza Vermes ("Balaam") shows that the story of Baalam, who was often identified with Laban, contains elements that link these disparate verses.

He points out that Balaam-Laban (who was regarded as a single individual) was an archvillain who lived hundreds of years. He first attempted to kill the child ancestor of the Messiah in Egypt. After he came out of Egypt (Hosea 11:1), there were further attempts during the next centuries. We have to piece this story together from fragments, especially in Targum Pseudo-Jonathan. The original readers would presumably be familiar with more details than the few that have survived. Rabbinic comments indicate a skeptical familiarity with these stories.

In the following, italics indicate where the targum departs significantly from the Hebrew text.

> As [Rachel's] soul departed—for *death came upon her*—she called his name "Son of my Agony"; but his father called him Benjamin. And Rachel died and was buried on the way to Ephrath—that is, Bethlehem. . . . *Jacob* journeyed on and pitched his tent beyond the Tower of the Flock, *the place from which the King Messiah will reveal himself at the end of days.* (Tg. Ps.-J. Gen. 35:18–21, based on McNamara)

> *It is* I who *in my Memra* will go down with you to Egypt. *I will look upon the misery of your son, but my Memra will exalt you there;* I will also bring *your son up from there.* (Tg. Ps.-J. Gen. 46:4, based on McNamara)

Matthew makes many links with this story. Mary, like Rachel, is to give birth in Bethlehem of Ephrath (Matt. 2:5–6), and her child will be king of the Jews (2:2) and the Messiah (2:4). Matthew quotes Mic. 5:2 but appends "he will shepherd" from v. 4 to juxtapose kingship and shepherding. This emphasizes the origin of this prophecy in the narrative of Gen. 35:19–21, where Rachel is buried at Bethlehem but Jacob pitches his tent nearby at the Tower of the Flock, which Micah links with the Messiah. Matthew links the mourning of Rachel in Jer. 31:15 with the mass infanticide of Herod, who consulted magi like Balaam-Laban. Indeed, he was the father of Pharaoh's two magicians (referred to in 2 Tim. 3:8) who were known as magi (Philo, *Moses* 1.92; Pliny, *Nat.* 30.11).

> And [Balaam] was riding on his *ass* and his two lads, *Jannes and Jam(b)res, were with him.* (Tg. Ps.-J. Num. 22:22, based on McNamara)

> *Jannes and Jambres, the chief magicians, opened their mouths* and said *to Pharaoh: "A son is to be born in the assembly of Israel, through whom all the land of Egypt is destined to be destroyed." Therefore Pharaoh,* the king of Egypt, *took counsel* and said to the *Jewish* midwives . . . (Tg. Ps.-J. Exod. 1:15 [McNamara])

The biblical Balaam later attempts to curse Israel in the wilderness but is forced instead to prophesy about a scepter and star. These have messianic interpretations in many streams of Judaism (Targum Onqelos; Targum Pseudo-Jonathan; Targum Neofiti; 1QM 11.5–9; CD 7.18–21; T. Jud. 24:1–5; T. Levi 18:3).

These Laban-Balaam stories were referred to by the rabbis, but mostly in negative ways. They criticized the idea of linking Laban with Balaam, which would imply that Balaam lived for about four hundred years.

> A Tanna taught: Beor, Cushan-rishathaim, and Laban the Syrian are identical; Beor denotes that he committed bestiality; Cushan-rishathaim that he perpetrated two evils upon Israel: one in the days of Jacob and the other in the days of the Judges. But what was his real name? Laban the Syrian.

> Scripture writes, "the son of Beor" [Num. 22:5; 31:8; etc.], [but also] "his son [was] Beor" [Num. 24:3, 15].

> R. Johanan said: His father was as his son in the matter of prophecy. . . .

> A certain heretic said to R. Hanina: Have you heard how old Balaam was? He replied: It is not actually stated, but since it is written, *Bloody and deceitful men shall not live out half their days* [Ps. 55:23], [it follows that] he was thirty-three or thirty-four years old. He rejoined: You have said correctly; I personally have seen Balaam's Chronicle, in which it is stated, "Balaam the lame was thirty years old when Phinehas the Robber killed him." (b. Sanh. 105a, 106b, based on Epstein)

The first paragraph is anonymous, so it was already old enough to be considered authoritative in the third century when it is being cited. It is familiar with the idea that Laban and "Balaam son of Beor" are identical, but it has found a way to reduce the length of his lifespan by saying that Laban was identical with Beor, not with his son Balaam. A later anonymous comment reduces the lifespan further by suggesting that Laban was Balaam's grandfather who was also called Balaam, because it says that "his son was Beor" (a possible translation at Num. 24:3, 15) and that he was "the son of Beor." Finally, R. Johanan bar Nappaha (mid-third century) completely removes the mystical element from this tradition by saying that Laban was an ancestor of

Balaam, and they were identical merely in a prophetic sense. By the time of the next generation (late-third century), R. Hanina supports Johanan by concluding that Balaam lived only thirty-three years—which may be a covert reference to Christ (Herford, 65–76, contra Ginzberg, 121n18).

Matthew's early readers were likely familiar with the fantastic stories about Laban-Balaam, unlike later generations. Matthew quotes the prophetic references that can be related to these stories in Micah, Hosea, and Jeremiah.

Blessing before Meals

Psalm 24:1—"The earth is the LORD's, and everything in it"—is quoted at 1 Cor. 10:26, apparently to support the preceding statement: "Eat anything sold in the meat market without raising questions of conscience" (v. 25). However, the context in the psalm does not relate to food, so this text does not appear to provide any force to Paul's reasoning, except to say (rather weakly) that God made everything.

The force of the quotation becomes clearer when we see it used as a blessing for food, as implied in a couple of sources: "One must not taste anything until he has [first] recited a benediction [over it], as Scripture states, *The earth is the Lord's and all that it contains* [Ps. 24:1]. One who derives benefit from this world [by eating its produce] without first having recited a benediction has committed sacrilege" (t. Ber. 4:1, based on Neusner). This undatable source quotes Ps. 24:1 in a similar way to Paul: the brief citation refers to saying grace before food. This Jewish tradition of giving thanks before eating is associated in the NT with Jesus (Matt. 14:19; 15:36; 26:27; Mark 6:41; 8:6; 14:23; Luke 9:16; 22:17, 19; John 6:11, 23; 1 Cor. 11:24) and Paul (Acts 27:35).

The actual recitation of Ps. 24:1 is not referenced until the end of the second century:

> R. Hiyya b. Abba [early second century] related: I was once a guest of a man in Laodicea, and a golden table was brought before him, which had to be carried by sixteen men; sixteen silver chains were fixed in it, and plates, goblets, pitchers, and flasks were set thereon, and upon it were all kinds of food, dainties, and spices. When they set it down they recited, *The earth is the Lord's, and the fullness thereof*[Ps. 24:1]; and when they removed it [after the meal] they recited, *The heavens are the heavens of the Lord, but the earth hath he given to the children of men* [Ps. 115:16]. (b. Shabb. 119a, based on Epstein)

Although this is relatively late, the purpose of the quotation is not to teach the use of blessing, but to indicate a meal had started, so it is referring to an established tradition.

This is a situation where we cannot be sure that the rabbinic material dates back to NT times, though it is reasonable to conclude that it does. None of the three sources in NT and rabbinic traditions demonstrates clearly that Ps. 24:1 was used as a prayer before meals, but each passage makes more sense if this was so.

The exegesis stated in the first rabbinic source also helps to explain Paul's reasoning. The rabbi reasons in a literal way that the words "The earth is the Lord's" indicate that all food belongs to God. Therefore, it would be sacrilege (i.e., stealing from the sacred) to eat without acknowledging this ownership and giving thanks for the gift.

This explains the reasoning behind Paul's use of this quotation. The "weaker" believer felt that eating something offered to a god implied worship of that god or at least partaking of something that belonged to that god. But Paul asserts that the meat does not belong to that god, even if it has been offered to him, because everything belongs to the Lord. Thanks must therefore be given to the Lord, and when someone does give thanks, they assert that the meat does indeed belong to the Lord, and therefore does not belong to the god it may have been offered to.

Mercy, Not Sacrifice

When the temple was destroyed, Judaism could have collapsed, because its soteriology and worship were dependent on sacrificial offerings and other rites in the temple. Even the alternate temple at Onias in Egypt was destroyed by Vespasian in AD 73. In any case, the rabbis did not consider offerings at that temple to fulfill one's obligations (m. Menah. 13:10), so even Philo sent offerings to Jerusalem on top of his offerings in Egypt (*Providence*, cited in Eusebius, *Praep. ev.* 8.14.64).

Simon the Just in the third century BC, a member of the priestly Onias family who established this Egyptian temple, left a saying that saved Judaism:

> Simon the Just was one of the last surviving members of the Men of the Great Assembly. He would say: The world stands on three things: on the Torah, on the [Temple] service [*ʿăbôdâ*], and on acts of kindness [*ḥesed*] [m. Avot 1:2].
>
> . . . On acts of kindness. How so? It says, *For I desire kindness* [*ḥesed*], *not sacrifices* [*zebaḥ*] (Hosea 6:6). The world was created from the very beginning with kindness, as it says, *For I have said that the world will be built on kindness, and the heavens will be established on Your faith* [Ps. 89:3].
>
> Once, Rabban Yohanan ben Zakkai left Jerusalem, and Rabbi Yehoshua followed after him. And he saw the Holy Temple destroyed. [Yehoshua said:] The place where all of Israel's sins are forgiven! [Yohanan] said to him: My son, do not be distressed, for we have a form of atonement just like it. And what is it? Acts of kindness, as it says, *"For I desire kindness, not sacrifices."* (Avot R. Nat. A 4.1, 5, based on Kasher)

The opening tradition of Simon from Avot is followed by a commentary linking this saying with Hosea 6:6.

It also tells a story of Yohanan ben Zakkai (late first century) when he cited the same text to explain how Judaism could continue without a temple. This same text is found on the lips of Jesus twice in Matthew (9:13; 12:7).

Like all biographical traditions, this story of Yohanan and Yehoshua should not be regarded as datable by the individuals named within it. However, it is unlikely that this OT quotation would have been given such prominence after its use within Christian communities had become well known. In the context of the destroyed temple, this text is especially dangerous because it appears to agree with the Christians' conclusion that sacrifices are not necessary.

This is similar to the danger first-century Jews perceived in the idea that the Ten Commandments might be considered more important than the others. This might lead to the conclusion that only the moral commands in the OT are important, as Christians believed. This would be an easy conclusion following the destruction of the temple. To avoid this, all Jews stopped reciting the Ten Commandments along with the Shema in their daily devotions. This former practice is evidenced in the second-century BC Nash Papyrus and tefillin found at Qumran (Vermes, "Phylacteries").

If they went to such lengths to avoid a mere implication that Christians might use, they would certainly not invent the idea that Yohanan regarded *ḥesed* as a replacement for temple sacrifices. It is therefore unlikely that this quotation would have been put into the lips of Yohanan unless a very strong tradition of him using it this way already existed.

We might assume from Avot Rabbi Nathan that Yohanan learned this text from the tradition by Simon. However, like most Scripture texts and proofs, this was likely added to Simon's saying at a later time. And there are good reasons to conclude that Simon did not originally refer to this text. Someone looking for a scriptural basis for Simon's threefold "Torah, worship [*ʿăbôdâ*], and kindness [*ḥesed*]" could have found it easily in the example of Josiah (2 Chron. 35:25–26) or Nehemiah (Neh. 13:14–15). Hosea 6:6 contains only one of these three—*ḥesed*. It is therefore likely that this text was added for a different reason, perhaps to give Yohanan an older tradition to stand on.

Hosea 6:6 fits perfectly with Yohanan's need to find a way to continue Judaism because instead of Simon's *ʿăbôdâ* ("worship") it refers to *zebaḥ* ("sacrifice"). This word is normally used of festival offerings such as Passover or Firstfruits (e.g., Exod. 12:27; 23:18), or optional peace offerings and vows (e.g., Lev. 3:1; 7:16)—that is, the sacrifices that the people themselves used to bring to the temple to demonstrate their devotion.

If this usage of Hosea 6:6 can indeed be traced to Yohanan ben Zakkai, and if Matthew accurately records Jesus's use of this same text (9:13; 12:7), we have an interesting possibility of a shared tradition. Yohanan taught in Galilee for eighteen years during the early first century (m. Shabb. 16:7; 22:3; y. Shabb. 16:8, 81b), which makes it likely that he and Jesus knew of each other, and perhaps even heard each other preach. They would certainly have heard reports of each other's teaching. Still, Jesus and Yohanan understood this verse in different ways.

Treasure in Heaven

Simon's message in the passage above is very different from Yohanan's message, though it is similar to another teaching of Jesus, about treasure in heaven.

The original message of Simon is obscured by the later addition of Hosea 6:6. The three things he named were famed for having two features in common: they are optional and they are without limit. A very old saying was used as the introduction to the tractate Pe'ah:

> These are things which have no measure: the *pe'ah* [harvest leftovers for the poor], and the *bikkurim* [firstfruits], and the *re'ayon* [festival "appearance" offerings], and acts of *ḥesed*, and study of Torah.
>
> These are things of which a man eats the fruit in this world, and the capital [comes] to him for the future world. (m. Pe'ah 1:1 AT)

This saying is so old that when it is discussed in the third century, they are no longer sure what *re'ayon* means (b. Hag. 7a). Most of this saying is entirely incidental to the topic of the tractate, so it likely functioned as an introductory famous quote that happened to include the term *pe'ah*. This tradition is arguably the source of Simon's saying. His version ignores *pe'ah* (because these rules applied only in "the Land" and not in Egypt, where he lived), and he combines the two forms of offering as "worship," thereby producing a list of "three things," as was appropriate for a memorable saying.

The significance of things with "no measure" is that most commands *had* to be obeyed, but these things could be done simply to please God. Doing such things built up "capital" for the "future world"—that is, "treasure in heaven" (Matt. 19:21 // Mark 10:21 // Luke 18:22). And this "capital" gains "fruit in this world"—that is, "interest," which is the same word as "fruit" in Hebrew/Aramaic. In other words, when you do good things voluntarily, you accumulate valuable treasure in heaven, and the interest from that capital is enjoyed during your life on earth.

As a result of this teaching, rich people were regarded as morally good, because their riches were assumed to be the interest from their accumulated treasure in heaven. This reward was not random or capricious: it was a natural outcome from the "capital" gained by doing good.

It is therefore significant that the rich young man, who is described as an exemplary keeper of the law, is the one to whom Jesus said, "Sell what you possess and give to the poor, and you will have treasure in heaven" (Matt. 19:21 ESV). He believed, along with everyone else, that his riches were earthly interest payments from the heavenly treasure built up by his piety. Jesus's response does not contradict the heavenly part of this theology but points out the fallacy in the earthly part: if he is really so keen on pleasing God, he will forgo this earthly reward.

Conclusion

Although few specific texts are exegeted in both the NT and rabbinic literature, when these shared texts are examined, they link to a much wider world of shared theology. The Christian use of the OT may come to different conclusions, but it starts in the same Jewish thought world. The differences are sometimes a deliberate contrast or reaction to the way the text is used in the Jewish world, and sometimes a different emphasis. The two worlds are interdependent, and their closeness, like that of rival siblings or neighbors, may have increased the resulting antagonism between them.

See also OT Use of the OT: Comparison with the NT Use of the OT; *other Mishnah, Talmud, and Midrashim articles; Dead Sea Scrolls articles; Philo articles; Septuagint articles; Targums articles*

Bibliography. Ellis, E. E., "A Note on First Corinthians 10:4," *JBL* 76 (1957): 53–56; Epstein, I., et al., *The Babylonian Talmud*, 18 vols. (Soncino, 1952); García Martínez, F., and E. J. C. Tigchelaar, *The Dead Sea Scrolls*, 2 vols. (Eerdmans, 1997–98);Ginzberg, L., "Some Observations on the Attitude of the Synagogue towards the Apocalyptic-Eschatological Writings," *JBL* 41 (1922): 115–36; Heineman, J., *Prayer in the Talmud*, SJ 9 (de Gruyter, 1977); Herford, R. T., *Christianity in Talmud* (Williams & Norgate, 1903); Instone-Brewer, D., "The Eighteen Benedictions and the Minim Before 70 CE," *JTS*, n.s., 54 (2003): 25–44; Instone-Brewer, *Techniques and Assumptions in Jewish Exegesis before 70 CE*, TSAJ 30 (Mohr Siebeck, 1992); Instone-Brewer, *Traditions of the Rabbis from the Era of the New Testament*, vols. 1, 2A (Eerdmans, 2004–11); Kasher, D., trans., Avot D'Rabbi Natan, Sefaria, accessed November 8, 2022, https://www.sefaria.org/Avot_D'Rabbi_Natan; McNamara, M., et al., *The Aramaic Bible*, 22 vols. (Liturgical Press, 1990–2007); Neusner, J., *Mishnah* (Yale University Press, 1988); Neusner, *The Tosefta Translated from the Hebrew*, 6 vols. (Ktav, 1977–86); Neusner, J., et al., *The Talmud of the Land of Israel*, 34 vols. (University of Chicago Press, 1982–95); Vermes, G., "Pre-Mishnaic Jewish Worship and the Phylacteries from the Dead Sea," *VT* 9 (1959): 65–72; Vermes, "The Story of Balaam," in *Scripture and Tradition in Judaism* (Brill, 1961), 127–77.

David Instone-Brewer

Mishnah, Talmud, and Midrashim: Thematic Parallels to the NT

The NT and rabbinic traditions grew out of the same culture of Palestinian Judaism and refer to the same Scriptures (the OT) as their foundation for beliefs. They use similar techniques to interpret these texts (see the article "Mishnah, Talmud, and Midrashim, OT Use in" elsewhere in the dictionary) and usually came to similar theological conclusions. Despite all this, it is difficult to find themes that both discuss at length because they left behind such completely different types of literature.

The NT was written to relatively uneducated individuals for the purpose of evangelism and discipleship while most rabbinic literature was written for highly educated lawyers to help them decide difficult cases. The areas of disagreement concern a few topics in theology, notably the Messiah, soteriology, eschatology, and the role of OT law. Unfortunately, neither the NT nor rabbinic traditions are theological treatises per se, so in both cases the theology of their authors has to be inferred and is often subject to disagreements even within their own communities.

Resurrection

Both the NT and rabbis before AD 70 were keen to show that the OT, and especially the Torah, teaches the resurrection. The Sadducees rejected this doctrine (Josephus, *J.W.* 2.164; Mark 12:18; Acts 23:8), but this movement did not survive Jerusalem's destruction, so any later debates are likely to be rehashes of previous ones.

Although there is a foundational agreement that "all Israel will be saved" (m. Sanh. 10:3; Rom. 11:26), disbelief in the resurrection creates an exception. It is unnecessary to tell those who do not believe in resurrection that they will not experience it, so the following tradition demonstrates the animosity engendered by this difference in theology.

> All Israel have a portion in the world to come, for it is written: *Your people are all righteous; they shall inherit the land forever, the branch of my planting, the work of my hands, that I may be glorified* [Isa. 60:21], but the following have no portion in the world to come: He who says that resurrection is not from Torah; [and who says] the Torah is not from heaven; and an Epicurean.
>
> R. Akiva [early second century] added: one who reads uncanonical books. Also one who whispers [a charm] over a wound and says, *I will bring none of these diseases upon thee which I brought upon the Egyptians: for I am the Lord that heals you* [Exod. 15:26].
>
> Abba Saul [mid-second century] says: also one who pronounces the Divine Name as it is spelt. (m. Sanh. 10:1, based on Epstein)

The list of exceptions grew with time, as seen later in the Mishnah and in both Talmuds. The first three likely originate in the first century, because they are already a fixed tradition by the start of the second century when Akiva adds to them. The first likely targets the Sadducees, who denied the resurrection, and the second those who lived in a secular way, such as Herodians (as in Matt. 22:16; Mark 3:6; 12:13). Both could be accused of using Epicurean philosophy to justify a lifestyle epitomized by their gold utensils (Avot R. Nat. A 5.1; cf. 1 Macc. 14:41–43).

The earliest rabbinic proof texts for the resurrection occur in a relatively late discussion, though it cites a mid-second-century debate involving R. Ishmael. The following omits the later rabbis in order to reconstruct the earlier debate.

> How is resurrection derived from the Torah? As it is written, *And you shall give the Lord's heave offering to Aaron the priest* [*and to his sons as a perpetual due*] [Lev. 7:34]. But would Aaron live forever—he did not even enter Palestine—so [could] heave offerings be given him? So it teaches that he would be resurrected, and Israel [would then] give him heave offerings. Thus, resurrection is derived from the Torah.
>
> The school of R. Ishmael [early second century] taught: *To Aaron* [means to one] like Aaron: just as Aaron was a *haber* [who can eat the heave offering], so *his sons* must [also] be *haberim*. . . .
>
> It has been taught: R. Eliezer, son of R. Jose [mid-second century], said: In this matter I refuted the books of the sectarians, who maintained that resurrection is not deducible from the Torah. I said to them: You have falsified your Torah, yet it has availed you nothing. For you maintain that resurrection is not a biblical doctrine. But it is written, *That soul shall utterly be cut off* [*hikkārēt tikkārēt*]; *his iniquity shall be upon him* [Num. 15:31]. Now, [seeing that] he shall *utterly be cut off* in this world, when shall *his iniquity be upon him*? Surely in the next world. . . .
>
> R. Ishmael said: But the verse has previously stated, *He reviles the Lord, and that soul shall be cut off* [*nikrĕtâ*] [Num. 15:30]. Are there then three worlds? But [interpret thus]: and [that soul] shall be cut off in this world: *hikkārēt*, he is to be cut off in the next; whilst as for [the repetition] *tikkārēt*, that is because the Torah employs human phraseology. (b. Sanh. 90b, based on Epstein)

These disputes presumably originate from debates with Sadducees before AD 70. The "books of the sectarians" that Eliezer tantalizingly mentions are likely to be the works of those Sadducees that are now completely lost. This may be identical to the Sadducean "Book of Decrees" mentioned in both ancient sources in the first-century Megillat Ta'anit (Tamuz 4).

Rabbi Ishmael is here seen rebutting some *derash* techniques that later rabbis were using to illustrate the resurrection. These techniques would not have convinced the Sadducees or anyone else who did not already want to find the resurrection in Torah, but the exegesis of Ishmael would have been harder to refute.

Rabbi Ishmael was known for the principle that "the Torah employs human phraseology." That is, it communicates in normal human language, and not in language that has to be interpreted in special ways. This is, in effect, a rejection of the newer *derash* techniques in favor of using nothing but *peshat*, as was normal before AD 70—though Ishmael's teaching is never presented in such a contentious way in Talmud.

Later unnamed rabbis interpret "to Aaron" in an ultraliteral way. Offerings were to be made to him and his sons forever, so they must live forever. However, Ishmael and his school consider this merely a human idiom.

Eliezer found a double verb—that is, an infinitive absolute form (*hikkārēt tikkārēt*)—and presumably interpreted this as a second death, which implies a second life. His actual reasoning is missing, but Ishmael refutes it and argues that this is merely normal human speech.

However, Ishmael shows that the text does indeed refer to a second death, because both v. 30 and v. 31 refer to him being cut off. Today we would regard this as normal human repetition. But Ishmael (and other Jews) regarded God as a perfect author, so needless repetition cannot occur. The literal meaning of these two verses would therefore imply being cut off after they have been cut off. In the language of Revelation, they suffer a "second death" (Rev. 20:6).

Jesus's proof of resurrection from Torah would have been much more convincing to the average Jew, because he relates it to a prayer that every Jew recites twice a day: the Eighteen Benedictions. The wording of this prayer was not fixed in the first century, and consequently survived in various versions. However, some wording is consistent and likely dates back to the first century (see Instone-Brewer, "Benedictions").

Jesus introduces his proof with "You do not know the Scriptures or the power of God" (Mark 12:24 // Matt. 22:29). After a comment about the much-married woman they asked him about, he cites Exod. 3:6: "I am the God of Abraham, the God of Isaac, and the God of Jacob." Jesus's teaching is memorable because it is based on the first two benedictions. The first benediction starts, "Blessed are you, Lord . . . God of Abraham, God of Isaac, and God of Jacob," and was consequently known as "the Fathers." The second benediction contains the words: "You are powerful . . . sustaining the living, reviving the dead. . . . Blessed are you, Lord, reviving the dead." This benediction is known as "the Powers" (cf. m. Rosh Hash. 4:5: "The order of the benedictions: One says the Fathers, the Powers, the Sanctification . . ."). Luke 20:27–49 does not include the reference to God's "power," perhaps because he did not understand it or thought his readers would not.

Jesus's proof refers to the plain meaning of the text, because even the abbreviated accounts in the Gospels emphasize that he is citing God's words spoken to Moses "in the passage about the bush" (Mark 12:26 // Luke 20:37 ESV). This reminds the readers that God speaks this long after Abraham, Isaac, and Jacob have died—and yet he says "I *am* the God of . . ."

This reasoning might be thought to depend on the LXX, which has *egō eimi* ("I am"), whereas the Hebrew merely has *ʾānōkî* ("I [am]"). However, for any Hebrew reader, the argument is just as convincing, because *ʾānōkî* always conveys the present tense when occurring without a verb, even in situations where a non-Hebrew reader might think a verb was essential (e.g., Gen. 27:24). When another tense is being communicated, a verb is supplied (e.g., Exod. 4:12, 15: "I will be"). Thus, a Hebrew reader would find this as convincing as a Greek reader.

Escaping Hell

Hell is an important topic in the Gospels, occupying about forty-five verses, compared to about sixty-six verses on God's love. On top of this are about twenty parables referring to two types of people or the "two ways" to heaven or hell. These are presumably a reaction against contemporary rabbinic teaching about the three ways. The earliest record of this doctrine is a school dispute:

> **The house of Shammai says:** [There are] three groups: one for *eternal life* to come; and one *for shame* [and] *eternal contempt* [Dan 12:2]. The one *for eternal life*—these are the perfectly righteous. The one *for shame* [and] *eternal contempt*—these are the perfectly evil.
>
> **Those who are balanced [between righteous and evil] go down to Gehenna and squeal and rise from there and are healed.** As it says: "*And I will bring the third through fire*" [Zech. 13:9].
>
> And about them Hannah said: "*The Lord kills and makes alive* [*bringing down to Sheol and he brings up*]" [1 Sam. 2:6].
>
> **The house of Hillel says: [He who is] *great in mercy*** [Exod. 34:6] **inclines towards mercy.** And about them it says: *I love the Lord because he hears . . .* [Ps. 116]. And the whole section speaks about them. (t. Sanh. 13:3 AT of the Vienna MS)

Both Hillel and Shammai agree there are three ways: the good go to heaven and the evil go to hell; and in-between Jews will also go to heaven, though there is a small disagreement about this. Shammai says they go to heaven after a brief punishment in hell, but Hillel disagrees, though his precise view is not clear in the records. He appears to say that God in his mercy lets them go straight into heaven, but the scriptural proof text implies they do visit hell.

The views expressed are likely genuine, though the original summarized record probably consisted of only the bold text. The scriptural supports were almost certainly added by later rabbis. Rabbis after AD 70 normally support Hillel, though in this case they record more of the Shammaites' scriptural support and possibly undermine the Hillelites' support.

Shammai appeals to the "third" in Zech. 13:9 who are refined by fire. The other "two thirds, they shall be cut off, they shall expire" (v. 8 AT). His followers apparently interpret this as "one third is cut off (*krt*) and one third expire (*gwʿ*)." Being "cut off" happens after a mortal sin (e.g., Exod. 30:38; Lev. 7:27), while "expire" is used for the good deaths of Abraham, Isaac, and Jacob (Gen. 25:8; 35:29; 49:33) as well as not-so-good deaths. This leads to the conclusion that one third go to hell, one third have a good death that leads to heaven, and the last third are refined by fire before going to heaven.

This is the kind of atomistic interpretation that Shammaites would accuse Hillel of when creating the "any cause" divorce, dividing a single phrase into two options in Deut. 24:1 (see my discussion in the article "Mishnah, Talmud, and Midrashim, OT Use in" under "Redundancy"). It is therefore possible that this proof was not originally used by Shammai, especially as it also helps the case of the later rabbis.

The later Hillelites (i.e., those who added the Scripture proofs) also undermine Hillel's conclusion. He appeals to the mercy of God as found in the grand self-description of God in Exod. 34:6, and he presumably denies Shammai's conclusion that the third group briefly visits hell. His contrary conclusion is presumably that God lets the third group go straight into heaven albeit without certain rewards (as Yohanan's tradition indicates, below).

And yet the proof text from Ps. 116 goes on to say, "The pangs of Sheol laid hold on me. . . . Then I called on the name of the LORD. . . . He saved me" (vv. 3, 4, 6 ESV). This implies the Shammaite view that they "go down to Gehenna . . . and rise from there," though perhaps without punishment—that is, they do not "squeal and rise." To emphasize that these later verses are important, they add, "and the whole section speaks about them" (t. Sanh. 13:3 AT of the Vienna MS). The principle that the context is important is normally taken for granted in *peshat* exegeses. In this tradition itself, the translation has to include extra words from the context of Zech. 13:9 and 1 Sam. 2:6 because they are required for the argument. Those words are not cited, but the reader is expected to remember how the passage continues. However, with regard to Ps. 116 the reader is specifically reminded to consider the verses that follow v. 1. Those verses undermine Hillel's original conclusion, so it is likely that later rabbis actually prefer the teaching of Shammai. They give Shammai a disproportional amount of scriptural support, and give Hillel a proof text the context of which ends up undermining him.

The NT refers to similar words in Ps. 16: "You will not abandon my soul to Sheol" (v. 10 ESV), but applies the quotation to Jesus rather than a third group (Acts 2:25–28). The next verse refers to the "path of life" (Ps. 16:11), which is likely alluded to in Matt. 7:14 as one of only two paths.

The teaching about two paths in Luke precedes a parable of the final banquet, which is also found in early rabbinic teaching. Yohanan ben Zakkai tells a parable that illustrates the early Hillelite teaching that the third group goes straight to heaven, though his parable also explains that they are treated differently from the perfectly good:

> This may be compared to a king who summoned his servants to a banquet without appointing a time. The wise ones adorned themselves and sat at the door of the palace; ["For,"] said they, "is anything lacking in a royal palace?" The fools went about their work, saying, "Can there be a banquet without preparations?" Suddenly the king desired [the presence of] his servants: the wise entered adorned, while the fools entered soiled. The king rejoiced at the wise but was angry with the fools. "Those who adorned themselves for the banquet," ordered he, "let them sit, eat, and drink. But those who did not adorn themselves for the banquet, let them stand and watch." (b. Shabb. 153a AT)

Most of the details in this parable are also found in various parables of Jesus (Matt. 22:2–13; 25:1–13; Luke 13:25–29; 14:17–24). The OT focus of these parables is Isa. 25:6–8, about a banquet when God "will swallow up death forever." However, this common origin cannot account for all the details shared between this rabbinic tradition and the Gospels. Both sets of parables include details not found in Isaiah: a king, invitations, an unknown start time, two groups (wise and foolish), some waiting expectantly, some continuing to work, and the king's anger against those who were late or inappropriately dressed.

The similarities are too close to occur without being linked. It is unlikely that Yohanan would retell a parable of Jesus or (if he did) that this would be recorded positively. In the early second century R. Eliezer b. Hyrcanus was arrested for heresy when he merely considered a teaching of Jesus to be interesting (t. Hul. 2:24). So it is unthinkable that Yohanan would retell a parable of Jesus. However, it is possible that the Gospel parables are a response to Yohanan's, because the various versions explore different elements of it, and because they all disagree with its conclusion in the same fundamental way.

In Yohanan's version, the tardy and inappropriately dressed guest is treated like a servant, who stands and waits to eat the leftovers. But in each of the Gospel versions, those who are late or who arrive inappropriately dressed are locked out and expelled to hell: "Throw him outside, into the darkness, where there will be weeping and gnashing of teeth" (Matt. 22:13); "I don't know you" (25:12); "'I don't know you or where you come from. Away from me, all you evildoers!' There will be weeping there, and gnashing of teeth" (Luke 13:27–28). Jesus may have been in Galilee at the same times as Yohanan, so it is possible that he would respond to a parable told or retold by Yohanan.

The language of hell that is used repeatedly in the Gospels comes partly from Isa. 66:24 (fire and worms) and partly from Jdt. 16:17 (pain and eternity), though these are also common in various intertestamental Jewish sources—especially Enoch, the Damascus Document, and the War Scroll. The most distinctive non-OT detail is the name Gehenna, which Jesus uses regularly and is found in a wide range of Jewish sources: targums (e.g., Ps. 37:20; 68:15; Isa. 66:24); the halakhic traditions (e.g., t. Sanh. 13:4, 5; m. Ed. 2:10); and Sibylline Oracles (1:103; 2:292; 4:186).

The reason for using this language is perhaps to make clear that Jesus is speaking about the same hell that other Jews were referring to. They regarded this as the fate of gentiles, who are clearly the subject of Isa. 66 because these are the enemies of Jerusalem (vv. 13–15) "who rebelled against me" (v. 24). They considered that a few extremely evil Jews would be counted among them (m. Sanh. 10:1–3), but generally Jews went to heaven.

Jesus, of course, teaches differently. He emphasized that there are only two paths and that those who do not repent will go to hell—including Jews. This dramatic contrast with virtually all other Jews accounts for the number of times this teaching is referred to in the Gospels.

Sabbath Work

The Sabbath created a theological and practical fault line between Jews and Christians shortly after NT times, but it is not clear what caused this. Believers in the NT apparently worshiped on the Sabbath (Acts 13:42, 44; 16:13; extending into the start of Sunday in Acts 20:7). There is also an emphasis that Jesus and his followers enter synagogues *on the Sabbath*—something that is predictable and unnecessary to mention (Mark 6:2; Luke 4:16, 31; Acts 13:14; 17:2; 18:4). Followers of Jesus are recorded observing Sabbath regulations (Matt. 28:1; Mark 16:1; Luke 23:54, 56; Acts 1:12), and there is an assumption that this will continue (Matt. 24:20). The only exception is Joseph of Arimathea (Mark 15:42; Luke 23:50–54), and other followers are contrasted with him: "But they rested on the Sabbath in obedience to the commandment" (Luke 23:56).

Sabbath conflicts concerned only two issues: preparing a snack in a field (Matt. 12:1–6 // Mark 2:23–26 // Luke 6:1–4) and healing (Matt. 12:10–13 [// Mark 3:1–5 // Luke 6:6–10]; Luke 13:10–17; 14:1–6; John 5:2–18; 7:22–23; 9:1–16). The only conflict recorded by Paul concerns celebrating the Sabbath with other Jewish rites (Col. 2:16).

The conflict about eating grain from a field on the Sabbath is unlikely to concern illegal labor such as harvesting and winnowing—that is, picking the heads and separating the grain from the husks. This type of meal was regarded as a "snack" (*ʿărāʾy*)—a technical term for a handful of harvest that has not yet been fully processed. Preparing an *ʿărāʾy* was exempt from Sabbath labor rules according to both Hillelites and Shammaites before AD 70, and this exemption was still accepted by the next generation, which tended to be stricter about the Sabbath (m. Ma'as. 2:4; 4:2–3; t. Ma'as. 2:1–2; 3:2).

However, Hillelites would have charged the disciples with breaking the law against tithing on a Sabbath. Even a snack needed basic tithing. More importantly, the heave-offering portion (a tenth of the tithe) had to be removed because only a priest could eat it (m. Ma'as. 2:4; 4:2). This would merely involve casting at least a hundredth of the grain to the ground before eating—but the decision to do this (not the act itself) was regarded as "labor," so they had to make this mental decision before the Sabbath started though they could enact it during the Sabbath (m. Demai 7:1).

Jesus's reference to David eating priestly food (1 Sam. 21:1–6) is therefore interpreting the plain meaning of that text: he is asserting that David's men were in the same situation. Both incidents took place on a Sabbath (1 Sam. 21:6—the bread was changed on the Sabbath: Lev. 24:8; 1 Chron. 9:32; m. Sukkah 5:7–8; m. Menah. 11:7). The disciples and David's men were "hungry," which can be interpreted as a danger to life that overrides the Sabbath (m. Yoma 8:6–7; cf. Matt. 12:1). Therefore, David's men could eat the priestly food, and Jesus's disciples could also eat the priestly portion of their snack.

All three accounts are followed by the claim that the Son of Man is greater than the Sabbath (Matt. 12:8 // Mark 2:28 // Luke 6:5). In Matthew the magnitude of this claim is made explicit: "Something greater than the temple is here" (12:6).

Healing on a Sabbath was a contentious matter among competing Jewish groups, which may explain why this provoked such animosity (Matt. 12:14; Mark 3:6; Luke 6:11; 13:17; John 5:16). Jesus is able to heal in one synagogue without opposition (Mark 1:21–27; Luke 4:31–36), and later that day he heals in a private home (Peter's mother-in-law). However, the crowd of others who are ill or need exorcism wait till that evening—that is, when the Sabbath is over (Mark 1:32; Luke 4:40–41)—which implies they knew that Sabbath healing was an issue for many. John records that this issue was potentially divisive among Jews (9:16).

The NT accurately reflects the situation in rabbinic Judaism, where everyone agreed that labor was forbidden on the Sabbath but disagreed about a few details, including tithing and especially the issue of healing. The definition of Sabbath labor had become encapsulated in a list of thirty-nine activities (m. Shabb. 7:2). This number reflected the thirty-nine lashes (Deut. 25:3), so it was difficult to add items. However, tithing and healing were missing, so those wanting to include these items had to vigorously defend their teaching. This new doctrine grew with time. Initially any act of healing that included an act of "labor" such as setting a bone was forbidden (m. Shabb. 22:6); then any medicine was forbidden that could not be regarded as food (m. Shabb. 14:3–4); finally, it was forbidden to pray even for healing (t. Shabb. 16:22a).

The only exception was when life was in danger. The origin of this principle is uncertain, but it did not exist in the mid-second century BC when the Maccabees were slaughtered because of their adherence to Sabbath laws. This tragedy prompted a change in practice (1 Macc. 2:41). The rabbinic phrase that encapsulated this decision was *danger to life overrides the Sabbath*. In the following passage it is italicized, as if it were Scripture, because the phrase was so universally accepted that they exegeted it in a similar way. Parts of this debate are late, but they are noteworthy because they reflect the different interpretive techniques used in different periods.

> R. Jose [b. Halafta, mid-second century] said: From where [do we know that] preserving *life overrides the Sabbath*?
>
> Since it is said: "[*Surely*] *you shall keep my Sabbaths*" [Exod. 31:13].
>
> Is it possible that circumcision or [Temple] service or preserving *life* [*override the Sabbath*]?
>
> Torah says: "*Surely*" [*'akh*—indicating an unwritten] exception—[that is, there are] times when you rest [on the Sabbath] and times when you do not rest [on the Sabbath].
>
> R. [E]liezer [b. Hyrcanus, late first century] says: Circumcision [proves that] one should *override the Sabbath* for it.
>
> Because of what? Because of their liability to extirpation for it [if they delay circumcision till] after the [specified] time.
>
> Behold, the rulings [can be argued on the basis of] *qal wahomer*: Now, [if] for one body-part of him one should override the Sabbath is it not logical that one must *override the Sabbath* for the whole of him? . . .
>
> R. Akiva [b. Joseph, early second century] said: And about what is Torah stricter: about [temple] service or about Sabbath [regulations]? It is stricter about [temple] service than about Sabbath [regulations], for [temple] service *overrides the Sabbath* and the Sabbath does not override it.
>
> Behold, the rulings [can be argued on the basis of] *qal wahomer*: Now [if temple] service overrides the Sabbath

> [and] *danger to lives overrides* it [the Sabbath], [then] the Sabbath which [temple] service overrides—is it not logical that *danger to lives overrides* it?
>
> Hereby you learn that: *Danger to lives overrides the Sabbath.* (t. Shabb. 15:16 AT)

Jose's second-century debate depends on the fact that Exod. 31:13 starts with *ʾak,* which indicates an unwritten exception according to the exegetical technique of limitation (*miut* [see "Lists of Exegetical Techniques" in the article "Mishnah, Talmud, and Midrashim, OT Use in" elsewhere in the dictionary]). This is a *derash*-style technique (i.e., it seeks hidden meanings in the text) that is hardly, if ever, used before AD 70.

Earlier, Akiva uses *qal wahomer,* which can be used to decide the plain meaning of a text, though his reasoning is fairly complex. He starts with the unspoken assumption that preserving life overrides temple regulations. Akiva points out that labor in the temple overrides the Sabbath, so if life is more important than the temple, it is also more important than the Sabbath.

Earlier still, Eliezer uses *qal wahomer* in a different way. He points out that circumcision overrides the Sabbath, and if fixing one body part is permitted, surely fixing the whole body is more important. This reasoning mirrors an argument in John: "If on the Sabbath a man receives circumcision, so that the law of Moses may not be broken, are you angry with me because on the Sabbath I made a man's whole body well?" (John 7:23 ESV). Eliezer taught just after AD 70, though the traditions he passes on are usually very conservative, as if he was the repository of the previous generation's teaching.

Even the strict sectarians at Qumran accepted the principle that danger to life overrides the Sabbath, though they warned that one should not rescue a drowning man with a tool that one might use for labor on any other day, and one certainly should not rescue an animal:

> A man must not bring up an animal which falls into water on the Sabbath day.
>
> But if it is a living man who falls into water on the Sabbath, he may throw to him his garment to bring him up, but he must not pick up a tool [to bring him up] on the Sabbath [day]. (4Q265 7.5–8 AT)

When justifying healing on a Sabbath, Jesus simply contradicts this Qumran teaching as absurd. Perhaps he is appealing to common sense ("Which one of you . . . will not . . ." [Matt. 12:11 // Luke 14:5 ESV; cf. Luke 13:15]), or perhaps to economic consequences ("if he had one sheep" [Matt. 12:11 NET]—i.e., his whole flock is at stake). However, this is more likely an allusion to Nathan's parable of a man with one sheep that he has loved since it was a lamb (2 Sam. 12:1–4). This appeals to the emotional attachment that people can have to their animals, which implies that Jesus's reasoning relies on mercy and relationship rather than legalism.

This kind of allusion, that relies on just a couple of words, is very common in rabbinic reasoning because the text of Scripture was so ingrained in their minds. Modern readers need to be aware that ancient readers had a far greater grasp of the OT text, because even an ancient rabbi would read less nonbiblical literature in a lifetime than we see in a day.

Conclusion

There is little overlap between the concerns of the NT and datable rabbinic writing, because the latter consists mainly of legal debates with little interest in theology. On the few occasions when themes overlap in these two sets of literature, they reflect similar concerns and use the OT in similar ways. Sometimes they even appear to be responding to each other. However, they can come to dramatically different conclusions because of the presuppositions each is based on.

See also OT Use of the OT: Comparison with the NT Use of the OT; *other Mishnah, Talmud, and Midrashim articles; Dead Sea Scrolls articles; Philo articles; Septuagint articles; Targums articles*

Bibliography. Epstein, I., et al., *The Babylonian Talmud,* 18 vols. (Soncino, 1952); Fee, G. D., *The First Epistle to the Corinthians,* rev. ed., NICNT (Eerdmans, 2014); García Martínez, F., and E. J. C. Tigchelaar, *The Dead Sea Scrolls,* 2 vols. (Eerdmans, 1997–98); Gerhardsson, B., *Memory and Manuscript,* ASNU 22 (Gleerup, 1961); Heineman, J., *Prayer in the Talmud,* SJ 9 (de Gruyter, 1977); Instone-Brewer, D., "The Eighteen Benedictions and the Minim Before 70 CE," *JTS,* n.s., 54 (2003): 25–44; Instone-Brewer, *Techniques and Assumptions in Jewish Exegesis before 70 CE,* TSAJ 30 (Mohr Siebeck, 1992); Instone-Brewer, *Traditions of the Rabbis from the Era of the New Testament,* vols. 1, 2A (Eerdmans, 2004–11); McNamara, M., et al., *The Aramaic Bible,* 22 vols. (Liturgical Press, 1990–2007); Neusner, J., *Mishnah* (Yale University Press, 1988); Neusner, *The Tosefta Translated from the Hebrew,* 6 vols. (Ktav, 1977–86); Neusner, J., et al., *The Talmud of the Land of Israel,* 34 vols. (University of Chicago Press, 1982–95); Strack, H. L., and P. Billerbeck, *Commentary on the New Testament from the Talmud and Midrash,* 3 vols. (Lexham, 2013–21), ET of *Kommentar zum Neuen Testament aus Talmud und Midrasch* (Beck, 1922–61).

David Instone-Brewer

Mission

Christian mission has as its center the saving message of the gospel, proclaiming Jesus's death for rebellious humanity. Properly conceived, therefore, mission is predicated upon the fall narrated in Gen. 3 and spans all of subsequent human history until Jesus's triumphant return and final judgment of the unbelieving world (Köstenberger with Alexander). Defined this way, mission is soteriological, Christocentric, and even cross- and resurrection-centered. Such a definition of Christian mission safeguards against efforts to conceive of mission more broadly as mere service to humanity or as God's activity in this world apart from the gospel of the saving cross-work of Christ.

While Scripture indicates that God's plan of salvation is grounded in eternity past, the first expression of the salvific initiative and intervention of God comes immediately following the fall in God's promise that the woman's offspring—the Messiah—would crush the serpent's (Satan's) head (Gen. 3:15; the so-called protevangelium). In this way, it is proper to speak of "God's mission"—the *missio Dei*—which is an expression of God's unconditional love for the human beings he created, despite their sinful rebellion. In due course, this divine mission takes clearer shape as centered in the mission of the Messiah, who would appear at the appointed time as God's chosen instrument of salvation (Wright). Following the death, burial, and resurrection of Christ—which form the heart of the gospel—God the Father and Jesus his Son jointly send the Holy Spirit from heaven in order to empower the witness of the new messianic community across the globe.

Thus, while God's mission spans the fall to the events surrounding Christ's return, the dynamic of that mission changes from OT to NT times. In OT times, the movement was essentially centripetal. The nation of Israel was to serve as an outpost of the worship of YHWH, a lighthouse for the nations, following a model of *attraction*. In this way, Israel, God's "treasured possession" "out of all nations" (Exod. 19:5), would serve as "a kingdom of priests and a holy nation" (19:6). In the late OT and Second Temple periods, and into NT times, we see this attractional model on display in form of the institution of the synagogue where the Jewish people met to worship on the Sabbath and where gentiles were welcome to join them as God-fearers and proselytes. At the same time, there is no clear evidence that Israel ever launched a centrifugal missionary movement to go to the nations for the sake of making converts (Jonah, the reluctant missionary to Nineveh, being a possible exception; Köstenberger with Alexander, appendix; McKnight; Dickson).

All this changes with the coming of Jesus. The Gospels narrate how Jesus gathers around himself a group of twelve apostles, mirroring the twelve tribes of Israel in the OT. This believing Jewish remnant serves as the nucleus of the church, Jesus's new messianic community. While the Jewish nation, represented by its leaders, rejects Jesus's messianic mission and spearheads his crucifixion, sanctioned by the Roman authorities, this new messianic community proclaims the saving message of Jesus's death, burial, and resurrection from Jerusalem to the "ends of the earth" (Acts 1:8). While this had been foreseen in OT times (e.g., Isa. 49:6), it is only after the ascension of Jesus that the green light is given for the church's mission to proceed. Just prior to the ascension, the risen Jesus commissions his followers to "go and make disciples of all nations, baptizing them in the name of the Father and of the Son and of the Holy Spirit, and teaching them to obey everything I have commanded you" (Matt. 28:19–20). It remains to trace the contours of the mission theme in the Bible in greater detail below.

Mission in the OT

The starting point of the biblical theology of mission is vital in setting a proper framework for the entire theme. If creation is adopted as the starting point, with new creation as its end-time counterpart, it is likely that mission is defined rather broadly along the lines of the cultural mandate given to the first humans to "be fruitful and multiply" and "to fill the earth and subdue it" (Gen. 1:28 ESV). Since "mission" as such is not a word used in Scripture, it can be defined in different ways. To speak of "*Christian* mission," however, in biblical terms has traditionally, and for good reason, been understood to entail a redemptive dimension. That is, "mission," biblically speaking, presupposes the predicament humanity incurred at the fall when the first man and the first woman rebelled against God and thus broke fellowship with God. As a result, humans are unable to save themselves and are desperately dependent upon God's gracious initiative to provide salvation by his own means apart from any merit on their part. This reality requires that salvation in the Lord Jesus Christ, the God-sent Messiah, occupy the central place in a biblical theology of mission, properly conceived, with Christ's death, burial, and resurrection at the center of the saving message of the gospel.

God's promise of a future deliverer and his covenant with Abraham. The opening chapters of Scripture set the stage for God's saving initiative (Köstenberger with Alexander, 11–42). Following God's creation of Adam from the ground and of Eve from Adam's side, the woman succumbs to the serpent's deception, transgressing God's command and leading Adam, too, into sin. Rather than serving as God's stewards of creation and enjoying their God-given marital union, the first man and the first woman are now alienated from their Creator and stand in dire need of reconciliation. They are expelled from the garden of Eden and have forfeited the privilege of serving God as specially appointed vice-regent over the world he had made. As a result, they were no longer able to manifest God's presence and glory across the globe as his image-bearers and divine representatives.

Nevertheless, while meting out proper discipline for their rebellion, God, true to his gracious, loving, and forgiving nature, raises the hope of future restoration of their relationship with him. The woman's offspring will subjugate the deceiver to whom the woman has succumbed, reversing the negative effects of the fall (Gen. 3:15). This promise of future redemption by a God-sent Messiah, as mentioned, provides the proper starting point for understanding the biblical teaching on mission. Rightly understood, mission is rooted in the loving heart and gracious initiative of God, and humans are the undeserving recipients of God's redemptive activity, which is shown to gradually unfold over the centuries and pages of Scripture that follow.

Specifically, we see that against the dark backdrop of human rebellion and apostasy from God a thread of descendants emerges, individuals that are chosen, called, and set apart for a special relationship with God. This messianic line prominently includes Noah, who, along with his family, is saved by God amid a universal flood that conveys God's judgment on the depraved, unbelieving world. While God establishes a covenant (sacred contract) with Noah promising never to send another universal flood, the vast majority of humanity persists in rebellion against their Creator.

The *missio Dei* reaches a vital early climax in the calling of Abram/Abraham, whom God promises a land, a seed (offspring), and a blessing (Gen. 12:1–3). In fact, all the nations will eventually be blessed through Abraham's descendant, the Messiah (17:4–8). This descendant of Abraham will be appointed to serve as God's set-apart viceregent, fulfilling the role originally bestowed on the first representatives of humanity (17:21; 22:17–18). The remainder of Genesis chronicles the continued progression of God's covenant with Abraham in and through his descendants Isaac, Jacob, and Joseph. Joseph's role in serving as a blessing for people from multiple nations as ruler in Egypt during a worldwide famine signals the even greater blessing that is to come through the ultimate descendant of Abraham, the Messiah.

The exodus as a typological pattern of salvation. The book of Exodus chronicles God's miraculous deliverance of the Israelites from slavery in Egypt through his servant Moses. The exodus, in turn, serves as a typological pattern for the redemptive mission of the Lord Jesus Christ. While the original exodus introduces the nascent Jewish nation to a special covenant relationship with God as his "treasured possession" "out of all nations" that would serve as "a kingdom of priests and a holy nation" (Exod. 19:5–6), the later "exodus" enacted in the Messiah (cf. Luke 9:31) will establish a new covenant relationship between God and a believing Jewish remnant that, in turn, will serve as representative believers from all the nations. Just as God delivers the Israelites from their bondage to the Egyptians (Exod. 6:6; 15:13), the Messiah will set believers free from their bondage to the deceiving serpent, Satan.

The Passover motif is an integral part and climactic feature of the exodus motif. During the original exodus, the sacrificial blood of an animal causes the "destroyer" to "pass over" a household, providing a ransom that saves the firstborn male Israelite from death (Exod. 12:21–23). At the second exodus enacted through the Messiah, Jesus will give his life as a ransom for many, and his blood will provide cleansing and forgiveness for all who trust in him for salvation. At the original exodus, the Israelites celebrate a sacred Passover meal in anticipation of their impending deliverance and the covenant God will establish with them (12:8–11; cf. 24:7–8). At the second exodus, Jesus will gather his new messianic community to establish a new covenant in his broken body and shed blood in anticipation of his impending sacrificial death for the sins of his people.

There is also an important element of escalation. While the original exodus and Passover in due course enable the Israelites to dwell in God's presence in the city of Jerusalem (Exod. 15:17), the second exodus will entail the transformation of the entire universe through the establishment of a "new Jerusalem" as the center of the new creation. This new creation will be inhabited by people from every tribe, tongue, and nation (Rev. 21:1–22:5). In this way, the *missio Dei* will fulfill God's covenant with Abraham, which includes the promise that Abraham would be the father of many nations (Gen. 12:1–3; 17:4–8; 22:16–18).

God's promise of a royal "son of David." Within the larger framework of God's promises to Abraham and God's deliverance of the people of Israel from bondage in Egypt through Moses, God's promise of a royal "son of David" takes center stage. Thus, the establishment of a Davidic regal dynasty is vital for the fulfillment of God's redemptive mission, culminating in the birth, ministry, sacrificial death, and resurrection of the Messiah. God's covenant with David to establish an eternal royal dynasty in him is narrated in the book of Samuel and repeatedly referenced in Psalms (2 Sam. 7:11–16; cf. Ps. 89:3–4, 19–37). The book of Kings assigns blame for the Babylonian exile to Israel's failure to keep the Sinai covenant established by God during the exodus through Moses. Nevertheless, Chronicles envisions the fulfillment of God's promise of an eternal dynasty to David. Psalms collectively presages the restoration of God's rule over his people through the Davidic messianic line.

Similarly, the messianic hope pervades a wide range of prophetic writings, both prior to the exile and in the period following the exile where no representative of the Davidic dynasty ruled in Jerusalem. Isaiah, in particular, casts the vision of a Davidic ruler who would bring righteousness and justice to a new creation as a result of the redemptive mission of YHWH's servant who would give his life for the transgressions of many (Isa. 52:13–53:12). This humble messianic servant will be anointed by God's Spirit and proclaim the good news of salvation and deliverance especially to the poor (42:1–4; 61:1–2). In addition, both Isaiah and Malachi speak of a future forerunner of the Messiah, who will prepare the way for him (Isa. 40:3; Mal. 3:1–2). With this, the stage is set for the mission of the Messiah who will carry out God's mission of establishing a new covenant with a believing remnant and of dying sacrificially for the sins of his people.

Mission in the NT

The NT writings have rightly been called "documents of a mission" (Marshall, 34–35). The central mission in the NT is the mission of Jesus, God's servant, who continues the *missio Dei* in his unique person and work (Wright, 105–35; Schnabel, *Mission*, 1:1–913). Jesus's mission, as mentioned, is preceded by that of his forerunner, John the Baptist, in keeping with Isaiah's vision of a herald of the new exodus inaugurated through the Messiah. Jesus's mission properly commences with his baptism by John, which marks the beginning of Jesus's public ministry. Jesus's mission spans a period of approximately three and a half years, during which he performs numerous messianic signs, gathers and equips his new messianic community, and establishes a new covenant in keeping with Jeremiah's prophecy (Jer. 31:31–34; cf. Ezek. 36:26–27; Köstenberger, *Missions*).

At the same time, Jesus is met with rejection by the Jewish nation represented by its leaders. He was crucified, buried, and on the third day rose from the dead, all in keeping with scriptural expectations (1 Cor. 15:3–4). The mission of the Spirit follows Jesus's ascension and exaltation. The Spirit witnesses to Jesus through the apostles, resulting in the spreading of Christianity to the farthest corners of the earth, despite human and supernatural opposition. The triune mission will be completed at the return of Christ, who will judge the nations. The new heavens and the new earth will be populated by people from every tribe, tongue, and nation, displaying the results of God's redemptive mission in and through the Messiah.

The Gospels. The four canonical Gospels all connect the coming of Jesus to OT messianic expectations regarding the mission of the son of David who would inherit David's royal office (Matt. 1:1; 20:30–31; Mark 10:47–48; Luke 18:38–39; John 7:42). At the heart of Jesus's mission stands his proclamation that in him the kingdom of God—God's spiritual rule in believers' hearts and his eventual rule over his people in a new heavens and new earth—has been inaugurated and will be consummated at his return. As the servant of YHWH, Jesus has been anointed by the Spirit to preach the good news of God's deliverance and forgiveness in himself. In God's sovereign providence, the world's rejection of Jesus—in an unholy alliance of Jews and gentiles (Acts 4:25–26; cf. Ps. 2:1–2)—resulted in the Messiah's substitutionary atonement for the sins of humanity. Jesus's sacrificial death on the cross, in turn, serves as the supreme demonstration of God's love for the people he has made (John 3:16; 13:1). Jesus's resurrection enables him to commission his followers to make disciples of all nations (Matt. 28:18–19; Luke 24:44–49; John 20:21). With this commission, God's promise to Abraham that in him all the nations of the earth would be blessed takes a massive step toward fulfillment.

Acts and Paul. Acts narrates the continuation of Jesus's mission through the apostles in the power of the Spirit (Schnabel, *Mission*, vol. 2). In keeping with Jesus's command, they serve as witnesses to the resurrection starting in Jerusalem and Judea and moving outward toward Samaria and ultimately the "ends of the earth" (Acts 1:8). The outpouring of the Spirit at Pentecost marks the beginning of the mission of the Spirit, who empowers the church's witness in the face of persistent opposition. As in Jesus's case, the mission is directed first to the Jews and subsequently also to the gentiles. The apostle Peter, who has previously been given the "keys of the kingdom" by Jesus (Matt. 16:19), preaches the inaugural sermon at Pentecost and is called to authenticate the reception of the Spirit by the Samaritans (Acts 8:14–25) and the gentiles. With regard to the gentiles, Peter receives a vision urging him not to regard gentiles as unclean and summoning him to the house of Cornelius, a gentile (chap. 10). Cornelius's conversion later becomes the subject of the Jerusalem Council (chap. 15), which ratifies the gentiles' reception of the gospel on par with the Jews. This, in turn, opens the door for the establishment of believing communities in places such as Philippi (chap. 16), Thessalonica (chap. 17), Corinth (chap. 18), and Ephesus (chap. 19). The presentation of Paul's mission, with an extended section devoted to the apostle's trials and defense before Roman governors (chaps. 21–26), evinces unmistakable parallels to the mission of Jesus, though there are differences as well (e.g., Paul is not divine and does not die a substitutionary death). Acts, with its narration of the ministries of Peter, John, Paul, and James, also serves as the framework for the NT writings that follow: the thirteen letters of Paul, the three letters of John, the two letters of Peter, and the letter of James, as well as Hebrews and Jude (Köstenberger with Alexander, chap. 5).

Paul's apostolic consciousness is grounded in his call by the risen Jesus on the road to Damascus (Acts 9; Schnabel, *Mission*, 2:923–41). Saul (renamed Paul) is God's chosen instrument to bring the gospel to the gentiles and to suffer for his name. The gospel Paul is called to preach is the gospel of God (Rom. 1:1), proclaiming God's gracious salvation of sinners to be appropriated by faith apart from any human merit or works (1:17; 3:21; Eph. 2:8–9; cf. Gen. 15:6). By accepting Christ's sacrifice on behalf of sinners, God is not only just but also the justifier of those who believed in Christ for salvation (Rom. 3:26). Paul fiercely defends his gospel against opponents such as the "Judaizers" who require "works of the law" (such as circumcision) for salvation (Gal. 1:6–9), rebuking even Peter and Barnabas when they succumb to external pressure, as well as those who came with alleged authorization from James, the Lord's half-brother and head of the Jerusalem church (Gal. 2:11–12). Paul understands himself to be a herald making first-time proclamation of the gospel in a given location, establishing communities of believers, and then pressing on toward regions where the gospel has not yet been preached (1 Tim. 2:7; 2 Tim. 1:11; cf. Rom. 15:19–21). His coworkers—the "Pauline circle" included individuals such as Timothy, Titus, Luke, Barnabas, Priscilla, and Aquila—partner with him in his mission, frequently following up as directed by the apostle (Bolt and Thompson). Paul understands his outreach to the gentiles as a priestly service presenting the nations as a pleasing offering to God (Rom. 15:16; cf. 2 Tim. 4:17). As part of his ministry, the apostle writes letters to churches and apostolic delegates that serve as substitutes for his presence and provide instructions concerning qualifications for leadership and various challenges faced by these congregations.

James, Hebrews, Jude, Peter, and John. James's letter is essentially a Jewish-Christian document that espouses a wisdom ethic largely derived from the OT; Jesus's name is mentioned only twice (James 1:1; 2:1). There is little direct information on mission. The (unknown) author of Hebrews asserts the supremacy of Christ and his priesthood over the old covenant system, urging believers not to revert to the old system. Jude calls on his readers to join him in defending the faith "once for all delivered to the saints" (Jude 3 ESV), which he proceeds to do over against false teachers who pervert the grace of God into a license for immorality (Jude 4). Peter, in his first letter, conceives of Christians as exiles and strangers in this world (1 Pet. 1:1; 2:11), urging them to Christlike suffering in view of his return. Peter also calls his readers to "proclaim the excellencies" of the one who called them "out of darkness into his marvelous light" (2:9; cf. Isa. 43:21) and enjoins them to be ready "to make a defense . . . for the hope" that is in them (1 Pet. 3:15). In his second letter, Peter likely adapts portions of Jude's letter and defends the faith against imposters who are denouncing his teaching regarding Jesus's second coming. John calls on believers not to love the world or the things in the world, espousing the need for radical spiritual separation from evil (1 John 2:15–17). He also warns the congregations under his apostolic jurisdiction not to extend hospitality to false teachers (2–3 John; Köstenberger with Alexander, chaps. 3–4).

Revelation. Revelation is a prophetic book encouraging believers toward the end of the first century of the Christian era to endure suffering at the hands of their Jewish and Roman opponents (see especially the letters to the seven churches in Asia Minor in Rev. 2–3; Köstenberger with Alexander, chap. 6). The book presents four visions (or possibly one vision in four parts) received by John "in the Spirit" (1:10: on the island of Patmos; 4:2: in the heavenly throne room; 17:3: in the wilderness; 21:10: on a high mountain). The first vision depicts the glorified Christ as the head of the church who calls on believers to stand firm until the end. The second vision—by far the longest in the book—presents God's judgment of the unbelieving world and the vindication of his saints. The third casts the world as a prostitute, "the whore Babylon," who commits sexual immorality and spiritual adultery with the rulers of this world. The fourth and final vision presents a magnificent vista of the "new Jerusalem," the new heavens and the new earth, where believers will dwell in God's presence at the culmination of history following God's judgment of the unbelieving world, including Satan and his demons. The presence of people from every tribe, tongue, and nation around God's heavenly throne attests to the fact that God's redemptive mission, centered on Jesus the Messiah—the sacrificial Lamb and the Lion of Judah—has now been fulfilled. While the book primarily serves as theodicy—the vindication of God's righteous judgment upon unbelievers—a small window remains for conversion as the end rapidly approaches. Sadly, however, it appears that the vast mass of unbelieving humanity only hardens in their opposition to God's purposes. Thus, the book primarily serves the purpose of urging believers to endure until the end.

Summary

The mission of God takes its point of departure from the rebellion of the human beings God fashioned in his image as his divinely commissioned representatives. The *missio Dei* spans from God's initial promise to send a deliverer who would crush the serpent's (Satan's) head to the coming and cross-work of the Messiah, the Lord Jesus Christ, and from there to the church's proclamation of the gospel to both Jews and gentiles in the power of the Spirit. God's initiative consists of his setting apart a faithful remnant, a messianic line that would become his instrument of blessing and salvation. This line includes righteous Noah, faithful Abraham, God's servant Moses, and King David. Through a series of covenants, God establishes a relationship with his chosen people. In these covenants, God gradually reveals who the Messiah will be with ever-greater specificity: a descendant of Abraham in whom all the nations of the earth will be blessed; a righteous ruler in the line of David; and, per Isaiah, the Servant of YHWH who will die for sinners' transgressions. Not only will he restore the fortunes of Israel, but he will also serve as a "light for the Gentiles" (Isa. 49:6).

The NT affirms that God's promises come to fulfillment in the person and work of the Lord Jesus Christ. Jesus is the Word who has been sent by God, accomplished his purpose while on earth, and subsequently returned to the Father who sent him (John's "sending Christology"; cf. Isa. 55:10–11). Jesus is the son of Abraham, the son of David, who fulfills Israel's destiny and opens the door for gentiles to be saved as well (Matt. 1:1, 2, 6, 17; 28:18–20). Jesus, the servant of YHWH who ushers in a new exodus, has given his life as a ransom for many (Mark 1:2–3; 10:45). In this way, Jesus serves as the culmination of God's plan of salvation, procuring redemption for both Jews and gentiles, as Luke affirms in his two-volume work (Luke-Acts) and as Paul proclaims throughout his apostolic mission. As a pioneer church planter, Paul established communities of believers across the Mediterranean, frequently writing letters to churches he planted (plus some churches he did not plant—e.g., the churches in Rome and Colossae) and instructing his apostolic delegates. From its early Jewish Christian beginnings (James) to its universal culmination (John), the early church's mission involved a wide range of activities including evangelism (e.g., Acts 2), apologetics (1 Pet. 3:15), and a robust defense of the faith against false teachers (e.g., Jude 3; 2 Peter; 1 John). Revelation brings satisfying closure to the mission of God carried out through the instrumentality of Jesus Christ, the Messiah and Son of God, in the power of the Holy Spirit.

See also Adam, First and Last; Creation; Glory of God; Image of God; Jews and Gentiles

Bibliography. Aune, D. E., and R. Hvalvik, eds., *The Church and Its Mission in the New Testament and Early Christianity*, WUNT 404 (Mohr Siebeck, 2018); Bolt, P., and M. Thompson, eds., *The Gospel to the Nations* (InterVarsity, 2000); Dickson, J. P., *Mission-Commitment in Ancient Judaism and in the Pauline Communities*, WUNT 2/159 (Mohr Siebeck, 2003); Köstenberger, A. J., *The Missions of Jesus and the Disciples according to the Fourth Gospel* (Eerdmans, 1998); Köstenberger, A. J., with T. D. Alexander, *Salvation to the Ends of the Earth*, 2nd ed., NSBT (InterVarsity, 2020); Köstenberger, A. J., and M. J. Kruger, *The Heresy of Orthodoxy* (Crossway, 2010); Marshall, I. H., *New Testament Theology* (InterVarsity, 2004); McKnight, S., *A Light among the Gentiles* (Fortress, 1991); Plummer, R. L., *Paul's Understanding of the Church's Mission*, PBM (Paternoster, 2006); Porter, S. E., and C. L. Westfall, eds., *Christian Mission*, MNTS (Pickwick, 2010); Schnabel, E. J., *Early Christian Mission*, 2 vols. (InterVarsity, 2004); Schnabel, *Paul the Missionary* (InterVarsity, 2008); Schnabel, "The Theology of the New Testament as Missionary Theology," in *Jesus, Paul, and the Early Church*, WUNT 406 (Mohr Siebeck, 2018), 505–34; Wright, C. J. H., *The Mission of God* (InterVarsity, 2006).

ANDREAS J. KÖSTENBERGER

Moses *See* Covenant; Sinai

Mystery

When readers encounter the term "mystery" in the NT, most think of Sherlock Holmes or Agatha Christie novels. The first entry for the term "mystery" in *The American Heritage Dictionary of the English Language* defines it as something "that is not fully understood or that baffles or eludes the understanding; an enigma" (Picket). But the biblical conception of "mystery," while it does contain some overlap with our contemporary understanding of the term, is wedded to the history of redemption and God's progressive disclosure of revelation.

The word "mystery" (*mystērion*) occurs twenty-eight times in the NT (counting the variant in 1 Cor. 2:1), but what makes the term significant is *where* we encounter it. Though occurring only three times in the Synoptics, the evangelists relate the term to the nature of the end-time kingdom (Matt. 13:11 // Mark 4:11 // Luke 8:10). The arrival of the kingdom (and, by implication, Jesus's messiahship) differs from first-century Jewish expectations, and these expectations, though varied, find their point of origin in the OT. The term "mystery" is one way the evangelists attempt to resolve the problem of why so many within Israel have rejected the very one they are expecting!

The majority of NT occurrences of "mystery," twenty-one instances, are in the Pauline corpus. Paul generally appropriates the term with regard to a dimension of the gospel itself (e.g., Rom. 16:25; 1 Cor. 2:1, 7) or the resulting relationship between Jews and gentiles (e.g., Rom. 11:25; Eph. 3:3). Paul also uses "mystery" to describe the nature of believers' resurrection (1 Cor. 15:51), the unity between Christ and the church (Eph. 5:32), the odd fulfillment of Daniel's "man of lawlessness" (2 Thess. 2:3–7), and general eschatological insight (1 Cor. 13:2; 14:2). Finally, Revelation mentions the word four times regarding the nature of the church (1:20), the unusual fulfillment of the prophecy of Dan. 11:29–12:13 (10:7), and the self-destructive behavior of Babylon (17:5, 7).

A host of scholars have surveyed mystery in the Bible and Second Temple Judaism (e.g., Bockmuehl; Brown; Gladd), so we need not retrace all of their discussions. There are also instances in the NT where the concept of mystery occurs without the word (see Carson, 424–36), but we will focus only on where the term "mystery" is explicit. We will begin with Daniel—the benchmark of mystery—and then venture into three prominent NT uses. Our primary concern here is to sketch, albeit in brief, the biblical conception of mystery and then consider how it relates to biblical theology and hermeneutics.

Mystery and the Book of Daniel

Though the word *mystērion* appears a few times outside of Daniel (e.g., Job 15:8 [θ′, σ′]; Ps. 24:14 [25:14 θ′, Quinta]; Prov. 11:13 [σ′]; 20:19 [θ′]), Daniel is the only book that translates the Aramaic term *rāz* as *mystērion*. The two Greek versions of Daniel—OG and Theodotion—consistently translate *rāz* as *mystērion* (2:18, 19, 27, 28, 29, 30, 47 [2x]; 4:9 [MT 4:6]), suggesting that the term "mystery" is a *terminus technicus* within the book of Daniel. Today, the majority of Qumran and NT scholars are convinced that "mystery" is a technical term, and they find its point of origin in Daniel. It is not a coincidence, then, that when mystery occurs in Jewish and Christian literature, allusions to Daniel are often in view.

Since Daniel is formative for grasping the biblical conception of "mystery," it is worth investigating the narrative in chap. 2. Nebuchadnezzar's dream *and* its interpretation compose the "mystery" in chap. 2 (Gladd, 33–38). Nebuchadnezzar envisions a magnificent colossus with a head of gold, chest and arms of silver, belly and thighs of bronze, legs of iron, and feet of a mixture of clay and iron (2:32–33). Despite its seemingly impregnable stature, a rock that is "cut out, but not by human hands," smashes the statue's feet, resulting in a total decimation of the colossus (2:34). The "rock" then grows into a mountain that fills the entire earth (2:35). The narrative progresses as Daniel unlocks the full meaning of the enigmatic dream. This is what Nebuchadnezzar is waiting for. The four parts of the statue symbolize four kingdoms (often interpreted as Babylon, Medo-Persia, Greece, and Rome). At the very end of history, God's eternal kingdom dramatically eclipses the fourth and final kingdom, the feet of iron and clay (2:45).

We can now make two critical observations. First, a twofold structure or form characterizes mystery—the initial symbolic revelation (2:31–35) and then a subsequent interpretative revelation (2:36–45; cf. Gen. 40–41). Elsewhere in Daniel, this structure appears in visions (Dan. 7, 8, 10–12) and writing (Dan. 5), and it is also seen in Jeremiah's prophecy (Jer. 9). The subsequent interpretation elucidates the former revelation. The twofold component of mystery signals the hidden nature of the revelation and its interpretation—largely hidden but now more fully revealed.

Commentators, though, often overlook an important dimension to the nature of wisdom in Daniel. Within the twofold structure, the narrative hints at Nebuchadnezzar possessing insight into the interpretation of his dream (see Beale and Gladd, 36–41). Recall that in 2:1 Nebuchadnezzar "had dreams; his mind was troubled." This may be something more than sleep deprivation. Perhaps he is "troubled" because he has some degree of insight into the meaning of his dream. The parallel account in chap. 4 is illuminating. Again, the king "had a dream" that made him "afraid," and the "images and visions . . . terrified" him (4:5; cf. 4:19). As Nebuchadnezzar rehearses the dream to Daniel (4:8–9), he appears to include a partial interpretation of the dream itself: "I looked, and there before me was a holy one. . . . He [the angel] called in a loud voice: 'Cut down the tree'" (4:13–14). Remarkably, the angel then interprets the dream: "Let *him* be drenched with the dew of heaven, and let *him* live with the animals. . . . Let *his* mind be changed . . . , till seven times pass by for *him*" (4:15b–16). The angel teases out the meaning of the tree by referring to it as a person. Embedded within the king's dream, an angel interprets the tree as a royal figure.

Although the Aramaic third-person pronoun remains the same throughout this passage (masculine singular), the angel interprets the tree as a prominent human figure in 4:15b–16. So, when Daniel delivers the formal interpretation to King Nebuchadnezzar in 4:19–27, he is *fully* interpreting what the king already knew *in part*. The OG version of 4:18 appears to confirm this observation: "I [Nebuchadnezzar] described the dream for him [Daniel], and he showed me *its entire interpretation* [*pasan tēn synkrisin autou*]" (Eng. 4:15 NETS). In contrast, Theodotion renders this phrase simply as "the meaning" or "interpretation." The OG appears to be mindful of the interpretative portion of Nebuchadnezzar's initial dream report, allowing Daniel to disclose the "entire interpretation" of the dream.

The second characteristic of mystery concerns the content of Nebuchadnezzar's dream in chap. 2 and is much more straightforward: the vision is eschatological. This is evident from 2:28, where Daniel informs Nebuchadnezzar that, in contrast to the false deities of Babylon, "there is a God in heaven who reveals mysteries, and he has made known to King Nebuchadnezzar what will take place *in the latter days* [MT: *bəʾaḥărît yômayyāʾ*; OG and θʹ: *ep' eschatōn tōn hēmerōn*]" (NASB). The expression "latter days" is highly eschatological (e.g., Gen. 49:1; Num. 24:14; Isa. 2:2; Jer. 23:20; 30:24; Hosea 3:5; Mic. 4:1), referring to events that will occur at the end of history (e.g., Beale, 13–19).

To summarize, mystery constitutes an eschatological revelation that was previously hidden but now has been revealed. This revelation is divulged in two stages. Within the initial revelation, the visionary has some degree of insight into the meaning of the dream. The second and final revelation fully unlocks the meaning of the first revelation.

Mystery and the NT

As we come to the NT's contribution to understanding mystery, we should bear in mind that this term played a significant role in the "history-of-religions school" in the late nineteenth and early twentieth centuries. Within this approach the mystery in the NT (especially in Paul's Letters) was thought to be derived from a pagan background. But a few decades later the tide shifted, and several scholars forcefully argued for an OT and Jewish background (e.g., Brown; Deden; Prümm). Today, the vast majority of scholars are convinced that the NT authors are indebted to Daniel and early Judaism in their conception of mystery.

Mystery appears in a variety of contexts and links to several cardinal doctrines in the NT, but we will restrict our investigation to three foci—kingdom, the crucifixion, and the relationship between Jews and gentiles. In limiting ourselves to these three, we can examine mystery in greater detail and get a better handle on how the two Testaments relate. Further, there appear to be two types of hiddenness: temporary and permanent.

Temporary hiddenness operates on a redemptive-historical plane and concerns the unveiling of end-time events, whereas permanent hiddenness refers to the persistent inability to understand revelation even after the mystery has been revealed. Only those who have spiritual "eyes to see" can grasp the full meaning of God's revelation in Christ. While this essay will discuss only temporary hiddenness in the NT, we should note that permanent hiddenness is also a constitutive part of the concept of mystery (see, e.g., Matt. 13:13–15 // Isa. 6:9–10; 1 Cor. 2:8–9 // Isa. 64:4; Eph. 1:17–18).

Kingdom. All three Synoptics employ the term in the same discourse on the nature of the kingdom (Matt. 13:1–52 // Mark 4:1–34 // Luke 8:1–18). Mark uses the singular "mystery [*to mystērion*] of the kingdom" (Mark 4:11 NASB), whereas Matthew and Luke use the plural "mysteries [*ta mystēria*] of the kingdom" (Matt. 13:11 // Luke 8:10 NASB). As most commentators argue, mystery in the Synoptics largely concerns the unexpected fulfillment of the eschatological kingdom (e.g., Ladd, 218–42). What precisely was "hidden" in the OT that has now been "revealed" in the NT? To state the matter differently, How does Jesus's teaching on the kingdom differ, to some degree, from the OT? Matthew's Gospel provides the fullest answer to these pressing questions.

The parables of the weeds (Matt. 13:24–30, 37–43) and of the net (13:47–50) communicate the same basic principle: the kingdom Jesus inaugurates generally differs from OT expectations in that one of the main tenets of the prophesied latter-day kingdom is the *consummate* establishment of God's kingdom, directly preceded by the ultimate destruction of unrighteousness and foreign oppression (e.g., Gen. 49:9–10; Num. 24:17–19; Dan. 2:44; 7:13–14). But paradoxically, Jesus teaches that two realms coexist simultaneously—one made up of those who belong to the kingdom and one of those who do not. The old age and the new age oddly overlap. The parables of the mustard seed (Matt. 13:31–32) and of the yeast (13:33) demonstrate that fulfillment of the end-time kingdom is slow but steady. While the OT predicted that the kingdom would arrive suddenly and all at once, Jesus claims that the kingdom is *gradual*. The eternal kingdom has been inaugurated, but its consummation remains a future reality.

If the above analysis of mystery in Daniel is correct, we should see traces of continuity between the OT and the unveiling of "mysteries of the kingdom" in the Synoptics. Recall that the revelation of mystery is not a radical disclosure. At the end of Matthew's discourse, Jesus even comments, "Every teacher of the law . . . is like the owner of a house who brings out of his storeroom new treasures *as well as old*" (13:52). To state the matter as a question, Where does the OT anticipate the already-not-yet aspect of the eternal kingdom? Perhaps we need not look any further than the most quoted OT passage in the NT—Ps. 110:1: "The LORD says to my Lord: 'Sit at my right hand *until I make your enemies a footstool for your feet*.'" All three Synoptics explicitly quote Ps. 110:1, so we can be confident that the passage is formative to their narratives (Matt. 22:44 // Mark 12:36 // Luke 20:42). While Ps. 110:1 itself is no stranger to debate, the text seems to claim Yahweh will appoint an enigmatic priestly figure (110:4) as ruler over the cosmos. Commentators often overlook the two-stage appointment of the rule of the "Lord"—"Sit at my right hand *until* [*ʿad*] I make your enemies a footstool." This psalm therefore hints, albeit enigmatically, at an already/not-yet rule, although the length of the inaugurated rule is unclear.

The revelation of the "mysteries of the kingdom" fits well with the paradigm we established in our investigation of mystery in Daniel, possibly explaining why allusions to Daniel pepper Matt. 13 (see Beale and Gladd). Jesus's conception of the latter-day kingdom is a legitimate fulfillment of the OT's expectation of the kingdom. It is "treasure hidden in a field" that the followers of Jesus must purchase at all costs (13:44). But the teaching on the kingdom also contains some new and surprising developments, and the disciples must await the pouring out of the Spirit at Pentecost to grasp these new dimensions of the kingdom more fully.

Crucifixion. The second chief use of mystery in the NT occurs in 1 Cor. 2:7, where Paul explains how the cross, the supreme manifestation of God's wisdom, is a mystery. The apostle states, "We declare [*laloumen*] God's wisdom, a mystery [*sophian en mystēriō*] that has been hidden and that God destined for our glory before time began." While it is not entirely clear whether the prepositional phrase *en mystēriō* modifies *laloumen* or *sophian*, many translations prefer the latter (e.g., NRSV, NLT, CSB). The content of the mystery is also not immediately obvious. Our first task is to note the general topic of chaps. 1–2: the content of wisdom (1:18–31), Paul's personal delivery of that wisdom (2:1–5), and the accessibility of that wisdom (2:6–16). Since wisdom (*sophia*) and mystery (*mystērion*) here are most likely interchangeable, as many scholars contend, all of 1:18–2:16 could be understood as a revealed mystery centering on the cross.

What elements of the cross were hidden in the OT? The reader is responsible to take inventory of several clues that Paul has left behind in chaps. 1–2. We can uncover the precise content of the mystery by focusing our attention on pregnant terms, titles, and phrases: for example, "Lord of glory" (2:8; cf. 1 En. 22:14; 27:3, 5), "Christ" or "Messiah" (1:17, 23; 2:2), "power" (1:18, 24), and the scandal of the cross (1:17–18, 22–25; 2:1–2, 8). The cumulative effect of the aforementioned points is striking. While Jesus is accursed and suffers a shameful death on the cross, he is simultaneously the supreme divine ruler—"the Lord of glory." He rules, as the Lord incarnate, in death and defeat. Two dimensions of the crucifixion appear to be "hidden," then, at least from the perspective of the OT: the ironic rule of the messiah and his identity as Israel's God in the flesh. Though a suffering messiah is anticipated (e.g., Isa. 52–53; Dan.

9:25–26; Zech. 12:10), a suffering messiah does not play a central role in the OT and early Judaism.

What about Christ's *ironic* rule at the cross? Is it utterly foreign to the OT that the messiah should rule at the moment of suffering? Probably not. For example, Ps. 22 describes intense persecution that has befallen King David. While he rules as Israel's king, he suffers at the hands of his enemies (Ps. 22:11–21). We would do well to recall that the evangelists frame portions of Jesus's suffering in accordance with Ps. 22 (e.g., Matt. 27:46 // Ps. 22:1; Mark 15:24, 29, 34 // Ps. 22:18, 7, 1; John 19:24 // Ps. 22:18). They draw points of continuity between David's suffering and Christ's suffering. Psalm 22 is, at least from the perspective of the NT, one example of the OT prophetically anticipating the ironic rule of Christ.

The same could be said for Christ's divine identity as Israel's Lord on the cross. Christ's preexistence is notoriously complex, and we do not have the space to wade into these deep waters. We only need to point out that the OT may not be silent on this issue. The enigmatic appearances of the "angel of the LORD" (e.g., Exod. 3:2; Judg. 2:1, 4), the role of wisdom in creation (Prov. 8), and prophetic texts such as Isa. 9:6 and Mic. 5:2 likely set a trajectory for this important NT doctrine. In the end, Paul's portrayal of the cross falls in line with what we have seen elsewhere: certain aspects of Christ's death were "hidden" from the vantage point of the OT but not completely so.

Jews and gentiles. The term "mystery" occurs six times in Ephesians (1:9; 3:3–4, 9; 5:32; 6:19). The disclosed mystery in Eph. 1 encapsulates the summation and unification of all things under the indomitable rule of Christ (1:9). Paul then gives a concrete example of such unification in Eph. 3: the equality and unity between Jews and gentiles in Christ (3:3–4, 9). Ephesians 5 presents a further example of unity about which Paul has received special insight—the union between Christ and the church mirrors the union between a husband and a wife (5:32). Finally, the last occurrence of "mystery" probably returns to the more general message of the gospel (6:19). In almost every case, mystery in Ephesians is tethered to the OT.

We will focus on Eph. 3, where Paul argues for the absolute unity between Jews and gentiles in Christ. The apostle articulates how the mystery involves gentiles participating in the new-covenant community and becoming equal members along with believing Jews in that new community—by faith in Christ. "The mystery [was] made known to me by revelation. . . . In reading this, then, you will be able to understand my insight *into the mystery of Christ* [*en tō mystēriō tou Christou*], which was not made known to people in other generations as it has now been revealed by the Spirit to God's holy apostles and prophets. This mystery is that through the gospel the Gentiles are heirs together with Israel, members together of one body, and sharers together in the promise in Christ Jesus" (3:3–6).

The unveiled mystery appears to be the unity between Jews and gentiles "in Christ Jesus." Many commentators argue that the mystery is the complete equality between the two parties, in that both make up true Israel (e.g., Caragounis, 140–41). But the thrust of the passage appears to be *how* the two stand on equal footing. OT authors, especially within the prophetic corpus, explicitly prophesy that gentiles will become part of true Israel in the latter days by adopting Israelite customs and outward covenantal signs (e.g., Isa. 56:3–8; 66:18–21; Zech. 14:16–19). Surprisingly, Paul claims that gentiles, together with Jewish believers, have now become true Israelites through faith alone in Christ, the embodiment of true Israel, and not by identifying with the externals of the Mosaic covenant.

Did the OT anticipate the admittance of gentiles into the people of God apart from adherence to the Torah? It appears so, at least at some level. Notice Paul's wording here: "The mystery of Christ . . . was not made known to people in other generations [OT writers] *as* it has now been revealed" (Eph. 3:4b–5). The term "as" (*hōs*) is key because it seems to indicate that OT authors had *some* insight into the unveiled mystery that was disclosed to Paul. While they lacked completely clarity on how gentiles could share in the covenant community by being identified with Israel's Messiah, a careful reading of several key passages seems to anticipate this doctrine (e.g., Gen. 7:2, 8; 15:6). Isaiah outlines, for example, the success of a "servant" figure who appears to embody Israel (42:1–9; 49:1–13; 50:4–11; 52:13–53:12). Isaiah 55–66 then switches to the plural "servants" to designate an obedient group within Israel that wholly identifies with the one faithful servant (e.g., 54:17; 56:6; Brendsel, 56–60).

Biblical-Theological and Hermeneutical Implications

Now that we have broadly surveyed the biblical concept of mystery, we will consider how it informs biblical theology and hermeneutics. The three NT passages we examined (Matt. 13; 1 Cor. 1–2; Eph. 3) all contain a key point of continuity—the person of Christ. With the possible exceptions of 2 Thess. 2:7 and Rev. 17:5, 7, all twenty-eight occurrences of "mystery" are tethered to the person of Christ. The "mysteries of the kingdom" entail the surprising arrival of the already/not-yet kingdom (Matt. 13:11–52 and pars.). Jesus establishes a kingdom that unexpectedly coexists with pagan empires and wickedness. Oddly, the kingdom is outwardly marked by suffering and death, not by political victory and success. Paul's use of mystery in 1 Cor. 1:18–2:16 fits remarkably well with the "mysteries of the kingdom" in the Synoptics and, in some sense, picks up where the evangelists leave off. The apostle argues that Christ rules as Yahweh incarnate at the moment of suffering and defeat. Indeed, this is precisely how he overcomes sin and the devil. According to Eph. 3:1–13, the mystery is how Jews and gentiles relate to one another.

Perhaps we can push further and attempt a synthesis of the three themes. While fulfilling OT expectations, albeit unexpectedly, Christ set in motion the end-time kingdom. Believers reign with Christ through suffering and death in their participation in the kingdom, just as he reigned through suffering and death in establishing the kingdom. Through union with Christ, Jews and gentiles share in the mysterious nature of the cross in the kingdom and enjoy complete access to the true end-time people of God. The horizontal relationship between Jews and gentiles is a consequence of Christ's work and establishment of the latter-day kingdom. Paul's "insight" (Eph. 3:4) into the mystery of the Jew-gentile relationship rests on Jesus's foundational teaching on "mysteries of the kingdom" (Matt. 13:11 NASB).

The biblical conception of mystery may also be a window into how the apostles understand the OT in relation to the coming of Christ. In our brief examination of Daniel, we saw that mystery is the full revelation of what has already been revealed in part. The full revelation is not radically new. Rather, the second revelation decodes or interprets the initial revelation; it is an unveiling of what is already "there" in the initial revelation. Daniel's interpretation of the colossus does not impose new meaning (Dan. 2:36–45)—it explains or clarifies what was largely unknown to Nebuchadnezzar. This fundamental observation may help us understand how the NT writers often perceive antecedent revelation. *If* our analysis of mystery in Daniel is correct and *if* the NT authors follow suit, then profound NT doctrines that are deemed a "mystery" are really "there" in the OT though generally hidden until the coming of Christ.

Contemporary hermeneutical discussions on the relationship between the OT and NT often invoke "mystery" in the debate. Richard Longenecker insists, for example, that NT authors resemble Qumran in their use of the OT and widely engage in "pesher exegesis," a technique where an OT passage is cited (lemma), the technical word "interpretation" (*pšr*) is used, and then the OT passage is eschatologically applied to the local situation (see 1QpHab 7.1–8). Qumran therefore views OT prophetic texts as a "vision" or something that requires decoding, much like the dreams and visions in Daniel. For Longenecker, much of the NT "approximates Qumran exegesis," and "the dominant manner in which the Old Testament is employed within these materials is that of a *pesher* treatment" ("Reproduce," 17). The hermeneutical payoff, for Longenecker, is that the NT writers engage the OT "more charismatically than scholastically" and, when necessary, "treated the [OT] passage in a creative fashion" ("Reproduce," 32). The point is that NT authors imitate the Qumran community and often set aside the original meaning of the OT in their use of it (see Longenecker, *Biblical Exegesis*, 113–16; Enns, 128–32).

The issue is that Longenecker builds his argument upon a misunderstanding of mystery. The disclosure of mystery in the NT is not a completely new revelation severed from the intent of the OT. This is not how the biblical conception of mystery works. Mystery, according to Daniel, is the full eschatological disclosure of what was revealed partially. It always comprises two parts—hidden revelation and interpreted revelation. The interpretation more fully reveals the initial revelation. Scholars such as Longenecker ignore the first half of mystery while seizing the latter. They fail to recognize that the symbols within the initial revelation possess meaning and that the subsequent revelation unveils the full meaning of those symbols. Further, we argued that the visionary in Daniel had some inkling of the meaning of the revelation even before the subsequent revelation. Perhaps this serves as a template of how OT authors may have grasped some of the fuller meaning of their oracles, knowing that their words would eventually be eclipsed by a fuller, more complete revelation.

Though we have examined only three NT uses of mystery (Matt. 13; 1 Cor. 1–2; Eph. 3), we have learned that on each occasion the unveiled mystery remains fastened to the OT and that the NT authors perceive meaning that is really "there" in the OT passage. It may not be a stretch to apply our understanding of mystery to the broad category of the NT use of the OT. While not every connection to the OT may be deemed a mystery, it appears to be a critical tool in the apostles' hermeneutical toolbox.

See also Biblical Theology; Literal Fulfillment.

Bibliography. Beale, G. K., *The Use of Daniel in Jewish Apocalyptic Literature and in the Revelation of St. John* (University Press of America, 1984); Beale, G. K., and B. L. Gladd, *Hidden but Now Revealed* (InterVarsity, 2014); Bockmuehl, M., *Revelation and Mystery in Ancient Judaism and Pauline Christianity*, WUNT 36 (Eerdmans, 1997); Brendsel, D. J., *"Isaiah Saw His Glory,"* BZNW 208 (de Gruyter, 2014); Brown, R., *The Semitic Background of the Term "Mystery" in the New Testament*, FBBS 21 (Fortress, 1968); Caragounis, C., *The Ephesian Mysterion*, ConBNT 8 (Gleerup, 1977); Carson, D. A., "Mystery and Fulfillment," in *The Paradoxes of Paul*, vol. 2 of *Justification and Variegated Nomism*, ed. D. A. Carson, P. T. O'Brien, and M. A. Seifrid (Baker Academic, 2004), 393–427; Deden, D., "Le 'Mystère' paulinien," *ETL* 13 (1936): 405–42; Enns, P., *Inspiration and Incarnation* (Baker Academic, 2005); Gladd, B. L., *Revealing the Mysterion*, BZNW 160 (de Gruyter, 2008); Ladd, G. E., *The Presence of the Future* (Eerdmans, 1974); Longenecker, R. N., *Biblical Exegesis in the Apostolic Period*, 2nd ed. (Eerdmans, 1999); Longenecker, "Can We Reproduce the Exegesis of the New Testament?," *TynBul* 21 (1970): 3–38; Picket, J. P., ed., *The American Heritage Dictionary of the English Language*, 4th ed. (Houghton Mifflin Harcourt, 2000); Prümm, K., "Mystères," in *Dictionnaire de la Bible: Supplément*, ed. L. Pirot, A. Robert, and A. Feuillet (Letouzey et Ané, 1960), 6:10–225.

Benjamin L. Gladd

N

Nahum, Book of

Nahum ("comfort") of Elkosh, a Judean town of uncertain location, wrote his book for a Judean audience near the middle of the seventh century. The book refers to the fall of Thebes (No-Amon, 3:8) that occurred in 663 BC as a past event but anticipates the fall of Nineveh, which took place in 612, placing its composition between these two events. The fact that Assyria was currently "at full strength" (1:12 ESV) suggests a date not much later than 652, when the rebellion of the province of Babylon began to sap the empire's strength. The book was thus likely composed during the long reign of Manasseh (ca. 698–642), whose resolute opposition to biblically normed religion (2 Kings 21:1–18; 2 Chron. 33:1–9) almost single-handedly made Judah's fall inevitable (2 Kings 21:10–13). Although most of the book focuses on Nineveh (1:1; etc.), its status as Assyria's capital city means that it also represents the empire as a whole.

Essential Features of the Book of Nahum

Composition. In keeping with a common pattern in the ancient Near East and especially with Deuteronomy's insistence that YHWH speaks only through designated prophets, the book derives from the prophet named in 1:1 (Hilber). Varying redactional approaches propose that the book developed from an early kernel (e.g., an early form of 2:4–3:19; Zapff, 256), or that it grew out of transformed judgment speeches originally directed against Judah (Wöhrle, 60–66, 161–64). The book's opening hymn is often thought to be late on the assumption that worldwide judgment that does not distinguish between Judah and the nations was a late development.

Redactional theories remain very hypothetical, especially as their complexity increases (Berman). Further, the criteria by which their practitioners find breaks and discontinuities in the text are often at odds with basic linguistic principles and presume that a perfect text would have little if any complexity or diversity (Gigon, 2). Both methodological and theological reasons, therefore, favor seeing Nahum as the book's seventh-century author and pursuing an understanding of the book that makes sense of all its parts taken as a whole (Landy).

Structure and message. The following structure is adapted from my commentary (Timmer, *Nahum*):

1:1	Introduction
1:2–8	Threat of global judgment
1:9–15 (MT 1:9–2:1)	Announcements of Assyria's destruction and Judah's deliverance
2:1–13 (MT 2:2–2:14)	Prophetic anticipation of Nineveh's fall
3:1–19	Deconstruction of Assyria's pride

The book's opening hymn establishes the eschatological horizon against which the rest of the book, focused on Assyria, should be seen. Nahum 1:2–8 describes a worldwide, definitive divine judgment of humanity that takes account not of individuals' ethnic or national identity but only of their trust in or opposition to YHWH (1:7–8). The addresses to Assyria and Judah in 1:9–15 contrast Assyria's present strength and earthly glory with the destruction and shame that will come upon king and empire alike. Judah, previously afflicted by God (1:12), will be liberated and experience God's deliverance (1:13, 15). Chapter 2 anticipates the fall of Nineveh, a city thought to be impregnable. The fall of Nineveh will bring an end to the Assyrian Empire's violent and rapacious domination of the ancient Near East, which Nahum compares to lions' violent killing and consumption of their prey (2:12–13). Chapter 3 uses a woe oracle (3:1–7), several taunts (3:8–17), and a dirge (3:18–19) to condemn Nineveh for its violence, idolatry, and oppression, and to further persuade the reader that it will fall before its attackers. Assyria's fall at the end of the seventh century fulfilled 1:9–3:19 but should also be seen as a very limited, partial fulfillment of YHWH's promise in 1:2–8 to bring final deliverance to those who fear him while destroying his enemies.

Nahum's Use of the OT

Nahum's use of the OT involves quotations as well as allusions and echoes. The most extensive survey dealing with Nahum's inner-biblical interpretation appears in Heinz-Josef Fabry (94–104, 113); Carl Armerding is also helpful. The instances of Nahum's interpretation of other OT texts examined here are roughly arranged in order of strength, from strongest to weakest. Because our method favors connections that are at least in part lexically defined rather than semantic structures like themes and patterns represented by a wider group of lexemes (e.g., "judgment on the oppressor" in Isa. 51–52 [Armerding, 454]), the former will receive special attention.

Isaiah 52:1, 7 and context in Nah. 1:15. Following the opening hymn, Nah. 1:9–15 presents four speeches that address, in alternation, Assyria (1:9–10, 14) and Judah (1:11–13, 15, *pace* NIV). The speeches to Assyria affirm that its plans against YHWH and his people will ultimately fail (1:9–10) and that the Assyrian king, his offspring, and the gods who purportedly empower him will come to an end (1:14). The contrasting speeches to Judah affirm in 1:11–13 that Judah's punishment will soon end, and in 1:15 that news has come that Judah's deliverance is on the point of being realized, so that vows and feasts should be celebrated.

This passage quotes repeatedly from Isa. 52 and its context (see table 1). There YHWH announces to exiled Jerusalem that he is bringing her punishment to an end (Isa. 51:22cd), and then calls exiled Jerusalem to arise in joyful expectation of the coming deliverance from all her foes, after which she will return to Judah with YHWH as her king.

Although several of these parallels lack shared lexemes, suggesting they are mere echoes (Isa. 52:1bc and Nah. 1:15cd; Isa. 51:8ab and Nah. 1:15f; Nurmela, 71, sees Nah. 1:15cd as compatible with Isa. 52:1b), the density of shared Isaianic lexemes and themes noted by Armerding (454) in Nah. 1:15 favors the conclusion that Nahum's use of Isa. 52 and its context is almost a running quotation or catena. Recognizing that the scope of Isaiah's prophecy extends to the return from exile and beyond (Watts), we can conclude that Nahum quotes a prophecy with an eschatological horizon in the context of Judah's deliverance from Neo-Assyrian oppression in order to identify this event as a partial fulfillment of the Isaianic promise. Since the celebration of Judah's feasts

Table 1. Comparison of Isa. 51–52 and Nah. 1:15

Isa. 51–52	Nah. 1:15
How beautiful on the mountains are the feet of those who bring good news, who proclaim peace! (52:7ab)	Look, there on the mountains, the feet of one who brings good news, who proclaims peace! (1:15ab)
Clothe yourself with strength, O Zion! Put on your garments of splendor, Jerusalem! (52:1bc)	Celebrate your festivals, Judah, and fulfill your vows! (1:15cd)
The uncircumcised and defiled will not enter you again. (52:1d)	No more will the wicked invade you. (1:15e)
The moth will eat them up like a garment; the worm will devour them like wool. (51:8ab)	They will be completely destroyed. (1:15f)

is retrospective and the payment of vows is clearly tied to Judah's deliverance from Assyria, Nahum himself probably recognized the limited nature of this fulfillment with respect to both Isa. 51–52 and the book's opening hymn. Although Nah. 1:9–15 deals with the downfall of Assyria and its monarch, God's judgment of Assyria in the seventh century BC is a limited, partial fulfillment of YHWH's promise to return to Zion and establish his righteousness punitively and savingly. And yet the passage simultaneously expresses confidence in the future full realization of God's judgment. This eschatological horizon for Nahum's message is corroborated by the NT use of Isa. 52:7–10, which ties it directly to God's work in Jesus Christ. (Spronk, 80, and others recognize the close relationship between the two passages but date Isaiah after Nahum, thereby reversing the direction of dependence.)

Nahum 1:2 and Exod. 20:5 or 34:14. The first connection in literary terms between Nahum and earlier portions of the OT appears in Nah. 1:2 ("A jealous [*qannô'*] and avenging God is YHWH" [AT]), which quotes part of Exod. 20:5 ("I, YHWH your God, am a jealous [*qannā'*] God") and/or part of Exod. 34:14 ("YHWH, whose name is Jealous [*qannā'*], is a jealous God" [AT]). These terms' identical semantics and shared root and referent make the minor orthographic difference between them insignificant (Reuter, 49, 53–55). The historical and textual priority of Exod. 20:5 favors seeing it as the source of the allusion/quotation, while the proximity of 34:14 to the divine self-description makes its use here equally plausible. Although no clear decision is possible, both potential source texts for the allusion/quotation in Nah. 1:2 emphasize YHWH's jealousy for his glory and honor. Since some uses of *qannā'* in the prophetic books show that the nations' behavior also bears directly on YHWH's honor and glory (Peels, 939), this concern is equally relevant to Israelites and non-Israelites, and so is well-suited to the global, nonethnic perspective of Nah. 1:2–8 (cf. Timmer, *Nahum*).

Nahum 1:3a and Exod. 34:6. After a meditation on YHWH's vengeance and wrath in the rest of 1:2, Nahum adds a second quotation from the Sinai pericope in 1:3a, "YHWH is slow to anger" (AT). Presumably drawing on Exod. 34:6 as the first biblical use of this description (cf. Num. 14:18; Pss. 86:15; 103:8; 145:8; Prov. 14:29; 15:18; 16:32; 19:11; contrast Cook), this facet of the divine character is notable for its connection to YHWH's renewal of the covenant that Israel broke by its idolatry while Moses was on Mount Sinai. Following God's gracious response to Moses's intercession for Israel at Sinai, this analogical reuse of earlier Scripture enriches the characterization of YHWH in Nah. 1 by adding that his wrath, repeatedly mentioned in 1:2, is not mercurial or arbitrary in his later dealings with his people. This gives those threatened by it time to repent and find shelter in him (1:7).

Nahum 1:3b and Exod. 32:11. The assertion that YHWH is "great in power" (*gədol-kōaḥ*) is most likely also drawn from the Sinai pericope, where it describes YHWH's deliverance of Israel from Egypt in Exod. 32:11 (*kōaḥ gādôl*, "great power"). This phrase occurs several dozen times in the OT, but even if Exod. 32:11 is not the earliest such reference in temporal terms, it is salient because of its rhetorical importance and because Nah. 1:2–8 includes other quotations from Exod. 32–34. Since Moses uses this description of YHWH's power to support his petition that YHWH would show them mercy (cf. Exod. 32:11; Num. 14:17–18; cf. Cook), the analogical reuse of this element is also positive in Nahum, as is "slow to anger" in the preceding line.

Nahum 1:3c and Exod. 34:7. A third element from Exod. 32–34 appears in the statement that YHWH "will by no means leave the guilty unpunished" (Nah. 1:3 AT // Exod. 34:7). In its original context this statement affirms that the guilty within Israel will not escape divine correction, and this morally based inner-Israel distinction makes possible its integration in Nah. 1:3, where the identity of those judged is unrestricted and unspecified. Nahum's reuse establishes an analogy between guilty Israelites and guilty sinners without distinction on the basis of YHWH's unchanging holiness and justice.

Nahum 1:4 and Ps. 106:9. The description of YHWH's coming in judgment begins in the last two lines of Nah. 1:3, where the pair "tempest . . . storm" may weakly echo other passages (Ps. 83:15; Isa. 29:6 adds "flame of fire" [all AT]; for similar pairs of storm terms, see Isa. 17:13; Hosea 8:7). Nahum 1:4 alludes more clearly to the crossing of the Sea of Reeds as described in Ps. 106:9, the only other text that uses the pair *gāʿar* + *yām* (rebuke + sea) (cf. Isa. 50:2; 51:10; Josh. 2:10; 4:23; 5:1). This reuse is typological, since Nahum makes the scope of this divine action global by absolutizing the "sea," much like "all the rivers" in the next line. The images of dried seas and rivers appear with some frequency in prophetic descriptions of deliverance or judgment that are too diffuse to tie directly to Nahum (Roberts, 51, lists numerous parallels; cf. Isa. 19:5–7; 42:15; 44:27; 51:10; Jer. 51:36; Zech. 10:11; the second-exodus connotations proposed by Baumann, 122, do not fit well here). The rest of the description of this future theophany lacks any close connection to particular texts, although it shares vocabulary, motifs, and other contextual factors with some, including several within the Twelve (esp. Baumann, 179–242; Kessler; see below).

Nahum 1:7 and Exod. 33:19. A final probable allusion to the Sinai pericope appears in the affirmation "Good [*ṭôb*] is YHWH" that begins a series of three salvific descriptors of YHWH (Nah. 1:7 AT). The same prominence is given to YHWH's reference to his own "goodness" (*ṭûb*) in Exod. 33:19 that introduces the comparable salvific descriptors "gracious" and "compassionate" as a "preface to the theophany" that culminates Exod. 34:6–7 (Timmer, *Creation*, 123). The shared referent, semantics, and use of the two terms outweigh the fact that they are not lexically identical, especially since *ṭûb* likely derives from *ṭôb* (Höver-Johag, 303). Nahum's reuse of this text as an authoritative description of YHWH asserts that his goodness as revealed to Moses is accessible to all who seek refuge in him amid a far more definitive judgment.

Conclusions regarding Exod. 20, 32–34 in Nah. 1. The probable presence of four allusions to or quotations from Exod. 32–34, and the possibility of a fifth (unless "jealous God" in Nah. 1:2 is drawn from Exod. 20:5), strongly suggest that Nahum has repeatedly drawn upon Exodus's presentation of the Sinai theophany as a whole segment, most likely because its presentation of the divine character is unparalleled and it integrates the themes of punishment and deliverance (cf. Boda, 27–52). Nahum brings to bear on all humanity the same divine character and attributes so powerfully presented in Exod. 32–34, affirming God's commitment to both justice and mercy. He thus interprets the divine judgment and salvation in the exodus-Sinai paradigm typologically, connecting those themes to later superlative divine interventions that punish sin and deliver God's people. This contextually sensitive approach shows that at least some OT inner-biblical interpretation exhibits awareness of "broad reference" (Turner, 578). This means, furthermore, that there are grounds on which to anticipate the same phenomenon in the NT's use of the OT (see below).

Nahum 1:9 and 2 Kings 18–19 // 2 Chron. 32 // Isa. 36–37. The feminine singular addressee in Nah. 1:11–13 is most likely Judah (*pace* NIV). This means that the "one who plotted evil against YHWH, a wicked counselor" (1:11 AT), is one who left Judah. This one is presumably identical to the one who "plotted against YHWH" in 1:9. The context, as with the only other use of "evil" in Nahum (3:19), makes clear that these expressions refer to Assyria. The following considerations make it likely that Sennacherib's siege of Jerusalem in 701 BC is in view in Nah. 1:9. This episode is a key conflict between Assyria and its gods and Judah and her God in 2 Kings 18–19, 2 Chron. 32, and Isa. 36–37; no other Assyrian interaction with Judah in Kings, Chronicles, or Isaiah is described in a similar way (e.g., 2 Chron. 33:11; Isa. 20:1); and Nah. 1:9 assures Nahum's audience that regardless of the size and skill of the Assyrian army ("at full force," 1:12 AT), YHWH is more than able to destroy it. The "going up from" Judah/Jerusalem mentioned in Nah. 1:11 is thus probably a reference to Sennacherib's lifting of his siege of Jerusalem and his abandoning of his campaign against Judah (2 Kings 19:36; 2 Chron. 32:21; Isa. 37:37).

Nahum 2:12–13; 3:18 and Isa. 5:25–30 and context. Nahum 2:12–13 exhibits both semantic/thematic and lexical connections to the predictive description of Judah's anonymous attackers in Isa. 5:29. There Isaiah describes the oncoming army as roaring "like a lioness" (*lābîʾ*) and "like young lions" (*kəpîrîm*) as it seizes (*ʾḥz*) and carries away (*plṭ*) its prey (*ṭerep*). Nahum 2:12–13 describes Assyria's habitual violence in terms of a pride of lions using similar or identical vocabulary: lioness (*lābîʾ*), prey (*ṭerep* and *ṭərēpâ*), and young lions (*kəpîrîm*). Nahum has taken an accurate depiction of Assyria's strength near the end of the eighth century and reused it, with irony, in his later, contrasting prediction of Assyria's fall (cf. discussion of 3:18 below). The irony is all the stronger since the texts use leonine imagery, which carries unparalleled ideological weight as the symbol of the Assyrian monarch's power. Looking beyond the phase in which Assyria punishes Judah (1:12), Nahum foresees in 2:12–13 the end of that empire despite its apparent strength.

Another connection to Isaiah appears in Nah. 3:18. Isaiah 5 predicts that various nations (surely including Assyria) will be summoned by YHWH to punish his people for the sins enumerated earlier in that chapter. In the late eighth century, Assyria's forces are described (accurately) as not suffering from weariness, stumbling, drowsiness, or sleepiness (Isa. 5:27), and as arriving "with great haste" in obedience to YHWH's summons (5:26). In Nahum's prediction of the empire's fall, by contrast, he foresees that its leaders will be "drowsy" (*nûm*, the same verb as Isa. 5:27) and "lie down (to sleep)," with the result that king and empire both come to an end (Nah. 3:18–19).

While Klass Spronk (142) suggests that Nah. 3:18 "reverses" Isaiah's *prophecy*, it is better to see this as an ironic inversion of Isaiah's *description* of eighth-century Assyria in a future context. Writing near the middle of the seventh century, Nahum knew that Assyria had been oppressing Judah for roughly a century (esp. in 701) and would thus have considered Isaiah's prophecy fulfilled (cf. Fabry, 95). His prediction concerns the next step in YHWH's dealings with Assyria, the final destruction of the empire. These examples lend further support to the conclusion that Nahum's use of earlier Scripture involves robust contextual awareness.

Nahum 3:7 and Isa. 51:19. There is likely an ironic allusion to Isa. 51:19 in Nah. 3:7. There (cf. also 3:19), Nahum rhetorically asks who will "grieve over" (*nûd*) Nineveh's fall and where one might find "comforters" (*nḥm*) for her. The irony arises from the fact that this rare pair of questions appears in Isa. 51:19, a context from which Nah. 1:15 has already quoted. There YHWH asks who will grieve over and comfort Judah, which has been overwhelmed by the punishment of exile. The answer to the question, and to Judah's troubles, is YHWH's promise of salvation. The case of Nineveh is the very opposite: although it considered itself to be supreme and untouchable, YHWH's destructive punishment of its violence and idolatry will reveal its abuse of the surrounding nations and so render impossible any grief over its fall or attempt to comfort Nineveh.

Nahum 1:2–8 and Mic. 7:18–20. Gerlinde Baumann (186–87) questions many of the verbal correspondences that James Nogalski (197) thinks bind Nah. 1:2–8 and Mic. 7:18–20 together redactionally, noting important differences between them. Baumann perceives the following links between the two passages, although their semantic weight is quite limited: divine wrath (Nah. 1:3, 6; Mic. 7:18), sea and rivers (Nah. 1:4; Mic. 7:12), Bashan and Carmel (Nah. 1:4; Mic. 7:14), the land or the earth (Nah. 1:5; Mic. 7:13) with its inhabitants, and darkness as the destiny of YHWH's foes (Nah. 1:8) or of Jerusalem's enemies (Mic. 7:8). The fact that Micah predates Nahum rules out literary dependence upon it, and Ruth Scoralick (188–96) argues that the two hymns are largely independent of one another but are both dependent upon Exod. 34:6–7.

Nahum 1:2–8 and Hab. 3:3–15. The hymn in Nah. 1:2–8 and the theophany report in Hab. 3:3–15 exhibit significant structural (theophany hymn joined to typical prophetic genres), semantic (YHWH eliminates enemies, saves his people/those who trust in him), and historical connections (Assyria in Nahum, Babylon in Habakkuk; Fabry, 100; Kessler). However, Nahum's hymn is oriented only toward the future, whereas Habakkuk uses YHWH's past theophanic appearances as indications of his plans for Judah and the world as a whole (Hab. 3:1–2, 16–19). There is no evidence of literary dependence between the two texts, but the similarity of their messages suggests that their authors share similar understandings of Judah's hybrid character, of the applicability of a similar distinction among non-Israelites, and of the interrelation of the fates of Judah and the nations.

Nahum and the NT

Despite the limited number of connections between Nahum and the NT, early Christian authors gave considerable attention to Nahum, as did the author of 4QpNah before them (Moyise, 110).

Nahum 3:1 and Rev. 17:5–6; 18:23–24; 19:2. The presentation of Nineveh in Nahum as a "city of blood" (Nah. 3:1), fully committed to sorcery and idolatry (3:4) that sustain the empire's project of world domination, is taken up typologically in Revelation's description of Babylon (17:5–6; 18:24; 19:2; Beale, 923). The fact that many OT prophetic texts condemn Assyria and Babylon for the same reasons highlights their nearly identical religious and moral profiles. Although its interaction with Israel preceded Babylon's, Assyria's destruction of the Northern Kingdom was less significant than Babylon's destruction of Judah, Jerusalem, and its temple—and the consequent ending of the Davidic dynasty and the theocracy (cf. Arnold, 57). After Babylon fell, its theological role and moral profile was eventually transferred to Rome, which regularly oppressed the early church. Nineveh's (and Assyria's) commitment to idolatry, divination, violence, and economic success through exploitation and domination thus places it at the beginning of the typological trajectory continued by Babylon (Isa. 47), then by Rome (Rev. 18 and passim), and finally by all opposition to Christ and his church (Rev. 17:2). Revelation's echoes of or allusions to Nah. 3 are thus examples of typological broad reference that draw upon the literary, theological, and redemptive-historical contexts of the Nahum text.

Nahum 1:6 and Rev. 6:17. The depiction of the world's end after the opening of the sixth seal in Rev. 6:12–17 is indebted first to Joel 2:10, 31 (Beale, 401), to which is appended the question "Who can stand?" This may be an echo of Nah. 1:6 or Mal. 3:2 (the LXX texts use a similar verb), with Nahum being slightly more likely due to its global horizon rather than Malachi's focus on Judah. If this is correct, it shows that NT writers understood Nahum's hymn as a prediction of eschatological judgment, although preliminary, partial fulfillments are not thereby ruled out.

Bibliography. Armerding, C. E., "Nahum," in *EBC*, 7: 447–89; Arnold, B. T., "Babylon," in *DOTPr*, 53–60; Baumann, G., *Gottes Gewalt im Wandel*, WMANT 108 (Neukirchener Verlag, 2005); Beale, G. K., *The Book of Revelation*, NIGTC (Eerdmans, 1999); Berman, J., "A Response: Three Points on Methodology," *JHebS* 10 (2010), https://doi.org/10.5508/jhs.2010.v10.a9; Boda, M., *The Heartbeat of Old Testament Theology*, ASBT (Baker Academic, 2017); Cook, G., "Power, Mercy, and Vengeance," *JESOT* 5, no. 1 (2016): 27–37; Fabry, H.-J., *Nahum*, HTKAT (Herder, 2006); Gigon, O., *Erwägungen eines Altphilologen zum Neuen Testament* (FETA, 1972); Hilber, J., "The Culture of Prophecy and Writing in the Ancient Near East," in *Do Historical Matters Matter to Faith?*, ed. D. Magary and J. K. Hoffmeier (Crossway, 2012), 219–42; Höver-Johag, I., "*ṭwb*," in *TDOT*, 5:296–307; Kessler, R., "Nahum-Habakuk als Zweiprophetenschrift," in *"Wort JHWHs, das geschah . . ." (Hos 1,1)*, ed. E. Zenger, HBS 35 (Herder, 2002), 149–58; Landy, F., "Three Sides of a Coin," *JHebS* 10 (2010), https://doi.org/10.5508/jhs.2010.v10.a11; Moyise, S., "The Minor Prophets in Paul," in *The Minor Prophets in the New Testament*, ed. M. J. J. Menken and S. Moyise, LNTS 377 (Bloomsbury Academic, 2009), 97–114; Nogalski, J., "The Redactional Shaping of Nahum 1 for the Book of the Twelve," in *Among the Prophets*, ed. P. R. Davies and D. J. A. Clines (JSOT, 1993), 193–202; Nurmela, R., *The Mouth of the Lord Has Spoken*, SJud (University Press of America, 2006); Peels, H. G. L., "*qn'*," in *NIDOTTE*, 3:937–40; Reuter, E., "*qn'*," in *TDOT*, 13:47–58; Roberts, J. J. M., *Nahum, Habakkuk, Zephaniah*, OTL (Westminster John Knox, 1991); Scoralick, R., *Gottes Güte und Gottes Zorn*, HBS 33 (Herder, 2002); Spronk, K., *Nahum*, HCOT (Kok Pharos, 1997); Timmer, D. C., *Creation, Tabernacle, and Sabbath*, FRLANT 227 (Vandenhoeck & Ruprecht, 2009); Timmer, *Nahum*, ZECOT (Zondervan Academic, 2019); Turner, I., "Going beyond What Is Written or Learning to Read?," *JETS* 61, no. 3 (2018): 577–94; Watts, R. E., "Echoes from the Past," *JSOT* 28 (2004): 481–508; Wöhrle, J., *Der Abschluss des Zwölfprophetenbuches*, BZAW 389 (de Gruyter, 2008); Zapff, B. M., *Redaktionsgeschichtliche Studien zum Michabuch im Kontext des Dodekapropheton*, BZAW 256 (de Gruyter, 1997).

Daniel C. Timmer

Nations *See* Jews and Gentiles

Nehemiah *See* Ezra-Nehemiah, Books of

New Areas for Exploration of the OT in the NT

Recent studies have turned more and more to the OT as the key source for understanding NT biblical theology. The very title of the epoch-making work by C. H. Dodd displayed a greater appreciation for the significance of this vital subject: *According to the Scriptures: The Substructure of New Testament Theology* (1952). Since Dodd's contribution, scholarly attempts have regularly been made to analyze all the various quotations of the OT in the NT. Especially noteworthy is the 1,200-page treatment of the subject in *CNTUOT*.

Yet new directions may provide fresh stimulation in exploring this subject. Two areas could provide productive investigation: (1) *general statements* in the NT indicating the significance of the OT in shaping the thought patterns of the NT and (2) the integration of *key word(s)* into the text immediately before and after quotations by various NT authors.

General Statements Indicating the Significance of the OT as Shaping New-Covenant Patterns of Thought

A number of passages in the NT affirm by general statements that the entirety of the OT has shaped the theology of the new covenant. Samples from various NT authors confirm this observation.

Matthew. Matthew's analysis of the various phases of the life of Christ by the phrase "that it might be fulfilled" has been regularly recognized. Jesus's infancy, his teaching ministry, his healing activity, and his betrayal unto death all occur in fulfillment of specific Scripture (1:22; 2:17; 4:14; 8:17; 12:17; 13:35; 21:4; 27:9). The treatment of these quotations by N. B. Stonehouse (127, 190, 191) is quite insightful. But beyond those particulars, summary statements in Matthew's Gospel indicate that everything associated with the passion of Christ occurred in fulfillment of the OT: "The Son of Man will go *just as it is written about him*. . . . Do you think I cannot call on my Father, and he will at once put at my disposal more than twelve legions of angels? But *how then would the Scriptures be fulfilled that say it must happen in this way*?" (26:24, 53–54).

Even his betrayal and arrest fall under the category of events anticipated by the OT. According to Jesus, "This has all taken place *that the writings of the prophets might be fulfilled*" (26:56).

These generalized statements do not refer to specific passages from the OT that anticipate the redemptive events of the life and death of Jesus. Instead, they draw into consideration the whole of the OT. Just as every thread of a handmade quilt makes its own contribution to the whole of the finished product, so every portion of the old-covenant Scriptures has its part to play in the prophetic presentation of the Christ.

Luke. In similar fashion, Luke concludes his Gospel with two all-encompassing affirmations about the role of the OT in anticipating the death and resurrection of Jesus. At his appearance to two disciples on the road to Emmaus, the resurrected Christ declares, "'How foolish you are, and how slow of heart to believe *all that the prophets have spoken*! Did not the Messiah have to suffer these things and then enter his glory?' And *beginning with Moses and all the Prophets, he explained to them what was said in all the Scriptures concerning himself*" (24:25–27).

In his final appearance to his disciples before his ascension, Jesus points them once more to the whole of the Scriptures: "He said to them, 'This is what I told you while I was still with you: *Everything must be fulfilled that is written about me in the Law of Moses, the Prophets and the Psalms*.' Then he opened their minds *so they could understand the scriptures*. He told them, '*This is what is written: The Messiah will suffer and rise from the dead on the third day, and repentance for the forgiveness of sins will be preached in his name to all nations, beginning at Jerusalem*'" (24:44–47).

The breadth of redemptive-historical elements encompassed in these two statements is remarkable. They include (1) all the various sufferings of the Christ, (2) his glorious resurrection on the third day, (3) the subsequent preaching of repentance and forgiveness, (4) the inclusion of all nations as recipients of the saving gospel, and (5) the beginning point of Jerusalem. All these key factors of the Christian gospel are declared to find their anticipation in the OT. In addition, all parts of the OT are identified by the phrase "the Law of Moses, the Prophets and the Psalms."

The effect of Jesus's opening the Scriptures about himself to his disciples on the road to Emmaus must be carefully noted. "Were not our hearts burning within us while he talked with us on the road *and opened the Scriptures to us*?" (24:32). The "burning heart," the heart elevated with wonder at God's redemptive working in the world, is not dependent on a visible sighting of the Savior. Even while their eyes are restrained from recognizing him, their hearts overflow with astonished amazement. What produces in them the "burning heart"? Not the recognition that the man speaking with them is the resurrected Christ. No, it is the opening of the whole of the Scriptures, the illumination of their minds concerning the revelation of Christ in the Law and all the Prophets—in all the Scriptures—that causes their exhilaration.

Every believer in Christ of every age and continent can experience the "burning heart." Physical sightings of the Savior are not the things that inspire. Understanding, believing the Scriptures as they reveal Christ, and doing what he commands are everything.

John. The Gospel of John begins by declaring this same generalized truth about the significance of the OT in relation to the NT. As Jesus begins to summon disciples who will join him in the publication of this saving gospel, Philip declares to Nathanael, "We have found *the one Moses wrote about in the Law, and about whom the prophets also wrote*" (1:45). By this testimony, the whole of the OT as summarized in the writings of Moses and the prophets has as its uniting subject the Messiah, here identified as Jesus.

John reports Jesus as making a sweeping claim about the OT in a simple parenthetical statement: "And the Scripture is not able to be broken" (10:35 AT). With the singular form of the word "Scripture," he speaks of the entirety of the OT. In its wholeness and in all its parts, Scripture can be appealed to as the basis for settling matters of theological controversy in the NT era.

On more than one occasion, the Gospel of John acknowledges the testimony of the OT concerning the Christ's resurrection from the dead. Only after Jesus is raised from the dead do the disciples believe "the scripture and the words that Jesus had spoken" regarding his resurrection (2:22). After Jesus is glorified the disciples finally realize "that these things had been written about him" (12:16). When receiving witness concerning the empty tomb, Peter and John run to the site. John enters, and "he saw and believed. *For not yet did they understand the Scripture that it was necessary for him to rise from the dead*" (20:8b–9 AT). A full knowledge of the OT actually should prove more effective in producing faith than being an eyewitness of the resurrected Christ, for an isolated appearance could be subject to many misunderstandings and subsequent doubts. But a faith generated from the whole of the OT may rise to a full comprehension of the redemptive and restorative intentions of God's saving work as displayed across both the old- and new-covenant epochs.

Acts. In the preaching of Acts, the apostles discourage the people from waiting until the resurrected Christ should appear to them before they believe. Instead, they point out that in God's good purpose the resurrected Jesus was to appear not to all the people but to witnesses that God had "hand-picked in advance" (*prokecheirotonēmenois*, 10:41 AT). As a consequence, the apostles ultimately base their case for Jesus's resurrection on the testimony of the OT. For, as Peter continues, "all the prophets testify about him" (10:43). As Paul indicates, his death and resurrection "fulfilled the words of the prophets" and consummate "all that was written about him." For "what God promised our ancestors he has fulfilled for us" (13:27, 29, 32–33).

Paul. Paul in Romans includes several general statements concerning the OT Scriptures. His opening words in Romans, along with his closing benedictory pronouncement, provide a framework for the use of the OT throughout the entire epistle. In speaking of Paul's initial reference to "the Gospel, which God promised of old by his prophets in the Holy Scriptures" (1:2 AT), C. H. Dodd comments, "That is to say, Paul's preaching of the Gospel loyally preserves continuity with the Old Testament tradition" (*Romans*, 4). All the essence of the "gospel of God" is found in the OT.

Similar observations may be made regarding the general statement about Scripture at the end of Romans (16:25–27). These two passages in Rom. 1 and 16 serve as "bookends" for Paul's masterful epistle. All the richness of theology in Romans has its roots in the OT Scriptures.

In this concluding benediction Paul contrasts the "mystery kept silent in ages past" with the revelation "now made manifest through the writings of the prophets" (16:25–26 AT). Though the prophets spoke the truth, it could not be properly understood until the reality actually came into being. As Peter explains, the prophets diligently inquired regarding the grace that the Spirit of Christ in them was pointing to for believers in the new-covenant era (1 Pet. 1:10–11).

What is it that the prophets wrote about? Paul sets forth the following items: (1) the person of Jesus Christ, who is able to make you strong (Rom. 16:25a); (2) the distinctives of "my"—that is, Paul's—gospel (16:25b); (3) the "mystery," which most likely refers to the inclusion of peoples from all nations as equal participants among the people of God (16:25c; cf. Eph. 3:6); (4) the critical nature of the "obedience of faith" (16:26b ESV); and (5) the truth that this gospel is for "all the nations" (16:26c NASB). How all-inclusive is Paul's concluding affirmation regarding the comprehensiveness of the OT in anticipating the message of the NT! Though the entirety of redemptive truth may be found in the new-covenant Scriptures, the simple fact of their brevity in comparison with the larger volume of the OT indicates that the anticipative elaboration of the OT provides invaluable service to the Christian church of today in its revelation of redemptive truth.

One example of this principle may make the point. Ezekiel's prophecies include eight chapters regarding Judah's neighboring nations (Ezek. 25–32). God repeatedly indicates that judgment will descend on all these nations without discrimination. But notice the reason for this divine judgment. Over and over, this judgment on Judah's national neighbors comes because of their mockery and mistreatment of God's people (25:3, 6, 8, 12, 15; 26:2). From the NT we know that the raging of the nations against the Lord and his Christ will be in vain (Acts 4:23–31; cf. Ps. 2:1–2). But do Christians today, in scanning the history of the rise and fall of nations, recognize that devastation of nations regularly comes from the Lord as a consequence of their mistreatment of God's people, the Christian church? Nations should take heed. Mockery or mistreatment of the disciples of Jesus could precipitate a nation's downfall.

Not only in the realm of the rise and fall of nations but even in the minutiae affecting personal relationships, the OT Scriptures speak into the era of the NT. In addressing the tensions between the "strong" and the "weak" brothers in Rome, Paul states, "For whatsoever was written before was written for our instruction, in order that through the patience and comfort of the Scriptures we might have hope" (Rom. 15:4 AT). The varied teachings of the OT will always provide both patience and comfort—patience in dealing with others who have a different opinion and comfort when you must be the one to suffer personal loss by pleasing others rather than yourself.

The general statements in the NT regarding the OT span the entirety of human relations, whether large or small, international or local. Many truths of a critical nature find elaboration in the OT that may be only briefly recognized in the NT.

Paul's pastoral letters to Timothy and Titus look beyond the time when living apostles will be available to offer a final word for any issue needing clarification among the new-covenant people of God. He reminds young Pastor Timothy that from infancy he has known the "sacred Scriptures" (AT), which possess the power to make him "wise for salvation through faith in Christ Jesus" (2 Tim. 3:15). Being himself a Pharisee as well as the son of Pharisees (Acts 23:6), Paul engages Timothy's cultural roots as the descendant of an Israelite mother and grandmother (2 Tim. 1:5) by a number of expressions. First, the phrase "sacred Scriptures" appears only here in the Bible, but it served as a standard expression for the whole of the OT in Greek-speaking Judaism, as attested in the writings of Philo and Josephus (Kelly,

Pastoral Epistles, 201). Second, "wisdom" was the most important thing a father in Israel could give to his son, as the repeated address to "my son" in Proverbs indicates. "My son" occurs over twenty times in Proverbs, including three times in the opening chapter to set the stage for the imparting of a father's wisdom to his son (1:8, 10, 15). Paul chooses exactly this form of address for Timothy four times over in his two letters (1 Tim. 1:2, 18; 2 Tim. 1:2; 2:1).

To capture the significance of this general statement about the capacity of the Scriptures to make a person "wise for salvation," consider an example from the final chapter of the wisdom book of Proverbs. In this case, a mother passes on her wisdom through the king to the king's son. Solomon most likely is the king represented by the pseudonym "Lemuel," and Bathsheba the mother, a circumstance that speaks volumes about God's grace (Prov. 31:1). The ancient mother's wisdom covers three critical areas of life—critical indeed if the son is to be "wise for salvation":

> [1] Do not spend your strength on women,
> your vigor on those who ruin kings.
> [2] It is not for kings . . .
> . . . to drink wine,
> not for rulers to crave beer,
> lest they drink and forget what has been decreed,
> and deprive all the oppressed of their rights.
> [3] Speak up for those who cannot speak for themselves,
> for the rights of all who are destitute.
> Speak up and judge fairly;
> defend the rights of the poor and needy.
> (Prov. 31:3–5, 8–9)

These three principles necessary for a young man bearing serious responsibilities can all be found in the NT. But nothing quite matches the comprehensiveness and conciseness of the mother's admonition formulated in the OT book of wisdom.

As a third Judaic element, Paul has previously made use of eight lines of poetical parallelism, so characteristic of prophetic and wisdom literature in the OT (2 Tim. 2:11–13). Now once more, Paul, the rabbinical teacher of Timothy, his son in the faith, uses this traditional form for transmitting godly instruction, this time with a chiastic A-B-B′-A′ arrangement:

> All Scripture is breathed out by God and has great usefulness
>
> A for teaching,
> B for rebuking,
> B′ for rectifying,
> A′ for instructing in righteousness. (2 Tim. 3:16 AT)

But can it actually be said that every portion of the OT has "great usefulness" for participants in the new covenant? What about the nine chapters of genealogy opening 1 Chronicles? How is it "useful" for believers today to plow through these nine chapters of mostly unknown names?

A comparison may be made with the Vietnam Veterans Memorial in Washington, DC. As you survey name after name of human casualties, the reality of it all overwhelms you. It really did happen. It's not a myth. The long list of names inscribed on the memorial does its work well.

Read the genealogies of humanity in Gen. 5 and Gen. 10. Read the genealogies of Jesus in Matt. 1 and Luke 3, going all the way back to Abraham and even to Adam. These chapters serve as "reality checks." They are not an Israelite version of the mythology of the gods. This listing represents the consistency of God's working of redemption in the realities of human history. For this reason, these genealogical Scriptures, along with all the rest of the OT, have "great usefulness."

Paralleling his reference to the whole of the OT by the traditional Judaic formula for "sacred Scriptures" (*hiera grammata*), Paul additionally employs a common designation for these same Scriptures: "All Scripture [*pasa graphē*] is breathed out [*theopneustos*] by God" (2 Tim. 3:16 AT). The term "God-breathed," used only here, is generally understood as affirming that the Scriptures of the OT are "in-spired" by God. In actuality, the phrase affirms that all Scripture is "breathed out by God," a creation of the Almighty's breath. The classic analysis of this text is still B. B. Warfield's ("Terms"; "God-Inspired").

What is the practical consequence of all Scripture being "God-breathed," a special product of the creative power of God's breath? Paul elaborates on the full benefit that comes from the Scriptures with the following phrases: "that the man of God may be amply supplied, having been fully equipped for every good work" (2 Tim. 3:17 AT). Now you know where to look for all the resources necessary for doing the work of God. Not only can the "sacred Scriptures" make you "wise for salvation" (2 Tim. 3:15). You may also look to all the Scriptures to make you competent, altogether equipped for all the work God has for you to do. One commentator says it well: "Do we hope, either in our lives or in our teaching ministry, to overcome error and grow in truth, to overcome evil and grow in holiness? Then it is to Scripture that we must . . . turn, for Scripture is 'profitable' for these things" (John Stott, as quoted in Knight, 450). So, Paul provides the means for making a modern theologian. In the areas of both doctrine and life, the OT will provide a firm foundation for new-covenant believers.

Peter. First and Second Peter contain several general statements about Scripture (1 Pet. 1:10–11, 22–25; 2 Pet. 3:2, 13). The classic statement of 2 Pet. 1:19–21 represents the fullest expression of what the new-covenant people of God may expect to find in the OT. A literal though somewhat amplified translation is as follows:

> Beyond that, we have the prophetic word, which is even more firmly established, to which you are well advised to give your most careful attention as to a lamp shining in murky darkness, until the day dawns and the morning star rises in your hearts. Understand this principle as of first importance: no prophecy of Scripture came by private insight. For never, ever by the determination of man was (any) prophecy ever borne along, but men spoke from God as they were being borne along by the Holy Spirit.

Peter has just informed his readers that he will soon be putting off the tent of his body (2 Pet. 1:13–14). What benefit will the prophetic word of the OT provide for those who believe in Jesus as the Christ after contemporary apostolic voices fade away? More certain than living eyewitnesses is the "prophetic word."

This certainty rests firmly on the ultimate source of the Scriptures themselves. Of first importance when dealing with biblical prophecy, it must be recognized that not a single prophecy of Scripture came by private insight. For never, ever was any prophecy "borne along" by "the determination of man." To the contrary, "men spoke from God as they were being borne along by the Holy Spirit" (2 Pet. 1:20–21). The verbal root is identical both in denying the human origin and affirming the divine origin of the inspired prophet. Being "borne along" describes first negatively and then positively the ultimate source of the prophet's every word. Just as the wind fills the sails of a ship, so the Holy Spirit actively filled the prophet as he inscribed the words of God.

On this solid basis of the ultimately divine origin of all Scripture, the believer throughout this extended time beyond the end of the apostolic age may have confidence regarding the "power" and the "appearing" of the Lord Jesus Christ (2 Pet. 1:16 AT). The dawning of the eternal day will have cosmic dimensions (2 Pet. 1:19b). At the same time, a total transformation of every believer's heart will accompany the "rising" of the "morning star" (2 Pet. 1:19c). According to one commentator, "Here the 'rising in our hearts' obviously points to something which happens, in a blessed and saving way, to Christians in their inner selves. The clause must be a pictorial description of the way in which, at His Coming, Christ will dissipate the doubt and uncertainty by which their hearts are meanwhile beclouded and will fill them with a marvellous illumination" (Kelly, *Peter*, 323). As a consequence, you are "well advised" to "give your most careful attention" to each and every aspect of the prophetic word (2 Pet. 1:19 AT). For the whole of the OT is like a "shining lamp," constantly available to guide every aspect of your life and thoughts.

Revelation. Revelation stands out as the NT book most saturated with the OT. Not so much in explicit quotation but more in total absorption of language and imagery, Revelation cannot be matched by any other portion of the NT. As has been well said, "No other book of the NT is as permeated by the OT as is Revelation. Although its author seldom quotes the OT directly, allusions and echoes are found in almost every verse of the book" (Beale and McDonough, 1081).

Revelation opens with a unique blessing not found in any other biblical book: "Blessed is the one who reads and those who hear the words of this prophecy" (1:3a AT). As it begins, so it concludes, with an open invitation for everyone to receive the Lord's blessing (22:14, 17). But in contrast with its opening chapter, the book's concluding words round out the age-old tradition of setting covenantal curse alongside covenantal blessing. This passage contains the severest of warnings to all its readers: "I offer this solemn witness to all people who hear the words of the prophecy of this book: If anyone should presume to add to them, God himself shall add to him the plagues that have been recorded in this book. And if anyone should take away from the words of the book of this prophecy, God himself shall take away his share in the tree of life and of the holy city which have been described in this book" (22:18–19 AT; cf. Deut. 27:9–28:68). As a covenantal document with its conclusion in blessings and curses, the words of Revelation are altogether sacrosanct. Consequently, God himself shall add all the plagues to, and God himself shall take away any share in the tree of life and the holy city from, anyone who tampers with a single word in this book.

These curses obviously apply to Revelation itself. Yet the distinctive position of these "Do not add" and "Do not take away" admonitions among the final words, the final verses, the final chapter of the final book of the Bible encourages a broader application to the whole of the God-breathed covenantal documents of the OT as well as the NT. These formulae encapsulate an ancient covenantal tradition going back to the earliest phase of God-breathed covenantal documents. (For a fuller treatment of the "Do not add" formula, see Robertson, *Final Word*, 64–67.)

"Do not add" and "Do not take away" first appear in Deuteronomy. During the covenant-renewal ceremony enacted in the plains of Moab, Moses warns the people, "Do not add to" and "do not take away from" the revelation that comes from the Lord (4:2; 5:22; 12:32). John, as the final author of God-breathed Scripture, joins Moses, the initial author of God-breathed Scripture. As Moses writes, "Do not add," and, "Do not take away," so John writes, "Do not add," and, "Do not take away."

With this comparable covenantal context in the writings of Moses and John, it seems perfectly appropriate to extend the application of both Moses's and John's words to the entirety of sacred Scripture. From both Deuteronomy, at the beginning of redemptive revelation, and Revelation, at the conclusion of redemptive revelation, the "Do not add" formula establishes the sacrosanct character of all Scripture. No one should ever presume to add a single word to any portion of Scripture, and no one should ever presume to take away a single word. These concluding words of the new-covenant Scriptures underscore the sacred nature of Scripture. Because God has said it all, all of it must forever stand as originally written.

Conclusion. This limited, selective representation of generalized statements in the NT about the OT in all its parts hardly exhausts the NT testimony regarding the role of the OT in the formulation of NT patterns of thought. The many specific passages from the OT quoted in the NT are only the tip of the iceberg. Not just the isolated texts but the larger, deeper streams of old-covenant theology also form the foundation for the theology of the new covenant. A full comprehension of the OT's role in defining the message of the NT will be grasped only by the absorption of the total message of the OT. To think like the apostles, a person must comprehend the total message of the old-covenant Scriptures as the apostles did.

Key-Word Methodology in NT Quotations

On the side of the minutiae of biblical quotations, the key-word methodology used by various NT writers when quoting OT passages represents a largely overlooked factor in understanding the way in which the OT has impacted the formation of NT biblical theology. Passages from Hebrews, Matthew, Acts, and 1 Peter may illustrate this distinctive methodology.

Hebrews 10:5–10. The author of Hebrews intends to establish the superiority of Christ's offering of himself in contrast with the multiple offerings under old-covenant legislation. At both the beginning and end of this discussion, he introduces a critical term: "once" (*hapax*, 10:2; *ephapax*, 10:10). The denial of the once-for-all character of animal sacrifices in contrast with the affirmation of the once-for-all character of Christ's sacrifice establishes the absolute superiority of the new-covenant provision for cleansing from sin's defilement.

To underscore this contrast, the writer quotes Ps. 40:6–8, following the LXX translation. The presentation of the quotation immediately below attempts to capture the parallelism of the OT poetry. The italicized words are the original author's key words, as his subsequent exposition indicates:

> [A] Sacrifice and *offering*
> [B] you did not desire,
> [C] but a *body* you prepared for me;
> [A] with whole burnt offerings and offering for sin
> [B] you were not pleased;
> (then I said)
> [C] Behold I come!
> (in the scroll of the book
> it is written of me)
> [C] I delight to do your *will*,
> O my God;
> [C] your law is within my heart. (Heb. 10:5–7 AT)

In his interpretive comments (10:8–10), the writer clearly demonstrates his understanding of the structures of Hebrew poetic parallelism. He first joins the "A" sections (v. 8a: "sacrifice and offering"; "whole burnt offerings and offering for sin") and then the "B" sections (v. 8b: "you did not desire"; "you were not pleased"). He then omits the two parenthetical phrases and joins the two of the four "C" sections that convey essentially the same idea of personal submission to God's will as a sacrifice far superior to the offering of animals (v. 9: "Behold I come!"; "I delight to do your will"). His interpretive remarks may be represented as follows, with italics indicating his echo of the key words that he is analyzing:

> First he said,
> "*Sacrifices and offerings, burnt offerings and sin offerings*
> you did not desire; you were not pleased with them"
> (though they were offered in accordance with the law). (Heb. 10:8 AT)
>
> Then he said,
> "Behold I come! I delight to do your *will*."
> He sets aside the first to establish the second.
> And by that *will*, we have been made holy
> through the *offering* of the *body* of Jesus Christ *once for all*. (Heb. 10:9–10 AT)

The author presumes to pluralize "sacrifices" and "offerings" (10:8). By his running exegetical comments, he emphasizes the drastic contrast between the singular, once-for-all sacrifice of Christ and the unending, multiple sacrifices of the old-covenant system. But still further, he directly analyzes the heart of his quotation by the deliberate repetition of three key words from his quoted material: "By that *will* we have been made holy through the *offering* of the *body* of Jesus Christ once for all" (10:10).

This smooth interjection of key words from the quoted material into the flow of his interpretive comments clearly demonstrates the methodology being discussed. It would be very easy to overlook the critical role of these key words if a reader were not familiar with the procedure. The NIV translates the word *prosphora* in the quotation in 10:5 as "offering" but then renders the same term as "sacrifice" in the interpretive comments in 10:10. In doing so, it fails to establish the direct connection between the key word and its interpretation. But for those who recognize the NT's use of key words in its quotations of the OT, a focus on these key words becomes a helpful aid in identifying the specific emphasis of the passage. The "will" of Christ in the "offering" of his "body" provides the key to the point stressed by the author. It is the "willingness" of Christ to "offer" his "body" as a supreme act of obedience that provides the key to understanding the acceptability of his sacrifice.

Other passages in Hebrews follow the same pattern of weaving interpretive remarks around selected key words. Note the examples in table 1.

Table 1. Use of Key Words in Heb. 2:6–4:11 (All AT)

OT Citation	Interpretive Key Words
"*everything under* his feet" (2:8a)	"*everything under* him" (2:8b)
"*made a little lower than*" (2:7a)	"*made a little lower than*" (2:9a)
"*crowned with glory and honor*" (2:7b)	"*crowned with glory and honor*" (2:9b)
"a *son of man*" (2:6c)	"many *sons*" (2:10a)
"with *glory*" (2:7b)	"to *glory*" (2:10a)
"*Today*" (3:7)	"while it is called *Today*" (3:13) "the seventh *day*" (4:4) "a certain *day*, calling it *Today*" (4:7a) "another *day*" (4:8)
"if you *hear* his voice" (3:7)	"they who *heard* and rebelled" (3:16) "the message they *heard*" (4:2a) "those who *heard*" (4:2b)
"do not *harden* your hearts" (3:8a)	"so none of you may be *hardened*" (3:13)
"in the *rebellion*" (3:8a)	"who heard and *rebelled*" (3:16)
"in the *desert*" (3:8c)	"fell in the *desert*" (3:17c)
"I was *angry*" (3:10)	"with whom was he *angry*" (3:17)
"I declared on *oath*" (3:11a)	"to whom did God *swear*" (3:18)
"never *enter* my *rest*" (3:11b)	"never *enter* his *rest*" (3:18) "promise of *entering* his *rest*" (4:1) "we . . . *enter* that *rest*" (4:3) "on the seventh day God *rested*" (4:4) "never *enter* my *rest*" (4:5) "some will *enter* that *rest*" (4:6) "if Joshua had given them *rest*" (4:8) "there remains a sabbath-*rest*" (4:9) "*enters* God's *rest* also *rests*" (4:10) "let us . . . *enter* that *rest*" (4:11)

Numerous other passages from Hebrews might be cited that employ this same methodology. The author skillfully weaves key words from a quoted passage of the OT into the very fabric of his exposition. Outstanding in this regard is the detailed exposition, word by word, of Ps. 110:4 in Heb. 7:1–28: "The LORD has sworn . . . , 'You are a priest forever in the order of Melchizedek.'"

The author first quotes this verse in Heb. 5:6 and then again in 5:10. After an interruption in which the author addresses the immaturity of his hearers (5:11–6:20a), the passage surfaces for the third time: "He has become a high priest forever after the order of Melchizedek" (6:20b AT). This multiple return to the same phrase climaxes with the author's exhaustive explanation, extending through the whole of Heb. 7, of every single word in this verse:

"this *Melchizedek*" (7:1–10)
"*in the order of* Melchizedek" (7:11–15)
"You are a priest *forever*" (7:16–19)
"*The Lord has sworn*" (7:20–25)
"*You are a priest*" (Heb. 7:26–28)

Few, if any, other places in the NT so thoroughly explain an OT passage. But only by a full awareness of the key-word methodology will this magnificent phrase-by-phrase exposition in Scripture become apparent. (For a fuller exposition of Ps. 110:4 in Heb. 7 based on the recognition of this key-word methodology, see Robertson, *Israel*, 53–83.)

Matthew 4:12–17. Matthew explains a Galilean rather than a Judean locale for Jesus's ministry by reference to both current circumstances and the OT. John the Baptist has been put into a Judean prison (Matt. 4:12). Jesus will later explain that as they did everything they wished to John, so the Son of Man will suffer at their hands (17:12). But by departing from Judean territory in the south, Jesus avoids a premature conflict with the leadership of that area (4:12; cf. 12:15, 19, 20). In Galilee he leaves his hometown of Nazareth and locates his ministry at the busy crossroads town of Capernaum, identified by Matthew as "by the sea, in the area of Zebulun and Naphtali" (4:13 AT). All major English translations properly render the phrase "by the sea" except the NIV, which reads "by the lake," apparently considering the fact that Capernaum is located by Lake Galilee while the phrase "the way of the sea" refers to the international highway that skirted Capernaum and then descended to Egypt along the shores of the Mediterranean Sea. This historic "way of the sea" connecting the three continents of Europe, Asia, and Africa went right by (or through) Capernaum. The present author well remembers noting a Roman milestone marker in Capernaum that read *Via Maris*, the "Way of the Sea."

Matthew explains this locale for Jesus's ministry in Galilee of the Nations as a fulfillment of Isaiah's prophecy (Isa. 9:1–2). In the narrative section, several key words or phrases anticipate Matthew's quotation (all AT):

Anticipative Key Words	OT Citation
"Galilee" (4:12)	"Galilee of the Nations" (4:15c)
"by the sea [*parathalassian*]" (4:13)	"the way of the sea [*hodon thalassēs*]" (4:15b)
"Zebulun and Naphtali" (4:13)	"Zebulun and Naphtali" (4:15)

By observing the key quote words in Matthew's anticipative comments, we see that the emphasis of his quotation becomes crystal clear. Not in Judea but in Galilee of the Nations, by "the way of the sea"—an international highway connecting the three continents of Africa, Europe, and Asia—Jesus begins his public preaching ministry. The summation of his proclamation underscores this same international scope for his ministry. Jesus does not declare, "Repent, for the kingdom of the Judeans is imminent." Instead, he underscores the universal character of his kingdom: it is the kingdom of heaven that he brings to the brink of its realization by his preaching (Matt. 4:17).

Matthew anticipates his quotation by integrating key words into his narrative. The recognition of these key quote words reinforces the point he wishes to make. The locale for the inauguration of Jesus's ministry embodies a major principle in Matthew's Gospel: the kingdom of the Messiah comes through the ministry of Jesus for all nations and peoples.

Acts 4:23–31. Luke reports that Peter and John are commanded by the Sanhedrin not to "utter a peep" (*phthengesthai*) in the name of Jesus (Acts 4:18). On being released, the two go back to their own people and raise their voices to God (Acts 4:23–24). In their prayer, they quote Ps. 2:1–2, and numerous key words and phrases appear. In the following extract, key words and phrases are italicized, and phrases subsequently exposited by the interpretive text that follows are underlined.

> Why do the *nations* rage
> and the *peoples* plot in vain?
> The kings of the earth take their stand,
> and the rulers are *assembled together*
> against the Lord
> and against his *Anointed One*. (Acts 4:25–26 AT)

The immediately following interpretive comments build on the key quote words:

- The *nations* (*ethnē*, v. 25) are identified as the various "*nations*" of the world (*ethnē*, v. 27) in contrast with the "*peoples*" (*laoi*) of Israel.
- The "*peoples*" (*laoi*, v. 25) are identified as the "*peoples* of Israel" (*laoi*, v. 27).
- "*Assembled together*" (*synēchthēsan*, v. 26) is underscored by the repetition of the same word in Peter's opening interpretive remarks (*synēchthēsan*, v. 27).
- "Against his *Anointed One*" (v. 26) is interpreted by the phrase "whom you *anointed*" (v. 27) and once again by "your holy child Jesus whom you *anointed*" (v. 27).

All standard English translations render *ethnē* as "nations" in the quotation of v. 25 and exactly the same Greek word as "gentiles" in v. 27. Consequently, the English reader fails to perceive the significant use of this key word. Most major English translations properly read "gathered together" both in v. 26 and v. 27. But the NIV obscures the emphasis by translating "band together" in v. 26 and "met together" in v. 27, apparently not perceiving that the identical verb appears in both the quotation and the interpretive remark and is positioned first in v. 27 for emphasis.

Peter weaves additional interpretive applications into his comments by specifically identifying "Herod" and "Pontius Pilate" (v. 27) as the people functioning in this historical circumstance as "kings of the earth" and "the rulers" (v. 26). Note also his extended exposition of the phrase "in vain" (v. 26). Peter observes that the nations and the peoples of Israel assembled together "to do exactly what your hand and purpose determined in advance would occur" (v. 28), which underscores the fact that their ragings against the Christ were "in vain."

How amazing is this running application and commentary as developed by Luke! Not a single concept in the quoted passage from Ps. 2 lacks interpretation. Clearly the whole procedure is intentional and must have served as a model for subsequent treatments of old-covenant passages by new-covenant believers.

First Peter 2:4–9. If a person is not yet a "believer" in the key-word methodology of the NT writers, perhaps 1 Pet. 2:4–9 will provide adequate persuasion. These verses are bristling with interpretive comments focusing on key words. The interpretive comments both anticipate as well as follow the quoted OT passages. As an additional feature, the most critical key word, "stone," makes its appearance in the first phrase of three successive passages quoted from the OT.

A verse-by-verse treatment may serve to underscore the extensive role of this key-word methodology. In this case, I provide a rather literal translation to make the role of the key words apparent:

1. In the two verses that anticipate the quotations, no less than eight key words appear, with the key word "stone" occurring once in the singular and once in the plural:

> . . . the living *stone*
> *rejected* by men
> but by God *elect*, *honorable*,
> and you yourselves as living *stones*
> are being *built up* into a spiritual house,
> into a *priesthood* that is *holy*. (1 Pet. 2:4–5)

2. In the first quotation that follows (Isa. 28:16), three of these key words reappear, while this verse introduces two new anticipative key words (underlined):

> Behold I lay in Zion a *stone*,
> the peak of the *corner*, *elect*, *honorable*,
> and the one who *believes* in him shall never
> be put to shame. (1 Pet. 2:6)

3. Peter's following explanatory comment draws on both the original and the newly introduced key words:

> To you therefore who *believe* (is) the *honor*.
> (1 Pet. 2:7a)

4. In the second quotation (Ps. 118:22), four previous key words reappear:

> The *stone* that was *rejected* by the *builders*,
> this one has become the head of the *corner*.
> (1 Pet. 2:7b)

5. In the third quotation (Isa. 8:14), one previous key word and one new key word appear:

> The *stone* that makes them <u>stumble</u>,
> and the rock that causes a scandal. (1 Pet. 2:8a)

6. The subsequent explanatory comments connect with four previous key words:

> They *stumble* by disobeying the word, unto which they were destined.
> But you are an *elect* race, a kingdom of *priesthood*, a *holy* nation, a people for his possession, that you might declare abroad the praises of the one who called you out of darkness into his awesome light. (1 Pet. 2:8b–9)

There are so many key words in this single passage—ten, to be exact!

stone	priesthood
stumble	holy
rejected	corner
elect	built up
honorable	believes

Ten different words deliberately repeated in the interpretive remarks provide insight into the rich theology of this passage. It is difficult to comprehend the whole of the theology being communicated. But without some awareness of the key-word methodology, attempting to comprehend the message of the text would be even more difficult.

Summary on the key-word methodology. The role of key words in connection with quotations from the OT in the NT is quite significant. Taking proper notice of this phenomenon can help the modern exegete better understand the meaning intended by the various authors. It may also help in determining the emphasis underlying the biblical text, which can be quite significant for a proper appreciation of the message of the inspired Scripture.

Conclusion

In this article, new areas for exploring the NT's perspective on the OT from both a macrocosmic and a microcosmic perspective have been proposed. On the one hand, a sample of general statements in the NT have displayed the NT's conviction that the totality of the OT Scriptures anticipates Christ and the realities of the new covenant. As a consequence, analyzing specifically quoted materials from the OT in the NT, even in light of their larger OT context, will not suffice to provide all the substance necessary for a full NT biblical theology. Instead, the whole of the OT must be investigated as anticipating the whole of NT realities. At the same time, the microcosmic details of NT quotations as seen in the key-word methodology indicate an additional area for exploration. The biblical author's purpose in his quotation will become clearer as the contemporary interpreter considers the specific key words on which the new-covenant writer focuses his attention.

It is hoped that this exploratory article may stimulate fresh research into the riches of the NT's perspective on the OT. May the continued investigation of these two covenantal documents reveal more and more of the fullness of the gospel embodied in the person and work of our Lord Jesus Christ.

Bibliography. Beale, G. K., and S. M. McDonough, "Revelation," in *CNTUOT*, 1081–1161; Dodd, C. H., *According to the Scriptures: The Sub-structure of New Testament Theology* (Nisbet, 1952); Dodd, *The Epistle of Paul to the Romans*, MNTC (Hodder & Stoughton, 1932); Kelly, J. N. D., *A Commentary on the Epistles of Peter and Jude* (Baker, 1981); Kelly, *A Commentary on the Pastoral Epistles* (Hendrickson, 1987); Knight, G. W., III, *The Pastoral Epistles*, NIGTC (Eerdmans, 1992); Robertson, O. P., *The Final Word* (Banner of Truth, 1993); Robertson, *The Israel of God* (P&R, 2000); Stonehouse, N. B., *The Witness of Matthew and Mark to Christ* (Grand Rapids: Eerdmans, 1944); Warfield, B. B., "'God-Inspired Scripture,'" in *The Inspiration and Authority of the Bible* (Presbyterian and Reformed, 1967), 245–96; Warfield, "The Terms 'Scripture' and 'Scriptures' as Employed in the New Testament," in *The Inspiration and Authority of the Bible* (Presbyterian and Reformed, 1967), 229–41.

O. Palmer Robertson

Numbers, Book of

Numbers supplies the fourth book of the Pentateuch, traditionally attributed to Moses (hence the common name, Fourth Book of Moses). The association with Moses places the book's events in the late second millennium BC, and the putative first audience would be the generation of Israel that followed Joshua across the Jordan River. Each subsequent audience should then see themselves as the heirs of this first audience.

Essential Features of the Book of Numbers

Composition. The question of how Numbers came to be composed is part of the larger question of how the Pentateuch came to be written and ascribed to Moses. A full review is not possible here, but several remarks are appropriate. First, the theories about the history of composition are driven by perceived tensions and contradictions, which lead to the conclusion that potentially disparate sources were put together with varying levels of success at smoothing (see, e.g., Friedman). If a sympathetic literary approach could show that the perceived tensions are actually compatible with a coherent reading, these tensions lose value as evidence for the composition process. Such literary approaches need not lead to a traditional position: for example, Roger Whybray argues for a single author, probably in the sixth century BC (the time of the Babylonian exile). Second, many of the reconstructed histories of composition point to features of the text that might seem more at home in an era much later than that of Moses, perhaps even as late as the exilic or postexilic eras. If, however, the material fits better with the period preceding Rehoboam's rule, then that also limits the role of a long process of composition. (For more discussion, see Wenham, *Exploring*, 159–85; Vogt, 130–36.) Third, the presentation in Ezra 3:2; 7:6, 10; Neh. 8:1–8 (to name no others) implies that the Torah is a known entity, and that Ezra is to expound and enforce something that already exists, rather than to create something new. The role of the Torah as canon means that it was to be read aloud in the regular worship gatherings of Israel and Judah, and this usage suggests that genuine inconsistencies are unlikely, and also that its authority is unlikely to be arbitrary (for a sociological defense of invoking the canon, see C. J. Collins, *Reading*, 201–4).

In any case, there is no disputing that Jews in the Second Temple era, as well as the early Christians, read Numbers as part of a coherent Pentateuch that originated from Moses, and that their use of the book reflects that reading.

Structure and message. Numbers in its present form serves as a portion of the Pentateuch, and any discussion of structure and message must start there. The name "Pentateuch" reflects the traditional division of the Torah into five books. Nevertheless, this division may obscure the connection between the books—namely, the narrative flow of the Pentateuch:

1. (Genesis) Backstory: creation, fall, Abraham's family winds up in Egypt
2. (Exodus–Numbers) Journey from Egypt to the border of Canaan
   Exodus: From Egypt to Sinai
   Leviticus: Encamped at Sinai
   Numbers: From Sinai to the Jordan River
3. (Deuteronomy) Exhortation before crossing the Jordan River

The connection between Exodus, Leviticus, and Numbers is so strong that Hendrik Koorevaar has argued that we should treat them as one book. On the other hand, there are clear boundaries at the beginning and close of each book—but Koorevaar's point helps to manage some of the perceived difficulties of Numbers. The differing components of the books also serve to distinguish them. The author (or compiler) has inserted into his accounts of events in Exodus-Leviticus-Numbers the laws that will govern Israel's corporate life, but in differing proportions: in Leviticus the laws dominate, in Exodus they are a major feature, and in Numbers they figure largely but not overwhelmingly. Genesis has very little of these laws, though a number of its events do explain the place of certain Israelite practices, and it offers the historical justification for Israel's claim to the land. Deuteronomy is largely sermonic in form, consisting of addresses preached by Moses to all Israel just before his death and not long before the conquest of the land under the leadership of Joshua. Its flavor is motivational, urging Israel's faithful and heartfelt obedience to the covenant laws given during the previous forty years; its theology is focused on convincing Israel to trust and obey, and to conquer the land.

The two most common outlines for the book follow either the geography or the chronology. The geographical outline observes the role of travel:

Text	Contents
1:1–10:10	Preparing to depart Sinai
10:11–25:18	Departing Sinai for the promised land, traveling
26–36	Preparing to enter from the plains of Moab

The chronological outline makes the two census-takings the key structuring device (see Olson, 5–6; Sakenfeld, 8–11):

Text	Contents
1–25	The old generation of rebellion
26–36	The new generation of hope

This chronological approach finds the first section, dealing with the generation that left Egypt, to be largely pessimistic about their faith and loyalty (they do, after all, rebel at the report of the ten scouts [chaps. 13–14]). Their children's generation is the focus of the second section, and "new life and hope, not rebellion and death, characterize this new generation's story" (Olson, 5).

Certainly the two census-takings (or military numberings) are key structural features, serving as key events in the overarching narrative of the Pentateuch. Further, the itinerary in Num. 33 recaps the Egypt-to-plains-of-Moab narrative from the perspective of locations. It is therefore simpler to say that the *demands of the narrative* provide the principle that explains the contents and organization that we find in Numbers. This principle also explains the sound insights of the geographical approach to structure; that structure derives from the itinerary, as the chronological approach does. The geographical approach captures better the nature of the narrative in the book.

The main action in 1:1–10:10 is predominately instructions, with the leading event being God speaking. Then in 10:11, *movement* gets under way. Then in 26:1 the action is again largely divine speech, delivering instructions (which begin with a census, as in chap. 1).

Within this narrative framework, the rebellion in Num. 14 is a decisive turning point, involving God's refusal to allow any members of the first generation (besides Joshua and Caleb) to enter the land, and his sentence that they must remain in the desert until that generation has all died out (another thirty-eight years). At the same time, because God heeds Moses's appeal on behalf of the people (14:19), he sustains Israel's existence and reaffirms his commitment to bless the world through them (14:20–21). The ten unfaithful scouts die immediately, but the majority of Israel remains alive to manage their families and flocks during the desert sojourn (14:37). Hence, while the overall evidence tells against Dennis Olson's structure for the book, many of his literary observations merit careful consideration. For example, this may be one reason why so few incidents from the additional thirty-eight years are recounted in Num. 15–20: the ratio of narration time to elapsed time drops off precipitously. Perhaps, then, the main thing to say about this period (other than the reaffirmation of the Aaronic priesthood [chaps. 16–17]) is that the generation died off. The narrator returns to recounting more details, with a higher narration-time to elapsed-time ratio, in 20:1, as the desert sojourn is ending.

Hermeneutics of Numbers

Numbers assumes the events and instructions of Genesis–Leviticus, and this can create problems in that it sometimes seems to offer different prescriptions for the sacrifices. Since the primary use of the Pentateuch is for public reading and exposition, it is unlikely that a flat contradiction will be the best explanation for these differences. For example, Num. 15:1–31 specifies grain and drink offerings that are supplements to the sacrifices; Lev. 1–7 does not include them. Although Jacob Milgrom (118) suggests that this difference reflects a development from the wilderness to a more agricultural setting, it is simpler to suppose that the Numbers texts elaborate those in Leviticus. Deuteronomy takes for granted the basic story line of Numbers, with some amplifications and slightly differing emphases in places. For example, Deut. 2:5 adds to Num. 20:14–21 the divine command to Israel not to contend with Edom; Numbers makes no mention of a similar command concerning Moab (Deut. 2:9).

Other texts in the Hebrew Bible cite the events in Numbers as facts with enormous significance. For example, the Transjordan tribes must fulfill their pledge and are praised for doing so (Num. 32:16–27; Josh. 1:12–18; 22:1–9). Caleb reminds Joshua of the special role the two men have as the faithful spies (Num. 14:24, 30; Josh. 14:6–15). Joshua obeys the requirement to allocate the land fairly (Num. 34:17–18; Josh. 14:1), and to set aside Levitical cities, including cities of refuge (Num. 35:1–8; Josh. 20–21; cf. also 1 Chron. 6:54–81). The cities of refuge find no further explicit mention in the rest of the canon (although such cities as Hebron and Shechem do figure in). Several passages in Psalms also reflect on the events in Numbers: for example, Pss. 78:15–16 and 95:8 link the water episodes (Exod. 17:6–7; Num. 20:10–13) as standard instances of both the people's unbelief and God's provision. Psalm 78:25–31 recalls God's sending of quail to supplement the manna (Num. 11:4–35): there must be something wrong with people who dislike that kind of food! Doubtless the suggestion of the cravers that the conditions were better in Egypt supports the psalm—their craving for something other than what God has provided will lead back to slavery by glamorizing the hideous conditions of their servitude. Psalm 95:10 recalls the forty years of discipline that Numbers recounts; and Ps. 106:24–33 remembers several episodes, such as the rebellion and its sentence (14:26–35), the incident with the Baal of Peor (25:1–15), and the water conflict at Meribah, which turned out poorly for Moses (20:1–13). The psalms repeatedly mention the rebellion and its punishment, together with the water conflicts, because their lessons about the dire consequences of unfaithfulness are worth hammering home.

Numbers in the NT

NT authors draw on Numbers in several modes: they accept its story of Israel's journey from Sinai to the Jordan River and refer to episodes in that story (generally for analogical purposes); they use terms and concepts influenced by Numbers; they build on the messianic ideas found here and elsewhere in the Hebrew Bible; and they cite or allude to particular texts in the course of their arguments, some of which require their own treatment.

Story. In 1 Cor. 10:1–11 Paul lists a series of things that happened "as examples" (v. 6, *typoi*; v. 11, *typikōs*), and the series includes several incidents from Numbers:

- "the Rock" (1 Cor. 10:4; cf. Num. 20:7–11)
- "overthrown in the wilderness" (1 Cor. 10:5 ESV; cf. Num. 14:16, 29, 37)
- "desire evil" (1 Cor. 10:6 ESV; cf. Num. 11:4; Pss. 78:24–31; 106:14–15)

- "sexual immorality," "twenty-three thousand fell" (1 Cor. 10:8; cf. Num. 25:1, 9)
- "snakes" (1 Cor. 10:9; cf. Num. 21:6–9)
- "grumble" (1 Cor. 10:10; cf. Num. 14:2)

Generally, these citations follow the way the Hebrew Bible has already referred to the incidents. This survey will add a few remarks to that discussion above and note some further examples.

The narrative of Eldad and Medad (11:26–29) provides the template for reporting an incident in the Gospels, in which Jesus must caution his disciples against narrowness as well (Mark 9:38–40; Luke 9:49–50, both of which use the same verb "stop" as in the LXX of Num. 11:28 [*kōlyō*]).

An incident of high prominence for NT writers is the report of the ten unfaithful spies, and the penalties that derived from it (Num. 14:29, 32). For Israel, the enduring message was to be sure that they, and those who lead their corporate life, are seeking genuine faithfulness (as Pss. 78; 95; 106 insist). The crucial distinction is between membership in the people, and actual belief in the Lord's promises (Num. 14:11). NT writers invoke the same principle in admonishing their young congregations: Paul warns his audience in Corinth not to imitate the example of the unbelieving (1 Cor. 10:5, 10, echoing Num. 14:2, 16 LXX). Hebrews similarly cautions its Jewish Christian readers to hold fast to their faith, likening their potential apostasy to the unbelief of that generation of Israel (Heb. 3:16–19; see also Jude 5). In traditional theological terms, this relates to the distinction between the sign and the thing signified: the sign should foster true faith and faithfulness, but one may have the sign and, tragically, lack the signified.

Another event is the rebellion led by Korah. The second census mentions this rebellion as a significant event, noting under its entry for the families descended from Reuben that the Reubenites Dathan and Abiram allied themselves with the Levite Korah (Num. 26:9–11). Some have inferred from the way that other texts mention the incident, that two originally discrete rebellions have been combined here (e.g., Milgrom, 415), but the evidence does not support this inference. For example, Deut. 11:6; Ps. 106:17 mention only Dathan and Abiram; but Ps. 106:18 goes on to refer to fire and their "company" (*ʿēdâ*, cf. Num. 16:5), which points to Korah's group as well. Logically, the nonmention of something is not the same as its denial; and the rhetorical purpose of Deut. 11:6 in context is more strengthened by reference to Dathan and Abiram's complaint and disposal than to Korah's. Ben Sira's account (Sir. 45:18) mentions all three. The NT refers only to Korah (Jude 11). Generally, these treat the incident as a noteworthy rebellion; the punishment on the rebels should serve as a warning against carrying out anything even remotely like it. Psalm 106 also celebrates God's persistent devotion to preserving Israel as a people.

It is possible that in 1 Cor. 10:4 Paul alludes to the water conflict at Meribah (Num. 20:2–13), perhaps with the earlier water conflict mixed in (Exod. 17:1–7): "They drank from the spiritual Rock that followed them, and the Rock was Christ" (1 Cor. 10:4 ESV). The Greek term "rock" (*petra*) occurs in the LXX of both incidents (Exod. 17:6, and cf. Ps. 104:41 [ET 105:41]; Num. 20:8, 10, 11). By Paul's placement (right after exodus and manna, 1 Cor. 10:3) the earlier account is more likely, but the additional "followed them" might suggest that there is some sense in which both rocks are in view. Roy Ciampa and Brian Rosner (724) document the rabbinic notion that the same rock accompanied Israel in the wilderness, but it is not certain that such a "legend" was available in the time of Paul (see the cautious conclusions in Thiselton, 727–30). For our purposes, we can simply note that *if* Paul alludes to a "legend" of some sort, that does not imply that he *believed* it as historical, any more than my referring to Paul Bunyan in an argument would imply I believe the legends about him. Paul's point is that the Corinthian Christians are in danger of committing an analogous kind of rebellion against the gracious Savior in their disrespect toward Paul.

As for Num. 21:4–9, perhaps the best-known allusion is Jesus's likening of his own being "lifted up" (*hypsōthēnai*) to Moses's "lifting up" of the serpent in the wilderness; the point of similarity is the benefit that comes to the one who would look with faith (John 3:14–15; cf. Wis. 16:7, 12). Although the Greek verb "lift up" does not appear in the LXX of our passage, Jesus's statement is a fair paraphrase for what Moses is to do ("set it on a pole," Num. 21:8–9 ESV) and fits well with the Johannine theme of Jesus anticipating his manner of death (John 3:14; 8:26; 12:32, 34), in which the humiliation of the cross is actually an exaltation.

Numbers presents Balaam as a complex person (Num. 22–24; 31:8, 16); he can sound very obedient to God, but ultimately that is undone by his advice to Balak. The further reflections on Balaam in the Hebrew Bible focus on him as the thwarted agent of Balak (Deut. 23:3–4; Josh. 24:9–10; Mic. 6:5; Neh. 13:2), or else as the sinister sorcerer and adviser of corruption (Num. 31:16; Josh. 13:22). NT authors tend to use the latter side (2 Pet. 2:15–16; Jude 11; Rev. 2:14). Mainstream Judaism likewise came to focus on the sinister side of Balaam, calling him "Balaam the wicked" and contrasting his disciples with those of Abraham (m. Avot 5:19). Josephus (*Ant.* 4.102–30), by contrast, allows more of Balaam's complexity to show through. (For a helpful survey, see Savelle.) Authors will emphasize one aspect or the other in light of their particular rhetorical goals; to stress one does not of itself deny the other. To set these two aspects over against each other, as Baruch Levine (2:154) seems to do, is to miss this basic point.

Concepts and terms. The Nazirite institution (Num. 6:1–21) is treated as known in the NT: John the Baptist is apparently to be a Nazirite from before birth (Luke 1:15), and Paul both took a Nazirite vow and sponsored several Jewish Christians who had taken such vows (Acts 18:18; 21:26). There are apparently two types of Nazirites: those who voluntarily become Nazirites by virtue of a "special vow" (usually for a limited stretch of time), and those who are dedicated before birth. The instructions in Numbers deal only with the former, but both appear in the biblical narratives. When the angel of the Lord announces to Manoah's childless wife that she will bear a son, he explicitly says that the child will be "a Nazirite to God from the womb"; not only shall no razor come upon his head, but the mother is to "drink no wine or intoxicating drink, and eat nothing unclean" (Judg. 13:3–5 ESV). There are slight differences from the expectations outlined in the law: in Num. 6:5 "no *razor* [*taʿar*] shall *pass over* [*ʿābar*] his head," while in Judg. 13:5 "no *razor* [*môrâ*] shall *go up* [*ʿālâ*] on his head"; the *mother* is forbidden wine and other intoxicants, with nothing said about Samson's practices; nor is there an exclusion of all grape products, nor any mention of uncleanness due to contact with a corpse. The birth of Samuel is preceded by his mother's vow that she will give him to the Lord all the days of his life and "no razor shall go up on his head" (1 Sam. 1:11 AT, as in Judg. 13:5). The LXX adds that he shall drink neither wine nor intoxicating drinks. Samuel, therefore, probably fits in the same category of Nazirite from before birth: that is how some rabbis cited in the Mishnah (m. Naz. 9:5) interpret his calling, as does Sir. 46:12 (in Hebrew, not in Greek; see further Chepey).

John the Baptist presents a similar case (Luke 1:13–17): the angel declares that he is appointed for a special calling, and that "he must not drink wine or strong drink" (v. 15 ESV), the Greek being very close to the LXX of 1 Sam. 1:11 and Judg. 13:4, 7, 14, and reminiscent as well of Num. 6:3.

The "voluntary" Nazirites appear in 1 Macc. 3:49 as "Nazirites who had completed their days" (cf. Num. 6:5, 13). It seems likely that Paul had also taken such a vow, after which he "shaved his head" (Acts 18:18 AT), although he did this "at Cenchreae" and not at Jerusalem (perhaps because his period was over, consistent with Num. 6:18). (In Numbers LXX the word for "shave" is *xyraō*, while in Acts 18:18 the word is *keirō*; but the reference to a "vow" in Acts, as well as the parallelism between *xyraō* and *keirō* in Mic. 1:16 LXX points to this being a Nazirite vow.) In Acts 21:23–26, Paul agrees to pay the expenses of men who "have a vow . . . so that they may shave their heads" (NASB). The Greek here echoes that of Num. 6:18, so the Nazirite vow is probably in view. Thus, some Jewish Christians continued to employ this institution, while there is little or no evidence that they applied it to gentiles—which also matches the way that m. Naz. 9:1 excludes gentiles (lit., "worshipers of stars") from the institution. Eusebius (*Hist. eccl.* 2.23.5) records a story from Hegesippus (d. ca. 175–89) about James the brother of Jesus that makes him sound like a Nazirite from the womb (although Chepey, 174–77, discusses the problems with this account that make it hard to accept).

Numbers uses the notion of the divine Spirit resting upon someone and empowering that person for service (11:17, 25), which clarifies what the Spirit is doing on the first Christian Pentecost (Acts 2:3) and in subsequent "gifts" (1 Cor. 12:1).

Numbers uses the intuitive concept of sinning "unintentionally" (15:22–31). The LXX rendering *akousiōs* has as its opposite *hekousiōs*, which the NT uses to designate not simply a willful sin but one that repudiates divine lordship. The author of Hebrews warns his Jewish Christian audience that they run the risk of committing the equivalent of the high-handed sin, for which there is no effective sacrifice, should they drop away from their Christian faith in order to avoid the trouble that comes from their fellow Jews (Heb. 10:26). He uses the expression "go on sinning *deliberately*" (ESV; *hekousiōs . . . hamartanontōn*), where the Greek corresponds to the opposite of "unintentionally" (but here with the nuance "willfully" or "defiantly"). This author's overall stance toward his audience mixes this genuine warning with a pastorally warm optimism (Heb. 10:19–25). The usage here resembles that of 2 Macc. 14:3, where the term carries not simply the nuance of "intentionally" but "defiantly" or "willfully."

The Greek rendering for the "tassels" that devout Israelites were to wear (*ṣîṣît*, Num. 15:38) is *kraspedon*, properly "fringe." Jesus wears such tassels (Matt. 9:20; 14:36; Mark 6:56; Luke 8:44), emblematic of his Jewish faithfulness, but he also condemns the ostentatious display of such scrupulosity (Matt. 23:5).

Hebrews 9:4 seems to suggest that "Aaron's rod" (Num. 17:10 AT) was actually placed inside the ark, and not simply inside the most holy place. If that is so, then for it to fit (Exod. 25:10), it would need to be the length of a familiar walking stick, rather than a staff the height of a man.

The Christian term "baptism" has a background in Jewish ceremonial usage, where Sir. 34:30 (NETS) uses this word for washing after contact with a dead body (Num. 19:11–13; cf. also Ezek. 36:25, using the same Hebrew verb for the application of the water, *zrq*; see C. J. Collins, "Baptism," 13). That shines light on the ceremonial function of baptism as presented in the NT, and why it can be the vehicle of a transition from death to life. Hence, Heb. 10:22 likely refers both to baptism and to Ezek. 36:25 ("clean/pure water"). The previous chapter (Heb. 9:13, 19) evokes the instructions from Num. 19 for cleansing in a straightforward fashion (see Num. 19:6, 9, 17).

Numbers has the first attestation of the expression "sheep without a shepherd" (27:17), which describes a body of people helpless and vulnerable for lack of a responsible leader. Such a leader, however, has more than a military function; he serves as a "shepherd," which can be used for a civic leader but also suggests the importance of leading the people in carrying out their calling as a holy congregation (e.g., Ezek. 34:23). "Sheep that have no shepherd" became a common way to describe Israel without such consecrated leadership (1 Kings 22:17 ESV; cf. Ezek. 34:5; Zech. 10:2; Matt. 9:36 // Mark 6:34). The Hebrew of these texts varies a little, which indicates that the phraseology is not fixed. Further, the Greek renderings are likewise not identical, and the Gospels use the explicit verb *echō* ("have") where the underlying Hebrew or Aramaic would use the dative (cf. Num. 27:17 MT and Peshitta for the Gospel texts). These other texts are therefore not "quotations" of Num. 27:17 as such; rather, they employ the same proverbial image.

Messianic expectation. Many take Num. 24:17 ("A star will come out of Jacob") as messianic, and this reading is common in the NT era (see J. J. Collins, *Scepter*, 71; Alter, 814; Wenham, *Numbers*, 179), and this may explain Jesus's self-designation (Rev. 22:16). The earlier oracles of Balaam anticipate Israel's eventual dominion over other nations, especially over those that opposed Israel (cf. 23:24; 24:8–9). This oracle takes the subject further, not only in listing some of the surrounding nations but also in referring to what seems like a particular person from Israel who will accomplish these things (24:17). This is highly consistent with earlier material that can be considered messianic, in the sense that it envisions an Israelite ruler ("scepter") who will subdue the gentiles into his empire (e.g., Gen. 49:10; see further Alexander, *Genealogies*, and *Observations*). This oracle, however, stresses the victory over the adversaries and leaves the topic of bringing God's light to them for other texts.

Specific texts. A handful of particular texts cite or allude to phrases in Numbers in an incidental fashion, and in some cases call for special comment.

Numbers 9:12 contains the prohibition against breaking the bones of the Passover sacrifice (cf. Exod. 12:46), and similar wording also appears in Ps. 34:20. John 19:36 interprets the fact that the Roman soldiers did not finish Jesus off by breaking his bones to be the fulfillment of "the Scripture": "Not one of his bones will be broken." Psalm 33:21 LXX is quite close to the Greek in John, with its passive "be broken" (*syntribēsetai*); this would emphasize that Jesus died as a righteous sufferer, whom God would certainly vindicate. At the same time, the LXX of Exod. 12:46 is also quite close, with its singular "bone" (*ostoun*), in which case the Gospel writer portrays Jesus as the Passover lamb. For the argument that John has combined both themes in John 19:36, see Köstenberger ("John," 503–4). The degree to which Passover imagery lies behind John's presentation of Jesus is, however, controversial, since "the Lamb of God, who takes away the sin of the world" (John 1:29) alludes to Jesus as the sin-bearing sacrifice using the Greek word for "lamb" found in places such as Isa. 53:7 (*amnos*) rather than the words found in Exod. 12:3–5 (*probaton* and *arēn*). The Passover is not an atoning sacrifice (see further C. J. Collins, "Eucharist," 21–23).

Numbers 12:7 describes Moses as "faithful in all my house." Hebrews 3:2, 5 use this phrase both to affirm Moses's role as a faithful servant in God's house and to identify Jesus as more than that—namely, the Son, who is also the builder of the house (3:3–6). To liken Jesus to the builder of the house, and then to note that the builder of all things is God, is consistent with this author's application to Jesus of biblical passages about God (as in 1:10–12). Hebrews does not play down Moses in order to promote Jesus; rather, it stresses that Jesus is the one whom Moses faithfully served, so that its audience of Jewish Christians will continue to follow Jesus without fearing that they are abandoning Moses.

In Num. 15:35–36 Israel executes a transgressor "outside the camp." The writer of Hebrews invites his readers to join Jesus in his place of reproach "outside the camp" (13:13), echoing the way the sentence on Jesus treated him (wrongly) as a blasphemer. Luke's narration of Stephen's death also echoes this theme (Acts 7:58).

Numbers 16:5 LXX reads, "The Lord knows those who are his." The MT has "make known" (*wəyōdaʿ*), a *hiphil*. The LXX (*kai egnō*) apparently read it as a *qal wayyiqtol* (*wayyēdaʿ*) or perfect with simple *waw* (*wəyādaʿ*). This Greek rendering appears in 2 Tim. 2:19, where the context invites Timothy to trust his ultimate vindication as a faithful teacher of the truth (as over against improper claimants) and therefore not to lose heart, which serves as an application of the ideas at work.

Numbers 25:9 presents us with "the missing thousand." Paul warns the Corinthian Christians not to commit whoredom (*porneuō*), "as some of them did, and twenty-three thousand fell in a single day" (1 Cor. 10:8 ESV; cf. Num. 25:1 LXX: *ekporneuō*). Paul apparently sees the same principles at work governing the Christian community as governed the ancient Israelite one, but his mention of twenty-three thousand rather than twenty-four thousand in Num. 25:9 presents a difficulty. (A few NT manuscripts do read twenty-four thousand, but they may be ignored.) Possibly Paul thought that the plague lasted more than a day, with its casualties spread out over time. Josephus reports the number as "no fewer than fourteen thousand" (*Ant.* 4.155: *ouk elattous tetrakischiliōn kai myriōn*). Or, possibly, Paul somehow fetched the number from the census of the Levites (Num. 26:62), whether for unknown symbolic reasons, or from memory. However, Paul's Greek is *eikosi treis chiliades*, which differs in format from the LXX of both Num. 25:9 (*tessares kai eikosi chiliades*) and 26:62 (*treis kai eikosi chiliades*), so neither Paul nor Josephus has offered a simple quotation from the LXX. It is also possible that these are both round numbers. For survey and analysis of the possibilities, see Anthony Thiselton (739–40).

Thiselton helpfully observes, "It is worth noting that the patristic writers seem to be untroubled by this verse." Rohintan Mody suggests that Paul has connected the three thousand who died in the golden-calf incident (Exod. 32:28) with the number that some Jewish interpreters infer have died by execution here; the result is probably too complicated for Paul to have expected his readers to understand it, but no simple solution has found favor. In any case, the Corinthian Christians (and all others) would do well, first, to refrain from congratulating themselves over their tolerance of what defiles the whole people (1 Cor. 5:6–8), and second, to be zealous for the better gifts, that they might build the body up in loyal service to the Lord (1 Cor. 12:31; 14:1, 12).

Numbers 33:55 warns that the Canaanites whom Israel allows to remain will be "barbs in your eyes and thorns in your sides" (ESV). These are far more than mere annoyances; they serve as a picture of something that, if allowed free reign, will destroy any possibility of continued life (because they will induce Israel to violate what is sacred). Even though we cannot be sure just what plants supplied the barbs and thorns (*śikkîm* and *ṣənînim*), the image is clear when we consider the texts that echo this one (Josh. 23:13; Judg. 2:3; Ezek. 28:24), which include the pictures of a snare and a trap. Further, if the LXX can guide, the thorns are serious: the words *skolops* and *bolis* indicate something sharp and spikey, likened to a stake or a javelin. The canonical testimony is that this seduction is just what happens (cf. Ps. 106:34–39), which does eventually lead to drastic judgments on the people (cf. 2 Kings 17:7–19; 23:26–27, for the historian's verdict on both Israel and Judah). Paul appropriates the image of the barbs and thorns, using the LXX rendering (*skolops*) for some experience of his, a "thorn in the flesh" (2 Cor. 12:7). Specialists on Paul have debated just what he means by this expression: Is it a temptation or sin, or some illness or disability, or hardships and persecutions, or demonic attack, or something else? The arguments are involved, and Paul's words do not enable those outside the original communication to identify his referent. Raymond Collins (239–40) wisely remarks, "In the end, it is impossible to know what Paul meant by this intriguing image. The Corinthians themselves may not have known the real meaning of the metaphor." But, to the extent that Paul's image is tied to the LXX usage, it denotes some kind of hindrance, whether to Paul's health, or faithfulness, or ministry (or some combination).

Bibliography. Alexander, T. D., "Further Observations on the Term 'Seed' in Genesis," *TynBul* 48, no. 2 (1997): 363–67; Alexander, "Genealogies, Seed, and the Compositional Unity of Genesis," *TynBul* 44, no. 2 (1993): 255–70; Alter, R., *The Five Books of Moses* (Norton, 2004); Chepey, S., *Nazirites in Late Second Temple Judaism*, AGJU 60 (Brill, 2005); Ciampa, R., and B. Rosner, "1 Corinthians," in *CNTUOT*, 695–752; Collins, C. J., "The Eucharist as Christian Sacrifice," *WTJ* 66 (2004): 1–23; Collins, *Numbers*, ZECOT (Zondervan, 2024); Collins, *Psalms*, ESVEC (Crossway, 2022); Collins, *Reading Genesis Well* (Zondervan, 2018); Collins, "What Does Baptism Do for Anyone? (Part 1)," *Presbyterion* 38, no. 1 (2012): 1–33; Collins, J. J., *The Scepter and the Star* (Eerdmans, 2010); Collins, R. F., *Second Corinthians*, Paideia (Baker Academic, 2013); Friedman, R. E., *The Bible with Sources Revealed* (HarperCollins, 2003); Koorevaar, H., "The Books of Exodus, Leviticus and Numbers, and the Macro-structural Problem of the Pentateuch," in *The Books of Leviticus and Numbers*, ed. T. Römer, BETL 215 (Peeters, 2008), 423–53; Köstenberger, A., "John," in *CNTUOT*, 415–512; Levine, B., *Numbers*, 2 vols., AB (Doubleday, 1993, 2000); Milgrom, J., *Numbers*, JPSTC (Jewish Publication Society of America, 1990); Mody, R., "'The Case of the Missing Thousand,'" *Chm* 121 (2007): 61–79; Olson, D. T., *Numbers*, IBC (John Knox, 1996); Sakenfeld, K. D., *Journeying with God*, ITC (Eerdmans, 1995); Savelle, C. H., "Canonical and Extracanonical Portraits of Balaam," *BSac* 166 (2009): 387–404; Thiselton, A., *The First Epistle to the Corinthians*, NIGTC (Eerdmans, 2000); Vogt, P. T., *Interpreting the Pentateuch*, HOTE (Kregel, 2009); Wenham, G. J., *Exploring the Old Testament* (InterVarsity, 2003); Wenham, *Numbers*, TOTC (InterVarsity, 1981); Whybray, R. N., *The Making of the Pentateuch*, JSOTSup 53 (Sheffield Academic, 1989).

C. John Collins

Obadiah, Book of

Attention attracted by Obadiah has mainly concerned the complex issues of authorship, date, unity, and canonical placement to the neglect of its inner-biblical connections and theology. This has been unfortunate, since Obadiah is replete with intertextual parallels to other parts of the OT, not least to the Jacob-Esau narrative in Genesis, which informs its theological message.

Literary Context

Literary composition and unity. The book of Obadiah reflects a diversity in grammatical style and imagery, as well as differing perspectives on Edom and Israel and their relations to surrounding nations. Critical scholarship has interpreted the diversity as reflecting composite layers in the book (cf. Allen, 133–37; Raabe, *Obadiah*, 16–17, for helpful overviews). However, the various difficulties put forth are not insurmountable. As Raabe (*Obadiah*, 17) notes, "It is precisely the nature of prophetic discourse to make sudden shifts on all levels of language, including style and imagery, and to juxtapose multiple, divergent, and even dissonant perspectives in much the same way as in the use of poetic parallelism." Indeed, a highly stylized, concatenated pattern reveals a coherent structural unity across each of the main sections of the book (cf. Raabe, *Obadiah*, 20).

Literary features. Obadiah is located in the literary context of the Twelve Prophets. More specifically, it fits within the prophetic subcategory of an "oracle against the nations" (cf. Raabe, "Oracles"), being in this case an oracle against Edom. The book presents itself as "the vision of Obadiah" (v. 1a), orienting the reader's interpretation in two main ways. First, the vision is singular, encouraging the reader to interpret the book as a coherent, unified whole. Second, the noun *ḥăzôn* is a *terminus technicus* for "a prophetic revelation," indicating that the vision comes directly from Yahweh, as seen in the messenger formula (v. 1b). According to the frequency of the so-called prose particles (direct-object marker, relative pronoun, and definite article), the book divides neatly into two genres: poetry (vv. 1–18) and prose (vv. 19–21).

Literary structure. A variety of opinions exists in Bible translations and commentaries concerning the structure of Obadiah. Three main sections are discernible (vv. 1–9, 10–18, 19–21), with the first two sections containing two units each (vv. 1–4, 5–9 and 10–14, 15–18). Clearly, vv. 1–18 are set off from vv. 19–21 due to the shift in genre from poetry to prose. This is reinforced by the marker of climax: "for the LORD has spoken" (v. 18 ESV). The two uses of "declares the LORD" (vv. 4, 8) may serve as structural markers to close their respective units (vv. 1–4, 5–9). The two units connect grammatically by the *ʾim* particle (vv. 4, 5) and rhetorical questions (vv. 3, 5); they also connect thematically by the verb "deceive" (*nšʾ*; vv. 3, 7). The third unit (vv. 10–14) is marked off by the introduction of a new topic: the hostile behavior by Esau-Edom against his "brother Jacob" (v. 10a). This unit focuses on two "days" of violence against Judah: one past (vv. 10–11), the other future (vv. 12–14). The string of eight negative exhortations gives the unit some internal coherence. Talk of the "day" (*yôm*) of Judah's calamity provides a natural segue for the introduction of the future day of the Lord (*yôm yhwh*) in the fourth unit (vv. 15–18). The day of the Lord will mean two different destinies for the "twin" nations: judgment for Esau-Edom, salvation for Jacob-Judah. The fifth and final unit (vv. 19–21) provides a prophetic commentary on the divine oracle (vv. 1–18) as the theme of land possession is brought to the fore. After the exile, Jacob-Judah will return to possess his land (v. 17c) and also the land of Esau-Edom (v. 19a). The unit climaxes with an affirmation of Yahweh's sovereignty, realized in the reversal of fortunes for Esau-Edom and Jacob-Judah in the unfolding divine economy.

Historical Context

Author. Obadiah's brief title contrasts with those of other Latter Prophets, which give information such as the prophet's place of origin, father's name, and occupation as well as the date and addressees of the prophetic messages. Obadiah's name, in both its short form (*ʿōbadyâ*) and long form (*ʿōbadyāhû*), means "servant of Yahweh." Some scholars have suggested that the name may simply be a symbolic title, "a pious invention to identify a prophetic fragment making up the Twelve" (Ackroyd, 2). However, given that the name Obadiah, in both its short and long versions, denominates twelve persons in the Hebrew Bible (1 Kings 18:1–16; 1 Chron. 27:19; 2 Chron. 34:12; 1 Chron. 7:3; 8:38 [= Neh. 9:44]; 12:9; 2 Chron. 17:7; Obad. 1; 1 Chron. 3:21; 9:16 [= Neh. 11:17]; Ezra 8:9 [= Neh. 10:5]; Neh. 12:25), it seems best to take this reference as a personal name. The Talmud (b. Sanh. 39b) identifies the prophet with the Obadiah in King Ahab's court, who met Elijah and saved many prophets from death (1 Kings 18:1–16). While this fits with the early date for the book of Obadiah, which is argued for below, the identification of these two Obadiahs can remain only at the level of proposal. What is certain, however, is that the Obadiah of this book was a devoted follower of Yahweh who "believed firmly in Yahweh's intervention in history and in the ultimate vindication of God's people" (Niehaus, 503).

Date. Three general positions on the historical setting of Obadiah have been proposed by scholars. The preexilic date locates Obadiah in the ninth century during the reign of Jehoram (852–841 BC; 2 Kings 8:20–22; 2 Chron. 21:16) or in the eighth century during the reign of Ahaz (732–716 BC; Amos 1:6, 9; 2 Chron. 28:16–18; cf. Keil and Delitzsch, 228–34; Niehaus, 497–99). The early to mid-exilic date views Obadiah as present during the fall of Jerusalem in 587 BC, which explains the prophet's impassioned outburst in vv. 12–14 (cf. Baker, 23; Wolff, 18–19). Several texts support the idea that the Edomites colluded with the Babylonians at the decisive moment in Judah's downfall (Ps. 137:7; Lam. 4:18–22; Ezek. 25:12–14; 35:1–15). The postexilic date generally situates Obadiah in the late sixth or early to mid-fifth century, when Edom had collapsed as a nation following the campaign of Nabonidus in 553 BC (Wellhausen, 214; Allen, 129–33), though some date it as late as the Nabatean Arab invasion that ended in 312 BC (Hitzig, 156).

The exilic and postexilic dates are attractive because they ground Obadiah's prophecy in recorded events in Judah's history. However, upon closer examination several problems surface with situating Obadiah in either of these two periods. First, the string of eight negative exhortations in vv. 12–14 makes little sense if the event to which the prohibitive commands refer—the fall of Jerusalem—is already in the past. As Niehaus (502) comments, "It would make no sense for Obadiah to command Edom *not* to do something it could not do, which is what Obadiah would be doing if he wrote during or after the exile." Allen's contention that the prophet is speaking rhetorically in a "highly imaginative fashion . . . of events in the past as if they were still present" (Allen, 156; cf. also Targum Pseudo-Jonathan) is unconvincing from the fact that this would be a unique use of negative *yiqtol* jussives in the Hebrew Bible.

Second, surrounding the string of eight negative exhortations are verses that concern Edom's violence against his brother Jacob in the past (vv. 10–11, 16), thus indicating that Obadiah writes at a point in history when Edom has already been guilty of violations against the fraternal relationship with Judah and still has potential to repeat such behavior in the future. Biblical data support the view that Edom's violence against Judah was not a one-off event but a pattern repeated over centuries. There were skirmishes during the reigns of David in the tenth century BC (2 Sam. 8:13–14; 1 Kings 11:15–18), Jehoram in the ninth (2 Kings 8:20–22; 2 Chron. 20:1–30; 21:8–17; cf. Pss. 79; 83), and Ahaz in the eighth (2 Kings 16:5–6; 2 Chron. 28:17). At different points, Philistines and Arabians invaded Judah, taking possessions and carrying away captives (cf. Amos 1:6, 9). Edom did likewise. Indeed, 2 Chron. 28:17 notes that by the time of Ahaz, Edom was at it "again" (*ʿôd*). Thus, locating Obadiah in the preexilic period (either in the ninth or eighth century) makes good sense of Obad. 10–14 regarding Edom's past and future actions against his twin-brother nation, Judah. As Keil and Delitzsch (234) comment, "If the act already performed was but one single outbreak of a prevailing disposition, and might be repeated on every fresh occasion, and possibly had already shown itself more than once, a warning against such an act could neither be regarded as out of place, nor as particularly striking." Moreover, strictly speaking, there is no explicit mention of Jerusalem's destruction in vv. 12–14; the expressions are general enough to be applicable to a hostile attack by foreign peoples on any occasion.

Third, while the placement of books in the Twelve is not strictly chronological, the books are generally placed in preexilic and postexilic groupings, with Obadiah among the older preexilic books. Obadiah's relation to Jeremiah further supports a preexilic dating. Significant overlap exists between Obad. 1–8 and Jer. 49:7–22, raising the question of the direction of dependence. Jeremiah's use of Obadiah seems most likely, rather than vice versa, for several reasons: (1) Jeremiah leans on earlier prophets for his oracles against the nations (e.g., Jer. 47 // Isa. 14:28–32; Jer. 48 // Isa. 15–16; Jer. 49:1–6 // Amos 1:3–5; Jer. 50–51 // Isa. 13–14); (2) Jeremiah has peculiar expressions and a characteristic style, none of which are found in Obadiah; (3) the overlapping material in Jeremiah is scattered and displays no coherent unit, unlike its appearance in Obad. 1–8 (Keil and Delitzsch, 229–30); and (4) Obad. 12–14 is most notably lacking in Jer. 49, which makes sense given that Jeremiah's oracle against Edom was written after the fall of Jerusalem (cf. Jer. 39). Since the prophet Jeremiah ministered in the late seventh century up to the early sixth century (627–587 BC), his selective use of Obadiah places the ministry of the latter prophet in an earlier period. Obadiah also predates Joel, as indicated by Joel's direct quotation of Obad. 17 followed by the words "as the Lord has said" (Joel 2:32). In sum, the position of Obadiah in the Twelve and its relation to Jeremiah and Joel support a preexilic date for the book.

Inner-biblical Interpretation in Obadiah

Possible examples. Paul Raabe (*Obadiah*, 32–33) observes that Obadiah exhibits parallel phraseology with twenty different books of the OT:

Obad. 1–4 // Jer. 49:14–16
Obad. 1e // Judg. 18:9; Jer. 6:4–5
Obad. 2a // Mal. 2:9
Obad. 3b // Jer. 48:28; Song 2:14
Obad. 3d // Jer. 21:13; 49:4
Obad. 4a // Job 39:27
Obad. 4b // Num. 24:21; Hab. 2:9
Obad. 4c // Amos 9:2
Obad. 5–6 // Jer. 49:9–10c
Obad. 7b–c // Jer. 20:10; 38:22
Obad. 7d // Ps. 41:9 (MT 41:10)
Obad. 7e // Deut. 32:28
Obad. 7e–8 // Jer. 49:7
Obad. 9b // Ezek. 25:13; 35:7
Obad. 10a // Joel 3:19
Obad. 10b // Mic. 7:10
Obad. 11c // Joel 3:3; Nah. 3:10
Obad. 12b–c // Ezek. 35:13, 15; Ps. 35:19–21; Lam. 2:16; 3:46
Obad. 15a // Isa. 13:6; Ezek. 30:3; Joel 1:15; 2:1; 3:14; Zeph. 1:7, 14
Obad. 15b // Jer. 50:15, 29; Ezek. 16:59; 35:11, 15
Obad. 15c // 1 Kings 2:33; Joel 3:4, 7; Ps. 7:16; Prov. 12:14
Obad. 17a // Joel 2:32
Obad. 17b // Joel 3:17
Obad. 18a–b // Isa. 10:17
Obad. 18e // Num. 24:19 [?]
Obad. 19a // Num. 24:18; Amos 9:12
Obad. 21b // Ps. 22:28; 1 Chron. 29:11.

Adopting the ninth-century date for Obadiah eliminates many of these parallel texts from the category of Obadiah's intentional reuse, since the other texts are dated later. In other cases, where the parallel text is earlier than Obadiah, the similarity may be explained by common parlance (stock vocabulary) or common themes rather than by inner-biblical quotation or allusion. Two significant passages for discussion are Jer. 38:22 and Jer. 49:7–22, which exhibit near-verbatim parallels with parts of Obadiah: in the first case, Obad. 7 // Jer. 38:22 and, in the second, Obad. 1–4 // Jer. 49:14–16; Obad. 5–6 // Jer. 49:9–10; and Obad. 7–8 // Jer. 49:7. How one dates Obadiah and Jeremiah answers the questions of directional dependence and intentional reuse (see Raabe, *Obadiah*, 22–31; Keil and Delitzsch, 228–29; Stuart, 403, for differing positions). Since this article proposes a preexilic, ninth-century date for Obadiah, as argued above, Jeremiah's dependence on Obadiah is the preferred position. This removes the parallels in Jeremiah from the discussion of Obadiah's inner-biblical interpretation.

Criteria for establishing intentional reuse. The following criteria help to distinguish between an intentional reuse of an earlier text and common parlance or themes shared between texts (cf. Gibson, 32–38): (1) the presence of lexical coordinates between two texts; (2) the frequency and distribution of shared lexemes; (3) peculiar occurrences of shared lexemes, such as rare words or lexical clusters; (4) shared phrases involving syntactical parallels; and (5) contextual and thematic correspondence. Such criteria provide a sound basis for proposing a formal correspondence that involves intentional reuse. The direction of dependence is determined by the availability of the source text and the plausibility of its reuse in the context of the quoting or alluding text. In the case of Obadiah, the mention of Esau and Jacob creates the formal correspondence with the Jacob-Esau narrative in Genesis, along with its central theme of divine reversal in their respective lives.

Lexical and syntactical parallels. A formal connection between Obadiah and the Jacob-Esau narrative in Gen. 25–36 is established through the use of their eponymous names. The name Esau (*ʿēśāw*) occurs seven times in the space of 21 verses (vv. 6, 8, 9, 18 [2x], 19, 21), the densest frequency in the OT outside of Gen. 25–27. The name Jacob (*yaʿăqōb*) is used three times in this short oracle (vv. 10, 17, 18). The phrase "your brother" (*ʾāḥîkā*) occurs twice (vv. 10, 12). In v. 10, "Jacob" is used in apposition to "your brother," indicating that the fraternal relationship between Jacob and Esau is intended as the backdrop to the oracle against Edom. Three other words may connect the two texts through possible wordplay: Obad. 2 speaks of God making Edom "small" (*qāṭōn*) and "despised" (*bāzûy*). Both words are used in the Genesis narrative, where Jacob is referred to as the "younger" (*qṭn*) brother (27:15, 42) and Esau is said to "despise" (*bzh*) his birthright (25:34). Furthermore, the name "Edom" (*ʾĕdôm*), situated among frequent references to Esau, is etymologically tied to the occasion when Esau sold his birthright for a pot of "red stuff" (*hā'ādôm hā'ādôm*, 25:30 NRSV).

Contextual and thematic parallels. Contextually, the reuse of the Jacob-Esau narrative in Genesis makes sense given that the oracle concerns the nations descending from the patriarchal twins. Edom descended from Esau (Gen. 36), while Judah descended from Jacob (Gen. 32:22–32). The context of hostility between the brothers—first begun in the womb (Gen. 25:22) and continued throughout their lives (Gen. 25:24–34; 27:41)—is recapitulated in the historical relations between Edom and Judah (e.g., 2 Sam. 8:13–14; 1 Kings 11:15–18; 2 Kings 8:20–22; 16:5–6; 2 Chron. 20:1–30; 21:8–17; 28:17). Obadiah addresses Edom's hostility against his "brother Jacob" directly, which serves as the basis for his condemnation (v. 10).

Thematically, the vision of Obadiah contains several reversals that connect with the divine reversal in the lives of the twin boys in Rebekah's womb (Gen. 25:23). Though Edom is high and seemingly impregnable in his lofty dwellings (v. 3b–c), he will be brought down low (v. 4c); though Edom is wise in his understanding (v. 8), he will be deceived internally by the pride of his heart (v. 3a) and externally by his allies (vv. 5–7); as Edom acted treacherously against his brother nation (v. 10a), so his allies will act treacherously against him (v. 7); just as Edom helped foreigners to cut off the remnant of Judah (v. 11), so Edom's remnant will be cut off (v. 10c) (cf. Magary, 995). The foreboding reversals for the nation of Edom are also set in contrast to favorable reversals for Judah: Esau's wealth will be lost (v. 6), while Jacob's wealth will be restored (v. 17); for Mount Zion there will be survivors, while for the house of Esau there will be no survivor (v. 18). These reversals are patterned after the divine reversal announced to Rebekah concerning her twin boys Esau and Jacob: "The older shall serve the younger" (Gen. 25:23).

Availability and plausibility. Since the Jacob-Esau narrative of Genesis originated in the time of Moses, the tradition and text would have been available to Obadiah in the ninth century BC. Acknowledging the descent of Edom and Judah from the patriarchal twin brothers Esau and Jacob, respectively, as well as the common contexts and shared themes between Gen. 25–36 and Obadiah, strengthens the plausibility for Obadiah's reuse of the Jacob-Esau narrative.

Interpretive significance. In Obadiah's first main section (vv. 1–9), Edom experiences reversal through deception from within (the pride of his heart) and from without (the betrayal of his allies). In the second main section (vv. 10–18), Esau's reversal is tied closely to *lex talionis*, executed on the day of the Lord: "As you have done, it shall be done to you" (v. 15 ESV). However, playing alongside these two thematic notes of reversal is a subtle background melody, which is communicated through the intertextual connection to the Jacob-Esau story: the reversal established in the decree of divine election (Gen. 25:23; cf. Mal. 1:2–5; Rom. 9:11–13). In other words, divine reversal will also, ultimately, occur in the life histories of Edom and Judah because Edom is Esau and Judah is Jacob—and the older must serve the younger. The third main section (Obad. 19–21) supports this, where the unexpected theme of land dominates and brings the motif of reversal to a climax: Jacob will have his land back (v. 17) and will also possess the land of Edom and rule Mount Esau (vv. 19, 21)—and all this because grace, not works, makes men differ. In this intertextual light, Obadiah's overarching theological message is brought into sharp focus: *the realization of Yahweh's sovereignty in the reversal of fortunes for Esau-Edom and Jacob-Judah.*

At the intertextual level, the equation of Edom with Esau and Judah with Jacob sheds light on how Obadiah recapitulates events from the story of Esau and Jacob in the history of Edom and Judah (cf. Robinson, 94). In particular, within the synonymity of Edom and Esau lies a profound ontology: Edom *is* Esau (Obad. 8–9; cf. Gen. 36:1, 8, 9, 19, 43). The nation is not just like Esau but *is* Esau, disclosing its inner nature, its rebellious core *ab origine*. In this sense, the heart of Esau in Genesis—including a propensity to deception (cf. Gen. 25:27–34) and a vengeful desire to eliminate the elect son and repossess his land (cf. Gen. 27:41–45)—has been passed down to his descendants: Esau *redivivus*. For example, as Esau was deceived (Gen. 25:30–34; 27:34–36), so too will Edom be deceived (Obad. 3, 7); as Esau experienced role reversal by the hand of Yahweh (Gen. 25:23) and those closest to him (Jacob and Rebekah; Gen. 25:30–34; 27:1–40), so too will Edom (Obad. 2, 4; 5–7, respectively); as Esau threatened to kill Jacob and then drove him from his land so that he could possess it for a time (Gen. 27:41–28:5), so too will Edom (Obad. 10–14, 19–20; cf. Ezek. 35:10; 36:2, 5). Conversely, if it is true that Edom *is* Esau, then Judah *is* Jacob—which means that lying behind Judah's favorable reversal of land restoration (Obad. 19–20) is the decree of divine election. For example, as Jacob returned to possess what was rightfully his after a period of "exile" from the land (Gen. 33:16–17; 36:43–37:1), so Judah will return from exile to "possess his possessions" (Obad. 17 AT; cf. vv. 19–20)—but only because he is Jacob, the chosen son, and not because of anything he has done. In short, corporate solidarity undergirds the life histories of Esau-Edom and Jacob-Judah.

Theologically speaking, Edom's violent behavior toward Judah is not simply an act of political treachery, nor yet even the betrayal of a brother, but, ultimately, a stroke against the divine plan. Edom's attack against his "brother Jacob" (v. 10) and subsequent aspiration to occupy areas in Israel (cf. Ezek. 35:10; 36:2, 5)—seen in the later migration of Edomites into the Negev following the fall of Jerusalem (cf. Bartlett, 127–28, 140–43)—is suggestive of his "wish to reverse the situation and restore the election and the birthright to Esau" (Assis, 12). The intertextual connections with Jacob-Esau thus cast Edom's actions in a new light: he has struck against the divine economy established in the tent of Rebekah (cf. Gen. 25:23). Indeed, this is the ground for his condemnation (Obad. 10). As long as this state of affairs continues on the world stage, Yahweh will not be seen to be king. In fact, only when the inversion of the divine economy is righted, as seen in the reversal of fortunes for Esau-Edom and Jacob-Judah, will Yahweh's sovereignty be finally realized. In that day, the older will serve the younger—and the kingdom will be the Lord's (v. 21). In sum, Obadiah's overarching message "is not simply [the] decimation of Edom nor the restoration of Israel" but rather the underlying truth that "Yahweh is king over all the world!" (Lillie, 21).

Obadiah and the NT

Obadiah is one of eight OT books (Ezra, Nehemiah, Esther [though see the article on Esther elsewhere in the dictionary], Song of Solomon, Lamentations, Obadiah, Nahum, and Zephaniah) not directly quoted or alluded to in the NT. Nevertheless, it may be said to be latent in two other OT texts that are cited: Acts 2:16–21 directly quotes Joel 2:32, a text that itself quotes Obad. 17, as seen by the divine-speech formula "as the LORD has said"; also, Acts 15:15–18 directly quotes Amos 9:11–12, a text that exhibits at least strong conceptual overlap with Obad. 19 if not an allusion. That Obad. 19 may even be in James's direct purview is supported by the fact that he speaks of "the words of the prophets [plural]" (Acts 15:15). Also of interest for biblical-theological purposes is the fact that the Herodian kings who bookend the life of Christ at his birth and trial (e.g., Matt. 2; Luke 23) are Idumeans (Edomites) and therefore descendants of Esau. The observation gives context and heightened drama to the animosity of these kings toward their "twin brother" Jesus. It also enriches Obadiah's intriguing prediction that saviors will go up to Mount Zion to rule Mount Esau. Reflection on how this is fulfilled in the ministry of the ascended Christ through the acts of his apostles, as his kingdom extends beyond the borders of Judea and Samaria, will prove fruitful for scholar and pastor alike (cf. Field, 102–18).

Bibliography. Ackroyd, P. R., "Obadiah, Book of," in *ABD*, 5:2–4; Allen, L. C., *The Books of Joel, Obadiah, Jonah and Micah*, NICOT (Hodder & Stoughton, 1976); Assis, E., "Why Edom?," *VT* 56 (2006): 1–20; Baker, D. W., "Obadiah," in *Obadiah, Jonah and Micah*, by D. W. Baker, T. D. Alexander, and B. K. Waltke, TOTC (InterVarsity, 1988); Bartlett, J. R., *Edom and Edomites*, JSOTSup 77 (JSOT Press, 1989); J. Barton, *Joel and Obadiah* (Westminster John Knox, 2001); Block, D. I., *Obadiah*, ZECOT (Zondervan, 2015); Cresson, B. C., "The Condemnation of Edom in Postexilic Judaism," in *The Use of the Old Testament in the New, and Other Essays*, ed. J. M. Efird and J. Durham (Duke University Press, 1972), 125–48; Field, D., *Obadiah*, ExpB (Day One Publications, 2008); Gibson, J., *Covenant Continuity and Fidelity*, LHBOTS 625 (Bloomsbury T&T Clark, 2016); Hassler, M. A., "The Setting of Obadiah," *JETS* 59 (2016): 241–54; Hitzig, F., *Die zwölf kleinen Propheten* (S. Hirzel, 1881); House, P. R., "Obadiah," in *DTIB*, 542–44; Keil, C. F., and F. Delitzsch, *Minor Prophets*, vol. 10 of *Commentary on the Old Testament* (Hendrickson, 2001); Krause, J. J., "Tradition, History, and Our Story," *JSOT* 32 (2008): 475–86; Lillie, J., "Obadiah—A Celebration of God's Kingdom," *CurTM* 6 (1979): 18–22; Magary, D., "Obadiah, Theology of," in *NIDOTTE*, 4:992–96; Mason, R., *Micah, Nahum, Obadiah*, OTG (JSOT Press, 1991); Niehaus, J., "Obadiah," in *The Minor Prophets*, ed. T. E. McComiskey (Baker, 1993), 2:495–542; Raabe, P. R., *Obadiah*, AB (Doubleday, 1996); Raabe, "Why Prophetic Oracles against the Nations?," in *Fortunate the Eyes That See*, ed. A. B. Beck et al. (Eerdmans, 1995), 236–57; Renkema, J., *Obadiah*, HCOT (Peeters, 2003); Robinson, R. B., "Levels of Naturalization in Obadiah," *JSOT* 40 (1988): 83–97; Stuart, D., *Hosea–Jonah*, WBC (Word, 1987); Watts, J. D. W., *Obadiah* (Alpha, 1969); Wellhausen, J., *Skizzen und Vorarbeiten*, vol. 5 (Reimer, 1893); Werse, N. R., "Obadiah's 'Day of the Lord,'" *JSOT* 38 (2013): 109–24; Wolff, H. W., *Obadiah and Jonah*, CC (Augsburg, 1986).

JONATHAN GIBSON

Orality

Literature has traditionally been thought of in written terms as a set of written texts (and in that regard orality cannot be discussed apart from the topic of written texts and literacy). This has been true especially since the Enlightenment but goes back much earlier than that. The recognition of the role of orality in the production of texts—oral texts or written texts—is therefore a phenomenon that has only relatively recently attracted significant attention. An indication of the significance of the issue is illustrated by Josephus, who observes that Homer did not write his poems (*Ag. Ap.* 1.11–12). Homer and his poems, the *Iliad* and the *Odyssey*, have constituted one of the most important areas for the study of orality. Throughout history, there have been those who have been interested in oral tradition, such as Erasmus, the Grimm brothers, and others. The subject was taken up with earnestness in the eighteenth century with the rise of historical criticism. The classicist François Hédelin doubted Homer's existence because he left no writings, while the British scholar Richard Bentley endorsed the oral growth of the Homeric poems. Robert Wood argued that Homer was an oral poet and could not write, while Friedrich Wolf, who instigated the analytic movement, argued for later redaction of written Homeric texts that originated from an oral poet. In the nineteenth century, the textual critic Karl Lachmann and then later Ulrich von Wilamowitz-Moellendorff argued for a composite Homeric text—that is, a mix of written and oral features—and a number of scholars began to recognize the formulaic and inexact remembrance of oral poetic composition. In the twentieth century, Milman Parry, followed by his student Albert Lord, argued for the oral-formulaic theory of composition based upon Yugoslavian folk singers (Foley, 2–10, supplemented by Ong, 16–20). This oral-formulaic composition theory is arguably one of the most important theories to have been developed regarding orality, and its influence continues in a variety of disciplines.

Whereas classicists were increasingly developing theories about orality, especially in relation to Homer's poems, there was a similar progression in NT studies. In the eighteenth century, J. G. von Herder recognized that Christianity originated with proclamation or preaching, rather than with written texts, and thus orality took precedence over the written, a view that has persisted in the development of modern linguistics. A concern for oral transmission was taken up in full force by the form critics of the 1920s (e.g., Martin Dibelius, Karl Ludwig Schmidt, Rudolf Bultmann) and the redaction critics of the 1950s (e.g., Günther Bornkamm, Hans Conzelmann, Willi Marxsen). Since that time, the oral dimension of the NT has flourished, with a variety of theories developed regarding orality, oral transmission, media studies, and memory studies (Loubser, *Oral*, 87; a slightly different accounting is offered by Dunn, *Jesus*, 192–210, although he focuses on individual NT scholars for the most part). This essay does not attempt to treat all contributors but rather summarizes major theories and potential avenues of exploration (for other treatments, see Iverson; Eve, both of whom categorize the subject differently than I do). A fuller range of theories than can be offered here has recently been produced by Eric Eve and many others.

The importance of the topic of orality for NT studies is multifaceted. In one sense, the study of the NT at almost any angle or perspective should probably be concerned with questions of orality. The content of many, if not most, of the NT books either overtly or covertly attempts to capture language that at one point was oral—whether that is through recording the speeches of others or capturing the dictation of authors. That was at least in part because the literary conventions of the time were based upon orality (as I will discuss further below). As J. A. Loubser states, "First-century literary conventions were still largely dependent on speech conventions. This compels us to take note of orality and oral conventions if we want to make any sense of first-century manuscripts" ("Orality," 62). However, orality extends beyond this. Within the books of the NT, many passages overtly represent themselves as instances of oral language, in the form of conversation, dialogue, speech, teaching, proclamation, or any number of other forms of oral language. Therefore, to study the NT one must be attuned to its orality, even though it is graphically represented by means of a written text. As Kelly Iverson (72) states, "Understanding of orality is essential for appreciating early Christianity." Having said that, even though we may recognize the oral dimension of, for example, the letters of the NT as specimens of dictated language, conveyed by means of a scribe taking dictation, or of a number of speeches such as are found in Acts, the most important or at least the best-developed area for the study of orality in the NT has been in the study of the Gospels (Iverson, 71–72). This does not mean that other areas of NT study cannot benefit from the study of orality—no doubt they can and should—but the Gospels have been the focal point of discussion, especially over the last century.

This essay explores the issue of orality as it relates to NT studies by focusing upon the major theories of orality and the challenges that they bring, along with opportunities to move in new directions.

Major Theories of Orality

As has already been intimated above, there are several different theories regarding orality that have significance in contemporary NT research. In NT studies, many of these are formulated in relationship to, and often reaction to, the form criticism of Dibelius, Schmidt, and Bultmann. Such theories are theories of orality or are at least represented as theories of orality, but they (as well as redaction theories) have often become linked with or used as theories of literacy in NT studies, with resulting confusion (cf. Güttgemanns, who has been followed by a number of scholars, especially those who advocate for oral tradition within NT studies). However, because form criticism is so well known, this essay will deal with theories that have presented alternatives to form criticism by appealing to the notion of orality—that is, the focus upon the orally transmitted sources of the NT. Theories of orality are closely linked with theories of transmission, by which we mean that we are concerned with how "texts," in this case oral texts, are transmitted within a community and over time. Several of these theories are currently being discussed in NT studies. Some are better known than others and some have already passed their major point of impact while others are gaining momentum. We will examine each briefly to gain insight into the major claims of the theory and its major continuing contributions to the discussion.

Oral-formulaic transmission. This theory is probably the best known and the most important theory of oral transmission that has been developed, at least to date. It was developed in the first half of the last century and is still widely used in a variety of disciplines, especially classical studies. This is widely known as the Parry-Lord hypothesis, after its developers, although others have also contributed to it, some of whom are noted below.

Parry (see Parry; this paragraph summarizes Ong, 20–30; for other useful summaries of Parry and Lord, see Foley, 19–56; Thomas, 31–36), the American classicist who died while only in his thirties, rejected the tendency to overidealize the Homeric poems and attempted to describe their fundamental character, developing further the trend already found in some previous scholarship on orality (see above). Parry's theory has been summarized by Walter Ong in this way: "Virtually every distinctive feature of Homeric poetry is due to the economy enforced on it by oral methods of composition. These can be reconstructed by careful study of the verse itself once one puts aside the assumptions about expression and thought processes engrained in the psyche by generations of literate culture" (21). Some of the oral features that guided the oral composition were the poetic meter, epithets, and formulas. Most of these ideas were contained in Parry's doctoral work, but he then died and his student, Lord, took up the mantle. Lord's great contribution was to witness and record the features that Parry observed in the orally composed poetry of Serbo-Croatian folk-epic singers, assuming that their experience is sufficiently similar to that of the ancient world to be used as a model (Lord, *Singer*). Eric Havelock extended these insights further into all classical cultures, including the influence of writing on thought and the introduction of written vowels on analytic thinking (*Preface*; *Origins*). Geoffrey Kirk reinforced much of Parry and Lord's work but retained more originality of the Homeric poet. The Parry-Lord hypothesis has been widely debated in classical studies (cf. Mary Sale, "Oral-Formulaic"; Merritt Sale, "Defense"), with advocates for and against it. Their theories have had an influence on a wide range of disciplines, including many of the world's languages and their literatures (see Ong, 28–29; Foley, 57–111).

The Parry-Lord hypothesis is often mentioned in NT studies, but it has not been as influential there as it has been in classical studies and some other disciplines. David Aune makes the interesting point that, at least at the time he wrote, oral tradition had been neglected in classical studies of the Hellenistic and Roman periods (he distinguishes study of oral tradition from the Parry-Lord hypothesis) *because* of the oral-formulaic hypothesis. He claims that this hypothesis has tended to romanticize oral tradition over literate culture so that when literate culture emerged, the importance of oral tradition retreated and hence was neglected (60). Nevertheless, there are a number of NT scholars who have accepted some of the premises and approaches of the Parry-Lord approach, and at least recognized its possibilities for NT studies. Some of these are Erhardt Güttgemanns (204–11), Werner Kelber (*Oral*, 78–80, but with reservations), and Craig Blomberg (28–30)—although none of them is a clear advocate for the approach.

If one wants clear advocacy of such an approach, examples are found in articles by Lord himself and by Pieter Botha. Lord was asked to participate in an interdisciplinary conference on the Gospels and he argued for the Gospels as "oral traditional literature" ("Gospels"; for response to Lord, see Talbert, 93–102). Lord defines oral tradition in terms of relatively fixed forms that express mythic material concerned with the lives of gods presented in a fluid yet sequential and unitized way. He finds such mythic life stories in Matthew and Luke. He also finds sequential patterns with verbal correspondence, and he examines the Gospels as variants on a pattern. He concludes that "the events in Jesus' life, his works, and teachings, evoked ties with 'sacred' oral traditional narratives and narrative elements that were current in the Near East and the eastern Mediterranean in the first century AD" ("Gospels," 91). Botha directly applies the "oral formulaic theory" of Lord to the Gospel of Mark as an attempt to overcome the shortcomings of form and redaction criticism ("Story"; cf. "Living"). He identifies in Mark the signs of oral traditional composition, including its formulaic style and its use of themes, two major features of such composition.

Informal controlled transmission. The theory of informal controlled transmission was developed within the field of biblical studies and has been adopted by a number of scholars to explain the features of orality within the NT. Kenneth Bailey uses the term to describe the kind of oral transmission that he believes functioned in the ancient Near East. Based upon his living in and observing traditions of transmission in the Near East for nearly forty years, Bailey first published his description in 1991 ("Informal"; "Middle"; cf. *Poet*, where he had already hinted at some of his theories). He distinguishes informal controlled transmission from other types of transmission, such as the informal uncontrolled oral tradition typical of form criticism (as seen in the work of Rudolf Bultmann) and the formal controlled oral tradition of the Scandinavian school of thought (as seen in the work of Harald Riesenfeld and Birger Gerhardsson). Bailey sees oral tradition as informal in that there were no established presenters or hearers of the tradition. Rather, the oral tradition was conveyed by those who participated in the process in informal gatherings and on varied occasions. The controlled element to the oral tradition is found in controls set by the community in which the transmission occurs. Bailey contends that there are three levels of flexibility within these controls. There is no flexibility for such things as poems and proverbs, some flexibility in parables and the recollection of historically significant people, and complete flexibility in more casual oral forms, such as telling jokes and conveying various events as they may happen. There is also a process by which new material is included within the tradition. Bailey relies upon the contemporary cultures that he observes, especially in Lebanon but also elsewhere, being identical with the NT environment.

In some ways, Bailey's view of oral tradition may appear somewhat naïve, but his theory is consistent with wider trends found in the post–World War II biblical theology movement regarding Israelite culture, seen here in terms of larger Near Eastern culture. Bailey's views, despite the relative lack of serious scholarly development of his ideas (compared, e.g., to the work on the oral-formulaic hypothesis), have become relatively significant in studies of orality in the NT over the last thirty or so years. One of the first to use Bailey for an extended exposition of a portion of the NT was N. T. Wright (133–37). He invoked Bailey's view of oral tradition in his exposition of the so-called parable of the prodigal son, although he did not draw many direct correlations to how Bailey's theory affected the telling of the parable. James Dunn is even more explicit in his use of Bailey. After summarizing various theories of oral tradition, Dunn adopts Bailey's view of informal controlled tradition as the basis for his study of "the Synoptic Tradition as Oral Tradition" (*Jesus*, 205–10; see also *Oral*, 248–64 [responding to Weeden]; "Altering"). Dunn has been followed by his student Terence Mournet, a computer scientist and biblical scholar who supports the findings of Bailey and Dunn further with statistical analysis (287–93). A major development of Bailey's approach is suggested by Richard Bauckham. He argues for a fourth typology of tradition, formal controlled transmission, in which there are controls on those who transmit and receive the oral tradition, in his case linked to the accounts of eyewitnesses (293; cf. 252–63).

Orality and rabbinic Judaism. Another view of orality has come to be called the Scandinavian school of thought. It is attributed mostly to the work of the Scandinavian scholar Birger Gerhardsson, but it has been continued by other scholars as well.

The development of the Scandinavian perspective on oral tradition was the product of several factors. These apparently include Harald Riesenfeld's interest in varying contexts of tradition and especially Gerhardsson's studying both with several NT scholars who were interested in the origins of the Gospels and with an OT scholar who raised for him questions about Jewish textual traditions (*Memory*; cf. Byrskog, "Introduction," 4–5, on the relationship of Riesenfeld's and Gerhardsson's thought). As a result, Gerhardsson's theory reflects the influence of Jewish and, more specifically, of rabbinic transmission of the Oral Torah—that is, not just the Torah but all of the traditional rabbinic teaching. Such transmission occurred within what Gerhardsson defines as a school context—that is, with teachers and students. The rabbinic schools were well known, and he seems to depict Jesus as a teacher in this light. The Oral Torah was passed on according to a number of factors. The primary factor was the role of memorization. Memorization was designed to preserve the authentic wording of the tradition. In order to do so, the tradition sometimes needed to be either condensed or abridged. There were a variety of ways that a student might preserve and transmit the authentic words of the teacher. These included various mnemonic devices, sometimes aided by written notes. The written form was not considered to be an authentic accounting of the tradition, and so memorization and constant repetition to solidify memory were required and emphasized. This was seen as the greatest means by which one could overcome the tendency to forget. Gerhardsson continued to develop and summarize his views in subsequent works (*Tradition*; *Origins*).

The influence of Gerhardsson and the Scandinavian school has been significant, even if not particularly widespread. Despite criticisms of it for adopting a model that is too dependent upon later rabbinic traditions, the notion that memory is the means by which oral tradition is preserved, with or without aids such as written notes, has become a major force within NT studies of orality. The first major treatment to develop Gerhardsson's ideas and take them further was a work on Jesus as a teacher by Rainer Riesner (*Jesus*; for the essence of Riesner's position, see "Orality," 94–105). This work, which has to date (so far as I know) appeared only in German, seeks to overcome the perceived limitation of Gerhardsson's work to rabbinic schools and show how other Jewish traditions also preserved oral tradition. It is also not surprising that one of Gerhardsson's students has taken up his approach. Samuel Byrskog, a fellow Scandinavian, has kept the school alive by taking up the challenge of accounting much more fully for the differences in the so-called "outer" tradition—that is, the "verbal, behavioural, institutional and material tradition"—that reflects the "inner" tradition (*Jesus*, 20). Byrskog has developed his ideas further in relation to historiography, in particular oral history, but he has retained an emphasis upon the importance of oral tradition so that he sees the Gospel writers as engaging in "a constant process of re-oralization" of the Jesus tradition in their process of transmission (*Story*, 305).

Orality and related fields of research. There are several current debates that link their studies with theories of orality. Several reflect more recent developments in the study of orality, while others are emerging or developing areas where there is a significant amount of current research. I have selected three for a brief discussion.

Orality and literacy. One of the major responses to the rise of the study of orality is to contrast orality with literacy or written texts. Discussion of these differences is sometimes referred to as media studies, with the two primary media being orality and literacy (Eve, 41–65). Seeing the contrast between them has been common in both orality studies outside of the NT and those within it. Ong is representative of those in orality studies who oppose orality and literacy. The fundamental premise of his work, especially his major work on orality, is that there is a diametric opposition between orality and literacy. He identifies what he characterizes as psychodynamic features of orality—namely, issues regarding memory and its devices, its accumulative rather than divisive characteristics, its conservatism, its ties to the world of humanity, its participatory nature, and its being situational, among others (Ong, 31–77). By contrast, Ong sees writing as restructuring human consciousness by creating what he calls "autonomous discourse," the result of oral texts becoming written artifacts (78–116). This kind of opposition is also found in the work of the NT scholar Werner H. Kelber. Kelber wishes to avoid a strong opposition between orality and literacy and has moderated his opposition through the years, but despite these efforts, he reacts to what he sees as the hegemony of literacy in NT studies and has been associated with what has been called "the great divide" between orality and literacy. He tends to see the two media less as a continuity than a bifurcation, by which the move from one medium to the other reflects a difference in origins and even conception (*Oral*, xix–xx, xxi–xxii; for the moderation of his views, see Kelber and Thatcher, "'Easy,'" 27–32; see also Güttgemanns).

Orality and the role of eyewitnesses. Discussion of the role of eyewitnesses in the origins and transmission of the Gospels has become a very important topic in recent NT research. This is not a development of work in orality studies outside the NT but an attempt to support orality by means of positing eyewitnesses as involved in the tradition-making and transmissional process. The two major figures in this research are Byrskog and Bauckham, already mentioned above. Byrskog, who in his volume on eyewitnesses is still working with an eye on the orality hypothesis of Gerhardsson, attempts to link oral history to eyewitnesses but in this work finds parallels within the practices of secular historians (Byrskog, *Story*). Byrskog posits eyewitness accounts (autopsy) as the source of oral tradition for both ancient historians and the NT writers. Bauckham, as mentioned above, introduces a fourth category regarding oral tradition, which he uses to distance his view from that of Bailey and Dunn because of his belief in the fundamental importance of eyewitnesses as the source of the oral tradition.

Orality and memory and performance. Memory studies and performance studies, often linked together, have become a major growth industry in the study of the Gospels. The claim is that one needs to appreciate the role of memory in the Gospel transmission process. (For performance criticism, see Rhoads.) As we have already observed above at several different places, memory has played a role in a number of different theories of orality. This is to be expected, since if transmission of knowledge is performed orally, then one should consider how those involved in the process remember what they are transmitting. Memory is often spoken of in relation to both individual memory and collective or social memory. Individual memory is often characterized by its general reliability, even if it requires means of structuring those memories. Memory studies are usually seen as a part of cognitive studies, where various terms are used of these schemas or scripts by which humans construe reality. Social or collective memory extends individual memory to represent the memories of various groups, socially or otherwise constructed. The group is involved in rehearsing its important memories. Besides Dunn and Kelber (esp. *Imprints*), two scholars whose works place varying degrees of emphasis upon memory are Rafael Rodriguez and Robert McIver. Rodriguez focuses upon two major elements: social memory and performance (39–113; cf. Horsley, Draper, and Foley). He tries to integrate individual and social memory, recognizes the relationship of the past and the present in memory, and acknowledges the social construction of reputation. Rodriguez acknowledges that we have no instances of performance of the Gospels, but he contends that performance actualizes the oral tradition. McIver takes a different approach to memory (5–94). The first half of his book is devoted to the discussion of memory, first individual memory and then collective memory. He discusses memory transience and patterns of forgetfulness for individuals but also introduces "flashbulb memories" as possible exceptions to transience. He then discusses how the complex notion of collective memory works, especially in an oral society, using Maurice Halbwachs as his major source.

Some Implications Regarding Orality

There are several implications of theories of orality for NT studies. Some of these can be briefly outlined.

The first concerns the Gospels. Recognition of orality—whether in its firm form as categorically different from literacy or in a softer form that recognizes a transition from orality to literacy—confirms a pre-Synoptic (as well as possibly pre-Johannine) oral period in the development of the Gospels and indicates that this stage may have had a dynamic role to play in the development, preservation, and transmission of that oral tradition (Dunn, "Altering," 59–74).

A second is that a robust view of orality, combined with eyewitness testimony, creates a major problem for traditional form and redaction, as well as source, criticism. This was first argued in a straightforward way for NT studies by Gerhardsson (*Memory*, 9–14) and then strongly and robustly extended by Kelber in his work on the oral gospel tradition (*Oral*, 2–8; cf. Iverson, 77–78). It has been reiterated and extended by many others, especially those who argue for eyewitness testimony, such as Bauckham (241–49; cf. Evans, 211–14).

A third possible implication concerns the reliability of the Jesus tradition, or at least the discussion of it by some scholars, even in light of some cautions expressed on the basis of memory studies. At least, this is what several recent advocates of oral tradition claim in their studies, even if they approach the discussion in slightly different ways. Some of these include Gerhardsson (*Memory*), Bailey ("Informal"), and Bauckham (305–18), among others.

A fourth implication concerns the orality of other parts of the NT, such as the Epistles. Most of the emphasis to date has been upon the oral tradition in the Gospels with implications for the study of Jesus. However, the oral nature of the Pauline Letters has also been raised as an important topic in light of the fact that orality was possibly involved at several stages in the epistolary process, such as dictation and reading to the original and even subsequent audiences (Loubser, "Orality," 64–73; Botha, "Letter," 17–34).

These (and no doubt other) implications could be explored in far more detail.

Final Thoughts regarding Orality

As orality studies continue to develop, one area that was introduced early into the discussion has been neglected in many, if not most, NT orality studies. This is the place of orality in relationship to literacy in linguistics. Ferdinand de Saussure states, "Language [by which he means oral language] and writing are two distinct systems of signs; the second exists for the sole purpose of representing the first. The linguistic object is not both the written and the spoken forms of words; the spoken forms alone constitute the object" (*Course*, 23–24). A statement such as this makes it understandable why biblical scholars have perhaps not taken a more linguistically attuned view of oral tradition, since Saussure appears to dismiss written language as a poor imitation. One of the major results of his formulation is that much of modern linguistics has focused upon speech rather than writing. As a result, of the theorists I have noted above regarding orality, the only one who mentions Saussure is Ong, who offers a brief summary of Saussure and then uses him as instigating a line of discussion of orality (5; cf. 7). Of the biblical scholars who mention orality, the only one I have found who addresses Saussure directly is Güttgemanns (59–65), while others refer to Güttgemanns mentioning Saussure (Eve, 48–51; Kelber, *Imprints*, 175, 319). Güttgemanns sees linguistics as the foundation of the humanities and lays out several fundamental assumptions of linguistics (e.g., *langage*, *langue* and *parole*, *valeur*). He points out that Saussure's thought always had a sociological dimension, which has come to be more widely recognized with the publication of others of Saussure's manuscripts as they have been discovered (e.g., *Writings*). This important point has sometimes been missed in modern linguistics with its typical focus upon *langue* over *parole* (or, as some linguists express it, competence over performance). This is especially the case for those who followed Saussure's Geneva school and the descriptivist structural linguistics in North America, such as Leonard Bloomfield and his followers. Not all linguists have shared this inclination (Ong, 17). One of the other major forces in the development of linguistics was the Prague school of linguistics that functioned between the two world wars. These Prague linguists had a much more socially oriented view of language as seen in their functional-sentence perspective (Vachek, 18–19). Their primary concern was to describe the functions of language, and in order to do that one had to understand language as it was used in social situations.

There have been other linguists who have tackled the issue of orality and literacy, but perhaps the most important is Michael Halliday. In a book on spoken and written language, Halliday makes it clear that he views the relationship between speaking and writing in a different way than Saussure when he states, "Written language never was, and never has been, conversation written down" (*Spoken*, 41). Even if there is a historical relationship between the two, they often, if not usually, develop differently. The result is that speaking and writing are instances "of a more general phenomenon of variation in language, that of register" ("Differences," 78), or language according to use, not user. Since they are two different varieties, they have different linguistic profiles. Halliday characterizes them in this way: "Spoken language is characterized by complex sentence structures with low lexical density (more clauses, but fewer high content words per clause); written language by simple sentence structures with high lexical density (more high content words per clause, but fewer clauses)" ("Differences," 77; for fuller exposition of these differences, see *Spoken*, 61–91). One can see that such a linguistic approach introduces a variety of new factors into the discussion of orality, its relationship with literacy, and the relationship between spoken and written texts. The challenge of applying such a framework in NT studies has been taken up by Ji Hoe Kim in a recent article (cf. Porter). He examines several passages in the Gospels (Matt. 21:12–17; Mark 11:15–19; Luke 19:45–48; John 2:13–22) and, by applying Halliday's criteria, concludes that the Markan account more typically conforms to spoken language than the other two accounts. His results show a continuum rather than a disjunction between spoken and written texts, one that varies according to the situational contexts in which language is used. Kim's results also thus dispute the great divide posited by such scholars as Kelber (at least in his earlier writings). This is an initial study, but a methodology that is able to address both spoken and written language along a continuum might suggest new possibilities for further exploration.

Conclusion

Theories of orality continue to be used in various ways in NT studies. Some of these theories have similarities to theories used in other disciplines, such as classical studies. However, several theories of orality, mostly responding to form criticism, are unique to NT studies.

These theories have developed in various directions, from initial reactions to written texts so as to emphasize orality, to theories that incorporate other social, cultural, and related phenomena. As a result, the resurgence in interest in orality has reopened some interesting questions, especially in Gospel studies. One area that remains neglected, however, is the role of linguistics in the NT discussion of orality. Although linguists have talked about this topic for some time, and although it is presented in some earlier work in reaction to form criticism, the use of linguistics in studies of spoken and written texts is a very recent phenomenon that merits further discussion.

See also Literacy in the Greco-Roman World; *Septuagint articles*

Bibliography. Aune, D. E., "Prolegomena to the Study of Oral Tradition in the Hellenistic World," in *Jesus and the Oral Gospel Tradition*, ed. H. Wansbrough (Sheffield Academic, 1991), 59–106; Bailey, K. E., "Informal Controlled Oral Tradition and the Synoptic Gospels," *Them* 20 (1995): 4–11; Bailey, "Middle Eastern Oral Tradition and the Synoptic Gospels," *ExpTim* 106 (1995): 363–67; Bailey, *Poet and Peasant and through Peasant Eyes* (repr., Eerdmans, 1983); Bauckham, R., *Jesus and the Eyewitnesses*, 2nd ed. (Eerdmans, 2017); Blomberg, C. L., *The Historical Reliability of the Gospels* (Inter-Varsity, 1987); Botha, P. J. J., "Letter Writing and Oral Communication in Antiquity," *Scriptura* 42 (1992): 17–34; Botha, "Living Voice and Lifeless Letters," *HvTSt* 49 (1993): 742–59; Botha, "Mark's Story as Oral Traditional Literature," *HvTSt* 47 (1991): 304–31; Byrskog, S., "Introduction," in *Jesus in Memory*, ed. W. H. Kelber and S. Byrskog (Baylor University Press, 2009), 1–20; Byrskog, *Jesus the Only Teacher*, ConBNT 24 (Almqvist & Wiksell, 1994); Byrskog, *Story as History—History as Story*, WUNT 123 (Mohr Siebeck, 2000); Dunn, J. D. G., "Altering the Default Setting," in *Oral Gospel Tradition*, 41–79; Dunn, *Jesus Remembered* (Eerdmans, 2003); Dunn, *The Oral Gospel Tradition* (Eerdmans, 2013); Evans, C. A., "The Implications of Eyewitness Tradition," *JSNT* 31 (2008): 211–19; Eve, E., *Behind the Gospels* (SPCK, 2013); Foley, J. M., *The Theory of Oral Composition* (Indiana University Press, 1988); Gerhardsson, B., *Memory and Manuscript*, trans. E. J. Sharpe, ASNU 22 (Gleerup, 1961); Gerhardsson, *The Origins of the Gospel Traditions* (SCM, 1979); Gerhardsson, *Tradition and Transmission in Early Christianity*, ConBNT 20 (Gleerup, 1964); Güttgemanns, E., *Candid Questions concerning Gospel Form Criticism*, trans. W. G. Doty (Pickwick, 1979); Halbwachs, M., *On Collective Memory*, trans. L. A. Coser (University of Chicago Press, 1992); Halliday, M. A. K., "Differences between Spoken and Written Language," in *Language and Education*, ed. J. J. Webster, CWH 9 (Continuum, 2007), 63–80; Halliday, *Spoken and Written Language* (Oxford University Press, 1989); Havelock, E. A., *Origins of Western Literacy* (Ontario Institute for Studies in Education, 1976); Havelock, *Preface to Plato* (Belknap, 1963); Horsley, R. A., J. A. Draper, and J. M. Foley, eds., *Performing the Gospel* (Fortress, 2006); Iverson, K. R., "Orality and the Gospels," *CurBR* 8 (2009): 71–106; Kelber, W. H., *Imprints, Voiceprints, and Footprints of Memory* (Society of Biblical Literature, 2013); Kelber, *The Oral and the Written Gospel* (repr., Indiana University Press, 1997); Kelber, W. H., and T. Thatcher, "'It's Not Easy to Take a Fresh Approach,'" in *Jesus, the Voice, and the Text*, ed. T. Thatcher (Baylor University Press, 2008), 27–43; Kim, J. H., "A Hallidayan Approach to Orality and Textuality and Some Implications for Synoptic Gospel Studies," *BAGL* 8 (2019): 111–38; Kirk, G. S., *The Songs of Homer* (Cambridge University Press, 1962); Lord, A. B., "The Gospels as Oral Traditional Literature," in Walker, *Relationships among the Gospels*, 33–91; Lord, *The Singer of Tales* (repr., Atheneum, 1960); Loubser, J. A., *Oral and Manuscript Culture in the Bible* (Sun, 2007); Loubser, "Orality and Literacy in the Pauline Epistles," *Neot* 29 (1995): 61–74; McIver, R. K., *Memory, Jesus, and the Synoptic Gospels* (Society of Biblical Literature, 2011); Mournet, T. C., *Oral Tradition and Literary Dependency*, WUNT 2/195 (Mohr Siebeck, 2005); Ong, W. J., *Orality and Literacy* (Routledge, 1982); Parry, M., *The Making of Homeric Verse*, ed. A. Parry (Oxford University Press, 1971); Porter, S. E., "Orality and Textuality and Implications for the New Testament," in *Linguistic Descriptions of the Greek New Testament* (T&T Clark, forthcoming); Rhoads, D., "Performance Criticism," *BTB* 36 (2006): 118–33, 164–84; Riesenfeld, H., "The Gospel Tradition and Its Beginnings," in *The Gospel Tradition* (Blackwell, 1970), 1–30; Riesner, R., *Jesus als Lehrer*, 3rd ed., WUNT 2/5 (Mohr Siebeck, 1988); Riesner, "The Orality and Memory Hypothesis," in *The Synoptic Problem*, ed. S. E. Porter and B. R. Dyer (Baker Academic, 2016), 89–111; Rodriguez, R., *Structuring Early Christian Memory*, LNTS 407 (T&T Clark, 2010); Sale, Mary, "The Oral-Formulaic Theory Today," in *Speaking Volumes*, ed. J. Watson, Mnemosyne Supplements 218 (Brill, 2001), 53–80; Sale, Merritt, "In Defense of Milman Parry," *Oral Tradition* 11 (1996): 374–417; Saussure, F. de, *Course in General Linguistics*, ed. C. Bally and A. Sechehaye, trans. W. Baskin (Fontana, 1959); Saussure, *Writings in General Linguistics* (Oxford University Press, 2006); Talbert, C. H., "Oral and Independent or Literary and Interdependent?," in Walker, *Relationships among the Gospels*, 93–102; Thomas, R., *Literacy and Orality in Ancient Greece* (Cambridge University Press, 1992); Vachek, J., *The Linguistic School of Prague* (Indiana University Press, 1966); Walker, W. O., Jr., ed., *The Relationships among the Gospels* (Trinity University Press, 1978); Weeden, T. J., Sr., "Kenneth Bailey's Theory of Oral Tradition," *JSHJ* 7 (2009): 3–43; Wright, N. T., *Jesus and the Victory of God* (Fortress, 1996).

STANLEY E. PORTER

OT Use of the OT: Comparison with the NT Use of the OT

The way that the NT authors use the OT does not exist in a vacuum. Long before the birth of Jesus the Jewish people engaged Scripture in multifaceted ways to explain the character of God, the unfolding of his plan for human history, and how his covenant people should live in this world. Within the OT itself later authors regularly use earlier OT Scripture to articulate what God is currently saying through them; indeed, "inner-biblical exegesis" is pervasive throughout the Hebrew Bible, appearing across the various literary genres (Fishbane; Schultz). Later biblical authors regularly draw upon key words, phrases, themes, motifs, and types found in previous texts of Scripture to articulate the relationship between what God is currently saying and what God has already said.

Thus, when the NT authors use the OT Scriptures they are joining an already ongoing conversation. Being steeped in the OT and likely familiar with many of the Jewish exegetical traditions surrounding OT texts, the NT authors' use of the OT often reflects a knowledge not just of the OT text itself but also of how that text is used and developed in later OT texts. Therefore, examining how later OT authors use earlier OT texts provides an important (and sometimes essential) backdrop for understanding how the NT authors use Scripture, both in general terms and in specific examples.

Given the broad scope of the subject, this essay will be representative rather than exhaustive. The goal is to describe several of the most prominent hermeneutical techniques that later OT authors use when drawing upon earlier Scripture and then briefly compare the results with how the NT authors engage the OT.

Promise-Fulfillment

The promise-fulfillment motif is fundamental not only to the way NT authors use the OT but also to how later OT authors use earlier Scripture. A good starting point is God's promise to Abraham, which within the context of the OT is the means by which God will one day restore humanity and even creation itself from the disastrous consequences of Adam's rebellion in the garden. The initial statement of the promise in Gen. 12:1–3 focuses on two primary themes: land (God will give Abraham a place to live) and line (God will multiply his descendants into a great nation). Through him God will bless all the families of the earth. The depth and scope of the promise frequently expand as God reiterates it to Abraham (15:1–6; 17:1–21; 22:17–18), Isaac (26:3–4, 24), and Jacob (28:13–15; 35:10–12; 46:3–4), though the focus on land and line remains consistent.

Exodus 1 shows how the promise to Abraham begins to be fulfilled. Despite entering Egypt as a family of seventy people (1:5), "the people of Israel were fruitful and increased greatly; they multiplied and grew exceedingly strong, so that the land was filled with them" (1:7 ESV; cf. vv. 12, 20; these verses in turn allude to Gen. 1:28). By the time they emerge from Egypt after four hundred years of bondage they number approximately two million strong. After forty years of wilderness wandering and the initial conquest of the land, "Joshua took the whole land, according to all that the LORD had spoken to Moses" (Josh. 11:23 ESV). Yet just two chapters later Yahweh tells Joshua, "You are old and advanced in years, and there remains yet very much land to possess" (13:1 ESV). Understood together these texts show the already/not-yet nature of fulfillment. A similar dynamic emerges when comparing Joshua's words to Israel before his death ("Not one word has failed of all the good things that the LORD your God promised concerning you. All have come to pass for you; not one of them has failed" [Josh. 23:14]) and the Lord not driving out certain nations from the land (Judg. 2:20–3:2).

Israel's history confirms the already/not-yet fulfillment of the promise to Abraham. At their zenith during the reign of Solomon, "Judah and Israel were as many as the sand by the sea," the king rules over his enemies, and Israel's borders stretch even beyond what God had promised Abraham (1 Kings 4:20–21; cf. Gen. 22:17–18). That fulfillment is short-lived, however, as both Israel and Judah spiral downward into idolatry, breaking Yahweh's covenant. Yet even in announcing the judgment of exile from the land, God reiterates his promise that he will multiply his people like the sand of the sea (Hosea 1:10–11). To fulfill this Abrahamic promise God will return his people from exile and transform creation itself through a suffering servant (Isa. 49–54; see further Harmon, 120–41). Thus, within the OT the promises to Abraham have an inaugurated fulfillment yet look forward to their ultimate consummation in a new creation.

God's promise to David reveals a similar already-not-yet dynamic. Building on the Abrahamic promise, God promises a line of royal descendants (i.e., a house) from David that culminates in a descendant who will rule over an eternal kingdom (2 Sam. 7:8–16). This descendant will build a temple (i.e., a house) where God will dwell with his people. That promise finds initial fulfillment in Solomon, who rules over a kingdom that extends beyond what God had promised Abraham (1 Kings 4:20–21; cf. Gen. 15:18–19; 22:17–18). Solomon also builds the temple in Jerusalem (1 Kings 6–8), which he explicitly acknowledges is the direct result of God fulfilling his promise to David (8:15–21).

Yet Solomon's failures make it clear that the ultimate fulfillment of God's promise to David awaits a future realization. As the kingdom splits and the line of Davidic kings continue their downward spiral into idolatrous disobedience, the prophets repeatedly point the faithful remnant toward a future Spirit-empowered Davidic king who will rule in righteousness (Isa. 11:1–10; Jer.

23:1–6) and shepherd his redeemed people in a renewed creation (Ezek. 34:23; 37:24–28). This future hope of a Davidic king is also prevalent in Psalms, showing its importance within the worship of God's people (e.g., Pss. 2; 8; 23; 89; 110). So, although there is a partial and initial fulfillment of God's promise to David in his son Solomon, the remainder of the OT makes it clear that the complete realization of that promise awaits a future fulfillment.

While other examples could be given, these two prominent promises are sufficient to demonstrate the already/not-yet dynamic of promise-fulfillment within the OT itself. In the NT the already/not-yet nature of promise fulfillment becomes even more prominent. The key difference is that in the OT the already/not-yet is not eschatological in nature, whereas in the NT it is fundamentally eschatological. That is, with the dawn of the latter days through Jesus Christ, the period of eschatological fulfillment has arrived. For example, those who are in Christ are a new creation (2 Cor. 5:17), yet believers still await the resurrection of their bodies (Rom. 8:23) and the arrival of the new heavens and new earth in which righteousness dwells (2 Pet. 3:13; Rev. 21–22). In 2 Cor. 6:16 Paul cites the well-known covenant formula "I will be their God and they will be my people" as having a partial fulfillment in the church, while Rev. 21:3 indicates the final fulfillment of that promise in a new creation (see discussion below). In response to the controversy over whether gentiles are required to be circumcised in order to become part of God's people, James concludes it is not necessary on the basis of Amos 9:11–12, which foresees a day when God will reestablish David's line and gather to himself "all the Gentiles who are called by my name" (Acts 15:14–21 ESV). The influx of gentiles in the present is only a partial fulfillment of that promise, as its final fulfillment awaits the reign of Christ in a new Eden, where he will reign over the nations (with his name written on their foreheads!) as they serve and worship him (Rev. 22:1–5). While explicit fulfillment language is more prevalent in the NT, promise-fulfillment is a fundamental framework by which later OT authors interpret Scripture, establishing a pattern for the NT authors to follow.

Typology

Typology rests on the conviction that God has so ordered history that people, events, institutions, and places reveal patterns that anticipate even greater realities later in redemptive history. Sometimes these patterns are evident within the type itself, while in other cases the typological nature of the original person, event, or institution is recognizable only when the antitype is revealed (Schnittjer, 855–56; Chase, 59–63), though increasingly scholars are finding that the OT contexts of these types sometimes reveal hints of their forward-looking function. While significant attention has been paid to how NT authors identify OT types and assert their fulfillment in an antitype, less attention has been paid to the presence of typology within the OT itself. But as several scholars have demonstrated, typology within the OT itself is an important feature of how later OT authors use earlier Scripture (see, e.g., Hummel; Fishbane, 350–79; Chase, 119–89; Hamilton, *Typology*). Space permits mention of only representative examples.

People. As the first human being, Adam is an individual who establishes a pattern for and foreshadows later figures. The following examples illustrate this. The commission given to Adam in Gen. 1:28 is reissued to Noah in modified form after the flood (9:1–6). Key elements of Adam's commission are taken up within God's promise to Abram in Gen. 12:1–3 as it expands and develops throughout the remainder of Genesis (13:14–18; 15:16–21; 17:1–16; 22:16–18). By describing Israel as a kingdom of priests (Exod. 19:5–6), God indicates that as a people they function as a corporate Adam, sent into the new Eden of the promised land. Embedded within God's covenant promise to David (2 Sam. 7:12–16) is the realization of God's original commission to Adam (cf. Pss. 1, 2, 8, 110). The NT, building on this OT pattern, repeatedly identifies Jesus as the true and final fulfillment of this Adam typology. Paul makes this claim both explicitly (Rom. 5:12–21; 1 Cor. 15:21–28, 35–49) and implicitly (e.g., Phil. 2:6–11; Col. 1:15–20). The Gospels, although often in more subtle ways, also portray Jesus as the last Adam, who fulfills not only God's original commission to Adam but also all subsequent developments of this commission given to Abraham, Israel, and David (see further Crowe).

Moses also functions as a type for later OT figures. Most immediately within the OT, Joshua, in the book that bears his name, is presented as a new Moses figure (Harmon, *Servant*, 61–78). As Moses's successor, Joshua follows a similar path. Both lead Israel to cross through a body of water on dry land (Exod. 14:1–15:21 // Josh. 3–4), encounter Yahweh in a theophany (Exod. 3:1–4:17 // Josh. 5:13–15), have victory in battle (Exod. 17:8–16 // Josh. 8:26), and write down the words of God (Deut. 31:24 // Josh. 24:26). Like Moses before him, Joshua is even called the servant of the Lord at his death (Deut. 34:5 // Josh. 24:29). Beyond Joshua, Moses is also the prophet who establishes the paradigm against which all later prophets are evaluated (Deut. 18:15–22; 34:10–12). Elijah's experience of Yahweh's presence on Mount Horeb is patterned after Yahweh passing by Moses and proclaiming his name on that very same mountain (1 Kings 19:9–18; cf. Exod. 34:1–9); in both passages God expresses his commitment to his people despite their covenant unfaithfulness. The last words of Malachi bring Moses and Elijah together as a call to covenant faithfulness in the present as Israel awaits the "great and awesome day of the LORD" (Mal. 4:4–6 ESV). The NT repeatedly presents Jesus as the ultimate Moses figure. Jesus is the long-promised prophet greater than Moses (Acts 3:22–24), who appears with Elijah at Jesus's transfiguration (Matt. 17:1–8). Rather than simply recording divine revelation, Jesus speaks it (Matt. 5–7). He leads his people in the ultimate exodus from sin, death, and the devil (John 6:1–59; Gal. 4:1–7).

Events. As mentioned in the section above, several events during the life of Joshua are patterned after earlier events in Israel's experience. Arguably the most prominent event that serves as paradigm for and pointer to a later event is the exodus (see esp. Estelle; Morales). Israel's physical deliverance from slavery in Egypt, their consecration as a nation under a covenant, and their eventual entry into the promised land form a pattern that anticipates an even greater redemption for God's eschatological people. As L. Michael Morales (119) notes, "In the second exodus proclaimed by the prophets, however, Yahweh God would do a work *within* the hearts of his people—the deliverance would include an inward, spiritual exodus . . . a true exodus toward God involves an inward dying to the old life of exile and how this had been Israel's original problem: though delivered physically from Egyptian bondage, the hearts of God's people had remained in spiritual bondage to the world, no different from the spiritual darkness of the nations."

While this promise of a new exodus occurs throughout the prophets, it is especially prominent in Isaiah. In the original exodus God made a path through the sea for his people (Exod. 14:1–31); in the new exodus God will lead his people through the waters of judgment (Isa. 43:2). As Israel wandered in the wilderness, God gave his people water to drink (Num. 20:2–13); in the new exodus Yahweh will cause water to spring forth in the wilderness not only to give his people water to drink but ultimately to transform creation itself (Isa. 43:16–21). Following an oracle that calls God's people to eagerly await the revelation of God's saving righteousness (51:1–8), Yahweh's actions in creation and the exodus are recalled as the basis for believing that God will bring his ransomed people to Zion with everlasting joy (51:9–11). But the extent of the new-exodus motif in Isaiah goes well beyond these specific texts where exodus imagery is explicitly employed. As Rikki Watts rightly notes, "Although other canonical writings appeal to the Exodus tradition, here [in Isaiah] it is elevated to its most prominent status as a hermeneutic, shaping the heart of [Isa.] 40–55 and even replacing the first Exodus as the saving event" ("Consolation," 32–33). Thus, within Isa. 40–55 the promised new exodus serves as an organizing framework within which other key themes such as the servant, new creation, and the fulfillment of the Abrahamic covenant must be understood. When one considers the larger use of exodus typology in the prophets, five major themes are consistently associated with the promise of a new exodus (Morales, 122–33): Yahweh's fame reaching the ends of the earth (Isa. 52:1–10; Jer. 16:21; Ezek. 36:20–23), a Davidic king (Isa. 55:3; Jer. 30:1–9; Ezek. 34:23–24), an Elijah figure to prepare the way for Yahweh's arrival (Mal. 3:1), the outpouring of God's Spirit on his people (Isa. 44:1–5; Ezek. 36:26–27), and resurrection from the dead (Ezek. 37:1–14; Hosea 13:14).

The NT authors build on this OT foundation in asserting that Jesus is the prophet greater than Moses, the promised Davidic king, and the Isaianic servant who leads his people in that promised new exodus (Estelle, 208–326). Mark begins his Gospel with a combined citation of Mal. 3:1 and Isa. 40:3 to position the work of Jesus within the framework of a new exodus to deliver his people from their bondage to sin, death, and the devil (Watts, *Exodus*; Marcus). The Isaianic new exodus plays a central role in shaping the way that Luke-Acts together presents the work of Jesus and the mission of the church (Pao). In John, Jesus is not only the greater Moses but also the Passover lamb of that new exodus whose resurrection reverses humanity's expulsion from Eden (Morales, 159–72). Throughout his letters Paul draws on new-exodus language to explain the significance of Jesus's work and help believers understand how they should live as God's people (e.g., Rom. 8:12–17; 2 Cor. 6:14–7:1; Gal. 4:1–7; see further Keesmaat). New-exodus motifs are also present in 1 Peter and Revelation (Estelle, 286–326). Based on the OT pattern of the exodus and the promise of a new and greater exodus, the NT demonstrates how Jesus has accomplished the new exodus through his death and resurrection, bringing into existence the eschatological people of God who are on their way to the new heavens and new earth.

Institutions. Several OT institutions take on a typological or forward-shaping significance as the OT unfolds. As but one example, later biblical authors see in the marriage union of Adam and Eve (Gen. 2:18–25) a pattern whose deeper significance is found in God's relationship to his people (e.g., Ezek. 16:1–14; Hosea 1:1–3:5; Song of Songs?). Of course, the NT extends this even further. As long as Jesus the bridegroom is with God's people they should celebrate, not fast (Mark 2:19–20; John 2:1–11). The relationship between Christ the bridegroom and the church as his bride forms the foundation for Paul's instructions for how husbands and wives are to interact with each other (Eph. 5:22–33). Part of how John describes the end of human history is the marriage supper of the Lamb, in which the church as the bride has made herself ready (Rev. 19:6–8). When the new Jerusalem descends from heaven, it is described as "a bride adorned for her husband" (Rev. 21:2 ESV).

Places. Given that Adam was a typological foreshadowing of figures who were to come, it should not be surprising that Eden as a place is a type for other places later in redemptive history. At various points the promised land is described in language evocative of a new Eden (e.g., Deut. 6:3; Josh. 23:13–16; see further Martin, 83–86). Edenic imagery in both the tabernacle and the temple indicates that these structures are God's sanctuary on earth, prototypes of God's heavenly sanctuary that point forward to greater realities (e.g., Exod.

25:17–21; 36:35; 1 Kings 6:23–30; see further Beale, *Temple*). Of course, in the NT the fulfillment of this type takes multiple forms. Jesus is both the true tabernacle (John 1:14) and the true temple (2:13–22). As God's Spirit indwells the church, they are the temple of the living God (1 Cor. 3:16; 6:19–20; Eph. 2:19–22). The new creation is described as the fulfillment of the hope of a new Eden (Rev. 22:1–5), which in its totality is the sanctuary of God such that no temple is needed (Rev. 21:22–27).

Abiding Authority

Later OT authors will often either cite or allude to earlier scriptural texts to ground the authority of what they are saying. Perhaps the most obvious example is Deuteronomy, which contains large sections of laws previously stated in Exodus, Leviticus, and Numbers. Yet in some cases these laws are not merely repeated verbatim; instead, these later statements contain slight variations. An obvious example is the restatement of the Ten Commandments in Deut. 5:1–21, where the fourth, fifth, and the tenth commandments differ from their original form in Exod. 20:1–17. As Gary Schnittjer (101) notes, "The repetition of the Ten Commandments points to the enduring authority of Yahweh's commanding will. The variations therein simultaneously signify Yahweh's sovereignty over his dynamic covenantal relationship with his people."

In addition to the repetition of specific laws, later OT authors repeat theological axioms as a source of abiding authority. Leviticus 18:5 states, "You shall therefore keep my statutes and my rules; if a person does them, he shall live by them: I am the LORD" (ESV). This text is picked up several times in Ezekiel to ground statements that Yahweh makes to his exiled people (Sprinkle, 34–40). Thus, in response to those who claim they are in exile solely because of their fathers' sins, Yahweh insists that those who walk in his statutes will in fact live (Ezek. 18:9, 17, 19, 21). In a prophetic oracle recounting Israel's history, Yahweh alludes to Lev. 18:5 three times to explain the demand for obedience and Israel's failure to obey (Ezek. 20:11, 13, 21). Ezekiel 33, in its description of a dying nation, uses language from Lev. 18:5 to portray Israel's failure to fulfill their covenant obligation of obedience (33:10, 19). An allusion to Lev. 18:5 in Nehemiah's summary of Israel's history performs a similar function. Despite Yahweh's repeated warnings Israel had persisted in disobeying the laws that would have brought them life (Neh. 9:29). Later OT authors see in Lev. 18:5 an abiding authority that explains Israel's exile. In the NT, Paul uses Lev. 18:5 to contrast an inadequate form of righteousness based on the law with the righteousness that God provides his people through the gospel (Rom. 10:5; Gal. 3:12).

The revelation of God's character/name in Exod. 34:6–7 serves as another theological axiom that later OT authors use as an abiding authority (Boda, 27–51). Yahweh reveals himself to Moses as "the LORD, the LORD, a God merciful and gracious, slow to anger, and abounding in steadfast love and faithfulness, keeping steadfast love for thousands, forgiving iniquity and transgression and sin, but who will by no means clear the guilty, visiting the iniquity of the fathers on the children and the children's children, to the third and the fourth generation" (ESV). Thus, when Moses intercedes for Israel after they refused to enter the promised land, he asks Yahweh to forgive the people based on Exod. 34:6–7 (Num. 14:17–19). In his prayer of confession, Nehemiah draws language from Exod. 34:6–7 to both acknowledge Yahweh's faithfulness and ask for mercy (Neh. 9:32). An ironic use of Exod. 34:6–7 occurs on the lips of the prophet Jonah. Expressing his frustration over God showing mercy to repentant Nineveh, Jonah explains that he initially fled to Tarshish because "I knew that you are a gracious God and merciful, slow to anger and abounding in steadfast love, and relenting from disaster" (Jon. 4:2 ESV). Repeated allusions and echoes of Exod. 34:6–7 throughout the OT show the importance of this text for later OT authors (see the catalog in Hamilton, *Judgment*, 133–37, and the chart in Boda, 45). In the NT, John echoes this text when he describes Jesus as "full of grace and truth" (John 1:14). Believers are encouraged to confess their sins to God, who is "faithful and just to forgive us our sins and to cleanse us from all unrighteousness" (1 John 1:9 ESV).

A final example of a theological axiom used as an abiding authority is the covenant formula that first occurs in Exod. 6:7: "I will take you to be my people, and I will be your God" (ESV; see Boda, 53–75). Variations of this formula appear throughout the OT, often at key points in redemptive history. Leviticus 26 articulates the covenant blessings for obedience (26:1–13) and the curses for disobedience (26:14–39). The culminating blessing is that Yahweh will dwell among them as their God and Israel will be his people (26:12). As part of his covenant with David, God promises to David's greater son, "I will be to him a father, and he shall be to me a son" (2 Sam. 7:14 ESV). When David prepares Solomon to build the temple, he repeats to Solomon what God had told him: "He shall be my son, and I will be his father, and I will establish his royal throne in Israel forever" (1 Chron. 22:10 ESV). At the heart of the new covenant announced in Jeremiah, God promises, "I will be their God, and they will be my people" (Jer. 31:33). Given the prominence of this covenant formula, it should be no surprise that it occurs in the NT as well. Paul exhorts the Corinthians to pursue holiness on the basis of this covenant formula (2 Cor. 6:14–7:1). In twice quoting Jer. 31:31–34, the author of Hebrews asserts that this axiom is true of believers because of their participation in the new covenant (Heb. 8:1–10:18). When the new heavens and new earth descend in Revelation, the angel announces, "Behold, the dwelling place of God is with man. He will dwell with them, and they will be his people, and God himself will be with them as their God" (Rev. 21:3 ESV).

More broadly considered, the prophets regularly draw upon the blessings and curses expressed in Lev. 26 and Deut. 28–30 to articulate both impending judgment for Israel's sin and God's eventual redemption of his people. Indeed, "The prophets had not the slightest sense they were creating any new doctrine but considered themselves spokespersons for Yahweh, who through them called his people *back* to obedience to the covenant he had given them many centuries before, and reminded them of its curses and blessings, which Yahweh had sworn to honor" (Stuart, xxxii). These covenant blessings and curses were regarded as the abiding authority undergirding the message of these prophets.

Summaries of Israel's Stories

At various points in the OT, biblical authors summarize the story of Israel up to that point (see the helpful list in Hood and Emerson, 340–43). The summaries highlight key events, individuals, institutions, divine promises, and divine acts that form the basis of Israel's identity. These summaries are, in essence, narrative creeds in which "we discover the history of God's redemption through finite action, that is, particular acts within specific times of history. While the emphasis is on God and his acts, these acts are directed toward a community and involve key leaders who play an important role. Thus, the human participants are part of this narrative theology that traces God's actions and human responses within the grand story of redemption" (Boda, 15). Such summaries appear in both narrative and poetic form. The biblical authors use these summaries to enable God's people to live faithful lives in the present as they await the fulfillment of God's promises in the future based on God's faithfulness in the past. Space permits noting just a few examples.

As Joshua comes to the end of his life, he gathers Israel together at Shechem. His summary begins with the call of Abraham and culminates in Israel's present situation dwelling in the land (Josh. 24:1–13). The account moves quickly from God's call of Abraham and the passing down of the promise through Isaac and Jacob on to the exodus from Egypt (24:1–7a). The pace slows to give attention to Israel's wilderness wanderings, highlighting the defeat of the Amorites and the efforts of Balak through the prophet Balaam (24:7b–10). Because God gave the inhabitants of the land into Israel's hands and sent the hornet ahead of them, Israel lives in houses they did not build and reaps fruit from fields they did not plant (24:11–13). Based on God's redemptive acts and faithfulness to his promises, Joshua calls Israel to serve Yahweh wholeheartedly and Israel vows to do so (24:14–24). Joshua confirms this commitment by making a covenant, writing it down in a book, and setting up a stone as a witness (24:25–28).

A similar scene appears much later in Israel's history. Nearly a century after a remnant of the Jews have returned from their Babylonian exile, Nehemiah gathers the people together for a time of mourning, confession, and worship (Neh. 9). Nehemiah begins at creation, stressing God as both Creator and Sustainer, who chose Abraham and fulfilled his promise to give his descendants the land (9:6–8). The exodus receives extended attention; God made a name for himself by bringing them out of their Egyptian bondage and revealing his law to them through Moses his servant (9:9–14). Despite their rebellion and idolatry with the golden calf (9:15–18), rather than forsake them God still led them in the wilderness and provided for them for forty years (9:19–21). He gave Israel possession of the land, subduing their enemies and multiplying them as the stars of the heaven (9:22–25). Despite showing Israel such staggering mercy, the people rebelled against Yahweh and his law (9:26). Thus began a lengthy cycle of God raising up saviors to deliver the people only to see them return to their rebellious ways despite repeated warnings from God's Spirit through the prophets (9:27–30). Yet in his great mercy God did not make an end of his people (9:31). Based on this centuries-long track record of God's covenant faithfulness and mercy, Nehemiah asks Yahweh to be mindful of their present pitiful state of living in the land under foreign oppression and leads the people to reaffirm the covenant (9:32–38).

These summaries of Israel's story are also embedded within Israel's worship. Psalm 106 opens with a call to thank God for his steadfast love and a plea to be remembered when God shows favor to his people (106:1–5). The people's sinfulness that the psalmist confesses begins with Israel's failure to remember Yahweh while they were slaves in Egypt; despite this God brought them out with a mighty hand and drowned their enemies in the sea (106:6–12). Despite this redemption, Israel repeatedly forgot Yahweh's works during their time in the wilderness, even going so far as to make a golden calf (106:13–33). Only Moses's intercession saved them from destruction (106:23), but even he failed to obey Yahweh (106:32–33). Israel's disobedience only intensified once they were in the land, culminating in their worship of the Canaanite idols (106:34–39). Because Yahweh was angry with his people he gave Israel into the hands of their enemies, and despite repeatedly delivering them Israel persisted in their rebellion (106:40–43). Yet in his steadfast love Yahweh caused Israel's enemies to pity them (106:44–46). The psalm concludes with a plea for God to restore them from their current exile so that his people may once again praise his name (106:47–48).

These examples demonstrate a consistent pattern. God's past redemptive acts are recounted with an emphasis on his faithfulness to his promises despite the repeated sin of his people. Despite some variation, key events such as God's covenant with Abraham, the exodus, Israel's wilderness wandering, and the conquest of the land are regularly highlighted. These summaries of Israel's stories are used to help God's people understand who they are and where they are in redemptive history, as well as provoke faithfulness to God as they wait for him to consummate his promises (see similarly Kee, 46).

A similar pattern is present in places where Israel's story is summarized and retold in the NT. The sermon summaries in Acts provide the most obvious examples (e.g., 7:1–53; 13:16–41; see further Bruno, Compton, and McFadden, 49–82). In Acts 7:1–53, Stephen responds to charges that he has spoken against the temple and the law by giving an extended survey of redemptive history. He moves through Israel's story in several phases: the call of Abraham through the birth of Jacob's twelve sons (7:2–8); the role of Joseph in preserving the family of promise (7:9–16); the birth and education of Moses (7:17–22); Moses's forty-year exile from Egypt in the wilderness (7:23–29); the commissioning of Moses, the exodus from Egypt, and wandering in the wilderness (7:30–43); and the presence of the tabernacle and the eventual building of the temple under Solomon (7:44–47). Based on this retelling of Israel's story, which consistently highlights their disobedience to God, Stephen reminds his hearers that God does not dwell in houses made by human hands (7:48–50). He concludes with a condemnation of the people as stiff-necked and resistant to the Holy Spirit, a posture that led them to betray and murder Jesus, God's Righteous One (7:51–53).

Although less explicit, Gal. 3–4 can also be regarded as a selective retelling of Israel's story (see Bruno, Compton, and McFadden, 83–114). God justifying Abraham on the basis of faith was an outworking of his promise to bless all the nations through Abraham (3:6–9). Those who rely on the Mosaic law to be right with God end up under a curse, but Christ redeems his people from that curse so that "in Christ Jesus the blessing of Abraham might come to the Gentiles, so that we might receive the promised Spirit through faith" (3:10–14). God's promise to Abraham, which is fulfilled in Christ, the promised seed of Abraham, was not nullified by the giving of the Mosaic law 430 years later (3:15–18). The Mosaic law was given to expose sin and function as a guardian over God's people until Christ, the promised seed, arrived (3:19–25). All who are in Christ are sons of God who inherit what God promised Abraham through their union with Christ, an inheritance that includes the Spirit of God's Son dwelling in God's redeemed people (3:26–4:7). After a personal appeal to remember their life before Christ and initial reception of the gospel through Paul (4:8–20), Paul brings his argument to its climax. God has fulfilled his promise to Abraham in Christ, the promised seed and suffering servant; through his resurrection the new/heavenly Jerusalem is now bringing forth children who live in the freedom that Christ has purchased for them, and in this way the gospel promise made to Abraham that "all the nations shall be blessed in you" (Gal. 3:8 ESV = Gen. 12:3) is being fulfilled (4:21–5:1).

As with the OT examples, NT summaries regularly highlight God's covenant with Abraham, the exodus from Egypt, the conquest of the land, and the people's persistent rebellion. Although not absent from the OT examples, God's covenant with David receives more prominence in the NT summaries of Israel's story. But most obviously the NT summaries stand out from their OT counterparts in their repeated assertions that the person and work of Jesus are the fulfillment of those promises and the inauguration of the last days that will one day culminate in the full realization of God's creational and redemptive purposes.

So, it is important to remember that uses of the OT may overlap. In the Galatians examples, summary of Israel's stories includes indication of direct prophetic fulfillment. Likewise, in Acts 7 above, the summary of Israel's history is interwoven with typology and indication of direct fulfillment of prophecy (on which, e.g., see Beale, *Temple*, 216–28).

Ironic or Inverted Use

On occasion, biblical authors use earlier Scripture in an ironic manner where the meaning of the source text is inverted for rhetorical effect. The men of Gibeah violating two women in the town square (Judg. 19:22–29) ironically picks up language from Lot's experience in Sodom (Gen. 19:1–29) to demonstrate that the Israelites have become just as wicked as the nations whom they have dispossessed from the land. Considered together, Mic. 4:8–10 and 5:2 promise a king for Jerusalem will come from Bethlehem Ephrathah despite its being small. These texts pick up language from the account of Rachel giving birth to Benjamin (Gen. 35:16–21), Saul's heritage as a Benjaminite (1 Sam. 9:21), and David's origins as an Ephrathite of Bethlehem (1 Sam 16:1; 17:12). "Micah seems to take advantage of the ironies of David an Ephrathite (1 Sam 17:12) coming from Bethlehem, associated with the birth of Benjamin, to get at ancient expectations for the Davidic ruler (Mic 5:2[1]). The reference to Bethlehem Ephrathah as small may further draw on the Saul and David traditions by evoking the sense of Saul's small family in a small tribe and David's youth. The same irony attaches to small Bethlehem Ephrathah, once again as an unlikely source of renewal" (Schnittjer, 413–14). Similar ironic use of previous Scripture also occurs in the NT. In Gal. 3:13 Paul cites Deut. 21:23 ("Cursed is everyone who is hanged on a tree" [ESV]) ironically to explain how Christ Jesus became a curse for his people to enable the blessing of Abraham to come to believers. The people worshiping the beast in Rev. 13:4 ("Who is like the beast?") echo Exod. 15:11 ("Who is like you, O LORD") to "mock [the beast's] efforts to assume the role of God" (Beale, *Handbook*, 92).

Summary Analysis and Conclusion

These representative examples demonstrate several of the ways that later OT authors use earlier Scripture to communicate fresh revelation from God. A similar dynamic is present in the NT, as the authors build on the foundations of their OT predecessors, though with some notable developments.

First, later biblical authors often do more than simply repeat language or wording from previous texts; they regularly interpret earlier texts in light of what God was presently doing and promised to one day do. On a macrolevel the most obvious OT example is 1–2 Chronicles, where the author selectively retells the history of Israel recounted in earlier texts (esp. 1–2 Samuel, 1–2 Kings) in order to interpret that history in a particular way. As but one example of this dynamic on the microlevel, one need only to trace the various iterations and expansions of the Abrahamic promise. NT authors similarly take OT texts and provide interpretation of those texts in light of the Christ-event (e.g., 1 Cor. 10:1–22).

Second, both OT and NT authors display a similar eschatological orientation. Within the OT itself the various divine promises intensify in both their scope and their specificity. The same is true for the various types and patterns as they build anticipation for their eventual fulfillment. The various covenants that God makes with his people encourage God's people not only to look back with gratitude to what God has already done but also to look forward with anticipation to the day when the blessings of those within the covenant will be fully realized. As one would expect, this eschatological orientation intensifies to a significant degree in the NT with the arrival of Christ, which ushers in the last days and inaugurates the age during which all of God's promises would eventually be fulfilled.

Third, the fulfillment of God's promises is a major emphasis of both OT and NT authors. In the most basic sense, this dynamic comes out in direct promises that are marked as fulfilled by a later biblical author. But it is also evident in the various types found in the OT, as later iterations of these "promise-shaped patterns" (Hamilton, *Typology*) fill up the significance of their precursors. Later biblical authors take great pains to both explicitly state and indirectly imply the fulfillment of God's promises and patterns as a means of encouraging God's people to remain faithful to the Lord. That emphasis on fulfillment takes on a heightened sense in the NT, with even more frequent explicit claims of fulfillment and a clear sense of escalation in light of Christ. Indeed, a key distinctive of fulfillment in the NT is its eschatological nature. In the OT, certain promises find a measure of fulfillment but then subsequently are reversed in some fashion. Thus, Israel's increase noted in Exod. 1 diminishes significantly by the time of Judah's return from exile in Ezra 2. Even more notably, God's promise that a descendant of David would build a house for him to dwell in finds partial fulfillment in the temple that Solomon builds. But its eventual destruction demonstrates that there is a greater, eschatological fulfillment yet to come, a fulfillment that the NT makes clear is the incarnate Jesus and the eschatological people of God indwelt by the Holy Spirit. Only with the arrival of the new covenant is fulfillment eschatological—that is, escalated, irreversible, and permanent.

Fourth, later OT authors and the NT authors demonstrate an already/not-yet understanding of God fulfilling his promises. As early as Joshua, texts affirm that God has fulfilled his promises to Israel to give them the land right alongside texts that note areas where the Israelites have been unable to drive out the Canaanites. Within 1 Kings we see Solomon and his building of the temple as a fulfillment of God's promise to David while at the same time recognizing that more fulfillment should be expected. This already/not-yet dynamic intensifies in the NT, where numerous OT promises and types/patterns find their fulfillment in Christ without exhausting the scope of the promise.

Lastly, a major difference between OT authors' use of earlier Scripture and that of NT authors is that the latter refocus and unite the numerous threads of the OT hope around the person and work of Jesus Christ. Although within the OT itself there is a narrowing of the hope to a remnant and a descendant from David's line, it is not until the NT that the OT hope is so singularly focused on Christ and through him to his people that Paul can say that all of God's promises find their "yes" in Christ (2 Cor. 1:20).

See also *Apocrypha articles; Dead Sea Scrolls articles; Mishnah, Talmud, and Midrashim articles; Philo articles; Pseudepigrapha articles; Septuagint articles; Targums articles*

Bibliography. Beale, G. K., *Handbook on the New Testament Use of the Old Testament* (Baker Academic, 2012); Beale, *The Temple and the Church's Mission*, NSBT 17 (IVP Academic, 2004); Boda, M. J., *The Heartbeat of Old Testament Theology* (Baker Academic, 2017); Bruno, C., J. Compton, and K. McFadden, *Biblical Theology according to the Apostles*, NSBT 52 (IVP Academic, 2020); Chase, M. L., *40 Questions about Typology and Allegory* (Kregel, 2020); Crowe, B., *The Last Adam* (Baker Academic, 2017); Estelle, B. D., *Echoes of Exodus* (IVP Academic, 2019); Fishbane, M., *Biblical Interpretation in Ancient Israel* (Oxford University Press, 1985); Hamilton, J. M., Jr., *God's Glory in Salvation through Judgment* (Crossway, 2010); Hamilton, *Typology* (Zondervan, 2022); Harmon, M. S., *The Servant of the Lord and His Servant People*, NSBT 54 (IVP Academic, 2020); Hood, J. B., and M. Y. Emerson, "Summaries of Israel's Story," *CurBR* 11 (2013): 328–48; Hummel, H. D., "The OT Basis of Typological Interpretation," *BR* 9 (1964): 38–50; Kee, H. C., "Appropriating the History of God's People," in *Pseudepigrapha and Early*

Biblical Interpretation, ed. J. Charlesworth and C. Evans (JSOT Press), 44–64; Keesmaat, S. C., *Paul and His Story*, JSNTSup 181 (Sheffield Academic, 1999); Kugel, J. L., *In Potiphar's House* (Harvard University Press, 1994); Kugel, *Traditions of the Bible* (Harvard University Press, 1998); Marcus, J., *The Way of the Lord* (Westminster John Knox, 1992); Martin, O. R., *Bound for the Promised Land*, NSBT 34 (IVP Academic, 2015); Miller, G., "Intertextuality in OT Research," *CurBR* 9 (2010): 283–309; Morales, L. M., *Exodus Old and New*, ESBT (IVP Academic, 2020); Pao, D. W., *Acts and the Isaianic New Exodus*, BSL (2000; repr., Baker Academic, 2002); Schnittjer, G. E., *The Old Testament Use of the Old Testament* (Zondervan, 2021); Schultz, R., *The Search for Quotation*, JSOTSup 180 (Sheffield Academic, 1999); Sprinkle, P. M., *Law and Life*, WUNT 2/241 (Mohr Siebeck, 2008); Stead, M. R., "Intertextuality and Innerbiblical Interpretation," in *DOTPr*, 355–64; Stuart, D., *Hosea–Jonah*, WBC (Thomas Nelson, 1987); Watts, R. E., "Consolation or Confrontation?," *TynBul* 41 (1990): 31–59; Watts, *Isaiah's New Exodus in Mark*, BSL (1997; repr., Baker Academic, 2000).

Matthew S. Harmon

[P]

Paraphrase *See* Quotation, Allusion, and Echo

Parousia *See* Consummation

Patristic Interpretation *See* History of Interpretation: Early Church

Peace *See* Shalom

Perspicuity of Scripture *See* Theological Interpretation of Scripture

Pesher *See* Dead Sea Scrolls, OT Use in

Peter, First Letter of

The author of 1 Peter, who identifies himself by the name Peter (1:1), relies heavily on the texts and traditions of the Jewish Scriptures, primarily in their Greek (LXX/OG) form. Peter explains the basis of his use of the OT in 1 Pet. 1:10–12, where he discloses that the gospel revealed in the life of Jesus Christ was the focus of the prophets of times long past. Their prophetic role was to serve a future generation, the generation contemporary with the death and resurrection of Jesus. Those ancient prophets had spoken of the gospel that has been preached to Peter's readers (1:12). Consequently, Peter, who has embraced Jesus as the Messiah (Matt. 16:16; Mark 8:29) and has witnessed his suffering, death, and resurrection, looks to the writings of the OT to make sense of the violent death of the Messiah.

To the extent that Acts is a source of information about the author of 1 Peter, Peter's reference to the "prophets" is broad, for from his first sermon on the day of Pentecost, Peter identifies King David as being among them and quotes various psalms as referring to Jesus (Acts 2:14–36, esp. v. 30). It is therefore not surprising that the Psalms, especially Ps. 34 (Ps. 33 OG), are important texts of OT Scripture in 1 Peter. The prophecy of Isaiah is a second major biblical source to which Peter turns in order to understand the suffering and rejection of Jesus Christ. Peter's speech in Acts primarily uses the Psalms, with few references to Isaiah; in contrast, 1 Peter primarily uses Isaiah, with fewer, but significant, references to Psalms (Moyise, *Writers*, 61).

Peter appropriates the OT for two purposes: first, to explain that Jesus was the Messiah, who, it was predicted, would suffer and die (prophetic interpretation) and, second, to explain how Christian believers are to live out their new lives in Christ (paraenetic application; Bauckham, 309). To that end, Peter quotes Leviticus (19:2), two psalms (118:22; 34:12–16), two proverbs (3:34; 11:31), and four passages from Isaiah (8:14; 28:16; 40:6–8; 53:9). Relative to its brief length, 1 Peter is comparable to Romans and Hebrews for its frequency of OT quotations (Moyise, "Isaiah," 175).

First Peter teaches Christology primarily through references to Isaiah, specifically in the "stone" passages of 1 Pet. 2:4–8 (Isa. 28:16; Ps. 118:22; Isa. 8:14) and Isaiah's suffering-servant prophecy in 1 Pet. 2:21–25 (Isa. 52:13–53:12, hereafter "Isa. 53"). Peter's Christology anchors Christian self-understanding and so informs Peter's instructions for Christian living. The objectives of both Christology and paraenesis in 1 Peter are distinguishable but integrally related. Since Peter is offering guidance for Christian living in a personal letter, not writing a theological tract, the paraenetic goal is at the forefront. Nevertheless, his Christology forms the indispensable basis of his paraenesis. Peter's use of the stone and suffering-servant passages from Isaiah indicates his understanding that Jesus directly fulfilled the prophetic aspect of those passages. Peter's paraenetic use of the OT often observes a continuity between Israel as God's people and the Christian communities to whom Peter writes.

OT Quotations in 1 Peter

Be holy: Lev. 19:2 in 1 Pet. 1:16. After praising God for the new birth through the resurrection of Jesus Christ (1 Pet. 1:3) and explaining that this gospel message is the culmination of the prophetic hopes of the OT (1:10–12), Peter begins to instruct his readers how to live their new lives begun through faith in Christ. The first quotation of the OT in the letter is found in 1:16, following the form of Lev. 19:2 LXX, and is an application of the OT hermeneutic that Peter presents in 1:10–12. Peter sees, at least for the purposes of his letter, that the OT prophets instruct a later generation—namely, those who would put their faith in Christ.

"Be holy, because I am holy" invokes the Leviticus Holiness Code, given to set Israel apart from the customs, rituals, and values of their surrounding culture. Peter draws continuity between the authority and holiness principle of the OT and the Christians to whom he writes. However, he does not enjoin the specifics of the Levitical code on his readers, such as the cultic purity rituals. His is a more complex hermeneutic that recognizes the difference between the historical location of ancient Israel and that of the Christian church. The Christians to whom Peter writes live after the resurrection of Jesus and the coming of the Spirit and within a different geopolitical context. Peter invokes OT Scripture as exhortation in a new context, reinforcing the OT's authority in and relevancy to the lives of Christians, though it is always to be viewed through the lens of Christ's coming (cf. Beale, 72–73). Accordingly, Christian holiness is centered not on the cultic rituals of temple sacrifice but on the moral transformation of those who have been born again through the resurrection of Jesus Christ. Peter sees Christian believers collectively as the new temple built on the cornerstone of the resurrected Christ (1 Pet. 2:4, 5).

Isaiah in 1 Peter. Although Peter quotes from all three sections of the Hebrew Bible—Pentateuch, Prophets, and Writings—more quotations of the OT are taken from Isaiah than from any other OT book.

The word of the Lord: Isa. 40:6–8 in 1 Pet. 1:24–25. The first quotation from Isaiah occurs in 1 Pet. 1:24–25, explaining that the word of the Lord, which is the seed of the new birth, is eternal, in contrast to the fleeting, weak transience of humankind and all its achievements. Even the glorious power of the Roman Empire confronting the Christians to whom 1 Peter was originally written has now fallen into the dust of the ages. But the gospel of Jesus Christ continues to flourish far beyond the former empire's boundaries (cf. Beale, 78).

There are a few textual differences of note between the MT of Isa. 40:6–8 and the OG: (1) in 40:6, "all their faithfulness [*ḥesed*]" is translated as "the glory of man" (*doxa anthrōpou*); (2) the phrase "when the breath of the LORD blows upon it" in 40:7 MT is omitted from the OG; and (3) the "fading" (*nābēl*) of the flower is translated as its "falling" (*ekpiptō*). The quotation in 1 Peter aligns more closely with the OG but departs from both by substituting "the word of the *Lord*" for "the word of God." This substitution is most likely a deliberate revision made by Peter, since Jesus is usually referred to as the "Lord" in 1 Peter and because it was the "Spirit of Christ" in the prophets who spoke God's word (1 Pet. 1:11). Where the prophets speak of "God," Peter (like other NT writers) often substitutes a reference to Jesus, indicating belief in the divinity of Jesus Christ.

The "stone" passages: Isa. 8:14 and 28:16. Two of the three OT passages that speak of a stone that God has laid in Zion are from Isa. 8:14 and 28:16 (the third is from Ps. 118:22 [117:22 OG]; see below). Isaiah 28:16 speaks of a foundation stone laid in Zion by God for the faith of the people. In the OG translation the prepositional phrase "on it/him" (*ep' autō*) is added as the object of faith, which allowed the stone to be interpreted in pre-Christian Jewish tradition as a metaphor for the Messiah. In Isa. 8:14 MT it is the Lord who will be a holy place and a stone that causes people to stumble, but in the Greek translation of Isa. 8:14, faith in the stone will protect one from stumbling. It remained for the apostles, who stood within the interpretive tradition of Judaism, only to identify Jesus as the Messiah (cf. Mark 12:10; Luke 20:17–18; Rom. 9:33; 10:11; Eph. 2:20).

The form of the quotation of Isa. 28:16 in 1 Pet. 2:6 agrees with the OG against the MT, personalizing the object of trust "in him" (*ep' autō*) to be Jesus, the Living Stone, and using the verb *kataischynō* (shame) in place of the MT's "panic" (*ḥîš*). But 1 Pet. 2:6 differs from the OG by replacing of the verb *emballō* with *tithēmi*, possibly because the semantic range of *tithēmi* includes the sense of appointment as well as that of putting or placing, perhaps resonating with "chosen" (*eklekton*) in 1 Pet. 2:4 and 2:9. Paul also combines these same two passages from Isaiah (8:14; 28:16) in Rom. 9:33, including some of the same differences from the OG (*tithēmi; kataischynō*). Although this was once argued to be evidence for a literary dependence between Peter and Paul, it is perhaps more likely that both were quoting from a source in earlier Christian tradition that had this textual form.

Peter's quotation of these verses in 2:6, 8 teaches that the resurrected Christ, the Living Stone, is the cornerstone of God's redemptive building project foreseen by Isaiah (cf. Beale, 56). The "living stones" who come to Christ in faith are built into this structure, joined and plumbed to the living cornerstone. While their Christian faith may have caused social ostracization, Isaiah's voice teaches that the living stones will never truly be put to shame, for they are on the side of God in history.

Peter includes a reference to the stone from Ps. 118:22 (117:22 OG) to show that the rejection of the stone by those building for merely human glory was predicted. Invoking this psalm, Peter teaches that response to the gospel message determines one's eternal destiny (see below).

An allusion to—or some may say an unmarked quotation of—Isa. 8:12 OG, "Do not fear what they [this people] fear" (*ton de phobon autou ou mē phobēthēte*), appears in 1 Pet. 3:14, suggesting that Peter has the fuller context of Isaiah's stone passages in mind. In both the MT and OG of Isa. 8:12, the antecedent of the third-person singular pronoun is "this people" of Jerusalem and Judah who feared the threatening alliance of Aram and the Northern Kingdom of Israel. God instructs them through Isaiah not to fear this threat. First Peter 3:14 contextualizes the meaning for a new situation by changing the pronoun to the plural *autōn*, referring to those who would harm Peter's readers: "Do not fear them." Both Isa. 8:13 and 1 Pet. 3:15 further command the reader to revere the Lord instead of fearing adversaries. Peter adds *ton Christon*, the Lord Christ, as the one Christians are to revere (*kyrion de ton christon hagiasate*).

The suffering servant: Isa. 53. Peter applies Isaiah's suffering-servant passage to Jesus more completely than any other NT writer (cf. Beale, 56). This significant christological teaching is, true to the objective of paraenesis, embedded within the so-called household code of 1 Pet. 2:18–3:7, drawing an analogy between the redemptive role of Jesus Christ and the least-empowered person in a Greco-Roman household, the slave (cf. Phil. 2:7). Addressing the household slave first and directly (1 Pet. 2:18), Peter dignifies the slave by showing that Jesus himself took on the role of the suffering servant to accomplish redemption through atonement for sin. Peter makes the point that every Christian is to be a slave to God (1 Pet. 2:16) and that every Christian is therefore called to this self-understanding of following in the footsteps of Jesus (2:21) as they live out new life in Christ.

Isaiah 53:9 OG is quoted precisely in 2:22 to remind readers that Jesus was sinless and innocent and yet nevertheless suffered to achieve God's purposes. That quotation invokes the fuller passage of Isa. 53 OG, from which Peter includes phrases that show Jesus responded without violence, retaliation, or threatening (Isa. 53:7 in 1 Pet. 2:23). Instead, he entrusted himself to God the Judge, who alone judges justly. This makes Jesus a role model for suffering Christians being ostracized and persecuted because of their faith, instructing them to respond without aggression and based on trust in God.

The atoning purpose of Jesus's suffering is clearly stated in 1 Pet. 2:24 using the words of Isa. 53:4 OG and amplifying them to specify Jesus's body on the cross as the atoning death. Even this substantial and profound christological statement forms the basis for the exhortation that the Christian might so die to sins and live for righteousness, showing how closely Christology is related to paraenesis in Peter's thinking. The wounds of Jesus, the suffering servant, heal the believer, echoing Isa. 53:5 OG in 1 Pet. 2:24. Furthermore, the Christian believer is like a sheep who had wandered astray from the flock but who, in coming to Christ, has now returned to the Shepherd and Overseer for healing and safety (Isa. 53:6 OG in 1 Pet. 2:25).

Psalms in 1 Peter. First Peter quotes two psalms: Pss. 34 and 118.

The rejected stone: Ps. 118. As noted above, the stone metaphor found in Ps. 118:22 (117:22 OG) describes the foundational cornerstone of God's redemptive building project as being rejected by the builders. When this verse is read together with the Isaiah stone passages, the reader learns that God has laid a stone in Zion that has become the cornerstone of God's redemptive project but that causes many to stumble. Those who do not stumble but trust will never be put to shame.

It is striking that these stone passages are cited by the apostle whom Jesus renamed the "rock," declaring he would build his church on "this rock" (Matt. 16:18). Yet Peter himself never hints that he considers himself to be the rock on which the church is built. But it is perhaps that memorable incident with Jesus that turns Peter's thoughts to the stone passages of the OT.

Peter appropriates the prophecy of Ps. 117:22 OG in 1 Pet. 2:7 to explain that the rejection of Jesus by the Jewish leaders of his day had been predicted in the Scriptures (cf. Beale, 56). Rejection of Christ disqualified from the work of God those who ironically thought they were building for God, for God's redemptive work is centered on the foundation of the living stone, the resurrected Jesus Christ. This statement about the essential importance of Jesus in God's purposes simultaneously forms a warning to readers not to reject the gospel. Again Peter weds Christology to paraenesis.

Deliverance of the righteous sufferer: Ps. 34. Peter instructs about the nature of the Christian life by invoking Ps. 33 OG (Ps. 34 MT), a psalm of praise for God, who delivers the one who suffers unjustly (1 Pet. 2:3; 3:10–12). When first inscripturated in the Hebrew Psalms, the psalm referred to the sufferings David experienced when he was driven out of Jerusalem to live among the Philistines (1 Sam. 21). When the psalm was translated into the context of the Greek Jewish diaspora, the sufferings of David in Ps. 33:5 OG were specified to be "sojournings" (*paroikiōn*), the same word found in 1 Pet. 2:11 describing those to whom Peter writes as "sojourners." Like David and like the Jews living in the Greek diaspora, Peter's readers were suffering from living among others who were not like them and who did not share their beliefs and values. Peter further recontextualizes Ps. 33 OG for his Christian readers, whom he has described as also sojourning. He exhorts them to turn from evil and do good *even* when suffering, for God delivers the *righteous* sufferer who suffers unjustly and, following the example of Jesus, does not retaliate or threaten.

Allusions to Ps. 33 OG appear pervasively throughout the paraenetic sections of 1 Peter as a scriptural basis for Christian ethics (Jobes, *1 Peter*, 221–23). The role of speech in returning good for evil and pursuing peace is emphasized, probably because Peter's readers are suffering from verbal abuse, insult, and ostracism.

The exhortation to turn away from evil is preceded by an allusion to Ps. 33:9 OG in 1 Pet. 2:3. Peter's readers have "tasted that the Lord is good." The Greek adjective *chrēstos* (good) is a play on the title *Christos* (Christ), differing by only one vowel. Since the readers have tasted the goodness of the Lord, Peter exhorts them to imbibe deeply for spiritual growth through ethical cleansing—putting off malice, deceit, hypocrisy, envy, and slander (2:1). Christians are to exhibit the good and holy character of the Lord Jesus because God is himself good and holy (1:16, quoting Lev. 19:2). When Jesus suffered unjustly, even to the point of being murdered, he did not sin and was a *righteous* sufferer. Peter points to the suffering Jesus as the role model for his readers in how they are to live out their lives, for Christians are called to suffer unjustly if necessary—that is, for no reason other than being Christian (1 Pet. 2:21; 3:9; 4:1). The call to repay suffering with blessing in 1 Pet. 3:9 introduces the extended quotation of Ps. 33:13–17 OG. The themes of Ps. 33 OG—namely, deliverance from shame (33:6 OG), and afflictions (33:7 OG), and want (33:10–11 OG)—are relevant to Peter's readers in the difficulties of their sojourning (cf. Beale, 67).

The text of Ps. 33:13–17 OG in 1 Pet. 3:10–12 is the most extensive quotation in the letter and, with one exception, closely follows the OG, which is itself a close translation of the Hebrew. The translator preserves many repetitions and parallelisms in Ps. 34 MT but does not attempt to imitate its Hebrew acrostic form. The question in Ps. 33:13 OG ("Who is the person . . . ?") has been revised in 1 Pet. 3:10 to be a statement introduced by *gar*, making it into a statement that can form the basis for Peter's exhortation in v. 9. The second-person imperatives have been replaced by third-person. The quotation ends in the middle of Ps. 33:17 OG with "the face of the Lord is against those who do evil." Of special interest is the difference between 1 Pet. 3:10a, which includes the infinitive *agapan* ("the one who wishes life *to love* and to see good days," AT), and Ps. 33:13 OG, which has the participle *agapōn* ("the person . . . *who loves* to see good days," AT). This difference hangs on one vowel, which may have been introduced by Peter to better suit his purpose, though such a difference may have arisen from a scribal error instead.

In addition to the quotation of Ps. 33 OG in 1 Pet. 3:10–12 and the allusion to it in 2:3, there are several possible echoes of the psalm in the first half of Peter's letter: Ps. 33:2 in 1 Pet. 1:3; 33:5 in 1:17; 33:6 in 2:6; 33:8 in 1:17; 33:10, 12 in 2:17; 33:18 in 3:12; 33:20 in 1:6; 33:23 in 1:18 (Jobes, *1 Peter*, 220–23). Such extensive echoes suggest that Peter was familiar with the full extent of Ps. 33 OG. Because this is the only place in the NT where Ps. 33 OG is quoted, its contribution to Christian ethics may have originated with Peter himself (Moyise, *Writers*, 43–44).

Proverbs in 1 Peter. There are two clear quotations from Proverbs in 1 Peter: Prov. 11:31 in 1 Pet. 4:18 and Prov. 3:34 in 1 Pet. 5:5. What at first appears to be a third quotation of Prov. 10:12 in 1 Pet. 4:8—"Love covers over a multitude of sins"—is probably not a textual reference. Peter's statement matches neither the MT reading nor the OG even though he otherwise follows the Greek OT consistently and closely throughout the letter. Therefore, 4:8 likely represents a proverbial use of Prov. 10:12 that was in circulation and may or may not have been familiar to Peter's readers (cf. Beale, 74).

What will become of the ungodly? Prov. 11:31. Peter's discussion of righteous suffering (1 Pet. 4:12–19) contrasts his readers' present suffering for being a Christian with the far greater suffering he believes will eventually come to those who reject ("do not obey") the gospel of God. This framing of the discussion in the context of eschatological judgment recognizes that living faithfully as a Christian can be difficult (v. 18) but that such suffering is of one piece with the judgment that begins with God's household (v. 17). For Peter, suffering because of Christian faith is evidence of future eschatological deliverance, and that recognition should produce joy. In light of that, Peter asks a rhetorical question: "What will the outcome be for those who do not obey the gospel?" He exhorts his readers to remain faithful in spite of suffering by contrasting the present sufferings of the Christian to the much greater future sufferings of those who do not believe. The quotation of Prov. 11:31 OG in 1 Pet. 4:18 responds to that rhetorical question in 1 Pet. 4:17 by pointing out that it has always been "hard" for the righteous to be saved, as the proverb acknowledges. This means not that God has difficulty saving the righteous but that authentic faith comes at a cost to the believer that may be hardship.

Peter's quotation follows the OG verbatim except for the absence of the conjunction *men*, possibly omitted by either Peter or his OG source because there is no expected *de* in the following clause. The MT reading is quite different: "If the righteous receive their due on earth, how much more the ungodly and the sinner!" In spite of its difference from the OG, which is more suitable for Peter's purpose, the MT does address the same issue of the difference between the righteous and the ungodly. Peter uses this ancient wisdom to encourage his suffering readers to recognize they are suffering *because* it is God's will that people should be Christ followers despite the cost. He exhorts them to entrust themselves to their faithful Creator, as Jesus himself did (1 Pet. 2:23), and continue to live their Christian life well. This use of Prov. 11:31 is consistent with the extensive use of Ps. 33 OG, which also speaks of the deliverance of the righteous sufferer as the basis for Christian ethics.

God opposes the proud: Prov. 3:34. Peter employs a second verse from Proverbs OG for a similar purpose in 5:5: to encourage submission to the elders of the church and humility toward one another. He grounds this exhortation in Prov. 3:34, which states God's posture toward two groups of people: the proud, who meet with God's opposition, and the humble, who receive God's grace (cf. Beale, 67). The quotation follows the OG reading exactly except that it replaces the subject of the verb, *kyrios*, with *theos*. This is most likely a deliberate change introduced by Peter, who in this letter typically reserves *kyrios* for Jesus Christ and refers to the Father as *theos*. Although Greco-Roman culture considered humility to be the attitude of a lowly slave and not suitable for a free citizen, this exhortation is consistent with Peter's exhortation that Christians live as slaves of God (1 Pet. 2:16).

Allusions to the OT in 1 Peter

In addition to the several recognizable quotations of the OT in 1 Peter, there are allusions to texts, events, and people that indicate Peter's belief that the Christian communities to which he writes are the post-Easter people of God.

In the opening address, Peter addresses his readers as "God's elect" (1 Pet. 1:1), which was the hallmark characterization of ancient Israel. The additional description of the elect as scattered exiles in 1 Pet. 1:1 and the closing mention of Babylon in 5:13 associate Peter's Christian readers with Israel's experience of exile and regathering. This frame suggests Peter understands his letter to function as a diaspora letter, a genre of letter previously known to the literature of Israel.

The first mention of Jesus Christ in the letter (1 Pet. 1:2) uses the covenantal language of *obedience* and *sprinkling* found in the narrative of Israel's establishment in Exod. 24:3–8, suggesting that Christians are brought into covenantal relationship with Israel's God through faith in Jesus Christ. In the Exodus account the newly formed people of Israel ratify their covenant with God first by pledging their *obedience* (24:3, 7) and then being *sprinkled* with the blood of the covenant sacrifice (24:8). The new covenant established by the blood of Jesus Christ is in view in 1 Pet. 1:2, and Christ is described as "a lamb without blemish or defect" (1:19), evoking the sacrificial system prescribed throughout the Pentateuch. Christ was "chosen before the creation of the world" (1:20) to redeem those who are God's "chosen people" (2:9). God's election and the Spirit's agency (1:2) have as their purpose bringing people into covenant relationship with God based on the blood sacrifice of Jesus Christ.

The people brought into that relationship are further described in 1 Peter as "a chosen people, a royal priesthood, a holy nation, God's special possession" (2:9). All of these descriptors are allusions to the OT. The phrase "a chosen race" echoes Isa. 43:3 OG, which announces that God himself is Israel's only savior, who will deliver his people from their exile in Babylon. The further description of Peter's readers as "a royal priesthood, a holy nation, a people for God's special possession" is language taken directly from Exod. 19:5–6 LXX. The holy nation of Israel was to have a mediating function as a priest between God and the nations. Peter declares that, collectively, Christian believers are to perform that same function with respect to the nations among which they are scattered. The modifier "royal" is apt, for this priesthood serves the King of the universe, who was revealed when Jesus Christ inaugurated the kingdom of God. The fourth descriptor, "a people for God's special possession," alludes both to Exod. 19:5 and to Isa. 43:20–21, where God refers to his chosen race in the context of the exodus and the Babylonian exile, respectively, as the people that he claims for himself. When God delivered his people from exile in Babylon, they were to declare the praises of God (Isa. 43:20–21 OG). Peter transfers that purpose of declaring God's praise to his Christian readers, who have been called out of darkness into God's wonderful light (1 Pet. 2:9).

Peter further describes his diverse readers from many nations and languages as once not a people and as those who had not received mercy. But now they are a people who have received God's mercy in Jesus Christ. This description is an allusion to Hosea 2:23 (2:25 OG). After ancient Israel had broken faith with God by acting like the pagans of the surrounding nations, God spoke through the prophet Hosea, promising a future restoration, a time when by unmerited love and mercy God would again constitute a people for his special possession who would declare the mighty act of God that brought them into existence. According to Peter, God's regathered royal priesthood and holy nation—his newly chosen race—are those reborn as the children of God himself through the resurrection of Jesus Christ (1 Pet. 1:3, 23). Although God is the Creator of all, he is in covenant relationship with those people who put their faith in Jesus Christ. Christians are to tell the nations about the mighty act of God in raising Christ from the dead, through which people can be born anew (1:3).

The Spirit of glory and of God rests on you: Isa. 11:2. First Peter 4:14 alludes to, or perhaps quotes, the messianic prophecy of Isa. 11:2. Peter understands the OT prophets, such as Isaiah, to have been inspired by the Spirit of Christ to predict the sufferings of the Messiah and the glories that would follow (1 Pet. 1:10–12). In 4:14 Peter associates that same Spirit with the believers who are willing to suffer for Christ. They should be encouraged by the presence of God in their suffering because they are blessed to share in the glories that followed Christ's suffering, beginning with the resurrection.

Whereas the verb in Isa. 11:2 OG is future, "will rest" (*anapausetai*), it is present tense in 1 Pet. 4:14, "rests" (*anapauetai*). In Isaiah the promise is that the Spirit "will rest on him," the messianic branch, but in 1 Pet. 4:14 the resting Spirit is "on you" (pl.), Peter's persecuted readers. Peter seems to be teaching that the same Spirit that accompanied and strengthened Jesus from his baptism to his execution is present in the lives of Christians, especially when they are persecuted for their faith in Christ. Because Jesus survived his sufferings through his resurrection into glories, Peter encourages his readers with the assertion that they, too, are enjoying the presence of God, who will deliver them from suffering to glory. They should rejoice in that they participate in the sufferings of Christ, and they will be overjoyed when his glory is revealed (4:13). This allusion to Isa. 11:2 as a source of encouragement for Christian life is consistent with the motivations behind Peter's use of Prov. 11:31 and of Ps. 33 OG, which exhort the readers to pursue righteousness because God delivers the righteous sufferer.

References to people and events of the OT. Not every mention of a person or event known to us from reading the OT is a reference to a *text* of the OT, for there is a long and rich Jewish interpretive tradition that NT writers draw upon (Sargent, 104). Consequently, interpretive tradition running true to Scripture is sometimes difficult to distinguish from references to the text of the OT itself.

Sarah and Abraham. The reference to Sarah and Abraham in 1 Pet. 3:6 probably does not cite a particular OT verse but instead refers to the Jewish interpretive tradition of Sarah's exemplary female role. In Gen. 18:12 LXX Sarah refers to Abraham as her lord (*kyrios*), but she does not address him by that term. This noun (*kyrios*) is the only connection between Gen. 18:12 and 1 Pet. 3:6, for the OT text does not speak of Sarah obeying Abraham. Rather, the Genesis story has Abraham obeying Sarah at three different points (Gen. 16:2, 6; 21:12). Nevertheless, the obedience of Sarah to Abraham became a long-standing element of Jewish tradition. In keeping with the overall goal of transforming readers' self-understanding, apparently Peter wishes his readers to look to the Sarah of Israel's religious tradition as the role model of the virtuous woman rather than admired women found in the Greek writings (e.g., Plutarch, *Conj. praec.* 48; Xenophon, *Oec.* 7.1–10.13). Christian women are to redefine themselves as Sarah's daughters and distance themselves from the virtuous woman as defined by Greco-Roman culture.

Noah and the flood. The remembrance of Noah and the flood functions similarly (1 Pet. 3:21) to draw readers into the heritage of ancient Israel, providing an analogy to Christian baptism that connects it to Israel's redemptive history. Water is the symbol that typologically associates the flood with Christian baptism, but Peter's correspondences are broader (Jobes, *1 Peter*, 252–53). Noah and his family "were saved *through* water" corresponding to Christian baptism, which "saves you" (pl., Peter's readers) *through* "the resurrection of Jesus Christ" (3:20–21). "Just as Scripture is understood to exist to serve the [Christian] communities . . . , so too are the events of history understood as bearing witness in some way to the climax of God's plan" in Jesus Christ (Sargent, 104).

Contributions of the OT References

Peter's inclusion of quotations of, allusions to, and references to the OT associates his thoughts with the long-standing literature of ancient Judaism, positioning his letter within the stream of interpretation that expects God to send a Messiah to his people. Christian interpreters take this for granted because the OT and NT are now bound within the same covers. But it is worth considering the significance of the fact that Peter and the other NT writers cite the Jewish Scriptures rather than the vast literature of the Greco-Roman world, with its philosophers, poets, and historians, to explain the significance of Jesus.

Peter and other NT writers believed in the historical continuity and the authority of the Jewish Scriptures as they sought to understand what God had done on the cross on which the Messiah had died. They understood the prophecies given by God in ancient times past to have been fulfilled by God in the times contemporaneous with Peter and the other apostles (1 Pet. 1:10–12). "The dominant hermeneutical idea in 1.10–12 is the notion in v. 12 that the prophetic witness was offered in service to an eschatological people standing at the climax of God's redemptive plan: the Christian communities addressed by 1 Peter" (Sargent, 99). Christianity did not originate as an ahistorical religion floating in thought above the realities of this life in which people live and die; rather, it was grounded in God's actions throughout human history.

The persistence of God's actions throughout the ages to give and to fulfill his prophecies and promises also implies the persistence of his authority, which became the authority on which the gospel of Jesus Christ stood. The citation of the Jewish Scriptures entailed and implied that the authority of Israel's mighty God stood behind the promises and prophecies of the Christian gospel that yet awaited fulfillment, such as the return of Christ, the resurrection of the dead, and the creation of the new heavens and earth.

The quotations, allusions, and references to the OT in 1 Peter also contribute specific content to Peter's thought, some of it distinctive and unique within the NT.

Contributions to Christology.

- Jesus is the foundation stone of God's redemptive project (Ps. 117:22 OG; Isa. 28:16).
- The rejection of Christ was predicted (Ps. 117:22 OG).
- The stone will cause people to stumble (Isa. 8:14).
- Jesus was the suffering servant foreseen by Isaiah (Isa. 52:13–53:12 OG).

- Jesus was sinless and innocent; his speech was without deceit (Isa. 53:9).
- Jesus did not retaliate or threaten (Isa. 53:7).
- Jesus's crucifixion atoned for sin (Isa. 53:4, 12).
- The wounds of Jesus heal us (Isa. 53:5).
- The Lord is good (Ps. 33:9 OG).

Instructions for Christian life.

- Like father, like child—that is, be holy (Lev. 19:2).
- Remember human life is transitory, but God's word is eternal seed (Isa. 40:6–8 OG).
- Those who trust in Christ will never be put to shame (Isa. 28:16 OG).
- One's response to Christ determines one's destiny (Isa. 8:14 OG).
- Do not fear adversaries of the Christian faith, but revere Christ as Lord (Isa. 8:12–13 OG).
- Christian believers are like sheep who had gone astray but who have returned to the Shepherd (Isa. 53:6).
- Christians are assured that God delivers the righteous, and they are therefore motivated to be righteous (Ps. 33 OG).
- Christians are sojourners who may suffer for their faith (Ps. 33:5 OG).
- Turn from evil, especially spoken evil (Ps. 33:14 OG).
- Do not repay evil with evil, but repay it with blessing (Ps. 33:13–17 OG).
- The Lord opposes the proud, so be humble (Prov. 3:34).
- The Christian life can be difficult but will be vindicated by God (Prov. 11:31 OG).

Conclusion

The various OT quotations, allusions, echoes, and references function in 1 Peter to orient its readers, both then and now, to see themselves drawn by faith in Jesus Christ into the long and magnificent heritage of Israel. They have been born again through the resurrection of Jesus Christ (1 Pet. 1:3) and must see themselves as new people with a new identity and way of life. The explanation of the significance of Jesus Christ (Christology) in 1 Peter is inseparable from the exhortations about how to live the new life in Christ (paraenesis).

Bibliography. Bauckham, R. "James, 1 and 2 Peter, Jude," in *It Is Written*, ed. D. A. Carson and H. G. M. Williamson (Cambridge University Press, 1988), 303–17; Beale, G. K., *Handbook on the New Testament Use of the Old Testament* (Baker Academic, 2012); Jobes, K. H., *1 Peter*, BECNT (Baker Academic, 2005); Jobes, "The Septuagint Textual Tradition in 1 Peter," in *Septuagint Research*, ed. W. Kraus and R. G. Wooden, SCS 53 (Society of Biblical Literature, 2006); Joseph, A. P., *A Narratological Reading of 1 Peter* (T&T Clark International, 2012); Moyise, S. "Isaiah in 1 Peter," in *Isaiah in the New Testament* (T&T Clark International, 2005), 175–88; Moyise, *The Later New Testament Writers and Scripture* (SPCK, 2012); Sargent, B. *Written to Serve*, LNTS 547 (T&T Clark, 2015); Woan, S., "The Psalms in 1 Peter," in *The Psalms in the New Testament*, ed. S. Moyise and M. J. J. Menken (T&T Clark International, 2004), 213–29.

Karen H. Jobes

Peter, Second Letter of

See Jude and the Second Letter of Peter

Philemon, Letter to

See Colossians and Philemon, Letters to the

Philippians, Letter to the

Because there are no explicit OT citations in Philippians, it is sometimes claimed that the OT has little influence on the content and argument of the letter. When compared to letters such as Romans, Galatians, Hebrews, and 1 Peter, Philippians certainly lacks the same level of direct engagement with Israel's Scriptures. But such a narrow focus on direct citations obscures the fact that despite the lack of explicit citations, the OT has a significant influence on this letter at numerous points. A careful reading of Philippians reveals a number of allusions, echoes, and key themes that are rooted in their OT background. Paul uses these OT references in connection with three topics in Philippians: (1) the person and work of Christ, (2) the identity of God's people, and (3) Paul's apostolic ministry.

The Person and Work of Christ

There are two passages where Paul uses a cluster of OT allusions, echoes, and thematic parallels to describe who Jesus is, what he has done, and what he will one day do: the so-called Christ hymn (2:5–11) and the depiction of Christ's eventual return (3:20–21). Despite the considerable distance between these two passages, the thematic and conceptual overlap between them suggests they are both part of a larger biblical-theological stream that begins in Genesis, ends in Revelation, and along the way incorporates several key texts that are echoed here in Philippians.

The Christ hymn (2:5–11). Much scholarly debate has centered on two possible OT backgrounds for the Christ hymn. The first is an Adam Christology that portrays Christ as the one who, through his obedience and suffering, receives the universal dominion over creation that Adam failed to accomplish. The second is the Isaianic servant; understood this way Christ fulfills the role of the suffering servant who is exalted by God. Each proposed background must briefly be summarized before the article explores a possible synthesis.

The case for an Adam Christology rests on the following considerations (see further Martin, 163–64; Dunn, 113–24; Wright, 90–97). Christ being "in the form of God" (2:6 ESV) recalls Adam's creation in the image of God. Unlike Adam, who grasped after equality with God, Christ, despite being equal with God, did not consider this status as something to be exploited (2:6). Christ made himself of no reputation (2:7), whereas Adam sought a greater reputation than God gave him. The servant role that Adam rejected when rebelling against God was gladly embraced by Christ, who took on the form of a servant (2:7). Whereas Adam sought to be like God, Christ took on the likeness of men (2:7). Instead of exalting himself as Adam did, Christ humbled himself (2:8). That humility led to Christ's obedience even to the point of death (2:8); by contrast, Adam disobeyed, and the result was death. As a result of his disobedience Adam was condemned, whereas Christ was exalted for his obedience (2:9). The universal dominion that Adam failed to exercise will one day be accomplished by Christ, to whom all creation will submit itself (2:10–11).

That Adam Christology is an important element of Paul's theology is beyond reasonable debate (see, e.g., Rom. 5:12–21; 1 Cor. 15:20–28, 42–49). But the challenge to considering references to Adam in Philippians is that the alleged connection rests entirely on conceptual parallels; indeed, except for the word "God" (*theos*) there is not a single meaningful linguistic parallel between the Greek text of Gen. 1–3 in the LXX and Philippians 2:5–11. Despite the number of conceptual parallels, the absence of actual verbal parallels to the key phrases in LXX Gen. 1–3 raises questions as to the prominence of an Adam Christology in the Christ hymn. Yet the conceptual parallels are significant enough to make such a background both possible and plausible.

The servant of Isa. 52:13–53:12 as the background rests on a combination of linguistic and conceptual parallels (see further Bauckham, 41–45; Harmon, *Philippians*, 62–63, 201–36; Krinetski, 157–93). In both texts God's servant moves from an initial state of exaltation, through a period of humiliation, to an even higher state of exaltation. Christ emptying himself (2:7) may echo the servant pouring out his soul to death (Cerfaux, 425–37). The emphasis on the appearance of the servant (Isa. 53:2–3) resonates with Christ being made in the likeness of man and "being found in appearance as a man" (Phil. 2:7–8). Christ's humble obedience to the point of death on a cross parallels the servant's humility in the face of brutal suffering culminating in his death (Isa. 53:3–12). In both Isa. 52:13–53:12 and Phil. 2:5–11, the work of the servant culminates in exaltation (Isa. 52:13; 53:12; Phil. 2:9–11). The Christ hymn concludes with an allusion to Isa. 45:22–23 that depicts the universal acclamation of Christ's reign as Lord and identifies him as Yahweh in the flesh. Based on these various allusions and echoes, Richard Bauckham concludes that Paul is reading Isaiah "to mean that the career of the Servant of the Lord, his suffering, humiliation, death and exaltation, is the way in which the sovereignty of the one true God comes to be acknowledged by all the nations" (43). Thus, the combination of verbal and conceptual parallels suggests the probability that Paul's description of Christ in Phil. 2:5–11 is shaped at least in part by the Isaianic servant of the Lord.

Christ's coronation (3:20–21). Philippians 3:20–21 overlaps with and expands upon the climax of the Christ hymn (2:10–11). As citizens of heaven, God's people await a Savior from heaven—the Lord Jesus Christ. The combination of "Lord" and "Savior" echoes Isa. 45:21 and corresponds to the allusion to 45:23 in Phil. 2:10–11. When Christ subjects all things to himself, he will accomplish the universal dominion envisioned in several OT texts. In Ps. 8:6, David reflects on God's original commission to Adam and marvels that "you have put all things under his feet" (ESV). Daniel 7:13–14 envisions universal dominion being granted to the Son of Man, a dominion that is shared with "the people of the saints of the Most High" (7:27).

Synthesis. Considered together, these two passages from Genesis and Isaiah are part of a larger biblical-theological framework. God commissions Adam to exercise universal dominion over creation (Gen. 1:26–31). Because of Adam's failure, God promises a descendant of Eve who will defeat the serpent through his vicarious suffering and accomplish the universal reign Adam cannot (Gen. 3:15). Through his promise to Abraham (Gen. 12:1–3) God will bring a new Adam. More specifically, this new Adam will come through the line of Judah (Gen. 49:8–10; Num. 24:17–19). In 2 Sam. 7:12–16 God promises that this new Adam will be a descendant of David who will rule over an eternal kingdom. Psalm 8 reveals that David understands this promise as the means by which God will accomplish humanity's universal dominion over creation (see also Ps. 110). The Isaianic servant further refines the picture. He will obey where Adam and Israel have failed (Isa. 42:18–25), suffer for the sins of his people (52:13–53:12), and redeem both Israel and the nations (49:5–6) in fulfillment of God's promises to David (55:3). This trajectory culminates in the individual Son of Man (an Adamic figure) described in Dan. 7:13–14, who shares his universal dominion with all God's people because they are identified with him (7:27). In summary, "the pattern that emerges from this survey is that of a priest king who through his sacrificial death and subsequent exaltation defeats his enemies and receives an eternal kingdom that he shares with all who are identified with him" (Harmon, *Philippians*, 65). Understood against this background, Paul presents Christ as the fulfillment of a biblical-theological framework (which consists of both direct promises and indirect typological patterns) that runs throughout the OT. At the same time, by borrowing language from Isa. 45:23 to describe the future universal acknowledgment of Christ's rightful reign over creation, Paul reaffirms the future fulfillment of the promise that all creation will recognize the universal authority of Yahweh. This kingdom will be consummated on the day of Christ. That is when God's work in believers will be completed (Phil. 1:6) and believers will be presented to God blameless (1:10). On the day of Christ, Paul will stand before God and give an account of his ministry (2:16). Yet the expression "day of Christ" cannot be understood properly without recognizing that it is a development of the day of the Lord described in the OT. As this theme emerges and develops within the OT, it centers on God judging his enemies and saving his people. Thus, it can refer to specific events in history (Isa. 13:6; Ezek. 13:5; Amos 5:18) and to the culmination of God's purposes at the end of human history (Joel 2:28–3:21; Zech. 14). Indeed, sometimes the two are so intertwined that it is difficult to distinguish easily between them (Zeph. 1:2–18). In any case, these individual events in history are, in essence, mini "days of the Lord" that build toward and anticipate the final and climactic day of the Lord at the end of human history. This dynamic continues into the NT, where events such as the crucifixion (Matt. 27:45–54) and Pentecost (Acts 2:1–41) are described in day-of-the-Lord language. But now that Jesus Christ has been revealed as Yahweh in the flesh, the day of the Lord is more specifically the day of Christ. The day of the Lord that took place at the crucifixion (Phil. 2:6–8), where we see both God's judgment on his enemies and the salvation of his people, anticipates the climactic day of Christ (2:9–11; 3:20–21), when God will execute both the final judgment of his enemies and the final salvation of his people. Thus, Paul sees in the day of Christ a fulfillment of the OT pattern of the day of the Lord, when God will judge his enemies and save his people.

The Identity of God's People

When Paul turns to describe the proper response to Christ's exaltation as the sovereign Lord (Phil. 2:5–11), he uses a cluster of OT allusions and echoes to portray believers. The first echo is in 2:12–13, where Paul asserts that believers must work out their own salvation because "it is God who works in you, both to will and to work for his good pleasure" (ESV). In describing God as the one working in believers, Paul may have in mind Ps. 68:28, which in the LXX uses the same verb found here to describe God's power at work for his people. As part of the new covenant, God promised that he would give his people a new heart (which includes the will of a person) and cause (i.e., empower) them to walk in obedience to God by putting his Spirit inside of them (Ezek. 36:26–27). Paul sees the fulfillment of these promises on display in the transformed lives of the Philippians.

Because God has now fulfilled that new-covenant promise, believers are able to avoid Israel's failures. Thus, Paul's command to "do all things without grumbling or disputing" (Phil. 2:14 ESV) is an exhortation to avoid Israel's persistent wilderness grumbling (Exod. 16:1–17:7; Num. 14:1–38; 16:1–17:13). By resisting the temptation to grumble as Israel did in the wilderness, believers will be "blameless and innocent" (Phil. 2:15 ESV), language that likely echoes God's command to Abraham in Gen. 17:1 to "walk before me, and be blameless" (ESV; Fee, 244). Unlike Israel in the wilderness, whom God describes as "no longer his children because they are blemished" and "a crooked and twisted generation" (Deut. 32:5 ESV), believers will be "children of God without blemish in the midst of a crooked and twisted generation" (Phil. 2:15 ESV). Paul inverts the OT language by applying negative descriptions of Israel to the pagan culture in Philippi and describing (largely gentile) believers as the opposite of what rebellious Israel was.

By living as children of God without blemish in a sin-darkened world, believers "shine as lights [or, perhaps better, "stars"] in the world" (Phil. 2:15 ESV). Paul adapts language from two different OT texts. The first is Isa. 49:6, where the messianic servant of the Lord is described as a "light for the nations, that my salvation may reach to the end of the earth" (ESV). But even more prominent is an allusion to Dan. 12:3, where God's resurrected people are said to "shine like the brightness of the sky above; and those who turn many to righteousness, like the stars forever and ever." Because believers are united to the resurrected Christ, they have experienced a spiritual resurrection that transforms them to such a degree that they stand out from the world. Through their faithful proclamation of the gospel, they turn many to the righteousness found in Jesus Christ (Phil. 1:9; 3:9) and thus participate in God's mission to take the light of salvation to the ends of the earth (Ware, 254–56). Thus, believers experience an initial and partial fulfillment of these promises in the present as they await their complete and final fulfillment in the consummated new creation.

At the close of the letter, Paul uses imagery that portrays the Philippians as priests who cause a pleasant aroma to ascend to God by making a sacrificial offering of financial assistance to Paul (Phil. 4:17–18). Numerous OT texts refer to the aroma from burnt offerings as pleasing to God (e.g., Gen. 8:21; Exod. 29:18, 25, 41; Lev. 1:9, 13, 17; Num. 15:3; etc.). The same is true of sacrifices being described as acceptable and pleasing (e.g., Lev. 19:5; 22:21, 29), though such language could also be extended to nonsacrificial acts, including prayer or even a person's way of life (Prov. 15:8; 16:7). Ezekiel 20:41 even foresees a day when God's redeemed people themselves will be a pleasing aroma to the Lord. But Paul's specific wording may echo Num. 28:2 (LXX), where the food offering is described as a pleasing aroma (Newton, 62–68). Such an echo would be consistent with Isa. 56:6–7, which anticipates a day when gentiles will join themselves to Yahweh as priests and present their gifts and offerings to him. Regardless of which OT texts are in view, it seems clear that Paul draws an analogy between OT sacrificial language and the generous gifts of the Philippians.

Paul's Apostolic Ministry

Immediately upon the heels of using OT allusions and echoes to describe believers, Paul pivots to describe his own apostolic ministry with OT imagery. If believers live out their identity as God's spiritually resurrected and transformed children, Paul will stand before Christ on the last day confident "that I did not run in vain or labor in vain" (Phil. 2:16 ESV). Because Paul sees himself as a fulfillment of the Isaianic servant of the Lord depicted in Isa. 49:1–6 (Acts 13:46–47; 2 Cor. 5:16–6:2; Gal. 1:15–16; see further Harmon, *Servant*, 179–93), he echoes the concern of the servant that his labor will be in vain (Isa. 49:4). This note of concern should be considered in light of Paul's more confident assertion in Phil. 1:19 that through the Philippians' prayers and the help of the Spirit, his current imprisonment "will lead to [his] salvation" (1:19 CSB). Although what Paul means by the expression is debated, there is less disagreement that Paul borrows this phrase from the LXX of Job 13:16 (Hays, 21–24). Regardless of whether he has in view his release from prison or eschatological salvation on the last day, Paul sees in Job's words an expression of his own confidence before the Lord. Thus, Paul seems confident when it comes to his own personal circumstances (Phil. 1:19) but more uncertain when it comes to the ultimate fruit of his ministry efforts (2:16).

Paul also portrays his ministry in cultic terms, using the language of the drink offering described in Num. 15:5–10 and 28:7 (cf. Exod. 25:29). Strong drink was offered twice each day (once in the morning, once in the evening) along with the food offering in the holy place. Paul uses this language to portray his life as wholly devoted to the service of the Lord, even to the point of his possible death. Like the Isaianic servant of the Lord, who poured out his life to death (Isa. 53:12), Paul is willing to lay down his life for the progress of the gospel (Bockmuehl, 159–60). The Philippians participate in this sacrificial act, as it is their lives that are laid on the altar before God (cf. Rom. 12:1–2). They are the living sacrifices upon which Paul, as the drink offering, is poured out by God himself to culminate the sacrificial act and produce an aroma pleasing to God. Paul's rhetorical use of OT cultic language not only highlights the significance of the Philippians' generosity but also helps them understand their identity as God's people set apart for his holy purposes.

Conclusion

Despite the initial impression one might have that Philippians contains little or no direct interaction with the OT, a closer look reveals sustained engagement at key points. This engagement takes the form of allusions, echoes, and thematic parallels. These allusions, echoes, and thematic parallels coalesce around the themes of the person and work of Christ, the identity of God's people, and Paul's apostolic ministry, a pattern that is evident elsewhere in Paul's use of the OT (see, e.g., Wilk). At least when it comes to the person and work of Christ, Paul's OT allusions and echoes seem to be part of a larger biblical-theological framework that presents Jesus as the one who, through his incarnation, suffering, exaltation, and return, redeems his people and accomplishes the universal dominion that Adam failed to achieve. As believers await his return, they are able to live in a manner that avoids Israel's failures, serve God as priests who offer their entire lives as a sacrifice, and extend the light of salvation in a sin-darkened world. Paul's role is to be poured out as a drink offering that culminates in the sacrificial lives of God's people. The ultimate goal is the universal recognition of God's reign in and through the suffering servant Jesus Christ.

Bibliography. Bauckham, R., *Jesus and the God of Israel* (Eerdmans, 2008); Beale, G. K., *Handbook on the New Testament Use of the Old Testament* (Baker Academic, 2012); Bockmuehl, M., *The Epistle to the Philippians*, BNTC (Hendrickson, 1998); Cerfaux, L., "L'hymne au Christ-Serviteur de Dieu," in *Recueil Lucien Cerfaux*, vol. 2, BETL 7 (Gembloux, 1954), 425–37; Dunn, J. D. G., *Christology in the Making* (Westminster, 1980); Fabricatore, D. J., *Form of God, Form of a Servant* (University Press of America, 2010); Fee, G. D., *Paul's Letter to the Philippians*, NICNT (Eerdmans, 1995); Fowl, S., "The Use of Scripture in Philippians," in *Paul and Scripture*, ed. C. D. Stanley (Society of Biblical Literature, 2012), 163–84; Harmon, M. S., *Philippians*, MentC (Christian Focus, 2015); Harmon, *The Servant of the Lord and His Servant People*, NSBT 54 (InterVarsity, 2020); Hays, R. B., *Echoes of Scripture in the Letters of Paul* (Yale University Press, 1989); Hofius, O., *Der Christushymnus Philipper 2,6–11*, WUNT 1/17 (Mohr, 1991); Keown, M. J., *Congregational Evangelism in Philippians*, PBTM (Paternoster, 2008); Krinetski, L., "Der Einfluss von Is 52,13–53,12 par auf Phil 2,6–11," *TQ* 139 (1959): 157–93; Martin, R. P., *A Hymn of Christ* (InterVarsity, 1997); Newton, M., *The Concept of Purity at Qumran and in the Letters of Paul*, SNTSMS 53 (Cambridge University Press, 1985); Silva, M., "Philippians," in *CNTUOT*, 835–40; Ware, J. P., *Paul and the Mission of the Church* (Baker Academic, 2011); Wilk, F., *Die Bedeutung des Jesajabuches für Paulus*, FRLANT 179 (Vandenhoeck & Ruprecht, 1998); Wright, N. T., *The Climax of the Covenant* (Fortress, 1992).

MATTHEW S. HARMON

Philo (1): Use of the OT

Philo was a biblical scholar and leader within the Jewish community in Alexandria, Egypt, ca. 20 or 15 BC–ca. AD 50. He is one of the most important sources of early Jewish thought—*the* most important single *writer*

(Hurtado, 73)—due to the volume of his extant writings and his references to wider practices and the thoughts and writings of others. Philo produced a tremendous amount of literature, primarily in the form of different types of commentaries on the Pentateuch. He is an invaluable conversation partner regarding Jewish uses of the OT.

Philo's Self-Understanding as an Exegete of Scripture in a Philosophical World

Philo is often described today as a Jewish philosopher. Many think of Philo's Platonic ideas before they think of his exposition of Moses's books. This is an error.

The primacy of Scripture in Philo's writings. Philo primarily sees himself as an exegete of Scripture (Runia, *Exegesis*; Borgen, *Philo*). Moses's writings, not Plato, are central to Philo (Nikiprowetzky). Philo considers philosophy a wonderful tool for rightly understanding and a necessary tool for responsibly communicating Scripture and the Mosaic doctrines of God, the world, and virtue in his context. Lévy (§6) writes that Philo "gathers concepts and themes of philosophy to free them, i.e., to bring them into the light of the God of the Torah. Like Moses who knew all the foreign sciences, Philo learned almost everything of philosophy, not in order to be a professional philosopher, but to demonstrate that the truth the Greeks looked for was where they did not imagine it to be." Indeed, whenever a philosopher's ideas (even Plato's) conflict with Philo's understanding of Moses's ideas, Scripture is always right—to the last detail.

Philo's Scripture is the Septuagint. He even recounts the story of the seventy translators (*Moses* 2.25–44). He thinks the translators used a divinely granted ability to simultaneously employ a word-for-word technique and a sense-for-sense technique, which contemporaries such as Cicero thought to be an impossible translation tactic. This "allows us to understand quite easily why he treats the Greek text as if it were the original, and dispenses with the Hebrew" (Kamesar, 71).

Philo's expositional studies are only on the Pentateuch. Around 98 percent of Philo's quotations are from the Pentateuch (Siegert). But this data does not mean that biblical texts outside the Pentateuch were not canonical for Philo or did not shape Philo's thinking significantly. In *Cherubim* 49, Philo explains that he is not only Moses's disciple but also "Jeremiah's disciple." Naomi Cohen provides a systematic study of Philo's use of the Latter Prophets, the Former Prophets, Psalms (cf. Runia, *Exegesis*, 102–21), Proverbs, and Job. She suggests the cyclical, liturgical use of the Prophets and the Writings in synagogues known as the haftarah may have been used in Philo's day and in his personal experience (see also Royse, 37; Gaster, 76–77; Marcus, xii–xv). It is possible that something like this practice took place in Palestine (Luke 4:17) and in the diaspora (Acts 13:15) (Cohen, 57n8).

In addition to seeing where he quotes or mentions nonpentateuchal Scriptures, one can see a broader impact of nonpentateuchal Scriptures on Philo's writing by analyzing, for example, how Prov. 8:22–31 and Ps. 8 affect Philo's interpretation of pentateuchal texts and themes. For Philo's use of Prov. 8:22–31 (and 8:23 in particular) to convey God's transcendent wisdom, see *Drunkenness* 30–31; *Virtues* 55–65; *Dreams* 2.242; *QG* 1.11; cf. *Flight* 94–102; *Worse* 54 (see Worthington, *Creation*; Laporte). For Philo's use of Ps. 8 to convey Adam's royalty in Gen. 1–2, see *Creation* 65–66, 83–88, 142–48 (Borgen, "Man's"; Worthington, "Gendered"). Regarding Philo's scriptural texts, then, the whole Septuagint was important to Philo—though especially the Pentateuch.

Philo's use of philosophy. Philo certainly engages philosophy, sometimes directly (e.g., *Good Person*; *Eternity*; *Providence* 1 and 2). Philo mentions by name Socrates, Plato, Aristotle, Zeno, Epicurus, and the pre-Socratics Pythagoras, Heraclitus, Anaxagoras, and Democritus. He refers to a Pythagorean book by Ocellos of Lucania. He clearly interacts with Skeptical ideas (see Lévy, §3.3). And, of course, Philo is well known for richly interweaving philosophical categories and terms throughout his numerous commentaries on Scripture (see Runia, *"Timaeus"*).

Philo was something of an eclectic with a clear Middle Platonic bent. As such, he employs significant aspects of Stoic philosophy throughout his commentaries, though not typically without modification due to his "transcendentalist and immaterialist perspective which is thoroughly inimical to Stoicism" (Dillon, "Philo," 79; cf. Lévy, §3.2): for example, the freedom of the good man (e.g., in *Good Person*), the virtuous one being a "citizen of the world" (*kosmopolites*, e.g., in *Creation* 3, 142–43; unless otherwise noted, translations of Philo's works are the author's), the psychology of the passions (e.g., throughout *Alleg. Interp.*, vol. 3), the doctrine of providence (e.g., in *Providence*, vols. 1–2), and the doctrine of mixture (*Confusion* 190–95).

For Philo, Aristotle's ability to categorize the corporeal and sense-perceptible creation into "genera" provides "the basis for identifying the essence of all things" (*Alleg. Interp.* 2.86) and is necessary for avoiding confusion (*Worse* 77). So, Philo applies Aristotle's categories to creation (*Heir* 133–40), virtues (*Alleg. Interp.* 1.56–65; *Names* 77–79), human affairs (*Names* 148; cf. Plato, *Resp.* 430b; Aristotle, *Hist. an.* and *Gen. an.*), and pentateuchal laws, organizing his major exegetical treatises on them (*Decalogue* 19, 50, 154; *Spec. Laws* 4.132–34; cf. *Heir* 168–73). (See Jastram, 14–36; Svebakken, 2–8; Baer, 26–27; Worthington, "Gendered," 202–5.)

Philo also relies heavily on Pythagorean arithmology (cf. *Creation* 8–9; *Spec. Laws* 3.180; *Posterity* 173; see Moehring; Lévy). He even incorporates the Skeptic idea that *paideia* cannot reach the telos of truth, for Philo thinks divine aid is necessary (*Drunkenness* 169–202). However, Philo tends to claim agreement with Plato more than with others, functioning as he was toward the beginning of the rebirth of Platonic thought in the form of "Middle Platonism" (Dillon, *Platonists*; cf. Runia, "Platonist?"). (For two fuller concrete examples of Philo's use of philosophical terms or ideas for his *exegesis* of biblical texts, see Worthington, *Creation* [for Plato]; "Gendered" [for Aristotle].)

Lévy cautions, "To say [Philo] was a Pythagorean, a Platonist, or a Stoic would have been for him to admit that he sought truth in spaces outside the Bible" (§3). "It is as if," Lévy argues, Philo's self-identity obligated him "not to coincide exactly with Greek philosophical doctrine" (Lévy, §3.3). He continues, "To comment upon the Bible with philosophical concepts was, in a certain way, to translate it into the language of the new cultural elite, the Roman as well as Greek. Regardless, the central idea was that the word of God had to be mediated to become accessible outside of Israel" (§4.2).

We certainly notice that many categories of Middle Platonism profoundly shape Philo's reading of Moses. Some of them, we might say, even control his reading of Moses. But it is also important to note that Philo sees himself most fundamentally not as a Platonist but as a "Moses-ist"—or, more properly, a follower of the covenant God as revealed by Moses—and Moses's texts (as Philo understands them) trump any other text when in conflict. It is also significant that almost all of Philo's uses of philosophic thought, terms, and themes occur in treatises that are not primarily philosophical treatises but systematic expositions of biblical texts.

The Organization of Philo's Writing on Scripture

We have all or portions of forty-six treatises by Philo. There is evidence of around seventy (see Sterling, "Place," 23n14). As Lévy (§1.2) outlines (though cf. Royse for a slightly different arrangement), Philo wrote at least thirty-nine allegorical commentaries on the Pentateuch, twelve expositions of the law, six treatises in the question-and-answer style on Genesis and Exodus, four historical and apologetic treatises, and five philosophical treatises. Lists of Philo's writings are usually placed in roughly canonical order according to texts he treats, with some clustering of "lives," "laws," and others following. But there is a more helpful organization.

Philo's three commentary series are "the heart of the Philonic enterprise" (Sterling, "General," xi). Philo seems to intend his expositional works (the first fifty-seven in the list above) to be treated as three different groups and types of commentaries, which likely have respective audiences in mind. Scholars generally agree on these three main groupings of Philo's writings on Scripture: exposition of the Law (the Pentateuch), allegorical commentary, and *Questions and Answers on Genesis and Exodus* (see Royse; cf. Cohn; Morris, 819–70; Runia, *Creation*, 2). Details are still debated, but in general the following list is the best way to understand Philo's exegetical project.

Exposition of the Law (Pentateuch). Philo himself argues that the Pentateuch has three genres—creation, history, legislation—and that he has treated them accordingly in his expositions (*Rewards* 1–3). These three genres in the Pentateuch align with his books in this expositional series. And since *On the Creation of the World* assumes the readers know who Moses is, Philo likely intended his two volumes on Moses's life to introduce his entire series of expositions. Then he begins with creation, runs through the lives, and comments on the generic and specific laws (see Runia, *Creation*, 5–8). This results in the following outline:

Introduction

- *On the Life of Moses*, vols. 1–2

1. Creation
   - *On the Creation of the World*, which provides the divine grounding and universal context of the law
2. History
   - *On the Life of Abraham* as "an exemplar of living the law" (Runia, *Creation*, 17), likely followed by lost commentaries on Isaac and Jacob
   - *On the Life of Joseph* as the statesman
3. Legislation
   - *Decalogue*, which focuses on the Ten Commandments as the genus
   - *Special Laws*, vols. 1–4, categorized and organized as species and particulars under each of the ten generic commands
   - *On the Virtues*, a more systematic treatment of themes related to the law
   - *On Rewards and Punishments*, a more systematic treatment of themes related to the law

Questions and Answers on Genesis and Exodus. This commentary series follows one of Philo's most prevalent styles in general (see below; Borgen and Skarsten). It is "zetetic," proceeding by inquiry (from *zētētikos*). Whether in his exposition of the law (see above) or in his allegorical commentaries (see below), Philo often asks a question or raises an important aporia—a seeming contradiction, a logical disjunction, an exegetical or theological/philosophical puzzle—sometimes one that others have observed and even mocked. (See *Confusion* 142–43 for Philo's record and response to someone using sarcasm to mock Gen. 11:5b.)

James Royse describes the long historical run this zetetic style of exegesis enjoyed before Philo in the preclassical era, in Plato's and Aristotle's work, in the Hellenistic era, and on into the imperial age (34–38). Philo's is the first biblical commentary series we have in the zetetic genre. His approach, as Royse (35) explains, "is to begin each section (as we may call the pair of question and its answer) by posing some problem in interpretation in the biblical text, or by more generally asking simply what is the meaning of a word or phrase found in it. This question is then followed by an answer that typically refers to the literal meaning of the text (sometimes perfunctorily) and to the allegorical meaning."

Here is the reconstructed structure of Philo's volumes in his *Questions and Answers* series, based on Armenian, Greek, and Latin manuscript evidence (see Royse):

Questions and Answers on Genesis, 6 vols., covering Gen. 2:4b–28:9

Questions and Answers on Exodus, 6 vols., covering Exod. 6:2–17:16 and 20:25b–30:10.

Allegorical Interpretation. This is Philo's more complex commentary series. It is on Genesis. It is more challenging to follow than his straightforward question-and-answer series (see above), so some suppose this allegorical series was designed for more advanced exegetical students while his zetetic series was an introduction to the Jewish text.

Greek writers already distinguished various levels of interpretation of important texts, not least between literal (or historical), ethical (or theological), and allegorical (Dillon, "Philo," 69; Kamesar, 72–91). Herodicus of Babylon (late 2nd century BC), a forerunner of Philo's younger contemporary Heraclitus (Denniston and Rusten), was a Stoic within a school of Homeric exegetes in Pergamene who tried to defend Homer's competency, piety, wisdom, and coherence by finding more meaning in Homer's wording than is at first evident (Dillon, "Philo," 73–74). Allegory—*allos* (other) and *agoria* (speaking)—was used for myths such as Homer's epics and Hesiod's cosmogony, both to distance the authors' intellects from actually believing such things as they wrote and to draw ethical implications from writing that was not designed to be didactic or ethical (Kamesar).

Philo used allegory toward similar ends, both to defend Moses and to cull out ethics. His allegorical commentaries include the following:

Allegorical Interpretation, on Gen. 2:1–17 (vol. 1); 2:18–3:1 (vol. 2); 3:8–19 (vol. 3)

On the Cherubim on Gen. 3:24–4:1

On the Sacrifices of Cain and Abel on Gen. 4:2–4

That the Worse Attacks the Better on Gen. 4:8–15

On the Posterity of Cain on Gen. 4:16–25

On the Giants on Gen. 6:1–4

That God is Unchangeable on Gen. 6:4–12

[In *Names* 53 Philo references two volumes he wrote on the covenants, likely on Gen. 6:13–9:19]

On Agriculture on Gen. 9:20a

On Planting on Gen. 9:20b–21

On Drunkenness on Gen. 9:21

On Sobriety on Gen. 9:24–27

On the Confusion of Tongues on Gen. 11:1–9

On the Migration of Abraham on Gen. 12:1–6

[In *Heir* 1 Philo references having written about rewards in his preceding book, likely on Gen. 12–14]

Who Is the Heir of Divine Things? on Gen. 15:2–18

On the Mating with the Preliminary Studies on Gen. 16:1–6

On Flight and Finding on Gen. 16:6–14

On the Change of Names on Gen. 17:1–22

On Dreams on Gen. 28:12 and 31:11–13 (vol. 1); 37:7–9; 40:9–11, 16–17; 41:11–17, 22–24 (vol. 2)

Philo's Exegetical Methods

The word most often associated with Philo's exegetical method is "allegory." As others have said, Philo's name is virtually synonymous with the idea of allegorical interpretation (Kamesar; Lévy). But Philo does not use only allegory. Also, why does Philo even use allegory, among his other exegetical methods?

We will explore Philo's zetetic, arithmological, literal, and allegorical approaches below. There is a cluster of reasons Philo employs each method of exegesis as he does. And words like "devotional," "pastoral," and "ethical" are more fundamentally fitting of Philo's exegetical methods than is allegory, for these qualities undergird each method. Fundamentally, Philo wishes for himself and his readers to be impacted in soul and action. This goal underlies all his interpretation, whether zetetic, arithmological, literal, or allegorical.

Zetetic. Philo's devotion to God drives his zetetic exegesis. The style of exegesis called "zetetic" (inquiry, from *zētētikos*) has a long history (Royse, 34–38). It involves raising a problem (an aporia) and then "seeking" a solution. Philo uses this as the overarching commentary structure and style in *QG* and *QE*. But he also uses it throughout his exposition of the Law and allegorical commentaries to resolve perceived textual or theological-philosophical issues.

The extent of this questioning method in Philo—beyond the obvious *Questions and Answers on Genesis* and *Questions and Answers on Exodus* commentary series as a whole—can be seen concretely in a big-picture overview of *On the Creation of the World,* in which Philo uses mainly the literal method (1–152, 170–72) but also the allegorical method (153–69). An example of Philo's zetetic method from each section demonstrates its influence.

During his non-allegorical interpretation of Gen. 1–2 (*Creation* 1–152), a particular detail in the third day raises an important aporia (a perceived problem): Why does Moses record the creation of plants (the third day) before the creation of the sun (the fourth day)? Without recourse to allegory, Philo resolves the aporia by turning to God's wisdom and sovereignty in this creative decision.

God chose that order intentionally, foreknowing the human propensity toward idolatry, so that humans would trust him and not creation's natural causes (45).

Philo's allegorical section of this commentary is launched by another textual aporia. Genesis 2:9 describes trees that bear virtues (good and evil, life) instead of fruit. This has "no resemblance to those trees in our experience" (153). Philo writes,

> These themes, it seems to me, are philosophized symbolically rather than in the proper sense of the words. No trees "of life" or understanding have ever appeared on earth in the past or are ever likely to appear in the future. Rather, it would seem that with the "garden of delights" [Moses] hints at the ruling part of the soul, which is filled with countless opinions just like plants, while with the tree "of life" he hints at the most important of the virtues, reverence for God, through which the soul is immortalized, and with the tree which "makes known good and evil things" at intermediate practical insight, through which things which are opposite by nature are discriminated. (*Creation* 153–54 [trans. Runia])

David Runia observes, "The allegorical method is not arbitrary, but is prompted by peculiarities of the text" (*Creation*, 374). Such non-ordinary textual details of Gen. 3 require an allegorical interpretation, because, in Philo's estimation, the sacred text is not "the fabrication of myths, in which the race of poets and sophists rejoice, but indications of character types which invite allegorical interpretation [*allegorian*] through the explanation of hidden meanings" (*Creation* 157 [trans. Runia]).

Outside of *Creation*, Philo's zetetic method is similar. Perceived problems or sticky points in the sacred text threaten to call into question God or his prophet Moses. "Moses therefore does well" when he writes exactly as he did (*Alleg. Interp.* 3.114–60; cf. *Sacrifices* 11–51). Philo's zetetic exegesis often runs in an apologetic direction, defending the wisdom of God and his servant Moses.

Arithmology. Philo's devotion to God also drives his frequent use of Pythagorean arithmology. It is an "exegetical tool" (Moehring), not an end.

Numbers matter for Philo in a more profound way than merely in whether a word is grammatically singular or plural (see *Alleg. Interp.* 2.79). As in the appropriation of the Pythagorean tradition in Plato, in the budding Middle Platonic practices, and in Hellenic thought more broadly, so too in Philo's writings: arithmology "wants to demonstrate the ordered, *rational* nature of noetic and sensible reality in universal terms. . . . Clearly Philo's adoption of this procedure was not only exegetically useful, but followed intellectually respectable, perhaps even rather fashionable trends of his day" (Runia, "*Timaeus*," 377–78).

When Philo uses arithmology, his comments are sometimes relatively brief. Deuteronomy 25:12 reads, "You shall cut off her hand." Philo uses this to explore the philosophical idea that the number two, being divisible, is an image of "the divisible matter that is worked upon," while the "unit," which cannot be divided (or cut), is the image of the first Cause (*Spec. Laws* 3.180; cf. *Creation* 8–9; *Alleg. Interp.* 1.3). The numbers prompted by this law suggest to Philo that we should honor God (the indivisible One) above divisible creation.

In *Alleg. Interp.* 1.3, Philo uses arithmology more fully. To explain God's completion of creation "on the sixth day" (Gen. 2:2 LXX), Philo explains that it does not refer to an amount of time. (For Philo, time is the "measured movement" of a body, which could not have existed before the body was formed and set in motion in Gen. 2:1, so the "days" before Gen. 2:1 must be a teaching tool of Moses, not literal days [*Creation* 26]). Rather, it refers to the perfection of the number six as a symbol for the sense-perceptible cosmos (*Alleg. Interp.* 1.3; cf. *Creation* 89). That is, six is two times three. Two and three both go beyond the "incorporeality which exists in the unit" (day one portraying God's creation of the incorporeal, noetic forms according to which God then made the corporeal, sense-perceptible [divisible] world on days two through six). Two and three go beyond because two is an image of matter in that it is divisible, and three is an image of a solid body since corporeal bodies are three-dimensional. Since two times three is six, six is (obviously) a perfect number to describe the completion of the material, corporeal, and therefore sense-perceptible cosmos.

Sometimes Philo uses arithmology more robustly. For example, regarding the seventh day in *Creation* 89–128, nearly a quarter of the entire commentary is dedicated to the significance of the number seven (Moehring). While Philo begins and ends this large section with specifically biblical content, this entire section on the beauty of the seven (and thus the seventh day) has a decidedly but subtly apologetic flavor, as can be seen not least in the number and type of nonscriptural texts he cites. Philo begins by describing how "the Father hallowed the seventh day, praising it, and calling it holy. For that day is the festival, not of one city or one country, but of all the earth; a day which alone it is right to call the day of festival for all people, and the birthday of the world" (*Creation* 89 [trans. Runia]). Rather than continuing to cite specific textual details or ideas from Genesis, from the rest of the Pentateuch, or from any other Scripture, Philo cites and alludes to numerous Hellenic authors and institutions. He refers to the Pythagorean Philolaus since he associated the seven with Zeus, the highest god (99–100). Philo quotes a poem by Solon, the Athenian lawgiver (104), and cites Hippocrates (105) on the seven ages of man. He cites Plato's *Timaeus* (119). He refers to the obstetric insights of Hippocrates (124), the seven vowels of language (126), and the etymologies for "seven" in Greek and Latin (127). Finally, he observes that the number seven is "honored by those of the highest reputation among both Greeks and barbarians who devote themselves to mathematical sciences" (128). Philo brings his reflections to a close with a return to the biblical textual reference to the seventh day that Moses "greatly honored" as "holy," to be used for the sake of ceasing work and "devoting that day to the single object of philosophizing with a view to the improvement of their morals" (128; see Moehring; cf. *Alleg. Interp.* 1.5–18)

In this long arithmological section, then, Philo is both devotional and apologetic. Moehring (218) observes, "Arithmology allows Philo to stress two points: (a) the cosmic and human order described by Moses is of universal validity . . . ; (b) this order is represented most clearly and purely in Jewish law, liturgy, and tradition; the Jewish religion is, therefore, the most 'natural' religion. . . . The superiority of the Jewish tradition is not esoteric in character: as can be shown through arithmology, it is reasonable and demonstrably so."

Literal. Out of devotion to God, Philo maintains literal exegesis—until he cannot. Philo distinguishes between "the proper sense of the words" (literal) and their philosophical or psychological symbolism (allegory) but uses both side by side. He argues that the family "continually devoted to the study of the holy scriptures, *both* in their literal sense *and* in the allegories figuratively contained in them," is "exempt from all injury" (*Rewards* 65 [trans. Yonge]). Both the literal and the allegorical are important to Philo.

In *Migration* 89–93, Philo interacts with the ideas of other interpreters of the Pentateuch. He attempts a both-and approach to exegetical techniques to maintain a balanced ethic in relation to God's Word: "It is right to think that this class of things [plain wording of laws] resembles the body, and the other class [figurative wording of laws] the soul. Therefore, just as we take care of the body because it is the abode of the soul, so also must we *take care of the laws that are enacted in plain terms*: for while they are regarded, those other things also will be more clearly understood, of which these laws are the symbols, and in the same way one will escape blame and accusation from men in general" (*Migration* 92–93; italics added).

However, sometimes the literal sense seems problematic. When it does, Philo's zetetic method pushes him into allegory. Two problems are common.

First, something in God's Word may seem to contradict reason. For example, Gen. 3:8 says that Adam and his wife hid from God. This is theologically impossible. Philo responds, "Let us in the next place consider how anyone is said to be concealed from God. But unless anyone receives this as an allegorical saying it would be impossible to comprehend what is here stated. For God has completed everything and has penetrated everything and has left no one of all his works empty or deserted. What kind of place then can anyone occupy in which God is not?" (*Alleg. Interp.* 3.4). Philo goes on to explain that sin causes a person to be shunned from God's holy presence, like a leper is shunned, hidden, or concealed from the community—though not "concealed" in the sense that the community does not know where they are. "We have shown, therefore, in what manner the wicked man is a fugitive, and how he 'conceals' himself from God" (3.28). (See other examples of this type of aporia in *Alleg. Interp.* 3.236 and *Planting* 32–36; see Kamesar, 78.)

Second, Scripture may say something that simply sounds too obvious and mundane to be *really* what it means. For Philo, God's Word is far above useless, petty details. This exemplifies a *theoprepeia* stance—that is, what is proper for God (Siegert, 185).

For example, in *Alleg. Interp.* 2.89, Philo mentions how Jacob (the supplanter of the passions) says, "For with my staff I passed over this Jordan" (Gen. 32:10). Philo reasons, "It is too low a notion to explain his saying literally; as if it meant that he crossed the river, holding his staff in his hand." It must carry a deeper meaning. Thus, "vice and passion are component parts of the lower, and earthly, and perishable nature; and the mind of the ascetic 'passes over' them in the course of its education" (he had already called the "rod" of Moses "instruction"). (See also *Prelim. Studies* 44–48.)

It is not that Philo doubted the record's historical or genealogical facts. Rather, such historical data was simply not strong enough in ethical compulsion to be worthy of God's Word—proper for God. With a pastor's devotional heart, Philo was convinced that every jot and tittle of God's Word is meant to help our souls, and bare migration or genealogical facts do not. Moses *must* have been pointing beyond the historical data too.

Allegory. Finally, because of Philo's devotion to God, he uses allegory toward psychological ethics. We can compare allegory in Philo's day to *a metaphor or simile functioning in reverse and in which the point of comparison is made explicit and argued textually*. To illustrate this, take a metaphor such as Jesus's "I *am* the bread of heaven" (A is B) or a simile such as Jesus's "The kingdom of God *is like* a grain of mustard seed" (A is like B). Adolf Jülicher has related parables to metaphors and similes, calling A (I, the kingdom) "the half about reality" while B (bread, grain) is "the half that is an image" (cf. Richards).

Jülicher explains that there is also a C: the *tertium comparationis*, or the point of comparison. Basic metaphors and similes tend to leave the *tertium comparationis* implied. Jesus's parables sometimes leave C implicit. But sometimes Jesus makes C explicit, as in Mark 4:30–32 (NLT): The "kingdom of God" [A] "is like a mustard seed" [B]. How so? "It is the smallest of all seeds, but it becomes the largest of all garden plants; it grows long branches, and birds can make nests in its shade" [C].

Philo's allegories tend to function with the same basic components—A, the real; B, the image; C, the *tertium comparationis*—but in reverse. That is, in a metaphor, simile, or parable, the subject A is known (the reality: I, the kingdom) while another object B is introduced (the image: bread, grain) to further illuminate something about the known subject. The *tertium comparationis* is either implicit or explicit (but brief). For Philo and other ancient allegorists, the text provides the image while the real must be discerned. But discerning the reality is not a free-for-all. The comparison must be reasonable and defensible, so the *tertium comparationis* is always explicit and developed, often at great length, in the allegorist's work. And it aims toward ethical living and, for Philo, devotion to God.

One example will suffice. In his allegorical commentary, even before what we have as *Allegorical Interpretation*, vol. 1 (see *Alleg. Interp.* 1.1), Philo refers to how he has already established that "man" and "woman" are Moses's vehicles in Gen. 1–2 for talking about the realities of "mind" and "sense-perception," respectively. He has already given numerous aspects of the *tertium comparationis* for each.

In *Alleg. Interp.* 2.71–73, then, Philo arrives at Gen. 3:1 and the serpent. He begins by explaining that in human moral psychology it is necessary for the "mind" and "sense-perception" to be united so as to appreciate and understand God's creation—and "pleasure" is the bond. It is of *pleasure* that Moses now speaks "symbolically under the name 'serpent'" (2.72). In the beginning of this union (i.e., in Gen. 3:1), "pleasure is *not* obtaining the dominion and mastery" but is ranked third: man (mind), then woman (sense-perception), then serpent (pleasure). It is easy for us to pass over the textual fact that "the Lord God made" the serpent, for we know the evil that is about to come, and we know later NT reflection on Satan's somewhat mysterious relationship with that serpent. But Philo maintains his theocentric and devotional focus: "God, who created all the animals on the earth, arranged this order very admirably" (2.73). The serpent is good, for God created him; and his third place after man and woman is admirable.

Philo continues, "And pleasure has been represented under the form of the serpent, for this reason. . . . And yet this is not the only reason. . . ." (2.74–76). Here Philo turns to the *tertium comparationis*, the point of the comparison, which must be responsible and defensible, between the textual image or vehicle (the serpent) and the proposed reality (pleasure). Philo even provides in 2.75–76 a breathtaking portrayal of the various forms of pleasure in this good world that wind and fold (in a non-evil serpentine manner) around our senses and mind.

But then the metaphor begins to shift. The same good pleasures in us can go askew, as they did for the children of Israel who craved the pleasures of Egypt while in the wilderness (*Alleg. Interp.* 2.77; Num. 21:5). So the Lord sent "deadly serpents" (note the connection: serpent—serpents), which bit the people so they died (21:6). Their death was "not that death which is a separation of soul and body, but that which is the destruction of the soul by vice," for "truly there is nothing which so much brings death upon the soul as an immoderate indulgence in pleasures!" (2.77). And such soul destruction remains "dead" until "it turns to repentance, and confesses its sin." How does Philo know this? "For the Israelites, coming to Moses, say, 'We have sinned'" (2.78; Num. 21:7).

The serpent (pleasure) that approached Eve (the senses) has morphed into serpents that bite and kill through immoderate indulgence in pleasures. And from this point on, Philo treats the serpent in Gen. 3 as problematic, evil pleasure even though at the beginning of his comments he had made room for good, God-given pleasure. Philo asks, "How, then, can there be any remedy for this evil?" (2.79). God commanded Moses to make a bronze serpent—another serpent—which is "self-control" since it is "a varied virtue" that readily repels pleasure (or, more likely, *overindulgence* in pleasure).

Philo then explores why the material is bronze (2.80–81) and concludes his exposition of Num. 21:5–9 by tying it back to Gen. 3 in this ethical way: "'And whomsoever the one serpent bites, if he looks upon the brazen serpent shall live' [Num. 21:9b]. Moses speaks truly, for if the mind that has been bitten by pleasure—that is by the serpent which was sent to Eve—shall have strength to behold the beauty of self-control—that is to say, the serpent made by Moses—in a manner affecting the soul, and to behold God himself through the medium of the serpent, it shall live. Only let it see and let it examine" (2.81 [trans. Yonge, with slight edits]).

Philo concludes his exegesis of Num. 21:5–9 by bringing his readers back to the main text, Gen. 3:1 (though now with the serpent of good pleasure representing uncontrolled pleasure-fulfillment). And he gives an ethical injunction. But Philo is not done with his *tertium comparationis* or his psychological-ethical exploration.

Philo uses other texts that mention serpents—the wilderness in Deut. 8:14; Moses's staff in Exod. 4:3; and Dan as the horse-biting serpent in Gen. 49:16–17—to treat a few nuanced issues in relation to pleasure. How can some people love self-control and yet still resist God, even going further away from him, and even when he is surrounding them with such beauty (2.82–85a)? What about his own experience, in which sometimes he is alone in a desert to contemplate life and God and yet his passions "bite" and distract him, while at other times he is in a crowd but God gives him refreshing focus? (Philo concludes that God was teaching him that "it is not the difference of place that is the cause of good and evil, but rather God, who moves and drives this vehicle of the soul wherever he pleases," 2.85b.) And "how can *anyone* believe God?" (2.89–93). Indeed, "it is impossible to take hold of and to master pleasure, unless the hand be first stretched out," as Moses did for his staff turned into a serpent—"that is to say, unless the soul confesses that all actions and all progress are derived from God, and attributes nothing to itself" (2.93).

Finally, in the midst of and after thinking about Dan as the "serpent in the path" who "bites the heel of the horse" so that the rider "falls backwards" and "awaiting the salvation of the Lord" (Gen. 49:17 in *Alleg. Interp.* 2.94–107), Philo confesses something personal (2.101) and then closes by spurring his readers (and his own mind too) on toward ethics and devotion (2.106–8):

> On which account Moses, approving of this backward fall from off the vices, adds further, "waiting for the salvation of the Lord" [Gen. 49:17]. For, in good truth, he who falls from the passions is saved by God, and remains safe after their operation. May my soul meet with such a fall as this, and may it never afterwards remount upon that horselike and restive passion, in order that it may await the salvation of God, and attain to happiness! . . .
>
> Fight then, O mind, against every passion, and especially against pleasure, for "the serpent is the most subtle of all the beasts that are upon the earth, which the Lord God has made" [Gen. 3:1]. . . . Therefore, array yourself against it the wisdom which contends with serpents; and struggle in this most glorious struggle, and labor to win the crown in the contest against pleasure, which subdues everyone else; winning a noble and glorious crown, such as no assembly of men can confer. (*Alleg. Interp.* 2.101, 106–108)

Philo understands himself as a pastor of souls and minds. And he primarily does his shepherding through exposition of the Pentateuch. He does this in a manner that constantly engages the philosophies of his day, often for apologetic reasons, though he never loses his covenantally theocentric and devotional approach to God, his Word, and his people. Every detail of God's Word (in the Greek) is purposeful and good, even when it may seem otherwise. This leads Philo to use a number of exegetical approaches, sometimes kept separate and sometimes in chorus. He uses a zetetic exegetical approach throughout, resolving perceived aporia. He uses arithmology to honor God's order and wisdom. To hold to God's honor and Moses's veracity, he maintains a nonmythic and literal approach to exegesis, until he cannot. But whether he can or cannot at any given textual point, Philo also explores what he and others in his day saw as the psychological-moral depths and riches of allegorical exegesis—all to help himself and others live rightly in devotion to God.

See also OT Use of the OT: Comparison with the NT Use of the OT; *other Philo articles*; *Mishnah, Talmud, and Midrashim articles*; *Pseudepigrapha articles*; *Septuagint articles*; *Targums articles*

Bibliography. Baer, R. A., *Philo's Use of the Categories Male and Female* (Brill, 1970); Borgen, P., "Man's Sovereignty over Animals and Nature according to Philo of Alexandria," in *Texts and Contexts*, ed. T. Fornberg and D. Hellholm (Scandinavian University Press, 1995), 369–89; Borgen, *Philo of Alexandria, An Exegete for His Time*, NovTSup 86 (Brill, 1997); Borgen, P., and R. Skarsten, "*Quaestiones et Solutiones*," *SPhilo* 4 (1976–77): 1–15; Cohen, N. G., *Philo's Scriptures*, JSJSup (Brill, 2007); Cohn, L., "Einteilung und Chronologie der Schriften Philos," *Philologus: Supplementband* 7 (1899): 387–436; Denniston, J. D., and J. S. Rusten, "Herodicus," in *OCD*, 674; Dillon, J., *The Middle Platonists* (Duckworth, 1977); Dillon, "Philo and the Greek Tradition of Allegorical Exegesis," in *SBL 1994 Seminar Papers*, SBLSP (Scholars Press, 1994), 69–80; Gaster, M., *The Samaritans* (Milford, 1925); Hurtado, L., "Does Philo Help Explain Christianity?," in *Philo und das Neue Testament*, ed. R. Deines and K.-W. Niebuhr, WUNT 172 (Mohr Siebeck, 2004), 73–92; Jastram, D., "Philo's Concept of Generic Virtue" (PhD diss., University of Wisconsin, 1989); Jülicher, A., *Die Gleichnisreden Jesu*, 2nd ed. (Mohr Siebeck, 1910); Kamesar, A. "Biblical Interpretation in Philo," in Kamesar, *The Cambridge Companion to Philo*, 65–94; Kamesar, ed., *The Cambridge Companion to Philo*, CCP (Cambridge University Press, 2009); Laporte, J., "Philo in the Tradition of Biblical Wisdom Literature," in *Aspects of Wisdom in Judaism and Early Christianity*, ed. R. L. Wilken (University of Notre Dame Press, 1976), 103–41; Lévy, C., "Philo of Alexandria," in *The Stanford Encyclopedia of Philosophy* (Spring 2018), ed. E. N. Zalta, https://plato.stanford.edu/archives/spr2018/entries/philo/; Marcus, R., *Quaestiones*, PLCL Suppl. I (Cambridge University Press, 1953); Moehring, H., "Arithmology as an Exegetical Tool in the Writings of Philo of Alexandria," in *SBL 1978 Seminar Papers*, SBLSP (Scholars Press), 191–227; Morris, J., "The Jewish Philosopher Philo," in *The History of the Jewish People in the Age of Jesus Christ (175 B.C—A.D. 135)*, by E. Schürer, ed. G. Vermes, F. Millar, and M. Goodman, vol. 3.2 (T&T Clark, 1987), 813–70; Nikiprowetzky, V., *Le commentaire de l'Écriture chez Philon d'Alexandrie*, ALGHJ 11 (Brill, 1977); Richards, I. A., *The Philosophy of Rhetoric* (Oxford University Press, 1936); Royse, J. R., "The Works of Philo," in Kamesar, *The Cambridge Companion to Philo*, 32–64; Runia, D., *Exegesis and Philosophy*, Collected Studies 332 (Variorum, 1990); Runia, *Philo in Early Christian Literature* (Fortress, 1993); Runia, *Philo of Alexandria: On the Creation of the Cosmos*, PACS 1 (Brill, 2001); Runia, *Philo of Alexandria and the "Timaeus" of Plato*, PhA 44 (Brill, 1986); Runia, "Was Philo a Middle Platonist?," *SPhilo* 5 (1993): 112–40; Siegert, F., "Philo and the New Testament," in Kamesar, *The Cambridge Companion to Philo*, 175–209; Sterling, G., "General Introduction," in Runia, *Philo of Alexandria: On the Creation of the Cosmos*, ix–xiv; Sterling, "The Place of Philo of Alexandria in the Study of Christian Origins," in *Philo und das Neue Testament*, ed. R. Deines and K.-W. Niebuhr, WUNT 172 (Mohr Siebeck, 2004), 21–52; Svebakken, H., *Philo of Alexandria's Exposition of the Tenth Commandment* (Society of Biblical Literature, 2012); Worthington, J., *Creation in Paul and*

Philo, WUNT 2/317 (Mohr Siebeck, 2011); Worthington, "Gendered Exegesis in Philo (*De opficio mundi*) and Paul (1 Corinthians)," in *Paul in the Greco-Roman Philosophical Tradition*, ed. J. R. Dodson and A. W. Pitts (Bloomsbury, 2017), 199–219; Yonge, C. D., trans., *The Works of Philo* (Hendrickson, 1993).

JONATHAN D. WORTHINGTON

Philo (2): Influence on the NT

The NT does not "use" Philo's writing (ca. 20 or 15 BC—ca. AD 50), at least not in the way it uses Scripture (the OT), other Jewish sources (e.g., in Jude 9), Hellenic sources (e.g., in Acts 17:28), or even other NT authors (e.g., in 2 Pet. 3:15–16). There are no references or allusions to his name or works. There is no *clear* implementation or criticism of his ideas by any NT author.

However, "Christianity emerged as a religious movement from the matrix of Second Temple Judaism, of which also Philo was a part" (Runia, "Testament," 64; cf. Sterling, "General," xiii). Philo also imprinted on Judaism "a particular stamp which makes him a distinctive example of the diaspora synagogue" (Runia, "Testament," 66). Thus, one might reasonably wonder whether NT authors and associates were influenced by Philo, his writings, or his followers—either directly or indirectly through synagogue relationships.

Possible Synagogue Contact with Philo or His Circles

Regarding the synagogues, Folker Siegert (175) writes, "The innumerable Greek-speaking synagogues of the Roman Empire, and especially those in the big cities, will have served as relay stations. They must have been places of learning in one way or another, and they did serve as the setting of one of Judaism's most important innovations, public sermons on Holy Scripture. If we assume that more than one teacher like Philo was active in the urban synagogues of antiquity, the diffusion of Philonic language and ideas can be explained by an appeal to oral forms of transmission." The chance of contact is increased still more when we consider Jewish travels throughout the Roman world, especially with its associated hospitality and sharing of ideas in synagogues and homes.

Philo's presence and activity in Jerusalem and Rome. Philo was in Jerusalem at least once (*Providence* 2.64, 107; see Haber, 187), maybe more. David Runia posits, "There must have been interchange [between Philo and Palestinian Judaism], if only because Philo himself tells us he regularly travelled to Jerusalem. The cross-currents between Philo's milieu and Haggadic and Halachic literature (and not to forget Qumran) are demanding continued investigation" ("Read," 185). If he went to Jerusalem later in his career, he likely would have been treated with special honor. For example, he may have been asked to speak in any number of synagogues (as the younger and less-known Jesus and Paul were) or invited to influential Jewish leaders' homes for meals.

Likewise, Philo spent up to two years in Rome during his embassy to Caesar Gaius Caligula (AD 38–40). One might wonder whether any of the Jewish Christians in or connected to Rome, such as the author of Hebrews or Aquila and Priscilla, may have "heard or met" Philo there (Siegert).

Alexandrian Jews in Jerusalem. On the day of Pentecost at some point in the early AD 30s, Jews from all over the diaspora were still in Jerusalem, including Jews from Egypt (Acts 2:10). Philo himself could have been present in Jerusalem at this time, though we have no way of knowing.

At some point later, still in Jerusalem, "opposition arose from members of the Synagogue of the Freedmen (as it was called)—Jews of Cyrene and Alexandria as well as the provinces of Cilicia and Asia—who began to argue with Stephen" (Acts 6:9). The Armenian translator of Philo's work (ca. 5th–6th centuries) suggests that Philo was one of these Alexandrian Jews (see Muradyan). It has been suggested more than once that Paul, from Tarsus of Cilicia, may have been associated in some capacity with the Synagogue of the Freedmen (Riesner, 204–6) and thus rubbing shoulders (and ideas) with Jews from Alexandria. One need not go that far to wonder if the Alexandrian Jews who took issue with Stephen were in some way acquainted with Philo, the eminent scholar of Scripture and community leader, with his writings directly, or with his ideas and synagogal and political influence more generally.

Apollos of Alexandria in Ephesus and Corinth. The most intriguing curiosity regards Apollos of Alexandria. Perhaps around the time of Philo's death (ca. AD 50), "a Jew named Apollos, a native of Alexandria, came to Ephesus. He was a learned man, with a thorough knowledge of the Scriptures" (Acts 18:24). He spoke in a synagogue in Ephesus and was further trained by Priscilla and Aquila (18:26). He went to Achaia (specifically Corinth), where "he vigorously refuted his Jewish opponents in public debate, proving from the Scriptures that Jesus was the Messiah" (18:27–28).

Apollos, an Alexandrian Jewish interpreter of Scripture, left a mark in a synagogue and formative Christian community in Ephesus, where both Paul and John ministered (Siegert). Apollos had an even more significant influence among the Jewish community at Corinth, and especially in the growth of the Corinthian Christian patterns of thinking (Pearson, *Pneumatikos-Psychikos*).

What we know, therefore, is that Apollos came from Alexandria having learned exegesis and theology. Perhaps Philo, his writings, or Philonic schools or followers in Alexandria shaped Apollos's exegesis and thought patterns—in what to believe and/or what to argue against. He then taught in Ephesus and Corinth. We notice similar key terms and texts arise in the Corinthian Christianity that Paul addresses, in John's Gospel (which may have arisen in Ephesus), and in Philo's commentaries, even if the substance is quite different. Paul addresses the Corinthians' errors, which were not exactly like Philo's teachings but shared some similarities (so Runia, "Testament"; Hurtado; Hultgren). John uses similar language and categories, most notably the *logos* active in creation, to resonate with and shape his (Ephesian?) readers. Runia finds the view "attractive" that such a link between Paul and Philo's writing may exist via Apollos, "though not devoid of speculative elements" ("Testament," 71). Indeed.

Possible Thematic Connections with Philo's Writings

As alluded to above, there are similar terms, possibly similar ideas, and some overlapping exegetical tendencies shared by some NT writers and Philo (see further the articles "Philo (3): Comparison with the NT Use of the OT" and "Philo (4): Thematic Parallels to the NT" elsewhere in the dictionary). For example, Philo and John both write about the *logos* that was active in creation. Philo and Paul both contrast "spirit" and "flesh"—Paul in 1 Corinthians (where Apollos had been) and Philo in *Giants* (and elsewhere)—and both use the language of "image of God" in multiple significant places. Philo and the author of Hebrews both have ideas comparable to a Platonic split between forms (in heaven) and earthly particulars (like shadows) (Thompson, 103–15; though see Ribbens, 234).

All these possible thematic correspondences (and many more) between NT authors and Philo are hotly debated. Note one example of the depth of debate. Some suppose a Philonic treatment of Gen. 1:27 and 2:7 is behind Paul's debate with the Corinthians in 1 Cor. 15, mediated through (and perhaps morphed by) Apollos's teaching (Pearson, *Pneumatikos-Psychikos*, 11–12, 17–21; "Gnosticism," 295–342; Horsley, "Pneumatikos"; "Wisdom"; "How," esp. 206–7; Davis, 49–62; Sellin, 156–89; Theissen, 353–67; Sterling, "Wisdom"; "Place," 41–43; and van Kooten). If so, some say Paul adopts and adapts a Philonic and/or Platonic interpretation of reality and Gen. 2:7 (and 1:27) in 1 Cor. 15:45–49. Others say the opposite: it was the Corinthians who adopted a Philonic interpretation of the anthropogonic texts in Genesis and Paul criticizes it. Still others, however, argue it was *neither* Philo *nor* Philonic ideas behind that debate, and that such interpretations misunderstand Paul and perhaps Philo too (e.g., Schaller, 53–72; Hultgren, 343–57; Asher, 112).

Similar debates arise related to Philo's treatment of Gen. 1:27 and 2:7 and Paul's language of Christ as "the image of the invisible God" in Col. 1:15 (Beale, *Colossians*, 119–26). For example, G. K. Beale (*Colossians*, 120) sees in Philo at least some sort of "precedent" for the idea that a being "could be thought to be in the image of God and not have bodily, visible existence before the creation of the earthly Adam in Gen. 1–2." There is debate about Col. 1:15 itself, of course. Some argue that in Col. 1:15 Paul is referring to Christ in his preincarnate invisible state when he calls him "the image of the invisible God." Interestingly, these scholars often use *Philo's* exegetical logic that the one who *is* "God's image" is a transcendent and bodiless being (e.g., the logos, the noetic paradigmatic human) while the man made from dust is specifically "*according to*" the image, not the image itself (*Heir* 231; italics added). Others think Paul is referring in Col. 1:15 to Christ in his resurrected and enthroned state (carrying on from 1:13–14) as God's visible image. Since Paul calls man "the image and glory of God" in 1 Cor. 11:7 (not "according to" a different image), and since it is the resurrected Christ with a glorified "face" in 2 Cor. 4:4–6 whom Paul labels "the image of God" (and not Christ in his bodiless preincarnate state), the second reading of Col. 1:15 has Pauline weight even if Philo would have argued that the "according to" is exegetically crucial. Beale leaves room for both readings of Col. 1:15, though he says Col. 1:15 seems to "stress" the incarnate, exalted Christ who reveals the invisible Father ("Colossians," 852–53). "However," he writes, "there appears to be no direct dependence of Paul on Philo at this point" anyway, "though presumably Paul may have been aware of Philo's writings" (*Colossians*, 123).

Siegert (175) writes that "the writings of the New Testament that reveal the clearest evidence of at least indirect Philonic influence are the Epistle to the Hebrews and the Gospel of John." He nevertheless demonstrates significant differences with Philo at every point and with each NT author (205–9). Hurtado (74) adds his caution: "If the question has to do with aetiology, that is, whether in Philo's writings we find the impetus, derivation, or causes for important features of earliest Christianity, then I think the correct judgement must be negative."

Hurtado (77) speaks specifically to comparisons between Philo and Paul: "It is in fact difficult to find any 'parallel' where Paul is echoing something that is unique to Philo, or that requires Philo's writings to account for it." He adds about Philo and John's Gospel, "The virtual consensus among scholars is that the Johannine prologue simply shows an independent appropriation and distinctive development of Jewish traditions about Wisdom/Word, and that Philo represents another, and very distinguishable appropriation" (78). And about Philo and Hebrews he writes, "Recently commentators and other observers of the debate have tended to agree that Hebrews and Philo independently witness to a broadly common milieu, with interesting linguistic and thematic correspondences, but marked differences in their respective thought and religious stance" (79).

Hurtado (79) concludes, "The many investigations of the relationship of Philo to various New Testament writings seem to justify only the modest and careful judgment that no direct relationship is plausible. These studies show that the main usefulness of Philo's writings is in providing further valuable illustration of the broad Jewish background of the time of the New Testament." We will stop here with any idea of the NT's "use" of Philo. We now turn, in the article "Philo (3): Comparison with the NT Use of the OT," to broader comparisons between the uses of shared Scripture by Philo and various NT authors.

See also OT Use of the OT: Comparison with the NT Use of the OT; *other Philo articles; Mishnah, Talmud, and Midrashim articles; Pseudepigrapha articles; Septuagint articles; Targums articles*

Bibliography. Asher, J., *Polarity and Change in 1 Corinthians 15*, HUT 42 (Mohr Siebeck, 2000); Beale, G. K., "Colossians," in *CNTUOT*, 841–70; Beale, *Colossians and Philemon*, BECNT (Baker Academic, 2019); Davis, J. A., *Wisdom and Spirit* (University Press of America, 1984); Haber, S., *"They Shall Purify Themselves"* (Society of Biblical Literature, 2008); Horsley, R., "'How Can Some of You Say That There Is No Resurrection of the Dead?,'" *NovT* 20 (1978): 203–31; Horsley, "Pneumatikos vs. Psychikos: Distinctions of Spiritual Status among the Corinthians," *HTR* 69 (1976): 269–88; Horsley, "Wisdom of Word and Words of Wisdom in Corinth," *CBQ* 39 (1977): 224–39; Hultgren, S., "The Origin of Paul's Doctrine of the Two Adams in 1 Corinthians 15:45–49," *JSNT* 25, no. 3 (2003): 343–70; Hurtado, L., "Does Philo Help Explain Christianity?," in *Philo und das Neue Testament*, ed. R. Deines and K.-W. Niebuhr, WUNT 172 (Mohr Siebeck, 2004), 73–92; Muradyan, G., "The Armenian Version of Philo Alexandrinus," in *Studies on the Ancient Armenian Version of Philo's Works*, ed. S. M. Lombardi and P. Pontani, SPhA 6 (Brill, 2010), 51–85; Pearson, B. A., "Philo and Gnosticism," in *Hellenistisches Judentum in römischen Zeit: Philon und Josephus*, ed. W. Haase, *ANRW* II.21.1 (de Gruyter, 1984), 295–342; Pearson, *The Pneumatikos-Psychikos Terminology in 1 Corinthians*, SBLDS 12 (Scholars Press, 1973); Ribbens, B. J., *Levitical Sacrifice and Heavenly Cult in Hebrews*, BZNW 222 (de Gruyter, 2016); Riesner, R., "Synagogues in Jerusalem," in *The Book of Acts in Its Palestinian Setting*, ed. R. Bauckham, BAFCS 4 (Eerdmans, 1995), 179–212; Runia, D., "How to Read Philo," in *Exegesis and Philosophy*, Collected Studies 332 (Variorum, 1990), 185–98; Runia, "Philo and the New Testament," in *Philo in Early Christian Literature* (Fortress, 1993), 63–86; Schaller, B., "Adam und Christus bei Paulus," in *Philo und das Neue Testament*, ed. R. Deines and K.-W. Niebuhr, WUNT 172 (Mohr Siebeck, 2004), 53–72; Sellin, G., *Der Streit um die Auferstehung der Toten*, FRLANT 138 (Vandenhoeck & Ruprecht, 1986); Siegert, F., "Philo and the New Testament," in *The Cambridge Companion to Philo*, ed. A. Kamesar, CCP (Cambridge University Press, 2009), 175–209; Sterling, G., "General Introduction to the Philo of Alexandria Commentary Series," in D. Runia, *Philo of Alexandria: On the Creation of the Cosmos*, PACS 1 (Brill, 2001), ix–xiv; Sterling, "The Place of Philo of Alexandria in the Study of Christian Origins," in *Philo und das Neue Testament*, ed. R. Deines and K.-W. Niebuhr, WUNT 172 (Mohr Siebeck, 2004), 21–52; Sterling, "Wisdom among the Perfect," *NovT* 37, no. 4 (1995): 355–84; Theissen, G., *Psychological Aspects of Pauline Theology*, trans. J. P. Galvin (T&T Clark, 1987); Thompson, J. W., *Beginnings of Christian Philosophy*, CBQMS (Catholic Biblical Association of America, 1981); van Kooten, G., *Paul's Anthropology in Context* (Mohr Siebeck, 2008).

Jonathan D. Worthington

Philo (3): Comparison with the NT Use of the OT

There are many ways one can compare Philo's uses of the OT with the NT's uses. The same Scriptures were vitally important to all authors involved. Philo could have given a hearty "Amen!" to Paul's statement that "all Scripture is God-breathed and is useful for teaching, rebuking, correcting, and training in righteousness, so that the servant of God may be thoroughly equipped for every good work" (2 Tim. 3:16–17; see Nickelsburg, 69). Of course, *how* exactly one derives instruction, reproof, correction, and training in righteousness from various Scriptures might be debated.

Paul wrote more of the NT documents than any other single author. His work is among the earliest we have, and some actually overlaps with Philo's life. Below I will suggest a few intriguing points of comparison between Paul's and Philo's exegetical practices. Then I will explore some particular comparable points between Philo's exegesis and some exegetical movements of Matthew and Jesus that are not as often explored.

Scripture's Word Choice Matters

For Philo, the Greek translation of Moses is so miraculously accurate that even its word choice reveals Moses's intention: thus every detail of the sacred (Greek) text matters to Philo. This is comparable to Paul's attitude toward Scripture. In *Worse* 104 Philo observes that Moses chooses the word "work" for Cain in Gen. 4:12: cursed Cain must "work" (*ergazomai*) the ground. In Philo's mind, Moses decided not to use the word "cultivate" or "farm" (*geōrgeō*). Cultivating and farming are useful arts requiring wisdom. Merely "working" the ground is dull and senseless, thus fitting for Cain. On the other hand, in Gen. 9:20 Moses wisely identifies Noah as a "farmer" (*geōrgos*), for he is a just and virtuous man.

In *Alleg. Interp.* 2.79, Philo compares the serpent in Gen. 3:1 to God's gift of pleasure and the fiery serpents of Num. 21 to an immoderate indulgence in pleasures (as the Israelites craved the food of Egypt). He observes that the remedy in Num. 21:8 is the bronze serpent of self-control. But Philo draws explicit attention to a pronoun, and a singular one at that, to make an important point of ethical devotion: "God says [to Moses], 'Make for yourself a serpent, and set it up for a sign.' Do you see that Moses makes this serpent for no one else but for himself? For God commands him, 'Make it *for yourself*,' in order that you may know that self-control is not a possession of everyone, but rather only of the one who loves God."

For Paul, it was profoundly important to his understanding of the entirety of redemptive history that at least one scriptural word was singular and not plural. "Now, the promises were spoken to Abraham and to *his seed*. He does not say 'and to *seeds*' as though referring to many, but referring to one, 'and to your *seed*,' who is Christ" (Gal. 3:16 AT; see DeRouchie and Meyer). When Paul sees the singular "seed," he understands that God made his covenant promise of inheritance to Abraham and *to Jesus himself*, Abraham's singular descendant, and *not* to Abraham's many descendants, the Israelites. This is profound: for Paul, *Jesus* is the rightful heir of everything most Jews thought was theirs by inheritance. To be sure, they *will* receive the inheritance *if* they are found in Christ, the true owner. This singular implies that God's covenant promise in Genesis holds true and remains guaranteed, even throughout the time of the law given to Abraham's many Israelite seeds, all the way "until *the seed* to whom it was promised [namely, Jesus] would come" (3:17–19 AT). If *any* are baptized into Christ—whether Jew or Greek, slave or free, male or female—they belong to Christ by faith and now "are Abraham's *seed*" and thereby "heirs according to promise" (3:27–29).

Scripture's Tense Matters

In *Migration* 43, Philo points out that Moses does not describe God's promise of the land in Gen. 12:1 as what "I *am showing* you," using the present (*deiknymi*). Rather, Moses records "which I *will show* you," using the future tense (*deixō*). This textual detail is important to Philo for giving us "a testimony to the faith with which the soul believed in God, showing its gratitude not by what had been already done, but by its expectation of the future."

Paul may be making a similar exegetical move in Rom. 4:17–21 (all AT). Paul quotes God's promise to Abraham: "In the manner [of the innumerable stars] shall your seed be" (4:18; quoting Gen. 15:5). And Paul quotes God's statement of a fact: "I have made you father of many nations" (4:17; quoting Gen. 17:5). But Abraham *did not* and *could not* have children, so how could God rightly say, "I *have* made you father"? For Paul, God has the prerogative to make a seemingly false statement to Abraham in Gen. 17:5 because of two divine qualities. First, while Abraham had a "corpsified body" (*sōma nenekrōmenon*) and Sarah had a "corpse-like womb" (*tēn nekrōsin tēs mētras*) (Rom 4:19), God is one who "makes alive the corpses" (*zōopoiountos tous nekrous*) (4:17c). Second, while Abraham had *no* nations existing at the time—not a single child with Sarah, not a single nation, certainly not "many nations"!—God uses the perfective "I have established" (*tetheika*) as the one who "calls things that do not exist as though they exist" (4:17d). The perfect tense in the Greek of Gen. 17:5 is meaningful to Paul (see Worthington, "*Nihilo*").

Scripture Must Cause One to Devote One's Life to God

Understanding Scripture is no mere intellectual pursuit, though it obviously includes substantial intellectual engagement. It is about knowing God better and being better devoted to him. Philo is at heart what we might call a pastor, a shepherd of souls. That is, his ultimate desire that manifests in his writing is for people—himself included—to live in a way that honors the one God.

For example, while exegeting the terms "depart," "to," and "from" regarding Abraham in Gen. 12:1–3, Philo inserts his own devotional experience:

> I am not ashamed to relate what has happened to me myself, which I know from having experienced it ten thousand times. Sometimes, when I have desired to come to my usual employment of writing on the doctrines of philosophy, though I have known accurately what it was proper to set down, I have found my mind barren and unproductive, and have been completely unsuccessful in my object, being indignant at my mind for the uncertainty and vanity of its then existing opinions, and filled with amazement at the power of the living God, by whom the womb of the soul is at times opened and at times closed up. (*Migration* 34; cf. *Alleg. Interp.* 2.85–93, 101)

Two repeated expressions also highlight Philo's devotional approach. Philo uses "O soul" at least twenty times: *Alleg. Interp.* 1.51; 3.11, 31, 52, 74, 158, 165; *Cherubim* 52; *Sacrifices* 20, 64, 101; *Posterity* 135; *Giants* 44; *Unchangeable* 114; *Migration* 169; *Flight* 213; *Names* 255; *Dreams* 1.149; 2.68; and *Providence* 2.7. Likewise, Philo uses "O mind" another eighteen times throughout each of his three types of exegetical treatises (though mostly his allegorical series): *Alleg. Interp.* 1.49; 2.91, 106; 3.17, 26, 47, 116; *Cherubim* 29; *Worse* 13; *Unchangeable* 4; *Migration* 222; *Heir* 71; *Dreams* 2.76, 176, 179; *Spec. Laws* 1.210, 299; *QE* 2.28. The former is sometimes translated as a self-stimulus, "my soul" or "O my soul." However, it could also be a direct address to his readers, a rhythmic appeal for them to turn their souls and minds toward God through Philo's exposition of the sacred text. He wanted to stimulate their devotion to God, and for this to manifest in ethics.

Paul likewise considers Scripture to be written "for us" (1 Cor. 9:9–10; 10:6, 11). The sacred writings (the OT) are "able to make you wise toward salvation in Christ Jesus" (2 Tim. 3:15 AT). All of them are, in fact, not only "breathed out by God" but also thereby "profitable for teaching, for reproof, for correction, and for training in righteousness, that the man of God may be complete, equipped for every good work" (3:16–17 ESV). Or, as Jesus points out to some Jewish leaders who undoubtedly would have agreed with Paul's theology of Scripture expressed in 3:16–17 (though not with 3:15), "You search the Scriptures because you think that in them you have eternal life; and it is they that bear witness about me, yet you refuse to come to me that you may have life" (John 5:39–40 ESV).

"Allegorizing": Hagar and Sarah

Paul seems to break his usual trend and "allegorizes" (*allēgoreō*) on at least one occasion, Gal. 4:21–31. The term "allegory" was quite flexible, and a term like "extended typology" may capture better what Paul is actually doing here. We can compare (and contrast) Paul's treatment of these two women from Genesis with what Philo writes about Sarah and Hagar as he interprets and applies the narrative on a number of occasions (*On the Preliminary Studies*).

Philo comments on a few occasions on the literal meaning of the Sarah/Hagar narrative (*QG* 3.20; *Abraham* 248–54). When Philo seeks the symbolic meaning toward which the details of the text point, Sarah is virtue. As Sarah was barren, we should see that "we are not as yet capable of becoming the fathers of the offspring of virtue, unless we first of all have a connection with her handmaiden; and the handmaiden of wisdom is the encyclical knowledge of music and logic, arrived at by previous instruction" (*Prelim. Studies* 9). As the handmaid of Sarah (virtue), Hagar is "grammar, geometry, astronomy, rhetoric, music, and all the other sorts of contemplation which proceed in accordance with reason" and function as a preface to virtue (11–18).

Philo wants to commend a pathway that carries on from education toward virtue. This has no apparent basis in the text, but the pattern of the text seems to be, for Philo, consistent with a true pattern in virtue ethics. Taking this approach, Philo ends up commending Sarah's gift of Hagar to Abraham, a very different reading from Paul's.

In terms of Paul's main exegetical movement, "the women are two covenants." Hagar is Mount Sinai and corresponds to the present Jerusalem, "for she is in slavery with her children" (Gal. 4:24–25 ESV). Sarah, meanwhile—the barren one who will yet, by God's promise, have many children (citing Isa. 54:1)—is "the Jerusalem above," which is "free" and "our mother" (4:26–27 ESV). Concluding the *tertium comparationis*—the point of the comparison between the A (the two covenants) and the B of the text (the two women)—Paul writes, "We are not children of the slave but of the free woman" (4:31 ESV).

By this point in his letter, Paul has already drawn attention to his overarching understanding of God's covenantal history. First, God gave a promise of inheritance to Abraham—namely, the blessing of righteousness by faith for all nations (3:8–9) and the promised Spirit for the nations through faith (3:14), which were to be distributed when Abraham's "seed" arrived, who is Christ (3:16). Second, it was 430 years after the promise that God introduced the law (at Mount Sinai), and God was purposeful in establishing it temporarily and in relation to transgressions until the arrival of Abraham's "seed" (3:17–24). Third, "now that faith has come, we are no longer under a guardian" (3:25 ESV; revisited in 4:1–3, 8). The promised Christ has arrived, so all God's previous promises—of righteousness by faith, of the Spirit, of sonship—are now present for all nations: "If you are Christ's, then you are Abraham's seed, heirs according to promise" (3:26–29 AT; revisited in 4:4–7, 9a). Fourth, many of the Galatian Christians are being tempted to move backward, contrary to God's redemptive-historical motion and his long-promised blessings in Christ, into the period of guardianship and slavery of the law (4:9b–21).

If Paul's readers were to think of the Sarah and Hagar narrative here, they might remember the moment God clarifies to Abraham that it is *not* through the slave Hagar but through his wife Sarah that the promised covenant inheritance will come (Gen. 17:15–21). Imagine if they responded to the narrative and said, "Regardless of God's promise and movement, we want to be Hagar's children and still be heirs of the promised inheritance." Such a response would make no sense. But that is the basic attitude and movement that the Judaizers in Galatia are pushing the Galatian Christians toward regarding Christ, the Spirit, the law, and gentiles in Christ.

And it is here that Paul brings up the story of Hagar and Sarah. He uses it to move the Galatians toward a sharp ethical injunction (though worded with the tremendous restraint of high-context communication): "Scripture says to throw them out!" (4:30 AT). Without naming the Judaizers explicitly in 4:29–31, and pursuing the story of Hagar from Gen. 16 into its extension with Ishmael in Gen. 21, Paul likens the abuse by Ishmael (the son born according to flesh) against Isaac (the son born by God's promise and according to God's Spirit) to the Galatian Christians' present experience of pressure from those who are focused on the flesh (circumcision) and the now-obsolete slavery of the law. Paul is strikingly clear while never saying explicitly that he means for the Galatian Christians to act according to Scripture: they should expel from their assembly all who would try to move them backward into the law, which is opposite of God's redemptive movement and gifts in Christ by the Spirit for all nations by faith.

Four points of comparison between Philo's and Paul's treatments of this narrative are noteworthy. First, Paul and Philo both use the story of Hagar and Sarah to move their readers toward ethical activity.

Second, Philo follows his usual pattern of identifying the *tertium comparationis* as psychological and ethical, while Paul is functioning with a primarily redemptive-historical approach.

Third, Philo's "real" (i.e., what the details of the text are about when read from a symbolic perspective; see the article "Philo (1): Use of the OT" elsewhere in the dictionary) is a psychological virtue ethic meant to transcend culture and be accepted by Jews and gentiles, though with clear roots in God's Word by Moses to the Jews. But Paul's real comparison is that his fellow Jews who wish to stay under the God-given but temporary law are "sons of Hagar, the slave woman." They are not even *really* heirs of Abraham! Otherwise, they would set aside the law's demands on gentiles who trust the Christ and accept them into God's community by virtue of their righteousness in Christ by faith and their possession of his Spirit. But as it is, since they oppose God's movement from promise through and beyond law to Christ, they have as much share in the covenant promises of God as the Ishmaelites—that is, none at all.

Fourth, Philo finds his "real" in his own ethical system that has little connection to the actual text other than in a comparable pattern. Philo must mediate the additional symbolic meaning of the text to people who could not have gotten there otherwise (since they may have seen a very different, though similarly defensible, "real"). Paul thinks his reading should be discernable in the text itself. "You who desire to be under the law, do you not listen to the law?" (Gal. 4:21 ESV).

For more on the comparison between Paul and Philo regarding the Sarah/Hagar narrative, see especially the article "Allegory" elsewhere in the dictionary; also cf. Barrett, "Allegory"; Di Mattei; Borgen; Rogers; Leemans.

Seeing God's Character Revealed in the Law: Oxen and Humans

Another rich point of comparison is in how Paul applies Deut. 25:4 in 1 Cor. 9. The passage is about oxen not being muzzled while working. Paul asks, "Is it about oxen that God is concerned?" He answers, "Surely [Moses] says this for us, doesn't he? Yes, this was written for us, because whoever plows and threshes should be able to do so in the hope of sharing in the harvest. If we have sown spiritual seed among you, is it too much if we reap a material harvest from you?" (1 Cor. 9:9–11).

Minimally, we can observe that Paul takes a *theocentric* stance, reading the law as revealing *what God personally cares about*. But even with such a stance, Deut. 25:4 seems to reveal more clearly God's care for oxen than for something not specified by the letter of the law. This prompts some to point out that Paul was taking a *theoprepeia* stance like Philo often does—that is, what is proper for God (Siegert, 185).

For Philo, minor details of the text, such as Jacob's crossing the Jordan with staff in hand (*Alleg. Interp.* 2.89) or a genealogical detail about Nahor's concubine (*Prelim. Studies* 44–46), are historically true but "too low a notion to explain Moses's saying literally." While not denying the literal truth of historical or genealogical details, Philo simply believes that God's Word *must* be saying something more meaningful for our ethical lives (cf. *Dreams* 1.52). God's Word helps our souls, and bare immigration facts do not.

Regarding Philo's reading of Deut. 25:4, he does believe it refers to the humane treatment of animals (*Virtues* 145), as it seems to. True, Philo can sometimes argue, "'The law was *not* established for the sake of irrational animals [*alogon*], but for that of those who have intellect [*nous*] and reason [*logos*].' So that the *real* object taken care of is *not* the condition of the victims sacrificed in order that they may have no blemish, but that of the sacrificers that they may not be defiled by any unlawful passion" (*Spec. Laws* 1.260 [trans. Yonge]; cf. *Dreams* 1.102). But in *Virtues* 145–46 Philo seems to stick closer to the overt meaning of Deut. 25:4 than does Paul. (It is typically the other way around.) That said, Philo does ultimately derive care for humans from this same law, even care for people from other nations, enemies, current enemies who will become friends, friends, and cities (*Virtues* 147–54).

Paul's hermeneutical assumption in 1 Cor. 9:9–11 could be like Philo's *theoprepeia* approach about what is "proper" or not for God. Alternatively, it may be like Philo's lesser-to-greater approach. David Instone-Brewer argues for the latter. Paul's approach is more like the *qal wahomer* in rabbinic literature (cf. Rosner, 128; Ciampa and Rosner, 720). If God cares for oxen (the lesser), then surely he cares for humans (the greater). Another position is argued by C. K. Barrett (*Corinthians*, 206). He takes Paul's "but for our sake" as *rejecting* any sense in which Deut. 25:4 may *also* be about oxen.

Yet Paul sometimes uses blunt language of "*not* this . . . but *rather* that" to refer to more nuanced situations that include "not *only* this" or "not *exactly* this": compare 2 Cor. 3:7–11; Phil. 2:4. What is more, 1 Cor. 9:11 shows that Paul is thinking in the categories of *qal wahomer*, though in reverse. Since Deut. 24:10–25:3 (the context leading up to 25:4) concerns God's care "for the fair and humane treatment of one's fellow human beings" (Rosner, 128), it is not surprising that Paul (1 Cor. 9:9–11) as well as Philo (*Virtues* 125–47) and Josephus (*Ant.* 4.233) all have a more human-centered reading of that law than the particular quoted law on its own suggests.

In this particular instance, then, Philo and Paul end up at a similar anthropological point through Deut. 25:4: God cares for humans through how people treat one another. Paul moves there quickly and bluntly while Philo moves there with greater subtlety. (Their reasons and genre of writing would influence their approach, of course. One is writing a treatise about an issue of his own choosing—in *Virtues*, anyway—the other writing an occasional epistle addressing many issues.)

Seeing God's Character Revealed in the Law: The Wilderness Rock

A final interesting point of comparison that we will explore here is found in Paul's comment on the wilderness era: the Israelites ate spiritual food and drank spiritual drink from the spiritual rock that "was Christ" (1 Cor. 10:4). This is another easy point of comparison because Philo comments on the same wilderness rock:

> God sends forth upon the soul the stream of his own accurate wisdom, and causes the changed soul to drink of unchangeable health. For the cut off rock is the wisdom of God, which is the highest and the very first of things he quarried out of his own powers [Prov. 8:23], and of it he gives drink to the souls that love God. And they, when they have drunk, are also filled with the most universal manna. For manna is called something which is the primary genus of everything [the "what is it," which gets at the essence of things]. But the most universal of all things is God. And in the second place the word of God. (*Alleg. Interp.* 2.86; cf. *Worse* 115–17; *Dreams* 2.221–22)

In 1 Corinthians Paul has already argued that God's wisdom (and power) is "Christ crucified" (1:23) and that Christ "has become for us wisdom from God" (1:30). One might be forgiven for some imagination here: Picture Paul and Philo having a textual-theological conversation about Exodus and the wilderness rock. Philo says, "The rock was God's wisdom, Paul, given as nourishment for those who love God." Paul replies, "Amen, Philo, and God's wisdom is the Christ, Jesus, who was crucified and raised for the glory of those who love God!"

In 1 Cor. 10, Paul exhibits a hermeneutical theory that the ancient sacred text was recorded for his contemporaries' ethical and devotional benefit (vv. 6, 11). Philo takes a fundamentally similar stance. Paul even demonstrates here a similar technique of stringing together numerous related biblical texts to make his ethical case: for example, 1 Cor. 10:1–14 uses passages like Exod. 32:6; Num. 11:1–34; 21:8–9; 25:1–9; and Ps. 106. Philo does this too, but on a grander scale, sometimes navigating scores and layers of texts he connects over extended sections of argumentation. For a fuller comparison of Paul's exegetical maneuvers in 1 Cor. 10 and Philo's corresponding passages, see treatments such as those by Bandstra; Meeks; Kreitzer; Ellis; Sandelin; Enns; Terrien; Aageson; Ciampa and Rosner; Fisk; Thiessen.

Below in the article "Philo (4): Thematic Parallels to the NT" we will return to compare a few key themes that arise in both Philo's and Paul's exegetical practices: in particular, theocentricity and certain anthropological considerations related to creation. Before that, though, we will shift from Paul to compare a few of Philo's typical uses of Scripture with two different types of NT passages: Matthew's arithmological genealogy and Jesus's exegetical use of a coin and inscription.

Philo's and Matthew's Arithmological Genealogies

Philo objected to taking genealogies merely literally (e.g., *Prelim. Studies* 44–46; see "Philo's Exegetical Methods" in the article "Philo (1): Use of the OT" elsewhere in the dictionary). He did not doubt their literal truth, but, taking a *theoprepeia* stance, Philo asserted that such historical data was not strong enough in ethical compulsion to be worthy of God's Word. Moses *must* have been pointing beyond the historical data too.

An interesting case in point comes in *On the Posterity of Cain*, Philo's commentary on Gen. 4:16–25. Philo comments on the significance of numbers of generations in a genealogy:

> On this account Abel, after having quitted the mortal body, departed to the better nature, and took up his abode with that. But Seth, as being the seed of human virtue, will never quit the race of mankind. But first of all he will receive his growth up to the number ten, that perfect number, according to which the just Noah exists; and then he will receive a second and a better growth from his son Shem, ending in a second ten, from which the faithful Abraham is named. And he will also have a third growth, and one more perfect than the number ten, extending from him to Moses, that man who is wise in all things, for he is the seventh from Abraham, not revolving, like an initiated worshipper, in the circle which is exterior to holy things, but like a hierophant, making his abode in the inmost shrines. (*Posterity* 173)

Philo demonstrates how "the seed of human virtue" grows perfectly into "justice," then grows perfectly again into "faithfulness," then again—even more perfectly—into being wise in all things, which involves not observing the deity from the outside but personally devoting oneself to, even entering into, God's presence.

To show how Moses is communicating this ethical and devotional point, Philo observes that the number ten is "a perfect number" (*arithmos teleios*). Noah is the tenth generation: Adam, Seth, Enosh, Kenan, Mahalalel, Jared, Enoch, Methuselah, Lamech, Noah (Gen. 5). Abraham is another ten generations from Noah: Shem, Arphaxad, Shelah, Eber, Peleg, Reu, Serug, Nahor, Terah, Abraham (10:10–26). To get to Moses from Abraham, however, it requires only seven generations: Abraham, Isaac, Jacob, Levi, Kohath, Amram, Moses (Exod. 6:16–20)—which is even more perfect (*teleoteron*) than ten!

Notice how Philo must count, however, to get these perfect numbers. Adam and Noah are both counted to get to the first ten. Noah is not counted again, for Philo counts ten from Shem to Abraham. But Philo must count Abraham a second time for the math to work: he is the tenth from Shem and again the first toward Moses.

But what is the point? We have already observed the ethical and devotional implications Philo thinks are embedded within Moses's recorded genealogies. He continues, "Consider the advances towards improvement made by the soul of the man who is eager for, and insatiable in, his craving after good things. And [consider] the illimitable riches of God, who gives the end of some things to be the beginnings of others. For the end of the *knowledge* that is according to *Seth* has become the beginning of the *righteous Noah*; and his perfection again is the beginning of the *education* of *Abraham*; and the most perfect *wisdom* of *Abraham* is *the first instruction of Moses*" (*Posterity* 174; italics added). Philo sees the genealogy as driving somewhere: toward Moses with the most perfect knowledge, justice, wisdom, and instruction, who enters the very sacred things of God. And both the significance of numbers and the number of generations (if counted in just the right way) help show God's order and deliberateness in giving his revelation to Moses. So, listen to Moses.

Matthew opens his Gospel with the genealogy of the Christ: "This is the genealogy of Jesus the Messiah the son of David, the son of Abraham. . . . Thus there were fourteen generations in all from Abraham to David, fourteen from David to the exile to Babylon, and fourteen from the exile to the Messiah" (1:1–17). As Philo draws special attention to Noah, Abraham, and ultimately Moses, so Matthew opens his narrative with a genealogy by drawing special attention to key points in God's redemptive history: the Christ, David, and Abraham, then again, at the end, Abraham, David, the exile, the Christ (see Bauckham; Johnson; Blair).

The fourteen-fourteen-fourteen scheme is obviously significant. It could be gematria of the name "David" (D [4] + V [6] + D [4] = 14), emphasizing the royal Davidic nature of Jesus as the anointed one (Christ, Messiah). And there is significant evidence that Matthew is doing a *lot* with gematria throughout his genealogy (Bryan, "Onomastics"). Or fourteen may be significant for the same arithmological reason that Philo explains: seven is the most perfect number, and its multiples carry the same intentionality and perfection (see Nolland, *Matthew*, 65–87). In this case, Matthew would be emphasizing the perfection and completeness of God's redemptive-historical plan that reaches its perfection in Jesus. There could be elements of both. Regardless, to get the perfect scheme, Matthew makes a few recording decisions. Matthew leaves out a number of kings in the second cluster to get fourteen generations (e.g., Ahaziah, Joash, and Amaziah consecutively, and Jehoiakim; see Nolland, "Jechoniah"). In addition, Matthew follows a counting principle similar to the one that Philo followed. Matthew counts Abraham and David as first and fourteenth in the first cluster. David is not counted in the second cluster, but Solomon is first and Jeconiah is fourteenth at the exile. For the final fourteen, however, Jeconiah is counted (again) as first so that "Jesus who is called the Christ" is fourteenth from the exile.

What is Matthew's point? While Philo attributes various virtues to each person, Matthew has no such psychological-moral reading at this point. His reading appears to be more covenantal-historical. First, God makes an epoch-shaping covenant with Abraham. Second, God makes an epoch-defining covenant with King David. Third, God sends the exiles to Babylon, which thus shrouds both covenants in questions and doubts. Fourth, God sends his Messiah—surely an epoch-defining moment!—everything happening at the *perfect* time. (In addition, though more subtle, Matthew may be repeating the phrase "X and his brothers" for a reason: "Judah and his brothers" [1:2] constitutes Israel; "Jeconiah and his brothers" [1:11] displays "Israel in its experience of national judgment and dissolution"; and "Jesus" and his "brothers" [cf. 1:16 and 28:10] may be using the entire Gospel narrative to complete the genealogy by representing Jesus and the Eleven as "Israel in its reconstitution" [see Bryan, "Missing"]. This itself has biblical precedent: Noah's genealogical formula begins in Gen. 5:32, but its conclusion is suspended until 9:28–29.) While Philo's genealogical moves end with the admonition to listen to Moses, Matthew's seem to end with the admonition to listen to this narrative of the Messiah.

Philo's and Jesus's Coins and Images

As recorded in the Synoptic Gospels, Jesus exegetes a Roman denarius. He interprets the "image" (*eikōn*) of Caesar and its associated inscription, which mark off the coin as "of" or "belonging to" the particular king portrayed by the image (Mark 12:16–17; cf. Matt. 22:20–21; Luke 20:24–25). He does this in order to navigate a weighty—even dangerous—political situation, while also delivering a rich theological and ethical punch. Jesus compares the coin's relationship to Caesar with humanity's relationship with God, so his exegesis of the coin carries with it an interpretation of Gen. 1:27 (see Nguyen, 177–78n128; Worthington, *Philo*, 140n8).

This taxation situation would have been intense for Jesus. He is being questioned in public within a shame-honor culture by the unlikely bedfellows of Pharisees and Herodians, each with their own agendas for popularity and politics. Even further, taxes had been a source of rebellion and imperial violence on Jews in Galilee during Jesus's boyhood (see background on Judas the Galilean in Acts 5:37; Caulley, 152–53). In addition, taxes in Jesus's day carried much more than merely monetary implications, which were heavy enough in a context of subsistence farming! Taxes also carried connotations of political-imperial subjugation and religious-cult pressures (see Taylor; Udoh; Kirkegaard; Shaw). The stakes were extremely high.

Philo himself had made statements about images on coins too. Philo describes the ancient process of stamping images on a wax tablet in *Heir* 180–81. And in *Alleg. Interp.* 3.95–96 and *Planting* 18–20, he relates this process of minting a coin directly to Gen. 1:27. This comparison between "stamping out" images on coins and wax tablets is ripe for Philo's (Platonic) theology of creation, for

Plato had discussed the demiurge "stamping out" creation in matter (*Tim.* 39e7, 50c–d). Even beyond Philo, the famous rabbi Hillel (Gamaliel's teacher) seems to have directly compared the statue of a god to himself in light of Gen. 1:27 (as attributed to Hillel in Lev. Rab. 34 [130d] in Str-B 1:654–55; cf. McCasland, 92). Thus, Jesus's comparison of the image of Caesar (stamped onto a coin) and the image of God (stamped onto a human) has historical precedent.

What is noteworthy, particularly in relation to Philo's exegetical insights about humanity "according to God's image" (see the article "Philo (2): Influence on the NT" elsewhere in the dictionary) is that Jesus does *not* say about the denarius, "Whose image is this *according* to?" He leaves all sense of the preposition out of discussion. Philo's three-tier understanding of how to relate (1) God to (3) humanity via (2) his image (the *logos*) is a different exegetical procedure from what Jesus uses. When Jesus asks, "Who's image *is* this?" (Mark 12:16–17), and the Pharisees and Herodians answer, "Caesar's," it is obvious that the intermediary stamp between Caesar's face and the metal substance had no place in this discussion. Some sort of intermediary stamp must be assumed, but his pithy statement simply involves Caesar's face (the image) and a coin (with his image on it)—a two-tier exegetical movement from Caesar to the coin, from God to the human.

In this truly life-or-death situation, Jesus puts forward a theocentric ethical implication to his exegesis—both his explicit exegesis of a denarius and his implied exegesis of Gen. 1:27. Humans are to "give" to God everything that has his image stamped on it, for he owns it anyway.

We will return to the theme of God's image in the article "Philo (4): Thematic Parallels to the NT."

See also OT Use of the OT: Comparison with the NT Use of the OT; *other Philo articles*; *Mishnah, Talmud, and Midrashim articles*; *Pseudepigrapha articles*; *Septuagint articles*; *Targums articles*

Bibliography. Aageson, J. W., "Written Also for Our Sake," in *Hearing the Old Testament in the New Testament*, ed. S. Porter (Eerdmans, 2006), 152–81; Bandstra, A. J., "Interpretation in 1 Corinthians 10:1–11," *CTJ* 6 (1971): 5–21; Barrett, C. K., "The Allegory of Abraham, Sarah, and Hagar in the Argument of Galatians," in *Rechtfertigung*, ed. J. Friedrich, W. Pöhlmann, and P. Stuhlmacher (Mohr Siebeck, 1976), 1–16; Barrett, *The First Epistle to the Corinthians*, BNTC (Hendrickson, 1996); Bauckham, R., "Tamar's Ancestry and Rahab's Marriage," *NovT* 37, no. 4 (1995): 313–29; Blair, H. A., "Matthew 1,16 and the Matthaean Genealogy," *SE* 2 (1964): 149–54; Borgen, P., "Some Hebrew and Pagan Features in Philo's and Paul's Interpretation of Hagar and Ishmael," in *The New Testament and Hellenistic Judaism*, ed. P. Borgen and S. Giversen (Aarhus University Press, 1995), 151–64; Bryan, S., "The Missing Generation," *BBR* 29, no. 3 (2019): 294–316; Bryan, "Onomastics and Numerical Composition in the Genealogy of Matthew," *BBR* 30, no. 4 (2020): 515–39; Caulley, T. S., "Notable Galilean Persons," in *Galilee in the Late Second Temple and Mishnaic Periods*, 2 vols., ed. D. A. Fiensy and J. R. Strange (Fortress, 2014–15), 1:151–66; Ciampa, R., and B. Rosner, "1 Corinthians," in *CNTUOT*, 695–752; DeRouchie, J., and J. Meyer, "Christ or Family as the 'Seed' of Promise?," *SBJT* 14, no. 3 (2010): 36–48; Di Mattei, S., "Paul's Allegory of the Two Covenants (Gal. 4.21–31) in Light of First-Century Hellenistic Rhetoric and Jewish Hermeneutics," *NTS* 52 (2006): 102–22; Ellis, E. E., "Χριστός in 1 Corinthians 10.4, 9," in *From Jesus to John*, ed. M. C. de Boer, JSNTSup 84 (Sheffield Academic, 1993), 168–73; Enns, P. E., "The 'Moveable Well' in 1 Cor. 10:4," *BBR* 6 (1996): 23–38; Fisk, B. N., "Pseudo-Philo, Paul and Israel's Rolling Stone," in *Israel in the Wilderness*, ed. K. E. Pomykala, TBN 10 (Brill, 2008), 117–36; Instone-Brewer, D., "1 Corinthians 9:9–11," *NTS* 38 (1992): 554–65; Johnson, M. D., "The Genealogy of Jesus in Matthew," in *The Purpose of the Biblical Genealogies*, 2nd ed. (Wipf & Stock, 2002), 139–228; Kirkegaard, B., "Rendering to Caesar and to God," *JLE* 6, no. 4 (2006), https://www.elca.org/JLE/Articles/605; Kreitzer, L., "1 Corinthians 10:4 and Philo's Flinty Rock," *CV* 35 (1993): 109–26; Leemans, J., "After Philo and Paul," in *Abraham, the Nations, and the Hagarites*, ed. M. Goodman, G. H. van Kooten, and J. T. A. G. M. van Ruiten, TBN 13 (Brill, 2010), 435–47; McCasland, S. V., "The Image of God according to Paul," *JBL* 69, no. 2 (1950): 85–100; Meeks, W. A., "'And Rose Up to Play,'" *JSNT* 16 (1982): 64–78; Nguyen, V., *Christian Identity in Corinth*, WUNT 2/243 (Mohr Siebeck, 2008); Nickelsburg, G., "Philo among Greeks, Jews and Christians," in *Philo und das Neue Testament*, ed. R. Deines and K.-W. Niebuhr, WUNT 172 (Mohr Siebeck, 2004), 53–72; Nolland, J., *The Gospel of Matthew*, NICNT (Eerdmans, 2005); Nolland, "Jechoniah and His Brothers," *BBR* 7 (1997): 169–78; Rogers, J., "The Philonic and the Pauline," *SPhiloA* 26 (2014): 57–77; Rosner, B. S., "Deuteronomy in 1 and 2 Corinthians," in *Deuteronomy in the New Testament*, ed. M. Menken and S. Moyise, LNTS 358 (T&T Clark, 2007), 118–35; Sandelin, K.-G., "Does Paul Argue against Sacramentalism and Over-Confidence in 1 Cor. 10:1–14? (1995)," in *Attraction and Danger of Alien Religion*, WUNT 290 (Mohr Siebeck, 2012), 77–93; Shaw, B., "Roman Taxation," in *Civilization of the Ancient Mediterranean*, vol. 2, ed. M. Grant and R. Kitzinger (Scribner's Sons, 1988), 809–27; Siegert, F., "Philo and the New Testament," in *The Cambridge Companion to Philo*, ed. A. Kamesar, CCP (Cambridge University Press, 2009), 175–209; Taylor, J., "Pontius Pilate and the Imperial Cult in Roman Judaea," *NTS* 52, no. 4 (2006): 555–82; Terrien, S., "The Metaphor of the Rock in Biblical Theology," in *God in the Fray*, ed. T. Linafelt and T. K. Beal (Fortress, 1998), 157–71; Thiessen, M., "'The Rock Was Christ,'" *JSNT* 36 (2013): 103–26; Udoh, F. E., *To Caesar What Is Caesar's*, BJS 343 (Brown

University Press, 2005); Worthington, J., "*Creatio ex Nihilo* and Romans 4:17 in Context," *NTS* 62, no. 1 (2016): 49–59; Worthington, *Creation in Paul and Philo*, WUNT 2/317 (Mohr Siebeck, 2011).

JONATHAN D. WORTHINGTON

Philo (4): Thematic Parallels to the NT

Many themes in Philo's writing can be compared with those in the NT. As George Nickelsburg (69) observes, "Early Christianity arose as a sect within the matrix of Judaism, and the books of the NT were written for communities that understood the religious language of the Hellenized world and, in some cases, the vocabulary and world view of Hellenistic Jewry." We should be shocked if there were *not* significant thematic overlaps, at least in terms of themes touched on by multiple authors if not in terms of themes understood similarly or agreed upon. (See fuller treatments in Williamson, *Philo*; "Christology"; Chadwick; Sandmel; Siegert; Runia, "Testament.")

Our Method of Exploring Themes

Sound and accessible resources already exist for gaining a broad and systematic understanding of key themes in Philo's writings. Marian Hillar introduces basic Philonic themes such as the contemplative life and philosophy (§4); how philosophy and wisdom relate as a path to ethical life (§5); ethics itself (§6); the transcendence of God and corresponding mysticism (§7); creation (§9); miracles (§10); and the Logos (§11). Carlos Lévy (§§4–5) adds the themes such as "negative theology" (i.e., describing what God is *not* and how he is *not* fully knowable); providence; God's various "powers" and his Logos; the law of nature; creation and anthropology; soul and body; virtue ethics according to *oikeiōsis* (kinship) and *homoiōsis* (likeness) to God; the movement from passions to virtue; virtues as the path to perfection; politics and contemplation; and the sage as the "divine man" (i.e., the one most like God). And there are full treatments of other (supposed) parallels such as Philo's dualism and what Hebrews is getting at (e.g., Williamson's *Philo* and "Christology").

There is one particular weakness in the works of Hillar and Lévy (and others)—namely, their treatment of Philo's "technique of exposition" (Hillar, §3). That is what the current articles on Philo within this dictionary are about. So, even as we end by exploring a few thematic parallels or touch points, we will maintain our focus on the use of the OT. We will not present a catalog either of Philo's key themes in general or of those that parallel NT themes.

Rather, we will explore the hermeneutical moves within a *few* important themes that run through Philo and some NT writings and that impact NT theology. In particular, we will address the themes of (1) Scripture's theocentricity; (2) humanity's inherent beauty (which tends to be a neglected theme in studies of both Philo's and Paul's anthropologies); and (3) humanity's sin and its consequences.

We will also heed Larry Hurtado's gentle warning (74–77) about this enterprise. He observes that "the real usefulness of studying" the sorts of "parallels" people sometimes see between Philo and NT authors—typically Paul, then John and Hebrews—"is that it enables us to see more clearly the distinctiveness and specificity of each text." This is why we will work hard to not force Philo or NT authors into a box fit for the other.

Scripture's Theocentricity

Scripture's theocentricity in Philo. Philo is fundamentally a God-lover. This comes out in one of his recurring exegetical moves: his theocentricity (Frick, 4). A few examples from *On the Creation of the World* will open a window to see this technique in his other commentaries.

When commenting on the third day of Gen. 1, Philo consistently turns his readers' attention to God, even in places the sacred text does not. For example, Moses's repetition in Gen. 1:11–12 of "according to its kind/their kinds" (4x in Gen. 1:11–12) and "according to likeness" (2x) suggests to Philo that God created in nature "the eternal genesis of likenesses" (*Creation* 43): seeds producing plants producing fruits producing seeds and around again, a sort of "immortalizing" and "eternity" of "the kinds" (44). While Philo is certainly making a textual observation (the repeated phrase) and a general ontological claim about the nature of beginning and end, he is also making a *theological* claim. As he words it, "*God* purposed . . . therefore *he* led and *he* spurred on . . . and *he* made to bend back around" (emphasis added). Even when nature (as secondary causes) can explain a perpetual process, Philo still sees and teaches that it is *God* being active in mind and work (cf. *Heir* 113–22; *Alleg. Interp*. 1.5–7).

Another textual detail at this point in Gen. 1 raises an important aporia for Philo (a seeming contradiction, logical disjunction, or puzzle): Why does Moses record the creation of plants (the third day) before the creation of the sun (the fourth day)? Philo defends the text, though not by resorting to allegory. Rather, he explores God's wisdom and sovereignty in this creative decision. According to Philo, Moses is showing that God intentionally delayed his adorning of heaven as "proof" of his "most evident power of rulership" (*Creation* 45). For God foreknew that humans would tend toward idolatry of the created order, specifically by attributing the "causes" of seasonal plant growth to the heavenly bodies themselves. Philo admits that seeing astral causation is somewhat "reasonable," but the danger is that people will admire the phenomena of all types of visible plant growth too much and thereby "believe in" or "trust" (*pisteuō*) the heavenly bodies rather than God. The third and fourth days transpire as the text says because of

God's foreknowledge and wise planning to undercut false trust beforehand! God is powerfully demonstrating that he does not *need* "his heavenly offspring" and that they are "not autonomous in their rule" (46), for it is *God himself* who, like a charioteer, "leads all natural processes *however he wishes*, each according to law and justice" (46 [emphasis added]). For Philo, the dignity of God's unique rule is at stake (47).

Finally, Philo's theocentric exegesis shines through at the end of his commentary. After completing his exposition on Gen. 1–3 (*Creation* 1–169), Philo suggests that *all* of Genesis's creation account teaches five key doctrines (170–72). And every doctrine involves God's nature and decisions for creation: (1) God really exists (which should convict agnostics and atheists); (2) God is one (which should convict polytheists); (3) God has created the cosmos (which should convict those depriving God of glory); (4) God created the cosmos to be one and complete (thus reflecting God's nature); and (5) God providentially cares for his creation. For Philo, *God* is the point of the text.

Scripture's theocentricity in Paul. Like Philo, Paul argues theocentrically about God's creative intentions and method: "What can be known about God is plain to them, because *God* has shown it to them. For his invisible attributes, namely, his eternal power and divine nature, have been clearly perceived, ever since the creation of the world, in the things that have been made *in order that* they would be without excuse" (Rom. 1:19–20 ESV adapted). God actively and intentionally set up creation in such a way that humans are morally obligated to honor him as Creator as they look at all the works of his hands. God did this for a purpose: in order that they would be (*eis to einai autous*) without excuse. For Paul, *God* is the focal point.

Interestingly, and again like Philo, Paul has a theocentric interpretation of the third day of creation. In 1 Cor. 15 Paul points out, "What you sow is not the body that is to be, but a bare kernel, perhaps of wheat or of some other grain. But *God* gives it a body *just as he wished*, and to each kind of seed its own body" (1 Cor. 15:37–38 ESV adapted). Paul sees God's desires and intentions as the thing to highlight from Gen. 1 as he moves the Corinthians' understanding of the nature of God toward the "how" and "in what type of body" God will resurrect them in Christ (15:35–49).

Paul carries forward this theocentric reading of God's creation of plants into the diversity of bodies, fleshes, and glories of the other earthly bodies (fish, birds, animals, humans) and heavenly bodies (sun, moon, stars; see 15:39–41). Since the beginning, God has always given bodies (various bodies, fleshes, glories) *just as he wished*, and "in this manner also is the resurrection of the dead" (15:42 AT).

In fact, Paul's notion of God's sovereign desire and activity can be seen in his understanding of God's creation of the human body (which, of course, is first recounted in Gen. 2:7). Earlier in his same letter Paul writes, "*God* arranged" the diversity of human body parts "*just as he wished*" (1 Cor. 12:18 AT). Paul applies this theocentric understanding of anthropology to ecclesiology: God has also arranged his Son's body, the church, just as he wished. *God* composed the parts, having given different gifts to different people, "*just as he purposed*" (12:11 AT; cf. vv. 27–30).

Moving backward in the same letter (1 Cor. 11:7–12b), Paul yet again shows a reading of creation that is theocentric. He describes the following four aspects of the nature of man and woman based in Gen. 1–2 before making a conclusion:

1. man as "God's image and glory" from Gen. 1:27 (1 Cor. 11:7);
2. the ontological creation of "woman *out of* man" from Gen. 2:21–23 (1 Cor. 11:8);
3. the purposive creation of "woman *on account of* man" from Gen. 2:18 (1 Cor. 11:9);
4. the ontological perpetuation of "woman *out of* man" from Gen. 2:21–23 (1 Cor. 11:12a);
5. the ontological perpetuation of "man through woman" from Gen. 4:1 until now (1 Cor. 11:12b).

He concludes with this theological statement of origins: "But *all things are from God*" (11:12c AT). The relationships within humanity—ontological and purposive, with ethical propriety based on both—are important primarily because they are "from" the creator.

And finally, still working backward in this letter, we see Paul's theocentric language applied to church growth with a botanical metaphor in 1 Cor. 3:5–9 (ESV): "What then is Apollos? What is Paul? Servants through whom you believed, as *the Lord assigned* to each. I planted, Apollos watered, but *God gave the growth*. So neither he who plants nor he who waters is anything, but *only God who gives the growth*. He who plants and he who waters are one, and each will receive his wages according to his labor. For we are *God's* fellow workers. You are *God's* field, *God's* building." Indeed, Paul applies this theocentric language to the entire new creation: "If anyone is in Christ, new creation! The old has passed away; behold, the new has come. But *all things are from God*" (2 Cor. 5:17–18 AT; cf. Heb. 2:10–11).

Paul and Philo share the theme of the theocentricity of creation. Thinking cosmically and redemptive-historically, Paul applies this creational theocentricity to the new creation in Christ, to God's activity in spreading the church, and to God's activity in equipping the church. Philo adds the dimension of theocentricity in our moral psychology. For Philo, "It is impossible to take hold of and to master pleasure . . . unless the soul confesses that *all actions and all progress are derived from God*, and attributes nothing to itself" (*Alleg. Interp.* 2.93 [emphasis added]). And for Paul, "*The God who said* 'Let light shine out of darkness' *has shone* in our hearts to give the light of the knowledge of *God's* glory in *Christ's* face. But we have this treasure in jars of clay, *so that* the surpassing power is *out of God* and not out of us" (2 Cor. 4:6–7 AT). For Philo and Paul, God is the point, for the Bible tells them so.

Humanity's Inherent Beauty

The oft-neglected positive side of Philo's anthropology. Philo's dualism is pervasive in his thought. It involves his cosmology with the noetic versus sensory worlds. It entails his anthropology with the mind versus the body, with "consisting of body and soul" serving as a general catch phrase for his anthropology (*Spec. Laws* 2.64; *Cherubim* 113; *Sacrifices* 126; *Drunkenness* 69; *Confusion* 62; *Giants* 33; see Runia, *Creation,* 325). And his dualism involves his ethics: virtue according to the mind or image versus vice according to the flesh or senses (*Planting* 44–46; see Tobin, 136–37; Levison, 86). Philo's deep dualistic convictions about reality are "the backbone of his anthropological views" (Van den Hoek, 65; cf. Runia, *"Timaeus,"* 262).

Just as scholars easily think only of Philo's use of allegory and miss his variegated ways of interpreting Scripture, so too scholars easily think that Philo is completely negative about the sense-perceptible world and bodies since he often elaborates on how far short they fall from the noetic world and minds. And it is true that for Philo the things that are perceptible to the senses are by nature corruptible, wasting away. This includes Adam's body as created in Gen. 2:7, for it is "by nature mortal," heading toward decay, having an inevitable propensity to dissipate to dust (*Prelim. Studies* 20; *Cherubim* 14; see Van den Hoek, 68; Runia, *Creation,* 325). For Philo, the bodily structure is inherently mortal and corruptible, even at creation.

This reading of the inherent mortality of the human body at creation has some weight in Gen. 2–3 itself. God acts "lest [Adam] reach out his hand and take also of the tree of life and eat, and live forever" (3:22 ESV). Eternal life is not inherently Adam's as a created being. Something extrinsic to his created frame must be added to change him into an immortal human, such as fruit from the tree of life. And when Adam sins, the text does not present the notion that something in Adam's anthropology dies but rather that his death is guaranteed by the deprivation of that external gift (3:23–24).

But saying that the physical world falls short of the noetic world is not the same as saying it is completely negative. Philo often gives a positive appraisal of the sensible world, as in *Prelim. Studies* 96–97 regarding the senses themselves: "To see, and to hear, and to smell, and to taste, and also to touch are divine gifts, for which it is our duty to give thanks. But not only are we taught to thank the Giver of all goodness for these earthly, and wooden, and corporeal things, and for the irrational animals, the outward senses, but also for the mind, which, to speak with strict propriety, is man in man, the better in the worse, the immortal in the mortal." With his standard theocentric reading of Scripture, Philo sees in Gen. 1–2 beauty in Adam's physical body (*Creation* 136–38) as well as soul (139). Adam is truly "most excellent" in "body" (136.1–3), "in truth beautiful and good" (136.6), and has "good form" (*eumorphian*) of body (136.7). And throughout *Creation* 140–44, Philo argues fiercely for Adam's surpassing features of body as well as cognition and rulership.

For Philo, Adam's body is surpassingly beautiful specifically because of *God's* skill: "The Craftsman was good, as well as in all else, in understanding to bring it about that each of the parts of the body [*hekaston ton tou sōmatos meron*] should have in itself individually [*idiai kath' heauton*] its due proportions, and should also be harmoniously fitted with accuracy toward the fellowship of the whole. And together with this symmetry [of the parts], God formed over the body good flesh [*eusarkian*], and adorned it with good color, purposing the first man to be the most beautiful [*kalliston*] to behold" (*Creation* 138; cf. *Virtues* 203). Due to God's skillful design and masterful execution, Adam's body parts work in harmony toward the "fellowship" of the whole body. (In 1 Cor. 12:12–30, Paul similarly describes God's creation of the human body; see Worthington, *Creation,* 176–80.)

Philo then explores the surpassing nature of Adam's soul as described in Gen. 2:7. "When God inbreathed [*empneusthenta*] into the man's face," it was then that "the human became an image and copy of [God's own Word]" (*Creation* 139; cf. *Worse* 86–87). Philo can import the "image" (*apeikonisma*) idea from Gen. 1:27 into Gen. 2:7 because in the latter Adam clearly has "the ruling mind in the soul" (cf. *Virtues* 204–5). Even though Philo has many negative things to say about the material world and the human body, especially in comparison to the noetic world and mind, it is not only God's granted "soul" but even God's chosen and formed "body" for the human that is of superior quality. And all is due to God's forethought, purpose, and skill.

The oft-neglected positive side of Paul's anthropology. For Paul, in Adam all die. This is very important for Paul's anthropology (and Christology, hamartiology, soteriology, eschatology, etc.). It is also not a simple idea in Paul's writings. All *actually* die in Adam because of Adam's transgression and our inclusion in his sin and exile from life (Rom. 5:12–21; cf. 1 Cor. 15:21–22). We also have inherited a frail mortality and perishability from Adam's created form, made from dust in Gen. 2:7. According to Paul, even Adam's *created* frame was not as full of glory and immortality as Christ's resurrected body (1 Cor. 15:42–47). Our inclusion in the resurrected last Adam by the life-giving Spirit guarantees to us a bodily incorruptibility, immortality, and glory that our inclusion in the first Adam, even in his pre-sin created dusty state, did not guarantee or give (15:48–49) (Worthington, *Creation,* 180–85; cf. Maston, "Crisis").

These are some of the negative sides of Paul's anthropology in Adam.

Because of Paul's just-mentioned contrasts between Adam and Christ, many Pauline scholars promote and perpetuate the idea that "the first Adam is *always* presented negatively while Christ is always presented positively" and that "Paul finds *nothing* positive in the depiction of Adam, and this suggests that Adam does not present an accurate understanding of true humanity" (Maston, "Christ," 285; cf. 279, 280, 288–89, 291, 292; see also Scroggs, 59, 91, 100; Dunn, 136n28; Kim, 264n1; Bouteneff, 45). But just as Philonic scholars often miss the positive aspect of Philo's anthropological reading of Gen. 1–2, so too such Pauline scholars miss the positive aspect of Paul's anthropological reading of Gen. 1–2. Here are some highlights as we explore thematic parallels (or at least touch points) with Philo.

For Paul, a contemporary Corinthian man exists as "God's image and glory," even as a contemporary Corinthian woman "is man's glory" (1 Cor. 11:7). Paul demonstrates that these positive statements of glory are currently true by arguing not christologically but textually. Genesis 1–2 gives Paul this understanding of the "glory" of contemporary man and woman. (This does not erase Paul's understanding of our guilt, shame, and death in Adam; we must not think simplistically about Paul's anthropology.) Paul's logic in 1 Cor. 11:7–9 works only if he believes Adam exists as God's image and glory in those texts (even though he never *explicitly* calls Adam God's image and glory). What is more, Paul's precise wording again only makes sense if he sees Adam not merely as *according to* another image but rather as *being* God's image and glory.

Paul's positive construal of man due to God's creation of Adam in 1 Cor. 11 makes sense of his later language about human bodies, flesh, and glory in 1 Cor. 15. There Paul writes that current earthly bodies and fleshes—including the human—truly "have glory" (15:39–41). And, again, based on v. 38, this creational and even anthropological "glory" is due to *God's* creative intentions and prowess in Gen. 1–2.

So, Samuel Sandmel's argument (38) that Philo and Paul "share a common reserved dualism, in which the material side of man is evil, the immaterial good" overlooks important data in both men's writings. Against scholars who do not see evidence of Paul writing positively about Adam and so deny it a place in his anthropology (e.g., Scroggs, Barrett, Dunn, Kim, Bouteneff, Maston), the evidence we have considered points to a place in his anthropology for inherent glory in humanity, even now, still rooted in God's creation of Adam.

What is more, noticing this feature of Paul's anthropology helps us see a broader christological reading of Scripture and another theological dynamic at play. For Paul, the "glory" of Moses's face and ministry is real and true (2 Cor. 3:7, 9, 11; interpreting Exod. 33–34), yet that glory can *also* be deemed as "no glory" when *compared* to the surpassing glory of the resurrected Christ and his ministry of the Spirit (3:10). Likewise, Adam's created glory is real and true (implied in 1 Cor. 11:7 and 15:39–41), as is ours in him, yet that true glory can *also* be deemed as no glory, even as "dishonor" (1 Cor. 15:42–43), when *compared* to the surpassing glory of the last Adam as resurrected by the Spirit, as well as our coming surpassing glory in him (15:42–49).

Humanity's Sin and Its Consequences

The well-known negative side of Philo's anthropology. Philo also teaches that Adam and Eve grievously sin in Gen. 3. They disobey God, and Philo does not take this lightly. Eating the fruit God had forbidden them "instantly changed" them. It immediately shifts them "out of a state of simplicity and innocence" and "into one of treachery"; and "the Father was sorely angry" (*Creation* 156).

For Philo, their deeds "were worthy of wrath," because "passing by the tree of immortal life—which is the consummation of virtue, by which they would have been able to bear fruit for a long-lasting and blessed life—they rather chose the daily and mortal 'time' (I cannot say 'life,' but rather merely 'time') full of unhappiness. [God] appointed for them the punishments that were fitting" (*Creation* 156). The "fitting" punishments that Philo describes branch out from the textual language and into the realm of slavery: Adam and Eve were "the first to become slaves of a hard and incurable passion" (*Creation* 167–68). Philo also thought of payment: Adam and Eve "immediately found the wages paid by pleasure." (This seems somewhat similar to Paul's reflections on the consequences of sin in Rom. 6. Riding on the heels of his reflection on Adam's sin in Rom. 5:12–21, Paul also uses language of slavery and payment: "slaves of sin," "wages paid by sin" [6:6–23 AT].)

Philo returns to the language of Gen. 3. Eve's "wages" were violent birth pangs and loss of liberty. Adam's "wages" were unceasing sweat, labors, and distress merely to gain life's bare necessities. Displaying a theocentric reading again, Philo observes that God saw that in this moment "evil began to get the better of the virtues," so *he* closed his "ever-flowing springs of graces" in order to no longer "bring supplies to those felt to be unworthy of them" (*Creation* 167–68). One might call these "natural" consequences, but Philo sees them as intended and enacted by God himself.

Philo believes it would have been "fitting justice" for God to completely wipe out the human race (Adam and Eve here). They have expressed "thanklessness toward God, who is the benefactor and savior." (This seems similar to Paul's comment in Rom. 1:32 ESV that "God's righteous decree" is "that those who practice such things deserve to die.") Yet God "took pity and moderated their punishment" and "permitted the race to continue"—that is, Adam and Eve remained alive and began having children—for God is "merciful by nature" (*Creation* 169).

Adam's thankless treachery even affects coming humanity. Specifically, God "no longer gave them food as he had done before from ready prepared stores" (*Creation* 169). So, everyone is affected in some way by Adam's sin—though not by bearing condemnation and being counted as transgressors because of "the one man" (which is Paul's language). Indeed, Cain's wickedness does not prove like-father-like-son, but actually renders him *unlike* Adam "in either body or soul," which is why Seth is given the honorable right of being Adam's firstborn and image in Adam's royal genealogy (*QG* 1.81).

For Philo, Adam tends to be a type of model for others. So Philo applies his language of "slavery" to *any* person who sins *like* Adam and Eve. As Adam succumbs to Eve and she to the serpent, so too whenever our own reason succumbs to our senses and desires, our "reason is immediately ensnared and becomes a subject instead of a ruler, and a slave instead of a master, and instead of a citizen an alien, and a mortal instead of an immortal" (*Creation* 165). Slavery, even mortality, is our lot *when* we sin like Adam. Only the person wholly submitted to God is truly free (*Good Person* 20). That said, even "soul death," which is *like* what Adam experienced, is neither inherited from him nor lasting (*Alleg. Interp.* 1.106–8). And for Philo, this death is due to sin's pervasiveness in this world and even in our lives.

The well-known negative side of the NT's and specifically Paul's anthropology. Philo is not the only one to use "slavery" language with regard to sin, of course. In John's Gospel, Jesus says that "everyone who commits sin is the slave of sin" (8:34 AT). The author of Hebrews describes "the devil" as "the one who has the power of death" and those living in "fear of death" as "subject to lifelong slavery" (2:14–15 ESV). And we noted above Paul's inclusion of "slavery" language for sin (Rom. 6:6–23).

Paul agrees that humans are in a dire place. But Paul sees it and expresses it more starkly and extremely than does Philo. In 1 Cor. 15:22, Paul writes that "in Adam all die." He does not elaborate there. But in Rom. 5:12–21 (ESV adapted), which he writes from Corinth and thus may have been thinking through similar themes, he does elaborate on our relationship to Adam and death in his sin. Not only did "sin enter the world" and "death through sin" generically, but also Paul takes pains to emphasize the personal responsibility of Adam and his effect on all humanity. Death's entrance was "through *one man*" (5:12a), "many died *by the trespass of the one man*" (5:15), "condemnation" came to all "*from the one trespass*" (5:16, 18 AT), "death reigned" over all "*because of that one man's trespass*" (5:17), and "the many were made sinners" because of "*one man's* disobedience" (5:19). This idea that all people are "sons of disobedience" and "by nature children of wrath" (Eph. 2:2–3 ESV) reaches into his other letters as well.

Conclusion

When finding thematic parallels between Philo and NT writers, we must be nuanced. Some words are similar. Some concepts are similar. Even some structures of thought are similar, such as the notion that something considered positive on its own can simultaneously also be considered negative in comparison to something better. And so there are thematic touch points, overlaps, and even some parallels in Philo's and Paul's thought. Yet with as horrible as Philo sees Adam's sin and its real and potential impact on humanity, his thought offers no parallel for Paul's treatment of the pervasive and deadly effects of Adam's sin. And no parallel theme can be found in Philo regarding a sense-perceptible, tangible, redemptive-historical upgrade from the glory of creation itself, or from the glory of Moses, due to the surpassingly glorious bodily resurrection of the Son of God, which God planned before creation and will give to those who love him by being found in Christ.

See also OT Use of the OT: Comparison with the NT Use of the OT; *other Philo articles; Mishnah, Talmud, and Midrashim articles; Pseudepigrapha articles; Septuagint articles; Targums articles*

Bibliography. Barrett, C. K., *From First Adam to Last* (Black, 1962); Bouteneff, P. C., *Beginnings* (Baker Academic, 2008); Chadwick, H., "St. Paul and Philo of Alexandria," *BJRL* 48 (1965–66): 286–307; Dunn, J. D. G., "1 Corinthians 15:45—Last Adam, Life-Giving Spirit," in *Christ and Spirit in the New Testament*, ed. B. Lindars and S. Smalley (Cambridge University Press, 1973), 127–41; Frick, P., *Divine Providence in Philo of Alexandria* (Mohr Siebeck, 1999); Hillar, M., "Philo of Alexandria," *Internet Encyclopedia of Philosophy*, https://iep.utm.edu/philo/#H3; Hurtado, L., "Does Philo Help Explain Christianity?," in *Philo und das Neue Testament*, ed. R. Deines and K.-W. Niebuhr, WUNT 172 (Mohr Siebeck, 2004), 73–92; Jervell, J. S., *Imago Dei*, FRLANT 76 (Vandenhoeck & Ruprecht, 1960); Kim, S., *The Origin of Paul's Gospel*, WUNT 2/4 (Mohr Siebeck, 1980); Levison, J. R., *Portraits of Adam in Early Judaism*, JSPSup 1 (Sheffield Academic, 1988); Lévy, C., "Philo of Alexandria," in *The Stanford Encyclopedia of Philosophy*, ed. E. N. Zalta, spring 2018 ed., https://plato.stanford.edu/archives/spr2018/entries/philo/; Loader, W., *The Septuagint, Sexuality, and the New Testament* (Eerdmans, 2004); Maston, J., "Anthropological Crisis and Solution in the *Hodayot* and 1 Corinthians 15," *NTS* 62, no. 4 (2016): 533–48; Maston, "Christ or Adam," *JTI* 11, no. 2 (2017): 277–93; McCasland, S. V., "The Image of God according to Paul," *JBL* 69, no. 2 (1950): 85–100; Nickelsburg, G., "Philo among Greeks, Jews and Christians," in *Philo und das Neue Testament*, ed. R. Deines and K.-W. Niebuhr,

WUNT 172 (Mohr Siebeck, 2004), 53–72; Runia, D., "Philo and the New Testament," in *Philo in Early Christian Literature* (Fortress, 1993), 63–86; Runia, *Philo of Alexandria: On the Creation of the Cosmos*, PACS 1 (Brill, 2001); Runia, *Philo of Alexandria and the "Timaeus" of Plato*, PhA 44 (Brill, 1986); Sandmel, S., "Philo Judaeus," in *Hellenistisches Judentum in römischen Zeit: Philon und Josephus*, ed. W. Hasse, ANRW II.21.1 (de Gruyter, 1984), 3–46; Scroggs, R., *The Last Adam* (Blackwell, 1966); Siegert, F., "Philo and the New Testament," in *The Cambridge Companion to Philo*, ed. A. Kamesar, CCP (Cambridge University Press, 2009), 175–209; Tobin, T., *The Creation of Man*, CBQMS 14 (Catholic Biblical Association, 1983); Van den Hoek, A., "Endowed with Reason or Glued to the Senses," in *The Creation of Man and Woman*, ed. G. P. Luttikhuizen, TBN 3 (Brill, 2000), 63–75; Williamson, R., "Philo and New Testament Christology," in *Studia Biblica 1978: III*, ed. E. A. Livingstone, JSNTSup 3 (JSOT Press, 1980), 439–45; Williamson, *Philo and the Epistle to the Hebrews*, ALGHJ 4 (Brill, 1970); Worthington, J., *Creation in Paul and Philo*, WUNT 2/317 (Mohr Siebeck, 2011).

JONATHAN D. WORTHINGTON

Postmodernism

See Theological Interpretation of Scripture

Powers and Principalities

See Divine Warrior; Satan

Presuppositions

See Apostolic Hermeneutics articles

Priest

The concept of priest may seem foreign, elitist, or disturbing (e.g., animal sacrifices) for contemporary Bible readers. Yet the presence of a special group who mediated between god(s) and people by offering sacrifices and maintaining sanctuaries was ubiquitous and unquestioned in the ancient world. It is not surprising, then, that the sanctuary and its priesthood are central in the Bible as well.

The most essential function of a priest in the Bible is to maintain holiness. Because of the gap between God's utter holiness and human sin, access to God's presence is extremely limited and must be guarded through an extensive system of regulations ensuring ritual purity. Failure to maintain this holiness can result in death. The second essential function of a priest is mediation, representing both God to the people and the people to God. In the OT, the priest is an essential element of Israel's covenantal relationship with God. In the NT, this office finds its fulfillment in the person and work of Jesus Christ and in his followers, who are identified as priests of his kingdom (e.g., Rev. 1:6).

The most common Hebrew word for "priest" in the OT, *kōhēn*, occurs 740 times (including references to non-Israelite priests; cf. *lēvî*, "Levite," which occurs about 350 times). The etymology of this word is uncertain. The word occurs 196 times in Leviticus, concentrated in Lev. 1–7, where priestly duties are outlined. No one term corresponds with "high priest" (cf. *hakkōhēn haggādôl*, "great priest," Num. 35:25, 28; *kōhēn hārō'š*, e.g., 2 Chron. 19:11). The term *kōhēn* is consistently rendered as *hiereus* ("priest") in the LXX. In the NT, *hiereus* occurs 31 times, with 14 occurrences in Hebrews; the term *archiereus* ("high priest") occurs 120 times.

This article traces the development of priests and the Levitical priesthood in the OT and the continuity and discontinuity of these entities as NT writers appropriate them. The origins and sources for Israel's priesthood are debated, with scholars considering questions about Canaanite parallels and purported pentateuchal sources (e.g., Wellhausen) as well as the impact these parallels and sources may have on reconstructions of Israel's history. These debates significantly impact one's understanding of priesthood in the Bible. The approach followed here, however, seeks to understand the office and role of priest as it develops in the final form of the OT and its appropriation in the NT. Hence, questions of sources will not be addressed.

Priest and the OT

Priests before the Aaronic priesthood. Priests in the OT are mostly associated with the Aaronic priesthood, although there are several important precursors to this priesthood, beginning with the creation account, the apex of which is the creation of those who bear the very image of God (Gen. 1–2). These image-bearers, Adam and Eve, dwell in God's presence in a special part of this creation, an abundant garden, best understood as a holy space. Adam and Eve are entrusted with extending God's rule and mediating his holy presence throughout the rest of creation. Moreover, the command to "rule over" (*rādâ*, Gen. 1:26) suggests a royal role, and the verbs "work" (*'ābad*, Gen. 2:15) and "take care of" (*šāmar*, Gen. 2:15) suggest a priestly vocation (the latter two verbs describe the Levite's work in the tabernacle [e.g., Num. 3:7–8]; Alexander, 20–31; Beale, 66–70).

Some suggest that the patriarchs performed priestly functions when they built altars or offered sacrifices (e.g., Abra[ha]m, Gen. 12:8; 22:13; Jacob, Gen. 28:18–19; 31:54; 46:1; cf. Abel, Gen. 4:4; Noah, Gen. 8:20; Job 1:5). Two early figures, however, are explicitly called priests. In Gen. 14:18–20, the enigmatic Melchizedek, introduced as a "priest of God Most High," appears to worship the same God as Abraham. Moreover, by receiving a blessing from and giving a tithe to Melchizedek, Abraham acknowledges Melchizedek as a legitimate priest. In Exod. 2:16, Reuel (2:18; called Jethro in 3:1; 18:1) appears as "a priest of Midian." It is unclear whom Jethro worships. Other clearly foreign priests are mentioned (e.g., Gen. 41:45, 50; 46:20; 47:22, 26). (The identity of the priests in Exod. 19:22, 24 is unclear. Some suggest they are Midianite, others that Exodus is not arranged chronologically and these are Aaronic priests.)

The Aaronic/Levitical priesthood. Following their miraculous deliverance from Egypt, God's people are brought to Sinai, where their identity as God's special possession out of all the nations (Exod. 19:5) and as a kingdom of priests and a holy nation (19:6) is revealed. The people are identified as priests, indicating that, as a nation, they are intended to mediate God's presence and holiness to other nations, thereby recalling the original vocation for God's image-bearers in the garden. The Sinaitic covenant and accompanying holiness regulations (Exod. 20–24) govern this special status of God's people. The people are strictly forbidden, however, from touching the foot of Sinai under penalty of death (19:12–13). Only Moses can speak with God directly (19:3–13) and represent God to the people. These restrictions reveal two important aspects of God's holiness. First, there are several levels of access to God's presence. The highest level is granted to Moses, and successively lower levels are granted to Aaron and his sons, the elders, and, finally, the people. This also indicates that holiness is closely related to priestly status. Second, there are clear dangers associated with God's holiness and severe consequences for violations of prescribed regulations.

Although the people are identified as "a kingdom of priests," a special class of individuals, Aaron and his descendants, are specifically set apart as priests (Exod. 28–29; Lev. 8). Set within the discussion of the tabernacle is the institution of the Aaronic priesthood (Exod. 28–29), indicating the organic connection between the two. Moreover, the extensive focus on the tabernacle (Exod. 25–31, 35–40) reveals its significance as the place where heaven and earth "meet" and where the Lord "dwells" in the midst of his people as they travel from Sinai to the land of Canaan.

Exodus does not indicate why God chooses Aaron and his sons to be his priests (Exod. 28:1), with Aaron designated as the "high priest" (Lev. 21:10; Ezra 7:5). The key priestly roles of maintaining holiness and acting as mediators are emphasized in Exod. 28–29 and Leviticus, which outline the five major offerings (burnt, grain, fellowship, sin, and guilt) that priests offer on behalf of the people before the Lord (Lev. 1–7) and the role of priests in maintaining cleanness among the people (Lev. 11–15). The importance of priestly obedience (e.g., Exod. 28:43) is underscored by the immediate death of Aaron's two older sons, Nadab and Abihu, who offer "strange" (i.e., unauthorized) fire (Lev. 10:1–3; cf. Num. 16), thus rendering Aaron's third son, Eleazar, his successor. Moreover, the faithfulness of Eleazar's son, Phinehas, results in a "lasting" priesthood (Num. 25:6–13).

Several additional elements indicate the consecrated nature of the priesthood: genealogical records, special clothing, and a special consecration ceremony. All priests are required to maintain ceremonial purity (Lev. 21:1–4, 7–8) and to be without physical defects (21:16–23), thereby indicating inner morality and purity through outward appearance. All priests are to avoid cutting their hair, trimming their beards, or cutting themselves (10:6; 21:5–10; likely because of parallel Canaanite practices) as well as consuming fermented drinks before entering the tent of meeting (10:8–11). The requirements for the high priest, however, are more restrictive, reinforcing the reality of restricted access to God's presence. Although all priests must descend from Aaron (Num. 3:10), the high priest has to descend from Aaron's son Eleazar (20:22–28). Whereas priests are restricted from touching a dead body except for that of an immediate family member (Lev. 21:3), the high priest can have no contact with any dead body (21:10–12). Whereas there are restrictions on whom a priest can marry (21:7), the high priest can marry only a virgin from his "own people" (21:13–15).

The high priest oversees the entire sacrificial system, the most important part of which is the Day of Atonement (Lev. 16), on which day (and only on this one day) he alone can enter the most holy place. First, the high priest sacrifices a bull as a sin offering for himself and his family. He then enters the most holy place to sprinkle the blood from this sacrifice on the mercy seat over the ark—the presence of the Lord being obscured by burning incense. Then he sacrifices a goat as a sin offering for the people and sprinkles the blood from this offering before God in the most holy place. Finally, he lays his hands on the scapegoat and sends it off to the wilderness with the sins of the people. Although the danger associated with God's holiness is emphasized in this ceremony (Lev. 16:2, 13; cf. Exod. 28:35), the high priest's entrance to the most holy place (filled with Edenic imagery) can also be understood in terms of a "cultic Adam," who symbolically returns to Eden (see Morales, 172–80).

The high priest is further distinguished by ornate clothing, which gives him "dignity and honor" (Exod. 28:2) and reflects the glory of the Lord. These items are made of gold, blue, purple, and scarlet yarn and fine linen (28:5). The ephod (28:6–14; 39:2–7) is like a vest that hangs over the shoulders by means of two onyx stones, engraved with the names of the twelve sons of Israel, six names on each stone, that serve as a memorial before the Lord. The breastplate "for making decisions" (28:15–30; 39:8–21) has twelve stones, in four rows of three stones, that bear the names of the twelve tribes of Israel. Together, the two onyx stones and the twelve individual stones indicate that the concerns of the people as a whole and of the individual tribes are represented before the Lord, and they perhaps symbolically depict the "kingdom of priests" (Cheung, 267). The

Urim and Thummim, which can be used to seek God's will for matters not covered explicitly in the law (e.g., 1 Sam. 23:1–5), are to be placed in the breastplate. The robe of the ephod (Exod. 28:33–35; 39:22–26) is worn underneath, with bells to indicate that the high priest is entering and leaving the presence of the Lord. A turban with a plaque inscribed "HOLY TO THE LORD," a tunic, and a sash (28:36–39; 39:27–31) complete the elaborate outfit. The precious materials used for the high priest's clothing parallel the construction of the tabernacle in many ways, further underscoring the close association of the two (Exod. 26–27; 28:5; 39:1) and their Edenic symbolism. This elaborate clothing, however, is not worn on the Day of Atonement, when simple linen clothing instead reflects humility and contrition for sin (Lev. 16:3–4, 23–24, 32). Like the high priest, priests also have distinctive (although not as elaborate) clothing to give them "dignity and honor" (Exod. 28:40).

The increased holiness of the high priest is further reflected in his special anointing (Exod. 28:41; 29:4–7, 29), also paralleling the tabernacle's consecration (Lev. 8:10–13). During this ceremony, a bull is sacrificed as a sin offering for Aaron and his sons (8:14–21), and the blood from it is used to cleanse the altar. This is followed by the making of a burnt offering that is completely consumed as a pleasing offering to the Lord. Finally, a ram is sacrificed—unique to this ceremony—and blood from it is applied to the right ear lobes, thumbs, and big toes of Aaron and his sons. This is followed by a wave offering and a covenant meal (8:31–36). The ceremony lasts for seven days, likely recalling the seven days of creation, furthering the Edenic imagery.

The Levites assist the priests. Because of the role of Levi and Simeon in avenging Dinah's rape by murdering the men of Shechem (Gen. 34), they were cursed by Jacob on his deathbed (49:5–7) and received no land allotment. Yet due to their role in siding with Moses against Aaron after the golden-calf incident and slaughtering three thousand idolators (Exod. 32:25–29), the Levites are set apart to assist the Aaronic priesthood (Num. 3:5–9; 8:5–26). In lieu of a land allotment, they receive forty-eight specially designated cities throughout the land (Num. 35:1–8; Josh. 21:1–42; 1 Chron. 6:54–81). They are supported by tithes and are able to partake of sacrificial offerings (Num. 18:21). Moreover, the Lord himself is their inheritance (18:20–24; Deut. 18:1–2). Additionally, the Levites function as a substitute for the firstborn males of other tribes (Num. 3:11–13; cf. Exod. 13:1–2).

The primary function of the Levites is to transport the tabernacle (Num 1:47–53), including the ark of the covenant (Exod. 6:26; 13:18). In the time of David, Levites carry the ark into Jerusalem (1 Chron. 15). They also guard the tabernacle, putting to death any non-Levite who tries to enter it (Num. 1:51–53); and they serve as gatekeepers in the temple (1 Chron. 23). Eventually their role includes playing music and offering worship (1 Chron. 16, 23).

The levels of holiness are reflected throughout the Aaronic priesthood. Levites and priests can enter the tabernacle's outer room, the holy place, but only the high priest can enter the most holy place, and then only on the Day of Atonement. These same restrictions are reflected in the placement of the Levites' camps, surrounding the tabernacle on the west, south, and north (Num. 3:23, 29, 35), thereby providing a physical buffer between God's presence in the tabernacle and the profane or unclean realms (Num. 1:53; cf. Lev. 10:8–11). Moses, Aaron, and their descendants, however, camp at the eastern entrance of the tabernacle (Num. 3:38). The Levitical priesthood ensures safe access to God and guards against infringements of that access.

Priests in Israel's later history and the prophetic corpus. The main functions of the Levitical priesthood are outlined in Exodus–Numbers. The general deterioration of Israel during the time of the judges is also reflected in the faithlessness of priests and the especially reprehensible actions of two (perhaps representative) Levites: a Levite who can be bought as a personal priest (Judg. 17–18) and the horrific account of a Levite and his concubine (Judg. 19–21). This same deterioration is evident with Eli and his evil sons (1 Sam. 2–4). Although Samuel is a descendant of Levi (1 Chron. 6:25–27, 33–34), his role as a prophet dominates 1 Samuel.

Toward the end of his life, David has Zadok the priest and Nathan the prophet anoint Solomon as king (1 Kings 1:32–35). Zadok remains faithful to David and his choice of Solomon as king (1:1–8), whereas the priest Abiathar sides with Adonijah. Zadok's faithfulness is reflected in the presence of the Zadokites in Ezekiel's vision of the restored temple (Ezek. 44:15–16). Moreover, David also assigns the Levites to oversee the temple's construction (1 Chron. 23:1–4), and both priests and Levites serve in the temple as officials, judges, gatekeepers, guards, and musicians (23:1–26:28; cf. 6:31–47; 1 Kings 4:1–19). The priests and the Levites bring the ark into the temple (1 Kings 8:3–11).

Condemnation of priestly corruption and defilement is a frequent theme in the Prophets (e.g., Isa. 28:7; Jer. 2:4–8; 5:31; Lam. 4:13; Ezek. 22:26; Hosea 4:4–9; Zeph. 3:4; Hag. 2:10–14; Mal. 3:1–4), although there is also hope for future restoration (Jer. 30–31; Ezek. 34–38), including the future role of gentiles as priests and Levites (Isa. 66:20–21). Josiah's reforms include removing idolatrous priests (2 Kings 23:1–20) and reestablishing the Levitical priesthood (2 Chron. 35:10–14). When the postexilic temple is rebuilt, priests and Levites offer the Passover lamb (Ezra 6:19–21), teach "the Law" (Neh. 8:7–8), and assist in the covenant renewal (9:38). As the monarchy becomes weakened, however, the role of the priesthood, especially the high priest, becomes more prominent (2 Chron. 19:11; 34:9), and this change is reflected in extensive genealogies (e.g., 1 Chron. 6:1–81; 9:10–34;

23:1–26; Ezra 2:36–54). The political significance of the high priest increased further in the Persian period (the sixth century through the fourth century BC).

John Hyrcanus (ruled 135–104 BC) was both high priest and political ruler. Later, a dispute between Aristobulus II (younger son of Alexander Jannaeus, son of John Hyrcanus) and Hyrcanus II (older son of Alexander Jannaeus) resulted in the Roman general Pompey's siege of Jerusalem and the temple's desecration. Political rule went to the Romans, although John Hyrcanus remained as high priest. Jewish writings of this time period reflect both condemnation of the current, often corrupt, high priesthood (e.g., 2 Macc. 4:12–15; Pss. Sol. 4) and hopes for a future, pious priesthood in which Zadokite priests feature significantly (1QS 5.2, 4, 9). Qumran writings express hope for priestly (Aaronic) and royal (Davidic) messianic figures (1QS 9.9–11; CD 12.23). In 11Q13, Melchizedek appears as an angelic priest who officiates the Day of Atonement (2.4, 11–14). Similar praise for the Aaronic priest is found in Sir. 45:6–13.

Priest and the NT

Priestly duties. In the first century, regular priests (e.g., Zechariah, Luke 1:5–23) and Levites performed temple duties following a regular rotation (1 Chron. 24:4, 10; Neh. 12:4, 17). These duties included burning incense (Luke 1:9) and performing purification rites (e.g., Mark 1:44). The corruption of the high priest under the Hasmoneans continued under Herod the Great (ruled 37–34 BC) and culminated in Herod's controlling over the selection of the high priest and access to his vestments. Following Herod's death, high priests were increasingly aligned with and accountable to Roman authorities, although the high priest continued to wield significant power. Cooperation with Rome led to splintering of the priesthood, including the continued rise of the Sadducees (begun under the Hasmoneans). The high priest, often a Sadducee, ruled over the Sanhedrin. "Chief" priests may have comprised former high priests (who no longer served for life) and members of priestly families in Jerusalem (e.g., Luke 19:47; 20:19).

The Gospels and Acts. Throughout his incarnation, Jesus affirms the role of the temple and its priesthood by requesting that healed individuals seek out priests to fulfill required regulations (Matt. 8:1–4; Mark 1:40–44; Luke 5:12–14; 17:11–14) and by affirming the temple tax (Matt. 17:24–27). Luke records that the infant Jesus is presented in the temple in accordance with prescribed laws (Luke 2:22–40).

Jesus's understanding of his own priestly calling is affirmed in various ways in the Gospels. As one from the tribe of Judah, Jesus is not qualified to be a Levitical priest (Heb. 7:13), yet he is clearly set apart for service to God and anointed with the Spirit (at his conception, Matt. 1:18–25; Luke 1:26–38; his baptism, Matt. 3:16; his temptation, Matt. 4:1; Luke 4:1). The allusions to Ps. 2:7 at Jesus's baptism (Matt. 3:17; Mark 1:11; Luke 3:22) and transfiguration (Matt. 17:5; Mark 9:7; Luke 9:35) suggest that Jesus understands this Davidic psalm as referring to himself, as he similarly understands Ps. 110 (Mark 12:35–37). Although Ps. 110:4 is cited only in Hebrews (5:6; 7:17, 21; cf. 5:10; 6:20), Jesus's awareness of the entire psalm also suggests a priestly self-understanding. Additionally, his understanding of Dan. 7:13–14 with reference to himself suggests that he understands himself to be both the promised eschatological king and the promised eschatological high priest (see articles by Fletcher-Louis).

Jesus's actions and teaching reveal a priestly self-understanding: he declares the standard of true cleanness (Matt. 15:1–11; Mark 7:1–23; cf. Acts 10:9–16, 28), presents himself as the true interpreter of the law (Matt. 5:17–48; Luke 24:27), reveals the true intent of the Sabbath (Matt. 12:1–13; Mark 2:23–3:6; Luke 6:1–11; 13:10–17; John 5:16–18), and demonstrates his zeal for God's holiness by clearing the temple (Matt. 21:12–17; Mark 11:12–19; Luke 19:45–48; John 2:13–22), thereby also revealing the priesthood's failure to perform its duties (see esp. Perrin). Moreover, Jesus renders the unclean clean without thereby becoming unclean (e.g., Luke 5:12–13; 8:40–48). Although it does not indicate a priestly function, Jesus's declaration that he will rebuild the temple in three days (John 2:19) indicates that he fulfills the intention of both the Levitical priesthood and the temple. His intercession for the disciples also suggests a priestly self-understanding (John 17; Luke 22:32).

Furthermore, Jesus understands the sacrifice of his own sinless life as a sin offering (Mark 10:45; Luke 22:19–20; cf. John 1:29). The priestly hierarchy's failure to recognize God's ultimate purposes for the priesthood and the temple accounts for their opposition to Jesus (Matt. 16:21; 21:23–27; Mark 8:31; 11:27–33; Luke 9:22; 20:1–8; John 11:45–57) and resistance to his teaching (e.g., Matt. 21:33–46; Luke 20:9–19). This opposition culminates in Jesus's trial before the Sanhedrin, the high priest Caiaphas (Matt. 26:57–68; Mark 14:53–65), and Caiaphas's father-in-law Annas (John 18:12–24). It extends to the early church (Acts 4:1–22; 5:17–42; 6:8–7:53), even though some (most likely "regular") priests come to faith (Acts 6:7).

Hebrews. Jesus's death is understood in cultic terms in several epistles (e.g., "sacrifice," Rom. 3:25–26; Eph. 5:1–2; 1 John 2:1–2; 4:9–10; "sin offering," Rom. 8:3; 2 Cor. 5:21 mg.; "Passover lamb," 1 Cor. 5:6–8; "the sinless, spotless Lamb," 1 Pet. 1:18–19 NLT). The opening vision of the risen Jesus in Revelation (1:12–16) also employs priestly images. Hebrews, however, is unique in its priestly understanding of Jesus's person and work, presenting him as the true high priest (2:17; 3:1; 4:14; 5:5, 10; 6:20; 8:1; 9:11) or priest (5:6; 7:11, 15, 17, 21, 24). That these titles are used without accompanying explanation suggests that this is not a new concept for the epistle's audience.

The epistle offers an extended comparison between Jesus's priesthood and the Levitical one. First, Jesus's priesthood belongs to an entirely different order—"the order of Melchizedek" (5:6, 10; 6:20; 7:11, 17); thus, his priesthood is based not on genealogy (Exod. 29:9) but on divine oath (Heb. 5:5 [Ps. 2:7]; 7:20–22 [Ps. 110:4]). This oath shows the inextricable link between his statuses as divine Son and great high priest (1:2–3; 4:14; 5:5–6). Additionally, although the offices of king and priest were distinct in Israel's history, Ps. 110 addresses one who is both king and eternal priest in the order of Melchizedek. This psalm's appropriation in Hebrews indicates that Jesus is the perfect priest and king. Finally, the lack of indication of the beginning or end of Melchizedek's days in Gen. 14:18–20 points typologically to Jesus's eternal life (Heb. 7:16, 24), permanent priesthood (7:24), and continual intercession (7:24–25). The presence of another priesthood confirms the provisional nature of the Levitical one (7:11–19).

Second, Jesus is the divine Son and the perfect human being. Because of Jesus's solidarity with his brothers and sisters (2:11–16), he can sympathize with those who are tempted, because he has been tempted in every way, although he remains sinless (2:17; 4:14–16; 7:26). His obedience and suffering during his incarnation perfected him to become the high priest who is the source of eternal salvation (5:7–10; cf. 2:17), unlike the Levitical high priest (7:28). Jesus had no need to sacrifice for his own sins (7:27) but instead offered himself as the perfect, once-and-for-all sacrifice (9:26, 28; 10:12; cf. 10:4), which resulted in eternal redemption (9:12), cleansed consciences (10:22), and sanctifying perfection (10:14; 11:40).

Third, the change in priesthood (Melchizedekian) effects a change in the law (7:11–12). Thus, Jesus is the mediator of the new, eternal covenant, where sins are remembered no more and God's laws are written on believers' hearts and minds (7:22; 8:1–13; 9:15; 13:20). In Jesus, the Levitical priesthood has become obsolete (8:13; cf. Matt. 27:51; Mark 15:38).

Fourth, unlike Levitical high priests, who had to enter the earthly sanctuary repeatedly (Heb. 9:25–26), Jesus has entered the heavenly most holy place (8:4–5; 9:23–28) once for all by means of his own blood (9:11–12; cf. 4:14; 6:19–20; 9:24). Having completed his work of purification, he sits exalted at the right hand of God (1:3; 10:11–14) as the great high priest over God's house (10:21).

First Peter and Revelation: The priesthood of all believers. Jesus's perfect priesthood also restores the original priestly, royal status to redeemed humanity. In the NT, titles applied to Israel at Sinai are now applied to believers (1 Pet. 2:9–10; cf. Exod. 19:5–6; Isa. 43:21; Hosea 1:6–9; Rev. 1:6; 5:10), including both Jews and gentiles. Just as Israel was sanctified by the blood of the Passover lamb (Exod. 12:21–23), so also believers are made holy by the Lamb's shed blood (cf. 1 Pet. 1:18–19). A new temple founded upon Jesus Christ, the cornerstone, is being built with believers as "living stones," who offer spiritual sacrifices (1 Pet. 2:4–5; cf. 1 Cor. 3:9–17; 6:19; 2 Cor. 6:16–18; Eph. 2:19–22), their bodies (Rom. 12:1–2), and thanksgiving (Heb. 13:15–16). As priests, believers proclaim the gospel (e.g., Rom. 15:16; cf. Isa. 66:19–21) and pour out their very lives (Phil. 2:17). Their prayers are incense before God's throne (Rev. 5:8). They are clothed with righteous acts (Rev. 19:8). Priestly service includes a ministry of reconciliation (2 Cor. 5:18), worshiping the living God now (Heb. 9:14) and forever before his throne (Rev. 7:9–17; 20:6; 22:5).

Biblical-Theological and Hermeneutical Implications

Apart from a biblical understanding of priesthood, the concept of a priest can be difficult to understand for contemporary readers. Yet God's intention of having his people dwell with him in his holy space permeates Genesis to Revelation. The first humans' decision to rebel against God results in an immense gulf between God's perfect holiness and their sin. Early accounts in Genesis show the need for mediation between God and fallen humans—accounts that prepare for the Levitical priesthood as outlined in Exod. 19–Num. 10. Exodus 19 indicates that this priesthood flows out of the peoples' identity as God's special possession. Thus, both the priestly and royal roles for God's people are based on their unique relationship and chosen status with God. In this way, the Levitical priesthood, its elaborate sacrificial system and tabernacle, is an object lesson that affirms God's original intention for humanity yet also reveals the gulf between God's holiness and humanity's sin.

This is perhaps especially true for the high priest, whose consecration and mediation offer a picture of restored humanity, with its glory and access to God's presence (Cheung, 267–68). Ultimately, a merely human high priest cannot bring about complete restoration but instead points typologically to the perfect high priest, Jesus Christ, who perfectly mediates God to his people and the people to God (1 Tim. 2:5). Because he is the perfect high priest who has offered the fully efficacious sacrifice of his body, he restores the original priestly, royal vocation intended for humanity.

Thus, in Christ, we see several strands of the biblical story coming together. First, we see the perfect mediation between God and his people. Second, we see the restoration of the priestly, royal vocation intended for humanity. Third, we see the ultimate fulfillment and restoration of God's holy space where God can dwell in glory with his people (Rev. 21–22).

Without this framework, there appears to be much discontinuity between the OT and NT, with the Levitical priesthood and temple suddenly being replaced by Jesus Christ and the church. Instead, however, the unchanging purposes of God (Heb. 6:17) have always been to have his people dwell with him in his holy space. Against this backdrop, one finds surprising continuity between the concept of priesthood in both the OT and NT. In Christ, the intentions of the Levitical priesthood are both revealed and ultimately fulfilled.

See also Adam, First and Last; Image of God; Temple

Bibliography. Alexander, T. D., *From Eden to the New Jerusalem* (Kregel Academic, 2009); Anizor, U., and H. Voss, *Representing Christ* (IVP Academic, 2016); Beale, G. K., *The Temple and the Church's Mission*, NSBT 17 (IVP Academic, 2004); Cheung, A. T. M., "The Priest as the Redeemed Man," *JETS* 29 (1986): 265–75; Compton, J., *Psalm 110 and the Logic of Hebrews*, LNTS 537 (Bloomsbury T&T Clark, 2015); Duke, R. K., "Priests, Priesthood," in *DOTP*, 646–55; Fletcher-Louis, C. H. T., *The High Priest as Divine Mediator in the Hebrew Bible*, SBLSP 36 (Scholars Press, 1997), 161–93; Fletcher-Louis, "Jesus as the High Priestly Messiah: Part 1," *JSHJ* 4 (2006): 155–75; Fletcher-Louis, "Jesus as the High Priestly Messiah: Part 2," *JSHJ* 5 (2007): 57–79; Hagner, D. A., "The Son of God as Unique High Priest," in *Contours of Christology in the New Testament*, ed. R. N. Longenecker (Eerdmans, 2005), 247–67; Jenson, P. P., *Graded Holiness*, JSOTSup 106 (JSOT Press, 1992); Malone, A. S., *God's Mediators*, NSBT 43 (InterVarsity, 2017); Mason, E. F., *"You Are a Priest Forever,"* STDJ 74 (Brill, 2008); McKelvey, R. J., *Pioneer and Priest* (Pickwick, 2013); Morales, L. M., *Who Shall Ascend the Mountain of the Lord?*, NSBT 37 (InterVarsity, 2015); Perrin, N., *Jesus the Priest* (Baker Academic, 2018); VanderKam, J. C., *From Joshua to Caiaphas* (Fortress, 2004); Vanhoye, A., *Old Testament Priests and the New Priest* (St. Bede's, 1986); Wellhausen, J., *Prolegomena to the History of Israel*, trans. J. S. Black and A. Menzies (Cambridge University Press, 2014).

Dana M. Harris

Promises

To promise is to assure that one will do a particular thing or that a certain thing will happen, whether good or bad. God's promises of blessing and curse play a key role in helping believers grow in sanctification (2 Pet. 1:4; cf. 2 Cor. 7:1; 1 John 3:2–3) and suffer with hope (Ps. 119:50). Promises are one of Scripture's unifying motifs, and some scholars have even argued that divine promise is *the* theological center of the Christian canon (Kaiser, *Theology*; *Promise-Plan*). This article considers the language and form of biblical promises, overviews the major divine promises in Scripture, examines the conditional yet irrevocable nature of promissory covenants like the Abrahamic (Gal. 3:17–18), and offers guidance on how Christians should appropriate all God's promises as yes in Jesus (2 Cor. 1:20).

The Language and Form of Biblical Promises

The OT employs the *piel* verb *dbr* ("to speak") or, less commonly, the *qal* verb *'mr* ("to say") in the sense of "to promise." Foster McCurley (402n2) and Walter Kaiser (*Theology*, 33) have identified the use of *dbr* in relation to the promises of land (Exod. 12:25; Deut. 9:28; 12:20; 19:8; 27:3; Josh. 23:5, 10), blessing (Deut. 1:11; 15:6), the multiplication of Israel (6:3; 26:18), rest (Josh. 22:4; 1 Kings 8:56), all good things (Josh. 23:15), and a Davidic dynasty and throne (2 Sam. 7:28; 1 Kings 2:24; 8:20, 24–25; 1 Chron. 17:26; 2 Chron. 6:15–16; Jer. 33:14). Scripture also employs the noun *dābār* ("word, thing") in relation to the Lord's promise to/through Abraham (Ps. 105:42) and Moses (1 Kings 8:56). The LXX uses the verb *epangellomai* ("to promise") and noun *epangelia* ("promise") rarely (but see Esther 4:7; Ps. 55:9 [LXX 56:8]; Prov. 13:12; Amos 9:6). Nevertheless, they are common in the NT, often being used in relation to the promises God gave the patriarchs and Israel in the OT (see Rom. 9:4; 15:8; Eph. 2:12; Heb. 7:6; 11:17; cf. 2 Cor. 1:20; Heb. 6:12), which in turn are made better in the new covenant through Christ (Heb. 8:6; 10:23). For example, the verb occurs in relation to God's varied promises concerning Abraham (Acts 7:5; Rom. 4:21; Gal. 3:19; Heb. 6:13; 11:11), eternal life (Titus 1:2; James 1:12; 1 John 2:25), believers' kingdom inheritance (James 2:5), and the day of his appearing as judge (Heb. 12:26). Kevin Conway convincingly argues that Paul is unique in his exclusive use of *epangelia* for divine promises and that the conceptual and linguistic correspondence with *euangelion* ("gospel") grounded in the Abrahamic promises drive the apostle's application.

God's Major Promises in Scripture

God's promises commonly relate to life and death, blessing and curse. Divine provision, protection, and presence characterize the blessing of life, whereas the Lord removes all three of these in the curse of death.

Prior to his establishing the old covenant with Israel, Yahweh promises hope and dread without any evident prophetic mediation. From Moses forward, however, human agents arbitrate most divine promises.

God's first explicit promise in Scripture clarifies the reason why he permits Adam and Eve to eat from every tree in the garden except the tree of the knowledge pertaining to good and evil: "When you eat from it you will certainly die" (Gen. 2:17). Following their disobedience, Adam and Eve's spiritual death and God's exiling them from the garden prove the Lord's faithfulness to his word (3:22–24). But even prior to punishing them, Yahweh curses the serpent and promises him that there will be enmity with the woman and between his offspring and hers and that one of her male descendants will, through tribulation, triumph over him, thus reconstituting creation under God (3:15). From this point forward, redemptive history discloses a progressive hope in this coming offspring and in the age of global reconciliation with God that he will ignite.

While there are earlier foreshadowings (e.g., Gen. 9:25–27), Scripture next anticipates the curse's reversal in God's promises to the patriarchs, which relate to (1) progeny (seed), (2) property (land), (3) blessing or curse, and (4) divine presence.

1. *Progeny.* God will grow the patriarchs into a great nation (Gen. 12:2; 18:18; 46:3), give numerous offspring (15:5; 17:2, 6; 22:17; 26:4, 24; 28:3, 14; 48:4, 16), and raise up kings from their midst who will exert influence over nations (17:6, 16; 25:23; 35:11; 49:10). In time, Abraham's fatherhood will expand adoptively to include not only the single nation of Israel but also the nations more broadly (17:4–6, 16) when a single, male descendant rises and blesses the world (22:18; cf. Acts 3:25–26; Gal. 3:14, 16, 29; Collins, "Syntactical"; "Galatians 3:16"; Alexander; DeRouchie and Meyer; DeRouchie, "Counting").
2. *Property.* The Lord promises not only that he will give the patriarchs the land of Canaan as their central state (Gen. 17:8), with their broader kingdom reaching from the river of Egypt to the Euphrates (15:18–21; cf. Deut. 1:7; 1 Kings 4:20–21; Ps. 80:11), but also that a royal deliverer will expand the kingdom turf to include the rest of the world (Gen. 22:17–18; 26:4–5; 28:14; cf. Ps. 2:7; Matt. 5:5; Rom. 4:13; Eph. 6:3). These realities are now inaugurated in Christ's first coming and will be consummated in the new heavens and new earth (Williamson, "Promise"; Martin).
3. *Blessing and curse.* God promises to bless Abraham and his offspring through Sarah (Gen. 12:2; 17:16; 22:17; 24:1; 25:11; 26:3, 12, 24, 29; 27:27–29; 28:3–4; 32:29; 48:3, 16, 20; 49:25–26). Moreover, the Lord will bless those who bless the patriarchs or those associated with them, whereas he will curse the one who curses them (12:3; 27:29). Ultimately, Yahweh will use one of Abraham's male offspring to overcome God's enemies (22:17b; 24:60; cf. 3:15) and to bless some from all the families/nations of the earth (22:18; cf. 12:3; 18:18; 26:4; 28:14; Schnabel; DeRouchie, "Blessing-Commission").
4. *Divine presence.* From the beginning, Scripture associates God's blessing with humanity's ability to represent God rightly in the world (Gen. 1:28). God's favor alone provides a context for flourishing; curse brings only tragedy. In such a context, Yahweh affirms that he will be present with the patriarchs and their offspring (9:27; 28:15, 20; 31:3, 5, 42; 46:4; 48:21).

Conway (48, 145–223) tags Gen. 12:1–3 "the keystone passage in all of Scripture for the promises of God" and rightly identifies how much these promises shape the NT understanding of the gospel. Indeed, nearly all other biblical promises from Genesis to Revelation in some way relate to these patriarchal promises. God fulfills some promises in a single event (e.g., the coming of a specific offspring), whereas others are realized progressively (e.g., the land[s] promise and the promise of blessing reaching the nations) (cf. Heb. 11:13, 33, 39). Most of the patriarchal promises are initially and partially fulfilled in the Mosaic covenant (e.g., nationhood in the promised land with various material blessings to neighboring nations), but all are ultimately and completely fulfilled through Christ and the new covenant (e.g., God's overcoming the curse with universal blessing and a global kingdom in the new heavens and new earth).

Genesis 12:1–3 already anticipates this two-stage fulfillment in the way it associates Yahweh's promises to Abraham with two different imperatives: "Go . . . and be a blessing" (AT). When Abra(ha)m "goes" to the land, the Lord will make him into a great nation, bless him, and make his name great (12:1–2), whereas only when he (or his representative) is a channel of God's blessing will Yahweh bless those who bless him and curse the one who curses him and ultimately bless all the families of the ground in him (12:2–3; for the syntax and theology, see Williamson, *Sealed*, 78–79; DeRouchie, *Understand*, 209–11, 247–50; Gentry and Wellum, 266–81). We then see that Abraham will shift from being the father of one nation in the land (Gen. 17:7–8) to the father of a multitude of nations in many lands (17:4–6; 26:4–5) only when the single, male offspring arises to overcome enemies and to bring the promised blessing (22:17b–18; 24:60). This coming royal deliverer will rise from the tribe of Judah (49:8–10), generate a second exodus and flourishing creation (Num. 24:5–9), execute global domination (24:17–19), be a prophetic covenant mediator like Moses (Deut. 18:15–19; 34:10–12), judge the ends of the earth on Yahweh's behalf (1 Sam. 2:10), operate as a priest-king forever over a sure dynasty (2:35), and reign eternally on the Davidic throne as God's son (2 Sam. 7:12–16). He will in every respect be "God with us" (Isa. 7:14), enjoying Yahweh's presence like a movable temple-palace, working peace, righteousness, and justice from Yahweh's holy mountain over a global and multinational kingdom and healing and instructing all who surrender (9:6–7; 11:1–10; 42:1–7; 50:1–11; 61:1–3; cf. Ps. 2:7). He will represent Israel and save some from both Israel and the other nations (Isa. 49:1–12) and will triumph through tribulation, counting sinners righteous while bearing their iniquities (53:11). These are the types of promises that the NT sees fulfilled in Jesus and teaches Christians to claim as their own through him (e.g., 2 Cor. 1:20 with 6:16–7:1).

A Conditional, Irrevocable Promissory Covenant

Because all divine-human relationships in Scripture include promises, they are, at one level, all "covenants of promise" (Eph. 2:12 ESV). At another level, however, aspects of the Abrahamic covenant bear a distinctive promissory quality that Paul identifies as different from the Mosaic law covenant (Gal. 3:17–18; cf. Rom. 4:13–14). Variances like this have long led scholars to wrestle with the level of conditionality and revocability in the biblical covenants and their relationship to ancient Near Eastern suzerain-vassal treaties and royal grants (e.g., Mendenhall; Freedman; Weinfeld; Kaiser, *Theology*, 86–94; Waltke; Dumbrell; Blaising; Knoppers; Horton, 23–110; Williamson, *Sealed*, 17–43; Gentry and Wellum, 68n60, 451, 455, 662–66). In suzerain-vassal treaties, a sovereign elected to enter into a relationship with a lower party and vowed to protect and provide for the vassal so long as the vassal remained loyal. Thus, the suzerain-vassal treaties were both conditional and revocable. Royal grants, too, bore obligation for every generation, but the promises that shaped the grant appear to have been irrevocable or perpetually binding and therefore ensured that the promised land or kingship would stay in the family, even if certain individuals forfeited their participation in the covenant blessings by disloyalty (cf. Weinfeld, 189–90, with Knoppers, 683–92).

Yahweh's use of two-part conditional constructions clearly identifies the qualified nature of certain Mosaic covenant promises: "If you obey, then I will bless" (Lev. 26:1–13; Deut. 28:1–14; cf. Lev. 18:5), but "if you disobey, then I will curse" (Lev. 26:14–39; Deut. 28:15–68). And because Israel is stubborn, unbelieving, and rebellious (e.g., Deut. 9:6–7, 23–24; 10:16; cf. 29:4) and will remain so (31:16, 27), Moses knows that the old covenant he mediates will only condemn Israel (31:17–18, 29; cf. 4:25–29; Rom. 7:10; 2 Cor. 3:7, 9) and that God will need to establish a better covenant through a new prophetic covenant mediator (Deut. 18:15–19; cf. 1 Tim. 2:5; Heb. 9:15; 12:24; see DeRouchie, "Condemnation"). Thus, built into the Mosaic covenant are restoration promises that anticipate a new covenant that will supersede the old, ultimately in Christ (Lev. 26:40–45; Deut. 4:30–31; 30:1–14; cf. Jer. 31:31–34; Gal. 3:23–26; Heb. 8:6–13; 10:11–18).

As for the Abrahamic covenant, we have already noted the conditional nature of Yahweh's initial promises: the patriarch needs to "go" to the land and there "be a blessing" for the curse to be overcome and the world blessed (Gen. 12:1–3). We see a similar structure when the Lord commissions Abra(ha)m to "walk before me, and be blameless, that I may make my covenant between me and you, and may multiply you greatly" (17:1–2 ESV; cf. 26:3). Abraham (or his representative) needs to follow God and remain above reproach in order for the covenantal promises to be realized. Nevertheless, other texts make equally explicit that the promises *will be* realized. Such is made clear through Yahweh's self-imprecatory oath sign and promise in Gen. 15:17–21 (see Kline, 16–17, 41–42; Hugenberger, 168–215; Gentry and Wellum, 286–94) and through his vow to Abraham in 22:16–18 following the patriarch's faith-filled, obedient willingness to sacrifice Isaac (cf. 26:3–5). The Lord affirms that he will fulfill both stage one (great nation) and stage two (the world blessed) of his covenantal promises, but he also stresses that the enjoyment of fulfillment is contingent on obedience (see esp. 18:18–19).

In light of the inherent wickedness of humanity both before and after the flood (e.g., 6:5; 8:21), and because we know the old covenant will ultimately fail due to the people's lack of faith and hardness of heart (Deut. 31:16–17, 27, 29; cf. 2 Kings 17:14), how can God justly justify the ungodly and fulfill what he promised to Abraham (see Exod. 34:7; Prov. 17:15)? From Genesis we know that Abraham's "offspring" will only multiply and Yahweh's blessing will only reach the nations in the days of the single, male "offspring" deliverer (Gen. 22:17b–18; cf. 17:4–6). Thus, God himself provides a faithful covenant Son who will perfectly obey on behalf of the many (Rom. 5:18–19; 8:3–4; cf. John 5:19; 8:29; 14:31; Phil. 2:8; Heb. 5:8–9; 10:5–10). Operating in representative headship, this offspring's active and perfect covenantal obedience secures forgiveness, righteousness, and the complete Abrahamic inheritance for all who are in him (Acts 10:43; Rom. 5:18–21; 2 Cor. 5:21; Gal. 3:8, 14, 16, 29; Phil. 3:9; see Gentry and Wellum, 775–82).

How All God's Promises Are Yes in Christ

Paul asserts, "For no matter how many promises God has made, they are 'Yes' in Christ" (2 Cor. 1:20), which in context suggests that through Jesus both OT and NT promises are for Christians (see 6:16–7:1). But how can believers today faithfully appropriate OT promises? (See esp. DeRouchie, "'Yes'"; cf. Starling.)

Four foundational principles. 1. Christians benefit from OT promises only through Christ. Paul is convinced that all who are in Christ inherit the OT's blessings promised to Abraham: God made promises to Abraham and his offspring (Gen. 22:18; cf. 3:15). → Christ is the offspring (Gal. 3:16). → Faith unites us to Christ, making us offspring with him (3:7–9, 29). → We thus become heirs of the promised blessing (3:29; see Parker). At base, this is how *in Christ* alone all of God's promises find their yes.

2. All old-covenant curses become new-covenant curses. As laid out in the Abrahamic covenant (Gen. 12:3), the era of the new covenant includes God's promise to curse enemies. Thus, immediately after Moses predicts when Yahweh will circumcise the heart of his people and empower their love (Deut. 30:6), the prophet pronounces that God will also "put all these curses on your enemies who hate and persecute you" (30:7). In the age of new-covenant heart circumcision (now realized in the church, Rom. 2:28–29; Phil. 3:3), God will take Deuteronomy's curses, which warn old-covenant national Israel, and pour them out on all the enemies of his restored community.

The NT displays these curses as warnings against apostasy and against all who oppose God and his people (see Matt. 25:31–46; Luke 6:20–26; 2 Tim. 2:12; Heb. 10:26–27; cf. Heb. 10:29–30; 2 Pet. 2:1). Those in Christ will not experience curses in a punitive way, for Christ bears upon himself God's curse against all believers (Gal. 3:13; cf. John 3:14–15; 2 Cor. 5:21; 1 Pet. 2:24). While we still experience God's fatherly discipline, no level of earthly discipline or consequence calls into question the eternal security of any believer (Rom. 5:9). Instead, new-covenant curses serve as a means of grace to the elect to generate within them reverent fear of God leading to greater holiness (cf. Lev. 26:18, 21, 23, 27; Rom. 2:4; Heb. 12:11).

3. As part of the new covenant, Christians inherit the old covenant's original and restoration blessings. In Leviticus and Deuteronomy, there are old-covenant conditional promises of blessing (Lev. 26:1–13; Deut. 28:1–14) and curse (Lev. 26:14–39; Deut. 28:15–68). The condition is perfect obedience. There are also restoration blessings (Lev. 26:40–45; Deut. 30:1–14) that point in part to the era of the church age following the curse of exile. Paul declares, "Therefore, since we have these promises, dear friends, let us purify ourselves from everything that contaminates body and spirit, perfecting holiness out of reverence for God" (2 Cor. 7:1). One of the promises to which the apostle refers combines an old-covenant original blessing (Lev. 26:11–12) and a restoration blessing (Ezek. 37:27): "What agreement is there between the temple of God and idols? For we are the temple of the living God. As God has said: 'I will live with them and walk among them, and I will be their God, and they will be my people'" (2 Cor. 6:16).

Because Israel does not fully obey what God instructed, the Mosaic covenant results in curse and condemnation, not blessing (2 Cor. 3:9). Nevertheless, Paul says that all those in Christ are enjoying the old covenant's original and restoration blessings. When Christ perfectly obeyed the Father, he satisfied God's demands for absolute loyalty and thus secured blessing for the elect he represents (cf. John 15:10; Rom. 5:18–19; 8:4; Eph. 1:3; Phil. 2:8; Heb. 5:8).

Two conclusions follow from how Paul applies OT promises in 2 Cor. 6:16: (1) The restoration blessings of the old covenant include all the original blessings but in escalation and without the chance of loss. The way Ezekiel's new-covenant promise reasserts the original old-covenant blessings from Lev. 26 supports this claim. (2) Through Christ, the original old-covenant blessings *and* the restoration blessings have direct bearing on Christians.

4. Through the Spirit, Christians already enjoy all the blessings of their inheritance but will enjoy them fully only at Christ's final coming. Paul stresses that God the Father "has blessed us in the heavenly realms with every spiritual blessing *in Christ*" and that he has sealed us with "the promised Holy Spirit, who is a deposit guaranteeing our inheritance until the redemption of those who are God's possession" (Eph. 1:3, 13–14). Most scholars believe "spiritual blessings" refers to all the blessings that the Spirit of Christ secures for the saints, including those like election, adoption to sonship, redemption, forgiveness, sealing, and all that we will enjoy completely when we gain our full inheritance (cf. 2 Cor. 1:20, 22; 1 Pet. 1:3–4; see also the citation of Ps. 34:12–16 [LXX 33:13–17] in 1 Pet. 3:9–12).

In this overlap of the ages, our battle with sin is still evident, but God has freed believers so that sin no longer enslaves and condemns (Rom. 6:16–18; 7:25; 12:2). So, too, we still battle brokenness and decay, but such sufferings only develop our dependent faith in God and heighten our longing for the future (Rom. 8:20–23; 2 Cor. 4:16–18). And while death looms over us all, Christ removes its sting, and death itself becomes the channel to great reward (Phil. 1:21; cf. Rom. 5:17; 6:23; Rev. 21:4).

Guidelines for Christians in appropriating OT promises. God's promises (old and new) are vital for Christians, and if we fail to appropriate OT promises, we will lose many of the life-giving words of truth that our trustworthy God has given us to nurture our hope. When Jesus "fulfills" the Law and Prophets, he is actualizing what Scripture anticipated and achieving what God promised and predicted (Matt. 5:17; cf. Matt. 11:13; Luke 16:16). But while every promise is indeed yes in Jesus, and while every blessing is now ours *in Christ*, the way Jesus fulfills the various OT promises and secures them as yes for us is not static. Thus, we must approach biblical promises through a salvation-historical framework that has Jesus at the center—as a lens that clarifies and focuses the lasting significance of all God's promises (see figure 1).

1. Christ maintains some OT promises (no extension). That is, Christ *maintains* certain promises without adding any further beneficiaries to the original promise. Many of these are explicit restoration promises that include a vision of a global salvation after Israel's exile. For example, Daniel envisions a resurrection of some to everlasting life and others to everlasting contempt (Dan. 12:2), and Jesus, alluding to this passage, sees the same and associates it with his second coming (John 5:28–29; cf. John 11:11, 25; 1 Cor. 15:20, 23). Daniel 12:2 gives Christians hope because "if we have been united with him in a death like his, we shall certainly be united with him in a resurrection like his" (Rom. 6:5 ESV). This resurrection has an already/not-yet dimension, for the redeemed beneficiaries of the resurrection promise are saints of both the OT and NT epochs.

2. Christ maintains some OT promises (with extension). When Christ fulfills some promises, he extends the parties related to those promises. For example, Isaiah portrays the coming royal deliverer as speaking in the first person and declaring that Yahweh has called him from the womb, named him "Israel," and told him that his mission as the individual person is to save some from Israel and the rest of the nations (Isa. 49:1, 3, 6), thus fulfilling God's earlier promises to Abraham (Gen.

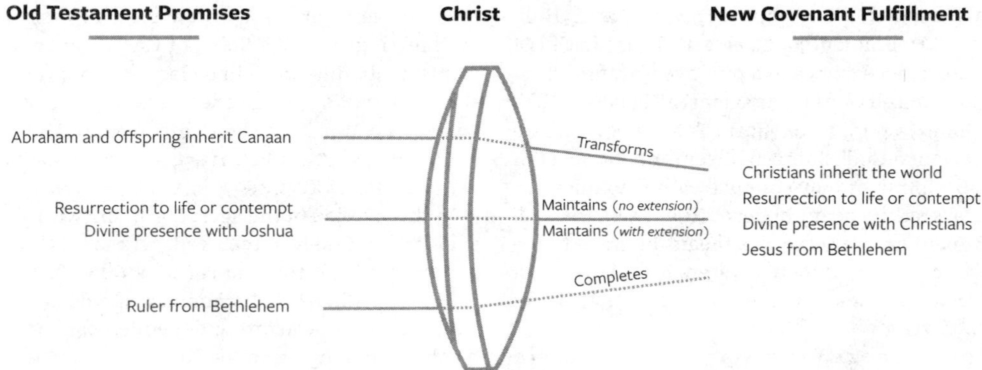

Figure 1. Old Testament Promises through the Lens of Christ

Source: Jason DeRouchie, "Is Every Promise 'Yes'?," 35.

12:3; 22:18). Paul sees Jesus as the most immediate referent to which Isa. 49:6 points (Acts 26:23). But he also sees the OT promises reaching further, to the mission of all who are in Christ (13:47). A promise related to the work of the servant Christ has now become a commission for all the servants identified with him (cf. Isa. 52:7 with Rom. 10:15; Ps. 2:9 with Rev. 2:26–27; 12:5; 19:15).

3. **Christ himself completes or uniquely fulfills some OT promises.** Such fulfillments prove to believers that God will certainly keep the rest of his promises (Deut. 18:22; Ezek. 33:33; cf. Rom. 8:32). For example, the prophet Micah predicts that a long-prophesied ruler in Israel will rise from Bethlehem (Mic. 5:2), and Christ exclusively fulfills that promise at his birth (Matt. 2:6). There is only one Christ, and he is born only once. Nevertheless, his birth is to spark a global return of "his brothers," and as king he will "shepherd his flock in the strength of the LORD," thus establishing lasting security and peace and enjoying a great name (Mic. 5:3–5). All these added promises continue to give Christians comfort and hope.

4. **Christ transforms some OT promises.** That is, he develops both the promise's makeup and its audience. These promises relate most directly to shadows that clarify and point to a greater substance in Christ or to OT patterns or types that find their climax or antitype in Jesus. Yahweh's promise to give the land to Abraham and his offspring as a lasting possession is of this kind (cf. Gen. 13:15; 17:8; 48:4; Exod. 32:13). The patriarch serves as the father of a single nation who would dwell in the land of Canaan (Gen. 17:8) and oversee an even broader geopolitical sphere (15:18). These realities are initially fulfilled in the period of the Mosaic covenant (Exod. 2:24; 6:8; Deut. 1:8; 6:10; 9:5; 30:20; 34:4) and realized in the days of Solomon (1 Kings 4:20–21). Nevertheless, Genesis already foresees Abraham becoming the father of not just one nation but *nations* (Gen. 17:4–6) and anticipates his influence reaching beyond the land to *lands* (26:3–4). This will happen when the singular, royal offspring rises to possess the gate of his enemies and when in him all the earth's nations are blessed (22:17b–18; cf. Ps. 2:7). Paul cites the Genesis land promises (Gen. 13:15; 17:8; 24:7) when he identifies Christ as the offspring to whom the promises were made (Gal. 3:16). The apostle then declares that all in Christ, whether Jew or gentile, slave or free, male or female, "are Abraham's seed, and heirs according to the promise" (3:28–29). Paul also stresses that the Christians' inheritance is *not* the present Jerusalem associated with the Mosaic covenant but is instead the heavenly Jerusalem (Gal. 4:24–26), which both Isaiah and John identify with the new earth (Isa. 65:17–25; Rev. 21:1–22:5; cf. Heb. 12:22).

In the new covenant, Christ transforms the type into the antitype by fulfilling the original land promise in himself and by extending it to the whole world through his people (Rom. 4:13); at the consummation the new earth will fully realize the antitype (see further Martin). While Christ maintains (without extension) Genesis's promises of the *antitypical* lands (plural), he does this by transforming the promises to Israel of the land (singular) as an "everlasting possession." The nature of his fulfillment identifies that the land (singular) is but a type, which he transforms into the antitype just as God has already foretold to the patriarchs.

Summary

God's promises are one of the central motifs that tie all of Scripture together. God's promises are often associated with life or death and conditioned on whether his covenant partner obeys. Whereas the old Mosaic covenant is conditional and revocable (and thus temporary in light of Israel's disobedience), the Abrahamic covenant is conditional and irrevocable, meaning that God will indeed realize all the promises but will do so only through an obedient Son. Representing Abraham and Israel, Jesus actively obeys and secures OT promises for all who are in him. At least four principles should guide Christians in appropriating OT promises: (1) Christians benefit from OT promises only through Christ. (2) All old-covenant curses become new-covenant curses.

(3) As part of the new covenant, Christians inherit the old covenant's original and restoration blessings. (4) Through the Spirit, Christians already enjoy all the blessings of their inheritance, but they do not possess them in their final fullness. Christ maintains some promises without extension, maintains others with extension, completes some, and transforms some.

See also Covenant; Land; Law; Literal Fulfillment; Mystery

Bibliography. Alexander, T. D., "Further Observations on the Term 'Seed' in Genesis," *TynBul* 48 (1997): 363–67; Blaising, C. A., "The Structure of Biblical Covenants," in *Progressive Dispensationalism*, by C. A. Blaising and D. L. Bock (BridgePoint, 1993), 128–211; Collins, C. J., "Galatians 3:16," *TynBul* 54 (2003): 75–86; Collins, "A Syntactical Note (Gen. 3:15)," *TynBul* 48 (1997): 139–47; Conway, K. P., *The Promises of God*, BZNW 211 (de Gruyter, 2014); DeRouchie, J. S., "The Blessing-Commission, the Promised Offspring, and the *Toledot* Structure of Genesis," *JETS* 56 (2013): 219–47; DeRouchie, "Counting Stars with Abraham and the Prophets," *JETS* 58 (2015): 445–85; DeRouchie, "From Condemnation to Righteousness," *SBJT* 18, no. 3 (2014): 87–118; DeRouchie, *How to Understand and Apply the Old Testament* (P&R, 2017); DeRouchie, "Is Every Promise 'Yes'?," *Them* 42 (2017): 16–45; DeRouchie, J. S., and J. C. Meyer, "Christ or Family as the 'Seed' of Promise?," *SBJT* 14, no. 3 (2010): 36–48; Dumbrell, W. J., "The Prospect of Unconditionality in the Sinaitic Covenant," in *Israel's Apostasy and Restoration*, ed. A. Gileadi (Baker, 1988), 141–55; Freedman, D. N., "Divine Commitment and Human Obligation," *Int* 18 (1964): 419–31; Gentry, P. J., and S. J. Wellum, *Kingdom through Covenant*, 2nd ed. (Crossway, 2018); Horton, M., *God of Promise* (Baker Academic, 2006); Hugenberger, G. P., *Marriage as a Covenant* (Baker, 1994); Kaiser, W. C., Jr., *The Promise-Plan of God* (Zondervan, 2008); Kaiser, *Toward an Old Testament Theology* (Zondervan, 1978); Kline, M. G., *By Oath Consigned* (Eerdmans, 1968); Knoppers, G. N., "Ancient Near Eastern Royal Grants and the Davidic Covenant," *JAOS* 116 (1996): 670–97; Martin, O. R., *Bound for the Promised Land*, NSBT 34 (InterVarsity, 2015); McCurley, F. R., Jr., "The Christian and the Old Testament Promise," *LQ* 22 (1970): 401–10; Mendenhall, G. E., "Covenant Forms in Israelite Tradition," *BA* 17 (1954): 50–76; Parker, B. E., "The Israel-Christ-Church Relationship," in *Progressive Covenantalism*, ed. S. J. Wellum and B. E. Parker (B&H Academic, 2016), 39–68; Schnabel, E. J., "Israel, the People of God, and the Nations," *JETS* 45 (2002): 35–57; Starling, D., "The Yes to All God's Promises," *RTR* 71, no. 3 (2012): 185–204; Waltke, B. K., "The Phenomenon of Conditionality within Unconditional Covenants," in *Israel's Apostasy and Restoration*, ed. A. Gileadi (Baker, 1988), 123–39; Weinfeld, M., "The Covenant of Grant in the Old Testament and the Ancient Near East," *JAOS* 90 (1970): 184–203; Williamson, P. R., "Promise and Fulfillment," in *The Land of Promise* (InterVarsity, 2000), 15–34; Williamson, *Sealed with an Oath*, NSBT 23 (InterVarsity, 2007).

Jason S. DeRouchie

Prophet

When we encounter prophets on the pages of Scripture, we may associate them with pop-culture references such as Nostradamus's ridiculous predictions in the supermarket tabloid *Weekly World News* or *The Daily Prophet* newspaper in the Harry Potter novels. But prophecy in the Bible is of the utmost seriousness. It is God's primary means of communicating with his people and the source of Scripture itself. Prophets speak on behalf of God and with his full authority.

In the OT, the primary word to denote prophecy is the verb *nbʾ* ("to prophesy," 115x) and the related noun *nābîʾ* ("prophet," 317x). Other words include *ḥōzeh* (16x) and *rōʾeh* (12x), both translated "seer" in most English translations. In the NT, the root *prophēt-* occurs a total of 195 times as a noun ("prophecy," "male prophet," "female prophet"), adjective ("prophetic"), and verb ("to prophesy"). In addition, the noun *pseudoprophētēs* ("false prophet") occurs 11 times. Although there are potentially many other references to prophetic activities and oracles in the Bible, we will restrict our discussion to texts containing these explicit terms.

Prophets in the OT

The essential role of a prophet is that of a spokesperson. In Exod. 4, Moses resists God's call to confront the Egyptian pharaoh over his enslavement of the Israelites. God responds that Aaron will be Moses's spokesman, "You shall speak to him and put words in his mouth. . . . He will speak to the people for you, and it will be as if he were your mouth and as if you were God to him" (4:15–16). Later, God says, "See, I have made you like God to Pharaoh, and your brother Aaron will be your prophet" (7:1). This use of the word "prophet" illustrates the definition of prophets who speak for God: "A prophet was chosen by God to receive his message and then to proclaim it to an audience in a particular historical situation" (Tully, 62).

Task. Moses puts forward the key elements of a prophetic "job description" in Deut. 18:15–22. First, Moses says, "The Lord your God will raise up for you a prophet like me from among you" (18:15). Because the word "prophet" is singular and because Moses was unique in that he spoke to the Lord face to face, this statement was often later understood as a prediction of a *particular* future prophet who would be like Moses (e.g., the prophetic office of the Messiah). However, the previous context in Deut. 17–18 introduces *institutions* that God was establishing for Israel, such as judgeship (17:8–13), kingship (17:14–20), and the priesthood (18:1–8). In the present passage, Moses announces the institution of prophecy or the succession of prophets of God (Block, 28–29). Any future prophet called by God would be "like Moses" because he or she would continue Moses's task. The primary point is that true prophets will be raised up by God—no one can choose to be a prophet; one can only respond to God's call. Second, Moses says that the prophet comes "from your brothers" (18:15 ESV)—that is, from within the covenant community. Third, he or she receives the words of God (18:18). The source of a prophet's words is not his or her own observations, insight, or conclusions; it is a special revelation from God. Fourth, the prophet re-speaks (or writes) the word of God to an audience (18:18).

As God's spokesperson, the word of the prophet carries absolute authority. Moses warns that God will hold accountable anyone who does not listen to the prophet who speaks in his name (Deut. 18:19). Many years later, God emphasizes that he will hold the prophet Ezekiel accountable if he does not report everything that God has said to the people with him in exile. If the people reject the prophetic word, they will bear the blame and face the consequences. But if Ezekiel does not accurately and faithfully deliver the authoritative word, *he* will face the consequences (Ezek. 3:16–21; 33:1–9).

Message. The oracles of the OT prophets were varied and tied to particular historical contexts, but they all contribute to a consistent message about God's character and expectations. Verbal oracles were collected and became written Scripture, so that future generations could know the works and ways of God like their ancestors (2 Kings 17:13). Prophets also provided kings with practical advice and wisdom in Israel's theocracy, urging them to be faithful to God's covenant. Unlike prophets in the surrounding nations, God's prophets were independent of the power structures and frequently critiqued kings for violating God's commands. The best-known example of this is the prophet Nathan, who confronted King David after he took Bathsheba and murdered her husband (2 Sam. 12).

Beginning with the prophet Elijah, prophets began to function as covenant "prosecutors." As God's representatives, they confronted the people of Israel and Judah for their violations of God's covenant stipulations. The people failed to love God and loved foreign idols instead (e.g., Jer. 2:23–25). They put confidence in foreign alliances (e.g., Hosea 5:13) and their own military power (e.g., 8:14) instead of in God's strength. They oppressed the poor and vulnerable that God had commanded them to protect (e.g., Isa. 3:14–15; Jer. 2:34; Amos 4:1). In response to these failings, the prophets called on the people to repent and announced future judgment if they refused. The author of 2 Kings looks back on the exile and states, "The LORD removed them from his presence, as he had warned through all his servants the prophets" (17:23).

However, the prophets were also preachers of hope. They looked back to God's promises to Abraham and forward through the sweep of redemptive history to a coming Davidic king who would put down God's enemies, establish a new covenant, and usher in a new heavens and earth where God's people from every nation would live in peace and abundance forever.

Opposition. Because the OT prophets proclaimed God's unchanging standards and called their listeners to forsake cherished idols, power, and all attempts at self-justification, they were continually ignored (Jer. 7:25), told to cease and desist (Isa. 30:10; Amos 2:12), called fools (Hosea 9:7), physically mistreated (Jer. 20:2; 38:6), and killed (1 Kings 18:4). Frequently speaking to a hostile audience, the prophets used a wide variety of rhetorical strategies to catch the attention of listeners and disarm their defensive posture. These strategies include parables, poetic imagery, and stories with surprise endings (e.g., Isa. 5:1–7; Ezek. 16). Another dramatic tool was the sign-act, in which the prophet role-plays the message (Ezek. 12:1–16) or uses some object lesson. In some cases, these were extreme, such as a prophet who purposefully wounds himself to make a point (1 Kings 20:35–43).

In addition, the OT prophets faced pressure from false prophets, who purported to speak on behalf of God but did so for their own benefit. Returning to Moses's instructions in Deut. 18, we see that anyone who makes up a message that God has not spoken and attributes it to God is a false prophet. But how would one know if a prophet is false? Moses provides two indications. First, if a prophet speaks in the name of another god, he or she is false and must receive the death penalty (18:20). Second, one can also recognize a false prophet if his or her prediction does not come true (18:22). This latter test allows a prophetic word to be falsified only in the case of a near-term predictive prophecy. Predictions of the distant, eschatological future were obviously not subject to this kind of verification. Perhaps this is why the prophets often combine and relate short- and long-range predictive prophecies. When short-term prophecies are verified, confidence in the prophet increases along with certainty in the validity of the long-term predictions. The stakes are high: if the true prophetic word required total obedience, the people had to be certain that it was actually from God. Nevertheless, the OT speaks of a number of false prophets who supported the status quo and the position of those in power, justifying evil behavior and allaying any fears that God's judgment would actually come (Jer. 27:16; Ezek. 22:28). At times, the true prophet of God stood alone against large groups of these counterfeits. Elijah faced 850 prophets of Baal and Asherah on Mount Carmel (1 Kings 18:19), and Micaiah was the sole dissenter against four hundred prophets who supported King Ahab (1 Kings 22:1–28).

References to the OT Prophets in the NT

The authors of the NT frequently cite or allude to the OT prophets as the authoritative spokesmen of God's enduring word to his people. Peter writes that the prophetic message is "completely reliable" and that we must pay attention to it (2 Pet. 1:19). He continues, "For prophecy never had its origin in the human will, but prophets, though human, spoke from God as they were carried along by the Holy Spirit" (1:21). Because the words of the OT prophets come from God, they are in continuity with God's work in the past, present, and future. Peter writes that we should observe the words spoken in the past by the holy prophets as well as the command by our Lord and Savior through the apostles (2 Pet. 3:2).

Message. The NT recognizes and repeats the major elements of the OT prophetic message discussed above. First, the OT prophets reveal God's character and expectations. Seven times NT authors connect the Law with the Prophets as twin foundations of theological truth. Jesus says that he has not come to abolish the Law or the Prophets, but to fulfill them (Matt. 5:17; see also 7:12 and 22:40). In Acts 24:14, Paul equates his Christian beliefs with "everything that is in accordance with the Law and that is written in the Prophets." Furthermore, Paul explains the kingdom of God from the Law of Moses and the Prophets (Acts 28:23).

Second, the NT cites or alludes to the OT prophets in order to establish that humanity, and the Jews in particular as God's people, have fallen short of his expectations and turned against him. In Matt. 15:7, Jesus quotes from Isa. 29:13, "These people honor me with their lips, but their hearts are far from me. They worship me in vain; their teachings are merely human rules." In Jesus's parable of the rich man and Lazarus, the rich man begs Abraham to send Lazarus to his family to warn them of Hades. Abraham replies, "They have Moses and the Prophets; let them listen to them" (Luke 16:29). However, the OT prophets also looked forward to God's salvation, which the NT authors announce has now been inaugurated (Luke 10:24). All the prophets foretold the days when God would begin to fulfill his promise to Abraham by bringing blessing to all people of the earth (Acts 3:24–25).

However, the OT prophets do not speak only in generalities. The NT authors demonstrate in quotation after quotation that the prophets anticipated specific details of God's redemptive plan through Jesus Christ. After Jesus is raised from the dead, he walks with two men on the road to Emmaus, a small village outside of Jerusalem. When the men express doubt that Jesus has really been raised, he says to them, "How foolish you are, and how slow to believe all that the prophets have spoken!" (Luke 24:25). Then, "beginning with Moses and all the Prophets, he explained to them what was said in all the Scriptures concerning himself" (v. 27). It would be overreading this statement to say that *every* verse of Scripture concerns Jesus directly. But clearly Jesus drew from all of Scripture as he spoke about himself. Jesus is the climax and means of God's redemption spoken of by the OT prophets.

The OT prophets anticipate John the Baptist as the forerunner of Jesus (Matt. 3:3 // Isa. 40:3). They announce that the Christ will come from the line of David (Luke 1:69–70; Acts 2:30). Matthew finds in the prophets support for Jesus's birthplace (Matt. 2:5–6 // Mic. 5:2), virgin birth (Matt. 1:22–23 // Isa. 7:14), sojourn in Egypt (Matt. 2:15 // Hosea 11:1), ministry of healing (Matt. 8:17 // Isa. 53:4) and justice (Matt. 12:17–21 // Isa. 42:1–4), preaching in parables (Matt. 13:35 // Ps. 78:2), entry into Jerusalem (Matt. 21:4–5 // Zech. 9:9), and arrest (Matt. 26:56). Peter preaches, "All the prophets testify about him that everyone who believes in him receives forgiveness of sins through his name" (Acts 10:43).

The OT prophets also taught that God's salvation was always intended to be offered to all peoples of the earth. When the early church is wrestling with the implications of gentiles coming to faith in Jesus, James quotes from Amos 9:11–12 in order to show that the restoration of David's line in Christ was so that "the rest of mankind may seek the Lord" (Acts 15:12–18). The mystery, made known to the OT prophets, is that "through the gospel the Gentiles are heirs together with Israel, members together of one body, and sharers together in the promise in Christ Jesus" (Eph. 3:5–6). The church, comprised of all nations and languages, is "built on the foundation of the apostles and prophets" (2:20).

Because the teaching of the OT prophets leads directly to NT theology and faith, the writers of the NT viewed themselves as "standing on the shoulders of the prophets" (Sandnes, 146). For example, Paul grounds his own apostolic authority in the gospel God "promised beforehand through his prophets in the Holy Scriptures" (Rom. 1:2). Similarly, in Revelation, John "was writing what he understood to be a work of prophetic scripture, the climax of prophetic revelation, which gathered up the prophetic meaning of the Old Testament scriptures and disclosed the way in which it was being and was to be fulfilled in the last days" (Bauckham, xi).

Opposition. Just as the Israelites consistently reject and persecute the OT prophets, Jesus and his followers face the same opposition. Jesus says in the Sermon on the Mount, "Blessed are you when people insult you, persecute you and falsely say all kinds of evil against you because of me . . . for in the same way they persecuted the prophets who were before you" (Matt. 5:11–12). The Pharisees who stand against Jesus insist that they would not have rejected and killed the OT prophets. But Jesus reminds them that, as the descendants of those who murdered the prophets, they continue in their ways (Matt. 23:29–31). Because Jesus is the culmination and ultimate referent of the prophetic message, the current generation will be responsible for the blood of all the prophets, shed from the beginning of the world (Luke

11:50–51). In his powerful speech before he is martyred, Stephen quotes from Deut. 18:15, “God will raise up for you a prophet like me from your own people” (Acts 7:37). He goes on to describe their ancestors’ rejection of Moses (7:39). Furthermore, they went on to reject all the prophets! “You are just like your ancestors. . . . Was there ever a prophet your ancestors did not persecute?” And now they have betrayed and murdered Jesus (7:51–52).

Jesus and the apostles reference the persecution of the OT prophets in order to make two points. First, the essential message of the OT prophets has not changed with the advent of Christ. In order to be right with God, one must still humbly accept God’s grace in the form in which it is offered. Second, rejection of Jesus is not a defense of OT orthodoxy but the rejection of it; it is the rejection of Moses and all the prophets who came after him.

Prophets in the NT

In addition to referring back to OT prophets, the authors of the NT also refer to specific individuals in the time of Christ and the early church as prophets. After a long period of prophetic silence after the ministry of Malachi, the birth of Jesus triggered a new phase in prophetism (Stronstad, 7). The first NT prophet is Zechariah, the father of John the Baptist. In Luke 1:67–79, he announces God’s salvation through the house of David and declares that his own son John will prepare the way for this Messiah. After Jesus is born, a prophetess named Anna meets Jesus and his family in the temple (Luke 2:36–38). She is spiritually enabled by God to recognize Jesus as the hope of Jerusalem after many decades of waiting (Reid, 44). John the Baptist is identified as a prophet both by his father Zechariah (Luke 1:76) and by Jesus, who says he is “more than a prophet” because of his unique role in introducing the Messiah (Matt. 11:9). The crowds also view John as a prophet like the OT prophets (21:26), and for this reason the Pharisees are hesitant to dismiss him explicitly as a fraud. Jesus himself is the ultimate prophet, not only in the NT but in all of Scripture. While Moses was the fountainhead and paradigm for biblical prophecy, Jesus embodies and teaches the word of God (Matt. 7:29; John 1:1), and represents God perfectly because he *is* God in the flesh (e.g., Matt. 9:6; 28:18; John 5:26–27).

Luke emphasizes Jesus’s prophetic role in a number of ways. In the synagogue in Nazareth, Jesus applies the words of Isa. 61:1–2 to himself: “The Spirit of the Lord is on me, because he has anointed me to proclaim good news to the poor . . . to proclaim the year of the Lord’s favor” (Luke 4:18–19). In Luke 4:25–27, Jesus relates his own ministry to that of Elijah and Elisha, who performed miraculous works for individuals outside of Israel. When Jesus raises a young man from the dead, onlookers conclude, “A great prophet has appeared among us” (7:16). Luke Timothy Johnson provides many other parallels, writing, “Luke makes particular use of prophecy as a way of giving coherence to his account—connecting the story of Jesus and the church to that of Israel in a specific way, as the continuation of God’s saving activity through prophetic utterance and deed” (*Prophetic Jesus*, 4).

In Deut. 18:15, Moses makes the prediction that “God will raise up for you a prophet like me from among you, from your brothers—it is to him you shall listen” (ESV). The relationship between this prediction and Jesus is debated by evangelical scholars. One view holds that Moses is anticipating a particular prophet—namely, Jesus Christ. As discussed above, Jesus fulfilled the role of prophet in addition to that of priest and king. The strongest evidence for this view is that many in Jesus’s day were anticipating a specific end-time prophet (Carson, 271). The crowds ask John if he is “the Prophet,” associated with the Messiah (John 1:21, 25), and he flatly denies it. When Jesus performs a dramatic miracle by feeding the crowd, they conclude, “Surely this is the Prophet who is to come into the world” (6:14). Similarly, when Jesus speaks about the gift of the Spirit as living water, some of the people say, “Surely this man is the Prophet” (7:40). This expectation is widely attested in the time period, such as in the Samaritan Memar Marqah 4:3 and at Qumran (4QTest 5–8) (Johnson, *Acts*, 70).

However, a second view (which I hold) is that Moses is using a generic singular in Deut. 18:15 when he says, “God will raise up for you a prophet,” and is anticipating the institution of prophecy more generally. The surrounding context of Deut. 18:9–22 contrasts true prophecy with magic and divination (which is strictly prohibited), explains the task of a prophet, and provides criteria for identifying false prophets. Deuteronomy 18:15 is quoted two times in the NT by two different speakers, and neither applies it to Jesus. In a sermon about the suffering and resurrection of Jesus, Peter argues that “all the prophets” foretold that the Christ would suffer (Acts 3:18). Then, after quoting from Deut. 18:15, 18, and 19, he repeats that “all the prophets who have spoken, from Samuel and those who came after him, also proclaimed these days” (Acts 3:22–24 ESV). In other words, the OT prophets (whom Moses anticipated) spoke with authority about Jesus Christ. To reject Jesus is to reject the prophetic testimony. Similarly, Stephen quotes Deut. 18:15 in Acts 7:37, highlighting that Moses was the peak of OT prophecy, even performing signs and wonders, and yet he was ultimately rejected by the people. Daniel Block (30) argues that if there is any link between Deut. 18:15 and Jesus, it is the long-standing pattern of rebellion against God’s agents, which now includes Jesus Christ. Therefore, in this view, Deut. 18:15 looks forward to the institution of OT prophecy that culminates in Jesus—the ultimate prophet—while the unified prophetic message anticipates Jesus’s saving work but it is not a direct predictive prophecy of Jesus.

Several other prophets are referenced in the narrative of the NT as well. Caiaphas, the high priest, prophesies (apparently without knowing it) about the ultimate significance of Jesus's death (John 11:49–52). In Acts 11:27–30, a prophet named Agabus predicts a severe famine throughout the entire Roman world, which was later fulfilled according to Luke. In Acts 21:10–11, this same Agabus performs a sign-act like the OT prophets: he takes Paul's belt, binds his own hands and feet, and makes a prediction that Paul will be bound and delivered over to the gentiles. Other prophets in the NT include Barnabas, Simeon, Lucius, Manaen, and Saul (Paul), who were also teachers (Acts 13:1), as well as the four unmarried daughters of Philip the evangelist (Acts 21:9). There is no indication that these prophets are unusual or have a different function than those who came before them.

Opposition. Like their counterparts in the OT, true prophets in the NT were subjected to rejection and persecution by those who did not recognize or accept God's standards or his means of salvation. After John the Baptist critiques King Herod for having Herodias, his brother's wife, Herod puts John in prison. Later, at a celebration for Herod's birthday, Herodias prompts her daughter to ask for John's head on a platter, and Herod grants the request that day by having John beheaded (Matt. 14:1–12).

In spite of Jesus's miraculous works, which both validate his authenticity as a prophet and actually meet the needs of the poor and the sick, he faces constant opposition. When the people of Nazareth are offended that Jesus, whom they know well, is speaking with authority, Jesus responds that "a prophet is not without honor except in his own town and in his own home" (Matt. 13:57). The Jewish leaders, especially those from Jerusalem, challenge him on the grounds that he is blaspheming, breaking the law of Moses, and leading the people astray. They scheme to have Jesus arrested and then, because they do not have the authority to kill him, convince the Romans to do so (John 18:31). Even Jesus's torture and death are infused with the mocking of his prophetic ability: as the Jewish leaders in the Sanhedrin spit on Jesus, strike him, and slap him, they say, "Prophesy to us, Messiah. Who hit you?" (Matt. 26:67–68).

Prophets in the NT also parallel OT prophets in that they compete with counterfeit prophets for the peoples' hearts and minds. Jesus warns that there will be *many* false prophets (Matt. 24:11), apparently with the ability to perform great signs and wonders so that they will be especially deceptive (24:24). Therefore, the people of God must "test the spirits . . . because many false prophets have gone out into the world" (1 John 4:1). In the next verse, John gives us the key to distinguishing between true and false prophets: every spirit that acknowledges that Jesus Christ has come in the flesh is from God. As in the OT, the teaching of false prophets does not encourage faith in the true God and does not conform to the certain truth that God has revealed previously.

The Gift of Prophecy in the NT Church

In Rom. 12:5–6, Paul writes that the church is one body and that its members have different gifts, including the gift of prophecy. In 1 Corinthians, he provides a list of gifts that come from the Spirit: healing, miraculous powers, prophecy, distinguishing between spirits, and speaking in different tongues (12:9–10). Two chapters later, Paul writes that prophecy is for the edification of the church (14:2–4). It involves the uncovering of information not widely known, convicts people of sin, and can bring unbelievers to faith in Christ (14:24–25).

The precise nature of this gift of prophecy in the church continues to be debated by scholars. Does the gift continue today or has it ceased? What implications does this gift have for the conviction that the biblical canon is closed? Due to the limitations of this article, we will briefly consider only the primary question in the debate: Is the gift of prophecy in the NT church the same phenomenon as OT prophecy, in which an individual proclaims a fully authoritative word from God, or is this spiritual gift a different kind of activity? We will examine three major views (also see Blaylock for a survey of views).

First, some scholars argue that the prophetic gift described in 1 Cor. 12–14 is a continuation of the fully authoritative prophecy in the OT. Rather than using different lexemes to signal that this is a new version of prophecy, NT authors use the same Greek words for OT prophecy, NT prophecy, and the spiritual gift in the church even though other potential terms were available. Therefore, Ulrich Luz (60) argues that early Christians saw their experiences as a continuation of the biblical tradition, speaking under the mandate of God. According to Luz (64), Paul's instructions to the Corinthians were not to the congregation in general (i.e., every believer) but to the *prophets* at Corinth. Similarly, R. Bruce Compton (72) concludes that there is only one type of NT prophecy: "the communication of special revelation that is inerrant and has divine authority."

A second view is that the gift of prophecy involves the faithful and effective interpretation and proclamation of Scripture (1 Cor. 14:19, 24). In the same way that OT prophets received a word from God and then spoke it to contemporaries, the gift of prophecy involves receiving God's word (in Scripture) and re-speaking it in the church. E. Earle Ellis (133) argues that the primary activity of a prophet in the church is the interpretation of Scripture. He notes that Luke pairs *prophētēs* ("prophet") with *parakaleō* ("exhort, encourage") in Acts 15:32 and that Paul relates the two concepts as well (1 Cor. 14:31). "For Paul, prophecy apparently is a formal term embracing certain kinds of inspired teaching" (Ellis, 141). David Hill calls prophecy "sustained utterance" (123). "The prophet . . . implants the Word of God into the life of a community" (127). David Garland (582) states that prophecy is the declaration of God's will to the people from the Scriptures. Slightly different is the view of Thomas Gillespie, who believes that NT prophecy is the proclamation of the gospel for the edification of the church. He writes, "According to the apostle Paul, the early Christian prophets were interpreting theologically the inherent implications of the kerygma when they were prophesying" (32).

A third view is represented by Wayne Grudem, who argues that it is NT *apostles* who are parallel to OT prophets as messengers of Christ, speaking the words of God with absolute divine authority (27–33). By contrast, ordinary congregational prophecy is "speaking merely human words to report something God brings to mind" (71). For Grudem, Paul's instructions in 1 Cor. 14:29 that two or three prophets should speak and others should weigh (*diakrinō*) what is said indicates that this is a new kind of prophecy that includes the possibility of error (see 1 Thess. 5:20–21). The prophetic word, "while it may have been prompted by a 'revelation' from God, had only the authority of the merely human words in which it was spoken. The prophet could err, could misinterpret, and could be questioned or challenged at any point" (69). Thus, Grudem understands the gift of prophecy as an opportunity to speak into specific contexts in the church and the life of the believer for encouragement and edification. However, these messages are subject to review because of the uncertainty as to whether a word from God is being delivered accurately.

Let us briefly evaluate these three views. The first view, that the NT gift of prophecy is a direct continuation of OT prophecy, has the advantage of lexical consistency. However, in the OT, prophecy is never presented as a spiritual gift widely distributed. Prophets are called to deliver a specific word from the Lord (sometimes many times over many years), often against their will (cf. Jer. 20:7–9). An OT prophet had to be obeyed without question; these high stakes were the reason that a false prophet was to receive the death penalty (Deut. 18:20). By contrast, the gift of prophecy in the NT is nearly universal (1 Cor. 14:31) and should be weighed (1 Cor. 14:29), suggesting that prophets may get things wrong; but there is no mention of a consequence as serious as the death penalty.

The third view takes seriously the NT gift of prophecy as a special means of encouragement and edification in the church. However, it requires some lexical shifting so that the word "prophet" or "prophecy" must have a different meaning than in the OT. It also assumes that some *new* revelation is involved for edification, although the NT passages that speak of the gift of prophecy do not actually claim this. Elsewhere in the NT, believers are encouraged in their faith and edified in much more mundane ways (cf. Rom. 1:12; Eph. 6:22; Phil. 2:1; Col. 4:8).

The second view is the most convincing. Just as an OT prophet received God's word and then proclaimed it in a specific time and context, NT believers are gifted by the Holy Spirit to receive God's word (from Scripture) and then to recontextualize it for their particular audiences. In this way, God gifts his people to bring his living word to bear in a variety of situations for proclamation of the gospel and strengthening the faith of believers. Thus, while the NT gift of prophecy may not involve new revelation, the task and action are analogous to OT prophecy.

Conclusion

Each time we encounter a prophet in the OT or NT, it is a reminder that God has spoken in many times and in various ways (Heb. 1:1), revealing himself to the people he has created. This revelation is not only general—in nature and conscience—it is a specific disclosure of the Lord's character, his commitment to justice, his love for the world, and his work of redemption through the death and resurrection of Jesus Christ. The prophets bring God's word to bear on specific contexts throughout the history of Israel and the early church, but their messages are also preserved in the pages of Scripture for the future people of God so that those of us who come after can respond to God's mercy and grow in faith and hope. True prophets speak for God and therefore demand an accounting from us. At the beginning of the NT, Jesus says, "Whoever welcomes a prophet as a prophet will receive a prophet's reward" (Matt. 10:41), and at the end of the NT, John says, "Blessed is the one who keeps the words of the prophecy written in this scroll" (Rev. 22:7). When we accept the true prophetic word, we accept the word of our great God, who is not silent.

See also Adam, First and Last; Covenant; Image of God

Bibliography. Bauckham, R., *The Climax of Prophecy* (T&T Clark, 1993); Blaylock, R. M., "Towards a Definition of New Testament Prophecy," *Them* 44, no. 1 (2019): 41–60; Block, D. I., "My Servant David," in *Israel's Messiah in the Bible and the Dead Sea Scrolls*, ed. R. S. Hess and M. D. Carroll R. (Baker Academic, 2003), 17–56; Carson, D. A., *The Gospel according to John* (InterVarsity, 1991); Compton, R. B., "The Continuation of New Testament Prophecy and a Closed Canon," *DBSJ* 22 (2017): 57–73; Ellis, E. E., *Prophecy and Hermeneutics in Early Christianity* (Mohr Siebeck, 1978); Garland, D. E., *1 Corinthians*, BECNT (Baker Academic, 2003); Gillespie, T. W., *The First Theologians* (Eerdmans, 1994); Grudem, W., *The Gift of Prophecy in the New Testament and Today* (Crossway, 2000); Hill, D., *New Testament Prophecy* (John Knox, 1979); Johnson, L. T., *The Acts of the Apostles* (Liturgical Press, 1992); Johnson, *Prophetic Jesus, Prophetic Church* (Eerdmans, 2011); Luz, U., "Stages of Early Christian Prophetism," in *Prophets and Prophecy in Jewish and Early Christian Literature*, ed. J. Verheyden,

K. Zamfir, and T. Nicklas (Mohr Siebeck, 2010), 57–75; Reid, B. E., "Prophetic Voices of Elizabeth, Mary, and Anna in Luke 1-2," in *New Perspectives on the Nativity*, ed. J. Corley (T&T Clark, 2009), 37–46; Sandnes, K. O., *Paul—One of the Prophets?* (Mohr Siebeck, 1991); Stronstad, R., "The Rebirth of Prophecy," *JBPR* 5 (2013): 3–28; Tully, E. J., *Reading the Prophets as Christian Scripture* (Baker Academic, 2022).

ERIC J. TULLY

Prosopological Exegesis

Prosopological, or prosopographic, exegesis (hereafter PE) refers to a method of scriptural interpretation that identifies distinct persons (*prosōpa*) speaking in texts. This concept is closely related to the practice of *prosōpopoiia* (Greek) or *prosopopoeia* (Latin): a literary or dramatic device that attributes speech to specific character(s) (LSJ). More specifically, as used by Christian exegetes, PE refers most often to distinct divine persons (i.e., Father, Son, Spirit) speaking in OT texts—or to prophets speaking in texts "in the person of" distinct divine persons. PE is amply attested in the exegetical practices of early Christian writers and is consistent with the widespread Christian belief in the preexistence of the Son—the Word of God—who was active and spoke in the OT, prior to the incarnation. The use of PE by Christian theologians also attests and assumes the unity and divine inspiration of the Scriptures. This method has been discussed by patristics scholars for many years (e.g., Andresen; Rondeau; Slusser; Trigg) but has recently become prominent in biblical studies, especially in light of the works of Matthew Bates (*Hermeneutics*; *Trinity*).

In this essay I first briefly consider historical precedents for PE. Second, I illustrate some clear examples of PE from the early centuries of the church. Third, I address possible instances of PE in the NT authors' appropriation of the OT. Fourth, I consider possible OT texts for further exploration. Fifth, I provide a preliminary assessment of PE.

Ancient Literary Precedents for PE

PE did not originate from the church fathers but was a reading strategy known more broadly both in the rhetorical training of the ancient world and in speeches in ancient drama (Rondeau, 12; Andresen, 14–15; Bates, *Hermeneutics*, 192–99; Pierce, *Discourse*, 6–8). It is not surprising that many church fathers employed PE, since their interpretive methods were greatly influenced by their educational contexts, and often methods utilized on classical texts would in turn be utilized on biblical texts as well (see, e.g., McCartney, 282–83). Thus, when the Bible became a focus of serious scholarship, it was natural to use the scholarly methods available and known to them—even though the Bible was, by common consent of Christians, understood to be an inspired book. PE was apparently known in the Alexandrian context, as it is attested, for example, by Philo (Grillmeier, 126; Slusser, 468–69) and perhaps even in Cicero (Slusser, 469–70). The educational context for the early church, however, does not determine whether such methods would have been utilized by NT authors themselves. It remains an open question how prominent such training would have been for NT authors (so also Gentry, 119).

One may also inquire about possible PE precedents from other Jewish exegetical traditions, including early rabbinic sources (see also Docherty). Though these sources are too late to provide evidence of direct influence on the NT, it has been argued that identifying speakers in texts where the Hebrew is ambiguous is a prominent concern in pentateuchal targumim (Gentry, 107, noting both Docherty and Samely). PE may also be found earlier, in 11Q13, from Qumran (Pierce, *Discourse*, 10–11). Such examples may also corroborate PE in the NT.

PE in the Early Church

Before looking at the NT, we turn to the clear presence of PE in the early church. The following examples are by no means exhaustive but are rather merely representative.

Apostolic Fathers. Perhaps the earliest extant example of PE in the postapostolic church comes from 1 Clement in the final decade of the first century. First Clement 36:4–5 speaks of the Father's speech to the Son, echoing the use of Pss. 2; 110 in Heb. 1:5, 13: "But of his Son the Master spoke thus: 'You are my Son; today I have begotten you. Ask of me, and I will give you the Gentiles for your inheritance, and the ends of the earth for your possession.' And again he says to him: 'Sit at my right hand, until I make your enemies a footstool for your feet'" (text and trans. Holmes). This second quotation is clearly speech directed to the Son ("again he says to him [*pros auton*]"). In light of this, the first quotation could also be translated, "But *to* his Son the Master spoke," taking *epi* in the phrase *epi . . . tō huiō autou* as indicating the one to whom the Master spoke (BDAG, s.v. *epi*, 14.a). In either case, the speech from the Father to the Son in 1 Clem. 36 is recorded in the words of Scripture (Pss. 2:7–8; 110:1), so these verses of 1 Clement can be categorized as PE. Additionally, in 1 Clem. 16 Christ is identified as the speaker of Isa. 53; Ps. 22.

Further evidence of PE comes from the second-century letter Barnabas, which in 5:5 reads, "If the Lord submitted to suffer for our souls, even though he is the Lord of the whole world, to whom God said at the foundation of the world, 'Let us make humankind according to our image and likeness,' how is it, then, that he submitted to suffer at the hands of humans?" (Holmes). The hortatory subjunctive "let us make" (from Gen. 1:26) is thus understood as the Father's speech to the Son. Similarly, Barn. 6:12 again references the Father's speech to the Son in Gen. 1:26. Here the author of Barnabas notes that the Genesis text speaks about (*peri*) those who have been forgiven in terms of new creation (see 6:11; cf. Prigent, 86), but the author again confirms that "these things he [i.e., the Father] said to the Son" (Holmes). In Barn. 6:16 the Son speaks the words of, most likely, Ps. 22:22, echoing Heb. 2:12. This might also be categorized as PE. The author's approach assumes that some words of Scripture can be attributed to distinct divine persons and that Scripture is the inspired speech of God. Further, it is striking that this is another example of PE of an OT passage that is also found in Hebrews. Other examples of PE in Barnabas may include the Son (= the Lord) speaking in Barn. 7:3–7.

Consistent with PE, 2 Clement attributes words of the OT to Jesus the Lord. In 2 Clem. 3:5 the words of Isa. 29:13 are attributed *to Christ* speaking in Isaiah, even though this passage is attributed to Isaiah himself in the Gospels (Matt. 15:7–8; Mark 7:6). Second Clement 3:5 assumes the preexistence of Christ and his speech in the OT (see also 9:5), which is also consistent with the programmatic statement in 2 Clem. 1:1. Second Clement 13:2 alludes to Isa. 52:5, and again the speaker is most likely Jesus, identified here as "Lord." Likewise, in 2 Clem. 17:4 the Lord who speaks the words of Isa. 66:18 is probably the Son.

More daunting is 2 Clem. 15:3–4: "Let us, therefore, in righteousness and holiness remain true to the things we have believed, in order that we may boldly ask of God, who says, 'While you are still speaking, I will say, "Behold I am here [Isa. 58:9]."' For this word is the sign of a great promise, for the Lord says that he is more ready to give than the one asking is to ask [see Isa. 65:1, 24]" (Holmes). Here one must unravel whether one or two divine persons speak the words of Isaiah. The quotation from Isa. 58:9 seems to refer to God the Father. However, the following phrase, which explains Isa. 58:9, is attributed to "the Lord," which elsewhere refers to Jesus in 2 Clement. This latter phrase probably also alludes to Isaiah (see esp. Isa. 65:1, 24). Here *God* and the *Lord* probably identify *two* divine persons speaking in Isaiah, since elsewhere "God" (*theos*) most often refers to God the Father and "Lord" (*kyrios*) elsewhere always seems to refer to the Son. Additionally, elsewhere in 2 Clement both the Father and the Son speak the words of Isaiah (e.g., 2:1; 3:5; 7:6; see Crowe, "Like Father," 260–61). Thus, in 2 Clement both the Father and the Son speak the words of the OT.

Justin Martyr. Justin looms large in discussions of PE, especially his statement in *1 Apol.* 36:

> But when you hear the utterances of the prophets spoken as it were personally, you must not suppose that they are spoken by the inspired themselves, but by the Divine Word who moves them. For sometimes He declares things that are to come to pass, in the manner of one who foretells the future; sometimes He speaks as from the person of God the Lord and Father of all; sometimes as from the person of Christ; sometimes as from the person of the people answering the Lord or His Father, just as you can see even in your own writers, one man being the writer of the whole, but introducing the persons who converse. (*ANF*, 1:175)

In other words, the OT prophets sometimes speak in the person of the Father, sometimes in the person of the Son, and the method of identifying speakers in texts is known to Justin's audience. Further, sometimes it is the *people who respond* who are presented as speaking in the text. Justin then proceeds in *1 Apol.* 37–39 to give examples of the Father speaking in Isaiah (perhaps 1:3–4, 11–15; 58:6–7; 66:1), the Son speaking in Isaiah (perhaps 50:6–8; 65:2) and/or Psalms (perhaps Pss. 3:5; 22:7–8, 16, 18), and the Spirit speaking in Isaiah (2:3–4) (Marcovich, *Apologiae*, 85–87).

Further examples of PE are found in Justin's *Dialogue with Trypho*. The Father speaks to the Son in Pss. 45; 110 (cf. Trigg, 320–21). The Son appears to Abraham, Isaac, and Moses and speaks with Moses from the bush (*Dial.* 59; cf. 75). The Son is the Word who speaks in the OT, including by Solomon in Prov. 8 (*Dial.* 61). Consistent with what we have seen, Justin also understands Gen. 1:26 to show that God "conversed with some one [*sic*] who was numerically distinct from Himself, and also a rational Being" (*Dial.* 62 [*ANF*, 1:228]). The Father speaks Ps. 96:2, but he speaks of Christ (*Dial.* 74; cf. Marcovich, *Dialogus*, 197–98). David speaks from the person (*apo prosōpou*) of Christ, to whom the Father speaks in Ps. 2 (*Dial.* 88).

Irenaeus of Lyons. Irenaeus also employs PE, in both *Demonstration of the Apostolic Preaching* and *Against Heresies*, though it has also been argued that PE is attenuated in Irenaeus given its prominence among his Gnostic opponents (Presley, "Exegetical Roots," 167–71). The Son of God is the preexistent Word who spoke through the prophets (*Epid.* 34; cf. 45) and spoke with Moses (*Epid.* 40, 46). The Father as Lord speaks to the Son as Lord in Pss. 2; 110; Isa. 45 (*Epid.* 48–49). Irenaeus explains this: "It is not David nor any other one of the prophets, who speaks from himself—for it is not man who utters prophecies—but [that] the Spirit of God, conforming Himself to the person concerned, spoke in the prophets, producing words, sometimes from Christ and at other times from the Father" (*Epid.* 49 [Behr]). He continues, "Christ says, by David, that the Father Himself speaks with Him" (*Epid.* 50 [Behr]; see also 51), this time quoting Isa. 49. From such passages Irenaeus writes that we can identify other passages that speak in a similar manner (*Epid.* 52). Irenaeus also includes Gen. 1:26, where the Father says to the Son, "Let us make man in our image" (ESV)—for the Son is the Wonderful Counselor of the Father (*Epid.* 55).

PE is also evident in *Against Heresies*: Gen. 1:26 (*Haer.* 4.20.1; 5.1.3, which include the Son and Spirit as addressees); Exod. 3:8 (*Haer.* 3.6.2); Ps. 110:1 (*Haer.* 3.6.1); Prov. 8:22–25 (*Haer.* 4.20.3). The Word himself spoke through the Law and the Prophets (*Haer.* 4.6.6; cf. 4.2.3). Indeed, the Lord himself (i.e., the Word) spoke "in His own person to all alike the words of the Decalogue" (*Haer.* 4.16.4 [*ANF*, 1:482]). Yet it is only in the NT that the Word is revealed as "the crucified and risen Jesus Christ" (Behr, 116, noting *Haer.* 4.34.1; cf. Behr, 112–13).

Tertullian of Carthage. In *Against Praxeas*, Tertullian points to the inconsistency of a modalistic understanding of God and to the reality that different persons speak to one another in Scripture—including in the OT (*Prax.* 11). He explains in great detail in *Prax.* 11–12: The Father speaks to the Son (Ps. 2:7; Isa. 42:1; 49:6), the Son speaks to the Father (Pss. 3:1; 71:18; Isa. 61:1), the Spirit speaks of the Father and the Son in the voice of a third person (Ps. 110:1), and the Spirit speaks to the Father about the Son (Isa. 53:1–2). These conversations thus require distinct persons in the Trinity. Tertullian argues that most of the psalms that predict the coming of Christ do so by representing the Son speaking to the Father. To these examples many more could be added: the Father speaks to the Son (e.g., Gen. 1:26 in *Res.* 6; Ps. 2:7 in *Prax.* 7 [also *Marc.* 3.20]; Isa. 52:14 in *Marc.* 3.17), the Son speaks (e.g., Pss. 22:22, 25; 68:26 in *Marc.* 3.22; Ps. 59:11 in *Marc.* 3.23; Prov. 8:22 in *Prax.* 6–7; Isa. 40:3 in *Marc.* 4.33; Isa. 50:4 in *Prax.* 22; Isa. 50:11 in *Marc.* 3.23; Isa. 61:1 in *Marc.* 4.11, 14; Isa. 61:10 in *Marc.* 4.11; Jer. 1:9 in *Prax.* 22; and by Jeremiah in *Marc.* 4.40—for the Son frequently speaks in the prophets [*Marc.* 4.13]), and the Holy Spirit speaks (e.g., Ps. 8:6 in *Marc.* 5.17; Isa. 49:18 in *Marc.* 4.11; Isa. 63:1 in *Marc.* 4.40).

Other early church fathers. I mention here a few more of the many examples of PE in the church fathers (see also Rondeau). Theophilus of Antioch practices PE with respect to Gen. 1:26 (*Autol.* 2.18; see also 2.10). Hippolytus of Rome views the Son speaking of himself in the OT prophets (e.g., Isa. 65:1; *Noet.* 12) and likely assumes PE in his understanding of Ps. 2 (*Noet.* 15). Novatian practices PE with respect to Gen. 1:26; Isa. 61:1 (*Trin.* 26, 29).

Clement of Alexandria practices PE with respect to the OT, where Jesus ("the Instructor") teaches about himself (*Paed.* 1.7), speaking through Moses, David, Solomon, Jeremiah, Isaiah, and Ezekiel (*Paed.* 1.9–10). Origen argues that Christ spoke already in the OT (*Princ.*, preface.1) and discusses PE explicitly in *Philoc.* 7.1 (Heine, 88–91). All this is consistent with the Alexandrians' view that the OT is "a continuous narrative of the Logos himself" (McGuckin, 189–90).

Hilary of Poitiers states that the "primary condition of knowledge" when reading Psalms is to determine who is speaking to whom—sometimes the Father is speaking, sometimes the Son; indeed, in the majority of psalms, the Son speaks (*Hom. Ps.* 1.1 [*NPNF*², 9:236]; see also Rondeau, 7). Augustine understands many of the psalms to be spoken by Christ, in his person, such as in Pss. 2; 3; 22 (*En. Ps.* 2.5; 3.1; 22.1); it is incumbent upon readers to identify the speaker in passages like Ps. 45 (*En. Ps.* 45.4–5). Jesus, our King, speaks in the character of his human nature in Ps. 16 (*En. Ps.* 16.1).

Summary of the early church. PE is common in many church fathers. This is consistent with belief both in Christ as the preexistent Word of God who spoke already in the OT and in the nature of Scripture as inspired prophecy. Some texts seem to be utilized with particular frequency in this regard, including Gen. 1:26; Pss. 2; 45; 110, along with prophetic texts like the suffering-servant passages from Isaiah. What I have not considered in much detail is whether there is exegetical warrant for these PE interpretations; I will say more about this in what follows.

PE in the NT

It remains now to consider whether the NT authors themselves utilize PE. If we do indeed find examples of PE in the NT, we may expect to find that some of the same OT passages will be read as divine conversations in the NT as among the church fathers—texts like Gen. 1:26; Pss. 2; 45; 110; Isa. 50; 53.

Hebrews. We have seen that 1 Clem. 36:4–5 attests to PE where it echoes Heb. 1:5, 13. Barnabas 6:16 also manifests PE when alluding to Heb. 2:12. Further, Hebrews clearly portrays biblical texts as conversations between Father and Son (e.g., Griffiths, 126–27). Hebrews is thus an important NT text to consider for PE.

In Heb. 1:5 (and 5:5) the Father speaks to the Son the words of Ps. 2:7, "You are my Son; today I have begotten you" (ESV), and he also speaks the words of 2 Sam. 7:14. The use of Ps. 2:7 is a strong candidate for PE, since the Father addresses the Son. This, however, does not solve the issue of *when* this conversation—or when the *begetting*—takes place. Is this a preincarnate or eternal conversation? Or is it spoken on the day of the resurrection and/or ascension of Christ? Proponents of PE often highlight the former view of Ps. 2:7 (e.g., Swain, 120; Bates, *Trinity*, 64–80; Pierce, "Hebrews 1," 127–31), though the latter option is clearer in Hebrews and coheres well with the parallels to Acts 13 (on which, see below; see also Calvin, 42). In other words, the primary context for the speech in Heb. 1:5 is the accomplishment of salvation. Even so, the sonship in view cannot be limited to the resurrection—as, for example, was the approach of the Socinians (Mastricht, 543)—for Heb. 1:1–4 emphasizes the preexistent divine sonship of Christ (so also Carson, 58–59). The Son is by nature divine; he was not designated Son *only* at the resurrection and/or ascension. Instead, the resurrection and/or ascension is the demonstration of Christ's preexistent divine sonship (Mastricht, 542–43; Turretin, 1:294–95; Bavinck, 3:435, 442). The use of Ps. 2:7 in Heb. 1:5 thus draws attention to the eternal Son's accomplishment of redemption "in these last days" (1:2).

The Father again speaks to the Son in 1:8–13, quoting Pss. 45:6–7; 102:25–27; 110:1. These OT texts further support PE in the NT. The preposition *pros* in Heb. 1:8, 13 (and assumed in 1:10) most likely refers to the Father speaking *to* the Son (so CSB, KJV), though in many translations this is rendered "of" or "about," perhaps in light of the usage of *pros* in 1:7. Again the emphasis is on the Son's accomplishment of salvation, but the context also speaks of the preexistent, divine Son. In Ps. 110:1 one Lord speaks to another Lord—the Father speaks to the Son. The NT specifies who the two Lords are (i.e., Father and Son) in a way that clarifies what is more opaque in the OT. Psalm 110 is spoken by David through the Spirit in the OT, prophesying Christ's exaltation. Psalm 110, like most of the psalm quotations in Heb. 1, draws attention to the eternal Father-Son relationship, even as its main focus is on the Son's accomplishment of redemption and his transition to the estate of glory (cf. 1:6 with 2:5). In Heb. 1 the Father speaks to the Son, as he also does in subsequent quotations of Ps. 110 in Heb. 7:17, 21 (Ps. 110:4). The Father also speaks the words of Jer. 31 in Heb. 8 (so Pierce, *Discourse*, 78–90).

The Son speaks the words of Scripture in Hebrews in two key passages. The first is Heb. 2:12–13, which portrays Jesus speaking the words of Ps. 22:22; Isa. 8:17–18. Psalm 22 was widely understood in the early church as a prophecy directly about Christ (or spoken in the person of Christ). This approach finds support in Hebrews, where Jesus is the one who announces God's name. The words of Isaiah are also attributed to Jesus. Jesus is not ashamed to call brothers those whose flesh and blood he shares. Jesus thus invokes Ps. 22 to speak of the congregation he shares with his family, and he quotes Isa. 8 to speak of his faith in God and of his solidarity with his people. Here again Hebrews focuses on the accomplishment of redemption, even as it is the words of the OT that are fulfilled. If this is PE, then the eighth-century BC prophet spoke in the person of the Son about what would happen when salvation was accomplished. It is also possible that a typological approach, in which the prophetic speech anticipates a greater fulfillment, sufficiently accounts for this text.

The second is the quotation of Ps. 40:6–8 in Heb. 10:5–7, a text in which many see a reference to the eternal covenant of salvation and a text that speaks of the Son's role in mediation—a body was prepared for him (Turretin, 2:242–43). When the preexistent Son comes into the world, he says that he has come as it is written of him in the book. This echoes the words of David from Ps. 40, where the book probably refers to Deut. 17. Even so, Ps. 40 looks ahead to the greater son of David and the greater salvation he will accomplish; it would thus be fitting to read Ps. 40 as the words of the Son, who came in the fullness of time but was Mediator even before the incarnation (cf. Turretin, 2:243). At the same time, reading Ps. 40 entirely as the words of the Son has limitations, since Ps. 40:12 also speaks of the sins of the Davidic speaker.

Also not to be missed is the Holy Spirit, who likewise speaks in the OT, according to Hebrews (3:7; 9:8; 10:15–17).

In summary, PE is a helpful category for understanding Hebrews, which records divine speech between persons *in the words of Scripture*. It is striking that Hebrews utilizes Pss. 2, 45, 110 to highlight the Father's speech to the Son, a use that is consistent with these texts' appropriation by many church fathers. At the same time, we need to exercise caution in order not to overread OT texts as *only* spoken in the past or in eternity in ways that would downplay eschatological fulfillment. We must respect the author of Hebrews' opening thesis that, in contrast to previous eras, it is now, in the last days, that God has spoken in his Son (1:2). Despite the continuity of divine speech in Hebrews (e.g., 3:7; 4:2), there must be something new to the speech as well. For the author of the (likely) third-century *Refutation of All Heresies* (traditionally attributed to Hippolytus), this newness was that in the last days the Son speaks directly, whereas he spoke through prophets in the OT (*Haer*. 10.33.14).

Gospels and Acts. Some of the same OT passages from Hebrews are also candidates for PE in the Gospels and Acts, including Pss. 2; 110. Psalm 2:7 is probably echoed in the baptism of Jesus (Matt. 3:17; Mark 1:11; Luke 3:22; see also John 1:34). The baptism is *not* the adoption of Jesus when he *becomes* Son of God. Instead, Jesus's baptism assumes his preexistent sonship. This does not directly support PE, but it does support Ps. 2:7 attesting the sonship of Jesus prior to his exaltation, which might indirectly support PE. The use of Ps. 2:7 in Acts 13:33 is slightly different. In Acts 13 the psalm is used primarily to support the enthronement of Christ (*pace* Bates, *Trinity*, 72–74), though the resurrection vindicates and demonstrates Christ's preexistent sonship (see Crowe, *Hope*, 58–61).

Even more relevant for PE is Ps. 110:1, which Jesus utilizes in the final week of his life to reveal his identity (Matt. 22:44; Mark 12:36; Luke 20:42). Jesus's question assumes that he is both David's son (from the line of David) and David's Lord (he is inherently greater than David). Indeed, part of Jesus's being David's Lord entails his preexistence, which means that Jesus is not only David's Lord at the installation to God's right hand but also must have been David's Lord already in David's own day. It is also worth noting that Jesus explicitly identifies *David* as the speaker of Ps. 110 (Matt. 22:43; Mark 12:36; Luke 20:42). Though PE certainly appreciates that the prophets themselves can speak "in the person" of the Son, might one expect Jesus to identify himself somehow as the actual speaker of the psalm if PE is correct? Perhaps, though we must also appreciate the "good and necessary consequences" of texts whereby the implications of texts lead to more robust doctrinal formulations. In one sense Jesus is Lord already at his birth (Luke 2:11), though at the exaltation Jesus is Lord in a new, redemptive-historical sense (Acts 2:36). In Peter's Pentecost sermon in Acts 2:34, Ps. 110:1 highlights this redemptive-historical realization that Christ is the heavenly Lord of whom David spoke. We again have a both-and approach: Ps. 110:1 speaks of a preexisting reality (the Son is David's Lord) while also pointing to the realization of lordship in redemptive history. Thus, Ps. 110:1 seems to support PE. Another possibility of PE is Ps. 16:8–11 in Acts 2:25–28. Here David, as a prophet, speaks about the resurrection of Christ (2:30–31), whose final deliverance David's own deliverance anticipated (see Crowe, *Hope*, 25–27). Typology is clear in this text, though PE is also possible.

Psalm 22 is another possibility for PE. On the cross Jesus quotes Ps. 22:1 ("My God, my God, why have you forsaken me?"; Matt. 27:46; Mark 15:34), and this is taken from a psalm that seems to be directly prophetic of the coming of the Messiah. Here it is possible that the inspired words of David were spoken in the person of the Son, anticipating his speech on the cross. The same is possible for Luke 23:46 ("Into your hands I commit my spirit," Ps. 31:5), though in each case Jesus may simply be echoing the words of the psalmist and fulfilling them in a greater typological way.

Sometimes OT texts that are quoted in the Gospels and understood as exhibiting PE by church fathers seem not to be clearly used as PE in the NT. For example, Origen understands the fulfillment quotation of Ps. 78:2 in Matt. 13:35 to be PE (Heine, 90–91, noting homily 1 on Ps. 77 [on 77:2; ET 78:2]). In *Marc.* 4.11 Tertullian points to the Son as the one who speaks the words of Isa. 61:1. Yet when Jesus quotes this passage (Luke 4:18), he does not explicitly point to himself as the speaker in Isaiah. Instead, he speaks of the fulfillment of Isa. 61 in his ministry. Similarly, John Calvin follows Nicholas of Lyra's double-literal sense when interpreting Isa. 61:1–2 and rejects the notion that the words were spoken only of Christ (see Muller, 223–24). In Matt. 13:35 and Luke 4:18 *fulfillment* does not necessarily equate to PE. In these cases, the appeal to PE is not compelling.

Additionally, though church fathers frequently take PE approaches to suffering-servant passages, the use of these passages in the NT does not provide clear evidence of PE. In the quotation of Isa. 53:1 (and 6:10) in John 12:38–41, PE is possible but seems unlikely, since Isaiah himself is identified as the one who spoke of (*peri*) Christ (12:41). This phrasing does not require that Isaiah spoke "in the person of" the Son. It may be better to find here a direct prophetic fulfillment in v. 38 and an indirect typological fulfillment in v. 40, the latter of which looks forward to a greater fulfillment in Jesus's day. A better candidate for PE with Isa. 53 comes in the exchange between Philip and the Ethiopian eunuch, who asks Philip in Acts 8:34 *who* the prophet is speaking about—himself or someone else. PE is possible here (e.g., Bates, *Trinity*, 110–13) but again is not certain—especially since Isaiah speaks in the third person and may simply be prophesying about the coming of the suffering servant. Luke's statements in this regard are not nearly as explicit in potential support of PE as are Clement of Rome's.

Pause in overemphasizing PE also comes from sweeping statements Jesus himself makes about the OT. In Luke 24:44 Jesus says that everything written "about me" (*peri emou*) in the Law, the Prophets, and the Psalms must be fulfilled; here Jesus does not seem to intimate PE as the primary reading strategy. Similarly, in another programmatic text about OT interpretation (John 5:39), Jesus speaks of the Scriptures bearing witness "about me" (*peri emou*). In these texts, along with John 12:41 (see above), we should be careful not to ask *peri* to bear more weight than it ought; these programmatic texts do not appear to require PE.

NT Letters. Perhaps supporting PE in the NT Epistles are references to the eternal plan of redemption (i.e., *pactum salutis*; see 1 Pet. 1:20; 2:4), which are consistent with the logic of PE (see also Swain, 118–21). This may also be assumed in Gal. 3:16, where the promise is made to Abraham's seed. This claim echoes Gen. 13:15; 17:8; 24:7 and seems to speak of an eternal or preincarnate promise made *to Christ*, who is Abraham's seed (see Gibson, 17–19). Psalm 110 is also used in Paul's Letters (1 Cor. 15:25; Eph. 1:20), but in a way that focuses on the exaltation of Christ rather than on the identity of the speakers.

Bates suggests other candidates for PE in Rom. 10:6–8 (Deut. 9:4; 30:12, 14; Ps. 107:26), 16 (Isa. 53:1); 11:9–10 (Ps. 69:22–23); 15:3 (Ps. 69:9), 9 (2 Sam. 22:50; Ps. 18:49); 2 Cor. 4:13 (Ps. 116:10) (*Hermeneutics*, 223–328). PE is a possibility for these, but one could also argue that speech-in-character (i.e., *prosopopoeia*) or typology—or maybe some combination thereof—may explain the texts just as well.

Summary of the NT. While the NT most likely does include examples of PE, some of the proposed examples are more indirect and, while possible, are not certain.

PE in the OT?

In light of the preceding discussions, it is also prudent to consider whether PE may be present in the OT itself. This is important because, often, the texts that the church fathers pointed to as examples of PE are not quoted, or are not used as examples of PE, in the NT. For example, Gen. 1:26; Prov. 8:22–25 are frequent examples of PE in the church fathers, but neither is quoted in this way in the NT. Yet if we understand the OT to be inherently forward-looking and the Son to be preexistent and speaking in the OT, then we may find PE in the OT. For example, Gen. 1:26 appears to be a strong candidate: "Let us make" most likely attests an intratrinitarian counsel rather than a heavenly court or royal "we," since the angels did not assist God in creation, nor are people made in the image of angels (see also Turretin, 1:273–74). Proverbs 8:22–25 enjoys a long exegetical tradition that says the Son is speaking about his role as Word of God—this is seen as a personification, and perhaps a hypostatization, of wisdom (see Turretin, 1:295–97; Emerson). In the NT, Christ is identified as the eternal Word and Wisdom of God, by whom all things were created (e.g., John 1:1; Col. 1:15–20), but it is unnecessary to conclude that Prov. 8 is an express proclamation about eternal generation (see also Bavinck, 2:274; Waltke, 127–30).

Frequently, Psalms is at the center of discussions about PE (Rondeau). This is evident in patristic expositions of Psalms and in frequently invoked texts for PE like Pss. 2, 22, 45, 110. Here we need to be circumspect, since Ps. 2 is used in the NT primarily to speak about the messianic sonship of Christ. Even so, the NT's clear teaching on the Son's eternality opens up the possibility of divine speech between persons in Psalms. This plurality of divine persons may also explain, at least in part, the relative dearth of attention given to Ps. 110:1 in the pre-NT context: its meaning becomes apparent only when the incarnation of the divine Son of God and the Son of David has occurred. In some texts, such as Pss. 2; 45; 110, we see conversations *in the texts themselves*. Given the application of these texts to Jesus in the NT, it is indeed appropriate to consider who is speaking in the original context and to whom the message is spoken. But this also requires the revelation of the NT to clarify who is speaking, and prophetic *prosopopoeia* remains a viable explanation (cf. Waltke and Houston, 493).

In sum, though PE may be comparatively rare in the OT, it does appear that we can identify distinct voices speaking in some OT texts, when the author speaks "in the person of" a member of the Godhead. Possibilities include Gen. 1:26; Pss. 2; 22; 45; 110; and (less likely) Prov. 8:22, 25—texts that are common in the church fathers as well. Possibilities can also be found in the Prophets. But a PE approach to the OT cannot be separated from the fuller revelation, including fuller insights into the persons of the Trinity, granted in the NT.

Summary and Assessment

That many early church fathers utilized PE is beyond cavil. But that does not solve all the questions about the extent of the method in the NT itself. While those with a high view of Scripture and Christology have often affirmed the method (e.g., Letham, 256–57), others have objected that the method wrests the texts from their original contexts and imports new meanings that could not have been understood by the original authors (Gentry, 120) or that the method is (at least with Origen) applied "arbitrarily and fancifully" (Waltke and Houston, 9). What follows is a brief, preliminary assessment of the method, recognizing that more work remains to be done.

PE is theologically consistent with the rule of faith. It remains unclear how and why PE first emerged, but that it emerged as a prominent tool in early Christian theology is clear. The orthodox believed from the beginning in the divine, preexistent Son who did not threaten the oneness of God. As the doctrine of the Trinity began to emerge more clearly in the early church, the supernatural inspiration of the Scriptures and the distinction between persons seem to have congealed into a more explicit PE approach, which may also have been influenced by contemporary rhetorical training. Early Christians appear to have read the OT in light of key presuppositions that led to identifying divine conversations in texts, even if those texts were not quoted in the NT or not quoted in a way that clearly attested PE. PE may thus be something that emerged as a "good and necessary consequence" of the teaching of Scripture rather than from a swath of examples of the NT use of the OT. In other words, it may be that in light of NT fulfillment, the fathers could look back and see that it was the Son speaking all along. The OT was opened to them as a rich reservoir of the words of Christ; it is not difficult to find conversations in the OT when one takes this approach.

PE thus follows on the conviction that Christ is the preexistent Word of God who was active in the OT and that the OT is the inspired speech of God. Further, PE assumes the fundamental unity of the Scriptures along with the unity of God's actions *ad extra*—including the unity of salvation. The Scriptures teach the implementation of the covenant of grace and imply an eternal covenant of redemption, which is manifested in speech between Father, Son, and Spirit (see also Richardson, 48–50); these speeches are sometimes alluded to (e.g., Luke 22:29; John 6:38; Heb. 5:5; 1 Pet. 1:20; 2:4) without being recorded explicitly (see also Swain, 119).

At the same time, heretics also used PE; the Gnostics appear to have used it quite commonly (Presley, *Intertextual*). PE can thus be used either faithfully or unfaithfully. We therefore ought not to anoint PE as a panacea for proper theological conclusions. Irenaeus may provide a helpful caution here, since his focus in PE is often on the identity of God rather than on "the multiplicity of divine persons speaking in the text" (as it is in Justin; see Presley, "Exegetical Roots," 170).

PE does not negate typology. While PE is likely present in the NT, we must be careful not to jettison typology for the sake of PE. Rather than categorizing texts as either prosopological or typological, it is better to take a both-and approach that recognizes typology as well as PE in some texts. We need a typological method that emphasizes "greater fulfillment" in the NT (see also Hays; Beale); we must not miss the NT's emphasis on the progress of redemptive history.

For example, Ps. 2 is spoken to the Davidic king about his enthronement and is thus a typological prophecy (so also Waltke and Houston, 180). The historical, earthly horizon is therefore important but not ultimate, for the details of Ps. 2 point to a greater sonship that transcends the merely human sphere. Thus, even if PE is a possibility in Ps. 2, it is not the only approach one needs. Likewise, while Ps. 16 may be an example of PE, it cannot be about *only* the Son (or only the words of the Son)—for David speaks of himself as the king who has been delivered (*pace* Bates, *Trinity*, 72). To illustrate further, a deliverance from death similar to David's in Ps. 16 is recounted by Hezekiah in Isa. 38:17–19, though there is little reason to understand Isa. 38 prosopologically, given its immediate reference to the events in Hezekiah's life. Instead, Hezekiah's historical deliverance anticipates the greater deliverance of Jesus in the NT—the king from Hezekiah's family line who is raised from the dead. The same is also true of Ps. 16: since David speaks of his own historical (though not *final*) deliverance, typology must not be dismissed for the sake of PE.

In short, we must give attention not only to the broader biblical and theological contexts but also to the near contexts of particular texts; *both* contexts are necessary. Without denying the Son's preexistence, eternal generation, or activity in the OT, we must be careful not to shortchange the exegetical process by opting for PE apart from sufficient attention to the more immediate contexts of a given passage. Indeed, while PE and typology may overlap in some texts, typology seems to be quite more common than PE in the NT (see next point).

PE does not appear to be a prominent method in the NT. Though the NT does indeed appear to attest to PE, we need to be careful not to overplay the role of PE in the NT. Further, given that part of the raison d'être for PE is to provide clarity about who is speaking in a text when it is unclear, we surely must be circumspect about reading trinitarian speakers or intratrinitarian statements into texts where these are not clearly revealed. As noted above, we may rightly ask whether PE, by working out the implications of biblical doctrines, is more developed than the NT itself. This does not mean the method is illegitimate, but as with doctrine in general, perhaps the method congealed more clearly in eras beyond that of the NT in light of the implications of texts.

The principles of *progressive* revelation should also caution us against overclaiming what is revealed in the OT. Only with the NT comes the fullest flowering of biblical revelation. It is in the latter days that the Father has definitively spoken in his Son (Heb. 1:2). This means that we are not always sure about who is speaking in the OT; texts may be intentionally opaque, and the NT may not always provide definitive clarity on the identities of speakers. It is also worth considering whether *prosopopoeia* may be a better option than PE in some cases.

Conclusion

Scripture speaks of the eternal Son of God who has always been active. In this sense, PE provides a welcome corrective to minimalistic (and sometimes unorthodox) readings of Scripture. Yet research on this important method with respect to biblical studies is still relatively young, and I anticipate many more studies in the coming years that will continue to clarify the issues.

See also Apostolic Hermeneutics articles

Bibliography. Andresen, C., "Zur Entstehung und Geschichte zur des trinitarischen Personbegriffes," *ZNW* 52 (1961): 1–39; Bates, M. W., *The Birth of the Trinity* (Oxford University Press, 2015); Bates, *The Hermeneutics of the Apostolic Proclamation* (Baylor University Press, 2012); Bavinck, H., *Reformed Dogmatics*, ed. J. Bolt, trans. J. Vriend, 4 vols. (Baker Academic, 2003–8); Beale, G. K., *Handbook on the New Testament Use of the Old Testament* (Baker Academic, 2012); Behr, J. *The Way to Nicaea*, FCT 1 (St. Vladimir's Seminary Press, 2001); Calvin, J., *Commentaries on the Epistle of Paul the Apostle to the Hebrews*, trans. J. Owen (repr., Baker Books, 2003); Carson, D. A., *Jesus the Son of God* (Crossway, 2012); Crowe, B. D., *The Hope of Israel* (Baker Academic, 2020); Crowe, "Like Father, like Son," *WTJ* 77 (2015): 251–64; Docherty, S. E., *The Use of the Old Testament in Hebrews*, WUNT 2/260 (Mohr Siebeck, 2009); Emerson, M. Y., "The Role of Proverbs 8," in *Retrieving Eternal Generation*, ed. F. Sanders and S. R. Swain (Zondervan, 2017), 44–66; Gentry, P. J., "A Preliminary Evaluation and Critique of Prosopological Exegesis," *SBJT* 23, no. 2 (2019): 105–22; Gibson, D., "'Fathers of Faith, My Fathers Now!,'" *Them* 40, no. 1 (2015): 14–34; Griffiths, J. I., "Hebrews and the Trinity," in *The Essential Trinity*, ed. B. D. Crowe and C. R. Trueman (Apollos, 2016), 122–38; Grillmeier, A., *From the Apostolic Age to Chalcedon (451)*, vol. 1 of *Christ in Christian Tradition*, trans. J. Bowden, 2nd rev. ed. (John Knox, 1975); Hays, R. B., "Christ Prays the Psalms," in *The Conversion of the Imagination* (Eerdmans, 2005), 101–18; Heine, R. E., *Origen*, Cascade Companions (Cascade, 2019); Holmes, M. W., ed., *The Apostolic Fathers*, 3rd ed. (Baker Academic, 2007); Hughes, K. R., *The Trinitarian Testimony of the Spirit*, VCSup 147 (Brill, 2018); Irenaeus, *On the Apostolic Preaching*, trans. J. Behr, PPS (St. Vladimir's Seminary Press, 1997); Letham, R., *Systematic Theology* (Crossway, 2019); Litwa, M. D., ed. and trans., *Refutation of All Heresies*, WGRW 40 (SBL Press, 2016); Marcovich, M., ed., *Iustini Martyris: Apologiae pro christianis*, PTS 38 (de Gruyter, 1994); Marcovich, *Iustini Martyris: Dialogus cum Tryphone*, PTS 47 (de Gruyter, 1997); Mastricht, P., *Theoretical-Practical Theology*, trans. T. Rester, ed. J. Beeke, vol. 2 (Reformation Heritage Books, 2021); McCartney, D. G., "Literal and Allegorical Interpretation in Origen's *Contra Celsum*," *WTJ* 48 (1986): 281–301; McGuckin, J. A., *St. Cyril of Alexandria* (repr., St. Vladimir's Seminary Press, 2004); Muller, R. A., *Post-Reformation Reformed Dogmatics*, 4 vols. (Grand Rapids: Baker Academic, 2003); Origen, *Homilies on the Psalms: Codex Monacensis Graecus 314*, trans. J. W. Trigg, FC 141 (Catholic University of America Press, 2020); Pierce, M. N., *Divine Discourse in the Epistle to the Hebrews*, SNTSMS 178 (Cambridge University Press, 2020); Pierce, "Hebrews 1 and the Son Begotten 'Today,'" in *Retrieving Eternal Generation*, ed. F. Sanders and S. Swain (Zondervan, 2017), 117–31; Presley, S. O., *The Intertextual Reception of Genesis 1–3 in Irenaeus of Lyons*, BibAC 8 (Brill, 2015); Presley, "Irenaeus and the Exegetical Roots of Trinitarian Theology," in *Irenaeus*, ed. S. Parvis and P. Foster (Fortress, 2012), 165–71, 247–49; Prigent, P., *L'Épître de Barnabé I–XVI et ses sources*, EBib (Gabalda, 1961); Richardson, G., "The Covenant of Redemption," in *Covenant Theology*, ed. G. P. Waters, J. N. Reid, and J. M. Muether (Crossway, 2020), 43–62; Rondeau, M.-J., *Les commentaires patristiques du Psautier (IIIe–Ve siècles)*, vol. 2, OCA 220 (Pont. Institutum Studiorum Orientalium, 1985); Samely, A., *The Interpretation of Speech in the Pentateuch Targums*, TSAJ 27 (Mohr Siebeck, 1992); Slusser, M., "The Exegetical Roots of Trinitarian Theology," *TS* 49 (1988): 461–76; Swain, S. R., "Covenant of Redemption," in *Christian Dogmatics*, ed. M. Allen and S. R. Swain (Baker Academic, 2016), 107–25; Trigg, J., "The Apostolic Fathers and Apologists," in *The Ancient Period*, vol. 1 of *A History of Biblical Interpretation*, ed. A. J. Hauser and D. F. Watson (Eerdmans, 2003), 304–33; Turretin, F., *Institutes of Elenctic Theology*, trans. G. M. Giger, ed. J. T. Dennison Jr., 3 vols. (P&R, 1992–97); Waltke, B. K., *The Book of Proverbs: Chapters 1–15*, NICOT (Eerdmans, 2004); Waltke, B. K., and J. M. Houston, *The Psalms as Christian Worship*, with E. Moore (Eerdmans, 2010).

BRANDON D. CROWE

Proverbs, Book of

Within the landscape of the OT, the book of Proverbs is a strange place. To adapt a well-known phrase from L. P. Hartley's *The Go-Between*, things are done differently here. The sages of Proverbs attend neither to Israel's formative traditions nor to God's mighty acts in history. Instead, they focus on ordinary life; and they infuse the ordinary with moral and theological significance through an exploration of the interrelations among creatures, creation, and the Creator.

The Structure and Message of Proverbs

Proverbs may be concerned with the ordinary, but the document is far from ordinary within the canon of Scripture. Similar to the Psalter, Proverbs is an anthology. The collections within the anthology are marked off by superscriptions, which serve as windows into the book's compositional history:

Proverbs 1–9: "The proverbs of Solomon son of David, king of Israel" (1:1)

Proverbs 10:1–22:16: "The proverbs of Solomon" (10:1a)

Proverbs 22:17–24:22: "Words of the wise" (22:17 AT)

Proverbs 24:23–34: "These also are of the wise" (24:23a AT)

Proverbs 25–29: "These also are proverbs of Solomon, which the men of Hezekiah king of Judah transcribed" (25:1 AT)

Proverbs 30: "The words of Agur son of Jakeh" (30:1a AT)

Proverbs 31: "The words of Lemuel, king of Massa" (31:1a AT)

At minimum, these superscriptions indicate that the discrete collections within Proverbs were produced by different individuals and incorporated in the anthology at different times.

The formation of the anthology, however, was far from haphazard. While scholars continue to debate whether or not the individual sayings in Prov. 10–29 are cast in coherent pairs or clusters, the arrangement of the collections evinces signs of deliberate design. Two features stand out. First, the preamble (1:1–7) and prologue (1:8–9:18) formally introduce the central collections within the anthology (10:1–29:27). They institute root metaphors, conventional character types, and prominent motifs that are nuanced and developed by the variegated materials in the central collections. Far from providing a detailed description of the wise life, the preamble and prologue introduce different virtues, vices, desires, and moral worldviews to illuminate the surpassing value of wisdom. Against this backdrop, the central collections profile the virtues, vices, appetites, and affections embodied in specific character types to form the character, and extend the moral vision, of readers in accord with wisdom.

Second, the preamble and prologue are intimately related to the materials in Prov. 30–31. Together, these collections situate the diverse materials in Prov. 10–29 within a formal, literary framework. This framework is formed through terms, expressions, and images characteristic of the preamble, prologue, and concluding collections. The motto of the book—"the fear of Yahweh" (AT)—occurs at the climax of the preamble (1:7), the conclusion of the prologue (9:10), and the end of the book (31:30), where it moves from the requisite posture of one seeking wisdom to a form of life embodied in the "valiant woman." The phrase "knowledge of the Holy One" occurs only in 9:10 and 30:3, at the conclusion of the prologue and within the words of Agur. The maternal voice mentioned in the prologue (1:8; 6:20) is given expression in the instruction of Lemuel's mother (31:1). Just as the book opens in the confines of the home, so also it concludes with a mother instructing her son in the home (31:1–9). And the poem devoted to the "valiant woman" (31:10–31) includes terms and expressions that are used elsewhere only to describe Lady Wisdom (see Camp, *Feminine*, 186–208; Yoder, *Woman*, 91–93). The female imagery, combined with the use of unique terms and expressions, suggests that Prov. 30–31 coalesces with the preamble and prologue to provide a literary framework within which to interpret the materials in the anthology.

Viewed within this literary framework and through the lens of the preamble (1:1–7), Proverbs seeks to (trans)form readers in accord with Yahwistic wisdom and virtue. That is, the book attempts to shape the character, sharpen the intellect, form the feelings, direct the desires, and attune the lives of readers in accord with divine wisdom.

In the light of the structure and message of Proverbs, this entry explores various texts, motifs, and concepts that influence and inform Proverbs' kaleidoscopic projection of the wise life; it follows the sequence of the Hebrew canon, moving from the Pentateuch to the Prophets to the Writings. And it concludes with some reflections on the use of Proverbs in the NT.

The Pentateuch

While the equation of wisdom with Torah does not become explicit until the work of Ben Sira (Sir. 19:20; 24:23), Proverbs exhibits at least five intertextual and conceptual affinities with the Pentateuch.

The first is the unique expression "tree of life." With the exception of Gen. 2–3 and certain aphorisms within Proverbs, the OT does not mention this phrase elsewhere (cf. LXX Isa. 65:22). Its use within Proverbs generates a fruitful dialogue with the Eden narrative. This dialogue is conducted through Proverbs' metaphorical use of "tree of life" (Prov. 3:18; 11:30; 13:12; 15:4). Though the indefinite form of the expression indicates that it does not match *the* tree of life in Gen. 2–3, it is organically and conceptually related to the primeval arbor.

As a metaphor nourished by the semantic field cultivated in Eden, "tree of life" conveys concepts of vitality, flourishing, and abundance within Proverbs. And the use of the image recasts aspects of the Eden narrative (see Yoder, "Tree"). Whereas the "way" to the tree of life was barred from human passage (Gen. 3:22–24), Lady Wisdom opens a network of "ways" to a tree of life that is accessible (Prov. 3:17–18). Whereas the tree of life was prohibited from human touch (Gen. 3:22), Lady Wisdom is a tree of life that one must grasp (Prov. 3:18). Whereas the fruit of the tree of life was excluded from consumption in Eden (Gen. 3:22–23), the righteous produce the fruit of a tree of life that the community may consume (Prov. 11:30a). And whereas the tree of knowledge that the woman found delightful brought death and dissatisfaction (Gen. 3:4–6), desire fulfilled is a tree of life, bringing vitality and gratification (Prov. 13:12). Taken together, the references to "tree of life" within Proverbs intimate that the form of life and the blessings enjoyed in the garden are now accessible east of Eden. The tree provides a rich metaphorical source domain that funds Proverbs' vision of the good life in God's good creation.

The second intertextual link with the Pentateuch is established through a unique sequence of prepositional phrases. The expressions "by wisdom," "by understanding," and "by knowledge" are reiterated in Prov. 3:19–20; 24:3–4; Exod. 31:3; 35:31 (see Van Leeuwen). According to Prov. 3:19–20, wisdom, understanding, and knowledge were the tools the divine architect employed to construct and fill the cosmos (cf. Jer. 10:12; 51:15). The mode and tools of Yahweh's creative work are reflected in the formation of human homes. By wisdom, understanding, and knowledge, humans found and fill domestic and social spheres (Prov. 24:3–4). And the mode and tools of Yahweh's creative work mirror the construction of the tabernacle. The microcosmic representation of Yahweh's heavenly house is formed and filled by Bezalel, a craftsman endowed with wisdom, understanding, and knowledge (Exod. 31:3; 35:31; cf. 1 Kings 7:14). This fixed sequence of prepositional phrases reveals an intertextual topos that links the formation of the tabernacle and human house-building with Yahweh's construction of the cosmic house (Van Leeuwen, 77–87). By virtue of wisdom, understanding, and knowledge, humans imitate the divine architect and the construction of the tabernacle through their ordering of domestic and social spheres.

The third intertextual link with the Pentateuch is formed through the motto of Proverbs: "the fear of Yahweh." While the expression possesses distinctive connotations across the Pentateuch and Proverbs, the fundamental posture conveyed by "the fear of Yahweh" clarifies their conceptual similarities. The fear of Yahweh is a disposition that recognizes one's place within the cosmos and dependence upon Yahweh (see Jindo). The perspectival knowledge of one's creaturehood and Yahweh's universal authority generates fear—that is, a moral ontology or "state of mind" that allows one to live in accord with Yahweh's will as well as the grain of creation (Jindo, 450). This mode of being is reflected in Israel's physical and verbal response to Yahweh's declaration of the Decalogue at Sinai (Exod. 20:18–20). It is the requisite posture for covenant fidelity within Deuteronomy (5:29; 6:2; 10:12–13). And it is the epistemological and ontological precondition for the acquisition of wisdom in Proverbs (1:7; 9:10; 15:33). Whether the physical, moral, covenantal, or cognitive connotations of "the fear of Yahweh" are foregrounded in its use across the Pentateuch and Proverbs, these discrete dimensions illuminate aspects of a perspectival posture necessary for both covenant fidelity and a wise life.

The fourth intertextual link with the Pentateuch is forged through Proverbs' use of language redolent of the Shema (Deut. 6:4–9; cf. 11:18–20; see Fishbane; Overland). Just as the Israelites were to "bind" Moses's words as a sign on their hands and "write" them on their doorposts (Deut. 6:8–9; 11:18, 20), so also the son is to "bind" kindness and faithfulness as well as parental commands on his body and "write them on the tablet" of his heart (Prov. 3:3; 7:3; cf. 6:21; Jer. 31:33). The combination of the verbs "bind" and "write" occurs only in these texts within the OT. And the use of the verb "bind" along with the expressions "when you walk about" and "when you lie down" in Prov. 6:21–22 (AT) is reminiscent of Deut. 6:7–8 (cf. Deut. 11:18–19). The shared terminology among these texts intimates that the exordia to the parental instructions in Prov. 3:1–12; 6:20–35; 7:1–27 appeal to Deut. 6:4–9 by means of intertextual allusion. These intertextual allusions not only indicate that the parental lectures of Proverbs concretize Moses's call to teach one's children the will of Yahweh (Deut. 6:7); they also suggest that the commandments of the parents are consonant with the commandments of Yahweh.

The fifth intertextual link between Proverbs and the Pentateuch surfaces in the words of Agur (Prov. 30). In the light of human finitude (30:1–3), Agur unleashes a barrage of rhetorical questions to accentuate the severe limits of human wisdom and power (30:4). Among these questions, Agur reiterates Moses's basic inquiry, "What is his name?" (cf. Exod. 3:13). And the implied answer to this question sets the stage for Agur's relational solution to the matter of human limits (Prov. 30:5–6; Waltke, 473–77). This relational solution is conveyed through composite quotations from David's victory song (2 Sam. 22:31 in Prov. 30:5; cf. Ps. 18:31) and Moses's sermons in Deuteronomy (Deut. 4:2 in Prov. 30:6; cf. Deut. 12:32). Proverbs 30:5 modifies David's victory song to focus attention on the reliability of divine revelation. Proverbs 30:6 draws on the initial half of the canon formula (Deut. 4:2), prohibiting one from adding to God's words. These composite quotations provide Agur with a grammar for his relational solution to the problem of human limits. This solution is found in whom you know, not what you know. That is, knowledge of the Holy One is discovered in relationship with Yahweh through his revealed will, not in human investigation (Moore, 100–101). The combination of these composite quotations captures the necessity of divine revelation in the pursuit of true wisdom (cf. Schipper, 250–55).

Together with common forms, expressions, and ethical visions (see Weinfeld), these intertextual links indicate that Proverbs is neither isolated from the Pentateuch nor adverse to its conception of covenant life. Instead, Ben Sira's equation of wisdom with Torah is latent in Proverbs' intertextual and conceptual links with the Pentateuch.

The Prophets

When Proverbs is read against the backdrop of the Prophets, it appears that Israel's historiographic and prophetic materials contribute little to the anthology's witness, since Proverbs exhibits a lack of concern with the formative events of Israel's history and prophetic revelation (though cf. Prov. 29:18). In an attempt to reconcile Proverbs with the Former and Latter Prophets, many have searched for signs of wisdom influence in the historiographic and prophetic works of the OT (see, e.g., Fichtner; Whybray; Macintosh). They explore the ways in which the sages influenced or shaped certain texts, but they do not reflect on how these texts may have influenced Proverbs. Did texts from the Former and Latter Prophets inform Proverbs? Although the signs of influence are minimal, a few deserve specific comment.

Former Prophets. First Kings 1–11 is an intertextual flashpoint for exploring affinities between Proverbs and the account of Solomon's reign. The attribution of "proverbs" to Solomon (1 Kings 4:32; Prov. 1:1; 10:1; 25:1), combined with the narrative's frequent attention to wisdom, opens an intertextual dialogue that clarifies the semantic range and variegated facets of wisdom in Proverbs (see Kynes). These facets include wisdom's association with building. As noted above, the unique sequence of prepositional phrases in Prov. 3:19–20; 24:3–4; Exod. 31:3 links Yahweh's construction of the cosmos with the construction of both human homes and the tabernacle. This intertextual topos recurs in 1 Kings 7:14, where Yahweh endows Hiram "with wisdom, with understanding, and with knowledge" to form and fill the temple. This stereotypical sequence connects the building of the temple with the building of the cosmos, the tabernacle, and human homes (Van Leeuwen, 83–87). Each is constructed with the same tools; and each, in different ways, serves as an earthly reflection of the heavenly reality. The recurrence of the topos reinforces a specific aspect of Proverbs' discourse on wisdom. Craftsmanship or skill in the various dimensions of life is a central component of wisdom (see Lemaire; Schwáb, 203–4).

In addition to building, 1 Kings 1–11 informs Proverbs' conception of wisdom as effective governance (see Lemaire; Kynes). Solomon asks for wisdom in order to govern Yahweh's people and to distinguish between good and evil (3:9); and he manifests this political-judicial wisdom through the organization of his administration (4:1–28), the institution of diplomatic and commercial relations with other countries (5:1–7; 10:1–13), and the adjudication of the case involving the two women (3:16–28; cf. 10:9). These political and judicial aspects of wisdom are dominant shades in Proverbs' definition of the concept (e.g., Prov. 8:15–16; 16:10; 20:28; 29:4). The political and judicial aspects of wisdom presented in 1 Kings 1–11 match and magnify the political-judicial dimensions of wisdom in Proverbs.

The narrative account of Solomon's reign illuminates the facets of wisdom in Proverbs. And the narrative account shares some particular intertextual connections with Proverbs (see Winkler). Just as Solomon received wisdom as a divine gift (1 Kings 3:12), so also Proverbs affirms that wisdom is a divine gift (Prov. 2:6). Just as

Solomon's wisdom is accompanied by gifts of wealth, honor, and long life (1 Kings 3:13–14), so also Lady Wisdom grants wealth, honor, and long life to her devotees (Prov. 3:16; 8:18). And just as Solomon falls prey to foreign women (1 Kings 11:1–13), so also the foreign woman poses a perennial threat to the addressee of Proverbs (Prov. 2:16–19; 5:1–23; 6:20–35; 7:1–27). These lexical and conceptual similarities suggest that 1 Kings 1–11 provides a rich intertextual resource for recognizing the blessings of wisdom, threats to the wise life, and the multifaceted dimensions of wisdom itself within Proverbs (see Camp, *Strange*, 166–83).

Latter Prophets. In addition to Proverbs' intertextual interaction with the Former Prophets, the book bears at least three similarities to the Latter Prophets. First, Lady Wisdom's initial discourse is painted with a prophetic brush (Prov. 1:20–33). This speech combines general prophetic diction with specific terms and phrases from Jer. 7; 20; Zech. 7 (Harris, 93–94). The confluence of these prophetic terms, images, and motifs not only indicates that Proverbs traffics in prophetic rhetoric in order to warn readers of the disastrous consequences associated with disregarding Wisdom's rebuke; the shared language also suggests that, like the prophets, Wisdom is an authorized authority. If one rejects her, then one rejects Yahweh (Harris, 99).

Second, Agur's words and the sayings of Lemuel's mother are cast in the form of a prophetic oracle (Prov. 30:1; 31:1; cf. Isa. 13:1; Hab. 1:1). They are "inspired utterances," which convey truths God has disclosed. The inclusion of this oracular form suggests that Proverbs is not indifferent to divine revelation. To the contrary, divine revelation is essential for acquiring genuine wisdom, because human investigation of the world is not enough.

Third, Proverbs employs images and ethical concepts that are consonant with the Latter Prophets. The "strange woman" functions as a polysemous symbol for sexual, social, and religious behavior that transgresses normative boundaries and awakens the power of desire (2:16–19; 5:1–23; 6:20–35; 7:1–27; 23:27). As a multivalent symbol, her portrait may be informed by Deuteronomic regulations concerning intermarriage with foreigners (Deut. 7:3–4; Ezra 10:9–44; Neh. 13:23–27; see Tan); equally, however, prophetic metaphors that depict Israel's covenant infidelity in terms of marital unfaithfulness involving foreign women may inspire Proverbs's portrait of this femme fatale (Hosea 2:8–13; Jer. 3:1–5; Ezek. 16:1–58; see O'Dowd). And similarly to its relationship with Israel's covenant ethics, Proverbs shares many similarities with prophetic ethics.

In the light of its concern with the (trans)formation of character in accord with Yahwistic wisdom and virtue, Proverbs may exhibit a lack of concern with the formative events of Israel's history as well as prophetic revelation. Its variegated affinities with the Former and Latter Prophets, however, indicate that Proverbs did not pursue this goal in a vacuum.

The Writings

As a document situated in the Writings, Proverbs exists in a fruitful intertextual friendship with several texts. Among these texts, its relationship with the Psalter and the Songs of Songs, as well as the interrelations between the collections in the anthology, deserve specific comment.

Whether "wisdom psalms" is a legitimate generic classification or an illegitimate child of form criticism, the shared language and forms between Proverbs and certain psalms are striking. The admonitions and advice of Ps. 37, for example, align with the wisdom of Proverbs (Cheung, 69–71). The call to "not . . . be envious" of evildoers (Ps. 37:1, 7, 8) reverberates throughout Proverbs (3:31; 23:17–18; 24:1–2), and the charge to "trust in Yahweh and do good" (Ps. 37:3 AT; cf. vv. 5, 27) mirrors several aphorisms in Proverbs (3:5; 16:20; 28:25). With the exception of one word, Prov. 24:19 matches Ps. 37:1, and several sayings bear a close resemblance to the instructions within the psalm (Ps. 37:5 and Prov. 16:3; Ps. 37:16 and Prov. 16:8; Ps. 37:30 and Prov. 10:31). These similarities, combined with the psalm's attention to the righteous and the wicked, suggest that Ps. 37 and Proverbs traffic in the same terminology and share a common ethical vision. Whereas the former focuses on the fate of the righteous and the wicked, the latter emphasizes the character of these figures (see Brown).

The relationship between the Psalter and Proverbs is apparent in several other poems. The opening words of Ps. 78 contain terms that mirror the exordia of the parental instructions in Prov. 1–9 (Ps. 78:1; Prov. 2:2; 4:5; 5:1). Proverbs maintains that one may grow in their understanding of the fear of Yahweh (Prov. 2:5), and several psalms seek to teach the fear of Yahweh, whether directly (Ps. 34:11) or indirectly (Pss. 111, 112). From a synchronic perspective, the lexical and formal correspondences between the Psalter and Proverbs indicate that these collections employ comparable rhetoric to achieve complementary didactic ends. The Psalter moves one to praise; Proverbs, on the other hand, moves one to grow in wisdom (Brown, 101–2).

This growth in wisdom includes the objects of one's desire. In the light of its assumption that humans are desiring creatures (see Stewart), it is not surprising that Proverbs shares many intertextual resonances with the Song of Songs. In addition to the variety of lexical parallels, Proverbs employs imagery evocative of the Song. Just as honey drips from the lips of the Shulammite (Song 4:11), so also the strange woman's lips drip honey (Prov. 5:3). Both Proverbs and the Song encourage intoxication with love (Prov. 5:19; Song 5:1), and both portray lovemaking through the metaphor of springs and cisterns (Prov. 5:15–18; Song 4:15). The language and imagery of love play a formative role in Proverbs' instruction; they serve as a didactic tool for directing one's desire to legitimate objects of love.

These intertextual affinities between Proverbs and the Writings, however, pale in comparison with the connections within the anthology itself. The phenomenon of "variant repetition" establishes these connections. Variant repetitions are cases in which proverbs or parts of proverbs recur "in identical or slightly altered form" (Heim, 3–5). Proverbs contains ninety-six variant sets—that is, 223 out of the 915 verses exhibit the phenomenon. Far from representing the work of a sloppy scribe, these variant repetitions are a deliberate editorial technique that contributes to the anthology's pedagogical agenda (Heim). They create innertextual coherence within and across the collections of Proverbs; and by virtue of the incorporation of distinctive elements within variant repetitions, these "twice-told proverbs" sharpen the intellect and hone the hermeneutical skills of the reader. While Proverbs shares affinities with texts throughout the OT, its own collections represent the anthology's closest intertextual partner.

Proverbs in the NT

Beyond the confines of the OT, the presence of Proverbs is felt in the NT. The NT cites its aphorisms to concretize particular theological and practical matters (Rom. 12:20; Heb. 12:5–6; James 4:6; 1 Pet. 4:18; 5:5; 2 Pet. 2:22). And several NT texts echo the theological and ethical sentiments of Proverbs. Peter's affirmation that "love covers a multitude of sins" (1 Pet. 4:8 ESV) resounds in Proverbs (10:12; 11:13; 17:9). Paul's rendering of retribution (Gal. 6:8) is illustrated throughout Proverbs (1:19; 10:16; 11:18–19). James's discourse on the limits of human wisdom (4:13–17) resonates with the anthropological and epistemological perspective of Proverbs (16:3, 9; 27:1). And the request for daily bread in the Lord's Prayer (Matt. 6:11) recalls Agur's prayer for sufficient sustenance (Prov. 30:8).

These explicit quotations and potential echoes of Proverbs in the NT represent only a portion of the anthology's influence. In addition to the striking similarities between the ethical vision of Proverbs and the NT (see Pennington), NT depictions of Jesus's nature and identity reflect Proverbs's portrayal of wisdom and Lady Wisdom. The unique clustering of common terms in Prov. 2:3–6 and Col. 2:2–3 suggests that Proverbs provides Paul with a lexicon to elucidate the mystery of God—a mystery that Christians understand on account of their union with the source of genuine wisdom: Christ. In the same way, the pregnant, poetic portrait of Lady Wisdom's cosmic preeminence, intimate relationship with God, and mediatorial position in Prov. 8 bears a striking resemblance to several NT texts (John 1:1–3; Col. 1:15–20; Heb. 1:2–3; Rev. 3:14). These texts capitalize on the semantic potential of the terms in Prov. 8 and Lady Wisdom's reception in the Second Temple period to delineate Christ's preexistence, cosmic preeminence, and agency in creation (see Beetham). They redeploy the language of "begotten," "beginning," and "before" all things as well as the concepts of "firstborn of all creation" and active personal agency in creation to illuminate Christ's divine nature. Proverbs' construal of wisdom and Lady Wisdom provides the NT with lexical and conceptual resources for its christological witness. Together with its contributions to the theological economy of the OT, Proverbs also funds the theological economy of the NT.

Bibliography. Baumann, G., *Die Weisheitsgestalt in Proverbien 1–9*, FAT 16 (Mohr Siebeck, 1996); Beetham, C. A., *Echoes of Scripture in the Letter of Paul to the Colossians*, BibInt 96 (Society of Biblical Literature, 2008); Brown, W. P., "'Come, O Children . . . I Will Teach You the Fear of the Lord' (Ps. 34:12)," in *Seeking Out the Wisdom of the Ancients*, ed. R. L. Troxel, K. G. Friebel, and D. R. Magary (Eisenbrauns, 2005), 85–102; Camp, C. V., *Wisdom and the Feminine in the Book of Proverbs*, BLS 11 (Almond, 1985); Camp, *Wise, Strange and Holy*, JSOTSup 320 (Sheffield Academic, 2000); Cheung, S. C.-C., *Wisdom Intoned*, LHBOTS 613 (T&T Clark, 2015); Dell, K., and W. Kynes, eds., *Reading Proverbs Intertextually*, LHBOTS 629 (T&T Clark, 2019); Fichtner, J., "Jesaja unter den Weisen," *TLZ* 74 (1949): 75–80; Fishbane, M., "Torah and Tradition," in *Tradition and Theology in the Old Testament*, ed. D. A. Knight (SPCK, 1977), 275–300; Harris, S. L., *Proverbs 1–9*, SBLDS 150 (Scholars Press, 1995); Heim, K. M., *Poetic Imagination in Proverbs*, BBRSup 4 (Eisenbrauns, 2013); Jindo, J. Y., "On the Biblical Notion of the 'Fear of God' as a Condition for Human Existence," *BibInt* 19 (2012): 433–53; Kynes, W., "Wisdom Defined through Narrative and Intertextual Network," in Dell and Kynes, *Reading Proverbs Intertextually*, 35–47; Lemaire, A., "Wisdom in Solomonic Historiography," in *Wisdom in Ancient Israel*, ed. J. Day, R. P. Gordon, and H. G. M. Williamson (Cambridge University Press, 1995), 106–18; Macintosh, A. A., "Hosea and the Wisdom Tradition," in *Wisdom in Ancient Israel*, ed. J. Day, R. P. Gordon, and H. G. M. Williamson (Cambridge University Press, 1995), 124–32; Moore, R. D., "A Home for the Alien," *ZAW* 106 (1994): 96–107; O'Dowd, R., "A Prophet in the Sage's House?," in *Riddles and Revelations*, ed. M. J. Boda, R. L. Meek, and W. R. Osborne, LHBOTS 634 (T&T Clark, 2018), 165–81; Overland, P., "Did the Sage Draw from the Shema?," *CBQ* 62 (2000): 424–40; Pennington, J. P., *The Sermon on the Mount and Human Flourishing* (Baker Academic, 2017); Schipper, B. U., *Hermeneutik der Tora*, BZAW 432 (de Gruyter, 2012); Schwáb, Z. S., *Toward an Interpretation of the Book of Proverbs*, JTISup 7 (Eisenbrauns, 2013); Stewart, A. W., *Poetic Ethics in Proverbs* (Cambridge University Press, 2016); Tan, N. N. H., *The "Foreignness" of the Foreign Woman in Proverbs 1–9*, BZAW 381 (de Gruyter, 2008); Van Leeuwen, R. C., "Cosmos, Temple, House," in *Wisdom Literature in Mesopotamia and Israel*, ed. R. J. Clifford, SBLSymS 36 (Society of Biblical Literature,

2007), 67–90; Waltke, B. K., *The Book of Proverbs: Chapters 15–31*, NICOT (Eerdmans, 2005); Weinfeld, M., *Deuteronomy and the Deuteronomic School* (Oxford University Press, 1972); Whybray, R. N., *The Succession Narrative*, SBT 9 (SCM, 1968); Winkler, M., *Das Salomonische des Sprichwörterbuches*, HBS 87 (Herder, 2017); Yoder, C. R., *Wisdom as a Woman of Substance*, BZAW 304 (de Gruyter, 2001); Yoder, "Wisdom Is the Tree of Life," in Dell and Kynes, *Reading Proverbs Intertextually*, 11–19.

CHRISTOPHER B. ANSBERRY

Psalms, Book of

Most people read psalms flatly, with little awareness of the time variations and literary contributions within a single psalm. But psalms are multidimensional, in both the chronological sense—past, present, and future—and the literary sense that involves multiple voices, including the psalmist, God, the psalmist's enemies, and other voices, especially the voices of other Hebrew Scriptures.

A study of Psalms through the lens of intertextuality seeks to identify and interpret the scriptural voices, thus contributing to the multidimensional perspective by recognizing scriptural voices from the past applied in various ways by the psalmists themselves. These include historical details, semantic phrases, metaphors, allusions to other Hebrew Bible texts, and even direct quotations from other sources of the Hebrew Bible.

Moreover, as even a cursory reading of the Psalms will show, they are not written in the language of prose but poetry. That means the reader must look for such literary features as metaphors, allusions, quotations, parallelisms, chiasms, *inclusios*, and other literary patterns that highlight ideas the psalmists want to emphasize. While a study of the Psalms does not require the reader to be an expert in recognizing and decoding all of these features, the reader who really wants to view the Psalms through multidimensional glasses will need to become aware of these literary features and make a firm effort to understand and use them in order to call forth the priceless treasures of the Psalter. Thus the object of any serious study of the Psalms is to explore all of their dimensions, and intertextual studies are a necessary endeavor for scholars, and for laypersons, too, who will accept the challenge.

Intertextuality

A chapter in the history of interpretation. Giving some credence to Qoheleth's famous decree that "there is nothing new under the sun," we should acknowledge that intertextuality has humble though respectable beginnings among the ancients, and, to the credit of modern hermeneutics, the development of this subdiscipline has enhanced our understanding of how the ancient writers thought and interacted with the texts they had at hand. It is a lesson in how they used Scripture, and a fascinating chapter in the history of interpretation. Thankfully, many portions of the Hebrew Bible have benefited from the well-deserved application of the rules of intertextuality, but the Psalter, by anyone's estimation, is the most blessed of them all.

As we look at the long history of biblical interpretation we discover that intertextuality, too, has a long history. Augustine (AD 354–430) describes this hermeneutical feature by saying that "Scripture interprets Scripture" (Augustine, *Doctr. chr.* 2.9), which is an acknowledgment that a difficult text of Scripture can and should be interpreted in light of a clearer text. David Emanuel (7) prefers to say "Scripture reworks Scripture," a turn of the phrase that will become clearer as our study moves along and that suggests a more complex understanding of intertextuality than Augustine's rule. In the modern era the cross-reference study of the Bible is probably a closer parallel to Augustine's hermeneutic than modern intertextuality, since cross-referencing is only a sliver of the intertextual hermeneutic. Certainly its objective is less comprehensive and its motive less complex than that of intertextuality.

A basic description. Intertextuality is all about texts shared by two sources—in the present study, Psalms and other books of the Hebrew Bible. One feature that we need to recognize right off is that the psalmists were steeped in biblical language. To illustrate this point, when one reads the prayers of the great English preacher Charles Spurgeon, the reader will notice that his prayers are often woven together with quotations, phrases, and images that are peculiar to the KJV. The psalmists afford us a similar opportunity to peer through the portholes of their language and thought and perceive the wider sea of texts from which the poets drew their verbal pictures and language of prayer. It is another layer of meaning that, once perceived, contributes to the multidimensional perspective that students of Psalms should seek to achieve.

At the same time, while we do not want to underestimate the written sources that may have been available to the psalmists, we must assume that the sources were mostly oral and were stored away in the poets' memories. These sources appear mostly as allusions (some prefer the term "echoes") and quotations. In this study we will refer to the Psalms text as the receiver text and the text alluded to as the source text. In terms of the dynamic between the two shared texts, the interpretation given by the receiver text may coincide with the meaning of the source text or it may take a different angle of meaning, thus Emanuel's turn of phrase, "Scripture reworks Scripture." Beth LaNeel Tanner (5) describes the dynamic as a bricolage in the sense that it is "an intersection of pieces, echoes, and allusions of other 'texts.'" As an example, Emanuel (73, 141–42) identifies at least fifteen source texts for Ps. 105 and twenty-three source texts for Ps. 106 from six different OT books. If we put a template of those texts down on the master template of Pss. 105 and 106, it would demonstrate the broad semantic and theological dependence of these psalms on other OT texts. Another psalm that illustrates the presence of allusions so well is Ps. 78, which has at least twenty-five allusions to persons, places, and events across five books of the Hebrew Bible (Bullock, *Psalms,* 2:47). We will discuss Pss. 105 and 106 below as examples of intertextual allusions.

Four functions. Before we go further, we should observe that the psalmists, not exclusively but unapologetically, wrote intertextually for practical and theological purposes. In regard to the psalms' titles, for example, Brevard Childs (521) says they do not tie the psalms to the ancient past but "have been contemporized and individualized for every generation of suffering and persecuted Israel." Based upon my own studies, I have identified four functions of intertextuality that stand out in Psalms. In addition to being important for understanding the function of intertextuality, these functions set the standard for the use of Psalms in synagogue and church. In his extensive and perceptive analysis of the NT interpretation of OT texts, G. K. Beale offers an extensive list of literary/hermeneutical categories of the NT writers (*Handbook,* 55–93), some of which can be applied to how Psalms interprets the OT. The following four functions are practical/theological responses that I have observed in my reading of Psalms. They may be subsumed under Beale's "rhetorical use of the OT."

First, the psalmists prayed with the ancients, stressing Yahweh's character and reviewing his actions in history, especially the historical-redemptive events, and sometimes entreating Yahweh to repeat those events. Or they may even acknowledge that Yahweh had indeed done so (Bullock, *Psalms,* 1:72). An occurrence of this feature is the use of Moses's words in Num. 10:35: "Arise, LORD," the first words of a longer prayer spoken when the ark was moved from one place to another.

Second, and quite natural for Psalms as a compendium of theology, the psalmists confess their faith with the ancients, or we might say, reaffirm their faith, especially faith in the God of the Sinai covenant. While this function is not peculiar to Psalms, it has a distinct place in that book.

Not surprisingly, a third function of intertextuality is that the psalmists exhort their own generation (and future generations as well) to moral and religious observance. This function, while also not peculiar to Psalms, finds a home in this book because one of its purposes is to teach readers how to pray, how to believe, and how to live.

Fourth, and perhaps the most frequent function of all, is that the psalmists engage in theological reflection, as we will demonstrate below from Ps. 8. The practical nature of these four functions, while not exhausting the purposes of intertextuality, opens real-world, hands-on avenues for those who read Psalms, and, on a microscopic scale, reveals the larger uses of the Psalter in the church and synagogue throughout the centuries. In that same vein of thought, Leslie C. Allen (545) comments on the Chronicler's model of David as the teacher of future generations: "David's generosity in his material provision for the Temple is presented as a model for Israel which the Chronicler surely intended his own generation to copy." And then Allen draws a conclusion about the rhetorical David: "It is by no means unreasonable to posit that in the Psalter also the ancient hero *mutatis mutandis* became a standard of spirituality for members of each generation of God's people" (Allen, 545; see also Beale's principle on the rhetorical use of the OT, *Handbook,* 78–79.)

By the same principle, Psalms not only teaches the ancient hearers how to pray, confess their faith, engage in moral action, and reflect theologically, but inherently it also provides the model for its use by church and synagogue from ancient times to the present. The title of an earlier version of this article captures this dimension well: "The Psalter and Intertextuality: Voices Once Heard and Still Speaking." Indeed, if we are to explore the depths of Psalms for the people of God, intertextual studies are not optional but mandatory. While these four basic functions are not the substance of this article, our discussion will recognize them as purposeful operations of the intertextual method of Psalms studies.

A Basic Taxonomy

Explicit Allusions. For the sake of simplicity, we may break down allusions into explicit and implicit allusions. They are not quotations as such, even though semantically they may share exact or similar terms with the source text.

Explicit allusions are texts that pick up commonly known historical details from their source texts, identified especially by personal and place names, and exact or close semantic terms. The historical psalms (Pss. 78; 105; 106; 136) contain many such illustrations. Psalm 105, for example, cites the personal names of Abraham, Isaac, Jacob, Israel, Joseph, Moses, and Aaron, and the place names of Canaan, Egypt, and Ham, and we may assume that each of these names carries a particular significance for the psalmist. A closer examination of Pss. 105 and 106 will clarify the role of explicit allusions in these texts.

Our first observation is that Ps. 105 is a celebration of Yahweh's "wonderful acts" (105:2; cf. 106:2: "mighty acts"), especially drawing out Yahweh's faithfulness to the Abrahamic covenant (105:7–11). In view is Yahweh's resolve to give Abraham and his descendants the land of Canaan (105:11). In fact, the entire psalm is dedicated to demonstrating Yahweh's faithfulness in giving Abraham's descendants the land of Canaan. There are other features of that covenant, of course, but the emphasis on the possession of Canaan is quite appropriate as Book 4 (Pss. 90–106) makes its transition to Book 5 (Pss. 107–150), where Israel's return from Babylonian captivity and entrance again to their homeland is celebrated as a historical/saving parallel to the exodus and Israel's entrance to Canaan (Ps. 107:2–3). Psalm 105 provides a historical log that demonstrates Yahweh's faithfulness to his covenant with Abraham, phase by phase, to give the land of Canaan to his descendants, relating

- the patriarchal sojournings (vv. 12–15),
- Joseph and Israel's sojourn in the land of Egypt (vv. 16-25),
- Moses and the plagues (vv. 26–36),
- the exodus from Egypt (vv. 37–38),
- the wilderness wanderings (vv. 39–41), and
- the closing caption, celebrating the exodus from Egypt (vv. 42–45).

The literary caption to the story is that Yahweh has remembered his holy promise given to his servant Abraham.

> He brought out his people with rejoicing,
> his chosen ones with shouts of joy;
> he gave them the lands of the nations,
> and they fell heir to what others had toiled for—
> that they might keep his precepts
> and observe his laws.
> Praise the LORD. (105:42–45)

Psalms 105 and 106 are tandem psalms. As such, Ps. 105 celebrates Yahweh's "covenant he made with Abraham" (105:9), while Ps. 106 celebrates the overwhelming power of Yahweh's love, despite Israel's rebellion (106:45): "For their sake he remembered his covenant and out of his great love he redeemed" ("love" [*ḥesed*] occurs three times, in 106:1, 7, 45). The psalmist continues:

> He caused all who held them captive [Babylonian captivity]
> to show them mercy.
> Save us, LORD our God,
> and gather us from among the nations [return from Babylonian exile],
> that we may give thanks to your holy name
> and glory in your praise. (106:46–47)

"The abundance of [Yahweh's] steadfast love" (ESV; NIV: "his great love") is an explicit allusion to the final phrase in the second Sinai revelation (the formula of grace) after the golden-calf debacle (Exod. 34:6), here using the plural noun rather than the singular. Thus, the two covenants, Abrahamic and Mosaic, are celebrated in these two companion psalms and the two exoduses, from Egypt and Babylonia, are the object of Yahweh's faithful remembering. Note that Yahweh's "love" (*ḥesed*; NIV: "many kindnesses" in 106:7) does not occur in Ps. 105 but occurs three times in Ps. 106 (vv. 1, 7, 45). Thus, Ps. 106 turns the positive description of Yahweh the covenant-keeper of Ps. 105 to the tragic story of Israel as the covenant-breaker in Ps. 106, and installs the all-encompassing truth of God's "love" as the overarching force of Israel's history. The obvious purpose of the review laid out in Pss. 105 and 106 is to move Israel to believe in Yahweh's salvation from their captors, praying for deliverance from the Babylonian captivity out of faith in Yahweh the covenant-keeper and the God of "love": "Save us, LORD our God, and gather us from the nations [return from exile], that we may give thanks to your holy name and glory in your praise" (106:47). This is the third function as outlined above.

Psalm 106, the concluding psalm of Book 4, keys into two decisive instances of God's mercy in the time span covered by Ps. 105: Moses's intervention for Israel on the occasion of the golden calf and Phinehas's intervention for Israel on the occasion of their sin with Baal of Peor (Num. 25). In a tactical move, Ps. 106 links the Mosaic era back to the Abrahamic (Gen. 15:6) as the psalmist describes Phinehas's bold and heroic reaction to the Baal of Peor apostasy, attributing to him the Lord's commendation of Abraham, "that it was counted to him as righteousness" (106:31 AT). This, of course, is the psalmist's reflection on Phinehas's heroic act, and since the reason for its highly acclaimed importance is not spelled out in the psalm, this absence calls the reader into hermeneutical service (the fourth function). One plausible way for the reader to look at this commendation is to remember that, just as Moses "stood in the breach" and saved the nation (v. 23), in like manner Phinehas performed an act that, though different from Moses's act, also saved the nation and merited the Abrahamic commendation. Moreover, both Moses and Phinehas stopped the plagues that would have destroyed Israel (vv. 23, 30).

The rehearsal of Moses's story is paraphrastic in style, telling the story quite beautifully and without any surprises. The story of Phinehas, in contrast, contributes a striking addition to the source narrative: the commendation attributed to Abraham in Gen. 15:6 is reapplied to Phinehas. The words are not an exact quotation but come close:

> Gen. 15:6 (AT): "And he [the LORD] accounted it [the fact that Abraham "believed the LORD"] to him as righteousness."
>
> Ps. 106:31 (AT): "And it [Phinehas's action] was accounted to him as righteousness."

This retelling integrates explicit and implicit allusions. In Numbers, the word "plague" (*maggēpâ*) describes the Lord's punishment of Israel for their apostasy with Baal of Peor, which is ended by Phinehas's intervention: "And the plague was stayed" (*wattēʿāṣar hammaggēpâ*, 25:8). The receiver text (Ps. 106) preserves these two words from the source text, a beautiful illustration of an explicit allusion, and then takes the liberty of applying to Phinehas the Lord's approval of Abraham for his faith. This could be attributed to midrashic sources or the psalmist's own hermeneutical discretion. I suspect the latter. Yet, this should not be seen as a license to add to the Word, but rather liberty to interpret it within one's own circumstances. In many instances this liberty is exercised in the form of implicit allusions, which reflect the idea of the source text in such a way that, despite the absence or near absence of shared semantic terms, the allusions take a different and often a memorable form. We must also remember that, while we take such liberties also, our resultant interpretations are authoritative only to the extent that they do not conflict with Scripture in general and the text at hand in particular.

Implicit allusions. The topic of implicit allusions by itself could fill a whole book, so we must be very selective. One of my favorites is Ps. 8:5 (AT): "Yet you have made him [man] a little lower than God [LXX: angels]." There are two features of the receiver text that lead us to the source text: shared themes and shared semantic terms. The shared theme in this case is the creation of humanity. No other OT text could qualify for the honor of source text outside of Gen. 1. In fact, the shared theme is the major pointer to the source text. The source text is further indexed by the use of semantic terms shared with Gen. 1: the earth (*hāʾāreṣ*), the heavens (*haššāmayim*), stars (*kôkābîm*), dominion (*mšl*), beasts (*bahămôt*), the sea (*hayyām*), and man (*ʾādām*). That is, our writer takes the vocabulary of the creation story and weaves it into his own narrative, thus reflecting the source text. Psalm 8 is thus an interpretation of Gen. 1, especially the creation of the cosmos and humanity, and it represents theological reflection on the truth of Scripture. Humankind's status is second only to God (or "third" if we accept the LXX rendering "angels"). Although the distinctive phrase "in our image [*bətsalmenu*], according to our likeness [*kidmutenu*]" (Gen. 1:26) occurs in only one other text (Gen. 5:3, with terms reversed and applied to Adam rather than God, *in his* [Adam's] *likeness, according to his* [Adam's] *image*), it logically follows that the magnificent statement "You have made him a little lower than God" was the poet's way of saying the same thing in his own words.

Yet the psalmist reflects on a puzzling paradox: In view of the wonder, mystery, and beauty of the cosmos, why is it that God lavishes so much care upon his human creatures? Psalm 8 then exhibits semantic liberties, yet theological truths, and provides us with an excellent example of the writer's reflection on the source text. To the question "What is mankind that you are mindful of him?" (8:4 ESV), the answer, perhaps to our surprise, is phrased in three ways: (1) God has made mankind a "little lower than God" and "crowned him with glory and honor" (v. 5 AT); (2) God has given humanity dominion over his creation ("the works of your hands," v. 6); and (3) for this favored status, as incredible as it seems, the psalmist engages in exultant praise of God: "LORD, our Lord, how majestic is your name in all the earth!" (v. 9). The mystery of God's creation of and attendant love for humanity is ultimately expressed best in the praise of God our Creator, which is all-encompassing as indicated by the *inclusio* (8:1, 9).

The use of Ps. 8 in Heb. 2 presents us with a good example of intertextual principles as applied in the NT. Psalm 8 uses two terms to refer to humanity: "mankind" (*ʾĕnoš*) and "son of man" (*ben-ʾādām*). In the OT the phrase "son of man" generally means "man/mankind" and is used in Ezekiel and elsewhere in the OT in that sense. Along with Matthew's use of Hosea 11:1, "Out of Egypt I called my son" (Matt. 2:15), this illustrates how a term with a historical meaning can project itself into the eschatological future. Both Hosea's "son" (*ben*) and the psalmist's "mankind" (*ʾĕnoš*) have an inherent predictive meaning. Even though the two terms in Ps. 8 are, semantically speaking, synonymous, the fact that the second term ("son of man") is specific and different from the first ("mankind") would be enough for a NT interpreter to project "son of man" into the future manifestation of Messiah Jesus, which is precisely what the writer to the Hebrews does (Heb. 2:5–9). The hermeneutical principle here is the direct fulfillment of an OT prophecy.

Quotations. Quotations, understandably, are the treasure trove of intertextual studies because they provide a substantive text that can be traced to its source, a text that, comparatively speaking, consists of exact or almost exact wording.

A quotation can be a mere phrase or brief clause, as in Ps. 3:7 (*qûmâ YHWH*, "Arise, O LORD"; cf. Num. 10:35); or a longer clause, as in Ps. 106:31, "this was credited to him as righteousness" (cf. Gen. 15:6); or a more expansive text, such as the formula of grace (*YHWH ʾēl raḥûm wəḥannûn ʾerek ʾappayim wərab-ḥesed weʾəmet,* Exod. 34:6), which occurs in Psalms in three theologically sensitive positions in Books 3 (86:15), 4 (103:8), and 5 (145:8). A quotation will include enough words to substantiate its duplicate nature. I consider a quotation to be comprised of at least two words from another text in the same order, allowing for some minor differences as with Gen. 15:6 and Ps. 106:31 (see Bullock, "Covenant," 20–21; Schultz).

As stated above, a frequent function of intertextual usage is to join the prayers of the psalmist to the prayers of the ancients. An obvious illustration is the liturgical prayer that Moses prays when the Israelites move the ark to a new place: "Arise, O LORD, and let your enemies be scattered" (Num. 10:35 ESV; see Kim; Bullock, "Covenant"). The instances of the entreaty, "Arise, O LORD," occur in the precise form of Moses's prayer (Pss. 3:7; 7:6; 9:19; 10:12; 17:13; 132:8; 2 Chron. 6:41), except for two instances where *ʾĕlōhîm* stands in place of *YHWH* (Pss.

74:22; 82:8). The frequent occurrence of this prayer suggests that it had become a standard petition in Israel's prayer book, especially when they were threatened by their enemies; and, not surprisingly, most of the occurrences are in Book 1, where David is constantly facing the threat of national and personal adversaries. That is, David prays with Moses, and Moses in effect prays with David. Of special significance is that this prayer is borrowed from Moses, one of Israel's boldest and most valiant prayer warriors (see Exod. 32:32). Still today we sometimes assume that putting our petitions in the form of the prayers of biblical worthies may get God's attention more readily than our own words. This practice is not a magic wand, nor should it be barred from our arsenal of prayer methodology when we are trying to bring our hearts in line with those who love and trust God (the first function). This interpretive principle is similar to Beale's "proverbial" use of the OT (Beale, *Handbook*, 75), and is in fact one of the standard uses of Psalms in Jewish and Christian prayer, established by the Psalter itself. The spiritual effect of this prayer is, "Do it again, Lord!" (Bullock, *Psalms*, 1:72).

Hee Suk Kim proposes that the three quotations of the formula of grace (Exod. 34:6) positioned in Books 3, 4, and 5 of Psalms follow a discernible pattern that widens from David the king to the kingdom of Yahweh. First, Ps. 86, the lone David psalm of Book 3, is an affirmation of Yahweh's steadfast love and faithfulness to King David. Second, Ps. 103, the final David psalm of Book 4, widens the presence of Yahweh's steadfast love to include the community of the faithful. Third, Ps. 145, the final David psalm in the Psalter, further widens the theme to the kingship and kingdom of Yahweh and applies Yahweh's steadfast love to that kingdom (Kim, 47). It certainly is the case that the image of David *as king* fades into David *as servant* in Book 5. The use of this formula is an excellent example of how the reflective function of intertextuality works on a more extended format in Psalms, in this case forming an arc across Books 3, 4, and 5.

I might add to Kim's keen observation that the strategic placement of the formula of grace in Books 3, 4, and 5 forms a threefold *inclusio* in the David psalms. Each engages a crucial moment of historical significance, always in advance of the event to which it applies. Psalm 86, as already mentioned, is the only David psalm in Book 3, so the formula of grace on the lips of David is critical for a nation wrestling with the demise of the Davidic dynasty, and thus with the Davidic covenant (2 Sam. 7). The editor of Book 3 evidently wants the readers/listeners to hear David's confession of faith in Moses's own words before he entertains the troubling question of Ps. 89:49 (ESV): "Lord, where is your steadfast love of old, which by your faithfulness you swore to David?" David's confession begins the arc and streaks across the "firmament" of Books 3, 4, and 5, announcing the overarching sky of God's steadfast love. The middle occurrence of the formula (103:8) anticipates the announcement in the concluding psalm of Book 4 that the exile is over and recalls Yahweh's steadfast love: "Nevertheless, he looked upon their distress, when he heard their cry. For their sake he remembered his covenant, and relented [lit., "repented"] according to the abundance of his steadfast love. He caused them to be pitied by all those who held them captive. Save us, O Lord our God, and gather us from among the nations, that we may give thanks to your holy name and glory in your praise" (106:44–47). Again, in anticipation of the announcement that the exile is ended, the editor of Book 4 assures us that Yahweh's steadfast love is the moving force of history that has saved Israel from the nation(s) who held them captive. The fact that this confession, as in Ps. 86, is made in David's name is a way to converge David's persona and God's covenant plan into the single movement of Yahweh's steadfast love. Then Ps. 107 begins Book 5 by fulfilling the intent of 106:47, the end of the exile: "Oh give thanks to the Lord, for he is good, for his steadfast love endures forever!" (107:1).

The third occurrence of the formula of grace, the end of the arc begun in Ps. 86, is positioned in the final David psalm of Book 5. At last David, now servant of Yahweh (see also titles of Pss. 18 and 36), confesses Yahweh as King (145:1) and takes the words of the formula of grace on his lips one last time (145:8) to celebrate Yahweh's everlasting kingdom: "Your kingdom is an everlasting kingdom, and your dominion endures throughout all generations" (145:13 ESV). The kingship that David represented and the kingdom-building that made him Israel's greatest king have now modulated to Yahweh's kingship and universal kingdom (146:10; 148:11–13; 149:5–9; 150:6). Thus, the editor has quoted the formula of grace as the marker for the progression of the kingdom, from David's kingdom, to the renewed kingdom anticipated by the return from exile, and finally to the universal kingdom of Yahweh that will include all humanity.

Conclusion

This study has sought to highlight an essential literary and theological phenomenon of Psalms, insisting that intertextual interpretation is essential for achieving a multidimensional perspective on Psalms. We have analyzed allusions, which are myriad, and quotations, which are not as prolific as allusions but certainly a theological treasure in Psalms. When the psalmists quote other texts of the Hebrew Bible, they in effect add another voice or voices (source texts) that the listeners/readers should be aware of; how they deal with these texts (receiver texts) constitutes a significant chapter in the history of biblical interpretation and, at the same time, becomes an important component of the interpretation of the psalm involved. Further, we have asserted that the psalmists use these voices for at least four practical functions: (1) praying with the ancients,

(2) confessing faith with the ancients, (3) exhorting the psalmists' contemporary and future generations to moral and religious observance, and (4) reflecting on theological truths. In the history of synagogue and church these functions, consciously and unconsciously, have provided a model for the use of Psalms through the centuries. Thus, our study of intertextuality has hopefully opened our ears to "voices once heard and still speaking."

Bibliography. Allen, L. C., "David as Exemplar of Spirituality," *Bib* 67, no. 4 (1986): 544–46; Beale, G. K., "Finding Christ in the Old Testament," *JETS* 63 (2020): 25–50; Beale, *Handbook on the New Testament Use of the Old Testament* (Baker Academic, 2012); Bullock, C. H., "Covenant Renewal and the Formula of Grace in the Psalter," *BSac* 170 (2019): 18–34; Bullock, *Psalms*, 2 vols., TTCS (Baker Books, 2015, 2017); Bullock, *Reading Ecclesiastes Intertextually* (Bloomsbury T&T Clark, 2014); Bullock, *Reading Proverbs Intertextually* (Bloomsbury T&T Clark, 2019); Childs, B. S., *Introduction to the Old Testament as Scripture* (Fortress, 1979); Dell, K., and W. Kynes, eds., *Reading Job Intertextually* (Bloomsbury T&T Clark, 2013); Emanuel, D., *From Bards to Biblical Exegetes* (Pickwick, 2012); Kim, H. S., "Exodus 34.6 in Psalms 86, 103, and 145 in Relation to the Theological Perspectives of Books III, IV, and V of the Psalter," in *Inner Biblical Allusion in the Poetry of Wisdom and Psalms*, ed. M. J. Boda, K. D. Chau, and B. L. Tanner (T&T Clark, 2019), 36–48; Kynes, W., *My Psalm Has Turned into Weeping* (de Gruyter, 2012); Schultz, R. L., *The Search for Quotation*, JSOTSup 180 (Sheffield Academic, 1999); Spurgeon, C., *The Pastor in Prayer* (Banner of Truth Trust, 2004); Stead, M. R., *The Intertextuality of Zechariah 1–8* (T&T Clark, 2009); Tanner, B. L., *The Book of Psalms through the Lens of Intertextuality* (Lang, 2001); Vassar, J. S., *Recalling a Story Once Told* (Mercer University Press, 2007).

C. Hassell Bullock

Pseudepigrapha: A Brief Introduction

The OT spawned a myriad of literary activity from the time of its closing verses through the first century AD, and indeed beyond. Among these are the Dead Sea Scrolls, the OT Apocrypha, and the so-called OT Pseudepigrapha. However, these categories of literature may be somewhat misleading. For although the Dead Sea Scrolls are identified with the ancient Jewish documents discovered in eleven caves in the environs of the ancient settlement of Khirbet Qumran, some of these documents are also attested among the Apocrypha and Pseudepigrapha. Furthermore, the Apocrypha are often identified as works present in the Septuagint but not in the Hebrew Bible, whereas the texts typically identified as Pseudepigrapha, even those originating from the Second Temple period, are not attested as collections in single manuscripts, manuscript collections, or even identified with a single Jewish group from antiquity. Also unlike the Apocrypha, which are preserved in Greek and many of which stem from a Semitic original, a variety of documents designated as Pseudepigrapha are extant also, and sometimes exclusively, in Latin, Syriac, Coptic, Ethiopic, and a number of other languages. Moreover, nearly all the documents in question are preserved exclusively in Christian traditions. Finally, unlike the works of the Apocrypha, which date prior to the Bar Kokhba revolt (AD 132–35), the dates of composition for most of these pseudepigraphic documents are often debated (Gurtner, 12–16).

For so vast an assortment of literature to stem from a Jewish context but be preserved in Christian traditions means that determining whether or not any given text is Jewish or Christian, early or late, is a complicated task. Even the categories of "Jewish" or "Christian" may be more fluid than one might expect. Such texts could be associated with Jews, Jewish Christians, gentile Christians, Samaritans, gentile God-fearers, gentiles sympathetic to Judaism, and pagans with some interest in Jewish traditions (Davila). Any one of these groups, and perhaps more, could lay claim to the interests contained in these documents. So here we aim to privilege texts suited to the scope of this article—namely, texts that are (1) demonstrably Jewish both in origin and in present form, and (2) dated to the Second Temple period (i.e., not later than AD 135). While a large assortment of texts suits this profile, no texts are representative of the whole in terms of their use of the OT since the pseudepigrapha are in no sense an organic "collection." Nevertheless, like many other Jewish texts from the Second Temple period they are shaped by the OT in numerous ways and some examples can illustrate their complexities.

A final problem with the OT Pseudepigrapha is the nomenclature. The English word "pseudepigrapha" (sing. "pseudepigraphon") transliterates a Greek term that refers to "falsely attributed writing," from *pseudēs* ("false") and *epigraphē* ("inscription, superscription"). It is often used to designate works falsely attributed to, or in some way related to, prominent individuals. In the case of the OT Pseudepigrapha, the individuals in view are featured in the body of literature contained in the Hebrew Bible. Yet the category can be misleading (Reed). First, the very notion of falsehood with respect to authorship conjures up negative prejudices, which can do injustice to the documents in their respective contexts. Second, some works within this category are associated not with an esteemed figure from antiquity, but with their real authors. Third, the category of Pseudepigrapha can be taken as implying a degree of coherence among its constituent parts, which, as shown above, is not typically the case.

The complexities of the utilization of the OT within the pseudepigraphic texts of Second Temple Judaism render finding more prominent hermeneutical and interpretive features a problematic task. The approach here will be to examine some of the more important texts among the Pseudepigrapha where engagement with the OT is prominent.

Book of Watchers (1 En. 1–36) and Gen. 6

Among the apocalypses of the OT Pseudepigrapha, the largest and most important is 1 Enoch, which comprises a set of distinct apocalypses, each associated with the biblical Enoch. The earliest of these is the Book of Watchers (1 En. 1–36), which expands on the biblical account from Gen. 6 in a manner indicative of its use of the OT. The setting is one in which Enoch, father of Methuselah (Gen. 5:18–23), features prominently. The deaths of important patriarchs in the Hebrew Bible are typically described explicitly (Abraham, Gen. 25:7–10; Moses, Deut. 34:5–7), but nothing is said of Enoch save that "Enoch walked faithfully with God; then he was no more, because God took him away" (Gen. 5:24). This ambiguity, perhaps not unlike the Melchizedek traditions (cf. Gen. 14:18–20; Ps. 110:4; Heb. 7:1–17), gave rise to a considerable creative flurry about Enoch himself. The Book of Watchers is a blessing said to be pronounced by Enoch upon the elect and righteous who would be present on the day of tribulation (1 En. 1:1). The important affinity with the OT for our purposes begins in 1 En. 6, which paraphrases Gen. 6 as follows: 1 Enoch follows Genesis in the account of the multiplication of humans (Gen. 6:1; 1 En. 6:1a), mentioning not only beautiful daughters but also handsome sons (1 En. 6:1b). The ambiguous "sons of God" (*bənê-hā'ĕlōhîm*, Gen. 6:2a) are explicitly said to be "angels" and "the children of heaven" (1 En. 6:2a *OTP*). Furthermore, whereas Genesis simply recounts that these figures were attracted to the daughters and took as their wives any they chose (Gen. 6:2b), 1 Enoch expands to a considerable extent, including their dialogue among themselves (1 En. 6:2b), identification of their leader (Semyaz, 1 En. 6:3a), and an oath in which they all swear to carry out the deed of taking human wives (1 En. 6:4–5). These angels, or watchers, are two hundred in number when they descend to the summit of Mount Hermon to swear their oath (1 En. 6:6). The names of the chiefs of these angels are then recounted (1 En. 6:7–8) before the description of their taking women occurs (1 En. 7:1a). The Enoch text then bypasses the Genesis statement about the Lord's limiting of human life to 120 years (Gen. 6:3) and any explicit reference to the Nephilim (Gen. 6:4a). It seems to rejoin the Genesis account when the "sons of God" (again, *bənê-hā'ĕlōhîm*) sire children by the women (Gen. 6:4b; 1 En. 7:1a). But the watchers also teach the women magical medicine, incantations, the cutting of roots, and about plants (1 En. 7:1b). The children born to them, whom Genesis calls the "mighty men . . . of old" (*haggibōrîm . . . mē'ôlām*) and "men of renown" (*'anšê haššēm*; Gen. 6:4 ESV), become in Enoch great giants, three hundred cubits in height (1 En. 7:2b). These beasts first devour produce, then resort to eating people, then birds, wild beasts, reptiles, and fish before devouring one another and drinking blood (1 En. 7:3–5). Where in Genesis the Lord regrets making humans and plans their demise (Gen. 6:5–7), the Book of Watchers lays blame elsewhere. The earth (1 En. 7:6) and people (1 En. 8:4) cry out and are heard by the angels Michael, Surafel, and Gabriel, who in turn report it to the Most High (1 En. 9:1–11). The Most High sends the angelic figures to act in response: First, Asuryal is to warn the son of Lamech (Noah) about the coming deluge (10:1–3). Second, Raphael is to bind Azazel and imprison him until the final judgment (10:4–8). Third, Gabriel is instructed to destroy the wicked, including the giants (10:9–10). Fourth, Michael is sent by God to inform the fallen Watchers of their doom and God's intent to rid the world of their wickedness (10:11–16a). God will then restore righteousness and purity, and his people will experience prosperity (10:16b–20). All the nations will come to worship God, and the earth will be cleansed from its pollution forever (10:21–22; 11:1–2). The result is that the OT narrative becomes a starting point from which considerable speculation derives.

The Animal Apocalypse (1 En. 85–90) and Israelite History

An innovative use of the OT is found in the Animal Apocalypse (1 En. 85–90), which dates from between 164 and 160 BC (Collins, *Apocalyptic*, 67; Nickelsburg, *1 Enoch 1*, 361). Here the ancient author offers an allegorical recounting of human history from Adam into the Hellenistic time, after which occurs the final judgment and the establishment of a newly created order (Nickelsburg, *1 Enoch 1*, 354). Much of this recasts the OT narrative in highly symbolic and condensed form.

It begins with a symbolic depiction of Adam and Eve and their children (1 En. 85:3–10; cf. Gen. 2–5), where Adam is depicted as a white bull, Eve as a young heifer, and Cain and Abel as black and red bull calves, respectively. The black calf strikes the red (85:4), grows, and has offspring like himself (85:5). The female grieves the absence of the red calf (85:6–7) and bears another white bull (Seth) and many more black bulls and cows (85:8). That white bull grows and fathers other white cattle like himself (85:9–10).

The next segment (1 En. 86:1–88:3) provides a symbolic account of the fall of the Watchers (cf. Gen. 6:1–4), largely following the narrative found in the Book of Watchers (1 En. 6–11). The fallen stars mentioned here are the fallen angels that become bulls, pasture among humans (depicted as cattle), sire destructive beasts (giants, 86:4; cf. 7:2–5), and fall under judgment by seven figures like white men (angels; 87:2–88:3).

The account of Noah and the flood is the subject of the next symbolic account (1 En. 89:1–8; Gen. 6:8–8:18), where a white man (angel) teaches a white bull (Noah) a mystery: he is born a bull but will become a man (89:1a). Noah builds a vessel for himself and three other bulls (his sons; 89:1b) before the great deluge overtakes the earth (89:2–5). The vessel floats safely while the bulls, elephants, camels, and donkeys perish (89:6), after which the waters recede, the vessel comes to rest, and darkness gives way to light (89:7–8).

The white bull departs from the vessel along with three other bulls (Shem, Ham, and Japheth; 1 En. 89:9–27; Gen. 8:18–21:3). From them descend other white bulls (Abraham and Isaac), then a white sheep (Jacob) who sires twelve sheep (the twelve tribes of Israel; 1 En. 89:10–12). These twelve hand over one of their own (Joseph) to wild donkeys (Ishmaelites), who in turn hand him over to wolves (Egyptians; 1 En. 89:13). That sheep becomes a ram and cares for the other eleven among the wolves (89:14; Gen. 37:2–50:26). When the wolves oppress the sheep, the Lord summons one of the sheep (Moses) to testify against the wolves (1 En. 89:15–17; Exod. 1–4). But that sheep (Moses), accompanied by another sheep (Aaron), is ignored by the wolves (1 En. 89:18–20; Exod. 5–11) and so leads the sheep to a swamp, which splits before them but devours the pursuing wolves (1 En. 89:21–27; Exod. 12–14). The sheep enter a desert and are cared for by the Lord (1 En. 89:28–31) but nevertheless are blinded by the Lord and go astray (89:32). The Lord's anger burns against them, but the lead sheep returns all the straying flock to their fold (89:33–35). The lead sheep builds a house for the Lord (89:36) and leads them to a river before all the large sheep (Moses and his generation) fall asleep (89:36–38; Exod. 15–Deut. 34).

After the departure of Moses, two sheep (Joshua and Caleb) arise to lead the flock to a pleasant land (1 En. 89:39–41). There the flock is devoured by wild animals until the Lord raises up a ram from among the sheep to lead them (King Saul; 89:42) and defeat those who harm the flock (89:43) until he himself is led astray (89:44; 1 Sam. 9–15). The Lord appoints another sheep to be the ram and rule the flock, but the first ram pursues the second ram until the former falls before the dogs (89:45–47). The second ram (David) leads the sheep (89:48), who have become numerous and feared among animals (89:49; 1 Sam. 16–2 Sam. 24). The ram sires other sheep and then falls asleep. One of the sheep becomes a ram and rules the sheep (Solomon; 1 En. 89:48b) and builds a house (the temple) for the Lord of the sheep (89:50; 1 Kings 1–10).

The sheep abandon the house of the Lord and go astray, so they fall into the hands of wild beasts (89:51–58; around the time of Manasseh; 1 Kings 11–2 Kings 20). The Lord then appoints seventy shepherds (guardian angels) to pasture the sheep and keep record of their deeds (1 En. 89:59–64; cf. 90:5; Deut. 32; Dan. 10; Jer. 25), each in their own period of time (roughly the Babylonian, Persian, Ptolemaic, and Seleucid eras; Collins, *Apocalyptic*, 69). The first account of the disobedient shepherds (1 En. 89:65–68a) runs from Manasseh (ca. 671/ 661 BC; 2 Kings 21) to the destruction of Jerusalem by Nebuchadnezzar and exile to Babylon (587/577 BC; 2 Chron 10–36). These shepherds abandon the sheep to lions (1 En. 89:65), who, along with leopards and boars, devour and destroy them (89:66–67; cf. 2 Kings 25:1–20; 2 Chron 36:17–20). This is followed by the writing of a report of these events (1 En. 89:68b–72a).

The second period of the shepherds' activities (1 En. 89:72b–90:1) covers from the return from exile and rebuilding the temple to Alexander the Great. Led by three sheep (Zerubbabel, Jeshua [Ezra 5:2; 1 Esd. 6:2], and likely Sheshbazzar [Ezra 1:8–10; 5:14–16; 1 Esd. 2:12–15; 6:18–20]; Nickelsburg, *1 Enoch 1*, 394), exiles return and commence rebuilding the temple (89:72b). The temple is rebuilt, but its sacrifices are polluted (89:73), both the sheep and their shepherds are blind (89:74a; cf. Mal. 1:7–8, 12; CD 4.17–5.19), and the sheep are scattered (89:75; cf. Ezek. 34:12). Though this ends the biblical narrative, it by no means concludes the story line of the Animal Apocalypse, which proceeds with the conquests of the Macedonians and the wars of the Diadochi (1 En. 90:2–5), the Seleucid era after 198 BC (90:6–19; cf. 1 Macc. 2:42–48; 7:13; 2 Macc. 11:6–12; 14:6), and a season of eschatological renewal (1 En. 90:28–42; cf. 2 Bar. 4:2–7; Dan. 7:14, 27).

Book of Jubilees and the "Rewriting" of Scripture

Another work that recasts OT accounts into different forms is Jubilees. This book, which dates between the 170s and 125 BC (VanderKam, *Jubilees* [2018], 1:37–38), is largely a retelling of Genesis and early parts of Exodus (chaps. 1–24). It is typically regarded as a classic example of "rewritten Scripture" in its recasting of the biblical narrative. However, it also answers many questions about those accounts, such as how humanity developed if Adam and Eve had only sons, when God chose Israel, where Abraham was when first spoken to by God, and why Levi was chosen for the priesthood in Israel. All of this is couched in an exhortation to the author's strict interpretation of the Law (Kugel, 272). The narrative generally follows the biblical order, sometimes reproducing the text verbatim, at other times omitting segments (e.g., Gen. 12:11–15a, 18–19a at Jub. 13:12; Gen. 13:5–10 at Jub. 13:17; Gen. 20 at Jub. 16:10; Nickelsburg, "Rewritten," 97), condensing stories (e.g., the plagues on Pharaoh, Exod. 7–10 = Jub. 48:4–11; Wintermute, "Jubilees," 2:35), explaining (e.g., Reuben's apparent incest, Gen. 35:22 = Jub. 33:2–20; Wintermute, 2:35), supplementing (e.g., tales of Abraham's youth, Jub. 12:1–8, 12–14, 16–21, 25–27; Wintermute, 2:35), or entirely recasting biblical episodes (e.g., Isaac's covenant with Abimelech, Gen. 26:23–33 = Jub. 24:21–33; Wintermute,

2:35), but typically recasting the narrative or making additions to it in line with the author's own interests (Nickelsburg, "Rewritten," 97n35). Its most distinctive characteristic is its chronological framework, including numbered months, 364-day years, seven-year periods ("weeks of years"), and units of seven seven-year periods (forty-nine years) called "Jubilees." The book traces biblical history from creation until the entry into the promised land as fifty Jubilees (2,450 years; VanderKam, *Jubilees* [2018], 1). Jubilees is a massive document, taking up nearly fifty-five thousand words in English translation (*OTP*). By way of comparison, the biblical text upon which it is based uses approximately forty-nine thousand words in English translation (NIV).

In its title Jubilees describes itself as an account of the division of days as the Lord gave Moses on Sinai. The first chapter sets the scene for the entire book. The narrative begins in the first year of the exodus from Egypt, when Moses is summoned up Mount Sinai, where he stays forty days and nights (Jub. 1:1–4a). There the Lord reveals to Moses the past and the future, the account of the division of all days "of the Law and the testimony" (1:4b). Moses is instructed to write what God dictates as witness to Moses's descendants that God has not abandoned them (1:5–6). First, Moses is told that Israel will enter the promised land but nonetheless turn to foreign gods and abandon the commandments of God (1:7–11). Then God will send witnesses whom Israel will reject and murder and so be cast into captivity where they will be removed from the land and forget God's ordinances (1:12–14). God then promises that when Israel repents, they will be restored and their sanctuary rebuilt (1:15–18). Moses prays that Israel will not be ensnared by their sin and pleads for God's mercy (1:19–21), and the Lord predicts their restoration (1:22–25). God tells Moses to write all that he will be told on the mountain from beginning to end (1:26) and tells the angel to write, or perhaps "dictate" (Kugel, 288), the history for Moses (1:27–28). This angel, which accompanied Israel from Egypt (cf. Exod. 14:19), takes the tablets, which tell of the divisions of years from the time of creation to the time of new creation (Jub. 1:29; cf. Isa. 65:17; 66:22).

It is the author's task of "rewriting" biblical accounts that has most intrigued scholars. In general, the author's interpretive methodology is unlike other methods, such as midrash or pesher, in that he does not set off the biblical text as distinct from his own contributions but rather melds the two into a new text entirely, all placed within the new setting of Moses at Sinai (Jub. 1). And so, the angel of the Presence, commanded by God, dictates the narrative to Moses in place of the anonymous narrator of Genesis (Segal, 21–23) and sets the whole within an explicit chronology. The modifications are generally additions and omissions, some of which function as what VanderKam calls enhancements and "defamation of characters" (*Jubilees* [2018], 1:23).

Additions take a number of forms, such as the clarification that the sin introduced by the fallen angels was so heinous as to justify the extent of God's judgment in the flood (Jub. 5:1–19). And even after the flood the offspring of the fallen angels continue to lead humanity into sin (10:1–13). The account of land allocated to Noah's descendants provides a basis for Israel's territorial claims (8:8–9:15; 10:28–34). After recounting the Genesis narrative of Abram's origins (11:27–32), Jubilees explains that he merited the ensuing favor with God (Gen. 12:1–3) by furnishing accounts of his youth in which he exhibits hostility toward idolatry while embracing monotheism (Jub. 11:15–12:21). Also, though Abraham and Jacob are contemporaries in Genesis, they never meet. Jubilees, however, depicts Abraham's recognition of Jacob as his promised heir, whom he blesses and instructs (19:16–29; 22:10–30). The author attempts to improve Levi's negative reputation in Genesis (Gen. 34; 49:5–7). His vengeance upon Shechem is seen as a righteous act (Jub. 30:17–20). He is blessed by Isaac (31:13–17) and learns by a dream of his appointment to the priesthood (32:1), for which he is anointed by Jacob (32:2–9). Jubilees also inserts an account of a war between Egypt and Canaan to explain why Joseph's bones remained in Egypt until after the exodus (46:4–11; cf. Gen. 50:24–26; Exod. 13:19; Josh. 24:32; VanderKam, *Jubilees* [2018], 1:22–23). Jubilees adds a number of speeches not found in the Hebrew Bible, such as the dialogue between Moses and God (Jub. 1), the legal topics explained by the angel (2:17–33; 5:13–19; 6:10–38; 15:25–34; 16:28–31; 23:8–31; 30:5–23; 32:10–15; 33:9–20; 41:23–28; 49:7–23; 50:6–13), and speeches or "testaments" from parents to their progeny (7:20–39; 20:1–22:30; 25; 35; 36; VanderKam, *Jubilees* [2018], 1:23). Still other additions pertain to characterization, both positively and negatively. Jacob, for instance, is an obedient and respectful son (Jub. 25; 29:15–20; 35–36), whereas Esau breaks his pledge to his parents and wages war against Jacob (37:1–38:14; VanderKam, *Jubilees* [2018], 1:23–24; see more extensively VanderKam, *Jubilees* [2001], 109–14).

It is worth considering why the author would introduce more laws into his narrative than one finds in Genesis and Exodus. In part the author may be intending to enumerate and identify the laws and commands that Abraham is said to have obeyed (Gen. 26:5). Secondly, Jubilees may try to resolve problems created by punishments indicated in Genesis for violating laws that were not yet revealed (VanderKam, *Jubilees* [2018], 1:79–80). Finally, the ascription of additional laws in the narratives and attributing them to the heavenly tablets establishes the eternality of the torah. Its statutes did not simply originate with Moses; rather, Moses was recording something that was established long beforehand (VanderKam, *Jubilees* [2018], 1:80). Presumably, Jubilees's omissions do not suit his purposes or perhaps conflict with them. These include the expulsion of Hagar (Gen. 16:6–14), two accounts of Abimelech (Gen.

20; 21:22–34), and the reductions of the lengthy search for a wife for Isaac (Gen. 24) and the preparations for Esau and Jacob to meet (32:1–33:17), each of which are reduced to a single verse (Jub. 19:10; 29:13; VanderKam, *Jubilees* [2018], 1:23). Also omitted are negative portrayals of people whom the author prefers to cast in a positive light, such as Abraham (Gen. 12:13, 19) and Jacob (27:19).

Beyond the obvious use of Gen. 1–Exod. 24, Jubilees exhibits familiarity with and usage of other portions of the Hebrew Bible. Teaching on the Sabbath (Jub. 2:17, 25) is drawn from features elsewhere in Exodus (Exod. 31:12–17), whereas Leviticus is particularly important for regulations used throughout Jubilees pertaining to sacrifices (Lev. 1–7), festivals (Lev. 16; 23), and sexual relations (Lev. 18; 20). Material regarding dates and offerings pertaining to festivals (Num. 9:1–14; cf. Jub. 49) is utilized in Jubilees, as is the priestly blessing (Num. 6:24–26; cf. Jub. 31:15). Deuteronomy serves as a sort of model for Jubilees, which draws from it in statements about the residing presence of God (Deut. 7:1–6; cf. Jub. 49:21) and regulations about tithes (Deut. 14:22–27; cf. Jub. 32:10–15; VanderKam, *Jubilees* [2018], 1:85).

Joseph and Aseneth and the Problems of Idolatry

Joseph and Aseneth, composed in a Jewish community in Egypt between 100 BC and AD 117/135, is a fanciful tale of the patriarch Joseph and his Egyptian wife Aseneth, daughter of Potiphera, priest of On (Gen. 41:45). She gives birth to two sons, Ephraim and Manasseh (Gen. 41:50; 46:20), but the biblical account says nothing else. Joseph and Aseneth expands on this material to create a narrative that describes Aseneth prior to her marriage to Joseph, how they met, and their subsequent marriage (Standhartinger, 353–54). How Joseph, an esteemed Jew, could marry the daughter of a gentile idolatrous priest, a notion strictly forbidden in Scripture (Gen. 24:3–4, 37–38; 27:46; 28:1; cf. Jub. 20:4; 22:20; 30:7–16), is a matter Joseph and Aseneth seeks to address. The answer lies in Aseneth's repentance, which is displayed in her rejection of idols and her prayer to God, and is recognized by an angelic visitor who declares her converted. With Pharaoh himself officiating, she marries Joseph who reigns in Egypt forty-eight years (*OTP*, 2:177).

Biblical Figures

Among the uses of the OT in the OT Pseudepigrapha, it is evident that key individuals from the Hebrew Bible are utilized in various ways in the literature. Here a few will be discussed. Clearly *Moses* has appeared as a pivotal figure throughout Second Temple Judaism, including the Pseudepigrapha (Tuval). In Jubilees he appears at Mount Sinai receiving additional instructions by revelation not found in the biblical Torah (Jub. 1:1–4). In the Animal Apocalypse he appears first as a "sheep" (Israelite) who is transformed into a "man" (angelic figure) upon his reception of the law at Sinai. Elsewhere in the Pseudepigrapha Moses is said to have been born circumcised (LAB 9:13). He is said to have been prevented from entering the promised land because he did not want to see the graven images that would lead Israel astray (LAB 19:7). Before his death Moses is given a vision of glorious things (LAB 19:10; cf. 2 Bar. 59:2–11), and after his death the angels cease their singing and he is buried by God himself (LAB 19:16). Moses is important in 2 Baruch, written after the destruction of the temple (AD 70) because Israel was then left only with God himself and the law given by Moses (2 Bar. 85:3).

Similarly, *Abraham* is revered among the OT Pseudepigrapha (van Ruiten, "Abraham"). He is said to be the first to believe in the one true God of Israel (Jub. 11:16–17; 12:2, 6–7; LAB 23:5). From his youth Abraham was exposed to idols, which to him are a mere illusion (Jub. 11:16; 12:1–3, 6–7; Apoc. Ab. 1:3). Ambiguities in the story of Abraham and Sarah in Egypt (Gen. 12:10–20) are resolved in Abraham's favor in the Pseudepigrapha. The deceit of claiming her as his sister is removed entirely (Jub. 13:10–16). Strikingly, Abraham is obedient not only to instructions from God such as circumcision (Gen. 17; cf. Jub. 15:23–24) but also to the law, which had not yet been given at Sinai, such as abstaining from idolatry (Jub. 12:2–5, 17–20) and observing the festivals (15:20–31). Furthermore, prior to his death he instructs Isaac regarding cultic practices (Jub. 20). He is regarded as the "plant of righteousness" from whom all the chosen ones of the righteous descend (1 En. 93:5).

A figure who receives considerable attention is *Enoch*, who appears in the OT as the seventh from Adam (Gen. 5:18–19, 21–24; cf. 1 Chron. 1:3; Stokes). The cryptic statement that Enoch "walked faithfully with God; then he was no more, because God took him" (Gen. 5:24) seems to have given rise to some extraordinary speculation in the Pseudepigrapha. Sometimes he is regarded as a scribe (1 En. 12:3–4; 15:1; cf. 72:1; 83:2; Jub. 4:17–19, 23). The ambiguity of the Genesis accounts gave rise to a tradition that Enoch did not die but, as a righteous person, ascended into heaven, received revelations from God (1 En. 12:1; 71:1–4, 5–16; 87:3–4; Jub. 4:23), and even was, in some sense, divinized (1 En. 12:1–4; 71–72).

Conclusion

Despite the problems posed by analyzing the use of the OT within the pseudepigraphic texts of Second Temple Judaism, we are able to survey some of the more prominent. In the Book of Watchers (1 En. 1–36), the narrative of Gen. 6 is the starting point from which considerable speculation derives. The Animal Apocalypse (1 En. 85–90) recasts much of the OT narrative in highly symbolic and condensed form. The author of Jubilees engages in the task of "rewriting" Scripture but not with any sense of replacing or denigrating it. Instead, his select modifications clarify and emphasize aspects of the biblical text to suit his own purpose of depicting his understanding of God's ordering of time according to units of "Jubilees." The difficulty of the patriarch Joseph's marriage to an Egyptian is addressed in Joseph and Aseneth, which expands considerably upon the biblical narrative to depict Aseneth's repentance, rejection of idols, and conversion to the God of Israel. A number of figures from the OT, such as Moses, Abraham, Enoch, and others, are pressed into new literary arenas in Second Temple literature. All this demonstrates that while the material defies simple classification according to OT usage, the OT nonetheless maintains a considerable influence on the proliferation of literary developments in Second Temple Judaism.

See also OT Use of the OT: Comparison with the NT Use of the OT; *other Pseudepigrapha articles; Dead Sea Scrolls articles; Mishnah, Talmud, and Midrashim articles; Philo articles; Septuagint articles; Targums articles*

Bibliography. Alexander, P. S., "From Son of Adam to Second God," in Stone and Bergren, *Biblical Figures*, 87–122; Chesnutt, R. D., *From Death to Life*, JSPSup 16 (Sheffield Academic, 1995); Clarke, K. D., "The Problem of Pseudonymity in Biblical Literature and Its Implications for Canon Formation," in *The Canon Debate*, ed. L. M. McDonald and J. A. Sanders (Hendrickson, 2002), 440–68; Collins, J. J., *The Apocalyptic Imagination*, 3rd ed. (Eerdmans, 2016); Collins, "Apocrypha and Pseudepigrapha," in *EDSS*, 1:35–39; Collins, "Testaments," in *Jewish Literature of the Second Temple Period*, ed. M. E. Stone (Fortress, 1984), 325–56; Davila, J. R., *The Provenance of the Pseudepigrapha*, JSJSup 105 (Brill, 2005); DiTommaso, L., "Pseudepigrapha Research and Christian Origins after the OTP," in *The Pseudepigrapha and Christian Origins*, ed. G. S. Oegema and J. H. Charlesworth (T&T Clark, 2008), 30–47; Donaldson, T. L., *Judaism and the Gentiles* (Baylor University Press, 2007); Endres, J. C., *Biblical Interpretation in the Book of Jubilees*, CBQMS 18 (Catholic Biblical Association of America, 1987); Falk, D. K., *The Parabiblical Texts*, LSTS 63 (T&T Clark, 2007); Fisk, B. N., *Do You Not Remember?*, JSPSup 37 (Sheffield Academic, 2001); Gruen, E. S., *Heritage and Hellenism* (University of California Press, 1998); Gurtner, D. M., *Introducing the Pseudepigrapha of Second Temple Judaism* (Baker, 2020); Gurtner, D. M., and L. T. Stuckenbruck, eds., *The T&T Clark Encyclopedia of Second Temple Judaism* (T&T Clark, 2020); Hillel, V., "Testaments," in *ESTJ*, 2:766–68; Jacobson, H., "Biblical Quotation and Editorial Function in Pseudo-Philo's Liber Antiquitatum Biblicarum," *JSP* 5 (1989): 47–64; Kolenkow, A. B., "The Literary Genre 'Testament,'" in *Early Judaism and Its Modern Interpreters*, ed. R. A. Kraft and G. W. E. Nickelsburg (Scholars Press, 1986), 259–67; Kugel, J. L., "Book of Jubilees," in *Outside the Bible*, ed. L. H. Feldman, J. L. Kugel, and L. H. Schiffman, 3 vols. (University of Nebraska Press, 2013), 272–465; Lierman, J., *The New Testament Moses*, WUNT 2/173 (Mohr Siebeck, 2004); Murphy, F. J., *Pseudo-Philo* (Oxford University Press, 1993); Murphy, "Retelling the Bible," *JBL* 107, no. 2 (1988): 275–87; Najman, H., *Seconding Sinai*, JSJSup 77 (Brill, 2003); Newman, J. H., *Praying by the Book*, EJL 14 (Scholars Press, 1999); Nickelsburg, G. W. E., "Abraham the Convert," in Stone and Bergren, *Biblical Figures*, 151–75; Nickelsburg, "The Bible Rewritten and Expanded," in *Jewish Writings of the Second Temple Period*, ed. M. E. Stone, CRINT 2/2 (Fortress, 1984), 89–156; Nickelsburg, *1 Enoch 1*, Herm (Fortress, 2001); Nickelsburg, *Jewish Literature between the Bible and the Mishnah*, 2nd ed. (Fortress, 2005); Nickelsburg, G. W. E., and J. C. VanderKam, *1 Enoch 2*, Herm (Fortress, 2012); Reed, A. Y., "The Modern Invention of 'Old Testament Pseudepigrapha,'" *JTS* 60, no. 2 (2009): 403–36; Segal, M., "Between Bible and Rewritten Bible," in *Biblical Interpretation at Qumran*, ed. M. Henze, SDSSRL (Eerdmans, 2005), 10–29; Stackert, J., *Rewriting the Torah*, FAT 52 (Mohr Siebeck, 2007); Standhartinger, A., "Recent Scholarship on *Joseph and Aseneth*," *CBR* 12, no. 3 (2014): 353–406; Stokes, R. E., "Enoch," in *ESTJ*, 2:239–42; Stone, M. E., and T. A. Bergen, eds., *Biblical Figures outside the Bible* (Trinity Press International, 1998); Stuckenbruck, L. T., "Apocrypha and Pseudepigrapha," in *EDEJ*, 143–62; Stuckenbruck, *The Myth of the Rebellious Angels* (Eerdmans, 2017); Tuval, M., "Moses," in *ESTJ*, 2:517–20; van Ruiten, J. T. A. G. M., "Abraham," in *ESTJ*, 2:4–6; van Ruiten, *Abraham in the Book of Jubilees*, JSJSup 161 (Brill, 2012); VanderKam, J. C., *The Book of Jubilees*, GAP (Sheffield Academic, 2001); VanderKam, *Jubilees*, 2 vols., Herm (Fortress, 2018); Wintermute, O. S., "Jubilees," in *OTP*, 2:35–142.

DANIEL M. GURTNER

Pseudepigrapha: Comparison with the NT Use of the OT

Comparing the use of OT texts in the NT with their use in the OT Pseudepigrapha is a worthwhile endeavor. The texts of the Pseudepigrapha furnish the student of the NT with a diverse array of literary material that, like the NT, is deeply indebted to the Hebrew Bible. Seeing how the authors of these extracanonical writings interpreted and utilized the very same text referenced in the NT can go a long way to grasping important facets about the Judaic contexts in which Christianity emerged and spread. Yet the task of comparing how the NT and Pseudepigrapha interpret the same OT text faces a number of problems.

First, whereas numerous studies have been undertaken to account for OT citation in the NT, and accounts charting this material are widely available even in a good study Bible, the same cannot be said for the Pseudepigrapha. Specific studies have been published on facets of OT texts in various pseudepigraphical books, like Jubilees or portions of the Book of Watchers (1 En. 1–36). But the OT Pseudepigrapha is not itself a coherent collection in any sense like the early Christian writings enshrined in the NT. This means that a complete analysis of the use of the OT in the Pseudepigrapha would be problematic. And scholars specializing in the Pseudepigrapha would be reticent to present such an analysis since it might suggest a degree of coherence that does not exist.

Second, reference tools that indicate where OT texts are cited in the Pseudepigrapha are unsystematic and sometimes unreliable. Steve Delamarter's *Scripture Index* cites marginal notations in the Charlesworth *Old Testament Pseudepigrapha* volumes, as well as those found in footnotes. Yet many of the works in the Charlesworth volumes do not belong properly to Second Temple Judaism but are in fact later Christian works. Also, there is no indication of any uniform methodology by the contributors in the Charlesworth volumes, so readers have little indication from the mere use of the *Scripture Index* whether there is a citation, allusion, or something else. Similarly, Armin Lange and Matthias Weigold's *Biblical Quotations and Allusions in Second Temple Jewish Literature* purports to indicate, as its title suggests, quotations and allusions and expands the corpus to all Second Temple literature, including not only the Pseudepigrapha but also the Apocrypha and the Dead Sea Scrolls. But here also the methodology of determining what constitutes a citation or allusion is by no means evident, nor is the volume without its inconsistencies. Finally, both resources cite OT texts that may do no more than cite similar ideas without an actual citation or allusion.

A third problem with comparing the use of the OT in the Pseudepigrapha and the NT comes from the differences of focus. For instance, though Ps. 110:1 is frequently cited in the NT (Matt. 22:44; Mark 12:36; Luke 20:42–43; Acts 2:34–35; 1 Cor. 15:25; Heb. 1:13), it is not listed among the citations in either of the two Pseudepigrapha reference works. Conversely, there are many texts cited in a variety of Pseudepigrapha that are not referenced in the NT at all.

Despite this impasse there is a way forward that begins with careful use of the indices mentioned above and laboriously turning through pages of text to ensure that the purported allusion or citation is warranted. This allows us to chronicle all the citations of OT texts that these two tools cite and that overlap with known OT citations in the NT. This yields a sizable list, but only some of these are actual citations or clear allusions. So, care must be taken to identify clear conceptual and/or linguistic points of correspondence between the Jewish text and its OT source. Here, too, a number of similarities are found, as table 1 illustrates. Though far from comprehensive, it represents a cross section of OT texts that the Pseudepigrapha and NT share in common.

Table 1. OT Texts Cited in the NT and in the Pseudepigrapha

OT Text	Citation in NT	Citation in Pseudepigrapha
Genesis		
2:7	1 Cor. 15:45	Sib. Or. 1:285
14:17–20	Heb. 7:1	Jub. 22:11; 25:11
15:5	Rom. 4:18	LAB 18:5; Jub. 14:5; Apoc. Ab. 20:5
15:13–14	Acts 7:6	LAB 9:3; 15:5; Jub. 48:8; Apoc. Ab. 21:1–4; 32:2, 4
22:17	Heb. 6:14	LAB 14:2; 18:5; 32:4; T. Mos. 3:9
25:23	Rom. 9:12	LAB 32:5
26:4	Acts 3:25	LAB 14:2; Jub. 24:8–9
28:12	John 1:51	Jub. 27:19–20
Exodus		
1:8	Acts 7:18	Sib. Or. 11:308; LAB 10:1
3:5	Acts 7:33	LAB 19:9
3:7–10	Acts 7:34	LAB 15:4
19:5–6	1 Pet. 2:9	Jub. 16:18
20:11	Acts 4:24; 14:15	LAB 11:8
20:12	Matt. 15:4; Mark 7:10; Eph. 6:2	LAB 11:9; 44:6–7; Jub. 7:20; Ps.-Phoc. 6–8, 179–80; Let. Aris. 228
20:14	Matt. 5:27; James 2:11	LAB 11:10; Ps.-Phoc. 3
20:17	Rom. 7:7	LAB 11:13; Ps.-Phoc. 6–7
24:8	Heb. 9:20	Jub. 6:11
25:40	Heb. 8:5	2 Bar. 4:2
32:1	Acts 7:40	LAB 12:2
34:34	2 Cor. 3:16	LAB 12:1
Leviticus		
18:5	Rom. 10:5; Gal. 3:12	Pss. Sol. 14:2–3; LAB 23:10
19:12	Matt. 5:33	Ps.-Phoc. 16–17
19:18	Matt. 5:43; 19:19; 22:39; Mark 12:31, 33; Luke 10:27; Rom. 12:19; 13:9; Gal. 5:14; James 2:8	Jub. 7:20; Let. Aris. 228
26:12	2 Cor. 6:16	Jub. 1:17
Deuteronomy		
4:35	Mark 12:32	Sib. Or. 3:760
5:16	Matt. 15:4; Mark 7:10; Eph. 6:2	Ps.-Phoc. 6–8, 179–80; Jub. 7:20; Let. Aris. 228
5:16–20	Matt. 19:18; Mark 10:19; Luke 18:20	Ps.-Phoc. 3–6, 12–13
5:17	Matt. 5:21; James 2:11	Ps.-Phoc. 4
5:18	James 2:11	Ps.-Phoc. 3
5:21	Rom. 7:7	Ps.-Phoc. 6–8
6:4	Mark 12:29, 32	LAB 23:2
17:7	1 Cor. 5:13	Pss. Sol. 4:3
29:17 (ET 29:18)	Heb. 12:15	LAB 25:3, 5
31:6	Heb. 13:5	Jub. 1:18
32:43	Rom. 15:10; Heb. 1:6	Sib. Or. 3:313
2 Samuel		
7:8	2 Cor. 6:18	Pss. Sol. 17:4

OT Text	Citation in NT	Citation in Pseudepigrapha
Psalms		
2:9	Rev. 2:27; 19:15	Pss. Sol. 17:23–24
14:1–3	Rom. 3:10–12	4 Ezra 8:58; Pss. Sol. 17:15
35:19	John 15:25	Pss. Sol. 7:1
44:23 (ET 44:22)	Rom. 8:36	4 Ezra 15:10
78:24	John 6:31	LAB 10:7
104:4	Heb. 1:7	Jub. 2:2
Proverbs		
25:21	Rom. 12:20	T. Job 7:11
Isaiah		
6:3	Rev. 4:8	4 Bar. 9:3; 1 En. 39:12
6:9 (LXX)	Matt. 13:14; Mark 4:12; Acts 28:26	Sib. Or. 1:360–61
26:19	Matt. 11:5; Luke 7:22	2 Bar. 29:8
40:3	Matt. 3:3; Mark 1:3; John 1:23	Pss. Sol. 8:17
40:3–5	Luke 3:4–6	Pss. Sol. 11:4; Sib. Or. 3:680
52:7	Rom. 10:15	Pss. Sol. 11:1
52:11	2 Cor. 6:17	Jub. 22:16
53:12	Luke 22:37; 1 Pet. 2:24	Pss. Sol. 16:2
54:1	Gal. 4:27	Pss. Sol. 1:3
65:17	2 Pet. 3:13	Jub. 1:29
66:1–2	Acts 7:49–50	Sib. Or. 1:139; 4:8
66:22	2 Pet. 3:13	Jub. 1:29
Ezekiel		
5:11	Rom. 14:11	Pss. Sol. 2:3
37:5	Rev. 11:11	Sib. Or. 2:221–24; 4:181
37:10	Rev. 11:11	Sib. Or. 4:181; 2:224
Daniel		
7:13	Matt. 24:30; 26:64; Mark 13:26; 14:62; Luke 21:27; Rev. 1:7	Sib. Or. 5:256
Hosea		
6:6	Matt. 9:13; 12:7	Sib. Or. 2:82
Joel		
3:1–5 (ET 2:28–32)	Acts 2:17–21	Sib. Or. 3:293
Micah		
7:6	Matt. 10:35–36; Luke 12:53	3 Bar. 4:17
Malachi		
1:2	Rom. 9:13	LAB 32:5

Genesis 15:5 in Rom. 4:18 and OT Pseudepigrapha

In Gen. 12 God calls Abram to leave for a land that the Lord will show him (12:1–6). Furthermore, the land of Canaan was promised to his offspring (12:7; 13:14–15, 17). When God appears in a vision, Abram, presumably recalling God's promises, raises the concern that despite God's repeated promises that his offspring will inherit land, he remains childless (15:1–3). The Lord then promises that Abram's "very own son" will be his heir (15:4 ESV). Then the Lord takes Abram outside and instructs him to look at the innumerable stars in the sky, promising, "So shall your offspring be" (15:5). The promise of numerous descendants is often repeated in Genesis, sometimes in comparison to stars (22:17; 26:4), or sand of the seashore (22:17; 32:12), or the dust of the earth (13:16; 28:14; Hamilton, 423). The striking aspect of this account is that, despite all outward appearances—a point about which Paul will make much—Abram simply takes God's word for it: "Abram believed the LORD, and he credited it to him as righteousness" (15:6).

Genesis 15:5 in Rom. 4:18. Genesis 15:5 is taken up by Paul in Rom. 4, where he explains that the blessings of justification are not only for the circumcised but also for the uncircumcised (Rom. 4:1–8). He uses the example of Abraham, to whom faith was counted as righteousness before he was circumcised (Rom. 4:9–11a). "So then," Paul insists, "he is the father of all who believe but have not been circumcised, in order that righteousness might be credited to them" (Rom. 4:11b). And so, Abraham becomes the father of all who walk in the footsteps of his faith, fulfilling the promise that God would make him the father of many nations (Rom. 4:12–17). This faith is demonstrated in his belief, against hope, that he would be the father of many nations, according to the promise of Gen. 15:5: "So shall your offspring be" (Rom. 4:18–25). Genesis goes on to assert that Abraham "believed the LORD, and he credited it to him as righteousness" (15:6), whereas Paul expands to illustrate that faith demonstrated in Abraham's later life: though his body was as good as dead at about a hundred years old and his wife barren, "he did not waver through unbelief" and remained "fully persuaded that God had power to do what he had promised" (Rom. 4:20–21). That is why, Paul insists, Abraham's faith was "credited to him as righteousness" (v. 22). For Paul, then, the promise of Gen. 15:5 is the very promise in which Abraham believed and so was justified. This startling assertion binds vv. 5 and 6 from Gen. 15 into a single unit that, as we will see, has almost no bearing on the use of this passage in the OT Pseudepigrapha, which make much of the promise but are silent on the accrediting of righteousness.

Genesis 15:5 in the Pseudepigrapha. The same text from Gen. 15:5 is also clearly cited in the OT Pseudepigrapha (e.g., LAB 18:5; Jub. 14:5; Apoc. Ab. 20:5). One citation occurs in the Book of Biblical Antiquities, transmitted erroneously in the name of Philo of Alexandria, hence attributed to Pseudo-Philo, and it dates between 50 BC and AD 150 (Gurtner, 259–60). It is often known by its Latin title, *Liber antiquitatum biblicarum*, abbreviated LAB. This work recasts biblical narratives from the time of Adam to King David, sometimes summarizing briefly or completely omitting, while at other times quoting specifically or paraphrasing. In still other instances the author inserts material, such as prayers, speeches, or narrative sections, not found in the Hebrew

Bible (Nickelsburg, 265–66), interweaving biblical accounts with legendary expansions of these accounts (see comments by Harrington in *OTP* 2:297). As such it is naturally replete with citations from the OT. For the present purposes, the citation of Gen. 15:5 appears in LAB 18:5, a section that does not draw primarily from Genesis (see table 2).

Table 2. OT Narratives in LAB

LAB 1–8	Genesis
LAB 9–12	Exod. 1–34
LAB 13	Exod. 35–40; Leviticus
LAB 14–18	Numbers
LAB 19	Deuteronomy
LAB 20–24	Joshua
LAB 25–48	Judges
LAB 49–65	1 Samuel; 2 Sam. 1

The context of the reference recounts Moses's defeat of the kings of the Amorites, while Balak rules as king in Moab and summons Balaam, an interpreter of dreams, to curse Israel for him, though the reader is told this is the plan of God (LAB 18:1–3; cf. Num. 21). Then God speaks not to Abraham but to Balaam at night and warns him against cursing those whom God has chosen (LAB 18:4–6). God explains that it was of these people, Israel, that he spoke to Abraham, saying, "Your seed will be like the stars of the heaven." At that time, God says that he "lifted [Abraham] above the firmament and showed him the arrangement of all the stars" (LAB 18:5 *OTP*). Though the wording is not precisely that of Gen. 15:5, it is clearly to this verse that the author refers. Yet, unlike Paul, who uses the verse to support his notion that Abraham's offspring will, by faith in Christ, include innumerable Jews *and* gentiles, Pseudo-Philo uses the verse as the grounds for protecting Israel from harm. Moreover, nothing is said in LAB 18 about the profound faith of Abraham, by which he is declared righteous by God, so central to Paul.

The promise to Abraham in Gen. 15:5 also appears in Jubilees, which is largely a retelling of Genesis and early parts of Exodus (chaps. 1–24) that dates sometime between the 170s and 125 BC (VanderKam, 1:37–38). It describes itself as an account of the division of days as the Lord gave Moses on Sinai into "Jubilees." After a first chapter in which a narrative at Sinai is recounted, Jubilees reviews accounts of creation and Adam (chaps. 2–4) and Noah (chaps. 5–10), respectively. Then the primary attention turns to Abraham (11:1–23:10). The Lord appears to Abram in a dream and, in language precisely like that of Gen. 15, tells Abram to look at the stars: "Thus shall your seed be" (Jub. 14:5 *OTP*). In the context of Jubilees, the narrative affirms what Abram was already told, that his descendants will be numerous as the sands of the earth (13:20). Moreover, Jub. 14:5 adds the explicit statement that Abram looked at the sky and saw the stars, an addition not found in Genesis but making explicit Abram's compliance (VanderKam, 1:492). Jubilees retains "And he believed the LORD and it was counted for him as righteousness" (Jub. 14:6 *OTP*) from Gen. 15:6 but proceeds from there into promises of the land of Canaan without reflection on Abram's belief. In his creative rewriting the author does not typically quote Scripture as distinct from his own contribution; rather, the two are melded into a new text entirely, all placed within the new setting of Moses at Sinai (Jub. 1). The author's rewriting of Gen. 15 in Jub. 14 is designed to underscore the general agreement between God and his human associates, here Abraham (VanderKam, 1:489).

A final citation of Gen. 15:5 is found in the Apocalypse of Abraham (Apoc. Ab. 20:5), which, like both 4 Ezra and 2 Baruch, is a Jewish apocalyptic writing from after the destruction of the temple in AD 70. Unlike those other works, however, it constitutes a first-person narrative of the patriarch's youth and pilgrimage from the idolatry of his fathers (Apoc. Ab. 1–8), and an apocalypse proper in which God makes revelations to him (Apoc. Ab. 9–32). The apocalypse is particularly "woven around the story of Abraham's sacrifice in Gen. 15" (Collins, *Apocalyptic*, 280). So it is natural that there are quotations (Apoc. Ab. 8:4 = Gen. 12:1; Apoc. Ab. 9:1–4 = Gen. 15:1; Apoc. Ab. 9:5 = Gen. 15:9; Apoc. Ab. 15:1 = Gen. 15:17; Apoc. Ab. 21:1–4 = Gen. 15:13–14; Apoc. Ab. 32:1–4 = Gen. 15:13–14) and allusions (Apoc. Ab. 20:4 = Gen. 18:27; Apoc. Ab. 20:6 = Gen. 18:30). In this context, God, "the Eternal, Mighty One," calls to Abraham and tells him, "Look from on high at the stars which are beneath you and count them for me and tell me their number!" (Apoc. Ab. 20:3 *OTP*). The reader is here aware that Abraham is in the midst of a heavenly ascent, and so must look not up to the stars but downward. God then tells Abraham, "As the number of the stars and their power so shall I place for your seed the nations and men" (Apoc. Ab. 20:5a *OTP*). But here the quote continues that Abraham's seed is "set apart for me in my lot with Azazel" (20:5b *OTP*). When Abraham objects to the involvement of Azazel, the fallen angel (20:6–7), the Eternal One commands him to look beneath his feet, where he sees the heavens, the earth, and the things therein (21:1–7), which God created good (22:1–2). There he also sees people divided into two groups: those prepared for judgment on one side and those set apart with Azazel on the other (22:3–5a). It is the latter, God says, that have been prepared to be born of Abraham and called to be God's people (22:5b). The point of the citation of Gen. 15:5 regarding the descendants of Abraham is integral to the main themes of the Apocalypse of Abraham. These are, first, the tension between Israel's status as God's covenant people and its fate at the hands of the gentiles and, second, the practicing of idolatry (Nickelsburg, 287–88) and the special role of Abraham and his descendants in rejecting it (Collins, *Apocalyptic*, 282). The inclusion of Azazel indicates that the world remains under the dominion of evil forces but is redeemed by the righteousness of God's chosen people (Box, 66). The point throughout rests on the identification of Israel as Abraham's descendants, since in the Apocalypse of Abraham the distinction between Israel and the gentiles, the antagonists of Israel since the fall, "is fundamental to the book" (Nickelsburg, 287). Thus, the citation from Gen. 15 has little interest in the faith of Abraham but instead is concerned with the identity of his progeny—namely, Israel.

Conclusion. In its original context Gen. 15:5 is a promise to Abram that, despite present appearances, he will not only have his own son as an heir but also have numerous descendants. Abram's belief in God and his promises is based on this promise (Gen. 15:6), which belief, the author says, was reckoned to him as righteousness. Paul is careful to see the promise of the numerous descendants in the context of faith, and insists that Abram is in fact a model of sorts for belief preceding the ascription of righteousness, and so naturally applies this likewise to those in Christ (Rom. 4:18–25). The same Gen. 15:5 text is cited in LAB 18:5 when God speaks to Balaam at night. God warns him against cursing Israel since they are the "seed [that] will be like the stars of the heaven" (*OTP*; italics omitted) spoken about to Abraham without reference to Abraham's faith. Similarly, in Jubilees the Lord makes the promise to Abram about his innumerable seed (14:5), underscoring God's promises to Israel for the land of Canaan. In the Apocalypse of Abraham (20:5), God's promise to Abraham of numerous descendants occurs in a context where the author is underscoring the distinction between Jew and gentile. All of these pseudepigraphical texts cite Gen. 15:5 as an authoritative promise from God, but each does so in a manner quite distinct from that of Paul in the NT.

Exodus 20:12 in the NT and the OT Pseudepigrapha

After Moses led Israel from Egypt, they arrived at Mount Sinai, which became wrapped in smoke and trembled at the presence of the Lord (Exod. 19:17–20a). From atop that mountain the Lord summoned Moses (19:20b). From there God spoke "all these things" (20:1), which culminate in the Decalogue, or Ten Commandments (20:2–17). Among these is the command, "Honor your father and your mother, so that you may live long in the land the LORD your God is giving you" (Exod. 20:12). This instruction is taken up in several places in both the NT (Matt. 15:4; Mark 7:10; Eph. 6:2) and the OT Pseudepigrapha (LAB 11:9–12; 44:6–7; Jub. 7:20; Ahiqar 138; Ps.-Phoc. 6–8, 179–80; Let. Aris. 228).

Exodus 20:12 in the NT (Matt. 15:4; Mark 7:10; Eph. 6:2). In Matthew's Gospel (chap. 15) the Pharisees and scribes question Jesus about his disciples breaking the traditions of the elders regarding washing their hands when they eat (15:1–2). In response Jesus asks why they break the commandment of God for the sake of their tradition (Matt. 15:3). As an example, Jesus cites the command, "Honor your father and mother" (15:4a; cf. Exod. 20:12a), which his opponents dismiss and, for the sake of their traditions, "nullify the word of God" (Matt. 15:5–6). Matthew also includes the threat of death for those not honoring their father and mother (Matt. 15:4b; Exod. 21:17). The same scene occurs in Mark's Gospel, where Jesus rebukes the Pharisees and scribes for their hypocrisy, citing a prophetic word from Isaiah (Isa. 29:13; Mark 7:5–7) and adding his own rebuke for their rejecting the commands of God in favor of their traditions (7:8–9). Jesus then cites the same command from Exod. 20:12a: "Honor your father and your mother" (Mark 7:10). Mark's text follows the parallel in LXX Deut. 5:16, reading *sou* twice. LXX Exod. 20:12 reads *sou* only after *patera*. This is followed by a further rebuke of his opponents for dismissing the command of God, "making void the word of God" by their traditions (Mark 7:11–13 ESV). The final NT citation of the Exod. 20:12 command is found in the "household codes" of Ephesians (6:1–9). Here Paul begins with an exhortation to children to obey their parents in the Lord (6:1). Then he commands them to honor their father and mother (6:2), citing Exod. 20:12a, and reminding the readers that this is "the first commandment with a promise" (6:2b). Paul then quotes the promise: "so that it may go well with you and that you may enjoy long life on the earth" (6:3; Exod. 20:12b). The NT citations, then, make it clear that the instruction given to Moses at Sinai remains in force as an expectation in the church.

Exodus 20:12 in the OT Pseudepigrapha (LAB 11:9–12; 44:6–7; Jub. 7:20; Ahiqar 138; Ps.-Phoc. 6–8, 179–80; Let. Aris. 228). The command to honor father and mother is found in a number of OT Pseudepigrapha texts. Pseudo-Philo cites the verse near the end of a segment that deals with material from Exodus (LAB 9–12). The entire biblical account of the rise of Moses, confrontation with Pharaoh, and plagues upon Egypt (Exod. 3–13) is summarized in a single verse (LAB 10:1). This is followed by the account of the crossing through the Red Sea (LAB 10:2–6; cf. Exod. 14) and the forty-year wilderness wandering (LAB 10:7; cf. Exod. 15–18). More attention is given to Moses's ascent of Mount Sinai where he receives the everlasting law (LAB 11:1–3; cf. Exod. 19). Amidst the clamoring of thunder and lightning, Moses brings the people before God, where he speaks the Ten Commandments (LAB 11:4–14; cf. Exod. 20). A careful comparison between the Exodus text and the LAB 11:9 illustrates the latter's expansion at a textual level:

> Honor your father and your mother, so that you may live long in the land the LORD your God is giving you. (Exod. 20:12)

> Love *your father and your mother,* and *you shall honor* them, and then your light will rise. And I will command the heaven, and it will give forth its rain, and the earth will give back fruit more quickly. And *you will live many days* and dwell *in* your *land,* and you will not be without sons, for your seed will not be lacking in people to dwell in it. (LAB 11:9 *OTP*; italics added)

To honoring one's father and mother is added loving them, with explicit promises from God tied to obeying this commandment: The statement that the readers' "light will rise" is ambiguous but likely refers to God's provision through nature (the sun) for the nurturing of their harvest. This is borne out in the following explanation, where God will bring forth rain and so produce a harvest more quickly. This is augmented by further promises of living many days in the land, numerous sons, and descendants to dwell in the land. The author has modified Exodus in characteristic ways, emphasizing God's control of nature and the correspondence between Israel's adherence to torah and the ensuing blessings through nature (Murphy, 67).

Later the author turns to the dark days of the judges (LAB 25–48). At a time when Israel had no leader and everyone did whatever they wanted, Micah, at the prompting of his mother, fashioned gods for whom he would be priest (44:1–5; cf. Judg. 17). And so all who wished to consult the idol came to Micah (LAB 44:5; cf. Judg. 17) until many Israelites had been led astray and provoked the anger of the Lord (LAB 44:6–7), who brings his jealous wrath upon Micah, his mother, and all who violate his laws (44:8–10). It is in the context of these provocations of God that the citation of Exod. 20:12 is found. Here, the commands issued to Israel are recounted, quoting God as saying, "I told them to honor father and mother, and they promised they would do it" (LAB 44:6 *OTP*). Then he recounts their violations: "Whereas I have told them to love father and mother, they have dishonored me, their Creator" (44:7 *OTP*). The context is one scathing rebuke for idolatry. The author uses the Ten Commandments as the "epitome of God's covenantal commands to Israel" and demonstrates, point by point, how Israel promised to obey and failed. Furthermore, idolatry is at the root of all this sin, and by her idolatry Israel has broken each of the Ten Commandments (Murphy, 175).

Exodus 20:12 is also cited in Jubilees, in a section (Jub. 5–10) that relates primarily to Noah. The command is cited in a testament of Noah in which he warns his progeny against fornication, blood pollution, and injustice, and instructs them on regulations on reserving the first fruits for the Lord (7:20–39). Among these specific instructions to his sons, Noah exhorts them to "bless the one who created them and honor father and mother" (7:20). VanderKam observes affinities with Leviticus (Lev. 19:3) and notes examples in Jubilees of Shem and Japheth honoring Noah, Isaac displaying respect for Abraham, and Jacob caring for both parents (Jub. 22; 29:15–20; 35:12–13; VanderKam, 1:342).

Further citation of this important verse is embedded in the Letter of Aristeas, which is widely regarded as a fictitious accounting for the origins of the Greek translation of the Torah from the Hebrew, dating not later than the last decade of the second century BC (Wright, 28). This work is presented as a letter from a certain Aristeas, a (gentile) figure of some importance in the court of Ptolemy II Philadelphus, king of Egypt (283–247 BC), to his brother, Philocrates, whose interest in religious matters furnishes the occasion for writing (§§1–8). It claims that the Egyptian king has instructed his librarian, Demetrius of Phalerum, to collect books for the library in Alexandria. Demetrius, desiring to include the Law of the Jews in Greek translation in this collection, dispatches a letter to the high priest in Jerusalem requesting men for the task. A delegation from Alexandria delivers the letter and secures the participation of seventy-two Jews from that region to return to Egypt to undertake the task of translation. Aristeas claims to be among that delegation. In the midst of the narrative is recounted Ptolemy's reception of the Jewish delegation (§§172–300), which includes a lengthy (about one third of the entire book) and tedious account of the king's questions to the translators and their replies during the seven days of the banquet (§§187–294). Among these is the question, "To whom must one show favor?" To this the Jewish delegate answers, "To his parents, always, for God's very great commandment concerns the honor due to parents" (§228 *OTP*). In this respect the regulation seems to be among the most essential instructions observed by diaspora communities.

Also in diaspora writings are two additional allusions to Exod. 20:12. These occur in the Sentences of Pseudo-Phocylides. This didactic wisdom poem of 230 verses is attributed to a popular Greek poet, Phocylides, who lived in the sixth century BC in Ionia (Miletus) (Collins, *Jewish,* 158) but was really written by a Hellenized diaspora (Alexandrian) Jew between ca. 30 BC and ca. AD 37 (Gurtner, 355–56). It is written in Greek and expounds upon a combination of ethical commands from the Greek translation (Septuagint) of the Law alongside non-Jewish Hellenistic writers of moral treatises (van der Horst, 2353). In doing this the author melds the Pentateuch with Wisdom literature to form "moral precepts" (Kampen, 823). Exodus 20:12 is referenced twice here: First, in the author's brief summary of the Ten Commandments (Ps.-Phoc. 3–8; cf. Exod. 20:2–17; Deut. 5:6–21), he briefly asserts the command, "Honor God foremost, and afterward your parents" (Ps.-Phoc. 8 *OTP*). Much later in the work, in a segment largely regarding the virtues of marriage and propriety in sexual behavior (ll. 175–206), the author writes, "Do not touch your stepmother, your father's second wife, but honor her as a mother, because she follows the footsteps of your mother" (ll. 179–80 *OTP*).

In both citations the author couches the instruction in the guise of Hellenistic moralists, though in accord with the teachings of torah, for the Sentences are characterized by their avoidance of any distinctly Jewish features, such as dietary restrictions, Sabbath observance, circumcision, cultic rituals, or any such aspects of Jewish religion that distinguish it from others (Gurtner, 354–55). Instead, emphasis lies squarely on moral precepts, and the instruction from Exod. 20:12 suits this purpose.

Conclusion. The straightforward command from Moses in Exod. 20:12 is widely shared in both NT and pseudepigraphic writings. While the NT and some of the OT Pseudepigrapha retain the concise and clear meaning of the original, other pseudepigraphic texts exhibit considerable expansions though the essential teaching remains largely unchanged in the respective contexts of the literature in which it is preserved.

Isaiah 6:3 in Rev. 4:8 and the OT Pseudepigrapha

In the famous scene in the year of King Uzziah's death, the prophet Isaiah sees the Lord, sitting on a throne, high and lifted up, "and the train of his robe filled the temple" (Isa. 6:1). The prophet sees seraphim calling to one another, "Holy, holy, holy is the LORD Almighty; the whole earth is full of his glory!" (6:2–3). At this and other portents of the theophany Isaiah cries out in woe for he has "seen the King, the LORD Almighty!" (6:4–5). This formulaic ascription of holiness, called the Trisagion, is found in the NT and some OT Pseudepigrapha.

Isaiah 6:3 in Rev. 4:8. The Isaianic vision lies behind a striking scene in Rev. 4, where John sees a door standing open in heaven and a voice like thunder beckoning him to come (4:1). John, then "in the Spirit," sees a throne in heaven and one seated on the throne (v. 2). John describes the one sitting on the throne (v. 3), who and what surround the throne (vv. 4, 6a), the flashes of lightning and peals of thunder issuing from the throne (v. 5), and finally the four living creatures on each side of the throne (vv. 6b–8a). It is these creatures who constantly say, "'Holy, holy, holy is the Lord God Almighty,' who was, and is, and is to come" (4:8). The language is clearly that of Isa. 6, yet with some modification:

> "Holy, holy, holy is the LORD Almighty; the whole earth is full of his glory." (Isa. 6:3)

> "Holy, holy, holy is the Lord God Almighty, who was, and is, and is to come." (Rev. 4:8)

The designation of God as "who was and is and is to come" (*ho ēn kai ho ōn kai ho erchomenos*; cf. Rev. 1:4) likely stems from Exod. 3:14: "I AM WHO I AM" (LXX *egō eimi ho ōn*). This may be merged with other "temporal descriptions" of God in Isaiah (e.g., Isa. 41:4; 43:10; 44:6; 48:12; Beale, 187). In the context of Revelation it is formulated into a statement about both the nature of God and his imminent return. Otherwise, Revelation takes the Trisagion in the Isaianic sense of a strict affirmation of the holiness of Israel's God.

Isaiah 6:3 in the OT Pseudepigrapha (1 En. 39:12; 4 Bar. 9:3). This distinctive passage from the Isaianic theophany appears in two OT Pseudepigrapha. The first is found in the Similitudes of Enoch, or Book of Parables (1 En. 37–71), which dates between the first century BC and the end of the first century AD. The Similitudes record Enochic visions and angelic interpretations as Enoch was borne up by clouds and wind (39:3; cf. 52:1) through God's throne room—where he sees the "Son of Man" enthroned (46:1–8; 61:8)—and the universe (41:3–8). In these experiences, Enoch learns the fate of the righteous and the wicked, and about the new order that is to come. Furthermore, Enoch sees the "Son of Man" (also called the "Anointed One" and "Elect One") acting as God's agent of judgment against the wicked before he ascends to the heavenly throne room (chap. 71), where he is told that he himself is the "Son of Man." In the scene in question Enoch ascends to heaven (39:3) and sees the dwelling places of the holy ones (39:4–5; cf. chap. 14). He also sees the "Elect One" (39:6a) and countless righteous and elect caught up in praise of the Lord of Spirits (39:6b–7). Then Enoch joins in the heavenly worship (39:8–14), blessing and praising God (39:9–10) and God's eternal nature and foreknowledge, and declaring the unceasing praise God receives from those who stand before his glory, saying, "Holy, Holy, Holy, Lord of the Spirits; the spirits fill the earth" (39:12 *OTP*). Whereas in Isaiah's context the glory of God fills the whole earth as well as the throne room, in 1 En. 39:12 it is restricted to the latter, while it is the Lord of Spirits who fills the earth with his spirits. That is, God's glory itself remains in heaven, and his presence on earth is mediated by his spirits, giving the citation of Isa. 6:3 a distinctly liturgical form (Nickelsburg and VanderKam, 128). Otherwise the Similitudes take the Trisagion in the Isaianic sense of a strict affirmation of the holiness of Israel's God.

The Isaianic formula is cited again in 4 Baruch, a work attributed to Baruch the scribe, also known as "Things Omitted from Jeremiah the Prophet" (*Paraleipomena Jeremiou*). It describes events at the time of the fall of Jerusalem to Nebuchadnezzar (586 BC) but before the death of Jeremiah by stoning. It is generally agreed that the fall of Jerusalem to "Babylon" is a contextual recasting of the destruction of Jerusalem by the Romans in AD 70. And so, the work as a whole is set after the destruction of the Jerusalem temple in AD 70 and before the completion of the Bar Kokhba revolt (ca. AD 135/36; Gurtner, 325–27). In the context of the citation, the narrative recounts the Lord leading Israel out of Babylon, and Jeremiah instructs only those who are willing to forsake their idolatrous ways to cross the Jordan to Jerusalem (8:1–5). Those who refuse turn back to Babylon, from which they are turned away only to establish their own city, called Samaria (8:6–12). Then Jeremiah and his companions travel a further nine days, rejoicing and offering sacrifices (9:1). On the tenth day Jeremiah offers a sacrifice (9:2) and prays, "Holy, holy, holy, incense of the living trees, true light that enlightens me until I am taken up to you; for your mercy I plead, for the sweet voice of the two seraphim I plead, for another fragrant odor of incense" (9:3–4 *OTP*). The prayer conflates several ideas with the Isaianic Trisagion, including a list of divine names that seem to tie Israel's God to aspects of the Yom Kippur festival (Torijano, 2676). This is why the author refers to the fragrant odor of incense (cf. LXX Lev. 16:12–13), where God is present in the smoke (Torijano, 2676). This usage retains the Isaianic ascription to God's supreme holiness.

Conclusion. The Isaianic Trisagion first appears in the context of a theophany for the prophet. It is utilized later in Rev. 4:8, where John has a similar theophanic vision in which four living creatures surround a throne in heaven, constantly crying, "'Holy, holy, holy is the Lord God Almighty,' who was, and is, and is to come." The usage here retains the Isaianic sense of the unique and ultimate holiness of God, while modifying a contextual element to indicate his imminent return. Pseudepigraphic texts make no such modifications toward any kind of coming of God but do utilize the Isaianic formula in like manner for affirmations of God's holiness. In the Similitudes, however, a slight modification is made so as to affirm that God's glory resides exclusively in heaven, rather filling the earth as in Isa. 6. Fourth Baruch utilizes the Trisagion in the context of Jeremiah's prayer while offering a sacrifice (4 Bar. 9:2–4) while melding the formulation with other aspects of God's divine names.

Conclusions

Comparing how the NT uses an OT text with how that same verse is cited in the OT Pseudepigrapha is complex. Authors of both the Pseudepigrapha and the NT clearly had occasion to appeal to the same OT texts for their respective purposes. Sometimes different emphases are found. For example, Paul finds a concern for faith and justification in Gen. 15, while the three pseudepigraphical texts cite Gen. 15 as a means of protecting Israel (LAB 18:5), laying claims to her rights to the land of Canaan (Jub. 14:5) or identifying Israel with respect to gentiles (Apoc. Ab. 20:5). In other instances, such as the command to honor one's father and mother (Exod. 20:12), the NT and the Pseudepigrapha largely present the text at face value with an apparent expectation that it be observed unchanged. Similarly, the Isaianic Trisagion, though used with some distinct contextual nuances in Revelation (Rev. 4:8), is largely preserved as a simple affirmation of the supreme holiness of God, whether in a heavenly vision (1 En. 39:12) or a prayer (4 Bar. 9:2–4), while melding the formulation with other aspects of God's divine names. These examples illustrate the diversity of usages within the contextual spheres of the NT authors. Though by no means representative, they do show that both the Christian traditions in the NT and the Jewish traditions in the OT Pseudepigrapha made use of the OT, though with their distinctive purposes largely governing their methodologies. It is important to note that this is merely a sampling, and so precludes one from claiming what "the Jews" believed about certain texts vis-à-vis the NT. It does give one a window, however, into what *some* Jews did with the texts preserved for us in the OT, and at least in some small degree displays some of the ways NT authors may differ from their contemporaries, even when citing the same text.

See also OT Use of the OT: Comparison with the NT Use of the OT; *other Pseudepigrapha articles*; *Dead Sea Scrolls articles*; *Mishnah, Talmud, and Midrashim articles*; *Philo articles*; *Septuagint articles*; *Targums articles*

Bibliography. Beale, G. K., *The Book of Revelation*, NIGTC (Eerdmans, 1999); Box, G. H., *The Apocalypse of Abraham* (SPCK, 1919); Collins, J. J., *The Apocalyptic Imagination*, 3rd ed. (Eerdmans, 2016); Collins, *Jewish Wisdom in the Hellenistic Age* (T&T Clark, 1997); Delamarter, S., *A Scripture Index to Charlesworth's* The Old Pseudepigrapha (Sheffield Academic, 2002); Dunn, J. D. G., *Romans 1–8*, WBC (Word, 1988); Gurtner, D. M., *Introducing the Pseudepigrapha of Second Temple Judaism* (Baker Academic, 2020); Hamilton, V. P., *The Book of Genesis: Chapters 1–17*, NICOT (Eerdmans, 1990); Kampen, J. I., "Wisdom Literature," in *ESTJ*, 2:822–24; Lange, A., and M. Weigold, *Biblical Quotations and Allusions in Second Temple Jewish Literature* (Vandenhoeck & Ruprecht, 2011); Murphy, F. J., *Pseudo-Philo* (Oxford University Press, 1993); Nickelsburg, G. W. E., *Jewish Literature between the Bible and the Mishnah*, 2nd ed. (Fortress, 2005); Nickelsburg, G. W. E., and J. C. VanderKam, *1 Enoch 2*, Herm (Fortress, 2012); Torijano, P., "4 Baruch," in *Outside the Bible*, ed. L. H. Feldman, J. L. Kugel, and L. H. Schiffman, 3 vols. (University of Nebraska Press, 2013), 2662–80; van der Horst, P. W., "Pseudo-Phocylides, *Sentences*," in *Outside the Bible*, ed. L. H. Feldman, J. L. Kugel, and L. H. Schiffman, 3 vols. (University of Nebraska Press, 2013), 2353–61; van der Horst, P. W., and J. H. Newman, *Early Jewish Prayers in Greek*, CEJL (de Gruyter, 2008); VanderKam, J. C., *Jubilees*, 2 vols., Herm (Fortress, 2018); Wright, B. G., III, *The Letter of Aristeas*, CEJL (de Gruyter, 2015).

Daniel M. Gurtner

Pseudepigrapha, NT Parallels in

The OT heavily influenced and shaped the writings of the Second Temple Period, including the NT and the OT Pseudepigrapha. This is true at a textual level, where verses are quoted or alluded to for the authors' respective purposes, but it is also true on the conceptual or thematic level. Many concepts found in the OT are, to varying degrees, explored, expanded upon, and utilized in these later writings. Yet some that are important for early Christianity receive little attention in the Pseudepigrapha, and some of the Pseudepigrapha reflect deeply on OT themes that are only sparsely addressed in the NT. Nevertheless, finding thematic parallels to the NT in the OT Pseudepigrapha that find their origin in the OT can provide an important window into the priorities and hermeneutics of the respective communities. The present analysis, then, is a sampling of important themes that may be compared at a conceptual level.

Creation

Creation and new creation in the OT. In the well-known narrative of Gen. 1 there was darkness, and the earth itself was without form and void (1:2). God speaks into existence light (v. 3), sky (v. 6), earth (v. 10), vegetation (v. 11), the sun, moon, and stars (vv. 14–19), living creatures of the sea and air (vv. 20–23), and living creatures of the earth (vv. 24–25). All these God creates in the formulaic "let there be . . . and there was" manner. All of these also God names, observes, and declares to be "good." Finally, God makes man in his image and likeness, male and female, blesses them, and gives them dominion over the earth (vv. 26–30). At the end of six days, God is finished and declares all that he has made "very good" (1:31). Then God "rested" on the seventh day (2:1–3). The narrative is marked by symmetrical pairing: the creation of light (1:1–5; day 1) and the sun and moon (1:14–19; day 4); the sky and seas (1:6–8; day 2) and the birds and fish (1:20–23; day 5); dry land (1:9–13; day 3) and living creatures upon the earth (1:24–31; day 6). The creation account of Gen. 1 is referenced elsewhere in the OT, most immediately in Gen. 2:4–3:24. This recounts not the entirety of creation but a single day, seeming to bring into focus one particular day in the making of heaven and earth, when the Lord God makes "man" (*hāʾādām*) from the dust of the ground (*min-hāʾădāmâ*) and he becomes a living creature (*wayəhî hāʾādām lənepeš ḥayyâ*; 2:4–7). This day also includes the creation of the garden in Eden, instructions concerning the forbidden tree, the creation of "woman," the serpent's temptation of Adam and Eve, and their subsequent fall and expulsion from the garden. Other places in the Hebrew Bible reflect on these accounts, but most particularly on Gen. 1 (e.g., Job 38–41; Pss. 8; 33; 74; 90; 102; 104; Prov. 8:22–31; Eccles. 1:2–11; 12:1–7; Isa. 40–55; Jer. 27; 32; Ezek. 28).

In a sense the creation is renewed after the flood, when God repeats his instruction to Noah and his sons, "Be fruitful and increase in number and fill the earth" (Gen. 9:1), just as he earlier instructed the first man and woman (1:28). Later Isaiah speaks of creating "new heavens and a new earth. The former things will not be remembered, nor will they come to mind" (Isa. 65:17). Presumably this is because the earth is "broken up" and "split asunder" (24:19) and "the heavens will vanish like smoke" (51:6; cf. 34:4). In Isaiah this re-creative act of God is his kingdom, where he dwells among a transformed people, devoid of sin, death, and destruction (48:13; G. Smith, 718). This promise of a "new heavens and new earth" is repeated for assurance in Isa. 66:22, in the final paragraph of the book describing the glorious coming of God (66:15–24; G. Smith, 744, 751–52). Both these Isaianic texts appear in a context (e.g., Isa. 65–66) where God's people take part along with creation in praise of their Creator (65:17, 18; Hubbard, 17). Here promises to those who become God's servants are realized in God's glorious kingdom, which recalls a setting in Eden prior to the fall (G. Smith, 716).

Creation and new creation in the NT. In the NT creation remains an important topic. John 1:1, recalling the "in the beginning" of Gen. 1:1, recounts the activity of "the Word" (*ho logos*), which was with God and was God, through whom all things came into being (John 1:1–3). In the Word was life, which was the light of humanity (1:4), and in fact the true light that gives light to all humanity was himself coming into the world that he created (1:9). Thus, the recounting of creation bears a decidedly Christocentric focus, ascribing to Christ the means by which creation came about (cf. also 1 Cor. 8:6; Col. 1:15; Heb. 1:2). In Romans, Paul affirms that ever since creation, creation itself has borne witness to God's attributes sufficiently for him to be known by humanity (Rom. 1:20). Later in this letter Paul explains that creation itself is in bondage to corruption and longs to be set free (8:19–23).

In the NT, the "new creation" (*kainē ktisis*) language explicitly refers to the transformation of the believer in Christ (2 Cor. 5:17; Gal. 6:15; cf. Jer. 31:31–34; Ezek. 36:26–27). But the concept can extend to the "new person" (*kainos anthrōpos*) in reference to the community of believers (e.g., Eph. 2:15; 4:23–24; Col. 3:9–10). For the present purposes, however, the primary concern for new creation in the NT refers to God's renewal or restoration of creation in the eschatological age to come. This is the creation depicted in its transitional longing at present as it awaits something in the future (Rom. 8:19–22). Hebrews also references the "coming world" (*tēn oikoumenēn tēn mellousan*) that is subject to humans (Heb. 2:5). The most explicit depiction of the new creation is in Rev. 21–22, where it is first described as "a new heaven and a new earth" (*ouranon kainon kai gēn kainēn*) but expanded on in terms of a new Jerusalem and the likes of a heavenly temple. In this dazzling account the visionary explains that the first earth has passed away (21:1) and sees the new Jerusalem descend (21:2). All the ensuing vision pertains to the holy city, the one seated on a throne, and the message to the church (21:3–22:21).

Creation and new creation in the OT Pseudepigrapha. Creation in the Pseudepigrapha in particular, and indeed Second Temple Judaism in general, is a significant theme presented not exclusively in terms of origins but in terms of its attestation to God's sovereignty over the world, and as such appears seldom in isolation from other theological concepts (Hogan, 2:176). To be sure, God is responsible for the beginning of the world as well as its end (4 Ezra 6:6; 2 Bar. 56:2–4). But also, after six days of creation God institutes the Sabbath, on which he chooses and blesses his people (Jub. 2:19–21; Mermelstein, 91–93). Similarly, Adam is mentioned at the end of the six-day creation account as a means of designating him ruler of the created order and ancestor to God's elect people (4 Ezra 6:54; Moo, 41–42). The author of 1 En. 2–5 calls upon his readers to observe the orderly manner in which creation adheres to its role in the created order, in stark contrast to the rebellious (Argall, 159–64). In eschatological contexts, particularly in apocalyptic writings, the reward for the righteous draws upon imagery of the original people in the garden of Eden (1 En. 25:3–6; 90:37–38; 2 Bar. 51:10–12; 4 Ezra 7:36; 8:52; cf. 4 Ezra 7:75; 2 Bar. 73–74; Gurtner, "Disaster").

Some works, however, give considerable attention not so much to the act of creation but to aspects of its ordering for a particular purpose. Foremost among these is surely the Book of the Heavenly Luminaries or Astronomical Book, which comprises part of 1 Enoch (1 En. 72–82; Gurtner, *Pseudepigrapha*, 22, 46–55). The central concern of this ancient work is the order of God's created celestial bodies depicted in their movements and corresponding calendrical concerns. The cosmological laws are unchanging and remain the same from creation until the establishment of a new creation (see, e.g., 1 En. 72:1). The constancy of the travels of the sun, moon, and stars seems to underscore the endurance of the 364-day solar calendar. As long as these patterns endure, the calendar they establish endures as well. The importance of the calendar is central to the work's advocacy for a 364-day calendar (1 En. 72:32). It is on this matter that a polemical tone is introduced. Typically, the importance of calendrical issues lies in the correct days for observing religious festivals. Changes in these patterns furnish the Jewish author with an eschatological turning point. The biblical prophets foresee that the heavens will vanish and the earth wear out (Isa. 51:6). The sun and moon will no longer give their light (Isa. 13:10; Ezek. 32:7–8; Joel 2:10) and will themselves be replaced by the radiance of the Lord (Isa. 60:19). For the author of the Book of the Heavenly Luminaries this change will inaugurate an eternal "new creation" (1 En. 72:1; cf. Isa. 65:17; 66:22). In Jubilees the "new creation" marks the completion of time, with the first creation (Gen. 1) being the first Jubilee of years and the new creation being the full number of Jubilees of years. Here too the author draws from Isaiah (65:17–18) but is more expansive than the brief mention in 1 En. 72:1 to connote the renewal of the entirety of the first creation—heaven, earth, and their creatures (Jub. 1:29). Their renewal occurs "until the sanctuary of the LORD is created" (Jub. 1:29 *OTP*). The first creation (Gen. 1), according to Jubilees, contained a sanctuary (the garden of Eden, Jub. 8:19). But the new creation will contain a sanctuary as God's eternal dwelling place "in Jerusalem upon Mount Zion" (1:29 *OTP*), which "will be sanctified in the new creation for the sanctification of the earth" (4:26 *OTP*). Moreover, this results in the sanctification of the earth "from all sin and from pollution throughout eternal generations" (4:26 *OTP*). Also, in this new creation lights will be renewed for healing, peace, and blessing for the elect of Israel (1:29). Here a stark contrast is evident with the depiction of the new Jerusalem in Rev. 22, where "the throne of God and of the Lamb will be in the city" (v. 3). Rather than a renewed light, like in Jubilees, in Revelation "they will not need the light of a lamp or the light of the sun, for the Lord God will give them light" (22:5).

Conclusion. The OT and NT, as well as the Pseudepigrapha, share the view that God has created the universe and that its creation reflects a purposeful ordering. In the NT the focus sharpens toward Christ, who is the instrument of God's creative activity and whose people, the church, are made new by virtue of their faith in Christ. Even the eschatological new creation finds Christ as its glorious centerpiece. In select Pseudepigrapha, the ordering of creation is foremost, precisely for the purposes of proper observing of Jewish religious festivals. The new creation, at least in the Book of Heavenly Luminaries, is a remotely distant and undefined hope that seems to have little bearing on the present.

Resurrection

Resurrection in the OT. There is little explicit material about resurrection in the OT. To be sure one finds narratives of people who have died coming back to life, such as the son of the widow of Zarephath (1 Kings 17:17–24). Here the prophet Elijah takes the woman's son, lays him down, stretches himself upon the child three times, and prays. "And the boy's life returned to him, and he lived" (17:22). The son lives, and the woman believes that Elijah is indeed a man of God (17:23–24). Here the author merely indicates that the boy "revived" (*wayyeḥî*) or "lived" (NIV) in a manner which, as will be seen, is quite distinct from "resurrection." Elisha performs a similar feat for the Shunammite woman Gehazi, whose son dies (2 Kings 4:31–37). Elisha prays and lies on the boy until he grows warm, sneezes, and opens his eyes (4:34–35). The prophet presents him to his mother alive (4:36–37), but nothing is said of resurrection, only that his life has returned to him. Briefly in 2 Kings, a dead man who was buried in the tomb of Elisha came to life when his body touched the bones of the prophet (13:20–21). These miraculous events likely serve to authenticate the prophetic ministries of Elijah and Elisha by showing how people are reanimated to their prior form of existence.

Other passages may hint at resurrection, such as the notion that God will not "let [his] faithful one see decay" (Ps. 16:10; cf. 49:14–15). Still others seem more clear, such as Job's affirmation that "after my skin has been destroyed, yet in my flesh I will see God" (Job 19:26) and especially Isa. 26:19: "But your dead will live, LORD; their bodies will rise—let those who dwell in the dust wake up and shout for joy—your dew is like the dew of the morning; the earth will give birth to her dead." The prophecy of Ezekiel (37:1–14) expresses hope of national rebirth in explicitly physical terms of resurrection. The prophet is led by the Lord to a valley full of very dry bones (37:1–2) and told to prophesy the word of the Lord over these bones (37:3–4). The prophecy is that the Lord will cause breath to enter the bones and they shall live, with graphically physical terms: the laying of sinews, covering of flesh, living and standing on their feet, opening of graves, and raising the dead from the graves and bringing them into the land of Israel (37:5–14; cf. Gen. 2:7).

Daniel foresees a time when people whose names are found written in a book will be delivered (12:1). The deliverance, then, is described in terms of "those who sleep in the dust of the earth shall awake," with some to everlasting life (cf. Isa. 65:20–22) and others to shame and contempt (Dan. 12:2; cf. Isa. 66:24). There remain unanswered questions regarding the identity of those who will be raised to life and the nature of the punishment (Goldingay, 545–49), but it seems clear to some degree that this is an affirmation of individual, bodily resurrection, particularly for vindication of unjustly persecuted righteous people.

Resurrection in the NT. Bodily resurrection is a central component to NT teaching, beginning foremost with the bodily resurrection of Jesus. This is articulated most fully and earliest in Paul's First Letter to the Corinthians (1 Cor. 15; ca. AD 55), which explains in some detail the nature and significance of the resurrection as well as its antiquity and importance in early Christianity. Here one must follow the argument of the author closely to gain his meaning, beginning with the statement that the teaching on this matter is something the Corinthians had already received from Paul's preaching (15:1, 3), presumably in reference to Paul's missionary activity in that city (Acts 18:1–18). Moreover, this is a teaching that Paul himself received (*ho kai parelabon,* 15:3) and is not peripheral but "as of first importance" (*en prōtois,* 15:3). This entails: Christ died for our sins (15:3), he was buried (15:4a), he was raised on the third day, "in accordance with the Scriptures" (*kata tas graphas,* 15:4b ESV), and he appeared to many, including Paul (15:5–8). Apparently, the Corinthians were claiming there is no resurrection of the dead (15:12), a claim that Paul shows to be wrong (15:13–19). He affirms Christ's resurrection as "the firstfruits of those who have fallen asleep" (*aparchē tōn kekoimēmenōn,* 15:20) by whom death is destroyed (15:26, 54–57). Paul then describes in some detail the nature of the resurrection body (15:35–53). The bodily resurrection of Christ is presumed elsewhere in the writings of Paul and other NT authors (Gal. 1:1; Eph. 1:20; Rom. 4:24; 1 Pet. 1:21) but is also a foundational historical event with profound implications for the Christian faith. It exhibits the defeat of death (Rom. 6:9; 1 Cor. 15:55; Heb. 2:14; Acts 2:24) and the basis on which Christians also may hope to be raised from the dead (1 Cor. 15:52).

Resurrection in the OT Pseudepigrapha. In Second Temple Judaism, the language of "resurrection" can be used in reference to a variety of concepts that relate to God's eschatological restoration of the dead to life (Elledge, "Resurrection," 2:656). Resurrection is sometimes depicted in contexts of persecution or repentance, giving rise to notions of postmortem recompense (Nickelsburg, *Resurrection,* 119–40). In the Book of Watchers (1 En. 1–36), Enoch is shown a mountain in the west, at the ends of the earth, where the spirits of the dead are held until judgment (1 En. 20–36). Some of these souls, his angelic guide Rufael explains, are the souls of wicked people who themselves died a violent death, which is sufficient recompense for their evil in life. And so, they "will not rise from" their place for judgment (22:13). Here the author has some kind of resurrection in mind in which the spirits of the wicked will not participate. Later (1 En. 24:5–25:1) it is evident that the righteous will be raised (Nickelsburg, *1 Enoch 1,* 306) to what seems to be an eschatological, and perhaps resurrected (as suggested by the presence of "bones," 24:6; see Nickelsburg, *1 Enoch 1,* 315), life that the righteous will experience on earth in a renewed Jerusalem (cf. Isa. 65–66). The Similitudes of Enoch (1 En. 37–71) anticipates a "change for the holy and the righteous ones" at the end of days, when "glory and honor shall be given back" to them, which may suggest resurrection (1 En. 50:1–2 *OTP*). Resurrection is more explicit in the First Epistle of Enoch (1 En. 91–108), which anticipates a future time when "the righteous one shall arise from his sleep" (91:10 *OTP*; cf. 92:3; 103:4; and possibly 104:1–2). An allusion to resurrection may be found in Jubilees, which speaks of the Lord healing his servants, causing them to "rise up and see great peace" (Jub. 23:30). Though the Psalms of Solomon sometimes indicate some sort of postmortem recompense for the pious (e.g., Pss. Sol. 3; 13; 14; 15), references to resurrection are few (e.g., 3:12) and ambiguous.

After the destruction of the temple by the Romans in AD 70, resurrection "remained crucial to the sophisticated explorations of theodicy undertaken" in 4 Ezra and 2 Baruch (Elledge, "Resurrection," 2:657). In the latter, Baruch, the scribe of Jeremiah, asks God about the way things will be in the eschatological world to come (2 Bar. 49:1–3). Among centerpieces of the eschaton is the fate of the righteous in resurrection. God tells Baruch that the earth "will surely give back the dead" in like form to how it received them (50:2a). God will himself raise them (50:2b). It will be evident that "the dead are living again" (50:3), and for that reason God will raise them in an appearance that is recognizable to others (50:4). They will not even appear aged by their time in the earth (51:9; see Gurtner, "Disaster"). Fourth Ezra discusses resurrection in two places. First, the angel Uriel uses impending childbirth as an analogy for the resurrection: "In Hades the chambers of the souls are like the womb. For just as a woman who is in travail makes haste to escape the pangs of birth, so also do these places hasten to give back those things that were committed to them from the beginning" (4 Ezra 4:41b–42 *OTP*; Moo, 42). Then later (4 Ezra 7:75–101), the author describes postmortem punishments and rewards for the wicked and righteous, respectively, as they await resurrection. Ezra asks to see what will occur with people when God renews his creation (7:75). He is told that when a person dies, the spirit leaves the body and "adores the glory of the Most High" (7:78). But if the person has despised God's law, his spirit shall wander in torment (7:79–87). Those who have kept God's law will see "with great joy the glory of him who receives them" and "they shall have rest in seven orders" (7:91). Among these orders are, fourth, the "glory which awaits them in the last days" (7:95) and, sixth, that they will become "incorruptible" (7:97).

A final occurrence of resurrection for the present discussion is found in the Book of Biblical Antiquities (or, in Latin, *Liber antiquitatum biblicarum*, abbreviated LAB; Gurtner, *Introducing*, 256). This work recasts biblical narratives, sometimes summarizing briefly or completely omitting, while at other times quoting specifically or paraphrasing. The mention of resurrection is found in the segment summarizing Genesis (LAB 1–8), specifically in the account of the flood (LAB 3; cf. Gen. 6:9–9:29). After the waters subside, God promises not to curse the earth again, with a considerable amplification in Gen. 8:21 (LAB 3:9). Added to this is an eschatological promise regarding the fulfillment of the appointed years, when light and dark will pass away (LAB 3:10a). Then God says that he "will bring the dead to life and raise up those who are sleeping from the earth," and "hell will pay back its debt, and the place of perdition will return its deposit" so that God may give to each according to his works (LAB 3:10b), an integral aspect of eschatological judgment in the book (Murphy, 35; cf. LAB 33:3).

Conclusion. Belief in bodily resurrection seems to be shared by the NT and at least some Jews as seen in the OT Pseudepigrapha. Yet the Christian authors are adamant about the resurrection of Christ as a foundational historical and theological event as a ground for the believers' hope. It is also a graphic anticipation of what the believer likewise will experience. Yet even here it is Christocentric, as the resurrection of believers occurs at the return of Christ. In the select Pseudepigrapha, in contrast, resurrection is a future reality in a rubric based on rewards and punishments related to individual behavior.

Temple

The Jerusalem temple was in many respects a formidable emblem of Jewish religious and cultural identity. From its earliest mention in the Hebrew Bible to the most vivid speculations in apocalyptic writings of Second Temple Judaism and early Christianity, it figures prominently as a place to commune with Israel's God, a location of controversy, and a symbol of eschatological hope. Indeed, while its function in Israelite life in the OT is fundamental, in the NT Gospels it is the centerpiece of not only Israelite religious practices but also societal structures and political conflicts for the environment in which Jesus lives, ministers, and dies. It is the setting for political controversy and strife, both among Jews themselves and with respect to the Roman overlords. Second Temple Judaism furnishes us with literature both before and after the destruction of the temple by the Romans in AD 70, providing some perspective that can be illuminating for the study of the NT.

Temple in the OT. From the time of the exodus from Egypt to the establishment of the monarchy, Israel worshiped their God in the tabernacle. King David sought to construct a permanent and more suitable dwelling for Israel's God (2 Sam. 7:2), patterned after the tabernacle. The temple, ultimately built by Solomon, was constructed on Mount Moriah (2 Chron. 3:1) or Mount Zion (1 Chron. 21:22–23). The structure was largely stone (limestone?) while the interior was lined with cedar overlaid with gold, graven with cherubim, palms, and flowers (1 Kings 6:15–29). It was divided into two main sections, the holy place (*hêkal*) and the most holy place or holy of holies (*dəbîr*; 6:16–18). Within the most holy place stood the ark of the covenant, with its two golden cherubim stationed atop its lid, wings outstretched so as to reach the walls of the room (6:23–28; 2 Chron. 3:10–13). Within the holy place there were various additional cultic furnishings (1 Kings 6:20–22; 7:23–49; 2 Chron. 4:1–19).

The temple was dedicated by Solomon (1 Kings 8:22–61; 2 Chron. 6:12–42), and the glory of the Lord dwelled within it (1 Kings 8:10–11; 2 Chron. 5:13–14). Religious decline began in Solomon's lifetime (1 Kings 11:1–8) and continued thereafter. Eventually, Nebuchadnezzar of Babylon looted the temple and palace (cf. 2 Chron. 36:7) and carried the king and a significant part of the population into captivity (2 Kings 24:1–17). The ruination was completed after an eighteen-month siege in 586 BC (25:1) with the destruction of Jerusalem and its temple, with only a few Jews left behind (25:11–12).

Putting an end to this captivity, Cyrus, king of Persia, permitted Jews to return to Jerusalem and rebuild their temple (2 Chron. 36:23; Ezra 1:1–4). The return began in 538 BC, and the ensuing temple was similar to that of Solomon, though apparently lacking its adornment (Ezra 3:12–13; Hag. 2:3). The temple was known as that of Zerubbabel, governor during that period, who restored the sacred vessels and provided for further building (Ezra 1:6–11; 6:3–8:36). Despite Zerubbabel's ongoing efforts (Ezra 3:7–13), the building project faced opposition and was suspended until 520 BC (Ezra 4). At the exhortation of the prophets Haggai and Zechariah, building resumed and was completed with celebration in 516 BC (Ezra 5–6). As was the case with the earlier temple, the temple grounds were again divided into a holy place and a most holy place, though the latter did not contain the ark (m. Yoma 5:2), and the contents of both rooms were more modest than those of their predecessor (cf. 1 Macc. 1:21–22). Subsequent history of the temple is found in 1 Maccabees and Josephus, though details are scant.

Daniel's vision (Dan. 7–12) anticipates a renewal of the temple as part of God's eschatological triumph (12:11–12). Other biblical prophets similarly look to the establishment of an enormous eschatological temple (cf. Ezek. 40–47), despite misgivings about cultic practices of the time (Ezek. 8–10). God would one day restore the fortunes of Jerusalem (Zech. 1:16–17; cf. Isa. 2:1–4). Its location, Zion, was the mountain of God (cf. Ps. 68:16; Isa. 40:9).

Temple in the NT. In the time of the NT the temple was expanded, this time under Herod the Great (37–4 BC). From the historical accounts furnished by Josephus (*Ant.* 15.380–402; *J.W.* 5.184–227; see also Let. Aris. 83–90), one can glean some important things about the temple. Herod began his work on the temple in 20–19 BC (cf. Josephus, *Ant.* 15.380–87; *J.W.* 1.401–2). Much of it was designed according to OT regulations, though on a considerably larger scale, and can be described here in less detail. The temple proper (*naos*) was finished in about eighteen months, although eight years were required for the courts and considerably longer for the entire complex (John 2:20 records forty-six years). It was not completed until AD 64. Its white marble and gold plating resembled a snow-covered mountain (Josephus, *J.W.* 5.222–27).

The size of the Herodian structure was nearly double that of the Solomonic temple (Josephus, *J.W.* 1.401–2), more broad on the north than south, surrounded by a stone wall with several gates (Josephus, *Ant.* 15.410–20; cf. m. Mid. 1:3), a porch on the east side (John 10:23; Acts 3:11), and open spaces where some commerce occurred (Matt. 21:12 par.; John 2:14–16). Here was the location where Jesus ministered to the blind and lame (Matt. 21:14) and overturned the money tables (Matt. 21:12 par.). Increasing the size required extensive topographic reconfigurations, including filling in the valleys to the west and north, and part of the Kidron Valley to the south. Modern archaeological analysis suggests that the retaining wall for the Temple Mount was 1,590 feet (west) by 1,035 feet (north) by 1,536 feet (east) by 912 feet (south). According to Josephus, the outside of the temple was adorned with so much gold that when the sun shone upon it, it virtually blinded those who looked at it. The structure was praised by Josephus as a building with a "magnificence never surpassed" (*J.W.* 1.401).

The temple naturally figures prominently in the ministry of Jesus, where one of his temptations occurs (Matt. 4:1–11; Luke 4:1–12) and sometimes participation in cultic worship seems to be presumed (Matt. 5:23–24; 8:4; cf. Mark 1:40–45; 5:43; 7:36; Luke 1:8–10; 2:24, 27; 5:14). But even this is in proper perspective as Jesus states that God desires "mercy, not sacrifice" (Matt. 9:13; 12:7) and insists that "something greater than the temple is here" (12:6; cf. 17:24–29).

It is also the scene of his "triumphal entry" into Jerusalem (Matt. 21:1–11; Mark 11:7–10; Luke 19:37–44), "cleansing" of the temple (Matt. 21:12–13; Mark 11:11–17; Luke 19:45–46; John 2:15), healings and teachings (Matt. 21:14–16; 21:23–24:1; 26:55; Mark 11:27–13:1; 14:49; Luke 19:47–21:38; 22:53; John 5:14; 7:14, 29; 9:2, 20–59; 18:20). Jesus is accused of threatening to destroy the temple (Matt. 26:61; 27:40; Mark 14:59; 15:29), but John clarifies that the temple about which he spoke was his body (John 2:19–21).

In Acts the Jerusalem temple was a frequent place for the meeting of early Christians (Acts 2:46–47) and the teaching of the apostles (3:1–10; 5:19–26; 21:26–31; cf. 25:8; 26:21). Elsewhere in the NT the church becomes God's temple (1 Cor. 3:16–17; Eph. 2:21). Revelation sees a temple in heaven where God dwells (Rev. 11:1–2, 19), from which angels issue forth (14:15–17), and from which God speaks (16:1, 17). Then in the new Jerusalem the Lord God Almighty and the Lamb become the temple (21:22).

Temple in the OT Pseudepigrapha. Among the OT Pseudepigrapha, a variety of apocalyptic traditions, likely drawing from Ezekiel's vision of a new temple, similarly looked to a future sanctuary (cf. 1 En. 90:28–29). Initially, it was widely held that Zerubabbel's structure paled in comparison to that of Solomon (cf. Hag. 2:9; Zech. 14:8–11; 1 En. 90:29) and was even considered ritually impure (1 En. 89:72–74; cf. T. Mos. 5:3–4). An earlier portion of 1 Enoch (ca. 200 BC) asserts that ever since the exile all of Israel was apostate, apparently because of its inability to rightly engage in cultic worship (1 En. 93:9). Others viewed any human structure as inferior to that which God showed Moses at Sinai (Exod. 25:8) and therefore anticipated the establishment of that heavenly sanctuary on earth (cf. 2 Bar. 4:5; Jub. 1:16, 27–28; 25:21; 49:18). Shortly after the destruction of the Herodian temple in AD 70, 2 Baruch anticipates a heavenly sanctuary (32:2) that will "be renewed in glory and perfected forever" (32:4; cf. 32:5; 68:5). Some of the cultic articles are said to have been removed prior to its destruction (6:7) in anticipation of their restoration in an eschatological cultic structure (6:8; cf. 10:19; 80:2; 2 Macc. 2:5).

Like 2 Baruch, the Apocalypse of Abraham is a Jewish apocalyptic writing from after the destruction of the temple in AD 70. In it Abraham sees the idolatrous practices of Israel, led by a man slaughtering in the temple who makes the Lord angry (25:1–6). Then Abraham sees that heathens will come and kill the people of Jerusalem and destroy its temple (26:1–27:5) and learns that it is his own seed that has provoked God to such judgment (27:6–12). But ultimately God promises that there will be some righteous among Abraham's seed, who will "strive in the glory" of God's name in a reconstituted temple where they will again offer sacrifices (29:18).

The Psalms of Solomon is a collection of eighteen pseudonymous hymns or poems, attributed to Solomon, that convey a Jewish community's response to persecution and a foreign invasion, likely in reference to the Roman general Pompey in 63 BC (Pss. Sol. 2:1–2; 8:18–22; 17:7–13; see Gurtner, *Introducing*, 340–52). But the polemic is not only against the gentile invaders but also against other Jews, the Hasmoneans. It is these, the Jewish Hasmoneans, who have "defiled the sanctuary of the Lord" (2:3) while the gentiles "walked on the place of sacrifice of the Lord" (8:12). The remedy for this defilement in the Psalms of Solomon lies in its conception of the messiah (esp. Pss. Sol. 17–18). In Pss. Sol. 17, the author recalls the promise of God to give David's kingship to his descendants (17:4). But Israel's sins have caused "sinners" to rise up against her and established a monarchy (Hasmoneans) while despoiling the throne of David in arrogance (17:5–6). But God raised a man "alien to our race" (i.e., the Roman general Pompey) who hunted them all down to bring about judgment upon them (17:7–10). This "lawless one" (Pompey entered the holy of holies; cf. Pss. Sol. 2:2; Josephus, *J.W.* 1.152; *Ant.* 14.72) laid waste the land and expelled its inhabitants (17:11–13), doing in Jerusalem what gentiles do for their gods elsewhere (17:14). Even the Israelites living among the "gentile rabble" adopted these practices (17:15). The pious did not remain in Jerusalem but fled to the wilderness (17:16–17), while the wicked in Jerusalem continued to practice their iniquity, appointing commoners to leadership and criminals to rule (17:18–20). The psalmist then implores the Lord to raise up the king, the son of David, to rule over Israel, asking God to empower him to destroy unrighteous rulers and purge Jerusalem of gentiles (17:21–30a). The purpose is to purge Jerusalem and make it holy so that nations will come from the ends of the earth to see its glory (17:30b–31) and, presumably, to resume pure sacrifices. Here the temple's restoration is at the heart of the psalmist's messianic longings (Pss. Sol. 17:32–46; 18:1–12).

Conclusion. Apocalyptic texts among the Pseudepigrapha envisioned a future sanctuary (cf. 1 En. 90:28–29). Sometimes this was because of its ritual impurity (1 En. 89:72–74; cf. Pss. Sol. 8:12) or the inability of apostate Israel to conduct cultic worship rightly (1 En. 93:9; cf. Pss. Sol. 2:3). For others only a heavenly sanctuary could replicate that shown to Moses at Sinai (Exod. 25:8; cf. 2 Bar. 4:5; Jub. 1:16, 27–28; 25:21; 49:18). For some the solution was messianic intervention for the purification of the temple and restoration of sacrifices (Pss. Sol. 17:32–46; 18:1–12). While Jesus is concerned that the temple should be a "house of prayer" (Mark 11:17), there is little compelling evidence that the NT authors sought a restoration of right sacrifices or any sense of a reconstituted temple. Instead, it is a location where Jesus has taught with authority, and for early Christians the sacrifices of the temple could never be ultimately efficacious (Heb. 10:4), but instead point to the perfect sacrifice of Christ (1 Pet. 1:19).

Exodus

Exodus in the OT. The departure (ἔξοδος, *exodos*) of Israel from bondage in Egypt is foregrounded in the calling of Moses, who encounters the Lord in a flame in the midst of a bush and is commissioned to announce God's deliverance of Israel from their affliction in Egypt to the land of the Canaanites, despite the resistance of the king of Egypt (Exod. 3:2–22; 4:1–31). Then Moses, accompanied by his brother Aaron, confronts Pharaoh with the Lord's command to release Israel. Upon Pharaoh's repeated refusals, corresponding plagues are unleased upon the Egyptians (Exod. 5–11). Finally, the Lord instructs Israel to celebrate a feast in anticipation of their impending deliverance at Passover, when the firstborn of the Egyptians is struck down but those of Israel are spared (12:1–30). Pharaoh and the Egyptians are forced to urge Israel to leave and so, after 430 years, the Lord brings Israel out of Egypt (12:31–51). After instructing Moses to consecrate every firstborn to him (13:1–16), the Lord led Israel in a pillar of cloud by day and pillar of fire by night (13:17–22). Changing his mind, Pharaoh then pursues Israel and backs them up against the Red Sea (14:1–20). Moses stretches out his hand over the sea and the Lord drives back the waters, enabling Israel to pass through on dry ground (14:21–22). When the Egyptians follow, the Lord causes the waters to return and cover them, saving Israel and causing great rejoicing (14:23–15:21). God's mighty deliverance is often evoked as a means of exhortation to Israel (esp. Pss. 77; 78; 80; 105; 106; 136; Ezek. 20; Dan. 9:15–16) and in a way replicated in the book of Joshua (Josh. 3–4). The exodus is used by Isaiah both to provide assurance of God's power (Isa. 43:1–11; 48:20–22) and in anticipation of a new, eschatological deliverance for God's dispersed people (51:9–11; 56:7–8; 57:14; 63:7–19; 66:7–9; 66:18–23; cf. Jer. 16:10–21; Hosea 11:1–11; Mic. 7:15–20; Zech. 10:10–12).

Exodus in the NT. Though there is little explicit mention of the exodus event itself, recognizable traces of it are found in the NT. This is especially the case in Mark, where the opening chapter (Mark 1:1–3) utilizes the notion of God sending an angel before Israel (Exod. 23:20) eschatologically in the framework of the good news for which John the Baptist prepares the way (cf.

Mal. 3:1; 4:5; Isa. 52:7; 61:1–2). Some regard Jesus's baptism as an exodus-like passing through the waters (Mark 1:10 pars.) and the declaration of the "beloved son" as an identification of Jesus as Israel's servant-deliverer (Mark 1:11 pars.; cf. Ps. 2:7; Isa. 42:1). Others include the depiction of Jesus as a new Moses bringing about a greater exodus-like deliverance (Matt. 4–7; Heb. 3:1–11) and departure from slavery (Rom. 6–8; cf. Eph. 1:7; Col. 1:13–14). In Revelation John evokes images of the exodus plagues to depict his scenes of judgment (Rev. 8:2–9:21; 15:1–16:21).

Exodus in the OT Pseudepigrapha. Despite its importance in Israel's history, the exodus finds comparatively sparse attention in the OT Pseudepigrapha. Instead, one finds many traditions about related matters, such as Sinai, the law, and Moses, but little on the exodus itself. Sometimes the event is only briefly summarized (Sib. Or. 3:248–64). In the Animal Apocalypse (1 En. 85–90), the story is recast with characters depicted as animals, where Israel are sheep and the Egyptians wolves. Eventually the wolves begin to fear the sheep and oppress them, and their cry reaches the Lord (89:15–16). The Lord summons one of the sheep (Moses) to testify against the wolves on behalf of the sheep (89:17). That sheep (Moses), accompanied by another sheep (Aaron), speaks to the wolves on behalf of the sheep (89:18). The wolves deal still more harshly with the sheep despite the Lord striking the wolves (89:19–20). The sheep depart and the wolves pursue them to a swamp of water (89:21–23), which splits before the sheep and devours the wolves (89:24–27). The sheep enter a desert, where the Lord cares for them (89:28).

The exodus narrative is also retold in the Biblical Antiquities (LAB), though the entire narrative of the rise of Moses, confrontation with Pharaoh, and plagues upon Egypt (Exod. 3–13) is summarized in a single verse (LAB 10:1). This is followed by the account of the crossing through the Red Sea (LAB 10:2–6; cf. Exod. 14) and the forty-year wilderness wandering (LAB 10:7; cf. Exod. 15–18). The emending of the biblical narrative simultaneously underscores the leadership of Moses and demonstrates the power of God to frustrate the efforts of even the mightiest of human forces (Murphy, 61–62).

Jubilees is more expansive. It devises its entire scheme of the division of time in terms of "Jubilees," with the narrative beginning in the first year of the exodus from Egypt, when Moses is summoned up Mount Sinai where he stays forty days and nights (Jub. 1:1–4a). But toward the end of the book the exodus event itself is recounted, though revised to show how Mastema, a Satan-like spirit, tried to assist the Egyptians. In the forty-ninth Jubilee Moses goes to the land of Midian and returns to Egypt in the fiftieth Jubilee (48:1). The narrative then infers that it is in Midian that Moses goes up Mount Sinai, which may allude to the account of God's encounter with Moses at the burning bush on Mount Horeb (Exod. 3:1–4:19). Where Exod. 4:24 mentions the Lord's intent to kill Moses, Jubilees attributes that plan to Prince Mastema to save the Egyptians from Moses's hand (Jub. 48:2–3). But God delivers Moses and sends him to Egypt to perform signs against Pharaoh (48:4), which are recounted in the plagues (Jub. 48:5–8; cf. Exod. 7:1–11:10). Prince Mastema tries to make Moses fall into the hand of Pharaoh by aiding the latter's magicians (Jub. 48:9–12), but the revealing angel stands between Egypt and Israel to deliver Israel by binding Mastema to prevent Egypt from pursuing Israel out of Egypt (48:13–15). Then Mastema is released so that the Egyptians might pursue Israel and be trapped in the midst of the sea (48:16–19). Moses's story ends in Jubilees 49–50, which contain a collection of laws pertaining to the Passover (Jub. 49), Jubilees (50:1–5), and the Sabbath (50:6–13). The book ends by declaring the "account of the division of days is finished here" (50:13; Gurtner, *Introducing*, 245).

Conclusion. Since the exodus event itself is described in such detail and referred to so often in the Hebrew Bible as a display of God's power and covenant fidelity to his people, it is perhaps surprising that more is not made of it in subsequent literature. Thematically one may find undercurrents in the NT, regarding the salvation accomplished in Christ as a theological new exodus from bondage to sin. But such a reading lies beneath the surface and is not made explicit. Mention of the event is found in the Pseudepigrapha, but there is little evidence that the authors paused to reflect on the monumental event.

Conclusions

These data represent only a very small cross section of some more prominent themes where comparisons can be drawn. Others that could be considered include the flood, exile and restoration, and even the origins of sin. Even notions of "salvation" vary from one text to another among the Pseudepigrapha and especially in comparison with the NT. What stands out to students of both the Pseudepigrapha and the NT is how decidedly unique the latter is in comparison with the former. While Second Temple Judaism in general is important for a contextual understanding of early Christianity, and there is perhaps more overlap than one may at times think, it is striking how uniquely Christocentric the NT is. That is, what unites the NT authors in their utilization of concepts from the OT is the person and work of Jesus Christ. No such pervasive unifying factor exists among the OT Pseudepigrapha.

See also OT Use of the OT: Comparison with the NT Use of the OT; *other Pseudepigrapha articles*; *Dead Sea Scrolls articles*; *Mishnah, Talmud, and Midrashim articles*; *Philo articles*; *Septuagint articles*; *Targums articles*

Bibliography. Alexander, T. D., and S. Gathercole, eds., *Heaven on Earth* (Paternoster, 2004); Argall, R. A., *1 Enoch and Sirach*, EJL 8 (Society of Biblical Literature, 1995); Bauckham, R., "Jesus' Demonstration in the Temple," in *Law and Religion*, ed. B. Lindars (James Clarke, 1988), 72–89; Beale, G. K., *Temple and the Church's Mission* (IVP Academic, 2004); Ben-Dov, J., *Head of All Years*, STDJ 78 (Brill, 2008); Blenkinsopp, J., *Creation, Un-Creation, Re-Creation* (T&T Clark, 2011); Busink, T., *Der Tempel von Jerusalem*, 2 vols. (Brill, 1970–80); Byron, J., "Exodus, The," in *ESTJ*, 2:261–62; Collins, J. J., "The Afterlife in Apocalyptic Literature," in *Judaism in Late Antiquity*, ed. A. Avery-Peck, J. Neusner, B. Chilton, Handbook of Oriental Studies: Section 1, The Near and Middle East 49 (Brill, 1999), 3.4:119–39; Collins, "Reinventing Exodus," in *Jewish Cult and Hellenistic Culture*, JSJSup 100 (Brill, 2005), 44–57; Cox, R., *By the Same Word*, BZNW 145 (de Gruyter, 2007); Elledge, C. D., "Resurrection," in *ESTJ*, 2:656–58; Elledge, *Resurrection of the Dead in Early Judaism 200 BCE–CE 200* (Oxford University Press, 2017); Evans, C. A., "Predictions of the Destruction of the Herodian Temple in the Pseudepigrapha, Qumran Scrolls, and Related Texts," *JSP* 10 (1992): 89–147; Goldingay, J., *Daniel*, rev. ed., WBC (Zondervan, 2019); Gray, T. C., *The Temple in the Gospel of Mark* (Baker Academic, 2008); Gruen, E. S., "The Use and Abuse of the Exodus Story," in *Heritage and Hellenism*, ed. E. S. Gruen (University of California Press, 1998), 41–72; Gurtner, D. M., *Introducing the Pseudepigrapha of Second Temple Judaism* (Baker, 2020); Gurtner, "Matthew's Temple and the 'Parting of the Ways,'" in *Built upon the Rock*, ed. D. M. Gurtner and J. Nolland (Eerdmans, 2008), 128–53; Gurtner, "On the Other Side of Disaster," in *This World and the World to Come*, ed. D. M. Gurtner, LSTS 74 (T&T Clark, 2011), 114–26; Gurtner, D. M., and N. Perrin, "Temple," in *DJG*[2], 939–47; Hahne, H. A., *The Corruption and Redemption of Creation*, LNTS 336 (T&T Clark, 2006); Haran, M., *Temples and Temple Service in Ancient Israel* (Clarendon, 1977); Hayward, C. T. R., *The Jewish Temple* (Routledge, 1996); Hogan, K. M., "Creation," in *ESTJ*, 2:176–77; Hubbard, M. V., *New Creation in Paul's Letters and Thought*, SNTSMS 119 (Cambridge University Press, 2002); Kerr, A. R., *The Temple of Jesus' Body*, JSNTSup 220 (Sheffield Academic, 2002); Mermelstein, A., *Creation, Covenant and the Beginnings of Judaism*, JSJSup 168 (Brill, 2014); Moo, J. A., *Creation, Nature and Hope in 4 Ezra*, FRLANT 237 (Vandenhoeck & Ruprecht, 2011); Murphy, F. J., *Pseudo-Philo* (Oxford University Press, 1993); Netzer, E., *The Architecture of Herod, the Great Builder*, TSAJ 117 (Mohr Siebeck, 2006); Nickelsburg, G. W. E., *1 Enoch 1*, Herm (Fortress, 2001); Nickelsburg, *Resurrection, Immortality, and Eternal Life in Intertestamental Judaism*, rev. ed., HTS 56 (Harvard University Press, 2007); Owens, M. D., "Isaiah's New Exodus in the Writings of Second Temple Judaism," in *As It Was in the Beginning* (Wipf & Stock, 2015), 187–92; Perrin, N., *Jesus the Temple* (Baker Academic, 2010); Ritmeyer, K., and L. Ritmeyer, "Reconstructing Herod's Temple Mount in Jerusalem," *BAR* 15 (1989): 23–43; Smith, D. L., "The Uses of 'New Exodus' in New Testament Scholarship," *CBR* 14 (2016): 207–43; Smith, G., *Isaiah 40–66*, NAC (Broadman & Holman, 2009); Stuckenbruck, L. T., "Messianic Ideas in the Apocalyptic and Related Literature of Early Judaism," in *The Messiah in the Old and New Testaments*, ed. Stanley E. Porter (Eerdmans, 2007), 90–116; Trafton, J. L., "What Would David Do?," in *The Psalms of Solomon*, ed. E. Bons and P. Pouchelle, SBLEJL 40 (SBL Press, 2015), 155–74; Walton, J. H., *Genesis 1 as Ancient Cosmology* (Eisenbrauns, 2011); Watts, R. E., *Isaiah's New Exodus and Mark* (Mohr Siebeck, 1997); Wold, B. G., "Revelation's Plague Septets: New Exodus and Exile," in *Echoes from the Caves*, ed. F. García Martínez, STDJ 85 (Brill, 2009), 279–98; Wright, N. T., *Resurrection of the Son of God* (Fortress, 2003).

DANIEL M. GURTNER

Pseudepigrapha, NT Use of

Discussing the use of the OT Pseudepigrapha in the NT is problematized by the scant and debated evidence. As we will see, Jude clearly quotes 1 Enoch, but there is debate as to how he regards the authority of that source with respect to the OT. Jude's familiarity with Pseudepigrapha is also evident outside of this quotation, but elsewhere in the NT there is considerable ambiguity. While one may find numerous points of parallel ideas, perhaps indicative of a shared Palestinian-Jewish context collated in such sources as the margins to the NA[28] or even *OTP*, none of these are clear quotations. Therefore, it is pertinent in the present discussion to begin with the clearest example before moving to some other considerations.

Book of Jude

It has been well documented that the book of Jude is deeply indebted to the OT, both in Greek and Hebrew. But, according to Richard Bauckham (8), the author's "real intellectual background is in the literature of Palestinian Judaism," whose works he uses at least as extensively as he uses the OT. Moreover, Jude is the only NT book to utilize a quotation from the Pseudepigrapha (Jude 14–15). Therefore, careful consideration of Jude's quotations and allusions to these traditions is the starting place for the use of the OT Pseudepigrapha in the NT.

Jude 5–7 (1 Enoch 10:4–6). The account of Jude 5–7 warns of "angels who did not keep their own domain, but abandoned their proper abode" whom God has "kept in eternal bonds under darkness for the judgment of the great day" (v. 6 NASB). Several traditions in Second Temple Judaism speak to the descent of the "sons of God" (Gen. 6:1–4) as angels transgressing their proper boundaries (e.g., 2 Bar. 56:10–16; CD 2.17–19; Sir. 16:7–10; 3 Macc. 2:4–7; Bauckham, 46; DeSilva, 108), but most immediately reflect God's command to the angel Raphael with respect to Azazel, the fallen angel, or Watcher, who falls under God's judgment: "And secondly the Lord said to Raphael, 'Bind Azaz'el hand and foot (and) throw him into the darkness!' And he made a hole in the desert which was in Duda'el and cast him there; he threw on top of him rugged and sharp rocks. And he covered his face in order that he may not see light; and in order that he may be sent into the fire on the great day of judgment" (1 En. 10:4–6 *OTP*). Azazel's fate will be shared by the other fallen Watchers held in a prison until final judgment (1 En. 18:14–16; 21:3, 10).

This narrative from 1 Enoch belongs to the Book of Watchers (1 En. 1–36), which may date as early as the fourth century BC. That larger narrative draws from the account of Enoch, father of Methuselah (Gen. 5:18–23), and paraphrases and expands upon Gen. 6. The ambiguous "sons of God" (*bənê-hāʾĕlōhîm*, Gen. 6:2a) are explicitly said to be "angels" and "the children of heaven" (1 En. 6:2a). Some two hundred fallen angels, or Watchers, take human wives (1 En. 6:4–5; 7:1a) with whom they sire children (Gen. 6:4b; 1 En. 7:1a). But the Watchers also teach the women magical medicine, incantations, the cutting of roots, and about plants (1 En. 7:1b). The children born to them, whom Genesis calls the "mighty men . . . of old" (*haggibōrîm . . . mēʿôlām*) and "men of renown" (*ʾanšê haššēm*; Gen. 6:4), become in Enoch great giants, three hundred cubits in height (1 En. 7:2b). These beasts first devour produce, then resort to eating people, then birds, wild beasts, reptiles, and fish before devouring one another and drinking blood (1 En. 7:3–5). Where in Genesis the Lord regrets making humans and plans their demise (Gen. 6:5–7), the Book of Watchers lays blame elsewhere, on the fallen Watchers, whose deeds are reported to the Most High (1 En. 9:1–11). The Most High sends the angelic figures to act in response. First, Asuryal is to warn the son of Lamech (Noah) about the coming deluge (10:1–3). Second, Raphael is to bid Azazel and imprison him until the final judgment (10:4–8). Third, Gabriel is instructed to destroy the wicked, including the giants (10:9–10). Fourth, Michael is sent by God to inform the fallen Watchers of their doom and God's intent to rid the world of their wickedness (10:11–16a). God will then restore righteousness and purity, and his people will experience prosperity (10:16b–20). Whereas the myth originally was used in reference to the origin of evil (1 En. 6–19) and is sparsely alluded to in the NT (e.g., 1 Pet. 3:19–20; 2 Pet. 2:4), the origin of evil in early Christianity focuses instead on the fall of Adam (Rom. 5; Bauckham, 51).

For Jude the illustration is poignant: if these angelic figures will not escape God's judgment, neither will the false teachers who have crept into the church (Jude 4; DeSilva, 108). Whether Jude envisions the judgment of the fallen Watchers as a "type" of the false teachers (Bauckham, 53) is not obvious. Regardless, the fate of eternal judgment to be faced by the fallen Watchers will inevitably be shared by Jude's false teachers. Since the Watchers have not "kept" (*tērein*, Jude 6a) to their divinely ordained position, they are now "kept" (*tērein*, v. 6b) in prison to await judgment. No doubt in Jude's context the purpose is to encourage the readers that the real threat their enemies pose to the church will not go unpunished by God's righteous judgment (v. 10).

Jude 9 and the body of Moses. Shortly thereafter, Jude underscores the audacity of the false teachers whom he opposes for reviling "angelic majesties" (Jude 8 NASB) or, more properly, "slander the glorious ones" (*doxas de blasphēmousin*). The "glorious ones" (*doxas*) are surely angels (cf. 1QH[a] 18.8; 2 En. 22:7, 10). However, the nature of the false teachers' slanderous disparagement of angels is obscure. It likely refers to the angels' role as givers of the Law to Moses (Jub. 1:27–29; Josephus, *Ant.* 15.136; cf. Acts 7:38, 53; Heb. 2:2) and so reflects the false teachers' antinomianism (Bauckham, 57–58). In response, Jude references a seemingly familiar tradition regarding "Michael the archangel" (Jude 9), who did not dare revile even the devil but said, "The Lord rebuke you" (Jude 9 NASB). The issue, according to Jude, pertains to a dispute Michael is said to have had with the devil about the body of Moses. In the OT Michael appears in Daniel (Dan. 10:13, 20–21; 12:1) but without reference to Moses. In the Enochic literature he intercedes on behalf of the oppressed (1 En. 9–10; 20:5) and may be the angelic scribe of the Animal Apocalypse (1 En. 89:61–64; 90:22; Hannah, 36–37). He is named as one of the four archangels in the War Scroll (1QM 9.15–17), and the War Scroll seems to attribute to him a position of some authority (1QM 17.6–8). Yet Jude here reports of Michael disputing with the devil regarding the body of Moses. Even Michael, the esteemed archangel, did not have the audacity to rebuke the devil, perhaps regarding accusations the devil has against Moses (Bauckham, 61). Instead, the archangel leaves such judgment in the (proper) hands of God.

This account most likely derives from the Testament of Moses. This work, also known as the Assumption of Moses, is a farewell exhortation given to Joshua by Moses before the transfer of leadership of the people of Israel. The ending of the book has been lost, and it is generally assumed that Moses's death was narrated at some point in the earlier text (Hillel, 2.766–68; Collins, *Apocalyptic*, 159). It dates from early in the first century AD (Gurtner and Stuckenbruck, 169). The beginning of the text is fragmentary, and likely refers to the year of Moses's life when he conveys his farewell speech to Joshua (cf. Deut. 31:2; 34:7; Collins, *Apocalyptic*, 161; Harrington, 59–68). The setting occurs after the exodus and when Israel had crossed the Jordan, and is couched as the prophecy of Moses in Deuteronomy (T. Mos. 1:2–5). Moses instructs Joshua regarding ministry in the tabernacle and leadership of Israel to the promised land (1:6–14) before informing Joshua of Moses's impending death (1:15–18).

Chapters 2–9 then give an extensive prophecy of the history of Israel, beginning with Moses predicting the entry into the promised land under Joshua and extending through the time of the exile (chaps. 2–3). Then comes the restoration (chap. 4) followed by a period (chap. 5) typically associated with the Hellenizing priests appointed during Seleucid rule (198–167 BC) or the priest-kings in place during the Hasmonean rule (142–37 BC). Chapter 6 then recounts events from the Hasmonean rulers up through 4 BC. In chap. 7 Moses foresees a crucial time of destructive rulers, likely the readers' own time, when events of chaps. 5 and 6 come to a climax. The author does not identify particular events, but they are characterized by rulers who are godless, deceitful, self-pleasing, false, devouring, gluttonous, and claim to be righteous (7:3–10). This is followed by a time of persecution and the heroics of a Levite named Taxo, who would rather die than transgress the laws of their ancestral God (chaps. 8–9).

Chapter 10 is a prophecy of the advent of God's kingdom in hymn form, which concludes with Moses announcing his impending death to Joshua (10:11–15). Despite his grief and inability to lead (11:1–12:1), Joshua is encouraged by Moses (12:2–9) and promised that good will come to those who observe God's commands (12:10–11). Furthermore, there will remain a segment of Israel through whom God will establish his ancient covenant (12:12–13). Then the text breaks off in the middle of a sentence, and the remainder of the manuscript is lost.

Several scholars have attempted to reconstruct the sizable material that must have comprised the now lost ending of the Testament of Moses (Bauckham, 73–76). But there is only a small amount that can be said with much certainty. First, the original ending must have contained some account of Moses's death by virtue of the dialogues and the testament form. Second, statements indicating that Moses expected his death (T. Mos. 1:15; 10:14) suggest some accounting of the event itself must have been in the original ending. Third, the concern about how Joshua could care for the body of such a revered figure as Moses (11:7) again suggests his death, and fragments of the lost ending (see below) suggest Michael the archangel may have been involved in the burial or perhaps, fourth, transported his body to heaven (Tromp, 270–71).

Fragments of Greek texts provide some indication of the lost ending, of which the most important are from the *Ecclesiastical History* of Gelasius Cyzicenus (d. ca. 476) and Jude. Gelasius, who elsewhere quotes from T. Mos. 1:14, includes additional quotations in reference to the dispute between the devil and Michael that are almost verbatim to those found in Jude. The Gelasius account reads, "In the book of the Assumption of Moses, the archangel Michael, in a discussion with the devil, says: 'For by his Holy Spirit, all of us have been created,' and further he says: 'God's spirit went forth from his face, and the world came into being'" (*Ecclesiastical History* 2.21.7). This is very much like the reading of Jude 9. Furthermore, Johannes Tromp (272–75) observes that the interchanges between Michael and the devil are nearly identical in Greek, suggesting that the original ending did indeed contain a dispute between Michael and the devil regarding the body of Moses (cf. also Origen, *Princ.* 3.2.1). And so it seems almost certain that the reference to events made by Jude was part of a now lost ending of the Testament of Moses. Nevertheless, the tradition was sufficiently familiar to Jude's readers to illustrate the point about the audacity of the false teachers.

Jude 12b–13 and "wandering stars." In his ongoing berating of the false teachers, Jude regards them as "clouds without water, carried along by winds; autumn trees without fruit, doubly dead, uprooted; wild waves of the sea, casting up their own shame like foam; wandering stars, for whom the black darkness has been reserved forever" (Jude 12b–13 NASB). Some contend that the metaphors and descriptions depicted here reflect those of the Testament of Moses (T. Mos. 10:5–6; see comments by Priest in *OTP* 1:924; cf. also Tromp, 275–81). But save for a reference to the sea (cf. Isa. 57:20), they share only a use of metaphors from nature. In other Jewish literature the order of nature rather than chaos is emphasized (1 En. 2:1–3), showing that all God's works properly obey him and function in their proper ways (1 En. 5:1–4). It therefore becomes poignant when Jude refers to the false teachers as "wandering stars" (*asteres planētai*; Jude 13). Such bodies were unreliable for navigation and so suitable for Jude's contention of the misdirection offered by his opponent (DeSilva, 109). These wayward stars are those "for whom the black darkness has been reserved forever" (Jude 13), where Jude may allude to the place of judgment for the fallen angels in the Book of Watchers (1 En. 18:3–6, 14; 21:3–6; DeSilva, 109). The connection is found in the thought that angels controlled the movement of heavenly bodies (1 En. 82; Bauckham, 89), and misdirection of stars was regarded as eschatological judgment (80:6–8; cf. 86:1–3; 88:1, 3; 90:24).

Jude 14–15 (1 En. 1:9). Having thus far displayed familiarity with traditions in the Pseudepigrapha, Jude next makes an explicit quotation from 1 Enoch. This citation, the only clear quotation of the Pseudepigrapha in the NT, raises a number of important hermeneutical questions. The context is one in which Jude continues his denunciation of the false teachers: "Enoch, the seventh from Adam, prophesied about them: 'See, the Lord is coming with thousands upon thousands of his holy ones to judge everyone, and to convict all of them of all the ungodly acts they have committed in their ungodliness, and of all the defiant words ungodly sinners have spoken against him'" (Jude 14–15). The quotation is taken from 1 En. 1:9, which is the very beginning of the Book of Watchers (1 En. 1–36), which is among the oldest of the Enochic literature and likely serves as an introduction to the entirety of the 1 Enoch corpus (Gurtner, 22). In that context, Enoch, who appears but briefly in the pages of Genesis (Gen. 5:19–24), receives a vision from

God (1 En. 1:1–2) announcing that God himself will come upon Mount Sinai and instill fear to the ends of the earth (1:3–7a). God will bring judgment upon all, but the righteous will receive blessing (1:7b–8). But the fate of the wicked is stated in v. 9, that quoted by Jude: "Behold, he comes with the myriads of his holy ones, to execute judgment on all, and to destroy all the wicked, and to convict all flesh for all the wicked deeds that they have done, and the proud and hard words that wicked sinners spoke against him" (trans. Nickelsburg, 142). While textual comparison between Jude 14–15 and 1 En. 1:9 is warranted, it is important to note that the translation from Jude is directly from its original language of composition (Greek). The Book of Watchers is widely held to be composed originally in Aramaic, which was then rendered into Greek and then Ethiopic (Geʾez; Gurtner, 23–24). The Nickelsburg translation is drawn principally from the Ethiopic but consults extant materials in Aramaic from Qumran that date no later than the first century BC (4Q201 and 4Q204; Milik 140–63, 178–79). Perhaps before the turn of the era the Book of Watchers was rendered into Greek. Yet only about twenty-eight percent of the entirety of 1 Enoch survives in that language (Nickelsburg, *1 Enoch 1*, 12). The Greek of 1:9 is found in Codex Panopolitanus, which dates from the fifth or sixth century AD. Like the remainder of 1 Enoch, the Book of Watchers is preserved in its entirety only in Ethiopic (Geʿez), translated from the Greek sometime between the fourth and sixth centuries (Knibb, 2:21–22). Of the forty-nine Ethiopic manuscripts, however, none date earlier than the fifteenth century. With these observations in view it is worth noting some points of comparison:

> Enoch, the seventh from Adam, prophesied about them: "See, the Lord is coming with thousands upon thousands of his holy ones to judge everyone, and to convict all of them of all the ungodly acts they have committed in their ungodliness, and of all the defiant words ungodly sinners have spoken against him." (Jude 14–15)

> Behold, he comes with the myriads of his holy ones, to execute judgment on all, and to destroy all the wicked, and to convict all flesh for all the wicked deeds that they have done, and the proud and hard words that wicked sinners spoke against him. (Nickelsburg, *1 Enoch 1*, 142)

Responsible comparison with Jude's source text must recognize that he may well have had readings at his disposal that differ from those represented in the Nickelsburg translation. Nonetheless, a few observations may be made. Enoch's "he" is clarified by Jude as "the Lord." The ambiguous "comes" in Enoch is the past tense "came" in Jude, surely in reference to the coming of Christ (Bauckham, 96). Enoch's "myriads" (cf. Deut. 33:2) of holy ones become "many thousands" in Jude. The first purpose, "to execute judgment on all," is identical in both texts. Yet Enoch's purpose, "to destroy all the wicked," is omitted by Jude. And Jude retains Enoch's third purpose, "to convict," but changes the object in Enoch, "all flesh," to "all the ungodly [*asebeis*]," clearly applying the utterance to Jude's opponents particularly. Furthermore, the "proud and hard" words of the wicked are reduced to "all the harsh things [*sklērōn*; "defiant words," NIV]" of the ungodly, and both in Enoch and Jude these are uttered against the Lord (cf. 1 En. 101:3; T. Mos. 7:9; Dan. 7:8, 20; Bauckham, 99).

It is worth commenting that Jude regards Enoch's utterance as prophecy (*proephēteusen*, Jude 14). Bauckham remarks that though this language connotes an understanding of divine inspiration, it need not imply that Jude regarded 1 Enoch as having canonical status (Bauckham, 96). Indeed, Second Temple apocalyptic literature often features prophecy as a key component of the revelatory experience of the visionary as divine mediator (Jassen, "Scribes"; *Mediating*), without claiming authoritative status for the document itself in its respective communities.

Conclusion on Jude. Jude presumes his readers are sufficiently familiar with the traditions referenced to make sense of them. An appeal to an unknown tradition surely would defeat the purposes for which he refers to it. Moreover, Jude's familiarity with at least 1 Enoch is more pervasive than these texts indicate. In his citations in vv. 6, 12–16, he seems to depend on the Aramaic text (vv. 6, 14) and the Greek as well (v. 15; Bauckham, 8). So Jude knows the Book of Watchers (1 En. 1–36 [vv. 6, 12–16]), but also the Astronomical Book (1 En. 72–82 [vv. 12–13]) and perhaps other portions as well (Bauckham, 8).

A more complicated matter pertains to the way in which Jude was received in the early church because of its use of these sources (Chaine, 263–67; Mason, 181–200). Jude is among works spoken against by some, precisely because of its use of 1 Enoch, though by "age and use" it is reckoned among the Holy Scriptures (Jerome, *Vir. ill.* 4). Similarly, Clement of Alexandria (fl. ca. AD 200) in his *Hypotyposes* includes Jude in his canonical list, though Eusebius (citing Clement) lists it among the disputed works (*Hist. eccl.* 6.14.1). In Clement of Alexandria's *Stromata* (again according to Eusebius, *Hist. eccl.* 6.13.6), Jude is among the "disputed Scriptures" (along with Wisdom of Solomon, Sirach, Hebrews, Barnabas, etc.). Yet elsewhere Clement of Alexandria (*Strom.* 3.2) cites Jude's words without question, and even as prophetic. For his part, Eusebius (*Hist. eccl.* 2.23.25) says that Jude, along with James, was disputed, by which he means not many of the "ancients" have mentioned it (cf. also *Hist. eccl.* 3.25.3; 6.25.3). Origen cites it without question (*Comm. Matt.* 10.17; 15.27; 17.30). Tertullian considered that Jude regarded 1 Enoch so highly that the church should afford it canonical authority (*Cult. fem.* 3.3; DeSilva 110). Though Jude was excluded from the Syriac NT (Peshitta) until the sixth century (DeSilva, 110), it was listed as Scripture in the Muratorian Canon and Athanasius's festal letter of AD 367 (Chaine, 263–67). The general consensus, then, is that Jude was widely, though not universally, regarded as authoritative Scripture.

Sufferings of Job in the Book of James

While Jude contains the clearest and most discussed citation of the Pseudepigrapha in the NT, many others are contested. The nature of the debate pertains to whether NT authors are demonstrably dependent upon the psuedepigraphical source or whether they share close points of correspondence by virtue of their shared milieu. Among the most prominent in this category of uncertainty, James exhorts his readers pertaining to the patient endurance exhibited by Job: "As you know, we count as blessed those who have persevered. You have heard of Job's perseverance [*hypomonēn*] and have seen what the Lord finally brought about. The Lord is full of compassion and mercy" (James 5:11).

There are points of similarity between this illustration of Job and the account found in the Testament of Job, which is itself an embellishment of the biblical book of Job. As a testament it presents Job imparting wisdom to his progeny prior to his impending death with particular emphasis on the virtue of patient endurance. Most of the work (T. Job 1:4–45:4) is Job's first-person account of the cause and consequences of his hardships; the work concludes with Job's death, the ascent of his soul, and his burial (T. Job 51–53). Of particular interest is how Job's legendary endurance and patience are emphasized throughout. He is patient at the outset (1:5) and his enduring patience will be rewarded with restored fortunes (4:6; 27:4). He exhibits patience toward those who owe him (11:10), and not even Satan can cause him to forgo his patience (20:1). His endurance and patience occur while he is seated on a dung heap (26:5; cf. 24:1) from which he exhorts his progeny to patience (27:7).

The key verse that is sometimes identified as a source for James is T. Job 1:5: "I am your father Job, fully engaged in endurance [*hypomonē*]. But you are a chosen and honored race from the seed of Jacob, the father of your mother" (*OTP*).

Relevant to whether James uses Testament of Job is the debate concerning the latter's date and provenance (Gurtner, 178–79). The Testament of Job, like nearly all pseudepigrapha, was preserved in Christian environments. Some have regarded the Testament of Job as a Christian writing, but there are no undisputed distinctively Christian (or Jewish) features. Others have argued that the work was a pre-Christian folk presentation of Jewish piety that informed the NT portrayal of Jesus as a sufferer (Spitta) or a pre-Christian work designed according to missionary interests of Hellenistic Judaism (Rahnenführer). Still others argue for a Jewish provenance with specific identification with the Essenes (Kohler). Most scholars attribute the Testament of Job to an Egyptian Jew writing at the turn of the era primarily based on its affinities with other Jewish writings from that date (Collins, "Structure"). Despite these uncertainties, Dale Allison shows that James's distinctive image of Job "matches the portrait in the Testament of Job" as a model for patient endurance (T. Job 1:3; 4:6; 5:1; 26:6; 27:10; Allison, 715) and presumes his knowledge of extracanonical traditions (Allison, 716; Nickelsburg, *Jewish*, 320).

Conclusions

This canvassing of two well-known NT texts that utilize traditions found in the OT Pseudepigrapha shows that at least some authors were familiar with these writings and, for their own purposes, made use of them with presumably some notion that they were in some way familiar to their respective readers. A host of other discussions on lesser points could be proposed. For instance, some regard the Testament of Moses, likely in the background to Jude, as lying behind other texts in the NT (e.g., 2 Pet. 2:13; Acts 7:36–43; Matt. 24:19–21 par.). In addition, it may be that Matthew was "sufficiently familiar" with 1 Enoch in his reference to the blessed inheriting the earth (Matt. 5:5), which David DeSilva (110) regards as cognizant of the promise to the "chosen" that they will enjoy "light and joy and peace, and they will inherit the earth" (1 En. 5:7). Similarly, DeSilva regards as an "echo" a segment from the parable of the wedding feast (Matt. 22:1–14) where the king orders his servants to take the one without a wedding garment and "bind him hand and foot and cast him into the outer darkness" (Matt. 22:13 ESV). This reflects the command in 1 En. 10:4 regarding the fallen watchers: "Bind Azazel hand and foot; cast him into the darkness" (AT). DeSilva regards Matthew's echo as "a phrase borrowed, perhaps unwittingly," from 1 Enoch (DeSilva, 111). Similarly, Amy Richter proposes a fallen Watcher's "template" behind a number of texts in Matthew. Some familiarity with Enochic traditions has also been suggested in the writings of Paul (1 Cor. 11:10), Peter (1 Pet. 3:18–22; 2 Pet. 2:4–5), and the Revelation of John (4:1; 12:8). That NT authors are familiar with and at times make use of these traditions need mean no more than that they were useful for their purposes, and original readers of the NT are well familiar with these authors' tendency to do so. Jesus makes use of nature, agricultural experiences, and home life in his parables. Paul even uses an inscription found on an altar that reads "To an unknown god" (Acts 17:23) as a starting point for his proclamation of the gospel in Athens. So, NT authors' use of this material need not mean they regarded it as authoritative or as Scripture, but rather it reflects authors who were attuned to the literary contexts in which they and their readers functioned.

See also OT Use of the OT: Comparison with the NT Use of the OT; *other Pseudepigrapha articles*; *Dead Sea Scrolls articles; Mishnah, Talmud, and Midrashim articles; Philo articles; Septuagint articles; Targums articles*

Bibliography. Allison, D. C., *James,* ICC (T&T Clark, 2013); Bauckham, R. J., *2 Peter, Jude,* WBC (Word, 1983); Chaine, J., *Les Épîtres Catholiques,* 2nd ed., EBib (Gabalda, 1939); Collins, J. J., *The Apocalyptic Imagination,* 3rd ed. (Eerdmans, 2016); Collins, "Structure and Meaning in the Testament of Job," *Society of Biblical Literature 1974 Seminar Papers,* 2 vols., SBLSP (Society of Biblical Literature, 1974), 1:37–52; DeSilva, D. A., *The Jewish Teachers of Jesus, James, and Jude* (Oxford University Press, 2012); Gurtner, D. M., *Introducing the Pseudepigrapha of Second Temple Judaism* (Baker Academic, 2020); Gurtner, D. M., and L. T. Stuckenbruck, eds., *The T&T Clark Encyclopedia of Second Temple Judaism* (T&T Clark, 2020); Hannah, D. D., *Michael and Christ* (Mohr Siebeck, 1999); Haralambakis, M., *The Testament of Job,* LSTS 80 (T&T Clark, 2012); Harkins, A. K., K. C. Bautch, and J. C. Endres, eds., *The Watchers in Jewish and Christian Traditions* (Fortress, 2014); Harrington, D. J., "Interpreting Israel's History," in *Studies on the Testament of Moses,* ed. G. W. E. Nickelsburg, SCS 4 (Society of Biblical Literature, 1973), 59–68; Hillel, V., "Testaments," in *ESTJ,* 2:766–68; Jassen, A. P., *Mediating the Divine,* STDJ 68 (Brill, 2007); Jassen, "Scribes, Visionaries, and Prophets," *HBAI* 5, no. 3 (2016): 233–54; Knibb, M. A., *The Ethiopic Book of Enoch,* 2 vols. (Clarendon, 1978); Kohler, K., "The Testament of Job," in *Semitic Studies in Memory of Rev. Dr. Alexander Kohut,* ed. G. A. Kohut (Calvary, 1897), 263–338; Mason, E. F., "Biblical and Nonbiblical Traditions in Jude and 2 Peter," in *Reading 1–2 Peter and Jude,* ed. E. F. Mason and T. W. Martin, RBS 77 (Society of Biblical Literature, 2014), 181–200; Milik, J. T., *The Books of Enoch* (Oxford University Press, 1976); Nickelsburg, G. W. E., *1 Enoch 1,* Herm (Fortress, 2001); Nickelsburg, *Jewish Literature between the Bible and the Mishnah,* 2nd ed. (Fortress, 2005); Nickelsburg, G. W. E., and J. C. VanderKam, *1 Enoch 2,* Herm (Fortress, 2012); Rahnenführer, D., "Das Testament Hiob und das Neue Testament," *ZNW* 62 (1971): 68–93; Richter, A. E., *Enoch and the Gospel of Matthew,* PrTMS (Pickwick, 2012); Spitta, F., "Das Testament Hiobs und das Neuen Testament," in *Zur Geschichte und Literatur des Urchristentums,* vol. 3, no. 2 (Vandenhoeck & Ruprecht, 1907), 139–206; Stuckenbruck, L. T., and G. Boccaccini, eds., *Enoch and the Synoptic Gospels,* EJL 44 (SBL Press, 2016); Tromp, J., *The Assumption of Moses,* SVTP 10 (Brill, 1992); VanderKam, J. C., *Jubilees,* 2 vols., Herm (Fortress, 2018).

Daniel M. Gurtner

Qumran *See Dead Sea Scrolls articles*

Quotation, Allusion, and Echo

This article explores the three literary modes of reference known as quotation, allusion, and echo. Their nature is discussed, some examples are presented—especially for allusion, which is the most misunderstood of the three—and definitions are provided. The article also briefly touches on these modes of reference and their relationship to and significance for biblical theology. Yet before beginning discussion of quotation, allusion, and echo, we must first situate them within the broader literary concept known as *intertextuality*.

Intertextuality

The literary critic Julia Kristeva is credited as having coined the term *intertextuality* (*intertextualité*) in her 1969 essay "Word, Dialogue, and Novel" (in Kristeva, *Sēmeiōtikē*; published in English in 1980 in Kristeva, *Desire*), although the concept is rooted in the earlier work of others, including the Russian literary critic M. Bakhtin, whose thought on this shaped Kristeva's own (Allen, 14–15; Orr, 25–27). Therefore, the concept originated squarely within the field of literary criticism, and *intertextuality* is a technical term of that discipline. Unfortunately, today the term "is one of the most commonly used and misused terms in contemporary critical vocabulary," even though it is "one of the central ideas in contemporary literary theory" (Allen, 2). Broadly speaking, intertextuality refers to theories that understand that a text can only ever be understood within its larger network of interconnected relations with other, prior texts (Allen, 1). All texts are intertexts because they dialogue with, refer to, recycle, and are dependent on preexisting texts; no text is an island (Kilbride).

Part of the problem with the term *intertextuality* is that it has come to encompass such a broad range of theories and ways of reading that its meaning has become vague. The critic wanting to conduct an "intertextual" study must therefore provide further explanation to clarify the actual type of approach to be taken in their work. Mary Orr (60) writes, "For interest groups [such as biblical scholars!] wanting to use such a capacious umbrella concept for strategic purposes, intertextuality offers rather small ideological leverage and surprisingly limited sites of operation before the need for distinctive terms re-emerges." Orr's "directory of alternative terms for 'intertext,' 'intertextuality'" at the end of her book demonstrates just how broad of an umbrella concept intertextuality is. She lists a magnificent and dizzying array of terms, ranging from "abridgement" to "hypertext" and from "midrash" to "prefiguration" and "worldwide web" (Orr, 238–46). It becomes obvious that any scholar claiming to conduct an "intertextual" study must further explain what he or she is doing, including providing clear definitions of the subset terms that are going to be employed in the research.

From the 1960s onward, the concept of intertextuality was developed most notably by poststructuralist, deconstructionist, and postmodern literary critics who questioned the authority of the author as originator of a text's meaning (e.g., Barthes). Intertextuality is therefore today predominantly understood as a text-oriented and/or reader-oriented enterprise. Yet literary critics continue to debate the nature of the complex relationships between meaning and the author, the text, and the reader. So even to the present day the concept of intertextuality, at least in theory, continues to have space under its vast canopy for the more modest and traditional author-oriented, diachronic approaches that typically limit study to intentional references to prior texts—such as quotations and allusions. Yet this space under the intertextual umbrella is often grudgingly conceded and vocally contested by many postmodern critics who argue that such author-focused studies are oppressive, privileging some texts or canons while silencing others (see Orr, 60–93). Many postmodern critics do therefore in fact desire the "death of the author" in intertextual study and reject author-oriented approaches.

Others, however, take exception to this postmodern coup d'état, which is viewed as just as much a grasp for power as all the prior ones that postmodern literary critics abhor. Atheist philosopher William Irwin argues that it is *intertextuality* instead that should be "stricken from the lexicon of sincere and intelligent humanists," as it dubiously "implies that language and texts operate independently of human agency," a theory riddled with issues ("Against," 240). He continues, "The term *intertextuality* is at best a rhetorical flourish intended to impress, at worst it is the signifier of an illogical position" (240). He argues it should therefore be dropped as a term (and, more fundamentally, as a credible theory of how literature works). The scholarly debate about this will no doubt continue for some time to come.

Quotation

Quotation stands at the most explicit end of the continuum among the three literary modes of reference explored in this essay. A quotation is an author-oriented, intentional, and overt act. An unintentional quotation is an oxymoron. An author creates a quotation when he or she chooses a selection of text from a prior author and embeds it into his or her own in an explicit and direct attempt to have the reader recognize the embedded material and then interpret the selection *in its new context*. ("Text," "author," and "context" here are broadly conceived, since a "text" could be, e.g., a speech, while an "author" would then be a speaker, not a literal writer.) A quotation of a previous text is normally verbatim or near verbatim, and the words quoted follow one another in what is typically an uninterrupted sequential order. In a successful quotation, the author quotes enough of the prior text for the ideal reader to recognize that the author has embedded words of another text into their own. Often the author provides an explicit marker of some kind to signal to the reader that a quotation has been embedded in the immediate context (typically called a *quotation formula* or *introductory formula*). It must be emphasized with a quotation that the author *wants* the reader to recognize that he or she is quoting a previous source. This should not be understated and is fundamental to quotation. It is an intentional, authorial act of referring to a prior text.

The NT contains 355 quotations according to NA[28]. Other tallies vary depending on the scholar, the text used, the method employed, and how one counts combined quotations (on combined quotations, see Adams and Ehorn). The statistics that follow are based on NA[28]. We use NA[28] as a base in this essay because it is the standard critical edition most used by scholarship, and its editors' identification of quotations will encompass in most cases those references to OT Scripture that would most qualify as quotations due to volume and the presence of explicit markers. The NA[28] italicizes text wherever its editors believe the NT text is quoting text from the OT. Of these 355 quotations, 240 have some sort of quotation formula, and 115 have no quotation formula. Thus, approximately 67 percent of the quotations of the OT in the NT have a quotation formula. A *quotation formula* (or *introductory formula*) is a marker that the author provides to signal to the reader that what follows (or immediately precedes) is a quotation of a prior text.

Table 1. The Longest and Shortest OT Quotations in the NT

OT Text	Location in the NT	Quotation Formula?	Number of Words (in Greek)
Longest Quotations			
Jer. 38:31–34 LXX [31:31–34]	Heb. 8:8–12	yes	131
Joel 3:1–5 LXX [2:28–32]	Acts 2:17–21	yes	95
Ps. 94:7–11 LXX [95:7–11]	Heb. 3:7–11	yes	67
Shortest Quotations[1]			
Exod. 20:15 LXX [20:13] // Deut. 5:18 LXX [5:17]	Matt. 5:21	yes	2
Exod. 20:13 LXX [20:14] // Deut. 5:17 LXX [5:18]	Matt. 5:27	yes	2
Jer. 7:11	Mark 11:17[2] // Luke 19:46[2]	yes	2
Gen. 15:6	Rom. 4:23	yes	2
Exod. 20:17 // Deut. 5:21	Rom. 7:7	yes	2
Deut. 9:19	Heb. 12:21	yes	2
Exod. 20:13 LXX [20:14] // Deut. 5:17 LXX [5:18]	James 2:11a	yes	2
Exod. 20:15 LXX [20:13] // Deut. 5:18 LXX [5:17]	James 2:11b	yes	2

[1] Each of the two-word quotations listed under this header has a quotation formula, which confirms they are quotations and not allusions or echoes.

[2] This quotation is part of a larger, combined quotation.

The NT authors most frequently quote Psalms (over 85x), Isaiah (over 70x), Deuteronomy (at least 35x; more if references to the Decalogue are attributed to Deut. 5 and not Exod. 20), Exodus (over 35x if all quotations of the Decalogue are attributed to Exod. 20 and not Deut. 5), Genesis (at least 27x), Leviticus (14x), Jeremiah (13x),

Hosea (10x), Daniel (8x), and Zechariah (8x). There are no quotations from Judges, Ruth, Ezra, Esther, Ecclesiastes, Song of Solomon, Lamentations, Obadiah, or Nahum. It is also worth noting that there are no quotations from the Apocrypha or deuterocanonical books. The most frequently quoted text is Lev. 19:18.

Table 2. The Most Frequently Quoted OT Texts in the NT according to NA28

OT Text	Number	Wording and Location
Lev. 19:18	9x	"You shall love your neighbor as yourself." Matt. 5:43; 19:19; 22:39; Mark 12:31, 33; Luke 10:27; Rom. 13:9; Gal. 5:14; James 2:8
Ps. 110:1[1]	6x	"The Lord said to my Lord: 'Sit at my right hand . . .'" Matt. 22:44; Mark 12:36; Luke 20:42; Acts 2:34; 1 Cor. 15:25; Heb. 1:13
Exod. 20:12 // Deut. 5:16	6x	"Honor your father and mother." Matt. 15:4; 19:19; Mark 7:10; 10:19; Luke 18:20; Eph. 6:2
Exod. 20:13 // Deut. 5:17	6x	"You shall not murder." Matt. 5:21; 19:18; Mark 10:19; Luke 18:20; Rom. 13:9; James 2:11
Exod. 20:14 // Deut. 5:18	6x	"You shall not commit adultery." Matt. 5:27; 19:18; Mark 10:19; Luke 18:20; Rom. 13:9; James 2:11

[1] If one includes allusions and echoes in the tally, Ps. 110:1 is by far the most frequently referenced text in the NT (Hays, 163–64).

The widespread use of quotation formulae in the NT shows that the phenomenon of quoting is not a modern invention. Ancient writers knew how to quote, and they did so in many ways that mirror our own ways of quoting and use of quotation formulas today. The hard data from the NT suggest that, in general, its authors employed a quotation formula when they wanted to ensure that the reader would recognize and understand that the text that followed (or immediately preceded) was a quotation of a prior text. As stated above, approximately sixty-seven percent of NT quotations have a quotation formula. That means thirty-three percent do not. Why do these latter quotations not have a quotation formula?

If a NT author can successfully quote a passage with or without a quotation formula and, as stated above, a quotation is an author's explicit attempt to have the reader recognize the embedded material in its new context, then one would be reasonably led to believe that a NT author would provide a quotation formula if his quotation was short and/or less explicit and thus in danger of not being detected by the reader. And at times this is true (see, e.g., the two-word quotations in table 2). But in fact, the evidence shows that the opposite is often the case. For every NT book with at least six OT quotations, the average word-count lengths of the quotations *with* a quotation formula are *longer* than the quotations *without* a quotation formula—at times much longer (see table 3).

Table 3. Average Word Counts of OT Quotations in the NT

NT Book	Total Quotations	With a Quotation Formula		Without a Quotation Formula	
		Number	Average Word Count	Number	Average Word Count
Matthew	59	40	14.25	19	7.84
Mark	30	17	13.05	13	8.53
Luke	29	20	12.70	9	6.88
John	17	13	8.15	4	6.25
Acts	32	27	25.37	5	12.80
Romans	51	43	12.95	8	11.12
1 Corinthians	19	13	8.61	6	6.50
2 Corinthians	12	8	9.12	4	6.25
Galatians	10	7	11.28	3	6.33
Ephesians	6	2	13.00	4	9.75
Philippians	0	0	-	0	-
Colossians	0	0	-	0	-
1 Thessalonians	0	0	-	0	-
2 Thessalonians	0	0	-	0	-
1 Timothy	3	2	n/a	1	n/a
2 Timothy	2	2	n/a	0	-
Titus	0	0	-	0	-
Philemon	0	0	-	0	-
Hebrews	43	35	16.09	8	11.00
James	7	5	5.60	2	4.00
1 Peter	18	2	10.50	16	9.60
2 Peter	1	0	-	1	n/a
1 John	0	0	-	0	-
2 John	0	0	-	0	-
3 John	0	0	-	0	-
Jude	1	1	n/a	0	-
Revelation	14	3	15.66	11	9.63

Note: Counts are of Greek words. The editors of the NA28 mark what they consider a quotation by setting text in italics. For the calculations in this table, based on the NA28, words of continuously running italics constitute one quotation. If *kai* ("and") or another word in roman font intervenes and breaks a quotation, and what follows is a quotation from a different OT text, then the material is counted as two quotations. If they come from the same OT text, then they are counted as one. So then, e.g., the catena of OT texts in Rom. 3:10–18 is counted as one quotation even though it is made up of at least six OT texts because the sequence runs continuously in italics with no breaks. Every NT book with a total of at least six OT quotations was included in the calculations.

For example, in Matthew, the average word count for a quotation *with* a quotation formula is 14.25 words, while the average word count for a quotation *without* a quotation formula is 7.84. For Acts, it is 25.37 to 12.80. The evidence thus leads in a different direction. Quotation formulae are used, on average, with the longest and most overt quotations because the author *is in fact always quoting* in these instances. With the quotations without quotation formulae, with their lower average word counts and less explicit nature, a measure of doubt begins to creep in with some or even many of them about whether NA[28] has labeled them correctly as quotations. Many could and probably should be classified as allusions or echoes instead (on which, see below). There are, of course, exceptions. There *are* references to the OT in the NT with no quotation formula that are truly quotations, and the author means for them to be understood as such. But the bottom line is that we can know for certain that a quotation would have been understood as a quotation by an original audience only if the author provides a quotation formula of some sort to indicate this. All other NT references to OT Scripture will simply have to be studied on a case-by-case basis to determine their nature and thus what label might best be used to classify each one. This is important, since each literary mode of reference—quotation, allusion, and echo—is different, with different implications for what the author was attempting to do and thus communicate. It is therefore important to determine as precisely as possible the nature of each literary mode of reference since it impacts one's understanding of the author's intended meaning as that meaning is embedded and encoded in the written text.

The NT includes a few puzzling instances of quotation that scholars continue to discuss. Some NT authors quote material in a way that suggests they believe that what they are quoting is Scripture, but the quotation doesn't match any specific text of OT Scripture as we have them today. For example, the author of John's Gospel has Jesus stating that "whoever believes in me, as Scripture has said, rivers of living water will flow from within them" (7:38). The quotation formula "as Scripture has said" (*eipen hē graphē*) is clearly a reference to the OT, but no specific text of the OT states anywhere exactly that "rivers of living water will flow from within them." It is possible that a collage of OT texts may be in view. In 1 Cor. 9:10 the NA[28] italicizes words that are nowhere found in OT Scripture ("Whoever plows should plow in hope and whoever threshes should thresh in hope of a share in the crop" [NRSV]). Scholars debate whether it should be considered a quotation at all and, if it is a quotation, from where it might originate. Another instance is found in Eph. 5:14, where the author uses the same quotation formula (*dio legei*) he used in 4:8 to introduce a quotation from Ps. 68:18. Yet the text quoted at 5:14—"Wake up, sleeper, rise from the dead, and Christ will shine on you"—is nowhere found in OT Scripture. A final example is found in James 4:5, where the author writes, "Or do you suppose that it is for nothing that the scripture says [*hē graphē legei*; cf. Rom. 4:3], 'God yearns jealously for the spirit that he has made to dwell in us'?" (NRSV). Yet no text of OT Scripture reflects these words.

The NT authors occasionally quote other writings as well. First Timothy 5:18 appears to quote material embedded in Luke 10:7—a NT text. Elsewhere, NT authors appear to quote early Christian hymns, liturgies, poetry, and confessional material (e.g., Phil. 2:5–11; Col. 1:15–20; 1 Tim. 3:16; 2 Tim. 2:11–13; cf. John 1:1–18; Rev. 4–5). Some NT authors quote Greco-Roman writings (e.g., Aratus, *Phaen.* 5 in Acts 17:28; a Greco-Roman proverb in 1 Cor. 15:33, possibly from Menander's *Thais*; Epimenides, a Cretan poet, in Titus 1:12).

What is the purpose or goal of quotation? Today we often place quotation marks around words to ensure we appropriately highlight sources we have borrowed and to avoid accusations of plagiarism. The Greco-Roman world, "contrary to some modern misstatements," also had a concept of plagiarism (Silk). Yet both ancient and modern writers quote for more reasons than merely to credit their sources for information borrowed. Ruth Finnegan (259) writes, "Given its variegated manifestations . . . quoting can be put to multiple uses, deployed for just about any purpose under the sun." Authors of nearly all genres from almost all periods quote in order to "do" all sorts of things within their writings.

Yet the NT authors hold a certain view of the OT that shapes their quotations of that corpus. They understand the OT to be sacred writings, inspired by God himself, and thus to be authoritative and normative. Its epic story is the true story of the whole world, its writings are divine self-disclosure, and its laws are just and true and to be fully obeyed. It is therefore unsurprising that the NT authors often quote Scripture to appeal to divine authority in order to provide support for a point being made in the new context. Yet other purposes can doubtless be detected, and each OT quotation in the NT must be explored on a case-by-case basis to determine the author's purpose for the quotation in its immediate literary context.

We conclude this section on quotation by offering the following definition for this literary mode of reference.

> **Quotation:** A verbatim or near-verbatim selection of a prior text that an author intentionally embeds into their own text in an explicit and direct attempt to have the reader recognize the embedded material and interpret it in its new context. Authors often signal the presence of a quotation by providing a quotation formula or introductory marker.

Allusion

It is true that an allusion is a mode of reference that stands between echo and quotation on the literary continuum of explicitness. Yet it is a fatal literary error to think of allusion merely in terms of a rhetorical hierarchy of overtness. For allusion is in fact a specific and brilliant literary device that an author intentionally employs to evoke a prior text in a new context, and true allusions are infrequently used in the NT (cf. Irwin, "Aesthetics," 530). Many references to the OT in the NT that are classified as "allusions" by NT scholars are in fact often just indirect references or heightened echoes that don't truly allude at all (cf. Coombs, 480). Biblical scholars rightly explore these so-called allusions but have not always attended carefully to those outside their discipline whose field of expertise involves the reasoned study of all sorts of questions about the nature of literature and how it works, including allusion. It therefore seems advisable to explore what literary specialists have to say about allusion rather than using the terminology while missing something essential about how it works. What follows has literary allusions specifically in view, but of course "allusions can and do occur outside of literature" (Irwin, "What," 294). Four elements are essential to the nature of allusion (what follows develops Beetham, 18–20).

Intentionality. An allusion is an author's intentional attempt to point a reader back to a prior text. John Hollander (64) writes that "intention to allude recognizably is essential to the concept" and that "one cannot allude unintentionally—an inadvertent allusion is a kind of solecism." Carmela Perri states that "the author *intends* that the allusion-marker's echo will identify the source text for the audience" (300, emphasis added). Irwin writes that "authorial intention is a necessary condition for allusion" and "an author must intend this indirect reference" ("What," 291, 293). Robert Alter asserts that "allusion implies a writer's active, purposeful use of antecedent texts" (112). Göran Hermerén argues that in allusion "the artist *intended* to make beholders think of the earlier work" (211; italics added). Stephanie Ross (63–64), discussing allusion in art, argues that intent is fundamental to allusion. Ziva Ben-Porat's entire essay on the nature of allusion presupposes that allusion is an intentional, conscious activity. For example, she writes that an allusion marker is "*for* the activation of independent elements from the evoked text" and that this activation of an allusion is "*for* the formation of intertextual patterns" (108–9; italics added).

Single identifiable source. Also fundamental to allusion is that it has "in each instance, a single identifiable source" (Miner, 39). In allusion the author attempts to point the reader to one specific predecessor. This precursor need not be a specific line of prior text; it could be a person, event, tradition, or thing—whether concrete or abstract—outside of any given literary text (cf. Miner, 38–40). In theory the allusion is "identifiable" since the nature of an allusion is such that its wording derives from a prior text or entity that the author has read or knows about and anticipates that his ideal audience will also know. Ben-Porat writes regarding allusion in literature that "allusion is a device for the simultaneous activation of [only] two texts," the alluding and the alluded (107). Yet although each such allusion alludes to one and only one prior text, an author can allude to several texts together in a tight cluster. Each of these would constitute a separate allusion, and each would need to be explored in terms of its essential interpretive links and meaning effects created in the new context (on which, see below).

Sufficient explicitness. While allusion itself is considered an indirect mode of reference, the marker embedded in the alluding text must be sufficiently explicit to be recognized by the ideal reader. Perri (290) writes that it is "generally assumed that allusion-markers are possible to recognize, an assumption which entails that [it] be sufficiently overt to be understood." This further presupposes that author and audience share a "high degree of cultural literacy" that includes "fixed literary canons and a high capacity for verbatim retention of texts" (Alter, 119). A "portable library" must be "shared by the author and his ideal audience" (Hollander, 64). Without this shared library, the audience will almost certainly fail to successfully interpret an allusion made within the assumed cultural-historical-canonical matrix. When this happens, the reader grasps only the surface-level meaning or the "un-allusive" sense of the text (Perri, 295). Yet, depending on the allusion, the reader may still be able to piece together a partial understanding of the author's overall meaning when this occurs. The amount of meaning lost will depend largely on the helps present in the immediate context. Yet an allusion can also miscarry because the author fails to provide a sufficiently explicit marker. An obscure marker renders the audience less likely to recognize the allusion and thus unable to fully grasp the author's meaning.

Essential interpretive link. This is the fundamental feature of allusion that uniquely distinguishes it from quotation and echo and gives it its brilliance and playful, artistic genius. In allusion, the author embeds a marker pointing to another, prior text, inviting the audience to recognize the marker, remember the other text's original context, and link "the appropriate components that the new context requires to be fully understood" (Beetham, 19). Perri (301) writes, "Recognizing, remembering, realizing, connecting: these are the effects of a successfully performed allusion for its audience" (cf. Ben-Porat, 109–11). Michael Thompson develops Perri's thought: "In order for the allusion to be successful, the audience must *recognize* the sign, *realize* that [it] is deliberate, *remember* aspects of the original text to which the author is alluding, and *connect* one or more of these aspects with the alluding text in order to get the author's point" (29). John Campbell (19) adds, "Allusions invite us to select from our mental library, knowledge which is not in the text itself and without which the writer's intention will not be fully communicated." Irwin agrees:

"For an allusion to be successful, in the sense of being understood, the reader must call to mind something not explicitly in the text" ("What," 293).

Yet further it must be emphasized that in allusion the author *intends the audience to connect very specific elements* from the source text to the new context. Irwin writes, "In a successful allusion an author manages to get the audience to fill the gap in just the way he or she intended" ("What," 293). The allusion marker "tacitly specif[ies] the property(ies) belonging to the source text's connotation relevant to the allusion's meaning" (Perri, 291). Michael Leddy (112) writes that allusion "invokes one or more associations of appropriate cultural material and brings them to bear upon a present context," and Irwin asserts that it is these very associations that are absolutely "necessary for correct and completed understanding" ("What," 288). Irwin states that a reader cannot just "call to mind anything at all in his or her 'library of knowledge' to complete the allusion" but must rather "call to mind what the author intended for him or her to call to mind" (293). Any other connections made between the source text and the new text apart from the author's intention we can call "accidental associations," but these are not part of the allusion itself because the author did not intend to create those associations (294).

OT example: Isa. 11:1 and the stump of "Jesse." A couple examples will demonstrate that allusion as outlined above is not a modern literary innovation anachronistically foisted on ancient biblical texts but is itself an ancient literary mode of reference. Our first example comes from Isa. 11:1, where a new oracle is introduced. It reads:

> A shoot shall come out from the stump of
> Jesse,
> and a branch shall grow out of his roots.
> (NRSV)

The allusion marker in this case is "Jesse." Jesse is obviously an individual's name and thus a reference to a person, but the verse itself provides no help contextually about who Jesse may be. The word "Jesse" occurs only once more in Isaiah, several verses later in v. 10, but it also provides no further help as to the identification of Jesse. We do get some help in the verses immediately after v. 1, however, as the imagery of "shoot"/"branch" is unpacked and refers to a powerful ruler full of God's Spirit who executes justice on the earth (vv. 2–5). Nevertheless, without knowing to whom the allusion marker "Jesse" refers, we are left with an allusion whose riddle remains unsolved. We need to know the prior "text" that holds the key to unlocking the meaning of Isa. 11:1. Even though we've pieced together a partial understanding of the passage (recall Perri's "un-allusive" sense above), the author's *intended* meaning is not fully understood. Someone unfamiliar with the historical-canonical matrix of the early stages of monarchy in Israel will not be equipped to unlock the allusion.

Yet for those who know 1 Sam. 16 and/or the tradition that it reflects (cf. Ruth 4:17–22), the allusion to Jesse evokes an entire theme of massive significance for OT theology and, indeed, for all Christian Scripture. In 1 Sam. 16 we read that Jesse is the father of David, who eventually becomes king of Israel and with whom God makes an everlasting covenant, promising that David's descendants will rule over Israel forever (2 Sam. 7:12–16). Over time this theme developed (see Beetham, 102–8, for texts), and what was implicit in seed form grew into a towering tree: this lineage of royal Davidic sons would someday culminate in an ultimate king who would rule the entire world forever. Isaiah 11 taps into and contributes midstream to the development of this theme, adding that all creation will be transformed and renewed at the arrival of this ultimate son of Jesse, this second David (Isa. 11:6–9). These are Isaiah's *intended* associations that he invites his audience to remember and connect to the new context of Isa. 11:1. Isaiah's audience must *recognize* the sign of "Jesse," *realize* that it is deliberate, *remember* aspects of the original text to which the author is alluding (i.e., 1 Sam. 16 and/or the tradition it reflects), and *connect* one or more of these aspects with the alluding text in order to grasp the author's point. Though in Isaiah's oracle the tree of Jesse has been violently cut down (it is, after all, "the *stump* of Jesse"; cf. 10:33–34), God will faithfully fulfill his promise to David, and a scion will grow out of the wreckage to rule the nations, execute justice, and transform creation. By his rule the earth "will be filled with the knowledge of the LORD as the waters cover the sea" (11:9).

NT example: 1 Pet. 5:13 and "Babylon." Our second example comes from the NT at 1 Pet. 5:13. The text reads:

> She who is in Babylon, chosen together with you, sends you her greetings.

Most Petrine specialists agree that, on the surface level, "Babylon" is a reference to the capital city of the powerful Neo-Babylonian Empire that stretched across Mesopotamia along the Euphrates River and that existed for about a century from ca. 626 to 539 BC (at which time the Persian king Cyrus conquered Babylon and brought its empire to an end). Yet in the immediate context of 1 Peter, a reference to the ancient (and all but extinct) capital city of Babylon makes little to no sense, and the author provides no other help in the immediate context as to what he means by this reference.

To make things more complex, most Petrine scholars also agree that "Babylon" is symbolic or figurative language for the city of Rome, the capital of the Roman Empire, in power at the time of writing and the likely place of the composition of the letter (Elliott, 131–32). This interpretation is probably on target and is helpful, but it still does not explain why the author chose the word "Babylon" for Rome. Why not "Nineveh" or "Athens" or "Jerusalem" or "Alexandria"? Why "Babylon"? Without knowing why Babylon was selected, we are left with not just figurative language but an allusion whose riddle remains unsolved. We need to know the prior "text" that holds the key to unlocking the meaning of 1 Pet. 5:13. Even though we have pieced together a partial understanding of the passage (recall Perri's "un-allusive" sense above), the author's fully intended meaning remains inaccessible.

The outsider unfamiliar with the historical-canonical matrix of the Babylonian Empire's subjugation of Judah, their destruction of Jerusalem and its temple, and their forced exile of its people to Babylonia in 587 BC will be unable to unlock the allusion. Yet Second Temple Jews knew this information all too well, as a significant portion of their Hebrew Bible records and is decisively shaped by these momentous historical events and was read regularly in their synagogues. (The historical event of this devastation was second in significance only to the exodus itself in terms of historical impact and memory.) Early gentile Christianity arose from such Jewish synagogues (see Acts) and therefore would likely have had at least some in its scattered communities who would have had rudimentary knowledge of Babylon's decisive role in shaping Israel's sacred history as recorded in the OT. The audience must *recognize* "Babylon" as an allusion marker, *realize* that it is deliberate, *remember* aspects of the original "text" to which the author is alluding (in this case, the "text" is a large thematic swath of OT material, where no one text is likely in view), and *connect* one or more of these aspects with the alluding text in order to grasp fully the author's meaning.

For those who do know this tradition, the allusion to "Babylon" in 1 Pet. 5:13 evokes this whole historical-canonical web of imperial oppression and subjugation, destruction of Jerusalem and the temple, and life in exile as God's chosen people in a harsh, foreign, idolatrous land. This lattermost association is likely the most obvious essential interpretive link that the reader is to remember and connect. Earlier in the letter, the author had written in his epistolary prescript that he was writing to "God's elect, *exiles* scattered throughout the provinces of Pontus, Galatia, Cappadocia, Asia and Bithynia" (1:1), and a bit later he urged them "as foreigners and *exiles*, to abstain from sinful desires, which wage war against your soul" (2:11). The author understands his gentile audience to be God's chosen people in Christ who are living in exile, scattered across the Roman Empire and living amid an uncertain and potentially oppressive period of pagan imperial rule. Life for the Israelite exiles under Babylonian rule provides an analogy (or, perhaps more accurately, a pattern or type) to help Peter's largely gentile audience grasp their own theological situation as Jesus-followers, as the new-covenant people of God.

Why allude? Yet why allude in the first place? Why not just communicate in a more direct mode of communication? Why risk an audience not recognizing an allusion or misconstruing its meaning? Irwin writes, "Allusions can be employed for several different purposes, including to instruct an audience, to generate an aesthetic experience in an audience, and to link or connect the author with a tradition by activating themes, motifs, and symbols" ("Aesthetics," 521). Yet further he writes that sometimes an author can purposely shape an allusion so that the historical-canonical matrix necessary to grasp it is not readily available to every reader of the text. "Allusions can reveal and conceal selectively depending on the audience in a way that straightforward statements ordinarily cannot" (523). Allusions can be crafted to include certain ideal readers who should know the prior "text," rendering them insiders when they successfully connect the essential interpretive link and unlock the allusion. But authors can also craft an allusion in such a way as to exclude certain readers, rendering them unknowing, alienated outsiders because they *don't* know the prior text. When an audience does successfully unlock the allusion, meaning is obviously conveyed, but it also "strengthens the connection between the author and the audience, cultivating intimacy and forging a sense of community. . . . The author and the audience become, in effect, members of a club who know the secret handshake" (523).

Recall the example of "Babylon" in 1 Pet. 5:13 above. Both Jewish and gentile house churches reading 1 Peter would likely have someone in their group who would know the historical-canonical significance of a reference to Babylon because of how those events so decisively shaped the story of OT Scripture. But unknowing, unbelieving Roman imperial governors, magistrates, centurions, and citizens would be much less likely to know OT Scripture and thus be more likely to brush past or misconstrue the allusion marker. The allusion conveys something theologically profound to the insider but conceals its meaning from the outsider, who, in this case, may also be a potential persecutor of the fledgling Christian communities who make up the intended audience.

We conclude this section on allusion by offering the following definition for this literary mode of reference.

> **Allusion:** A literary device that an author intentionally employs to point a reader back to a single identifiable source, of which one or more components must be remembered and brought forward into the new context in order for the alluding text to be fully understood (Beetham, 20).

Echo

An echo is the least explicit mode of reference in the "rhetorical hierarchy" of quotation, allusion, and echo (Hollander, 44). What follows has literary echoes specifically in view. Like allusion, four essential items must be understood in order to grasp the nature of echo (what follows develops Beetham, 20–24).

Indeterminate intentionality. Unlike allusion, an echo may be an intentional or unintentional act. Intention implies a conscious activity, and echo can be but is not always or even often a considered choice. Echo is by nature a subtle reference, and it is difficult if not impossible to discern whether any given instance was intentionally generated. Hollander (64) writes that "in contrast with literary allusion, echo . . . does not depend on conscious intention. The referential nature of poetic echo, as of dreaming . . . may be unconscious or inadvertent."

Single identifiable source. Like allusion, echo has in each instance a single identifiable source (Hollander, 48). When the reference is a literary echo, the wording originates from a specific text that the author has read in the past. In theory the echo is "identifiable" since the nature of an echo is such that its wording derives from a prior text that the author has read or knows. (See further the corresponding discussion under "Allusion.")

Subtle nature. Unlike allusions, echoes are by nature faint and subtle. An author must render an allusion sufficiently explicit for the audience to recognize the allusion, but echoes are more like whispers, understated and elusive. Carlos Baker (8) quips that an echo is a "flash in the brainpan." Perri (304) writes concerning echo that "such subtle incorporations of markers may appear to be for the poet himself, something we 'overhear,' thereby contributing to a quality of lyrical privacy." Yet a reader deeply familiar with the literary canon prized by the author may overhear the author's otherwise private whispers and "flashes in the brainpan" with his or her well-attuned ear. An author typically generates echoes in a text because his or her mind is saturated with the source text(s). For the NT authors, the Scriptures of Israel, the OT, constituted such a sacred, prized canon.

No essential interpretive link. Unlike allusion, an echo can be understood independently of the original meaning of the echoed text. A reader can overlook the presence of an echo but still grasp the author's meaning. This is simply not true for allusion, where a reader must "recognize, remember, realize," and then "connect" the appropriate elements of the alluded text to the alluding text. Hollander (64) writes that "a pointing to, or figuration of, a text recognized by the audience is not the point" of echo. Unlike allusion, echo is a linking of texts without intention to highlight that another, prior text is in play.

Moreover, with echo, the original context may or may not have been taken into consideration. Baker (8) writes that echoes occur "with or without their original contexts" in mind. Therefore, again, a reader may miss an echo yet still grasp the author's meaning in the echoing text. "We cannot speak of a loss of intended-for-the-*public* authorial meaning" when a reader misses an echo. "The component intended as public communication is adequately conveyed apart from recognition of the echo" (Beetham, 22).

Despite this fact, significant reasons exist for why readers will want to explore the original context of an echoed text. Among the most important is that discovery of an echo can unveil a vast textual and symbolic world lying behind and suffusing the new context of the echoing text. Hollander shows repeatedly in *The Figure of Echo* how exploration of the original context of the echoed text uncovers unexpressed links of otherwise unnoticed insight that enhance and deepen a reader's understanding of the echoing text. Richard Hays (20), who builds on Hollander's work, writes that echo often "places the reader within a field of whispered or unstated correspondences." These evoked resonances are discovered only when the echoed and the echoing texts are compared and the original context of the echoed text explored. (For examples of echoes with discussion, see the works of Hollander, Hays, and Beetham in the bibliography.)

We conclude this section on echo by offering the following definition for this literary mode of reference.

> **Echo:** A subtle literary mode of reference that is not intended for public recognition yet derives from a single identifiable source and that an author generates either consciously or unconsciously and contextually or noncontextually (Beetham, 24).

Quotation, Allusion, Echo, and Biblical Theology

Quotations, allusions, and echoes of the OT in the NT play an essential role in constructing a canonical biblical theology of Christian Scripture because they provide the fundamental pillars on which a whole-Bible biblical theology can be built. They are explicit connections between the two Testaments and thus function as bridges that span and link them together. Apostolic interpretation of the OT is central to grasping how the NT relates to the OT. The NT authors' quotations, allusions, and echoes show how they interpreted hundreds of OT texts and thus how they understood those texts in light of the dawning of the new age in Christ. Those same references also often reveal both important unspoken *hermeneutical presuppositions* of the NT author concerning the OT text as well as clues as to how the NT author understood *the original OT context* of the referenced text (see Beetham, 23–24). For example, exploring all the OT quotations, allusions, and echoes in Rom. 9–11 reveals much about how the apostle Paul understood the OT realities of Israel, election, and the remnant in light of the arrival of Messiah Jesus. In my own work in *Echoes* I have tried to show how the theme of new creation quietly suffuses Colossians by virtue of its allusions to and echoes of Gen. 1, Isa. 11, and Prov. 8 (Beetham, passim; see table on 267).

Conclusion

This article has explored the three literary modes of reference known as quotation, allusion, and echo. Their nature has been discussed, some examples have been presented—especially for allusion, the most misunderstood of the three—and definitions have been provided. The article also briefly touched on these modes of reference and their significance for biblical theology. Before beginning our discussion of quotation, allusion, and echo, we first situated them within the broader literary concept known as *intertextuality*. (For an introduction to the study of Scripture's use of prior Scripture that is often called *inner-biblical interpretation* or *inner-biblical exegesis*, see Lester.)

See also Method

Bibliography. Adams, S. A., and S. M. Ehorn, eds., *Composite Citations in Antiquity*, 2 vols., LNTS 525, 593 (T&T Clark, 2016, 2018); Allen, G., *Intertextuality*, 2nd ed. (Routledge, 2011); Alter, R., "Allusion," in *The Pleasures of Reading in an Ideological Age* (Norton, 1996), 111–40; Baker, C., *The Echoing Green* (Princeton University Press, 1984); Barthes, R., "The Death of the Author," in *Image-Text-Music*, trans. S. Heath (1967; repr., Hill & Wang, 1977), 42–48; Beetham, C. A., *Echoes of Scripture in the Letter of Paul to the Colossians*, BIS 96 (Brill, 2009); Ben-Porat, Z., "The Poetics of Literary Allusion," *Poetics and Theory of Literature* 1 (1976): 105–28; Campbell, J., "Allusions and Illusions," *French Studies Bulletin* 15, no. 53 (1994): 18–20; Chandler, J. K., "Romantic Allusiveness," *Critical Inquiry* 8, no. 3 (1982): 461–87; Coombs, J., "Allusion Defined and Explained," *Poetics* 13 (1984): 475–88; Elliott, J., *1 Peter*, AB (Doubleday, 2000); Finnegan, R., *Why Do We Quote?* (Open Book, 2011); Hay, D., *Glory at the Right Hand*, SBLMS 18 (Abingdon, 1973); Hays, R., *Echoes of Scripture in the Letters of Paul* (Yale University Press, 1989); Hermerén, G., "Allusions and Intentions," in *Intention and Interpretation*, ed. G. Iseminger (Temple University Press, 1992), 203–20; Hollander, J., *The Figure of Echo* (University of California Press, 1981); Irwin, W., "The Aesthetics of Allusion," *Journal of Value Inquiry* 36, no. 4 (2002): 521–32; Irwin, "Against Intertextuality," *Philosophy and Literature* 28, no. 2 (2004): 227–42; Irwin, "What Is an Allusion?," *Journal of Aesthetics and Art Criticism* 59, no. 3 (2001): 287–97; Kilbride, L., "Byatt: Intertextuality," Cambridge Authors, accessed May 20, 2022, www.english.cam.ac.uk/cambridgeauthors/byatt-intertextuality; Kristeva, J., *Desire in Language* (Columbia University Press, 1980); Kristeva, *Sēmeiōtikē* (Editions du Seuil, 1969); Leddy, M., "The Limits of Allusion," *British Journal of Aesthetics* 32, no. 2 (1992): 110–22; Lester, G. B., "Inner-biblical Interpretation," in *Oxford Encyclopedia of Biblical Interpretation*, ed. Stephen L. McKenzie, 2 vols. (Oxford University Press, 2013), 1:444–53; Miner, E., "Allusion," in *The New Princeton Encyclopedia of Poetry and Poetics*, ed. A. Preminger and T. Brogan (Princeton University Press, 1993), 38–40; Orr, M., *Intertextuality* (Polity, 2003); Perri, C., "On Alluding," *Poetics* 7 (1978): 289–307; Ross, S., "Art and Allusion," *Journal of Aesthetics and Art Criticism* 40, no. 1 (1981): 59–70; Silk, M. S., "Plagiarism," in *The Oxford Classical Dictionary*, 3rd ed., ed. S. Hornblower and A. Spawforth (Oxford University Press, 1996), 1188; Thompson, M., *Clothed with Christ*, JSNTSup 59 (JSOT Press, 1991).

Christopher A. Beetham

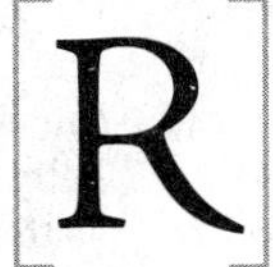

Rabbinic Literature *See Mishnah, Talmud, and Midrashim articles*

Race *See* Jews and Gentiles

Reader-Response Criticism *See* Theological Interpretation of Scripture

Redemptive History *See* Biblical Theology

Remnant *See* Israel and the Church, The Story of

Resurrection

The resurrection of Jesus is not only central to the Christian faith; it is scripturally necessary. The risen Jesus tells his disciples that his resurrection on the third day was necessary to fulfill the Scriptures (Luke 24:44–46; cf. 24:26–27). Similarly, Paul states that Jesus was raised on the third day according to the Scriptures (1 Cor. 15:4). And yet these summaries provide no specific texts. Where does the OT teach the resurrection?

Resurrection teaching does not occur in only a handful of texts; the OT is replete with it. In this essay we'll look first at resurrection in the OT, then at the fuller teaching of resurrection in the NT. The NT authors do not illegitimately import new meanings into OT texts but rightly develop in more detail the OT teaching on the resurrection of the body.

Resurrection in the OT

Pentateuch. Seeing the resurrection in the OT requires the proper framework. The old covenant already speaks about spiritual blessings, including the hope of immortality (Calvin, §2.10). The Pentateuch speaks of God as the Creator, the only true God who kills and makes alive (cf. Deut. 32:39). This theological principle is central to the scriptural rationale for the resurrection: If God can give life in the first place, he can restore to life those who have died. Additionally, not only is God the creator of all, but he is also the covenant Lord of Israel who makes inviolable promises to his people. God does not cease to be the God of Abraham, Isaac, and Jacob when they die, but the covenant relationship continues (Exod. 3:14–15). Further, promises are made to the patriarchs that are yet unfulfilled at the death of the patriarchs (e.g., Gen. 12:1–3), which means there must be a future realization of the covenant promises (Heb. 11:10, 13–16). When Abraham set out to sacrifice Isaac, he recognized that God can raise the dead (Heb. 11:19). This is perhaps evident when Abraham tells his servants that he *and Isaac* will return to them (Gen. 22:5).

"The third day," restoration, and the prophets. Both Jesus and Paul speak of "the third day" as the day of the resurrection, and we may find anticipations of this in the OT where life is restored on the third day, perhaps also in association with the temple theme (Dempster). Restoration to life on the third day is in some sense experienced in Genesis by the cupbearer in prison with Joseph (Gen. 40:12–13) and by Joseph's imprisoned brothers (42:17–18, 20), and later by King Hezekiah, who is restored to life, after the imminent threat of death, on the third day (2 Kings 20:1–6). Jonah is delivered from the great fish after three days and nights (Jon. 1:17). It is on the third day that Israel sees the glory of God at Sinai (Exod. 19:1, 11, 15–16). Hosea likewise speaks of Israel's restoration after three days (Hosea 6:2).

On this point, the OT speaks of Israel's corporate restoration in terms of resurrection. Prominent in this regard is Ezekiel's vision of the valley of dry bones coming back to life (Ezek. 37:1–14). This passage is largely about the restoration of God's people, but it nevertheless assumes that God can raise the dead (Calvin, §2.10.21). The NT shows further how the restoration of God's people and resurrection are closely related. Not every OT passage that looks forward to Jesus's resurrection on the third day is directly *predictive*; often the OT uses types and historical precedents to anticipate the coming eschatological fullness. Other anticipations of the resurrection include the translation of Enoch (Gen. 5:24), the miraculous resuscitations performed by Elijah and Elisha (1 Kings 17:17–24; 2 Kings 4:32–37), and Elijah's fiery chariot (2 Kings 2:11).

The prophets also speak of the hope of new, bodily resurrection life, such as in Isa. 26:19 and perhaps 25:8 (cf. 66:24; Hosea 13:14). Daniel 12:2 contains probably the most explicit text teaching physical resurrection in the OT. Though it may be remarkable for its clarity, it is far from unique in its theology.

Psalms and Wisdom literature. Psalm 16 speaks with clarity about the hope of immortality. David, as a prophet, expresses confidence that the grave will not have the final word (16:10). Though David ultimately speaks about the resurrection of Christ (Acts 2:30–31; cf. 2 Sam. 7:12–13), his confidence expresses hope in life after death and his belief in resurrection life (Turretin, §12.5.6, 15). David even states that his flesh will dwell in security (16:10 [15:9 LXX: "My flesh will dwell in hope" (AT)]; cf. Acts 2:26). David himself had experienced deliverance from death (Ps. 18:4; 116:3), yet he also anticipates final deliverance from death through his greater Son. A similar prayer to David's is expressed by Hananiah, Mishael, and Azariah when they are delivered from the fiery furnace in Dan. 3:88 LXX (OG/θ′).

Wisdom literature also assumes life after death. Proverbs assumes that the righteous will be rewarded in the end (Waltke, *Proverbs*, 104–7). Historically, Job 19:25–26 has been understood to teach physical resurrection ("For I know that my Redeemer lives, and at the last he will stand upon the earth. And after my skin has thus been destroyed, yet in my flesh I shall see God" [ESV]). This passage involves textual difficulties in the MT. Many OT scholars doubt this text speaks of physical resurrection (Martin-Achard, 166–80); others are more open to the possibility (Waltke, *Theology*, 935–36, 968). The NT does not quote Job 19 to support the resurrection (but cf. John 19:30 in NA[28]), though it was invoked in early Christianity to speak of the resurrection of the flesh (1 Clem. 26:3).

Noncanonical literature. Building on OT teaching, several noncanonical Jewish texts attest the resurrection (Elledge). The resurrection features in 2 Macc. 7:9, 11, 22–23 (cf. 4 Macc. 18:17) and 1 En. 22:13; 25:6; 90:33. At Qumran, expectations of the resurrection can be seen in 4Q521, and in fragments of Pseudo-Ezekiel (4Q385; 4Q386; 4Q388), which echo Ezek. 37 (Elledge, 160–69). Other texts that seem to speak of resurrection include 2 Bar. 50:1–3; Sib. Or. 4:181–82; Liv. Pro. 3:12; LAB 3:10; Pss. Sol. 3:12; T. Jud. 25:1; T. Benj. 10:6–11 (see also Haacker). Collectively, such texts illustrate that "expressions of resurrection are deeply rooted in the language of earlier prophetic hopes" (Elledge, 201)

Resurrection according to the Scriptures in the NT

Gospels. The NT grounds the resurrection in the OT. In the Synoptic Gospels, Jesus speaks about giving his generation the sign of Jonah (Matt. 12:38–41; Luke 11:29–32), the sign of the resurrection. Just as Jonah was in the belly of the sea beast for three days and three nights, so the Son of Man will be in the heart of the earth three days and three nights (Matt. 12:39). The background of Jonah, who was delivered from the fish and spewed out on the land (Jon. 2:10), ensures that we are to understand that Jesus will emerge from the heart of the earth after three days. In Luke, Jonah himself became a sign to the people of Nineveh, just as the Son of Man will be a sign to his own generation (11:30). Further, Jesus predicts his resurrection at least three times in the Gospels (Matt. 16:21; 17:22–23; 20:17–19 and pars.); he knows he will be delivered from death more fully even than Jonah. Early church fathers (e.g., Justin Martyr, Athanasius of Alexandria) understood the sign of Jonah to refer to Jesus's resurrection.

In the week leading up to his crucifixion, Jesus addresses some Sadducees' opposition to the resurrection; the debate revolves around the proper way to interpret the OT. The Sadducees' premise was that the teaching of Deut. 25:5–6 could not be reconciled to the doctrine of the resurrection. Jesus responds that they know neither the Scriptures nor the power of God (Matt. 22:20; Mark 12:24). Jesus points out the covenantal formula of Exod. 3:6 ("I am . . . the God of Abraham, the God of Isaac and the God of Jacob") and assumes that the covenantal promises to the patriarchs remain in effect, even though the patriarchs have died, for God is the God not of the dead but of the living (Matt. 22:32; Mark 12:27; Luke 20:38). Jesus's answer demonstrates that the resurrection is indeed rooted in the OT (cf. Luke 20:39).

Similarly, the parable of the rich man and Lazarus (Luke 16:19–31) assumes the OT roots of the resurrection. The rich man pleads with Abraham that he might visit his family and warn them. Abraham responds that Moses and the Prophets are sufficient, and that if they do not believe the Scriptures, neither would they believe if someone were to rise from the dead (16:29–31). This anticipates the scriptural message of the resurrection in Acts, and the lack of belief from many who should have known the teaching of Moses and the Prophets.

In John, the resurrection explains the nature of eternal life. Jesus's interactions with Martha in John 11 make sense in light of the OT teaching on the resurrection. Lazarus has died, and Jesus tells Martha that her brother will rise again (11:23). When Martha affirms that her brother will rise again in the general resurrection on the last day (11:24), Jesus pronounces himself to be (*already*) the resurrection and the life (11:25–26). Jesus does not introduce the resurrection for the first time. Instead, Jesus announces that the end-time hope of Israel has broken into the present age, and is already present in himself (Carson, 412–14; Wright, 444). The raising of Lazarus is the most impressive sign to this point in John, and all of the signs of John revolve around life, which John clarifies is *resurrection* life (see 5:24–29; 20:30–31). When Jesus himself was raised on the first day of the week, this nevertheless came as a surprise to his disciples (Peter and John), who did not yet understand the scriptural necessity that the Messiah must rise again (20:9).

Jesus's identity as the Son of Man may also recall the OT hope of resurrection. As Son of Man, Jesus endures suffering and rejection; but the title Son of Man also has a future glorification in view. Drawing on Dan. 7:13–14, the Son of Man's glorification is manifested in Jesus's resurrected state, with all authority in heaven and on earth (Matt. 28:18–20), and the resurrected Son of Man reigns over an everlasting kingdom.

Jesus speaks of the scriptural necessity of his resurrection on the road to Emmaus (Luke 24:44–47). Earlier, Jesus chides Cleopas and his companion because they were foolish and slow to understand the Scriptures (24:25). He then shows them the necessity of the Messiah's entering into glory (24:26), and thus the scriptural necessity of the resurrection.

Acts. The resurrection of Christ as the fulfillment of the OT is one of the key emphases of Acts. I have argued that one of the purposes of Acts is to provide a defense of the Scriptures, and this is done in large measure by emphasizing the resurrection of Jesus (Crowe, 149–74). Acts thus helps us understand OT teaching on the resurrection and Jesus's summary in Luke 24:44–47.

Peter's sermon at Pentecost (Acts 2:14–36) explains the outpouring of the Holy Spirit through a christological lens: the crucified Jesus has been raised as both Lord and Christ (2:36). To defend the scriptural rationale for Christ's exaltation (which entails the resurrection, ascension, heavenly session, and future return of Jesus), Peter invokes several OT passages. Psalm 16:9–11 predicts that the holy one of God will not see decay (Acts 2:25–28), and Ps. 110:1 supports the exaltation of Jesus to the right hand of God (Acts 2:34–35). "Loosing the birth-pains of death" in Acts 2:24 likely draws from Pss. 18:5; 116:3; this is an appropriate idiom to refer to the resurrection (Anderson, 203–8). The everlasting dynasty offered to David hovers in the background throughout much of Luke and Acts (cf. 2 Sam. 7:12–13) and is probably in view when Peter in Acts 2:30 echoes Pss. 89:4; 132:11. In this context restoration recalls the resurrection and reunification of Ezek. 37: the resurrected and exalted Jesus now reigns over a reunited people (see also Acts 2:24–36).

Later Peter invokes language of the servant from Isa. 53 to speak of the exaltation of Jesus (Act 3:13, 26) and sees Jesus's "raising up" in glory as the ultimate fulfillment of Deut. 18:15, 18 and the raising up of a prophet like Moses (3:22). The raising of Jesus in Acts 4:11 is communicated in language from Ps. 118:22: Jesus is the stone who was rejected but has been raised as the cornerstone. Peter tells Cornelius and those gathered that Jesus, the one who was crucified on the tree, has been raised on the third day and forgiveness of sins is offered in his name, for the prophets spoke of him (10:39–43).

Likewise, Paul emphasizes the resurrection of Jesus and its scriptural foundation. After Paul's encounter with the risen Christ on the road to Damascus, he soon begins to demonstrate from the Scriptures that Jesus is the Christ (cf. Acts 9:22). Given the experience of the *risen* Christ in the shaping of Paul's thinking (Kim), Paul certainly would have been demonstrating (at least) the resurrection from the Scriptures. This is quite clear in Paul's longest speech (13:16–41). Paul explains the scriptural rationale for God raising Jesus from the dead (13:30–33) from Pss. 2:7; 16:10; and Isa. 55:3 (Acts 13:33–35). Paul's logic also assumes he has the promise of an everlasting dynasty of the Davidic covenant squarely in view (cf. 2 Sam. 7:12–13; see also Amos 9:11–12 in Acts 15:16–18). Paul's sermon at Pisidian Antioch provides an epitome of the sort of argument Paul likely would have made in other contexts.

For example, Paul also teaches the resurrection of Jesus from the OT in Thessalonica (Acts 17:1–3; cf. 17:7). Though there are mixed reactions there (17:4–5), the Bereans are more noble (17:10–12): they search the Scriptures to see if Paul's message is true. Since Paul has just been preaching the resurrection (17:1–3), the Bereans surely are searching the Scriptures for the resurrection. Luke surely wants us to understand that they found it amply attested. In Athens Paul does not explicitly quote the OT, but his argument rooting the unity of humanity in the progenitor Adam (17:26) demonstrates a biblical framework for articulating Jesus as resurrected Lord of all (17:30–31).

When on trial, Paul often points to the pristine scriptural heritage of his resurrection message. He is on trial for his belief in the resurrection (23:6); this divides the Pharisees and Sadducees, reinforcing the point that the debate about the resurrection centers on the interpretation of Scripture (contrast 5:34–39 with Luke 20:27–40). Paul proclaims to Felix that the resurrection is clearly taught in the Law and Prophets (Acts 24:14–15). Later Paul urges King Herod Agrippa II to recognize that Christ's resurrection was the fulfillment of the hope of their fathers and that Paul has spoken nothing contrary to their traditions or scriptural heritage (26:6–8, 22–23, 27). Paul sums up the resurrection as the hope of Israel (28:17–20). If Paul is on trial for the resurrection of Jesus, and if the resurrection is amply demonstrated to be a scriptural message, then Scripture itself is on trial (and thus God's faithfulness to his word) along with Paul.

In Acts the resurrection of Jesus demonstrates that the Scriptures are true. To believe the Scriptures is to believe in the resurrection; to resist the scriptural message is to resist the resurrection message.

Paul's Epistles. The resurrection is one of the key emphases of Paul's theology (Gaffin), and Paul often relates this to the fulfillment of the OT. In Rom. 1:1–4 Paul speaks of the gospel of Jesus Christ, which was promised beforehand by the prophets in Scripture and includes the resurrection. Thus, as part of the gospel message the resurrection is a scriptural message. These introductory verses relating the resurrection to the OT provide context for understanding other resurrection passages in Romans (e.g., 4:24–25; 6:4–5, 8). In Rom. 10:6–9 Paul invokes Deut. 9:4; 30:12–14; Ps. 107:26 (106:26 LXX) to speak of the realities of Christ's incarnation and resurrection, and the call to respond in faith to the message that Jesus is the resurrected Lord of all.

Similarly, in Paul's summary of the gospel message in 1 Cor. 15:1–4 he includes Jesus's being raised on the third day according to the Scriptures (15:4). Later Paul expounds upon the resurrection, identifying Jesus's risen glory to be that of the last Adam, in contrast to the first Adam (15:45–49). Whereas the first Adam became (passively) a living being (Gen. 2:7), Christ as the last Adam became life-giving Spirit. Paul also leans on Pss. 8:6 (8:7 LXX); 110:1 (109:1 LXX) to explain the authority of the resurrected and ascended Christ in 1 Cor. 15:25, 27 and Eph. 1:20. Though Paul does not use the title Son of Man for Jesus, one detects the influence in his description of the glorious, risen Son-of-Man-like-Adam who reigns over an everlasting kingdom. All things will finally be subjected to the resurrected Christ as the second and last Adam. By his resurrection Jesus enables us to be clothed in immortality, for he has swallowed up death in victory (Isa. 25:8; Hosea 13:14; 1 Cor. 15:53–55). Paul also speaks of the exaltation of Jesus after his suffering (Phil. 2:9–11), noting that every tongue will confess the risen, exalted Jesus in language that echoes Isa. 45:23.

Hebrews. Not only is the OT central to Hebrews, but so is the resurrection (cf. 13:20). Though much attention in Hebrews is given to the blood and death of Christ, the assumption throughout is that Jesus has risen from the dead and been exalted as the heavenly high priest in the heavenly sanctuary. To make this point, the author often invokes the OT.

The catena of quotations in Heb. 1:5–13, distinguishing the Son from the angels, brings the resurrection into view. The first quotation, in Heb. 1:5 (quoting Ps. 2:7), speaks of the "today" of the Son's begottenness. This "today" is most likely the day of Jesus's resurrection and/or installation to the right hand of the Father (Bavinck, 3:435). Psalm 2:7 is quoted again in Heb. 5:5 to speak of Jesus's appointment as high priest, and Heb. 1:5 also cites the promise of the Davidic covenant in 2 Sam. 7:14, which speaks of an everlasting kingdom that is fulfilled by means of the resurrection. Similarly, the quotation of Ps. 45:6–7 (44:7–8 LXX) in Heb. 1:8–9 makes reference to the everlasting kingdom of the divine Son with an eye to his victory in redemptive history. Psalm 45:6–7 also speaks of the actions of "your God" toward the "God" who sits on the throne—perhaps echoing the divine interplay of persons seen in "the LORD said to my Lord" from Ps. 110:1. The firstborn's entering the world in Heb. 1:6 is the occasion for the angels of God worshiping him (Deut. 32:43 LXX; cf. Ps. 97:7 [96:7 LXX]) and most likely refers to the Son's exaltation and entrance into the heavenly world (Moffitt, 53–69). If so, the resurrection is in view. The catena concludes with Ps. 110:1, which speaks of the exaltation of the resurrected Christ to the place of honor at the right hand of the Father (1:13; also 10:12–13). Psalm 110:4 is quoted in Heb. 5:6; 7:17, 20 (cf. 5:10) to speak of the exalted, resurrected Christ's priesthood after the order of Melchizedek (cf. 7:17). The prevalence of Christ's serving as a high priest in the heavenly sanctuary throughout Hebrews also assumes that Christ rose to new life to serve as an ongoing high priest in a way that excels the sacerdotal ministry of the old covenant (e.g., 7:24–8:4; 9:11–14, 23–28).

The discussion of Christ's humanity in Heb. 2 also builds a resurrection argument on the OT. Psalm 8:4–6 (5–7 LXX) in Heb. 2:6–8 invokes the divine design that all things be put under humanity's feet. Though we don't see this at present, we do see Jesus who has been crowned with glory and honor after his suffering of death (2:9). Jesus has become the forerunner or pioneer (*archēgos*, 2:10), a term that is always used in the NT to refer to the resurrection (cf. Acts 3:15; 5:31; Heb. 12:2; see also Ellingworth, 160). It is unclear whether this term comes from any particular OT passage, but the idea of Jesus as an exalted, resurrected man reigning over all things is intimated by the citation of Ps. 8, which itself is often paired with Ps. 110:1 to speak of Jesus's resurrection. Thus, the means by which Jesus has been crowned with glory and honor must include the resurrection. The vindication of Jesus (and his people) is likely in view, in some way, in the quotations of Ps. 22:22 (21:23 LXX); Isa. 8:17, 18 in Heb. 2:12–13. Though Jesus suffered, this was fitting in order that he might be raised to defeat the one who has the power of death and that he might bring many sons and daughters to glory (2:10, 14–18).

The examples of faith from the OT in Heb. 11 also feature the resurrection. Abraham was willing to offer Isaac as a sacrifice because he knew that God could raise the dead (11:17–19). Indeed, Sarah's faith in the birth of Isaac earlier manifested belief that God can give life even when one is as good as dead (11:11–12). Some women in the OT received back their dead by anticipatory resurrections (11:35). Elsewhere in Heb. 11 the translation of Enoch (11:5), hope in future rewards (patriarchs, 11:16; Moses, 11:26), and indeed the tenor of the passage as a whole point to a coming life beyond the present age. This was already a conviction in the OT.

Catholic Epistles. The resurrection is also foundational in the Catholic Epistles (James through Jude). This is apparent in their emphasis on the return of Christ: if Jesus is going to return, then he lives today. When James 2:1 speaks of Jesus as the Lord of glory, this fits with the broader NT emphasis on the resurrected glory of Jesus as Lord (cf. 1 Cor. 2:8; 2 Pet. 3:18). James 2:1 does not cite any specific OT passage, but it likely invokes the glory of the Lord from the OT.

In 1 Pet. 1:10–12 the OT prophets looked forward to the specifics about the sufferings of Christ and his coming glory; this must include the resurrection of Christ. First Peter 3:18–22 clearly brings Jesus's resurrection into view alongside a discussion of Noah, though many of the details of this passage remain challenging. Jesus is the chief shepherd, who lives and will appear at the end of the age (5:4), which may build on the imagery of God as shepherd (Ps. 23:1–6; Ezek. 34:11–16; see also Clowney, 199–200).

The return of Christ is crucial to 2 Peter as well. This finds support in the glorious unveiling of Jesus on the Mount of Transfiguration (1:16–18). The transfiguration previewed the glory that will be manifested when Christ returns (cf. 1 Pet. 4:13), which also finds support from the OT prophets (2 Pet. 1:19–21).

Revelation. Jesus as the resurrected Son of Man is introduced early in Revelation (1:7, 12–18) and assumed throughout (e.g., 1:5; 2:1–3:22), building on Dan. 7:13–14. As with so much of Revelation, the OT is woven into the fabric of the book even though no OT passage is quoted explicitly. Jesus is the one who was pierced (1:7; cf. Zech. 12:10–12) but who now lives. As the firstborn from the dead Jesus holds the keys of Death and Hades (1:18), which demonstrates his authority over death in a way that builds on the authority of Eliakim (Isa. 22:20–25; Beale, 215). Jesus is the risen, conquering Lion from the tribe of Judah, the Root of David, building on messianic prophecies (e.g., Gen. 49:9–10; Isa. 11:1–10). Later Jesus is the risen, living Lamb, who will guide his people and wipe away every tear from their eyes (Rev. 7:15–17; cf. Isa. 25:8; Rev. 21:4). The kingdom of the risen Christ is an everlasting kingdom (Rev. 1:6; 5:13; 11:15; cf. 21:7), fulfilling the Davidic covenant (2 Sam. 7:12–16). All told, the exalted Christology of Revelation, like the book as a whole, is steeped in OT language.

Conclusion: The Resurrection according to the Scriptures

The resurrection of Christ is one of the central teachings of the NT. Jesus spoke of his resurrection as necessary to fulfill the Scriptures, and the apostolic gospel that features the resurrection is in full accord with the Scriptures. Yet to understand the pluriformity of ways that the OT speaks of the resurrection requires us to appreciate patterns and prefigurations of the resurrection in addition to more direct prophecies. Jesus is the messianic representative who sums up and represents his people. His resurrection fulfills expectations for Israel's corporate restoration, for the rebuilding of the Davidic dynasty, and for the restoration of life after death, for indeed, the resurrection is "the hope of Israel" (Acts 28:20).

See also Adam, First and Last; Consummation; Image of God

Bibliography. Anderson, K. L., *"But God Raised Him from the Dead,"* PBM (Wipf & Stock, 2006); Bauckham, R., "The God Who Raises the Dead," in *The Resurrection of Jesus Christ*, ed. P. Avis (Darton, Longman & Todd, 1993), 136–54; Bavinck, H., *Reformed Dogmatics*, ed. J. Bolt, trans. J. Vriend, 4 vols. (Baker Academic, 2003–8); Beale, G. K., *The Book of Revelation*, NIGTC (Eerdmans, 1999); Calvin, J., *Institutes of the Christian Religion*, ed. J. T. McNeill, trans. F. L. Battles, 2 vols., LCC 20–21 (Westminster, 1960); Carson, D. A., *The Gospel according to John*, PNTC (Eerdmans, 1991); Clowney, E., *The Message of 1 Peter*, BST (InterVarsity, 1988); Crowe, B. D., *The Hope of Israel* (Baker Academic, 2020); Dempster, S. G., "From Slight Peg to Cornerstone to Capstone," *WTJ* 76 (2014): 371–409; Elledge, C. D., *Resurrection of the Dead in Early Judaism, 200 BCE–CE 200* (Oxford University Press, 2017); Ellingworth, P., *The Epistle to the Hebrews*, NIGTC (Eerdmans, 1993); Gaffin, R. B., Jr., *The Centrality of the Resurrection* (Baker, 1978); Gowan, D. E., *Theology of the Prophetic Books* (Westminster John Knox, 1998); Haacker, K., "Das Bekenntnis des Paulus zur Hoffnung Israels nach der Apostelgeschichte des Lukas," *NTS* 31 (1985): 437–51; Keener, C. S., *Acts*, 4 vols. (Baker Academic, 2012–15); Kepple, R. J., "The Hope of Israel, the Resurrection of the Dead, and Jesus," *JETS* 20 (1977): 231–41; Kim, S., *The Origin of Paul's Gospel*, WUNT 2/4 (Eerdmans, 1982); Levenson, J. D., *Resurrection and the Restoration of Israel* (Yale University Press, 2006); MacArthur, H. K., "On the Third Day," *NTS* 18 (1971/1972): 81–86; Marguerat, D., "Quand la résurrection se fait clef de lecture de l'histoire (Luc-Actes)," in *Resurrection of the Dead*, ed. G. Van Oyen and T. Shepherd, BETL 249 (Peeters, 2012), 183–202; Martin-Achard, R., *From Death to Life*, trans. J. P. Smith (Oliver & Boyd, 1960); Moffitt, D. M., *Atonement and the Logic of Resurrection in the Epistle to the Hebrews*, NovTSup 141 (Brill, 2011); Novakovic, L., *Raised from the Dead according to Scripture*, JCT 12 (Bloomsbury T&T Clark, 2012); Peterson, D. G., "Resurrection Apologetics and the Theology of Luke-Acts," in *Proclaiming the Resurrection*, ed. P. M. Head (Paternoster, 1998), 29–57; Turretin, F., *Institutes of Elenctic Theology*, trans. G. M. Giger, ed. J. T. Dennison Jr., 3 vols. (P&R, 1992–97); Waltke, B. K., *The Book of Proverbs: Chapters 1–15*, NICOT (Eerdmans, 2004); Waltke, B. K., *An Old Testament Theology*, with Charles Yu (Zondervan, 2007);

Wright, N. T., *The Resurrection of the Son of God*, COQG 3 (Fortress, 2003).

BRANDON D. CROWE

Retribution *See* Justice

Revelation *See* Mystery

Revelation, Book of

No book in the NT is as saturated with OT imagery as Revelation. Nor is this a question of numerous but incidental details: Revelation cannot be understood apart from its forebears in the Law and the Prophets. Since an exhaustive list of the OT citations and allusions is impossible in a brief article, we will focus on the OT books that make the most critical programmatic contributions to Revelation: Genesis, Exodus, Daniel, the Prophets (with particular attention to Isaiah, Jeremiah, Ezekiel, and Zechariah), and Psalms. (Often more than one OT text will be in play in Revelation, and so there will be inevitable overlaps as we move from one OT book to another.)

Before getting into the individual texts, we may briefly consider *how* Revelation uses the OT. There is one fairly consistent rule of engagement: the *universalization* of texts once focused on Israel (cf. Beale, *Book of Revelation*, 91–92). This does not necessarily preclude the idea that God might have a place in his plan for ethnic Israel or the land, but it does mean that John typically sees promises made to the *people* of Israel in terms of the universal church, and promises about the *land* of Israel in terms of the whole earth, and indeed the whole cosmos. Thus, in Rev. 1:6 the whole church without ethnic distinctions receives the designation once reserved for Israel: "a kingdom and priests" (cf. Exod. 19:6). Likewise, Ezekiel's promise that the renewed Israel will contain trees with "leaves for healing" (Ezek. 47:12) is expanded by John to read "healing *for the nations*" (Rev. 22:2). The worshipers before God's throne include "a great multitude that no one could count, from every nation, tribe, people and language" (Rev. 7:9), and their worship is reminiscent of the Israelite Feast of Booths (see Ulfgard; cf. Zech. 14:16–19). Most obviously, the promises made to the earthly Jerusalem find their fulfillment in Revelation in the new Jerusalem "coming down out of heaven" (Rev. 21:2), which is said to fill an enormous space of twelve thousand cubic stadia (about 1,300 cubic miles—rather larger than the original Jerusalem!).

While this basic principle holds true, what John is doing with an OT reference in any given instance must be resolved on its own terms.

Genesis

Direct citations of Genesis are relatively sparse, but allusions to the book play a crucial role in Revelation's theological outlook. The most transparent allusion comes at Revelation's climactic vision of the new Jerusalem (Rev. 22:1–2): "Then the angel showed me the river of the water of life, as clear as crystal, flowing from the throne of God and of the Lamb down the middle of the street of the city. On each side of the river stood the tree of life, bearing twelve crops of fruit, yielding its fruit every month. And the leaves of the tree are for the healing of the nations."

The river and the tree of life represent the eschatological fulfillment of Gen. 2:10–14 and Gen. 2:9 respectively. The images are enhanced with contributions from Ezek. 47: the mention of the river flowing from the throne is an almost certain allusion to 47:1 (cf. Ps. 46:4), while the detail that the leaves of the tree are for healing comes from 47:12 (John himself appears to add the detail that they are for the healing *of the nations*). Since the allusions represent the fulfillment of God's eschatological plan, they hold a disproportionate importance for understanding God's overall message: God, the maker of heaven and earth (Rev. 4:11; 14:7), will bring the forfeited blessings of Eden back to humanity at the consummation.

Genesis also contributes to John's portrayal of the great antagonist of God, the dragon. In Rev. 12:9 we read: "The great dragon was hurled down—that ancient serpent called the devil, or Satan, who leads the whole world astray. He was hurled to the earth, and his angels with him." Multiple OT texts are in play here: the dragon-serpent hearkens back to, inter alia Isa. 27:1, and his role as the "devil"—the slanderer or *diabolos*—recalls Job 1–2 and Zech. 3. But the juxtaposition of the "ancient" serpent with the messianic birth in 12:5 surely recalls the promise that the offspring of the woman will bruise the serpent's head (Gen. 3:15; see Buisch).

Further allusions might be teased out. For instance, the judgment cycles of the seals (Rev. 6; 8:1–5), trumpets (8:6–9:21; 11:15–19), and bowls (chap. 16) may be explicit acts of "de-creation": six destructive events followed by an interim period and culminating in a seventh unit of absolute judgment—a kind of inverse Sabbath (see McDonough). But the two texts cited capture John's theological foundation in a nutshell: despite the efforts of humanity's primeval antagonist, God will bring his creation project to fruition.

Exodus

If Genesis provides the theological underpinnings of Revelation, Exodus provides its fundamental plotline: through mighty acts of judgment, God is bringing his people out from the oppression of wicked rulers and into the freedom of the promised land. The story is enhanced by other OT books (e.g., the beasts of Dan. 7 and the Zion theology of the prophets) but this is the central narrative thread. The significance of Exodus emerges most clearly in the trumpet and bowl judgments. God's people have cried out for deliverance (Rev. 6:10) and he answers with devastating Exodus-like signs: hail and fire (Rev. 8:7; hail alone 11:19; 16:21; cf. Exod. 9:22–25); water turning to blood and/or becoming undrinkable (Rev. 8:8–11; 16:3–4; cf. Exod. 7:20–25); darkening of the heavenly bodies (Rev. 8:12; 9:2; cf. Exod. 10:21–23); and locust plague (Rev. 9:1–11; cf. Exod. 10:12–15; see Beale, *Book of Revelation*, 465).

The centrality of Exodus is reinforced by the appearance of the two witnesses in Rev. 11: while the figures of Joshua and Zerubbabel may have shaped their narrative in part, the wonder-working activity of the two witnesses most resembles that of Moses and Elijah (cf. Bauckham, *Theology*, 84–88; and remember that Elijah himself is a Moses-figure in the narrative of 1 Kings).

Just as the original exodus culminated in the Song of the Sea after the destruction of Pharaoh and his minions (Exod. 15), so the ultimate exodus finds the redeemed saints celebrating their salvation by the heavenly "sea of glass" (Rev. 15:2). While the sea of glass draws from OT cosmological images of the heavenly sea before the divine throne (see Gen. 1:2; Exod. 24:10; Ezek. 1:22), it is noteworthy that Jewish commentators say that the sea at the exodus became like glass (Mek. Rab. Ishmael, Beshallaḥ 5.15 [on Exod. 14:16–21] and Avot R. Nat. 30a; see Beale, *Book of Revelation*, 791–92). In case someone missed the allusion to Exod. 15, John makes it crystal clear in the ensuing verse: "And [the victorious saints] sang the song of God's servant Moses and of the Lamb" (Rev. 15:3). It is worth noting that the song that follows is drawn from a compilation of OT texts (Jer. 10:6–7; Ps. 86:8–10), not simply from the Song of the Sea (cf. Bauckham, *Theology*, 99–101). But the biblical-theological point is clear: God's people praise him for his works of deliverance in the end just as they did at his seminal work of deliverance at the exodus. The declaration in the vision of Rev. 21:1 that "there was no longer any sea" thus signals (among other things) that the barrier between God's people and their promised land in the presence of God has been removed (see Moo).

We might finally make note of the frequent allusions to temple and priesthood themes throughout Revelation (1:6; 3:12; 5:10; 7:15; 11:1–2, 19; 14:15–17; 20:6; 21:22). Naturally these motifs draw upon any number of OT analogues, along with Jewish traditions surrounding the historical temple(s) in Jerusalem. Nonetheless, Exodus does formally introduce the Israelite cultus and its priesthood in the instructions for the tabernacle (Exod. 26–27) and for the installation of Aaron and his sons as priests (28:1). Amongst the many allusions we may single out Rev. 1:5–6: "To him who loves us and has freed us from our sins by his blood, and has made us to be a kingdom and priests to serve his God and Father—to him be glory and power for ever and ever! Amen." The key is the phrase "a kingdom and priests," which is derived from Exod. 19:6: "You will be for me a kingdom of priests and a holy nation" (cf. LXX: "priestly kingdom"). The strategic deployment of the phrase here at the beginning of Revelation indicates its programmatic importance for the book (which is fitting, since it is equally crucial to the understanding of Israel's role in Exodus). All the depictions of the saints as priests in Revelation go back to this primal text: from their white linen garments (Rev. 3:4, 18) to their songs of praise, to their appearance in God's temple (3:12) (on priesthood in Revelation, see Schüssler Fiorenza). Likewise, the central theme of the saints reigning (sometimes paradoxically in the midst of their sufferings [2:10, 26–27; 3:21; 6:10–11; 7:14]; in the eschaton more straightforwardly [5:10; 15:2; 19:14; 20:4–6; 22:5]) ultimately depends upon Exod. 19:6.

Daniel

While Daniel can of course be grouped with the prophets, we follow the Hebrew canon here and treat him on his own. As G. K. Beale has demonstrated (*Daniel*, 154–305), Daniel was such a formative influence on Revelation that it is difficult to overestimate his importance for the book. We might say that if the central narrative thread of Revelation is Exodus, much of the surrounding tapestry is dominated by Danielic images.

John's inaugural vision of Jesus in Rev. 1 owes much to Daniel's vision of the son of man receiving dominion from the Ancient of Days. While Ezek. 1 has also contributed to John's vision (see below), the images of Christ on the clouds of heaven, hair like white wool, and fiery flames derive from Dan. 7:9–10, 13–14. The fact that John sees the risen Christ clothed in the splendor of the Ancient of Days is one of the most powerful examples of his high Christology (cf. Mounce, 58).

Daniel 7 (again in conjunction with Ezek. 1, with an equally important contribution from Isa. 6) also forms the basis for another controlling image of Revelation: the throne room of God, especially as it is described in Rev. 4–5. One of the most important moments in the book—the Lamb's reception of the scroll, representing the achievement of God's kingdom (Rev. 5:6–6:1)—is predicated upon the son of man's reception of rule from the Ancient of Days (Dan. 7:13–14; cf. Aune, 336–38).

If John's portrait of God and his Christ owes much to Daniel, this is even more true of the great antagonist of the saints, the beast of Rev. 13. This antichrist figure represents an amalgam of the four beasts emerging from the sea in Dan. 7: whereas Daniel sees beasts "like a lion . . . like a bear . . . like a leopard" along with a "terrifying and frightening and very powerful" fourth beast (Dan. 7:3–7), John sees one beast (presumably Daniel's fourth beast) which combines the traits of the first three: the creature he sees "resembled a leopard, but had feet like those of a bear and a mouth like that of a lion" (Rev. 13:2).

It is fitting that the dragon—whose appearance with seven heads and *ten horns* is a back-formation from the description of the beast in Dan. 7:7, 24—acts in keeping with the rampaging beast of Dan. 8:10: "Its tail swept a third of the stars out of the sky and flung them to the earth" (Rev. 12:4). John deliberately expands the scope of Daniel's beast imagery to create a nightmare vision of a "satanic trinity" that dominates the action of the central chapters of Revelation: the dragon, who represents the false "father" and would-be ruler of the cosmos; the first beast, the dragon's authorized ruler on earth, and thus in the strict sense his antichrist (though John does not use that explicit term); and the second beast, the mockery of the Holy Spirit who propagandizes on behalf of the first beast and the dragon. Together they raise up the counterfeit city Babylon and seek to seduce people from the worship of the true and living God (see McDonough).

Revelation 12–20 as a whole can thus be seen as a chiastic representation of the rise and fall of the satanic empire: the figures of the dragon, the beasts, and Babylon are marched onto the stage in chaps. 12–14 and then summarily marched off it in reverse order in chaps. 15–20 (judgment of Babylon, chaps. 16–19; judgment of beasts in chap. 19; judgment of Satan in chap. 20; cf. Beale, *Book of Revelation*, 622–23).

Daniel also provides one of the key numerical schemes for Revelation. When Daniel asks the "man clothed in linen," "How long will it be before these astonishing things are fulfilled?" he is told, "It will be for a time, times, and half a time" (Dan. 12:6–7). John translates this figure to "three and a half years" and elsewhere describes it as "forty-two months" and "1,260 days" (Rev. 11:2–3). While this unit of time has been taken literally and projected onto a variety of last-days scenarios, the fact that John describes it in three different ways augurs for a symbolic interpretation: the "end time" Daniel foresees begins with the death, resurrection, and ascension of Jesus, and represents the entirety of the church age. John's differentiation of the "time, times and half a time" into years, days, and months can then be seen as a brilliant technique to tease out the complex reality of the church age: the church is subject to persecution or "trampling" for forty-two months (Rev. 11:2); yet during this *very same time* it serves as God's powerful prophetic witness (1,260 days, Rev. 11:3; cf. Beale, *Book of Revelation*, 565–68).

Many of the images of *judgment* in Revelation have roots in Daniel. The most striking perhaps is the note in Rev. 20:4: "I saw thrones on which were seated those who had been given authority to judge"; this recalls Dan. 7:9–10: "As I looked, thrones were set in place, and the Ancient of Days took his seat. . . . The court was seated, and the books were opened." This text is also the proximate source for the "books" that appear in Rev. 20:12: "And I saw the dead, great and small, standing before the throne, and books were opened. Another book was opened, which is the book of life. The dead were judged according to what they had done as recorded in the books." Finally, while fire is frequently associated with judgment in the OT (e.g., Ps. 80:16, Jer. 51:25), this is a concentrated image in Dan. 7: God's throne is described as "flaming with fire"; its wheels "were all ablaze"; and "a river of fire was flowing, coming out before him" (Dan. 7:9–10).

The Prophets

Chief among the concerns of Israel's prophets was the fate of Jerusalem, especially after its devastation at the hands of the Babylonians in 586 BC. Whether they were foretelling its doom (early chapters of Jeremiah) or searching for hope amidst its ruins (Isaiah, Zechariah, et al.), the destiny of the holy city overshadows virtually all else. The prophet John follows in their train, seeing himself as a prophet (cf. esp. Rev. 10 discussed below), such that Richard Bauckham has aptly titled his book on Revelation *The Climax of Prophecy*. While John universalizes the theme beyond the confines of ethnic Israel, the future of God's city provides yet another way of getting at the core message of Revelation: God is determined to establish his city, the new Jerusalem, on earth, and no human or satanic opposition will stop him. It remains to see how John weaves material from the individual prophets into this central theme.

Isaiah. Isaiah is arguably the most important book in the OT for the shaping of NT theology: it looks back to the traditions of creation and exodus, while looking forward to the redemption of Israel and the nations through the work of God's servant. It is not surprising that Isaiah is a pillar of Revelation as well.

We have noted the importance of Daniel for the central throne-room vision of Rev. 4–5. Isaiah is almost as critical to understanding these chapters. The wings of the "living creatures" in Rev. 4 associate them with the seraphim of Isa. 6. More importantly, the song of the seraphim in Isaiah—"Holy, holy, holy is the LORD Almighty; the whole earth is full of his glory" (6:3)—has been subtly changed in Rev. 4:8, which reads, "'Holy, holy, holy is the Lord God Almighty,' who was and is and is to come." The substitution of "who was and is and is to come" for "the whole earth is full of his glory" indicates that in the throne vision of Rev. 4 God's glory is not yet fully present on earth (hence the need for him to *come*); this will await the advent of the Messiah and the beginning of his messianic reign (Bauckham, *Theology*, 140–43). The lamb-like nature of that reign (Rev. 5:6), while evoking images of the Passover and the temple cult, is also likely derived from the quintessential suffering-servant passage in Isa. 52–53: "He was oppressed and afflicted, yet he did not open his mouth; he was led like a lamb to the slaughter, and as a sheep before its shearers is silent . . ." (53:7).

Isaiah also furnishes imagery for two of the other prime characters in the book. The rendering of Satan as "the dragon" has its most obvious roots in Isa. 27:1: "In that day, the LORD will punish with his sword—his fierce, great and powerful sword—Leviathan the gliding serpent, Leviathan the coiling serpent; he will slay the monster of the sea" (LXX: *epi ton drakonta ophin skolion kai anelei ton drakonta*). The fact that this comes in the midst of Isaiah's "Little Apocalypse" solidifies the case that John has it in mind. John draws from this same setting to label the collective character "the inhabitants of the earth" (e.g., Rev. 3:10; 13:8, 14). Far from being a neutral category of "everyone who happens to be in the world," it instead describes the idolatrous "worldlings" subject to the divine wrath (see Isa. 24:5–6: "The earth is defiled by its people; they have disobeyed the laws, violated the statutes and broken the everlasting covenant. Therefore a curse consumes the earth; its people must bear their guilt"; cf. Bauckham, *Climax*, 239–41).

Perhaps Isaiah's most enduring legacy to Revelation lies in the description of the new Jerusalem. Just after the servant song of chaps. 52–53, Isaiah describes the glorious restoration of the holy city; this includes its adornment with jewels (Isa. 54:11–12: "I will rebuild you with stones of turquoise, your foundations with lapis lazuli. I will make your battlements of rubies, your gates of sparkling jewels, and all your walls of precious stones"). This vision lies at the heart of John's glittering description of the new Jerusalem in Rev. 21:18–21 (though in typical fashion John melds Isaiah's imagery with other OT texts; cf. Koester, 817–20). This fulfills the promise of Isa. 65:17: "See, I will create new heavens and a new earth" (cf. Rev. 21:1).

Jeremiah. Jeremiah is of chief interest to us for its lengthy portrayal of the judgment of Babylon in Jer. 51. The destruction of Babylon and its replacement by the new Jerusalem is at the heart of John's message, and Jeremiah plays an important role in furnishing images for that destruction. The practical message of Revelation is summed up most succinctly in the exhortation to flee Babylon: "Come out of her, my people, so that you will not share in her sins, so that you will not receive any of her plagues; for her sins are piled up to heaven, and God has remembered her crimes" (18:4–5). This is clearly drawn from Jer. 51:6 (cf. v. 45): "Flee from Babylon! Run for your lives! Do not be destroyed because of her sins. It is time for the LORD's vengeance; he will repay her what she deserves." The maddening wine Babylon has given the nations (Rev. 18:3) recalls Jer. 51 (v. 7), as does the note that Babylon will become a haunt of unclean beasts (Rev. 18:2; cf. Jer. 51:37).

The most important detail for us, however, may be the note in Jer. 51:25 that the "destroying mountain" Babylon will be "roll[ed] . . . off the cliffs" and become a "burned-out mountain"; the image is reinforced in Jeremiah's acted parable where he ties his book to a stone, throws it into the Euphrates, and declares, "So will Babylon sink to rise no more" (51:64). In light of the importance of Jer. 51 elsewhere, it hardly seems coincidental that the language of Rev. 8:8–11 features a burning mountain being thrown into the sea, with dire consequences for the world:

> The second angel sounded his trumpet, and something like a huge mountain, all ablaze, was thrown into the sea. A third of the sea turned into blood, a third of the living creatures in the sea died, and a third of the ships were destroyed.
>
> The third angel sounded his trumpet, and a great star, blazing like a torch, fell from the sky on a third of the rivers and on the springs of water—the name of the star is Wormwood. A third of the waters turned bitter, and many people died from the waters that had become bitter.

While the trumpet judgments are among the hardest things to account for in all Revelation, the parallels with Jeremiah suggest at a minimum that John has the judgment of Babylon in mind long before he names the city in Rev. 14 (cf. Caird, 114).

Ezekiel. The inaugural vision of Ezek. 1 plays an important role in establishing John's portrait of God in Revelation. The fiery advent of God in Ezek. 1:4 recalls Christ's appearance in Rev. 1:16: "His face was like the sun shining in all its brilliance." An even more obvious connection is the "four living creatures" before the divine throne in both Ezek. 1:5–14 and Rev. 4:6–9. Though the particulars differ, the presence of human, ox, lion, and eagle faces betray John's indebtedness to Ezekiel (as we noted above, Isaiah's portrayal of the seraphim adds to the picture). Unlike Ezekiel, John does not describe in detail the glory of the enthroned God. But he does note the presence of the sea of glass before him (Rev. 4:6; cf. Ezek. 1:22). He also picks up the image of the rainbow around God's throne from the prophet (Rev. 4:3; cf. Ezek. 1:28). Bauckham sees this as a sign that God will not abandon his creation, but will bring it to full flourishing (Bauckham, *Theology*, 51–53).

The opening chapters of Ezekiel also provide the template for John's self-understanding of his prophetic-apocalyptic mission. Whether John on Patmos saw himself as analogous to Ezekiel in exile by the Chebar River in Babylon is open for debate, though it seems likely in light of John's identification with Ezekiel and his emphasis on Babylon (cf. Bauckham, *Theology*, 2–5). In Rev. 10:8–11, John is commanded to eat a scroll, which is sweet as honey in his mouth but bitter in his stomach; the angel then explains, "You must prophesy again about many peoples, nations, languages and kings." This is taken practically verbatim from Ezekiel's prophetic commissioning in Ezek. 3:1–3: "Son of man, eat what is before you. Eat this scroll; then go and speak to the house of Israel. . . . So I ate it, and it tasted as sweet as honey in my mouth." This passage also aids our understanding of the pivotal scroll in Rev. 5 (Bauckham, *Climax*, 246–53). The scroll in Rev. 5:1 is said to be an opisthograph, having writing on the inside and outside, just like the scroll in Ezekiel (2:10). Although John does not explicitly note that his scroll contains "written words of lament and mourning and woe" (Ezek. 2:10), this is a fair summary of the contents of Revelation.

The vision of divine judgment on Jerusalem in Ezek. 9 may indirectly help us with the *hermeneutics* of

Revelation. There is an obvious connection between the "sealing" of the saints with a mark on the forehead in Rev. 7:3 and the similar marking of the foreheads of repentant Israelites in Ezek. 9:4. What is of chief interest, however, is the relationship of Ezekiel's vision to the historical reality it represents and how that might influence our interpretation of Revelation. Ezekiel 9 is clearly referring to the ravaging of Jerusalem by the Babylonians in 586 BC. In the vision, the slaughter is done by six presumably angelic agents who start in the temple and spare only the righteous. Yet the historical conquest was of course done by the Babylonians, who would have begun slaughtering people on the perimeter of the city and only then moved into the temple. Nor is there any evidence that the righteous were miraculously spared in the invasion and only the wicked killed: the spiritual obduracy of the Israelites in exile, well known to Ezekiel and Jeremiah, confirms this. The vision thus informs us of important *spiritual* truths concerning the punishment of Jerusalem—but it is not meant to be a blow-by-blow depiction of events on the ground. This would appear to provide a sensible reading strategy for Revelation as well. We certainly need to consider the historical context of Revelation as we study the book, just as we need to consider the historical context of the fall of Jerusalem when we study Ezekiel. But this does not mean that things happening in the vision will exactly match things happening in John's day or at some point in the future.

Ezekiel finally plays a foundational role for the structure and imagery of the final chapters in Revelation, to the extent that a thoughtful examination of Ezekiel becomes essential for a responsible approach to the admittedly vexing problem of the millennium in Rev. 20. The key lies in the unfolding of events in Ezek. 38–40 (cf. Stewart, 571–74). Ezekiel 38 features a prophecy against "Gog, of the land of Magog" (38:2), which involves an attempt by Gog to assault Israel, only to meet with a devastating defeat engineered by God. Curiously, Ezek. 39 repeats the prophecy against Gog, albeit with differing details. After this dual narration of the defeat of Gog, Ezek. 40–48 reports the restoration of the land of Israel and the temple.

Revelation 19–20 appears to mirror Ezekiel's structure and includes specific allusions to Ezek. 38–48. The battle (and note that the Greek of 19:19, as in 16:14 and 20:8, features the definite article, suggesting that *one* battle, *the* battle, is in view in all three places) in which the two beasts are conquered includes a heavenly voice calling for the birds to "come, gather together for the great supper of God, so that you may eat the flesh of kings, generals, and the mighty" (Rev. 19:17–18), an echo of Ezekiel 39:17–20. The (same?) battle against the dragon in Rev. 20:7–10 contains an explicit mention of Gog and Magog (20:8). Shortly after this, John reports that an angel "carried [him] away in the Spirit to a mountain great and high, and showed [him] the Holy City, Jerusalem, coming down out of heaven from God" (21:10); this is obviously mirroring Ezek. 40:2: "In visions of God he took me to the land of Israel and set me on a very high mountain, on whose south side were some buildings that looked like a city." The parallels continue with the aforementioned reference to the river of the new Jerusalem recalling Ezek. 47.

We have in Ezekiel, then, an initial Gog battle narrative, a second Gog battle narrative, and a mountain vision of the eschatological temple. Revelation offers a battle narrative referencing the Gog story, a second battle narrative overtly speaking of Gog (and Magog), and a mountain vision of the eschatological city, which is said to have no temple. The similarities hardly seem coincidental. While the likeness of the patterns does not guarantee that the visions in Rev. 19–20 represent the same events seen from different perspectives, it strongly suggests that this could be the case.

Truly, all Revelation is saturated with allusions to Ezekiel (on which, see Kowalski).

Zechariah. Since Zechariah shares with other prophets an emphasis on the restoration of Jerusalem (with a particular emphasis on the eschatological nature of that restoration in Zech. 14) it is difficult in places to know whether John is influenced by Zechariah or another OT text. But Zechariah's distinctive voice may be discerned at some key junctures in the book (see Jauhiainen), and we may say that Zechariah's relatively compact book, with its consistent focus on the restoration of Jerusalem, would have made it a particularly important source for John.

John draws on Zechariah right from the first chapter, where he previews what is to come with a quotation from Zech. 12:10: "'Every eye will see him, even those who pierced him'; and all peoples on earth 'will mourn because of him.' So shall it be! Amen" (Rev. 1:7). The inaugural appearance of Christ amid the seven golden lampstands is likely drawn from Zech. 4 (cf. Beale, *Book of Revelation*, 206–7). While Exod. 25 is surely the base for the visions of both John and Zechariah, the fact that Zech. 4 concerns the Davidic ruler Zerubbabel and his role in rebuilding the temple makes it an ideal text for John to deploy. In addition to providing an OT rationale for directing his message to *seven* churches, the interpretation of the lamps as the "eyes of the LORD" (Zech. 4:10; cf. 3:9) may have influenced John's unusual note of the "seven spirits before [God's] throne" in the trinitarian formula of Rev. 1:4 (Beale, *Book of Revelation*, 189).

Zechariah is also the source of one of Revelation's best-known images, the notorious "four horsemen of the apocalypse" (Rev. 6:1–8). After a brief introduction, Zechariah begins with a vision of four horsemen of different colors sent out by God to patrol the earth (1:7–12); later he sees a quartet of chariots likewise drawn by multicolored horses (6:1–8). John apparently has blended the two visions (and added his own distinctive elements), since the horsemen of Zech. 1 are messengers or spies, and the martial element emerges only with the chariots of Zech. 6, whereas John's four individual horsemen are emblems of war (cf. Beale, *Book of Revelation*, 372).

Zechariah not only provides *seven* spirits and *four* horsemen but also supplies the proximate source for the image of the *two* witnesses in Rev. 11. We have seen that the activity of the witnesses best matches the ministries of Moses and Elijah; and the traditional OT demand for two witnesses (Deut. 19:15) is also surely relevant. But when John tells us in 11:4 that "they are 'the two olive trees' and the two lampstands, and 'they stand before the Lord of the earth,'" it is impossible to miss the connection with Zech. 4:11–14. Since the context of Zech. 4 concerns the reestablishment of God's temple, it is not surprising to see that John's reference to the olive-tree witnesses follows hard on the heels of a depiction of the church as a temple in Rev. 11:1–2.

The well-known battle of Armageddon (Rev. 16:16) is at least partially related to Zechariah (with a considerable assist from Isaiah). The plain of Megiddo was a convenient battle location in Israel, as can be seen in Judges 5:19 and 2 Kings 9:27. But even more intriguing is Zech. 12:11: "On that day the weeping in Jerusalem will be as great as the weeping of Hadad Rimmon in the plain of Megiddo." The near context features the eschatological battle of the nations against Jerusalem, which profoundly shapes John's vision of the end in Rev. 16–20. And we have already seen that the immediately preceding verse, "They will look on me, the one they have pierced" (Zech. 12:10), is of programmatic importance for Revelation.

In light of the pervasive importance of Zechariah for John, the prophet's climactic vision in Zech. 14 is likely a primary source for John's vision of the nations besieging Jerusalem (Rev. 16:16; 20:9). There is undoubtedly a mélange of texts adding to the vision: we have already noted Ezekiel's contribution, and we could add to that Joel 3 (e.g., v. 12: "Let the nations be roused; let them advance into the Valley of Jehoshaphat, for there I will sit to judge all the nations on every side"). But the peculiar detail in Zech. 14 that the nations will celebrate the Feast of Booths in the eschaton seems to find its fulfillment in the worship of the saints in Rev. 7, and Zech. 14 has a cluster of features that resonate with Revelation: the eschatological earthquake (Zech. 14:4–5; Rev. 6:12; 8:5; 11:13; 16:18); the Lord himself fighting on behalf of Israel (Zech. 14:3; Rev. 19:11); perpetual light (Zech. 14:7; Rev. 21:25); living waters flowing from Jerusalem (Zech. 14:8; Rev. 22:1); and no curse in Jerusalem (Zech. 14:11; Rev. 22:3).

Psalms

Given their anthological nature, the Psalms do not make a thematic contribution to Revelation in quite the same way as Genesis, Exodus, or the prophets. Yet they are still critical to the book: Revelation's repeated depictions of worship and song make the Psalms an obvious and frequently alluded-to resource. As much as any set of texts they inform the mood of Revelation, as well as adding sundry items of independent theological interest. Despite the scattered nature of the references, then, it is helpful to at least make note of some of the most important uses of the Psalms in Revelation.

Since this is the "revelation of Jesus *the Messiah*" (Rev. 1:1 AT), it is natural that the messianic psalms play an important role in the proceedings. Psalm 2 is of particular note. The message to Thyatira contains a quotation from Ps. 2:8–9: the one who overcomes "will rule them [= the nations] with an iron scepter and will dash them to pieces like pottery" (Rev. 2:27). In the psalm, this pertains to the son's rule, a point that is affirmed in Rev. 12:5 and 19:15, where Ps. 2:8–9 is applied to Jesus; in Rev. 2, that authority extends to the Messiah's followers. Psalm 2 also underlies the general opposition to the Messiah's reign that characterizes Rev. 12–20. The psalm begins, "Why do the nations conspire and the peoples plot in vain? The kings of the earth rise up and the rulers band together against the LORD and against his anointed" (Ps. 2:1–2). John picks up the phrase "the kings of the earth" (e.g., Rev. 17:18; 19:19), a sign that the warfare in the final chapters of Revelation draws in significant measure from the psalm. Note too that the Messiah is established on "Zion, my holy mountain" (Ps. 2:6), just as the Lamb stands on Mount Zion in Rev. 14:1.

Psalm 89 focuses on David and his dynasty, and thus it is not surprising to see it factor in the introduction of Jesus in Rev. 1:5. The notion that Jesus is "*firstborn* from the dead" is derived from Ps. 89:27, while the preceding phrase, "the faithful witness," is at least in part derived from the nearby Ps. 89:37 (cf. Moyise, "Psalms," 250–51; while it is used there of the "faithful witness" of the moon, it appears John has taken this as a messianic image [cf. Exod. Rab. 19:7 and note that the very next verse in the psalm mentions the casting off and rejection of *the anointed one*]). While the NT's favorite messianic psalm, Ps. 110, does not make an overt appearance in Revelation, it is almost certainly in the background of the tableau in Rev. 4–5, where the Lamb receives the scroll from God in the throne room—note that the scroll is in God's right hand (cf. Ps. 110:1).

The pot-smashing king in Ps. 2 presents a rather sobering view of God's rule over the nations. This is mitigated in at least two important ways in Revelation, with the assistance of the psalms. First, God's relationship with his people is presented in intimate, caring terms in Rev. 7:17: "For the Lamb at the center of the throne will be their shepherd; 'he will lead them to springs of living water.' 'And God will wipe away every tear from their eyes.'" The image of the loving shepherd is drawn from the opening lines of the beloved Ps. 23: "The LORD is my shepherd, I lack nothing. He makes me lie down in green pastures, he leads me beside quiet waters" (vv. 1–2). With respect to the nations, the harsh language of

Ps. 2 may be balanced by the positive vision of the nations worshiping—for example, Rev. 15:3–4: "Great and marvelous are your deeds, Lord God Almighty. Just and true are your ways, King of the nations. Who will not fear you, Lord, and bring glory to your name? For you alone are holy. All nations will come and worship before you, for your righteous acts have been revealed." While some see this as a grudging acknowledgment of God's power by nations soon to perish in judgment, Bauckham has made a strong argument that John views this as positive worship, drawing on the OT texts most optimistic about the fate of the nations (Bauckham, *Theology*, 98–104). These texts include Pss. 111:2 ("Great are the works of the LORD"); 139:14 ("Your works are wonderful"); 145:17 ("The LORD is righteous in all his ways"); and most tellingly, 86:9 ("All the nations you have made will come and worship before you, Lord; they will bring glory to your name").

Lastly, the Psalms find a natural place as the means of communication with God, through prayer and worship. The saints offer prayers as incense (Rev. 5:8; Ps. 141:2), cry out to him for justice (Rev. 6:10; Ps. 79:5), and long to see his face (Rev. 22:4; Ps. 17:15).

Conclusion

As we noted up front, space will fail us to detail all the contributions made by the OT to Revelation, and so we must pass over Joel, Amos, the historical books, and others that have helped shape John's theological vision. (This is not to mention other early Jewish texts, such as the Enoch material, which shaped the apocalyptic genre and thus had an influence on Revelation.) Revelation depicts the purpose of God to complete the creation project he had started in Gen. 1, and the story of God's beleaguered people is best mapped onto the Exodus narrative, especially as that has been reshaped by the visions of Daniel, Isaiah, and Ezekiel. Alternatively, one might describe Revelation as the fulfillment of the prophets' visions concerning the restoration of Jerusalem.

Bibliography. Aune, D., *Revelation 1–5*, WBC (Word, 1997); Bauckham, R., *The Climax of Prophecy* (T&T Clark, 1993); Bauckham, *The Theology of the Book of Revelation*, NTTh (Cambridge University Press, 1993); Beale, G. K., *The Book of Revelation*, NIGTC (Eerdmans, 1999); Beale, *The Use of Daniel in Apocalyptic Literature and in the Revelation of St. John* (University Press of America, 1984); Buisch, P. P., "The Rest of Her Offspring," *NovT* 60, no. 4 (2018): 386–401; Caird, G. B., *The Revelation of Saint John*, BNTC (Hendrickson, 1999); Jauhiainen, M., *The Use of Zechariah in Revelation* (Mohr Siebeck, 2005); Koester, C. R., *Revelation*, AB (Yale University Press, 2014); Kowalski, B., *Die Rezeption des Propheten Ezechiel in der Offenbarung des Johannes*, SBB 52 (Katholisches Bibelwerk, 2004); McDonough, S., "Being and Nothingness in the Book of Revelation," in *Creation ex Nihilo*, ed. G. A. Anderson and M. N. A. Bockmuehl (University of Notre Dame Press, 2018), 77–98; Moo, J., "The Sea That Is No More," *NovT* 51 (2009): 148–67; Mounce, R. H., *The Book of Revelation*, NICNT (Eerdmans, 1998); Moyise, S., "The Language of the Psalms in the Book of Revelation," *Neot* 37, no. 2 (2003): 246–61; Moyise, *The Old Testament in the Book of Revelation* (Sheffield Academic, 1995); Schüssler Fiorenza, E., *Priester für Gott* (Aschendorff, 1972); Stewart, A. E., "The Future of Israel, Early Christian Hermeneutics, and the Apocalypse of John," *JETS* 61, no. 3 (2018): 563–75; Ulfgard, H., *Feast and Future* (Almqvist & Wiksell, 1989).

SEAN McDONOUGH

Rhetoric

The place of rhetoric in biblical studies emerged strongly in the 1980s, grew to its peak interest probably in the late 1990s, and began to trail off in the early 2000s (cf. Watson and Hauser; Watson). Since then, rhetoric has retreated as a biblical analytic, although it continues to make itself known in some ways, as we will discuss below. Rhetoric began in the ancient world, and rhetoricians were orators who called upon their oratorical abilities (for a concise history of rhetoric in NT studies, see Olbricht, 325–26; Hughes, 20–27; for a concise history of classical rhetoric, see Kennedy, "Historical"). As a result, handbooks on rhetoric were written by some rhetoricians (Aristotle and Quintilian being perhaps the most famous, but certainly not the only ones) to aid those being educated as rhetors. Various church fathers show some familiarity with the rhetoricians and use them in biblical interpretation, and rhetoric grew to prominence in the Reformation and Renaissance. Then, with the rise of historical criticism, rhetoric was discussed by some of the leading figures in the criticism of the time, culminating perhaps in the scholarship of scholars such as Friedrich Blass on Asianism and Eduard Norden on ancient prose. Then a resurgence in interest in classical rhetoric occurred within both classical studies and NT studies on the basis of an important essay by James Muilenburg (1–18), several works in classical studies by the classicist George Kennedy (*Art*; cf. *Interpretation*), some articles by Wilhelm Wuellner (448–63), and an important commentary by Hans Dieter Betz on Galatians (see also *Corinthians*; "Literary"). The amount of literature written from a rhetorical standpoint on the NT alone is significant (for a good survey, see Classen, "Theory," 14–19).

This essay outlines the field of rhetoric in NT studies by addressing some major issues, including its various approaches and practitioners, some of the strengths and weaknesses of the approach, Paul's education, and then some of its possibilities for examination of the use of the OT in the NT, before turning to some potential future developments.

Major Issues

There are a variety of issues to discuss regarding the relationship of rhetoric, in particular ancient rhetoric, to NT studies. I have identified four of importance here: the variety of methods, their validity, Paul's education, and the use of rhetoric for studying the relationship of the OT to the NT.

The variety of rhetorical methods. One of the major issues in the discussion of rhetoric in relation to the NT is the question of what is meant by rhetoric. The common understanding is that rhetoric is defined as means of persuasion. It may be true that good rhetoric persuades, but what about bad rhetoric? And are there other ways to persuade besides rhetoric? This provides a functional definition focusing on a major way in which rhetoric is used, but it is not the only one nor is it exclusive to what we might call rhetoric, at least as a discipline.

As a result, several further definitions of rhetoric have been offered. These can be identified as classical rhetoric, handbook rhetoric, the New Rhetoric, and socio-rhetorical criticism, although these categories are not always distinguished and discrete, as the discussion below will make clear.

Classical rhetoric. Classical rhetoric is rhetoric fashioned after the great rhetoricians of the ancient world. A tradition of oration grew up in the ancient Greek world in the fifth century BC and then developed further in the Roman world. In a culture that relied heavily upon orality, those who were masters of oratory became important. This was especially true within Greece, where there were many occasions for public oration. As a result, three types of rhetoric came to be identified (and defined by Aristotle in his *Rhetoric*): forensic, associated with disputation over past actions and the courtroom; deliberative, associated with future actions and influencing public behavior especially in the assembly; and epideictic, ceremonial rhetoric often found in funeral orations and other public events. The rhetorical tradition arguably reached its apex in the so-called Ten Attic Orators, ten orators associated with Athens who gave speeches and sometimes wrote speeches for others to deliver and were later canonized as setting the standards for classical rhetoric. Demosthenes is probably the most famous of these orators. These rhetoricians had a major influence upon the rhetorical handbook tradition, as authors attempted to codify elements of oratory, especially arrangement, invention, style, delivery, and memory, along with genres and sometimes style. Handbooks were written from the time of Aristotle until long past the writing of the NT. Besides Aristotle's *Rhetoric*, many other writers and writings may be noted: for example, the pseudo-Aristotelian *Rhetoric for Alexander*, anonymous *Rhetorica ad Herennium*, Cicero (many works), Demetrius (on style), Dionysius of Halicarnassus, Aelius Theon (*progymnasmata*), Quintilian, Longinus (on the sublime), Hermogenes of Tarsus, and Menander Rhetor (see Kennedy, "Historical," 19–37, for a complete list, with description and bibliographical information). This field of rhetorical studies has had the largest influence upon NT studies (see Martin).

Handbook rhetoric. I use the term "handbook rhetoric" to describe not the ancient handbooks themselves but the approach generated by such handbooks in later study. The ancient handbook tradition was important for ancient education, as the handbooks appear to have been used in grammar school and rhetorical education, both of which were reserved for the elite who were intending to move into public service. While some of the handbooks did not survive or survived only through descriptions by other authors, a number of handbooks were preserved and continued to influence later education. Rhetoric was a part of the traditional liberal arts, divided into the *trivium* (rhetoric, grammar, and logic) and the *quadrivium* (arithmetic, geometry, music, and astronomy) that formed the basis of the medieval university curriculum (on medieval rhetoric, see Murphy). As a result, others also wrote rhetorical handbooks, such as Peter Ramus in the sixteenth century. Rhetoric continued to be a part of education into the modern period and was initially a part of the university curriculum (see Connors). Rhetoric faded in importance within the modern university and has in many ways been replaced by speech departments, although there are some institutions that retain a place for rhetoric. The major influence of handbook rhetoric is often seen not only in the teaching of speech but also in the teaching of writing and even literary study (the history of modern rhetoric, with its foundation in the ancients, is found in Dixon; Richards; Vickers). Some of the classical works in this respect are Brooks and Warren's *Modern Rhetoric*, Edward Corbett's *Classical Rhetoric for the Modern Student*, and Heinrich Lausberg's *Handbook of Literary Rhetoric*. Although a few NT scholars have shown some interest in the history and development of rhetoric in the handbook tradition (e.g., Augustine, Melanchthon), not much work engages with this field.

The New Rhetoric. I use the term "New Rhetoric," after a book published by Chaïm Perelman and Lucie Olbrechts-Tyteca, to describe various forms of rhetoric that clearly show their dependence upon classical rhetoric, even the handbook tradition, but wish to go much further and show the influence, effects, and possibilities of rhetoric in a wider variety of aspects of life. In that sense, a book by Sonja Foss, Karen Foss, and Robert Trapp captures what I have in mind. They offer a discursive account of major scholars who have had a major influence upon contemporary rhetoric. These include the British literary scholar I. A. Richards, the Italian philosopher Ernesto Grassi, the Belgian professor Perelman and his collaborator Olbrechts-Tyteca mentioned above, the British philosopher Stephen Toulmin, the American literary scholar Richard Weaver, the American polymath Kenneth Burke, the German social scientist Jürgen Habermas, the American feminist Black writer bell hooks, the French sociologist Jean Baudrillard, and the French philosopher Michel Foucault. Others could be added to this list as well (e.g., Jakobson, for his theory of communication). This list of scholars—who are well-known in a variety of areas, many of them beyond what is usually designated as rhetoric—illustrates that rhetoric is still a vibrant field in which some of the leading intellectual figures of our age are engaged, even if they do not all use the same terminology or display the same level of comfort with the term "rhetoric." These scholars show that questions of rhetoric, communication, symbolic systems, or whatever language they use are recurrent ones as humans engage in their interaction with each other and their environment and attempt to persuade or explain their worlds. Though some of these scholars are occasionally referenced, few have had much influence upon NT rhetorical studies, apart possibly from Perelman and Olbrechts-Tyteca and Burke (cf. Burke, *Grammar*; *Rhetoric*).

Socio-rhetorical criticism. A more recent arrival on the rhetorical scene is what has come to be called socio-rhetorical criticism, or more recently socio-rhetorical interpretation. By that, I do not mean a convention of commentary writing but an approach to rhetoric put forward by Vernon K. Robbins, first in a book on Mark (*Jesus*). Robbins is very familiar with the categories of classical rhetoric, having coauthored a book on the *progymnasmata* with Maynard Mack. However, in his socio-rhetorical criticism, he attempts to provide a comprehensive critical interpretive model that unites Christianity and its texts to a number of factors that he identifies (*Tapestry*; *Texture*). These are context, theology, and language. In order to do this, he recognizes that the interpreter is ideologically situated and then designates several different "textures." By textures, Robbins seems to indicate not only levels or strata of analytic interpretation but also subcategories of features within these textures. These various textures include inner texture, concerned with the inner workings of a text; intertexture, concerned with the social, cultural, and historical dimensions of a text (what others might call situational context); social and cultural texture, concerned with larger cultural questions (what others might call cultural context); ideological texture, concerned with the complex set of beliefs within a text; and sacred texture, concerned with the relationship of humans to the world in its cosmic and divine dimensions. Three more recent additions to socio-rhetorical interpretation are attention to cognitive studies (including conceptual metaphor theory and related ideas), attention to critical-space theory, and appreciation of art in terms of "visual exegesis" (see Robbins, von Thaden, and Bruehler, xv–xxv; Robbins, Melion, and Jeal). Recently, some NT studies have pursued socio-rhetorical interpretation.

The validity of applying Greco-Roman rhetoric to the NT. Two of the biggest questions in the rhetorical study of the NT (and OT, perhaps even more so) are, What is meant by rhetoric? and What are the limitations of its use in the study of the Bible? Much of the debate over the use of rhetoric in biblical studies has been over clarifying its methods, especially as there are various approaches that are available. The second point of clarification concerns whether one is speaking of macro- or micro-rhetoric. In other words, is one speaking of the influence of rhetoric upon the overall shape and form of the text in question, such as its arrangement of the individual parts of the text, invention, and genre, or is one speaking of the possible use of rhetorical devices, such as chiasm, inclusion, and chreiai (anecdotes attributed to a character), what one might call style? These questions come out in the long-standing debate over the question of whether it is appropriate to use Greco-Roman rhetoric to interpret the NT. There have been two sides to the debate, those in favor and those opposed (cf. Classen, "Theory," 14–19).

Those who favor the use of categories of Greco-Roman rhetoric include a wide variety of scholars in NT studies, including George Kennedy, Hans Dieter Betz, Richard Longenecker, and Ben Witherington. The basic argument is that ancient culture was primarily oral, and so most communication took place in terms of speaking, rather than writing, and hence required that people be able to orally persuade others of their cause. As a result, the use of ancient rhetoric pervaded the surrounding culture, was institutionalized into the educational system, and could legitimately expect to be encountered in the course of daily life. It has even been expressed that rhetoric was "in the air" (Longenecker, 10). The argument sometimes further posits that Paul knew the rhetorical handbooks. The typical course of an argument for the use of ancient rhetoric is to identify the genre of the work (forensic, epideictic, or deliberative) or describe its macro-rhetorical structures, such as its arrangement, often with an appeal to other rhetorical critics who have used similar approaches. Sometimes such studies also appeal to various stylistic features. Some rhetorical critics have noted problems with such a supposition for NT books that do not resemble ancient orations (which is admittedly most of them) and so have gone so far as to posit, for example, that letters are speeches that have had epistolary openings and closings attached to them (Witherington, *Rhetoric*, 1–9).

Many arguments have been marshaled against such a theory, not least that few if any of the NT books present themselves as orations (Hebrews being a possible exception) (see, among many, Porter, "Theoretical"; Porter and Dyer, "Oral," 328–38). Acts arguably contains the greatest number of orations, by Peter and by Paul, and these are subject to examination as orations, but they are relatively short when compared to ancient speeches, even in the Greco-Roman historians. Further criticism attacks the emphasis upon orality at the expense of literacy. One cannot simply state that the ancient world was an oral culture as a justification for oratory and rhetorical criticism (see the article "Orality" elsewhere in the dictionary). While relatively few may have been formally literate, the Greco-Roman world was a literate culture that depended upon written documents. Even if a person could not read or write, that person was required to move in a world of written documentation, in which letters and other written documents played a vital part. Further, some question whether it is appropriate to use categories of ancient rhetoric to analyze the NT writings, whether these categories are found in the rhetorical handbooks or garnered elsewhere. Scholars express a variety of opinions as to the appropriate categories to use in such analysis, with some emphasizing the genres, others arrangement, and still others invention, while some reserve the category of style for their rhetorical analysis. Whereas the ancients appear to have followed relatively standard patterns in all of these, the NT books are often seen to be mixtures of these various categories. Further, scholars often have great disagreement when applying these macro-rhetorical categories, disagreeing on genres and organization of the NT books, including Paul's Letters. The use of the rhetorical genres is especially problematic in this regard, as it creates a circular argument when the category dictates the exegesis. The use of rhetorical arrangement can also have the effect of imposing a rhetorical structure on a text that may defy such categories. Betz's arrangement of Galatians is criticized for his needing to invent a category not found in any of the classical rhetorical handbooks. There is the further major question of whether the use of such categories is even appropriate for critical analysis since the ancients themselves do not appear to have used the categories of rhetoric in their own examination and analysis of literature but only in the creation of their speeches. As Jeffrey Reed (322) states, "*Functional* similarities between Paul's argumentative style and the rhetorical handbooks do not prove a *formal* relationship between them." So far as is known, works like gospels or letters were not subject to rhetorical analysis. In fact, as Carl Classen states, "Rhetoric (oratory) and epistolography were regarded as two different fields in antiquity" (*Rhetorical*, 26), with letter types entering discussion only in the fourth century, long after the writing of the NT. Finally, one must wonder where the NT authors gained their rhetorical education when it was not commonly available to all but was elitist and, for the most part, reserved for the elite (I will discuss education further below). There seems to be a residual belief that, if one performs rhetorical criticism by means of ancient Greco-Roman rhetorical categories, one is approaching a more definitive interpretation because such interpretation is something with which the ancients would be familiar. There is no evidence that this is the case. One can use rhetorical criticism based on ancient categories if one wishes, but it is no more privileged as an interpretive strategy than many other forms of criticism and would not have been recognizable to the ancients themselves.

Paul's education. It is difficult to calculate, but probably Paul's Letters have been the major target of NT rhetorical criticism. If Paul was an accomplished rhetor, as such rhetorical critics contend, then the question must be raised of where Paul acquired his rhetorical education. Kennedy claims that the evidence is "ambivalent" whether Paul may have been formally trained in rhetoric. Paul did not need formal rhetorical education because he could not escape his rhetorically charged environment (Kennedy, *Interpretation*, 9). This environment included rhetorical handbooks to which he apparently would have had easy access. Witherington goes further and, following Martin Hengel (Hengel and Deines, 57–58), contends that Paul learned Greco-Roman rhetoric when he was studying with Gamaliel in Jerusalem since other Jews supposedly had availed themselves of such education (Witherington, *Paul*, 97–98; he later backs away but is no less generous in his accolades for Paul's rhetoric; see *Rhetoric*, 131–32). Some scholars attempt to bolster this evidence by citing evidence at the micro- and macro-levels for Paul's rhetorical knowledge. They cite Paul's use of words that may have indicated formal knowledge of rhetoric, although these words may well have only been part of the vocabulary of an intelligent, literate user of Greek of the time (for such a list, see Classen, *Rhetorical*, 29–44).

Paul can on occasion rise to rhetorical heights in his language, but there is no indication that what he writes is influenced by formal rhetorical education. Paul may well have mastered reading and writing, the writing of letters, and even some of the rhetorical exercises (*progymnasmata*) while he was in grammar school (for a recent treatment of the *progymnasmata*, see Parsons and Martin). It is entirely likely that Paul was educated in a grammar school, probably in Tarsus, although Jerusalem is also a possibility, depending on one's interpretation of Acts 22:3 (see Pitts, 27–33). However, because rhetorical education was elitist and designed for those contemplating entering into public service, and mostly because there is no evidence of a Greek rhetorical school being located in Jerusalem during the first century (as there was in Tarsus), it is unlikely that Paul was formally educated in rhetoric (Pitts, 44–50, arguing against Hengel, the only one, he claims, to have argued for a rhetorical school in Jerusalem).

The OT in the NT from a rhetorical perspective. A recent development worth discussing at this point is the possible relationship between rhetoric and the use of OT quotations in the NT. Some scholars who examine the use of the OT in the NT may implicitly understand that such usage had a "rhetorical" effect, however that is defined. However, that is not the same as examining the use of quotations from a rhetorical perspective. Two scholars appear to have been working on the question of how Paul uses his scriptural quotations rhetorically: Dennis Stamps and Christopher Stanley, both of whom knew of the other's work.

Stamps and Stanley take two different approaches to rhetoric and the use of OT quotations. Stamps takes a classical rhetoric approach. He begins by offering a survey of many of the major methodological issues in the study of the OT in the NT. These include terminological issues regarding the OT, what constitutes a citation, and the Jewish background that is assumed by most scholars; and hermeneutical issues, such as historical questions regarding authorial or audience perspective from which to analyze citations and theological developments in the NT, literary dimensions, literary issues, and theological considerations. Having weighed these various issues, Stamps then discusses the use of the OT as a rhetorical device. Rather than looking to the Jewish background of the NT, he turns to rhetoric as important within the Hellenistic culture of the NT. He defines rhetoric following Aristotle as "the faculty of discovering the possible means of persuasion in reference to any subject whatever" (*Rhet.* 1.2.1), in line with Cicero (*Inv.* 1.5) and Quintilian (*Inst.* 2.14–15), both of whom also emphasize persuasion even if focusing on different means. Stamps acknowledges that various Jewish authors, such as Philo, use the OT for persuasive purposes. He, however, examines the use of "authoritative tradition" in Greco-Roman writings (27). Stamps believes that Greco-Roman authors drew upon authoritative collections of citations, such as Homer, and used these to teach and instruct others. The ancients do not say a lot about the use of authoritative citations, but they are one form of proof or evidence noted by Aristotle (*Rhet.* 1.15.1–3, 13–19). Quintilian seems to agree (*Inst.* 2.7.4; 1.8.12), while Longinus (*Subl.* 13.2–3; 14.1) sees them also as emphatic. Stamps notes that Stanley sees Homeric quotation play the same role as the OT plays in the NT (citing Stanley, "Paul"). Stamps sees the same pattern in post-NT writings.

Stanley begins from the standpoint that Paul writes "to motivate specific first-century Christians to believe and/or act (or stop believing or acting) in particular ways." To this end, "quotations are meant to affect an audience; otherwise, there is no reason to include them in a literary work" (*Arguing*, 3) With this premise, he attempts to lay out the rhetorical use of OT quotations in Paul's letters. After noting the minimal amount of secondary literature on the rhetorical use of quotations, Stanley turns to the New Rhetoric, and in particular to a follower of Perelman, Eugene E. White, for his "model of rhetorical communication" (Stanley, *Arguing*, 14; cf. White). White (11) defines rhetoric as "the purposive use of symbols in an attempt to induce change in some receiver(s), thereby derivatively modifying the circumstances that provoked, or made possible, the symbolic interaction between persuader(s) and receiver(s)" (cited in Stanley, *Arguing*, 15; cf. also Burke, *Rhetoric*, 41). Stanley emphasizes from White's definition that "all rhetorical acts are situational," based upon a "provoking rhetorical urgency," or what is often known as a "rhetorical situation" (Stanley, *Arguing*, 15, again citing White and referring to Bitzer). One determines the author's intention in light of the author's presentation of ideas and his or her attempts to affect others' beliefs on the basis of coherence between the author's beliefs and those of the audience. Stanley further invokes J. L. Austin's speech-act theory to account for the purposive use of language, although Austin does not deal with quotations. After surveying several theories of the function of quotations, including the dramaturgical view of the linguist Anna Wierzbicka, the proteus principle of the literary scholar Meir Sternberg, and the demonstration theory of the psycholinguist Herbert Clark and psychologist Richard Gerrig, Stanley adopts the parodic approach of Gillian Lane-Mercier, in which quotations are used as proof and to put forward the ideas of the user. Stanley uses Lane-Mercier's approach as a defense of his well-known audience-oriented approach to quotations, because they affect the audience (he has always tended to shy away from treating allusions and other indirect citations, because of his focus on the audience). However, Stanley uses this as a means of focusing upon Paul's audiences. He devotes an entire chapter to raising and then examining nine assumptions regarding Paul's audiences, especially regarding their recognition of, access to, and understanding of quotations of the OT and Paul's own faithfulness to their biblical contexts. Stanley concludes, "It seems unlikely that many of the people in Paul's congregations knew the Jewish Scriptures well enough to evaluate his handling of the biblical texts. It seems equally implausible that Paul expected them to do so" (*Arguing*, 60).

On the basis of these methodological studies, Stanley develops his method for analysis of the rhetorical effect of Paul's quotations. He focuses upon two fundamental questions: (1) How do Paul's quotations promote his advancing argument within his letters? (2) How does Paul's argumentative strategy with these quotations cohere with what can be ascertained regarding the audience's understanding? (For Stanley's understanding of the audience, using terminology from Fish, see Stanley, *Arguing*, 67; cf. Fish, 174.) As a result, Stanley examines both the quotations themselves and the biblical knowledge of the letters' recipients. With this in place, Stanley devotes the second part of his volume to examining quotations in 1 and 2 Corinthians, Galatians, and Romans (one may question the validity of Stanley's return to Baur's *Hauptbriefe*; he uses the same corpus in Stanley, *Paul*). He typically describes the situation of the given letter with regard to Paul's relationship to the audience and/or their biblical literacy before turning to particular passages quoted within the individual books. Finally, in his conclusion, Stanley draws together his work. He notes, first, that each letter situation was different and hence reflected a different "provoking rhetorical urgency" (to use

White's terms). Even though Paul used the OT, he wrote to primarily gentile audiences but did not discuss their background but instead often invokes a narrative, even though some may have understood the quotations more than others. Paul clearly respects the Jewish Scriptures, and they play a variety of roles in his letters, even though he adapts them to his own use, usually not developing the meaning of their original OT contexts. Second, regarding the effectiveness of the quotations, Paul tries to make their meaning clear to his readers, who respected the OT. He probably also realizes that their view of him influences their responses to his arguments, possibly even using quotations to help himself in relation to them. However, third, there are some indications that Paul may not have been as effective as he may have wished. Paul's letter audiences were diverse, and he probably would not have known which quotations would be known to them. His use of quotations may have been undermined if they distrusted him.

Stamps is clearly not as well-developed as Stanley in his argument, as he recognizes. Still, he attempts to show that the NT authors use OT citations in a way similar to other ancient Greek authors and as discussed by the handbook writers. Stanley, on the other hand, presents a much fuller argument, based upon a much broader and more diverse theory of rhetoric that moves well beyond classical rhetoric and possibly even the New Rhetoric in some ways. Because the theory is so closely linked to audience response—not untypical for those who wish to speak of the persuasive power of rhetoric—it is difficult to test a hypothesis that Paul was successful in his rhetorical use of OT quotations.

Potential Developments for Rhetorical Study

Stanley's approach to the use of OT quotations in the Pauline Letters has some recognizable linguistic features to it. White's theory of rhetoric has many characteristics of theories of communication, in which the dynamic between author and audience is mediated by language. Stanley recognizes this in his appeal to the speech-act theory of Austin. One of the clear challenges of Stanley's approach is the ability to assess the reaction of the audience. This will probably always be a problem in studies of this sort. However, much more can probably also be done from a linguistic standpoint to deal with the persuasiveness of the speaker or author.

To date, linguistics has not proven to be a highly productive approach to rhetoric and the NT. There have been some attempts to discuss rhetorical study in relationship to linguistics (the following modifies Porter, "Linguistics"). (1) Various grammatical theories have been integrated into some theories of rhetoric. The range of grammars varies, from traditional grammar to structuralism (developed from the thought of Ferdinand de Saussure) to the generative grammar of Noam Chomsky (see Winterowd, 66–128, drawing attention to Fries; Chomsky). In some ways, traditional grammar may appear more conducive to dealing with classical rhetorical categories, while structuralism and generative grammar may appear to be limited in their relations to rhetoric because the sentence and its structure tend to be the highest level of analysis, whereas rhetoric tends to be about the force of texts. (2) Tagmemics, the linguistic model of Kenneth Pike, has proven perhaps more successful in rhetorical study, at least more successful than the various grammatical theories. This is because tagmemics reconceptualizes the rhetorical task linguistically in terms of strata and function (in which slots of function are filled by higher-level elements), rather than trying to meld together two dissimilar approaches. Further, tagmemics takes a holistic view of its task that is compatible with the notion of rhetoric as the persuasive force of a discourse. For tagmemics, style is also a part of the linguistic model and hence integrated within the scope of rhetoric. (3) Communication theory also has some possibilities for rhetoric, especially the model of Roman Jakobson. His six-part conceptual framework to describe communication provides a role for both addresser and addressee, as well as the message. Jakobson's model, as influential as it has been, relies upon two layers of conception, and it is not clear how the two relate to each other or to language, although it is clear that they capture the functions of language. (4) Discourse analysis has been proposed as a way to think of rhetoric. The various approaches to discourse analysis differ in significant ways, so it is difficult to speak on behalf of all of them. However, the general emphasis is to move beyond the clause or sentence to the entire discourse and hence to capture the semantics of the text as a whole. Nevertheless, most of the models also have some limitations that make it unclear how they can become models of rhetoric. (5) Systemic functional linguistics, which thinks of language as a set of networks of semantic choices, is not a theory of rhetoric, but it recognizes the place of rhetoric within its architecture (see Halliday; for an attempt to conceptualize rhetoric in systemic functional linguistic terms suitable for study of the Greek NT, see Porter, *Linguistic*, chap. 4). The systemic functional linguistic architecture is relatively complex, so it is sometimes unclear whether rhetoric is better thought of as a part of the interpersonal or the textual component of a text. Nevertheless, some recent explorations have suggested that certain features of systemic functional linguistics address some of the same concerns as rhetoric and do so by means of providing lexicogrammatical and semantic realizations that enable rhetoric to become a more finely tuned concept for the critical analysis of texts. There is much more unexplored potential in the discussion of the relationship between rhetoric and linguistics.

Conclusion

The field of rhetoric has captivated the imaginations of those who have been concerned with the Bible ever since the early church. A variety of proposals have been developed in relationship to the NT. Some of these are grounded in ancient classical practices, and others are more modernly conceived, to the point that some still newer rhetorical models are being proposed. The relatively recent flurry of activity examining the NT on the basis of the categories of ancient rhetoric has diminished to a large extent, but more work has been done here than in probably any other area of rhetorical study of the NT. One of the areas that has been explored recently has been that of the rhetorical force of the use of the OT in the NT. Although much work has been done in this area, there is still room for more extended discussion. An area that is still relatively untapped is a rigorous approach to rhetoric that attempts to ground persuasive force in clear linguistic description.

See also Letter Couriers; Literacy in the Greco-Roman World; *Septuagint articles*

Bibliography. Austin, J. L., *How to Do Things with Words*, 2nd ed. (Harvard University Press, 1962); Betz, H. D., *Galatians*, Herm (Fortress, 1979); Betz, "The Literary Composition and Function of Paul's Letter to the Galatians," *NTS* 21 (1975): 353–79; Betz, *2 Corinthians 8 and 9*, Herm (Fortress, 1985); Bitzer, L., "The Rhetorical Situation," *Philosophy and Rhetoric* 1 (1968): 1–14; Brooks, C., and R. P. Warren, *Modern Rhetoric*, 2nd ed. (Harcourt, Brace, 1958 [1949]); Burke, K., *A Grammar of Motives* (repr., University of California Press, 1945); Burke, *A Rhetoric of Motives* (repr., University of California Press, 1950); Chomsky, N., *Syntactic Structures*, JLSM 4 (Mouton, 1957); Classen, C. J., "Can the Theory of Rhetoric Help Us to Understand the New Testament, and in Particular the Letters of Paul?," in *Paul and Ancient Rhetoric*, ed. S. E. Porter and B. R. Dyer (Cambridge University Press, 2016), 13–39; Classen, *Rhetorical Criticism of the New Testament*, WUNT 128 (Mohr Siebeck, 2000); Connors, R. J., "Rhetoric in the Modern University," in *The Politics of Writing Instruction*, ed. R. Bullock and J. Trimbur (Boynton/Cook, 1991), 55–84; Corbett, E. P. J., *Classical Rhetoric for the Modern Student*, 3rd ed. (Oxford University Press, 1990 [1965]); Dixon, P., *Rhetoric*, Critical Idiom 19 (Methuen, 1971); Fish, S., "Interpreting the *Variorum*," in *Reader Response Criticism*, ed. Jane Tompkins (Johns Hopkins University Press, 1980), 164–84; Foss, S. K., K. A. Foss, and R. Trapp, *Contemporary Perspectives on Rhetoric*, 3rd ed. (Waveland, 2002); Fries, C. C., *The Structure of English* (Harcourt, Brace, 1952); Halliday, M. A. K., *Language as Social Semiotic* (Edward Arnold, 1978); Hengel, M., and R. Deines, *The Pre-Christian Paul* (Trinity Press International, 1991); Hughes, F. W., *Early Christian Rhetoric and 2 Thessalonians*, JSNTSup 30 (JSOT Press, 1989); Jakobson, R., "Concluding Statement," in *Style in Language*, ed. T. A. Sebeok (Wiley & Sons, 1960), 350–77; Kennedy, G. A., *The Art of Persuasion in Greece* (Princeton University Press, 1963); Kennedy, "Historical Survey of Rhetoric," in *Handbook of Classical Rhetoric in the Hellenistic Period 330 B.C.–A.D. 400*, ed. S. E. Porter (Brill, 1997), 3–41; Kennedy, *New Testament Interpretation through Rhetorical Criticism* (University of North Carolina Press, 1984); Lane-Mercier, G., "Quotation as a Discursive Strategy," *Kodikas* 14 (1991): 199–214; Lausberg, H., *Handbook of Literary Rhetoric*, ed. D. E. Orton and R. D. Anderson, trans. M. T. Bliss, A. Jansen, and D. E. Orton (Brill, 1998 [1960]); Longenecker, R. N., *Galatians*, WBC 41 (Word, 1990); Mack, B. L., and V. K. Robbins, *Patterns of Persuasion in the Gospels* (Polebridge, 1989); Martin, T. W., ed., *Genealogies of New Testament Rhetorical Criticism* (Fortress, 2014); Muilenburg, J., "Form Criticism and Beyond," *JBL* 88 (1969): 1–18; Murphy, J. J., *Rhetoric in the Middle Ages* (University of California Press, 1974); Olbricht, T. H., "Rhetorical Criticism," in *Dictionary of Biblical Criticism and Interpretation*, ed. S. E. Porter (Routledge, 2007), 325–27; Parsons, M. C., and M. W. Martin, *Ancient Rhetoric and the New Testament* (Baylor University Press, 2018); Perelman, C., and L. Olbrechts-Tyteca, *The New Rhetoric*, trans. J. Wilkinson and P. Weaver (University of Notre Dame Press, 1969 [1958]); Pike, K. L., *Language in Relation to a Unified Theory of the Structure of Human Behavior*, 2nd ed., JLSM 24 (Mouton, 1967); Pitts, A. W., "Hellenistic Schools in Jerusalem and Paul's Rhetorical Education," in *Paul's World*, ed. S. E. Porter, PaSt 4 (Brill, 2008), 19–50; Porter, S. E., *Linguistic Descriptions of the Greek New Testament* (T&T Clark, forthcoming); Porter, "Linguistics and Rhetorical Criticism," in *Linguistics and the New Testament*, ed. S. E. Porter and D. A. Carson, JSNTSup 168 (Sheffield Academic, 1999), 63–92; Porter, "The Theoretical Justification for Application of Rhetorical Categories to Pauline Epistolary Literature," in *Rhetoric and the New Testament*, ed. S. E. Porter and T. H. Olbricht, JSNTSup 90 (JSOT, 1993), 100–122; Porter, S. E., and B. R. Dyer, "Oral Texts?," *JETS* 55 (2012): 323–41; Reed, J. T., "Using Ancient Rhetorical Categories to Interpret Paul's Letters," in *Rhetoric and the New Testament*, ed. S. E. Porter and T. H. Olbricht, JSNTSup 90 (JSOT, 1993), 292–324; Richards, J., *Rhetoric*, New Critical Idiom (Routledge, 2008); Robbins, V. K., *Exploring the Texture of Texts* (Trinity Press International, 1996); Robbins, *Jesus the Teacher* (Fortress, 1984); Robbins, *The Tapestry of Early Christian Discourse* (Routledge, 1996); Robbins, V. K., W. S. Melion, and R. R. Jeal, eds., *The Art of Visual Exegesis* (SBL Press, 2017); Robbins, V. K., R. H. von Thaden Jr., and B. B. Bruehler, eds., *Foundations for Sociorhetorical Exploration* (SBL Press, 2016); Stamps, D. L., "The Use of the Old Testament in the New Testament as a Rhetorical Device," in *Hearing the Old Testament in the New Testament*, ed. S. E. Porter (Eerdmans, 2006), 9–37; Stanley, C. D., *Arguing with Scripture* (T&T Clark, 2004); Stanley, "Paul and Homer," *NovT* 32 (1990): 48–78; Stanley, *Paul and the Language of Scripture*, SNTSMS 74 (Cambridge University Press, 1992); Vickers, B., *In Defense of Rhetoric* (Clarendon, 1988); Watson, D. F., *The Rhetoric of the New Testament* (Deo, 2004); Watson, D. F., and A. J. Hauser,

Rhetorical Criticism of the Bible, BibInt 4 (Brill, 1994); White, E. E., *The Context of Human Discourse* (University of South Carolina Press, 1992); Winterowd, W. R., *Structure, Language and Style* (Brown, 1969); Witherington, B., III, *New Testament Rhetoric* (Cascade Books, 2009); Witherington, *The Paul Quest* (InterVarsity, 1998); Wuellner, W., "Where Is Rhetorical Criticism Taking Us?," *CBQ* 49 (1987): 448–63.

Stanley E. Porter

Romans, Letter to the

There are significantly more citations from the OT in Romans than in any other Pauline letter. This is due partly to the length of the document but mostly to the nature of the argument. Christopher Stanley (*Arguing*, 142) identifies forty-two quotations that are marked by introductory formulas such as "as it is written," "what does Scripture say?," "David says," "(God) says to Moses," "(God) says in Hosea," "Isaiah cries out," "Moses writes," and "says the Lord" (1:17; 2:24; 3:4, 10–18; 4:3, 7–8, 17, 18; 7:7; 8:36; 9:9, 12, 13, 15, 17, 25–26, 27–28, 29, 33; 10:5, 6–8, 11, 15, 16, 19, 20, 21; 11:3, 4, 8, 9–10, 26–27; 12:19; 13:9a, 9b; 14:11; 15:3, 9, 10, 11, 12, 21). Several of these passages join two or more biblical texts together. Three further citations can be recognized by contextual means (4:22; 9:7; 10:18). Nine more are unmarked, and Stanley suggests they would have been "unrecognizable to the Romans unless they happened to know the original passage (2:6; 3:20; 9:20; 10:13; 11:2, 34, 35; 12:17, 20)." In fact, there may be more than sixty-eight citations and ninety-one allusions or verbal parallels with the OT and Apocrypha, depending on how they are evaluated (Kruse, 77). Criteria for identifying quotations and their functions are examined by Steve Moyise (15–28), while Stanley Porter (29–40) considers the difference between allusions and echoes of Scripture (cf. Hays, 29–32).

Scripture and the Purpose of Romans

Stanley observes that "explicit quotations from Scripture are not dispersed evenly across the letter; fully three-quarters of them are concentrated in three passages: 4:1–25; 9:6–11:36; and 15:1–12" (*Arguing*, 142). In other major sections of the letter, Paul is said to develop his argument "with little or no biblical reference and mostly to reinforce points that he has already made in his own words." Since all the passages that use Scripture extensively concern God's plan to create a chosen people that would contain believing Jews and gentiles, Paul's "rhetorical urgency" was to affirm this and challenge "what he perceived as an attitude of superiority on the part of Gentile Christians in Rome towards their Jewish colleagues (11:18)" (*Arguing*, 143n19). J. Ross Wagner (36) adds that Paul may also "have intended his argument to be *overheard* by Jewish Christians in the Roman congregations."

Romans begins with Paul's self-introduction as "a servant of Christ Jesus, called to be an apostle and set apart for the gospel of God—the gospel he promised beforehand through his prophets in the Holy Scriptures" (1:1–2). Paul is keen to preach this gospel in Rome (1:8–15), even though he knows there are already many committed believers in that city (16:3–16). "To preach the gospel" sums up Paul's lifelong obligation and can embrace "the whole range of his ministry, including his explication of the gospel in this very letter" (Dunn, *Romans 1–8*, 33–34). Paul writes to minister to the believers in Rome in anticipation of his visit and to gain their support for the next stage of his missionary activity to Spain (15:14–33). The opening verses of the letter affirm that his exposition of the gospel will be a development of significant biblical themes and expectations.

Paul returns to this linkage in his concluding wish-prayer (16:25–26), where he claims that his proclamation of Jesus Christ is "in keeping with the revelation of the mystery hidden for long ages past, but now revealed and made known through the prophetic writings by the command of the eternal God, so that all the Gentiles might come to the obedience that comes from faith" (16:25–26; cf. 1:5–6). Paul's gospel announced the fulfillment of prophetic predictions, but there was an element of mystery about what was promised that needed to be disclosed and explained (cf. Eph. 3:1–13; Col. 1:24–28). So, he regularly pauses in his exposition of the gospel to address disputed issues, using a more defensive style and arguing more obviously from Scripture (Peterson, 10–19). In the defensive strand of the letter, there is a focus on matters relating to the Mosaic law and God's purpose for Israel (Rom. 2:1–3:20; 3:27–4:25; 5:12–21; 7:1–25; 9:1–11:36).

Stanley identifies a number of significant assumptions that Paul might have had about the biblical knowledge of the Roman Christians (*Arguing*, 139–42) and offers three explanations for his elaborate use of Scripture in the apologetic or argumentative strand of the letter. "First, if the letter represents a veiled attempt to resolve tensions that Paul knew were dividing the Jewish and Gentile Christians in Rome (whether individuals or entire congregations), he might have felt that the authoritative Jewish Scriptures offered the only common ground from which he could argue effectively with both sides" (143). Second, if the letter was written to commend Paul's ministry and gain the support of the Roman Christians for his mission to Spain, "his negative experiences with 'Judaizers' elsewhere might have led him to think that he should defuse any potential problems in this area with a series of preemptive arguments from the authoritative Scriptures" (144). Third, if the letter represents an anticipation of Paul's defense of his ministry in Jerusalem before visiting Rome (15:31), he would have known that the chief bone of contention was "his claim that God was now accepting Gentiles on equal terms with Jews" (144).

Scripture and the Gospel

Paul's first reference to the gospel (1:2–4) describes its essence in terms of the prophetic promises fulfilled in the Son. His second definition (1:16–17) builds upon the first by describing the gospel's function in terms of its saving power, the righteousness of God, and faith (Calhoun, 143). The first summary is christological in focus and the second is soteriological. Paul's claim that in the gospel the righteousness of God is revealed "from faith to faith" (1:17, *ek pisteōs eis pistin*) means that this revelation is received by faith to encourage a life of faith. The need for faith is supported by Paul's first biblical citation (Hab. 2:4: "The righteous will live by faith"; cf. Gal. 3:11; Heb. 10:38). This establishes the continuity of God's way of salvation before and after Christ, while emphasizing the newness of the revelation of God's righteousness in the gospel. Habakkuk proclaimed that the righteous Israelite would be preserved through the terror of an enemy invasion because of his or her faith. When Paul cites this text, he omits the personal pronoun (MT: "The righteous by *his* faith[fulness] will live"; LXX: "The righteous by *my* faith[fulness] will live"), so that the emphasis falls on faith generically as trust or reliance upon God and his word, rather than "faithfulness" (Seifrid, 608–11; Peterson, 107).

Habakkuk's message concerned deliverance through judgment, and Paul echoes that perspective when he turns to explain how "the wrath of God is being revealed from heaven against all the godlessness and wickedness of people who suppress the truth by their wickedness" (Rom. 1:18). The truth human beings suppress is "what may be known about God" (1:19–20; cf. Job 12:7–9). They give themselves over to idolatry, exchanging "the glory of the immortal God" for images of their own making (Rom. 1:21–23; cf. Ps. 106:20; Jer. 2:11). God expresses his wrath against their refusal to glorify him by abandoning them to the moral consequences of their rebellion (Rom. 1:24–32; cf. Lev. 18:1–23). Here Paul reflects on the outcome of the fall as portrayed in Gen. 3–11 and subsequently. Three further passages take up the issue of God's ultimate judgment against sin (Rom. 2:1–6; 2:17–29; 3:20), employing a range of biblical texts to show why Jews and gentiles alike need the salvation he proclaims. This strand of his argument is examined below.

The exposition of the gospel in 3:21–26 involves no explicit citations, though Paul relates important biblical themes to the achievement of God in Christ. The righteousness of God is now revealed "apart from the law," though the Law and the Prophets attest to it (3:21). Paul stresses the continuity of divine revelation, even as he proclaims the newness of God's saving intervention through Christ. In 3:5–6, God's righteousness is an attribute that he demonstrates as he rules his creation with justice and subdues all forms of opposition to his rule (cf. Pss. 96:10–13; 97:2, 6–9; 98:7–9). But "his righteousness" in 3:25–26 has a more positive, salvific meaning (cf. Pss. 51:14; 71:15–16; Isa. 46:13), referring to his justice in presenting Jesus as "a sacrifice of atonement" for sins and justifying those who have faith in him (3:21–22; Peterson, 61–66, 187–88). An Isaianic basis to Paul's argument is suggested when he says "all are justified by his grace through the redemption that came by Christ Jesus" (3:24; cf. Isa. 43:14–21; 48:20–21; 52:1–12). Isaiah presents Israel's exile and oppression as the result of sin, so that the liberation of the nation necessitates God's forgiveness (Isa. 42:25; 44:22–23; 53:11). This imagery is radicalized by Paul, so that "Israel's exile becomes an image of human sin and alienation from God (cf. Rom. 2:24; 3:9)" (Seifrid, 619; cf. Peterson, 193–94). Paul uses the term "sacrifice of atonement" (*hilastērion*, 3:25; cf. Exod. 25:17–22; Lev. 16:2–15 ["atonement cover on the ark"]; Heb. 9:5) to portray Jesus as the new-covenant antitype of the old-covenant "place of atonement" for sin in the tabernacle/temple (Seifrid, 619–21; Peterson, 194–97; cf. Rom. 8:3, "a sin offering").

Paul begins to explain the present implications of his gospel in 5:1–11, where he introduces the theme of peace or reconciliation with God, together with references to suffering, endurance, glory, the love of God, and the Holy Spirit. When these terms reappear in 8:18–39, a large inclusion is formed between these passages. In the structure of the letter as a whole, 5:1–8:39 has a central role with its focus on living in the light of what God has already accomplished for us in Christ while we await the consummation of his purpose for us (Moo, 293–94; Wright, 508–14). Scripture is quoted only when Paul returns to a more defensive sort of argument about the law (7:7, citing Exod. 20:17; Deut. 5:21) or uses Ps. 44:22 (43:23 LXX) to show that facing death "all day long" has always been the lot of God's people (8:36). But biblical allusions can be discerned throughout (e.g., Ps. 22:5 in 5:5; Ps. 118:6 in 8:31; Ps. 110:1 in 8:34; Isa. 50:8 in 8:34). Paul clearly reflects on Gen. 3:1–6, 19 when he develops his comparison between Adam and Christ (Rom. 5:12–21) and considers the relationship between sin and the law (7:7–11). Genesis 3:17–19; 5:29 is in mind when he mentions "present sufferings" and the creation being "subjected to frustration, not by its own choice, but by the will of him who subjected it, in hope" (8:18–21; cf. Eccles. 1:2). Both the developing strand of gospel exposition (5:1–11; 6:1–23; 8:1–39) and the apologetic strand that is interwoven with this (5:12–21; 7:1–25) continue to show how OT themes and expectations can be given new significance when applied to the person and work of Jesus.

Scripture and Specifically Jewish Issues

Judgment, the law, and the obedience of faith. The first defensive section of this letter (2:1–3:20) focuses attention on Jewish beliefs and practices, though Paul's rhetorical strategy dictates that Jews are not named until 2:17 (Gathercole, 197–200). As he considers "the day of God's wrath" when God's righteous judgment will be fully revealed, the apostle deals with the failure of his fellow Jews to live up to their calling. In 2:1–5, the second-person singular is used in a diatribe to address the sort of person who passes judgment on those who practice the things listed in 1:29–31 but acts in a similar way (Stowers, 93–96, 110–12). Paul assumes that his readers will agree that "God's judgment against those who do such things is based on truth" (2:2) and warns that those who refuse to repent are storing up wrath against themselves (2:5). Scripture is then quoted to confirm that "God will repay each person according to what they have done," apparently conflating portions of Ps. 62:12 (62:13 MT; 61:13 LXX) and Prov. 24:12. In such texts, "Paul sees the pattern of divine judgment, which has taken place in many instances in the past, as anticipatory of the final judgment that is coming upon the world of human injustice and cruelty" (Seifrid, 611–12). Judgment will come "for every human being who does evil: first for the Jew, then for the Gentile," while "glory, honor and peace" will be God's gift "for everyone who does good: first for the Jew, then for the Gentile" (2:9–10).

This twofold reference to Jew and gentile leads Paul to a statement about the judgment of those who sin "apart from the law" and those who sin "under the law" (2:12). In preparation for the denunciation of the disobedient Jew in 2:17–24, he makes it clear that "it is not those who hear the law who are righteous in God's sight, but it is those who obey the law who will be declared righteous" (2:13). The fundamental issue is whether (lit.) "the work of the law" (*to ergon tou nomou*, 2:15) is written on human hearts (2:14) and reflected in human behavior. The final judgment of God, which according to Paul's gospel will take place "through Jesus Christ," will expose the secrets of the human heart and reveal those whose hearts are set on doing what God requires (v. 16).

The diatribe with an imaginary opponent continues in 2:17–29, though the person addressed is now explicitly a Jew, who approves what the law teaches, commends it to others, but fails to obey it (vv. 17–20). Four rhetorical questions challenge whether he is guilty of the very sins he condemns in others (vv. 21–22). A summary statement clarifies that Paul has been speaking about Jews who boast in the law but dishonor God by breaking it (v. 23). A modified portion of Isa. 52:5 LXX is cited to highlight the implications (v. 24, "God's name is blasphemed among the Gentiles because of you"). At the time of the Babylonian exile, gentiles denigrated the God of Israel because his people had become subject to them, making their God seem weak and ineffective. But the prophet insists that the Lord is actively judging his people for their unfaithfulness and continuing transgression of his law (Isa. 40:2; 42:24–25; 43:22–28; 50:1). Although the immediate context relates to the prospect of deliverance and blessing rather than rejection and judgment (Stanley, *Arguing*, 147–48), the behavior Paul has been exposing recalls the disobedience to God that the broader context in Isaiah identifies as the reason for the exile. "Paul's appeal to Isa. 52:5 is typical in nature. Israel's disobedience in the past has been repeated in the present" (Seifrid, 613; cf. Wagner, 176–78).

Paul's argument in 2:25–29 focuses on circumcision as a particular reason for Jews to boast in the law and have confidence about their relationship with God. "Circumcision has value if you obey the law," he says, "but if you break the law, you have become as if you had not been circumcised" (v. 25). Surprisingly, however, an uncircumcised person who keeps the law may be regarded by God "as though they were circumcised" (v. 26). This anticipates the argument in 4:9–17 that gentiles may be justified by faith together with Jews who trust in Jesus, and thus be reckoned as Abraham's true descendants. Paul contrasts a person who is (lit.) "a Jew outwardly" with a person who is "a Jew inwardly," the difference being that the latter has experienced "circumcision of the heart, by the Spirit, not by the written code" (2:28–29). This recalls God's promise in Deut. 30:6 to circumcise the hearts of his people and prophetic expectations that God would write his law on their hearts (Jer. 31:33) and place his Spirit within them to enable them to observe his ordinances (Ezek. 36:26–27).

Paul continues his debate with an imaginary Jewish opponent in 3:1–8. Two introductory questions express objections that might be made to his preceding argument: "What advantage, then, is there in being a Jew or what value is there in circumcision?" (vv. 1–2). Paul's emphatic response ("Much in every way!") leads him to affirm the fundamental truth that "they have been entrusted with the very words of God" (*ta logia tou theou* [lit., "the oracles of God"]; cf. Num. 24:4, 16 LXX; Acts 7:38; Heb. 5:12; 1 Pet. 4:11). Two more questions take up the issue of Jewish unfaithfulness and God's faithfulness (v. 3). The claim that God must be true, even though every human being is a liar (Ps. 116:11 [115:2 LXX]), is supported with a quote from Ps. 51:4 (MT 51:6; LXX 50:6; "so that you might be proved right when you speak and prevail when you judge" [AT]). Although there is debate about the best way to interpret the text in its original context, in the sequence of Paul's argument, it relates God's faithfulness to his righteousness in judgment (Moo, 188; cf. Neh. 9:32–33). The verb *dikaioō* ("justify") is a key term in Romans (2:13; 3:20, 24, 26, 28, 30; 4:2, 5; 5:1, 9; 6:7; 8:30, 33) with different applications. Here, God is justified or "proved to be right" (BDAG) in his "words" (*en tois logois sou*), which means that he will "triumph" when he "judges" you (*nikēsēs en tō krinesthai se*).

A final series of questions concerning God's righteousness in judging sinners leads Paul to conclude that his aim has been to charge that "Jews and Gentiles alike are all under sin" (3:9; cf. Isa. 50:1; Rom. 7:14). Biblical texts are woven together in 3:10–18 to reinforce his message about the universality of sin and its impact on every aspect of human life. The opening statement in 3:10–12 is probably a rephrasing of Ps. 13:1–3 LXX

(14:1–3 MT/ET), with words from Eccles. 7:20 included ("There is no one righteous"). This effectively defines unrighteousness in terms of not understanding or seeking after God (Seifrid, 616). Two lines from Ps. 5:10 LXX (5:9 MT/ET) focus on the deadly effects of speech (Rom. 3:13ab, "Their throats are open graves; their tongues practice deceit"). A line from Ps. 139:4 LXX (140:3 MT/ET) reinforces this (Rom. 3:13c, "The poison of vipers is on their lips"), and an adaptation of Ps. 9:28 LXX (10:7 MT/ET; Rom. 3:14, "Their mouths are full of cursing and bitterness") adds to the picture. An abridgment of Isa. 59:7–8a LXX identifies the violence that brought God's judgment on Israel (Rom. 3:15–17, "Their feet are swift to shed blood; ruin and misery mark their ways, and the way of peace they do not know"). A slight modification of Ps. 35:2b LXX (36:1b MT/ET) restates in different terms the idea of not seeking God (Rom. 3:18, "There is no fear of God before their eyes").

As Paul prepares to explain the divine solution to humanity's captivity to sin, he contends that God's law was given to speak "to those who are under the law, so that every mouth may be silenced and the whole world held accountable to God" (Rom. 3:19). Psalm 142:2 LXX (143:2 MT/ET) is adapted to read, "No one will be declared righteous in God's sight *by the works of the law*" (Rom. 3:20). Paul's explanation for this ("Rather, through the law we become conscious of our sin") remains to be unpacked in 7:7–12.

Justification by faith and the blessing of the nations. The defensive section in 3:27–4:25 arises directly from the exposition of the gospel in 3:21–26. Paul reaffirms that justification is by faith and reinforces this by adding "alone" and "apart from the works of the law" (3:28). This must be so, because there is only one God (Deut. 6:4), whose concern for Jews and gentiles alike means that he must "justify the circumcised by faith and the uncircumcised through that same faith" (Rom. 3:29–30). Far from canceling the law, Paul claims that his gospel upholds the law (v. 31). The explanation for this in 4:1–25 focuses on Abraham's righteousness and the identity of his true descendants. The matter of boasting, which is raised in 2:17–23 and 3:27, is picked up again in 4:3. "Paul reads the story of Abraham in the light of Gen. 15:6, setting 'boasting' in the context of the human relationship with God and inverting the early Jewish image of Abraham" (Seifrid, 622–23; cf. Gathercole, 232–51). In 4:9–25, he shows how the covenant promises to Abraham are fulfilled in Christ, enabling Jews and gentiles to trust in the Messiah and benefit from his saving work together. Fundamentally, then, Paul means that the law is upheld in its prophetic role (3:31), as a preparation for the gospel era, "in which both Jews and Gentiles will be justified by grace through faith" (Rosner, 154).

Jewish evaluations of Gen. 15:6 in Paul's era emphasized that Abraham's faithful obedience was counted as righteousness by God (Gathercole, 237–38). But Paul understands this text differently. The "crediting" on view (*elogisthē*) was a reckoning of something that was not inherently true of Abraham. Indeed, Paul implies that Abraham was "ungodly" when his faith was "credited as righteousness" (4:5). Abraham responded to God's promise with trust and he "believed the LORD" (Gen. 15:4–6). The apostle follows a rabbinic pattern of biblical interpretation called *gezerah shawah* (analogy), citing another passage to confirm his interpretation of Gen. 15:6, where the term "credited" is also used (Ps. 31:2 LXX [32:2 MT/ET], *logisētai* [NIV: "count"]). As the human author of this passage, David is portrayed as an ungodly and sinful Israelite, who speaks of "the blessedness of the one to whom God credits righteousness apart from works" (Rom. 4:6). The word "blessed" occurs twice in the quotation, referring first to the forgiveness of transgressions and then to his sin not being reckoned in judgment.

Paul goes on to ask, "Is this blessedness only for the circumcised, or also for the uncircumcised?" arguing from the context in Genesis that faith was credited to Abraham before he was circumcised (4:9–10). Abraham received circumcision "as a sign, a seal of the righteousness that he had by faith while he was still uncircumcised," so that he might become "the father of all who believe," whether circumcised or not (4:11–12). Abraham's God-given faith was the means by which God's plan to bless the nations was advanced in his own lifetime (Gen. 12:3; 17:4–5; 18:18). The ultimate fulfillment of God's promises occurred through Christ, who has made it possible for believing Jews and gentiles to share his resurrection glory and reign with him in the world to come (4:23–25; 5:2, 17; 8:11, 17, 19–23). The final citation of Gen. 15:6 in Rom. 4:22 leads Paul back to the gospel: "The words 'it was credited to him' were written not for him alone, but also for us, to whom God will credit righteousness—for us who believe in him who raised Jesus our Lord from the dead" (4:23–24). A confessional statement in 4:25 ("He was delivered over to death for our sins and was raised to life for our justification"; cf. Isa. 52:13–53:12) forms the basis for the argument in 5:1–11, where the gospel is further expounded and applied.

Jews, gentiles, and Paul's apostolic mission. Since many Israelites had not believed the gospel and experienced the promised messianic blessings when Paul wrote to the Romans (9:1–5), he sets out in 9:6–11:32 to explore the double issue of "the gospel's apparent failure with respect to Israel *and* its paradoxical success with respect to the Gentiles" (Byrne, 282). Biblical quotations comprise more than 30 percent of the argument and play a critical role in addressing this issue. The apostle's firm belief is that God's word has not failed (9:6), because "not all Israelites truly belong to Israel, and not all of Abraham's children are his true descendants" (NRSV). Paul illustrates this process of election with reference to God's choice of Isaac rather than Ishmael (9:7, citing

Gen. 21:12; then 9:9, citing Gen. 18:10, 14) and Jacob rather than Esau (9:12–13, citing Gen. 25:23 and then Mal. 1:2–3). God's elective calling expresses his mercy and grace, and this is unrelated to what people have done in the past or might do in the future.

Next, Paul responds to the charge that God is unjust to act in this way: "For he says to Moses, 'I will have mercy on whom I have mercy, and I will have compassion on whom I have compassion'" (9:15, citing Exod. 33:19). This revelation came after Israel rebelled against God at Sinai and made a golden calf (Exod. 32:1–6). The continuing implication is that God's mercy cannot be earned or deserved by what one desires or does (Rom. 9:16). Paul moves on to assert that God cannot be charged with injustice, even when he uses those who oppose him to fulfill his plan. What "Scripture says to Pharaoh" (9:17), the enemy of God's people, continues to reveal a vital aspect of his character and way of operating in human history. Paul's interpretive translation of Exod. 9:16 emphasizes that God caused Pharaoh to appear on the stage of history for positive reasons, "that I might display my power in you and that my name might be proclaimed in all the earth." Paul concludes that the sovereign God "has mercy on whom he wants to have mercy, and he hardens whom he wants to harden" (Rom. 9:18).

Paul imagines an opponent saying, "Then why does God still blame us? For who is able to resist his will?" (9:19). He responds by drawing attention to the creaturely status of his challenger and questioning the appropriateness of contending against God (9:20, "But who are you, a human being, to talk back to God?"). He also uses the familiar biblical image of the potter and the clay to make the point that God has the right "to make out of the same lump of clay some pottery for special purposes and some for common use" (9:21; cf. Isa. 29:16; 45:9; Jer. 18:1–12). God has shown his wrath to some and made "the riches of his glory known to the objects of his mercy, whom he prepared in advance for glory—even us, whom he called, not only from the Jews, but also from the Gentiles" (9:22–24). Several texts are brought together to illuminate this argument. Hosea 2:23 addresses the Northern Kingdom of Israel just before the Assyrian invasion, when God treated them as "not my people" and as "not my loved one," yet through the prophet he promises that he will again call them "my people" and "my loved one." A citation from Hosea 1:10 confirms God's focus on the restoration of this relationship: "In the very place where it was said to them, 'You are not my people,' there they will be called 'children of the living God'" (Rom. 9:26). Since Paul has just mentioned God's calling of Jews and gentiles (9:24), some would argue that the Hosea texts relate to the conversion of many gentiles while the Isaiah texts that follow in 9:27–28 (Isa. 10:22–23; 1:9) anticipate the comparatively small number of Jews in the Christian community. Gentiles are certainly now included among those whom God calls "my people" and may be called "sons of the living God" (Rom. 8:14–17; cf. 1 Pet. 2:10), but Paul's concern here is to demonstrate how the word of God to ethnic Israel has not failed (9:6). So, he juxtaposes Hosea's predictions about a comprehensive restoration of God's covenant people with Isaiah's prophecies about only a remnant being saved (Peterson, 364–66; Stanley, *Arguing*, 157–59; Wagner, 78–116). This he applies to a remnant of ethnic Israelite believers. Ministry to gentiles then becomes the focus in 11:11–24.

Paul brings his overview of God's relationship with Israel to a climax by claiming that "they stumbled over the stumbling stone," who is their Messiah (9:32b–33). This happened because they pursued righteousness through the law as if it were by works, rather than by faith (9:31–32a). At the same time, Paul celebrates the fact that "the Gentiles, who did not pursue righteousness, have obtained it, a righteousness that is by faith" (9:30). These two approaches are highlighted again in 10:3, where the contrast is expressed in terms of "the righteousness of God" and "their own [righteousness]." Isaiah encourages the people of Jerusalem to trust in the Lord and the "stone" he is putting in Zion (Isa. 28:16). When Paul cites this text, he removes the words "a tested stone, a precious cornerstone for a sure foundation" and inserts a warning from Isa. 8:14 ("a stone that causes people to stumble and a rock that makes them fall"), concluding with a version of the promise in 28:16 ("and the one who believes in him will never be put to shame"). The LXX contains the important words *ep' autō* ("in him"), which are not found in the MT but allow for the development of a messianic interpretation (Stanley, *Language*, 119–25; Wright, 649–51).

Arising directly from his argument in 9:30–10:4, Paul's implication is that there are two different ways of reading and responding to God's law (10:5–10). The first simply takes Lev. 18:5 as the key ("The person who does these things will live by them"). The second perceives the significance of Deut. 30:12–14, understood in its context and in the light of its fulfillment in Christ. This passage points to the need for the righteousness that comes by faith, which is the message the apostle has been proclaiming. The biblical argument fuses two voices, a "speech-in-character" and a Hebrew interpretive translation, "with Moses 'writing' in the initial text from Leviticus, and a personified 'righteousness by faith' 'speaking' the next five citations" (Jewett, 622; cf. Tobin, 343). God's intention to save Jews and gentiles through faith in the risen Lord is confirmed in Rom. 10:11–13 with citations from Isa. 28:16 and Joel 2:32. As Paul outlines the process by which people are saved (10:14–17), he cites Isa. 52:7 regarding "those who bring good news" and draws attention to Israel's unbelief and failure to obey the gospel, just as Isaiah had predicted (Isa. 53:1). Then he uses a collection of texts to confirm that dispersed Israel has indeed heard the good news, because God's words have gone "to the ends of the world" (Ps. 19:4). Israel has failed to understand God's plan to make them jealous (Deut. 32:21) by revealing himself to gentiles who did not ask for it (Isa. 65:1). But God continues to hold out his hands to Israel through the preaching of the gospel, even though they remain "a disobedient and obstinate people" (Isa. 65:2).

The apostle denies that God has rejected his people and points to himself as a true Israelite (11:1). He refers to what Elijah said about Israel's apostasy in his era (1 Kings 19:10, 14) and highlights God's response concerning a faithful remnant (19:18), concluding that, "so too, at the present time there is a remnant chosen by grace" (Rom. 11:5). The rest of Israel has been hardened by God in spiritual obduracy "to this very day," recalling Deut. 29:4 (29:3 LXX, modified with words from Isa. 29:10). David's imprecatory prayer in Ps. 69:22–23 presents this as a curse. In answer to his own rhetorical question (11:11, "Did they stumble so as to fall beyond recovery?"), Paul recalls the message of Deut. 32:21 (cited in 10:19): "Not at all! Rather, because of their transgression, salvation has come to the Gentiles to make Israel envious." He contemplates the "full inclusion" (11:12, *plērōma*) of elect Israelites, as he continues his ministry as apostle to the gentiles, hoping that he might somehow arouse his own people "to envy and save some of them" (11:14; cf. 15:20–21, citing Isa. 52:15). The climax of this argument comes in 11:25–27 with the revelation of a "mystery" to his readers: "Israel has experienced a hardening in part until the full number [*plērōma*] of the Gentiles has come in, and in this way all Israel will be saved." Israel's salvation is certified by a combination of divine promises from Isa. 59:20–21 ("The deliverer will come from Zion; he will turn godlessness away from Jacob. And this is my covenant with them") and 27:9 ("when I take away their sins"). The MT has the deliverer coming "to Zion," while the LXX has "for the sake of Zion." Paul's "from Zion" may refer to the Messiah's future return from heaven, but it more likely means that the deliverer has already come from heaven or from the midst of God's holy people to accomplish Israel's salvation (Peterson, 425–27; cf. Wagner, 276–94).

Scripture and Pastoral Issues

Romans 12:1–15:13 details the lifestyle that should flow from experiencing God's mercy through Christ and the gospel. As Paul deals with ministry in the body of Christ and relationships with outsiders (12:3–21), he urges his readers not to take revenge, because Deut. 32:35 promises that God will avenge and repay. Proverbs 25:21–22 is applied to this situation also, as an example of how to overcome evil with good. When the apostle talks about being subject to the governing authorities and fulfilling social responsibilities (13:1–10), he describes love as fulfilling the law, cites four commandments, and concludes that these are summed up by Lev. 19:18.

The need for love among believers, rather than a judgmental attitude, is reiterated in 14:1–15:7, as Paul reflects on what will promote peace and edification in the Roman situation. References to disputes about food and the observance of certain days in honor of the Lord suggest that some were concerned to keep aspects of the Jewish ceremonial law. Christ as Lord is presented as the key to everything (14:4, 6–8, 14, 15, 18; 15:3, 5–7). Two biblical citations play a significant role in the argument. Isaiah 45:23 is quoted to confirm that "each of us will give an account of ourselves to God" (14:11–13). As a motivation for pleasing others "for their good, to build them up" (15:1–3), Ps. 69:9 is applied to Christ, who "did not please himself." Paul concludes that "everything that was written in the past was written to teach us, so that through the endurance taught in the Scriptures and the encouragement they provide we might have hope" (15:4). Endurance and hope are then linked to the challenge for believers to have this Christ-like attitude toward one another and to praise God together for his mercy (15:5–12). A final catena of texts in 15:7–13 (2 Sam. 22:50/Ps. 18:49; Deut. 32:43; Ps. 117:1; Isa. 11:10) functions "both as a conclusion to the exhortations of 12:1–15:6 and as a summation of the principal themes of the letter as a whole" (Wagner, 307).

Conclusion

Paul uses Scripture in this letter *didactically* in relation to God's character, his response to Israel's failure, his covenantal commitment to Abraham and his offspring, and the saving message of the gospel. He interprets it *prophetically* in relation to the Messiah, Israel, and the nations, particularly in view of the coming judgment of God. He employs it in a *hortatory* way, to encourage Christians to make appropriate responses to God and his will, *missiologically* to explain his own ministry agenda, and *doxologically* to encourage celebration of God's saving achievement through his Son. Most of the modifications Paul makes to LXX citations are simply "adaptations in grammar or syntax or wording to fit the text most appropriately to the syntax and rhetoric of the letter" (Dunn, *Theology*, 171). Although it is possible that he sometimes uses a different version of the LXX from those now extant, or is translating freely from the Hebrew himself, he mostly modifies the LXX for rhetorical and theological reasons (Wagner, 344–52). Sometimes he adds words and phrases from other contexts to give an interpretive rendering of a text. Both Greco-Roman and Jewish literature provide "strong evidence for a general cultural and literary ethos in which incorporating interpretive elements into the wording of a quotation was considered a normal and acceptable means of advancing one's argument" (Stanley, *Language*, 337). In Paul's case, a conviction that God's long-standing plan of salvation has been fulfilled in Jesus Christ gave him a hermeneutical principle by which to read and explain Scripture (Kruse, 88–92).

Bibliography. Byrne, B., *Romans*, SP 6 (Liturgical Press, 1996); Calhoun, R. M., *Paul's Definition of the*

Gospel in Romans 1, WUNT 2/316 (Mohr Siebeck, 2015); Dunn, J. D. G., *Romans 1–8*, WBC (Word, 1988); Dunn, *Romans 9–16*, WBC (Word, 1988); Dunn, *The Theology of Paul the Apostle* (T&T Clark, 1998); Gathercole, S. J., *Where Is Boasting?* (Eerdmans, 2001); Harrington, D. J., "Paul's Use of the Old Testament in Romans," *SCJR* 4 (2009): 1–8; Hays, R. B., *Echoes of Scripture in the Letters of Paul* (Yale University Press, 1989); Jewett, R., *Romans*, Herm (Fortress, 2007); Kruse, C. G., "Paul's Use of Scripture in Romans," in *Paul and Scripture*, ed. S. E. Porter and C. D. Land, PS 10 (Brill, 2019), 77–92; Kujanpaa, K., *The Rhetorical Function of Scriptural Quotations in Romans*, NovTSup 172 (Brill, 2019); Moo, D. J., *The Epistle to the Romans*, NICNT (Eerdmans, 1996); Moyise, S., "Quotations," in *As It Is Written*, ed. S. E. Porter and C. D. Stanley, SymS 50 (Society of Biblical Literature, 2008), 15–28; Peterson, D. G., *Commentary on Romans*, EBTC (Lexham, 2021); Porter, S. E., "Allusions and Echoes," in *As It Is Written*, ed. S. E. Porter and C. D. Stanley, SymS 50 (Society of Biblical Literature, 2008), 29–40; Rosner, B. S., *Paul and the Law*, NSBT 31 (InterVarsity, 2013); Seifrid, M. A., "Romans," in *CNTUOT*, 604–97; Stanley, C. D., *Arguing with Scripture* (Clark, 2004); Stanley, *Paul and the Language of Scripture*, SNTSMS 74 (Cambridge University Press, 1992); Stowers, S. K., *The Diatribe and Paul's Letter to the Romans*, SBLDS 57 (Scholars Press, 1981); Tobin, T. H., *Paul's Rhetoric in Its Contexts* (Hendrickson, 2004); Wagner, J. Ross, *Heralds of the Good News*, NovTSup 101 (Brill, 2002); Witherington, B., III, with D. Hyatt, *Paul's Letter to the Romans* (Eerdmans, 2004); Wright, N. T., "The Letter to the Romans," in *NIB*, 10:395–770.

DAVID G. PETERSON

Ruth, Book of

Set in the tumultuous period of the judges, a time without a king, the book of Ruth tells the story of a family who leaves Bethlehem because of famine to sojourn outside the promised land. In Moab, Elimelech and his sons die, leaving behind three widows. Upon hearing that YHWH had broken the famine in Bethlehem, Naomi, the widow of Elimelech, sets out to return home. Ruth, the foreign widow of one of her sons, returns with her (chap. 1), and so sets in motion a train of events through which God preserves Elimelech's family line. Ruth providentially meets Boaz in his field, where he showers upon her kindness after kindness (chap. 2). Naomi sends Ruth to the threshing floor to propose marriage to him, where he informs her there is a closer kinsman who has the first right of refusal (chap. 3). At the town gate, the closer kinsman declines the right to redeem Naomi's property and marry Ruth, leaving Boaz to do so. God grants Boaz and Ruth a son, Obed, who becomes the grandfather of King David (chap. 4).

Essential Features of the Book of Ruth

Composition. Like most historical narratives in the OT, its author is unknown. The date of composition is also unknown, with the time of David (4:17–22) being the earliest possible date. Two general historical periods are most likely. If written during the monarchy, it could have supported King David's line (against the line of Saul, for instance). If it was written in the early restoration period (soon after the Jews returned from Babylonian exile), it could have presented a voice against the ban on ethnic intermarriages (cf. Ezra-Nehemiah). Either date is consistent with a high view of Scripture, and thankfully, the authorship and date of composition are not crucial to understanding the book's message.

Structure and message. The four chapters of the Ruth narrative can be structured as a chiasm, reflecting the reversal structure of the plot. Each scene corresponds to another symmetrically.

- A End of a family line in Moab (1:1–6)
  - B En route: Naomi, Orpah, and Ruth dialogue (1:7–19a)
    - C Town gate: Naomi laments before the townswomen of Bethlehem (1:19b–22)
      - D Home: Naomi accepts Ruth's plan (2:1–3)
        - E Boaz's field: Encounter between Ruth and Boaz (2:4–17)
          - F Home: Naomi and Ruth debrief (2:18–23)
          - F′ Home: Ruth accepts Naomi's plan (3:1–5)
        - E′ Threshing floor: Encounter between Ruth and Boaz (3:6–15)
      - D′ Home: Naomi and Ruth debrief (3:16–18)
    - C′ Town gate: Boaz redeems before the elders of Bethlehem (4:1–12)
  - B′ Home: Naomi, neighborhood women dialogue (4:13–17)
- A′ Beginning of a royal line in Israel (4:18–22)

The first scene (A) is a prologue that describes the tragic death of Elimelech and his sons in Moab. They live there for ten years, during which his sons marry Moabite women without bearing any children. Elimelech's family line is left under threat, and the widows are left destitute. Naomi faces a life of poverty and shame. The corresponding scene (A′) is a genealogical epilogue that lists ten generations from Perez to David and includes Obed, who will continue the family line of Elimelech (4:17). The seeming end of a family line ends up producing the greatest Israelite king! And Naomi's shame has been reversed to honor.

The two central panes of the chiasm (DEF-F′E′D′) comprise corresponding scenes based on location and conversation partners. The central scene of the first pane (E) takes place in Boaz's field during the day. Ruth "just happens" to stumble into Boaz's field, where her and her mother-in-law's fortunes start to turn around. Boaz's words and actions reveal him to be a godly, kind, and generous Israelite, willing to go beyond the basic requirements of the charity laws. Ruth is astounded by his show of generous provision and protection, which he explains is in response to the loyalty she had shown her mother-in-law by turning her back on her native land and people to throw in her lot with Naomi. He asks YHWH to reward her kindness since she has taken refuge under his wings, although we see God already doing so through the man praying the prayer. The extraordinary amount of grain she gleans is material evidence that she is on the path to fullness. The corresponding scene of the second pane (E′) takes place on the threshing floor during the night. Under instruction from Naomi, Ruth waits for the designated time to lie at Boaz's feet. When he wakes up, she asks him to marry her because he is a "kinsman-redeemer." Boaz does not say yes because he cannot—there is a more closely related clansman who has the first right of refusal. Nonetheless, Ruth secures her future by receiving Boaz's promise that he will ensure her (and as it turns out also Naomi's) redemption, either from him or the nearer kinsman. The reversal of the widows' destitution is assured.

The crucial turning point of the narrative is the pair of scenes at its center (F-F′). In the first scene, Ruth debriefs with Naomi at home after Ruth's first day of gleaning (F). Ruth reveals that she gleaned in Boaz's field, to which Naomi responds enthusiastically by praying a benediction upon him and detailing his significance for them—"He is one of our kinsman-redeemers" (2:20 AT). With this renewed hope in the form of Boaz, Naomi is transformed from bitter and withdrawn to rejuvenated and resourceful. And it is her threshing-floor scheme that forms the second of the turning-point scenes (F′). In this scene, also at Naomi and Ruth's home, the mother-in-law devises a risky scheme to arrange a marriage between her daughter-in-law and Boaz.

This structure highlights human initiative at the core of the narrative, but two mentions of God's activity bookend the narrative action (1:6 [strictly speaking, hearsay]; 4:13). The reversal for Naomi (and also Ruth, Boaz, and the nation of Israel) is ultimately under God's hand, although his hand appears mostly hidden. However, the characters' comments about God and prayers to him throughout the narrative ensure that the audience does not forget his role in the proceedings.

Ruth and the OT

Ruth and antecedent legal texts. Whether Ruth was written in the monarchic or postexilic period, it is likely that the legal texts, or at least their contents, were already well known. If OT law prescribes the baseline ethical requirements, then OT narratives help us understand the ideal behavior (Wenham, 4). In the Ruth narrative this can be demonstrated in relation to five laws: gleaning, redemption, levirate marriage, intermarriage, and exclusion from the assembly.

The gleaning law (Lev. 19:9–10; Deut. 24:19–22) was one aspect of social security in ancient Israel. Landowners were not allowed to harvest the edges of their fields nor to return to harvest a sheaf that had been missed. They were to leave it for those people who did not have access to the produce of the land: the resident alien, the fatherless, and the widow. Two reasons are given: First, God is the landowner, and all Israelites are tenants on his land. Second, the Israelites were to remember that they were slaves in Egypt, with the implication that they were not to enslave others in their poverty. In the book of Ruth, Boaz goes beyond the requirements of the gleaning law. He not only allows her access to his field, but also offers her protection, water to drink, and food to eat while she gleans in the field. He even instructs his workers to deliberately pull out stalks for her to glean, so that she gleans enough on the first day to feed herself and Naomi for at least a week. He prays that YHWH would repay her for her loyal actions to her mother-in-law (2:11–12), and he becomes one through whom YHWH blesses her.

Based on the law, a kinsman-redeemer was a relative who wholly restored that which has been lost, usually at his own personal cost. When a relative in need of redemption could not help themselves, the redeemer would act out of family solidarity—every Israelite is linked by a series of widening networks: father's house, clan, tribe, and nation. If a relative was in need, there was an obligation to help: the closer the kinship relation, the stronger the obligation. The law outlined four main roles for a kinsman-redeemer: (1) buying back property that was lost outside the clan for an indebted relative (Lev. 25:25–30); (2) buying back a relative who had sold themselves into slavery (25:47–55); (3) executing murderers of relatives as an "avenger of blood" (Num. 35:12, 19–27; Deut. 19:6, 11–13); and (4) receiving restitution money on behalf of a deceased relative (Num. 5:8). Only the first of these is relevant to the book of Ruth. Although the details are debated, it seems that Naomi was selling the right to redeem the property of Elimelech (4:3–4). Boaz first offers the land to the nearer kinsman-redeemer, since he had the first right of refusal under the law (cf. Lev. 25:48–49). He accepts. However, when Boaz informs him that Ruth is part of the package, he reneges. On the one hand, his response is understandable since marriage to a widow is not a stated legal requirement of a kinsman-redeemer. On the other hand, the elders, the legal quorum at the town gate, do not object to Boaz's application of the law under the particular circumstances; in fact, the whole throng at the town gate give their blessing. Boaz could have applied the redemption law according to the "moral logic" underlying the law: if the role of a kinsman was to restore wholeness, in this case, that role required marrying the widow (cf. Isa. 54:4–5). Or he could have expanded the application of the redemption and levirate laws. Since in this case there was no heir to continue the name of the dead on his landed inheritance, the application of the redemption law could have triggered the levirate law (Deut. 25:5–10). The allusions to the levirate custom in the book of Ruth (1:11–13; 2:20; 3:9–13; 4:7–12, 16–17) suggest that this is likely, although not conclusively. If so, since Naomi is past childbearing age, Ruth is substituted for her to produce an heir to continue Elimelech's name on his inheritance. Some scholars accuse Boaz of underhanded tactics, but his application of the two laws is consistent with the principles underlying those laws.

On first reading, it seems that Boaz's marriage to Ruth the Moabite contravenes the law prohibiting intermarriage (Deut. 7:3–4). Strictly speaking, this law prohibits an Israelite from marrying any Canaanite, those incumbent in the promised land. The reason for this prohibition is crucial: the hearts of God's people must not be turned aside to follow foreign gods. The assumption was that all non-Israelites worshiped their own gods, not YHWH—ethnic groups both in and outside the promised land. Generally speaking, ethnic intermarriage with Moabites should also be prohibited. Yet Ruth had sworn her allegiance to Naomi's God, and her self-imprecatory oath in YHWH's name reinforced the authenticity of her pledge (Ruth 1:16–17). In short, her ethnicity plus worship of her god would have rendered her off-limits to Boaz, but her ethnicity plus worship of YHWH do not. And her ethnicity should have excluded her from the assembly of YHWH, since "no Ammonite or Moabite or any of their descendants may enter the assembly of the Lord, not even in the tenth generation," because they did not show hospitality, and they hired Balaam to curse God's people (Deut. 23:3–6). Again, a surface reading of this law would lead to Ruth's exclusion (and perhaps King David's, since Ruth was his great grandmother), but an examination of the principle underlying the law leads to another application. When an Israelite family sought hospitality outside the promised land, Ruth the Moabite obliged, even marrying an Israelite son, and so can be seen to "bless" instead of "curse" God's people (cf. Gen. 12:3).

The application of these antecedent laws in the Ruth narrative encourages an expansive rather than a restrictive application, based on the principles underlying the laws rather than strict adherence to the specifics of the laws. In NT terms, one should follow the spirit of the law rather than the letter. The Ruth narrative promotes the virtue of kindness, and concerning the law, this is expressed in its generous application toward those in need—especially the widow and the resident alien.

Ruth and OT allusions. Ruth contains many innerbiblical allusions. The major ones will be detailed here. (For those pertaining to Ezra-Nehemiah, Prov. 31, and Psalms, see Lau and Goswell, 5–18, 37–70.)

Ruth is set in the time of the judges (1:1). In the Christian canon, Ruth follows immediately after Judges, which ends, "In those days Israel had no king; everyone did as they saw fit" (Judg. 21:25). Reading the Ruth narrative after Judges leads us to expect a time of political and moral anarchy, as vividly depicted in the distressing vignettes that conclude Judges (chaps. 17–21). On the whole, however, the narrative has a gentle feel, which might indicate that Ruth took place in one of the intermittent peaceful periods. All is not well, however, since there is famine and death and infertility, leading one Israelite family to abandon the promised land. And the unruly spirit of the age of the judges intrudes on the narrative, as seen in Ruth's need to glean in a field where the owner will allow her (2:2) and in Boaz's need to protect Ruth from physical harassment and verbal assault (2:9, 22). Reading Ruth after Judges also increases anticipation for a king, and the first allusion is found in the father of the family, Elimelech (1:2), whose name most likely means "my God is king." Ironically, he does not live with God as his king, as he leaves the land to seek blessing in the land of Chemosh. Hope for a king soon emerges, since Elimelech's family are Ephrathites from Bethlehem in Judah, the same clan as David (1 Sam. 17:12). The last time Bethlehem was mentioned in the OT, it described Rachel's burial place: "Ephrath (that is, Bethlehem)" (Gen. 35:16, 19; 48:7). By the end of Ruth, there is a prayer for greatness in Ephrathah/Bethlehem (4:11), fulfilled in King David. This motif is picked up by Micah, who looks forward to another messianic ruler from "Bethlehem Ephrathah" (5:2–5 [5:1–4 MT/LXX]). The kindness of the characters in the book of Ruth is all the more striking against a backdrop of violence and anarchy.

David's birth at the end of Ruth draws a direct connection with the book of Samuel. Several episodes, words, and phrases further link the books. To escape Saul, David and his parents go to Moab, where the Moabite king shelters them (1 Sam. 22:3–4). Ruth gleans "an ephah" of barley to offer her mother-in-law (Ruth 2:17), while Hannah offers "a three-year-old bull, an ephah of flour and a skin of wine" to God to give thanks for her son (1 Sam. 1:24). The women of the town judge Ruth as "better . . . than seven sons" (4:15), while Hannah's husband asks, "Don't I mean more to you than ten sons?" (1 Sam. 1:8).

Allusions to and the mention of ancestors invite us to read Ruth within the matrix of the Genesis narratives. For instance, the famine in Bethlehem leading to a sojourn outside the promised land recalls the famines that drove Abraham and Isaac from Canaan (Ruth 1:1; Gen. 12:10; 26:1; see Lau and Goswell, 71–74). Ruth's abandoning her homeland and people to journey to

Judah parallels Abraham's journey (Ruth 2:11; Gen. 12:1), although Ruth's decision is more remarkable because she does not depart with a promise from God. As such, the correspondence between Ruth and Abraham in this sense can be viewed as biographical typology (Fishbane, 372). The theme of seed/offspring is prominent in both books, with the associated threat to a family line. The author's use of the *tôlədōt* formula ("this is the family line of") suggests that the Ruth narrative continues the story line from Genesis (Ruth 4:18; Gen. 5:1; 6:9; 10:1; 11:10, 27; 25:12, 19; 36:1, 9; 37:2; cf. also Gen. 2:4; Num. 3:1), particularly the line of Judah.

The presence of ancestors in the blessings for Boaz and Ruth (Ruth 4:11–12) forges deeper connections with three Genesis narratives in particular. The Ruth genealogy begins with Perez instead of his more illustrious father Judah, and his three mentions in Ruth (4:12, 18 [2x]), compared to his father's single mention (4:12), suggest that his selection is not accidental. There are correspondences between the Judah-Tamar (Gen. 38) and Ruth-Boaz (Ruth 3) narratives, but also contrasts. The Judah-Tamar narrative is the only OT narrative occurrence of the levirate custom, and the Ruth narrative likely alludes to this custom. In both cases, a family line is under threat, and when Judah refuses to give his last son to his daughter-in-law Tamar, she takes matters into her own hands. She pretends to be a prostitute to entice her father-in-law to impregnate her. Like the Ruth narrative, this breaks social mores (it is apt that the offspring of this union is called Perez, meaning "breach"), but in the end, Judah recognizes that his withholding his son was wrong; indeed, he proclaims that Tamar "is more righteous than I" (Gen. 38:26). Driven by desperation, both foreign women take huge (though calculated) risks: Ruth her reputation and Tamar her life. But while Judah is impetuous, Boaz is restrained; while Tamar entices her father-in-law to have sexual intercourse before confronting him with his responsibilities, Ruth is upfront with the latter without engaging in the former (cf. Eskenazi and Frymer-Kensky, xxii). We can thus view Boaz as a more righteous version of his ancestor, or, in Michael Fishbane's terminology, a typological reversal (Fishbane, 373).

Similarly, in light of Moab's contemptible origins (Gen. 19), Ruth can also be seen to "redeem" the shame of her ancestors. Seven correspondences between Lot and his daughters and Ruth have been identified (Zakovitch, 50). The three main correspondences are an encounter between a man and a woman whose husband had died; all women are called "daughters"; and an older man encounters a woman at night after he has been drinking (Ruth 3:7). Similarly driven by desperation, Lot's daughters produce incestuous children who become the ancestors of Ammon and Moab. Yet their stated motivation was to preserve a threatened family line (Gen. 19:32, 34), similar to Tamar and Ruth. And they are resourceful, just like Tamar and Ruth. Ruth not only turns her back on Moab but also commits herself to Naomi and YHWH. Her actions driven by kindness model a core Israelite virtue. And reading the three narratives together reveals a greater purpose within the story line of the OT.

All three narratives recount the history of a single family (Fisch). Lot is the father of Moab, the ancestor of Ruth. Judah is the father of Perez, the ancestor of Boaz. The single clan of Abraham and Lot, which separated early in OT history, is now brought together in Ruth and Boaz.

Ruth and the NT

The book of Ruth is not quoted in the NT, but some of its characters are mentioned in the genealogies of Jesus Christ (Matt. 1:1–6; Luke 3:31–34). The Matthean genealogy not only completes the messianic line from David to Jesus but also expands on and completes interlocking themes from Ruth. In Ruth, Perez begins the ten-generation genealogy, a typical pattern of ancient Near Eastern king lists, and places Boaz and David at prominent positions—seventh and tenth. The effect of the genealogy links the Ruth narrative with the grand narrative of the OT, from Genesis to Kings, in which kingship is a major theme. Perez transports the audience back to the patriarchal stories of Genesis (esp. Gen. 38); then we move forward to David, whose last days are recorded in 1 Kings 1–2. The Ruth genealogy thus establishes a continuity between earlier biblical history and the beginning of the Davidic monarchy. The Matthean genealogy continues and completes this grand messianic narrative, pointing to its fulfillment in "Jesus the Messiah the son of David, the son of Abraham" (Matt. 1:1).

The Matthean genealogy also continues the trajectory of foreign females building the messianic line. Among OT books, Ruth is noted for its uniquely female focus. Elimelech and his sons die early in the narrative, leaving Naomi and Ruth as the main characters (1:3–5). We, as the audience, are concerned about the plight of Naomi. Will her emptiness be filled? We side with Ruth as she gleans and as she proposes marriage. Boaz is the center of attention in the legal case, but although he speaks of the male issues of property and progeny, he also acts for the sake of and on behalf of the women. Soon, attention returns to the women and we again hear their perspective (4:13–17). Ruth, of course, is a foreign woman, a reality of which she is sorely conscious (2:10), and of which the narrator reminds us (Ruth's designation "the Moabite" is found in 1:22; 2:2, 6, 21; 4:5, 10). Yet, remarkably, by the end of the Ruth narrative, a foreign woman not only belongs as a full member of God's people but even contributes to the building of the Davidic dynasty. In the NT, foreign women who contribute to dynasty-building are listed in the genealogy of Jesus Christ, the greatest son of David: Tamar, Rahab, "the wife of Uriah [the Hittite]" (Bathsheba), and Ruth (Matt. 1:1–17).

Each of these women has a questionable background or behavior: Tamar dressed up as a prostitute, Rahab was a prostitute, Bathsheba was not a foreigner but was married to one and was involved in an adulterous relationship, and Ruth snuck onto the threshing floor at night (if prostitutes frequented threshing floors [cf. Hosea 9:1], she could have been mistaken as one also). Canonically, these women pave the way for Mary's scandalous conception of Jesus (Matt. 1:18–19). Moreover, their incorporation is in fulfillment of God's promise of blessing to "all peoples" through Abraham (Gen. 12:3). And the acceptance of these foreigners into Israel in the OT anticipates the acceptance of gentiles into the church in the NT (e.g., Acts 10:34–48; Rom. 1:16). The kingdom of David's son will accept all who seek refuge under the Lord Jesus; all peoples from everywhere are one in him (Gal. 3:28).

We can trace other themes and motifs from the Ruth narrative through to the NT. Kindness is a central theme in Ruth, but it is too general to trace explicit connections to the NT. The other central theme is redemption. The book of Ruth reveals four aspects of redemption that can be traced through to the NT (Lau and Goswell, 117–39).

First, the redeemed are in desperate straits. Naomi and Ruth were in material poverty, but Elimelech's family line was also under threat of extinction.

Second, it was costly for the redeemer, an issue raised by the nearer kinsman-redeemer. He was willing to pay the initial cost of redeeming the property (Ruth 4:4), but not the ongoing cost of feeding Naomi and Ruth, and any children through Ruth, especially since the redeemed property would be transferred to a son produced with Ruth. His refusal highlights the cost Boaz was willing to bear.

Third, the redeemer's actions are characterized by generosity and self-sacrifice; in other words, traits closely aligned with kindness. In the OT, God is the great Redeemer, with kindness being one of his core characteristics (see esp. Exod. 34:6–7). He redeemed his people from not only physical bondage (esp. the exodus from Egypt) but also spiritual bondage (e.g., Ps. 130:7–8; Isa. 52:13–53:12). In the NT, such spiritual bondage is fatal for all humanity. All people are slaves to sin, which leads to death (e.g., Rom. 5:12; 6:16–20, 23). Because of shameful sin, all people lack God's glory (Rom. 3:23). Like the widows in Ruth, we cannot save ourselves (cf. Eph. 2:5; Col. 2:13). Thankfully, in kindness God has paid the redemption price—the precious blood of Christ (e.g., Rom. 3:24–25; Eph. 1:7; 1 Pet. 1:18–19). Those who trust in Christ will no longer face shame (Rom. 10:11; 1 Pet. 2:6–7). In this sense, the kind actions of Boaz foreshadow the greatest kindness of God in providing Jesus Christ. Boaz can be considered a type of Christ. His redemption was temporary; Christ's redemption is eternal.

Fourth, there is a kinship connection between the redeemer and the redeemed. Boaz and "Mr. So-and-So" (*pəlōnî ʾalmōnî* [Ruth 4:1]) have an obligation to redeem because they are relatives of Elimelech. God redeemed Israel to be his covenant people, related to him as his own family by the covenant (Exod. 6:6–7; 15:13). They were God's "firstborn son" (4:22–23). Isaiah describes God as Israel's "Father" and "Redeemer" (63:16), "Maker," "husband," and "Redeemer" (54:5). Just as marriage followed Ruth's redemption, so the Sinai covenant followed Israel's redemption (McKeown, 125). The NT explains that Jesus had to be incarnated as a human to redeem humanity (e.g., John 1:14; Rom. 8:3; Phil. 2:7), and so could redeem us as our kinsman (cf. Heb. 2:10–17). We who are now "in Christ" are adopted in God's family as Jesus's brothers and sisters (e.g., Rom. 8:29; Gal. 4:3–7; Heb. 2:11–13). What a great honor it is to be a member of God's family (Rom. 8:15–18)! Jesus is thus the kinsman-redeemer par excellence, bringing all peoples into God's household (cf. Gal. 6:10).

Bibliography. Eskenazi, T. C., and T. Frymer-Kensky, *Ruth*, JPSBC (Jewish Publication Society, 2011); Fisch, H., "Ruth and the Structure of Covenant History," *VT* 32 (1982): 425–37; Fishbane, M., *Biblical Interpretation in Ancient Israel* (Clarendon, 1985); Lau, P. H. W., and G. Goswell, *Unceasing Kindness*, NSBT (InterVarsity, 2016); McKeown, J., *Ruth*, THOTC (Eerdmans, 2015); Wenham, G. J., *Story as Torah* (T&T Clark, 2000); Zakovitch, Y., *Das Buch Rut*, trans. A. Lehnardt, SBS 177 (Katholisches Bibelwerk, 1999).

Peter H. W. Lau

S

Sabbath and Sunday

The Sabbath bookends the story of history and belongs to the crossroads of sacred space and time. Israel's Sabbath in the observance of days and years led to a world that is "wholly Sabbath rest for eternity" (m. Tamid 7:4; Neusner, 873). That final day was inaugurated by Christ and remains as a hope for the consummation. The Lord's Day originated apart from Sabbath law and practice. After the NT era, Sunday came to be a Christian Sabbath.

Sabbath in the OT

The Sabbath within Gen. 2:1–3 (cf. Exod. 20:8–11; 31:17) is God's; no command is expressed. The completion of creation is marked; God ceases from work, and he blesses the day and makes it holy. God's *rest* and *refreshment* are explicit in the Exodus texts (20:11; 31:17). Comparisons of Gen. 1–2 to ancient Near Eastern cosmogonic/theomachic myths (Baal Epic, Enuma Elish, Atrahasis Epic, some Egyptian sources), which involve conflict and erection of a temple where the victorious god *rests*, suggest both parallels and discontinuities with Israel's creation Sabbath and her tabernacle/temple. Israel's God is the sole author of all creation, there are no contending gods, humans do not free God from toil, God does not flee creation's turmoil, nor does God remove himself from the rule of creation. Yet, viewed with this lens, Israel's subsequent tabernacle/temple as God's resting place echoes and highlights language of Gen. 1–2 that hints at the garden as sacred space and divine rest (Sabbath); there is also a note of anticipation. That the creation Sabbath is God's own and that it falls within an unrepeatable week of permanent effects could seem to distance it from human affairs, but that God blesses that day, a day within the created world, and makes that day holy, further suggests a goal toward which creation moves (Timmer, 37, 45, 56, 66–74, 86; Laansma, *Rest*, 61–76). That movement is disrupted by the act of disobedience that follows in Gen. 2:4–3:24; rather than work leading to rest, there is a curse.

Israel's Sabbath enters with Exod. 16 as a test of Israel's obedience to the divine word, foreshadowing the Sabbath year and Jubilee (Lev. 25:21; cf. Deut. 8:3). Exodus 20:8–11 grounds and parallels Israel's Sabbath with Gen. 2:2–3, suggesting that it partakes, through Israel's obedience to keep it holy, of the holiness of the seventh day of creation. The humanitarian interest indicated elsewhere (Exod. 23:12) is left implicit; the Sabbath intended for all creation is indicated as a weekly sign. Deuteronomy 5:12–15 amplifies this aspect and grounds it in God's deliverance from slavery, while retaining the echo of Gen. 1:1–2:3 in the six-seventh pattern. Each week, Israel itself is enlisted in ensuring that the freedom and rest of this salvation are denied none; all are on equal footing. Reading Exod. 20 and Deut. 5 stereoscopically parallels the plight of the curse and the plight of slavery; God's Sabbath equals consecrating salvation. The parallel also evinces the exodus as a new act of creation.

By dint of Gen. 2, Exod. 20, and Deut. 5, the Sabbath looms large in the OT. Its importance is likewise underscored by Michael Burer's comment about Lev. 23: "The Sabbath is the basis, both calendrically and theologically, for the whole system of Israelite feasts and festivals" (Burer 38).

A relationship between the tabernacle/temple and the Sabbath was approached in Laansma's study (*I Will Give You Rest*), concentrated on the shared theme of rest: God's promise of a resting place for his people, where he would have his own resting place in the temple, echoed the same cosmogonic and theomachic myths noted for the Sabbath above. The relationship between the themes in the canonical texts themselves is not verbally direct, but exegetical studies such as Daniel Timmer's and Jared Calaway's draw the fact and nature of those relations into focus.

For Timmer, Exod. 25–40 is about how God dwells within Israel; it is interrupted by the calf disaster and the covenant's restoration, framed by two Sabbath texts (31:12–35:3). These texts (31:12–17 and 35:1–3) are reminders of Yahweh's commitment to maintain the covenant and to sanctify Israel. The allusion to Gen. 2:2–3 in Exod. 31:12–17 expresses "the eschatological or anticipatory nature of Yahweh's commitment to sanctify Israel, a trajectory which intersects the consummation of the Sinai covenant itself" (Timmer, 176). "It is significant that the sabbath . . . frames Israel's horrible failure . . . , for in doing so the literary structure of Exodus subordinates the ravages of sin to Yahweh's redemptive purpose and gracious forgiveness" (Timmer, 102). The tabernacle is "an intermediate point on the spectrum of God's presence with humanity. . . . Its association with the sabbath accentuates the expectation that God will act eschatologically to resolve his people's insurmountable lack of full sanctification and bring those whom he forgives and sanctifies into the full enjoyment of his rest" (Timmer, 145). In the later prophets, Timmer (179) finds a "consistent interest in the themes of rest, divine presence, and the eschatological enjoyment of the cosmos's intended fruitfulness as manifestations of a restored and consummated covenant relationship with God," in terms that are consistent with the Sabbath frame of Exod. 31:12–35:3 (see Laansma, *Rest*, 65–67).

Calaway arrives at insights potentially complementary to Timmer's: Certain OT writers (designated "Priestly" by Calaway) developed how the sacred is accessed so that the Sabbath and sanctuary overlap as expressions of God's holiness. "Because of this interrelationship, God's holiness could be experienced spatially through the sanctuary and temporally through the Sabbath," ultimately by anyone keeping covenant on the seventh day (Calaway, 21). Isaiah 56 worked out the implications, making "the Sabbath literally the temporal entry to the physical temple in post-exilic Yehud" (Calaway, 179). The land's Sabbath and the Day of Atonement—both Sabbaths (cf. Lev. 16:31; 23:32)—acted as correlates that explained the exile and how to dwell in the land. "Both the sanctuary and the land could be defiled and had a Sabbath to restore it. . . . As the Day of Atonement restores the sanctuary and as the land's Sabbath restores the land, so Sabbath observance restores the people. When all elements of the system are operative, God can dwell in the temple, in the land, and among the people" (Calaway, 179).

The land was to enjoy a Sabbath every seventh year; it was not to be worked, and only what it produced of itself was to be eaten (Lev. 25:1–7; Exod. 23:10–11). As with the weekly Sabbath, this free provision was for all equally, including slaves, sojourners, and domesticated and wild animals. God's concern for overlooked people challenges Israel to adopt the same concern. According to Deut. 15:1–11, debts were forgiven. The Jubilee (Lev. 25:8–55; 27:16–25; Num. 36:4; Ezek. 46:17) every fiftieth year added the return of each Israelite to their land and clan—for the land belonged not to them to possess but to God—and the freeing of Hebrew slaves: "because the Israelites are my servants, whom I brought out of Egypt" (Lev. 25:42). Letting the land lie fallow was for the sake of the poor with creation as its background. The year was to be devoted to the study of Torah (Deut. 31:10–11), upon which Israel's security hung.

Observance of these years would lead to prosperity nationally and internationally; the blessings of Lev. 26:2–13 are expansions of Jubilee promises (cf. Lev. 25:6–7, 12, 18–22; Deut. 15:4–6). Disobedience would bring a curse in the form of redemptive punishment, scattering Israel among the nations, so that "the land will enjoy its sabbath years all the time that it lies desolate and you are in the country of your enemies; then the land will rest and enjoy its sabbaths. All the time that it lies desolate, the land will have the rest it did not have during the sabbaths you lived in it" (Lev. 26:34–35; cf. v. 43; Jer. 25:12; Dan. 9:2; 2 Chron. 36:21; Ezra 1:1). Accordingly, the Jubilee lent itself to eschatological expectations, particularly in Isa. 61:1–2 (cf. 58:6), a passage taken up by Jesus in Luke 4:16–30 (see below and esp. Sloan, 12–18).

Sabbath was of ultimate significance for Israel, enlisting her in recalling and realizing the conditions brought about by God in creation and salvation. She would deny herself, be still and know that Yahweh is God, give her full attention to his ways and will, and enact the truth of Deut. 8:3. Thus, the Israelites received the sign that Yahweh sanctifies them.

Sabbath in Judaism

For Israel's enemies, the Sabbath was to be exploited militarily. In addition to the Seleucid campaigns, Gerhard Hasel (853) notes earlier evidence of the same for the Assyrians and Neo-Babylonians. The disasters of exile and Hellenization brought a sharpened sense of national self-definition for the Jews, including an emphasis on Sabbath (Scott, 126). The Sabbath's observance was chiefly a matter of abstention from work, synagogue attendance, and common meals. So great was the Sabbath that much of the rest of the week was structured around it (cf. Safrai, 806). Calendrical disputes developed out of reverence for the day and related festivals, as did stipulations as to what constituted observance or violation of the Sabbath within the new historical contexts of Jewish life (e.g., CD 10.14–12.5; Jub. 2:25–33; 50:6–13; Philo, *Moses* 2.4; m. Shabbat; m. Betzah 5:2; m. Eruv.; allowing that it is always necessary to distill pre–AD 70 traditions from later writings). The day was observed devoutly by many, and certain cases allowed for exceptions to the work prohibitions, either for humanitarian reasons or because of a commandment related to something too sacred to violate (e.g., Jub. 50:10–11; m. Shabb. 16:1–7; 18:3; m. Pesah. 6:1–2; m. Yoma 8:6–7). Adherence was sufficiently well-known to cause the Romans to exempt Jews from military service because it would be impossible to allow for the Sabbath (Schürer, 474–75).

The Jubilee Year was obligatory only when the land was duly occupied and divided, but it was expected that the Sabbatical Year would be observed (Josephus, *Ant.* 11.338; 14.201, 320–28). Following Bar Kokhba, the observance of the Sabbatical Year became sporadic (Safrai, 826).

Two conceptual developments of Sabbath are noteworthy: With John 5:17 in mind, Burer delineates several respects in which some such idea of divine Sabbath work had precedent in Judaism. Some texts state outright that God's Sabbath does not preclude certain kinds of work (Burer, 27–102; e.g., Gen. Rab. 11:10; Mek. Shabb. 1:120–25). Several passages imply the same (e.g., Exod. 20:8–11 and Deut. 5:12–15). In differing ways, the Sabbath is a sign of the eschatological renewal, being featured as part of the calendar of the eschaton and as a shorthand for the age to come ("the day that is wholly Sabbath rest for eternity," m. Tamid 7:4; cf. Mek. Shabb. 1:38–41; see further on this Laansma, *Rest*, 122–29), and in several texts either God's agent or a righteous person does things on the Sabbath that would normally be disallowed and yet without censure.

With an eye on Hebrews, Calaway (88) explores how OT priestly thought and then subsequent Second Temple literature "integrated rest, Sabbath, land, and sanctuary to form a nexus of holiness and defilement that determined how the divine presence dwelled among people." In opposition to several scholars, he avers that Philo of Alexandria—in spite of his intrinsically important cosmic, social, and philosophical speculations related to the Sabbath—has little to offer as illuminating background for Hebrews (for further on Philo, see Laansma, *Rest*, 113–22). Jubilees extensively develops the OT's Sabbath, Sabbath Year, and Jubilee Year, organizing itself by them (esp. 2:17–33). For this work, the Sabbath is "a heavenly institution given to earth, and humans do it at the command of God and in imitation of the angels and, thereby, become angelic in holiness and blessedness" (Calaway, 91). The Songs of the Sabbath Sacrifice (second c. BC to first c. AD) found at Qumran and Masada go further than Jubilees in directly aligning the Sabbath observances of humans and angels, conjoined with the heavenly tabernacle. Its thirteen songs move from the creation Sabbath to the heavenly sacrifice in the tabernacle. Ultimately, one experiences the heavenly tabernacle through the Sabbath: "The Sabbath is the temporal entrance into heavenly reality" (Calaway, 94). Though differences with Hebrews are noted, among the parallels is the appearance that "the *Songs of the Sabbath Sacrifice* and Hebrews are the only works after the Pentateuch to bring the Sabbath and tabernacle back together, and both do so in a heavenly setting" (Calaway, 97).

Sabbath in the NT

In Matt. 11:28–30 an explicit offer of rest by the Son of David, the new Moses, the something-greater-than-temple, the "Lord of the Sabbath," follows up on an announcement couched in Sabbath/Jubilee imagery (Matt. 11:5; cf. Isa. 61:1–2, noted above) of good news preached to the poor, and abuts directly on Matthew's two Sabbath pericopes (Matt. 12:1–14), in which Jesus argues that his healing messianic work is appropriate to *that* day. Matthew's interests are not with law disputes or Christian Sabbath observance but with Christology and salvation. The true Sabbath rest was dawning (see Laansma, *Rest*, 229–31).

Mark absorbs the Sabbath into the larger question of Jesus and his authority. The Sabbath as salvation is not highlighted, but its humanitarian intention is (Mark 2:23–3:6; cf. 1:21–31; 6:1–6). For Mark, the "Sabbath offers the supreme test of Jesus' lordship over religious practice—and he passes," and by making himself Lord of the Sabbath he assumes Yahweh's role of Lev. 23:3 (Gundry, 143, 148). Sabbath is the day for bringing about (i.e., doing the *work* of) God's salvation.

In Luke 4:16–30, Jesus enters the synagogue of Nazareth and applies to himself Isaiah's announcement of the eschatological Jubilee (Isa. 61:1–2), thereby casting himself as God's kingly/prophetic agent (see Sloan). Since Luke features this event as programmatic for Jesus's ministry, and given the overshadowing importance of Sabbath in the Scriptures and life of the Jews, there is justification for hearing Jubilee themes in the surrounding narrative. Arguably, much of Luke 6:20–38 draws from the ideals of the Sabbath Year and Jubilee, especially as in Isa. 58 and 61, if not also Lev. 25 and Deut. 15; a similar argument could be made for the Lord's Prayer in Luke 11:2–4 (Sloan, 121–46). Joel Green detects a Jubilee allusion in Luke 1:68–71 (116–17). In these and other ways, Luke's message of Jesus's salvation is an announcement of the all-encompassing advent of God's Sabbath.

Specifically, in his examination of Luke 13:10–17, Burer (112–20) observes both that Jesus, who emphatically initiates this healing, shifts the focus from law to the character and nature of the Sabbath, and that Jesus is acting from the primary aim of his mission. Jesus's entrance into the synagogue and the concept of a "release" both bring to mind Luke 4:16–30. The woman is identified in terms of her relationship to God as a member of the covenant community, and her release from bonds is cast apocalyptically. Jesus's argument is that the Sabbath is the right day for this woman to know "release" from the bonds of Satan, just as God had earlier freed Israel from slavery (Deut. 5:15). By virtue of the echoes of Luke 4:16–30, this healing functions as a foretaste of the age to come. Similar commentary is possible for Luke 14:1–24, in which a Sabbath meal is made an occasion for living with a view to the resurrection of the righteous and so remembering the poor, and also as a time for anticipating the great feast in the kingdom of God.

John 5 is distinctive in explicitly drawing on the concept of God's Sabbath work (see Burer, 120–35, pointing especially to Philo, *QE* 2.68; Laansma, *Rest*, 323–24). Specifically, God is performing the Sabbath work of his creative and ruling powers through Jesus, who, by dint of his unique Sonship, is in fact acting in the role of God himself.

Paul's comments about Sabbath, which require contextualizing in a larger framework of law and gospel, will be referenced in the next section, except to mention the pregnant phrasing of Col. 2:16–17. Though I disagree with G. K. Beale's sabbatarian conclusions in regards to Lord's Day observance (see below), his discussion of this Colossians passage (*Colossians*, 214–24) is noteworthy: "The idea [of 2:17] is that the things mentioned in Col. 2:16 are typological foreshadowings of Christ, and these foreshadowings have found the substance to which they point in Christ. . . . As a consequence, the observance of these holy days is not obligatory in the new-covenant age." Sabbath is henceforth not calendar, but Christ.

Conceivably in awareness of the Christian traditions just noted, perhaps as attested in Matt. 11:28–12:14 in particular or in Luke, Heb. 3–4 draws together the two major OT streams related to God's promise of rest—on the one hand, the promise of a resting place and rest for his people, where God would appoint his own resting place in the temple (Ps. 95:11), and, on the other hand, the Sabbath of Gen. 2:2–3—as a way of expressing the goal of all salvation history that is attainable only for a life run to the end by faith (for this, see esp. Laansma, *Rest*, surveying evidence from the ancient Near East through the second c. AD). The linkage of Ps. 95 and Gen. 2 goes beyond merely a Greek hook word to deep-running currents of relations between Sabbath and tabernacle already at work in the OT. The work of Calaway on both the OT and Second Temple literature, noted above, attests the survival of distinct forms of those OT currents into the first century at Qumran. For Hebrews, the ideas of the resting place (*katapausis*) and Sabbath celebration (*sabbatismos*) are not made synonymous and interchangeable but rather joined dramatically (*pace* Calaway and others), so that entrance into God's resting place, closely related conceptually to entrance into the most holy place, is to enter into the goal of salvation as the locale of a great celebration of God's creation Sabbath. For pastoral-rhetorical purposes, this entrance is conceptualized as the yet-future and final arrival of the traveling people of God, though Hebrews' already/not-yet eschatology would be consistent with a form of present participation. Following this apocalyptic vision of salvation designed to motivate perseverance in faith (Heb. 3:7–4:11), Hebrews both slows down the story and backs up to the key moment of the priestly work and sacrifice that makes entrance into God's holy presence possible (4:14–10:25). Neither the resting place nor the Sabbath reappear verbally after Heb. 4:11, but both are evoked through God's subjugation of his enemies (10:13; cf. Deut. 12:10; 2 Sam. 7:1–2; 1 Kings 5:3–4), the land and city hoped for (Heb. 11:10, 14–16; 13:14), the vision of Mount Zion (Heb. 12:22–24), and, not least, the Day of Atonement, itself a Sabbath (Lev. 16:31; 23:32). The pivotal pronouncement of Heb. 10:18 summarizes the whole development of 5:1–10:18 as "release, forgiveness" (*aphesis*; also 9:22; cf. 8:12; 10:17). This is striking both because the more characteristic language for salvation has been that of cultic cleansing and perfection, and because *aphesis* is not used straightforwardly for "forgiveness of sins" in the LXX, on which Hebrews has so strongly relied. It is used for the release of the goat on the Day of Atonement (Lev. 16:26), but its most characteristic use is for the Jubilee and Sabbath Year (e.g., Lev. 25; 27; Deut. 15). Yet, forgiveness and release are already intermingled in Jewish tradition (Sloan, 166–94).

Thus, the crossroads of sacred time and space, Sabbath and temple, merge and find their goal as the ultimate hope of the people of God. It is possible, given the range and depth of the above, that Sabbath theology underlies other NT texts as well (e.g., 1 Cor. 7:22–23; cf. Lev. 25:42, 55).

Lord's Day

The rise within Christianity of what would be called the Lord's Day, Sunday, is properly treated as a separate history that only later was conflated with Moses's Sabbath (for this, with further bibliography, see Laansma, "Lord's Day" and "Sunday Letter"). In fact, when we turn to the NT for the roots of weekly Sunday meetings, we find only a small group of passages that can at best be interpreted, and not without justified disagreements, as hints, not positive evidence, of an early custom—with a variety of qualifications quickly following. The key passages from a historical perspective are 1 Cor. 16:2; Luke 24:1; Acts 20:7; John 20:1, 19; Rev. 1:10 (for early post-NT texts, note Did. 14:1; Ign. *Magn.* 9:1; Barn. 15:9; Justin, *1 Apol.* 67; Gos. Pet. 35, 50; Pliny, *Ep.* 10.96). A theological angle is afforded by Gal. 4:8–11; Rom. 14:5–6; Col. 2:16. Other relevant passages include John 5:17; 7:23; Matt. 11:28–12:14; Heb. 3:7–4:11. In general, the NT hints that Lord's Day observance arose as an early, nonmandatory custom in at least some Christian churches, apparently in correlation with the day of Christ's resurrection. It was not thought of as a Sabbath or in terms of Sabbath law (including a one-in-seven principle); (Saturday) Sabbath observance according to Jewish customs may have continued among some churches alongside Sunday Christian gatherings, while being discontinued or never initiated among others. Christians probably met on other days for gatherings as also on Sunday, in whatever way Sunday was demarcated. How the day was marked out and observed (possibly morning and/or evening from an early date, probably incorporating the Eucharist if in the evening) will have varied. Naturally, Sunday would have been a day of regular work. Nothing in the NT evidence verbally supports the formalized picture of Sunday that is projected by later sabbatarian traditions.

In his surveys of the postapostolic period through the Protestant tradition, Richard Bauckham finds no evidence that Sunday was regarded as a day of rest in the second century, though the regard for Sunday as a festival might have led to the desire that it be a work-free day (for the following, see Bauckham, "Sabbath and Sunday in the Post-Apostolic Church"; "Sabbath and Sunday in the Medieval Church in the West"; "Sabbath and Sunday in the Protestant Tradition"). Sabbath and Sunday were in that century infrequently compared, though there were hints toward a correlation of them. The OT Sabbath command was interpreted metaphorically or eschatologically rather than transferred to Sunday. The legislation of Constantine (AD 321) is the earliest clear reference to Sunday as a work-free day, in the interest of Sunday observance and without a theological, let alone specifically sabbatarian, rationale. The first known transference of Sabbath to Sunday is Eusebius of Caesarea's commentary on Ps. 91 (dated to after AD 330). True sabbatarianism was, however, "a medieval, not a patristic, development" (Bauckham, "Post-Apostolic," 287) and was not a theological development in the first place; it "grew from below, from popular sentiment, and was imposed from above, by legislation. It was a long time before the theologians provided much more than a means of accommodating it" (Bauckham, "Medieval," 302). The greatest impetus may have been the Christianization of Germanic tribes who saw a similarity between their own taboo days and the Sabbath. Bauckham summarizes: "Medieval Sabbatarianism grew in the context of theocratic kingship and of church discipline of an increasingly juridical character. Its legalistic quality derives less from its OT model than from its origin in an attempt to legislate for a Christian society. The laws for Sunday rest had a minimum of genuinely ethical content and existed for several centuries as rules in search of a theological context and justified by a divine authority curiously difficult to locate" ("Medieval," 303). The sabbatarian doctrine was accepted unanimously among the Scholastics, reversed somewhat by the Reformers, and then renewed among Puritans and in English, Scottish, and American Protestantism.

Though the Lord's Day cannot technically be construed as a Christian Sabbath day or tied directly to Exod. 20 or Deut. 5, and while it is not grounded in an alleged creation mandate for a weekly human practice, the gospel's freedom permits a linkage in practice that is in keeping with faith, love, and hope. This would involve not so much a set of practices distinct from the rest of Christian life as an intensification and concentration, instructed by the Sabbath's meaning for Israel and for the church, for the sake of reminder, discipline, proclamation, and righteousness.

Biblical-Theological and Hermeneutical Implications

Sabbatarianism—that is, the belief that Christians inherit the Sabbath mandate to observe a *weekly* day of rest, whether operating with a one-in-seven principle or otherwise—is by now a respected option within Christian faith. It has many defenders, and the work of G. K. Beale (*Theology*, 775–801) both summarizes and expands its exegetical and theological basis in Gen. 2, Exod. 20, and elsewhere. The present treatment shares with Beale and others the conviction that the Sabbath, rooted in Gen. 2, was ultimately meant for all. The balance of NT and later evidence, however, favors the view that apostolic churches were *by design* not mandatorily sabbatarian, though they did view their practice as entering and fulfilling the Sabbath along with the rest of the law. Ultimately, then, the nonsabbatarian view of the present author can accept much of the exegetical detail advanced in an argument such as Beale's without reaching the specifically sabbatarian conclusion; where the OT evidence is pressed for the sabbatarian conclusions, those readings are not more probable than the contrary view. As the temple was finally understood in a radically new and universalizing fashion (though actually this was a return to the original), so also Sabbath.

In sum, at the heart of Israel's law, life, and hope stands the Sabbath as the observance of the seventh day (Saturday) of every week, as well as Israel's festivals, the Day of Atonement, the Sabbath Years, and the Jubilee. To declare Moses's law abrogated or sustained runs afoul of both sides of Jesus's assertion in Matt. 5:17. He neither canceled and discarded, nor renewed the Mosaic covenant, but founded a new covenant in which Moses's law was brought to fulfillment. As the law (1 Cor. 9:21) and commandment of Christ (allowing for differences of idiom and intention: Matt. 28:20; John 13:34; 1 John 3:23–24), the law of Moses—in its parts and as a whole—is upheld and satisfied (Matt. 22:40; Gal. 5:14; cf. Col. 2:16–17; Hebrews). The expression of the righteousness of God in Moses, as provision and command, is as necessary as ever "until heaven and earth disappear" (Matt. 5:18). Henceforth, the Sabbath commandment finds that fulfillment not in the observance of a calendrical day but in the acceptance of and obedience to the whole of the gospel of freedom in the totality of one's life, all as a foretaste of the future unending day that is wholly Sabbath rest in which his people are wholly sanctified. Rightly grasped, this is a higher standard and greater righteousness. Obedience to this command is of greater consequence now than ever. It is this to which the Sabbath always pointed, and what it realized in type "until the time of the new order" (Heb. 9:10). From this we can see what is true of all of the Mosaic commandments.

See also Covenant; Feasts and Festivals; Jews and Gentiles; Law

Bibliography. Bauckham, R., "Sabbath and Sunday in the Medieval Church in the West," in *From Sabbath to Lord's Day*, ed. D. A. Carson (Zondervan, 1982), 299–309; Bauckham, "Sabbath and Sunday in the Post-Apostolic Church," in *From Sabbath to Lord's Day*, ed. D. A. Carson (Zondervan, 1982), 251–98; Bauckham, "Sabbath and Sunday in the Protestant Tradition," in *From Sabbath to Lord's Day*, ed. D. A. Carson (Zondervan, 1982), 311–41; Beale, G. K., *Colossians and Philemon*, BECNT (Baker Academic, 2019); Beale, *A New Testament Biblical Theology* (Baker Academic, 2011); Burer, M. H., *Divine Sabbath Work*, BBRSup 5 (Eisenbrauns, 2012); Calaway, J., *The Sabbath and the Sanctuary*, WUNT 2/349 (Mohr Siebeck, 2013); Green, J., *The Gospel of Luke*, NICNT (Eerdmans, 1997); Gundry, R. H., *Mark* (Eerdmans, 1993); Hasel, G., "Sabbath," in *ABD*, 5:849–56; Laansma, J. C., *I Will Give You Rest*, WUNT 2/98 (Mohr Siebeck, 1997); Laansma, "Lord's Day," in *DLNTD*, 679–86; Laansma, "Sunday Letter," in *Early New Testament Apocrypha and Pseudepigrapha*, ed. J. C. Edwards, ALNTS 9 (Zondervan, forthcoming); Neusner, J., *The Mishnah* (Yale University Press, 1988); Safrai, S., "Religion in Everyday Life," in *The Jewish People in the First Century*, vol. 1.2, ed. S. Safrai et al., CRINT (Fortress, 1976), 793–833; Schürer, E., *The History of the Jewish People in the Age of Jesus Christ*, vol. 2, rev. and ed. G. Vermes, F. Millar, and M. Black (T&T Clark, 1979); Scott, J. J., *Customs and Controversies* (Baker, 1995); Sloan, R. B., Jr., *The Favorable Year of the Lord* (Schola Press, 1977); Timmer, D., *Creation, Tabernacle, and Sabbath*, FRLANT 227 (Vandenhoeck & Ruprecht, 2009).

Jon C. Laansma

Sacrifices and Offerings

The NT employment of OT sacrificial concepts and practices binds the two Testaments together in ways that are important for understanding Jesus Christ, what he has done for us, and what this means for living the Christian life well. The writers of the NT assumed that the reader would know about the OT practices and procedures, since they and the earliest church were largely Jewish, and their first Bible was the OT (in Hebrew and/or Greek), whether they were Jews or gentiles. It is not possible to deal with all the specific details and rationale of these various offerings and sacrifices. We are limited here to points that are particularly relevant for the NT use of elements of the OT system (for more on the OT system itself, see Averbeck, "Sacrifices and Offerings," and the literature cited there; see also Averbeck, "Leviticus," 178, and "Offerings and Sacrifices," 1020–21, for relatively detailed charts of the five main kinds of offerings and sacrifices in Lev. 1–7).

There are three main categories of references to OT sacrifices and offerings in the NT. First, some NT passages simply recount the continuing performance of OT ritual sacrifices and offerings as part of Jewish practice (as well as references to pagan practices of this sort). We are not able to deal with this category of references here. Second, other passages apply various OT sacrifices and offerings, or elements of them, to the sacrifice of Christ in the NT, sometimes comparing them and at other times contrasting the sacrifice of Christ with the sacrifices in the OT. Third, the NT also applies the OT sacrifices and offerings to the life of the church and the believer. Due to lack of space, the second category receives the most attention in this entry. The third category is treated very briefly in the conclusion.

NT Application of OT Sacrifices and Offerings to Jesus Christ

The sacrifices and offerings of the OT were active in the Jewish world of NT times, and the NT authors applied that background to understanding the purpose and work of Christ. Christ's sacrificial death typologically takes the OT sacrifices to a new level. It focuses attention on certain features of the offerings that apply his work on the cross to us (Paul, 508). For example, as our Passover sacrifice, Jesus did not become a literal lamb, nor was his blood applied to the doorposts of houses (Exod. 12:1–28). Yet, he was still crucified at the time of Passover, and, by applying his blood to the lives of those who put their trust in him, God grants them his gift of eternal life by his grace (see more on this below). The fact that it is typological does not make it any less true or important. On the contrary, it highlights the features of the OT sacrificial system that help us to understand the wonders of what Jesus has done for us. In terms of typology, the OT sacrifices and offerings are the types and the sacrifice of Jesus is the antitype. The former anticipates, foreshadows, or prefigures the latter, which takes it further on a new level (Treier, 823–24). This has the effect of unifying the biblical theology of sacrifices and offerings from the OT into and through the NT. The specific connections from NT references to Jesus as our sacrifice back to the OT sacrifices and offerings, however, are not always clear from the text. We are not always sure which OT offering or sacrifice the NT passage is referring to, or if perhaps the NT is referring back to the system or some part(s) of it in a more general way.

Jesus as our Passover sacrifice. The Passover sacrifice is not among the five major kinds of offerings in Lev. 1–7 but is instituted in Exod. 11–12 as part of the exodus from Egypt. It was a kind of peace offering sacrifice (*zebaḥ*), since the people ate the meat of the lamb (see, e.g., Deut. 16:2, 5–6). According to the Synoptic Gospels, Jesus and his apostles celebrated the Passover together in the upper room the evening before the day of his trial and crucifixion (Matt. 26:17–30; Mark 14:12–26; Luke 22:7–23). On this occasion, Jesus instituted what we know as the "Last/Lord's Supper," "Communion," or the "Eucharist" as an extension to the Passover meal itself. There is a major scholarly debate over how this relates to John's chronology in John 13–19, where he apparently has Jesus being crucified at the time of the slaughter of the Passover lambs (see, e.g., John 18:28; 19:14, and the helpful summary and discussion in Carson, *John*, 455–58, 589, 603–5, and Köstenberger, 500).

John 19:31–37 tells us that when the soldiers came to break the legs of the three men on the crosses, they found Jesus already dead so they did not break his legs: "Not one of his bones" was "broken" (v. 36). Some consider this a powerful link to Jesus as the Passover sacrifice, since the regulations for eating the Passover lamb included, "Do not break any of the bones" (Exod. 12:46; cf. Num. 9:12; see Köstenberger, 503–4). Others connect this to Ps. 34:20, which refers to God's protection of the righteous, "He protects all his bones, not one of them will be broken."

Some scholars believe that 1 Pet. 1:19 refers specifically to Jesus as our Passover lamb. We have been redeemed from our empty life not with silver or gold "but with the precious blood of Christ, a lamb without blemish or defect" (see, e.g., Marshall, 55–56; cf. Exod. 12:5). Others take this to be an indefinite reference to unblemished sacrificial lambs in the sacrificial system more broadly, and to the suffering servant in Isa. 53 (esp. v. 7), in addition to the Passover lamb (see, e.g., Carson, "1 Peter," 1019; Osborne, 163).

Jesus as our Passover lamb is most clear in the exhortation to purity in 1 Cor. 5:7: "Get rid of the old yeast, so that you may be a new unleavened batch—as you really are. For Christ, our Passover lamb, has been sacrificed." Paul uses this to rebuke the Corinthians for not removing an evil man from their church fellowship, since the celebration of the Passover required removing all yeast from the house (Exod. 12:15, 19–20; cf. also the reference to no leaven in the grain offering in Lev. 2:11). The rabbinic tradition develops this requirement in significant detail (m. Pesah. 1–3).

Jesus as our burnt and peace offering. As noted above, in the Synoptic Gospels the Passover celebration in the upper room was the context in which Jesus instituted what we refer to as the "Lord's Supper" as a new ritual for those who would follow him after his death, burial, and resurrection (Matt. 26:26–29; Mark 14:22–25; Luke 22:17–20). The bread is a symbol of his body, and the wine his blood. As Mark puts it, Jesus says, "This is my blood of the covenant, which is poured out for many" (14:24), alluding to the ratification of the Mosaic covenant in Exod. 24:3–8, where Moses splashed the blood of the burnt and peace offerings on the people and pronounced in a very similar way, "This is the blood of the covenant that the LORD has made with you" (v. 8; see the helpful explanation in Watts, 229–32). Matthew adds that the blood was "poured out for many for the forgiveness of sins" (Matt. 26:28). Luke makes it more specific to the new covenant in Jer. 31:31–34: "This cup is the new covenant in my blood, which is poured out for you" (Luke 22:20; cf. 1 Cor. 11:25). In Jeremiah the Lord said that this covenant "will not be like the covenant I made with their ancestors when I took them by the hand to lead them out of Egypt" (i.e., the Mosaic covenant), which they had broken (31:32). It would be a "new covenant" (31:31). The passage goes on to explain how it was "new." Zechariah seems to make an abbreviated reference back to Exod. 24:8 in Zech. 9:11: "As for you, because of the blood of my covenant with you, I will free your prisoners from the waterless pit."

As noted, the blood of the ratification ritual for the old covenant in Exod. 24 came from the combined burnt and peace offerings presented there (vv. 5–6). The burnt offerings (Lev. 1:3–17; MT *ʿōlâ*, LXX *holokautōma*) were completely consumed on the altar. They constituted a gift that made atonement (1:4) as an "aroma pleasing to the LORD" (1:9, 13, 17). The peace offerings (*šəlāmîm*) were not only "offerings" but also "sacrifices" (*zebaḥ*; see, e.g., 3:1), since the worshipers ate the meat in fellowship with the Lord and one another (7:11–34). Like the whole carcass of the burnt offering, however, the fat of the peace offering served as "an aroma pleasing to the LORD" (3:5; cf. v. 16).

Normally, according to the tabernacle regulations, all the blood of a burnt or peace offering would have been splashed against the altar (see, e.g., Lev. 1:5; 3:2, 17). In Exod. 24:6–8, however, Moses splashed only half of the blood against the altar, and the other half he splashed on the people. Thus, the people were purified and consecrated by blood to be his covenant people, a "kingdom of priests" (Exod. 19:6). A more distinct application of the blood of the ordination offering to Aaron and his sons (Exod. 29:19–34; Lev. 8:22–35) made atonement for them (Exod. 29:33; Lev. 8:34) to serve as priestly mediators for the people. Thereby they became the priests for the kingdom of priests.

These burnt and peace offerings were likely accompanied by grain offerings of various sorts (loaves or cakes that were baked or fried in a pan, always with oil; Lev 2:4–7) and drink offerings (i.e., wine) to provide a meal for the priests and the worshipers (Lev. 7:12–15; Num. 15:1–12), along with the meat of the peace offerings. It should be assumed that, after the blood ratification ritual in Exod. 24:6–8, the people ate a covenant meal before the Lord with this meat, bread, and wine. This same food also supplied the covenant meal that Moses, Aaron, Nadab, Abihu, and the elders of Israel ate on top of the mountain with the Lord, who was visibly present there (Exod. 24:9–11; cf. vv. 1–2; see Sarna, 152–53). Thus, the covenant was ratified by a blood covenant ritual and a covenant meal.

The eating of the bread of the Last Supper represented the eating of the new-covenant meal. The wine represented the blood of the covenant ritual. Jesus's elaboration on the bread and the cup was not part of the Passover celebration proper but was built from it on this occasion to initiate the ritual remembrance of what he was about to do on the cross. As Jesus said, "This cup is the new covenant in my blood, which is poured out for you" (Luke 22:20). We are to do this "in remembrance" of Jesus and what he did to make the new covenant available to us through his sacrificial death that was coming soon (Luke 22:19, "Do this in remembrance of me"; cf. 1 Cor. 11:24, 26). Jesus intended that the ongoing practice of the Lord's Supper would become a means of regularly renewing our remembrance of what he did for us and our commitment to covenant faithfulness.

Beyond the core allusion to the burnt and peace offerings in Exod. 24:1–11, Jesus may also be incorporating elements from other related OT sacrificial passages (see the discussions in Watts, 229–32; Pao and Schnabel, 381–83). For example, according to Mark, Jesus "poured out" his blood "for many" (Mark 14:24; cf. Luke 22:20, "poured out for you"), and Matthew adds to that, "for the forgiveness of sins" (Matt. 26:28). The expression "poured out for many" most naturally recalls the combination of expressions in Isa. 53:12, "because he poured out his life unto death, and was numbered with the transgressors. For he bore the sin of many" (cf. also v. 11 and 52:15). The addition "for the forgiveness of sins" in matthew may be a reference to Jer. 31:34, "For I will forgive their wickedness and will remember their sins no more," or it could allude to the forgiveness that came through the sin offering in Lev. 4:1–5:13 (e.g., 4:20, 26, 31, 35; 5:10, 13).

Jesus as our sin offering. In OT Hebrew the regular term for "sin" is the same as that for "sin offering" (MT *ḥaṭṭā't*, LXX *hamartia*; Lev. 4:3). According to Lev. 4:3, for example, "If the anointed priest sins to bring guilt on the people, he shall present for his sin [*ḥaṭṭā't*] that he has sinned a bull of the herd without blemish to the LORD for a sin offering [*ḥaṭṭā't*]" (AT). One determines from the context which meaning of the word is intended. The same is true in NT Greek—for example, Rom. 8:3 reads, "For what the law was unable to do in that it was weak through the flesh, God sent his own Son in the likeness of sinful flesh and for a sin offering [*hamartia*] to condemn sin [*hamartia*] in the flesh" (AT). Consider also perhaps 2 Cor. 5:21, "God made him who had no sin to be sin [or "a sin offering"?] for us."

Like the burnt and peace offerings discussed above, the sin offering also included "an aroma pleasing to the LORD" when the fat of the animal was offered up on the altar as part of the ritual procedure (stated explicitly in Lev. 4:31; cf. also vv. 10, 19, 26, 35). The priest, however, manipulated the sin offering blood in a very different manner. Setting aside the more specific details, we note that he would dip his finger into the blood in order to sprinkle it before the curtain of the tabernacle and/or rub it on the horns of the incense or burnt offering altar (Lev. 4:5–7, 16–18, 25, 30, etc.). This purified the altar and the tabernacle from the impurity caused by the sin for which the sinner brought the offering (see Averbeck, "Reading," 141, and below). The priest simply disposed of the rest of the blood in a sanctified way by pouring it out on the ground at the base of the burnt offering altar (vv. 7, 18, 25, 30, 34). This was not part of the atonement proceedings (Milgrom, 238–39; *pace* Hoskins). The handling of blood was always a sensitive matter whether it was used to make atonement or not (see, e.g., Gen. 9:4–5; Lev. 17:8–14; Deut. 12:15–16).

Meanwhile, by means of the blood manipulation at the altar and the burning of the fat on the altar as an aroma pleasing to the Lord, the priestly mediator would make atonement for the one who brought the offering and he or she would be forgiven (Lev. 4:20, 26, 31, 35; 5:10). In addition, there is good reason to believe that the priest's atoning work included "bearing the culpability" (*nāśā' 'āwōn*) for the sin committed (Averbeck, "Reading," 142; Sklar, 88–99). The priestly mediator took the sinner's responsibility and culpability for the sin upon himself (contrast, e.g., Lev. 5:1, where the sinner "bore his own culpability" [AT]). Later, in the scapegoat ritual on the Day of Atonement, therefore, the high priest would place all the culpability for all the sins of the people for the whole year on the head of the goat so that it "bore all their culpabilities" away from the camp far into the wilderness, never to return again (Lev. 16:22 AT).

Specific atonement terminology appears six times in the NT (*hilaskomai* in Luke 18:13 and Heb. 2:17; *hilasmos* in 1 John 2:2 and 4:10; and *hilastērion* in Rom. 3:25 and Heb. 9:5). Romans 3:25 in the NIV reads, "God presented Christ as a sacrifice of atonement [*hilastērion*], through the shedding of his blood—to be received by faith," but the text note tells us this word refers to the "mercy seat" or "atonement cover" (= Heb. *kappōret*) over the ark, which is clearly what it means in Heb. 9:5 (cf. Lev. 16:2, 13–15 LXX). The debate continues over the correct rendering in Rom. 3:25 (see, e.g., Longenecker, 424–29, supporting "sacrifice of atonement," and Seifrid, 619–22, supporting "mercy seat"). It seems that "atonement cover" or "mercy seat" is most likely the basic meaning here. The place of atonement in the OT is being metaphorically applied to Jesus as the person of atonement in the NT.

Jesus is not only the place of atonement but also the sin offering atonement sacrifice itself, according to Rom. 8:3: "God sent his own son in the likeness of sinful flesh and for a sin offering [*hamartia*] to condemn sin [*hamartia*] in the flesh" (AT; see above). There has been considerable debate about whether the atonement worked for us by Jesus Christ as our sin offering should be understood as effecting "propitiation," the aversion of God's wrath, or "expiation," the removal of sin and impurity, or both (see the helpful discussions in Longenecker, 427–29; Moo, 255–58). The OT word "to atone, make atonement" (*kipper*) includes both (Sklar; Averbeck, "*Kpr*"). The emphasis in the sin offering is "expiation" because of the special way the priest would manipulate the blood as a means of cleansing, although the burning of its fat on the altar also contributed as an aroma pleasing to the Lord. Normally, the blood of the burnt, peace, and guilt offerings was simply splashed against the sides of the altar. Thus, it became part of the ransom gift that was offered up to God, calling for his favor rather than wrath or judgment (see the clarity in Gen. 8:20–21).

On the Day of Atonement, the priest purified and (re) consecrated the altar for the coming year (Lev. 16:19). In doing this, he "made atonement on behalf of [*ba'ad*] himself, and on behalf of his household, and on behalf of the whole community of Israel" (v. 17b AT, all indirect objects of *kipper*). Verse 20 summarizes the effect of the slain sin offerings differently: "So he finished atoning [i.e., purging] the holy place and the tent of meeting and the altar" (AT, all direct objects of *kipper*). The summary at the end of the chapter shows the same shift: the priest purged directly the most holy place, the tent of meeting, and the altar, and he did this for (i.e., on behalf of) the priests and the people of the congregation (v. 33) as their mediator.

The point is that the combined offerings in the OT accomplished both propitiation and expiation. The same is true for Christ's work of atonement in the NT. The noun "atoning sacrifice" (*hilasmos*) in 1 John 2:2 and 4:10 captures the picture as a whole, without breaking it down into parts. Jesus is the "atoning sacrifice for our sins," making propitiation and expiation. The corresponding verb "to make atonement" (*hilaskomai*) appears in Heb. 2:17 and likewise captures the whole idea: Jesus became "fully human in every way, in order that he might become a merciful and faithful high priest in service to God, and that he might make atonement for the sins of the people."

Hebrews 5–7 develops Jesus's high priesthood according to the order of Melchizedek, since Jesus was not born into the Levitical Aaronic line of the OT priesthood. Hebrews 8–10 develops this special high priesthood of Jesus further in terms of how he is not only our high priest but also, at the same time, the sacrifice that he offers as our high priest. This includes speaking of Jesus as our sin offering, but his giving of himself also corresponds to other features of the OT system of offerings and sacrifices.

First, Jesus serves as our high priest in the true tabernacle, the throne room of God in heaven, as a priest according to the order of Melchizedek (Heb. 8:1–2; cf. chaps. 5–7). The tabernacle on earth was only a copy of the one in heaven. The Lord showed Moses the tabernacle in heaven so that he could fabricate the earthly tabernacle according to it (8:3–5; 9:1–5; cf. Exod. 25:9, 40, and see Guthrie, 968–70). The tabernacle in heaven is a better tabernacle.

Second, the priestly service in the copy on earth consisted of "external regulations" (9:10) and used the blood of animals and the ashes of the red heifer to "cleanse the flesh" (9:13 AT), whereas Christ offered his own blood in the heavenly tabernacle to "cleanse our consciences" (9:14) for our eternal redemption (Heb. 9:6–14). Such cleansing corresponds to the OT practice of making atonement through sin offerings to purge the sanctuary so that people could be clean. The red heifer ashes mixed with water were also a kind of "sin offering" (Num. 19:9, 17 ESV). The sin offering of Christ is a better sin offering.

Third, Jesus is the mediator of a new covenant with an eternal inheritance (Heb. 9:15–20; cf. 8:6–13, citing Jer. 31:31–34). Moses ratified the Sinaitic covenant with burnt and peace offerings (Heb. 9:18–20; cf. the discussion of Exod. 24:1–11 above), but Christ ratified and initiated the new covenant with his own death on the cross (Heb. 9:15–17). In this way, Jesus served as our new-covenant burnt and peace offering. His blood was applied to us like Moses applied the sacrificial blood to the people in Exod. 24:8. The new covenant is a better covenant.

Fourth, when Moses consecrated the earthly tabernacle he used sin offering blood to purify the altar for the purpose of making atonement upon it (Heb. 9:21–22; cf. Lev. 8:14–15). Similarly, when Jesus entered the heavenly tabernacle he offered his own blood as a sin offering to consecrate the heavenly tabernacle and its altar (Heb. 9:23–24). As our high priest he entered heaven itself, into the very presence of God, to offer his own blood as a sin offering. Jesus is a better high priest who offers a better sin offering.

Fifth, the OT priests had to offer the Day of Atonement sin offering sacrifices every year, year after year (Lev. 16:11–19, 29–34), but Christ sacrificed himself only once for all, never to do it again (Heb. 9:25–28). Since the Day of Atonement sacrifices in the OT had to be repeated annually, they could never take sin away permanently. Jesus, however, offered himself once for all with eternal effect, taking sin away permanently, consummately, so there is no longer any need for sacrifice (Heb. 10:1–4). Jesus is a better sin offering than those sin offerings presented by the high priest on the Day of Atonement in the OT.

Sixth, the sacrificial work of Christ has set aside the whole OT system of sacrifices. The atoning work is completely finished, all our sins have been forgiven, and those who know Jesus are holy to the Lord (Heb. 10:5–18; cf. Jer. 31:33–34). We have open and direct access to God (Heb. 10:19–21). This is clear. However, the meaning of "through the veil, that is, his body" (v. 20 AT) is debated. According to Heb. 6:19–20, Jesus entered through the veil as our high priestly forerunner. How could he enter through the veil and, at the same time, his body be the veil (Cockerill, 468–71)? Some take the verse to mean that we have access to God "through the veil, that is, (by means of) his flesh"—that is, through his incarnation on earth that continues in heaven (Moffitt, 281–83).

The simplest rendering, however, is "through the veil, that is, (through) his flesh," which is the veil that was torn when he suffered and died on the cross, giving us open access to God. So, again, how then can he both enter through the veil into God's presence for us (Heb. 6:19–20) and, at the same time, be the veil itself in this passage? On this interpretation, the answer is in the typological nature of the biblical theology of sacrifice and offering as it is applied to Jesus. Just as Jesus is the mercy seat in Rom. 3:25 and yet applied his sin offering blood to the mercy seat, he is the veil in Heb. 10:20 and yet entered into the holy of holies through the veil. Through Christ, therefore, we can draw near to God within the veil with a pure heart and clean conscience (v. 22). What Jesus accomplished for us is better than the whole OT system of offerings and sacrifices put together.

In recent years an old view of Christ's atonement in Hebrews has gained renewed support, according to which the death of Jesus on the cross was preliminary to his presentation of his blood in the heavenly tabernacle, which was the true atoning moment (Moffitt, 215–96). We cannot discuss this issue in detail here. Some scholars have accepted this reading of Hebrews, others have rejected it, and still others are cautious about it (Kibbe). The major objection to this view is that the death of Jesus on the cross often appears to be at the center of what he did for us in the NT (see, e.g., Rom. 6:10; 1 Pet. 3:18). It is certainly a big part of the story in all four Gospels, and it stands at the core of the gospel message.

Jesus as our guilt offering. Finally, the guilt offering enters into this discussion in a different kind of way through Isa. 53:10, "Yet it was the LORD's will to crush him and cause him to suffer, and though the LORD makes his life *an offering for sin*, he will see his offspring and prolong his days, and the will of the LORD will prosper in his hand." Underlying the rendering "an offering for sin" is the regular Hebrew term for "guilt (reparation) offering" (*ʾāšām*; see Lev. 5:14–16 and the details in Averbeck, "Interpretations," 45–60).

There is a good deal of scholarly debate about the interpretation of Isa. 53, but it is clear that the NT takes it to refer to the vicarious suffering, death, resurrection, and exaltation of Jesus Christ. Isaiah 53:10 itself is never cited directly in the NT, but other parts of the passage are. One of the clearest examples is Acts 8, where Philip encounters the Ethiopian eunuch, who is reading Isa. 53 and asks who the passage is talking about. At that point, "Philip began with that very passage of Scripture and told him the good news about Jesus" (Acts 8:35; cf. also, e.g., Luke 22:37; John 12:37–38; 1 Pet. 2:18–25).

The purpose of the guilt offering was to make atonement for desecration of sancta—that is, for the mishandling or mistreatment of holy (sacred) things as if they were common (see esp. the basic instructions in Lev. 5:14–6:7 [5:14–26 MT]). The proper management of the distinction between things that are holy versus common is one of the two core principles in the priestly sacrificial regulations, as the Lord made clear to Aaron in the wake of the death of his two sons, Nadab and Abihu (Lev. 10:1–9): "You must distinguish between the holy and the common, between the unclean and the clean" (Lev. 10:10 AT).

Applying this background understanding of the guilt (reparation) offering to Isa. 53:10 contributes substantially to the interpretation of the servant's ministry as described in Isa. 53 and Isa. 40–66 overall. Historically, therefore, the meaning and message of Isa. 53 are intimately bound up with the realities of the Babylonian exile of the day. The exile from the promised land amounted to a desecration of sancta—the specific sancta being Israel itself as the Lord's "kingdom of priests" and "holy nation" (Exod. 19:6). In this way, the sacrificial suffering of the servant as a guilt offering makes perfectly good sense in the context of Isa. 40–66. Reparation for the violation of sancta needed to be made so that they could be restored.

Furthermore, the suffering of this servant provides redemption and restoration for "many nations" and their "kings" (Isa. 52:15, cf. 53:11–12). The Lord's concern for the nations, not just Israel, is also declared elsewhere in the larger context (e.g., 49:6–7; 56:6–7). The vicarious sacrifice of Isa. 53 would apply to them as well. The Jews were in exile in that day. Gentiles who do not know the Lord are in "exile" too even today. We all need restoration to the Lord our God. As a "guilt offering," Jesus Christ made this restoration possible for all of us.

Conclusion

The NT writers also apply many of the principles and practices of the OT sacrificial system to the lives of those who believe in Jesus. Christ offered himself up as a sacrifice, and if we are going to become like him and follow in his footsteps, we must do the same (see Treier, 826–27; Averbeck, "Reading," 147–48). There are differences, of course. The offerings and sacrifices of the believer do not make atonement for us or anyone else. That was accomplished fully and permanently for us through the sacrificial work of Jesus Christ. Thus, as believers we never become a sin or guilt offering, so to speak.

We are priests called to offer "spiritual sacrifices acceptable to God through Jesus Christ" (1 Pet. 2:5; cf. Heb. 13:15–16). As is well known, the exhortations to live the Christian life well in Rom. 12–15 begin with "I urge you, brothers and sisters, in view of God's mercy, to offer your bodies as a living sacrifice, holy and pleasing to God—this is your true and proper worship" (12:1). According to Rom. 15:16, God gave Paul "the priestly duty of proclaiming the gospel of God, so that the Gentiles might become an offering acceptable to God, sanctified by the Holy Spirit." In Phil. 2:17 he regards himself as one "being poured out like a drink offering on the sacrifice and service" of the faith of the believers at Philippi (cf. Num. 15:1–12). These are just a few examples.

See also Feasts and Festivals; Priest; Sin; Temple

Bibliography. Averbeck, R. E., "Christian Interpretations of Isaiah 53," in *The Gospel according to Isaiah 53*, ed. D. L. Bock and M. Glaser (Kregel, 2012), 33–60; Averbeck, "*kpr*," in *NIDOTTE*, 2:689–710; Averbeck, "Leviticus," in *NIV Biblical Theology Study Bible*, ed. D. A. Carson (Zondervan, 2018), 172–216 [= 2015: 189–238]; Averbeck, "Offerings and Sacrifices," in *NIDOTTE*, 4:996–1022; Averbeck, "Reading the Ritual Law in Leviticus Theologically," in *Interpreting the Old Testament Theologically*, ed. A. T. Abernethy (Zondervan, 2018), 135–49; Averbeck, "Sacrifices and Offerings," in *DOTP*, 706–33; Averbeck, "Tabernacle," in *DOTP*, 807–26; Bock, D. L., *Acts*, BECNT (Baker Academic, 2010); Carson, D. A., "1 Peter," in *CNTUOT*, 1015–45; Carson, *The Gospel according to John*, PNTC (Eerdmans, 1991); Cockerill, G. L., *The Epistle to the Hebrews*, NICNT (Eerdmans, 2012); Guthrie, G. H., "Hebrews," in *CNTUOT*, 919–95; Hoskins, P. M., "A Neglected Allusion to Leviticus 4–5 in Jesus' Words concerning His Blood in Matthew 26:28," *BBR* 30, no. 2 (2020): 231–42; Kibbe, M., "It Is Finished?," *JTS* 65 (2014): 25–61; Köstenberger, A. J., "John," in *CNTUOT*, 415–512; Longenecker, R. N., *The Epistle to the Romans*, NIGTC (Eerdmans, 2016); Marshall, I. H., *1 Peter*, IVPNTC (InterVarsity, 1991); Milgrom, J., *Leviticus 1–16*, AB (Doubleday, 1991); Moffitt, D. M., *Atonement and the Logic of the Resurrection in the Epistle to the Hebrews*, NovTSup 141 (Brill, 2011); Moo, D. J., *The Letter to the Romans*, NICNT (Eerdmans, 2018); Osborne, G. R., *James, 1–2 Peter, Jude*, CornBC (Tyndale House, 2011); Pao, D. W., and E. J. Schnabel, "Luke," in *CNTUOT*, 251–414; Paul, I., "Metaphor," in *DTIB*, 507–10; Sarna, N., *Exodus*, JPSTC (Jewish Publication Society, 1991); Seifrid, M. A., "Romans," in *CNTUOT*, 607–94; Sklar, J., *Sin, Impurity, Sacrifice, Atonement* (Sheffield Phoenix, 2005); Treier, D. J., "Typology," in *DTIB*, 823–27; Watts, R. E., "Mark," in *CNTUOT*, 111–249.

Richard E. Averbeck

Samuel, Books of

Both thematically and chronologically (from a narrative, story line point of view), 1–2 Samuel follows closely on the heels of Judges and Ruth. Judges ends with Israel in a disastrously disobedient situation, far removed from the hope of blessing in the land created by the story line in Genesis–Joshua. The story implies the question, "Who will save them from this mess?" The answer is David, introduced in Ruth and emerging as the central human character in 1–2 Samuel. Yahweh, as David Firth (21) notes, is the true central character of 1–2 Samuel. The other characters have subservient roles in the narrative. Samuel—judge, priest, and prophet—serves as the transition from the rule of the judges to the inauguration of the monarchy, which he implements. Saul, the first king, is a foil to David, demonstrating the weaknesses that arise when the king is selected according to the peoples' criteria instead of Yahweh's criteria. David, on the other hand, is at the center of the story. In contrast to the repeated unfaithfulness of Israel in Judges and the unfaithfulness of the first king, Saul, in 1 Samuel, David is faithful to Yahweh, restoring Israel to a proper worship of Yahweh. Likewise, David finally completes the conquest, and Yahweh establishes an eternal covenant with David, a covenant that promises a righteous king and kingdom. This promise will continue beyond David, providing hope for the future for Israel even after David, who starts off so well but later commits such terrible acts of sin and disobedience regarding Bathsheba and Uriah and consequently becomes inept as the ruler of Israel. Tragically, and ironically, in the closing chapters of 2 Samuel (chaps. 13–20), David and his family are depicted as paralleling the disastrously sinful behavior that characterized the people in the ending of Judges (chaps. 19–21) (Chisholm, 3).

Ultimately, 1–2 Samuel underscores the kingship of Yahweh, who often chooses to mediate his authority through human kings and his relationship with them. The monarchy of Israel that Yahweh establishes, however, is always subservient to his presence, represented often in 1–2 Samuel by the ark of the covenant, and apart from him, the monarchy has no authority (see Firth, 43; and Duvall and Hays, 66–71).

In 1–2 Samuel, more than anywhere else in the OT, except perhaps Jeremiah, there are numerous significant and complex textual variations between the MT and LXX. The Dead Sea Scrolls can be helpful in determining the most likely original reading, but the four Samuel scrolls discovered at Qumran are only partially preserved and their fragmentary nature limits their usefulness to a small number of textual problems. In discussing 1–2 Samuel's use of earlier canonical material, this article will rely primarily on the readings of the MT while still recognizing that the MT might not reflect the best reading in all cases. Yet when one moves to discuss how the NT uses 1–2 Samuel, then the readings of the LXX must be given more consideration.

First and Second Samuel can be outlined thematically as follows (from Hays and Duvall, 167–68):

I. From Corrupt Priests to Corrupt King: The Transition from Judges to Monarchy (1 Sam. 1:1–15:35)

A. Hannah and her son, Samuel, contrasted with Eli and his wicked sons (1:1–3:21)
B. The ark narrative: Yahweh defeats Philistia by himself (4:1–7:1)
C. Samuel anoints and establishes Saul as king (7:2–12:25)
D. Saul disqualifies himself through disobedience (13:1–15:35)

II. Who Will Be the Proper King? The Contrast between Saul and David (1 Sam. 16:1–31:13)
A. David is anointed by Samuel and empowered by the Spirit of Yahweh (16:1–23)
B. David slays Goliath, acting like a king empowered by the Spirit (17:1–58)
C. The decline of Saul (and his increasing madness) versus the rise of David (and his increasing greatness) (18:1–31:13)

III. The Inauguration of King David and the Restoration of Israel (2 Sam. 1:1–10:19)
A. David becomes king and reunites the kingdom politically (1:1–5:25)
B. Through David, Israel is restored to covenant relationship with Yahweh (6:1–7:29)
C. David completes the conquest and restores Israel to military prominence (8:1–10:19)

IV. The Collapse of David—the Bathsheba and Uriah Affair (2 Sam. 11:1–12:31)

V. The Consequences of David's Sin: The Unraveling of His Kingdom (2 Sam. 13:1–20:26)

VI. A Positive and Negative Summary of David and His Kingdom (2 Sam. 21:1–24:25)

The Use of Genesis–Ruth in 1–2 Samuel: An Overview

First and Second Samuel frequently alludes to people, patterns, and events in the preceding canonical books, Genesis to Ruth. As demonstrated below, these allusions are expressed both explicitly, through direct reference or citation, and, more frequently, implicitly, through subtle, suggestive, and often ironic reference.

Numerous scholars, although often with differing views on literary dependence and sequential dating of sources, have nonetheless noted similar literary connections such as themes, catchwords, and phrases between 1–2 Samuel and the patriarchal narratives of Genesis. This is particularly true regarding David and his family in comparison with the patriarchs and their families. These scholars often conclude that the comparison is intentional and significant in regard to the meaning of the text (see Schnittjer, 151–52, 170–71; Ho; Rendsburg; Biddle, 617–38; Zakovitch, 149–51).

In a broader study, R. D. Bergen (46–50) presents dozens and dozens of examples indicating 1–2 Samuel's historical and legal "interconnections" to the Pentateuch as a whole. Likewise, he notes (51–53) several literary motifs from the Pentateuch that also appear in 1–2 Samuel: the barren wife who, with God's help, bears a child of great significance (Gen. 11:30 [Sarah]; 25:21 [Rebekah]; 29:31 [Rachel]; 1 Sam. 1–2 [Hannah]); the shepherd as a great leader (Gen. 4:2 [Abel]; 12:16 [Abraham]; 26:14 [Isaac]; 30:29–31 [Jacob]; Exod. 3:1 [Moses]; 1 Sam. 9 [not Saul]; 16:11, 19; 17:15, 20 [David]); the outwitted Philistine king (Gen. 20 [Abraham and Abimelek]; 26:1–11 [Isaac and Abimelek]; 1 Sam. 27:1–28:2 [David and Achish]); the sibling who murders a sibling (Gen. 4:8–11 [Cain and Abel]; 2 Sam. 13:23–29 [Absalom and Amnon]; 14:5–7 [widow's two sons]); the sinner who goes into exile eastwardly (Gen. 3:23–24 [Adam and Eve]; 4:16 [Cain]; 2 Sam. 17:22 [David]); and the younger sibling who surpasses his elder sibling (Gen. 4:26 [Seth]; 17:18–21 [Isaac]; 25:23 [Jacob]; 37:3–9 [Joseph]; Exod. 6:20 [Moses]; 1 Sam. 16:11–12 [David]).

Not surprisingly, 1–2 Samuel also contains several allusions to the exodus events (Auld, 16). Interestingly, while 1–2 Samuel mentions numerous leaders by name, such as Moses, Aaron, and several of the judges, it does not refer explicitly to the person Joshua (Auld, 17), although subtle allusions to Joshua as exemplary leader of the conquest have been suggested. Likewise, there are several probable allusions to the book of Ruth. For example, Hannah's husband states, "Don't I mean more to you than ten sons?" (1 Sam. 1:8), echoing the words of Naomi's neighbors, who tell her, "[Ruth] is better to you than seven sons" (Ruth 4:15). Likewise, the description of Hannah in 1 Sam. 1:10 as *mārat nāpeš* ("weeping bitterly") resonates with Naomi's reference to herself as *mārāʾ* ("Mara," i.e., "bitter," Ruth 1:20; Auld, 20).

Yet while 1–2 Samuel often alludes to people, patterns, and events in the Pentateuch, Judges is the book echoed the most frequently and prominently in 1–2 Samuel. Indeed, 1–2 Samuel serves as the sequel to Judges (Chisholm, 8). The narrator of 1–2 Samuel frequently employs the patterns and parallels of the book of Judges to characterize (both to praise and to judge) Samuel, Saul, and David. Thus David, for example, follows the positive pattern of Caleb and Othniel early in his story but ends up in the negative pattern of Samson, leading his kingdom into the chaos pattern that ended the book of Judges (Chisholm, 2–3).

In Judges the refrain "In those days Israel had no king; everyone did as they saw fit" is repeated numerous times as commentary on the disastrous situation in Israel depicted in the final chapters (17:6; cf. 18:1; 19:1), even appearing as the final, concluding verse of the book (21:25). This leads naturally into 1–2 Samuel, which describes the establishment of the monarchy, but which also underscores the challenge in the second part of the refrain ("everyone did as they saw fit") as King Saul, and ultimately even King David, struggles with obedience to Yahweh.

Methodologically, it is important to underscore that 1–2 Samuel is an extremely complex and artistically constructed narrative. Firth comments, "This is not a dry recounting of events. The narrative is meant to grip those who hear and read it, and attention to the narrative skill employed is a vital interpretative element, since it is through the narrative's artistry that the theological themes are developed" (Firth, 22). Meir Sternberg's insight is helpful, for he notes that complex Hebrew narratives in the Bible like 1–2 Samuel are concerned with a triad of three important and interconnecting aspects: history, ideology (or theology), and aesthetics (Sternberg, 41–57). Sternberg uses the term "aesthetics" in a fashion similar to Firth's use of "artistry," both of them recognizing that the narrator is presenting an exciting, entertaining, and sophisticated story (in an artistic sense), yet using this artistry/aesthetics as the means for conveying theology/ideology.

It is at this level that the narrator can be very subtle, especially in his use of irony (see, e.g., the discussion below on slings, David, and the Benjaminites). Thus, while the manner of allusion in 1–2 Samuel can sometimes be explicit and clearly identifiable, it can also be easily missed. Traditional exegetical approaches, which frequently focus on the historical aspects, important as they are, often miss the subtle allusions, and thus also miss some of the embedded (but still "author-intended") meaning. Furthermore, we should also recognize that while careful reading of 1–2 Samuel in the constant context of Genesis–Ruth can help us as readers to identify the subtle, colorful, and often ironic allusions, it does not automatically identify the point of the allusion. That is, although these allusions are playing a role in conveying theology, sometimes determining that theology can be subjective, as is often the case when interpreting artistic works.

Use of Genesis–Ruth in 1–2 Samuel: Specific Examples

There are dozens and dozens of allusions and interconnections between 1–2 Samuel and the canonically previous books of Genesis–Ruth. The scope of this article allows for only a few examples and a very brief explanation of each.

Samuel compared and contrasted with Samson. The story of Hannah and the divinely enabled birth of Samuel in 1 Sam. 1 echoes the similar birth accounts of the patriarchs Isaac and Jacob, who were also conceived by previously barren women (Gen. 18:10–15; 21:1–7 [Isaac]; 25:21 [Jacob]). Yet a connection between the birth of Samuel and the birth of Samson in Judg. 13 seems to be even more direct. Both stories start out with a similar introduction ("A certain man of Zorah, named Manoah," Judg. 13:2; "There was a certain man from Ramathaim . . . whose name was Elkanah," 1 Sam. 1:1). Both stories involve a previously barren woman who gives birth to a special son due to the intervention of God. Samson's mother is instructed to dedicate the boy as a Nazirite (Judg. 13:5), while Hannah, Samuel's mother, includes the Nazirite dedication as part of her vow to Yahweh (1 Sam. 1:11). Compare her words, "No razor will ever be used on his head" (1 Sam. 1:11), with Samson's words to Delilah, "No razor has ever been used on my head" (Judg. 16:17; Polzin, 24). In the Dead Sea Scrolls (4QSam[a]), Hannah actually says, "I have dedicated him as a Nazirite—all the days of his life" (1 Sam. 1:22). Hannah's vow concerning the dedication of her son as a Nazirite is also probably ironically contrasted with the vow of Jephthah (Judg. 11:31), which ultimately involved the dedication of his daughter as a sacrifice (Polzin, 23).

As a leader (both are called "judges," Judg. 16:31; 1 Sam. 7:15) Samuel is everything that Samson is not, truly living as one dedicated to Yahweh, leading Israel toward Yahweh, and defeating Israel's enemies (especially the Philistines), both directly through his own leadership and indirectly through the leadership of King David, whom Samuel anoints (Chisholm, 9–10).

Numerous aspects in the story of Hannah, Samuel's birth, and Samuel's childhood reflect the background setting described in the Pentateuch; the nature of the sin by Eli's sons, the Nazirite vow, annual pilgrimages, the offerings, the three-pronged offering fork, the perpetual lamp, et cetera (see Bergen, 48–49; Schnittjer, 307, 352).

More subtle is the opening mention of "the hill country of Ephraim" (1 Sam. 1:1), geographically locating this story in the same location as the final terrible events in Judg. 17–21. This phrase ("the hill country of Ephraim") is mentioned seven times in Judg. 17–21 (17:1, 8; 18:2, 13; 19:1, 16, 18), and referencing this again in the introductory verses for Samuel creates a negative anticipation in the reader, an anticipation which is ironically reversed as Hannah, Elkanah, and Samuel turn out to be models of piety, in stark contrast to the characters in the final chapters of Judges (Firth, 54).

The ark narrative. In 1 Sam. 4:1 the ark narrative opens with the statement, "The Israelites went out to fight against the Philistines." This opening alludes back to Judges, especially to the Samson story, where fighting against the Philistines is a dominant part of the story. Indeed, the Samson story opens with the declaration, "The Israelites did evil in the eyes of the LORD, so the LORD delivered them into the hands of the Philistines for forty years" (Judg. 13:1). The ark narratives in 1 Sam. 4–6 also imply the same power of Yahweh's presence associated with the ark that was evident in Exodus and Joshua. Even the Philistines are aware of the exodus tradition (1 Sam. 4:8; Exod. 7–14). Note also the comment by the Philistine sorcerers, "Why do you harden your hearts as the Egyptians and Pharaoh did?" (1 Sam. 6:6; cf. Exod. 8:15, 32; 9:34; Polzin, 58, 66). In contrast to the situation in Judges, where Yahweh raises up various leaders to deliver Israel (especially Samson, who was supposed to deliver Israel from the Philistines), in the ark narrative of 1 Sam. 4–6 Yahweh invades and defeats the Philistines (and their gods) by himself.

The mention of the city of Kiriath Jearim in 1 Sam. 6:21–7:2 reminds the reader of Josh. 9:17, where this city is identified as a *Gibeonite* city. The Gibeonites (inhabitants of the land who tricked Joshua during the conquest) will surface again as important characters in 2 Sam. 21 (Saul had tried to annihilate them; David seeks to make restitution). Here in 1 Sam. 6:21–7:2 the irony is rich: this city is blessed by Yahweh as his ark resides there for twenty years.

Samuel and the end of the Judges cycle. The cycle of disobedience summarized in Judg. 2:11–19 is the background context for understanding 1 Sam. 7, which appears to conclude the era of the judges (note 7:15–17 and the anointing of the king in chap. 8). "Baals and Ashtoreths" are specifically mentioned in 1 Sam. 7:4 as in Judg. 2:13, making the connection quite explicit. The critical difference between Judges and 1 Sam. 7 is that Israel truly repents in 1 Sam. 7:2–4 and thus is able to defeat the Philistines (7:13–14; Polzin, 72–76).

Saul the Benjaminite and the ending of Judges. Israel's call for a king in 1 Sam. 8 connects back to the requirements for the king in Deut. 17:14–20, and Samuel's words of warning prophetically anticipate the indictment of Solomon in 1 Kings 11.

Furthermore, the selection of Saul and his anointing, as well as his initial battle and his confirmation (1 Sam. 9–11), contain numerous ironic allusions to Judg. 19–21 (the episode of the Levite, his concubine, and the annihilation of the Benjaminites). Recall that at the end of Judges the Israelites have ceased trying to destroy the Canaanites and are instead seeking to annihilate their fellow tribe of Benjamin. Thus, here in 1 Sam. 8, when Israel calls for a king, is it not with irony (even perhaps a bit of poetic justice) that Yahweh gives them a Benjaminite as a king (1 Sam. 9:1)? Further indicating that the narrator of 1 Samuel intends a comparison back to Judg. 19–21 is the repeated reference to the two towns of Jabesh-Gilead and Gibeah (1 Sam. 10:5, 10, 26; 11:1, 4, 9), two towns that are also paired together and mentioned repeatedly in Judg. 19–21 (19:12–16; 20:4–43; 21:8–12). Saul the Benjaminite from Gibeah rescues Jabesh-Gilead. When read against Judg. 19–21, the specificity of this two-city relationship is quite remarkable (see the extensive development of this connection in Polzin, 111–14).

Samuel's farewell speech. In 1 Sam. 12, as part of his farewell speech, Samuel gives a historical summary of Israel's history from the exodus to the time of the judges, mentioning Jacob, Moses, Aaron, Jerub-Baal (Gideon), Barak, Jephthah, and Samuel (some variants read "Samson") and underscoring the cycle of disobedience, oppression, deliverance by Yahweh, and then disobedience again that characterizes Judges.

Samuel's imperative in 12:20 to "serve the LORD with all your heart" not only picks up this theme from Deuteronomy (e.g., 10:12; 13:1–3) but also points forward, as this theme continues throughout 1–2 Samuel and 1–2 Kings.

The exodus and the conquest in reverse. First Samuel 13 begins the story of Saul's disobedience and his demise. In this context the narrator mentions that "they hid in caves" (13:6–7), recalling the situation in Judg. 6:2 (Chisholm, 82), and that "some Hebrews even crossed the Jordan to the land of Gad and Gilead" (1 Sam. 13:7), a subtle suggestion perhaps that the conquest of the land is going backward (see Polzin, 127). Likewise, God's command to Saul to destroy the Amalekites (1 Sam. 15:3) alludes back to the events of the exodus in Exod. 17:8–14 and Deut. 25:17–19.

Saul's foolish vow. After Yahweh delivers Israel and gives them victory, Saul makes a foolish vow (1 Sam. 14:24), bringing to mind the equally foolish vow made by Jephthah (who was just mentioned in 1 Sam. 12:11) back in Judg. 11:30–31 (Firth, 164–65).

Judah, Benjamin, David, Saul, and victory with a sling and stone. The tribes of Judah and Benjamin are placed in stark contrast to each other, both at the beginning of Judges (cf. 1:8 with 1:21) and at the end (19:1–2, 14, 16, 18; 20:4, 10–25, esp. 20:18). Thus, in 1 Samuel, when the first king, a Benjaminite, fails, it comes as no surprise that his replacement is from Judah.

Interestingly, in Judg. 20:1–25 the outnumbered Benjaminites defeat the Israelites who were led by the tribe of Judah (20:18). One of the reasons provided for this upset victory is the "seven hundred select troops" of Benjamin (from Gibeah) who were left-handed (a pun on the meaning of Benjamin—"son of my right hand"), "each of whom could sling a stone at a hair and not miss" (20:16). No other tribe is mentioned as having soldiers who fought with slings, yet apparently the Benjaminites from Gibeah are famous for their ability with slings. Thus, in 1 Sam. 17 note the irony as David from Judah, and not Saul, the Benjaminite from Gibeah, defeats the enemy of Israel with a sling. Samuel Meier (156–74) provides a good discussion of the narrator's artistic use of weaponry in the story. Likewise, Benjamin Giffone (23–25) tracks the narrative use of the skill that the Benjaminites in particular had with certain weapons (like slings).

David captures Jerusalem and defeats the Philistines. David's capture of Jerusalem (2 Sam. 5:6–10) brings to mind the struggle for Jerusalem in Judges. The tribe of Judah captured it in Judg. 1:8, but apparently the tribe of Benjamin lost it and was unable to recapture it (Judg. 1:21; 19:10–12). Further reversing the negative events of Judges, after capturing Jerusalem David then defeats the Philistines (2 Sam. 5:17–25).

David moves the ark to Jerusalem. In 2 Sam. 6 David moves the ark to Jerusalem. The entire chapter is filled with allusions and references to texts, items, and events from Exodus, Leviticus, Deuteronomy, and Joshua. These include the ark (Exodus, Joshua), the name of Yahweh (Deuteronomy), the cherubim above the ark (Exodus), moving the ark (Exodus), the ephod (Exodus; perhaps also in contrast to Judg. 8:27 [Gideon] and 17:5–18:20 [Micah]), offerings (Leviticus), and references to the presence of Yahweh ("before the LORD," used 60x in Leviticus and 30x in Numbers).

Yahweh's covenant with David and the completed conquest. In 2 Sam. 7 Yahweh makes a covenant with David. Throughout the chapter, texts and events from Genesis–Judges are assumed as well-known background context. These include the tabernacle and its wandering (Exodus–Numbers), "rest" (Deuteronomy), references to "my people" (Exodus), a "place" for them (Deuteronomy), "my Name" (Deuteronomy), and the phrase "make your name great" (Genesis).

Then in 2 Sam. 8, David completes the conquest, expanding his kingdom to the limits promised to Abraham in Gen. 15:18–21, thus fulfilling much of the Abrahamic covenant (Firth, 399–400). Dedicating his silver and gold to Yahweh (2 Sam. 8:11–12), along with hamstringing captured horses instead of creating a large chariot force (2 Sam. 8:4), portrays David as obeying Deut. 17:14–20 and will contrast with the extravagant disobedience of Solomon in 1 Kings.

David's sin and its consequences. David's terrible sin with Bathsheba and his murder of her husband Uriah reflect clear and blatant violations of several of the Ten Commandments (Exod. 20:13–15, 17; Deut. 5:17–19, 21; Chisholm, 236). Brevard Childs (64) posits that often the OT narratives serve as commentary on the Ten Commandments, noting that the narrative of David and Uriah "goes right to the heart of the crime of murder."

Allusion back to Judg. 9:50–53 occurs in 2 Sam. 11:21 when Joab says, "Who killed Abimelek . . . ? Didn't a woman drop an upper millstone on him from the wall?" Joab (and the narrator) may be suggesting more than just the issue of Uriah's death and getting too close to enemy walls. Joab may be implying and warning about the possible downfall of David, brought about by a woman but ironically with him on the wall and her down below.

The narrator describes the unraveling of David's kingdom in 2 Sam. 13:1–20:26, but the focus of the crisis is frequently on the family of David. As noted above, numerous scholars have observed the close connection between events in this part of 2 Samuel and those in the Jacob/Joseph narratives of Genesis. Gary Schnittjer notes that the failures of Jacob's four oldest sons have strong parallels with the struggle for power seen in four of David's sons (Amnon, Absalom, Adonijah, and Solomon). Reuben sleeps with his father's concubine (Gen. 35), while Absalom sleeps with several of his father's concubines (2 Sam. 16). Like Simeon and Levi in Gen. 34, in 2 Sam. 13 Absalom avenges the rape of his sister. Numerous phrases are similar: "such a thing should not be done in Israel" (2 Sam. 13:12; cf. Gen. 34:7); "he raped her" (2 Sam. 13:14; cf. Gen. 34:2); "disgrace" (2 Sam. 13:13; Gen. 34:14). Both David and Jacob know, but do nothing, becoming angry later (2 Sam. 13:21; cf. Gen. 34:30–31). Both David and Jacob mourn over their sons for many days (2 Sam. 13:37; Gen. 37:34; see Schnittjer, 151–52; Auld, 489; Zakovitch, 149–51).

Reuse of Material in 1–2 Samuel within 1–2 Samuel

Although it is outside the scope of this article, it should be noted in brief that there is a tremendous amount of intertextual allusion and connection within 1–2 Samuel. Themes from Hannah's song in 1 Sam. 2 (such as the reversal of fortune), for example, echo throughout 1–2 Samuel. Likewise, her song finds a parallel in David's song of 2 Sam. 22, forming an *inclusio* (Polzin, 33–35). Another good example of intertextual use within 1–2 Samuel is the role played by the Amalekites. Saul disobeys Yahweh by refusing to destroy them completely (1 Sam. 15), a destruction David is accomplishing in 1 Sam. 30 as Saul meets his end. Then, in 2 Sam. 2, it is an Amalekite who claims to have killed Saul and then is executed by David, finally ending the Amalekite problem.

Use of 1–2 Samuel in the NT

Numerous scholars note the parallels between Hannah's song in 1 Sam. 2:1–11 and Mary's song in Luke 1:46–56 (Firth, 63; Brueggemann, 21; Bock, 148; Goulder, 225–29). Yet undoubtedly it is God's covenant promise to David in 2 Sam. 7 and the messianic connotations associated with David that are cited and alluded to the most frequently, both throughout the following canonical OT books and throughout the NT. This trajectory goes from 1–2 Samuel through the prophets (e.g., Jer. 23:5; 33:17–26; Ezek. 34:23–24; 37:24–25) and Psalms (e.g., 89:3; 132:11) into the NT, where David is mentioned over fifty times (e.g., Matt. 1:1; 12:23; 20:30–31; 21:15; Mark 11:10; Luke 1:32; John 7:42; Rev. 22:16).

Interestingly, in Luke 18:38 it is a blind beggar who first publicly announces that Jesus is the long-awaited Son of David (Pao and Schnabel, 353). In light of the observation that this story is embedded within Jesus's climactic journey to Jerusalem, a central theme in the middle of Luke, it is intriguing to note that it is in 2 Samuel that Jerusalem receives its special status and that in 2 Samuel David also journeys to Jerusalem, in his case to capture it. In 2 Sam. 5:6 the Jebusites in Jerusalem declare, "Even the blind and the lame can ward you off." It is fascinating to note that as Jesus travels to Jerusalem at the climax of his ministry, he heals the lame (Luke 13:10–13) and the blind (18:35–43), being called the Son of David by the blind man.

When the Pharisees accuse Jesus's disciples of breaking the Sabbath, Jesus refers to 1 Sam. 21:1–7, where David, along with his companions, had eaten from the bread of the Presence while fleeing from Saul (Matt.

12:3; Mark 2:25; Luke 6:3). While probably demonstrating that very special people (i.e., Jesus and David) in very special circumstances can override the Sabbath rules, this complex use of 1 Samuel is probably suggesting other interconnections as well (Jesus as the fulfillment of the Davidic promises; the anointed king not being accepted, but being sustained by the presence of God, etc.; see Watts, 139–42).

Numerous other allusions to and direct quotations from 1–2 Samuel are found throughout the NT. For example, in Acts 13:22 Paul refers to David as a man after God's own heart, no doubt alluding to 1 Sam. 13:14. Likewise, 2 Cor. 6:18 ("I will be a Father to you") and Heb. 1:5 ("You are my Son; today I have become your Father") allude back to 2 Sam. 7:14 ("I will be his father, and he will be my son"), perhaps via Ps. 2:7 ("He said to me, 'You are my son; today I have become your father'"). In addition, 2 Sam. 22:50, repeated in Ps. 18:49, is quoted in Rom. 15:9, "Therefore I will praise you among the Gentiles; I will sing the praises of your name." Finally, 1 Samuel states repeatedly that David was from Bethlehem, often also specifying Bethlehem in Judah (16:1, 4, 18; 17:12, 15, 58; 20:6). Micah 5:2 alludes back to this, and the NT Gospels underscore this connection, stressing Bethlehem in Judea as the birthplace of Jesus (Matt. 2:1–16; Luke 2:4, 15; John 7:42).

Bibliography. Auld, A. G., *I & II Samuel*, OTL (Westminster John Knox, 2011); Bergen, R. D., *1, 2 Samuel*, NAC (Broadman & Holman, 1996); Biddle, M. E., "Ancestral Motifs in 1 Samuel 25," *JBL* 121 (2002): 617–38; Bock, D. L., *Luke 1:1–9:50*, BECNT (Baker, 1994); Brueggemann, W., *First and Second Samuel*, IBC (John Knox, 1990); Childs, B. S., *Old Testament Theology in a Canonical Context* (Fortress, 1985); Chisholm, R. B., Jr., *1 & 2 Samuel*, TTCS (Baker Books, 2013); Duvall, J. S., and J. D. Hays, *God's Relational Presence* (Baker Academic, 2019); Firth, D. G., *1 & 2 Samuel*, AOTC (IVP Academic, 2009); Giffone, B. D., "'Special Forces,'" *SJOT* 30, no. 1 (2016): 16–29; Goulder, M. D., *Luke*, vol. 1, JSNTSup 20 (JSOT Press, 1989); Hays, J. D., and J. S. Duvall, *The Baker Illustrated Bible Handbook* (Baker Books, 2011); Ho, C. Y. S., "The Stories of the Family Troubles of Judah and David," *VT* 49, no. 4 (1999): 514–31; Meier, S. A., "The Sword from Saul to David," in *Saul in Story and Tradition*, ed. C. S. Ehrlich and M. C. White, FAT 47 (Mohr Siebeck, 2006), 156–74; Pao, D. W., and E. J. Schnabel, "Luke," in *CNTUOT*, 251–414; Polzin, R., *Samuel and the Deuteronomist*, part 2, *1 Samuel* (Indiana University Press, 1989); Rendsburg, G. A., "David and His Circle in Genesis XXXVIII," *VT* 36, no. 4 (1986): 438–46; Schnittjer, G. E., *The Torah Story* (Zondervan, 2016); Sternberg, M., *The Poetics of Biblical Narrative* (Indiana University Press, 1987); Watts, R. E., "Mark," in *CNTUOT*, 111–249; Zakovitch, Y., "Through the Looking Glass," *BibInt* 1, no. 2 (1993): 139–52.

J. Daniel Hays

Sanctification *See* Gospel

Satan

"Satan" is labeled in a number of ways in the NT. The word "Satan" itself is a transliteration of the Hebrew *śāṭān*, which can represent an adversary in a general sense (see, e.g., Num. 22:22; 1 Sam. 29:4; 1 Kings 11:14; Ps. 109:6) or specifically the opponent of God's people in God's heavenly throne room (e.g., Job 2:1; Zech. 3; 1 Chron. 21). He can also be termed in Greek the *diabolos*. While the word would typically be rendered "slanderer" (and is used in this strict sense of human slanderers in, e.g., Esther 7:4 LXX; 2 Tim. 3:3; Titus 2:3), this precise nuance is seldom felt in the NT, and it is deployed as a general term for the enemy of God and his people. A key exception is Rev. 12, where "the one called the devil, and the Satan" (v. 9 AT) is then described as "the accuser [*ho katēgōr*] of the brethren, the one who accuses them night and day" (v. 10 AT, on which see below). Other epithets include "the evil one" (1 John 5:18); "the ruler of this world" (John 14:30 ESV); "the god of this world" (2 Cor. 4:4); (likely) "the ruler of the power of the air" (Eph. 2:2 AT); and Beelzebul (Luke 11:15–19). The latter may be a deliberate corruption of the Philistine god Baal-Zebub, "Lord of Flies" (see 2 Kings 1:2); Beelzebul itself might signify "lord of heaven" or "temple" (from *baʿal zəbûl*); or "lord of the territory" (from *baʿal gəbûl* [Wahlen, 125–26]; on names for Satan in general, see Farrer and Williams).

We must also account for the common idea that the Satan figure develops over the course of the Hebrew canon, and thence into the NT era (see Kelly). Such putative development is not easy to trace within the OT itself, though Satan certainly plays a more visible role in world events in the NT and many early Jewish texts. While the figure in Job and Zechariah does not bear full resemblance to the "ruler of the world" in John 14:30, neither is he necessarily a mere court functionary: his ability to afflict Job is worrisome, as is his apparent desire to thwart God's purposes for the restoration of Israel in Zech. 3 (cf. Page, 23–33). Likewise, the idea that he is a "world ruler" (cf. John 12:31; 14:30; 16:11) may not seem to square with the figure slithering through the grass in Gen. 3 until one considers the consequences of his action in the narrative for humanity and the world. The gap between the admittedly diverse portrayals of the adversary in the OT and the devil in the NT is not so wide as sometimes thought. Still, the devil familiar to NT readers becomes more recognizable in the literature of early Judaism.

Satan as Deceiver

Assuming, as the NT does, that the snake in Gen. 3 is indeed the devil (Genesis itself is silent on the matter), Satan's initial move in the canon is to call into question the veracity of God's word. Deception remains his calling card in the NT.

Satan's penchant for deception is seen in the sharpest relief in Revelation, particularly in the dramatic visions of chaps. 12–20. There he appears primarily in the guise of the dragon, the eschatological foe of God whom God promises to slay in Isa. 27:1. Isaiah may well have the insidious serpent of Gen. 3 in mind (cf. Motyer, 222). John certainly does. He reports in Rev. 12:9: "And the great dragon was thrown down, that ancient serpent, who is called the devil and Satan, the deceiver of the whole world" (ESV). Deception is at the heart of the devil's enterprise in Revelation (cf. 13:14; 18:23; 19:20; 20:3, 8, 10). The dragon is presented as the first member of the "satanic trinity" that dominates earth in Rev. 12–13 and meets its demise in the ensuing chapters (cf. Bauckham, *Revelation*, 89–91). The dragon deputizes the beast as his ruler on earth (antichrist in the strict sense, though John does not use the term). The portrait of the beast is most heavily indebted to the wicked rulers of Dan. 7, with additional shading from Pharaoh. The beast's rule is in turn propped up by a second beast, the false prophet, the *ne plus ultra* of the false prophets who abound on the pages of the OT (see, e.g., Jer. 23:9–40; Ezek. 13; 22:28). This satanic trinity gives rise to the counterfeit city Babylon, a blasphemous counterpart to God's city, the new Jerusalem (cf. the portraits of Babylon in Rev. 17 and the new Jerusalem in 21:9–27; see Rossing); Babylon is of course based on the chief superpower of the OT, again supplemented with images from Egypt, the other great antagonist of the OT. Satan's deceptive activity reaches a climax in his efforts to gather all the nations in a battle against God and the Lamb: "And when the thousand years have finished, Satan will be loosed from his prison and he will go out to deceive [*planaō*, Revelation's standard term for deception] the nations that are in the four corners of the earth, Gog and Magog, to gather them for the battle" (Rev. 20:7–8 AT; cf. Ezek. 38–39).

Paul offers a similar take on the centrality of satanic deception in the eschaton in 2 Thess. 2, where the appearance of "the lawless one" is said to arise from "the working of Satan," who proffers various signs and wonders to lead astray the reprobate (v. 9 NRSV). The mention of signs and wonders may recall the tricks of the Egyptian magicians in Exod. 7–8. Even more interesting is the follow-up comment that *God* sends the wicked a "powerful delusion" (2 Thess. 2:11). As is regularly the case in the OT, the activity of Satan is strictly circumscribed by God, such that the satanic activity of deception can in some sense be said to be sent by God. This is reinforced by Paul using the same word, *energeia*, to describe the "working" of Satan in v. 9 and the "powerful" delusion sent by God in v. 11. The paradox is apparent in the OT in the juxtaposition of 2 Sam. 24, where God incites David to take the census, and 1 Chron. 21, where Satan is said to incite David to the same act. For the idea that God could "send a delusion," compare 1 Kings 22:23, where the prophet Micaiah tells Ahab, "The Lord has put a spirit of deception in the mouths of all the prophets." (Of course, the fact Micaiah *is telling Ahab about this deception* adds another layer of complexity to the situation.)

John's Gospel and Letters also emphasize Satan's deception. Truth and falsehood form one of the key antinomies in 1 John, starting in 1:6: "If we say we have fellowship with him while we walk in darkness, we lie and do not practice the truth" (ESV; cf. 1:8, 10; 2:4, 22, 26–27). Thus, when John says that the devil "has been sinning from the beginning" (3:8), we may reasonably suspect that his role as deceiver is at least partly in view (cf. Brown, 405–6). This is confirmed by Jesus's searing words to his murderous opponents in John 8. After declaring that the devil, not Abraham, is their father, he says, "He was a murderer from the beginning, and does not stand in the truth, because there is no truth in him. When he lies, he speaks out of his own character, for he is a liar and the father of lies" (8:44 ESV). The notion that the devil was a *murderer* from the beginning may stem from the fact his deception leads ultimately to the death of Adam and Eve (Gen. 2:17; 3:19; cf. Page, 125–28), though it is just possible that it refers to his presumed role in instigating Cain's murder of Abel (see 1 John 3:12 ESV: "We should not be like Cain, who was of the evil one and murdered his brother").

Paul overtly draws on the Gen. 3 narrative to warn the Corinthians against accepting a different gospel: "But I am afraid that as the serpent deceived Eve by his cunning, your thoughts will be led astray from a sincere and pure devotion to Christ" (2 Cor. 11:3 ESV). He goes on to point out that Satan now uses false prophets and teachers as his instruments in deception; these deceivers seem pleasant, which should not catch believers off guard: "For even Satan disguises himself as an angel of light. So it is no surprise if his servants, also, disguise themselves as servants of righteousness. Their end will correspond to their deeds" (11:14–15 ESV). The notion that Satan would appear as an angel of light is not found in the OT but is in LAE (*Vita*) 9:1: "Then Satan was angry and transformed himself into the brightness of angels [Lat. *transfiguravit se in claritatem angelorum*] and went away to the Tigris River to Eve" (*OTP*; cf. Apoc. Mos. 17:1; see Harris, 774–75).

Satan as Tempter

Closely related to his role as deceiver is Satan's involvement in temptation, which is in essence the proffering of false benefits based on a renunciation of the true God and his ways. He maintains this primeval role of tempter in the NT. This is seen most dramatically in the Synoptic accounts of Jesus's temptation in the wilderness, passages awash in OT imagery. (Matt. 4:1 and Luke 4:2 ascribe the temptation to "the devil"; Mark 1:13 has "Satan" [*satanas*].) It is likely no coincidence that the temptation of Jesus arises at the beginning of his public ministry, just as it arises at the beginning of the Hebrew canon: Jesus represents a new start for humanity, and Satan once more tries to subvert the process (cf. Hendriksen, 233–34). This is seen most clearly in Matthew, who begins his Gospel with the words *biblos geneseōs Iēsou Christou,* which is generally (and understandably) rendered "the genealogy of Jesus Christ" (ESV) but which could more woodenly be translated as "the book of Genesis of Jesus Christ." Most critically for us, it is an allusion to Gen. 5:1 LXX: *biblos geneseōs anthrōpōn,* "the genealogy of *humanity* [Heb. *ʾādām*]" (cf. Hagner, 9). Luke makes a similar point by tracing the genealogy of Jesus back to Adam just prior to his recitation of the temptation story. Mark has no genealogy, but he does mention that Jesus was "with the animals" (1:13 AT), which many have seen as a reference to the pre-fall state of natural harmony enjoyed by Adam (cf. Gruelich, 38–40).

If the creation and fall lie at the foundation of the temptation narrative, however, the more obvious OT connection is to the story of Israel (cf. Page, 92). Matthew again shows this most clearly. Jesus passes through the water in baptism (with the Jordan doing double duty as a proxy for the Red Sea of the exodus and as a reminder of the conquest under Joshua) and is then brought into the wilderness to be tested for forty units of time. The connection to the wilderness generation is clear and is reinforced when Jesus thwarts Satan's deceptively "biblical" temptations by recourse to Deut. 6 and 8, chapters concerned precisely with Israel's failed test in the desert. Jesus does not simply repel Satan by a generic use of Scripture; he shows himself to be the true Israelite who will redo the nation's history in his own person. Since Israel represents God's plan to redeem all of humanity, Jesus in so redoing Israel's history also sets the world as a whole on a new course.

Satan's role in temptation is reinforced in other NT texts. In 1 Cor. 7:5, Paul says that Satan may leverage people's preexisting lack of self-control into (presumably sexual) temptation (cf. CD 4.13–21, T. Reu. 6:1–4; see Garland, 221). While the overt language of temptation is not used in the story of Ananias and Sapphira, Peter does assert in Acts 5:3 that it is Satan who has "filled their hearts" to lie about their withheld property; the fact that it is a couple who fall for Satan's temptations echoes Gen. 3 (cf. Fitzmyer, 319–20).

While James makes it quite clear that people are responsible for the sin they commit (James 1:13–15), he can still warn them to beware of the wiles of the devil (4:7). Such a tension between human responsibility and satanic influence likewise marks the final form of 1 Enoch, with the Book of the Watchers (chaps. 1–36) laying emphasis on the role of evil forces leading people into sin while the Epistle of Enoch (chaps. 91–108) locates the problem in the "folly" of human hearts (1 En. 99:7–9; see Stokes, 134–41).

Satan as the Adversary

In the opening chapters of Job and Zech. 3, Satan both accuses God's people and seeks in various ways to inhibit their flourishing. He is the adversary in at least these two senses. His general superintendence of opposition to God's people is reinforced and developed in early Jewish texts (e.g., 1 En. 54:6; Jub. 10:8; LAE [*Vita*] 16:1).

Both accusation and general antagonism feature prominently in NT depictions of the devil. He is often said to employ humans in his oppositional work, most famously in Peter's assertion that Jesus should never go to the cross, to which Jesus sternly replies, "Get behind me, Satan!" (Matt. 16:22–23). The narratives concerning Judas likewise highlight the devil's active hand in his betrayal of Jesus (e.g., Luke 22:3; John 6:70; 13:2, 27).

We may also note the role of Satan in the parable of the sower (Matt. 13 and pars.), where he snatches the seed of the kingdom message from uncomprehending hearts. This aligns well with two texts from the book of Jubilees. In Jub. 10:8 (*APOT*) we read: "And the chief of the spirits, Mastema, came and said: 'Lord, Creator, let some of them remain before me, and let them harken to my voice, and do all that I shall say unto them; for if some of them are not left to me, I shall not be able to execute the power of my will on the sons of men; for these are for corruption and leading astray before my judgment, for great is the wickedness of the sons of men.'" In the next chapter the specific imagery of seed appears: "And the prince Mastema sent ravens and birds to devour the seed which was sown in the land, in order to destroy the land, and rob the children of men of their labours. Before they could plough in the seed, the ravens picked [it] from the surface of the ground" (11:10 *APOT*).

First Peter 5:8 specifically labels the devil as an *antidikos,* a word that could mean either an accuser or a more general opponent. He goes on to compare him to a "roaring lion," an image likely drawn from Ps. 21:14 LXX, where the psalmist laments, "They have opened their mouths against me like a lion that snatches and roars" (AT). The fact that this psalm was a core text for the passion narrative likely explains its appearance here in 1 Peter (Michaels, 297–99).

Satan and his minions are regularly implicated in physical suffering. Thus, the bent-over woman in Luke 13 is said to have been "bound by Satan for eighteen years" (13:16 AT; cf. Acts 10:38). In Job 2:7, it is Satan who afflicts Job's body with loathsome sores, and so this text may lie behind the idea that Satan causes physical suffering. A connection with the prologue of Job is detectable in Paul's phrase "handing someone over to Satan" (see Dillon). In 1 Cor. 5:5, Paul urges the Corinthians to "hand . . . over to Satan for the destruction of the flesh" the man living with his mother-in-law, while in 1 Tim. 1:20 Paul himself has "handed over to Satan"

Hymenaeus and Alexander with the goal that they learn not to blaspheme. In both cases, Paul's language echoes the Septuagint of Job 2:6, where God says to Satan, "I will hand [Job] over to you." The parallel to Job suggests that the "destruction of the flesh" in the case of the Corinthian sinner refers to some bodily affliction enacted by the devil that will awaken the sinner to his spiritual plight.

Satan may also be the "destroyer" mentioned in 1 Cor. 10:10 and Heb. 11:28. While the identification is not certain, Paul and the author of Hebrews may be equating Satan and the "destroyer" of Exod. 12:23 LXX (see Farrer and Williams, 54–56). Note that the root for "the destroyer" in Exodus is the same as that used in the "destruction" of the flesh in 1 Cor. 5 (*olethr-*).

One of the more curious episodes of Satan's opposition is Jude 8–10, where Jude rebukes those who slander angelic majesties. "But Michael the archangel, when he was disputing with the devil and arguing about the body of Moses, did not dare to condemn him for slander [following Bauckham's translation], but instead said, 'The Lord rebuke you!'" (AT). Making sense of this requires considerable effort. One will search in vain for this story in the OT, though the quote "The Lord rebuke you!" likely comes from an analogous scene in Zech. 3:2, where Satan stands to accuse Joshua the high priest. It stems instead from a traditional story that may have formed the now-lost ending of the Testament of Moses, which in turn draws upon a number of stories concerning disputes between Satan and a chief angel, traditions concerning the unusual circumstances of Moses's burial (Deut. 34), and accounts of Satan's specific opposition to Moses (e.g., Jub. 48; CD 5.17–18). The tale seems to be preserved in garbled form in later Christian sources, but the essence of it is that Satan seeks to prevent Moses from being given an honorable burial on the grounds that he murdered the Egyptian in Exod. 2:11–15. Michael resists this *slander* on Moses's good name, though he entrusts the case to God as the final judge. This admittedly reconstructed background justifies Bauckham's rendering of the text as a question of a slander directed toward Moses, as opposed to conventional translations that make the unusual suggestion that Michael did not wish to speak ill of Satan (e.g., NRSV: "He did not dare to bring a condemnation of slander against him [i.e., the devil]"; on all this, see Bauckham, *Jude*, 56–63).

Satan as False World Ruler

While Satan is always subordinate to God in Scripture, the NT regularly ascribes to him some type of rulership, based on his evident ability to powerfully shape events in the world. First John 5:19 states that "the whole world lies in the power of the evil one" (ESV). This is a strong claim even when we recognize that *kosmos* here likely refers to the corrupt world system that enchains sinful humanity (cf. Stott, 101–3). Jesus can likewise refer to Satan as "the ruler of this world" in John 12:31 (ESV). Satan's "rule" is, of course, highly qualified: while he may hold sway over evil people now ("You are of your father the devil, and your will is to do your father's desires," John 8:44 ESV), he will be "cast out" by the death of Jesus (John 12:31 ESV). John uses the Synoptic verb for "casting out" demons here (*ekballō*), though he himself studiously avoids reporting any confrontations between Jesus and demons in his Gospel. This is John's subtle way of indicating that Jesus's death represents the ultimate exorcism, as he looses Satan's accusatory stranglehold on mankind (cf. van Oudtshoorn). In this same chapter John also indicates that Jesus is the ultimate parable by citing Isa. 6, while deliberately omitting parables in his reports of Jesus's teaching; we find instead the famous "I am" statements. As John says elsewhere, Jesus's incarnation can be seen as a move to counter Satan the usurper: Jesus "came to destroy the works of the devil" (1 John 3:8 AT).

This motif of destroying the works of the devil may be connected with the protevangelium in Gen. 3:15, where the seed of the woman will crush the head of the serpent. Paul certainly seems to have this verse in mind when he tells the Romans that God "will soon crush Satan beneath your feet" (Rom. 16:20 AT). (The verb for "crush" here, *syntribō*, would represent Paul's independent rendering of the Heb. *šûp*, "bruise" or "strike," since the LXX uses *tēreō*, "keep.")

As a part of his "shadow empire," Satan employs demonic henchmen to do his bidding. The Greek word *daimonion* shows up from time to time in the LXX (e.g., Deut. 32:17; Pss. 95:5; 105:37; Isa. 34:14; 65:11), though various beings discussed in the OT also fit the profile of what the NT will later label demons (see, e.g., the "evil spirit" that plagues Saul in 1 Sam. 16). But the idea that Satan would employ demonic spirits is present in intertestamental Judaism (see Stokes, 48–99): for example, Jub. 11:4–5 (cf. 10:8) discusses the activities of "the prince of Mastema [= hostility]" or "prince Mastema," who is identified with Satan in 10:11: "And the prince Mastema exerted himself to do all this, and he sent forth other spirits, those which were put under his hand, to do all manner of wrong and sin, and all manner of transgression, to corrupt and destroy, and to shed blood upon the earth."

Hebrews 2:14 asserts that the devil "holds the power of death," another claim that seems to go well beyond OT precedent. But Wis. 2:23–24 offers a clue as to how the notion arose, as well as providing us with a possible source text for the author of Hebrews: "For God created us for incorruption, and made us in the image of his own eternity, but through the devil's envy death entered the world, and those who belong to his company experience it" (cf. Lane, 60–63). The author of Wisdom here works with a traditional motif that the devil was envious of Adam at his creation (e.g., in the Greek Life of Adam and Eve); this envy led to his temptation of Adam and the death that resulted from it. In this sense, perhaps, Hebrews says the devil holds the power of death: through his primal temptation to sin, and his ongoing practice of temptation, he works death in the human race.

The assertion of Satan's "rule" is, of course, regularly qualified by assurances of his ultimate demise, sometimes seen in the image of his "falling" from heaven. In Luke 10:18, Jesus says after the return of the disciples from their mission, "I saw Satan fall like lightning from heaven." It is likely that this is an allusion to Isa. 14:12, "How you are fallen from heaven, shining one, star of the dawn" (AT). While the context concerns the temporal destruction of the king of Babylon, the text seems to include the spiritual underwriters of Babylon's power. Thus, the demise of the ruler implies a "fall" for the demonic forces behind his throne, which provides a good match for the mission in Luke 10: deliverance of suffering humans represents a "fall" for Satan's kingdom. In Rev. 12:7–9, meanwhile, we see an image of Michael and his angels casting Satan and his angels out of heaven. We should not think of this in terms of Milton's depiction of a primordial fall of Satan from heaven in *Paradise Lost*. The end of Rev. 12 explains that this apparent military engagement is in fact a picture of a judicial rebuke. "Now the salvation and power and kingdom of our God and the authority of his Messiah have come, because the accuser of the brothers has been cast out, the one who accuses them before God day and night. And they conquered him through the blood of the Lamb and through the word of their testimony, and they did not love their lives even unto death" (12:10–11 AT). Thus, the most relevant OT texts for Rev. 12 are the accusatory scenes (e.g., Zech. 3; Job 1–2). Jesus's death and resurrection spell the end of Satan's courtroom accusations.

Conclusion

Although there are distinct points of emphasis in the OT and NT portrayals of Satan, a consistent portrait emerges. While Satan makes only a few explicit appearances on the stage of the OT, he proves himself to be a relentless opponent of God's people, as is most clearly revealed in his savage and unprovoked attack on Job. By the same token, while Satan's role seems to expand in the NT, the texts never portray the devil as some independent power broker who operates outside the sphere of divine sovereignty. While he may not typically be depicted in the divine throne room (but cf. Rev. 12:7–9), he remains under God's sovereign control, and he is no match for the incursion of God's kingdom in the person of the Messiah Jesus.

See also Divine Warrior; Serpent and Antichrist

Bibliography. Bauckham, R., *Jude, 2 Peter*, WBC (Word, 1983); Bauckham, *The Theology of the Book of Revelation*, NTTh (Cambridge University Press, 1993); Brown, R. E., *The Epistles of John*, AB (Doubleday, 1982); Farrer, T. J., and G. J. Williams, "Diabolical Data," *JSNT* 39, no. 1 (2016): 40–71; Fitzmyer, J. A., *The Acts of the Apostles*, AB (Yale University Press, 1998); Garland, D. E., *1 Corinthians*, BECNT (Baker Academic, 2003); Gruelich, R. A., *Mark 1–8*, WBC (Zondervan, 2018); Hagner, D. A., *Matthew 1–13*, WBC (Zondervan, 2018); Harris, M. J., *The Second Epistle to the Corinthians*, NIGTC (Eerdmans, 2005); Hendriksen, W., *Exposition of the Gospel according to Luke* (Baker, 1978); Kelly, J. F., *Who Is Satan?* (Liturgical Press, 2013); Lane, W., *Hebrews 1–8*, WBC (Word, 1991); Michaels, J. R., *1 Peter*, WBC (Word, 1988); Motyer, J. A., *The Prophecy of Isaiah* (InterVarsity, 1993); Page, S. H. T., *Powers of Evil* (Baker, 1995); Rossing, B. R., *The Choice between Two Cities* (Trinity Press International, 1999); Stokes, R. E., *The Satan* (Eerdmans, 2019); Stott, J. R. W., *The Epistles of John*, TNTC (Inter-Varsity, 1987); Thornton, D. T., "Satan as Adversary and Ally in the Process of Ecclesial Discipline," *TynBul* 66, no. 1 (2015): 137–51; van Oudtshoorn, A., "Where Have All the Demons Gone?," *Neot* 51, no. 1 (2017): 65–82; Wahlen, C., *Jesus and the Impurity of Spirits in the Synoptic Gospels* (Mohr Siebeck, 2004).

SEAN MCDONOUGH

Sensus Plenior

See Allegory; Hosea, Book of

Septuagint: Background

Few areas of biblical studies have recently experienced a more dynamic development than Septuagint research. Considered for too long merely as a handmaid for textual criticism of the Hebrew Bible, the Septuagint has seen a change in fortunes in the last few decades. The wealth of recent publications confirms this trend. The projected six volumes of *Handbuch der Septuaginta*, under the editorship of S. Kreuzer, are off to a commendable start with an introductory volume (Kreuzer, *Introduction*) and one on the Septuagint language (Bons and Joosten, *Sprache*) to be followed by volumes on textual history, historical context, theology, and reception history of the Septuagint. J. K. Aitken's volume (*Companion*), which has already set a new standard in the field, is now accompanied by A. Salvesen and M. Law's *Oxford Handbook of the Septuagint*. Indispensable tools, such as T. Muraoka's volumes (*Lexicon, Index*, and *Syntax*), have been published in the last decade or so. The barren field of commentaries on the Greek OT is being populated by the multivolume *Brill Septuagint Commentary Series* (ed. Porter et al.), with fifteen volumes in print. Septuagint translation projects continue unabated, with completed works in English (NETS), French (*La Bible d'Alexandrie*), German (*Septuaginta Deutsch*), Spanish (*La Biblia griega*), Italian (*La Bibbia dei Settanta*), and Romanian (*Septuaginta*). Equally steady is the stream of monographs and dissertations dedicated to the Septuagint. E. Tov and

A. Lange's outstanding, multivolume reference work *Textual History of the Bible* needs to be mentioned here as well. Though not dealing primarily with the Septuagint, it includes coverage of the Septuagint and its textual history second to none. Septuagint research has come of age and has grown into a field of biblical studies legitimate in its own right.

The Septuagint, the first large-scale translation of the Hebrew Bible, reveals in a unique way the interpretive mindset and techniques current in Second Temple Judaism. No project of this magnitude emerges in a vacuum. The Septuagint stands as the most accurate reflection of the hermeneutical milieu that characterized the communities that produced and used the translation. An investigation of its theological profile provides a fuller understanding of the multifaceted context of the Septuagint, one of the most important cultural and religious enterprises of all time.

Any such study must commence with elucidating the meaning of its subject matter. There are at least three denotations for the term "Septuagint" (Wevers, 87). First, in its narrowest and probably original sense, the term was attributed to the Greek Pentateuch, the original translation of the Hebrew Torah, which some scholars still prefer. Second, as the translation project expanded to include other books of the Hebrew Bible, "Septuagint" became associated with an emerging collection of translated books, to which several writings originally composed in Greek were added. To avoid confusion, the term "Old Greek" replaced the original terminology, leaving "Septuagint" to designate generically the Greek sacred writings of the Jewish people (Dines, *Septuagint*, 2). A third ascription emerged when "Septuagint" was used for the OT section of various Greek Bibles of the church. The famous codices of the fourth and fifth centuries are an acknowledgment that, historically, the Septuagint survived primarily because of the work of Christian scribes who were responding to Christianity's growing reliance on and preference for the Greek OT. For the purposes of this article, "Septuagint" is used broadly to denote the collection of Greek sacred writings of the Jewish people.

The Septuagint is not a uniform collection of religious writings (Greenspoon, 80–81). It brings together translated writings and works originally composed in Greek. Any analysis of the LXX use of the OT must differentiate between the two categories. With regard to the former group, the investigation of the LXX use of the OT is not preoccupied with the phenomenon of biblical intertextuality. The early Jewish exegetical dynamic of *traditum* and *traditio* (Fishbane, 6) dominates any investigation of the OT / Hebrew Bible use of the OT. For the translated books of the Septuagint, however, the translators' *Vorlage* is an assumed datum; it is an already existent text. The translators' interaction with the OT is quintessentially different than that of the writers of the original Greek compositions. Herein lies the distinctiveness of the LXX use of the OT, which sets the Septuagint apart from other corpora treated in this volume (the Dead Sea Scrolls, the targumim, the OT Apocrypha, the Pseudepigrapha, etc.).

The present enquiry focuses on the LXX use of the OT by exploring the historical, literary, and theological dimensions of the Septuagint, a suitable investigative approach in dealing with the most complex hermeneutical venture in antiquity (N. T. Wright, 31). While every aspect related to the LXX and its use of the OT fits under these headings of the hermeneutical triad, space considerations allow room for tracing only the most consequential ones.

The Historical Dimension

To affirm that the Septuagint is a product of history, more precisely of Second Temple Judaism, is a truism. The events that preceded, accompanied, and followed the translation have a quintessentially historical determination: the project's location and time; its origin, rationale, and outcome; its promoters and beneficiaries; the final collection of books, its sequence, authority, and subsequent canonical status; the translators (their socio-religious-ethnic profile, linguistic and literary abilities, and theological competence and propensities); the biblical texts involved (the actual source and target texts); the evolution of the finalized text (the changes during its transmission, including its revisions and recensions). These all are historically laden aspects of a complex process explorable primarily through a rather meager cache of surviving manuscripts. While many aspects of the historical dimension deserve close scrutiny, the following selection focuses on the most consequential cases: the translators and their task, and the texts and their transmission.

The translators and their work. The Letter of Aristeas offers a conventional starting point in the analysis of the historical process. While the pseudepigraphic document, second in fame only to the Septuagint itself, is of limited historical value, it need not be dismissed entirely (B. Wright, 6–14). It traces the genesis of the Septuagint to the request for a translated copy of the Law of Moses (Let. Aris. 9–12) for the library in Alexandria. This happened during the reign of Ptolemy Philadelphus (285–247 BC), when the library was under the custodianship of Demetrius (Let. Aris. 9–12). Eleazar, the high priest in Jerusalem (Let. Aris. 9–11), granted the request and entrusted the task to seventy-two elders, six from each tribe (46), the probable origin of the name "the seventy" *(hoi hebdomēkontes)*. The project, completed in seventy-two days (Let. Aris. 307), was assessed and approved by the Jewish community (308–9), who issued a firm warning against any future revisions or alterations (310).

Although it is notoriously difficult to untangle historical reality from fiction in Aristeas (Rajak, 24–29), several details regarding the translators and their work deserve a closer look (Aejmelaeus, *Trail*). First, the perception of the kind of work undertaken by the translators is noteworthy. At one end of the spectrum stands Philo's appreciation, given at a time when embellishments had already been attached to the Aristeas. Philo considered the translators "not as translators but as prophets and priests of the mysteries, whose sincerity and singleness of thought has enabled them to go hand in hand with the purest of spirits, the spirit of Moses" (*Moses* 2.40), an accolade reflected in many religious traditions that use the Septuagint as their authoritative Scriptures. Various rabbinic traditions take the opposite end of the spectrum and give the Septuagint a less glorious assessment. A post-talmudic treatise, for example, excoriates the entire process: "It happened once that five elders wrote the Law in Greek for King Tolmai; and that day was a hard day for Israel, like the day on which Israel made the Golden Calf, because the Law was not capable of being interpreted according to all its requirements" (Mas. Sop. 1.7–10, quoted in Thackeray, 90). Jerome, who was himself engaged in a translation project of similar magnitude, expressed a more reasonable judgment: "They [did not] prophesy. For it is one thing to be a prophet, another to be an interpreter" (*Pref. Gen.*, quoted in Thackeray, 115). Regardless of these various perceptions of the translators' role, it is important to underline the indisputable fact that, through their work, the translators made the Jewish Scriptures available for a larger and ethnically diverse audience, who were thus able to read them for the first time in the lingua franca.

An equally important aspect about the translators and their work relates to the participants in the process. The Septuagint is not a one-man translation, a detail with significant implications for the LXX use of the OT. Even the Pentateuch, the original project, was translated by multiple translators, most probably five in number, each in charge of one book (Kim, 159). The resulting diversity found in the Pentateuch was replicated in the subsequent translations of the entire collection of the Hebrew Scriptures. Herein lies the premise for the heterogeneity of the Septuagint, a translation that varies from book to book, each one with its intrinsic literary and theological profile, shaped by the translator's linguistic abilities and theological predispositions.

One last historical aspect pertains to the chronological factor inherent in the project as a whole. The Pentateuch, once translated, became antecedent Scripture in the translation of the rest of the books, a status with important implications. The Greek Pentateuch provided the standard, the model, and the resource for the ensuing translations. Emanuel Tov lists vocabulary, lexical equivalences, phraseology in quotations or allusions, and exegetical guidelines as among the most important domains affected in the process (Tov, "Impact"). Evidently, this aspect has reverberations through the literary dimensions as well. In fact, the partition between the historical and literary dimensions might be artificial, since they are so intertwined, as evidenced in Aitken's study linking the translators' Jewish-Greek identity to the dialect they used (Aitken, "Language").

The texts and the history of their transmission. The Letter of Aristeas narrative ends with a decree-like statement, "It is right that it should remain in its present form and that no revision should take place" (Let. Aris. 310), issued by the priests and elders to shield the translation from any future alterations. The following centuries, however, attest to the futility of the decree, as numerous efforts were undertaken to provide a Greek text that corresponded more faithfully to the Hebrew text. The desire of subsequent Septuagint users, Jewish and non-Jewish alike, to improve the original translation meant that the LXX, throughout its history, was perceived as a rectifiable translation, always in need of improvement. In other words, one might postulate *Septuaginta semper transformanda est* (Septuagint must always be transformed), to build on Mogens Müller's phrase *Biblia semper interpretanda est* (The Bible must always be interpreted). This complex historical process must be understood both in terms of quantity and quality. As to the quantity, it meant an expansion in volume to include eventually the translation of all books of the Hebrew Scriptures and the later compositions in Greek. With regard to the quality, it meant repeated attempts at *diorthosis*, the corrective process that brings the translation to a higher degree of conformity with the Hebrew text. Participating in the process were Jewish and non-Jewish communities, driven by various underlying motivations.

Setting the stage is the earliest traceable revision, brought to light by the Minor Prophets Scroll from Naḥal Ḥever. Dated in the first century BC, the so-called Kaige recension was a Copernican moment in Septuagint studies (Barthélemy). The scrolls display an unmistakable effort at "isomorphic-Hebraizing adaptation" (i.e., aligning the translation to reflect ever so closely the form as well as the content of the Hebrew parent text) (Kreuzer, 27), with significant implications for the evolution of the Greek text.

Two revision movements, both in the wake of the Kaige recension, deserve separate treatment. First, the so-called Septuagint revisions are a group of Jewish translation projects aimed at providing a Greek Scripture that distances itself from the current LXX text. Given the importance attributed to the LXX by the nascent Christian church, including the NT authors and the apostolic and Eastern church fathers, these Jewish revisions were an effort to reclaim a Greek text that was no longer associated with the LXX, which had become part of the Christian Scriptures. Three such revisions are documented in the history of the Greek text: Aquila (early second c.), known for its consistent literalism, dutifully concordant and isomorphic (Kreuzer, 33); Symmachus (late second c.), noted for its refined phraseology; and Theodotion (late second c.), with a status, unfortunately, yet to be fully elucidated (Kreuzer, 34).

Second, Christian contributions in this respect are known as Septuagint recensions. Having already adopted the Septuagint as their OT Scriptures, early Christians engaged in such activities for several reasons, not least out of apologetic fervor in defending their Scriptures and interest in text-critical matters. Towering among them stand Origen and the Hexapla, the reproducing of the OT text in six parallel columns. The first two columns, reserved for the Hebrew text in unvocalized Hebrew script and in Greek phonetic transcription, are followed by the translations of Aquila, Symmachus, Origen's text of the LXX, and Theodotion (Jobes and Silva, 48). Whether praised or contested, the Hexapla stands as the greatest text-critical enterprise of antiquity, available today only in extremely fragmentary fashion. Its destruction can be deemed as one of the greatest textual tragedies of all times. Outside of the Hexapla and the Caesarian Greek text of Origen, the space permits only a brief mention of the recensions by Lucian and Hesychius, both late third century, to account for the so-called *trifaria varietas,* the threefold variations of the Septuagint text known to Jerome (Marcos, 223–46).

The historical evolution of the LXX is not a linear process. The useful display of textual relationships and influences (the simplified and the complex versions) in Jobes and Silva (48–54) allows insight into the complexity of the Septuagint's evolution. The relationship between events, texts, and participants continues to provide great intramural debates, which are not easily resolved in light of the meager manuscript evidence that has survived. Noteworthy in this respect is the *Textual History of the Bible* project gathering the most comprehensive manuscript and textual evidence of the prehexaplaric, hexaplaric, and posthexaplaric groups (Tov and Lange, 191–235).

What might these historical trajectories of the Greek text say about the LXX use of the OT? Three considerations are in order. First, the Kaige recension is an implicit witness to the process of standardization of the Hebrew text itself, reflecting a new hermeneutic and understanding of the Holy Scriptures. The authority of the Hebrew text was to be upheld and communicated only by a Greek text that matched it perfectly, both in content and in form. Changes had to be made to the word order, verbal tenses, and phrase constituents in the Greek text to mirror the Hebrew text. Guided by the new mentality, the Hebrew text "was supposed to shine through and become recognizable in the Greek translation" (Kreuzer, 27).

A second consideration relates to the periods of quasi-textual fluidity among the Greek textual traditions, mirroring the Hebrew textual traditions. "From uniformity to pluriformity," Paul Lagarde's hypothesis for the LXX origin, was countered by Paul Kahle's hypothesis, "from pluriformity to uniformity." Both are being replaced by Tov's more realistic synthesis: "from uniformity to pluriformity and back to unity" (Marcos, 53–103). The important inference from this complex aggregation of textual evidence must be the need for caution in sorting it out. When facing incongruities between the Hebrew and Greek texts, it is more prudent to consider every available aspect of textual evidence, rather than charge the translators with a cavalier or careless approach to their *Vorlage.*

A notable spin-off of the considerations above is the deuterographa, the doublets in the Hebrew and Greek Scriptures, which are thoroughly tallied by Armin Lange and Matthias Weigold (*Quotations*). The phenomenon surfaces most visibly in the Pentateuch, in the books of Kingdoms and Chronicles, and in Psalms and Proverbs. More work awaits to be done in the Septuagint deuterographa, with direct implications for understanding both the history and evolution of the texts as well as the reciprocal literary dependence in the translation process. The similarity of the translations of Psalms' choruses (Pss. 42:6, 11; 43:5 [LXX 41:6, 12; 42:5]), doublets (Pss. 14 and 53 [13 and 52]; 57:7–11 and 108:1–5 [56:8–12 and 107:2–6]), and liturgical phrases (106:1, 48; 117:2; 135:21; 136:3–5 [105:1, 48; 116:2; 134:21; 135:1–3], etc.), as well as doublets in Psalms and other books (Ps. 18 [17] and 2 Sam. 22 [2 Kgdms. 22]), is best explained by postulating a level of literary dependence during translation.

Last, but not least, one must acknowledge that texts develop not in a vacuum but in vibrant religious traditions. It should be no surprise to find reciprocal influences and cross-pollination between various textual traditions, such as the Septuagint and the NT. Given the predominant phenomenon of the NT quoting from the Septuagint, often passages in the LXX and NT traditions are preserved with identical textual variants. Text-critical decisions must be taken with great care in these cases, to assess the real direction of influence between passages (Gheorghita, "Influence").

Habakkuk 2:4 and its textual metamorphoses stand as a good example for the phenomena presented above (Gheorghita, *Role*). Below are the main textual traditions of the Greek text:

ὁ δὲ δίκαιος ἐκ πίστεώς μου ζήσεται (Old Greek, Göttingen LXX)

καὶ δί]καιος ἐκ πίστεως αὐτοῦ ζήσετ[αι] (Kaige recension, Naḥal Ḥever)

και δικαιος εν πιστει αυτου ζησεται (Aquila and Theodotion, α' and θ', cf. Hexapla)

ο ‹δε› δικαιος τη εαυτου πιστει ζησει (Symmachus, σ', cf. Hexapla)

‹ο δικαιος› εκ πιστεως αυτου ζησεται (the rest of the *hermeneutai,* cf. Jerome)

ὁ δὲ δίκαιος ἐκ πίστεως ζήσεται (Rom. 1:17, NT)

ὁ δὲ δίκαιος ἐκ πίστεως ζήσεται (Gal. 3:11, NT)

ὁ δὲ δίκαιός μου ἐκ πίστεως ζήσεται (Heb. 10:38, NT)

The Literary Dimension

The Septuagint is a collection of texts. Alongside the paramount importance of its religious content or of its unprecedented and unsurpassed status among ancient translations, the Septuagint is also a literary artifact, with a complex and rich literary dimension. Contributing to this dimension is a tapestry of issues including the nature of the target language, literary genre and style, textuality, translation technique, rhetoric, and intertextuality. Each one of these aspects is determined preeminently by the origins of the books in the collection.

The starting point for assessing the literary dimension must be the varying provenance of the Septuagint books, some as translations and others as original Greek composition, succinctly presented by de Troyer (268). The writings belonging to the two groups differ from each other, not only in their literary distinctiveness but also in their approaches to the OT. The translated books follow the parent text, which, essentially, is the factor responsible for their content. The LXX use of the OT in these writings, be they translations of the Hebrew canonical books or noncanonical books (e.g., Ben Sira), focuses exclusively on the translation process itself.

Conversely, the books composed originally in Greek are bound to no parent text. These writings use biblical material for their theological reflection, as they quote, allude to, echo, retell, explore, expand, apply, and actualize the Jewish Scriptures. The elaborate exploration of wisdom and its role in creation (Wis. 7–8) and in the Egyptian exodus (Wis. 11–19), the constant theological anchoring of the books of the Maccabees in the Mosaic covenant and its legislation, and the pathos of Ps. 151 all exemplify the creative ways in which the Apocrypha uses the OT. Since the Apocrypha is treated separately in this volume, no further attention is given to it here.

The nature of Septuagint Greek. The nature of the Greek language in the translated books of the Septuagint has been a perennial bone of contention among scholars and is intrinsically tied to the literary dimension of the LXX use of the OT. The nineteenth century set the stage by considering the LXX Greek as sui generis, a Holy Ghost language, uniquely suited to the Greek Scriptures. At the end of that century, the discovery of a significant cache of papyri, ostraca, and inscriptions caused a swing in the opposite direction. In light of new evidence, Adolf Deissmann concluded that the LXX language was not a special type of Greek (Marcos, 7); it was the marketplace Hellenistic Greek at the time. Words previously believed to be reserved for divinely inspired texts were also found in the common vocabulary of the masses. Any distinct flavor that might be attached to the Septuagint Greek was explained away as the direct, inevitable result of translation. Deissmann's assessment regarding the lexical stock was subsequently confirmed by Albert Thumb and James Moulton in the area of Greek syntax and phraseology (Marcos, 9).

Yet another evaluation was generated by work of Gehman and Turner, proponents for the so-called Jewish Greek, a language influenced at its core by features not characteristic of Koine Greek (Marcos, 11). The dialectal idiosyncrasies were not the result of translation but were characteristic of the language spoken by the translators and their community, a living dialect of Greek, an Alexandrian "Jewish-Greek." The tussle over the nature of LXX Greek has continued unabated, with ever increasing nuance and methodological precision. In his survey, Stanley Porter ("History," 31, 33) discusses, inter alios, Georg Walser, an advocate for a distinctive Semitic Greek arising from synagogue life, and Moisés Silva, who, starting from an analysis of bilingualism, astutely observes that the tension between the two camps can be resolved by taking into account the linguistic dichotomy of *langue* (style) versus *parole* (grammar).

The literary dimension of the LXX use of the OT is inherently linked with the nature of Septuagint language. In the translation process, the source language influenced the target language at all levels: vocabulary, morphology, syntax, rhetoric, and discourse. There are loanwords, especially cultic, such as *sabbaton* (Sabbath) and *pascha* (pesach); loan phrases, *lamnaṣṣēaḥ* (to the choir director) translated *eis to telos* (to the end); and adjustments of semantic range, *tôrâ* (instruction, direction, teaching) as *nomos* (law, custom), *ḥesed* (loving-kindness, covenantal loyalty) as *eleēmosynē* (mercy), *bṭḥ* / *beṭaḥ* (to trust / confidence) as *elpizō* / *elpis* (to hope / hope). The phenomenon extends to include various syntactical features, such as the replication of Semitic parataxis (Jobes and Silva, 114–19), and multitudes of other syntax adjustments, which are treated almost exhaustively in Muraoka's epochal study on the syntax of Septuagint Greek (*Syntax*).

Translation technique. The systematic analysis of translational features is the subject matter of translation technique, one of the most exciting and debated aspects in Septuagint research. Briefly stated, translation technique is the discipline that analyzes, describes, quantifies, and assesses the Septuagint qua translation. At the risk of oversimplification, there are two schools of thought regarding the legitimacy of the enterprise itself and the validity of its results. The advocates in favor of the method highlight the descriptive nature of this approach, confining it to an investigation of translation patterns, statistically analyzed, compared, and tallied, usually with the help of digital databases. The goal of a translation technique investigation is to uncover "patterns that guided the translation," without implying that translators' habits are necessarily intentional (Aejmelaeus, "Intention," 65).

The opposing perspective disregards the translation technique approach on account of several perceived systemic flaws. From a textual-criticism point of view, there is perennial uncertainty with regard to the source and target texts analyzed. Any assessment of translation technique presupposes a thorough knowledge of the actual texts, both the source and target texts. This is seldom the case in working with LXX manuscripts. A more fundamental criticism is leveled against the naive perception of the true nature of translation involving religious texts. Translators are not automatons; they are people deeply influenced by religious beliefs and cultural factors, which ultimately determine their translation habits. In evaluating a translation, mapping these factors is a more reliable guide than any metrics that translation technique could provide (Schaper, *Eschatology*, 16–20).

Regardless of the reservations some might have, translation technique methodology has had success when applied to Septuagint studies, particularly in assessing the literality of translation, a characteristic of paramount importance in Septuagint studies. Each translator finds his place on the continuum between *verbum de verbo* and *sensus de sensu*. Two approaches to Septuagint literality have proved to be most helpful. Tov proposes five criteria to assess the literalness of a translation: internal consistency, textual isomorphism, word order, quantitative representation, and adequacy of lexical choices (*Use*, 18–31). Though the criteria were designed with text-critical objectives in sight, they are equally useful in probing other facets of literality. The alternative approach is the taxonomy proposed by T. A. W. van der Louw, emerging from the interface of Septuagint studies and translation studies. It is an example of methodological complexity that leaves no room to chance. The uneven literality is one of the most palpable characteristics of the Greek Scriptures. The books are spread on a continuum ranging from translations characterized by a high degree of literalness (the Pentateuch, with perhaps the exception of Exodus; Psalms; the Minor Prophets) to those with a high degree of translational freedom (Proverbs; Job; Isaiah). For an acquaintance with the book-by-book Septuagint literality, J. M. Dines's volume is a good starter (*Septuagint*, 14–24). For an in-depth assessment, however, Aitken's *Companion* and Kreuzer's *Introduction* are unsurpassed.

The translation technique approach has more recently been extended to the area of rhetorical and literary devices in the Septuagint. In E. Bons and T. J. Kraus's volume dedicated to this topic (*Sapienter*), J. Joosten argues that grammatical variations in the Septuagint are often for rhetorical ornamentation ("Ornamentation"). Similarly, Dines points to the wide use of synonyms and rearranged word order to enhance the rhetorical impact of the translation ("Stylistic"), while Bons detects various rhetorical devices in the Greek Psalter absent in the Hebrew. Cumulatively, one can assert that rhetoric, discourse, and other literary considerations, while secondary in the translation process, were never altogether absent. Even in books exhibiting literal translation (e.g., Ecclesiastes), rhetorical features are present (Aitken, "Ecclesiastes").

Finally, the translation technique approach facilitates evaluation of different types of exegesis undertaken by translators. Joosten distinguishes between several types of exegetical procedures: spontaneous exegesis, deliberate exegesis, accidental exegesis, and quotation-based exegesis ("Interpretation"). In a similar vein, Tov detects evidence of theologically motivated exegesis (especially when the translators refer to God and his saving acts), midrash-type exegesis (in the translators' attempt to clarify pentateuchal laws), and actualizations of lexical units and phraseology, all done to render a more accessible and comprehensible translation ("Septuagint," 176–78). Ample textual evidence is provided in a separate article (Tov, "Exegesis"). The topic of theologically motivated exegesis, in fact, leads us to the theological dimension of the LXX use of the OT.

The Theological Dimension

The third dimension engages in the theological interpretation of the observations culled from the exploration of the previous two dimensions. This process has far-reaching implications for constructing a distinct theology of the Septuagint.

While there are reservations with regard to the pursuit of LXX theology or even its legitimacy, there are ardent defenders of the cause. T. M. Law criticizes the doublespeak of some scholars who, even while admitting significant divergence between the LXX and MT, still dispute that the two textual traditions have divergent theologies (169). Similarly, M. Rösel defends the writing of an LXX theology, an endeavor warranted by the perceived differences between the source and target texts. T. McLay (608) even charts the fundamental principles that should guide such an effort, which must not be limited to the differences between the presumed source texts and the target texts but should follow "the same basic principles as a theology of the OT/HB or the New Testament." The fascinating dialogue between the two positions must continue.

Two caveats should be mentioned. First, since individual books are the modules of translation, the theological profile of the LXX has to be investigated on a book-by-book basis. No theological *Tendenz* should automatically be assumed for all the books. Second, the distinct LXX theological nuances cannot be unequivocally ascribed to the translators; they could have been caused by a variety of reasons, not least the use of a different *Vorlage*. The translation versus interpretation divide must be considered with more methodological precision than in other instances (Brock, 87). Regardless of the real cause for the LXX theological nuances, it is unavoidable to conclude that the LXX use of the OT has substantial theological implications. The translation stands on its own theological trajectory, with or without the explicit intention of the translator.

Tracing the theological dimension of the LXX use of the OT can be approached in several ways. The approach could be primarily textual, in which all the textual constituents of the target text (words, morpho-syntactical constructions, phrases, sentences, structural markers, paragraphs, pluses and minuses, and translation equivalencies) are used to outline a theology of the target text. Alternatively, one could approach the task thematically, by focusing on passages that display distinct theological nuances. The discussion below follows this latter approach, concentrating on the areas of LXX eschatology and messianism.

Septuagint eschatology. In its incipient stages, OT eschatology was limited to the topics of resurrection and judgment of the dead, and the ensuing rewards and punishment (Collins, 597). Later developments, however, included other end-times aspects, primarily the expectation of future events and processes that move creation toward its goal of a "golden age of peace, righteousness and prosperity" (Evans and Flint, 2).

Septuagint eschatology is a subgenre of Jewish eschatology, which emerged from and was shaped by the Greek Scriptures. Its legitimacy is still debated, as typified by the *Handbook of Christian Eschatology*, which makes no mention of it (Mühling). Yet, just as other Judaic communities shaped their own distinct eschatologies (e.g., Qumran eschatology), it is reasonable to surmise that the Greek Scriptures were conducive to the emergence of a distinct Septuagint-shaped eschatology. The main shapers of Septuagint eschatology are passages in which the Greek text exhibits a more pronounced eschatological focus than its Hebrew counterpart, often due to significant textual divergencies. Moreover, the Apocrypha plays a significant part in shaping the distinct eschatological outlook of the Greek Scriptures. (See the articles on the Apocrypha elsewhere in the dictionary.)

Eschatological nuances can be detected at various levels. They can be found at the level of individual phraseology, such as the enigmatic phrase *eis to telos*, the translation of the musical term *lamnaṣṣēaḥ*, used fifty-five times in the Psalter's liturgical notes (Pss. 4:1; 5:1; 6:1; 44:1; etc.). Inadvertently or not, the net result is an eschatological orientation in the Greek psalms, which is not found in the Hebrew text. The same Hebrew phrase surfaces at the end of Hab. 3:19, where it is translated as an articular infinitive *tou nikēsai*, which reorients the Greek passage toward the goal of a future victory, an accent that does not exist in the corresponding text. These phrases, spread throughout the Septuagint and enhanced by the analogical principle *gezerah shawah* ("equal statute"), infuse the Greek Scriptures with distinct eschatological nuances not discernible in the Hebrew text. Furthermore, F. F. Bruce (52) draws attention to a similar eschatological surplus in the colophons of the Greek Psalter, especially the historical psalms, which have no correspondent in the Hebrew Psalms.

Individual books also display similar phenomena. I. L. Seeligmann's classic study on LXX Isaiah demonstrates that the translation was influenced both by the biblical text and popular Jewish traditions outside the Bible. As to the eschatology of the translator, Seeligmann (116) concludes that the translator "combined Isaiah's expectations regarding the future with his own." The distinct Isaianic eschatological nuances have been confirmed by others (see Baer; Troxel; De Sousa). D. H. Gard reaches similar conclusions on the eschatology of Job. Even though the translator's presumed *Vorlage* and the MT are very similar, "the concept of the future life in the book of Job M [MT] and G [LXX] differ significantly" (Gard, 17). The differences are traceable to the translator's tendency "to introduce [his] theological point of view" (18). The eschatological tendencies are even more pervasive in the LXX Psalter. J. Schaper argues that the LXX develops eschatological themes beyond the boundaries set by the Hebrew Psalter. The linguistic and thematic translation choices in the Psalter, and especially their similarity to other extracanonical contemporary writings, demonstrate that "the second century is witness to a continual development of the formulation of eschatological and messianic hopes, with the Greek Psalter as one of its main monuments" (*Eschatology*, 20). Almost identical conclusions are reached by J. H. Sailhamer's study on the translation technique in the LXX Psalter, even when using a methodology diametrically opposed to the one that guided Schaper. Sailhamer (21) observes that "the [verb] tense is . . . at the heart of one of the central social and religious issues of early Judaism, eschatology."

It is important not to overstate the case for a distinct LXX eschatology. The vast majority of passages in the LXX preserve faithfully the eschatological perspective underlying the Hebrew textual tradition; the Septuagint did not invent Jewish eschatology. Both the Hebrew *bəʾaḥărît hayyāmîm* and the Greek *en tais eschatais hēmerais* ("in the last days") equally point forward. The coming of a prophet like Moses (Deut. 18), the anticipation of a new covenant (Jer. 31 MT / 38 LXX), and the cataclysmic events of the end times (Hag. 2), to sample some classic passages, are as clearly future-oriented as their Greek counterparts. Yet, when various nuances of multiple eschatological passages in the Greek text are assessed, one cannot escape the conclusion that the exegetical details, whether lexical or morphological, syntactical or ideological, carry a more pronounced eschatological orientation.

Septuagint messianism. The shape of the Septuagint messianism can be assessed in an analogous way, as in W. Horbury's insightful analysis of messianic overtones in the OT Apocrypha and Pseudepigrapha ("Apocrypha"). A working definition for messianism should start with the cardinal characteristics of the messiah. The title is given to an eschatological figure, a "divinely appointed and anointed supernatural man" (Charlesworth, "Christology," 4), whose task is to establish God's kingdom on earth. The human yet transcendent savior is awaited as the long-expected royal Davidic redeemer (Lust, 10).

At the risk of oversimplification, the two schools of thought are representative. On the minimalist side, Charlesworth draws this basic profile: messianology in Jewish Scripture is limited, and it was developed much later than previously thought, being neither a coherent nor a normative doctrine. In his assessment, the Second Temple period was not characterized by the expectation of a coming messiah ("Christology," 35). On the maximalist side, Horbury challenges this interpretation. He construes the textual data very differently: "Messianism grew up in Old Testament times; the Old Testament books, especially in their edited and collected form, offered what were understood in the post-exilic age and later as a series of messianic prophecies; and this series formed the heart of a coherent set of expectations which profoundly influenced ancient Judaism and early Christianity" (*Cult*, 6).

The positions regarding the LXX's role in the development of Jewish messianism are similarly divided. J. Charlesworth's groundbreaking volume *The Messiah* contains no specific treatment of messianism in the Septuagint. The opening chapter, tracing the diachronic growth of Jewish messianism, does not even mention the Septuagint among the various corpora of contemporary Jewish literature. The reexaminations of the relevant texts by M. A. Knibb, J. Lust (*Messianism*), Schaper ("Messianism"), and Horbury (*Jewish Messianism*) attempt to rebalance the record.

The number of passages supporting the LXX messianic tendencies is impressive and spans the entire Tanakh. While the tally differs from author to author, the following is a standard list: Gen. 3:15; 49:10; Num. 24:7, 17; 2 Sam. 7:16; Isa. 7:14; 9:6–7; 11:4; 14:29–32; Ezek. 21:30–32; 43:3; Dan. 7:13; Hosea 8:10; Amos 4:13; Zech. 9:10; Ps. 110:3 (Lust, 9). Harl includes an even larger list of potential texts (Dorrival, Harl, and Munnich, 222).

The interpretation of the textual data varies among scholars. Lust discards many potential LXX proof texts, claiming that the relevant Greek texts have diminished messianic characteristics. He points to texts that the LXX construes corporately even though their Hebrew counterparts allude to an individual person; or to LXX passages that ascribe victory to God when the Hebrew text attributes it to a messianic figure; or to eschatological dimensions in the Hebrew text that are historically actualized in the Greek text ("Messianism," 10). He concludes that "one cannot say that the LXX as a whole displays a messianic exegesis" ("Messianism," 12). These charges are countered by Horbury ("Monarchy"), who combines the exegetical data of the relevant passages with the larger historical-religious context in which the Septuagint emerged. Horbury further strengthens his case by pointing to the similarities between the LXX and Qumran types of messianism. The position expressed by van der Woude (510)—"In definite deviations from the Hebrew original the LXX proclaims the messianic hope in Hellenistic Judaism"—considered once to be indisputable, will need to be perennially revisited.

Here, then, is a tripartite perspective on the LXX use of the OT. Either individually or collectively, the historical, literary, and theological layers of the Septuagint and its way of engaging with the OT establish the Greek textual tradition as *primus inter pares* among the Hebrew Bible offspring. The Septuagint is a pillar in the history of the biblical text, without which much would be unknown, hidden, or misunderstood, both in Judaism and in Christianity. For Second Temple Judaism, the Septuagint represents a genuine and veritable reflection of its hermeneutical milieu. For Christianity, the Septuagint offers not only an authoritative confirmation of the Hebrew Scriptures but also a conceptual framework in preparation for a much-anticipated event, which, in the fullness of time, was fulfilled "according to the Scriptures" (*kata tas graphas*).

See also OT Use of the OT: Comparison with the NT Use of the OT; *other Septuagint articles*; *Dead Sea Scrolls articles*; *Mishnah, Talmud, and Midrashim articles*; *Philo articles*; *Targums articles*

Bibliography. Aejmelaeus, A., *On the Trail of the Septuagint Translators* (Kok Pharos, 1993); Aejmelaeus, "Translation Technique and the Intention of the Translators," in Aejmelaeus, *On the Trail of the Septuagint Translators*, 65–77; Aitken, J. K., "The Language of the Septuagint and Jewish-Greek Identity," in *Jewish-Greek Tradition in Antiquity and Byzantine Empire*, ed. J. K. Aitken and J. C. Paget (Cambridge University Press, 2014), 120–34; Aitken, "Rhetoric and Poetry in Greek Ecclesiastes," *BIOSCS* 38 (2007): 55–78; Aitken, ed., *T&T Clark Companion to the Septuagint* (Bloomsbury, 2015); Baer, D. A., *When We All Go Home* (Sheffield Academic, 2001); Barthélemy, D., *Les devanciers d'Aquila* (Brill, 1963); Bockmuehl, M., and J. C. Paget, eds., *Redemption and Resistance* (T&T Clark, 2007); Bons, E., "Rhetorical Devices in the Septuagint Psalter," in Bons and Kraus, *Et sapienter et eloquenter*, 69–82; Bons, E., and J. Joosten, eds., *Die Sprache der Septuaginta* (Gütersloher Verlag, 2016); Bons, E., and T. J. Kraus, eds., *Et sapienter et eloquenter* (Vandenhoeck & Ruprecht, 2011); Brock, S. P., "Translating the Old Testament," in *It Is Written*, ed. D. A. Carson and H. G. M. Williamson (Cambridge University Press, 1988), 87–98; Bruce, F. F., "The Earliest Old Testament Interpretation," in *The Witness of Tradition*, by M. A. Beek et al. (Brill, 1972), 36–52; Charlesworth, J. H., "From Messianology to Christology," in Charlesworth, *The Messiah*, 3–35; Charlesworth, ed., *The Messiah* (Fortress, 1992); Collins, J. J., "Eschatology," in *EDEJ*, 594–97; De Sousa, R. F., *Eschatology and Messianism in Septuagint LXX Isaiah 1–12* (T&T Clark, 2010); de Troyer, K., "Septuagint," in *New Cambridge History of the Bible*, vol. 1, *From the Beginnings to 600*, ed. J. C. Paget and J. Schaper (Cambridge University Press, 2013), 267–88; Dines, J. M., *The Septuagint* (T&T Clark,

2004); Dines, "Stylistic Invention and Rhetorical Purpose in the Book of the Twelve," in Bons and Kraus, *Et sapienter et eloquenter*, 23–48; Dorival, G., M. Harl, and O. Munnich, *La Bible grecque des Septante* (Cerf, 1988); Evans, C. A., and P. W. Flint, "Introduction," in *Eschatology, Messianism, and the Dead Sea Scrolls*, ed. C. A. Evans and P. W. Flint (Eerdmans, 1997), 1–9; Fishbane, M., *Biblical Interpretation in Ancient Israel* (Clarendon, 1985); Gard, D. H., "The Concept of the Future Life according to the Greek Translator of the Book of Job," *JBL* 73 (1954): 137–43; Gheorghita, R., "The Influence of the Septuagint on the New Testament," in *Thematic Studies*, vol. 1 of *Early Christian Literature and Intertextuality*, ed. C. A. Evans and H. D. Zacharias (T&T Clark, 2009), 165–83; Gheorghita, *The Role of the Septuagint in Hebrews* (Mohr Siebeck, 2003); Greenspoon, L., "Hebrew into Greek," in *The Ancient Period*, vol. 1 of *A History of Biblical Interpretation*, ed. A. J. Hauser and D. F. Watson (Eerdmans, 2003), 80–113; Horbury, W., "Biblical Interpretation in the Greek Jewish Writings," in *New Cambridge History of the Bible*, vol. 1, *From the Beginnings to 600*, ed. J. C. Paget and J. Schaper (Cambridge University Press, 2013), 289–320; Horbury, *Jewish Messianism and the Cult of Christ* (SCM, 1998); Horbury, *Messianism among Jews and Christians* (T&T Clark, 2003); Horbury, "Messianism in the Old Testament Apocrypha and Pseudepigrapha," in Horbury, *Messianism among Jews and Christians*, 35–64; Horbury, "Monarchy and Messianism in the Greek Pentateuch," in *The Septuagint and Messianism*, ed. M. A. Knibb (Peeters, 2006), 79–128; Jobes, K. H., and M. Silva, *Invitation to the Septuagint*, 2nd ed. (Baker Academic, 2015); Joosten, J., "Interpretation and Meaning in the Septuagint Translation," in *Translation, Interpretation, Meaning*, ed. A. Aejmelaeus and P. Pahta (Helsinki Collegium for Advanced Studies, 2012), http://hdl.handle.net/10138/34744; Joosten, "Rhetorical Ornamentation in the Septuagint," in Bons and Kraus, *Et sapienter et eloquenter*, 11–22; Kim, H., *Multiple Authorship of the Septuagint Pentateuch* (Brill, 2019); Knibb, M. A., ed., *The Septuagint and Messianism* (Peeters, 2006); Kraus, W., and R. G. Wooden, eds., *Septuagint Research* (Brill, 2006); Kreuzer, S., ed., *Einleitung in die Septuaginta* (Gütersloher Verlag, 2016); Kreuzer, ed., *Introduction to the Septuagint*, trans. D. Brenner and P. Altmann (Baylor University Press, 2019); Lange, A., and M. Weigold, *Biblical Quotations and Allusions in Second Temple Jewish Literature* (Vandenhoeck & Ruprecht, 2011); Law, T. M., *When God Spoke* (Oxford University Press, 2013); Lust, J., "Messianism and Septuagint," in Lust, *Messianism and the Septuagint* (Peeters, 2004), 10–26; Marcos, N. F., *The Septuagint in Context* (Brill, 2000); McLay, T., "Why Not a Theology of the Septuagint?," in *Die Septuaginta—Texte, Theologien, Einflüsse*, ed. W. Kraus, M. Karrer, and M. Messer (Mohr Siebeck, 2010), 607–20; Mühling, M., *T&T Clark Handbook of Christian Eschatology* (Bloomsbury T&T Clark, 2015); Muraoka, T., *The Greek-English Lexicon* (Peeters, 2009); Muraoka, *The Greek-Hebrew Two-Way Index* (Peeters, 2010); Muraoka, *The Syntax of Septuagint Greek* (Peeters, 2016); Philo, *De Vita Mosis*, trans. F. H. Colson, in *Philo*, vol. 6, LCL 289 (Harvard University Press, 1984); Porter, S. E., "History of Scholarship on the Language of the Septuagint," in Bons and Joosten, *Die Sprache der Septuaginta*, 15–38; Porter, S. E., et al., eds., *Brill Septuagint Commentary Series* (Brill, 2004–); Rajak, T., *Translation and Survival* (Oxford University Press, 2009); Rösel, M., "Towards a Theology of the Septuagint," in Kraus and Wooden, *Septuagint Research*, 239–52; Sailhamer, J. H., *The Translational Technique of the Greek Septuagint for the Hebrew Verbs and Participles in Psalms 3–41* (Peter Lang, 1991); Salvesen, A., "Messianism in Ancient Bible Translations in Greek and Latin," in Bockmuehl and Paget, *Redemption and Resistance*, 245–61; Salvesen, A., and M. Law, *The Oxford Handbook of the Septuagint* (Oxford University Press, 2021); Schaper, J., *Eschatology in the Greek Psalter* (Mohr Siebeck, 1995); Schaper, "Messianism in the Septuagint of Isaiah and Messianic Intertextuality in the Greek Bible," in Knibb, *The Septuagint and Messianism*, 371–80; Seeligmann, I. L., *The Septuagint Version of Isaiah* (Brill, 1948); Thackeray, H. St. J., *The Letter of Aristeas* (SPCK, 1917); Tov, E., *The Greek and Hebrew Bible* (Brill, 1999); Tov, "The Impact of the Septuagint Translation of the Torah on the Translation of the Other Books" in Tov, *The Greek and Hebrew Bible*, 183–94; Tov, "Septuagint," in *Mikra*, ed. M. J. Mulder (Van Gorcum, 1988), 161–88; Tov, "The Septuagint Translation of the Torah as a Source and Resource for the Post-Pentateuchal Translators," in Bons and Joosten, *Die Sprache der Septuaginta*, 316–28; Tov, *Text Critical Use of the Septuagint in Biblical Research*, 3rd ed. (Eisenbrauns, 2015); Tov, "Theologically Motivated Exegesis Imbedded in the Septuagint," in Tov, *The Greek and Hebrew Bible*, 257–69; Tov, E., and A. Lange, eds., *The Textual History of the Bible*, 3 vols. (Brill, 2016–); Troxel, R. L., *LXX-Isaiah as Translation and Interpretation* (Brill, 2007); van der Louw, T. A. W., *Transformations in the Septuagint* (Peeters, 2007); van der Woude, A. S., "*chriō*: C. Messianic Ideas in Later Judaism: II. Septuagint," in *TDNT*, 5:510; Wevers, J. W., "The Interpretative Character and Significance of the Septuagint Version," in *Hebrew Bible / Old Testament: The History of Its Interpretation*, vol. 1, part 1, *Antiquity*, ed. M. Sæbø et al. (Vandenhoeck & Ruprecht, 1996), 84–107; Wright, B. G., *The Letter of Aristeas* (de Gruyter, 2015); Wright, N. T., *The New Testament and the People of God* (SPCK, 1992).

RADU GHEORGHITA

Septuagint: Comparison with the NT Use of the OT

This essay focuses on the use of the LXX in the NT. To introduce the topic we will briefly discuss the LXX and the important role it plays in the NT authors' use of the Hebrew Scriptures. However, the main focus of the essay is on a selection of passages that the LXX translator renders in a manner that differs from and develops to varying degrees the meaning of the corresponding MT and that are subsequently employed by the NT authors. The translators' rendering of the texts will be categorized and compared with the NT authors' appropriation of them.

The term "LXX" originally referred to the translation of the Pentateuch into Greek in Alexandria, Egypt, in the third century BC, as allegedly described in the Letter of Aristeas. However, the term is often used more generally to refer to the Greek Jewish Scriptures, consisting mainly of translations of the books of the Hebrew Bible but also including additions to some of the books of the Hebrew Bible as well as other independent works (Glenny, "Biblical Theology," 264–65; McLay, 6; Jobes and Silva, 13–15). This general use of the term "LXX" is similar to the way we might refer to the "German Bible" or "English Bible," without having a particular translation in mind. The use of the term "LXX" in this article follows this general usage, referring to the Greek Jewish Scriptures, consisting mainly of the books of the Hebrew Bible. The LXX text that will be used is the Rahlfs-Hanhart edition (2006).

The LXX has a complex history. The books in it that were translated from the Hebrew Bible were translated by various translators in Egypt and Palestine between the third century BC and about the first century AD. As time passed these translations were often revised and edited, usually to conform more closely to the proto-MT (e.g., the Naḥal Ḥever Greek Minor Prophets scroll). There are different translations for many books and different versions in the manuscript tradition (e.g., Daniel and Esther; see Aitken, 2).

There is evidence from all over the Roman Empire that in the first century AD the LXX was the Bible of choice for many Jews. There is no indication in the writings of the early Jewish authors Aristeas, Aristobulus, Philo, or Josephus that the Greek version should be considered secondary or incomplete, and for Philo and Josephus it was "an accurate version of the same authority as the Hebrew text. In principle, this meant that they accepted two 'original' texts on an equal footing" (Müller, 66). In fact, several times Philo and Josephus call the LXX the "sacred writings" (Philo in *Moses* 2.290, 292; Josephus in *Ant.* 1.13; 10.210; and *Ag. Ap.* 1.54; 1.127), employing the same phrase Paul uses to refer to the Hebrew Scriptures in 2 Tim. 3:15 to remind Timothy that from a child he has known the "sacred writings" (*hiera grammata*).

Any translation from one language to another involves changes in the precise meaning of the passage translated and a certain degree of interpretation of the source material. The LXX is no exception to these patterns, and, although overall it could be called a faithful translation, it does differ from and at points offer interpretive renderings of its source text. The faithfulness and character of the translation vary between translation units. Beyond the very nature of translation, the differences between the LXX and its source text can be attributed to several factors, including different *Vorlagen* (source texts), lack of clarity in the source text manuscripts, errors in transmission of texts, additions or subtractions in the translation, errors of the translator, and paraphrastic and interpretative renderings by the translator.

Often we cannot have absolute certainty concerning the cause of a difference between the LXX and its *Vorlage*. This is especially true with regard to the possibility of a different *Vorlage* or changes resulting from the transmission of one of the texts (Hebrew/Aramaic and Greek). However, with regard to different *Vorlagen*, when there is no evidence in the manuscript tradition of a possible source for the difference in the LXX rendering, it will be assumed that the difference could have been introduced by the translator. In this study I have tried to avoid passages where there is textual evidence that a major difference between the Hebrew and LXX is the result of a different *Vorlage*.

A further complication in interpreting differences between the Semitic source text and the Greek translation involves the question of the intention of the translator (see Glenny, "Septuagint and Theology," 320–23). For some, if the translator's normal translation technique or a mistake in his reading of the source text could account for the difference, it should not be considered intentional. However, it is very difficult to separate completely the translator's ideas and beliefs from any aspect of his translation, even from mistakes he makes. Furthermore, it is unlikely that the translations were done in isolation; they apparently reflect the ideas and beliefs of communities. Therefore, I will mention the apparent reasons for the differences between the Hebrew and Greek texts, but the translators' intentions will not be used to eliminate or exclude some of the differences from our discussion. Our focus will be on the Semitic and LXX texts *as we have received them* and not on the intentions of the translator.

After an analysis of the representative examples of the translation of the Hebrew Bible in the LXX and the appropriation of those LXX passages in the NT, the ways the LXX translates the Hebrew and the ways the NT appropriates the OT text will be placed into hermeneutical categories to compare them. The hermeneutical categories employed are taken from Beale (55–102) and include the following: (1) direct fulfillment; (2) indirect fulfillment of typological prophecies; (3) affirmation that a not-yet-fulfilled prophecy will assuredly be fulfilled in the future; (4) analogical or illustrative use; (5) symbolic use; (6) to indicate abiding authority; (7) to indicate a proverbial use; (8) to indicate a rhetorical use; (9) to indicate a segment of Scripture as a blueprint or prototype for a later LXX or NT segment; (10) to indicate an alternate textual use of the text; (11) to indicate an assimilated use of the text; (12) to indicate an ironic or inverted use of the text (see also the categories in Fishbane, 354–79).

Each passage of Scripture considered will be analyzed in its respective contexts in the Hebrew Bible, the LXX, and the NT in order to compare its meaning in all three contexts. Most attention will be given to the relationship of the LXX to the MT and then to the comparison of the use of the OT passage in the NT. The passages to be analyzed are Amos 9:11–12 in Acts 15:16–18; Ps. 40:6–8 in Heb. 10:5–7; and Isa. 40:6–8 in 1 Pet. 1:24–25.

Amos 9:11–12 in Acts 15:16–18

Amos 9:11–12 in the MT. In the Hebrew Bible the prophecy in Amos 9:11–15, which concludes the book, is the only positive message for Israel in the book (9:9b is positive in the LXX; see Glenny, *Finding*, 215). In this concluding paragraph the Lord promises to restore Israel as God's people, so they will dwell in their own land and never again be removed (9:14–15). Verses 11–12, the focus of our attention, describe that restoration in terms of rebuilding and military and political domination: "In that day I will restore David's fallen shelter—I will repair its broken walls and restore its ruins—and will rebuild it as it used to be, so that they may possess the remnant of Edom and all the nations that bear my name." Although translators differ on their interpretations of the "booth of David" that will be raised up in the last days, the context points to the fallen and weakened dynasty and kingdom of David, which the Lord will rebuild again as it was "in the days of old" (9:11 ESV). To "possess the remnant of Edom and all the nations who are called by my name" (ESV) apparently refers to Israel's subjection (under Judah's leadership) of their neighboring enemies to Davidic rule. The fact that the other nations are "called by" the Lord's name indicates at least his authority and power over them and could even refer to those nations having a covenant relationship with the Lord (Glenny, *Finding*, 217–20; "Apostolic," 3–4). Thus, in the Hebrew Amos 9:11–12 refers to the restoration of the fallen house of David to its status in days of old for the purpose that Israel may possess other nations and apparently influence them for the Lord.

Amos 9:11–12 in the LXX. The LXX is more polished than the Hebrew, especially in v. 11, and it differs from the Hebrew in several important particulars that require our attention, especially in v. 12 (for more on 9:11, see Dines, 301; Glenny, *Finding*, 220–28; "Apostolic," 4–10; *Amos*, 158–60). The Hebrew in 9:12, referring to the rebuilt "booth of David" (9:11), reads, "that they may possess the remnant of Edom and all the nations" (*ləmaʿan yîrəšû ʾet-šəʾērît ʾĕdôm wəkol-haggôyim*). The corresponding Greek reads "that the remnant of people and all the nations may seek [me]" (*hopōs ekzētēsōsin hoi kataloipoi tōn anthrōpōn kai panta ta ethnē*). In the Hebrew the Lord is going to rebuild the dynasty and kingdom of David so the Israelites can possess the remnant of Edom and the nations, but in the Greek the Lord will rebuild it so the remnant of people and all the nations may seek him (Glenny, "Apostolic," 4–6).

The LXX translation reflects a different reading of the Hebrew, and it is possible that the translator felt his Hebrew text offered him different possible translations, or he simply read it differently than our understanding of the MT. The translator apparently read the second *yod* in *yîrəšû* ("possess") as a *dalet*, resulting in *yidrəšû* ("seek"); the LXX translation also involves reading the Hebrew *ʾĕdôm* ("Edom") as *ʾādām* ("man, mankind"), which could have been a matter of vocalization if the vocalic *vav* in *ʾĕdôm* was not in the translator's *Vorlage*. This rendering could have also involved interpretation of the text, since it is an example of the logical hermeneutical method *qal wahomer*, or the argument from major to minor. Edom often functioned as a representative of all the nations in the Jewish Scriptures (see Isa. 34:1–15; 63:1–6; and Obad. 15–21). Thus, if Edom, Israel's perpetual enemy, is able to seek the Lord as Edomites, then all the gentiles are surely able to seek the Lord as gentiles (Jobes and Silva, 195). It is also possible that the particle *ʾet* was not in the *Vorlage*, or if it was the translator ignored it, perhaps because it did not make sense with the way he had read the verb (*yîrəšû*); as a result, he understood the Hebrew direct object (*šəʾērît*, "remnant") to be the subject in his translation.

A different Hebrew Vorlage could be the cause of the differences between the Greek and the Hebrew (Kreuzer, 234; Schart, 177), but there is no direct textual evidence to support this. Anthony Gelston ("Misreadings") argues that the translator was reading an obscure copy of the Hebrew text, and that caused him to misread one letter in the Hebrew verb (*yîrəšû*, "possess"), as described above; then the translator employed other exegetical possibilities in the text to make sense of the verse, resulting in the LXX rendering. His suggestion that the cause of this rendering was an obscure copy of the Hebrew source text is questionable, since similar interpretive rendering of the Hebrew is found elsewhere in LXX Amos (see Glenny, "Misreadings," for a response to Gelston). It is also possible that the initial motivation for this rendering came from the translator himself. Jobes and Silva (195) suggest, "Since the Hebrew preserved in the MT is not particularly difficult, we may consider the possibility that the LXX translator—whether or not he made a mistake in reading the Hebrew characters—was primarily motivated by hermeneutical concerns" (see also Dines, 302). There is evidence to support the latter explanation of the differences, both from the translation technique employed by the translator of LXX Amos and from the theology of the book (Glenny, *Finding*).

The theology of LXX Amos 9:12 is very similar to that found in other prophetic writings. J. M. Dines notes the similarity of vocabulary and theology with Zech. 8 and 14. The latter, a passage describing the defeat of the "nations" and their later recognition of the Lord, contains phrases similar to Amos 9:12 (*panta ta ethnē* in Zech. 14:2 and *kataleiphthōsin ek pantōn tōn ethnōn* in 14:16). Zechariah 8:22 is even closer to Amos 9:12: "And many peoples and many nations will come to seek the face of the Lord Almighty in Jerusalem" (AT) (*kai hēxousin laoi polloi kai ethnē polla ekzētēsai to prosōpon kyriou pantokratoros en Ierousalēm*). It is possible that the references in this text to the "nations" that "seek" the Lord influenced the translator's change from "possess" to "seek" discussed above. Another passage that could have influenced the translation of Amos 9:12 is Isa. 19:16–25, which also emphasizes the inclusion of gentiles. (Several passages in LXX Amos suggest the translator was interested in the inclusion of gentiles [see 4:13; 9:15; and Glenny, *Finding*, 216–28].) The translator's Hebrew text of Amos may have offered him several possibilities, and in light of theology elsewhere in the Hebrew Bible, he perhaps was influenced in his reading of Amos. The LXX's difference from the Hebrew in Amos 9:12 could have involved misreading the Hebrew, a theological rendering, or an attempt to correct the text (see also McLay, 21; see Glenny, "Apostolic," for further discussion of the hermeneutics employed by the translator).

Amos 9:11–12 is a direct prophecy in the Hebrew and in the LXX. The hermeneutical category that this LXX text fits best is "an alternate textual use" of the Hebrew in order to "amplify the meaning of the original OT prophecy" by choosing a different way to read the Hebrew consonants (Beale, 89–91). There may be a theological motive involved in the different reading of the Hebrew text, or the LXX reading could be based on a different understanding of the source text, which might mean the translator did not know he was adjusting the meaning.

Amos 9:11–12 in Acts 15. It is also important to consider how this passage is employed in the NT in Acts 15:16–18 at the Jerusalem Council. The purpose of this council is to consider if it is necessary for gentiles to be circumcised and keep the law of Moses in order to be saved. After Peter gives testimony of the conversion of Cornelius's house (15:7–11) and Paul and Barnabas recount the work of God among the gentiles through their ministry (15:12), James confirms their testimony and settles the discussion with an OT quotation from "the words of the prophets" (15:13–21), which he says agree with "this"—that is, the work of God through Peter. With his use of the words "as it is written" to introduce his quotation from Amos, James is appealing to divine authority and indicating this prophecy speaks directly to and is being fulfilled through the events among the gentiles previously recounted by Peter, Paul, and Barnabas.

The message of James recorded in Acts 15:13–21, including the scriptural citation in 15:16–18, is Luke's summary of the words of James on this occasion. The citation evidences dependence on the LXX and is apparently an abridgment of it, although it varies from it in several particulars without changing the overall sense of the passage. The most important differences are the addition of the opening words, "after this I will return" (*meta tauta anastrepsō*), and the last words, "things known from long ago" (*gnōsta ap' aiōnos*). The opening words "after this" (*meta tauta*) are usually understood to reflect Hosea 3:5, and the source of "I will return" (*anastrepsō*) could be Zech. 8:3 or Jer. 12:15. There are also several other possible sources of these words in the prophets. The source of the last words "things known from long ago" (*gnōsta ap' aiōnos*) is apparently Isa. 45:21. What is important is that the "words of the prophets" that comprise the citation in Acts 15:16–18 are from several different prophets, as James said when he introduced the citation (see Glenny, "Apostolic," 10–16, for more specific details about the text quoted in Acts 15:16–18).

There is no shortage of interpretations concerning the referent of the restored "tent of David" in Acts 15 (see Glenny, "Apostolic"). However, if we take seriously the purpose clause in Acts 15:17 "that the rest of mankind may seek the Lord" (*hopōs an ekzētēsōsin hoi kataloipoi tōn anthrōpōn ton kyrion*), it eliminates many of the suggested options (Glenny, *Finding*, 218–24). The interpretation that makes the most sense of the purpose clause is that the restored "tent of David" refers to "the restoration of the Davidic dynasty accomplished through the life, death, resurrection, and exaltation of Jesus" (Strauss, 190). However, whether one agrees with this exact interpretation of the phrase, in its context in Acts it has to be connected in some way with the work of Christ. And James's introductory words "as it is written" indicate that the restoration of the tent of David for the purpose of gentiles coming to the Lord fulfills the Scriptures he cites and refers to in Acts 15:16–18, most explicitly Amos 9:11–12. Thus, Luke is telling his readers that the salvation of gentiles apart from circumcision or the law, which the apostles are witnessing, is a direct fulfillment of Amos 9:11–12. However, the text being employed by Luke is LXX Amos 9:11–12, which is an alternate textual use of the Hebrew of Amos 9:11–12, as we saw above. Thus, if we follow Beale's categories, the NT author is not only employing Amos 9:11–12 to point to its fulfillment in the Christ events but also amplifying the meaning of the OT prophecy in the Hebrew original "to understand better how it is beginning to be fulfilled in Christ" (Beale, 89).

Psalm 40:6–8 in Heb. 10:5–7

Psalm 40:6–8 in the MT. Psalm 40 is a prayer of thanksgiving and lament attributed to King David. The psalm has two main units: the first contains the psalmist's praise and thanksgiving for past deliverance (vv. 1–10), and in the second the psalmist expresses lament and confidence in a present crisis (vv. 11–17). Because of the distinction between the two main units of thanksgiving and lament and because vv. 13–17 closely correspond to the words of Ps. 70, it is common to identify Ps. 40 as the combination of two initially independent works. However, Peter Craigie (314) argues convincingly that that theory must be rejected on the basis of the intimate relationship between the language in the two parts of the psalm and especially because the "form and setting" of the psalm make sense as part of a "royal liturgy of supplication" (cf. Eaton, 42–44).

The focus of our study, Ps. 40:6–8, is in the middle of the psalm's first main unit. This unit begins with David's praise to the Lord for his past deliverance of him (40:1–4) and for his many wonderful works on behalf of Israel (40:5). Then in 40:6–8 the king describes the proper response to the Lord's deliverance and acts on behalf of his people. It is not "sacrifice and offering" or "burnt offerings and sin offerings" but rather dedication to the Lord's will and delight in it. In the last two verses of the unit (40:9–10 ESV) David refers to his declarations of praise to the Lord in the "great congregation" (an assembly for worship or a national assembly) for his "deliverance."

Verse 6 is sometimes read as a rejection of sacrifices and offerings, but that makes no sense, since the Lord instituted the sacrificial system in the law (Kaiser, 27–28). This language must mean that obedience is more important than sacrifice (1 Sam. 15:22), and that to offer sacrifice without obedience is worthless. The phrase "my ears you have opened" in 40:6 could also be rendered "you have given me an open ear" (ESV) or "you have dug two ears for me" (Craigie, 312), and it likely has a sense similar to Isa. 50:4–5: the Lord "has opened my ears; I have not been rebellious" (see also 48:8). In Ps. 40 this language must refer to more than the Lord giving David the ability to hear with his physical ears; it is more the idea of hearing with the intent and desire of obeying (cf. Jer. 6:10). The idea is parallel to Ps. 40:8: "I desire to do your will, my God; your law is within my heart." Verse 6 describes the Lord's work in David's life to prepare David to do his will; he opened David's ears to be receptive and responsive to his law.

There is a sequence from v. 6 to v. 7 ("then"), and David's statement in 40:7 follows and results from the open ears the Lord gave him to go beyond the outward formalities of the cult to obey the Lord from his heart. Because of the Lord's work in his life, David can now say, "Here I am, I have come—it is written about me in the scroll." This verse likely refers to the king going to the sanctuary to present himself before the Lord to fulfill his obligations and offer the sacrifices required or prescribed for him in the law. The last clause, "it is written about me in the scroll," is generally understood to refer to the law, perhaps with special reference to the instructions the Lord has given for the king in Deut. 17:14–20. Those instructions stipulate that he is to put his confidence not in wealth, military might, or treaties, but in the Lord (17:16–17). Furthermore, he is to make a personal copy of the law and read it to learn to fear the Lord and keep all that is written in the law (17:18–20); this suggests the kind of internalizing of the law referred to in Ps. 40:8: "I desire to do your will, my God; your law is within my heart."

Psalm 40:6–8 in the LXX (39:7–9). LXX Ps. 39:7–9 follows MT Ps. 40:6–8 closely in sequence and meaning, with only minor differences (unlike our other two LXX passages, which differ more distinctly from the Hebrew). However, that does not mean the LXX text of these verses is without its difficulties. There is some question about the rendering of the Hebrew *ʾoznayim* ("ears") in 40:6, because in several of the main LXX manuscripts (the codices Vaticanus [B], Sinaiticus [S], and Alexandrinus [A]) the corresponding noun is rendered *sōma* ("body"; cf. Swete's Greek text and Brenton's English translation in Brenton). However, the critical editions Rahlfs-Hanhart and Göttingen both have *ōtia* ("ears"), following the Hebrew, the Old Latin manuscript G, and Jerome's Gallican Psalter, as well as the Jewish-Greek versions Aquila, Theodotion, and Symmachus. (The editors of the critical editions think the reading *sōma* in the Christian codices [B, S, and A] was influenced by this reading in Heb. 10 [see Grelot for a fuller discussion of this issue]).

There is a slight adjustment of the Hebrew verb "you have opened, dug out" (*kārîtā*) in MT 40:7 in its corresponding rendering in the LXX "you prepared" (*katērtisō*), a rendering that is unusual enough that Hatch and Redpath (vi) mark it with an obelus indicating that "the identification of the Greek and Hebrew is doubtful, or at least that a student should examine the passage for himself"; here it appears the translator has confused two homonymous verbal roots (I and III *krh*, meaning respectively [I] "hollow out, dig" and [III] "give, prepare a feast"; see *HALOT*, 2:496–97; *pace* Kaiser, 28–29). The LXX translation of the verb works with either "body" ("a body you prepared") or "ears" ("ears you prepared"), while the Hebrew reading, "opened, dug," is not appropriate with "body." The conclusion concerning this brief examination of the LXX rendering of Ps. 40, if we follow the critical editions with the reading *ōtia* ("ears"), is that the LXX represents the Hebrew well, and the translator has interpreted the Hebrew text literally, with only minor differences in the sense of a few words. The closest hermeneutical category, if we go beyond calling this a literal reading of the Hebrew, is that the translator is indicating "an abiding authority" carried over here from the Hebrew; the translator is underscoring the authority of the Hebrew original and for him it is "just as true and authoritative" as it was when first spoken by David (Beale, 72–73).

Psalm 40:6–8 in Heb. 10. The author of Hebrews employs Ps. 40:6–8 to bolster his argument that Christ's new-covenant offering of himself for sins is superior to the sacrifices offered under the old covenant and ends the need for those Levitical sacrifices (Heb. 8:3–10:18). George Guthrie (975) notes three contrasts in this section between the Levitical sacrifices and Christ's: (1) they were offered in an earthly tabernacle rather than a heavenly one; (2) they involved the blood of animals rather than the blood of Christ; and (3) they were made year after year rather than once for all. The last of these contrasts is the main point the author emphasizes in 10:1–18. The law by its very nature was only a shadow of the true realities and could never make perfect those who offered the sacrifices it required, as is evidenced by their perpetual nature (10:1–2). These sacrifices of bulls and goats could never take away sin but were actually a continual reminder of it (10:3–4). For these reasons (*dio*, 10:5), in Heb. 10:5–7 the author of Hebrews puts the words of Ps. 40:6–8 in Christ's mouth at the time of his first advent and uses them to contrast Christ's perfect once-for-all offering with the perpetual and inadequate Levitical offerings. The text of Heb. 10:5–7 does not explicitly say it is referring to Christ, but the preceding and following contexts clarify that the author of Hebrews is applying it to him (see esp. 10:10–12).

Consistent with his quotations from the OT elsewhere in Hebrews, the author employs the LXX here, with four variations (Jobes, 182–83; Guthrie, 977). The NT text has the following: (1) *sōma* ("body") in 10:5c rather than *ōtia* ("ears"); (2) *holokautōmata* ("burnt offerings," pl.) in 10:6 rather than *holokautōma* ("burnt offering," sing.); (3) *eudokēsas* ("you were [not] pleased") in 10:6 rather than *ētēsas* ("you [did not] demand"); and (4) two changes in 10:7: the NT word order is *ho theos to thelēma sou* ("O God, your will" [AT]) rather than the LXX *to thelēma sou, ho theos mou* ("your will, my God"), and the rest of LXX Ps. 39:9, "and your law is within my belly [heart]" (*kai ton nomon sou en mesō tēs koilias mou*), is not included in the NT. In the NT the infinitive *poiēsai* ("to do") functions as the purpose of the verb "I have come" (*hēkō*), rather than as the complement of "I desired" (*eboulēthēn*), as in the LXX.

Most of the differences between the LXX and the NT are minor and not hard to explain. The major modification is the reading *sōma* ("body") rather than the LXX's *ōtia* ("ears") in Heb. 10:5c. This could be explained by a different rendering of the Hebrew, a different source text, a scribal error, a loose citation/adaptation of the text to the NT context, or adjustments of the text to achieve phonetic assonance (see Jobes, 183–90; Swete, 394). There is no explicit evidence of a Hebrew textual basis for the LXX rendering, and likely the rendering *sōma* ("body") in some LXX manuscripts was influenced by Heb. 10. Scribal error is possible but unlikely. Karen Jobes argues for the last of the listed options (to achieve phonetic assonance), but she allows that other factors may have been involved, since adaptation for phonetic assonance would have been linguistic ornamentation to reinforce the author's argument (Jobes, 189–91). Thus, it is likely that the NT author is the source of the rendering *sōma*, and that he adapted or paraphrased the Hebrew and LXX reading ("ears"), employing synecdoche, the figure of speech in which the whole refers to a part (or vice versa); here the whole (a prepared "body") represents a part ("ears" to hear and obey). Both the prepared "body" (the whole) and the "ears" (the part) describe obedience, and perhaps the author of Hebrews chose a "culturally meaningful dynamic equivalent" that supported his argument (Kaiser, 29–32; see also Jobes, 188–89).

The author of Hebrews applies and explains the importance of the quotation from Ps. 40 in the following verses (esp. 10:8–10). For him the psalm refers ultimately to Christ and not David, and the words are the words of Christ when he entered the world at his first advent (Guthrie, 977). Two of the modifications of the LXX text are especially important for his argument. Based on the reading *sōma* ("body") he argues that the once-for-all offering of Christ is the fulfillment and end of the Levitical sacrificial system. His body could only be offered one time, and that offering has satisfied God once-for-all (10:10). Also, the omission of part of the psalm in Heb. 10:7 is important for the NT meaning. In Heb. 10:9–10 the offering of Christ's "body" is connected with the "will" of God he came "to do"; the arrangement of the words in 10:7 explicitly spells out that the will of God is the offering of Christ's body. Furthermore, in Hebrews the "scroll of the book" (ESV), where God's will for Christ is written, refers to the Hebrew Scriptures and their prophecies about Christ, as demonstrated throughout Hebrews. Also crucial to the use of Ps. 40 in the reported words of Christ in Heb. 10:5–7 is the connector "then" (*tote*) in 10:7. It indicates a temporal and logical progression from a preliminary state, which was characterized by the Lord's dissatisfaction with the provisional old-covenant offerings and the anticipation of a better covenant by means of the "body" that was prepared for Christ (10:5b–6), to the present situation under the new covenant, which was inaugurated when Christ came into the world to do God's will by giving his body (10:7). According to Heb. 10:9, "He abolishes the first in order to establish the second" (NRSV).

For the author of Hebrews it is Christ's fulfillment of Ps. 40:6–8 that inaugurates the new covenant and provides complete and final salvation. However, the words of Ps. 40:6–8 are not a direct prophecy, and the fulfillment in Hebrews is not a direct fulfillment. Instead, the fulfillment is indirect or typological fulfillment of the pattern established in the psalm. The opening of King David's ears to obey described in the psalm foreshadows the obedience of his greater Son, Christ, who in obedience to God's will gives his body. Not only are there analogies between the two contexts, but the psalm also has a forward-pointing aspect and Hebrews escalates its meaning. In the psalm David's obedience was incomplete (Ps. 40:12), God's will for David involved the instructions for kings (40:7), and the psalmist followed the Hebrew convention of using absolute language to describe relativities ("you did not desire," "you did not require," 40:6). In contrast, Christ's obedience was complete, and God's will for him was to give his life and offer his blood to inaugurate the new covenant. Furthermore, by the work of Christ the absolute language of the psalm, which foreshadows his work, is fully realized. David offered sacrifices, which were a mere formality apart from obedience to the divine will, but Christ obeys the divine will and offers himself as a sacrifice that ends all sacrifices (Craigie, 317).

Isaiah 40:6–8 in 1 Pet. 1:24–25

The Letter of 1 Peter evidences an "extraordinary dependence on the OT" (Schutter, 3). In fact, for its size it is difficult to find another Christian document that incorporates as much OT material. One of the main portions of the OT that the author draws on is Isaiah (e.g., Isa. 40:6–8 in 1:24–25; Isa. 28:16 in 2:6; Isa. 43:21 in 2:9; Isa. 53:4–6 in 2:24–25; Isa. 8:12–13 in 3:14–15; Isa. 11:2 in 4:14), and in this section we will focus on the quotation from Isa. 40:6–8 in 1 Pet. 1:24–25.

Isaiah 40:6–8 in the MT. Isaiah 40:6–8 is part of the prologue (40:1–11) to the second main section of the book (chaps. 40–55). The chapters that follow contain a message directed to the Jews in exile in Babylon who are questioning God's willingness and ability to deliver them. God assures his people that he is sovereign and will be faithful to them and deliver them.

The structure of the prologue is straightforward. In 40:1–2 Yahweh exhorts his heralds to comfort his people; the comfort involves the renewal of God's covenant relationship with Israel. The terminology "my people"/"your God" in 40:1 recalls the covenant formula, "I will be your God and you will be my people" (e.g., Lev. 26:9–13). The "hard service" (40:2) with which Yahweh disciplined his people for their violation of the Mosaic covenant has come to an end, and now he will return to them. In the remainder of the prologue three "voices" (vv. 3–5, 6–8, 9–11), likely the same heralds in view in 40:1–2, explain how the comforting promise of the first two verses will be fulfilled. In the first strophe (40:3–5), using exodus imagery, the voice commands the Jews in Babylon to make royal preparations for Yahweh to return across the wilderness to his people (see 40:10–11). Obstacles will be removed (40:4), and Yahweh's return will reveal his glory to all (40:5). The promise of Yahweh's return is certain because "the mouth of Yahweh has spoken" it (40:5c AT).

The second strophe (40:6–8) is the focus of this study. After a voice commands, "Cry out," Isaiah asks, "What shall I cry?" (MT has "another asks"; LXX, Vulgate, and 1QIsa[a] have "And I [Isaiah] said"). The answer to the query follows in vv. 6–7a: he is to cry out that all humankind is frail and transitory; in 40:7b Israel, "the people," is specifically in focus. Their failure is indirectly attributed to Yahweh, who blows on them as the wind that blows on and withers the grass. In contrast, the "word of our God" (40:8), which refers to the promise in 40:1 but is not limited to that, is certain and permanent. Thus, the foundations for the promised deliverance "do not lie in human capacities [which are ultimately thwarted by Yahweh and have disappointed God's people in the past] but depend solely upon the word of God" (Watts, 83).

The third strophe (40:9–11) gives more details about the coming of Yahweh announced in vv. 3–5. The Lord enlists Zion/Jerusalem to herald the good news to the cities of Judah that Yahweh is returning in power with the exiles to rule and in tenderness to shepherd his people (so ESV and NRSV; *pace* NIV and ASV, which understand others to be heralding the good news to Zion/Jerusalem in 40:9; see Carson, 1021).

Isaiah 40:6–8 in the LXX. The LXX text of Isa. 40:1–11 differs from the MT in several details. The most important are as follows: (1) In 40:1 "your" modifying God is omitted, and in 40:2 the heralds who are commanded to announce "comfort" to God's people are identified as "priests." (2) In 40:2 the "hard labor" of the exiles is called "humility," and their sin is softened by omitting the adjective "all," which modifies "sin" in the MT. (3) The LXX also omits or changes several anthropomorphisms. The most important is probably the omission of "in the desert," which is the location of the "highway" (MT) or "path" (LXX) for God in 40:3b (note also the LXX's "the Lord" for MT's "the mouth of the LORD" in 40:5, the omission of "his" with "arm" in 40:10, and the omission of the phrase "his bosom" in 40:11; but the LXX includes "his arm" in 40:11, following the Hebrew). (4) In 40:5 the LXX adds "the salvation of God" to clarify what "all flesh will see"; in the MT the implied object is the "glory of the LORD" from the previous clause. (5) The LXX changes "*ḥesed* [faithfulness] of it [flesh]" to "glory of man" (40:6). (6) The LXX has paraphrastic or general renderings, translating the phrase "the flower of the field" in 40:6 as "the flower of the grass [*chortou*]," and in 40:7a rendering the clause "the flower withers away" as "the flower has fallen off" (*exepesen*). (7) The LXX omits 40:7b–8a in the MT (likely resulting, whether intentionally or not, from identical phrases at the start of 40:7 and 40:8 MT). (8) In v. 11b the LXX combines the last two clauses ("and he will carry them in his bosom, and he will gently lead those nursing young") to read, "He will comfort those who are pregnant."

The omission of "in the desert" (40:3b) and the addition of "salvation of our God" (40:5) in the LXX suggest that for the translator this passage speaks of God coming to Babylon to deliver the exiles from their "humility" (*tapeinōsis*, 40:2) in Babylon rather than him coming across the desert to Jerusalem. Other factors suggest that these changes could also be part of a universalizing of the message of Isa. 40:1–11. The omission of "your" modifying God (40:1), the change of "all people will see it [the glory of the LORD] together" to "all flesh shall see the salvation of God" (40:5), the omission of

40:7b–8a (which in the MT apparently refers to Israel as God's "people"), and the change from "all their [Heb. "its"] faithfulness [*ḥesed*]" to "glory [*doxa*] of man" (40:6) all contribute to a universalizing of the message of Isa. 40:1–11. Thus, in this passage the translator leans toward the same universalizing tendency combined with an emphasis on Jewish preeminence that David Baer found in his study of LXX Isa. 55–66. Jewish preeminence is implicit in the LXX text in the downplaying of Israel's sin and frailty (40:2) and the avoidance of reference to God thwarting Israel's undertakings (40:7). The universalizing tendency in LXX 40:1–11, especially in the clause "all flesh shall see the salvation of God" (40:5), is supported in 40:6–8 by the LXX omission of "surely the people are grass"—an allusion to Israel (40:7). And the phrase "glory of man" in the LXX (40:6) shifts the sense slightly, suggesting a contrast between the best of humanity (what is valued in human culture) and "the word of our God" (40:8), rather than the MT's contrast between the faithfulness/loyalty (*ḥesed*) of man and "the word of our God." As far as hermeneutical categories go, although the context contains promises of deliverance, Isa. 40:6–8 is not a direct promise in the MT or LXX, and there does not seem to be an escalation of meaning that signifies an indirect fulfillment in the LXX. Yet it is more than a literal use, simply indicating the abiding authority of the text. It fits best in the analogical category; the translation emphasizes the basic principle found in the source text, but it adapts it slightly to fit a new context.

Isaiah 40:6–8 in 1 Pet. 1. First Peter 1:24–25a follows LXX Isa. 40:6b–8 closely in words and word order: (1) It omits the MT's 40:7b–8a. (2) It renders the MT's "faithfulness" (*ḥesed*) as "glory" (*doxa*, 40:6; this is the only time *ḥesed* is so rendered in the LXX). (3) It agrees with the LXX's rendering "the flower of the grass" (*chortou*) for the MT's "the flower of the field" (40:6). (4) It follows the LXX's clause "the flower has fallen off" (*exepesen*) rather than the MT's "the flower fades" (40:7). (For a fuller treatment of Isa. 40 in 1 Pet. 1:24–25, see Glenny, "1 Peter," 83–102.)

Despite the obvious dependence on the LXX in 1 Pet. 1:24–25, there are important differences from the LXX. In 1:24 the text of 1 Peter adds *hōs* after *sarx*, possibly to clarify or emphasize the comparison between "flesh" and "grass" in the verbless clause. Also, in 1:24 1 Peter has *autēs* instead of the LXX's *anthrōpou* (i.e., glory of "it" [referring to "flesh"] rather than "glory of man"); this is an important two-step change from the masculine noun of the LXX to the feminine pronoun of the NT. In addition, 1 Pet. 1:25a has *kyriou* for the LXX reading *tou theou hēmōn*, which changes the reference from the LXX's "word of our God" to "word of the Lord." These changes in 1 Peter have been attributed to the OT text used (Hort, 93–94) or quotation from memory (Selwyn, 152). These are possibilities, but the correlation of the changes with the context and message of 1 Peter suggests that these changes were designed to enhance the author's message (see Schutter, 125, on the reading *anthrōpou*).

The quotation from Isa. 40 in 1 Pet. 1:24–25 follows an exhortation for the recipients to grow in sincere love for one another (1:22–23). Such love is possible because they have been begotten "not of perishable seed, but of imperishable, through the living and enduring word of God" (1:23; cf. 1:25). Peter supports his claim that the word of God is "living and enduring" with a quotation from Isa. 40:6–8 in 1 Pet. 1:24–25, which he introduces with the causal conjunction "for" (*dioti*). Most important in this quotation are the words in 1:25: "'The word of the Lord endures forever.' And this is the word that was preached to you." The word of the Lord is contrasted with "all people" (lit. "all flesh" [*pasa sarx*]), who wither and fall like the grass and flowers of the field (1:24).

The expression "all flesh" (*pasa sarx*) in the Isaiah quotation in 1 Pet. 1:24 is commonly taken to mean "all men" or "every person" as in Isa. 40:5–6 (e.g., BDAG, 915; *TDNT*, 7:106, 143). For example, the NIV renders it "all people." However, this interpretation of "all flesh" in 1 Peter raises questions for several reasons. First, the preceding context is contrasting two spheres of human existence: the corruptible and the incorruptible (1:4, 18, and esp. 23; see also 3:4). Verse 23 states that the recipients have been begotten not of perishable but of imperishable seed, by means of the dynamic, everlasting word of God. That description hardly allows them to be included in a reference to withering flesh in 1:24. Furthermore, the other occurrences of *sarx* in 1 Peter do not have the idea of "human being." Instead, in 1 Peter *sarx* is a realm in which Christ and Christians live (4:2), suffer, and die (3:18; 4:1), where they are confined to physical bodies (3:21), and which has standards by which it judges and decides that are contrasted with God's standards (4:6). Often it is contrasted with the "spirit" (3:18; 4:6). In 1 Peter "flesh" (*sarx*) is not evil nor is it people; it is instead "human existence yoked to death" (Goppelt, 156; see also Michaels, 116, who defines it as "the realm of physical life"). Its meaning is closer to the realm in which people live in this age than the people who inhabit it. Therefore, the use of *sarx* elsewhere in 1 Peter, the emphasis on "glory" for Christians in the future (1:7; 5:4), the contrasts between corruption and incorruption (esp. 1:23), and the eschatological emphasis of 1 Peter raise questions concerning the interpretation of "all flesh" as "all people" in 1 Pet. 1:24.

However, the main indicators that "all flesh" in 1:24 is not to be interpreted as "all people" are the subtle changes in 1 Peter in the citation of the LXX. Two changes are especially important. First, with the substitution of *autēs* for the LXX's *anthrōpou*, "all the glory of it" (with "it" referring to "all flesh"), instead of "all the glory of man," is likened to the "flower of the grass," which withers and falls off. Thus, Peter does not connect "all flesh" with "man," as the LXX does. The result of this change is that while Isa. 40:6–8 (both MT and

LXX) contrasts people with God and encourages Israel with the fact that God will keep his promise to deliver them, 1 Pet. 1:24–25 contrasts the inability of the natural, corruptible man without God with the dynamic, new life and power of the incorruptible person born again into God's family by means of the dynamic and eternal word of God. In the LXX the "glory of man" refers to the strength and honor of people; in 1 Peter "the glory of it" refers to the strength, honor, and all the rest that is attractive in the culture and society of this world. Fenton Hort (95) comments regarding *doxa* in 1 Pet. 1:24, "The significance of the word here . . . consists in the attractiveness and pride which made heathen life in Greek cities of that time a real temptation to men wavering in their spiritual allegiance" (see also Scharlemann).

The second important change that the author of 1 Peter makes to the text of the LXX is to change "the word of our God" to "the word of the Lord." The change from *theou* to *kyriou* makes no sense as a scribal error or a move closer to the Hebrew *ʾĕlōhîm* in MT Isa. 40:8. Nor does it seem like this change is because of a loose quotation from memory, since in 1:23, the author is aware of the reading of the original text and introduces the quotation with an "iterative allusion" to 1:25a, using the word *theou* ("the living and enduring word of God"; see Schutter, 125). The bottom line is that Peter is responsible for the change from *theou* to *kyriou* in 1 Pet. 1:25a.

There is strong evidence that for Peter *kyriou* in 1:25a refers to Christ and not God. First, the presence of "God" in the introductory "iterative allusion" in 1:23 ("word . . . of God") suggests that "God" would be used again in 1:25 unless some change in meaning or emphasis were intended. Second, the words of 1:25b, "This is the word that has been preached to you," hearken back to the message of Christ referred to in 1:10–12. Note especially the repetition of the verb *euangelizō* in 1:12 and 1:25. Finally, and most importantly, *kyriou* in 1:25a prepares the hearer for the clear reference to Christ as *kyrios* in 2:3 (quoting Ps. 34:8) and in the description of Christ from the OT in the context that follows (2:4–8).

The "word from God" of Isa. 40:8 (genitive of source or subjective genitive) has become the "word about the Lord" (objective genitive) in 1 Peter (1:25a; cf. 1:10–11 on Christ in the OT; McCartney, 72; Schutter, 126–27), and the message about Christ that Peter finds in Isaiah (and elsewhere in the OT), which is living and eternal, is preached as the gospel to 1 Peter's recipients (1:25b; see 1:12 on the OT revelation about Christ being for Peter's recipients, not for the OT readers).

The context of Isa. 40 matches closely the historical situation of Peter and his recipients, who are respectively in "Babylon" (5:13) and "strangers" and "exiles" in the "diaspora" (1:1 AT; 2:11). Both the OT and NT contexts contain promises of good news proclaimed by evangelists (Isa. 40:9; 1 Pet. 1:12, 25), and both exhort the recipients to trust in God's eternal promise amid the changing trials of this life. The Lord promised a glorious deliverance of the exiles from Babylon (esp. in LXX Isa. 40:5 [*to sōtērion*]) that would be known by all, as he also promised to come and deliver the recipients of 1 Peter to glory (1:5 [*sōtēria*], 7, 13; 5:10). But most important for Peter's application of Isa. 40 to the situation of his recipients, Peter writes that the OT prophets, who prophesied concerning the deliverance of Judah from Babylon, "spoke of the grace that was to come to you"—that is, to Peter's recipients (1:10). The adjustments in the OT text cited in 1 Peter allow Peter to apply the promise of the Lord's deliverance of captives from Babylon to eschatological deliverance through Christ from the corruption of this realm of existence that ends in death. The promise has now become the life-giving, eternal "word about Jesus Christ," the gospel.

God's word of "good news" of deliverance from Babylonian captivity in Isa. 40 is a direct prophecy of the word of "good news" of the gospel of Jesus Christ. According to 1 Pet. 1:25b, "This [the word in Isa. 40] is the word that was proclaimed as good news to you." The category of usage of Isa. 40:6–8 in 1 Pet. 1:24–25 is direct prophetic fulfillment. The fulfillment of Isaiah's prophecy in the NT clarifies the OT meaning in that it finds its final fulfillment in Christ and the gospel, God's ultimate word.

Summary

In this essay I have sought to compare and classify with hermeneutical categories the manner in which the LXX and then the NT employ three passages from the Hebrew Bible. In Amos 9:11–12 the LXX translator amplifies the meaning of the Hebrew prophecy with an alternate use of the Hebrew text, and the author of Acts picks up that amplified meaning and points to the direct fulfillment of that meaning in Christ. The translator of Ps. 40:6–8 (LXX 39:7–9) translates the Hebrew with only small differences, indicating its abiding authority, but the author of Hebrews adapts the text to fit his argument and sees it fulfilled indirectly or typologically in Christ. The LXX of Isa. 40:6–8 employs the text in an analogous manner, emphasizing the basic truth found in the Hebrew but adapting it slightly; according to 1 Pet. 1:24–25, the message of good news in Isa. 40 finds direct fulfillment in the gospel message about Christ. The interpreter's journey from the Hebrew Bible to its fulfillment in Christ can take different routes, but on the way it is always wise to make sure one spends some time in the LXX, because time spent there always enhances the journey and often it is the most direct route.

See also OT Use of the OT: Comparison with the NT Use of the OT; *other Septuagint articles; Dead Sea Scrolls articles; Mishnah, Talmud, and Midrashim articles; Philo articles; Targums articles*

Bibliography. Aitken, J. K., "Introduction," in *T&T Clark Companion to the Septuagint*, ed. J. K. Aitken (T&T Clark, 2015), 1–12; Baer, D. A., *When We All Go Home*, JSOTSup 318 (Sheffield Academic, 2001); Beale, G. K., *Handbook on the New Testament Use of the Old Testament* (Zondervan, 2012); Brenton, L. C. L., *The Septuagint Version, With Apocrypha, Greek, and English* (repr., Zondervan, 1976); Carson, D. A., "1 Peter," in *CNTUOT*, 1015–45; Craigie, P. C., *Psalms 1–50*, WBC (Word, 1983); Dines, J. M., "The Septuagint of Amos" (PhD diss., University of London, 1991); Eaton, J. H., *Kingship and the Psalms*, 2nd ed. (JSOT Press, 1986); Fishbane, M., *Biblical Interpretation in Ancient Israel* (Clarendon, 1985); Gelston, A., "Some Hebrew Misreadings in the Septuagint of Amos," *VT* 52, no. 4 (2002): 493–500; Glenny, W. E., *Amos*, SCS (Brill, 2013); Glenny, *Finding Meaning in the Text*, VTSup 126 (Brill, 2009); Glenny, "Hebrew Misreadings or Free Translation in the Septuagint of Amos?," *VT* 57 (2007): 524–47; Glenny, "The Hermeneutics of the Use of the Old Testament in 1 Peter" (ThD diss., Dallas Theological Seminary, 1987); Glenny, "The Septuagint and Apostolic Hermeneutics," *BBR* 22 (2012): 1–26; Glenny, "The Septuagint and Biblical Theology," *Them* 41, no. 2 (2016): 263–78; Glenny, "The Septuagint and Theology," in *T&T Clark Handbook of Septuagint Research*, ed. W. A. Ross and W. E. Glenny (T&T Clark, 2021), 313–27; Goppelt, L., *A Commentary on 1 Peter* (Eerdmans, 1993); Grelot, P., "Le texte du Psaume 39,7 dans la Septante," *RB* 108 (2001): 210–13; Guthrie, G. H., "Hebrews," in *CNTUOT*, 919–95; Hatch, E., and H. A. Redpath, *A Concordance to the Septuagint* (repr., Baker, 1983); Hort, F. J. A., *The First Epistle of St. Peter I.1–II.17* (repr., James & Klock, 1976); Jobes, K. H., "The Function of Paronomasia in Hebrews 10:5–7," *TJ* 13 (1992): 181–91; Jobes, K. H., and M. Silva., *Invitation to the Septuagint*, 2nd ed. (Baker Academic, 2015); Kaiser, W. C., "The Abolition of the Old Order and Establishment of the New," in *Tradition and Testament*, ed. J. S. Feinberg and P. D. Feinberg (Moody, 1981), 19–37; Kreuzer, S., "From 'Old Greek' to the Recensions," in *Septuagint Research*, ed. W. Kraus and R. G. Wooden, SBLSCS 53 (Society of Biblical Literature, 2006), 225–38; McCartney, D. G., "The Use of the Old Testament in the First Epistle of Peter" (PhD diss., Westminster Theological Seminary, 1989); McLay, R. T., *The Use of the Septuagint in New Testament Research* (Eerdmans, 2003); Michaels, J. R., *1 Peter*, WBC (Word, 1988); Müller, M., *The First Bible of the Church*, JSOTSup 206 (Sheffield Academic, 1996); Rahlfs, A., and R. Hanhart, eds., *Septuaginta*, 2nd ed. (Deutsche Bibelgesellschaft, 2006); Scharlemann, M. H., "Why the *Kuriou* in 1 Peter 1:25?," *CTM* 30 (1959): 354–56; Schart, A., "The Jewish and the Christian Greek Versions of Amos," in *Septuagint Research*, ed. W. Kraus and R. G. Wooden, SBLSCS 53 (Society of Biblical Literature, 2006), 157–78; Schutter, W. L., *Hermeneutic and Composition in 1 Peter*, WUNT 2/30 (Mohr Siebeck, 1989); Selwyn, E. G., *The First Epistle of St. Peter*, 2nd ed. (repr., Baker, 1983); Strauss, M., *The Davidic Messiah in Luke-Acts*, JSNTSup 110 (Sheffield Academic, 1995); Swete, H. B., *An Introduction to the Old Testament in Greek*, rev. R. R. Ottley (repr., Hendrickson, 1989); Watts, J. D. W., *Isaiah 34–66*, WBC (Word, 1987).

W. EDWARD GLENNY

Septuagint, NT Use of

Although the Septuagint is unfamiliar to most English Bible readers today and is discussed primarily within the world of biblical scholars, it was Holy Scripture to the early Christian church of the Greco-Roman world. At the time of Jesus, the ancient Greek translation of the Hebrew Scriptures known as the Septuagint (LXX) was Scripture to the Greek-speaking Jewish diaspora in the Greco-Roman world. When the NT writers took up pens to proclaim in the Greek language the significance of Jesus Christ, it was fitting they should often quote and otherwise refer to the Jewish Greek Scriptures. Martin Hengel (22) remarks, "The use of the LXX as Holy Scripture is practically as old as the church itself. For NT writings, beginning with Paul, it is the rule." The ancient Greek Bible used by the Christian church for centuries was comprised of the Greek translation of the Hebrew Scriptures and the Greek NT. Therefore, the Greek Bible is part of the rich heritage of the church's history. Laypeople today could benefit from knowing about it, but for biblical scholars in general, and NT exegetes in particular, it is an essential area of study.

Defining Terms: The "Septuagint"

The term "Septuagint" is often used in modern English to refer to any of the ancient Greek translations of the Hebrew Scriptures, of which there were several (Jobes and Silva, 14–17). Strictly speaking, the term refers to the first of these ancient translations made of the Hebrew Pentateuch in the third century before Christ and most likely in Egypt. Through the centuries Greek translations were made of the rest of the books of the Hebrew canon, and the term was extended to refer to those books as well, though some scholars prefer the term "Old Greek" (OG) for those initial translations of the biblical books beyond the Pentateuch. The designation LXX/OG denotes what is presumed to be the oldest translation of a given biblical book, as distinguished from subsequent revisions and later Greek versions.

At the time of Jesus, there was more than one Greek translation in circulation, much as there are many English translations of the OT today. Although in general English usage the term "Septuagint" is commonly used somewhat inaccurately to refer to any ancient Greek translation of the Hebrew Bible, specialists would want to reserve the term to refer to the original Greek translation in distinction from its revisions and other known translations, such as Aquila (α′), Theodotion (θ′), and Symmachus (σ′).

The LXX/OG in the NT: Methodological Thoughts

It is clear to any reader of the Bible that the NT writers referred to the Jewish Scriptures by adopting their vocabulary, embracing their theological concepts, and including allusions and quotations from them in their own writings. English readers may be puzzled when checking a quotation in the NT with its OT source text only to find that sometimes the two do not agree. In many cases the reason for the discrepancy is that the NT writers, writing in Greek, often quote from a Greek version of the OT, whereas modern English Protestant Bibles are translated from the Hebrew Masoretic Text (MT). In many places the Hebrew text and its corresponding Greek translation do not agree, sometimes in small ways and sometimes quite drastically. In addition to differences introduced at its origin by the Greek translators for various reasons, the complex history of textual transmission of each of the three texts involved—the Hebrew text, the Greek translation, and the NT text itself—makes it difficult to explain with certainty the differences between the MT and the LXX/OG and between both of those and the NT. There were plenty of opportunities for copyist errors, interpretive differences, and deliberate modifications to slip in during the transmission of these biblical texts through the centuries when manuscripts were copied by hand.

The use of the OT in the NT is a complex field of study that encompasses not only quotations of the OT in the NT but also allusions, references to OT people, places, and practices, conceptual parallels, and typology (see the article "Quotation, Allusion, and Echo" elsewhere in the dictionary). This essay addresses not the general use of the OT in the NT but, more narrowly, the use of the Septuagint in the NT. The determination of whether the NT writer is quoting a Hebrew source text by producing his own Greek translation of it or is quoting one of the preexisting Greek versions of the OT is an important distinction for exegetical methodology even if uncertainty persists.

First, if a NT writer quotes or alludes to a preexisting Greek version of the OT that was in circulation, it would be a methodological error to turn immediately to the Hebrew MT as the source text for use in NT exegesis. This is true even where the Greek quotation in the NT aligns reasonably well with the corresponding Hebrew of the MT, for sometimes the immediate context in the Greek OT passage is different from the immediate context of the source text in the MT. One of the reasons a NT author quotes the OT "is to create a certain set of associations in his reader, because the quotation evokes a bundle of ideas connected with its context, and/or its interpretation and usage" (Hartman, 134). If, as often seems to be the case, the NT writer intends to evoke the larger immediate context of the OT source text, then it is important for the exegete to know which immediate context is intended, the Hebrew or the Greek. On the other hand, if the NT writer himself is translating a Hebrew source text into Greek, then the quotation sits in relative isolation from any preexisting Greek version and the immediate context of the MT should probably be assumed for exegetical purposes.

Second, there is little exegetical significance to differences between the Hebrew and Greek OT texts if a NT writer is simply quoting a preexisting Greek version of the OT (although those differences are possibly of great significance for textual criticism of the LXX/OG and the MT). The NT context in which the OT is quoted alone governs the significance of its inclusion. Sometimes a NT writer will deliberately introduce a difference between the OT source text and the NT quotation by revising the syntax of a quotation to fit its new linguistic context. Perhaps differences arise because the NT writer is paraphrasing either the Hebrew or the Greek OT text, perhaps due to a lapse in memory. But if a NT writer has deliberately modified the OT Hebrew or Greek quotation for his own rhetorical or theological purposes, then that textual difference becomes exegetically significant in understanding how the NT writer was thinking about the OT source text and what it contributes to the immediate NT discourse. Even a NT author's choice and unmodified quotation of a Hebrew or Greek OT reference implies a hermeneutical intent.

The Septuagint in the NT

Lexical influence. It has long been understood that biblical Greek is not, as once thought in the nineteenth century, a Semitized dialect of Greek unto itself, but represents the widely used Koine Greek of its time. Lexical studies of the Greek words unique to the LXX/OG and NT have shown that except for theological and religious terms and perhaps terms referring to Jewish customs and practices, the language of the Greek Bible was the same as that found in the vast corpus of secular Koine Greek literature (Jobes and Silva, 202–3). In the case of specific terms from Jewish culture that had no equivalent in Greek language at the time the first Hebrew-to-Greek translation was made, the translators used some rationale unknown to us to find or create a Greek word with which to represent the Hebrew term (Lee, 173–209). Perhaps they chose Greek words already in spoken use by Greek-speaking Jews in the diaspora communities, such as the Sabbath (*sabbaton*) or Passover (*pascha*, from Heb. *pesaḥ*). The choices that subsequent translators found in the Septuagint Pentateuch, or possibly in word lists available to subsequent translators, likely set the conventions followed by later Hebrew-to-Greek translators of the other biblical books (Lee, 202–8).

Some common Hebrew words were essentially transliterated into Greek letters in the LXX (cf. *pascha* and *sabbaton* above). In other cases, a Greek word was chosen whose semantic range only partially overlapped with that of the Hebrew word. An example of this is the use of the Greek word *nomos* to refer to the Hebrew *tôrâ*. The semantic ranges of *nomos* and *tôrâ* overlap in meaning only in legal contexts where *tôrâ* refers to Mosaic legislation. But *tôrâ* has a much larger semantic range that includes the concept of "instruction," and the term is also used to refer to the Pentateuch. These usages fell far outside the native semantic range of the Greek word *nomos*. A native Greek speaker who encountered *nomos* in these broader contexts might have puzzled over its sense, but by exposure to common Jewish usage would have come to understand the Hebrew background of the word.

The concept of "covenant" (*bərît*) also presented a translation issue. Whatever their rationale, the Septuagint translators chose the Greek word *diathēkē*, which in classical Greek referred to a last will or testament. Greek readers would have had to learn the sense of the word *diathēkē* when used in Hebrew contexts on the basis of the Hebrew texts and not from the Greek lexicon. Other terms in the NT, such as *dikaiosynē*, *klēronomia*, *pneuma*, and *hilastērion*, must be understood with attention to their Hebrew counterparts as mediated through the Greek Jewish Scriptures. (See Lee, 184–200, for discussion of other such words.)

Theological concepts. There can be no doubt that the Greek Jewish Scriptures form an important literary and theological context in which the NT must be interpreted. The NT is not a conceptually unrelated, independent Greek work but was intended by its authors to be the second act of the story of redemption that began in the Hebrew Bible. There is a unity to the two parts of our Bible despite their origin in two different languages. That historical fact justifies reading the NT in light of the OT and assuming an organic relationship between the two Testaments. Just as a seed contains in some mysterious way everything that will grow from it, the OT contains the material from which the message of the NT will grow in the light of the coming of Jesus Christ.

In the many centuries after the Hebrew Bible was written and before the NT writers took up their pens, the Septuagint translators contextualized the message of the Hebrew Bible for Greek-speaking Jewish readers living in diaspora. Adolf Deissmann (95) once commented that Greek Judaism had with the Septuagint plowed the furrows for the gospel seed in the Western world. F. F. Bruce (50) adds that it was the Christian preacher quoting the Septuagint who sowed that seed of the gospel. Bruce notes several places "in which the Septuagint translators used a form of words which (without their being able to foresee it, naturally) lent itself to the purposes of the NT writers better than the Hebrew text would have done." One famous example is Matt. 1:23 quoting Isa. 7:14, where the OG translates the MT's "young woman" (*ʿlmh*) with the Greek *parthenos*, a word that tilts toward underscoring the virginity of the young woman. Matthew elaborates and interprets Isa. 7:14 in light of the circumstances of Jesus's birth. The OG Isaiah also amplifies the concept of atonement for sin, making it more amenable to its identification by NT writers as a prophecy fulfilled by Jesus Christ. For instance, where the Hebrew text of Isa. 53:4 reads, "Surely he took up our pain and bore our suffering," the OG reads, "This one *bears our sins* and suffers pain for us" (NETS; italics added). Furthermore, in Isa 53:11–12 the OG translates the Hebrew verbs and their corresponding direct objects in the phrases "he will bear their iniquities" (53:11) and "he bore the sin of many" (53:12) with the same Greek verb, *anapherō* ("bear"), and noun, *hamartia* ("sin"), in both phrases, even though the Hebrew words are not the same in both phrases. The collocation of this particular Greek verb and noun is found in only three other places in the canonical books of the OG that refer to atonement (Lev. 9:10; 16:25; 2 Chron. 29:21).

In the centuries that intervened between the writing of the Hebrew biblical books and the NT, the theological concepts, practices of Judaism, and interpretation of the OT narratives developed as Judaism in diaspora contemplated its Scriptures in new times and circumstances. The Septuagint provides a glimpse into some of those interpretive developments, which in some cases were later adopted by the NT writers. As an example, in Num. 14:12 MT God tells Moses that he will smite his rebellious people with a pestilence (*deber*) and disinherit (*yrš*) them. The LXX translators rendered "pestilence" with *thanatos* (death) and the Hebrew verb *yrš* with the Greek *apollymi* (destroy), apparently representing an interpretation that is also found in the rabbinic writings. The Septuagint's understanding of Num. 14:12 is then reflected in Jude 5, "Jesus, who saved a people out of the land of Egypt, afterward destroyed those who did not believe." Jude not only adopts the interpretation of the LXX translators but also makes Jesus the subject of the sentence in place of God. Substituting a reference to Jesus where the OT text referred to God in allusions and quotations of the OT was a common way the NT writers created both continuity and discontinuity between the OT and the NT, joining their writings to the preexisting Jewish Scriptures but expressing their unique Christology of the divinity of Christ. This example also represents that large class of differences between the Septuagint and MT that are due to the interpretation of the Septuagint translators, giving us a glimpse of how the Hebrew Bible was understood at the time the translation was made.

Allusions. It is universally agreed that the NT writers allude to the OT, invoking names, places, events, and ideas, but there is little agreement on what constitutes an allusion, how many allusions the NT contains, or whether any alleged allusion refers to the OT text or more broadly to the tradition of Judaism that had been largely shaped by the Hebrew Scriptures. Despite these difficulties, interpretation of the NT message can be significantly enriched by attention to probable allusions to the OT.

But there is debate about what constitutes an allusion. As a rule of thumb, most scholars insist on at least three words in common between a NT text and the OT before a phrase is counted as an allusion. However, other factors may be considered. "The telltale key to discerning an allusion is that of recognizing an *incomparable or unique parallel in wording, syntax, concept, or cluster of motifs in the same order or structure*" (Beale, 31; italics original). But if distinctive enough, even one word could constitute an allusion, especially when combined with a cluster of shared motifs.

An example of a very unusual, distinctive word that should probably count as a one-word allusion is the feminine vocative form of *moichalides* ("adulteresses") found in James 4:4. Though often translated as "adulterous people," or "adulterers," or even "adulterers and adulteresses" (which misses James's point entirely), the Greek word is the *plural, feminine* vocative form. It is striking because James appears to address his readers in general, not just the women, and points out their moral shortcomings in various areas of their lives, not just the sexual. This vocative is likely a metaphorical reference to the image of the adulterous wife as found in the book of Hosea to show how God views his people's covenant breaking. A second connection to Hosea occurs nine verses earlier, where James 3:13 asks the question, "Who is *wise* and *understanding* among you?" a paraphrase of Hosea 14:9, "Who is *wise*? Let them realize these things. Who is discerning? Let them *understand*." This combination increases confidence in thinking that James does in fact allude to Hosea with just one Greek word, *moichalides*. Just as Hosea was calling adulterous Israel back to covenant faithfulness, James is raising a prophetic voice to point out that Christians, too, can be "adulterous" violators of the new covenant in Christ by being friends with the world. Even though translating *moichalides* in James 4:4 as "adulteresses" might be too confusing to the average English Bible reader, and even misleading, that one word does seem to be an allusion pointing back to Hosea (Jobes, "Greek Minor Prophets," 147–58).

Remembering that the Twelve were considered as one book, if the word *moichalides* in James 4:4 and the rhetorical question in 3:13 together allude to the OT theme of spiritual adultery introduced in Hosea, the first of the Minor Prophets, then we can discern several other echoes of Malachi, the last of the Twelve through the technique of lexical clustering of distinctive words. James echoes, but does not quote, Mal. 3:5–6 OG by including several distinctive words or concepts that link the passages together: Mal. 3:5 presents an array of five concepts from which James picks up the thought of the Lord drawing near (James 2:12–13) to judge the "adulteresses" (4:4) and condemns swearing oaths (5:12), defrauding workers (5:4), and oppressing widows and orphans (1:27). From Mal. 3:6, James 1:17 echoes the idea that God does not change. These two verses from Mal. 3 have been refracted into James's message in five different places, without any quotations or explicit references to either Hosea or Malachi.

This pervasive influence of the Septuagint in the NT even in those NT books that contain no explicit quotations of the OT is also observed in Philippians. While the book includes no direct OT quotations, Paul's "language and thought patterns are heavily dependent on Scripture and particularly in its Greek form" (Silva, "Philippians," 835–36). A clear allusion to Isa. 45:23 is found in Phil. 2:10–11 where the hymn to Christ's exaltation declares "every knee should bow . . . and every tongue confess" (ESV). The immediate context in Isa. 45:22–23 OG concerns God's role in salvation and reads, "Turn to me, and you shall be saved, you who are from the end of the earth! I am God, and there is no other. By myself I swear, 'Verily righteousness shall go forth from my mouth; my words shall not be turned back, *because to me every knee shall bow and every tongue shall acknowledge God*'" (AT; italics added). In Isaiah the knee bows and the tongue confesses to the God of whom "there is no other." The striking use of this OT language in reference to Christ clearly shows Paul's view of Jesus Christ's divinity and equality with God, whether or not Paul penned or simply included these words of the Christ hymn. Words originally in reference to God in the OT are often used in reference to Jesus Christ in the NT.

Furthermore, in Phil. 1:19 there are five words that are easily overlooked as an allusion to, or possibly a quotation of, Job 13:16 OG: *touto moi apobēsetai eis sōtērian* ("This will lead to salvation for me" [AT]). Paul does not introduce or otherwise indicate he is quoting Job, and the syntax of the sentence is so natural that readers would not suspect an allusion or echo of the OT here. Paul apparently does not feel it important to draw his reader's attention to the OT source text, if indeed Paul is deliberately alluding to Job. Whether or not the allusion is recognized, there is uncertainty about the significance of this sentence in Philippians. Was Paul expressing hope for a release from prison, taking *sōtērian* in its sense of deliverance? Later in the immediate context Job does describe himself metaphorically as a prisoner (Job 13:27), and there may be further resonances between Job's and Paul's situations (Hays, *Echoes of Scripture*, 22–23). Or perhaps Paul is thinking of his spiritual destiny regardless of whether he is released or not from prison (Silva, "Philippians," 836). In this case Paul is making the point that "his adversity *will result* in his deliverance . . . whether through life or death" (Silva, "Philippians," 836). Despite the question of its exegetical significance, five identical words from Job 13:16 OG in Paul's writing show that the language of this OT verse had influenced Paul's thinking at some point.

The influence of the Greek OT in these two cases from Philippians is clear, and the lexical correspondences suggest they are both references to the *text* of the Greek

OT, not simply to Jewish tradition more broadly. These two cases represent two ends of the spectrum in terms of the significance of the LXX/OG in the NT. In the case of Phil. 2:10–11 the doctrine of the deity of Jesus Christ is taught; in Phil. 1:19, the language refers to Paul's individual personal experience, if it is an allusion at all (cf. Beale, 91). These two examples from a NT book in which there are no explicit, marked quotations of the OT demonstrate both the pervasiveness of the OT in the NT as well as the range of exegetical impacts allusions can make.

Metaleptic Echoes. In intertextual studies of the OT within the NT, some scholars use the terms "echo" and "allusion" as practically synonymous. However, there may be methodological payoff for considering echoes as a class of intertextual reference distinct from allusion. Whereas an allusion is an intentional authorial act, an echo may be conscious or unconscious in the mind of the author and need not be recognized by the reader (Beetham, *Echoes*, 20–24). Although echoes are subtle references to an antecedent text, they may be nevertheless important for more deeply understanding the echoing text, for revealing the author's unstated hermeneutical assumptions about the original text, and for hinting at how the author understands the OT context of the echoed text (Beetham, *Echoes*, 23–24).

A metaleptic echo is an *unstated* resonance between a later text, in this case the NT, and an earlier source text, the OT. When a reference in the NT links the text to an earlier text, "the figurative effect . . . can lie *in the unstated or suppressed (transumed) points of resonance between the two texts*" (Hays, 20; italics added). Metaleptic echoes are triggered by a direct reference to an OT quotation or allusion and create resonances between the immediate context of the NT passage and the immediate context of the OT passage evoked by the quotation or allusion.

For example, consider the quotation of Ps. 69:9 in John 2:17, "Zeal for your house will consume me." The context in John is that Jesus has caused a ruckus in the temple courts by overturning the tables of moneychangers and of those selling sacrificial animals. In response, the Jewish leaders challenge his authority to do such a drastic act. The quotation of Ps. 69:9 (68:10 OG) in John 2:17 is slightly revised from the original statement in the Hebrew text, where the Hebrew verb is in the perfect and translates into English as "consumes/has consumed." Psalm 68:10 OG translates as expected with an aorist, *katephagen*, which carries the same sense as the Hebrew verb. However, in John 2:17, the verb is "quoted" in the *future* tense, *kataphagetai*, "will consume." This small revision in the quotation transforms an assertion into a prophecy, even though the original statement in the psalm was not prophetic. Furthermore, the quotation evokes metaleptic echoes of elements elsewhere in Ps. 68 OG that are *not* quoted, but that contribute to the exegetical significance of the quotation in John. One such metaleptic echo is found roughly ten verses later, in Ps. 69:21 MT, "They . . . gave me vinegar to drink," translated in Ps. 68:22 OG as, "For my thirst they gave me vinegar to drink" (AT). The word "vinegar" in Ps. 69:21 MT (68:22 OG) immediately brings the crucifixion of Jesus to mind for those who know the details of Jesus's death. In fact, John likely includes that detail in his telling of it to draw the reader's attention to the psalm (John 19:28–29). The further mention of "thirst" in the psalm strengthens the echo, as that word is also found to describe Jesus in John's crucifixion account (19:28). The quotation of Ps. 68:10 OG early in John's story of Jesus (2:17) points forward to the crucifixion story many chapters later where in John 19:28–29 Jesus thirsts and is given vinegar to drink. Through this unstated metaleptic echo, John signals the incident in the temple to be the first step of Jesus's path to the cross, as John remembers it (regardless of whether it occurred early in Jesus's ministry or during the last week).

The detection of such *unstated* inferences was not unknown to the rhetorical skill of the ancient world, and those who did perceive the echo perhaps felt especially rewarded. In a discussion of persuasive rhetoric, Pseudo-Demetrius, following Theophrastus, explains, "Not all possible points should be punctiliously and tediously elaborated, but some should be left to the comprehension and inference of the hearer. . . . When he perceives what you have left unsaid [he] becomes not only your hearer but your witness, a very friendly witness too" (Pseudo-Demetrius of Phaleron, *De eloc.* 4.222).

Therefore, metaleptic echoes would likely have been valued by hearers and readers in the ancient world and would have increased admiration for the author's expertise by those able to detect them. And in fact, it probably has the same effect on modern Bible readers, as their increasing knowledge of the OT is rewarded when they see echoes of the OT in the NT that they had previously not recognized.

Scholars take differing views on the value of metaleptic echoes for NT exegesis, and admittedly, the criteria for identifying them may not lead the exegete to certainty about their presence, especially for those that present less volume from the OT (Beale, 32–35; Hays, 29–32). "The volume of intertextual echo varies in accordance with the semantic distance between the source and the reflecting surface. Quotation, allusion, and echo may be seen as points along a spectrum of intertextual reference, moving from the explicit to the subliminal" (Hays, 23). The probability of the NT author's intent decreases with the volume of the echo and in some cases may be the exegete's own projection into the text. However, it would be surprising indeed if there were *not* these small, but exegetically interesting, resonances between the immediate contexts of the NT discourse and the OT source text. After all, NT writers were not prooftexting from the OT but were building a coherent, organically connected continuity between the OT and the significance of Jesus Christ.

Quotations. There are various enumerations of the quotations of the OT in the NT, but most counts are about four hundred (Beale, 30). The number is debatable and varies from scholar to scholar who takes the time to count. The uncertainty is because the definition and identification of quotations in the NT is not as simple as it may sound to those English Bible readers whose printed editions nicely set off quotations in italics or display format.

Often a NT writer will introduce a quotation by a formula, such as "it is written," that clearly marks the OT source text as such. Of course, unlike modern editions of the NT with their cross-references, the biblical manuscripts did not include chapter and verse numbers, and so even when an introductory formula identifies some text as a quotation from the OT, it may not be immediately obvious from where in the OT it came until scholarly editors locate and provide that information. Other quotations, while not introduced by a formula, consist of such a number of words obviously in agreement with an OT text that a quotation is clearly intended. At this point in the reading history of the NT, most interpreters agree on where the quotations are and from where in the OT they were drawn, giving the impression that quotations are obvious.

How quotations work. Quotations are found in the literature of all literary cultures and function in a number of ways, but every instance of quotation brings together two separate and independent discourse events: the original statement, with its own historical context, and the later event in which the source is quoted by a subsequent author.

Given that "context is king" over meaning, even when a quotation is word for word with its source text, the semantic effect it has in the quoting text may, intentionally or not, be different from its contribution in the source text. Meir Sternberg (107–8) observes, "However accurate the wording of the quotation and however pure the quoter's motives, tearing a piece of discourse from its original habitat and recontextualizing it within a new network of relations cannot but interfere with its effect." Furthermore, when quoting a previous source, the network of illocutionary intentions of the original quotation within its source is subordinated "to another network [of intentions, attitudes, and acts] which represents the potential illocutionary force expressed by the quoter" (Lane-Mercier, 205).

And so, when interpreting a quotation of the OT in the NT one must ask how the quotation connects to its new context and with what illocutionary effect. When a NT writer invokes an OT quotation, putting it into a new network of discourse relationships, he creates new discursive space in which to develop his own illocutionary purposes, possibly including echoes that must inform our exegesis of the NT passage. Various NT writers who quote the OT—even if they all quote the same OT verse—are putting the quotation to a different use and embedding it in a different textual context, and therefore are creating a discursive space unique to their own illocutionary purposes. (An illocutionary purpose is the purpose for which a statement is made, such as commanding, requesting, promising, warning. For instance, the locution, "'There's a spider under your chair,' has the illocutionary purpose of warning" [*Merriam-Webster*, s.v. "illocutionary"].)

Quotations carry with them an implicit authority or relevance that can presumably be recognized by both author and readers. In the NT the large number of quotations—almost all drawn from the Jewish Scriptures and from almost every book of those Scriptures—indicates the high value and authority NT writers put on the OT. In this case of biblical texts, voices from Israel's distant past reappear in later biblical texts as authoritative voices speaking into a new temporal (first c. AD), geopolitical (Roman rule), and theological (post-Easter) context. The quotations of the OT in the NT allow the voice of the authoritative OT writers to speak into the new setting following the incarnation and resurrection of Jesus Christ.

In order to bring the distant voices of OT biblical writers into dialogue with texts produced in a later stage of redemptive history, the NT writers often revise or amplify the original voice. Sometimes the revision is simply in order to produce a grammatical Greek sentence when the clause is embedded in its new context. For instance, Isa. 52:7 in both the MT and OG texts speaks of a singular messenger who brings good news, hence the singular participle in the OG, *euangelizomenou*. But when the verse is quoted in Rom. 10:15, the feet referred to are those of Christian messengers, plural. Accordingly the participle was revised to its plural form, *tōn euangelizomenōn*, simply for grammatical agreement.

But often revisions are made in order to reinterpret the past understanding of the OT writer putting it both in continuity with and in contrast to the new reality in Christ. Even if the revision of the original voice is slight or not revised at all, the new context into which an old voice is brought—for instance, Isaiah's voice (Isa. 53) brought into 1 Peter (2:21–25)—imparts new nuances of meaning. Because the NT writers recognize the incarnation, life, death, and resurrection of Jesus as a hermeneutical event of epoch-making import, they proceed to interpret Israel's ancient Scriptures in light of that event and vice versa.

When a previous source is quoted, the original intention of the OT author is subordinated to the thoughts, intents, and purposes of the NT writer. The original intention of the OT text within its own historical context remains important to understand in comparison to the way the quotation functions in the NT text because of the organic relationship between the OT and NT. In the NT, the OT is quoted often as a source of authority and theological context for the new thoughts about Jesus Christ being presented. But quotation as proof of authority or truth is only one aspect of the use of quotation. Quotations also afford the quoting author a space in which to revise, advance, or otherwise engage the source text, as would be needed when explaining Christ's relationship to the Jewish Scriptures. Quotations of the OT in the NT are generally used not as proof texts but as triggers to evoke an entire pericope of the source text and to create space in which the relevance of the quotation for the Christian gospel can be developed.

The quotations of the OT in the NT explain, either directly or indirectly, the significance of Jesus Christ in terms that would have been understandable to readers of the Jewish Scriptures of the first century. To that end there are several discernable ways OT quotations in the NT function (for one enumeration, see Beale, 55–93). The Gospels and Acts demonstrate the use of OT quotations to point out the fulfillment of prophecy by the events and circumstances surrounding Jesus. For instance, Matt. 2:17 quotes Jer. 31:15 in reference to the slaughter of the innocents; Matt. 4:14–16 quotes Isa. 9:1–2 (OG) in reference to Jesus's location in Galilee; Luke 4:18–19, 21 quotes Isa. 61:1–2 to indicate the ways Jesus is the fulfillment; John 13:18 quotes Ps. 41:9 to show that the betrayal of Judas was not unexpected; John 19:24 quotes Ps. 22:18 concerning the disposition of Jesus's garment at the crucifixion; Acts 2:16–21 quotes Joel 2:28–32 to show that the Pentecost event was foreseen by the prophet. The Gospel writers often introduce such quotations with a fulfillment formula—for instance, "this was to fulfill" or "this is what was spoken by the prophet." Some of these quotations would have been understood at the time of Jesus to be messianic prophecies (such as Mic. 5:2, 4 quoted in Matt. 2:5–6). Other christological prophecies emerged only when the NT writers identified them as such (e.g., Hosea 11:1 in Matt. 2:15).

The First Gospel also presents a second way the NT uses the OT—namely, to indicate a typological historical event during OT times as recapitulated in the life of Jesus, such as the famous Matt. 2:15, quoting Hosea 11:1 in reference to the relocation of the infant Jesus to Egypt. (See Beale, 57–66, for further examples; also Hays, 95–104, for the Israel/church typology.)

OT quotations and allusions are sometimes used to form an analogy between ancient Israel and Christian believers, which some interpreters consider a typological use. The exodus from Egypt into the promised land forms a prophetic analogy with the Christian exodus from sin into the kingdom of God. The exodus and its attendant events often form a negative pole of an analogy with expected Christian belief or behavior. The NT writers exhort Christians not to follow the example of ancient Israel's rebellions—for example, Heb. 3:7–11, 15; 4:7 quoting Ps. 95:7–8, "Today, if you hear his voice do not harden your hearts as you did in the rebellion."

The NT writer, especially Paul (e.g., Rom. 1:1–6), often takes an OT text as his theological basis for building an argument for the gospel of Jesus Christ as the telos of redemptive history. The allusion to Isa. 45:23 found in Phil. 2:10–11 is an example of taking a given theological concept from the OT, here the sovereign kingship of God, and extending it to develop the unique Christology of the NT. In 1 Cor. 2:16 Paul discusses the role of the Holy Spirit making it possible for the believer to know God, and concludes with a quotation of Isa. 40:13 OG, "Who has known the mind of the Lord?" In its original context this was a rhetorical question with the expected answer, "No one." But the apostle then answers the question in a stunning way, "But we have the mind of Christ," asserting that the crucified Christ is the Lord and further that the Holy Spirit makes it possible for us to know God (the focus of 1 Cor. 2). "The use of the word 'mind' here links this last comment with the LXX quotation, but the Hebrew original, as well as the context of Paul's discussion more generally makes clear that what the apostle means is, 'We have the Spirit of Christ and therefore we really know Christ'" (Silva, "Old Testament in Paul," 634).

The writer of Hebrews displays a distinctive use of the OT by putting the words of the OT directly into the mouths of God the Father and Jesus Christ (Jobes, "Putting"). All NT writers demonstrate their belief in the continuing authority of the OT in the life of the Christian church, but the writer of Hebrews most clearly displays a belief similar to the modern evangelical doctrine of Scripture, that the OT texts are the very word of God. The author of Hebrews uses words from the OT to allow the reader to overhear a dialogue between the Father and the Son. The dialogue begins in Heb. 1 with God the Father speaking various excerpts of the OT, reappropriating them from their original historical contexts to describe the work of the Son by whom God has spoken once and for all (Heb. 1:2). Although we find no parables, beatitudes, or teachings from the earthly ministry of Jesus in Hebrews, he does speak twice, in 2:11–13 and 10:5–7, where we find the words—from Ps. 22:22 (21:23 OG) and Isa. 8:17–18, and from Ps. 40 (Ps. 39 OG), respectively—put directly into Christ's mouth. In Hebrews, Jesus Christ speaks *only* words of the OT, and in both places they are words that reveal and clarify the mission of his incarnation. Remarkably, in this dialogue we hear the agreement between God the Father and the Son to establish the new covenant based on Christ's blood!

For instance, the "misquote" of Ps. 39:7–9 OG in Heb. 10:5–7 contains several small but exegetically significant differences that provide an excellent example of the two "speakings" mentioned in Heb. 1:1. A thousand years after David spoke the psalm, Christ the Son—both Son of God and son of David—spoke it. David says, "To do your will, my God, I desire" (Ps. 40:8 AT). But David's desire exceeded David's ability. When the words are put in Christ's mouth in Heb. 10:7, a transposition and truncation of the quotation locates the accomplishment of God's will as the purpose for the preceding "I have come." When Christ comes into the world he says, "I have come to do, O God, your will" (AT). What David could only desire, Christ accomplished. The transposition and truncation introduce an efficacy and finality to Christ's words that are appropriately lacking in David's.

Quotations and the language of Jesus. Quotations of the LXX/OG in the Gospels and Acts raise the complicated question of whether Jesus and others themselves used the Septuagint, despite Aramaic being the probable language of first-century Palestine. In Matthew, the evangelist's quotations of the OT usually follow the Hebrew text, but when Jesus quotes Scripture the quotation most often follows the LXX/OG reading (Jobes and Silva, 213). Of the approximately eighty quotations and allusions in Matthew, about thirty follow the Septuagint, and of those most occur in the direct speech of Jesus and John the Baptist.

In Luke 4:18, when Jesus reads Isa. 61:1 in the synagogue at Nazareth, the phrase "recovery of sight to the blind" is found instead of the Hebrew reading, "release from darkness for the prisoners." Was Jesus reading from a Greek scroll of Isaiah? Did he himself substitute the LXX reading for the Hebrew to give prophetic fulfillment to his miracles of healing the blind? Or did Luke simply quote the version of Isa. 61:1 that was accessible to him?

Of even greater interest is the case in Acts 15:13–18 of James's quotation of Amos 9:11–12 during the Jerusalem Council. The quotation clearly follows the OG version, "so that the rest of mankind and all the nations may seek me." Was the council conducted in Greek, even though it was held in Jerusalem, where Aramaic was the local language? Was Greek used in consideration of the visitors from Greek-speaking Antioch?

This classic case of Amos 9:11–12 in Acts 15:13–18 demonstrates how the Septuagint reading is often more congenial to the gospel message, displays common reasons for differences between the LXX/OG and the MT, and raises interesting questions about the Protestant doctrine of Scripture concerning inerrancy and authority. The Hebrew text of Amos 9:12 reads, "so that they may *possess* the remnant of *Edom* and all the nations," while the OG reads, "so that the rest of *mankind* and all the nations may *seek* me" (AT). One explanation of the difference between the verbs *possess* and *seek* in Hebrew is that at some point either during the transmission of the Hebrew or at the point when the translator (mis)read the Hebrew, the *yod* of *yrš*, "to inherit, possess," was read as a *dalet*, yielding the verb *drš*, "to seek." To make better sense of the verse after the inadvertent verbal change occurred, the name Edom was read as *ʾādām* (mankind), a difference of only one inferred vowel (a *qamets* or a *holem*), making either alternative reading possible (Jobes and Silva, 214–15).

An alternative explanation would be that the Hebrew *Vorlage* of Amos had been deliberately revised when the Hebrew version of the Twelve was redacted to place Obadiah, with its oracle against Edom, immediately after Amos, implying that the OG Amos may in fact preserve the original Hebrew reading.

A third explanation is that the difference was introduced by the Greek translator in order to contextualize Amos 9:12 for an audience for whom Edom symbolized one pagan nation representing "all the nations." Then, in line with the rest of the verse, "upon whom my name is called," the translator interpreted and contextualized the concept of possessing Edom in terms of *seeking* God, a more general pagan response.

In the absence of early manuscripts the answer to this puzzle will probably never be known with certainty. Which of these explanations most appeals may depend primarily on the sensitivities of the modern interpreter. Regardless, it is certain that in Acts 15, at a highly significant moment in Christian history, James is presented as quoting the OG text of Amos that either represented the original pre-MT Hebrew in the first place, or was the result of a misreading of the Hebrew text by the OT Greek translator, or was an interpretation of the Hebrew text by the Greek translator. In any case, James apparently presumes full scriptural authority in support of his argument.

Doctrinal Issues: The Authority of the OT in the NT

The many interesting cases of the use of the Septuagint by the NT writers raise thorny issues concerning the doctrine of Scripture, especially inerrancy. Because of the inspiration and authority of the original Hebrew texts as divine revelation, the authority of its translation in the Septuagint and the further authority of the Septuagint as quoted in the inspired NT, such as in Acts 15:13–18, has been discussed with respect to the relationships of the text forms. Where the Septuagint text form quoted in the NT does not match its corresponding Hebrew text, various attempts have been made to explain how divine authority is preserved.

One approach is to declare that the NT quotation "means" the same as the MT text, but this is problematic because the reappropriation of a text as quotation in a different time and for different illocutionary purposes implicitly confutes this approach. Whether or not the NT authors recognized any differences between the text they quote and the corresponding Hebrew, we must respect the words they wrote, even if they don't say exactly what the MT says.

A second approach throughout church history has been to declare the Septuagint translation to be divinely inspired. Christian debates over whether the Septuagint was inspired or not date back at least to the time of Augustine and Jerome and assume the authority of the *Greek* quotation is derived from its origin in the inspired

Hebrew text. Augustine argued that the Septuagint, and the Septuagint alone (in distinction from later Greek versions such as Theodotion, Symmachus, and Aquila), was inspired. Furthermore, he understood the differences between the Septuagint and the Hebrew text as progressive revelation (*Doctr. chr.* 2.15 [*NPNF*[1] 2:542–43]).

A different and more satisfying approach is found by conceptualizing the quotations of the OT in the NT as part of a new divine speech-act. This may clear the way for seeing how quotations, primarily from the Septuagint or other Greek version, can carry normative, divine authority even when they don't agree with the corresponding extant Hebrew text. This is because the divine authority of the quotations of the OT in the NT is derived not from the textual relationship between the Greek and its corresponding Hebrew but from hearing the NT writer's use of the Septuagint as a new divine speech-act.

The divine inspiration of the NT in its entirety means it is the Father's locution (statements) given for the Father's illocutionary purposes (informing, warning, promising, commanding, etc.) through human authors who wrote under various influences. "Scripture is itself a mighty speech act by which God reveals himself in his Son Jesus Christ. . . . Scripture is neither simply the recital of the acts of God nor merely a book of inert propositions. Scripture is rather composed of divine-human speech acts that through what they say accomplish several authoritative cognitive, spiritual and social functions" (Vanhoozer, 131). The illocutionary intent of the NT writers who quote the OT was, generally speaking, to persuade their readers of the truth of the gospel of Jesus Christ. The NT writers wanted to explain how the gospel of Jesus Christ and the Christian belief that developed around it were not new inventions but were the culmination of the work and word of God as inscripturated in the Hebrew sacred texts. NT authors quote the Septuagint, sometimes with amazing accuracy, sometimes with intriguing differences, but in all cases with an illocutionary intent that recontextualizes the quotations for postresurrection readers.

This means locutions once spoken by God through the OT writers in the past are spoken anew through the inspired NT author. So, rather than assuming the NT quotation's authority derives primarily from the inspiration of the autograph of its *source* text, we should see its authority as the result of its being part of a new, divine speech-act through the NT writers that happens to include a locution from previous Scripture. Since the texts of both the OT and NT are divine speech-acts in their own right, when the NT quotes the OT, there is an appropriation of a previous speech-act of God in a new speech-act that potentially, and in fact often, does not have the same illocutionary purpose as the original, even though the locution (the quoted text) may be identical or nearly so. The interaction between the discourse that frames the quotation and the quotation itself may in effect change perspective (by putting the quotation in a different mouth), participants (by ambiguating or reassigning antecedents of pronouns), tone (by using words that occur in the quotation differently in the frame), and so on. The quotation may or may not be comprised of the expected, translated wording of the Hebrew; its wording may or may not agree precisely with known ancient Greek translations; and it may or may not be used in a way that matches its contribution to the OT context.

This means that the divine inspiration and authority of the quotation, presented in Greek translation in the NT, does *not* depend only on its relationship to the Hebrew. The question of whether the Greek translators were inspired becomes moot, as does the question of how the textual form of the Greek quotation originated. This is not to say that the relationship of the Greek to its corresponding Hebrew is not an interesting and important question. Nor is it to deny that it is exegetically significant to determine if the form of the quotation was created by the NT author or was simply the text in the Greek OT available to him. But *theologically*, God's restatement in the NT of a previous locution of the OT, whether in the same or in a different form, does not threaten the doctrine of inspiration. Therefore, we need not be troubled by the inclusion of the uninspired Septuagint text as an authoritative source in the NT.

See also OT Use of the OT: Comparison with the NT Use of the OT; Quotation, Allusion, and Echo; *other Septuagint articles*; *Dead Sea Scrolls articles*; *Mishnah, Talmud, and Midrashim articles*; *Philo articles*; *Targums articles*

Bibliography. Beale, G. K., *Handbook on the New Testament Use of the Old Testament* (Baker Academic, 2012); Beetham, C., *Echoes of Scripture in the Letter of Paul to the Colossians*, BIS 96 (Leiden: Brill, 2008); Bruce, F. F., *The Canon of Scripture* (InterVarsity, 1988); Deissmann, A., *New Light on the New Testament* (T&T Clark, 1908); Hartman, L., "Scriptural Exegesis in the Gospel of St. Matthew and the Problem of Communication," in *L'Évangile selon Matthieu*, ed. M. Didier, BETL 29 (Duculot, 1970), 131–52; Hays, R. B., *Echoes of Scripture in the Letters of Paul* (Yale University Press, 1989); Hengel, M., *The Septuagint as Christian Scripture* (T&T Clark, 2002); Jobes, K. H., "The Greek Minor Prophets in James," in *The Letters and Liturgical Tradition*, vol. 2 of *"What Does the Scripture Say?,"* ed. C. A. Evans and H. D. Zacharias (T&T Clark, 2012), 147–58; Jobes, "Putting Words in His Mouth," in *So Great a Salvation*, ed. J. Laansma, G. H. Guthrie, and C. L. Westfall (T&T Clark, 2019), 40–50; Jobes, K. H., and M. Silva, *Invitation to the Septuagint*, 2nd ed. (Baker Academic, 2015); Lane-Mercier, G., "Quotation as a Discursive Strategy," *Kodikas* 14 (1991): 199–214; Lee, J. A. L., *The Greek of the Pentateuch* (Oxford University Press, 2018); *Merriam-Webster Dictionary*, s.v. "illocutionary," https://www.merriam-webster.com/dictionary/illocutionary; Silva, M., "Old Testament in

Paul," in *DPL*, 630–42; Silva, "Philippians," in *CNTUOT*, 835–39; Sternberg, M., "Proteus in Quotation-Land," *Poetics Today*, 3, no. 2 (1982): 107–56; Vanhoozer, K. J., *First Theology* (InterVarsity, 2002).

KAREN H. JOBES

Septuagint: Thematic Parallels to the NT

Around 280–250 BC, the Jewish community living in Alexandria, Egypt, translated the Hebrew Torah into Greek (Let. Aris. 309; Philo, *Moses* 2.31–40; Josephus, *Ant.* 12.11, 106–9). The accounts attribute the translation of the Torah to seventy-two translators (six from each of the twelve tribes of Israel), which was simplified to seventy (e.g., Sef. Torah 1.8, assimilating to the number of elders at Sinai or the Sanhedrin), hence the popular title, Septuagint (LXX). By the time of Justin Martyr (d. ca. 165), Christians believed that the Seventy had translated the whole OT, presumably interpreting *nomos* in the primary sources to refer to the whole OT (Gallagher, 93). The prologue to Ben Sira (ca. 130 BC) indicates that most of the Greek translations of the Law, the Prophets, and the other books were completed by then, but a few translations were probably produced just before the turn of the era (e.g., Esther). At this time, the Jews were also composing new works in Greek (e.g., 2 Maccabees) and translating books not traditionally included in the Hebrew canon (e.g., Ben Sira; Tobit). Eventually, in some Christian quarters, Tobit, Judith, Wisdom, Sirach, and 1–2 Maccabees were included in canons of the western church, even though their relationship to the Seventy would remain fuzzy (e.g., Augustine, *Doctr. chr.* 2.22; cf. *Civ.* 18.43; for Augustine's knowledge of the Maccabees' work after the time of the Seventy, see *Civ.* 18.36), while some church fathers neither included them among the books of the biblical canon nor considered them translated by the Seventy (e.g., Cyril of Jerusalem, *Cat. Lect.* 4.33, 35; Gallagher and Meade, 112–14). Thus, defining the Seventy's corpus in the Second Temple period and Late Antiquity remains complex (Meade, "Septuagint," 226–27). Below, I include these books in reconstructing the thematic parallels between the NT and the LXX. A further complicating factor in defining the oeuvre of the Seventy is that some Jewish communities began to revise already existing translations soon after the original translations were completed. One such tradition known as the Kaige recension is dated to just before the turn of the era and gained some prominence among some Jews.

The Greek translations reflect exegesis (see Tov, 197–98, for categories that vary from linguistic to theological exegesis), but whether LXX exegesis or theology is substantially different from the Hebrew Bible remains debated. Some conclude that a theology of the LXX would be more or less identical with a theology of the Hebrew OT (Wagner, 21), while others are more optimistic that a distinctive theology of the LXX can be written based on the Greek translators' own hermeneutical and theological ideas that influenced their work (Rösel, "Toward," 239, 251; Law, 170). Since Origen, Christians have known about differences between the Hebrew and Greek copies of the OT. Origen himself, for example, defended the Greek copies of the churches and described some of the larger transpositions vis-à-vis Hebrew copies "as though the thought [*dianoia*] does not seem to be equal [*paraplēsia*]" (*Ep. Afr.* 7–8). Although debates and uncertainties over this matter persist, the analysis below surveys thematic parallels between the HB (Hebrew Bible), LXX, and NT.

Resurrection

The teaching that God would raise individuals from the dead at the eschaton is a prominent theme in the NT that has its roots in the Hebrew Scriptures, the Greek translations, and Jewish Greek works.

HB. The HB often depicts death as a place or realm where someone descends and does not return (e.g., Sheol in Job 7:9–10; Block, 44–46; Johnston, 69–124). But Yahweh is praised as the one who kills and makes alive (Deut. 32:39; cf. 1 Sam. 2:6). He is the all-powerful God upon whom resurrection is based. In polemic against religious syncretism, Elijah, "the man of God," confesses both that Yahweh brought the calamity of death on the widow's son (1 Kings 17:20) and that he is the one who can revive him (17:21–22). Yahweh is the God who brings the dead to life, exhibiting his power over the Canaanite god of death, Mot. He also promises not to abandon David and his dynasty to Sheol and to prevent him from seeing the pit (Ps. 16:10). Yahweh makes the dry bones of the nation of Israel live again by opening the graves, bringing the bones out, and placing his spirit (*rûaḥ*) in them (Ezek. 37:1–14). In Isa. 26:12–19, the community's prayer refers to the "lords" who ruled them as the dead who will not see, as shades who will not rise (v. 14). But their prayer ends with an affirmation that God's dead ones will live and their corpses will rise (v. 19). This reference to resurrection comes after the prophet has already sounded death's defeat or death's being swallowed (cf. 25:8, the opposite of the Canaanite myth in which Mot swallows Baal; see Coogan and Smith, 139). (See the section "The Servant of the Lord" below for the theme of death and resurrection in the context of the servant.) Daniel 12:2 depicts the eschatological resurrection of those who are asleep, some to everlasting life, and some to shame and everlasting contempt. The HB, therefore, describes Yahweh as the God who makes alive, a theme further developed by the LXX and NT.

LXX. Both the Greek translations of the Hebrew Scriptures and the Jewish Greek compositions continue and amplify the theme of resurrection in the Hebrew text. OG Deut. 32:39 translates the Hebrew straightforwardly as *egō apoktenō kai zēn poiēsō* ("I will kill and I will make alive"). According to HRCS, LXX Dan. 12:2 is the only place where *anistēmi* ("to rise") translates II *qyṣ* ("to wake up"; cf. Ps. 3:6), amplifying the meaning of resurrection already latent in the Hebrew. The translator used the same Greek verb for *ʿmd* ("to stand") in 12:13, further elucidating the notion of resurrection in the Hebrew.

In LXX Isa. 26:14 ("The dead will not see life, nor will physicians raise [them]"), the translator renders the *qal* intransitive *qwm* ("to rise") with the active/transitive *anistēmi* ("to raise"), denying Israel's "lords" resurrection. In Isa. 26:19, the Greek amplifies the Hebrew: "Your dead will rise [*anistēmi* for *ḥyh*, "to live," as in 38:9], and those in tombs will be raised, and those in the earth will rejoice." The Hebrew of the middle clause is difficult (*nəbēlātî yəqûmûn*, "the corpse(s) of mine [i.e., the people] will rise"), since the noun is singular (though often used in a collective sense; cf., e.g., Isa. 5:25) and the verb is plural. Furthermore, the identity of the Hebrew's first-person pronoun is not obvious with either the Lord or the people in view, depending on whether v. 19 concludes the people's prayer or opens a new discourse with the Lord as speaker, though the division between vv. 19 and 20 is traditional and makes good sense (de Waard, 113). Against this background, some scholars have concluded the OG has been lost and only an early Christian interpolation ("those in tombs") from the Gospels remains (cf. Matt. 27:52–53; John 5:28–29), or OG offers a more elaborate translation of the Hebrew (see Barthélemy, 187, for brief survey). In either case, the Greek translation amplifies the theme of bodily resurrection from the dead. As taken up below (see "The Servant of the Lord"), OG Isa. 53:11 attests the original Hebrew text ("He will see light") and envisions the Lord "showing light" to the servant.

In Job 14:14, the Hebrew poses the question, "If a man dies, will he live (again)?" (AT). The Greek removes the question, "For, if a man dies, he will live (again)." Though the Hebrew of Job 19:26 remains obscure, OG Job 19:25–26 envisions Job praying in response to God who is about to undo him on earth, "May my skin, which patiently endures these things, rise up." OG Job has two additions to the Hebrew (42:17a and 42:17b–e), both considered to be part of the early transmission of the OG text—not part of the Old Greek itself (Cox, 386). The first addition says, "Now it has been written that he will rise again with those the Lord raises up," referring to the resurrection of the dead. Theodotion revises the latter part: *meth' hēmōn hoti theos anastēsei* ("with us because God will raise"), which shows that the longer text must have been added before the first century AD in order for Theodotion to revise it (Meade, *Hexaplaric*, 398–99). Beyond the Greek translations of the Hebrew, in several texts in 2 Maccabees (7:9, 11, 14, 23, 29, 36; 12:44; 14:46), the theme of the resurrection of the dead is prominent.

However, caution in the interpretation of some texts is required. For example, Schaper (47; cf. Wright, 148) interprets the translation of *qwm* with *anistēmi* in Ps. 1:5 as follows: "The Greek . . . altered the psalm's nature as a whole by reinterpreting a single word. The usage of *anistēmi* as an intransitive verb referring to the future state of a group of individuals clearly confers the idea of 'rising from the dead,' 'be resurrected.'" But this interpretation has been rightly challenged (Jobes and Silva, 342). Before giving some positive examples, for this first example, it is worth showing in some detail why OG Ps. 1:5 does not develop the theme of the eschatological resurrection and should serve as a caution to further missteps. *Qwm* is used forty-six times in Psalms, and the translator renders it in various ways (cf. table 1).

Table 1. Greek Equivalents of *qwm* in Psalms

Hebrew	Greek	Examples (LXX versification)
qwm qal (35x)	*anistēmi* (21x)	
	epanistēmi (7x)	3:2; 26:3, 12; 53:5; 85:14; 108:28; 123:2;
	histēmi (3x)	17:39; 23:3; 35:13
	exegeirō (1x)	118:62
	egeirō (1x)	126:2
	egersis (1x)	138:2
	hyphistēmi (1x)	139:11
qwm piel (2x)	*bebaioō* (1x)	118:28
	histēmi (1x)	118:106
qwm hiphil (7x)	*histēmi* (2x)	39:3; 118:38
	anistēmi (2x)	40:11; 77:5
	antilambanō (1x)	88:44
	epitassō (1x)	106:29
	egeirō (1x)	112:7
qwm hithpalel (2x)	*anthistēmi* (1x)	16:7
	epanistēmi (1x)	58:2

For *qwm*, the translator employs semantic differentiation. For example, the translator chooses *(ex)egeirō* and cognates when the psalmist would rise up after lying or sitting down or when God raises the poor from the ground. He normally uses *epanistēmi* + *epi*/simple dative to render the qal + *ʿal*/*b* to convey "rising up against" someone. Furthermore, he renders the factitive and causative stems in Hebrew with suitable, transitive Greek equivalents. The translator reserves the middle-passive of *anistēmi* for the many places where the Hebrew has *qwm* in the *qal* with an intransitive meaning. At several places the psalmist implores God to rise up (LXX 3:8; 7:7; 9:20 et al.). He depicts a generation rising up and telling God's law to their sons (LXX 77:6), and he enquires who will rise up for him against the wicked (LXX 93:16). Significantly, in LXX Ps 87:11, the translator deviates from his usual approach and renders *qwm qal* (intransitive) with an active form of *anistēmi* (transitive): "Surely, you shall not work wonders for the dead? Or will physicians *raise up* [the dead], and they [i.e., the dead] acknowledge you?" (NETS). Here, the translator understands the Hebrew to say the psalmist does not expect doctors to raise the dead and, subsequently, the dead to acknowledge God. The active voice implies a resurrection of the dead. The translator's lexical equivalents and overall approach must be analyzed in order to determine the probability that the translator has attempted a significant exegesis. In the case of Ps. 1:5, given the translator's normal approach in rendering intransitive *qwm* with the middle-passive of *anistēmi*, one should not conclude, at least not with any certainty, that the translator intends to convey the eschatological resurrection of the dead.

NT. Resurrection of the body, especially of the Messiah, in the NT is a central theme and clearly develops the theme from the OT (Wright). Jesus taught that it was necessary for him to be killed and to be raised on the third day (Matt. 16:21). All four Gospels attest that Jesus was raised from the dead (Matt. 28:6; Mark 16:6; Luke 24:6; John 20:1–10). From the beginning of Acts, Peter announces that David prophesied about the resurrection of the Christ (2:31). The rest of Acts attests that the resurrection of Jesus was central to apostolic preaching of the gospel (e.g., 4:2, 33; 17:31–32). In 24:15, 21, Paul testifies that he is on trial for a belief shared with his accusers that God will raise both the just and the unjust from the dead. The resurrection of the Messiah and all people is such a crucial doctrine that Paul includes it among matters of chief importance (1 Cor. 15:3), concluding that if Christ has not been raised, then his followers are still in their sins (15:17; cf. Rom. 4:24–25).

Conclusion. The concept of resurrection is found in the HB, and the Greek translations preserve it and often amplify it or make it explicit by their renderings. Second Maccabees clearly teaches the resurrection of the dead. The NT illuminates this theme (e.g., 2 Tim. 1:10) since the authors bear witness that God raised Jesus from the dead.

Creation

Creation is a major theme found on the Bible's opening page and the last pages of Revelation. This theme is prominent in the HB, LXX, and NT.

HB. The HB begins with a clear and straightforward account of the creation of the cosmos in six days. It climaxes in the creation of humanity as God's image according to his likeness on day six (Gen. 1:26–31). Before this, God speaks into existence the following: light (vv. 3–5), sky (vv. 6–8), earth (vv. 9–10), earth's vegetation (vv. 11–13), sun, moon, and stars (vv. 14–19), living creatures of sea and sky (vv. 20–23), and living creatures of the earth (vv. 24–25). Days one to five have the formulaic expression "And God said . . . And it was so. . . . The ___ day." But day six has a different form to set it off from the other days (*yôm haššiššî*, "the sixth day"). All was very good. Genesis 2 continues the theme of the creation by focusing on the creation of the man (2:7) and his wife (v. 22) with only minor mention of the creation of the animals (v. 19). Genesis 3 tells the fall and expulsion of the man and his wife from the garden and the tree of life. Other than Gen. 2:20; 3:17, 21, the Hebrew has *hāʾādām* ("the human"). In those three places, the Hebrew is indefinite (i.e., *ləʾādām*). Thus, it is difficult to know when *ʾādām* is first used as the personal name "Adam" (Wenham, 32).

Many other places in the HB reflect on the creation (e.g., Job 38–41; Pss. 8; 33; 74; 102; 104; 146:6; Prov. 8:22–31; Eccles. 1:2–11; 12:1–7; Isa. 40–55; 65:13–25; Jer. 4:19–26; Ezek. 28). Jeremiah 4:19–26 envisions the judgment and exile of Judah as a horrifying unmaking of Gen. 1 (e.g., the earth is described as formless and void, and heaven has no light). Isaiah's new heavens and new earth (65:17) and the new Jerusalem (v. 18) are undoubtedly dependent on the old creation, but only Yahweh's servants (now given "another name," v. 15) will dwell in the new creation and the new Jerusalem (65:13–14; cf. 54:17; 56:6–7). These servants are contrasted with rebellious Israel who will leave their name for Yahweh's chosen remnant to use in cursing; Yahweh will put the rebellious ones to death and give his chosen ones a new name.

LXX. The Greek translations maintain the same emphasis on creation as the HB, often bringing the source into sharper focus. In LXX Gen. 2:19, the Greek translator (or a prior Hebrew scribe) smooths out a difficulty in the original text since the Hebrew records the creation of the animals coming *after* the creation of humanity, the reverse order of chap. 1. The Greek translation clarifies the Hebrew: "And out of the earth God *furthermore* [*eti*, likely translating *ʿôd*] formed all the wild beasts . . . and he led them to Adam." Perhaps the sense is that God is creating more animals in the garden for Adam to name and to be his helper.

Although the reader of MT Gen. 2–3 may encounter a few disputed instances of the proper noun Adam as noted above, the LXX reader encounters the name much earlier and more often in the narrative. Beginning in 2:16 and continuing through chap. 5, the translator transliterates the Hebrew (*ʾādām*; cf. 1 Chron. 1:1). LXX Deut. 32:8 says, "When the Most High was apportioning the nations, as he scattered Adam's sons," reading the Hebrew (*bənê ʾādām*) as referring to Adam. The name "Adam" also appears in other Jewish Greek works from the Second Temple period. In Tob. 8:5–6 (AT), Tobias prays, "Blessed are you, O God of our fathers. . . . You made Adam and gave him his wife, Eve, as a helpful support, and from these two the descendants of humans have sprung. You said, 'It is not good that man be alone, let us make for him a helper like him.'" The author here depends on LXX Genesis. Sirach 40:1 (AT) notes, "Hard work was created for every human and a heavy yoke was placed upon Adam's sons." After tracing the OT's history, Sir. 49:16 (AT) says, "Above every living thing in the creation was Adam." Adam as a personal name does not appear outside of these references in the Greek translations and works.

OG Isaiah's vision of the new heaven and the new earth differs slightly from the Hebrew. In 65:17, the new heaven and the new earth will simply exist (*estai*) instead of the Hebrew's focus of God newly creating them. But the explanatory conjunction (*gar*) is maintained, and therefore, the translation conveys that only "those who serve [the Lord]" (vv. 13–14) will inhabit it. Although OG Isaiah varies its equivalents for Hebrew *ʿăbādîm* ("servants"; *tois therapeuousin* in 54:17; *eis doulous kai doulas* ["as male and female slaves"] in 56:6; *hoi douleuontes moi* ["those who serve me"] in 65:13), the reader still understands that only the Lord's servants will inhabit the new creation. In 65:15, OG Isaiah presents Israel as leaving their name for fullness to the Lord's elect ones. But the Lord will do away with them, while a new name will be called over those who serve him. This new name will be blessed on the earth because the servants will bless the true God, and those who swear upon the earth will swear by the true God (v. 16). OG Isaiah envisions a new people of God for the new creation.

During the period of Seleucid occupation (ca. 160 BC), the doctrine of creation encouraged the people to fear God—not the tyrant—and to cling to the future hope of resurrection. Second Maccabees 7:23 (AT) states that God is "the Creator [*ktistēs*] of the world who formed the origin of mankind and devised the origin of all things." Since he is the Creator, the text goes on to affirm that God by his mercy will return life and breath to the one who dies for his laws. In 7:28 (AT), the mother of the final son to be martyred encourages him from a doctrine of creation, "Look at the heaven and the earth and see everything that is in them and know that God did not make them out of things that existed" (*ouk ex ontōn epoiēsen auta ho theos*). Sometime later, commenting on the word "beginning" in John 1:1, Origen affirms that "God made the things that are from that which does not exist" (*ex ouk ontōn ta onta epoiēsen ho theos*), citing the teaching of "the mother of the seven martyrs in Maccabees" (*Comm. Jo.* 1.103).

NT. The NT authors ground their doctrine of creation in the Hebrew canon and reflect other early Jewish opinion on the topic (e.g., Matt. 19:4; John 1:1–3; Acts 14:17; 17:24–26; Rom. 4:17; Col. 1:15–16; Heb. 11:3; Rev. 4:11; 10:6). The NT continues to affirm that God has created heaven and earth and all things in them (e.g., Acts 17:24; cf. Ps. 146:6). Jesus grounds his teaching on marriage and divorce in God's creation of humanity as male and female (Matt. 19:4; cf. Gen. 1:27; 2:24). Paul grounds his fall and redemption narrative in the first Adam and second/last Adam (1 Cor. 15:22, 45–49; cf. Rom. 5:14), reading "the human" in Hebrew Genesis as "Adam," a connection LXX Genesis (2:16) and Theodotion (cf. 2:7) have already made. The incarnation and subsequent exaltation of the Son clarify previous reflection on the relationship between God and his Word and Wisdom in creating the world (John 1:1–3; Col. 1:15–16; cf. Ps. 33; Prov. 8:22–31; Wis. 7:21).

When describing the call and faith of Abraham and his subsequent family, Paul compares this miracle to God's creation as he calls the things that do not exist into existence (*kalountos ta mē onta hōs onta*, Rom. 4:17). Paul's language resembles that of 2 Macc. 7:28 and that of Herm. Mand. 26:1 (*poiēsas ek tou mē ontos eis to einai ta panta*). Hebrews 11:3, though using different terms, also appears to follow the logic that God's word created the universe "so that what is being seen did not come out of visible things" (*eis to mē ek phainomenōn to blepomenon gegonenai*). These passages teach that God created the universe from nothing, drawing inferences from passages like Gen. 1:1 and Isa. 45:7 as well as later Jewish reflection.

The NT also depends on the Hebrew canon and Greek translations for its promise of the new creation (e.g., 2 Cor. 5:17; Eph. 2:10, 15, 3:9; Rev. 21:1–3; 22:3–5). Paul depends on the language of Isa. 65:16–17 to communicate the passing away of the old and the coming of the new (2 Cor. 5:17). Revelation 21:1–3 envisions the new Jerusalem coming out of heaven as the new heaven and the new earth. That is, the new city is coextensive with the new cosmos, which is probably what Isaiah intends when he juxtaposes the creation of the new heavens and the new earth with the creation of the new Jerusalem in 65:17–18 (Gentry and Wellum, 521–23). Paul identifies Isaiah's servants who will receive a new name and inhabit the new creation with the church in Christ (Eph. 2:10) and the one new humanity created in him (2:15).

Conclusion. The Jewish Greek translations and compositions develop and amplify the theme of creation between the HB and the NT. The Greek translations further clarify themes of the historical person of Adam, the eternal Son, God's creation of things that exist from what did not exist, and the new creation, which are already latent in the Hebrew. The NT generally adopts these developments. But the NT further clarifies that it is Christ, the incarnation of the eternal Son, through whom and for whom all things were created, and whose resurrection is the beginning of the new creation. Furthermore, the church is the new creation in Christ. That development does not appear altogether clear from the HB or LXX (Beale and Gladd, 164).

Exodus

After the Hebrews' 430 years in slavery in Egypt, Yahweh finally fulfills his promise to the patriarchs when he leads his people out of Egypt in a grand display of his power and faithful character. The exodus is not an isolated event of God's redeeming power and love but is a type of God's future mighty acts of redemption. Thus, the exodus is a rich theme across the HB, LXX, and NT.

HB. God foretells to Abram Israel's sojourning, hardships, and eventual return to the land of the patriarchs' sojourning in Gen. 15:13–16. In Exod. 6:2–8, God speaks to Moses and says, "I am Yahweh." He confirms he is the God who appeared to Abraham, Isaac, and Jacob as El Shaddai, but by his name Yahweh he did not make himself known to them. Yahweh has remembered his covenant confirmed with the patriarchs. Therefore, he will bring Israel out of Egypt, deliver them, and redeem them with an outstretched arm and with terrible judgments. He will take them as his people and be their God. And finally, he will bring them into the land which he swore to the patriarchs.

After the mighty acts of God in the ten plagues or signs, Pharaoh releases Israel. The final wonder performed against Egypt is God's triumph over Pharaoh's armies at the Sea of Reeds (*yam sûp*) or the Red Sea (Exod. 13:18). Moses stretches out his hand over the sea, and the waters part. Israel walks through them on dry ground, but the Egyptian armies and chariots go in after them and drown when the waters come crashing down on them. This event is immediately memorialized in Moses's song in Exod. 15. The song does not merely describe the historical exodus but anticipates God's deliverance of his people into the land of promise (vv. 12–17; cf. Lohfink, 83–84). In fact, the song does not mention the people crossing through the Sea of Reeds on dry ground as the narrative account did (cf. 14:22). Rather, the song describes them as walking through the peoples of the land of Canaan (Philistines, Edom, Moab), silent as stone (v. 16), as Yahweh leads them into the land of promise, now envisioned as God's holy settlement (v. 13) and his inherited mountain, dwelling place, and established sanctuary (v. 17). In sum, the exodus was both a historical event and a prophetic type of God's future acts of redemption.

Before moving to the new exodus in some of the prophets, important to note is the great, faithful, covenant love of Yahweh as the ground for the exodus and care of Israel through the wilderness and entrance into the promised land (Exod. 34:6–7). Moses glimpsed the hinder parts of God's glory (Exod. 33:18, 23) from the rock and heard the revelation of God's name as "compassionate and gracious, slow to anger, and great of loyal love and truth" (34:6 AT). Yahweh's glory expressed in the greatness of his loyal and faithful love (*rab ḥesed we'ĕmet*) remains the ground for the first exodus and all other mighty, salvific acts of God.

The Song of the Sea typifies the way in which Yahweh will lead them across the Jordan River as a second exodus (Josh. 3:17) and also how Isaiah's new exodus out of Babylon will unfold (cf. the highway in the wilderness in 40:3–5; the exodus from Babylon in 48:20–21; the new entry into the promised land in 49:8–12; the new victory at the sea in 51:9–10; the new exodus in 52:11–12). Furthermore, the exodus from Egypt would typify the exodus out of sin and death accomplished by Yahweh's servant, his Messiah (Isa. 49:1–6; 52:13–53:12; on "the sure mercies performed by [the future] David" in Isa. 55:3 AT as located in the Servant Songs, especially the fourth, cf. Gentry, "Rethinking," 294). The physical return from exile or the new exodus would also typify this greater exodus by which God would restore the corrupt Jerusalem of the old creation as the new city of truth in the new creation (cf. Motyer, 326, 352, on Isaiah's national and spiritual redemptions and the different servants of Yahweh who accomplish the great and greater deliverances, respectively). Jeremiah 16:14–18 predicts people will no longer say, "As Yahweh lives who brought up Israel from the land of Egypt," but "As Yahweh lives who brought Israel from the land of the north and from all the lands where he drove them" (AT). Thus, the new exodus, patterned after the old one, will surpass it. Before this, Jeremiah had already announced that each of the nations would undergo their own exodus and return, and even be built or restored in the midst of his people (12:14–17), probably indicating that the nations will be included in this new exodus also (Gentry and Wellum, 532).

LXX. LXX Exodus attempts to remain faithful to its Hebrew source while also making sense of it by introducing some harmonizations (Salvesen, 35). Thus, the exodus in chaps. 14 and 15 is presented very similarly to the Hebrew text. But instead of a song about "Yahweh, a man of war," the LXX has *kyrios syntribōn polemous*, "the Lord, shattering wars" (15:3). This title is not so much an avoidance of anthropomorphism as a statement that "God is always victorious" (Salvesen, 35), or, less likely, the translator reverts the meaning of the Hebrew (Rösel, "Translators," 86). Yahweh's triumphs are clearly seen in Exod. 14 and 17. This same theme appears in Isa. 42:13 (AT): "The Lord God of armies will come and crush the war" (*kyrios ho theos tōn dynameōn exeleusetai kai syntripsei polemon*). Here, Isaiah commands, "Sing to the Lord a new song" (42:10 AT), assuming the audience is already acquainted with the old Song of the Sea. Thus, OG Isaiah continues the exegesis of LXX Exodus when it comes to Yahweh's epithet given to him at the Exodus.

Yahweh's *rab ḥesed* ("abounding loyal love") in Exod. 34:6 is rendered *polyeleos* ("much mercy"). And in 34:7, *nōṣēr ḥesed* ("guarding steadfast love") is rendered with a double translation: "guarding righteousness and doing mercy" (*dikaiosynēn diatērōn kai poiōn eleos*). The translator employs the double translation because *ḥesed* appears in contexts where love or mercy conforms to a norm, thus faithful or righteous mercy. The Greek translation highlights this nuance here as Yahweh's faithful character forms the basis of the exodus out of Egypt and all subsequent exoduses.

Aspects of the new exodus in OG Isaiah are muted. Although OG Isaiah still predicts a new exodus out of Babylon (e.g., 48:20–21), a return of those in Assyria and those in Egypt accompanied with great trumpet blast

(27:13), and the servant's role (52:13–53:12), OG Isaiah at times appears to modify texts like 19:24–25 (cf. Van der Kooij, 490): "On that day, Israel will be third among the Assyrians and among the Egyptians, blessed in the land that the Lord Sabaoth has blessed, saying, "Blessed be my people *that are in Egypt and are among the Assyrians, even Israel my heritage*" (NETS). OG Isaiah sees exiled Israelites in Egypt and Assyria as returning from Egypt, not Egypt and Assyria (representatives of the nations) coming in as equal members of the new people of God as Hebrew Isaiah envisions. I will treat the servant's role in the Isaianic new exodus below, but the NT authors do not transmit some of the more nationalistic elements of OG Isaiah's interpretation of the new exodus.

NT. The new-exodus theme permeates the entire NT. The new exodus frames Jesus's miracles, teachings, sufferings, death, and resurrection (e.g., Mark 1:1–3; cf. Watts, 90 and passim). For example, Mark frames Jesus's healing of the deaf and mute (7:37) and especially the stammerer (7:32) according to the new exodus described in OG Isa. 35:5–6.

Furthermore, the language of the exodus determines the apostles' own language in the NT Epistles as they describe God's grand salvation in Christ as their return from exile. For example, Peter's *kata poly autou eleos* ("according to his great mercy," 1 Pet. 1:3) depends directly on LXX Exod. 34:6 even as Peter states that the church's new birth through Christ's resurrection from the dead becomes the means for entering into the imperishable inheritance kept in heaven (1:4). The same "great mercy" of God undergirds the move from type to antitype, inheritance of the land to inheritance of the new, permanent creation.

In Col. 1:12–14, Paul's language of "share of the allotment," "saints," "light," "deliverance out of," and "redemption" betrays dependence on the exodus (Beale, 848–49). *Meris* ("share") and *klēros* ("allotment, inheritance") are often used together in Deuteronomy and Joshua to describe land allotments in the promised land. In Deuteronomy, the language often applies to the Levites, who have no share or allotment in the land (e.g., 12:12). Furthermore, Israel is first called "holy" in Exod. 19:6 (cf. "holy men" in LXX 22:30). Paul's language of "redemption" (*apolytrōsis*) comes from the many places in Exodus where the Lord redeems (*lytroō*) Israel out of Egypt.

Conclusion. The LXX's language of the exodus permeates the NT's own lexicon as the authors used it to describe the Christ event and salvation in terms of the exodus. However, it would be a mistake to conclude that the NT authors simply took over the older Greek translations' interpretations at every turn. The Isaiah translator had a nationalistic *Tendenz* and affinity for the Jewish community in Egypt that influenced certain international passages in the Hebrew. The NT authors do not follow OG Isaiah in these places but rather the Hebrew itself.

The Servant of the Lord

The "servant of the Lord" theme is found concentrated in relatively few passages (i.e., Isa. 40–55) but underlies many concepts of the biblical metanarrative (Dempster, 128). Charles Scobie (93, 95–96) chose "God's Servant" as one of four major themes for grouping related subthemes. This theme is also particularly interesting since the LXX reflects the older, original Hebrew in places (e.g., Isa. 53) where the MT has become corrupt. The LXX also shows contemporary interpretation at key points in the development of this theme as redemptive history climaxes in the advent of Christ. Study of this theme is not restricted to the presence of the word but includes the wider concept of the servant (Dempster, 135). This brief treatment, however, will only touch on clear instances of the terms across the HB, LXX, and NT.

HB. "Servant of the Lord" (*ʿebed YHWH*) along with pronominal constructions (e.g., "my servant") is applied only to Abraham (Gen. 26:24), Moses (e.g., Deut. 34:5), Joshua (e.g., Josh. 24:29), David (e.g., Ps. 18 subtitle), Jacob/Israel (e.g., Isa. 41:8), Job (e.g., 1:8), Solomon (e.g., 1 Kings 3:7), anonymous Israelites who do not worship Baal (e.g., 2 Kings 9:7), and finally "the servants of Yahweh" who follow the suffering servant (Isa. 54:17). The phrase denotes a human being who is in a subordinate relationship to Yahweh and given the special task to do God's bidding. For example, in Num. 12:6–8, Yahweh contrasts "my servant Moses" with normal prophets. Yahweh will make himself known in a vision or speak with them in a dream. But Moses, his servant, is faithful in all of God's house, and Yahweh speaks with him face to face. This usage and meaning can be easily seen with respect to Joshua and David, who are clearly entrusted with specific tasks by Yahweh. According to Psalms (89; 132; and the praise psalms at the end of the Psalter), "my servant David" will be exalted, then humbled, only to be exalted in the end (Dempster, 162).

Job is also Yahweh's servant (Job 1:8; 2:3; 42:7, 8 [3x]), "and it is precisely because of this fact that he suffers. In his suffering, he learns that Yahweh's ways for righting the wrongs in the world often pass through the vale of suffering and weakness rather than strength" (Dempster, 162). Job, too, goes from exaltation to humiliation back to exaltation.

The fulfillment of the OT usage of *ʿebed YHWH* is found in the Servant Songs of Isa. 40–55 (Zimmerli and Jeremias, 23). The identity of Isaiah's servant has been debated, with options ranging from the corporate nation to an individual, either a king or prophet, with many favoring a prophet (Zimmerli and Jeremias, 24–26; cf. Acts 8:34–35). The Servant Songs, however, contain "royal motifs" (Dempster, 156–57), which ultimately explain how the servant can be both identified with Israel (Isa. 49:3) and be the agent who restores Israel (49:5). Only the king can be referred to as the nation and yet be distinct from the nation (cf. Gentry and Wellum, 495).

This explains why the servant, who is numbered with the transgressors, suffers not for his own sins but for the sins of the nation (53:12; cf. Dempster, 156n88).

The original Hebrew text cannot be equated with the MT in several places in Isa. 53, and these places are crucial for reconstructing the theme of the suffering servant in the NT. In Isa. 53:8, the original text should be reconstructed from the Hebrew parent text of the LXX and 1QIsa[a] to read, "He was stricken to death"; that is, 1QIsa[a] and LXX attest *nûgaʿ* ("was stricken"), while the LXX attests *lammāwet* ("to death" = *eis thanaton*) not the MT's *lāmô*, "to/for them" (cf. Barthélemy, 397–99; de Waard, 194–95). Thus, the servant was stricken to death, a theme taken up in the NT. In 53:9, 1QIsa[a]'s *bomŏtô* ("his tomb") indicates that God assigns the servant's tomb with a rich man, not as the MT's "in his deaths" or the facilitated rendering in LXX, "in his death" (Gentry, "Part 3"). In 53:11–12, three crucial variants to the MT show that there was an ancient textual form (attested in 1QIsa[a], 1QIsa[b], 4QIsa[d], and LXX's Hebrew parent text) and therefore reveal secondary modification to the MT: (1) the servant will see *light* (omitted in the MT); (2) the servant will bear the *sins* of the many (*ḥăṭāʾê*, "sins of"; *ḥēṭʾ*, "sin of" in the MT), and (3) the servant will intervene *on the occasion of the transgressions* of the many (*ləpišʿêhem*, "at their transgressions"; *lappōšəʿîm*, "for/against transgressors," in MT; cf. Meade, "Part 4"; Barthélemy, 405; de Waard, 196–97). Each of these will be explained in connection with the NT below. The reading "he will see light" probably means the servant who died and was laid in a tomb will come back to life or be resurrected. To see light indicates life (e.g., Job 3:20), while not seeing light indicates death (e.g., Job 3:16; Ps. 49:19). Job 33:28, 30 probably describe life as seeing light. In Ps. 36:9, seeing light is in parallel with "the fountain of life." Thus, the servant's glimpse of light after he has died (Isa. 53:8) and been placed in a tomb (53:9) probably means he will be resurrected.

The "servant of the Lord" theme in the HB comes into the LXX and NT, and we must turn to the developments of the theme that are found there.

LXX. The OG translators use various terms to render *ʿebed*: (1) *pais* (*paidion, paidarion*), "child, servant"; (2) *doulos* (*douleia, douleuōn*), "slave"; (3) *oiketēs* (*oikos*), "household slave"; (4) *therapōn* (*therapeia, therapeuōn*), "attendant"; (5) *huios*, "son"; (6) *hyperetēs*, "helper" (Zimmerli and Jeremias, 35–40).

Most of Greek usage is straightforward and aligned with the Hebrew designations. But the Greek translations do reveal some nuance as they make connections between certain figures who are referred to using *therapōn*. In a passage not in the MT, LXX Gen. 24:44 calls Isaac "his [the Lord's] attendant," thus associating the term with the patriarch (cf. LXX Deut. 9:27, where Abraham, Isaac, and Jacob are called God's "attendants"). Moses is first called the Lord's attendant in LXX Exod. 4:10 (cf. 14:31; Num. 11:11; 12:7–8; Deut. 3:24; Josh. 1:2; 8:31, 33). The Greek term is not used for David or the other servants of Yahweh (*ʿabdê YHWH*) until one comes to Job, who is called "my servant" (1:8; *pais*) at first and then "my attendant" on five other occasions (2:3; 42:7, 8 [3x]). One wonders at the translator's choice here because now Job is grouped with the patriarchs and is perhaps cast in a Mosaic shadow as he must mediate between the anger of the Lord and his friends who are in the wrong (42:7–10) as Moses mediated between the anger of the Lord and the people's idolatry (Exod. 32:10–14).

The servant passages in Isa. 40–55 use *pais* (42:1; 52:13; cf. *paideia* in 50:4) and *doulos* (49:3) to refer to *ʿebed YHWH*, and the translator does not seem to imply a distinct identity by the use of these terms alone. OG Isaiah portrays the servant in similarly intriguing ways as the Hebrew. But in 53:2, the translator tips his hand to an individual messianic interpretation by rendering *yônēq* ("sapling") as *paidion* ("child"), a rendering that intentionally links the servant here with the messianic child in 9:6 (LXX 9:5; cf. 11:6) and the root with the two references to the Davidic root in 11:1 (Zimmerli and Jeremias, 41). OG Isaiah renders the two instances of *yānaq* ("to suck") in 60:16 with *thēlazō* ("to suck") and *esthiō* ("to eat") and the occurrence in 66:11 with *thēlazō* (cf. *trophos*, "nursing mother," for the *hiphil* of *yānaq* in 49:23). The only other occurrence of *yônēq* (11:8) is rendered with the unique double translation *paidion nēpion* ("nursing child") and thus should not be confused with 53:2. Likewise, *paidion* ("child") in Isaiah elsewhere renders *naʿar* ("lad"; e.g., Isa. 3:5), *yeled* ("child"; e.g., 8:18), *bēn* ("son"; 38:19), *raḥam* ("womb"; 46:3), and *ʿûl* ("nursing child"; 49:15). Thus, only in 53:2 does the translator render *yônēq* with *paidion*, linking the Davidic son with the suffering servant.

Joseph Ziegler's conjecture (99) of *aneteile men*, "he rose" (MSS: *anēngeilamen*, "we announced"), in Isa. 53:2 should be followed (cf. Zimmerli and Jeremias, 41). If so, the Greek text could harken to the messianic servant's "rising" (*anatolē* for *tsemaḥ*, "growth") in Zech. 3:8 and 6:12. Thus, the verb form in Isa. 53:2 would support a messianic interpretation of the suffering servant, which would explain why several NT authors allude to and quote the fourth Servant Song in their writings.

NT. The NT continues to mention David as servant (*pais*; cf. Acts 4:25) and Moses as *therapōn* (only in quotation; Heb. 3:5, quoting Num. 12:7), even as the theme now also includes Jesus's followers as God's *douloi* ("servants"; Acts 4:29; Rom. 1:1, etc.). However, the overwhelming majority of references to the servant of the Lord in the NT concern the quotations and allusions to the suffering servant of Isa. 53 (Dempster, 165). Dependence on 53:4–6, 9, 12 in 1 Pet. 2:22, 24–25 casts Jesus's atoning work in the mold of the vicarious suffering servant. Luke 22:37 quotes part of Isa. 53:12 ("and he was reckoned among the rebels") to show the Messiah's solidarity with fallen, rebellious Israel as a prerequisite to rescuing Israel.

In addition to direct references, allusions to the suffering servant in the NT abound. Mark 10:44–45 (note the progression from servant to Son of Man) alludes to Isa. 53:10–12's portrayal of the servant's sacrifice for the many. Matthew's narrative of the Last Supper includes Jesus's blood being "poured out for the many for the forgiveness of sins" (26:28; cf. Isa. 52:15; 53:12).

Paul's treatment of the one righteous man and the many sinners in Rom. 5 (see esp. vv. 15, 19) is crafted according to Isaiah's individual, messianic servant whose work is on behalf of the many (Isa. 52:14–15; 53:11–12). In his approach to Rom. 5, Paul alludes to the servant's work in 4:25. *Hos paredothē dia ta paraptōmata hēmōn* agrees almost entirely with OG Isaiah with the exception that OG has *hamartias* ("sins") instead of *paraptōmata* ("transgressions"). But here Paul probably does not depend on the OG directly (the translator used *hamartia* for both *ḥăṭāʾê* ["sins of"] and *pišʿêhem* ["their rebellions"] in the verse) or the MT's "transgressors" (*pōšəʿîm*); rather, he provides his own rendering of the Hebrew text form *pišʿêhem* ("their rebellions") evidenced in three Dead Sea Scrolls (1QIsa^{a}; 1QIsa^{b}; 4QIsa^{d}). Since other LXX translators rendered *pešaʿ* ("transgression") with *paraptōma* (e.g., Job 36:9; Ezek. 14:11; 18:22), Paul probably follows suit here. Furthermore, the last line of Rom. 4:25, "he was raised," appears to be Paul's interpretation of Isa. 53:11's "to see light" or even the LXX's "to show him light," indicating the servant was resurrected from the dead.

The tradition that Paul received according to 1 Cor. 15:3–4 confessed that the Christ died for our sins according to the Scriptures (cf. LXX Isa. 53:8), was buried, and that was raised on the third day according to the Scriptures. Early Christian tradition depended on Isaiah's suffering servant as preserved in a more ancient Hebrew text to which the LXX often attests clearly. Unpacking this early text form leads to more connections with the NT and its development of this important theme.

Conclusion. The servant of the Lord is an important theme not only for its development in the OT but also for how it binds the Testaments together. Interpreters will continue to discover NT allusions to the OT, especially as research into the textual history of the HB and LXX continues.

See also OT Use of the OT: Comparison with the NT Use of the OT; *other Septuagint articles*; *Dead Sea Scrolls articles*; *Mishnah, Talmud, and Midrashim articles*; *Philo articles*; *Targums articles*

Bibliography. Barthélemy, D., *Isaïe, Jérémie, Lamentations*, vol. 2 of *Critique textuelle de l'Ancien Testament* (Vandenhoeck & Ruprecht, 1986); Beale, G. K., "Colossians," in *CNTUOT*, 841–70; Beale, G. K., and B. L. Gladd, *Hidden but Now Revealed* (InterVarsity, 2014); Block, D. I., "The Old Testament on Hell," in *Hell under Fire*, ed. C. W. Morgan and R. A. Peterson (Zondervan, 2004), 43–65; Coogan, M. D., and M. S. Smith, *Stories from Ancient Canaan*, 2nd ed. (Westminster John Knox, 2012); Cox, C. E., "Job," in *T&T Clark Companion to the Septuagint*, ed. J. K. Aitken (Bloomsbury T&T Clark, 2015), 385–400; Dempster, S. G., "The Servant of the Lord," in *Central Themes in Biblical Theology*, ed. S. J. Hafemann and P. R. House (Baker Academic, 2007), 128–78; de Waard, J., *A Handbook on Isaiah* (Eisenbrauns, 1997); Gallagher, E. L., *Patristic Biblical Theory* (Leiden, 2012); Gallagher, E. L., and J. D. Meade, *The Biblical Canon Lists from Early Christianity* (Oxford University Press, 2017); Gentry, P. J., "Part 3: The Servant's Burial according to the Scriptures," Text & Canon Institute, April 6, 2022, https://textandcanon.org/part-3-the-servants-burial-according-to-the-scriptures/; Gentry, "Rethinking the 'Sure Mercies of David' in Isaiah 55:3," *WTJ* 69 (2007): 279–304; Gentry, P. J., and S. J. Wellum, *Kingdom through Covenant*, 2nd ed. (Crossway, 2018); Jobes, K. H., and M. Silva, *Invitation to the Septuagint*, 2nd ed. (Baker Academic, 2015); Johnston, P. S., *Shades of Sheol* (InterVarsity, 2002); Lange, A., and E. Tov, eds., *Textual History of the Bible*, 3 vols. (Brill, 2016–); Law, T. M., *When God Spoke Greek* (Oxford University Press, 2013); Lohfink, N., *The Christian Meaning of the Old Testament* (Bruce, 1968); Meade, J. D., *A Critical Edition of the Hexaplaric Fragments of Job 22–42* (Peeters, 2020); Meade, "Part 4: Who Does the Servant Intercede For?," Text & Canon Institute, April 13, 2022, https://textandcanon.org/part-4-who-does-the-servant-intercede-for/; Meade, "The Septuagint and the Biblical Canon," in *T&T Clark Handbook of Septuagint Research*, ed. W. A. Ross and W. E. Glenny (Bloomsbury T&T Clark, 2021), 207–28; Motyer, J. A., *The Prophecy of Isaiah* (InterVarsity, 1993); Rösel, M., "Toward a 'Theology of the Septuagint,'" in *Septuagint Research*, ed. W. Kraus and R. G. Wooden (Society of Biblical Literature, 2006), 239–52; Rösel, "Translators as Interpreters," in *A Companion to Biblical Interpretation in Early Judaism*, ed. M. Henze (Eerdmans, 2012), 64–91; Salvesen, A., "Exodus," in *T&T Clark Companion to the Septuagint*, ed. J. K. Aitken (Bloomsbury T&T Clark, 2015), 29–42; Schaper, J., *Eschatology in the Greek Psalter* (Mohr Siebeck, 1995); Scobie, C. H. H., *The Ways of Our God* (Eerdmans, 2003); Tov, E., "Greek Translations," in Lange and Tov, *Textual History of the Bible*, 1A:191–211; van der Kooij, A., "Isaiah: Septuagint," in Lange and Tov, *Textual History of the Bible*, 1B:489–92; Wagner, J. R. "The Septuagint and the 'Search for the Christian Bible,'" in *Scripture's Doctrine and Theology's Bible*, ed. M. Bockmuehl and A. J. Torrance (Baker Academic, 2008), 17–28; Watts, R. E., *Isaiah's New Exodus and Mark* (1997; repr., Baker Academic, 2000); Wenham, G. J., *Genesis 1–15*, WBC (Word, 1987); Wright, N. T., *The Resurrection of the Son of God* (Fortress, 2003); Ziegler, J., ed., *Isaias*, vol. 14 of *Septuaginta*, 3rd ed. (Vandenhoeck & Ruprecht, 1983); Zimmerli, W., and J. Jeremias, *The Servant of God* (SCM Press, 1957).

John D. Meade

Serpent and Antichrist

Who doesn't love a good dragon-slaying story? The classic dragon-slaying story in English literature is *Saint George and the Dragon*. *Beowulf* is an Old English epic in which Beowulf slays monsters and a dragon. In John Bunyan's *The Pilgrim's Progress*, Christian battles Apollyon. In C. S. Lewis's *The Chronicles of Narnia*, the White Witch is the main serpent figure, and others include the evil Queen of Underland in *The Silver Chair*. J. R. R. Tolkien's *The Hobbit* features a dragon named Smaug, and in *The Lord of the Rings*, Sauron is the primary serpent figure. In J. K. Rowling's *Harry Potter*, Voldemort is the primary serpent figure: he was in the House of Salazar Slytherin, whose mascot is a serpent; he unleashes a Basilisk, a monstrous serpent; he speaks the language of snakes; and the terrifying Nagini is his loyal pet snake.

We love good dragon-slaying stories because they echo the greatest story (Naselli, 19–31). The Bible is an epic dragon-slaying story. The serpent and his offspring have been opposing the Messiah since the garden of Eden. That is what antichrists are doing now, and that is what the antichrist will do.

Serpent

Serpent is an umbrella term that includes both snakes and dragons (Naselli, 17–19). The Greek word *drakōn* refers simply to an enormous serpent—not to a fire-breathing creature with wings and claws. As a general rule, the form a serpent takes depends on its strategy. Snakes deceive, tempt, lie, and backstab. Dragons devour, attack, murder, and assault. Snakes are subtle. Dragons are not.

A pithy way to summarize the Bible's story line is "Kill the Dragon, get the girl!" The story line features three main characters: the serpent (the villain—Satan), a damsel in distress (the people of God), and the serpent slayer (the protagonist and hero—Jesus).

The story begins with bliss. The damsel enjoys a beautiful garden in a pristine world. (Adam and Eve enjoy the garden of Eden.) But the serpent employs the strategy to deceive. (The snake deceives Eve.) As the story develops, the serpent craftily alternates between deceiving and devouring. (Sometimes Satan attempts to deceive God's people with false teaching. Other times Satan assaults God's people with violent persecution.) At the climax of the story, the dragon attempts to devour the hero but fails. (Satan murders Jesus but merely bruises his heel while Jesus decisively crushes the Serpent's head.) For the rest of the story, the dragon furiously attempts to devour the damsel. (Satan attempts to deceive and destroy the church.) The hero's mission is to kill the dragon and get the girl. And he will accomplish that mission. (The Lamb will consummate his kingdom for God's glory by slaying the dragon and saving his bride.)

The deceitful snake in Gen. 3. Genesis 3 teaches at least ten notable truths about the snake (Naselli, 33–47). (1) The snake is deceitful (3:1a). That is what "crafty" connotes. (2) The snake is a beast that God created (3:1a). Therefore, the snake is not God's equal since God is uncreated. Like every other creature, the snake is not independent of God. (3) The snake deceives by questioning God (3:1b–3). That is the snake's initial strategy. (4) The snake deceives by contradicting God (3:4–5). The snake intensifies his deceitful assault by blaspheming God as having selfish motives. (5) The snake deceives Eve into rebelling against God, and Adam follows Eve (3:6, 13; cf. 2 Cor. 11:3; 1 Tim. 2:14). God had commissioned his image-bearers to rule over the beasts of the field (Gen. 1:26–27), but instead his image-bearers committed treachery. Instead of obeying the King, they follow the snake (cf. Beale, *Temple*, 34–35). Eve was not alone. Adam "was with her" (3:6). So, when Adam ate, he rebelled against God not only by failing to obey what God commanded but also by failing to lead and protect his wife. When God calls to "the man" and asks, "Where are you [sing.]?" (3:9), he directly addresses Adam—not both Adam and Eve. Adam is primarily responsible because he is the head of the husband-wife relationship. That is why later Scripture blames Adam for the fall into sin (Rom. 5:12–21; 1 Cor. 15:21–22). Adam should have killed the dragon and rescued the girl.

(6) As a result of the snake's deceit, Adam's and Eve's sins separate them from God (Gen. 3:7–13). (7) As a result of the snake's deceit, God curses the snake and promises a snake crusher (3:14–15). God humiliates the snake by forcing it to slither on its belly in the dust. God curses not only the snake but also the snake's offspring. The rest of the Bible's story line traces the ongoing battle between the snake's offspring and the woman's offspring. The first seed of the serpent is Cain, who kills his brother Abel (4:1–16). The serpent, Jesus explains, "was a murderer from the beginning" (John 8:44), and Cain was the first human murderer. Humans are either children of God or children of the devil (Matt. 13:38–39; John 8:33, 44; Acts 13:10; 1 John 3:8–10). Instead of continuing through Abel, the seed of the woman continues through Seth (Gen. 4:25; 5:1–3). That line continues through Noah (6:9) and then through Abraham, Isaac, Jacob, and Judah, and eventually through David all the way to Jesus the Messiah and his followers. The woman's offspring can refer to a group of people (the people of God collectively; cf. Rom. 16:20) and to a particular person (the Messiah; cf. Gal. 3:16). Although the serpent will bruise the Messiah's heel (Jesus dies on a tree), Jesus is the ultimate seed of the woman who will mortally crush the serpent (cf. Gal. 3:16; Heb. 2:14–15; 1 John 3:8; see Hamilton, 30–43). (8) As a result of the snake's deceit, God punishes Eve and Adam with pain and mortality (Gen. 3:16–19). (9) As a result of the snake's deceit, God banishes Adam and Eve from the garden of Eden (3:22–24).

(10) The snake is Satan. Genesis 3 does not explicitly identify the snake as Satan. Some scholars concede that the NT identifies the snake as Satan yet are reluctant to interpret Gen. 3 in that way. Some insist that the snake in Gen. 3 is *not* Satan but instead embodies life, wisdom, and chaos. But when we read Gen. 3 in light of the whole Bible, we must identify the snake as Satan (see Rev. 12:3, 9, 10, 12). The Bible does not specify the precise way Satan and the snake in the garden of Eden relate, but Satan somehow uses the physical body of a snake in the garden of Eden. He may have transformed into a snake-like creature, or he may have entered and influenced one of the existing snakes to accomplish his devious plan. Regardless of the precise means, the Bible presents the story of the talking snake as real history—not as a myth or legend or fable.

Snakes and dragons between the Bible's bookends. At the story's beginning, the snake is deceitful. As the story progresses, the serpent's strategy alternates between deceiving as a snake and devouring as a dragon (Naselli, 49–103).

Satan is not the only serpent in the Bible. There are lots of other snakes and dragons in the story. Satan is the most powerful and important snake and dragon, and all the other evil snakes and dragons are Satan's children. Satan helps them try to trick and destroy God's people.

Snakes try to trick God's people. False teachers tell people what is not true about God and his world. They are sneaky snakes among God's people. The most famous snakes in the Bible are certain Pharisees and Sadducees. Both John the Baptist and Jesus call them a "brood of vipers" (Matt. 3:7–12; 12:33–37; 23:29–36; Luke 3:7–9). What they teach is poisonous, and God will judge them. Like their spiritual father—Satan the Snake—the Pharisees and Sadducees first *tempt* Jesus (Matt. 16:1; 19:3; 22:18, 35; Mark 8:11; 10:2; 12:15; Luke 11:16) and finally *murder* Jesus. The snake's children act like the snake. That is why Jesus told some of the snake's children, "You belong to your father, the devil, and you want to carry out your father's desires. He was a murderer from the beginning, not holding to the truth, for there is no truth in him. When he lies, he speaks his native language, for he is a liar and the father of lies" (John 8:44).

Dragons try to destroy God's people. Satan has many dragon-children. Three of Satan's most famous dragon-children are Pharaoh, Goliath, and Herod.

Pharaoh. The dragon hates Eve's children, so he intensely hates babies. Pharaoh king of Egypt acts like the dragon when he commands his people to murder all the Hebrew baby boys (Exod. 1:8–22). God sends Moses to free his people from the Egyptians, and one of the miracles God does is change Moses's staff into a snake (4:3–4; 7:8–13). Why a snake? Pharaoh wears a special crown with a snake carved into it. To the Egyptians, that snake symbolizes that the gods made Pharaoh powerful, magic, wise—even a god himself! Egypt worships the snake; it is one of their gods (cf. Currid, 89–94). So, when Moses's staff becomes a snake that swallows the snakes of Pharaoh's magicians, the true God is making fun of Pharaoh as weak. Egypt thinks Pharaoh is a mighty snake that will never die, but God can easily swallow him up. And that is exactly what God does to the Egyptian army in the Red Sea: "Who among the gods is like you, LORD? Who is like you—majestic in holiness, awesome in glory, working wonders? You stretch out your right hand, and the earth *swallows* your enemies" (15:11–12; cf. 14:16, 26; Ps. 74:12–14; Isa. 51:9–11). A short time later God's people are impatient and ungrateful. They complain that God delivered them from Egypt so that they would die in the wilderness. So, God sends poisonous snakes among them (Num. 21:4–9). It is as if God says to the complaining Israelites, "So you miss Egypt? Here, have some snakes—the animal that Egypt worships." God kindly provides a bronze snake that symbolizes bearing the curse in the place of snake-bitten Israelites who trust God. Jesus later explains, "Just as Moses lifted up the snake in the wilderness, so the Son of Man must be lifted up, that everyone who believes may have eternal life in him" (John 3:14–15). Jesus bears the curse in the place of people who deserve it (2 Cor. 5:21; Gal. 3:13; 1 Pet. 2:24). The Bible later makes fun of Egypt as a toothless dragon—someone God's people should not bother trusting (Isa. 30:1–3, 6–7). God taunts Pharaoh by calling him "the great dragon that lies in the midst of his streams" (Ezek. 29:3 ESV), and God warns that he will destroy Egypt (29:3–9; cf. 32:2–9).

Goliath (1 Sam. 17). The story of David and Goliath is a dragon-slaying story (cf. Verrett, 46–66). Goliath terrorizes God's people as a giant serpent who "wore a coat of scale armor" (1 Sam. 17:5). The Hebrew word translated "scale" (*qaśqeśet*) occurs seven other times in the OT, and every time it refers to the scales of fish—including the dragon in the sea (Lev. 11:9, 10, 12; Deut. 14:9, 10; Ezek. 29:4 [2x]). God calls Pharaoh "the great dragon" with "scales" (Ezek. 29:3–4 ESV). It is also significant that the word appears twice in Ezek. 29:4 because 1 Sam. 17 and Ezek. 29 parallel each other in at least three important ways: (1) They are the only two passages in the Bible that describe a *person* as having scales (1 Sam. 17:5; Ezek. 29:3–4). (2) They use these parallel statements: "I will give the carcasses of the Philistine army to the birds and the wild animals" (1 Sam. 17:46); "I will give you as food to the beasts of the earth and the birds of the sky" (Ezek. 29:5). (3) They also use these parallel statements: "The whole world will know that there is a God in Israel" (1 Sam. 17:46b); "All who live in Egypt will know that I am the LORD" (Ezek. 29:6a). The story in 1 Sam. 17 describes Goliath's armor as if he is a dragon with dragon scales. But the battle is the Lord's. The Lord slays dragons, and he helps David (one of Eve's children) crush Goliath (one of the dragon's children).

Herod (Matt. 2:1–18; cf. Rev. 12:4b–5). After Jesus is born in Bethlehem of Judea, King Herod talks to some wise men about this baby. Herod tries to kill Jesus. He orders his soldiers to murder all the boys in and around Bethlehem who are two years old and under. This story repeats the story at the beginning of Exodus. Pharaoh was a murderous dragon when he killed baby boys. But God helped Moses escape and deliver his people from Egypt. Here King Herod is a murderous dragon when he kills baby boys. But Jesus—the new and greater Moses—escapes and delivers his people from their sins. At the climax of the Bible's story, the dragon tries to destroy Jesus but fails. Satan the dragon murders Jesus on the cross, but Jesus rises from the dead and crushes the serpent's head.

The devouring dragon in Rev. 12 and 20. Revelation bookends the deceitful snake in Gen. 3 by referring to Satan in apocalyptic terms as the dragon (cf. Beale, *Revelation*, 50–69; Osborne, 15–18). The end of the Bible's story teaches at least ten notable truths about the dragon (Naselli, 105–22). (1) The dragon is the ancient serpent (12:9–10). Six labels apply to the same evil person: the dragon (*ho drakōn*), the ancient serpent (*ho ophis ho archaios*; alludes to Gen. 3), the devil (*diabolos*—the slanderer), Satan (*ho satanas*—the adversary), the deceiver (*ho planōn*), and the accuser of our brothers (*ho katēgōr tōn adelphōn hēmōn*). (2) The dragon is powerful and "enormous" (12:3). The ten horns symbolize great power and ruling authority (cf. Dan. 7:7–8, 19–27), and the seven diadems symbolize that his great power extends over the entire earth. The dragon "leads the whole world astray" (Rev. 12:9). (3) The dragon plans to devour the Messiah (12:1–4). The male child is Jesus the Messiah, who rules with a rod of iron (Ps. 2:9; Rev. 2:27; 19:15). The dragon plans to thwart God's master plan in Gen. 3:15 by devouring the Messiah. This passage portrays in apocalyptic terms what was happening when Herod tried to murder the Messiah (Matt. 2:1–18). (4) The dragon fails to devour the Messiah (Rev. 12:5b)—at his birth and then later at the cross. The Messiah rises from the grave and later ascends to the Father's right hand. (5) The dragon and his angels get thrown down to earth (12:7–10). Satan can no longer accuse God's people directly to God like he used to (e.g., Job 1–2). He no longer has direct access to God (cf. John 12:31; Col. 2:15). (6) The dragon furiously persecutes God's people (Rev. 12:6, 12b–17). (7) The dragon cannot destroy God's people (12:6, 14–16). The wilderness symbolizes a place where God tests, protects, and miraculously nourishes his people. God gives his people "the two wings of a great eagle" (12:14), which symbolizes that God protects and delivers his people (cf. Exod. 19:4; Isa. 40:31).

(8) The dragon is bound for a thousand years (Rev. 20:1–6). At minimum this entails that *God is more powerful than the dragon*. The dragon cannot bind God, but God can send one of his angels to bind Satan. (9) The dragon attempts to deceive the nations (20:2–3, 7–10). (10) The dragon is tormented forever in the lake of fire and sulfur (20:9b–10). Never again will the dragon, that ancient serpent, accuse or deceive or persecute God's people. God will sovereignly and perfectly enforce justice—justice for which we now yearn and for which we will eternally praise God. As Isaiah puts it, "In that day, the LORD will punish with his sword—his fierce, great and powerful sword—Leviathan the gliding serpent, Leviathan the coiling serpent; he will slay the monster of the sea" (Isa. 27:1). God will sovereignly destroy the most powerful evil monster in the universe. Consequently, snakes will no longer be deadly (Isa. 11:8; 65:17, 25). God will defang the snake. Snakes will no longer harm people. God's people will be safe and secure.

Antichrist

Serpents deceive as snakes and devour as dragons, and antichrists deceive as false teachers and devour as beasts. Paul explicitly connects the serpent with false teachers in two passages (2 Cor. 11:3–4, 13–15; Rom. 16:17–20). Satan the snake deploys false teachers to infiltrate God's people as intruding snakes. That is why the NT repeatedly warns God's people to beware of false teachers (e.g., Matt. 7:15; Gal. 2:4–5; 5:1; Col. 2:8; 1 Tim. 4:1–3; Titus 1:9–14; 2 Pet. 2:1–20; 1 John 2:18–27; 4:1–3; 2 John 7; Jude 3–4).

Antichrist in 1–2 John. Those passages in 1 and 2 John (see previous paragraph) contain all five NT uses of the words *antichrist* or *antichrists*:

> *1 John 2:18 [2x], 22:* Dear children, this is the last hour; and as you have heard that the *antichrist* is coming, even now many *antichrists* have come. This is how we know it is the last hour. . . . Who is the liar? It is whoever denies that Jesus is the Christ. Such a person is the *antichrist*—denying the Father and the Son.
>
> *1 John 4:3:* Every spirit that does not acknowledge Jesus is not from God. This is the spirit of the *antichrist*, which you have heard is coming and even now is already in the world.
>
> *2 John 7:* I say this because many deceivers, who do not acknowledge Jesus Christ as coming in the flesh, have gone out into the world. Any such person is the deceiver and the *antichrist*.

John teaches at least five notable truths about antichrists and the antichrist: (1) Antichrists are distinct from *the* antichrist. Many antichrists have already come, but the antichrist will come. Antichrists are here right now; the antichrist is not yet here. Antichrists are forerunners of the antichrist; they have *the spirit of* the antichrist. (2) The presence of many antichrists now signifies that it is the last hour. The expression "last hour" signals that the antichrists are inaugurally fulfilling what Daniel prophesied (cf. OG Dan. 8:17, 19; 11:35, 40; 12:1). (3) Antichrists are liars (1 John 2:22), false prophets (4:1), and deceivers (2 John 7; cf. Dan. 7:25; 8:12, 23–25; 11:30–34). They deny that Jesus is the

Messiah. They deny both the Father and the Son. They deny that Jesus is from God. They deny that Jesus has come in the flesh. This suggests that the prefix *anti* signifies that antichrists *oppose* Jesus, not merely that they attempt to *replace* Jesus. Antichrists are children of the snake. Satan is *the* snake, the ultimate deceiver. His human and demonic minions are his offspring—other snakes with the mission to infiltrate and deceive God's people. One of the snake's strategies to accomplish that evil plan is through false teachers and false teaching. (4) Antichrists attempt to infiltrate and deceive God's people, but they are only superficially attached to God's people: "They went out from us, but they did not really belong to us. For if they had belonged to us, they would have remained with us; but their going showed that none of them belonged to us" (1 John 2:19). (5) Antichrists do not have the Father: "No one who denies the Son has the Father; whoever acknowledges the Son has the Father also" (2:23; cf. Kruse, 106–10).

Antichrist in Daniel, Matt. 24 and Mark 13, 2 Thess. 2, and Revelation. The BDAG entry for *antichristos* says to see 2 Thess. 2:1–12 and Rev. 12–14 "for the general idea in the NT without the word." We could add to that Matt. 24 and Mark 13. All these NT passages develop themes from Daniel and seem to correspond with the already/not-yet antichrist paradigm in 1–2 John.

Antichrist in Daniel. Daniel records a vision he saw in the late 500s BC about what kings would do in the future (Dan. 11). Evangelical scholars typically recognize these future kings and kingdoms as the Persians, then Alexander the Great's Greeks, then the Seleucids and the Ptolemies, then the end of time. The "contemptible person" (11:21) refers to Antiochus IV Epiphanes, a Hellenistic king who ruled the Seleucid Empire from 175 BC until he died in 164 BC. (He may correspond to an evil figure in Dan. 7:20–25; 8:8–12; 9:26–27.) The Jews suffered intensely under Antiochus IV Epiphanes, who plundered the Jerusalem temple and blasphemously sacrificed pigs there (Dan. 11:31). Daniel 11:21–35 refers to Antiochus IV Epiphanes, and 11:36–45 seems to shift to the antichrist "at the time of the end" (11:40). If that is the case, then the evil Antiochus IV Epiphanes is an antichrist who prefigures the future antichrist who persecutes and deceives.

Antichrist in Matt. 24 and Mark 13. Forces from Antiochus IV Epiphanes "set up the abomination that makes desolate" (Dan. 11:31b ESV; see also 9:27; 12:11). The Greek translation of that phrase is *to bdelygma tēs erēmōseōs*—that is, "the abomination of desolation." In 1 Macc. 1:54, that phrase refers to what Antiochus IV Epiphanes did. Jesus warns people who "see standing in the holy place 'the abomination that causes desolation,' spoken of through the prophet Daniel" (Matt. 24:15; cf. Mark 13:14). A plausible way to interpret what Daniel prophesies is to recognize a typological pattern: (1) in 167 BC, Antiochus IV Epiphanes desecrated the temple; (2) in AD 67/68, Jewish Zealots desecrated the temple, and in AD 70, Rome destroyed it; and (3) at the end time, shortly before the Son of Man returns, the antichrist will claim divine authority and demand obedience and worship. The way Jesus warns people corresponds with the already/not-yet antichrist paradigm in 1–2 John since many antichrists will appear throughout history: "Watch out that no one deceives you. For many will come in my name, claiming, 'I am the Messiah,' and will deceive many" (Matt. 24:4–5). "Many false prophets will appear and deceive many people. Because of the increase of wickedness [*anomia*—i.e., lawlessness], the love of most will grow cold" (24:11–12). "At that time if anyone says to you, 'Look, here is the Messiah!' or, 'There he is!' do not believe it. For false messiahs and false prophets will appear and perform great signs and wonders to deceive, if possible, even the elect" (24:23–24; cf. Schnabel, 153–57).

Antichrist in 2 Thess. 2. "The man of lawlessness [*anomia*]" (2 Thess. 2:3; cf. Dan. 12:10–11; Matt. 24:12) seems to correspond to the future antichrist that Daniel describes: "He will oppose and will exalt himself over everything that is called God or is worshiped, so that he sets himself up in God's temple, proclaiming himself to be God" (2 Thess. 2:4; cf. Dan. 9:27; 11:31, 36–37; 12:11). The way Paul warns believers corresponds with the already/not-yet antichrist paradigm in 1–2 John: "The secret power of lawlessness is already at work. . . . And then the lawless one will be revealed, whom the Lord Jesus will overthrow with the breath of his mouth and destroy by the splendor of his coming" (2 Thess. 2:7–8). Second Temple Judaism had two types of antichrist figures who oppose God and God's people: a false prophet who deceives people and a political tyrant who oppresses people. The man of lawlessness combines both of them and supremely embodies all previous antichrists—Antiochus IV Epiphanes, Herod, Nero, Domitian, Pope Innocent III, Adolf Hitler, and others (cf. Beale, *Thessalonians*, 203–11; Beale, *Temple*, 269–92; Beale and Gladd, 215–36; Schnabel, 159–62).

Antichrist in Revelation. The beast from the sea in Rev. 13 (cf. 11:7; 14:9–10; 16:2, 10, 13; 17:3–17; 19:19–20; 20:10) shares characteristics of the four beasts in Dan. 7. The beast arises, receives power, and destructively wields that power. This beast in Revelation seems to correspond both to the world empires in Dan. 7 and to the future antichrist that Dan. 11:36–37 describes. It is difficult to sharply distinguish between the beast as an individual person and the beast as a system. Likely the beast is an individual that corporately represents a system composed of many people. As an individual, the beast is a political and military genius who counterfeits the true Trinity as part of an unholy trinity: the dragon (Satan), the beast from the sea (the antichrist), and the beast from the land (the false prophet). As a system, the beast from the sea deceitfully leads people to oppose God through politics, economics, culture, and religion. The way John warns believers corresponds with the already/not-yet antichrist paradigm in 1–2 John: the beast is already here in various resuscitated manifestations, and the beast is coming in the future (cf. Beale, *Revelation*, 690–92; Osborne, 493–95; Schnabel, 163–83).

So what should God's people do? Do not imitate the poisonous serpent or follow antichrists (John 8:44). Beware and fight the serpent as the deceiving snake and devouring dragon (1 Pet. 5:8–9; James 4:7). "Walk in love" *because* "many deceivers"—antichrists who are children of the serpent—"have gone out into the world" (2 John 6–7). Trust the serpent slayer. "The Lord is faithful, and he will strengthen you and protect you from the evil one" (2 Thess. 3:3). "The one who is in you is greater than the one who is in the world" (1 John 4:4).

Bibliography. Beale, G. K., *The Book of Revelation*, NIGTC (Eerdmans, 1999); Beale, *1–2 Thessalonians*, IVPNTC 13 (InterVarsity, 2003); Beale, *A New Testament Biblical Theology* (Baker Academic, 2011); Beale, *The Temple and the Church's Mission*, NSBT 17 (InterVarsity, 2004); Beale, G. K., and B. L. Gladd, *Hidden but Now Revealed* (InterVarsity, 2014); Currid, J. D., *Ancient Egypt and the Old Testament* (Baker, 1997); Hamilton, J. M., Jr., "The Skull Crushing Seed of the Woman," *SBJT* 10, no. 2 (2006): 30–55; Kruse, C. G., *The Letters of John*, PNTC (Eerdmans, 2000); Naselli, A. D., *The Serpent and the Serpent Slayer*, SSBT (Crossway, 2020); Osborne, G. R., *Revelation*, BECNT (Baker Academic, 2002); Schnabel, E., *40 Questions about the End Times*, 40 Questions (Kregel, 2011); Verrett, B. A., *The Serpent in Samuel* (Resource, 2020).

ANDREW DAVID NASELLI

Sexuality *See* Marriage

Shalom

All people have stories, which arise from their interactions with each other and their environments. In fact, story is fundamental to personal existence. We know people by their stories. The God of the Bible has his story too and in so having shapes ours as well. As the Nobel laureate Elie Wiesel said, "God made man because he loves stories" (Wiesel, front matter). The canon of Scripture relates God's story. According to Aristotle, every story has a beginning, a middle, and an end (*Poet.* 7). The canon of Scripture is no different in its storytelling. The Bible's story begins in harmony (Gen. 1–2), then come sin-caused strife and disruption (Gen. 3–Rev. 20), until in the end a new world is created as the conflict resolution (Rev. 21–22). Nothing less will do. Stephen Sykes finely captures the narrative thrust of Scripture: "In Christian narrative, God's world is the *setting*, the *theme* is the rescue of the fallen world and of humankind; the *plots* are the biblical narratives, from creation, election, to incarnation, crucifixion, resurrection and ascension; the *resolution* is the last judgment, heaven and hell, and the new creation" (Sykes, 14). The new creation will be a world of shalom, not strife. But exactly what is this shalom or peace?

Shalom: The Concept

According to Charles Scobie (881), "Life in its fulness is characterized by 'peace' or *shalom*, a word that is extremely difficult to translate into English." This article uses "shalom" and "peace" interchangeably. In the Hebrew Bible, depending on usage in situ, shalom (*šālôm*) positively can mean "well-being, safety, and contentment," and negatively, it can mean "a status absent of warfare and violence" (Smith-Christopher, 211). T. J. Geddert (604) adds, "It covers health, prosperity, security, friendship and salvation." Wholeness and completeness, too, are dimensions of shalom (Schaeffer, 597). Shalom may be experienced by both the individual and the community. The psalmist, as an individual, can pray for shalom (Ps. 122:6–7). As for the community, one of the many kinds of sacrifice practiced in ancient Israel speaks to the communal dimension. The "peace offering" (*šelem*) is "where sacrifice and a common meal symbolize right relationships with both God and one's fellow worshippers" (Scobie, 882). In the LXX and NT, *eirēnē* is its equivalent (Geddert, 604). The word *šālôm* occurs around 240x in the OT, and *eirēnē* occurs about 90x in the NT (Swartley, 583). With the exception of 1 John, every NT book refers to peace.

But in contrast to the ancient Greeks, "the great innovation of the OT is to make peace a religious idea: it is a gift of God. 'Gideon built an altar to Yahweh and called it Yahweh-Peace' (*eirēnē Kyriou*, Judg 6:24); 'I am Yahweh—I bring peace' (Isa 45:7); 'Great is Yahweh, who wishes peace for his servant' (Ps 35:27)" (*TLNT*, 1:426–27; cf. 424–38). The Aaronic blessing in Num. 6:24–26 provides further evidence of the gift nature of shalom (Scobie, 881–82). William Klassen (207) argues, "The Jewish concept of *šālôm* undergirds the Christian view of peace." By way of contrast, "in classical Greek, *eirēnē* means little more than absence of war" (Geddert, 604; cf. Laansma, 893). Moreover, whereas the Greeks could view peace in terms of inner tranquility as well as the absence of war, the Hebrews saw it mostly in interpersonal or social interaction terms (Klassen). Nicholas Wolterstorff suggests that "flourishing" is a better rendering of the Hebrew *šālôm* than "peace": "To experience shalom is to flourish in all one's relationships—with God, with one's fellow human beings, with non-human creation, with oneself" (Wolterstorff, 19–20). Interestingly, in the Judaism of Jesus's day, "shalom" was a common greeting and farewell term (John 20:19, 21, 26; Mark 5:34).

Edenic shalom. Although the word "shalom" does not appear in the story of the world's beginnings, the world depicted there is one of shalom. After God's working week is over (Gen. 1:1–2:4a), we see the man placed in a paradise entrusted with the care and control of the garden environment (2:15). There is enormous freedom, with only one prohibition. All the fruit of the trees, except one, are for God's image-bearer to enjoy (2:16–17). There is harmony and unity. There is no hint of discord. The creator and creature are in communion, as are the man and woman. There is not only the absence of strife. There is also relational richness. Nakedness brings no shame (2:25).

Rupture and promise. The idyllic picture in Gen. 2 is one of harmony between God and Adam, between Adam and Eve ("one flesh"), and between the pair and their environment. However, the shalom inside the garden paradise comes under threat from an intruder (3:1, a "beast of the field" [ESV]). The serpent proves a spoiler, sowing doubts about the good character of God with the subtlety of a question, rather than a statement (Gen. 3:1 ESV): "Did God actually say . . . ?" First, the woman falls to its wiles, and before long the man joins in disobeying God's explicit prohibition. The realization of their sin leads to their hiding from God out of shame (3:7–8). Flight from God replaces fellowship with God. Judgment is swift. Man and woman are exiled from paradise (3:22–24). The relationship with God is ruptured, as are the relationships between man and woman and between both and the environment (3:16–19). The harmony that once existed has been shattered by the catastrophe of the fall. The cherubim with their flaming swords symbolize a paradise lost with the possibility of reentry blocked (3:24). Yet there is hope. God makes a promise. The serpent will be defeated and a progeny of the woman will be its defeater (3:15, the famous protevangelium, "first gospel"). In many ways, the story told in the canon from this point on is the outworking of this programmatic promise, culminating in the devil/serpent being thrown into the lake of fire (Rev. 20:10).

The quest for shalom. What ensues from the fall and how the promise of Gen. 3:15 is realized may be characterized in many complementary ways. God's project is to reclaim creation for himself. God's project is to secure his people living under his reign in the place he provides. God's project is to show his wisdom and glory through the recovery of creation for himself and the judgment of all who oppose it, whether human or angelic. God's project is to establish true worship, and with it shalom, throughout the created order.

Through the quest for shalom, God will restore order throughout his creation. Communion will replace conflict. For some this will mean reconciliation with God; for the rebellious it will mean pacification by God. One period in Israel's history in particular anticipates the shalom to come. Solomon is now king. Potential threats and discontent have been eliminated. Adonijah, Joab, and Shimei have been put to death (1 Kings 2:13–46), and so, tellingly we read, "The kingdom was now established in Solomon's hands" (v. 46). Good kings are wise kings, wise like God. Solomon soon shows the depths of his wisdom by praying for it and then showing it in the thorny matter of the two prostitutes and the one living baby (1 Kings 3). Officials are appointed, wealth increases, God's temple is built, then Solomon's own palace, God appears to him twice, and the queen of Sheba comes to experience his wisdom and is not disappointed. As for Israel and the nations, "The people of Judah and Israel were as numerous as the sand on the seashore; they ate, they drank and they were happy" (4:20). In addition, Solomon rules over all the kingdoms from the Euphrates River to the land of the Philistines, as far as the border of Egypt. These countries bring tribute and are Solomon's subjects all his life (4:21). As the reference to "the sand on the seashore" suggests, the promises to Abram are coming to pass (Gen. 12:1–3; 22:17).

But shalom does not last. Solomon embraces the women of the surrounding nations, women who came with political advantage (1 Kings 11:1). Such alliances had consequences: "The LORD became angry with Solomon because his heart had turned away from the LORD, the God of Israel, who had appeared to him twice. Although he had forbidden Solomon to follow other gods, Solomon did not keep the LORD's command" (11:9–10). After Solomon's death, the kingdom splits into a northern one (under Jeroboam) and a southern one (under Rehoboam, Solomon's son). Much wickedness is evinced in both kingdoms. Kings, priests, prophets, and sages fail repeatedly, with some notable exceptions (e.g., King Josiah and the prophet Isaiah). For such failures there is no shalom (Isa. 48:22). False prophets arise in Jerusalem who proclaim shalom when the reality is forthcoming divine judgment in the form of defeat in war and exile (Jer. 6:14, 22–23).

The hope of shalom. The OT prophets hoped for shalom. Likewise, the psalmist hoped that the king of the universe would bless his people with shalom (Ps. 29:11). According to D. A. Carson (505–6), "*Peace* is one of the fundamental characteristics of the messianic kingdom anticipated in the Old Testament (Nu. 6:26; Ps. 29:11; Is. 9:6–7; 52:7; 54:13; 57:19; Ezk. 37:26; Hg. 2:9) and fulfilled in the New (Acts 10:36; Rom. 1:7; 5:1; 14:17)." A number of them envisage a time to come in which war would cease. Micah expresses this hope in striking terms (Mic. 4:1–5; cf. Isa. 2:1–5). In this time to come the nations will say, "Come, let us go up to the mountain of the LORD, to the temple of the God of Jacob. He will teach us his ways, so that we may walk in his paths" (Mic. 4:2). The hoped-for consequence follows: "They will beat their swords into plowshares and their spears into pruning hooks. Nation will not take up sword against nation, nor will they train for war anymore" (v. 3). Such shalom is not merely negative (i.e., the absence of war). It is also positive: "Everyone will sit under their own vine and under their own fig tree, and no one will make them afraid, for the LORD Almighty has spoken" (v. 4). The chaos of Babel will be no more.

For the prophet Isaiah, there is an intimate connection between shalom and justice. He foresees a day when after judgment the Spirit will be poured out, wilderness and field will burgeon with life, and God's people will live in quietness and trust. The effect of righteousness will be shalom (Isa. 32:15–18). The psalmist, too, longs for shalom and likewise sees the nexus between justice and shalom. Psalm 85:4–6 calls upon Yahweh to restore and revive his people. The psalmist hopes that God will speak shalom to his people (v. 8), anticipating a time when "love and faithfulness meet together; righteousness and peace kiss each other" (v. 10). Wolterstorff (20) comments in relation to Ps. 85, "There can be no doubt that justice was seen by biblical writers as an indispensable component of flourishing in one's social relationships."

God promises to establish for his people a covenant of shalom (*bərît šālôm*). God will not abandon his people (Isa. 52:7; 54:9–10; Ezek. 34:25; 37:26). The key agent in this scenario is a Davidic king who will bear God's rule as the Prince of Shalom (Isa. 9:6–7; Ezek. 37:25). According to Zechariah, this ruler will be a humble king who will preach shalom to the nations (Scobie, 832). "The battle bow will be broken. . . . His rule will extend from sea to sea and from the River to the ends of the earth" (Zech. 9:10). It is to this humble king we now turn our attention.

The Prince of Shalom. One of the expectations entertained by ancient Israel was that of a coming leader who would be the Prince of Peace. This title was one of a number predicated of this figure in Isa. 9:6: "And he will be called Wonderful Counselor, Mighty God, Everlasting Father, Prince of Peace." This Davidic personage would reign at some future date. The government he would bring would be characterized by justice and righteousness. All this would come to pass because of divine action: "The zeal of the LORD Almighty will accomplish this" (Isa. 9:7).

Multiple NT testimonies make it clear that Jesus is this Davidic figure (e.g., Matt. 1:17, 20; Luke 1:32–33; Rom. 1:1–6). The shalom motif is in the foreground in many contexts, including the infancy narratives. Zechariah, the father of John the Baptist, predicts that the Davidic figure will "guide our feet into the path of peace" (Luke 1:79). The angelic revelation to the shepherds in the field displays both the Davidic and shalom motifs (2:11 and 2:14, respectively). In Acts 10:36, Jesus is the preacher of shalom. Likewise, in Eph. 2:13–18, Jesus is the proclaimer of peace who unites both Jew and gentile in one new *anthrōpos* ("human"). He brings about this peace through his blood shed on the cross.

On the individual level, Jesus promised those disciples gathered in the upper room that he would leave them a peace that the world could not give (John 14:27). Carson comments, "The world promises peace and waves the flag of peace as a greeting; it cannot give it." The peace Jesus is offering is more than a sense of inner peace. It is freighted with "messianic and eschatological" import (Carson, 505–6). He is offering more than any Pax Romana could. Under the old covenant, it is Yahweh who gives the blessing of peace (Num. 6:24–26). Under the new covenant, it is Jesus.

Shalom in between. The NT writers place the follower of Christ in a specific time frame and place. The time frame is "these last days" (Heb. 1:1–2) and the place is the "groaning" creation (Rom. 8:18–25). In the NT, features of the age to come can be experienced in the here and now (e.g., justification, eternal life). This is the well-known already/not-yet phenomenon, summed up as inaugurated eschatology. Within this time frame, in this location and eschatological frame of reference, shalom shows itself in a variety of ways, including benefits and obligations, with the best yet to be.

First, the chief way shalom is experienced in this life is by our having peace with God (Rom. 5:1–2): "Therefore, since we have been justified through faith, we have peace with God through our Lord Jesus Christ, through whom we have gained access by faith into this grace in which we now stand" (cf. Dunn, 246–47; Osborne, 126–29; Longenecker, 555–56). This peace with God comes about through Christ and his saving work. In fact, the phrase "through our Lord Jesus Christ" occurs in four important places in Paul's argument from Rom. 5:1–7:25 (5:1, 21; 6:23; 7:25; Longenecker, 555–56). Three of these places mention a blessing of the age to come: justification (5:1) and eternal life (5:21; 6:23).

The locus classicus for Paul's understanding of how peace comes through Christ is Rom. 5:6–11. Paul describes the human predicament in stark terms (vv. 6–10): "powerless," "ungodly," "sinners," and "enemies." However, God has intervened. Motivated by love, God has provided a rescuer—namely, Jesus Christ (v. 8). Christ's death and resurrection are the keys to the rescue (v. 10). The result is reconciliation. Enemies have become friends, and divine wrath has been averted (vv. 9–10). In that light, Paul could write to the Corinthian church and describe himself as an ambassador for Christ passing on the message of reconciliation (2 Cor. 5:18–20). The word "peace" does not appear in Rom. 5:6–11, but the idea is there in the language of reconciliation.

Second, the good news of peace is not only vertical in direction. There is a horizontal dimension as well. Paul is our guide once more. He writes to the Ephesians about Jewish and gentile Christian relations, which were poor in the Greco-Roman world. There was between these two groups what Paul describes as "the dividing wall of hostility" needing to be broken down. Christ and his death are the keys once more (Eph. 2:14–16): "For he himself is our peace, who has made the two groups one and has destroyed the barrier, the dividing wall of hostility, by setting aside in his flesh the law with its commands and regulations. His purpose was to create in himself one new humanity out of the two, thus making peace, and in one body to reconcile both of them to God through the cross, by which he put to death their hostility." Here are the notes of peace and reconciliation. In fact, Paul sums up Christ's mission in shalom terms (vv. 17–18): "He came and preached peace to you who were far away and peace to those who were near. For through him we both have access to the Father by one Spirit."

Third, the gospel of peace brings with it a particular role and blessing for us. William Swartley (585) puts it well: "Peace is God's gift first and foremost, but it is also a task, seeking peace within Christ's body and witnessing to peace in the world." Jesus famously said (Matt. 5:9): "Blessed are the peacemakers [*eirēnopoios*], for they will be called children of God." The term "blessed" in this context "refers to those who are and/or will be *happy, fortunate*, or those 'to be congratulated' because of God's response to their behavior or situation" (Blomberg, 97–98). This text contains the only reference to "peacemakers" in the NT (Morris, 100–101). The role of peacemaking is predicated upon divine blessing and not the other way around. In this, Jesus follows the classic structure of Jewish ethics (e.g., Exod. 20:1–17). Halakah (the walk before God) is predicated on haggadah (the story of God's initiative). To be a peacemaker is to act like the God for whom shalom is an eschatological goal. Thus, the peacemaking child is like his or her parent in kingdom terms.

Fourth, unsurprisingly if the divine project aims to establish a state of shalom, peace is to be pursued with all as an interpersonal goal. Paul understood this desideratum (Rom. 12:17–18): "Do not repay anyone evil for evil. Be careful to do what is right in the eyes of everyone. If it is possible, as far as it depends on you, live at peace with everyone [*meta pantōn anthrōpōn*]." Paul counsels the Romans not to repay evil with evil but to leave vengeance up to God (12:17, 19). Indeed, peace is a characteristic of the kingdom of God, as are righteousness and joy (14:17). Consequently, Paul exhorts both the Romans and himself (14:19), "Let us therefore make every effort to do what leads to peace and to mutual edification." At Rome, there appears to have been strife between Jewish and gentile Christ followers, and so Paul is encouraging a practice without which interpersonal communion is endangered (14:1–16). This fruit of the Spirit was sorely needed (Gal. 5:22).

As in the OT testimony, the nexus between justice and shalom was thematized in the NT. James 3:18 provides a case in point: "Peacemakers [*tois poiousin eirēnē*, lit., "by the ones making peace"] who sow in peace [*eirēnē*] reap a harvest of righteousness." In this text, James echoes the Sermon on the Mount (Matt. 5:9) in citing peacemaking as a desideratum. The wise person with wisdom from above is one who makes peace and, therefore, stands in marked contrast to those who cause quarrels and fights (James 4:1; Davids, 155).

Shalom realized. Peace is a human desideratum (international, national, local, and personal). The Scriptures, too, know of the quest for peace. Indeed, God has his reconciliation project underway, which makes peace or shalom through the shed blood of Christ. This shalom finds its apogee in the world to come. The last two chapters of the canon show harmonies restored (Rev. 21–22). The ruptures in Gen. 3 are mended. Significantly, there is no longer any sea (Rev. 21:1). The sea, of course, represented chaos and threat to the Jewish mind. Tears are wiped away; death is no more. Nor is there mourning, crying, or pain. The order of disharmony has given way to the new order of harmony (Rev. 21:1–4). God and his people are at home with each other. The refrain from Exod. 6:7 to Rev. 20:3 is realized ("I will be their God, and they will be my people," Jer. 31:33).

The glorified people of God live with God and one another in the city of God in the context of the new heavens and a new earth. All is sacred space, or temple space as the cubical shape of the new Jerusalem suggests—the only other cubical space the canon mentions is the holy of holies. Hence, there is no need for a physical temple (Rev. 21:22). In this world to come, redeemed humankind are kings and priests (22:3–4). Thus, the original Adamic roles are realized in this new frame of reference. There is no need for prophets, as prophecy belongs to the east of Eden world, where sin needs to be challenged. There is not only the absence of strife but also richness of communion, glory, and light (21:22–26). Augustine in his classic work *Confessions* was right to claim, "You made us for yourself and our hearts find no peace until they rest in you" (*Conf.* 1.1). In this new reality, there is rest indeed. The peace mission of the God of peace has been completed (Rom. 15:33; 1 Cor. 14:33; 2 Cor. 13:11; Phil. 4:9; 2 Thess. 3:16; Heb. 13:20). Satan, the architect of strife, has been crushed by the God of peace (cf. Gen. 3:15; Rom. 16:20).

Conclusion

Shalom is a rich biblical concept that has many dimensions of meaning: health, prosperity, security, friendship, salvation, wholeness, and completion. The concept of flourishing may be the best way to capture the multiplicity of dimensions. Shalom is a desideratum in both the OT and NT. As a state of being, it will be a defining characteristic of the world to come when reconciliation has been realized throughout the created order. It is God in Christ through the Spirit who gives shalom. This is not surprising since the NT repeatedly describes God as the God or Lord of peace. For those living in this age, shalom is to be pursued in relationships. Peacemakers are blessed by God and are God-like in character as children of a peacemaking God should be. Peacemaking is wise. Strife-making is foolish. For the wicked there is no shalom.

See also Covenant; Law

Bibliography. Aristotle, *Poetics*, trans. S. H. Butcher (Dover Thrift Editions, 1997); Augustine, *Confessions*, trans. R. S. Pine-Coffin (Penguin, 1977); Blomberg, C., *Matthew*, NAC (Broadman & Holman, 1992); Carson, D. A., *The Gospel according to John*, PNTC (Eerdmans, 1991); Davids, P. H., *The Epistle of James*, NIGTC (Eerdmans, 1982); Dunn, J. D. G., *Romans 1–8*, WBC (Word, 1998); Geddert, T. J., "Peace," in *DJG*[1], 604–5; Klassen, W., "Peace: New Testament," in *ABD*, 5:207–12; Laansma, J. C., "Peace," in *DLNTD*, 893–900; Longenecker, R. N., *The Epistle to the Romans*, NIGTC (Eerdmans, 2016); Morris, L., *The Gospel according to Matthew*, PNTC (Eerdmans, 1992); Osborne, G. R., *Romans*, IVPNTC (InterVarsity, 2004); Schaeffer, G. E., "Peace," in *Evangelical Dictionary of Biblical Theology*, ed. W. A. Elwell (Baker, 1996), 597–98; Scobie, C. H. H., *The Ways of Our God* (Eerdmans, 2003); Smith-Christopher, D. L., "Shalom," in *NIDB*, 5:211–12; Swartley, W. M., "Peace," in *Dictionary of Scripture and Ethics*, ed. J. B. Green (Baker Academic, 2011), 583–86; Sykes, S., *The Story of Atonement* (Darton, Longman & Todd, 1997); Wiesel, E., *The Gates of the Forest* (Holt, Rinehart & Winston, 1966); Wolterstorff, N. P., "Justice and Peace," in *New Dictionary of Christian Ethics and Pastoral Theology*, ed. D. J. Atkinson and D. H. Field (InterVarsity, 1995), 17–22.

GRAHAM A. COLE

Shame

The concept of shame is referenced in the OT by lexemes such as *bwš*, *klm*, *ḥpr*, *bzh*, *zll*, *qlh*, *qll*, and *ḥrp*, and in the NT by lexemes such as *aidōs*, *entropē*, *atimia*, *deigmatizō*, *aischynē*, and *kataischynō*. The absence of these lexemes does not imply the absence of shame, since the concept referenced by these lexemes may be invoked by contextual clues such as spitting in the face (Num. 12:14; Deut. 25:9; Job 17:6; 30:10), shaving the beard (2 Sam. 10:4; Isa. 7:20; 15:2; 50:6), treating captives as animals (2 Kings 19:28; Ezek. 19:4), fleeing naked (Mark 14:51–52), or refusing to look up (Luke 18:13).

Although there are variations, the above shame lexemes collectively take three different uses in the Bible (Lau, 150). Their meanings and English glosses are as follows:

1. A disposition or inhibitory emotion that prevents a person from committing something dishonorable or ignominious—*modesty, reserve, sense of shame, sense of honor*, or *shamefastness*.
2. The subjective feeling that is experienced after doing something objectionable or ignominious—*shame, compunction*, or *remorse*. In this sense, shame is the painful emotion that arises when one is aware of one's inadequacies under the gaze of another person, real or imagined.
3. The objective state of disgrace—*humiliation, dishonor, shame, ignominy*, or *disgrace*. In this sense, shame is contrasted with honor and glory. It refers to the public acknowledgment of a person's disgrace or lack of worth as a result of his or her failure to embody qualities and values that are valued by the group. A person's shame, like honor, can be ascribed or attained. Ascribed shame is obtained simply for being who you are (e.g., born as a slave); attained or acquired shame results from one's action (e.g., throwing away one's shield and fleeing in a battle).

The biblical concept of shame is intimately connected to the motif of sin, judgment, and redemption. In this essay, I draw out biblical-theological implications of shame as I sketch its concept in the OT and NT. Since shame is frequently contrasted with glory and honor, I also highlight these themes as necessary.

Shame in the OT

Our survey of shame in the OT will be selective. We first examine its presence in Gen. 1–3. We then examine its use within the covenant community of Israel, the Deuteronomic covenant, and prophetic literature.

Created for glory, mired in shame. Our story necessarily begins in Gen. 1–3, for the earliest occurrence of shame in Scripture is in these chapters. In the beginning, God created the heavens and the earth for his glory (Pss. 19:1–4; 50:6; 89:5). God also created humankind for his glory (Isa. 43:7), creating Adam and Eve in his image (Gen. 1:26–27). As image-bearers, they are to reflect God's righteousness, love, justice, integrity, and above all his glory and honor (Ps. 8:5). They are to be fruitful and multiply, filling the earth as representatives of God's presence, rule, and glory (Gen. 1:28; Ps. 8:6–9). Faithfulness, obedience, and recognizing the honor that solely belongs to God the Creator are essential to carry out this mandate.

In the state of goodness before the entrance of sin, Adam and Eve live in unimpeded freedom with each other and with God. They were "both naked and were not ashamed" (Gen. 2:25 ESV). However, when they disobey God and eat the fruit, their eyes are opened. They perceive not only their physical nakedness but also their spiritual poverty. In wanting to "be like God" (3:5) they became idolaters and usurped God's glory. In arrogating glory for themselves they repudiated the glory that God intended for them as image-bearers and heaped shame on themselves—they exchanged their glory for shame. The shame they experienced was not just relegated to their nakedness; it was also bound to their exile from the garden and from the presence of God (3:23). God "drove [them] in disgrace from the mount of God" (Ezek. 28:16).

The Genesis narrative highlights several aspects of shame (Lau, 64–67). (1) Shame is a relational concept and is generated by a fractured relationship. Adam and Eve's desire to hide and conceal themselves reflects their disunion with God and with each other. (2) Shame is a function of sin. Shame can arise as the direct consequence of one's sin, of the sin of others, or from living in a fallen world. (3) Shame is the necessary condition of sinful humanity. Since all humans sin (Ps. 51:5; 58:3; 143:2; Rom. 3:23) and bear the death of Adam (Rom. 5:12; 1 Cor. 15:22), so also all bear the shame of Adam. Shame persists as long as sin exists. (4) Creation shares in the shame of humanity. As a result of Adam's sin, creation is defiled and cursed (Gen. 3:17; Isa. 24:5–6). It groans in frustration, unable to accomplish fully its purpose (Rom. 8:20, 22). If shame stems from the failure to meet one's ideal and if shame is linked to defilement and curse (as we will see later), we can then say that creation suffers shame along with humanity. (5) Only God is adequate to redress humanity's shame. Adam and Eve sew skimpy loincloths (*ḥăgôrâ*, 3:7) out of fig leaves to cover their shameful nakedness. God, however, in his mercy deals with their pitiful efforts. He provides long tunics (*kuttōnet*, 3:21; cf. 37:3, 23, 31–33) made from animal skins, thereby addressing the shame that they were incapable of addressing. The death of the animal points forward to the sacrifice of the Lamb of God who takes away not only the sin (John 1:29) but also the shame of the world.

Shame and purity in the wilderness community. The Genesis account shows how shame relates to moral categories. The cultic regulations surrounding the community in the Pentateuch also show that shame is related to the language of purity and defilement. Purity is embraced and honored, defilement shunned and shamed. Applying this framework to the wilderness community, the area within the camp must be kept holy, for the glory of God resides in the tabernacle within the center of the camp. Moreover, the Lord walks within the camp, and he must not see any "shameless deed" in its midst (Deut. 23:14 AT). Thus, things that are shameful, indecent, or defiling must be put outside the camp. That is where lepers are consigned (Num. 5:2–3), executions take place (Lev. 24:14, 23; Num. 15:33–36), bodies of sacrificial animals are burned (Exod. 29:14; Heb. 13:11), and latrines are kept (Deut. 23:12). Banishment from the community to this area of impurity is shameful. It diminishes one's social status and marks one out as persona non grata. When Miriam was struck with leprosy and ordered to stay outside the camp for seven days, she was said to be "in disgrace for seven days" (Num. 12:14).

Shame and the Deuteronomic covenant. The language of shame permeates the Deuteronomic covenant. The consequences associated with covenantal faithfulness can be understood in honor-shame categories. If Israel fully obeys Yahweh, the blessing they receive is honor. Yahweh will set them "high above all the nations on earth" (Deut. 28:1). Their enemies will scatter in fright as cowards; Israel will be "the head, not the tail"; they will "always be at the top, never at the bottom" (28:7, 13). However, if Israel does not obey all the words of the law, the curse they will receive is shame. They, not their enemies, will flee from battle in disgrace (28:25). They will be denied a dignified burial, and their carcasses will be devoured by scavenging animals and birds (28:26). They will be objects of ridicule (28:37) and serve their enemies in nakedness and poverty (28:48). They will sink lower, but their enemies will rise higher (28:43). They will be the tail, but their enemies will be the head (28:44). They will sink to a status lower than that of slaves—they will be *unwanted* slaves (28:68).

Apart from its consequences, the criteria for covenantal faithfulness can also be understood in honor-shame categories. Deuteronomy 28:58 brings this out clearly, for the failure to "revere this glorious and awesome name—the LORD your God"—parallels the failure to obey all the words of the law. Consequently, the Deuteronomic covenant can be understood in a reciprocal honor-for-honor and shame-for-shame dynamic. This principle of *lex talionis* is explicitly affirmed in 1 Sam. 2:30: "Those who honor me I will honor, and those who despise me shall be treated with contempt" (NRSV).

Shame, judgment, and redemption. Within the prophetic literature, the language of shame is frequently tied to sin, judgment, repentance, and salvation. When Israel rushes after false idols, they dishonor God. They rob God of the glory that is rightfully his; they "turn [his] glory into shame" (Ps. 4:2). Israel was formed to bring glory to God (Isa. 49:3), but they bring shame to God instead.

Israel's sin also brings shame upon themselves. Hosea portrays the Northern Kingdom as an adulterous wife who runs after many lovers (2:2–13). The Southern Kingdom fares no better. She degrades her beauty and spreads her legs with promiscuity to anyone who passes by (Ezek. 16:25). So deplorable is her conduct that even other nations are shocked by her lewdness (16:27). In response to such shameful behavior, God lifts up her skirt over her face and exposes her shameful nakedness (Jer. 13:26; Nah. 3:5). He pours forth his shaming judgment on her such that she is disgraced before the nations of the world. Her people wet themselves with urine (Ezek. 7:17; 21:7 LXX), their faces are covered with shame and their heads shaved (7:18), they become a laughingstock to all the nations (22:4), and their shame is great (Jer. 9:19).

Israel was supposed to reflect the glory of God. By trusting in the glory of humanity (be it military might or economic power) rather than the faithfulness of God, they "exchanged their glorious God for worthless idols" (Jer. 2:11). As a result of Israel's unfaithfulness, God divorces her. He forsakes her and hides his face, fulfilling the ultimate curse of the Deuteronomic covenant (Deut. 31:17–18). As God's glory departs the temple (Ezek. 10), Israel is left only with shame, for whatever honor they have is derivative from their relationship with God. In their idolatry, they become what they worship (Ps. 115:8; Beale, *Become*). They no longer reflect the glory of God but reflect the shame of idols. "They changed their glory into shame" (Hosea 4:7 NRSV).

Shame, however, is not to be the last word, for the purpose of shaming judgment is redemptive and doxological. The psalmist Asaph urges God to act against Israel's enemies. He prays, "Cover their faces with shame, LORD, so that they will seek your name" (Ps. 83:16). The purpose of God's shaming judgment is that people might turn toward God for salvation and acknowledge that he alone is "the Most High over all the earth" (83:18). If this thought is true for Israel's enemies, how much more is it true for God's people? If Israel internalizes their objective shame such that they acknowledge how far they have fallen short of God's standard, the resultant experience of shame should move them toward contrition and penitential confession of their sin (Jer. 3:25; 31:19; Dan. 9:7). Repentance leads to the forgiveness of sins and deliverance (Deut. 30:1–5). God will bring the exiles back to their land; he will make them prosperous; he will replace their shame with honor, praise, and joy (Isa. 61:7; Zeph. 3:19–20). If "judgment brings disgrace, salvation leads to the removal of shame" (Hadjiev, 334). But Israel's salvation does not result only in the restoration of honor for Israel. It ultimately brings glory to God, for nations will be drawn to Israel and will come "proclaiming the praise of the LORD" (Isa. 60:6). The above sequence of events can be diagrammed as follows: disobedience of covenantal obligations → covenantal curses and shame before other nations → internalized shame concerning one's sin → repentance → restoration → objective honor for Israel → glory to God.

The prophets, however, present a dire picture. Instead of feeling remorse for her shameful behavior, Jerusalem remains hardened and does not know how to blush (Jer. 3:3; 6:15; 8:12; Zeph. 3:5). She is shameless. Jerusalem's exile, however, brings shame not only on herself but also on God. Jerusalem's exile impugns the name of the Lord, for the fate of a nation is positively correlated with the prestige of its god (cf. Exod. 32:11–12; Deut. 32:26–27; Ezek. 36:20). As Jerusalem remains in exile, God is himself put to shame before the other nations so much so that he "felt sorry for [his] holy name" (Ezek. 36:21 AT). God cannot experience shame from doing anything shameful or from failing to accomplish any of his purposes, for he is the sovereign God. Nevertheless, God so intimately identifies with his people through the covenant that their humiliation becomes his. God will thus act on behalf of his name, and he will restore his people back from exile. He will remove their disgrace (36:30). But he will do something more: he will give them a new heart and a new spirit so that they will have a renewed knowledge of themselves and of him. With a transformed perspective, they will now be able to remember their sin in light of his compassion and loathe themselves for their wickedness (36:31). They will now be able to experience a healthy subjective shame that is indicative of true restoration (16:53–63; 20:43–44; 36:31–32; 39:26; 43:10–11; 44:9–14). And God will bring all this through the work of his Son, Jesus.

Shame in the NT

Our survey of shame in the NT will have to be selective. We first examine its presence in Jesus's crucifixion and in Paul's presentation of the gospel in Romans. We then analyze its significance within the life of the church and its final reversal in Rev. 20–22.

Shame and Jesus's crucifixion. Crucifixion was the most degrading form of public execution in the Roman world, and its purpose was to humiliate the victim. The place of execution is typically public or along major thoroughfares so that everybody can gawk at the spectacle. The victim was stripped naked and suffered a protracted death. In many cases, the corpse was left on the cross and devoured by birds and animals. Crucifixion is also inherently shameful from a Jewish perspective, for anyone who is hung on a tree is cursed (Deut. 21:23; Gal. 3:13).

The Synoptics highlight the disgrace of Jesus's crucifixion. The crowds mock and despise him (Matt. 27:38–43; Mark 15:27–32; Luke 23:35–38; cf. Isa. 49:7; 50:6; 53:3). Yet surely what Jesus experiences most acutely is not the ridicule of the crowds but the shame of divine abandonment. To be abandoned by God is the ultimate covenantal curse (Deut. 31:17); it invites scorn and derision (Ps. 42:3, 10; Joel 2:17). As Jesus hangs on the cross, he questions not the taunt of the crowds but the silence of God. He cries out with a loud voice, "My God, my God, why have you forsaken me?" (Mark 15:34; cf. Ps. 22:1). But there is no immediate answer (Ps. 22:2). What Jesus experiences most painfully on the cross is the shame of divine abandonment as he takes upon himself our guilt and our shame.

Through his shameful death on the cross, Jesus reverses the shame of his people and "[brings] many sons and daughters to glory" (Heb. 2:10). He enacts the new exodus (Mark 1:3; cf. Isa. 40:3), thereby ending the shame of Israel's spiritual exile—their separation from God. Even though Israel had already returned to the promised land years earlier under Zerubbabel, the postexilic community remains in spiritual exile for they continue to dishonor God and despise his name (Mal. 1:6–8). Jesus accomplishes the hope of restoration foretold by the prophets, not least that of Ezekiel, for it is through his death on the cross that the Holy Spirit will be given to all. This Spirit convicts rebellious Israel and the nations of their sin (John 16:8), enabling them to experience the shame that is necessary for true repentance.

Shame and the gospel in Romans. In Rom. 1–3, Paul relates the sin of all humanity to a fundamental distortion of honor and shame that suppresses the truth that God alone is the one who deserves honor (Jewett). The gentiles are under God's judgment for dishonoring God. They "neither glorified him as God nor gave thanks to him" (1:21). Instead of praising the Creator, they worship and serve created things (1:25). God therefore judges these idolaters with shame. He hands them over to the degradation of their bodies, to shameful lusts, and to a depraved mind (1:24, 26, 28). Jews fare no better for they also "dishonor God" (2:23). By their disobedience to the law "God's name is blasphemed" (2:24). God therefore shames them by giving them trouble and distress rather than glory and honor (2:9–10). Both Jew and gentile alike are guilty of dishonoring God. As a consequence of their sin, both "fall short of the glory of God" (3:23). They fail to measure up to the glorious image of God for which they were created.

If the nature of sin, as demonstrated by sinful humanity, is to dishonor God, the nature of faith, as demonstrated by Abraham, is to consider God trustworthy and give glory to him (4:20). Through this posture of faith, humanity is justified (3:22). But if sin results in shame, justification results in glory. Thus, Paul declares, "Everyone who trusts in him will not be put to shame" at the final judgment (10:11 AT; cf. 1 Pet. 2:6; Isa. 28:16 LXX; 49:23; Pss. 25:3; 34:5). God rescues and honors those who call on him (Ps. 91:15). By being united with Christ through faith, believers no longer share in the shame of the first Adam but share in the glory of the second (Rom. 5:12–21). They can boast in the hope of sharing in God's glory (5:2), for they are now able through Christ to recover the image of God in them.

The recovery of the image of God in believers is described by Paul via a clothing metaphor. Although nakedness and clothing typically symbolize shame and honor respectively, clothing can also be used as a metaphor for *both* shame and honor. What matters is the kind of clothing with which one is attired. Filthy clothes signify shame (e.g., with Joshua in Zech. 3:3–5), while royal robes signify honor (e.g., with Joseph in Gen. 41:42 and Mordecai in Esther 6:7–9). Thus, one can be clothed with shame (Job 8:22; Pss. 35:26; 109:29; 132:18) or with dignity, honor, and righteousness (Job 40:10; Ps. 104:1; Prov. 31:25; Isa. 61:10). Now, Paul remarks that believers have stripped off the old self (Adam) and clothed themselves with the new self (Christ) that is renewed according to the image of God (Col. 3:9–10; Gal. 3:27; Rom. 13:14). This clothing imagery probably alludes to Gen. 3 (Beale, *Theology*, 452–55). Believers have discarded the inadequate loincloths of the old Adam, which are inherently shameful and unable to hide the shame of their nakedness. They have instead clothed themselves with the attire of the last Adam (Christ), an attire that Adam proleptically received from God in Eden (Beale, *Theology*, 455). By putting on Christ, by identifying themselves with the second Adam rather than the old, fallen Adam, believers clothe themselves with the glory that Christ himself has. They restore to themselves the glory that God originally intended for his children. Although the restoration of God's glory in humanity is consummated on the last day (Rom. 5:2; 8:17–18, 21, 30), believers are now progressively transformed from one degree of glory to another as they are conformed to the image of God's Son through the power of the Spirit (Rom. 8:29–30; 2 Cor. 3:18).

Shame and the church. Honor and shame are values whose specific content needs to be determined by the respective court of opinion. The pagan court of opinion values strength but disparages weakness, especially that displayed on the cross. The Jewish court of opinion values Torah obedience (Sir. 44:1–50:21) but considers the cross to be blasphemous. The manifestation of God's glory in and through the cross, however, invalidates these two courts of opinion. Honor is no longer found in human power, human wisdom, or even in obedience to the Torah. On the contrary, honor is henceforth to be solely based on the cross and the crucified Messiah. That which the world considers shameful is now esteemed by God. In the eyes of the pagan and Jewish courts of opinion, the message of a crucified Messiah is scandalous—it is "a stumbling block to Jews and foolishness to Gentiles" (1 Cor. 1:23). In the eyes of God, however, the crucified Messiah is the power and wisdom of God (1:24). He will use the cross and those who are aligned with the crucified Messiah "to shame the wise" and "to shame the strong" of the world (1:27).

Living in the already/not-yet framework where the glory of the cross is not embraced by all, the church must remind itself that God is the judge whose opinion ultimately matters. They must calibrate their honor and shame values to cohere with the divine court of opinion. Here are several ways in which this is done:

First, the church must not be ashamed of their crucified Messiah. If they are ashamed of him, he will be ashamed of them when he returns in glory (Mark 8:38; Luke 9:26). Moreover, if Jesus "is not ashamed to call them brothers and sisters" (Heb. 2:11), the church should not be ashamed of identifying with him and "bearing the disgrace he bore" (13:13).

Second, the church must not be ashamed of the gospel concerning a crucified Messiah (Rom. 1:16). "The message about the cross is foolishness to those who are perishing, but to us who are being saved it is the power of God" (1 Cor. 1:18). Consequently, the church must proclaim this message with boldness (Acts 4:29; Eph. 6:19).

Third, the church must remember that the only basis of their honor is Christ. Believers cannot be driven by vain conceit (Phil. 2:3); they must repudiate society's passion for ambition, considering their accomplishments as dung and liabilities (3:7–9). Christ alone possesses true, lasting honor (2:9–10). Consequently, any honor that believers hope to attain can come only through their association with Christ.

Fourth, the church must live in "a manner worthy of the gospel" (Phil. 1:27). They must maintain a proper sense of shame, being careful to do nothing that will dishonor Christ (1 Cor. 6:15), the church (5:1), or other believers (11:22). Moreover, they must maintain the holiness of the community. Since the Holy Spirit dwells within the church (Eph. 2:19–22), there must not be anything shameful in its midst. Following the example of the wilderness community, the church must expel anything that is indecent or defiling. The church must remove anyone who persistently and unrepentantly brings shame to the name of Christ (1 Cor. 5:5, 11). They must not associate with them so that they might be ashamed and turn back from their sin (2 Thess. 3:14).

Fifth, the church must not "shrink back" and succumb to society's pressure to conform (Heb. 10:38–39). Believers will face marginalization and scorn as they bear witness to the crucified Messiah. Nevertheless, they must remember the example of Jesus. For just as the shame of Jesus's suffering preceded his glory (Phil. 2:5–11), so also the shame of our "momentary light affliction produces for us an eternal weight of glory beyond all measure" (2 Cor. 4:17 AT). When persecuted for the name of Christ, the church should not retaliate but should care for their enemies. For in so doing, they will heap "burning coals" on the heads of their enemies (Rom. 12:20; cf. Prov. 25:21–22). Their enemies will experience pangs of shame that may produce remorse and contrition (1 Pet. 3:16).

From shame to glory. Our story of shame ends in Rev. 20–22. Christ's return ushers in the final stage of the new creation as there will be a metamorphosis of shameful matter into glorious matter. He will transform the "body of humiliation" of his people to be like "his body of glory" (Phil. 3:21 AT; cf. 1 John 3:2). That which is "sown in dishonor" will be "raised in glory" (1 Cor. 15:43). But not only are the bodies of God's people transformed into glory, so also is creation; for the former things that are stained with sin, death, curse, defilement, and shame pass away (Rev. 21:3). Instead of the old creation, John sees in Rev. 21:1 an incorruptible new heaven and new earth. The old cosmos that shared in the shame of Adam is renewed and transformed so that it now shares in the glory of God's redeemed people (Rom. 8:21).

John envisions the new heavens and the new earth as the "Holy City" (Rev. 21:2). Just as the OT wilderness community cannot allow anything indecent or shameful within its midst, so also to a much greater degree this holy city. "Nothing impure will ever enter it, nor will anyone who does what is shameful" (21:27). Believers who have "washed their robes and made them white in the blood of the Lamb" (7:14) have every right to enter through its gates "into the city" (22:14). The wicked, however, are consigned to the area of shame "outside" the city (22:15)—they are burned in the lake of fire (20:15; 21:8). In the words of Dan. 12:2, they are resurrected not to eternal life but "to shame and everlasting contempt."

This holy city is also called the "new Jerusalem" (Rev. 21:2). The collocation of "Holy City" and "Jerusalem" echoes Isa. 52:1, a passage where God's people no longer suffer the shame of exile. Instead, God says to his people as he gathers them back to himself in Zion, "Do not be afraid, for you will not be put to shame; do not feel humiliated, for you will not be disgraced. For you will forget the shame of your youth and the reproach of your widowhood" (Isa. 54:4 AT). In Rev. 21:4, John further notes that the holy city will fulfill the vision of Isa. 25:8. God will wipe every tear from their eyes, and death will exist no more. Isaiah 25:8 goes on to say that "[God] will remove the disgrace of his people from all the earth" (AT). As God gathers his people back to himself in the new Jerusalem, he definitively and completely removes their shame.

John depicts the reversal not only of Israel's shame as they return back from exile to Jerusalem but also of humanity's shame as they return back from exile to the garden of Eden. John's language of water, curse, and the tree of life in Rev. 22:1–3 recalls Gen. 1–3. In so doing, John tells us that God's people are now no longer banished from his presence in the garden. God again dwells among his people. He again walks in their midst, but they no longer need to hide in shame as Adam once did. On the contrary, they see his face and their foreheads are inscribed with his name (Rev. 22:4), signifying that they reflect not the image of the beast but the image of God. God's people at last fully reflect not the shame of idols, but the glory of God as originally intended. In so doing, the restoration of humanity abounds to God's glory.

See also Image of God

Bibliography. Beale, G. K., *A New Testament Biblical Theology* (Baker Academic, 2011); Beale, *We Become What We Worship* (IVP Academic, 2008); Hadjiev, T. S., "Honor and Shame," in *DOTPr*, 333–38; Jewett, R., "Honor and Shame in the Argument of Romans," in *Putting Body and Soul Together*, ed. V. Wiles, A. R. Brown, and G. F. Snyder (Trinity Press International, 1997), 258–73; Lau, T.-L., *Defending Shame* (Baker Academic, 2020).

TE-LI LAU

Sin

Sin in the OT

Creation. God, who is perfect in holiness, creates all things good. He creates a good cosmos with good humans. Of all his creatures, God makes only humans in his image. They are like him in unique ways and are created with minds to know him and do his will. He makes them morally upright and puts them over the other creatures to steward and care for them (Gen. 1:26–2:25). God makes man from the dust of the ground, but man is more than dust—his life comes from the very breath of God (2:7). God plants a garden and provides a delightful and sacred space in which humans enjoy a harmonious relationship with him, each other, the animals, and the land. The story of creation reveals that sin is not created or authored by God. Further, it shows that sin is not original—there was a time when there was no sin.

The fall. Obviously, sin exists now. What went wrong? "The Bible begins with God creating the heavens and the earth (Gen. 1–2). Repeatedly, God's verdict is that all of his handiwork is 'very good.' There is no sin and no suffering," writes D. A. Carson (41). He adds, "But the first human rebellion (Gen. 3) marks the onset of suffering, toil, pain, and death. A mere two chapters later, we read the endlessly repeated and hauntingly pitiful refrain, "then he died . . . then he died . . . then he died . . . then he died."

The first couple are given only one prohibition: they must not eat of the tree of the knowledge of good and evil. Sadly, Gen. 3 informs us that they listen to Satan rather than God, and sin enters human history. Nothing, except God himself, is the same after the fall. Indeed, the fall occurs when "Adam . . . acts in willful, autonomous rebellion against God and thus, tragically, turns the created order upside down" (Gentry and Wellum, 621).

The primal sin is many things: disobedience, unbelief, infidelity. But most profoundly, the fall is human creatures seeking to usurp their Creator's prerogatives. God gave Adam and Eve every tree in the garden except one. The prohibition of Gen. 2:17 "made explicit for Adam and Eve the distinction that existed between creature and Creator, and the necessity that the relationship between them and God had always to be defined from God's side and not from theirs" (Dyrness, 100). In seeking to blur this distinction, our first parents violated the order defined by God's word.

The results are catastrophic, as a comparison of the pre-fall and post-fall situations shows: sin enters the picture and disrupts each human relationship—with God, self, one another, and creation (Morgan, *Christian*, 202). Paul House answers his own question, "How important is the prevalence of sin in the rest of the Old Testament canon? In a very real sense, the rest of Scripture deals with the solution to the sin problem" (67). Genesis 3:15 provides more than a hint of that solution when it makes the first promise of redemption.

The flood. The effects of Adam's sin multiply swiftly and relentlessly, as Bruce Waltke (276) explains: "Sin spreads like wildfire. . . . Cain murders his brother and fears being killed. In turn, Cain's offspring repeatedly kill in unbridled revenge. . . . Sin is like a lethal lion crouching at the door, wanting to devour. . . . Unless checked by faith, sin is like yeast that works through the whole batch of dough. . . . The depth and comprehensiveness of human depravity prior to the flood portends the end of history at the Parousia."

Indeed, some of Scripture's saddest words tell why God brings the judgment of the flood: "The LORD saw how great the wickedness of the human race had become on the earth, and that every inclination of the thoughts of the human heart was only evil all the time" (Gen. 6:5).

Abraham. With few exceptions (Enoch, Noah), Gen. 3–11 paints a gloomy picture of humanity's mutiny against its Maker. Genesis 3 and 11 form an *inclusio*, with the former portraying the fall of humans and the latter the fall of human society as city builders seek security and architectural fame in Babel apart from God. Thankfully, God brings hope amid this darkness (Gen. 12:1–3). In grace he responds to the human dilemma, replacing curses with blessings. As with Noah, God makes a new beginning with Abraham, whom he calls from idolatry and to whom he makes great promises through which he will eventually solve the sin problem (Dumbrell, 60–61, 66).

Moses. When God gives Moses the law on Mount Sinai he codifies his will in writing. From then on sin is exposed for what it is—violation of divine command. Though God gives the law to express his covenant love, and his people swear obedience, they are a defiant, stiff-necked people whom the law condemns (Exod. 32:9; Jer. 7:26; Acts 7:51). How quickly Israel forgets God's redemption from Egyptian bondage! Alarmingly, while Moses communes on the mountain with God, Aaron leads the people in idolatry, breaking the commandments before God finishes giving them.

The Mosaic law accentuates accountability and sin's seriousness. Graciously, God provides the sacrificial system, and "for the pious Israelite, sacrifice was . . . an effective means of actual forgiveness for sins committed within the covenant," as Leviticus shows (Dumbrell, 111). Israel is blessed beyond all nations, but the repetitive sacrifices and annual Day of Atonement point to the future, for the law offers no lasting solution to the sin problem.

Historical Books. The key question is "Will Israel be faithful to following God in the Promised Land as spelled out in Deuteronomy?" (Pate, 51). The sad answer is a booming "No!" When conquering the promised land, Israel disobeys God and fails to destroy the Canaanites with grave consequences. "Israel's lack of faith leads to debauching Canaanization" (Waltke, 617). Though many see a recurring cycle in Judges of sin, repentance, rescue, and repeated sin, the truth is worse: we see "a descent into an ever-deepening moral abyss that threatens the existence of Israel in the land" (House, 215). The contrast between the opening chapters of Joshua and the closing ones of 2 Kings is telling: in the former Israel seizes Jericho by God's power as they begin to possess the promised land, but in the latter the Babylonians seize the land (Pate, 51).

Two landmarks in the Historical Books are Jeroboam's sin and God's covenant with David. Jeroboam commands

Israel to worship two golden calves at Bethel and Dan (1 Kings 12:25–33). The sins of the subsequent kings of the Northern Kingdom are measured as to whether they "walked in the ways of Jeroboam" (1 Kings 15:34 and passim). Ultimately, Jeroboam's idolatry leads to exile (2 Kings 17:21–23). The most important historical narrative tells of God's covenant with David, in which he promises to care for Judah (1 Kings 15:3–5) and foretells the eternal reign of David's descendent (2 Sam. 7:13, 16).

Psalms and Proverbs. OT poetry underscores the ugliness of sin and the beauty of God's grace. Psalms and Proverbs reveal the subjective character of the law's objective demands. They trace sin's outward manifestations to inborn depravity (Ps. 51:5). "Even from birth the wicked go astray; from the womb they are wayward, spreading lies" (58:3). Though the locus of sin is in the heart, it manifests itself in all that people do; they abound in transgressions (Prov. 29:22; Dyrness, 107). In agreement with the law, Psalms portrays sin's universality: "If you, LORD, kept a record of sins, Lord, who could stand?" (Ps. 130:3; cf. Eccles. 7:20).

Sin is foolish and oppresses human minds, hearts, and wills, as Waltke (278) explains: "With regard to the Wisdom Literature, Roger Whybray speaks of 'the doctrine of original folly' (Prov. 22:6, 15). . . . Sin enslaves humanity, obscuring our minds, degrading our feelings, and enslaving our wills to love self, not God and others." All sin is ultimately sin against God himself, even adultery and murder (Ps. 51:4), but because of God's "unfailing love" and "great compassion," all who repent and confess their sins to him find forgiveness, cleansing, and a renewed spirit (Ps. 51:1–10).

Prophets. Along with the rest of the OT, the prophets confess sin's universality. They focus on collective sins, especially Israel's violation of the covenant in ritual and social sins. They attack ritual formalism as empty and vain. God hates, and his prophets ruthlessly condemn, sacrifices brought with a sinful attitude rather than sincerity and contrition (Isa. 1:10–15).

All sin is unfaithfulness to the Lord, which Hosea powerfully reviles as spiritual adultery (Hosea 1:2). Knowing the law's protection of the poor and defenseless, Amos attacks social sins of class exploitation, oppression, and injustice (Amos 4:1; 8:2–6; Dumbrell, 168).

"Above all else, the text [of the Prophets] focuses on Yahweh. God allows no rivals, because to do so would allow people to believe and live a lie" (House, 399). Thus, although Isaiah attacks wanton luxury (Isa. 2:7), drunkenness (5:11), pride (2:11), greed, and oppression (5:23), he views sin most profoundly as robbing God of glory (8:19). The prophets strongly denounce sin. Jeremiah likens Israel's strong compulsion to idolatry to the drive of an animal in heat (Jer. 2:23–25; Dyrness, 109). And Isaiah likens our "righteous deeds" to "a polluted garment" (Isa. 64:6 ESV).

Idolatry and covenant infidelity lead to exile (2 Kings 17). Still the Davidic promise in 2 Sam. 7 provides future hope, and Isa. 53 links OT sacrifices and NT teaching concerning Jesus's atoning death (House, 131).

Sin in the NT

Every NT corpus continues and intensifies the OT's view of sin.

Synoptic Gospels. We see this first in the preaching of John the Baptist and Jesus. As the OT prophets repeatedly confronted Israel with its need to repent, so John and Jesus sound the same notes. "The word of God came to John" the Baptist, and he preached "a baptism of repentance for the forgiveness of sins" (Luke 3:2–3). John considers himself the precursor to the Messiah, who will pour out the Holy Spirit. But John also calls Israel's covenant people to repentance to avoid the Messiah's "unquenchable fire" (v. 17). John denounces Israel's leaders as a "brood of vipers" heading for "the coming wrath" (Matt. 3:7). Being Abraham's offspring will not spare them. Rather, they must yield "fruit in keeping with repentance" (v. 8). OT prophets pronounced "woes" against Israel's leaders as false shepherds (e.g., Ezek. 34:2), and Jesus does the same: "Woe to you, teachers of the law and Pharisees, you hypocrites!" (Matt. 23:13 and six more times). While the Pharisees and scribes acknowledge God with their lips, "their hearts swerved in another direction" (Schreiner, 511; see Matt. 15:8–9).

Although the leaders deserve special censure, all are "a wicked and adulterous generation" (Matt. 16:4) like their OT forebears (Hosea 1:2). Jesus sweeps aside unbiblical Jewish traditions and insists on obedience to God's Word. Contrary to the tradition of the elders, people are defiled not by what enters the body through the mouth but by what comes "out of a person's heart"—namely, "sexual immorality, theft, murder, adultery, greed, malice, deceit, lewdness, envy, slander, arrogance and folly" (Mark 7:20–22).

Jesus paints stinging pictures of sinners and their sins. He likens them to "the sick," for sin is a debilitating illness requiring a spiritual "doctor," or savior (Matt. 9:12–13). Sin is a massive debt owed God, the creditor, that no one can pay, implying the need for deliverance (Matt. 18:23–35). Each sinner is a "bad tree" that can only produce "bad fruit" and is headed for "the fire" of God's judgment (Matt. 7:17–19). Sinners need a change of nature; a "bad tree" must become a "good tree," something beyond human ability.

The Synoptics' doctrine of sin, then, reflects OT teaching. Is there anything new besides the messengers? The answer is yes—the covenant people despised, rejected, and murdered their Messiah! Even this fits OT Israel's persecution of the prophets. But this is far worse, because the incarnate Son came to the covenant people. Thomas Schreiner (514) is right: "In the story line of the Gospels, the sin of Israel culminated in the . . . crucifixion of Jesus the Messiah. . . . Israel as a whole failed to embrace Jesus." Frank Thielman (98) shows that Jewish opposition to Jesus was comprehensive and lifelong: "Every type and rank of leader opposed Jesus. They opposed him, moreover, not sporadically or gradually, but unremittingly from cradle to grave."

Gospel of John. John's vocabulary of sin differs from that of the Synoptics. Lost people live in and love darkness "because their deeds [are] evil" (John 3:19; cf. 12:46). They belong to the "world," the sinful system opposed to God (7:7; 15:19). By hating Jesus (15:19, 24), they reveal that they are not children of God but of the devil, whom they obey (8:44). They are "condemned already," "God's wrath remains on them," and they "will die in [their] sins" (3:18, 36; 8:24). John links sin to unbelief, as is seen by juxtaposing 12:37 with his purpose statement in 20:30–31:

> Even after Jesus had performed so many signs in their presence, they still *would not believe* in him. (12:37)

> Jesus performed many other signs in the presence of his disciples, which are not recorded in this book. But these are written that you may *believe* that Jesus is the Messiah, the Son of God, and that by *believing* you may have life in his name. (20:30–31)

As was true of the Synoptics, so for John, as Schreiner says, "the betrayal of Jesus and his death is the apex of evil" (516). All four Gospels exhibit a problem, and John most clearly. They agree that God stands behind humans' rejection of Jesus as Isaiah foretells (6:9–10). Yet unbelievers are also guilty for their unbelief. Luke is succinct, speaking of Judas: "The Son of Man will go as it has been decreed. But woe to that man who betrays him!" (Luke 22:22). John teaches that in God's plan, unbelievers "could not believe" (John 12:39). Thielman explores this problem (190–96) and concludes, "The gospel authors do not formalize a philosophical answer to the question of inability and culpability, any more than does Paul. They simply affirm, alongside their conviction that those who rejected Jesus 'could not believe,' that they were nevertheless culpable for their own disbelief" (190).

In sum, for the Gospels, Jesus's hearers, like their OT ancestors, need to know "the Son of Man" who "came to seek and to save the lost" (Luke 19:10).

Acts. After Jesus ascends and sends the Spirit in newness and power at Pentecost, the early church explodes, as God converts large numbers of Jews. The apostles preach the gospel, churches are planted, and persecution ensues. The preaching in Acts to Jews shows continuity with the OT and Gospels in condemning Israel for their stubbornness and unbelief, as Stephen's speech illustrates: "You stiff-necked people! Your hearts and ears are still uncircumcised. You are just like your ancestors: You always resist the Holy Spirit! Was there ever a prophet your ancestors did not persecute? They even killed those who predicted the coming of the Righteous One. And now you have betrayed and murdered him—you who have received the law that was given through angels but have not obeyed it" (Acts 7:51–53). Acts thus shows continuity with the OT and Gospels in denouncing Israel's sins. However, Paul's ministry also draws attention to the sins of the gentiles, including idolatry and sexual immorality. In Athens Paul "was greatly distressed to see that the city was full of idols" (Acts 17:16; cf. 19:26–29). Among the sins that the Jerusalem Council wrote for gentile Christians to avoid was "sexual immorality" (15:29). Paul's ministry also draws attention to the fact that, as Peter told the council, "it is through the grace of our Lord Jesus that we [Jews] are saved, just as they [gentiles] are" (15:11).

Just as the Gospels portray Jesus's crucifixion as the greatest evil, so does Acts. Peter contrasts the Jewish leaders' estimation of Jesus with that of God: "You, with the help of wicked men, put him to death by nailing him to the cross. But God raised him from the dead" (2:23–24). Again, "You killed the author of life, but God raised him from the dead. We are witnesses of this" (3:15; cf. Paul in 13:29–30). Nevertheless, in the flow of redemptive history, Acts goes beyond the Gospels. In fulfillment of Jesus's predictions, the Jews' and gentiles' persecution of the apostles shows their rebellion against God. Objects of persecution include Peter and John (Acts 4:18, 21), the apostles (5:17–18, 33, 40), Stephen (7:54, 58), and Paul (16:19–24; cf. 2 Cor. 11:23–26). All without Christ are headed for judgment (Acts 10:42; 17:31). Therefore, all need to repent and believe the gospel (10:43; 17:30).

Paul. The apostle Paul gives Scripture's broadest and deepest treatment of sin. At sin's source is humans' refusal to glorify God and give him thanks, with the result that their "thinking became futile and their foolish hearts were darkened" (Rom. 1:21). In Rom. 1:21–32 idolatry is seen as the root of all sin (e.g., 1:25–26 AT: "They worshiped and served the creature rather than the Creator. . . . For this reason God gave them over to degrading passions"). Paul argues that sin is all-encompassing (1:18–3:30), and he concludes with a chain of quotations from the OT (3:10–18). In doing so, Paul stresses that sin is universal and that its corruption is pervasive, from head to toe, as it were. It includes the mind, will, throat, tongue, mouth, and feet. Schreiner (273) adds, "For Paul sin plagues all social groups and dominates every individual within those groups." Pride comes in for special censure by the apostle, for bragging contradicts the gospel. Pride appears everywhere, even with the Corinthians bragging about God's gifts to them. Sin is the opposite of faith that glorifies God, for sin refuses to believe and "everything that does not come from faith is sin" (Rom. 14:23).

Paul condemns sinful attitudes, words, and acts, but he emphasizes how sin dominates human beings. Ever since Adam's primal sin, death reigns over the human race (Rom. 5:14, 17, 21), and as a result all humanity is in bondage to sin. Indeed, before conversion we were in slavery under the elemental spiritual forces of the world (demons, Gal. 4:3), "slaves to those who by nature are not gods" (Gal. 4:8), "slaves to impurity and to ever-increasing wickedness" (Rom. 6:19), and "slaves to sin, which leads to death" (Rom. 6:16; cf. vv. 17, 20). Although Paul views the law as "holy, righteous and good" (Rom. 7:12), he sometimes regards the law as our enemy, stirring up sin, and condemning us (Rom. 4:15; 5:20; 7:5–9; Col. 2:14). Schreiner (535) clarifies, "Sin has wrapped its tentacles so tightly around human beings that it brings the law under the orbit of its influence." Thankfully, the Holy Spirit sets us free from sin and fear and brings about our adoption to sonship (Rom. 8:15). Although we continue to struggle, by God's grace believers "have been set free from sin and have become slaves of God" with benefits of holiness and eternal life (Rom. 6:22).

Paul usually points to the actual sins that humans commit to prove their guilt before God (Rom. 1:29–32; 3:23; Gal. 5:19–21). However, in Rom. 5:12–21 he traces sin, death, and condemnation to their roots in the original rebellion of Adam. I have written elsewhere, "Although clarity on the reason(s) for Adam's sin remains out of reach, Scripture does indicate that Adam's sin not only results in his own punishment but also has dire consequences for all of humanity. Adam sins not merely as the first bad example but as the representative of all humanity." Thus, "in Adam all are sinners; all die; all are under the domain of death; and all are condemned" (Morgan, *Christian*, 204–5). Thankfully, Rom. 5:12–21 is not only about original sin but especially Christ's "one righteous act" (v. 18), his "obedience" as the basis of believers' justification. Sin abounds, but grace abounds much more. To show this, Paul contrasts Adam and Christ and their effects: "In Adam there is sin, death, and condemnation. In Christ there is righteousness, life, and justification. In Adam there is the old era, the dominion of sin and death. In Christ there is a new reign, marked by grace and life (cf. 1 Cor. 15:20–57)" (Morgan, *Christian*, 204; cf. Ridderbos, 78–86).

In Eph. 2:1–3, Paul digs a deep pit from which sinners cannot escape. They are spiritually dead, devoid of the life of God. They spend their lives in the sphere of sin. They obey the dictates of the world system opposed to God. Worse, without knowing it, they do the will of the devil, who is at work in them. They pursue their hearts' evil desires without thought of God. In addition, they are born guilty before a holy God, "by nature deserving of wrath" (v. 3). Henri Blocher puts it creatively: "Sinfulness has become our quasi-nature while remaining truly our anti-nature" (30). Other passages also teach that people are unable to rescue themselves. A person without the Holy Spirit "does not accept the things that come from the Spirit of God but considers them foolishness, and cannot understand them because they are discerned only through the Spirit" (1 Cor. 2:14). The devil "has blinded the minds of unbelievers, so that they cannot see the light of the gospel that displays the glory of Christ" (2 Cor. 4:4). Left to themselves, therefore, people are hopeless. But miraculously, "because of his great love for us, God, who is rich in mercy, made us alive with Christ even when we were dead in transgressions—it is by grace you have been saved" (Eph. 2:4–5).

As in the previous NT corpora, so in Paul's Epistles the ultimate expression of humans' rebellion against their Maker is their crucifixion of his beloved Son. Thielman (686) explains, "Since the time of Adam all human beings have been in a state of rebellion against God, who created them. This rebellion reaches its climax when both Jewish and Gentile rulers crucify God's Son."

Furthermore, Paul teaches that sin also has cosmic effects. He finds our present sufferings insignificant in comparison to the glory God will give us. He personifies the creation, saying it "waits in eager expectation" for our final revelation in Christ (Rom. 8:19). And the apostle longs for the day when Christ's death and resurrection will redeem the creation itself so that it "will be liberated from its bondage to decay and brought into the freedom and glory of the children of God" (v. 21).

Hebrews. Sin is unbelief, disobedience, and apostasy. Readers are not to follow the bad example of the OT Israelites in the wilderness (4:1–11). They lacked faith (v. 2), and the readers must be diligent "so that no one will perish by following their example of disobedience" (v. 11). Although Satan enslaves humans in sin and the fear of death, the Son of God incarnate is Christus Victor, who breaks Satan's power and frees believers from fear of judgment (2:14–15). The writer warns of the sin of apostasy and encourages professing Hebrew Christians to persevere in faith in the face of persecution: "But we do not belong to those who shrink back and are destroyed, but to those who have faith and are saved" (10:39).

James. James blames sin on wayward human hearts, not on the holy God (1:13–15). He teaches that all sin, especially in speech (3:2–12). Because even one sin is rebellion against the Lawgiver (2:9–10), all need God's mercy (v. 13). Sin's folly is evident in our inconsistency (3:9–12). Using OT language, James labels unfaithfulness as spiritual adultery (4:4). Sin displays itself in various forms, including double-mindedness, friendship with the world, and refusal to submit to God (1:8; 4:4–10). Sin has serious consequences, producing disorder in the church, damage to individuals, and enmity with God (3:16–4:4). For the wicked, it leads to a just final punishment (5:1–6; Morgan, *James*, 156–59).

First Peter. Peter writes to gentiles, who formerly lived "in debauchery, lust, drunkenness, orgies, carousing and detestable idolatry" (4:3). Christ has delivered them from ungodliness (vv. 1–4). They should not be surprised at their "fiery ordeal" of persecution as Christians (vv. 12–15) but can rejoice that their handling of trials results "in praise, glory and honor when Jesus Christ is revealed" (v. 7). They are to fear and obey God their Father, not indulging their evil desires but seeking to be holy as God is holy (vv. 14–17). They are to honor Christ and graciously share the gospel with the lost (3:15–16), lest they perish (4:17). They are to resist the devil, who is like a roaring lion on the prowl (5:8–9). Their final goal is "eternal glory in Christ" (v. 10).

Second Peter. Through God's promises we may be like him, "having escaped" the world's corruption "caused by evil desires" (1:4). The world is "a dark place," filled with sin, and we need the light of the "completely reliable" Word of God for guidance until Christ returns (v. 19). Peter warns that "false teachers" will come even as "false prophets" plagued OT Israel (2:1). He condemns them for introducing "destructive heresies" that lead others astray (vv. 1–3). The false teachers sin sexually (vv. 13–14) and are greedy "slaves of depravity" who enslave others (vv. 18–19). In contrast, believers must "live holy and godly lives" as they look for the new earth (3:11).

First John. John writes to protect his readers from teachers who failed to persuade his audience of their bad teaching and practice and then rejected them. The false teachers deny the incarnation (4:1–3) and do not take sin seriously (1:8–10). John labels them "antichrists" whose greatest sin is their rejection of Christ (2:18–23). Although the lost are under Satan's sway, faith in Christ overcomes the world (5:4–5, 19). John teaches that sin is lawlessness (3:4), urges Christians to live righteously, and acknowledges their need to confess their sins.

Jude. Jude admonishes his readers "to contend for the faith" because false teachers, who pervert God's grace "into a license for immorality and deny Jesus," have infiltrated their churches (vv. 3–4). As God judged humans and angels who rebelled in the OT, he will cast the wicked into hell (vv. 5–7, 13). The false teachers are ungodly, engage in sexual sin, and rebel against authority (v. 8). Jude transports them into the scenes of Cain, Balaam, and Korah, infamous OT villains, and condemns them (vv. 11). By contrast, the readers are to build themselves up in the faith, pray in the Spirit, and remain in God's love (vv. 20–21).

Revelation. At its heart, sin is idolatry committed by individuals (9:20) and societies (chap. 18). The wicked refuse to repent, even while experiencing God's judgments (16:8–9). The lake of fire will be the destiny of "the cowardly, the unbelieving, the vile, the murderers, the sexually immoral, those who practice magic arts, the idolaters and all liars" (21:8). Sin does not have the last word, for God creates a new heaven and new earth (21:1).

Synthesis

In sum, sin is a failure to glorify God and is rebellion again him. It is an offense against God and violation of his law. Sin is a willful act and the present state of human existence. Sin is both personal and social. It involves commission, omission, and imperfection. Sin is an intruder in creation yet never beyond God's sovereignty. Sin is a failure to image the Creator to the world. Indeed, the root of all sin is idol worship. Sin includes both guilt and pollution. It includes thoughts, words, and actions. It is foolish and deceitful. Sadly, sin had a beginning in history, but wonderfully, sin will have an end. Sin will be judged and defeated (Mahony; Morgan, *Christian*, 195–201). Whereas sin abounds, grace superabounds (Rom. 5:12–21). In the biblical story, God has the first word (Gen. 1) and the last (Rev. 20–22; cf. 1 Cor. 15:55–57).

See also Adam, First and Last; Gospel; Justice; Sacrifices and Offerings

Bibliography. Blocher, H., *Original Sin*, NSBT (Eerdmans, 1997); Carson, D. A., *How Long, O Lord?* (Baker, 1990); Dumbrell, W. J., *Covenant and Creation* (Nelson, 1985); Dyrness, W., *Themes in Old Testament Theology* (InterVarsity, 1979); Gentry, P. J., and S. J. Wellum, *Kingdom through Covenant* (Crossway, 2012); House, P. R., *Old Testament Theology* (InterVarsity, 1998); Mahony, J. W., "A Theology of Sin for Today" in Morgan and Peterson, *Fallen*, 187–217; Morgan, C. W., *Christian Theology*, with R. A. Peterson (B&H Academic, 2020); Morgan, "Sin in the Biblical Story," in Morgan and Peterson, *Fallen*, 131–62; Morgan, *A Theology of James* (P&R, 2010); Morgan, C. W., and R. A. Peterson, eds., *Fallen*, TC 5 (Crossway, 2013); Pate, C. M., J. S. Duvall, J. D. Hays, E. R. Richards, W. D. Tucker Jr., and P. Vang, *The Story of Israel* (InterVarsity, 2004); Ridderbos, H., *Paul*, trans. J. R. de Witt (Eerdmans, 1997); Schreiner, T. R., *New Testament Theology* (Baker Academic, 2008); Shuster, M., *The Fall and Sin* (Eerdmans, 2004); Thielman, F., *Theology of the New Testament* (Zondervan, 2005); Waltke, B. K., *Old Testament Theology* (Zondervan, 2007).

CHRISTOPHER W. MORGAN

Sinai

Sinai is the mountain of God in the wilderness. It is where Israel enters into covenant with God, where the law is revealed, where the tabernacle is built, and where God meets humanity through an encounter recalling Adam's experience in Eden. Even more, Sinai is a typological Eden: the mountain looks back to the beginning (*Urzeit*) and also forward to Zion and Israel's anticipated end (*Endzeit*). As the place of intersection between heaven and earth (*axis mundi*), between the supernatural and the natural, this mountain is the place of mediation. This is evident when Moses intercedes on Israel's behalf to save them from destruction upon Sinai's summit, indicating the necessity of a perpetual high priesthood to save Israel and later the church from annihilation. The mountain is the place of worship, not Israel's anticipated ultimate site of worship (which is instead Zion, Exod. 15:17) but rather a midpoint in the wilderness, between Egypt and Canaan, where the newly constituted nation builds the tabernacle allowing them to take God's presence with them into the promised land. The Sinai narrative occupies the structural center of the Pentateuch (Exod. 19:1–Num. 10:10), and NT authors often echo and allude to the story in their writings.

Sinai as a Cosmic Mountain

We are unable to pinpoint Sinai's location. While the mountain's location is lost, the revelation received there is preserved, and, therefore, it is more important to focus on what took place at Sinai and what the mountain represents rather than trying to pinpoint its location. This ambiguity of location, nonetheless, is significant: it is in no-man's-land, outside the reach of the Egyptian state and outside the domain of the Midianite people (Levenson, 19–23). In contrast to common ancient Near Eastern ideology, God's domain is not identified with any preexisting state and is portrayed as a cosmic mountain rivaling all other sites of divine locale throughout the world. It is a place identified not with the kingship of any man but rather with the kingship of God alone—the divine abode and the place of intersection between heaven and earth (*axis mundi*).

Many scholars argue that Sinai should be understood within the complex of ancient Near Eastern cosmic mountain ideology, the common characteristics of which are identified as follows: "the meeting place of the gods, the source of water and fertility, the battleground of conflicting natural forces, the meeting place of heaven and earth, the place where effective decrees are issued" (Clifford, 3). By portraying Sinai as a cosmic mountain, the biblical author places Sinai in contrast to all other sacred elevations throughout the world. This would have powerfully resonated with the ancient Israelites, who were familiar with such concepts.

The meeting place of the gods. Sinai is God's dwelling place and the meeting place between God and humanity (Exod. 3–4; Exod. 19:1–Num. 10:10). This recalls Eden, where God is said to "walk" (*hlk*, Gen. 3:8) among Adam and Eve. God will later also "walk" (*hlk*, Lev. 26:12; Deut. 23:14 [MT: 23:15]) among his people in the tabernacle—the divine sanctuary, a portable Sinai, and the means whereby Israel is able to make a typological return to Eden and experience the divine presence.

The source of water and fertility. Sinai/Horeb is the place where Moses drives his flock while in the wilderness (Exod. 3:1), suggesting that it was an oasis and could sustain life, presumably a place with access to water and grazing land. Why else would Moses drive his flock to Sinai/Horeb? If it were a desolate place, then he would have avoided it. This recalls Eden, which is the fountainhead of the four cosmic rivers (Gen. 2:6, 10–14) and a place identified with fertility and life (2:8–9).

The battleground of conflicting natural forces. Many scholars understand Sinai to have volcano-like attributes since it emanates fire and smoke, and trembles (Exod. 19:18). Unlike in the ancient Near Eastern mythological accounts, however, Sinai is not a place where God engages in combat with other deities to try to obtain supremacy. He is supreme by nature. He does, nonetheless, engage in combat with Pharaoh and his army at the Sea of Reeds before leading Israel to the mountain (Exod. 14).

The meeting place of heaven and earth. Sinai is the means whereby humanity is able to cross over from the realm of the earth into the realm of the heavens. By ascending and descending this mountain, Moses mediates God's heavenly instructions to his people on earth. It is also the means whereby Moses is able to commune with God in the heavens (see esp. Exod. 24:15–18). Sinai is an *axis mundi*.

The place where effective decrees are issued. Sinai is the place of theophany and the locus of revelation, where God reveals himself to Moses and Israel, and the place from which he reveals his law and instructions for building the tabernacle. This recalls Eden, where God revealed his law to Adam concerning his priest-like dietary restrictions (Gen. 2:16–17).

Sinai as the Place of Mediation

As the place of intersection between heaven and earth (*axis mundi*), Sinai is the place of mediation, where Moses intercedes on Israel's behalf. He is the only person able to ascend Sinai. He alone is called by God to ascend the mountain and enter the shekinah glory cloud where he will experience the fullness of the divine presence (Exod. 24:12–18). He intercedes on Israel's behalf when they sin (Exod. 32–34), and it is only through his intercession that Israel is saved from destruction. Like the later high priest of the tabernacle cultus, he stands in the gap between God and his people and saves them from annihilation.

The narrative structure of Exod. 25–40 highlights the centrality of Moses's intercessory role at Sinai by situating his mediatorial act at the center of a chiasm concerning the tabernacle building project: (A) tabernacle instructions, 25–31:11; (B) Sabbath legislation, 31:12–18; (C) golden calf and Mosaic intercession, 32–34; (B′) Sabbath legislation, 35:1–3; (A′) tabernacle construction, 35:4–40:38 (Park). The account of Mosaic intercession (Exod. 32–34) is, therefore, one of the great literary and theological high points of the Sinai narrative. If narrative structure is intended to highlight points of theological significance, then the structure of Exod. 25–40 highlights both the severity of Israel's transgression and the importance of Moses's intercession.

This is also highlighted by the intentional parallels between Exod. 32:7–10 and Gen. 6:11–12, wherein Moses is identified as the means of ensuring Israel's survival from a possible new deluge-like event (Moberly, 83–95). In Gen. 6:11–12, God decides to destroy the cosmos with a flood and start anew with Noah (new humanity), while in Exod. 32:7–10, God decides to destroy Israel through divine judgment and start anew with Moses (new nation). In both cases, God decrees judgment because the people "corrupt" (*šḥt*) the "way" (*drk*) of God: in Gen. 6:12, it is written that "all flesh had corrupted [*šḥt*] his [i.e., God's] way [*drk*] upon the earth," while in Exod. 32:7–8, God echoes these words to Moses when he says that "your people have corrupted [*šḥt*] . . . they have turned quickly from the way [*drk*] which I commanded them."

Israel's sin is, therefore, likened to humanity's sin that led to the deluge. Just as God wiped out an infant humanity because of their sin, so too does an infant Israel deserve to be wiped out. Such judgment, however, is averted because of Moses's intercession (Exod. 32:11–14). He stands in the gap between God and humanity upon Sinai's summit and convinces God to relent from his decision to judge the new nation (Exod. 32:14). Moses, therefore, typifies the later high priest of the tabernacle and temple cultus, and ultimately the high-priestly ministry of Jesus Christ. Without a perpetual high priest ministering then for Israel and now for the church, the people of God would face certain extinction (cf. Heb. 5; 7–10). It is, therefore, not surprising that Heb. 12:18–24 compares Jesus's mediation upon the heavenly mountain to Moses's mediation upon Mount Sinai. Moses's act of intercession has become paradigmatic.

Moses's intercession upon Sinai's summit also results in tabernacle construction. While the blueprints for the tabernacle were given in Exod. 25–31, Israel's worship of the golden calf threatened to thwart the building of this divine dwelling place. It is only because of Moses's intercession that construction of the tabernacle may commence—a structure through which Israel will be able to return (typologically) to Eden and dwell in the divine presence, a reality experienced by no one since Adam. Moreover, Moses clearly understands that his intercession is not merely for the sake of preserving Israel's existence but even more for the sake of allowing them to experience God's presence (see Exod. 33). Existence in the promised land without God is worthless. It would be better to remain in the wilderness.

Sinai as the place of worship. Israel comes to Sinai through a historicized experience of the creation pattern, whereby the nation undergoes the threefold redemption/recreation process: (1) through the waters, (2) to the mountain of God, (3) for worship in the divine presence (Morales, *Tabernacle*). This pattern is prefigured in the Genesis creation story, wherein man (*'dm*), through his association with the ground (*'dmh*), is delivered through the primeval waters and is then "rested" (*nwḥ*) upon Eden (Gen. 2:15), where he worships God as his priest. The pattern is later mimicked in the deluge narrative (6:9–9:17), wherein Noah (a new Adam) is likewise delivered through the floodwaters and is then "rested" (*nwḥ*) upon Ararat (8:4), where he builds an altar and offers sacrifices (8:20).

While not undergoing an ordeal by water, Abraham's westward entrance into Canaan—a reflex of humanity's eastward expulsion from Eden (Gen. 3:24; 4:16)—is also marked by worship: like Noah, he builds an altar (12:7–8). Some scholars argue that the altar represents the cosmic mountain (Kang), and, therefore, Adam, Noah, and Abraham all undergo an ordeal culminating with the worship of God upon a mountain: Adam upon Eden, Noah upon Ararat, and Abraham at various altar sites within Canaan. Redemption/recreation is for the sake of worship within the divine presence atop his holy mountain (Morales, *Ascend*).

Just as Eden, Ararat, and the various altar sites in Canaan (most likely upon mountaintops) were the designated places of worship, so does Sinai become the designated place of worship in the wilderness. Before Israel is ever brought to this place, Moses is first brought here through the threefold redemptive/recreation pattern: he is (1) brought safely through the waters of the Nile (2) to the mountain of God (Horeb/Sinai) (3) for worship in the divine presence. Just like Adam and Noah, Moses's deliverance from the waters of death in the Nile River results in him coming to Sinai/Horeb, where he worships God. Accordingly, Moses's deliverance from the Nile and his later high-priestly ministry upon Sinai intentionally recall Adam's deliverance from the primeval waters and his later high-priestly ministry in Eden.

Moses's arrival at Sinai also recalls Noah's journey to Ararat. While Pharaoh commands that all male children be drowned in the Nile (Exod. 1:22), Moses is delivered from this execution through an "ark" (*tbh*, Exod. 2:3, 5). The only two places in the OT where the word "ark" (*tbh*) is used are in Gen. 6–9 concerning Noah's vessel of deliverance and in Exod. 2:3, 5 concerning Moses's vessel of deliverance. The more common modern translation of "basket" (e.g., NIV, NASB, ESV) is, therefore, not helpful. Like Adam, Noah, and Abraham, Moses eventually comes to a mountain (Sinai/Horeb) where he experiences God's presence and worships (Exod. 3:1–6). Also, note that Moses is placed in the ark "among the reeds" (*bswp*, Exod. 2:3, 5) of the Nile, foreshadowing Israel's deliverance through the Sea of Reeds (*ym swp*).

Like Moses, Israel is delivered from Pharaoh's army (1) through the waters of the Sea of Reeds, after which they are (2) brought to Mount Sinai (3) for worship in the divine presence. In this deliverance account, Israel passes through the sea on "dry land" (*ybšh*, Exod. 14:16, 22, 29; 15:19), the same word used in the Genesis creation story to describe the emergence of "dry land" (*ybšh*, Gen. 1:9–10). A great "wind" (*rwḥ*) from God is also instrumental in the Genesis creation story (1:2) and the deluge narrative (8:1), and it is the means whereby the Sea of Reeds is parted in the exodus account (Exod. 14:21). Accordingly, Israel's redemption through the Sea of Reeds is intentionally identified as a new creation event wherein the primordial creation pattern has been historicized.

The goal of Israel's redemption/recreation is the worship of God (Exod. 3:12, 18; 4:23; 5:1, 3; 7:16; 8:1, 20 [MT 7:26; 8:16]; 9:1, 13; 10:3), experienced in part at Sinai. Note, in particular, that the Hebrew word *'bd*, which is translated in most modern editions of the OT as "to serve," can also be translated as "to worship." While the Israelites previously were forced to serve/worship Pharaoh by building the storage cities of Pithom and Rameses in order glorify the city of humanity (*ʿbd*, Exod. 1:13–14), they will instead be delivered to serve/worship (*ʿbd*) God by building the tabernacle and its furnishings in order to glorify the city of God. Like Adam, Noah, and Abraham, Israel is saved for the sake of worship.

Sinai and the tabernacle. The goal of redemption is worship in the divine presence, first at Sinai and then through the tabernacle cultus. The Sinai narrative (Exod. 19:1–Num. 10:10), most of which is devoted to the regulation of worship, stands at the center of the Pentateuch and comprises roughly 42 percent of these five books (Balentine, 67–68). The amount of narrative time devoted to tabernacle building instructions and worship regulations stresses the central importance of worship within the Sinai narrative. Programmatic statements such as Exod. 25:8; 29:45–46 also indicate that Israel's redemption/recreation is for the sake of constructing the tabernacle so that God might dwell among Israel and that Israel may worship God through divinely ordained means.

The blueprints for the tabernacle are revealed upon Sinai's summit, and it is subsequently built in the vicinity of the mountain. The relationship between the tabernacle and Sinai, however, is more than merely that of proximity and location; instead, the tabernacle becomes Sinai. In particular, it becomes a portable Sinai and the means whereby Israel is able to take the presence of God with them from the wilderness into the promised land. Without the tabernacle, the presence of God would remain at Sinai, unable to be transferred to Zion (as in 1 Kings 8:10–11). This proposed correspondence between Sinai and the tabernacle is primarily indicated through (1) the parallels between geography and architecture and (2) the relocation of the divine presence from atop Sinai into the tabernacle.

Geographical and architectural parallels. Mount Sinai is presented as having three distinct geographical boundaries, each corresponding to the three geographical boundaries of the world (heaven, earth, Sheol) and also the three architectural boundaries of the tabernacle (holy of holies, holy place, outer court). First, the base of the mountain where only commoners are permitted (Exod. 19:12–13) corresponds to the outer court where likewise only commoners are permitted. Second, the midsection of the mountain where only Moses, Aaron, Nadab, Abihu, and the seventy elders of Israel are permitted (Exod. 24:1–2, 9–11) corresponds to the holy place where only certain Levitical priests are permitted. Third, the summit of the mountain where only Moses is permitted (Exod. 24:12–18) corresponds to the holy of holies where only the high priest is permitted to enter once a year on the Day of Atonement (Rodríguez).

Relocation of the divine presence. Through a dramatic series of events, God relocates his special presence from atop Sinai to within the tabernacle. Similarities in vocabulary and syntax between Exod. 24:15–16 and Exod. 40:34; Lev. 1:1 indicate that the biblical author intended for readers to make a connection between Sinai and the tabernacle (Weinfeld, 504). Just as God once called to Moses from atop Sinai (Exod. 19:3), so does he call to Moses from within the tabernacle (Lev. 1:1). The locus of revelation has changed because the place of God's presence has changed (Knohl, 73). The stone tablets are also given to Moses by God atop Sinai (Exod. 24:12; 31:18; 32:15–16; 34:28–29), and they are subsequently deposited within the holy of holies in the tabernacle (Exod. 25:21; Deut. 10:2, 5).

Sinai and the covenant. The word "Sinai" primarily recalls ideas related to covenant. It is the place where Israel enters into covenant with God and where the covenant's stipulations are given. While it was assumed that these stipulations would be broken, the Sinai covenant could always be renewed through repentance (Lev. 26:40–45). Later OT authors stress the importance of the Sinai covenant, though they also anticipate a time when a new and greater covenant will be instituted through a new exodus event (e.g., Jer. 31:31–34; cf. Matt. 26:28; Mark 14:24; Luke 22:20; 1 Cor. 11:25; Heb. 8:6–13). Just as Sinai was a midpoint in the wilderness between Egypt and Canaan—a temporary stopping place—so did NT authors understand the covenant to have a limited duration, eventually being subservient to the promises made to Abraham and David (e.g., Gal. 3–4).

Sinai in the NT. Outside of the Pentateuch, the use of the title "Sinai" is rare in the OT, used only on four other occasions (Judg. 5:5; Ps. 68:8, 17 [MT 68:9, 18]; Neh. 9:13). The title "Horeb" is equally rare, used in only five other places (1 Kings 8:9; 19:8; Mal. 4:4 [MT 3:22]; Ps. 106:19; 2 Chron. 5:10). In these passages, Sinai/Horeb is primarily remembered as the place where God visited his people in power, revealed his law, and entered into covenant with Israel. In the NT, the title "Horeb" never appears and "Sinai" is used only four times (Acts 7:30, 38; Gal. 4:24, 25). Although Sinai is rarely mentioned by name in the NT, ideas related to Sinai and the tabernacle appear throughout. Through echoes and allusions, NT authors interpret events and persons in light of the Sinai event, thus calling upon readers both to look back to the mountain in the wilderness and to interpret their texts in light of earlier texts attesting to Israel's great experience.

The Sermon on the Mount (Matt. 5–7) recalls Sinai: Jesus goes up on a mountain and then teaches and explains laws that were previously given at Sinai (5:21–26 [cf. Exod. 20:13; Deut. 5:17]; 5:27–30 [cf. Exod. 20:14; Deut. 5:18]; 5:33–37 [cf. Lev. 19:12]; 5:38–42 [cf. Exod. 21:24; Lev. 24:20]; 5:43–48 [cf. Lev. 19:18]). Jesus is, therefore, identified as a new Moses delivering a new law to the people. Later, at the end of the Gospel, Jesus will ascend another mountain where his disciples engage in worship and where he will deliver further instructions

(Matt. 28:16–20). Jesus's ministry in Matthew's Gospel, therefore, begins and ends with Jesus upon a mountain delivering instructions, recalling Moses upon Sinai. Accordingly, the evangelist is identifying Jesus as a new and greater Moses couched in the language and imagery of Sinai. Even more, the author is identifying Jesus with Yahweh, since he is the recipient of worship and the ultimate source of this new law.

John 1:17 further identifies Jesus's ministry with Moses's ministry: "For the Law was given through Moses; grace and truth were realized through Jesus Christ" (NASB). This positive correlation not only indicates that Jesus's ministry is modeled on Moses's ministry but also identifies his ministry as far superior to that of Moses. While Moses revealed the law to Israel at Sinai, experienced the glory of God, and interceded on Israel's behalf, Jesus himself, God incarnate, has descended from his heavenly abode to dwell among his people: "And the *logos* became flesh and dwelt/tabernacled [*skēnoō*] among us, and we saw his glory, glory as the only begotten from the Father, full of grace and truth" (John 1:14 AT). In a text couched in the language and imagery of Sinai (note esp. the use of the word "glory" [Heb. *kbwd*, Exod. 24:16–17; 33:18, 22; 40:34–35; Lev. 9:23]), the Gospel writer attests that what he has witnessed in the person and ministry of Jesus far exceeds anything Moses experienced.

The transfiguration accounts (Matt. 17:1–8; Mark 9:2–8; Luke 9:28–36; cf. 2 Pet. 1:16–18) further draw upon the language and imagery of Sinai wherein Jesus is presented as superior to both Moses and Elijah. The event takes place on a mountain (Matt. 17:1; Mark 9:2; Luke 9:28) and Jesus's face shines, paralleling Moses's shining face upon Sinai (Exod. 34:29–35). To further strengthen these parallels, the gospel writers inform readers that Jesus was conversing with both Moses and Elijah upon the mountain—the only two people who ever experienced a direct encounter with God upon Sinai/Horeb (Exod. 32–34; 1 Kings 19).

There are also parallel sequences of events between the transfiguration accounts and Exod. 24, indicating that the Gospel writers intentionally drew upon the Sinai tradition (Mauser, 108–19). As has been noted, within both the OT and NT passages, "(1) three named people accompany the primary figure; (2) there is an ascent up a mountain; (3) a cloud covers the mountain; (4) a time period of six days is mentioned; and (5) the participants hear somebody speaking from the cloud" (Miller, 499–500). Accordingly, Jesus is identified as a new and greater Moses and is imbued with divine authority. Even more, as God's Son, he is identified with Yahweh. The disciples must listen to Jesus just as Israel listened to Moses.

Finally, just as Moses had to undergo an ordeal by water through the Nile River before he was able to lead Israel to Sinai and mediate the covenant, so too has Jesus followed the same pattern. Before he could lead the church through a new exodus event and mediate the new covenant, he first went through the waters of the Jordan at his baptism and later had to undergo the ordeal of the crucifixion, identified as a baptism in Luke 12:50, resulting in his ascent to the heavenly Jerusalem/Zion (Luke 24:51; Acts 1:9; Phil. 2:9–11; etc.). Hebrews 12:18–24 identifies Jesus's mediation of the new covenant with his current position upon the heavenly Jerusalem/Zion in contrast to Moses's mediation of the old covenant upon Sinai. Through the ordeal of baptism, the church likewise joins in this redemption/re-creation process (Rom. 6:3–7), which terminates upon the mountain of God (Heb. 12:22–24).

Both Jesus and the church, therefore, undergo the same redemption/re-creation pattern experienced by both Moses and Israel through the exodus and at Mount Sinai: through the waters of judgment (baptism/crucifixion), to the mountain of God (heavenly Jerusalem/Zion), for the worship of the triune God. Accordingly, Moses's and Israel's experiences at Sinai prefigure Jesus's and the church's experiences in this present age, or rather, Jesus's and the church's experiences are patterned upon Moses's and Israel's experiences at Sinai (or perhaps it is both). What happened at Sinai has become paradigmatic, and NT authors intentionally present Jesus and his ministry in language and with imagery recalling this great event. They call upon readers to both interpret new events in light of former events and understand these new events as having far surpassed the former events upon which they are patterned.

See also Covenant; Exodus, The; Israel and the Church, The Story of; Jerusalem; Law; Revelation, Book of

Bibliography. Balentine, S. E., *The Torah's Vision of Worship* (Fortress, 1999); Clifford, R. J., *The Cosmic Mountain in Canaan and the Old Testament*, HSM 4 (Wipf & Stock, 1972); Kang, S. I., "The 'Molten Sea,' or Is It?," *Bib* 89 (2008): 101–3; Knohl, I., "Two Aspects of the 'Tent of Meeting,'" in *Tehillah Le-Moshe*, ed. B. Eichler, M. Cogan, and J. Tigay (Eisenbrauns, 1997), 73–79; Levenson, J. D., *Sinai and Zion*, NVBS (HarperOne, 1985); Mauser, U. W., *Christ in the Wilderness*, SBT (SCM, 1963); Miller, D. M. "Seeing the Glory, Hearing the Son," *CBQ* 72 (2010): 498–517; Moberly, R. W. L., *At the Mountain of God*, JSOTSup 22 (JSOT Press, 1983); Morales, L. M., *The Tabernacle Pre-figured*, BTS 15 (Peeters, 2012); Morales, *Who Shall Ascend the Mountain of the Lord?*, NSBT 37 (InterVarsity, 2015); Park, C. H., "From Mount Sinai to the Tabernacle" (PhD diss., University of Gloucestershire, 2002); Rodríguez, A. M., "Sanctuary Theology in Exodus," *AUSS* 24 (1986): 127–45; Weinfeld, M., "Sabbath, Temple, and the Enthronement of the Lord," in *Mélanges bibliques et orientaux l'honneur de H. Cazelles*, ed. A. Caquot and M. Delcor, AOAT 212 (Butzon & Bercker, 1981), 501–12.

Andrew M. Gilhooley

Song of Songs, Book of

Song of Songs is perhaps the most difficult book in the OT to interpret, much like the book of Revelation in the NT. Its use of metaphorical and symbolic language throughout allows for a wide range of interpretations that have challenged commentators throughout its expansive history (Garrett, 352–58; Hess, 22–29; Longman, 200–247; Pope, 89–229; Provan, 237–48). Before describing the use of this book in the rest of Scripture, we must first discover what it means and how it functions in the larger context of Scripture.

We begin with what we know. First, the Song appears in the Writings, the third section of the Hebrew Bible, a section containing a number of books that describe life in the covenant (Van Pelt, introduction, 33–34, 38–39). Second, at some level, the Song is about marriage and sexual intimacy in the context of that relationship. Third, Solomon, the son of David, plays a key role in the Song and its interpretation.

Canonical Context

The Hebrew canon's position of Song of Songs in the Writings is strategic, providing key information for its interpretation. It appears after Ruth, which appears after Proverbs. Proverbs contains a collection of wisdom literature originally assembled for the instruction of young men in the royal court. In general, the "my son" poems located in Prov. 1–9 present a young man with a choice between two women: Lady Wisdom and Lady Folly. Both women entice and allure, but one leads to life while the other leads to death. In these chapters, the father and the mother work to persuade this son to embrace wisdom and reject folly. Proverbs 5 and 7 provide us with important examples that relate closely with Song of Songs. Proverbs 5 begins with a warning against the allure of Lady Folly and then follows with an exhortation to the faithful embrace of Lady Wisdom as a covenant partner. Verses 3–5 are part of the allure and warning found in vv. 1–14:

> For the lips of a stranger drip honey,
> and her palate is smoother than oil [the allure];
> but her end is bitter like wormwood,
> sharp like a double-edged sword.
> Her feet go down to death,
> her steps lead to Sheol [the warning]. (AT)

Note that lips dripping with honey (Song 4:11), a palate or mouth (2:3; 5:16; 7:10), a sword (3:8), a woman's feet (5:3), and death and Sheol or the grave (8:6) all appear in Song of Songs. This section in Proverbs is followed by a contrasting exhortation in vv. 15–20 to embrace Lady Wisdom as a marriage covenant partner, the language of which also parallels that of Song of Songs in many ways (Kaiser):

> May your spring be blessed,
> and may you rejoice in the wife of your youth.
> A lovely doe and a graceful she-goat,
> may her breast enliven you all of the time;
> may you stagger in her love continually.
> Why would you stagger, my son, with a strange woman,
> and embrace the bosom of a foreign woman? (vv. 18–20 AT)

It is no surprise, therefore, that Proverbs concludes with a description of the ideal marriage partner, a partner described in 31:10 as "a woman [wife] of strength" (AT). Ruth follows Proverbs and provides a living illustration of what this wife might look like. Ruth is the only woman in the Hebrew Bible to be identified as a "woman of strength" (Ruth 3:11 AT), and the man who finds her is known as "a man, mighty in strength" (2:1 AT). Song of Songs follows Ruth and constitutes the correlate to Proverbs' search for wisdom and rejection of folly in the context of marriage. In Song of Songs, the woman is presented with a similar choice. She must choose between the life of luxury in the harem of Solomon (Song 6:8), a clear violation of the marriage standard presented in Gen. 2 (cf. Matt. 19:4–9), or the more difficult life of faithful marriage to her beloved shepherd (see below), a choice between folly and wisdom.

Marriage and Sexual Intimacy

Song of Songs is filled with erotic imagery employed to entice, protect, and sustain love and lovemaking in the context of marriage. However, because of humanity's fall into sin in Gen. 3, the covenant of marriage (Mal. 2:14) will experience the effects of sin (Gen. 3:16) just like every other aspect of life in this fallen world. Thus, some invitations to love and lovemaking in Song of Songs are illicit temptations for the woman. For example, in the beginning of the song, the woman is encouraged to participate in harem life, "Would that he would kiss me with some of the kisses of his mouth, for your lovemaking will be better [i.e., more intoxicating] than wine" (1:2 AT). Or later in the song, "Eat, friends, drink, and be drunk with lovemaking" (5:1 AT). All the imperatives in this verse are plural in form, not singular.

In other contexts, sexual imagery is used in a positive way, as a means of resisting the temptation of harem life. For example, in the two poetic dream accounts (Song 3:1–4; 5:2–7), the woman longs to be sexually united to her beloved in order that she might become unqualified for harem life with the king. The language employed in these dreams is metaphorical and euphemistic, but it does not overreach. For example, when searching for her beloved in the first dream, she desires to bring him into "the chamber of my conceiving" (3:4 AT)—that is, to engage in sexual union in order to terminate her status as a virgin and so become unqualified for entering into the harem of the king. The second dream functions in the same way, though it is even more explicit, "My beloved sent his 'hand' through the 'hole' and my body roared over him" (5:4 AT). Song of Songs does not shy away from describing the powerful force of sexual intimacy for those created in the image of God as male and female (Gen. 1:27).

Finally, the wisdom presented in the Song also uses sexual imagery as one of the means for sustaining the exclusive marriage covenant. For example, in 8:10, the woman states, "I am a wall and my breasts are like the towers, and so in this way I have become in his eyes like one who both brings forth [for him] and finds [for myself] wholeness [*šālôm*]" (AT). As we consider Song of Songs in the context of the Christian canon, we will discover a close relationship between the covenant of marriage, the power of sexual intimacy, and the covenantal way in which the Lord relates to his people in each of the ways detailed above.

Solomon and the Song of Songs

The role of Solomon in the Song is debated and will depend largely upon the interpretation adopted by a reader (Van Pelt, "Song of Songs," 421–23). The superscript may suggest that Solomon is the author of the Song, "The Song of Songs, which is *by* Solomon" (1:1 AT; cf. the superscripts for Pss. 72; 127). Others, however, legitimately argue that the Song's superscript may constitute a dedication, "*for* Solomon," or describe its general content, "*about* Solomon." In addition to the superscript, Solomon is mentioned by name six more times in the Song (1:5; 3:7, 9, 11; 8:11–12) and a male figure is identified as the "king" five other times (1:4, 12; 3:9, 11; 7:5). Regardless of one's interpretation, the close relationship between the figure of Solomon and the Song presents several challenges. Is the male figure Solomon himself or simply a personification of the king? Is the king the only male figure in the Song, or is there another? How does the life of Solomon presented in 1 Kings 1–11, especially the account of his sizable harem (11:1–8), impact the interpretation of the Song? If the Song celebrates the exclusive covenant of marriage and the sexual intimacy experienced within that covenant, then Solomon is the worst possible canonical example to employ, for "Solomon loved many foreign women. . . . He had seven hundred royal wives and three hundred concubines and his wives corrupted his heart" (1 Kings 11:1, 3 AT). For those who hold to an allegorical interpretation of the Song, the infidelity of Solomon presents a serious challenge since the king is connected with YHWH in Jewish interpretation and with Jesus in Christian interpretation.

Interpretation of the Song

The Song of Songs is best understood as a wisdom composition associated with Solomon in the tradition of Proverbs (1:1; 10:1; 25:1) and Ecclesiastes (1:1, 12). Like other wisdom compositions, the key to the message is often located toward the end of work (e.g., Job 42; Eccles. 12:13–14), requiring readers to return to the beginning and reread the work in light of the message found in the conclusion. With Song of Songs, the message is located in 8:6–10 and may be contextualized in the following way. *Song of Songs teaches that the covenant of marriage should be rock solid in terms of commitment and white hot in terms of sexual intimacy. A marriage that works to sustain both of these realities will better endure hardship, resist temptation, and promote satisfaction and wholeness.* Table 1 connects this message with the text of Song 8:6–10.

Table 1. Message of the Song

Verse	Translation (AT)	Instruction
8:6a	Place me like the seal on your heart, like the seal on your arm; for love is strong like death, obstinate like the grave with zeal.	The commitment of marriage should be rock solid.
8:6b	Its flames are flames of fire, the very flame of the LORD [or "the hottest possible flame"].	The intimacy of marriage should be white hot.
8:7a	Many waters cannot extinguish this love, and rivers cannot flood it.	This type of love endures hardship.
8:7b–9	If a man would give all the wealth of his house for this love, it would utterly scorn him. We have a younger sister . . .	This type of love resists temptation.
8:10	I am a wall and my breasts are like the towers, and so in this way I have become in his eyes like one who both brings forth [for him] and finds [for myself] wholeness [*šālôm*].	This type of love promotes satisfaction and wholeness.

Source: Taken from M. V. Van Pelt, "Song of Songs," in *A Biblical-Theological Introduction to the Old Testament*, edited by M. V. Van Pelt. Copyright © 2016, p. 433. Used by permission of Crossway, a publishing ministry of Good News Publishers, Wheaton, IL 60187, www.crossway.org.

While the message of the Song is relatively straightforward, the way in which the author sets forth this message is more complicated and elusive, as the history of interpretation demonstrates. The following interpretation is just one of the possible interpretations set forth in the Song's long history (cf. Ginsburg, 4–11; Kaiser; Provan, 245–48; Stoop-van Paridon, 469–79; Van Pelt, "Song of Songs"). In my view, the woman of the Song represents the main voice in the composition. She has been taken into the harem of Solomon (6:8–9; cf. Esther 2), wherein she is tempted by the allure of wealth and fame well known to us from 1 Kings 10–11. In the end, the woman of the Song rejects the illicit temptation of Solomon and his harem and remains steadfast in her devotion to her beloved shepherd, who must wait for her until her ordeal in the harem complex comes to an end (Song 2:17; 8:5, 14). This rejection is made explicit in 8:11–12, where the woman rejects Solomon's vineyard (i.e., his "harem") in Baal-Hamon, which is not a place, but a characterization of the harem, translated from Hebrew as "a husband of a multitude." This interpretation finds support in Prov. 5 and 7, as well as Prov. 1–9 in general as stated above. Just as the young man in Proverbs is confronted with the choice of two women, so also is the woman of the Song presented with two men: the beloved shepherd in a marriage corresponding with Gen. 2 or Solomon and his wealth in a gross violation of that standard as portrayed in 1 Kings 11. The structure of the Song accords with this interpretation:

I. Introduction—The Temptation of Solomon's Harem (1:1–2:7)
II. The Arrival (and Departure) of the Beloved Shepherd (2:8–3:5)
III. The Arrival of Solomon and His Enticements (3:6–8:4)
IV. The Arrival of the Woman with Her Beloved and Wisdom Instruction (8:5–14)

Each section pivots or transitions with the woman's so-called adjuration of the daughters of Jerusalem, who are the virgins preparing for harem life (Song 6:8–9), in 2:7; 3:5; and 8:4. Each adjuration is followed by the arrival of a different character in 2:8 (the beloved shepherd); 3:6 (Solomon); and 8:5 (the woman with her beloved).

Inner-Biblical Connections

The institution and significance of marriage play a major role in the canon of Scripture. It is instituted by God in Gen. 2, corrupted by sin in Gen. 3, and ultimately perfected in Rev. 21. Additionally, the Lord uses the analogy of the covenant of marriage to speak about his covenantal relationship with his own people, especially in terms of their infidelity to that covenant. Thus, while Song of Songs neither quotes nor is quoted by other Scripture (cf. Schnittjer, 591), its content and message are central to the message of the Bible and the history of redemption.

Law. Though Song of Songs does not quote or explicitly allude to any antecedent Scripture, the topic and significance of marriage and sexual intimacy in this current world order permeate this first part of the canon, especially Gen. 1–3.

In Gen. 1:27, humanity was created in the image of God, "male and female he created *them*." This harmonious, interdependent male-female image was designed to function as one of the primary ways in which the cultural mandate was to be carried out. Only in the context of the marriage covenant could humanity "be *fruitful* and *increase* and *fill* the earth" (1:28 AT).

Genesis 2:4–25 backs up and returns to Gen. 1 by rehearsing the events of day six in the creation narrative with greater attention to detail. We know from Gen. 1:31 that God set apart day six from the previous five days with the designation of this day as "very good." In Gen. 2, therefore, it is shocking to read that there was a point in time when this day was, in fact, "not good" (v. 18). One thing that brings the condition of day six from "not good" to "very good" is the creation of the woman and the institution of the marriage covenant in 2:21–25. This creation of the woman and the marriage covenant serves as the climax not only of day six but also of the six creation days collectively. Marriage, as created and instituted by God himself, is a pre-fall institution designed to serve as the basis of civilization through which the cultural mandate would be carried out. While humanity, through sin, has corrupted this institution, the institution itself is *not* corrupt.

Later in Genesis, two intrusions of the eschatological judgment ethic (Kline)—the flood in Gen. 6–9 and the destruction of Sodom and Gomorrah in Gen. 19—are flanked by terrible violations of the marriage covenant as established in Gen. 2. The account of the flood begins with the illicit union of the sons of God with the daughters of man in 6:1–4 (angelic beings with humans; cf. Job 1:6; 2:1; 38:7) and ends with Ham uncovering the nakedness of his father (maternal incest; cf. Lev. 18:7, 14). Similarly, the account of the destruction of Sodom and Gomorrah begins with the men of Sodom coming to sexually violate the angels who had come to Lot's house (angelic beings with humans) and ends with the daughters of Lot violating their father to produce offspring (paternal incest).

These extreme accounts of judgment flanked by violations of the marriage covenant serve to highlight the significance God had intended for marriage as it was instituted in creation. It may even be observed that the whole of Genesis is stitched together by the institution of marriage. The *tôlədōt* (generations) introductions to its ten sections come to pass through marriage and the bearing of offspring and serve to identify and contrast the seed of the serpent with the seed of the woman as the kingdom of God advances in this first book of the Bible (Gen. 2:4; 5:1; 6:9; 10:1; 11:10, 27; 25:12–13, 19; 36:1; 37:2; cf. 10:32; 36:9; see DeRouchie).

Former Prophets. As stated above, Song of Songs is closely connected with the life of Solomon as recorded in 1 Kings 1–11. As indicated above, Solomon is the only person mentioned by name in the Song. Additionally, he is addressed as the king on several occasions, and the abundance of spices, mentioned throughout the Song, is also associated with his reign (1 Kings 10:10, 25). It is also recorded that Solomon wrote three thousand proverbs and 1,005 songs (1 Kings 4:32). The title "Song of Songs," meaning "the best song," may constitute one of those numbered in this account. Solomon's famous wisdom (1 Kings 3:9; 4:29–34; 10:23–24), a divine gift, may also connect with the Song as an outstanding wisdom composition.

Solomon's association with the Song has also occasioned a number of challenges for interpreters. The Song appears to uphold and celebrate marriage as instituted by God in Gen. 2, an exclusive, lifelong commitment between one man and one woman who have become "one flesh" in the context of sexual union (Gen. 2:24; Matt. 19:5; Mark 10:8; 1 Cor. 6:16; Eph. 5:31). We know from the account of the life of Solomon that he, in spite of his unsurpassed wisdom, violated this standard in an unparalleled manner. It is recorded in 1 Kings 11 that the women of Solomon's harem, some one thousand in number, turned his heart to follow other gods so that he was not wholly devoted to YHWH alone (11:4, 9; cf. Song 6:8). Thus, Solomon "did what was evil in the sight of YHWH" (11:6 AT), a designation familiar to us from Deuteronomy (4:25; 31:29) and Judges (2:11; 3:7, 12; 4:1; 6:1; 10:6; 13:1), characterizing the violation of the covenant with persistent idolatry. Solomon's violation of the marriage standard and his corresponding fall into idolatry become the flash point for the division of Israel into the Northern and Southern Kingdoms (1 Kings 11:11–13). Consequently, Solomon is not idealized in the Song; rather, he parallels Lady Folly in terms of her allurements and enticements, all the while retaining his wisdom as the means by which his vanity was measured (Eccles. 2:1–11).

Latter Prophets. In the Latter Prophets, the marriage covenant and fidelity to it become one of the ways in which YHWH characterizes his own covenantal relationship with Israel. In this case, YHWH stands as the faithful husband while Israel is portrayed as the unfaithful wife who whores after other gods (cf. Ortlund). In Song of Songs, the woman resists temptation and remains faithful to her beloved shepherd: "I belong to my beloved and my beloved belongs to me" (6:3 AT). In the Latter Prophets, Israel gives in to temptation and plays the whore. For example, Jeremiah asks, "If a man divorces his wife and she leaves him and goes to another man, will he return to her? Would not that land become truly defiled? You [Israel] have whored after many companions and would you return to me?" (Jer. 3:1 AT). Perhaps most famously, Ezek. 16 and Hosea 1–3 employ the analogy of the marriage covenant to the relationship between YHWH and his people in a way that is intended to first condemn and then to provoke repentance.

In Ezek. 16, the word of the YHWH came to the prophet in order that he might "make known Jerusalem's abominations" (16:2 AT). In this account, Israel is characterized as an infant female abandoned at birth and found at the precipice of death (vv. 3–5). Upon discovery, she is revived to life and raised by YHWH himself (vv. 6–7). YHWH then enters into a covenant of marriage with her and so becomes her faithful husband (vv. 8–14). The beauty and splendor of this woman become known among the nations because of the Lord's great kindness to her. Tragically, however, the great kindness of YHWH's covenant love is met with the woman whoring after all who would have her. The woman's unfaithfulness is highlighted by the appearance of the Hebrew root for "whoring" (*znh*), which appears nineteen times in this brief account (Ezek. 16:15–17 [4x], 20, 22, 25–26 [3x], 28–31 [5x], 33–36 [6x], 41). In the end, however, YHWH leaves his people with the hope that he will one day atone for his unfaithful wife and so make possible the renewal of the marriage covenant (vv. 59–63).

The language of Ezek. 16 also connects at many points with Song of Songs. This includes words like "breasts" and "hair" (v. 7), "love" and "lovemaking" (v. 8), as well as references to oils, jewelry, precious metals, garments, and various fine foods (vv. 9–13). Again, because marriage is a covenant, it is well suited to characterize the covenantal relationship between YHWH and his people, both in terms of the commitments required of that covenant and the nature of the intimacy experienced in that relationship.

Hosea 1 and 3 record two enactment prophecies (also called sign-acts) whereby the prophet performs a certain action representing a prophetic message, something like a real-life sermon illustration. YHWH commands Hosea, "Go, take for yourself a wife of prostitution and children of prostitution, for the land has indeed prostituted itself by departing from YHWH" (1:2 AT). Again, in 3:1, YHWH commands Hosea, "Go, love a woman loved by another and an adulteress, like the love of YHWH for the children of Israel, even though they have turned to other gods and love cakes of raisins" (AT). In each case, the marriage of Hosea to Gomer serves as an illustration of the covenantal relationship between YHWH and his people. Once again, like in Ezek. 16, YHWH is portrayed as the faithful husband and Israel as the unfaithful wife. The covenant of marriage serves as the point of reference for the covenant between YHWH and his people. The full significance of the relationship between the human institution of marriage and YHWH's relationship with his people does not become clear until we arrive at the NT.

Writings. As described above, Song of Songs is located in this third section of the Hebrew Bible, and it occupies a strategic position as the fifth book in this collection with a strong connection to Israel's wisdom tradition that includes Proverbs, Ruth (a wisdom narrative), and Ecclesiastes.

Psalm 45 is also cited with some frequency with reference to the Song. The superscript designates this psalm as a maskil. It further describes it as a "love song" to be conducted "according to the lilies." The term "maskil" appears thirteen times in the superscriptions of Psalms and may characterize these poetic works as belonging to a wisdom tradition. The designation "love song" uses the same word for "song" as Song of Songs has in its superscription (1:1). Additionally, the term for "love" is related to the Hebrew word commonly translated as "beloved" and "lovemaking" in the Song, appearing thirty-nine times (e.g., 1:2, 4). Finally, the enigmatic reference to "lilies" or "Shoshanim" (a transliteration of the Hebrew word) also finds its place in the Song on numerous occasions (2:1–2, 16; 4:5; 5:13; 6:2–3; 7:3; see also the superscripts for Pss. 69; 80). In terms of content, Ps. 45 appears to describe the marriage of a king exalted by God (v. 7) to a beautiful woman (v. 11; see also vv. 12–16). The psalmist also writes about the king's own beauty, "You are more beautiful than the sons of man; favor [grace] has been poured upon your lips. Therefore, God has blessed you forever" (45:2 AT).

In the book of Esther, the woman Esther (Hadassah) is taken into "the house of the king" and placed in "the house of the women" (2:8 AT) in order that she might be prepared, trained, and considered for a life in the king's harem. This process of preparation and beautification took a year to complete with "six months for oil of myrrh and six months for spices and the cosmetics of women" (2:12). Though we do not know what this process might have looked like in the harem of Solomon, we can only imagine that it occurred on an unparalleled scale. Song of Songs 6:8 records that, at that time, Solomon's harem included sixty queens, eighty concubines, and *virgins without number*. We know from 1 Kings 11 that this number grew through the reign of Solomon, but the brief description of harem preparation in Esther 2 provides context for understanding what it might have been like for the woman of the Song of Songs as a virgin preparing for the possibility of harem life.

NT. In the Gospels, Jesus upholds the covenant of marriage instituted in Gen. 2 when he answers the Pharisees regarding the question of divorce, "Have you not read that, from the beginning, the Creator made them male and female? And he said, 'For this reason a man will leave his father and mother and be joined to his wife, and the two will become one flesh,' so that they are no longer two but one flesh" (Matt. 19:4–6 AT). Similarly, Paul admonishes believers to avoid illicit sexual conduct because of its covenantal implications: "Do you not know that the one who is joined to a prostitute becomes one body [with her]? For it is said, 'The two will become one flesh'" (1 Cor. 6:16 AT). Paul explicitly connects sexual union with a prostitute to the one-flesh state brought about by sexual union in Gen. 2. The act of sexual union is never neutral. It is either covenant making, covenant renewing, or covenant breaking (Hugenberger, 216–79). Likewise, the author of Hebrews exhorts, "Marriage is to be honored by all and the marriage bed [or sexual activity] is to be undefiled, for God will judge the sexually immoral and the adulterer" (Heb. 13:4 AT). The importance of marriage, sexual intimacy, and fidelity to that covenantal relationship is at the heart of the message of Song of Songs, and that message carries over unchanged into the NT.

However, when it comes to the interpretation of Song of Songs and the significance of marriage in the context of the whole Bible, no text is more important than Eph. 5:32. After exhorting wives to submit to their husbands (Eph. 5:22–24) and husbands to love their wives (5:25–30), Paul grounds his commands by quoting Gen. 2:24 and then states, "This mystery is great, and I am speaking about Christ and the church" (5:32 AT). Note that Paul grounds the love of a husband for his wife in their one-flesh, covenantal union instituted by God in Gen. 2, and then identifies that marriage covenant as a type of the relationship that Christ desires with his people, the church. In other words, the marriage covenant of Gen. 2 was always intended as a type of the marriage covenant of Rev. 21 (cf. 19:7–9; 22:17). This connection has led some scholars to identify possible allusions to Song of Songs in Revelation, but each one must be evaluated individually (cf., e.g., the Scripture indexes in Beale and in Leithart). There is probably a specific allusion to Song 5:2 in Rev. 3:20, which compares Christ to the husband of the Song and the church to the Song's bride (see Beale, 308). However, in terms of the general message of the book, all the longing, desire, and intimacy in the context of human marriage portrayed in the Song will find their ultimate satisfaction, meaning, and fulfillment in the marriage of Rev. 21. In Gen. 1, creation occurs by way of division in days one through three and then the filling of those divided kingdoms in days four through six. In Gen. 2, the woman is created by way of separation. Then, in the marriage covenant immediately following, that which was once divided is reunited by becoming "one flesh." In the same way, the dawning of the eschatological age takes place when the visible and invisible kingdoms separated in the beginning (cf. Gen. 1:1; Col. 1:16) are reunited as husband and wife (Rev. 21:1–4) for all eternity. As such, the language of consummation is altogether fitting when speaking about the moment at which the human covenant of marriage begins, as well as the dawning of the eternal, eschatological age.

Bibliography. Beale, G. K., *The Book of Revelation*, NIGTC (Eerdmans, 2008); DeRouchie, J. S., "The Blessing-Commission, the Promised Offspring, and the *TOLEDOT* Structure of Genesis," *JETS* 56, no. 2 (2013): 219–47; Garrett, D. A., *Proverbs, Ecclesiastes, Song of Songs*, NAC 14 (Broadman, 1993); Ginsburg, C. D., *The Song of Songs* (Longman, Brown, Green, Longmans, and Roberts, 1857); Hess, R. S. *Song of Songs*, BCOTWP (Baker Academic, 2005); Hugenberger, G. P., *Marriage as a Covenant*, VTSup 52 (Brill, 1993); Kaiser, W. C., Jr., "True Marital Love in Proverbs 5:15–23 and the Interpretation of Song of Songs," in *The Way of Wisdom*, ed. J. I. Packer and S. K. Soderlund (Zondervan, 2011), 106–16; Kline, M. G., "The Intrusion and the Decalogue," *WTJ* 16, no. 1 (1953): 1–22; Leithart, P. J., *Revelation 1–11*, ITC (Bloomsbury T&T Clark, 2018); Leithart, *Revelation 12–22*, ITC (Bloomsbury T&T Clark, 2018); Longman, T., III, *Song of Songs*, NICOT (Eerdmans, 2001); Murphy, R. E., "The Unity of the Song of Songs," in *Poetry in the Hebrew Bible*, ed. D. E. Orton, BRBS 6 (Brill, 2000),

148–55; Ortlund, R. C., *God's Unfaithful Wife*, NSBT 2 (IVP Academic, 2016); Pope, M. H., *The Song of Songs*, AB (Doubleday, 1977); Provan, I., *Ecclesiastes, Song of Songs*, NIVAC (Zondervan, 2001); Schnittjer, G. E., *Old Testament Use of the Old Testament* (Zondervan, 2021); Stoop-van Paridon, P. T. W., *The Song of Songs* (Peeters, 2005); Van Pelt, M. V., introduction to *A Biblical-Theological Introduction to the Old Testament*, ed. M. V. Van Pelt (Crossway, 2016), 23–42; Van Pelt, "Song of Songs," in *A Biblical-Theological Introduction to the Old Testament*, ed. M. V. Van Pelt (Crossway, 2016), 419–38.

MILES V. VAN PELT

Son of David

See Kingdom and King; Messiah

Son of God

Jesus is God's Son. This statement is eminently biblical and undeniably Christian. Yet, as the ecumenical councils (e.g., Nicaea, Constantinople, Chalcedon) illustrate, Jesus's sonship is one of the most misunderstood propositions in the history of the church. Even more, when we open the Bible, Jesus is not the only "son of God." In fact, Graeme Goldsworthy (31–32) finds no fewer than fifteen different uses of "son of God" in Scripture. D. A. Carson also demonstrates how this "christological title" has been, in the words of his book's subtitle, "often overlooked, sometimes misunderstood, and currently disputed." Acknowledging a diverse semantic range, he shows how "son of X" is not always biological, is often vocational (i.e., your father defines your work), and is applied variously across the OT and NT.

For instance, Carson (29–34) lists seven different "sons" of God. In chronological order, they are (1) Adam (Luke 3:38), (2) Israel (Exod. 4:22–23), (3) David (2 Sam. 7:14), (4) God's covenant people (Deut. 14:1; Isa. 43:6; 45:11; 63:8; Jer. 3:19; Rom. 8:14; Gal. 3:26; Phil. 2:15; 1 John 3:1), (5) those adopted by God (in Christ) (Rom. 8:15, 23; 9:4; Gal. 4:5; Eph. 1:4–5), (6) imitators of God (Matt. 5:44–45), and (7) believers who will receive the kingdom of God (Rom. 8:23; Rev. 21:7). He also recognizes that "son of God" is used of angels (e.g., Job 1:6; 2:1; 38:7; cf. Gen. 6:4), a textual feature we will consider in passing.

When we add up all these different uses of "son of God," we can see why this title is sometimes misunderstood. It does not have to be, though. As the OT unfolds and the NT interprets the progressive revelation of God's Son (see Heb. 1:1–3), we can see clearly how the manifold use of "son of God" comes to rest on Christ and those who are in Christ.

In what follows, I will identify the way Adam, Israel, and David are explicitly identified as sons of God. Additionally, I will show how the office of the high priest functions as God's "son." From these four "sons of God," we can better understand Jesus as *the* "Son of God." By way of divine revelation, each OT "son of God" is formed in the likeness of the divine Son. The eternal Son of God is the divine archetype, by which all sons of God come into being. Yet, in redemptive history these sons of God serve as biblical types for Jesus Christ, the antitype, who will come in the fullness of time.

Indeed, one way to understand the relationship between God the Son, the eternally begotten God (John 1:18), and Jesus Christ, the Son of God, is to look at the way "son of God" is used typologically in the OT. By comparing the OT types and the NT antitype, we come to understand "son of God" in all of its manifold glory. In what follows, we will compare the sons of God (Adam, Israel, Aaron, David) to Jesus Christ. And then, once God the Son incarnate is granted the title "Son of God" in his resurrection (see Acts 13:32–33; Rom. 1:4), we will see how Jesus's sonship is applied to all of God's new-covenant children.

Adam

Luke 3:38 is unmistakable: Adam is the "son of God." Coming at the end of Jesus's genealogy (3:23–38), Luke identifies Jesus as Adam's offspring by means of Abraham's family line. Placed at the beginning of his public ministry, this genealogy identifies Jesus as "son of Adam" and "son of God." Brandon Crowe (29) explains the background to this connection in Gen. 5:1–3:

> The correlation of Adam and divine sonship is found not only in Luke 3:38 but already in the genealogy of Genesis 5. We read in Genesis 5:1 that God created Adam in his own likeness (Hebrew: *damut*; Greek: *eikon*), and in 5:3 we read that Adam begat a son in his likeness (*damut*) and image (*selem*; see also Gen. 1:26). The implication is that, in a way analogous to Adam's fatherhood of Seth (and on down the line), God is Father to Adam, and therefore Adam should be understood as son of God. This also seems to be a clear implication of the conclusion to Luke's genealogy in 3:38 ("son of Adam, son of God").

The theological significance of this connection between Jesus and Adam is developed in the Gospels, by Paul, and by the author of Hebrews (cf. Crowe). Most explicitly, Paul introduces Adam as a prophetic type of Christ in Rom. 5:14. Picking up Adam typology in 1 Cor. 15, he again calls Jesus the "last Adam" (v. 45) and alludes to Seth, the "image" of Adam in Gen. 5:3, when he says in v. 49, "Just as we have borne the image of the man of dust, we shall also bear the image of the man of heaven" (cf. Gladd, 308). Colossians 1 also uses "image"

This article is modified with permission from David Schrock, "Jesus as the Son of God," The Gospel Coalition, accessed February 22, 2023, https://www.thegospelcoalition.org/essay/jesus-as-the-son-of-god/.

to express sonship when it declares Jesus to be "the image of the invisible God, the firstborn of all creation" and "the firstborn from the dead" (vv. 15, 18). And Heb. 1:2–3 introduces the Son as "the radiance of the glory of God and the exact imprint of his nature."

From these verses, we find a strong connection between sonship and image, a point well-developed by Emadi (25–35) as he conjoins sonship with image, as well as kingship and priesthood. As many have shown (e.g., Gentry and Wellum, 86–91), Adam's sonship entails kingship and priesthood. As "the son of God," Adam's kingship is seen explicitly in Gen. 1:26–28 and Ps. 8, as he receives dominion over all creation (Dempster, 56–62). Likewise, Gen. 2:15–17 portrays Adam as a priest who serves in God's garden-temple (Beale, *Temple*, 66–70; Schrock, *Royal Priesthood*, 27–34). Put together, "Adam should always best be referred to as a 'priest-king,' since it is only after the 'fall' that priesthood is separated from kingship" (Beale, *Temple*, 70). Indeed, before sin, the glory of man was found in the indivisible office of sonship, priesthood, and kingship.

After the fall, God divided these roles in Israel. Priests came from the sons of Levi (Deut. 33:8–11) and kings came from the sons of Judah (Gen. 49:8–12). Yet, this separation of priesthood and kingship was not meant to be everlasting. Rather, the division anticipated the arrival of the true Son who would be king *and* priest (Ps. 110; Heb. 7). In the last Adam, therefore, the true radiance of God was seen in Christ's royal priestly glory.

To be more precise, the eternal glory of the divine Son (John 17:5) is now seen through Jesus's glorified humanity (17:24). This glorified humanity was veiled while Christ dwelt on the earth, but now Scripture testifies to the glorified humanity of the Son (see the "Son of God" in Rev. 1:12–16; 2:18). As last Adam, the Son of God enjoys his heavenly glory (1 Cor. 15:35–49), even as he leads all God's children to glory (Heb. 2:10). By means of his resurrection, the divine Son is now understood to be the true Son of God. And importantly, as a son of God like Adam, all that was true of the first man is true of Jesus—only to an even greater extent (Schrock, "Restoring," 31–33). This includes Adam's priestly and kingly functions, two roles that will be developed through Aaron and David's sons, respectively.

Israel

Israel is identified as God's "firstborn son" (Exod. 4:22–23). In context, Yahweh identifies Israel as his firstborn when he threatens to kill Pharaoh's firstborn in order to deliver his people (i.e., his son). What follows in Exodus is a competition to see who is God's true son. In Egypt, the firstborn of Pharaoh presumably would become the next son of God, a title reserved for the king of Egypt (Gentry and Wellum, 76–77; Emadi, 27–29). Yet, in delivering the children of Abraham from Egypt, Yahweh is showing who the true son of God is.

Later revelation identifies the exodus as the place where God became the father of Israel (Deut. 32:18; Ps. 80:15; Jer. 31:9; Hosea 11:1). This corporate identification explains how Israel relates to Adam. As G. K. Beale has put it, Israel is a "corporate Adam" (*Temple*, 120–21). What began in Eden—God's relationship with his son—is picked up again with his covenant people. And, as we will see with the priests below, the relationship between God and his mediators is always fatherly. As a son does the bidding of his father on earth, so the sons of God do the bidding of their Father in heaven.

In Exodus, we see God's fatherly relationship with Israel when we compare 4:22–23 and 19:1–8. Identified as his firstborn, Israel will be brought through a series of trials, including the redemption of all firstborn sons in the Passover (Exod. 12–13) and the baptism of Moses in the Red Sea (Exod. 14–15; cf. 1 Cor. 10:1–2). By this process of sanctification, the son of God (Israel) will be identified as his treasured possession (*səgullâ*) and a "kingdom of priests" (19:5–6). Importantly, Israel's exodus is what enabled the firstborn of Yahweh to approach God's holy mountain (Exod. 19–24) and then his tabernacle (Exod. 25–40). In all of this, God was beginning the process of restoring to Israel what Adam lost by his sin in Eden—namely, as God's son, Israel is called to be a royal priesthood. These vocations (priest and king) identify who Israel is and what they are to do. This connection of sonship, priesthood, and kingship goes back to Adam and prepares the way for a greater son.

When we compare Israel with Adam, we discover that both sons of God are royal priests. Not by accident does Moses present Adam as a son of God who is priest and king. Indeed, Israel's triple identification as son, priest, and king reflects the way in which Israel, as God's son, is a "corporate Adam" and the means by which a new humanity will come from their lineage (cf. Gal. 3:16). Accordingly, whenever we see "son of God" language in Scripture, we should recognize that priesthood and kingship are close at hand. Even as the sons of Aaron (Exod. 28:1) and the sons of David (2 Sam. 7:9–14) become Israel's priests and kings, respectively, the aim is always a reunion of the offices (see, e.g., Ps. 110:1–7; Zech. 6:9–15).

Confirming this reading of Exodus, Matthew identifies Jesus as the true Israel when he appropriates Hosea 11:1 ("Out of Egypt I called my son") in Matt. 2:13–15. By taking the designation of God's son and applying it to Jesus, he explains how Jesus is God's Son (Beale, *New Testament*, 406–12). But to be precise, the language of sonship here identifies Jesus as true Israel. Similarly, when Jesus is led by the Spirit into the wilderness for forty days (Matt. 4:1–11), he repeats the events of Israel, which Matthew employs to identify the kind of son Jesus is—a son like Israel. Moreover, the locations at the temple (v. 5) and over all the nations (v. 8) are not accidental; they conjoin sonship with priesthood and kingship. Even more, the devil tempts Jesus to prove his sonship, saying, "If you are the Son of God . . ." (Matt. 4:3, 6). As Jesus recites Scripture related to Israel's identity as a son (see Deut. 8:3–5), Jesus is recapitulating the events of Israel's temptation in the wilderness. Yet, simultaneously, he is also proving himself a true "Son" of God like Adam.

Similarly, when the Father identifies Jesus as his true Son at his baptism ("This is my beloved Son, with whom I am well pleased," Matt. 3:17 ESV), he takes up OT references and applies them to his Son. Whether Matthew is recalling Gen. 22 or Isa. 42 or both, the point is certain: Jesus is the true Son of God, just as Israel was God's son. This does not deny the ontological deity of the Son or the fact that he is, and has always been and will always be, the divine Son. But at Jesus's baptism such a theological designation is still premature. Instead, this event, like all of Jesus's life, is revealing the multifaceted nature of his sonship. Portraying Jesus as a son, as true Israel, reveals his functional redemptive-historical role in relation to doing what Adam and, especially, Israel should have done in obeying God.

At this point, the modern reader may be tempted to ask, How do we know which facet is being revealed? For instance, is Jesus's temptation proving that he is a son of God like Israel? Or a son of God like Adam? And the biblical answer is yes. As Israel, the corporate Adam, fails in the wilderness, their disobedience points back to Adam's failure in the garden. Simultaneously, Israel's experience in the wilderness also points forward to a son of Israel, who is the true Son of God. Thus, when Matthew recounts Jesus's forty days in the wilderness, he is not restricting himself to one type. Instead, he is conjoining shadows as he bears witness to their substance—Jesus Christ, the Son of God.

The High Priest

If Israel, as a kingdom of priests (Exod. 19:6), is called the son of God (Exod. 4:22–23), it follows that priests are also sons of God. As noted with Adam, the relationship of sonship to priesthood is inherent to the image of God (Schrock, *Priesthood*, 19, 33; Emadi, 30–35). Following this, when God chose Aaron and his sons to serve in his house, he clothed them with glory and beauty (Exod. 28:2), just like the first man (Emadi, 73–74). As the living embodiment of the Lord (i.e., the image of God), the high priest would serve in his Father's house and bring blessing to everyone else (Num. 6:22–26; Ps. 133). Indeed, even before Exodus, the sons of promise made altars (Gen. 26:25; 33:2; 35:1, 3, 7; cf. Exod. 17:15) and worshiped God in ways that anticipated the corporate worship of Israel (Schrock, *Royal Priesthood*, 34–45). That is to say, before the Mosaic and Levitical covenants, the sons served as priests among the patriarchs (Hahn, 136–42; Morales, 8–12). This is suggested by the presence of pre-Aaronic priests at Sinai (Exod. 19:22, 24), the service of young men offering sacrifices (Exod. 24:5), and the replacement of firstborn sons with Levites due to the golden-calf incident (Schrock, *Royal Priesthood*, 51–55). In other words, before God chose Aaron's sons to be priests, priesthood came by way of sonship.

Admittedly, the phrase "son of God" is not directly applied to the sons of Aaron, but when God set them apart for service, he effectively adopted them as sons. Peter Leithart (77) even likens priestly ordination to a kind of adoption. Moreover, priestly service before God's altar on earth mirrored the service of angels in God's heavenly temple (Leithart, 68). In other words, if "sons of God" is a term used for angels (see Job 1:6; 2:1; 38:7), and "sons of God" is also used for the human mediators of Israel, it is worth asking if there is any connection. One possibility is that sons of God, angelic or human, are those who serve in God's presence.

Angels are not priests per se, but the analogy is this: the human sons of God on earth do what the angelic sons of God do in heaven. Going one step further, the OT looked to a day when the nations, who were subjected to angelic powers (i.e., "sons of God" in Deut. 32:8–9 ESV; cf. Dan. 10:13), would be subjected to a human son of God. Indeed, what Adam lost in the garden, God promised to restore when the true Son of God came from heaven to earth. In fact, it is significant that when Christ sat down as high priest, thus fulfilling Ps. 110:1, all things in heaven, both visible and invisible were put under the feet of the one who was declared "Son of God" (Rom. 1:4).

In multiple ways, this vision of human sons of God replacing other angelic sons of God is confirmed by Hebrews. In this priestly epistle, Jesus is presented as the true man (2:5–9, citing Ps. 8:4–6) and the true Son over God's house (3:1–6). Because he is the true Son, he will be accepted into his Father's house as the true priest. Indeed, Heb. 5:5–6 says that Jesus receives his priesthood because of his perfect sonship, an eschatological reality that fulfills Ps. 110. Even more, because of his glorious ascension, he has purified heaven (Heb. 9:23) and made a place for the sons of God to enter into glory with him (2:10; 11:39–40). As a result, heaven is now populated by the church of the firstborn (*ekklēsia prōtotokōn*), as well as the angels who are dressed in festival clothing (12:22–24).

Hermeneutically, this association of priesthood and sonship reminds us that "son of God" is a biblical-theological concept that exceeds the collocation of "son" and "of God." Instead, the phrase "son of God" is one part of a threefold cord, and just as kingship implies sonship, so does priesthood (Leithart, 118; Perrin, 85). As Hebrews unveils, sonship, priesthood, and kingship must be read together (Emadi, 169–204). In both Testaments, these three titles are mutually interpretive, and we should not restrict our understanding of "son of God" to a mere word search. This will be proven especially true as we consider the Son of God as David's son.

David

Another OT passage that is associated with Jesus's baptism is Ps. 2:7 ("You are my Son; today I have begotten you" [ESV]). As a psalm of David (see Acts 4:25), Ps. 2 identifies the son who will be set on Zion's throne (vv. 6–8). In its original context, however, this statement is a poetic expansion of God's covenant with David in 2 Sam. 7, not a direct statement about Jesus's divinity (Wellum, 99–101).

In 2 Sam. 7, when David seeks to build a house (i.e., a temple) for Yahweh, God turns around and promises to build a house (i.e., a dynasty) for David. In this covenant with David, God promises a son who will sit on an eternal throne (vv. 12–14). Even more, this eternal throne comes with the offer that David's son will be God's son: "I will be to him a father, and he shall be to me a son" (v. 14 ESV).

In the immediate history of Israel, this son of God was Solomon. He ruled with wisdom and justice, bringing peace and blessing to the people by leading the nation to keep covenant with God. In this way, the fate of Israel as God's collective son would depend upon David's son.

At the same time, the role of priesthood was not far removed from the royal government of David and Solomon, either. Though neither was a son of Aaron, David and Solomon often worshiped Yahweh like priests (see 2 Sam. 6:14; 1 Kings 8). Both oriented their kingdom toward the temple of God and established the priesthood in Israel. Though they were inconsistent in their rule, these two kings did not act like the kings of the nations (cf. 1 Sam. 8). Instead, like the earlier priest-king Melchizedek, they served God Most High with priest-like obedience (cf. Perrin, 143–65)—that is, they served God like true sons.

Sadly, the obedience of David's sons was short-lived. Solomon turned his heart away from God to serve idols. And later, David's heirs, with a few exceptions, broke their covenant with God and lost their right to sit on the throne (Ps. 89). Still, the mold for a Davidic king who was the son of God was set, and as the prophets lamented the fall of David's house, God began to promise a son of David whose righteousness would restore the kingdom to Israel (Isa. 9:6–7; 11:1–10; Jer. 23:5–6; Ezek. 34:23–24; Hosea 3:5; Amos 9:11–12; Mic. 5:2; Zech. 6:9–15).

Indeed, in the NT, the Son of God is the son of David, whose righteousness under the law makes possible the new covenant. In fact, Paul's gospel is based on God's promises to David (Rom. 1:3; 2 Tim. 2:8). To limit ourselves to one passage, Rom. 1:2–4 shows how Jesus, as David's son, is the Son of God and the hope of salvation.

Paul speaks of Christ receiving the title "Son of God" at his resurrection. Romans 1:3–4 reads, "concerning his Son, who was descended from David according to the flesh and was declared to be the Son of God in power according to the Spirit of holiness by his resurrection from the dead, Jesus Christ our Lord" (ESV). This passage is best understood as the eternal Son of God taking on a human nature, through the line of David, and receiving the honor of being called the "Son of God in power" when he rose to life (cf. Acts 13:32–33). As Thomas Schreiner (*Romans*, 42) notes, "The title [*huiou theou*] in verse [4] is a reference not to Jesus' deity but to his messianic kingship as the descendent of David (cf. 2 Sam. 7:14; Ps. 2:7)," a messianic kingship that was given to him "upon his resurrection." While Jesus is the Son of God throughout his entire human life, his resurrection assigns him the title "Son of God."

This exalted title goes back to 2 Sam. 7:14. Only now, it is applied to Jesus, who has proven himself to be God's true Son and worthy of an eternal throne. As Hebrews confirms, it is only after Jesus's humanity is "perfected" that he receives the title "Son of God." This is why Hebrews argues that it was necessary for the Son to learn obedience through suffering (5:8). In other words, when Christ rose from the dead and ascended to the Father's right hand (cf. Ps. 110), all creation was put under his feet (Ps. 8), so that he received the right to rule over heaven and earth *as the son of David* (Gentry and Wellum, 194–95).

In summary, what Adam, Israel, Aaron, and David all failed to do—prove their sonship—Jesus accomplished. And marvelously, his resurrection proves to be the moment when he is "declared," or better "appointed" (*horizō*), the "Son of God," while his ascension proves to be the moment of his glorious coronation. Paul identifies this at the beginning of Romans and defines it as the core of the gospel message (Rom. 1:1–7). Truly, this is the way that God in Christ unites all things in heaven and on earth (Eph. 1:10), as the eternal Son of God is finally recognized as the "Son of God" who fulfilled once and for all what Adam, Israel, and David's sons should have done.

Jesus

When the divine Son assumed human nature, he fulfilled all the purposes of God. That is to say, Jesus is the now *the* Son of God, who is the better Adam, the true Israel, the perfect high priest, and the eternal king. And what unites all of these vocations is his sonship. God the Son incarnate, exalted to God's right hand, is both God the Son and the Son of God. And this truth brings us full circle to the way Scripture articulates what the historic creeds confess—namely, that the Son of God is fully God and fully man. In what follows, we will look at John's Gospel to see the divine glory of the Son.

While the divinity of the Son is perceivable in other Gospels, the Fourth Gospel is most explicit. Beginning in his prologue (John 1:1–18), we find John calling Jesus the divine Son. In declaring that the eternal Word took on flesh and dwelt among us, John identifies Jesus as "the only Son from the Father" (v. 14 ESV). This word *monogenēs* has been translated "only begotten" (KJV, NASB), "one and only" (NIV), or "only" (ESV). It has a unique meaning within the Johannine corpus (see 1:14, 18; 3:16, 18; 1 John 4:9) and has posed many challenges to interpreters and theologians (see Köstenberger and Swain, 76–79; Irons, 98–116). Whether or not this word by itself supports eternal generation, it clearly identifies Jesus as God's divine Son. He is a son unlike any other son of God, and throughout his Gospel John returns to the divine nature of Jesus as God's Son.

For instance, John 5:18 identifies the Son as "equal" with the Father, which led the Jewish leaders to desire Jesus's death. John 5:19–29 goes on to explain the relationship of the Father to the Son. And while stressing the human obedience of the Son to the Father, the cumulative effect of these verses identifies Jesus's divine sonship. As John 5:26 indicates, "For as the Father has life in himself, so he has granted the Son also to have life in himself." In the context of John, "this claim to divine aseity [i.e., life in himself] must refer to the Son's eternal ontology, not to a function of his incarnation" only (Wellum, 162).

Supporting this interpretation, John 8:58 identifies Jesus as the divine Son when Jesus, speaking of his Father, goes on to say that "before Abraham was, I am." The "I am" (*egō eimi*) recalls the Lord's divine name ("I AM WHO I AM," Exod. 3:14), and Jesus's antecedent existence ("before Abraham") surely identifies Jesus as the eternal Son.

To mention just one more place, Jesus addresses his Father in John 17. Praying that God would glorify him on earth (v. 1), he describes the glory he shared with his Father before creation (v. 5). When Jesus says he will show his glory with his disciples (v. 24), it is apparent that what his disciples will see is the reflection of the glory he has shared eternally with the Father. In other words, Jesus, as God's Son, shares in his Father's divine glory, and that uncreated glory is the source of the glory that God will bring into the world through the ministry of the Son. All in all, John's Gospel shows us how Jesus is not only the son of God according to his humanity; he is also the Son of God according to his eternal divinity.

Church

Finally, "son of God" also refers to Christians. Yet, there is no mistaking the follower for the Master, the saint for the Savior. Rather, as Gal. 3:26–29 makes plain, we are sons of God and coheirs with Christ, *because of Jesus, the only-begotten Son of God*.

The male title "son" is applied to women too in order to stress the theme of inheritance, not to confuse or conflate the two genders—male and female. As Larry Hurtado (906) explains, "Paul consistently refers to the sonship of Christians as derived sonship, given through and after the pattern of Jesus, whereas Jesus is the original prototype, whose sonship is not derived from another."

Typology is the right way to speak of Christ's sonship and ours. Indeed, Jesus Christ is the true substance of what it means to be a son of God. In other words, the divine Son lives out his perfect sonship in a human form for all to see and to achieve God's original commission to Adam. The person of the divine Son demonstrates what it means to be God's Son through his human nature. And because of his human obedience, he also makes a way for sinful children to become sons and daughters and inherit the righteousness of the last Adam (see 2 Cor. 6:18). By union with Christ, the exalted Son of God confers on his new humanity the right to be priests and kings—the original design for the image of God.

In this way, we see how central sonship is to the story of the Bible and to every biblical doctrine. For truly, Jesus Christ is the Son of God, and all who have the Son have the life that he has gained in his resurrection. When he received the right to be called the "Son of God" in his human nature, God the Son reveals to mankind the full glory of the Father (cf. Luke 10:22). And thus to all who recognize Jesus as God the Son incarnate, they will discover what it means to be God's children, as God the Father conforms them into the image of his Son, by means of the Spirit.

See also Adam, First and Last; Kingdom and King; Messiah

Bibliography. Beale, G. K., *A New Testament Biblical Theology* (Baker Academic, 2011); Beale, *The Temple and the Church's Mission* (InterVarsity, 2004); Carson, D. A., *Jesus the Son of God* (Crossway, 2012); Crowe, B. D., *The Last Adam* (Baker Academic, 2017); Dempster, S. G., *Dominion and Dynasty*, NSBT (InterVarsity, 2003); Emadi, M., *The Royal Priest*, NSBT (IVP Academic, 2022); Gentry, P. J., and S. J. Wellum, *God's Kingdom through God's Covenant* (Crossway, 2015); Gladd, B. L., "The Last Adam as the 'Life-Giving Spirit' Revisited," *WTJ* 71 (2009): 297–309; Goldsworthy, G., *The Son of God and the New Creation*, SSBT (Crossway, 2015); Grudem, W., *Systematic Theology* (Eerdmans, 2000); Hahn, S. W., *Kinship by Covenant* (Yale University Press, 2009); Hurtado, L. W., "Son of God," in *DPL*, 900–906; Irons, C. L., "A Lexical Defense of the Johannine 'Only Begotten,'" in *Retrieving Eternal Generation*, ed. F. Sanders and S. R. Swain (Zondervan, 2017), 98–116; Köstenberger, A. J., and S. R. Swain, *Father, Son, and Holy Spirit*, NSBT 24 (InterVarsity, 2008); Leithart, P. J., *The Priesthood of the Plebs* (Wipf & Stock, 2003); Morales, L. M., *Who Shall Ascend the Mountain of the Lord?*, NSBT (InterVarsity, 2015); Perrin, N., *Jesus the Priest* (SPCK, 2018); Schreiner, T. R., *Romans*, BECNT (Baker Academic, 1998); Schreiner, "Son of God," in *New Testament Theology* (Baker Academic, 2008), 233–48; Schrock, D., "Restoring the Image of God," *SBJT* 22, no. 2 (2018): 25–60; Schrock, *The Royal Priesthood and the Glory of God* (Crossway, 2022); Wellum, S. J., *God the Son Incarnate*, FET (Crossway, 2016).

David S. Schrock

Son of Man

"Son of man" is at one level a standard Hebrew idiom referring to a human being, like the expression "one born of woman" (Job 25:4; cf. 14:1; 15:14; Matt. 11:11; Luke 7:28; Gal. 4:4). The phrase often appears in parallelism with "man" when this term means "human" (rather than specifically *adult male*). The first occurrence in the OT is a typical one: "God is not a man, that he might lie; or a son of man, that he might change his mind" (Num. 23:19 CSB). Such "son of man" phraseology often causes difficulties for Bible translators who are aiming for gender-accurate translation: the Hebrew phrase *ben-ʾādām* (or in Daniel's Aramaic, *bar ʾĕnāsh*) does not mean "man" insofar as this English word increasingly in standard usage means "adult male," while in poetry the language of "human being" and "humankind" can seem clunky or prosaic.

The phrase is especially common, in both singular and plural, in the poetic books of the OT, and most of all in God's address to Ezekiel as "son of man" (93x). It is sometimes said of the idiom that it has connotations of weakness, but this is not especially true. Sometimes it is used in contexts of human frailty (e.g., Isa. 51:12), but not markedly more so than other expressions for humanity. The Semitic idiom of "son of man" referring to a human being is used several times in the NT (e.g., Mark 3:28; Eph. 3:5; Heb. 2:6, quoting Ps. 8:4). Most significant, however, is the usage of the phrase as a self-designation by Jesus in the Gospels.

Son of Man in the OT

Psalm 8. The statement about humanity's position in creation in Ps. 8 is a well-known instance of the expression: "When I consider your heavens, the work of your fingers, the moon and the stars, which you have set in place, what is man that you are mindful of him, the son of man that you care for him? You have made him a little lower than the angels and crowned him with glory and honor" (8:3–5 AT; cf. 144:3). This passage is an eloquent expression of the position of humanity in God's created order, echoing the facts that humanity exclusively is made in the image of God and rules over the rest of the creaturely realm (Gen. 1:26–27).

The "one like a son of man" in Dan. 7. The most influential usage of the phrase in the OT is that of Dan. 7: "In my vision at night I looked, and there before me was one like a son of man, coming with the clouds of heaven. He approached the Ancient of Days and was led into his presence. He was given authority, glory and sovereign power; all nations and peoples of every language worshiped him. His dominion is an everlasting dominion that will not pass away, and his kingdom is one that will never be destroyed" (7:13–14). Although the phrase is used here, we are not necessarily dealing with a human being but with "one *like* a son of man." This is a figure of immense majesty: his appearance "with the clouds of heaven" suggests that he is a heavenly and indeed divine figure (cf., e.g., Deut. 33:26: "There is no one like the God of Jeshurun, who rides across the heavens to help you and on the clouds in his majesty"). At the same time, he is not simply alone God, because he stands in the presence of God ("the Ancient of Days") in heaven, rather like the Lord who is addressed by the Lord in Ps. 110:1. He has a position of authority over all humanity, who worship him. He is also an immortal king, whose rule will never end ("His dominion is an everlasting dominion").

The approach of this figure is the climactic appearance in a vision. Before the son of man, there are four beasts: the first like a lion with the wings of an eagle (7:4), the second like a bear with three ribs in its mouth (7:5), the third like a winged, four-headed leopard (7:6), and a fourth beast with iron teeth and ten horns (7:7). These creatures are all violent, destructive forces, symbolic of a succession of human kings and empires who precede the arrival of the one like a son of man. Unlike the man-like figure's everlasting dominion, these human rulers and the empires they represent are merely temporary and destroyed by God at their appointed time. As Daniel says of the fourth and last beast, "I kept looking until the beast was slain and its body destroyed and thrown into the blazing fire. The other beasts had been stripped of their authority, but were allowed to live for a period of time" (7:11–12).

As is common in accounts of visions, an interpretation follows (7:16–27). There is a clear heading: "The four great beasts are four kings that will rise from the earth" (7:17). Most modern scholars take the four kingdoms to be Babylon, Media, Persia, and Greece, partly on the basis of an interpretation of the textual details and partly because (on a date of Daniel in the second century BC) the author would not be able to prophesy into the first century BC or AD. Historically, however, the standard interpretation has been to combine Media and Persia into a single empire, making the sequence Babylon, Medo-Persia, Greece, and *Rome*. (Greeks also conflated Media and Persia, as for example where "Medizing" means siding with Persia or adopting Persian customs.) This interpretation goes back to about AD 100, when the Jewish apocalypse of 4 Ezra identifies the unclassified fourth beast as an *eagle* with twelve wings that symbolize twelve Caesars from Julius to Domitian (4 Ezra 11–12). The attraction, in the Christian history of interpretation, of seeing the fourth beast as Rome has been that in the vision of Dan. 7:9–14 and especially in the interpretation in 7:23–27, the one like a son of man appears not after the destruction of the fourth beast but during its dominion. Hence it fits better to see the son of man, Jesus, as arriving during the Roman Empire.

Whatever the historical reference in the beasts, there is probably an implied contrast with the creation narrative in Gen. 1:

> Then God said, "Let us make mankind in our image, in our likeness, so that they may rule over the fish in the sea and the birds in the sky, over the livestock and all the wild animals, and over all the creatures that move along the ground."
>
> So God created mankind in his own image,
> in the image of God he created them;
> male and female he created them.
>
> God blessed them and said to them, "Be fruitful and increase in number; fill the earth and subdue it. Rule over the fish in the sea and the birds in the sky and over every living creature that moves on the ground." (Gen. 1:26–28)

There is a clear distinction in the creation narrative between man and beast, and human beings are to steward creation, to take responsibility for animals and manage them. In the vision of Dan. 7, however, human rulers have become beasts and subdue human beings. Rather than being "crowned with glory and honor," as in Ps. 8, the humanity ruling creation is animalistic and shameful. This has already been graphically illustrated in Daniel, when Nebuchadnezzar moved away from other human beings, "ate grass like an ox," growing "hair . . . like the feathers of an eagle and . . . nails like the claws of a bird" (Dan. 4:33); elsewhere he is called a lion (Jer. 50:17) and an eagle (Ezek. 17:3). Against the background of this bestial takeover of creation, it is notable that rule is wrested from the animals and given over to one like a son of *man*. Thus, the order of creation expressed in Gen. 1 and Ps. 8 is restored.

Perhaps surprising, however, is the way in which the son of man is interpreted in the second half of Dan. 7. The fourth beast opposes God as follows: "He will speak against the Most High and oppress his holy people and try to change the set times and the laws. The holy people will be delivered into his hands for a time, times and half a time. But the court will sit, and his power will be taken away and completely destroyed forever. *Then the sovereignty, power and greatness of all the kingdoms under heaven will be handed over to the holy people of the Most High. His kingdom will be an everlasting kingdom, and all rulers will worship and obey him*" (Dan. 7:25–27). Here, then, what was granted to the man-like figure in Dan. 7:14 (authority, glory, sovereign power, worship from all nations, and an everlasting dominion) is in fact granted to the saints of the Most High—that is, God's people (cf. also 7:18). This is not as much of a shift as it might first seem. At the beginning of the interpretation, the beasts are identified as four kings, and the one like a son of man in Dan. 7:13–14 certainly appears as an individual as well. However, at various points through both the vision and the interpretation the images clearly represent both rulers and their empires. In the case of the fourth, for example, the last beast is not a single king who by himself crushes and devours his victims singlehandedly (7:7, 19). Additionally, this beast's ten horns are ten kings who will in turn be succeeded by an eleventh king; hence, the fourth beast is not simply one king but an empire ruled by a succession of kings. The same might apply to the bear's three ribs and the leopard's four wings and heads. These beasts are kingdoms and not just kings. In the light of this, the interpretation of the one like a son of man is not so strange. This figure, while in possession of dominion over the whole world, rules in a special way over one particular people as their representative.

The Interpretation of Dan. 7 in First-Century Judaism

Christians were not the first to identify the figure in Dan. 7 as the Messiah. There are three particular works, dated to the first or early second centuries AD, which are known to make use of Dan. 7. The Parables of Enoch (a section of the larger 1 Enoch) is of uncertain date but comes from the time frame between 50 BC and AD 100, or possibly into the early second century AD. Fourth Ezra comes more securely from around AD 100, and 2 Baruch was probably written shortly after that. There is no strong evidence that the use of Dan. 7 or the phrase "Son of Man" in the Gospels and Revelation is directly influenced by any of these works, although it is possible.

In the Parables of Enoch, the Messiah of the Lord of Spirits (1 En. 48:10) is one and the same as "that son of man" (48:2). This refers on the one hand to a human being already mentioned, but the clear allusions to Dan. 7 and the frequency of the expression in the Parables of Enoch mean that "that son of man" refers to Daniel's man-like figure. In any case, Dan. 7 exerts a clear influence on 1 Enoch. In 1 En. 46, for example: "There I saw one who had a head of days, and his head was white like wool, and with him was another being whose countenance had the appearance of a man, and his face was full of grace, like one of the holy angels. And I asked the angel who went with me and showed me all the hidden things, about that son of man, who he was, and where he came from, and why he went with the Head of Days" (46:1–2, trans. Nickelsburg and Vanderkam). This messianic figure in 1 Enoch is also preexistent: he was "hidden in his [i.e., God's] presence before the world was created," and "from the beginning the son of man was hidden" (1 En. 48:6; 62:7, trans. Nickelsburg and Vanderkam).

In 4 Ezra, the angel announces that he is giving Ezra the interpretation of Daniel's vision (4 Ezra 12:10–12). What Daniel saw was "one like a man . . . on the clouds of heaven" (13:2–3 AT), therefore making clear the identification of the Messiah and one like a son of man. This figure who confronts the fourth beast, the "eagle" mentioned above, is "he whom the Most High has been keeping for many ages" and "the Messiah whom the Most High has kept until the end of days" (12:25–26, 32 AT). Since the world is referred to as the Messiah's creation, there may well be an implication that he was involved in making it (13:26). There are also several allusions to Dan. 7 in the vision with the anointed one in 2 Baruch. The focus is on the Messiah as an eschatological judge revealed in the last days (2 Bar. 29:30). Following the pattern of Daniel's four beasts, the angel gives Baruch the interpretation of his vision: "Behold, days are coming when this kingdom which once destroyed Zion [i.e., Babylon, the first beast] will be destroyed, and it will be subjected to that which comes after it. And after a time that kingdom will in turn be destroyed, and another, a third, will arise. . . . After these things a fourth kingdom will arise. . . . And when the time for the completion of its downfall has approached, the dominion of my Messiah will be revealed" (2 Bar. 39:3–7 AT). Jewish messianic usage of Dan. 7 continues later into the Talmud (fifth c. AD), where, for example, the glorious Danielic figure is one depiction of the Messiah, which is contrasted with Zech. 9's picture of the lowly Messiah on a donkey (b. Sanh. 98a), and the passage is popular in designations of the messiah elsewhere, in the targumim (Aramaic paraphrases of the Hebrew Bible) and in rabbinic exegetical works.

Son of Man in the NT

Only Revelation employs Daniel's phrase "one like a son of man" in the NT (Rev. 1:13; 14:14). Elsewhere, the shorter phrase "the son of man" / "the Son of Man" is used. In all but one saying of Jesus, the Gospels use the Greek article, which signals the phrase as "definite" or defined. In other words, the son of man is introduced as a known quantity: as one scholar (Moule) has glossed the phrase, "the Son of Man" is "*the* Son of man [whom you know from that vision]" in Dan. 7. As a result, the "Son of Man" title is employed to draw attention not to Jesus's humanity but to the authority given to him by God as referred to in the Danielic vision.

Mark. In the Gospels, the accent on Jesus's authority as Son of Man is obvious. The first two references in Mark's Gospel show this very clearly: "The Son of Man has authority on earth to forgive sins" (2:10) and "The Son of Man is Lord even of the Sabbath" (2:28). The Son of Man is therefore revealed at the outset as an authoritative figure. Although Dan. 7 does not mention the forgiveness of sins or the Sabbath particularly, the dominion of the one like a son of man is universal. His superhuman, divine identity (echoing, e.g., the clouds in Dan. 7) is also evident in the fact that the Son of Man claims a divine prerogative (forgiveness) and jurisdiction over a divine institution (the Sabbath).

Mark's Gospel continues in a different vein, of course. Jesus does not sweep majestically through Galilee and Judea, conquering all before him. Instead, his authority as Son of Man is rejected. The next set of cases of the title in Mark is focused in the three passion and resurrection predictions (cf. also Mark 8:38): "He then began to teach them that the Son of Man must suffer many things and be rejected by the elders, the chief priests and the teachers of the law, and that he must be killed and after three days rise again" (8:31). The language of the other two predictions is also important: "The Son of Man is going to be delivered into the hands of men" (9:31) and "The Son of Man will be delivered over to the chief priests and the teachers of the law. They will condemn him to death and will hand him over to the Gentiles" (10:33). There is an interesting connection here with Dan. 7—not with the glorious vision of the man-like figure, but with the maltreatment of the saints of the Most High who are attacked by the fourth beast and "will be delivered into his hand for a time, times and half a time" (Dan. 7:25). Jesus's passion predictions here share similarities with Daniel in (1) the verb "giving" / "handing over" (*didōmi* in Daniel, *paradidōmi* in Mark), (2) the "into the hand(s) of" idiom, and (3) the temporary three days / three and a half "times." Hence, for Jesus in Mark's Gospel, the Son of Man endures the projected suffering of the saints of the Most High. Or to put it another way, the saints of the Most High do go through their suffering, but they endure it in the person of the Son of Man, their representative.

While the Danielic background suggests a more representative role for the Son of Man, a more substitutionary note is sounded just after the three passion-resurrection predictions in the so-called ransom saying: "For even the Son of Man did not come to be served, but to serve, and to give his life as a ransom for many" (Mark 10:45). There is a paradox here, in that the Son of Man in Dan. 7 comes precisely in order to be served—by every nation in the world. This part of the divine design is to wait, however. The Son of Man must be killed as a life-for-life exchange.

If Mark's Gospel begins with a *revelation* of Jesus's authority and centers on the *rejection* of that authority, then the final chapters accentuate its *vindication*. Two of the last references to the Son of Man in Mark make this clear. In the eschatological discourse in Mark 13, it is Jesus as Son of Man who will be seen "coming in clouds with great power and glory. And he will send his angels and gather his elect from the four winds, from the ends of the earth to the ends of the heavens" (13:26–27). Here the connection with Dan. 7 is obvious in the coming with clouds. As Son of Man, Jesus is obviously a figure of great authority: the angels are called "his angels" and the people of God are "his elect."

The final reference in Mark to the Son of Man is in Jesus's appearance before the high priest: "The high priest asked him, 'Are you the Messiah, the Son of the Blessed One?' 'I am,' said Jesus. 'And you will see the Son of Man sitting at the right hand of the Mighty One and coming on the clouds of heaven'" (Mark 14:61–62). Here again the Son of Man is clearly the figure from Dan. 7, and it is notable here that the "Son of Man" title has some kind of equivalence to the "Messiah" title, as well as to "Son of God" (here, "Son of the Blessed One").

In sum, the pattern of the sayings in Mark makes it clear that the "Son of Man" title, unlike the titles of "Son of God" or "Lord," is not merely a way of describing Jesus in a glorious or authoritative manner but is also a way of pointing to Jesus's destiny—his suffering at the hands of the fourth beast like the saints of the Most High and his subsequent vindication.

Matthew and Luke-Acts. Matthew and Luke do not have such an obvious pattern of usage of the "Son of Man" title. They both reproduce most of this part of the Markan sayings tradition. They also, however, have additional material. The first "Son of Man" saying in Matthew is about the foxes and birds who have their dwelling places, "but the Son of Man has no place to lay his head" (Matt. 8:20). By comparison with Mark, however, Matthew perhaps in general accentuates the role of Jesus the Son of Man as the eschatological judge seated on his "glorious throne" (Matt. 19:28; 25:31). This glorious throne is a motif also paralleled in 1 Enoch. Matthew also alludes to Dan. 7 at the climax of the Gospel, though without using the "Son of Man" title: Jesus says, "All authority in heaven and on earth has been given to me," which gives the basis for his entrusting the disciples with their mission among all the nations (Matt. 28:18–19). This probably means that at his resurrection he is exalted to a new kind of rule that comes into effect with this new era of salvation history (cf. Rom. 1:4; Acts 2:36; Rev. 12:10).

Luke makes use of additional sources besides Mark. One of the most memorable Lukan sayings is his conclusion to the Zacchaeus episode: "For the Son of Man came to seek and to save the lost" (Luke 19:10). Luke does not have the "ransom" saying present in Mark and Matthew but has this reference to the Son of Man coming in order to carry out his earthly mission, thereby probably implying his preexistence. Most distinctive in Luke's presentation of the Son of Man material is the rather enigmatic cluster of references to the "day" or "days" of the Son of Man. The singular is more straightforward: "For the Son of Man in his day will be like the lightning, which flashes and lights up the sky from one end to the other" (17:24). Jesus is probably drawing attention simply to the moment of his future coming, "the day the Son of Man is revealed" as he puts it shortly afterward (17:30). Luke also uses the plural, however, indicating a future time of the Son of Man: "The time is coming when you will long to see one of the days of the Son of Man, but you will not see it" (17:22) and "Just as it was in the days of Noah, so also will it be in the days of the Son of Man" (17:26). The best explanation of this is that these sayings draw on a way of speaking about the future era of the Messiah. The idiom "the days of the Messiah" is common in rabbinic literature. One rabbinic commentary states the opinion that "Edom, Moab, and the chief of the children of Ammon are the three nations that were not given to them in this world, as it is said, 'For I will not give you of their land . . .' (Deut. 2:5). But *in the days of the Messiah* they shall once again belong to Israel, in order to fulfil God's promise" (Gen. Rab. 44:23, trans. Freedman and Simon). This way of speaking is also common in the Talmud.

Luke also has an instance of the "Son of Man" title in Acts, where Stephen as he is dying states, "Look, I see heaven open and the Son of Man standing at the right hand of God" (Acts 7:56). This is unusual both because it does not occur on the lips of Jesus, as almost all usages do, but also because the Son of Man is *standing* rather than sitting: Luke earlier said that "from now on, the Son of Man will be seated at the right hand of the mighty God" (Luke 22:69). The point here may be that the Son of Man, although exalted, is still active. Specifically in this context, the activity is receiving Stephen's spirit (Acts 7:59).

John's Gospel. A number of scholars have argued that John has an idea of the Son of Man fundamentally different from that of the Synoptics. This has been greatly exaggerated, and the Danielic framework for understanding the Son of Man in John remains. The "Son of Man" phrase is used of Jesus first as the ladder between heaven and earth (1:51) and next as the one who came from heaven (3:13). It is therefore extremely unlikely that the title is thought by John to emphasize Jesus's humanity. One argument sometimes made for this view is that John records the saying, "And he has *given him authority* to judge because he is the *Son of Man*" (5:27). The missing premise could be that Jesus has been a human being, endured temptation and yet did not sin (cf. Heb. 4:15), and therefore has the moral authority to judge. This is improbable, however, because the background to John 5:27 is much more likely to be Dan. 7, which states that the one *like a son of man was given authority* by the Ancient of Days.

Revelation. In two places in Revelation Jesus is described not as "the Son of Man" of the Gospels but with the phrase from Daniel. In the former, John sees among the lampstands "someone like a son of man" (Rev. 1:13). The echo of Dan. 7 in the following verse is surprising because Christ is described as having hair "white like wool" (1:14), which is an attribute of the Ancient of Days in Daniel's vision (Dan. 7:9). The focus of Revelation's use of Daniel is to depict the one like a son of man not as a representative of the people of God but as a victorious, divine figure. The vision goes on to talk of him as holding the seven stars (symbols for the angels of the seven churches) and the keys of death and Hades (1:13–18).

The second instance where Jesus is depicted in the language of Dan. 7 is in a similarly transcendent context: "I looked, and there before me was a white cloud, and seated on the cloud was one like a son of man with a crown of gold on his head and a sharp sickle in his hand" (Rev. 14:14). The passage describes him as on a cloud three times, evoking the clouds of Dan. 7. Jesus then swings his sickle over the earth to bring in the harvest. There is dispute among scholars over whether Jesus's harvesting in Rev. 14:14–16 is an image of the ingathering of the saints, a punishment of the wicked, or a general depiction of judgment encompassing both. It is very difficult to decide. On the one hand, the picture is very similar to what happens immediately afterwards, where the imagery is clearly punitive judgment (14:17–20). There are differences, however: while the angel in the latter passage harvests grapes whose juice turns out to be blood, Christ harvests grain that is elsewhere used positively; additionally, some earlier in the chapter are described as the "firstfruits" (14:4), which may point to a full grain harvest here. Furthermore, the main point at which the harvest scenes differ is the lack of explicit reference in the first scene to the trampling and the blood. Overall, however, it is perhaps more likely that both the action of Christ in 14:14–16 and that of the angel in 14:17–20 depict the same kind of judgment. What points in this direction is the dramatic imagery of Jesus wielding the sickle, which is probably a threatening image.

Conclusion

As noted in the discussions of Ps. 8 and Dan. 7, the original created order consisted of human beings—under God—ruling over creation and its birds of the air and beasts of the field. With the fall, there was a reversal, in which imperial "beasts" took charge—the bestial rulers of Dan. 7, and most especially the fourth beast, whose iron teeth oppressed the saints of the Most High. After the succession of monsters in his vision, Daniel saw "one like a son of man" (Dan. 7:13). The beasts were images both of kings and of the kingdoms they ruled (cf. 7:17, 23). In the same way, this "son of man" figure is a king, the individual person Jesus Christ, but he also represents the saints of the Most High, the people of God (cf. 7:13–14, 27). In fulfillment of the vision, the Son of Man came to the earth where these brutes had held sway. In his first advent, he came not to be served but to serve and pay the ransom price to rescue God's people by dying for their sins (Mark 10:45; Matt. 20:28). When that Son of Man, Jesus Christ, thereby defeated sin on the cross, the beastly empires were defeated (Dan. 7:26). He therefore restores the order of creation: the human figure once again rules over the beasts, as in Gen. 1–2. Indeed, this vindication is not just a restoration of the original created order but an escalation of it. In this new creation, the people of God are incorporated into Christ and thereby receive a share in his glorious dominion in the new Jerusalem, which, unlike the garden in Genesis, can never be disfigured by the rule of feral overlords or subject to the power of sin and death. Unlike in his first coming, after the Son of Man's return he will be served and "given authority, glory and sovereign power" over every nation (Dan. 7:14).

See also Adam, First and Last; Consummation; Kingdom and King; Messiah

Bibliography. Burkett, D., *The Son of Man Debate*, SNTSMS 107 (Cambridge University Press, 1999); Collins, J. J., "The Son of Man in First-Century Judaism," *NTS* 38 (1992): 448–66; Evans, C. A., "Jesus' Self-Designation 'The Son of Man' and the Recognition of his Divinity," in *The Trinity*, ed. S. T. Davis, D. Kendall, and G. O'Collins (Oxford University Press, 1999), 29–47; Freedman, H., and M. Simon, eds., *Midrash Rabbah* (Soncino, 1939); Gathercole, S., "The Son of Man in Mark's Gospel," *ExpTim* 115 (2004): 366–72; Hooker, M. D., *The Son of Man in Mark* (SPCK, 1967); Horbury, W., "The Messianic Associations of 'The Son of Man,'" *JTS* 36 (1985): 34–55; Hurtado, L. W., and P. L. Owens, eds., *"Who Is This Son of Man?"* (Bloomsbury, 2011); Kim, S., *The "Son of Man" as the Son of God* (Mohr Siebeck, 1983); Moule, C. F. D., "'The Son of Man': Some of the Facts," *NTS* 41 (1995): 277–79; Nickelsberg, G. W. E., and J. C. VanderKam, *1 Enoch: A New Translation* (Fortress, 2004); Reynolds, B. E., *The Apocalyptic Son of Man in the Gospel of John* (Mohr Siebeck, 2010); Reynolds, *The Son of Man Problem* (Bloomsbury, 2018).

SIMON GATHERCOLE

Sonship *See* Son of God

Stanley, Christopher D.

See Rhetoric

Talmud

See *Mishnah, Talmud, and Midrashim articles*

Targums: A Brief Introduction

The following three essays address the targums and their connection to the NT. This first essay provides an overview of the various surviving targums, as well as a comparison of targumic and rabbinic hermeneutics. In the second essay, the NT use of select OT passages is compared to their targumic interpretation. This comparison is preceded by a discussion regarding the dating of targumic and rabbinic traditions, as well as their relationship to the NT. The third essay offers a comparison of thematic parallels between the targums and the NT (e.g., the kingdom of God, eschatology).

Terminology

The word "targum" occurs in both Aramaic and later forms of Hebrew as a noun that means "translation." The quadriliteral verb *tirgēm* ("to translate") appears once within Scripture. Introducing the Aramaic portion of the book, Ezra 4:7 refers to a letter that had been "translated" (*məturgām*) in Aramaic. For the purposes of these targumic essays, the word "targum" will identify Jewish Aramaic translations of the OT that were produced during the rabbinic period. This is a common approach to targumic literature, the rationale for which has been nicely described by Paul Flesher and Bruce Chilton (7–8).

Historical Context—Synagogue as *Sitz im Leben*

Though they are a rabbinic corpus of translations, the targums stem from earlier traditions, which may reach as far back as Ezra and Nehemiah. The earliest reference to translating Scripture might be found in Neh. 8:8, which states, "They read from the book, from the Law of God, clearly [*məpōrāš*], and they gave the sense [*śôm śekel*], so that the people understood the reading" (ESV). Some commentators, both ancient and modern, believe this verse refers to translating the biblical text into a more familiar language—namely, Aramaic (cf. Le Déaut, 29–30; y. Meg. 4:1.9; b. Meg. 3a). Though it is not entirely clear if Neh. 8:8 provides a description of public translation, Martin McNamara's description of this "as the prototype of synagogue liturgy" is reasonable (*Testament*, 64).

In the NT, we see Jesus teaching in the synagogues, reading Scripture and interpreting its meaning (Matt. 13:53–58; Luke 4:14–30). Though the text does not provide the *ipsissima verba* of Jesus, translation into Aramaic is a possibility. In Acts, we see that the synagogue was a primary location for preaching the gospel and reasoning with both Jews and Greeks (Acts 14:1; 17:17; 18:4). Similar descriptions are found in both Josephus and Philo. According to Josephus, Moses established that the people should abandon their work and gather publicly to hear the reading of the Law so that they might "examine it closely with precision" (*Ag. Ap.* 2.175; unless otherwise indicated, all translations of ancient Jewish texts are my own). Philo describes the people at the weekly assembly sitting silently with all attention as they listen to instruction (*Spec. Laws* 2.61–62). Elsewhere, Philo writes that "a certain priest is present or one of the elders reads the holy laws to them and expounds [*exēgeomai*] them individually until about the late afternoon" (preserved in Eusebius, *Praep. ev.* 8.7.13).

From the Persian period until the era of the NT, in addition to the public reading of the Law, it was vitally important for its meaning to be discussed and clarified for the people. If the hearers had insufficient knowledge of Hebrew, it is difficult to imagine that translation did not occur in such a setting.

Rabbinic Testimony of the Targums

In rabbinic literature, not only do we find the same emphasis upon the reading and exposition of the Scripture but we also find ancient testimony regarding the translation of the Hebrew OT into Aramaic. From the perspective of the rabbis, the original Hebrew text took priority over its translation. The earliest picture we see of the public reading and translating of Scripture comes from the Mishnah. A call-and-response structure is described in m. Meg. 4:4, where the Torah is first read and then the meturgaman (translator) responds with its translation. According to the Talmud, the Hebrew would be read twice and the translation recited once (b. Ber. 8a). In m. Meg. 4:6 and t. Meg. 3:27 we learn that it is acceptable for a man with ragged clothing to translate but he is not allowed to "read in the Torah, pass before the ark, or raise his hands." Thus, stricter standards were set for the Hebrew original than for its Aramaic translation. Additionally, the passage goes on to state that it is acceptable for a blind man to translate publicly but, for obvious reasons, he would not be allowed to read from the scroll. This would suggest that translating was performed from memory or in an impromptu manner. The translator would listen to the Hebrew text being read aloud and then offer his translation.

Subsequent rabbinic law confirms the idea that translations were offered without the aid of a manuscript. In the Palestinian Talmud, Rabbi Samuel confronts a scribe who reaches for the targum as he reads from the scroll: "He said to him, 'That is forbidden to you! Words which were spoken by mouth [should, in turn, be spoken] by mouth and words said in writing [should, in turn, be said] in writing'" (y. Meg. 4:1.4). Thus, a written targum should not be used in conjunction with the Hebrew original. Instead, the Hebrew should be read and then the translation should be delivered orally (*bappeh*) and not in writing (*biktāb*). We see in this passage that targum manuscripts were, in fact, available to the meturgaman. Further evidence of written targums comes from the Babylonian Talmud, which occasionally cites known targums. For example, in b. Sanh. 106b, Rabbi Ashi makes the case that Doeg the Edomite (1 Sam. 22:9) was stricken with leprosy. Citing the phrase *laṣṣəmîtut* ("forever") from Lev. 25:30, he comments, "which we translate *laḥlûṭîn*" (making an etymological connection with *ʾaḥlaṭ* ["to sentence a leper"]). In any case, we see the Talmud quoting directly from Targum Jonathan to aid in the understanding of the Hebrew original. Additional examples of this may be found elsewhere (b. Naz. 39a; b. Git. 68b; and b. B. Qam. 116b). The Talmud even refers to "our translation" (*targûm dîdan*), which is to serve as a guide to navigate the pitfalls of translating (b. Qidd. 49a).

Types of Targums

Except for Ezra-Nehemiah and Daniel, there is at least one targum for every book of the OT. There are multiple targums for the Pentateuch and Esther. The various extant targums may be separated into groups based upon Aramaic dialect and nature of translation.

Targum Onqelos. There are three main types of pentateuchal targums—namely, Targum Onqelos, the Palestinian Targums, and Targum Pseudo-Jonathan. The oldest and most famous Aramaic translation is Targum Onqelos. Its dialect (and Targum Jonathan to the Prophets) is Jewish Literary Aramaic. The most popular theory for the targum's provenance is that it originated in Palestine during the second or third century AD and then developed further in Babylonia (see Flesher and Chilton, 151–66). An alternative perspective has been suggested by Edward Cook, who proposes a dialect geography for "Central Aramaic" dialects and places both Targum Onqelos and Targum Pseudo-Jonathan in this group, dating them to a period before AD 200. Targum Onqelos's dialect would then reflect only one geography instead of two (i.e., Palestinian and Babylonian). In any case, its dialect is unique in that it shares characteristics with Jewish Palestinian and Jewish Babylonian Aramaic.

As a translation, Targum Onqelos may be characterized as literal. Unlike the later Pentateuch targums, it rarely adds to the text. Instead, its translation corresponds evenly with the Hebrew. However, it should not be regarded as a wooden translation. Rather, it is consistent with early rabbinic attitudes toward translation. In the Tosefta, Rabbi Judah argues, "The one translating a verse literally [*kəṣûrātô*, according to its form], behold, this one is a liar; and the one adding to it, behold, this one is a blasphemer" (t. Meg. 3:41). A primary example of this dual concern would be the avoidance of anthropomorphisms. Wherever the MT reads that "the LORD appeared" or "the LORD came down," Targum Onqelos will read that "the Lord was revealed" (e.g., Gen. 12:7; 17:1; Exod. 19:20; Num. 16:9; and Deut. 31:15). As is normally the case in Targum Onqelos, the text is neither literally translated nor expanded.

The Palestinian Targums (Pentateuch). The Palestinian Targums cover the Pentateuch. They include Targum Neofiti, the Cairo Genizah Targum, and the Fragmentary Targums. Though they differ from each other to some degree, their agreement places them in the same family of manuscripts. Among the Palestinian Targums, Targum Neofiti is the most complete, even containing extensive marginal notations. It is missing only nineteen verses (Gen. 29:5; 35:10; 36:22–30, 41; 39:13; Exod. 12:26; 21:17; Lev. 26:42–44; Num. 32:18). The Cairo Genizah Targum is fragmentary due to its deterioration. Roughly speaking, one-sixth of the Pentateuch appears in the Cairo Genizah Targum (955 extant verses out of 5,853). The Fragmentary Targums are also incomplete, but this is by nature of their composition. They consist of *selections* more than fragments. Their five groups of manuscripts contain a portion of the Pentateuch similar in size to the Cairo Genizah Targum (1,050 verses).

The language of the Palestinian Targums is that of Jewish Palestinian Aramaic, a western dialect that is related to rabbinic literature from Palestine (cf., e.g., the Palestinian Talmud, Genesis Rabbah, Lamentations Rabbah, Pesiqta of Rab Kahana). In light of their dialect and rabbinic parallels, they are speculated to have originated in Palestine during the third or fourth century AD (McNamara, *Neofiti*, 1–46).

Similar to Targum Onqelos, the Palestinian Targums often follow the MT closely, replacing certain words or phrases for interpretative reasons. However, unlike Targum Onqelos, the Palestinian Targums will often expand the text. Take, for example, the expansion of Gen. 4:8 in Targum Neofiti. In this verse, the beginning and end of the MT is translated literally, but a large expansion is inserted in between, where Cain and then Abel speak at length, debating the justice of God.

MT	And Cain said to his brother Abel. And while they were in the field . . .
Tg. Onq.	And Cain said to his brother Abel. And while they were in the field . . .
Tg. Neof.	Then Cain said to Abel, "Come and let us go to the open field." And it came about when they had gone out into the open field that Cain answered and said to Abel, "I understand that the world was not created by mercy and is not conducted upon the fruit of good works and there is partiality in judgment . . ."

After Cain and Abel speak at length, debating the justice of God, the text returns to a literal translation of the MT, "and Cain arose against Abel his brother and killed him." The expansions of the Palestinian Targums occur consistently throughout the Pentateuch and vary in size. Using the Targums Wordmap module within Accordance Bible Software, we can determine that there are approximately 144,510 words in Targum Neofiti. Of these, 27,244 have no parallel equivalent in Targum Onqelos. Thus, roughly 19 percent of Targum Neofiti may be considered targumic expansions.

Targum Pseudo-Jonathan (Pentateuch). The dialect of Targum Pseudo-Jonathan is Late Jewish Literary Aramaic. This is a later dialect that borrows from previous dialects and is thought to be a literary dialect (see Kaufman). This dialect is related to the later eastern dialects of Jewish Babylonian Aramaic and Mandaic. The date for Targum Pseudo-Jonathan is a matter of debate. For linguistic reasons, scholars such as Stephen Kaufman and Edward Cook would date it to a period after the Islamic conquest. Scholars such as Avigdor Shinan and Moise Ohana make a similar argument in light of tradition history. Alternatively, scholars such as Paul Flesher would date it to a period before the Islamic conquest (for a survey of the issue, see Flesher and Chilton, 87–89). Flesher holds that the impetus for its creation was the intended rebuilding of the temple by Julian in AD 362 ("Literary Legacy"). Among the Pentateuch targums, Targum Pseudo-Jonathan is the most expansive.

The expansions of Targum Pseudo-Jonathan occur consistently throughout the Pentateuch and vary in size. Using the Targums Wordmap module within Accordance Bible Software, we can determine that there are approximately 160,617 words in Targum Pseudo-Jonathan. Of these, 40,664 have no parallel equivalent in Targum Onqelos. Thus, about 25 percent of Targum Pseudo-Jonathan may be considered targumic expansions.

Targum Jonathan (Former and Latter Prophets). The dialect of Targum Jonathan and the nature of its translation are very much the same as Targum Onqelos. Though similar in nature, the number of expansions within Targum Jonathan is greater than within Targum Onqelos. In particular, Hosea, Nahum, and Habakkuk have undergone significant expansions.

Targums of the Writings. The dialect of the Targums of the Writings and the nature of their translation are very much the same as Targum Pseudo-Jonathan (see Litke, 3–19). Regarding expansions, with the exception of Targum Chronicles, all of these targums are *more* expansive than Targum Pseudo-Jonathan. Most notably, Targum Songs of Songs and the Second Targum of Esther expand the biblical text by factors of four and five, respectively.

Rabbinic Hermeneutics and the Targums

Targumic hermeneutics are fundamentally rabbinic hermeneutics. The two main sources of influence for the targums are the MT and the Beth Midrash (i.e., the house of study). When the targums depart from the MT, the paraphrases and expansions offered consistently correspond with rabbinic interpretation. There are, however, occasional nonrabbinic elements within the targums. Some of these are unique to the targums, like the concept of Memra (see "Memra and Logos" in the article "Targums: Thematic Parallels to the NT" elsewhere in the dictionary), while others appear in later Jewish folklore (see Shinan, "Aggadah"). Some nonrabbinic elements are related to non-Jewish traditions, such as a reference to Adisha and Fatima in Tg. Ps.-J. Gen. 21:21 or the appearance of an "antichrist" named "Armilus" in Tg. Ps.-J. Deut. 34:3 (see Everson, "Comparison," 87–89). Despite such elements, the hermeneutics of the targums are consistently related to rabbinic hermeneutics. Consequently, what follows here is a survey of targumic hermeneutics reflected in rabbinic literature as well as rabbinic hermeneutics reflected in the targums.

Targumic hermeneutics reflected in rabbinic literature. A number of introductions classify the general techniques or characteristics of the targums. The following categories are gleaned from three such arrangements (Alexander, 226–29; Flesher and Chilton, 38–53; McNamara, *Testament*, 101–19).

Adherence to the biblical text. The basic hermeneutic of the targums is to accompany the original text and to clarify its meaning. Whereas the other ancient versions (e.g., the LXX, the Vulgate, and the Peshitta) seek to replace the MT, the targums seek to accompany it. Because of this fact, they are less free to deviate from the original text. For Targum Onqelos and Targum Jonathan, this means regularly corresponding to the Hebrew. When a paraphrase is introduced, it evenly replaces the antecedent, creating an elegant counterpart to the Hebrew. For the later targums, such as the Palestinian Targums or Targum Pseudo-Jonathan, the expansions do not confuse or distract the reader/listener from the original. Generally speaking, it is clear when a targum breaks from the original text and when it returns. Thus, it is a simple matter to distinguish the expansion from the translation.

As discussed above, the priority of the Hebrew text is evident in rabbinic attitudes toward the public reading and translating of Scripture. The importance of the text is further expressed through the rabbis' stated affection for the Torah. In the Mishnah, Ben Bag-Bag famously regards the Torah in this way: "Turn it over and turn it over again, for everything is in it. Look into it. Grow old and gray in it. Do not turn from it for you can have no better rule than it" (m. Avot 5:22). The Mishnah goes on to say that the Torah is greater than the priesthood or the kingship (m. Avot 6:6). According to the Talmud, the study of Torah (*talmûd tôrâ*) is greater than saving a life, building the temple, or honoring your father and mother (b. Meg. 16b).

Multiple senses. The targums often take advantage of a word's semantic range, translating one Hebrew word with more than one Aramaic word. For example, the rabbis often understood the Hebrew word *ʿqb* as "heel" (*ʿāqēb*), but at other times they understood it as "end" (*ʿēqeb*). Within rabbinic literature, the *ʿēqeb* in Gen. 3:15 refers not only to this world but also to the eschatological world to come. Accordingly, Targum Neofiti and Targum Pseudo-Jonathan translate this noun twice: first, with reference to the snake biting the heel, and second, with reference to "the end, in the days of the King Messiah." This draws together the eschatological ideas of the ancient serpent and the coming Messiah. The serpent of the garden being judged in the messianic age to come also appears in Gen. Rab. 20:5, which reads, "In the [messianic] future to come, all things will be healed except for the serpent and the Gibeonite." The rabbinic association of *ʿāqēb* with the Messiah has its origin in Ps. 89:52, which refers to the footsteps (*ʿiqqəbôt*) of the Lord's anointed. This passage is used by the rabbis to understand the coming messianic age (b. Sanh. 97a; Song Rab. 2:33; and Pesiq. Rab. 15.39).

Converse translation. Occasionally, the targums will reverse the meaning of the original text in its translation. In Num. 12:1, though the text states that Moses married a Cushite woman, both the targums and the rabbis seek to assert that he did not. Targum Onqelos removes "Cushite woman" from the text and replaces it with "beautiful woman." Roger Le Déaut has suggested that this was accomplished through a gematria of the name Zipporah and the phrase "beautiful of appearance" (*yəpat-marʾeh*; see McNamara, *Testament*, 105–6). Targum Neofiti goes a step further and adds, "Just as the Cushite is distinct from all creatures so was Zipporah, the wife of Moses, lovely in form and pleasing in appearance." A similar interpretation can be found in b. Mo'ed Qat. 16b and Pirqe R. El. 53.5. However, in their interpretation, Zipporah is distinguished by her words and good deeds.

Treatment of anthropomorphisms. The rabbis and the targums alike were uncomfortable with anthropomorphic portrayals of God. Physical language for God is often interpreted or translated with less anthropomorphic language. For example, the Hebrew phrase "in the eyes of the LORD" is almost always translated as "before the LORD" (e.g., Gen. 6:8; 38:7; Lev. 10:19; Num. 32:13; Deut. 4:25; Judg. 2:11; 1 Sam. 12:17; 1 Kings 11:6; Isa. 49:5; Jer. 52:2; Mal. 2:17). Likewise, the targums often avoid a literal translation of "the hand of the LORD." Instead, translations read "plague" (Exod. 9:3; Deut. 2:15; Judg. 2:15; 1 Sam. 5:6), "power" (Josh. 4:24; Isa. 19:16; 25:10), "hand of the Memra [word] of the Lord" (Josh. 22:31), or "spirit of prophecy" (Ezek. 1:3; 8:1). "The mouth of the LORD" is rendered by "the Memra [word] from before the Lord" (Deut. 8:3; Isa. 1:20; 40:5; Jer. 23:16; Mic. 4:4).

The targums also avoid making God the direct object or subject of certain actions. For example, in Gen. 1, Targum Neofiti often translates the phrase "God saw" with "it was revealed before the Lord" (Gen. 1:4, 10, 18, 25). Targum Onqelos also does this in Gen. 31:42 and Exod. 2:25, as does Targum Jonathan in 2 Kings 14:26 and Isa. 59:15. Similarly, "God heard" or "the LORD heard" is usually rendered with the passive, "it was heard before" God or the Lord (Gen. 21:17; Exod. 2:24; Num. 11:1; 12:2; Deut. 1:34; 5:28; 2 Kings 19:4; Ps. 34:6; 78:21, 59). According to Targum Chronicles, the Lord did not "hear" Hezekiah's prayer; rather, "he received the prayer of Hezekiah" (2 Chron. 30:20).

An interesting anti-anthropomorphism is found in the story of Jacob's ladder. In the MT of Gen. 32:31 (ET 32:30), Jacob names the place "Peniel," because he has seen God face to face. Targum Onqelos, however, reads, "I have seen the angel of the Lord face to face." Though the angelic identity of Jacob's opponent is commonly asserted within rabbinic literature (Gen. Rab. 78:2; Lam. Rab. 3:8; Song Rab. 3:9), this verse and the place name "Peniel" are essentially ignored within the rabbinic corpus (see Hyman and Hyman, 1:64). The widespread rabbinic boycott, as it were, of this passage and place name is a good indication of the rigorous resistance to or avoidance of the anthropomorphic portrayal of God.

Another interesting example is found in Exod. 25:8. The MT reads, "Let them build for me a sanctuary so that I might dwell among them." Making use of the Hebrew verb for "dwell" (*šākan*), Targum Onqelos and Targum Pseudo-Jonathan read, "so that my shekinah might dwell among you" (Targum Neofiti has "the glory of my shekinah"). The same exposition of this verse appears in Gen. Rab. 3.9.

Targumic doublets. In the targums, a single word in the MT is often translated with two words. This targumic hermeneutic usually stems from the biblical text itself. Take, for example, the phrase "sojourner and foreigner," which appears in the MT of Gen. 23:4; Lev. 25:23, 35, 47. This phrase or a variation of it appears as a doublet translation of "sojourner" in the Palestinian Targums of Gen. 15:13 and Exod. 2:22, and in Tg. Ps.-J. Exod. 18:3 (cf. Gen. Rab. 58:6). The Aramaic doublet "thanks and praise" is used to translate the Hebrew "worship" on a number of occasions in Targum Neofiti (Gen. 24:26, 52; 47:31; Exod. 34:8). The phrase itself appears to come from Dan. 2:23. The targumic doublet "grace and loving kindness" appears nearly twenty times as a translation for the Hebrew word "grace" in the Palestinian Targums (e.g., Gen. 6:8; 18:3; 33:8; 39:4; Exod. 33:12; 34:9; Num. 11:11; Deut. 24:1). This doublet has its origin in Esther 2:17. In the case of doublets, we see the influence of the MT upon the targums. Even though these doublet phrases may also be found within rabbinic literature, they originate from the biblical text itself.

Respect for the elders of Israel. The moral shortcomings of biblical figures could generate rabbinic interpretations seeking to mitigate unbecoming portrayals. The story of Judah and Tamar is one such example. According to the Palestinian Targums of Gen. 38:25, Tamar was unable to find the witnesses needed to confront Judah. Two Cairo Genizah Targum fragments explain that Sammael (a rabbinic alias for Satan) had hidden them. In her distress, Tamar prays for help, declaring that she will establish for God three righteous descendants (i.e., Hananiah, Mishael, and Azariah). This results in an angel being dispatched to help Tamar acquire the witnesses. Presenting the witnesses, she willingly faces execution but refuses to identify Judah as the father. Furthermore, Judah becomes morally convicted, confesses his guilt, and readies himself for execution. Just then a *bat qôl* (i.e., a heavenly voice) is sent to declare their innocence. In b. Sotah 10b, the Talmud offers a similar interpretation. However, in its version, Judah's hypocrisy remains secret and, thus, he is portrayed as magnanimous in sparing Tamar, such that God promises to spare his descendants from the flames as well (i.e., Hananiah, Mishael, and Azariah).

A second example of respecting the elders of Israel is found in the episode of the golden calf. For the rabbis, it was difficult to explain why the Israelites would abandon God for an idol so soon after leaving Egypt. According to Targum Pseudo-Jonathan, it is the work of Satan. Thus, Tg. Ps.-J. Exod. 32:1 reads, "Then Satan went and made them stray, and their heart returned to pride." Then, at 32:19 we read, "When Moses came near to the camp, he saw the calf and the musical instruments in the hands of the wicked ones, dancing and bowing before it. And Satan was within it, leaping and jumping before the people." Even though a number of rabbinic sources portray Satan as the instigator of Exod. 32:1 (Exod. Rab. 41:7; Tanh. [Buber], Ki Tissa 13; and b. Shabb. 89a), it is only in later rabbinic literature or even Islamic folklore that we find Satan possessing the golden calf (Pirqe R. El. 45; Shelah, Toledot Adam 34; and the Islamic tale of al-Sāmirī; see Everson, "Angels," 318–21). In this way, Israel is portrayed in a more flattering light, for their sin was prompted by Satan himself.

A third example of respecting the elders of Israel may be found in the treatment of Leah. In Gen. Rab. 70:16, Rabbi Johanan states that Leah's weak eyes are a sign of her piety, not a physical disability. "She would weep and say [to God], 'May it be your will that I would not fall to the lot of a wicked man.'" A similar interpretation is offered in Tg. Neof. Gen. 29:17, which reads, "The eyes of Leah were lifted up in prayer seeking to marry Jacob, the righteous." The Fragmentary Targums and a marginal note in Targum Neofiti add that Leah's eyes are "weak" from weeping and praying. This same language is used in Gen. Rab. 70:16.

Derogatory translation. Just as the targums seek to portray the elders of Israel in a flattering light, they also seek to portray the opponents of Israel in an unflattering light. This can be seen in the phrase "Balaam the wicked" (Tg. Ps.-J. Num. 22:30; 23:10, 21; 24:25; also in the Palestinian Targums). This title is also used in rabbinic literature (Exod. Rab. 20:5; Deut. Rab. 3:4; b. Ta'an. 20a; b. Sanh. 105b). Other examples include "Jeroboam the wicked" (Tg. Ruth 4:20; Tanh., Ki Teitzei 4.1), "Vespasian the wicked" (Tg. Lam. 1:19), and "Nebuchadnezzar the wicked" (Tg. Lam. 5:5; Exod. Rab. 30:1; b. Pesah. 117a).

Resolving difficulties. If there is something unexplained within the MT (or perceived to be so), the targums may seek an interpretative solution. One such difficulty occurs in the story of Jacob's dream at Bethel. Because the MT of Gen. 28:11 states that "Jacob took from the stones" in acquiring his pillow, the rabbis felt that multiple stones were used. However, in Gen. 28:18, it is clear that, by morning, there is only *one* stone under his head. The solution is found in Gen. 28:10 of the Palestinian Targums and Targum Pseudo-Jonathan. Accordingly, "when he arose in the morning, he found all of them as one stone" (Targum Neofiti). The targums identify this as one of the five miracles that were performed for Jacob (cf. Gen. Rab. 68:11; Tanh., Wayeitzei 1; b. Hul. 91b).

Another textual difficulty is found in Exod. 26:28, which describes the middle bar of the tabernacle as thirty cubits in length. Where would the Israelites have acquired such a long piece of wood? According to Targum Pseudo-Jonathan, it was taken from the tamarisk tree that Abraham had planted in Beersheba (Gen. 21:33). The targum adds two extraordinary facts concerning this bar. First, when Israel was crossing the Red Sea, angels felled the tree, threw it upon the sea, and announced its significance so that the Israelites might acquire it. Second, while the tabernacle was disassembled, it was straight and seventy cubits in length (i.e., forty cubits longer than the tabernacle itself). However, whenever the tabernacle would be assembled, the bar would miraculously wind around the various other planks of the tabernacle so as to fit within the tabernacle.

Within rabbinic literature, these last two extraordinary features of the bar are unique to Targum Pseudo-Jonathan (see Shinan, *Embroidered*, 263n102). In comparison, Gen. Rab. 94:4; Song. Rab. 1:56; and Yal. Shimoni, Nach 983.14 all assert that the middle bar of the tabernacle had been taken from the tree that Abraham had planted in Beersheba. However, using Gen. 46:1 as a proof text, these state that Jacob had cut down the tree that Abraham planted. This wood, along with other wood used in the tabernacle, was carried into Egypt and brought out during the exodus. Regarding the miraculously winding middle bar, Num. Rab. 18:14 expresses a contrary opinion to that of Targum Pseudo-Jonathan by comparing the bar to Moses and Aaron, who are like iron. That is, the center bar stretches from one end to the other and does not move. Another opinion is found in Zohar 2.233b, where, as part of the holy chariot, the boards of the tabernacle arrange themselves in their proper order. Thus, it appears that Targum Pseudo-Jonathan has built upon a midrashic tradition, adding to it the intervention of angels and miraculous timber.

Rabbinic hermeneutics reflected in the targums. The rabbis were thoughtful and diligent interpreters of the Bible. The method and content of their interpretation developed over the course of hundreds of years. They would often discuss and debate correct and incorrect methods of interpreting Scripture. At various times, the approved methods were collected into lists. The first and most famous of these is attributed to Hillel the Elder, the central ancestor of Rabbinic Judaism (1st c. BC). The seven rules of Hillel are first mentioned in t. Sanh. 7:11. The second set of rules is attributed to Rabbi Ishmael, who was central to Tannaitic Judaism (2nd c. AD). The thirteen middot of Ishmael are first mentioned in the Baraita of Rabbi Ishmael. With the inclusion of one additional rule, these are essentially an expansion of Hillel's seven rules. It should be noted that these first two lists appear early in the rabbinic corpus. A later list of thirty-two middot, attributed to Eliezer ben Yose Hagelili, is included in the Midrash Hagadol. Speculated dates for this list range from the third to the eighth century AD (see Strack and Stemberger, 22–30). These rules are never cited within the targums themselves. The targums are focused upon providing the meaning of the text, not upon the means of acquiring that meaning. However, the rabbinic interpretations that are based upon these hermeneutical rules are often reflected within the targums.

Qal wahomer (*a minori ad maius*). The rabbinic hermeneutic of *qal wahomer*, or "from the lesser to the greater," is the first on Hillel and Ishmael's lists and appears frequently within rabbinic literature. In Num. 5:11–32, we read of a jealousy ritual that was to be conducted concerning marital infidelity. In v. 22, the woman is to reply, "Amen, amen." For the rabbis, nothing within the text is superfluous, which means that repeated words require separate interpretations. Thus, Num. Rab. 9:35 offers a separate interpretation for each amen, stating that "these are matters of *qal wahomer*." Targum Neofiti and the Fragmentary Targums do likewise, expanding the verse with, "Amen that I have not been defiled. Amen that I will not be defiled." Targum Pseudo-Jonathan expands the text further with "Amen, I have not been defiled while betrothed. Amen, I have not been defiled when married." Some maintain that Jesus makes use of this hermeneutic in his exposition in Matt. 6:30 (see Notley and García, 352).

Gezerah shawah (equal ordinance). The second of Hillel and Ishmael's rules, *gezerah shawah*, may be employed when the Torah makes use of an identical word or phrase. Thus, the meaning of one passage may be applied to another if the expressions are identical. According to b. Sanh. 54a, the unknown method of punishment in Lev. 20:11 is supplied by v. 27 through the rule of *gezerah shawah*. Since both passages contain the phrase "their blood is upon them," the execution by stoning is supplied to Lev. 20:11. Targum Onqelos renders "their blood is upon them" with "they are liable for execution." Making use of both Targum Onqelos and the *gezerah shawah*, Targum Pseudo-Jonathan reads, "They are liable for execution by the throwing of stones." Some maintain that Jesus makes use of this rule in his exposition of Isaiah in Luke 4:18–19 (see Notley and García, 355–56).

Kelal uferat (the general and the particular). This is the fifth of Hillel's rules and is divided into rules 4–11 within Ishmael's list. According to this rule, something from the general may be added to the particular. In the Mekilta, there is a debate regarding the gender of the firstborn who must be consecrated to God (Pischa 16). Citing this rule, the Mekilta uses Exod. 13:2 as the general statement (*kəlāl*), which does not specify gender, and 34:19 as the specific statement (*pərāṭ*), which does. As a result, those consecrated would include firstborn males. With the insertion of the phrase "of the males," Targum Pseudo-Jonathan reflects this interpretation.

Ribbui (increase or inclusion). This is the first of Eliezer's thirty-two middot. The rule of *ribbui* allows the reader to expand meaning wherever the Hebrew original uses *ʾap, gam*, or *ʾēt* (Strack and Stemberger, 23). In b. Arakh. 7a, the rabbis are debating if there should be a stay of execution for a pregnant mother in Deut. 22:22, so that the child might be delivered. Applying this rule, Rabbi Abbuha maintains that the judgment should "include the child." He infers this from the use of *gam* in Deut. 22:22. In translating this verse, Targum Pseudo-Jonathan inserts the following expansion: "and even if she is pregnant, you should not delay until she should give birth but, in that hour, you should execute them."

A sentence supplemented from its parallel. This rule is the twenty-second of Eliezer's thirty-two middot. It allows the interpreter to supplement meaning from a parallel. Exodus 23:1 reads, "You shall not join hands with a wicked man to be a malicious witness" (ESV). Employing this rule, Rabbi Nathan translates, "Set not thy hand: do not let the wicked testify, do not let the malicious testify" (Mek. R. Ishmael, Kaspa 2.49). A similar interpretation is offered in Tg. Ps.-J. Exod. 23:1, which reads, "Do not receive the false words from a man who slanders his neighbor before you and do not set your hand with the wicked that he should become a false witness."

Gematria. This rule is the twenty-ninth of Eliezer's thirty-two middot. Gematria is a method of interpreting the biblical text based upon the numerical values of letters. Accordingly, *aleph* = 1, *bet* = 2, *gimel* = 3, and so on. An example of this may be found in the interpretation of Gen. 14:14, where Abraham's servants are said to have numbered 318. In the Pesiqta of Rab Kahana, Rabbi Shimon ben Laqish comments that Abraham brought forth just one man with him—namely, Eliezer, because "in the name of Eliezer is three hundred eighteen" (i.e., *aleph* = 1, *lamed* = 30, *yod* = 10, *ayin* = 70, *zayin* = 7, *resh* = 200; Pesiq. Rab Kah. 8.2). This interpretation appears in both Targum Pseudo-Jonathan and the marginalia of Targum Neofiti. Interestingly, a Christian gematria of this number also appears in Barn. 9:8, where 10 (I) + 8 (H) = IH (Jesus) and 300 (T) = the cross. There is also reverse gematria that occurs within rabbinic interpretation called the *atbash*, where values are assigned in reverse order—namely, *tav* = 1, *shin* = 2, *resh* = 3, and so on (cf. Song Rab. 3:6).

If the MT of Jer. 25:26 is accurate, this method of interpretation goes back to the prophet Jeremiah himself. The end of that verse reads, "The king of Sheshach shall drink after them" (NASB). Among the ancient versions, only Targum Jeremiah translates "King of Sheshach" as "King of Babylon." Within rabbinic literature, this interpretation may be found in Tanh., Qorah 12.2, which states, "Sheshach in gematria is Babylon."

Notarikon (division of a word into two or more). This is the thirtieth rule of Eliezer's thirty-two middot, which allows the interpreter to divide one word into two or more meanings. An example of this may be found in Gen. Rab. 90:4, which comments upon the name that Pharaoh gave to Joseph in Gen. 41:45. Accordingly, the name Zaphenath-paneah is interpreted to mean, "the hidden things [*ṣəpûnôt*] are revealed [*môpîaʿ*] and they are easy [*nôḥôt*] to speak." All of the extant targums (including the targum on Genesis from the Cairo Genizah Targum) translate this name as "the man to whom hidden things are revealed." Targum Onqelos alone includes both the original name and the translation.

Regarding and disregarding mishnaic law. Within the Mishnah, the tractate Megillah discusses rules concerning the reading of Esther at Purim and the reading of Scripture in general. Several biblical passages are prohibited for public reading and/or translation. Sometimes, the targums disregard these prohibitions. For example, m. Meg. 4:10 forbids translating the second reading-portion of the golden calf (Exod. 32:21–24). This is translated by Targum Onqelos, Targum Neofiti, and Targum Pseudo-Jonathan. A similar disregard for the Mishnah occurs regarding the story of David and Amnon in Tg. Jon. 2 Sam. 13 (cf. m. Meg. 4:10).

There are two instances where Targum Onqelos and Targum Neofiti respect the mishnaic ruling but Targum Pseudo-Jonathan does not. First, m. Meg. 4:9 forbids the translating of Lev. 18:21 so that reference is made to sexual intercourse. Anyone who would do so should be "silenced with rebuke." This prohibition is preserved and discussed in both Talmuds (b. Meg. 25a; y. Meg. 4:10.7). Targum Onqelos and Targum Neofiti both abide by the mishnaic ruling. Targum Pseudo-Jonathan, however, disregards the ruling with its translation: "You should not give of your seed in copulation to a daughter of the nations." Second, m. Meg. 4:10 forbids the reading or translating of the priestly benediction (Num. 6:24–26). Abiding by the ruling, Targum Onqelos and Targum Neofiti offer no translation. Instead, these targums simply reproduce the Hebrew. Targum Pseudo-Jonathan, on the other hand, translates and expands the text to include protection from various types of demons, a blessing for Torah study, and a blessing for prosperity.

Conclusion

The targums are an integral part of an extensive and enduring rabbinic tradition. They served the important role of facilitating the public communication of Scripture along with its interpretation. The rabbinic approach of the targums is sometimes creative, sometimes surprising, but always carefully examined. Theologically, they are primarily concerned with preserving the dignity of Israel's God and his Torah. They are also concerned with preserving the dignity of Israel's elders and displaying the disgrace of her enemies.

See also OT Use of the OT: Comparison with the NT Use of the OT; *other Targums articles; Dead Sea Scrolls articles; Mishnah, Talmud, and Midrashim articles; Philo articles; Septuagint articles*

Bibliography. Alexander, P. S., "Jewish Aramaic Translations of Hebrew Scriptures," in *Mikra,* ed. M. J. Mulder, CRINT 2/1 (Fortress, 1988), 225–28; Cook, E. M., "A New Perspective on the Language of Onqelos and Jonathan," in *The Aramaic Bible,* ed. D. R. G. Beattie and M. J. McNamara, JSOTSup 166 (JSOT Press, 1994), 142–56; Everson, D. L., "Angels in the Targums" (PhD diss., Hebrew Union College, 2009); Everson, "A Brief Comparison of Targumic and Midrashic Angelological Traditions," *AS* 5 (2007): 75–91; Flesher, P. V. M., "The Literary Legacy of the Priests?," in *The Ancient Synagogue from Its Origins until 200 CE,* ed. B. Olsson and M. Zetterholm (Almqvist & Wiksell, 2003), 467–508; Flesher, P. V. M., and B. Chilton, *The Targums,* SAIS 12 (Brill, 2011); Hyman, A., and A. B. Hyman, *Torah Hakethubah Vehamessurah,* 3 vols., 2nd ed. (Dvir, 1998 [Hebrew]); Kaufman, S. A., "Targum Pseudo-Jonathan and Late Jewish Literary Aramaic," *AS* 11 (2013): 1–26; Le Déaut, R., *Introduction à la littérature targumique* (Biblical Institute Press, 1966); Litke, A. W., *Targum Song of Songs and Late Jewish Literary Aramaic,* SAIS 15 (Brill, 2019); McNamara, M., *Targum and Testament Revisited,* 2nd ed. (Eerdmans, 2010); McNamara, *Targum Neofiti 1: Genesis,* ArBib 1A (Liturgical Press, 1992); Notley, R. S., and J. P. García, "Hebrew-Only Exegesis," in *The Language Environment of First Century Judaea,* ed. R. Buth and R. S. Notley, JCPS 26 (Brill, 2014), 349–74; Ohana, M., "La polémique judéo islamique et l'image d'Ismaël dans Targum Pseudo-Jonathan et dans Pirke de Rabbi Eliezer," *Augustinianum* 15, no. 3 (1975): 367–87; Shinan, A., "The Aggadah of the Palestinian Targums of the Pentateuch and Rabbinic Aggadah," in *The Aramaic Bible,* ed. D. R. G. Beattie and M. J. McNamara, JSOTSup 166 (JSOT Press, 1994), 203–17; Shinan, *The Embroidered Targum* (Magnes, 1992 [Hebrew]); Strack, H. L., and G. Stemberger, *Introduction to the Talmud and Midrash,* trans. M. Bockmuehl (T&T Clark, 1991).

DAVID EVERSON

Targums: Comparison with the NT Use of the OT

The targums and the NT have much in common regarding the interpretation of the OT. In this essay, I compare the respective hermeneutics of a number of OT passages in the targums and the NT.

Past and Present Perspectives on the Targums and NT

The dating of rabbinic and targumic traditions is a thorny issue. Regarding rabbinic literature, there was once great interest and confidence in its relevance to early Christian thought. Rabbinic traditions, which the Mishnah or Talmud assigned to a period prior to or contemporary to Christ, were comfortably understood as such. There was little skepticism in this regard. A primary example of this would be Hermann Strack and Paul Billerbeck's *Kommentar zum Neuen Testament aus Talmud und Midrasch,* whose publication spans from 1922 to 1961. This approach faded, however, with the scholarship of Jacob Neusner. Showing the inconsistencies of attested traditions and disallowing material that cannot be distinguished as early, Neusner questioned whether the rabbinic literature provides much useful information for early Christianity. The popularity of this new approach, coupled with scholars' general unfamiliarity with the rabbinic corpus, has led many to avoid rabbinic literature altogether.

A similar development can be seen within targumic scholarship. In the middle of the twentieth century, Paul Kahle (208) held that the Palestinian Targums contain "material coming from pre-Christian times which must be studied by everyone who wishes to understand the state of Judaism at the time of the birth of Christianity." Likewise, though he concedes to later accretions within the text, Martin McNamara maintains that most of the material within the Palestinian Targums may be assigned to "an early, even pre-Christian, date" (McNamara, *Palestinian,* 35). During this period, much of targumic scholarship was devoted to the intersection of the targums and Christianity. However, in the following decades, these positions were confronted by Anthony York, Preben Wernberg-Møller, and others, with the result that the enterprise of comparing the NT and the targums became suspect. According to Paul Flesher and Bruce Chilton, this was an unfortunate development, "for even though the similarities between the two documents do not indicate historical dependence between written texts, there is no denying that there are literary, interpretive, and thematic parallels between them" (385).

Despite the reluctance of many to explore the intersection of the NT and rabbinic/targumic traditions, numerous scholars have persisted in doing so. Regarding rabbinic literature, a broader and more cautious approach has been adopted by Craig Keener (among others). With the hope of creating a "broader range of uncertain but possible data," Keener (194) concludes, "Neusner's claim, 'What we cannot show, we do not know,' works with a minimalist objective; for our objective, the better principle is, 'Some evidence is better than no evidence,' even if some evidence is less than certain." Regarding targumic literature, a similar perspective is held by Craig Evans. He writes, "Whereas much, even most, of the Messianic tradition in the Targums derives from times after the New Testament, a fair portion of it reflects interpretative traditions and ways of speaking from the first century and even earlier. Bruce Chilton's work on the Isaiah Targum has shown how at many points Jesus' utterances, as well as his general concept of the kingdom of God, cohere with targumic language and themes. Jesus research cannot, therefore, neglect the Targums" (181). Or, as McNamara puts it,

"It becomes obvious that [the targums'] greatest use for the student of the NT lies in their provision, not of antecedents, but analogies" ("Targum," 395).

It is beyond the scope of the current article to evaluate the direction or degree of influence between rabbinic/targumic traditions and the NT. To that end, the reader may consult the perspectives of McNamara; Keener; Günter Stemberger; and Flesher and Chilton (389–404). Instead, by isolating similar passages and concepts in the targums and NT, I hope to compare and contrast interpretative use.

Interpretive Comparison of Selected Passages

The Golden Rule: Matthew and Targum Pseudo-Jonathan. In Matt. 5:43–44, Jesus comments upon Lev. 19:18, saying, "You have heard that it was said, 'You shall love your neighbor and hate your enemy.' But I say to you, Love your enemies and pray for those who persecute you" (ESV). Later in the sermon Jesus teaches his disciples the Golden Rule: "So whatever you wish that others would do to you, do also to them, for this is the Law and the Prophets" (Matt. 7:12 ESV). Targum Pseudo-Jonathan offers a similar interpretation of Lev. 19:18. The targum reads, "Do not be ones who take revenge or ones who hold enmity against the sons of your people but love your neighbor. *That which is hateful to you [ʾant], do not do to him.* I am the Lord" (the expanded text is italicized; unless otherwise indicated, all translations of ancient Jewish texts are my own). Targum Pseudo-Jonathan's interpretation is similar to the command given by Jesus but is reversed. Prompted by the command of Moses to love one's neighbor, it broadens the command to include treating others the way one would like to be treated. Commenting on Luke's version of this command, Flesher and Chilton write, "Luke shows that the stock of proverbial wisdom Jesus drew on goes back to the first century, while Pseudo-Jonathan shows that it continued to be reused until the date of its composition. The targumic echo is therefore most certainly not the immediate source of Jesus' statement, but it may help us to understand the nature and general character of Jesus' statement within Judaism" (Flesher and Chilton, 387).

In addition to relying on a first-century stock of proverbial wisdom, Targum Pseudo-Jonathan possibly relies upon a later talmudic tradition, which may be found in b. Shabb. 31a: "A certain heathen came before Shammai. He said to him, 'Proselytize me on the condition that you teach me the entirety of the Torah, while I am standing on one foot.' [Shammai] chased him away with the builder's cubit that was in his hand. [When] he came before Hillel, he converted him. [Hillel] said to him, 'That which is hateful to you, do not do to another. This is the entirety of Torah and the other is its interpretation. Go, study.'" Notice that the language of Targum Pseudo-Jonathan closely parallels that of the Talmud. Linguistically speaking, the second-person pronoun used by Targum Pseudo-Jonathan (i.e., "you," *ʾant*) is a geminate form, a feature of Jewish Babylonian Aramaic and Mandaic (see Cook, 127–29). It is also interesting to note the similarity between Hillel and Jesus. In addition to his own version of the Golden Rule (reversed in form), Hillel asserts that this rule is "the entirety of the Torah," a statement that is reminiscent of Jesus's words in Matt. 7:12: "For this is the Law and the Prophets" (ESV).

Creation and the Son: John and Targum Neofiti. In Targum Neofiti, the text of Gen. 1:1 reads, *milqadmîn bəḥokmâ bərāʾ da-yyy šaklēl yāt šəmayāʾ wəyāt ʾarʿāʾ*, which may be translated, "From the beginning, with wisdom, the Son of Yahweh completed the heavens and the earth." This is how the text appears in the *editio princeps* and how it was first translated (Macho, 3:497). The Hebrew/Aramaic word *brʾ* is usually translated "created." However, in Targum Neofiti, it is followed by the relative particle *dalet*, which would indicate that *bərāʾ* is from the noun *bar* (i.e., "the son") and is further described by *da-yyy* (i.e., of Yahweh / the Lord). The construction *bərāʾ d-* appears elsewhere in Targum Neofiti to indicate "the son of . . ." (e.g., Gen. 36:10; Exod. 23:12; Deut. 21:16). Though a manuscript erasure is visible before the verb *šaklēl*, the phrase *bərāʾ da-yyy* is clearly original to the manuscript (see https://digi.vatlib.it/). Many targumic scholars feel the text should read *bərāʾ yyy wəšaklēl* ("Yahweh created and completed"; see McNamara, *Neofiti*, 52n1).

The idea that the world was created through wisdom first appears in the OT. Twice, the prophet Jeremiah declares that the Lord "established the world by his wisdom" (Jer. 10:12; 51:15 ESV). Likewise, in Prov. 8:22–31, wisdom is described as the "craftsman" (*ʾāmôn*) who established the heavens, marked out the foundations of the earth, and was with God in the beginning (*rēʾšît*). Proverbs 3:19 states that the Lord founded the earth in wisdom. In Ps. 104:24 we read, "O LORD, how manifold are your works! In wisdom have you made them all; the earth is full of your creatures" (ESV).

Early on in the rabbinic corpus, we see the wisdom of Prov. 8:22 (who was with God in the beginning) identified as the Torah. Using this verse, the Mishnah and the Mekilta identify the Torah as one of five possessions that the Holy One set aside for himself (m. Avot 6:10; Mek. R. Ishmael, Shirata 9.123). In Sifre Deut. 37.5, we read, "The Torah is loved [by God] before all things. It was created before all things, for it says, 'The Lord possessed me at the beginning of his work.'" Commenting on Prov. 3:19, the Tanhuma reads, "'Wisdom' [here] is nothing other than Torah" (Wayelech 2.1). Also, Genesis Rabbah begins its commentary by comparing God to an architect (*ʾāmôn*; cf. Prov. 8:30) who consults his plans before building. Accordingly, God "looked into the Torah and created the world" (Gen. Rab. 1:1).

John 1:1 echoes the words of Gen. 1:1. In John, Jesus, as the *logos*, is identified with the Word or speech of God, through which the world came into being. John's language also reminds us of "the word of the LORD" in the OT. The Lord declares, "So shall my word be that goes out from my mouth; it shall not return to me empty, but it shall accomplish that which I purpose, and shall succeed in the thing for which I sent it" (Isa. 55:11 ESV).

John, Targum Neofiti, and rabbinic literature have striking parallels in this description of creation. First, all three traditions agree that God is the creator of the universe and that the universe was created in wisdom. Second, Targum Neofiti and rabbinic literature together agree that wisdom was *not* the agent of creation. For the rabbis, the Torah or the Word of the Lord (as it is sometimes called; see Lev. Rab. 2:1; b. Sanh. 99a) was separate from God and used as a blueprint to aid in creation. For John and the people of the NT, however, the Word, the Wisdom of God (*theou sophia*, 1 Cor. 1:24) was the agent of creation. Third, Targum Neofiti and John agree that the Son of God was the agent of creation.

Jannes and Jambres: 2 Timothy and Targum Pseudo-Jonathan. In 2 Tim. 3:8, warning Timothy about difficult times ahead, Paul compares the opponents of truth to the opponents of Moses—namely, Jannes and Jambres. These two figures are also mentioned in Targum Pseudo-Jonathan as the opponents of Moses (Exod. 1:15; 7:11) and as the servants of Balaam (Num. 22:22). Jannes and Jambres appear frequently within Second Temple literature (see Pietersma and Lutz, 427–36). Rabbinic literature is thought to preserve the original spelling of the pair—namely, "Johana and Mamre" (see b. Men. 85a; Yal. Shimoni, Torah 182.1; 235.1)—although the Hellenized forms are also attested (see Tanh., Ki Tassa 19; Zohar 2.191a; 3.194a). In later rabbinic sources, Jannes and Jambres are identified as the sons of Balaam (Dibrê ha-yamim shel Moshe [Jellinek, 2:5]; Yalkut Shimoni on Torah 168.2; 176.4; Tikunei ha-Zohar 142a; and Zohar 2.191a–192a).

Based on the use of Hellenized names and the similarity of tradition, McNamara maintains that Tg. Ps.-J. Exod. 1:15 and 7:11 are "old midrashim of pre-Christian origin" and are preserved "as they existed in the [Palestinian Targums] in NT times" (McNamara, *Palestinian*, 96). However, if Targum Pseudo-Jonathan is an example of first-century midrash, one might expect Semitic forms. As Lester Grabbe puts it, "Rather than being a mark of antiquity, the form of the names may actually be a sign of lateness" (Grabbe, 398). Another mark of antiquity would be Targum Pseudo-Jonathan identifying Jannes and Jambres as the servants of Balaam. Nowhere within pre-Islamic rabbinic literature are Jannes and Jambres associated with Balaam. In any case, the length and breadth of attestations regarding these two is a striking example of the endurance of an interpretive tradition. What we find in 2 Tim. 3:8 is roughly similar to what we find in Tg. Ps.-J. Num. 22:22. However, in light of Grabbe's criticism and the medieval association with Balaam, it is unlikely that Targum Pseudo-Jonathan preserves a first-century tradition.

The fire of Gehenna. During the period of the Second Temple, the Hinnom Valley (*gê-hinnōm*, Neh. 11:30) became known as the location for God's final judgment. In the NT, the term "Gehenna" (*geenna*) appears a dozen times, always as reference to hell. On four occasions, it is associated with fire (Matt. 5:22; 18:9; Mark 9:43; James 3:6). Similar language appears in 4 Macc. 12:12, as well as the Pseudepigrapha (T. Zeb. 10:3; 2 Bar. 85:13, cited in Maher, 30). Such language appears early on in the rabbinic corpus. Using Isa. 66:23 as a proof text, Rabbi Akiva believed the unrighteous would suffer in Gehenna for twelve months (m. Ed. 2:10). Commenting on the hellish vision of Isa. 66:24, Rabbi Yosé says, "The fire of Gehenna [*ʾēš gēhinām*] was created on the second day and it will never grow dim" (t. Ber. 5:31; also in b. Pesah. 54a). Some rabbis understood the fires of Gehenna as noneternal. In Gen. Rab. 48:8, it is said to last "for a short while" (see also b. Avod. Zar. 3b–4a). Gehenna is avoided through good works. In b. B. Metz. 85a, Rabbi Eleazar is said to have fasted one hundred days so that the "fire of Gehenna" (*nûrāʾ dəgêhinām*) might not overcome him.

Though the term never appears in Targum Onqelos, it appears more than fifty times in Targum Jonathan and the Targums to the Writings as a designation for hell (e.g., 1 Sam. 2:8–9; Isa. 26:19; 33:17; 53:9; Jer. 17:13; Hosea 14:10 [ET v. 9]; and Nah. 1:8). The targums contain multiple references to a fiery Gehenna. Targum Isaiah speaks of a fire in Gehenna that burns all day and forever (Isa. 33:3, 14; 65:15; 66:24). In the Tg. Job 28:5, Gehenna is described as the place "where the cold of snow becomes like fire." In Tg. Neof. Gen. 15:17, Abraham has a terrible vision of hell: "And behold, Gehenna, which is comparable to a furnace [*ʾattûn*; cf. Dan. 3:6], to an oven surrounded by sparks of fire, flaming fire, into the midst of which the wicked fell, since the wicked rebelled against the Torah during their life on this world." Expanding Deut. 32:35, where the Lord declares, "Vengeance is mine," Targum Neofiti adds that the "fire of Gehenna" has been prepared for the wicked, bringing them retribution in the world to come. "The fire of Gehenna" also appears in Tg. Song 8:6 and Tg. Eccles. 10:11. The "burning of Gehenna" appears in Tg. Ps.-J. Gen. 27:33.

Strack and Billerbeck maintain that the term "Gehenna" appears suddenly within Palestinian Judaism during the second century BC, just as the term "Sheol" disappears as a technical term for the place of punishment (4:1022). The targums and the NT are consistent with this development. It is interesting to note that this term predominantly occurs within the more Judaic sources of Matthew and James. The phrase "fire of Gehenna" appears only in Matthew, certain targums, and rabbinic literature.

Seeing and perceiving: Mark 4:12 and Targum Isaiah. In Mark 4:10–12, Jesus explains to his disciples why he speaks in parables. In doing so, he quotes from Isa.

6:9–10. However, Mark 4:12 is closer to Tg. Isa. 6:9–10 than to any other ancient versions. Mark 4:12 reads, "so that 'they may indeed see but not perceive, and may indeed hear but not understand, lest they should turn and be forgiven'" (ESV). The other ancient versions end with some version of "lest they turn and be healed" (MT, LXX, Vulgate). The Peshitta reads "lest it be forgiven him" but this is likely the influence of Mark (*dəlā'* . . . *neštəbeq leh*; see Chilton, 91). Additionally, the purpose clause in Mark, "so that they might see [*blepōsin*] and not perceive [*idōsin*]," makes use of third-person verbs. The MT uses second-person verbs (perfect and imperative). The targum makes use of participles, leaving the subject in the third person: "this people who indeed hear but do not understand." Although it is not a word-for-word citation, Bruce Chilton (92) comments, "Mark presents the fullest parallel to the specifically Targumic form of Isaiah 6:9, 10 and seems to be reliant on it."

Be merciful: Luke and Targum Pseudo-Jonathan. In Luke 6:36, Jesus says, "Be merciful, even as your Father is merciful" (ESV). This passage closely parallels Lev. 19:2: "You shall be holy, for I the LORD your God am holy" (ESV). In the previous verse in Luke, Jesus provides his alternative to Lev. 19:18—namely, "Love your enemies" (cf. Matt. 5:44). Jesus's teaching in Luke 6:36 finds its closest parallel in Tg. Ps.-J. Lev. 22:28, which reads, "My people, children of Israel, just as I am merciful in heaven, so should you be merciful on earth." Interestingly, the paraphrase of Lev. 22:28 is quoted twice, nearly verbatim, in the Palestinian Talmud as a forbidden translation. Such a translation is forbidden since it reduces the "measures" (*midôt*; y. Ber. 5:3.2) or "decrees" (*gəzērôt*; y. Meg. 4:10.3) of God to mere mercy. McNamara believes Targum Pseudo-Jonathan's paraphrase "is certainly a very old one, and probably dates from NT times" (*Palestinian*, 136). Chilton comes to a similar conclusion (Flesher and Chilton, 386).

Parable of the vineyard owner: Matthew, Mark, Luke, and Targum Isaiah. An interesting parallel occurs in the parable of the vineyard owner (Matt. 21:33–46; Mark 12:1–12; Luke 20:9–19) and Tg. Isa. 5:1–7. In all three of the Gospel accounts, Jesus teaches this parable after cleansing the temple and being confronted by the chief priests, scribes, and elders. After hearing this parable, the chief priests, Pharisees, and scribes desire to arrest Jesus but stop short of doing so for fear of the crowd. In beginning of the parable, Jesus uses language that is reminiscent of Isa. 5:1–7. Matthew 21:33 reads, "There was a master of a house who planted a vineyard and put a fence around it and dug a winepress in it and built a tower and leased it to tenants, and went into another country" (ESV). In Isa. 5:2, we read, "He dug it and cleared it of stones, and planted it with choice vines; he built a watchtower in the midst of it, and hewed out a wine vat in it; and he looked for it to yield grapes, but it yielded wild grapes" (ESV). The connection between these two passages has long been recognized. David Pao and Eckhard Schnabel (360) write that "the intertextual relationship with Isa. 5:1–7, the Song of the Vineyard, informs the meaning of the parable."

The Isaiah passage is presented as an indictment against the house of Israel, specifically Judah. Why would a parable built upon an allusion to Isa. 5 anger Jewish leaders such that they wished to seize Jesus? An interpretive tradition preserved in Targum Isaiah may help answer that question. In Tg. Isa. 5:2, we read, "And I made them holy and I honored them and I established them like the planting of a choice vine and I built my sanctuary [*maqdaš*] in their midst and I even gave my altar to make atonement for their sins. I said that they should do good deeds, but they made their deeds evil." This interpretation of Isaiah is a clear indictment against the cultic leadership of Israel. Within rabbinic Judaism, this interpretation appears early on. Just as the targum has done, the Tosefta identifies the "watchtower in the midst of it" as the temple (*hêkāl*) and the winepress as the altar (*mizbēaḥ*; t. Me'il. 1:16). This interpretation appears later in both Talmuds (b. Sukkah 49a; y. Sukkah 4:6.5). Accordingly, Evans and Chilton conclude that the Synoptic texts present us with a parable "whose emphasis fell unmistakably (against its targumic background) on the guilt of the cultic authorities in the treatment of the prophets" (Evans and Chilton, 306).

Conclusion

Neusner's critique of those who view rabbinic sources as preserving the *ipsissima verba* of the first-century rabbis is valid. Nevertheless, I would not endorse such a positivist approach to tradition history. I would grant to Neusner's perspective that we cannot have certainty in connecting rabbinic traditions to the first century. However, we cannot certainly disconnect them from the first century either. As it stands, we can only speculate a reasonable probability of their connection. To that end, we should consider the testimony of Josephus regarding the Pharisees (i.e., the predecessors of the rabbinic tradition). In his *Antiquities*, we see a prototype of the rabbinic doctrine of the Oral Torah (*tôrâ šebə'al-peh*; see Sifre Deut. 351). He writes that "the Pharisees have handed down certain laws [*nomima*] from the succession of their fathers, which have not been written in the laws of Moses" and that, for this reason, these laws are rejected by the Sadducees (*Ant.* 13.297). Josephus goes on to say that, in this dispute, the Sadducees persuade only the rich but the Pharisees have the multitude as "fighting allies" (*Ant.* 13.298). If Josephus is to be believed, the Pharisees were concerned with preserving their traditions and disseminating them among the multitudes. It is reasonable to suspect that subsequent rabbinic literature would preserve many of these traditions. Therefore, since there is the possibility of a relationship between them, it is a useful endeavor to identify and consider targumic and rabbinic parallels to the NT.

In our analysis here, we have seen targumic traditions that are uniquely paralleled in the NT: (1) the expression "Be merciful" in Luke 6:36 and T. Ps.-J. Lev 22:28; (2) the language of "seeing and perceiving" in Mark 4:10–12 and Tg. Isa. 6:9–10; and (3) the creation of the world through the Son of God in John 1 and Tg. Neof. Gen. 1. We have also seen targumic/NT parallels that are a part of a larger Jewish tradition: (1) the Golden Rule as it appears in Matthew and Targum Pseudo-Jonathan; (2) the creation of the world through the wisdom of God; (3) the tradition of Jannes and Jambres; (4) the eschatological fire of Gehenna; and (5) the parable of the vineyard. Though the direction and degree of influence between these traditions is difficult to determine, their examination may help us better understand the NT.

See also OT Use of the OT: Comparison with the NT Use of the OT; *other Targums articles; Dead Sea Scrolls articles; Mishnah, Talmud, and Midrashim articles; Philo articles; Septuagint articles*

Bibliography. Chilton, B., *A Galilean Rabbi and His Bible* (Glazier, 1984); Cook, E. M., "Rewriting the Bible" (PhD diss., University of California, 1986); Evans, C. A., "Early Messianic Traditions in the Targums," in *Jesus and His Contemporaries,* AGJU 25 (Brill, 2001), 155–81; Evans, C. A., and B. Chilton, "Jesus and Israel's Scriptures," in *Studying the Historical Jesus,* ed. B. Metzger and B. Ehrman, NTTS 19 (Brill, 1994), 281–335; Flesher, P. V. M., and B. Chilton, *The Targums,* SAIS 12 (Brill, 2011); Grabbe, L. L., "The Jannes/Jambres Tradition in Targum Pseudo-Jonathan and Its Date," *JBL* 98 (1979): 393–401; Jellinek, A., *Bet ha-Midrasch,* 6 vols. (Friedrich Nies, 1853); Kahle, P. E., *The Cairo Geniza,* 2nd ed. (Praeger, 1960); Keener, C. S., *The Gospel of John,* 2 vols. (Hendrickson, 2003); Macho, A. D., *Genesis,* vol. 1 of *Neophyti 1* (Consejo Superior de Investigaciones Científicas, 1968); Maher, M., *Targum Pseudo-Jonathan: Genesis,* ArBib 1B (Liturgical Press, 1992); McNamara, M., *The New Testament and the Palestinian Targums to the Pentateuch,* AnBib 27 (Pontifical Biblical Institute, 1966); McNamara, "Targum and the New Testament," in *The New Testament and Rabbinic Literature,* ed. R. Bieringer et al., JSJSup 136 (Brill, 2010), 387–427; McNamara, *Targum Neofiti 1: Genesis,* ArBib 1A (Liturgical Press, 1992); Neusner, J., *The Rabbinic Traditions about the Pharisees before 70,* 3 vols. (Brill, 1971); Pao, D. W., and E. J. Schnabel, "Luke," in *CNTUOT,* 251–606; Pietersma, A., and R. T. Lutz, "Jannes and Jambres," in *OTP,* 2:427–42; Stemberger, G., "Dating Rabbinic Traditions," in *The New Testament and Rabbinic Literature,* ed. R. Bieringer et al., JSJSup 136 (Brill, 2010), 79–96; Strack, H. L., and P. Billerbeck, *Kommentar zum Neuen Testament aus Talmud und Midrasch,* 6 vols. (Beck, 1961); P. Wernberg-Møller, "An Inquiry into the Validity of the Text-Critical Argument for an Early Dating of the Recently Discovered Palestinian Targum," *VT* 12, no. 3 (July 1962): 312–30; York, A. D., "The Dating of Targumic Literature," *JSJ* 5, no. 1 (1974): 49–62.

David Everson

Targums: Thematic Parallels to the NT

The targums and the NT have much in common with regard to biblical ideas and language. In what follows, I will compare and contrast some of the shared language and themes of the targums and the NT. For a discussion on past and present perspectives on the targums and the NT, see the other Targums articles.

Similarities in Language

Living by the sword. Bruce Chilton sees a possible connection between Jesus's proverb about living by the sword and Targum Isaiah. In Matt. 26:52, Jesus says, "Put your sword back into its place. For all who take the sword will perish by the sword" (ESV). Though the MT of Isa. 50:11 makes no reference to swords, the targum translates the verse so: "Behold, all of you who kindle fire, who grasp the sword. Go, fall on the fire that you have kindled and on the sword that you have grasped." Chilton sees a strong affinity between the two passages (Flesher and Chilton, 391–92).

Second death. Another interesting example comes from Revelation and Targum Onqelos. In Revelation, the phrase "second death" (Rev. 2:11; 20:6, 14; 21:8) is used for those who are sent to the lake of fire when the day of judgment comes. The same language and meaning appear in Tg. Onq. Deut. 33:6, which reads, "May Reuben live in eternal life and may he not die the second death [*môtāʾ tinyānāʾ*]" (unless otherwise indicated, all translations of ancient Jewish texts are my own). Interestingly, this language occurs virtually nowhere else within rabbinic literature (Pirqe R. El. 34.1 is an exception). A similar interpretation with different language appears in an early halakic midrash. Quoting the words of Moses in Deut. 33:6, "may he not die," Sifre Deut. 347 comments, "And did he not die? What is the teaching regarding 'and may he not die'? It is regarding the world to come" (*hʿwlm hbʾ*; see also b. Sanh. 92a). "Second death" also appears four times in Targum Jonathan (Isa. 22:14; 65:6, 15; Jer. 51:57). Martin McNamara suggests that Rev. 20:14 may be referring to Tg. Isa. 65:15, stating that "in this section of the Targum . . . we are in the presence of pre-Christian paraphrases which have influenced the thought and terminology of the Apocalypse" (*Targum and Testament,* 227). G. K. Beale suggests that Targum Isaiah provides an interpretive background to Rev. 20:14. Accordingly, as the "second death" of Tg. Isa. 65:14–18 appears before the new creation of 66:22–24, so also it appears in Rev. 20:14 before the new creation of 21:1 (Beale, *Revelation,* 1036–37).

Measure by measure. In Mark 4:24 (also Matt. 7:2), Jesus says, "With the measure you use, it will be measured to you" (ESV). Similar language is used in Tg. Isa. 27:8, which reads, "With the measure by which you were measuring, they will measure you." The MT simply reads "measure by measure." Similar language appears in m. Sotah 1:7, which reads, "By the measure with which a man measures, they will measure him" (see also Mek. R. Ishmael, Shirata 4.80, and Amalek 2.10; b. Sotah 8b; b. Sanh. 100a; and y. Sotah 1:7.1).

Unrighteous mammon. There are four occurrences of the loanword "mammon" in the NT (Matt. 6:24; Luke 16:9, 11, 13). In Luke 16:9 we find the phrase "mammon of unrighteousness" (AT). The Greek *mamōnas* transliterates the Aramaic word *māmônāʾ*, which means "wealth." Mammon appears frequently in rabbinic literature, sometimes associated with greed (y. Ber. 9:2.12; Exod. Rab. [Margulies] 10:1; Lev. Rab. 22:1; Eccles. Rab. 5:6). Mammon appears commonly in all of the targums. The phrase "mammon of falsehood" (*mamōn dišqar*) appears ten times in Targum Jonathan (e.g., 1 Sam. 8:3; Isa. 5:23; Ezek. 22:27; Hosea 5:11; Amos 5:11), twice in the Targums of the Writings (Job 27:8; Prov. 15:27), and once each in Targum Neofiti and Targum Pseudo-Jonathan (Exod. 18:21). Sperber's edition of Tg. Hab. 2:9 contains the phrase "mammon of wickedness" (*māmôn diršaʿ*), which more closely resembles the "mammon of unrighteousness" in Luke 16:9.

"Blessed is the womb." In Luke 11:27, an anonymous woman raises her voice in praise of Jesus and declares, "Blessed is the womb that bore you, and the breasts at which you nursed!" (ESV). McNamara maintains that this blessing has parallels dating back to Tannaitic times (*Palestinian*, 131–33). A similar blessing is found in the Palestinian Targums of Gen. 49:25, which reads, "Blessed are the breasts from which you nursed and the womb in which you laid." According to Gen. Rab. 48:20, Jacob blessed Rachel using this same formula.

Sin as debt. In the Lord's Prayer, sin and sinner are referred to as debt (*opheilēma*) and debtor (*opheiletēs*), respectively (Matt. 6:12). In similar fashion, Luke 11:4 makes use of *opheilō* for "debtors." Such language for sin is used nowhere else in the NT. This language does, however, appear commonly throughout all of the targums. The Aramaic word *ḥôb* ("debt") is used regularly to translate the Hebrew *ʿăwōn* ("sin" or "guilt") and sometimes to translate *ḥaṭāʾt* ("sin"). It appears in most Aramaic dialects as a word for "sin." Within rabbinic literature, this term persists as an Aramaic term for sin (e.g., Gen. Rab. 11:4; Lev. Rab. 5:8; and b. Qidd. 13a).

The Kingdom of God

With its roots in the OT, the kingdom of God is perhaps the central teaching of Jesus. The rabbinic conception of the kingdom of heaven is similar to that of the NT and appears regularly within the targums (see Strack and Billerbeck, 1:172–84). First, in both traditions we find the prioritizing of the heavenly kingdom over earthly kingdoms. Quoting from Ps. 2, Peter confronts the Sadducees in Acts 4:25–26, declaring that earthly kings and rulers rage against God's Messiah. However, this is done in vain. In Tg. Onq. Gen. 25:23, Jacob and Esau are identified as two kings within one womb. One kingdom will be made stronger and the other will be made subject to it (cf. b. Meg. 6a). God's love for Israel over Esau, often understood as Rome in rabbinic literature, can be seen in Gen. Rab. 68:3.

Second, those who enter the kingdom of God swear allegiance to one king, as it were, and follow his commands. For the rabbis, the reciting of the Shema was a means of acknowledging both the existence of only *one* God and obedience to the Torah. This prayer of confession, then, became the means of receiving the "yoke of the kingdom of heaven" (*ʿôl malkût šāmayim*; b. Ber. 14b–15a; a similar tradition is found in Tanh. [Buber], Lek Leka 1). The Shema and kingdom appear together in Tg. Neof. Gen. 49:2. In that passage, after the twelve tribes recite the Shema, Jacob responds with, "Blessed be the glorious name of his kingdom forever and ever" (cf. Gen. Rab. 108:3; Deut. Rab. 2:31, 35). Interestingly, in Mark 12:28–34, we also see the juxtaposition of the Shema and kingdom. There Jesus identifies the greatest commandments as Deut. 6:4–5 (i.e., the Shema) and Lev. 19:18. After a scribe approves of this teaching, Jesus tells him, "You are not far from the kingdom of God."

Third, God's people wait for or long to see his kingdom. In the Synoptics, Jesus encourages his followers, telling them that some of them will see the kingdom of God before they taste death (Luke 9:27; Matt. 16:28; Mark 9:1). In John 3:3, Jesus tells Nicodemus that he must be born again if he would like to see the kingdom of God. Looking toward the messianic age, we read in Tg. Isa. 24:23 that "the kingdom of the Lord of hosts" will someday be revealed in glory on Mount Zion. This will take place before the elders and the people of God (see also Tg. Isa. 31:4; 40:9; 53:10).

Fourth, related to this visible kingdom is the idea of an eschatological kingdom. In Heb. 1:8, we read, "Your throne, O God, is forever and ever, the scepter of uprightness is the scepter of your kingdom" (ESV). Likewise, in Rev. 11:15, we read, "The kingdom of the world has become the kingdom of our Lord and of his Christ, and he shall reign forever and ever" (ESV). In Tg. Neof. Exod. 15:18, we read that God's kingdom was created "from before the world" and will last forever and ever. Likewise, in Tg. Ps.-J. Exod. 15:18, God is described as the king of kings in this age and, in the age to come, his kingdom will last for ever and ever. This idea appears frequently in rabbinic literature as well. For example, Rabbi Eleazar looks forward to the day when "God will become the One throughout the world and His kingdom will last for ever and ever and ever" (Mek. R. Ishmael, Amalek 2.157).

Memra and Logos

In the targums, the word *mêmərāʾ* is the emphatic form of *mêmar* (from *ʾămar*), which means "word" or "command." In each set of targums, Memra occurs hundreds of times (e.g., 199x in Tg. Onq.; 297x in Tg. Neof.; 330x in Tg. Ps.-J.; 660x in Tg. Jon.; 379x in Tg. Ket.). To avoid the isolated use of the Tetragrammaton, the targums will frequently insert Memra into the text, so the text reads, "the Memra of the Lord." Accordingly, the activities of the Memra are as varied as those of the Lord—for example, acting, speaking, punishing, and receiving worship. Despite its ubiquity in the targums, Memra never appears within rabbinic literature. Similar concepts may still be found. In the Mishnah, the world was said be created by "ten statements" (*ʿăśārâ maʾămārôt*; m. Avot 5:1). Similarly, b. Sanh. 42a states that God created the heavens by "his word" (*maʾămārô*) and all their hosts "by the breath of his mouth" (*bərûaḥ pîw*).

Numerous passages describe the Memra in separate or personal terms. For example, in all of the targums of Exod. 3:12, the Lord says to Moses from the burning bush, "My Memra will be your help." When Joseph swears his oath at Bethel, he says "If the Memra of the Lord will be my help." In light of these personal descriptions and the close connection to God, the association of Memra with the *logos* of John has been a matter of great interest over the years. Years ago, G. F. Moore concluded that Memra is a "buffer-word," instead of a personal being. It occurs as a circumlocution used where God is personally active (Moore, 52–54). Memra as a personification of God or a hypostasis would be difficult to reconcile with the term not being limited to God alone (e.g., Gen. 22:16; 45:21; Exod. 38:21; Deut. 17:6 of Tg. Onq., Tg. Neof., and Tg. Ps.-J.; Exod. 15:25 of Tg. Neof. and Tg. Ps.-J.; Num. 4:27 of Tg. Onq. and Tg. Ps.-J.; Deut. 21:5 of Tg. Ps.-J.). Strack and Billerbeck (2:329) maintain that Memra is a "paraphrasing substitute" (*umschreibender Ersatz*) and should not be viewed as a divine hypostasis. As such, they argue, it is unsuitable to serve as the starting point of John's Logos theology (2:333). Craig Keener arrives at a similar conclusion. Quoting C. K. Barrett, he writes, "*Memra* is a blind alley in the study of John's logos doctrine" (Keener, 1:350).

Martin McNamara argues to the contrary, pointing out that such criticism reflects an opinion that was formed before the discovery of Targum Neofiti. In his survey of the topic, McNamara points to the scholarship of Diez Macho, Robert Hayward, Bruce Chilton, and John Ronning (among others), making the case that Targum Neofiti's Memra theology may have pre-targumic roots and may have contributed to John's Logos theology (*Targum and Testament*, 154–66). He concludes his treatment of the matter with an expansion found in Exod. 12:42 of the Palestinian Targums, which describes the first night of creation. The passage reads, "The world was formless and void, and darkness was spreading over the surface of the deep, and the Memra of the Lord was the light and it shined forth [*mêmərêh da-yyy hăwâ nəhôrāʾ ûnhar*]." McNamara points out that, in John's prologue, the activity of the Logos is the same as that of the Memra here. He writes, "It is legitimate to assume that the author of the Fourth Gospel was under the influence of the targums in the formulation of his doctrine of the Logos" (*Targum and Testament*, 164).

The Sacrifice of the Son

The binding of Isaac, or the Akedah, is found in Gen. 22:1–19 (*ʿăqêdâ* = binding of a sacrifice; cf. m. Tamid 4:1). This story features prominently in rabbinic thought and Christian thought. Hayward (73–74) points out several striking commonalities in Jewish and Christian thought throughout the history of interpretation. "The parallel between Isaac carrying the wood and a man carrying his cross is oft-repeated; Isaac is portrayed as one dead and resurrected in both Jewish and Christian texts; and both Jews and Christians speak of Abraham as a priest." Among the targums, the Palestinian Targums and Targum Pseudo-Jonathan add interpretive expansions concerning the binding of Isaac. In Gen. 22:8 of the Palestinian Targums, when Isaac inquires about the location of the lamb, Abraham tells him that God will reveal the sacrifice to them but then adds, "If not, you are the lamb of the offering." The verse then adds that the two of them "went together with a peaceful heart." In Gen. 22:10 of the Palestinian Targums and Targum Pseudo-Jonathan, Isaac is very concerned that he be bound well, lest he become an unfit sacrifice and "be pushed into the pit of destruction." The idea of Isaac, the son of Abraham, becoming a willing sacrifice is similar to the idea of Jesus, the Son of God, becoming a willing sacrifice.

In Targum Pseudo-Jonathan and rabbinic literature, it is not clear if Isaac was nearly sacrificed or actually sacrificed and then resurrected. In Tg. Ps.-J. Gen. 22:20, we read, "Satan went and told Sarah that Abraham had sacrificed Isaac." Given the context and the reputation of the one speaking, the targum probably seeks to portray Satan as a liar. However, in rabbinic literature, there are references to Isaac being cut or killed by Abraham. The (rabbinic) Targum Job identifies Isaac as "the servant of the Lord" (*ʿabdāʾ da-yyy*) and, thus, may seek to identify him with Isaiah's suffering servant (Tg. Job 3:19). Isaac being harmed during the Akedah appears in a number of rabbinic sources. According to Mek. R. Ishmael, Pischa 7.78, when the Lord looked upon the doorposts of the Israelites (Exod. 12:13), he would see "the blood of the binding of Isaac." (Apart from late sources [Lekach Tov, Exod. 12:13.4; Yal. Shimoni on Torah 182.1], I have not found this idea elsewhere in rabbinic literature.) Pirqe Rabbi Eliezer appears to depend on Targum Pseudo-Jonathan in describing the sacrifice and resurrection of Isaac (31.10) and how Satan brought about the death of Sarah (32.8). In the NT, the possibility of

Isaac's resurrection appears in Heb. 11:19, which reads, "[Abraham] considered that God was able even to raise him from the dead, from which, figuratively speaking [*en parabolē*], he did receive him back" (ESV). Isaac is viewed as a type or foreshadowing of Christ. Considering Heb. 11:19 in light of the targums, Paul Flesher and Bruce Chilton write, "Event, intention, possibility, and promise are all mixed together, somewhat in the manner of rabbinic interpretation, because the significance of Genesis 22, in the epistle to the Hebrews' conception, is that the sacrifice of Isaac was truly completed in the crucifixion and resurrection of Jesus" (468). Flesher and Chilton, as always, would not propose a direct targumic influence upon Hebrews. In their perspective, similarities between the targums and the NT are best explained by understanding both traditions as being downstream of earlier traditions (see Flesher and Chilton, 385–86). However, Michael Maher and Roger Le Déaut see a possible direct connection between the two traditions (see Maher 77n2).

The Angelology of the NT and the Targums

The angelology of the NT and that of the targums have a great deal in common. In both traditions, angels were seen as created beings (Col. 1:16; Tg. Ps.-J. Gen. 1:6; see also Gen. Rab. 1:3). A basic function or role of angels is the praise of God (Luke 2:13–14; Rev. 5:8–14; Tg. Ps. 29:1; Tg. Job 35:10; and Tg. Song 2:3; see also Gen. Rab. 12:11; Exod. Rab. 15:6; b. Hul. 91b). In the NT, angels are often described as having human appearance (Mark 16:5; Acts 12:15; Heb. 13:2). In the targums, angels are sometimes described as appearing in the likeness of a man (*bidmût gĕbar* in Tg. Neof. Gen. 18:2; 32:25; 37:15; Tg. Esther II 6:1). In ancient Judaism, there was a belief that one could have a guardian angel that was identical in appearance to oneself. In Acts 12:15, when Rhoda informs the others that Peter is at the door, they are in disbelief and say it must be "his angel." In Tg. Ps.-J. Gen. 33:10, Jacob says to Esau, "I have seen the expression of your face and it seems to me like seeing the face of your angel." In light of rabbinic interpretation of Esau, it is probable that Targum Pseudo-Jonathan believes Esau and his angel to be of the same appearance (cf. Gen. Rab. 77:3; Pirqe R. El. 37; Song Rab. 3:9; Zohar 2.163b). Though they are sometimes described as human in appearance, the NT also describes angels as being glorious in appearance (Luke 2:9; 9:26; Acts 12:7; 2 Pet. 2:10; Jude 8). Though this is less common in the targums, angels are occasionally described with such language (e.g., Tg. Ps.-J. Gen. 22:10). In the NT, angels are often cause for fear (Matt. 28:1–8; Mark 16:5–8; Luke 24:5; Acts 10:4). In Targum Pseudo-Jonathan, Eve is fearful before "Sammael, the angel of death" (Gen. 3:6), and Moses is fearful before two angels named Anger and Fear (Deut. 9:19). According to both the NT and the targums, angels had been present or instrumental in the giving of the Law at Sinai (Acts 7:38, 53; Gal. 3:19; Heb. 2:2; Palestinian Targums and Tg. Ps.-J. Deut. 33:3–4; see also Jub. 1:27–29; Josephus, *Ant.* 15.13; Song Rab. 5:9; b. Hag. 16a; Num. Rab. 2:3). Paul seems to assert that angels have their own language in 1 Cor. 13:1. In Gen. 22:11, the Fragmentary Targums describe the angels as speaking "in the language of the sanctuary." This is consistent with the Talmud, which describes angels as speaking Hebrew but able to understand Aramaic (b. Hag. 16a; b. Shabb. 12b).

The NT and the targums differ from each other in two key respects on angels—namely, the belief in fallen angels and the use of angels as a literary foil. First, within the NT, the belief in a heavenly rebellion, led by Satan, can be seen in a number of passages (Matt. 25:41; 2 Pet. 2:4; Jude 6; Rev. 12:7–9). Among the Pentateuch targums, the idea of a heavenly rebellion is completely rejected by both Targum Onqelos and the Palestinian Targums (see Everson, 431–32, 443–45). This idea, however, is enthusiastically endorsed by Targum Pseudo-Jonathan. For example, Tg. Ps.-J. Gen. 6:4 reads, "Shamhazai and Azael fell from heaven and . . . went in to the daughters of man and bore children for them" (cf. 1 En. 6:3–7). Additionally, though no angels are named within the MT of the Pentateuch, sixteen named angels appear within Targum Pseudo-Jonathan, including figures such as Gabriel, Michael, Metatron, Uriel, Sammael, and Satan (see Everson, 471–73). Second, in the NT, angels function as important pieces within the larger historical narrative. They are not introduced as a literary foil to make a theological point. This is not true with respect to rabbinic literature. Some feel that the rabbis, including targumists, were scandalized by the disgraceful behavior of pseudepigraphical angels and, as a result, the angels' role was reduced to an exegetical device (Shapiro, 42, 117–20; Urbach, 135–36). For example, Targum Pseudo-Jonathan resolves the tensions created by the "Let us" statements in Gen. 1:26 and 11:7–8 by the introduction of angels (cf. Gen. Rab. 8:4). Likewise, in Gen. 35:7, instead of God revealing himself at Bethel, the Cairo Genizah Targum (frg. C) states that angels were revealed (as does b. Sanh. 38b).

Eschatology

The world to come. A common dichotomy within rabbinic literature is the idea of "this world" (*haʿôlām hazzeh*) and "the world to come" (*haʿôlām habbāʾ*; cf. m. Avot 4:1). The latter is associated with the messianic age and/or the resurrection of the dead. Occasionally, three ages are described. In Tg. Ps.-J. Exod. 17:16, we read, "He will destroy them [i.e., the house of Amalek] for three generations: from the generation of this world [*ʿalmāʾ dên*] and from the generation of the Messiah and from the generation of the world to come [*ʿalmāʾ dəʾātê*]. Sifre Deut. 47.1 also lists these three ages: this world, the days of the Messiah, and the world to come. In Tg. Neof. Gen. 4:8, Cain foolishly declares that there is no reward for the righteous, no "other world" (*ʿôlām ḥôrān*). According to the Song of Moses in Targum Neofiti, however, retribution will come to the wicked "in the world to come." The NT uses similar language in the story of the rich man (Mark 10:30; Luke 18:30). Accordingly, Jesus says that those who have suffered for his sake and the sake of the gospel will be rewarded "in the age to come." In Matt. 12:32, Jesus warns that one who speaks against the Holy Spirit will not be forgiven in this age or the age to come. Also, Heb. 6:5 speaks of "the powers of the age to come." All these NT passages use the Greek word *aiōn*, which is commonly used to translate the Hebrew word *ʿôlām* in the LXX.

The day of judgment. The phrase "the day of judgment" appears in both the NT (Matt. 10:15; 11:22, 24; 12:36; 2 Pet. 2:9; 3:7; 1 John 4:17) and in Targum Onqelos and Targum Jonathan (Gen. 4:7; Deut. 32:34; 1 Sam. 2:9; Isa. 30:8). In Targum Neofiti, Targum Pseudo-Jonathan, and the Targums of the Writings, the phrase appears as "the great day of judgment" (Gen. 3:19; 4:7; 39:10; 49:22; Exod. 15:12; 20:7; Num. 14:18; 15:31; 31:50; Deut. 5:11; Job 1:6; 10:15; Pss. 50:3; 73:20; 92:9). This is similar to the phrase "the judgment of the great day," which appears in Jude 6 (ESV). Paul also speaks of "the day of wrath when God's righteous judgment will be revealed" (Rom. 2:5). Often in the NT and more so in the targums, "the day of judgment" concerns those who will be found guilty. In Tg. Isa. 2:9, the phrase refers to the wicked who "will be judged in Gehenna." In Tg. Ps. 92:9, the Lord "will be repaid by the debtors [i.e., sinners] in the world to come, on the great day of judgment." In Matthew, Jesus gives warning that the day of judgment will be unbearable for those who reject his message. Second Peter 3:7 describes the day of judgment as a time when the ungodly will be destroyed. On the other hand, "the day of judgment" sometimes refers to those who will not receive punishment. In Tg. Ps. 73:20, on judgment day the righteous will be vindicated by their God. Likewise, John writes that we may have confidence or boldness on the day of judgment (1 John 4:17).

The resurrection of the dead. Within the rabbinic tradition, the idea of the resurrection of the dead (*təḥiyayt hamētyīm*) was affirmed early on (m. Sanh. 10:1; m. Avot 4:22; Mek. R. Ishmael, Shirata 1.9). However, exactly who would be raised and to what end was a matter of debate. Some thought it would be limited to Israel (e.g., Gen. Rab. 13:6) or to the righteous (e.g., b. Ta'an. 7a) or to only the righteous who were buried in Israel (e.g., b. Ketub. 111a). Others thought all would be raised but with different outcomes, either paradise or Gehenna (see Strack and Billerbeck, 1:1174–77). Like rabbinic literature, the targums lack a clear opinion regarding the nature of the resurrection. In Gen. 3:19, Adam is told that he is destined to return (Tg. Neof.) or rise (Frag. Tg. and Tg. Ps.-J.) from the dust so that he might give "judgment and account" for all that he has done. Targum Pseudo-Jonathan adds that this will occur "on the day of great judgment" (cf. Heb. 9:27). In Tg. Zech. 3:7, we read that if Joshua should walk in the Lord's ways and keep his Memra, then he will be made alive "at the resurrection of the dead." This suggests that the righteous will be resurrected. However, in Tg. Song 8:5, it seems that only the dead of Israel who are buried at the Mount of Olives will be raised. According to this passage, the righteous will come in peace whereas the wicked will be thrown away like a stone.

The NT is distinct from the targums with regard to the resurrection of the dead in two particulars. First, the NT understanding of this concept is founded upon the life, death, and resurrection of Jesus Christ. In John 11:25, Jesus states that he is the resurrection and the life. As death entered the world through Adam, so shall all be made alive in Christ. He is the firstfruits of the resurrection of the dead (1 Cor. 15:22–23). Second, those who are raised to glory are those who belong to Christ (1 Cor. 15:23). Or, as Paul writes in Rom. 8:11, "He who raised Christ Jesus from the dead will also give life to your mortal bodies through his Spirit who dwells in you" (ESV).

In several other particulars, the NT and targums are similar. First, both demonstrate a hope or longing for the resurrection. In Luke 14:14, Jesus teaches that those who are generous will be repaid "at the resurrection of the just" (ESV). The resurrection of the dead was Martha's hope for the deceased Lazarus (John 11:24). Second, we also learn from the NT that the resurrection is not limited to the people of God. In John 5:29 a distinction is made between the "resurrection of life" and the "resurrection of judgment." Thus, the NT teaches that the resurrection is something that awaits all of humanity. Third, it is possible that the interpretation behind Targum Hosea may provide background to Paul's statement that Jesus "was raised on the third day in accordance with the Scriptures" (1 Cor. 15:4 ESV). What Scriptures are being referred to here? We could understand this as a general reference (see Ciampa and Rosner, 744) or this may refer to something more specific. Paul may have an interpretation of Hosea 6:2 in mind. Here is the passage, juxtaposed with the MT:

MT (trans. ESV)	Targum
After two days he will revive us;	He will bring us to life [*yəḥayênanā'*] for the days of consolation that are to come;
on the third day he will raise us up,	on the day of the resurrection of the dead he will raise us up,
that we may live before him.	and we will live for him.

"Consolation" (*neḥāmâ*) as possible resurrection terminology is found Gen. 49:1 of the Palestinian Targums, where Jacob is revealing the secrets of hidden times. Likewise, Tg. 2 Sam. 23:1 mentions David's prophecy about "the days of consolation." In the MT of Hosea 6:2, the object of resurrection or revival is the people of Israel. However, a typological interpretation of Jesus as the embodiment of Israel would provide a possible parallel. Accordingly, McNamara maintains that the passage Paul is referring to "is probably Hosea 6:2, but as interpreted midrashically in the Targum, in keeping with rabbinic Judaism" (*Targum and Testament*, 208).

The eschatological paradise of Eden. As the prophets look forward to the salvation of God, they use images of Eden. In Isa. 51:3 we read, "For the LORD comforts Zion; he comforts all her waste places and makes her wilderness like Eden, her desert like the garden of the LORD" (ESV; see also Ezek. 28:13; 31:8–9). As David Pao and Eckhard Schnabel write, such descriptions of paradise are "understood as an eschatological image of new creation, a place of expected bliss, the abode of the righteous after death" (398). In the Pseudepigrapha, the garden of Eden is understood eschatologically. In 1 Enoch, we read that the chosen dwell in the "garden of life" (1 En. 61:2; see also 32:3–6; 60:8, 23). In Jub. 4:21–26, Enoch is brought to the garden of Eden, where he writes down the condemnation and judgment of the world and all the wickedness of the children of men.

The eschatological understanding of Eden continues throughout rabbinic literature and the targums. According to Gen. 3:24 of the Palestinian Targums and Targum Pseudo-Jonathan, two thousand years before creation, God "prepared the garden of Eden for the righteous, so that they might eat and enjoy the fruit of the tree, because they had kept the commands of the torah in this world." The garden of Eden and the Torah are among the seven things that preceded creation (Tanh. [Buber], Nasso 19; b. Pesah. 54a; b. Ned. 39b). The garden of Eden is the home of the righteous (Tg. Pss. 50:10; 56:14; Tg. Song 8:2) and those who keep the torah (Tg. Eccles. 1:15; 6:8). Upon death, their souls are escorted to Eden by angels (Tg. Song 4:12; cf. Deut. Rab. 11:10). It is a place of feasting and drinking (Tg. Eccles. 9:7; cf. b. Ber. 17a; Num. Rab. 13:2). The garden of Eden is enormous in size and decorated with precious stones (Tg. Job 28:6; 38:18).

The NT speaks of heaven in similar ways. First, in Luke 23:43, Jesus tells the thief on the cross that they would soon be together "in paradise." The word used here for "paradise" (*paradeisos*) is also used by the LXX to translate the Hebrew word "garden" (*gan*). As Pao and Schnabel (398) put it, Jesus asserts "that he has the key to paradise." Second, Paul also uses the language of paradise with respect to heaven. In 2 Cor. 12:3–4, Paul writes of a man that was caught up into "the third heaven," which he then refers to as "paradise." This parallels rabbinic teaching. In Targum Job, when the Lord speaks from the whirlwind, he asks Job, "Who can count the seven heavens?" (Tg. Job 38:7). The rabbis typically speak of seven heavens or firmaments (b. Rosh Hash. 32a; Deut. Rab. 2:32) but some speak of three heavens (Midr. Pss. 114.2). Third, the clearest description of the eschatological garden of Eden is found in Revelation. In Rev. 22:1–2, we read of healing fruits, a flowing river, and the tree of life. As G. K. Beale and Sean McDonough (1150) put it, this is a description of "an end-time Eden." Similar to the targumic vision of Eden, Rev. 19:7–10 speaks of great feasting in the world to come. Both the targums and the NT have an eschatological vision where the last things are made like the first.

The days of the Messiah. The term "messiah" (*məšîḥāʾ*) appears frequently within targums, usually as an insertion into the text. For the rabbis, the coming of the Messiah signaled the transition from this world into the world to come. After a period of warfare and messianic kingship, God would bring about the consummation of salvation (b. Sanh. 97b; Exod. Rab. 15:21). There are a number of similarities between the targums and the NT concerning the nature and purpose of the Messiah. First, the most common depiction of the Messiah within the targums is that of a warrior (e.g., Tg. Neof. Gen. 49:10; Tg. Ps.-J. Num. 24:7, 20, 24; Tg. Isa. 14:29). In Tg. Onq. Num. 24:17, Balaam prophesies that the Messiah will come and conquer Israel's enemies. In Gen. 49:11–12 of the Palestinian Targums and Targum Pseudo-Jonathan, the eschatological Messiah will arise from the house of Judah, "slaughtering kings with rulers, making red the mountains from the blood of their slain . . . his clothing soiled from blood, resembling one who treads grapes." The Messiah's eschatological victory over Gog and Magog appears in Tg. Jon. 1 Sam. 2:10 and Tg. Neof. Num. 11:26 (cf. Ezek. 38:2; Rev. 20:8). This language echoes the description of the warrior in Rev. 19. This rider of war has clothes dipped in blood (19:13). He is followed by the armies of heaven (19:14). He will strike down nations and "tread the winepress of the fury of the wrath of God the Almighty" (19:15 ESV). There are additional examples of the warrior Messiah within the targums.

Second, the targums speak of the Messiah as a fulfillment of prophecy. In Tg. 1 Kings 5:13, Solomon prophesies about the kings who would rule "in this age and in the age of the Messiah." Targum Isaiah 11:1 reads, "And the king will come forth from the sons of Jesse and the Messiah will be exalted from his sons' sons" (cf. Acts 13:22–23). The targums associate the coming of the Messiah with the appearance of Elijah (Tg. Ps.-J. Deut. 30:4; Tg. Ruth 1:1; Tg. Lam. 4:22; cf. Matt. 11:14; Mark 6:15). The targums also say the Messiah will come from Ruth (Tg. Ruth 3:15; cf. Matt. 1:5) and be born in Bethlehem (Tg. Mic. 5:1; cf. Matt. 2:5–6; John 7:42). In Num. 24:17, the star (*kôkāb*) coming out of Jacob is interpreted messianically by all the pentateuchal targums. The NT imagery of "morning star" seems to be a messianic interpretation of this passage (2 Pet. 1:19; Rev. 2:28; 22:16). Rabbi Akiba viewed the leader of the Second Jewish Revolt (AD 132–35) as the fulfillment of this passage (Lam. Rab. 2:4; y. Ta'an. 4:5.13). Thus, the revolt came to be known as the Bar Kokhba Revolt (*bar kôkəbāʾ* = Aramaic, "Son of the Star"). Rabbinic literature, however, names him Bar Koziba (*bar kôzîbāʾ*), "Son of the Lie" (b. Sanh. 93b; Midr. Lam. 2:9).

Third, the targums often speak of the Messiah or the time of his coming being revealed (e.g., Tg. Jer. 30:21;

Tg. Zech. 3:8; 6:12; Tg. Eccles. 7:24; Tg. Song 8:1). In Tg. Mic. 4:8, the coming of the Messiah and his kingdom is imminent but he is presently hidden by "the sins of the congregation of Zion." According to the Tg. 1 Chron. 3:24, "the King Messiah who will be revealed" is named "Anani" (see also Tanh. [Buber], Toledot 20). According to Tg. Ps.-J. Gen. 35:21, at the end of days, the King Messiah will be revealed beyond the tower of Eder. In similar fashion, the NT often speaks of Christ Jesus or his identity being revealed (Matt. 16:16–17; Luke 2:25–26; 17:30; John 1:29; 2 Thess. 1:7).

Fourth, the targums speak about the Messiah bringing the redemption and consolation of Israel. The idea of the consolation of Israel stems from Isaiah. The Hebrew terms used for "comfort" in Isa. 40:1–2; 57:18; 66:11 are *niḥam*, *niḥumîm*, and *tanḥûm* (LXX uses *parakaleō* and *paraklēsis*). This same language is used in Tg. 2 Sam. 23:1 and Luke 2:25. In the Tg. 2 Sam. 23:1, David prophesies "about the end of the world, about the days of consolation [*yômê naḥāmātā'*]." In v. 3, David speaks of the Messiah who will arise and rule over mankind (cf. y. Ber. 2:4.12; Midr. Prov. 19.2). Similarly, in Luke 2:25–26, righteous Simeon has been waiting to see the Christ, "the consolation of Israel" (*paraklēsis tou Israēl*). The targums also speak of the Messiah bringing about the redemption of Israel (Tg. Ps. 61:9; cf. Luke 24:21), ushering in an era of peace (Tg. Isa. 11:6; cf. Luke 2:14; John 14:27), and bringing the dead to life (Tg. Hosea 14:8; cf. John 11:25).

Fifth, the targums and Rom. 16:20 both interpret Gen. 3:15 messianically. Both the Palestinian Targums and Targum Pseudo-Jonathan teach that "in the days of the King Messiah" those who keep the Torah will "strike" (*məḥî*) the head of the serpent. In this passage, Michael Shepherd (52–53) sees the targums participating in an OT theme—namely, crushing the head of God's enemy. OT examples include Num. 24:17; Judg. 5:26; Hab. 3:13; Pss. 68:21; 110:6. Paul, then, continues this theme when he writes, "The God of peace will soon crush Satan under your feet" (Rom. 16:20 ESV). Shepherd (53) concludes, "Both Paul and the Palestinian Targum tradition associate the defeat of the enemy and the deliverance of God's people with the time of the Messiah." An important distinction between these traditions is the one who strikes the serpent. For Paul, it is the Messiah. For the targums, it is those who keep the Torah. Obedience to the Torah in the days of the Messiah appears elsewhere in the targums (see Tg. Isa. 4:2; 53:10; Tg. Song 7:14; 8:1).

Conclusion

In this essay, as in the previous one, we have seen uniquely targumic traditions that are paralleled in the NT: (1) "living by the sword," (2) "unrighteous mammon," (3) describing sin as "debt," (4) the Memra, and (5) messianic consolation. We have also seen targumic/NT parallels that are a part of a larger Jewish tradition: (1) the "second death," (2) the blessing of the womb in Luke 11:27 and Palestinian Targums Gen. 49:25, (3) the kingdom of God, (4) the sacrificial son, (5) angelology, (6) the eschatological world to come, (7) the eschatological garden of Eden, and (8) the Messiah.

Within this analysis, there are two distinctions worth noting. First, the rabbis and most of the targums reject the idea of fallen angels and a heavenly rebellion. The NT and Targum Pseudo-Jonathan, on the other hand, support this idea. Second, with regard to eschatology, the NT views the Messiah, Christ Jesus, as central to the fulfillment of the eschaton. For the rabbis, however, the Messiah is not viewed in this way. The "days of the King Messiah" are considered a necessary eschatological step but will not bring about the absolute consummation of salvation (see Strack and Billerbeck, 4:799–976, esp. 816–21).

See also OT Use of the OT: Comparison with the NT Use of the OT; *other Targums articles; Dead Sea Scrolls articles; Mishnah, Talmud, and Midrashim articles; Philo articles; Septuagint articles*

Bibliography. Beale, G. K., *The Book of Revelation*, NIGTC (Eerdmans, 1999); Beale, G. K., and S. M. McDonough, "Revelation," in *CNTUOT*, 1081–158; Chilton, B. D., *The Glory of Israel*, JSOTSup 23 (JSOT Press, 1982); Ciampa, R. E., and B. S. Rosner, "1 Corinthians," in *CNTUOT*, 695–752; Everson, D. L., "Angels in the Targums" (PhD diss., Hebrew Union College, 2009); Flesher, P. V. M., and B. Chilton, *The Targums*, SAIS 12 (Brill, 2011); Hayward, C. T. R., *Targums and the Transmission of Scripture into Judaism and Christianity*, SAIS 10 (Brill, 2010); Keener, C. S., *The Gospel of John*, 2 vols. (Hendrickson, 2003); Maher, M., *Targum Pseudo-Jonathan: Genesis*, ArBib 1B (Liturgical Press, 1992); McNamara, M., *The New Testament and the Palestinian Targums to the Pentateuch*, AnBib 27 (Pontifical Biblical Institute, 1966); McNamara, *Targum and Testament Revisited*, 2nd ed. (Eerdmans, 2010); Moore, G. F., "Intermediaries in Jewish Theology: Memra, Shekinah, Metatron," *HTR* 15, no. 1 (1922): 41–85; Pao, D. W., and E. J. Schnabel, "Luke," in *CNTUOT*, 251–606; Shapiro, M. D., "The Philosophy Implicit in Rabbinic Angelology" (PhD diss., Hebrew Union College, 1977); Shepherd, M. B., "Targums, the New Testament, and Biblical Theology of the Messiah," *JETS* 51 (2008): 45–58; Strack, H. L., and P. Billerbeck, *Kommentar zum Neuen Testament aus Talmud und Midrasch*, 6 vols. (Beck, 1961); Urbach, E. E., *The Sages* (Harvard University Press, 1975).

DAVID EVERSON

Temple

This is one of the more substantial topical essays in this dictionary, since significant parts of other essays refer to

This essay is an abbreviated summary and revision of G. K. Beale, *A New Testament Biblical Theology* (Baker Academic, 2011), 614–48, wherein are found secondary sources in support.

this essay as a basis for their discussions. The first tabernacle and temple existed long before Israel happened on the scene. Indeed, it is apparent that the first sanctuary is discernible from the very beginning of history.

The Garden of Eden Is a Temple in the First Creation

The first sanctuary was in Eden. But how could we possibly know this? There was no architectural structure in Eden, nor do the words "temple" or "sanctuary" occur as a description of Eden in Gen. 1–3. Such a claim may sound strange to the ears of many. But a number of scholars recently have argued this from one angle or another.

Eight observations supporting the notion that Eden was a sanctuary. (1) The temple was the unique place of God's presence later in the OT, where Israel had to go to experience that presence. The same Hebrew verbal form (*hithpael*) used for God's "walking back and forth" in the garden (Gen. 3:8) also describes God's presence in the tabernacle (Lev. 26:12; Deut. 23:14 [23:15 MT]; 2 Sam. 7:6–7; Ezek. 28:14).

(2) God places Adam in the garden "to cultivate it and keep it" (Gen. 2:15 NASB). The two Hebrew words for "cultivate" and "keep" (respectively, *ʿābad* and *šāmar*) usually are translated "serve" and "guard." These two words have this meaning without exception every other time they occur together in the OT, referring either to Israelites serving and guarding/obeying God's word (about 10x) or to priests who serve God in the temple and guard it from unclean things entering it (Num. 3:7–8; 8:25–26; 18:5–6; 1 Chron. 23:32; Ezek. 44:14). Adam also is portrayed as wearing priestly attire in Ezek. 28:13. Some identify this figure as Satan, but the description points to this figure being Adam. The jewels that are his "covering" (NASB) have correspondence to those listed in Exod. 28:17–21 (though most of the Hebrew words for the jewels are different, some translations [e.g., NASB] give the same names for the jewels, seeing them as synonyms for the jewel names in Exod. 28). The jewels in Exod. 28 describe the jewels on the ephod of Israel's high priest, who is a human, not an angel. Either the Ezekiel list is an allusion to the human priest's bejeweled clothing in Exod. 28 (which is likely; so Block, 106–9) or Exod. 28 has roots in an earlier tradition about Adam's apparel, which is represented by Ezekiel. Furthermore, since Ezek. 28:11–19 is likely addressed to a figure standing behind "the king of Tyre" (v. 11), who has sinned like the human king, it is more likely that the figure in Eden is also human. (Alternatively, the king of Tyre is painted with Adamic colors in order to explain his own fall as a king.) Not only does the LXX clearly identify Adam as the glorious figure dwelling in the primeval Eden in Ezek. 28:14 (as does Tg. Ezek. 28:12), but also it is plausible that the Hebrew text does so as well. And Ezek. 28:18 identifies Eden as having "sanctuaries," identifying it as a temple (which I will discuss further below).

Therefore, Adam is to be the first priest to serve in and guard God's temple. When Adam fails to guard the temple by sinning and admitting an unclean serpent to defile the temple, he loses his priestly role, and the two cherubim take over the responsibility of guarding the garden-temple: God "stationed the cherubim . . . to *guard* the way to the tree of life" (Gen. 3:24 NASB). Their role becomes memorialized in Israel's later temple when God commands Moses to make two statues of angelic figures and station them on either side of the ark of the covenant in the holy of holies inside the temple. Like the cherubim, Israel's priests are to "keep watch" (the same word as "keep" in Gen. 2:15 NASB) over the temple as "gatekeepers" (2 Chron. 23:19; Neh. 12:45).

(3) The "tree of life" itself is probably the model for the lampstand placed directly outside the holy of holies in Israel's temple: it looks like a small tree trunk with seven protruding branches, three on one side and three on the other, and one branch going straight up from the trunk in the middle.

(4) Israel's later temple has wood carvings that give it a garden-like atmosphere and likely are intentional reflections of the garden of Eden (1 Kings 6:29, 32, 35; 7:18–20), which suggests that Eden is the original/first temple.

(5) Just as Israel's later temple and the end-time temple of Ezekiel rest on mountains with entrances facing east (Exod. 15:17 [Zion]; Ezek. 40:2; 43:12), so Eden is situated on a mountain (Ezek. 28:14, 16) with its entrance facing east (Gen. 3:24).

(6) Just as a river flows out from Eden (Gen. 2:10), so the postexilic temple (Let. Aris. 89–91) and the eschatological temple in both Ezek. 47:1–12 and Rev. 22:1–2 have rivers flowing out from the center (likewise Rev. 7:15–17 and, probably, Zech. 14:8–9). Ezekiel 40–47 generally depicts latter-day Mount Zion (and its temple) with descriptions of Eden to show that the promises originally inherent in Eden will be realized in the fulfillment of his vision (cf. Ps. 36:8–9; Jer. 17:7–8, where fertility and rivers also describe Israel's temple).

(7) Like Israel's later temple, we can discern a tripartite sacred structure in the garden of Eden: (a) Eden, the source of the rivers (the holy of holies); (b) the actual garden adjacent to the water source (the holy place, where most priestly activity occurs); (c) the outer, uninhabited area of the world (the outer court). Similarly, in the end-time temple of Rev. 22:1–2 there is "a river of the water of life . . . coming *from the throne of God and of the Lamb*" and flowing into a garden-like grove modeled on the first paradise in Gen. 2, as is much of Ezekiel's portrayal.

(8) In the light of these numerous conceptual and linguistic parallels between Eden and Israel's tabernacle and temple, it should not be surprising that Ezek. 28 refers to "Eden, the garden of God . . . the holy mountain of God" (vv. 13–14 NASB) and says it contains "sanctuaries" (v. 18), which elsewhere is a plural way of referring

to Israel's tabernacle (Lev. 21:23) and temple (Ezek. 7:24; so also Jer. 51:51).

The inherent purpose of Eden being a sanctuary. All these observations together point to the likelihood that the garden of Eden was the first sanctuary in sacred history. Adam was to "guard" this sanctuary. He was also to subdue the earth: "God blessed them. . . . 'Be fruitful and multiply, and fill the earth, and subdue it; and rule over the fish of the sea and over the birds of the sky, and over every living thing that moves on the earth'" (Gen. 1:28 NASB). He was to extend the geographical boundaries of the garden as he began to rule over and subdue the earth until Eden covered the whole earth. the presence of God that was limited to Eden was to be extended throughout the whole earth. God's presence was to "fill" the entire earth.

As we know, Adam was not faithful and obedient in subduing the earth and extending the garden sanctuary. Thus, not only was the garden-temple not extended throughout the earth but also Adam himself was cast out of the garden and no longer enjoyed God's presence. He lost his function as God's priest in the temple.

Humanity becomes worse and worse after Adam's fall and expulsion from the garden-temple, and only a small remnant of the human race is faithful. God eventually destroys the whole earth by flood because it has become so thoroughly wicked. Only Noah and his immediate family are spared. As a result, God starts the creation of the world over again.

It is possible that God has started building another temple for his people to dwell in and to experience his presence during Noah's time. Noah and his sons, however, are not faithful and obedient, so if God has begun another temple-building process, it is immediately stopped because of the sin of Noah and his sons. They follow in Adam's sinful footsteps. In fact, Noah's "fall" is reminiscent of Adam's, as both sin in the context of a garden. "Noah began farming and planted a vineyard. And he drank of the wine and became drunk," and this led to further sin by his sons (Gen. 9:20–21).

After the disobedience of Noah and his family, God starts over again and chooses Abraham and his descendants, Israel, to reestablish his temple.

Adam's Commission as a Priest-King to Rule and Expand the Temple Is Passed On to the Patriarchs

After Adam's failure to fulfill God's mandate, God raises up other Adam-like figures to whom his commission was passed on. Some changes in the commission occur as a result of sin entering the world. However, Adam's descendants fail like him. Failure continues until a "last Adam" arises, who finally fulfills the commission on behalf of humanity.

The passing on of Adam's commission to his descendants. Adam's commission is passed on to Noah, to Abraham, and to his descendants. The following references in Genesis are a sample of this (all NASB):

> Gen. 1:28: "*God blessed them*; and God said to them, '*Be fruitful and multiply, and fill the earth*, and *subdue it; and rule* over the fish of the sea and over the birds of the sky and over every living thing that moves on the earth.'"
>
> Gen. 9:1, 7: "And God blessed Noah and his sons and said to them, '*Be fruitful and multiply, and fill the earth. . . . Be fruitful and multiply; populate the earth abundantly and multiply in it.*'"
>
> Gen. 12:2–3: "And I will make you a great nation, and *I will bless you*, and make your name great; and so you *be a blessing*; and *I will bless those who bless you*, and the one who curses you I will curse. And in you *all the families of the earth* will be blessed."

See likewise Gen. 17:2, 6, 8, 16; 22:17–18; 26:3–4, 24; 28:3–4, 13–14; 35:11–12; 47:27.

In fact, the same commission given to the patriarchs is restated numerous times in subsequent OT books both to Israel and to the true, eschatological people of God. As we have seen, like Adam, Noah and his children fail to perform this commission. God then gives the essence of the commission to Abraham (Gen. 12:2–3; 17:2, 6, 8, 16; 22:18), Isaac (Gen. 26:3–4, 24), Jacob (Gen. 28:3–4, 14; 35:11–12; 48:3, 15–16), and to Israel (see Deut. 7:13 and Gen. 47:27; Exod. 1:7; Ps. 107:38; Isa. 51:2, the latter four passages of which state the initial fulfillment of the promise to Abraham in Israel). Recall that the commission in Gen. 1:26–28 involves the following elements, especially as summarized in 1:28: (1) "God blessed them;" (2) "be fruitful and multiply"; (3) "fill the earth;" (4) "subdue" the earth; (5) "rule over" all the earth.

The commission is repeated, for example, to Abraham: "I will greatly *bless you*, and I will greatly *multiply your seed* . . . ; and *your seed shall possess the gate of their enemies* [= "subdue and rule"]. In your seed all the nations *of the earth* shall be *blessed*" (Gen. 22:17–18). God expresses the universal scope of the commission by underscoring that the goal is to bless "all the nations of the earth." It is natural, therefore, that in the initial statement of the commission in Gen. 12:1–3 God commands Abraham, "Go forth from your country. . . . And so *you shall be a blessing*. . . . And in you all the families of the earth will be blessed."

The passing on of Adam's commission together with temple building. Commentators apparently have overlooked something interesting: the Adamic commission is repeated in direct connection with what looks like the building of small sanctuaries. Just as the Gen. 1:28 commission was initially to be carried out by Adam in a localized place, enlarging the borders of the arboreal sanctuary, so the restatement of the commission to Israel's patriarchs results in the following: (1) God's appearance (except in Gen. 12:8; 13:3–4); (2) pitching a tent (LXX: "tabernacle"); (3) a mountain; (4) altars and worship (i.e., "calling on the name of the LORD," which probably includes sacrificial offerings and prayer) at the place of the restatement; (5) the place name "Bethel," meaning the "House of God." (The only case of altar-building not containing these elements nor linked to the Gen. 1 commission is 33:20.) The combination of these five elements occurs elsewhere in the OT only in describing Israel's tabernacle or temple.

There seems to be more significance to the construction of these sacrificial sites than merely a theophany and a move to a new site. The patriarchs appear also to have built these worship areas as impermanent, miniature forms of sanctuaries that symbolized the notion that their progeny were to spread out from a divine sanctuary to subdue the earth in fulfillment of the commission in Gen. 1:26–28. Although the patriarchs constructed no buildings, these sacred spaces can be considered sanctuaries comparable to the first nonarchitectural sanctuary in the garden of Eden, particularly because a tree often is present at these sites. A holy piece of geography or a sacred area can be considered a true sanctuary or temple even when no architectural building is constructed there, as we have seen with Eden, which will be important to recall later.

Thus, the patriarchs' commissions involve the building of sanctuaries, like Adam's commission connects with the garden-temple. These informal sanctuaries in Genesis point to Israel's later tabernacle and temple from which Israel is to branch out over all the earth reflecting God's presence.

The only *architectural* feature designating a sacred space prior to Moses's construction of the tabernacle was an altar. This suggests that the miniature sanctuaries of the patriarchs adumbrated the later temple, which is further pointed to by the observation that later altars were installed into the bigger sacred spaces of the tabernacle and temple.

Abraham, Isaac, and Jacob building altars at Shechem between Bethel and Ai, at Hebron, and near Moriah resulted in Israel's future land becoming dotted with shrines. This pilgrim-like activity was probably symbolic of claiming the land for God and Israel's future temple, where God would take up his permanent residence in the capital of that land. All these smaller sanctuaries pointed to the greater one to come in Jerusalem.

The preparations for the reestablishment of a larger-scale tabernacle, and then temple, began at the exodus. Again, God brought about chaos in creation on a small scale (in Egypt as a microcosm) and delivered Israel to be the spearhead for his new humanity. Upon them was placed the temple-building commission originally given to Adam. The patriarchal altars point to the altars in Israel's tabernacle and temple, where sacrifices are offered because of Israel's sin.

Israel's Tabernacle in the Wilderness and Later Temple Reestablish the Garden of Eden's Sanctuary

What was implicit with the patriarchs and with Moses at Sinai becomes explicit with Israel's tabernacle and temple. First Chronicles narrates David's preparations for building the temple that Solomon will complete. David's preparatory actions include all the same elements found within the fivefold small-scale temple building activities of Abraham, Isaac, and Jacob. (1) David begins the preparations on a mountain (Mount Moriah). (2) David experiences a theophany (he sees "the angel of the LORD standing between earth and heaven" [1 Chron. 21:16 NASB; cf. 2 Chron. 3:1]). (3) At this site "David built an altar to the LORD." (4) There he "offered burnt offerings . . . and he called to the LORD" (1 Chron. 21:26 NASB). (5) David calls the place "the house of the LORD God" (1 Chron. 22:1) because this is the site of Israel's future temple. These parallels make clear that the altar-building activities of the patriarchs were constructions of small-scale sanctuaries that climax with the larger-scale construction of Israel's temple.

The following considerations show that Israel's tabernacle and subsequent temple were both new temples of a new creation. The dwelling place of God among Israel is explicitly called a "tabernacle" and then a "temple" for the first time in redemptive history. God's unique presence with his covenant people has never been formally called a "tabernacle" or "temple" (though see Gen. 28:10–22). We have seen how, nevertheless, the garden of Eden has essential similarities with Israel's temple, which shows that Israel's temple is a development of the sanctuary implicit in Gen. 2.

The temple as a symbol of the cosmos. Not yet mentioned is the fact that the Eden temple also serves as a little earthly model of God's temple in heaven that eventually would encompass the whole earth. This is seen most clearly in Israel's temple in the following ways.

Psalm 78:69 says something amazing about Israel's temple: God "built His sanctuary like the heights, like the earth which He has founded forever" (NASB; see also Exod. 25:9, 40). This tells us that God modeled the temple to be a little replica of the entire heaven and earth. Yet God says, "Heaven is My throne, and the earth is My footstool. Where then is a house you could build for Me?" (Isa. 66:1 NASB). God never intended for Israel's little, localized temple to last forever, since, like the Eden temple, Israel's temple was a small model of something much bigger: God and his universal presence, which could never be contained eternally by any localized earthly structure.

Israel's tabernacle and temple are a miniature model of God's huge cosmic temple that is to dominate the heavens and earth at the end of time. The temple is a symbolic model pointing not merely to the present cosmos but also to the new heaven and earth that will be perfectly filled with God's presence. The figurative features of the three sections of the temple—the holy of holies, the holy place, and the outer courtyard—are evidence that the temple is a miniature, symbolic model: the holy of holies represents the invisible heavenly dimension, the holy place represents the visible heavens, and the outer courtyard represents the visible sea and earth, where humans live. I will elaborate on this symbolism in the following sections.

The holy of holies as a symbol of the unseen heaven. That the holy of holies represents the invisible heaven where God and his angels dwell is suggested by the following:

1. The statuette cherubim around the ark of the covenant and the figures of the cherubim woven into the curtain that guards the holy of holies reflect the real cherubim in heaven who stand guard around God's throne.
2. The fact that no image of God is in the holy of holies and that it "appears" empty further point to it representing the invisible heaven.
3. The holy of holies is the place where the heavenly realm extends down to the earthly, explaining why the ark of the covenant is called God's "footstool." God is pictured sitting on his throne in heaven with his invisible feet on the ottoman of the ark of the covenant.
4. The holy of holies is separated from the holy place and the outside courtyard by a curtain. It symbolizes the separation of the invisible heavenly dimension from the physical.
5. Even the high priest, who could enter only once a year, is prohibited from viewing the light of God's glorious presence by an incense cloud. This underscores again the separateness of this most holy inner space, which represents the holy, invisible heavenly sphere. The incense cloud itself may have a further association with the clouds of the visible heaven, which itself points to the invisible heaven.

The holy place as a symbol of the visible heaven. Based on the following, the holy place likely represents the visible heavens that are still separated from the earth:

1. The curtains of the holy place are blue, purple, and scarlet, representing the variegated colors of the sky, and figures of winged creatures are woven into all the curtains throughout the tabernacle, enforcing the imagery of the visible heavens.
2. The lampstand has seven lamps on it, and in Solomon's temple there are ten lampstands. Thus, if people were to peer into the holy place, they would see seventy lights, which would resemble the heavenly light sources (stars, planets, sun, and moon) against the darker setting of the curtains of the tabernacle and temple.
3. This symbolism is enhanced by observing that the Hebrew word for "light" (*mā'ôr*) is used ten times in the Pentateuch for the lamps on the lampstand. The only other place in the Pentateuch where the word occurs is in Gen. 1:14–16 (5×), where it refers to the sun, moon, and stars. The tabernacle appears to have been designed to represent the creative work of God, who "stretches out the heavens like a curtain and spreads them out like a tent to dwell in," and "who has created these stars" to hang in this heavenly tent (Isa. 40:22, 26 NASB). Likewise, Ps. 19:1–5 (NASB) says that in "the heavens" God "placed a tent for the sun." This connection may plausibly explain why the holy place was covered with gold (1 Kings 6:20–21), on the ceiling, floor, and walls; the sheen of the precious metal would mimic the reflection of the stars of heaven (as was true in ancient Near Eastern temples, especially in Egypt).
4. Perhaps because of this biblical evidence, the seven lamps on the lampstand in the holy place were understood by first-century Jews (particularly Josephus and Philo) to represent the seven light sources visible to the naked eye of the ancient person, underscoring that this second section of the temple symbolizes the visible heavens (Josephus, *Ant.* 3.145; *J.W.* 5.217; Philo, *Heir* 221–25; *Moses* 2.102–5; *QE* 2.73–81). Later Judaism equated the seven lamps on the lampstand with the "lights in the expanse of heaven" mentioned in Gen. 1:14–16 (so Tg. Ps.-J. Exod. 40:4; Num. Rab. 15:7; 12:13). Furthermore, the first-century Jewish historian Josephus, who had firsthand acquaintance with the temple, said that the outer curtain of the holy place had needlework on it of stars, representing the heavens.

The courtyard as a symbol of the visible sea and earth. The courtyard probably represents the visible sea and earth. This identification of the outer court is suggested further by the OT description, where the large metal washbasin and the altar in the temple courtyard are called respectively the "sea" (1 Kings 7:23–26) and the "bosom of the earth" (Ezek. 43:14 AT; the altar also likely was identified with the "mountain of God" in 43:16). The altar was also to be an altar of earth (in the early stages of Israel's history) or of uncut stone (Exod. 20:24–25), thus identifying it even more with the natural earth. Thus, both the sea and the altar appear to be cosmic symbols that may have been associated in the Israelite mind with the seas and the earth (cf. the ten smaller washbasins, five on each side of the holy place [1 Kings 7:38–39]). The bronze sea was seven feet high and fifteen feet in diameter, holding ten thousand gallons of water, and would not be convenient for priestly washing, indicating its symbolic nature (in this respect, the ten waist-high washbasins would have been the ones for daily practical cleansings). The arrangement of the twelve bulls "entirely encircling the sea" and the lily blossom decorating the brim also seem to present a partial miniature model of land and life surrounding the seas of the earth (2 Chron. 4:2–5 NASB). The twelve bulls also support the washbasin and are divided into groups of three, facing to the four points of the compass, which could reflect the four quadrants of the earth. Twelve oxen are pictured holding up the "sea" and designs of lions and oxen are on the washbasin stands, further pointing to an "earthly" identification of the outer courtyard. All Israelites, representing humanity at large, could enter the outer court and worship, which intimates its relationship with the visible earth.

The purpose of the temple as a symbol of the cosmos. The cumulative effect of these observations is that Israel's temple serves as a little earthly model of God's temple in heaven that will eventually encompass the whole earth. Specifically, the inner sanctuary of God's invisible presence will extend to include the visible heavens and earth. The latter two sections in the temple—the holy place and courtyard—symbolize the visible sky and earth, respectively, to show that they will be consumed by God's holy of holies presence.

The tripartite structure of the tabernacle is modeled on Mount Sinai's tripartite structure as a mountain temple. The very top of Sinai is the "holy of holies," where Moses as the high priest receives God's special revelatory law. The middle of Sinai is comparable to the "holy place," since Aaron and Israel's elders can enter there along with Moses. The base of Sinai is where all Israelites are and also where sacrifices were offered; this is equivalent to the outer court of the tabernacle.

Architectural models do not function only as models. They point to a bigger task, creating a bigger structure in the future. Israel's temple serves precisely the same purpose. The temple is a small-scale model and symbolic reminder to Israel that God's glorious presence will eventually fill the whole cosmos, and that the cosmos, not merely a small architectural structure, will be the container for God's glory. This probably was to serve as a motivation to the Israelites to be faithful witnesses to the world of God's glorious presence and truth, which was to expand outward from their temple.

The temple is a symbol to Israel of the task that God wants carried out. Israel is to execute the same task that Adam (and likely Noah) should have carried out but did not: to "multiply, and fill the earth, and subdue it" (Gen. 1:28 NASB). They are to execute this by expanding the local boundaries of the temple (where God's special revelatory presence is) to include the entire earth. That is, Israel is to spread God's presence throughout the whole earth. Interestingly, Israel, the land of promise, is repeatedly called the "garden of Eden" (cf. Gen. 13:10; Isa. 51:3; Ezek. 36:35; Joel 2:3), partly perhaps because Israel is to expand the limits of the temple and of its own land to the ends of the earth in the way that Adam should have. This is Israel's ultimate task, as is apparent from a number of OT passages prophesying that God will finally cause the sacred precinct of Israel's temple to expand and first encompass Jerusalem (Isa. 4:4–6; 54:2–3, 11–12; Jer. 3:16–17; Zech. 1:16–2:11), then the entire land of Israel (Ezek. 37:25–28), and then the whole earth (Dan. 2:34–35, 44–45; cf. Isa. 54:2–3).

Similarly, as we have seen, God gives to Israel the same commission that he has given to Adam and Noah. For example, God says to Abraham, the progenitor of Israel, "I will greatly bless you, and I will greatly multiply your seed . . . ; and your seed shall possess the gate of their enemies" (Gen. 22:17). Interestingly, Gen. 1:28 becomes both a commission and a promise to Abraham, Isaac, Jacob, and Israel.

Israel, however, does not carry out this great mandate to spread the temple of God's presence over the whole earth. The contexts of Isa. 42:6 and 49:6 express that Israel should have spread the light of God's presence throughout the earth, but it has not. Exodus 19:6 says that Israel collectively is to be "a kingdom of priests and a holy nation" going out to the nations and being mediators between God and the nations by bearing God's light of revelation. Instead of seeing the temple as a symbol of their task to expand God's presence to all nations, the Israelites wrongly view it as symbolic of their election as God's only true people and as an indication that God's presence is to be restricted to them as an ethnic nation. They believe that the gentiles will experience God's presence primarily through judgment.

Thus, God sends them out of their land into exile, which Isa. 45 compares to the darkness and chaos before creation in Gen. 1 (cf. Isa. 45:18–19). So God starts the process of temple-building all over again, but this time he plans that the local spiritual boundaries of all the past temples of Eden and Israel will be irreversibly expanded finally to circumscribe the boundaries of the entire earth. How does this occur?

Christ and His Followers Are a Temple in the New Creation

Christ is the temple that all earlier temples look toward and anticipate (cf. 2 Sam. 7:12–14; Zech. 6:12–13). Christ is the epitome of God's presence on earth as God incarnate, thus continuing the true form of the old temple, which was a foreshadowing of Christ's presence throughout the OT era. Jesus's repeated claim that forgiveness now comes through him and no longer through the sacrificial system of the temple suggests strongly that he is taking over the function of the temple. In fact, the forgiveness that he now offers is what the temple had imperfectly pointed to all along. Indeed, the ultimate redemptive-historical purpose of the temple sacrifices was to point typologically to Christ as the ultimate sacrifice, which he has offered for the sins of his people as a priest, at the cross, in the heavenly eschatological temple (see Rom. 3:25). In this respect, Christ refers to himself in the Synoptic Gospels as the "cornerstone" of the temple (Mark 12:10; Matt. 21:42; Luke 20:17). John 1:14 says that he became God's tabernacle in the world. Jesus is the sinless last Adam, who, partly on this basis, is able to inaugurate the expansion of the true temple, along with his followers, because their sin has been forgiven at the cross and Christ's Spirit has entered into them.

John 2:19–21 reports this exchange between Jesus and Jewish leaders: "Jesus answered them, 'Destroy this temple, and in three days I will raise it up.' The Jews then said, 'It took forty-six years to build this temple, and will You raise it up in three days?' But he was speaking of the temple of His body" (NASB). It is important to recognize that the Jews think that he is speaking of the physical temple that he has just cleansed, since the subject of the directly preceding verses is his unusual activity in the temple (2:14–17). The Jews are asking Jesus to adduce a sign to demonstrate his authority in cleansing the temple (2:18). But Jesus is referring to himself as the temple. He will be the end-time temple-builder by raising it up in the form of his body, in line with OT prophecies that predict that the Messiah will build the latter-day temple (again, see 2 Sam. 7:12–14; Zech. 6:12–13).

As alluded to earlier in this section, Jesus begins to take over the function of the old temple during his ministry, so that when he is crucified, he is being "destroyed" as the temple. The "raising up" of the temple in "three days" is an obvious reference to his resurrection (John 2:22a: "When He was raised from the dead, His disciples remembered that He said this" NASB). Again, we see the notion of new creation expressed in this, since we have seen repeatedly that new life and resurrection are none other than new creation. Relevant for understanding John 2 is my earlier observation that the OT temple symbolizes the entire creation and points forward to the entire new creation. In this light, Christ refers to his resurrection as a "raising up" of the temple to show that the purpose of the old temple all along was to point symbolically toward the time when God's special revelatory presence in the old temple would break out of the holy of holies and fill the entire new creation as his cosmic temple. Accordingly, Christ's precrucifixion life begins to fulfill this (see John 1:14), and his resurrection especially as the beginning of the new creation is the initial escalated fulfillment of the symbolic purpose of Israel's temple: the new creation has begun in Christ, so he is God's tabernacling presence of the new creation, which is to expand further until it is completed at the very end of the age by the whole cosmos becoming the temple of God's consummate presence.

Incidentally, if Jesus is what the temple prophetically pointed to all along, then it is doubtful that we can think of a possible future physical temple as anything more than a secondary fulfillment, though even this is unlikely. Second Corinthians 1:20 says, "For as many as are the [OT] promises of God, in Him [Christ] they are yes" (NASB). Christ is the major beginning fulfillment of the prophecies of the end-time temple. Likewise, Israel's architectural temple was a symbolic shadow pointing typologically to the eschatological substance and "greater and more perfect tabernacle" (Heb. 9:11) in which Christ and the church would dwell and form a part. If so, it would seem to be the wrong approach for Christians to hope for the building of another architectural temple in Jerusalem composed of earthly "bricks and mortar" as a fulfillment of the OT temple prophecies. Is it too dogmatic to say that such an approach confuses the shadow with the end-time substance? Would this approach not seek to possess the cultic picture alongside the true christological reality to which the picture points (on which, see Heb. 8:2, 5; 9:8–11, 23–25)? And would it not posit a retrogression or reversal in the progress of redemptive history? It would be inconsistent to agree with the overall approach of this chapter and still hold to some expectation of an architectural temple.

The church as the temple in Acts. Although neither "temple," "sanctuary," nor other synonyms are used in Acts 2, the concept of the descending heavenly temple is woven throughout the narrative and forms part of its underlying meaning. The strongest evidence that a temple is present in the Acts 2 narrative is the image of the descent of the Holy Spirit in the form of "tongues as of fire" (2:3 NASB). Isaiah depicts God's tabernacling presence in his heavenly temple as God's "tongue like a consuming fire" (30:27–30 NASB). Isaiah 5:24–25 is similar, referring to an emblem of judgment, but not explicitly referring to a heavenly tabernacle (the Hebrew text has "tongue of fire," and the LXX versions of Theodotion, Aquila, and Symmachus have the Greek equivalent, *glōssa pyros*).

The repeated use of the image of "tongues of fire" in 1 En. 14 and 71 forms part of the heavenly temple and contributes to the overall effect of the burning theophany in the holy of holies, where "the flaming fire was around about him [God], and a great fire stood before him" (14:22). In addition, Qumran says the high priest's Urim and Thummim shone gloriously with "tongues of fire" (1Q29 1.3; 2.3). Therefore, we once more have the "tongues of fire" as a phenomenon occurring within the "holy of holies" or, more probably, the "holy place" of the temple as an expression of God's revelatory presence.

In the light of these OT and Jewish uses of "tongues of fire," the use of the same image in Acts 2 likely depicts God's presence from his heavenly temple descending upon his people and making them a part of it. These people then are to go out into the unbelieving gentile world representing God's tabernacling presence in order to make some of them part of that tabernacle. Acts 2 is the commencement of the church as the new temple.

The church as the temple in Paul. After Pentecost, when people believe in Jesus, they become a part of Jesus and the temple, since Jesus himself is the locus of that temple. According to Eph. 2:20–22, believers are then "built on the foundation of the apostles and prophets, Christ Jesus Himself being the cornerstone, in whom the whole building, being fitted together is growing into a holy temple in the Lord [Jesus], in whom you also are being built together into a dwelling of God in the Spirit" (NASB adapted). The Christian's identification with the temple is also affirmed by other statements (all NASB):

1. "Do you not know that you are a temple of God and that the Spirit of God dwells in you?" (1 Cor. 3:16, speaking of the corporate church).
2. "Do you not know that your body is a temple of the Holy Spirit who is in you?" (1 Cor. 6:19, referring to the individual Christian).
3. "For we are the temple of the living God" (2 Cor. 6:16a; cf. also 1 Pet. 2:5; Rev. 3:12; 11:1–2; all with reference to the corporate church).

This last verse is one of Paul's most explicit references to believers' identification as a temple. In 2 Cor. 6:16–17, Paul cites several texts from the OT to support the notion that the Corinthian believers are a temple in fulfillment of OT prophecy (e.g., Lev. 26:11–12; Ezek. 37:26–27 in 2 Cor. 6:16b; and Isa. 52:11; Ezek. 11:17; 20:41 LXX in 2 Cor. 6:17). Thus, we have a staccato rattling off of temple prophecies by Paul. Is Paul saying that the Corinthian church has begun to *fulfill* these prophecies, or is he merely saying that the church is *like* what these OT passages prophesy about the temple? Paul's application of these prophecies to the Corinthians makes it highly likely that this is actual inaugurated fulfillment.

One of the most theologically pregnant statements in all of Paul's writings occurs in 2 Cor. 1:20a (a verse noted earlier): "For as many as are the promises of God, in Him [Christ] they are yes" (NASB). The "promises" certainly refer to OT promises whose fulfillment began in Christ. Surely the end-time temple is among the prophetic promises that Paul has in mind. Both 1:20 and 7:1 refer to "promises" plural (the latter introduced with "therefore"), indicating that Paul expounds prophetic fulfillment of more than one prophecy in the intervening text. As is well known, the establishment of a new temple is prophesied to be part of Israel's restoration (e.g., Ezek. 37:26–28; 40:1–48:35). The "therefore" introducing 2 Cor. 7:1 shows that the promises fulfilled among the Corinthians are especially the temple promises in the directly preceding verses.

Christ initially fulfilled the temple promise (cf. 1:20), and the readers participate in that fulfillment also, as they are ones "having these promises" (7:1 NASB). The reason they and Paul fulfill the same promise that Christ fulfills is that God "establishes us with you in Christ" by "sealing" believers and giving the "Spirit in our hearts as a down payment" (1:21–22 NASB adapted). As Paul says in 1 Corinthians, the church is "a temple of God" in which "the Spirit of God dwells" (3:16 NASB [cf. 6:19]). They have only begun to fulfill the eschatological expectation of the temple, but a time will come when they perfectly realize that hope.

John's Vision of a New Creation, a New Jerusalem, and Eden Portrayed as a Cosmic Temple

The new heaven and the new earth in Rev. 21:1–22:5 are described as a temple because the temple, which equals God's presence, encompasses the whole earth due to the work of Christ. At the end of time, the true temple will come down completely from heaven and fill the whole creation (as 21:1–3, 10; 21:22 affirm). Revelation 21:1 commences, as we have seen, with John's vision of "a new heaven and a new earth" followed by his vision of the "new Jerusalem, coming down out of heaven" (v. 2). He then hears a loud voice proclaiming that "the tabernacle of God is among men, and He will tabernacle among them" (v. 3 NASB adapted). It is likely that the second vision in v. 2 interprets the first vision of the new cosmos, and that what is heard about the tabernacle in v. 3 interprets vv. 1–2. If so, the new creation of v. 1 is identical to the new Jerusalem of v. 2, and both represent the same reality as the tabernacle of v. 3.

Consequently, the new creation and the new Jerusalem are none other than God's tabernacle. This tabernacle is the true temple of God's special presence portrayed throughout Rev. 21. This cultic divine presence, formerly limited to Israel's temple and then the church, will fill the whole earth and heaven and become coextensive with it. Then the eschatological goal of the temple of the garden of Eden dominating the entire creation will finally be fulfilled (so 22:1–3).

John says in his portrayal of the consummated condition of the new heavens and earth in Rev. 21:22, "I saw no temple in it, because the Lord God the Almighty and the Lamb are its temple" (NASB). Unlike the OT where the container for the divine glory was often an architectural building, in the new age this old physical container will be shed like a cocoon and the new physical container will be the entire cosmos. The ultimate essence of the temple is the glorious divine presence. If such is the case in the consummated form of the cosmos, would this not begin to be the case in the inaugurated phase of the latter days? The glorious divine presence of Christ and the Spirit among his people composes the beginning form of the eschatological temple.

Thus, we see temple prophecies such as Ezek. 37; 40–48; and Isa. 54 fulfilled by the Rev. 21:1–22:5 vision prophetically depicting the time when the intended universal cosmic design of OT temples, including that of Eden, will be completed or accomplished.

Conclusion

The essence of the temple, the glorious presence of God, sheds its OT architectural cocoon by emerging in Christ, then dwelling in his people, and finally dwelling eternally throughout the whole earth. Thus, again, we see a major NT idea: Christ and the church are the end-time temple, another facet of the already/not-yet new creation.

See also Adam, First and Last; Image of God

Bibliography. Beale, G. K., *The Temple and the Church's Mission* (Apollos, 2004); Block, D. I., *The Book of Ezekiel: Chapters 25–48*, NICOT (Eerdmans, 1998); Clifford, R. J., "The Temple and the Holy Mountain," in *The Temple in Antiquity*, ed. T. G. Madsen, RSMS 9 (Brigham Young University Press, 1984), 107–24; Clowney, E. P., "The Final Temple," *WTJ* 35 (1992): 156–89; Cody, A., *Heavenly Sanctuary and Liturgy in the Epistle to the Hebrews* (Grail Publications, 1960); Cole, A., *The New Temple* (Tyndale, 1950); Gärtner, B., *The Temple and the Community in Qumran and the New Testament*, SNTSMS 1 (Cambridge University Press, 1965); Gurtner, D. M., *The Torn Veil*, SNTSMS 139 (Cambridge University Press, 2007); Heil, J. P., "The Narrative Strategy and Pragmatics of the Temple Theme in Mark," *CBQ* 59, no. 1 (1997): 76–100; Kerr, A. R., *The Temple of Jesus' Body*, JSNTSup 220 (Sheffield Academic, 2002); Koester, C. R., *The Dwelling of God*, CBQMS 22 (Catholic Biblical Association of America, 1989); Levenson, J. D., "The Temple and the World," *JR* 64 (1984): 275–98; McKelvey, R. J., *The New Temple* (Oxford University Press, 1969); Morales, L. M., ed., *Cult and Cosmos*, BTS 18 (Peeters, 2014); Morales, *The Tabernacle Pre-Figured*, BTS 15 (Peeters, 2012); Spatafora, A., *From the "Temple of God" to God as the Temple*, TGST 27 (Gregorian University Press, 1997); Wenham, G. J., "Sanctuary Symbolism in the Garden of Eden Story," in *Proceedings of the Ninth World Congress of Jewish Studies, Division A* (World Union of Jewish Studies, 1986), 19–25; Woudstra, M. H., "The Tabernacle in Biblical-Theological Perspective," in *New Perspectives on the Old Testament*, ed. J. B. Payne (Word, 1970), 88–103.

G. K. Beale

Testimony Hypothesis

See History of Interpretation: 1800 to Present

Theological Interpretation of Scripture

Scripture is the soul of theology, including the theology of the NT. The NT authors were saturated in Scripture—namely, the OT. Rudolf Bultmann directed his famous question, "Is exegesis without presuppositions possible?" (Bultmann, 145–54) to twentieth-century biblical interpreters, but it's worth posing to the first-century apostles too: "Is NT use of the OT without presuppositions possible?" Specifically, which *theological* presuppositions—convictions about God's relationship to the authors, words, and readers of the Bible—inform the apostles' exegesis, and should they also inform ours? How is that ancient practice, the NT use of the OT, related to the contemporary practice known as theological interpretation of Scripture (henceforth TIS)—namely, reading the two Testaments to hear the one word of God for the one people of God, yesterday and today?

We begin by asking whether the NT authors were themselves theological interpreters. We then examine ways in which TIS stretches the notion of the "proper context" for exegesis. This sets the stage for a consideration of how these expanded contexts enable a reading of the NT use of the OT in a trinitarian framework.

NT Use or Theological Interpretation of the OT?

The "theological" qualifier to "interpretation of Scripture" signals what enthusiasts of TIS have in common: a prevailing interest in deploying theological categories more fundamentally than hermeneutical and philosophical ones to describe the agents, matter, process, and aims of reading Christian Scripture. Three initial questions bring into focus TIS's particular interest in the NT use of the OT.

OT and TIS. Does the OT refer to Jesus Christ and, if so, how? Paul says it is "of first importance" that Christ died for our sins and was raised on the third day "according to the Scriptures" (1 Cor. 15:3–4). He does not say which Scriptures, "but the point is that he can presuppose that it is sufficient for his argument merely to allude to the *possibility* of adducing scriptures. And this implies that they are common ground between him and his readers" (Lindars, 59).

Marcion's rejection of the OT and its wrathful God precipitated a theological crisis in the early church: Do OT texts qualify as Christian Scripture? Tertullian rightly rejected Marcion's claim that Jesus's teaching about the Father's love is incompatible with the malignant acts of the God of the OT, by pointing out the extent to which NT authors draw on the OT to identify Jesus Christ and explain his saving work.

Jesus himself asks his disciples, "Who do you say I am?" (Matt. 16:15). It was no final exam, but what if it were an open-book exam, the book in question being the OT? Should they have been able to prove from the Scriptures that Jesus was the Christ, and could they have said whose son he was?

Jesus describes events in his own life as "fulfilling" Scripture. After his resurrection, he "explained to them what was said in all the Scriptures concerning himself" (Luke 24:27). We can rephrase our final exam question: What did the OT authors know (about Jesus), and when did they know it? Do the prophets intend their discourse to be taken as predictive, as types prefiguring

NT antitypes, or would they repudiate the use the NT authors make of it? "It would be no exaggeration to understand the hermeneutical problem of the Old Testament as *the* problem of Christian theology, and not just as one problem among others" (Gunneweg, 2).

Recent scholarship has made great strides in understanding the NT use of the OT: how pervasive it is; how it resembles Jewish ways of reading in the context of Second Temple Judaism; how varied it is (e.g., direct quotes, allusions, echoes). What TIS brings to the discussion is an interest in theological presuppositions and contexts other than those of the original historical authors, on which more below.

NT and TIS. Are the apostles theological interpreters of Scripture? The NT identifies Jesus largely by relating his person and work to OT precedents, including names (e.g., "Son of Man"), symbols (e.g., "lamb"), and events (e.g., his death as "exodus" [Luke 9:31]). Scholars have disagreed, however, as to whether the OT authors meant everything the NT authors find in their texts. Stated pointedly: Does the NT use of the OT count as genuine interpretation? There is a difference, after all, between employing a text for one's own purposes and reading it to discover its author's communicative intention. "Users" may coerce a text to say something against its will; by way of contrast, "interpreters" are respecters of authorial persons and their intentions (Vanhoozer, 155–58).

TIS helps clarify the NT use of the OT by posing three questions about the notion of *use*. Most importantly, *whose* use counts as the real meaning: the prophets', the apostles', or the Holy Spirit's, who according to the Nicene Creed "spoke by the prophets" and who guides later readers into all truth (John 16:13)? Second, *what kind* of use? David Kelsey has examined how contemporary theologians appeal to Scripture to prove doctrine, but the biblical authors' use of Scripture merits further attention. Are the apostles using the OT as proof texts, predictions, prophecies, typological patterns, or something else? Third, *why* are the apostles using the OT? Is their final purpose apologetic, doctrinal, moral, pastoral, or something else?

All these queries pose the key question: How did the NT authors read the OT? At one end of the spectrum are those who argue that the NT writers changed the meaning of the OT, *using* it for their own purposes rather than attempting to hear the OT writers on their own terms. At the other end of the spectrum are those who contend that the NT writers always respected the original intentions of the OT authors, even as they applied their texts to new situations. Everything depends on clarifying the hermeneutical presuppositions of the NT authors, which for proponents of TIS are primarily theological.

Whatever we finally decide about the NT use of the OT, we still have to face the follow-up question: Should readers today go and do likewise? Can we, should we, may we interpret the OT the way the apostles do? The NT writers lived in a reading culture that employed Jewish exegetical techniques that modern biblical scholars view as either illegitimate or difficult to imitate. However, some think that because the apostles were inspired, their teaching is nevertheless authoritative: "Our commitment as Christians is to the reproduction of the apostolic faith and doctrine, and not necessarily to the specific apostolic exegetical practices" (Longenecker, 219).

Can we hold to the apostles' doctrine without imitating their exegesis? The same question arises in connection with the church fathers. Some biblical scholars would like the apostles and church fathers alike to subscribe to the old adage: "Do what I say (i.e., trust my doctrine), not what I do (i.e., beware my hermeneutic)." Parents can be embarrassing, to be sure. The question is whether we can maintain the apostolic tradition, and the patristic doctrine of the Trinity, without their respective biblical hermeneutics: "Theologies which are unable to sustain the broad premodern Catholic tradition of reading Scripture will also find it difficult to sustain dense engagement with the doctrinal heritage they may uphold" (Ayres, 421).

Neither the apostles' nor the church fathers' ways of interpreting Scripture are obvious or familiar to contemporary readers, but that alone does not make their readings arbitrary or illegitimate (Beale, 7–10).

Earlier we asked whether the OT refers to Jesus. Perhaps the real question is how Jesus refers to the OT, for the status of the apostles as rightful theological interpreters of the OT ultimately rests on our verdict concerning Jesus's own use of the OT. C. H. Dodd (126–27) famously suggested that the NT authors likely learned their hermeneutics from Jesus. If Christians should hold the doctrine of Scripture that Jesus himself held (Wenham, 7), should they not also read the OT the way Jesus read it? Perhaps we need a new quest, one for the theological presuppositions of the historical Jesus (see Barrett).

NT use of OT and TIS. Does the NT use of the OT imply a trinitarian frame of reference? Many of the leading voices in TIS take their cue not from the apostles' use of the prophets but from the church fathers' use of the prophets and apostles. One of the characteristic features of TIS is its determination to retrieve Nicene orthodoxy and, to some extent, what we might call Nicene hermeneutics. This "retrieval" of patristic modes of reading has more in common with the NT use of the OT than it does with modern grammatical-historical exegetical methods. David Steinmetz may have been thinking of the contrast between medieval and modern biblical interpretation when he declared the "superiority of precritical exegesis," but surely this phrase encompasses the NT use of the OT too. What TIS admires in precritical authors is precisely their use of the OT as the hermeneutical key that unlocks the meaning of Jesus Christ (and vice versa).

The most important question TIS puts to the NT use of the OT concerns the right frame of reference, that coordinate system with which to connect the canonical dots. For example, should we read the OT according to the original author's historical frame of reference exclusively, or may one employ the redemptive-historical frame of reference the NT authors used to connect OT dots (e.g., types) to the story of Jesus? The signature move of TIS is to say that Christians can read the OT with a redemptive-historical or even canonical frame of reference. Those who do so do not deny the role of context for proper interpretation; rather, they expand it.

Theology is the attempt to understand everything, including the NT use of the OT, in relation to God. The most radical theological issue pertaining to the NT use of the OT therefore concerns theology proper, the doctrine of God: "Who is the God of the whole Bible? and How do we read the Bible in light of this God?" (Rowe, "Biblical," 295).

The Ways of TIS: Expanding "Proper Context"

TIS is best understood as both retrieval and reaction. Proponents of TIS assert the superiority of precritical exegesis not because medieval interpreters were smarter than their modern counterparts but because they were explicitly Christian in their approach to hermeneutics. TIS is a reaction to what its proponents take to be an undue restriction of meaning to the historical horizons of the original authors (i.e., the world "behind" the text). They do not object to historical criticism per se, only to the reductionist assumption that its meaning is limited to the communicative intention of its original authors. TIS reckons modern biblical studies to be more likely right in what it affirms (e.g., the historical sense) than in what it denies (e.g., a "spiritual" sense).

TIS reacts negatively to a certain form of modern academic biblical theology for the sake of retrieving another kind of biblical theology. Modern academic biblical theology, of the kind promoted by James Barr and Krister Stendahl, aims to provide historically accurate descriptions of the biblical authors' ideas of God in their own terms and stages of development. Often this involves a strict distinction between saying "what it meant" and "what it means" (see Stendahl). Practitioners of this kind of biblical theology strive to be objective historians who refrain from invoking their own faith commitments, and from using any categories drawn from postbiblical creedal or confessional theology, in order to concentrate on the ways Israel and the early church expressed their beliefs and experiences.

One result of such historical description is the recognition that there is not one theology but many theologies represented by the various biblical authors, a diversity that threatens the unity of the canon and widens the gulf between church and academy even further. When biblical theologians propose a unifying concept like covenant (Eichrodt) or God's elusive presence (Terrien), critics object that it is an extrabiblical construct drawn from confessional theology or philosophy (Fowl, 27).

Proponents of TIS resist the idea that biblical interpretation is a two-step dance, with exegesis (historical description) leading and systematic theology (doctrine) always following. Instead of viewing theology as an application of the results of a prior exegesis, TIS views biblical interpretation itself as thoroughly theological. TIS looks through and not merely at doctrines such as sin, sanctification, and the church as it examines readers and the process of reading Scripture.

How, then, might representatives of TIS approach the three questions above, and with what theological resources? Much depends on judgments about the proper context in which to interpret previous Scripture. If exegesis is a historical investigation into what a human author meant (Fee), then is anything but an investigation into the original historical and literary context to be written off as eisegesis? Or may there be other kinds of context that bear on textual meaning? TIS challenges biblical studies precisely here, in its concept of which context is decisive for right reading. TIS thinks about context theologically and, in so doing, expands what may be considered "proper context" in the three following ways.

Ecclesial context: Rule of faith. The NT authors interpreted the OT as Christian Scripture with the intent of building up the early church. TIS seeks to go and do likewise. In the context of the early church, perhaps the most important hermeneutical principle was to read according to the rule of faith. Modern biblical scholars cry foul, however, when such "ruled readings" appear to impose a grid taken from church tradition onto the texts—the very opposite of their own discipline's aim.

There is a case to be made for viewing "ruled reading" as less a postapostolic tradition that unlocks an otherwise hidden meaning of the OT than a precritical form of biblical theology, where making inner-biblical (canonical) connections matters more than recovering details about the original context. The rule of faith does not supply supplementary material content to the Bible. On the contrary, it was used in the early church as a summary of the apostolic teaching, usually in the context of preparing candidates for baptism. What was confessed was not the subjective faith of the individual catechumen, but the objective "good deposit" (2 Tim. 1:14) of faith—namely, the apostolic teaching handed on in the context of the church. In this sense, the rule of faith may be seen as something internal to Scripture.

There is no such thing as "the" rule of faith in the sense of a single authorized version. Instead, there are diverse second- and third-century formulations by Justin Martyr, Tertullian, Irenaeus, Hippolytus, and others, all of which bear a family resemblance to the Apostles' Creed. Each variation has a broadly narrative form that begins with a confession of God the Creator and goes on to recount how this God sent his Son to become man to suffer and rise from the dead for us and our salvation. Indeed, the most important rule was to read in ways that hold the OT and NT together. And yet, the rule is more than just a CliffsNotes summary of the biblical story line.

The rule functioned for early Christians as a guide to right reading. Tertullian and Irenaeus appealed to the rule in their writings against heretics. In his *Against Heresies*, Irenaeus equates the rule with apostolic preaching, suggesting that it functions both as a rule for right reading and a criterion for "sound doctrine" (1 Tim. 1:10). In a justly famous passage (*Haer.* 1.8.1), Irenaeus compares the heretical Valentinian reading of the Bible to a person who puts the tiles of a mosaic together in the wrong way to form the image of a dog rather than the true image, a portrait of a king. What the heretics lack is the key or plan (*hypothesis*) for laying out the tiles in their proper arrangement. According to Irenaeus, the rule of faith is the *hypothesis* that guides the right (i.e., Christian) reading of Scripture. That Jesus fulfills the OT is the key that unlocks the whole: "The whole content of the apostolic preaching is derived, for Irenaeus, from the OT" (Behr, 8).

Something like the rule may be implicit in the NT authors' use of the OT to preach Christ and proclaim the gospel. Proponents of TIS therefore protest when the rule is dismissed as postapostolic tradition. The rule is neither imposed *on* the biblical texts nor deduced *from* them, but rather describes an underlying pattern of theological judgment present *in* the biblical texts (Treier, 60). The rule rules Christian reading of Scripture, even as Scripture rules the rule (Long).

Irenaeus exemplifies what I am here calling precritical biblical theology. Irenaeus reads with Christian faith, seeing the OT as preparing the way for Jesus Christ, and Jesus's birth, life, death, resurrection, and ascension as fulfilling the promised substance of the OT. Irenaeus's hypothesis, his key for showing how the OT and NT fit together, is christological: the king's face is Scripture's christological referent. God's plan for the fullness of time is to unite all things, including both Testaments, in Christ (Eph. 1:10). Christ is before all biblical things, and in him all biblical things hold together (cf. Col. 1:17). The rule is thus "a basic 'take' on the subject matter and plot of the Christian story" (Greene-McCreight, 704) and, as such, rules out heretical readings that fail to see the *skopos* or essential subject matter of the Bible: Christ the king.

There is another sense in which ecclesial context and the rule of faith bear on TIS and the NT use of the OT. The most important Augustinian hermeneutical principle for reading Scripture in the context of the church is to prioritize interpretations that foster love of God and neighbor. Some in TIS have taken this to heart, making the "rule of faith" into a virtual "rule of love." Rather than appeal to historical context to ascertain the correct meaning, these interpreters appeal to ecclesial context in order to reorient the aims and ends of interpretation—namely, to encourage communion with God and the communion of the saints. Augustine himself believed it was important to ascertain authorial intent, if possible. His advice to prefer the reading that most fosters love of God and neighbor must therefore not become a wax nose, especially if we let the life, teaching, and death of Christ serve as its standard and criterion (1 John 4:10; 2 John 6).

Other proponents of TIS likewise insist that the rule of faith, understood as the underlying pattern of theological judgments implicit in the Scriptures themselves, is the church's interpretive norm. Still others regard the rule as an interpretive norm in a broad sense regarding the ecumenically received *skopos* of Scripture while nevertheless acknowledging the normative force of the verbal textual sense as well.

Canonical context: The one Bible. The Christian canon is more than a list of authorized books. Although the OT was more or less complete by Jesus's time, the NT developed alongside the rule of faith as the early church sought to delimit the gospel, both formally and materially. TIS thinks about the process of canon formation in theological as well as historical terms: the books eventually included are a sign not of the power of an ideological majority but of the Spirit speaking and convicting the church that God in person speaks in these very texts.

Brevard Childs explores the theological significance of the canon by calling attention to its role as a context for interpretation. Unlike traditional exegetes, Childs is interested in recovering the intention of the original author not for its own sake, but as an aspect of what most interests him—namely, what we find at the end of the process of canonical development: the final form. The final form is a kind of commentary on the text's prehistory, which is why the canonical approach can accommodate form, redaction, and tradition criticism. The final form is not simply a means to an authorial end; it is the final form itself that the church acknowledges as canonical. Hence his rule for right reading: interpret each text in its canonical context. Childs's theological exegesis is at once fully academic in its willingness to trace the historical development of the canon with source and redaction criticism yet fully ecclesial in its insistence that what counts is the "canonical intentionality" that is a function of the final form and that enables Scripture to serve future generations.

Whereas Steinmetz proclaims the superiority of precritical exegesis, Childs proclaims the superiority of the final form of the Christian Scripture, which of course is made up of OT and NT. According to Driver, the canon is for Childs a theological, not just historical, phenomenon: "The historically shaped canon of scripture, in its two discrete witnesses, is a christological rule of faith that in the church, by the action of the Holy Spirit, accrues textual authority" (4). The canonical whole is more than the sum of its parts, for the final form arranges those parts in a way that allows them to enrich one another and be meaningful to succeeding generations.

Any canonical approach poses to its users the challenge of doing justice to the two discrete witnesses (OT and NT) in the one canon. In what sense is the OT a discrete voice? Do the NT authors respect it as such, or are the prophets merely a ventriloquist's dummies through which the apostles project their own voices, in which case the discrete witness of the OT gets swallowed up by its NT reception? The debate over how rightly to respond to this question continues, as does the debate over Childs's canonical approach in general.

The chief task of the canonical approach is "the theological interpretation of the plain sense witness of two testaments" (Seitz, "Canonical," 104). Childs's critics often miss the extent to which theology funds his canonical approach. What makes the final form the focus of Childs's study is not its literary features but its divine referent: God's self-communication in Israel's history and, climactically, in Jesus Christ. Canonical interpretation attends to the final form of Scripture in order to apprehend the reality of God, a subject matter that providentially orders its own form and calls forth its own prophetic and apostolic witnesses.

Some read Childs's commendation of the canonical context as a direction to attend to the Bible's theological content more than its literary context, its divine subject matter more than its canonical form. At the heart of the one Bible is the one God, and the Bible is God's word for the church. The NT bears witness to this theological subject matter precisely by offering commentary on the prior OT witness. Yet both witnesses point, in their respective ways, to the one God known in the face of Jesus Christ.

While some see the canon as a context for giving guidance to successive generations of interpreters by providing witness to a theological subject matter, other proponents of TIS emphasize the canon's divine authorship. On this view, the unity of the canon is intrinsic rather than being a function of the community's reception. This intrinsic canon is "the corpus of writings commissioned by God to be the 'rule' or 'standard' of Christian faith and practice" (Peckham, 19).

To read canonically on this view is to read for the divine authorial intention, which, while it does not go against the prophets' intent, may go beyond it, insofar as it intends a referent the human authors could not have known: "God speaks dynamically through the words of Scripture, here and now, according to the contours of redemptive history, and in a manner consistent with but not fully constituted by the original sense" (Lee, 216).

One way to interpret the canon *theologically* is to view it as the unified work of its divine author, God's magnum opus: "To authorize a sequence of words *as a work* is to declare that one wants one's readers to read it as a totality" (Wolterstorff, 226). "Discourse" pertains to illocutionary acts—what authors *do* with words—and the canon provides the appropriate context within which to determine what God is doing in the human discourse of Scripture. Instead of being a rival to Childs's canonical approach, authorial discourse may provide its proper warrant. The canon, taken as a whole, is the context within which to give "thick descriptions" of God's central illocutionary acts (Barker, 237).

Redemptive-historical context: Typology and figural interpretation. The third way TIS expands the notion of proper context is by revisiting the meaning of "historical." Typically, those who read the Bible "like any other book" limit meaning to what the human author could have known at the time of writing. History, on the standard critical view, is a horizontal temporal continuum, where time moves forward in a linear sequence, closed off to God's presence and activity. By way of contrast, TIS views history as the stage on which the living and active God executes his plan of salvation. To read biblical texts in their redemptive-historical context is to be attuned not only to history's length, but also to history's breadth and depth, as it were, and to the fulcrum on which the ages turn, the event of Jesus Christ. Moreover, attending to redemptive history collapses the distance between the apostles and contemporary readers, for the church today in an important sense inhabits the same context, theologically speaking, as the early church: after Pentecost, awaiting the return of Christ.

Some see redemptive history as providing theological warrant for typology, perhaps the distinctive template governing the NT use of the OT. Typology involves more than the fulfillment of an earlier promise. Christ is the second Adam, but the first Adam is not, strictly speaking, a promise; rather, he is a type, the first member in a correspondence relation ("pattern" = Gk. *typos* in Rom. 5:14). Some scholars see no distinction between typology and allegory; in both cases, one thing (e.g., Noah's flood) symbolizes something else (e.g., baptism [1 Pet. 3:20–21]). However, allegorical associations float free of historical anchors in a way that typology does not. Typology requires redemptive history as its necessary framework, preserving a narrative coherence between referents that is absent in allegory. Typology, then, involves both a historical and a theological correspondence between persons, things, or events, though the antitype belongs to a later stage of redemptive history. There is therefore theological continuity (God is at work in substantially the same way) yet historical discontinuity (the antitype displays eschatological intensification).

What is hermeneutically significant, and undeniable, is that the NT authors interpret Jesus's history as continuing and fulfilling earlier patterns in Israel's history. Yet typology is less a method of exegesis than a way of thinking about the relationship between events in redemptive history (Seitz, *Figured*). Typology requires a theological view of history that sees God acting consistently, *only more so*. There is a single continuous redemptive process that becomes more glorious as it reaches its realization in Jesus Christ.

The preferred term in TIS for thinking of how one biblical event, person, or thing anticipates another is "figure." The key issue in figural interpretation is not the verbal meaning of a type, which usually presents no problem, but rather its *referent*. The challenge in interpreting a passage like Isa. 53:7–8 lies not in determining the semantic range of the Hebrew for a sacrificial "lamb." Rather, it lies in determining whether or not this "lamb" refers to Jesus and, if so, whether it was the OT prophet, Jesus himself, a NT apostle, the Holy Spirit, or the early church who first made the figural connection. The issue, in other words, is *how* to identify the referent of OT types and *whose* identification decides the matter (Dawson).

Some of the leading scholars in TIS argue that the Christian interpretation of the OT, and by extension the NT use of the OT, is figural (Radner; Collett; Hays). Unlike allegorical interpretation, figural reading requires theological presuppositions—in particular, the assumption that redemptive history is the outworking of a divine intention to transform humanity over time in Christ through the Spirit. Figural reading is a way of identifying what the biblical authors are talking about by referring everything back and forth to the story of Jesus—and of seeing the church today, the new and expanded Israel of God (Gal. 6:16), as part of that story. There remains disagreement in the TIS ranks as to whether figural interpretation is a matter of reading forward (from OT to NT, with Christ as the anticipated end) or backward (from NT to OT, with Christ as the assumed content), or both: "We learn to read the OT by *reading backwards* from the Gospels, and—at the same time—we learn how to read the Gospels by *reading forwards* from the OT" (Hays, 4).

The key concern in TIS is not to smother the discrete voice of the OT with Christian interpretations, as if its "real" meaning sleeps until awakened by an apostolic kiss: "The NT is not somehow 'closer' than the OT to the theological reality it renders, since the two testaments speak of one theological subject matter, rather than two" (Collett, 157). The connection between the divine promise in the OT and the divine fulfillment in the NT is not arbitrary but due entirely to God's providential and redemptive ordering of history.

The Trinity as Content and Context of the NT Use of the OT

If exegesis without presuppositions is not possible, is the Trinity one of the right presuppositions? Modern biblical scholars have typically resisted this suggestion on the grounds that the goal of exegesis is to recover what the biblical authors meant in their original historical contexts. To read either the OT or the NT through a Nicene lens, they object, is to impose dogma where it has no business being. This makes perfect sense if one reads the Bible like any other book, where what human authors know reflects their historical and cultural situation. In contrast, TIS reads the Bible *unlike* any other book, for no other collection of texts comprises the Spirit's inspired and illumined word of God for the people of God.

TIS views OT theology as the task of reading the OT as Christian Scripture: "Christian reading needs to be attentive to the meaning of the text in its pre-Christian frame of reference; on the other hand, it must simultaneously take with full seriousness the recontextualization of the material in a frame of reference not its own" (Moberly, 30).

The doctrine of the Trinity thus provides a fitting case study for reading the text in canonical, ecclesial, and redemptive-historical context. TIS suggests that to read the Bible as the word of God, as Christians, is to read it in a trinitarian frame of reference, as the word of the one who is Father, Son, and Spirit.

Canonical pressure. The crucial Nicene concept *homoousios,* which asserts that the Son is of the "same substance" as the Father, clearly falls outside the horizons of the world of the OT authors. Nevertheless, "the church's struggle with the Trinity was not a battle *against* the OT, but rather a battle *for* the OT" (Childs, 376). As noted above, one of the first theological crises pertained to the NT use of the OT: Was the early church right to read the OT as Christian Scripture—that is, as testimony to Jesus Christ, the eternal Son of God made flesh?

Though counterintuitive, it is nevertheless safe to say that "the doctrine of the Trinity would never have arisen on the basis of the Old or the New Testament taken in isolation" (Rowe, "Biblical," 299). It is precisely the dynamic of OT monotheism combined with NT confession of Christ's lordship that generates and governs trinitarian theology. In the beginning was God (YHWH): one maker of heaven and earth, distinct from all else. The LXX consistently renders YHWH—the personal, covenant name for God—as *kyrios,* the very name the NT authors ascribe to Jesus (cf. Joel 2:32 and Rom. 10:13).

The NT authors take care to distinguish the Lord who is Son from the Lord who is the Father who sends him (see, e.g., John 5:19–24). Both Father and Son are named *kyrios,* yet the Father is not the Son: "This pressure moves us to the conclusion that YHWH is not the Father alone" (Rowe, "Biblical," 303). A similar dynamic obtains between the Son and the Spirit. "Now the Lord is the Spirit" (2 Cor. 3:17), and yet the NT also distinguishes between the Son and Spirit (Luke 3:22): "Read canonically, then, the full unity of God as expressed through the name *kyrios* is that of Father, Son, and Spirit" (Rowe, "Biblical," 304).

It is precisely such NT uses of the OT that exert the canonical pressure that led the early church to formulate the doctrine of the Trinity. The use of the same divine name for different persons indicates that both Testaments are talking about the same divine identity. It was the NT use of the OT that ultimately led the church to think through the ontology implied by the divine names. The biblical narrative raises questions that only ontology (or systematic theology) can answer. The monotheism of the OT (Deut. 6:4) makes sense only if Father, Son, and Spirit are *different persons who share the same nature.* From the perspective of TIS, the canonical pressure that led the church to Nicene theology is actually "God's own testimony to himself as Trinity" (Rowe, "Biblical," 309).

An economic rule. From examining the Bible's witness to God's acts in history, we move now to the postapostolic inference as to who God is in himself. Expressed in terms of dogmatic theology, we turn from considering the economic Trinity (God at work in history) to the ontological Trinity (God in himself). The question is whether Christians ought to read the whole Bible in a trinitarian framework once they know who YHWH really is. To answer in the affirmative is to see the doctrine of God as itself a hermeneutic (Rowe, "Doctrine").

Interpreting Scripture in a trinitarian framework casts new light on the NT use of the OT. Context is indeed king when it comes to determining meaning, but TIS holds that Christian readers should consider the divine economy as a proper context too. It is only in the context of the triune God's historical work, for example, that we are able to see what the prophets are really talking about—not just an indeterminate messiah, but the God-man Jesus Christ. The context of the divine economy stretches the literal sense, not by altering its verbal meaning but by specifying its definitive referent. The rule of faith is thus a rule for reading the Bible in this overarching "economic" context. The rule now states that the meaning of an OT passage is ultimately determined by its location in the triune economy (Rae, 40).

Trinitarian figures. The ontological Trinity also plays a role in the way TIS views the NT use of the OT. Although the Trinity was not apparent to the prophets, Christian readers now know who YHWH *always* was: Father, Son, and Spirit. The question is whether interpreters today can read this reality back into the discrete witness of the OT and, if so, how. To ask whether it can ever be legitimate to read the Bible in light of later trinitarian dogma is to ask whether it can ever be legitimate to read the Bible in light of God's reality. Can it?

Several studies have recently retrieved the patristic practice of prosopological exegesis—interpretation done with particular attention to who (Gk. *prosopon* = "face") is speaking. Here, too, the focus is not the verbal sense but the referent, though the "referent" in question is not *what* is being talked about but *who* is doing the talking. What makes this exegesis theological is the suggestion that there are places in the OT where specifying the speaker—as alternately Father, Son, or Spirit (and sometimes even the church, Christ's "body")—clarifies the meaning. Typological interpretation stems from redemptive history, but prosopological interpretation is based on the concept of person (whose words?).

Tertullian deploys prosopological exegesis against the Monarchians of his day who want to collapse Son and Spirit into the Father: "The one who speaks and the one about whom he speaks and the one to whom he speaks cannot be seen as one and the same" (quoted in Slusser, 464). Consider, for example, who is speaking to whom in Ps. 2:7: "He said to me, 'You are my son; today I have become your father.'" Augustine uses prosopological exegesis in his homilies on Psalms, yet the phenomenon is also present in the NT use of Psalms (Pierce). The suggestion, then, is that Jesus not only prayed psalms but also, as preexistent Son, was the one who *spoke* them. There is evidence that the doctrine of the Trinity, in particular the concept of the three "persons," emerged from this reading practice of identifying different divine speakers in the text (Bates).

Conclusion

When viewing the two Testaments as separate anthologies, each with its own authors and cultural-historical horizons, it is often difficult to make sense of the NT use of the OT. TIS insists that they belong together, two witnesses united formally in a single canon and materially by their common subject matter. When two magnets are kept apart, they appear to be inert. When put together, however, as in the canon, they exert a strong attractive force. The OT and NT are twin poles in a triune magnetic field, with Jesus Christ, in whom all things hold together, its magnetic center.

See also Biblical Theology; Canonical Interpretation; Method; Prosopological Exegesis; Rhetoric; Typology; *Apostolic Hermeneutics articles*

Bibliography. Ayres, L., *Nicaea and Its Legacy* (Oxford University Press, 2004); Barker, K., "Speech Act Theory, Dual Authorship, and Canonical Hermeneutics," *JTI* 3, no. 2 (2009): 227–39; Barr, J., *The Concept of Biblical Theology* (Fortress, 1999); Barrett, M., *Canon, Covenant and Christology* (InterVarsity, 2020); Bates, M. W., *The Birth of the Trinity* (Oxford University Press, 2015); Beale, G. K., ed., *The Right Doctrine from the Wrong Texts?* (Baker, 1994); Behr, J., "Introduction," in Irenaeus, *On the Apostolic Preaching* (St. Vladimir's Seminary Press, 1997), 7–26; Childs, B., *Biblical Theology of the Old and New Testaments* (Fortress, 1992); Collett, D. C., *Figural Reading and the Old Testament* (Baker Academic, 2020); Dawson, J. D., *Christian Figural Reading and the Fashioning of Identity* (University of California Press, 2002); Dodd, C. H., *According to the Scriptures* (Nisbet, 1952); Driver, D., *Brevard Childs, Biblical Theologian* (Mohr Siebeck, 2010); Eichrodt, W., *Theology of the Old Testament*, 2 vols. (SCM, 1961); Fee, G., *New Testament Exegesis*, 3rd ed. (Westminster John Knox, 2002); Fowl, S. E., *Theological Interpretation of Scripture* (Cascade, 2009); Greene-McCreight, K., "Rule of Faith," in *DTIB*, 703–4; Gunneweg, A. H. J., *Understanding the Old Testament* (Westminster, 1978); Hays, R., *Reading Backwards* (Baylor University Press, 2014); Kelsey, D., *Proving Doctrine* (Trinity Press International, 1999); Lee, G. W., *Today When You Hear His Voice* (Eerdmans, 2016); Lindars, B., "The Place of the OT in the Formation of NT Theology," *NTS* 23, no. 1 (1976): 59–66; Long, V. P., "Irenaeus, Scripture, and the 'Rule of Truth,'" *Crux* 54, no. 2 (2018): 13–25; Longenecker, R., *Biblical Exegesis in the Apostolic Period* (Eerdmans, 1975); Moberly, R. W. L., *Old Testament Theology* (Baker Academic, 2013); Peckham, J. C., *Canonical Theology* (Eerdmans, 2016); Pierce, M. N., *Divine Discourse in the Epistle to the Hebrews* (Cambridge

University Press, 2020); Radner, E., *Time and the World* (Eerdmans, 2015); Rae, M., "Text in Context," *JTI* 1, no. 1 (2007): 23–45; Rowe, C. K., "Biblical Pressure and Trinitarian Hermeneutics," *ProEccl* 11, no. 3 (2002): 295–312; Rowe, "The Doctrine of God Is a Hermeneutic," in *The Bible as Christian Scripture*, ed. C. Seitz (Society of Biblical Literature, 2013), 155–70; Seitz, C. R., "The Canonical Approach and Theological Interpretation," in *Canon and Biblical Interpretation*, ed. C. Bartholomew (Zondervan, 2006), 58–110; Seitz, *Figured Out* (Westminster John Knox, 2001); Slusser, M., "The Exegetical Roots of Trinitarian Theology," *TS* 49, no. 3 (1988): 461–76; Steinmetz, D. C., "The Superiority of Pre-Critical Exegesis," in *ThTo* 37, no. 1 (1980): 27–38; Stendahl, K., "Biblical Theology, Contemporary," in *IDB*, 1:418–32; Terrien, S., *The Elusive Presence* (HarperCollins, 1983); Treier, D. J., *Introducing Theological Interpretation of Scripture* (Baker Academic, 2008); Vanhoozer, K. J., *Is There a Meaning in This Text?* (Zondervan, 1998); Wenham, J., *Christ and the Bible* (InterVarsity, 1972); Wolterstorff, N., "The Unity behind the Canon," in *One Scripture or Many?*, ed. C. Helmer (Oxford University Press, 2004), 217–32.

KEVIN J. VANHOOZER

Theophany *See* Sinai

Thessalonians, First and Second Letters to the

As is often noted, 1–2 Thessalonians do not include any explicit quotations of the OT. Still, as is true with every NT book whether it has explicit quotations or not, 1–2 Thessalonians are significantly influenced by the OT. These two books contain themes, allusions, specific vocabulary, and implicit assumptions deriving from the OT. This significant OT influence is not surprising given Paul's Jewish background (see, e.g., Acts 22:3; Phil. 3:5), his view that "Christ is the culmination of the [OT] law" (Rom. 10:4; cf. Acts 26:22–23; 1 Cor. 15:3–4), and his use of explicit OT quotations in some of his letters (e.g., Rom. 3:10–18; 2 Cor. 6:16–18; Eph. 4:8–10). Further, if one considers God the divine author of all of Scripture—let alone the providential controller of all events, especially those in the OT and NT—then having many OT connections is certainly expected.

Through the twentieth century and into the present, scholarship has not uniformly agreed to the above. Of course, all agree that Paul lived in a Greco-Roman culture and was aware of the OT along with various syncretistic Hellenistic and Second Temple Judaism views. But in addition to his interaction with other Christians, what were the significant theological influences that affected his understanding of the Christ-event? Some deny that the OT per se is a significant influence on Paul, and others, agreeing that the OT is significant, tend to concentrate on only the explicit quotations.

A sizable portion of critical scholarship in the first half of the twentieth century argued strongly that Paul was not significantly influenced by the OT. This was associated primarily with the history-of-religions school and its assumed syncretistic Hellenistic emphases upon Paul (e.g., Bousset, 21; Koester, 97–99). The implications of this view were exacerbated in Pauline books such as 1–2 Thessalonians because there were no explicit OT quotations to ameliorate this tendency even partially. With the advocacy of the *Heilsgeschichte* (redemptive-historical) school (e.g., Cullmann, 26–27; Ridderbos, 44–49; Ladd, 432–34; cf. the earlier Vos, 9–14), the OT's influence on Paul gained prominence again among many in the mid-twentieth century and up to the present. Also in the mid-twentieth century, the Dead Sea Scrolls were discovered, fostering a renewed interest in the influence of Second Temple Judaism upon Paul. Unfortunately, for many scholars who posited strong Second Temple influence, Paul's understanding of the OT is very closely identified with the Second Temple's understanding. That is, Paul does not fundamentally distinguish between the OT and the interpretations of Second Temple Judaism, especially on the topic of a grace-oriented religion as opposed to a works-salvation religion. Recent supporters of this notion label themselves as the "radical new perspective" or "Paul within Judaism" (e.g., Nanos and Zetterholm), while a softer version may be attributed to the New Perspective on Paul (e.g., Sanders).

For those in the twentieth century who saw the OT as having a significant influence upon Paul, many concentrated only on the explicit quotations. Leonhard Goppelt complained in 1939 that "far too much emphasis has been placed on the actual quotations. . . . The NT use of Scripture is not restricted to the direct quotation of OT passages" (198). Hays's well-known scholarship on the OT allusions and echoes in Paul was a large step in the correct direction. In fact, he notes the "pervasiveness of scriptural allusion in Paul's discourse, including 1 Thessalonians" (195n16). Now, in the twenty-first century, a sizable portion of scholarship admits to significant OT influences upon Paul, both through the quotations and more broadly (Stuhlmacher, xix, 273–82). In his summary of 1–2 Thessalonians scholarship, Nijay Gupta concurs that past scholarship has too often "discounted" OT influences on 1–2 Thessalonians, and he too advocates for considering the OT a "significant influence" (36–37, 192). Following the recent trend to see pervasive OT influences upon Paul beyond the explicit quotations, several recent commentaries on 1–2 Thessalonians emphasize this (e.g., Beale; Cara, *1 and 2 Thessalonians*; Johnson, *1 and 2 Thessalonians*; Weima, *1–2 Thessalonians*), and, preeminently, Jeffrey Weima's commentary in *CNTUOT*.

The situation for 1–2 Thessalonians is complicated not only by the absence of explicit quotations but also because most critical scholarship questions the Pauline authorship of 2 Thessalonians (for an extended discussion of the state of current authorship arguments, see Gupta, 197–220). For the purposes of this article, Pauline authorship of 2 Thessalonians is assumed based ultimately on 2 Thess. 1:1.

Weima's Commentary in *CNTUOT*

Any discussion considering the OT as a significant influence upon 1–2 Thessalonians must begin with Weima's article in *CNTUOT*. He notes twenty-one possible OT connections in 1 Thessalonians (Steele [12–15] sees seven) and fifteen in 2 Thessalonians. For each, Weima includes informed discussions of the OT and Thessalonian contexts in addition to possible Greco-Roman and Second Temple Judaism influences. For the vast majority of possible connections, he concludes that the OT did influence the Thessalonian text, although not always (e.g., "peace and safety" [1 Thess. 5:3] is from Roman influence and not Jer. 6:14).

Examples of Weima's work in 1 Thessalonians include the following: "Church" (*ekklēsia*) in 1 Thess. 1:1 (and 2 Thess. 1:1) reflects the LXX usage and connects the predominantly gentile Thessalonians to the OT/NT people of God (871–72). Paul's description of the Thessalonians as having "turned to God from idols to serve the living and true God" (1 Thess. 1:9) is informed by the OT background for "turned," "idols," "serve," and "living and true" (872). The difficult text related to the "Jews who killed the Lord Jesus and the prophets . . . [and] heap up their sins to the limit" (1 Thess. 2:15–16) is related to Gen. 15:16 but also to a broader theme found in both the OT and Second Temple Judaism that some Jews are faithless to other Jews (874). Concerning "when our Lord Jesus comes with all his holy ones [*hagiōn*]" (1 Thess. 3:13), Weima sees Paul alluding to Zech. 14:5 but expanding the implied "angels" of Zechariah to refer either to only human "saints" or to both human "saints" and angels (875). First Thessalonians 4:3–8 relates to the OT theme of "holiness," especially as found in Lev. 17–26 (876). In the two eschatological passages, 1 Thess. 4:13–18 and 5:1–11, Paul makes many connections to the OT "day of the LORD," including "trumpets," "clouds," "day"/"night," "breastplate," and "helmet" (880–82).

Examples from 2 Thessalonians include the following: "God . . . will pay back trouble to those who trouble you" (2 Thess. 1:6) relates to the OT *lex talionis* principle (883). God as avenging judge in Isa. 66:15–16 "is transferred to the returning Christ" in 2 Thess. 1:7–8 (884). The eschatological 2 Thess. 2:1–12 again connects broadly to the OT "day of the LORD" and also includes both wording from Dan. 11:36, which is related to Paul's comment that an evil figure will "exalt himself over everything that is called God" (2 Thess. 2:4), and wording from Isa. 11:4, which is related to the statement that "the Lord Jesus will overthrow with the breath of his mouth" (2 Thess. 2:8) (887–88). The ending prayer for "peace" (3:16) "echoes the Aaronic blessing of Num. 6:26" (888).

In sum, Weima's "analysis demonstrates [that] Paul's vocabulary, metaphors, and theological framework . . . betray the influence of the OT in both small and significant ways" (871). Weima's detailed analysis confirms a significant OT influence upon 1–2 Thessalonians.

A Complementary Analysis of Major Themes

To state the obvious, Weima's commentary in *CNTUOT* is very useful for assessing OT influences. His analysis marches in order through the text, concentrating on specific words/phrases and strong allusions that have clear or reasonably clear connections to the OT. What follows complements this by noting major themes and considering, when appropriate, any OT connections, whether broader or more specific.

As to major themes in 1–2 Thessalonians, scholars typically emphasize the following: (1) eschatology (1 Thess. 1:3, 10; 2:12; 3:13; 4:13–5:11; 2 Thess. 1:5–2:12) along with the associated Divine Warrior theme (2 Thess. 1:7–8; 2:8); (2) calling and election (1 Thess. 1:4; 2:12; 4:7; 5:9, 24; 2 Thess. 1:11; 2:13–14); (3) holiness/sanctification (1 Thess. 1:5, 6; 3:13; 4:3, 4, 7, 8; 5:23, 26; 2 Thess. 1:10; 2:13); (4) working versus idleness (1 Thess. 4:11–12; 5:14; 2 Thess. 3:6–15); (5) kinship/family (1 Thess. 2:7, 11; 4:9–10; 5:12–15, 26; 2 Thess. 3:15; plus the numerous "brothers" references); and (6) imitation (1 Thess. 1:6–7; 2:14; 3:12; 2 Thess. 3:7, 9; cf. 1 Thess. 2:3 // 4:7; 2:4 // 4:1; 2:8 // 4:9; 2:9 // 4:11; 2:10 // 5:23; 1 Cor. 11:1).

Many agree that several of the above have significant OT influence—for example, the themes of eschatology / Divine Warrior and calling/election. Others are more debated. For example, is the imitation theme most strongly connected to Greek moral philosophers (Malherbe, 52–60), to Paul's view of the cross (Fowl), or to *imago Dei* and Lev. 11:44 implications (Cara, "1 Thessalonians," 328–29; see also the discussion of holiness/ethics below)?

In my view, all of the above themes have OT influence, although with varying intensity. What follows considers the holiness/sanctification theme and its plausible OT connections. Broadly considered, this theme also touches on some of the other above-mentioned themes (cf. Johnson, 228–56).

Holiness/Ethics

As noted above, *hagiasmos* (holiness/sanctification) and its cognates, *hagios* (holy), *hagiōsynē* (holiness/holy), and *hagiazō* (to sanctify / make holy), occur often in 1–2 Thessalonians. One key verse is 1 Thess. 4:3: "It is God's will that you should be sanctified [*hagiasmos*]." In context, this relates to "We instructed you how to live in order to please God" (4:1) and has the sense of an overarching statement that sets the stage for the ethical specifics in the following verses. In addition to the lexical frequency of *hagiasmos* and its cognates, 1–2 Thessalonians (like all of Paul's Letters) include many explicit and implicit ethical statements. These conceptually tie into the holiness theme.

Given the prominence of the holiness/ethics theme in the OT, I will simply look at two well-known sections of the OT with plausible connections to 1–2 Thessalonians: (1) the Ten Commandments (Exod. 20:1–17 // Deut. 5:6–21) and (2) Lev. 17–27, the so-called Holiness Code plus Lev. 27. The Ten Commandments are pertinent as the core of OT ethical principles. Leviticus 17–27 is also pertinent because, similarly to 1–2 Thessalonians, it has a significant concentration of the word "holy" (MT *qādôš*, LXX *hagios*) and its cognates (e.g., Lev. 19:2; 20:7–8; 21:8; 22:2; 23:2; 24:9; 25:10; 27:14), along with many connections to the Ten Commandments (e.g., Lev. 19:1–4; 20:10; 23:3; 24:17; 26:1; 27:2). Briefly, "holy" in Lev. 17–27 refers to moral purity, separation, or a combination of the two. In all cases, it is based on the Lord's character/actions and/or his revealed will.

The well-known phrase from the Holiness Code "Love [LXX *agapaō*] your neighbor as yourself" (Lev. 19:18) is clearly included conceptually in 1–2 Thessalonians (cf. Gal. 5:14; Rom. 13:9): "Now about your love for one another [*philadelphia*], . . . you yourselves have been taught by God to love [*agapaō*] each other" (1 Thess. 4:9; cf. Rom. 12:10). "May the Lord make your love [*agapē*] increase and overflow for each other and for everyone else" (1 Thess. 3:12; cf. 4:18; 5:11). "Always strive to do what is good for each other and for everyone else" (1 Thess. 5:15; cf. 2 Thess. 3:15). In addition, this emphasis on love and specifically "brotherly love" (*philadelphia*) dovetails with the kinship/family theme (see Burke, though he does not tie in Lev. 19:18), which in turn connects to the fifth commandment (using the Jewish/Protestant numbering system) and Lev. 19:3, 32; 20:9.

The condemnation of various sexual sins is prominent in the Holiness Code (Lev. 18:1–23; 20:10–21) and connects to the seventh commandment. First Thessalonians also prominently condemns sexual sins in a pericope that emphasizes holiness (1 Thess. 4:3–8; cf. 5:22). Interestingly, immediately following both discussions of sexual sins in the Holiness Code, Paul comments that these sexual sins are the customs of the nations. "Do not defile yourselves in any of these ways [sexual sins], because this is how the nations (MT *gôyim*, LXX *ethnē*) that I am going to drive out before you became defiled" (Lev. 18:24; cf. 20:23). Paul makes a very similar comment amid his discussion of sexual sins: "not in passionate lust like the pagans [*ethnē*]" (1 Thess. 4:5). The seventh commandment clearly influences Paul (cf. Rom. 13:9; 1 Tim. 1:10), and the Holiness Code likely does also.

"Be holy because I, the LORD your God, am holy" (Lev. 19:2; cf. 11:44–45; 20:7, 26; 21:8; 1 Pet. 1:16) is the baseline for Lev. 17–27. When an attribute (or action) by God is the basis for a positive character trait (or action) by a believer, portions of the Christian tradition have termed this a "communicable attribute" (Bavinck, 2:135–37, 216–21). Here the divine attribute of being holy is the basis and goal for the holiness of believers. Similarly, "You shall sanctify [MT *qiddaš*, LXX *hagiazō*] him [the priest], for he offers the bread of your God. He shall be holy [MT *qādôš*, LXX *hagios*] to you, for I, the LORD, who sanctif[ies] [MT *qiddaš*, LXX *hagiazō*] you, am holy [MT *qādôš*, LXX *hagios*]" (Lev. 21:8 ESV). Note that the Israelites are told to "sanctify" the priest because it is the Lord who "sanctifies" Israel—that is, "to sanctify" is a communicable action. In 1 Thess. 5:8, Paul also uses this communicable-attribute-and-action pattern. He alludes to Isa. 59:17, where God is a warrior with a breastplate and helmet, and he appropriately relates this communicable aspect of God/Christ (cf. 2 Thess. 1:7–8; 2:8) to believers also being warriors. This communicable-attribute-and-action pattern also dovetails well with the above-mentioned imitation theme in 1–2 Thessalonians. "You became imitators of us and of the Lord" (1 Thess. 1:6). Paul asks others to imitate him and other Christians, all under the rubric of imitating, and being in the sphere of the lordship of, Christ (Cara, "1 Thessalonians," 328–29). This communicable-attribute-and-action pattern in both Leviticus and 1–2 Thessalonians (and elsewhere in the Bible) is broadly connected to humanity being made in the image of God (Gen. 1:27), but it is also evidenced by the refrain "Be holy for I am holy."

In addition to affirming God's will that believers be holy, both the Holiness Code and 1–2 Thessalonians strongly assert that God will graciously effect their holiness. "I am the LORD, who makes you holy [MT *qiddaš*, LXX *hagiazō*]" is another constant refrain in the Holiness Code (Lev. 20:8; cf. 21:8, 15, 23; 22:9, 16, 32; Exod. 31:13; Ezek. 20:12; 37:28). Paralleling this emphasis and using *hagiazō* or its cognates, Paul explicitly affirms that all three persons of the Trinity effect the holiness of believers: "May God himself, the God of peace, sanctify [*hagiazō*] you" (1 Thess. 5:23); "May he [the Lord Christ] strengthen your hearts so that you will be blameless and holy [*hagiōsynē*]" (1 Thess. 3:13); and "God chose you as firstfruits to be saved through the sanctifying [*hagiasmos*] work of the Spirit" (2 Thess. 2:13). The Spirit is explicitly termed holy (*hagios*) in 1 Thess. 1:5, 6; 4:8. This emphasis by Paul on the Spirit being holy is plausibly connected directly to the Holiness Code, but it is certainly connected to the OT broadly considered.

Working versus idleness is a major theme in 1–2 Thessalonians. "The one who is unwilling to work shall not eat" (2 Thess. 3:10). There are many OT verses broadly related to this command (e.g., Gen. 2:2, 15; 3:17–19; Deut. 25:4; Ps. 128:2; Prov. 10:4; 12:11; 19:15; cf. Sir. 33:27; Did. 12:1–5; Gen. Rab. 2:2). Is Paul's command significantly influenced by the fourth commandment and/or the Holiness Code? Sabbath is certainly emphasized in the Holiness Code (e.g., Lev. 19:3; 23:3; 26:2). It is especially connected to feasts and resting from work so that the "sacred assembly" (MT *miqrāʾ qōdeš*, LXX *klētē hagia*) may gather and worship (e.g., Lev. 23:7–8, 21, 35, 37). Obviously, the fourth commandment emphasizes rest on the Sabbath, but it also strongly implies that working six days is proper because God created/worked six days

(Exod. 20:8–11; cf. Gen. 2:2), which is another communicable action. In addition, working is shown as positive within the Festival of Weeks section of the Holiness Code and its Sabbath associations. The command to aid the poor by not completely harvesting one's field immediately follows the command not to work relative to the festival ceremonies (Lev. 23:21–22; cf. Lev. 19:10–11). Hence, the understanding that God worked and so should able-bodied humans is plausibly implicit in Paul's discussion.

The terms "defect" (MT *mûm*, LXX *mōmos*) and "without defect" (MT *tāmîd*, LXX *amōmos*; NT *amemptos/amemptōs*) occur often in Leviticus. In the Holiness Code there is a clear parallel between priests being without blemish (Lev. 21:17–24) and sacrificial animals being without blemish (Lev. 22:18–25; 23:12, 18). Both of these are within the explicit context of God accomplishing the priest's holiness: "I am the LORD who sanctifies" (Lev. 21:23 ESV; 22:32 ESV). In 1 Thessalonians, all three of Paul's uses of "blameless" (*amemptos/amemptōs*) have an adjacent "holiness" cognate (1 Thess. 2:10; 3:13; 5:23). Paul's use of "blameless" broadly includes forgiveness of sins by Christ's work, initial and progressive change in this life, and an eschatological complete change. Certain aspects of this broad concept are then highlighted in various contexts (Cara, *1 and 2 Thessalonians*, 97). These overlaps with Leviticus further confirm Paul's view that God both desires for believers to be holy and has a resolve to accomplish this.

Other connections with 1–2 Thessalonians worth briefly mentioning include (1) idols (second commandment; Lev. 19:4; 26:1; 1 Thess. 1:9), (2) proper oaths and vows (third commandment; Lev. 19:12, 15; 27:2, 14, 17–19, 26, 28; 1 Thess. 5:27), (3) lying (ninth commandment; Lev. 19:11, 15, 16; 1 Thess. 2:3, 5; 2 Thess. 2:2; cf. 2 Thess. 2:12–13), and (4) coveting (tenth commandment; 1 Thess. 2:5).

In sum, the above analysis of the holiness/ethics theme in 1–2 Thessalonians compared to the Ten Commandments and Lev. 17–27 further confirms that Paul is significantly influenced by the OT and adds exegetical insight to 1–2 Thessalonians (e.g., Paul's use of the communicable-attribute-and-action pattern).

Bibliography. Bavinck, H., *Reformed Dogmatics*, 4 vols. (Baker Academic, 2003–8); Beale, G. K., *1–2 Thessalonians*, IVPNTC (InterVarsity, 2003); Bousset, W., *Kyrios Christos*, trans. J. E. Steely (Baylor University Press, 2013); Burke, T. J., *Family Matters*, JSNTSup 247 (Continuum, 2003); Cara, R. J., *1 and 2 Thessalonians*, EPSC (Evangelical Press, 2009); Cara, "1 Thessalonians," in *A Biblical-Theological Introduction to the New Testament*, ed. M. J. Kruger (Crossway, 2016), 321–35; Cullmann, O., *Christ and Time*, trans. F. V. Filson, 3rd ed. (Wipf & Stock, 2018); Fowl, S. E., "Imitation of Paul/of Christ," in *DPL*, 428–31; Goppelt, L., *Typos*, trans. D. H. Madvig (Wipf & Stock, 2002); Gupta, N. K., *1 and 2 Thessalonians*, ZCINT (Zondervan Academic, 2019); Johnson, A., *1 and 2 Thessalonians*, THNTC (Eerdmans, 2016); Hays, R. B., *Echoes of Scripture in the Letters of Paul* (Yale University Press, 1989); Koester, H., *History and Literature of Early Christianity*, vol. 2 of *Introduction to the New Testament* (de Gruyter, 1982); Ladd, G. E., *A Theology of the New Testament*, ed. D. A. Hagner, rev. ed. (Grand Rapids: Eerdmans, 1993); Malherbe, A. J., *Paul and the Thessalonians* (Sigler, 2000); Nanos, M. D., and M. Zetterholm, eds., *Paul within Judaism* (Fortress, 2015); Ridderbos, H., *Paul: An Outline of His Theology*, trans. J. R. DeWitt (Eerdmans, 1975); Sanders, E. P., *Paul and Palestinian Judaism* (Fortress, 1977); Steele, E. S., "The Use of Jewish Scriptures in 1 Thessalonians," *BTB* 14 (1984): 12–17; Stuhlmacher, P., *Biblical Theology of the New Testament*, trans. and ed. D. P. Bailey (Eerdmans, 2018); Vos, G., *The Pauline Eschatology* (1930; repr., P&R, 1994); Weima, J. A. D., "1–2 Thessalonians," in *CNTUOT*, 871–89; Weima, *1–2 Thessalonians*, BECNT (Baker Academic, 2014).

ROBERT J. CARA

Timothy and Titus, Letters to

My previous treatment of the use of the OT in the Pastoral Epistles (*CNTUOT*, 891–918) introduced the relevant texts and examined their biblical "pre-texts" in a consecutive manner. The goal of this essay will be to delineate patterns of this inner-biblical use of OT materials (and other traditions) within the three letters. In the first part I briefly overview several familiar categories of use. The second part describes the use of the OT for purposes of literary characterization of the opponents, Paul, and Timothy. It is here, as polemical response to opponents, on the one hand, and in constructing images of Paul and Timothy in 2 Timothy, on the other, that a uniquely creative use of the OT in the Pastoral Epistles can be seen. For the most part, I will summarize my detailed treatments of the texts in *CNTUOT* (891–918) and elsewhere (*Letters*; "Cowardice"; "Ethical"), as well as those of other scholars.

Categories of OT Use

Use of the OT in theological statements and doxologies. Theological statements. A distinctive feature of the Pastoral Epistles is the expression of aspects of theology in "set" theological statements. While, in part or whole, these may have preexisted the letters in which they appear, they tend to include elements that occur elsewhere in the letters, suggesting at the very least that the author adapted or revised them for specific application (Towner, *Letters*, 32). Such statements are presented as authoritative and Pauline, and therefore reliable, sometimes identified by the *pistos ho logos* formula (1 Tim. 1:15; 4:8–10; 2 Tim. 2:11–13; Titus 3:4–8a), which the English versions have rendered in various ways (NRSV: "The saying is sure"; NIV: "trustworthy saying"; etc.). Each saying, in its own way and context, asserts that salvation (properly understood) is a present reality.

It is partly the "properly understood" factor just mentioned that explains the function of OT citation or allusion (so, too, the inner-biblical contact made with earlier Paul and the Jesus-tradition). So, in 1 Tim. 2:5–6, the epithet "God is one" explicitly echoes Deut. 6:4 (and Jewish/Christian reflections on this theme), the founding statement of Israel: "Hear, O Israel: . . . the LORD is one." But the intention of the echo proves to be complex, designed to call up the Shema for reflection in the light of Christ: "God is one and the Mediator between God and humankind is one, the human Christ Jesus" (AT). The latter phrase, "the human Christ Jesus," itself a complex echo (Num. 24:7; Isa. 19:20; see Towner, "1–2 Timothy," 892–93; *Letters*, 182), draws together two strands of OT reflection on the "messianic man," a way of legitimating the christological recalculation of Jewish monotheism for the church.

Elsewhere, in 1 Tim. 4:10, the epithet "the living God" is a thoroughly OT description of God (Ps. 84:2; Isa. 37:4, 17; Hosea 1:10). This may be an example of "latent intertextuality" (unconscious), but it implies nonetheless that the salvation (in Christ) announced in the Pauline gospel is the very salvation promised in the OT. Theological statements in 2 Timothy (1:9–10; 2:11–13) are given in the theological vernacular of either Paul or the early church.

The two theological pieces in Titus are closely linked by the theme of epiphany and allusion to Ezekiel. The first theological statement in Titus (2:11–14) consciously engages with Greco-Roman rhetoric (epiphany, grace, *paideia*) to undermine a secular ideology: the statement begins in the Greek conceptual world (2:11–12: "For the grace of God has appeared, bringing salvation to all, training us to renounce impiety and worldly passions, and in the present age to live lives that are self-controlled, upright, and godly" [NRSV]) but finishes unmistakably in the Jewish-Christian conceptual world (2:13–14: "while we wait for the blessed hope and the manifestation of the glory of our great God and Savior, Jesus Christ. He it is who gave himself for us that he might redeem us from all iniquity and purify for himself a people of his own who are zealous for good deeds" [NRSV]; see Towner, "Ethical"; *Letters*, 740–66). In the course of this movement, a catena of inner-biblical echoes applies Jewish/OT content (e.g., Exod. 19:5; Deut. 7:6; Ps. 129:8; Ezek. 36:25–33; 37:23) to gloss and denature local (Cretan) wider Greek and imperial ideologies of "epiphany," co-opting the concept to interpret a Christian theology of God's grace in Christ and showing the new possibilities this presents to be the outworking of OT prophetic promise. This strategy is particularly served by a complex engagement with texts in Ezekiel to explore further the meaning of salvation through prominent metaphors: cleansing by God, sprinkling with water, removal of uncleanness, and being made into the people of God (Towner, "1–2 Timothy"; *Letters*). In this way, "an OT hermeneutical line" is established "that allows Christ's death to be viewed as Yahweh's ultimate act of deliverance, and the results to be seen in terms of the new-covenant perspective that emerged especially in Ezekiel" (Towner, "1–2 Timothy," 915). The ethical conclusion of the piece ("zealous for good deeds"), especially in light of the Ezekiel allusions, foreshadows the gift of the Holy Spirit, which will come into view in the theological expression of Titus 3.

In the latter, as the Greek text is structured (NA[28]), salvation is described in terms of "the washing of regeneration" and "renewal by the Holy Spirit, who was poured out upon us" (3:5d–6a AT). A complex echo of OT sources is indicated. From the same range of Ezekiel texts at play in Titus 2:14 comes the core image of renewal by the "ingiving of the Spirit" (36:27 AT), so that what was conspicuously absent above now becomes visible in Titus 3:5–6 (further accented by the allusion to Spirit-outpouring in Joel 3:1): "He saved us, not because of any works of righteousness that we had done, but according to his mercy, through the water of rebirth and renewal by the Holy Spirit. This Spirit he poured out on us richly through Jesus Christ our Savior" (NRSV). The language of this formulation should perhaps be understood as the Christian (or Pauline) assimilation of OT prophecies. In either case, "in a way continuous with 2:14, the promise of the Joel text is combined creatively with the Spirit texts in Ezekiel and new-covenant prophecy to locate the Cretan Christians within redemptive history" (Towner, "1–2 Timothy," 917).

The OT in the doxologies of 1 Timothy (1:17; 6:15–16). Within the Pastoral Epistles, only 1 Timothy employs doxological statements, at 1:17 and 6:15–16. Apart from matters of content, these attract attention for their structural effect in bracketing the entire letter. Each is constructed of OT and Jewish-traditional materials, but their rhetorical function is more to make well-known assertions about God, strengthened by their combination into distinct doxologies, than to invite hearers to reconsider specific OT texts or traditions. Thus, they combine elements that were standard in the Hellenistic-Jewish critique of pagan claims and some probably recycled for the Christian appraisal of Rome (see Towner, *Letters*, 152–54, 420–23). What stands out, however (it is not a theme in 2 Timothy or Titus), is the monotheistic stress ("the only God," 1:17; "only Ruler," 6:15; to these should be related "there is one God and one Mediator," 2:5), which stems ultimately from the foundational Shema of Deut. 6:4 ("Hear, O Israel: . . . the LORD is one") as mediated in various ways down through the centuries and taken up by the early church (see above and Towner, *Letters*, 153). This monotheistic thrust may have been designed and positioned to challenge the claims of local (the Artemision and its cult) and imperial ideologies, perhaps taken up in some way also by the opponents troubling the church in Ephesus.

The church's ontology, administration, and (community) ethics. Ontology of the church. Two texts that relate to the church's "ontology" are 1 Tim. 2:8 and 2 Tim. 2:19–20. The first text leads into the section that addresses the adornment and teaching of wives in the community. A rather light intertext, "in every place," either evokes Mal. 1:11, 14 in relation to the theme of prayer to God offered by all the nations (the church as the fulfillment of this vision; Towner, "1–2 Timothy"), or it adapts the OT theme of the irresistible spread of YHWH's rule throughout the world (the church in Ephesus being an eschatological case in point; e.g., Ps. 103:22; Prov. 15:3; Jer. 8:3; 24:9; 45:5; 3 Macc. 7:12; Towner, "Resonance," 71). In 2 Tim. 2:19–20, in the midst of a complex inner-biblical engagement with Numbers and Isaiah designed primarily to characterize the false teachers (see below), a second payoff takes the form of the assertion of the church's permanence (see Towner, *Letters*, 530–32).

Administration and an example of community ethics (1 Tim. 2:8–15; 5:18–25; 6:1). Overt citation of OT texts comes into play in three texts concerned with aspects of church practice and community ethics. First, in the case of 1 Tim. 2:8–15, the use of Genesis creation materials to support restricting Christian wives from teaching has been examined in detail elsewhere (Towner, *Letters*; "1–2 Timothy"; "Resonance"). The question in my mind continues to be the effect intended by the more creative (and allusive) intertext in 2:15a (an allusion to the protevangelium of Gen. 3:15–16, and thereby to the birth of Jesus Christ). If the intertext is present, the restrictions based on references to Gen. 2 in 1 Tim. 2:11–14 may, in the subsequent allusion to the promise of Gen. 3, be eschatologically mitigated: that is, the restrictions of 1 Tim. 2:11–14 may have a "limited shelf life" conditioned on the gospel promise.

> The allusions to Genesis 2 in [1 Tim.] 2.13–14 are normally taken as proof texts and in isolation from what follows, with the text being analyzed almost as if the verse numbers in our scholarly editions of the Greek text were full stops. However, if 2.15a with its reference to childbearing is taken instead within the flow of what precedes, it does not allow one to stop the discursive process (choosing this but rejecting that) until the Protoevangelium (Gen. 3.15–16) has been proclaimed into that primal imperfection of the Fall. Moreover, if the resonance of the closing promise of salvation calls to mind the birth of Jesus, the note of eschatological fulfillment sounded in the opening, at 2:8, receives reinforcement at the closing. (Towner, "Resonance," 76–77)

Second, within 1 Tim. 5:18–25, an extensive engagement with the OT provides a detailed paradigm of "legal" procedures in the church of Ephesus by establishing (OT) precedents. The citation formula that introduces 5:18a suggests it grounds the instructions concerning material support of elders in 5:17 by establishing a precedent in Scripture (Deut. 25:4; cf. 1 Cor. 9:9–10) to which is added a citation of the Jesus-tradition (Luke 10:7) whether "for Scripture says" extends to this or not. Then, 5:19–21 shifts to disciplinary measures concerning elders. Here, the author creatively rewrites Deut. 19:15–20 (concerning the assessment of accusations, legitimate evidence, witnesses, judges, etc.) to suit the present situation in which an opposition movement in the church has resulted in the capitulation of some church leaders. The inner-biblical contact is evident in the framing of an evaluative process that produces a just outcome, has a positive effect on the community, excludes partiality, and is overseen by a triad of witnesses (see Fuller; and Wolfe, 207–8). The technique, though here applied to ground a church administrative function, is similar to other instances of OT inner-biblical exegesis in the Pastoral Epistles in which initial contact with the OT pre-text opens out on a more complex engagement with the OT (see below on 2 Tim. 2:18–19; 4:9–18).

Third, it is worth noting that in 6:1 contact is made with the allegation in Isa. 52:5 (that God's name is blasphemed among the nations because of Israel's disobedience) to motivate slaves to honor their masters (cf. the "mission" motive in Titus 2:5, 10).

Inner-Biblical Exegesis and Characterization

To a degree not seen in the earlier Pauline Letters, engagement with the OT, Jewish traditions, earlier materials from Paul's Letters, and the Jesus-tradition (as well as other local discourses) becomes a means of literary characterization. It constructs a deeper understanding or interpretation of the "players" and their concerns by allowing the audience to see them within the mélange of stories that either form or compete/interfere with the redemptive narrative that structures Paul's thought. I will organize the discussion as follows: (1) examples of the characterization of the opponents and their concerns; (2) examples of the characterization of Paul and Timothy and their concerns. The reader will find detailed treatments of the texts in my chapter in *CNTUOT*, subsequent studies (Towner, *Letters*; "Cowardice"), and in relevant publications of other scholars cited.

Characterization of the opponents: 2 Tim. 2:17–19; 3:1–9; Titus 1:10–16. Within the broader passage—2 Tim. 2:14–21, which is designed to guide Timothy in responding to opponents and their harmful doctrines—v. 19cd is a complex intertext that reaches into the story of the rebellion of Korah, Dathan, and Abiram. Verse 19c cites Num. 16:5 LXX ("The Lord knows those who are his"). Verse 19d echoes a mix of traditions taken up with "naming the name of the Lord" (e.g., Isa. 26:13; Joel 2:32 [3:5 LXX]) and "separating from wickedness" (e.g., Sir. 17:26; Isa. 52:11; cf. 2 Cor. 6:17), while, however, staying within the frame of the Numbers story by an additional echo of the verb for "separation" that describes the people's compliance with Moses's command to "separate" from the rebels (Num. 16:27; see Towner, *Letters*, 530–37). By comparing the co-texts of the Numbers pre-text and of the intertext in 2 Timothy, two things become clear. First, this engagement with the OT does more than simply underscore the surety of God's election and permanence of the church. Second, the efficiency of the complex OT engagement can be readily seen. The technique characterizes the opponents more thoroughly than naming alone (they are in fact reprising the sin of Korah, Dathan, Abiram); their chief sin is thematized (repudiating Paul's God-given authority as Moses and Aaron's opponents did theirs); the appropriate response of the believers endangered by the opponents' false teaching is indicated ("separate" from the rebels); and Paul and Timothy may be seen as the counterparts of Moses and Aaron (see Martin).

Second Timothy 3:1–9 is overtly designed to characterize the opponents: it locates them prophetically ("in the last days," 3:1; cf. 4:3; 1 Tim. 4:1); excoriates their behavior with a long vice list (vv. 2–4); and exposes their false piety (v. 5), destructive tactics (vv. 6–7), and ultimate downfall (v. 9). The characterization reaches a colorful crescendo in the allusion to the story of Moses's contest with the magicians of Pharaoh (Exod. 7:1–12, 22): "As Jannes and Jambres opposed Moses . . ." The intertext is complex, evoking both the Exodus narrative and later Jewish elaborations that supply names for the unnamed characters in Exodus (CD 5:17–19; cf. Jude 11; see further Towner, *Letters*, 563–66). Coming on the heels of the reference to the two false teachers and their association with those who rebelled against Moses and Aaron (2:17–19), the naming of the *two* magicians again suggests the intertext is further characterizing Hymenaeus and Philetus. When this is appreciated, the further association of Paul with Moses cannot be far behind.

The approach to the false teachers taken in 1 Tim. 4:1–5 (all AT) is similar. It identifies the false teachers with the prophetic theme ("The Spirit explicitly says") of the appearance of false teachers/prophets in "the later times" (= "the last days" in 2 Tim. 3:1; cf. 4:3). In contrast to the Spirit's prophetic word, the author characterizes their teachings (or prophecies) in terms of devotion to "deceiving spirits and teachings of demons" (v. 1), and the heretics themselves as hypocritical liars with ruined consciences (v. 2). Further characterization comes by way of a rare glimpse of two aspects of their teaching (forbidding marriage, abstaining from foods; v. 3), the latter of which elicits an intervention in two parts by appeal to the OT. The intervention reaches back first, by reference to "foods" (*brōmatōn*), to Gen. 9:3 (which specifically invalidates any such food abstinence) and a broader tradition about the divine provision of foods (Gen. 1:29; 2:9, 16; cf. Deut. 26:1–11). Then, the subject-verb combination in the correction, "foods, which *God created*," and the subsequent explanation ("for the whole creation of God is good"; v. 4) combine to recall the creation account and God's concluding assertion that all things that he has created are "very good" (Gen. 1:31; for details, see Towner, *Letters*, 299–301). By calling up that divine pronouncement, Paul is able to give his unequivocal response ("and nothing is to be rejected, if it is received with thanksgiving"; cf. 1 Cor. 10:26, 30 for the same logic). While providing Timothy and other church leaders with the scriptural precedent necessary to correct the erroneous ascetic practice, the OT allusive intervention also supports and extends the characterization of the opponents' dangerous incompetence as "teachers of the law" (1:7, etc.).

For comparison, Titus 1:12 provides another example of characterization of the opponents (in Crete) by means of an intertextual thrust. In this case, however, Paul, drawing from cultural narrative, deploys the well-known "Cretan reputation" for dishonesty and depravity, which he epitomizes in citing a maxim of one of their "prophets" (perhaps a combination of Epimenides and Callimachus) to vilify the opposition. The intertextual allusion is graphic and the intention unmistakably simple, showing no regard for the philosophical conundrum (the "liar's paradox") involved in the "prophecy," capitalizing rather on the biting three-part criticism (Towner, *Letters*, 699–703; cf. Merz, 37–38).

The characterization of Paul and Timothy through an OT lens: 2 Tim. 1:6–14; 4:9–18. Paul. Although Pauline self-reflection is somewhat thematic in the Pastoral Epistles, deployed to underscore the link between the apostle and the authentic gospel (1 Tim. 1:11–16; 2:7; Titus 1:1–3), 2 Timothy is virtually structured around it (1:9–14; 2:8–13; 3:10–12; 4:6–8, 16–18) and its corollary, suffering. The definitive reflection is the final one, 4:9–18. It appears at first as a closing commentary (people's movements, his situation in prison), though the reference to Demas's desertion, hardly business as usual, puts the audience on alert. When the discourse reaches its climax (vv. 16–18), a portrait of Paul in the image of Jesus Christ emerges, subtly constructed by intertextual engagement with the passion psalm (Ps. 22 [21 LXX]; Mark 15:34; Matt. 27:46). That psalm's opening verb of abandonment (*enkataleipō*), used first of Demas (v. 10), is now repeated in reference to the desertion of "everyone" at Paul's "first defense" (v. 16). The double occurrence of the verb is the spark leading into the psalm. Although the hearer/reader might wonder what exactly had been entered, once inside, echoes of the psalm come fast and strong, leaving no doubt: (1) the distinctive metaphor of delivery in 4:17, "I was delivered from the lion's mouth" (Ps. 22:21 [21:22]); (2) the pairing of the verbs *rhyomai* and *sōzō* in 4:18, which is thematic in the psalms and occurs in Ps. 21:5–6, 9, 21–22 LXX; (3) the occurrence of references to the "kingdom" (*basileia*) in 4:18 and Ps. 22:28 (21:29), in each case associated with the Lord (*kyrios*);

and (4) Paul's proclamation to "all the nations," which picks up the psalmist's assertion that all the families of the nations will worship the Lord, who has dominion over the nations (22:27–28 [21:28–29]). Thematic coherence is also notable, as Paul's experience of the Lord's presence and empowerment/help echoes the psalmist's repeated cry for God's presence and help (Towner, "1–2 Timothy"; *Letters*, 635–49; Merz, 46–57).

If one were to memorialize the apostle Paul, or if this was rather the apostle bent on leaving a lasting impression (the theological meaning of his suffering and martyrdom in Rome) for his successor, constructing the final scene around the passion psalm and on the model of Christ's experience of suffering and abandonment would certainly be an effective device. In the context of the letter, this concluding OT depiction invites a quick return to similar but less well-developed self-reflective texts that are also constructed through inner-biblical means, though the pre-texts are not exclusively OT texts. Three texts (1:7–12; 2:8–13; 3:10–11) reflect on the Pauline persona, the first and last, which we will consider briefly, engaging with the OT. Within the larger discourse of the command to Timothy concerning his gift (1:6–7), his shame and suffering (1:8), and the command to "guard the good deposit" (1:13–14), classic Paul emerges through at least two intertexts. The first is a contracted version of the threefold descriptor in 1 Tim. 2:7, but it is loud and nearly verbatim in what is taken over from a generic statement about Paul's calling in 1 Timothy. Its reapplication in 2 Tim. 1:11 is specifically linked to suffering (v. 12), as it is adapted to the problem of gospel entrustment, proclamation, and suffering in 2 Timothy. The second intertext replays Paul's gospel/shame discourse in Rom. 1:16 for the commissioning sequence in 2 Tim. 1. As the intertexts play their part in the developing discourse, the themes of gospel entrustment, proclamation, suffering, and the thematic pairing of gospel/shame combine to interpret the Pauline self-description: ". . . or of me, his [Christ's] prisoner." Paul's situation is the outcome of his willing association with Christ and the gospel.

Finally, closing a list of experiences and places that have defined Timothy's life with Paul (3:10–11) is another reference to the trials and sufferings that Paul underwent. The statement "and the Lord delivered me from them all" (AT) makes strong contact with the discourse on the suffering of the righteous in Ps. 34:19–21 (see Towner, "1–2 Timothy"), as it also foreshadows Paul's climactic concluding self-characterization (4:17–18).

Timothy. The counterpart to the complex characterization of Paul in the image of Jesus in 2 Tim. 4:9–18 is the characterization of Timothy as a Joshua-figure in 1:6–14. As the detailed argumentation would show (Towner, "Cowardice"), this introductory exhortation to Timothy is essentially about renewal of his commitment to fulfill his commission to succeed Paul (to continue the Pauline mission). Inner-biblical cues indicate that Paul is "sending" Timothy back to the story of Moses's commissioning of Joshua in Deut. 31 and beyond. The text is a complex web of images (Timothy's character mirrors Paul's) and allusions, involving a critical echo of Rom. 8:15 within which occurs an instance of paronomasia that, in combination with other relevant OT links, triggers the allusion to the Moses-Joshua story. But upon arrival at Deut. 31, it becomes clear that the commissioning sentence is itself an intertext, taking the hearer/reader back to Deut. 1 and then outward into what I have called the "cowardice" topos. This movement through OT and intertestamental traditions, which I can only summarize here, is crucial to the characterization of Timothy.

Contact with the Moses-Joshua story (for details, see Towner, "Cowardice"; Wolter, 222–41; cf. Martin, 25–27) depends on the following main findings: (1) comparable status of the characters, Moses/Paul anticipating death, Joshua/Timothy as successors; (2) the role of the Moses/Joshua paradigm in Jewish tradition; (3) "laying on of hands" to communicate some necessary capability/authority to the successors (Deut. 34:9; Num. 27:18, 20, 23; 2 Tim. 1:6); (4) the language of the commissioning/renewal paraenesis to Timothy, which incorporates components of the formulaic (positive/negative) exhortation in Deut. 31 directed first to the people and then to Joshua (positive: empowerment, bravery; negative: cowardice, fear); (5) the surprising appearance of "cowardice" (*deilia*) in 2 Tim. 1:7, which picks up its use in Deut. 31:8 in the commissioning of Joshua; (6) other themes in the terms "guard/keep/observe," "understanding" (2:7), and "desert/abandon," which show further the inclination toward the Moses/Joshua story.

At the center of Paul's intertextual thrust into the Moses/Joshua paradigm, within which Timothy is to find understanding for his own ministry as successor, is the surprise occurrence of *deilia* (cowardice). Here, an echo and reshaping of Rom. 8:15 for reconsideration in 2 Tim. 1:7 involves the replacement of *douleias* (slavery) in the Romans pre-text with *deilias* (cowardice) in the later text. A kind of pun, this instance of inner-NT wordplay (paronomasia) functions by raising the specter of "cowardice" in the exhortation to Timothy, calling to mind the language of the Moses/Joshua paradigm. But once Joshua's commission comes into view, the occurrences of the *deilia* word group in the charge to Joshua create a next echo to Deut. 1. There it transpires that "cowardice" is defined by the disobedience and cowardice of the first generation of Israel, who, having known the presence, power, protection, and provision of God and God's promise to be present with them as they go up into the land, nevertheless refused to enter the land. The meaning of "cowardice" comes therefore to be equated with rebellious unbelief. And in the context of the commissioning of Joshua, this negative side of the formula ("do not be cowardly or fear"), more than simple encouragement, implies that the one commissioned has taken an oath of absolute faithfulness to God. "Cowardice," from Deut. 1 outwards, becomes an admonitory topos: applied to the new situation of Maccabean suffering and martyrdom, *deilia* is logically extended and associated with denial of the faith to avoid pagan torture; in the NT, *deilia* describes the cowardice of the disciples (despite the close proximity of Jesus) and of those who will recant their faith (Rev. 21:8); in the Apostolic Fathers, it will again be associated with denial of the faith to escape martyrdom.

In this letter of exhortation to Timothy, in a turbulent time of opposition and abandonment of the faith, and with the challenge to "rekindle his gift" and to take up his part in (the apostolic) suffering, the subtle and complex intertextual strategy invites the characterization of Paul/Timothy by association with Moses/Joshua. But it also taps into the "cowardice topos" to underscore the absolute requirements of boldness, suffering, and faithfulness and to warn of the extreme consequences of "turning back" in unbelief and cowardice.

Bibliography. Fuller, J. W., "Of Elders and Triads in 1 Timothy 5:19–25," *NTS* 29 (1983): 258–63; Martin, S. C., *Pauli Testamentum: 2 Timothy and the Last Words of Moses,* TGST 18 (Editrice Università Gregoriana, 1997); Merz, A., *Die fiktive Selbstauslegung des Paulus,* NTOA 52 (Vandenhoeck & Ruprecht, 2004); Towner, P. H., "The Ethical Agenda of Titus," in *"Ready for Every Good Work" (Titus 3:1),* ed. R. Zimmermann and D. I. Manomi, WUNT 484, CNNTE 13 (Mohr Siebeck, 2022); Towner, "1–2 Timothy and Titus," in *CNTUOT,* 891–918; Towner, *The Letters to Timothy and Titus,* NICNT (Eerdmans, 2006); Towner, "Resonance, Dissonance, Resistance and 1 Timothy 2.8–15," *MOP* 3, no. 53 (2021): 67–84; Towner, "2 Tim. 1:7, Cowardice, and the Specter of Betrayal," *Bib* 101, no. 4 (2020): 577–601; Wolfe, B. P., "The Sagacious Use of Scripture," in *Entrusted with the Gospel,* ed. A. J. Köstenberger and T. L. Wilder (B&H, 2010), 199–218; Wolter, M., *Die Pastoralbriefe als Paulustradition,* FRLANT 146 (Vandenhoeck & Ruprecht, 1988).

PHILIP H. TOWNER

Typology

Typology is the study of patterns (types) in the Bible that escalate over time until they find their intended fulfillment in Christ and his church. Like seeds planted in the soil of the OT, biblical types are persons, places, events, and institutions that develop across redemptive history until they reach full flower in God's climactic revelation in Christ. God designed types as a form of revelation to prepare the way for his Son, and in the fullness of time, biblical types are an important way NT authors demonstrate that Jesus is the Christ.

Typology is not merely simplistic correspondence between two episodes of Scripture—an occasional literary feature of biblical stories. Instead, typology is part of the very framework of Scripture; typology is often how the biblical authors make theological claims. Scripture thus presents us with a complex web of patterns that intersect with one another and with the promises, prophecies, and teachings of Scripture. This article, therefore, refers to this complex web of patterns and promises as "typological structures" (Gentry and Wellum, 129–37).

In what follows, we observe typology as it occurs in the Bible and examine how both Testaments teach us to understand biblical types. While scholars have often debated whether types are prospective (an element of predictive prophecy) or retrospective (something later authors recognized and applied in their works), a better approach affirms both. As this dictionary attempts to relate the two Testaments, this article delimits its scope to the biblical canon, then demonstrates how typology works prospectively and retrospectively, before concluding with a final section on discerning biblical typology by reading with the grain of Scripture.

Clarifying the Scope of Investigation

Typology is a vast subject. Therefore, we must define the scope of the approach taken here. First, while typology has gathered the attention of literary theorists, we restrict our focus to typology in the Bible. This focus on typology in the text of Scripture prevents us from considering typology as a purely academic discipline, especially one that owes its understanding to postmodern methods of interpretation whereby readers create typological connections through the process of reading. Though consultation with typology outside the Bible may alert us to ways that language works, this article intends to illustrate how the biblical authors understood typology.

Second, while the early church, the Reformers, and various biblical theologies contribute to a history of typological approaches with their various schools of thought, this article focuses on the way the prophets and apostles employed typological structures to communicate God's Word. By paying attention to the intentions of the biblical authors, we will best understand how typology works across the biblical canon. While we are dependent on pastors and scholars who have gone before us, this article joins with them in studying the text of Scripture itself.

Finally, while we can speak of typology as a singular study, each biblical author, depending on his place in redemptive history, employs types differently. In other words, it is appropriate to speak of biblical typologies. These typologies are unified by the Spirit of Christ, who inspired what the biblical authors wrote, but typologies in Moses and Matthew are not the same. Therefore, careful attention to the author and his place in covenant history is necessary to understand how typology is applied throughout the Bible.

With these caveats in place, we are ready to see typology across the biblical canon.

Prospective Typology: Typology in the OT

Typology in Gen. 1–3. Scripture's typological structures are established as early as the creation narrative itself. Adam, the garden, and other aspects of creation are prototypical patterns of later persons, places, events, and institutions in biblical history. Moses makes this point explicit by describing the events of primeval history in a way that would evoke for his original readers the exodus and then records the exodus events and Israel's subsequent history in ways that echo the creation narrative.

Almost every major biblical typology emerges from the prototypical patterns established in Gen. 1–3 and the covenant God makes with Adam (Carson, "Genesis"). For instance, two of Scripture's most prominent types begin in Adam: kingship and priesthood. God creates Adam in his own image (*ṣelem*), an ANE term with royal connotations. By coupling "image" (*ṣelem*) with "likeness" (*dəmût*), Moses indicates that Adam bears a filial relationship with the Creator (cf. Gen. 5:1–3)—he is a son of God (cf. Luke 3:38). These hints at Adam's royal occupation are made explicit in his commission to "subdue" and "rule" over creation (Gen. 1:28; cf. Ps. 8).

Adam's priestly identity is seen in God's command that he "serve" (*ʿābad*) and "guard" (*šāmar*) the garden—two words that when coupled later in the Pentateuch refer to priestly service in the temple (Num. 3:7–8; 8:26; 18:5–6). Moses also emphasizes Adam's priestly identity by depicting Eden as a garden sanctuary—a prototype of Israel's tabernacle (cf. Ezek. 28:13–16).

The typological structures of Scripture emerge in the creation narrative and in the Adamic covenant. Kingship, priesthood, and sanctuary remain as prominent throughout the rest of Scripture as they are in the creation narrative. Yet these features of the creation story are only a part of the typological structures present in the text. Other elements of Gen. 1–2 also foreshadow later redemptive-historical developments. As the Pentateuch unfolds, Moses makes clear that other elements of the creation narrative—such as separating the dry land from the water or the Sabbath—also establish a pattern of God's acts in history (cf. Exod. 14:21; 20:8–11).

Moses signals that these features of the creation narrative are prospective, even before the fall, not just by evoking these patterns later in the Pentateuch, but by showing within the creation narrative itself that God's work, his covenant with Adam, and Adam's commission are eschatological—that is, they point forward toward a consummate state. As Adam and Eve carry out God's mandates, they should create other image-bearers who themselves will continue the pattern of Adam's royal priesthood. These image-bearers follow the *type* of work Adam himself does: ruling creation, serving in God's garden-sanctuary, multiplying image-bearers, and expanding the borders of Eden until the whole earth serves as God's sanctuary and humanity enters an eternal Sabbath rest.

Of course, Adam's path to eschatological rest is disrupted by the fall. He fails to carry out his commission and pollutes God's holy mountain with his sin. Yet, even as God judges Adam and Eve, his curse against sin includes a promise of a seed who will crush the serpent's head (Gen. 3:15)—the implication being that this seed will consummately fulfill the Adamic commission, do what Adam failed to do, and restore what was lost in Eden.

The promise of a future seed who will undo Adam's failures creates a prospective orientation to both the creation narrative and those that follow. Even as the fall corrupts the created order, God's purposes for creation and the path to eschatological rest follow the patterns God established with Adam. The protevangelium signals to the reader that Adam and other features of creation are prospective; they represent a pattern readers should anticipate later in redemptive history. Another Adam will emerge, a priest-king able to cleanse God's garden sanctuary so that the whole earth will be filled with his glory.

Typology in the rest of the Pentateuch. Moses's subsequent writings in the Pentateuch confirm this interpretive perspective. Moses portrays later biblical characters as "new Adams"—ectypal figures modeled after the Adamic prototype. These new Adam figures emerge particularly as God establishes covenant heads through whom he intends to advance the story of redemption. For instance, Moses portrays Noah as a "new Adam," a figure connected with the Adamic hope of rest and deliverance from the curse (Gen. 5:29). As with Adam, God establishes a covenant with Noah and repeats to him the original Adamic commission in Gen. 1:28 (9:1, 7). Noah, like Adam, serves as a priest-king (cf. 8:20–21) who ultimately fails God by acting unrighteously in a vineyard (9:20–27).

Like Noah, Abraham is also patterned after Adam. He is the father of a new humanity, one that will, in turn, restore the blessing Adam forfeited for all creation (Gen. 12:3) and reclaim a garden sanctuary where they dwell with God (12:6–8; cf. Exod. 15:17). Like Adam, Abraham receives God's blessing (Gen. 12:1–3; cf. 1:28), only this time God himself promises to fulfill through him the command he gave to Adam to "be fruitful and multiply" (17:2, 6; 22:17).

Israel is also patterned after Adam. In covenant with the Lord, they are both God's son (Exod. 4:22) and royal priests (19:6), as well as a people whom God promises he will make "fruitful and multiply" (Lev. 26:9; cf. Exod. 1:7). This pattern of "new Adams" throughout the Pentateuch is instructive for understanding typology in the OT. Divinely inspired types are one means by which God reveals himself to the people created in his image. Just as the words of Moses are inspired by God, so too are the typological structures that stand between the first Adam and the last Adam.

Similarly, the tabernacle, the centerpiece of Israel's national identity, recalls God's first dwelling place—the garden of Eden (Beale, *Temple*)—as well as the heavenly dwelling of God. On Sinai, God revealed to Moses a vision of heaven, on which the tabernacle was "patterned" (Exod. 25:9, 40; Heb. 8:5). Thus, the tabernacle is a "vertical" type that is patterned after heavenly realities, but as Moses received this pattern for Israel's earthly replica of heaven, it became a "horizontal" type as well (cf. Davidson, 336–67). The earthly tabernacle/temple looks up and looks forward.

Furthering our understanding of typological structures, the tabernacle serves as a touchpoint for vertical and horizontal types. In other words, when God gives his people a place to meet with him, the tabernacle does not simply recall the garden sanctuary in Eden; it also reveals something of God in heaven. The tabernacle, then, prepares the way for God to come to earth in the person of Christ, who is the true antitype of the tabernacle (John 1:14; 2:19). In this way, we can see in God's revelation to Moses the ontological priority of the antitype, even as the type comes first in the story line of redemption.

Moses's interpretation of redemptive history will become the normative pattern that later biblical authors embrace. Adam and the covenant of creation are prototypes, molds that shape and give meaning to the future biblical story line. As the Pentateuch develops, we find numerous "seeds" patterned after Adam, what we might call ectypes. Each ectype advances redemptive history and God's reclamation of humanity from sin while also falling short of total restoration, usually on account of each figure repeating an Adam-like "fall." Thus, each instantiation in the pattern creates further expectation of a coming fulfillment. These repeated patterns and the corresponding promises of eschatological salvation (e.g., Gen. 3:15; 5:29; 12:1–3; 17:1–8; 49:8–12; Num. 24:17–19) show that Moses sees Adam, Noah, Abraham, and Israel as prophetically foreshadowing a greater antitype in the future—one who will recapitulate the patterns of the past while not succumbing to the failures of these patriarchs.

Furthermore, Moses's typological portrayal of persons, places, events, and institutions in redemptive history is expansive, going well beyond the obvious Adam-Noah-Abraham-Israel connections. Even shorter, less prominent narratives are repeatedly patterned after previous stories or connected with promises that demonstrate that these narratives portend future, antitypical fulfillment. For instance, Moses's description in Gen. 12:10–20 of Abraham's sojourn in Egypt on account of a famine (along with accompanying "plagues" on Pharaoh's house) clearly foreshadows Israel's own exodus from Egypt. Likewise, Moses signals that both Joseph and Judah foreshadow a coming messiah by describing this king from Judah's line as recapitulating the events of the life of Joseph (Gen. 49:8; Emadi, 57–82).

In the Pentateuch, then, redemptive history is typological. God ordains patterns in history that foreshadow future, greater works. We discern these patterns as we read each story in light of what comes before and interpret them in light of God's covenant promises. The Pentateuch itself ends on a note of typological anticipation of a new Moses (Deut. 18:15–18; 34:10–12) and a new exodus (30:1–10) that will transform Israel from the inside out, making them obedient from the heart (30:6).

Typology in the Former Prophets. The authors of the Former Prophets imitate Moses's interpretive perspective and recognize their own narratives or the narratives they record as part of the pattern of typological anticipation Moses began in the Pentateuch. For instance, the author of Joshua, picking up the typological expectation established by Deut. 18:15–18, portrays Joshua as a new Moses and the conquest of Canaan as a new exodus. Joshua, like Moses, is a "servant of the LORD" (Deut. 34:5; Josh. 1:1; 24:29), experiences God's presence (Josh. 1:5), and leads Israel through the Jordan in a Red Sea–like crossing (Josh. 3; 4:23–24) to reenter Canaan—a land guarded by a heavenly figure resembling the cherubim stationed at the boundary of Eden (Josh. 5:13–15; cf. Gen. 3:24).

These patterns in Joshua reveal that the author understood Moses's interpretive perspective and embraced that same typological understanding of redemptive history. He records the events of the conquest to highlight the correspondences between his own story and the exodus, thus creating anticipation for even further typological fulfillment in the future. For instance, the author of Joshua records the Rahab narrative (Josh. 2) in a way that echoes the story of the Passover, inviting readers to see Rahab's story as a recapitulation of Israel's (Schrock, "Valid," 11–12). These correspondences between Moses's and Joshua's ministries highlight an important point. As types develop throughout redemptive history, they undergo escalation. Whereas Moses's Passover and water crossing simply redeemed people from slavery, Joshua's "Passover" and water crossing result in possessing the promised land, fulfilling God's promises to Abraham, and even include gentiles like Rahab as part of the covenant community.

Scripture's typological structures further develop in David. A king from the line of Judah (Gen. 49:8–12), he enters redemptive history beheading a seed of the serpent (1 Sam. 17:5; cf. Gen. 3:15). In fact, much of his life is modeled on the prophetic expectations found in Deut. 17, and David, like Adam and Israel before him, functions as a priest-king throughout the books of Samuel (cf. 1 Sam. 2:35; 2 Sam. 6). God's covenant with David clearly builds upon the typological patterns already established in the Adamic, Abrahamic, and Mosaic covenants, echoing elements from each of these covenants and from the life of Joshua as well (2 Sam. 7:1; cf. Deut. 12:9–11; Josh. 1:13).

Further, David himself understands his own place in redemptive history and the place of his children as part of the typological structures previously established, patterns that reach as far back as Adam in the garden

(2 Sam. 7:19). In fact, as we will see below, David's assessment of his own life moves him to identify his own experiences as prophetically forecasting those of his greater, messianic son. Similarly, all of David's sons are compared to him (see, e.g., 1 Kings 2:12, 24; 11:6, 33; 14:8; 15:3, 11), as royal "types" that either deepen or distort the divinely ordained pattern of kingship in redemptive history.

Typology in the Latter Prophets. The Latter Prophets, in light of Israel's failure to keep covenant with Yahweh, project God's future deliverance according to typological structures already established in the Pentateuch and in the Former Prophets. The prophets, for instance, regularly employ the exodus as paradigmatic for God's future deliverance (Isa. 11:16; Jer. 16:14–15; Hosea 11:1). Ezekiel further identifies this new exodus and return from exile as a picture of resurrection from the dead—salvation from the Adamic curse itself (Ezek. 37:7–12; cf. Gen. 2:16–17; 3:14–19). Similarly, the prophets anticipate a day when God will establish a new covenant that supersedes previous covenants and renders the old covenant obsolete (Isa. 54–55; Jer. 31:31–34; Ezek. 36:22–38; Hosea 3).

Notably, these prophetic expectations also focus on the coming of a new David, who will restore the people of Israel and mediate covenant blessing to the nation. Thus, the prophets indicate the new covenant has a Davidic shape. It simultaneously fulfills OT expectations while at the same time recapitulating the same patterns found in David's own reign (Isa. 9:6–7; 11:1; 55:3; Jer. 23:5–6; Ezek. 34:23–24; Hosea 3:5; Amos 9:11–12; Mic. 5:2; Zech. 6:9–15).

Typology in the Writings. In the Writings, the biblical authors continue to describe the narratives they record as developments of a God-ordained pattern expecting eschatological fulfillment. Following the expectations of the Prophets, much of the Writings create this sense of anticipation by focusing on how the historical David's life typifies an eschatological king. In fact, David himself develops this line of thought, speaking in ways that blur the distinction between him, his children, and his eschatological seed.

For instance, David in Ps. 2:7 (cf. Acts 4:25) applies to himself the promise that his future seed would be God's son (2 Sam. 7:14). In so doing, he signals that his own life is a pattern for the messianic king who will emerge from his line. David's understanding also explains the enigmatic statement from David that his coming "Lord" would be both king and priest (Ps. 110:4). David understands God's covenant promises to him in light of the typological patterns previously established with Adam, Noah, Abraham, and Israel—each of whom was a royal priest. Therefore, as David reflects on his eschatological son, he sees him as the fulfillment of the patterns God established in previous covenants. Just as Adam and Israel were both God's "son" and a royal priest before God, so too David's son will be God's "son," who will embody both the Adamic commission and Israel's corporate identity as royal priests.

The Writings conclude with Chronicles, a book that focuses on David and the prophetic expectation his life creates for the nation of Israel after their return from exile. Chronicles highlights David's successes and Israel's prosperity under his reign so as to sustain and promote the expectation that David's life foreshadows a coming work of the Lord (cf. 1 Chron. 17). A greater David, who will reign eternally and unfailingly mediate God's new-covenant promises, is coming just as God promised through the prophets.

Furthermore, despite being perceived as detached from Scripture's covenantal story line, the Wisdom literature actually develops Scripture's typological structures. A few lines of evidence demonstrate this development. For instance, the author of 1 Kings portrays Solomon and the exercise of his kingly wisdom as recapitulating God's ideal for humanity in Adam. Just as Ps. 8 identifies the Davidic king as a new Adam, so also Solomon carries out the Adamic commission to rule creation and have dominion over the land (1 Kings 4:21–24)—a rule that reinstates Edenic conditions for those under his authority (4:25). Further, Solomon's wisdom extends to all creation. Just as Adam named the animals, so Solomon speaks "of beasts, and of birds, and of reptiles, and of fish" (4:33 ESV; cf. Gen. 1:28–30; 2:19–20). Solomon's wisdom therefore is "Adamic." It both reflects God's design for how image-bearers can flourish, while at the same time suggesting that the king of Israel, particularly the eschatological king, will be a new Adam who embodies wisdom.

Given these connections between Solomonic wisdom and Adam, it's not surprising to find echoes of Eden peppered throughout the Wisdom literature. Proverbs, especially the first nine chapters, is written to give sons wisdom to rule in righteousness. As a royal son himself (Prov. 1:1), Solomon equips his sons with wisdom necessary for them to rule in Israel. Likewise, the Song of Solomon describes an idealized marriage between the king of Israel and his bride, one that overturns the curses of Gen. 3 that plague marriage relationships (Hamilton, "Music"). Ecclesiastes also has numerous allusions to Adam, Eden, and the fallen condition of humanity (Webb, 103–4). Picking up types from Gen. 1–11, Solomon teaches his son how to fear God and keep his commandments (Eccl. 12:12–13). These connections between wisdom, Adam, Eden, and the Davidic king forged in the Wisdom literature create an anticipation that Israel's end-time king will not only take up Adam's commission to reign but also will do so embodying the wisdom necessary to fulfill that commission with righteousness and justice (1 Kings 3:28; cf. Matt. 12:42; 1 Cor. 1:30).

OT typology: A summary. This survey of the OT demonstrates that typology is not a reading method but rather a phenomenon within the text itself. The biblical authors, following Moses's example, understand certain persons, places, events, and institutions in their writings as representing patterns that anticipate God's future work. These types escalate throughout redemptive history but by the end of the OT remain unfulfilled.

This survey also shows that Scripture's primary typological structures correlate with and are contoured by the biblical covenants (Gentry and Wellum, 135–37). The covenants with Adam, Noah, Abraham, Israel, and David all develop the same sets of promises and patterns in Israel's history. Each covenant builds on previous ones, advancing the biblical story line to the next stage of redemptive history. In turn, these covenants provide the hermeneutical grid for understanding the events of Scripture and the typological relationships between them. As patterns emerge in Scripture between persons, places, events, and institutions, the promises of the covenants provide the theological significance for those patterns.

As we turn from the OT to the NT, it is vital to see that the NT authors also read the OT in this way. Not only did they learn to see the patterns of redemption from Moses and the prophets who followed him, but also they saw the Spirit of Christ leading these men to write inspired Scripture filled with types and shadows. For this reason, they could record Jesus saying, "[Moses] wrote of me" (John 5:46), and could affirm that Isaiah "spoke of him" (12:41). Yet, whereas the OT prophets employ typology prospectively, the NT authors fill their writings with typology that looked back on the OT, showing how Christ and his church fulfill God's typological patterns.

Retrospective Typology: Typology in the NT

Just as Moses wrote his five books after the exodus culminated in God's revelation on Sinai, so the NT apostles and prophets wrote inspired Scripture after Christ had ascended to heaven and sent his Holy Spirit. As the Spirit of Christ enabled Moses and the prophets after him to interpret God's acts of redemption (2 Pet. 1:19–21), so the Spirit led the NT authors to interpret the meaning of Christ's life, death, and resurrection (John 14:26). As in the OT, NT authors understood God's acts in redemptive history as typological.

There is a difference, however, between OT typology and NT typology. OT typology points forward to the coming Messiah with varying degrees of opaqueness—what Scripture calls "mystery" (cf. Rom. 16:25; 1 Cor. 2:1, 7). NT typology, however, considers the culmination of Scripture's types in Christ and his church. With Christ's arrival, the light of the world brought not only salvation to the lost but also epistemological clarity to OT typological structures awaiting fulfillment.

Accordingly, the NT often speaks plainly about biblical types (cf. Rom. 5:14; 1 Cor. 10:6; Heb. 8:5; 1 Pet. 3:20). It also affirms the prospective nature of OT types (1 Pet. 1:10–12), as the NT repeatedly employs typological structures from the OT to introduce Jesus and his work of redemption. Eschatology underlies all typology, such that the forward-looking types of the OT find fulfillment in Christ, the church, and Christ's second coming (Davidson, 404–5). These three fulfillments—the "Christological," "ecclesiological," and "apocalyptic" (Davidson, 405)—each occur throughout the NT. In this article, however, we use these headings as a heuristic model, noting how the Gospels emphasize christological typology, the Epistles emphasize ecclesiological typology, and 1–2 Peter and Revelation emphasize eschatological typology.

This rubric will help us see how typology serves our understanding of Christ's identity in the Gospels, ethics, and church life in the Epistles, and how it strengthens suffering saints in Revelation. Indeed, in the NT typology is neither esoteric nor academic but ubiquitous and intensely practical.

Christological typology. In the Gospels, typology provides the basic framework for understanding the theological claims of the authors. From the macrostructures of each book to smaller dialogues and discourses, each evangelist identifies Jesus by way of typology. This pattern mirrors Jesus's own teachings. He constantly identifies himself by way of OT types. The evangelists follow suit, presenting Christ according to the persons, places, events, and institutions established across the OT canon. In what follows, we sample representative typologies from Matthew and John.

Matthew. Matthew opens, closes, and fills his Gospel with biblical types. In Matt. 1:1 he introduces his Gospel, "The book of the genealogy of Jesus Christ, the son of David, the son of Abraham." Identifying Jesus with David makes Jesus the long-expected heir to David's throne (cf. 2 Sam. 7:9–14); identifying him with Abraham makes him the promised offspring who would bless all nations (cf. Gen. 12:1–3; 22:18). Additionally, Matthew's use of Gen. 5:1 in Matt. 1:1 ("the book of the genealogy," *biblos geneseōs*) associates Jesus with Adam and the creation narrative of humanity (cf. Gen. 2:4). Loaded into this one verse are at least three biblical types that provide background for understanding the person of Christ.

In this way, Matt. 1:1 employs metalepsis, "a literary technique of citing or echoing a small bit of a precursor text in such a way that the reader can grasp the significance of the echo only by recalling or recovering the original context from which the fragmentary echo came and then reading the two [or more] texts in dialogical juxtaposition" (Hays, *Gospels*, 11). The Spirit-inspired words of Matthew identify Christ, therefore, with multiple types. This combination of types finds its substance in Christ, the antitype.

Matthew's introduction to his Gospel illustrates NT retrospective typology: Matthew writes his Gospel selecting events from Jesus's life that most clearly fulfill the patterns set forth in the OT. By presenting Christ on the basis of previously revealed types, he makes clear Jesus's identity.

On the other end of his Gospel, Matthew concludes his book with a depiction of eleven disciples worshiping Jesus (28:16–17) and Jesus making his famous Great Commission (28:18–20). What is important to observe is the way that this closing narrative mirrors the closings of Genesis and 2 Chronicles. In Gen. 50:15–21, Joseph is surrounded by his eleven brothers, while their exalted brother pronounces forgiveness. Likewise, 2 Chron. 36 concludes with a statement from Cyrus that prefigures Jesus. Cyrus recognizes the authority given to him by Yahweh to build God's temple in Judah, and he offers a blessing of God's presence to be with those who go up to Jerusalem (v. 23). Such narrative similarities are more than accidental. Matthew writes his Gospel, as do the other evangelists, with deliberate use of OT patterns, both in literary form and christological content.

Related to christological content, we find associations between Jesus and many OT types. Some are explicit and obvious, some implicit and obscure. More explicitly, Matthew records how Jesus likens himself to Solomon (Matt. 12:42) and indicates that Jonah's three days in the fish forecast his own death and resurrection (12:39–41). More implicitly, Matt. 3:17 and 17:5 both record the voice of God. In both cases, the Father speaks of the Son with the idiom of OT types. For readers familiar with Gen. 22, Isa. 42, Ps. 2, and Deut. 18, these statements from heaven identify who Jesus is by means of typology rooted in the text of Scripture.

At the same time, these texts contribute to two other christological typologies in Matthew. First, Matthew presents Jesus as a new Moses. From the birth narrative of Jesus, who escapes death at the hand of Herod like Moses escaped death from Pharaoh (Matt. 2:1–12; Exod. 2:1–11), to the authoritative instruction of the Sermon on the Mount (5:1–7:29), Matthew introduces Jesus with events and actions that recall Moses. Likewise, Jesus feeding the five thousand in the wilderness (14:13–21) and the Father's use of Deut. 18:15's "Listen to him!" on the Mount of Transfiguration (Matt. 17:5) confirm that Matthew is intentional with his Moses-like portrayal of Jesus (cf. Allison, 137–270).

Second, and closely related, Jesus recapitulates many of the experiences of Israel. Identified as God's Son in his flight to and from Egypt (Matt. 2:15–17; cf. Hosea 11:1–11) and then again at his baptism (Matt. 3:17), Jesus is presented as the embodiment of Israel. Like God's covenant people, the Spirit leads Jesus into the wilderness to be tested by the devil for forty days (4:1–11), but unlike Israel, who grumbled and broke faith with God, Jesus proves his sonship by clinging to God's promises. Such a dramatic moment of testing is not simply for Christian imitation; it is first and foremost an example of christological typology identifying Jesus as the true Israel.

To those who might not intuitively recall these OT texts or see Christ's actions as typological fulfillments, Matthew telegraphs his message with the repeated use of "fulfill" (*plēroō*; see 1:22; 2:15, 17, 23; 3:15; etc.). This technical term helps us understand how Matthew understands and uses the OT. While many of his fulfillment quotations cite an OT passage, not all do (e.g., 2:23). Thus, Matthew's use of the OT is far from simplistic. He recognizes patterns related to the end of exile brought about by the arrival of David's promised son, and he applies them to Jesus (Piotrowski). Accordingly, his "fulfillment quotations" refer not to a prediction qua prediction, but to a pattern that Christ has fulfilled to the highest degree. This way of reading the OT does not deny the predictive element of the OT (see above), but it demonstrates that the typological structures escalating throughout the OT have come to their telos.

John. John also employs typology throughout his Gospel. For instance, the temple and the sacrificial calendar in Israel frame his entire book. Such cultic themes reveal the importance of Christ's replacement of the temple (John 2:19–21; see Hoskins). Temple typology plays a central role in understanding John's presentation of the person and work of Christ. For instance, John 1:29—"Behold, the Lamb of God, who takes away the sin of the world!" (ESV)—requires readers to understand Jesus according to the sacrificial typology established in books like Exodus and Leviticus.

John 3:14 is another text that beckons readers to understand Christ's person and work through a biblical type. While John 3:16 is more famous, it functions as a supporting explanation for what Jesus has just said in 3:14 concerning the serpent being lifted up in the wilderness (John 3:14–15; cf. Num. 21:4–9). Only with an understanding of the relationship between Moses's bronze serpent lifted up on a pole and God's lifting up his Son on the cross does the meaning of John 3:16 possess its true significance. Once again, John, following Jesus, is dependent on OT types to explain who Jesus is and what he has done.

In sum, christological typology follows OT typological threads through to their fulfillment in Jesus. Because of their focus on fulfillment, NT authors stress retrospective reading more emphatically than do OT authors. Distinct from the forward-looking, predictive typology of the OT, the apostles are instead demonstrating how Christ has fulfilled OT types and shadows. In almost every chapter of the Gospels we find Jesus presented in accordance with OT patterns.

Ecclesiological typology. Because of their ecclesial provenance, the Epistles not only identify Jesus as the Christ but also emphasize how the body of Christ, the church, shares in his fulfillment of the OT's typological structures. As Richard Hays has observed, the ecclesiocentric nature of Paul's Letters is "a consequence of the historical contingency of his writings as pastoral letters" (*Paul,* 162). Likewise, Richard Davidson (400) has noted the presence of ecclesiological types, which address "the individual worshipers, the corporate community, and/or the sacraments of the church." In the Epistles, we find a multitude of types applied to the church by virtue of their union with Christ. Again, the Epistles also contain christological typology, but more than the Gospels they emphasize how those fulfilled types also become part of the church's identity.

Paul. Speaking to those who are "in Christ," Paul's Letters call Christians to work out their salvation by seeing themselves as the people on whom the end of the ages has come (1 Cor. 10:11). In other words, everything written *to* Israel was ultimately *for* the church, a covenant people composed of believing Jews and gentiles (Eph. 2:11–22). Through a plethora of biblical metaphors, Paul employs typology to identify churches and Christians as God's temple (1 Cor. 3:16–17; 6:19; 2 Cor. 6:16–18; 1 Tim. 3:15; cf. 1 Pet. 2:5–10), suffering servants (Phil. 2:5–11; cf. Acts 13:47–48), and sons of God (Rom. 8:14–25; Gal. 4:6–7). These titles are not inventions of Paul. Each has a long history that escalated through the covenants of Israel and found ultimate fulfillment in Christ. Now Paul applies these biblical types to the church in order to secure their identity and ethics in Christ.

Paul regularly dips his pen into the inkwell of the OT to identify the people of God according to various typological structures found therein. For instance, when Paul identifies two kinds of people in Rom. 5 as those "in Adam" and those "in Christ," he makes a direct contrast between the heads of two opposing humanities. This passage is founded on christological typology, but it serves the purpose of ecclesiology—identifying two kinds of people. This focus on ecclesiological typology continues throughout Romans as Paul speaks of slaves of sin and slaves of righteousness (Rom. 6:16–19), vessels of wrath and vessels of mercy (9:22–23), and natural and grafted branches (11:17–24). To understand Paul's argument in each of these cases, we must first understand the OT typological structures of Israel's slavery, election, and status as God's vineyard.

Similarly, in 1 Cor. 10:1–22, Paul urges the Corinthians to flee idolatry. Again, he uses the events of Israel's past as examples (*typoi*) to instruct the Corinthian church (vv. 1–11). Paul's point is ethical, but his means of argument is typological. This appeal to a divinely intended pattern in Israel's history is commonplace in Paul. For instance, in Gal. 4:24, Paul is not spinning an allegory when he speaks of Hagar and Sarah, Sinai and Zion. Rather, he sees in Genesis and Exodus an inspired contrast between these historical figures—a contrast illustrating a typological structure that runs through covenantal history (Caneday; Emerson). With careful attention to Moses's own words, Paul urges the churches in Galatia to walk in the freedom of faith like Sarah, not the bondage of works like Hagar. These examples show that Paul understands OT historical patterns as ultimately culminating in both Christ and the people united to him.

Hebrews. Arguably, the book with the most explicit use of typology in the NT is Hebrews. In this book, we find an all-encompassing argument for why Jesus is greater than the angels (1:1–2:4), greater than Adam and Abraham (2:5–18; 6:13–20), greater than Moses (3:1–6), greater than Joshua (3:7–4:13), and greater than Aaron (4:14–7:28). As a priest after the order of Melchizedek (7:1–28), Jesus inaugurates a better covenant (8:1–13), makes a better sacrifice (9:1–28), and serves at a better altar in a better temple (8:1–10:18). From start to finish, the argument of Hebrews turns on typology. But that typology is not only christological; it is also ecclesiological.

The author exhorts the "Hebrews" to trust Christ and abide in his church (see 10:19–25) and to see themselves as children of God, heirs of his kingdom, and priests serving at his altar—all elements of OT typology. Intriguingly, Hebrews begins by identifying Christ as God's Son, God's true priest, and God's righteous king (see 1:1–3), and it concludes by applying these same titles to God's people in the final three sections of the book (12:1–17, 18–29; 13:1–19). In short, Hebrews models how christological typology leads to ecclesiological typology—a pattern that repeats throughout the NT.

Apocalyptic typology. In one sense, all typology is eschatological; historical types prefigure God's culminating work of redemption in his Son. Furthermore, Christ, in his death and resurrection, has ushered in "the last days" and Israel's eschatological hopes. Yet, in another sense, certain typological structures relate to the final and future return of Christ and the eternal state, which Scripture describes as the new heavens and new earth (Isa. 65:17; 66:22; 2 Pet. 3:13; Rev. 21:1). These apocalyptic types are prominent in 1–2 Peter and Revelation, and they remind us that not all typological patterns were exhausted by Christ's first advent.

First and Second Peter. In 1 Pet. 3:21, Peter says baptism corresponds to (i.e., is an antitype [*antitypon*] of) Noah's flood. Just as God saved Noah and his family through the judgment of water, so God saves all those who safely pass through the judgment of God in Christ. This mention of Noah's ark, however, does not exhaust Peter's use of the flood narrative. In his second letter, Peter cites the watery judgment again and compares it to the fiery judgment that will come on the last day (2 Pet. 3:5–7). Instead of simply speaking of God's final judgment, he employs a biblical type of salvation and judgment to emphasize the point. Those who deny God's judgment have been wrong before and they will be wrong again, if they ignore God's dire warning. In this way, typology underscores the gospel message and points to God's future judgment of all nations (Yoshikawa).

Revelation. John employs apocalyptic typology in his apocalypse. As others have observed, John rarely cites passages from the OT explicitly. Rather, he weaves biblical types and allusions into every portion of his book. To select only one illustration, Rev. 21–22 concludes with a glorious vision of the new creation. In this section, John presents the new heavens and the new earth as a radiant bride and a bejeweled city. Employing types from all across the biblical canon, John shows how the final state of the world is like the garden of Eden, only better.

The placement of this final vision is not accidental. In the final book of the Bible, John fittingly laces his writing with biblical types that began as early as the first pages of Scripture and continued developing throughout the biblical canon (Dumbrell). Such a Bible-saturated presentation may not be easily discerned or digested by those unfamiliar with typology. But for those attuned to Scripture's typological structures and who have embraced Scripture's own terms, concepts, and images as their primary interpretive lens, Revelation is a fitting capstone to the inspired types that bring the whole message of Scripture together in Christ and his church, both now and until the Lord comes again.

NT typology: A summary. In the NT, the biblical authors employed typology to make theological claims about the person and work of Christ, the church, and God's consummate work in the return of Christ. Christ, his people in union with him, and his return are the culmination of Israel's history and all the patterns that began in the garden of Eden. In this way, the NT, in multiple ways, gives us the antitype and fulfillment of all the promises and patterns written down long ago.

Notably, this survey of both the OT and the NT demonstrates that typology in Scripture is not merely superficial connections between two verses. Instead, the biblical authors develop a complex web of interrelated historical patterns that span redemptive history and move from prototype through various ectypes and ultimately culminate in an antitype.

Since these typological structures develop throughout redemptive history and terminate in new-covenant realities, readers must interpret types with an eye for how they develop previous patterns and in light of their divinely intended telos—Christ and his church. The shape of biblical history requires us to interpret biblical types along three horizons: textual, epochal, and canonical—respectively, the type in its own context, as a development of previous redemptive-historical patterns, and finally in view of its fulfillment in Christ and his church (see Lints, 290–311).

Typology in Practice: Reading with the Grain of Scripture

Typology is both prospective and retrospective. Typology is *ontologically* prospective: God ordained persons, places, events, and institutions in redemptive history to prophetically witness to new-covenant realities. At the same time, typology is also *epistemologically* retrospective: a complete understanding of Scripture's typological structures could be discerned only after the fullness of God's revelation in Christ.

The NT authors, given their privileged interpretive location after the resurrection of Christ, understood the fullness of God's purpose in Christ and interpreted the OT according to its intent, both human and divine. Their typological readings are not fabrications, imaginative rereadings of Israel's Scripture through the lens of the Christ event. Instead, the NT authors consistently witness to the fact that their proclamation is "in accordance with the Scriptures" (1 Cor. 15:3–4 ESV). They understand that the mystery of the OT has now been revealed in Christ. The OT bore witness to Christ (Rom. 1:2; 3:21; 15:8; Gal. 3:8) even as that witness was a "mystery that was kept secret for long ages" (Rom. 16:25–27 ESV). B. B. Warfield (141–42) helpfully explains the relationship between ontological prospection and epistemological retrospection by likening the OT to a well-furnished room dimly lit. The NT flips the light switch, allowing inhabitants to see the furniture that was already there but hidden in shadow.

Typological retrospection in the NT is not an imposition of the author on the OT text but a Spirit-led unfolding of the true meaning of the OT. Similarly, typological reading today, modeled after Scripture's own pattern, is not a rereading of the OT through a christological lens, creating correspondences where none exist, but a right reading of the OT in light of the fullness of God's revelation in Christ. Typological reading, if it is even best to call it that, is not an interpretive "method" but an effort to understand Scripture according to authorial intent and on its own terms.

This conclusion mirrors the interpretive assumptions of Jesus and the apostles throughout Scripture. Jesus indicates that the Scriptures testify of him (John 5:39), and he rebukes the Jews for not seeing that Moses's writings are ultimately about him (5:46–47). Similarly, after his resurrection Jesus "beginning with Moses and all the Prophets . . . interpreted to them in all the Scriptures the things concerning himself" (Luke 24:27 ESV). In that same conversation Jesus says, "These are my words that I spoke to you while I was still with you, that everything written about me in the Law of Moses and the Prophets and the Psalms must be fulfilled" (Luke 24:44–45 ESV).

Similarly, Paul tries to convince others "about Jesus both from the Law of Moses and from the Prophets" (Acts 28:23 ESV), and Apollos "powerfully refuted the Jews in public, showing by the Scriptures that the Christ was Jesus" (18:28 ESV; cf. 9:22). Paul in his defense before Agrippa indicates that his preaching consists of "saying nothing but what the prophets and Moses said would come to pass: that the Christ must suffer and that, by being the first to rise from the dead, he would proclaim light both to our people and to the Gentiles" (26:22–23 ESV).

Jesus and the apostles saw their christological reading of the OT as honoring the very intent of "Moses and the prophets." The message of the OT prophetically anticipated their own. The OT, in its types, patterns, prophecies, and promises, proclaims a crucified and third-day-risen Savior (1 Cor. 15:3–4), even as that message remained "hidden in plain view" (Carson, "Mystery,"

427)—a mystery awaiting God's climactic revelation of himself in Christ.

Today, as the church seeks to interpret God's Word on its own terms and obey all Christ has commanded, typology is necessary for understanding Scripture, formulating sound doctrine, and cultivating Christ-like disciples. With that in mind, we offer this two-part definition of biblical types and biblical typology that pulls together the threads of this essay. *Biblical types* are historical persons, places, events, and institutions that are prophetic by nature, often identified retrospectively from the full revelation of God's Word; they are held together in typological structures that progress across the canon and find their terminus in organically related ectypes and antitypes. *Typology* is the study of how types escalate in their meaning as God's covenantal history progresses toward Christ, his church, and the consummation of all things. Typology that accords with Scripture will always consider the individual types *and* their corresponding typological structures that run through the OT and NT.

See also Apostolic Hermeneutics: Description and Presuppositions; Contextual and Noncontextual NT Use of the OT; Literal Fulfillment; OT Use of the OT: Comparison with the NT Use of the OT

Bibliography. Allison, D. J., *The New Moses* (Fortress, 1993); Beale, G. K., *Handbook on the New Testament Use of the Old Testament* (Baker Academic, 2012); Beale, *The Temple and the Church's Mission*, NSBT 17 (InterVarsity, 2004); Caneday, A., "Covenant Lineage Allegorically Prefigured," *SBJT* 14, no. 3 (2010): 50–77; Carson, D. A., "Genesis 1–3," *TJ* 39 (2018): 143–65; Carson, "Mystery and Fulfillment," in *Justification and Variegated Nomism*, ed. D. A. Carson, P. T. O'Brien, and M. A. Seifrid, WUNT 181 (Baker Academic, 2004), 2:393–436; Daniélou, J. *From Shadows to Reality*, trans. W. Hibberd (Newman, 1960); Davidson, R., *Typology in Scripture*, AUSDDS (Andrews University Press, 1981); Dumbrell, W., *The End of the Beginning* (Wipf & Stock, 2001); Emadi, S., "Covenant, Typology, and the Story of Joseph" (PhD diss., Southern Baptist Theological Seminary, 2016); Emerson, M., "Arbitrary Allegory, Typical Typology, or Intertextual Interpretation?," *BTB* 43, no. 1 (2013): 14–22; Gentry, P., and S. Wellum, *Kingdom through Covenant*, 2nd ed. (Crossway, 2018); Goldsworthy, G., *Christ-Centered Biblical Theology* (InterVarsity, 2012); Goppelt, L., *Typos*, trans. D. Madvig (Eerdmans, 1982); Greidanus, S., *Preaching Christ from the Old Testament* (Eerdmans, 1999); Hamilton, J., "The Messianic Music of the Song of Songs," *WTJ* 68 (2006): 331–45; Hamilton, "The Typology of David's Rise to Power," *SBJT* 16, no. 2 (2012): 4–25; Hamilton, *What Is Biblical Theology?* (Crossway, 2014); Hays, R., *Echoes of Scripture in the Gospels* (Baylor University Press, 2017); Hays, *Echoes of Scripture in the Letters of Paul* (Yale University Press, 1989); Hoskins, P. M., *Jesus as the Fulfillment of the Temple in the Gospel of John*, PBM (Wipf & Stock, 2006); Lints, R., *The Fabric of Theology* (Eerdmans, 1993); Piotrowski, N., *Matthew's New David at the End of the Exile*, NovTSup 170 (Brill, 2016); Ribbens, B., "A Typology of Types," *JTI* 5 (2011): 81–96; Schrock, D., "From Beelines to Plotlines," *SBJT* 21, no. 1 (2017): 35–56; Schrock, "What Designates a Valid Type?," *STR* 5, no. 1 (2014): 3–26; Sequeira, A., and S. C. Emadi, "Biblical-Theological Exegesis and the Nature of Typology," *SBJT* 21, no. 1 (2017): 11–34; Vanhoozer, K. J., "Ascending the Mountain, Singing the Rock," in *Heaven on Earth*, ed. H. Boersma and M. Levering (Wiley-Blackwell, 2013), 207–29; Warfield, B. B., "The Biblical Doctrine of the Trinity," in *The Works of Benjamin B. Warfield: Biblical Doctrines*, vol. 2 (Baker Books, 2003), 133–72; Webb, B., *Five Festal Garments*, NSBT 10 (InterVarsity, 2000); Yoshikawa, S., "The Prototypical Use of the Noahic Flood in the New Testament" (PhD diss., Trinity Evangelical Divinity School, 2004).

Sam Emadi and David S. Schrock

Unity of Scripture *See* Canonical Interpretation

Wilderness

OT Background

The wilderness is an important theme in the NT, but it derives its significance largely from the background of the OT, where it is frequently the pivotal place for divine encounter. It is remarkable that such a location, hostile to civilization and population settlements, would achieve such significance in the biblical narrative. But the reasons for this become clear upon further reflection.

A number of words in the Bible are used to describe this particular geographical location often translated as "wilderness" in English. The main term is *midbar* (cf. *yĕšîmôn* and *ʿărābâ*), and its Greek equivalent is frequently *erēmos*. Although it could sometimes refer to sparsely pastured and semiarid areas, "wilderness" usually signified a barren, desert-like area, with scant water and food, a haunt for wild animals, serpents, and scorpions, unsuitable for human habitation.

The OT provides the essential background, both positive and negative, for the development of the wilderness theme in the NT. Positively, it is the place of Israel's "honeymoon" with Yahweh as his people live with him without diversions after the exodus and are completely dependent on him (Jer. 2:1–3). As such it will be a place in the future where God and his people will have intimate relations without any distractions (Hosea 2:14–23). It is also the place of revelation, for it is here that Moses experiences his call and God reveals his name (Exod. 3:1–15). Here too Israel receives its call to be a kingdom of priests and hears the voice of God thundering from the mountain (Exod. 19–24). Later in Israelite history a "wilderness ideal" becomes important. For example, the Rechabites eschew the distractions of urbanized life in order to be faithful to their ancestor Jonadab, who renounced these in order to live authentically as a follower of Yahweh (Jer. 35). But even in these positive examples the wilderness is not intended as a permanent destination. It is regarded as a transitional zone, an intermediate space, which will eventually lead to a place where people can flourish, a land of "milk and honey."

While the wilderness has spiritual advantages with its freedom from distractions, for the most part, it has negative associations as the haunt of wild animals and demonic creatures, the place of infertility and death, a place ill-suited for human habitation. Hagar is banished twice to the wilderness, where she nearly died (Gen. 16; 21:9–21). While Israel experiences its call as the people of God in the wilderness ("In a desert land [God] found [Israel], in a barren and howling waste," Deut. 32:10), it is explicitly contrasted with their destination in the promised land of "milk and honey." And thus it becomes the place of judgment par excellence. Indeed, the words of Moses about Israel's experience in the wilderness leave no doubt about such a view: "He led you through the vast and dreadful wilderness, that thirsty and waterless land, with its venomous snakes and scorpions. He brought you water out of hard rock" (Deut. 8:15). And even though God leads Israel through the wilderness, an entire generation of Israelites, even the great Moses, perish there as a result of disobedience (Num. 14:31–35; 20:1–13). Similarly, Jeremiah describes God's future judgment on the land as a return to pre-creation chaos, "formless and empty" (*tōhû wābōhû*; cf. Gen. 1:2), which will transform the once fertile Mount Carmel into a barren wilderness (Jer. 4:23–26). Thus, future salvation from judgment for Israel is described in terms where the wilderness, a place of present desolation, will blossom like a rose and waters will burst forth in the desert (Isa. 35:1–7), so that even a valley of desolation will become a door of hope (Hosea 2:15; Ezek. 36:33–36).

NT Development

The Gospels. This theological ambivalence of the wilderness carries over into the NT. It is a place of revelation and relationship but also one of danger, temptation, and failure. One does not have to read the NT long before this wilderness theme appears. John the Baptist, the last of a line of OT prophets, appears in the wilderness, announcing the coming of the kingdom of God. His words are like a trumpet blast, or a voice crying "in the wilderness," to prepare the way for God's coming reign (Matt. 3:1–5; Mark 1:2–7; Luke 3:3–20). Citing Isa. 40:3, he thunders, "Prepare the way for the Lord, make straight paths for him." In Isaiah's context the announcement is given to divine messengers who are to prepare for the vanguard of God's parade leading the exiles home from Babylon through the wilderness to the promised land. While this happened in 539 BC, John considers it a preview of the coming kingdom of God, and therefore the need for a greater exodus from the exile of sin. People need to ready themselves for the coming of the great king. Consequently, John fittingly appears in the wilderness to make this announcement. It is bad news for the proud ("Every mountain and hill will be abased") and good news for the humble ("Every valley will be exalted," Isa. 40:4 AT).

The wilderness is thus a place of *preparation* for the kingdom of God. Everyone realizes that John is the forerunner of the kingdom, and his call to repentance clearly shows the ramifications of the preparation for a highway in the desert. This is probably one of the main reasons the Qumran community saw the desert as a place to reside. They were preparing for the coming kingdom.

The wilderness is a place of *revelation* as well. This is where the messiah, the king, will appear. Just as Moses (Exod. 3) and Israel (Exod. 19–24) receive their revelation and their marching orders from God in the wilderness of Sinai, Jesus receives his commission in the wilderness of Judea. Here he is baptized with the Holy Spirit at the Jordan River and not at the temple site in Jerusalem! The baptism in the wilderness coincides with the divine imprimatur as he hears his Father's voice appointing him for his mission as his Messiah: "You are My beloved Son, in whom I am well pleased" (Mark 1:11 NJKV; cf. Matt. 3:17; Mark 1:11; Luke 3:22). When he retreats to the wilderness, he communes with his Father for forty days and nights, fasting and listening to the divine voice. His use of Scripture toward the end of his stay shows that he is not only fasting but also meditating on and consuming the divine word (Matt. 4:4, 7, 10). The wilderness can be a place where all the distractions of village and city life are avoided, so that one might more clearly hear the divine word. In his later ministry Jesus retreats to such places for dialogue with God (Mark 1:35; Luke 5:16).

The wilderness in Israel's experience is also a place of *testing*. In fact, Moses reminds his people that one of the reasons why God had brought them into the desert was to see if they would remain true to their God: "Remember how the LORD your God led you all the way in the wilderness these forty years, to humble and test you in order to know what was in your heart, whether or not you would keep his commands" (Deut. 8:2). Similarly, Jesus, the Son of God, is tested for his fitness to be the divine representative. Will he fail the test as Israel often did in the wilderness? Will he hold to the bedrock truth that he has just learned at his baptism, that he is the divine Son, commissioned by God and empowered with his Spirit to trust God above all else? At least three times the tempter tests him with temptations to which Israel in the past has yielded repeatedly. Will he rely on the Word of God for his food instead of using his miraculous power like some genie? Will he rely on God's affirmation of his identity rather than invoking divine power for spectacular miracles to show everyone once and for all his credentials as Messiah? Will he remain true to his divine mission with the cross ahead of him rather than taking a shortcut to inherit the mantle of the king of the nations?

Repeatedly he depends on his Father, rebuffing his enemy only with the words of Deuteronomy. Whereas old Israel failed the test in the wilderness and was condemned to forty years there, this new Israel succeeds in the wilderness in forty days! Mark's reference to this testing is oblique. Jesus spends his time with the wild animals, but they do not hurt him while angels minister to him (Mark 1:12–13). Jesus tames the wild beasts and rules over them as the new Adam (cf. Gen. 2:18–20).

In several places in the Synoptics and in John, the wilderness is a place of *provision*, where Jesus uses his miraculous power to provide for people. He feeds not just a few individuals but multitudes in the wilderness, a place where no sustenance is possible without his supernatural provision. This is the point of the feeding of the four thousand (Matt. 15:32–39; Mark 8:1–9) and five thousand (Matt. 14:13–21; Mark 6:30–44; Luke 9:10–17; John 6:1–15). He is the good shepherd who looks after the hungry and straying flock. Whereas Israel laments that God cannot provide a table in the wilderness (Ps. 78:19), Jesus does this very thing! Whereas Elisha fed a hundred men with twenty loaves of bread with some left over in a fertile area (2 Kings 4:42–44), Jesus feeds thousands with much less fare and more excess in the wilderness! John develops this point at length when Jesus directly compares himself to the manna given to Israel in the wilderness (Exod. 16). Indeed, the manna was given daily to teach the people that without God's word they could never survive in the desert (Deut. 8:1–3). While this manna provides temporary life, Jesus is the true bread of life who provides eternal life (John 6:22–58).

John also points out that just as God provided salvation in the wilderness to a rebellious people being bitten by fiery serpents, he similarly provides salvation for those afflicted with a lethal spiritual disease. Thus, Jesus remarks, "No one has ever gone into heaven except the one who came from heaven—the Son of Man. Just as Moses lifted up the snake in the wilderness, so the Son of Man must be lifted up, that everyone who believes may have eternal life in him" (John 3:13–15). The story in Num. 21:4–9 describes divine judgment in the wilderness as a result of the people constantly complaining about lack of provision. As divine judgment God sends fiery serpents to bite the people with their lethal venom. Salvation from the judgment consists in Moses erecting a bronze serpent on a pole so that those who look at the snake may be healed. Jesus uses the same story to indicate that he brings salvation from a spiritual death, where people have been afflicted by the lethal venom of sin. Consequently, when he is lifted up (on the cross), those who trust in him will be healed.

Acts and Paul. In his speech before the Sanhedrin in Acts, Stephen suggests that the wilderness was a place of *failure* for the Israelite nation. He mentions the wilderness journey as a time when Israel provoked God with idolatry. He is probably thinking not only of texts like Amos 5:25–27 (cf. Acts 7:42–43) but also Exod. 32 (cf. Acts 7:40–41), where Israel made a golden calf at Sinai as an idol. This theme is resumed by Paul and emphasized in 1 Corinthians. While Paul mentions that Christ was present with the Israelites in the desert as the rock in the wilderness where water flowed for the people and they were nourished by the word of God, this was a place of transition between their baptism at the Red Sea and their entrance into the promised land. As such it became preeminently the place where Israel failed to trust God and was judged accordingly. In a short span Paul mentions a catalog of wilderness experiences:

> Nevertheless, God was not pleased with most of them; their bodies were scattered in the wilderness. Now these things occurred as examples to keep us from setting our hearts on evil things as they did. Do not be idolaters, as some of them were; as it is written: "The people sat down to eat and drink and got up to indulge in revelry." We should not commit sexual immorality, as some of them did—and in one day twenty-three thousand of them died. We should not test Christ, as some of them did—and were killed by snakes. And do not grumble, as some of them did—and were killed by the destroying angel. (1 Cor. 10:5–10)

Paul uses four examples from Israel's wilderness experience to warn the Corinthian believers: idolatry at Sinai (Exod. 32); sexual immorality with Moabite women at Shittim (Num. 25); complaints leading to lethal snake bites (Num. 21:4–9); and grumbling punished by an angel of death. The fourth example may refer to the judgment of the unbelieving spies in Num. 14 or more generally to judgment for the pattern of complaint throughout the entire wilderness journey (Exod. 15:24; 16:1–17:7; Num. 11:1, 10, 18; 14:2, 26–36; 17:5; 20:3, 13; 21:5). Paul warns the Corinthians that they could just as easily perish as did their Israelite forebears in the wilderness if they do not withstand the temptations in Corinth. Paul is probably thinking of the twin dangers of sexual immorality and idolatry in a city notorious for both (e.g., the verb "to corinthianize" was a synonym for "to fornicate"). As the "exodus church" that has not yet reached the promised land, the Corinthian Christians have to be alert to the temptations in the wilderness of this present age, knowing, as Paul later states, that no temptation has ever overtaken a person from which Christ has not prepared a way of escape (1 Cor. 10:13).

Hebrews and Revelation. The writer to the Hebrews has a similar perspective but he writes to a church facing a different temptation—namely, to give up their Christian faith because of intense persecution and return to Judaism. The writer reminds his audience of the situation of ancient Israelite believers in the wilderness on the verge of entering the promised land. They failed to enter the land because of unbelief and were destroyed in the desert. Psalm 95 is used to confirm the point:

> Today if only you would hear his voice,
> "Do not harden your hearts as you did at Meribah,
> as you did that day at Massah in the wilderness,
> where your ancestors tested me;
> they tried me, though they had seen what I did.
> For forty years I was angry with that generation;
> I said, 'They are a people whose hearts go astray,
> and they have not known my ways.'
> So I declared on oath in my anger,
> 'They shall never enter my rest.'" (Ps. 95:7b–11; cf. Heb. 4:1–13)

As Ps. 95 states, the Israelites failed to enter the promised rest of the land of Canaan because of their unbelief. The analogy is crystal clear. The audience of Hebrews will enter the promised rest of salvation in the consummated kingdom of God only if they remain faithful: "We should do our best to enter that place of rest, so none of us will disobey and miss going there, as they did" (Heb. 4:11 CEV). In a profound sense Christians constitute a "wilderness church" that lives between the exodus of their salvation and the promised land of the new heavens and new earth. This clearly shows the concept of the overlap of the ages. The church has been delivered into the new age and the kingdom of light through the events of the cross, resurrection, and Pentecost. But that new age has not completely arrived yet. The kingdom has not been consummated, and thus the church makes its trek in the wilderness of this present age as it heads for the promised land of the city of God.

Finally, Revelation presents a positive example of the wilderness theme, as a place of *protection and insight*. The church is delivered from the clutches of the dragon by being spirited off to the wilderness (Rev. 12:1–6, 13–16). When the dragon tries to drown the people of God, the wilderness opens up in front of them and drains the deadly waters away. The wilderness is a type of sanctuary from evil. And it is also in the desert, free from distractions, that the apostle John can see the antichrist truly in all his clarity as the embodiment of evil (17:3–5). Such an emphasis may eventually have led many in the early church to move to the wilderness to flee the entanglements of the world so that they could draw closer to God. But in the end, the final destination of the people of God is not the wilderness. It is the garden city, flowing with the waters of life, lush with trees of life for the healing of the nations (22:1–4).

Thus, the wilderness theme is used in multiple ways in the NT. It functions as a place for the preparation of God's people, for the locus of divine revelation, for the testing of character, for the provision of bodily needs, and for the description of failure and disobedience. In the wilderness God protects his people and grants them new insight for life.

See also Covenant; Exodus, The; Israel and the Church, The Story of; Sinai; Typology

Bibliography. Caneday, A. B., "Mark's Provocative Use of Scripture in Narration," *BBR* 9 (1999): 19–36; Coetzee, N. J., "Wild God in the Wilderness" (PhD diss., University of Birmingham, 2016); Davies, G. I., "Wilderness Wanderings," in *AYBD*, 6:912–14; Ferris, P. W. J., "Judah, Wilderness of," in *AYBD*, 3:1037; Gaffin, R. B., Jr. "Christ, Our High Priest in Heaven," *Kerux* 1, no. 3 (1986): 17–27; Gibson, J. B., "Jesus' Wilderness Temptation according to Mark," *JSNT* 53 (1994): 3–34; Kelly, H. A., "The Devil in the Desert," *CBQ* 26 (1964): 202–23; Lewis, J. J., "The Wilderness Controversy and Peirasmos," *Colloq* 7 (1974): 42–44; Matthewson, D., "Reading Heb. 6:4–6 in Light of the Old Testament," *WTJ* 61 (1999): 209–25; Mauser, U. W., *Christ in the Wilderness* (SCM, 1963); Miller, D. M., "Seeing the Glory, Hearing the Son," *CBQ* 72 (2010): 498–517; Seely, D. R., "Sin, Wilderness of," in *AYBD*, 6:47; Sun Wook, K., "The Wilderness as a Place of the New Exodus in Mark's Feeding Miracles," *BTB* 48 (2018): 62–75.

STEPHEN G. DEMPSTER

Wisdom

Wisdom in the Bible has distinct theological entailments. Principles for a wise life and theology interface across the canon. Furthermore, in both Testaments, wisdom can personify a divine attribute or the divine person. As a result, wisdom's role in OT biblical theology is vitally important (Clements, 277); moreover, there are "many significant connections between wisdom and the NT that remain to be explicated and integrated by biblical theologians" (Estes, "Wisdom," 858). This essay argues that wisdom bridges creation, revelation, and salvation. Wisdom invites people to a virtuous life in harmony with the created order, divine revelation, and God's saving work, first in Israel and then finally in Christ.

Wisdom: From OT to NT

Overview. It is now generally recognized that Job, Proverbs, Ecclesiastes, Song of Solomon, and select psalms reflect a shared worldview (Kynes). OT prophets, priests, and sages can write in the wisdom genre (Sneed, 40–42; Longman, 276–82). Even when addressing enigmas common to ancient Near Eastern wisdom, the OT operates from its own religious context (Crenshaw, 82–83).

Israel's covenant with the Lord shapes OT wisdom. While the word "covenant" is rare (once in Proverbs and several times in Job and Psalms), the covenant is always the underlying assumption. Israel's wisdom gravitates around two foci, the fear of the Lord and his law (Prov. 1:7; Ps. 111:10; Eccles. 12:13; Job 1:1, 8). Instruction in the fear of the Lord is key for Proverbs: it is defined as the beginning of wisdom in 9:10, bookmarks the collection at 1:7 and 31:30, and occurs another fourteen times. Fear of the Lord within the Mosaic covenant results in worship and obedience (Deut. 10:12; Josh. 24:14). This is the path of wisdom that leads to life.

A transition to the messianic age and the new covenant is anticipated by Israel's prophetic and typological hope framed against an increasing sense of failure. This double strand of failure and hope marks much of OT history, including covenant, land, city, king, and more. The same can be said of Israel's wisdom. Solomon is preeminently identified with OT wisdom. In the end, his life becomes a prototype of wisdom and folly, at once a type of Christ and a picture of human failure (1 Kings 3–4; 11:4; Estes, *Message*, 64–74). OT prophets reveal how Israel's wisdom is distorted (Jer. 8–9; Estes, *Message*, 75–84; Isa. 29:14). One greater than Solomon with the eschatological Spirit of wisdom was needed (Isa. 11:1–10; Matt. 12:42). This is the cry of Ps. 53. The fool says, "There is no God" (v. 1). God looks "to see if there are any who understand (NRSV: are wise), any who seek God" (v. 2). Verse 6 concludes in hope, "Oh, that salvation for Israel would come out of Zion!"

With the coming of Christ, wisdom finds its eschatological fulfillment, a reconfiguration within the new covenant. It is the same Lord, known more fully, still worthy of fear and obedience (e.g., Luke 1:50; Acts 9:31; 10:34–35; 2 Cor. 5:11; Phil. 2:12; Heb. 12:28–29; Longman, 250–51). But the center of gravity has shifted from fear and law to the gospel and Christ—the full and final locus of divine wisdom.

This NT wisdom can reflect the literary features and content of OT wisdom. Jesus's life models the wisdom of Proverbs (Luke 2:40, 47, 52). His teachings, as the one greater than Solomon, reflect the style and content of OT wisdom (Matt. 12:42; Luke 11:31). A distinct wisdom genre and content also characterize the Epistle of James, which reflects both Proverbs and the teachings of Jesus (Moo, 8; Carson, 997).

As we will see, wisdom in the NT is not limited to the wisdom genre and the word "wisdom." Such wisdom, deep-rooted in the OT, has become an entailment of Christ and the gospel, revealing a new understanding of the created order, God's self-revelation, and his saving work. The literature of the OT, including its wisdom material, is unified by its covenantal context; in the NT, Christ and the gospel undergird the documents, including its wisdom teaching.

Caveat about "Lady Wisdom." A long-debated question in the movement between Testaments has been the identity of personified wisdom and the figure's relationship to Christ (Prov. 8; Murphy). The use and abuse of "Lady Wisdom" in contemporary theology continues to require a close reading of the biblical material. Some approaches serve agendas of constructive theology, where questions of ecology, a gendered identity of God, or various liberation motifs—however valid in themselves—become the controlling hermeneutic (e.g., Douglas). Such readings can deviate from wisdom's canonical development and reorient Christology around exaggerated "Lady Wisdom" narratives (Ebert, "Wisdom," 303–5). Tremper Longman argues for an "association" of Christ with personified wisdom but not an "identification" (245–50; cf. Fee). The OT and Second Temple backgrounds are complex. Other figures, such as the angel of the Lord, have arguably melded together with the wisdom motif (Günther). It is best to see personified wisdom as part of the typological movement between the Testaments, with the sapiential linguistic and conceptual material as a share in the complex of OT motifs that inform NT Christology (Jobes).

Wisdom and the gospel. The reconfiguration of OT wisdom in Christ does have ontological implications for Christ's deity since OT wisdom is identified with the Lord. But the NT stress is functional. In Paul's opposition to false wisdom at Corinth, he locates wisdom in God's plan that climaxes in Christ and the gospel. In 1 Corinthians the apostle explicitly calls Christ "wisdom"; however, the focus is not on the nature of Christ per se but on the significance of his work (1:23–24). Christ as wisdom is defined by the gospel: righteousness, holiness, and redemption (1:30). Paul's wisdom teaching is about Christ and the eschatological drama unfolding in him. With the coming of Christ and the Spirit, the early church arrives at a fresh perspective on wisdom—the gospel and its application in the life of the Christian community (1 Cor. 2:7–16).

Paul's understanding of wisdom is amplified in Ephesians and Colossians. Here lexical parallels to Proverbs reveal the OT's influence on Paul's language (e.g., Prov. 2:3–6). God has "lavished on" believers the saving grace of the gospel in "all wisdom and understanding" (Eph. 1:8). In Christ God grants "the Spirit of wisdom" (Eph. 1:17). The OT links wisdom with God's Spirit; this association continues in the NT (Longman, 250, 254–55). For the apostles, however, the Spirit of God is the Spirit of Christ (Rom. 8:9; cf. 1 Pet. 1:11). Paul prays that God would fill the saints "with the knowledge of his will through all the wisdom and understanding that the Spirit gives" (Col. 1:9). Paul proclaims Christ, "teaching everyone with all wisdom." His desire is to "present everyone fully mature in Christ" (Col. 1:28), "in whom are hidden all the treasures of wisdom and knowledge" (Col. 2:3; cf. Rom. 11:33).

To unpack this "christological wisdom," the balance of this article explores three OT themes related to wisdom that are fulfilled in Christ: creation, revelation, and salvation. Despite some methodological problems, these three themes also surface in Eva Günther's work on Matt. 23:37–39. She identifies the OT and Second Temple functions of wisdom in God's work of creation (Prov. 1), in the sending of prophets (Wis. 10), and in protecting Israel (Sir. 24). We will briefly consider each motif in the OT, then in its NT context, and then more fully by select NT texts. A final passage illustrates how such new-covenant wisdom informs the life of the church.

Wisdom and Creation

Four points about the OT wisdom-creation relationship are relevant here. First, the OT provides an "order of creation" grounded in a personal God who has created everything in wisdom (Ps. 104:24; Prov. 3:19). Second, the Lord's creational wisdom is famously personified in Prov. 8:22–31 (cf. 3:19) as well as in apocryphal texts (Sir. 24:3–22; Wis. 6–10; Fee, 252). Third, wisdom's creational role spills over into a providential saving role. Creation and salvation form a common pair in the OT narrative (e.g., Deut. 10:14–22; O'Dowd, 62). Fourth, while creation, and this creation-salvation pairing, are related to wisdom, these motifs are not reducible to wisdom. God creates and saves not only by wisdom but also by his word and Spirit. This complex of themes, however, including the structure of creation, is significant for the NT's understanding of wisdom.

Wisdom and creation in the NT. There is a widespread confession in the NT that Christ played a role in creation (1 Cor. 8:6; Col. 1:15–20; John 1:1–3; Heb. 1:2). Appropriated in early Christian worship, this conviction is assumed rather than argued (McDonough, 2). Linguistic and conceptual parallels from the first-century religious context were appropriated to serve this confession, including wisdom language. The prologues to John and Hebrews are classic examples (Ebert, *Christology*, 47–49, 153–54). In addition to wisdom, other figures are identified in Jewish literature as God's intermediaries in creation, including the messiah, God's spirit, God's word, God's creative power, and God's son (for references, see Ellingworth, 96). As a result, the role of God's Word in John or the Son in Hebrews cannot simply be explained in terms of a wisdom background.

An association between Christ's creative work and OT wisdom is most explicit in 1 Corinthians and Colossians (cf. 1 Cor. 8:6 with 1:24, 30, and Col. 1:15–17 with 2:3). But the connections are carefully nuanced. Paul calls Christ the "wisdom and power" of God, though his attention is on the gospel (1 Cor. 1:24, 30). In 1 Cor. 8:6, where both Christ and creation are in focus, the confession essentially embeds Christ in the Shema (Bauckham, 140–41). For the early church, Jesus is the crucified Messiah *and* "the Lord of glory" (1 Cor. 2:8; cf. 12:3). Wisdom is an entailment of Christ's lordship and the gospel. The order is important. It is not that Jesus is confessed as wisdom, leading to Christ's identification with deity; rather, Jesus is confessed as "Lord," leading to his identification with the cosmological function of OT wisdom (Ebert, "Wisdom," 206–25). God's wisdom in the "order of creation" is implicitly captured by Paul's christological confession: "There is but one Lord, Jesus Christ, through whom all things came and through whom we live" (1 Cor. 8:6).

Wisdom and creation in Col. 1:15–20. The concentrated Christology of Col. 1:15–20 artfully presents Christ at the center of creation's eschatological order. It is one of several NT texts that speak of "the cosmic Christ" (John 1:1–18; 1 Cor. 8:6; Phil. 2:6–11; Heb. 1:1–4). The conceptual center in all these creation texts is God's Son as the Messiah (McDonough, 66–94). Here, too, is the received tradition of Christ as Lord (Col. 2:6, 9–10). While wisdom should not be given too much explanatory value here, this confession is arguably a portrayal of Christ as God's mystery in whom are hidden "the treasures of wisdom" (Col. 2:2–3).

Colossians 1:15–20 also speaks of revelation (the Son is "the image of the invisible God," v. 15) and salvation ("peace through his blood, shed on the cross," v. 20). Furthermore, the combination of creation and redemption repeats the common OT pattern. This illustrates how tightly integrated OT themes are in NT theology and cautions against overinterpreting the influence of a single motif. As with the prologues to John and Hebrews, so here in Col. 1:15–17, the Son's role in creation cannot simply be explained in terms of a wisdom background (for an argument against verbal allusions to wisdom here, see Fee and the balanced discussion in Beale, 121–24). In sum, the background is more complex and the connection with wisdom theology more subtle.

In the OT, God's wisdom defines the "order of creation." In Colossians, Paul places Christ at the center of both creation (1:15–17) and redemption (1:18–20). Verses 17–18a hold Paul's composition together and reveal the order of creation in Christ: "He is before all things, and in him all things hold together. And he is the head of the body, the church" (on the hymn's structure, see Bauckham; Ebert, *Wisdom*, 89–93). Echoes of OT wisdom function within this messianic framework. The confession identifies Christ with God and points the church to the power and wisdom of the gospel in the inaugurated new creation.

Wisdom and Revelation

Wisdom and revelation in the OT. The Lord's voice is heard in the voice of wisdom: "Blessed are those who listen to me" (Prov. 8:34). Wisdom reveals God's will and ways. This revelation is embedded not only in the created order (Prov. 8; Job 38), but also in the law, and in Israel's covenant history (Deut. 4:6; cf. Sir. 24:23). Two themes echo back and forth between Wisdom literature and law. First, wisdom calls people to walk in the ways of the Lord (e.g., Ps. 1; Deut. 8:6), the way of life rather than the way of death (e.g., Prov. 2; Deut. 30:15–20). Second, wisdom is identified with the fear of the Lord and his instruction (e.g., Prov. 1:7; Deut. 4:5–6). This identification is stressed in extracanonical literature (e.g., Sirach; rabbinic passages citing Prov. 8:22; see Enns, 225n15).

Wisdom and revelation in the NT. As with other OT phenomena, the revelatory function of wisdom reaches its apex in Christ. Wisdom's call to the path of life and wisdom's identification with the law are reframed in him. The call to life is heard in Jesus's parable of the wise and foolish builders (Matt. 7:24–27). Jesus's words are the words of divine wisdom ("everyone who hears these words of mine," 7:24, 26). The rock on which the wise build has shifted from the law to Christ. NT passages that are dense with Christology and ostensibly related to wisdom feature not only creation but also God's revelation in Christ (Matt. 11:25–30; John 1:1–18; Heb. 1:1–4; Col. 1:1–20).

Scholars often interpret the prologues of John and Hebrews against a wisdom background, but the extent of influence is contested (Jobes). The wisdom strand in early Christology is so integrated into the church's confession that isolating distinct wisdom motifs is challenging (Ebert, *Christology*, 39–55, 145–71). Clearly both prologues emphasize God's revelation in the Son (John 1:1, 14, 18; Heb. 1:2–3). In this sense, the voice of wisdom calling is unmistakable—only now, God is speaking in the Son. The wise respond properly to this call when they receive him and attend to the revelation (John 1:12; Heb. 2:1). Both prologues also assume a hermeneutical shift of wisdom from law to Christ (John 1:17; Heb. 1:1; cf. 10:1).

Wisdom and revelation in Matt. 11:25–30. As with the prologues to Hebrews and John, it is tempting to overinterpret the wisdom motif in Matthew (e.g., Witherington). Its presence is tightly interwoven with other christological motifs. Avoiding an exaggerated "Lady Wisdom" approach, however, should not rule out wisdom's revelatory function. The putative wisdom passages in Matthew portray Jesus in messianic and eschatological terms (Günther). They emphasize the forward movement in redemptive history ("something greater . . . is here"): Jesus identifies himself typologically in relation to the temple (12:6), Jonah (12:41), and Solomon (12:42). Matthew's focus is on the Son's role as the promised manifestation of the Lord, whose conduct, along with that of the Lord's forerunner, will be vindicated (11:1–19). This Jesus, identified as God's Son, is qualified to reveal the Father (11:27).

Wisdom, as divine teaching, is referred to in this passage as "these things" (11:25), "all things" (11:27), and the things that can be "learned" from Jesus (11:29). What the wise in the ordinary sense cannot grasp, the Father reveals (11:25). This revelation involves Jesus's teaching (11:1), his works (11:2, 20), and his identity in relationship to the Father (11:27). God has given this wisdom to the Son, and the Son invites his disciples to receive it (11:27–30). It is in this context that we have wisdom's call: "Come to me, all you who are weary and burdened, and I will give you rest" (11:28; cf. Prov. 8:1–6; 9:5).

Wisdom's relationship to the law is implicit in what follows, "Take my yoke upon you and learn from me. . . . My yoke is easy and my burden is light" (11:29–30). Second Temple literature is significant here. Sirach explicitly identifies wisdom with the law (6:37; 24:23) and describes the yoke as belonging to wisdom (6:25; 51:26). Jesus provides a restful alternative to the heavy yoke of the law and yet, in Matthean terms, takes up the law and fulfills it.

Other texts shed light on Matt. 11:29–30, showing the NT's complex use of the OT. In Jeremiah the Lord says, "Ask where the good way is, and walk in it, and you will find rest for your souls" (6:16). The clearest example is in Isaiah: "This is the resting place, let the weary rest" (28:12). The context is messianic, "See, I lay a stone in Zion, a tested stone, a precious cornerstone for a sure foundation" (28:16). This background indicates that Jesus is being presented as the culmination of God's word, the eschatological wisdom bringing rest. He is the fulfillment of covenant-law and true wisdom (Sirach); he is the promised cornerstone (Isaiah) and the good way leading to rest (Jeremiah). Exodus 33:14 can be read typologically: "My Presence will go with you, and I will give you rest." In calling people to himself for rest, Jesus is bringing both wisdom and law to their culmination (Ebert, "Wisdom," 117–41).

Pauline reflections on law and wisdom. This reading of wisdom and law as fulfilled in Christ informs Paul's use of the OT in Rom. 10:1–10. The apostle argues that his kinsmen are without true knowledge (Rom. 10:1–2)—namely, the wisdom of the gospel (Eph. 1:17). Paul then describes the provision of the law as a prefiguration of God's revelation in Christ (Deut. 30:12–13; Rom. 10:5–10). Baruch also comments on the law's reception in Deut. 30, where he identifies the law with wisdom. Baruch is calling Israel to Torah fidelity (Bar. 3:9–4:4). Paul's call, in contrast, is a call to faith in Christ. The gospel has brought the law and wisdom to their culmination, providing righteousness and salvation (Rom. 10:4, 8–10; Ebert, "Wisdom," 162–85). We find a similar case in Galatians, where Paul responds to those tempted to submit again to the law's yoke (4:4–5; cf. 3:1; 5:1; Ebert, "Wisdom," 185–97).

Wisdom and Salvation

Wisdom and salvation in the OT. In the literature of Israel, along with roles in creation and revelation, personified wisdom provides guidance and providential care. This is "redemptive" only in a general sense rather than in providing atonement for sin. To read wisdom's OT role as "mediating God's redemptive presence" runs the risk of slipping categories (e.g., Ringe, 59). A specified role for personified wisdom in the OT's sacrificial system does not exist. This is true even in Wisdom of Solomon, where wisdom's reconciling work (Wis. 7–9) is "fundamentally educative," with no reference to sacrifice for sin (Lane, 15). The OT identification of wisdom with creation, combined with the creation-salvation pairing, does suggest a general salvific role for wisdom. This arguably is a typological structure for Christ's saving work in the more redemptive sense. Care, however, is needed. The creation-salvation pairing is a common OT feature, not simply a wisdom motif.

Wisdom and salvation in the NT. The creation-salvation pairing, the teaching role of wisdom, and the identification of wisdom with God all align OT wisdom with salvation more broadly (Günther). Wisdom is the source of life. Whoever finds it "finds life and obtains favor from the LORD" (Prov. 8:35 ESV). The NT reads this typologically of Christ: "In him was life, and the life was the light of men" (John 1:4 ESV). Christ both fulfills and far surpasses this saving role of wisdom. With the forward step in salvation history, wisdom in Christ is now shown to be sacrificially redemptive.

The one NT text that explicitly calls Jesus the wisdom of God highlights this redemptive work of the cross (1 Cor. 1:23–24, 30). Indeed, for all the NT passages that interweave sapiential themes of creation, revelation, and salvation, the atonement is central. Colossians confesses that reconciliation is through the Son's "blood, shed on the cross" (Col. 1:20). For the Philippian hymn the pivotal line is "even death on a cross" (2:8). John's prologue is followed by the cry of John the Baptist, "Look, the Lamb of God who takes away the sin of the world" (1:29).

Wisdom and salvation in Heb. 1:1–4. The main contribution of Hebrews is its exposition of Christ's priestly sacrificial work. This theme is subtly introduced in the author's prologue ("he had provided purification for sins," 1:3). How does this relate to OT wisdom?

The author of Hebrews is an exceptionally skilled interpreter of Scripture. His prologue arguably captures wisdom motifs. The primary investigation of a direct literary wisdom influence has focused on v. 3 and an alleged dependence on Wisdom of Solomon. According to William Lane (12), this wisdom tradition provides Hebrews with "categories and vocabulary with which to interpret the person and work of Christ." This must not be overinterpreted (see Ebert, "Wisdom," 54–63). Christ does fulfill OT revelatory roles, including that of wisdom, but he also far surpasses these.

The primary theological influence on Hebrews is the church's confession of Christ. As in Matt. 11:27 and John's prologue, Hebrews declares that God "has spoken to us by his Son" (1:2). The literary structure of Heb. 1:1–4 draws attention to the revelatory function of the Son: he is better than prophets (1:1–2) and angels (1:4), and uniquely participates in the revelatory capacity of the divine identity (1:3). Like John 1:3 and Col. 1:16, Hebrews confesses that it is through the Son that God "made the universe" (1:2). As the supreme revelation of the Father, and as the divine agent of creation, the Son accomplishes his atoning work.

The author is celebrating the Son not only as the Davidic king but also as the high priest who makes atonement for sin. The author's reflection on the creation-salvation pairing may, in part, echo OT wisdom functions. In two parallel lines, the author subtly links creation and salvation. After alluding to a messianic psalm about the Son's inheritance (Ps. 2), the author states that God through the Son "made the universe." The Greek here is not "created" (*ktizō*), but "made" (*poieō*). In the parallel line, before alluding to a second messianic psalm about Christ's enthronement (Ps. 110), the author states that the Son "made purification of sins" (NASB). Significantly, the author does not use the typical verb (*katharizō*); rather, he uses the unique compound expression "made [*poieō*] purification." This results in a direct correlation of creation and salvation, specifically in terms of Christ's atonement (Ebert, *Christology*, 46–49).

In presenting Christ to us, the author gathers up common confessional elements found in the early church and weaves them together to give us an application of the wisdom of God in Christ. This is a Christology that advances the OT typological role of wisdom. Wisdom's OT saving role in Christ has become redemptive and provides atonement for sin.

Wisdom and Virtue

Wisdom and virtue from OT to NT. This exploration of biblical wisdom concludes by illustrating how the NT fulfillment of wisdom in Christ relates to life and virtue. Several insights in biblical theology have been helpful: (1) OT wisdom is integral to covenant life in fear of the Lord; (2) wisdom is reconfigured in Christ; and (3) the NT draws attention not so much to personified wisdom as to wisdom's fulfillment in the gospel. It is the eschatological revelation in the Son, the christological order of creation, and Christ's atoning work, including the sending of the Spirit, that are the framework for a life of wisdom and virtue. The moral teaching of the NT documents, in all their variety, is set within this framework.

The virtuous life begins with the knowledge of Scripture that can make one "wise for salvation through faith in Christ" (2 Tim. 3:15). The gospel is both the power and wisdom of God for salvation (Rom. 1:16; 1 Cor. 1:24; John 1:12). This saving wisdom leads to Christian formation and the virtuous life (Treier, 61–62).

The new life is to be lived after the pattern of Christ. The primary NT texts that echo OT wisdom motifs typically address problems in the community, providing christological wisdom (Ebert, *Christology*). Colossians 1:15–20 is a response to the so-called Colossian heresy, calling believers in the face of worldview challenges to hold fast to the head, which is Christ (1:9, 28; 2:3). The prologue to Hebrews is a response to a persecuted church's wavering faith, calling believers to hold fast to the priestly sacrifice and saving mediation of Christ (1:1–4; 2:1–4).

Other examples of life shaped by christological wisdom are embedded in the NT. The Corinthian church suffered from a divisive spirit caused by pride in human wisdom. In response Paul calls Christ "the wisdom of God." This wisdom reflects the Son's identity as "the Lord of glory" (1 Cor. 2:8; cf. 8:6), but it is also defined by the Son's sacrificial death. The content of this wisdom is the cross-centered gospel of the incarnate one. Identifying "Christ crucified" as God's wisdom sets aside all human wisdom and points to life shaped by the cross.

Wisdom and virtue in Phil. 2:5–11. A remarkable application of christological wisdom is found in the Philippians confession (2:6–11). All three wisdom motifs occur here: the creation will confess Christ as Lord (v. 11); being "in the form of God" qualifies the Son as the revealer of God (v. 6 ESV); and the Son's saving obedience extends "to the point of death—even death on a cross" (v. 8 ESV). This is an explicit (but easily overlooked) application of Christology as wisdom for the problem of discord in the church (4:2). Primary attention is given to the christological issues of the hymn itself (2:6–11), without careful attention to verses 1–5. One can also miss the lexical relationship of "insight" (*phronēsis*) and "wisdom" (*sophia*). These terms can be near synonyms (e.g., Eph. 1:8). When Paul calls on the Philippians to be "like-minded," to have "one mind" (2:2), and to "have the same mindset as Christ" (v. 5), he is leading believers into the wisdom of Christ. This is the hortatory context for the Philippian confession, with the cross of Christ at its literary center (v. 8). This confession in context illustrates what is arguably an apostolic pattern of applying Christology as wisdom in the life of the church (Ebert, *Christology*, 113–44). OT wisdom has found its fulfillment in the redemption of the cross and the pattern of the cross has become the way of wisdom.

See also Adam, First and Last; Covenant; Ethics; Israel and the Church, The Story of

Bibliography. Bauckham, R., "Confessing the Cosmic Christ," in *Monotheism and Christology in Greco-Roman Antiquity*, ed. M. V. Novenson, NovTSup (Brill, 2020), 139–71; Beale, G. K., *Colossians and Philemon*, BECNT (Baker Academic, 2019); Carson, D. A., "James," in *CNTUOT*, 997–1013; Clements, R. E., "Wisdom in Old Testament Theology," in *Wisdom in Ancient Israel*, ed. J. Day, R. P. Gordon, and H. G. M. Williamson (Cambridge University Press, 1995), 269–86; Crenshaw, J. L., *Old Testament Wisdom*, 3rd ed. (Westminster John Knox, 2010); Douglas, S., *Early Church Understandings of Jesus as the Female Divine*, LNTS (T&T Clark, 2016); Ebert, D. J., IV, *Wisdom Christology*, EBT (P&R, 2011); Ebert, "Wisdom in New Testament Christology with Special Reference to Hebrews 1:1–4" (PhD diss., Trinity International University, 1998); Ellingworth, P., *The Epistle to the Hebrews*, NIGTC (Eerdmans, 1993); Enns, P., "Wisdom of Solomon and Biblical Interpretation in the Second Temple Period," in Waltke, Packer, and Soderlund, *The Way of Wisdom*, 212–25; Estes, D., *The Message of Wisdom* (InterVarsity, 2020); Estes, "Wisdom and Biblical Theology," in *DOTWPW*, 853–58; Fee, G. D., "Wisdom Christology in Paul," in Waltke, Packer, and Soderlund, *The Way of Wisdom*, 251–77; Günther, E., *Wisdom as a Model for Jesus' Ministry*, WUNT 2/513 (Mohr Siebeck, 2020); Jobes, K. H., "Sophia Christology," in Waltke, Packer, and Soderlund, *The Way of Wisdom*, 79–103; Kynes, W., *An Obituary for "Wisdom Literature"* (Oxford University Press, 2019); Lane, W. L., *Hebrews*, WBC (Zondervan, 1991); Longman, T., *The Fear of the Lord Is Wisdom* (Baker Academic, 2017); McDonough, S. H., *Christ as Creator* (Oxford University Press, 2009); Moo, D. J. *The Letter of James*, 2nd ed., PNTC (Eerdmans, 2021); Murphy, R. E., "The Personification of Wisdom," in *Wisdom in Ancient Israel*, ed. J. Day, R. P. Gordon, and H. G. M. Williamson (Cambridge University Press, 1995), 222–33; O'Dowd, R., "Creation Imagery," in *DOTWPW*, 60–63; Ringe, S. H., *Wisdom's Friends* (Westminster John Knox, 1999); Sneed, M. R., "'Grasping after the Wind,'" in *Was There a Wisdom Tradition?*, ed. M. R. Sneed (SBL Press, 2015), 39–67; Treier, D. J., *Virtue and the Voice of God* (Eerdmans, 2006); Waltke, B., J. I. Packer, and S. Soderlund, eds., *The Way of Wisdom* (Zondervan, 2000); Witherington, B., *Matthew*, SHBC (Smyth & Helwys, 2006).

Daniel J. Ebert IV

Worship

Worship commonly refers to the devotional practices of a religion or culture. In Christian circles, it often substitutes for "what we do in church" or more narrowly "prayer and praise." In the Bible, however, worship has a more profound and extensive meaning, revealing how we may relate to God appropriately and do his will. This article will first examine the terminology of worship used in the OT and show how it is adapted and employed in the NT. The focus will then be on OT teaching about worship, how it is fulfilled in the person and work of Christ, and how this enables us to engage with God "on the terms that he proposes and in the way that he alone makes possible" (Peterson, *Engaging*, 20).

OT Terms for Worship

Worship as homage or grateful submission to God. Most commonly, the Hebrew root *ḥwh* is translated "worship," although it literally means "bow (down), make/do obeisance" (Fretheim; Block, 12–17). In the MT, it is often used in combination with other terms expressing similar gestures (e.g., Ps. 95:6). The LXX almost always renders this verb with some form of *proskyneō*. Both the Hebrew and the Greek terms express the custom of bowing down or casting oneself on the ground, kissing the feet, the hem of a garment, or the ground, as a total bodily gesture of respect before a superior (Gen. 18:2; Exod. 18:7; 2 Sam. 14:4). Applied to pagan gods, this meant bending over or falling down before an image or making some physical gesture of homage to the god. In relation to the living and true God, this gesture expresses surrender or submission. Sometimes it is an immediate and spontaneous reaction to a divine intervention or revelation, specifically motivated by awe and gratitude (Gen. 24:26–27, 52; Exod. 4:31; 34:8; Judg. 7:15). Bending over before the Lord as a gesture of homage or grateful submission also became associated with sacrifice and public praise in Israel. In such contexts, it could be a formal way of expressing devotion to or dependence on God (Deut. 26:1–11; Ps. 95:1–7; 1 Chron. 29:20–21; 2 Chron. 7:3–4; 29:28–30; Neh. 8:6). But the gesture was only meaningful if it reflected a recognition of God's majesty and holiness and a desire to acknowledge him as king in all of life (Jer. 7:1–8).

Worship as service to God. Another Hebrew term that is often translated "worship" is *ʿbd*, which literally means "serve" (Carpenter; Block, 17–23). When this verb refers specifically to the service offered to God, the LXX often renders it with *latreuō*. The purpose of Israel's redemption from slavery in Egypt was to release the people for exclusive service to the Lord (Exod. 3:12; 4:23; 8:1). When the parallel expressions "to offer sacrifices to the Lord" (3:18; 5:3; 8:8, 25–29; cf. 5:8, 17) and "to hold a festival" (5:1) are used, it is clear that some form of cultic service is in view. A complex system of sacrifices, rituals, and festivals was instituted by God so that Israel as a nation could serve him appropriately (Ross, 197–208, 223–41). In family life, the Passover meal was a particular "service" (ESV) to be observed each year in remembrance of the Lord's saving work at the time of the exodus (Exod. 12:25–26; 13:5; Ross, 160–61). The ministry of priests and Levites was a specialized form of service to God, generally indicated in the LXX by the verb *leitourgeō* and related terms, mostly translating forms of Hebrew *šrt*. Yet it is important to note that many passages set such service within the broader framework of fearing God, walking in all his ways, and observing all his commands and decrees. A total lifestyle of allegiance to God was clearly required of God's people (Deut. 10:12–13; Josh. 22:5; 24:14–24). Consequently, bowing down and serving aspects of the creation or other gods was strictly forbidden (Deut. 4:19; 5:9; 7:4, 16), and provisions were made for removing every temptation to idolatry (Beale, *Worship*, 71–126).

Worship as reverence or respect for God. A third group of terms are used to indicate the fear, reverence, or respect due to God. In Greek, these are words based on the *seb-* stem or words in the *phobeō* group, generally translating forms of the Hebrew *yrʾ* (Van Pelt and Kaiser; Block, 8–12). Such fear involved keeping God's commandments (Deut. 5:29; 6:2, 24; Eccles. 12:13), obeying his voice (1 Sam. 12:14; Hag. 1:12), walking in his ways (Deut. 8:6; 10:12; 2 Chron. 6:31), turning away from evil (Job 1:1, 8; 2:3; 28:28; Prov. 3:7), and serving him (Deut. 6:13; 10:20; Josh. 24:14). Sacrifice and other rituals were clearly a way of expressing reverence for God, but faithfulness and obedience to the covenant demands of God in every sphere of life were the distinguishing marks of true religion (Exod. 18:21; Ps. 25:14; Mal. 3:16; 4:2).

Significant OT Perspectives on Worship

Saved to serve. Exodus records the great saving event whereby the Lord acted to rescue his people from captivity and to begin the next stage in fulfilling his covenant purpose for them. They were saved to serve God (Exod. 3:7–12), to obey him fully and keep his covenant, so that out of all nations they might be his "treasured possession . . . a kingdom of priests and a holy nation" (19:1–6). To facilitate this, God manifests his power and glory at Sinai and speaks to Moses and Aaron at the top of the mountain, while the people wait below (19:9–25). They are given the Ten Commandments, calling upon them to have no other gods, resist bowing down to or serving other gods, honor the Lord's name, keep the Sabbath, and honor God in family and societal relationships (20:1–17). The worship that God desires is based on this definitive revelation of his character and will. Homage and service to God are to be formally expressed at the tabernacle instituted by God (chaps. 25–27) through the mediation of a divinely consecrated priesthood (chaps. 28–29; Ross, 210–15). Three annual festivals would also be the means of celebrating both their redemption from Egypt and God's continuing provision for them in the cycle of nature (23:14–19; cf. Deut. 16:1–17; 26:1–15). Leviticus reveals more about the pattern of sacrifice and cleansing rituals needed to maintain them as a holy people in the land given to them by God (Lev. 1–17; cf. Deut. 14:1–21; Block, 62–73, 81–107).

Tabernacle and temple. The focal point of the tabernacle was the ark (Exod. 25:10–22), which contained the tables of the covenant, expressing God's rule over his people and his presence with them to bless them. The tabernacle had an outer court where the people could gather, a tent for priestly ministry called "the holy place," and an inner sanctuary called "the holy of holies," which only the high priest could enter and only on the annual Day of Atonement (Lev. 16). All this was designed to manifest the holiness of God and how to approach him. In concrete form it indicated that human beings could not come into his presence on their own terms. The complex provisions for sacrifice in connection with the tabernacle were the cultic means for acknowledging God's kingship over their lives and drawing near to him through priestly mediation. The whole system was designed to keep a sinful people in an exclusive relationship with the Holy One (Ross, 82–89, 187–96).

Deuteronomy stresses the need to establish a central place for worship in the promised land, where the Lord would choose "to put his name there for his dwelling" (12:5). God's presence is linked to the "name," by which his character is revealed and acknowledged (Exod. 3:13–17; 33:19–20; 34:4–7). In the presence of the Lord their God, the Israelites were to bring their offerings and sacrifices, their tithes and special gifts, to eat together and rejoice in God and his blessings (Deut. 12:7). They were to be united in observing the pattern of worship he had revealed to them and so avoid every temptation to idolatry (12:1–4, 8–32). Conquest of the land made possible the building of a more permanent "house" for God than the tabernacle. When David became king and Jerusalem was established as his capital, he sought to build a temple, but God gave that honor to his son Solomon (2 Sam. 7:1–17; 1 Kings 6–8). The temple was built with the same basic design as the tabernacle, though on a much grander scale. At its dedication, Solomon questions whether God can really dwell on earth (1 Kings 8:27). Nevertheless, conscious of being in God's presence (lit., "before your face," 8:28), he requests that prayers directed toward "this place" might be answered by God from heaven, his dwelling place (8:30). The temple signified that there was a future for Israel as the people of God, because the building itself expressed the continuation of God's covenant promise to be with them and bless them (8:56–61).

Apostasy and division. At the end of Solomon's reign, pagan practices are introduced into Jerusalem, and the Lord responds in judgment by announcing the division of Solomon's kingdom (1 Kings 11:4–13). A rival form of idolatrous worship is established by the breakaway tribes in the north (12:25–33), while the worship in Jerusalem goes through alternating periods of corruption and reform (Ross, 308–28). In addition to condemning such unfaithfulness, the prophets attack the hypocrisy of those who participated in temple worship without genuine repentance or a desire to live in obedience to God's moral law (e.g., Isa. 1:10–17; 66:1–4; Mic. 6:6–8; Ross, 329–39). The prophets might argue that the Lord's presence with his people in his sanctuary on Mount Zion means that he will defend them against their enemies and bless them (Isa. 31:4–5; 37:33–35), but they make it clear that God's promise to protect them is not unconditional (Isa. 29:1–4; Jer. 7:1–15). Should the people remain disobedient to the covenant and neglectful of worship that truly honors God, terrible judgment will come from the hand of the Lord himself (Ezek. 11:1–12).

The renewal and transformation of worship. God's judgment on the northern tribes comes with the Assyrian invasion (2 Kings 17:5–41). Then Jerusalem and the temple are destroyed by the Babylonians, and many of the people are taken into exile (24:10–25:21). Although the prophets proclaim the justice of these judgments, they also predict that God will act in forgiveness and restoration, allowing a remnant to return to their homeland (Isa. 40:1–11), a new covenant to be established (Jer. 31:31–34), and the worship of his people to be purified (Ezek. 20:39–44; 36:24–38). A new temple will be established and become the spiritual center not only of Israel but also of the nations (Isa. 2:2–3; 44:28; cf. Mic. 4:1–3; Jer. 3:17–18). The coming of the gentiles to Zion will be the means by which God adorns his sanctuary and city in the coming age and glorifies himself in their midst (Isa. 60; Zech. 2:10–13; 8:1–23). The purifying and sanctifying influence of this ideal temple will renew both land and people (Ezek. 47:1–12), because God will be with them in his fullness (48:35). When successive groups of exiles return to Jerusalem to reestablish the city, rebuild the temple, and renew the worship (Ezra; Neh. 8–9, 13), it soon becomes evident that this is only a first step in the fulfillment of God's promises concerning their future (see Hag. 2:1–9 and all of Malachi; Ross, 347–55).

Prayer, praise, and thanksgiving. From Genesis to Malachi, godly Israelites engage in individual and corporate expressions of prayer, praise, and thanksgiving (Peterson, *Encountering*, 101–3, 110–16). Sometimes this arises from personal encounters with God or from individual concerns (e.g., Gen. 18:22–33; 24:26–27; Exod. 33:12–20; 1 Sam. 1:9–11; 2 Sam. 7:18–29). At other times, prayer and praise are offered more broadly on behalf of God's people to advance his covenant purpose for them (e.g., 1 Chron. 29:10–20; Ezra 9; Dan. 9:4–19). Psalms contains many forms of prayer, praise, and thanksgiving, including individual laments (e.g., Pss. 3; 5; 7; 13) and songs of thanksgiving (e.g., Pss. 30; 32; 41; 116) but also communal hymns of praise (e.g., Pss. 100; 145–50) and laments (e.g., Pss. 44; 74). Debate continues about the extent to which these were linked with the rituals of the temple, though it is recorded that musicians and choirs were appointed to lead the people in public worship from the time when the ark was brought to Jerusalem (1 Chron. 16:1–36; Ross, 253–89). Many of Israel's songs were written to keep the people faithful to God and his covenant, dependent on his grace, and committed to serving him in everyday life and relationships (cf. Wenham).

NT Terms for Worship

Key terms for worship found in the OT are also used in the NT, sometimes with reference to the ongoing activity of the temple in Jerusalem or the practices of the nations, but mostly in new ways, because of the coming of Christ.

Worship as homage or grateful submission to Christ. The verb *proskyneō* is employed in some contexts to show that the Son of God deserves the homage and devotion due to the Lord God of Israel (e.g., Matt. 14:33; 28:9, 17; Luke 24:52; John 9:38; Heb. 1:6; Rev. 5:14). Even where such terminology is not used, it could be argued that apostolic preaching aimed to bring people to worship Christ in the sense of yielding their allegiance to him as Savior and Lord (Acts 2:36–39; 10:36–43). Such worship involved calling upon his name (Acts 9:14; Rom. 10:9; 1 Cor. 1:2; Phil. 2:9–11), praying to him (Acts 7:59–60; 1 Cor. 16:22; 1 Thess. 3:11), and praising him (Col. 1:15–20; 1 Tim. 3:16; Rev. 5:9–14).

Homage terminology dominates Jesus's discussion with a Samaritan woman about whether Jerusalem is the place to offer to God acceptable worship (John 4:19–24; cf. Peterson, *Engaging*, 95–102). Her question reflects the ancient division in Israel concerning the place and manner of true worship. Jesus affirms that the worship associated with the Jerusalem temple was based on divine revelation and was therefore honoring to God (4:22, "We worship what we do know, for salvation is from the Jews"). However, he indicates that "a time is coming and has now come when the true worshipers will worship the Father in the Spirit and in truth, for they are the kind of worshipers the Father seeks" (v. 23). Under the new covenant, Jesus is the means by which the Father obtains "true worshipers" from every nation (4:23; cf. 12:32). "True" (*alēthinos*) means "real" or "ultimate" in comparison with the anticipatory provisions of the old covenant (cf. "true light" [1:9], "true bread" [6:32], "true vine" [15:1]). In the context of John's Gospel, worship "in truth" involves acknowledging Jesus as the ultimate, eschatological revelation of God (14:6) and responding with faith to what he reveals about the Father and his purposes for them (8:45; 18:37). Worship "in the Spirit" means homage directed by the end-time Spirit, who is given to all who believe in the Son (7:37–39; cf. 3:5–8; Acts 2:38–39). Jesus is not the object of worship in John 4 but the *means* to God-honoring worship. God as Trinity makes the worship of the messianic eschatological era possible, no longer tying it to any earthly sanctuary or prescribed ritual (Frame, 25–36).

Worship as service to God through Christ. The language of service is also adapted to identify the response we are to make to Jesus and the gospel. Essentially, because of his saving work, we are to present ourselves as "a living sacrifice, holy and pleasing to God" (Rom. 12:1). The sacrifice in question is our "bodies," meaning ourselves as a totality (6:13, 16, "offer yourselves"). As those who have been brought from death to life through Jesus's death and resurrection (6:4–11), we have been made "holy and pleasing to God," so that our self-offering becomes "true and proper worship" (12:1, *logikēn latreian* [lit., "understanding service"]). Christian worship is the devoted service to God rendered by those who truly believe the gospel and want to live out its implications in every sphere of life (12:2–21; cf. Col. 3:9–10; Eph. 4:22–24). The rest of Romans indicates what that service involves in the church and in the world.

Paul indicates that his own particular service (*latreuō*) to God takes place in the sphere of gospel ministry (Rom. 1:9). Intercessory prayer is part of this (1:8–10), but gospel preaching is the focus and goal of all his activity (1:11–15; Peterson, *Engaging*, 179–88). As a "minister [*leitourgos*] of Christ Jesus to the Gentiles," he has "the priestly duty [*hierourgounta*] of proclaiming the gospel of God, so that the Gentiles might become an offering acceptable to God, sanctified by the Holy Spirit" (15:16). The apostle's service to God makes it possible for others to "serve" (*leitourgeō*), in this case by offering financial support to "the poor among the Lord's people in Jerusalem" (15:26; cf. 2 Cor. 9:12 [*leitourgia*]; Phil. 2:25, 30). Such service is clearly a ministry that will glorify God (2 Cor. 9:13). Indeed, these gifts are "a fragrant offering, an acceptable sacrifice, pleasing to God" (Phil. 4:18).

Hebrews similarly teaches that the sacrifice of Christ can "cleanse our consciences from acts that lead to death, so that we may serve the living God" (9:14). We should be grateful for receiving "a kingdom that cannot be shaken" and "so worship [*latreuō*, "serve"] God acceptably, with reverence and awe, for our 'God is a consuming fire'" (12:28–29). Hebrews 13 outlines what acceptable service means in everyday relationships and responsibilities. No earthly "cult" is prescribed in NT teaching about worship, because Jesus has fulfilled the pattern of approach to God established in the OT, opening a new way to God for us. This enables us to offer ourselves to God in adoration and gratitude.

Reverence or respect for God. Paul uses "fear" terminology negatively when describing those who exchange the truth about God for the lie of idolatry, so that they "worshiped [*esebasthēsan*, "reverenced"] and served created things rather than the Creator" (Rom. 1:25; cf. Matt. 15:9, citing Isa. 29:13; Acts 19:27 [*sebomai*]). But the terminology is used positively when Peter encourages his readers to live out their lives in this world "in reverent fear" (1 Pet. 1:17, *en phobō*), and Hebrews calls upon believers to serve God acceptably "with reverence and awe, for our 'God is a consuming fire'" (Heb. 12:28–29). Appropriate fear of God is commended in a variety of contexts (e.g., Matt. 10:28; Luke 1:50; Col. 3:22; Heb. 10:31; Rev. 14:7 [*phobeomai*]; Ross, 52–53).

Significant NT Perspectives on Worship

Jesus replaces the temple. The Gospels give various hints that Jesus replaces the temple in the plan and purpose of God. For example, Matthew records his claim that one "greater than the temple is here" (12:6), and John declares that "the Word became flesh and made his dwelling among us" (1:14; cf. Joel 3:17; Zech. 2:10). As the incarnate Son of God, Jesus represents God's royal presence and authority more fully than the temple. Moreover, his cleansing of the temple expresses God's imminent judgment against those who are abusing it (Mark 11:12–21). The resurrected Lord Jesus indicates that he will continue to draw many into relationship with himself through the witness and teaching of his disciples, thus becoming the center of salvation and blessing for the nations (Matt. 28:18–20; Luke 24:46–49; cf. John 4:23; 12:20–33). The prophetic hope that people from every nation would unite with the faithful in Israel to acknowledge and serve the Lord is fulfilled in Christ (Beale, *Temple*, 169–200).

Jesus's cleansing of the temple in John 2:13–22 more explicitly reveals him as the one sent to replace the institutions of the Mosaic covenant. "Destroy this temple," he claims, "and I will raise it again in three days" (v. 19). The insight that this saying referred to his resurrection body came only after he had been raised and the disciples "believed the scripture and the words that Jesus had spoken" (v. 22). Jesus's zeal (or the religious leaders' ungodly zeal to try) to establish the purpose of God for Jerusalem and the temple would "consume [i.e., destroy]" him (Ps. 69:9, cited in John 2:17), but God would enable him to take up his life again. The function of the temple is fulfilled in John's perspective by the death and resurrection of the incarnate Son of God, securing liberation from sin and bringing believers to eternal life. Paul extends the image of the new temple to include the community of those who are united to the glorified Christ by faith and whose bodies are indwelt by his Spirit (e.g., 1 Cor. 3:16–17; 6:19–20; 2 Cor. 6:16–18; Eph. 2:20–22; Beale, *Temple*, 245–92).

Jesus fulfills and replaces the sacrificial system. Paul describes Jesus's death as "a sacrifice of atonement, through the shedding of his blood—to be received by faith" (Rom. 3:25; cf. Eph. 5:2). The word translated "sacrifice of atonement" (*hilastērion*) is used twenty-one times in the LXX to refer to the golden cover over the ark in the inner sanctuary of the tabernacle (Exod. 25:17–22; Heb. 9:5). Animal blood was sprinkled there by the high priest on the annual Day of Atonement (Lev. 16:2, 13–15) as part of the ritual to make atonement for the whole assembly of Israel (16:17). Paul uses it to portray Jesus as the new-covenant antitype to the old covenant "place of atonement" and, "derivatively, to the ritual of atonement itself" (Moo, 232). Only by this sacrifice can the wrath of God be averted (Rom. 1:18–28; 2:5; 8:3 ["a sin offering"]) so that believers have peace with God and the hope of sharing in the glory of his eternal kingdom (5:1–11). Reflecting OT teaching about the sacrificial system, Paul indicates that it is God who provides the means of forgiveness, cleansing, and sanctification under the new covenant (Rom. 6:4–11; 1 Cor. 1:30; 6:11). The atoning work of Jesus as servant of the Lord is also described in terms suggesting the fulfillment of the sacrificial system in 1 Pet. 2:24–25;

3:18 (cf. Isa. 53:10; Mark 10:45; Luke 22:37) and 1 John 2:2; 4:10 (*hilasmos*, "atoning sacrifice").

Hebrews uses a related verb to describe the self-offering of Jesus in suffering and death to "make atonement for the sins of the people" (2:17, *hilaskesthai*). His "reverent submission" to the will of his Father "perfects" him as the high priest of the new covenant, enabling him to become "the source of eternal salvation for all who obey him" (5:7–10). The author proclaims the fulfillment of Ps. 40:6–8 by "the sacrifice of the body of Jesus Christ once for all," satisfying every provision of the sacrificial system formerly instituted by God (10:5–10). Jeremiah 31:33–34 is fulfilled when a uniquely sufficient sacrifice for sin is offered by this high priest (10:11–18). Psalm 110:4 is fulfilled when he is exalted to heaven to reign at God's right hand and "to save completely those who come to God through him, because he always lives to intercede for them" (7:25; cf. Peterson, *Engaging*, 228–37).

Jesus provides direct access to the heavenly sanctuary. Hebrews develops a typology of worship based on the details of the tabernacle in Exod. 25–27 and its function in the ritual of the Day of Atonement (Lev. 16). The author first argues that the exalted Christ "serves in the sanctuary, the true tabernacle set up by the Lord, not by a mere human being" (Heb. 8:2; cf. 6:19–20). It is the "true" tabernacle in the sense that it is the genuine or real (*alēthinos*) tabernacle, of which the earthly tabernacle was only "a copy and shadow" (8:5; cf. 10:1). God required this earthly structure to be built by Moses according to the pattern shown to him (citing Exod. 25:40), but the Lord alone established the sanctuary in which his Son now reigns and serves as high priest. Although the heavenly sanctuary is portrayed in apparently concrete terms in Hebrews, the image simply means that Christ has definitively opened the way for sinners to approach God and live in his holy presence for ever (12:22–24). This is clarified when a description of the two divisions of the tabernacle and their purpose under the old covenant is given (9:1–10). Then Christ as "high priest of the good things that are now already here" is identified as definitively fulfilling the ritual of the Day of Atonement by his death on the cross and his heavenly ascension (9:11–12, 24).

As "the great high priest who has passed through the heavens" (4:14 AT), Jesus is able to apply the benefits of his once-for-all sacrifice to believers in every trial and temptation (4:15–16). But they must hold fast to the "confession" that gives them hope and keep on "drawing near" to God with confidence (4:16 AT; cf. 10:19–23). The verb *proserchomai* ("draw near") is used in some OT contexts to signify approaching God in prayer (e.g., LXX Jer. 7:16; Ps. 33:6 [ET 34:5]). More broadly, it is used to describe the people who come before the Lord to receive his words through Moses (Heb. 12:18; cf. Exod. 16:9; Lev. 9:5–6) and subsequently to offer sacrifices through the mediation of priests. The people could draw near to stand before the Lord at a distance, and priests without defects could draw near to the altar to make offerings on the people's behalf (Lev. 9:7, 8; 21:17, 21, 23; 22:3). So, Hebrews makes the extraordinary claim that those who have drawn near to God in his heavenly sanctuary through Jesus the mediator of a new covenant (12:22–24) may continue to draw near with confidence to be sustained in that relationship until they reach their heavenly destination (Peterson, *Engaging*, 238–41, 250–52).

Anticipating the worship of heaven. Like Hebrews, Revelation focuses on the realm where Jesus the crucified Messiah reigns in glory. The whole of life is to be lived in relation to the new Jerusalem and the victory of "the Lamb who was slain" (5:12). Visions of heaven consistently portray the offering of adoration and praise to God and the Lamb, and the language of worship pervades the whole document. Most significantly, the term *proskyneō* is used twenty-four times, indicating the centrality of this theme to the author's message. In most passages, it describes some form of homage to the living and true God by heavenly beings or by those redeemed from earth (4:10; 5:14; 7:11; 11:1, 16; 14:7; 15:4; 19:4, 10; 22:9; Ross, 473–500).

However, Revelation also concentrates on the earthly scene. Various forms of idolatry are portrayed (9:20; 13:4, 8, 12), together with prophecies of the awful judgment coming upon those who bow to false gods and refuse to acknowledge the living and true God. John effectively divides humanity into two categories: the worshipers of the dragon and the beast and the worshipers of God and the Lamb (14:1–12). His vision of the new creation (21:9–22:9) portrays the future of the faithful in the city where God himself dwells (21:22), and where his servants serve him unceasingly (22:3 [*latreuō*]; cf. 7:15). This fulfills the biblical ideal, which was only partially realized for Israel in the prescriptions of the Mosaic law. Meanwhile, faithful service to God as "a kingdom and priests" on earth is called for (1:4–6; 2:1–3:22; 14:12; cf. Exod. 19:6; 1 Pet. 2:5, 9; Peterson, *Engaging*, 261–79).

More than any other NT book, Revelation stresses the importance of praise and acclamation as a means of honoring God and encouraging his people to trust him and obey him. The pattern of the heavenly assembly suggests that singing the praises of God and the Lamb is a way of affirming fundamental gospel truths and of acknowledging God's powerful but gracious rule over nature and history. Together with teaching and various forms of exhortation (Heb. 3:13; 5:12–14; 10:24–25), it can strengthen Christians to maintain their confidence in God and in the outworking of his purposes in a world devoted to idolatry and every kind of God-rejecting activity. Testifying to the goodness and power of God in the congregation of his people can be a means of encouraging faithful testimony before unbelievers in everyday life (Acts 2:42–47; Col. 3:16–17; 4:2–6; Heb. 13:13–16). In Revelation, "the sovereignty of God and Christ in redeeming and judging brings them glory, which is intended to motivate saints to worship God and reflect his glorious attributes through obedience to his word" (Beale, *Revelation*, 151; see Rev. 14:7).

See also Adam, First and Last; Glory of God; Temple

Bibliography. Beale, G. K., *The Book of Revelation*, NIGTC (Eerdmans, 1999); Beale, *The Temple and the Church's Mission*, NSBT 17 (IVP Academic, 2004); Beale, *We Become What We Worship* (IVP Academic, 2008); Block, D. I., *For the Glory of God* (Baker Academic, 2014); Carpenter, E., "*ʿbd*," in *NIDOTTE*, 3:304–9; Frame, J., *Worship in Spirit and Truth* (P&R, 1996); Fretheim, T. E., "*ḥwh*," in *NIDOTTE*, 2:42–44; Moo, D. J., *The Epistle to the Romans*, NICNT (Eerdmans, 1996); Peterson, D. G., *Encountering God Together* (P&R, 2013); Peterson, *Engaging with God* (IVP Academic, 1992); Ross, A. P., *Recalling the Hope of Glory* (Kregel, 2006); Van Pelt, M. V., and W. C. Kaiser Jr., "*yrʾ*," in *NIDOTTE*, 2:527–33; Waltke, B., and J. Houston, *The Psalms as Christian Worship* (Eerdmans, 2010); Wenham, G. J., *The Psalter Reclaimed* (Crossway, 2013).

DAVID G. PETERSON

Wrath

The concept of a wrathful God is a theological allergen for some in the church and for many outside it. With regard to the former, H. Richard Niebuhr in *The Kingdom of God in America* made a famous observation about the social gospel: "A God without wrath brought men without sin into a Kingdom without judgment through the ministrations of a Christ without a Cross" (193). However, the concept of divine wrath makes sense when the gravity of human sin is appreciated in its full depth (Anselm, 138). Without such a recognition, the biblical plotline from Gen. 3 to Rev. 22 becomes incomprehensible.

To address this theme of wrath, we need to consider how God is rendered in the biblical testimony. Attention also needs to be paid to the biblical plotline in its unfolding. The discipline of biblical theology provides a canonical reading strategy for such exploration. Word and concept need to be carefully distinguished. The idea of wrath may be present in the text even if the language of wrath is not explicit.

The concept of wrath will be our first consideration with special reference to its connection with divine emotion.

The Concept of Wrath and Divine Emotion

In some texts, both a common Hebrew term for wrath and a number of the metaphors for wrath are in view as in Isa. 30:27: "See, the Name of the LORD comes from afar, with burning anger [*ʾap*] and dense clouds of smoke; his lips are full of wrath, and his tongue is a consuming fire." Burning, dense clouds, smoke, lips, tongue, and fire convey the awesome nature of divine wrath.

Is this wrath a divine emotion? According to Stephen Voorwinde (24), it can be: "The Hebrew Old Testament contains some 842 references to the emotions of God." The most common of these emotions, he argues, is that of anger/wrath (447x). Next comes compassion (101x). In the NT, he maintains, there are more references to divine love (53x) than divine anger/wrath (29x). Wrath is both *affectus* ("feeling" or "emotion") and *effectus* ("event" or "outcome") (Lane). Whether wrath is to be understood as *affectus* or *effectus* is contextually determined.

In OT Hebrew, a variety of terms express the concept of divine anger at sin. The most frequent term is *ʾap*. It occurs well over two hundred times. This is the word used for the nostril or nose (e.g., Isa. 2:22). It may be that anger is shown in the flaring of the nostrils and that this is the anthropomorphism underlying the usage (e.g., Job 4:9 with reference to God). Another term is the noun *ḥārôn*, which is used exclusively to refer to divine wrath (e.g., Exod. 15:7). The related term *ḥārâ* means "to burn." When *ʾap* and *ḥārâ* are paired, the sense is that of intense anger (literally, "burning nose"). Still another relevant term is *ḥēmâ*, which Grant suggests "may derive from a root meaning 'to be hot.'" For example, divine wrath shoots out like a flame in Jer. 21:12 (Grant, 932–33). Fire can also express anger (e.g., Lev. 10:1–2; cf. Rev. 14:10). In the LXX, wrath is poured out (*ekcheō* with *thymos*) by God like a liquid to signify judgment against both those who disobey the covenant and those who persecute the people of the covenant (e.g., Jer. 10:25; Ps. 69:24 [68:25 LXX]). The NT uses similar language. In Rev. 14:9–11, the wine of God's wrath (*thymos*) is poured unmixed (*akratos*)—that is to say, not watered down—into the cup of divine anger (*orgē*) (Aune, 833–36). The objects of such wrath are those who worship the beast. In the LXX, the Greek terms *thymos* and *orgē* "render all the Hebrew anger-words" (Packer, "Anger," 381–83). In NT usage, *thymos* and *orgē* are, generally speaking, synonyms (Borchet, 991).

We turn next to the canonical story line.

The Canonical Story Line

"In the beginning God . . ." The Scriptures open by introducing the reader to God. The majestic Creator God of Gen. 1:1–2:4 creates by speech act. Divine benevolence is on view in the successive creative acts. The creation of the man and the woman show a God who is generous. Permission is given for great freedom of choice (2:15–16): "The LORD God took the man and put him in the Garden of Eden to work it and take care of it. And the LORD God commanded the man, 'You are free to eat from any tree in the garden.'" There is a warning though and with it the hint that this God is not to be trifled with (2:17): "But you must not eat from the tree of the knowledge of good and evil, for when you eat from it you will certainly die." All trees and their fruit are there for human pleasure, except this one. To eat of this tree is to die. The pair eat, and death ensues. The death on view takes the form of exile from the divine presence (3:24): "After he drove the man out, he placed on the east side of the Garden of Eden cherubim and a flaming sword flashing back and forth to guard the way to the tree of life." Sin brings judgment. The Creator is also the Judge. Divine wrath and divine judgment are connected.

But who is this God? The theophany on Sinai is the highpoint of revelation when it comes to understanding something of the divine character. Moses learns that this God who made creatures is also the maker of Israel. Yahweh is "the compassionate and gracious God, slow to anger, abounding in love and faithfulness. . . . Yet he does not leave the guilty unpunished; he punishes the children and their children for the sin of the parents to the third and fourth generation" (Exod. 34:6–7). To use much later language found in the NT, this God is light (holy) and this God is love (cf. 1 John 1:5 and 4:8). Both ideas are on display in the Sinai revelation. Indeed, "In God's innermost being, his attributes are perfectly united. There is no love of God that is not holy and no holiness of God that is not loving" (Lane). This God of holy love is no celestial Santa Claus. He abounds in love but will punish sin.

The God revealed in the OT is the same God as revealed in the NT. Irenaeus saw this in the second century. Marcion, living in the same century, did not. Marcion argued that the God of the OT was not the father of Jesus. Tertullian satirized Marcion's view of God: "A better god has been discovered, who never takes offence, is never angry, never inflicts punishment, who has prepared no fire in hell, no gnashing of teeth in the outer darkness!" (*Marc.* 1.27, quoted in Stevenson, 105). Anthony Thiselton (852) rightly argues, "At all events, the old-fashioned liberal notion [and that of Marcion] that the OT portrays a wrathful God whereas the NT portrays a God of love is thoroughly misguided." The 101 OT references to divine compassion support Thiselton's contention. Moreover, wrath is not incompatible with divine love. The opposite of love is not anger but indifference (Thiselton, 851). The God of the Bible is not indifferent to sin and evil.

God's wrath expressed in judgment. From Gen. 3 to Rev. 20, the canonical narrative renders God as not only a savior, but also a judge: "God's wrath in the Bible is always judicial—that is, it is the wrath of the judge, administering justice" (Packer, *Knowing God*, 137). The story of divine judgment begins with the exiling of the primal pair from the paradise zone of Eden. Exile means separation, and separation in biblical texts is death. The exiles do not stop with Adam and Eve. Cain, the killer of his own brother, is also judged and exiled (Gen. 4). The most spectacular act of judgment in the early chapters of the Bible is that of the great flood. Humankind is wiped out except for Noah's family (Gen. 6–8). This is no arbitrary act, for it is the divine response to out-of-control human wickedness. Indeed, according to the Genesis text, God is grieved to his heart by human wickedness (Gen. 6:6). Human arrogance is also judged in the story of the tower of Babel (Gen. 11).

By Gen. 12:1–3 and the call of Abram, a pattern has emerged of divine action. There is grace and mercy (e.g., Noah and Abram), but there is also judgment (e.g., the flood and Babel). This same pattern comes before the reader when the story of Israel's bondage in Egypt is considered. God graciously rescues the children of Abraham and in so doing judges Pharaoh, his people, his army, and his gods (Exod. 1–15). That Israel has a special covenanted relationship to God is plain, but so also is Israel's folly. A whole generation misses out on entry into the new Eden, the land flowing with milk and honey, because of their ingratitude and idolatry. Israel too is judged, and that judgment expresses divine wrath as the incident of the golden calf makes clear (Exod. 32–34). In the wilderness, Israel continues its rebellious ways, as the events at Meribah and Massah show. Divine wrath is a consequence (Ps. 95:8–11). Judgment can extend to families. Achan and his family serve as an example (Josh. 7:10–26). Wrath can fall on individuals, as the story of Nadab and Abihu and their offering of "unauthorized fire" shows. Their "unauthorized fire" is met with divine fire from the Lord (Lev. 10:1–2). Indeed, whole cities may experience divine wrath as Sodom and Gomorrah did (Gen. 19:23–29), even the people of God (Ps. 95:8–11). The wrath of God, the divine warrior, can envelop the nations (Rev. 19:15).

Israel's fate in the land of promise is contingent upon covenant fidelity (Deut. 28:15–68). It is the Northern Kingdom that falls first, and Assyria becomes the instrument of divine wrath (Isa. 10:5, "the rod of my anger"). Wrath, therefore, on occasion can be mediated rather than direct. As a consequence, the Northern Kingdom is no more. The Southern Kingdom also fails and is judged with exile to Babylon (Jer. 52:24–30). Again, we find that the divine wrath was mediated rather than direct. Upon the exiles' return to the land of promise, the temple is rebuilt, but even so there is disappointment (Ezra 3:12–13). The Hebrew OT ends subtly with God's people to some extent seeming to be in exile still despite the return to the land (cf. 1 Chron. 9:1–2 and 2 Chron. 36:22–23). The Protestant OT canon ends more clearly on the note of hope. A day is coming when judgment will set things right. This is the day of the Lord. God is coming (Mal. 4:5). But before the Lord comes, Elijah will be sent to prepare the way (4:5–6). The pattern of grace with the obverse side of judgment is also found in the last chapter of the OT canon. Fire awaits evildoers, burning "like a furnace," but for those who reverence the divine name, there is healing (Mal. 4:1–3).

Divine wrath is provoked chiefly by idolatry. Deuteronomy links divine anger and divine jealousy. Yahweh will not share his glory with another (Deut. 6:14–15): "Do not follow other gods, the gods of the peoples around you; for the LORD your God, who is among you, is a jealous God and his anger will burn against you, and he will destroy you from the face of the land." The golden-calf incident is a case in point (cf. Exod. 20:4–6; 32:10, 22–24). Social injustice is the other important cause of such a wrathful reaction (e.g., Isa. 45:18–25; Thiselton, 852).

Wrath and John the Baptist. Jesus identifies John the Baptist as the Elijah figure to come (Matt. 11:13–14). An important aspect of his preaching ministry was to warn. Warn of what? The wrath to come: "But when he saw many of the Pharisees and Sadducees coming to where he was baptizing, he said to them: 'You brood of vipers! Who warned you to flee from the coming wrath?'" (3:7). The appropriate response to John's warning was repentance, a return to the way of the covenant (3:8).

John the Baptist was not the focus, however. He was the precursor, and he knew it: "I baptize you with water for repentance. But after me comes one who is more powerful than I, whose sandals I am not worthy to carry. He will baptize you with the Holy Spirit and fire" (3:11). John elaborates with a farming image: "His winnowing fork is in his hand, and he will clear his threshing floor, gathering his wheat into the barn and burning up the chaff with unquenchable fire" (3:12). The fire imagery suggests both purification for some and judgment for others. The farming analogy presents both wheat worthy of preservation and chaff worthy only of everlasting destruction. D. Turner and D. L. Bock (59) capture the double aspect well: "So it is best to conclude that the one eschatological outpouring of the Spirit through Jesus will purify and judge." Once more we see the pattern we saw first in the OT. Divine action saves some on the one hand, and judges some on the other.

Wrath and Jesus. Jesus was the coming one whom John the Baptist foretold of and identified with at the Jordan. Jesus begins his public ministry within weeks after his baptism by John. He preaches from Isa. 61:1–2 in the synagogue in Nazareth, and his message proves controversial. The passage he quotes references the anointing of the Holy Spirit, the proclamation of good news to the poor, liberty to the captives, the recovery of sight to the blind, and the liberation of the oppressed. Indeed, he is proclaiming the year of the Lord's favor. Significantly, he omits the reference in Isaiah to "the day of vengeance of our God." He had come to save. However, he will come again to judge. The pattern we have seen in the OT of salvation and judgment is now phased. The Johannine witness captures the phases (John 12:47–48): "If anyone hears my words but does not keep them, I do not judge that person. For I did not come to judge the world, but to save the world. There is a judge for the one who rejects me and does not accept my words; the very words I have spoken will condemn them at the last day."

Wrath, Jesus, and the cross. The canonical presentation of divine wrath cannot be accurately told without reference to the cross of Christ and what took place there. It was a place of salvation and also of judgment. In the garden of Gethsemane, Jesus refers to his impending death in terms of a cup to be drunk (Mark 14:36). In the OT, the cup in some places symbolizes the divine wrath (Isa. 51:22; Jer. 25:15). Jesus, who knew the OT intimately, most probably had divine wrath in view in referring to the cup he was to drink. Paul is the great interpreter of the cross, which for him was the place of propitiatory sacrifice: "God presented Christ as a sacrifice of atonement, through the shedding of his blood—to be received by faith" (Rom. 3:25). The wider context of the Pauline claim makes the NIV's "sacrifice of atonement" seem far too vague. Paul thematizes divine wrath in Rom. 1:18 ("the wrath [*orgē*] of God is being revealed from heaven"); 2:5 ("the day of God's wrath [*orgē*]"); 2:8 ("wrath and anger [*orgē kai thymos*]"); 3:5 ("his wrath [*orgē*]"); 4:15 ("the law brings wrath [*orgē*]"); and 5:9 ("God's wrath [*orgē*]"). Romans 2:8 is of particular interest. In this text, Paul employs the two words in Greek (*orgē* and *thymos*) that express the variety of Hebrew terms for wrath (Grant, 936; Thiselton, 852). Paul also teaches the Romans that the death of Christ goes beyond expressing divine love. The propitiatory sacrifice of Christ also saves them from divine wrath (5:6–9).

The wrath of the Lamb. The NT not only presents Jesus as the Lamb of God who takes away the sin of the world (John 1:29). It also thematizes the wrath of the Lamb. This is not surprising since the NT often presents Christ in "the role of eschatological judge (John 5:22, 27; Acts 10:42; 17:31; Rom. 2:16; 2 Cor. 5:10; 2 Thess. 2:8; 2 Tim. 4:1; [also] *Barn.* 15:5)" (Aune, 421).

Revelation is the NT locus classicus for this idea (cf., e.g., Rev. 6:16, "the wrath of the Lamb [*tēs orgē tou arniou*]"). For "lamb" and "wrath" to appear in the same sentence is striking. However, it is not the disposition of a lamb in view but the one who was sacrificed like a lamb, who is also an apocalyptic warrior (Carson, 58). This text posits a coming day in which the wrath of the Lamb and that of the one who sits on the throne will be expressed (cf. Rev. 6:12–17 [6:17, *tēs orgēs autōn*]). This describes the day of the Lord, which is a day of wrath that reveals God's righteous judgment (Rom. 2:5).

Wrath and the earliest church. Wrath and judgment are connected, and although Acts does not explicitly speak of the wrath of God, the judgment of God is very much in evidence. Ananias and Sapphira lied to God, and judgment fell (Acts 5:1–11). Herod's pride is also judged (12:20–23). Elymas opposed the gospel and was judged for it (13:4–12). The Corinthian church was a pastor's nightmare: party spirit leading to division, lawsuits, immorality, and wrong doctrine about the resurrection among other problems. Startlingly, some of the Corinthians had misbehaved at the Lord's Supper, and according to Paul, were judged with death for it (1 Cor. 11:29–32).

Wrath in today's world? There is salvation now, and there is a day of wrath to come. But is there wrath now?

"The wrath of God is being revealed from heaven against all the godlessness and wickedness of people, who suppress the truth by their wickedness" (Rom. 1:18). Paul then proceeds to describe the pagan world of his day: idolatry (1:22–25), sexual license (1:26–27), and many other evils (1:28–31). How does the Creator react to such folly? He shows his wrath by giving humankind up to what it sets its foolish heart on (1:24, 26, 28, *paredōken*). In this context wrath seems to be one of the ways judgment works rather than an expression of divine passion. However, since Paul argues that this wrath is revealed (*apokalyptetai*) from heaven (1:18) and that it is God who gives the sinner up to wrath, God is indeed involved in the process, and the process cannot be reduced to an impersonal one (contra Dodd, 22–24).

Divine wrath may also be delivered in a mediated way. Governing authorities can act as agents of the divine purpose when it comes to crime and punishment: "For the one in authority is God's servant for your good. But if you do wrong, be afraid, for rulers do not bear the sword for no reason. They are God's servants, agents of wrath [*orgē*] to bring punishment on the wrongdoer" (Rom. 13:4).

There is a place for righteous human anger, but one must guard against sin (Eph. 4:26–27). After all, Jesus was righteously angry on more than one occasion (e.g., at Pharisaic indifference to suffering as in Mark 3:1–5, the abuse of the temple as in Mark 11:15–17, and even at death per se as in John 11:33–38). However, there is no place for vengeful anger in the Christian's life. The matter of fitting punishment is to be left to God and to the divine wrath, so Paul argues (Rom. 12:19).

The question may be asked as to why the day of wrath has not already come. It is not a new question. The promise of the return of Christ was questioned in the NT era (2 Pet. 3:4): "They will say, 'Where is this "coming" he promised? Ever since our ancestors died, everything goes on as it has since the beginning of creation.'" Peter compares his day to that of Noah's. Judgment did come (3:5–6) and will come (3:7): "By the same word the present heavens and earth are reserved for fire, being kept for the day of judgment and destruction of the ungodly." How then can God's seeming inaction be explained? Peter has his answer (3:9): "The Lord is not slow in keeping his promise, as some understand slowness. Instead he is patient with you, not wanting anyone to perish, but everyone to come to repentance." But make no mistake, he warns (3:10): "The day of the Lord will come like a thief. The heavens will disappear with a roar; the elements will be destroyed by fire, and the earth and everything done in it will be laid bare." Second Peter does not use the word "wrath," but "the day of the Lord" phrase captures the idea.

The wrath to come. D. A. Carson correctly observes, "The primary emphasis in the New Testament is on the eschatological wrath of God" (Carson, 39). John the Baptist, Jesus, and Paul all taught that wrath is coming. Paul, for example, summed up the gospel he preached to the Thessalonians and that they believed in these words (1 Thess. 1:9–10): "You turned to God from idols to serve the living and true God, and to wait for his Son from heaven, whom he raised from the dead—Jesus, who rescues us from the coming wrath." Humankind does not need mere enlightenment. It needs rescue. In Paul's theology, the agent of rescue for some and the agent of judgment for others is the same: Jesus (cf. Acts 17:30–31; 1 Thess. 1:10).

The wrath to come as judgment was appreciated by early Christianity as the Niceno-Constantinopolitan Creed of 381 shows: "He will come again in glory to judge the living and the dead, and his kingdom will have no end" (1975 ecumenical text). Judgment occupies the second place in the four last things in traditional systematic theology. The traditional order is death, judgment, heaven, and hell. However, though each of these elements has biblical warrant, the ultimate eschatological horizon offered by the canon is that of a new heavens and a new earth in which righteousness is at home (2 Pet. 3:13).

A Residual Question: Is Wrath a Divine Attribute?

The biblical witness does raise the question whether wrath is an attribute of God or an expression of an attribute of God. I favor the latter. Within this camp, some argue that wrath is an expression of divine holiness (e.g., Stephen Charnock, J. I. Packer, John Murray, Sinclair Ferguson, and D. A. Carson). Others maintain that wrath expresses divine righteousness (e.g., Herman Bavinck, Gerald Bray, and Jeremy J. Wynne). Still others contend that wrath is an expression of divine love (e.g., Tony Lane). On any of these views, wrath is not an eternal attribute of God. An eternal attribute has neither beginning nor end. Strictly speaking, unlike divine love or holiness or righteousness, wrath is aeviternal and not eternal. That is to say that wrath has a beginning but no end, given an enduring hell. God is essentially love and essentially holy, but his wrath presupposes a creation gone awry. As we have seen, the biblical narrative as it unfolds is unflinching in presenting the ways in which human creatures have indeed gone astray.

Conclusion

Divine wrath is not the temper tantrum of a deity not getting his own way. Nor is wrath arbitrary. It is how holiness responds to evil in a moral universe. Creatures are judged, whether human or angelic. Humankind reaps what it has sown. There is a restorative-justice strand in the canonical presentation, both OT and NT (e.g., Exod. 22:1; Luke 19:8), but with regard to wrath, it is retributive justice that is at work. This is a hard word for modern ears to hear and a bracing one. However, Hebrews is clear (10:31): "It is a dreadful thing to fall into the hands of the living God." And again, its message is bracing (12:29): "For our 'God is a consuming fire.'"

See also Consummation; Day of the Lord; Gospel; Justice

Bibliography. Anselm, "Why God Became Man," in *A Scholastic Miscellany*, ed. and trans. E. R. Fairweather (Westminster, 1956); Aune, D. E., *Revelation 6–16*, WBC (Word, 1998); Borchet, G., "Wrath, Destruction," in *DPL*, 991–93; Carson, D. A., "The Wrath of God," in *Engaging the Doctrine of God*, ed. B. L. McCormack (Baker Academic, 2008), 37–63; Cole, G. A., *God the Peacemaker* (InterVarsity, 2009); Dawkins, R., *The God Delusion* (Mariner, 2008); Dodd, C. H., *The Epistle of Paul to the Romans* (Harper & Row, 1932); George, T., "No Squishy Love," *First Things*, July 29, 2013, https://www.firstthings.com/web-exclusives/2013/07/no-squishy-love; Grant, D., "Wrath," in *NIDB*, 5:932–37; Lane, T., "The Wrath of God as an Aspect of the Love of God," https://www.uniontheology.org/resources/author/tony-lane; Niebuhr, H. R., *The Kingdom of God in America* (Harper & Row, 1959); Packer, J. I., "Anger," in *NDBT*, 381–83; Packer, *Knowing God* (Hodder & Stoughton, 1973); Stevenson, J., ed., *A New Eusebius*, rev. W. H. C. Frend, 3rd ed. (Baker Academic, 2013); Thiselton, A. C., *The Thiselton Companion to Christian Theology* (Eerdmans, 2015); Turner, D., and D. L. Bock, *Matthew and Mark*, CornBC (Tyndale, 2005); Voorwinde, S., "Does God Have Real Feelings?," *Vox Reformata* 67 (2002): 24–51; Wynne, J. J., *Wrath among God's Perfections* (T&T Clark, 2010).

Graham A. Cole

Z

Zechariah, Book of

The book of Zechariah is often known as the "little Isaiah" since it has more to say about the messianic shepherd-king than any other OT prophetic book except Isaiah. Zechariah's message was one of rebuke, exhortation, and encouragement—a tract for troubled times. For several reasons, those were vexing days for the Hebrews who had returned to Judah and Jerusalem after the Babylonian exile. The people were not only faced with the daunting task of rebuilding the city and temple of Jerusalem, but they were also still the pawn of a Mesopotamian superpower—now Persia instead of Babylonia. In addition, doubt and despair over the seeming failure of God's earlier promises for restoration after the exile made by prophets like Jeremiah (e.g., Jer. 23:5–6) and Ezekiel (e.g., Ezek. 38:14–23) spawned disillusionment, cynicism, and apathy among the people.

The pastoral tone for the messages of Zechariah is established in his exchange with the interpreting angel commissioned to relay the "kind and comforting words" from the Lord (1:13). The hortatory character of his sermons is seen in charges like "take courage" and "don't be afraid" (e.g., 8:15). Zechariah's hope for his people in troubled times was bound up in the servant-deliverer, a shepherd-king who was of humble station in life (9:9; 13:7), who would serve as shepherd to a scattered and wandering people (10:2), deliver Israel from their enemies, and rule as king in peace and righteousness in Jerusalem (9:9–10; 14:1–5, 9, 16).

It is assumed that the *prophetic word* formula ("The LORD gave this message," 1:1 NLT) signifies that Zechariah penned his own oracles. Nehemiah lists Zechariah as the head of the priestly family of Iddo (Neh. 12:4, 16; cf. Ezra 5:1; 6:14). This suggests that Zechariah was a member of the tribe of Levi and that he served in Jerusalem as both a priest and a prophet. It also helps explain Zechariah's thorough knowledge of God's previous revelation to the Hebrews by numerous messengers.

We learn from Ezra that Haggai and Zechariah were contemporary prophets of the early postexilic period (Ezra 5:1–2), during the reign of the Persian king Darius I (522–486 BC). The date formulas in the book indicate that Zechariah began preaching in Jerusalem in 520 BC, about two months (Zech. 1:1) into Haggai's brief four-month ministry (Hag. 1:1; 2:20). The two sermons of Zechariah (chaps. 7, 8), likely a pastiche of his preaching over the two-year period, are dated to 518 BC (Zech. 7:1).

Haggai and Zechariah were also complementary prophets in that Haggai exhorted the people to rebuild the Jerusalem temple while Zechariah summoned the community to repentance and spiritual renewal. His task was to prepare the people for proper worship in the temple once the building project was completed. The reference to Haggai and Zechariah in Ezra 5:2 suggests that they both continued to support and encourage the people until the Second Temple was completed and rededicated to the worship of YHWH with the celebration of the Passover in 515 BC (Ezra 6:13–22).

Zechariah's repeated appeals to the words of "earlier prophets" authenticate his own ministry and assure his audience that they have not misinterpreted God's previous revelations (1:4; 7:7, 12). Rex Mason (*Preaching*, 234) summarizes the ministry of all three of the postexilic prophets—Haggai, Zechariah, and Malachi—as one of preaching "the hopes of the [earlier] prophets to a people who could have easily become cynical about their lack of fulfillment, assuring them of both the present degree to which they had been and were being fulfilled and the certainty of their ultimate triumph."

Like his predecessors and his contemporaries, Zechariah understood that a return to the Lord, genuine repentance, is the key to establishing and maintaining right relationship with the God of Israel (Zech. 1:3; cf. Isa. 30:15; 44:22; Jer. 3:12, 14; Hosea 14:1–2; Joel 2:12–13; Mal. 3:7). The pericope containing Zechariah's call to repentance serves as the introduction to the entire book (Zech. 1:1–6; see Wenzel, 55–58). The citation of the message of the "earlier prophets" (1:4) lays the groundwork for his sustained appeal to previous divine revelation to both reinforce his own word from YHWH and counter the spiritual malaise of his people. Careful study of the brief (generically marked) quotation of the earlier prophets suggests Zechariah may have several precursor texts in mind, including 2 Kings 17:13; Jer. 18:11; 25:5; 35:15; and Ezek. 33:11 (see Wenzel, 59–65). Heiko Wenzel (63) and Michael Stead (31–32) prefer Jer. 25:5, 7 as the primary reference text for Zech. 1:4. The ambiguity of the intratextual citation (i.e., the OT appeal to the OT) is intentional, allowing the audience to make connections with that portion of previous divine revelation with which they were most familiar.

Outline of the Book

The book of Zechariah divides neatly into two major units (see table 1). The first section includes the introductory verse (or superscription) with the call to repentance (1:1–6), the eight night-visions (1:7–6:15), and two sermons addressing the topic of fasting (chaps. 7–8). The second part of the book consists of prophetic oracles subdivided into two sections: the word of the Lord concerning the land of Hadrach (or Aram, chaps. 9–11), and the word of the Lord concerning Israel (chaps. 12–14). (On the literary history and structure of Zechariah, see further Boda, *Haggai, Zechariah*, 36–45.)

Literary analysis of Zechariah's prophecy has identified an elaborate chiastic structure underlying each of the two halves of the book (Baldwin, 75–81, 85–86; Dorsey, 318–19).

Repeated themes serve to unify Zechariah's collection of visions, sermons, and oracles. Prominent among these unifying themes are (1) the call to repentance, (2) the promise of divine presence in the midst of Israel, (3) the enabling work of the Holy Spirit, (4) God's judgment of the nations, (5) the call for social justice, (6) the establishment of divinely appointed leadership, and (7) the ultimate triumph of righteousness and the blessing of peace for Jerusalem. In some instances, the prophet's appeal to select earlier messages from God to Israel also contributes to the thematic unification of the book. For example, Wenzel summarizes the message of Zechariah as a call and response anticipating YHWH's complete fulfillment of his earlier promises. The dialogical orientation of his preaching reinforces the prophet's "theology of transition and of waiting" (258). Mark Boda identifies God, leadership, sin, and restoration as themes unifying the book (*Zechariah*, 42–44).

Meredith Kline's (179–84, 192–93) analysis of the book as a diptych bound together by a triple-hinge mechanism further supports the overall unity of the work. The primary hinge, Zech. 6:9–15, provides the key theme of the messianic priest-king that unifies the book. The two secondary hinges (chaps. 3 and 11) tie the prophet's visions and oracles together and reinforce the chiastic structure of the entire book. Such elaborate literary artistry and sharp thematic focus suggest an original master plan and argue for a unified book of Zechariah composed by a single author.

Table 1. Outline of Zechariah

I. Prelude: A call to return to the Lord (1:1–6)
II. Zechariah's visions (1:7–6:15)
  A. A man among the myrtle trees (1:7–17)
  B. Four horns and four blacksmiths (1:18–21; MT 2:1–4)
  C. Future prosperity for Jerusalem (2:1–5; MT 2:5–9)
  D. The exiles are called home (2:6–13; MT 2:10–17)
  E. Cleansing for the high priest (3:1–10)
  F. A lampstand and two olive trees (4:1–14)
  G. A flying scroll (5:1–4)
  H. A woman in a basket (5:5–11)
  I. Four chariots (6:1–8)
  J. The crowning of Joshua (6:9–15)
III. Zechariah's messages (7:1–8:23)
  A. A call to justice and mercy (7:1–14)
  B. Promised blessing for Jerusalem (8:1–23)
IV. Zechariah's oracles (9:1–14:21)
  A. First oracle (9:1–11:17)
    1. Judgment against Israel's enemies (9:1–8)
    2. Zion's coming king (9:9–17)
    3. The Lord will restore his people (10:1–11:3)
    4. Good and evil shepherds (11:4–17)
  B. Second oracle (12:1–14:21)
    1. Future deliverance for Jerusalem (12:1–14)
    2. A fountain of cleansing (13:1–6)
    3. The scattering of the sheep (13:7–9)
    4. The Lord will rule the earth (14:1–21)

Overview of Inner-Biblical Allusion in Zechariah

Biblical scholars rightly note the importance of the introduction for understanding the book of Zechariah (Zech. 1:1–6; see Wenzel, 55). The prologue orients the audience to both the key theme of repentance (1:3) and the role earlier divine revelation plays in the prophet's message (1:4). This appeal to the previous word of the God of Israel is described variously as inner-biblical allusion (i.e., relationships between the words of Zechariah and the prophets who preceded him in form and language; see Boda, *Zechariah*, 39–40), or inner-biblical exegesis (i.e., an approach to Scripture that investigates the reinterpretation and reapplication of earlier biblical texts by later texts; cf. Fishbane, 10–13), or intertextuality (i.e., the linkage of Zechariah with other scriptural texts both by way of allusion and citation; e.g., Meyers and Meyers, *Haggi, Zechariah 1–8*, 35).

Beyond the question of taxonomy is the problem of defining what constitutes an allusion or citation to an earlier scriptural message by a later biblical spokesperson or author. Such analysis is further complicated by lack of consensus in biblical scholarship regarding the historical dating of many OT texts. Which text is actually the precursor text? This analysis will employ the broad-based taxonomy of inner-biblical allusion, recognizing the category includes both allusion and citation.

Considerable literature on inner-biblical allusion in Zechariah has been generated in recent years. Several layers or types of use of earlier divine revelation in Zechariah may be discerned. Three specific types are examined here: (1) a broad approach emphasizing theme and literary form; (2) Zechariah's use of prophetic speech formulas; and (3) select textual parallels between Zechariah and other OT literature.

Boda (*Zechariah*, 39–41) discerns numerous examples of earlier divine revelation shaping and influencing Zechariah 1–8:

Zech. 1:1–6; 7:1–8:23 are shaped by Jer. 26; 36; 37–41.
Zech. 1:7–6:15 reflects the influence of Amos 7; 9; Jer. 1; 24; Ezek. 1; 2; 8; 10; 37; 44.
Zech. 1:7–17; 3:1–10; 4:1–14 (the divine-council motif) are influenced by 1 Kings 22:19–21; Isa. 6; Job 1–2.
Zech. 3:1–10; 6:9–15 (prophetic sign-acts) demonstrate similarities to Jer. 13; 16; 19; 27–28; Ezek. 3; 4–5; 6; 12; 24.

In addition, Boda (*Zechariah*, 40) recognizes the influence of earlier prophetic form traditions in Zechariah 9–14:

the summons to joy (9:9; cf. Hab. 3:18; Zeph. 3:14);
the entrance liturgy (11:1; cf. Isa. 26:2; Ps. 24);
the call to lament (11:2; cf. Isa. 14:31; Jer. 6:26; Joel 1:12–14);
the report of prophetic sign-act (11:4–16; cf. Jer. 13; 16; 19; 27–28; Ezek. 3; 4–5; 6; 12; 24);
the woe oracle (11:17; cf. Isa. 5);
and the sword oracle (11:17; 13:7–9; cf. Jer. 50:35–38).

Zechariah conforms to the other postexilic prophets, Haggai and Malachi, in the repetitive use of standard prophetic speech formulas found widely in the prophetic literature of the OT. Prominent among them are the following:

the prophetic-word formula ("the word of the LORD came," 1:1; 6:9; 7:8; cf. 8:1);
the messenger formula ("so said the LORD," 1:3 AT [20x in Zech.]);
the divine-utterance formula ("oracle of the LORD," 12:1 AT [20x in Zech.]); and
the divine epithet ("LORD of Hosts," 1:3 AT [over 50x in Zech.]).

The *messenger formula* is common in prophetic speech and signifies the oral transmission of a message by a third party. The phrase suggests participating in the divine assembly or council of the gods in ancient Near Eastern thought. The messenger of the council stands as an observer in council sessions and then reports what he has heard as an envoy of the council to others (see *ABD*, 2:214–17; Walton, 53–57). For this reason, the verb of speaking is better rendered according to its past tense form: "Thus said the LORD of Hosts" (so NJPS). The expression places emphasis on the divine source and authority of the message, and the heavy repetition of the formula in the postexilic prophets serves to connect their ministries and messages to the earlier Hebrew prophetic tradition. Calling attention to such continuity may have been helpful in defusing a possible crisis concerning the prophetic word in the minds of some in Haggai's audience. The people had returned to the land of Judah more than twenty years ago and yet the promises of Jeremiah and Ezekiel regarding Israel's restoration after the Babylonian exile remained unfilled (cf. Jer. 31:31–33; 33:14–16; Ezek. 34:23–24; 37:24–28).

The divine title "LORD Almighty" is prominent in the postexilic prophetic literature. The expression is often understood as a construct-genitive relationship: "the LORD of Hosts" (KJV; the Heb. word *ṣəbāʾôt* means "host, army, warrior"). More precisely, the construction is one of absolute nouns in apposition, perhaps conveying a verbal force: "YHWH *creates* [angel] armies" (*TDOT*, 5:515). In either case, the epithet emphasizes "the invincible might behind the Lord's commands" (Baldwin, 39). This reaffirmation of God's sovereign rule of the nations was important for the Hebrew restoration community since they remained under the control of a foreign power during the postexilic period.

Inner-Biblical Allusion in Zechariah

The quest for a reliable method for detecting inner-biblical allusion within the OT remains an important issue for biblical interpretation. Michael Stead seeks to develop a broader-based hermeneutic that accommodates both the thematic allusion emphasis of the tradition-history approach (e.g., Mason, "Relation") and the more restrictive understanding of intertextuality based on verbal parallels (e.g., Nurmela; Schultz).

Stead examines five specific case studies to develop a method for detecting Zechariah's reuse of other OT texts: (1) Zech. 1:4c and Jer. 25:5–7; (2) Zech. 6:15 and Deut. 28:1; (3) Zech. 2:10 [MT 2:14] and Isa. 12:6 and/or Zeph. 3:14–15; (4) Zech. 8:21–22 and Isa. 2:3; and (5) Zech. 2:5–6 and Ezek. 40:3.

Based upon his analysis, Stead (37) makes three observations that inform his methodology for identifying inner-biblical allusion in Zechariah—namely, the use of loose quotation (example 3), the weaving of multiple sources into a new composite text (example 5), and variations or the reworking of a theme (example 4). He then proceeds to discuss nearly forty "intertexts" in the visions and sermons of Zech. 1–8.

Among the helpful contributions Stead makes to the understanding of inner-biblical allusion in the OT are the features of the sustained allusion and the composite metaphor. Sustained allusion consists of repeated references to a given background passage stretching across multiple passages (e.g., the sustained allusion to Lam. 2 in Zech. 1–2). Composite metaphor is defined as "the simultaneous allusion to imagery from multiple source passages" (Stead, 248). Both have implications for the NT use of the OT. For example, the quotation of the text referencing the priest-king Melchizedek informing the discussion of the priesthood of Jesus the Messiah in Heb. 7:1–8:6 is a type of sustained allusion. The multiple OT sources drawn on in Paul's discussion of faith, justification, and the law in Gal. 3:6–16 have affinities to the composite metaphor.

Further, thematic ties between Zech. 1–6 and 7–8 establish a relationship between the visions and the sermons of Zechariah. The continuity of themes in Zech. 1–8 and 9–14, supporting the earlier analysis of Mason ("Relation," 238, as cited in Stead, 262), identify a clear line of tradition between the two literary units.

Carol Meyers and Eric Meyers catalog more than eighty inner-biblical allusions in Zech. 9–14, including intertextual relationships with each of the major divisions of the Hebrew Bible (*Zechariah 9–14*, 41–43). The handy chart format also references the specific language or theme tying Zech. 9–14 to other biblical texts. Zechariah utilizes a great variety of exegetical strategies typically employed by the OT prophet(s) in the allusions to earlier biblical materials. According to Meyers and Meyers (*Zechariah 9–14*, 44–45), "nearly always, the Zecharianic usage represents a transformation of genres: for example, a Pentateuchal curse or blessing emerges in an oracular statement [Deut. 28:28 // Zech. 12:4], or a legal prescription is reworked into an eschatological forecast [Deut. 12:2–3 // Zech. 13:3]. The range and creativity of the intertextual process are striking," showcasing "the extraordinary skill of figures such as 'Second Zechariah,' who managed to set forth an eloquent and hopeful message to a beleaguered community while holding fast to the revelatory authority of his forebears."

The reference to "earlier prophets" (Zech. 1:4; cf. 7:7, 12) "reveals that Zechariah and/or his secretary-compiler were well aware of the legacy of classical prophecy. Both the prophet and his followers saw themselves as belonging to the long line of true prophets" (Meyers and Meyers, *Haggi, Zechariah 1–8*, 101). There is great artistry in Zechariah's use of early materials, not simply a cut-and-paste pastiche. Rather, "original minds responded to the profound tension between past and present. They transformed existing authoritative predictive prophecies, without negating their sanctity or validity, into equally valid formulations that could erase the prevailing sense of hopelessness and powerlessness while simultaneously sustaining traditional community values and beliefs" (Meyers and Meyers, *Zechariah 9–14*, 45). The interpretive strategies of inner-biblical allusion practiced by the OT prophets establish precedents for the variety of ways the later writers of the NT appeal to the OT. Broadly understood, inner-biblical allusion assumes a process of selection (including marked and unmarked citations), arrangement, and reshaping (if any; see the discussions in Hays; Hill, "Patchwork"; Kaiser, *Uses*; Porter, "Further").

Zechariah's use of other OT texts has correspondence to several of Michael Fishbane's categories of inner-biblical exegesis. These intertextual associations in Zechariah are precursors of later rabbinic interpretation and help to illustrate the transition between biblical interpretation during the Second Temple period and later Jewish traditions for interpreting the dual Torah (i.e., written and oral). Naturally, the historical development of Jewish biblical interpretation has significant implications for the NT interpretation of the OT.

For example, Fishbane's category of legal exegesis aims at applying and clarifying OT ethical instruction for the purpose of defining community action and involvement (Fishbane, 108). Stead (232–33) recognizes intertextual overtones of several OT passages in the prophet's exhortation to postexilic Judah to obey the commands of God and avoid a repeat of the Babylonian exile (Zech. 7:9–10; cf. Deut. 24:14, 17–18; Jer. 7:5–6). Stead (235) also identifies intratextual connections, the self-referential appeal to material within the primary document, in the allusion of Zech. 8:16–17 to 7:9–10. More broadly, Stead (230–31) understands Zech. 7–8 as a recapitulation of Zech. 1–6, another interpretive strategy typical of later rabbinic inner-biblical exegesis.

Unlike legal exegesis, which focuses on preexisting legal texts, Fishbane's category of haggadic exegesis explores the full range of the inherited Jewish written and oral tradition for the sake of new theological insights, attitudes, and moral and practical speculations (282). Haggadic reinterpretation and reapplication show how a particular law or teaching can transcend its original focus and take on new meaning (283). Haggadic reapplication transforms an "old guarantee" into "a new warrant of hope in a later time" (350)—as in the case of the Branch, who will rebuild the temple of the Lord (Zech. 6:12; cf. Jer. 23:5–6).

Fishbane identifies several categories of haggadic inner-biblical exegesis, including the use of simile, metaphor, and a variety of typologies. Zechariah's development of analogical relationships between pentateuchal and prophetic material may take the form of simile in the comparison of the disobedient posture of his postexilic audience to that of their preexilic counterparts (Zech. 1:4–6; cf. 2 Kings 17:23; Jer. 44:4–6). Or the prophet may make a metaphorical transformation of an earlier text, as in the reinterpretation of the pipes of the golden lampstand of the tabernacle with Zerubbabel and Joshua, the leaders of the restoration community (Zech. 4:1–6; cf. Exod. 25:31–40; see Fishbane, 303–4). The typologies Fishbane identifies are as follows:

1. Cosmological-historical typologies tend to portray a cosmological event as the prototype or warrant for a historical redemption to come (see Fishbane, 352–53). This category is eschatological in nature and is illustrated in Zechariah's vision of the new creation (Zech. 14:6–9; cf. Isa. 60:19–22; 65:17–19; Ezek. 47:1–12; Rev. 21:1–2).

2. Historical typologies employ a historical paradigm with the prototype, whether event, person, office, or institution, providing the terms or configuration for the way the later referent is presented and understood (see Fishbane, 359–60). Fishbane discerns two kinds of historical typologies. One is retrospective in nature (cf. Zech. 1:2–6), while the second is projective in nature. Zechariah appeals projectively to the events of the Assyrian and Babylonian exiles as the basis for hope in Israel's regathering—a type of second exodus (Zech. 10:9–12; cf. Petterson, 236). A second example of projective historical typology is Zechariah's reference to the "house of David" and God's timely enablement of the postexilic Hebrew community to defend Jerusalem with the prowess of the warrior-king David (Zech. 12:7–9; cf. 1 Sam. 17:50; 18:7, 13–16).

3. Spatial typologies focus attention on the diverse loci of ancient Israel's sacred geography, those places where the powers of heaven and earth conjoin (Fishbane, 368). These sacred places provide the prototype for later events and institutions associated with the given locale. The restoration of the glory of Jerusalem as God's habitation and the worship center for all humanity is a central theme across Zechariah's visions, sermons, and oracles (Zech. 1:14–17; 2:1–10; 8:1–3; 12:1–9; 14:16–21; cf. Isa. 65:17–19; 66:19–20).

4. Biographical typologies feature the correlation of biblical persons and tend to focus on the character of an individual life (Fishbane, 372). Zerubbabel's faith, courage, and obedience in response to the word of the Lord were deemed exemplary (Zech. 4:6–10)—perhaps an echo of Hag. 1:12–15 (cf. Meyers and Meyers, *Haggai, Zechariah 1–8*, 242–44, 250–52).

Fishbane (443) defines the category of mantological exegesis as the interpretation and reinterpretation of prophecies and oracles over time. The mantological materials are part of the ongoing prophetic tradition in Israel and are important to its reception by next generations—assurance that God's word has not failed (444). One example of this reinterpretation of earlier prophetic oracles is the envisioned restoration of divine presence in the Second Temple (Isa. 60:1–7; 62:1–5; Ezek. 43:1–9; 44:4; Mic. 4:1–5). The eschaton will witness ironic reversal in the response of the nations to the God of Israel and his people. The nations who destroyed Judah and Jerusalem (Zech. 1:18–21) will seek to firmly grasp even the hem of the robe of a Jewish person because God is once again with Israel, living amid his people (8:20–23; cf. 2:10–13). Zechariah's correlations between what is seen in the present (the return of Israel from Babylonian exile) and what is unseen in the future (the Lord's return to Jerusalem [Zech. 1:16]) provide hope and encouragement for the restoration community of Judah to build the Second Temple and obey the instructions of the Lord (Zech. 6:15; cf. Hag. 1:12).

Zechariah and Jesus the Messiah in the NT

The index of Scripture in *CNTUOT* (1196) lists more than 180 references to the book of Zechariah in the NT. The extensive NT appeal to Zechariah is especially aimed at identifying Jesus of Nazareth as Messiah in fulfillment of OT prophecies (see Jauhiainen; Kaiser, *Messiah*). For example, the Messiah will:

be the capstone (Zech. 4:7) or cornerstone (Ps. 118:22–23) rejected by the builders (Matt. 21:42; Mark 12:10; Luke 20:17);

come in a low and humble station of life (Zech. 9:9; 13:7; cf. Matt. 21:5; 26:31, 56);

restore Israel by the blood of his covenant (Zech. 9:11; cf. Mark 14:24);

serve as shepherd to a people scattered and wandering like sheep (Zech. 10:2; cf. Matt. 9:36; Mark 6:34);

be rejected as good shepherd, betrayed and sold (Zech. 11:12–13; cf. Matt. 26:14–16; 27:6–10);

be pierced and struck down (Zech. 12:10; 13:7; cf. Matt. 26:31, 56; John 19:37);

return in glory and deliver Israel from their enemies (Zech. 14:1–5; cf. Matt. 25:31);

rule as priest-king in peace and righteousness in Jerusalem (Zech. 6:9–15; 9:9–10; 14:9, 16; cf. Heb. 7; Rev. 11:15; 19:6);

establish a new world order (Zech. 14:6–19; cf. Rev. 21:25; 22:1, 5).

The Messiah mysteriously presented by Zechariah as both a suffering shepherd (13:7) and a righteous king (13:9) will produce a redeemed people who testify of their covenant loyalty to the God of Israel (13:9). Zechariah sees a day when the long-awaited kingdom of YHWH will be established over all the earth and righteousness will fill the earth (9:9–10), and all peoples will worship the King, YHWH Almighty (14:9, 16, 21).

The Message of Zechariah

Zechariah's essential message is an exhortation to repentance and spiritual renewal—a return to loyal covenant relationship with God (1:1–6). The central theme of Zechariah's preaching is encouragement, as he explicitly states his duty as one of comforting (1:13) and strengthening the people (8:9, 13, 15). Zechariah also reinforced Haggai's summons to the people to rebuild the Jerusalem temple (8:9, 13). Yet his message extended beyond the material reconstruction of the Jerusalem temple. He called for the moral and spiritual rebuilding of the Hebrew people so that they might be a holy people unto the Lord and offer appropriate worship in the Second Temple (7:8–10; 8:14–17, 19; cf. 8:3). Such worship is the ultimate goal of God's redemptive history (Ps. 86:9; Isa. 66:23; Rev. 7:9).

Zechariah reminds his audience of the certainty of God's sovereign rule over the nations (1:11, 18–21 [MT 2:1–4]; 2:7–9 [MT 2:11–13]; 8:20–22; 12:1–6; 14:16–19). Given the horrors of the Babylonian conquest and exile, and the continued domination of restoration Judah by the Persians, prophetic pronouncements of God's oversight of the raging nations rang hollow (cf. Mal. 1:2–3; 3:14–15). Yet, like Daniel, Zechariah understood that it was God who had delivered Judah into the hands of King Nebuchadnezzar (Dan. 1:2) and that his punishment of Judah's sin was justified (Lam. 1:18). As Boda (*Zechariah*, 42) notes, YHWH passionately pursues his rule over the nations, including both judgment on rebellious nations and opportunities for repentance and submission so that the nations may benefit from the righteous rule of God (cf. Zech. 1:14–15; 6:8; 8:20–23; 14:16–19). The people of God today need this reminder as the nations continue to rage in our world: "The One enthroned in heaven . . . scoffs at them" (Ps. 2:4).

Boda correctly observes that Zechariah is part of the OT prophetic tradition that is used in the NT to shape the faith response of the people of God and inform their ethical behavior. This includes the admonition to practice social justice, demonstrating mercy and compassion for one another (Zech. 7:8–10; 8:16–17). Thus, Boda concludes: "The book highlights patterns to avoid, those patterns which threaten the first (love the LORD your God) and second (love your neighbor as yourself) commandments which underlie Israel's covenantal law and express the moral vision of Christ" (*Zechariah*, 44).

Bibliography. Baldwin, J. G., *Haggai, Zechariah, Malachi*, TOTC (Tyndale, 1972); Boda, M. J., *The Book of Zechariah*, NICOT (Eerdmans, 2016); Boda, *Haggai, Zechariah*, NIVAC (Zondervan, 2004); Boda, M. J., and M. H. Floyd, eds., *Bringing Out the Treasure*, JSOTSup 370 (Sheffield Academic, 2003); Dorsey, D. A., *The Literary Structure of the Old Testament* (Baker, 1999); Fishbane, M., *Biblical Interpretation in Ancient Israel* (Clarendon, 1988); Hays, R. B., *The Conversion of the Imagination* (Eerdmans, 2005); Hill, A. E., *Haggai, Zechariah, Malachi*, TOTC (InterVarsity, 2012); Hill, "Patchwork Poetry or Reasoned Verse?," *VT* 33, no. 1 (1983): 97–101; Jauhiainen, M., *The Use of Zechariah in Revelation*, WUNT 2/99 (Mohr Siebeck, 2005); Kaiser, W. C., *The Messiah in the Old Testament* (Zondervan, 1995); Kaiser, *The Uses of the Old Testament in the New* (Moody, 1985); Kline, M. G., "The Structure of the Book of Zechariah," *JETS* 34 (1991): 179–93; Mason, R. A., *Preaching the Tradition* (Cambridge University Press, 1990); Mason, "The Relation of Zech. 9–14 to Proto-Zechariah," *ZAW* 88 (1976): 227–39; Mason, "The Use of Earlier Biblical Material in Zechariah 9–14," in Boda and Floyd, *Bringing Out the Treasure*, 1–208; Meyers, C. L., and E. M. Meyers, *Haggai, Zechariah 1–8*, AB (Doubleday, 1987); Meyers and Meyers, *Zechariah 9–14*, AB (Doubleday, 1993); Nurmela, R., *Prophets in Dialogue* (Åbo Akademis Förlag, 1996); Petersen, D. L., *Haggai and Zechariah 1–8*, OTL (Westminster, 1984); Petterson, A. R., *Haggai, Zechariah and Malachi*, AOTC (IVP Academic, 2015); Porter, S. E., "Further Comments on the Use of the Old Testament in the New Testament," in *The Intertextuality of the Epistles*, ed. T. L. Brodie, D. R. MacDonald, and S. E. Porter, NTM 16 (Sheffield Phoenix, 2006), 98–110; Porter, "The Use of the Old Testament in the New Testament," in *Early Christian Interpretation of the Scriptures of Israel*, ed. C. A. Evans and J. A. Sanders, JSNTSup 14, SSEJC 5 (Sheffield Academic, 1997), 79–96; Schnittjer, G. E., *Old Testament Use of Old Testament* (Zondervan, 2021); Schultz, R. L., *The Search for Quotation*, JSOTSup 180 (Sheffield Academic, 1999); Stead, M. R., *The Intertextuality of Zechariah 1–8*, LHBOTS 506 (T&T Clark, 2009); Walton, J. H., *Ancient Near Eastern Thought and the Old Testament*, 2nd ed. (Baker Academic, 2018); Wenzel, H., *Reading Zechariah with Zechariah 1:1–16 as the Introduction to the Entire Book*, CBET 59 (Peeters, 2011).

ANDREW E. HILL

Zephaniah, Book of

Zephaniah prophesied in Judah to support King Josiah's reforms, and he likely did so soon after the discovery of the Deuteronomic book of the law (2 Kings 22–23) but before much spiritual and societal change was evident (ca. 622 BC) (Robertson, 33, 254–56). He warns of Yahweh's impending day of wrath and urges the remnant in Judah and beyond to seek the Lord together and to wait upon him to avoid punishment and to enjoy satisfying salvation. The prophet envisions Yahweh's fiery fury overcoming all unrepentant sinners in the world, yet he also foresees a multiethnic, transformed community of worshipers who would celebrate the presence of God in Zion amid a new creation and whom the Lord would take pleasure in and deliver from all their oppressors.

Composition, Structure, and Message

The superscription identifies the prophecy as "the word of the LORD that came to Zephaniah . . . in the days of Josiah the son of Amon, king of Judah" (Zeph. 1:1 ESV). Nothing in the book suggests anyone other than Zephaniah penned his message. The book witnesses an antiphonal-like character switching between the voices of Yahweh and his prophet (see Wendland and Clark). Nevertheless, the lack of introductory speech formulas and the sustained cohesion and coherence of the whole show that the frequent shift in person neither governs the flow of the argument (so Sweeney, "Reassessment" and *Zephaniah*; Floyd; contra House) nor distinguishes levels of authority.

Following the superscription in 1:1, Yahweh invites all who will listen to be saved through surrender. A single oracle runs from 1:2–3:20b and includes two parts: The *setting* of the Savior's invitation occurs in 1:2–18, and here the prophet calls those in Judah and beyond to revere the Lord in light of his coming day of punishment. The reality of coming punishment provides the context for the call (1:2–6), and then the makeup of the call includes a further unpacking of the fury Yahweh will pour out on both Jerusalem (1:7–13) and the world at large (1:14–18). The main body or *substance* of the book then comes in 2:1–3:20b, as the prophet charges the people to patiently pursue God together. Stage one of this summons initially urges those in Judah and beyond to gather together (2:1–2) and then commands those who have heeded to seek the Lord in righteousness and humility (2:3). A foundational reason why they must pursue Yahweh in this way relates to the lamentable state and fate ("woe") of the rebels from both the foreign nations (2:4–15) and Jerusalem (3:1–7). God intends to bring global destruction that will implode on Jerusalem itself. Building on this reasoning, stage two of the Savior's invitation directs the remnant to wait on the Lord in order to enjoy satisfying salvation (3:8–20b). The charge to wait stands as an inference from what precedes ("therefore," 3:8) and is grounded in the certainty that Yahweh will both put an end to all his enemies (3:8) and preserve and restore a single yet global community of worshipers, reversing the effects of the tower of Babel (3:9–10). Motivating the call to wait are promises that "on that day" the Lord will not put Jerusalem to shame (3:11–13) but will instead save completely (3:16–20b)—realities that should result in fearless joy among the saved (3:14–15). The book closes in 3:20c where it began in 1:1—by affirming the whole as God's word.

Table 1. Outline of Zephaniah

I. The *superscription* of the Savior's invitation to satisfying salvation (1:1)
II. The *setting* of the Savior's invitation to satisfying salvation: a call to revere God in light of the coming day of the Lord (1:2–18)
   A. The context for the call to revere God: coming punishment (1:2–6)
   B. The makeup of the call to revere God (1:7–18)
III. The *substance* of the Savior's invitation to satisfying salvation: charges to patiently pursue the Lord together (2:1–3:20b)
   A. Stage 1: the need to seek the Lord together in order to avoid punishment (2:1–3:7)
   B. Stage 2: the need to wait on the Lord in order to enjoy satisfying salvation (3:8–20b)
IV. The *subscription* to the Savior's invitation to satisfaction (3:20c)

The Hermeneutics of Zephaniah

Zephaniah views the day of the Lord as a climactic decreation and re-creation that will both echo and reverse all negative effects of the primeval curses associated with the garden of Eden, the flood, and the tower of Babel. He also portrays the day of wrath as a new divine conquest by which God will put an end to rebellion and reestablish a new promised land with global scope.

Examples of OT allusion. Coming fires of judgment parallel the waters of judgment at the flood. Zephaniah's oracle opens with a promise of encroaching punishment that will result in Yahweh's destroying mankind on the earth. He will gather "everything from on the face of the ground" for judicial assessment: "man and beast . . . the birds of the heavens and the fish of the sea, and the rubble with the wicked" (Zeph. 1:2–3 AT). The phrase "from on the face of the ground" (1:2–3) consistently occurs in contexts of divine punishment (e.g., Gen. 4:14; Exod. 32:12; Deut. 6:15; 1 Kings 9:7; 13:34; Jer. 28:16; Amos 9:8), and the use of "ground" recalls the sphere of the original curse (Gen. 3:17–19). Zephaniah is probably linking the coming global judgment with the past flood by which the Lord punished the whole earth (Gen. 6:7; 7:3–4, 23; 8:8) (see esp. DeRoche). Nevertheless, because Zephaniah includes "fish" (Zeph. 1:3), the scope of Yahweh's new assessment will be even wider, for the sea creatures were never explicitly targeted in the great deluge. The prophet is not here subverting, replacing, or even qualifying God's earlier promise to never "again strike down every living creature as I have done" (Gen. 8:21 ESV) (contra DeRoche, 105–6; Berlin, *Zephaniah*, 82). Indeed, Yahweh himself had specified, "Never again shall all flesh be cut off *by the waters of the flood*" (Gen. 9:11 ESV; cf. Isa. 54:9–10). Furthermore, the most natural reading of Zeph. 1:2–3 is that the Lord promises to "gather" *all* creatures but to "cut off" only mankind (cf. Zeph. 1:18; 3:8; DeRouchie, "Ingathering").

The day of the Lord as a new conquest to claim a global promised land. The prophet alludes several times to the original conquest of Canaan, suggesting that he envisions the day of the Lord to be a greater divine conquest by which God will atone for sin and establish his kingdom on a global scale. First, in Zeph. 1:11b, the prophet declares that Jerusalem's inhabitants would wail when Yahweh silenced "all the people of Canaan" (NIV: "merchants"). These were most likely the Philistine traders (see 2:5) who were negatively influencing Judah with both their worldly goods and perspectives (cf. Isa. 2:6–8; Hosea 12:7). In declaring that God would destroy these "Canaanites," Zephaniah recalls the original conquest, wherein their wickedness matched by God's choice of their land demanded their extermination (Deut. 7:1–2; 9:4–5; 20:16–17; cf. Gen. 9:25–27). Similarly, the prophet carries on his conquest motif when he mentions the "trumpet blast" of war and of God's overpowering "unassailable cities" (Zeph. 1:15–16 AT)—all likely allusions to the Canaanite strongholds (Num. 13:28; Deut. 1:28; 3:5; 9:1) and to Israel's subduing them (Deut. 6:10–11; Josh. 6:5, 20; cf. Neh. 9:25).

Second, the prophet depicts Jerusalem as spiritually deaf, heedless, faithless, and motionless (Zeph. 3:2; cf. 1:6, 12)—those who had lost sight of Yahweh's greatness and had sourced their strength and affluence in the Canaanite traders. These foreigners had reshaped Judah's worship (1:4–5), dress (1:8), and lifestyle (1:6, 9) so much that Zephaniah could tag these Judeans as "the remnant of Baal" (i.e., the chief god of the Canaanites, 1:4b ESV). And having identified with Canaan, they will receive the same punishment (Deut. 8:19–20; cf. 20:18).

After highlighting how Yahweh would seek to destroy all those in Jerusalem who were complacent (Zeph. 1:12), the prophet stresses the futility of the nation's future by alluding to the conquest: "Their goods shall be plundered, and their houses laid waste. Though they build houses, they shall not inhabit them; though they plant vineyards, they shall not drink wine from them" (1:13 ESV). Zephaniah's descriptions and vocabulary regarding the loss of possessions and hopeless deprivation recall Mosaic covenant curses, which foretold that one evidence of divine wrath would be sustained futility in building, planting, and other endeavors (Deut. 28:30, 39; cf. Amos 5:11; Mic. 6:15). Even more, the language identifies that God is reversing his original covenant blessings and treating Israel as Canaanites. He had pledged that Israel would enjoy "great and good cities that you did not build, and houses full of all good things that you did not fill, and cisterns that you did not dig, and vineyards and olive trees that you did not plant" (Deut. 6:10–11; cf. Jer. 29:5–7). Now they are the ones who will experience substantive loss, as Yahweh will reestablish a new promised land for his earthly kingdom and faithful remnant.

Third, what was an original blessing of the Mosaic covenant will become a restoration blessing for "the remnant of the house of Judah" who survive the day's tribulation unto triumph: "In the houses of Ashkelon [the remnant of the house of Judah] shall lie down at evening" (Zeph. 2:7 ESV; cf. Isa. 65:18, 21–22; Ezek. 28:26). Thus, Zephaniah recalls the original conquest to stress how the day of the Lord will both cleanse the earth of its defilements and provide a context wherein God can establish a restored, now global kingdom.

Cush, the Table of Nations, and the reversal of the tower of Babel judgment. Several features from the early chapters of Genesis appear to have conceptually and literarily guided Zephaniah's portrayal of devastation and deliverance in 2:1–3:20b. In 2:5–3:7, Zephaniah sketches Yahweh's object of wrath like a compass of punishment around Judah that will implode upon them—Philistia to the west, Moab and Ammon to the east, Cush and Assyria to the south and north. Adele Berlin (*Zephaniah*, 120–24; "Oracle") helpfully argues that the prophet chose and described the particular nations in 2:5–15 based on the Table of Nations in Gen. 10, thus highlighting that their pride arose from Babel (Gen. 11:1–9). Zephaniah "made the reality of his time fit the pattern in Genesis 10 by choosing the countries from Genesis 10 that were important [Philistia, Assyria], omitting those that were obscure [e.g., Put], and adding crucial ones, lacking in Genesis 10, in terminological equivalents to those in Genesis [Moab, Ammon]" (Berlin, *Zephaniah*, 121).

While Berlin fails to appreciate enough that God, showing no ethnic favoritism, promises to destroy the nation of Judah and its capital city Jerusalem (3:1–7) right alongside their neighbors (2:5–15), the prophet does hold out hope—not for the nation of Judah as a whole but for a remnant from it (2:3, 7, 9) and from the foreign nations (2:9, 11; 3:9–10). Specifically, the phrase "the remainder of my nation will inherit them [i.e., some from the foreign nations]" (2:9d AT) points to a multiethnic community arising out of the fires of Yahweh's wrath. Furthermore, peoples from the farthest reaches of the planet will "bow down" to the Lord, some in worship and others in defeat (2:11c). Finally, by smiting Cush (2:12) God begins what will become a universal eradication of the human pride dispersing from the tower of Babel (Gen. 10:32–11:9) (see Floyd, 210–13). The prophet declares that on the very day when Yahweh gathers the world for judgment (Zeph. 3:8), he will "change the speech of the peoples to a pure speech" and generate a community of "worshipers, the daughter of my dispersed ones" that will rise from "beyond the rivers of Cush" (3:9–10 ESV). The imagery of speech purification implies the overturning of judgment (Ps. 55:9) and likely alludes to a reversal of the tower of Babel episode, where a communal pride against God resulted in his confusing of "language/speech" and "dispersing" the rebels across the globe (Gen. 11:7, 9). As if following the rivers of life back to the garden of Eden for fellowship with the great King (Gen. 2:13; cf. Rev. 22:1–2), the prophet envisions that even the most distant lands upon which the Lord has poured his wrath (Zeph. 2:11–12) will become one with "those who are left in Israel" (3:13), compelled by the presence of the saving God. As many prophets anticipate (e.g., Isa. 2:2–3; Jer. 3:17; Zech. 8:23), the people of the new covenant—here described as a "daughter" of the dispersed—will include a worldwide, multiethnic community descending from the seventy families that the Lord "dispersed" in punishment at Babel after the flood (Gen. 11:8–9). Indeed, even some from Cush, Zephaniah's own heritage (Zeph. 1:1), would gain new birth certificates declaring that they were born in Zion (Ps. 87:4; Isa. 18:7; 45:14).

Zephaniah's hermeneutical and theological strategy. Three factors appear to have guided Zephaniah's hermeneutical use of Mosaic covenant blessings and curses and of the accounts of the flood, the Table of Nations, the tower of Babel, and the conquest: (1) typology, (2) redemptive-historical reversal, and (3) event as blueprint.

Typology. Zephaniah likely portrays the scope of the coming day of judgment with imagery of the flood not only to draw an analogy between the two events but also to highlight the coming destruction of mankind as an indirect fulfillment of what the flood itself anticipated. Two reasons suggest that typology and not just analogy is at play: (1) Following the fall, God foretold that he would ultimately overthrow the source of all evil and reconstitute creation through a male deliverer (Gen. 3:15). Thus, we must read the pentateuchal narratives seeing every defeat of serpent-like hostility against God as an intentional foretaste of the ultimate deliverance to come. (2) Because the same inherent wickedness that sparked the need for the flood punishment (Gen. 6:5–7) continued after the deluge (8:21), the biblical author portrays the original flood account as anticipating a greater global destruction that would bring about a more lasting new creation.

A similar hermeneutical step appears evident in the use of the conquest and blessing/curse materials. Israel enjoyed the land God promised Abraham (Gen. 15:18; 17:8) in the Mosaic covenant period (Exod. 2:24; 6:8; Deut. 1:8; 6:10; 9:5; 30:20; 34:4), as realized in the days of Solomon (1 Kings 4:20–21). Nevertheless, hope always existed for the time when the "land" of the single nation would extend to "lands" of a multitude of nations (Gen. 17:4–6; 26:3–4), when Yahweh's royal deliverer would perform a greater conquest of evil and bring God's blessing to the ends of the earth (Gen. 3:15; 22:17–18; cf. 24:60; 49:8–10; Num. 24:7–9, 17–19). Zephaniah's use of the conquest narrative indicates not only that God continues to fulfill his original covenant curses against rebellious Judah (Deut. 8:19–20; cf. 28:15–68) but also that he is working out Deuteronomy's curses in an eschatological era against all his enemies, including unrepentant Israel/Judah (30:7). What the Canaanites were in the original conquest, all the evil ones of the world are to Yahweh. Thus, God "will bring distress on mankind . . . because they have sinned against the LORD" (Zeph. 1:17 ESV), and as he does, there is heightened hope for a worldwide purified kingdom.

Redemptive-historical reversal. Zephaniah sees the intrusion of the day of the Lord as inaugurating the definitive reversal of the tower of Babel and as reconstituting a people who are more concerned with his name than with their own (cf. Gen. 4:26; 11:4; Zeph. 3:9). God portrays the faithful remnant as "the daughter of my dispersed ones" (Zeph. 3:10 ESV)—that is, the offspring of those whose language Yahweh once altered and whom he scattered across the globe away from Babylon (Gen. 11:8–9). Noah's grandson Nimrod, a Cushite, built Babel (10:8, 10), and then following Yahweh's punishment, the Cushites established their kingdom in what the ancients considered the southernmost region on the planet—near the convergence of the Blue and the White Nile in modern-day Sudan. Zephaniah envisioned the Lord's day of wrath as already starting with Cush (Zeph. 2:12), and he utilized a remnant from this region to represent the global restoration that God was going to accomplish (3:10). Whereas Yahweh once countered the unity of hostility by confusing the "lip/language" of the earth (Gen. 11:8–9), he now would purify the "lip/speech," not by recreating a common language but by joining the profession and partnership, so "that all of them may call upon the name of the LORD and serve him with one accord" (Zeph. 3:9 ESV). Zephaniah's use of redemptive-historical reversal signals that God will inaugurate the new creation that he first anticipated in Gen. 3:15 and then predicted in his promises to Abraham that he would bless all the families of the earth (e.g., 12:3; 18:18; 22:18; 26:4).

Event as blueprint. As Berlin identifies (*Zephaniah*; "Oracle"), the Table of Nations in Gen. 10 may have supplied a blueprint for the structure of Zeph. 2:5–15. With this, Zephaniah's likely biracial link to the Cushites (Zeph. 1:1) may have drawn him to Gen. 10, which focuses heavily on the Hamitic line (Gen. 10:6–20), from which the Philistines, Canaanites (= Sodom and Gomorrah), Cushites, and Assyrians all arose. That the Table of

Nations precedes the account of the tower of Babel also works to the prophet's advantage, for he first addresses the scope of God's judgment (Zeph. 2:5–3:7) and then identifies the way the Lord's blessing will counter the effects of the Babel judgment and restore a lasting age where all survivors of Yahweh's day worship his name forever (3:9–20).

Zephaniah and the NT

The eschatological ingathering to punish and save. Using the root *'sp* ("to gather"), Zephaniah depicts Yahweh's day as a time of eschatological "ingathering"—a divine harvest that will result in his punishing the wicked (Zeph 1:2–3, 8; cf. Isa. 24:22; Jer. 8:13; Hosea 4:3, 6; Zech. 14:2) and in his delivering those seeking him (Zeph 3:8–10, 18; cf. 2:3; Isa. 11:11–12; 49:5, 12; Ezek. 11:17; Mic. 2:12; 4:6) (see DeRouchie, "Ingathering"; "Seek"). Both Jer. 3:8 and Zech. 14:2 may intentionally echo Zephaniah's materials, but Matt. 13:24–30 appears to deliberately allude to Zeph. 1:2–3 (cf. Matt. 3:12; 25:32, 46).

While comparing the kingdom of heaven to a field mixed with wheat and weeds (Matt. 13:24–30), Jesus stresses how both must "grow together until the harvest, and at harvest time I will tell the reapers, '*Gather* the weeds first and bind them in bundles to be burned, but *gather* the wheat into my barn'" (13:30 ESV). Later, in his explanation of the parable to the disciples, he says, "Just as the weeds are *gathered* and burned with fire, so will it be at the end of the age. The Son of Man will send his angels, and they will *gather* out of his kingdom all *causes of sin* and all *law-breakers*, and throw them into the fiery furnace. In that place there will be weeping and gnashing of teeth" (13:40–42 ESV). Clearly parallel with Zeph. 1:2–3; 3:8, 18 is the theme of "ingathering," which Matthew describes through the verbs *syllegō* ("to gather by plucking or picking") and *synagō* ("to gather up"), both of which are fine free renderings of the Hebrew *'sp* (cf. 1 Kings 10:26; Deut. 16:13) but the latter of which is found in 8HevXii gr (col. 20) at this point. The second parallel, this time with the Hebrew text of Zeph. 1:3, is the mention of the *skandala* ("stumbling blocks"; ESV: "causes of sin") and the *anomian* ("lawless") (Matt. 13:41). While the LXX does not render Zephaniah's phrase "the stumbling blocks with the wicked" in 1:3, Symmachus does, using the wooden *ta skandala syn [tois] asebesi* ("the stumbling blocks with the wicked"). It seems very likely that Jesus is alluding to the Hebrew text, identifying the great eschatological ingathering of which he speaks with that of Zephaniah (so too Robertson, 259–60; France, 536; Carson, 374).

The inauguration of the day of the Lord in the death and resurrection of Christ and the birth of the church. Zephaniah 3:8–10. Several links between God's ingathering of a multiethnic group of worshipers in Zeph. 3:8–10 and the early chapters of Acts suggest that Luke saw the events of Pentecost and of God's saving work among the nations as directly fulfilling Zephaniah's vision of Babel's reversal and of the new creation's inbreaking at the day of the Lord (Butcher; cf. Davis; Keener, 840–44; see too Jub. 10:22; T. Jud. 25.3; Rev. 5:9; 7:9).

The following are noteworthy connections: (1) Using similar vocabulary, both Joel 2:32 and Zeph. 3:9 foresee the faithful remnant calling on the name of Yahweh during his day of ingathering. While Peter cites Joel 2:28–32 in Acts 2:17–21, the Greek version of Zeph. 3:9 renders the term for "speech/lip" with *glōssa* ("tongue"), a term important to both the tower of Babel episode (Gen. 11:7; cf. 10:5) and the Pentecost narrative (Acts 2:3–4, 11, 26; cf. 10:46; 19:6) but not found in Joel. The "calling on Yahweh's name" in Zeph. 3:9 counters the quest for a name in Gen. 11:4 and links with Acts 2:21. (2) With Joel 2:31 and Acts 2:20, Zeph. 3:9 also employs the verb *metastrephō* ("to turn, cause a change in state or condition") with respect to God's new-creation work, though with reference to the speech change and not the altering of the atmosphere and heavenly bodies. (3) Pentecost is a harvest feast of ingathering, which conceptually aligns with the ingathering motif in Zephaniah. (4) The image of serving the Lord *in unity* (Zeph. 3:9) may have influenced Luke to include the comment in Acts 2:42–47 regarding the early saints' corporate surrender and worship. (5) For Zephaniah, Yahweh's future transforming of speech (Zeph. 3:9) will happen in direct association ("then") with his ingathering of the "nations" for judicial assessment (3:8; cf. Isa. 66:5). As for Luke, he stresses that the Jews present in Jerusalem at Pentecost who heard the gospel in their own tongues came "from every nation under heaven" (Acts 2:5), and it is this reality that will help fulfill Jesus's global commission to be his witnesses "in Jerusalem, and in all Judea and Samaria, and to the ends of the earth" (1:8). (6) Strikingly absent from the list of nations in Acts 2:9–11 is "Ethiopia," the Hellenistic title for OT "Cush." I propose the reason Luke did not identify any Jews from this region is because he wanted to wait until later to highlight that the story of God's saving the Ethiopian eunuch (Acts 8:26–40) signals the Lord's initially fulfilling Zephaniah's prediction that worshipers from the region of Cush would lead the ingathering of the nations to Yahweh at the end of the age (Zeph. 3:9–10).

One implication of Luke's apparent use of Zephaniah is that he must have envisioned Christ's wrath-bearing, substitutionary work on the cross as fulfilling in part Zephaniah's vision of God's sacrificial fires of punishment on his day of fury (Zeph. 1:7, 18; 3:8; for more, see DeRouchie, "Zephaniah," 565–68). Supporting this was Luke's conviction that the astronomical manifestations were to happen "before the day of the Lord comes" (Acts 2:20 ESV; cf. Matt. 27:45; Mark 15:33; Luke 23:44; cf. Ortlund and Beale), whereas in Joel's prophecy the Spirit's outpouring flows out of Yahweh's visitation (see "afterward" in Joel 2:28). Further support is found in the allusion to Zeph. 3:14–15 in John 12:13, 15.

Zephaniah 3:14–16. Interpreters commonly recognize that John cites Ps. 118:25–26 and Zech. 9:9 in his account of Jesus's triumphal entry: "So they took branches of palm trees and went out to meet him, crying out, 'Hosanna! Blessed is he who comes in the name of the Lord, even the *King of Israel*!' And Jesus found a young donkey and sat on it, just as it is written, '*Fear not, daughter of Zion*; behold, your king is coming, sitting on a donkey's colt" (John 12:13–15 ESV). What some miss, however, is that the psalm does not include the phrase "King of Israel" and that Zechariah's opening charge is actually "rejoice" rather than "fear not." Christopher Tachick argues strongly that these differences identify that John is also alluding to Zeph. 3:14–16, which is the only place in the OT where we find the grouping "King of Israel," "Fear not," and "daughter of Zion." Within Zephaniah, this exhortation intrudes into his depiction of Yahweh's cleansing and renewal of his creation that he will accomplish "on that day" of his judgment (3:11, 16).

So how does John use Zephaniah both hermeneutically and theologically? As Tachick identifies (155–208), John's primary hermeneutical purpose was to identify Jesus's triumph through tribulation as directly fulfilling the prophet's prediction of God's end-time reign. In Christ, Zephaniah's eschatological day of the Lord has dawned. Theologically, John's use of Zephaniah closely associates Yahweh with King Jesus, and through his narrative he incorporates Zephaniah's motifs of both the warrior-king (John 12:13, 31) and gentile ingathering (12:19–20, 32). The very structure of Zeph. 3:8–20b may have informed John's narrative account.

Bibliography. Berlin, A., *Zephaniah*, AB (Doubleday, 1994); Berlin, "Zephaniah's Oracle against the Nations and an Israelite Cultural Myth," in *Fortunate the Eyes That See*, ed. A. B. Beck et al. (Eerdmans, 1995), 175–84; Butcher, J. D., "The Significance of Zeph. 3:8–13 for Narrative Composition in the Early Chapters of the Book of Acts" (PhD diss., Case Western Reserve University, 1972); Carson, D. A., "Matthew," in *EBCRE*, 9:23–670; Davis, J., "Acts 2 and the Old Testament," *CTR* 7, no. 1 (2009): 29–48; DeRoche, M., "Zephaniah 1:2–3: The 'Sweeping' of Creation," *VT* 30 (1980): 104–9; DeRouchie, J. S., "Who Should Seek YHWH Together?," *BBR* 30 (2020): 183–207; DeRouchie, "YHWH's Future Ingathering in Zephaniah 1:2," *HS* 59 (2018): 173–91; DeRouchie, "Zephaniah," in *Daniel–Malachi*, ESVEC (Crossway, 2018), 561–604; Floyd, M. H., *Minor Prophets, Part 2*, FOTL 22 (Eerdmans, 2000); France, R. T., *The Gospel of Matthew*, NICNT (Eerdmans, 2007); House, P. R., *Zephaniah*, JSOTSup 69 (Almond, 1989); Keener, C. S., *Introduction and 1:1–2:47*, vol. 1 of *Acts* (Baker Academic, 2012); Ortlund, D. C., and G. K. Beale, "Darkness over the Whole Land," *WTJ* 75 (2013): 221–38; Robertson, O. P., *The Books of Nahum, Habakkuk, and Zephaniah*, NICOT (Eerdmans, 1990); Sweeney, M. A., "A Form-Critical Reassessment of the Book of Zephaniah," *CBQ* 53 (1991): 388–408; Sweeney, *Zephaniah*, Herm (Fortress, 2003); Tachick, C. S., *"King of Israel" and "Do Not Fear, Daughter of Zion,"* RAD 11 (P&R, 2018); Wendland, E. R., and D. J. Clark, "Zephaniah: Anatomy and Physiology of a Dramatic Prophetic Text," *JOTT* 16 (2003): 1–44.

Jason S. DeRouchie

Zion

See Jerusalem

Index of Scripture and Other Ancient Writings

Old Testament

Genesis

Exodus

Leviticus

Numbers

Deuteronomy

Joshua

Judges

Ruth

1 Samuel

2 Samuel

1 Kings

2 Kings

1 Chronicles

2 Chronicles

Ezra

Nehemiah

Esther

Job

Psalms

Proverbs

Ecclesiastes

Song of Songs

Isaiah

Jeremiah

Lamentations

Ezekiel

Daniel

Hosea

Jonah

Micah

Nahum

Habakkuk

Zephaniah

Haggai

Zechariah

Malachi

New Testament

Matthew

Mark

Luke

John

Acts

Romans

1 Corinthians

2 Corinthians

Galatians

Ephesians

Philippians

Colossians

1 Thessalonians

2 Thessalonians

1 Timothy

2 Timothy

Titus

Philemon

Hebrews

James

1 Peter

2 Peter

1 John

2 John

Jude

Revelation

Old Testament Apocrypha / Deuterocanonical Books

Baruch

Bel and the Dragon

1 Esdras

2 Esdras

Judith

2 Kingdoms (= 2 Samuel)

3 Kingdoms (= 1 Kings)

Letter of Jeremiah (= Baruch chap. 6)

1 Maccabees

2 Maccabees

Prayer of Azariah

Prayer of Manasseh

Psalm 151

Sirach (Ecclesiasticus)

Song of the Three Jews

Susanna

Tobit

Wisdom (of Solomon)

Old Testament Pseudepigrapha

Ahiqar

Apocalypse of Abraham

Apocalypse of Moses

Apocalypse of Zephaniah

2 Baruch (Syriac Apocalypse)

3 Baruch (Greek Apocalypse)

4 Baruch (Paraleipomena Jeremiou)

1 Enoch (Ethiopic Apocalypse)

2 Enoch (Slavonic Apocalypse)

4 Ezra

Jubilees

Liber antiquitatum biblicarum (Pseudo-Philo)

Letter of Aristeas

Life of Adam and Eve

Lives of the Prophets

3 Maccabees

4 Maccabees

Pseudo-Phocylides

Psalms of Solomon

Sibylline Oracles

Testament of Adam

Testament of Job

Testament of Moses

Testament of Abraham

Testaments of the Twelve Patriarchs

Testament of Benjamin

Testament of Gad

Testament of Judah

Testament of Levi

Testament of Naphtali

Testament of Reuben

Testament of Zebulun

Dead Sea Scrolls

Qumran

ALD

CD

CD–A

CD–B

1QH[a]

1QIsa[a]

1QIsa[b]

1QM

Wadi Murabbaʿat

Naḥal Ḥever

Mishnah, Talmud, and Related Literature

Babylonian Talmud

Philo

Papyri